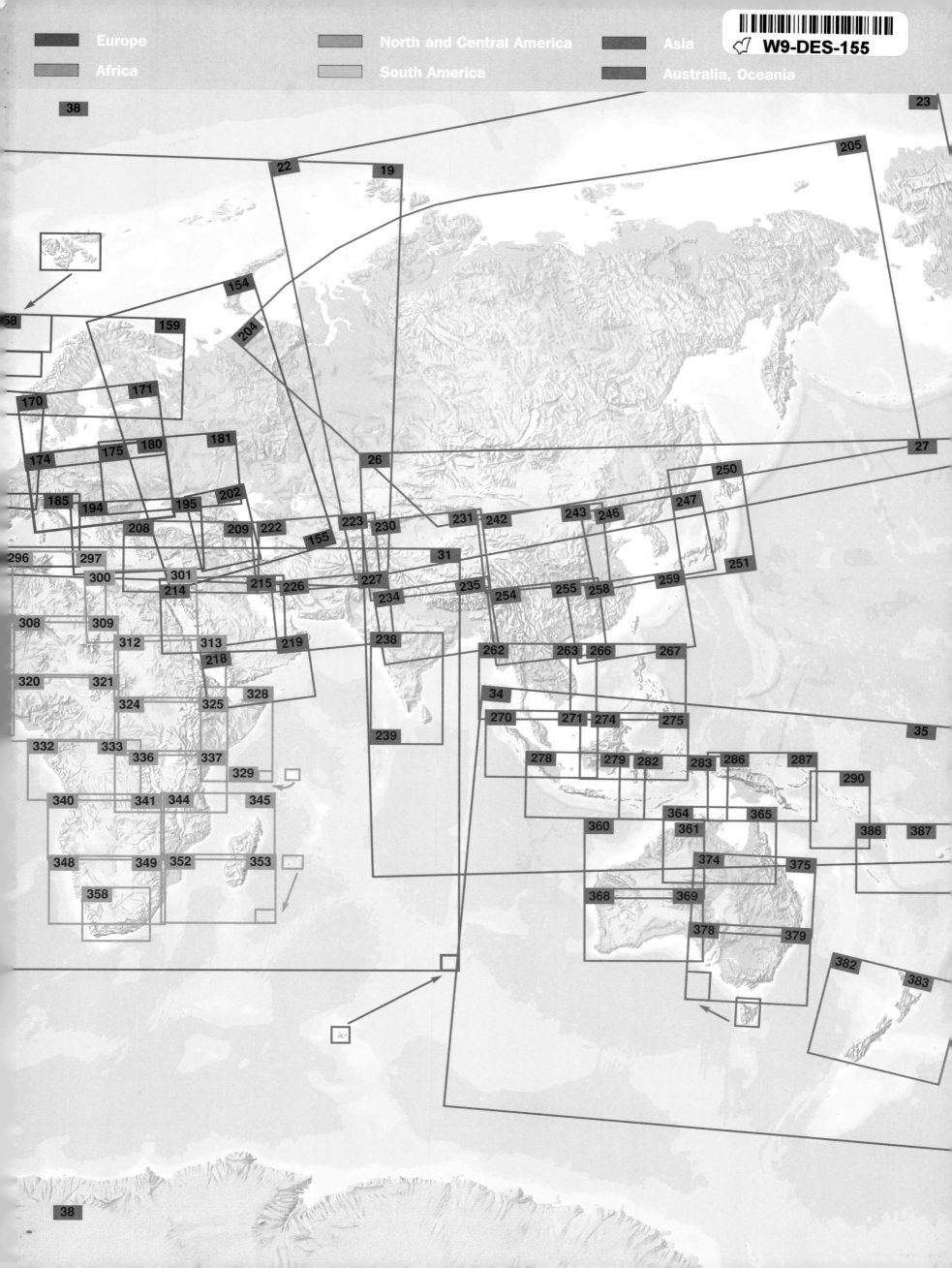

Europe

Africa

North and Central America

South America

Asia

Australia, Oceania

SATELLITE
WORLD ATLAS

2006 Barnes & Noble

ISBN-13: 978-0-7607-8530-0
ISBN-10: 0-7607-8530-9

Printed and bound in Spain

1 3 5 7 9 10 8 6 4 2

SATELLITE
WORLD ATLAS

UPDATED MAPS AND AMAZING DIGITAL IMAGES OF THE EARTH

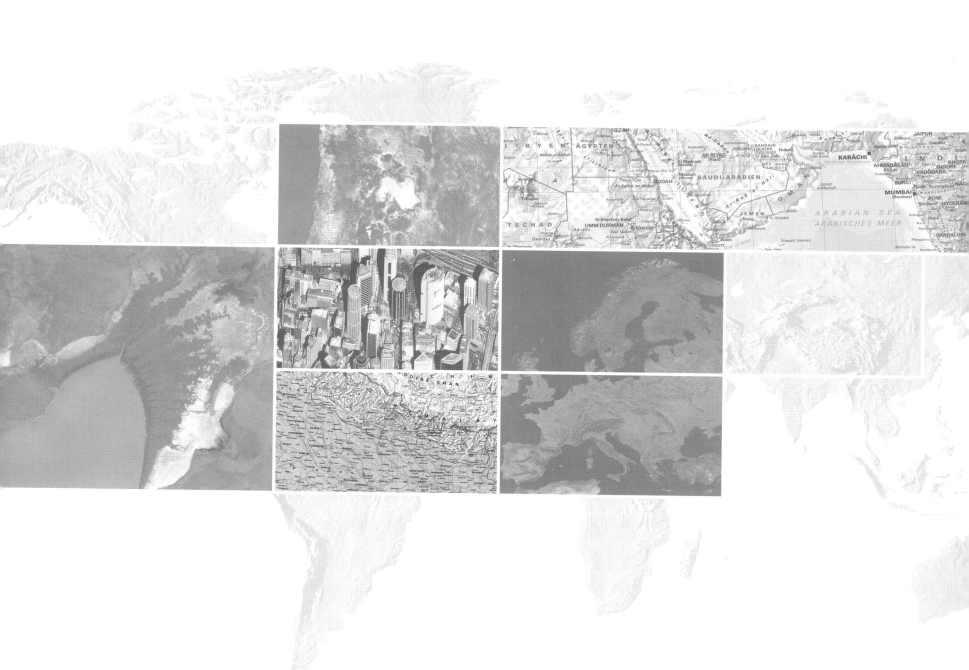

BARNES & NOBLE

NEW YORK

Contents

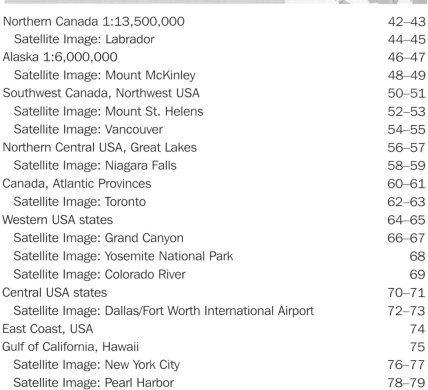

Asia 1:4,500,000

Africa 1:4,500,000

Australia and Oceania 1:4,500,000

Landscapes and water

1. Coast, shoreline
2. Island, archipelago
3. Coral reef
4. River, permanently water-bearing
5. River, only seasonally water-bearing
6. Waterfall, rapids
7. Lake, permanently water-bearing
8. Lake, only seasonally water-bearing
9. Reservoir with dam
10. Spring, oasis
11. Marsh, swamp
12. Desert
13. Plateau
14. Hill and mountain country
15. Mountains, mountain ranges
16. Mountain with altitude
17. Pass with altitude
18. Glacier

Contour level —————

Depth contour —————

Height
m
3000
2000
1000
600
300
100
0
< 0
200
1000
2000
4000
6000
8000
10000
m
Depth

Traffic routes, towns, borders

Traffic routes

1. Highway/multi-carriageway—under construction
2. Highways
3. Main road
4. Side road
5. Trail, piste
6. Railroad
7. National—international airport

Town designations

8. Over 5,000,000 inhabitants
9. 1,000,000–5,000,000 inhabitants
10. 500,000–1,000,000 inhabitants
11. 100,000–500,000 inhabitants
12. 50,000–100,000 inhabitants
13. 10,000–50,000 inhabitants
14. 5000–10,000 inhabitants
15. Fewer than 5000 inhabitants

Borders

16. State border
17. Disputed border
18. Capital city of a sovereign state
19. Administrative border
(federal state, region, province, autonomous area)
20. Region with indication of sovereign state
21. Restricted area
22. Reservation
23. National park
24. Cultural monument—particularly worth visiting
25. Natural monument—particularly worth visiting

Place markings

NEW YORK	Over 5,000,000 inhabitants
SURABAYA	1,000,000–5,000,000 inhabitants
LIVERPOOL	500,000–1,000,000 inhabitants
MOMBASA	100,000–500,000 inhabitants
Périgueux	50,000–100,000 inhabitants
San Vicente	10,000–50,000 inhabitants
Ban Dung	5000–10,000 inhabitants
Lakohembi	Fewer than 5000 inhabitants

Sundry markings

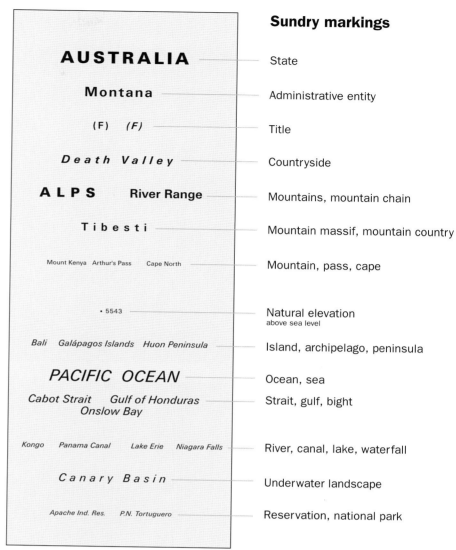

AUSTRALIA	State
Montana	Administrative entity
(F) *(F)*	Title
Death Valley	Countryside
ALPS **River Range**	Mountains, mountain chain
Tibesti	Mountain massif, mountain country
Mount Kenya Arthur's Pass Cape North	Mountain, pass, cape
• 5543	Natural elevation above sea level
Bali Galápagos Islands Huon Peninsula	Island, archipelago, peninsula
PACIFIC OCEAN	Ocean, sea
Cabot Strait Gulf of Honduras *Onslow Bay*	Strait, gulf, bight
Kongo Panama Canal Lake Erie Niagara Falls	River, canal, lake, waterfall
Canary Basin	Underwater landscape
Apache Ind. Res. P.N. Tortuguero	Reservation, national park

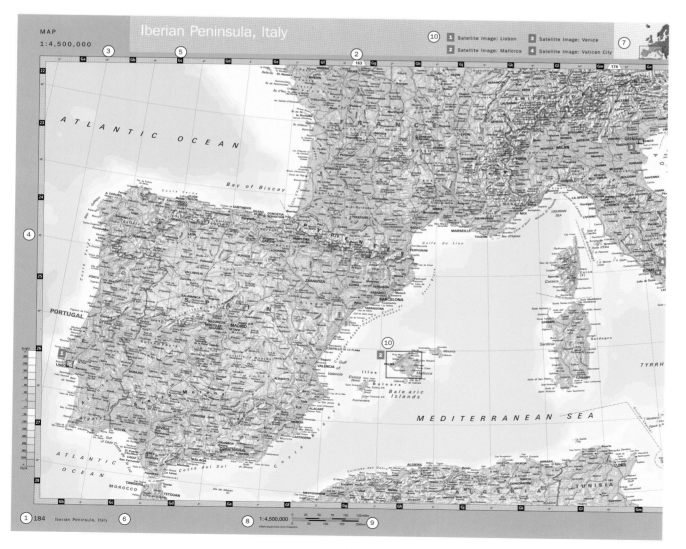

Map borders

- ① Page number
- ② Page reference
- ③ Geographical longitude
- ④ Geographical latitude
- ⑤ Search field indication
- ⑥ Column, page title
- ⑦ Page overview, pictogram
- ⑧ Scale and projection
- ⑨ Scale in km
- ⑩ Reference to satellite image

Satellite images and resolution

The resolution of a satellite image is determined by how great a surface area a pixel (or cell) of the imager can see. If an image's resolution is 1 m (3.3 ft), this means that a single pixel of the image can show a surface area of 1 x 1 m (3.3 x 3.3 ft). This is particularly remarkable for a camera that is located some 681 km (423 miles) above the earth's surface.

While the highest image resolutions have the greatest eye appeal, when printing, it is often necessary to alter the resolution of the images. For example: An area 10 x 10 km (6.2 x 6.2 miles) at a resolution of 1 m (3.3 ft) would comprise 10,000 x 10,000 pixels. If such an image were to be reproduced at the standard print resolution of 300 dpi (dots/pixels per inch), then the finished image would be 83.5 x 83.5 cm (33 x 33 in) in size. This is hardly a practical format for most books or newspapers. To fit a whole image on a smaller page, such pictures are generally edited, or brought into line with a predetermined page layout and format. When an image like this needs to fit into an area of 20 x 20 cm (8 x 8 in), it must be reduced by a factor of 4: This means 2500 x 2500 pixels or a resolution of 4 m (13 ft) per pixel.

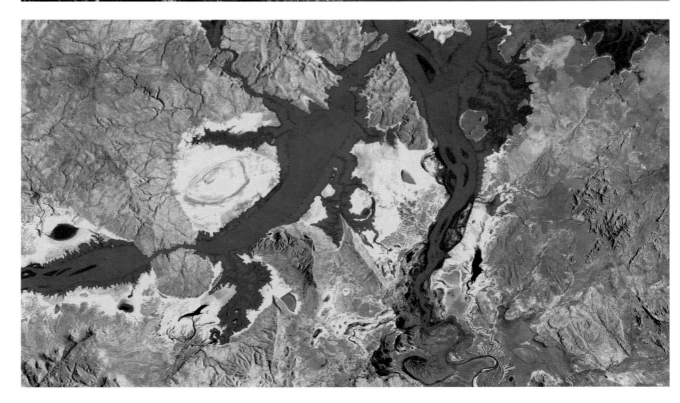

top: **resolution: 10,000 m**

middle: **resolution: 250 m**

bottom: **resolution: 100 m**

It must nevertheless be emphasized that an image with an original resolution of 4 m (13 ft) does not give the same amount of detail as an edited image with a resolution of 1 m (3.3 ft), viewed at the lower resolution. For this reason most images have been reduced to $\frac{1}{4}$ or $\frac{1}{10}$ of their original resolution. Some images, however, appear here at their original resolution.

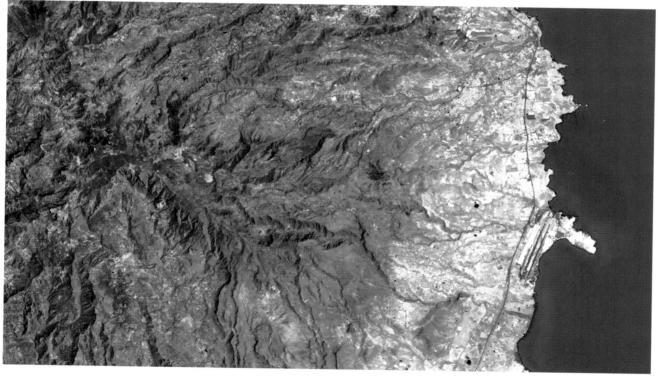

top: **resolution: 30 m**

middle: **resolution: 15 m**

bottom: **resolution: 1 m**

Satellite images and the underlying technology

Satellite images can be divided by means of two major criteria: by their **resolution** or by their **frequency band** or spectral colors.

Resolution

The resolution of a satellite image *(see information on pages VIII and IX)* is defined by the smallest point or pixel of which the image is made up. If a satellite sensor's resolution is at 5 m (16.4 ft), for example, this means that each dot (pixel) in the image corresponds to a surface area of 5 x 5 m (16.4 x 16.4 ft). With some exceptions, the rule of thumb is this: Objects that are smaller than the resolution capability cannot be clearly identified in a satellite image.

Modern commercial satellites supply data with a resolution of between 60 cm (23.6 in) and 1 km (0.6 miles) per pixel. At 60 cm (23.6 in), people can still be recognized as such, even when they cannot be identified. A resolution of 1 km (0.6 miles) per pixel is useful only when you want to capture whole countries in one view.

Color bands

The overall impression of a satellite image is largely determined by the choice of individual colors used. The sensors record separate data for each segment of the color spectrum. Printed out all together, the three data sets for the segments red, green, and blue, depending on how they are combined, give a natural color rendering. In fact, most satellites record four or more color segments, of which many lie outside the visible color spectrum. As a result, with the help of satellites, numerous discoveries and a great deal of information have been garnered for research and development purposes that could not have been achieved by any other means.

Not all satellites, however, record multiple colors. Where color is not important, it is easier to achieve a higher resolution in black

Satellites, such as Spacelmagings's, collect data from all around the globe

and white than in color. When a satellite supplies images in black and white, it is called panchromatic data. Of course, a combination of the two is best: the high resolution of panchromatic data together with the color rendering of lower resolution imagery. WorldSat has developed its own method, in which color images with lower resolution are combined with high-resolution panchromatic pictures, and the result is a high-definition image in color. Incidentally, the raw data from a satellite rarely gives the "true" or "natural" view that we recognize from our everyday reality. Only after a process of digital editing on a computer is a realistic color rendering achieved.

All satellite pictures are then saved as a scene or extract with a standardized size. A satellite records a strip of a given width by "scanning" the earth's surface. Normally, the size of a scene is defined as a quadrant of this strip width. Therefore, if a satellite maps a strip 60 km (37.3 miles) wide, a scene has a surface of 60 x 60 km (37.3 x 37.3 miles). In general, such a

small extract is not sufficient so two or more such scenes are put together to form a mosaic. This can be a problem when the individual scenes of a mosaic come from different seasons or even from different years. In such mosaics, when rendered in natural color, not only must the given data be edited, but the color values of the individual scenes must also be standardized and balanced.

Balancing gives rise to yet another difficulty: the dissimilarity between pictures with different resolutions. If, for example, one wishes to zoom in from a view from outer space to a particular house on earth, it is necessary to mount at least five different image layers one behind the other. If the colors of these layers are not balanced, then the realistic zoom effect is lost, because the overlap becomes visible. WorldSat is one company that has succeeded in creating a color match between data sets with different resolutions. Thus, an apparently natural zoom from the edge of our atmosphere to a single car on the road is possible.

Digital elevation data and reliefs

Digital elevation or relief data (digital terrain data, DTED) show the height profile of a landscape. For each point inside an image, the elevation above sea level is available. On the basis of this data, land models can be created. Information on the vegetation, road traffic, deserts, etc. cannot however be obtained in this way. But if this data is combined with satellite images it is possible to create realistic models of the earth's surface. With the corresponding software one can even simulate flights through virtual landscapes.

The World

KUWAIT
Tābuk
Ad Dahna
Bandar-e Abbas
Khūzdar
Sukkur
Bikaner
Aligarh
Jodhpur
JAIPUR
Agra
Fīrozābād
LUCKNOW
Patna
Ajmer
Gwalior
KANPUR
Jhānsi
Allahābad
VĀRĀNASI
Jabalpur
Bandar-e Chāh Bahār
KARĀCHI
Tropic of Cancer
Haidarābād
Udaipur
Madhya
Rājasthan
Uttar Pradesh
Jharkhand
Rānchi
KOL
(Ca
Buraydah
Ad-Dammām
Manama
BAHRAIN
QATAR
Doha
Dubai
Abu Dhabi
UNITED ARAB EMIRATES
RIYADH
Al Hufuf
Medina
Rājkot
AHMADĀBĀD
Ujjain
BHOPAL
INDORE
Chhattisgarh
Raipur
Raurkela
Orissa
Muscat
Porbandar
VADODARA
Bharuch
Dhūlia
Amrāvati
Nāgpur
Bhavnagar
Mecca
At-Ta'if
JIDDAH
SAUDI ARABIA
Rub' al Khālī
Gulf of Oman
OMAN
SURAT
Nashik
Aurangābād
NĀGPUR
Maharāshtra
Būr Sūdān
Al-Qunfudhah
Masira
MUMBAI (BOMBAY)
PUNE
Nizamabad
Vishākh
Abhā
Salalah
Sholāpur
HYDERĀBĀD
Sāngli
Krishna
Vijayawāda
Najrān
YEMEN
Al Ghaydah
ARABIAN SEA
Kolhāpur
barga
Guntur
Ba
Be
Seiwan
Shibām
Sanaa
Hubli
Kurnool
Nellore
Mitsiwa
Al Hudaydah
Al Mukallā
Goa
Davangere
Asmara
Aksum
Ta'izz
Mangalore
BANGALORE
CHENNAI (MADRAS)
Mekele
4620
Aden
Gulf of Aden
Socotra (Yemen)
Amīndīvi Is.
Calicut
Erode
Mysore
Vellore
Gondar
Kelay Tana
Dese
DJIBOUTI
Tadjoura
Raas 'Asayr
Lakshadweep
Cochin
Alleppey
Tamil Nadu
Kumbakonam
Dindigul
Pondicherry
Madurai
Sri Jawaharlal Markos
Djibouti
Barbera
Haafuun
Lakshadweep Is.
Quilon
Tirunel veli
Trincomalee
Jima
Dire Dawa
Hargeysa
Eight Degree Channel
Nagercoil
Trivandrum
SRI LANKA
ADDIS ABABA
Harer
Ogādēn
COLOMBO
Kandy
Awasa
Goba
Gaalka'yo
Sri Jayawardhanapura
Kotte
Moratuwa
ETHIOPIA
Gaarowe
Islands

The World, Physical Overview

1:85 000 000

0	500	1000	1500	2000	2500	3000 miles
0	1000	2000	3000	4000		5000 km

Van der Grinten Projection

1:85 000 000

0	500	1000	1500	2000	2500	3000 miles
0	1000	2000	3000	4000	5000 km	

North America

1:30,000,000

Van der Grinten Projection

North America

1:30,000,000

Van der Grinten Projection

| 0 | 250 | 500 | 750 | 1000 | 1250 miles |
| 0 | 500 | 1000 | 1500 | 2000 km |

Height
m
3000
2000
1000
600
300
100
0
< 0
200
1000
2000
4000
6000
8000
10000
m
Depth

1:30,000,000

0   250   500   750   1000   1250 miles

0   500   1000   1500   2000 km

Van der Grinten Projection

1:30,000,000

Van der Grinten Projection

0	250	500	750	1000	1250 miles
0	500	1000	1500	2000 km	

Ab 160° Ba 150° Bb 140° 10 Ca 130° Cb 120° Da 110° Db 100

10°

P A C I F I C

9

Line Islands

Palmyra
(USA)

Teraina
Tabuneran

Kiritimati

0°

Equator
Jarvis
(USA)

O C E A N

Clipperton I.
(F)

R i s e

Malden

10

K I R I B A T I

Starbuck

Penrhyn

Penrhyn
(Tongareva)

Vostock Carolina

Rokahanga

Manihiki B a s i n Flint

Hatutea

Nuku Hiva **Marquises Is.**
Ua Huka
Ua Pou Hiva Oa
Tahuata

Fatu Hiva

Bauer
Basin

35

Suwarrow

11

**Cook
Islands**

(NZ)

Palmerston

Aitutaki Hervey
Mitiaro

Atiu Maute

Rarotonga

Mangaia

Society Islands

Bora
Bora Huchine
Raiatea Papeete
Tahiti

Mataiva
Rangiroa

Niau Fakarava Katiu
Makemo
Anaa Marutea Tatakoto
Amanu

Marokau Hao
Nengonengo

Ahunui

F r e n c h

Îles du
Roi Georges Napuka

T u a m o t u   I s l a n d s

Pukapuka

Pukarua

Reao

Tiki B a s i n

20°

**P o l y n e s i a
(F)**

Maria Rurutu

Mangaia

Tropic of Capricorn

Austral Islands

Vanavana
Turéia Ténarunga

Tematangi Mururoa Marutéa
Group Acteon

Gambier Is.

Mangareva

12

Rimatara Tubuai

Raivaveé

Rapa

Oeno Henderson Ducie
Pitcairn
Pitcairn Islands
(U.K.)

Sala y Gomez
(Chile)

Rapa Nui
Easter I.
(Chile)

P

S O U T H

P A C I F I C

O C E A N

P a c i f i c

13

30°

40°

Height
m
3000
2000
1000
600
300
100
0
<0
200
1000
2000
4000
6000
8000
10000
m
Depth

14

50°

E a s t

15

170° Ab 160° Ba 150° Bb 140° Ca 130° Cb 120° Da 110°

1:30,000,000

0 250 500 750 1000 1250 miles

0 500 1000 1500 2000 km

Van der Grinten Projection

Caribbean Sea

Ea 90° **Eb** 80° **Fa** 70° **11** **Fb** 60° **Ga** 50° **Gb** 40° **Ha**

Guatemala EL SALVADOR NICA- RAGUA
St. Ana Tegucigalpa
San Salvador
León Esteli
I. Providencia (CO)
I. San Andrés (CO)
de France Fort Martinique (F)
Castries ST. LUCIA
ST.VINCENT
Kingstown BARBADOS
Bridgetown

Manaqua COSTA RICA Puntarenas
S. José Limón
Colón
PANAMÁ
Panamá David
Gulf of Panama
Chitré
Santa Marta
BARRANQUILLA Cartagena
Sincelejo
Montería
MARACAIBO Maracay
CARACAS
Valencia
Barquisimeto
Cumaná
Barcelona
Maturín
Port of Spain Tobago
TRINIDAD AND TOBAGO
Trinidad
Curaçao (NL)
Willemstad
Lesser
Antilles
GRENADA
St. George's

8

Guiana
Basin

Isla del Coco (CR)
Cocos
Ridge

Turbo
C. Ojeda
Cabimas
Valera
S. Cristóbal
Barinas
S. Fernando
El Tigre
Ciudad Guayana
Ciudad Bolívar
Orinoco
Georgetown
New Amsterdam
Paramaribo
Kourou
Cayenne
GUYANA
SURINAME
French Guiana
Guiana
Highlands

10°

Isla Malpelo (CO)
MEDELLIN Manizales Cartago Pereira
Tunja
Bucaramanga
Cúcuta
Bello
BOGOTÁ
Ibagué
Kuru- pukari
Boa Vista
Roraima
9

Buena ventura
CALI
Popayán
Guaviare
Pico da Neblina 3013
Içana
Amapá

Tumaco
ECUADOR
QUITO
Pasto
Macapá
Ilha do Marajó
Equator
Bragança
Equator

Manta
Portoviejo
GUAYAQUIL
Chimborazo 6310
Riobamba
Rio Negro
Rio Putumayo
Amazon
Manacapuru
MANAUS
Amazon
Óbidos
Santarém
Cametá
Tucurui
BELEM
São Luis
Parnaiba
FORTALEZA
Rémidos
Fernando de Noronha

0°

Machala
Cuenca
Iquitos
Leticia
Rio Juruá
Itaituba
Altamira
Marabá
Imperatriz
Tocantinópolis
Sobral
Crateús
Iguatu
Rio Grande do Norte
Natal
Campina Grande
Paraiba
João Pessoa

10°

Sullana
Piura
CHICLAYO
Cajamarca
Pucallpa
Rio Ucayali
Cruzeiro do Sul
Labrea
Humaitá
Rio Madeira
Rio Tapajós
Rio Xingu
Rio Araguaia
Rio Tocantins
Miracema
Juazeiro do Norte
Caruaru
Petrolina
RECIFE
Maceió
Olinda

TRUJILLO
Chimbote
Rio Branco
Porto Velho
Abunã
Araripina
Senhor do Bonfim
Juazeiro
Atalaia
Sergipe

Callao Huan- cayo
LIMA
La Montaña
Brasiléia
Riberalta
Rio Madre de Dios
Serra dos Parecis
Rondônia
BRAZIL
Barreiras
SALVADOR
Bahia de Todos os Santos

10°

Pisco
Ica
Cuzco
Abancay
Trinidad
Rio Guaporé
Mato Grosso
Rio Teles Pires
Porangatu
Feira de Santana
Ilhéus

Nazca
Lago Titicaca
Illampu 6362
Llanos de Mojos
Diamantino
Goiás
Aracaju
Belmonte

Arequipa
Camaná
LA PAZ
Cochabamba
SANTA CRUZ
Pantanal
Cuiabá
Rondonópolis
BRASILIA
Distrito Federal
Anápolis
Montes Claros
Teófilo Otoni
11

Mollendo
Arica
Oruro
Sucre
Potosí
Corumbá
Mato Grosso do Sul
GOIÂNIA
Uberlândia
Uberaba
Divinó polis
Governador Valadares
BELO HORIZONTE
Vitória

Iquique
Salar de Uyuni
BOLIVIA
Campo Grande
Barretos
Ribeirão Preto
Represa de Furnas
Juiz de Fora
Campos

20°

Antofagasta
Salar de Atacama
Tartagal
Salvador de Jujuy
Concepción
Rio Paraguay
Aracatuba
Bauru
Represa de Tres Marias
Campinas
Sorocaba
Sto. André
Volta Redonda
Petrópolis
RIO DE JANEIRO
Niterói
Tropic of Capricorn

Chañaral
Copiapó
C. Ojos 6864
Catamarca
La Rioja
Salta
San Miguel de Tucumán
Santiago del Estero
Resistencia
Formosa
Asunción
Foz do Iguaçu
Londrina
SÃO PAULO
CURITIBA
Paranaguá
Santos
Santos Plateau

Coquimbo
Viña del Mar
Aconcagua 6962
San Juan
San Luis
Mendoza
Santa Fe
Corrientes
Rio Paraná
Uruguaiana
Passo Fundo
Caxias do Sul
Joinville
Itajaí
Florianópolis
Lages
Tubarão
Santa Catarina

12

Valparaíso
Tupungato 6800
Rancagua
CORDOBA
Villa María
Rio Cuarto
Paraná
Rosario
Salto
URUGUAY
Rio Negro
Santa Maria
Canoas
PORTO ALEGRE

30°

Curicó
Talca
San Rafael
Luis
SANTIAGO DE CHILE
Bernardo
Godoy Cruz
S. Isidro
Morón
BUENOS AIRES
La Plata
Lomas
MONTEVIDEO
Pelotas
Rio Grande
Mirim Lagoon
Ratos Lagoon
30
Rio Grande Rise

Chillán
Concepción
Talcahuano
Santa Rosa
Tandil
Mar del Plata
13

Temuco
Valdivia
Neuquén
Bahía Blanca
Bahía Blanca
Buenos Aires
Pampa

Osorno
Puerto Montt
Nahuel Huapi
Rio Negro
Rio Colorado
Zapala
Rio Negro

40°

A T L A N T I C

Argentine

Isla Grande
Archipiélago de los Chonos
Viedma
San Matías Gulf
Valdés Peninsula
Rawson
Argentine Plain
Basin

O C E A N

Península de Taitao
Golfo de Peñas
4058
Comodoro Rivadavia
Gulf of San Jorge
Cabo dos Bahias
Cabo Tres Puntas

14

Isla Wellington
Lago S. Martín
Santa Cruz
Lago Viedma
Lago Argentino
Lago Buenos Aires
Valentín
Chubut
Rio Chubut

50°

Archipiélago Reina Adelaida
Puerto Natales
Rio Gallegos
Bahia Grande
Falkland Islands (U.K.)
Mt. Adam
Stanley
West Falkland
Darwin
East Falkland
Falkland Plateau

Punta Arenas
Str. of Magellan
Strait of Magellan
Isla S.ta Inés
Tierra del Fuego
Ushuaia
Isla de los Estados
Shag Rocks (GB)
South Georgia (GB)
2931 Mt. Paget
Grytviken
Scotia Ridge
15

S o u t h e a s t
Pacific
Basin
Cape Horn
Yaghan Basin
Scotia Sea

Ea 100° 90° **Eb** 80° **Fa** 70° **Fb** 60° **Ga** 50° **Gb** 40° **Ha**

South America

160°   150°   140°   12   130°   120°   110°

0°

10°

20°

30°

40°

50°

160°   150°   140°   130°   120°   110°

1:30,000,000

| 0 | 250 | 500 | 750 | 1000 | 1250 miles |

| 0 | 500 | 1000 | 1500 | 2000 km |

Van der Grinten Projection

1:30,000,000

0   250   500   750   1000   1250 miles

0   500   1000   1500   2000 km

Van der Grinten Projection

Europe

1:30,000,000

Van der Grinten Projection

| 0 | 250 | 500 | 750 | 1000 | 1250 miles |
| 0 | 500 | 1000 | 1500 | 2000 km |

Asia

1

A R C T I C

o. Ušakova

O. Schmidta

O. Komsomolefs

o. Vize

O. Oktyabr´skoy
Revolyutsii

O. Bol´shevik

S e v e r n a y a   Z e m l y a

m.Čeljuskin

O. Malyy Taymyr

zal. Faddeja

K a r a   S e a

L a p t e v   S e a

Belkowski-H.

New Siberian Is.

Anjou Is.

o. Ber

o. Russkiy

arch. Nordensköld

B y r r a n g a

Marii Pronščevoj

o. Bol. Begičěv

o. Ben

o. Faddejevskij

2

o-va Izvestij CIK
Ostrova
Arkticheskogo
Instituta

g o r y
g o r y   B y r

T a y m y r   p e n i n s u l a

Chatangskiy Zal.

Nordvik

Olenekskiy
Zal.

L e n a
D e l t a

Prol. Sannikova

o. Maly Ljachovskij

o. Bol. Ljacho

Prol. Dmitriya Lap

K

o. Svedtrup

ozero Taymyr

Syndassko

Tit-Ary

Yanskiy Zal.

Yano-Indigirskaya Nizmenn

o. Belyy

o. Vil´kickogo

Dickson

Pyasina

N o r t h   S i b e r i a n   L o w l a n d

Chatanga

Tiksi

Kjusjur

Kazačje

o. Sibirjakova

Gydanskaya Guba

Yeniseyskiy Zal.

Karaul

Chatanga

Kotuj

Olenjok

Lena

Khrebet

o. Olenij

70°

Y a m a l

Gydanskiy

oz. Pjasino

p l a t o   P u t o r a n a

Žigansk

Verkhoyanskiy Khr.

Jana

Pol.

Sjojacha

P o l u o s t r o v

Dudinka

Norilsk

Jessei

Verkhoyanskiy

19

Mys-
Kamennyi

Tazovskiy
Pol.

Igarka

Njurba

Champa

Sangar

Batamaj

Khr.

Chandyga

Novyj
Port

Nyda

Arctic Circle
Tazovskij

Yenisey

Turuhansk

Niž. Tunguska

Tura

Viljujskoje
vdhr.

Botulu

Njurba

Mirnyj

Suntar

Yakutsk

El´dikan

3

W e s t

Taz

Nižneimatskoje

C e n t r a l

S I B E R I A

S i b e r i a n

Lena

Marcha

Chandyga

Sun

Chanty-
Mansijsk

Ob´

Surgut

Nizhnevartovsk

Kuz´movka

Podkamennaja

R U S S I A

P l a t e a u

Lensk

Mača

Aldan

60°

S i b e r i a n

Kolpaševo

Jenisej

Angara

Kežma

Kirensk

Ivanuškova

Aldan

A l d a n s k o y e

Tobol´sk

Irtys

Ob´

Ilimsk

Ust´-Kut

N a g o r ´ y e

Aldan

Height
m
3000

Išim

Tara

Jenisejsk

Bratsk

S t a n o v o y e

Slovarodima

2000

OMSK

Barabinsk

Tomsk

Ačinsk

**KRASNO-
YARSK**

Bratskoye
Res.

S t a n o v o y e
N a g o r ´ y e

Khrebet Dzhug

Čumikan

1000
600

Petro-
pavlovsk

NOVOSIBIRSK

Kemerovo

Kansk

Tulun

S t a n o v o y   K h r.

Šantar-
o-va

300

Kokshetau

Prokopjevsk

Abakan

N a g o r ´ y e

Zlatoust

100

Atbasar

Pavlodar

Barnaul

Novokuznetsk

Balagansk

Lena

Lake Baykal

Yablonovvy Khr.

4

0

Astana

Ekibastuz

Bijsk

Usol´e-
Sibirskoe

Pangu

<0

Temirtau

Semey

Rubcovsk

W e s t e r n   S a y a n

E a s t e r n   S a y a n

Kyzyl

Jenisej

Angarsk

Irkutsk

Čita

Belogorsk

200

Quaraghandy

Oskemen

K A Z A K H S T A N

A l t a y

Ölgiy

Ulaangom

Usol´e-

Ulan-Ude

Süchbataar

Blagoveščensk

Čegdomyn

Komsomol´sk
na-Amure

1000

S a r y a r k a

Lake
Zaysan

Hovd

Mörön

Manzhouli

2000

Ayakoz

Zaysan

Burchun

Süchbataar

Heilongjiang

4000

Balqash

Altay

Ulaanbaatar

Cöjbalsan

Khabarovsk

5

Lake Balqash

M O N G O L I A

QIQIHAR

6000

Džambul

Yining

Shihezi

Saynshand

Hegang

8000

Shymkent

ALMATY

ÜRÜMQI

HARBIN

Jiamusi

10000

Angren

Namangan

Bishkek

Přzevalsk

Gobi Desert

Dalandzadgad

Erenhot

Jixi

m
Depth

KYRGYZSTAN

TIAN SHAN

C H I N A

Hami

Mudanjiang

JILIN

6

TASHKENT

Andijon

Oos

Fergana

Korla

Lop nur

Anxi

N e i

Huhehaote

Jining

Zhang-
jiakou

Fuxin

Siping

Changchun

Vladivosto

Dushanbe

Pamir

X i n j i a n g   U y g u r   Z i z h i q u

Kashi

Anxi

Ikanbujmal

Charchan

M o n g o l

Zhang-

**SHEN
YANG**

Biaoyuan

Fushun

T A J I K S T A N

T a k l a   M a k a n   D e s e r t

Yumen

BAOTOU

6

Kunduz

1:30,000,000

0   250   500   750   1000   1250 miles

0   500   1000   1500   2000 km

Van der Grinten Projection

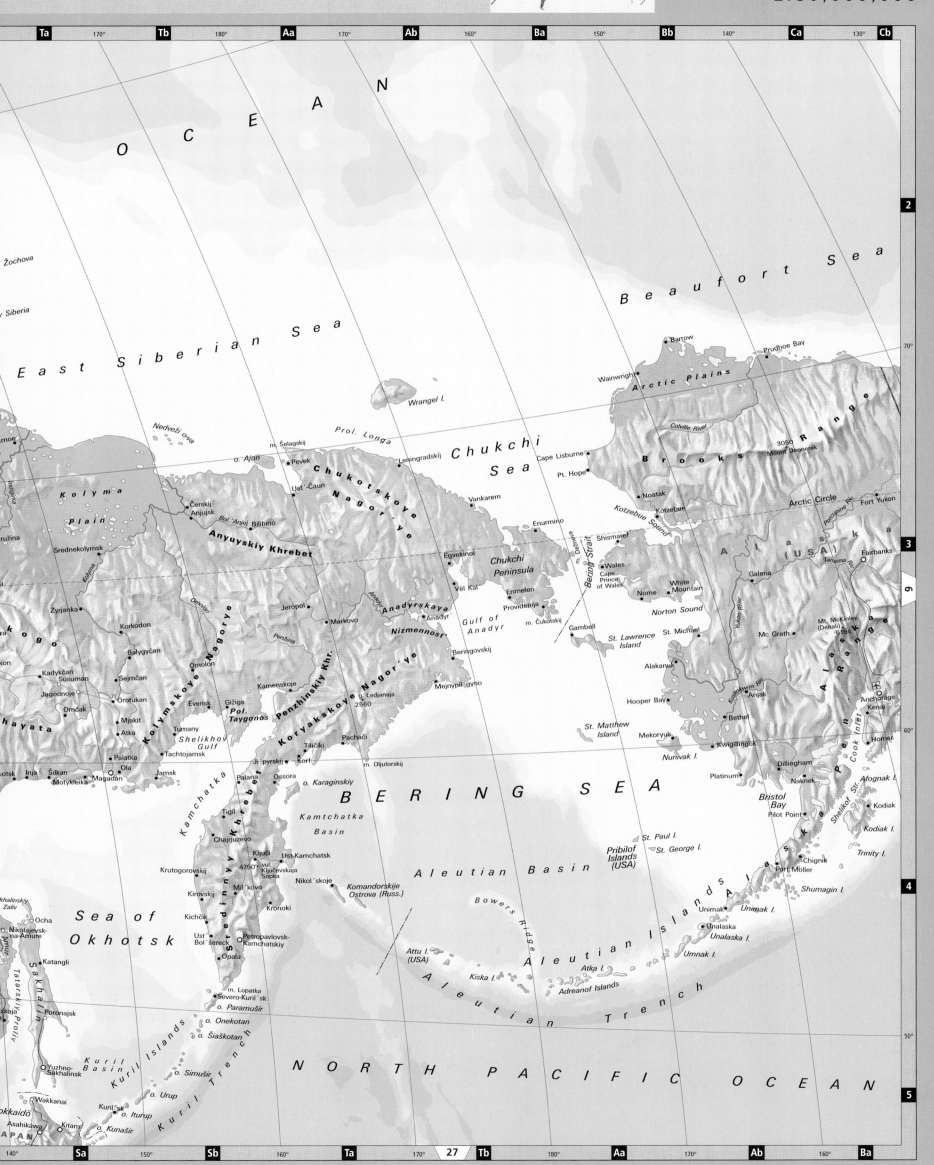

Ta | Tb | Aa | Ab | Ba | Bb | Ca | Cb
170° | 180° | 170° | 160° | 150° | 140° | 130°

O C E A N

Žochova

Siberia

E a s t   S i b e r i a n   S e a

Nedveži o-va

B e a u f o r t   S e a

Barrow
Prudhoe Bay

Wainwright
Arctic Plains

Wrangel I.

Prol. Longa

Colville River

m. Šelagskij
o. Ajon
Pevek
Leningradskij
Cape Lisburne
B r o o k s   R a n g e
3050
Mount Doonerek

C h u k c h i
S e a
Pt. Hope

Ust'-Čaun
Chukotskoye
Nagor'ye
Vankarem
Noatak
Arctic Circle

Kolyma
Čerskij
Anjujsk
Bol'Anjuj Bilibino
Enurmino
Kotzebue Sound
Kotzebue
Fort Yukon
Porcupine Riv.

Plain
Anyuyskiy Khrebet
Shismaref
A l a s k a
(USA)

Srednekolymsk
Egvekinot
Chukchi
Peninsula
Wales
Cape
Prince
of Wales
Nome
Galena
Fairbanks
Tanana Riv.

ružina
Zyrjanka
Jeropol
Vel'Kaj
Enmelen
Providenija
White
Mountain

Anadyrskaja
Anadyr
m. Čukotskij
Norton Sound
Mt. McKinley
(Denali)
6194

kogo
Korkodon
Markovo
Nizmennost'
Gulf of
Anadyr
Gambell
St. Lawrence
Island
St. Michael
Mc Grath
A l a s k a   R a n g e

Balygyčan
Penžina
Beringovskij
Alakanuk
Kuskokwim Riv.
Anjak
Anchorage

Kadykčan
Susuman
Sejmčan
Kolymskoye Nagor'ye
Omolon
Evensk
Kamenskoje
Mejnypil'gyno
g. Ledjanaja
2560
Hooper Bay
Bethel
Kenai

Jagodnoje
Omčak
Mjakit
Gižiga
Penzhinskiy Khr.
Koryakskoye Nagor'ye
St. Matthew
Island
Mekoryuk
Homer

hayata
Atka
Tumany
Pol.
Taygonos
Tiličiki
Pachači
St. Matthew
Island
Nunivak I.
Kwigillingok
Dillingham
Cook Inlet

kon
Palatka
Shelikhov
Gulf
Ji'pyrskij
Korf
m. Oljutorskij
Platinum
Naknek
Afognak I.

otsk
Inja
Šilkan
Ola
Tachtojamsk
Palana
Ossora
o. Karaginskij
Kodiak

Motykleika
Magadan
Jamsk
B E R I N G   S E A
Bristol
Bay
Pilot Point
Kodiak I.

Kamchatka
Tigil
Kamtchatka
Basin
St. Paul I.
Chignik
Trinity I.

Chajrjuzevo
Pribilof
Islands
(USA)
St. George I.
Port Moller

Ključi
Ust'-Kamtsak
Aleutian   Basin
Shumagin I.

Sea of
Okhotsk
Krutogorovskij
4750
vul.
Ključevskaja
Sopka
Nikol'skoje
Komandorskije
Ostrova (Russ.)
Bowers Ridge
Unimak I.
Unimak I.

khalinskij
Zaliv
Ocha
Nikolajevsk-
na-Amure
Kirovskij
Mil'kovo
Kronoki
Unalaska
Unalaska I.

Sedinnyy Khrebet
Kichčik
Umnak I.

Katangli
Ust'-
Bol'šereck
Petropavlovsk-
Kamchatskiy
Opala
Attu I.
(USA)
Kiska I.
Aleutian Islands
Atka I.
A l a s k a   P e n i n s u l a
Umnak I.

Sakhalin
Poronajsk
m. Lopatka
Severo-Kuril'sk
o. Paramušir
Adreanof Islands
A l e u t i a n   T r e n c h

Tatarskij Proliv
skaja Proliv
Kuril
Basin
o. Onekotan
o. Šiaškotan
Kuril Islands

Yuzhno-
Sakhalinsk
o. Simušir
N O R T H   P A C I F I C   O C E A N

Wakkanai
o. Urup
Kuril Trench

Hokkaidō
Kuril'sk
o. Iturup
Asahikawa
Kitami
o. Kunašir
J A P A N

140° | 150° | 160° | 170° | 180° | 170° | 160°
Sa | Sb | Ta | 27 | Tb | Aa | Ab | Ba

1:30,000,000

0   250   500   750   1000   1250 miles

0   500   1000   1500   2000 km

Van der Grinten Projection

Southeast Asia

24

33

36

1:30,000,000

0	250	500	750	1000	1250 miles
0	500	1000	1500	2000 km

Van der Grinten Projection

150°   160°   170°   180°   170°   160°   150°

40°

30°

20°

10°

10°

0°

10°

150°   160°   170°   180°   170°   160°

37

1:30,000,000

Van der Grinten Projection

0	250	500	750	1000	1250 miles
0	500	1000	1500	2000 km	

TURKEY
Konya
Antalya
Mersin ADANA Gaziantep Diyarbakir
Rhodes Iskenderun Orümiyeh Rasht Gorgan Mazar-e Sharif Kunduz Baghlan
Nicosia Latakia Mosul Maymanah Karakoram Xizang Jang Than
CYPRUS Homs ALEPPO Kirkuk Hamadan TEHRAN MASHHAD Srinagar CHINA
SEA Beirut DAMASCUS Qom Kermanshah Herat KABUL Peshawar HIMALAYA
LEBANON Haifa SYRIA BAGHDAD IRAN Rawalpindi Transhimalaya
Jerusalem AMMAN IRAQ Esfahan Dasht-e Kavir AFGHANISTAN Islamabad Lhasa
ALEXANDRIA ISRAEL An Najaf Khorramabad Birjand Gujranwala CHANDIGARH
JORDAN Karbala Dasht-e Lut Kandahar LAHORE Jalandhar Meerut
CAIRO Port Said Suez Sinai Ahvaz Kerman FAISALABAD Ludhiana Uttaranchal
GIZA Tanta SHIRAZ Abadan Zahedan Bahawalpur Rohtak
Al Fayyum Al Basra Bushehr PAKISTAN Multan New Delhi DELHI
Al Minya Asyut Kuwait Kuwait Bandar-e Baluchestan Khuzdar Bikaner JAIPUR
EGYPT Mut Luxor KUWAIT Ad-Dammam Bandar-e Abbas Panjgur Sukkur Jodhpur Gwalior KANPUR PATNA
Kharga Aswan Buraydah Manama BAHRAIN Dubai Gulf of Oman Ajmer Jhansi INDIA
Wadi Halfa QATAR Doha Abu Dhabi Haidarabad Udaipur Allahabad VARANASI
Toshka Lakes Medina Ad Dahna Al Hufuf UNITED ARAB EMIRATES Muscat Rajasthan BHOPAL KOLKATA
Marsa Sha'b JIDDAH Mecca RIYADH SAUDI ARABIA KARACHI Ahmadabad INDORE Jabalpur DHAKA
Nubian Desert At-Ta'if Rub' al Khali OMAN Tropic of Cancer VADODARA Chhattisgarh BANGLA-DESH
Bur Südan Al-Qunfudhah Abha OMAN SURAT Nashik Amravati NAGPUR Raipur Cuttack
Abu Hamad YEMEN Masira PUNE Aurangabad Bhubaneswar
Atbara Sanaa Shibam Salalah SHOLAPUR HYDERABAD Brahmapur
Khartoum North Kassala Mitsiwa Al Hudaydah Al Mukalla Al Ghaydah MUMBAI (BOMBAY) Vishakhapatnam
OMDURMAN Asmara ERITREA Ta'izz Aden Gulf of Aden Kolhapur Maharashtra Rajahmundry
Khartoum Aksum Mekele DJIBOUTI Socotra (Yemen) Hubli Kurnool Vijayawada Bay of Bengal
SUDAN Al-Damazin Gonder Dese DJIBOUTI Raas 'Asayr Davangere Nellore CHENNAI (MADRAS)
Sennar Debre Markos ETHIOPIA Haafuun Mangalore BANGALORE
Malakal ADDIS ABABA Barbera Bur Amindivi Is. Mysore Vellore Cuddalore
Jima Harer SOMALIA Lakshadweep Calicut Erode Kumbakonam
Wau Rumbek Awasa Goba Ogaden Lakshadweep Is. Cochin Alleppey Madurai Dindigul
Yambio Juba Dolo Gaalka'yo Quilon Tirunelveli Yapanaya
Mega Beled weyne Alleppey SRI LANKA
UGANDA Kelem Lake Turkana Baydhabo Nagercoil Trincomalee
Arua Marsabit Eight Degree Channel COLOMBO Kandy
Isiro KENYA Wajir Muqdisho (Mogadishu) Sri Jayawardhanapura Kotte Moratuwa
Kampala Eldoret Marka Male
Jinja Nakuru Jilib Somali MALDIVES
Kisumu Basin Maldives Addu Equator
RWANDA Nyeri NAIROBI Kismaayo
BURUNDI Kigali Lake Victoria Musoma Voi
Bukoba Arusha Moshi Malindi
Mwanza Kilimanjaro 5895 Mombasa Carlsberg Ridge Chagos Archipelago (U.K.)
TANZANIA Singida Tanga Pemba I. Amirantes Victoria Mahé Diego Garcia
Tabora Dodoma Wete SEYCHELLES Coëtivy Mid-Indian
Mpanda Morogoro Zanzibar I. Alphonse
DAR ES SALAAM Aldabra Is. Cosmoledo Is. Farquhar Is. Agalega (MS) Basin
Iringa Mtwara Providence I. Mascarene Plateau INDIAN
ZAMBIA Mbeya Lindi COMOROS Moroni Njazidja Mayotte (F) Maramokotro 2876 Mascarene
Lubumbashi Kasama Songea Palma Moçimboa da Praia Antsiranana Basin
Mansa Mzuzu MALAWI Lichinga Pemba Antalaha Cargados OCEAN
Kitwe Chipata Lilongwe Nacala Ambanja Tromelin (F) (MS)
Ndola Kabwe Cuamba Mahajanga Antsirabe Carajos
Mutare Blantyre Nampula Maroantsetra Rodrigues (MS)
HARARE Zomba Quelimane Mocuba Marovoay Mascarene Is. MAURITIUS
ZIMBABWE Chinhoyi Bindura Tete Ambatondrazaka Toamasina Port Louis
Kwekwe Mutare Cabora Bassa Res. Morondava Ambositra Réunion (F)
BULAWAYO Gweru Masvingo Mozambique Channel Mananjary St-Denis
Beira ANTANANARIVO Manakara St. Paul (F)
MOZAMBIQUE Vilanculos Morombe Fianarantsoa Farafangana MADAGASCAR
Chiredzi Chicualacuala Bassas da India (F) Ihosy
Messina Inhambane Europa (F) Manakara Tropic of Capricorn
Polokwane (Pietersburg) Guijá Toliara Cape Vohimena
Tshwane (Pretoria) Xai-Xai Tôlañaro Madagascar Basin
Johannesburg Komatipoort Manzini SWAZILAND Maputo Mbabane
Germiston Vereeniging Maseru
Bethlehem LESOTHO Richard's Bay Natal Basin
Ladysmith Pietermaritzburg
Kroonstad Drakensberg Durban
Umtata Crozet Basin Kerguelen (F) Mt. Ross 1850
Queenstown Amsterdam (F)
Buffalo City (East London) St. Paul (F)
Port Elizabeth

Africa

1:30,000,000

Van der Grinten Projection

0	250	500	750	1000	1250 miles
0	500	1000	1500	2000 km	

1:30,000,000

Van der Grinten Projection

| 0 | 250 | 500 | 750 | 1000 | 1250 miles |

| 0 | 500 | 1000 | 1500 | 2000 km |

Australia and Oceania

1:30,000,000

0	250	500	750	1000	1250 miles
0	500	1000	1500	2000 km	

Van der Grinten Projection

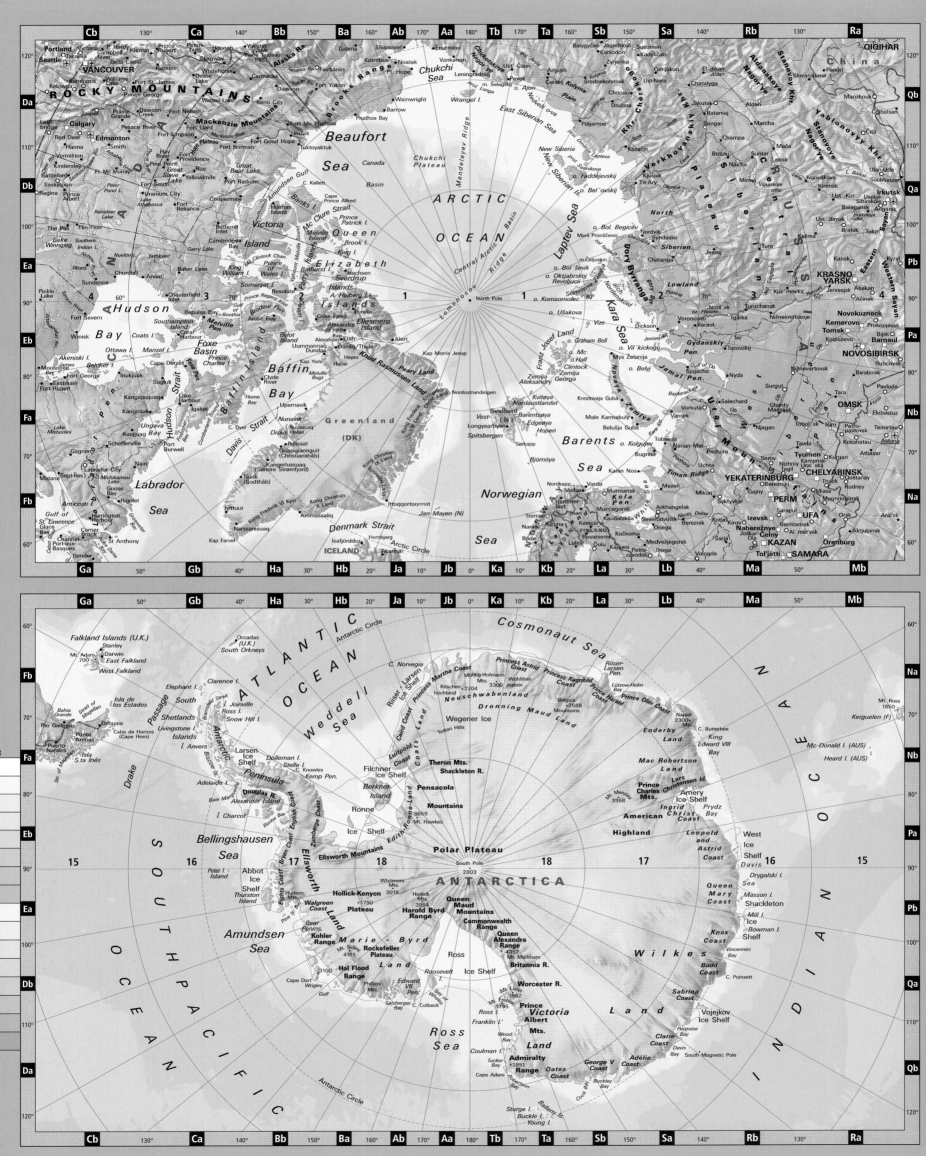

1:36,500,000

| 0 | 250 | 500 | 750 | 1000 miles |

| 0 | 500 | 1000 | 1500 | 2000 km |

Van der Grinten Projection

The Arctic, Antarctica

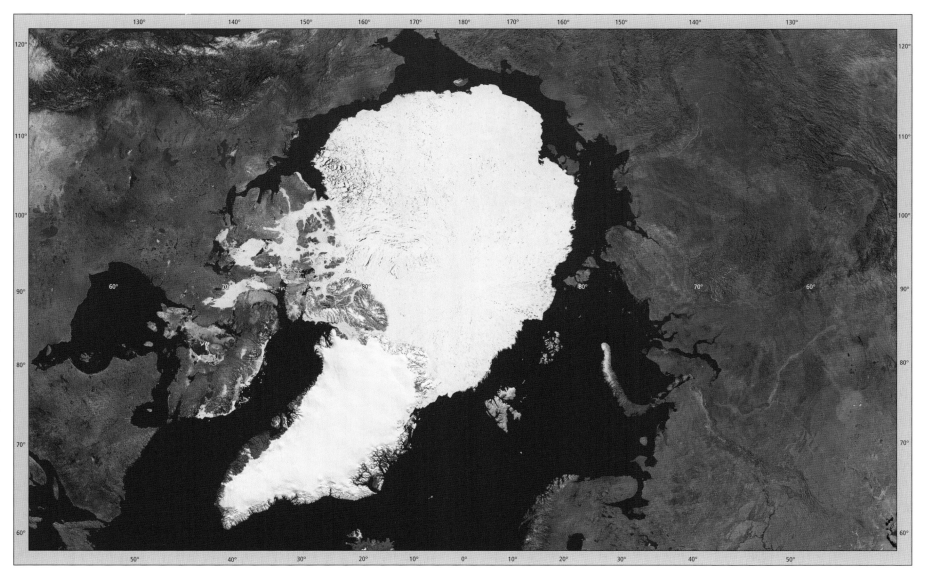

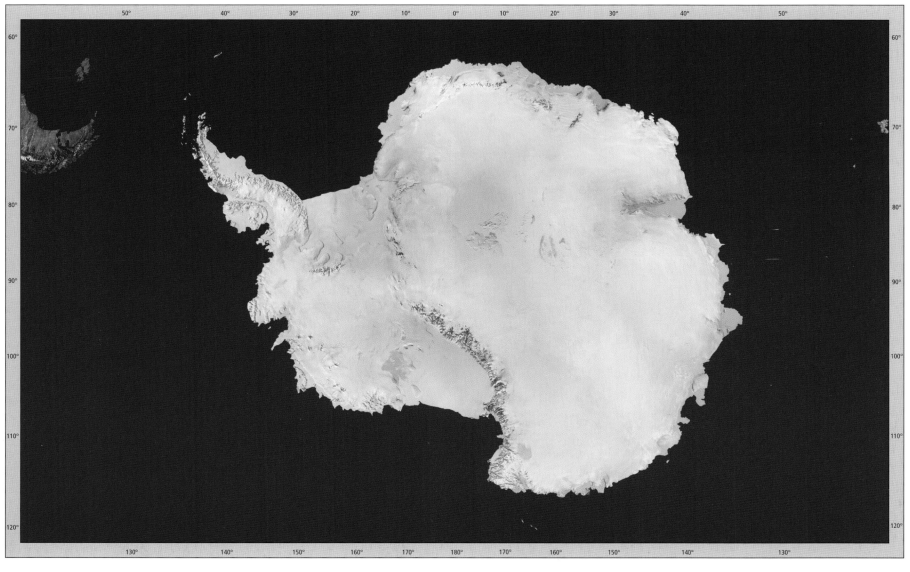

1:13,500,000

0   100   200   300   400miles
0   100   200   300   400   500km

Stereographic Projection

Labrador

Labrador, a large peninsula flanked by the Hudson Bay and the Labrador Sea, encompasses an area of about 1.6 million km² (617,600 square miles). It was discovered around AD 1000 by the Icelandic explorer Leif Eriksson, one of the first Europeans to reach North America. The Portuguese navigator João Fernandez, who sailed to Greenland in about 1500, named the island Tierra de Lavrador, and this name later passed to the whole peninsula. Administratively, the greater part of Labrador belongs to the Canadian province of Quebec and the smaller portion to the province of Newfoundland. The satellite image shows the eastern part of Labrador, between Ungava Bay in the west and the Labrador Sea in the east. The peninsula is virtually uninhabited and is still largely unexplored. Its climate is Arctic to sub-Arctic, with long winters and short summers. Snow falls from September to the end of June. The greater part of Labrador is covered by tundra.

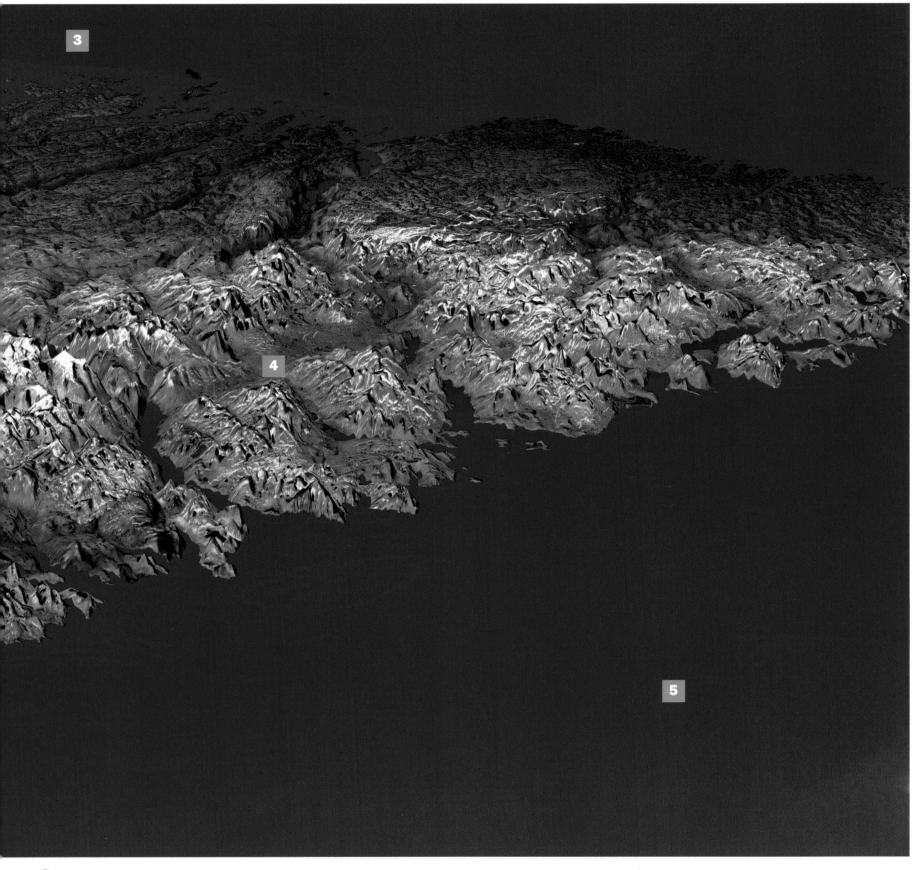

① **Saglek Bay** ←
This photograph shows a sunset on Saglek Bay, in northern Labrador. The uninhabited islands and islets that line this part of the peninsula lie in the calm waters of the fjords that cut deep inland. Saglek Bay was once the home of the Dorset Inuit, who migrated here about 2500 years ago. Archeological explorations have unearthed artifacts such as harpoon spikes and small knife blades.

② Hebron

In about 1700, the Boehm brothers founded several mission stations on the east side of the Labrador Peninsula, as part of a movement of religious reform that had developed before the time of Martin Luther, Ulrich Zwingli, and John Calvin. Hebron, a mission located at about 58° 12' north and 62° 24' west, was founded in 1831 with the aim of converting the native Inuit to Christianity. In 1959, following pressure from officials in charge of the province, the station was closed, and the small number of residents were moved farther south, although they did not easily adjust to city life. The buildings of the former mission—the church, living quarters, storerooms, and workshops—are still maintained today and are occasionally visited by passengers of passing cruise ships.

③ Ungava Bay

Ungava Bay, in the Hudson Strait, is some 20 km (12 miles) wide and extends inland for about the same distance. It divides the Labrador Peninsula into two unequal halves. The coastline here slopes gently down to the sea, and the bay itself is the habitat of many species of Arctic animals. The world's largest herds of caribou travel through Labrador, along with elks, wolves, lynx, grizzly bears, and even polar bears. Southern Labrador, where pine forests grow, is also home to North American porcupines, which are similar to tree-dwelling porcupines.

④ Mount Eliot

Mount Eliot is one of the highest peaks in the Torngat Mountains, and was surveyed for the first time in July 1900 by an expedition of scientists from Harvard University. The Torngat Mountains stretch from north to south through the eastern part of the Labrador Peninsula, forming a rough boundary between the provinces of Quebec in the west and Newfoundland in the east. A multitude of free-standing rock formations characterize the northern part of the mountain range: Here, sheer rock faces rise from the ocean to heights of up to 1500 m (4900 ft), creating a breathtaking sight.

⑤ Labrador Sea

The Labrador Sea, which lies between the southwestern coast of Greenland and the northeastern coast of the Labrador Peninsula, is part of the North Atlantic. It is the source of the Labrador Current, a very cold ocean current that influences the climate of eastern Canada. Along the continental shelf, the current supports a vast wealth of fish, since its cold waters are rich in oxygen. The Gulf Stream joins the Labrador Sea at Newfoundland.

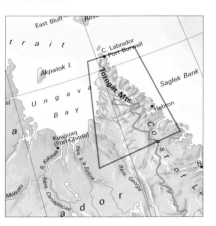

1:6,000,000

Albers Equal Area Conic Projection

2

Mount McKinley

Denali National Park and Preserve, in southern Alaska, consists of about 24,000 km² (9264 square miles) of wilderness, making it the second-largest nature reserve in the USA after Wrangell-St. Elias National Park, also in Alaska. Its landscape consists of broad tracts of tundra with wide river valleys that are the habitat of grizzly bears, wolves, reindeer, and elk, as well as high alpine mountain chains. In the center of the national park stands Mount McKinley: Peaking at 6194 m (20,328 ft), it forms part of the Alaska Range, a mountain chain whose average height is around 4000 m (13,130 ft). Mount McKinley's original name, Denali, comes from the Athabaskan Native American language and aptly describes it as "The High One."

1 Mount McKinley ↑

Denali or Mount McKinley? The confusion over the mountain's name has historical significance. In 1896 a gold prospector renamed it McKinley after William McKinley, who later became the 25th president of the United States. Since this time there have been protests over the name, although in 1980, the mountain was formally recorded as Denali in the Alaska National Interest Lands Conservation Act.

2 North Peak

The first ascent of Denali's 5934 m (19,475 ft) north peak was made in April 1910, when the polar researchers Tom Lloyd, Peter Andersen, Charley McGonagall, and Bill Taylor reached the summit. Although an earlier polar researcher, Dr. Frederick Cook, claimed to have climbed the peak in 1906, and described this undertaking in his book, *To the Top of the Continent*, later research confirmed that Cook had never even set foot on the summit of Mount McKinley.

3 South Peak

As early as 1912, another race to the summit of the higher south peak began, and was al-

most successful when an expedition came to within 45 m (150 ft) of the summit. However, just a year later, on June 7, 1913, this impressive peak was finally scaled. The first to stand on the south peak of Mount McKinley were the Episcopal superintendent of Yukon, Hudson Stuck, and his fellow-climbers Harry Karstens, Robert Tatum, and Walter Harper. Many other expeditions followed, and in June 1947, Barbara Polk became the first woman to conquer this bitterly cold terrain.

4 Glaciers

Compared to the Himalaya, Denali is not particularly high, but some of its features make the ascent to its summit extremely difficult. It is the northernmost mountain over 6000 m (19,700 ft) in the USA, and standing just outside the Arctic Circle, it is said to be the coldest in the world. Above the 4000 m (13,000 ft) mark, even average summer temperatures rarely rise over an average temperature of –25°C to –30°C (–13°F to –22°F). Additionally, due to its sub-Arctic, exposed location, and its proximity to the wet, cold Bering Sea, it is subject to dramatic weather changes accompanied by high winds.

The largest glaciers are located on the south side of the peak, where there is high rainfall. The longest and widest of these is the 73 km (45 mile) Kahiltna Glacier, which also serves as a track for mountaineers en route to Denali's summit. In technical terms, the ascent is not difficult. However it is the extreme weather conditions and the low pressure that prevail in the north—corresponding to barometric pressure in the Himalaya at altitudes over 7000 m (23,000 ft)—that often make climbing impossible due to shortness of breath. Many lives have been lost in these harsh conditions on the mountain.

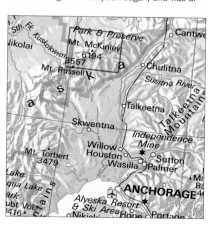

1 Satellite Image: Mount St. Helens

2 Satellite Image: Vancouver

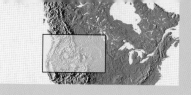

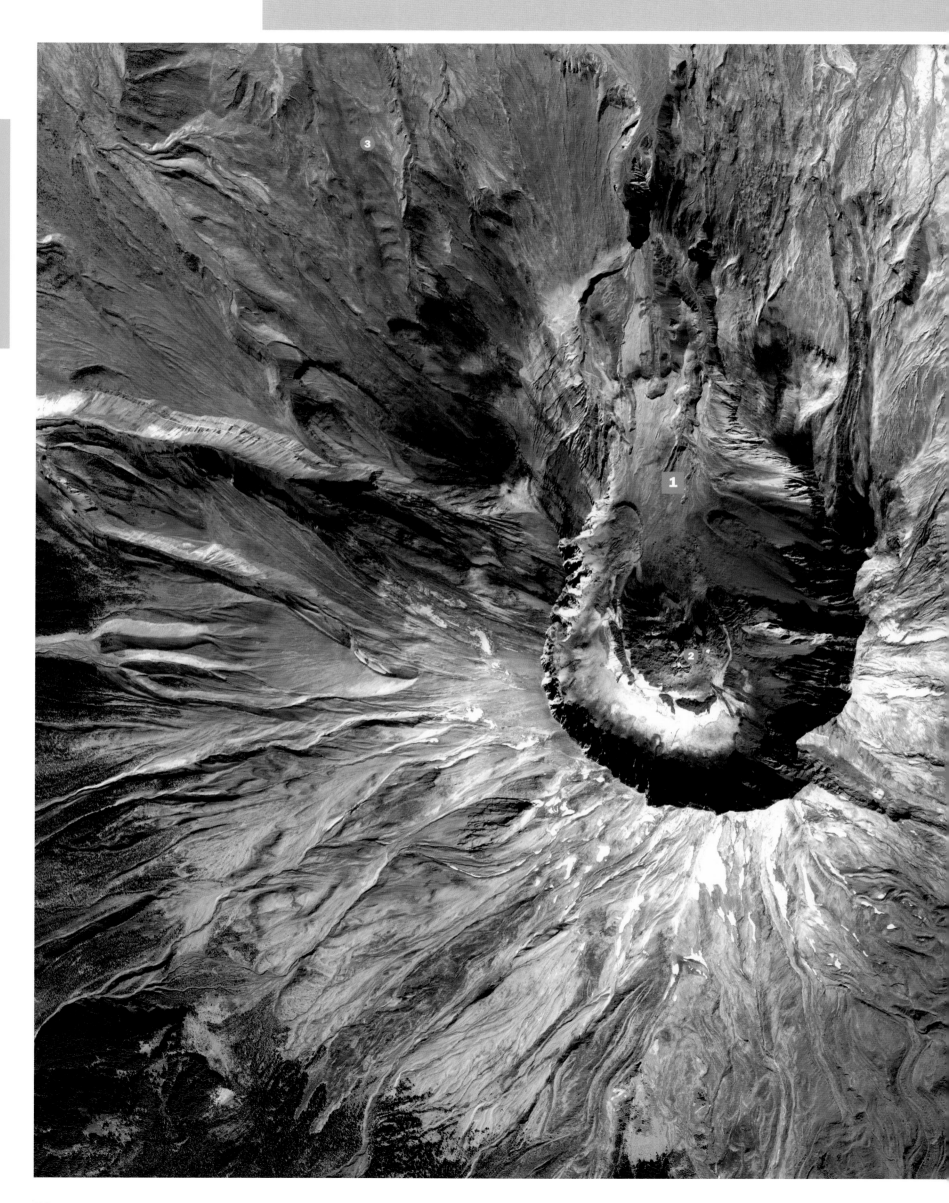

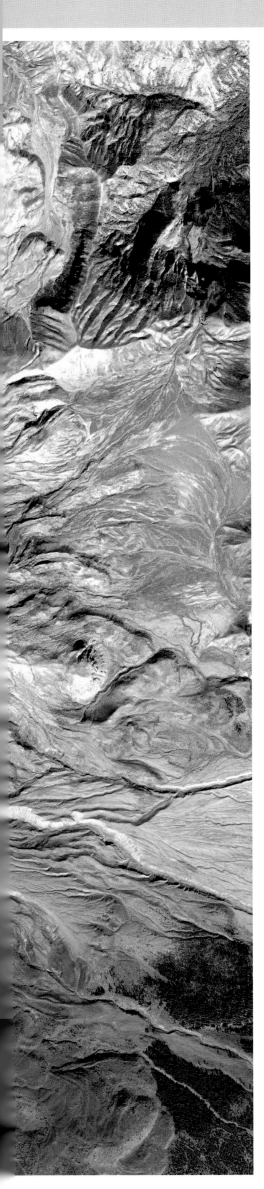

Eruption, May 1980

The first minor tremors and small eruptions began in March 1980. In mid-April the north face began to bulge out above the mountain, and on May 18, the summit was blown away by an enormous explosion. As a massive avalanche of molten rock hurtled down the valley at great speed, a plume of steam and ash rose 25 km (15 miles) into the stratosphere and hot gases gushed out over the north flank of the volcano. The impact of the blast destroyed almost everything in its path. Trees, 2 m (6 ft) in diameter, were torn apart and those left standing were scorched. Repeated flows of lava at temperatures of more than 800°C (1500°F), consisting of gases and hard particles, raced down toward the valley. The area to the east of the volcano was covered in ash up to a distance of 10 km (6 miles) away.

Mount St. Helens

Mount St. Helens, in Washington State, forms part of the Cascade Range, a chain of volcanoes that stretches from Northern California to Canada. In this section of the Pacific Ring of Fire (a zone of frequent earthquakes and volcanic eruptions), the volcanoes are situated at intervals of about 50 km (30 miles). Having erupted several times in recorded history, Mount St. Helens was already considered to be the most active volcano of the Cascade Range. But its eruption in May 1980 was on a far larger scale than any of its previous eruptions and, following a debris avalanche, the mountain's height was reduced from 2900 m (9520 ft) to 2550 m (8366 ft), some 350 m (1154 ft). Later, the area—440 km² (170 square miles)—was preserved and placed under protection as the Mount St. Helens National Volcanic Monument.

② *Lava Dome in the Crater ↑*

Three and a half weeks after the great explosion, hot lava began to rise slowly from the center of the 700 m (2300 ft) deep crater, mushrooming into a dome as it grew. The dome, 300 m (985 ft) across and 65 m (213 ft) high, exploded on July 22, 1980 (see picture). This process was repeated several times. Today the lava dome is about 900 m (2954 ft) across and some 300 m (985 ft) high.

This type of volcanic eruption is typical of the seismic activity that occurs within subduction zones, where tectonic plates collide, forcing one to slip beneath the other. In the Mount St. Helens region, the Pacific Juan de Fuca plate is being pushed under the continental North American plate. Scientists have calculated that, before the

eruption, the volcano's magma chamber was located 7–13 km (4–8 miles) below the surface of the earth and that, measuring 1.5 km (1 mile) across, it contained almost 20 km³ (5 cubic miles) of molten rock. The magma has a temperature of 940°C (1724°F).

③ *The Aftermath of the Volcanic Eruption →*

The far-reaching consequences of the eruption were only fully recognized once the volcanic activity had ceased. On the north side of the mountain a crater 700 m (2300 ft) deep had been created and the peak of the volcano now reached a height of only 2550 m (8366 ft). All around, in an area with a radius of up to 20 km (12 miles), rock debris filled valleys to a depth of 50–60 m (165–195 ft), and at the foot of the volcano, where the rock debris had accumulated, the ground level had risen by about 70 m (230 ft). Over a distance of up to 20 km (12 miles) to the north of the volcano, trees no longer stood as they had been uprooted and swept away. Mudslides followed the course of channels formed by the lava, especially on the south side of the volcano. Even now, more than 25 years after the eruption, mudslides still run down the steeper flanks of the volcano as debris landslides, forming a horseshoe outline.

Despite the violence of the eruption, only 57 lives were lost. This was both because settlement within a 50 km (30 mile) radius of the volcano was sparse and because the area was sealed off before the eruption. The David Johnson Cascades Volcano Observatory was established after the

eruption and is dedicated to, among other things, scientific experiments for the regeneration of plants and animals in the affected area. Since the 1990s the number of tourists visiting Mount St. Helens has recovered: The national park recently reiceived over one million visitors in a single year.

Vancouver

Bordered by ocean and mountains, criss-crossed by rivers, and fringed by deep fjords, Vancouver is ideally located, and is one of the most beautiful cities in Canada. Although not the capital of British Columbia, it is this province's largest city, and its 1.6 million inhabitants comprise almost half of the total population. Vancouver, a young city, is like most other cities in North America in that it is surrounded by a ring of suburbs.

The first European explorer to reach the coast where the city now stands was the Spanish navigator José María Narváez, in 1791. Canada's first settlement, Vancouver was named for the British explorer George Vancouver (1757–98). Its greatest period of expansion occurred after 1884, when it became the terminus of the Canadian Pacific Railway. The city's harbor too became a major shipping terminal and is still the most important on the west coast of North America. Today it is generally used for trade within Canada but, as Vancouver lies just 40 km (25 miles) north of the border with the USA, it also provides convenient trade links with the northwestern states of the USA, as well as with Japan and other Asian countries.

1 Strait of Georgia

Vancouver owes its protected location to the large, 460 km (290 mile) long Vancouver Island, which seals the coast off like a dam. The city itself is not located directly on the Pacific coast, but on the Strait of Georgia, a waterway 50 km (30 miles) wide at its broadest point, and which lies on a southeast–northwest axis like a wedge between Vancouver Island and the mainland.

2 Fraser River

The Fraser River, which divides into several widely spread streams running for over 1370 km (850 miles) to the south of Vancouver, is the longest river in British Columbia. Its source lies at the foot of Mount Robson, which rises to a height of 3954 m (12,977 ft) in Mount Robson Provincial Park, and it flows across the rugged interior of British Columbia into the Strait of Georgia. Its estuary is a large swamp and marshland, an ideal breeding ground and gathering place for sedentary and migratory birds. Because of this, certain areas of the estuary have been declared a nature reserve. The river is named for Simon Fraser (1776–1862), a trapper of the fur-trading North West Company who, in 1808, became the first white man to navigate the river from its source to its estuary.

3 *Downtown ↓*

Vancouver's business district is located on a peninsula that is separated from the south of the city and its residential areas by a narrow inlet, False Creek. High-rise buildings dominate the southern part of the peninsula, while the green areas of Stanley Park occupy the north. Downtown Vancouver has a popular nightlife and an attractive shopping area, especially around Canada Place, on the Burrard Inlet, the estuary north of the peninsula. Many elegant shopping centers are also located in the nearby Harbour Centre. Downtown also includes two special districts of Vancouver—Gastown and Chinatown.

Gastown is the historical center of Vancouver. It is here that Gassy Jack Deighton opened a saloon for sawmill workers in the mid-19th century. The saloon became a great success and the center of a small settlement—Gassy's Town, which was later contracted to "Gastown." Today, bars, boutiques, and galleries have sprung up in many of the small Victorian houses. Chinatown, the former settlement center of Chinese immigrants, is located on its eastern boundaries. With a population of 35,000, Chinatown is an authentic small Chinese city, with Chinese street names, Chinese signs on all the shops, restaurants where roast ducks and chickens hang in the windows, and
where Chinese supermarkets and pharmacies are open virtually round the clock.

4 *Stanley Park ↑*

Stanley Park, on a peninsula north of downtown Vancouver, was opened to the public by Lord Stanley, governor-general of Canada, in 1888. Covering 404 ha (990 acres), the park has more than 80 km (50 miles) of hiking trails, including the Seawall, a 9 km (6 mile) path that runs all the way round the peninsula: Such accessibility makes this expanse of tamed wilderness one of the city's favorite open spaces. The park's attractions include a small zoo and an aquarium, as well as various restored Native American totem poles. The 847 m (2780 ft) long Lions Gate Bridge starts from the north shore of the park and spans the Burrard Inlet.

5 Grouse Mountain

Grouse Mountain, which rises to 1211 m (3793 ft) on the north side of Vancouver, commands one of the most beautiful panoramas of the city. This vantage point also emphasizes its unique location. On a clear day, the view from the summit of Grouse Mountain extends westward all the way over the Strait of Georgia to Vancouver Island, southward to Mount Baker volcano (in US territory), and northward to the Coastal Mountains, which are often shrouded in clouds.

6 Lighthouse Park

The northeastern entrance into Burrard Inlet, which reaches into the hinterland, and on which Vancouver's harbor is also located, has been marked by a manned lighthouse since 1874 (the present one dates from 1912). The lighthouse stands in the middle of a 75 ha (185 acre) coastal park in which Douglas firs, western hemlock, and red cedars grow, some of them the largest trees in the region. The park also supports a variety of mosses, pines, wildflowers, and mushrooms, and is a haven for insects, amphibians, birds, and marine animals such as starfish, crabs, and mussels. *Arbutus Menzies*, the only evergreen broad-leafed tree in Canada, grows on the shores of the Strait of Georgia and is a special feature of the park. Related to the arbutus, it does not shed its leaves but instead loses its reddish-brown bark in autumn.

7 Vancouver Museum and Vancouver Maritime Museum

The largest civic museum in Canada, the Vancouver Museum houses extensive collections detailing British Columbia's diverse and colorful past as well as archeological finds from the region, mostly from ancient settlements of the Salish people. Its main focus, however, is on the story of the European settlement of the region.

The Maritime Museum, nearby, documents European sea voyages to the north of British Columbia. It also displays the *St. Roch*, the first ship to sail through the fabled Northwest Passage (from the Pacific to the Atlantic oceans) in both directions.

8 Museum of Anthropology

The University of British Columbia Museum of Anthropology presents an excellent collection of objects illustrating the culture and lifestyles of peoples from all over the world. However, its main focus is on the Native Americans of coastal British Columbia.

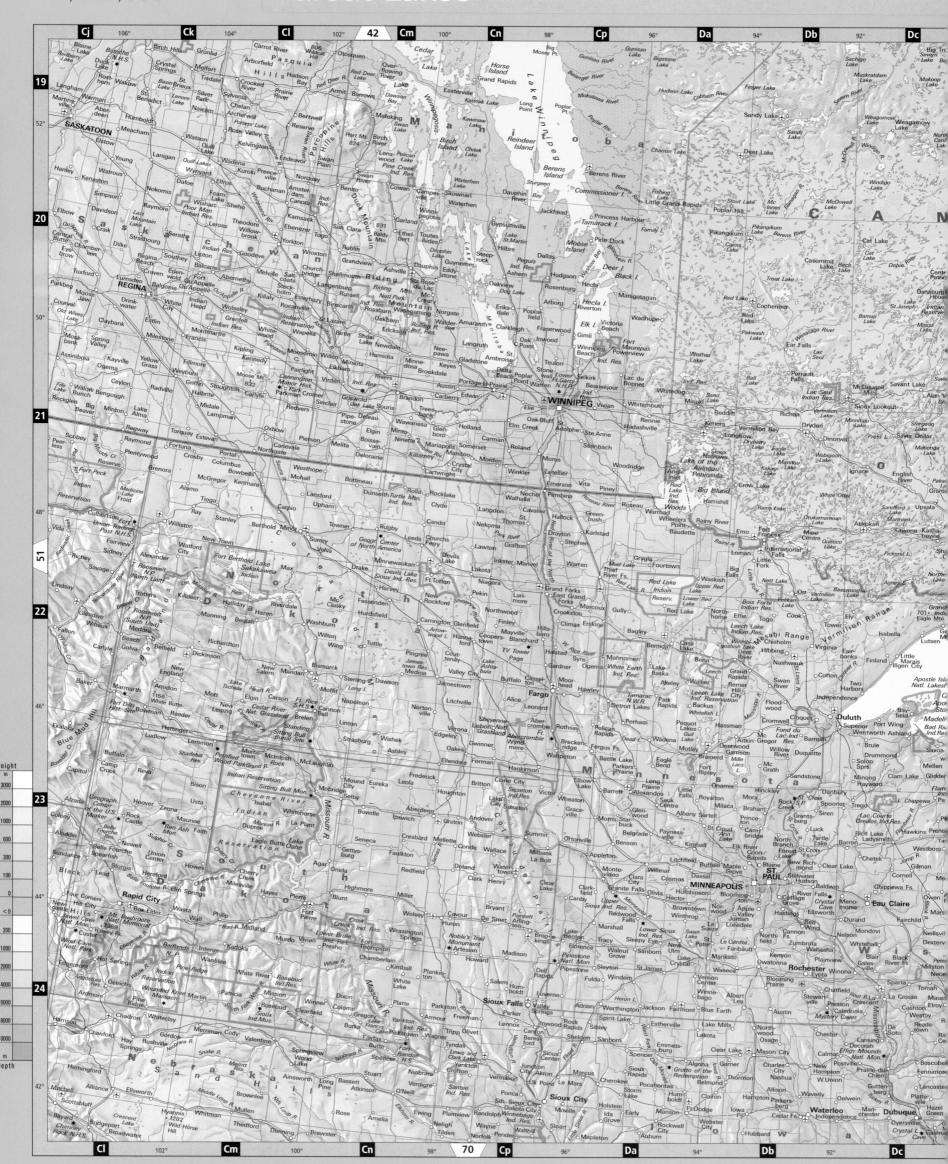

1:4,500,000

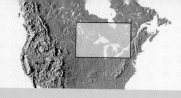

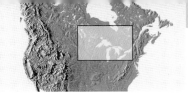

N

Niagara Falls

"Niagara," meaning "Thundering Water" in the language of the region's Native American inhabitants, is a fitting name for one of the largest waterfalls in the world. The first European to discover the Niagara Falls was the French Franciscan monk Louis Hennepin, in 1678. This gigantic natural wonder now attracts more than 12 million visitors a year. The area around the falls is no longer as densely forested as it was when Brother Hennepin came upon them: The falls are now flanked by two cities, both of which make the most of this tourist attraction. Nevertheless, the spectacle of nature remains impressive. As 186,000 m³ (22 million cubic ft) of water per minute hurtles over the precipice, the torrent creates a raging roar, the pool below churns, and the rising foam envelops everything in a fine mist. In clear weather, thousands of small rainbows light up the chasm. The falls are located on the border between the USA and Canada, but their larger part is on the Canadian side. It is from here, where the cascade is illuminated after dark, that the best panoramic view can be enjoyed.

1 Niagara River

Just 45 km (28 miles) long, the Niagara is a short river, but one of the wildest in the world. On its course between Lake Erie and Lake Ontario, it descends 109 m (360 ft) and, gathering speed, it finally plummets spectacularly at Niagara Falls. Although the river is more than 1 km (0.5 mile) wide above the falls, further down its course it passes through a deep and impressive gorge, where its width contracts to 80–300 m (260–985 ft).

2 Niagara Falls

Two towns named Niagara Falls flank this natural attraction, one in Ontario (Canada), the other in New York State (USA). They are connected by a bridge with a border station, and both of-

who attempted to navigate the falls in barrels or boats, or who crossed them on high wires.

3 *Horseshoe Falls ↓*

The Horseshoe Falls is the larger of the two falls over which the torrent of the Niagara River cascades. The precipice is 645 m (2117 ft) wide at the top, with a 52 m (179 ft) high drop. The horseshoe shape of the precipice is relatively recent: It was formed about 100 to 150 years ago by the erosive action of the turbulent, plunging water, which wore away the soft strata of sand and slate that lay beneath the 25 m (80 ft) thick layer of surface rock. As, over time, cavities in the rock became enlarged, the surface layer collapsed and the falls gradually moved backward. Between 1842 and 1905 the Horseshoe Falls

fer visitors similar parking facilities, observation towers and viewpoints, boat trips up to the falls, and amusement parks. On the Canadian side there is a museum dedicated to those daredevils

regressed by some 80 m (260 ft) in their central section. Since then, human intervention has mostly stopped this erosion. For example, one step taken is that, upstream of the falls, both Canada and the USA channel water away from the river to generate energy, so that a smaller volume of water now plunges over the precipice. Another is that the softer rock has been artificially reinforced with concrete.

4 American Falls

The smaller of the two falls is named the American Falls. Here the torrent plunges over a precipice just 330 m (1100 ft) wide, although the drop is 55 m (180 ft). Because access is easier, these falls are also more convenient to visit. On the US side, a bridge leads to Goat Island, located between the two falls, and footbridges lead directly below the water from there.

1:4,500,000

Albers Equal Area Conic Projection

① City Hall ↓

Toronto's distinctive City Hall was designed by the Finnish architect Vilio Revell, and its unusual design is best viewed from the air. The concept behind the building is that it should symbolize the "Eye of Government." It consists of two concave towers enclosing a circular building, which in turn encloses a central council chamber—the "pupil" of the "eye." Completed in 1965, this innovative building, and the idea behind it, was highly controversial among the residents of Toronto. Today, however, it is considered to be a pioneering design and also a symbol of the city's development from sleepy backwater to exciting cultural metropolis of international renown, with a population of one million. The southern forecourt of City Hall is an open-air concert and theater arena, as well as a meeting point and picnic area in summer; it al-

Toronto

Toronto's boom began during the 1970s, when the city became the largest in Canada. Innovative architects built theaters, concert halls, and music clubs, and, due to the separatist tendencies in the French-speaking state of Quebec, international companies settled here. The current metropolis rapidly developed to become the most multi-cultural city in the world, an accolade bestowed on it by the United Nations in 1988, in recognition of the fact that here every culture retains its identity. Founded in 1720, Toronto is now home to people of over 100 different nationalities, who have created a vibrant culture. As "Toronto" means "meeting place and gathering point" in the language of the Native Americans who originally inhabited the locality, its modern character perfectly matches its ancient name.

so serves as an arena for skaters in winter. The Old City Hall, a Victorian brick building, is located on its eastern side.

② Chinatown

In this district, the street names are written in Roman as well as in Chinese characters. The whole quarter glows with colorful Chinese advertising signs, and vendors display everything from plastic bowls and dried seahorses to ivory carvings (as well as plastic imitations), silk clothing, slippers, incense, plastic Christmas trees, aluminum cooking pots, and high-tech items. As in other Chinese urban districts all over the world, roast and fried ducks hang in shop windows and large barrels of dried crabs can be found on the pavements. Chinatown, a rectangle of a dozen blocks, is Toronto's largest residential quarter, with a population of more than 350,000 Chinese inhabitants.

③ Yonge Street

Toronto's main shopping street is probably the longest street in the world. Starting from the shore of Lake Ontario in the east, it leads straight through the city, reaching its western limits after some 20 km (12 miles). In its continuation beyond the city limits, it becomes Highway 11, which proceeds through villages and small towns, and finally ends on the northern shores of Lake Superior, approximately 2000 km (1245 miles) from its starting point. Although Yonge Street is not Toronto's most fashionable thoroughfare, it is one of its liveliest. The thousands of small shops that line the street include specialty and designer boutiques, bakeries, antique shops as well as snack bars, and bric-a-brac shops. Eaton Centre, Toronto's largest inner-city shopping mall, is a giant complex under a 450 m (1480 ft) long glass roof, with more than 300 shops as well as restaurants and theaters.

④ Lake Ontario

About 310 km (190 miles) long and 85 km (50 miles) wide, Lake Ontario is the smallest of the five Great Lakes that straddle the border between the USA and Canada. The other four, each larger than the other, are Lake Erie, Lake Huron, Lake Michigan, and Lake Superior. All five were formed during the last ice age, approximately 13,000 years ago. The main tributary of Lake Ontario is Lake Erie, to which it is linked by the Niagara River, and which empties spectacularly into the Niagara Falls (see p59). Its outflow is formed by the Saint Lawrence River, which empties into the North Atlantic after about 1290 km (800 miles). The northern coast of Lake Ontario is the most densely populated area in Canada. The Toronto Islands, a small group of islands used as a local recreation area, lie off the shoreline of the lake opposite Toronto.

⑤ CN Tower ↓

A famous Toronto landmark, the CN Tower serves as a visual expression of a city for which the sky is the limit. It was built between 1973 and 1976 and remains the highest free-standing building in the world. In the form of a giant tapering needle rising to a height of 553 m (1815 ft), the tower is visible from a distance of over 100 km (60 miles). The observation platform, at a height of 447 m (1467 ft), offers a breathtaking panorama of the city, which stretches out over an area of about 800 km² (309 square miles). There is also a revolving restaurant, at a height of 335 m (1099 ft). Next to the tower stands the Skydome, Toronto's baseball and football stadium, which has capacity for 70,000 spectators. The retractable roof is opened during good weather, and closed when shelter from rain and snow is needed. As well as restaurants, this sports complex also features a hotel, with rooms looking onto the playing field.

Western USA states

1:4,500,000

Albers Equal Area Conic Projection

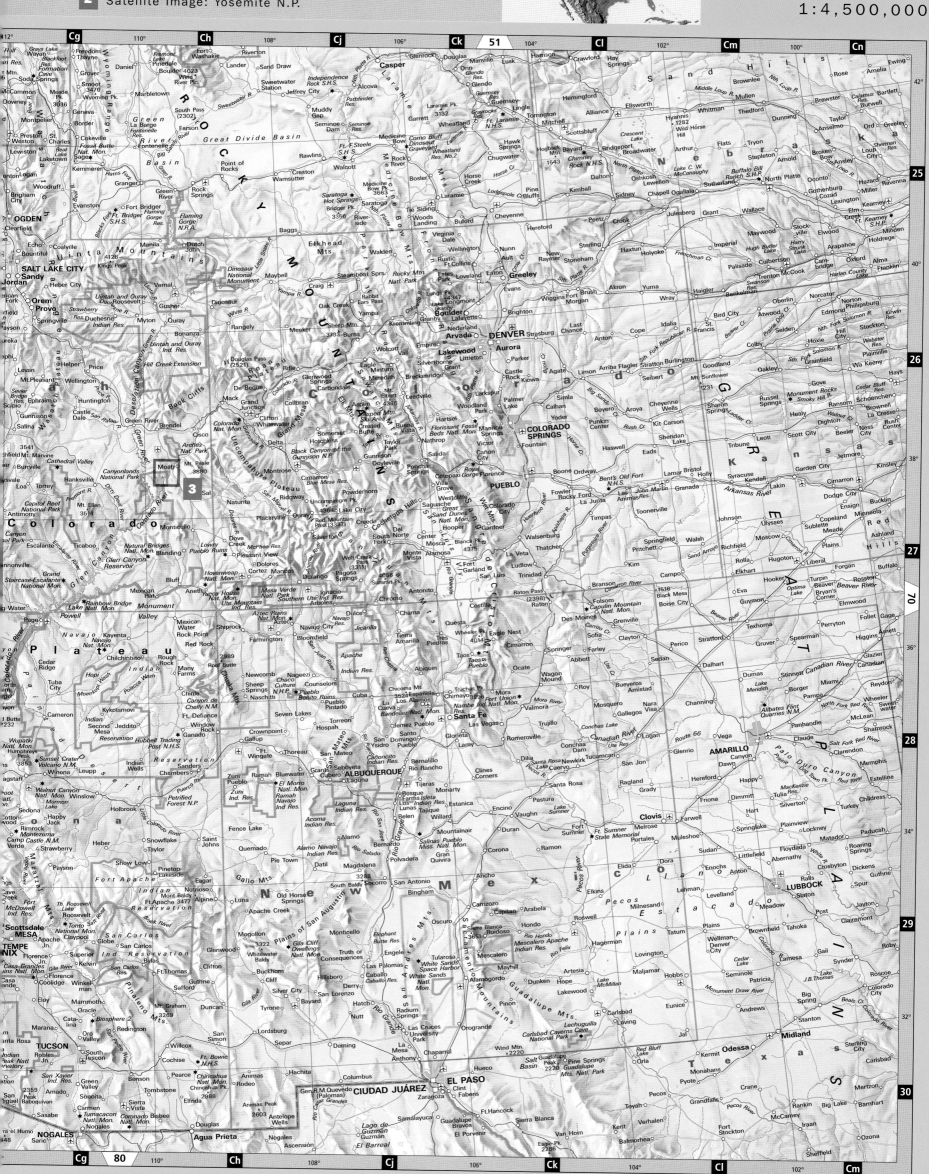

1 *Grandview Point* ↓

Stunning picture-postcard views of the Grand Canyon may be enjoyed at several points along Rim Drive, a panoramic road that begins at Grand Canyon Village and leads along the rim of the canyon westward and eastward. West Rim Drive, 13 km (8 miles) long, is closed to private vehicles during the summer so as to avoid congestion. East Rim Drive, 40 km (25 miles) long, ends at the eastern entrance to the 5000 km² (1930 square mile) national park. There are various observation points along the way: Yaki Point, Grandview Point, Moran Point, Lipan Point, and finally Navajo Point. Probably the most popular observation point is Grandview Point, but as it becomes crowded at peak times during the summer, visitors must stand in line for the best panorama. The sides of the deeply carved canyon are tinged

Grand Canyon

Carved out by the Colorado River over millions of years, the Grand Canyon, in Arizona, is one of the greatest natural wonders of the world. On its winding course across the Kaibab Plateau, the river covers just under 450 km (280 miles). The canyon that it has dug into the plateau ranges in width from about 6 km (4 miles) at its narrowest point to 29 km (18 miles) at its broadest. It is up to 1500 m (4923 ft) deep at its southern rim and 1800 m (5908 ft) deep at its northern rim. "The canyon is entirely useless, so I will probably be the last white person to visit it," wrote a US lieutenant about the Grand Canyon in 1857. His prediction could not have been less accurate: In 1919 it was declared a National Preserve, and today about four million people come to the canyon each year.

with reddish, bluish-green, and yellowish hues. Black shadows obscure the view into the depths of the canyon, where the Colorado River foams some 2 km (1 mile) below. By 1880, the first tourists had started to come to the Grand Canyon, and in response to this, the first hotel was opened at Grandview Point in 1892. Further to the east are the Tusayan Ruins, vestiges of the settlements of a community of Pueblo people, who lived here in the 12th century. However, the inhospitable-looking canyon was settled more than 4000 years ago as archeological discoveries have proved.

2 Grand Canyon Village and Visitor Center

The village on the canyon's southern rim offers the best access into the national park. Most accommodation for visitors to the canyon is located here, but, because of the throng of tourists, it must be reserved in advance during the summer season. All hotels and camping sites are usually fully booked for weeks ahead. Guided tours to

various observation points start at the national park's Visitor Center. Lectures on the geology and history of the Grand Canyon—the finest example of erosion in arid areas in the world—are given daily. There are also mule rides, bus tours, and helicopter trips.

Although geologists are unsure of the precise process of its formation, it is thought that the canyon developed over the last nine million years. As such, it is one of the oldest visible rock formations on the planet. Wide at the top and narrowing into a wedge shape at the bottom, the canyon has been carved through rock that, at its base, is about 1.7 billion years old. From the bottom to the top of the canyon's cliffsides, various periods in the history of the earth may be traced in the horizontally layered strata of rock and sediment that vary in hardness. The strata of sand and limestone, which date from the Devonian, Cambrian, and Permian periods, glow in colors that change according to the sun's position in the sky.

3 North Rim Inn and Grand Canyon Lodge

For the best experience of this stunning natural phenomenon, a UNESCO World Heritage Site, visitors to the Grand Canyon should view it from both rims. The northern rim lies approximately 300 m (985 ft) higher than the southern, so that each offers a completely different perspective. North Rim Inn and the Grand Canyon Lodge, near the beginning of the North Kaibab Trail, are the starting point for tours. The trail leads 23 km (14 miles) down into the canyon, descending from an altitude of 2512 m (8244 ft) above sea level to the bottom of the canyon, where the river flows at 730 m (2396 ft) above sea level. The hiking trail is aptly named: Local Native Americans called the canyon Kaibab, meaning "inverted mountains."

4 *Colorado River* ↓

The 2334 km (1450 mile) long river, which has carved its way into the Colorado Plateau in such a spectacular manner, essentially originates west of Denver, Colorado. Initially flowing southwest, it then turns southward near Las Vegas, and finally flows into the Gulf of California. Despite its large drainage basin, the Colorado is not a fast-flowing river in its lower reaches: This is partly because of rapid evaporation and partly because much of its water is diverted to Los Angeles and other towns and cities of the west coast.

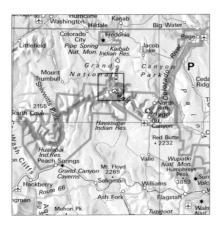

Yosemite National Park

This famous national park, founded in 1890 and covering 3084 km² (1190 square miles) of the Sierra Nevada mountain range, in eastern California, offers visitors isolation and excitement in equal measure. With extensive forests, breathtakingly beautiful lakes and wide rivers, as well as fascinating wildlife, the park attracts over four million visitors a year. Most of them venture no further than the Yosemite Valley, an area 12 km (7 miles) long, and which comprises just 1 percent of the park's entire area. Only a small number of visitors explore the park's majestic mountains, with their vertically soaring granite crags, and its giant waterfalls, alpine lakes, and snowfields.

1 Merced River
The Merced River, a small river whose source lies on Mount Leyell, within the national park, flows through the Yosemite Valley. Several of the most spectacular rock formations for which the park is so famous may be found along its course: Among them is the Half Dome, a monolith 1695 m (5560 ft) high in the form of a vertically split dome.

2 El Capitan ←
With a smooth wall of granite almost 1000 m (3282 ft) high, El Capitan is the most famous climbing mountain in the USA. The mountain was scaled for the first time in 1958, when the ascent took 47 days. Today, most climbers take less time, but still have to spend one night halfway up the granite wall.

3 Royal Arches and Washington Column
Several impressively tall, sheer rock faces can be found in the eastern part of the Yosemite Valley. These include the Royal Arches and, farther east, the Washington Column, a stunning granite column that was conquered for the first time in 1964, since when it has been virtually overrun by rock-climbers.

4 Visitor Center
Every aspect of the park of interest to visitors is covered by displays at the Visitor Center.

5 Yosemite Falls
The highest waterfalls in North America and the second-largest in the world, the Yosemite Falls cascade down a 739 m (2425 ft) drop in three stages, and can be reached only after a 12 km (7 mile) hike.

1 Colorado Plateau

The Colorado Plateau stretches over southeastern Utah and northeastern Arizona. A semi-arid, desert-like plateau lying at an altitude of 1800–3000 m (5900–9846 ft), it is almost featureless, with few elevations. The two larger rivers, the Green River and the Colorado River, which flow through Canyonlands National Park, have carved deep canyons into the plateau. The most famous and perhaps also the most impressive of all these canyons is the Grand Canyon (see pp66–7). Because the plateau was pushed up very gradually, there was time, especially over the last 10 million years, for the river to cut slowly through the rock as it continuously altered its course. Most of the fascinating features of the landscape here may be traced to the river's meanderings, which have left behind dried-up ancient river beds. The plateau is now divided into several well-known national parks—including the Zion, Bryce Canyon, and Capitol Reef national parks—as well as reservations for Native Americans.

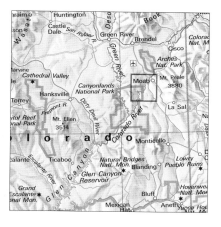

2 Colorado River ↘

The Colorado River can probably be said to hold an unchallenged world record: As it crosses the Colorado Plateau, it flows through one national park after another. Over millions of years the river has carved deep channels into the plateau's sandstone. Because the sandstone consists of varying degrees of hardness, it has eroded at different rates, producing curious rock formations as well as deep, inaccessible, and inhospitable canyons. Today, the Colorado River is also used by sports enthusiasts. White-water rafting expeditions follow the swirling river, which is very fast-flowing in some stretches, while mountain bikers tackle demanding trails and routes on the plateau and in the deeply carved valley.

Colorado River

The Mormon town of Moab, located south of the Colorado River (partly out of shot in the satellite image), is the best starting point for a visit to Utah's most famous national parks. These are the Arches National Park to the north, and the Canyonlands National Park to the southwest. Both are aptly named: The first has bizarre natural sandstone sculptures, the second has countless canyons, mesas, and buttes. With a great variety of landscapes, ranging from the picturesque to the dramatic, areas of southeastern Utah have often been used as locations for movies. *Rio Grande*, with John Wayne, as well as parts of the *Indiana Jones* trilogy, were filmed here.

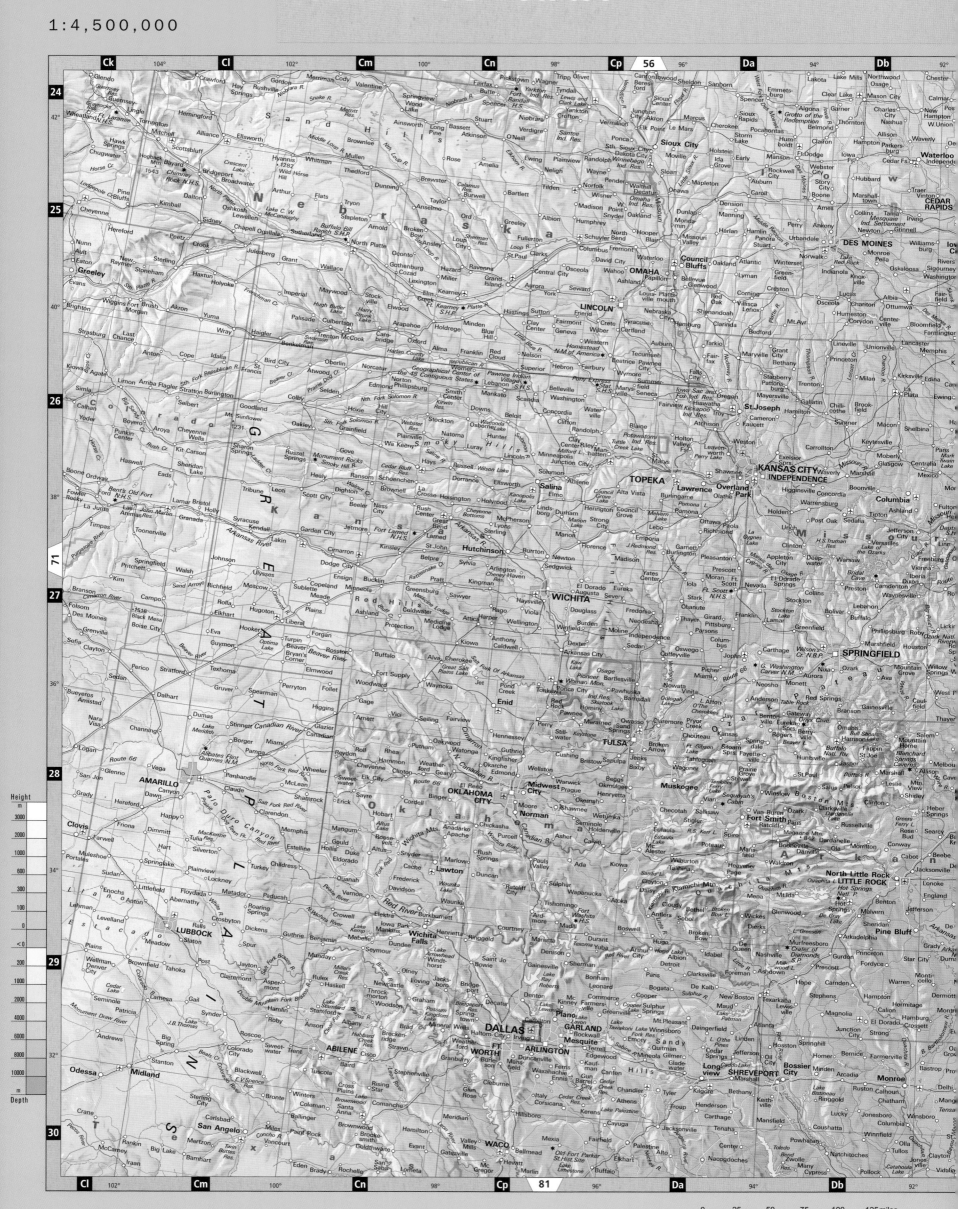

1:4,500,000

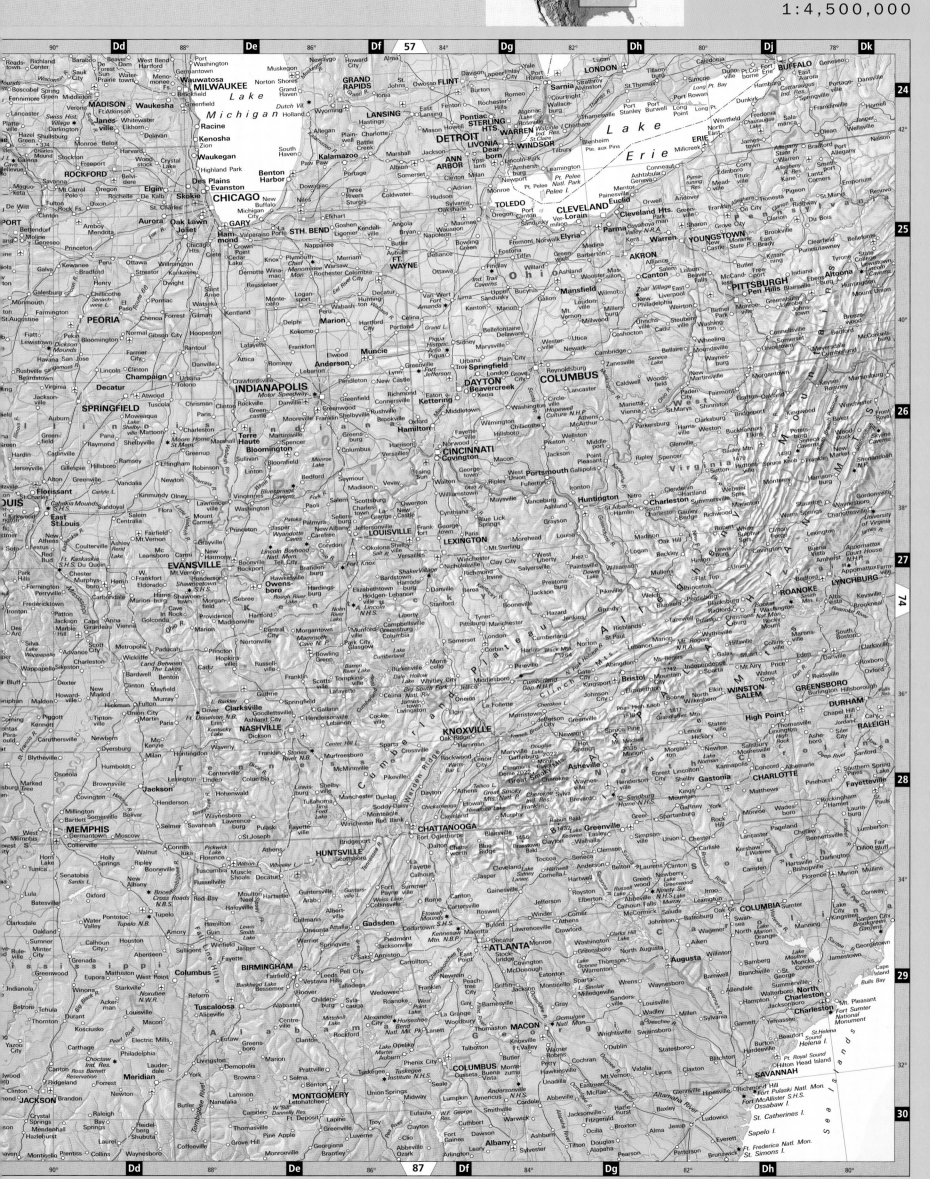

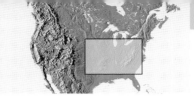

Dallas/Fort Worth International Airport

Dallas and Forth Worth, in Texas, together form one of the largest urban agglomerations in the USA. While the cities themselves have a relatively modest population (Dallas with only one million residents and Fort Worth with barely 0.5 million), their environs are home to almost 4.5 million people. The base of international oil companies, of aircraft and missile manufacturers, and of electronics corporations, Dallas is one of the largest financial and economic centers in the American southwest. To maintain this economic base, excellent national and international air connections are essential. Dallas/Fort Worth International Airport opened in 1974 and has been gradually expanding ever since. Handling more than 50 million passengers a year, the airport is now the fourth-largest in the USA.

1 *Dallas Skyline* ↓

The Dallas cityscape is similar to that of any other typical American city. Great skyscrapers tower prominently above a sea of lower, indistinguishable buildings. The impressive high-rises house the offices of well-known banks and large corporations, while the flat residential and industrial districts stretch far into the surrounding areas.

will be located opposite Terminal E, is still under construction. The customs halls are located in Terminal D. Altogether there are about 180 boardings gates, and passengers board all planes directly from the building.

From Dallas, airplanes fly non-stop to around 160 destinations, 50 of which are in Canada, Mexico, Central and South America, and the

2 Runways

The airport has seven runways, five of which lie on a north–south axis, and two of which lie diagonally on a northwest–southwest axis. A further runway is planned and will be constructed over the next few years. With a length of 2.5 km (1.5 miles), even the shorter runways make it possible for international wide-bodied jets to use Dallas Airport. During take-off and landing, air passengers can enjoy outstanding aerial views of Dallas.

3 Terminals

Dallas/Fort Worth International Airport is laid out to a near-symmetrical plan, with semi-circular terminal buildings arranged on either side of a central axis. Currently the airport has five terminals: In the east wing, from north to south, are terminals A, C, and E, while in the west wing, Terminal B is located opposite Terminal A, and Terminal D opposite Terminal C. Terminal F which

Caribbean, as well as Asia and Europe. The city's central location in the USA makes it possible for passengers arriving at Dallas/Fort Worth to catch connecting flights that will allow them to reach any US destination (except for Alaska and Hawaii) within four hours. This may be the reason why the US carrier American Airlines has made this airport its central hub.

In terms of the number of flights that it handles, Dallas/Fort Worth International Airport is the third-largest in the world, after Chicago and Atlanta. It is also the region's economic engine: Statistics show that the airport earns the North Texan economy more than $11 billion a year. A total of 1800 people work directly for the airport administration and more than 200,000 jobs in this region depend on it.

4 Freeways

The airport, owned jointly by the cities of Dallas and Fort Worth, was built after a long pre-planning period. As early as 1927—when both cities were planning to build their own separate airports—Fort Worth, Dallas's neighbor and rival, proposed building a joint airport. It was not until the mid-1960s that joint planning began, and in 1974 the airport—then the most expensive in the world—was finally opened. It was built on a huge area of land as, even at this first planning stage, there were optimistic visions of further phases of expansion in the future. Comprehensive transport networks were also laid out. This is why the airport is surrounded by a dense network of highways and freeways that lead in many different directions. One highway even passes the terminals, running north–south right through the center of the airport complex.

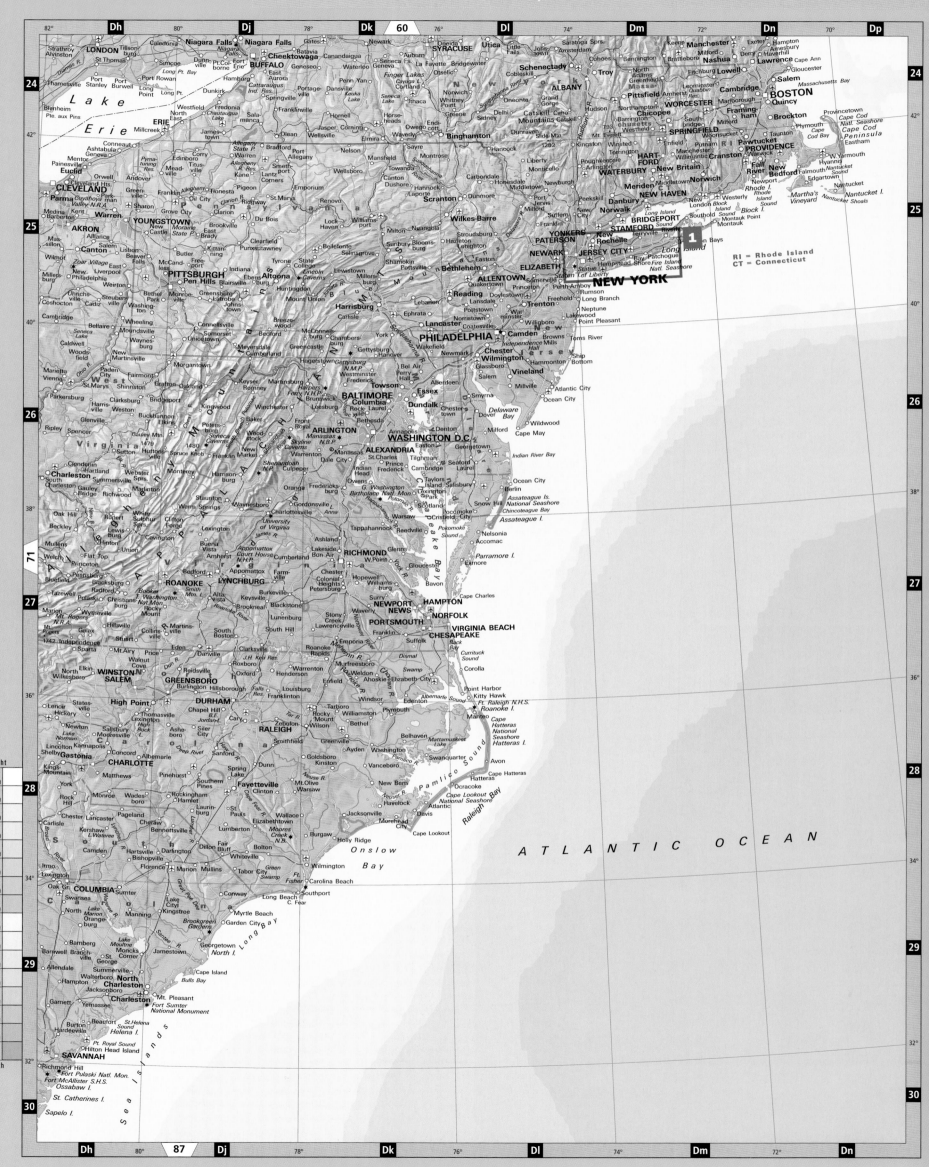

1:4,500,000

Albers Equal Area Conic Projection

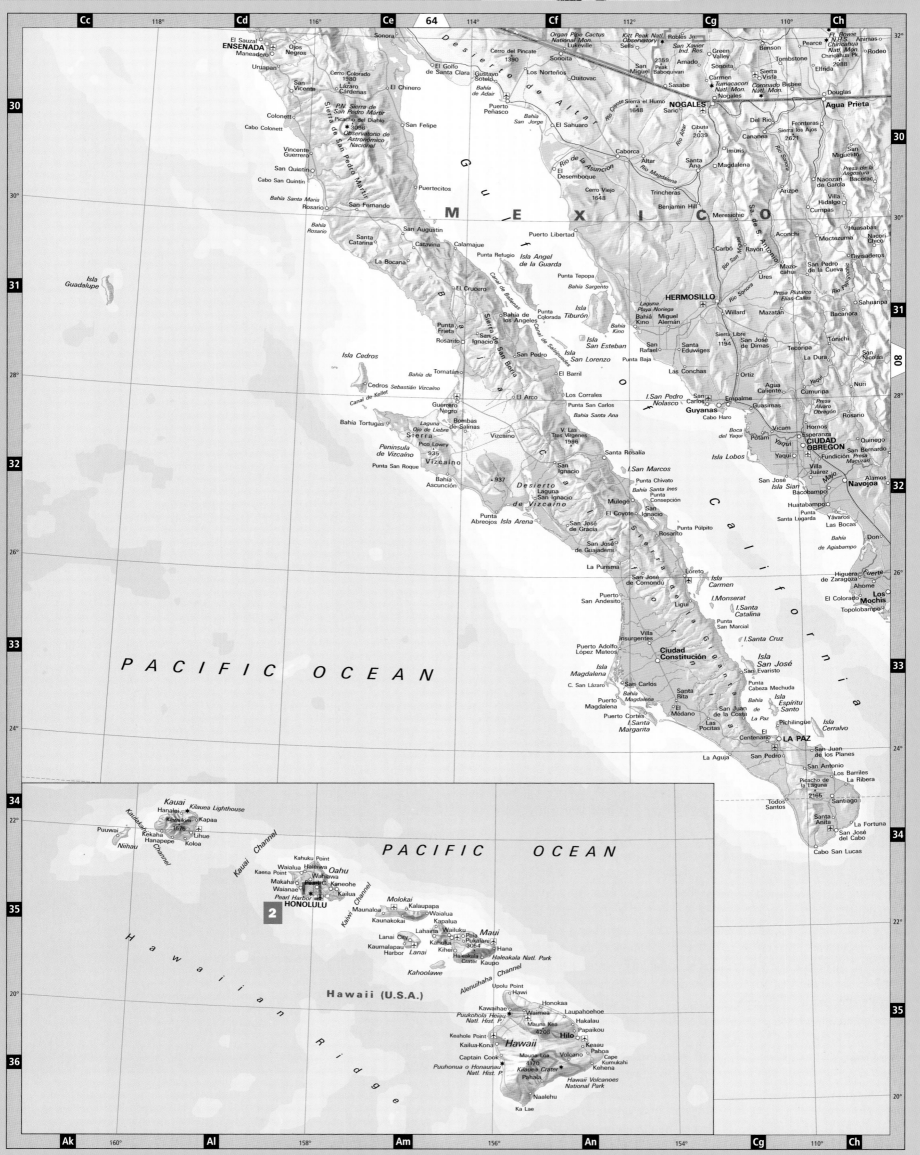

| | | | 64 | | | | |
|Cc|Cd|Ce| |Cf|Cg|Ch|

MEXICO

ENSENADA

NOGALES

Agua Prieta

HERMOSILLO

GUYANAS

CIUDAD OBREGON

Navojoa

Los Mochis

LA PAZ

P A C I F I C   O C E A N

Hawaii (U.S.A.)

Kauai

Niihau

Oahu

HONOLULU

Pearl Harbor

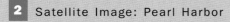

Molokai

Lanai

Maui

Kahoolawe

Hawaii

Hilo

Hawaiian Ridge

Hawaiian Channel

Kauai Channel

Kaiwi Channel

Alenuihaha Channel

Haleakala Natl. Park

Hawaii Volcanoes National Park

| | | | | | | |
|Ak|Al|Am|An|Cg|Ch|

New York City

A huge, densely populated metropolis, New York City covers a wide area. The satellite image here also provides a clear picture of its layout and population distribution. More than 7.3 million people live in the central urban area alone; but when the greater metropolitan area, which takes in parts of New Jersey and New York State, is taken into consideration, the population figure stands at 18 million. New York City is surrounded by water: It is in close proximity to the mouth of the Hackensack River, which flows westward into Newark Bay, as well as the Hudson River and the East River, which flow into Long Island Bay. Larger, undeveloped areas can be made out only in the eastern part of Long Island and on Staten Island.

In 1626 Dutch settlers, who purchased the peninsula from the Manna-Hatta tribe of Native Americans, founded a settlement here, which they named Nieuw Amsterdam. Britain conquered it in 1664 and renamed it New York. Developing into a city, New York was for a time the capital of the USA, and by 1820, it had become its largest metropolis, a distinction that it has retained to this day.

1 *Bridges over the East River*
Two bridges spanning the East River link southern Manhattan and Brooklyn: One is Manhattan Bridge (left) and the other Brooklyn Bridge. With a span of 1834 m (6019 ft), Brooklyn Bridge was designed *according to plans by the German engineer John A. Roebling. He died in 1869, and construction was then undertaken by his son, Washington. In the foreground of the photograph the FDR drive can be seen.*

Manhattan and Central Park

2 The island of Manhattan is the heart of New York City. Although it is not the city's most populous district, 1.5 million people live here in close proximity. Manhattan is also the location of New York's most important museums and theaters, and of its largest and best-known skyscrapers. Wall Street, in Lower Manhattan, location of the New York Stock Exchange, is the world's foremost center of finance. The headquarters of the United Nations, meanwhile, is in Midtown Manhattan. Overall, Manhattan island covers just 57 km² (22 square miles), and this densely populated area swarms with a mixture of many ethnic groups. Reflecting this, there are neighborhoods with names such as Chinatown and Little Italy, as well as fashionable quarters such as Greenwich Village. The city's finest museums are located on the Upper East Side, and the area around Fifth Avenue is a hub for its wealthiest inhabitants. Harlem, north of 110th Street, is the African-American quarter. Central Park is an island of greenery in an ocean of buildings: 4 km (3 miles) long and 500 m (550 yards) wide, it was laid out in 1859–70 as part of an extensive program of city planning.

An inner-city recreation area, Central Park is a popular place for walking or jogging. It also serves as a venue for open-air concerts, and part of it is a bird sanctuary.

New Jersey and Staten Island

3 The Hudson River, west of Manhattan, separates New York State from the neighboring state of New Jersey. New Jersey is known as the Garden State, but in the metropolitan area it is hard to tell why: The smell of the docks at Newark and Hoboken are carried on the breeze. To the south lies Staten Island which is the least densely populated area of New York City.

4 *Statue of Liberty* ←

Standing about 4 km (3 miles) from the southern tip of Manhattan, the Statue of Liberty raises her torch in a symbolic gesture. Presented to the city by liberty-loving French citizens in 1886, the statue was erected on a small rocky island. It remains a symbol of the freedom that New York City in particular, and the USA in general, promises to all its inhabitants, whether native-born or immigrant.

Long Island

5 Although this cannot be seen in the satellite image, Long Island, as its name implies, is completely surrounded by water. New York City's two largest districts—Brooklyn, with more than

2.3 million inhabitants, and Queens, with 2 million inhabitants—are located here.

LaGuardia and J. F. Kennedy Airport

6 New York has two major airports: LaGuardia and John F. Kennedy (JFK). While LaGuardia is located on the north side of Long Island, JFK is north of Jamaica Bay.

USA   **77**

N

Pearl Harbor

Pearl Harbor, site of a US air force base, located on the south coast of the island of Oahu, Hawaii, is best known today for the surprise attack that was launched on it by Japanese forces in 1941. Made without a declaration of war, the attack happened early in the morning of December 7, and more than 2400 people lost their lives. This offensive was the main reason for the USA entering into World War II. Despite its distance from the American mainland—the Hawaiian archipelago lies about 4000 km (2485 miles) west of Los Angeles—the USA already had a strategic interest in it in the mid-19th century. In 1898, this previously independent kingdom was annexed by the USA, and finally in 1959, the group of islands became its 50th state.

1 Ford Island Naval Station

Ford Island is a small island in the deep, well-sheltered bay that gives Pearl Harbor its ideal location. Since 1887 the USA had maintained the sole right to use this bay, although it was not until 1898, after the islands' annexation, that work on building the marine base began. Following the dredging of a channel between the narrow bay and open waters in 1911, larger ships were able to anchor here.

For decades Pearl Harbor was used not only as a marine base, but also as a military air base. Even today aircraft carriers of the US Pacific Fleet,

the naval dockyard also remained intact. After the attack, the American people agreed to the USA's joining in the war.

2 USS Arizona and USS Missouri ↓

A memorial in Pearl Harbor marks the place where 1100 soldiers lost their lives when the battleship USS Arizona sank during the Japanese attack. The USS Missouri, anchored next to it, honors naval officers who died in World War II (1939–45), in the Korean War (1950–53), and in Operation Desert Storm (1991), the US-led operation to liberate Kuwait from Iraq. This photograph shows the

as well as destroyers and submarines, are still stationed here. Having built an airport on Ford Island, the USA is in possession of an "unsinkable aircraft carrier" in the Pacific. Strategically significant, Ford Island and Pearl Harbor protect the west coast of the USA from potential attack by eastern Asian countries, and act as a military presence in the Pacific.

It was for this reason that the Japanese, who wanted to break US domination of the Pacific, attacked Pearl Harbor in 1941. Even though both the US secret service and intelligence provided by allies of the USA warned several times of the possibility of such an attack by Japan, the offensive still came as a surprise. Japanese forces succeeded in destroying a large part of the US Pacific Fleet, but none of its aircraft carriers, since they were not anchored at Pearl Harbor at the time of the attack. The enormous fuelstore and

USS Arizona in a cloud of smoke on December 7, 1941, after the Japanese attack.

3 Pearl City

Located on the bay, this small town, with a population of about 30,000, is the main residential base of troops stationed in Hawaii. In addition to the military presence, the town derives revenue from agriculture—the cultivation of fruit and vegetables—and the processing of this produce. A typical small US town, Pearl City is mostly residential, with several shopping centers and a small college. Pearl City is located on Highway 1, which leads to Honolulu, the capital of Hawaii.

Submarine USS Nevada ↓
On December 7, 1991, marines marked the 50th anniversary of the attack on Pearl Harbor and those who died in it.

Height
m
3000
2000
1000
600
300
100
0
< 0
200
1000
2000
4000
6000
8000
10000
m
Depth

1:4,500,000

0   25   50   75   100   125 miles
0   50   100   150   200km

Albers Equal Area Conic Projection

1 Satellite Image: El Paso

2 Satellite Image: Rio Grande

Portales
Elida
Dora
Sudan
Plainview
Lockney
Matador
Paducah
Crowell
Elektra
Ringgold
Courtney
Marietta
L. Texoma
Yuba
Red River
Detroit
Clarksville
Foreman
Ashdown
Hope
Camden
Hampton
Calion
El Dorado

Milnesand
Enochs
Littlefield
Floydada
Roaring
Springs
Dickens
Guthrie
Benjamin
Iowa Park
Mankins
Henrietta
Windt-
horst
Saint Jo
Bowie
Gainesville
Bonham
Sherman
Denison
Paris
Bogata
De Kalb
New Boston
Maud
Texarkana
Lewis-
ville
Magnolia
Stephens
Bernice

Lehman
Levelland
Anton
Crosbyton
Spur
Munday
Seymour
Olney
Jacks-
boro
Decatur
Denton
Commerce
Cooper
Farmers-
ville
Sulphur Springs
Pittsburg
Mt.Pleasant
Linden
Homer

c o l o i n o
LUBBOCK
Slaton
Post
Jayton
Millers
Creek Res.
Newcastle
Throck-
morton
Graham
Bridge-
port
Plano
GARLAND
Rockwall
Mineola
Gilmer
Glade-
water
Cedar
Springs
Bethany
Long-
view
SHREVEPORT
Bossier
City
Minden
Arcadia

29

l l a n o
E s t a c a d o
P l a i n s
Tatum
Meadow

Slaton
Aspermont
Clairemont
Jayton
Hamlin
Roby
Anson
Stamford
Albany
Breckenridge
Strawn
Granbury
Weather-
ford
FT.
WORTH
ARLINGTON
Mans-
field
Burle-
son
DALLAS
HALTOM CITY
Irving
Mesquite
Terrell
Kaufman
Canton
Gun
Barrel
City
Chandler
Tyler
Kilgore
Henderson
Carthage
Center
Tenaha
Nacogdoches
Toledo
Bend
Res.
Many
Zwolle
Natchitoches
Powhatan

Lovington
Hobbs
Maljamar
Seminole
Patricia
Lake
J.B. Thomas
Snyder
Colorado
City
Blackwell
Roscoe
Sweet-
water
Trent
Cisco
Stephenville
Glen
Rose
Cleburne
Italy
Waxahachie
Ennis
Corsicana
Cedar Creek
Res.
Athens
Palestine
Jacksonville
Troup
32°

Red Bluff
Lake
Orla
Kermit
Odessa
Midland
Sterling
City
Carlsbad
Winters
Ballinger
Coleman
Santa
Anna
Brownwood
Comanche
Hamilton
Meridian
Mexia
Old Fort Parker
St.Hist.Site
Elkhart
Alto
Crockett
Diboll
Lufkin
Pinelane
Hodges
Gardens
Res.
Florien
Bend
Leesville

86

Pecos
Toyah
Monahans
Pyote
Andrews
Stanton
Big
Spring
Miles
Paint Rock
San Angelo
Bronte
Sterling
City
Eden
Brady
Goldthwaite
Brooke-
smith
Evant
Gatesville
Mc
Gregor
Hewitt
WACO
Bellmead
Marlin
Temple
Rosebud
Cameron
Hearne
Franklin
Madisonville
Buffalo
Madison
Trinity
Woodville
Livingston
Alabama and
Coushatta I.R.
Corrigan
Kountze
Evadale
Kirbyville
Marry-
ville
Ragley
Moss Bluff
Sulphur
30

Pecos River
T e x a s
McCamey
Rankin
Big Lake
Barnhart
Mertzon
Vancourt
Menard
Mason
Llano
Lampasas
Burnet
George-
town
Taylor
Rockdale
Milano
Bryan
College
Station
Navasota
Huntsville
Lake
Conroe
Cleveland
The Woodlands
Conroe
Lake
Livingston
Lake
Houston
Kingwood
Orange
Vidor
BEAUMONT
Liberty
Nederland
P. Arthur
Calcasieu
Lake
Lake
Charles

Iraan
Grandfalls
Crane
Verhalen

Fort
Stockton
S t o c k t o n
P l a t e a u
Sheffield
Ozona
Sonora
E d w a r d s
Eldorado
Fort McKavett
Junction
Llano River
Cherry
Spring
Fredericksburg
Lake Lyndon
B. Johnson
Lake
Travis
Johnson
City
Marble
Falls
Leander
Round Rock
AUSTIN
Elgin
Bastrop
Giddings
Somerville
Lake
Brenham
Hempstead
Katy
HOUSTON
Sealy
Sugar Land
Missouri
City
PASADENA
BAYTOWN
La Porte
Texas
City
Port Bolivar
High Island
Winnie
Sabine
N.W.R.
Cameron

Marathon
Sanderson
Dryden
Pandale
Juno
P l a t e a u
Rocksprings
Camp
Wood
Leakey
Comfort
Boerne
New
Braunfels
San
Marcos
Blanco
Lockhart
Luling
Seguin
Gonzales
Yoakum
Schulen-
burg
La
Grange
Columbus
Rosenberg
Pearland
Alvin
Angleton
Clute
Freeport
Galveston
Island
Bolivar
Port Bolivar

Alpine
2092
Cathedral Mt.
McKinney
Mtn.
1528
Marathon
Langtry
Comstock
Del Rio
Brackettville
Uvalde
Hondo
Castroville
Devine
Poteet
Pleasanton
Floresville
Stockdale
Nixon
Cuero
El Campo
Louise
Wharton
West
Columbia
Bay City
Lake
Jackson
Matagorda
Galveston
31

Study
Butte
Big Bend
Ft. Davis
Fort Davis
M.N.S.
Ft Davis
Santiago
Pk
1988
Emory Pk
2386
Boquillas
del Carmen
Parque Int.
del
Big Bend
Nat.
Park
Manuel
Benavides
Boquillas
del Carmen
Ciudad
Acuña
Spofford
Knippa
Universal City
La Vernia
Victoria
Goliad
Tivoli
Port Lavaca
Port O'Conner
Matagorda
Bay

SAN ANTONIO
Jourdanton
Pearsall
Charlotte
Kenedy
Port
Lavaca

X I C O
Emory Pk
2386
Alamos de
Márquez
Piedras
Negras
Ciudad
Acuña
Jiménez
San Carlos
La Pryor
Dilley
Three
Rivers
Beeville
Refugio
Woodsboro
San Antonio River
San
Antonio Bay

S i e r r a
d e l
C a r m e n
Morelos
Zaragoza
PIEDRAS
NEGRAS
Eagle Pass
Normandy
Crystal City
Big Wells
Cotulla
Fowlerton
Tilden
George
West
Mathis
Sinton
Portland
CORPUS
CHRISTI
Corpus Christi Bay
Mustang Island

os de los
los Mesteños
La Babia
La Encantada
Rio Bravo
San
Miguel
El Milagro
El Remolino
Zaragoza
Morelos
Allende
Villa
Union
Encinal
Freer
San
Diego
Robstown
Ingleside
Aransas Pass
San Jose Island

X
S i e r r a
La Sabia
La Encantada
El Guaje
La Mora
El Reyes
La Rosita
Palau
Nueva Rosita
Sabinas
Benavides
Alice
Kingsville
Baffin
Bay
Matagorda Peninsula

El Guaje
Laguna
El Guaje
El Zacate
Acebuches
Múzquiz
Colombia
NUEVO
LAREDO
Laredo
Oilton
Hebbronville
Riviera
Falfurrias
Encino
Padre
Island
National Seashore

M E X I C O
Cenzontle
Sierra
Mojada
Don Martin
Juárez
Minas
de Barroterán
STA. Elena
Progreso
Los
Rodríguez
Hermanas
Rio Salado
Ciudad
Anáhuac
Jarita
Randado
Zapata
Agua
Nueva
Rachal
Norias
Baffin
Bay
G u l f

mi
Laguna
del Rey
Ocampo
Cuatro
Ciénegas
San
Buenaventura
Lampazos
de Naranjo
Falcon
Reservoir
La
Gloria
Guerrero
Lynn
Raymondville
Port
Mansfield
o f

San
Ignacio
Laguna
del Rey
Candela
Sabinas
Hidalgo
Villaldama
Nueva Cd.
Guerrero
Paras
Mier
Roma
Cd.
Aleman
Camargo
Los
Guerra
Valadeces
Agualeguas
General
Treviño
Edinburg
Elsa
MCALLEN
Mission
Pharr
Merce-
des
Harlingen
San Benito
Port Isabel
Island

MONCLOVA
Candela
Castaños
La
Referma
Vallecillos
Cerralvo
Dr.
González
REYNOSA
Rio Bravo
Río
Bravo
Valle
Hermoso
BROWNSVILLE
Playa Lauro Villar
Gulf
32

La Margarita
del Norte
Charcos
de Risa
Estanque
del León
Las
Coloradas
General
Bravo
China
El Miguelito
MATAMOROS
Santa
Teresa
Barra los Americanos
Boca Sta. María

San
GOMEZ
PALACIO
TORREON
Francisco
I.Madero
Bermejillo
dena
San Pedro
de las Colonias
Paila
Hipólito
Santa
Catarina
S.NICOLAS
GARZAS
STA.
CATARINA
Garcia
GUADALUPE
San Rafael
MONTERREY
SALTILLO
Santiago
General
Terán
Montemorelos
Méndez
Guadalupe
Victoria
Francisco
Villa
Francisco
Madero
La Carbonera
El Temascal
33

Jimulco
Viesca
Parras
de la Fuente
General
Cepeda
Agua
Nueva
Allende
Rio San Lorenzo
Galeana
San Rafael
Iturbide
Villa
Muinero
San
Fernando
Cruillas
M e x i c o

Peñón
Blanco
Cuencamé
Cedros
Concepción
del Oro
El Salvador
San Roberto
San José
de Raíces
San Carlos
La Coma
Santander
Jiménez
La Pesca

Ignacio Allende
General
Simón Bolívar
San Juan
de Guadalupe
Camacho
Ascensión
Hidalgo
Abasolo
Soto
La Marina

Miguel
Auza
Juan Aldama
Nieves
Norias
San Tiburcio
Huertecillas
La
Escondida
Padilla
Vicente
Guerrero
Presa
Vicente
Guerrero
Casas
Tropic of Cancer

La Ochoa
La
Colorada
Vanegas
Cedral
Cerro Peña Nevada
4054
Doctor
Arroyo
Miquihuana
Llera
Agua Nueva
San Rafael
Barra del
Tordo
34

Suchil
Sombrerete
Cañitas
Matehuala
CD. VICTORIA
Jaumave
Palmillas
La
Ventana
Tula
Xicotencatl
González
El Limón
Aldama
Laguna de
San Andrés

Candela
Saín Alto
Villa
de Cos
El Rucio
Santo Domingo
Illescas
Charcas
El Reventón
Ocampo
Xicoténcatl
González
Manuel
3080

Jiménez
de Teul
Víctor Rosales
Morelos
Moctezuma
Pozas de
Santa Ana
Ciudad
del Maíz
Guadalupe
Antiguo
Morelos
Las
Aztecas
Altamira
22°

FRESNILLO
Valparaíso
Jerez
de García
Salinas
Guadalupe
Troncoso
Salinas
Espíritu Santo
Guadalcazar
Ciudad
del Maíz
Lag.
Chila
Mezquital
Pánuco
CIUDAD MADERO
TAMPICO

Monte
Escobedo
ZACATECAS
Victor Rosales
Pinos
El Potosí
San Vicente
Tancuayalab
Chicayan
Isla Juana
Ramírez
La Laja
Laguna de
Tamiahua

AGUASCALIENTES
SAN LUIS
POTOSI
Ojocaliente
Salinas
San
Nicolás
Tolentino
CIUDAD
VALLES
San Vicente
Tancuayalab
Tamuín
35

Northern Mexico 81

1 Rio Grande

Although the Rio Grande, which is known as the Rio Bravo on the Mexican side of the border, is spanned by five bridges along its course through the urban agglomeration, it is still a physical barrier between El Paso, in the north, and Ciudad Juárez, in the south. On either side of the bridges, this frontier between the USA and Mexico is reinforced partly with barbed wire and partly with a high wall, which is rigorously guarded. It prevents Mexicans from crossing illegally into the USA, in order to look for work: For this reason it is sometimes, and somewhat cruelly, referred to as the Tortilla Curtain. Originating in the Rocky Mountains, the Rio Grande flows south for about 1000 km (620 miles) before it reaches El Paso, where it becomes a slow-running river. A few kilometers west of El Paso and Ciudad Juárez, the river

El Paso

With 500,000 inhabitants, El Paso, in western Texas, is the largest US city on the border with Mexico. It was established in the 16th century by the Spanish conquistadors for strategic reasons: Here the Rio Grande could be forded quite easily and the Franklin Mountains nearby could be quickly crossed. For this reason the town was called El Paso del Norte (The Pass to the North) in its early days. From El Paso, the conquistadors traveled northward into what is now New Mexico, in order to subdue the Pueblo Native Americans. Today the city, which is laid out to a grid-like plan, relies for its revenue on the clothing and food industries, oil refining, and copper mining. Indirect sources of revenue are provided by tourism, the University of Texas, which has a campus here, and the presence of Fort Bliss air force base.

reaches the US–Mexican border, and for some 2000 km (1250 miles) beyond this point, it marks the border between these two countries, finally flowing into the Gulf of Mexico at Brownsville.

2 El Paso ↑

For many, El Paso epitomizes a town of the American Wild West, since it entirely matches the cliché of a Texan border settlement. The city center is filled with country and western clubs, there are rodeo competitions, as well as ubiquitous statues of well-known cowboys and gunslingers such as Wyatt Earp and Pat Garrett.

3 El Paso Museum of Art

This art museum displays not only Mexican colonial art from the 17th to the 19th centuries, but also US art from the 19th century to the present. The collection also includes pre-Columbian and other Native American artifacts dating from several centuries. However, the most valuable aspect of the museum's exhibits is the Kress Collection. Samuel H. Kress, a successful businessman, collected European art and donated it to many museums in the USA, including the National Gallery of Art, in Washington, DC.

4 Ciudad Juárez

El Paso's larger counterpart south of the Rio Grande, and across the border with Mexico, Ciudad Juárez is a city of 1.5 million inhabitants. Like El Paso, its streets are laid out in a grid pattern. Although neither particularly well-kept nor beautiful, Ciudad Juárez offers everything that cannot be obtained in conservative Texas. Besides traffic chaos and deafening music, it holds such attractions as cheap doctors (who are popular with uninsured Americans), bargain shopping, gambling, and prostitution. Ciudad Juárez is in fact the original El Paso del Norte. When the latter became the twin city on the US side of the border, the old El Paso was renamed Ciudad Juárers for Benito Juárez García, who was president of Mexico from 1861 to 1871.

5 Fort Bliss

Fort Bliss is the largest military air base in the Western world. Established in 1854, it was named for Lt. Col. William Wallace Smith Bliss. Fort Bliss is a training site for anti-aircraft forces and it houses the Army's Sergeants Major Academy. The German air force maintains a missile school here jointly with the USA.

6 Franklin Mountains State Park

The Franklin Mountains State Park, located in the center of El Paso, is the largest inner-city park in the USA. It was laid out in 1979 with the aim of preventing urban development from further endangering the habitat of numerous birds, reptiles, and small mammals, and threatening the particular desert vegetation, which is unique to this area. The Franklin Mountains, whose highest point in El Paso's urban area is Ranger Peak, at 1723 m (5655 ft), were once the largest settlement area of various Native American tribes. Surviving traces of their presence include cave paintings and rock art, which are in the vicinity of waterholes.

7 Downtown ↓

Downtown El Paso—the view here is from the town hall into the inner city—is very similar to other large US cities. Once no more than a huddle of tents and barracks, it is today the fourth-largest city in Texas. However it was only during the mid-19th century, with the construction of Fort Bliss, that the town grew into a city.

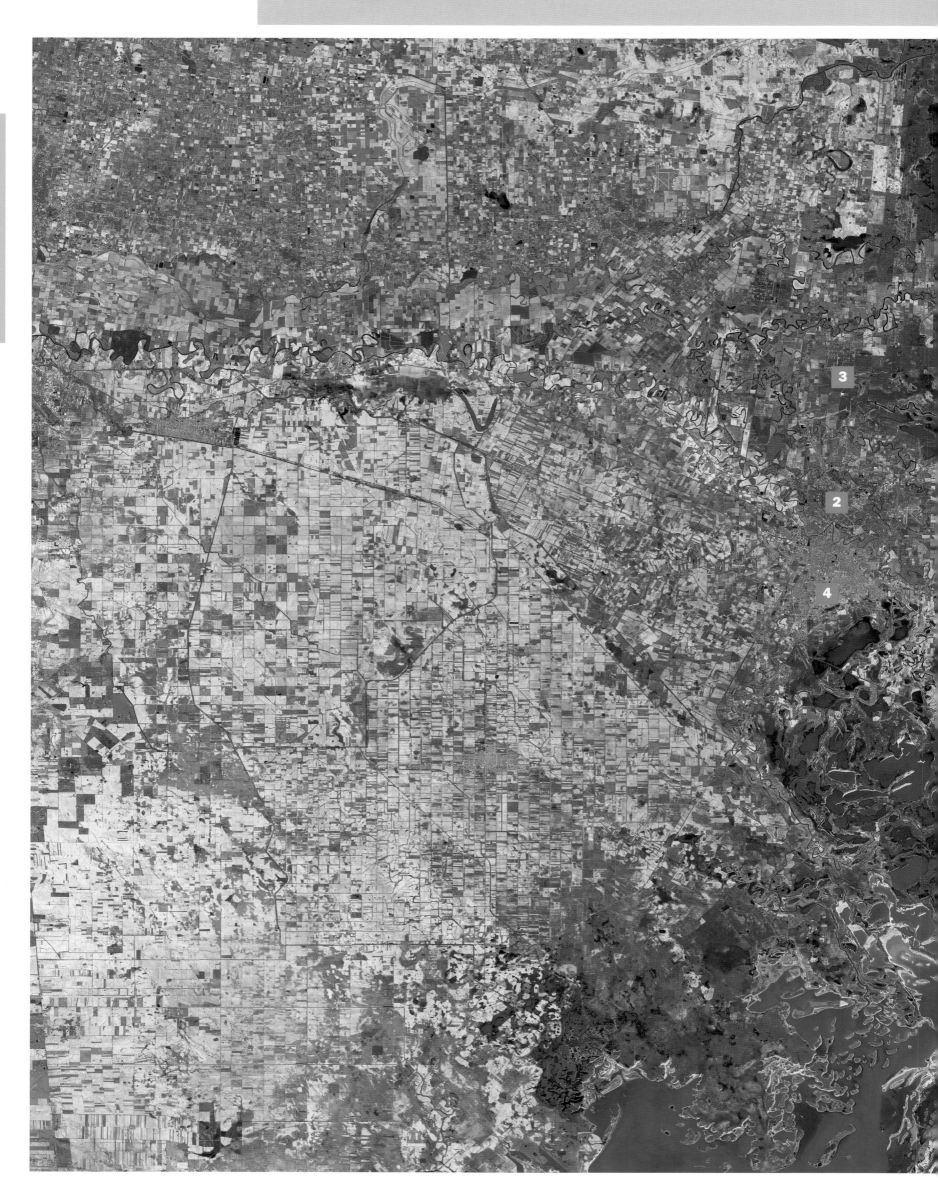

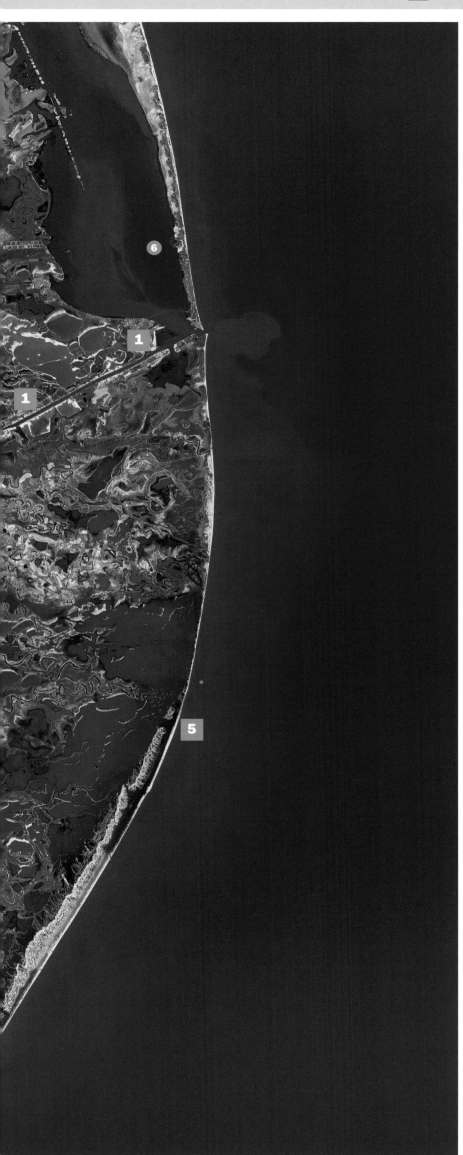

Rio Grande Estuary

Along the 2000 km (1250 miles) of its course between El Paso, in the north, and its estuary at Brownsville, on the Gulf of Mexico, the Rio Grande marks the border between the USA and Mexico. Along this stretch, it has two names: the Rio Grande on the US side of the border, and the Rio Bravo on the Mexican side. Seen from the air, the frontier is barely distinguishable at the estuary, however. This is because the river branches out into countless smaller streams, which can create floodplains and further subdivide into rivulets. The national border is most obvious within towns and cities, as the river often runs through channels here. Outside urban areas, the border is marked by barbed wire or tall steel walls, erected to prevent immigrants from illegally entering the USA.

1 Brownsville Ship Channel
A 27 km (17 mile) long shipping channel connects the harbor, located northeast of the city of Brownsville, with the Gulf of Mexico. The port of Brownsville is an inner deep-draft harbor with a railroad connection.

2 Brownsville
The southernmost city in the state of Texas, and location of the University of Texas at

Brownsville, this is one of the fastest-growing cities in the state, with almost 300,000 people living in the metropolitan area. Brownsville is also well-known in the USA as a historic site. When Mexico won independence in 1821, border conflicts with its northern neighbors began. Texas was then part of Mexico, but in 1835, it began its fight for independence, and in 1845, it became the 28th state of the United States. Mexico considered this annexation to be a declaration of war: This in turn led to the Mexican War (1846–8), in which US and Mexican forces fought partly on battlefields near Brownsville.

3 Palo Alto Battlefield
This historic battlefield is now a memorial park, with a tourist center that traces the history and outcome of the conflict. The first battle in the Mexican War took place on May 8, 1846, in the Palo Alto prairie, north of what is now Brownsville. Hostilities ended in 1848, when the Treaty of Guadalupe Hidalgo was signed. Under the terms of the treaty, in exchange for $18 million US, the USA was granted the area that today comprises the states of New Mexico, Colorado, Arizona, Utah, Nevada, Northern California, and Texas. Brownsville, together with the adjacent region to the north, was also granted to the USA. Since

that time, the Rio Grande has marked the definitive border between the two countries.

4 Matamoros
The Mexican port city of Matamoros, on the south bank of the Rio Grande (or Rio Bravo) is connected to Brownsville, its counterpart on the north bank of the river, by two bridges. With more than half a million inhabitants, Matamoros is the larger city, and it continues to grow: According to

official predictions, the city's population is expected to exceed one million within 15 years. The reason for this growth is the special economic zone that has been established in Matamoros. US-run assembly plants located on Mexican soil, where lower wages make manufacturing cheaper than in the USA, are known as *maquiladoras*. The lure of jobs here is the main reason for the steady influx of people from southern Mexico into this border city.

5 Playa Lauro Villar
This stretch of the Mexican coastline, the continuation of South Padre Island, on the US side of the border, lies 38 km (24 miles) east of Matamoros, on Highway 2. The residents of Matamoros like to spend their weekends here, enjoying beaches where the surf is gentle and where fish swim close to the shore.

6 South Padre Island ↓ ↑
South Padre Island, which takes the form of a narrow spit of land lying parallel to the coast, has the most beautiful beaches on Texas's Caribbean coast. Although it is not a nature reserve, it is a haven for sea turtles, and home to 350 species of birds.

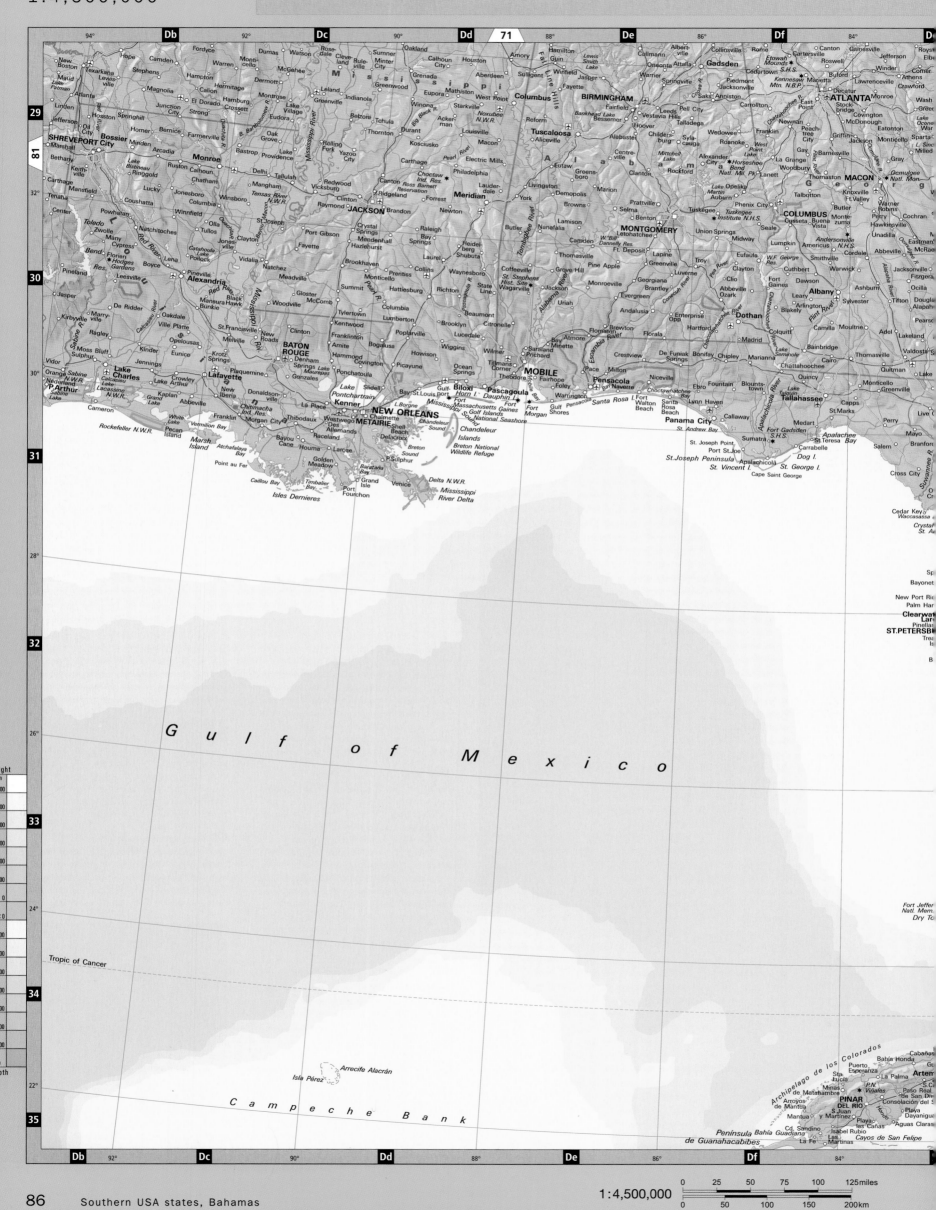

Gulf of Mexico

Tropic of Cancer

Campeche Bank

Height
m
3000
2000
1000
600
300
100
0
< 0
200
1000
2000
4000
6000
8000
10000
m
Depth

0   25   50   75   100   125 miles
0   50   100   150   200 km

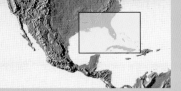

Dh 74 80° Dj 78° Dk 76° Dl 74° Dm 72° Dn

COLUMBIA

Augusta

SAVANNAH

Blake

JACKSONVILLE

Florida

Plateau ATLANTIC OCEAN

DAYTONA BEACH

ORLANDO

Lakeland

B *a* *h*

West Palm Beach

Great Bahama Island

Little Bahama Bank

Cooper's Town

Marsh Harbour

FT. LAUDERDALE
HOLLYWOOD

Northwest Providence Channel

Abaco Island
Eight Mile Bay

HIALEAH
MIAMI
Miami Beach
Kendall

Bimini Islands

North Bimini

a
m
a

Southwest Point

BAHAMAS

1 *Everglades*
Florida Bay National

Biscayne National Park

Great Harbour Cay
Bullock's Harbour
Berry Islands
Hoffman's Cay
Little Harbour
Bonds Cay
Whale Cay
Chub Cay

Dunmore Town
Royal I. Alice Town
Current I.
Eleuthera I.
Governor's Harbour

2

NASSAU

Rock Sound

s

Cape Sable

East Cape

Florida Keys

Great Bahama Bank

Straits of Florida

Joulter Cays
Nichols Town
New Providence I.
Rose I.

San Andros

Coral Heights
Andros Town

Staniard Creek

Andros Island

Highborn Cay

Norman's Cay

Powell Point
Bannerman Town
Flamingo Point

Arthur's Town
Cat Island

Tongue of the

East End Point
Little San Salvador I.

New Bight

Key West

Nicholas Channel

Archipelago de Sabana

Damas Cays

Cay Sal

Anguilla Cays

Williams I.

Wide Opening

Big Wood Cay
Moxey Town

Kemps Bay

Exuma Cays Land and Sea Park

Great Guana Cay

Black Point

Exuma Sound

Devil's Pt.

Port Howe

San Salvador

Cockburn Town
Columbus Monument

Conception I.
Cape Santa Maria
Rolleville
Stella Maris

Rum Cay
Port Nelson

Tropic of Cancer

CUBA

Archipelago de Camagüey

Guinchos Cay

South Andros I.

Cistern Point

Green Cay

Curly Cut Cays

Great Exuma Island

George Town

Little Exuma I.

William's Town

Deadman's Cay
Clarence Town

Long Island

Samana Cay

Gordon's

Pitts Town
Colonel Hill

Crooked Island

Pinefield

The Bight of Acklins

Snug Corner
Albert Town

Samana Passage

SANTA CLARA

CIENFUEGOS

CIEGO DE AVILA

Nurse Cay
Raccoon Cay

Ragged Island

Duncan Town
Little Ragged Island

Salina Point

Acklins Island

Castle Island

Mira Por Vos

Little Inagua Island

29
30
31
32
33
34
35

32°
30°
28°
26°
24°
22°

Dh 100 80° Dj 78° Dk 76° Dl 74° Dm

Everglades

Established in 1947, the Everglades National Park covers almost the entire tip of southern Florida. But, although it has a surface area of nearly 6000 km² (2200 square miles), it comprises only a fraction of the Everglades, an enchanting aquatic landscape of sawgrass punctuated by sparse islands on which trees grow. The Seminole, an indigenous people who once lived here, called the region *Pay-hay-okee,* meaning "river of grass." An English survey-or later named it the River Glades, while the region's present name—the Everglades—came about as a result of a printing error on maps. Its Seminole name, however, is more fitting, as the region is truly defined by a river: The River Glades flows very slowly southward from Lake Okeechobee, a 1800 km² (695 square mile) lake in central Florida lying at the same altitude as Fort Myers and West Palm Beach. The gradient descends by only 4–5 m per 100 km (12–15 ft per 60 miles), and the water flows at a rate of just 800 m (0.5 miles) per day. Overground, via the Glades, the lake drains into the Gulf of Mexico, while below ground, water from the lake seeps through porous limestone, flowing eastward to the Atlantic.

1 *Wilderness Waterway*

The best way to explore the Everglades is by canoe. The Wilderness Waterway, almost 160 km (100 miles) long, leads along canals, through mangrove swamps, past countless islands, and across bays and open expanses of sawgrass. The waterway is waymarked all along its length, and it takes about nine days to cover the entire stretch by canoe, with overnight stops at designated camping sites, some of which are located on artificial islands. For a pleasant canoe trip along this unique and spectacu-lar waterway, three pieces of equipment are essen-tial: a good map, a permit from the National Parks Administration, and effective insect protection.

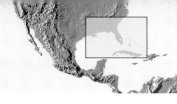

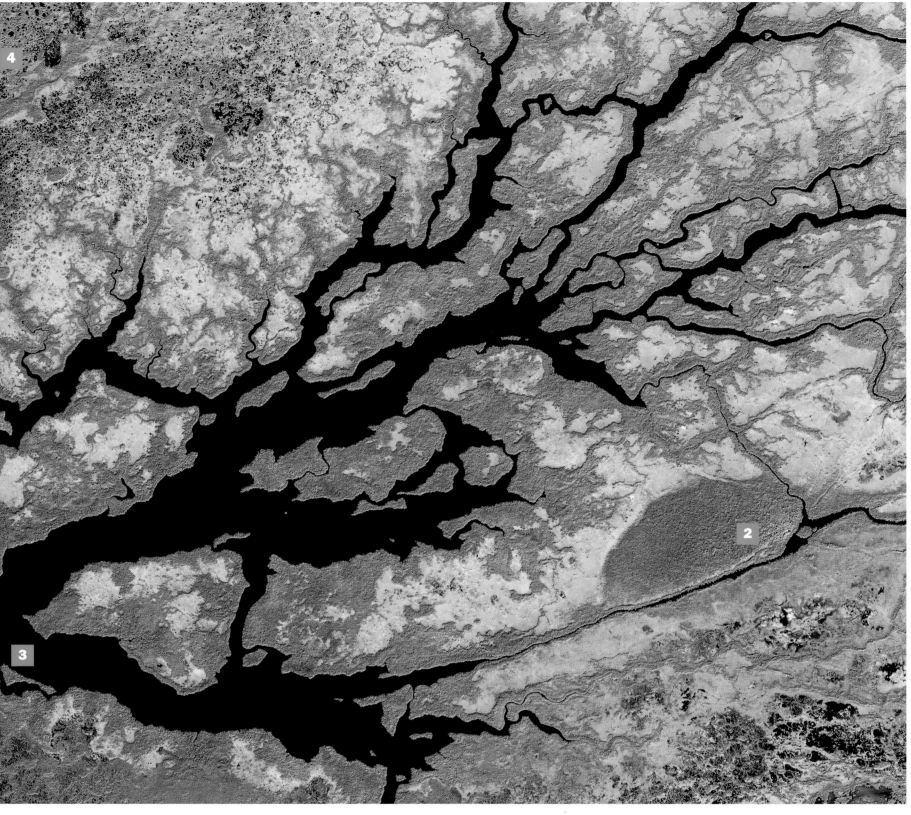

Hardwood Tree Islands

This "sea of grass" is dotted with sparse and scattered islands known as hammocks, which vary in size. Most of the larger islands are covered with hardwood trees: Here cabbage palms, West Indian mahogany, gumbo-limbo trees, and other woody plants grow. During the high-water season, they provide a safe refuge for the Everglades' population of mammals, which includes bobcats, raccoons, skunks, white-tailed deer, and otters.

Bayhead Tree Islands

The smaller islands are flatter than the larger, hardwood-covered islands. They support laurel and myrtle, and they are often surrounded by meadows of sawgrass. "Gator" holes, water-holes that attract alligators, are frequently found in the swampy undergrowth: The Everglades provides a habitat for thousands of alligators. They are easy to spot during canoe trips or walking tours on the raised walkways constructed through the swampy region. Despite their apparent indifference, they are dangerous creatures: Up to 5 m (15 ft) long, these great reptiles, which live primarily in subtropical North America, can strike very suddenly and pose a real danger to humans.

Wetland Prairie

The River Glades, which slowly washes through the Everglades, flows for 320 km (200 miles) into the Gulf of Mexico. The river bed is more than 100 km (62 miles) wide, but its average depth is only 15 cm (6 in). The water level, however, rises and falls depending on the season. Humans have had a destructive impact on this watery wilderness, especially in the 20th century. The only area in the USA with a sub-tropical climate, the Everglades once stretched from West Palm Beach over almost all of southern Florida. As a result of regular rainfall of up to 1500 mm (59 in) a year, the sawgrass swamps were once submerged for months. This was a paradise for waterfowl and wading birds, and countless minute life forms, as well as for crabs and fish in the brackish belt along the mangrove coast.

However, the first settlers considered southern Florida to be a worthless, mosquito-infested land, and at the beginning of the 20th century, many people envisioned draining the wetland prairie in order to use the land more effectively. To control the water and drain the swamps so as to create farmland, dikes were built and canals dug, especially in the 1920s and in the years following World War II. In total, around half of the Everglades was drained. As a result of southern Florida's inexorable development and the growth of its cities, with their heavy demands for fresh water, the "river of grass" was deprived of water and allowed to dry up. In spring, the Glades now dries up to such an extent that fires break out, and during the rainy season, from May to October, precious fresh water flows unused through canals into the Atlantic. "There are no other Everglades in the world. They are, they have always been, one of the unique regions of the earth... They are unique also in the simplicity, the diversity, the related harmony of the forms of life they enclose." Journalist Marjorie Stoneman Douglas wrote this in the late 1940s in her book The Everglades—River of Grass. Even back then she wrote: "This rare ecosystem is threatened with extinction."

Today, environmentalists demand that pumping stations should be set up, canals filled in and new ones excavated. Basically, all obstructions to an unimpeded water flow should be removed. Not everyone in Florida embraces this idea. The sugar-cane farmers have mounted strong protest, and even the tourist industry is divided: While some see the Everglades as a precious natural environment that should be preserved as an economic asset, others fear that reconstruction would result in loss of income for the sunshine havens on the coast.

USA **89**

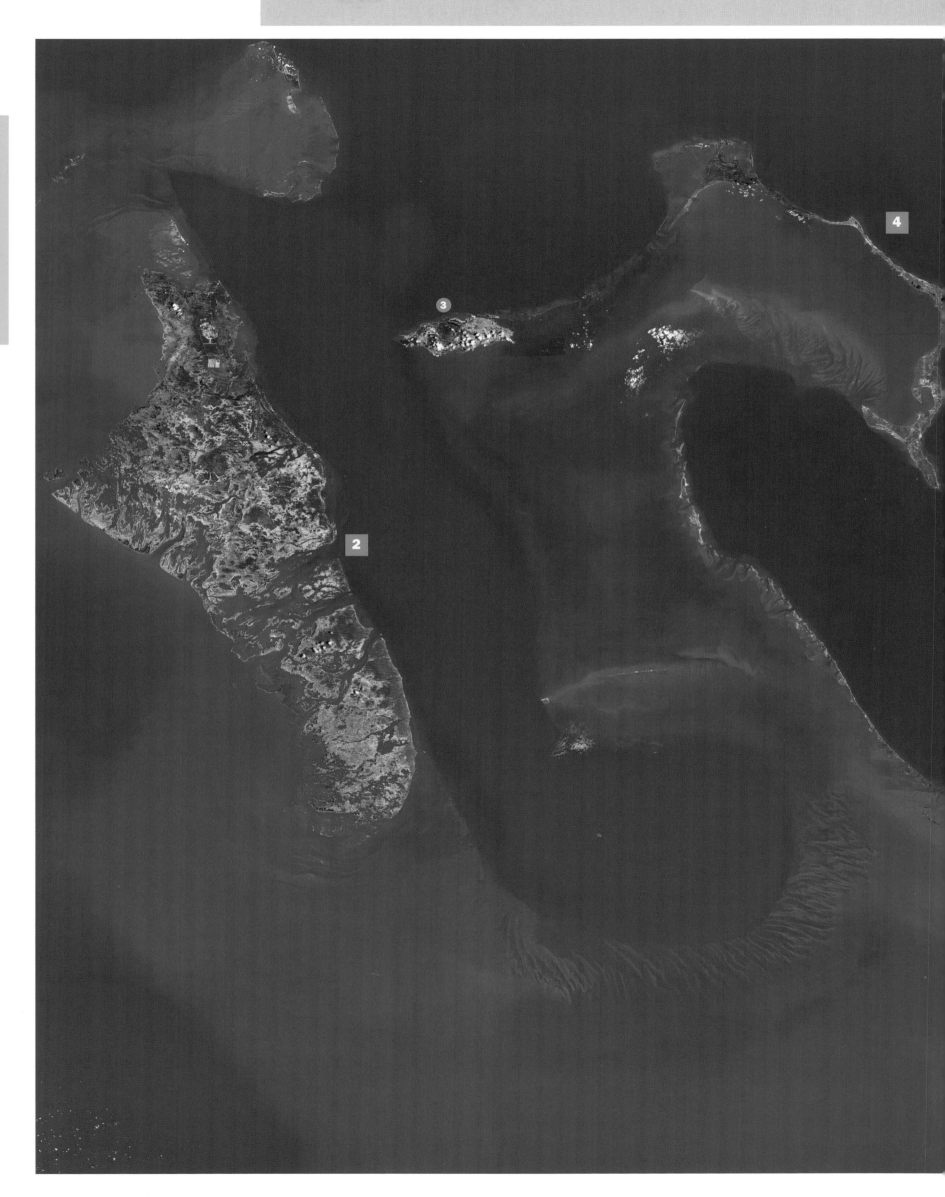

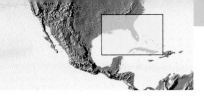

Bahamas

The Bahamas, an island state in the Caribbean Sea, form part of the West Indies. The islands, of which there are about 700, form an arc that stretches for 1200 km (750 miles) from the east coast of Florida to Haiti. These islands, 30 of which are permanently inhabited, are very low-lying and rise only a few meters above the azure ocean. Built of coral, they are located on the sandy Bahama Banks. Until 1873, the Bahamas were a British colony. After independence, tourism became the islands' main source of revenue. With long beaches fringed with palm trees, warm tropical waters that are a paradise for divers, and a high-class tourist infrastructure, the Bahamas particularly attract American holidaymakers and are a popular port of call for cruise-ship passengers. In earlier times, extensive freedom from taxation and liberal banking regulations helped the Bahamas to gain a reputation as an international center of finance.

1 Long Island ↑

Long Island has countless, often deserted and completely unspoilt white-sand beaches and crystal-clear water warmed by the Gulf Stream. While the water along the island's eastern shore, which faces the Atlantic Ocean, is quite rough, on its western side the coast is a tropical paradise, with sheltered beaches for sunbathing, and with clear, calm waters for diving and snorkeling. The island is almost completely covered in low scrub. Rum Cay, in the east of the island, was once an important source of salt production.

2 Andros Island

The largest island in the Bahamas, Andros lies 160 km (100 miles) southeast of Florida. About 230 km (145 miles) long and covering 5950 km² (2297 square miles), Andros is the second-largest barrier reef in the world. It is also a stunning diving site and forms an attractive area for anglers.

3 New Providence Island ↙

Nearly two-thirds of all Bahamians live on New Providence Island, which covers an area of 207 km² (80 square miles). This is also the location of the capital, Nassau, where the population is concentrated. Nassau's historic center has many reminders of its British colonial past. There is also a statue of Christopher Columbus, who set foot in the New World for the first time in San Salvador. Reflecting the fact that Americans make up over 85 percent of all tourists who visit the Bahamas, the lifestyle in Nassau, and the range of goods offered for sale in its shops, are strongly Americanized. Sun, sand, sea, and gambling define the rhythm of life at Paradise Island and Cable Beach.

4 Eleuthera Island

In terms of its landscape, Eleuthera, which covers 518 km² (200 square miles), is the most diverse island of the Bahamas. In 1648, Eleuthera Island and Harbour Island were the first bases for English settlers, who came here from England for religious reasons. By 1870, Dunmore Town, in the bay on the island's northern tip, had become the second-largest Bahamian town after Nassau.

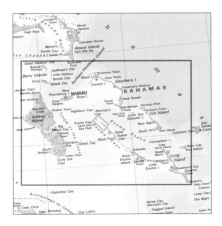

PACIFIC

OCEAN

Height
m
3000
2000
1000
600
300
100
0
<0
200
1000
2000
4000
6000
8000
10000
m
Depth

1:4,500,000

0   25   50   75   100   125miles
0   50   100   150   200km

Lambert Azimuthal Equal Area Projection

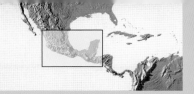

Da   96°   Db   94°   Dc   92°   Dd   90°   De   88°

24°

Gulf of Mexico

Tropic of Cancer

34

Mexico Basin

Isla Desterrada   Arrecife Alacrán
Isla Pérez

22°

Cayo
Arenas   Campeche Bank

Punta
Holohit   Isla   Cabo Catoche
Río Lagartos El Cuyo Holbox   Isla
Arrecife Madagascar   Dzilam   San Felipe   Contoy
Telchac   de Bravo   Isla
Arrecife Sisal   Progreso   Puerto   Panabá   Tizimín   Yucatán   Chiquilá   Blanca
Sisal   Temax   Buenaventura   Cancún
Hunucma   Conkal Motul   Cenotillo   Puerto
MÉRIDA Hoctún Izamal   Juárez
Celestún   Kinchil Umán Acancéh Dzitás   El Ideal   Isla
Punta Nimún   Tecoh Kantunil Piste★   Valladolid   Playa   de Cozumel
La Costa   Maxcanú   Sotuta Yaxcaba Chichén Chemax   del Carmen   Punta
Becal   Ticul Oxkutzcab   Itzá   Akumal   Molas
Calkiní Muna★   Yucatan   Cozumel
Hecelchakán   Uxmal   Tekax   Celarain
Tenabó Bolonchén Peto Tihosuco Tulum   Punta Celarain
CAMPECHE Lerma   de Rejón Tzucacab   Cenote
Chencoyi   Ichmul   Azul   Vigia
Punta Morro   Hopelchén Becanchén Dziuche   Chico
Champotón   Tixmucuy Pich Vicente   Xyatil Chichancanab   Punta Allen
Guerrero Polyuc   Felipe Carrillo Bahía de la Ascensión
Pustunich Dzibalchén   Puerto   Reserva de
Pixtun   Meseta Valle Hermoso   Sian Ka'an
Península Sabancuy Pixoyal   Peninsula Petcacab   Bahía del Espíritu Santo
El Palmar   de Zohlaguna   Punta Herrero
Isla del Carmen   Escárcega   Escondido   Puerto Madero
CIUDAD   Isla   Pital Centenario   Lázaro Cárdenas
DEL CARMEN de Aguada Conhuas Xpujil   Bahía   Cayo Norte
Punta Frontera Laguna de   Candelaria   Bacalar   de   Banco
Frontera   Términos   Majahual Centro   Chinchorro
Chiltepec   Monclova   CHETUMAL
Laguna del Carmen Tupilco Paraíso Jalpa   El Vapor Caribe   Chetumal Cayo Lobos
Sánchez de Mendoza   Palizada Tomás Garrido   Corozal   Xcalak
COATZACOALCOS Magallanes Comalcalco Laguna   La Unión   Orange Walk   Ambergris
Cosoleacaque Agua Cunduacán del Este   Cay
MINATITLÁN Dulce Cárdenas VILLAHERMOSA Nueva Coahuila Villahermosa Agua Azul Falls San Pedro
Las Choapas La Venta   Ciudad   Chablé Balancán   BELIZE Hick's Cays
Pemex Macuspana Catazajá   Dos Lagunas   Belize Turneffe Northern Cay
Francisco Chontalpa Emiliano   Lago del Tigre P.N. Río Azul City Islands Lighthoue Reef
Rueda   Juárez Teapa Zapato   Parque   San   Belmopan Blue Hole
Nacional   Carmelita Ignacio   Barrier-Reef Res. Long Cay
El Tigre La Palma   Dangriga
Palenque   Tenosique   Tikal P.N.
Palenque Gregorio   Sierra de Lacandón Tikal Melchor   Victoria Peak Glover
calco Yajalón Méndez   de Mencos   1120   Reef
Nezahualcóyotl Malpaso   Parque   San Pedro   Tobacco   Gulf
Nacional   San Benito   El   Range
Temó Lacandón   Cruce   Riversdale   of
Altamirano Bonampak   Marigo Creek   Honduras
Ocosingo   Lacanjah★   Dolores   Isla de Roatán
Lacantún Pasión   Poptún   Maya   Ranguana Cay Roatán
Las Margaritas Comitán   Sayaxché   Mountains
Las Maravillas Presa de la   Lagunas Lacantún San Luis Punta Negra   Sapodilla Cays Isla de Utila Utila
Angostura   de Montebello   San   Tres Puntas
La Trinitaria   Santa Isabel Antonio Punta Gorda Gulf of Bahía de Omoa Puerto Bahía de Tela
Concordia Tziscao   Sarstún Modesto   Amatique Puerto de Omoa Cortés P.N. Punta Sal La Ceiba
Parque   Santa Isabel Méndez El Golfete Omoa   Tela

36

18°

37

Gulf
of
Honduras

16°

Da   94°   Db   92°   Dc   90°   Dd   88°   De

Acapulco de Juárez

Its location on the sheltered Pacific Bay was central to Acapulco's history and growth, and ultimately the key factor in its modern-day status as the hub of Mexico's tourist industry. In the mid-16th century, the Spanish built a harbor here that served mainly as a transit point for trade with the East. Oriental spices, silk, and porcelain were unloaded here, and were transported to Vera Cruz, on the Gulf of Mexico, to be shipped to Europe. The city flourished until the early 19th century when the Spanish empire collapsed and other trade routes to the East became more attractive. However, after 100 years of obscurity, the bay was discovered by foreign tourists. Today this resort city derives its revenue mainly from tourism.

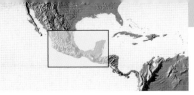

N

1 *Acapulco Bay* ←

The blue waters, white-sand beaches, and sheltered location, between two peninsulas that em-
brace the bay in broad arcs, as well as small islands (the largest being the uninhabited Isla La
Roqueta) had already made Acapulco an ideal
holiday destination in Mexico by the early 20th
century. Although, in the 1930s and 1940s, the
only foreign visitors were Hollywood stars, the city
underwent a systematic program of expansion,
particularly in 1946 under the presidency of
Miguel Aleman. To cater for mass tourism, large
hotels and apartment blocks bordering the
seafront were built, but the bay and the city itself
have retained their allure as well as their international sophistication.

2 City Center

Little evidence of international tourism
can be seen in the city center. The Zócalo—the
central square where the most important public
buildings, such as the city council, are located—
is a traffic-free oasis of calm, although it has
many coffee shops and restaurants. Here you can
enjoy a view of the cathedral and observe the
everyday life of the city. Nearby is the Fuerte de
San Diego, a fort built in 1615 and restored after
it suffered damage in an earthquake in the 18th
century. This is the only surviving relic from Acapulco's colonial days, when it was a center of
world trade, and it offers a grand view of the entire bay. A museum provides information about
the city's history.

3 Cliff-Diving

This is a breathtaking spectacle: Launch-
ing themselves from cliffs more than 40 m (130 ft)
high, Acapulco's world-famous *clavadistas*, or
cliff-divers, fly through the air and dive head-first
into the waters of the bay. This is a dangerous
sport, since the divers must watch the wave
activity and carefully time their jump so that they
enter the water when it is at its deepest.

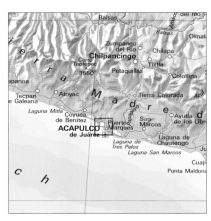

Central America

Height
m
3000
2000
1000
600
300
100
0
< 0
200
1000
2000
4000
6000
8000
10000
m
Depth

1:4,500,000

0   25   50   75   100   125 miles
0   50   100   150   200 km

Lambert Azimuthal Equal Area Projection

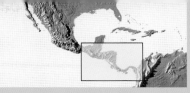

Df	**Dg**	**Dh**	**Dj**	**Dk**		
84°	82°	80°	78°	76°		

Islas
Santanilla
(HN)

Pedro Bank

Pedro Cays

Rosalind Bank

37

Cabo Camarón
Rio Platano
Reserve
Cerro Payas
1083
Laguna de Brus
La Mosquitia
Montañas de Colón
Puerto
Cabo Falso
Lempira
*Arrecifes de la
Media Luna*

Auasbila
Rus
Leimus
Rus
Waspam
Cabo de Gracias a Dios

C A R I B B E A N

Bonanza
La Rosita
Baká
Alamikamba

Cerro Saslaya
1650
P.N. Saslaya
Siuna

Arrecife Edinburgh

38

Puerto Cabezas

Cayos Miskitos

S E A

San Pedro
del Norte
Serranías Huapí
Laguna
de Wounta

*Isla de Providencia
(CO)*

14°

N A R A G U A

Cayos Guerrero

Cayo Tyara

Cayo King

Laguna
de
Perlas
Punta Perlas
Cayos Perlas

San
Andrés
*Isla de San Andrés
(CO)*

39

12°

Cordillera Chontaleña
Santo Domingo
Mico
La
Gateada
Rama
Muelle
de los Bueyes
Bluefields
Bahía de Bluefields
Isla del Venado

Islas
del
Maíz
(NIC)
Isla de Maíz Pequeña

Isla del Maíz Grande

*Cayos de Albuquerque
(CO)*

aragua
de
ame
San Carlos
Upala
Los Chiles

Nueva Guinea

Punta Mono

*Bahía
Punta Gorda*

40

Volcán Miravallas
2028 San
Rafael
Tilarán
Fortuna
Volcán Arenal
1633
Montevede
Juntas
Zarcero
Naranjo
Carlos
Boca Arenal

Barra del
Colorado

10°

colorado
S.Ramón
Heredia
Alajuela
SAN JOSÉ
Puntarenas
Caldera
Orotina
Colón
San Ignacio
Puerto Viejo
Horquetas
Guápiles
Siquirres

Moín
Limón

*Gulf
of Nicoya*
Jacó
Parrita
Sta. María
Villa Mills
Cartago
Paraíso
Turrialba
Asunción
Cahuita
Bribrí
P.N. Cahuita
Sixaola

Isla Colón
Bocas del Toro
*Archipiélago
de Bocas del Toro*

P.N.
Portobelo
Portobelo

Palenque
El Porvenir
Santa
Colón
Fuerte
S.Lorenzo
Alajuela
Cerro Jefe
*San Blas
Islands*
Ustupo
Yantupo
Mandinga

Gulf of Darién

Islas de San Bernardo
Pta.San Bernardo
Golfo de Tolú
San Bernardo
del Viento

Lorica

P.N. Chorales del
Rosaria
Báru
Punta Baru

RICA
Blanco
Chirripó
Cima
3819
Cerro Kamuk
Parque
Internacional
de La Amistad
3549
Almirante
*Laguna
de Chiriquí*
Pen.
Valiente

Mosquito Gulf
Boca del
Río Indio
Lago Gatún
Arenosa
Gatún

Chépo
Miguel
PANAMA CITY
920
Balboa
Pacora
Bahía de Panamá
935
L.Bayano
Pico Columna

Chimán
Cañazas

Mandinga
Cord.
de San
Blas
Ailigandi

Puerto
Obaldia
Acandi
*Golfo de
Urabá*
Caribia
Necocli
Titumate

MONTERIA
Tres Palmas
Arboletes

Ca.
Grande
Cereté

P.N. Manuel Antonio
Dominical
Buenos
Aires
Quepos
Punta Catedral
San Isidro
Palmar Norte
Puerto Cortés
Coronado
Piedras
Blancas
Golfito
San
Vito
Ciudad
Neily
La Concepción
Potrerillos
Vol.Barú
P.N.
Abajo
Volcán Barú
3477
Cerro Santiago
2826
*Reserva
Indígena*
Santa Fé 1518
Cerro Negro
La Pintada
Cope
San Cristóbal
Tambo
El
Valle
Cerro Gaital
Chame
San Carlos
1219

Santa
Rita
*Archipiélago
de las
Perlas*

San Miguel

Santa Fé
Meteti
Puerto
Quimba
La Palma
Yaviza
Pucuro

San Pedro
de Urabá

La Caña

Planeta
Rica

*Osa
Peninsula*
P.N.
Corcovado
Sirena
*Golfo
Dulce*
Rincón
*I. de
Parida*
Puerto
Armuelles
David
Santo
Tomás
Horconcitos
Remedios
Tolé
Cañazas
Santiago
Divisa

Calobre
Olá
Penonomé
Anton
Río Hato

Aguadulce
*Bahía de
Parita*
Parita

PANAMÁ

*Isla
del
Rey*
*Gulf of
San Miguel*
Isla
San José

Taimatí
Pinogana
Garachiné

Darién
Cerro Piña
1581
Cerro Pirré
1445
Arretí
Uraba
Turbo

Alto
Quimarí
2000
Tierralta

8°

Punta Burica
I. de
Jicarón
Gulf of Chiriquí
Isla Brincanco
Isla Uvas
*Islas
Secas*
El María
Soná
Puerto
Mutis
Ponuga
El Tigre
I.de
Cébaco
*Golfo
de Montijo*
Ocú
Macaracas

Los
Santos
Chitré

Las Tablas

Gulf of Panama

Parque
Nacional
Serranía del Sapo
Cerro
Piña
1561
Jaqué
de Darién

P.N.
Los Katíos
Riosucio
Sucio

Parque
Nacional
Río Sucio

Domingodé

Paramillo
3340
Ituango
3960
Peque

Cocos Ridge
*Isla
Montuosa*
*Isla de
Coiba*
416
*Bahía
Damas*
Punta Anegada
Espaveita
Tonosí
Cambutal
Valle
Rico
Los Asientos
Pedasí

*Azuero
Peninsula*

Aguacate
Puerto Piña
Nacional
(Ciudad Mutis)

Jurado
Cupica

Nudo de
Paramillo
3960
4080

San Andrés
Sabanalarga
Cañasgordas
Belmira
Antioquia

42

Punta Mariato

Punta Marzo
Punta Cruces
Vigia del Fuerte
Golfo de Cupica

Páramo Frontino
4080

Uramita
Dabeiba
P.N.
Las Orquídeas

106

Punta Solano
*Bahía Solano
(Ciudad Mutis)*

MEDELLÍN
ITAGÜÍ
Caldas

6°

P.N.
Ensenada
de Utría
Tribugá
*Golfo de
Tribugá*

Bebarama
Bolívar

C O L O M B I A

Nuquí
*Golfo de
Tribugá*

Quibdó
Virudó

Andes
Supia
Riosucio

43

Cabo Corrientes
Pie de Pepé
Las Animas
Istmina

Df	**Dg**	**Dh**	**Dj**	**Dk**
84°	82°	80°	78°	76°

N

Panamá

When the Spanish explorer and conquistador Vasco Nuñes de Balboa reached the Pacific Ocean on September 29, 1513, it was finally proven that the early European navigators of the age of Christopher Columbus had not, as had been thought, made landfall in India. At the same time, it was evident that the land bridge between North and South America was very narrow: Somewhat surprisingly, it was not until the end of the 19th century that a channel was cut through the isthmus, thus providing a shipping lane between the Atlantic and Pacific oceans. From then on, avoiding the long journey round Cape Horn, ships could shorten their journey by about 8000 nautical miles, or some 15,000 km (9300 miles). Today, guided by pilot boats, ships take eight to ten hours to pass through the 82 km (51 mile) long waterway.

1 *Miraflores Lock* ↑

The Panamá Canal is not simply a channel cut through the isthmus of Panamá. Because of the gradient, it has several different levels, which ships on their way from the Pacific to the Atlantic and vice versa negotiate by passing through locks. Besides the two-stage Miraflores lock, which raises ships by 12.5 m (41 ft), ships must pass through the Pedro-Miguel lock, with an elevation of 9.4 m (31 ft), and lastly the three-stage Gatun lock, with a descent of 26 m (85 ft). Each of these locks is 300 m (985 ft) long, 33 m (108 ft) wide, and 12.5 m (41 ft) deep. They are built as adjoining pairs, so that shipping can pass in both directions at the same time.

2 Panamá

Panamá City, capital of the state of Panamá, is the country's economic hub. This is where four out of ten of the country's industrial companies are located and where 60 percent of the country's economically active population work. The city, which continues to expand inexorably, has a population of almost 800,000 in the metropolitan area. The city stretches for about 10 km (6 miles) along the Pacific coast, from Panamá Vieja in the east, the old city founded by the Spanish in 1519 and destroyed by the English buccaneer Henry Morgan in 1670, to the mouth of the canal in the west. Panamá offers a mixture of different cultural, ethnic, and architectural contrasts. The old city has beautiful colonial buildings, while the modern district is dominated by a skyline of high-rise buildings.

3 Panamá Canal

In 1882 a French company under the management of Ferdinand de Lesseps (the engineer responsible for the construction of the Suez Canal) began work on the trans-American waterway. It was a fiasco, and not only due to corruption in the French parliament: 22,000 workers died of malaria or yellow fever, and after seven years the work was stopped, the project having incurred losses reaching into millions. In 1901 the USA secured the sole right for the construction of the canal, under the terms of a contract with Great Britain. Only after Panamá had won independence from Colombia in 1903 and had assured the USA sovereign rights over the Canal Zone, did construction resume, in 1904. The canal was completed in 1914, by which time the USA had invested $352 million. In the 1960s unrest occurred when the transfer of the canal and the Canal Zone to Panama was demanded. Since January 1, 2000, the Panamanian Autoridad del Canal de Panamá has had sole responsibility for the canal, which is used by about 14,000 freighters a year: The cargo that they carry, totaling 230 million metric tons (254 million tons), corresponds to about 4 percent of global commercial cargo. Panamá is planning to widen the canal over the next few years. However, for this Panamá needs foreign investments, particularly to fund the renewal of the locks' mechanism and electronic controls as well as for the parallel railroad and roadway along the canal.

4 Puente de las Américas

A bridge about 117 m (385 ft) high and 1653 m (5425 ft) long spans the Bahía de Panamá at the entrance of the canal. Replacing a ferry boat when it was completed in 1962, the bridge restores the land connection, broken by the canal, between the western and eastern parts of the country. Known as the Puente de las Américas, the bridge forms part of the Pan-American Highway.

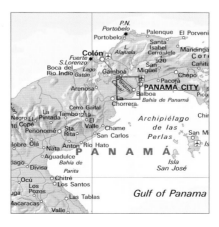

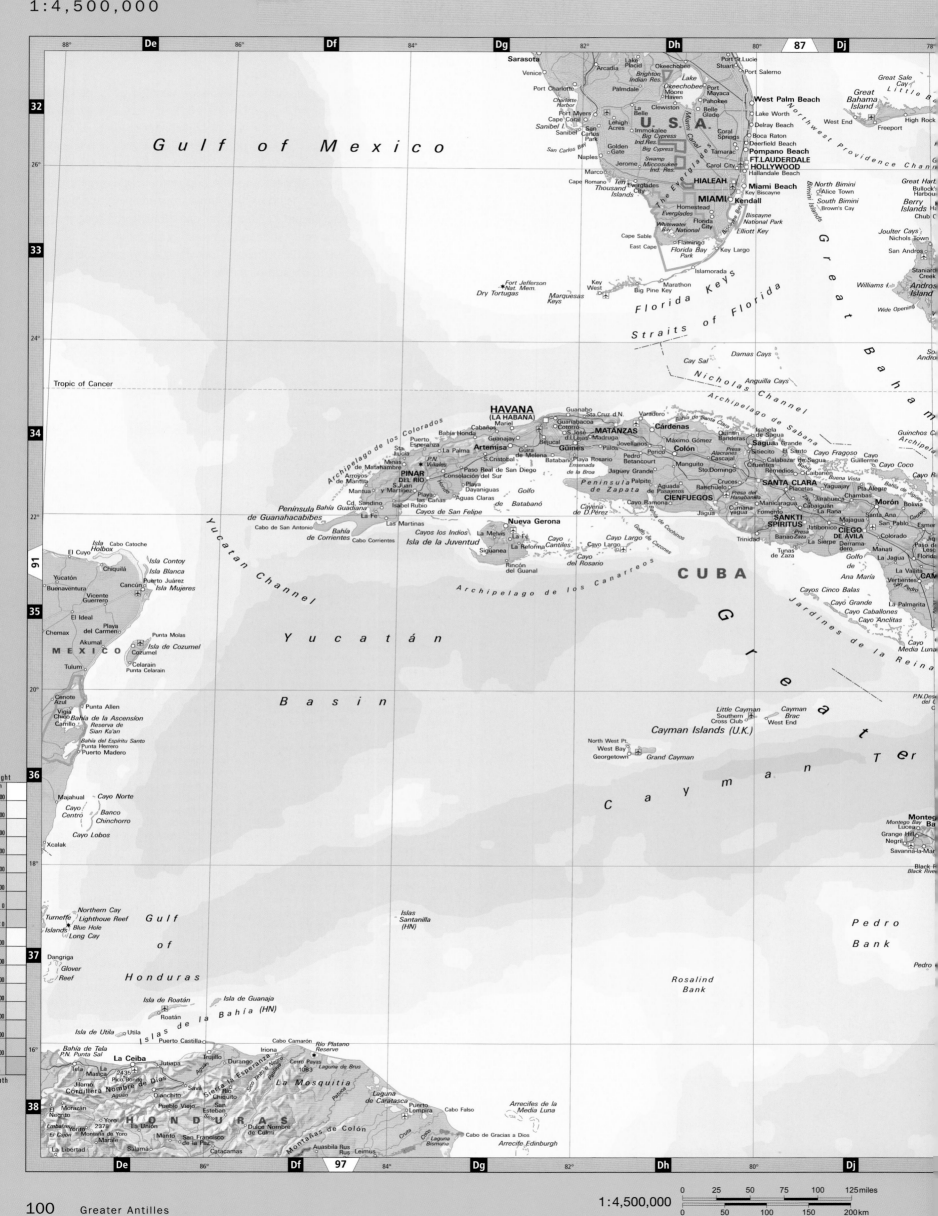

De · Df · Dg · Dh · Dj

32
33
34
91
35
36
37
38

Gulf of Mexico

Tropic of Cancer

U.S.A.

Sarasota
Venice
Arcadia
Lake Placid
Brighton Indian Res.
Port St.Lucie
Stuart
Port Salerno
Port Charlotte
Palmdale
Okeechobee
Port Mayaca
Lake Okeechobee
Moore Haven
Pahokee
Belle Glade
West Palm Beach
Lake Worth
Charlotte Harbor
Cape Coral
Sanibel I.
La Belle
Clewiston
West End
Freeport
High Rock
Great Sale Cay
Lehigh Acres
Coral Springs
Boca Raton
Deerfield Beach
Great Bahama Island
Lee
Cape Coral
San Carlos Park
Immokalee
Big Cypress Ind.Res.
Delray Beach
Fort Myers
Naples
Golden Gate
Big Cypress Swamp
Pompano Beach
FT.LAUDERDALE
HOLLYWOOD
Hallandale Beach
San Carlos Bay
Miccosukee Ind.Res.
Carol City
Marco
Cape Romano
Ten Thousand Islands
The Everglades National
Biscayne Bay
HIALEAH
Miami Beach
Key Biscayne
North Bimini
Alice Town
South Bimini
Brown's Cay
Great Harbour
Bullock's Harbour
Berry Islands
Homestead
MIAMI
Kendall
Bimini Islands
Everglades City
Florida City
Chub C.
Whitewater Bay
Biscayne National Park
Elliott Key
Cape Sable
Flamingo
Florida Bay Park
Key Largo
Joulter Cays
Nichols Town
East Cape
Florida Bay
Islamorada
San Andros
Fort Jefferson Nat. Mem.
Dry Tortugas
Marquesas Keys
Key West
Big Pine Key
Marathon
Williams I.
Staniard Creek
Andros Island
Florida Keys
Wide Opening
Straits of Florida
Great Bahama

Damas Cays
Cay Sal
Anguilla Cays
Nicholas Channel
Archipelago de Sabana

HAVANA (LA HABANA)
Guanabo
Sta.Cruz d.N.
Varadero
Mariel
Guanabacoa
Cabañas
Bahía Honda
Cotorro
S.José d.L.Lajas
Madruga
Jovellanos
MATANZAS
CÁRDENAS
Bahía de Santa Clara
Isabela de Sagua
Quinto Banderas
Guinchos Cay
PINAR DEL RÍO
Artemisa
Guira de Melena
Güines
Palos
Perico
Colón
Máximo Gómez
SAGUA
Sitiecito
El Santo
Cayo Fragoso
Cayo Guillerme
Archipela
Puerto Esperanza
La Palma
S.Cristobal
Paso Real de San Diego
Batabanó
Pedro Betancourt
Presa Alacranes
Cascajal
Cifuentes
Remedios
Caibarién
Cayo Coco
Sta.Lucia
Minas
Consolación del Sur
Playa
Aguada de Pasajeros
Manguito
Sto.Domingo
Calabazar de Sagua
Bahía Buena Vista
Arroyos de Mantua
de Matahambre
P.N. Viñales
S.Juan y Martinez
Playa
Dayaniguas
Aguas Claras
Golfo
de Batabanó
Península de Zapata
Presa del Hanabanilla
Manicaragua
SANTA CLARA
Placetas
Yaguajay
Chambas
Morón
Bolivia
Cd. Sandino
Isabel Rubio
Cruces
Jarahueca
Península Bahía Guadiana de Guanahacabibes
La Fe
Las Cañas
de
CIENFUEGOS
Ranchuelo
Cabaiguán
La Rana
Santa Ana
Cabo de San Antonio
Las Martinas
Cayos de San Felipe
Cayo Ramona
Jagua
Cumana-yagua
Fomento
SANKTI SPÍRITUS
Majagua
Esmer
Nueva Gerona
Bahía de Corrientes
Cabo Corrientes
Cayos los Indios
La Melvis
Cayería de D.Pérez
Golfo de Cochinos
Jatibonico
Barao Zaza
CIEGO DE ÁVILA
Colorado
La Reforma
Cayo Cantiles
Cayo Largo
Trinidad
La Sierpe
Derrama-dero
Manati
La Jagua
Paso de
Les
Siguanea
La Fé
Isla de la Juventud
Rincón del Guanal
Cayo del Rosario
Cayo Largo
Tunas de Zaza
Golfo de
Ana María
Cayos Cinco Balas
La Palmarita
CUBA
Archipelago de los Canarreos
Greater
Cayó Grande
Cayo Caballones
Cayo Anclitas
Cayo Media Luna
Jardines de la Reina
Vertientes

P.N.Dese del C
MEXICO
Isla Holbox
Cabo Catoche
El Cuyo
Chiquilá
Isla Contoy
Isla Blanca
Yucatán
Buenaventura
Vicente Guerrero
Puerto Juárez
Cancún
Isla Mujeres
El Ideal
Chemax
Playa del Carmen
Akumal
Cozumel
Isla de Cozumel
Celarain
Punta Celarain
Tulum
Cenote Azul
Punta Allen
Vigia Chico
Bahía de la Ascensión
Reserva de Sian Ka'an
Carrillo
Bahía del Espíritu Santo
Punta Herrero
Puerto Madero

Yucatan Channel

Yucatán

Basin

Little Cayman
Southern Cross Club
Cayman Brac
West End
Cayman Islands (U.K.)
North West Pt.
West Bay
Georgetown
Grand Cayman

Cayman

Greater

Majahual
Cayo Norte
Cayo Centro
Banco Chinchorro
Cayo Lobos
Xcalak

Turneffe Islands
Northern Cay
Lighthouse Reef
Blue Hole
Long Cay
Gulf of Honduras
Islas Santanilla (HN)
Pedro Bank

Dangriga
Glover Reef
Rosalind Bank
Pedro

Isla de Roatán
Isla de Guanaja
Roatán
Islas de la Bahía (HN)
Isla de Utila
Utila
Puerto Castilla
Montego Bay
Lucea
Grange Hill
Negril
Savanna-la-Mar
Black R.
Black River

Bahía de Tela
P.N. Punta Sal
La Ceiba
Tela
La Masica
Pico Bonito 2435
Jilomo
El Porvenir
Yorito 2379
Montaña de Yoro
Marale
Jutiapa
Durango
Trujillo
Aguán
Cabo Camarón
Iriona
Río Plátano Reserve
Cerro Payas 1083
Laguna de Brus
Arrecifes de la Media Luna
La Mosquitia
Laguna de Caratasca
Olanchito
Sava
San Esteban
Dulce Nombre de Culmi
Puerto Lempira
Cabo Falso
Cabo de Gracias a Dios
Arrecife Edinburgh
El Cajón
Yoro
El Morazán
Negrito
Cortito
La Unión
Manto
San Francisco de la Paz
Catacamas
Montañas de Colón
Cruta
Ausabila Rus Rus Leimus
Laguna Bismuna
Cordillera Nombre de Dios
HONDURAS
La Libertad
Salamá

Sierra de la Esperanza
Sierra Tierra Negra
Pueblo Viejo
San Chiquito
Río
Patuca

MEXICO
86°
Df
97
Dg
Dh
80°
Dj

Height
m
3000
2000
1000
600
300
100
0
< 0
200
1000
2000
4000
6000
8000
10000
m
Depth

1:4,500,000
0   25   50   75   100   125 miles
0   50   100   150   200 km
Lambert Azimuthal Equal Area Projection

Dk 76° **Dl** 74° **Dm** 72° **Dn** 70° **Dp** 68° **Ea**

32

33

34

35

36

104

37

38

A T L A N T I C

O C E A N

26°

24°

Tropic of Cancer

22°

20°

18°

16°

Marsh Harbour
Cherokee Sound
Abaco Island
Eight Mile Bay
West

BAHAMAS
Dunmore Town
Royal I.
Alice Town
Current I.
Eleuthera I.
Governor's Harbour
Rock Sound
José I.
NASSAU
Powell Point
Bannerman
Flamingo Point
Norman's Cay
East End Point
Little San Salvador I.
Arthur's Town
Cat Island
New Bight
Devil's Pto.
Port Howe
San Salvador
Cockburn Town
Columbus Monument
Conception I.
Cape Santa Maria
Rolleville
Stella Maris
Rum Cay
Port Nelson
Great Exuma Island
George Town
William's Town
Long Island
Little Exuma I.
Deadman's Cay
Clarence Town
Gordon's
Pitts Town
Colonel Hill
Crooked Island
Pinefield
Plana Cays
Samana Cay
Long Cay
Albert Town
The Bight of Acklins
Snug Corner
Betsy Bay
Abraham's Bay
Mayaguana I.
Nurse Cay
Raccoon Cay
Ragged Island
Duncan Town
Little Ragged Island
Salina Point
Acklins Island
Castle Island
Columbus Bank
Mira Por Vos
Exuma Cays
Great Guana Cay
Black Point
Green Cay

Bahama Cays
Land and Sea Park

Lobos

Bank

BAHAMAS

Bahamas National Trust Park
Little Inagua Island
Providenciales Islands
West Caicos I.
Blue Hills
Bottle Creek
North Caicos
Grand Caicos
Lorimers
East Caicos
Caicos Islands (U.K.)
South Caicos
Cockburn Harbour
Caicos Passage
Turks Islands (U.K.)
Cockburn Town
Grand Turk
Turks Island Passage

Northeast Point
Great Inagua Island
Northwest Point
Matthew Town
Lake Rosa

Mouchoir Passage
Mouchoir Bank
Silver Bank
Silver Bank Passage
Hispaniola Trough

Miguel
Baga
Manati
Mayanabo
maro
Vázquez
San Andrés
LAS TUNAS
Vado del Yeso
Buenaventura
MANZANILLO
BAYAMO
Jiguaní
Media
Contramaestre
Guisa
Yara
San Luis
La Maya
Bartolomé
Guisa
Turquino
Pico 1974
Chivirico
S.Pedro de la Roca
Daiquirí
El Portillo
Bahía de Santiago de Cuba
Sierra
Maestra
Pto.Padre
Jesús Menéndez
Gibara
Punta Lucrecia
La Canela
Rafael Freyre
Banes
Bahía de Banes
HOLGUÍN
Báguanos
Antilla
Bahía de Nipes
Cayo Mambí
Cueto
Sabana P.N.
Heche
wama
Urbano
Noris
Mayari
Los Indios
Sagua de Tánamo
Grupo Sagua Baracoa
Moa
Alejandro de Humboldt P.N.
Cayo Guín
Baracoa
Limonar
Punta de Maisí
Maisí
PALMA SORIANO
SANTIAGO DE CUBA
Manuel Tames
Arroyo Bueno
Jauco
GUANTÁNAMO
San Antonio del Sur
Cuero
Guantánamo (U.S.A.)
Bahía de Guantánamo Bay

DOMINICAN REPUBLIC

Île de la Tortue
Pointe Ouest
Port-de-Paix
Le Borgne
Monte Cristi
Bahía de La Isabela
Cabo Isabela
Luperon
Puerto Plata
Sosúa
Cabarete
Villa Vásquez
Los Cinuelos
San Juan del Norte
Cabrera
Guayubín
Mao
Cap-Haïtien
Port
Terrier Rouge
Caracol
Acul do Nord
La Citadelle N.H.P.
St Michel
Ennery
Dajabón
Moca
Nagua
Samaná Peninsula
Pte.Rivde
L'Artibonite
St.Marc
Hinche
Bánica
Restauración
P.N.
Armando Bermúdez P.N.
La Vega
Bonao
Cotui
Yuna
SANTIAGO DE LOS CABALLEROS
SAN FRANCISCO DE MACORIS
Bahía de Samaná
Sabana de la Mar
Miches
Sta. Barbara
Cabo Samaná
Escocesa
Gonaïves
Montrouis
Thomonde
Mirebalais
Comendador
Carmen
Ramírez
Pico Duarte
Maimón
Constanza
Yamasá
Monte Plata
Cordillera Oriental
El Macao
Cabo Engaño
Dame Marie
Cap Dame Marie
Jérémie
Roseaux
Corail
Île de la Gonâve
Île Grande Cayemite
Anse-à-Veau
Miragoâne
L'Asile
Petit Goâve
Léogâne
PORT-AU-PRINCE
Pétionville
La Tolson
Sierra de Neiba
San José de Ocoa
San Cristobal
Bajos de Haina
SANTO DOMINGO
Boca Chica
SAN PEDRO DE MACORÍS
Salvaleón de Higüey
San Rafael
Punta Cana
Tiburon
Massif de la Hotte
Baraderes
Barahona
Côtes de Fer
Jacmel
Marigot
Belle Anse
Cabral
Neiba
Rosario
Bahía de Ocoa
Bahía de Neiba
Sabana Grande de Palenque
Punta Palenque
La Romana
Bahía de Yuma
Saona Island
Parque Nacional del Este
Port-à-Piment
Aquin
Île-à-Vache
Port Salut
Les Cayes
Lago Enriquillo
Duverge
Jimaní
Vicente Noble
Jobillos
Pedernales
Massif de la Selle
Sierra de Bahoruco
Capo Falso
Oviedo
Cabo Beata
Beata Island

HAITI

Channel of Saint Marc
Channel of Gonâve
Montagnes Noires
Gulf of Gonâve
Windward Passage
Cheval Blanc

Ile Mona

OchO Rios
Port Maria
Annotto Bay
Port Antonio
Manchioneal
Linstead
Mts.
KINGSTON
Harbour View
Spanish Town
Portmore
Manchioneal
Morant Point
Golden Grove
Morant Bay
Spanish Alley
Portland Bight
Portland Pt.
JAMAICA

H i s p a n i o l a

Beata Ridge

C A R I B B E A N   S E A

J a m a i c a   C h a n n e l

A n t i l l e s

Lesser Antilles

In the 15th century, in the time before Christopher Columbus began his great voyages of discovery, the garland-shaped chain of islands then known as Antillia Insula was thought to lie between Asia and Europe. The Lesser Antilles, as these islands are known today, comprise the Windward Islands, which separate the Caribbean Sea from the Atlantic Ocean, the Leeward Islands, which tail south toward South America, Barbados, and the Netherlands Antilles. The islands are a colorful Caribbean paradise and a dream-holiday destination. But they are also a melting pot of cultures: Over several centuries the islands' original inhabitants have become integrated with colonists from several European countries, and also with immigrants from Africa, who were brought to the islands during the slave era. The natural scenery of the inner arc of the archipelago, with mighty volcanic islands, and that of the outer arc, with flatter, limestone islands, is shaped by a tropical climate.

1 St. Kitts and Nevis ↑
These two volcanic islands, part of the Leeward Islands, constitute the state of St. Kitts-Nevis, which gained its independence from Britain in 1983. The islands stretch for just 3.2 km (2 miles) and are separated by The Narrows, a strait running between their cliffs. In contrast to the neighboring islands of Antigua and Dominica, St. Kitts and Nevis have few beaches (such as Pinney's Beach on St. Kitts, seen here). Because of this, tourism is of only minor importance to the islands' economy.

2 Antigua and Barbuda
In geological terms, Antigua, Barbuda, and Redonda are in the transitional zone between the Lesser Antilles' limestone and volcanic islands. As elsewhere in the Caribbean, the economy of these islands was based on sugarcane cultivation until this was replaced by tourism. Covering about 160 km² (62 square miles), Barbuda is a designated nature reserve, with fascinating plants and animals, both on land and in the sea around its coastline.

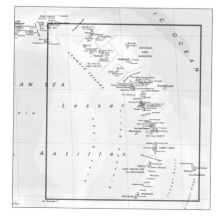

3 Guadeloupe
Consisting of two main islands, Grande-Terre and Basse-Terre, which are separated by a narrow strait, Guadeloupe resembles a giant butterfly when seen from the air. Grande-Terre, the eastern island, has long beaches and its interior is characterized by cirques—steep-sided semicircular basins formed by erosion. In the 19th century, the islands' rain forests were gradually destroyed to make way for sugar-cane plantations. Basse-Terre, by contrast, is an island of volcanic mountains and lush, tropical rain forests. The 1500 m (4923 ft) high Mount Soufrière volcano is still active today.

4 Dominica
When Christopher Columbus discovered this island, he named it for the day of the week—Sunday—that he set foot on its shores. Dominica has impressive natural scenery: Of volcanic origin, the island is covered in lush rain forest, which thrives in the predominantly tropical climate. The largely unspoilt island attracts holidaymakers, who come to trek in the forest. Several hundred Caribs, descendants of the island's original inhabitants, still live in Dominica. It is from them that the Caribbean takes its name.

5 Martinique ↗
Martinique, the second-largest island in the Lesser Antilles, with an area of 1090 km² (421 square miles), is similar to its sister island, Guadeloupe. Since 1946 the island has been an overseas region of France: Its official language is French and its administration is closely linked to that of France. Bordered by steep cliffs, the north of the island is covered with volcanoes. The 1397 m (4585 ft) high Mount Pelée (seen in the background in this view) last erupted in 1902, claiming over 38,000 lives. The flatter south of the island is used for agriculture and is fringed with beautiful beaches.

6 St. Lucia
Petit Piton and Gros Piton, two volcanoes in the shape of giant sugar loaves, dominate St. Lucia. This small island state in the Windward Islands was a colony of both French and British powers, until 1979, when it gained its independence. Today, tourism is becoming increasingly important to the island's economy.

7 Barbados
Over three-quarters of this island, the easternmost of the Lesser Antilles, is made up of limestone plateaus that have been eroded to form cirques. Some parts of the island's interior are also dominated by sugar-cane plantations. A British colony until it gained independence in 1966, Barbados has a political system and economic structure closely modeled on Britain's. Since it became independent, Barbados has become increasingly popular as a destination for British tourists. Compared to the other islands of the Caribbean, it has a developed infrastructure and a high standard of living, and is thus a model for the entire Central American region.

8 Grenada ↓
This island of volcanic origin, once known as the Spice Island, is one of the poorer states of the Caribbean. Despite abundant natural resources, such as nutmeg, cacao, and bananas, Grenada is still a developing country with a feeble economy and poor living standards. However, with its lush, tropical vegetation, a beautiful capital, St. George's (seen here), attractive harbors, and the idyllic Grand Anse Beach, this volcanic island has much to offer visitors. "Purchased" by the French in 1650 from the indigenous peoples, it was ceded to the United Kingdom in 1763, and eventually gained its independence from Britain in 1974.

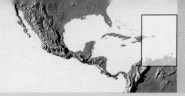

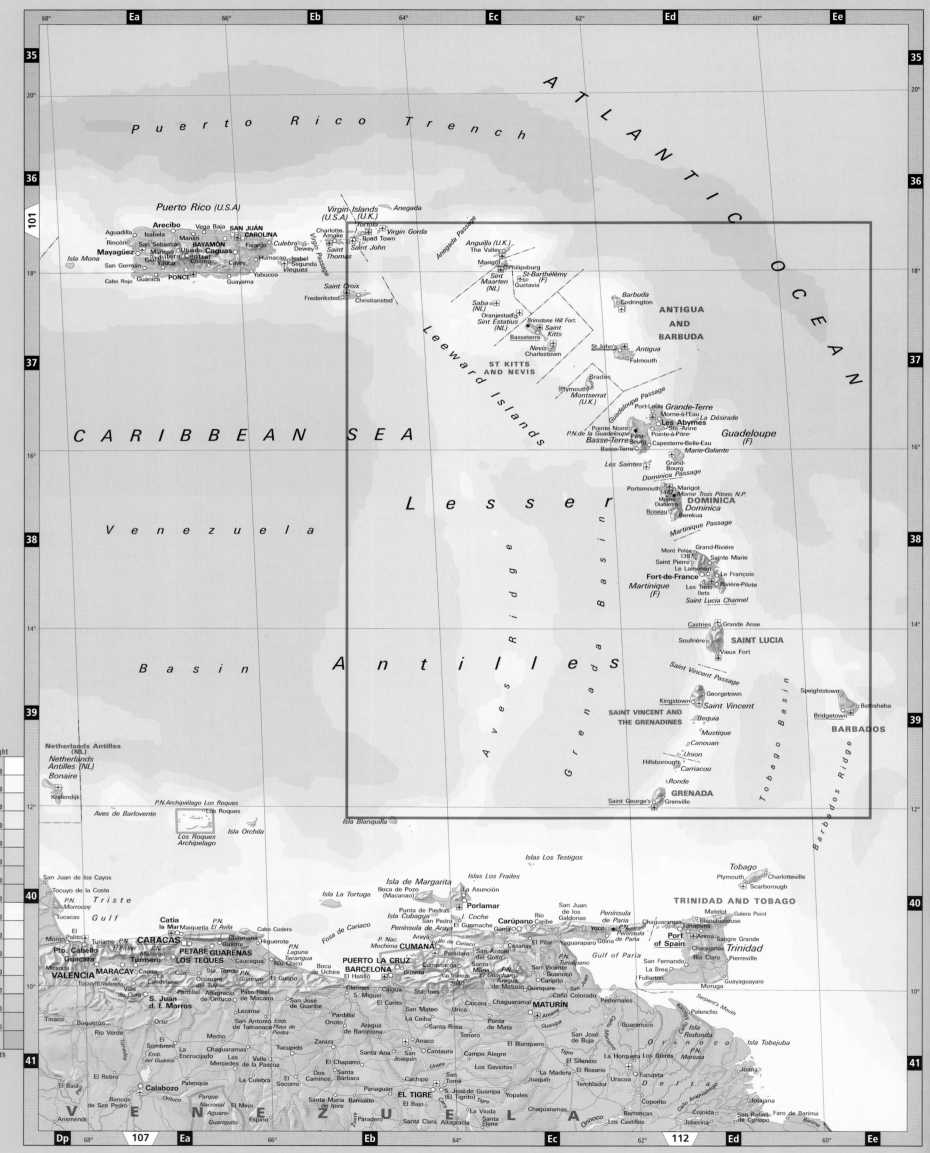

ATLANTIC OCEAN

Puerto Rico Trench

Puerto Rico (U.S.A)

Aguadilla
Arecibo
Vega Baja
SAN JUÁN
CAROLINA
Isabela
Manati
Rincón
San Sebastián
Utuado
Caguas
Mayagüez
Maricao
Cordillera Central
Yauco
Comío
Cayey
Humacao
Isabel
Segunda
San German
Guánica
PONCE
Yabucoa
Vieques
Cabo Rojo
Guayama

Isla Mona

Virgin Islands
(U.S.A)
Charlotte-
Amalie
Saint Thomas
Saint John
Dewey
Culebra
Fajardo

Tortola
Road Town
Virgin Gorda

Anegada

Anegada Passage

Saint Croix
Frederiksted
Christiansted

Virgin Passage

Anguilla (U.K.)
The Valley
Marigot
Sint
Maarten
(NL)
St-Barthélemy
(F)
Gustavia
Philipsburg

Saba
(NL)
Oranjestad
Sint Estatius
(NL)
Brimstone Hill Fort.
Saint
Kitts
Basseterre
Nevis
Charlestown

Barbuda
Codrington

ANTIGUA
AND
BARBUDA

St.John's
Antigua
Falmouth

ST KITTS
AND NEVIS

Brades
(Plymouth)
Montserrat
(U.K.)

CARIBBEAN SEA

Venezuela

Leeward Islands

Guadeloupe Passage

Port-Louis
Grande-Terre
Morne-à-l'Eau
La Désirade
Ste-Anne
Les Abymes
Pointe Noire
Pointe-à-Pitre
Guadeloupe
(F)
P.N.de la Guadeloupe
Petit-
Bourg
Basse-Terre
Capesterre-Belle-Eau
Basse-Terre

Marie-Galante

Les Saintes
Grand-
Bourg

Lesser

Dominica Passage

Portsmouth
1447
Morne Trois Pitons N.P.
Morne
Diabletin
DOMINICA
Roseau
Dominica
Berekua

Martinique Passage

Aves Ridge

Grenada Basin

Mont Pelée
Grand-Rivière
1397
Sainte Marie
Saint Pierre
Le Lamentin
Fort-de-France
Le François
Martinique
(F)
Les Trois
Ilets
Rivière-Pilote
Saint Lucia Channel

Guadeloupe Passage

Antilles

Castries
Grande Anse
Soufrière
SAINT LUCIA
Vieux Fort

Basin

Saint Vincent Passage

Kingstown
Georgetown
Saint Vincent
SAINT VINCENT AND
THE GRENADINES
Bequia
Mustique
Canouan
Union
Hillsborough
Carriacou

Speightstown
Bathsheba
Bridgetown
BARBADOS

Tobago Basin

Barbados Ridge

Netherlands
Antilles
(NL)
Bonaire
Kralendijk

Ronde
Saint George's
GRENADA
Grenville

Aves de Barlovente
P.N.Archipiélago Los Roques
Los Roques
Isla Orchila
Isla Blanquilla
Los Roques
Archipelago

Isla Los Testigos

Tobago
Plymouth
Charlotteville
Scarborough

Height
m
3000
2000
1000
600
300
100
0
< 0
200
1000
2000
4000
6000
8000
10000
m
Depth

Isla de Margarita
Islas Los Frailes
La Asunción
Boca de Pozo
(Macanao)
Porlamar
Isla La Tortuga
Isla Cubagua
Punta de Piedras
San Pedro
El Guamache

TRINIDAD AND TOBAGO

San Juan de los Cayos
Tocuyo de la Costa
P.N.
Triste
Morrocoy
Gulf
Tucacas
El
Morón
Palito
Turiamo
P.N.
Catia
la Mar
Maiquetía
El Avila
Cabo Codera
Pto. Cabello
Guacara
Turmero
Chirimena
Higuerote
VALENCIA
MARACAY
Cagua
Cúa
Sta. Teresa
P.N.
Villa
de Cura
Ocumare
del Tuy
Laguna
Tacarigua
Río Chico
Boca
de Uchire
Clarines
Caigua
CARACAS
PETARE
GUARENAS
LOS TEQUES
Guatopo
S. Juan
d. l. Morros
Altagracia
de Orituco
Paso Real
de Macaira
Lezama
San José
de Guaribe
Pardillal
Sta. Inés
El Chaparro
El Socorro

San Juan
de los
Galdonas
Carúpano
Río
Caribe
Península
de Paria
Chaguaramas
Matelot
Galera Point
Blanchisseuse
Yaguaraparo
Güiria de Paria
Arima
Tunapuna
Sangre Grande
Guiria
P.N.
Turuépano
Port
of Spain
Río Claro
Trinidad
Pierreville
Araya
Guaca
Casanay
El Pilar
San Fernando
La Brea
Guayaguayare
Fullarton
Moruga

Península de Araya
Boca
de Uchire
PUERTO LA CRUZ
BARCELONA
El Hatillo
Guanta
Mochima
Cumaná
CUMANÁ
Cariaco
Golfo de Cariaco
San Antonio
del Golfo
Casanay
P.N.
El Guácharo
Caripito
Maturín
Guanoco
Aragua
de Maturín
Quiriquire
Pedernales

El Tigre
San José de Guanipa
(El Tigrito)
Yopales
Guanoco
Barrancas
Tucupita
Isla
Redonda
Isla Tobejuba
Delta

VENEZUELA

Orinoco

Caño Araguabisi
Curiapo
Faro de Barima

0 25 50 75 100 125 miles

1:4,500,000

0 50 100 150 200km

Lambert Azimuthal Equal Area Projection

Colombia, Venezuela

C A R I B B E A N

SANTA MARTA
P.N.Tayrona de Gua
Cabo
San Di

BARRANQUILLA
Baranoa **SOLEDAD**
Galerazamba Sabanalarga Sitionuevo
Cga. Grande
de
Sta. Marta

CARTAGENA
P.N.Chorales del
Rosaria
Baru Turbaco San Felipe
Punta Baru Arjona Sincerin
Calamar
Chivolo

Islas de San Bernardo
Pta.San Bernardo San Onofre Plato
San Juan
Nepomuceno
El Carmen
de Bolívar
El Piñal
Santa
Cruz de
Mompós
Chimi

Golfo de
Morrosquillo Tolú **SINCELEJO**
Moñitos Lorica S. Andres Corozal
Sahagún San Jorge
MAGANGUÉ
Barranco
de Loba

Arboletes Cereté
MONTERIA
Tres Palmas
Caimito San Marcos Achí

La Caña
La Ye
San Benito
Abad Sucre
Pinillos

P.N.Cahuita Bribri Puerto Viejo
Sixaola
Guabito Parque
Internacional
de la Amistad Almirante Isla Colón
Bocas del Toro
Archipiélago
de Bocas del Toro Pen.
Valiente Mosquito Gulf **Gulf of Darién**
Golfo de
Uraba Ayapel Nechi

Chigorodó Caucasia
Planeta
Rica La Gl

Sabalito Volcán Baru
P.N. 3475
Vn.Baru
San Potrerillos Laguna
de Chiriqui San Cristóbal Turbo Riosucio Sucio Montelibano Piamonte El Bagre
Vito
La Concepcion Abajo 2826
Cerro Santiago Reserva
Indigena Puerto
Obaldia Acandi Pavarando Alto de Tamar
2350
Ciudad Chiriqui Grande Cordillera Central Santa Fé 1516 Copé Cariba
Necocli Caribana 2000 Alto
Quimari Tierralta
Neily **David** Cerro Negro El La
Pintada Penonome Meteti Metetí

Santo
Tomás Horconcitos Cañazas Sta. Calobre Olá Natá Anton Rio Hato Garita
Puerto Remedios Tolé Maria Santiago Divisa Pinogana Tucurá La Honda
Armuelles Divisa

Punta I. de
Parida El Maria Soná Puerto
Mutis Ponuga Ocú Los
Pozos Chitré Santa Fé Gulf of
San Miguel Yaviza 1875 Santo Riosucio Alto de
Carrizal

Gulf of Chiriquí El Tigre Macaracas Valle
Rico Las Tablas **Gulf of Panamá** Parque
Puerto Piña
Nacional
Jaque
de Darién Triundo Paramillo
3960 3960 Peque Segovia

Isla de Coiba Golfo de
Montijo Espaveita Tonosi Pedasí Jurado Dabeiba Santa
de Patamu Ituango Valdivia El Tigre

I.de
Cébaco 416 Bahia
Damas Cimbutal Azuero
Peninsula Aguacate
Punta Marzo P.N.
Las Orquideas Camisgordas Yali **BARRANCABERMEJ**
Punta Mariato Cupica Belmira Don
Matias Cisneros

Isla
Jicarón Punta Anegada Punta Vigia del Fuerte Bolivar Carolina Pto. Berrio Pto. Olaya
Cupica Golfo de Cupica Páramo Frontino
4080 Antioquia Copacabana San Puerto Nare

BELLO
Urrao **MEDELLÍN** Rionegro San
Luis Puerto Boyaca
ITAGÜÍ La Ceja
Vigia del Fuerte **Envigado** Cocorna

Punta Solano Bahia Solano
(Ciudad Mutis) Bebarama Caldas La Ceja Puerto Gutierez **Chiquinq**
P.N.
Ensenada
de Utria Tribuga Bebarama Fredonia Sonsón Muzo
Punta Arico Catedral d
Golfo de
Tribugá Nuquí **Quibdó** Andes Aguadas **La Dorada**
Bolivar Supia Salamina Pensilvania Victoria La Palma

Cabo Corrientes Virudo Riosucio Las Manzanares Mariquita Pacho
Animas 4900 Apia Chinchina Honda Guaduas Utica Zipaquir
Istmina Cerro Tamana 3980 **MANIZALES** Armero Alban Chia
Pie de Pepé Tatamá La
Virginia Nevado
del Ruiz Guarne Facatativa
P.N.Tatamá Ansermanuevo 5400 Nevado Cambao
de Santa Isabel Libano Funza
Punta Pizarro Noanama **PEREIRA** Los Nevados La Mesa **BOG**
Punta Manglares **ARMENIA** Nevado Alvarado Caquez
Manglares Cartago Quimbaya Tolima
5225 **Soacha**
Roldanillo Galeras Buenos Tocaima **VIL**
Zarzal Aires **Girardot** **VIC**
IBAGUÉ Fusagasuga A
Sevilla Caicedonia Chicoral Cunday 4560
Togoromá Pta. Charambirá Chaparral Guamo Co. Nevado
Espinal Saldaña Cabrera Shi
Istmo Palestina **TULUÁ** Ortega P.N.
Malaga Coyaima Purificacion Sumapaz

Punta Magdalena Bahia
de Buenaventura Llanobajo Buga Coyaima Santa Ana P.N.
BUENAVENTURA Isla Cayambe El
Cerrito Rioblanco Dolores Sumapaz

Isla Aji Yumbo Palmira Planadas Baraya
Veneral P.N.
Farallones
de Cali **PALMIRA** Florida Colombo
Boca **CALI** Jamundi Pto. Tejada Uribe
Candelaria Timba Santander d Neiva 3520 P.N.
Cali Lopez Mondomo Nevado del Huila Palermo Cerro Leiva Cord.
de los
Picachos
P.N. Isla Gorgona Punta Coco 5750 Paez Teruel
Gorgona Piendamo Campoalegre P.N.
Isla Soledad Uribe Argelia Silvia Inza Tierradentro Hobo Tinigua

Punta Reyes P.N.
Sanquianga Munchique **POPAYÁN** La Garzón San Vicente
Punta Guasacama Guapi El Tambo Plata Guacamayas del Caguan
Mosquera Argelia Rosas 4580 4546 Pto. Seco
El Carmen Sanabria Sotara Vn. La Altamira
Purace Argentina Lusitania Tagua
El Bordo La Vega P.N. de Puracé El Doncello
Ensenada de Tumaco P. Arqueologico Morelia
Tumaco San Antonio Pisanda San Agustin **Florencia** Cartagena
Patia Bolivar Santa Rosa Pitalito P.N. del Chaira
Cabo Manglares Barbacoas La Union San José (Albán) de los
Guacharos Sabaneta La Chaira
Terán 4070 Sabaneta
Isla Santa Rosa Sotomayor Buesaco Puerto Limón
Isla San Luis Junin La Florida Mocoa Valparaiso San Antonio
La Tola 4764 **PASTO** Laguna de Getucha
Punta Verde Guachucal de la Cocha Pto. Humbria Tres
Esmeraldas Nev.
de Cumbal Ilies Monopamba Solita
Punta Galera 4764 Maldo- Orito Mecaye
Atacames nado Tulcán Ipiales Pto. Asis Caguan
S. Mateo Lita El Monopamba
Galera Muisne **ECUADOR** Maldo- La Concepcion Mira S. Gabriel

P A C I F I C   O C E A N

I. Malpelo

Height
m
3000
2000
1000
600
300
100
0
< 0
200
1000
2000
4000
6000
8000
10000
m
Depth

1:4,500,000

Albers Equal Area Conic Projection

0   25   50   75   100   125 miles
0   50   100   150   200 km

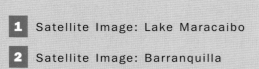

1 Satellite Image: Lake Maracaibo

2 Satellite Image: Barranquilla

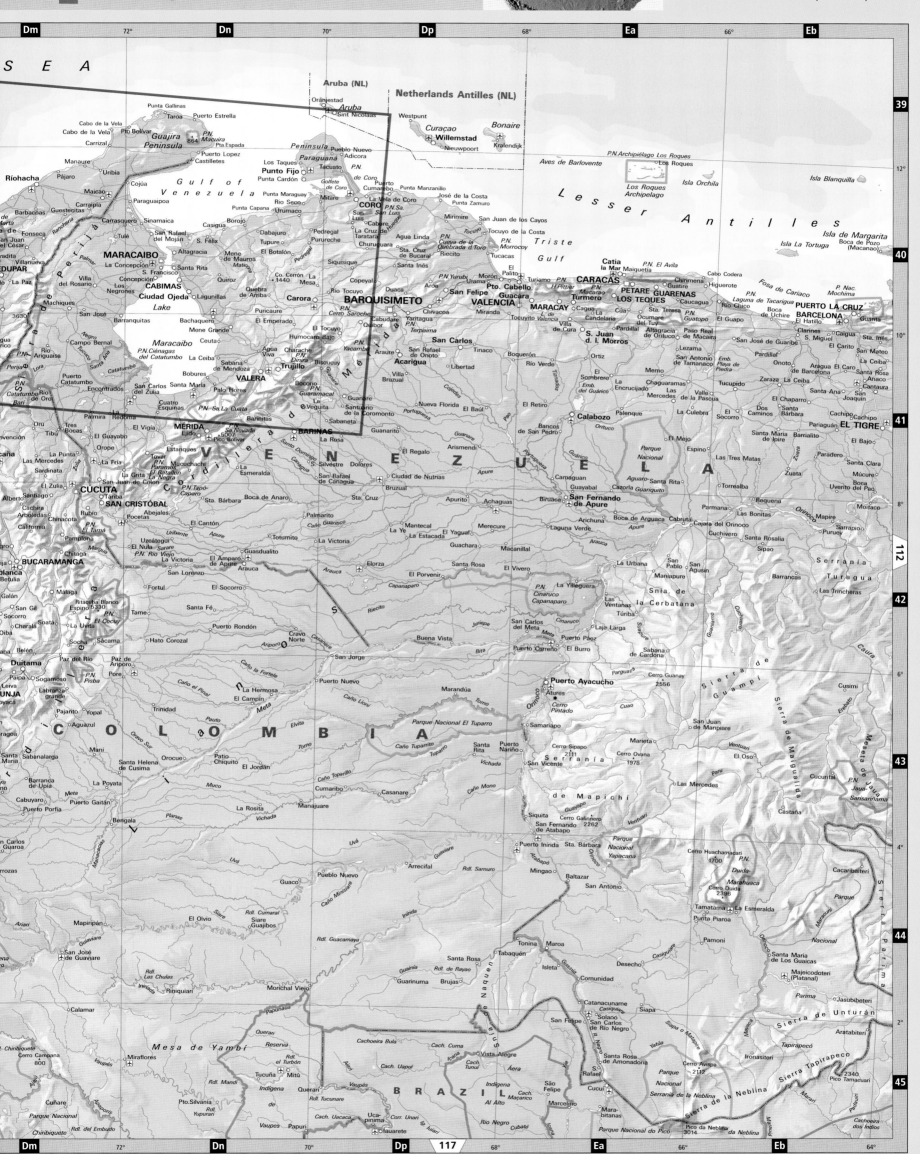

S E A

Dm   72°   Dn   70°   Dp   68°   Ea   66°   Eb

39

Punta Gallinas
Cabo de la Vela   Taroa   Puerto Estrella
Cabo de la Vela   Pto Bolívar
Carrizal   Pta.Espada
                    Guajira   864   P.N.Macuira
Manaure   Peninsula
Ríohacha   Uribia
        Pájaro   Puerto Lopez
Maicao   Cojúa   Castilletes
Carraipia   Los Taques
Barbacoas Guestecitas   Sinamaica   Punta Cardón
San Juan de   Rancherías

Aruba (NL)
Oranjestad   *Aruba*
        Sint Nicolaas   Westpunt

Netherlands Antilles (NL)
                Curaçao   Bonaire
            Willemstad
        Nieuwpoort   Kralendijk

Aves de Barlovente

L e s s e r   A n t i l l e s

P.N.Archipiélago Los Roques
        Los Roques
    Los Roques
    Archipelago   Isla Orchila   Isla Blanquilla

12°

Peninsula
Paraguaná   Isla de Margarita
                    Isla La Tortuga   Boca de Pozo
                                (Macanao)

40

MARACAIBO
    La Concepción
CABIMAS
Ciudad Ojeda
    Lake
    Maracaibo

BARQUISIMETO

CARACAS
    PETARE **GUARENAS**
    LOS TEQUES   **PUERTO LA CRUZ**
VALENCIA   **BARCELONA**
MARACAY

10°

VALERA
MÉRIDA
BARINAS

V E N E Z U E L A

Calabozo

41

CÚCUTA
SAN CRISTÓBAL

112

BUCARAMANGA

8°

San Fernando
de Apure

42

Puerto Carreño

Puerto Ayacucho

6°

C O L O M B I A

Parque Nacional El Tuparro

43

4°

La Esmeralda

44

2°

Dm   72°   Dn   70°   Dp   117   68°   Ea   66°   Eb   64°

45

B R A Z I L

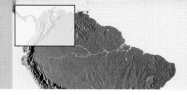

Lake Maracaibo

It is thanks to Lake Maracaibo that Venezuela received its name. When Alonso de Ojeda landed here in 1499, he named this watery environment Venezuela, meaning "Little Venice." The area around Lake Maracaibo is now one of the richest parts of the country. Crude oil has been extracted here since 1914: Extraction is concentrated on the lake's northern shore and many oil platforms stand right in the water. The Maracaibo Basin also contains Venezuela's most productive agricultural land. Marked by a chain of high mountains, the border between Venezuela and Colombia can be clearly seen in the satellite image. This mountain chain is the Sierra de Perijá, which rises to a height of 3630 m (11,909 ft) and is covered in a bank of clouds.

① *Sinamaico Lagoon* ↓

The lagoon lies just off the coast on the south-western side of the Gulf of Venezuela. It was the dwellings on stilts built here by the native inhabitants that reminded Alonso de Ojeda of Venice, although some might consider this an unflattering comparison for the Italian city. Today, indigenous people still live here in stilt dwellings, built either directly on the flat-bottomed lagoon or in the numerous side canals, where mangrove swamps predominate.

② Guajira Peninsula

Almost all of the Guajira Peninsula, on the western side of the Gulf of Venezuela, lies in

④ Lake Maracaibo

Some 155 km (96 miles) long and 120 km (75 miles) wide, Lake Maracaibo is the largest lake in South America. It is connected to the Gulf of Venezuela and the Caribbean Sea by a narrow waterway. Over recent decades, the canal has been enlarged so as to facilitate access for large oil tankers, which sail into the lake to reach the oil-loading areas there.

Lake Maracaibo is fed by numerous streams and rivers that flow down from the Andes, whose two eastern ridges (the Sierra de Perijá in the west and the Cordillera de Mérida in the southeast) extend along each side of the lake like two gigantic arms. These rivers bring a sufficient volume of fresh wa-

neighboring Colombia. Most of this inaccessible island has a semi-desert landscape. Like the rest of the border region, it is inhabited mainly by semi-nomadic people of the Guajiro tribe, who number around 23,000. They pay little heed to the national border that divides Venezuela from Colombia, and wander freely across it. Macuira National Park, which covers 250 km² (97 square miles), extends along the east side of the peninsula. The national park is a mountainous region and, unlike the arid semi-desert all around, it is covered in moist evergreen forest.

③ Paraguaná Peninsula

The peninsula is connected to the mainland by the Isthmus of Los Médanos. This narrow stretch of land is covered in dunes, some of which rise to a height of 20 m (66 ft). The peninsula itself is mostly a semi-desert landscape, with a small forested area in the interior. It is almost uninhabited, but, surprisingly, some attractive vestiges of the region's colonial period survive: These include the houses in the fishing village of Adicora and the churches in Muruy and Santa Ana. The largest town on the peninsula is Punto Fijo, in the southwest.

ter to the lake to prevent it from becoming too saline (salt water washes in from the open ocean), allowing it to support plant and animal life.

⑤ *Maracaibo* ↓

Although Caracas is the capital of Venezuela, the country's economic hub is the city of Maracaibo, which lies in one of the hottest areas of the country. About two-thirds of all of Venezuela's export revenue originates here. It was founded in 1574 and, when the San Carlos Fortress was completed in 1683, it was relatively safe from attacks by pirates. In the first 350 years of its existence, the sleepy little town grew very slowly, deriving its revenue from trade with the Netherlands Antilles. After oil was discovered beneath the lake, Maracaibo expanded to become a city inhabited by millions, with dazzling office buildings, large banks, and tall apartment blocks. The city has retained its original colonial character only in a small number of streets in the old town around the harbor, a district that escaped rebuilding and modern city planning. Here there are some amazing sights, most notably picturesque houses in elegant architectural styles dating from the time when Venezuela was still a Spanish colony.

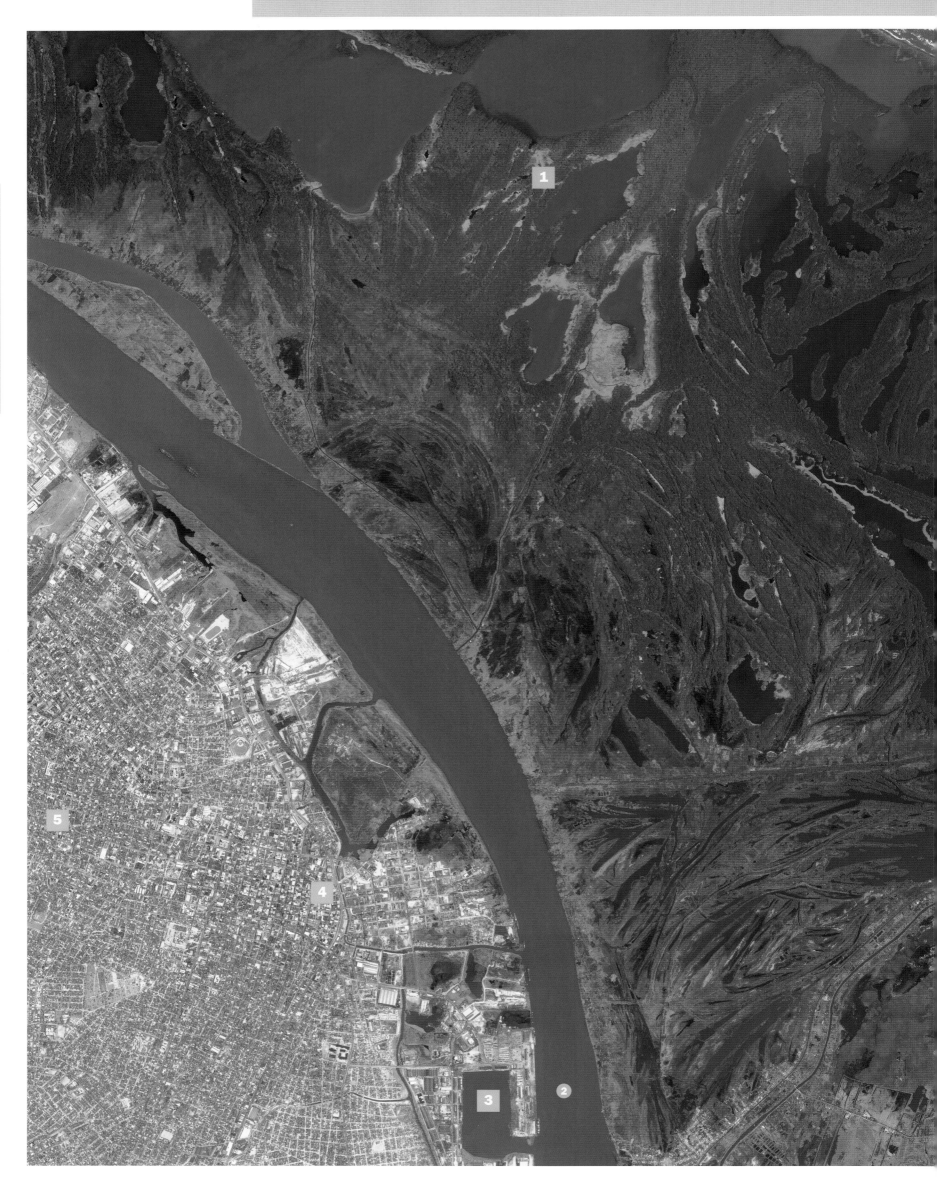

1 Salamanca Island National Park

Salamanca Island, which has been made a national park, extends to the east of the Magdalena's estuary. Despite its name, it is not in fact a single island but a group of islands and islets surrounded by lakes or separated by a network of canals and small tributaries of the Magdalena. As the tides come in, the fresh water of the lakes and rivers mixes with the salt water from the Caribbean Sea: The resultant brackish water creates a perfect environment in which mangroves can thrive. Thanks to their stilt-like roots, mangroves are the only type of land-based vegetation able to live in both fresh and salt water. The mangrove forests create a delicate ecosystem: They grow only along narrow coastal strips and also provide an ideal habitat where certain types of fish and marine animals—such as mudskippers, turtles, prawns, roaches, and sharks—can breed and flourish. With the largest expanse of mangrove swamps in Colombia, Salamanca Island National Park is a haven for these animals. The

Barranquilla

Barranquilla is the capital of the Atlántico region, one of the 24 provinces and nine administrative districts that make up Colombia. The city, which lies in the subtropical belt, where hot, sultry weather predominates all year round, is located on the Magdalena River, about 15 km (9 miles) south of the point where it flows into the Caribbean Sea. With a population of more than a million, the city is the fourth-largest in Colombia and is the country's leading industrial port and commercial city. Barranquilla was founded in 1629, but did not start to grow until the 19th century, soon developing into Colombia's hub of foreign trade and becoming its point of contact with the wider world. Colombia's first commercial airline, the Sociedad Colombo-Alemana de Transportes Aereos, was founded in Barranquilla in 1919. It was the predecessor of Avianca, the present-day Colombian national airline. Barranquilla is famous for its carnival, the largest and most exuberant in the whole of Colombia. In the five days leading up Ash Wednesday, work in the city comes to an almost complete halt.

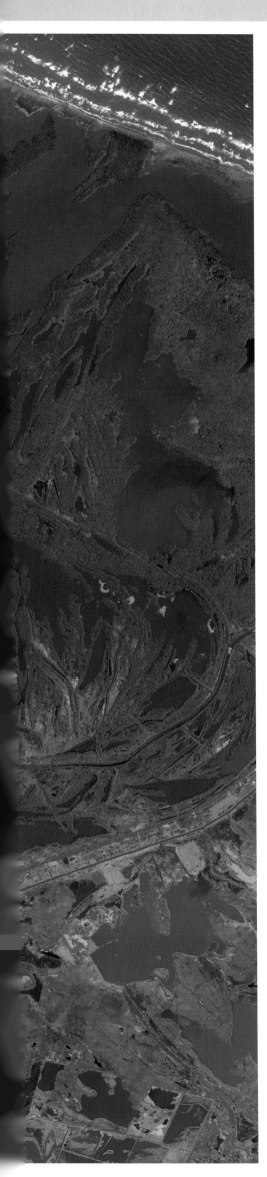

mangrove swamps here are so densely forested that they are impenetrable for human beings. Despite this, the environment is under threat. This is because the Straits of Barranquilla, which lead to Santa Marta and which can be seen in the southern part of the satellite image, form a barrier against fresh water entering the mangrove swamps. As a consequence, the exchange of fresh and salt water is insufficient to support the mangroves. However, channels have been dug below the straits to solve this problem.

2 Magdalena River ↑

The Magdalena is Colombia's longest river. It rises on the western slopes of the Central Cordillera—in Colombia the Andes divide into three almost

parallel mountain chains (the Western, Central, and Eastern cordilleras)—and flows northward through a valley lying between the Eastern and Central cordilleras. In the northern lowlands, the river splits into several branches, joins the Cauca River, which is almost as long as the Magdalena, and finally flows into the Caribbean Sea through a wide delta. The course of the Magdalena River is 1540 km (957 miles) long, 1300 km (808 miles) of which are navigable.

3 Port

Despite its accessible location just 15 km (9 miles) from the coast and the fact that it is connected to the hinterland by a navigable river, Barranquilla became a major port city at a relatively late stage in its history. Until the end of the 19th century, boatmen who transported cargo along the Magdalena used the coastal town of Cartagena, some distance southwest of Barranquilla, as a port. They sailed down the Magdalena to Calamar, a town located about 100 km (60 miles) south of Barranquilla, and from there made their way along the Dique Canal, which starts at Calamar and flows into the Caribbean Sea just to the south of Cartagena. At that time the Magdalena's delta could be navigated only with great difficulty, but at the end of the 19th century, changes made to the river alleviated the problem. This, and the simultaneous expansion of the port of Barranquilla, transformed it into Colombia's busiest port city. Coffee beans, one of Colombia's main exports, are shipped from here to all parts of the world.

4 Plaza de Bolívar

The square, named for Simon Bolívar (1783–1830), Latin America's most celebrated fighter for freedom from Spanish rule, gives Barranquilla's old city center its character, although neither the cathedral nor the most important administrative buildings are located here. Plaza de Bolívar is principally a market square, where every imaginable type of merchandise, including a wealth of goods smuggled in via the port, is bought and sold.

The city's cathedral is located somewhat to the west of Plaza de Bolívar. Completed in 1982, it has a modern design. While from the outside it has a closed, severe appearance, it is worth visiting for its interior, which is lit by beautiful stained-glass windows

5 El Prado

The wealthier and smarter face of Barranquilla is focused on an area of the city to the west of the historic center. This is El Prado, a district of tall apartment blocks and office buildings, where the streets are lined with boutiques and restaurants rather than market stalls and snack bars. The large number of hotels here provide accommodation for tourists, many of whom come to Barranquilla during the lively carnival period. Both of the city's finest museums are also located in the El Prado district: While the Museo Romántico is dedicated to the history of Barranquilla, the Museo de Antropología focuses mainly on artifacts from pre-Columbian times.

Guyana, Suriname, French Guiana

1:4,500,000

Albers Equal Area Conic Projection

0	25	50	75	100	125miles
0	50	100	150	200km	

39

12°

A T L A N T I C

40

10°

O C E A N

41

8°

42

6°

ey
arlborough
harity
Anna Regina

Tiger Island
Leguan Island
arika

GEORGETOWN
Vreed- Buxton
a-en-Hoop Clonbrook
imehrie Mahaicony

u Keria Fort Wellington
al Landing
iperu Rosignol Port Maurant
New Amsterdam
ine Linden Mara Leeds, Nieuw
Corriverton Amsterdam
Skeldon PARA-
Matali N Takama Groot MARIBO
mãkwa Nickerie Henar Totness Boskamp Saramaccan Tamanredjo
Kalkuni Wageningen Groningen Meerzorg Pt. Aouara
Ituni Kwakwani Batavia Lelydorp Wriedjk Galibi Mana
Wasjabo Jenny Onverwacht Paranam Moengo Organabo Iracoubo
Epira Apoera Zanderij Joden- Albina Saint Laurent- Sinnamary
Berg savanne Armina- Maroni du Maroni
Bitagron en Dal Phedra vallen Apatou Malmanoury Îles du Salut
Corantijn Loksiati Brokopondo Mana Centre Kourou
Avanavero Brownsweg Mobaka Langatabiki Spatial
Toekornstig- Kamp 52 Raleigh- Prof. Gare Tigre Guyanais Tonate
stuwmeer Blanche- vallen van Cayenne
Marievallen 240 Blommestein Lake Montsinéry Rémire
Kabalebo Voltsberg N.P. Saint-Élie Matoury
Umeru Bronsweg Mgnes. Roura
Rapids Central Françaises Pointe Béhague
Tonkensval Boto-Pasi Lely Gebergte 630 Baye de
Mt. Tafel Pokigron 669 Cacao l'Oyapock
1026 Asindonhopo Grand-Santi F r e n c h Régina Cabo Orange
Wilhelmina Gran Rio Cottica Papaichton Ouanary Parque
Lucie Mountains Pikin Rio Benzdorp Saint-Léon G u i a n a (F) Saint- Ponta Posto do Costa
Amotope Mt. Juliana De Goeje- Mt. Bellevue Dégrand Georges dos Indio Uaçá Cabo Caçiporé
Coeroeni 1280 gebergte de l'Inini 851 Saut Oiapoque Nacional
Nature Res. Apetina Maripasoula Grd.Canori São João do Caçiporé
Rosevelt Piek Área do Cabo
Paloemeu 710 Antécume Pata Indígena
Pelelu Tepu Oelemari Massif Uaçá Ponta Cambu
Kayser Geb. Awara Soela Saut Camopi Vila Orange
Kamani Oranje Mts. Macaque Camopi Vehla Cunani
New River Oronoque Majoli Litani Tabulaire Euca
Kwamalasamutu Calcoene
Tumu Cach. Lourenço Bela Nazaré
Great Falls Humac - Mountains Mananá Vista Ponta da Pescada
ruwini Sipaliwini Parque Amapá Maracá Ilha de Maracá
Johi Marapi Cach. Sucuriju Cabo do Norte
do Tatu Tartarugalzinho
Área São
Indígena Felício Amapá
Parque A.I. Ilha
Indígena Waiãpi Novo Apoema
ama Área Uruguinha São
Uruguiana Miguel Ponta do Guará
Ilha do Bailique
Serra do Navio Estuário do
Tauini Terceiro S. Luzia Ilha do Curuá
Trombetas Acampamento Porto Grande Ferreira do Paçuí Limão do Curuá
Gomes Punta de Santarém
Paru de Leste Gaivota Matapí Ilha Janaucú Rio Amazonas

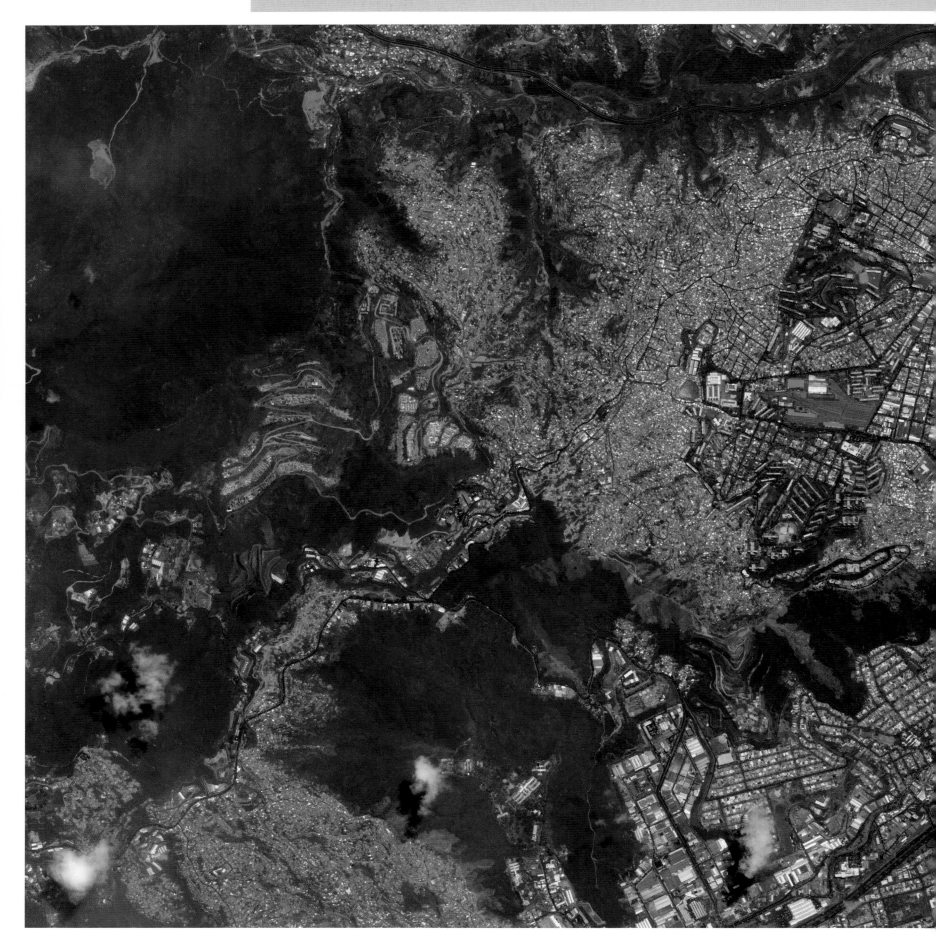

Caracas

Caracas, Venezuela's capital, is its uncontested center. Already a huge metropolis with a population of almost five million, its borders are continuously expanding. Modern high-rise buildings where multi-national companies have their smart, air-conditioned offices stand in stark contrast to the city's poorest quarters, which line arterial roads. The city's origins go back to the 16th century. In 1567, after bitter struggles, Spanish colonists snatched a settlement from the indigenous people and founded Santiago de León de los Caracas, which was subsequently destroyed several times by earthquakes. Caracas prospered, however, particularly in the 20th century, and it is still booming as the result of the discovery of oil beneath Lake Maracaibo *(see pp108–9)* in 1914.

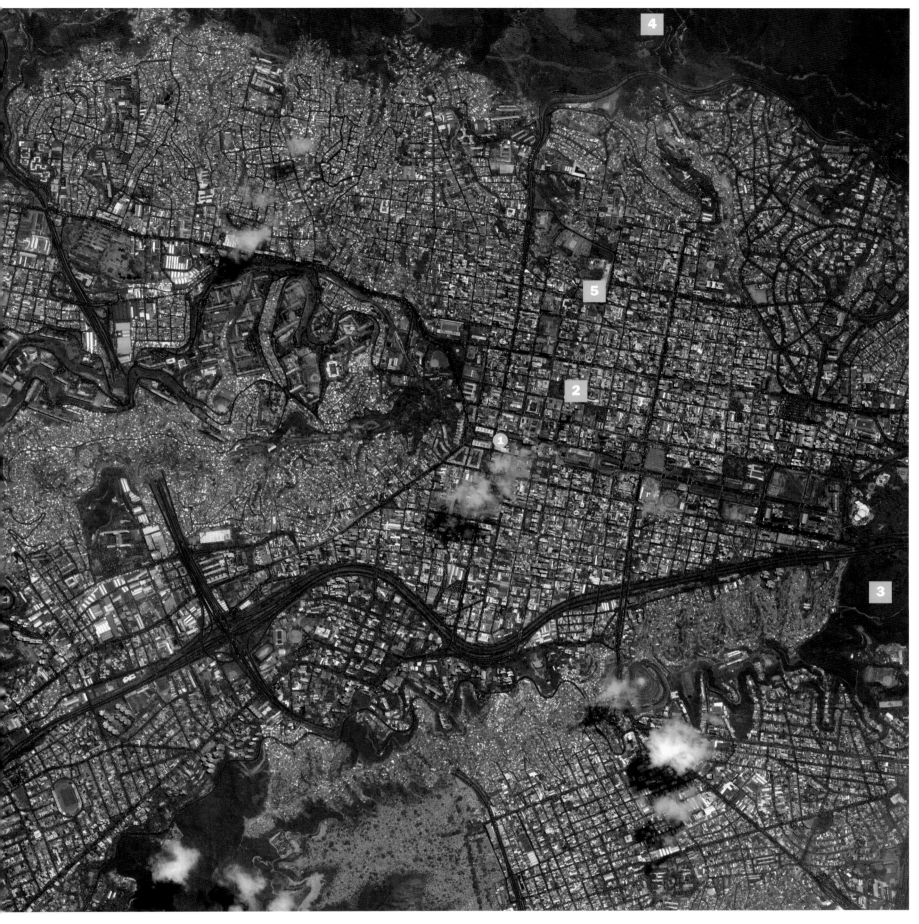

1 *Las Torres* ←

Two 32-story skyscrapers known as Las Torres ("The Towers") mark the western end of Avenida Bolívar, which was laid out in 1953. The main traffic artery through the city center, this great thoroughfare symbolizes the wealthy, cosmopolitan face of Caracas. Today, many high-rise buildings dominate the city's skyline. Caracas is not only Venezuela's commercial and administrative capital, but also its academic and cultural heart.

2 Plaza Bolívar

The historical center of Caracas spreads out around Plaza Bolívar, a large square lined with trees. Only a few colonial buildings survive here. The cathedral is located on the east side of the square, and the town hall and archbishop's palace stand on its southern side. The focal point of the square is a statue of Simon Bolívar, erected in 1874. Bolívar was born in Caracas in 1783 and the site of his supposed birthplace is one block to the south of the square. A celebrated national hero, Bolívar was a soldier and liberator who freed Venezuela, Colombia, Ecuador, and Peru from Spanish rule, although he failed in his attempt to set up a republican federation.

3 Jardín Botánico

The Botanical Gardens is a large, very well-kept park, located close to the city center. It provides an overview of the tropical plants native to Venezuela in the center of the capital.

4 Parque Nacional El Ávila

Monte Ávila rises to a height of 2159 m (7083 ft) to the north of the city. This mountain is the focal point of an extensive nature reserve. Although it was once possible to reach the summit by cable car, today this can be done only on foot, and entails a five-hour walk.

5 Panteón Nacional

In 1874, the Church of the Holy Trinity (Iglesia de la Santísima Trinidad) was converted into a national mausoleum and place of remembrance. The mortal remains of great Venezuelans rest here, including those of Simon Bolívar, who died in 1830.

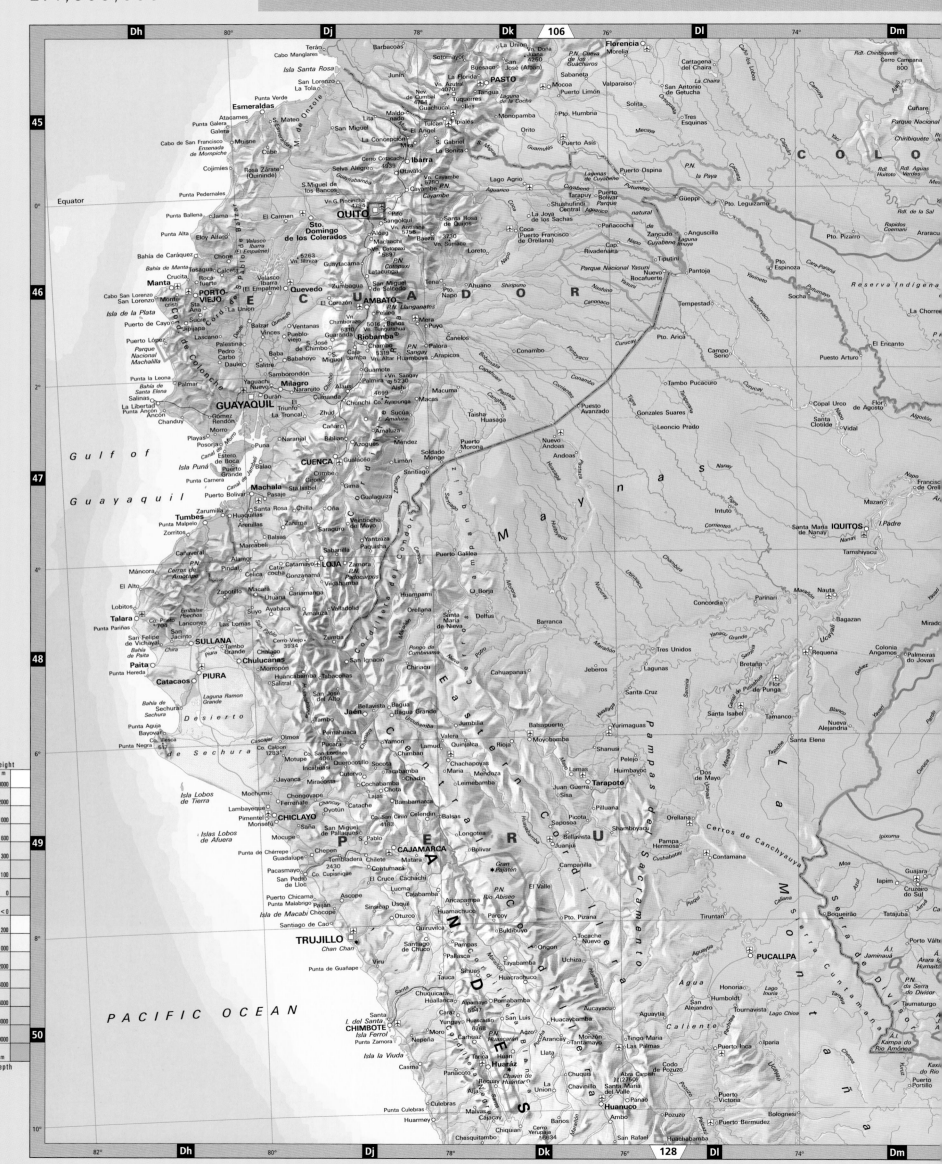

1:4,500,000

Albers Equal Area Conic Projection

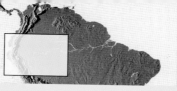

Quito

Lying at an altitude of more than 2800 m (9186 ft), Quito, capital of Ecuador, is the second-highest city in South America after La Paz, in Bolivia. It is located in the center of what the German scientist Alexander von Humboldt (1769–1859) called the Avenue of the Volcanoes, a high north–south valley located between both chains of the Andes, which here reach heights of 4000–5000 m (13,000–16,400 ft). The city is about 4 km (2.5 miles) wide, and it can expand only northward or southward: From its historic heart it has spread for more than 30 km (19 miles) up and down the valley. But with barely 1.5 million inhabitants, Quito is neither Ecuador's largest city nor its most important industrial center. This distinction goes to the port city of Guayaquil.

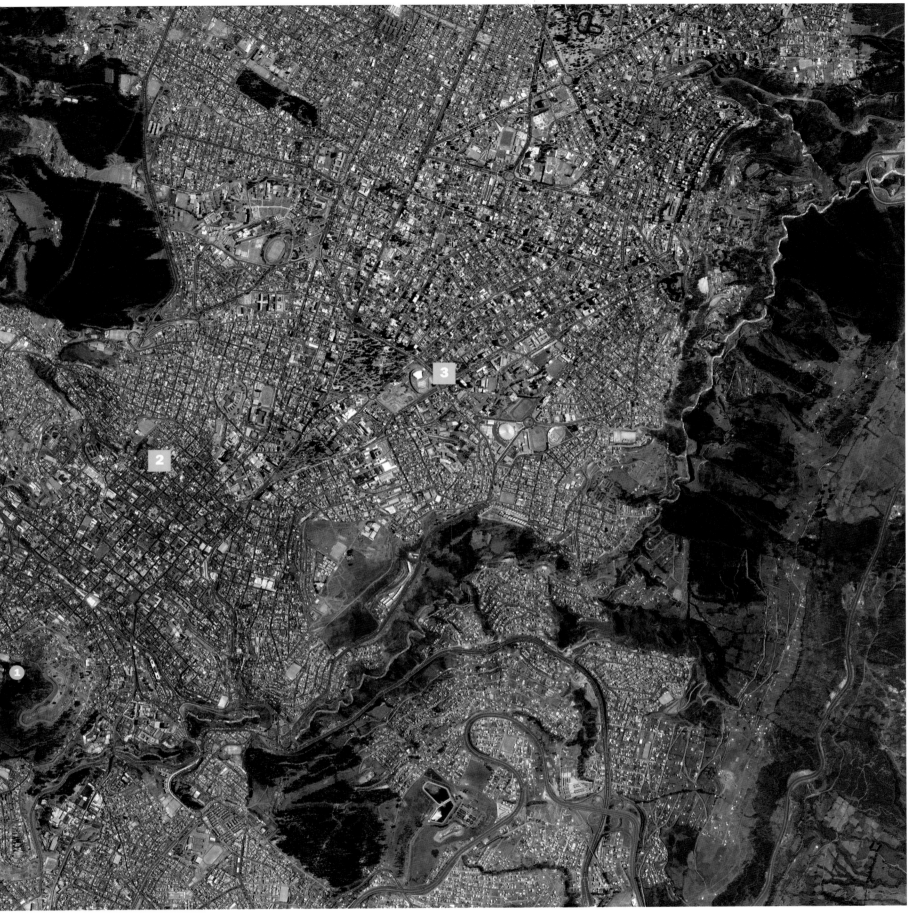

① *Panecillo* ←

The summit of Panecillo, the volcano that rises to the east of Quito's Old Town, provides the best view over the city. From the vantage point of the monumental statue of an angel that stands here, there is a splendid view to the north, far beyond both the Old Town and the new district, and across to Cayambe, a volcano that rises to 5790 m (18,996 ft) far in the distance.

② Plaza de la Independencia

This square is the central point of Quito's Old Town, which was made a UNESCO World Cultural Heritage Site in 1979. Covering an area no larger than 1 km² (less than 0.5 square mile), the Old Town has a concentration of important archi-

tectural and historical sights. The square itself is dominated by the cathedral, which was begun in 1755. The Governor's Palace is located beside the cathedral, and a little way farther on is the Iglesia de la Compañía: With its elaborate carvings and exuberant decoration, this Jesuit church is a masterpiece of Baroque architecture. Farther north is Plaza San Francisco, a square with a Franciscan church. It was completed in 1605 and its interior is covered with polychrome decoration and gilt woodcarvings.

③ Casa de la Cultura Ecuatoriana

This circular building houses Ecuador's finest museum. Divided into four sections, its collections document the artistic and cultural history of Ecuador from the earliest indigenous culture,

known as the Valdivia culture (3500–600 BC), to the present day. The Sala del Oro, with its displays of gold jewelry from pre-Columbian times, has some exquisite pieces, while the Sala de Arte Colonial contains masterpieces by the Quito School, one of the most renowned groups of painters of the New World's colonial period.

④ Guaga Pinchincha

One of Quito's best-known mountains is the Guaga Pinchincha, an active volcano that last erupted in 1999. Its two peaks rise to heights of 4790 m (15,715 ft) and 4794 m (15,728 ft). Small farmers' fields stretch from the outskirts of Quito out toward the volcano, and on upward, covering even its slopes.

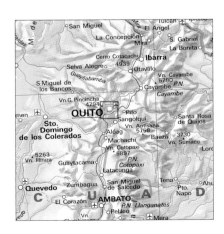

1:4,500,000

Albers Equal Area Conic Projection

A T L A N T I C   O C E A N

Mouths
of the
Amazon

Equator

Ilha de Marajó

BELÉM

Z   r   á

Z I L

M a r a n h ã o

T o c a n t i n s

The Amazon at Manaus

The confluence of two great rivers at Manaus is an impressive sight, especially when viewed from the air. At this point, the Negro, flowing southeast from Colombia, joins the Solimões, flowing eastward from Peru, to form the Amazon. Both the Negro and the Solimões are several kilometers wide at this point; their waters, which meet at different speeds and temperatures, flow alongside each other for about 8 km (5 miles) without blending. Along this stretch, the dark waters of the Negro (the Black River) are quite distinct from those of the Solimões, and two-tone whirlpools and streaks are formed. Only after about 30 km (20 miles) do the waters of the two rivers become completely blended. From the confluence at Manaus, the Amazon flows for a further 1600 km (994 miles) before it reaches the Atlantic.

1 Manaus

The settlement founded in the mid-17th century by Portuguese traders has been known as Manaus since 1856. In 1840, when the American inventor Charles Goodyear (1800–60) developed a process for vulcanizing rubber, Manaus underwent an unexpected transformation. At that time, rubber trees grew only in the Amazonian rain forest, and rubber traders in Manaus derived great wealth from this monopoly. As revenue poured in, money was quickly spent, and Manaus became a metropolis of decadent luxury in the jungle. Municipal palaces were built and, the ultimate crowning glory, a 700-seat opera house was constructed: All the building materials were shipped from Europe, and its opening was celebrated in 1896. However, Manaus's golden age was short-lived. In 1876, the Englishman Henry Wickham succeeded in smuggling rubber seeds out of Brazil and, within a few decades, huge rubber plantations had been created in southeast Asia.

Its monopoly broken, Manaus sank into poverty. However, the town's economic recovery began in the 1960s, when the Brazilian government granted tax concessions for the establishment of industrial settlements in the forest. Manaus was made a free trade zone. Today, about one million people live along the banks of the river here, and Manaus is the ninth-largest city in Brazil.

2 The Amazon ↑

The Amazon is 6400 km (3977 miles) long and, with a surface area of more than 7 million km²

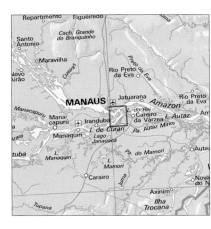

(2.7 million square miles), it drains two-fifths of the South American continent. It has about 1000 tributaries, 15 of which are themselves more than 2000 km (1240 miles) long.

Francisco de Orellana was the first European to sail the entire course of the river. At Christmas in 1541, together with 60 other Spaniards, he set off from Ecuador, sailing downstream from the confluence of the Coca and Napo rivers, with the aim of finding El Dorado, the fabled land of the Golden King of whom the indigenous people had spoken. He failed to find El Dorado, but, after eight exhausting months traveling down the river, during which they allegedly met war-like Amazons, the voyagers reached the Atlantic Ocean. Whether the river was named after the Amazons that the expedition encountered remains the subject of debate: The word "Amazon" is derived from amacunu, which in the language of a local indigenous people means either "water cloud sound" or "water bridge."

3 Negro River

About 1600 km (994 miles) long, the Negro River, which rises in southeastern Colombia as the Guainía River, is one of the longer tributaries of the Amazon. The Negro is appropriately called the Black River because it is a typical black-water river. These very clean rivers rise in rain forests, where the soil has only a very thin layer of humus. Decayed leaves, branches, and trees, and every other type of vegetable material, give the water its color, which is similar to black tea. Because of their high acidity, very little vegetable or animal life can grow in black-water rivers. This also means that there are hardly any mosquitoes found there.

4 Solimões River

By contrast, the Amazon (as it is called in Peru) or the Solimões (as it is called in Brazil, on the stretch of its course from the Peruvian border to the confluence with the Negro at Manaus), is a white-water river. A wide range of plants and animals live in these types of rivers, whose waters are murky and rich in minerals. The water's apparently milky color, which is really light brown, is created by the sediment it carries. Most of the sources and tributaries of South America's white-water rivers rise in the Andes.

Eastern Brazil

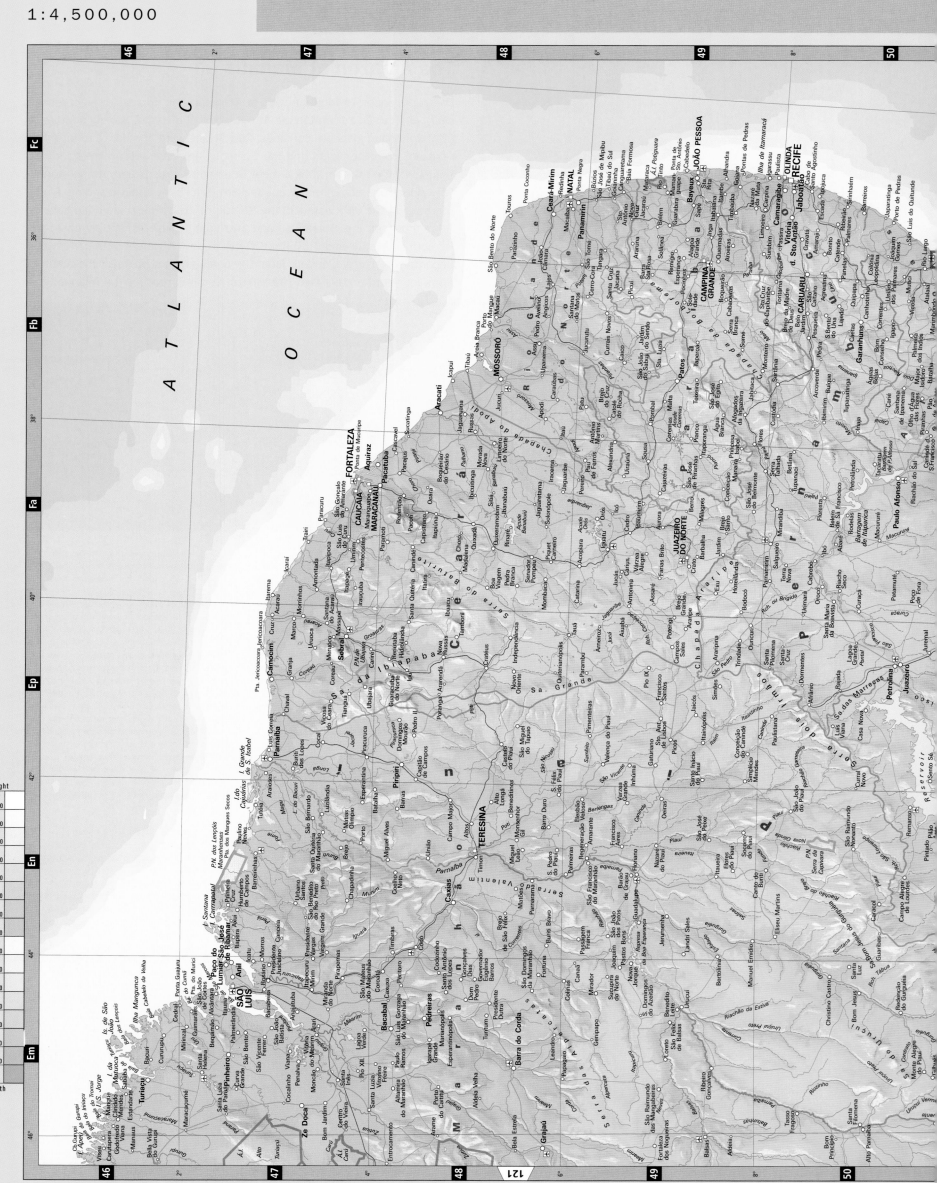

1:4,500,000

Albers Equal Area Conic Projection

A T L A N T I C

O C E A N

Abrolhos

A b r o l h o s   B a n k

SALVADOR

FEIRA DE SANTANA

ITABUNA
ILHÉUS

VITÓRIA DA CONQUISTA

Jequié

MONTES CLAROS

GOV. VALADARES

IPATINGA

Coronel Fabriciano

Teófilo Otoni

Linhares

São Mateus

Colatina

Sete Lagoas

ARACAJU
Nossa Senhora do Socorro

ALAGOINHAS

Lauro de Freitas

Camaçari

Maceió

This seaport on the Atlantic coast is the capital of the Brazilian state of Alagoas. Besides its importance as an administrative city, Maceió is also a major industrial center. One of the main industrial activities here is processing the agricultural produce, such as sugar and cotton, that is brought in from the surrounding areas where it is grown. Because of Maceió's attractive location on a beautiful stretch of coastline, as well as its proximity to Recife, the great metropolis to the northeast, the town has also recently begun to develop into an important center of tourism, and its tourist infrastructure offers visitors a full range of facilities. Maceió, with some 800,000 inhabitants, is increasingly benefiting from this industry.

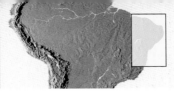

1 Coast ←

Maceió is reputed to have the most beautiful beaches in Brazil, and this is one reason why the city has become one of the most attractive and most popular holiday resorts in the country. Besides these beaches, which are lined with palm trees and have clear blue water, Maceió has a well-developed tourist infrastructure: Its newly built seafront promenade is lined with restaurants, bars, and shops, all of which attract many visitors. Average temperatures of 25 °C (77 °F) combined with sunny weather, beautiful lagoons and natural swimming pools contribute to the region's popularity as a travel destination. To the northeast of Maceió, coral reefs lie off the coastline. Where these coral reefs reach the coast,

basins known locally as piscinas naturais (natural swimming pools) are formed.

2 Port

Maceió's setting, in a long bay opening onto the Atlantic Ocean, provided favorable conditions for the location of a port. Although it is neither one of the largest nor one of the busiest ports on Brazil's Atlantic coast, Maceió is important as a transit point for the export and import of cargo and as a terminus for passenger services. Maceió also has an international airport.

3 City Center

Because it has relatively few attractive architectural features, the city center attracts few

visitors, who come to Maceió mainly for its beaches and vacation facilities. However, some picturesque houses from the city's colonial era still remain in the area around the cathedral, and there are shops specializing in local art and handicrafts. But the city center is still a lively place, particularly in February, when exuberant carnival celebrations, with dancing, floats, and music, take place.

4 Mundaú Lagoon

With a surface area of 23 km² (9 square miles), Mundaú Lagoon stretches out to the west of the Maceió Peninsula. The lagoon is dotted with nine islands, which are thickly covered with palm trees. The water channels that run in between the islands are popular for fishing and sailing.

Peru, Bolivia

PACIFIC

OCEAN

Nazca Ridge

Peru-Chile Trench

Height
m
3000
2000
1000
600
300
100
0
< 0
m
Depth

200
1000
2000
4000
6000
8000
10000
m

PERU

CHILE

Galapagos Islands
(EC)

Parque Nacional
de Galápagos

Equator

I.Pinta

Can. de Pinta

I.Marchena

I. Genovesa

I.San Salvador

Cerro
Cowan
905

Bahia
Banks
Darwin
1280

Wolf
1707

La
Cumbre
1494

I.Fernandina

Bahia
Elisabeth

1097

Cerro
Azul
1689

Santo Tomás
1490

Punta
Cristóbal

I.Isabela

Can. de
San Salvador

I. Baltra

I. Santa Cruz

Co.
Chacras
884

Puerto
Ayora

I. Santa Fé

Co.San
Joaquin
896

I. San
Cristóbal

Puerto
Baquerizo
Moreno

C. Norte

C. Norte

Puerto
Velasco
Ibarra

I. Santa Maria

I. Española

Can. de
Pinzon

I.Pinzon

1:4,500,000

0   25   50   75   100   125 miles

0   50   100   150   200 km

Albers Equal Area Conic Projection

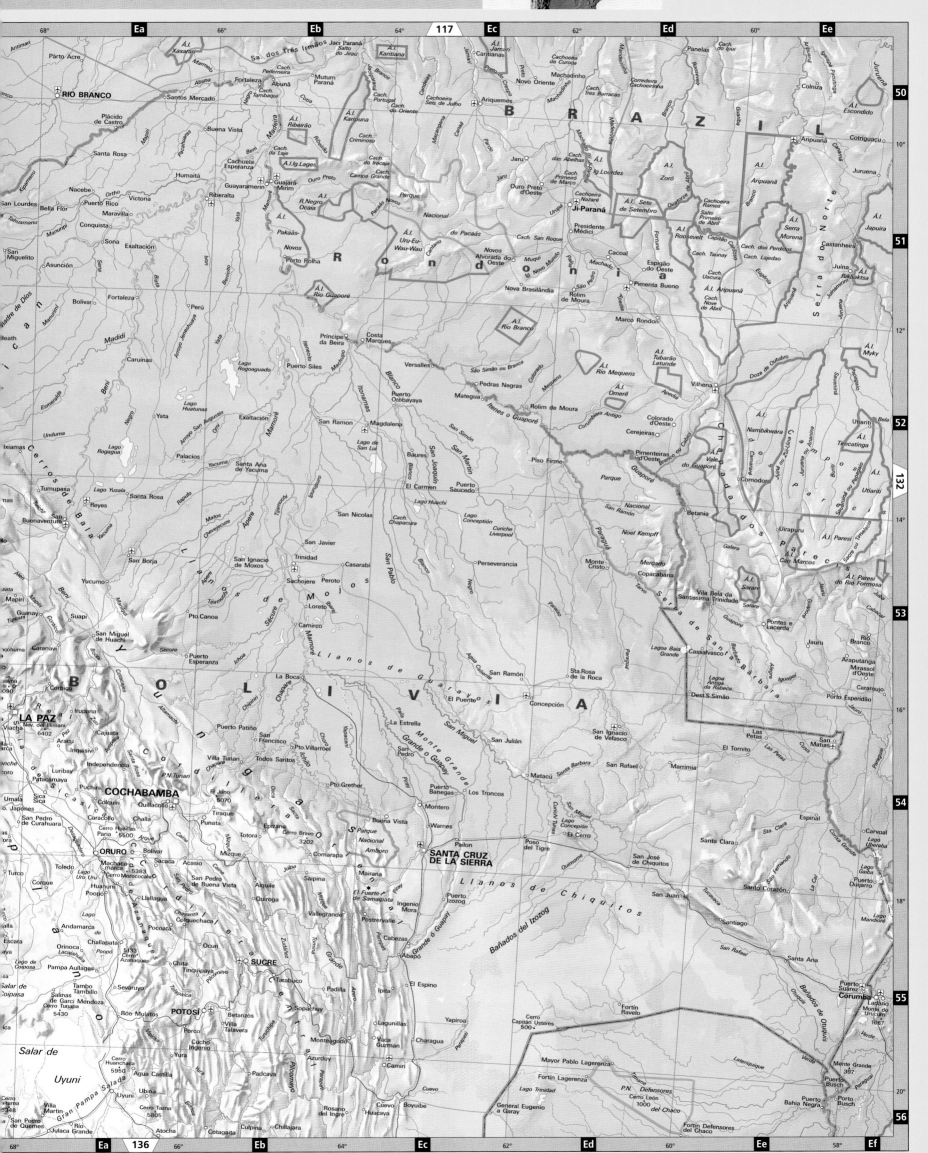

Urubamba

A river that divides a landscape into two distinct halves makes a striking sight. On the right-hand side of the river, in this satellite image, there are fertile plots of cultivated land, while on the left is a brown, apparently barren and uncultivated expanse of terrain. This is the Urubamba Valley, in the heart of Peru. This is also where the small town of Urubamba is located, about halfway between Cuzco, the former Inca town and Spanish colonial city, and Machu Picchu, the most spectacular of all the Inca ruins. Lying at an altitude of 2863 m (9393 ft), Urubamba is a quiet, picturesque town. Because of its moderate altitude, it enjoys a much more pleasant climate than that of Cuzco, the better-known city a short distance to the south. Urubamba is the main town in what is known as the Sacred Valley of the Incas, and thus has a large and very lively market square. The small cultivated plots of land that surround it extend up the mountain sides. Divided into tiny terraces, every last bit of the land is under cultivation.

1. Urubamba River

The Urubamba River rises near Urcos, about 80 km (50 miles) southeast of the section shown in the satellite image. As it flows northeast, the river has carved out a very narrow valley through the mountains. In Atalaya, about 400 km (250 miles) from its source, the Urubamba joins the Tambo: At this confluence the two rivers become the Ucayali River. After flowing for 1900 km (1181 miles), the Ucayali joins the Marañón River. This is where the Amazon (see pp 122–3) begins.

2. *Machu Picchu* ←

High above the Urubamba, about 40 km (25 miles) to the west of the section shown in the satellite image, lies Machu Picchu, the most famous and mysterious Inca ruins in South America. Set between near-vertical rock faces at an altitude of about 2300 m (7546 ft), Machu Picchu lay forgotten for centuries after the Spanish conquest of Peru. The city, by then in ruins, was accidentally rediscovered by the US explorer Hiram Bingham in

1911. In the following years it was excavated by a team of archeologists from Yale University. Machu Picchu was built in the mid-15th century. The terraced city consists of three main areas: a temple precinct, the Royal Quarter, and a residential quarter for the bulk of the population. The temple precinct contains the Intihuatana (meaning "Place Where the Sun is Tied" in Quechua): This was clearly a shrine dedicated to the sun, although its precise function is still not fully understood. The Royal Quarter contains the Princesses' Palace, and the Inca Palace, whose entrance is marked by a trapezoidal gate, covered by a heavy lintel weighing about 3 metric tons (3.3 tons). Behind the residential quarter lie terraced plots, which are thought to have been planted with maize (Indian corn).

A jagged granite peak known as Huayana Picchu rises like a giant sugar loaf behind the ruined city. It is 2720 m (8924 ft) high, and a steep hiking trail leads up the mountain to an altitude of 360 m (1181 ft) above Machu Picchu.

3. Urubamba

Before the arrival of the Spanish, Urubamba was an important settlement in the midst of agricultural land. After the Spanish conquest, it grew to become one of the most attractive colonial towns in the region. Around Plaza de Armas, the square that still marks the center of the modern town, are some beautiful colonial buildings and a massive cathedral. The fountain in the square is crowned by a sculpture of a large maize (Indian corn) cob, symbolizing the staple food on which the local population relies.

4. Road to Chinchero

On the left bank of the river lies an expanse of steep, barren land, parts of which, especially in precipitous areas and in small valleys, have been heavily eroded. The only link between the town and the left bank of the river is a small bridge, followed by a road that leads up into the bare mountains. Winding round a series of hairpin bends, this steep road connects Urubamba with

Chinchero, located at an altitude of about 3800 m (12,467 ft), almost 1000 m (3281 ft) higher than Urubamba.

Central Brazil

Height
m
3000
2000
1000
600
300
100
0
< 0
200
1000
2000
4000
6000
8000
10000
m
Depth

1:4,500,000

0   25   50   75   100   125 miles
0   50   100   150   200 km

Albers Equal Area Conic Projection

① Praça dos Três Poderes ↓

The "cockpit" area is filled by Praça dos Três Poderes (Three Powers' Square), named for the country's parliamentary, presidential, and legal systems. The Congreso Nacional (Parliament), Palácio do Planalto (president's official residence), and Supremo Tribunal Federal (Supreme Court) are located here. All three were designed by Oscar Niemeyer. The parliament building consists of two 28-story towers, which are connected from their 11th to their 13th floors. In front of these towers are two hemispherical buildings, which contain the two chambers of Brazil's bicameral parliament— the Chamber of Deputies and the Senate. While the Senate building consists of an upturned hemisphere in the shape of a cupola, the Chamber of Deputies takes the form of a downturned hemisphere in the shape of a shell: The two halves symbolically form a spherical whole. By contrast, the presidential residence, a low, flat building, is somewhat insconspicuous. The Supreme Court, in front of which stands a statue of Justice, is so light that it seems to float. Two platforms are connected by columns tapering upward. A cube with darkened windows stands between them; it is here that the offices are located.

Brasília

It was in the late 19th century that the idea of moving Brazil's capital to the center of the country was first put forward. The purpose of this radical move was to counteract the superior power of the large, prosperous urban centers—such as Recife, São Paulo, and Rio de Janeiro, the existing capital—that had developed along the coast of the Atlantic. Another reason for moving the capital inland was to promote the development of Brazil's central region. In 1956, the Brazilian government launched a competition for the design of the new city, which was to be called Brasília. The winner was Lúcio Costa, who was to be responsible for its layout. The architect Oscar Niemeyer was to design its buildings. Work began that year, and on April 21, 1960, the new city was completed.

Designed on the drawing board, Brasília's overall plan can best be appreciated from the air. The ground plan that Costa devised is based on the shape of an airplane. In the "cockpit" area are the parliament building, the supreme court, and the presidential palace; in the "fuselage"—a central north–south axis 6 km (3.7 miles) long and 250 m (820 ft) wide—are government ministries, the Senate and Chamber of Deputies, and the cathedral; and in the "wings" are the residential districts.

The Historical Museum of Brasília (the long, white building on the left in the photograph) is located on the square. It documents the city's history, which began in 1891, when Brazil received a new constitution that paved the way for transferring the capital from Rio de Janeiro into the center of the country. It was not until 1956, however, that plans for the transfer were finalized, the decision being made by President Juscelino Kubitschek de Oliveira, who made the creation of Brasília a central plank in his development program.

Work on building Brasília began in 1956. Almost immediately, thousands of poor agricultural workers from neighboring rural locations flocked to the area in search of work on its building sites.

As the first building materials were flown in, overland routes to the industrial center on the Atlantic coast were gradually created. The construction of the city cost several billion dollars: For many critics of this ambitious project, it is one reason for Brazil's existing huge foreign debt.

② Ministry of Foreign Affairs

The Ministry of Foreign Affairs is widely referred to as the Palacio do Itamarati. This is a reference to the old foreign ministry in Rio de Janeiro, which was housed in the former palace of Baron Itamarati. There are no similarities, however, between the modern building in Brasília and its predecessor in Rio de Janeiro. This is a concrete structure with huge glass facades divided by columns. Reflected in an artificial lake it seems to float weightlessly on the water. The building's interior is decorated with works by contemporary Brazilian artists.

③ Cathedral

The cathedral is one of Oscar Niemeyer's most beautiful buildings. With its circular ground plan and tapering concrete ribs, which soar upward, clustering together then flaring outward, the cathedral has a crown-like appearance: Niemeyer's intention was that the building should suggest Christ's crown of thorns. Although the cathedral looks stark from the outside, the interior has a completely different atmosphere. Here, the concrete ribs seem to soar toward heaven, an impression reinforced by natural light flooding down onto glass surfaces,

some of which are colored. Because the entrance to the cathedral and a part of its interior space are located below ground, the building seems much larger when experienced from within.

④ Television Tower

The 218 m (715 ft) high Torre de Televisão (Television Tower) offers the best view over the city. From its 75 m (246 ft) viewing platform, it is possible to make out Lúcio Costa's plan. However, the city was originally designed for a population of 800,000 and it now contains 1.6 million: As it has expanded, its original shape and edges have become increasingly indistinct. Planning flaws typical of the 1960s are visible from above. With broad avenues and long distances between its constituent parts, Brasília was built not with pedestrians in mind but as a city for private transport by car, and it is still without an overground public transport system today. The city's huge, empty squares, which were intended to be used and enjoyed by the populace, do not convey a pleasant atmosphere.

⑤ Lago do Paranoá

Like almost everything else about Brasília, the lake beside which the city lies is artificial. It was created by the construction of a dam on the Paranoá River, a tributary of the Paraná. The lake has a surface area of about 40 km² (15 square miles), and is surrounded by several development areas and recreational centers.

Height
m
3000
2000
1000
600
300
100
0
< 0
200
1000
2000
4000
6000
8000
10000
m
Depth

1:4,500,000

0   25   50   75   100   125 miles

0   50   100   150   200 km

Albers Equal Area Conic Projection

O C E A N

C H I L E

2

Northern Chile and Bolivia

With the deep blue of the Pacific Ocean, the arid coastal region of northern Chile, the high peaks of the western Andes, which rise to 6000 m (19,685 ft) and mark the border between Chile and Bolivia, the Altiplano—an extensive plateau with salt lakes—and the Central Cordillera, which runs through Bolivia, this satellite image shows landscapes that could hardly be more different from each other. However, distinct as they are, one thing unites them: Although they are all largely inhospitable environments, they are also rich in valuable natural resources. The whole region has a very broad range of minerals, from saltpeter, which is extracted from the Chilean desert and used to make gunpowder and artificial fertilizer, through to sulfur, which is mined on the Altiplano and used to make sulfuric acid and fungicides, and employed in the vulcanization of rubber. There are also large deposits of phosphate and manganese here, as well as lesser-known minerals such as molybdenum, rhenium, and lithium. The Central Cordillera was once Spain's main source of silver.

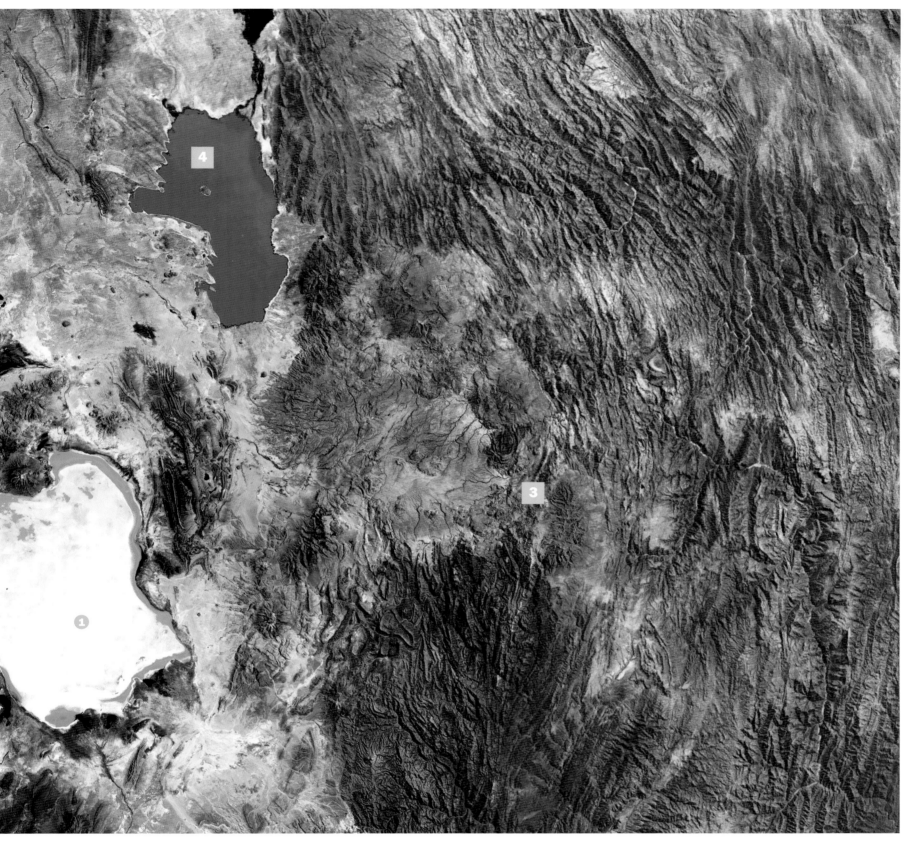

① *Uyuni Salt Lake* ←

With a surface area of about 12,000 km² (4633 square miles), the Uyuni is the largest salt lake in the Andes. It lies in the center of the Altiplano, at an altitude of more than 2600 m (8530 ft), between the Western and Central cordilleras. In the dry season, when the water level is at its lowest, the lake is covered in pure white salt crystals, which form a web-shaped pattern. Wide fluctuations in temperature, and the water that seeps out at some points, create fantastic shapes and patterns on the surface of the salt. The smaller Coipasa Salt Lake joins Uyuni Salt Lake in the north.

② Iquique

With over 150,000 inhabitants, Iquique is the largest city in northern Chile. It lies along a narrow coastal shelf between the Pacific Ocean and the foothills of the Andes, which rise up immediately east of the city. Iquique was at its apogee between the late 19th and early 20th centuries: This was when its finest buildings, such as the Teatro Municipal and the Centro Español,

were constructed. Also at this time, Iquique was a transit point from which saltpeter and, later, guano, were sent to destinations all over the world. Today, the city relies for its revenue on the large free trade zone in its port, and on fishing.

③ Potosí

In 1545 the Spanish discovered huge deposits of silver on a 4829 m (15,843 ft) mountain that they named Cerro Rico (Rich Mountain). Because of this they established the town of Potosí nearby. Lying at an altitude of 4040 m (13,255 ft), Potosí soon grew to become the most important city in the Americas. Almost three-quarters of all the world's silver once came from here. In the mid-17th century, Potosí had over 20,000 inhabitants, and today it has around 110,000. The town's royal mint and its numerous churches recall its heyday.

④ Poopó Lake

This large salt lake lies northeast of Uyuni Salt Lake, at an altitude of 3690 m (12,106 ft).

With a surface area of approximately 2800 km² (1081 square miles), this highly saline lake has a maximum depth of 3 m (10 ft) and is what is known as an end lake (a lake from which no water flows): Lake Titicaca drains into it via the Desaguadero River.

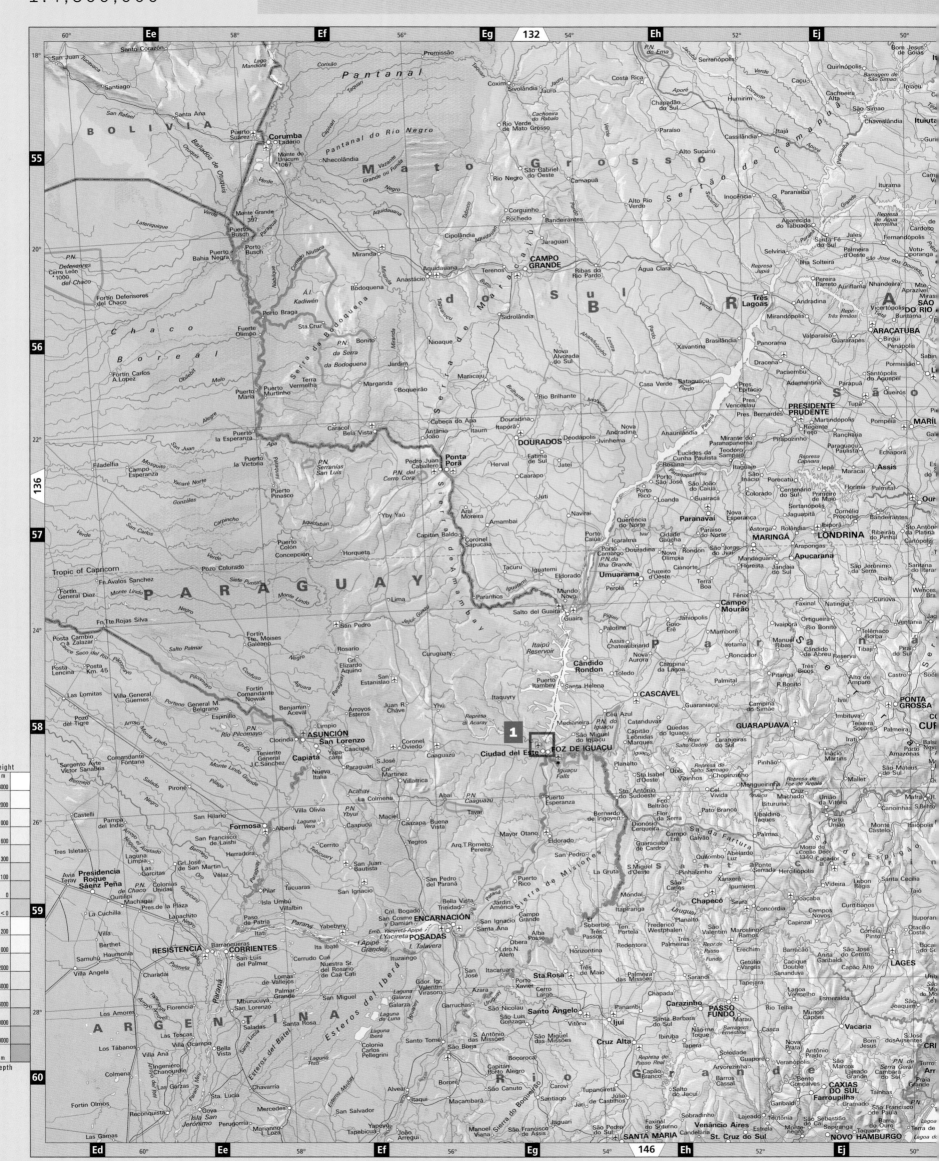

1:4,500,000

Albers Equal Area Conic Projection

| 0 | 25 | 50 | 75 | 100 | 125 miles |
| 0 | 50 | 100 | 150 | 200 km |

Itaipú

In 1973, Paraguay and Brazil embarked on an ambitious project. The waters of the Paraná River, which marks the border between the two countries, were to be harnessed for the production of electricity. The decision to build a dam and a power station came about only after long negotiations that started in the 1960s. After almost 20 years of construction work, the Itaipú hydroelectric power station opened in May 1991. It was then, and still is, the largest hydroelectric power station in the world, a great feat of engineering but also a monument to bad planning and soaring costs. While the cost of building the power station was originally estimated at $3 billion, final costs were almost $20 billion. Because Brazil itself provided most of the funds for the project, it accounts for a large part of the country's foreign debt.

① Reservoir and Dam ↓

In 1982, when the dam, which is 8 km (5 miles) long, and the main wall, which is 1.2 km (0.7 miles) long and up to 100 m (328 ft) wide, were completed, the sluices of the bypass canal were closed and the reservoir was filled. Today it has a surface area of 1350 km² (521 square miles) and an average depth of 22 m (72 ft): At the wall of the dam itself, the water is up to 170 m (558 ft) deep. This reservoir, or lake, is dotted with 66 small islands, 44 on the Brazilian side of the border and 22 on the Paraguayan side. The dam's operators

However, the lake does have its critics. Scientists have observed that it is the perfect breeding ground for malaria-carrying mosquitoes. Another disadvantage, where tourism is concerned, is that the Sete Quedas Falls—a waterfall on the Paraná that was even more spectacular than the Iguaçú Falls, on the border between Brazil and Argentina—was flooded when the lake was created.

② Paraná River

Almost 4000 km (2485 miles) long and draining an area of about 2.5 million km²

huge waterfalls, join together to form a single wall of water when the river is at its fullest. These are the famous Iguacú Falls, which are about 2700 m (8858 ft) wide, and which cascade in two levels to depths of up to 72 m (236 ft). At this point, a high basalt plateau, over which the Iguaçú flows into southern Brazil, ends abruptly in a precipice. Depending on the season and on the amount of rainfall or degree of drought, the water flows at a rate ranging from 300 m³ (10,594 cubic feet) to 6500 m³ (229,545 cubic feet) per second, the average being 1500 m³ (52,972 cubic feet) per second.

his beloved Naipur in a canoe along the Iguaçú, from the snake god M'Boi, who also loved Naipur. Incensed, the snake god beat the river bed with his strong tail. The earth opened up and a ravine was created, so that the water crashed down and pulled the canoe down, with both lovers in it. Naipur was turned into a stone at the foot of the waterfalls, while Caroba was transformed into a very tall tree. For Don Alvar Núñez Cabeza de Vaca, however, who came upon the falls in 1541—the first European to set eyes on them—they were less of a marvel of nature than a troublesome obstacle, because from this point onward the river was no longer navigable for him and his canoe.

③ Hydroelectric Station ↑

With an output of 14,000 megawatts, Itaipú is the largest hydroelectric station in the world. Its 20 turbines, each of which produces 700 megawatts, are the largest ever built, and the station generates more than eight times as much energy as the Aswan Dam in Egypt. For example, the energy it produced in 1997 (89.2 billion kilowatts per hour) was sufficient to supply Brazil's electricity needs for three months. The hydroelectric station now supplies a quarter of all the energy produced in Brazil's southern, southwestern, and central western areas. While Brazil is the largest consumer of energy generated at Itaipú, Paraguay takes 4 percent of the station's output. The electricity travels over a distance of more than 1000 km (620 miles) to supply Brazil's centers of industry along the Atlantic coast.

④ Iguaçú Falls ↓

The Iguaçú Falls, which have been declared a UNESCO World Natural Heritage Site, are located on the border between Brazil and Argentina. The larger part of the falls lies in Argentinian territory. Although the best view of the entire falls is from the Brazilian side, the individual waterfalls that make up this great natural spectacle can also be enjoyed from the Argentinian side. The Garganta del Diablo (the Devil's Gorge), the largest of all the waterfalls, can be reached on foot via footbridges: It is a raging cauldron, enclosed on three sides.

claim that its construction caused no ecological damage. In fact, two nature reserves and five environmentally sensitive biosphere areas were created on the shores of the lake, and a huge area of land was replanted with trees. The lake's existence also helps the economies of Brazil and Paraguay: With its beautiful artificial beaches, parks, and marinas, it attracts tourists and thus provides the local population with a means of living other than agriculture, which is relatively unprofitable.

(965,255 square miles), the Paraná is the seventh-largest river in the world. It begins at the confluence of the Paranaíba and Rio Grande, along the borders of the Brazilian states of Minas Gerais, São Paulo, and Mato Grosso. From there it flows in a southwesterly direction across the triangle formed by Brazil, Paraguay, and Argentina, marking the border between Paraguay and Argentina farther on, and flowing into the River Plate through a large delta. It is Argentina's major navigable river. In its upper reaches it has been dammed so as to harness its waters for hydroelectricity.

One of the Paraná's major tributaries is the Iguaçú (as it is known in Brazil), or Iguazú (its name in Argentina). In Guaraní, the word means "big water." It joins the Paraná only a few kilometers above the Itaipú hydroelectric power station. About 1300 km (808 miles) long, the Iguaçú is not only the Paraná's longest tributary, but also the tributary that covers the largest area. The Iguaçú begins at the confluence of the Iraí and Atuba rivers, in the Curitiba area.

A few kilometers downstream from this confluence, and just a few kilometers south of the area shown in the satellite image, the Iguaçú creates one of South America's greatest natural wonders. More than 250 separate cascades, including 19

The Guaraní people who inhabit this region have a legend that explains how the waterfalls were created. The Guaraní warrior Caroba was fleeing with

N

Rio de Janeiro

On New Year's Day, 1502, the Portuguese navigator André Gonçalves entered a wide bay, now known as Guanabara Bay. Struck by the beauty of the scenery, Gonçalves believed that he had sailed into a river estuary rather than a bay: He named it Rio de Janeiro, meaning January River. Even after it had been found that the putative river was in fact a bay, the name stuck, and on March 1, 1564, a settlement—Cidade de São Sebastão do Rio de Janeiro—was founded. It became the capital of Brazil, and is known throughout the world as Rio. As early as the 18th century the city was booming thanks to deposits of gold that had been discovered in the state of Minais Gerais. Since then Rio has continued to grow, with a steady development of new residential areas. Today the city's population stands at about 12 million, 10 percent of its inhabitants living in *favelas*, or slums.

① *Sugar Loaf Mountain* ↑

A granite mountain 396 m (1299 ft) high guards the entrance to Guanabara Bay. Its name came about because of a misunderstanding on the part of the early Portuguese explorers. Hearing the region's indigenous inhabitants speak of paundaçuqúa, a word they actually used to describe the rugged coastline here, the Portuguese interpreted it as pão de açúcar, meaning "sugar loaf," and took it to refer to the mountain. By coincidence, the mountain bears a striking resemblance to a sugar loaf. Visitors can reach the summit by cable car, and from here get the best panoramic view over Rio and Guanabara Bay.

② Copacabana Beach

The most famous beach in Brazil, Copacabana Beach stretches out along 4 km (2.5 miles) of the Atlantic coast. This beach, with its fine sand and ideal swimming conditions, is located south of the former town and present suburb of Copacabana. Lined with tall apartment blocks, Copacabana Beach is one of Rio's trademarks. It is synonymous with a hedonistic beach culture, a place where music is made and football played, and a parade ground where ogling and flirting take place openly.

③ Corcovado

The highest mountain in metropolitan Rio, Corcovado rises to a height of 709 m (2326 ft) southwest of the city. The mountain is crowned by a statue of Christ, his arms outstretched protectively over the city and the bay. Consisting of concrete and granite, the statue stands 38 m (125 ft) high. One

of Rio's most famous sights, it welcomes visitors to the city, and is floodlit at night. From the foot of the statue, there is a wide panorama of the fashionable areas of Copacabana, Ipanema, and Leblon. Corcovado, meaning "hunchback," forms part of Tijuca National Park. This nature reserve extends far into the municipal area and provides a protected environment for a wealth of tropical plants.

④ City Center

The center of Rio is not located directly on the Atlantic but in sheltered Guanabara Bay, to the north of Corcovado and Sugar Loaf Mountain. As well as banks, businesses, and elegant boutiques, central Rio contains the city's most important sights. These include the church of São Francisco da Penitência, the Teatro Municipal, which was built in 1909, and a modern cathedral, which was begun in 1964 and completed in 1976. In the shape of a hemisphere 80 m (262 ft) high, the cathedral is an impressive sight: Its modernistic design is so striking that it almost seems like an alien entity in the old city.

The Rua Marquês de Sapocaí is also located in the city center. The architect Oscar Niemeyer, who designed many of the buildings in Brasília (see pp 134–5), constructed a 600 m (1969 ft) roof over the street, transforming it into what is now the Sambódromo Stadium. With a capacity for some 60,000 people, the Sambódromo is a focal point of the city during the Rio Carnival. The venue for the famous parades put on by Rio's samba schools, its arena is filled with colorfully attired male and female dancers, who perform their lively dances with great agility, despite wearing very heavy costumes.

⑤ Niterói

Opposite Rio, on the other side of the bay, lies the town of Niterói. It was founded in 1573 and, although its colonial atmosphere has almost disappeared, it boasts a gem of modern architecture. This is the Museu de Arte Contemporânea, designed by Oscar Niemeyer. With a filigree-like construction, the building takes the form of an apparently floating disk rising from a cylindrical base. Today Niterói has become almost completely joined to Rio, particularly since 1974, when the Costa e Silva Bridge was completed. About 13.5 km (8.4 miles) long and 60 m (197 ft) high, the bridge allows access for ocean-going ships.

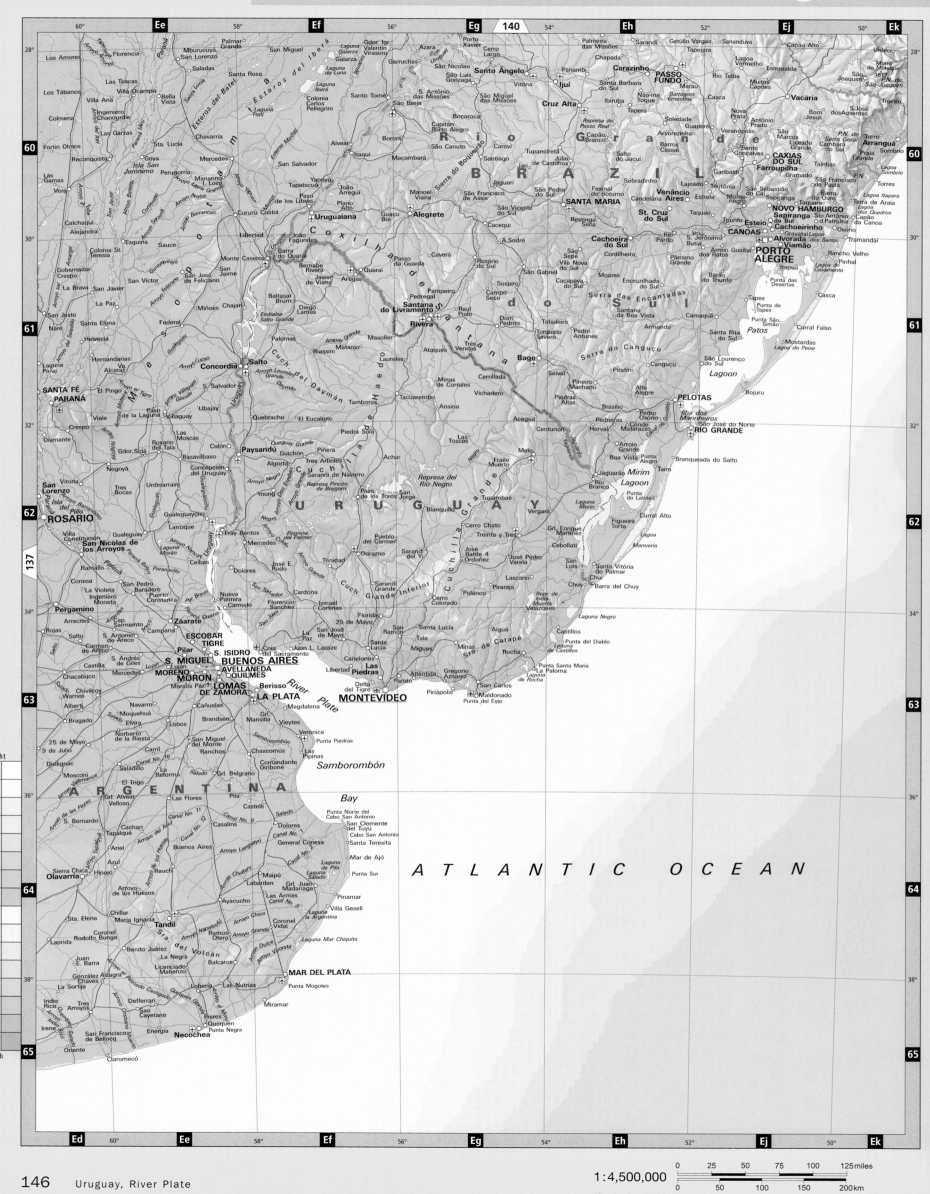

1:4,500,000

| | 0 | 25 | 50 | 75 | 100 | 125 miles |

Albers Equal Area Conic Projection

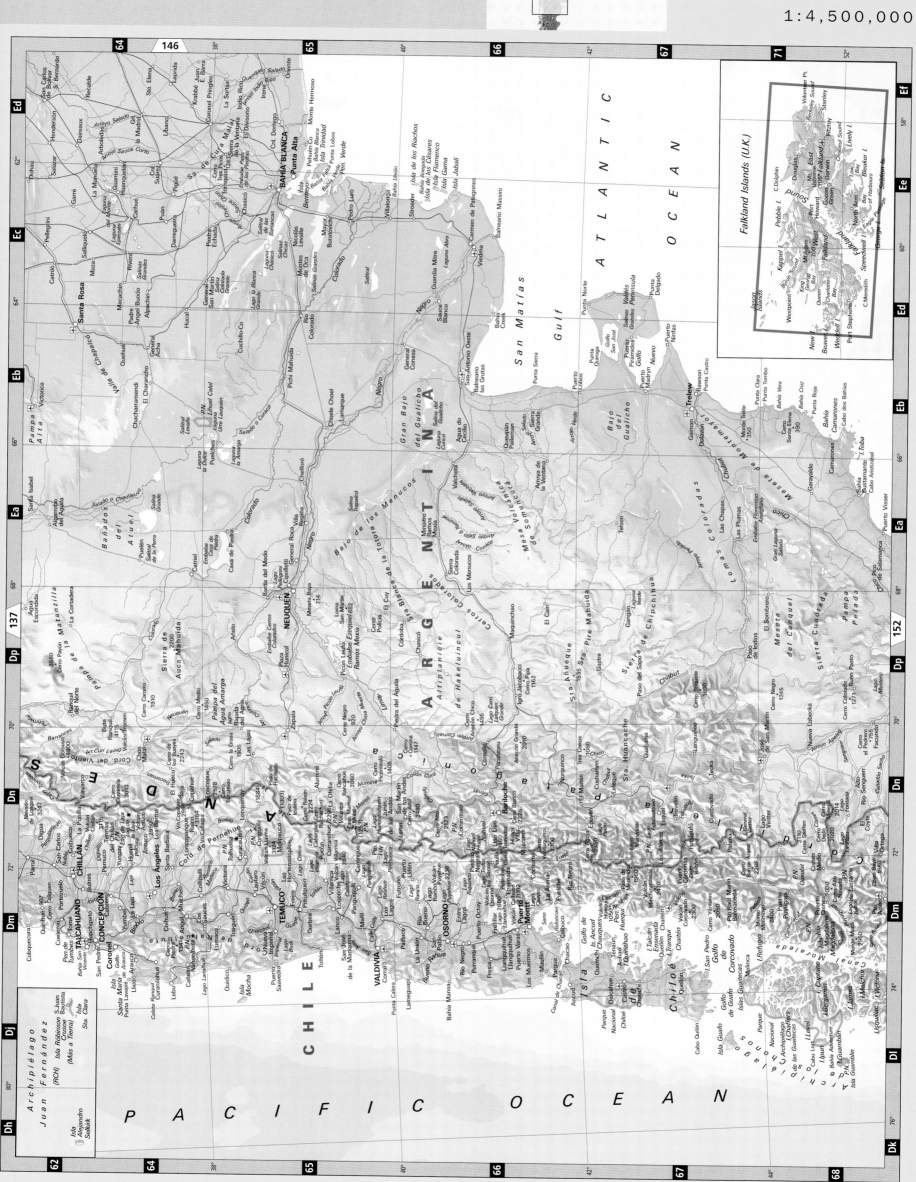

Falkland Islands (U.K.)

PACIFIC OCEAN

ATLANTIC OCEAN

ARGENTINA

CHILE

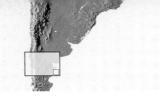

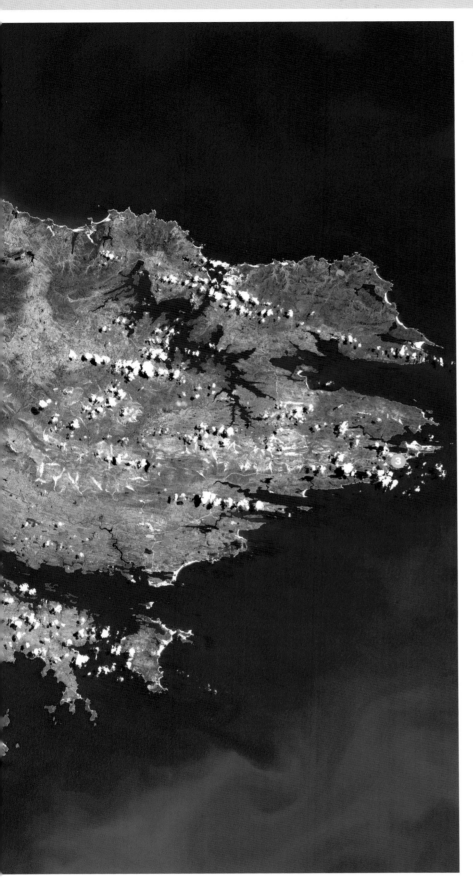

Falkland Islands

The Falkland Islands, known as the Islas Malvinas in Spanish, are located in the South Atlantic, about 500 km (300 miles) off the east coast of Patagonia. They consist of two main, hilly islands separated by Falkland Sound, as well as countless smaller islands. The whole archipelago covers an area of 12,173 km² (4700 square miles), and its highest mountain, Mount Usborne on East Falkland, peaks at 705 m (2313 ft).

Since their discovery by European navigators in about 1600, controversy has surrounded ownership of the islands. Initially the object of dispute between France, England, and Spain, the question of their sovereignty escalated when Argentina gained independence in 1816: From that time, the dispute was between Argentina and Britain. The British Empire defeated Argentina in a battle in 1833 and for almost 100 years Argentina then attemped to stake its claim to the islands by diplomatic means. However, in 1982 Argentina's military government tried to secure the islands by force. This led to the Falklands War, a brief conflict in which Britain defeated Argentina and which briefly drew international attention to these remote and tiny islands. The Falkland Islands thus remain a UK Overseas Territory, ruled by a governor appointed by the British government in London.

1 Port Stephens ←

Despite its name, Port Stephens, on the southwestern side of West Falkland, is in fact little more than a small settlement. Nestling in a bay sheltered from the stormy South Atlantic, it is set in some of the most beautiful scenery in the whole archipelago.

With little more than 2900 inhabitants, the Falkland Islands are very sparsely populated. But they are an important breeding ground for many species of seabird. Colonies of penguins and King cormorants (Phalacrocorax atriceps) come to nest here. Cormorants are always found in large colonies, often of several thousand pairs. They build mound-shaped nests out of dry seaweed, and although a colony's nests are clustered together, they are far enough apart to prevent the birds from pecking each other. Cormorants defend their nests against birds of the same species by lashing out with their beaks, but they readily join forces to defend their colony against preda-

tors such as seagulls or foxes. King cormorants are also found along the coastline of Patagonia and Tierra del Fuego, and around Cape Horn. They feed on fish, which they catch by diving deep down into the ocean, swallowing their catch whole when they return to the surface.

2 Weddell Island

The third-largest island in the archipelago, Weddell Island is covered by a single, large sheep farm. The island's highest mountain is the 410 m (1345 ft) high Mount Weddell. However, the island is also the habitat of many species of indigenous animals, such as Magellanic penguins, herons, and southern giant petrels. Like all species of penguin, Magellanic penguins live in large colonies, where they build their nests. Mature Magellanic penguins stand up to 76 cm (2 ft 6 in) high and are distinguished from other species of penguin by a white stripe above their eyes, which arches downward to their neck. Besides the Falkland Is-

lands, Magellanic penguins can be found along the whole of Patagonia's Atlantic coast and along the Pacific coast as far as southern Chile.

3 Port Stanley ↑

Capital of the Falkland Islands, Port Stanley is the only sizeable settlement on the archipelago. With a population of fewer than 2000, it is, however, little more than a small village with half a dozen streets running parallel to the coast and many streets set at angles to them. Port Stanley's most striking feature is Christ Church Cathedral, built in 1892, with its metal roof. There is also a monument to those who fell in the Falklands War and a museum documenting the islands' history. Port Stanley was founded in 1844, on the eastern side of East Falkland. With deep inlets, the coastline here is well-sheltered, providing favorable conditions for the establishment of a harbor. Port Stanley was used as a port of call for ships on their journey round Cape Horn, and it is still a loading station for the wool produced on the islands' sheep farms. Today, the town and the port also derive revenue from the fishing fleets that come to fish in the deep waters around the islands and which dock in the harbor.

4 Keppel Island

In 1853, the South American Missionary Society established a mission station on Keppel

Island so as to convert the Yaghan, an indigenous people whom the missionaries had brought from Tierra del Fuego. There, the Yaghan had lived as hunters and gatherers, but the missionaries began to teach them how to grow crops, particularly potatoes. The project was controversial because the British government doubted that the Yaghan had come to the Falkland Islands voluntarily. However, it continued until 1898, when the mission station was closed. Today Keppel Island is inhabited by only a small number of sheep farmers, although the mission's buildings still stand. The former chapel now serves as a warehouse for cotton.

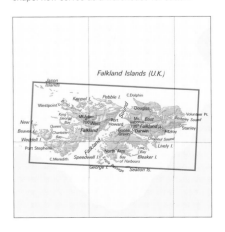

Falkland Islands (U.K.)

San Rafael Lagoon

Patagonia, known as Chile's Great South, is a wild, arid tableland that constitutes the southernmost tip of the South American continent. This is a region
of glaciers and islands, fjords that cut deep inland, dense forests and snow-
capped mountain peaks, stormy winds and icy climates, and of adventures for
intrepid explorers. Only a few small, sparse settlements dot the landscape.
They are located either along the Carretera Austral, Chile's Southern Highway,
or take the form of tiny fishing villages, which nestle beside lonely fjords and
are intermittently plied by ships bringing essential supplies. Covering 109,000
km² (42,085 square miles), Patagonia has a population of about 90,000.
More than half its inhabitants live in Coihaique, the only town.

1 *San Rafael Lagoon* ↓

*San Rafael Lagoon, behind which lies the great
San Rafael Glacier, is the only accessible part of
the San Rafael Lagoon National Park. But, because the lagoon can be reached only by plane
and then by boat, even the trip itself is an adventure. From the air, there are views of a lonely
wilderness, apparently endless narrow fjords, high,
precipitous cliffs and primeval forests, and mountains permanently capped with snow and ice. The
final stage of the journey is by boat along the Tem-
pano River. This narrow, natural canal connects the
San Rafael Lagoon with the Estero Elefantes, a
fjord about 120 km (75 miles) long that begins
south of Puerto Aisén. Here, blue, shimmering ice-*

ty, the glacier slowly moves down the valley at a
speed of no more than 1–2 cm (0.4–0.8 in) an
hour. At the point where the glacier meets a lake
or sea, the glacier calves, or fragments into
huge pieces that drift in the water. On the San
Rafael Lagoon, braver passengers can leave the
boat and board rubber dinghies. Watched by sea
lions, black-necked swans, and, occasionally,
dolphins, visitors can get to within a few hundred meters of the San Rafael Glacier, which rises up like a forbidding wall of ice. Welcome
glasses of whiskey, offered by the shipping companies, with ice freshly broken from the glacier,
help keep out the cold wind that blows across
the icefield.

*bergs drift along in the water and, as the walls of
the canal grow ever narrower, the icebergs become
increasingly larger until the huge lagoon finally
comes into view. It covers 170 km² (66 square
miles) and beyond it is the San Rafael Glacier, a
bluish-white wall of ice 3 km (2 miles) wide and 60
m (197 ft) high.*

2 San Rafael Glacier

Of all the glaciers in the world, the northernmost ridge of the Patagonian Ice Sheet is the
closest to the equator, and it calves into the sea.
Glaciers are rivers of ice formed by an accumulation of snow, which when subjected to a continu-
ous process of thawing and freezing become
compacted and form rivers of ice, or glaciers, that
generally form in valleys. Under the force of gravi-

3 San Quintin Glacier

The tip of the San Quintin Glacier lies to
the south of the San Rafael Glacier. However,
because it does not reach into the lagoon, it
has not developed such a spectacular tongue
as the San Rafael Glacier. Signs that the glacier
is retreating are clearly visible. Its former extent
is marked by a series of dark green terminal
moraines, or rocky debris deposited by the glacier,
and by gray areas covered in boulders brought
down by the glacier.

4 Patagonian Ice Sheet

Excluding those at the North and South
poles, the largest body of ice in the world is found
in Patagonia. It extends along the border between
Argentina and Chile, and the Southern Patagonian
Ice Field alone covers about 22,000 km² (8494
square miles).

The satellite image shows the Northern Patagonian Ice Field and the San Valentín Ice Field. These
cover an area of about 3000 km² (1158 square
miles) but are cut off from the Southern Patagonian
Ice Field by several fjords, which reach deep inland.
Both the Northern Patagonian Ice Field and the San
Valentín Ice Field form the core of the gigantic San
Rafael Lagoon National Park: Lying west of Lake
General Carrera and the Carretera Austral, the park
stretches as far as the Pacific Ocean and covers an
area of more than 17,000 km² (6564 square
miles). Within the park, and a little to the south of
the area shown in the satellite image, is Mount San
Valentín, which at 4058 m (13,314 ft) is the highest mountain in the southern Andes.

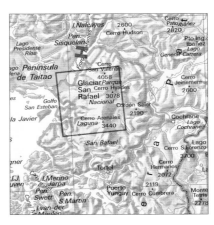

1:4,500,000

Albers Equal Area Conic Projection

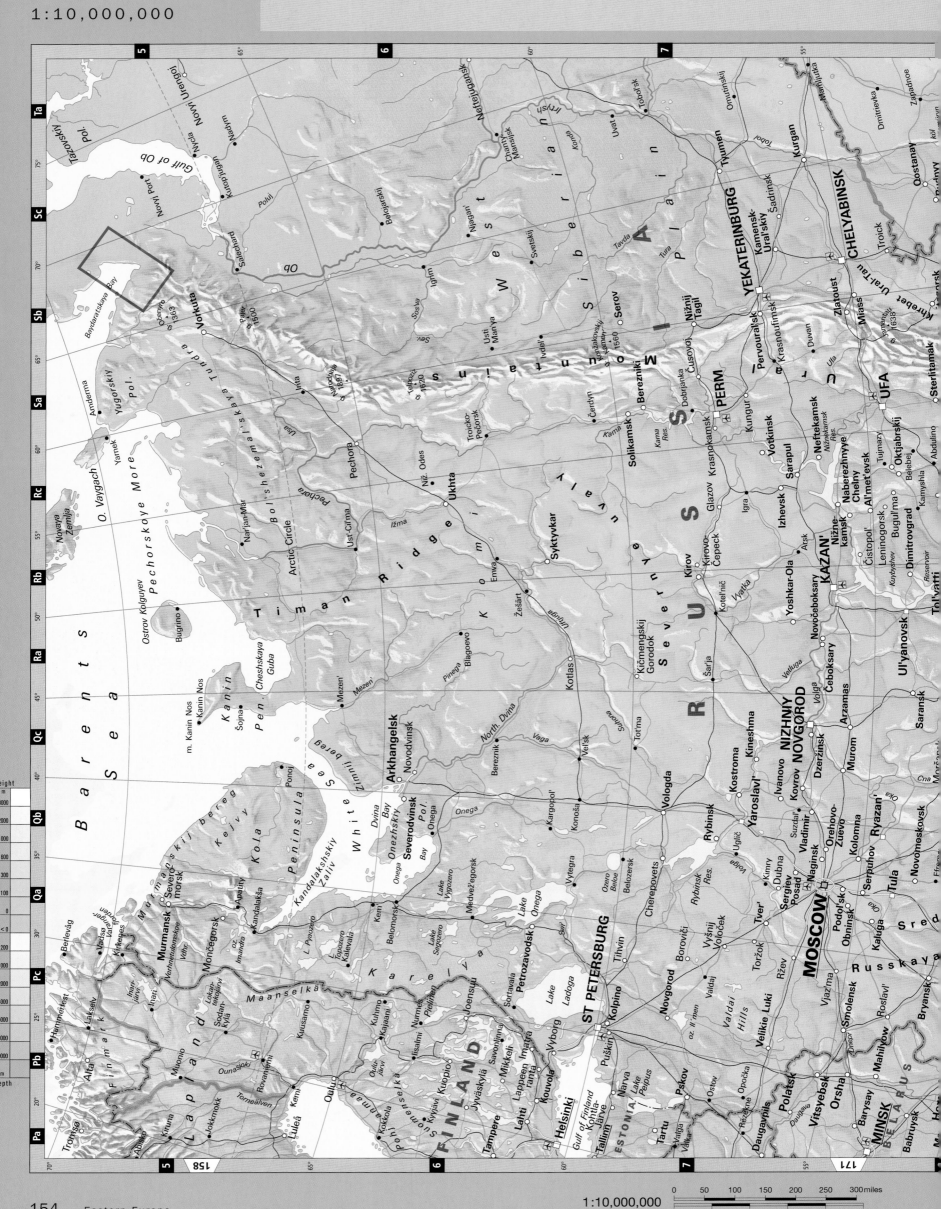

1:10,000,000

Stereographic Projection

| 0 | 50 | 100 | 150 | 200 | 250 | 300 miles |
| 0 | 100 | 200 | 300 | 400 | 500 km |

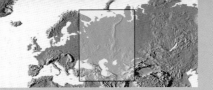

KAZAKHSTAN

UZBEKISTAN

TURKMENISTAN

Aral Sea

Caspian Sea

Black Sea

Sea of Azov

UKRAINE

KIEV

ODESSA

KHARKIV

DNIPRO-PETROVS'K

DONETS'K

ROSTOV-NA-DONU

VOLGOGRAD

Saratov

Orenburg

Astrakhan'

BAKU

AZERBAIJAN

GEORGIA

T'BILISI

ARMENIA

YEREVAN

CAUCASUS

TEHRAN

IRAN

MASHHAD

TABRIZ

TURKEY

ANKARA

Pontic Mountains

Taurus Mountains

Southeastern Taurus

IRAQ

BAGHDAD

Mosul

SYRIA

DAMASCUS

ALEPPO

LEBANON

BEIRUT

ISRAEL

Jerusalem

AMMAN

Nicosia

Elbruz

Koppe Dağ

Baydaratskaya Bay

Baydaratskaya Bay, situated in northwest Siberia, may be enormous, but it comprises only one small part of the vast Russian tundra. Yet it is interesting nonetheless—numerous powerful rivers flow from here into Lake Kara, an Arctic sea shelf. The northern end of the 2500 km (1553 mile) long Ural mountain range lies just south of the region shown, and the 10°C (50°F) July isotherm, acknowledged as the border of the Arctic Circle, runs through the area. During the summer, this region is an endless landscape of swamps and moors, and access is difficult: During the winter, it is an inhospitable desert of ice. The Nenets (Samoyeds)—a Finno-Ugric nomadic people numbering around 20,000—use the area of the Yamal Peninsula as summer grazing for their reindeer herds.

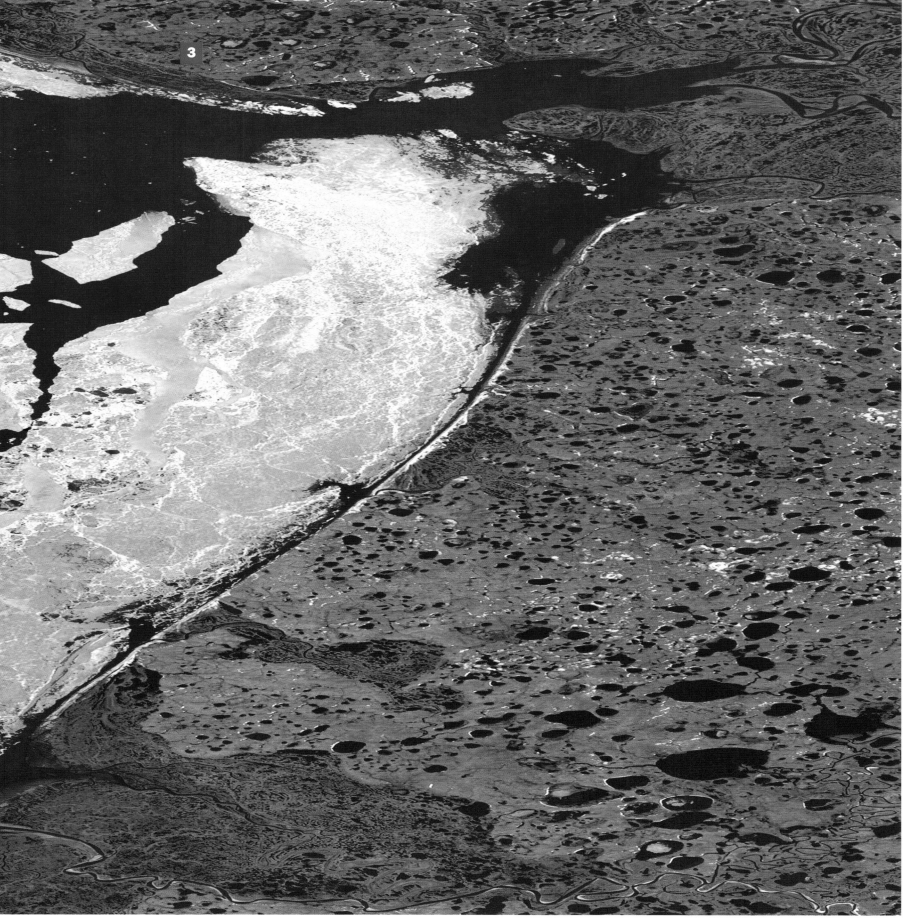

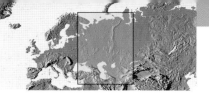

① Sea Ice Drift ←

If seawater cools to below -1.8°C (28.8°F), sea ice forms, which is then driven by wind and current systems. The continental sea shelf ice in Lake Kara, caught up by the transpolar drift, clogs many important routes—including those to southern Greenland and Labrador—making them impassable. This pack ice, however, melts away in the spring.

② Lake Kara

The flat sea shelf of the European North Sea stretches between the Russian mainland and the elongated and crooked island of Novaya Zemlya in the west, and the Severnaya Zemlya island group in the east. Across the narrow waterway of Karskiye Vorota, to the south of Novaya

Zemlya, lies Lake Kara, which is famous for its large proportion of ice in contrast to other Arctic ice shelves.

③ Yamal Peninsula

At the top edge of the image is the southwest coast of the 80 km (50 mile) long Yamal Peninsula, which is purported to contain the largest natural gas reservoir on earth. The nomadic inhabitants, the Nenets (Samoyeds), spend the winter in dwellings shielded by the *taiga* (forest), this side of the Gulf of Ob'. In the spring they often travel over 1000 km (600 miles) to the other side of the Yamal with their 1000-strong reindeer herds—some of the largest herds in the world. Many of them, however, choose to make

these treks by the most direct route, over the 50 km (31 mile) wide, icy Ob' Basin, in order to reach the pasturelands of the Yamal before the snow begins to melt.

④ Permafrost Terrain

Permafrost conditions are present over almost a fifth of the earth's surface and are found over large areas of Siberia, where the ground is often frozen to a depth of up to 0.5 m (1.6 ft) all year round. During the short summers only the uppermost layer of the earth thaws out. When the thaw begins in the late spring the water collects in countless small ponds and puddles, but it cannot be absorbed due to the underlying ice, and runs off into the sea.

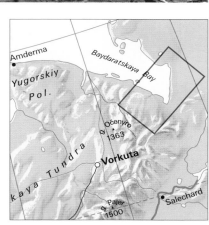

1:4,500,000

0   25   50   75   100   125 miles

0   50   100   150   200km

Albers Equal Area Conic Projection

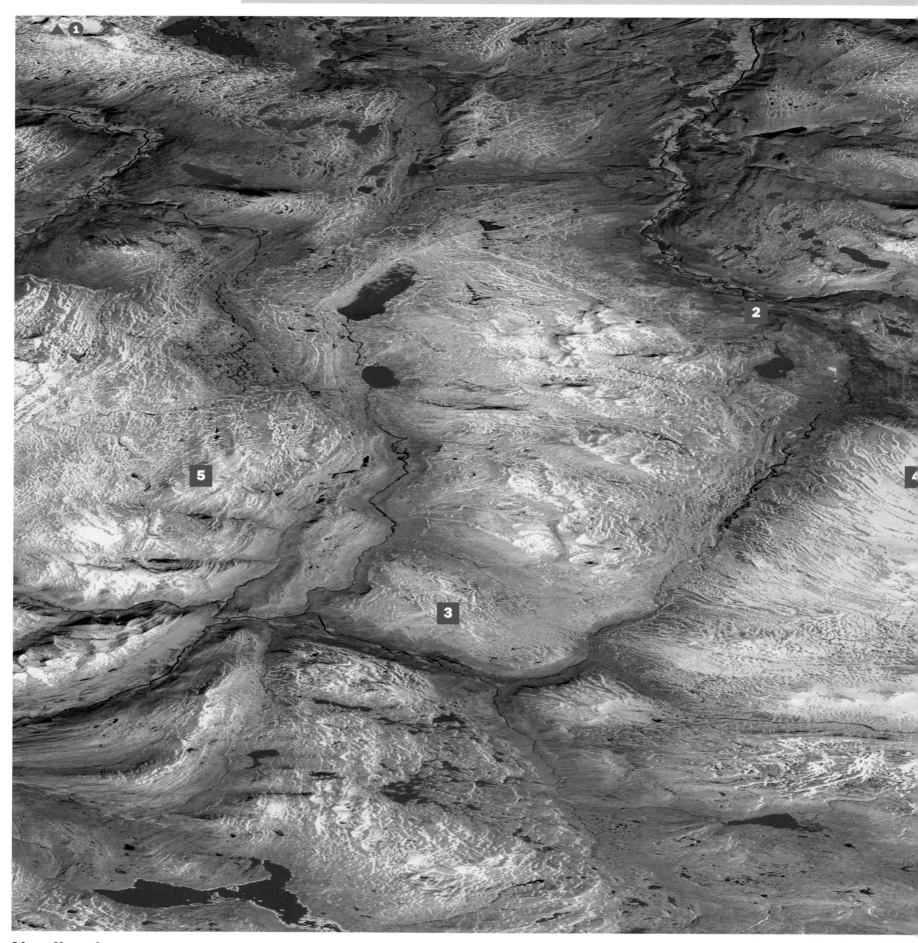

Nordland

Short plants such as lichen, moss, dwarf birches, and willows are typical of Nordland, the mountainous province of northern Norway, which is situated to the north of the Arctic Circle, at the lower edge of the image. While the tree line in the southern Norwegian mountains reaches up to 1000 m (3280 ft), in the north it falls to just 300 m (984 ft), hence the low-level landscape. It is only in the Norwegian fjord valleys that trees grow to a "standard" height, and, in many places, into complete forests. While the fauna of the southern Scandinavian Peninsula barely differs from that of central Europe, in the northern latitudes of the Scandinavian mountains, Arctic animals such as reindeer, wolverines, ice foxes, and lemmings make their homes.

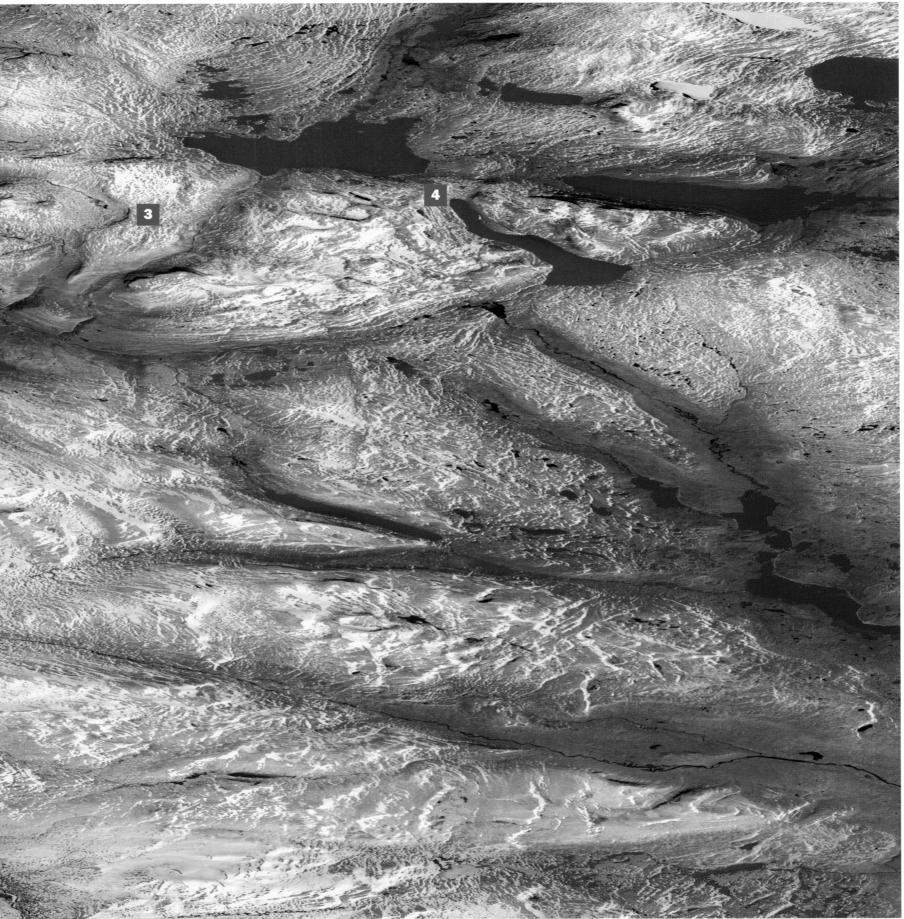

① *Moskenes, Lofoten Islands* ←

The colorful houses of the picturesque village of Moskenes are typical of Nordland. Moskenes, to the northwest of the satellite image, is located on the island of Moskenesøya, at the southern end of the Lofoten Islands. The community comprises approximately 1200 inhabitants. The islands, connected by numerous bridges and tunnels, are a popular tourist destination.

2 Storjord

To the south of Storjord, at the northern end of the Løns Valley, is one of the most beautiful waterfalls in the country, the Kjemåga. Highway 95 stretches to the east from here in the direction of Jäkkvik in Sweden.

3 Saltfjellet

The image shown is of the Svartisen-Saltfjellet National Park—about 1300 km² (500 square miles) of the Saltdal are environmentally protected. The sparse and treeless high plains of the Saltfjellet are part of the national park area, as well as the Junkerkal-Balvatn plant protection area seen in the top right section of the image. The Junker Valley is one of the most impressive parts of the Saltfjellet, and the mountain areas are justifiably popular with hikers.

4 Watersheds

In 1751, Sweden and Norway decided to adjust their national borders to follow the natural watersheds. Determining the watersheds was a difficult task, but the 1619 km (1006 mile) long border is certainly one of the least contested. At the top right edge of the image, the border runs between the Norwegian lake Balvatn (left) and the Swedish lakes of Ikesjaure (center) and Mavasjaure.

5 Scandinavian Mountains

The Scandinavian Mountains divide the Scandinavian Peninsula into a western Norwegian part, and an eastern Swedish part. Even though the Scandinavian Mountains may not seem that high, at a height of 1000 m (3280 ft), climatic conditions are comparable to those at 2500 m (8200 ft) in the Alps. In the section shown, the elevations range from between 1300 and 1700 m (4265 and 5577 ft).

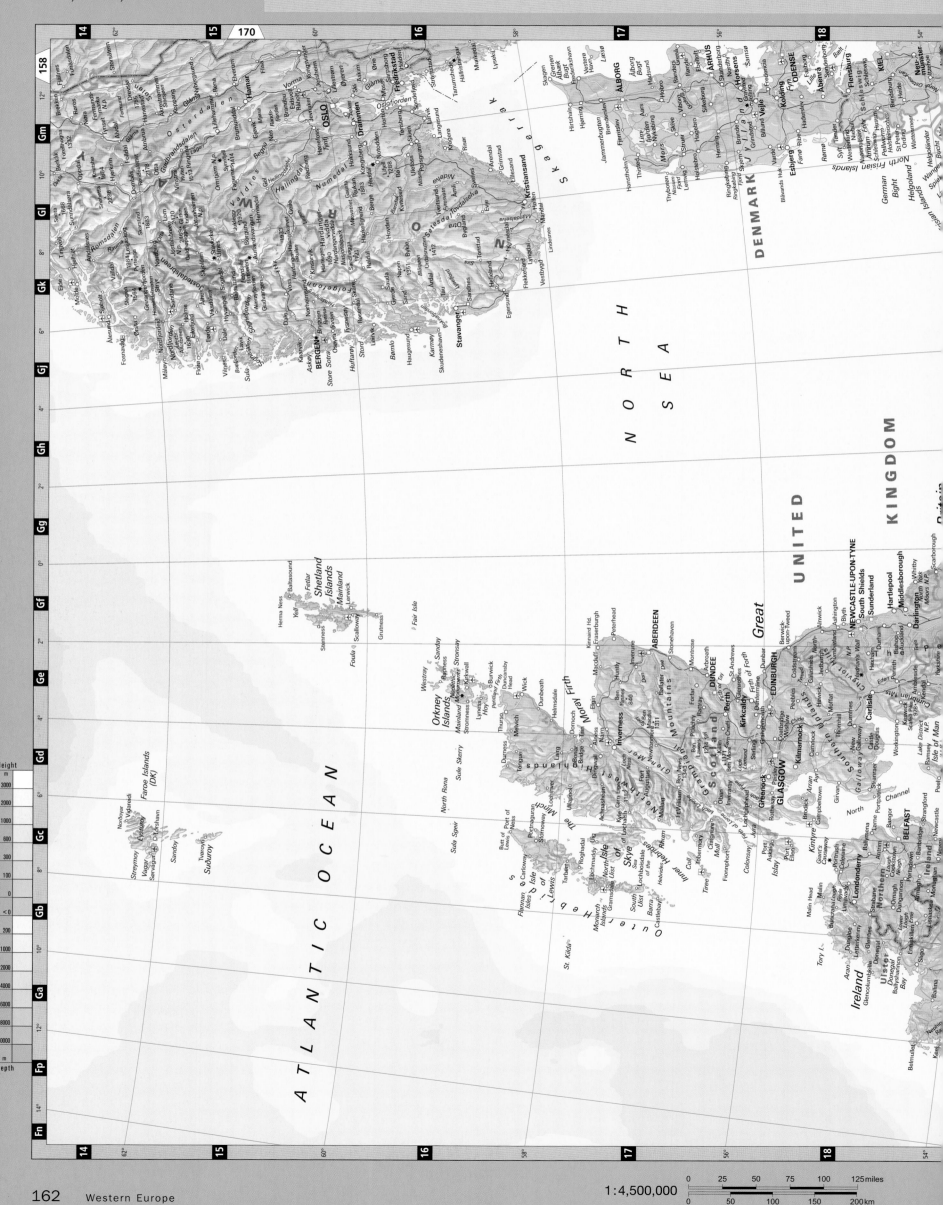

Height
m
3000
2000
1000
600
300
100
0
< 0
200
1000
2000
4000
6000
8000
10000
m
Depth

1:4,500,000

| 0 | 25 | 50 | 75 | 100 | 125 miles |

| 0 | 50 | 100 | 150 | 200 km |

Albers Equal Area Conic Projection

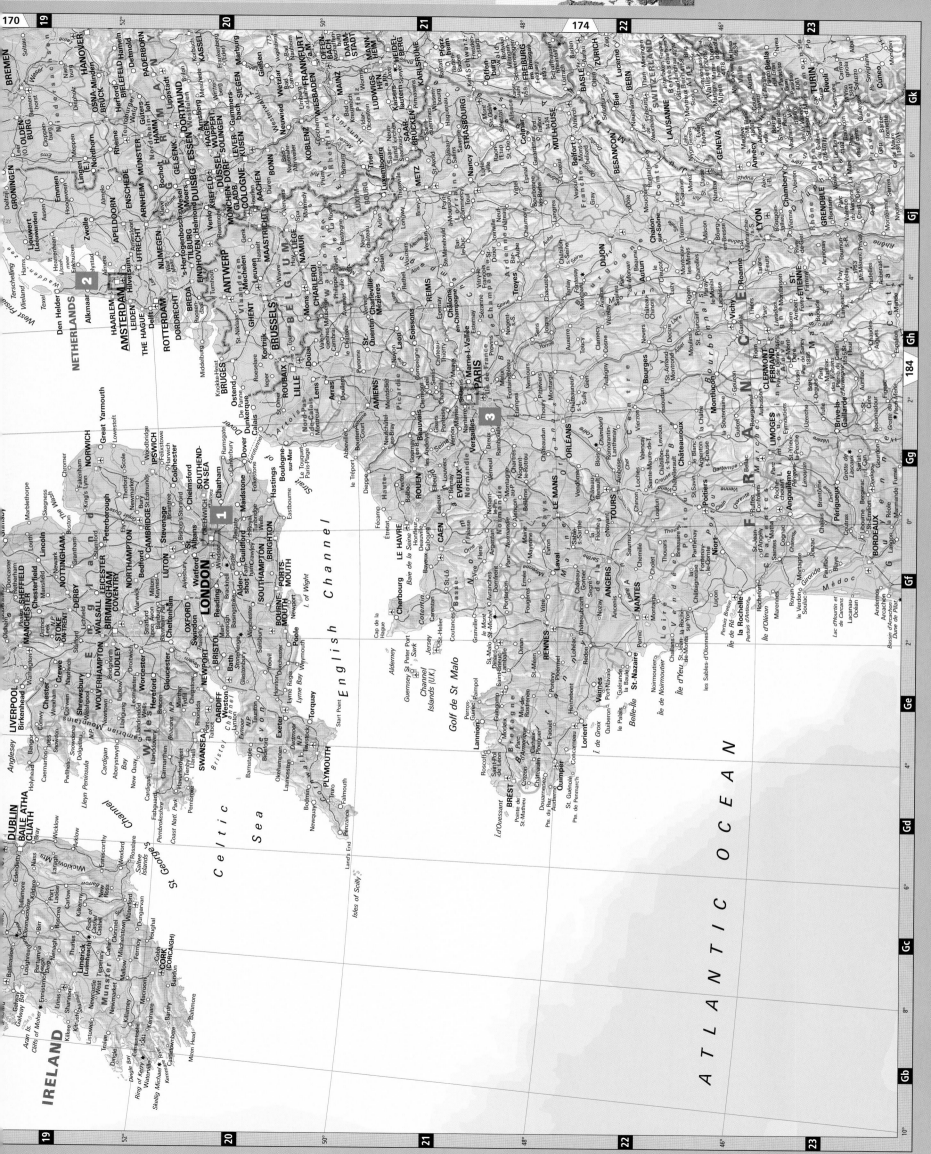

London

The capital of the United Kingdom and its largest city is a vast metropolis, yet its growing size has not harmed its many original features, especially its numerous smaller neighborhoods, all of which have particular quirks. London, divided in two through its heart by the mighty River Thames, also has another peculiar anomaly, standing as a no-man's-land between east and west. The Greenwich Meridian, at 0° longitude, transects the inner city neighborhood of Greenwich and geographically "divides" the earth into an eastern and a western half. This cosmopolitan city of some 7.5 million inhabitants is a hub of modern culture thanks to its museums, theaters, orchestras, and galleries, yet it is also one of the most important economic centers in the world, due to its busy Stock Exchange.

1 *The Houses of Parliament and Big Ben ↑*
The official name of the parliament building is the Palace of Westminster, in reference to the former royal palace that previously occupied the same location. After the latter's destruction by fire in 1834, the Neo-Gothic parliamentary building was built according to a design by Charles Barry (1840–88) and Augustus Pugin (1812–52). It boasts a facade nearly 300 m (984 ft) long, which overlooks the Thames and is grouped around 11 interior courtyards. In all it contains nearly 1100 rooms.

The parliamentary building is dominated by the 96 m (316 ft) high clock tower, known as "Big Ben." Originally only the 13.8 metric ton (15.2 ton) clock bore that title, but today the entire structure is generally afforded the nickname. The clock was supposedly named for the then very popular Labor Minister Benjamin Hall, who was responsible for public buildings, although other theories also abound. The tolling of "Big Ben," the so-called "Westminster Peal," is famous the world over, not least because the BBC World Service uses its chimes as a time signal on its radio broadcasts. A total of 334 steps lead to the top of the tower, where a lamp burns while Parliament is in session, and is extinguished only when the sessions come to a close.

2 The Thames
The most important river in England runs through the British capital from west to east, and flows into the North Sea from the east of the city through an estuary 148 km (92 mile) long and up to 9 km (6 mile) wide. In the inner city area the river is spanned by 14 bridges, of which the most famous is undoubtedly Tower Bridge. The image here, from upstream, includes seven of these: Waterloo, Hungerford (railway), Westminster, Lambeth, Vauxhall, Grosvenor (railway), and Chelsea bridges.

3 Tate Britain
Sir Henry Tate (1819–99) made his fortune in sugar via the Henry Tate & Sons company (later Tate & Lyle), then indulged his passion by spending it on art. Ten years before his death he donated his collection to the country, on the condition that it be adequately displayed in gallery space, and he provided a substantial sum toward the construction of such a place. The result was the Tate Gallery, built on the site of the former Millbank Prison and opened in 1897. The original Tate Gallery, today called Tate Britain, has three main collections: British paintings from 1500 to the present, modern paintings from America and Continental Europe, and 19th- and 20th-century sculpture. The work of British painter Joseph

Mallord William Turner (1775–1851) has been housed in the purpose-built Clore Gallery, designed by the architect Sir James Stirling, since 1987. London also houses Tate Modern, Britain's national museum of modern art.

4 Victoria Station and Waterloo Station
London is very much a commuter city—nearly 12 million people live in the Greater London area, but as most work in the city center, daily train travel is a necessity. Nearly 400,000 people work in the City of London alone, the financial district to the east of the image, which gives some idea of the number of commuters who come from the surrounding areas into London on a daily basis. So it is no surprise that the city has one of the oldest and most comprehensive subway systems in the world (the "Tube"). In addition, overland train tracks entering the city from the outlying areas end in numerous hub stations, the most important and largest of which are Victoria Station and Waterloo Station.

5 Trafalgar Square
On October 22, 1805, the British fleet, under the leadership of Admiral Horatio Nelson, defeated the combined Spanish and French forces at Cape Trafalgar off the southwest Spanish coast. Nelson died in the attack but was posthumously ennobled and a central London square was created in honor of his victory between 1829 and 1845. Its most prominent point is the 56 m (184 ft) high granite column topped with a 5.5 m (18 ft) tall statue of the admiral. The four bronze lions on the square were installed in 1868, and the fountains have bubbled here since 1939. On the north side, the square is bordered by the National Gallery, which displays masterpieces by Dürer, Raphael, Rubens, Constable, Gainsborough, Degas, and others. The Church of St. Martin-in-the-Fields stands on the northeast side.

6 British Airways London Eye
What began as a competition for the millennium festivities has developed into one of London's major tourist attractions: The architectural team of David Marks and Julia Barfield introduced the "London Eye" concept in 2000, the largest Ferris wheel in the world. The 135 m (443 ft) high steel construction stands across from the Houses of Parliament, directly on the banks of the Thames. A total of 32 glass capsules (known as "pods") are attached to the exterior of the wheel, and the view from the top stretches far out over the city.

7 *Buckingham Palace ↓*
The palace at the west end of St. James's Park, built in 1703 for John Sheffield, Duke of Buckingham, has been the London residence of the British royal family since Queen Victoria moved here in 1837. Today, the palace supposedly contains over 600 rooms yet only a small section is open to the public. In summer, visitors may view the Queen's Gallery, which displays artwork from the royal family's collection, the Royal Mews, and the Royal Stables, where the coaches, carriages, and even the royal automobiles are displayed. The main attraction for visitors, however, is the Changing of the Guard in front of the palace.

Amsterdam

The capital of the Netherlands is neither the seat of government nor the permanent residence of the Dutch royal family—The Hague holds both these honors. However, with just under 750,000 residents, Amsterdam is the largest city in the country, and its greater metropolitan area is home to nearly 1.5 million people. It is also one of the economic centers of the Netherlands, and, above all, is the most culturally important. The city lies within an expansive marsh and polder landscape, the result of a centuries-long battle between the Dutch people and the water, during which the sea and the rivers have been subjugated through tremendous effort. Large parts of the region lie up to 5 m (16 ft) under sea level and were once vast lakes. Today intensive agriculture is practiced here by highly specialized small companies.

1 *Amsterdam City Center* ↑

As the satellite image clearly shows, the inner city of Amsterdam lies on the IJmeer, a bay off the IJsselmeer, and has developed in semi-circular form around the core settlement since its founding in 1270. In the 17th century, known as the Golden Age of Amsterdam, the carefully planned canals (grachten) were created as fortifications, running in four rings around the city center. The Singel, Herengracht, Keizersgracht, and Prinsengracht, with their multitude of beautiful patrician houses, still give an impression of the city's previous wealth. Somewhat later the outlying Singelgracht was built to conclude the development. These concentrically built canals are traversed by a number of perpendicular streets and smaller canals, and the city is divided into numerous small islands that are all connected by bridges. Of the more than 1000 bridges, the Magere Brug ("skinny bridge"), a wooden drawbridge over the Amstel, is by far the most famous. Originally built in 1670, it was later rebuilt many times, and was due to have been replaced in 1929 with a modern electric bridge. Luckily it was decided that it should be reconstructed instead—its last rebuilding was completed in 1969.

2 Port
The port of Amsterdam is the second largest in the Netherlands after Rotterdam. In the early days the Zuidersee was used as a water passage for trading ships, but by the 17th century most international trade was being funneled through the port of Amsterdam on the IJsselmeer. Today the port boasts an area of about 3000 ha (7413 acres).

3 North Sea Canal
In 1876 the North Sea Canal was opened. Due to its present width of 270 m (918 ft) and depth of 15 m (49 ft), it is accessible to seafaring ships along its entire length of 15 km (9 miles); it has thus created an important link between the city and the North Sea. The canal also benefits from a complicated sluice system, which means that it is not dependent upon the flow of the tides.

4 Amstel
Amsterdam was originally founded at the Amstel Delta of the IJ, on both sides of the small river. The Amstel's source is found only a few kilometers to the south of the greater Amsterdam metropolitan area and is directed into the city area via extensive canals.

5 *Polder Regions* ↓
Amsterdam's environs have been constantly changing over the past few hundred years. As early as the 17th century, necessary land reclamation measures were begun: Entire lakes were laid dry in order to create more agricultural areas. A small dike was typically built around the region to be reclaimed, then the water was pumped into newly dug canals. Windmills drove the pumps in the pre-Industrial era, although today electric pumps are used. Land reclaimed in this manner is extremely fertile, and has resulted in the dominance of horticulture as well as agriculture. Indeed, the Netherlands leads the world in this market, and tulips are one of the country's most important exports.

Paris

"Charm, flair, spirit, haute couture"—these words apply above all to the French capital. In addition, Paris offers some of the most famous landmarks in the world. The cityscape is made up not only of architectural showpieces but also of beautifully designed green spaces such as the Tuileries Garden, the Luxembourg Gardens, and the Bois de Boulogne. Important chapters in French history have also been witnessed, perhaps the most dramatic being the storming of the Bastille in 1789, which marked the start of the French Revolution. A great sporting event also engulfs the city once a year, when the world casts its eye on Paris as the best cyclists on the planet converge on the Champs-Élysées for the last leg of the Tour de France.

1 *Arc de Triomphe ↑*

The Arc de Triomphe stands in the center of the Place de l'Étoile, so named because 12 streets converge here in a star (étoile) formation. Napoleon Bonaparte commissioned its construction to celebrate the victory at the Battle of Austerlitz, and building began in 1806, to be completed 30 years later. The 51 m (167 ft) high Arc de Triomphe also acts as France's cenotaph and is home to the Tomb of the Unknown Soldier.

2 The Eiffel Tower

The emblem of the city was built for the World Fair in 1889 and was the tallest building in the world at 300 m (984 ft), until this honor was "stolen" by the construction of the Chrysler Building in New York in 1930. The Eiffel Tower is one of the most frequently visited monuments in the world—around six million people climb the tower each year, using either the stairs or the elevator to reach the top. From one of the three observation platforms—the highest is at 274 m (899 ft)—some of the most beautiful views of Paris can be enjoyed. At night, artistic light shows turn the tower into the city's most spectacular sight.

3 The Seine

A blue band of water crosses the pulsating city from east to west—the sedate and tranquil River Seine. It is spanned by 27 bridges as it follows its course through Paris, and it surrounds a

number of islands, some of which are inhabited. The most famous is the Île de la Cité, which contains the cathedral of Notre Dame. In the city center many book and antiques stalls line the banks of the Seine and numerous excursion boats ply the river, offering tourists the opportunity to take in the romantic sights from the water.

4 The Louvre

The Louvre, housed in a former palace dating from the 12th century on the right bank of the Seine, is the French national art museum. The whole establishment contains more than 300,000 exhibits, some of which are of inestimable value. It is here that the most famous painting in the world, Leonardo da Vinci's *Mona Lisa,* has found a worthy setting. The glass pyramid at the entrance was built in 1989 by the renowned architect I. M. Pei.

5 *Champs-Élysées ↓*

This magnificent boulevard and promenade is, without contest, the most famous avenue in the world. The 3 km (2 mile) long Champs-Élysées is, in essence, the pride of the city and a worthy site for victory parades, processions, and other national and international events. The legendary avenue, running a straight majestic route between the Place de la Concorde and the Arc de Triomphe, is lined with rows of trees, fountains, and numerous street cafes. A stroll here is a must for every visitor to Paris.

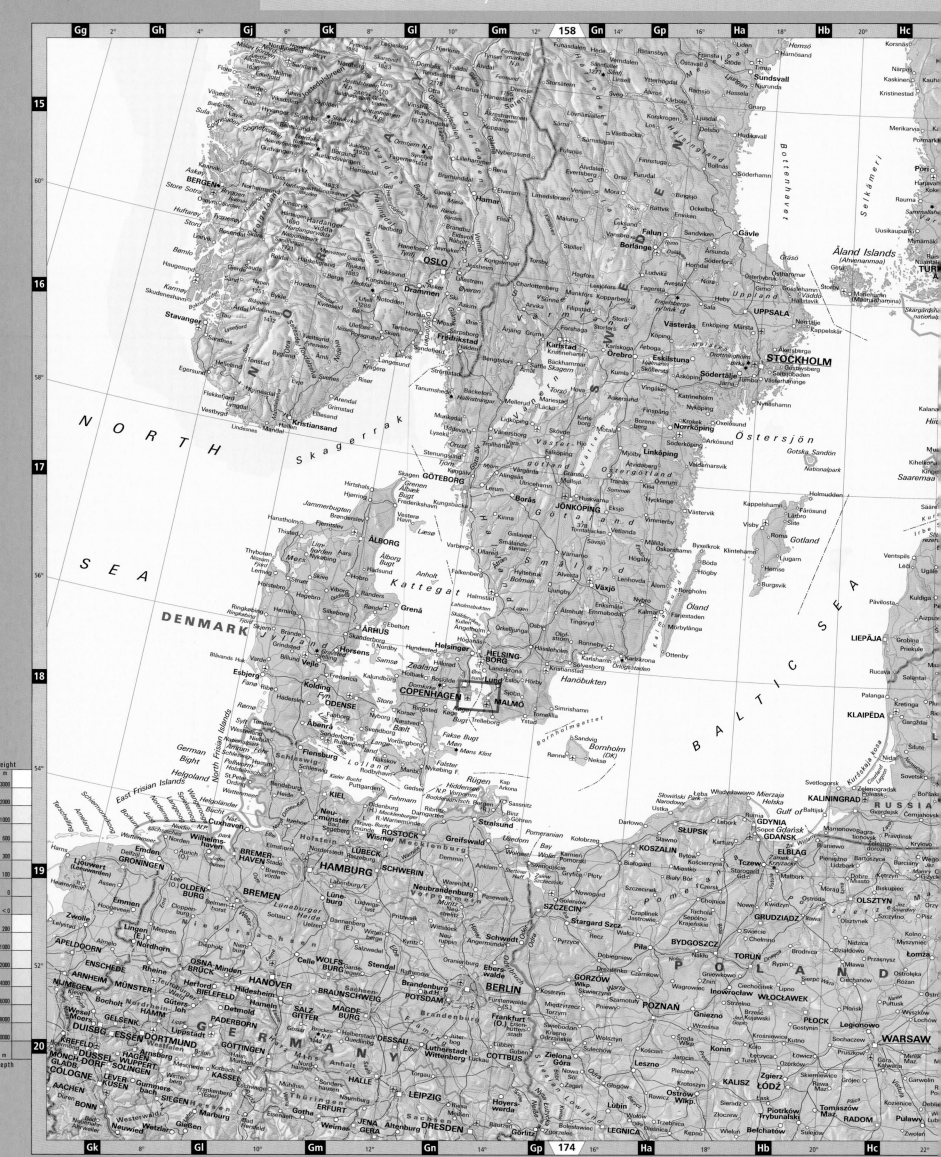

1:4,500,000

Albers Equal Area Conic Projection

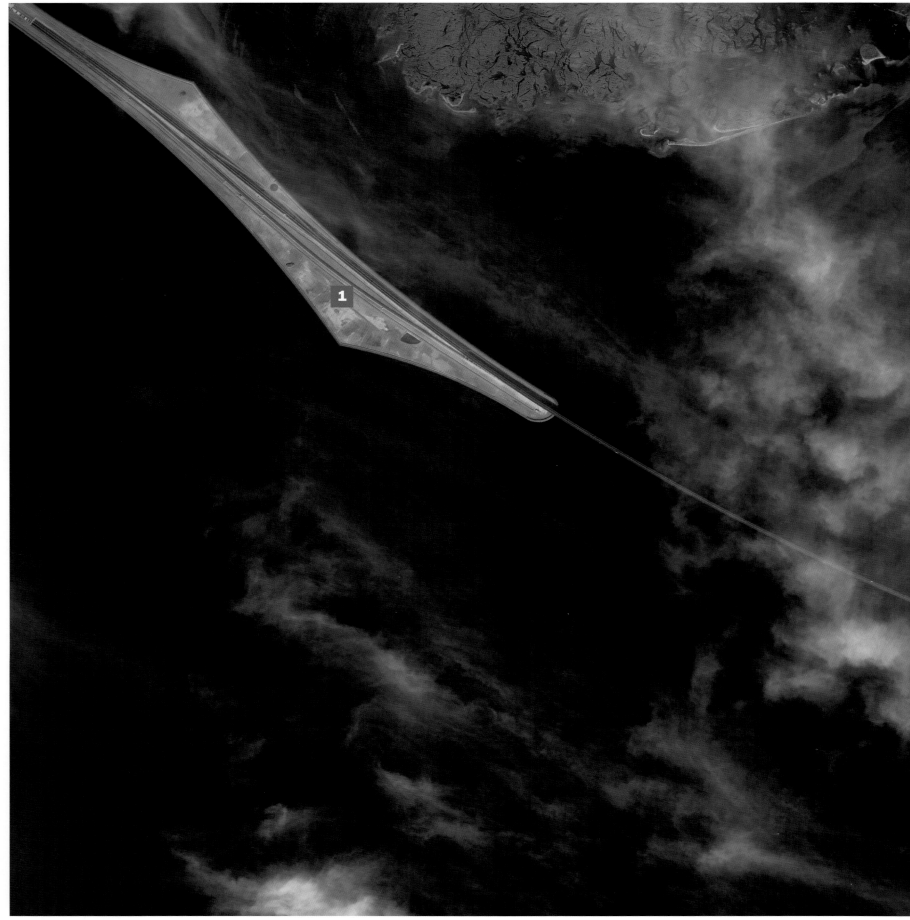

Øresund Bridge

Only a few years ago, anyone wishing to travel from Copenhagen in Denmark to Malmö in Sweden in their own vehicle had to take a ferry and would be subjected to long delays. However, since July 1, 2000, the travel time is only 15 minutes: On that day the official inauguration of the new bridge took place with Danish Queen Margrethe II, and her Swedish counterpart King Carl XVI Gustaf, presiding. The structure, 16 km (10 mile) long, combines a variety of construction styles, and has created a completely new cross-border economic area between Kastrup and Malmö, with 3.2 million residents. The concerns of numerous conservationists that the mammoth bridge could change bird migration patterns and currents have as yet proven to be unfounded.

1 Peberholm Island

The Øresund connection begins with the longest combined automobile and railway tunnel in the world (4 km/2.5 miles); two channels per mode of transport lead to the 4 km (2.5 mile) long manmade Peberholm Island, which was constructed from material taken from the bottom of the Øresund Sound. Its striking contours were designed to protect the structure from natural water currents.

2 High Bridge ←

The western ramp, more than 3014 m (9888 ft) long, follows the core piece of the construction: a 1092 m (3583 ft) long double deck suspension bridge that is supported by 80 pairs of cables.

The 4–204 m (13–669 ft) high bridge pylons are seated in the sea bed, and are linked by the road sections. The high bridge spans the Flinterenden waterway on the Swedish side of Øresund Sound. The light bridge height is 57 m (187 ft), with automobiles occupying the upper deck and trains the lower. The eastern ramp is nearly 4 km (2.5 miles) long.

3 The Lernacken Toll Gate

The central toll gate is located in Lernacken, Sweden, southwest of Malmö, with 11 lanes that can accommodate up to 2600 vehicles in each direction. Guides work in the control center, regulating the speed limits according to the traffic situation.

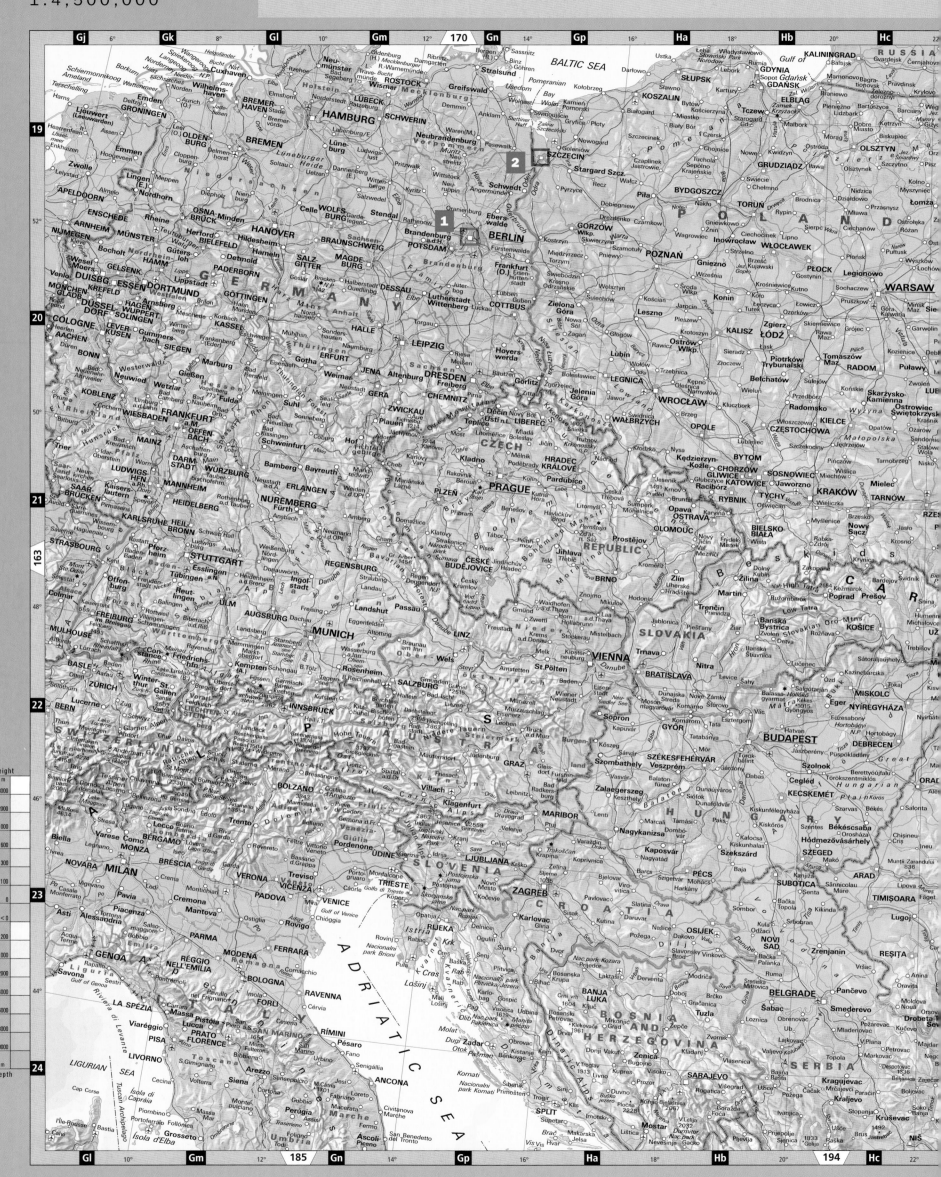

1:4,500,000

Albers Equal Area Conic Projection

1 Satellite Image: Berlin
2 Satellite Image: Szczecin

He 24° **Hf** 26° 28° **Hg** 171 30° **Hh** 32° **Hj** 34° **Hk** 36° **Hl** 38° **Hm** 40°

RUSSIA

BELARUS

VILNIUS
MINSK
HRODNA
BARANAVICHY
PINSK
BREST

ORSHA
MAHILYOW
BABRUYSK
BRYANSK
OREL
LIPECK
ELEC
VORONEZH

Slutsk
Salihorsk
Svyetlahorsk
Rechytsa
HOMYEL
Zhlobin
Klincy

KURSK
Gubkin
LISKI
OSTROGOŽK

MAZYR
ČERNIHIV
SUMY
BELGOROD

Korosten'
Nižyn
Romny
Pryluky

KHARKIV

L'VIV
RIVNE
LUC'K
ŽYTOMYR
KIEV
Brovary
Bila Cerkva
ČERKASY
POLTAVA

TERNOPIL'
Chmel'nyc'kyj
VINNYCJA

UKRAINE
KREMENCHUK
DNIPROPETROVS'K
IZUM
SLOVJANS'K
KRAMATORS'K
LYSYČANS'K
SEVERO-DONEC'K

IVANO-FRANKIVS'K
KAM'JANEC-PODIL'S'KYJ
Kolomyja
ČERNIVCI

Uman'
KIROVOHRAD
KRYVYJ RIH
ZAPORIŽŽJA
DONETS'K
KRASNOARMIJS'K
PAVLO-HRAD
KOSTJANTYNIVKA

MOLDOVA
BOTOŞANI
SUCEAVA
BĂLŢI
CHIŞINĂU
TIGHINA
TIRASPOL
MYKOLAJIV
KHERSON
Nova Kachovka
MELITOPOL'
MARIUPOL
BERDJANS'K

IAŞI
BACĂU
VASLUI
BÂRLAD
ODESSA
Bilhorod-Dnistrovs'kyj

Sea of Azov

KERCH

PIATRA-NEAMŢ
ROMAN
FOCŞANI
GALAŢI
BRĂILA
BUZĂU
Izmajil
TULCEA
Danube Delta

JEVPATORIJA
SIMFEROPOL'
SEVASTOPOL'
Yalta

Crimea
Feodosija

SIBIU
BRAŞOV
PLOIEŞTI
TÂRGOVIŞTE
BUCHAREST
CONSTANŢA

PITEŞTI
RÂMNICU VÂLCEA

RUSE
DOBRIČ

PLEVEN
ŠUMEN
VARNA

BLACK SEA

He 24° **Hf** 26° 28° **Hg** 30° **Hh** 32° **Hj** 195 34° **Hk** 36° **Hl**

19 52°
20
21 50°
48°
22 46°
23 44°
24

181

Berlin

The neighborhoods of Charlottenburg, Tiergarten, Wilmersdorf, and Schöne-berg, with their many parks and water features, are the "Green Lung" of Berlin, and have always been desirable residential and commercial locations. Despite heavy damage inflicted on Berlin during World War Two, many origi-nal rows of houses have remained intact: oases of peace amidst the expan-sive and traffic-ridden German capital. However, some aspects have changed in the four Berlin districts since reunification: Numerous new purpose-built structures have appeared and development has become denser, while the pulsing life from the pre-unification era has moved to Berlin's new center—Potsdamer Platz and around Unter den Linden.

1 *Exhibition Center* ←
All large Berlin exhibitions and conventions take place in Charlottenburg's "West End." The international congress center, built in 1979, and the 368 m (1207 ft) tall TV tower (1924–6) are seen as the modern symbols of Berlin.

2 Schloss Charlottenburg
Berlin's largest castle was completed in 1701 as a summer residence for the Princess Elect Sophie Charlotte. It was the preferred residence of Frederick the Great until the completion of Schloss Sanssouci. In 1943 the castle was badly damaged by air raids; so badly, in fact, that demolition was considered. It was eventually rebuilt and now serves as a museum.

3 River Spree
The 400 km (249 mile) long River Spree originates in the Lusatian Hills of Saxony. In Berlin's Spandau district, it empties into the Havel.

4 Schloss Bellevue
The castle was built in 1786, and serves as the residence of the federal president.

5 Tiergarten
The landscape architect Lenné formed the 200 ha (494 acre) park in the English style, but because the freezing population of post-war Berlin cleared the park after 1945 to use the trees as firewood, its original layout can only be speculated upon today.

6 June 17th Avenue
This beautiful avenue is a memorial to the East Berlin workers' rebellion of 1953.

7 Zoological Garden
In 1844, Friedrich Wilhelm IV bequeathed his animal collection from the Tiergarten to the population of Berlin, and it eventually developed into the most visited zoo in Europe.

8 Kurfürstendamm
The great thoroughfare, affectionately known as the "Ku'damm," was laid in the mid-16th century as a connecting road to the Grunewald hunting lodge. Today it is one of the city's most elegant shopping streets.

3

Szczecin

The Szczecin Lagoon (also called the Oder Lagoon) is divided by the German-Polish border into the German "Little Lagoon" and the Polish "Great Lagoon." It is up to 9 m (30 ft) deep, 51 km (31 miles) long, and up to 14 km (9 miles) wide. The German-Polish island of Usedom and the Polish island of Wolin seal it off from the Baltic Sea. Three branches of the River Oder—Peene, Swina, and Dziwna—are spread around its area and connect the lagoon with the sea. The city of Szczecin, Polish since 1945, was previously called Stettin in German. It lies at the southern end of the Szczecin Lagoon, 65 km (40 miles) from the Baltic Sea, and not far from the Oder Delta. After World War Two, the city quickly began to "polonize" the largest city in western Pomerania and the newly acquired surrounding area. The names of areas, lakes, and rivers were changed from German to Polish and numerous residents moved out. Today the university and port city of Szczecin has over 400,000 residents.

1 *Port ↑*

Szczecin's fate had already been determined before its entry into the Hanseatic League in 1278 by Baltic trade and ship-building. Yet ports and dockyards were greatly expanded during that period, and again in 1870. Until 1945, Szczecin was Prussia's largest port. Although 90 percent of its facilities were destroyed during World War Two, it quickly developed into the most important Baltic port in Poland.

2 River Oder

Nearly 750 km (466 miles) of the German-Polish border river are navigable. With many islands and branches, the Oder first empties into Lake Dąbie at Szczecin, then into the lagoon.

3 Lake Dąbie

Lake Dąbie, through which the Oder flows, is the fourth largest lake in Poland, measuring 56 km² (22 square miles). In the Góry Bukowe mountain range surrounding it are to be found some former chalk quarries and additional lakes.

4 Puszca Bukowa

The "metropolis in the countryside," as Szczecin is often called, lies in a moraine region and is surrounded by dense forests, heaths,

lakes, and small waterways. The primeval Bukowa forest is a popular excursion destination.

5 The Old Town

After 1871, when Szczecin became part of the unified German state, it was recreated according to the "Parisian model." During World War Two, however, 60 percent of the city was destroyed, so that little was left of its once-elegant parks and boulevards, and the star-shaped squares.

6 *The Ducal Palace ↓*

Most of the tourist attractions in Szczecin are located close to each other in the Old Town, on the steep west bank of the Oder. The most important structure in the city is the highly visible Gothic Ducal Palace of the dukes of Pomerania, remodeled in the Renaissance style. It is founded on the ruins of a Slavic fort and contains Pomeranian sarcophagi from the Middle Ages. Following heavy war damage, it was reconstructed in the original style in 1980, and today serves as a museum and events center.

Height
m
3000
2000
1000
600
300
100
0
< 0
200
1000
2000
4000
6000
8000
10000
m
Depth

1:4,500,000

0 25 50 75 100 125 miles
0 50 100 150 200 km

Albers Equal Area Conic Projection

MAP

1 : 4,500,000

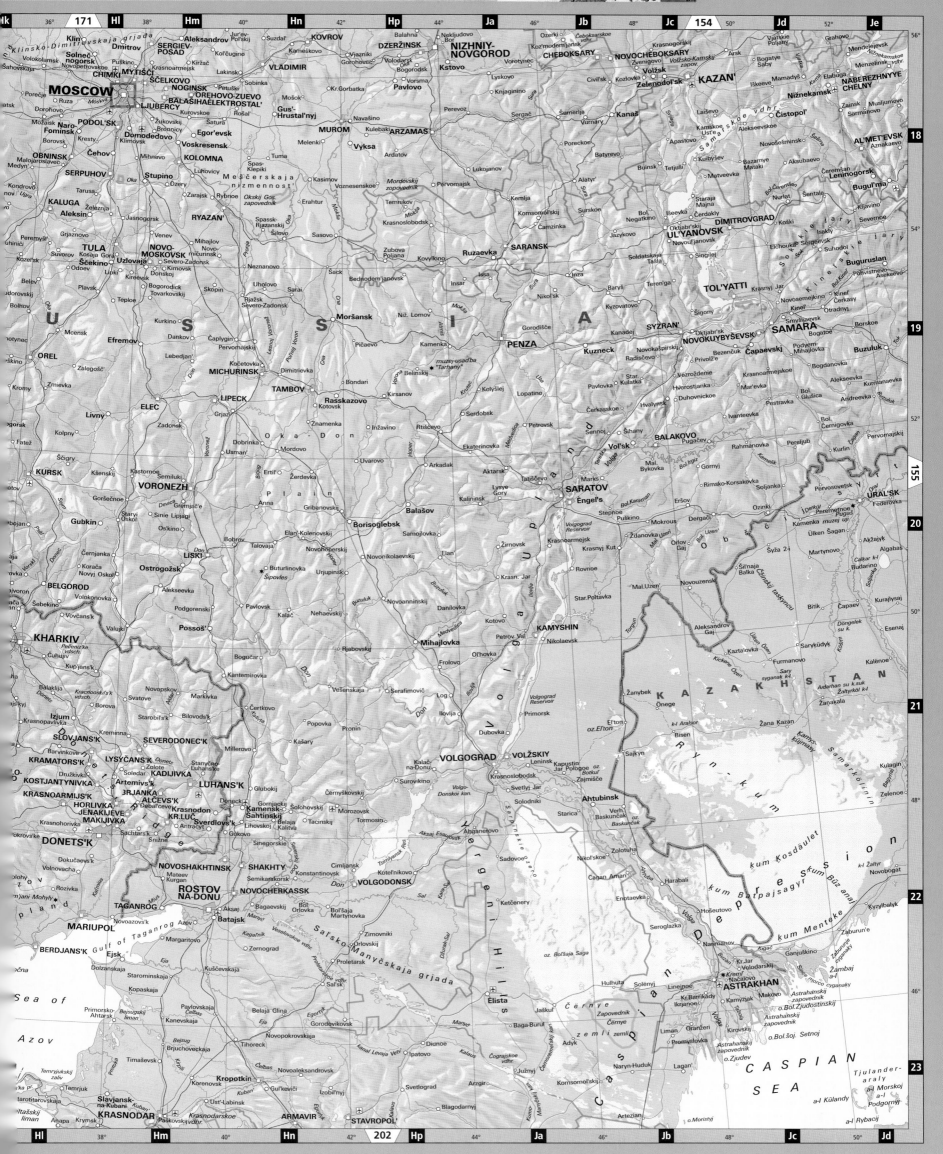

1 The Moskva
The 503 km (312 miles) long tributary of the Oka is navigable starting from Moscow, the most important and the most frequently used Russian river port. Links with the Baltic Sea, the Black Sea, the Caspian Sea, the White Sea, and the Arctic Ocean are reached via the 128 km (80 miles) long Moskvy Canal (1932–7) and other waterways.

2 Rossija Hotel
With 21 storys, 3200 rooms, and 6000 beds, the finest hotel in Russia is also the largest hotel in Europe. The best view of Red Square can be had from the hotel restaurant located on the 21st floor.

3 Alexander Gardens
When the Neglinnaya River, which used to be located along the northwestern side of the Kremlin, was driven underground, the site was built over and made into a park in 1821 in honor of Tsar Alexander I.

4 *Red Square and St. Basil's Cathedral* →
Red Square, which adjoins the northwestern part of the Kremlin, is 400 by 150 m (1312 by 492 ft) in size, and consists of a menage of buildings in different styles and with different functions. In addition to the Museum of History, the GUM department store, and the Lenin Mausoleum, the bizarre St. Basil's Cathedral dominates the image.

5 Bolshoi Theater
A visit to the "Great Theater" founded in 1776 is a must for every visitor to Moscow. The Neo-Classical building dating from 1825 (and renovated after a fire in 1856) has seats for more than 2000 spectators and a unique atmosphere. The Classical ballets and operas staged here are generally considered to be the pinnacle of perfection.

6 *Moscow Kremlin* ↓
Moscow's city fortress is encircled by a 2235 m (7333 ft) long fortified wall with 20 towers. Although the Kremlin also contains museums, cathedrals, palaces, and other functional and cultural buildings, it is synonymous with being the seat of the Russian government. The highest structure within the Kremlin is the 81 m (266 ft) high "Ivan the Great" belltower, which provides a view up to 40 km (25 miles) over the city.

Moscow

With over 10 million inhabitants—and in the Moscow conurbation, 12 to 14 million—Moscow is the most populated city in Europe. It also lies at the center of a country with the most varied peoples and landscapes on earth. Mentioned for the first time in 1147, Ivan the Terrible was the first to make the city, located by the River Moskva, the focal point of Tsarist Russia in the 16th century. Although St. Petersburg was the capital during the period 1703–1917, Moscow became the Russian capital during Soviet times, after the Russian Revolution of 1918. Architecturally, the city lost many of its pre-19th-century buildings to fire, started by the Muscovites themselves as they fled from Napoleon's troops in 1812. It also suffered from the rigorous implementation of Stalin's idea of a functionalist city. As a result, Moscow's center is characterized mainly by pompous propagandist and utilitarian buildings and those in the Classical and Baroque styles are rare. So while St. Petersburg blossomed, Moscow became known as an "architectural Sleeping Beauty."

7 Old Circus
The Old Circus building has room for 2000 spectators and was built at the end of the 19th century. Although a New Circus building has existed since 1973, most Muscovites prefer the older entertainment venue situated in the city center.

1935, Moscow has had a highly efficient metro system with nine lines and 150 train stations, carrying up to seven million passengers per day. Its ring line roughly corresponds to the course of the Garden Ring. A second metro ring is planned and is to connect Moscow's uniform satellite towns to the traffic network.

8 Ring Roads and the Metro Network
Numerous main roads leading to the Kremlin cut through Moscow's concentric, bowl-shaped city center. Ring roads follow the direction of the former city walls, and include the 9 km (6 miles) long Boulevard Ring. In its original form of fortified white stone walls, it encircled the "White City," home to those exempt from tax: these were subjects who directly served the Tsars, the aristocracy, and the Church. The white walls were dismantled at the end of the 1700s and replaced by the Boulevard Ring. The Garden Ring, truncated by the bottom left-hand edge of the image, was a 14 km (8 miles) long earth wall with towers, which ran to the south of the Moskva. Since

9 Arbat
This area was a playground for the Moscow intelligentsia and artists until the 20th century. Having degenerated over a period of time, numerous restored town houses, villas, and museums once again bear witness to the return of the erstwhile inhabitants. The Arbat Uliza has been transformed into a pulsating pedestrian zone.

10 Cathedral of Christ the Savior
Like 150 other churches in Moscow, the Cathedral of Christ the Savior, built during the years 1839–83, fell victim to the Communists and was destroyed to make way for the Palace of Soviets. Following the fall of the Soviet Union, the biggest of all of Moscow's churches was rebuilt in the years 1994–7.

1 Satellite Image: Lisbon 3 Satellite Image: Venice
2 Satellite Image: Mallorca 4 Satellite Image: Vatican City

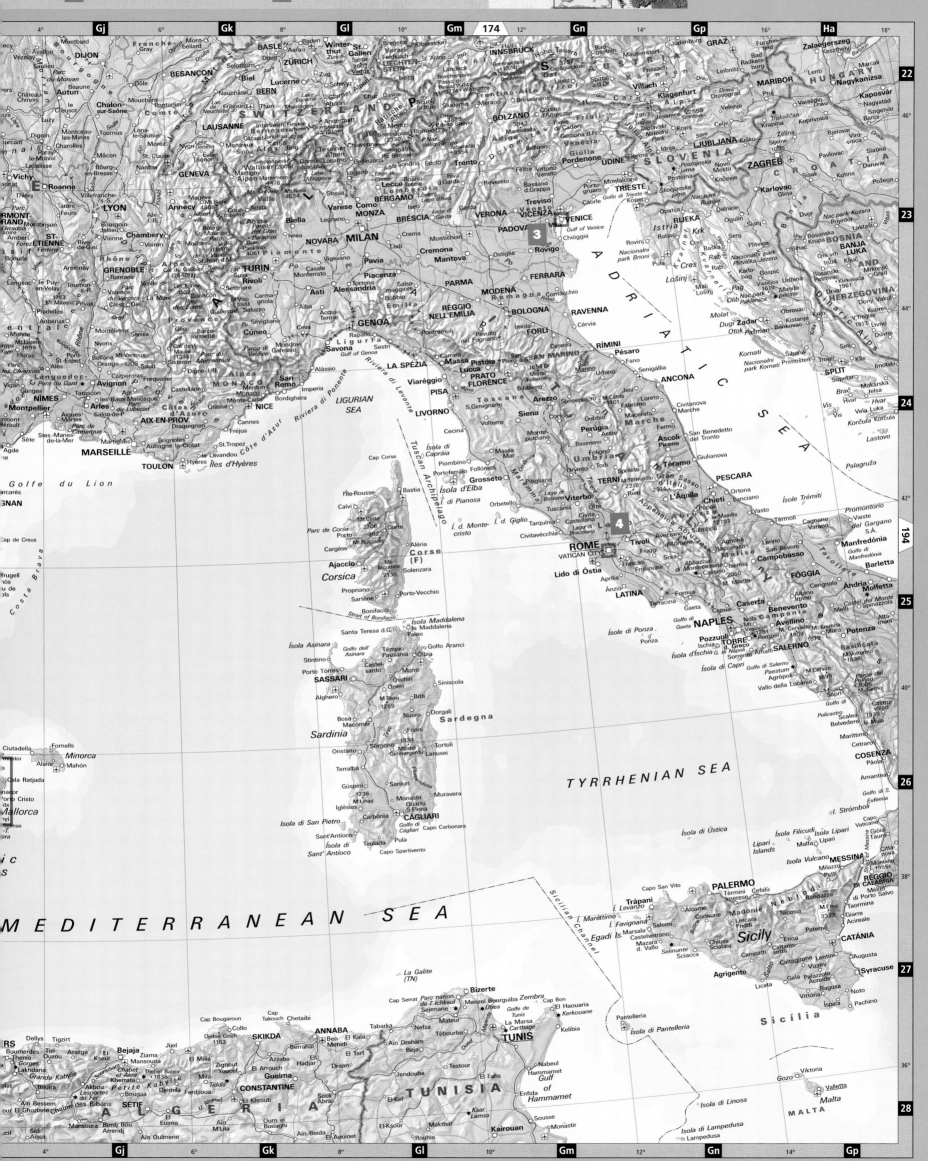

1 Alfama

Today, the name and the outlines of Alfama, the oldest part of the city, still recall its Moorish builders. The nucleus of the capital is located on the highest hill. The Romans built a castle here in 205 BC, and in 1255 the Castelo de São Jorge became the residence of the Portuguese kings. Today there is a breathtaking view from here over the Alfama area, Baixa in the west, with its checkered pattern streets, and the green Avenida da Liberdade, which extends to the northwest.

2 *Padrão dos Descobrimentos* →

Wherever one goes in Lisbon, there are monuments that recall the country's great seafaring traditions. The most impressive are without a doubt the Torre de Belém and the Padrão dos Descobrimentos (Monument to the Discoverers). It was here, on the banks of the Tagus, in the suburb of Belém, that the caravels of Vasco da Gama and other great navigators set off to sea and laid the foundations for the success of this former world power. In 1960, the Monument to the Discoverers was officially opened in the marina on the 500th anniversary of the death of Henry the Navigator. It resembles a caravel and its sides are decorated with 9 m (30 ft) high sculptures of important Portuguese explorers, in particular Henry the Navigator. Tribute is also paid to cartographers, sailors, artists, and scientists.

3 Belém

Located to the west of the city center, this area is indelibly linked with Portugal's golden era. The magnificent buildings and churches date from the time of Manuel I and bear witness to this important period. The most important examples, both of which are protected as UNESCO World Heritage Sites, are the Torre de Belém (1515–21), to the west of the yacht port, and the Mosteiro dos Jerónimos (from 1501 onward), a church built to commemorate Vasco da Gama's trip to India. Both the interior of the church and the beautiful cloisters are worth a visit.

Lisbon

The heart of Portugal continues to beat strong and firm in its capital Lisbon (Lisboa). The city's heyday was during the 16th century. At that time Lisbon even surpassed Venice as the richest city in Europe. Good fortune was soon to come to an end, however. The metropolis had its darkest hour on November 1, 1755, when, within the space of a few minutes, an earthquake reduced the city to rubble and killed more than 50,000 of its 270,000 inhabitants. For centuries after, Lisbon was in a state of decline, but on joining the European Union in 1986, this charming capital rightly received international recognition once again. In 1994, it became the European Capital of Culture; in 1998, it played host to the Expo World Exhibition under the "Ocean" banner; and, in 2004, it was one of the cities in which the European Football Championships were held. The wounds from the terrible Great Fire of 1988 have also healed following the restoration of many of its historical buildings.

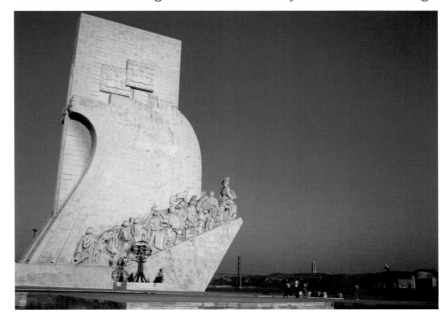

4 River Tagus

Lisbon's size and importance are closely linked to the Tagus, the longest river on the Iberian Peninsula, with a total length of 1100 km (690 miles). The river, which is known as the Tejo in Portuguese, and Tajo in Spanish, rises on the border between Aragón and Castilla-La Mancha in the Sierra de Albarracín, and has been dammed at several points in both Spain and Portugal. All 210 km (130 miles) of its lower reaches are navigable. The river joins the Mar de Palha a good 10 km (6 miles) before it flows into the Atlantic, here forming the ocean's largest natural port. Ferries, which ply the river and provide spectacular views of the city, form part of the rhythm of life of the Lisboetas.

5 *Ponte 25 de Abril* ↑

Ponte 25 de Abril, seen from the south. This impressive suspension bridge connects the city of Almada in the south with Lisbon's Alcântara district. The steel construction that is the huge Ponte 25 de Abril suspension bridge, modeled on the Golden Gate Bridge in San Francisco, extends over the river for a distance of 2277 m (7470 ft). Orginally named for Antonio de Oliveira Salazar, the former Portuguese dictator, it was renamed in honor of the day, in 1974, on which the revolution took place and the country once again became a democracy.

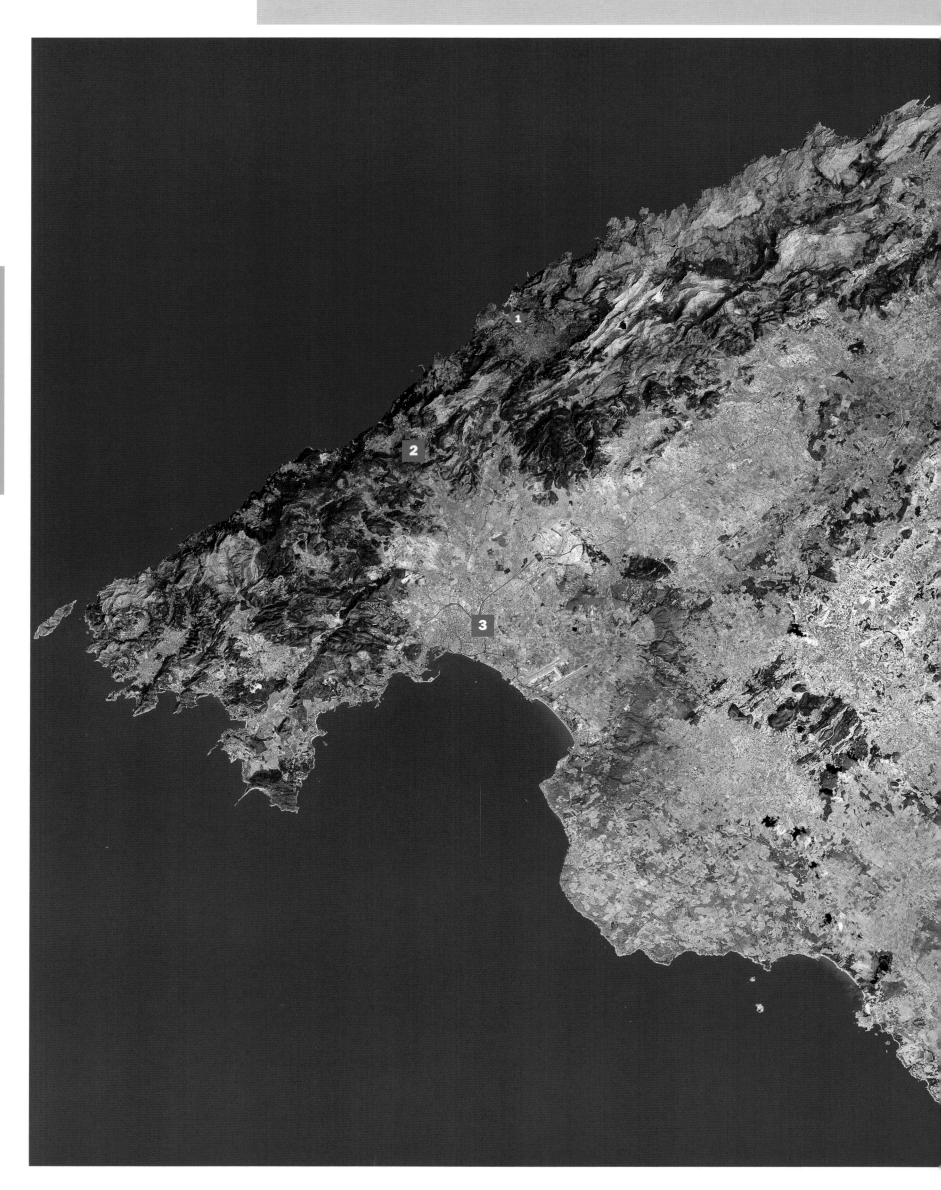

Mallorca

At 3684 km² (1422 square miles) the largest of the Balearic Islands—which also consist of the smaller islands of Minorca, Ibiza, and Formentera—Mallorca blossomed into the most popular holiday island in Europe in the 1960s. There is something here for everyone: sun-worshipers, night owls, nature-lovers, culture vultures, or those just in search of a little rest and relaxation. It is a mountainous island in the west, with more than ten peaks over 1000 m (3281 ft) high and a steep coastline; this is in contrast to the northeast, where flatter hills taper out to wide beaches. The central part of the island is a flat, fertile plain in which up to four harvests are possible each year due to the Mediterranean subtropical climate. The largest bay in the Balearics is the Badia d'Alcúdia.

1 *Port de Soller* ↑

On the fissured, steeply rising northwest coast of the island there is only one natural port, Port de Soller. It is still a fishing port today as well as a port for the small town of Soller, located about 5 km (3 miles) inland, to which it is linked by the "Orange Express," a rickety old tram. Approximately 7000 inhabitants live in the city of Soller, which serves as an administrative center for the community of the same name. Close to Soller are the villages of Fornatlutx and Biniaraix, both situated in a fertile valley of orange and olive trees.

2 Valldemossa

In 1399, a Carthusian monastery was established on the estates of a former king's palace. After secularization in 1835, the monks were driven out and the former cells sold to private individuals. The writer George Sand and the composer Frédéric Chopin lived in cells 2 and 4 in the winter of 1838 and were eyed suspiciously by the Mallorcans. During those months Sand wrote her book *Winter on Mallorca*, while Chopin composed several works, including his *Raindrop Preludes*.

3 Palma de Mallorca

About 320,000 people, almost half of all the inhabitants of the islands, live in Palma de Mallorca, the capital of the Balearic Islands. Palma is the economic, political, and cultural center of the Balearics and, despite the fast rate at which it has grown in the last decades and the rise in tourism, it has been able to retain much of its original character, in particular in the old town. The island, originally Roman, was conquered by the Saracens in 902 and later, at the beginning of the 13th century, was taken over by the Christian rulers from the House of Aragón.

The dominant building in the city center is the cathedral, La Seu, built on the ruins of the main Moorish mosque. Designed in the French Gothic style, the building work began in 1230 and was completed in 1604. The Palau d'Almudaina is located opposite the cathedral; the former building was once the seat of the Moorish viziers, and was used by the Spanish kings as their residence in Majorca. A walk through the capital also reveals numerous beautiful buildings from the 20th century in the Art Nouveau style, while a visit to the market hall, which is a bold iron structure, is also to be recommended.

4 Portocristo

This seaside resort is not visited so much for its beaches but for its system of caves, known as the Coves del Drac (Dragon's Caves). A huge dripstone cave has been made accessible by means of footbridges and pathways, and inside it can be found the Lago Martel, the largest subterranean lake in Europe at a length of 177 m (581 ft), which is navigated by small rowing boats.

5 Parc Natural de s'Albufera

The 2500 ha (6178 acre) area of swampland and marshland was declared a national park in 1988. It is separated from the sea by a strip of sand with a length of about 8 km (5 miles) and a breadth of 250–500 m (820–1640 ft), which is criss-crossed by many channels. About 230 species of birds are protected here, many of which have their breeding grounds among the reeds or which gather here on their migration south to their winter quarters. Other inhabitants include eels, watersnakes, and the European pond turtle.

[map of Mallorca and the Balearic Islands with labels: Ciutadella, Cap de Formentor, Pollença, Alcúdia, Inca, Sóller, Puig Major 1445, Artà, Cala Ratjada, PALMA, Manacor, Porto Cristo, Llucmajor, Felanitx, Santanyi, Cabo de Salinas, Mallorca, Cabrera, P.N.M.-T. de Cabrera, Balears, Balearic Islands, Alaior, Joan, britja, Eulària d.R., Francesc d.F.]

Venice

So much beauty in such a small space—what other city can compare with Venice in this respect? This northern Italian city's Centro Storico (historic center)—excluding the industrial part of the city, Marghera, located on the mainland, and the modern port—is a car-free, waterlogged wonderland of alleyways, canals, bridges, palaces, cathedrals, and cafes. But the city is in peril: The water level is rising and the ground is sinking. In the 20th century alone the city lost 23 cm (9 in) to the sea. Since 1984, the Consorzio Venezia Nuova has been working on the MOSE project, the Modulo Sperimentale Elettromeccanico, which involves raising huge metal gates as barriers at the entrance to the lagoon when the water is high. Only in 2003 did the Commissione di Salvaguardia di Venezia agree to this rescue plan.

① Grand Canal ↑
Taking a 4 km (2.5 mile) trip in a vaporetto on the Grand Canal from the Stazione Ferrovia to Piazza San Marco offers the chance to go on a journey through the most beautiful "museum" of Venetian architecture, from the Gothic, through to the colorful marble of the High Renaissance, and to the Baroque. On the former river bed of the Brenta around 200 palaces and churches are lined up one after the other. The most spectacular is doubtless the Santa Maria della Salute (see above on the right). However, the daily life going on along the Grand Canal, the most beautiful waterway in the world, is a sight in its own right and is always full of surprises.

② Piazza San Marco
The legend of St. Mark originates from the robbery of relics by two Venetian merchants/adventurers in the year AD 828, who are also said to have taken the mummified corpse of the saint from Alexandria in Egypt to their native city. A church was built in St. Mark's honor in the square where the Basilica di San Marco would later stand, and Venice from this point on became known as the "Republic of St. Mark." One comes across countless illustrations of the saint and his heraldic animal, the lion, in this lagoon city. The

Basilica di San Marco, dating from the 11th century, dominates Piazza San Marco (St. Mark's Square) with the brilliance of its mosaics, while its 95 m (312 ft) high belltower looms over the pigeon-filled area. On the opposite side of the square it opens onto the lagoon affording spectacular views; on the piazzetta it is flanked by the arcades and rows of pointed arches of the Palazzo Ducale (Doge's Palace).

③ Teatro La Fenice
It might have taken some years, but in 2003, the curtain once again went up in Venice's most famous opera house. The Teatro La Fenice, on the Campo San Fantin, dates from the 18th century, and when burnt down in 1836, was immediately restored in 1837. It has a strong Neo-Classical aspect to its facade, and the auditorium is filled with rich golden and stucco decorations. La Fenice fell victim to another fire in 1996—two electricians were sentenced to prison for the event. True to the original, and correspondingly expensive, it was rebuilt. To add to the atmosphere, audience members can arrive at the theater in true Venetian style, by motorboat or by gondola, because it has its own "water entrance."

④ San Michele Cemetery Island
There is limited space in Venice for the living, let alone the dead. Anyone who is not wealthy, or a member of those families who have maintained their marble mausoleums for centuries, will find his or her final resting place on San Michele in a double man-sized stone wall unit piled eight to twelve storys high. However, the island cemetery, once a monastic island for the Benedictine Camaldolites, with its high trees and stones overgrown with moss, has a festive, even a romantic atmosphere. The graves of prominent native Venetians and visitors to Venice can be found here, including those of Sergei Diaghilev, Igor Stravinsky, Ezra Pound, and many more.

⑤ Bridge of Sighs ↓
Darkness amidst the brightness of Venice, the beautifully ornamented Ponte dei Sospiri—the so-called Bridge of Sighs (coined by Byron)—dates from the 16th century and marks the course that convicts would take from the Doge's Palace and the courtroom located there to the Prigioni, the state jail in Venice with its notorious lead roofs. Few people have succeeded in breaking out of this jail—the account of his escape in autumn 1755 by Giacomo Casanova in The Story of My Life still makes for an exciting read today. In the top left of the image below is a partially obscured drunken Noah beneath the grapevine, a work dating from the 15th century.

⑥ Rialto Bridge ↓
With a total of 12 arcades—six to the right and six to the left of the central portico—the Ponte di Rialto is immediately recognizable in every photograph, and has been a symbol of Venice since 1591 (a wooden bridge used to be here). In the face of doubts and protests from his contemporaries, Antonio da Ponte, the architect with an appropriate name, completed his bold, single-arched construction with a span of 28 m (92 ft) and a height of 9.5 m (31 ft), and it is still here today. The Rialto Bridge is certainly the most used of only three bridges spanning the Grand Canal.

Vatican City

With a surface area of only 0.44 km² (0.17 square miles), the Vatican is the smallest state in the world, and the only one whose head of state is vested with absolute power according to the constitution. The head of state is the Pope, who is also the Bishop of Rome and head of the Roman Catholic Church, and who is elected by a body of delegates made up of cardinals in strict isolation (conclave). About 800 people live in the Vatican, only about half of whom possess citizenship of the country. It has its own army, known as the Swiss Guard, as well as numerous educational institutions, its own radio station, which broadcasts throughout the world in many languages, a newspaper, a post office, and a railway station linked to the Italian rail network. Financially, the Vatican lives off donations from the Catholic faithful as well as income from capital investments.

Some pilgrim churches in Rome, located outside of the city state, and Castel Gandolfo, the Pope's summer residence in the town of the same name, located on Lake Albano, are also part of the territory of the Vatican.

1 Vatican Gardens
From the satellite image one can clearly see that about half of the territory of the Vatican is taken up by gardens. The extensive park can only be visited as part of a guided tour. It contains numerous buildings as well as the radio station (Radio Vaticano) and the Academy of Sciences.

2 St. Peter's Basilica ↓
St. Peter's is the symbol of the Vatican and the largest church in Christendom. Its interior of more than 23,000 m² (247,570 square feet) provides space for 60,000 believers. Work commenced in 1506 on the site of a basilica that had been built on the grave of the apostle St. Peter by Emperor Constantine the Great in the 4th century. The first architect to work on

3 Vatican Museums
The Vatican museums, which also comprise parts of the Vatican Palace and the Sistine Chapel, contain some of the most important art collections in the world and house the world's largest collection of antiquities. Among the most important works of art from the ancient world are the Laocoon Group, one of the main classical Greek artworks, and the Apollo of Belvedere, the Roman copy of a Greek bronze statue. In the palace, the *stanze* (state rooms) of Pope Julius II, which were painted by Raphael and his pupils, are worth a special look. However, the real tourist magnet is the Sistine Chapel, decorated with Michelangelo's spectacular frescoes, including the famous *Creation of Adam* on the ceiling.

St. Peter's was Bramante, who originally designed a central structure in the form of a Greek cross. Raphael and Sangallo continued with Bramante's work after his death. However, from 1564 onward, the church was given its present-day character by the fourth architect, Michelangelo, who added a nave in the eastern section and designed the 120 m (394 ft) high cupola. Michelangelo's famous Pietà statue can also be admired (behind glass) here, in the interior of the church.

4 St. Peter's Square ↑
In the years 1656–67, the Baroque sculptor and architect Gian Lorenzo Bernini brilliantly fulfilled the task he had been entrusted with—to create a square that would be monumental, but not too overwhelming, and that would include the broad facade of St. Peter's Basilica. The result was two semi-circular colonnades of 284 columns, crowned by 140 religious statues that lead one's eye directly to the church. An Egyptian obelisk has adorned the center of the square since 1586.

5 Audience Hall
The huge Audience Hall, commissioned by Pope Paul VI and designed by Pier Luigi Nervi, on which work began in 1966, is located close to the Campo Santo Teutonico, the German Cemetery in the Vatican. It provides seating for up to 25,000 people during the traditional general audiences, which take place on Wednesdays.

6 Cortile di San Damaso
Every year on May 6, the day of the "Sacco di Roma" (the Plundering of Rome), the new recruits to the Papal Swiss Guard swear their solemn oath in the prestigious St. Damasus Courtyard. The Swiss Guard is the smallest army in the world; its duty is to protect the Pope and the institutions of the Vatican.

Greece, Turkey

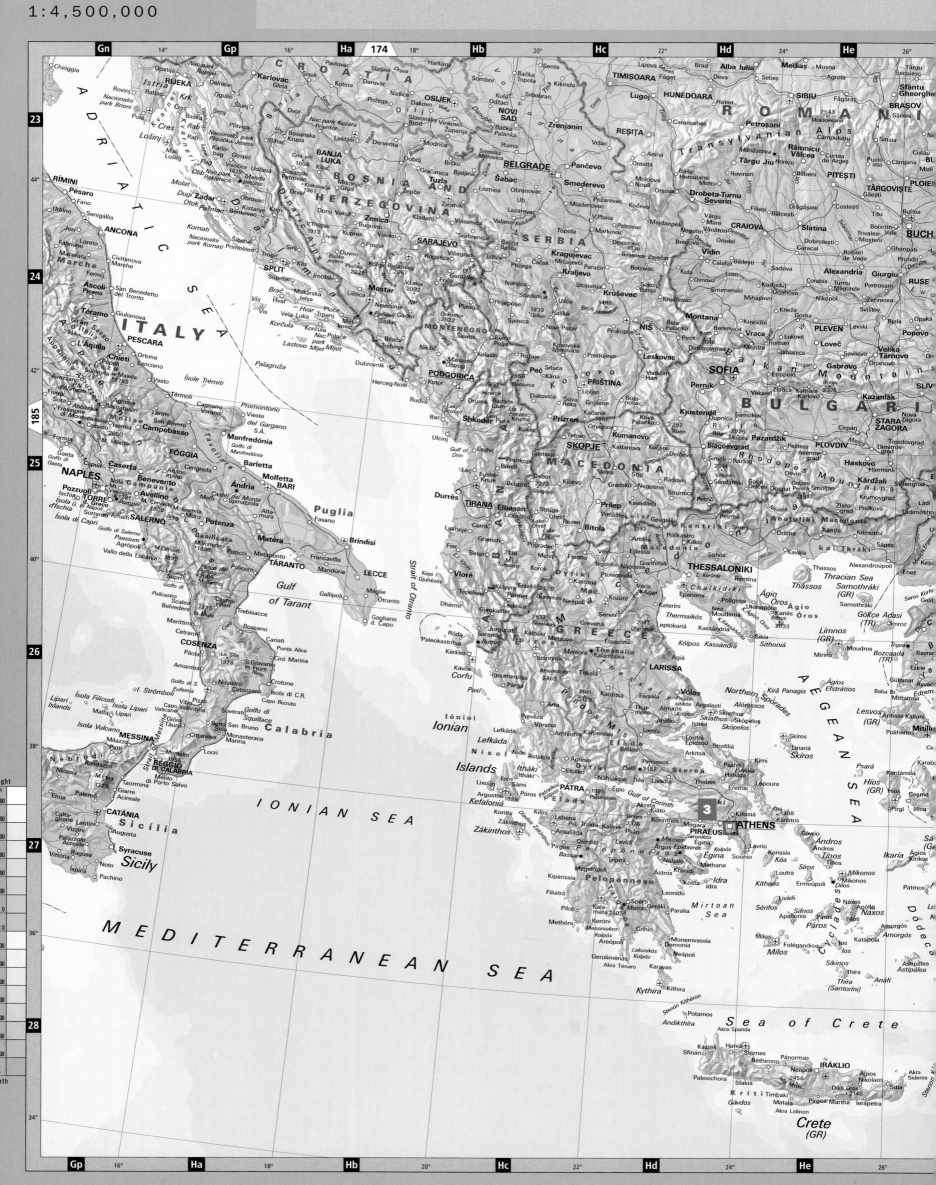

1:4,500,000

Albers Equal Area Conic Projection

BLACK SEA

Sea of Azov

UKRAINE

Crimea

Karkinit Gulf

RUSSIA

KRASNODAR

MAYKOP

KERCH

NOVOROSSIYSK

SOCHI

SOKHUMI

JEVPATORIJA

SIMFEROPOL

SEVASTOPOL'

Yalta

ARMAVIR

KROPOTKIN

CONSTANŢA

VARNA

BURGAS

ISTANBUL

Bosporus

ÜSKÜDAR

Sea of Marmara

BURSA

KOCAELI (IZMIT)

SAKARYA (ADAPAZARI)

ZONGULDAK

Ereğli

Karabük

Kastamonu

SAMSUN

ORDU

TRABZON

Giresun

Sinop

Pontic Mountains

ANKARA

ÇORUM

Amasya

Tokat

SIVAS

ERZINCAN

KIRIKKALE

Yozgat

ELAZIĞ

ESKİŞEHİR

KÜTAHYA

AFYON

KAYSERİ

MALATYA

ADIYAMAN

T U R K E Y

UŞAK

BALIKESİR

Nevşehir

Aksaray

KONYA

KAHRAMAN-MARAŞ

SANLI URFA

AYDIN

DENİZLİ

ISPARTA

BURDUR

Karaman

GAZI ANTEP

Kilis

ANTALYA

Gulf of Antalya

ADANA

TARSUS

İÇEL (MERSIN)

OSMANİYE

İSKENDERUN

ALEPPO

Alanya

Silifke

HATAY (ANTAKYA)

Idlib

Taurus Mountains

Rhodes

Rhodes(GR)

Turkish Part

CYPRUS

NICOSIA (LEFKOSIA)

LEMESOS

AL LĀDHIQĪYAH (LATAKIA)

Tartūs

HAMĀH

HOMS

S Y R I A

TRIPOLI

LEBANON

175

214

23

202

24

25

26

209

27

28

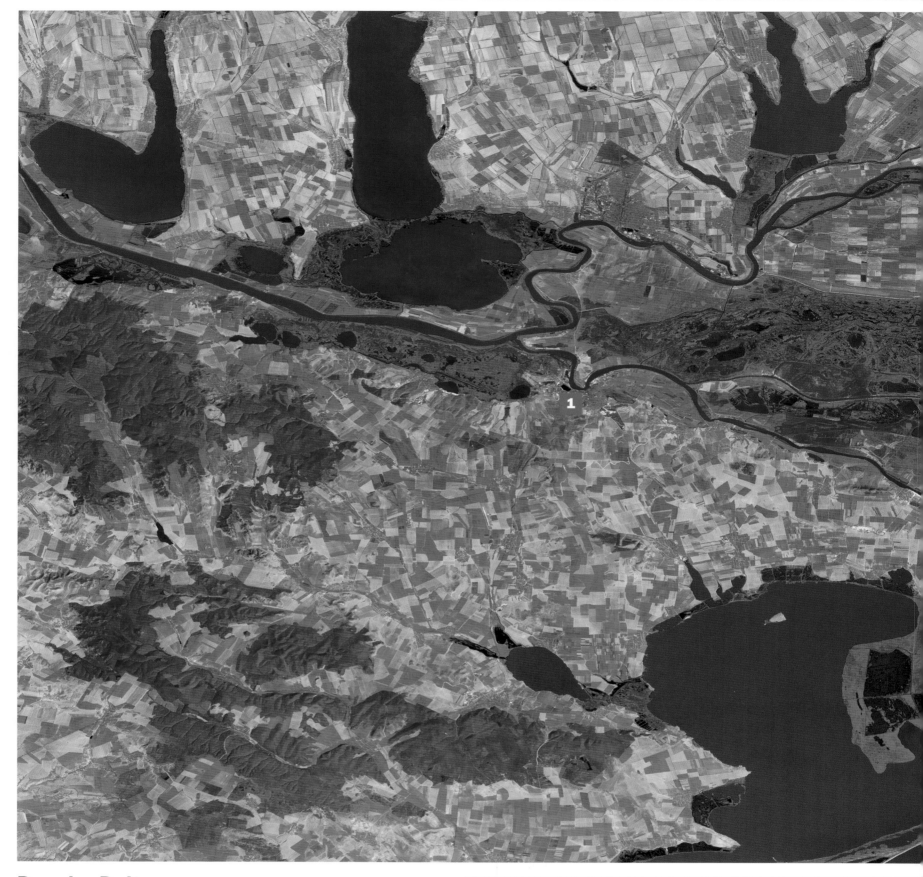

Danube Delta

The Danube is the only great river of Europe that flows from west to east. Rising in the Black Forest in Germany, it flows 2852 km (1772 miles) into the Black Sea, on the border between Romania and the Ukraine. It is second only to the Volga as the largest river delta in Europe: Of its total area of at least 5700 km² (2200 square miles), 15 percent of the delta is located in Ukrainian territory and 85 percent in Romanian territory. In addition, 70 million metric tons (77 million tons) of alluvium ensure that it advances a further 50 m (164 ft) into the Black Sea every year. The amphibious area, 80 percent of which is covered in water, came into existence at the end of the Ice Age some 10,000 years ago. Birdwatchers are the principal visitors to the region. The area is home to 300 species of birds, among them the pink-backed and white-backed pelican, the spoonbill, the glossy ibis, herons, and sea eagles.

Endangered Flora and Fauna ↑
About 1100 species of plants and more than 110 species of fish have been found in the Danube Delta, which also contains an astonishing variety of birds, insects, amphibians, reptiles, and mammals. However pollution flowing into the delta from the ten countries through which the Danube flows, hydraulic engineering errors, poaching, and *the burgeoning tourism industry have all contributed to a significant reduction in their numbers. Romania, Bulgaria, the Ukraine, Moldova, and the World Wildlife Fund (WWF) have recently come to an agreement with regard to a "Green Corridor" along the Danube, which will in the future become the largest transnational nature reserve in Europe.*

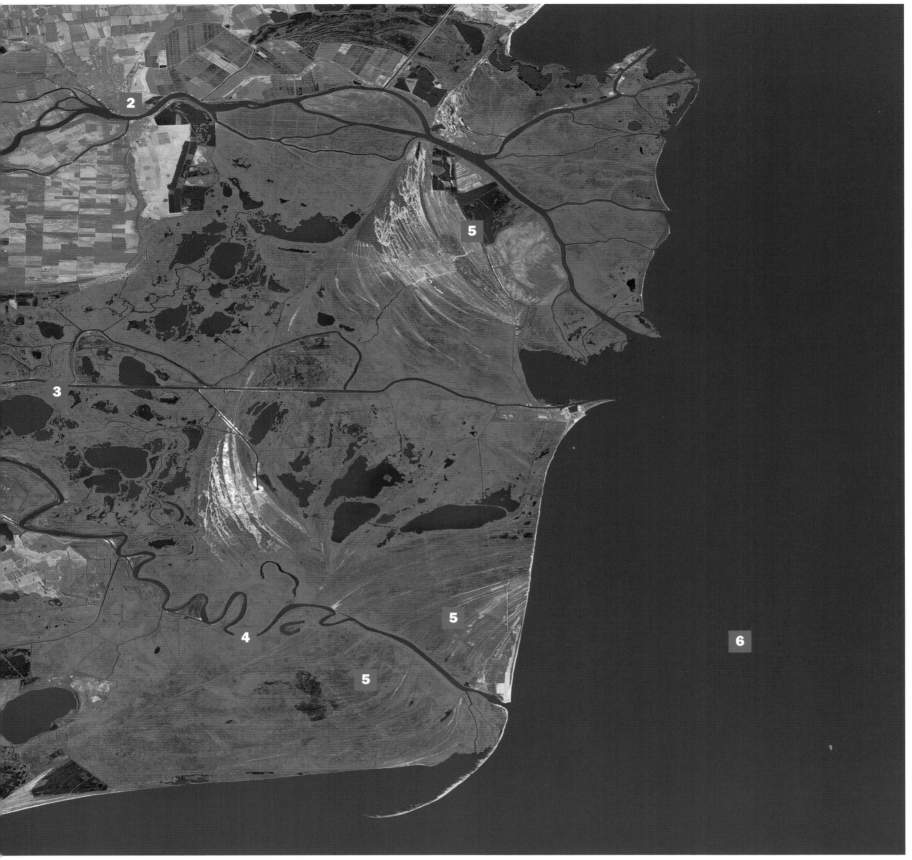

1 Tulcea
Shortly before the town of Tulcea, the "Gate to the Danube Delta," the river splits into three main branches: the Chilia, Sulina, and Sfîntu-Gheorghe. An important port, Aegyssus, was also located here as far back as ancient times, at the point of intersection of Phoenician, Greek, and Roman shipping lanes. Even today, things are still lively in the river port, and the town, which has a population of 110,000, nestles into the bank like an amphitheater.

2 Chilia Arm
The most northern, and at 116 km (72 miles) the longest, arm of the delta carries two-thirds of the water of the Danube and forms the border with Romania and the Ukraine. With around 40 estuaries, this area is almost a "delta within the delta." The high-sea naval port of Kiliya (marked on the map) has a varied history. Found-ed by the Romans and Byzantines, it belonged to

Moldova from the 14th century onward, but was conquered by the Ottomans in 1484. After several changes of rule, including Russian and Romanian, it has been part of the Ukraine since 1991.

3 Sulina Arm
Almost 17 percent of the water of the Danube flows through the Sulina arm, whose course was straightened in the 19th century by reducing its original length from 92 km (57 miles) to the present day 64 km (40 miles). The other branches cut off during this process are still easy to identify. The very bleak port of Sulina at the mouth of the river is located 3.5 m (11 ft) above sea level and is the lowest-lying area in Romania.

4 Sfîntu-Gheorghe Arm
After a distance of 109 km (68 miles), the southernmost arm of the Danube flows into the Black Sea. It has many twists and turns and flows through particularly beautiful scenery. The

1200 or so inhabitants of the Romanian village of Sfîntu-Gheorghe, a former Turkish base located at the mouth of the river, live on sturgeon catches, caviar production, and hunting and fishing.

5 Delta Sediment Structures
The Danube carries moving and suspended alluvium and deposits it in the form of belts, which can be seen clearly in these sediment structures. They have formed due to the diminished carrying power of the water, which interacts with the current of the Black Sea. Since the sediment acts as a barrier to the river, it must split up and branch out in a way that is typical of the delta.

6 Black Sea
This minor part of the Mediterranean Sea, which is up to 2245 m (7365 ft) deep in places, owes its somber name to the fact that fog and storms frequently occur over its waters. From a depth of 100–200 m (328–656 ft), its oxygen

content is greatly reduced, but the surface water is rich in fish, which provide a major source of food and trade for the seven countries surrounding the Black Sea.

Istanbul

This international city has a unique position, with one foot in Europe and one foot in Asia. Two towering bridges span the Bosporus, separating the two continents. A city with a long and complex history, Istanbul has over the centuries been a Greek colony and the capital of three vast empires—Roman, Byzantine, and Ottoman. It has also been known in turn as Byzantium, and then later Constantinople. In 1923, the Turkish leader Mustafa Kemal Pasha, known as Atatürk, made the more central Ankara the capital of the young republic, but the cosmopolitan heart of Turkey still beats in Istanbul, and the city even now retains a very European style. In only two decades the number of inhabitants in Istanbul has doubled to over 11 million people.

1 *Süleymaniye Mosque* ↓

One of the most important symbols of Istanbul is the dome of the Süleymaniye Mosque—built for Süleyman the Magnificent on the Golden Horn—with its four prominent minarets set around a cloister of arcades. The mosque was built by the great architect Sinan, the man in charge of all building works for the great sultan (reigned 1520–66), who led the Ottoman Empire to the peak of its power. The mosque complex includes the Sinan Mausoleum as well as foundation buildings, which today are partly used as a museum, but also as schools, universities, a hospital, a swimming pool, a fountain, a public kitchen, and a library.

wheels. The most attractive places are Büyükada ("First Island"), Heybeliada, Burgazada, and Kınalıada. Yassıada, in contrast, is used as a military prison. The islands take their names from the Byzantine period, when princes who were thought to present a threat to the throne were exiled in monasteries here.

4 Bosporus

This maritime highway, a 33 km (20 mile) long link extending from the Black Sea to the Sea of Marmara, made Istanbul's rise into a metropolis possible from its earliest days. However, the idyll of green hilly banks, Ottoman parks and gardens,

2 Topkapı Palace

At the tip of the peninsula separating the Golden Horn from the Sea of Marmara, the conqueror of Christian Byzantium, Sultan Mehmed II (reigned 1451–81), ordered the Topkapı Palace to be built as his main residence. In English the name means "cannon gate," on account of the guns that safeguarded the port. Due to its location above the sea, its elegant pavilions and rich gardens, its jewels, and historical tales of harem life and sultanate power struggles, the palace remains the embodiment of Ottoman splendor, greatness, and political machinations.

3 Princes' Islands

Residents of Istanbul only need to make a short journey by boat across the Sea of Marmara to find peaceful refuge in nature. The Princes' Islands are dotted with villas, pine groves, bays overlooked by cliffs, and traditional wooden houses. Furthermore there are no noisy car horns here, only the clatter of hooves and the gentle rolling of carriage

and summer palaces are a thing of the past. Due to the sheer amount of growth, the banks of the Bosporus have been increasingly subject to land speculation and construction. However, architectural and museum highlights such as the luxurious Dolmabahçe Palace, tea gardens, and restaurant terraces still attract visitors, and a short trip on the Bosporus remains delightful.

5 *Bosporus Bridges* ↓

The Bosporus has been connecting the European bank with the Asian bank since 1973, when the first Bosporus bridge, constructed to a height of 64 m (210 ft) above the water level, allowed ships to pass beneath it. The increased amount of motor traffic, however, meant that a second bridge, the Fatih Sultan Mehmet Bridge, had to be built. One of its pillars was built on the European bank, close to the Ottoman castle of Rumeli Hisari dating from 1452, also known as the Fortress of Europe. Istanbul is currently waiting for a tunnel to be built under the Bosporus in the next few decades.

① Acropolis ↓

The temple district, which developed after 480 BC on the ruins of the city castle destroyed by the Persians, is the most important example of Classical art. The Parthenon, the largest temple of its kind in Greece, was built around 447 BC as a temple to Athena, with 46 Doric marble pillars. Also in the temple district and dating from the same century are the Propylaea, the entrance gate to the Acropolis; the Ionic Temple of Athena Nike; and the Erechtheum, a combination of temples to Athena, Poseidon, and the fabled King Erechtheus. The clearly visible half-circle of the Theater of Herodes Atticus and the Theater of Dionysus, in which the tragedies of Aeschylus, Euripides, and Sophocles were performed, are located on the southern slope of the Acropolis.

Athens

The cityscape of the Greek capital is characterized by two hills—the Acropolis and the Lykavittós Hill, shown on the upper right-hand edge of the image—rising above a mass of buildings. Athens is the cradle of classic European culture and had its heyday in the 4th and 5th centuries BC, when artists such as Pheidias created the Classical style of architecture and sculpture, writers Aeschylus and Sophocles invented Greek tragedy, and Socrates, Plato, and Aristotle founded their schools of philosophy. Classical art is omnipresent in the metropolis, but the city is also very much a thriving modern capital. Since more than one-third of all Greeks—almost four million people—live in the conurbation of Athens, the capital has to fight constantly against noise, dirt, traffic congestion, and smog.

② Agora

The Agora, a market square and the center of ancient Athens, was located to the north-west of the Acropolis. This was not only a trading area, but also the political heart of Athens *(polis)* and a gathering place for important announcements. Here, Socrates explained his philosophical theories, public debates were held, and laws were promulgated. The most well-maintained building from the ancient Agora is the Hephaesteum, built around 440 BC—a Doric temple whose frieze depicts the deeds of Theseus and Heracles. The 116 m (380 ft) long Stoa of Attalos, a wonderfully restored ancient building, once served as a market hall for the bourgeoisie, but now houses a museum displaying ancient finds from the site.

③ Kerameikos

Kerameikos is an archeologist's dream. Situated to the northwest of the Acropolis, it was used as a cemetery for 16 centuries by rich Athenian families. As a result of excavations carried out in the 1900s, a wealth of gravestones from as far back as 1200 BC to 400 AD was revealed. These finds facilitated an excellent reconstruction of the

cult of the dead practiced in Athenian society in what is now known as the Street of Tombs. Here, commemorative stones (stelae), particularly from the 4th century, can be admired.

④ Pláka

To the north of the Acropolis and to the west of the National Gardens extends the maze of houses and alleyways that constitute the Pláka region, Athens's "Old Town." It is not only the epitome of tourism-related hustle and bustle, with good-value restaurants and traditional music bars, all purporting to display Greek folk culture, but also a residential area for many Athenian citizens. Step down any of the side alleys, however, and you're likely to escape the hurly-burly and find quiet corners and squares with small churches and Classical buildings.

⑤ Vouli and Syntagma

After Greek independence in 1822, the National Assembly elected Otto of Wittelsbach, the son of Ludwig I of Bavaria, as king of Greece in 1832. From 1832–8, King Otto had his palace built by Friedrich von Gärtner, masterbuilder to the court, and it remained the royal residence until 1924, when a referendum abolished the monarchy. Since 1926 it has been used as the seat of the Greek parliament (Vouli). Syntagma Square, situated in front of the parliament and home to the Tomb of the Unknown Soldier, is patrolled by the National Guard dressed in their traditional white skirts and red pompoms. The square is adjoined to the south by the National Gardens, the "green lung" of the city and the favorite place of refuge for stressed city dwellers in the hot summer months. A Botanical Museum is also located in the gardens.

⑥ Kallimarmaron Stadium

When the first modern Olympic Games were held in 1896 there was no discussion con-

cerning where the games were to be held—their natural home was, of course, Greece. Sponsors were quickly found, including a rich Athenian who had a 70,000-seat marble replica of the ancient Olympic Stadium built exactly in the place where the original arena once stood.

⑦ Temple of the Olympian Zeus ↓

The Temple of the Olympian Zeus is the largest temple in Greece. Covering a basic land area of 107 by 41 m (351 by 135 ft), its roof was held aloft by 104 Corinthian pillars, which were 17 m (56 ft) high and had a base diameter of 1.7 m (5.5 ft). Today, only 15 of these pillars, which taper upward, still remain. Building work began on the temple as early as the 6th century BC, but was only completed under Emperor Hadrian (AD 117–38) and officially opened in AD 131–2. Hadrian's Arch rose close to the temple, a triumphal structure of which parts still remain. It marked the transition from the old town of Athens to what became known as Hadrian's city, the Roman "new town."

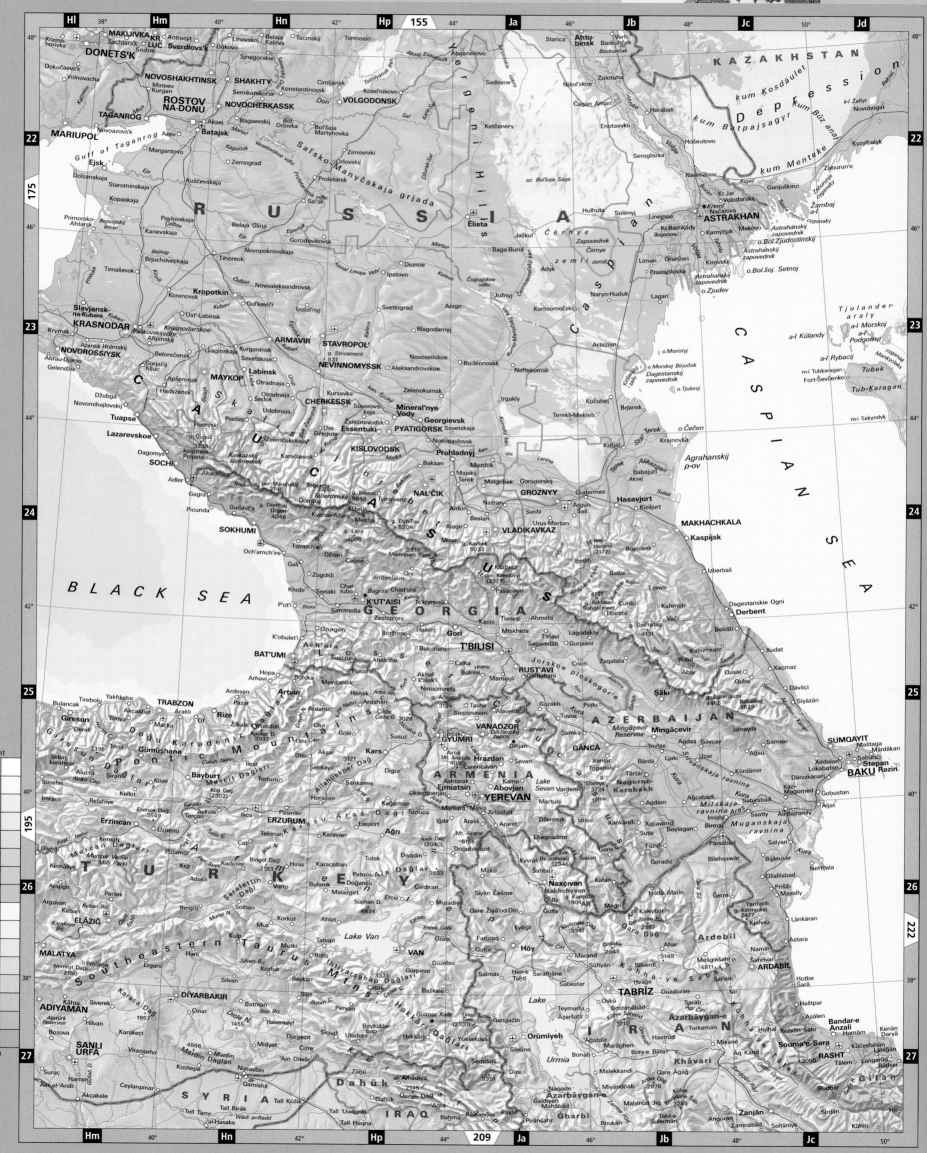

KAZAKHSTAN

kum Kosdäulet *De pre ss io n*
kum Batpajsagyr *kum Büz aral*
kum Menteke

MAKIJIVKA
KR
Sverdlovs'k
DONETS'K
NOVOSHAKHTINSK
SHAKHTY
ROSTOV NA-DONU
NOVOCHERKASSK
TAGANROG
MARIUPOL
Gulf of Taganrog
Azov
Batajsk

R U S S I A N

VOLGODONSK

ASTRAKHAN

KRASNODAR
NOVOROSSIYSK

STAVROPOL'
NEVINNOMYSSK
MAYKOP
CHERKESSK
Mineral'nye Vody
Georgievsk
PYATIGORSK
Essentuki
KISLOVODSK
TUAPSE
SOCHI

C
A
U
C
A
S
U
S

NAL'ČIK
GROZNYY
VLADIKAVKAZ
Hasavjurt
MAKHACHKALA
Kaspijsk

SOKHUMI

B L A C K   S E A

C A S P I A N   S E A

Derbent

K'UT'AISI
G E O R G I A
BAT'UMI
Gori
T'BILISI
RUSTAVI

TRABZON
Giresun
Rize
Artvin

VANADZOR
GYUMRI
Hrazdan
A R M E N I A
Ejmiatsin Abovjan
YEREVAN

AZERBAIJAN
GANCA
Mingačevir Reservoir
Nagorno-Karabakh
SUMQAYIT
BAKU

ERZINCAN
ERZURUM
Kars
Ağrı
Mt. Ararat
Naxçıvan
Nakhchyvan
T U R K E Y
Lake Van
VAN
TABRÎZ
I R A N
ARDABÎL

MALATYA
ELÂZIĞ
DİYARBAKIR
ADIYAMAN
ŞANLI URFA

S Y R I A
I R A Q
RASHT

Height
m
3000
2000
1000
600
300
100
0
< 0
200
1000
2000
4000
6000
8000
10000
m
Depth

1:4,500,000
Albers Equal Area Conic Projection

0   25   50   75   100   125 miles
0   50   100   150   200 km

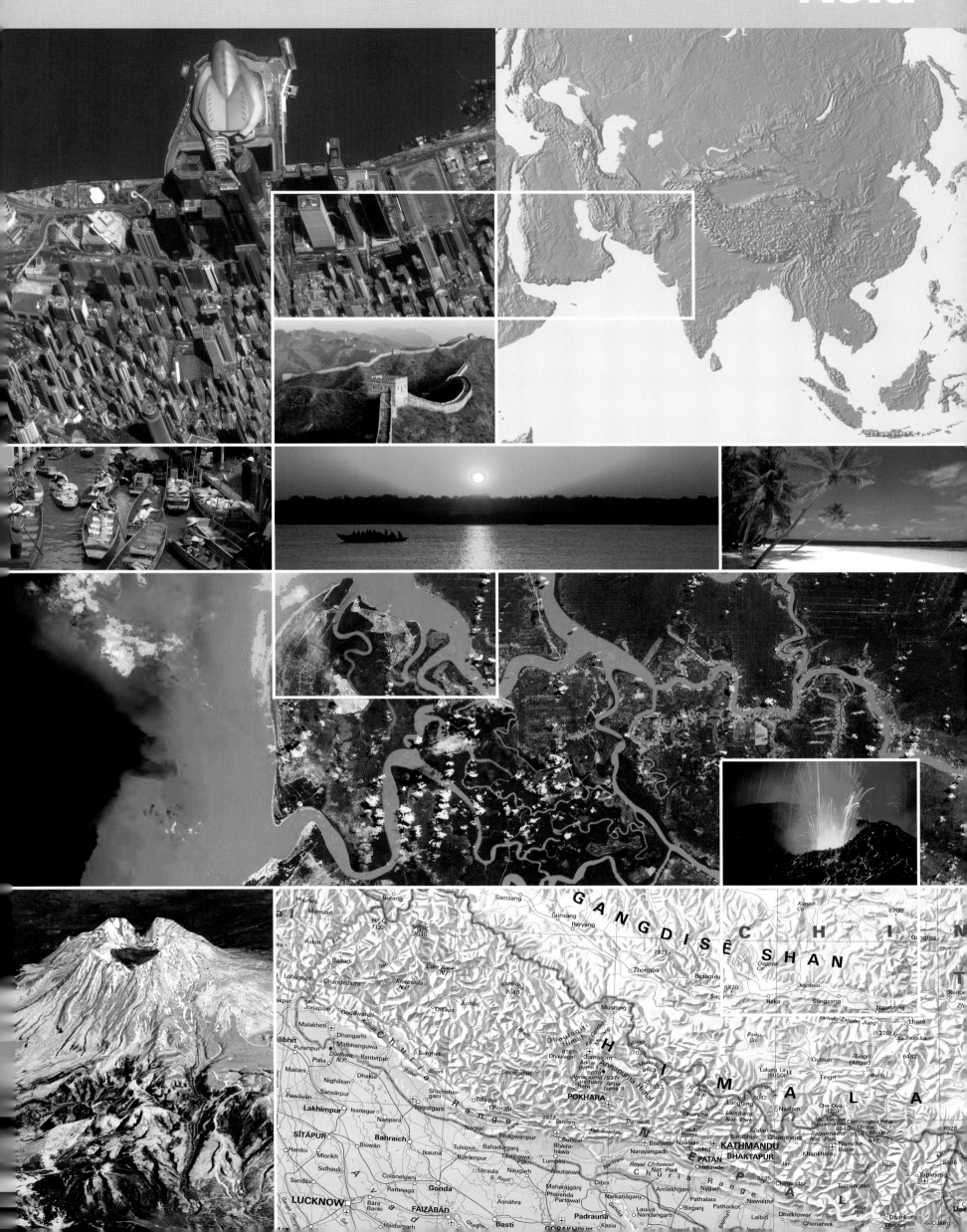

Northern Asia

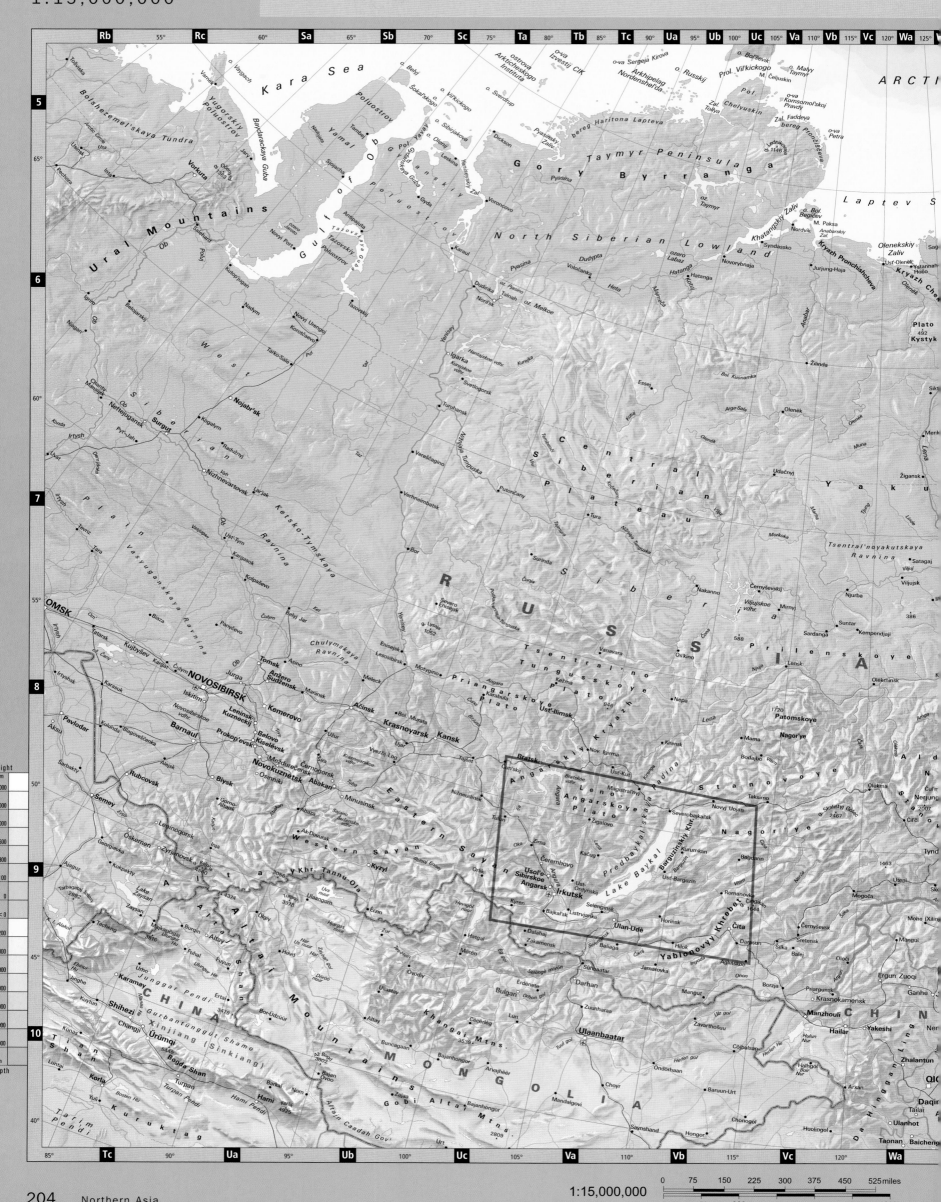

1:15,000,000

| 0 | 75 | 150 | 225 | 300 | 375 | 450 | 525 miles |

| 0 | 150 | 300 | 450 | 600 | 750 | 1000 km |

Stereographic Projection

Height
m
3000
2000
1000
600
300
100
0
<0
200
1000
2000
4000
6000
8000
10000
m
Depth

| | | | | | | | | | | | | | |
|Xa 140°|Xb 145°|Xc 150°|Ya 155°|Yb 160°|Yc 165°|Za 170°|Zb 175°|Zc 180°|Aa 175°|Ab 170°|Ac 65°|

EAN

New Siberian Islands

ostrova de-Longa

Anjou Islands

o. Bennetta

o. Žohova

ostrov Faddeevskij

Blagoveshchenskiy Prol.

New Siberia

el'kovskij

ostrov Kotel'nyj

Zemlja Bunge

o. Stolbovoj

Proliv Sannikova

o. Mal. Ljahovskij

Ljahovskie ostrova

o. Bol. Ljahovskij

Prol. Dmitriya Lapteva

M. Svjatoj Nos 394

oz. Bustah

M. Buor-Haja

Yanskiy Zaliv

uba

Khaya

Haiyr

Yano-Indigirskaya Nizmennost

Ust-Jansk

Ust-Kuiga

Kryazh Poulousnyy

Depyatskij

Topolovo

oz. Mogotoevo

Poljarnyj

Verhojansk

Yana

Batagaj

Džargalah

Arctic Circle

Khrebet Kular

Indigirka

Kolymskaya Guba

Longašinko

Alazeja

Medvežka

Medvež'i o-va

East Siberian Sea

Ayon

Ayon

Chaunskaja Guba

Pevek

Wrangel Island

zal. Krasn

Proliv Longa

m. Billingsa

Šelagskij

Leningradskij

Vaukarem

Arctic Circle

Chukchi Peninsula

Cape Dezhneva

Naukan

Prince of Wales

King I.

Bering Strait

Enurmino

Uelen

6

Čerskij

Nižne-kolymsk

Krestovkj

Ryēuš

Pljavaam

Tromsaboro

Pevek

Polavnyj

Ilirneyskiy Kryazh

Amguēma

Egvekinot

Eqvekinot

Ermelen

Nunligran

Providenija

St. Lawrence (U.S.A.)

Gambell

Savoonga

Batamaj

Druzina

Arpahtan

Mal. Anjuj

Bilibino

Stadunho

Anyuyskiy Khrebet

Kurinskiy Kryazh

Mandrikovo

Bol. Anjuj

Omolon

Anadyrskaya Nizmennost'

Šmidt

Mejnypil'gyno

m. Navarin

60°

Hatyngnah

Kolyma

Lobaj

Oloyskiy Khrebet

Oloj

Olonna

Uelkal

Kanchalan

Krasnoe

m. Geka

Upēr'ye Koř.

Hatyrka

Khrebet Ush.-Urekchen

Penžina

Ananka

Gulf of Anadyr

Alazeyskoye Ploskogor'ye

Ožogina

Bulun

Korkodon

Omolon

Pēnžina

Golaja 1437

Anadyr

Everek

Ledvanaja 2001

Momskiy Khr.

Honuu

Moma

Zyrjanka

Omsukchanskiy Khr.

Ichigemskiy Khrebet

Oklanskoe plato

Manily

Kamenskoe

Korvakskoye Nagor'ye

1853

Pobeda 3147

Predporožnyj

Ust-Nera

Sejmčan

Omsukčan

Talovka

Oklan

Taygonos

Avekova Pol.

Pachach

Koř.

7

Oymyakonskoye Nagor'ye

Artyk

Kujdusun

Mus-Hala 2959

Topolinde

Susuman

Ototukan

1964

Penžinskiy Khr.

Talovka

Koř.

Kor.

Olyutorskiy Zaliv

m. Olyutorskij

Bering Sea

Khrebet Suntar Khayata

Kulu

2688

Ust-Omēug

Shelikhov Gulf

Gižiginskaya Guba

Pol.

Palana

o. Karaginskiy

Karaginskiy

Kamchatka Basin

55°

Namcy

Aldan

Teplyj Ključ

Handyga

Yakutsk

Čurapča

Amga

Ust-Maja

Utahan-Bom

Kemkara

m. Ènkèn

Ohotsk

Yamskaya Guba

Yama

Talon

Pol. Pyagina

Magadan

Yamskaya Guba

Pol. Pyagina

Sokol

Zaliv

o. Beringa

o. Mednyi

Komandorskije ostrova (RUS)

Attu I.

8

Kutana

Maja

1900

Ulinskiy Khr.

Pribrezhnyj Khr.

Khrebet Dzhugdzhur

2243

Chofa

Pol. Lisyanskogo

Tauyskaya Guba

Sea of Okhotsk

Kronotskaya

Atlasovo

Ključi 4750

Ust-Kamchatsk

Kamchatskiy Zaliv

Petropavlovsk-Kamchatskiy

3621

Kronotskiy Zaliv

50°

Kutana

Handyga

Šimanovsk

Svobodnyj

Belogorsk

Blagoveshchensk

Zavitinsk

Bureinskiy Khrebet

2167

Čegdomyn

Bureinskoe vdhr.

Amgun

Nikolaevsk-na-Amure

Lazarev

Sahalinskiy Zal.

Bol. Šantar

m. Aleksandra

Šantarskie o-va

Udskaya Guba

Tugur

Čumikan

Uda

2384

Akademii Zal.

Sakhalinskiy Zal.

Oha

m. Elizavety

Atlasova

Ojtjabr'skij

2476

m. Lopatka

o. Šumšu

o. Paramušir

9

O'lginsk

Fevral'sk

Duki

Sofijsk

Komsomol'sk-na-Amure

Amursk

Nogliki

Tymovskoe

Aleksandrovsk-Sahalinskij

1609

Lopatino

o. Onekotan

o. Šiaškotan

Kuril Basin

45°

Birofel'd

Birofel'd

Birakan

Obluč'e

Tyrma

Fuyuan

Khabarovsk

Vjazemskij

Slavjanka

Sovetskaya Gavan

Sihote Alin

Sahalin

Sahalin

Tatarskiy proliv

Poronajsk

Uglegorsk

Zaliv Terpenija

mys Terpenija

o-va Černye Brat'ja

o. Ketoj

o. Simušir

1840

Kuril Islands (RUS)

Kuril Trench

PACIFIC OCEAN

Leninskoe

Puzino

Tēli

Yichun

Hegang

Fujin

Shuanyashan

Raohe

Bikin

Bikin

Dal'nerečensk

Samarga

Holmsk

Yuzhno-Sakhalinsk

Korsakov

Nevel'sk

mys Aniva

Zaliv Aniva

o. Monaron

La Pérouse Strait

Wakkanai

o. Urup

o-va Černye

Kuril'sk

o. Urup

Kunašir

o. Iturup

10

ARBIN

Qitaihe

Jiamusi

Jixi

Vostok

Rebun-tō

Rishiri-tō

Shiretoko (hinto)

o. Kunašir

Lake Baykal

Lake Baykal, close to the Russian-Mongolian border in southern Siberia, is both the deepest and the most voluminous lake in the world. Protected by UNESCO as a World Natural Heritage Site since 1996, the lake has a length of 636 km (395 miles), a maximum breadth of 80 km (50 miles), and an average depth of 730 m (2395 ft). It is thought to have been created between 20 and 25 million years ago in the form of a rift valley combining one-fifth of the world's freshwater supply. The northern part of Lake Baykal is often frozen for eight months of the year, whereas the southern part is frozen for only three months a year. The shores of the lake are covered with a wide variety of landscapes and most of the area is still a wilderness.

N

1 *Lake Fauna* ←

Hundreds of indigenous species live in the lake, including the salmon-like omul and the golomyanka, an almost transparent, scaleless fish with no air-bladder. The best-known creature is the Baykal seal, although fish and seal numbers have fallen markedly in the southern part of Lake Baykal. The main cause of this is the discharge from paper and cellulose plants where production methods dating from the Soviet Union are still being used.

2 Angara River

Hydroelectric power stations and dams have brought the 1850 km (1149 mile) long single outlet of Lake Baykal and tributary of the Yenisey River under control.

3 Irkutsk

As early as the 17th century this industrial town was an assembly point for people seeking their luck and fortune in Siberia. The capital of East Siberia has churches and museums that explain the area's history and it is also a university town.

4 Bratsk and the Bratsk Dam

Bratsk is located on the Baykal Amur Magistrale (BAM), south of the Trans-Siberian Railroad. It has made possible the exploitation of the southern part of East Siberia, which is rich in mineral resources. The main sight in the industrial town is the 557 km (346 mile) long dam, the building of which destroyed numerous settlements along the Angara River.

5 River Lena

The 4300 km (2672 mile) long river has its source close to the lake and flows into the Arctic Ocean. The River Lena is one of the most important traffic routes in the rough landscape of East Siberia.

6 Olchon

The largest of the 30 islands in Lake Baykal is inhabited by a Mongolian tribe known as the Buryat and is covered by forests and steppes. The deepest point of Lake Baykal, at 1637 m (5370 ft), is located close to the island.

7 Selenga

The most important of the 336 tributaries of Lake Baykal is 1024 km (636 miles) long.

MAP

1 : 4,500,000

Middle East

1:4,500,000

Albers Equal Area Conic Projection

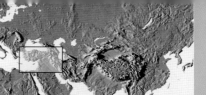

1 Satellite Image: Ararat

2 Satellite Image: Karbala

1 Ararat Mountains

Christians have traditionally regarded Mount Ararat as a holy mountain because of its relevance to Noah's Ark. However, in the Bible, at the end of the great flood, it says that the ark "…rested upon the mountains of Ararat" (Genesis, Chapter 8). It can therefore be argued that the ark landed in the Biblical land of Ararat, now called Urartu, and not on the actual mountain summit itself. In the first millennium before Christ the region extended as far as present-day Armenia, but even at that time all endeavors to find remnants of the ark on Ararat were fruitless.

2 İshak Paşa Sarayı

This fortress, built around 1700 in a deep gorge at the foot of the Ararat Mountains, was one of the most beautiful Oriental palaces in Turkey. It was built so that its lords could take road tolls from the bands of caravans that traveled the route here. The fortress offers a fantastic view of Little Ararat, while the renovated architecture with the relief decor featuring entwined leaves is magnificent. The people who built the fortress, which once allegedly contained 366 rooms, were the Cıldıroğlus, who were of Georgian, Armenian, and Kurdish origin.

3 Doğubayazıt →

For the numerous long-distance truck drivers, as well as adventurous mountain climbers and, un-doubtedly, smugglers, Doğubayazıt is the last stop in Turkey, located close to the borders of Iran and

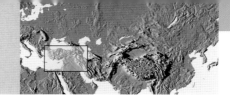

Ararat

The highest mountain in Turkey is a dormant volcano that towers in Eastern Anatolia, the region that forms a border between Turkey, Armenia, and Iran. At a height of 5165 m (16,945 ft), the summit, which is covered in glacial ice, is around 300 m (984 ft) higher than Mont Blanc in the Alps. The imposing massif also includes the 3896 m (12,782 ft) high Little Ararat, which is also volcanic in origin, as well as remnants of huge lava streams that extend along the saddle between both peaks. These lava streams bear witness to the last time the volcano erupted, in 1840, destroying an Armenian Dominican monastery and a village. Despite the severe climate, with very snowy winters and temperatures as low as -43°C (-45.4°F), followed by summer heat as high as 38°C (100.4°F), shepherds live on the slopes and on the dry steppe, as far down as the foot of the mountains. The bottom half of their houses are built into the ground like ramparts, for protection against the unfavorable climatic conditions.

Black Sea and the Caspian Sea. To the southeast of Kars in Turkey and to the west of Yerevan in Armenia, the Araks (known in Persian as Rud-e Aras, in Russian as Araks, and in ancient times as Araxes) takes up the smaller Ahurjan and becomes the river forming the border for around 600 km (373 miles). Only close to the Caspian Sea does it flow into the Kura River. Although the Araks is not navigable it is important for agriculture, in particular in the areas to the north and northwest of the Ararat massif. The course of the river, which meanders in certain points, can clearly be made out on the northern sides of the image.

⑤ *Ararat Summit ↑*
The main peak of Mount Ararat, which is 5165 m (16,945 ft) high and covered in an icecap, rises from the eastern, beautifully shaped 3896 m (12,782 ft) high Küçük Ağrı Dağı (Little Ararat). Scientists were the earliest to chronicle their ascent to the summit of Ararat, the first being a French botanist, Joseph Pitton de Tournefort, who climbed the mountain in 1707. More than 100 years later, in 1829, he was followed by the doctor and physicist Dr. Johann Jakob Parrot, from Karlsruhe in Germany, who worked as a professor in Dorpat and was accompanied by a Russian astronomer. Today Mount Ararat is popular with recreational mountain climbers, particularly in the most favorable months of July, August, and September. Every year several thousand people undertake the four- to five-day climb up and down the mountain. The first base camp is located at a

height of about 2800 m (9183 ft), up to which point the climb is one long walk for those with some experience and good fitness levels. The second base camp, however, from which guides set out with their groups before sunrise, is at a height of 4200 m (13,779 ft), and the thinner air requires acclimatization. Knowledge of how to use crampons and icepicks is also required to reach the summit.

⑥ Saz Gölü and Seynlı Gölü
The swampy lakes located in the southwest of the Ararat Mountains are of interest to biologists, especially ornithologists, who have found the breeding grounds of many rare species here, such as the citrine wagtail.

Armenia. This "passing through" atmosphere is reflected in the poverty of the people and the ugliness of the city, laid out at a height of 1700 m (5577 ft). Doğubayazıt has actually only existed since the 1930s: At that time, old Bayazıt, which directly neighbors İshak Paşa Sarayı, was destroyed by artillery fire during a military campaign against insurgent Kurds, and a settlement was built 7 km (4 miles) farther on. On a mountain ledge above the plain, criss-crossed by herds of sheep, there are remnants of a castle founded by the Urartu people, which was later developed by the Islamic Seldshuks. The town itself may not be pretty, but it does have magnificent views of both summits in the Ararat mountain range, with a difference in height of around 4000 m (13,123 ft).

Due to the broad plains, with its swamps and lakes, parts of which are silted up and which extend across the area, this mountainous panorama looks all the more impressive and, when the view is clear, is doubtless one of the highlights of a trip through Anatolia.

④ Araks River
When the 1072 km (666 mile) long Araks River flows around the Ararat Mountains, it has already been flowing for hundreds of kilometers from its source high in the Bingöl Dağları ("Mountains of a Thousand Lakes") to the south of Erzurum. This is where the watershed extends between the Firat Nehri (Euphrates), which flows into the Persian Gulf, and the rivers that flow into the

Karbala

Since the death of Mohammed, Islam has been split into the Sunni and Shiah faiths. In the city of Karbala, located 100 km (60 miles) southwest of Baghdad, this bloody split began in 632, according to the Christian calendar, when a close friend of the prophet Mohammed—and not his grandson, Hussein—was elected as caliph. The Shiite movement requested that one of Mohammed's descendants be their leader, but in 680, in the Battle of Karbala, all of Mohammed's direct male descendants were killed. About 10 percent of all Muslims in the world, and about 65 percent of all Iraqis, are Shiites. However, they have never reached an agreement over who is the rightful successor.

1 *Mausolea of the Imam Hussein and of his Brother Abbas* ←

The magnificent tomb of the third Shiite Imam, Hussein, and of his grandfather, Mohammed, is embellished with a golden cupola and two minarets. At the end of Moharran, the month of mourning, their deaths are remembered here during ritual processions. The tomb of Abbas is also the subject of much worship. Abbas was the brother and advisor of Hussein and was laid to rest close to Hussein's tomb in a similarly ostentatious manner. When Saddam Hussein ruled Iraq, mass pilgrimages to Karbala were prohibited, but in 2004, after he was deposed, about one million people took part in the pilgrimage. Sadly it was overshadowed by a massive bomb attack in which hundreds of pilgrims were killed.

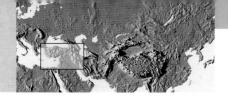

2 **Karbala al-Qadimah**

A Christian cemetery is said to be located beneath the holy, old town district of Karbala al-Qadimah. In order to expand the city, parts of the historic city walls were pulled down from 1868 onward, but in the north the beginning of the route the walls once took can still be seen in the form of an "indentation."

3 **Surrounding Countryside**

A city of 300,000 inhabitants is located around 50 km (30 miles) to the southeast of Baghdad, on the banks of the Husainiya desert river, which flows into the Euphrates. The city extends farther and farther into the wooded surrounding countryside in a northerly and easterly direction. Important branches of industry located in the south of what was once Mesopotamia are oasis cultures and tobacco growing.

4 **Karbala al-Jadid**

According to the Shiah faith, all believers who die in the holy city of Karbala go to heaven. This is why there are so many cemeteries and religious libraries, at least 100 Islamic schools (madrassahs), and just as many mosques in Karbala, some of which are located in the new districts of the city (al-Jadid means "new city").

5 **Desert**

The Syrian-Arabian Desert begins just to the west of Karbala and is a high steppe-like and desert-like chalky limestone plateau with few sandy areas, extending to Syria, Jordan, and the north of Saudi Arabia. Important roads and pipelines traverse the inhospitable region, which is mainly inhabited by nomads. It is drained as far as the Euphrates by wadis, some of which are 400 km (248 miles) long. These are dry river beds that contain water only during times of heavy rainfall. The salt lake of Bahr al-Minh is located to the northwest of Karbala and, with a total area of around 1000 km^2 (386 square miles), it is the third-largest stretch of inland water in the country.

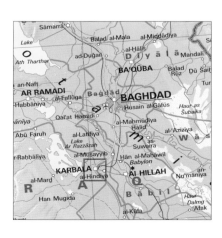

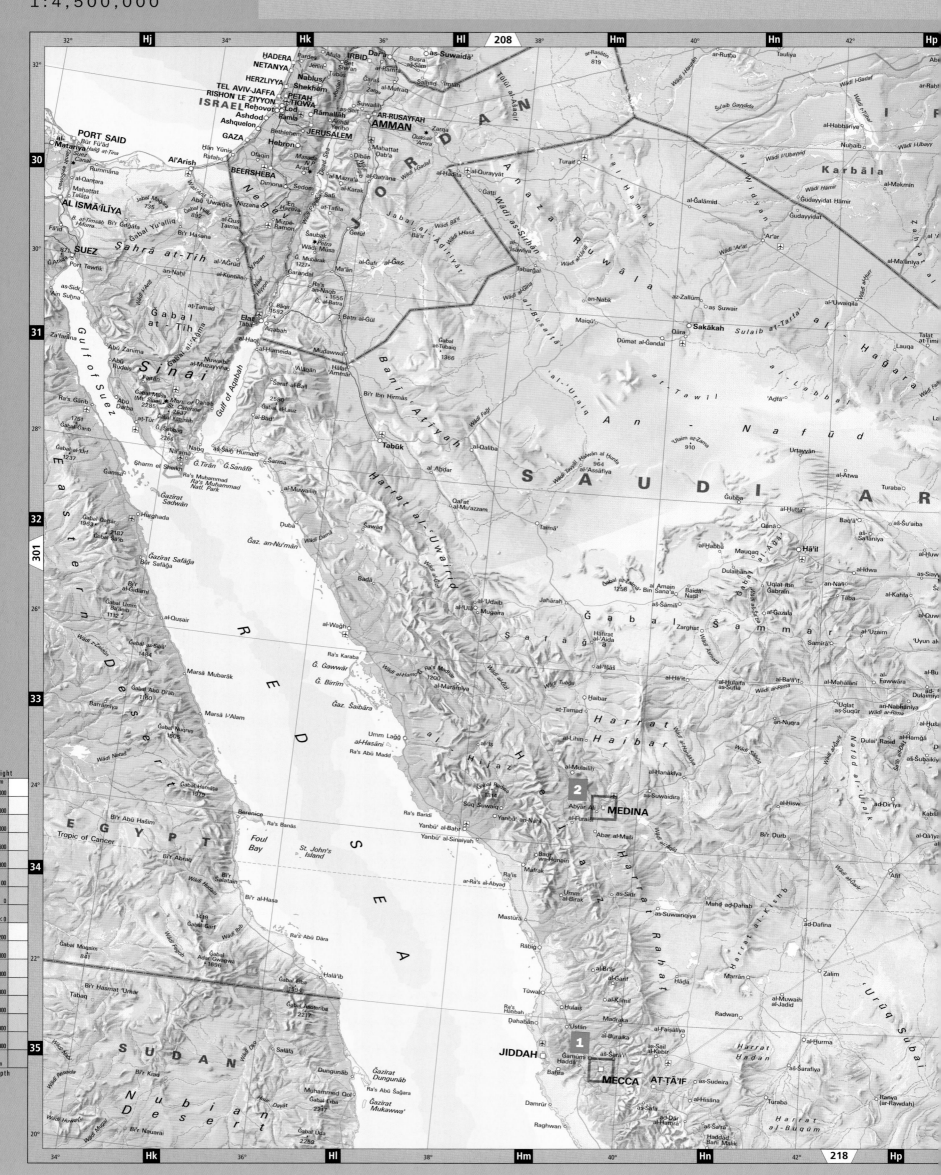

1:4,500,000

Albers Equal Area Conic Projection

Ja   46°   Jb   48°   Jc 209   50°   Jd   52°   Je   54°   Jf

29
32°
30
30°
31
28°
226
32
33
26°
34
24°
35
22°

Mecca

The Saudi Arabian city of Mecca, which has a population of two million, is the religious center of the Islamic world. It owes its significance to a stipulation in the Koran, which calls on all believers to make the pilgrimage (known as the hajj) to the holy sites of the prophet Mohammed at least once in their life, on the condition that they can afford it and that they are healthy enough to undertake it. Since there are more than one billion Muslims in the world today, and with the advance in air travel as well as land routes, this means that around four million pilgrims currently visit Mecca every year.

1 **Great Mosque**

The Saudi government published its plans for a necessary extension to the Great Mosque as early as 1955 and, after decades of work, the space covered by the mosque has now grown to 160,000 m² (1,722,225 square ft). This is mainly the result of the construction of a second ring of colonnades around the first ring from the era of the Abbasids and Ottomans. This new ring of colonnades has two storys, which is why the Kaaba looks as if it has sunk into a big pit.

2 **Kaaba** ←

The stone building covered in black encircles an empty, 15 m (49 ft) high, windowless room, while the base is 12 by 10 m (39 by 33 ft) in size. The roof is supported by three wooden pillars. The building is the most sacred in Islam and the direction in which Muslims pray is the direction from any point to the Kaaba. Long before Islam was established, the Kaaba was the destination for pilgrims from the desert tribes and it contained Bedouin idols. A holy meteorite (hajar) is fixed into the southeastern corner of the wall.

3 **The "Saỳ" Rite**

After the pilgrims have walked around the Kaaba, they climb up to Safa Hill and cross the valley to Marwa Hill. The route looks like a hall today, with a broad roof, and is divided up into four lanes. The outer broader lanes are for pedestrians walking in both directions, while the inner narrower lanes are for people in wheelchairs. The faithful must walk back and forth seven times. The rite recalls the Biblical story of the maid Hagar, who bore a son Ishmael to Abraham, and was cast out at the request of Abraham's wife Sarah. She wandered the desert in search of water for the child and found the fountain of Zamzam with the help of the Angel Gabriel.

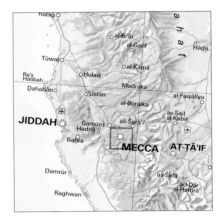

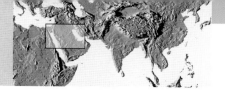

1 Old Town

A generation ago, as those who knew Medina remember, the city "was like a big garden with majestic palms lining houses and market-places, which created an impression of richness and wealth" (Seyyed Hossein Nasr). A large part of the old town, however, was torn down to create space for the enlarged mosque area and the oval ring of the roads leading to it. The whole complex of buildings now covers an area of around 247,500 m² (2,644,068 square ft).

2 *Great Mosque* ↘

The regularly ordered cupolas above the halls of the greatly enlarged mosque area can clearly be seen on the image. A closer look reveals the six uniform minarets on the corners and above the main gate. Pilgrims pray here under the open sky, as seen in the image, upon a richly ornamented, bright marble floor. Since the time of the hajj (pilgrimage) changes according to the lunar year, and because the weather can be extremely hot when it takes place, air-conditioning systems were installed in the building, which was enlarged in 1995. The Great Mosque (located in the center of the complex of mosques) still has Ottoman characteristics and two tower-sized and two smaller minarets.

The prophet's mosque (pictured), surrounding the tomb of the prophet, is one of three holy Muslim mosques (the other two are located in Jerusalem and in Mecca) that the prophet Mohammed and his companions are said to have touched with their hands when they were being built. There is room for 300,000 pilgrims to pray in the Great Mosque at any one time.

Medina

Mohammed's sojourn in the oasis city of Medina in around 622–32, the last decade of his life, was his most successful ten years from a religious and political point of view, and today the tomb of the prophet here makes Medina the second most important place of pilgrimage for Muslims. The green cupola above his tomb also crowns the Great Mosque (originally built in 707–9) and is the symbol of Medina. Today, more than half a million people live in Medina. As in Mecca, non-Muslims are not permitted to enter the city and the roads are laid in such a way that they cannot see the holy sites.

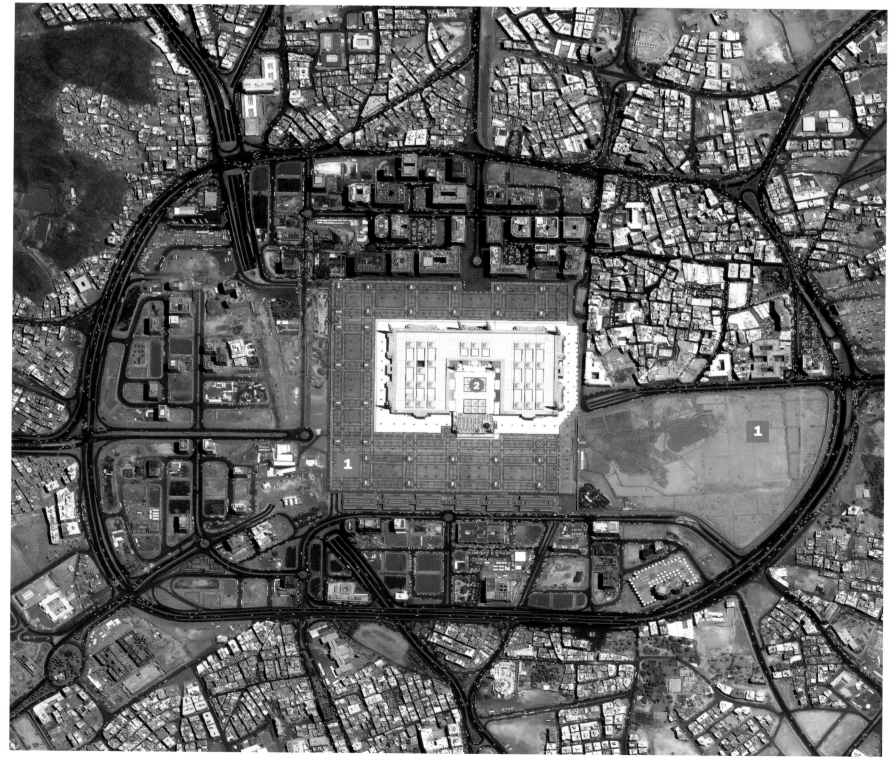

Arabian Peninsula

Height	
m	
3000	
2000	
1000	
600	
300	
100	
0	
<0	
200	
1000	
2000	
4000	
6000	
8000	
10000	
m	
Depth	

1:4,500,000

| 0 | 25 | 50 | 75 | 100 | 125 miles |
| 0 | 50 | 100 | 150 | 200 km |

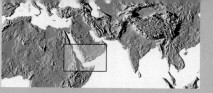

Jc 50° Jd **215** 52° Je 54° Jf 56° Jg **226** 58° Jh

as-Sanām

al-Mahākik

al-Mihrād

al-Kidan

Wādi al-'Ayn

al-Aswad

Natih

Nuhaida

Adam

al-Musallā

Ramlat
al-Wahiba

22°

al-Ubaila

O M A N

Al Huwaysah

W. Musallim

Ghaba

Wādi Andam

'Urūq

Hibāka

Ramlat al-Gāfa

Umm as
Samin

35

al-Hibāk

al-Hibāk

al-Urūq al-Mu'tarida

73

20°

Ghaba

al-Huqf

al-Watā

Sirāb

Filim

al-Kalbān

Ra's Abū Rasās

Masıra Channel

Gulf of
Masira

Ad Dikāka

Haimā'

Ĝiddat al-Harāsīs

al-Agā'iz

Duqm

36

Muqšin

Wādi Muqšin

Ra's Madrakah

miyāt

Fasad

Wādi Atina

Dauka

W. Ghadūn

al-Khalil

Sawqirah
Bay

18°

as-Sišar

as-Šisar

Šalim

Wādi Rikat

Sauquira

Marmul

220

Ra's Šarbitāt

Qafa

as-Šuwaimiya

Gulf of
as-Saudā'

al-Hallānīyāt

37

Sanāw

Makinat
Sihan

Dho.

419

Ĝaza'ir Huriyā Muriyā
(al-Hallānīyāt)

hfri

Tamūd

Habarūt

Dhofar (Zufār)

Mudayy

Burg

Tamarit

Ĝal-Qarā

Hadbaram

Hallānīyāt

Wādi Hidā

Sārif

ad-Dibin

Ĝal-Qamar

Qahnin

1463

Ĝebel Simhān

Mirbāt

Sadh

Raisūt

Salalah

SALĀLAH

Mughsail

Tāqa

Wādai Mauba

Wādi al-'Ūz

al-Gaida

al-Mahra

Ardin

Jadib

Ra's Sāgir

al-Faidami

Garūb

16°

Fāghmah

Tarim

Sana

Wadi Hadramaut

Wādi Qargarat

Zabūt

Ništūn

Ra's Fartak

38

Sūna

Marahayy

Maqrat

Saqr

Qišn

al-Gail

Saihūt

Ra's Šarwan

al-Ouza

Al Quaiti

Tamnūn

Sarār

14°

al-Gaida

al-Hāmi

as-Suhair

Al Mukallā

Burum

Zulūma

I N D I A N

O C E A N

39

Aden

12°

Qalansiya

Hadibū

Qadub

Ra's Mami

Ra's Šu'b

Gebel al-Ghir

Sigira

Aden

'Abd al-Kūri

The Brothers

Socotra
(YEMEN)

Samhah

Darsah

Raas Caluula

40

Caluula

Bereeda

Raas Caseyr

Geesaley

Hooda

Bandar Murcaayo

Dhurbo

1402

togga Wayne

Raas Binna

Qandala

Ceel Gaal

Bargaal

Boosaaso

Karin

Cal Miskaat

togga Glael

10°

ilayo

Xanda

iwaco

togga Dhud

Ufeyn

Hurdiyo

Raas Xaafuun

Meeladeen

Jaceel

Xaafuun

Iskushuban

Gacanka
Xaafuun

Samaysa Dheer

41

Jc 50° Jd 52° Je 54° Jf 56° Jg

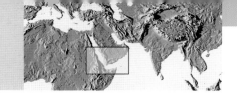

Hadramaut

The image shows the region of Hadramaut, located on the south coast of the Arabian Peninsula. The narrow coastal plain, whose main town is al Mukalla, is adjoined by the desert-like plateau of the Djol, which is criss-crossed by fertile valleys such as the Wadi Doan and the Wadi Hadramaut. Shibam and Tarim are the largest areas in the hinterland. Yemen was created in 1991 by the amalgamation of the Democratic People's Republic of Yemen (South Yemen) and the Yemen Arab Republic (North Yemen). Traditions and cities like those found in the *Thousand and One Nights* characterize the agrarian country, which remained almost untouched by the oil boom that changed its neighbors from the poorest into the richest countries on earth.

1 *Wadi Doan ↑*

Yemen is the only country on the Arabian Peninsula to have a small number of river valleys, which carry water all year round. However, toward the coast and the northeast the rocky plateaus of the highland are furrowed by dry valleys, which can be transformed into raging rivers with immense erosion power when downpours occur. Oases covered in acacias, date palms, and tamarisks are found in the steep-walled wadis and their alluvial chambers, located along the coast.

2 Ramlat al Sab'atayn

The desert located between Marib in the west and Shibām in the east forms the most southern end of the large Ar Rub 'al Khali sand desert, known as the "Empty Quarter." The Incense Road (see Shibām) ran between Marib and the Hadramaut oasis on the southern edge of the Ramlat.

3 Wadi Hadramaut

This is the second-largest river valley in Arabia after the Wadi Rum in Jordan. In the densely populated oasis valley, which is as much as 10 km (6 miles) wide, about 200 km (124 miles) long, and inhabited by around 200,000 people, cereals and dates are the main produce, cultivated by simple methods. From the 1st century BC until the Middle Ages, the valley, parts of which lie at a height of 2100 m (6890 ft), was an important area in terms of culture, with influential towns such as Shibām, Sayun, and Tarim.

4 Shibām

One of the important transregional caravan routes in pre-Christian southern Arabia was the Incense Road, which, in the image shown, ran from the coast, over the Ramlat as-Sab'atayn along the western side of the Arabian Peninsula, in the direction of Jordan and Egypt. The legendary kingdom of the Queen of Sheba owed its riches to the incense obtained from the resin of the Boswelia bush. Well-fortified, inhabited towers, with the typical geometrical outline, were built along the Incense Road, while the 500 clay and brick houses in the 2000-year-old town of Shibām, many of which lean against each other and which are as much as ten storys high, today still bear witness to this architectural style.

5 Tarim

In the old town of Tarim, located at the crossroads of old trade routes, there are many mosques and palaces whose facades and minarets also contain elements of Asian architectural styles. In the town's heyday there were 365 mosques and 300 Koran schools here.

6 Djol Plateau

The Djol Plateau, which is as high as 2185 m (7169 ft) in places, forms part of the Arabian Table. Steep-walled wadis up to 300 m (984 ft) deep are carved into this plateau. The largest is the Wadi Hadramaut.

7 Gulf of Aden

Africa and Arabia split apart from each other about five million years ago and today the Gulf of Aden, located on the south coast of the Arabian Peninsula and the Somali Peninsula, is part of a rift valley several thousand kilometers long. It is 2500 m (8202 ft) deep in parts and linked to the Red Sea via the Bab al Mandab Strait.

8 Al Mukallā

The capital of the province of Hadramaut is an important port and fishing center. With around 300,000 inhabitants, the city is the fourth-largest in the country. Qasr al-Ghuweizi is located on a rock shelf on the edge of the city; it was once a customs point on the road to the Wadi Hadramaut.

1:4,500,000

Albers Equal Area Conic Projection

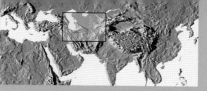

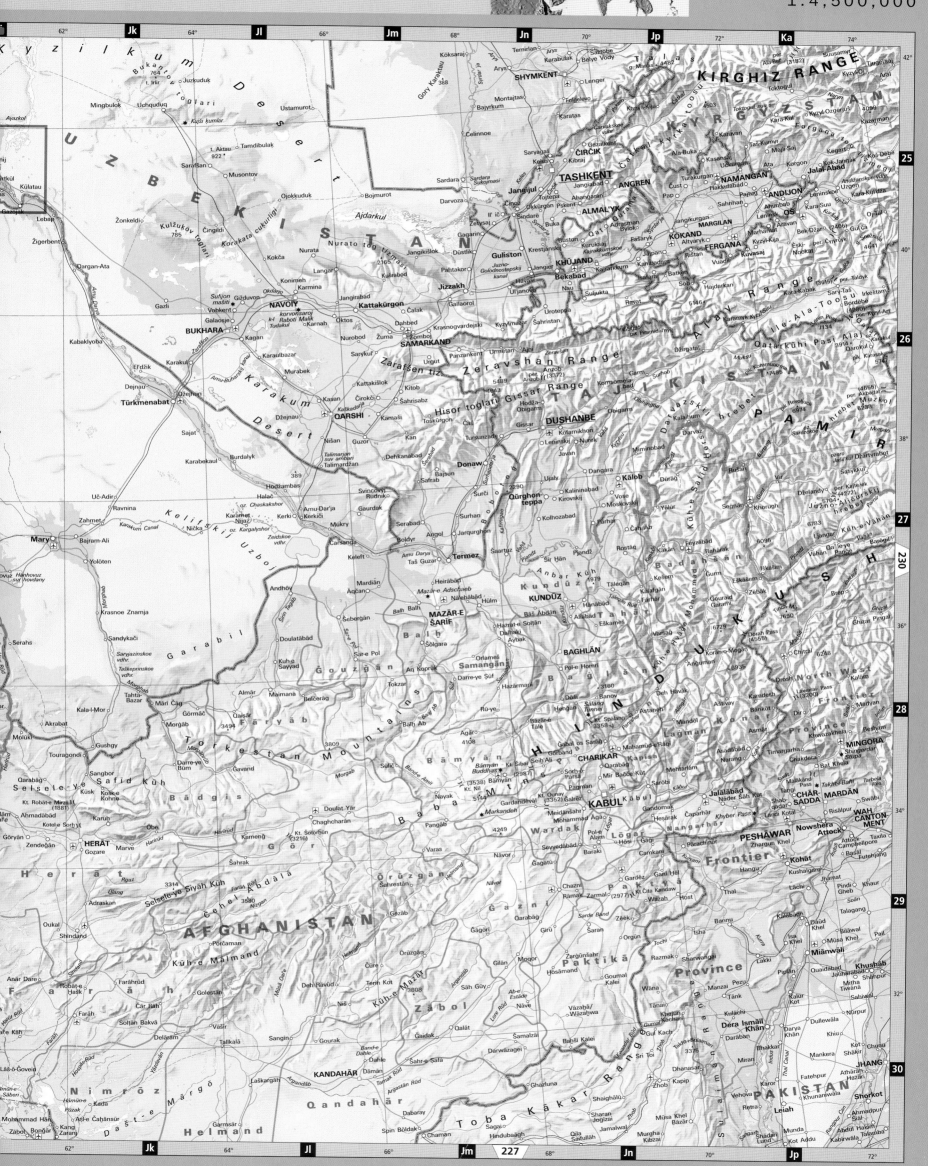

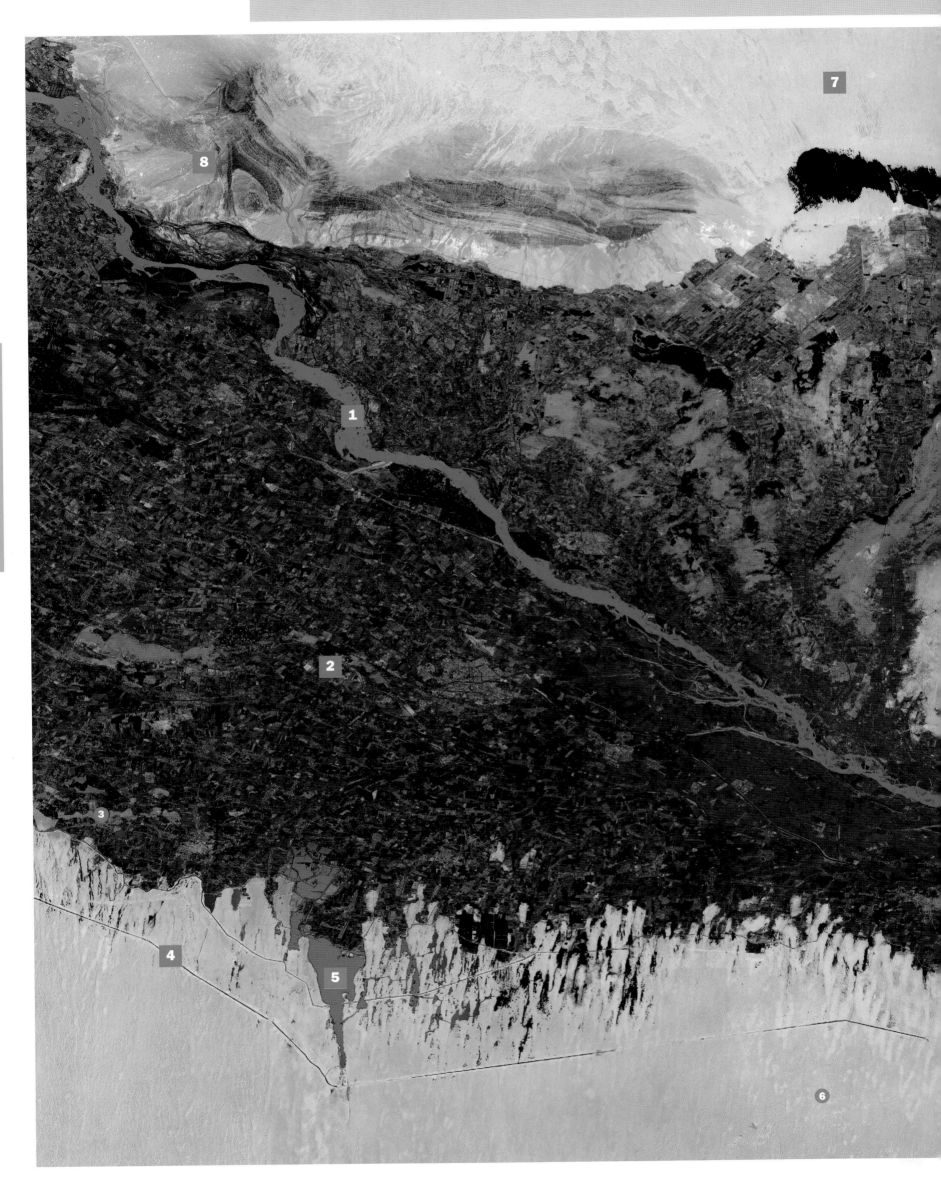

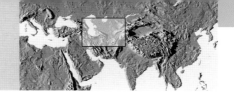

Amu Darya

The lowlands of Turan, which extend from the Caspian Sea and Iran as far as southern Kazakhstan, are covered in huge deserts. Two desert rivers— the Amu Darya and the Syr Darya—flow through the thinly populated region and into Lake Aral. Extremely important hydroelectric engineering measures made in the Soviet era paid little thought to the environmental impact. Fertile and densely populated river oases in the river valleys, such as the one around Urganch in the image shown here, were created, but dams and the diversion of large quantities of water from both external rivers have caused the level of Lake Aral to fall by 14 m (46 ft) in only 40 years. The lake is now only half as big as it was 50 years ago and has lost 70 percent of its content.

1 Amu Darya
The river, which was called the Oxus in ancient times and "the end of the world" by the Greeks, is a total of 2640 km (1641 miles) long and flows through Tajikistan, Turkmenistan, and Uzbekistan. The image shows the course it takes between Kulatau and Gurlan, shortly after the river has crossed the border of Turkmenistan, which is located to the south of the river, into Uzbekistan. Its source rivers are located in the Hindu Kush; in the Pamir region, around 200 km (124 miles) to the north of the section of the image shown, it flows into Lake Aral. In the image several islands can also be seen located in the broad river.

2 Urganch
Until its destruction by the Mongolians in the 13th century the Uzbek oasis city of Urganch was an important trading center and the capital of the kingdom of Choresm. The remnants of a minaret, a mosque, and a mausoleum from the 11th century are reminders of this era.

4 Pipelines
Turkmenistan, most of whose border corresponds with the border between the southern desert of Karakum and the irrigated areas, has enormous deposits of natural gas. Since the country is hesitant about its obligations to pay for the use of old Russian pipelines, however, extraction of the gas is declining. In the future Turkmenistan would like to become independent of Russia, with its own new pipelines. Uzbekistan is also rich in fossil mineral resources.

5 Reservoirs
The irrigated land around Urganch and Beruniy, located on the other shore, is characterized by numerous artificial lakes and canals, where cotton and rice are the most highly cultivated products. Some natural, albeit salty lakes (right edge of image) can be seen in the desert. A hydroelectric power station is located in the northern part of the Tuyamuyun Reservoir (lower right corner of image).

3 Khiva ↑
A visit to the old town of Itchan Kala in Khiva, which has been declared a World Cultural Heritage Site by UNESCO, has been compared to a fairy tale from the Thousand and One Nights. *Huge town walls made of clay, impressive town gates, and a citadel protect the old town with its mosques, minarets, madrassahs (Koran schools), and mausolea, which date from the 16th to the 19th centuries.*

6 Karakum
The "black desert," which covers about 90 percent of Turkmenistan and a total of 350,000 km² (135,136 square miles), is actually mainly a white and extremely hot salt and sandy desert. It is 81 m (266 ft) at its lowest point and has an extreme continental climate—even snow now falls in winter. Camels are the most important means of transport here.

7 Kyzylkum
The "red desert" is flanked by the Amu Darya in the south and the Syr Darya in the north. Mountains, some of which are as high as 900 m (2953 ft), rise from the desert, which covers an area of 300,000 km² (115,831 square miles). Precipitation is between 100 and 200 mm (3.9 and 7.8 in). The nomads' Karakul sheep are their most valuable possessions, prized for their meat, milk, and wool.

8 Gora Ačcitov
The Gora Ačcitov in the Sultan Ubays mountainous region is around 473 m (1552 ft) high and the only hill worth mentioning near Urganch, which is about 150 m (492 ft) above sea level.

MAP

1 : 4,500,000

Gulf of Oman, Indus Valley

Height
m
3000
2000
1000
600
300
100
0
< 0
200
1000
2000
4000
6000
8000
10000
m
Depth

1 : 4,500,000

| 0 | 25 | 50 | 75 | 100 | 125 miles |

| 0 | 50 | 100 | 150 | 200 km |

Albers Equal Area Conic Projection

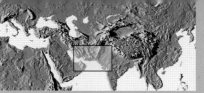

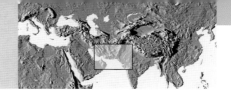

Zagros Mountains

Iran covers the region between the Caspian Sea and the Persian Gulf. Large parts of the country comprise sand, rock, or salt deserts at an average of 1000–1500 m (3281–4921 ft) above sea level, which are often lined with towering chains of fold mountains more than 4000 m (13,123 ft) high, with internal basins located between them. The 1500 km (932 mile) long Zagros Mountains form the longest mountain range in the country and, in geological terms, are part of the young, alpidic chains of mountain ranges. Iran is located within the sphere of influence of many tectonic plates moving in different directions and is thus among the zones in the Near East most at risk from earthquakes.

① *Kuh-e Kharman* ↓

One of the most striking peaks on the northern sides of the Zagros Mountains (see image), which rise as high as 4548 m (14,921 ft) and whose foothills located by the Strait of Hormuz extend almost to the Persian Gulf, is the fissured hump known as Kuh-e Kharman at 3201 m (10,502 ft) high.

consequent erosion, and permanent damage caused by small domestic animals mean that no new vegetation worth mentioning has been able to grow for centuries. The area under consideration, located on the edge of the mountain range, is also practically empty of vegetation. Some connected green areas extend around the town of Eştahban.

② Salt Lakes

When precipitation occurs in zones where there is a great deal of evaporation, minerals located in the depths force their way to the surface of the rocks as salt solutions. While they are washed farther on in semi-arid regions, they often completely crystallize in very arid regions to form huge layers of salt. If the inflow of water and the evaporation balance each other out, salt lakes are then formed. The lakes shown here are located 100 km (60 miles) to the east of the metropolis of Shīrāz in a longitudinal valley situated between two chains of the Zagros Mountains. The western lake (Daryāce-ye Task) and the eastern lake (Daryāce-ye Bahtegan) are situated at a height of about 1500 m (4921 ft) and are temporarily connected together. The mountains between both lakes reach a height of as much as 2575 m (8448 ft).

③ Ore Mining

Iran has enormous deposits of mineral oil and natural gas. In addition, a large amount of its copper, lead, chromium, zinc, and manganese deposits have not yet been mined or have only been mined in a very primitive fashion, after the mining industry began to decline during the years of the Revolution post-1979. Some of the mining areas worked in the 1980s are shown in the image.

④ Vegetation

Iran's lack of woods and forests is not caused by the scarcity of water. Deforestation,

⑤ Sarvestan

Many important archeological sites are located around Shīrāz. The tiny village of Sarvestan contains the gravestone of a sheikh dating from the 13th century and, just outside the village, are remarkable Sassanid ruins from the 5th century.

⑥ Agricultural Areas

Only a very small percentage of the land in Iran can be farmed. In the arid Zagros Mountains cattle are raised and land is farmed mainly for personal use, often by nomads from the Bakhtiar, Khamseh, and Qashqai tribes. The inhabitants have laid out plantations on the valleys and on the mountainsides. Figs and pistachios are almost the only products that can be wrested from the ground.

⑦ *Rivers and Mountains* ↓

The chains of mountains in Iran constitute huge weather barriers and guarantee that the climate on the highlands is dry and low in precipitation. Temperatures of around 45°C (113°F) are common in summer. In contrast, dry, cold conditions predominate in winter. Parts of the highlands are among the regions of the world with the lowest atmospheric humidity. The rivers flowing from the mountains into the interior of the country are mainly dry rivers or carry water only periodically. The few oases provide a stark contrast in the barren landscape. Thanks to constant water supply even palm trees can flourish here.

Height
m
3000
2000
1000
600
300
100
0
< 0
200
1000
2000
4000
6000
8000
10000
m
Depth

1:4,500,000

| 0 | 25 | 50 | 75 | 100 | 125 miles |

| 0 | 50 | 100 | 150 | 200 km |

Albers Equal Area Conic Projection

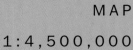

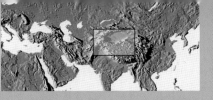

Kg Kh Kj Kk Kl Km

84° 86° 88° 90° 92° 94° 96°

Be Shan

iqa
Luntai
KORLA
Yuli
Qongkol
Tikanlik
Hongliuyuan
Anxi
25
Bai Shan
2014
Kong He
2809
Kuruktag
Konqi He
Loulan Gucheng
Shule He
40°
Argan
Lop Nur
Yumenguan Yumenguan
Minghoshan
Yulin Ku
Yueyaguan Mogao Ku
Mingshashan
BASIN
984
Ikanbujimal
Luobuzhuang
Miran
Donglük
Baxkorgan
26
Altun Shan
Subei
Yema Manshan
Aksay (3520)
Dangin Shankou
Altun Shan
5796
4612
esert
Ruoqiang
Yandakxak
Dingzikou
Lenghu
Huahaizi
Qarqan He
Aktaz
Waxxari
Xorkol
Tsagaan Chulunta
Altun
Yugia
38°
Yusupalik Tag
Mangnai Zhen
Tomorlog
Youdunzi
Gebituolatuo
Chalengkou
Ige
Da Qaidam
Qiemo (Qaran)
6062
Huatugou
Qaidam Pendi
Higen gol
gaztarim
Hadilik
Gas Hu
Mangnai
Dong Taijnat Hu
Dabsen Hu
Qarhan
27
Andirlangar
Shudanzhuang
Tura
Sinkiang
Ayakkuru Hu
Gansen
Dong Taijnat Hu
ongguzlangar
Aqqan
Quimantag
Haya'er
Gashunchaka
Bostan
Aqqikkol Hu
5251
Golmud
Ak Tag
6749
Arka Tag
Muztag
7723
Jingyu Hu
KUNLUN Qingshai
Dabsen Hu
AN
AN
5798
5464
Bukadaban Feng
6862
Hoh Sai Hu
Xiaopanchuan
Naij Tal
Qagan Tahoi
36°
242
Hoh Xil Shan
Huiten Nur
(4850) Kunlun Shankou
6302
Budongquan
Manni
Hoh Xil Hu
Elsen Nur
Qumar Heyan
Qumar He
28
CHINA
Xijir Ulan Hu
Ulan Ul Hu
Wuli
Quicigou
Tongtren He (Jiqu)
Tukola Tolha
34°
Laxong Co
6460
Dogai Coring
Tuotuo He
Tuotuo Heyan
Gormo Co
Kulanhor
Lugu
Geladaindong
6559
Wenquan
Dam Qu
Kili Bulak
Zh Qu (Makong)
29
Plateau of Tibet
Tanggula (Dangla Shan)
Tanggula Shan
6240
Tanggula Shankou
(5180)
6580
Shan
Gêrzê
Dong Co
6300
Amdo
Monza
Nyainrong
Boqen
32°
Zhaxi Co
Lagkor Co
Dongco
Co Nag
Xagquka
Sog Xian
Dagzê Co
Nyima
Dongqiao
Nagqu
Nu Jiang
6280
Tangyung Tso
Urru Co
Siling Co
Doba
Dôgen Co
Banbar
Tarok Tso
Gyaring Co
Bong Co
Tibet
30°
bia
Lunggar
Chunt Tso
Coqên
Tangra Yumco
Gomang Co
Namco
NYAINQÊNTANGLHA SHAN
Alamdo
ka
Karong Tso
Zhari Namco
Ngangzê Co
Zangdo
Xainza
Nam Co
Atas Gompa
Lhari
Moerkesung
7100
Luxikegongba
Yengchang
Kyogchi La (4900)
Horra
Yigong Zangbo
Xung Co
Dêqên
Nyainqêntanglh F.
7114
Damxung
Reting
Yigong Co
30°
ANGDISÊ SHAN
6200
6059
Qungfao
Yangbajain
Yangbajain
Maizho Kungqar
Gongbo'gyamda
Bayzhan
Suge La (5300)
31

Kg Kh Kj 235 Kk Kl Km

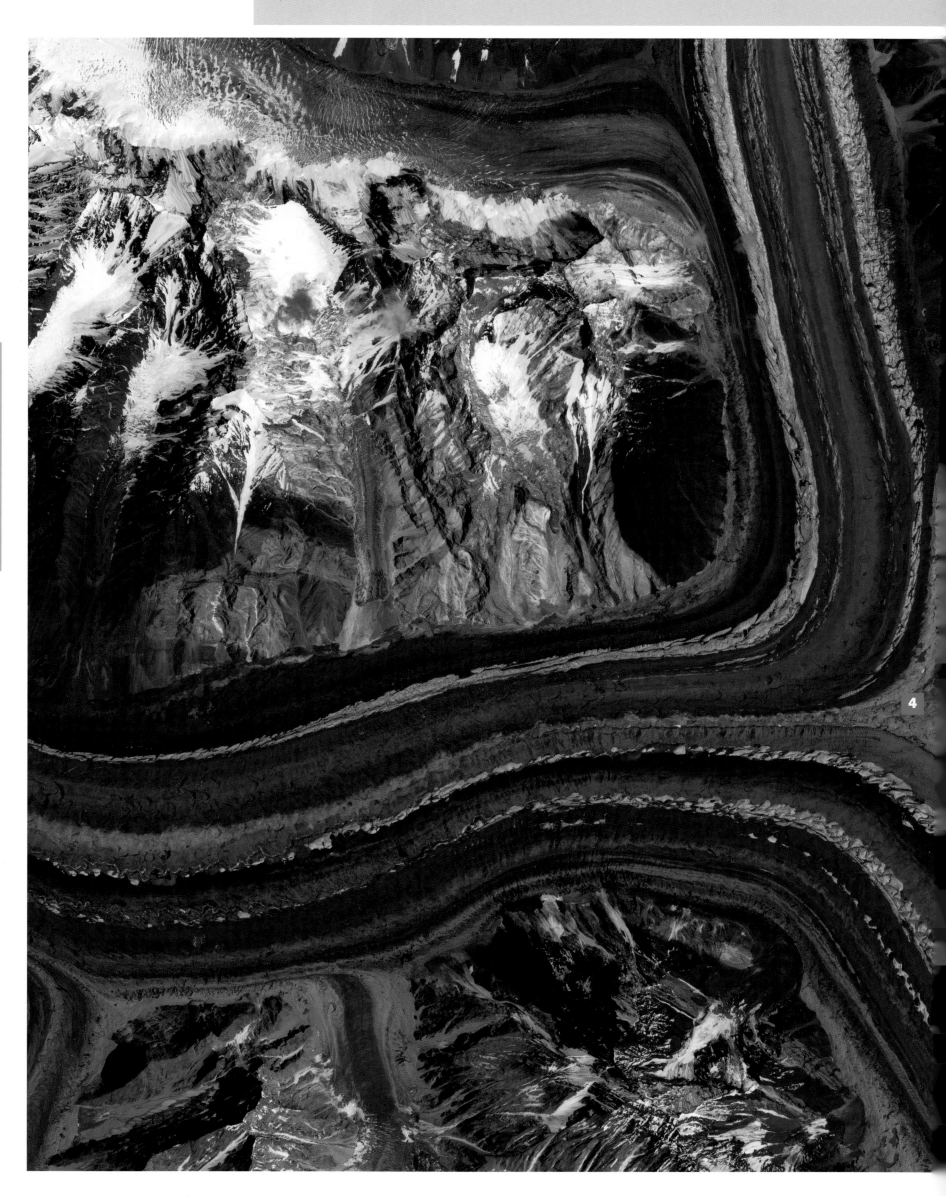

4

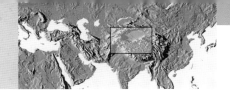

Baltoro Glacier

The 480 km (298 mile) high mountain range located in Baltistan in the north-east of Pakistan contains four impressive mountains at least 8000 m (26,247 ft) high: K2 (Mount Godwin-Austen) at 8611 m (28,251 ft), Gasherbrum I (8068 m [26,470 ft]) and Gasherbrun II (8035 m [26,361 ft]), and Broad Peak (8047 m [26,401 ft]). The mountain range also includes the largest collection of mountains between 6000 and 7000 m (19,685 and 22,966 ft) high, and huge glaciers. They all form a natural amphitheater at the confluence of the Godwin-Austen and Baltoro glaciers. Some of the 7000 and 8000 m (22,966 and 26,247 ft) high mountains are considered to be harder to climb than the mountains of the Eastern Himalaya.

1 *Karakoram* ↑

In 1958 the famous Italian climber Fosco Mariani described the Karakoram mountain range as "the world's greatest museum in shape and form." The high mountain range was discovered and measured in 1856 by the Survey of India. At 8611 m (28,251 ft), K2, located outside the upper right edge of the image, is the highest mountain in the Karakoram and the second-highest mountain on earth. The mountain, which was originally called K2 because it was the second peak in the Karakoram mountain range to be surveyed, has a distinct pyramidal shape and was later renamed in memory of the English surveyor Henry Godwin-Austen, who was in charge of the first surveys of the region. The Balti people who live in the Karakoram mountains immigrated from Tibet 600 to 800 years ago and today provide support during large expeditions, such as the shown expedition to K2.

2 Broad Peak

The "Broad Peak," at 8047 m (26,401 ft), is the twelfth-highest mountain on earth. It is located right beside K2 and was given its name in 1892 by W. Martin Conway: Its native name, Phalchen Kangri, is hardly known at all. In 1934, the International Himalaya Expedition called it "almost unclimbable" due to its steepness. However, after a number of failed attempts, it was in fact climbed for the first time in 1957 by Markus Schmuck, Hermann Buhl, Kurt Diemberger, and

Fritz Wintersteller, members of a four-man Austrian expedition.

3 Baltoro Glacier

The area around what, at 62 km (39 miles) is the second-longest glacier outside the polar regions, can be reached only arduously by taking a flight to Skardu, situated in the politically disputed region of Jammu and Kashmir in the Indus Valley, to the southwest of the Karakoram mountain range. From there, visitors travel by jeep to Askole Village, where helpers from the Balti tribe take over the heavy loads, some of which weigh as much as 25 kg (55 lbs), required for continuing the march along the 93 km (58 mile) long Baltoro Glacier Trek into the heart of the Karakoram Mountains. This impressive trek leads to the base camp for K2, Broad Peak, and Gasherbrum I and II. Impressive icy and rocky peaks such as the Masherbrum (7821 m [25,659 ft]) and the Muztagh [Muztagh] Tower line the arduous route to the glacier. The first destination is Concordia Place, where 10 of the 30 highest peaks on earth are jammed together. The Godwin-Austen Glacier, which is loaded with detritus, flows into the Baltoro Glacier here and is fed by the massif of K2. The Godwin-Austen Glacier is the largest secondary glacier of the Baltoro Glacier, which comes from the south, and is in turn fed by countless smaller glaciers from the massif formed by Gasherbrum I and II. Both glacier rivers are almost completely loaded with detritus and rocks; the lighter color of the central moraines can be clearly made out.

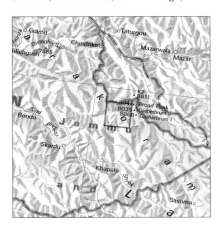

4 Concordia Place

After more than one week of traveling along the Baltoro Glacier, mountain climbers reach Concordia Place, located at a height of 4650 m (15,256 ft), the "largest amphitheater in the world," whose impressive rocky frame is broken only by the large Godwin-Austen Glacier and additional smaller glaciers. This confluence of both powerful glacier rivers was named after Konkordiaplatz on the Swiss Aletsch Glacier. Concordia Place offers the first view of the impressive pyramid of K2, which rises 3657 m (11,998 ft) high above Baltoro Glacier. The American mountain climber Galen Rowell described Concordia as the "Throne Room of the Mountain Gods."

1:4,500,000

Albers Equal Area Conic Projection

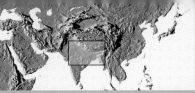

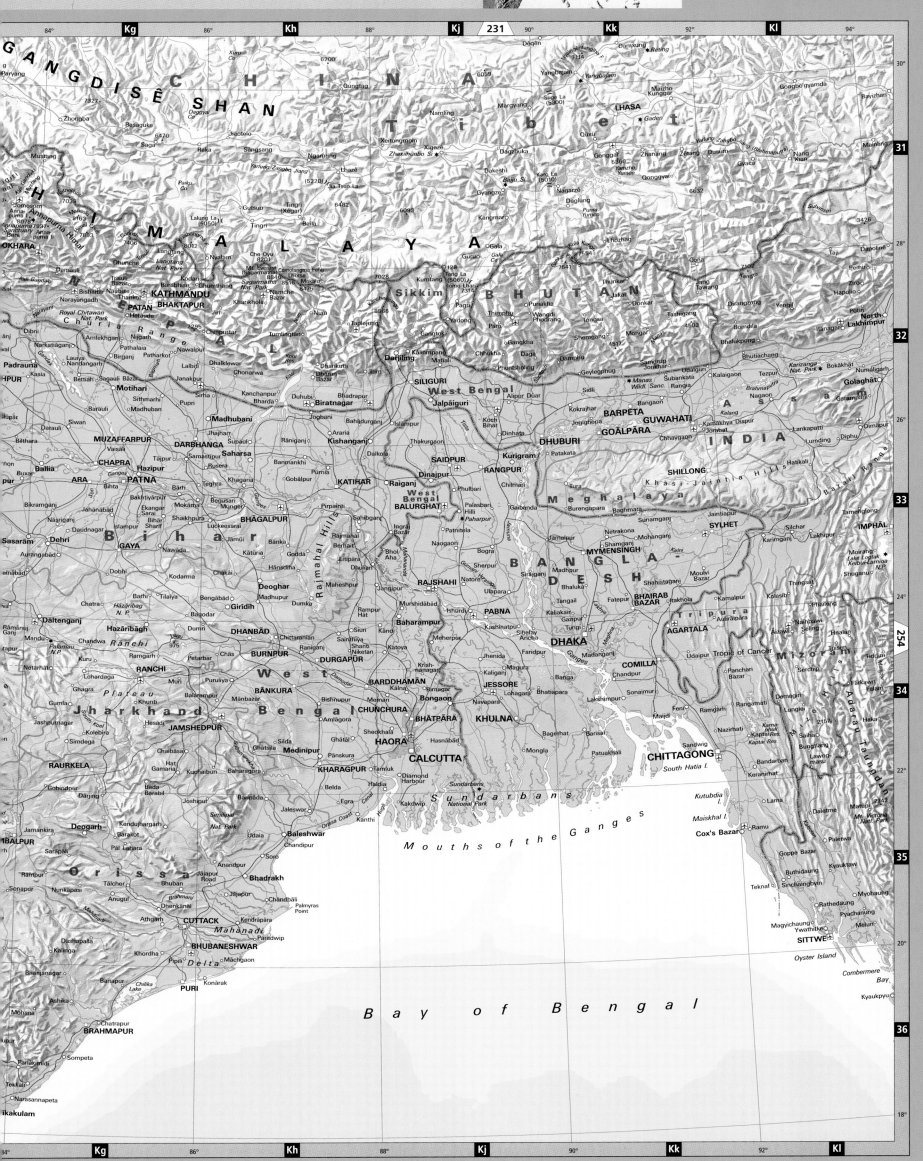

Taj Mahal

India's Taj Mahal is one of the most famous and most admired manmade sights on the planet. The first travelers from Europe to see the Taj Mahal ranked it among the world's greatest buildings: In this respect, the Frenchman François Bernier wrote in 1663 that the Taj Mahal "deserves to be counted among the wonders of the world, more so than the uniform masses of the Egyptian pyramids." The 74 m (243 ft) high domed structure on the Yamuna River was completed in 1654, 23 years after the death of Mumtaz Mahal, the beloved wife of the Great Mughal Shah Jahan (1592–1666). Unusual for the time, Mumtaz Mahal ("The Exalted One of the Palace") spent her short life accompanying her husband on his military campaigns against the Hindu princedoms, offered him advice, and gave birth to 14 children during their 19 years of marriage. She died while giving birth on June 17, 1631, at the young age of 37, in the encampment near Burhānpur in central India.

❶ *Mausoleum* ←

It is not just the famous silhouette of the onion-shaped dome above the bright marble cube that contributes to the beauty of the Taj Mahal. The symmetry and clarity are also impressive; the division of the whole unit with both of the ancillary buildings flanking it and their three cupolas can also clearly be seen from a bird's-eye view. However, what is most worthy of admiration is the play of light and shadow at the entrances, which are similar to halls, and which the architect used to soften the harsh aspect of the mausoleum. The cool light from the marble makes the monument appear lighter and wonderfully graceful despite its size. The marble also shimmers in a different way whenever the light changes. The name of the architect is not known for certain, but it is assumed to be one Ustadh Ahmadh from Lahore, who later also built the Red Fort in Delhi. It is estimated that more than 20,000 craftsmen and workers helped build the site.

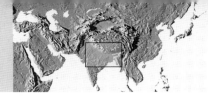

2 Paradise Garden

The geometrically laid out garden, known as a *charbagh,* is entered via a 30 m (98 ft) high arched gateway, which was once covered in silver plate. It is only here that it is possible to get a glimpse of the full glory of the Taj Mahal and see its reflection in the long, extended water basin. And only on closer inspection does the visitor notice that there are in fact four canal-shaped basins, which collect in a central basin. According to Muslim tradition, this symbolizes the "Basin of Fullness," into which the four rivers of paradise flow.

The Koran *surahs* (chapters) on the exterior and interior walls of the Taj Mahal are also part of the heavenly symbolism of the garden basin. The verse of the Koran on the main gate promises heavenly life after death: "You who have found peace in your faith! Return happily and safely to your Lord. Join the circle of my servants and come into my heaven."

The master craftsmen responsible for the *pietra dura* (inlaid stone) in the Taj Mahal added the floral decorations and grapes and fruits made from precious stones to the blooming gardens; these compete with the beauty of the calligraphy. The thousands of agates, turquoises, jade stones, amethysts, and malachites have been fitted perfectly into the marble. These blossoms bloom most magnificently around the majestic sarcophagi of Mumtaz Mahal and Shah Jahan.

3 Amarvilas Hotel

Amarvilas means "God's pleasure" or "immortal pleasure," and in Agra it is the name of a new Oberoi Palace Hotel located to the south of the hilly bushland of the Taj City Forest. Situated within walking distance of the Taj Mahal, the Amarvilas offers a clear view of the marble monument from all of the guestrooms. Every luxury is provided, from the spa to the bar; the Mughal tradition lives on in the form of magnificent craftsmanship.

4 Red Fort

Three Mughal rulers were responsible for the construction of the Red Fort—Akbar the Great, who moved the capital of his kingdom from Delhi to Agra in 1565, and who had the first buildings constructed; his grandson Shah Jahan, who increased the number of palaces and had the Moti Masjid, the famous Pearl Mosque, erected; and then his son, Aurangzeb, who had the fortifications strengthened even more. Agra remained the capital for 70 more years until Delhi became the residence of the Mughals in 1658. The Red Fort is now a UNESCO World Cultural Heritage Site.

5 Yamuna River

From the pavilions of the Red Fort is the best view over the broad river, which today is unfortunately very polluted, to the Taj Mahal and to the region along the northern banks, still undeveloped to a great extent. The bright zone with the green banks, shown in the image, is a flood plain; paths and fields can be made out in the shallow water. The 1376 km (855 mile) long Yamuna River is the most important tributary of the Ganges.

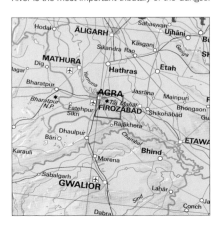

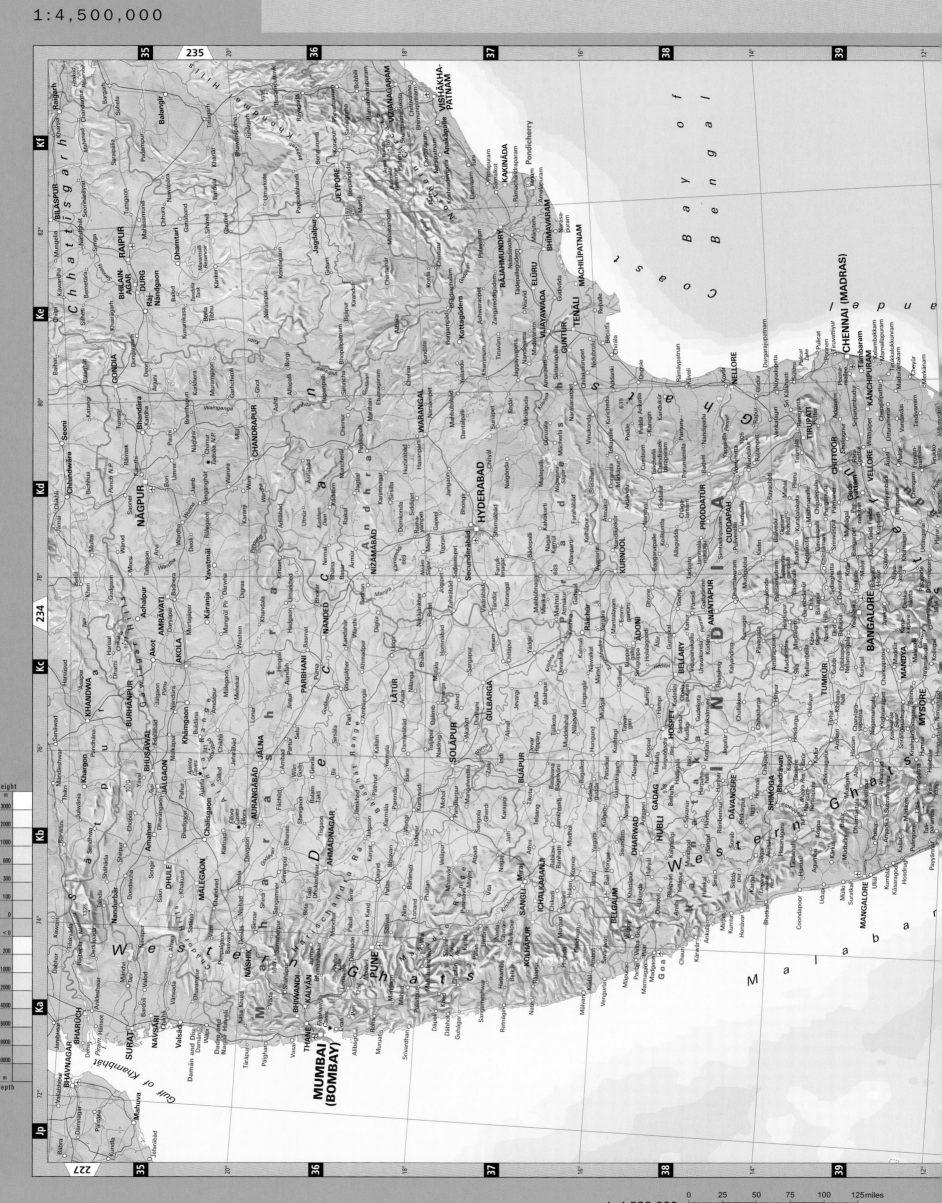

1:4,500,000

Albers Equal Area Conic Projection

| 0 | 25 | 50 | 75 | 100 | 125 miles |
| 0 | 50 | 100 | 150 | 200 km |

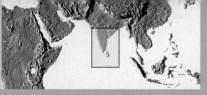
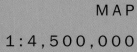

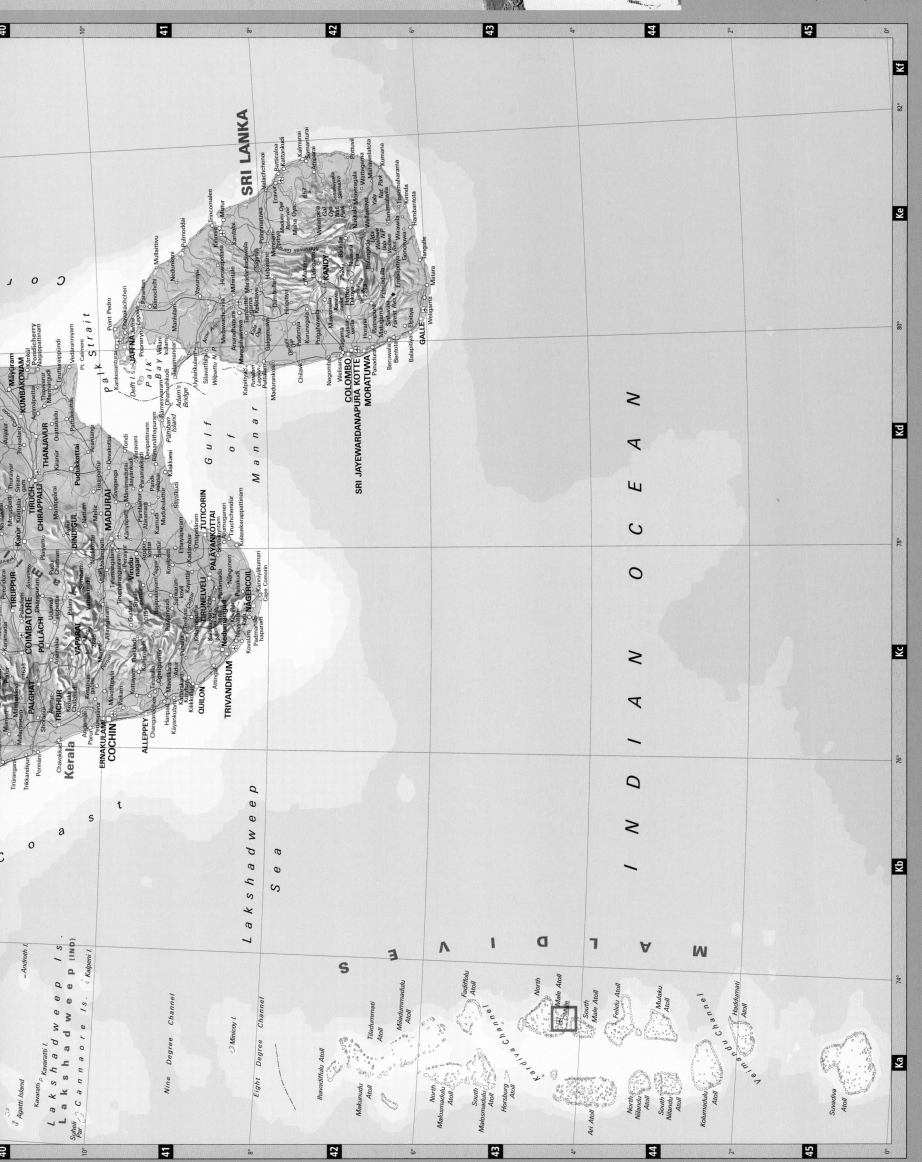

SRI LANKA

JAFFNA

KANDY

COLOMBO
SRI JAYEWARDANAPURA KOTTE
MORATUWA

GALLE

Palk Strait

Palk Bay

Gulf of Mannar

INDIAN OCEAN

Lakshadweep Sea

MÁYÚRAM
KUMBAKONAM
THANJAVUR
TIRUCH CHIRAPPALLI
PUDUKKOTTAI
MADURAI
DINDIGUL
TUTICORIN
PALAYANKOTTAI
TIRUNELVELI
NAGERCOIL
VIRUDU-nagar
VAPARAI
COIMBATORE
POLLÁCHI
TIRUPPUR
PALGHAT
TRICHUR
ERNAKULAM
COCHIN
ALLEPPEY
QUILON
TRIVANDRUM

Kerala

Coast

Lakshadweep Is.
Lakshadweep (IND)
Cannaore Is.

Nine Degree Channel

Eight Degree Channel

M A L D I V E S

Tiladummati Atoll
Miladummadulu Atoll
Fadiffolu Atoll
North Male Atoll
South Male Atoll
Felidu Atoll
Mulaku Atoll
Haddumati Atoll

Thavadiffulu Atoll

Makunudu Atoll

North Malosmadulu Atoll
South Malosmadulu Atoll

Horsburg Atoll

Ari Atoll

North Nilandu Atoll
South Nilandu Atoll

Kolumadulu Atoll

Kardiva Channel

Veimandu Channel

Suvadiva Atoll

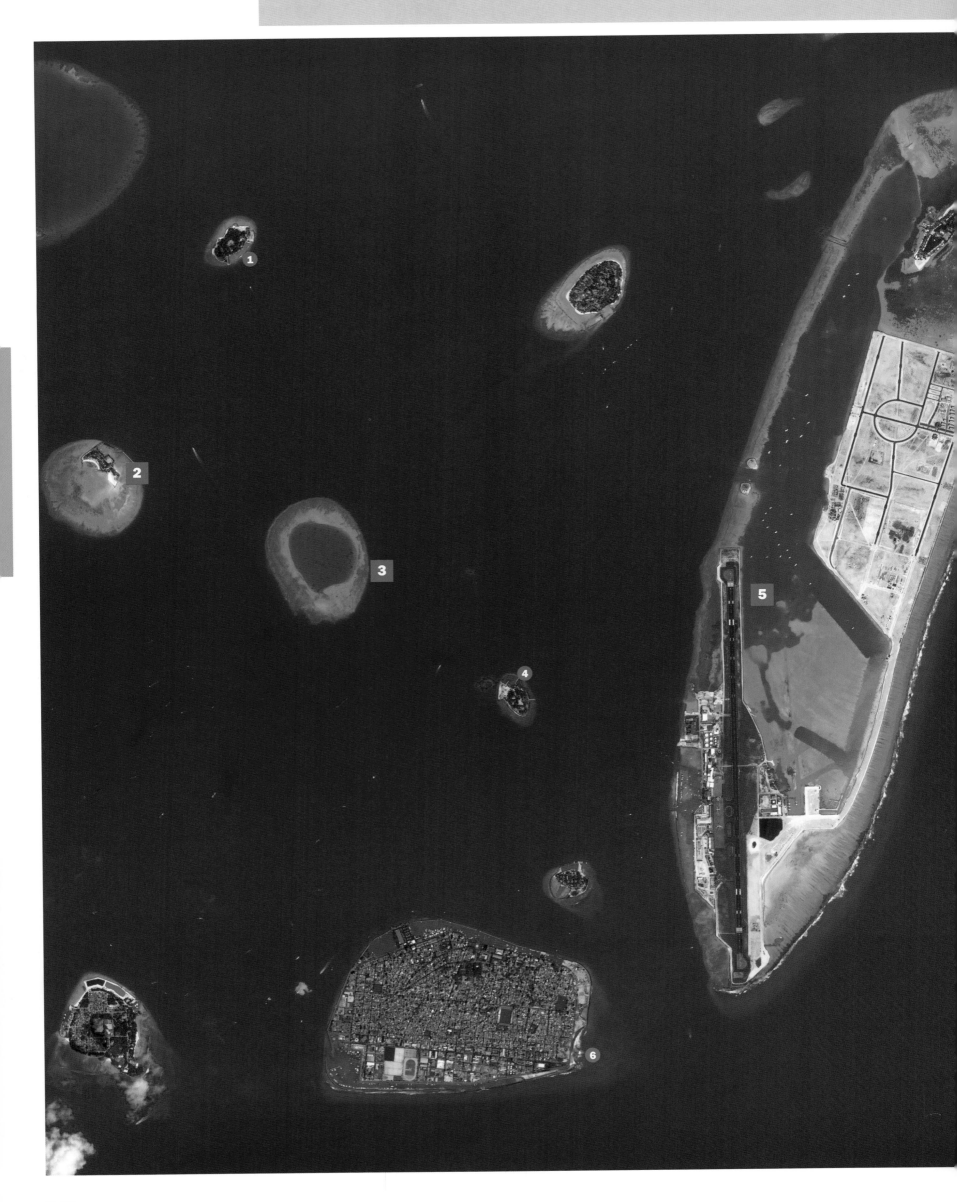

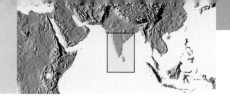

Maldives

The islands that make up the Maldives look like spots of color on a dark blue canvas. The radiant white of the sandy beaches forms an intense contrast to the turquoise of the surrounding sea. The island chain of the Maldives comprises around 2000 islands; about 200 or so are inhabited. The overall area of all of the islands is less than 300 km² (116 square miles), a fact that makes the island group the smallest country in Asia. The climate of the country located close to the equator is tropically warm the whole year round, but the monsoons, some of which are very violent, bring large amounts of rain. The official language, Maldivian, is an Indo-Germanic language; the natives have Indian, African, and Arabic ancestors. Their cultural roots are correspondingly varied. However, unity exists where religion is concerned—almost every Maldivian professes a faith in Islam. The economic backbone of the country is the fishing industry.

4 *The Maldives as a Tropical Diving Paradise* ↑
The tropical areas of the Indian Ocean are shallow close to the coast, rich in oxygen, and flooded with light. In addition, the currents of the ocean bring an inexhaustible supply of food— ideal living conditions for a large variety of fish. For several decades, tourists, mainly Europeans, have been discovering the exotic paradise as a holiday destination. In addition to the fine sandy beaches, holidaymakers are attracted by ideal conditions for diving and snorkeling. The crowds of visitors are channeled to certain islands that are open to holidaymakers, which means that tourists rarely come into contact with locals who do not work in the tourism industry. Jetties several meters long, which bridge over the flat reefs around the islands, allow boats to bring diving tourists to the holiday islands located on the South Male Atoll.

1 *Palm Beaches* ↑
Coconut palms are among the plants typically found within the tropical latitudes. They also characterize the appearance of many islands in the Maldives. The trunks of some trees sway toward the sea and bring a little bit of shade to the virtually white sandy beaches, which completely surround many of the islands. Some specimens can grow as high as 30 m (100 ft). The coconut palm is used in many ways—the flesh of the coconuts is a valued food in both its raw and prepared forms, and when dried it serves as a raw material for oils, soaps, and candles. In addition, mats and baskets, among other things, are woven from palm leaves, while rope is produced from coconut fibers.

2 Tropical Island Paradise
Round, oval, crescent-shaped—the forms the islands and isles take are varied. However, as fascinating as the island world may be, the idyll's existence is under threat. Most of the islands rise only a few meters above sea level, while around 80 percent of the whole area lies less than

1 m (3 ft) above sea level, and this is why the topography of the islands is relatively uniform. This phenomenon results in natural advantages when roads are being laid, but, on the other hand, the island archipelago could become a victim of continued global warming. The sea level has been rising for some time and some of the flattest islands are already in danger of being completely submerged. Many Maldivians are concerned that their islands could disappear from the map eventually.

3 Coral Reefs
In the Indian Ocean some coral reefs rise above sea level. The reefs consist of the chalky skeletons of the corals and are restricted to the tropical oceans because the water temperature does not sink below 20°C (68°F). Reefs grow very slowly, only a few centimeters a year. Reefs that line an almost completely circular lagoon are called atolls.

5 Hulule Airport Island
Scarcely anywhere else in the world does an airport stand out so impressively amid its surroundings. The airport spans two islands joined by reclaimed land. The cost of the expansion has been worthwhile because the take-off and landing strips can be used by large-capacity, international jets. A small barrier reef extends along the whole eastern outer side of the island and protects the islands and land areas to the west of it from the destructive power of the white breakers.

6 *Male* ↓
With at least 70,000 inhabitants, the capital Male, located in the southeast of the North Male Atoll, is without a doubt the metropolis of the Maldives because every fifth inhabitant of the country lives here. The city is not only the largest settlement in the archipelago but also contains the most important port in the island country. From here there are shipping links with many additional islands in the Maldives as well as with Sri Lanka. In addition to tourism, fishing and fish processing play a large role. Thousands of fishermen sail to sea on a daily basis and return home in the evening, often with large catches. The trade in wood and products derived from the coconut palm is also important for the capital in an economic sense. Many of the buildings in Male were built using wood from coconut palms and from coral limestone.

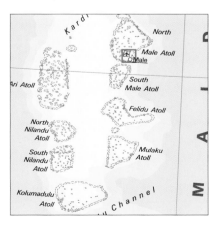

Northern China

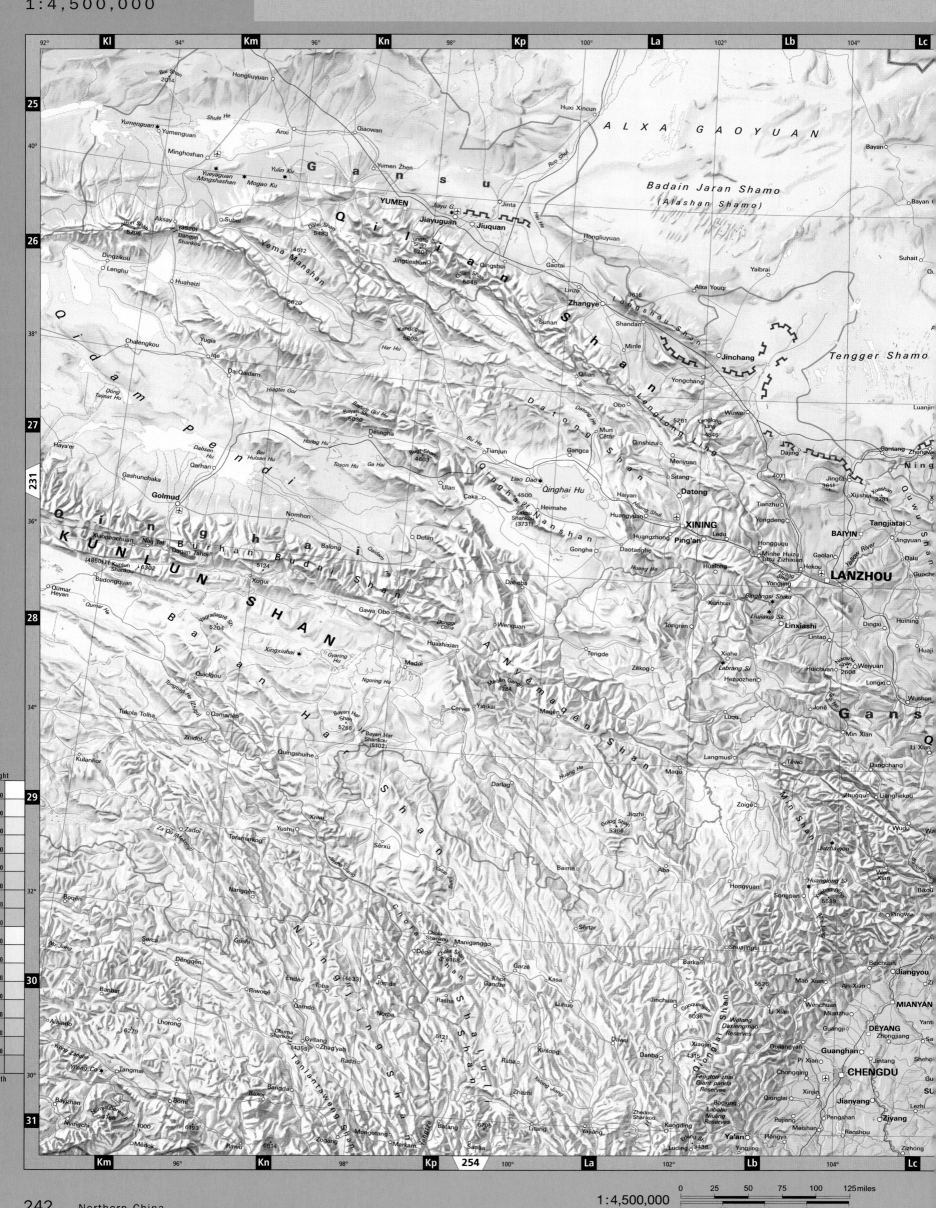

1:4,500,000

Albers Equal Area Conic Projection

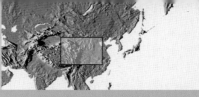

Ld 108° Le 110° Lf 112° Lg 114° Lh 116° Lj 118° Lk

ang Shan
Urad Huoqi
YIN SHAN
1807 Darhan Mumingan Lianheqi
Qahar Youyi Houqi
Siziwang Qi
Qahar Youyi Qianqi
Zhangbei
2131 Fenghning
Guicheng
Luanping
CHENGDE
Pingquan
Kuancheng
Qinglong

25 40°

Wuyuan
Urad Zhongqi
Daqing Shan 2173
Wuchuan
Guyang
JINING
Huangqi Hai
ZHANG-JIAKOU
Xuanhua
2286
Huailai
Mutianyu
Yanqing
Badaling
Beijing Shi
2051
Jinshanling
Xinglong
Zunhua

Linhe
Xamba
Ulansuhai Nur
Dalad Qi
Tumd Youyi
HOHHOT
Horinger
Zhuozi
Fengzhen
Zuoquan
Huaian
Haoshaoying
Xiayuanshui
Changping
BEIJING
Ji Xian
Fengrun

BAOTOU
Ulansuhai Nur
2129
Urad Qianqi
Yellow River
Togtoh
Qingshuihe
DATONG
Yangyuan
Ying Xian
Lingqiu
Zhoukoudian
Yasanke
Zhuozhou
Langfang
Ninghe
TANGSHAN
Leting

26 38°

WUHAI
Wuda
Zhuozi Shan 2148
Xindhao Shan 2516
Hanggin Qi
Sishiliang
Dongsheng
Ejin Horo Qi
Jungar Qi
Dafanpu
Lamadong-zhaoban
Pinglu
Shanyin
Hunyuan
Hengshan 2016
Wutai
Fuping
Quyang
Dingzhou
TIANJIN
Tianjin Shi
TANGGU
Bazhou
Tangguantun
Bohai Wan

Shizuishan
Sanbei
Yangchang
Narin Nur
Qagan Nur
Otog Qi
Uxin Ju
Tug
Bag Nur
Fugu
Baode
Wuzhai
Dongzhai
Yuanping
Yi Xian
Xu-cheng
Xushui
BAODING
Renqiu
Heijian
Anguo
Huanghua
Changcheng
DONGYING

ZUISHAN
Pingluo
ORDOS
Qab
Uxin Ju
Shenmu
Kelan
Jingle
Xinzhou
Dingxiang
Xiaxiyu
Xingtang
Pingshan
Shen Xian
Dachenzhuang
Botou
Yanshan
CANGZHOU
38°

Helan
YINCHUAN
(MU US SHAMO)
Bulanghee
Yulin
Gaojiabu
Xing Xian
Lan Xian
Lishi
Shouyang
YANGQUAN
Cangyanshan
Gaoyi
Jingxing
Nangong
Hengshui
DEZHOU
Shanghe
Huimin
Ningjin
Leling
BINZHOU

ing
Lingwu
Wuzhong
Yanchi
Otog Qian Qi
Wuding He
Jia Xian
Jia Xian
Yuhe
Suide
Wubu
Liulin
Wenshui
Qingxu
YUCI
Xiyang
Zuoquan
Longyao
Wei Xian
Qinghe
Linging
Gaotang
Jiyang
Zouping
ZIBO
27 36°

zu Zizhiqu
Hu'anpu
Dingbian
Dashuikeng
Haotan
Mizhi
Zizhou
Baiyan Si
Panguangou 1832
Lan Xian
Xuanzhong Si
Jin Si
TAIYUAN
Taigu
2302
Yangqu Shan
Heshun
Zuoquan
XINGTAI
Linging
JINAN
Taishan 1099
Yiyuan
LAIWU
Lishi
Shigong Si
Zichang
Long'an
Ansal
Qingjian
Yongping
Yang-quangu
Fenyang
Shuanglin Si
Jiexiu
Yushe
Tongyu
Shahe
Wu'an
HANDAN
Guantao
Shen Xian
Pingyin
TAI'AN
XINTAI
Mengyin
PINGYI

wan
wuliang
Fanxue
Wugi
Zhidan
Yaodian
Yanchang
Daning
Xi Xian
Lingshi
Qin Xian
Guodao
Licheng
She Xian
Xiangtangshan Shiku
LIAOCHENG
Fan Xian
Nanjie
Wen Shang
Kong Fu
Sishui
Suncun
QUFU
Fei Xian
246

Guyuan
HUANGTU GAOYUAN
YAN'AN
Mubo
Maojing
Qianshanghongyuan
Ganquan
Linzhen
Ji Xian
Yichuan
Jishan
Hejin
Huozhou
Guangsheng Si
Beizhandian
Lucheng
Lin Xian
ANYANG
HEBI
Hua Xian
Xun Xian
Puyang
Juye
Jiaxiang
JINING
Nanyang Hu
Chengqian
Tengzhou
ZAOZHUANG
Weishan
Weishan Hu
28 36°

Pingliang
Qingyang
Xifengzhen
Zhenyuan
Ning Xian
1688
Fu Xian
Huangling
Huanglong
LINFEN
Xianfeng
Yicheng
Xiangning
Wenxi
Lishan
Yangcheng
CHANGZHI
JINCHENG
Gaoping
Anze
Hongdong
XINXIANG
Weihui
Changyuan
Fengliu
HEZE
Dingtao
Cao Xian
Lankao
Minquan
Shan Xian
Xiao Xian
Dangshan
XUZHOU
HUAIBEI
Lingbi

Pingliang
Jingchuan
Lingtai
Bin Xian
Changqie Si
1846
Yijun
Hancheng
Heyang
Houma
Lishan
Yuanqu
Yima
Gong Xian
Song Xian
Song He
Zhumashan
KAIFENG
Weishi
Sui Xian
SHANGQIU
Xiayi
Yongcheng
Guzhen

Shan
Changle Si
Zhao Ling
Qian-Ling
Sanyuan
Baishui
Pucheng
Chengcheng
Dali
Yuncheng
Sanmenxia
Yongle Gong
Ruicheng
Yima
Luoning
LUOYANG
Longmen Shiku
Dengfeng
Heng Xian
Mangshan
ZHENGZHOU
Yanling
Taikang
Zhecheng
Luyi
Bozhou
Mengcheng
SUZHOU
29 34°

TONGCHUAN
Yao Xian
Qianyang
Xunyi
Jing Hao River
Fuping
Huayin
Tong'guan
Xiao Shan 2093
Yichuan
Yuzhou
XUCHANG
Xihua
Guoyang
BENGBU
Huaiyuan
HUAINAN
Fengyang

BAOJI
Mei Xian
Fufeng
Fengxiang
Qian'an
XIANYANG
Mao Ling
Huaqingchi
Lintong
Lantian
Xionger Shan
Song Xian
Ruzhou
Xiangcheng
Jia Xian
Huai-yang
Danchen
Zhangcunpu
Jieshou
Linquan
Lixin
Guzhen
HEFEI
Feixi

UI
Wei He
Taibai Shan 3768
Taibai
Zhouzhi
XI'AN
Hongmenhe
Shangzhou
Luanchuan
Fuing
Wuligou
2191
Nanzhao
PINGDING-SHAN
Ye Xian
Wuyang
LUOHE
Xiping
Shang-cheng
Yejie
Nianyu-wan Shuiku
Xiang-hongdian Shuiku
Heishan Shuiku
LU'AN
Shucheng

ling
Jing Shan
Shanyang
Shangnan
H e n a n
ZHOUKOU
Fugou
Dancheng
30 32°

Feng Xian
Liuba
Fuping
Jinyu Shan 3014
Zhen'an
Shang-nan
Nanzhao
Yunyang
Yahekou
Fangcheng
Shangcai
Chunshui
Runan
Huaibin
Huaiyang
Huaiyang
Changfeng

HANZHONG
Liuba
Chenggu
Ningqiang
Mian Xian
Shiquan
Hanyin
Ziyang
Ningshan
Zhushan
Fujin Shan
NANYANG
Neixiang
Xichuan
Zhenping
ZHUMADIAN
Biyang
Zhengyang
Luoshan
XINYANG
Shangcheng
Huwan
Shawo
Huoshan
Lujiang

NGYUAN
Nanjiang
Wangcang
Qishu
Daxba Shan
Xixiang
Pingli
Zhenba
Baihe
SHIYAN
Danjiangkou
Wudang-shan
Laohekou
Minggang
Tongbai
Tongbai Shan 1141
Shang-shui
Dawu
Macheng
Yuexi
Huoshan

Bazhong
Wenchang
Tongjiang
Wanyuan
2916
Zhushan
Zhuxi
Pingli
ZAOYANG
Gucheng
Shuang-gougou
Xinye
Tanghe
Dengzhou
HUANGCHUAN
Shang-cheng
Qianshan
Xiang-hongdian Shuiku
1728
Tiantangzhai
Tongcheng
ANQING

NANCHONG
Yilong
Lishan
Shuangba
Baiyi
Xuanhan
Wuxi
Daning
Shennongjia 3106
Julong Shan
XIANGFAN
Baokang
Nanzhang
1852
Yicheng
Suizhou
Hongshan
Guangshui
Anlu
Yunmeng
Zhongxiang
Guangling
Huangpi
Songzi
Fenghuan
Sanlitun
Qianshan
Huaning-qiao Si
Zongyang
ANQING
Dadukou
30°

Changle
Huaqiao
Dazhu
Kai Xian
Kaixian
Yunyang
Fengjie
Baidi Cheng
Daning
Wushan
Badong
711
Zhanghe Shuiku
Yuguanshan
JINGMEN
Tianmen
Licheng
Jingshan
Yingcheng
Xiaogan
Huangpi
WUHAN
Wuchang
Huanggang
Huangshi
Daye
Zhezhen
Wangjiang
Dongzhi

ong
QU XIAN
Quxian
Dazhu
Liangping
Zhong Xian
Gangchang
Three Gorges Reservoir
Lucongdian
Zigui
Jianshi
Wufeng
Yuan He
SHASHI
Qianjiang
JIANGLING
Xintao
Honghu
Jiayu
Wuxue
Huangmei
Chang Jiang
Ruichang
Lushan N.P.
JIUJIANG
Hukou
Tianfanjie

NANCHONG
WAN XIAN
Shizhu
Lichuan
ENSHI
Xuan'en
Renhe
Yuelai
Gangxiang
Zhichengshi
Zhijiang
Wufeng
Liujiachang
Songzi
Gong'an
YICHANG
Gezhou Ba (Gezhou Dam)
Zhijiang
JINGZHOU
Shadaogou
31 30°

Hechuan
Tongliang
Jiangbei
Changshou
Fengdu
Shizhu
Changshou
ong
Linshui
Renhe
Yuelai
Shizhu
Hefeng
Nishi
Jinshi
Nanping
Huarong
Linxiang
Chongyang
Lushui
Tongshan
Qiujin

Ld 108° Le 255 110° Lf 112° Lg 114° Lh 116° Lj

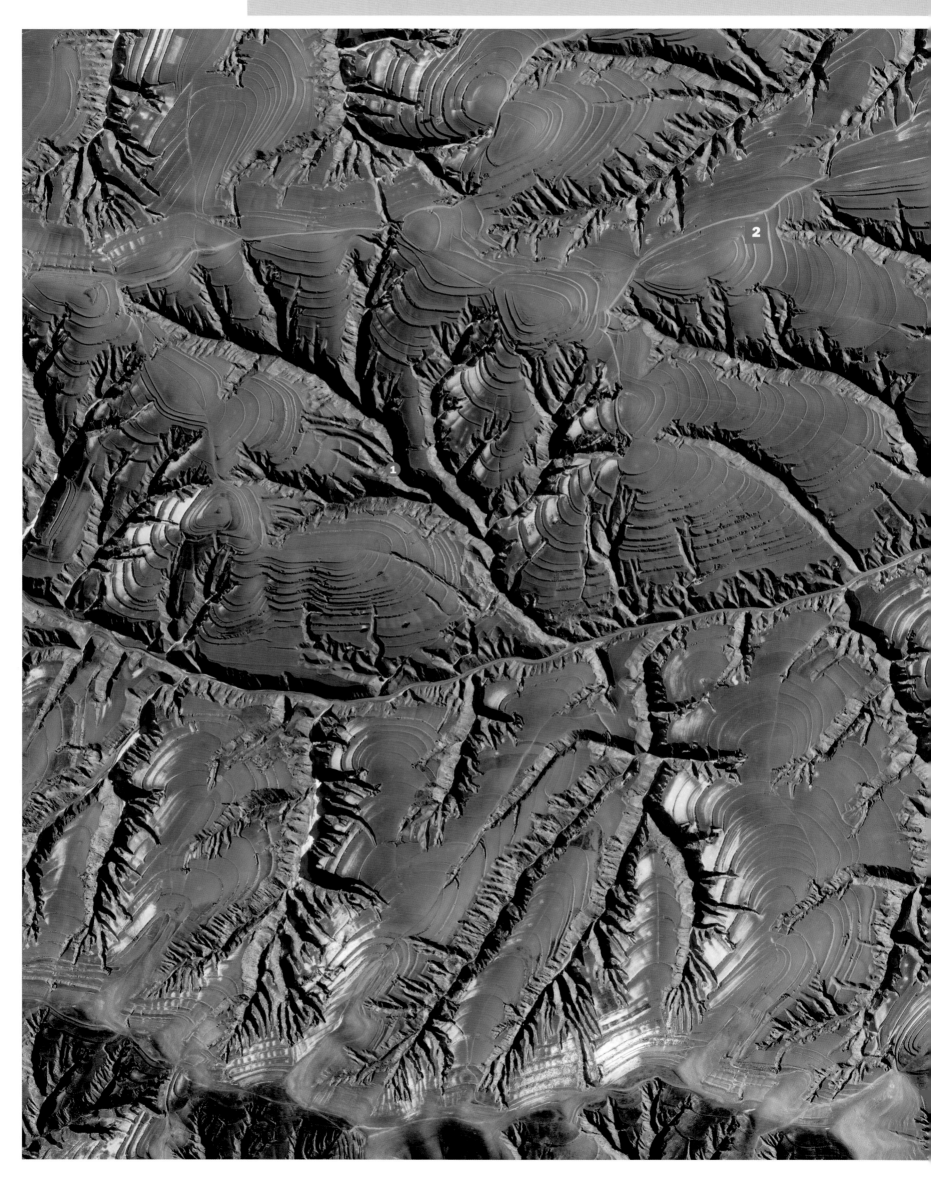

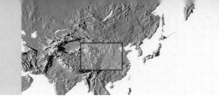

Kelan

A highland with an average height of 2000 m (6562 ft) stretches across the northwest of the province of Shanxi in the People's Republic of China, at about 39 degrees north. Its uniform brown coloring comes from the layer of loess covering the area. The image, taken in winter, shows terraced slopes on which snow is still lying. The river moving from west to east in the image, which flows into the Huang He, or Yellow River, along with its numerous tributaries and streams, has greatly eroded the loess-covered mountainous region. The plateau, which contains many ravines, has very few roads and is thinly populated. Some 2000 years ago 50 percent of this ancient Chinese settlement was covered in forest.

1 *Loess Plateau* ↓

The Chinese word shanxi *means "western mountains" because the province's mountain chains, which stretch from the southwest to the northeast, are located to the west of the Chinese lowlands. Their base is formed by a bedrock on which flat, paleozoic and mesozoic layers of stone lie. These can be seen in the quarry located to the north of the settlement in the upper right edge of the image. A huge layer of loess, an average of 100 m (328 ft) thick, lies above this layer of rock. Northwest winds from the Gobi*

ward direction. The terracing of the slopes can moderate and hinder this process, but it cannot wholly prevent it.

3 Terrace Agriculture

Farming people have been deforesting the fertile loess-covered moutainous region since at least the 3rd century BC and it has continued unabated since then at heights of up to 2400 m (7874 ft), although agriculture is disadvantaged here in several respects. As a rule, there are only 140 to 180 frost-free days a year in this region,

Desert have deposited this fine, loosely structured substance throughout the millennia. Wherever the layer of loess is exposed to wind and water, it is eroded and cut into pieces; deep, steep-walled ravines are then created.

2 Retrograde Erosion

The summer rains can transform the small rivers on the loess plateau into raging torrents that destroy everything in their path while the narrow valleys cover them in layers of mud. The loess reaches the streams and rivers in the Huang He, which owes its name, Yellow River, to the erosion of the loess-covered mountainous region. In the lower reaches, its water contains sediment weighing 35 kg per cubic meter (2.2 lb per cubic foot). The image impressively shows how the erosion progresses inexorably in a back-

which has a cold, wintry, steppe-like climate. In January, the temperature falls as low as -12°C (10.4°F), while in July it rises to 22–27°C (71.6–80.6°F). However, the real enemy of the people in the semi-arid region is unreliable precipitation. An average of 400 mm (15.7 in) of rain falls in summer, but at very irregular intervals: In some years the inhabitants are afflicted by the feared floods, which wash away the soil, while in other years they may be affected by extreme drought.

The main crops cultivated are millet, sorghum, spring wheat, oats, and soya beans, a fact reflected in a cuisine that predominantly contains carbohydrates. The rural population suffers from a lack of fuels, feed for the animals, and fertilizers, and the per capita income in the agricultural sector is very low compared to the average for the country as a whole.

4 Relics from a People's Commune

The rulers of the province of Shanxi were early supporters of initiatives stemming from the Communist agricultural policies. This is why land reforms were carried out here as early as the 1940s and were followed by collectivization in 1953. In 1958, the People's Commune became a reality: Huge stables, barns, machine halls, accommodation, and canteens were built. As had been the case with individual farmsteads in the past, the collective facilities were walled in. Decollectivization occurred in 1978, and today individual families once again farm the land that they rent.

1:4,500,000

Albers Equal Area Conic Projection

Changbai
2750 Baitou Shan (Paektu-san)
Samjiyon
Linjiang
Chunggang

1284
Huchang
HYESAN
Changbai
Odaejin
Kimjongsuk-up

1846
Chasong
Musan
Kanggye
Kapsan
Kilju
Musu Dan

Chosan
Sansu-ri
Hoeryong
Honggun-ri
Pabal-Ri
GIMCHAEK
2309
Chongchon
2522
Tanchon

2187
Changjin
Hoban

NORTH KOREA

Sea of Japan

HAMHEUNG
Sinhung
Pukchong

Alkawa

Sado-shima

Yamato
Basin

Yamato Rise

JAPAN

Honshū

SOUTH KOREA

SEOUL

DAEGU

BUSAN

GWANGJU

Jeju Do

Kyūshū

KAGOSHIMA

MIYAZAKI

PACIFIC OCEAN

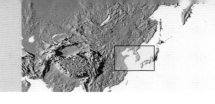

Baitou Shan

The highest mountain in the northeast of China is the 2744 m (9003 ft) high Baitou Shan, located in the province of Jilin at 42 degrees north; its uppermost parts are covered in snow. Baitou Shan ("White Head") is the Chinese name, while Paektu-san is the Korean name for the relatively unknown volcano across which the border between the People's Republic of China and North Korea runs. It is part of the Changbai Shan Natural Park named for the mountain range, and is very important to the Koreans, who regard it as a holy mountain.

The volcano massif has formed above the subduction zone as part of the circum-Pacific ring of fire. The Pacific Plate sinks below the lighter Asian Continental Plate in this zone. The last huge explosion proven to have taken place here occurred in around 1000 BC, when volcano ash made up of rhyolithe and trachyte was scattered as far as North Japan. In AD 965 the volcano erupted again, this time spreading pyroclast with a high pumice content. The last known eruptions, with lesser impact, occurred in 1413, 1597, 1668, and 1702. Since then, gas has been observed escaping close to the summit several times and hot springs have opened out on the slopes. From time to time, the surrounding area is shaken by small, volcanic earthquakes.

① Tian Chi ↑

Baitou Shan's 4.5 km (3 mile) wide crater summit is filled by the 384 m (1260 ft) deep Tian Chi lake ("Heavenly Lake"), which is the second-largest interior lake in North Korea. Its water level is located 2257 m (7405 ft) above sea level and the lake is covered in ice between the middle of October and the middle of June. The steep walls of the caldera were formed when the summit of the volcano fell into a cavity underneath the crater. The walls consist mainly of pyroclastic

flows welded together. Several rivers have their sources on the slopes of the volcano and have cut their valleys into the ash cone. These rivers include the Yalu Jiang, Tumen, and Songhua.

② Changbai Shan

The largest massif in the province of Jilin has average heights of 800 to 1000 m (2625 to 3281 ft). Remnants of the forests, which used to stretch across much greater distances, are found here and are a rarity in China. The coal deposits also make the region interesting from an economic point of view for both China and Korea.

③ Agricultural Areas

A Korean-speaking people live in the mountains on both sides of the border, most of whom are farmers. They cultivate the land here; soya beans, maize, millet, potatoes, wheat, and oil plants can be grown due to the black types of soil covering the plateau, although these are only found on the Chinese side. Only one crop cycle a year can be harvested because a semi-humid, cold to temperate, continental climate predominates here. In fact, only 120 to 140 days of the year are frost-free. In January the temperature falls to -10°C (14°F), while it reaches 23°C (73.4°F) in July.

MAP

1 : 4 , 5 0 0 , 0 0 0

Japan

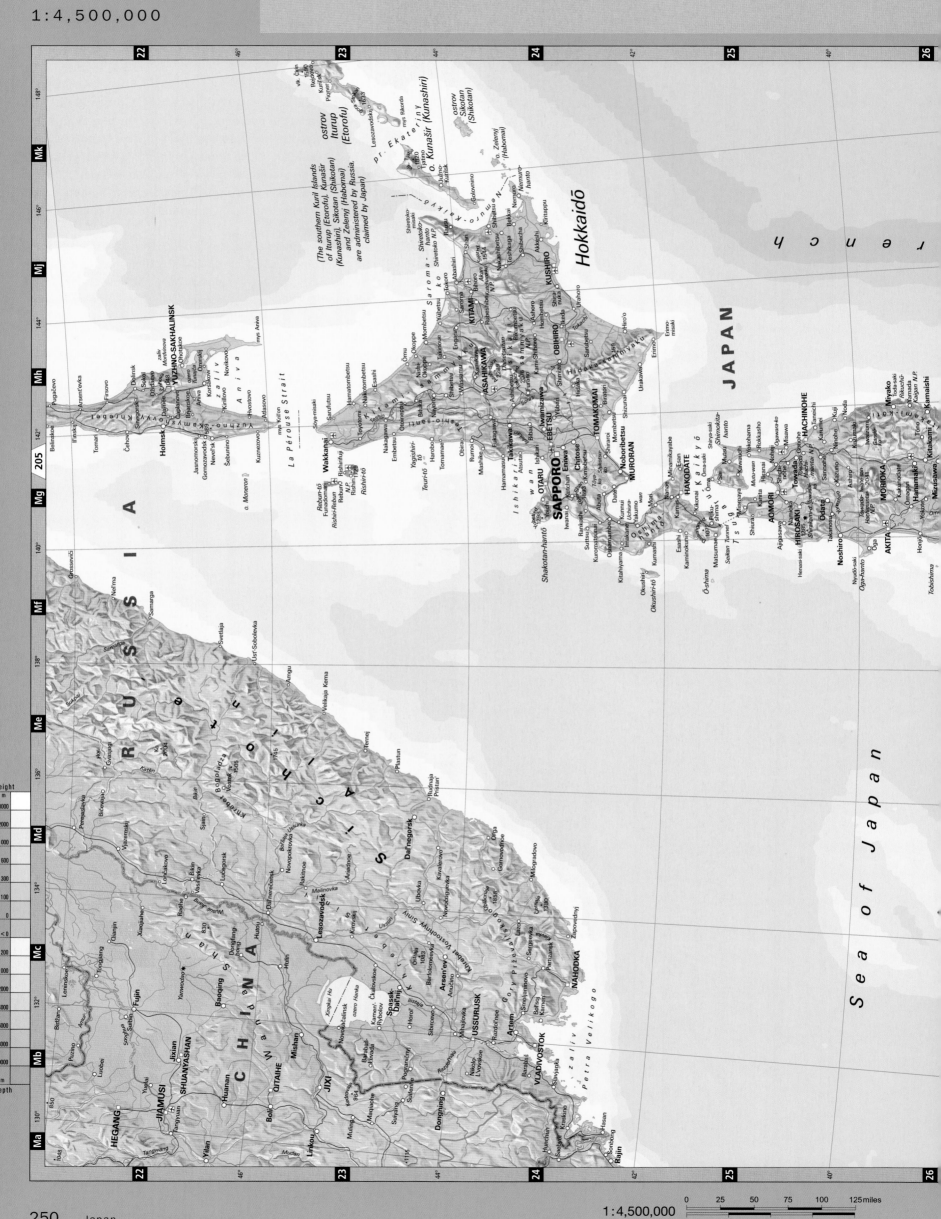

205

The southern Kuril Islands of Iturup (Etorofu), Kunašir (Kunashiri), Šikotan (Shikotan) and Zelenyj (Habomai) are administered by Russia, claimed by Japan.

R U S S I A

C H I N A

Sea of Japan

Hokkaidō

J A P A N

SAPPORO

Height
m
3000
2000
1000
600
300
100
0
< 0
200
1000
2000
4000
6000
8000
10000
m
Depth

1:4,500,000

| 0 | 25 | 50 | 75 | 100 | 125 miles |

| 0 | 50 | 100 | 150 | 200km |

Albers Equal Area Conic Projection

Japan

J a p a n

I z u   T r e n c h

Hachijyo-shima

Aogashima

P A C I F I C   O C E A N

Yamato
Basin

Yamato

Honshū

Sado-shima

Oki-shoto
Dōgo
Nishino-shima

Dokdo
(Takeshima)
(Admin. by South
Korea, claimed
by Japan)

Ullungdo
(South Korea)
Ulling

ISHINOMAKI
Shiogama
SENDAI
IZUMI
Haramachi
Namie
Tendō
FUKUSHIMA
KORIYAMA
YAMAGATA
Sukagawa
IWAKI
HITACHI
KITAIBARAKI
KATSUTA
MITO
TSUCHIURA
Sawara
Chōshi
FUNABASHI
KASHIWA
KAWASAKI
URAWA
TOKYO
YOKOHAMA
HIRATSUKA
YOKOSUKA
AIZU
WAKAMATSU
KIRYU
ASHIKAGA
KŌNOSU
OMIYA
KAWAGOE
HACHIŌJI
ODAWARA
NUMAZU
FUJI
KŌFU
MAEBASHI
TAKASAKI
UTSU
NOMIYA
Ōshima
SHIMIZU
SHIZUOKA
FUJIEDA
NAGAOKA
NIIGATA
NAGANO
UEDA
MATSUMOTO
Shiojiri
HAMAMATSU
TOYOHASHI
JŌETSU
TAKAOKA
TOYAMA
Uozu
KANAZAWA
KOMATSU
FUKUI
Takefu
Tsuruga
GIFU
NAGOYA
TOYOTA
OKAZAKI
ANJO
HANDA
MATSUZAKA
ISE
TSU
YOKKAICHI
SUZUKA
KARIYA
NANAO
Himi
Takayama
Ōno
Seki
TAJIMI
Ōmi-NOMIYA
OGAKI
HIKONE
KYŌTO
NARA
ŌTSU
HIGASHI-ŌS.
ŌSAKA
SAKAI
KOBE
AMAGASAKI
TAKATSUKI
WAKA
YAMA
TANABE
KISHIWADA
HIMEJI
KAKO
GAWA
KASAI
TOTTORI
MATSUE
YONAGO
OKAYAMA
KURASHIKI
FUKUYAMA
SOJA
HIGASHI-
HIROSHIMA
ONOMICHI
IMABARI
MATSUYAMA
KURE
HIROSHIMA
IWAKUNI
TOKUYAMA
YAMAGUCHI
HŌFU
HAGI
Masuda
Hamada
TOKU
SHIMA
Anan
TAKAMATSU
Sakaide
NIIHAMA
KŌCHI
Muroto
HYUGA
NOBEOKA
ŌITA
BEPPU
Usa

Honshū

Shikoku

Kyūshū

Noto-hantō
Wajima

Izu-hantō

Bōsō-hantō

Izu - shotō
Miyake-shima
Mikura-shima
Niijima
Kōzu-sh.

38°
36°
34°
32°
30°
30°
31°
144°
142°
140°
138°
136°
134°
132°

27
28
29
30
31
Mi
Mh
Mg
Mf
Me
Md
Mc

▽247

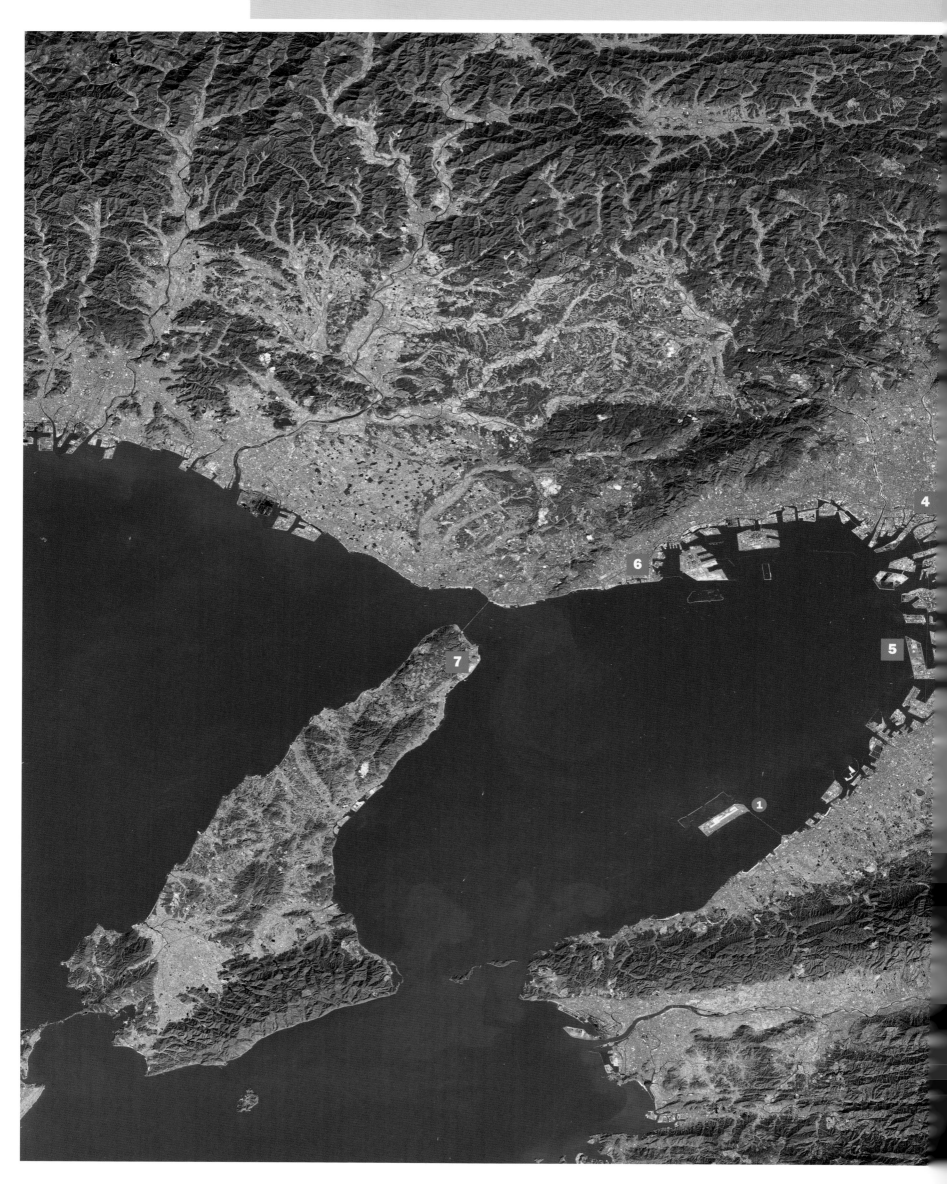

Ōsaka

Ōsaka is the cultural center of western Japan and, after Tokyo and Yoko-hama, the third-largest city in the country. The home of 2.8 milllion inhabitants, it extends across a huge area and is surrounded by Ōsaka Bay. Its convenient location on the Yodo River, between the sea and wooded hills, was the reason why the reigning monarchs founded the first settlement here as early as the 4th century. Although Ōsaka is overshadowed by Tokyo where tourism is concerned, the city warrants a visit, not least for its famous nightlife and culinary delights. Due to the provision of many English-language signs, Ōsaka is easier to travel around for European visitors than most other cities in Japan.

1 *Airport* ↑
Ōsaka is an important hub for international air traffic. Kansai International Airport in the city is located on an artificial, rectangular island, which lies off the coast in Ōsaka Bay and is linked to the mainland via a bridge. The Nikko Kansai Airport Hotel was built on the same island as the airport and is directly linked to the terminal building. Thanks to building projects such as these, Ōsaka had developed into a very modern metropolis by the beginning of the 21st century.

2 Ōsaka Castle
The castle is by far the most famous sight in the city and is considered to be the nucleus of Ōsaka. The original building was completed in 1586, and at that time it was the largest castle in Japan. During the reign of the Shogun Tokugawa dynasty, however, the well-fortified structure was initially besieged and then, in 1615, largely destroyed. The current building was completed in 1931: Only a few gates and annexes remain of the original castle. However, these areas are considered to be the most important cultural shrines in Japan. An exhibition on the history of the city as well as collections of weapons and traditional Bunraku puppets are today housed on a number of floors.

3 Shitennoji Temple
This building is considered to be the birthplace of Buddhism in Japan. The original

structure was built at the end of the 6th century and was completely restored several times after it was wrecked by fires. The current building was constructed in 1965. The five-story pagoda is its most striking feature. Tennoji Park extends to the southwest of the gates, some of which are well-preserved, and surround the building. In addition to botanical gardens and a zoo, Tennoji Park contains the Ōsaka Municipal Museum of Art, with its impressive collection of both Japanese and Chinese paintings.

4 Yodo River
Ōsaka is located in Ōsaka Bay, at the confluence of several rivers, but the Yodo is the most important, winding through the city and taking up a number of tributaries as it does so. With more than 1000 bridges spanning its many canals, Ōsaka was given the nickname "Venice of the East," but in recent decades some of the canals have been filled in.

5 Port
Cargo ships, ferries, and fishing fleets jostle for attention in Ōsaka Bay—the largest city in western Japan owes it economic significance to its port. Many goods produced in Ōsaka are exported from here, while the port also plays a big role in supplying the city and the surrounding areas with imports.

6 Kobe
The university city founded at the end of the 19th century has one of the largest sea ports in the country. The 931 m (3054 ft) high Rokko Mountain rises behind the city. On January 17, 1995, one of the most devastating earthquakes in Japanese history, measuring 7.2 on the Richter scale, destroyed large parts of the city.

7 Awaji-shima
The island of Awaji, located in Ōsaka Bay, is linked to the city of Kobe in the northeast via the almost 4 km (2.5 mile) long Akashi Kaikyo suspension bridge.

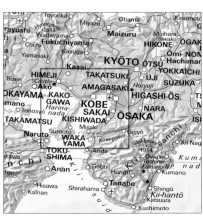

1:4,500,000

| 0 | 25 | 50 | 75 | 100 | 125 miles |

| 0 | 50 | 100 | 150 | 200 km |

Albers Equal Area Conic Projection

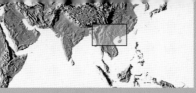

3

1

Hanoi

As the image clearly shows, Hanoi is a waterfront city. Even its name, Hanoi, in use since 1831, can be translated as "in the river." Numerous small and large lakes and the reddish-brown waters of the Sông Hông determine the cityscape of the Vietnamese capital, situated in a horseshoe bend of the Red River on whose western bank it nestles. The city was founded in 1010, but during the course of the centuries Hanoi was conquered repeatedly, lost its function as the capital for an interim period, and was renamed several times. Compared to other Asian capitals, which have developed into metropolises with a western character, Hanoi, with its roughly three million inhabitants, is a latecomer with a very Asian feel.

1 *Ba Dinh Square and Ho Chi Minh Mausoleum* ←
The huge Ba Dinh Square radiates an austere functionality because the political center of Vietnam is located here. Together with the parliament and some ministries, important institutions forming part of the government district are grouped around the square. Many government agencies are today located in the beautiful buildings formerly occupied by the colonial government. In 1945, President Ho Chi Minh read the Declaration of Independence from here and today the site is marked by the imposing building containing the Ho Chi Minh Mausoleum. The palace of the former French governor general and the simple residence of Ho Chi Minh are located close to the

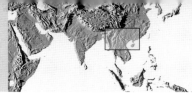

mausoleum. The monumental Ho Chi Minh Museum, which adjoins the mausoleum, was a gift from the Soviet Union. Many villas from the colonial era line the surrounding avenues and are used mainly as embassy buildings.

2 *Old Town* ←

Each block in the old town is occupied down to the last square centimeter: Whole villages open up behind facades and impenetrable walls. Most of the old brick houses come from the 19th century and are held together only by sand, lime, and sugar cane syrup. There is a significant lack of accommodation in the old part of Hanoi. Today, four or five families often live in houses designed for one. Houseboats, still a very common

form of accommodation, lie moored by the banks of the river and along the canals.

3 West Lake

The Ho Tay, also know as West Lake, is a dead branch of the Red River and, with a circumference of almost 14 km (9 miles), is the largest lake in Hanoi. The well-to-do area of the city has been spreading out along its shores for centuries. While kings and members of the aristocracy originally built their summer palaces here, in the 20th century it was high-ranking officials who had their Communist party buildings and holiday homes built on its shores. Today, a huge construction boom has broken out: Office buildings and hotels are being constructed at great speed.

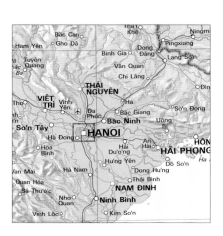

Southern China, Taiwan

Height
m
3000
2000
1000
600
300
100
0
< 0
200
1000
2000
4000
6000
8000
10000
m
Depth

1:4,500,000

0   25   50   75   100   125 miles
0   50   100   150   200 km
Albers Equal Area Conic Projection

HANGZHOU
Xiaoshan
Shaoxing
Cixi
Yuyao
Zhoushan
Haining
Haiyan
Wangpang
Yang
Daqu Shan
Dai Shan
Zhoushan
Qundao
Qiandao
Zhoushan
Dao
Putuoshan
Hemudu
Yizhi
Zhongzhai
NINGBO
Shenjiamen
Wenhua
Fenghua
Oikou
Liuheng
Dao
Zhuji
Sheng Xian
Xinchang
Xiangshan
Dongyang
Ninghai
Shipu
Pan'an
Tiantaishan
Sanjiaotang
Niutou
Shan
Tiantai
Sanmen
Linhai
Xianju
1382
Huangyan
JIAOJIANG
Jinyun
Yantou
Dangshanshan
Daxi

East China Sea

Tokara-rettō
Kuchino-shima
Nakano-shima
Suwanose-
shima
Akuseki-
shima
Takara-
shima
Yokate-shima

Satsunan Islands

Kasari
Amami
Ō-shima
Kikai-shima
Naze
Setouchi

Tokuno-shima
Tori-shima
Tokunoshima
Okinoerabu-shima
Wadonari

Amami Islands

Ryukyu Islands

Iheya-shima
Iheya
Izena-shima
Yoron
Yoron-shima
Ie-shima
Oku
Aguni-shima
Motobu
Nago
Okinawa-
shima
Kume-shima
Gusuku sites
Kin
Ishikawa
Gushikawar
Ishikawa
NAHA
OKINAWA

Okinawa Islands

Kerama-
rettō

Uotsuri-shima
Sekibisho-shima
Senkaku-shotō

Pengchia Yü
Huaping Yü
Fukuei Chiao
Keelung
Miyako-rettō (J)
Miyako-
Shima
Hirara
TAIPEI
Yangmingshan N.P.
Tanshui
HSINCHU
TAOYUAN
Wulai
Ilan
Suao
Yaeyama-rettō (J)
Tarama-
shima
Hirado
Miao Li
Chilan
Yonaguni-Shima
Ishigaki
Otomi
Ishigaki-Shima
FENGYUAN
Tungshih
Taroko N.P.
Iriomote-Shima
Kuro Shima
CHANGHUA
TAICHUNG
Poli
Taroko
Hateruma-shima
YUANLIN
Nantou
Toulu
Sun
Moon
Lake
Kuangfu
Fengpin
CHIAYI
Alishan
3951
Alishan N.P.
Changpin
Hsinying
Yuli
Tungho
Chiasien
Fuli
Taiwan

Ryukyu Trench

Tropic of Cancer

Tropic of Cancer

HUALIEN

PINGTUNG
TAITUNG
Lü Tao
FENGSHAN
Fangliao
Tawu
TAIWAN
Fangshan
Tajen
Checheng
Lan Yü
Kenting N.P.
Lan Yü
Hengchun
Oluanpi

PACIFIC OCEAN

Luzon Strait

Itbayat I.

Batan Islands
Batan
Island
Sabtang I.

35

Balingtang Channel

Calayan
Island
Babuyan
Island

PHILIPPINES

Dalupiri
Island
Babuyan Islands
Camiguin
Island
Fuga
Island

Philippine

Sea

Mayrara Pt.
Claveria
Palaui I.
Bangui Bay
Escarpade Pt.
Pansian
Pamplona
Abulug
Santa Ana
Laoag
Aparri
Bawa
Iligan Pt.
Buguey
Lal-lo
Solsona
Kasa
Alcala

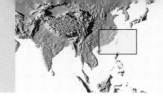

1 Hong Kong Island: Central District

The British established their capital, Victoria, here and the government is today still based in what is known as the Central District. Huge skyscrapers such as Exchange Square, Jardine House, the Bank of Hong Kong and Shanghai, the silver, shimmering Bank of China—until 1992 the tallest building in Asia—and many other high-rises made of steel and glass house financial institutes, the stock exchange, and information and administrative centers. Although it is not obvious at first glance, most of these modern structures were constructed in accordance with the rules of geomancy (feng shui) handed down through the generations.

2 Wooded Slopes

Despite the initial impression of the dominating skyscrapers, there are a number of green spaces in the area, as well as restaurants, galleries, nightclubs, and, only a few minutes' walk to the west, the Hillside Escalator, which, at a length of 800 m (2625 ft), is the longest escalator in the world. It carries about 30,000 people a day, downward from 6 to 10 in the morning, and upward from 10 in the morning to 10 at night. Directly behind the strip of skyscrapers and street canyons located parallel to the coast begins the steep ascent of the hills, some of which are covered in dense growth. Here it is possible to see that the rocky island of Hong Kong, with all of its bays, is a continuation of the southern Chinese mountainous region. This is why the coastline has, from 1870 to the present, constantly been widened to create land for building on as well as for traffic, and industrial and port areas. Many traffic problems are caused by the cramped space available.

3 Wan Chai

The former nightclub district of Wan Chai can be reached by tram. Today, its main attraction is the curved Convention and Exhibition Center building. The ceremony for the handing over of Hong Kong to the government of the People's Republic of China took place here on July 1, 1997. In Golden Bauhinia Square there is a giant sculpture of the bauhinia flower, the symbol of Hong Kong.

4 Happy Valley

To the south of Causeway Bay lies Happy Valley; the Happy Valley Sports Ground, with its horseracing track, can clearly be seen in the image. The fact that such a large open-air area was able to survive in a city known for its lack of space is due to the Hong Kong Jockey Club, founded in 1894. The original plan was to use the valley for a settlement, but heat and malaria drove out the English and the area was then given over to horseracing, which received additional impetus due to the Chinese passion for gambling. Today, the modern complex is characterized by luxurious clubhouses, stands, and betting offices. All of Hong Kong has betting fever on racing days; a large amount of the revenue from gambling is used for the benefit of social institutions.

5 *Causeway Bay* ⬎

Double-decker trams have linked the western and the eastern parts of the city since 1904. Japanese institutions predominate in the district adjoining Wan Chai to the east, while dozens of boats

Hong Kong

Hong Kong means "fragrant bay" in Chinese and it was the name given to a rocky island located 70 km (43 miles) from Guangzhou (Canton), on which incense sticks were made in a village until the 19th century. After the British occupied the island in 1842, a profitable trade in opium was carried on from here, and in 1860 they also took possesson of Kowloon Peninsula located opposite the island. In 1898, they leased the new territories from the Chinese for an agreed period of 99 years and the British Crown Colony of Hong Kong developed into one of the largest trading, financial, and services centers in the world. In 1997, however, the 1103 km^2 (426 square miles) that make up Hong Kong (Xianggang in Mandarin) were handed back to the People's Republic of China, although it was initially to be ruled by its own form of government. The motto of "One State–Two Systems" applies to the 6.7 million inhabitants until 2047. Hong Kong distinguishes itself from China by means of its form of government, its economy, and its currency (the Hong Kong dollar). Strict security precautions prevent Chinese living on the mainland from emigrating to this special administrative zone.

are moored in Causeway Bay, beside the Royal Hong Kong Yacht Club, and are protected from the feared typhoons behind a breakwater. Although the densely populated northern side lacks beautiful, quiet bathing beaches, walking trails, and pleasure parks, they are abundant on the southern side of the island.

6 *Hong Kong Cultural Center* ⬆
The Cultural Center is located close to the waterfront promenade and contains museums with classical Chinese masterpieces and contemporary

art, as well as the Hong Kong Space Museum and the planetarium. There is a superb view of Hong Kong Island from Kowloon Pier. Victoria City, which is located on the other side of Victoria Harbour, can be reached in just a few minutes on the Star Ferry.

7 Kowloon

The name Kowloon means "Nine Dragons" and is so called because of a chain of hills adjoining the peninsula in the north. The southernmost tip, Tsim Sha Tsui, is shown here. The central axis of Nathan Road leads northward and thousands of businesses are lined up alongside each side of this road. Many businesses operating in the export industry are also located here, but the textile and electrical industries, as well as the toy and watch industries, are currently struggling with high wage and property costs.

Kowloon was once notorious for its Walled City, a Chinese enclave in what was then a British Colony, which became synonymous with crime, prostitution, and drug trafficking because the Hong Kong police were not allowed to enter. The labyrinthine corridors were eventually pulled down in 1992. The area is now occupied by Kowloon City Park, with its sculpture park, swimming pool, and the Chinese Garden, which breaks up the sea of houses.

Height
m
3000
2000
1000
600
300
100
0
<0
200
1000
2000
4000
6000
8000
10000
m
Depth

INDIAN

OCEAN

Rajang Yoma (Arakan Mts.)

Combermere Bay
Yebok
Kyaukpyu
Letpan
Rambré (Ramree I.)
Cheduba I.
Rambre
Man'aung Kyun (Cheduba Island)
Meinmagwe
Man'aung
Haywood Channel
SANDOWAY
Ngapali

Dalangyun
Egayit
Mindon
Thayetmyo
Allanmyo
Thagaya
PROME
Shwedaung
Oktwin
TOUNGOO

Lewe
Ngwedaung

Kawlipoli
Kwedalkon
Pasawng

Loi-kaw

Na Wai
Mae Suya
Sop Huai
Thoeng
Muang Hongsa

Doi 2175
Chiang Dao
Phan
Chun
Chiang Kham
Thung Muang

CHIANG MAI

Mae Hong Son
Doi Suthep Poi Nat. P.
Mae Khajan
Mae Tieng
Ngao
Chian Muan
Hae
Tha Wang Pha

Paukkaung
Kyungon
Taungup
1390
Man'aung

BASSEIN

Ngathainggyaung
Yegyi

HENZADA
Kyangin
Gyobingauk
Penwegon
Theme

Doi Inthanon Nat. Park
Doi Inthanon 2890
Lamphun
Mae Su
Mae Chaem
Hot

Chon Tong

LAMPANG
Long
Phrae
Den Chai
Wiang Sa
Ban Pa Daeng

Sirikit Res.
1072
Rong Kwang
Nan
Ban Chirim

18°

Gwa

Zigon

Mezaligon
Myanaung
Kyeintali

Lemyethna

Nyaunglebin

Minhla
Letpadan

Hinthada
Kanyidaung

Kyaunggon
Taikky
Danubyu

Nyaungkhashe

Shegyin

Hlegu
Thanatpin

Mae Sariang
Mae Pok

Mae Sot

Sop Moei

Thung Salaeng Luang N.P.

Sop Prap
Si Satchanalai Nat. P.
1285

Uttaradit
Si Satchanalai

Phu Yen 1031

Ban Pak Bat

Na Haeo
Pong Chi
Lom Sak

Bogale
Phapon

Magugon
Mawdin
Ama

Ye

Winyaw

Gulf of

Martaban

Tavoy

Nam Chon Res.

Peinedaw
16°

Mouths of the Irrawaddy

MYANMAR

(BURMA)

Andaman

Basin

Andaman

Sea

Ten Degree Channel

37

38

39

40

41

42

262   Thailand, Cambodia, Southern Vietnam

1:4,500,000

0   25   50   75   100   125 miles
0   50   100   150   200 km
Lambert Azimuthal Equal Area Projection

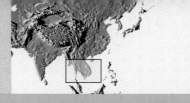

Gulf of

Tonkin

HAINAN
(China)

H a i n a n

South China Sea text areas:

SANYA

HUÊ

DÀ NẴNG

Amphitrite Group
Xishaqundao
(Paracel Is.)
(Admin. China)
Crescent Group

QUY NHON

Tuy Hòa

L A O S

VIENTIANE

UDON
THANI

KHON KAEN

Kalasin

Savannakhét

UBON
RATCHATHANI

Surin

C A M B O D I A

PHNOM PENH

Angkor Wat

Bătdămbăng

Tonle

Sap

Cardamom Mtns.

Phanom Dong Rak

Chuŏr Phnum Dângrek

V I E T N A M

Buôn Me Thuột

NHA TRANG

Hòn Tre

Đà Lạt

Cam Ranh

THỦ DẦU MỘT

BIÊN HÒA

HO CHI MINH
(SAIGON)

Phan Thiết

Tân An

MỸ THO

VŨNG TÀU

Bên Tre

LONG XUYÊN

Sa Đéc

Vĩnh Long

Hà Tiên

CẦN THƠ

Trà Vinh

Rạch Giá

Sóc Trăng

Đảo Phú Quốc

Cà Mau

Minh Hải

Côn Đảo

Côn Đảo

Spratly
Island

S O U T H   C H I N A   S E A

Mouths of the Mekong

Quân Đảo Nam Du

Hòn Thổ Chu

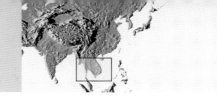

Bangkok

Krung Thep, "City of Angels," is what the Thais call their capital, Bangkok. Under King Rama I, this previously insignificant city became capital of the Kingdom of Thailand in 1782, and today it is a vast, bustling place with contradictory atmospheres of chaos and peace. The city is large, highly populated, noisy, and full of cars. However, it also has its quiet corners, oases of tranquillity in the midst of the turmoil, and quiet little streets lined with old teak wood houses. The magnificent palaces and monasteries of Bangkok, with their colorful and golden hues, are evidence of this fast-growing metropolis: Bangkok is an Asian melting pot in which more than six million people live.

1 *Wat Phra Kaeo* ↑

By far the most impressive sight in Bangkok is the large royal palace district. This is also where the most important shrine in the country is located, the Wat Phra Kaeo, with the famous Emerald Buddha. A special ceremony takes place here three times a year during which the king himself personally changes the Buddha's clothes. In addition to the large number of temples, the palace district also encompasses a broad range of royal museums and administrative buildings. It is used by the king as the traditional backdrop for state receptions and special ceremonies.

2 Wat Pho

The oldest and largest temple in Bangkok has been the site of a sanitorium and pharmacy since time immemorial. Today, the head offices of the world-famous school of reflexology zone foot massage is situated in the temple district. A total of 91 *prangs* (spires) and *chedis* (stupas) stand in the courtyard in front of the shrine that houses the famous Reclining Buddha. This 45 m (148 ft) long and 15 m (49 ft) high monumental figure is gold-plated and liberally decorated with mother-of-pearl on its eyes and also its feet, which are considered to be the most sacred part of the human body.

3 Wat Suthat

The Wat Suthat is one of the oldest and, at the same time, one of the most beautiful Buddhist temples in Bangkok. Three kings had this

temple built, starting in 1782. In addition to its delightful architecture, it contains very interesting wall paintings. One of the most striking structures in Bangkok is located in the center of a busy square, directly in front of the Wat Suthat temple complex. The 27 m (89 ft) high teak wood frame is the Giant Swing, and was the focus of the Swing Festival, a royal new year ceremony that continued from the 18th century until 1935. After each rice harvest, daring monks came here to have themselves swung through the air on a narrow board in order to try to catch a bag of coins in their teeth.

4 Klong

The once numerous canals of Bangkok are called *klongs* and, in the past, were used as floating markets. However, in recent decades most of the canals running through the city have been filled in, partly because of the danger of cholera and partly because urgently needed roads had to be built. Today, numerous boat owners invite visitors on an interesting tour on the Menam Chao Phraya River and then through what is still a complicated network of small and large canals. Life is at its most varied here in the morning and late afternoon.

5 Wat Prayun

The artificial hill at the entrance to the temple was the idea of King Rama III, who was inspired by the wax of a burning candle to create this shape. *Chedis, prangs,* and small temples adorn the hill, which stands at the heart of a manmade pond.

6 *Wat Arun* ↓

According to legend, the "Temple of the Dawn" was built on the spot where, in 1767, after a long march with the last survivors, General Taksin saw the sun rise after the destruction of the old Thai capital, Ayutthaya, by the Burmese army. The 86 m (282 ft) central prang of this temple has now become a symbol of Bangkok. The outer sides of the brick building are decorated with countless porcelain pieces. The top of the prang provides a wonderful view over the city. And spectacular sunsets can be seen over the Wat Arun from the opposite bank of the Menam Chao Phraya River, which flows through Bangkok.

108°   110°   112°   114°   116°   118°

Le   Lf   Lg   Lh   Lj

36

Haitou   Dan Xian   Chengmai   Wenchang
Chancheng   Yaxing   Tunchang   Huangzhu   Penglai
    Baisha
Dongfang   Changjiang   Qionghai
    Tongshi   1868   Qiongzhong
Ledong   Daben   Wanning
Yinggehai   Jiusuo   Yacheng   Lingshui   Dazhou Dao
Tianyahaijiao   Tuqu Gang   HAINAN
    SANYA   (China)

H a i n a n

W u z h i   S h a n

18°

37

16°   DÀ NẴNG
    Chan
    Hôi An
    Thăng Bình
    Quê Sơn   Tam Kỳ
    Bin Lâm
    Núi Thân
    Mũi Nam Trâm
Trà My   Bình Sơn
    Trà Bồng   Mũi Ba Làng An
    Quảng Ngãi

Amphitrite Group

Xishaqundao
(Paracel Is.)
Crescent Group   (Admin. China)

263

38

    Thạch Tru
    Dức Phổ
    Thạch Tru
Ba Tơ   Hoài Nho'n
Gia Vức
Kon Plông   1079
    Mũi Vĩnh Kim
    Diêm Tiêu
    Phù Cát

S O U T H   C H I N A   S E A

Scarborough
Shoal

14°   An Khê   Bình Định
    Tây Sơn
Giang Trung   Vân
1331   Canh   QUY NHON
Cheo   Song Cầu
Reo   Chí Thanh
    La Hai
    Krông Pa   Tuy Hòa

39   Krong Buk   Tây Sơn
B.E. Klô'p   Vạnh Ninh
M' Drac
    Đưc Mỹo   Ninh Hòa
Chu
Dang Sin   Diên Phu'ở'c   NHA TRANG
2403   Sơn Hiệp   Hòn Tre

12°   Đà Lạt   Cam Ranh
    Ninh   Vĩnh Hy
Đưc Trong   Sơn
    Văn Lâm   Phan Rang

V I E T N A M

West York
Island
    Thitu Island
Loaita   Flat Island
Island   Nanshan Island

Itu Aba I.

Namyit
Island

Height
m
3000
2000
1000
600
300
100
0
<0
200
1000
2000
4000
6000
8000
10000
m
Depth

40   Sóng Lũy   Tuy Phong
    Bắc Bình   Mũi La Gan

Phù Quý

Sin Cowe I.

S p r a t l y   I s l a n d s

Malat
Bay
    Eran
    Bay
Malabungan   Banua Mantalingajan
    Mt   2100   Bro
    San Antonio Bay

41

Cuarteron
Reef

Commodore
Reef

Cape Bulikyan   Coral
Pandanan I.   Bay
North Balabac Strait   Bugsuk Island
Ramos I.   Balabac

Spratly
Island

Lizzie
Webber
Reef

Mariveles
Reef

S p r a t l y   I s l a n d s

P a l a w a n   P a s s a g e

8°
Amboyna
Cay

42

Le   Lf   Lg   Lh   Lj

110°   112°   114°   116°

Balabac Island
Cape Melville
B a l a b a c   S t r a i t

274

0   25   50   75   100   125 miles
0   50   100   150   200 km

1:4,500,000

Lambert Azimuthal Equal Area Projection

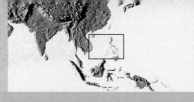

Manila

The east coast of Luzon, the largest island in the Philippines, is broken up by numerous peninsulas and islands, deep bays, steep cliffs, and flat beaches. On the east coast of Manila Bay, on both sides of the confluence of the River Pasig, the largest densely populated area in the island kingdom has developed—metropolitan Manila, with five cities, more than twenty communes, and a total of well over ten million inhabitants. Since the Spanish colonial era the present-day city of Manila has been the administrative center and educational center of the country. Due to its port, the city also became the most important trading and industrial center in the Philippines. The Filipinos take the threat posed to the island kingdom by seismic and volcanic activities in a calm manner.

① *Manila* ↑

In 1571, the Spaniards built the walled old town quarter of Intramuros to the south of the River Pasig. After the port city had resisted the attempts to conquer it by the Dutch, English, and then the Portuguese, the Americans finally conquered the city in 1898. Manila was occupied by the Japanese from 1942 to 1945 and suffered an enormous amount of bomb damage, but much of the area was restored in the 1980s and still bears witness to former Spanish colonizers in its architecture.

② Manila Bay

In times of war the entrance leading from Manila Bay to the South China Sea was hotly disputed. Terrible battles were fought, in particular during World War Two between the Americans and the Japanese, for the island of Corregidor.

③ Laguna de Bay

With an area of 922 km² (356 square miles), Laguna de Bay is the largest lake in the Philippines. It used to be directly linked to Manila Bay but, due to tectonic processes, the land was raised and the lagoon was thus cut off from the sea. Today, Laguna de Bay drains into Manila Bay via the River Pasig. Numerous short tributaries provide the continental lake with a large amount of suspended matter, which explains the light color of the water. The island of Talim has an area of 28 km² (11 square miles).

④ Lake Taal

Lake Taal, a huge caldera covering an area of 127 km² (49 square miles) is located about 65 km (40 miles) to the south of Manila. The volcanic island located in the lake points to the volcanic character of this collapsed basin, whose water-filled main crater has a diameter of 1.3 km (0.8 miles). The central volcanic cone is only 311 m (1020 ft) high and is still active. In 1901, an eruption claimed the lives of 2000 victims; it has most recently erupted in 1965 and 1977.

⑤ Bataan Peninsula

Two other volcanoes, Mount Bataan at 1388 m (4554 ft) and Balanga at 1253 m (4111 ft), shown on the image, are considered to be extinct. They are located on Bataan Peninsula, along a tectonic line in this area to the northwest of Lake Taal, on the other side of the entrance to Manila Bay. They can be recognized by the vegetation covering them and the radial channels.

⑥ *Slum Shacks* ↓

In some areas of the city to the north of the River Pasig the population density is as high as 60,000 inhabitants per km² (156,000 per square mile) making for slum-like conditions.

Malaysia, Sumatra

Height
m
3000
2000
1000
600
300
100
0
<0
200
1000
2000
4000
6000
8000
10000
m
Depth

0 25 50 75 100 125 miles
1:4,500,000
0 50 100 150 200 km
Lambert Azimuthal Equal Area Projection

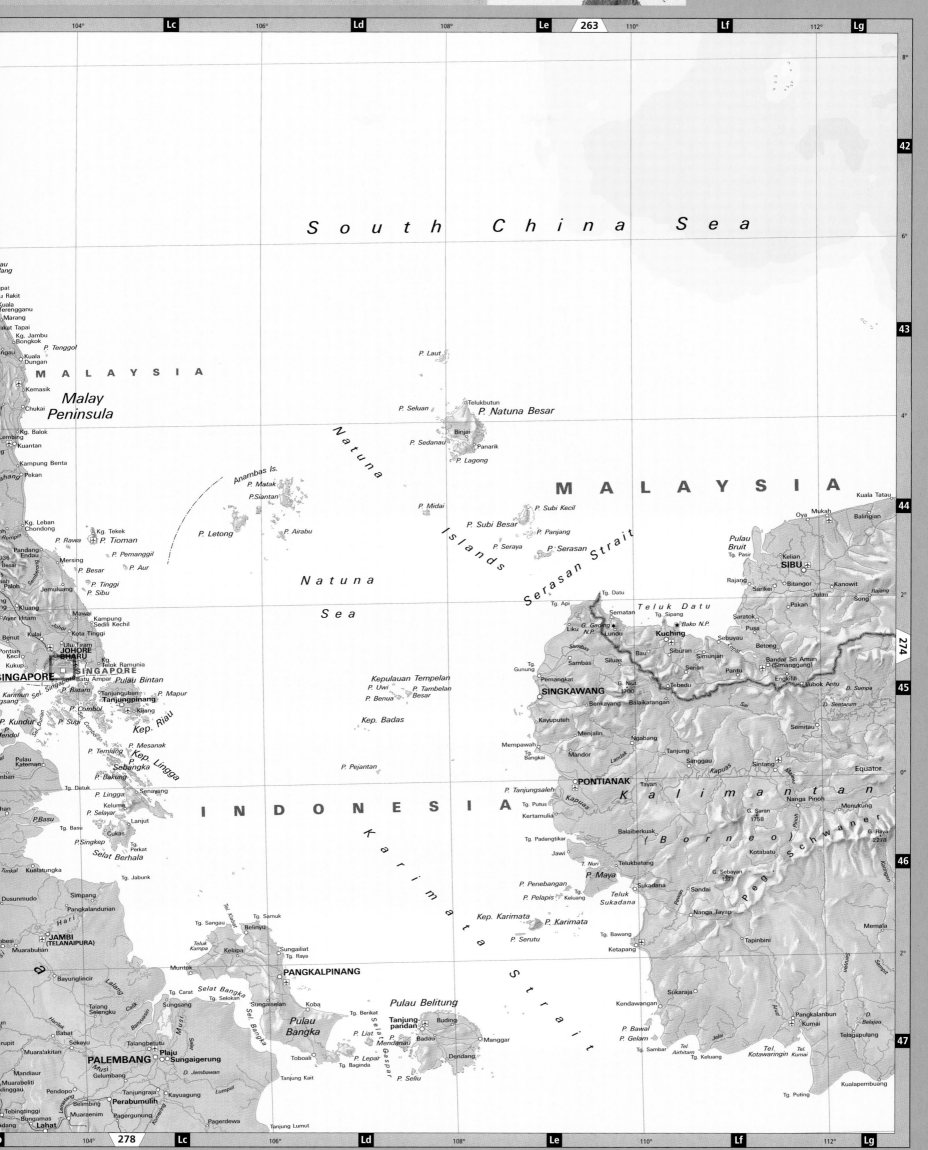

Singapore

On most maps the small city-state of Singapore is hardly bigger than a pin-head. However, the little island located in the Strait of Malacca is the largest business center in southeast Asia. Singapore's meteoric rise began in 1819, when Sir Stamford Raffles established a trading post in the name of the East India Company here. Strategically and conveniently located along the most important west–east trade routes, an important harbor quickly established itself in Singapore, which profited above all from the boom in rubber and the opening of the Suez Canal. Its economic rise attracted many immigrants from China, India, and Malaysia, who transformed the sleepy little town into a pulsating, multi-cultural metropolis within the space of just a few decades.

1 *Boat Quay* ↓

Today, the oldest part of Singapore is a place of contrasts. Where there was once a protected natural port at the mouth of the Singapore River, quaint houses from the colonial era now snuggle close to one another. The former business houses, which were lovingly restored in the 1980s, today contain mainly restaurants and cafes. The picturesque look of these houses is in stark contrast to the skyscrapers of the banking and financial district located directly behind them, but makes for a breathtaking landscape, particularly at night.

city. The largest and best shops in the city were located here up until the 1960s. Today, however, the former Victorian charm of this square has given way to modernity and the square is surrounded by glittering high-rises housing international banks and the headquarters of other large companies.

4 Chinatown

The economic rise of Singapore to the leading port and business center in the region led to a significant influx of foreign workers, most of

2 Former Colonial Quarter

According to historical records, the point at which Sir Stamford Raffles is said to have first set foot on land in 1819 and the place where the city of Singapore is said to have been founded is located on the opposite side of the river to Boat Quay. The former colonial quarter of the city is located in this area. Today, in addition to the parliament, the ministries, and the courts, it contains museums and other cultural institutions.

3 Raffles Place

Raffles Place, located in the heart of the banking and financial district, was once one of the most important market and trading squares in the

whom came from China. Raffles's plans for the city provided for the division of the immigrant peoples into ethnic groups. This is why its Chinatown came into being as early as the 1820s to the northwest of the present-day banking district.

5 Marina Bay

While high-rises are crowded together in the banking district around Raffles Place, the open spaces of Marina Bay extend across the south of the city. In the coming years office and residential buildings are to be built in this area, which has been created by reclaiming new land.

6 Suntec City

The extensive complexes that make up Suntec City, a huge multi-functional center located on the southern edge of the historic city center, extend across an area created from new land. Among other things, Suntec City contains a huge shopping center, hotels, a theater, a conference center, and the largest fountain in the world.

7 Kampong Glam

In addition to the Indians, who also have their own ethnic area, the mainly Muslim Malays are among the smaller ethnic groups living in Singapore. Kampong Glam has been the traditional heart of Singaporean Muslim life since the 19th century, and the Sultan Mosque is its focal point.

Height
m
3000
2000
1000
600
300
100
0
<0
200
1000
2000
4000
6000
8000
10000
m
Depth

1:4,500,000

| 0 | 25 | 50 | 75 | 100 | 125 miles |

| 0 | 50 | 100 | 150 | 200 km |

Lambert Azimuthal Equal Area Projection

Sea

Ll 122° Lm 124° **267** Ln 126° Lp 128° Ma

Sindangan Bay Sindangan Mt. Malindang Tudela **ILIGAN** **Malaybalay** **Bislig** Sanco Pt.
Labason Liloy Lala Marawi Trento Lingig
Siraway *Zamboanga Peninsula* Aurore Kalatungan Mts. Cateel
Ipil Sibuguey *Slay* San Miguel *Pagadian Bay* 2896 Pulangi Monkayo Boston Bay
Kabasalan Madamba Lake Valencia Cateel
Sibuguey Bay Margosatibug Lanao Maramag Sto. Tomas Compostela Baganga
Tungawan Talusan Tabina Balabagan Mt. Ragang Kibawe Caraga
Sibuco Olutanga I. Flecha Pt. Parang Malabang 2316 Panabo **TAGUM** Maco Manay
Buenavista Seboto Pt. Datu **Mindanao** Baguio Samal Manay
Sacol I. Midsayap Kidapawan **DAVAO** Samal I. Pantukan Tarragona
ZAMBOANGA **COTABATO** Sultan Kudarat M'lang Mt. Apo Lupon **Mati** Mayo Pt.
Pilas Group Basilan I. Upi Datu 2954 Sulop Governor
Isabela Piang Kabacan **Sta. Cruz** Generoso
Pilas I. Lamitan Tacurong Isulan **Digos** Cape S. Agustin
Maluso Matalan Pt. Lebak Buluan **Koronadal**
Tapiantana Channel Norala Buluan Malita
Tapiantana Tapiantana Palimbang Banga **GENERAL** Kalian
Samales Group Polomolok **SANTOS**
Group Mt. Busa 2083 Jose Abad
Jolo Tungkil I. Kiamba Malapatan Santos
Cap I. Parang Talipaw Jolo I. Maasim **Glan**
Tapul I. Pata I. Tinaca Point *Sarangani* Miangas
Lugus I. Cabingaan Balut I. *Islands*
Tapul Group Lapac Siasi
Siasi I. **P H I L I P P I N E S**
Sugbai Passage
Tawi Tawi *Kepulauan Nanusa*
Group P. Merampi
Sulu Archipelago *Kepulauan Talaud*

8°

Moro Gulf Basilan Strait

42

Samales
Group

6°

C e l e b e s   S e a Geme
Essang P. Karakelong
Beo

43

Niampak
Lirung
P. Salibabu
G. Awu P. Kaburuang
1320 Tahuna *P. Toade*
P. Sangihe

4°

Ngalipaeng

Kepulauan

Sangihe

I N D O N E S I A P. Siau

Mahuneni

44

P. Tahulandang Tg. Sopi
Tahulandang Pangeo
P. Biaro P. Morotai
P. Rau Berebere
Kep. P. Doi
Loloda Utara Wayabula
P. Dagasuli

2°

P. Mantehage P. Talisei Gamkana Soluta
P. Monadotua P. Bangka Sabatai
P. Kahatola Galela Tg. Dehegila
Tg. Pulisan Tel. Galela
P. Lembeh Tahafo Katana P. Miti
MANADO Wori P. Mayu Baru P. Tolonuu Tg. Lelai
Tomohon Bitung Tobelo Akelamo
Airmadidi Sahu Kao Dorolomo
Amurang Tondano Tahuta Jailolo Lolobata
Kawangkoan D. Tondano Sidangoli Dodaga
Peg. Paleleh Tg. Arus Santigi Leok P. Tifore Ternate Majid Wasile Tg. Wayamli
Tg. Kandi Lunguto Belang P. Halmahera
Tolitoli Biau Inobonto Totok Kusu
Bukaka Paguyaman Boroko **Ternate** Payahe Buli
2304 Pinamula Kuandang Maelang Kotamobagu **P. Halmahera**
Tembito Limboto Bone-Dumoga P. Tidore Sidangoli
Ongka Taopa Moutong Issimu National Park Payaheisalam

45

Pinogu P. Moti
GORONTALO Nuangan Ngofakiaha Sepo Waci
Tel. Gorontalo Imandi P. Makian Kobe P. Sayafi
Tg. Santigi Molibagu Tg. Flesko Kep. Goraici P. Kayoa Patani
Taludaa Maidi Mafa Tel. Weda
M o l u c c a   S e a

0°

Gulf of *Togian Is.* P. Taneti
Tomini P. Waleakodi P. Waleabahi P. Muari P. Yu
P. Unauna P. Latalata Dolit P. Gebe
Liang Ruta Akelamo Kacepi
Tg. Talatakoh Walea Gorogoro Saketa
Beriteng P. Poat *Halmahera*
Lakagon Walea Selat P. Moeilijk *Sea*
Selat P. Kasiruta P. Bacan Songa Lemolemo Kep. Widi
Batudaka Boalemo P. Vrooiljk
Tanjung Api Reserve 2400 Siuna Tumputiga Teku Labuha Gani
Sausu Ampana Uebonti Peh Rangaranga 1590 Opang P. Liboboo
Pagimana Balo Tg. Santigi Tabulo P. Damar

283

Tobamawu Selat P. Mandioli P. Hasil
2835 Lobu Tg. Tapat P. Bisa Pulau
Tongku Pandiri P. Peleng P. Belangbelang Laiwui Torobi
Poso Tobadak P. Tumpu Messeleak Luksagu P. Belangbelang Kep. Boo

46

Tentena Mapane Pemali P. Obilatu P. Obi
2508 Kayuku Batui P. Banggai Menganga P. Pisang
Malino Toili Banggai Todeli Dofa P. Mangoe P. Lawin
2560 Kembani Mumulusan Limbo Wayhayu P. Obi
Banggai Masoni Fagudu
Peg. Tineba Baturube Taduno P. Labobu Matang Timpaus Capalulu Tg. Dehekolano
Is. Bangkulu P. Melihis Wendi Mangole Flukk P. Gomumu
Tompira Salue Besar Dofa Tg. Fet Dome
Gulf Kolonedale Sana P. Labengke *Kepulauan Sula* P. Sanana
of Garitma Salonsa Wata P. Sago Kabau Tg. Santigi
Tolo P. Salue Kecil P. Sanana Waka P. Taliabu Sanana
D. Matano Kep. Bowokan Waygai
Bungku 142 Losoni *C e r a m   S e a*
3016 D. Towuti G. Karoni Mangkutana *Sulawesi*
Mangkutana *(Celebes)* *Pulau Seram (Ceram)*
Malili Tg. Lasoni P. Labengke Lasahata Paoni Wahai
Bulupulu Leleng Kep. Salabangka P. Boano Kawa
Palopo Langkobale Pombungi Lasolo Kep. Salabangka *North Banda* Tg. Paipetu Piru Sawai
Ponrang Jenemaju P. Padea- Wapotih *Pulau Buru* Hulane Masohi Mariasuela
Cimpu Besar Bara Namlea Teluk Piru Serikambelo Amahai Tg. Haya
Gulf *Peg. Abuki* G. 2790 P. Manui Fogi K. Kaplamada 2730 Rumahkai Saparua
of P. Bahubulu P. Rana Natabori Hila Tulehu P. Saparua
Bone Waimenda Wawotobi *B a s i n* Wakatin P. Manipa Tutu P. Haruku P. Nusa Laut
Latoma 2790 Lembo Tifu Oki P. Ambon Laha **AMBON**
Susua Nipanipa Namrole P. Ambelau P. Lia P. Haya
Siwa Wowewu Mowewe **Kendari**

45

2°

Ll 122° Lm 124° **282** Ln 126° Lp 128° Ma

Rajang Delta

Borneo is a part of the Malayan Archipelago, a group of islands located between the Indian and the Pacific oceans. After Greenland and New Guinea, Borneo is the third-largest island in the world. Three countries have a share in this island—the lion's share is part of Indonesian territory, the northwestern part encompasses the Malaysian states of Sabah and Sarawak, while the independent Sultanate of Brunei is located between them. As a result of its productive mineral oil and natural gas deposits, the Sultanate is one of the richest countries in the world. The island, which is also called Kalimantan, is located in the inner tropics, which is why broad areas of Borneo are covered in rain forest.

1 Sibu

Sibu, located 130 km (80 miles) from the coast, in the interior of the country, on the Rajang River, is the second-largest city in Sarawak and has the largest harbor in the Malaysian state. The harbor, located on the confluence of the Rajang and Igan rivers, is the trading center for tropical timber, which is cut in the jungle of Sarawak and driven down the Rajang River on large rafts. The main sight in the area is the seven-story pagoda of the Tua Pek Kong Temple. Sibu is the the starting point for tourists taking river journeys along the Rajang into the interior of the country.

← *Iban hunters with blowpipes*

2 Cultivation on Plantations

In the regions where the rain forest was cut down by timber companies, some of the de-forested areas are, after a number of years, once again being used for agricultural purposes. The most important agricultural product supplied to the people is rice. Another typical cultivated plant is pepper; Sarawak is responsible for around 90 percent of all of Malaysia's pepper production. Cocoa is also grown on plantations.

3 Tropical Rain Forest

The rain forest begins only a short distance from the coastal plain. The thick timber stands provide living space for a whole host of animal species. The mammalian fauna includes, among others, orang-utans, proboscis monkeys, and tree shrews, also known as tupaias. Timber is one of the most important raw materials; a total of more than 50 different usable types of timber thrive in the forests of Sarawak. However, the size of the forest has decreased significantly in recent decades. In addition to much clearance, the main cause was the devastating forest fires that occurred in 1997.

4 Rajang Delta

Annual precipitation is very high. In wet years there can be more than 4500 mm (177 in). In Sibu, the 500 km (311 mile) long Rajang River begins to split up into five main arms and a network of smaller canals and tributaries.

Java, Lesser Sunda Islands

1:4,500,000

0	25	50	75	100	125 miles
0	50	100	150	200 km

Lambert Azimuthal Equal Area Projection

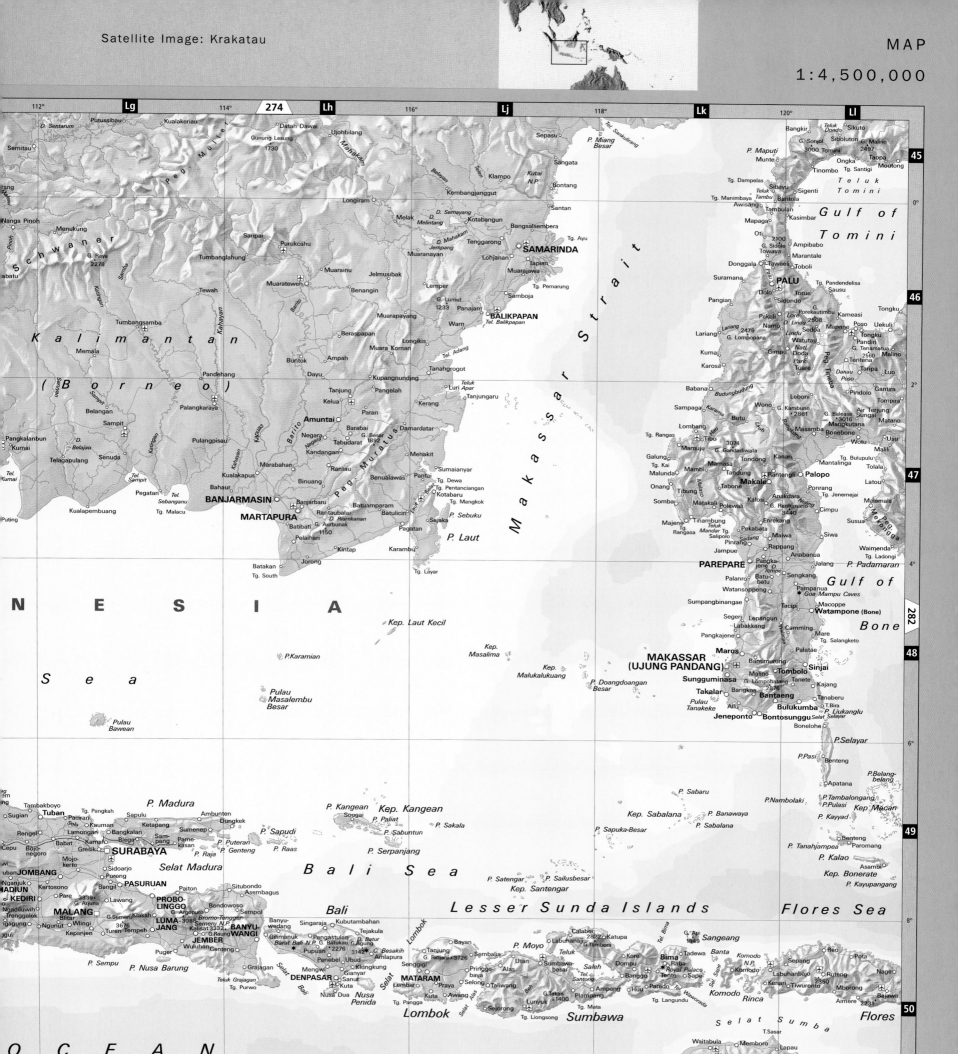

112° **Lg** Putussibau 114° **274** Kualakerian Datah Dawai **Lh** 116° **Lj** 118° **Lk** 120° **Ll**

D. Sentarum
Kualakerian
Putussibau
Ujohbilang
Bangkir
Teluk
Dondo
Sikutu
45

Semitau
Datah Dawai
Sepasu
P. Miang
Besar
Tel. Sankulirang
P. Maputi
Munte
G. Sonei
3000
Tinombo
Tomini
Onga
Taopa
Moutong

Nanga Pinoh
Menukung
Longiram
Gunung Lesung
1730
Klampo
Kutai
N.P.
Sangata
Bontang
Santan
Tg. Dampelas
Sibayu
Sigenti
Manimbaya
Awisang
Tumbuan
Kasimbar
Gulf of
Tomini
0°

Schwaner
G. Raya
2278
Saripai
Purukcahu
Tumbanglahung
Muaratewen
Melak
D. Melintang
Kotabangun
Bangsalsembera
Mapaga
Oti
2100
G. Siddii
Ampibabo
Towaya
Donggala
Marantale
Toboli
Suramana
PALU
Torue
Pandendelisa
Sausu

Borneo
Kalimantan
Longiram
D. Semayang
Muarainu
Jelmusibak
Lemper
Tenggarong
Tg. Ayu
Muarajawa
Lohjanan
SAMARINDA
Pangian
Dolo
Sidondo
Pakuli
Lindu
Watutau
Namo
G. Lompobana
2508
Porekautimbu
Kameasi
Poso
Uekuli

Menukung
Tewah
Benangin
G. Lumut
1233
Panajam
Warn
BALIKPAPAN
Tel. Balikpapan
Lariang
2479
Natl.
Park
Tuare
Doda
Tentena
Danau
Poso
Taripa
Luo
Gantura

Nanga Pinoh
Tumbangsamba
Beraspapan
Muarapayang
Muara Koman
Tanahgrogot
Babana
Budungburdung
Wono
Leboni
G. Kambuno
2861
Pindolo
Tompira
Matano

Kalimantan
Memala
Buntok
Dayu
Ampah
Longikis
Tel. Adang
Sampaga
Karama
Butu
Tibo
3074
G. Gandadiwata
Mangkutana
Bonebone
Usu
Matano

Pangkalanbun
Kumai
D.
Belajau
Senuda
Palangkaraya
Belangan
Sampit
Pulangpisau
Buntok
Kupangnunding
Teluk
Luri Apar
Galung
Tg. Rangas
Mamuju
Mamasa
Tondong
Tandung
Masamba
Wotu

Tel.
Kumai
Telagapulang
Belangan
Negara
Kandangan
Damardatar
Kupangnunding
Pangelah
Tanjungaru
Tg. Kai
Malunda
Onang
Tibung
Matakali
G. Rantemario
3440
Cimpu

Puting
Kualapembuang
Pegatan
Tel.
Sebanganu
Bahaur
Banjarbaru
Binuang
Marabahan
Rantau
Sumaianyar
Pantai
Benualawas
Tg. Dewa
Somba
Tabone
Makale
Palopo
Ponrang
Kalosi
G. Jenemejai
Matemala

Amuntai
Barabai
G. Besar
1892
Mehakit
Kotabaru
Majene
Enrekang
Maiwa
Siwa

BANJARMASIN
Batuamparam
Pentanciangan
Tinambung
Teluk
Mandar
Sadang
Pekabata
Waimenda

MARTAPURA
Rantaubalai
D. Riamkanan
C. Aruhbak
1150
Pelaihari
Kintap
Jorong
Batakan
Tg. South
Pagatan
Karambu
Sejaka
Pelaihari
P. Sebuku
Salipolo
Pinrang
Rappang
Jampue
Tg. Ladongi

P. Laut
PAREPARE
Pangka-
jene
Jalang
P. Padamaran
Tg. Layar
Palanro
Batu-
batu
Sengkang
4°

NESIA
Watansoppeng
Sumpangbinangae
Segeri
Pangkajene
Tacipi
Macoppe
Mare
Cimming
Pampanua
Goa Mampu Caves
Watampone (Bone)
Tg. Salangketo
Gulf of
Bone
282

Kep. Laut Kecil
Kep.
Masalima
Kep.
Malukalukuang
Lepangung
Labakkang
Maros
Bantimurung
Palatae
Salangketo
48

S e a
P.Karamian
Kep.
Masalima
Kep.
Malukalukuang
P. Doangdoangan
Besar
MAKASSAR
(UJUNG PANDANG)
Sungguminasa
Malino
G. Lompobatang
2876
Bangkeng
Maros
Sinjai
TOMBOLO
Tanete
Kajang
Tanaberu
T. Bira

Pulau
Masalembu
Besar
Takalar
BANTAENG
Bulukumba
P. Liukanglu

Pulau
Bawean
Pulau
Masalembu
Besar
Jeneponto
Bontosunggu
Pulau
Tanakeke
Allu
Selat Selayar
P. Selayar
6°

P. Selayar
P.Pasi
Benteng
P.Belang-
belang

P. Madura
Tuban
Tg. Pangkah
Sapulu
Ambunten
Dungkek
Kep. Kangean
P. Paliat
P. Sabaru
P.Nambolaki
P.Tambalongan
P.Pulasi
Kep Mecan

Tambakboyo
Sugian
Paciran
Kauman
Ketapang
Sumenep
Sougai
P. Sakala
Kep. Sabalana
P. Banawaya
P. Kayyad
Benteng
Paromang
49

Rengel
Lamongan
Bangkalan
Sampang
Pamekasan
P. Sapudi
P. Sabuntun
P. Sapuka-Besar
P. Sabalana
P. Kalao
Tanahjampea

Cepu
Bojo-
negoro
Babat
Gresik
Blega
P. Puteran
P. Genteng
P. Serpanjang
Kep. Bonerate

uban
JOMBANG
Mojo-
kerto
SURABAYA
Sidoarjo
Porong
P. Raja
P. Raas
B a l i   S e a
P. Satengar
P. Sailusbesar
Kep. Santengar
Flores Sea
P. Kayupangang

MADIUN
Nganjuk
KEDIRI
Kertosono
Bangil
PASURUAN
Paiton
Situbondo
Asembagus
Bali
Lesser Sunda Islands

Nganjuk
Pare
G. Arjuna
Lawang
PROBO-
LINGGO
Bondowoso
Banyu-
wedang
Singaraja
Kubutambahan
Calabai
2822
Katupa
Sangeang
8°

Trenggalek
MALANG
Blitar
Wlingi
G. Semeru
3676
Klakah
Bromo-Tengger
Semeru N.P.
BANYU-
WANGI
Gilimanuk
Pengastulan
D. Batur
Bayan
P. Moyo
Labuhanaji
Tg. Tambera
Tel. Bima
G. Api
1949
Sangeang

LUMA-
JANG
Kalisat
Tempeh
JEMBER
Wuluhan
Genteng
Barat Bali N.P.
Pupuan
G. Batukau
2276
Tanjung
Rinjani
3726
Sembalia
Teluk
Utan
Sumbawa-
besar
Kore
Bima
Tadewa
Banta
Komodo
N.P.
Sepang
Red
Pota

Ngunut
Kepanjen
Turen
Puger
Grajagan
Mengwi
Penebel
Ubud
G. Batukau
G. Agung
3142
Amlapura
Praya
Pringga-
baya
Alas
Dompu
Banggo
Raba
Royal Palace
Sape
Komodo
Ruteng
Nage

MADIUN
P. Sempu
P. Nusa Barung
DENPASAR
Sanur
Kuta
Nusa Dua
Klungkung
Gianyar
C. Besakih
MATARAM
Selong
Taliwang
Teluk
Saleh
Santonga
Parado
Wawo
Rinca
2350
Tiwuronto
Aimere
2231

OCEAN
Teluk Grajagan
Tg. Purwo
Nusa
Penida
Lombok
Selat
Bali
Lembar
Awang
Lunyuk
G.Takan
1400
Plampang
Ampang
Tg. Langgudu
Komodo
Waitabula
Memboro
Lapau
T.Sasar

Lombok
Sejorong
Tg. Liongson
Tg. Mata
Sumbawa
Selat Sumba
Flores
50

Lombok   B a s i n
Waikabubak
Kodi
Waimangura
Waibakul
Kapaku
Waingapu
Payeti
Lakohembi

Sumba
1225
G. Wanggameti
Kaliuda
Baing
Kananggar
Melolo

112° **Lg** 114° **Lh** 116° **Lj** 118° **Lk** 120° **Ll**

J a v a   T r e n c h

51

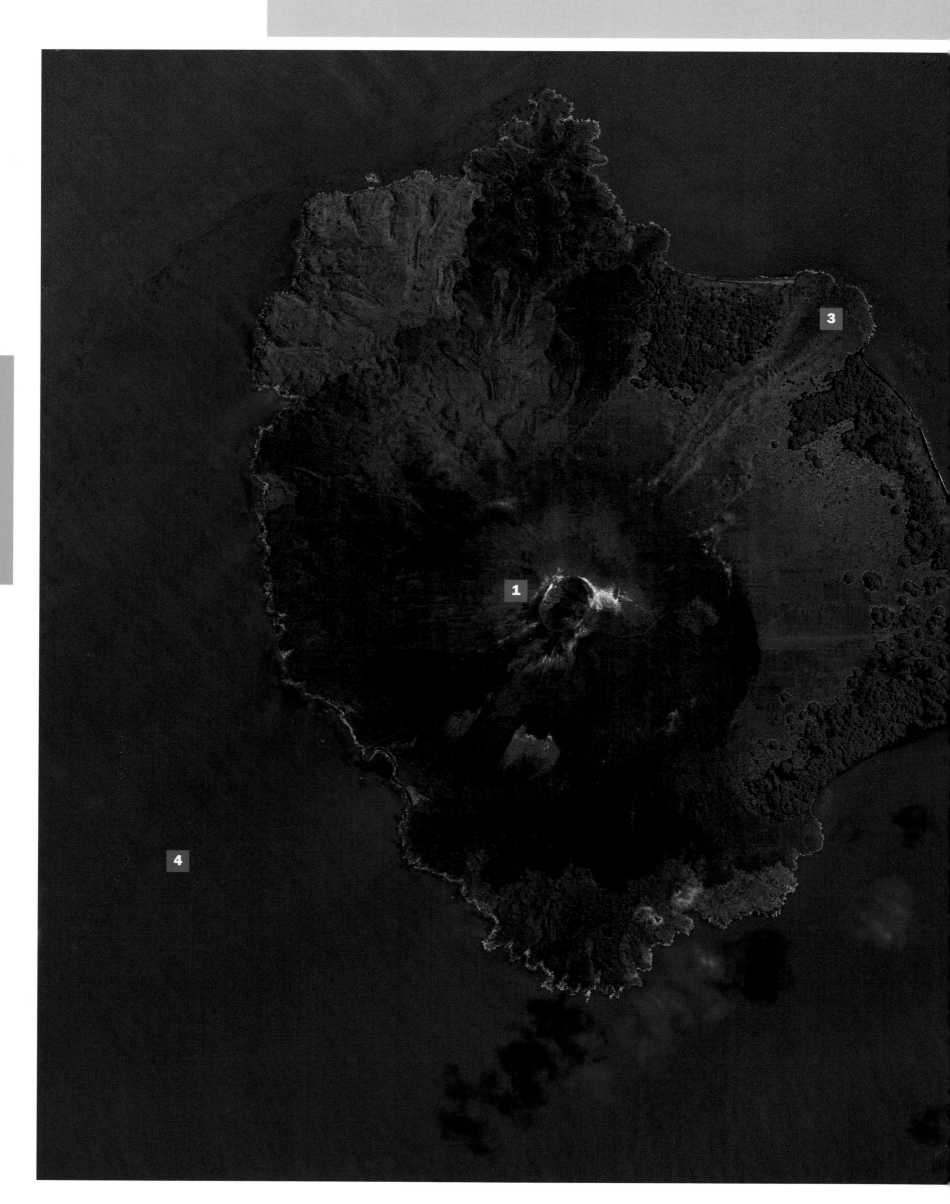

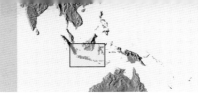

1 Anak Krakatau

The volcano did not remain quiet even after the eruption of 1883. Beginning in 1927, constant eruptions of new magma and volcanic rock formed the youngest volcano, Anak Krakatau—the "Child of Krakatau." This new volcano island is located about 3 km (2 miles) to the north of the remnants of the old Krakatau. The opening on the Anak is located more or less right above the center of the subterranean magma chamber. The Anak Krakatau was very active in 1960, when explosions occurred at intervals of half a minute to ten minutes. Since then there have been more than a dozen phases of activity, most of which, however, lasted less than one year. In the meantime the island has been growing from year to year and now rises 400 m (1312 ft) out of the sea. It can be visited during periods when the volcano is quiet. In 1991, UNESCO declared the whole Krakatau National Park a World Natural Heritage Site.

Krakatau

The remnants of the volcano island of Krakatau rise out of the sea between both of the large Indonesian islands of Java and Sumatra. After a long dormant phase of around 1500 years, Krakatau erupted on August 26, 1883, with such force that the explosion could be heard on Madagascar and in Australia, thousands of kilometers away. Around two-thirds of the island sank into the Sunda Sea. Of the three volcanoes that once stood on Krakatau, only the Rakata volcano remained. Huge quantities of volcanic rock and ash were hurtled up to 80 km (50 miles) high into the atmosphere when the explosion occurred, the sky darkened over large areas of the earth, and a tsunami occurred, which reached as far as the east coast of Africa. When the magma was projected outward, a subterranean vacuum was created, which collapsed the whole mountain in on itself. The explosion cost a total of 36,000 people their lives.

2 Return of Plant and Animal Life

Almost all of the island of Krakatau was completely sterilized and all life extinguished by the explosion in 1883. This event gave scientists the opportunity to examine in detail how an isolated ecosystem recovers, how new species are added, and how they behave. The unique location of the islands between the Indian and the Pacific oceans also provided the best conditions for doing so. Even the tropical rain forests have returned to cover the islands once again after a very short period of time. And today, dense forests cover the slopes of the Rakata volcano once more. In 1953, 70 years later, another explosion occurred, extinguishing all life on the small island of Anak Krakatau. Scientists were able to observe the whole process again with

even better knowledge and equipment. The wind and water carried the first spores to the island, and animals followed soon thereafter. However, although they are located only a few kilometers from each other, each of the four islands developed in a different way due to the different species that settled there.

3 Lava Streams

The Anak Krakatau is a typical shield volcano whose shape is due to the thin masses of lava that flowed out of the crater in a radial direction. Whenever the Anak Krakatau erupts, the lava flows down the valley in long streams until it reaches the sea and cools off. If the eruption stops, the masses of lava solidify and a lava tongue remains, which has increased the height of the volcano by a few meters. The interior of the Anak Krakatau has been seething up until the present day, and many accidents have already occurred as a result of overly adventurous tourists. Not surprisingly, the water around the island is hot and sulfurous vapors rise everywhere.

4 Sunda Strait

The Sunda Strait is a strait located between the main Indonesian islands of Java and Sumatra. The strait is only 22 km (14 miles) wide at its narrowest point, and links the Indian Ocean to the Java Sea, one of the seas bordering the Pacific Ocean. The Sunda Strait, which is named after an early Indonesian people who lived on West Java and had a highly developed culture, is characterized by a particularly high density of vol-

canoes. Like beads on a necklace, one volcano is located after the other, as on the neighboring islands of Java and Sumatra. The reason for this accumulation of volcanoes is the location close to the edge of two large continental plates, which rub against each other at a great depth. The resultant tension built up inside the earth is released in the form of earthquakes and volcanic eruptions. While this process is taking place, the southern Indo-Australian Plate is being forced under the Malayan Archipelago. The rock is melted in the depths and appears on the surface of the earth again in the form of volcanic lava.

Consequences of the Volcanic Eruption ↑
The explosion on Krakatau was the most powerful volcanic eruption observed on earth to date, and the consequences of this enormous outburst in 1883 were significant outside the region of southeast Asia. The ash spread out at great heights above the whole northern hemisphere, resulting in climatic changes in the following period. The dust from Krakatau circled the earth several times and caused more than just spectacular sunsets in the northern hemisphere—after the eruption, irradiation from the sun was significantly reduced and average temperatures the following year were about 1.2ºC (2.2ºF) colder than in many previous years throughout the world. It took years for the atmospheric conditions to normalize themselves once again. The image shows a still-active volcano in Ujung Kulon National Park, which is located on the southern part of Krakatau Island.

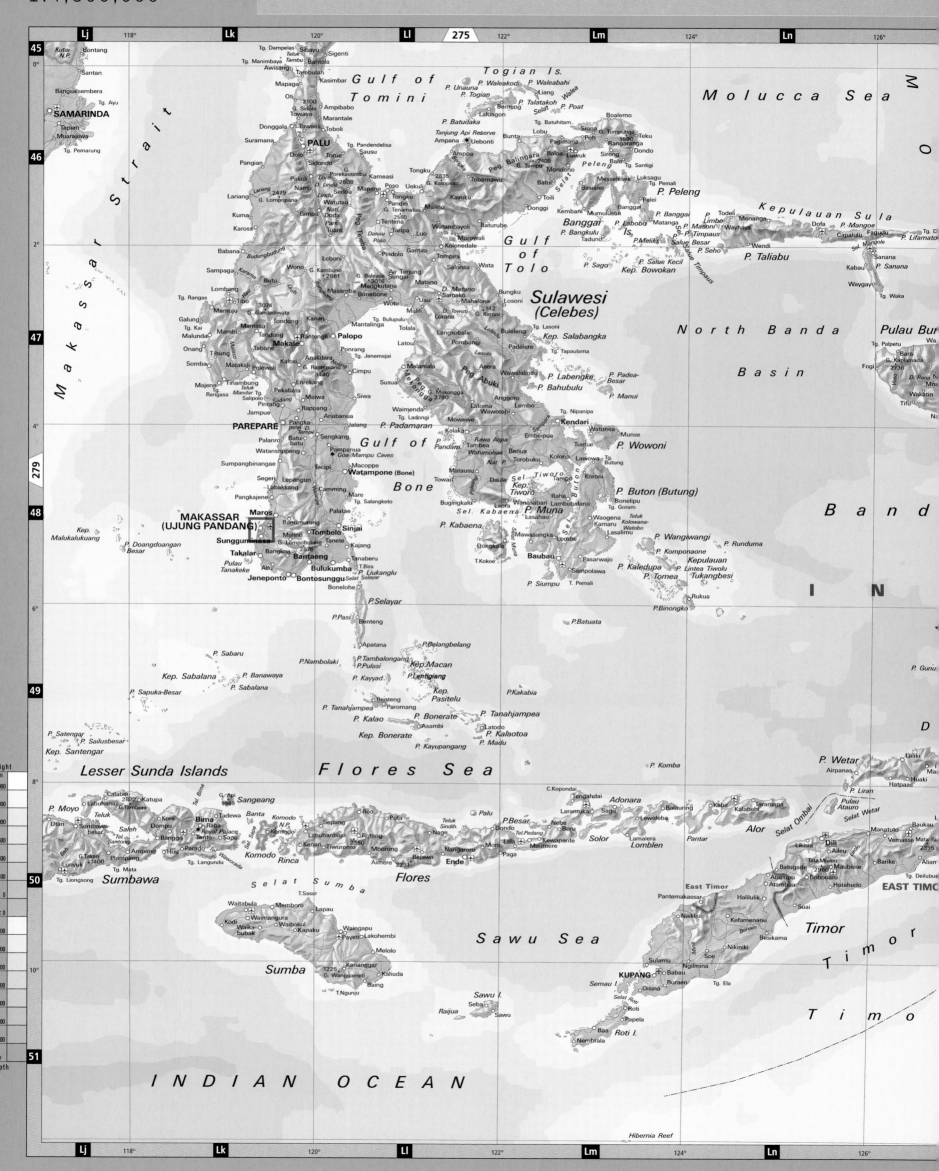

Height
m
3000
2000
1000
600
300
100
0
<0
200
1000
2000
4000
6000
8000
10000
m
Depth

1:4,500,000

0 25 50 75 100 125 miles

0 50 100 150 200km

Lambert Azimuthal Equal Area Projection

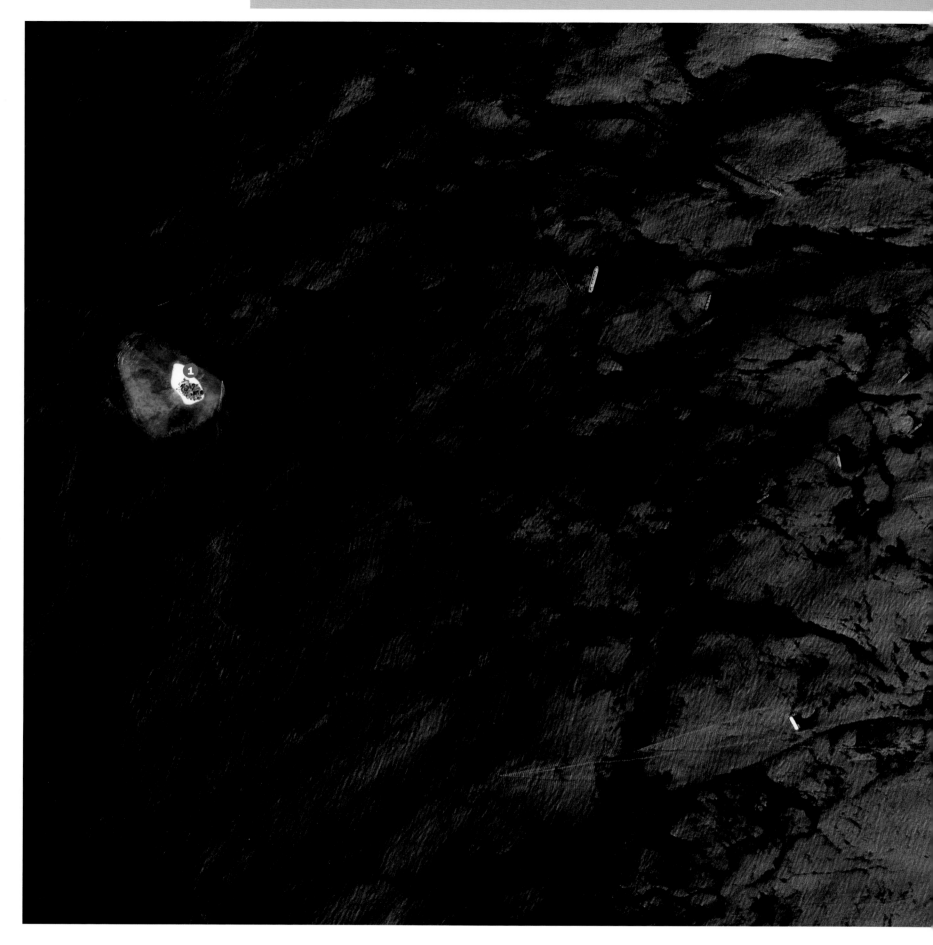

Makassar (Ujung Pandang)

With just one million inhabitants, Makassar (Ujung Pandang) is the largest city on the Indonesian island of Sulawesi and the sixth-largest in the whole country. After independence in 1971, the city was called Ujung Pandang until 1999, when, not least for tourism-related reasons, it returned once more to its old and more well-known name of Makassar. This was the name the Dutch gave it after they had conquered the Portuguese Kingdom of Goa. Today, with all of its administrative buildings, it is the capital of the province of South Sulawesi and the intersection between the western and eastern islands. Due to the multitude of ethnic groups living in the city area, Makassar is one of the most colorful cities in the country.

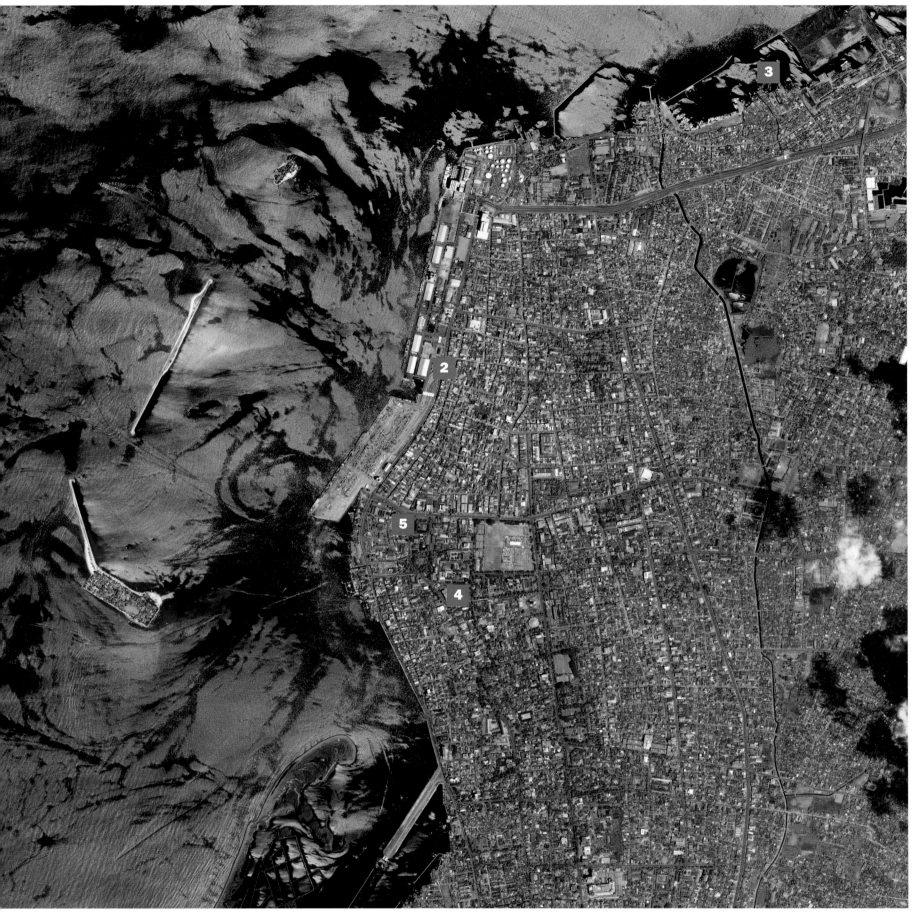

1 Samalona Island ←

The small island of Samalona is located opposite the harbor and, after a short boat trip of 45 minutes, offers good opportunities for diving, snorkeling, water-skiing, and sport fishing. The accommodation available on the island, however, is basic.

2 Overseas Port

Due to the convenient location of its port, Makassar was a spice port and trading center much fought over between the Portuguese and Dutch during the era of the European colonial powers. Today, the sea port is one of the most important in the country. The large, new port areas on pre-laid subsoil are striking and are used to anchor giant craft.

3 Northern Port

The northern part of the port is characterized by the traditional *bugis* and *prahus*—sailing ships and schooners—whose teak wood designs have not changed for centuries. They are used for transportation around the islands.

4 City Center

Chinese residences from the 16th century are located beside Dutch colonial houses from the 17th century in the old heart of the city. Special attractions are the Mussel Museum and the Orchid Garden, both of which are worth seeing. The northern part of the old town, which has a stronger Chinese character, contains some centuries-old Buddhist temples with impressive col-

ored paintings and stone and wood carvings. The *bugis* coming into the port can be observed from the Losari Esplanade, one of the most attractive riverside roads in Indonesia.

5 Fort Rotterdam

In the place where an old fortification of the Sultan of Goa once stood, the Portuguese built a fortress of their own in 1545, which was taken over by the Dutch in 1608. Under their rule the fort was strengthened with walls as thick as 2 m (7 ft) and as high as 7 m (23 ft). Some of the best-maintained examples of Dutch colonial fortified architecture are located around the fort. Eleven of the total of 13 buildings go back to the Dutch era.

Papua New Guinea

1:4,500,000

| | 0 | 25 | 50 | 75 | 100 | 125 miles |
| 0 | 50 | 100 | 150 | 200 km |

Lambert Azimuthal Equal Area Projection

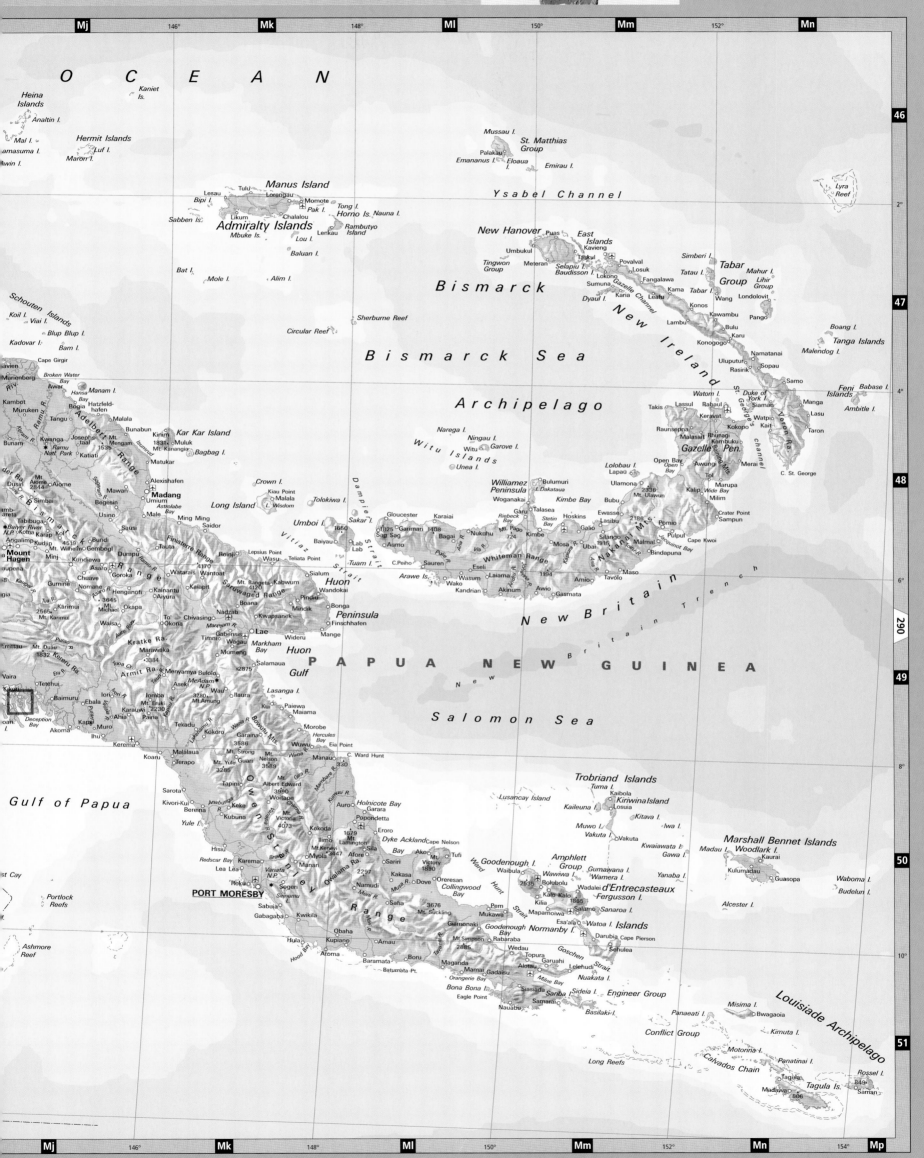

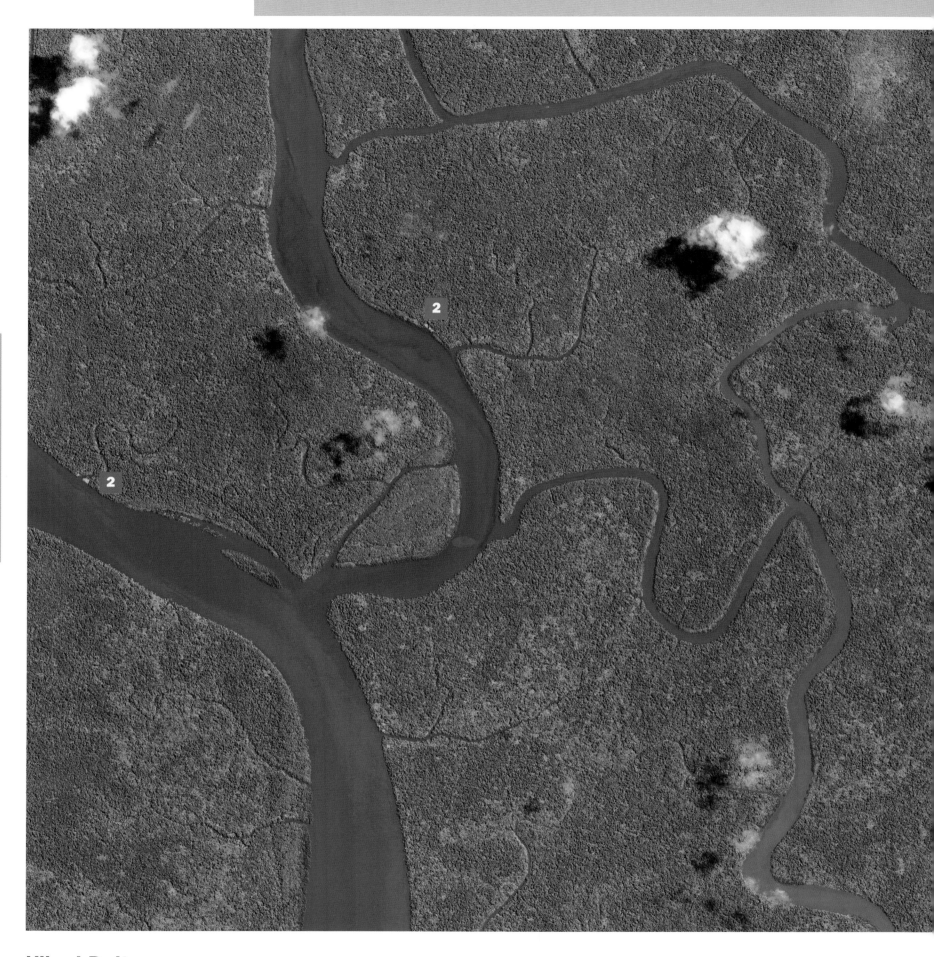

Kikori Delta

The image shows a part of the delta into which the Kikori flows. The Kikori rises in the foothills of the central mountain chain in Papua New Guinea and, while forming a delta, flows into the Gulf of Papua, which is located to the south of the main chain. As it does so, it exhibits the typical characteristics of rivers rising in the central chain of mountains and flowing southward: In the precipitous and steep relief of the mountain range, a river initially flows at high speed and, later on, it forms a broad delta before flowing into the sea. Broad stretches of mangrove forests, which find ideal conditions for growing in the brackish water, are typical of the delta area. Mangroves, which are unique ecosystems, host a wide variety of organisms such as algae, oysters, and sponges.

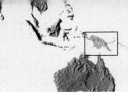

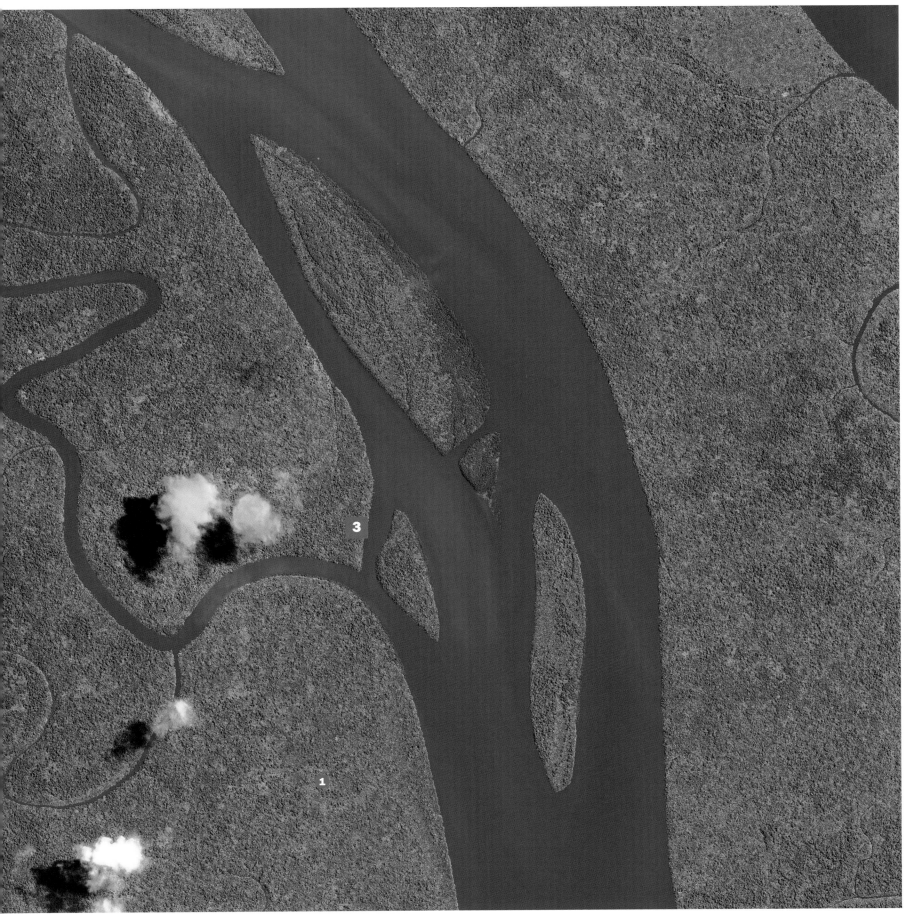

3

1

 Mangrove Forests ←

Mangroves develop in the shape of particular copse formations in the flat water of protected bays along tropical coasts and, in the brackish water of tropical estuaries, in the shape of low tree and bush vegetation. The latter, with strongly branched stilt roots, special breathing roots soaring upward, and lateral feeding roots, have adapted to the muddy subsoil, which is poor in oxygen and nutrients, found in these coastal areas. In this respect, they merely use the subsoil to embed themselves, while they get most of the nutrients they require from the water, to whose fluctuating salt content they are very resistant. Their fruits often germinate before falling so that some roots can grow very quickly and establish

themselves in the mud. The restrictive effect of the thick stilt root structure on the streaming water leads to increased sedimentation in the mangroves so that land is acquired here by natural means and, at the same time, the land behind it is protected. Outside the sphere of influence of the salt water, mainland vegetation can establish itself on this land.

2 Use of Mangroves

The impenetrable thickets of tropical mangrove forests are favorable breeding grounds for fish, crabs, amphibians, and birds, and have thus been used by people for millennia. The complexity of this landscape offers everything required for a modest life close to nature, but, so that its

stock is not endangered, it also requires concessions and some adaptation, such as houses built on stilts and the renunciation of permanent paths and roads.

3 Delta Formation

When they cross over onto the coastal plain, the speed at which the rivers from the mountain ranges travel decreases abruptly, the large amount of sedimentation is deposited and hinders the river itself. The river is forced to meander across a wide area and to form lateral branches, as demonstrated here by the watercourses of the Nabui, a tributary of the Kikori. The deposited sediment builds up to form the coastal plain.

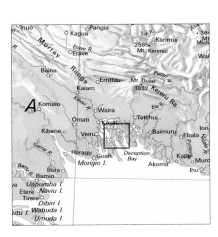

Solomon Islands

P A C I F I C   O C E A N

Lyra Reef

Malum Islands

Nuguria Islands

Boang I.

Tanga Islands

Malendog I.

Samo

Manga

Lasu

Taron

Babase I.

Feni Islands

Ambitle I.

Pinipel I.

Green Islands

Nissan I.

Kilinailau Is.

Mortlock Is.

Nukumanu Islands

C. St. George

Cape Hanpan

Lemankoa

Gagan

Buka Island

Hutjena

Siara

Tinputz

Taiof I.

Kunua

Wakunai

Koripobi

Mt.Balbi

Tarara

Bougainville

Island

Arawa

Kieta

Atopa

Empress Augusta Bay

Panguna

Mt. Taraka

Otong Java Islands

Kella

Leuanrua

Roncador Reef

PAPUA
NEW GUINEA

2219

Boku

Aku

Buin

Liuliu

Ovau I.

Chirovanga

Nukiki

C. Alexander

Susuka

SOLOMON ISLANDS

Moija Pt.

Balalai I.

Western

Fauro I.

Korovou

Zarepe

Mt. Maitabi

Panggoe

Shortland I.

Choiseul

980

Korasa

Luti

Mono I.

Maloaini

Poro I.

Taora

Sikopo I.

Ghaghe I.

Maanong

Treasury Is.

Vella Lavella I.

Rob Roy I.

Vaghena I.

Vaha

Kia

Papatura Fa.

Sorezaru Pt.

Barora Ite I.

Suavanao

Baolo

Paraso

1010

Santa

Filuo

287

Mbava

Maravari

Tuki Pt.

Kolombangara I.

Visuvisu Pt.

Isabel

Ghoveo

Ranongga

Mbarakoma

Kula

Jejevo

Fera I.

Buala

Maana'oba

Dai I.

750

Gulf

Hovoro

Mt. Kubonitu

Kilokaka

Mahu

Kwailibesi

1788

Ghizo I.

Ringgi

1128

New Georgia

Kaevanga

Tatamba

Fo'ondo

Fouia

Ghizo

Mbanga

Kaolo

Vilavu

Stewart I.

Simbo I.

Vonavona

Munda

820

Dala

New Georgia

Egholo

Vanunu I.

San Jorge I.

Vikenara Pt.

1310

Olomburi

Rendova

1080

Mbatuna

Auki

Atori

Malaita

Seghe

Mt.Vangunu

Marshall

Tavara Channel

Mbulo I.

1045

Russell Islands

Buena Vista I.

Nggela

Sule

Mt.

Bennet Islands

Tetepare

Nggatokae I.

Mbokonumbeta

Mburna

Kolourat

Woodlark I.

Group

Mborokua

Yandina

Savo I.

Pavuvu

395

Siota

Maasupa

Guasopa

Waboma I.

Alokan I.

Mbanika I.

Chapuru

Nggela Pile

Hauhui

Maru'ura

Budelun I.

Tambea

Lambi

Honiara

Ruavatu

Aola

Marapa I.

610

Maramasike

Tangarare

Tetere

Kaoka

Apio

(Small Malaita)

Mt.Makarakomburu

2447

Mt.

Aroaha

Louisiade Archipelago

Mbambanakira

Kauchui

Avu Avu

1921

Makina

Sa'a

Cape Zele'e

Kimuta I.

Mbalo

Guadalcanal

Ulawa I.

Marou

Poi I.

Three Sisters Islands

Panatinai I.

Tadahadi

Uki I.

Rossel I.

Tagula

Tetere

Kirakira

Madawa

849

Saman

Watee

Tagula Is.

806

San Cristobal

1248

Arite

Nasuraghena

Haurana

C. Sta Ana I.

Surville

Bellona I.

Peka

San Cristobal Trench

Manggautu

Rennell I.

Lavanggu

Pocklington Trough

Lake
Te Nggano

Tinggoa

North Reef

S o l o m o n   S e a

S o l o m o n   I s l a n d s

New Georgia Sound

Indispensable Strait

Middle Reef

Indispensable Reefs

South Reef

Height
m
3000
2000
1000
600
300
100
0
<0
200
1000
2000
4000
6000
8000
10000
m
Depth

0   25   50   75   100   125 miles

1:4,500,000

0   50   100   150   200km

Lambert Azimuthal Equal Area Projection

Africa

Canary Islands, Morocco, Algeria

Height

m	
3000	
2000	
1000	
600	
300	
100	
0	
< 0	
200	
1000	
2000	
4000	
6000	
8000	
10000	

m

Depth

1:4,500,000

0	25	50	75	100	125 miles
0	50	100	150	200 km	

Albers Equal Area Conic Projection

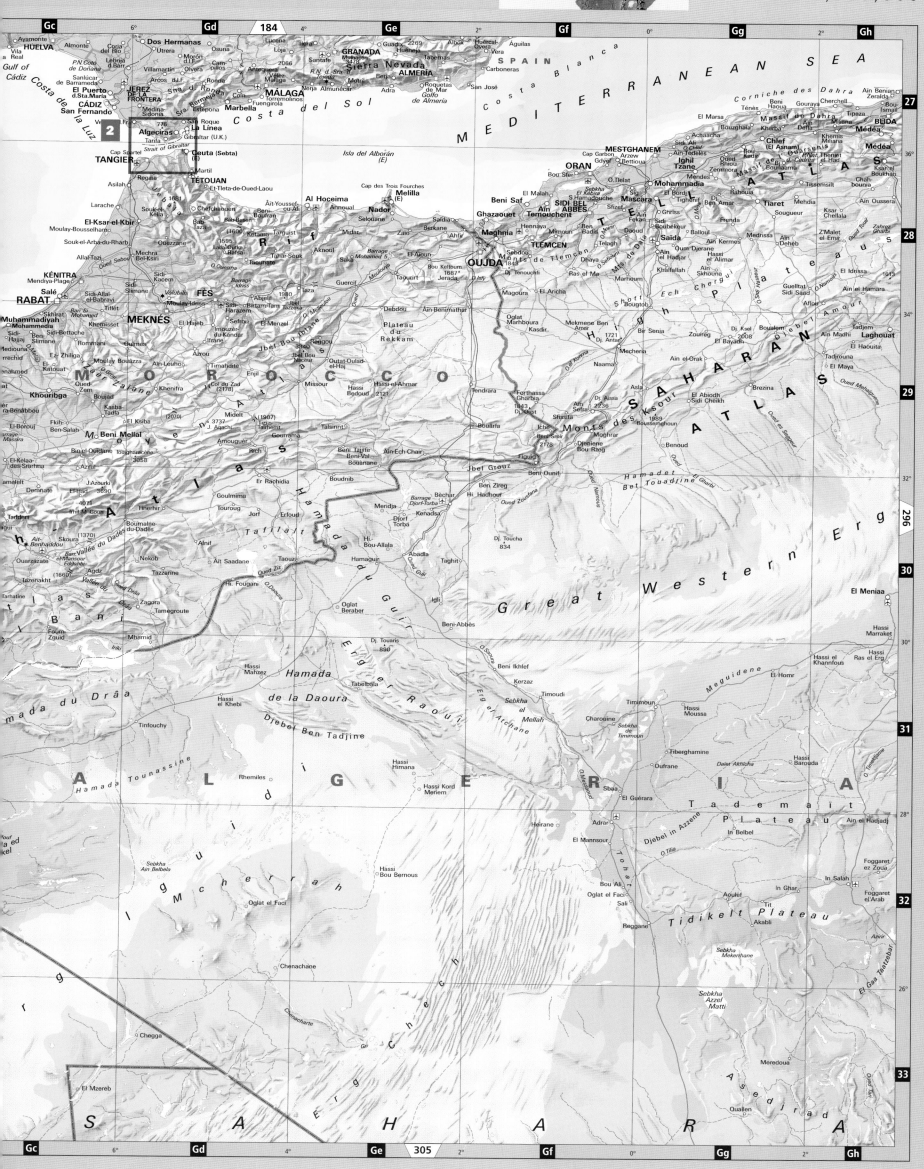

MEDITERRANEAN SEA

SPAIN

HUELVA
Ayamonte
Almonte
Coria del Río
Dos Hermanas
Utrera
Osuna
Lucena
Loja
Illora
GRANADA
Guadix
Huéscar
Albox
Huércal-Overa
Vera
Águilas
Costa Blanca
Vila Real
P.N. Coto de Doñana
Lebrija
d.Barr.
Villamartín
Carmona
d.I.F.
Santafe
Sierra Nevada 2269
Tabernas
Gulf of Cádiz
Sanlúcar de Barrameda
Arcos d.I.F.
Ronda
Antequera
2086
ALMERÍA
Roquetas de Mar
San José
Costa Blanca
JEREZ DE LA FRONTERA
Medina Sidonia
Estepona
Coín
Nerja Almuñécar
Motril
Berja
Golfo de Almería
CÁDIZ
d.Sta.María
MÁLAGA
Torremolinos
Adra
San Fernando
776
Marbella
Costa del Sol
MESTGHANEM
Algeciras
La Línea
Cap Garbon
Arzew
Cap des Trois Fourches
ORAN
Tarifa
Gibraltar (U.K.)
TANGIER
Ceuta (Sebta) (E)
Melilla (E)
Nador
Beni Saf
MOHAMMADIA
Asilah
TÉTOUAN
El-Tleta-de-Oued-Laou
Martil
Ghazaouet
Aïn Temouchent
MASCARA
Larache
Chefchaouen
Al Hoceima
Annoual
Seloune
Maghnia
TLEMCEN
SAÏDA
El-Ksar-el-Kbir
Rif
OUJDA

MOROCCO

SAHARAN ATLAS

RABAT
FÈS
MEKNÈS

ALGERIA

Great Western Erg

Hamada du Guir
Erg er Raoui
Erg el Archane

SAHARA

Tidikelt Plateau

Gran Canaria

The third-largest of the Canary Islands, Gran Canaria is striking because of its compact, almost circular shape. The island consists of the tip of a partly submerged mountain, the summit of which, known as the Pico de las Nieves, reaches an altitude of 1949 m (6394 ft). Gorges (known as *barrancos*) cut all the way down the mountainside, from the peak to the coastline. Some are very deep, and can be clearly seen in the satellite image. In the south and east of the island the terrain flattens out into broad coastal plains. This is where most of the island's population is concentrated.

1 Pico de las Nieves

The Pico de las Nieves (meaning "Snowy Peak") rises in the center of the island. This great mountain divides Gran Canaria into two distinct regions, each one with completely different landscapes. The northern part, which in winter is occasionally affected by rain-bearing Atlantic troughs, is relatively moist and thus thickly covered in subtropical vegetation. By contrast, the southern part is much drier and has a steppe- and desert-like terrain. The deeply cut valleys that are so characteristic of the island are particularly pronounced in the west and south. There are also a few deep craters, vestiges of past volcanic activity. The mountainous area of the island is deeply fissured and extremely rugged in parts.

2 Maspalomas Dunes ←

Gran Canaria is very near the Sahara. The island's proximity to the biggest desert in the world is particularly evident at its southern tip, which is covered in dunes. Although this landscape is very reminiscent of the Sahara, the sand that makes up the Maspalomas Dunes did not originate in the African mainland but comes instead from the sea bed. In the distant past sand from windswept beaches was carried inland by the wind, forming dunes that rise to heights of 1 m (3 ft).

3 Las Palmas de Gran Canaria

Las Palmas de Gran Canaria is by far the largest town on the Canary Islands. With almost 400,000 inhabitants, it is one of the ten largest cities in Spanish territory: It is in fact the country's eighth-largest metropolis. The port of Las Palmas is of prime importance to the island's economy. Located at the intersection of major shipping routes between Europe, Africa, and South America, it has developed into one of the largest ports in the Atlantic Ocean.

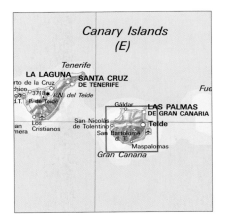

1 Tangier

1 Tangier

Because of the strategic importance of the Strait of Gibraltar, settlements were established on the coastal plains on either side of the water from very early times. In 1600 BC, Tangier was founded in a sheltered bay north of the foothills of the Rif, a mountainous region in northern Morocco. Later, the greatest powers in the Mediterranean world fought for control of the city. Today, Tangier is one of the liveliest and most colorful port cities in Morocco.

2 Ceuta

Paradoxically, Ceuta, a Spanish exclave, is the port city on the African continent located closest to Europe. A few kilometers to the west of the port area rises Monte Hacho, or Jebel Musa. Known as Abila in Greek mythology, this mountain and the Rock of Gibraltar on the European side were the twin Pillars of Hercules. While executing one of his Twelve Labors, the eponymous hero came to a mountain that was once Atlas: Rather than climb it, he split it in half, thus creating the strait. In Greek times, this legendary portal marked the limits of the known world.

3 *Rock of Gibraltar* →

This huge, high cluster of rocks rises impressively from the Mediterranean Sea. Like the city of Gibraltar located on its western side, it forms part of the British colony of Gibraltar. Despite its small size Gibraltar is an important naval base, and has its own airport. A large part of the colony is thus dominated by military installations. The Rock of Gibraltar is 426 m (1398 ft) high. While its eastern side forms a sheer drop, its western side slopes down in a succession of terraces. The interior of the rock contains several caves, which were formed as water seeped through the permeable Jurassic limestone, slowly dissolving it and creating cavities.

Strait of Gibraltar

Both a vital shipping link and the topographical eye of a needle, the Strait of Gibraltar is a narrow passage between the Mediterranean Sea and the Atlantic Ocean. Here, Europe and Africa are very close, the strait being just over 14 km (9 miles) wide. The strategic significance of the strait has always been immense. From ancient times, its control also meant domination of all trade in the western Mediterranean. The strait was named for the Rock of Gibraltar, which was in turn named Gebel al-Tarik (meaning "Tarik's Mountain") for the Arabian military leader Tarik.

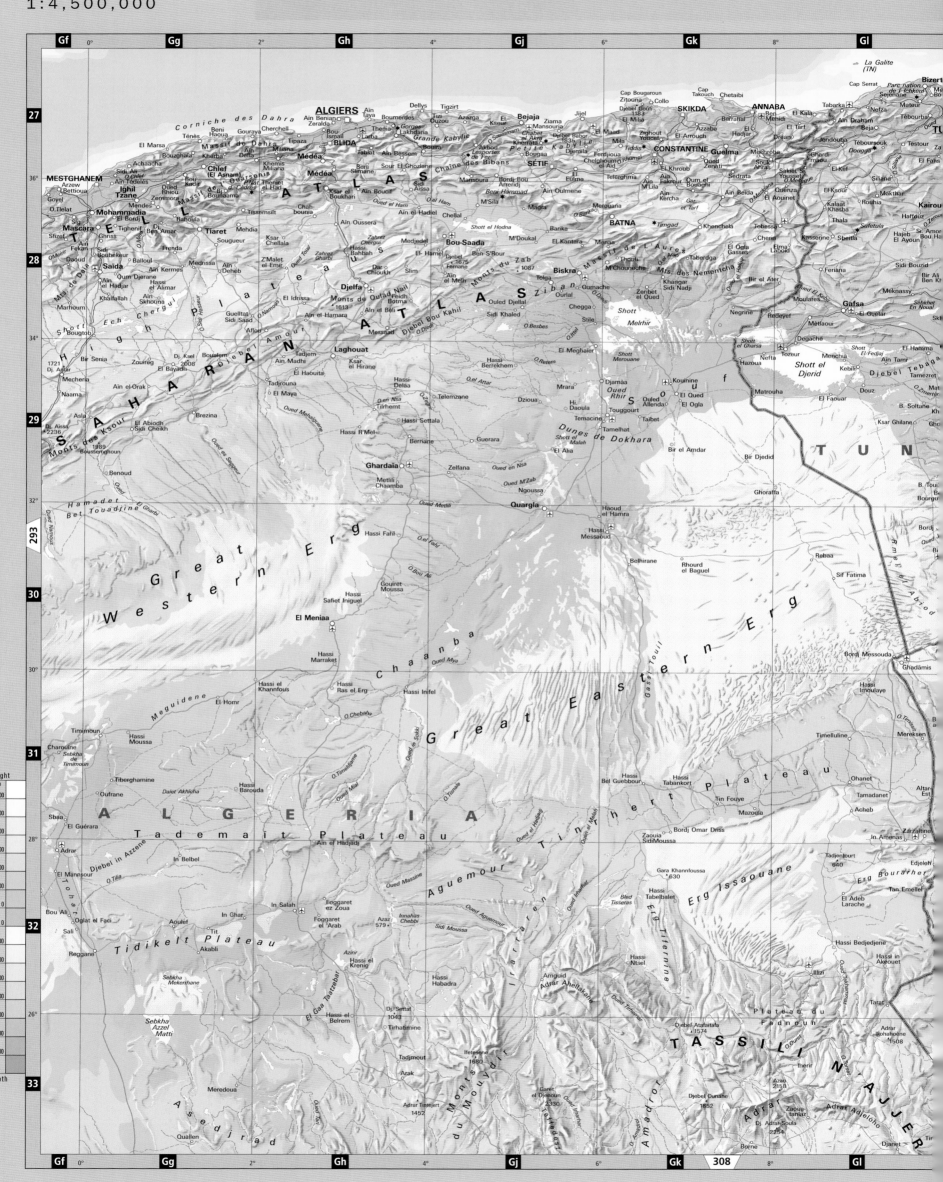

1:4,500,000

Albers Equal Area Conic Projection

Height
m
3000
2000
1000
600
300
100
0
< 0
200
1000
2000
4000
6000
8000
10000
m
Depth

0   25   50   75   100   125 miles
0   50   100   150   200 km

MEDITERRANEAN SEA

ITALY

Sicily

CATÁNIA

Agrigento

SIRACUSA

MALTA

Malta

Valletta

Gozo · Viktoria

Isola di Pantelleria

Isola di Linosa

Isola di Lampedusa
Lampedusa

Cape Bon
El Haouaria
Kerkouane
Kelibia
Menzel
Temime
Nabeul
Hammamet
Gulf of
Hammamet
Sousse
Monástir
Moknine
Beni
Hassan
Mahdia
Ksour Essaf
El Jem
Chebba
Jebiniana
Kerkenah
SFAX
Sidi Youssef
Er-Remla
Gulf
Gabès
Jerba Island
Houmt Souk
(Jerba)
Aghir
Zarzis
Neffatia
Ben
Guerdane
Rass Ajdir
Bu Kammásh
Zuwárah
AZ-
ZÁWIYAH
TRIPOLI
Tájúra'
Al Garabulli
Raqdalin
Al'Assah
Sabrátha
Al Wittyah
Al 'Aziziyah
Bir al
Ghanam
Bir
Müdákim
Gharyán
Abu
Zayyán
Al Jaws
al Kabir
Bir A'yád
Sidi as Sayd
Tarhúnah
AL KHUMS
Lapdah
(Leptis Magna)
Qasabát
MISRATAH
Qasr Ahmad
Zlitan
Al Faid
Majir
Al Kararim
Táwurghá'
BENGHAZI
Ad Darsia
Túkrah
Al Marj
Sidi Khalifah
Madinat
al Abyar
Baninah
Taykan
Qaminis
Suluq
Záwiyat
Masus
Al Maqrún
Antlat
Ajdábiyá
Ras Lanuf Marsá al Buráyqah
As Sidr
Bin Jawwad
Annofliyah
Al 'Uqaylah
Barqah al Baydá
Sabkhat
Shunayn
Hisn as Sahábi
Wádi al Fárigh
Marsá al Buráyqah
Mabrúk
Siltar
Gulf of Sidra
Surt
(Sirte)
Qasar
bu Hadi
Bu'ayrat
al Hsun
Bi'r al
'Utaylah
Abugrin
Bani Walid
Al Qala'a
Qaryat
Shumaykh
Wádi Targhalil
Bir Dhu'fán
Sabkhat Umm al 'Izám
Sabkhat al Hayshah
Tripolitan
Jabal Nafúsah
Jádú
Al Rahibat
Wamis
Mizdah
Nasmah
Fassanu
Bi'r Alláq
Al
Harabah
Hamadah al Hamrá'
W. Maymún
Bi'r Názsirah
Bi'r al Guzayil
Assdadah
Wádi Zamzam
Bi'r Bin 'Isa
Wádi Qarayh
Wádi Tághrir
Qaryat Abú
Nujaym
Al Qaryah
ash Sharqiyah
Wádi al Kabir
Sahrá'
Surt
Dahrá
Wádi Hárúnah
Wádi al Awrá
Wádi Tamat
Abyar ash Shuwayrif
Bi'r al
'Alaqah
Bi'r al
Kammúniyah
Bi'r Oaryás
Bi'r al Fátiyah
Ra's az Zallim
Jabal Waddán
973
Húm
Waddán
Sawkanah
Wáhát
al Jufrá
Marúdah
Ar Raqúbah
Sabkhat
Ghuzayyil
Zaltan
Jabal
Zaltan
Bi'r Zaltan
Al Wáhah
Jabal al Hasáwinah
Bi'r
al Qát
Sewdáyah
Zillah
Jabal as Sawdá'
839
Qárat al Hárah
Al Fuqahá'
Wádi Kunayr
Qárarat al
Hayyirah
Calanscio
Sand
Sea
Ubári Sand Sea
Hásy in Agiuel
Adiri
Barqin
Birak
Al Marúqah
Ashkida
Wash Shás
Samnú
Tamanhint
Sabhá
Sarir al Qattúsah
Ramlat Zalláf
Bi'r Khalaf Alláh
Qasr Khulayf
Awbári
Al Ghrayfah
Qasr Larocu
Bi'r Tin Abundq
Ghaddúwah
Sarir Umm'Illah
W. an Nashú
Zawilah
Qárarat
al Kalb
Tmassah
Qárat
as Sabáh
1200
Al Haruj al Aswad
Qárat Khalaf Alláh
762
Thamad Bú Hashishah
Wadi Shuhaymah
Msak Mustafit
Wádi Irawan
ithtsa
Bi'r Taziet
Tsawah
Umm al Aranib
Al Hufrah ash Sharqiya
Marzuq
Taräghin
Al Ghomode
Iwadi Barjúj
Bi'r al Mastútah
Sahra Marzuq
Al Qatrún
Jabal Bin Ghanimah
Wáw al Kabir
Jabal al Maruf
Wáw an Námús
Rebiana Sand Sea

LIBYA

El Gheraia

The oasis of El Gheraia is located about 700 km (435 miles) south of Tripoli, in the middle of the Fessan, a desert wilderness within the northern Sahara. El Gheraia forms part of a chain of oases that follow the course of a wadi, or seasonal watercourse. Today, the oases are connected by a wide tarred road, which also provides a link with Tripoli (Tarabulus), on the Mediterranean coast to the north, and with Ghat, to the southwest, near the border between Libya and Algeria. With settlements and gardens, each oasis lies in an area where the groundwater is close to the surface. From ancient times, the presence of water made it possible, using skillful irrigation methods, for large palm groves to grow in the arid desert.

1 El Gheraia

This oasis, which lies 597 m (1959 ft) above sea level, is connected to the groundwater by a natural channel. The heart of the settlement consists of small farmsteads, whose square outlines are clearly seen in the satellite image. The oasis is inhabited mainly by Tuareg and Tubu, the majority of whom are sedentary farmers, with only a few having a nomadic lifestyle as cattle herders.

2 *Palm Groves* ←

As early as the Middle Ages, the land around the oasis was being successfully cultivated, thanks to a carefully managed system of irrigation. Cereals, melons, olives, and citrus fruits were grown in the oasis gardens. After their discovery in the New

World, potatoes and tomatoes were also cultivated. Dates were another major crop, but the bulk of the harvest was sent along the trade route. *The thousands of palm trees that grow here have roots that reach down to the water table, which is fed by periodic rainfall.*

3 Land Reclamation

In order to turn areas of desert into agricultural land, new oasis gardens were systematically laid out and agricultural cooperatives founded. However, the existing groundwater here was insufficient to support crops. Deep wells were therefore sunk into the ground, and these pump fossil groundwater from a depth of 400 to 1500 m (1312 to 4921 ft).

4 Ramlat Zallaf

With dunes 80 to 100 m (262 to 328 ft) high, this large sandbank reaches the edge of the fields around the oasis. It consists of several large ridges of sand, which are divided by deep valleys and which lie parallel to each other. These ridges are in turn made up of a multitude of smaller dune systems, which lie in different directions. The inhabitants of the oasis have dug away the sand here, so as to lower the ground level and allow the palms' roots to reach the groundwater. Because their upkeep is very labor-intensive, many of these small oases are being abandoned: Left to the mercies of wind and drought, they become engulfed in sand with the passage of time.

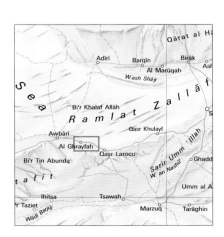

Ha 18° Hb 20° Hc 22° Hd 24° He 26° Hf

M E D I

Gulf of Sidra

BENGHAZI

Al Jabal al Akhdar

Hamamah
Al Haniyah Shahat
(Chrenej)
Al Bayda
Ad Darsia
Süsah Ra's al Hilāl
Darnah
Al Qubbah
Martūba
Bümbah
Khalij al Bümbah
At Tamimi
Tükrah Taknis
Maräwah
Suluntah
Qaryat al Fa'idiyah
Al Marj
Sidi Khalifah
Madinat al Abyar
Qasr al Kharrübah
Samalusi
Zāwiyat al Mukhayla
Al Qardabah
Tubruq
Baninah
Taykan
Ayn al Ghāzalah
Al 'Adam
Kambüt
Qasr al Jady
Al Bardi
Umm Sa'ad
Qaminis
Sulüq
Zāwiyat Masus
Bi'r al Qatif
Bi'r Jubni
Sidi Barrāni
Al Maqrün
Ḥaliğ as-Sallüm
as-Sallüm
Marsā
Antlat
Ajdābiyā
Bir Baili
Qasr ash Shaqqah
Bi'r Fuād

Siltar
Annofliyah
Bin Jawwad
As Sidr
Ras Lanuf Marsā al Buraygah
Al 'Uqaylah
Barqah al Baydā
Sabkhat Shunayn
Wādi al Farigh
Hisn as Sahābi
Bü Athlah
Gardabah
Sanyat ad Daffah
Qasr al Qarn
ad Diffa
Al Jaghbüb
Qārā
Qatt

Wādi Harawah
Sahrā Surt
Dahra
Sabkhat Ghuzayyil
Wādi al Harnim
al Wāhāt Siwa
Siwa
'Ain Tabagbug

Mabrük
Wādi al Awra
Marādah
Ar Rāqübah
Ijkharrah
Awjilah
Wāhāt al Jalu
Jalu
Great Sand Sea
Weste

Zaltan
Jabal Zaltan
Bi'r Zaltan
Al Wahah
y
r
e
n
Libyan Desert

Sewdāyah
Qārat as Sab'ah
1200
Al Haruj al Aswad
C a l a n s c i o
S a n d   S e a
a
i
c
a
Bi'r Abü M

Qārat Khalaf Allāh
762
Thamad Bü Hashishah

L I B Y A
Ad Dahāwah Tāzirbü
Zighan
Jabal al Gardah
Jabal al Hawa'ish

Height
m
3000
2000
1000
600
300
100
0
<0
Wāw an Nāmüs
Jabal al Maruf
R e b i a n a   S a n d   S e a
Al Huari
Al Hawwari
Wāhāt al Kufra
Al Jawf
Rabyanah
At Tullab

200
1000
2000
4000
6000
8000
10000
m
Depth

Tropic of Cancer
S a r i r
Jilf Kabir Plateau

T i b e s t i
S A H A
Jabal Nuqay

Ennedi Yebbi
1660
Ma'tan
4866
Jabal Tarhuni
Jabal Arknu
1436
Jabal Uweinat
Uweinat 1908
Abü

Karnaou
1840 Aozou
Bikübü
2266
Ouri
Ma'tan as Sarah

Aderké
Ornchi
Tarso Emissi
3876
C H A D
Yebbi Bou
Aozi
Yebbi Souma

Ha 18° Hb 20° Hc 22° Hd 24° He 26° Hf

312

M E D I T E R R A N E A N   S E A

DAMASCUS

Sayda
(Sidon)   Gizzin   at-Tall   Duma

Nabatiya t-Tahta   Qatana   S Y R I A

Tyre   Q.Shemona   al-Quanaitira   ad-Dimas

Nahariyya   Bint   az-Zabadani   as-Sanamin   qz-Zalaf

Ma'alot-Tarshiha   Zefat   ar-Rafid   Izra'   as-Suwaida'

HAIFA   Acre   'Ain   Teverya   Dar'a

NAZARETH   Afula   Bet She'an   Busra   Salhad   Imtan

HADERA   Pardes   Jenin   Garaq   al-Mafraq

NETANYA   Tubas   Suwailih   Quasair
                                                                                  Amra

HERZLIYYA   Nablus/   ar-Rusayfah

TEL AVIV-JAFFA   Shekhem   AMMAN

PETAH
TIQWA   Ramallah   Tall al-
RISHON LE ZIYYON   Ramla   817

I S R A E L   JERUSALEM   al-Azraq

Ashdod   Bet Lehem   Mahattat
Ashquelon   (Bait Lahm)   Dab'a

GAZA   Hebron   Qatrana   al-Qurayyat

Han Yunis   Masada   al-Mazra'a   Wadi 'l-Gadal   al-Hadita
Rafah   N.P.   as-Safi   al-Karak

al-'Aris   Dimona   Sedom   Gerut   al-Gafr

Rummana   Nizzana   'En Hozeva   at-Tafila   al-Gafr

al-Qantara   Gabal Magara   at-Tih   al-Qus   al-Tuwaiq   Ma'an

ISMA'ILIYA   735   Bir Grigafa   Bir Hasana   Ra's
                                                                                  an-Naqb   al-Batra

Fa'id   Sahra at-Tih   al-'Agrud   al-Kuntilla   Elat   al-Aqaba

B. at-Timsah   Bir Hasana   at-Tamad   Ma'an

SUEZ   Port Tewfik   Jabal   at-Tih   al-Haqi   al-Humeida   Mudawwa

G. Ataqa   as-Sidr   Gabal Sitt   Nuwaibi   'Alagan   Halat
                                                                                  al-Muzayyina   'Ammar

'Ain Suhna   Sinai   Saraf Bu'ai   Bir Ibn Hirmas

Gabal al-Galala   Abu Zanima   2580   al-Bad
al-Bahriya   Abu   Firan   Gabal

Za'farana   Rudeis   Mon. of Dahab   al-Lauz   SAUDI ARABIA
                                                                                  2286   al-Abdar

1103   Abu   St. Caterine   Sarma

Gabal al-Galala   Darba   Jabal Katherina   Nabq   Taima'
al-Qibliya   2285   2266

Ra's Garib   1751   Na'ama   al-Muwailih

Gabal Garib   Sharm el-Sheikh   G. Sanafir   Wagh

1237   Ra's Muhammad   G. Tiran   Duba

Gamsa   Ra's Muhammad   Gaz. an-Nu'man

Natl. Park   Taima'

Gazirat   Bada

Sadwan

Al Ghurdaqah   al-Udaib
                                                                                  Mugaira

R E D   S E A   SUDAN

Giza

According to experts, Cairo's infrastructure is sufficient to support a population of three million. However, the city's population is estimated to be more like 18 million. Here, in the capital of Egypt and the largest city on the African continent, people live in extremely cramped conditions. Because of immigration and high birth rates, Cairo's expanding population has spilled out into areas on its outskirts, but these new settlement areas cannot expand further because they are hemmed in by the desert. On its southwestern side, however, Cairo merges seamlessly into Giza. Its western suburbs closely border the famous Pyramids of Giza. These are the last of the Seven Wonders of the Ancient World to survive to this day and are a UNESCO World Heritage Site.

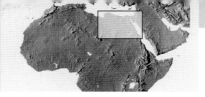

5

---

1 *Pyramids of Giza* ←

The pyramids of the pharaoh Khufu, his son Khafra, and the ruler Menkaura were built in around 2500 BC on a rocky plateau at the edge of the Libyan desert. The Great Pyramid of Khufu (the northern-most of the three) is the largest of all Egyptian pyramids. Although it was originally 146 m (479 ft) high, the Great Pyramid now stands only 137 m (449 ft) high. To its left is the Pyramid of Khafra, which is just 136 m (446 ft) high, although it appears to be taller because it was built on a hill. It was once clad entirely in limestone. At 65 m (213 ft) high, the Pyramid of Menkaura is the smallest of the three. Still smaller pyramids are aligned on the south side of the Pyramid of Menkaura and on the east side of the Great Pyramid of Khufu.

2 The Sphinx

About 20 m (66 ft) high and 74 m (243 ft) long, the Sphinx is the largest manmade sculpture ever created. While the body was hewn from a natural outcrop of rock, the legs and paws were carved from separate blocks of stone and added to the rock. Traces of pigment on one of its ears indicate that the Sphinx was once painted in different colors.

3 Cairo's Satellite Towns

So as to safeguard farmland around Cairo and to relieve its population problem, the Egyptian government embarked on a program of building several "relief towns" around the city. This program began in 1977 but has met with limited success.

4 Mena House Oberoi Hotel

Once a royal hunting lodge, Mena House was subsequently converted into a hotel. For more than a century, it has been one of Cairo's finest luxury hotels.

5 Canals

To make it possible for crops to be grown all year round, hydraulic engineering measures were implemented along the Nile, particularly in the 19th century. The Nile runs for about 8 km (5 miles) to the east of the satellite image. Traces of areas that are deliberately flooded can still be seen at the edge of the built-up area. Water is channeled along the Mansuria Canal, in the west, and the Mariotia Canal, in the east.

Mauritania, Mali

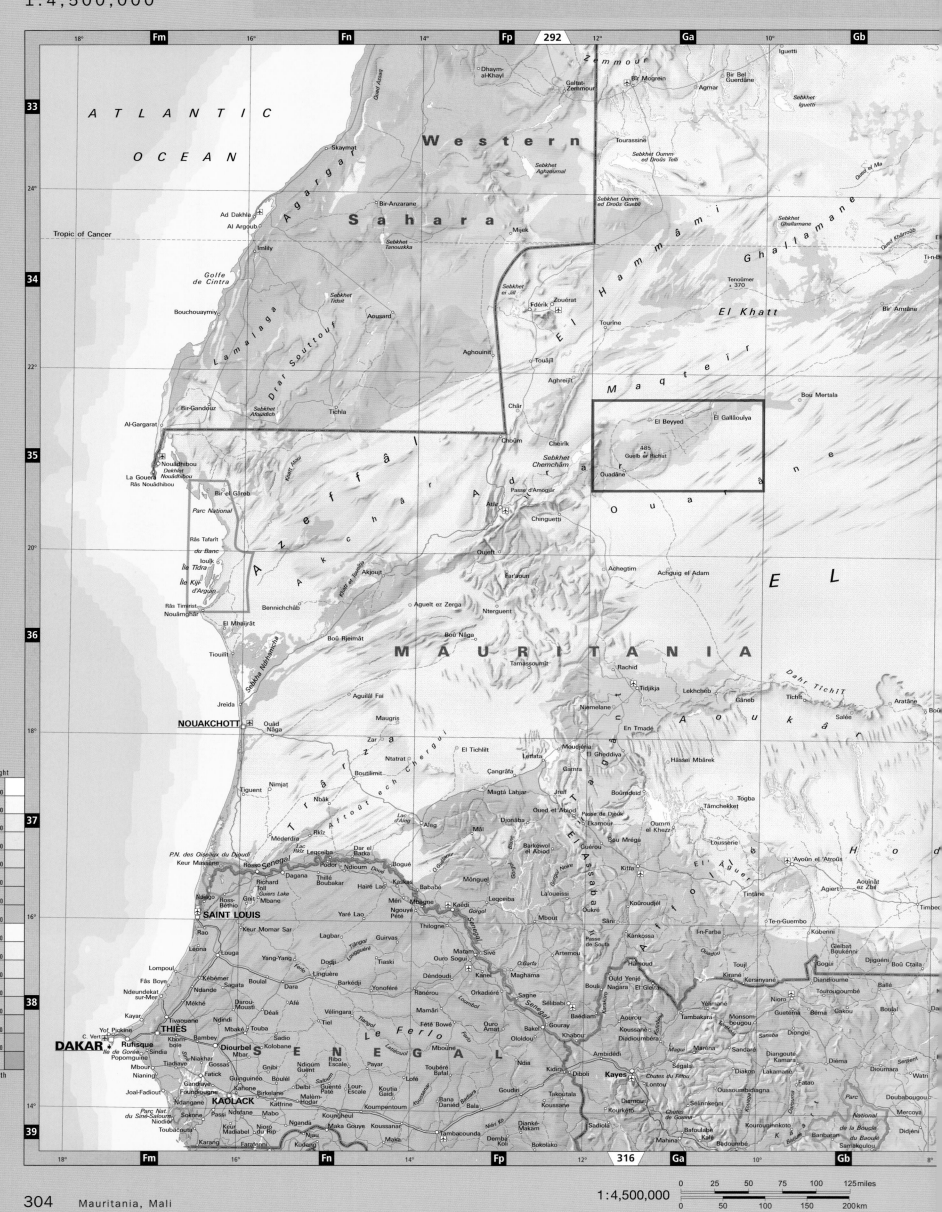

1:4,500,000

Albers Equal Area Conic Projection

Height
m
3000
2000
1000
600
300
100
0
<0
200
1000
2000
4000
6000
8000
10000
m
Depth

| 0 | 25 | 50 | 75 | 100 | 125 miles |

| 0 | 50 | 100 | 150 | 200km |

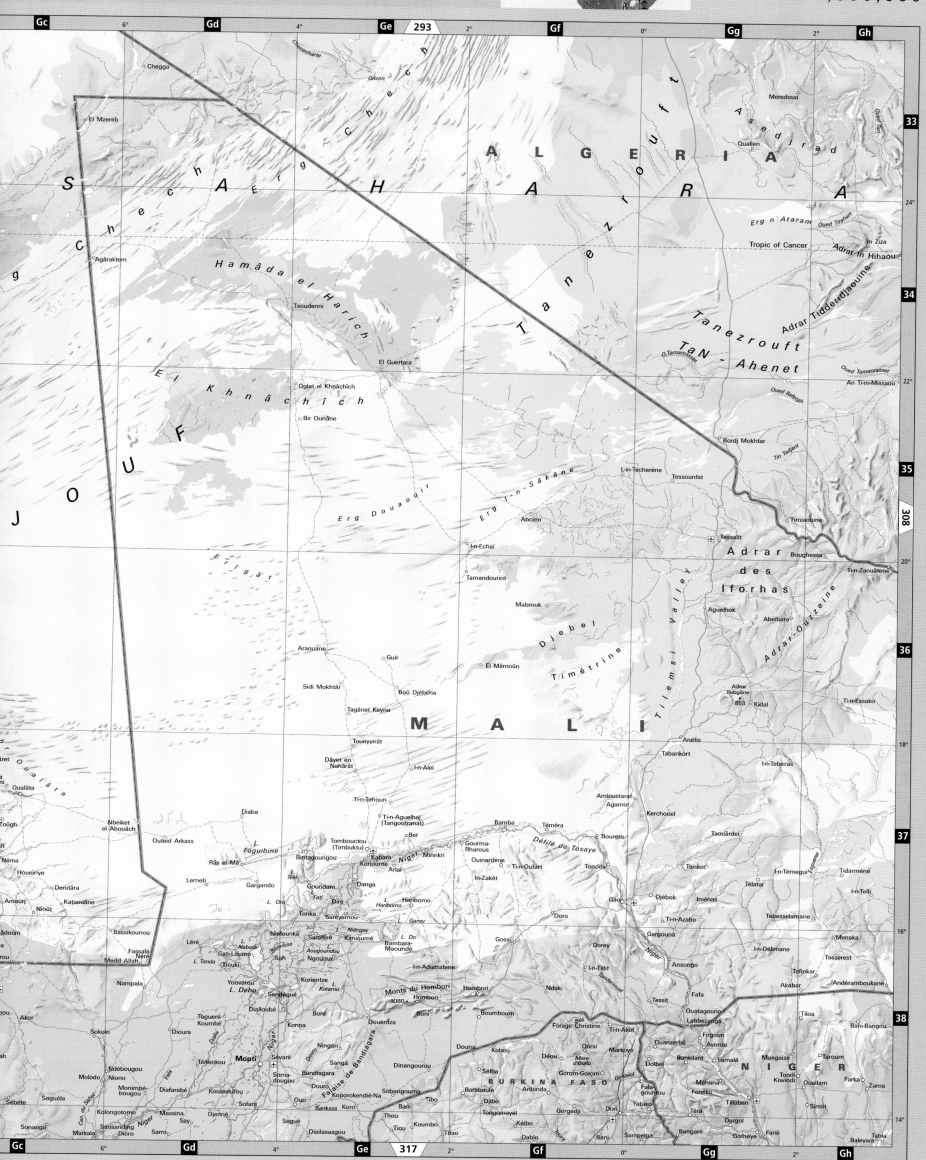

33

24°

34

22°

35

308

20°

36

18°

37

16°

38

14°

Guelb er Richat

One of the most spectacular geological formations in the Mauritanian Sahara is Guelb er Richat, a volcano visible from space and known as the Eye of Africa. It is located in the center of Mauritania, a country largely comprising the western part of the Sahara. As a result of long periods of drought and inappropriate farming methods, the western edge of the Sahara has steadily advanced toward the Atlantic. In the distant past, however, the landscape here was very different: Archeological finds and prehistoric rock paintings and engravings show that this was once a fertile region. Today, though, vast areas of it are uninhabited. The interior of Mauritania has only a few large settlements, clustered around oases.

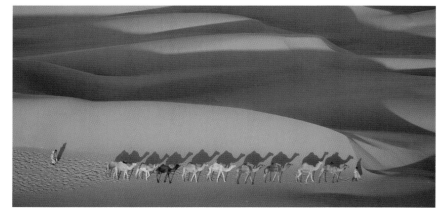

① *Maqteir* ←

An immense expanse of dunes, some as much as 1 km (0.6 mile) long, stretches out north of the Adrar Plateau. Wherever the desert is too hot and too dry even for simple types of vegetation, such as grass, to grow, the upper layer of soil is blown away by strong winds. But the curious shapes created by wind-blown sand are not permanent. Blowing unimpeded across vast tracts of open desert, the winds constantly reshape these sand formations according to their speed and direction. If wind consistently blows in one direction for a period of time, for example, a characteristically long formation, like the one shown in the image, is created. These long dunes are a major obstacle for wheeled vehicles but not for caravans of camels.

② Guelb er Richat

Among the most striking features of the Mauritanian Sahara are the concentric rings of Guelb er Richat, located to the northeast of the Ouadane oasis. Clearly visible on the satellite image, they can also be made out on the map (see p304). Geologists initially believed that they were created when a huge meteor hit the earth, but more recent research carried out under the guidance of Théodore Monod, an expert on the French Sahara, suggested that these circular hills are the vestiges of a volcano, which imploded as it was about to erupt. The outer ring has a diameter of 45 km (28 miles), while the circular rims are only a few meters high. The landscape here is eerily barren, broad, and empty. The center of what would have been the volcano's crater can be reached by climbing up a slope, which leads through a landscape of salt lakes and silica deposits.

③ Ouadane Oasis

This oasis settlement is located 30 km (19 miles) from the southwestern edge of Guelb er Richat. Approaching it from the northwest, some of its clay buildings can be seen from a distance, and its palm trees stand out against the yellow sandy desert. This is a fine example of an oasis town dating from the era of the trans-Saharan caravan trade of the 11th and 12th centuries, when Ouadane, Chinguetti, and other oasis towns supplied passing caravans. It has been declared a UNESCO World Heritage Site.

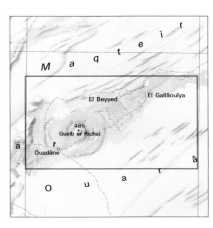

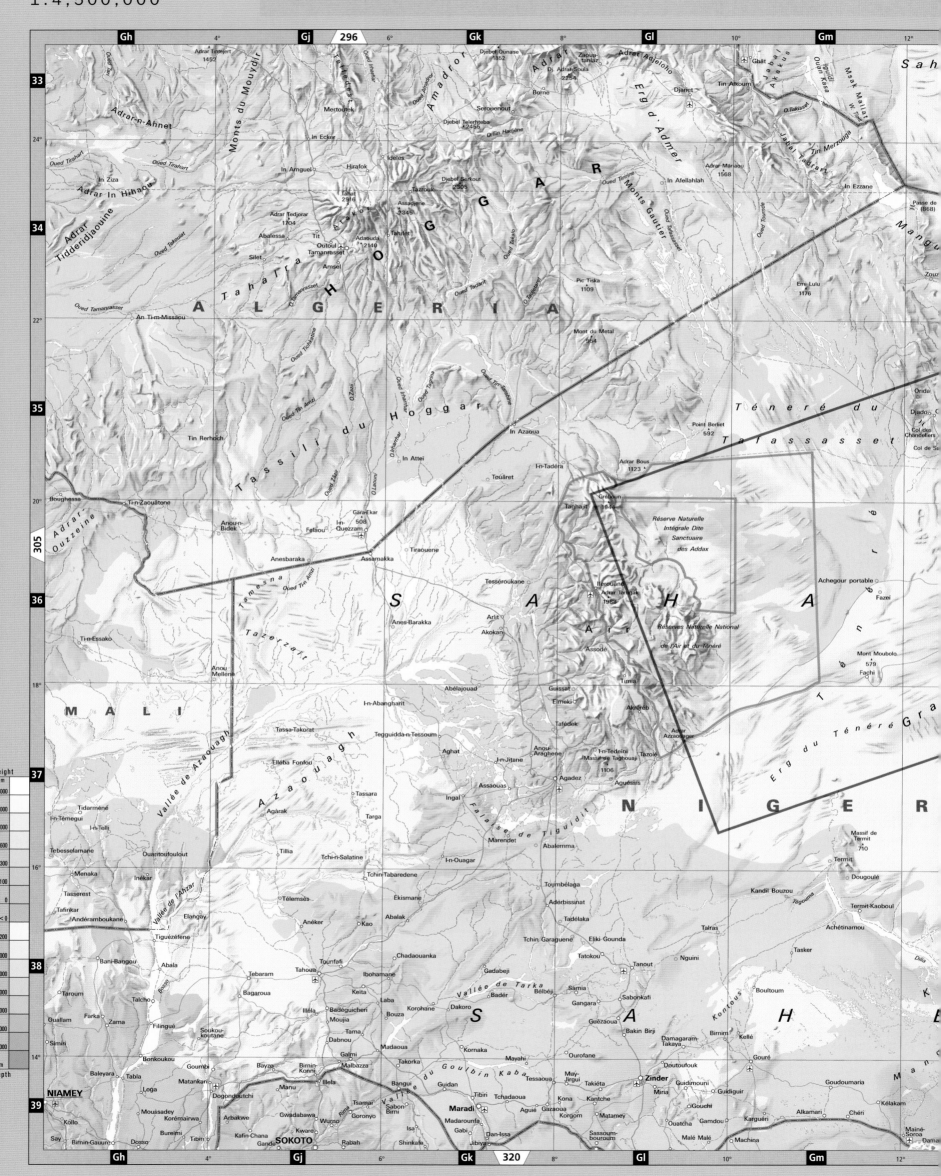

Height
m
3000
2000
1000
600
300
100
0
< 0
200
1000
2000
4000
6000
8000
10000
m
Depth

1:4,500,000

| 0 | 25 | 50 | 75 | 100 | 125 miles |

| 0 | 50 | 100 | 150 | 200 km |

Albers Equal Area Conic Projection

Marzuq

Al Qatrūn   Jabal Bin Ghanīmah

Tahrami   Al Wigh

) (Murizidié Pass

Sarīr   **L I B Y A**

Rebiana Sand Sea

Jabal al Hawa'ish   33

Al Huari

Rabyanah   Al Hawwari   Al Khufra   At Tullab

Tropic of Cancer   24°

T i b e s t i

Wāw an Nāmūs

Ma'tan   34

1660   Jabal Nuqay

ateau   Jabal Timmū   1022

Passe de Kōrizo

Enneri Yébigué

Enneri Bardagué   Karnasaï   1640   Aozou

Bikubiti   2786

Ouri   Yanggera   22°

4866   Jabal Tarhuni

do   Madama

Emi Fezzane   1000

Massif d'Atafi

Massif d'Abo

W. Wour   Wour

Bardai

Aderké   Omchi   Tarso Emisu   3376

Kozi   Ma'tan as Sarah

odemi

Mabrous

Col de Yéi Lulu

Pic Toussidé   3315

Yebbi Souma

Yebbi-Bou

Enneri Mi   Zouar

T i b e s t i   Tarso Teroko   2675

Jef-Jef el Kébir   35

Monts Totomaï

Dao Timi   Yat

Col de Gobo

Sherda

Falaise de Mguer-Tay   Bini-Erde   Tarso Laman   20°   312

guédine

uebo

Enneri Tegenam   Enneri Ké

Emi Koussi   3415

Gouro   Tékro

mba   Baba

473   Rond-Point de Gaulle

Ouniinga Kébir   Lac Yoa

Ouniinga Sérir   Nabar   *E r d i*   36

A   *Erg de Bilma*

Tigui   Oyé Yeska

Bédo

B o r k o u

Yen   Dépression du Mourdi   18°

djigo   Ain Galaka

Faya (Largeau)   *Mourdi*

Falaise d'Angamma

Palmeraie du Borkou   *E n n e d i*

ifem   ezzé Denga   Homodji

Yogoum

Fada   Basso   1450   37

Koussa Arma

Chicha   Tchie

Bodélé   *Erg du Djourab*

Broulkou

Menou

nimma   aram

Tanga   Ourini   16°

Moul   oufey

Aziz

Toungour

Koro Toro

Kouba Olanga   Oum-Chalouba   O. Ouangat   *Zaghaou*

Nédéley

Ouadi Achim   O. Fama

Bakaoré   1220   Inba   Massif du Kapka

ri   Dabwa   *L*   Nokou   Ntiona   Beurkia   Arada   Tini

Nguigmi   Nokou   Mao   Tellis   **C   H   A   D**   O. Haddad

asso   Bisagana   Liwa   Mondo   Ziguéy   Salal   Safi   Ouadi Enné   Biltine   Guéréda   Kulaykil   Koulbous

Baga Sola   Rig Rig   Méchirneré   Babi al Ghazal (Soro)   Am-Zoer   Ardémi   38   14°

Doum Doum   Kouri Koutr   Moussoro   Am Raya   Rime   Haraz-Djombo   Abou Goulem   Adré   Birkat Saira   39

Lake Chad   Mouzarak   Ngarangou   Ngouri   El Ouadey   Ifenat   Ouadi Rime   Am Sak   Abéché   Abou Goudem   El Gemeina

Baga   Am Djemena   Ati   Djédaa   Am Himédé   Oum-Hadjer   Dérèssa   Koulbo   Wadi Kauo   Misterei   Nurei

Batha   Koundijourou   Assinet

Ténéré

In the southern Sahara lie the Aïr mountain range and the Ténéré, a sandy desert. Located between 18° and 21° latitude north, both lie in an arid belt in what are known as the horse latitudes, which are characterized by winds, calms, and high barometric pressure. This area of desert and semi-desert consists partly of open sandy or stony deserts, and partly of arid mountain ranges. Being so inhospitable, the region has always been very sparsely populated, and because it can be crossed only with difficulty, it forms a barrier between North and Central Africa. It is, however, dotted with a few small oases, which are barely visible in the satellite image. Today, as in ancient times, these oases are important stopping places for travelers, whether they are journeying with a caravan of camels or in motorized vehicles.

1 *Aïr* ↑

The Aïr's lowest mountain range rises 1800 m (5906 ft) above the Ténéré, causing the German explorer Heinrich Barth (1821–65) to describe it as the "Alps of the Sahara." The ancient massif consists of crystalline rock, with outcrops of gneiss, granite, and crystalline slate. The upward-curving peneplain (an area of land flattened by erosion) reaches an average height of 700 m (2297 ft). Massifs of younger volcanic rock tower above it, rising to a height of 2300 m (7546 ft). Vestiges of volcanic craters and of basalt lava line the valleys.

2 Koris

In contrast to the surrounding deserts, the Ténéré receives up to 100 mm (4 in) of rainfall a year. This makes it possible for many species of plants and animals to thrive here, including several species of gecko. The rivulets that periodically carry water are called *koris* in local parlance. The groundwater in the *koris* also provides irrigation for many oases, where date palms grow. The Timia oasis can be seen in the satellite image.
The Tuareg graze their flocks on the scrub that covers the areas around the oasis and the mountain sides. They belong to the Berber ethnic group, speak a Berber language, and have their own script. Rock drawings dating back to the Stone Age show that the Aïr mountain range has been inhabited for thousands of years.

3 Sandstone Ridge

A ridge of sandstone rises about 100 m (328 ft) above the dunes in the Ténéré. Lying on a north–south axis, it divides the desert into a western and an eastern region. At the foot of the ridge is an alignment of oases.

4 *Ténéré* ↓

The word "Ténéré" means "The land out there" in the language of the Berbers. It broadly describes the inhospitable, empty plain that covers the northwestern part of the huge Chad Basin (see pp322–3). Its uniform colors and level surface make this desert an apparently boundless ocean. While in the north it consists mainly of stony terrain, in the south it is made up of an area of dunes that merge into each other.

Those who know the Sahara advise any travelers who dare venture into the Ténéré to go there only in reliable and well-maintained vehicles. As well as a complete set of spare mechanical parts, essential supplies and equipment should include large reserves of fuel and sufficient supplies of water, as journeys through the desert are often much longer than anticipated. They may, for example, involve wide detours to find a safe passage through the dunes. Another hazard is soft sand: Toward the middle of the day, when it is whipped up into ripples by the wind (as seen in this photograph), it loses its firmness and becomes treacherous for vehicles.

Sudan, Eritrea

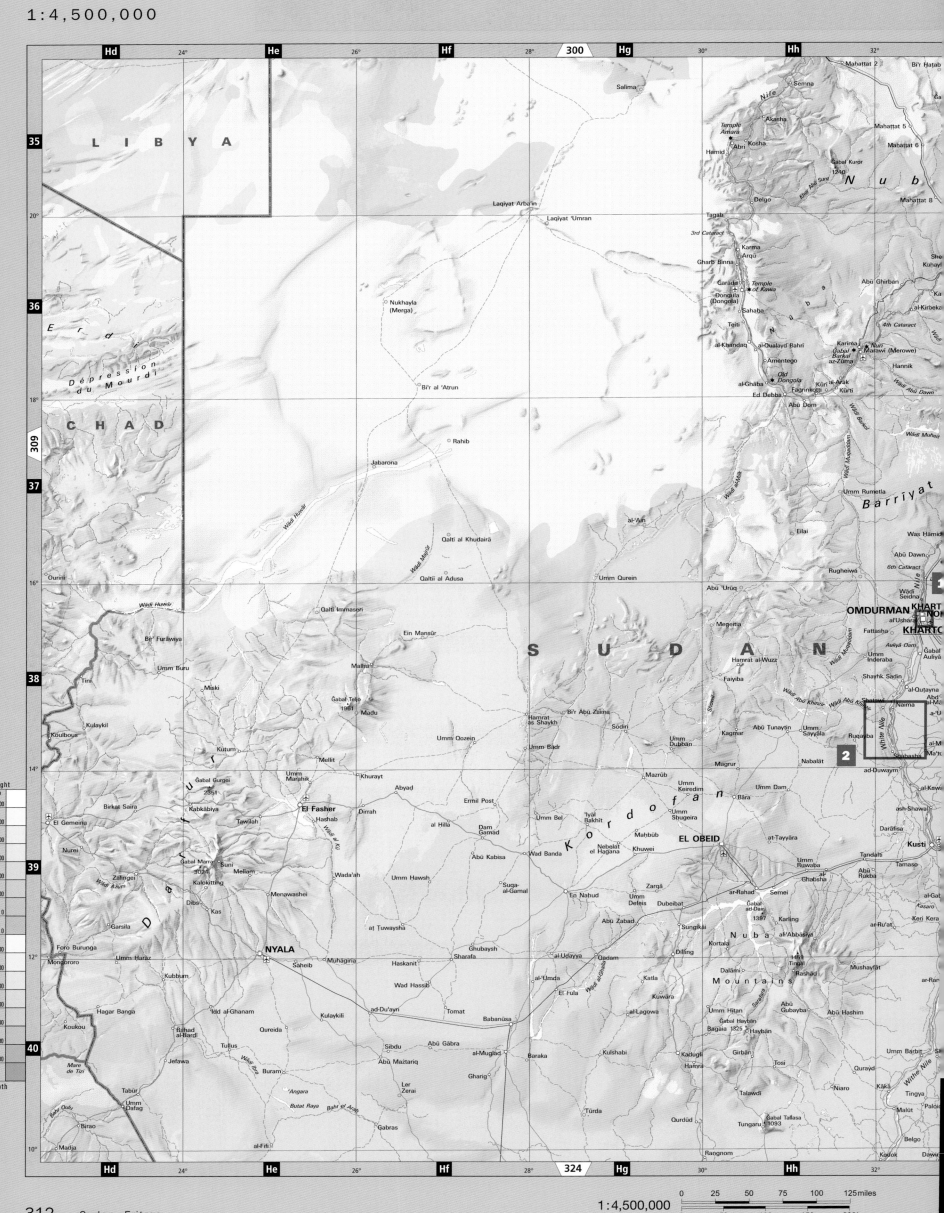

1:4,500,000

0   25   50   75   100   125 miles

0   50   100   150   200 km

Albers Equal Area Conic Projection

Khartoum

Khartoum

Established at the confluence of the Blue Nile and the White Nile, Khartoum became the political, cultural, administrative, and economic center of Sudan, the largest country in Africa. At this point, where the rivers form a vital link with the outside world and provide a transportation route, three large cities with a total population of almost five million form an agglomeration in a desert region: They are Khartoum, on the left bank of the Blue Nile, with 2.7 million inhabitants; Umm Durman, on the left banks of the White Nile and the Nile, with 1.3 million inhabitants; and Khartoum North, with 0.7 million inhabitants.

1 The Nile

The volume of water carried by the Nile, which flows for 6671 km (4145 miles) between Khartoum and its delta on the Mediterranean Sea, is subject to seasonal fluctuations. After summer rainfall in the highlands of Ethiopia, the Blue Nile carries up to 50 times more water than it does during the dry season. Water and silt carried down by the Blue Nile make up 80 percent of the volume of water in the Nile when it is in flood. When the water is low, the White Nile makes up about 80 percent of the volume of water at its confluence with the Blue Nile. The distribution of the water of the White Nile indicates that the satellite image was taken when the water was low.

2 Irrigated land

Irrigated land, visible as patches of green in the satellite image, covers the banks of the White Nile and the Blue Nile that have not been claimed by urban development.

3 Khartoum ←

In the street markets of Khartoum groceries such as rice, beans, vegetables, eggs, and spices are sold. Despite temperatures of over 40° C during most of the year business life is taking place outdoors.

4 Khartoum North

A road and rail bridge, which was built in 1910, spans the Nile here. It connects the capital with Khartoum North, which is an important industrial area.

5 Khartoum

The English laid out Khartoum, on a grid system typical of many British cities, at the end of the 19th century. Ministerial buildings and the university are located along the riverbank.

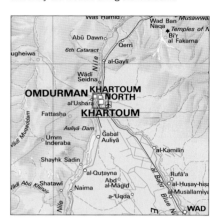

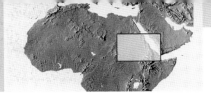
1 Manaqil Canal

So as to increase the extent of the irrigated land of Gezira, work began in 1939 on the Manaqil Canal, which is fed by the main canal near the Blue Nile. However, it was not until 1958 that this new tract of land, covering 336,000 ha (830,274 acres), could be cultivated with water supplied by the dense network of irrigation channels. Millet and cotton are the main crops here, although these have tended to be replaced by wheat and rice in recent years. The land is divided

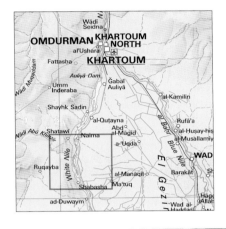

into 2.1 ha (5 acre) fields. These are leased in units of three, which the lessee cultivates in rotation over several years. A typical cycle would be to plant cotton one year, let the land lie fallow the next, and plant millet and beans the year after; then forage plants, followed by fallow land, then cotton. The rotation system is prescribed by law and can be clearly seen in the satellite image, where parcels of fallow land appear as brownish patches. Tens of thousands of farming families earn their living in this way.

2 Dune Belt in the Sahel Zone

Scrub land and desert, marked by long lines of dunes, extend as far as the White Nile. Fluctuations in annual rainfall are very wide here. From June to the end of September average rainfall is about 300 mm (12 in). This is enough to support sparse vegetation, which protects the dunes from wind and prevents them from drifting.

3 *White Nile →*

Both banks of the White Nile have been inhabited since very ancient times. Here, early farmers grew millet, sesame, and peanuts, which they traded. The crops that appear as green strips in the satellite image below are irrigated by means of water pumps.

Gezira

This satellite image of part of Sudan shows three distinct geographical features, which divide the land into three longitudinal bands: On the left is a sandy, desert-like area; near the center, a stretch of the White Nile, which bisects the terrain like a blue ribbon; and on the right a wide expanse of irrigated land. This verdant landscape forms part of Gezira, meaning "island" in Arabic. It is the largest irrigated region in Africa, and spreads out between the White Nile and the Blue Nile, southeast of Khartoum. Work on creating Gezira began in 1925, after the waters of the Blue Nile had been dammed.

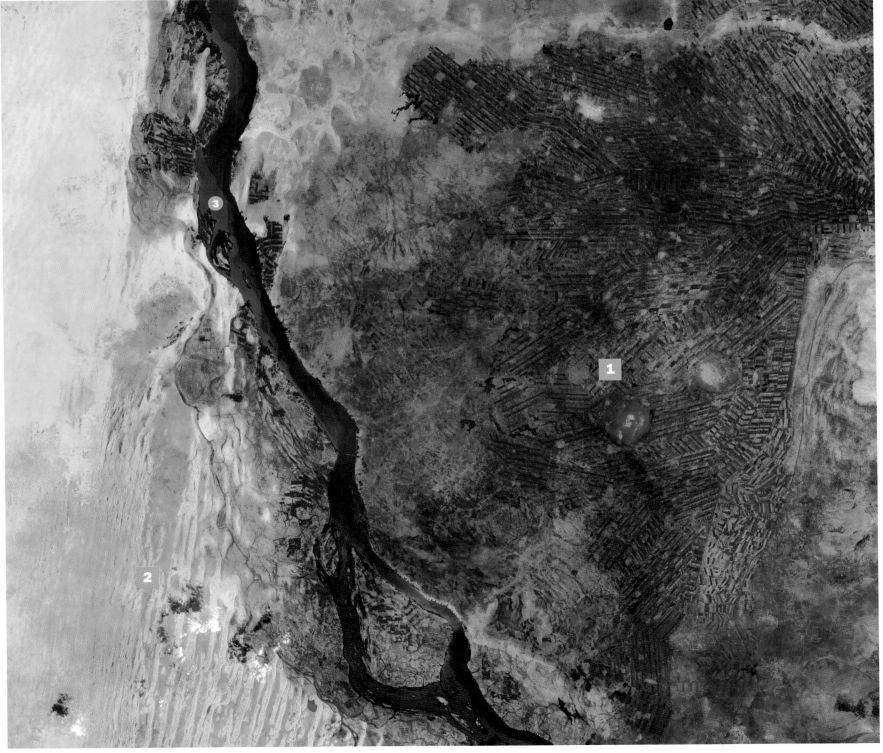

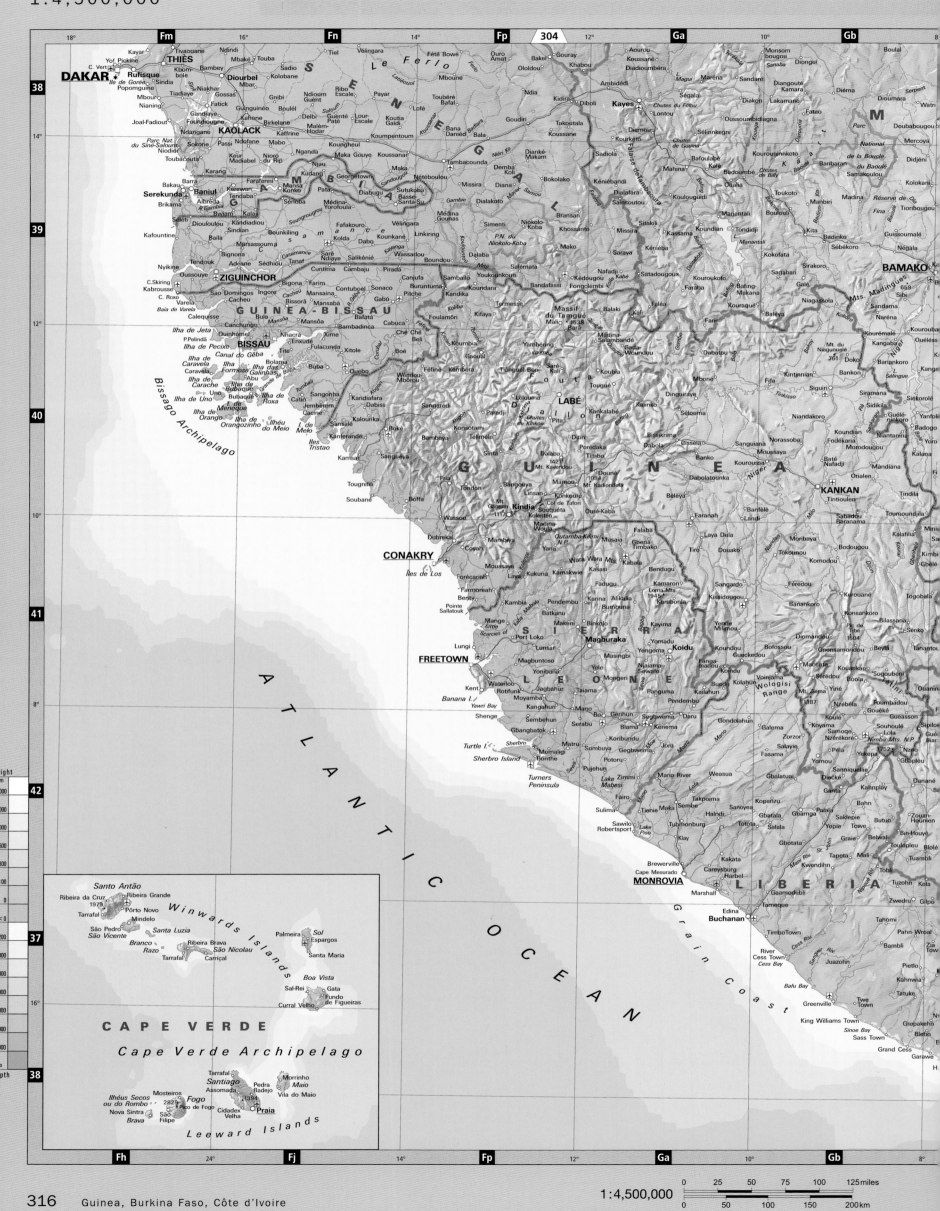

1:4,500,000

Albers Equal Area Conic Projection

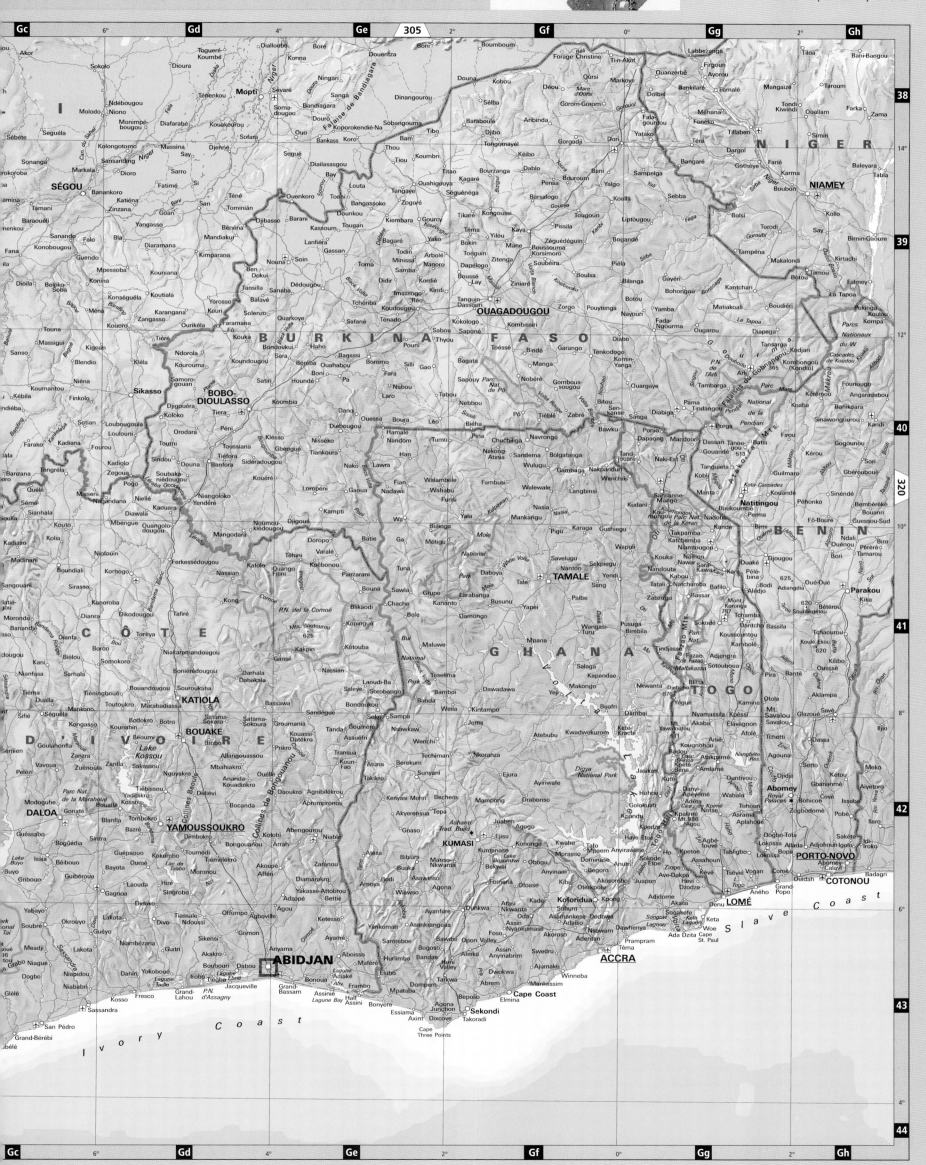

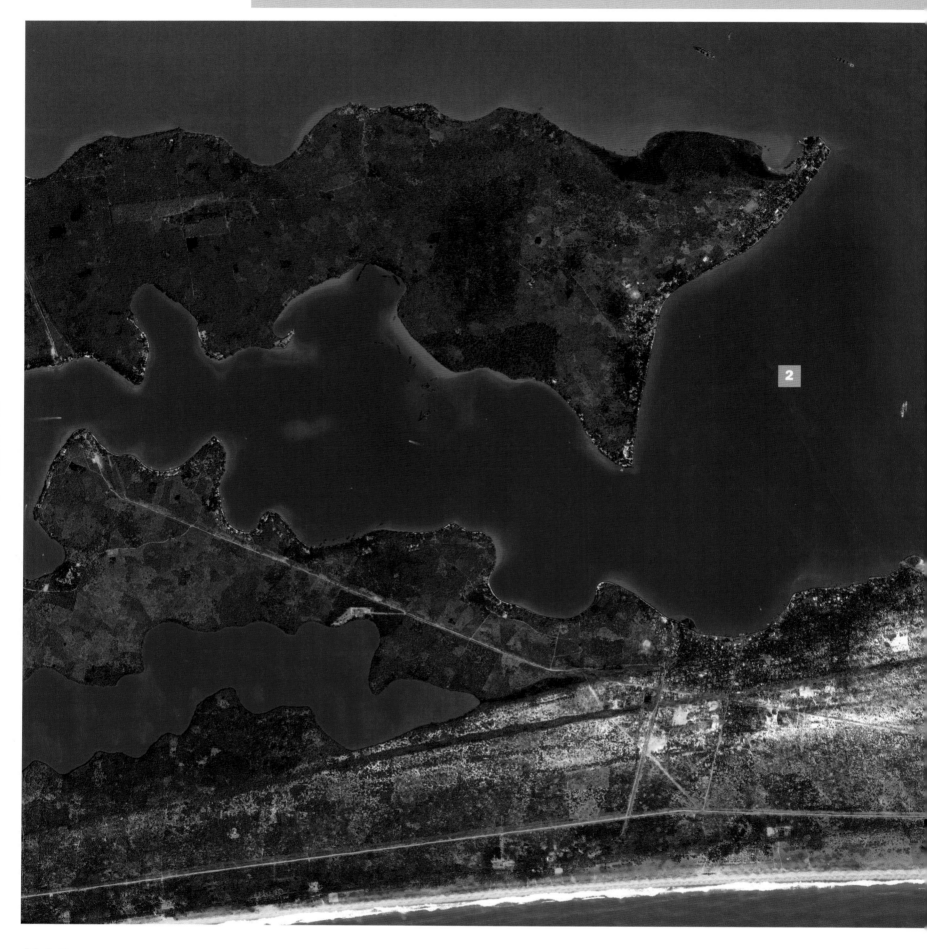

Abidjan

With more than three million inhabitants, Abidjan is the largest city in Côte d'Ivoire. It extends along the Ébrié Lagoon, across a series of islands and headlands that are connected to each other by bridges. Although some districts have prestigious buildings and elegant shops, the city has some typically African areas, which make up its true heart. In 1934, Abidjan became the capital of what was then a French colony. After Côte d'Ivoire won independence, in 1960, Abidjan remained the capital. In 1983, the seat of government was transferred to Yamoussoukro, but Abidjan remains the country's undisputed commercial metropolis. It is a melting pot for people with a great variety of ethnic origins.

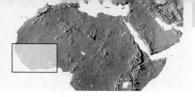

1 Le Plateau ←

Abidjan's skyline is in keeping with the modern
face of Africa. With magnificent avenues, skyscrapers, and shopping centers on a par with
those of major European or North American
cities, Abidjan is often referred to as the Manhattan of Africa. In the past three decades in particular, Le Plateau, the city's commercial district
(north of the section shown in the satellite image), has experienced tremendous growth, culmi-
nating in spectacular construction projects. In addition to functional high-rise office buildings, a
number of prestigious buildings have also been
unveiled. The range of goods on offer in the
shops lining Le Plateau's boulevards is similar to
that found in Paris or New York.

2 Ébrié Lagoon

This sheltered lagoon stretches from Abidjan's seafront for about 150 km (93 miles) farther to the west. Only a narrow strip of land separates the lagoon from the Gulf of Guinea, a bay
on the Atlantic Ocean. Although Ébrié Lagoon is
very narrow—it is 7 km (4 miles) wide at its
broadest point—it is very deep: Its average depth
is 4.8 m (15.7 ft), but close to Abidjan it plunges
to 15–20 m (49–66 ft).

3 Vridi Canal

Vridi Canal, completed in 1950, is an
important waterway. It links Ébrié Lagoon with the
Atlantic Ocean, thus connecting areas of the city
that are some distance from the coast to Port

Bouet, in the east. About 90 percent of Côte
d'Ivoire's exports (particularly cocoa and oil) pass
through this port.

4 Treichville

The spirit of West Africa is vigorously alive
in areas of the city such as Treichville. This district
stands in particularly marked contrast to the
modern part of Abidjan. There is always plenty
going on in the maquis, as Treichville's countless
cafes and restaurants are called. In contrast to
those in the Europeanized areas of the city,
prices in the shops here are affordable to the
local population. The gloriously colorful Treichville
Market is legendary: To European eyes, it is like
an African bazaar.

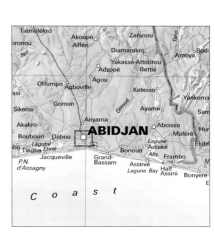

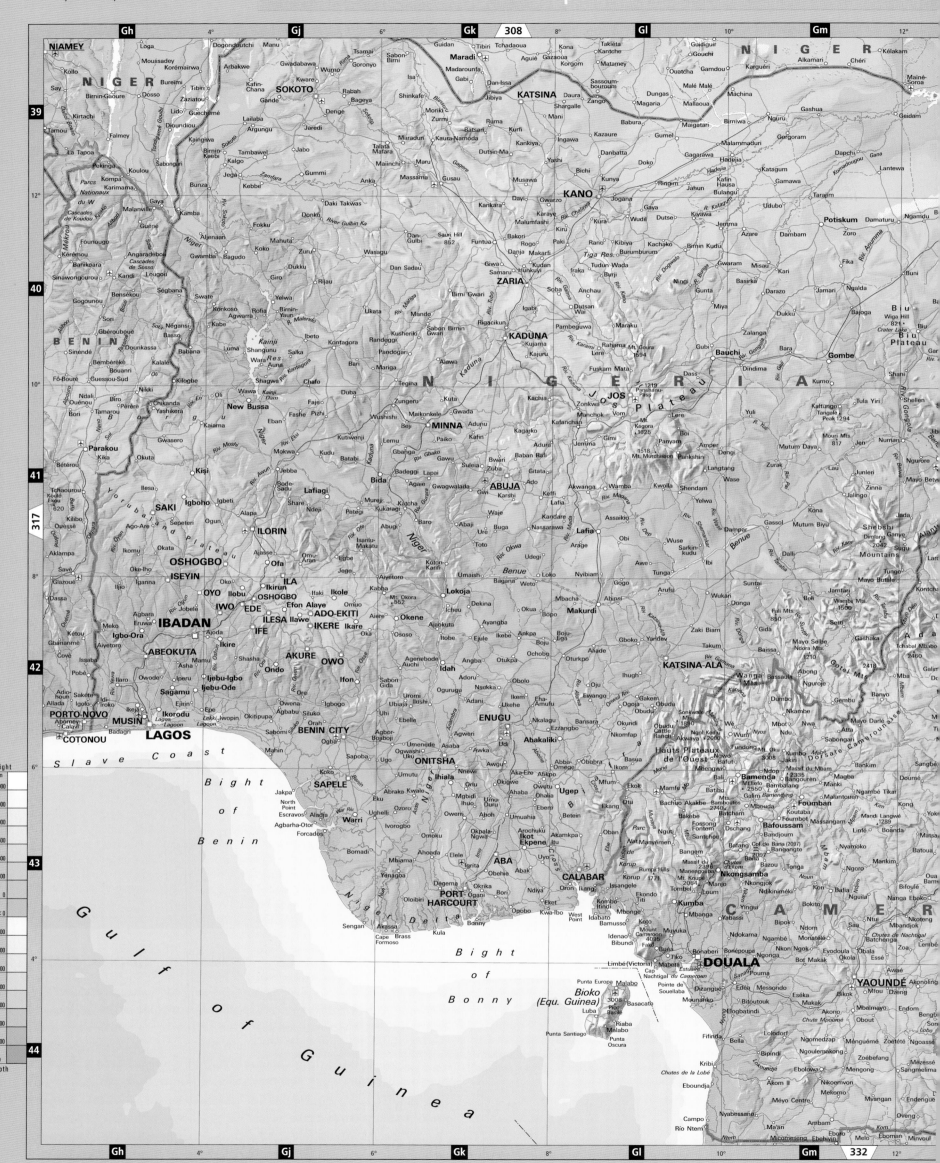

1:4,500,000

0   25   50   75   100   125 miles
0   50   100   150   200 km

Albers Equal Area Conic Projection

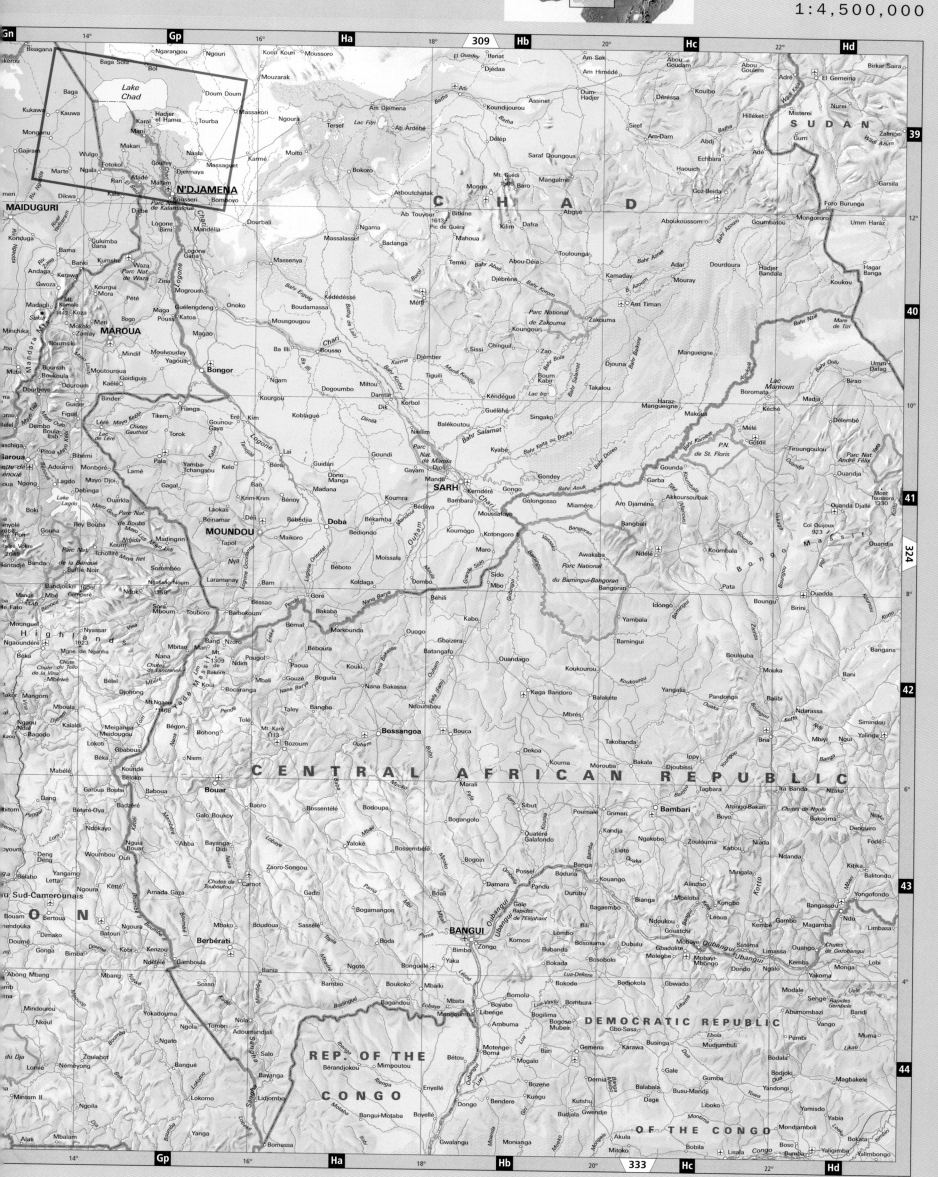

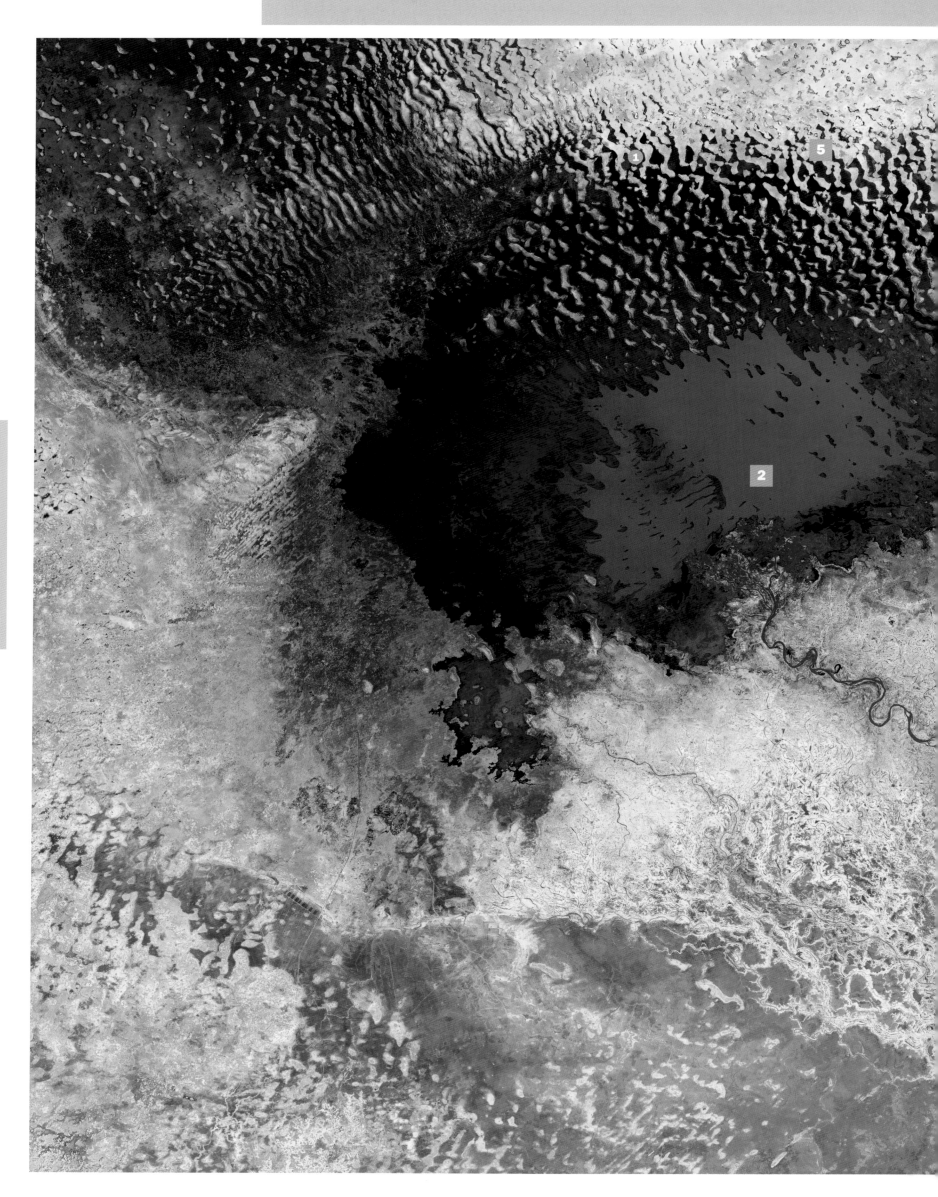

Lake Chad

Lake Chad, south of the Sahara, lies in the deepest part of the southern Chad Basin. It is fed by rivers that flow from the hills to the south, but has no apparent outlet. No rivers feed it from the north, because this side of the lake is bordered by arid desert. In the past, between about 9500 and 4500 BC, the climate here was humid, with heavy rainfall, and the lake covered an enormous area. Since then, it has progressively shrunk, although it has also periodically expanded during periods of increased rainfall. In the second half of the 19th century, when the water level was 2 m (7 ft) higher than it is today, what is now Lake Chad's northern shore was under water. The northern part of the lake bed has been dry since 1972.

1 *Natron Extraction in Baga Sola ↓*

The waters of Lake Chad contain natron in concentrations of up to 400 mg per liter. But the technology needed to extract it, and the costs involved, have made the exploitation of this resource impractical. However, fossil beds of natron have been successfully mined around the Baga Sola area north of Lake Chad, and this photograph shows blocks of natron stacked in rows along the lakeshore to dry. Natron is a mineral that consists of hydrated sodium carbonate. A white crystalline substance, it reacts with carbon dioxide when it is exposed to heat or acids, and is used to make baking powder and sherbet. It is also used in glass-making and silk-weaving, and in the manufacture of washing powder, cellulose, and artificial colorants.

3 Chari River

Rainfall accounts for only 10 percent of the water in Lake Chad. The rest is brought mainly by the Chari, the largest of the rivers that feed the lake. The Chari brings water from southern Chad, where rainfall is heavy, to this semi-arid region, where scrub vegetation predominates. Here annual rainfall can reach 400 mm (16 in), although evaporation can reduce the lake's water level by 2000 mm (79 in). The Chari River, which is 1400 km (870 mile) long, forms a delta at the point where it enters the lake. It provides 90 percent of the annual volume of water that feeds the lake and carries the greatest volume of water from August through to the end of December, when it is navigable. From June to September, the period

2 Islands in Lake Chad

With a maximum depth of 7 m (23 ft), Lake Chad currently has a surface area of 24,000 km² (9266 square miles). It is surrounded by a marshland that covers 6800 km² (2625 square miles), and which is mainly covered in reeds in the north and papyrus in the south. The many islands that dot Lake Chad are old dunes. The Buduma, a Muslim tribe who live in conical-roofed huts on these islands, live by raising cattle and catching fish.

of the rainy season, it breaks its banks, flooding broad tracts of land.

4 N'Djamena

N'Djamena, capital of Chad, was founded in 1900, when it was known as Fort Lamy. It lies at an altitude of 294 m (965 ft), and grew from a settlement that was established on the west, reed-covered bank of the Chari River, opposite its confluence with the Logon. In 1945 N'Djamena had only 7000 inhabitants, but since then it has developed into a city with a population of half a million. With an international airport, good road connections, and facilities for handling river traffic, this major metropolis is an important hub for transportation.

5 Land Reclamation in Bol

To the east and northeast of Lake Chad—including the center of Bol—wide areas of previously unusable terrain have been turned into fertile agricultural land. This transformation was brought about by the construction of dikes. Cotton, wheat, millet, sugar cane, rice, and vegetables are now cultivated on this reclaimed land. Intensive cattle farming also takes place here. Irrigation is carried out by means of artesian wells and irrigation canals.

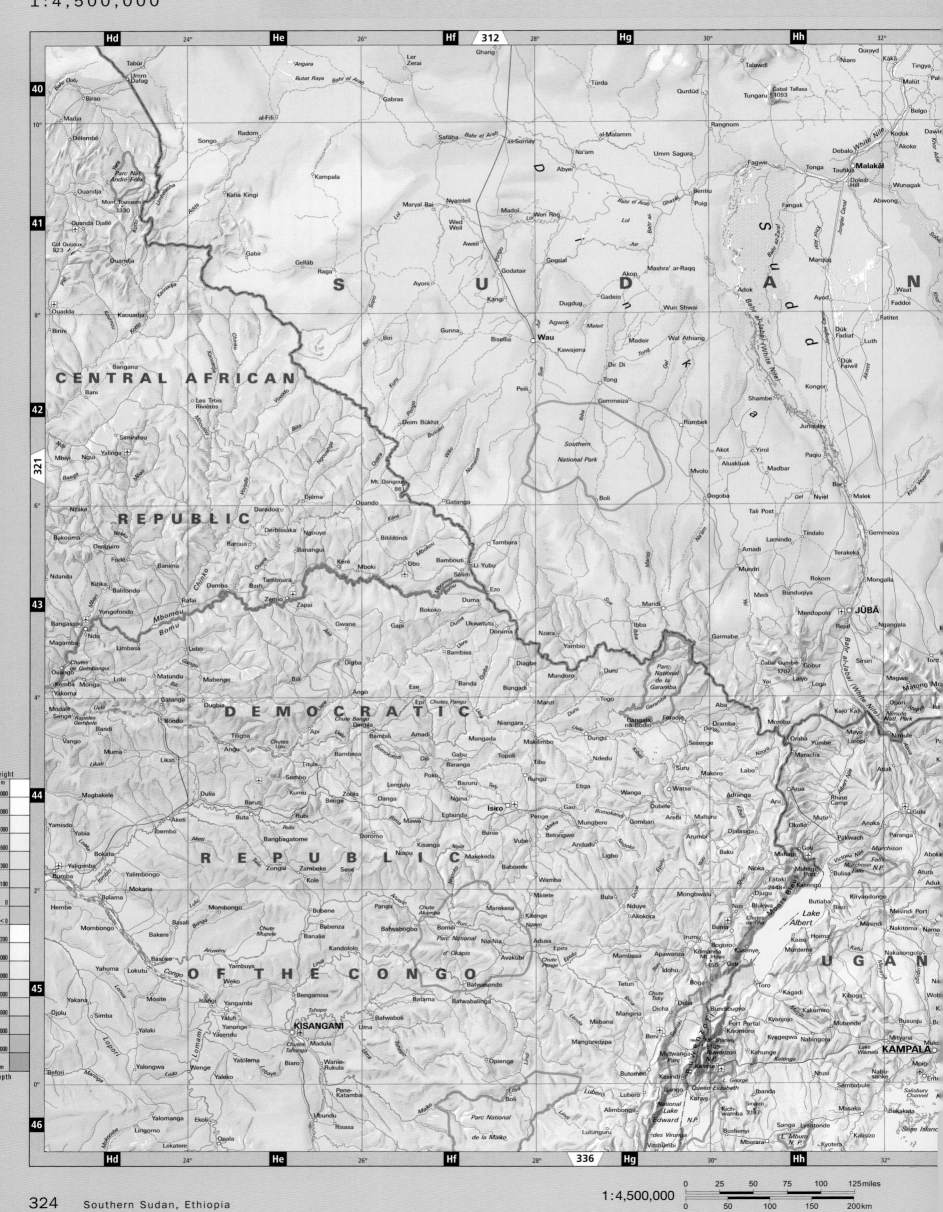

1:4,500,000

0   25   50   75   100   125 miles

0   50   100   150   200 km

Albers Equal Area Conic Projection

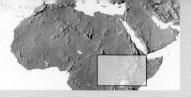

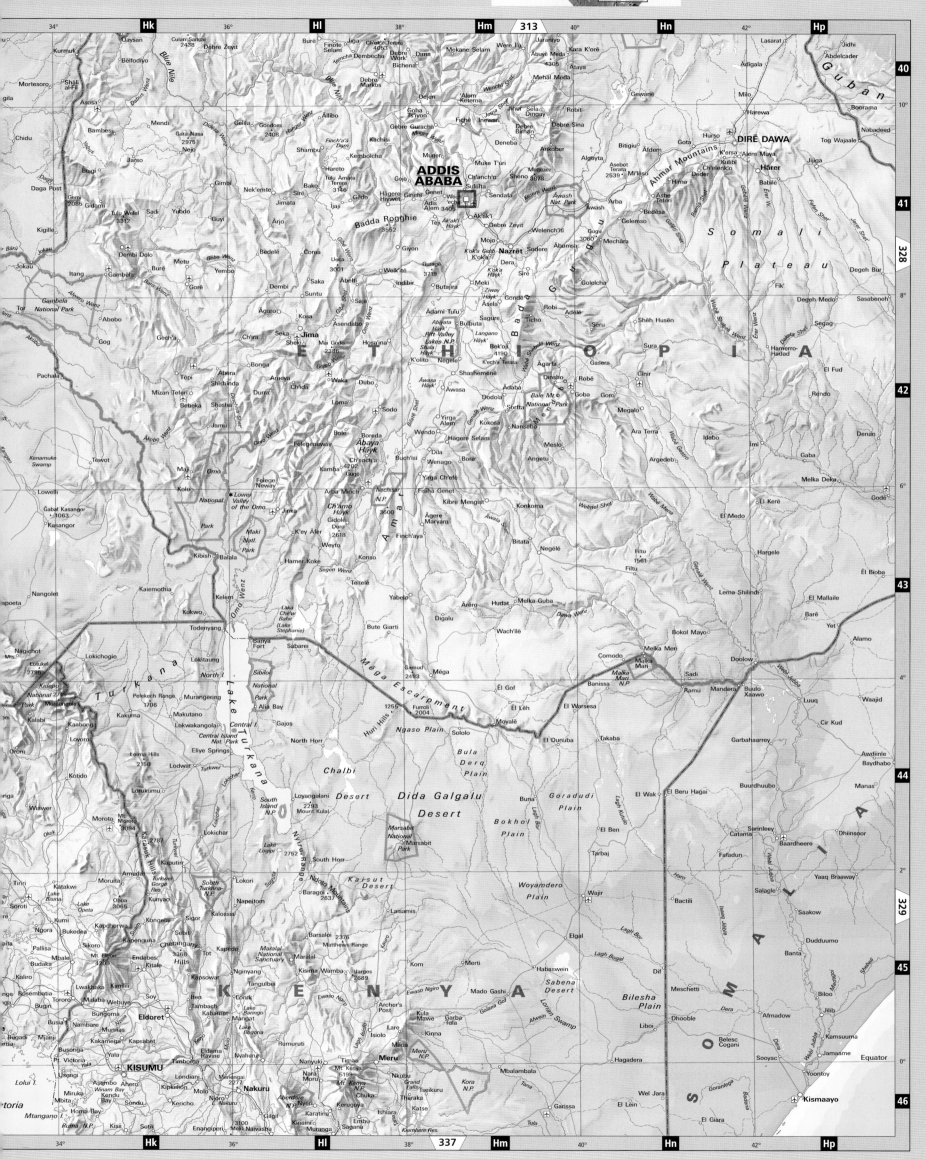

Addis Ababa

Addis Ababa means "new flower" in Amharic, the official language of Ethiopia. It was the name that the wife of the emperor of Ethiopia gave to the small settlement that was established near hot springs. In 1886, emperor Negus Menelik built a palace here. The city of Addis Ababa originated in the neighboring army camp. As a result of famine, which drove people from the countryside, the city's population increased, with many immigrants settling wherever they could around the town. The settlements that sprang up were the precursors of Addis Ababa's present-day districts. Although some of the forests that separated them survived for a time, they were eventually cleared, allowing the settlements to merge into a single city.

1 ## Old Ghibbi

Old Ghibbi is the oldest district of Addis Ababa. It is enclosed by fences and is not open to visitors. This is where the hot springs, which led to the establishment of the early settlement, are located. The governor's palace is set in parkland, and the Kidus Taaka Negest Beata Maryam Church, built in 1911, stands on the southern edge of the park. Members of the former imperial family are buried in the church's mausoleum.

2 ### Churchill Avenue ←

This avenue shows Addis Ababa as a modern African metropolis. It is the central thoroughfare through a district of wide boulevards, with several lines of traffic, paved roads, and pavements. The modern district is filled with prestigious buildings made from steel, glass, and concrete, where insurance companies and banks have their offices. The modern district also contains theaters and large hotel complexes. Most of these buildings originated in the 1960s and 1970s. The other face of Addis Ababa can be seen only a few hundred meters away: Outside the modern district, the city spreads out in a mass of small, flimsy, single-story houses and shacks. This is where the city's poorest people live and work, in cramped and unsanitary conditions. The congested streets and tightly packed dwellings stretch into the distance as far as the eye can see.

3 ## Mercato

The Mercato, or Market, is located in the west of Addis Ababa. The largest open-air market in Africa, it constitutes a district in itself. Goods of every kind—from spices and scrap metal, to jewelry and designer clothing, blocks of salt, and saddles—are bought and sold here. Visitors who venture into the throng without a guide can easily lose their bearings. Additional hazards to be aware of here are pickpockets and traffic: Cars are carelessly driven through the throng of people with little regard for safety. The impressive Anwar Mosque as well as the catholic cathedral of the Holy Family are located in Abidjan's Merkato district.

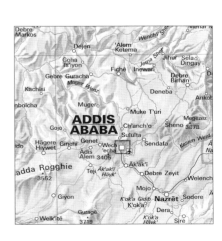

MAP

1:4,500,000

Height
m
3000
2000
1000
600
300
100
0
< 0
200
1000
2000
4000
6000
8000
10000
m
Depth

Gulf of Aden

Bāb al-Mandab

Gulf of Tadjoura

DJIBOUTI

Cal Madow

Cal Miskaat

Bannaanka Saraar

Guban

Somali Plateau

ETHIOPIA

Ogaden

ADDIS ABABA

DIRĒ DAWA

Hārer

NAZRĒT

Desē

Berbera

Hargeysa

1:4,500,000

0 25 50 75 100 125 miles
0   50   100   150 200km

Albers Equal Area Conic Projection

MAP

1 : 4,500,000

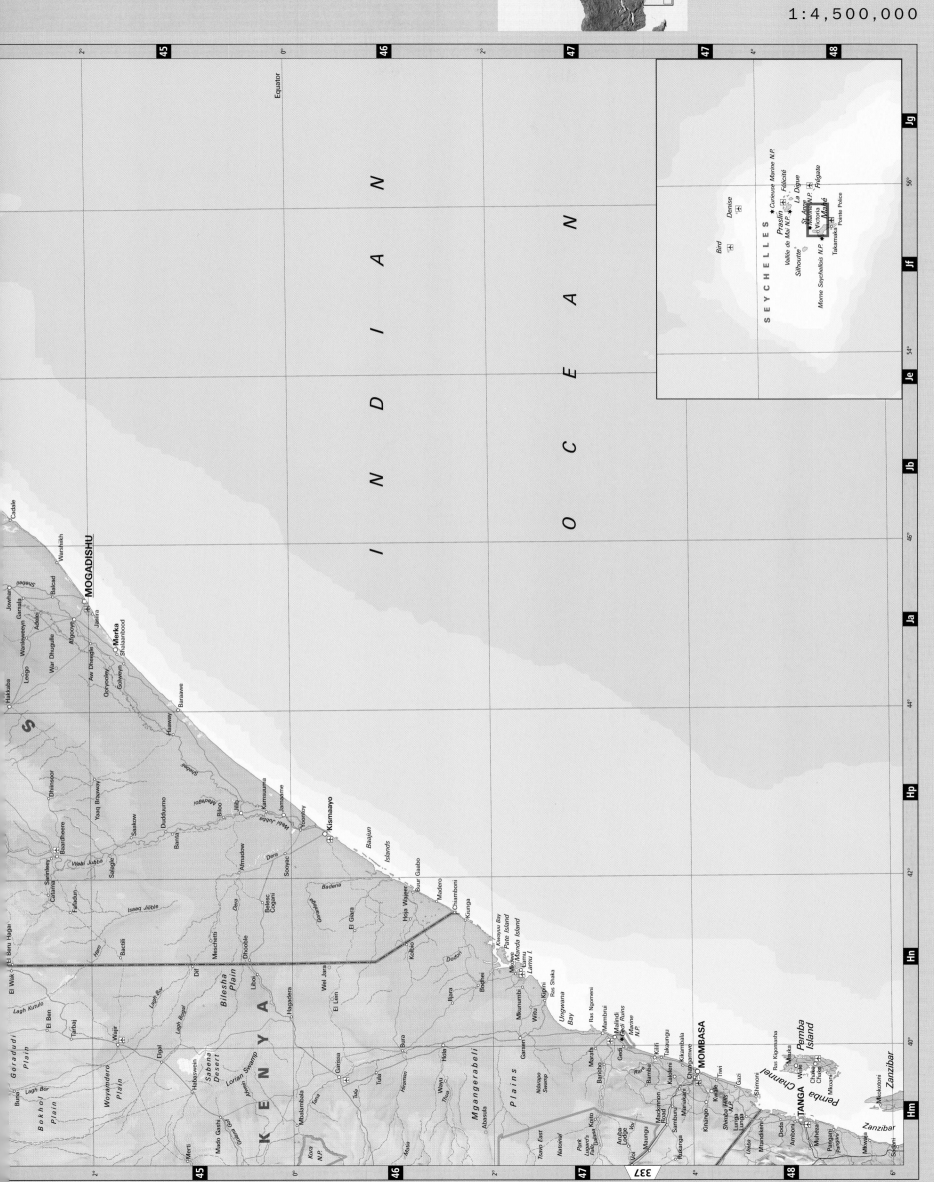

45 0° 46 2° 47 47 4° 48

Equator

I N D I A N

O C E A N

SEYCHELLES

Bird

Denise

Curieuse Marine N.P.
Praslin ★ Félicité
Vallée de Mai N.P. La Digue
Silhouette St. Anne ★
North Marine N.P. Victoria **Mahé** Frégate
Morne Seychellois N.P. ★
Takamaka Pointe Police

Jg

Jf

56°

Je

54°

Jb

46°

Cadale

Warshiikh

MOGADISHU
Jowhar
Balcad
Shabeelle

Ja

44°

Garsaale
Wanlweweyn
Addan
Algooye
Merka
Shalaanbood
Aw Dheegle
Golweyn
Ooryooley
Baraawe
Leego
War Dhugulle
Haakaba
Haawey

Hp

42°

Dhimmspor
Yaaq Braawe
Saakow
Dudduumo
Biloo
Jilib
Kamsuuma
Jamaame
Shiirinleey
Banta
Yoontoy
Kismaayo
Webi Jubba
Salagle
Atmadow
Afmadow
Sooyac
Baajun
Dera
Islands
Catama
Fafadun
Isaaq Jilible
Badena
Buur Gaabo
Dera
Geraharei
Madero
El Wak
El Beru Hagia
Bacuti
Meschenti
El Giara
Hoja Wajeer
Chiamboni
Dif
Dhoobie
Kolbio
Kiunga
Libo
Kiwayu Bay
Pate Island
Haro
Lagh Bor
Liboi
Hagadera
Dodori
Manda Island
Lamu I.
Moowe
Lamu

Hn

K E N Y A
Bilesha Plain
Lagh Kutulo
El Ben
Wel Jara
El Lein
Iljara
Bodhei
Kipini
Ras Shaka
Tarbaj
Wajir
Bura
Hola
Mkunumbi
Witu
Ungwana
Bay
Ras Ngomeni
Eipal
Garissa
Tula
Hieima
Wayu
Garsen
Malindi
Gedi Ruins
Gedi
Kilifi
Marafa
Baricho
Bamba
Merti
Mado Gashi
Galana Gof
Mtalambula
Tana
Mackinnon
Road
Takaungu
Mombasa
Burra
Lagh Bor
Goradudi Plain
Woyandero Plain
Sabena Desert
Habaswein
Loriani Swamp
Abasula
Mangerabeli Plains
Mwango Swamp
Mariakani
Kikambala
Charngamwe
MOMBASA
Tiwi
Buna
Bokhol Plain
Lagh Bogal
Aweyn Swamp
Aruba Lodge
Mala
Koito
Voi
Kinango
Kwale
Shaba Hills N.P.
Gazi
Pemba Island
Mvia
Ras Kiponasha
Meaka
Kora
N.P.
Tsavo East
National
Park
Lugard's
Falls
Samburu
Muingu
Mackinon
Mariakani
Lunga
Lunga
Shimoni
Chako
Chiaso
Wete
Pemba
Channel
Rukanga
Mtaindikeni
Mariakani
Doda
Amboni
TANGA
Mkoani
Zanzibar
Mtandika
Muheza
Pangani
Pangani
Mkokotoni
Zanzibar
Sadani
Mtwala

Hm

45 0° 46 2° 47 4° 48 6°

337

African Horn, Northern East Africa   329

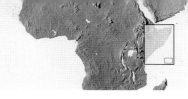

Seychelles

The group of islands known as the Seychelles lies in the Indian Ocean, northeast of Madagascar. The islands number over 100, only a third of which are inhabited. With their idyllic beaches and picture-postcard scenery, many are tropical paradises. But the archipelago also has its surprises. One is the Morne Seychellois, on the island of Mahé: The highest mountain in the island group, it rises to a height of 905 m (2969 ft). Another is the coco de mer, or sea coconut. These huge palm nuts, which grow only in the Seychelles, can be up to 50 cm (20 in) long: They contain a two-lobed edible kernel. The islands' culture is a blend of European colonial elements and black African traditions. The popular religion consists of a blend of Christian practices and voodoo rites.

Palm Beach on La Digue ↑

A visit to the island of La Digue reveals the full beauty of the Seychelles. Located about 50 km (30 miles) northeast of the area shown in the satellite image, La Digue is one of the largest islands in the archipelago. Its appeal lies in its white-sand beach and turquoise water with fish of every hue, as well as its secluded bays and granite cliffs, and the lines of coconut trees picturesquely inclined toward the sea. Although the Seychelles lie between the tropics, the islands enjoy a pleasantly warm climate that is tempered by cooling sea breezes. On La Digue, as on many other of the Seychelles islands, the average annual temperature is about 27°C (80.6°F), with only slight fluctuations. Rainfall, by contrast, varies greatly according to the time of year. It can reach an annual figure of 3000 mm (118 in), and the period of heaviest precipitation is between November and the end of April.

1 Mahé, the Largest Island

Most of the Seychelles' inhabitants, who number about 80,000, live on Mahé. Covering 148 km² (57 square miles), this is the largest island in the archipelago. The international airport, completed in 1971, is situated on Mahé's east coast. Most of the tourists who come to the Seychelles to go diving in the in-shore waters arrive at this airport: Tourism has developed into the most important source of revenue for the Seychelles. Other economic activities include the cultivation of coconuts, which are grown in plantations, some of which are extensive. Mangroves also line parts of the coast of Mahé, while the interior is mainly hilly or mountainous, with mountaintops often shrouded in clouds. The island's interior is thickly forested.

2 Victoria

Victoria is the capital of the republic of the Seychelles. It is located in a bay on the northeast coast of Mahé, and is backed by mountains on its western side. Victoria's historic center has some fine 19th-century colonial buildings.

3 Sainte Anne Marine Park

The small island of Sainte Anne is located about 5 km (3 miles) east of Mahé. The coastal waters around the island make up the Sainte Anne Marine Park, a conservation area that is also open to divers. In addition to hotel staff, only 150 tourists may stay overnight on the island, most of which is uninhabited.

Pineapple Plantations ↓

Pineapples thrive in the tropical climate of the Seychelles. They are grown in plantations and sold in the market in Victoria.

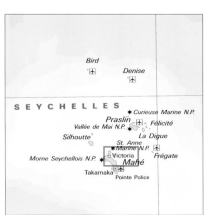

320

330

340

44

2°

45

0° Equator

46

2°

47

4°

48

6°

8°

49

50

Gk 8° Gl 10° Gm 12° Gn 14° Gp 16°

ATLANTIC OCEAN

CAMEROON

EQUATORIAL GUINEA

SÃO TOMÉ AND PRÍNCIPE
São Tomé
Príncipe
Pedras Tinhosas
São António
Neves
São Tomé
Pico de São Tomé 2021
Porto-Alegre

LIBREVILLE

PORT-GENTIL

GABON

REPUBLIC

OF THE

CONGO

Franceville

BRAZZAVILLE

KINSHASA

POINTE-NOIRE

Cabinda
(ANGOLA)

MATADI

Boma

Height
m
3000
2000
1000
600
300
100
0
<0
200
1000
2000
4000
6000
8000
10000
m
Depth

1:4,500,000

0 25 50 75 100 125 miles
0 50 100 150 200 km
Albers Equal Area Conic Projection

DEMOCRATIC REPUBLIC OF THE CONGO

MBANDAKA

KISANGANI

KIKWIT

KANANGA   MBUJI-MAYI   Kabinda

Gandajika

Mwene-Ditu

Kamina

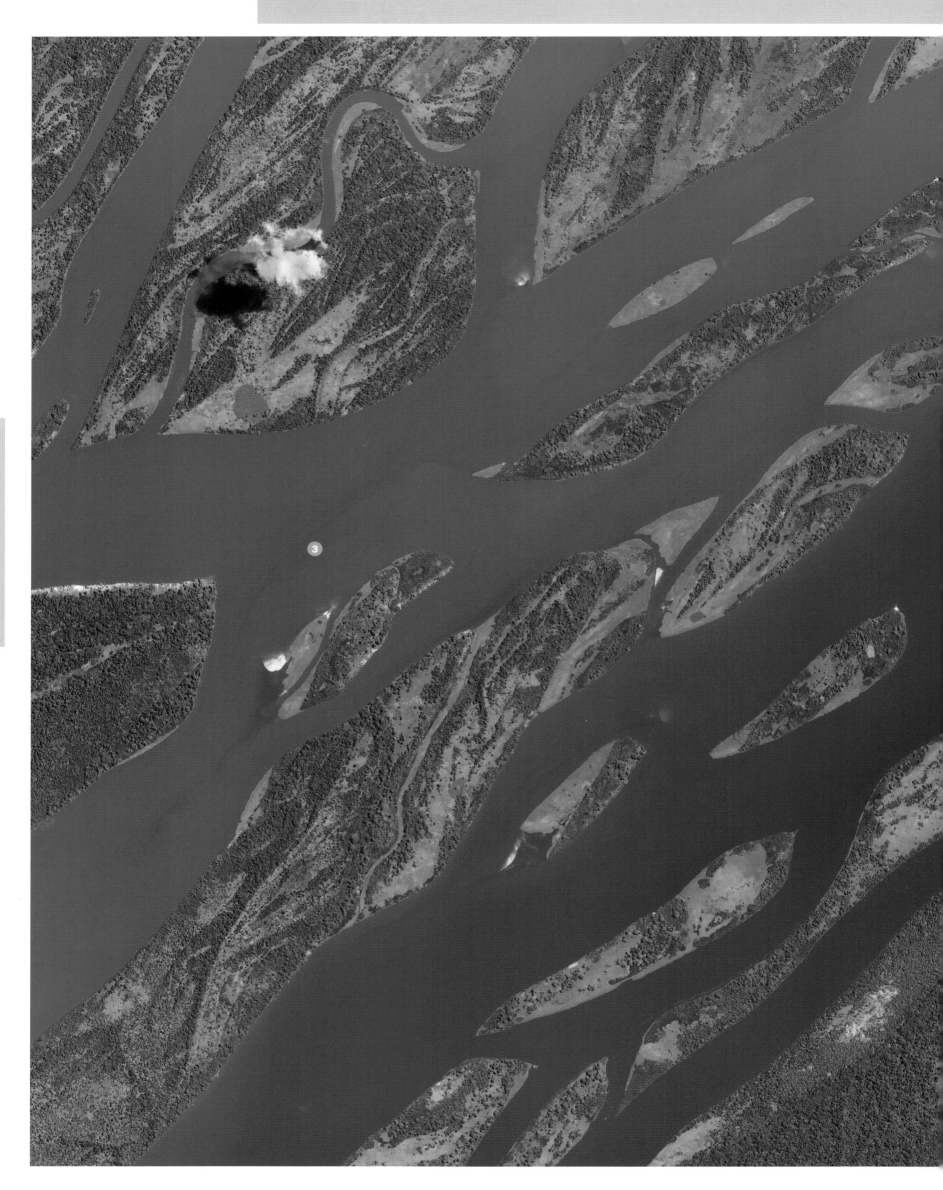

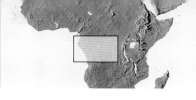

Congo

The satellite image shows the branches into which the Congo divides, a short distance upstream of the point where it is joined by the Ubangui. Covering 2300 km (1429 miles), the Ubangui is the Congo's longest tributary and, on account of the huge volume of water that it carries, it is its second-largest tributary. Here, the Ubangui also marks the border between the Democratic Republic of the Congo, formerly Zaïre, to the east, and the Republic of the Congo, to the west. The flat, low-lying land in the center of the Congo Basin allows the Ubangui to form a large inland delta here: The delta, which is several dozen kilometers wide, has created the Ngiri swamplands. South of this huge delta, the Ubangui flows into the Congo. As a transportation artery, the Congo is of great importance to the economy of the Democratic Republic of the Congo. Logging is one of the country's major economic activities, and the river serves as a crucial transport route for timber.

① Congo ↑

The word "Congo" is derived from the name of the Bakongo, a tribe whom European explorers encountered in the region around the river's estuary on the Atlantic coast. "Zaire", the other name by which the river is known, goes back to early Portuguese explorers: While searching for a southern route round the Horn of Africa in the 15th century, they reached the Congo's estuary, and gave it the name Zaire, from nzadi, the Bantu word for "river." Because of the volume of water that it carries, the Congo is the second-largest river in the world after the Amazon (see pp122–3). Flowing through the huge Congo Basin, it drains an area of about 3,659,000 km² (1,412,750 square miles). Because its tributaries flow through regions on either side of the equator, where rainy seasons occur in tandem, the Congo is fed at a constant rate, and so carries roughly the same amount of water all year round. Large volumes of water brought by the northern tributaries counterbalance small amounts simultaneously brought by the southern tributaries, and vice versa.

② River Island

In the area shown in the satellite image, the Congo broadens to a maximum width of 14 km (9 miles). As it widens, the river splits into increasingly smaller watercourses divided by a multitude of narrow islands, some of which are more than 10 km (6 miles) long. While the smaller river islands are permanently susceptible to flooding,

the larger ones are relatively safe. The settlements that have grown up on these islands reflect the importance of the river, as a central transport and supply route, to the local population.

③ The Congo as a Traffic Route ↑

Their slow-moving, steady flow, and the extremely level terrain through which they pass, make the Congo and its tributaries some of the best natural shipping networks in the world. These two factors cause the river to divide into many branches, whose course may change within a relatively short period of time. As a result, the river does not cut a deep bed into the land. The many shallows and sandbanks that form along its course are a hindrance to river traffic.

Southern East Africa

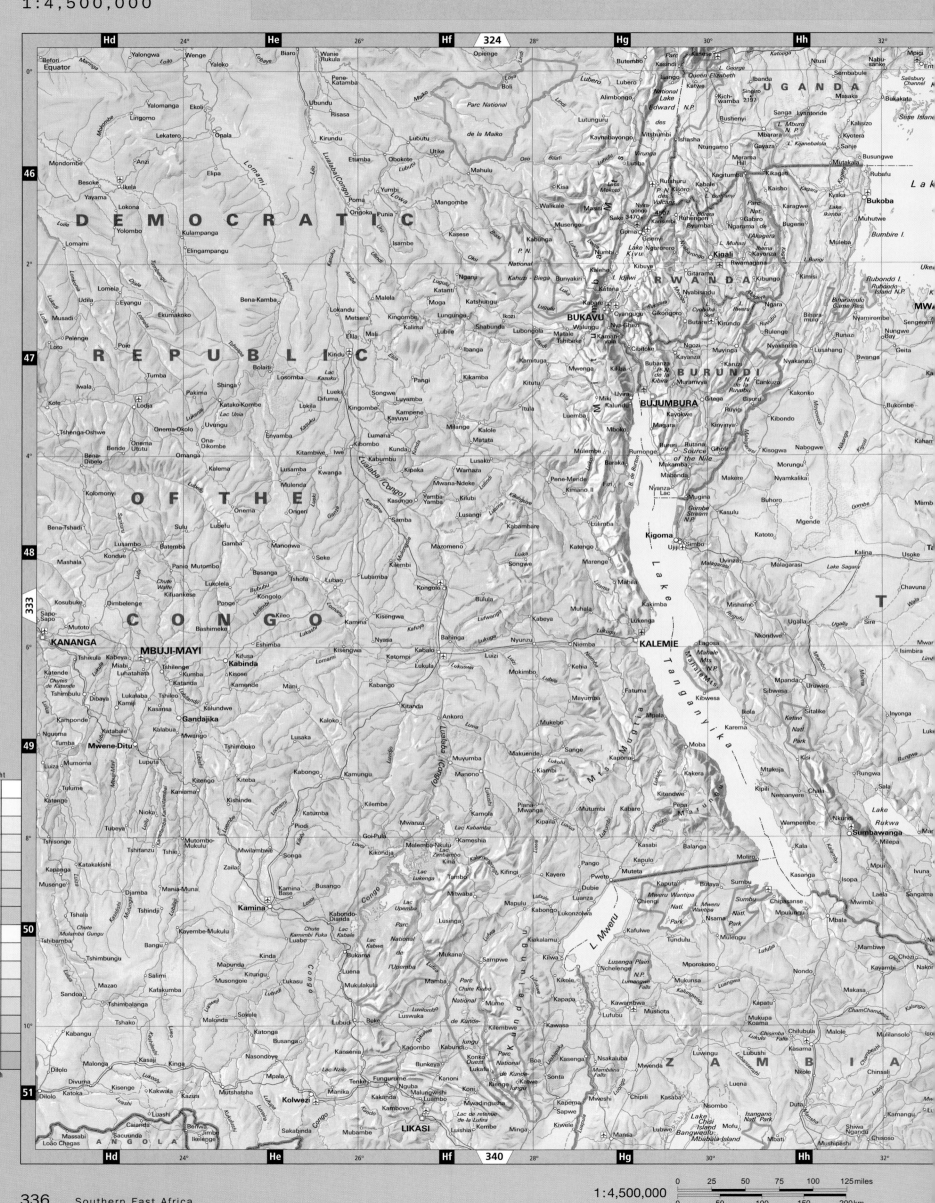

1:4,500,000

0   25   50   75   100   125 miles

0   50   100   150   200 km

Albers Equal Area Conic Projection

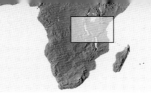

Ngorongoro Crater

East Africa's northern region is marked by an extraordinary physical feature, the Ngorongoro Crater. One of many craters that dot the Crater Highlands, it lies southeast of Lake Victoria. This volcanic basin is 700 m (2297 ft) high and has a diameter of about 22 km (14 miles). It is located in the center of the Ngorongoro Crater Conservation Area, which covers an expanse of 8288 km² (3200 square miles). Because of its unique character, the area was declared a UNESCO World Natural Heritage Site and International Biosphere Reserve in 1979. The graves of the German zoologist Bernhard Grzimek (1909–87) and his son Michael, who both worked tirelessly for the protection of East Africa's wildlife, are in the reserve.

1 *Ngorongoro Crater* ↑

The Ngorongoro Crater is part of a long-extinct volcano, which collapsed into itself, forming a huge basin. The edges of the crater are roughly 2400 m (7874 ft) above sea level, and they tower above the ground at a height of about 700 m (2297 ft). The crater is remarkable for its wildlife. It is impressive not only on account of the number of animals there—about 40,000—but also because of the great variety of species, the largest of which are the elephants. Because the crater is a secluded haven, the population of elephants in the Ngorongoro Crater was not decimated by poaching, unlike those living in the neighboring Serengeti National Park.

2 Mount Lodmalasin

At a height of 3600 m (11,811 ft), Mount Lodmalasin, an extinct volcano, is the highest point in the area around the Ngorongoro Crater. Along with other volcanoes in the vicinity, it forms part of East Africa's Great Rift Valley system, which is 6000 km (3728 miles) long and was created by the earth's crust drifting apart along the tectonic fault line. Extinct and active volcanoes line the edges of the valleys and the Ngorongoro Crater Conservation Area.

3 Lake Magadi

Lake Magadi lies at the bottom of the Ngorongoro Crater. Water from the small amount

of annual rainfall that the region receives accumulates here, at the crater's lowest point, and the size of the lake varies depending on the season. It provides a resting place for flamingoes and many other species of bird.

4 Olmoti Crater

The Olmoti Crater is the principal source of water for the wildlife of the Ngorongoro Crater Conservation Area. Covered with grass, the crater's flat bottom also provides pasture for the Maasai's herds—mainly cattle—as well as for eland and bushbuck. The Munge River rises here and drops sharply down at the point where it flows out of the basin.

5 *Empakaai Crater* ↓

In the center of this crater, which is 6 km (4 miles) wide and 300 m (984 ft) high, lies a deep-blue lake. Its waters, with a maximum depth of 85 m (279 ft), are slightly alkaline. Antelope, gazelle, buffalo, apes, and rhinoceros, as well as several species of bird live in the crater.

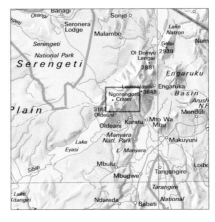

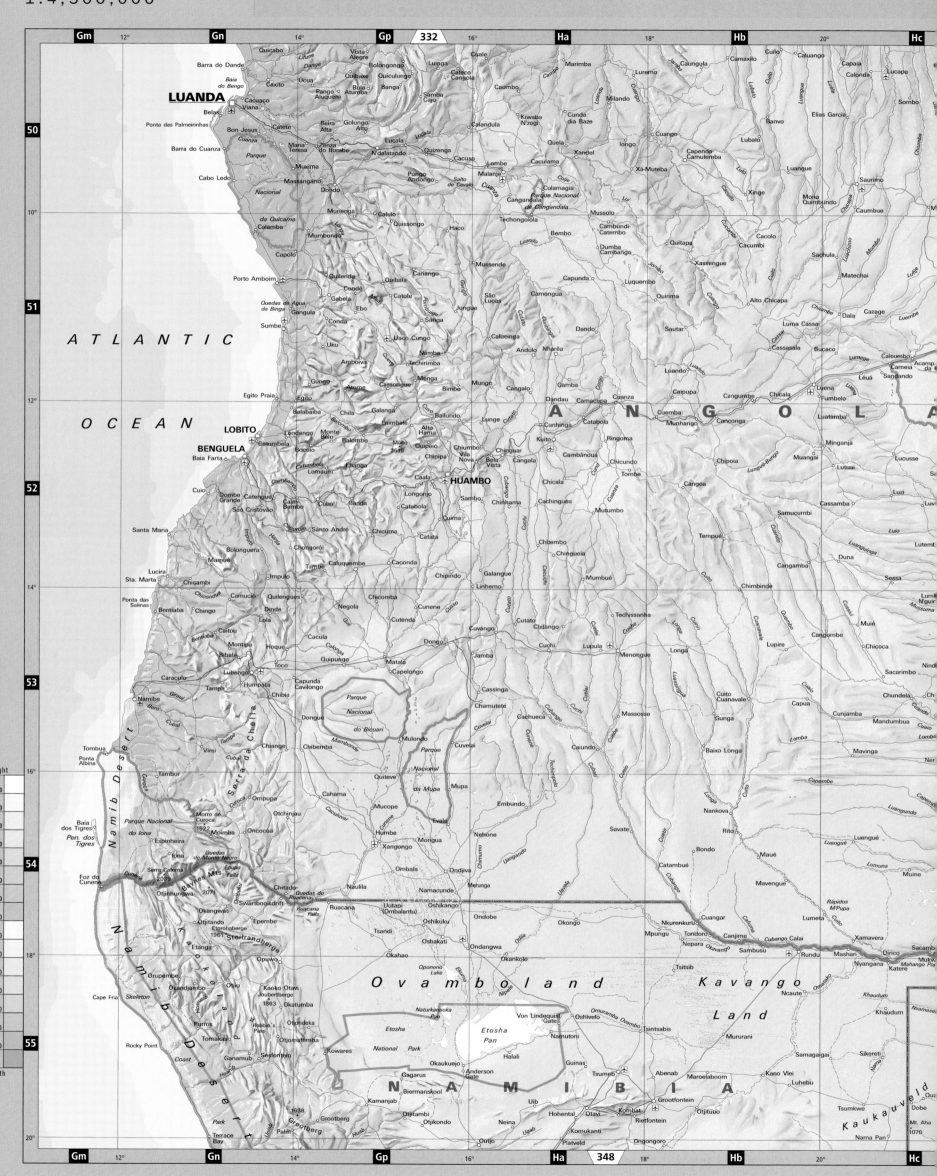

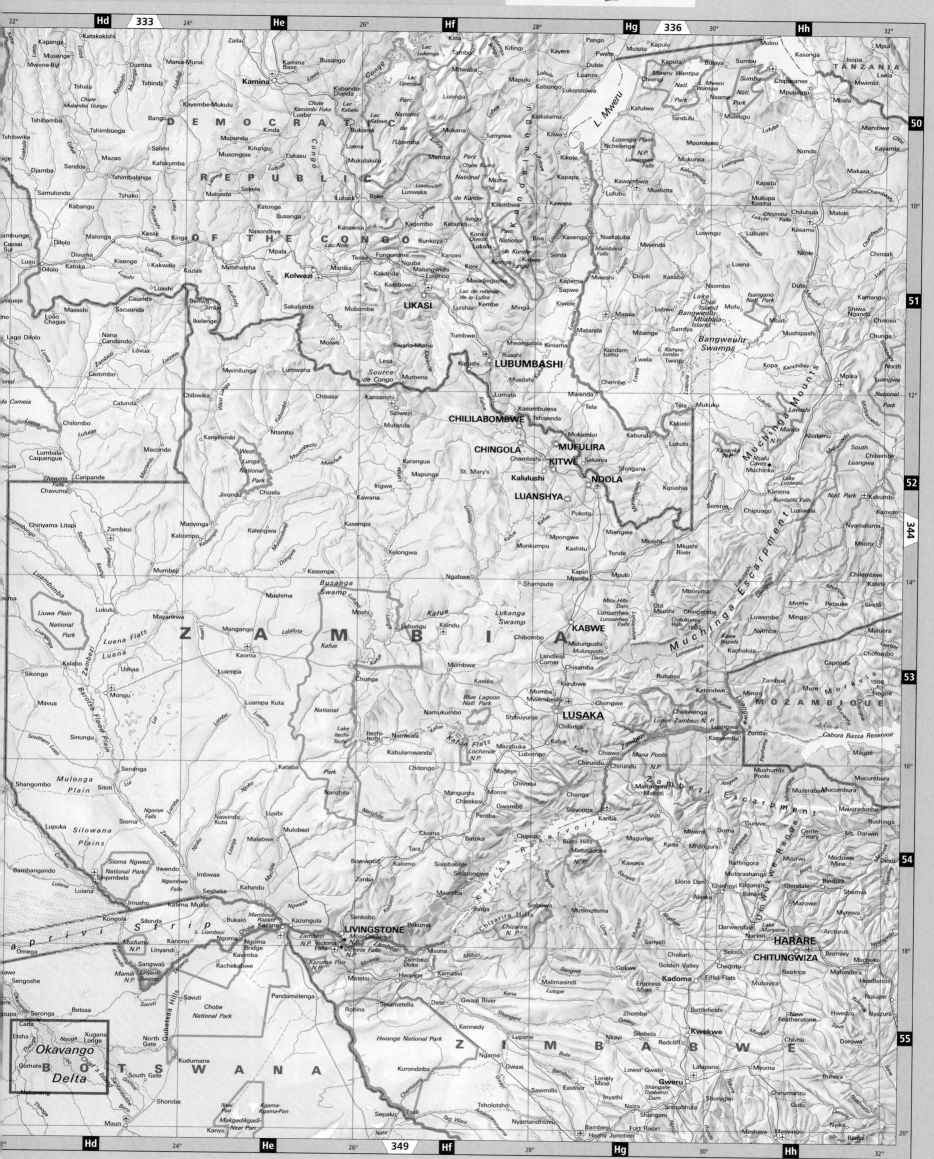

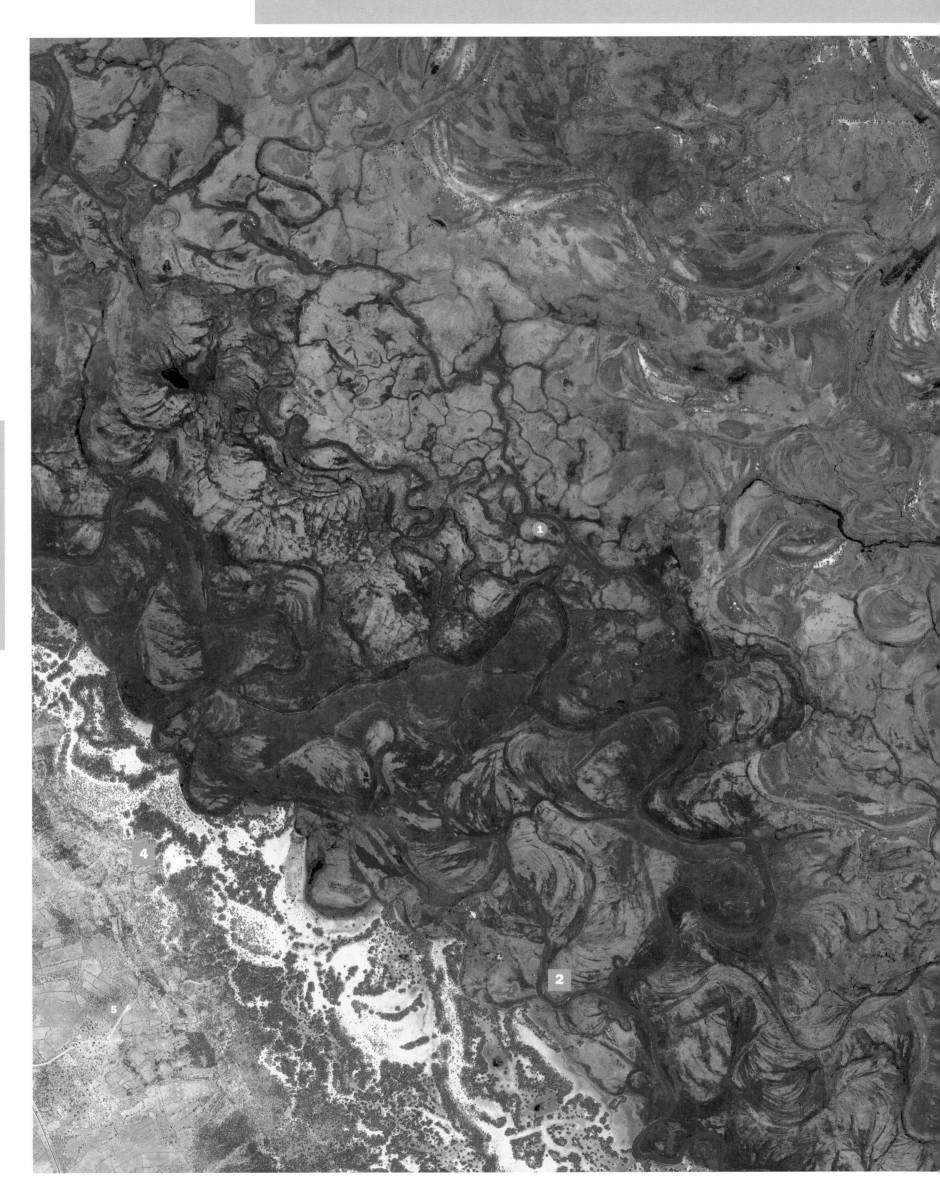

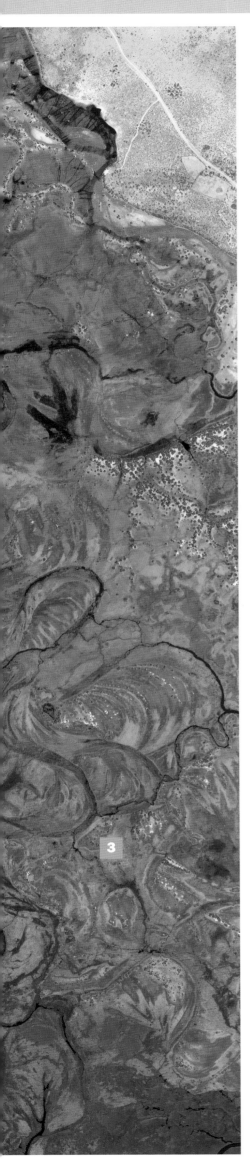

1 Riverbanks ↓

The delta is dotted with many permanent islands. Many originated as termite mounds, which survived regular flooding thanks to the concrete-like nature of the material, a mixture of earth and saliva, produced by the termites. As the mounds accumulated sediment washed down by the sluggish river, they gradually grew, eventually becoming islands. Trees, including mopanis and tall acacias, also grow on their banks. Beds of swaying papyrus that line the banks of the watercourses are often mistaken for solid islands, but they are in fact floating clumps of vegetation, drifting like cushions in the shallow streams, where hippopotamus grass and water lilies grow. Reedbuck, antelope the size of deer, with curved horns, live on the banks of the islands. Covered in sedge and acidic grass, they also provide grazing grounds for hippopotamus, while other animals come here to drink the water.

Okavango Delta

Forming a huge inland delta in northern Botswana, the Okavango River has created one of the largest swamplands not only in Africa but in the whole world. Winding through the arid landscape of northwestern Botswana, the Okavango reaches flat lowlands to the south. Here it spreads out into a delta that creates a verdant paradise of watercourses divided by islands, some of which are covered in trees. The Okavango Delta spreads out over an area of 17,000 km² (6564 square miles) and is one of the most beautiful wetlands in the world. Lying in an otherwise arid environment, this unique swampland is similar to a desert oasis. The river is fed by rivulets from the mountains of Angola. As it reaches the flat Kalahari Plain, it loses speed, which causes it to spread out and form a huge inland delta, and as it advances toward the Kalahari Desert the water dries up.

2 River Courses as Traffic Routes

Because of the decreasing speed at which the water flows, the river divides into sluggish watercourses, which spread out like tentacles across the deep sand of the Kalahari Desert. The river's many troughs are also the only traffic routes here. Passable roads on dry land, such as those visible in the top right-hand corner of the satellite image, are rare.

3 Tributaries of the Okavango

The main course of the Okavango is determined by the Great Rift Valley, which extends from Syria, through East Africa, and on to Mozambique, and whose fault lines are responsible for seismic activity here. Earthquakes occur

at an average rate of three a year, and their epicenters are usually beneath the Okavango. These cause constant alterations to the course of the river, and to its many branches and tributaries. Another factor affecting its course is the sandy subsoil, which is highly susceptible to erosion: This facilitates the rapid shifting of the course of its branches, a process that occurs several times a year.

4 Edges of the Delta

In Botswana, where the climate ranges from semi-arid to arid, water is a scarce commodity, and there are strict controls on its use for agricultural purposes. By contrast, in the watery environment of the delta, only a small amount of land can be cultivated because of a surplus rather than a shortage of water. In the face of these two extremes, attempts are being made to convert previously uninhabitable areas into usable land. Unlike the native population, however, whose traditional way of life goes back thousands of years, immigrant farmers with modern attitudes are exploiting the delta area without regard for its ecological balance. Their attempts to create favorable conditions for intensive cattle farming by draining areas of the delta have caused the soil to become exhausted and over-saline, particularly near centers of habitation. Desertification often results. The tsetse fly, which carries a virus that causes sleeping sickness and the fatal nagana disease in human beings, has still not been exterminated, and this continues to limit the use of the delta for agricultural purposes.

5 Settlements ↓

The banks of the Okavango have been inhabited for about 100,000 years. The first people to live here were the baNoka, the river bushmen, whose clans were widely spread throughout the area. Since the 18th century, the baNoka have been joined by the baYei, who came from the Caprivi swampland and who were thus accustomed to surviving in such an environment. Living in harmony with nature, they inhabit a territory that stretches from the edges of the delta as far as the inhospitable expanses of the Kalahari Desert, which they roam as hunters and gatherers. Besides hunting and collecting fruits and honey, the original inhabitants of the Okavango Delta also live by fishing.

1:4,500,000

Albers Equal Area Conic Projection

50

Providence I.
Providence
Atoll

Bancs Providence

F a r q u h a r   G r o u p
(S e y c h e l l e s)

Aldabra Group
Picar   Malabar
Grande Terre
Assomption

Menai
Grande Île

Astove

Farquhar Atoll   Île du Nord
Goëlettes   Île du Sud

10°

I N D I A N   O C E A N

51

Îles Glorieuses
(Réunion)

Mitsamiouli
Ngazidja   M'Beni
Hahaya
Moroni   Kartala   C O M O R O S
2361
Foumbouni

Cape Bobaomby
Andranovondronina
Mangôaka   Ramena
Antsiranana
Ambohitra
Cape
Anorontany   Ampombiantambo   Parc Nat. de la
Montagne d'Ambra
Nosy Ankao

12°

Mutsamudu   Ndzouani
Miringoni   Fomboni   Sima 1595 Domoni
Moili

Nosy Mitsio

Antsohimbondrona

C o m o r o s   A r c h i p e l a g o

Mamutsi
Mayotte   Dzaoudzi
(F)   Sada   Pamanzi-Bé

Nosy Be   Betsiaka   Daraina
Djamandjary   Ambilobe   Amborondolo
Andoany   Beramanja   Iharana
Antsahampano   Ambanja
Milanoa   Fanambana

52

Saikanosy   Ambato   Andrafainkona
Ampasindava   Maromokotra   Antsirabe Avaratra
Nosy
Radama   Marovato   2876 Bemarivo   Antsirabe Avaratra
Maromandia   Magindrano   Sambava
Doany   Maroiezy 2133   Farahalana

14°

Analalava
Baie
de
Narinda   Antsohihy   Antsahabe   Ambalapaiso   Andapa   Antsambalahy
Antsakabary   Befandriana Ava.   Antalaha
Antonibe   Anahidrano   Maromandia   Antsirabato

53

Baie
de
Mariarano   Mahajamba   Antsakanalabe   Ambohitralanana
Borizny   Maroala   Maroantsetra   Cape Angontsy
Antsilanitia   Ambanjabe   Bandabe   Mahalevona
Mahajanga   Ambalabe   Marovato   Saikanosy
(Majunga)   Katsepy   Boronono   Ambalakiraly   Mandritsara   Masoala
Bolriamary   Ankazombororona   Rantabe   Antogila
Namakia   Mampikony   Rantabe   Bay
Mitsinjo   Marotandrano   Manambolosy   Cape Masoala
Manambolosy   Manara Ava.

16°

Cape Vilanandro   Soalala   Marovoay   Sandrakatsy
Ambohipaky   Bekipay   Tsaramandroso   Antanambe
Madirovalo   Miarinarivo 1301   Lembalemban'i   Manompana
Besalampy   Andranomavo   Ambato   Marovoalavo   Nosy Boraha
Sitampiky   Boeny   Kamoro   (Sainte-Marie)
Marovoay   Ambalajana-   Andilamena   Betty-Plage
komba   Soanierana   Ambodifotatra
Bekodoka   Maevatanana   Tsaratanana   Ivongo
Mahabo   1316   Betalevana   Ambasimba

54

Île Juán de Nova
(Réunion)   Kandreho   Ampasimena
Mahazoma   Tanambe   Vohilengo
Tambohorano   Ambataminty   Amparafaravola   Ambatosoratra   Fenoarivo Atn.
Andriba   Vohimena   Fenoarivo Atn.   Mahambo
M A D A G A S C A R   Manakana   Anjahambe
Morafenobe   Ambatomainty   1549   Morrano   Ambatondrazaka
Lembai   Didy   Andranomena   *Toamasina*
Maintirano   Beravina   Fiadanana   Anjay   Ambodiriana   (Tamatave)

18°

Betanantanana   Kiranomena   Ambatomanoina   Ambalarondra   Lac Nosive
Antsondrodava   Fenoarivo Be   Andaingo
Antsalova   Ankazobe   Moramanga
Tsiroanomandidy   Gara   Ambalarondra
Tsingy de   Fiadanana   Maroseranana
Bamaraha N.R.   Morurano   Ankazondandy   P.N. de   Lac Rasoabe
Belo Tsiribihina   Maiadrivazo   Mahatsy   Mantadia   Ampasimanolotra
Tsimafana   Bekopaka   Ambohi   Miarinarivo   Andasibe   Andovoranto
Kinangay   ratrimo   *ANTANANARIVO*   Manjakan-
Ampely   Anjomonamo   driana   Moramanga
Belobaka   Mahasolo   Manjakan-   Vatomandry
Babetville   Soavinandriana   driana

55

Ankavandra   Arivonimamo   Andapa
Soavinandriana   Faratsiho   Antananbe
Kinangay   Antananbe
1519   Iaratsiho   2642   Ambatolampy   Ilaka
Mandoto   Antsiranmanatsy   Manampotsy
Belo Tsiribihina   Antanifotsy   Mahanoro
Tsimafana   Betafo   Antanjombo-
Ambatolahy   Antanjombo-   lamena
Ankotrofotsy   2034   lamena
Antsoha   Vondrandry   Mahanoro
2254   Fandriana

20°

Hp   44°   Ja   46° 353 Jb   48°   Jc   50°   Jd   52°

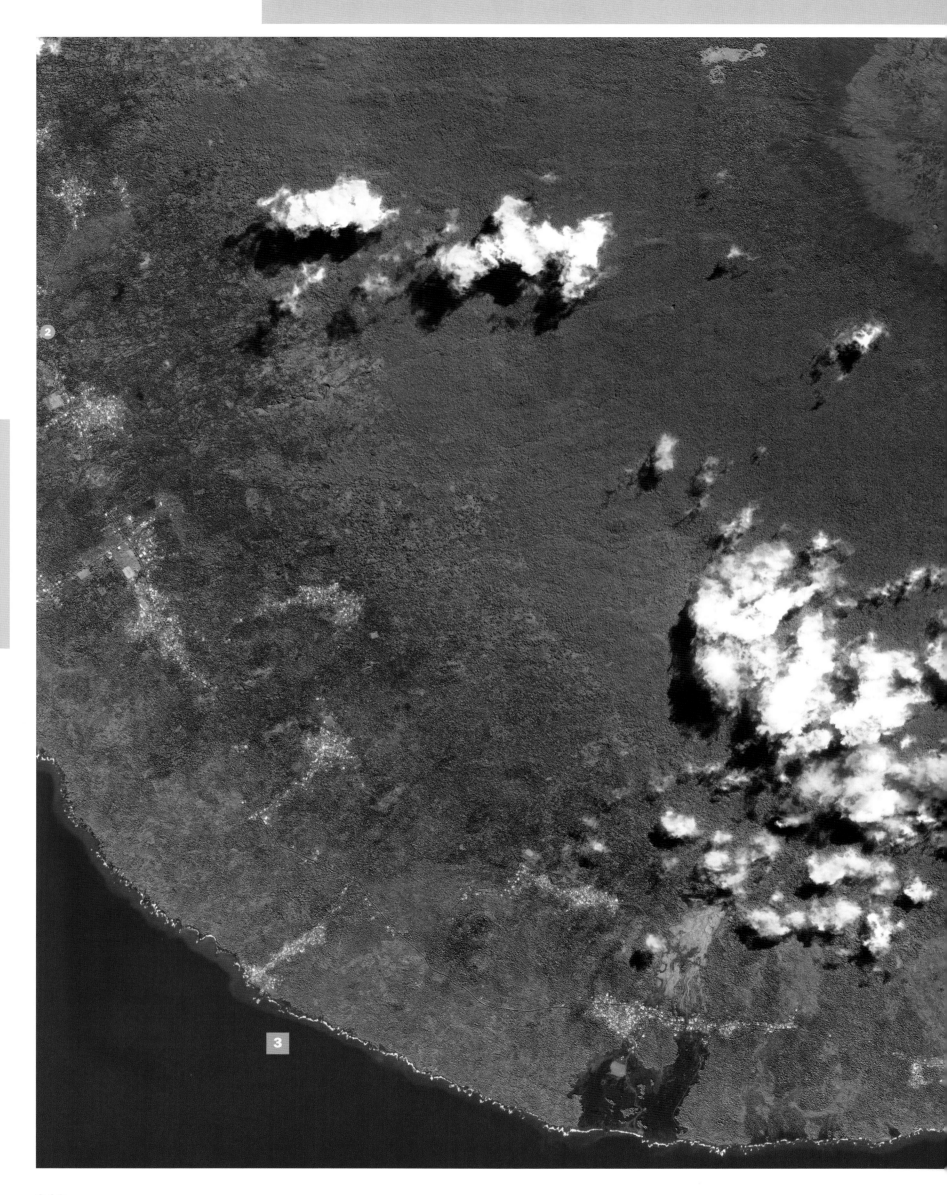

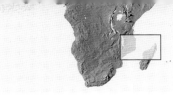

Comoros

The islands that make up the Comoros archipelago rise up out of the Pacific Ocean roughly midway between East Africa and Madagascar. Volcanic in origin, the islands are mainly mountainous and are covered in large expanses of dense tropical vegetation. Although they form a geographical entity, and were once a French territory, the islands are now politically divided. Since 1975 three of them—Ngazidja (formerly Grande Comore), Ndzouani (Anjouan), and Moili (Mohéli)—have made up the independent republic of Comoros. Another, Mayotte, remains a French overseas territory. Although the islands are gradually opening up to tourism, their native inhabitants still have a traditional lifestyle, dependent mainly on agriculture and fishing.

1 Karthala

Ngazidja is the largest and northernmost of the Comoros islands. It is mainly mountainous and, like the other islands, volcanic in origin. It consists of two volcanoes, whose tall peaks rise in the interior. The southern, higher volcano is Karthala, which rises to a height of 2361 m (7746 ft). Its crater, which has collapsed several times, is 3 by 4 km (2 by 2.5 miles) in diameter, and a crater lake, clearly visible in the satellite image, has formed on its floor. Since the 19th century more than 20 eruptions have been recorded, either from the summit or from the volcano's sides.

3 Coast

Because large parts of the island's interior are inaccessible, most of its larger towns, such as Hahaya and M'Beni, are located on the coast. The population is concentrated in the alluvial plains: Thanks to irrigation brought by rivers, farming is possible on the relatively level terrain here. The island's rocky coastal areas stand in sharp contrast to these verdant areas. Dark green forests, which are so dense that they almost hide the coastline in places, make up a unique kaleidoscope of colors together with the white beaches and the dazzling blue of the

2 Moroni ↑

Moroni is the capital of Comoros and, with a population of roughly 40,000 inhabitants, is also its largest town. It is located on the west coast of Ngazidja, the main island. The island's main port and an international airport are also located in Moroni. Agricultural produce grown on the island is exported from the port. Almost all Ngazidja's inhabitants are Muslim, and a large number of mosques dot the capital. Among the largest is the Friday Mosque, seen here, located close to the port. Moroni is also known for its lively markets, where food, arts and crafts, fabric, and everyday commodities are bought and sold.

ocean. Some parts of the coast are lined with coral reefs.

4 Direction of Roads

Roads on the island link individual settlements, but, dictated by Ngazidja's rugged topography, these run not along the coast, but along the clifftop of the island.

5 Rain Forest

The summits of the island's volcanoes are often shrouded in clouds. Annual rainfall on the windward side of the mountains can reach 4000 mm (157 in) in particularly wet years. After a long period of intensive deforestation, only small areas of the rain forest that once covered wide stretches of the island remain today. Plantations were laid out on clearance areas. Coffee, coconuts, and ylang-ylang trees, from whose blossoms an oil is extracted for use in the production of perfume, are the most important crops. Spices are another major export, and the Comoros were once known in Europe as the Spice Islands or Perfume Islands. The climate of the Comoros is ideal for cultivating vanilla, which is grown in huge plantations. A species of orchid, the only one used in food for human consumption, vanilla produces an aromatic fruit. The pods are picked when they are unripe, then fermented and dried. The export of vanilla brings Comoros vital revenue for the import of basic foodstuffs.

MAP

1 : 4,500,000

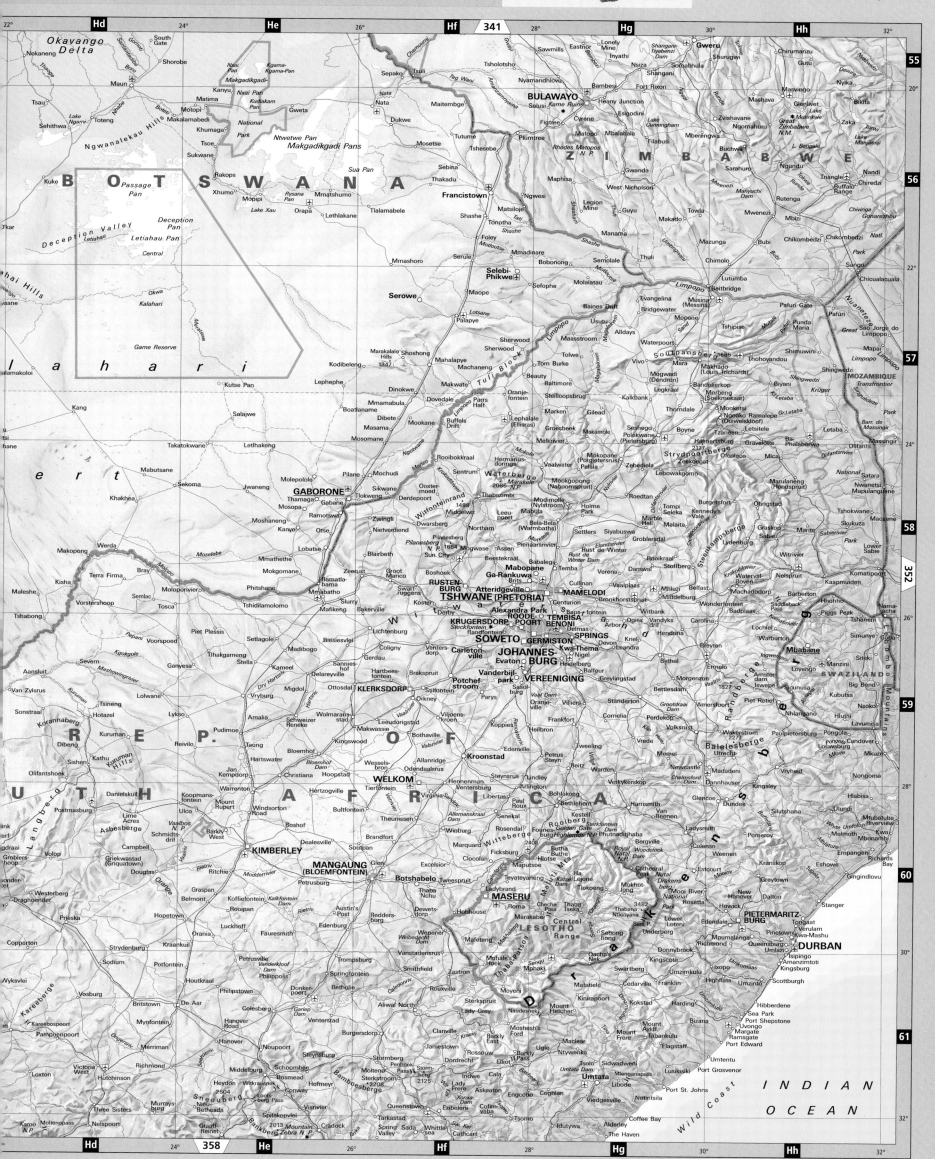

Namib

The geography of Namibia, a country that lies along the southwestern coast of Africa between the Atlantic Ocean and the Kalahari Desert, is extraordinary in many ways. A large part of the country consists of the Namib Desert, one of the most arid regions in the world. Some 2000 km (1243 miles) long and 150 km (93 miles) wide at its broadest point, the Namib Desert forms a narrow strip that lies parallel to the Atlantic coast, extending the length of the country. In the north, the Namib is mainly a stony desert, while in the south it is mostly sandy with impressive dunes. Morning swathes of fog, which sweep eastward across the desert from the cool ocean, are its only appreciable source of moisture. The desert is rich in minerals and this makes Namibia, which achieved independence from South Africa in 1990, one of the world's foremost mineral producers.

1 *Sossusvlei* ↑
Sossusvlei is a spectacular area of dunes situated about 200 km (124 miles) south of the area shown in the satellite image. The dunes, which rise as high as 300 m (984 ft), form part of the Namib Naukluft Park, which is the country's largest national park.

2 ## Goboboseb Mountains
In this part of Namibia, thick strata of basalt covering an area 30 by 50 km (19 by 31 miles) bear witness to a long phase of volcanic activity during the Cretaceous period. The lava came from the Messum Crater (seen on the left in the satellite image) and flowed mainly toward the north and west. The Goboboseb Mountains are one of the principal sources of amethyst and cairngorm, a variety of quartz.

3 ## Uis
Until 1990, tungsten and tin were mined in the small town of Uis, which is located on the southeastern edge of the Brandberg Massif. Although it is unprofitable, tantalite is still extracted here. Uis is also the location of the only gas station in operation for miles around.

4 ## Brandberg Massif
This oval mass of granite 30 km (19 miles) long and 23 km (14 miles) wide protrudes from the earth's crust, and has been greatly eroded over time. Namibia's tallest peak is the König-

stein (King's Peak), which rises about 2000 m (6562 ft) from the coastal plain and whose peak soars to 2573 m (8441 ft) above sea level. Ancient rock engravings show that this rugged plateau was inhabited 30,000 years ago. The desert vegetation that grows here can withstand long periods of drought: It includes the quiver tree, which grows to a maximum height of 10 m (33 ft) and which can store water in its trunk. A species of aloe, which belongs to the family of succulents, the quiver tree owes its name to the fact that its branches, which are easy to hollow out, were once used as quivers, cases in which to carry arrows. The Bushmen who, until very recent times, inhabited this area used arrows for hunting the animals they depended on for food.

5 ## Ugab River
Only the rivers on Namibia's northern border flow all year round. All Namibia's other rivers, including the unusually long Ugab River, which rises to the south of the Etosha Pan, are what is known as dry rivers (*riviere* in Afrikaans). That is, they are dry throughout large parts of the year and carry water only after periods of unusually heavy rainfall.

6 ## Skeleton Coast
The wrecks of countless ships line the Skeleton Coast, which was feared by navigators because of its fierce storms and dense fog. In the past, sailors who were stranded here stood little chance of survival because the coast is lined by a strip of desert 40 km (25 miles) wide and extending from the confluence of the Ugab River, in northwestern Namibia, to Angola, across the border to the north.

7 ## Cape Cross
This promontory owes its name to the crucifix that the Portuguese explorer Diego Cão erected here in 1486. The first European to set foot in what is now Namibia, Cão encountered Damara tribesmen and Bushmen here. The Cape Cross seal colony, populated by some 200,000 individuals, is one of the largest in Africa, and this scenic and historic region is a popular tourist destination.

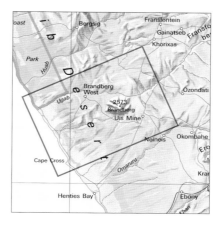

1:4,500,000

Height
m
3000
2000
1000
600
300
100
0
< 0
200
1000
2000
4000
6000
8000
10000
m
Depth

I N D I A N

1:4,500,000

| 0 | 25 | 50 | 75 | 100 | 125 miles |
| 0 | 50 | 100 | 150 | 200 km |

Albers Equal Area Conic Projection

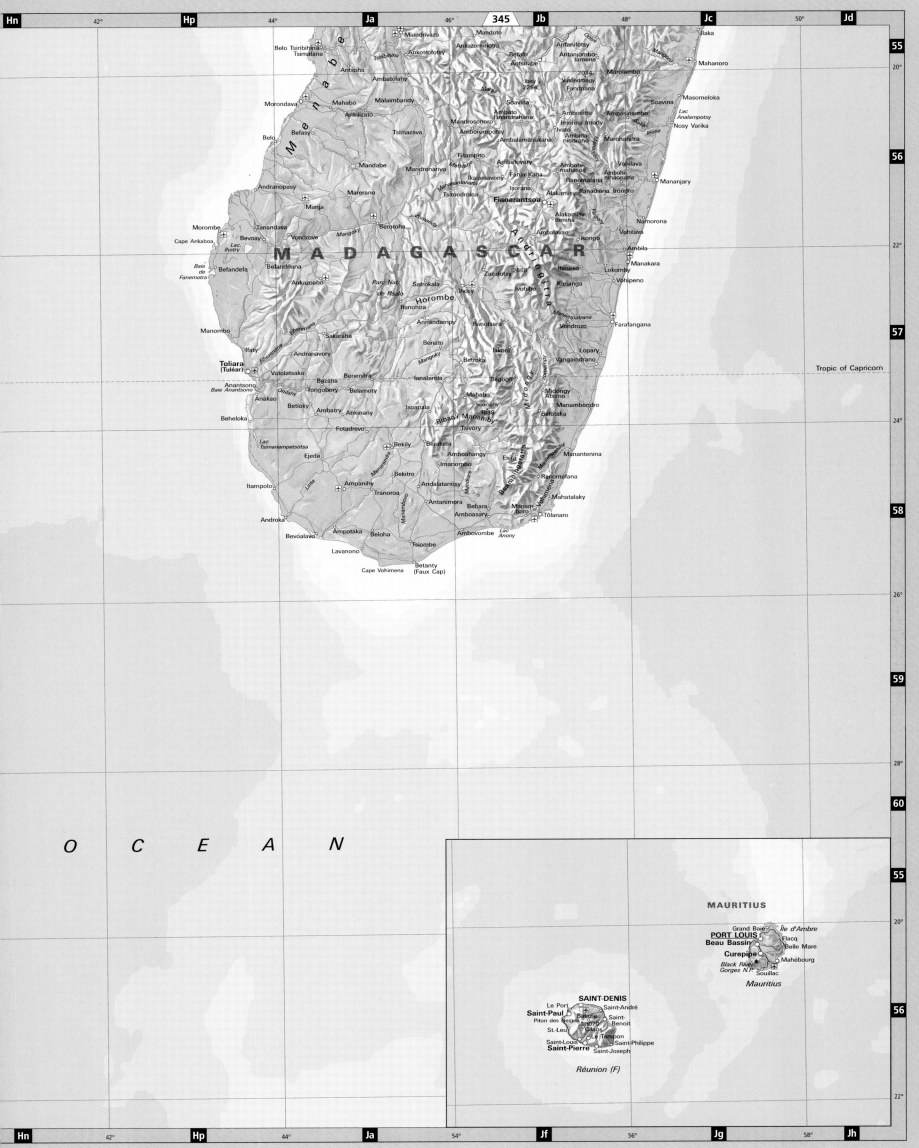

| Hn | 42° | Hp | 44° | Ja | 46° | 345 | Jb | 48° | Jc | 50° | Jd |

Miandrivazo
Mandoto
Belo Tsiribihina
Tsimafana
Ilaka
Antsoha
Tsiribihina
Ankotrofotsy
Ankazomiriotra
Betafo
Antanifotsy
Antanjombo
Iamena
Mahanoro
55
Ambatolahy
Antsirabe
Marolambo
20°
Morondava
Mahabo
Malaimbandy
Ibity
2254
Vohindrany
Fandrana
Soavina
Masomeloka
Ankilizato
Mandrosonoro
Ambato
Finandrahana
Imerina Imady
Ambositra
Ampasinambo
Lac
Analampotsy
Mandabe
Amborompotsy
Ivato
Ambina
nindrana
Maroharatra
Isona
Nosy Varika
Mandronarivo
Ambalamanakana
Ambanovory
56
Befasy
Tsimazava
Fitampito
Ikalamavony
Fanja Kana
Amboni-
mahasoa
Ambohi
nihaona
Vohilava
Belo
Isorana
Tsitondroina
Ranomafana
Mananjary
Andranopasy
Marerano
Fianarantsoa
Alakamisy
Ifanadiana Irondro
Manja
Alakamisy
Itenina
Namorona
22°
Morombe
Beroroha
Ambalavao
Ikongo
Vohilava
Cape Ankaboa
Tanandava
Lac
Ihotry
M A D A G A S C A R
Zazafotsy
Ifanirea
Ambila
Manakara
Baie
de
Fanemotra
Bevoay
Befandriana
Parc Nat.
de l'Isalo
Safrokala
2658
Ivohibe
Kananga
Lokomby
Vohipeno
Befandefa
Ankazoabo
Horombe
Ihosy
Ranohira
Anriandampy
Ranotsara
Vondrozo
Farafangana
57
Manombo
Sakaraha
Benato
Ilaty
Ambalavao
Ikongo
Ihosy
Toliara
(Tuléar)
Fihorenena
Andranavory
Mangoky
Betroka
Ivohibe
Vangaindrano
Tropic of Capricorn
Vatolatsaka
Bezaha
Benenitra
Bekora
Lopary
Anantsono
Baie Anantsono
 Onilahy
Tongobory
Belamoty
Ianabinda
Mahabo
Midongy
Atsimo
Anakao
Betioky
Ambatry
Ankinany
Isoanala
Ivakoany
1938
Manambondro
Behaloka
Fotadrevo
Tsivory
Befotaka
24°
Lac
Tsimanampetsotsa
Bekily
Beraketa
Ranomafana
Ejeda
Bekitro
Amboahangy
Esira
Manantenina
Itampolo
Ampanihy
Tranoroa
Andalatanosy
Androka
Antanimora
Behara
Manam
baro
Mahatalaky
58
Bevoalavo
Ampotaka
Beloha
Ambovombe
Tôlanaro
Lavanono
Tsiombe
Lac
Anony
Betanty
(Faux Cap)
Cape Vohimena
26°

O   C   E   A   N

| 55 | 20° |
| MAURITIUS |
Grand Baie
Île d'Ambre
PORT LOUIS
Flacq
Beau Bassin
Belle Mare
Curepipe
Mahébourg
Black River
Gorges N.P.
Souillac
Mauritius
56
SAINT-DENIS
Le Port
Saint-André
Saint-Paul
Sainte-
Saint-
Piton des Neiges
3070
Benoit
St-Leu
Le Tampon
St-Louis
Saint-Philippe
Saint-Pierre
Saint-Joseph
22°
Réunion (F)

| Hn | 42° | Hp | 44° | Ja | 54° | Jf | 56° | Jg | 58° | Jh |

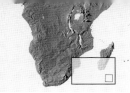

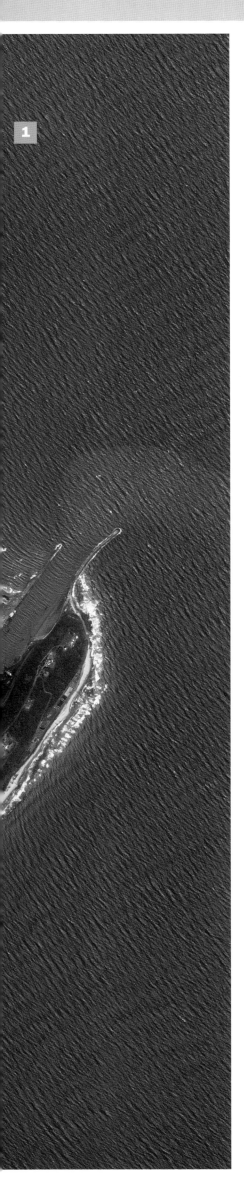

1 Indian Ocean

With 318 days of sunshine a year and a mild, subtropical climate, Durban is a popular resort. Water temperatures remain above 20°C (68°F) all year round, but the breakers can occasionally be very strong. This is why only some sections of the beach are reserved for swimmers or are watched by lifeguards. Around 100 species of shark live off South Africa's 3000 km (1864 mile) coast, and since KwaZulu-Natal's waters are some of the most shark-infested in the world, 44 km (27.3 mile) nets were laid in the ocean off Durban so as to protect swimmers from attacks. The project began in the early 1960s and the nets are checked on a daily basis. With very few exceptions, they have been effective.

2 Beachfront

About two million tourists a year spend their vacations on Durban's Golden Mile. This is the city's seafront promenade, which is lined with hotels, restaurants, nightclubs, cafes, swimming pools, and fountains. Stretching for 8 km (5 miles), it is thought to be the longest seafront resort in the whole of Africa.

3 Port →

Durban's port lies in a sheltered bay between a spit of land known as The Point, in the north, and a stretch of dunes known as The Bluff, in the south. The port complex covers a total area of 2000 ha (4942 acres). Not only is it the busiest port in South Africa, it is the largest in the whole of Africa, and the ninth-largest port in the world. As the point from which South African produce such as fruit, vegetables, and sugar is exported, it is of great importance to Durban's economy. In terms of the monetary value of its exports, it is closely followed by the ports of Richards Bay, north of Durban, and Saldanha Bay in Cape Town (see pp356–7).

4 Ocean Terminal

Large cruise and passenger ships dock at this pier. The shipping channel here had to be dredged to a depth of about 13 m (43 ft) to allow ships with deep drafts to sail into Durban's harbor.

5 Sugar Terminal

One of the largest market places for trading sugar in the world is located here. Every hour, up to 800 metric tons (882 tons) of sugar are traded and loaded onto ships. About 500,000 metric tons (551,156 tons) of cane sugar are temporarily stored in silos.

6 Indian Quarter

In cosmopolitan Durban, one in three of the city's inhabitants is Indian or of part-Indian descent, and a fifth are Muslim. The magnificently decorated Jumah Mosque, completed in 1880, is one of the largest mosques in the southern hemisphere. Directly beside it are the market halls, which were rebuilt after a fire in 1973. They can hold almost 200 stalls, and a fascinating range of Afro-Oriental, Indian, and Far Eastern goods is offered for sale. The migrants who came to the city in the 19th century included the political and spiritual leader and social reformer Mahatma Gandhi: Over 21 years, he successfully fought for the rights of the Indian community in Durban. He left

Durban

At Christmastime in 1497, the Portuguese navigator Vasco da Gama sailed round the Cape of Good Hope. On the east side of the cape, he came to a bay, which he named Port Natal, meaning "Christmas Harbor." A settlement was established here in 1823, but it only received the name Durban, that of a British governor called Benjamin d'Urban, 12 years later. In the mid-19th century the British began settling thousands of Indians here, whom they put to work in the sugar cane plantations. The descendants of these workers, who form part of Durban's population today, have shaped the city's character. The capital of the province of KwaZulu-Natal, Durban is also South Africa's third-largest city. It has only about three million inhabitants, but, in terms of population growth, it is the second-fastest growing city in the world after Mexico City. With magnificent beaches, historic sights, a wide range of entertainments and, not least, an exceptionally well-developed infrastructure, Durban is a mecca for South African vacationers.

South Africa in 1914, but his experience here, with the practical application of his doctrine of passive resistance, laid the basis for the fight for home rule for India that he subsequently led.

7 Greyville Racecourse

For horse-racing enthusiasts, the Rothman's Durban July Handicap is an important event. Held on the first Saturday in July, it takes place at South Africa's most famous racetrack.

8 Durban Botanical Gardens

Durban has many public parks, but the Botanical Gardens are a particular highlight. Covering 20 ha (49 acres), they are located on a hill in the northwestern part of the city center. They were laid out in 1849, and some of the rarer specimens are as old as the park itself.

9 Killie Campbell Museum

This ethnographical museum and the library that forms part of it are devoted to the history and the crafts of KwaZulu-Natal. The museum's holdings are considered to be one of the best private collections of anthropological artefacts in Africa.

10 FitzSimons Snake Park

A rich variety of entertainment is offered along the Golden Mile. The Snake Park houses almost 120 species of South African snakes, including highly poisonous cobras and mambas, which are mainly kept for research and as a source of serum. One of the few ice stadiums in Africa, a real tourist attraction, is located beside the Snake Park.

11 Sea World

More than 1000 species of animals can be seen in this marine aquarium. Sea World is al-

so the base for many of the world's leading institutes of marine research.

12 City Hall

Despite the numerous high-rise buildings that surround it, Durban's City Hall is still an impressive structure. It was built in 1910, and was modeled on the town hall in Belfast, Northern Ireland. The City Hall is not only the base of the city council: It also houses a natural history museum, a municipal library, and Durban Art Gallery, which is South Africa's second-largest art museum. It contains works by both African and well-known European artists, and was the first gallery to display the work of black artists.

Park and fountain in Durban ↓

Cape Town

Cape Town extends along a promontory that juts out into the Atlantic Ocean on the western side of the Cape of Good Hope. Backed by Table Mountain and facing both the Atlantic and Pacific oceans, it has been described as the city with the most beautiful location in the world. But Cape Town has also been described as the Gateway to the Antarctic. The cold Benguela Current, which flows north from the Antarctic, and the warm Agulhas Current from the Indian Ocean determine Cape Town's climate. These currents bring cold, damp weather in July and August, and warm, sunny weather in November and December. Whereas the Cape's coastline is always green, the Little Karoo, a desert that lies immediately behind the chain of mountains at the edge of the city, acts as a shield against the weather. The people of Cape Town are as diverse as the climate. The first European settlement in South Africa, Cape Town is the only city in sub-equatorial Africa in which black people constitute a minority.

1 Table Mountain ↑

The flat-topped mountain that rises to the south of the city is 1087 m (3566 ft) high. The slate and sandstone of which it consists are about 600 million years old. Even on sunny days, clouds pour over the mountain, creating an effect known as the Tablecloth. Table Mountain receives a great deal of rainfall, and about 2000 different species of plants grow on this high plateau. The summit of the mountain that makes Cape Town's silhouette so distinctive can be reached on foot, involving a strenuous climb, or in minutes by cable car.

2 Signal Hill
This mountain, 350 m (1148 ft) high, owes its name to the cannon shot fired from it at noon every Sunday. From the summit at night there is a spectacular view over the city's glittering sea of lights.

3 Victoria and Alfred Waterfront
Until a few years ago, the port area named after Queen Victoria and her son was very run down. As a result of radical redevelopment, it is now a pleasant place to explore. Besides hotels, its attractions includes museums, restaurants, shops, theaters, cinemas, and an aquarium, which are among the best in the world and draw millions of visitors each year. However, Long Street, an attractive traditional Victorian shopping street, has since become deserted.

4 Castle of Good Hope
Completed in 1679, the Castle of Good Hope is South Africa's oldest colonial building. It is surrounded by deep moats and well-fortified walls. Once the administrative nucleus not only of Cape Town but the whole of South Africa, the castle is now a museum and army barracks.

5 Malay Quarter
A population of 50,000 Cape Malays, also known as Cape Muslims, the descendants of Indonesian slaves, are concentrated around Signal Hill. This district is characterized by mosques and small pastel-painted houses. Its restaurants and street stalls sell such typically Mayalan dishes such as gorengs and curries.

6 Lion's Head
This mountain, which rises to 669 m (2195 ft) near the coast, separates the suburbs of Sea Point and Camps Bay. Seen from the air, its outline resembles the shape of a lion's head.

7 Port ↓
In terms of the volume of cargo that passes through it, Cape Town's port is only the fourth-largest in South Africa. However, its fishing fleet and the quantity of fruit traded here are both important. A constant stream of cruise ships also berth in the port, with the fascinating backdrop of Table Mountain in the distance.

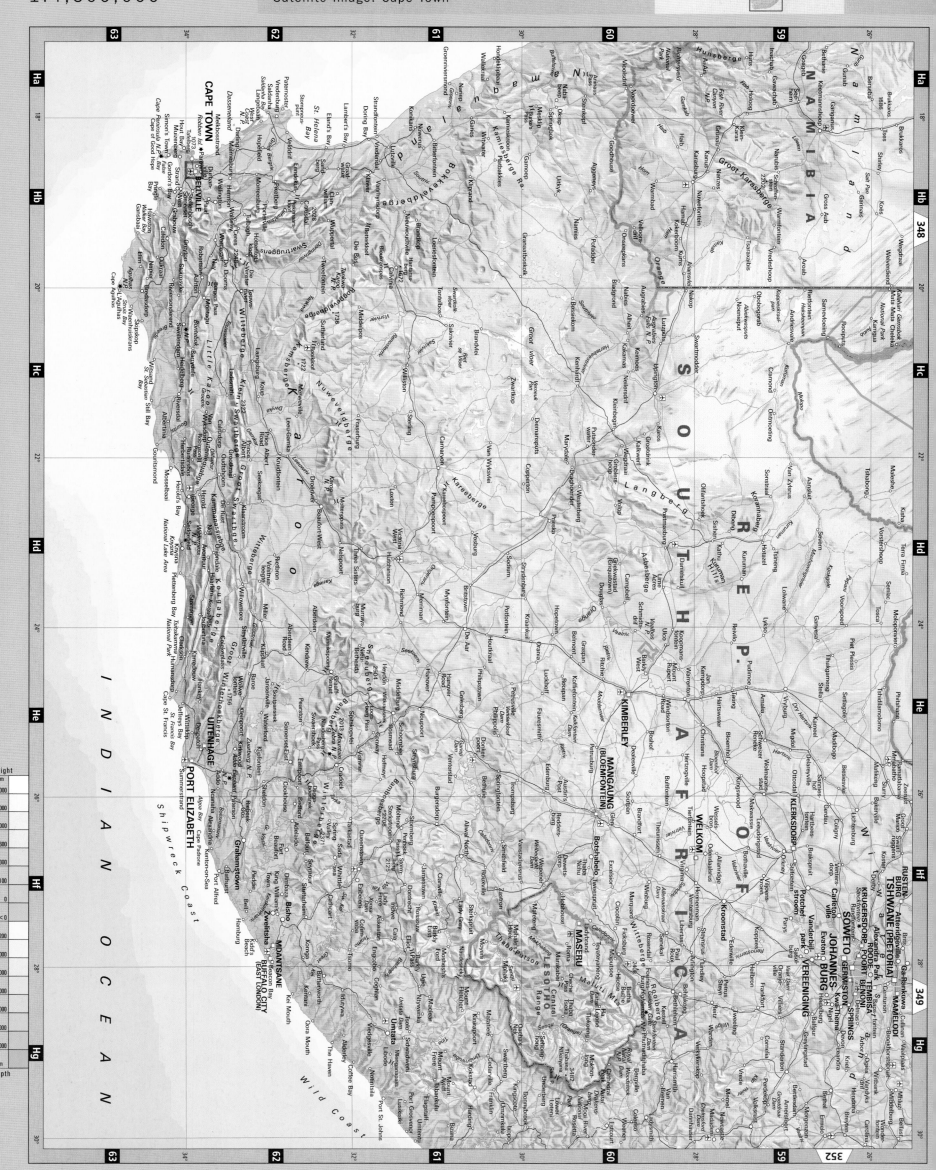

Height
m
3000
2000
1000
600
300
100
0
<0
200
1000
2000
4000
6000
8000
10000
m
Depth

INDIAN OCEAN

1:4,500,000

0   25   50   75   100   125miles
0   50   100   150   200km
Albers Equal Area Conic Projection

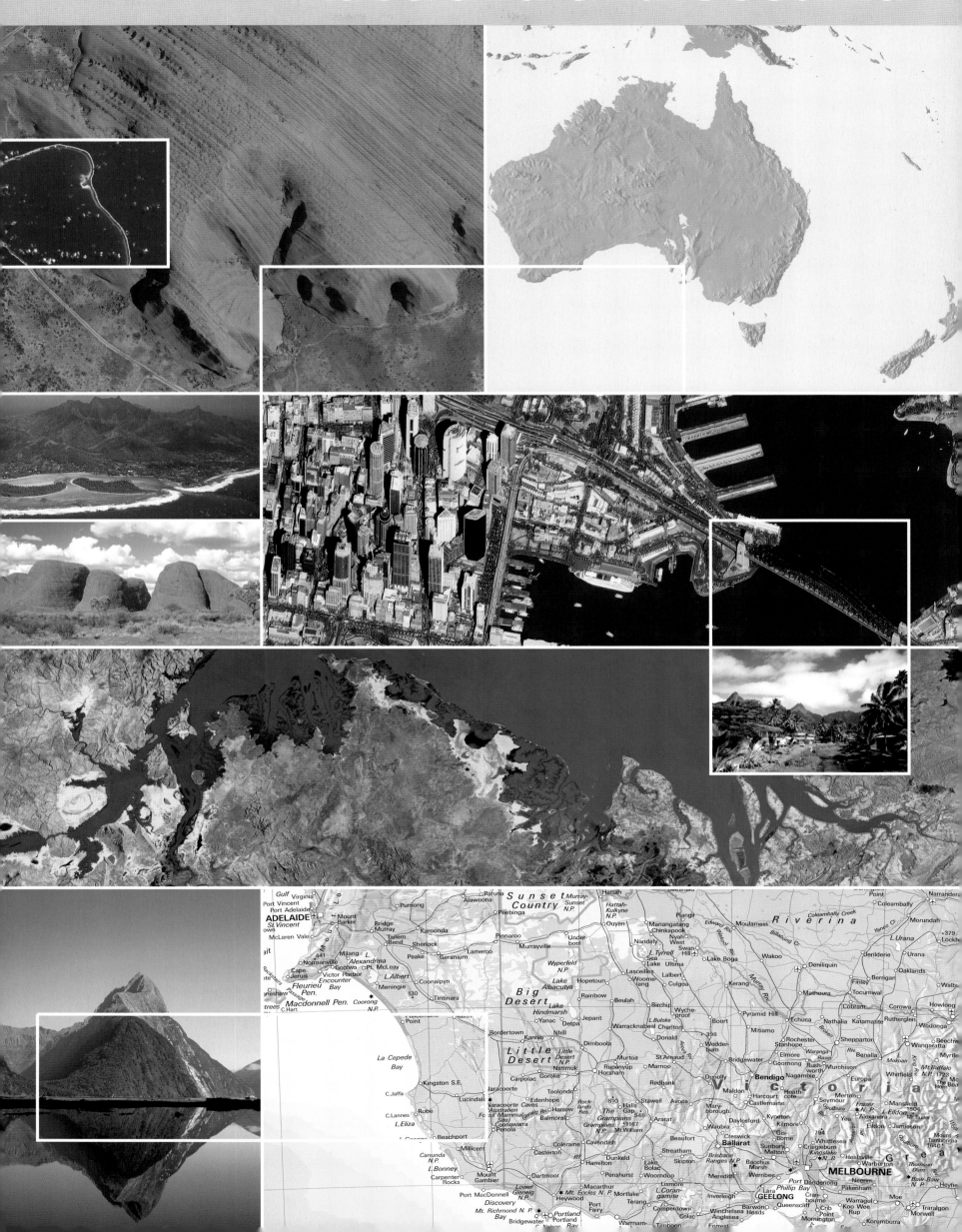

Lg 114° Lh 116° Lj 118° Lk 120° Ll 122° Lm

52   14°

53

INDIAN   OCEAN   16°

54   18°

North Australia

Basin

Seringapatam Reef

Scott Reef

Lynher Reef

C.Leveque
Lombadina, Abor.
Pender
Emeriau Pt. Bay
Lacepede Is. Baagle Bay
Beagle Bay
Aboriginal
C.Baskerville Reser
Carnot Bay
Coulomb Pt.

Dampier
Land

Rowley Shoals
Mermaid Reef
Clerke Reef
Imperieuse Reef

Gantheaume Pt. Broome
Roebuck
Roadhouse
Roebuck
Bay
Thangoo

Rowley Shelf

C.Latouche Treville

Lagrange
Bay
C.Bossut
Lagrange
Mission

Nita Downs
Anna Plains

Beach

Mile

Wallal Downs
Eighty
Poissonnier
Point
Larry Pt.
Spit Pt.
C.Keraudren
Pardoo
Port
Hedland
Goldsworthy

Mandora
Sandfire
Roadhouse

Grea

Exmouth

Plateau

20°

Montebello Is.
Dampier
Archipelago
Enderby I.
C.Dupuy
Barrow I.
Boodie I.
South End
Pasco Island
Mardie I.
Mary Anne Passage
Mary Anne
Group
Thevenard I.
Muiron Islands
North West C.

Legendre I.
Sloping
Pt.
Nickol
Bay
C.Lambert
C.Preston
Depuch I.
Wickham
Cossack
Roebourne
Karratha
Roadhouse
Karratha
Wapet Camp

Dampier

Mundabul-
langana
Whim Creek

Strelley
Pippingarra
Pippingarra
Abor.Reserve
Carlindi
Warralong
Wallareenya Abor.Reserve
Lalla Rookh
Mallina
Gillam

132°
Goldsworthy
Mount

Shay Gap
Yarrie
Muccan
Eginbah
Bamboo
Creek

Callawa

Warrawagine

Marble Bar

Mt.Edgar
Mount
Edgar

372

L.Waukarlycarly

G r e a

W e s

Height
m
3000
2000
1000
600
300
100
0
< 0
200
1000
2000
4000
6000
8000
10000
m
Depth

56   22°

Exmouth
Mt.Hollister
Learmonth
Exmouth
Gulf
Minderoo

C.Dupuy

Mardie
Fortescue
Roadhouse
Pannawonica
Millstream
Chichester N.P.
Millstream

Yarraloola
Beadon Pt.
Onslow

Peedamulla

Red Hill

Yandeyarra
Yandeyarra
Mt.
Gratwick
394
Aboriginal

Mount
Florance

673
Mt.Elvire

Mt.Margaret
Pk.Hester
551
882

Reserve

Abydos

Pilga
Hillside

Nullagine

Mt.Edgar

Bonney
Downs

Coral Bay

57   Tropic of Capricorn

Warroora

Ningaloo
Cape
Range
N.P.
Ningaloo

Bullara
Giralia

North

Yanrey
Nanutarra
Roadhouse

418
Uaroo

Barradale
Roadhouse

Winning

Towera
Minilya
Roadhouse

Cane
Cane Riv.

Mount
Stuart
Ashburton

Wyloo

Kooline

Duck Cr.

Pilbara

Mount
Brockman
1132
Mt.Brockman

Mt.Wall
957

1080
Mt.
Samson
1084
Rocklea

Hamersley
Mt.
Frederick Karijini
1176
1235
N.P.
Mt.Bruce
826
Tom
Price

Wittenoom
Wittenoom
Gorge

Roy Hill
458
Roy Hill

Balfour Downs
Ethel Creek

Talawana

Rudall River

National Park

Hanging Rock
638

L.Di

L.

Rudall

L.B

58   24°

West

Basin

Quobba
L.MacLeod
Pt.Quobba
C.Ronsard
Bernier I.

Carnarvon

Geographe
Channel

Gnaraloo

Wandagee
Williambury
Lyndon

Lyons Riv.
Binthalya

Marroonah
Ullawarra

Mt.Palgrave
696

Yarraloola

Gooch Range

Minnie
Creek

Gifford
Creek
Cobra
Mt.Augustus
N.P.

Lyons Riv.
Mount
Augustus
1105
Mt.Augustus

Yinnietharra

Kennedy Range

Mt.
Sandiman

Lyons River
Waldburg Range

Mt.Gascoyne
769

Wanna

Mt.Bennett
June Downs
Range N.P.
Mt.Meharry
1253
1158
Mt.Robinson

Paraburdoo

Ashburton
Downs

683
Mt.Bresnahan

Mount
Vernon

Tangadee

Kenneth Range

Ophthalmia Range
805
Shovelanna Hill
Newman

Prairie
Downs

Turee
Creek

Angelo

Collier Range

N.P.

Waldburg
Mt.Egerton
994

Wood-
lands
Mulgul

Spearhole
Cr.

Bullo
Downs
Lofty Range

731

Woolung-
unna
Hill

Mt.Essendon
910

Little

Sandy

Desert

Sylvania
Jiggalong Aboriginal
Land

Mundiwindi

Weelarrana

Kumarina

Walgun

Jiggalong

A u s t

L.Disappointme

McKay Ra.

Throssell Range

Gregory Range

Paterson Range

Telfer

De Grey Riv.
Yule Riv.
Shaw Riv.
Oakover Riv.
Davis Riv.
Rudall Riv.
Nullagine Riv.
Shenley Riv.
Fortescue Riv.
Harding Riv.
George Riv.
Rose Riv.
Cane Riv.
Ashburton Riv.
Henri Riv.
Barlee Range
Lyons Riv.
Thomas Riv.
North
Ethel Riv.
Ashburton
Seavry Riv.
Rail

0   25   50   75   100   125 miles
1:4,500,000
0   50   100   150   200km
Albers Equal Area Conic Projection

Lg 114° Lh 116° Lj **368** 118° Lk 120° Ll 122° Lm

Sahul Shelf

Patterson Noonaman Humpty
Fog Darwin River Doo
Bay Run Jungle
Wagait Batchelor Litchfield Sargents 215
North Peron I. Abor. Res. Bark
South Peron I. Hut Inn
Anson Bay Adelaide River
C. Ford Hayes Creek

West Holothuria Reef
Holothuria Troughton I. C.Talbot C. Londonderry
Reef C.Ruthieres
Cassini I. C.Bougainville Vansittart
Montesquieu Is. Napier C. Bernier
Broom
Admiralty Kimberley Kalumburu
Bigge I. Montague Gulf Abor. Abor.
C.Voltaire Land Kalumburu
Sound Land

Joseph Bonaparte Gulf

C.Scott

Hyland Bay

Daly River
230
Wadeye

Daly River
Elizabeth
Downs
Tipperary
Oolloo
Pine Creek

Jindare
Edithvale
Claravale

Douglas

Katherine

Mt.Lambell
318
Fergusson
River
Nitmiluk
Katherine Gorge
N.P.
Eva Valley

Beswick

Bamyili
Aboriginal
Land

Pearce Pt. C.Dussejour
Cambridge
Gulf

Aboriginal Land Wingate Mts.

Dorisvale

Wambung

Beswick

Mataranka

Elsey N.P.
Moroak
Elsey

Port Warrender Mt.Connor
Mitchell 312
River

Drysdale
River
Natl.P.
Forrest River
360
Aboriginal Reserve

Adolphus
Island

Legune

Bullo River

Quoin I.

Queens Channel
Keyling Inlet
Fitzmaurice Riv.

Yambarran Range

Larrimah
Birdum
Maryfield
Killarney

Gardner
Plateau

Drysdale
River
Mt.Hann
779

Ellenbrae

Mt.
Cockburn
671
Kununurra
Hidden
Valley
N.P.

Keep River
N.P.

Auvergne

Fitzroy

Timber
Creek

Victoria River
Roadhouse

New
Delamere
Old
Delamere
Birrimba
Out Station

Gorrie

Kimberley

Beverley
Springs

Gibb River

Mount
Barnett

Pentecost
Downs
(Karunjie)

El Questro

Dunham
River

Lake Argyle
Newry

Rosewood
West Baine

Lissadell

Mt.Behn
428

Waterloo
Kildurk

National
Gregory
Bullita
Out Station

Humbert River
Park

Victoria
River Downs
Pigeon Hole

Mt.Sullivan
267
Yingawunarri
Aboriginal Land
Top
Springs

Mooloolooo
Out Station

Daly Waters

Hidden Valley

Dunmarra

Napier Downs
Kimberley
Downs

Mt.Herbert
762
947
Mt.Ord

Windjana
Gorge
N.P.

Tableland

Bedford
Downs

590
Mt.Remarkable
778
Mabel
Downs

Turkey Creek
(Warmun)
Mt.Parker
Bungle Bungle
(Purnululu)
N.P.

Mistake
Creek

Mt.Sanford

Limbunya

Camfield

Mount Sanford

Mt.Napier

Dagaragu-Kurintji
Kalkaringji

Wave Hill
Cattle Cr.

Cattle Creek
Out Station

Newcastle
Waters

Beetaloo

Elliott

Leopold
Downs

Geikie Gorge
N.P.

Fitzroy
Crossing
Gogo

Fossil Downs

Little Gold Rh.

O.Donnell
Mueller Range

Springvale

Ord River
490

Kirkimbie
Inverway

Mt.Farquharson
444

Hooker Creek
Aboriginal
Land

Lajamanu
(Hooker Creek)

288

Aboriginal

Walmanpa-Warlpiri

L.Woods

Powell
Creek

Nerrima
Noonkanbah

573
Mt.Ball

Margaret Rv.

Mary Rh.

Halls Creek
Flora
Valley

Sturt Cr.

Nicholson

Nongra L.

Birrindudu

Central Desert

Northern

Helen
Springs

Muckaty

Cherrabun

312

Christmas
Creek

Cummins Range

Louisa Downs
500
Mt.Dockrell

Wolf Cr.

McClintock Ra.

Mount
Amhurst

Koongie Park

Ruby Plains

Gordon
Downs

628
Mt.Junction

Supplejack
Downs

Aboriginal Land

Banka
Banka

andy Desert

Wolf Creek
Meteorite
Crater N.P.

Carranya
Billiluna

L.Jones

L.Betty

L.McLerron

L.Lanagan

Sturt Creek

Mt.Buck

497
Mt.Tanami

Rabbit Flat
Roadhouse

Tanami Desert

Phillip Creek

Warego
Mine

Tennant Creek

Territory

Kaititja-Warlpiri

ern

Percival Lakes

Tobin Lake

No.35 Well

Balgo

Gregory L.

Godfreys Tank
315
Mt.Elliott

Djakanan
Balwina
Aboriginal
Reserve

Lewis Range

L.Dennis

L.White

450

L.Wills

Mt.Davidson
464

Mt.Theo
583

Aboriginal

Stirling

McLaren
Creek

Wauchope
Roadhouse

Auld

top

Gibson Desert

alia

Southesk
Tablelands

Stansmore Range

Wilbrunga Range

L.Mackay
Aboriginal
Land

Central

Mt.Webb
532

Australia

546

Mt.Singleton
808

Vaughan
Springs
817

Mt.Cockburn
847

Gurner

L.Bennett

Mount Doreen

860

Treuer Range

Yuendumu
Yuendumu
Abor.Land

Yunkanjini Aboriginal
Land

Newhaven
Mount Wedge
Mt.Wedge
Central
1094

Chilla Well

Mt.Leichhardt
1142

Mount Denison

Napperby

Pine Hill

Reynolds Range

Stuart Bluff Range

Vaughan Springs

Wirliyajarrayi
Abor.Land

Willowra

Lander Riv.

Barrow
Creek

Neutral
Junction

Mt.Stuart
845

Ti-Tree

Woola
Downs

Woodgreen

Red Cliff
660

Mt.Octy
695
Mount
Skinner

Aileron

Bushy Park

Alcoota

Percival Lakes

McPhersons Pillar
532

L.Hancock

L.Cobb

L.Newell

Rawlinson Range

Kiltmore Range
901
Mt.Leisler

L.MacDonald

L.Anec

L.Hopkins

Haasts Bluff
Johnstone Hill
704

Aboriginal Land

Kings Canyon

Bloods Range

840
Mt.Harris
1001
Docker Creek
(Kaltukatjara)
Petermann

Schwerin Mural Cres.

L.Neale

Watarrka
N.P.
George Gill Range

L.Amadeus

Carmichael Creek
906

Finke Gorge
N.P.

Haast Bluff
Mt.Zeil
1511
Mt.Soder
1349
Simpsons
Ormiston Gorge
Natl. P.
Glen Helen
Hermannsburg

Papunya
Derwent

Narwietooma

Mt.Liebig
1525

Mt.Hoy

1063
Mt.Prizner

Yambah

Hamilton
Downs

1170
Mt.Laughlen

1249

Alice Springs

Owen Springs

Ross River

James

Range

Santa Theresa
Aboriginal Land

Henbury
Henbury Meteorite
Craters

Orange
Creek

Santa
Theresa

Deep Well

Joseph Bonaparte Gulf

Joseph Bonaparte Gulf, on the north coast of Australia, lies southwest of Darwin and Arnhem Land and east of the Kimberley Plateau. Four large rivers empty into the gulf: From west to east, they are the Pentecost River, the Ord River (which flows out of Lake Argyle), and the Victoria River, all of which flow from the south; and the Fitzmaurice River, which flows from the east. The foothills of the Kimberley Plateau and the Kimberley Range rise on the west side of the gulf, giving it a rugged character. By contrast, the east side of the gulf is much flatter. The gulf also lies on the border between Western Australia and the Northern Territory. This border, established in 1824, is marked by the 129th meridian and runs on a north–south axis.

1 ## Vegetation and Settlements

The region of the Victoria and Ord rivers is comparatively barren. The only significant deposits of soil are found in river valleys, something that has had an effect on the area's natural vegetation. Since the earliest European settlements were established here in the late 19th century, great efforts were made to cultivate the land, despite its naturally unpromising condition. Even attempts at cattle breeding were thwarted by continual setbacks. The area is still sparsely populated today, which is reflected in the very few settlements seen in this satellite image. They include Wyndham, on the Pentecost River, and Kununurra, on the Ord River, visible at the lower edge, with a mosaic of cultivated fields.

2 ## Salt Marshes

The Pentecost, Fitzmaurice, and Victoria rivers all end in long estuaries. While the estuary of the Ord has been formed by the sediment that its waters deposit as it flows into the ocean, tides in the Queens Channel, the estuary of the Victoria, have created mud flats, salt marshes, and mangrove swamps. At high tide, sea water flows far upstream, flooding the flat, low-lying estuary area and mixing with the river's water. This creates saline, brackish water, conditions that the vegetation along the river banks can withstand.

3 ## Sand Deposits

From their sources far to the south of the gulf, these rivers carry large volumes of sand and

sediment, washed from the terrain that their waters erode as they flow down toward the coast. The waters of the Ord are particularly rich in sand. The Cambridge Gulf is lined with patches of infertile red sand, which supports no more than a sparse covering of vegetation.

4 ## *Kimberley Range* ←

This rocky mountain range has a very varied topography, with strange rock formations that have been created by the wind and rain, and deep valleys with almost vertical sides cut by fast-flowing rivers. It is from the Kimberley Range that the Ord, which has now been dammed to create the Argyle Reservoir, flows down, slowing as it reaches the flatlands of the gulf.

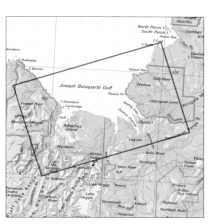

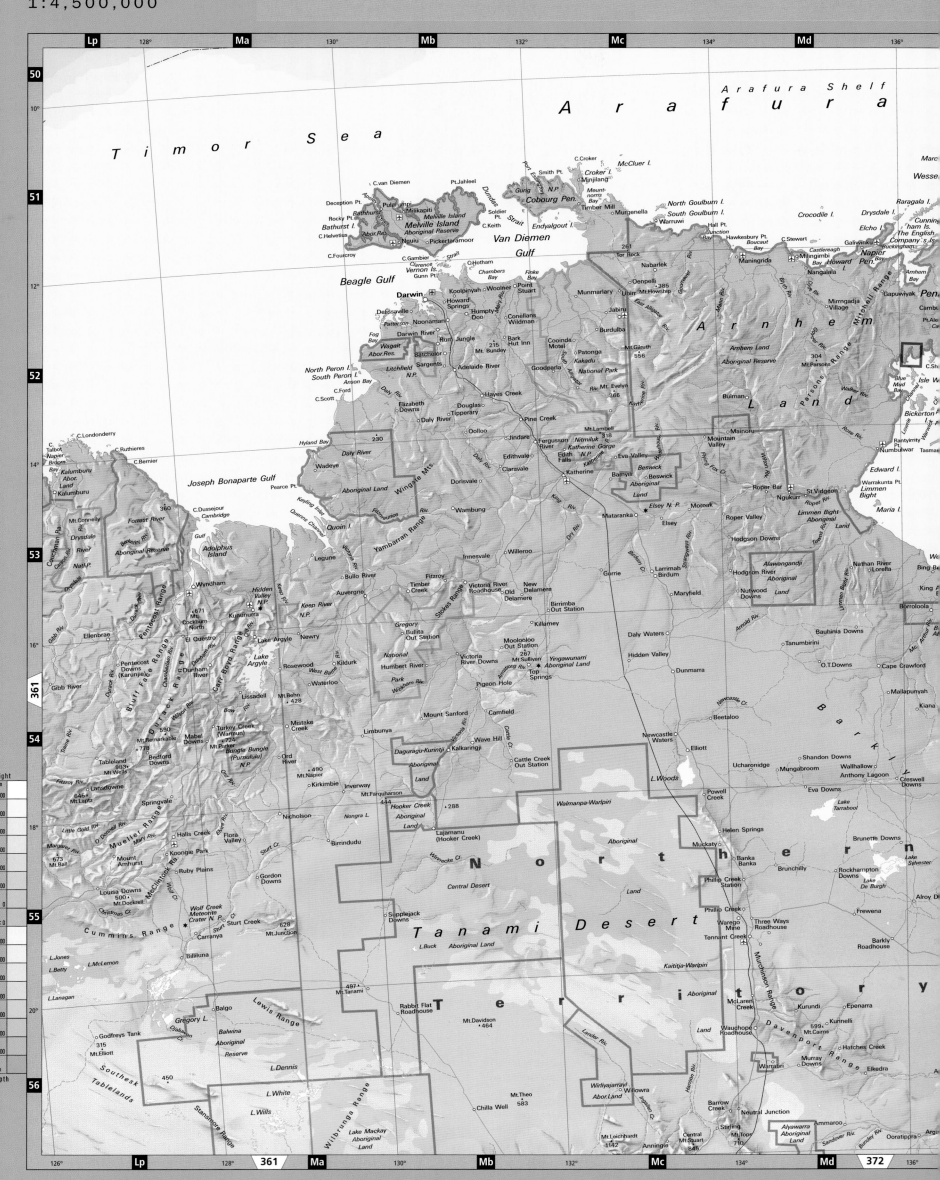

Arafura Shelf

A r a f u r a

T i m o r   S e a

Timor Sea

Deception Pt.

C.van Diemen

Pt.Jahleel

Smith Pt.

C.Croker

McCluer I.

Croker I.

Minjilang

Gurig

N.P.

Cobourg Pen.

Mount-

norris

Bay

North Goulburn I.

South Goulburn I.

Timber Mill

Crocodile I.

Raragala I.

Drysdale I.

Elcho I.

Cunning

ham Is.

The English

Company's Is.

Buckingham

Marc

Wesse

Rocky Pt.

Bathurst

Apsley

Pularumpi

Milikapiti

Melville Island

Melville Island

Aboriginal Reserve

Bathurst I.

C.Helvetius

Abor.Res.

Nguiu

Pickertaramoor

C.Keith

Soldier

Endyalgout I.

Port Essington

Murgenella

Warruwi

North Goulburn I.

Hawkesbury Pt.

Boucaut

Bay

Maningrida

Milingimbi

Bay

Howard

Bay

Nangalala

Galiwinku

Arnhem

Bay

Castlereagh

Bay

Gapuwiyak

Napier

Pen.

Pt.Ale

Ca

C.Fourcroy

C.Gambier

Clarence

Strait

Dundas Strait

Van Diemen

Gulf

Tor Rock

261

Nabarlek

Junction

Bay

Hall Pt.

C.Stewart

Pt

Numbulwar

Tasman

Mirrngadja

Village

Cambu

Pt

Beagle Gulf

C.Hotham

Chambers

Bay

Finke

Bay

Point

Stuart

Munmarlary

Ubirr

Mt.Howship

Oenpelli

385

Darwin

Delissaville

Koolpinyah

Howard

Springs

Humpty

Doo

Woolner

Cooinda

Motel

Wildman

Jabiru

Burdulba

Patonga

Kakadu

Goodparla

Mt.Giruth

556

Arnhem Land

Aboriginal Reserve

304

Mt.Parsons

Bulman

A r n h e m

L a n d

Mitchell Range

Parson's Range

Blue

Mud

Ba

Isle W

C.Sh

Fog

Bay

Noonamah

Bark

Hut Inn

215

Mt.Bundey

National Park

Mt.Evelyn

366

Rantyirrity

Pt

Bickerton I

Wagait

Abor.Res.

Darwin River

Rum Jungle

Batchelor

Sargents

Adelaide River

Hayes Creek

Douglas

Tipperary

Mainoru

Walker Riv.

Rose Riv.

C.Sh

North Peron I.

South Peron I.

Litchfield

N.P.

Anson Bay

C.Ford

Daly River

Ooloo

Jindare

Fergusson

River

Mt.Lambell

318

Nitmiluk

Katherine Gorge

N.P.

Mountain

Valley

Edward I.

Maria I.

C.Scott

Elizabeth

Downs

Daly River

Pine Creek

Edith

Falls

Beswick

Aboriginal

Land

Eva Valley

Roper Bar

Ngukurr

St.Vidgeon

Warrakunta Pt.

Limmen

Bight

Joseph Bonaparte Gulf

C.Londonderry

C.Talbot

Napier

Broom

C.Ruthieres

C.Bernier

Hyland Bay

230

Daly Riv.

Edithvale

Claravale

Katherine

Bamyili

Elsey N.P.

Elsey

Moroak

Roper Riv.

Roper Valley

Limmen Bight

Aboriginal

Land

Kalumburu

Abor.

Land

C.Dussejour

Cambridge

360

Wadeye

Wingate Mts.

Dorisvale

Wambung

Mataranka

Hodgson Downs

Kalumburu

Pearce Pt.

Keyling Inlet

Daly Riv.

Stokes Range

Innesvale

Willeroo

Gorrie

Larrimah

Birdum

Hodgson River

Aboriginal

Alawanganji

Nathan River

Lorella

Bing Be

Mt.Connelly

Drysdale

Forrest River

Aboriginal Reserve

Quoin I.

Adolphus

Island

Legune

Fitzroy

Timber

Creek

Victoria River

Roadhouse

New

Delamere

Old

Delamere

Maryfield

Nutwood

Downs

King A

Borroloola

Courtman Ra.

Mt.Connelly

Nat'l.P.

Drysdale

Quenns Channel

Gulf

Bullo River

Auvergne

Yambarran Range

Birrimba

Out Station

Daly Waters

O.T.Downs

Bauhinia Downs

Tanumbirini

Cape Crawford

Mallapunyah

Kiana

Wyndham

Hidden

Valley

N.P.

Kununurra

Keep River

N.P.

Gregory

Bullita

Out Station

Killarney

Hidden Valley

Dunmarra

Ellenbrae

671

Mts.

Cockburn

North

Newry

Rosewood

West Baines

Kildurk

Moolooloo

Out Station

Victoria

River Downs

Mt.Sullivan

267

Yingawunarri

Aboriginal Land

Top

Springs

B

a

r

k

l

y

Gibb River

El Questro

Lake Argyle

Waterloo

Wickham Riv.

Pigeon Hole

Newcastle Cr.

Gibb River

Lake

Argyle

590

Mt.Remarkable

778

Mistake

Creek

Limbunya

Mount Sanford

Camfield

Newcastle

Waters

Elliott

Shandon Downs

Wallhallow

Anthony Lagoon

Creswell

Downs

Pentecost

Downs

(Karunjie)

Mabel

Downs

Turkey Creek

(Warmun)

Mt.Parker

772

Wave Hill

Cattle Cr.

Cattle Creek

Out Station

Eva Downs

Fitzroy Riv.

Tableland

883

Mt.Wells

Bedford

Downs

Bungle Bungle

(Purnululu)

N.P.

490

Mt.Napier

Daguragu-Kalkaringji

Kalkaringi

Walmanpa-Warlpiri

Powell

Creek

Lake

Tarrabool

Lansdowne

646

Mt.Laptz

Ord

River

Kirkimbie

Inverway

Mt.Farquharson

444

Hooker Creek

Aboriginal

Land

288

L.Woods

Brunette Downs

Little Gold Riv.

Springvale

Halls Creek

Flora

Valley

Nicholson

Nongra L.

Birrindudu

Wennecke Cr.

Lajamanu

(Hooker Creek)

Aboriginal

Helen Springs

Muckaty

Lake

Sylvester

Margaret Riv.

573

Mt.Ball

Mount

Amhurst

Koongie Park

Ruby Plains

Gordon

Downs

Suplejack

Downs

Central Desert

N o r t h e r n

Phillip Creek

Station

Banka

Banka

Brunchilly

Rockhampton

Downs

Lake

De Burgh

Alroy Di

Louisa Downs

500

Mt.Dockrell

Wolf Creek

Meteorite

Crater N.P.

Sturt Cr.

628

Mt.Junction

Tanami Desert

L.Buck

Aboriginal Land

Phillip Creek

Warego

Mine

Three Ways

Roadhouse

Tennant Creek

Barkly

Roadhouse

Frewena

Christmas Cr.

Carranya

Billiluna

Cummins Range

497

Mt.Tanami

Kaititja-Warlpiri

Aboriginal

McLaren

Creek

Kurundi

Epenarra

Kurinelli

L.Jones

L.Betty

L.McLemon

Lewis Range

Balgo

Rabbit Flat

Roadhouse

T e r r i t o r y

Mt.Davidson

464

Wauchope

Roadhouse

599

Mt.Cairns

Hatches Creek

L.Lanagan

Godfreys Tank

315

Mt.Elliott

Gregory L.

Djaluan Cr.

Balwina

Aboriginal

Reserve

Landu Riv.

Land

Davenport Range

Murray

Downs

Elkedra

Southesk

Tableland

450

L.Dennis

L.White

Wilbrunga Range

Wirliyajarrayt

Abor.Land

Willowra

Chilla Well

Mt.Theo

583

Warrabri

Hanson Riv.

Barrow

Creek

Neutral Junction

Stanmore Range

L.Wills

Lake Mackay

Aboriginal

Land

Mt.Leichhardt

1142

Anningie

Central

Mt.Stuart

845

Stirling

Mt.Tops

710

Alyawarra

Aboriginal

Land

Ammaroo

Sandover Riv.

Oorratippra

Arga

Height
m
3000
2000
1000
600
300
100
0
<0
200
1000
2000
4000
6000
8000
10000
m
Depth

1:4,500,000

0   25   50   75   100   125miles

0   50   100   150   200km

Albers Equal Area Conic Projection

50

10°

S e a

Orman Reef
Gabba I.
Zagai I.
Mabuiag I.
Murray I.
Portlock Reefs

Badu I.
Moa I.
Sassie I.
Abor.Land
Abor.Land

Ashmore Reef

Thursday I.
Thursday Island
Horn I.
Strait
York
Somerset
Somerset Aboriginal Reserve

Prince of Wales I.
Endeavour
Cowal Creek
Bamaga
Slade Pt.
Jardine
Jardine River
N.P.
McHenry Riv.

51

G u l f

Mapoon Aboriginal Reserve
Dulhunty Riv.

Shelburne Bay
C. Grenville

C.Arnhem
Port Musgrave
Mapoon
Cape

Bertiehaugh
Bramwell
Temple Bay
Fair C.
Weymouth Bay
C.Weymouth
Iron Range N.P.
Portland Roads

12°

Duyfken Point
Andoom
Wenlock
Moreton
Weipa
Weipa South
Batavia Downs

Albatross Bay
Lloyd Bay
C.Direction
Lockhart River

Thud Point
Merluna
York
Mt.Carter 667
Lockhart River Aboriginal Reserve
C.Sidmouth

Archer Bay
Watson
Wenlock
508
Cone Peak

Aurukun
Aurukun
Archer Bend N.P.
Archer River Roadhouse
Rokeby-Croll Creek

o f

Archer Riv.
Aboriginal
Merapah
Rokeby N.P.
Mt White 450
Coen

Groote Eylandt
C.Keer-weer
Reserve
Kendall
Peninsula

Cape Beatrice
Edward River
Holroyd Riv.
Moojeeba
Princess Charlotte Bay
Flinders Group
C.Melville

52

14°

C a r p e n t a r i a

Kowanyama
516
Mt.Ryan
Strathburn
Marina Plains
Cape Melville N.P.
Howick Group

Pormpuraaw (Edward River)
Strathgordon
Strathhaven
Musgrave
Breeza Plains O.S.
Lakefield
C.Bowen

Osprey Reef

Aboriginal
Coleman Reserve
Riv.
New Dixie
National Kalinga Park
Lakefield
Lizard I.
Lizard I. N.P.
Lookout Pt.

Sir Edward Pellew Group
Kowanyama
Mitchell and Alice Rivers N.P.
Oroners
Fairview
Laura
Battle Camp
C.Flattery
Aboriginal Hopevale Res.
C.Bedford
Hope Vale

53

Vanderlin I.
Nassau Riv.
Rutland Plains
Koolatah
Kimba
Palmer Riv.
King Junction
Strathleven
Palmerville
148
Rossville
Mt.Goole N.P.
Cooktown

Wellesley Islands
Dunbar
Drumduff
Palmer Riv.
Lakeland Downs
Bloomfield River
Cedar Bay N.P.

Seven Emu
Mornington I.
C.Van Diemen
Inkerman
Galbraith
Staaten Riv.
Highbury
Mount Mulgrave
Woods Peak
Cape Tribulation N.P.
Alexandra Bay
Daintree

Robinson River
Pungalina
Gununa
Forsyth I.
Macaroni
Staaten River N.P.
Bellevue
Mount Mulgrave
Daintree N.P.
Mossman
Port Douglas

16°

Calvert Hills
Wollogorang
Denham I.
Bentinck I.
Bountiful Is.
Point Austin
Delta Downs
Vanrook
Wrotham Park
Lynd Riv.
Bulimba
Blackdown
Mount Molloy
Mareeba
Palm Cove
Yorkeys Knob

Sweers I.
Allen I.
Stirling
Miranda Downs
Red Riv.
Bibohra
Tinaroo
Falls Res.
Gordonvale
Green I.
Fitzroy I.

Westmoreland
Karumba
Maggieville
Torwood
Tate Riv.
Chillagoe
Mungana
Dimbulah
Cairns

54

Seigals Creek
Burketown
Normanton
Abingdon Downs
Almaden
Atherton
Bellenden Ker N.P.
Malanda
Babinda

Waanyi-Garawa Aboriginal Reserve
Doomadgee Aboriginal Reserve
Doomadgee
Nicholson
Armraynald
Glenore
East Haydon
Blackbull
Strathmore
Minnies
Dagworth
Mount Garnet
Herberton
Millaa 1022
Innisfail
Johnstone South

18°

Spring Vale
Highland Plains
Lawn Hill
Gregory Downs
Inverleigh
Wernadinga
Milgarra
Croydon
Gilbert River
Forest Home
Georgetown
Mount Surprise
Meadowbank
Ravenshoe
Koombooloomba
Tully
Dunk I.

Lawn Hill N.P.
Australian Fossil Mammal Site
Silver Star Mine
Planet Downs
Augustus Downs
Macalister
Talawanta
Claraville
Mittagong
Candlour
North Head
Einasleigh
Spring Creek
Kinrara
Lumholtz N.P.
Cardwell
C.Sandwich
Hinchinbrook I. N.P.

Old Herbert Vale
Riversleigh
Lorraine
Iffley
Esmeralda
Glenora
Forsayth
The Lynd Junction
Oak Hills
Abergowrie
Halifax
Palm Is.

Gallipoli
Burke and Wills Roadhouse
Myola
Prospect
Bairds Table Mtn. 912
Conjuboy
Greenvale
Ingham
Toobanna
Great Palm I.

Herbert Vale
Kamileroi
Boomarra
Canobie
Victoria Vale
Kidston
Gilberton
Lyndhurst
Pandanus
Camel Creek
Halifax Bay

55

Morstone
Thorntonia
Alsace
Arizona
Pelham
Mt.Lookout
Hidden Valley
Clarke River
Magnetic Island

Gunpowder
Dobbyn
Alcala
Kalmeta
Numil Downs
Bellfield
Black Braes
Mt.Oweenee
Crystal Creek N.P.
Magnetic I. N.P.
Bluewater

Cloncurry
Camooweal
Camooweal Caves N.P.
Yelvertoft
Calton Hills
Clonagh
Dalgonally
Bunda Bunda
Saxby Riv.
Middle Park
Mount Norman
Stopem Blockem Range
Craigie
Maryvale
Reedy Springs
Eumara Springs
TOWNSVILLE

Soudan
Avon Downs
Pipah Range
Barkly Downs
Quamby
Ford Constantine
Manfred Downs
Runnymede
Burleigh
Doncaster
Mt.Dick 899
Great Basalt Wall N.P.
Mt.Stewart 1002
Baffes Creek
Dotswood
Fanning River

20°

Austral Downs
Lake Nash
Hilton
L. Moondarra
Julia Creek
Nelia
Maxwelton
Richmond
Porcupine Gorge N.P.
Pentland
Homestead
Brookville

Georgina Downs
Bullecourt
Mount Isa
Cloncurry
Malbon
Oorindi
Gilliat
Yorkshire Downs
Edith Downs
Marathon
Prairie
Torrens Creek
Mingela
Charters Towers
Ravenswood
Millaroo

Mt.Hogart 345
Headingly
Sheila
Oban
Black Mtn. 567
Kuridala
McKinlay
Dimora
Nottingham Downs
Stamford
Oxenhope
Longton
Dalrymple Lake
Harvest Home
Campaspe

56

Warwick Downs
O.S.
Duchess Butru
Selwyn
Beau Desert
Kynuna
Whitewood
Sutton Downs
Bogunda
Ulva
Yarrowmere
Hidden Valley
Mount Coolon

Walgra
Dajarra
The Mounment
Dagworth
Corfield
Woolfield
Tangorin
Uanda
Alberfoyle
L.Buchanan
Mount Douglas

Carandotta
Carandotta
Chatsworth
Cuckadoo
Olio
Birricannia
Disney

Ranges Valley
Q u e e n s l a n d

Blue Mud Bay

The Northern Territory's eastern coastline runs from Arnhem Land in the west, and southward round the Gulf of Carpentaria, which is bordered by the Cape York Peninsula on its eastern side. Indented by small bays, this stretch of the Northern Territory's coastline is rugged and uneven in places. The inshore waters here are dotted with islands, the largest of which was named Groote Eylandt, meaning Great Island, by Dutch navigators. The satellite image shows the northern part of Blue Mud Bay, which lies at the southern end of the Gove Peninsula. This area, with impressively wild coastal scenery, narrow, unspoilt beaches, and extensive areas of rocky hinterland, forms part of a reserve for Aborigines. Visitors may enter it only with special permission.

1 *Arnhem Land ↑*

Arnhem Land owes its name to a Dutch sailing ship that was lost along this stretch of the coast of Australia in 1623. For several hundred years, white people made no attempt to explore the rocky landscape beyond the coast. However, at the beginning of the 20th century, whites began to penetrate the hinterland to extract minerals such as uranium. Arnhem Land has been inhabited by Aborigines for thousands of years, and in 1931, when little was known about the region's deposits of bauxite and uranium, its western section, in the form of Kakadu National Park, was declared a reserve for Aborigines. Today, Arnhem Land is one of the last areas of Australia that is still relatively untouched by European culture. The 30,000 Aborigines who live here have control over the issue of permits for the mining of its rich mineral resources. A distinctive feature of the landscape is its tall termite mounds, which are visible for great distances across the savannah.

Some stand as high as 7 m (23 ft): They are constructed in such a way that as little of their surface as possible is exposed to the scorching sun.

2 Erosion Gullies

Blue Mud Bay lies in the tropical zone, where heavy, monsoon-like rain falls in summer. As a result, the rocky landscape around the bay has been heavily eroded. In particular, the action of water on the softer stone of the sandstone plateau has carved out valleys where tropical vegetation has taken root. However, few trees will grow in areas that are flooded in summer: The vegetation consists mostly of grassland, which together with the tree-covered areas, contribute to the landscape's savannah-like character.

3 Mangrove Swamps

The rivers that flow down from the high peaks of the Mitchell Range and of its southern continuation, the Persons Range, empty into the sea in the bays along a stretch of coastline known as Gulf Country. Climatic conditions here lead to the formation of a highly saline mud, particularly around Blue Mud Bay, and to a lesser extent around Limmen Bight, in the south, and Caledon Bay, in the north. The edges of these mud flats support grasses and bushes that can withstand saline conditions. The mud is formed by the combination of salt crystals created by the rapid evaporation of water and by sediment carried down by the rivers. It has a bluish color, which has given the bay its name. Mangrove-like plants and swamp-dwelling animals are found here. The brackish waters at the mouths of Arnhem Land's rivers are a suitable habitat for the Australian saltwater crocodile, which also swims far out to sea.

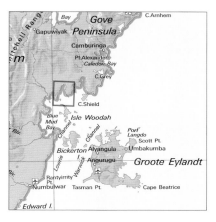

1:4,500,000

Albers Equal Area Conic Projection

Height	
m	
3000	
2000	
1000	
600	
300	
100	
0	
<0	
200	
1000	
2000	
4000	
6000	
8000	
10000	
m	
Depth	

ern

534
Mt.Madley

L.Hancock
McPhersons Pillar
532

L.Cobb

L.Anec
L.Hopkins

Johnstone Hill
704
Aboriginal Land

Mb

Mc

MacD
Haast
Bluff
Ormiston Gorge · 1349
Mt.Soder
Mt.Hoy
Hamilton
Downs
N.P.
Mt.Harris

Alice Springs
Iwupataka
James
Ranges
Deep
Well

Aboriginal

Reserve

McPhersons Pillar

L.Newell

L.Christopher

Rawlinson
Range

Bloods Range
840

L.Neale

Undandita
Hermannsburg
Owen Springs

L.Jones
Hoar
eene

L.Farnham

Schwerin Mural Creek
1001

Docker Creek Petermann
(Kultukatjara)
Aboriginal Land

Carmichael Creek
Kings Canyon ★
Watarrka
N.P.

Finke Gorge
N.P.

Orange
Creek
Range

Maryvale

Mt.William
Lambert
516

Everard
Junction
L.Sprenger
L.Gruzka

534

Mt.Johnson

530
Mt.Beadell
L.Breaden

Giles
Meteorological
Station

T218

Warakurna
Mt.Deering

Petermann
Ranges

L.Amadeus

Henbury Meteorite
Craters

Henbury

Indacowra

ame Range

Herbert
Wash

Mt.Charles
533

Mann
Ranges

Yulara
1066
Mt.Olga
(Kata Tjuta)

Katiti
Aboriginal
Land

Curtin
Springs

Mount
Ebenezer

Erldunda

Engoordina

Uluru N.P.

· 863
Uluru
(Ayers Rock)

2

Blyth Lagoon
Warburton Ra.
594 ·
Aboriginal Land

Scamp Hill
Mt.Rawlinson
605

Stevensons
Peak
1032

Kulgera

L.Gillen

Warburton · 823
Warburton Range

Mt.Talbot
Mt.Squres
705

Mt.Hinkley
1058

Pipalyatjara

Mann
Ranges

Amata

Musgrave Range

Mt.Cecil
· 551

Tieyon

Warburton Range
Aboriginal Reserve

Permits only area

Tomkinson Ranges

Pukatja
(Ernabella)

Iwaninyi
(Kenmore Park)

Aparawatatja
(Fregon)

1436
Mt.Woodroffe

Pitjantjatjara

Lake
Baker

Mt.Kintore
1073

Mt.Lindsay
817

Aboriginal Land

Everard Ranges

Mt.Illbillee
917

Mimili

Iwantja

Mintabie

Marla

Saunders Pt.
528

Waigen Lakes

Cheesman Peak
654

Great Victoria Desert

L.Throssel

Yamama

Yeo L.

Pt.Salvation
Aboriginal
Reserve

Neale
Junction

Rason L.

alia

Wanna Lakes

L.Meramangye

San Marino

L.Gidgi
Jubilee L.

Blue Robin Hill

Plumridge
Lakes

Shell
Lakes

L.Ilma

Forrest
Lakes

Wyola Lake

L.Dey-Dey

Maralinga-Tjarutja

Aboriginal Land

Mabel
Creek
Coober Pedy

Garford

Comet

ell L.

L.Maurice

Wilkinson
Lakes

Indooroopilly

Nullarbor   Plain

Mound
352

Premier
Downs

Seemore
Downs

Yarle L.

Maralinga

Ooldea Range

Half
Moon L.

Durkin
Outstation

Carnes

Kitchener
Aboriginal
reserve

Haig

Loongana

Reid
Forrest

Deakin

Cook

Fisher

Watson

Bates

Wynbring

Malbooma

Rawlinna

E   u   c   l   a   B   a   s   i   n

Ifould L.

Tarcoola

Noondoonia

Caiguna

Madura

Mundrabilla

Mundrabilla
Motel

Cocklebiddy

Eucla

Nullarbor National Park

Nullarbor
Roadhouse

Travellers
Village

Yalata

Yalata
Aboriginal   Land

Head of
Bight

Nundroo

Penong

C.Nuyts

Fowlers Bay

Coorabie

Fowlers Bay

Coduna

Maltee

Lake
Everard

Russel Range

Twilight Cove

Peperndicular Cliffs
Pt.Dover
Pt.Culver

St.Peter I.

Denial Bay

Smoky
Bay

Smoky Bay

Hiltaba

Manambinia

Nuyts Archipelago
St. Francis
Islands

Pt.Brown

C.Bauer

Streaky
Bay

Poochera

Streaky Bay

Israelite Bay

Israelite Bay

C.Blanche

C.Radstock

Port Kenny

Pk.

Pt.Malcom
Cape Pasley

Oaw I.
Eastern
Group

Anxious
Bay

Mt.
Wedge

arche
South
East Is.
ry I.

Waldegrave I.

Flinders I.
C.Finnis

Elliston

Pearson I.

Great   Australian   Bight

Pt.Sir Isaac

Greenly I.
Coffin Bay
N.P.

Sheringa

Perth

Perth was founded in 1829 by Governor James Stirling as a town for settlers as well as the capital of the new colony of Western Australia. The place that he chose was 18 km (11 miles) upstream of the mouth of the Swan River. Surrounded by mosquito-infested swamps, the location was unfavorable, and this hampered the city's construction. However, with the impetus provided by the gold rush that began in 1890, Perth prospered, developing into one of Australia's richest cities, with wealthy suburbs spreading out onto the rolling hills along the Swan River. Laid out on a grid pattern, the city was planned and built by John Septimus Roe. Today, Perth covers 5500 km^2 (2123 square miles) and its inhabitants number one million.

N

1 *South Perth and Mill Point ←*

South of Kings Park is Narrow Bridge, which links the northern and southern districts of the city. South Perth begins on the promontory to the south of the city. Resembling a peninsula, the promontory was created by the meandering course of the Swan River. At Mill Point there is a historic windmill and a small museum that documents the role that the mill played in early colonial days. The expressway leads to the elegant suburb of Fremantle, located at the mouth of the river.

2 Swan River

Perth's old town is located at the mouth of the Swan River, which flows into the Indian Ocean at Fremantle, 18 km (12 miles) downstream. Fer-

ries from the terminal in Riverside Drive provide a link between the city center, on the north bank of the river, and South Perth, on the south bank.

3 Kings Park

Covering 440 ha (1087 acres), Kings Park was created at the end of the 19th century, and is considered to be one of the most beautiful landscaped parks in Australia. Laid out in the English style, it covers a rocky spit of land at the foot of Mount Eliza, which rises steeply in the city center. Most of the indigenous natural bushland that covers the promontory was preserved, and each spring it becomes a stunning carpet blooming with flowers. The park also includes a botanical garden.

4 St. George's Terrace

Perth's main commercial artery is St. George's Terrace, in the old town. Lined with skyscrapers, it is the location of the headquarters of oil and mining companies. To the west, St. George's Terrace ends at Parliament House, behind which is Kings Park. Along the green, southern side of the street, which faces the river, are Government House, St. George's Anglican Cathedral, and the Supreme Court. The latter contains the old court: Dating from 1836, it is the oldest building in Perth.

5 Burswood

The 100 ha (247 acre) Burswood International Resort Casino Complex was created on a peninsula jutting out into the Swan River.

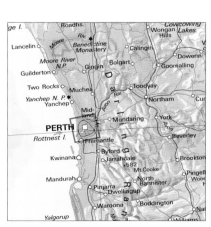

Uluru/Ayers Rock

The large monolith, Uluru/Ayers Rock, lies in the red heart of Australia. It consists of red arkose, a kind of sandstone, and its proportions are huge. It is about 3.6 km (2 miles) long and 2.4 km (1.5 miles) wide, it covers an area of 3.3 km² (1.3 square miles), and it has a circumference of 8 km (5 miles). The mountain, whose outline resembles that of a turtle shell, rises 318 m (986 ft) above its flat surroundings. The Aborigines, to whom the rock is sacred, called it Uluru, meaning "Place that Creates Shadows." The surveyor William Gosse, who was the first white man to see the monolith at close quarters in 1873, named it Ayers Rock, after Sir Henry Ayers, the chief secretary of South Australia. Today more than 40,000 people visit it every year. The gigantic Yulara Tourist Resort was built for this purpose, and can handle 5000 visitors a day. The stream of tourists is channeled through the resort, keeping the ecological impact to a minimum.

1 *The Rock at Sunrise* ↑
At dawn, as the sun rises above the horizon, Uluru/Ayers Rock appears to change color. An indistinct gray by night, at first light it changes to a dark reddish brown. As the sun climbs, it takes on a glowing red color, and in broad sunlight it is a light reddish orange.

2 Climbing Uluru/Ayers Rock
From the nearby parking lot, hikers begin the 1.6 km (1 mile) climb to the summit of Uluru/Ayers Rock. Along the steepest sections of the route there is a chain for hikers to hold on to. At the summit, which is flat, the wind blows fiercely and the sun burns with a relentless heat. But the climb is rewarded by breathtaking views of the vast semi-desert, where red spinifex and mulga grow, and of Kata Tjuta (a group of rocks also known as The Olgas) to the west. In 1985, in recognition of its mythical importance to the Aborigines, Uluru/Ayers Rock was returned to the Anangu, a local tribe. This was a triumph for Australian champions of Aboriginal rights and for environmental campaigners.

3 Mutitjulu
Those who choose not to tackle the climb to the summit of Uluru/Ayers Rock can walk all the way round the foot of the rock in three to four hours. The walk reveals many fascinating rock formations created as a result of heavy erosion by the penetration of moisture along the base of the monolith. Walkers also come to Mutitjulu, a watering hole that never dries up. According to an Aboriginal myth, Wagampi, the snake god, resides here, and anyone who dives into the water is

supposed to die as the result of a magical poison. Above the pool lives Kapi Agaiyu Wanambijarra, the holy rainbow snake. A rock known as The Brain—a part of the cliff that has been eroded into a shape resembling a human brain —can also be spotted among the smaller rock formations.

4 Taputji
Taputji, or Little Ayers Rock, is a hill on the track of the Earth Mother Cult that runs around Uluru/Ayers Rock. It is the place from which Aborigines witness the rituals that are performed on certain religious occasions. Visitors are expressly prohibited from climbing it.

5 *Rock Art* ↓
The rock's steep-sided base is pitted with several caves. As they are sacred to Aborigines, many of the caves are closed to visitors. The walls of most of the caves are decorated with Aboriginal paintings and drawings, some of which are extremely old. The custom of Aboriginal cave painting took place here from ancient times and continued into the 1930s. The artists used the chewed ends of strips of bark as brushes, with which they created sometimes abstract forms and patterns using earth-based pigments. Among important motifs are depictions of the Dreamtime and of primordial, mythical events. The paintings also give an insight into Aboriginal life, such as hunting.

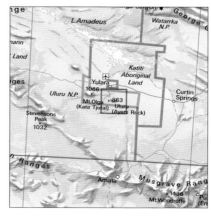

1:4,500,000

Albers Equal Area Conic Projection

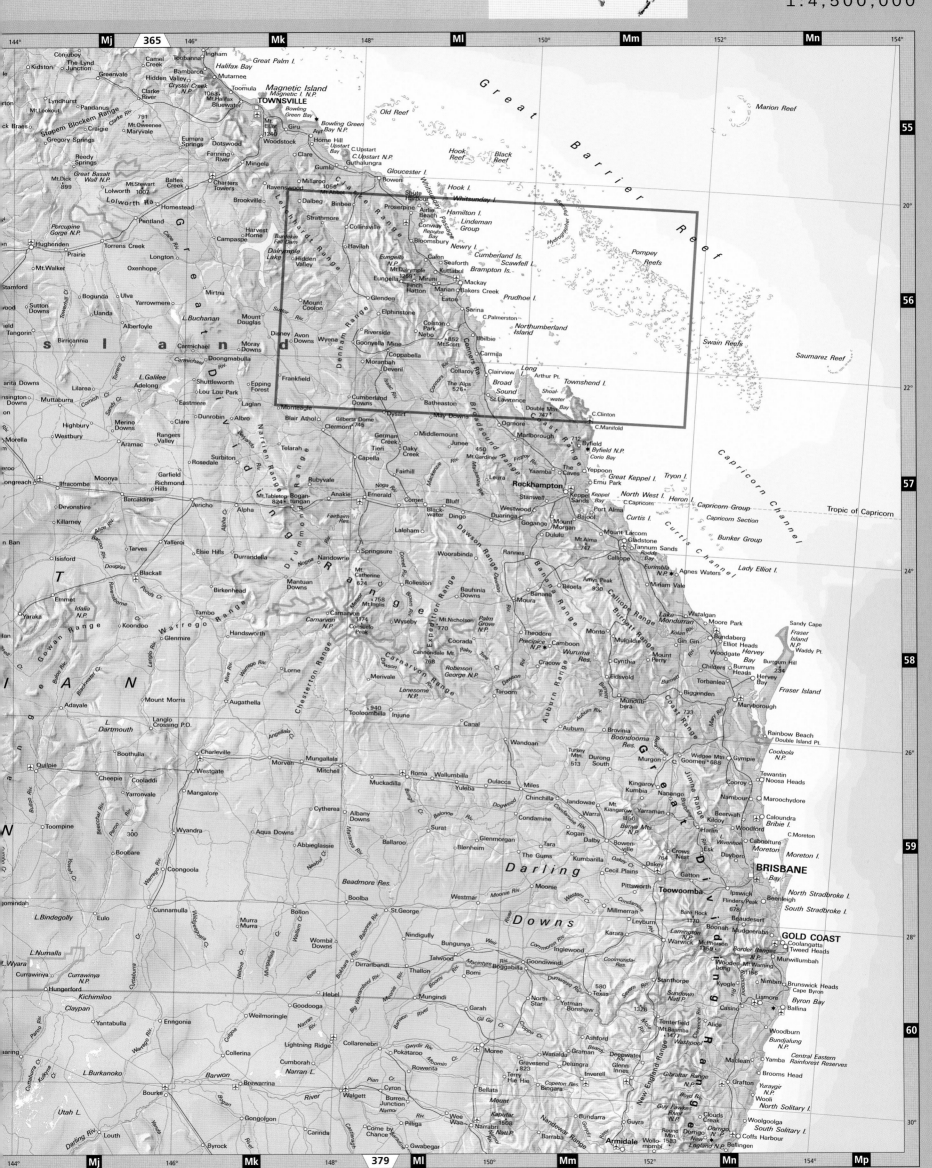

Great Barrier Reef

The Great Barrier Reef has been described as the Eighth Wonder of the World and as the largest living thing on earth. Consisting of about 2500 individual reefs, it forms a natural breakwater that stretches 2027 km (1259 miles) from the Torres Strait in the north to the Tropic of Capricorn in the south. As an underwater national park, the entire reef is a protected area, and was made a UNESCO World Natural Heritage Site in 1981. The reef as it is today has existed since the end of the last Ice Age, about 10,000 years ago. But it overlies dead, older reefs, which are thought to contain oil deposits. About a quarter of this fascinating marine environment is under threat of destruction both by natural forces and human activity.

N

5

1 Whitsunday Islands ←

The rain forest-covered Whitsunday Islands, which lie off the coast of Queensland, are one of the most popular holiday destinations in Australia. Many of the 74 islands that make up the group are uninhabited and are protected as national parks: They include Whitsunday Island, the largest, and the Lindeman Islands, which lie further south. Others, such as Hamilton Island have idyllic beaches that are a paradise for swimmers, and some also have luxurious resorts. Under the constant influence of trade winds, the islands' inshore waters are among the best in the world for sailing. Direct flights to Hamilton Island from Sydney, Melbourne, Brisbane, and Cairns contribute to the region's popularity as tourist destination.

2 Mackay

Mackay is set on an inlet on the coast of Queensland between Cairns and Brisbane. With beautiful beaches, it is popular with swimmers, but it is also known as the "sugar capital" of Australia: Extensive plantations of sugar cane cover the undulating land around the town.

3 Eungella National Park

Coastal Queensland contains many small national parks. They were created to protect the region's rain forest. One of these parks is Eungella National Park, an ancient volcanic region. "Eungella" means "Land of Clouds" in the language of the Aborigines, and the park comprises the subtropical rain forest of the Clarke Range.

4 Mineral Resources

Since the 1960s, the service industry and mining have been the main planks of Australia's industrial activity. Queensland is particularly rich in mineral resources, not only in terms of quantity but also because of the great variety of its minerals. Extracting them is, however, often both difficult and costly.

5 The Pompey Reefs

The Pompey Reefs, and the Swain Reefs adjoining them to the south, constitute the southern extremity of the Great Barrier Reef. Reefs that lie just beneath the surface of the ocean appear as light blue areas. This outer reef lies about 150 km (93 miles) off the coast.

Albers Equal Area Conic Projection

Mj	146°	Mk	148°	Ml	375	150°	Mm	152°	Mn	154°	Mp

L.Numalla

Currawinya
Currawinya N.P.

Hungerford
Kichimiloo
Claypan

Yantabulla

L.Burkanoko

Bourke

Louth

Byrock

New

Mt.Nymagee
519

South Wales

Cobar

Hermidale

Nyngan

Barnato

Nymagee

Trangie

Dubbo

Wombil Downs
Nindigully
Bungunya
Talwood
Macintyre Riv
Goondiwindi
Inglewood
Warwick
McPherson
Border Ranges N.P.
Coolangatta
Tweed Heads
Murwillumbah

Dirranbandi
Thallon
Bomi
Boggabilla
Stanthorpe
Woodenbong
Mt Warning
Kyogle
Nimbin
Brunswick Heads
Cape Byron

North Star
Texas
Casino
Lismore
Ballina

Hebel
Garah
Yetman
Bonshaw
Tenterfield
Woodburn
Bundjalung N.P.

Goodooga
Mungindi
Ashford
Graman
Deepwater
Gibraltar Range N.P.
Maclean
Yamba

Weilmoringle
Narran
Collarenebri
Moree
Gravesend
Delungra
Inverell
Glen Innes
Grafton
Yuraygir N.P.

Lightning Ridge
Wee Waa
Narrabri
Bellata
Terry Hie Hie
Bingara
Copeton Res
Wooli
North Solitary I.

Collerina
Pokataroo
Mount Kaputar Nat.P.
Barraba
Guyra
Dorrigo
Woolgoolga
South Solitary I.

Come by Chance
Pilliga
Boggabri
Bundarra
Uralla
New England N.P.
Coffs Harbour

Brewarrina
Walgett
Cumborah
Gwabegar
Baradine
L.Keepit
Manilla
Armidale
Bellingen

Gongolgon
Carinda
Coonamble
Gunnedah
Tamworth
Walcha
Nambucca Heads
Macksville

Darling River

Coolabah
Gulargambone
Mulaley
Werris Creek
Quirindi
Nundle
Yarrowitch
Smoky Cape
Hat Head Natl. P.
Kempsey
Crescent Head

Budda-buddah
Gilgandra
Blackville
Willow Tree
Murrurundi
Blue Knob
Wauchope
Port Macquarie

TASMAN SEA

NEWCASTLE

SYDNEY

WOLLONGONG

CANBERRA
Queanbeyan

A.C.T.

MELBOURNE

GEELONG

Bass Strait

King Island

Flinders Island

Furneaux Group

Cape Barren Island

Clarke Island

Sydney

In 1788, the British founded a settlement on Jackson Bay, which they named after Lord Sydney, the British home secretary who had authorized the establishment of a colony. Thanks to its location at the mouth of the Parramatta River, the inlet now known as Sydney Cove was an excellent place to drop anchor as it was protected from floods. The city's early nucleus centered on the peninsula now known as The Rocks, between Sydney Cove and Walsh Bay. Later the city's business and administrative districts developed nearby, between Darling Harbour in the west and the city's green spaces in the east. These open spaces—Hyde Park, The Domain, and the Royal Botanic Gardens—are the setting for several historical buildings, including Government House.

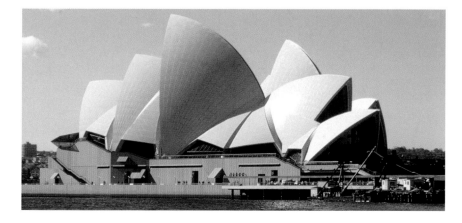

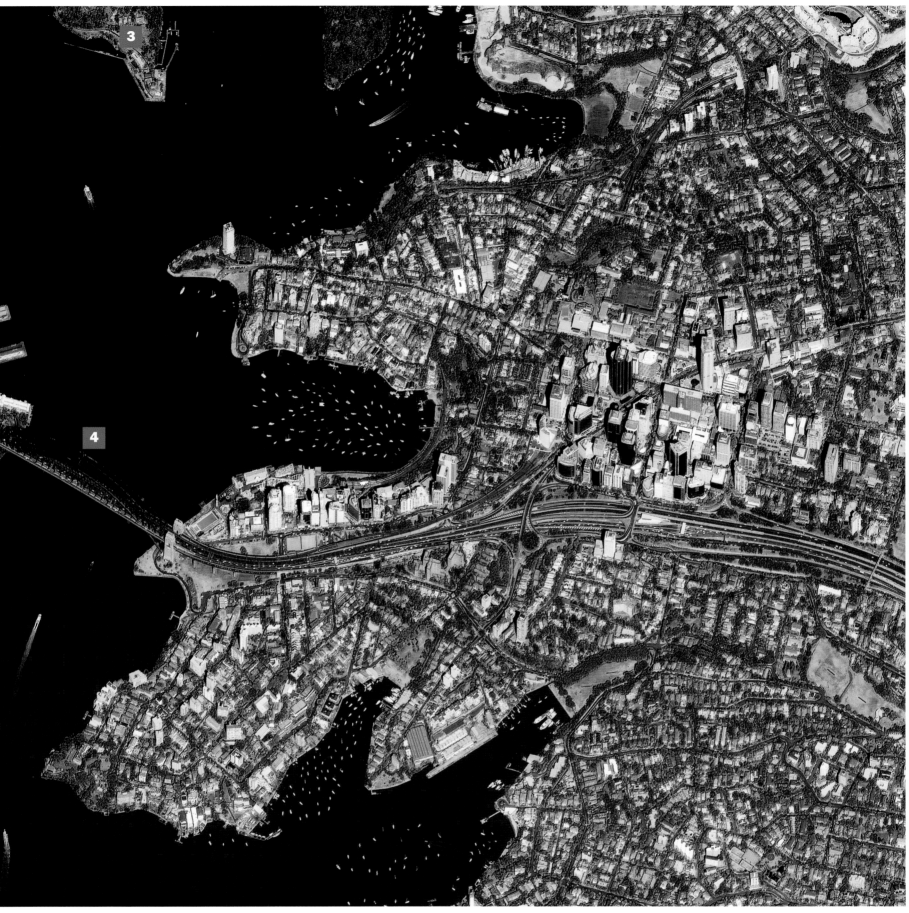

3

4

1 *Sydney Opera House* ←

Set at the end of Bennelong Point, the Opera House has become Sydney's most famous symbol. It was designed by the Danish architect Jörn Utzon, and work began in 1957. However, the construction of this bold steel-girder building became the subject of a long-drawn-out controversy. It was originally to have cost only $7 million AUS to build, but in 1973, after Utzon had abandoned the project, it was taken on by the architects Ove Arup and Partners, who completed it at a final cost exceeding $100 million AUS. Despite these setbacks, Sydney Opera House is one of the world's finest modernist buildings. The roof structure is supported by 350 km (217 miles) of steel cables, and it contains 6225 km² (2403 square miles) of glass.

2 Central Business District (CBD)

The area that now makes up Sydney's Central Business District (CBD) was once an area of low-rise buildings. They were replaced by skyscrapers, where today newspaper, television, and financial companies have their offices, and by the 304 m (997 ft) high Sydney Tower. The CBD is also the city's shopping center and administrative hub, and has been described as the Manhattan of the South Seas. A banking district has been created around Martin Place and a hotel district around Circular Quay. Several schools and universities, libraries, and museums are also concentrated in the CBD, as are numerous wholesale traders, near Darling Harbour.

3 The Rocks

The Rocks, the spot where Sydney was founded, takes its name from its hilly topography. Thanks to a regeneration initiative, the character of this historic district has been preserved: Its old buildings have been restored and have not been swept away by skyscrapers. In addition to old warehouses and residential buildings, many restaurants and boutiques are also located here.

4 Harbour Bridge

The Sydney Harbour Bridge, with a span of 503 m (1650 ft) and eight traffic lanes, was opened in 1932. From the top of the east pier there is a magnificent view over the city and of the harbor.

	Ba		150°		Bb		140°		Ca		130°		166°		Nf		168°		Ng		170°		Nh

10

160°

K I R I B A T I

Hatutea
Nuku Hiva *Marquises Is.*
Ua Huka
Ua Pou *Hiva Oa*
Tahuata
Fatu Hiva

10°

Penrhyn
(Tongareva)

Vostock *Carolina*

Flint

F r e n c h

11

Îles du *Napuka*
Roi-Georges
Society Islands *Mataiva* *Pukapuka*
Rangiroa

T u a m o t u   I s l a n d s

Bora *Fakarava* *Katiu*
Bora *Niau* *Makemo*
Raiatea *Huchine* *Marutea* *Tatakoto*
Papeete **2** *Anaa* *Amanu*
Tahiti *Marokau* *Pukarua*
Nengonengo *Hao* *Reao*

Ahunui

20°

Hervey
Mitiaro *Turéia*
Atiu *Vanavana* *Ténarunga*
Maute *Mururoa* *Marutéa*
Rarotonga *Tematangi* *Group   Acteon*
Mangaia *Maria* *Rurutu*
Rimatara *Mangareva*
Tropic of Capricorn *Tubuai* *Gambier Is.*
P o l y n e s i a
(F) *Oeno*
Raivaveé *Henderson*
A u s t r a l   I s l a n d s *Pitcairn*
Pitcairn Islands
12 *(GB)*

PACIFIC OCEAN

Rapa

30°

1:30,000,000

0	250	500	750 miles
0	500	1000	1500 km

C h a l l e n g e r

P l a t e a u

65

40°

Height	
m	
3000	
2000	
1000	
600	
300	
100	
0	
<0	
200	
1000	
2000	
4000	
6000	
8000	
10000	
m	
Depth	

42°

66

T A S M A N   S E A

Westport
Cape Foulwind
Charleston
Paparoa
N.P.
Punakaiki

Pancake Rocks

Greymouth Stillwa

SOUTH

Hokitika Kumata

ISLAND

67

Haritari

Franz Josef
Fox Glacier 2795
Mt Tasman
Westland Mt Cook Mount
N.P. Mt Sefton N.P. Hutt
Lake Mt Cook Mt Somers
Paringa Lake
Tekapo
Lake Ashburto
Cascade Point Pukaki Tekapo

Haast Geraldine

Awarua Point Mt Aspiring Lake
N.P. 3027 Ohau Fairlie
Makarora
Mt Aspiring Lake Twizel
Milford Sound N.P. Wanaka Lake Cave Timaru
Mitre Peak Mt Tutoko Benmore
1692 2746 2819 Lake Hawea Omarama
Milford
Sound Glenorchy Tarras Waitaki
George Sound Lake Linda Pass Duntroon
Fiordland Wanaka
Queenstown Frankton Cromwell Kyeburn
Secretary I. Lake Omakau Waikati
Doubtful Sound Wakatipu 2324 Alexandra
National Te Anau Garston Middlemarch Palmerston
Breaksea Lake 2035
Sound Te Anau Boxburgh Moeraki
Resolution I. Park Lake Waikaia Raes Oamaru
Dusky Sound Manapouri Junction Mosgiel
Manapouri Mossburn 1211 Mahinerangi Port Chalmers
Caroline Peak Monowai Otago
1722 Lake Lumsden Lawrence Peninsula
Chalky Inlet Hauroko Clifden Tapanui DUNEDIN
Preservation Inlet Winton Gore Clinton Milton
Waikaka Balclutha Kaitangata
Te Edendale Mólyneux
Waewae Riverton Tokanui Bay
Bay Invercargill Mokoreta Owaka
Solander I. Bluff Fortrose Waikawa Long Point
Foveaux Strait Tokanui
Codfish Mt Anglem Ruapuke Island
Island 850 Halfmoon Bay (Oban)
Mason Bay Paterson Inlet
Doughboy Bay Mt Allen Stewart
750 Island

44°

67

46°

68

	Nb		160°		Nc		162°		Nd		164°		Ne		166°					168°				170°		Nh

Southwest Cape 168°

NEW ZEALAND

NORTH ISLAND

NORTHLAND PLATEAU

TAKAPUNA
AUCKLAND

Bay of Plenty

Hamilton

North Taranaki Bight

South Taranaki Bight

New Plymouth

Napier

Palmerston North

WELLINGTON
Lower Hutt

Cook Strait

Hikurangi Trench

P A C I F I C   O C E A N

CHRISTCHURCH

Mernoo Bank

Chatham Rise

Chatham Islands (NZ)
Chatham Island
The Forty Fours
Pitt Island
Mangore Island   Rangátira Island

Canterbury Bight

1:4,500,000

0	25	50	75	100	125 miles
0	50	100	150	200km	

Alber's Conical Equal-Area Projection

Mount Cook

The Southern Alps, on New Zealand's South Island, contain the highest mountain in the country: This is Mount Cook, which rises to a height of 3754 m (12,316 ft). Popularly referred to as the Roof of New Zealand, the peak was known to the Maoris as Ao-raki, meaning "Cloud-Piercer." It was renamed Mount Cook by Captain J. L. Stokes, who surveyed the region in 1851, and named the peak after the British navigator and explorer Captain James Cook (1728–79). The mountain and its surroundings are now an officially protected area—the Aoraki/Mount Cook National Park, which became a World Natural Heritage Site in 1986. About 40 percent of the park is glaciated, and it contains 22 mountains over 3000 m (9842 ft) high.

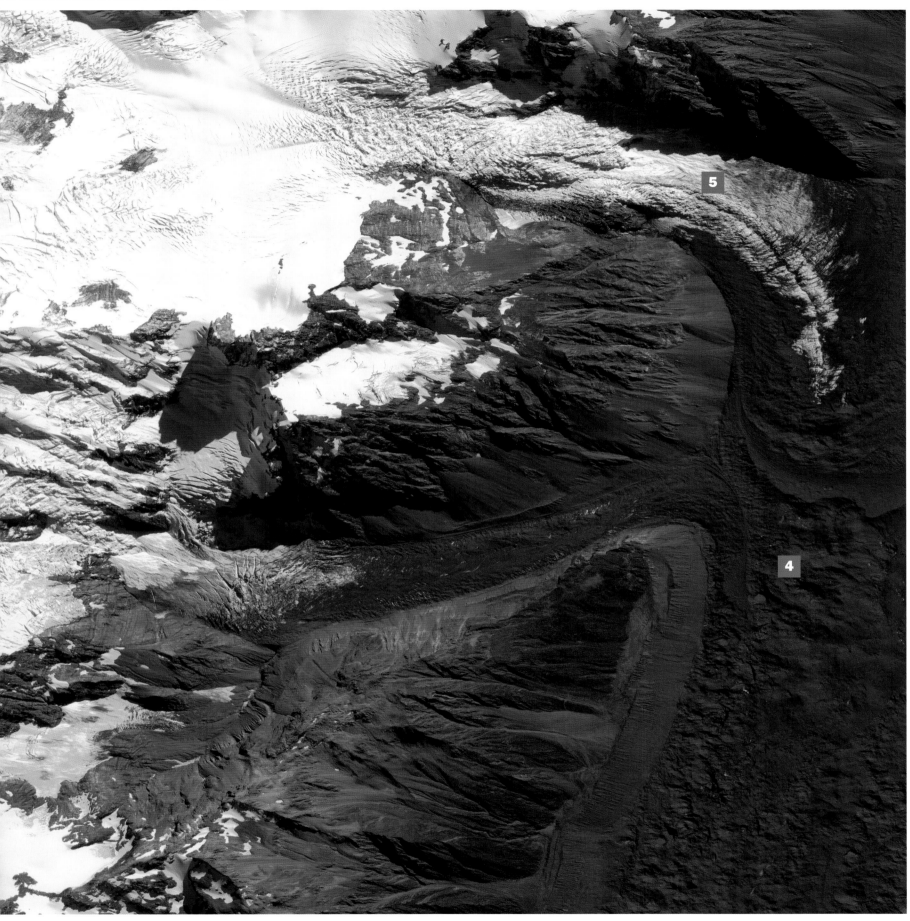

① *Mount Cook Massif* ←

The Tangata Whenua regard the mountain as the dwelling place of their ancestors. This is why, for them, Aoraki is a sacred mountain and one that they must not climb. Both as a sacred mountain for the Maori, and as a mountaineering challenge for New Zealand's European immigrants, it has inspired many legends. It is awesomely bleak and wild: Because of its exposed location, the mountain experiences severe weather conditions and long-lasting storms.

② Mount Cook Range

The high alpine environment of the Mount Cook Range is one of New Zealand's main tourist attractions. Many hiking trails, most of which start at Mount Cook Village, on the southwestern edge of the Mount Cook Range, lead up into the higher mountains and to dramatic glaciers.

③ Summit of Mount Cook

In January 1992, ice and rocks broke off the summit, reducing the height of the mountain by 20 m (66 ft), so that its present height reaches 3754 m (12,316 ft). The crest of the mountain is deeply fissured, and consists of three main peaks. The first expedition to reach the summit did so in December 1894. Since then, other attempts have been made, although sudden changes in weather conditions, as well as avalanches and crevasses, have claimed many lives.

④ Tasman Glacier

The Mount Cook Massif contains five large glaciers, and the peak itself is encircled by two long outlet glaciers. The Hooker Glacier lies on the west side of the mountain. The Tasman Glacier lies on its eastern side; it is fed by several glaciers from Mount Cook.

⑤ Hochstetter Icefall

The spectacular Hochstetter Icefall flows from the huge Grand Plateau (the brilliant white ice field visible to the east of the summit of Mount Cook in the satellite image) into the Tasman Glacier. The Hochstetter Icefall is a huge amphitheater consisting of ice cut into by deep crevasses.

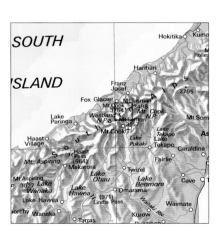

Vanuatu, New Caledonia, Fiji

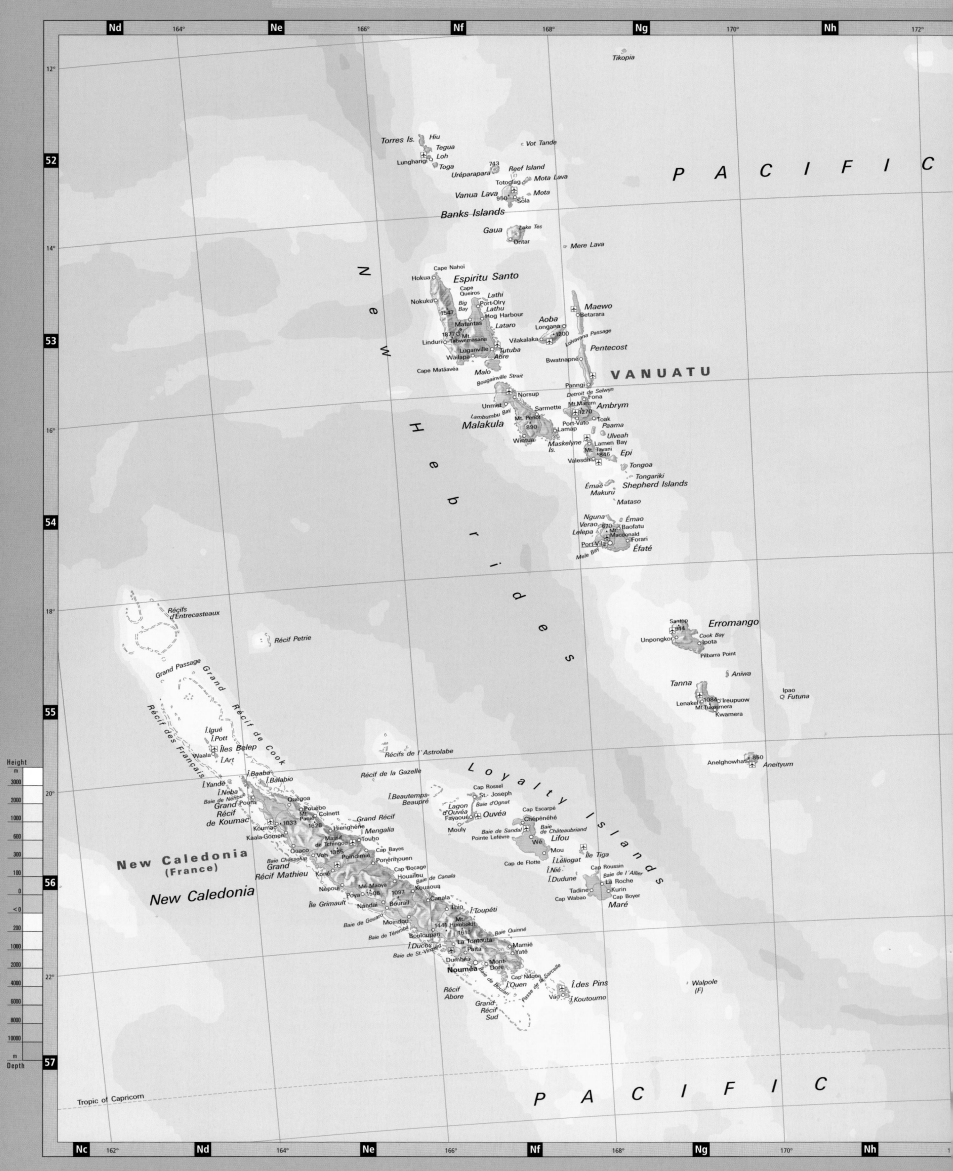

Nd 164° **Ne** 166° **Nf** 168° **Ng** 170° **Nh** 172°

12°

P A C I F I C

Tikopia

52

Torres Is.   Hiu
                Tegua   Vot Tande
         Loh
Lunghangir Toga   743   Reef Island
         Uréparapara   Mota Lava
                Totoglag   Mota
         Vanua Lava 950 Sola

Banks Islands

14°   Gaua Lake Tes
                Ontar   Mere Lava

N   Cape Nahoi
e   Hokua   *Espiritu Santo*
w   Cape
             Queiros   Lathi
     Nokuku   Port-Olry
             Big   Lathu
             Bay   Hog Harbour   Maewo
         1547   Lataro   Betarara
             Matantas   Aoba
53   1879 Mt. Longana
     Linduri Tabwemasana   Vilakalaka 1200 Lolowana Passage
         Luganville Tutuba   *Pentecost*
         Wailapa   Aore
                        Bwatnapné
     Cape Matáavéa   Malo
             Bougainville Strait   Panngi
                    Detroit de Selwyn   *V A N U A T U*
             Norsup   Fona
         Unmet   Mt.Marum   *Ambrym*
H   Sarmette 1270
e   Lambumbu Bay Mt. Pendi   Toak
b   *Malakula* 890   Port-Vato Paama
r   Wiantua   Lamap   *Ulveah*
i   Maskelyne   Lamen Bay
d   Is.   Mt. Tavani *Epi*
e   Valesdir   846   Tongoa
s   Tongariki
             Émaé   *Shepherd Islands*
             Makurú   Mataso

16°

54   Nguna   *Émao*
         Verao 670 Baofatu
         Lelepa Mt. Macdonald
         Port-Vila Forari
         Mele Bay   *Éfaté*

18°   Récifs
     d'Entrecasteaux   Santop   *Erromango*
                    914
                Unpongkor   Cook Bay
         Récif Petrie   Ipota

                        Pilbarra Point

     Grand Passage   *Tanna*   Aniwa
                            Ipao
G   Futuna
r   Î.Igué
a   Récif des Français Î.Pott   L   Lenakel 1084 Ireupuow
n   Îles Belep   o   Mt.Tukosmera
d   Waala   Î. Art   y   Kwamera
         Î.Baaba   Récif de l'Astrolabe a
R   Î.Yandé   l
é   Î.Noba Î.Balabio Récif de la Gazelle t   Anelghowhat 850 Aneityum
c   Baie de Néhipu Grand Poum   y
i   Quégoa   Cap Rossel
f   Récif Pouébo Colnett   St.- Joseph I
     de Koumac Mt.Panié   Î.Beautemps-   Lagon   s
d   Koumac 1628 Beaupré d'Ouvéa Ouvéa l
e   Kaala-Gomen 1033   Fayaoué Mouly a
C   Hienghéne Grand Récif Baie de Sandal n
o   Touho   Baie de Châteaubriand d
o   Voh Mengalia   Pointe Lefévre We   s
k   Massif   Cap Escarpé   Lifou
     Ouaco de Tchingou Pouindimié   Mou
             Poindimié   Î.Tiga
     New Caledonia   Poindimié   Cap de Flotte Î.Léliogat
     (France)   Kone Ponérihouen   Î.Nié
         Houailou   Î.Dudune Cap Roussin
     Grand   Baie de Bocage   Baie de l'Allier
     Récif Mathieu   Me Maoya Baie de Canala Tadine La Roche
     New Caledonia Nepoui   Kouaoua   Cap Boyer
         Poya 1508 1097   Canala Cap Wabao   *Maré*
     Île Grimault Nandai Bourail   Thio
                Î.Toupéti
         Moindou   Baie Quinné
         Boulouparis Mt.Humboldt
         Î.Ducos 1441 1618 La Tontouta Mamié
     Baie de Térembé   Plaita Yaté
     Baie de St-Vincent   Dumbéa Mont-
         Nouméa Dore
                Cap Ndoua Î.des Pins *Walpole*
     Récif   Î.Ouen   (F)
     Aboré   Grand   Passe de la Sarcelle
         Récif   Vao Î.Koutoumo
         Sud

20°

22°

Tropic of Capricorn

P A C I F I C

Height
m
3000
2000
1000
600
300
100
0
< 0
200
1000
2000
4000
6000
8000
10000
m
Depth

0 25 50 75 100 125 miles
1:4,500,000
0 50 100 150 200km
Albers Equal Area Conic Projection

Nc 162° **Nd** 164° **Ne** 166° **Nf** 168° **Ng** 170° **Nh**

Nj   174°   Nk   176°   Nl   178°   Nm   180°   Aa   178°   Ab

Rotuma

O C E A N

Wallis and Futuna (F)

14°

Futuna
Alofi

52

53

Thikombia

Vetauua

Great Sea Reef   Great Sea Reef   Udu Point   Nggelelevu
Kia   Mali   Lagalaga
Yaqaga   Nabavatu   Naravuka   Labasa   Rabi   Yanuca
Nadun   Nalewa Bay   Nanuku Passage
Yadua   Vanua Levu   Buca   Kioa   Thakaundrove
Bua   Nasorolevu   Peninse   Laucala
Matacawa Levu   Yasawa   Bua   1032   Somosomo   Qamea
Yasawa   Nacula   Bay   Nabouwalu   Savusavu   Somosomo   1241   Taveuni
Group   388 Yaqeta   Bligh Water   Ulunggalau   Naitaba
Viwa   Naviti   Vanua
579   Vatukira Channel   Yacata   Malima   Balavu
Waya   Koro   Kanacea   Lomaloma

54

Mamanutha   Nailaga   Tavua   Rakiraki   Vatu Vara   Mago
   Mana   Ba   Vatukoula   Natovi   Wakaya   Northern Lau Group
Group   Malolo   Nadi   Tomanivi   Korovou   Levuka   Batiki   Koro Sea
    Keiyasi   1323   Ovalau   Cicia
     Viti Levu   Moturiki   Nairai   Nayau
Sigatoka   Korolevu   Lami   Nausori   Sawaleka   Ngau   Lakemba Passage

18°

Lakemba   Tabou
Suva   Vanua Vatu   Oneata
Beqa   FIJI   Moala   Southern
Vatulele   Kandavu Passage   Lau Group   Moce
    Bulia   Moala   Komo
   Kandavu   Ono   Group   Totoya   Tavu Na Sici   Namuka-i-Lau
   Tavuki   Vunisea   372   363   Kabara
   840   Bay   Matuku   Fulanga   Ogea Levu
Cape Washington   Ogea Oriki

390

55

Vatoa

20°

Onoilau

56

22°

O C E A N

Tropic of Capricorn

57

24°

Nj   174°   Nk   176°   Nl   178°   Nm   180°   Aa   178°   Ab

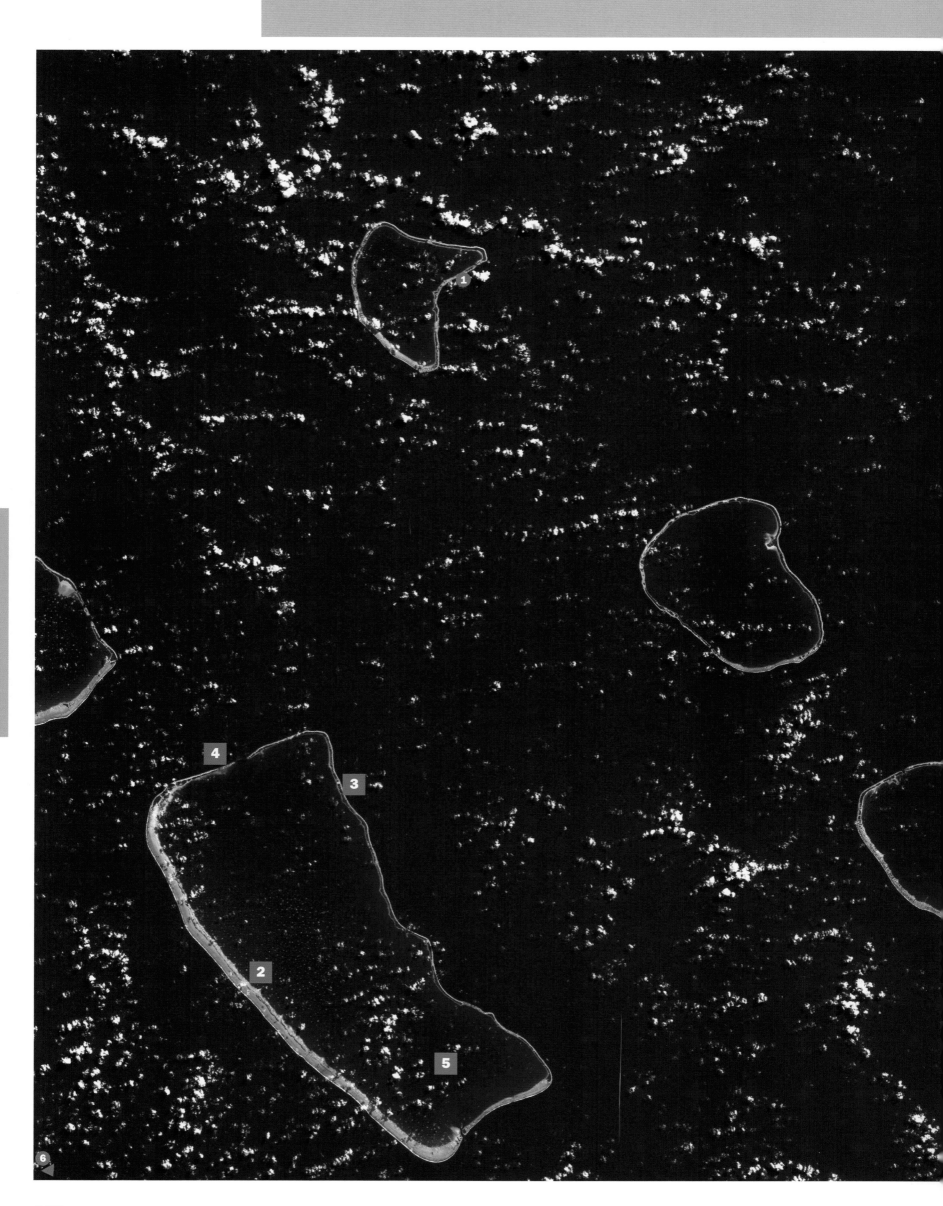

N

1 *Atolls* ↓

The section of the Tuamotu Archipelago shown in the satellite image includes some of its flat, low-lying atolls, which rise only slightly above sea level. The word "atoll" is derived from atolhu, a word in the language of the inhabitants of the Maldive Islands, and is a circular coral reef enclosing a lagoon. Over several hundred years, coral can grow to form high, sometimes mountainous reefs. Preconditions for the growth of coral are clear water that is rich in oxygen and nutrients, sufficient salinity, light, and water temperatures of not less than 20°C (68°F).

Atolls are created in different ways. Some are formed when coral grows on the craters of extinct volcanoes that are submerged below the surface of the ocean. Volcanoes may become submerged either as the result of erosion by waves and

Tuamotu Islands

The South Sea Islands that are now French overseas territories are among the most beautiful islands in the world. French Polynesia, in the middle of the Pacific Ocean, consists of several groups of islands, or archipelagoes. The main group is the Society Islands, and of these Tahiti is the best known. North of the Society Islands lie the Marquesas Islands: Between these two groups are the 76 atolls that make up the Tuamotu Islands. Partly because of their isolated location and partly because of their feeble economies, all the Polynesian Islands are heavily dependent on France, their old colonial power. For reasons of military defense and as a reflection of the country's self-image as a world power, France assures the Polynesian Islands' economic survival through financial support and other forms of investment.

weather or because of tectonic processes affecting the sea bed. Since coral requires a certain amount of light to grow, it is found only up to a depth of 40 m (130 ft). As the coral grows, the reef spreads all around the volcanic crater, building up into an increasingly high atoll.

2 Fakarava

Fakarava, the main island of the Tuamotu Archipelago, lies some 450 km (280 miles) northeast of Tahiti. It is one of the most beautiful atolls in the world. About 60 km (37 miles) high and 25 km (16 miles) wide, it is the second-largest atoll in Polynesia. Two villages are located on it: Rotoava, in the northeast, and Tetamanu, once the main town, in the south. The atoll is largely unspoilt, and most of its buildings are in the traditional style. Because dead coral does not

produce very fertile soil, the atoll has only a small area of land that is suitable for agriculture. This is why its inhabitants, who number some 400, rely mainly on fishing for their livelihood. Other sources of revenue are the cultivation of black pearls and a modest tourist industry supported by the small number of tourists who come for the island's spectacular diving opportunites.

3 Rotoava Diving Center

Rotoava, an atoll that is a UNESCO Biosphere Reserve, is comparatively unspoilt. Rare species of birds, forests of coconut trees, and a unique underwater world make up its almost pristine ecosystem. Although it is relatively remote from the well-known tourist destinations in French Polynesia, Rotoava is being discovered by growing numbers of foreign visitors, who come to enjoy its beaches and to dive in its warm waters. Beyond its almost deserted, white-sand beaches, the edges of the atoll drop sharply: The deep waters here teem with colorful marine plants and animals. There is a diving center in Rotoava and, somewhat unusually for an atoll, a very comfortable hotel.

4 Reef Passes

The lagoon on the north side of Fakarava atoll is connected to the open ocean by an underwater channel, the Garuae Pass. About 800 m (2625 ft) wide, this is the widest reef pass in Polynesia. The channel leading from the lagoon on the south side of Fakarava is the Passe Sud or Tumakohua Pass, which is no more than 200 m (656 ft) wide.

5 Lagoon

The Fakarava atoll encircles a 1121 km² (433 square mile) lagoon. As in most lagoons, the water is shallow here. Because of its sheltered location, the lagoon is particularly attractive to snorkelers.

6 *Moorea* ↓

The topography of the islands of French Polynesia ranges from low-lying coral atolls to imposing volcanic mountains. A fine example of the latter is Moorea, a mountainous island that can be seen from Tahiti. Moorea is a raised island, on which old coral was deposited as a result of volcanic activity above sea level. It consists of several rocky massifs.

French

Tuamotu Islands

Îles du
Roi- Georges   Napuka
taiva   Pukapuka
Rangiroa
        Fakarava
Niau   Katiu
        Makemo
chine   Marutea Tatakoto
Papeete   Anaa   Amanu
Tahiti   Pukarua
        Marokau   Hao
    Nengonengo
            Ahunui
                    Turéia
            Vanavana   Tén
lynesia
(F)   Tematangi   Mururoa
                Acteon

Tonga, Samoa

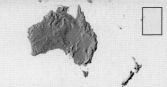

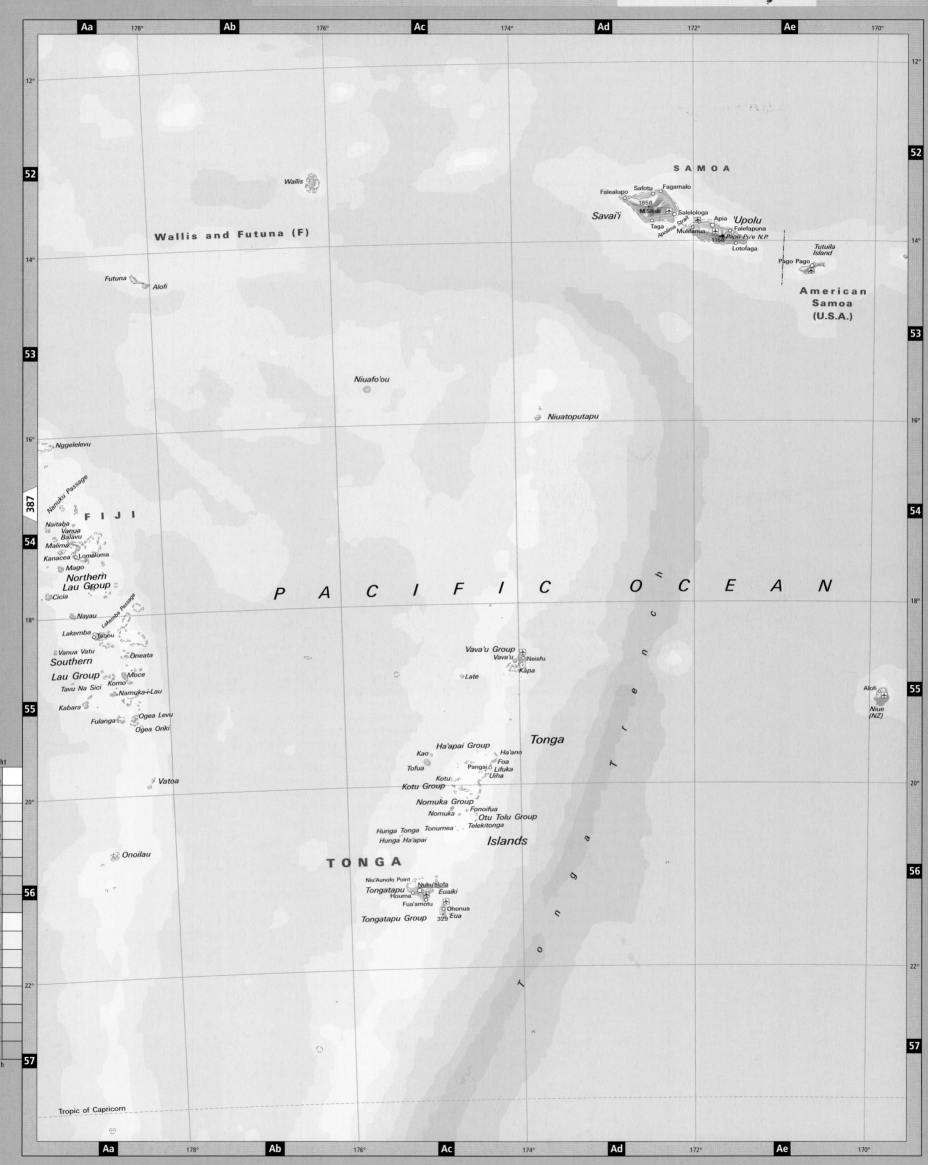

Aa · 178° · Ab · 176° · Ac · 174° · Ad · 172° · Ae · 170°

12°

52

S A M O A

Wallis

Falealupo Safotu Fagamalo
1858
Savai'i M. Silisili Salelologa
Taga Apolima Strait Apia 'Upolu
Mulifanua Falefapuna
Wallis and Futuna (F) Papū Pu'e N.P.
Lotofaga
14°

Futuna Alofi *Tutuila Island*

Pago Pago

**A m e r i c a n
S a m o a
(U.S.A.)**

53

Niuafo'ou

16°

Niuatoputapu

16° Nggelelevu

Namuku Passage
387

F I J I

Naitaba
Vanua
Balavu
Malima
Kanacea Lomaloma
Mago
**Northern
Lau Group**
Cicia

54

Nayau
18° Lakemba Tabou

P A C I F I C   O C E A N

18°

Vanua Vatu Oneata
**Southern
Lau Group** Moce
Tavu Na Sici Komo
Namuka-i-Lau

Kabara

Vava'u Group
Vava'u Neiafu
Late Kapa

Alofi

*Niue
(NZ)*

55

Fulanga Ogea Levu
Ogea Oriki

Tonga

Ha'apai Group
Kao Ha'ano
Tofua Foa
Pangai Lifuka
Uiha
Kotu Kotu
Vatoa **Kotu Group**
20° **Nomuka Group**
Nomuka Fonoifua
Otu Tolu Group
Telekitonga
Hunga Tonga Tonumea
Hunga Ha'apai **Islands**

56

T O N G A

Onoilau

Niu'Aunofo Point
Tongatapu Nuku'alofa
Houma Euaiki
Fua'amotu
Ohonua
Tongatapu Group 325 Eua

22°

Tropic of Capricorn

Aa · Ab · 178° · 176° · Ac · 174° · Ad · 172° · Ae · 170°

Height
m
3000
2000
1000
600
300
100
0
< 0
200
1000
2000
4000
6000
8000
10000
m
Depth

0 25 50 75 100 125 miles
1:4,500,000
0 50 100 150 200km
Albers Equal Area Conic Projection

A

Abb.	Abbay (Fr.) abbey
Abor.	Aboriginal (Engl.)
Ad.	Adasi (Turk.) island
Ág.	Ágios (Gr.) saint
Á.I.	Área Indígena (Port.) Indian reservation
Arch.	Archipiélago (Span.) archipelago
Arr.	Arroyo (Span.) brook
Austr.	Australia (Engl.)
Aut.	autonomous (Engl.)
Aut.Reg.	autonomous region (Engl.)

B

B.	Baie (Fr.) bay
Ba.	Bahía (Span.) bay
Bal.	Balka (Rus.) gorge
Ban.	Banjaran (Mal.) mountains
Bel.	Belo,-yj, -aja, -oe (Rus.) white
Bk.	Bukit (Mal.) mountain
Bol.	Bolšoj, -aja, -oe (Rus.) big
Bol.	Boloto (Rus.) swamp
Bot.	Botanical (Engl.)
B.P.	Battlefield Park (Engl.)
Bras.	Brasil (Port.) Brazil
Brj.	Baraj (Turk.) dam
Buh.	Buhta (Rus.) bay

C

C.	Cape (Engl.)
C.	Cap (Fr.) cape
C.	Cabo (Port., Span.) cape
C.	Candi (Indon.) gate
Cach.	Cachoeira (Port.) rapids
Can.	Canal (Span.) canal
Cast.	Castello (Ital.) castle, palace
Cd.	Ciudad (Span.) city
Cga.	Ciénaga (Span.) swamp
Chr.	Chrebet (Ukr.) mountains
Co.	Cerro (Span.) mountain
Col.	Colonia (Span.) colony
Cord.	Cordillera (Span.) mountain chain
Corr.	Corredeira (Port.) rapids
Cpo.	Campo (Port.) field
Cr.	Creek (Engl.)

D

D.	Dake (Jap.) mountain
D.	Danau (Indon.) lake
Dagl.	Daglar (Turk.) mountains

E

Emb.	Embalse (Span.) reservoir
Ens.	Ensenada (Span.) small bay
Esp.	España (Span.) Spain
Est.	Estación (Span.) railway station
Est.	Estrecho (Span.) strait, sound

F

Fin.	Finland (Engl.)
Fk.	Fork (Engl.)
Fr.	France (Engl.)
Fs.	Falls (Engl.) falls, waterfall
Ft.	Fort (Engl.)

G

G.	Gunung (Indon.) mountain
G.	Gora (Rus.) mountain
G.	Gabal (Arab.) mountain
Gde.	Grande (Span.) big
Gds.	Grandes (Span.) big
Gr.	Greece (Engl.)
Gr.	Grove (Engl.)
Grd.	Grand (Fr.) big
Grl.	General (Span.) general

H

H.	Hora (Ukr.) mountain
Harb.	Harbour (Engl.)
Hist.	Historic (Engl.)
Hr.	Hrebet (Rus.) mountains
Hte	Haute (Fr.) high
Hts.	Heights (Engl.)

I

I.	Ilha (Port.) island
I.	Island (Engl.)
I.	Isla (Span.) island
Î.	Île (Fr.) island
Igl.	Iglesia (Span.) church
Ind.	Indian (Engl.)
Ind.	India (Engl.)
Ind.Res.	Indian reservation (Engl.)
Is.	Islands (Engl.)
Îs.	Îles (Fr.) islands
It.	Italia (Ital.) Italy

J

Jct.	Junction (Engl.)
Juz.	Juznyj, -aja (Rus.) southern

K

Kan.	Kanal (Ger.) canal
Kep.	Kepulauan (Indon.) archipelago
Kg.	Kampung (Indon.) village
K-l.	Küli (Uzbek.) lake
K-l.	Kölí (Kazakh.) lake
Kör.	Körfez (Turk.) bay, gulf
Kp.	Kólpos (Gr.) bay, gulf
Kr.	Krasno, -yj, -aja, -oe (Rus.) red

L

L.	Lac (Fr.) lake
L.	Lake (Engl.)
Lag.	Laguna (Span.) lagoon
Lag.	Laguna (Rus.) lagoon
Lev.	Levje, -aja (Rus.) left
Lim.	Liman (Rus.) lagoon
Lim.	Limni (Gr.) lake
Lte.	Little (Engl.)

M

M.	Mys (Rus.) cape
Mal.	Malaysia (Engl.)
Mal.	Malo, -yj, -aja, -oe (Rus.) little
Man.	Manastir (Bulg.) monastery
Man.	Manastir (Turk.) monastery
Man.	Manastire (Rom.) monastery
Mem.	Memorial (Engl.)
Mgne	Montagne (Fr.) mountains
Mi.	Misaki (Jap.) cape
Mñas.	Montañas (Span.) mountains
Mon.	Monasterio (Span.) monastery
Mt	Mont (Fr.) mountain
Mt.	Mount (Engl.)
Mte.	Monte (Span.) mountain
Mti.	Monti (Ital.) mountains
Mtn.	Mountain (Engl.)
Mtns.	Mountains (Engl.)
Mtn.S.P.	Mountain State Park (Engl.)
Mts.	Mountains (Engl.)
Mts.	Montes (Span.) mountains
Mus.	Museum (Engl.)

N

Nac.	Nacional (Span.) national
Nac.	National'nyj, -aja, -oe (Rus.) national
Nat.	National (Engl.)
Nat.Mon.	National Monument (Engl.)
Nat.P.	National Park (Engl.)
Nat.Seas.	National Seashore (Engl.)
Naz.	Nazionale (Ital.) national
N.B.P.	National Battlefield Park (Engl.)
N.B.S.	National Battlefield Site (Engl.)

Ned. ...

Ned.	Nederland (Neth.) Netherlands
N.H.P.	National Historic Park (Engl.)
N.H.S.	National Historic Site (Engl.)
Niz.	Nize, -nij, -naja, -neje (Rus.) lower
Nizm.	Nizmenost' (Rus.) lowlands
N.M.P.	National Military Park (Engl.)
Nov.	Novo, -yj, -aja, -oe (Rus.) new
N.P.	National Park (Engl.)
Nth.	North (Engl.)
Nva.	Nueva (Span.) new
Nvo.	Nuevo (Span.) new
N.W.R.	National Wildlife Refuge (Engl.)
N.Z.	New Zealand (Engl.)

O

O.	Ostrov (Rus.) island
Obl.	Oblast (Rus.) district
O-va.	Ostrova (Rus.) islands
Oz.	Ozero (Rus.) lake

P

P.	Parque (Span.) park
P.	Passe (Fr.) pass
P.	Pico (Span.) peak
P.	Port (Engl.)
P.	Pulau (Indon.) island
Peg.	Pegunungan (Indon.) mountains
Pen.	Península (Span.) peninsula
Per.	Pereval (Rus.) pass
Pk.	Peak (Engl.)
P.N.	Parque National (Span.) national park
Po.	Paso (Span.) pass
Pol.	Polska (Pol.) Poland
Por.	Porog (Rus.) rapids
P-ov.	Poluostrov (Rus.) peninsula
Pr.	Proliv (Rus.) strait, sound
Presq.	Presq´île (Fr.) peninsula
Prov.	Provincial (Engl.)
Prov. P.	Provincial Park (Engl.)
Pso.	Passo (Ital.) pass
Pt.	Port (Engl.)
Pt.	Point (Engl.)
Pta.	Punta (Span.) cape, point
Pte.	Pointe (Fr.) cape, point
Pto.	Puerto (Span.) port, pass

R

Río	Río (Span.) river
R.	Rio (Port.) river
Ra.	Range (Engl.)
Rdl.	Raudal (Span.) stream
Rep.	Republic (Engl.)
Repr.	Represa (Port.) dam
Rère	Rivière (Fr.) river
Res.	Reserva (Port.) reservation
Res.	Reservoir (Engl.)
Resp.	Respublika (Rus.) republic
Rib.	Ribeiro (Port.) small river
Rib.	Ribeira (Port.) shore
Riv.	River (Engl.)

S

S.	São (Port.) saint
S.	San (Jap.) mountain
S.	San (Span.) saint
Sa.	Serra (Port.) mountains
Sa.	Saki (Jap.) cape
S.Afr.	South Africa (Engl.)
Sal.	Salar (Span.) salt desert
Sanm.	Sanmyaku (Jap.) mountains
Sd.	Sound (Engl.)
Sel.	Selat (Indon.) strait, sound
Sev.	Sever, -nyj, -naja, -noe (Rus.) north
Sh.	Shima (Jap.) island
S.H.P.	State Historic Park (Engl.)
S.H.S.	State Historic Site (Engl.)
S.M.	State Monument (Engl.)
Sna.	Salina (Span.) salt flat
Snía.	Serranía (Span.) ridge
S.P.	State Park (Engl.)
Sprs.	Springs (Engl.)

Sr. ...

Sr.	Sredne, -ij, -aja, -ee (Rus.) central
Sra.	Sierra (Span.) mountains
St.	Saint (Engl.)
Sta.	Santa (Span.) saint
Sta.	Staro, -yi, -aja, -oe (Rus.) old
Ste.	Sainte (Fr.) saint
Sth.	South (Engl.)
St. Mem.	State Memorial (Engl.)
Sto.	Santo (Port.) saint
Str.	Strait (Engl.)
Suh.	Suho, -aja (Rus.) dry
Sver.	Sverige (Swed.) Sweden

T

T.	Take (Jap.) peak
Tel.	Teluk (Indon.) bay
Tg.	Tanjung (Indon.) cape

U

U.K.	United Kingdom (Engl.)
Ukr.	Ukraine (Engl.)
Urug.	Uruguay (Engl.)
U.S.	United States (Engl.)
USA	United States of America (Engl.)

V

V.	Vallée (Fr.) valley
Va.	Villa (Span.) town
vdchr.	vodohranilišče (Rus.) reservoir
vdsch.	vodoschovyšče (Ukr.) reservoir
Vel.	Veliko, -ij, -aja, -oe (Rus.) big
Verh.	Verhnie, -yj, -aja, -ee (Rus.) upper
Vill.	Village (Engl.)
Vly.	Valley (Engl.)
Vod.	Vodopad (Rus.) falls, waterfall
Vol.	Volcán (Span.) volcano
Vul.	Vulcano (Philip.) volcano

W

W.	West (Engl.)

Y

Y.	Yama (Jap.) mountains

Z

Zal.	Zaliv (Rus.) gulf, bay
Zap.	Zapadne, -ji, -aja, -noe (Rus.) west
Zapov.	Zapovednik (Rus.) protected area

Index of Map Names

② Icons

▫ .... Country	⌂ .... Island	≈ .... Ocean, Sea	⚲ .... National park
▣ .... Capital city	⌂⌂ .... Mountain range	∼ .... Lake, River	••• .... Reservation
⊙ .... Administrative unit	△ .... Mountain	v .... Undersea topography	★ .... Point of major interest
○ .... Place	⌒ .... Cape	▲ .... Glacier	⌂ .... Landscape

③ Sovereign States and Territories

AFG .... Afghanistan	DOM .... Dominican Republic	LT .... Lithuania	RSM .... San Marino
AL .... Albania	TP .... East Timor	L .... Luxembourg	STP .... São Tomé and Principe
DZ .... Algeria	EC .... Ecuador	MK .... Macedonia	KSA .... Saudi Arabia
AND .... Andorra	ET .... Egypt	RM .... Madagascar	SN .... Senegal
ANG .... Angola	ES .... El Salvador	MW .... Malawi	SCG .... Serbia
AG .... Antigua and Barbuda	GQ .... Equatorial Guinea	MAL .... Malaysia	SY .... Seychelles
RA .... Argentina	ER .... Eritrea	MV .... Maldives	WAL .... Sierra Leone
ARM .... Armenia	EST .... Estonia	RMM .... Mali	SGP .... Singapore
AUS .... Australia	ETH .... Ethiopia	M .... Malta	SK .... Slovakia
A .... Austria	FJI .... Fiji	MA .... Marocco	SLO .... Slovenia
AZ .... Azerbaijan	FIN .... Finland	MH .... Marshall Islands	SOL .... Solomon Islands
BS .... Bahamas	F .... France	RIM .... Mauritania	SP .... Somalia
BRN .... Bahrain	G .... Gabon	MS .... Mauritius	SA .... South Africa
BD .... Bangladesh	WAG .... Gambia	MEX .... Mexico	ROK .... South Korea
BDS .... Barbados	GE .... Georgia	FSM .... Micronesia	E .... Spain
BY .... Belarus	D .... Germany	MD .... Moldova	CL .... Sri Lanka
B .... Belgium	GH .... Ghana	MC .... Monaco	SUD .... Sudan
BH .... Belize	GR .... Greece	MNG .... Mongolia	SME .... Suriname
DY .... Benin	WG .... Grenada	MON .... Montenegro	SD .... Swaziland
BHT .... Bhutan	GCA .... Guatemala	MOC .... Mozambique	S .... Sweden
BOL .... Bolivia	RG .... Guinea	MYA .... Myanmar	CH .... Switzerland
BIH .... Bosnia and Herzegovina	GNB .... Guinea Bissau	NAM .... Namibia	SYR .... Syria
RB .... Botswana	GUY .... Guyana	NAU .... Nauru	RC .... Taiwan
BR .... Brazil	RH .... Haiti	NEP .... Nepal	TJ .... Tajikistan
BRU .... Brunei	HN .... Honduras	NL .... Netherlands	EAT .... Tanzania
BG .... Bulgaria	H .... Hungary	NZ .... New Zealand	THA .... Thailand
BF .... Burkina Faso	IS .... Iceland	NIC .... Nicaragua	RT .... Togo
BU .... Burundi	IND .... India	RN .... Niger	TO .... Tonga
K .... Cambodia	RI .... Indonesia	WAN .... Nigeria	TT .... Trinidad and Tobago
CAM .... Cameroon	IR .... Iran	DVRK .... North Korea	TN .... Tunisia
CDN .... Canada	IRQ .... Iraq	N .... Norway	TR .... Turkey
CV .... Cape Verde	IRL .... Ireland	OM .... Oman	TM .... Turkmenistan
RCA .... Central African Republic	IL .... Israel	PK .... Pakistan	TUV .... Tuvalu
TCH .... Chad	I .... Italy	PAL .... Palau	EAU .... Uganda
RCH .... Chile	JA .... Jamaica	PA .... Panama	UA .... Ukraine
VRC .... China	J .... Japan	PNG .... Papua New Guinea	UAE .... United Arabian Emirates
CO .... Colombia	JOR .... Jordan	PY .... Paraguay	GB .... United Kingdom
COM .... Comoros	KZ .... Kazakhstan	PE .... Peru	USA .... United States of America
RCB .... Congo	EAK .... Kenya	RP .... Philippines	ROU .... Uruguay
CR .... Costa Rica	KIR .... Kiribati	PL .... Poland	UZB .... Uzbekistan
CI .... Côte d'Ivoire	KWT .... Kuwait	P .... Portugal	VU .... Vanuatu
HR .... Croatia	KS .... Kyrgyzstan	Q .... Qatar	V .... Vatican City
C .... Cuba	LAO .... Laos	RO .... Romania	YV .... Venezuela
CY .... Cyprus	LV .... Lativa	RUS .... Russia	VN .... Vietnam
CZ .... Czech Republic	RL .... Lebanon	RWA .... Rwanda	YE .... Yemen
RDC .. Democratic Republic of the Congo	LS .... Lesotho	KN .... Saint Kitts and Nevis	Z .... Zambia
DK .... Denmark	LB .... Liberia	WL .... Saint Lucia	ZW .... Zimbabwe
DJI .... Djibouti	LAR .... Libya	WV .... Saint Vincent and the Grenadines	
WD .... Dominica	FL .... Liechtenstein	WS .... Samoa	

1-9

100 Mile House ○ **CDN** 50 Cb 20
150 Mile House ○ **CDN** 50 Cb 19
1959 Earthquake Area ★ **USA** 51 Cg 23
1st Cataract 〜 **ET** 301 Hj 33
25 de Mayo 〜 **RA** 137 Dp 63
25 de Mayo ○ **RA** 137 Ed 63
25 de Mayo ○ **ROU** 146 Ef 63
31 de Janeiro ○ **ANG** 332 Gp 49
3rd Cataract 〜 **SUD** 312 Hg 36
4th Cataract 〜 **SUD** 313 Hj 36
5th Cataract 〜 **SUD** 313 Hj 36
5th Cataract 〜 **SUD** 313 Hj 36
6th Cataract 〜 **SUD** 312 Hj 37
9 de Julio ○ **RA** 137 Ed 63

A

A. Panal 〜 **RI** 270 La 44
A. Sodré ○ **BR** 146 Eg 61
Aachen ○ **D** 163 Gk 20
Aadan Yabaal ○ **SP** 328 Jb 44
Äänekoski ○ **FIN** 159 He 14
Aansluit ○ **ZA** 349 Hd 59
Aarau ○ **CH** 174 Gl 22
Aare 〜 **CH** 163 Gk 22
Aars ○ **DK** 170 Gl 17
Aba ○ **VRC** 242 La 29
Aba ○ **WAN** 320 Gk 43
Aba ○ **RDC** 324 Hh 44
Abā ad-Dūd ○ **KSA** 215 Hp 32
Abā ar-Ruḩām ○ **KSA** 218 Ja 36
Abacaxis 〜 **BR** 120 Ee 48
Abacaxis ○ **BR** 120 Ee 49
Abaco Island ⌂ **BS** 87 Dk 32
Âbâdân ○ **IR** 215 Je 30
Âbâdeh-ye Ṭašk ○ **IR** 215 Je 31
Abadhara ○ **GE** 202 Hn 24
Abadia dos Dourados ○ **BR** 133 El 55
Abadla ○ **DZ** 293 Ge 30
Abaeté ○ **BR** 133 Em 55
Abaeté 〜 **BR** 133 Em 55
Abaetetuba ○ **BR** 121 Ek 46
Abaí ○ **PY** 140 Eg 58
Abaida △ **DJI** 328 Hp 40
Abaíra ○ **BR** 125 Ep 52
Abaji ○ **WAN** 320 Gk 41
Abak ○ **WAN** 320 Gk 43
Abakaliki ○ **WAN** 320 Gk 42
Abakan ○ **RUS** 204 Tc 8
Abakan 〜 **RUS** 204 Tc 8
Abala ○ **RN** 308 Gh 38
Abala ○ **RCB** 332 Gp 46
Abalak ○ **RN** 308 Gk 38
Abalemma ○ **RN** 308 Gk 37
Abalessa ○ **DZ** 308 Gj 34
Abancay ○ **PE** 128 Dn 52
Abanga 〜 **G** 332 Gm 45
Abapó ○ **BOL** 129 Ec 55
Abar al-Maši ○ **KSA** 214 Hm 33
Abaré ○ **BR** 124 Fa 50
Abarqū ○ **IR** 215 Je 30
Abashiri ○ **J** 250 Mj 23
Abasolo ○ **MEX** 80 Ck 33
Abasolo ○ **MEX** 92 Cn 34
Abasula 〜 **EAK** 337 Hm 46
Abaucán 〜 **RA** 136 Ea 60
Abaura Island ⌂ **PNG** 286 Mh 50
Ābaya Hāyk' 〜 **ETH** 325 Hl 42
Abaza ○ **RUS** 204 Tc 8
Abba ○ **RCA** 321 Gp 43
Abba-Omege ○ **WAN** 320 Gl 42
Abbâsâbâd ○ **IR** 222 Jg 27
Abbāsābād ○ **IR** 226 Jf 30
Abbazia di Montecassino ✶ **I** 185 Gn 25
Abbeville ○ **USA** 71 Dg 28
Abbeville ○ **USA** 86 Db 31
Abbeville ○ **USA** 86 Df 30
Abbeville ○ **F** 163 Gg 20
Abbey ○ **CDN** 51 Cn 20
Abbieglassie ○ **AUS** 375 Mk 59
Abbot Ice Shelf ⬟ **⚑** 38 Ea 17
Abbotsford ○ **CDN** 50 Ca 21
Abbotsford ○ **USA** 56 Dc 23
Abbott ○ **USA** 65 Cx 27
Abbottābād ○ **PK** 230 Ka 28
'Abd al-Kūri ⌂ **YE** 219 Je 39
Abd al-Māgid ○ **SUD** 312 Hj 38
Âbdân ○ **IR** 215 Jd 31
Abdânân ○ **IR** 209 Jb 29
Abdelcader ○ **SP** 328 Hp 40
Abdj ○ **TCH** 321 Hc 39
Abdul Hakim ○ **PK** 227 Jp 30
Abéché ○ **TCH** 309 Hc 39
Ab-e Estâde 〜 **AFG** 223 Jm 29
Abeibara ○ **RMM** 305 Gg 36
Abejales ○ **YV** 107 Dn 42
Abélajouad ○ **RN** 308 Gk 37
Abelardo Luz ○ **BR** 140 Eh 59
Abel Tasman ⚑ **NZ** 383 Nj 66
Åbeltī ○ **ETH** 325 Hl 41
Abemarre ○ **RI** 286 Mg 49
Abenab ○ **NAM** 340 Hb 55
Abenelang ○ **GQ** 332 Gm 45
Abengourou ○ **CI** 317 Ge 42
Abenójar ○ **E** 184 Gg 24
Àbenrå ○ **DK** 170 Gl 18
Abeokuta ○ **WAN** 320 Gh 42
Abepura ○ **RI** 286 Mg 47
Abercrombie ○ **USA** 56 Cp 22
Abercrombie 〜 **AUS** 379 Ml 63
Aberdare ⚑ **EAK** 337 Hl 46
Aberdeen ○ **USA** 50 Ca 22
Aberdeen ○ **CDN** 51 Cj 19
Aberdeen ○ **USA** 56 Cn 23
Aberdeen ○ **USA** 74 Dk 26
Aberdeen ○ **USA** 86 Dd 29
Aberdeen ○ **ZA** 358 Hd 62
Aberdeen Lake 〜 **CDN** 42 Fb 6
Aberdeen Road ○ **ZA** 358 Hd 62
Àbergelê ○ **ETH** 313 Hm 39
Abergowrie ○ **AUS** 365 Mj 55
Abernathy ○ **USA** 70 Cm 29
Abernethy ○ **CDN** 51 Cl 20
Aberystwyth ○ **GB** 163 Gd 19

Āb-e Seimarre 〜 **IR** 209 Jb 29
Âb-e Sirvân 〜 **IRQ** 209 Ja 28
Âb-e Zimkân 〜 **IR** 209 Jb 28
Abganerovo ○ **RUS** 181 Ja 21
Abgué ○ **TCH** 321 Hb 40
Abhā ○ **KSA** 218 Hp 36
Abhāna ○ **IND** 234 Kd 34
Abhar 〜 **IR** 209 Jc 27
Âbhê Bad 〜 **DJI** 328 Hp 40
Åbhê Bid Hãyk' 〜 **ETH** 313 Hn 40
Abīdīya ○ **SUD** 312 Hj 36
Abidjan ○ **CI** 317 Ge 43
Abiekwasputs ○ **ZA** 348 Hc 59
Abilene ○ **USA** 70 Cn 29
Abilene ○ **USA** 70 Cp 26
Abingdon ○ **USA** 71 Dg 27
Abingdon Downs ○ **AUS** 365 Mh 54
Abinsi ○ **WAN** 320 Gl 42
Abinsk ○ **RUS** 202 Hm 23
Abiquin ○ **USA** 65 Cj 27
Abiramam ○ **IND** 239 Kd 41
Abisko ◉ **S** 158 Hb 11
Abisko ◉ **S** 158 Hb 11
Abitibi River 〜 **CDN** 57 Dh 20
Âbīy Âdī ○ **ETH** 313 Hm 39
Abīyata Hãyk' 〜 **ETH** 325 Hm 42
Abjelil ○ **MA** 293 Gd 28
Abminga ○ **AUS** 374 Md 59
Abnūb ○ **ET** 301 Hh 32
Aboabo ○ **RP** 266 Lk 41
Abobo ○ **ETH** 325 Hk 42
Aboh ○ **WAN** 320 Gk 43
Abohar ○ **IND** 230 Kb 30
Aboine 〜 **WAN** 320 Gk 42
Aboki ○ **EAU** 324 Hj 44
Abolo ○ **RCB** 332 Gn 45
Abomey ○ **DY** 317 Gg 42
Abomey-Calavi ○ **DY** 317 Gh 42
Âbomsa ○ **ETH** 325 Hm 41
Abong Mbang ○ **CAM** 321 Gn 44
Aboriginal Hopevale Reserve ••• **AUS** 365 Mj 53
Aborlan ○ **RP** 267 Lk 41
Aboua ○ **RCB** 332 Gp 45
Abou-Déïa ○ **TCH** 321 Hb 40
Abou Goulem ○ **TCH** 309 Hc 39
Aboukoussom ○ **TCH** 321 Hc 40
Aboun ○ **G** 332 Gl 45
Abovjan ○ **ARM** 202 Ja 25
Abra Carpish △ **PE** 116 Dl 50
Abraham Lincoln N.H.S. ★ **USA** 71 Df 27
Abraham's Bay ○ **BS** 87 Dm 34
Abra Huashuaccasa △ **PE** 128 Dm 53
Abraka ○ **WAN** 320 Gk 43
Abra la Cruz Chica △ **BOL** 136 Eb 56
Abrams ○ **USA** 57 Dd 23
Abrantes ○ **P** 184 Gb 26
Abra Pampa ○ **PY** 136 Eb 57
Abrau-Djurso ○ **RUS** 195 Hl 23
Abre Campo ○ **BR** 141 En 56
Abregro ○ **DY** 317 Gh 42
Abrem ○ **GH** 317 Gf 43
Abreu ○ **MOC** 344 Hl 55
Abrolhos Bank ⎍ **BR** 141 Fa 55
Abrud ○ **RO** 175 Hd 22
'Abs ○ **YE** 218 Hp 37
Absaroka Range ⚠ **USA** 51 Cg 23
Ab Touyour ○ **TCH** 321 Ha 40
Abu ○ **GNB** 316 Fn 40
Abu al Abyad ⌂ **UAE** 215 Je 33
Abū' Alī ⌂ **KSA** 214 Hk 28
Abū ' Arîš ⌂ **KSA** 218 Hp 37
Abū 'Ammār ○ **SUD** 313 Hh 37
Abū Ballās ○ **ET** 300 Hf 33
Abū Darba ○ **ET** 301 Hj 31
Abū Dariha ○ **SYR** 208 Hj 28
Abū Dawn ○ **SUD** 312 Hj 37
Abū Dhabi ▣ **UAE** 215 Je 33
Abū Dīs ○ **SUD** 312 Hj 36
Abū Dom ○ **SUD** 312 Hh 37
Abū Dulayq ○ **SUD** 313 Hj 38
Abufan ○ **BR** 117 Ce 48
Abū Faruh ○ **IRQ** 209 Hp 28
Abū Gâbra ○ **SUD** 312 Hf 40
Abū Ghirban ○ **SUD** 312 Hh 36
Abugi ○ **WAN** 320 Gk 41
Abū Gisra ○ **IRQ** 215 Ja 30
Abugrin ○ **LAR** 297 Gp 30
Abū Gubayba ○ **SUD** 312 Hh 40
Abū Hamad ○ **SUD** 312 Hj 36
Abū Hashim ○ **SUD** 312 Hh 40
Abū Hugar ○ **SUD** 313 Hj 39
Abuja ▣ **WAN** 320 Gk 41
Abū Kabīr ○ **ET** 301 Hh 30
Abū Kabisa ○ **SUD** 312 Hf 39
Abū Kamâl ○ **SYR** 209 Hn 28
Abukuma 〜 **J** 251 Mg 27
Abū Ḳuraḩ ○ **RP** 267 Ll 36
Abulung 〜 **RP** 267 Ll 36
Abū Maẕtariq ○ **SUD** 312 Hf 40
Abū Mendi ○ **ETH** 313 Hk 40
Abū Mina ★ **ET** 301 Hg 30
Abumombazi ○ **RDC** 321 Hd 44
Abuna 〜 **BR** 117 Ea 50
Abunã ○ **BOL** 117 Eb 50
Âbune Yosêf △ **ETH** 313 Hm 39
Abū Oir ○ **ET** 301 Hg 30
Abū Ouarqâs ○ **ET** 301 Hh 32
Abū Road ○ **IND** 227 Ka 33
Abū Rudeis ○ **ET** 301 Hj 31
Abū Rubua ○ **SUD** 312 Hh 39
Abū Șaffâr ○ **SUD** 313 Hj 37
Abū Simbel ★ **ET** 301 Hh 34
Abū Ṣuwayyir ○ **IRQ** 215 Jb 30
Abuta ○ **J** 250 Mg 24
Abū Tig ○ **ET** 301 Hh 32
Abū Ṭunaytin ○ **SUD** 312 Hh 38
Abū 'Urūq ○ **SUD** 312 Hh 38
Âbuyê Meda △ **ETH** 313 Hm 40
Abuyog ○ **RP** 267 Ln 40
Abū Zabad ○ **SUD** 312 Hg 40
Abū Zanīma ○ **ET** 301 Hj 31
Abū Zayyân ○ **ET** 297 Gn 29
Abwong ○ **SUD** 324 Hj 41
Abyad ○ **SUD** 312 Hf 39
Abyâr Ali 〜 **KSA** 214 Hm 33
Abyâr ash Shuwayrif ○ **LAR** 297 Gn 31

Abydos ○ **AUS** 360 Lk 56
Abyei ○ **SUD** 324 Hg 41
Âbyek ○ **IR** 222 Jd 28
Ac. Jacurici 〜 **BR** 125 Fa 51
Acacias ○ **CO** 106 Dm 44
Acadia National Park ⚑ **USA** 60 Dp 23
Acadia Valley ○ **CDN** 51 Cg 20
Acahay ○ **PY** 140 Ef 58
Açailândia ○ **BR** 121 El 48
Acajutla ○ **ES** 93 Dc 39
Acala ○ **MEX** 92 Da 37
Acámbaro ○ **MEX** 92 Cm 35
Acampamento Grande ○ **BR** 120 Eh 45
Acampamento da Cameia ○ **ANG** 340 Hc 51
Acancéh ○ **MEX** 93 Dd 35
Acandi ○ **CO** 106 Dk 41
Acangatá ○ **BR** 121 Ej 47
Acapetagua ○ **MEX** 93 Db 38
Acaponeta ○ **MEX** 92 Ck 34
Acaponeta 〜 **MEX** 92 Ck 34
Acapu 〜 **BR** 120 Ef 46
Acapulco de Juárez ○ **MEX** 92 Cm 37
Acará 〜 **BR** 117 Ec 49
Acará ○ **BR** 121 Ek 46
Acará 〜 **BR** 121 Eh 47
Acarai 〜 **BR** 121 Ek 47
Acará-Mirim 〜 **BR** 121 Ek 47
Acaraú ○ **BR** 124 Eg 47
Acaraú 〜 **BR** 124 Ep 47
Acaré 〜 **BR** 121 Ek 47
Acari ○ **BR** 120 Ee 48
Acari 〜 **BR** 120 Ee 49
Acari ○ **PE** 128 Dl 53
Acarigua ○ **YV** 107 Dp 41
Acari Mountains ⚠ **BR** 120 Ee 45
Acasio ○ **BOL** 129 Eb 54
Acatlán ○ **MEX** 92 Cn 36
Acatlán ○ **MEX** 93 Cp 36
Acayucan ○ **MEX** 93 Da 37
Accomac ○ **USA** 74 Dl 27
Accomac ○ **USA** 74 Dl 27
Accra ▣ **GH** 317 Gf 43
Acebuches ○ **MEX** 81 Cl 31
Acegua ○ **ROU** 146 Eg 61
Achaacha ○ **DZ** 293 Gg 27
Achacachi ○ **BOL** 129 Dp 53
Achaguas ○ **YV** 107 Dp 42
Achalpur ○ **IND** 234 Kc 35
Achao ○ **RCH** 147 Dm 67
Achar ○ **ROU** 146 Ef 62
Ach'ara ◉ **GE** 202 Hn 25
Acheb ○ **DZ** 296 Gl 31
Achegmine ○ **RIM** 304 Ga 36
Achelóos 〜 **GR** 194 Hc 26
Achelouma 〜 **RN** 309 Gn 35
Acheng ○ **VRC** 205 Wb 9
Acheron 〜 **AUS** 379 Mj 64
Achétimaonu 〜 **RN** 308 Gm 38
Achguig el Adam 〜 **RIM** 304 Ga 36
Achi ○ **CO** 106 Dl 41
Achibueno Longavi 〜 **RCH** 137 Dn 63
Achill Island ⌂ **IRL** 162 Ga 19
Achiras ○ **RA** 137 Eb 62
Achiri ○ **BOL** 128 Dp 54
Achnasheen ○ **GB** 162 Gd 17
Achoma ○ **PE** 128 Dn 53
Achouka ○ **G** 332 Gl 46
Acigöl 〜 **TR** 195 Hg 27
Ačinsk ○ **RUS** 204 Ua 7
Acıpayam ○ **TR** 195 Hg 27
Acireale ○ **I** 185 Gp 27
Ackerman ○ **USA** 86 Dc 29
Acklins Island ⌂ **BS** 87 Dl 34
Acobamba ○ **PE** 128 Dl 52
Acoma ••• **USA** 65 Cj 28
Acomayo ○ **PE** 128 Dn 52
Aconchi ○ **MEX** 80 Cg 31
Acopiara ○ **BR** 124 Fa 49
Acora ○ **PE** 128 Dk 51
A Coruña ○ **E** 184 Gb 24
Acos ○ **PE** 128 Dk 51
Acostambo ○ **PE** 128 Dl 52
Acqui-Terme ○ **I** 185 Gl 23
Acre ◉ **BR** 116 Dm 49
Acre 〜 **BR** 117 Ea 50
Acre ○ **IL** 208 Hk 29
Acreúna ○ **BR** 133 Ej 54
Actinolite ○ **CDN** 60 Dk 23
Actopan ○ **MEX** 92 Cn 35
Açuã 〜 **BR** 117 Ec 49
Açude Banabuiú 〜 **BR** 124 Fa 48
Açude Coremas 〜 **BR** 124 Fb 49
Açude Orós 〜 **BR** 124 Fa 49
Acul do Nord 〜 **RH** 101 Dm 36
Acultzingo ○ **MEX** 92 Cp 35
Acurenan ○ **GQ** 332 Gm 45
Aczo ○ **PE** 116 Dk 50
Ada ○ **USA** 70 Cp 28
Adaba ○ **ETH** 325 Hm 42
Ada Dzita ○ **GH** 317 Gg 43
Adaïm al-Hulay 〜 **KSA** 218 Hn 35
Adaiso ○ **GH** 317 Gf 43
Adaja 〜 **E** 184 Gd 25
Adaklı ○ **TR** 202 Hn 26
Adam ○ **OM** 226 Jg 34
Adamantina ○ **BR** 140 Ej 56
Adamarca ○ **BOL** 129 Ea 55
Adamawa Highlands ⚠ **CAM** 320 Gn 42
Adamello △ **I** 174 Gm 22
Adaminaby ○ **AUS** 379 Ml 64
Adāmī Tulu ○ **ETH** 325 Hm 42
Adams ○ **CDN** 50 Cc 20
Adam's Bridge ⌂ **IND** 239 Kd 41
Adams Lake ○ **CDN** 50 Cb 20
Adams Lake 〜 **CDN** 50 Cc 20
Adam's Peak △ **CL** 239 Ke 42
Adana ○ **TR** 195 Hk 27
Adan as-Șughra 〜 **YE** 218 Ja 39
Adane ○ **G** 332 Gm 46
Adaoudia △ **DZ** 308 Gj 34
Adapazari ○ **TR** 195 Hh 25
Adar ○ **TCH** 321 Hc 40
Adarama ○ **SUD** 313 Hk 37
Adarau Taungdan ⚠ **MYA** 254 Kl 34
Adarot ○ **SUD** 313 Hl 37
Adaut ○ **RI** 283 Mb 50
Adayale ○ **AUS** 375 Mj 58

Adda 〜 **I** 174 Gl 22
Adda 〜 **SUD** 324 He 41
Ad-Dab'a ○ **ET** 301 Hg 30
Ad Dahwar ○ **LAR** 300 Hc 33
Ad Dahnā ⌂ **KSA** 215 Ja 32
Ad-Daid ○ **ET** 301 Hj 33
ad-Dair ○ **ET** 301 Hj 33
Ad Dakhla ○ **MA** 304 Fm 34
ad-Damman ○ **KSA** 215 Jd 32
Addanki ○ **IND** 238 Kd 38
ad-Dār al-Ḩamrā' ○ **KSA** 218 Hn 35
ad-Darsia ○ **LAR** 300 Hc 29
ad-Dawwar ○ **ET** 301 Hg 30
ad-Diddiba ○ **KSA** 215 Jb 31
ad-Diffa ⌂ **LAR** 300 He 30
ad-Dikāka ⌂ **KSA** 219 Jd 36
ad-Dir'īya ○ **KSA** 214 Hp 33
ad-Dir'īya ○ **KSA** 215 Jb 33
ad-Diwâniya ○ **IRQ** 215 Ja 30
Addo ○ **ZA** 358 Hd 62
Addo Elephant ★ **ZA** 358 He 62
Addu ⌂ **MV** 31 Nb 10
ad-Du'ayn ○ **SUD** 312 Hf 40
ad-Dubai'a ○ **KSA** 215 Jb 33
ad-Dubai'a ○ **UAE** 215 Je 33
ad-Dulaimīya ○ **KSA** 214 Hp 33
ad-Duwaym ○ **SUD** 312 Hh 39
Adé ○ **TCH** 321 Hc 39
Adéane ○ **SN** 316 Fm 39
Adel ○ **USA** 86 Dg 30
Adelaide ○ **ZA** 358 Hf 62
Adelaide ▣ **AUS** 378 Me 63
Adelaide Island ⌂ **⚑** 38 Ta 16
Adelaide Peninsula ⌂ **CDN** 42 Fb 5
Adelaide River ○ **AUS** 364 Mb 52
Adel Bagrou ○ **RIM** 305 Gc 38
Adelbert Range ⚠ **PNG** 287 Mj 48
Adêlê ○ **ETH** 325 Hm 42
Adelei ○ **SP** 329 Ja 44
Adelia María ○ **RA** 137 Ec 62
Adélie Coast 〰 **⚑** 38 Sa 16
Adelong ○ **AUS** 375 Mj 57
Ademuz ○ **E** 184 Gf 25
Aden ○ **YE** 218 Ja 39
Adentan ○ **GH** 317 Gf 43
Aderbissinat ○ **RN** 308 Gk 38
Aderké ○ **TCH** 309 Ha 35
Âdêt ○ **ETH** 313 Hl 40
Adéta ○ **RT** 317 Gg 42
Aḏi Abun ○ **ETH** 313 Hm 38
Adiaké ○ **CI** 317 Ge 43
Adiangdia ○ **DY** 317 Gg 41
Aḏi Ark'ay ○ **ETH** 313 Hl 39
Adicora ○ **YV** 107 Dp 40
Aḏi Da'iro ○ **ETH** 313 Hm 38
Adidoma ○ **GH** 317 Gg 42
Adige 〜 **I** 174 Gm 22
Âḏigrat ○ **ETH** 313 Hm 38
Aḏi Gudom ○ **ETH** 313 Hm 39
Aḏik'eyih ○ **ER** 313 Hm 38
Aḏikwala ○ **ER** 313 Hm 38
Adilābād ○ **IND** 238 Kd 36
Adin ○ **USA** 64 Cb 25
Adinsoone ○ **SP** 328 Jc 41
Adipala ○ **RI** 278 Le 49
Aḏī Ramets' ○ **ETH** 313 Hl 39
Adirī ○ **LAR** 297 Gn 32
Adirondack Mountains ⚠ **USA** 60 Dl 23
Adis Ababa ▣ **ETH** 325 Hm 41
Âdis ○ **ETH** 325 Hm 41
Âdīs Zemen ○ **ETH** 313 Hl 40
Aḏī Ugri ○ **ER** 313 Hm 38
Adiyaman ○ **TR** 195 Hm 27
Adjengré ○ **RT** 317 Gg 41
Adjohoun ○ **DY** 317 Gh 42
Adjud ○ **RO** 175 Hf 22
Adler ○ **RUS** 195 Hm 24
Admiralty Gulf 〜 **AUS** 361 Ln 53
Admiralty Gulf Aboriginal Reserve ••• **AUS** 361 Ln 53
Admiralty Inlet 〜 **CDN** 43 Ga 4
Admiralty Island ⌂ **USA** 47 Bj 17
Admiralty Island National Park ⚑ **USA** 47 Bj 17
Admiralty Islands ⌂ **PNG** 287 Mk 47
Admiralty Range ⚠ **⚑** 38 Ta 17
Ado ○ **WAN** 320 Gk 41
Âdobed Hãyk' 〜 **ETH** 313 Hn 40
Ado-Ekiti ○ **WAN** 320 Gj 42
Adok ○ **SUD** 324 Hj 41
Adolfo López Madero ○ **MEX** 80 Cj 31
Adolphus Island ⌂ **AUS** 364 Ma 53
Adonara ⌂ **RI** 282 Lm 50
Âdoni ○ **IND** 238 Kc 38
Adorf ○ **D** 174 Gn 20
Adoru ○ **WAN** 320 Gk 42
Adoumandjali ○ **RCA** 321 Gp 44
Adoumri ○ **CAM** 321 Gn 41
Adour 〜 **F** 184 Gd 24
Adra ○ **E** 184 Ge 27
Adranga ○ **RDC** 324 Hh 44
Adrar ⌂ **DZ** 296 Gf 33
Adrar ⚠ **DZ** 296 Gh 33
Adrar Ahellakane ⚠ **DZ** 296 Gj 33
Adrar Azzaouager △ **RN** 308 Gj 37
Adrar Bous △ **RN** 308 Gl 35
Adrar des Iforhas ⚠ **RMM** 305 Gg 35
Adrar Ilebgâne △ **RMM** 305 Gg 36
Adrar In Hihaou △ **DZ** 305 Gh 34
Adrar Mariaou △ **DZ** 308 Gj 34
Adrar-n-Ahnet △ **DZ** 308 Gh 33
Adrar-n-Aklim △ **MA** 292 Gb 30
Adrar Ouârâne △ **RIM** 304 Fp 35
Adrar-Ouzzeine △ **RMM** 305 Gg 34
Adrar Tamgak △ **RN** 308 Gl 36
Adrar Tedjorar △ **DZ** 296 Gj 33
Adrar Tidderidjaouine △ **DZ** 305 Gg 33
Adrar Tintejert △ **DZ** 296 Gh 33
Adraskan ○ **AFG** 223 Jk 29
Adré ○ **TCH** 321 Hd 39
Adreanof Islands ⌂ **USA** 10 Aa 4
Adrian ○ **USA** 56 Da 24

Adrian ○ **USA** 71 Dg 25
Adrianópolis ○ **BR** 141 Ek 58
Adriatic Sea ◥ **▩** 185 Ge 23
Adua ○ **RI** 283 Ma 46
Aduana ○ **ET** 313 Hn 63
Aduku ○ **EAU** 324 Hj 44
Adunu ○ **WAN** 320 Gk 41
Adur ○ **IND** 239 Kc 41
Adusa ○ **WAN** 320 Gk 43
Adusa ○ **RDC** 324 Hg 45
Advance ○ **USA** 71 Dd 27
Adwa ○ **ETH** 313 Hm 38
Adwana ○ **IND** 227 Kb 33
Adyča 〜 **RUS** 205 Xa 5
Adzopé ○ **CI** 317 Ge 42
Aegean Sea 〰 **GR** 194 He 26
Aekanopan ○ **RI** 270 Kp 44
Ael ○ **USA** 50 Cb 24
Aera Indigena Al Alto Rio Negro ••• **BR** 117 Dp 45
Aesakes Laggon 〜 **PNG** 286 Mg 49
Afadé ○ **CAM** 321 Gp 39
'Afak ○ **IRQ** 209 Ja 29
Âfambo ○ **ETH** 313 Hn 40
Âfambo Hãyk' 〜 **ETH** 313 Hn 40
Af Barwaargo ○ **SP** 328 Jc 42
Afdem ○ **ETH** 325 Hn 41
Afé ○ **SN** 304 Fn 38
Afféri ○ **CI** 317 Gd 42
Affon 〜 **DY** 317 Gg 41
Afghanistan ■ **AFG** 223 Jk 29
Afgooye ○ **SP** 329 Ja 44
Afikpo ○ **WAN** 320 Gk 43
Afîpinskij ○ **RUS** 202 Hm 23
Áfjord ○ **N** 158 Gn 13
Aflou ○ **DZ** 293 Gg 28
Afmadow ○ **SP** 329 Hp 45
Afobaka ○ **SME** 113 Eg 43
Afogados da Ingazeira ○ **BR** 124 Fb 49
Afognak Island ⌂ **USA** 46 Ba 15
Afolé ○ **RT** 317 Gg 42
Afore ○ **PNG** 287 Ml 50
Afrânio ○ **BR** 124 Ep 50
Afredo Wagner ○ **BR** 140 Eh 59
Âfrêra Terara △ **ETH** 313 Hn 39
Âfrêra Ye Che'ew Hãyk' 〜 **ETH** 313 Hn 39
Afrin ○ **SYR** 195 Hl 27
Afton ○ **USA** 70 Da 27
Aftoût ech Chergui 〜 **RIM** 304 Fn 37
Afua ○ **BR** 121 Ej 46
Afua 〜 **BR** 121 Ek 46
'Afula ○ **IL** 208 Hk 29
Afwein 〜 **EAK** 325 Hm 45
Afyon ○ **TR** 195 Hh 26
Âgâbšīr ○ **IR** 209 Ja 27
Agadem ○ **RN** 309 Gn 37
Agadez ○ **RN** 308 Gl 37
Agadir ○ **MA** 292 Ga 30
Âğã Gâri ○ **IR** 215 Jc 30
Agaho ○ **J** 251 Mf 27
Agaie ○ **WAN** 320 Gk 41
Agalega ⌂ **MS** 31 Mb 11
Agamor ○ **RMM** 305 Gf 37
Agar ○ **USA** 56 Cm 23
Agâr ○ **AFG** 223 Jm 28
Agar ○ **IND** 234 Kc 34
Agàrak ○ **RN** 308 Gj 37
Ağaraktem ○ **RMM** 305 Gc 34
Agarfa ○ **ETH** 325 Hm 42
Agargar ○ **MA** 304 Fn 34
Ağârgar ○ **MA** 304 Fn 34
Agaro ○ **ETH** 325 Hl 42
Agarsararën ○ **ETH** 328 Ja 42
Agaru ○ **SUD** 313 Hk 38
Agastya Malai △ **IND** 239 Kc 41
Agate ○ **USA** 65 Ck 26
Agats ○ **RI** 286 Mf 48
Agatti Island ⌂ **IND** 239 Ka 40
Agattu Island ⌂ **USA** 205 Zb 8
Agawa Bay 〜 **CDN** 57 Df 22
Agawa Bay ○ **CDN** 57 Df 22
Agbabu ○ **WAN** 320 Gj 42
Agbara ○ **WAN** 320 Gj 42
Agbarha-Otor ○ **WAN** 320 Gj 43
Agbélouvé ○ **RT** 317 Gg 42
Agbo-Bojiboji ○ **WAN** 320 Gk 42
Agboville ○ **CI** 317 Gd 43
Aĝçabâdi ○ **AZ** 202 Jb 25
Agdam ○ **AZ** 202 Jb 25
Aĝdaş ○ **AZ** 202 Jb 25
Agde ○ **F** 185 Gh 24
Agdz ○ **MA** 293 Gc 30
Agen ○ **F** 184 Gg 23
Agenebode ○ **WAN** 320 Gk 42
Ägere Maryam ○ **ETH** 325 Hm 43
Aggeneys ○ **ZA** 348 Hb 60
Aghat ○ **RN** 308 Gk 37
Aghir ○ **TN** 297 Gm 29
Aghiyuk Island ⌂ **USA** 46 Al 17
Aghor ○ **PK** 227 Jf 33
Aghouinit ○ **MA** 304 Fp 34
Aghrẽïjît ○ **RIM** 304 Fp 35
Agiá ○ **GR** 194 Hd 26
Agía Marína ○ **GR** 194 Hf 27
Agī Čây 〜 **IR** 209 Jb 27
Agiert ○ **RIM** 304 Gb 37
Agio Óros ◉ **GR** 194 He 25
Agío Óros ⌂ **GR** 194 He 25
Ágios Efstrátios ⌂ **GR** 194 He 26
Ágios Kírikos ○ **GR** 194 Hf 27
Ágios Nikólaos ○ **GR** 194 He 28
Ágios Triáda ○ **GR** 194 Hd 28
Agíos Nikólaos ○ **GR** 194 He 28
Aglinskoe ○ **RUS** 204 Vb 8
Agmar ○ **RIM** 292 Ga 33
Agnes Lake 〜 **CDN** 56 Dc 21
Agness ○ **USA** 50 Bp 24
Agnes Waters ○ **AUS** 375 Mm 58
Agnew ○ **AUS** 368 Ll 60
Agnibilékrou ○ **CI** 317 Ge 42
Agnita ○ **RO** 175 He 23
Agno 〜 **RP** 267 Ll 37
Agno ○ **RP** 267 Ll 38
Ago ○ **J** 251 Me 28
Ago-Are ○ **WAN** 320 Gh 41
Agogo ○ **GH** 317 Gf 42
Agoitz ○ **E** 184 Gf 24
Agona ○ **GH** 317 Gf 42
Agona Junction ○ **GH** 317 Ge 43

Agou ○ **CI** 317 Ge 43
Agoueïnît ○ **RIM** 305 Gc 37
Agouna ○ **DY** 317 Gg 42
Agra ○ **IND** 234 Kc 32
Agrahanskij p-ov ⌂ **RUS** 202 Jb 24
Agrestina ○ **BR** 124 Fb 50
Âgri ○ **TR** 202 Hp 26
Agrigento ○ **I** 185 Gn 27
Agrihan ⌂ **USA** 27 Sa 8
Agrio 〜 **RA** 147 Dp 65
Agrópoli ○ **I** 194 Gp 25
Ağsu ○ **AZ** 202 Jc 25
Água Azul Falls 〜 **MEX** 93 Dd 37
Agua Blanca ○ **YV** 112 Ec 42
Agua Boa ○ **BR** 125 En 54
Agua Boa ○ **BR** 133 Eh 54
Agua Boa do Univiní 〜 **BR** 120 Ed 45
Água Braga ○ **BR** 133 Ek 52
Água Branca ○ **BR** 124 Fb 49
Água Caliente ••• **USA** 64 Cd 29
Agua Caliente ○ **MEX** 80 Cg 31
Agua Caliente ○ **PE** 116 Dl 50
Agua Caliente 〜 **BOL** 129 Ec 53
Agua Castilla ○ **BOL** 136 Ea 56
Aguacate ○ **CO** 106 Dk 42
Aguadilla ○ **USA** 104 Ea 36
Água do Cecilio 〜 **RA** 147 Eb 66
Água Doce do Norte ○ **BR** 141 Ep 55
Agua Dulce ○ **MEX** 93 Da 36
Aguadulce ○ **PA** 97 Dh 41
Agua Escondida ○ **RA** 137 Dp 64
Água Fria ○ **USA** 65 Cf 28
Agua Fria ○ **BR** 125 Fa 51
Agua-Fria ○ **BR** 133 Ej 52
Aguaí ○ **BR** 141 El 56
Agualeguas ○ **MEX** 81 Cl 32
Agua Linda ○ **YV** 107 Dp 40
Aguán 〜 **HN** 96 De 38
Aguanaval ○ **MEX** 81 Cl 33
Aguanaval 〜 **MEX** 92 Cl 34
Agua Negra 〜 **RA** 137 Dp 61
Agua Nueva ○ **USA** 64 Cd 29
Agua Nueva ○ **MEX** 81 Cm 33
Agua Nueva ○ **USA** 81 Cn 32
Agua Nueva ○ **MEX** 92 Cn 34
Aguanus 〜 **CDN** 61 Ec 20
Aguapey 〜 **RA** 146 Ef 60
Agua Preta 〜 **BR** 117 Eb 46
Agua Prieta ○ **MEX** 80 Ch 30
Agua Quente 〜 **BR** 133 Em 51
Aguara 〜 **PY** 140 Ef 58
Aguaray ○ **PY** 136 Ec 57
A Guarda ○ **P** 184 Gb 25
Aguarico 〜 **EC** 116 Dk 45
Aguarico 〜 **EC** 116 Dk 46
Aguaro-Guariquito ⚑ **YV** 107 Ea 41
Aguas Belas ○ **BR** 124 Fb 50
Aguas Blancas ○ **RCH** 136 Dp 58
Aguas Blancas ○ **PY** 136 Eb 57
Aguas Claras ○ **C** 100 Dg 34
Aguas Formosas ○ **BR** 125 Ep 54
Agua Viva ○ **YV** 107 Dn 41
Aguaytía ○ **PE** 116 Dl 50
Aguaytia 〜 **PE** 116 Dl 50
Aguazul ○ **CO** 107 Dn 43
A Gudiña ○ **E** 184 Gc 25
Agueda ○ **E** 184 Gb 25
Aguelhok ○ **RMM** 305 Gg 36
Aguelt ez Zerga 〜 **RIM** 304 Fp 36
Aguemour ○ **DZ** 296 Gj 32
Aguéssis ○ **RN** 308 Gl 37
Aguga 〜 **EAU** 325 Hj 44
Aguié ○ **RN** 320 Gk 39
Aguijan ⌂ **USA** 27 Sa 8
Aguilâl Faï ○ **RIM** 304 Fn 36
Aguilar d. C. ○ **E** 184 Gd 24
Aguilares ○ **ES** 93 Dd 39
Águilas ○ **E** 184 Gf 27
Aguililla ○ **MEX** 92 Cl 36
Aguiz ○ **ER** 313 Hn 38
Âgula'i ○ **ETH** 313 Hm 39
Agulhas △ **ZA** 358 Hb 63
Agulhas Plateau 〰 **⚑** 31 La 13
Agumbe ○ **IND** 238 Kb 39
Aguni-shima ⌂ **J** 259 Lp 32
Agurá Grande ○ **RA** 137 Ed 61
Agusan 〜 **RP** 267 Ln 41
Agustin Codazzi ○ **CO** 107 Dm 40
Agutaya Island ⌂ **RP** 267 Ll 40
Agwampt 〜 **SUD** 313 Hk 36
Agwarra ○ **WAN** 320 Gj 40
Agwei 〜 **SUD** 325 Hj 42
Agwok ○ **SUD** 324 Hg 42
Ahaba ○ **WAN** 320 Gk 43
Aḩad al-Masāra ○ **KSA** 218 Hp 37
Aḩad Rāfida ○ **KSA** 218 Hp 36
Ahalcihe ○ **GE** 202 Hp 25
Ahanduizinho 〜 **BR** 140 Eh 56
Ahangaran ○ **UZB** 223 Jn 25
Ahar ○ **IR** 209 Jb 26
Ahero ○ **EAK** 337 Hk 46
Ahfir ○ **MA** 293 Ge 28
Ahia ○ **PNG** 287 Mj 49
Ahillio ○ **GR** 194 Hd 26
Ahititi ○ **NZ** 383 Nk 65
Ahklun Mountains ⚠ **USA** 46 Al 15
Ahlat ○ **TR** 202 Hp 26
Ahmadābād ○ **AFG** 223 Jj 28
Ahmadābād ○ **IND** 227 Ka 34
Ahmadnagar ○ **IND** 238 Kc 36
Ahmadpur East ○ **PK** 227 Jp 31
Ahmadpur Lamma ○ **PK** 227 Jn 31
Ahmadpur Siāl ○ **PK** 227 Jp 30
Ahmar Mountains ⚠ **ETH** 325 Hn 41
Ahmeta ○ **GE** 202 Ja 24
Ahoada ○ **WAN** 320 Gk 43
Ahome ○ **MEX** 80 Ch 33
Ahoskie ○ **USA** 74 Dk 27
Ahram ○ **IR** 215 Jd 31
Ahraura ○ **IND** 234 Kf 33
Ahtuba 〜 **RUS** 181 Jb 22
Ahtubinsk ○ **RUS** 181 Jb 21
Ahty ○ **RUS** 202 Jb 25
Ahuacatlan ○ **MEX** 92 Cn 35

Ahuachapán ○ ES 93 Dd 39
Ahualulco ○ MEX 92 Cm 34
Ahualulco de Mercata ○ MEX 92 Ck 35
Ahuano ○ EC 116 Dk 46
Ahufjan ~ ARM 202 Hp 25
Ahunui ◬ F 35 Bb 11
Ahvāz ○ IR 215 Jc 30
Ahwa ○ IND 238 Ka 35
Ahwar ○ YE 218 Jb 39
Ai-Ais ○ NAM 348 Ha 59
Aialik Cape ⌓ USA 46 Ba 15
Aiapuá ○ BR 120 Ed 48
Aiari ~ BR 117 Dp 45
Aidar ~ UA 181 Hm 21
Aiddejavrre ○ N 159 Hd 11
Aiduna ○ RI 283 Md 48
Aiema River ~ PNG 286 Mh 49
Aiere ○ WAN 320 Gj 42
Aigai ★ GR 194 Hd 25
Aiguá ○ ROU 146 Eg 63
Aigues-Mortes ○ F 185 Gj 24
Aija ○ PE 116 Dk 50
Aikawa ○ J 251 Me 26
Aiken ○ USA 71 Dh 29
Ailao Shan △ VRC 254 La 33
Aileron ○ AUS 361 Mc 57
Aileu ○ TP 282 Ln 50
Ailigandí ○ PA 104 Dk 41
Ailinginae ◬ MH 27 Ta 8
Ailuk ◬ MH 27 Tb 8
Aimere ○ RI 282 Ll 50
Aimogasta ○ RA 136 Ea 60
Aimorés ○ BR 141 Ep 55
Ain ~ F 163 Gj 22
Ain al-'Arab ○ SYR 209 Hm 27
'Ain al-Bakra ○ KSA 215 Jb 34
'Ain an-Naft ○ IRQ 209 Hp 29
Ainaži ○ LV 171 He 17
Aïn Beïda ○ DZ 296 Gk 28
Aïn Benian ○ DZ 296 Gh 27
Aïn-Benimathar ○ MA 293 Ge 29
Aïn Ben Tili ○ RIM 292 Gb 33
Aïn Bessem ○ DZ 296 Gh 27
Aïn Boucif ○ DZ 296 Gh 28
Ain Dār ○ KSA 215 Jc 33
Aïn Defla ○ DZ 293 Gg 27
Aïn Deheb ○ DZ 293 Gg 28
Ain Diwār ○ TR 202 Hn 27
Aïn Draham ○ TN 296 Gl 27
Aïn-Ech-Chair ○ MA 293 Ge 29
Aïn el Béli ○ DZ 296 Gh 28
Aïn el Hadiel ○ DZ 296 Gh 28
Aïn el Hadjadj ○ DZ 296 Gh 32
Aïn el Hadjar ○ DZ 293 Gg 28
Aïn el Hamara ○ DZ 296 Gh 28
Aïn el Melh ○ DZ 296 Gj 28
Aïn el-Orak ○ DZ 293 Gg 29
Aïn Fakrour ○ DZ 296 Gk 27
Aïn Fekan ○ DZ 293 Gf 28
Aïn Galaka ○ TCH 309 Hb 36
Ainggyi ○ MYA 254 Km 35
'Ain Hamūd ○ IRQ 215 Ja 30
'Ain Ibn Fuhaid ○ KSA 215 Ja 32
'Ain 'Īsā ○ SYR 209 Hm 27
Aïn Kercha ○ DZ 296 Gk 28
Aïn Kermes ○ DZ 293 Gg 28
Aïn-Leuho ○ MA 293 Gd 29
Aïn Madhi ○ DZ 296 Gh 29
Aïn M'Lila ○ DZ 296 Gk 27
Aïn Oulmene ○ DZ 296 Gj 28
Aïn Oussera ○ DZ 296 Gh 28
Ainsa ○ E 184 Gg 24
Aïn Saadane ○ MA 293 Gd 30
Aïn Sefra ○ DZ 293 Gf 29
Aïn Skhouna ○ DZ 293 Gg 28
'Ain Suhna ○ ET 301 Hh 31
Ainsworth ○ USA 56 Cm 24
'Ain Tabağbuğ ○ ET 300 Hf 31
Aïn Tamr ○ TN 296 Gl 29
Aïn Taya ○ DZ 296 Gh 27
Aïn-Tédelès ○ DZ 293 Gg 28
Aïn Temouchent ○ DZ 293 Gf 28
Aiome ○ PNG 287 Mj 48
Aiquile ○ BOL 129 Eb 55
Aiquiri ~ BR 117 Ea 50
Aïr ⛰ RN 308 Gl 36
Airbangis ○ RI 270 Kp 45
Airdrie ○ CDN 50 Cf 20
Aire ~ F 163 Gj 21
Aire-s.-l'Adour ○ F 184 Gf 24
Air Force Island ◬ CDN 43 Ha 5
Airlie Beach ○ AUS 375 Ml 56
Airmadidi ○ RI 275 Ln 45
Airpanas ○ RI 282 Ln 49
Air Terjung Sungai ○ RI 282 Ll 47
Aisne ~ F 163 Gj 21
Aitape ○ PNG 286 Mh 47
Aït-Baba ○ MA 292 Gb 30
Ait-Benhaddou ★ MA 293 Gc 30
Aitkin ○ USA 56 Db 22
Aït-Mellou ○ MA 292 Gb 30
Aitutaki ◬ NZ 35 Ab 11
Aït-Youssef-ou-Ali ○ MA 293 Gd 28
Aiuabá ○ BR 124 Ep 49
Aiuanã ~ BR 117 Eb 46
Aiuruoca ○ BR 141 Em 56
Aix-en-Provence ○ F 185 Gj 24
Aix-les-Bains ○ F 185 Gj 23
Aiyetoro ○ WAN 320 Gh 42
Aiyetoro ○ WAN 320 Gk 42
Aiyura ○ PNG 287 Mj 49
Aizawl ○ IND 254 Kl 34
Aizpute ○ LV 170 Hc 17
Aizuwakamatsu ○ J 251 Mf 27
Ajaccio ○ F 185 Gl 25
Ajacuba ○ MEX 92 Cn 35
Ajaguz ○ KZ 204 Tb 9
Ajajú ~ CO 116 Dm 45
Ajalpán ○ MEX 92 Cp 35
Ajan ○ RUS 22 Rb 4
Ajana ○ AUS 368 Lh 59
Ajanka ○ RUS 205 Za 6
Ajanta ○ IND 234 Kb 35
Ajanta Caves ★ IND 234 Kb 35
Ajanta Range ⛰ IND 234 Kb 35
Ajaokuta ○ WAN 320 Gk 42
Ajarani ~ BR 112 Ed 45
Ajasse ○ WAN 320 Gj 41
Ajdābiyā ○ LAR 300 Hb 30
Ajdarkul ~ UZB 223 Jm 25
Ajigasawa ○ J 250 Mf 25
Ajman ○ UAE 226 Jf 33
Ajmer ○ IND 234 Kb 32
Ajni ○ TJ 223 Jn 26
Ajo ○ USA 64 Cf 29
Ajoda ○ WAN 320 Gj 42
Ajon ○ RUS 205 Za 5
Ajtos ○ BG 195 Hf 24
Ajumaku ○ GH 317 Gf 43
Ajuruteua ○ BR 121 El 46
Ajuy ○ RP 267 Lm 40
Akaba ○ RT 317 Gg 42
Akaba Pass △ SUD 313 Hl 36
Akabar ○ RMM 305 Gg 38
Akabli ○ DZ 293 Gg 32
Akadomari ○ J 251 Mf 27
Aka-Eze ○ WAN 320 Gk 43
Akagera ~ RWA 336 Hh 47
Akagi ○ J 251 Mc 28
Akaishi-sanchi ⛰ J 251 Me 28
Āk'ak'ī ○ ETH 325 Hm 41
Āk'ak'ī Hāyk' ~ ETH 325 Hm 41
Akakro ○ CI 317 Gd 43
Akalkot ○ IND 238 Kc 37
Akamkpa ○ WAN 320 Gl 43
Akan ⚘ J 250 Mj 24
Akanous ○ NAM 348 Hb 58
Akaroa ○ NZ 383 Nj 67
Akasame ○ PNG 286 Mh 47
Akasha ○ SUD 312 Hh 35
Akāshāt ○ IRQ 209 Hn 29
Äkäslompolo ○ FIN 159 Hd 12
Akassa ○ WAN 320 Gk 43
Akat Amnuai Phang Khon ○ THA 263 Lb 37
Akatsi ○ GH 317 Gg 42
Akbaba D. △ TR 202 Hp 25
Akbarpur ○ IND 234 Kf 32
Akbou ○ DZ 296 Gj 27
Akçaabat ○ TR 195 Hm 25
Akçadağ ○ TR 195 Hl 26
Akçakale ○ TR 195 Hm 27
Akçakoca ○ TR 195 Hh 25
Akçakoca Dağları ⛰ TR 195 Hh 25
Akçalı Dağları ⛰ TR 195 Hj 27
Akchâr ⌒ RIM 304 Fn 36
Ak Dağlar △ TR 195 Hg 27
Ak Dağlar ⛰ TR 195 Hk 26
Akdağmadeni ○ TR 195 Hk 26
Ak-Dovurak ○ RUS 204 Tc 8
Akel ~ RI 275 Ma 45
Akelamo ○ RI 275 Ma 45
Akelamo ○ RI 283 Lp 46
Akélataka ○ RCB 332 Gp 46
Akeley ○ USA 56 Da 22
Akeonik ○ USA 46 Aj 9
Åkersberga ○ S 170 Hb 16
Aketi ○ RDC 324 Hd 44
Aketi ~ RDC 324 He 44
Akhalk'alak'i ○ GE 202 Hp 25
Akhiok ○ USA 46 An 17
Akhisar ○ TR 195 Hf 26
Akhmim ○ ET 301 Hh 32
Akhnoor ○ IND 230 Kb 29
Aki ○ J 251 Mc 29
Akiachak ○ USA 46 Aj 15
Akiéni ○ G 332 Gn 46
Akimiski Island ◬ CDN 57 Dh 19
Akinum ○ PNG 287 Ml 49
Akita ○ J 251 Mf 26
Akjoujt ○ RIM 304 Fn 36
Akka ○ MA 292 Gb 31
Akkajaure ~ S 158 Ha 12
Akkeshi ○ J 250 Mj 24
Akkoursoulbak ○ RCA 321 Hc 41
Aklampa ○ DY 317 Gh 41
Aklavik ○ CDN 47 Bg 11
Aklera ○ IND 234 Kc 33
Akmeqit ○ VRC 230 Kc 27
Aknoul ○ MA 293 Ge 28
Akō ○ J 251 Md 28
Ako ○ PNG 287 Ml 50
Äkobo Wenz ~ ETH 325 Hk 42
Akodia ○ IND 234 Kc 34
Akoga ○ G 332 Gm 45
Akoka ○ SUD 324 Hj 41
Akokan ○ RN 308 Gk 36
Akoko ○ G 332 Gl 45
Akokora ○ RDC 324 Hg 45
Akola ○ IND 234 Kc 35
Akoma ○ PNG 287 Mj 49
Akom II ○ CAM 320 Gm 44
Akono ○ CAM 320 Gm 44
Akonolinga ○ CAM 320 Gn 44
Akop ○ SUD 324 Hg 41
Akor ○ RMM 305 Gc 38
Āk'ordat ○ ER 313 Hl 38
Akoroso ○ GH 317 Gf 43
Akosombo ○ GH 317 Gf 42
Akot ○ IND 234 Kc 35
Akot ○ SUD 324 Hh 42
Akou ○ G 332 Gp 46
Akoupé ○ CI 317 Gd 42
Akpatok Island ◬ CDN 43 Hb 6
Akpınar ○ TR 195 Hk 26
Akqi ○ VRC 230 Kd 25
Akrabat ○ TM 223 Jj 28
Akra Lidinon ⌓ GR 194 He 28
Akranes ○ IS 158 Fj 13
Akra Sideros ⌓ GR 194 Hf 28
Akra Spanda ⌓ GR 194 Hd 28
Akrata ○ GR 194 Hd 26
Akra Ténaro ⌓ GR 194 Hd 27
Akréréb ○ RN 308 Gl 37
Åkrestrømmen ○ N 158 Gm 15
Akron ○ USA 56 Cp 24
Akron ○ USA 65 Cl 25
Akron ○ USA 71 Dh 25
Aksaj ○ RUS 181 Hm 22
Aksaj ~ RUS 202 Jb 24
Ak Saj ~ KS 230 Kc 25
Aksaj Esaulovsk ~ RUS 181 Hp 21
Akşar ○ TR 202 Hp 25
Aksaray ○ TR 195 Hk 26
Aksay ○ VRC 242 Km 26
Aksay Qin ⌒ IND 230 Kd 28
Aksayqin Co ~ IND 230 Kd 28
Akşehir ○ TR 195 Hh 26
Akşehir Gölü ~ TR 195 Hh 26
Akseki ○ TR 195 Hh 27
Aks-e Rosta ~ IR 226 Jf 31
Aksu ○ KZ 204 Ta 8
Aksu ~ TJ 230 Kb 27
Aksubaevo ○ RUS 181 Jd 18
Aksu Çayı ~ TR 195 Hh 27
Aksūm ○ ETH 313 Hm 38
Ak Tag △ VRC 231 Kg 27
Aktarsk ○ RUS 181 Ja 20
Aktau ○ KZ 155 Rb 10
Aktau △ UZB 223 Jf 25
Aktaz ○ VRC 231 Kh 26
Aku ○ PNG 290 Mp 49
Akūbū ○ SUD 324 Hj 42
Akūbū ~ SUD 325 Hj 42
Akui ○ BR 124 En 47
Akula ○ RDC 321 Hc 44
Akumal ○ MEX 93 De 35
Akune ○ J 247 Ma 29
Akure ○ WAN 320 Gj 42
Akureyri ○ IS 158 Fl 13
Akuseki-shima ◬ J 259 Ma 31
Akwanga ○ WAN 320 Gl 41
Akwaya ○ CAM 320 Gl 42
Akwot ~ SUD 324 Hh 42
Akyerensua ○ GH 317 Ge 42
'Alābād ~ IR 226 Jj 30
Alabama ◉ USA 71 De 29
Alabama ~ USA 86 De 30
Alabama and Coushatta I.R. ••• USA 81 Da 30
Alaban ○ RI 270 Kn 44
Alabaster ○ USA 71 De 29
Alabat Island ◬ RP 267 Lm 38
al-'Abbāsīya ○ SUD 312 Hh 39
Alabo ~ GH 317 Gg 42
al-'Abr ○ YE 218 Jb 37
Ala-Buka ○ KS 223 Jp 25
Alaca ○ TR 195 Hk 25
Alacam ○ TR 195 Hk 25
Alacant ○ E 184 Gf 26
Alachua ○ USA 87 Dg 31
Aladağ △ TR 195 Hh 26
Ala Dağlar ⛰ TR 195 Hk 27
Ala Dağlar ⛰ TR 202 Hp 26
Al ,Adam ○ LAR 300 Hd 30
Aladdin ○ USA 51 Ck 23
Aladé ○ CAM 321 Gp 39
Aladja ○ WAN 320 Gj 43
al-'Ağā'iz ○ OM 219 Jg 36
Alaganik ○ USA 46 Bc 15
Alagē △ ETH 313 Hm 39
Alagir ○ RUS 202 Hp 24
Alagoa Grande ○ BR 124 Fc 49
Alagoas ◉ BR 124 Fb 50
Alagoinhas ○ BR 125 Fa 52
Alagón ~ E 184 Gc 26
Alagón ○ E 184 Gf 25
al-'Ağrūd ○ ET 214 Hk 30
Alah ~ RP 275 Ln 42
Alahanpanjang ○ RI 270 La 46
al Ahdar ○ KSA 214 Hl 31
Alah-Jun' ~ RUS 205 Xa 6
al-Ahmadī ○ KWT 215 Jb 31
Alaïli Dadda ○ DJI 313 Hp 39
al-'Ain ○ SUD 312 Hg 37
Alaior ○ E 185 Gh 26
Alajärvi ○ FIN 159 Hd 14
Alajuela ○ CR 97 Df 41
Alakamisy ○ RM 353 Jb 56
Alakamisy Itenina ○ RM 353 Jb 56
Alakanuk ○ USA 6 Ab 3
Alakanuk ○ USA 46 Ag 13
Alakurtti ○ RUS 159 Hg 12
Al 'Alamayn ○ ET 301 Hg 30
Alalaú ~ BR 120 Ed 46
al-'Amādīya ○ IRQ 209 Hp 27
Alamagan ◬ USA 27 Sa 8
al Amain Bin Sana'a ○ KSA 214 Hm 32
al'Amār ○ KSA 215 Ja 33
Al-'Amārah ○ IRQ 215 Jb 30
Alā Marv Dašt ~ IR 215 Je 32
Alamat'ā ○ ETH 313 Hm 39
Alamdo ○ VRC 242 Km 30
Alamikamba ○ NIC 97 Df 39
Alaminos ○ RP 267 Lk 37
al-'Āmirīya ○ ET 301 Hg 30
Alamo ○ USA 51 Cl 21
Alamo ○ USA 64 Ce 27
Alamo ○ USA 65 Cj 28
Alamo ○ MEX 81 Cp 34
Alamo ○ SP 328 Hp 43
Alamogordo ○ USA 65 Ck 29
Alamo Lake ~ USA 64 Cf 28
Alamo Navajo ••• USA 65 Ch 28
Alamor ○ EC 116 Dh 47
Alamos ○ MEX 80 Ch 32
Alamosa ○ USA 65 Cj 27
Alamos de Márquez ○ MEX 81 Cl 31
al-'Amūda ○ IRQ 215 Ja 30
Al-Anbār ◉ IRQ 209 Hn 29
Aland ○ IND 238 Kc 37
Åland Islands Ahvenanmaa ◬ FIN 170 Hb 15
Alaniemi ○ FIN 159 He 13
Alantika Mountains ⛰ WAN 320 Gn 41
Alan Water ○ CDN 56 Dc 20
Alanya ○ TR 195 Hj 27
Alapa ○ WAN 320 Gj 41
Alapaha ○ USA 86 Dg 30
Alapaha ~ USA 86 Dg 30
al-'Aqaba aṣ-Ṣagīra ○ ET 301 Hj 33
,Alāqān ○ KSA 214 Hk 31
al-'Aqīq ○ KSA 218 Hn 35
Alaquines ○ MEX 92 Cn 34
Al Argoub ○ MA 304 Fm 34
al Ārida ○ KSA 218 Hp 37
al-'Arīš ○ ET 301 Hj 30
al-Artawī ○ KSA 215 Ja 33
Alas ~ RI 270 Kn 44
Alas ○ RI 279 Lj 50
Alashan Shamo ⌒ VRC 242 La 25
al-Ashara ○ OM 226 Jh 35
Alaska ◉ USA 46 Aj 13
Alaska ○ ZW 341 Hg 54
Alaska Peninsula ◬ USA 46 Aj 17
Alaska Range ⛰ USA 6 Ba 3
Alaska Range ⛰ USA 46 An 15
al-'Assāfīya ○ KSA 214 Hm 31
Al'Assah ○ LAR 297 Gm 29
Alássio ○ I 185 Gl 23
al 'Ašūrīya ○ IRQ 214 Hp 30
al-Atawala ○ KSA 218 Hn 35
Alati ○ CAM 321 Gn 44
Alatna River ~ USA 46 An 11
al-Atshan ~ SUD 313 Hk 39
Alatskivi ○ EST 171 Hf 16
Ālattur ○ IND 239 Kc 40
al-Atwa ○ KSA 214 Hp 31
Alatyr' ○ RUS 181 Jb 18
Alausí ○ EC 116 Dj 47
Alaverdi ○ ARM 202 Ja 25
Alavus ○ FIN 159 Hd 14
Alawa ○ WAN 320 Gk 40
Alawangandji Aboriginal Land ••• AUS 364 Md 53
Alawoona ○ AUS 378 Mg 63
Al 'Ayn ○ UAE 226 Jf 33
al-Ayn ○ OM 226 Jg 34
Alay Range ⛰ TJ 223 Jp 26
Alazeja ~ RUS 205 Ya 4
Alazeyskoye Ploskogor'ye ⛰ RUS 205 Xc 5
al-'Azīzīya ○ IRQ 209 Ja 29
Al ,Azīzīyah ○ LAR 297 Gn 29
Alba ○ I 185 Gl 23
al-Ba'āğ ○ IRQ 202 Hn 27
al-Ba'ā'it ○ KSA 214 Hn 32
Al Bab ○ SYR 195 Hl 27
Albacete ○ E 184 Gf 26
al-Bad' ○ KSA 214 Hk 31
al-Badā'i' ○ KSA 214 Hp 33
al-Badārī ○ ET 301 Hh 32
Alba de Tormes ○ E 184 Gd 25
al-Bādī ○ IRQ 209 Hn 28
al-Badī' ○ KSA 218 Jb 35
al-Badī'a ○ KSA 218 Hp 37
al-Bāha ○ KSA 218 Hn 35
al-Bahra ○ KWT 215 Jb 31
al-Bahrīya ⛰ ET 301 Hh 31
al-Baida' ○ YE 218 Ja 39
Alba Iulia ○ RO 175 Hd 22
Albaka ○ IND 238 Ke 36
Ålbæk Bugt ~ DK 170 Gm 17
al-Balyana ○ ET 301 Hh 32
Albán ○ CO 106 Dl 43
Alban ○ CO 116 Dk 45
Albania □ AL 194 Hc 26
Albany ○ USA 50 Ca 23
Albany ○ USA 56 Da 23
Albany ○ USA 60 Dl 24
Albany ○ USA 70 Cn 29
Albany ○ USA 86 Df 30
Albany ○ AUS 368 Lj 63
Albany ○ NZ 383 Nk 64
Albany Downs ○ AUS 375 Ml 59
Albany Island ◬ CDN 57 Dh 19
Albany River ~ CDN 43 Gb 8
Albany River ~ CDN 57 De 20
Alba Posse ○ RA 140 Eg 59
Al Bardī ○ LAR 300 He 30
Albarracín ○ E 184 Gf 25
al-Barun ○ SUD 313 Hj 40
al-Başirī ○ SYR 208 Hl 28
al Başra ◉ IRQ 215 Jb 30
Albatros Plateau ▾ 11 Db 8
Albatross Bay ~ AUS 365 Mg 52
al-Bauga ○ SUD 312 Hj 36
al-Bawītī ○ ET 301 Hg 31
al-Bayad ⌒ KSA 218 Jb 35
Al Bayda ○ LAR 300 Hc 29
Albay Gulf ~ RP 267 Ln 39
al-Begeir ○ SUD 312 Hj 36
Albemarle ○ USA 71 Dh 28
Albemarle Sound ~ USA 74 Dk 27
Alberdi ○ PY 140 Ee 59
Alberfoyle ○ AUS 375 Mj 56
Albergaria-a-Velha ○ P 184 Gb 25
Alberge Creek ~ AUS 374 Md 59
Alberta ◉ CDN 50 Ce 20
Alberti ○ RA 137 Ed 63
Albert I land ◬ N 158 Gm 6
Albertinia ○ ZA 358 Hc 63
Albert Lea ○ USA 56 Db 24
Albert Nile ~ EAU 324 Hh 44
Albert Town ○ BS 87 Dl 34
Albertville ○ USA 71 De 28
Albertville ○ F 185 Gk 23
Albi ○ F 184 Gh 24
Albia ○ USA 70 Db 25
al-Bi'ār ○ KSA 214 Hm 34
al-Biğādīya ○ KSA 214 Hp 33
Albina ○ SME 113 Eg 43
Albion ○ USA 60 Dj 24
Albion ○ USA 64 Bp 26
Albion ○ USA 70 Cp 25
Albion ○ USA 70 Da 29
Albion ○ USA 71 Df 24
al-Birk ○ KSA 218 Hn 36
Ålborg ○ DK 170 Gm 17
Ålborg Bugt ~ DK 170 Gm 17
Albox ○ E 184 Ge 27
Albreda ○ WAG 316 Fm 39
Albro ○ AUS 375 Mk 57
Albufeira ○ P 184 Gb 27
al-Bukairīya Riyāḍ ○ KSA 214 Hp 32
Albuquerque ○ USA 65 Cj 28
Albuquerque ○ E 184 Gc 26
al-Buraika ○ KSA 218 Hm 35
al-Buraimī ○ OM 226 Jf 33
Albury ○ AUS 379 Mk 64
al-Busaitā' ⌒ KSA 214 Hm 30
Alcácer do Sal ○ P 184 Gb 26
Alcala ○ RP 267 Ll 37
Alcala ○ AUS 365 Mg 55
Alcalá d. H. ○ E 184 Ge 25
Alcalá d.J. ○ E 184 Gf 26
Alcalá de Xivert ○ E 184 Gg 25
Alcalá la Real ○ E 184 Ge 27
Álcamo ○ I 185 Gn 27
Alcañices ○ E 184 Gc 25
Alcañiz ○ E 184 Gf 25
Alcantara ○ BR 121 Em 47
Alcántara ○ E 184 Gc 26
Alcaraz ○ E 184 Ge 26
Alcaudete ○ E 184 Gd 27
Alcázar de San Juan ○ E 184 Ge 26
Alcester Island ◬ PNG 287 Mn 50
Alčevs'k ○ UA 181 Hm 21
Alcira ○ RA 137 Eb 62
Alcobaça ○ P 184 Gb 26
Alcol ○ E 184 Gf 26
Alcoota ○ AUS 374 Md 57
Alcorcón ○ E 184 Gd 25
Alcorta ○ RA 137 Ed 62
Alcova ○ USA 65 Cj 24
Alcubierre ○ E 184 Gf 25
Alcúdia ○ E 185 Gh 26
Alcurve ○ CDN 51 Cg 19
Aldama ○ MEX 80 Cj 31
Aldama ○ MEX 92 Cn 34
Aldan ○ RUS 204 Wa 7
Aldan ~ RUS 205 Wc 6
Aldan ~ RUS 205 Wc 7
Aldanskoye Nagor'ye ⛰ RUS 22 Ra 4
Aldanskoye Nagor'ye ⛰ RUS 204 Wa 7
Aldeia ○ BR 121 El 49
Aldeia ○ BR 133 El 51
Aldeia Velha ○ BR 121 Em 48
Aldeia Viçosa ○ ANG 332 Gp 50
Aldeia Vila Batista ○ BR 120 Ed 46
Alder ○ USA 51 Cf 23
Alder Creek ○ USA 60 Dl 24
Alder Flats ○ CDN 50 Ce 19
Alderley ○ ZA 358 Hg 62
Alderley ○ AUS 374 Mf 57
Alderney ◬ GB 163 Ge 21
Aldershot ○ GB 163 Gf 20
Alédjo ○ DY 317 Gg 41
Aléeria ○ F 185 Gl 24
Aleg ○ RIM 304 Fp 37
Alegre ~ PY 140 Ee 56
Alegre ○ BR 141 Ep 56
Alegrete ○ BR 146 Eg 60
Alegria ○ RP 267 Lm 41
Alegria ○ RP 267 Lp 40
Alëhovščina ○ RUS 171 Hj 15
Aleiandia ○ CO 106 Dl 41
Alejandra ○ RA 146 Ee 60
Alejsk ○ RUS 204 Tb 8
Aleknagik ○ USA 46 Al 15
Aleksandrov ○ RUS 171 Hm 17
Aleksandrov Gaj ○ RUS 181 Jc 20
Aleksandrovskoe ○ RUS 202 Hp 23
Aleksandrovsk-Sahalinsij ○ RUS 205 Xb 8
Alekseevka ○ RUS 181 Jd 19
Alekseevskoe ○ RUS 181 Jc 18
Aleksin ○ RUS 171 Hl 18
Alem ○ RA 140 Eg 59
Ålem ○ S 170 Ha 17
Alèmbé ○ G 332 Gm 46
'Alem Ketema ○ ETH 313 Hm 40
'Alem Maya ○ ETH 325 Hn 41
Além-Paraíba ○ BR 141 En 56
Alençon ○ F 163 Gg 21
Alen Nkoma ○ G 332 Gm 45
Alenquer ○ BR 120 Eg 46
Alenquer ○ P 184 Gb 26
Alentejo ⌒ P 184 Gb 27
Alenuihaha Channel ~ USA 75 Am 35
Aleppo ○ SYR 195 Hl 27
Alert ○ CDN 7 Fb 1
Alerta ○ PE 128 Dn 51
Alés ○ F 185 Gj 23
Alešd ○ RO 174 Hd 22
Aleskseevka ○ RUS 181 Hm 20
Alessandria ○ I 185 Gl 23
Ålesund ○ N 158 Gj 14
Aleutian Basin ◬ USA 23 Tb 4
Aleutian Islands ◬ USA 10 Aa 4
Aleutian Range ⛰ USA 46 Al 17
Aleutian Trench ▾ 10 Aa 4
Alexander ○ USA 51 Cl 22
Alexander Archipelago ◬ USA 42 Cc 7
Alexander Bay ○ ZA 348 Ha 60
Alexander City ○ USA 86 Df 29
Alexander Island ◬ 38 Fa 16
Alexander Wall Sadd-e Eskandar ★ IR 222 Jf 27
Alexandra ○ USA 74 Dk 26
Alexandra ~ AUS 365 Mg 55
Alexandra ○ AUS 379 Mj 64
Alexandra ○ NZ 382 Ng 68
Alexandra Bay ~ AUS 365 Mj 54
Alexandra Channel ~ MYA 262 Kl 38
Alexandra Fjord ○ CDN 43 Gc 3
Alexandra Park ○ ZA 349 Hf 58
Alexandria ○ USA 56 Da 23
Alexandria ○ CDN 60 Dl 23
Alexandria ○ USA 86 Db 30
Alexandria ○ BR 124 Fa 49
Alexandria ○ RO 194 He 24
Alexandria ○ ET 301 Hg 30
Alexandria ○ ZA 358 Hf 62
Alexandrina ○ AUS 365 Me 55
Alexandroúpoli ○ GR 194 He 25
Alexeck ~ NAM 348 Hb 56
Alexis Creek ○ CDN 50 Ca 20
Alexishafen ○ PNG 287 Mj 48
al-Faidamī ○ YE 219 Je 36
Al Faid Majir ○ LAR 297 Gp 29
al-Faiṣalīya ○ KSA 218 Hn 35
al-Fallūga ○ IRQ 209 Hp 29
al-Faq' ○ UAE 226 Jf 33
al-Farāfira ⌒ ET 301 Hg 32
al-Farda ○ YE 218 Jc 38
al-Farša ○ KSA 218 Hp 37
al-Fašn ○ ET 301 Hh 31
al-Fath ○ OM 226 Jg 34
al-Fāw ○ IRQ 215 Jc 31
al-Fawwāra ○ KSA 214 Hp 32
Al-Fayyum ○ ET 301 Hh 31
Alfenas ○ BR 141 Em 56
al-Fifi ○ SUD 312 He 40
Ålfotbreen ○ N 158 Gj 15
Ålfotbreen △ N 158 Gj 15
Alfred Chaves ○ BR 141 Ep 56
Alfredo M. Terrazas ○ MEX 92 Cn 35
al-Fuhaihil ○ KWT 215 Jc 31
al-Fula ○ SUD 312 Hg 40
Al Fuqahā' ○ LAR 297 Ha 32
al-Furaišī ○ KSA 214 Hm 33
al-Gabalayn ○ SUD 312 Hj 39
al Gadida ○ ET 301 Hg 31
al-Gafara ○ KSA 215 Ja 34
al-Ğāfāt ○ OM 226 Jg 34
al-Ğafr ○ JOR 214 Hl 30
al-Ğafr ~ JOR 214 Hl 30
al-Ğāfūra ⌒ KSA 215 Jd 33
al-Gahra ○ KWT 215 Jb 31
al-Gaida ○ YE 219 Je 38
al-Gaida ○ YE 219 Jd 37
al-Gail ○ YE 219 Jd 38
al-Ğalāmid ○ KSA 214 Hn 30
al-Gamalīya ○ ET 301 Hh 30
al-Ganad ○ YE 218 Ja 39
al-Ganamīya ○ KSA 215 Jb 33
Al Garabulli ○ LAR 297 Gn 29
al-Garef ○ SUD 313 Hk 40
Al-Gargarat ○ MA 304 Fm 35
al-Garif ○ KSA 214 Hm 34
Algarrobal ~ RCH 136 Dn 60
Algarrobo ○ RCH 137 Dm 62
Algarrobo del Aguila ○ RA 137 Ea 64
Algarve ⌒ P 184 Gb 27
al-Ğāt ○ KSA 215 Ja 33
al-Gaura ○ SUD 313 Hk 37
al-Gawār ⌒ KSA 215 Jc 33
al-Gaylī ○ SUD 312 Hj 37
al-Gazala ○ KSA 214 Hn 32
Algeciras ○ E 184 Gd 27
Al Gedaref ○ SUD 313 Hk 38
Algena ○ ER 313 Hm 37
Alger ○ USA 57 Df 23
Algere ~ BR 132 Ee 53
Algeria □ DZ 296 Gg 31
Algeyta ○ ETH 325 Hn 41
al-Ghāba ○ SUD 312 Hh 36
al-Ghabsha ○ SUD 312 Hh 39
Alghero ○ I 185 Gk 25
Al Ghomode ○ LAR 297 Gm 33
Al Ghrayfah ○ LAR 297 Gn 32
Al Ghurdaqah ○ ET 301 Hj 32
Algiers ▣ DZ 296 Gh 27
al-Gišā ○ KSA 215 Jc 33
Algoa Bay ~ ZA 358 He 62
Algodón ~ PE 116 Dm 47
Algoma Upland ⛰ CDN 57 Dg 22
Algona ○ USA 56 Da 24
Algona ○ USA 57 De 23
Algonac ○ USA 57 Dg 24
Algonouin Upland ⛰ CDN 60 Dj 23
Algonquin Provincial Park ⚘ CDN 60 Dj 23
Algorta ○ RCH 136 Dp 57
Algorta ○ ROU 146 Ef 62
al-Gubail ○ KSA 215 Jc 32
al-Haba ○ UAE 226 Jf 33
al-Ḥabbā ○ KSA 214 Hn 32
al-Ḥabbānīya ○ IRQ 209 Hp 29
al-Ḥabbārīya ○ IRQ 209 Hn 29
al-Ḥābūra ○ OM 226 Jg 34
al-Ḥadar ○ IRQ 209 Hp 28
al-Ḥadd ○ OM 226 Jh 34
al-Ḥaddār ○ KSA 218 Ja 34
al-Ḥadīta ○ KSA 214 Hl 30
al-Ḥağara ⛰ KSA 214 Hn 30
al-Ḥağarain ○ YE 218 Jc 38
al-Ḥağr ○ KSA 215 Jb 33
al-Ḥā'it ○ KSA 214 Hn 33
al-Haiz ○ ET 301 Hg 31
al-Ḥālis ○ IRQ 209 Ja 29
al-Hallānīyāt ◬ OM 219 Jf 37
al-Ḥamād ⛰ KSA 214 Hm 30
Al Hamadah al Hamrā' ⌒ LAR 297 Gm 31
Alhama de Murcia ○ E 184 Gf 27
al-Ḥamar ○ KSA 215 Jb 34
al-Ḥamāsīn ○ KSA 218 Ja 35
al-Ḥamğā ○ KSA 214 Hp 33
al-Ḥāmī ○ YE 219 Jc 38
al-Ḥammām ○ IRQ 215 Hp 30
al-Ḥammām ○ ET 301 Hg 30
al-Ḥamrā ◬ OM 226 Jg 34
al-Ḥanākīya ○ KSA 214 Hn 33
Alhandra ○ BR 124 Fc 49
Al Ḥanīyah ○ LAR 300 Hc 29
al-Ḥaql ○ KSA 214 Hk 31
al-Ḥaqw ○ KSA 218 Hp 37
Al Harabah ○ LAR 297 Gm 30
al-Ḥarf ○ YE 218 Ja 37
al-Ḥarğ al Kharj ○ KSA 215 Jb 33
al-Ḥāriğa Kharga ○ ET 301 Hh 33
Al Ḥaruj al Aswad ⛰ LAR 297 Ha 32
al-Ḥasā' ⛰ KSA 215 Jc 32
al-Ḥaṣab ○ OM 226 Jg 32
Al Hasaka ○ SYR 202 Hn 27
al-Ḥasānī ◬ KSA 214 Hl 33
al-Ḥasī ○ YE 219 Jc 38
al-Ḥātim ○ UAE 226 Jf 33
al-ḤauĞā ○ YE 218 Hp 39
al-'Ḥaura ○ YE 218 Jb 39
al-Ḥawātah ○ SUD 313 Hk 39
Al Ḥawwari ○ LAR 300 Hd 33
al-Ḥazm ○ YE 218 Ja 37
Alheit ○ ZA 348 Hc 60
al-Ḥibāk ⛰ KSA 219 Je 35
al-Ḥibāk ⛰ KSA 219 Je 36
al-Ḥijaz ⌒ KSA 214 Hl 33
al Ḥilla ○ SUD 312 Hf 39
Al Ḥillah ○ IRQ 209 Ja 29
al-Hindīya ○ IRQ 209 Hp 29
al Ḥisāna ○ KSA 218 Hn 35
al-Ḥisw ○ KSA 214 Hn 34
Al Hoceima ○ MA 293 Ge 28
Al Huari ○ LAR 300 Hd 33
al-Ḥubar ○ KSA 215 Jd 32
al-Ḥudaida ○ YE 218 Hp 38
al-Ḥufayyira ○ KSA 215 Ja 33
Al Hufrah ash Sharqiya ⌒ LAR 297 Gp 32
al-Hufūf ○ KSA 215 Jc 33
al-Hulaifa as-Suflā ○ KSA 214 Hn 33
al Ḥulwa ○ KSA 215 Jb 34
al-Ḥumeida ○ KSA 214 Hk 31
al-Ḥuqf ⌒ OM 219 Jg 35
al-Ḥurma ○ KSA 218 Hp 35
Ålhus ○ N 158 Gk 15
al-Ḥušaibī ○ KSA 214 Hp 33
al-Ḥuṣay-hiṣa ○ SUD 313 Hj 38
al-Ḥuwair ○ KSA 214 Hp 32
al-Ḥuwaymī ○ YE 218 Jb 38
Al Ḥuwaysah ○ OM 226 Jg 34
Ali ○ PNG 286 Mh 49
Aliābād ○ IR 222 Jf 27
Aliābād ○ AFG 223 Jn 27
Alia Bay ○ EAK 325 Hl 44
Aliade ○ WAN 320 Gl 42
Aliağa ○ TR 195 Hf 26
Aliákmonas ~ GR 194 Hd 25
Aliambata ○ TP 282 Lp 50
Aliança do Tocantins ○ BR 133 Ek 51
Aliantan ○ RI 270 La 45
'Alībād ○ IR 226 Jf 31
Alībāg ○ IND 238 Ka 36
Ali-Bajramly ○ AZ 202 Jc 26
Alibates Flint Quarries N.M. ★ USA 70 Cm 28
Alibori ~ DY 317 Gh 40
Alice ○ USA 56 Cp 22
Alice ○ USA 81 Cn 32
Alice ~ AUS 365 Mh 53
Alice ~ AUS 375 Mj 57
Alice ○ AUS 379 Mn 60
Alice Springs ○ AUS 361 Mc 57
Alice Town ○ BS 87 Dj 33
Alice Town ○ BS 87 Dk 33
Aliceville ○ USA 86 Dd 29
Alicia ○ RP 267 Ll 37
Alicia ○ RP 267 Ln 41
al-Idwa ○ KSA 214 Hp 32
Aligarh ○ IND 234 Kc 32
Aligūdarz ○ IR 209 Jc 29
Ali Hasan ○ OM 226 Jh 34
Alikalia ○ WAL 316 Ga 41
Alikkod ○ IND 238 Kb 40
Alima ~ RCB 332 Ha 46
Alimbongo ○ RDC 336 Hg 46
Alim Island ◬ PNG 287 Mk 47
Alindao ○ RCA 321 Hc 43
Alingar ~ AFG 223 Jp 28
Alingly ○ CDN 51 Cj 19

394 Ahuachapán - Alingly

Alingsås ○ S 170 Gn 17
Alīpur ○ PK 227 Jp 31
Alipur Dūar ○ IND 235 Kj 32
Aliquisanda ○ MOC 344 Hk 52
Āli Rāipur ○ IND 234 Kb 34
Alīrājpur ○ IND 235 Kf 34
al-ʿIrqa ○ YE 218 Jb 39
al-ʿIṣ ○ KSA 214 Hm 33
Ali Sabiet ○ DJI 328 Hp 40
al-ʿIšāš ○ KSA 214 Hm 32
al-ʿIsāwīya ○ KSA 214 Hl 30
Aliseda ○ E 184 Gc 26
Alishan ○ RC 259 Ll 34
Alishan ★ RC 259 Ll 34
Aliwal North ○ ZA 349 Hf 61
Al Jabal al Akhdar ⛰ LAR 300 Hc 29
Al Jaghbūb ○ LAR 300 He 31
al-Jamlīyah ○ Q 215 Jd 33
Aljat ○ AZ 202 Jc 26
Al Jawf ○ LAR 300 Hd 33
Al Jaws al Kabīr ○ LAR 297 Gm 29
Aljenaari ○ WAN 320 Gh 40
Aljezur ○ P 184 Gb 27
Aljustrel ○ P 184 Gb 27
al-Kadada ○ SUD 313 Hj 37
al-Kahfa ○ KSA 214 Hp 32
al-Kalbān ○ OM 219 Jh 35
al-Kamak Thebes ★ ET 301 Hj 33
Alkamari ○ RN 308 Gm 39
al-Kāmil ○ KSA 214 Hm 34
al-Kāmil ○ OM 226 Jh 34
al-Kamilīn ○ SUD 313 Hj 38
al-Karak ○ JOR 214 Hk 30
Al Kararim ○ LAR 297 Gp 29
Al Kathiri ⌓ YE 218 Jc 37
al-Kawa ○ SUD 312 Hj 39
Al Khalil ○ OM 219 Jg 36
al-Khandaq ○ SUD 312 Hh 36
Al Kharj al-Ḥarǧ ○ KSA 215 Jb 33
al-Khiran ○ KWT 215 Jc 31
Al Khums ○ LAR 297 Gp 29
Al Khuwayr ○ OM 226 Jf 34
al-Kidan ⌓ KSA 215 Je 34
al-Kirbekan ○ SUD 312 Hj 36
Alkmaar ○ NL 163 Gj 19
al-Kūfa ○ IRQ 209 Ja 29
a-l Kūlandy ⊿ KZ 202 Jc 23
al-Kumait ○ IRQ 209 Jb 29
al-Kuntilla ○ ET 214 Hk 31
al-Kūt ○ IRQ 209 Ja 29
al-Labbal ⌓ KSA 214 Hn 31
Allada ○ DY 317 Gg 42
Al Lādhiqīyah Latakia ○ SYR 208 Hk 28
Allagash ~ USA 60 Dp 22
al-Lagowa ○ SUD 312 Hg 40
Allagudda ○ IND 238 Kd 38
Allahābād ○ IND 234 Ke 33
Allāhganj ○ IND 234 Kd 32
Allahüekber Dağ ⛰ TR 202 Hp 25
Allakaket ○ USA 46 An 11
Allal-bou-Fenzi ○ MA 292 Gb 30
Allal-Tazi ○ MA 293 Gc 28
Allangouassou ○ CI 317 Gd 42
Allanmyo ○ MYA 254 Km 36
Allanridge ○ ZA 349 Hf 59
Allapalli ○ IND 238 Ke 36
Allardville ○ CDN 61 Eb 22
Allatar ○ BG 195 Hf 24
al-Latifiya ○ IRQ 209 Hp 29
Alldays ○ ZA 349 Hg 57
Allegan ○ USA 57 De 24
Allegeny State Park ♀ USA 74 Dj 25
Allegheny ~ USA 74 Dj 25
Allegheny Mountains ⛰ USA 71 Dg 27
Allegheny Reservoir ~ USA 74 Dj 25
Allemanskraal Dam ~ ZA 349 Hf 60
Allen ○ RP 267 Ln 39
Allendale ○ USA 71 Dh 29
Allende ○ MEX 81 Cm 31
Allende ○ MEX 81 Cm 33
Allen Island ⊿ AUS 365 Mf 54
Allentown ○ USA 74 Dl 25
Alleppey ○ IND 239 Kb 41
Allgäu ⌓ D 174 Gl 22
Allgäu ○ D 174 Gm 22
Alliance ○ CDN 51 Cg 19
Alliance ○ USA 51 Cl 24
Alliance ○ USA 71 Dh 25
Allibo ○ ETH 325 Hl 41
Allier ~ F 185 Gh 23
Alligator Pond ⊿ JA 101 Dk 37
al-Līhīn ○ KSA 214 Hm 33
Allinagaram ○ IND 239 Kc 41
Allipen ~ RCH 147 Dn 65
Allison ○ USA 56 Db 24
Allison ○ USA 70 Db 28
al-Līt ○ KSA 218 Hn 35
al-Liwā' ⌓ UAE 215 Je 34
al-Liwā' ○ OM 226 Jg 33
Allu ○ RI 279 Lk 48
Al Luhayyah ○ YE 218 Hp 38
Alma ○ USA 57 Df 24
Alma ○ CDN 60 Dn 21
Alma ○ CDN 61 Eb 23
Alma ○ USA 70 Cn 25
Alma ○ USA 87 Dg 30
Alma ~ UA 175 Hj 23
al-Maʿānīya ○ IRQ 214 Hp 30
al-Madaniqa ○ KSA 218 Hp 37
Almadén ○ E 184 Gd 26
Almaden ○ AUS 365 Mj 54
al-Mafāza ○ SUD 313 Hk 39
al-Mafraq ○ JOR 208 Hl 29
al-Maǧardal ○ KSA 218 Hn 36
al-Maǧārim ○ YE 218 Jb 38
al-Maǧma'a ○ KSA 215 Ja 33
Almagro Island ⊿ RP 267 Ln 40
al-Maḥābiša ○ YE 218 Hp 37
al-Maḥākik ⌓ KSA 219 Jd 35
al-Maḥālānī ○ KSA 214 Hp 32
Al Maḥalla Al Kubrā ○ ET 301 Hh 30
al-Maḥariq ○ ET 301 Hh 33
Almahel ○ ETH 313 Hk 40
al-Maḥfid ○ YE 218 Ja 37
al-Maḥmūdīya ○ IRQ 209 Ja 29
al-Mahra ⌓ YE 219 Jd 38
al-Maḥwa ○ KSA 218 Hn 36
al-Maḥwīt ○ YE 218 Hp 38
al-Makmin ○ IRQ 214 Hp 30
al-Malamm ○ SUD 324 Hg 41
Almalyk ○ UZB 19 Na 5
Almal'yk ○ UZB 223 Jn 25
al-Manādir ⌓ UAE 226 Jf 34
al-Manāqil ○ SUD 312 Hj 38
Almansa ○ E 184 Gf 26
al-Manšāh ○ ET 301 Hh 32
Al Man-Sūra ○ ET 301 Hh 30
al-Manṣūrīya ○ YE 218 Hp 38
Al Maqrūn ○ LAR 300 Hb 30
Almār ○ AFG 223 Jl 28
al-Marāmīya ○ KSA 214 Hl 33
al-Marāšī ○ YE 218 Ja 37
al-Marāwi'a ○ YE 218 Hp 38
al-Marḍ ○ IRQ 209 Hp 29
al-Marfa' ○ UAE 215 Je 33
Al Marj ○ LAR 300 Hc 29
Al Marūqah ○ LAR 297 Gn 32
Almas ~ BR 133 Ek 52
Almas ~ BR 133 Ek 53
Almas ○ BR 133 El 51
al-Masāiqa ○ OM 226 Jg 34
al-Masna'a ○ OM 226 Jg 34
al-Masqa ○ KSA 218 Hp 37
al-Maṭāmah ○ YE 218 Ja 37
al-Matamma ○ SUD 313 Hj 37
al-Matarīya ○ ET 301 Hh 30
al-Matmarfag ○ MA 292 Fp 32
al-Matna ○ SUD 313 Hk 39
Almaty ○ KZ 22 Nb 5
al-Mayādin ○ SYR 209 Hm 28
Almazán ○ E 184 Ge 25
al-Mazra'a ○ JOR 214 Hk 30
Almeida ○ E 184 Gc 25
Almeirim ○ BR 121 Eh 46
Almeirim ○ P 184 Gb 26
Almel ○ IND 238 Kc 37
Almelo ○ NL 170 Gk 19
Almenara ○ BR 125 Ep 54
Almenar d. S. ○ E 184 Ge 25
Almendralejo ○ E 184 Gc 26
Almendrillo ○ RCH 137 Dn 62
Almere ○ NL 163 Gj 19
Almería ○ E 184 Ge 27
Al'met'evsk ○ RUS 154 Rb 7
Al'metevsk ○ RUS 181 Jd 18
Älmhult ○ S 170 Gp 17
al-Miḍnab ○ KSA 215 Hp 33
al-Mihrād ⌓ KSA 219 Je 35
al-Mintirib ○ OM 226 Jh 34
Al-Minyā ○ ET 301 Hh 31
al-Miqdādīya ○ IRQ 209 Ja 28
Almirante ○ PA 97 Dg 41
Almirós ○ GR 194 Hd 26
Almodôvar ○ P 184 Gb 27
Almodóvar del Rio ○ E 184 Gd 27
Almonte ○ CDN 60 Dk 23
Almonte ○ E 184 Gc 27
Almora ○ IND 234 Kd 31
Almora ○ AUS 365 Mf 55
a-l Morskoj ⊿ KZ 202 Jd 23
Al Mubarrez ○ KSA 215 Jc 33
al-Muḍailif ○ KSA 218 Hn 36
al-Muḍairib ○ OM 226 Jh 34
al-Muglad ○ SUD 312 Hf 40
Al-Muhammadiyah ○ MA 293 Gc 29
Al Muharraq ▣ BRN 215 Jd 32
Al Mukallā ○ YE 219 Jc 38
Al Mukhā ○ YE 218 Hp 39
al-Mulailiḥ ○ KSA 214 Hm 33
Almuñécar ○ E 184 Ge 27
al-Munqaṭi' ○ YE 218 Ja 38
al-Muṣallā ○ OM 226 Jg 34
al-Musallamīya ○ SUD 313 Hj 38
al-Mušarifa ○ SYR 209 Hm 27
al-Musayyib ○ IRQ 209 Hp 29
al-Mutannā ◉ IRQ 215 Ja 30
al-Muti'a ○ ET 301 Hh 32
al-Muwailiḥ ○ KSA 214 Hk 32
al-Muzāḥimīya ○ KSA 215 Jb 33
Alness ○ GB 162 Gd 17
Alnif ○ MA 293 Gd 30
al-Nuwaisib ○ KWT 215 Jc 31
Alnwick ○ GB 162 Gf 18
Alóag ○ EC 116 Dj 46
Alô Brasil ○ BR 133 Eh 52
Alofi ⊿ F 390 Ab 53
Alofi ○ NZ 390 Ae 55
Aloi ○ EAU 325 Hj 44
Aloja ○ LV 171 He 17
Alokan Island ⊿ SOL 290 Nb 50
Alónissos ⊿ GR 194 Hd 26
Alor ⊿ RI 282 Ln 50
Aloro ~ BOL 136 Ea 56
Alor Setar ○ MAL 270 La 42
Alota ○ BOL 136 Ea 56
Alotau ○ PNG 287 Mm 51
Alpachiri ○ RA 137 Eb 64
Alpamayo △ PE 116 Dk 50
Alpasinche ○ RA 136 Ea 60
Alpena ○ USA 57 Dg 23
Alpercata ~ BR 121 Em 49
Alpha ○ AUS 375 Mk 57
Alpha Creek ~ AUS 375 Mk 57
Alpine ○ USA 51 Cg 24
Alpine ○ USA 51 Ch 23
Alpine ○ USA 65 Cf 29
Alpine ○ USA 81 Cl 30
Alpinópolis ○ BR 141 El 56
a-l Podgornyj ⊿ KZ 202 Jd 23
Alpouro ~ DY 320 Gh 41
Alps ⛰ 185 Gk 23
Alpu ○ TR 195 Hh 26
Al Qa'āmīyāt ⌓ KSA 218 Jc 37
al-Qādisīya ◉ IRQ 215 Ja 30
al-Qaffāy ⊿ UAE 215 Jd 33
al-Qahmah ○ KSA 218 Hn 36
al-Qā'iya ○ KSA 214 Hp 33
Al Qala'a ○ LAR 297 Gp 30
al-Qalība ○ KSA 214 Hl 31
Al Qamishli ○ SYR 202 Hn 27
al-Qanṭara ○ ET 301 Hj 30
Al Qardabah ○ LAR 300 Hd 29
Al Qaryah ash Sharqīyah ○ LAR 297 Gn 30
al-Qaryatain ○ SYR 208 Hl 28
Al Qaṣabāt ○ LAR 297 Gp 29
al Qaṣr ○ ET 301 Hg 33
al-Qaṭīf ○ KSA 215 Jc 32
al-Qaṭn ○ YE 218 Jc 38
al-Qaṭrāna ○ JOR 214 Hl 30
Al Qatrūn ○ LAR 297 Gp 33
al-Qawz ○ SUD 313 Hj 37
al-Qibliya ⊿ ET 301 Hj 31
al-Qišla ○ IRQ 215 Jc 31
al-Qrṭāwīya ○ KSA 215 Ja 32
Al Quaiti ⌓ YE 219 Jc 38
al-Qualayd Bahrī ○ SUD 312 Hh 36
Al Qubbah ○ LAR 300 Hd 29
al-Qunaiṭira ○ SYR 208 Hk 29
al-Qunfuḍa ○ KSA 218 Hn 36
al-Qurayyāt ○ KSA 214 Hl 30
al-Qurna ○ IRQ 215 Jb 30
al-Quṣair ○ SYR 208 Hl 28
al-Quṣair ○ IRQ 215 Ja 30
al-Qus Ṭaima ○ ET 214 Hk 30
al-Quṭaifa ○ SYR 208 Hl 29
al-Quṭayna ○ SUD 312 Hj 38
al-Quwair ○ IRQ 209 Hp 27
al-Quwaisi ○ SUD 313 Hk 39
al-Quwāra ○ KSA 214 Hp 32
al-Qūz ○ KSA 218 Hn 36
al-Quza ○ YE 219 Jc 38
Al Rahibat ○ LAR 297 Gm 30
al-Ramta ○ JOR 208 Hk 29
Alroy Downs ○ AUS 364 Me 55
a-l Rybacij ⊿ KZ 202 Jc 23
Alsace ◉ F 163 Gk 21
Alsace ⌓ F 163 Gk 22
Alsace ○ AUS 365 Mf 55
al-Samha ○ UAE 226 Jf 33
Alsask ○ CDN 51 Ch 20
Alsasua ○ E 184 Ge 24
Alshi ○ EC 116 Dj 47
Al Socorro ○ CO 107 Dn 42
al-Subiya ○ KWT 215 Jc 31
Alta ○ N 159 Hd 11
Altaelva ~ N 159 Hd 11
Alta García ○ RA 137 Eb 61
Altagracia ○ YV 107 Dn 40
Altagracia ○ YV 112 Eb 41
Altagracia de Orituco ○ YV 107 Ea 41
Altai Mountains ⛰ MNG 204 Tc 9
Altaj ○ MNG 204 Ub 9
Altajn Caadah Gov' ⌓ MNG 204 Ub 10
Altaj Shan ⛰ VRC 204 Tc 9
Altamachi ~ BOL 129 Ea 54
Altamaha ~ USA 87 Dg 30
Altamira ○ MEX 81 Cp 34
Altamira ○ CO 106 Dl 44
Altamira ○ BR 121 Eh 47
Altamira ○ RCH 136 Dn 58
Altamira do Maranhão ○ BR 121 Em 48
Altamirano ○ MEX 93 Db 37
Altamont ○ USA 50 Cb 24
Altamonte Springs ○ USA 87 Dh 31
Altamura ○ I 194 Ha 25
Altar ○ MEX 80 Cg 30
Altar-Est ○ DZ 296 Gl 31
Altata ○ MEX 80 Ch 33
Alta Vista ○ USA 70 Cp 26
Altavista ○ USA 74 Dj 27
Altay ⛰ RUS 22 Pa 4
Altay ○ VRC 204 Tc 9
Altay ⛰ KZ/RUS 204 Tc 9
Altdorf ○ CH 174 Gl 22
Altea ○ E 184 Gg 26
Altenburg ○ D 174 Gn 20
Alter do Chão ○ P 184 Gc 26
Altéro do Chão ○ BR 120 Eg 47
Alterosa ○ BR 141 El 56
Altese d. S. ○ E 184 Gg 25
Altevatnet ~ N 159 Hb 11
Altiplanicie de Hakeluincul ⌓ RA 147 Dp 66
Altiplano ⌓ PE/BOL 128 Dp 54
Altkirch ○ F 163 Gk 22
Altmühl ~ D 174 Gm 21
Alto ○ USA 81 Da 30
Alto Alegre ○ BR 112 Ed 44
Alto Alegre ○ BR 146 Eh 61
Alto Anapu ~ BR 121 Ej 47
Alto Araguaia ○ BR 133 Eh 54
Alto Chandless ~ PE 128 Dn 51
Alto Chicapa ○ ANG 340 Hb 51
Alto de Amparo ○ BR 140 Ej 58
Alto de Carrizal △ CO 106 Dk 42
Alto de la Sierra ○ PY 136 Ec 57
Alto del Carmen ○ RCH 136 Dn 60
Alto de los Colorados ⛰ RA 136 Dp 59
Alto de Tamar △ CO 106 Dl 42
Alto Floresta ○ BR 120 Eg 50
Alto Garças ○ BR 132 Eh 54
Alto Hama ○ ANG 340 Gp 52
Alto Jurupari ~ BR 117 Dn 50
Alto Ligonha ○ MOC 344 Hm 53
Alto Longá ○ BR 124 En 48
Alto Madre de Dios ~ PE 128 Dn 52
Alton ○ USA 60 Dk 24
Alton ○ USA 70 Dc 27
Alton ○ USA 71 Dc 26
Altoona ○ USA 74 Dj 25
Alto Pacaja ~ BR 121 Ej 47
Alto Paraguai ○ BR 132 Ef 53
Alto Paraíso de Goiás ○ BR 133 El 53
Alto Parnaíba ○ BR 121 El 50
Alto Pencoso ○ RA 137 Ea 62
Alto Purús ~ PE 128 Dn 51
Alto Quimarí △ CO 106 Dk 41
Alto Río Mayo ○ RA 152 Dn 68
Alto Río Senguerr ○ RA 152 Dn 68
Alto Río Verde ○ BR 132 Eh 55
Altos ○ BR 124 En 48
Alto Sucuriú ○ BR 133 Eh 55
Alto Taquari ○ BR 132 Ef 52
Altotonga ○ MEX 92 Cp 35
Altötting ○ D 174 Gn 21
Altun ○ VRC 231 Kj 26
Altun Küprü ○ IRQ 209 Ja 28
Altun Shan ⛰ VRC 231 Kh 27
Altun Shan ⛰ VRC 231 Kk 26
Altun Shan △ VRC 231 Kl 26
Alturas ○ USA 64 Cb 25
Altus ○ USA 70 Cn 28
Altus Lake ~ USA 70 Cn 28
Altyaryk ○ UZB 223 Jp 25
Alua ○ MOC 344 Hm 52
Aluakluak ○ SUD 324 Hh 42
al-ʿUbaila ○ KSA 219 Jd 35
Alucra ○ TR 195 Hm 25
al-ʿUdaib ○ KSA 214 Hl 32
al-ʿUdaid ○ KSA 215 Jd 33
al-Uḍayya ○ SUD 312 Hg 39
Alūksne ○ LV 171 Hf 17
al-ʿUlā ○ KSA 214 Hl 32
al-ʿUmda ○ SUD 312 Hg 40
Aluminé ○ RA 147 Dn 65
Aluminé ~ RA 147 Dn 65
A Lu'ō'i ○ VN 263 Ld 37
Alupka ○ UA 175 Hj 23
al-ʿUqair ○ KSA 215 Jc 33
Al ,Uqaylah ○ LAR 300 Hb 30
Alūr ○ IND 238 Kb 39
Ālūr ○ IND 238 Kc 38
al-ʿUraiq ⛰ KSA 214 Hm 31
al-ʿUrūq al-Mu'tarida ⌓ KSA 219 Je 36
al'Ushara ○ SUD 312 Hj 38
Alušta ○ UA 175 Hk 23
al-ʿUtayshān ○ SUD 313 Hk 37
al-ʿUwaiqīla ○ KSA 214 Hn 30
Al Uwaynāt ○ LAR 297 Gm 33
al-ʿUyaina ○ KSA 215 Jb 33
al-ʿUẓaim ○ KSA 214 Hp 32
al-ʿUzair ○ IRQ 215 Jb 30
Alva ○ USA 70 Cn 27
Alvarado ○ MEX 93 Da 36
Alvarado ○ CO 106 Dl 43
Alvarães ○ BR 117 Eb 47
Alvarenga ○ BR 141 Ep 55
Ålvdal ○ N 158 Gm 14
Älvdalen ○ S 158 Gn 15
Alvear ○ RA 146 Ef 60
Alvesta ○ S 170 Gp 17
Alvin ○ USA 57 Dd 23
Alvin ○ USA 81 Da 31
Alvinston ○ CDN 57 Dh 24
Alvorada ○ BR 133 Ek 52
Alvorada ○ BR 146 Ej 61
Alvorada do Oeste ○ BR 129 Ec 51
Alvorado do Norte ○ BR 133 El 53
Alvord Desert ⌓ USA 50 Cc 24
Alvord Valley ⌓ USA 50 Cc 24
Älvros ○ S 158 Gp 14
Älvsbyn ○ S 159 Hc 13
al-Wafra ○ KWT 215 Jb 31
al-Waǧh ○ KSA 214 Hl 32
Al Wahah ○ LAR 300 Hb 31
al Wāhāt Sīwa ⌓ ET 300 He 31
Alwar ○ IND 234 Kc 32
Alwās ○ IND 230 Kc 29
al-Wāsiqa ○ KSA 218 Hn 35
al-Wāsiṭā ○ ET 301 Hh 31
al-Waṭā ⌓ OM 219 Jg 35
Alwero Wenz ~ ETH 325 Hk 41
al-Widyan ⛰ IRQ 214 Hn 30
Al Wigh ○ LAR 309 Gp 33
Al Wiṭṭyah ○ LAR 297 Gm 29
Alxa Gaoyuan ⌓ VRC 242 La 25
Alxa Youqi ○ VRC 242 La 26
Alxa Zuoqi ○ VRC 242 Lc 26
Alyangula ○ AUS 364 Me 52
al-Yāsāt ⊿ UAE 215 Je 33
Alyawarra Aboriginal Land ••• AUS 374 Md 56
Alyeska Resort&Ski Aera ★ USA 46 Ba 15
Alytus ○ LT 171 He 18
Alzada ○ USA 51 Ck 23
Alzagra ○ RA 137 Ed 64
Alzazani ~ GE 202 Jb 25
Alzira ○ E 184 Gf 26
Ama ○ MYA 262 Km 38
Ama ○ PNG 286 Mg 48
Amaciā ○ BR 117 Eb 48
Amacuro ~ YV 112 Ed 41
Amacuzac ~ MEX 92 Cn 37
Amada Gaza ○ RCA 321 Gp 43
Amadi ○ RDC 324 Hf 44
Amadi ○ SUD 324 Hh 43
Amadjuak Lake ~ CDN 43 Ha 6
Amado ○ USA 80 Cg 30
Amadror ⌓ DZ 296 Gk 33
Amagasaki ○ J 251 Md 28
Amagi ○ J 247 Mb 29
Amahai ○ RI 283 Ma 47
Amajac ~ MEX 92 Cn 35
Amaki ○ PNG 286 Mh 48
Amakusa ★ J 247 Ma 29
Amakusa-nada ~ J 247 Ma 29
Amakusa-shima ⊿ J 247 Ma 29
Åmål ○ S 170 Gn 16
Amala ~ EAK 337 Hk 46
Amalapuram ○ IND 238 Kf 37
Amalfi ○ I 194 Gp 25
Amalia ○ ZA 349 He 59
Amaliáda ○ GR 194 Hc 27
Amalner ○ IND 234 Kb 35
Amaluza ○ EC 116 Dj 47
Amaluza ○ EC 116 Dj 48
Amamá ○ RA 136 Ec 59
Amamapare ○ RI 286 Me 48
Amamba ○ MOC 352 Hj 56
Amambai ○ BR 140 Eg 57
Amami Islands ⊿ J 259 Ma 32
Amami Ō-shima ⊿ J 259 Ma 31
Amana ~ YV 112 Ec 41
Amanã ~ BR 120 Ef 48
Amanab ○ PNG 286 Mg 47
Amancio ○ C 101 Dk 35
Amānganj ○ IND 234 Ke 33
Amaniú ○ BR 125 Ep 51
Amankaragaj ○ KZ 154 Sa 8
Amantea ○ I 185 Gp 26
Amantogaj ○ KZ 155 Sb 8
Amanu ⊿ F 35 Bb 11
Amanzamnyama ~ ZW 341 Hf 55
Amanzimtoti ○ ZA 349 Hh 61
Amapá ◉ BR 113 Eg 45
Amapá ○ BR 113 Ej 44
Amapa Grande ~ BR 113 Ej 44
Amapari ~ BR 113 Eh 45
Amar ⛰ ETH 325 Hl 43
Amaraji ○ BR 124 Fc 50
Amarante ○ BR 124 En 49
Amarante do Maranhão ○ BR 121 El 48
Amaranth ○ CDN 56 Cn 20
Amarapura ○ MYA 254 Kn 35
Amarapuram ○ IND 238 Kc 39
Amaravati ○ IND 238 Ke 37
Amaravati ~ IND 239 Kc 40
Amarga ~ RUS 250 Mf 22
Amargosa ~ USA 64 Cd 28
Amargosa ○ BR 125 Fa 52
Amargosa Range ⛰ USA 64 Cd 27
Amarillo ○ USA 65 Cl 28
Amarkantak ○ IND 234 Ke 34
Amasya ○ TR 195 Hk 25
Amata ○ AUS 369 Mb 59
Amatari ○ BR 120 Ee 47
Amatitlán ○ GCA 93 Dc 38
Amatlán de Cañas ○ MEX 92 Ck 35
Amatura ○ BR 117 Dp 47
Amau ○ PNG 287 Mk 51
Amazon ~ PE 116 Dm 47
Amazon ~ BR 120 Ed 47
Amazon ~ BR 120 Eh 46
Amazonas Para ◉ BR 117 Dp 48
Amazon Basin ⌓ BR 117 Ea 48
Amazones ~ BR 121 Ej 46
Ambad ○ IND 238 Kb 36
Amba Farit △ ETH 313 Hm 40
Amba Gīyorgīs ○ ETH 313 Hl 39
Ambājogāi ○ IND 238 Kc 36
Ambakireny ○ RM 345 Jb 54
Ambala ○ IND 230 Kc 30
Ambalabe ○ RM 345 Jb 53
Ambalajanakomby ○ RM 345 Jb 54
Ambalakirajy ○ RM 345 Jc 53
Ambalamanakana ○ RM 353 Jb 56
Ambalamanasy ○ RM 345 Jc 53
Ambalapaiso ○ RM 345 Jc 53
Ambalarondra ○ RM 345 Jc 55
Ambalavao ○ RM 353 Jb 56
Ambam ○ CAM 320 Gm 44
Āmba Maderīya ○ ETH 313 Hm 39
Ambanja ○ RM 345 Jc 52
Ambarawa ○ RI 278 Lf 49
Ambargasta ○ RA 137 Ec 60
Ambarnyj ○ RUS 159 Hj 13
Ambato ○ EC 116 Dj 46
Ambato-Boeny ○ RM 345 Jb 54
Ambato Finandrahana ○ RM 353 Jb 56
Ambatolahy ○ RM 353 Ja 56
Ambatolampy ○ RM 345 Jb 55
Ambatomainty ○ RM 345 Ja 54
Ambatomanoina ○ RM 345 Jb 55
Ambatondrazaka ○ RM 345 Jc 54
Ambatosoratra ○ RM 345 Jc 54
Ambatovory ○ RM 353 Jb 56
Ambatry ○ RM 353 Ja 57
Ambe ~ RDC 333 He 47
Amberg ○ D 174 Gm 21
Ambergris Cay ⊿ BH 93 De 36
Amberley ○ CDN 57 Dg 23
Ambert ○ F 185 Gh 23
Ambidédi ○ RMM 304 Ga 38
Ambikāpur ○ IND 234 Kf 34
Ambila ○ RM 353 Jc 57
Ambil Island ⊿ RP 267 Ll 39
Ambilobe ○ RM 345 Jc 52
Ambinanindrano ○ RM 353 Jb 56
Ambinaninony ○ RM 345 Jc 55
Ambitle Island ⊿ PNG 287 Mn 48
Ambleside ○ GB 162 Ge 18
Ambo ○ PE 128 Dk 51
Amboahangibe ○ RM 345 Jc 53
Amboahangy ○ RM 353 Jb 58
Amboasary ○ RM 345 Jb 55
Amboasary ○ RM 353 Jb 58
Ambodifotatra ○ RM 345 Jc 54
Ambodiriana ○ RM 345 Jc 54
Ambohidratrimo ○ RM 345 Jb 55
Ambohimahasoa ○ RM 353 Jb 56
Ambohinihaonana ○ RM 353 Jb 56
Ambohipaky ○ RM 345 Ja 54
Ambohitra ○ RM 345 Jc 52
Ambohitralanana ○ RM 345 Jd 53
Amboise ○ F 163 Gg 22
Amboiva ○ ANG 340 Gp 51
Amboli ○ IND 238 Ka 38
Ambon ○ RI 283 Ma 47
Ambondromamy ○ RM 345 Jb 54
Amboni ○ EAT 337 Hm 48
Amborompotsy ○ RM 353 Jb 56
Amborondolo ○ RM 345 Jc 52
Amboseli ♀ EAK 337 Hl 47
Ambositra ○ RM 353 Jb 56
Ambovombe ○ RM 353 Jb 58
Amboy ○ USA 64 Ce 28
Amboy ○ USA 71 Dd 25
Amboyna Cay ⊿ MAL 274 Lg 42
Ambriz ○ ANG 332 Gn 49
Ambrolauri ○ GE 202 Hp 24
Ambrym ⊿ VU 386 Ng 54
Ambuaki ○ RI 283 Mc 46
Ambulong Island ⊿ RP 267 Ll 39
Ambuma ○ RDC 333 Hb 44
Ambunten ○ RI 279 Lg 49
Ambunti ○ PNG 286 Mh 48
Am-Dam ○ TCH 321 Hc 39
Amdāpur ○ IND 234 Kc 35
Amdasa ○ RI 283 Mb 49
Amderma ○ RUS 154 Sa 5
Am Djaména ○ RCA 321 Hc 41
Am Djemena ○ TCH 321 Ha 39
Amdo ○ VRC 231 Kk 29
Ameca ○ MEX 92 Ck 35
Ameca ~ MEX 92 Ck 35
Amecameca ○ MEX 92 Cn 36
Ameland ⊿ NL 163 Gj 19
Amelia ○ USA 56 Cn 24
Amelie ○ USA 56 Cn 24
Amellougui ○ MA 293 Gc 30
Amentego ○ SUD 312 Hh 36
ʿAmerī ○ IR 215 Jd 30
América Dourada ○ BR 125 Ep 51
Americana ○ BR 141 El 57
American Falls ○ USA 64 Cf 24
American Falls Reservoir ~ USA 64 Cf 24
American Fork ○ USA 65 Cf 25
American Highland ⌓ 38 Nb 17
Americus ○ USA 86 Df 29
Amerikanisch-Samoa ◉ USA 390 Ae 53
Amersfoort ○ NL 163 Gj 19
Amersfoort ○ ZA 349 Hg 59
Amery Ice Shelf ▲ 38 Nb 17
Ames ○ USA 70 Db 25
Amesbury ○ USA 60 Dn 24
Ameson ○ CDN 57 Df 21
Amethi ○ IND 234 Ke 32
Amett ○ USA 70 Cn 27
Amfilohia ○ GR 194 Hc 26
Amga ~ RUS 204 Wa 7
Amga ○ RUS 205 Wc 6
Amgu ○ RUS 250 Me 23
Amguéma ~ RUS 205 Zc 5
Amguid ○ DZ 296 Gj 32
Amgun ○ RUS 205 Xa 8
Amherst ○ USA 60 Dm 24
Amherst ○ CDN 61 Eb 23
Amherst ○ USA 74 Dj 27
Amherstburg ○ CDN 71 Dg 24
Amherst Island ⊿ CDN 60 Dk 23
Am Himédé ○ TCH 321 Hb 39
Amidon ○ USA 51 Cl 22
Amiens ○ F 163 Gh 21
Amīndīvī Islands ⊿ IND 239 Ka 40
Aminga ○ RA 137 Ea 60
Aminius ○ NAM 348 Hb 57
Amino ○ J 251 Md 28
Amio ○ PNG 287 Mm 49
Amirābād ○ IR 222 Je 27
Amir Chāh ○ PK 226 Jk 31
Amistad ○ USA 65 Cl 28
Amistad Reservation ~ USA 81 Cm 31
Amite ○ USA 86 Dc 30
Amizmiz ○ MA 292 Gb 30
Amkunj ○ IND 262 Kl 34
Amlāgora ○ IND 235 Kh 34
Amlamé ○ RT 317 Gg 42
Amlapura ○ RI 279 Lh 50
Amlekhganj ○ NEP 235 Kg 32
Āmli ○ N 170 Gl 16
Amloustarat ○ RMM 305 Gf 37
Amma ○ IND 238 Kc 40
Amman ▣ JOR 214 Hk 30
Ammänsaari ○ FIN 159 Hg 13
Ammāpettai ○ IND 239 Kd 40
Ammarnäs ○ S 158 Ha 13
Ammaroo ○ AUS 374 Md 56
Ammassaliq ○ DK 43 Kb 5
Ammersee ~ D 174 Gm 21
Ammochostos ○ CY 195 Hj 28
Amnat Charoen ○ THA 263 Lc 38
Amnok Gang ~ DVRK 246 Ln 25
Āmol ○ IR 222 Je 27
Amoltepec ○ MEX 92 Cp 36
Amon ○ MA 292 Ga 31
Amontada ○ BR 124 Fa 47
Amorgós ○ GR 194 He 27
Amorgós ⊿ GR 194 He 27
Amorinópolis ○ BR 133 Ej 54
Amory ○ USA 71 Dd 28
Amos ○ CDN 60 Dj 21
Amotope ○ SME 113 Ef 44
Amou ~ RT 317 Gg 42
Amouguèr ○ MA 293 Gd 29
Amourj ○ RIM 305 Gc 37
Amoya ○ GH 317 Ge 42
Amozoc ○ MEX 92 Cp 35
Ampah ○ RI 279 Lh 46
Ampana ○ RI 282 Ll 46
Ampang ○ RI 279 Lk 50
Ampanihy ○ RM 353 Ja 58
Amparafaravola ○ RM 345 Jb 54
Amparai ○ CL 239 Ke 42
Amparo ○ BR 141 El 57
Ampasimanolotra ○ RM 345 Jc 55
Ampasimbe ○ RM 345 Jc 54
Ampasinambo ○ RM 353 Jb 56
Ampefy ○ RM 345 Jb 55
Amper ○ WAN 320 Gl 41
Amphithéâtre ★ TN 297 Gm 28
Amphitrite Group ⊿ VRC 263 Lf 37
Amphlett Group ⊿ PNG 287 Mm 50
Ampibabo ○ RI 282 Ll 46
Ampisikinana ○ RM 345 Jc 52
Ampiyacu ~ PE 116 Dm 47
Ampoa ○ RI 282 Ll 46
Ampombiantambo ○ RM 345 Jc 52
Ampotaka ○ RM 353 Ja 58
Amqui ○ CDN 60 Ea 21
Amrān ○ YE 218 Hp 38
Amrāvati ○ IND 234 Kc 35
Am Raya ○ TCH 309 Ha 38
Amreli ○ IND 227 Jp 35
Āmri ○ PK 227 Jm 32
ʿAmrīt ○ SYR 208 Hk 28
Amritsar ○ IND 230 Kb 30
Amroha ○ IND 234 Kd 31
Amrum ⊿ D 170 Gl 18
Am Sak ○ TCH 321 Hb 39
Amsel ○ DZ 308 Gj 34
Amsterdam ⊿ F 31 Nb 13
Amsterdam ○ CDN 51 Cl 20
Amsterdam ○ USA 60 Dl 24
Amsterdam ▣ NL 163 Gh 19
Amsterdam ○ ZA 352 Hh 59
Amstetten ○ A 174 Gp 21
Am Timan ○ TCH 321 Hc 40
Amu-Buharskij kanal ~ UZB 223 Jl 26
Amuda ○ EAU 325 Hk 45
Amu-Dar'ja ○ TM 223 Jl 27
Amu Darya ~ UZB 19 Na 5
Amu Darya ~ UZB 223 Jm 27
Amund Ringnes Island ⊿ CDN 42 Fb 3
Amundsen Gulf ≈ CDN 42 Db 4
Amundsen Sea ≈ 38 Db 16
Amuntai ○ RI 279 Lh 47
Amur ~ RUS 204 Wa 8
Amur ~ RUS 205 Xa 9
Amur ~ RUS 205 Xb 8
Amur ~ RUS 250 Mb 22
Amurang ○ RI 275 Ln 45
Amursk ○ RUS 205 Xa 8
Amyo ○ J 251 Me 28
Amys Peak △ AUS 375 Mm 58
Am-Zoer ○ TCH 309 Hc 38
ʿĀna ○ IRQ 209 Hn 28
Anaa ⊿ F 35 Bb 11
Anabanua ○ RI 282 Ll 47
Anabar ~ RUS 204 Vb 4
Anabarskiy Zaliv ≈ RUS 204 Vb 4
Anabat ○ RP 267 Ll 37
Anabunga River ~ PNG 287 Mk 50
Anaco ○ YV 112 Eb 41
Anaconda ○ USA 51 Cf 22
Anacortes ○ USA 50 Ca 21
Anadarko ○ USA 70 Cn 28
Anadyr' ○ RUS 205 Zc 6
Anadyr' ~ RUS 205 Zc 6
Anadyrskaya Nizmennost' ⌓ RUS 205 Zc 5
Anáfi ⊿ GR 194 He 27
An-Agaf ◉ IRQ 215 Hp 30
Anaghit ○ ER 313 Hm 37
Anaheim ○ USA 64 Cd 29
Anahidrano ○ RM 345 Jb 53
Anahim Lake ○ CDN 50 Bp 19
Anáhuac ○ MEX 80 Cj 31
Anaimālai ○ IND 239 Kc 40
Anai Mudi △ IND 239 Kc 40
Anajás ○ BR 121 Ek 46
Anajatuba ○ BR 121 Em 47
Anajé ○ BR 125 Ep 53
Anaka ○ EAU 324 Hh 44
Anakao ○ RM 353 Hp 57
Anakāpalle ○ IND 238 Kf 37
Anakch ○ MA 292 Fp 32
Anakdara ○ RI 279 Lk 47
Anakie ○ AUS 375 Mk 57
Anaktuvuk Pass ○ USA 46 An 11
Analatava ○ RM 345 Jb 53
Analavory ○ RM 345 Jb 55
Analtin Island ⊿ PNG 287 Mj 46
Anamā ○ BR 120 Ed 47
Anambas Islands ⊿ RI 271 Lc 44
Anambra ~ WAN 320 Gk 42
Anamosa ○ USA 70 Dc 24

Alingsås - Anamosa 395

□Country ▣Capital city ⊙Administrative unit OPlace ♁Island ⩓Mountain range △Mountain ⌒Cape ≈Ocean, Sea ~Lake, River ♆Undersea topography ▲Glacier ♀National park •••Reservation ★Point of major interest ⌓Landscape

Anamu ~ **BR** 113 Ef 45
Anamur O **TR** 195 Hj 27
Anan O **J** 251 Md 29
Ananás O **BR** 121 Ek 49
Ananda-Kouadiokro O **CI** 317 Gd 42
Anandpur O **IND** 235 Kh 35
Ananindeau O **BR** 121 Ek 46
Ananjiv O **UA** 175 Hh 22
Anantnag O **IND** 230 Kb 29
Anantsono O **RM** 353 Hp 57
Anapa O **RUS** 195 Hl 23
Anápolis O **BR** 133 Ek 54
Anapu ~ **BR** 121 Ej 46
Anapu ~ **BR** 121 Ej 47
Ânâr Inari O **FIN** 159 Hf 11
Anār O **IR** 226 Jf 30
Anārak O **IR** 222 Je 29
Anār Dare O **AFG** 223 Jj 29
Ånarjohka ~ **N** 159 He 11
Anarjokka ♀ **N** 159 He 11
Anastácio O **BR** 140 Ef 56
Anathan ♁ **USA** 27 Sa 8
Anatolia ⌓ **TR** 195 Hh 26
Anatoliki Macedonia ⊙ **GR** 194 He 25
Anatone O **USA** 50 Cd 22
Añatuya O **RA** 136 Ec 60
Anauá ~ **BR** 120 Ed 45
Anaurilândia O **BR** 140 Eh 57
Anaza Ruwāla ⩓ **KSA** 214 Hl 30
Anbar Kūh ⩓ **AFG** 223 Jn 27
Anbyon O **DVRK** 247 Lp 26
Ancenis O **F** 163 Gf 22
Anchau O **WAN** 320 Gl 40
Ancho O **USA** 65 Ck 29
Anchorage O **USA** 6 Bb 3
Anchorage O **USA** 46 Ba 15
Anchorena O **RA** 137 Eb 63
Ancien O **RMM** 305 Gf 35
Ancón O **EC** 116 Dh 47
Ancon O **PE** 128 Dk 51
Ancona O **I** 185 Gn 24
Ancuabe O **MOC** 344 Hm 52
Ancuaze O **MOC** 344 Hk 54
Ancud O **RCH** 147 Dl 66
Anda O **VRC** 205 Wb 9
Andacollo O **RCH** 137 Dn 61
Andado O **AUS** 374 Md 58
Andaga O **WAN** 321 Gn 40
Andahuaylas O **PE** 128 Dm 52
Andai O **RI** 283 Mc 46
Andaingo Gara O **RM** 345 Jc 55
Andalatanosy O **RM** 353 Ja 58
Andalgala O **RA** 136 Ea 59
Åndalsness O **N** 158 Gk 14
Andalucia ⊙ **E** 184 Gd 27
Andalusia O **USA** 86 De 30
Andaman Basin ♆ **IND** 262 Km 39
Andaman Islands ♁ **IND** 262 Kl 40
Andaman Sea ≈ 262 Km 40
Andamarca O **PE** 128 Dl 51
Andamooka ⩓ **AUS** 378 Me 61
Andamooka Opal Fields O **AUS** 378 Me 61
Andapa O **RM** 345 Jc 53
Andaraí O **BR** 125 Ep 52
Andasibe O **RM** 345 Jc 55
Āndeba Ye Midir Zerf Ch'af ⌒ **ER** 313 Hn 38
Andeiá ~ **BR** 133 Em 55
Andenes O **N** 158 Gp 11
Andéramboukane O **RMM** 305 Gh 38
Ånderdalen ★ **N** 158 Ha 11
Andermatt O **CH** 174 Gl 22
Andernos O **F** 184 Gf 23
Anderson O **USA** 46 Ba 13
Anderson O **USA** 64 Ca 25
Anderson O **USA** 70 Da 27
Anderson O **USA** 71 De 25
Anderson O **USA** 71 Dg 28
Anderson Gate O **NAM** 340 Gp 55
Anderson River ~ **CDN** 47 Bl 11
Anderson River ~ **CDN** 47 Bn 11
Andersonville N.H.S. ★ **USA** 86 Df 29
Andes O **CO** 116 Dj 49
Andes ⩓ **PE** 128 Dk 51
Andes ⩓ **RA** 137 Dn 64
Andes ⩓ **RCH** 147 Dn 65
Andfjorden ~ **N** 158 Ha 11
Andhōy O **AFG** 223 Jl 27
Andhra Lake ~ **IND** 238 Ka 36
Andhra Pradesh ⊙ **IND** 238 Kd 36
Andijon O **UZB** 230 Ka 25
Andijskoe Kojsu ~ **RUS** 202 Ja 24
Andikthíra ♁ **GR** 194 Hd 28
Andilamena O **RM** 345 Jc 54
Andīmešk O **IR** 209 Jc 29
Anding O **VRC** 258 Lg 31
Andirá ~ **BR** 117 Ea 48
Andira ~ **BR** 120 Ef 47
Andirlangar O **VRC** 231 Kf 27
Andižan O **UZB** 22 Nb 5
Andjogo O **G** 332 Gn 46
Andoain O **E** 184 Gf 24
Andoany O **RM** 345 Jc 52
Andoas O **PE** 116 Dk 47
Andong O **ROK** 247 Ma 27
Andoom O **AUS** 365 Mg 52
Andorinha O **BR** 125 Fa 51
Andørja ♁ **N** 158 Ha 11
Andorra □ **AND** 184 Gg 24
Andorra la Vella ▣ **AND** 184 Gg 24
Andover O **USA** 56 Cp 23
Andover O **USA** 71 Dh 25
Andovoranto O **RM** 345 Jc 55
Andøya ♁ **N** 158 Gp 11
Andrade O **BR** 117 Ec 48
Andradina O **BR** 140 Ej 56
Andrafainkona O **RM** 345 Jc 52
Andramasina O **RM** 345 Jb 55
Andranavory O **RM** 353 Ja 57
Andranomavo O **RM** 345 Ja 54
Andranomena O **RM** 345 Jc 55
Andranopasy O **RM** 353 Hp 56
Andranovondronina O **RM** 345 Jc 52
Andreafsky River ~ **USA** 46 Aj 13
Andrée land ♁ **N** 158 Gp 6
Andrelândia O **BR** 141 Em 56
Andrequicé O **BR** 133 Em 55
Andrews O **USA** 65 Cl 29
Ándria O **I** 194 Ha 25
Andriamena O **RM** 345 Jb 54
Andriba O **RM** 345 Jb 54
Andriesvale O **ZA** 348 Hc 59
Andringitra ⩓ **RM** 353 Jb 56
Androka O **RM** 353 Hp 58
Androranga ~ **RM** 345 Jc 53
Ándros O **GR** 194 He 27
Ándros ♁ **GR** 194 He 27
Androscoggin ~ **USA** 60 Dn 23
Andros Island ♁ **BS** 87 Dj 33
Andros Town O **BS** 87 Dk 33
Androth Island ♁ **IND** 239 Ka 40
Andru River ~ **PNG** 287 Ml 49
Andselv O **N** 158 Ha 11
Andudu O **RDC** 324 Hg 44
Andújar O **E** 184 Gd 26
Andulo O **ANG** 340 Ha 51
Anduradhapura O **CL** 239 Kd 41
Anecón Grande △ **RA** 147 Dn 66
Anéfis O **RMM** 305 Gg 36
Anegada ♁ **GB** 104 Eb 36
Anegada Passage ≈ 104 Ec 36
Aného O **RT** 317 Gg 42
Aneityum ♁ **VU** 386 Ng 56
Anekal O **IND** 238 Kc 39
Anéker O **RN** 308 Gj 38
Anelghowhat O **VU** 386 Ng 56
Añelo O **RA** 147 Dp 65
Anesbaraka O **DZ** 308 Gj 36
Anes Barakka O **RN** 308 Gk 36
Aneth O **USA** 65 Ch 27
Aney O **RN** 309 Gn 36
Anfu O **VRC** 258 Lh 32
Angalimp O **PNG** 287 Mj 48
Angamāli O **IND** 239 Kc 40
Angangueo O **MEX** 92 Cm 36
Angara ~ **RUS** 204 Ub 7
Angara ~ **RUS** 204 Uc 8
'Angara ~ **SUD** 312 He 40
Angaradebou O **DY** 320 Gh 40
Angarsk O **RUS** 204 Uc 8
Angarskiy Kryazh ⩓ **RUS** 204 Uc 7
Angastaco O **RA** 136 Ea 58
Angaston O **AUS** 378 Mf 63
Angatuba O **BR** 141 Ek 57
Angba O **WAN** 320 Gk 42
Angeles O **RP** 267 Ll 38
Ängelholm O **S** 170 Gn 17
Angélica O **RA** 137 Ed 61
Angelina ~ **USA** 81 Da 30
Angellala Creek ~ **AUS** 375 Mk 59
Angelo ~ **AUS** 360 Lj 57
Angels Camp O **USA** 64 Cb 26
Angereb O **ETH** 313 Hl 39
Angereb Wenz ~ **ETH** 313 Hl 39
Ångermanälven ~ **S** 158 Ha 14
Ångermanland ⌓ **S** 158 Ha 14
Angermünde O **D** 170 Gn 19
Angers O **F** 163 Gf 22
Ängesån ~ **S** 159 Hd 12
Angetu O **ETH** 325 Hm 42
Anggoro O **RI** 282 Ll 47
Angical O **BR** 133 Em 51
Angicos O **BR** 124 Fb 48
Angikuni Lake ~ **CDN** 42 Fb 6
Angīra O **PK** 227 Jm 31
Anğīre O **IR** 222 Jf 29
Angkor Wat ★ **K** 263 Lc 39
Angle Inlet O **USA** 56 Da 21
Anglesea O **AUS** 379 Mh 65
Anglesey ♁ **GB** 163 Gd 19
Angleton O **USA** 81 Da 31
Ango O **RDC** 324 He 43
Angoche O **MOC** 344 Hm 54
Angohrān O **IR** 226 Jg 32
Angol O **RCH** 137 Dm 64
Angol O **UZB** 223 Jm 27
Angola O **USA** 71 Df 25
Angola □ **ANG** 340 Ha 50
Angola Basin ♆ 30 Ka 11
Angoon O **USA** 47 Bj 17
Angoram O **PNG** 287 Mj 48
Angostura Reservoir ~ **USA** 51 Cl 24
Angoulêrne O **F** 184 Gg 23
Angpawing Bum ⩓ **MYA** 254 Km 33
Angra dos Reis O **BR** 141 Em 57
Angren O **UZB** 19 Na 5
Angren O **UZB** 223 Jp 25
Ang Thong O **THA** 262 La 38
Ang Thong Marine ♀ **THA** 262 Kp 41
Angu O **RDC** 324 He 44
Anguilla ♁ **GB** 104 Ec 36
Anguilla Cays ♁ **BS** 100 Dh 34
Anguille Mountains ⩓ **CDN** 61 Ee 22
Anğuman O **AFG** 223 Jp 28
Anguo O **VRC** 243 Lh 26
Angūrān O **IR** 209 Jb 27
Anguran O **IR** 226 Jf 32
Angurugu O **AUS** 364 Me 53
Anguscilla O **PE** 116 Dl 46
Angwa ~ **ZW** 341 Hh 54
An Hài O **VN** 255 Ld 35
Anholt ♁ **DK** 170 Gm 17
Anhua O **VRC** 255 Lf 31
Anhui ⊙ **VRC** 246 Lj 29
Aniak O **USA** 46 Al 15
Aniakchak National Monument & Preserve ★ **USA** 46 Al 17
Aniakshak Bay ~ **USA** 46 Al 17
Ania River ~ **PNG** 287 Mm 48
Anicuns O **BR** 133 Ek 54
Anié ~ **RT** 317 Gg 41
Aniéo O **RT** 317 Gg 42
Anil O **BR** 121 Em 47
Animas O **USA** 80 Ch 30
Animas Peak △ **USA** 80 Ch 30
Animas River ~ **USA** 65 Cj 27
Anina O **RO** 174 Hc 23
Aninaus Pass △ **ZA** 348 Ha 60
Aninos ~ **BR** 132 Ef 52
Añisok O **GQ** 332 Gm 45
Anita Garibaldi O **BR** 140 Ej 59
Aniva O **RUS** 250 Mh 22
Aniwa ♁ **VU** 386 Ng 55
Anjahambe O **RM** 345 Jc 54
Anjalankoski O **FIN** 159 Hf 15
Anjar ★ **RL** 208 Hk 29
Anjār O **IND** 227 Jn 34
Anji O **VRC** 246 Lk 30
Anjombony ~ **RM** 345 Jc 53
Anjou ⌓ **F** 163 Gf 22
Anjou Islands ♁ **RUS** 22 Sa 2
Anjou Islands ♁ **RUS** 205 Xa 3
Anjozorobe O **RM** 345 Jb 55
Anju O **DVRK** 247 Ln 26
Anjujsk O **RUS** 205 Yc 5
Anka O **WAN** 320 Gj 39
Ankang O **VRC** 243 Le 29
Ankara ▣ **TR** 195 Hj 26
Ankaratra ⩓ **RM** 345 Jb 55
Ankavanana ~ **RM** 345 Jc 53
Ankavandra O **RM** 345 Ja 55
Ankazoabo O **RM** 353 Ja 57
Ankazobe O **RM** 345 Jb 55
Ankazomborona O **RM** 345 Jb 54
Ankazomiriotra O **RM** 345 Jb 55
Ankazondandy O **RM** 345 Jb 55
Ankeny O **USA** 70 Db 25
An Khê O **VN** 263 Le 39
Ankilizato O **RM** 353 Ja 56
Ankinany O **RM** 353 Ja 57
Anklam O **D** 170 Gn 19
Ankleshwar O **IND** 238 Ka 35
Ankober O **ETH** 325 Hm 41
Ankobra ~ **GH** 317 Ge 42
Ankola O **IND** 238 Kb 38
Ankoro O **RDC** 336 Hf 49
Ankotrofotsy O **RM** 345 Ja 55
Ankpa O **WAN** 320 Gk 42
Anliu O **VRC** 258 Lh 34
Anlong O **VRC** 255 Lc 33
Ânlóng Vêng O **K** 263 Lc 38
Anlu O **VRC** 243 Lg 30
Anmyŏn Do ♁ **ROK** 247 Ln 27
Anna O **USA** 71 Dd 27
Anna O **RUS** 181 Hn 20
an-Na'ān O **KSA** 215 Jb 34
Annaba O **DZ** 296 Gk 27
an-Nabhānīya O **KSA** 214 Hp 33
an-Nabk O **RL** 208 Hl 28
an-Nabk O **KSA** 214 Hm 30
An Nafūd ⌓ **KSA** 214 Hm 31
an-Naḫl O **ET** 301 Hj 31
Annai O **GUY** 112 Ee 44
An Najaf O **IRQ** 215 Hp 30
Anna Plains O **AUS** 360 Ll 55
Annapolis O **USA** 74 Dk 26
Annapolis Royal O **CDN** 61 Eb 23
Annapurna Himal ⩓ **NEP** 235 Kf 31
Annapurna I △ **NEP** 235 Kf 31
Annapurna II △ **NEP** 235 Kf 31
Annapurna Sanctuary ★ **NEP** 235 Kf 31
Ann Arbor O **USA** 71 Df 24
Anna Regina O **GUY** 113 Ee 42
An Nasiriyah O **IRQ** 215 Jb 30
Annecy O **F** 185 Gk 23
Annigeri O **IND** 238 Kb 38
Anning O **VRC** 254 Lb 33
Anningie O **AUS** 361 Mc 56
Anniston O **USA** 86 Df 29
Annitowa O **AUS** 374 Me 56
Ann Lake ~ **USA** 56 Db 23
Annofliyah O **LAR** 297 Ha 30
Annonay O **F** 185 Gj 23
Annotto Bay O **JA** 101 Dk 36
Annoual O **MA** 293 Ge 28
an-Nu'airīya O **KSA** 215 Jc 32
an-Nu'mānīya O **IRQ** 209 Ja 29
an-Nuqra O **KSA** 214 Hn 33
Año Nuevo Point ⌒ **USA** 64 Ca 27
Anori O **BR** 120 Ed 47
Anosibe An'Ala O **RM** 345 Jc 55
Anou-Araghene O **RN** 308 Gk 37
Anou Mellene O **RMM** 308 Gj 36
Anou-n-Bidek O **DZ** 308 Gj 36
Anpo Gang ~ **VRC** 255 Le 35
Anqing O **VRC** 246 Lj 30
Anqiu O **VRC** 246 Lk 27
Anquincila O **RA** 136 Eb 60
Anriandampy O **RM** 353 Ja 57
Ansal O **VRC** 243 Le 27
Ansbach O **D** 174 Gm 21
Anse à Galets O **RH** 101 Dm 36
Anse-à-Veau O **RH** 101 Dm 36
Ānseba Shet' ~ **ER** 313 Hm 37
Anselmo O **USA** 70 Cn 25
Ansermanuevo O **CO** 106 Dk 43
Anse Rouge O **RH** 101 Dm 36
Anshan O **VRC** 246 Lm 25
Anshi O **IND** 238 Kb 38
Anshun O **VRC** 255 Lc 32
Ansina O **ROU** 146 Eg 61
Ansley O **USA** 70 Cn 25
Anson O **USA** 70 Cn 29
Anson Bay ~ **AUS** 364 Ma 52
Ansongo O **RMM** 305 Gg 38
Ansus O **RI** 283 Md 46
Answer Downs O **AUS** 374 Mg 56
Anta O **PE** 128 Dm 52
Antabamba O **PE** 128 Dm 53
Antakya O **TR** 195 Hl 27
Antalaha O **RM** 345 Jd 53
Antalya O **TR** 195 Hh 27
Antanambao-Manampotsy O **RM** 345 Jc 55
Antanambe O **RM** 345 Jc 54
Antananarivo ▣ **RM** 345 Jb 55
Antanifotsy O **RM** 345 Jb 55
Antanimora O **RM** 353 Ja 58
Antânio João O **BR** 140 Eg 57
Antanjombolamena O **RM** 345 Jb 55
Antantapur O **IND** 238 Kc 38
Antarctica ⊙ 38 Da 18
Antarctic Peninsula ♁ 38 Ga 16
Antas O **BR** 125 Fa 51
Antécume Pata O **F** 113 Eg 44
Antelope Island ♁ **USA** 64 Cf 25
Antelope Wells O **USA** 80 Ch 30
Antequera O **E** 184 Gd 27
Anthony O **USA** 65 Cj 29
Anthony O **USA** 70 Cp 27
Anthony Lagoon O **AUS** 364 Md 54
Anti-Atlas ♁ **MA** 292 Gb 31
Anticosti Island ♁ **CDN** 61 Eb 21
Antigo O **USA** 57 Dd 23
Antigonish O **CDN** 61 Ed 23
Antigua ♁ **AG** 104 Ed 37
Antigua and Barbuda □ **AG** 104 Ed 37
Antigua Guatemala O **GCA** 93 Dc 38
Antiguo Cauce del Rio Barmejo ~ **RA** 136 Ec 58
Antiguo Morelos O **MEX** 92 Cn 34
Antilla O **C** 101 Dl 35
Antimari ~ **BR** 117 Dp 50
An Ti-m-Missaou O **DZ** 305 Gh 35
Antimony O **USA** 65 Cg 26
Antioquia O **CO** 106 Dl 42
Antipajuta O **RUS** 154 Sc 5
Antipodes Islands ♁ **NZ** 35 Tb 14
Ántissa-Kalloní O **GR** 194 He 26
Antlat O **LAR** 300 Hc 30
Antlers O **USA** 70 Da 28
Antofagasta O **RCH** 136 Dn 57
Antofagasta de la Sierra O **RA** 136 Ea 59
Antogila Bay ~ **RM** 345 Jc 53
Anton O **USA** 65 Cl 26
Anton O **USA** 65 Cl 29
Anton O **PA** 97 Dh 41
Antonibe O **RM** 345 Jb 53
Antonina O **BR** 124 Fa 49
Antonina O **BR** 141 Ek 58
Antonio de Biedma O **RA** 152 Ea 69
Antônio Dias O **BR** 141 En 55
Antônio Gonçalves O **BR** 125 Ep 51
Antônio Lemos O **BR** 121 Ej 46
Antônio Martins O **BR** 124 Fa 49
Antõnio Prado O **BR** 146 Ej 60
Antonito O **USA** 65 Cj 27
Antracyt O **UA** 181 Hm 21
Antrim O **GB** 162 Gc 18
Antsahabe O **RM** 345 Jc 53
Antsahampano O **RM** 345 Jb 52
Antsakabary O **RM** 345 Jc 53
Antsakanalabe O **RM** 345 Jc 53
Antsalova O **RM** 345 Ja 55
Antsambalahy O **RM** 345 Jc 53
Antschihy O **RM** 345 Jb 53
Antsiafabositra O **RM** 345 Jb 54
Antsianitia O **RM** 345 Jb 53
Antsirabato O **RM** 345 Jd 53
Antsirabe O **RM** 345 Jb 55
Antsirabe Avaratra O **RM** 345 Jc 52
Antsiranana O **RM** 345 Jc 52
Antsoha O **RM** 345 Ja 55
Antsohimbondrona O **RM** 345 Jc 52
Antsondrodava O **RM** 345 Ja 55
Anttis O **S** 159 Hd 12
Antuco O **RCH** 137 Dn 64
Antufaš ♁ **YE** 218 Hp 38
Antwerp O **B** 163 Gj 20
Anučino O **RUS** 250 Mc 23
Anugul O **IND** 235 Kg 35
Anum O **GH** 317 Gf 42
Anūpgarh O **IND** 227 Ka 31
Anūpshahr O **IND** 234 Kd 31
Anvak Island ♁ **USA** 46 Aj 17
Anvik O **USA** 46 Aj 13
Anxi O **VRC** 231 Km 25
Anxi O **VRC** 258 Lh 31
An Xian O **VRC** 242 Lc 30
Anxious Bay ~ **AUS** 378 Md 62
Anyama O **CI** 317 Ge 43
Anyang O **VRC** 243 Lh 27
Anyang O **ROK** 247 Lp 27
A'Nyêmaqên Shan ⩓ **VRC** 242 Kp 28
Anyer-Kidul O **RI** 278 Lc 49
Anyinam O **GH** 317 Gf 42
Anyirawase O **GH** 317 Gf 42
Anykščiai O **LT** 171 He 18
Anyuan O **VRC** 258 Lh 33
Anyue O **VRC** 242 Lc 30
Anyuskiy Khrebet ⩓ **RUS** 205 Yc 5
Anze O **VRC** 243 Lg 27
Anžero Sudženskk O **RUS** 204 Tc 7
Anzi O **RDC** 333 Hd 46
Ánzio O **I** 185 Gn 25
Anzob O **TJ** 223 Jn 26
Aoba ♁ **VU** 386 Nf 53
Ao Ban Don ~ **THA** 262 Kp 41
Aoga-shima ♁ **J** 251 Mf 29
Aola O **SOL** 290 Nc 50
Aomen O **VRC** 258 Lg 34
Aomori O **J** 250 Mg 25
Ao Phangnga ♀ **THA** 262 Kp 41
Aore ♁ **VU** 386 Nf 53
Ao Sawi ~ **THA** 262 Kp 40
Aosta O **I** 185 Gk 23
Ao Trat ~ **THA** 263 Lb 40
Aouînât ez Zbil O **RIM** 304 Gb 37
Aoukalé ~ **TCH** 321 Hc 40
Aoukâr ⌓ **RIM** 304 Ga 36
Aoulef O **DZ** 293 Gg 32
Aoulouz O **MA** 292 Gb 30
Aourou O **RMM** 304 Ga 38
Aousard O **MA** 304 Fn 34
Aozi O **TCH** 309 Hb 35
Aozou O **TCH** 309 Ha 35
Apa ~ **PY** 140 Ef 57
Apache ••• **USA** 65 Cj 27
Apache O **USA** 70 Cn 28
Apache Creek O **USA** 65 Ch 29
Apache Junction O **USA** 65 Cg 29
Apacheta Cruz Grande △ **BOL** 136 Eb 56
Apaikwa O **GUY** 112 Ed 42
Apalachee Bay ~ **USA** 86 Df 31
Apalachicola ~ **USA** 86 Df 30
Apalachicola O **USA** 86 Df 31
Apam O **MEX** 92 Cn 36
Apaporis ~ **CO** 116 Dm 45
Apaporis ~ **CO** 117 Dn 46
Aparawatatja Fregon O **AUS** 369 Mc 59
Aparecida de Goiana O **BR** 133 Ek 54
Aparecida do Tabuado O **BR** 140 Ej 56
Aparri O **RP** 267 Ll 36
Apastovo O **RUS** 181 Jc 18
Apatana O **RI** 282 Ll 49
Apatity O **RUS** 159 Hj 12
Apatou O **F** 113 Eg 43
Apatzingán O **MEX** 92 Cl 36
Apauwar O **RI** 286 Mf 46
Apauwar ~ **RI** 286 Mf 47
Apawanza O **RDC** 324 Hg 45
Apaxtla O **MEX** 92 Cm 36
Ape O **LV** 171 Hf 17
Apedia ~ **BR** 129 Ed 51
Apediá ~ **BR** 129 Ed 52
Apeldoorn O **NL** 170 Gk 19
Apennines ⩓ **I** 185 Gl 23
Apere ~ **BOL** 129 Eb 53
Apetina O **SME** 113 Eg 44
Api O **RDC** 324 He 44
Apia O **CO** 106 Dl 43
Apia ▣ **WS** 390 Ae 52
Apiacás O **BR** 120 Ef 50
Apiaí O **BR** 141 Ek 58
Api La △ **NEP** 230 Ke 30
Apinajes O **BR** 121 Ek 48
Apio O **SOL** 290 Nc 50
Apishapa River ~ **USA** 65 Ck 27
Apitpac O **MEX** 93 Db 37
Ap'khazet'l ⊙ **GE** 202 Hn 24
Aplahoue O **DY** 317 Gg 42
Aplao O **PE** 128 Dm 54
Apódaca O **MEX** 81 Cm 33
Apodi ~ **BR** 124 Fa 49
Apodi O **BR** 124 Fb 48
Apoera O **SME** 113 Ef 43
Apoko O **RCB** 332 Gp 46
Apolima Strait ≈ **WS** 390 Ad 52
Apolinario Saravia O **RA** 136 Ec 58
Apóllo O **GR** 194 He 27
Apollo Bay O **AUS** 379 Mh 65
Apollonia O **GR** 194 He 27
Apolo O **BOL** 129 Dp 53
Apopka O **USA** 87 Dh 31
Aporá O **BR** 125 Fa 51
Aporé ~ **BR** 133 Eh 55
Aporé ~ **BR** 133 Ej 55
Apo Reef ♀ **RP** 267 Lk 39
Aporema O **BR** 121 Ej 45
Apostle Island Natl. Lakeshore ★ **USA** 56 Dc 22
Apostle Islands ♁ **USA** 56 Dc 22
Apostolovc O **UA** 175 Hj 22
Apoteri O **GUY** 113 Ee 43
Apozol O **MEX** 92 Cl 35
Appalachian Mountains ⩓ **USA** 71 Dh 27
Appennino Abruzzese ⩓ **I** 185 Gn 24
Appleton O **USA** 56 Da 23
Appleton City O **USA** 70 Da 26
Apple Valley O **USA** 56 Db 23
Apple Valley O **USA** 64 Cd 28
Appomattox O **USA** 74 Dj 27
Appomattox Court House N.H.P. ★ **USA** 74 Dj 27
Approuague ~ **F** 113 Eh 43
Approuague ~ **F** 113 Eh 44
Apraksin Dvor O **RUS** 171 Hh 16
Aprilia O **I** 185 Gn 25
April River ~ **PNG** 286 Mh 48
Aprompronou O **CI** 317 Ge 42
Apšeronsk O **RUS** 202 Hm 23
Apsley O **CDN** 60 Dj 23
Apsley ~ **AUS** 379 Mn 61
Apsley Strait ~ **AUS** 364 Mb 51
Apt O **F** 185 Gj 24
Apu ~ **RI** 282 Lp 47
Apucarana O **BR** 140 Ej 57
Apuí O **BR** 120 Ee 49
Apuka O **RUS** 205 Za 6
Apurahuan O **RP** 266 Lj 41
Apure O **CO** 106 Dl 41
Apure ~ **YV** 107 Dn 42
Apure ~ **YV** 107 Dp 41
Apure ~ **YV** 107 Ea 42
Apurimac ~ **PE** 128 Dm 52
Apurito O **YV** 107 Dp 42
Āqā Bāba O **IR** 209 Jc 27
Aqabah O **JOR** 214 Hk 31
Āqčan O **AFG** 223 Jl 27
'Aqdā O **IR** 222 Je 29
'Aqiq O **SUD** 313 Hm 36
Āq Kand O **IR** 209 Jc 27
Aq Koprūk O **AFG** 223 Jm 27
Āq Qal'e O **IR** 222 Jf 27
Aqqan O **VRC** 231 Kg 27
Aqqikkol Hu ~ **VRC** 231 Kj 27
Aqra O **IRQ** 209 Hp 27
Aqtöbe O **KZ** 19 Mb 4
Aqtöbe O **KZ** 155 Rc 8
Aqua Downs O **AUS** 375 Mk 59
Aquarius Mountains ⩓ **USA** 64 Cf 28
Aqueduct ~ **USA** 64 Cb 26
Aquidabán ~ **PY** 140 Ef 57
Aquidauan ~ **BR** 140 Eg 56
Aquidauana ~ **BR** 132 Ef 55
Aquidauana O **BR** 140 Eg 56
Aquila O **USA** 64 Cf 29
Aquin O **RH** 101 Dm 36
Aquiraz O **BR** 124 Fa 47
Aquitaine ⊙ **F** 184 Gf 23
Ara O **IND** 235 Kg 33
Arab O **USA** 71 De 28
Arab ~ **SUD** 313 Hk 37
'Arabābād O **IR** 222 Jg 29
Araban O **TR** 195 Hl 27
Arabati O **ETH** 313 Hm 40
Arabela O **USA** 65 Ck 29
Arabian Desert ⌓ **ET** 301 Hh 31
Arabian Sea ≈ **OM** 226 Jj 34
Arabopó O **YV** 112 Ed 43
Araç O **TR** 195 Hj 25
Araçá ~ **BR** 117 Ec 45
Arā ah O **UAE** 215 Je 34
Aracaju O **BR** 125 Fb 51
Aracati O **BR** 124 Fb 48
Aracatu O **BR** 125 Ep 53
Araçatuba O **BR** 132 Eg 52
Araçatuba O **BR** 140 Ej 56
Aracena O **E** 184 Gc 27
Araci O **BR** 125 Fa 51
Aracruz O **BR** 141 Ep 55
Araçu ~ **BR** 120 Ee 48
Aracu O **BOL** 129 Ea 54
Araçuaí O **BR** 125 En 54
Araçuai ~ **BR** 125 En 54
Arad O **RO** 174 Hc 22
Arad O **IL** 214 Hk 30
Arada O **TCH** 309 Hc 38
Ārādān O **IR** 222 Je 28
Arafale O **ER** 313 Hm 38
Arafura Sea ≈ **RI** 283 Mc 50
Arafura Shelf ♆ 364 Md 51
Arage O **WAN** 320 Gl 41
Aragón ⊙ **E** 184 Gf 25
Araguacema O **BR** 121 Ek 50
Araguaçu O **BR** 133 Ek 52
Aragua de Barcelona O **YV** 112 Eb 41
Aragua de Maturín O **YV** 112 Ec 40
Araguaia ~ **BR** 121 Ek 49
Araguaia ~ **BR** 121 Ek 50
Araguaia ~ **BR** 133 Eh 54
Araguaia ~ **BR** 133 Ej 52
Araguaia ~ **BR** 133 Ej 53
Araguaiana O **BR** 133 Eh 53
Araguaína O **BR** 121 Ek 49
Araguanã O **BR** 121 Ek 49
Araguapaz O **BR** 133 Ej 53
Araguari ~ **BR** 121 Ej 45
Araguari O **BR** 133 Ek 55
Araguari ~ **BR** 133 Ek 55
Araguatins O **BR** 121 Ek 48
Arai O **J** 251 Mf 27
Araias do Araguaia ~ **BR** 121 Ej 50
Araioses O **BR** 124 En 47
Arāk O **IR** 209 Jc 28
Arak O **DZ** 296 Gh 33
Arakaka O **GUY** 112 Ee 42
Arakan Mountains ⩓ **MYA** 235 Kl 35
Arakawa O **J** 251 Mf 26
Araklı O **TR** 202 Hn 25
Arak's ~ **ARM** 202 Hp 25
Aral O **KZ** 19 Na 5
Aral O **KZ** 155 Sa 9
Ara Lake ~ **CDN** 57 De 20
Aralık O **TR** 202 Ja 26
Aral Moreira O **BR** 140 Eg 57
Aral Sea ~ **KZ/UZB** 155 Rc 9
Aramac O **AUS** 375 Mj 57
Arame O **BR** 121 Em 48
Aramia River ~ **PNG** 286 Mh 49
Aran ♁ **IRL** 162 Gb 18
Ārān O **IR** 222 Jd 28
Arancay O **PE** 116 Dk 50
Aranda de Duero O **E** 184 Ge 25
Arandai O **RI** 283 Mc 47
Arandas O **MEX** 92 Cl 35
Arandis O **NAM** 348 Gp 57
Ārani O **IND** 238 Kd 39
Aran Islands ♁ **IRL** 163 Ga 19
Aranjez O **E** 184 Ge 25
Aranos O **NAM** 348 Hb 58
Aransas Pass O **USA** 81 Cp 32
Arantangi O **IND** 239 Kd 40
Aranyaprathet O **THA** 263 Lb 39
Araouane O **RMM** 305 Ge 36
Aráoz O **RA** 136 Eb 59
Arapahoe O **USA** 70 Cn 25
Arapay Grande ~ **ROU** 146 Ef 61
Arapgir O **TR** 195 Hm 26
Arapicos O **EC** 116 Dk 46
Arapiraca O **BR** 124 Fb 50
Arapiuns ~ **BR** 120 Eg 47
Arapongas O **BR** 140 Ej 57
Arapunya O **AUS** 374 Md 57
Araputanga O **BR** 132 Ee 53
Ar'ar O **KSA** 214 Hn 30
Araracuara O **CO** 116 Dm 46
Araraquara O **BR** 141 Ek 56
Araras O **BR** 141 El 57
Ararat O **ARM** 202 Ja 26
Ararat O **AUS** 378 Mh 64
Ararendá O **BR** 124 Ep 48
Arari O **BR** 121 Em 47
Araria O **IND** 235 Kh 32
Araripe O **BR** 124 Ep 49
Araripina O **BR** 124 Ep 49
Araruama O **BR** 141 En 57
Araruna O **BR** 124 Fc 49
Aras ~ **AZ** 202 Jc 26
Aras ~ **IR** 209 Jb 26
Arasālu O **IND** 238 Kb 39
Aras Nehri ~ **TR** 202 Hn 26
Aratabiteri O **YV** 112 Eb 45
Aratâne O **RIM** 304 Gb 36
Ara Terra O **ETH** 325 Hn 42
Araticu ~ **BR** 121 Ek 47
Arauá ~ **BR** 117 Eb 48
Araua ~ **BR** 117 Eb 50
Arauca O **CO** 107 Dn 42
Arauca ~ **YV** 107 Dp 42
Arauca ~ **YV** 107 Ea 42
Araucána O **BR** 140 Ek 58
Arauco O **RCH** 137 Dm 64
Araure O **YV** 107 Dp 41
Aravalli Range ⩓ **IND** 227 Ka 33
Aravan O **KS** 230 Ka 25
Aravete O **EST** 171 He 16
Arawa O **PNG** 290 Mp 49
Arawe Islands ♁ **PNG** 287 Ml 49
Araxa O **BR** 133 El 55
Araya O **YV** 112 Eb 40
Arba O **ETH** 325 Hn 41
Arbakwe O **WAN** 308 Gj 39
Arba Minch O **ETH** 325 Hl 43
'Arbat O **IRQ** 209 Ja 28
Arbat Dāġ △ **IR** 209 Jb 27
Arbau O **RI** 283 Mb 48
Arbīl ⊙ **IRQ** 209 Hp 27
Arbīl O **IRQ** 209 Ja 27
Arbolé O **BF** 317 Ge 39
Arboledas O **CO** 107 Dm 42
Arboledas O **RA** 137 Ed 64
Arboles O **USA** 65 Cj 27
Arboletes O **CO** 106 Dk 41
Arbon O **USA** 51 Cf 24
Arbor O **ZA** 349 Hg 59
Arborfield O **CDN** 51 Cl 19
Arborg O **CDN** 56 Cp 20
Arborga O **S** 170 Gp 16
Arboutchatak O **TCH** 321 Ha 39
Arbroath O **GB** 162 Ge 17
Arcabuco O **CO** 107 Dm 43
Arcachon O **F** 184 Gf 23
Arcadia O **USA** 70 Db 29
Arcadia O **USA** 87 Dh 32
Arcahaie O **RH** 101 Dm 36
Arcas ~ **RCH** 136 Dp 56
Arcata O **USA** 64 Bp 25
Arcelia O **MEX** 92 Cm 36
Archaringa O **AUS** 374 Md 59
Archer ~ **AUS** 365 Mg 52
Archer Bay ~ **AUS** 365 Mg 52
Archer Bend ♀ **AUS** 365 Mh 52
Archer River Roadhouse O **AUS** 365 Mh 52
Archer's Post O **EAK** 325 Hl 45
Archerwill O **CDN** 51 Cl 19
Arches ♀ **USA** 65 Ch 26
Archipelago de Camagüey ♁ **C** 100 Dj 34
Archipelago de los Canarreos ♁ **C** 100 Dg 35
Archipelago de Los Chonos ♁ **RCH** 152 Dl 69
Archipelago de los Colorados ♁ **C** 100 Df 34
Archipelago de Sabana ♁ **C** 100 Dh 34
Archipelago of the Recherche ♁ **AUS** 368 Lm 63
Archipiélago de Bocas del Toro ⌓ **PA** 97 Dg 41
Archipiélago de la Reina Adelaida ♁ **RCH** 152 Dl 71
Archipiélago de las Perlas ⌓ **PA** 97 Dj 41
Archipiélago de Solentiname ♁ **NIC** 97 Df 40
Archipiélago Guayaneco ⌓ **RCH** 152 Dl 69
Archipiélago Los Roques ♀ **YV** 104 Ea 39

396 Anamu - Archipiélago Los Roques

Arckaringa Creek ~ AUS 374 Md 59
Arčman ○ TM 222 Jg 26
Arco ○ USA 50 Cf 24
Arco ○ P 184 Gc 25
Arcos ○ BR 141 Em 56
Arcos d.l.F. ○ E 184 Gd 27
Arcoverde ○ BR 124 Fb 50
Arctic Bay ○ CDN 43 Ga 4
Arctic Ocean ≈ 22 Qb 1
Arctic Plains ⌓ USA 46 Al 11
Arctic Red River ○ CDN 47 Bj 11
Arctic Red River ~ CDN 47 Bj 11
Arctic Village ○ USA 46 Bc 11
Arcturus ○ ZW 341 Hh 54
Arcyz ○ UA 175 Hg 23
Ardabīl ○ IR 209 Jc 26
Ardahan ○ TR 202 Hp 25
Ardakan ○ IR 215 Jd 30
Ardakān ○ IR 222 Jf 29
Årdal ○ N 170 Gk 16
Ardanuç ○ TR 202 Hn 25
Ardarhan su k. suk ~ KZ 181 Jd 21
Ardatov ○ RUS 181 Hp 18
Ardavidu ○ IND 238 Kd 38
Ardebil ⊙ IR 209 Jb 26
Ardeche ~ F 185 Gj 23
Ardee ○ IRL 162 Gc 19
Ardémi ○ TCH 309 Hc 38
Ardennes ⛰ B 163 Gj 20
Ardeşen ○ TR 202 Hn 25
Ardestān ○ IR 222 Je 29
Ardilea ○ RA 136 Eb 59
Ardīţ ○ OM 219 Je 36
Ardlethan ○ AUS 379 Mk 63
Ard Miri △ SP 328 Jb 40
Ardmore ○ USA 51 Cl 24
Ardmore ○ USA 70 Cp 28
Ardmore ○ AUS 374 Mf 56
Ardon ○ RUS 202 Ja 24
Ardrossan ○ AUS 378 Me 63
Área Indígena 9 de Janeiro ••• BR 117 Ec 49
Área Indígena Al Tikuna Evare ••• BR 117 Dp 47
Área Indígena Alto Rio Guama ••• BR 121 El 47
Área Indígena Alto Rio Purus ••• BR 117 Dn 50
Área Indígena Alto Turiaçú ••• BR 121 El 47
Área Indígena Amaneyé ••• BR 121 Ek 47
Área Indígena Andirá Marau ••• BR 120 Ef 47
Área Indígena Apurinã ••• BR 117 Ec 48
Área Indígena Apurinã Peneri ••• BR 117 Ea 50
Área Indígena Aracá ••• BR 112 Ed 44
Área Indígena Arara ••• BR 120 Eg 48
Área Indígena Arara Ig. Humaitá ••• BR 116 Dm 50
Área Indígena Araribóa ••• BR 121 El 48
Área Indígena Araweté Igarapé Ipixuna ••• BR 121 Eh 48
Área Indígena Areões ••• BR 133 Ej 53
Área Indígena Aripuanã ••• BR 129 Ed 51
Área Indígena Awa Gurupi ••• BR 121 El 47
Área Indígena Bakairi ••• BR 132 Eg 53
Área Indígena Batovi ••• BR 132 Eg 52
Área Indígena Baú-Mekragroti ••• BR 120 Eg 49
Área Indígena Betânia ••• BR 117 Dp 47
Área Indígena Caititu ~ BR 117 Eb 49
Área Indígena Camicuã ••• BR 117 Ea 50
Área Indígena Campinas ••• BR 116 Dm 49
Área Indígena Campo do Rio Amônea ••• BR 116 Dm 50
Área Indígena Cap Marcos ••• BR 132 Ee 53
Área Indígena Capoto ••• BR 120 Eh 50
Área Indígena Carú ••• BR 121 El 47
Área Indígena Cateté ••• BR 121 Ej 49
Área Indígena Coatá Laranjal ••• BR 120 Ee 48
Área Indígena Deni ••• BR 117 Ea 49
Área Indígena Escondido ••• BR 120 Ee 50
Área Indígena Gomes Cameiro ••• BR 132 Eg 54
Área Indígena Igara Lages ••• BR 129 Eb 51
Área Indígena Ipixuna ••• BR 117 Ec 49
Área Indígena Jacamim ••• BR 112 Ed 44
Área Indígena Jamari ••• BR 117 Ec 50
Área Indígena Jaminauá ••• BR 116 Dm 50
Área Indígena Jaminavá Arara ~ BR 117 Eb 49
Área Indígena Jaminavá Arara ••• BR 116 Dm 50
Área Indígena Japuira ••• BR 132 Ee 51
Área Indígena Jarina ••• BR 132 Eh 51
Área Indígena Juruá ••• BR 117 Ea 48
Área Indígena Kadiwén ••• BR 140 Ef 56
Área Indígena Kajabi ••• BR 120 Ef 50
Área Indígena Kanamari do Rio Juruá ••• BR 117 Dp 49
Área Indígena Kararaô ••• BR 121 Eh 48
Área Indígena Karipuna ••• BR 129 Eb 51
Área Indígena Karitiana ••• BR 117 Eb 50
Área Indígena Kaxarari ••• BR 117 Ea 50
Área Indígena Kaxinauá Nova Olinda ••• BR 117 Dn 50
Área Indígena Kaxinawá do Rio Humaitá ••• BR 117 Dn 50
Área Indígena Kaxinawá do Rio Jordão ••• BR 117 Dn 50
Área Indígena Kayabi ••• BR 132 Ef 51
Área Indígena Kayapó ••• BR 121 Eh 49
Área Indígena Kontinemo ••• BR 121 Eh 48
Área Indígena Kulina do Médio Juruá ••• BR 117 Dn 49
Área Indígena Lameirão ••• BR 117 Dn 48
Área Indígena Lourdes ••• BR 129 Ed 51
Área Indígena Mamoadate ••• BR 128 Dn 51
Área Indígena Manoá Pium ••• BR 112 Ed 44
Área Indígena Merure ••• BR 133 Eh 53
Área Indígena Miratu ••• BR 117 Eb 47
Área Indígena Mundurucu ••• BR 120 Ef 49
Área Indígena Myky ••• BR 132 Ee 52
Área Indígena Nambikwara ••• BR 132 Ee 52
Área Indígena Nhamundá Mapuera ••• BR 120 Ee 46
Área Indígena Omerê ••• BR 129 Ed 52
Área Indígena Pakaás-Novos ••• BR 129 Eb 51
Área Indígena Parabubure ••• BR 133 Eh 53
Área Indígena Paracanã ••• BR 121 Ej 48
Área Indígena Paraguassu ••• BR 125 Ep 53
Área Indígena Paresi ••• BR 132 Ee 53
Área Indígena Paresi do Rio Formosa ••• BR 132 Ee 53
Área Indígena Paru de Leste ••• BR 113 Eg 45
Área Indígena Paumari ~ BR 117 Eb 49
Área Indígena Pimentel Barbosa ••• BR 133 Ej 52
Área Indígena Pirahã ••• BR 117 Ec 49
Área Indígena Potiguara ••• BR 124 Fc 49
Área Indígena Raposa Serra do Sul ••• BR 112 Ed 43
Área Indígena Ribeirão ••• BR 129 Eb 51
Área Indígena Rikbaktsa ••• BR 132 Ee 51
Área Indígena Rio Branco ••• BR 129 Ec 52
Área Indígena Rio Gregorio ••• BR 117 Dn 50
Área Indígena Rio Guaporé ••• BR 129 Eb 51
Área Indígena Rio Mequens ••• BR 129 Ed 52
Área Indígena Rio Negro Ocaia ••• BR 129 Eb 51
Área Indígena Roosevelt ••• BR 129 Ed 51
Área Indígena Sangradouro ••• BR 132 Eh 53
Área Indígena São Marcos ••• BR 112 Ed 43
Área Indígena São Marcos ••• BR 133 Eh 53
Área Indígena Sarare ••• BR 132 Ee 53
Área Indígena Serra Morena ••• BR 132 Ee 51
Área Indígena Sete de Setembro ••• BR 129 Ed 51
Área Indígena Tapirapé Karajá ••• BR 133 Ej 51
Área Indígena Tenharim/Igarapé Préto ••• BR 120 Ed 50
Área Indígena Tenharim/Transamazônica ••• BR 120 Ed 50
Área Indígena Tikuna de Feijoal ••• BR 117 Dp 48
Área Indígena Tikuna São Leopoldo ••• BR 117 Dp 48
Área Indígena Tirecatinga ••• BR 132 Ee 52
Área Indígena Trocatá ••• BR 121 Ek 47
Área Indígena Tubarão Latunde ••• BR 129 Ed 52
Área Indígena Uaçá ••• BR 113 Ej 44
Área Indígena Uai-Uai ••• BR 112 Ee 45
Área Indígena Uati- Paraná ••• BR 117 Ea 47
Área Indígena Umutina ••• BR 132 Ef 53
Área Indígena Uneiuxi ••• BR 117 Ea 46
Área Indígena Uru-Eu-Wau-Wau ••• BR 129 Ec 51
Área Indígena Utiariti ••• BR 132 Ee 52
Área Indígena Vale do Guaporé ••• BR 129 Ed 52
Área Indígena Vui-Uata Nova Itália ••• BR 117 Dp 47
Área Indígena Waiãpi ••• BR 113 Eh 45
Área Indígena Waimiri Atroari ••• BR 120 Ed 46
Área Indígena Xerente ••• BR 121 Ek 50
Área Indígena Zoró ••• BR 129 Ed 51
Área Indígena Zuruahã ••• BR 117 Ea 49
Áreas Indígenas do Vale do Javari ••• BR 117 Dn 48
Áreas Indígenas Rio-Biá ••• BR 117 Ea 48
Arebi ○ RDC 324 Hg 44
Arecibo ○ USA 104 Ea 36
Areco ~ RA 146 Ee 63
Aredo ○ RI 283 Mc 47
Areia ~ BR 133 Em 53
Areia Branca ○ BR 124 Fb 48
Arelas ○ BR 121 Ej 46
Arenales ○ RCH 136 Dp 57
Arenápolis ○ BR 132 Ef 53
Arendal ○ N 170 Gl 16
Arenillas ○ EC 116 Dh 47
Arenosa ○ PA 97 Dh 41
Areópoli ○ GR 194 Hd 27
Arequipa ○ PE 128 Dn 54
Ārēro ○ ETH 325 Hm 43
Arévalo ○ E 184 Gd 25
Āreza ○ ER 313 Hm 38
Arezzo ○ I 185 Gm 24
'Arğa ○ KSA 215 Ja 33
Argadargada ○ AUS 374 Me 56
Argahtah ○ RUS 205 Ya 5
Argalasti ○ GR 194 Hd 26
Argan ○ VRC 231 Kj 25
Argandāb ~ AFG 223 Jm 29
Argao ○ RP 267 Lm 41
Arga-Sala ~ RUS 204 Va 5
Argastān Rūd ~ AFG 227 Jm 30
Argedeb ○ ETH 325 Hn 42
Argelès ○ F 185 Gh 24
Argelia ○ CO 106 Dk 44
Argentan ○ F 163 Gf 21
Argentina ○ RA 137 Ec 60
Argentina □ RA 147 Dn 66
Argentine Basin ▽ 15 Ga 14
Argentine Plain ▽ 15 Ga 14
Argenton-sur-Creuse ○ F 163 Gg 22
Argeş ~ RO 175 Hf 23
Argoim ○ BR 125 Fa 52
Argonne ○ USA 57 Dd 23
Árgos ○ GR 194 Hd 27
Argostóli ○ GR 194 Hc 26
Argun ○ RUS 202 Ja 24
Argun ~ RUS 202 Ja 24
Argun ~ RUS 204 Vc 8
Argungu ○ WAN 320 Gj 39
Argu Tso ~ VRC 230 Kf 30
Arguvan ○ TR 195 Hm 26
Arhavi ○ TR 202 Hn 25
Århus ○ DK 170 Gm 17
Ariadnoe ○ RUS 250 Md 23
Ariake-kai ~ J 247 Mb 29
Ariamsvlei ○ NAM 348 Hb 60
Ariano Irpino ○ I 194 Gp 25
Ariari ~ CO 106 Dm 44
Aria River ~ PNG 287 Ml 48
Arias ○ RA 137 Ec 62
Ari Atoll △ MV 239 Ka 44
Ariaú ○ BR 120 Ef 47
Aribinda ○ BF 305 Gf 38
Arica ○ RCH 128 Dn 55
Aricapampa ○ PE 116 Dk 49
Arichat ○ CDN 61 Ed 23
Arichuna ○ YV 107 Ea 42
Arida ○ J 251 Md 28
Aridéa ○ GR 194 Hd 25
Ariel ○ RA 146 Ee 64
Ārifwāla ○ PK 230 Ka 30
Arīhāl Yerīho ○ JOR 214 Hk 30
Arihanha ~ BR 132 Eh 54
Arikawa ○ J 247 Ma 29
Arima ○ TT 104 Ed 40
Arimu Mine ○ GUY 112 Ee 42
Arinas ~ BR 132 Eg 53
Arinos ~ BR 132 Ee 51
Arinos ~ BR 132 Ef 52
Arinos ○ BR 133 El 53
Ariogala ○ LT 171 Hd 18
Arion ○ B 163 Gj 21
Ariporo ~ CO 107 Dn 42
Aripuanã ○ BR 120 Ed 48
Aripuanã ~ BR 120 Ee 50
Aripuanã ○ BR 132 Ee 51
Aripuanã ~ BR 132 Ee 51
Ariquemes ○ BR 117 Ec 50
Aris ○ NAM 348 Ha 57
Arismendi ○ YV 107 Dp 41
Arissa ○ ETH 313 Hn 40
Aristazabal Island △ CDN 50 Bm 19
Aritao ○ RP 267 Ll 37
Arite ○ SOL 290 Nc 51
Arivonimamo ○ RM 345 Jb 55
Ariyadka ○ IND 238 Kb 39
Ariyalur ○ IND 239 Kd 40
Arizona ⊙ USA 64 Cf 28
Arizona ○ AUS 365 Mg 55
Arizona ○ AUS 374 Mg 56
Arizpe ○ MEX 80 Cg 30
Ārjāng ○ S 170 Gn 16
Arjawinangun ○ RI 278 Le 49
Arjeplog ○ S 158 Ha 12
Arjo ○ ETH 325 Hl 41
Arjona ○ CO 106 Dl 40
Arjona ○ CO 106 Dl 41
Arjuni ○ IND 234 Ke 35
Arkadak ○ RUS 181 Hp 20
Arkadelphia ○ USA 70 Db 28
Arkalgūd ○ IND 238 Kb 39
Arkansas ~ USA 70 Cn 26
Arkansas ⊙ USA 70 Db 28
Arkansas City ○ USA 70 Cp 27
Arkansas Post Nat. Mem. ★ USA 70 Dc 28
Arkansas River ~ USA 65 Cj 26
Arkatag ⛰ VRC 231 Kh 27
Arkhangelsk ○ RUS 154 Qc 6
Arkhangelsk ○ RUS 159 Hn 13
Arkhipelag Nordenshel'da △ RUS 22 Pb 2
Arkhipelag Nordenshel'da △ RUS 204 Ua 3
Arkitsa ○ GR 194 Hd 26
Arklow ○ IRL 163 Gc 19
Arkona ★ D 170 Gn 18
Arkonam ○ IND 238 Kd 39
Arkösund ○ S 170 Ha 16
Arlal ○ RMM 305 Ge 37
Arlandag △ TM 222 Jf 26
Arlanza ~ E 184 Ge 24
Arlanzon ~ E 184 Gd 24
Arlee ○ USA 50 Ce 22
Arles ○ F 185 Gj 24
Arli ○ BF 317 Gg 40
Arlington ○ USA 50 Ca 21
Arlington ○ USA 50 Cb 23
Arlington ○ USA 56 Cp 23
Arlington ○ USA 70 Cn 27
Arlington ○ USA 70 Cp 29
Arlington ○ USA 74 Dk 26
Arlington ○ USA 74 Dm 25
Arlington ○ USA 86 Df 30
Arlington ○ ZA 349 Hf 60
Arlit ○ RN 308 Gk 36
Arltunga ○ AUS 374 Md 57
Armagh ○ GB 162 Gc 18
Armagnac ⌓ F 184 Gf 24
Armahua ○ PE 128 Dl 52
Armanda ○ BR 146 Eh 61
Armant ○ ET 301 Hj 33
Armavir ○ RUS 202 Hn 23
Armenia ○ CO 106 Dl 43
Armenia □ ARM 202 Hp 25
Armenien ⌓ TR 202 Hn 26
Armería ○ MEX 92 Ck 36
Armero ○ CO 106 Dl 43
Armidale ○ AUS 379 Mm 61
Arminavallen ~ SME 113 Eg 43
Armit ○ CDN 56 Cm 19
Armit Range ⛰ PNG 287 Mj 49
Armjans'k ○ UA 175 Hj 22
Armour ○ USA 56 Cn 24
Armraynald ○ AUS 365 Mf 54
Armstrong ○ CDN 50 Cc 20
Armstrong ○ CDN 57 Dd 20
Armstrong ~ AUS 364 Mb 54
Ārmūr ○ IND 238 Kd 36
Arnedo ○ E 184 Ge 24
Arneiroz ○ BR 124 Ep 49
Arnhem ○ NL 163 Gk 20
Arnhem Bay ~ AUS 364 Me 52
Arnhem Land ⌓ AUS 364 Md 52
Arnhem Land Aboriginal Reserve ••• AUS 364 Md 52
Arno ~ I 185 Gm 24
Arno Bay ○ AUS 378 Me 62
Arnold ○ USA 57 De 22
Arnold ○ USA 70 Cm 25
Arnold ~ AUS 364 Md 54
Arnold's Cove ○ CDN 61 Eg 22
Arnøya △ N 159 Hc 10
Arnprior ○ CDN 60 Dk 23
Arnsberg ○ D 163 Gk 20
Arntfield ○ CDN 60 Dj 21
Aroa ○ YV 107 Dp 40
Aroab ○ NAM 348 Hb 59
Aroaha ○ SOL 290 Nc 50
Aroana ○ AUS 378 Mf 61
Arochuku ○ WAN 320 Gk 43
Aroeiras ○ BR 124 Fc 49
Aroma ○ RCH 128 Dp 55
Aroma ○ PNG 287 Mk 51
Aroma ○ SUD 313 Hk 38
Aroostock ~ USA 60 Dp 22
Aropa ○ PNG 290 Mp 49
Aroroy ○ RP 267 Lm 39
Aroya ○ USA 65 Cl 26
Arpa Acambuco ~ PY 136 Eb 57
Arpa Çayı ~ TR 202 Hp 25
Arq. T. Romero Pereira ○ PY 140 Eg 59
Arqalyk ○ KZ 155 Sb 8
Arqū ○ SUD 312 Hh 36
Arque ~ BOL 129 Ea 54
Arquipélago da Madeira △ P 292 Fm 29
Arquipélago de Quirimbas △ MOC 344 Hn 51
Arquipélagos dos Abrolhos △ BR 125 Fa 54
Arra ~ PK 227 Jl 32
ar-Radīsīya Baḥrī ○ ET 301 Hj 33
ar-Rafīd ○ SYR 208 Hk 29
Arraga ○ RA 136 Eb 60
Arrah ○ CI 317 Ge 42
ar-Rahad ○ SUD 312 Hh 39
ar-Rahad ~ SUD 312 Hj 38
ar-Raḥḥālīya ○ IRQ 209 Hp 29
ar-Rāhida ○ YE 218 Ja 39
Arraial do Cabo ○ BR 141 En 57
Arraias ~ BR 132 Eg 51
Arraias ○ BR 133 El 52
Ar Ramadi ○ IRQ 209 Hp 29
Arran △ GB 162 Gd 18
Arranguá ○ BR 140 Ek 60
ar-Rank ○ SUD 312 Hj 40
ar-Raqqah ○ SYR 209 Hm 28
Ar Rāqūbah ○ LAR 300 Hb 31
Arras ○ CDN 47 Ca 17
Arras ○ F 163 Gh 20
ar-Ra's al-Abyad ⌓ KSA 214 Hm 34
ar-Rasātin △ JOR 209 Hm 29
ar-Rass ○ KSA 214 Hp 33
ar-Rastān ○ SYR 208 Hl 28
ar-Rauḍa ○ KSA 215 Ja 33
ar-Rauḍa ○ YE 218 Jb 38
ar-Rauḍa ○ ET 301 Hh 32
ar-Rauḍatain ○ KWT 215 Jb 31
ar-Rawdah ○ KSA 218 Hp 35
ar Rayyān ○ Q 215 Jd 33
Arrecifal ○ CO 107 Dp 44
Arrecife ○ E 292 Fp 31
Arrecife Alacrán △ MEX 93 Dd 34
Arrecife Edinburgh △ NIC 97 Dg 38
Arrecife Madagascar △ MEX 93 Dc 35
Arrecifes ~ RA 146 Ee 63
Arrecifes de la Media Luna △ HN 97 Dg 38
Arrecife Sisal △ MEX 93 Dc 35
Arrecifes Triángulos △ MEX 93 Db 35
Arrecife Tanhuijo △ MEX 81 Cp 34
Arrecites ○ RA 137 Ed 63
Arreti ○ PA 104 Dk 42
Arriaga ○ MEX 93 Da 37
Arriba ○ USA 65 Cl 26
ar-Ribāṭ ○ SYR 209 Hn 28
Arrieros ~ RCH 136 Dp 57
ar-Rifā'i ○ IRQ 215 Jb 30
Arrifó ○ RA 137 Ed 61
Arroio Grande ○ BR 146 Eh 62
Arrojado ~ BR 133 Em 52
Arrojo dos Ratos ○ BR 146 Ej 61
Arrojolândia ○ BR 133 Em 52
Arrowie ○ AUS 378 Mf 61
Arrowrock Reservoir ~ USA 50 Ce 24
Arrowwood Lake ~ USA 56 Cn 22
Arroya de Jaucha ~ RA 137 Dp 63
Arroya de la Ventana ○ RA 147 Ea 66
Arroyito ○ RA 137 Ea 62
Arroyito ○ RA 137 Ec 61
Arroyo al Pedacido Castigado ~ RA 137 Ed 64
Arroyo Amores ~ RA 140 Ee 59
Arroyo Apeleg ~ RA 152 Dn 68
Arroyo Avalos ~ RA 146 Ee 60
Arroyo Barrancas ~ RA 146 Ee 60
Arroyo Barrancoso ~ RA 137 Ed 62
Arroyo Batelito ~ RA 146 Ee 60
Arroyo Bueno ○ C 101 Dl 35
Arroyo Chasicó ~ RA 147 Ec 65
Arroyo Chazón ~ RA 137 Ec 62
Arroyo Chelforo ~ RA 146 Ee 64
Arroyo Chico ~ RA 146 Ee 64
Arroyo China Muerte ~ RA 147 Dn 65
Arroyo Cololo ~ ROU 146 Ef 62
Arroyo Comallo ~ RA 147 Dn 66
Arroyo Comicó ~ RA 147 Ea 66
Arroyo Covunco ~ RA 147 Dp 65
Arroyo Cristiano Muerto ~ RA 146 Ee 65
Arroyo Curi Leuvú ~ RA 137 Dn 64
Arroyo d. Saladillo ~ RA 137 Ed 61
Arroyo de la Barda ~ RA 137 Ea 64
Arroyo de la Iglesia ~ RA 137 Dp 61
Arroyo de las Flores ~ RA 137 Ed 64
Arroyo del Austado ~ RA 140 Ee 59
Arroyo del Azul ~ RA 146 Ee 64
Arroyo del Medio ~ RA 137 Ed 62
Arroyo de los Huesas ~ RA 146 Ee 64
Arroyo de los Huesos ○ RA 146 Ee 64
Arroyo del Rey ~ RA 146 Ee 60
Arroyo Don Esteban ~ ROU 146 Ef 62
Arroyo Dulce ~ RA 146 Ee 64
Arroyo el Moro ~ RA 146 Ee 65
Arroyo el Tigre ~ RA 146 Ee 61
Arroyo el Toba ~ RA 137 Ed 60
Arroyo Feliciano ~ RA 146 Ee 61
Arroyo Grande ○ USA 64 Cb 28
Arroyo Grande ~ RA 146 Ee 64
Arroyo Grande ~ ROU 146 Ef 62
Arroyo Indio Rico ~ RA 147 Ed 65
Arroyo Itiyuro ~ PY 136 Ec 57
Arroyo Jeneshuaya ~ BOL 129 Ea 52
Arroyo Langueyú ~ RA 146 Ee 64
Arroyo Laureles Grande ~ ROU 146 Ef 61
Arroyo Lucas ~ RA 146 Ee 61
Arroyo María Grande ~ RA 146 Ee 60
Arroyo Monte Lindo ~ RA 140 Ee 58
Arroyo Moreira ~ RA 146 Ee 61
Arroyo Nancay ~ RA 146 Ee 62
Arroyo Napaleofú ~ RA 146 Ee 64
Arroyo Negro ~ ROU 146 Ef 62
Arroyo Nogoyá ~ RA 146 Ee 62
Arroyo Pavon ~ RA 137 Ed 62
Arroyo Perdido ~ RA 147 Ea 67
Arroyo Picún Leufú ~ RA 147 Dp 65
Arroyo Sal. Amargo ~ RA 137 Ed 61
Arroyo Salado ~ RA 137 Ed 64
Arroyo Salado ~ RA 147 Ea 66
Arroyo Salado ~ RA 147 Eb 66
Arroyo Saldaillo ~ RA 137 Ed 62
Arroyo San Augustin ~ BOL 129 Ea 52
Arroyo San Carlos ~ RA 137 Dp 63
Arroyo Santa Catalin ~ RA 137 Eb 62
Arroyo Sarandi ~ RA 146 Ee 61
Arroyo Sauce Corto ~ RA 137 Ed 64
Arroyos de Mantua ○ C 100 Df 34
Arroyo Seco ó Yaminué ~ RA 147 Ea 66
Arroyos Esteros ○ PY 140 Ef 58
Arroyo Tapalqué ~ RA 137 Ed 64
Arroyo Valchera ~ RA 147 Ea 66
Arroyo Vallimanca ~ RA 137 Ed 63
Arroyo Verde ~ RA 147 Eb 66
Arroyo Villaguay Grande ~ RA 146 Ee 61
Arroyo Vivoratá ~ RA 146 Ef 64
Arroyo Yaguari ~ RA 146 Ee 60
Arrozal ○ YV 112 Ec 41
ar-Ru'at ○ SUD 312 Hh 39
ar-Rubai'iyah ○ KSA 215 Ja 32
ar-Rub'al-Hālī ⌓ KSA 218 Ja 37
Arruda ○ BR 132 Ef 53
ar-Ruqai ○ KSA 215 Jb 31
ar-Rusāfa ○ SYR 209 Hm 28
Ar-Rusayfah ○ JOR 214 Hl 29
ar-Ruṣayris ○ SUD 313 Hk 40
Ar Rustāq ○ OM 226 Jg 34
ar-Rutaimī ~ SYR 209 Hm 28
ar-Ruṭba ○ IRQ 209 Hn 29
ar-Ruwaida ○ KSA 215 Ja 33
Ar Ruways ○ Q 215 Jd 32
Arsen'ev ○ RUS 250 Mc 23
Arsengān ○ IR 215 Je 31
Arsikeri ○ IND 238 Kc 39
Arsk ○ RUS 181 Jc 17
Årsunda ○ S 158 Ha 15
Artá ○ E 185 Gh 26
Árta ○ GR 194 Hc 26
Arta ○ DJI 328 Hp 40
Artashat ○ ARM 202 Ja 26
Arteaga ○ MEX 92 Cl 36
Arteaga ○ RA 137 Ec 62
Artem ○ RUS 250 Mc 24
Artemisa ○ C 100 Dg 34
Artemivs'k ○ UA 181 Hm 21
Artemou ○ RIM 304 Fp 38
Artesia ○ USA 65 Ck 29
Artesian ○ USA 56 Cp 23
Artezian ○ RUS 202 Jb 23
Arthur ○ CDN 57 Dh 24
Arthur ○ USA 64 Ce 25
Arthur ○ USA 70 Cm 25
Arthur City ○ USA 70 Da 29
Arthur Point ⌓ AUS 375 Mm 57
Arthur River ○ AUS 368 Lj 62
Arthur's Pass ○ NZ 382 Nh 67
Arthur's Pass ♀ NZ 382 Nh 67
Arthur's Town ○ BS 87 Dl 33
Artigas ○ ROU 146 Ef 61
Artik ○ ARM 202 Ja 25
Artillery Lake ~ CDN 42 Ec 6
Artois ⌓ F 163 Gg 20
Artux ○ VRC 230 Kc 26
Artvin ○ TR 202 Hn 25
Artyk ○ RUS 205 Xc 6
Artyk ○ TM 222 Jh 27
Aru ○ RDC 324 Hh 44
Aruã ~ BR 120 Ef 47
A Rúa ○ E 184 Gc 24
Arua ○ EAU 324 Hh 44
Aruanã ○ BR 133 Ej 53
Aruba △ NL 107 Dp 39
Aruba Lodge ○ EAK 337 Hm 47
Arud ~ RI 279 Lf 47
Arufi ○ PNG 286 Mg 50
Arufu ○ WAN 320 Gl 42
Aruja ○ BR 141 El 57
Arumã ○ BR 117 Eb 47
Arumã ○ BR 117 Ec 48
Arumbi ○ RDC 324 Hg 44
Arumuganeri ○ IND 239 Kd 41
Arun ~ NEP 235 Kh 32
Arunachal Pradesh ⊙ IND 235 Kl 31
Arupukottai ○ IND 239 Kc 41
Aruri ~ BR 120 Eg 48
Arusha ○ EAT 337 Hl 47
Arusha ♀ EAT 337 Hl 47
Arusha Chini ○ EAT 337 Hl 47
Aruvi Aru ~ CL 239 Ke 41
Aruwimi ~ RDC 324 He 45
Aruwin ~ RDC 324 Hf 45
Arvada ○ USA 51 Cj 23
Arvada ○ USA 65 Ck 26
Arvajhèèr ○ MNG 204 Uc 9
Arvand Kenār ○ IR 215 Jc 31
Arvi ○ IND 234 Kd 35
Arviat ○ CDN 42 Fc 6
Arvidsjaur ○ S 158 Hb 13
Arvika ○ S 170 Gn 16
Årviksand ○ N 159 Hb 10
Arvin ○ USA 64 Cc 28
Arvorezinha ○ BR 146 Eh 60
Arwin Island △ PNG 287 Mh 46
Arxan ○ VRC 204 Wa 9
Arzamas ○ RUS 181 Hp 18
Arzana △ UAE 215 Je 33
Arzew ○ DZ 293 Gf 28
Arzgir ○ RUS 202 Ja 23
Asa ~ RDC 324 He 43
Asab ○ NAM 348 Ha 58
Asaba ○ WAN 320 Gk 42
Asadābād ○ IR 209 Jb 28
Asadābād ○ IR 222 Jh 29
Asadābād ○ AFG 223 Jp 28
Aşağı Pinarbası ○ TR 195 Hj 26
Asahi ○ J 251 Me 27
Asahi-dake △ J 250 Mh 24
Asahikawa ○ J 250 Mh 24
Asalayeng ○ GQ 332 Gl 45
Āsalē ○ ETH 313 Hn 38
Asālen ○ IR 209 Jc 27
Asamankese ○ GH 317 Gf 43
Asambi ○ RI 282 Ll 49
Asankranguaa ○ GH 317 Ge 43
Asan Man ~ ROK 247 Lp 27
Asapur ○ IND 234 Kc 35
Āsār ○ IR 226 Jj 32
Asariamas ○ BOL 129 Dp 53
Asaro ○ PNG 287 Mj 49
Asaro River ~ PNG 287 Mj 49
Asawinso ○ GH 317 Ge 42
Āsayita ○ ETH 313 Hn 40
Asbesberge ⛰ ZA 349 Hd 60
Asbestos ○ CDN 60 Dn 23
Āsbe Teferi ○ ETH 325 Hn 41
Ascension △ UK 30 Ja 10
Ascensión ○ MEX 80 Cj 30
Ascensión ○ MEX 81 Cm 33
Aschaffenburg ○ D 174 Gl 21
Ascochinga ○ RA 137 Eb 61
Áscoli ○ I 185 Gn 24
Ascope ○ PE 116 Dj 49
Ascotán ○ RCH 136 Dp 56
Asebot Terara △ ETH 325 Hn 41
Asedirad ⛰ DZ 293 Gg 33
Aseki ○ PNG 287 Mk 49
Āsela ○ ETH 325 Hm 42
'As 'Ēla ○ DJI 328 Hp 40
Asele ○ S 158 Ha 13
Asembagus ○ RI 279 Lh 49
Asembo ○ EAK 337 Hk 46
Asendabo ○ ETH 325 Hl 42
Asenovgrad ○ BG 194 He 25
Asera ○ RI 282 Ll 47
Åsgårdfonna ~ N 158 Ha 6
Asha ○ WAN 320 Gh 42
Ashaldn ○ USA 70 Cn 27
Āshāne ○ IR 222 Jg 27
Ashangē Hayk' ~ ETH 313 Hm 39
Ashanti Trad. Building ★ GH 317 Gf 42
Ashburn ○ USA 86 Dg 30
Ashburton ~ AUS 360 Lj 57
Ashburton ○ NZ 382 Nh 67
Ashburton Downs ○ AUS 360 Lj 57
Ashdod ○ IL 214 Hk 30
Ashdown ○ USA 70 Da 29
Asheboro ○ USA 74 Dj 28
Asher ○ USA 70 Cp 28
Ashern ○ CDN 56 Cn 20
Asheville ○ USA 71 Dg 28
Ash Flat ○ USA 70 Dc 27
Ashford ○ AUS 375 Mm 60
Ash Fork ○ USA 64 Cf 28
Ashgabat ▣ TM 222 Jh 26
Ashibetsu ○ J 250 Mh 24
Ashihik ○ CDN 47 Bg 15
Ashihik Lake ~ CDN 47 Bg 15
Ashika ○ IND 235 Kg 36
Ashikaga ○ J 251 Mf 27
Ashington ○ GB 162 Gf 18
Ashiro ○ J 250 Mg 25
Ashizuri-Uwakai ★ J 251 Mc 29
Ashkida ○ LAR 297 Gp 32
Ashland ○ USA 50 Ca 24
Ashland ○ USA 56 Dc 22
Ashland ○ USA 60 Dp 22
Ashland ○ USA 70 Cp 25
Ashland ○ USA 70 Db 26
Ashland ○ USA 71 Dg 25
Ashland ○ USA 74 Dk 27
Ashland City ○ USA 71 De 27
Ashley ○ USA 56 Cn 22
Ashley ○ USA 71 Dd 26
Ashmont ○ AUS 378 Mh 62

Arckaringa Creek - Ashmont 397

Ashmore Reef ⌂ **AUS** 360 Lm 52
Ashmore Reef ⌂ **PNG** 365 Mj 51
Ashmyany ○ **BY** 171 He 18
Ashoknagar ○ **IND** 234 Kc 33
Ashoro ○ **J** 250 Mb 25
ash-Shawal ○ **SUD** 312 Hj 39
ash-Shuheit ○ **SUD** 313 Hk 39
ash-Shurayk ○ **SUD** 312 Hj 36
Ashta ○ **IND** 234 Kc 34
Ashtabula ○ **USA** 71 Dh 25
Ashtarak ○ **ARM** 202 Ja 25
Ashti ○ **IND** 234 Kd 34
Ashton ○ **USA** 51 Cg 25
Ashton ○ **ZA** 348 Hb 62
Ashwaraopet ○ **IND** 234 Ke 37
Asia ○ **PE** 128 Dk 52
'Asid Gulf ≈ **RP** 267 Lm 39
Âsifâbâd ○ **IND** 238 Kd 36
Asilah ○ **MA** 293 Gc 28
Asillo ○ **PE** 128 Dn 53
Asindonhopo ○ **SME** 113 Eg 43
Asi Nehri ∾ **TR** 195 Hl 27
Asino ○ **RUS** 204 Tc 7
Aşkale ○ **TR** 202 Hn 26
'Askarān ○ **IR** 222 Jd 29
Aškazar ○ **IR** 215 Je 30
Askeaton ○ **ZA** 349 Hf 61
Asker ○ **N** 170 Gm 16
Askersund ○ **S** 170 Gp 16
Askia △ **IS** 158 Fm 13
Askim ○ **N** 170 Gm 16
Åskira ○ **WAN** 321 Gn 40
Åsköping ○ **S** 170 Ha 16
Askot ○ **IND** 234 Ke 31
Askøy ⌂ **N** 158 Gj 15
Asla ∾ **DZ** 293 Gf 29
Asmãr ○ **AFG** 223 Jp 28
Asmara ■ **ER** 313 Hm 38
Åsnähra ○ **IND** 234 Kf 32
Åsni ○ **MA** 293 Gc 30
Aso ○ **J** 247 Mb 29
Aso ★ **J** 247 Mb 29
Åsori ○ **RI** 283 Md 47
Aspen ○ **USA** 65 Cj 26
Aspen Cove ○ **CDN** 50 Cb 21
Aspen Mountain Ski Area ★ **USA** 65 Cj 26
Aspermont ○ **USA** 70 Cm 29
Aspy Bay ≈ **CDN** 61 Ed 22
Asquith ○ **CDN** 51 Cj 19
Asrama ○ **RT** 317 Gj 42
Assa ○ **MA** 292 Gb 31
Assab ○ **ER** 313 Hp 39
aš-Šabb ○ **IRQ** 215 Hp 30
aş-Şabrūm ○ **IRQ** 215 Hp 30
aş-Şadâra ○ **YE** 218 Jb 38
aş-Şadâra ○ **YE** 218 Jc 38
as-Sadawî ○ **KSA** 215 Jb 31
Assadjene △ **DZ** 308 Gk 34
aš-Šafa ○ **KSA** 215 Jc 32
aš-Šafallaḥīya ○ **KSA** 215 Jc 32
as-Şaff ○ **ET** 301 Hh 31
aš-Šafrā ○ **KSA** 218 Hn 35
Assa Gaîla ○ **DJI** 313 Hp 39
as-Sahba ○ **KSA** 215 Jb 33
Assahoun ○ **RT** 317 Gg 42
aš-Šaiḫ Humaid ○ **KSA** 214 Hk 31
aš-Šaiḫ 'Uṯmān ○ **YE** 218 Ja 39
Assaikio ○ **WAN** 320 Gl 41
as-Sail al-Kabîr ○ **KSA** 218 Hn 35
Assaka ○ **MA** 292 Gb 31
as-Sālâbîḏ ○ **UAE** 226 Jf 33
As Salamîya ○ **KSA** 215 Jb 33
As Salamîyah ○ **SYR** 208 Hl 28
as-Sa'lânîya ○ **KSA** 214 Hp 32
aš-Šālimiyah ○ **KWT** 215 Jc 31
as-Sallûm ○ **ET** 300 He 30
as-Salmân ○ **IRQ** 215 Ja 30
as-Salt ○ **JOR** 214 Hk 30
as-Salwâ ○ **KSA** 215 Jd 33
Assam ◉ **IND** 235 Kl 32
aš-Sa'm ○ **UAE** 226 Jf 32
Assamakka ○ **RN** 308 Gj 36
aş-Şamâwa ○ **IRQ** 215 Ja 30
aš-Şamilî ○ **KSA** 214 Hn 32
aš-Šāmīya ○ **IRQ** 215 Ja 30
aš-Šamsîya ○ **KSA** 215 Ja 32
aš-Šanâm ○ **KSA** 219 Jd 35
aš-Sanamain ○ **SYR** 208 Hl 29
Assaouas ○ **RN** 308 Gk 37
aš-Şaša' ○ **KSA** 215 Ja 33
aš-Şa'râ ○ **KSA** 218 Hn 34
aš-Şarâfiya ○ **KSA** 218 Hn 35
aš-Şarâ'î ○ **KSA** 218 Jb 37
aš-Saraura ○ **KSA** 218 Jb 37
Assaré ○ **BR** 124 Fa 49
aš-Şarqat ○ **IRQ** 209 Hp 28
aš-Şarrâr ○ **KSA** 215 Jc 32
Assateague Is. National Seashore ⚲ **USA** 74 Dl 27
Assateague Island ⌂ **USA** 74 Dl 27
aš-Şaṭra ○ **IRQ** 215 Jb 30
as-Saudâ' ○ **OM** 219 Jf 37
as-Sawâdîya ○ **YE** 218 Ja 38
Assdadah ○ **LAR** 297 Gp 30
Asse ○ **WAN** 320 Gk 43
Assegai ∾ **SD** 352 Mh 59
Assen ○ **NL** 170 Gk 19
Assen ○ **ZA** 349 Hf 58
As Sfire ○ **SYR** 195 Hl 27
as-Siayyira ○ **KSA** 214 Hp 32
as-Sîb ○ **OM** 226 Jg 34
as-Siba ○ **IRQ** 215 Ja 31
as-Sibt ○ **KSA** 218 Jc 38
As Sidr ○ **LAR** 300 Hb 30
as-Sidr ○ **KSA** 214 Hm 34
as-Sidr ○ **ET** 301 Hj 31
aš-Şiḥr ○ **YE** 219 Jc 38
as-Şikr ○ **IRQ** 215 Hp 30
aš-Šināfîya ○ **IRQ** 215 Ja 30
Assin Anyinabrim ○ **GH** 317 Gf 43
Assina River ∾ **PNG** 286 Mh 47
Assinet ○ **TCH** 321 Hb 39
Assiniboia ○ **CDN** 51 Ck 20
Assiniboine △ **CDN** 51 Cl 19
Assiniboine River ∾ **CDN** 56 Cm 20
Assinié ○ **CI** 317 Ge 43
Assin Nyankumase ○ **GH** 317 Gf 43
Assis ○ **BR** 140 Ej 57
as-Şişar ○ **OM** 219 Je 36
Assis Brasil ○ **BR** 128 Dp 51

Assis Chateaubriand ○ **BR** 140 Eh 58
Assisi ○ **I** 185 Gn 24
Assodé ○ **RN** 308 Gl 36
Assok Begua ○ **G** 332 Gm 45
Assu ○ **BR** 124 Fb 48
Assu ∾ **BR** 124 Fb 48
aš-Šu'aiba ○ **KSA** 214 Hp 32
aš-Šu'ba ○ **KSA** 215 Ja 31
aš-Šubaikīya ○ **KSA** 214 Hp 33
as-Sudeira ○ **KSA** 218 Hn 35
Assuéfri ○ **CI** 317 Ge 42
aš-Şuğūr ○ **SYR** 208 Hl 28
as-Şuḥna ○ **SYR** 209 Hm 28
aš-Şuḥna ○ **YE** 218 Hp 38
as-Sūkî ○ **SUD** 313 Hj 39
as-Sulaimānīya ◉ **IRQ** 209 Ja 28
As Sulaymanyah ○ **IRQ** 209 Ja 28
as-Sulayyil ○ **KSA** 218 Ja 35
aş-Şulb ○ **KSA** 215 Jc 32
as-Şumay ○ **SUD** 324 Hf 41
aş-Şummãn △ **KSA** 215 Ja 32
aš-Şuqaiq ○ **KSA** 218 Hn 37
aš-Şuqqân ○ **KSA** 219 Jc 35
aš-Šūra ○ **IRQ** 209 Hp 28
aş-Şurra ○ **YE** 218 Jb 39
as-Suwaidâ ○ **OM** 219 Jf 37
as-Suwâr ○ **KSA** 214 Hn 30
as-Suwaira ○ **IRQ** 209 Ja 29
as-Suwaidira ○ **KSA** 214 Hn 33
as-Suwaimît ○ **OM** 219 Jf 37
aş Şuwair ○ **KSA** 214 Hn 30
as-Suwaira ○ **IRQ** 209 Ja 29
as-Suwairiqîya ○ **KSA** 214 Hn 34
as-Suwâr ○ **SYR** 209 Hn 28
Astakós ○ **GR** 194 Hc 26
Astana ■ **KZ** 19 Na 4
Astaneh ○ **AFG** 223 Jn 28
Astara ○ **AZ** 202 Jc 26
Asti ○ **I** 185 Gl 23
Astipalea ○ **GR** 194 Hf 27
Astipálea ⌂ **GR** 194 Hf 27
Åštivay ○ **AFG** 223 Jp 28
Åštiyān ○ **IR** 209 Jc 28
Åštiyān ○ **IR** 209 Jc 28
Astorga ○ **BR** 140 Ej 57
Astorga ○ **E** 184 Gc 23
Astoria ○ **USA** 50 Ca 24
Astrahanskij zapovednik ♥ **RUS** 202 Jc 22
Astrahanskij zapovednik ♥ **RUS** 202 Jc 23
Astrakhan ○ **RUS** 202 Jc 22
Astrolabe Bay ≈ **PNG** 287 Mj 48
Åstros ○ **GR** 194 Hd 27
Asturias ◉ **E** 184 Gc 24
Asunción △ **USA** 27 Sa 8
Asunción ○ **CR** 97 Dg 41
Asunción ○ **BOL** 129 Ea 55
Asunción ■ **PY** 140 Ef 58
Aswa ∾ **EAU** 325 Hj 44
Aswân ○ **ET** 301 Hj 33
Asyma ○ **RUS** 205 Wb 6
Asypovichi ○ **BY** 171 Hg 18
Asyût ○ **ET** 301 Hh 32
Ata ○ **TO** 35 Aa 12
Ata ⌂ **KS** 230 Ka 25
Atabapó ∾ **CO** 107 Ea 44
Atacama Desert ⌂ **RCH** 136 Dn 58
Atacames ○ **EC** 116 Dh 45
Atafu ⌂ **NZ** 35 Aa 10
'Ataîye ○ **IR** 222 Jh 28
Atakor ○ **DZ** 308 Gj 34
Atakora Mountains △△ **DY** 317 Gg 40
Atakpamé ○ **RT** 317 Gg 42
Atalaia ○ **BR** 124 Fb 50
Atalaia do Norte ○ **BR** 117 Dn 48
Atalaya ○ **PE** 128 Df 51
Ataléia ○ **BR** 125 Ep 55
Atambua ○ **RI** 284 Ln 50
Atami ○ **J** 251 Mf 28
Atapupu ○ **RI** 282 Ln 50
Ataques ○ **ROU** 146 Eg 61
Atâr ○ **RIM** 304 Fp 35
Atascadero ○ **USA** 64 Cb 28
Atas Gompa ○ **VRC** 231 Kl 30
Atasi Nkwanta ○ **GH** 317 Gf 42
Atasta ○ **MEX** 93 Db 36
Ataya ○ **ETH** 313 Hm 40
Atauba ○ **BR** 120 Eb 48
Ataya ○ **ETH** 313 Hm 40
Atbara ○ **SUD** 313 Hj 37
'Atbara ○ **SUD** 313 Hk 37
'Atbara ∾ **ETH** 313 Hl 39
Atbasar ○ **KZ** 19 Na 4
Atchafalaya Bay ≈ **USA** 86 Dc 31
Atchison ○ **USA** 70 Da 26
Atebubu ○ **GH** 317 Gf 42
Ateiku ○ **GH** 317 Gf 42
Aten ○ **BOL** 129 Dp 53
Atenango del Río ○ **MEX** 92 Cn 36
Atencingo ○ **MEX** 92 Cn 36
Atenguillo ○ **MEX** 92 Ck 35
Ateppi ∾ **SUD** 324 Hj 43
Atesa ○ **GH** 317 Ge 42
Athabasca ○ **CDN** 42 Eb 7
Athabasca Lake ∾ **CDN** 42 Eb 7
Athabasca River ∾ **CDN** 6 Da 4
Athamanon △ **GR** 194 Hc 26
Athârân Hazâri △ **PK** 227 Jp 30
Åtharî ○ **FIN** 159 He 14
Athens ○ **USA** 70 Da 29
Athens ○ **USA** 71 De 28
Athens ○ **USA** 71 Df 28
Athens ○ **USA** 71 Dg 26
Athens ○ **USA** 71 Dc 26
Athens ■ **GR** 194 Hd 27
Atherton Tableland △△ **AUS** 365 Mj 54
Athgarh ○ **IND** 235 Kg 35
Athi ○ **EAK** 337 Hl 46
Athi ~ **EAK** 337 Hl 46
Athi River ∾ **EAK** 337 Hl 46
Athlone ○ **IRL** 163 Gc 19
Athni ○ **IND** 238 Kb 37
Athlone ○ **IRL** 163 Gc 19
Athens ○ **USA** 50 Cd 22
Athos △ **GR** 194 He 25
Ati ○ **TCH** 321 Hb 39
Atiak ○ **EAU** 324 Hj 44
Atiamuri ○ **NZ** 383 Nl 65
Ati Ardébé ○ **TCH** 321 Ha 39
Atibaia ○ **BR** 141 El 57
Atico ○ **PE** 128 Dm 54
Atikameg River ∾ **CDN** 57 Df 20
Atikokan ○ **CDN** 56 Dc 21
Atimonan ○ **RP** 267 Ll 38

Atiu ⌂ **NZ** 35 Ba 12
Atka ○ **RUS** 23 Sb 3
Atka Islands ⌂ **USA** 10 Aa 4
Atkinson ○ **USA** 56 Cn 24
Atkot ○ **IND** 227 Jp 35
Atkri ○ **RI** 283 Ma 46
Atlacomulco ○ **MEX** 92 Cn 36
Atlanta ○ **USA** 50 Ce 24
Atlanta ○ **USA** 57 Df 23
Atlanta ○ **USA** 70 Da 29
Atlanta ■ **USA** 71 Dh 29
Atlantic ○ **USA** 70 Da 25
Atlantic ○ **USA** 71 Dh 29
Atlantic City ○ **USA** 74 Dl 26
Atlantic Ocean ≈ **USA** 70 Da 25
Atlántida ◉ **ROU** 146 Eg 63
Atlasovo ○ **RUS** 205 Yb 7
Atlasovo ○ **RUS** 250 Mh 22
Atlin ○ **CDN** 47 Bj 15
Atlin Lake ∾ **CDN** 47 Bj 15
Atlixco ○ **MEX** 92 Cn 36
Åtmakur ○ **IND** 238 Kc 37
Åtmakur ○ **IND** 238 Kd 38
Atmis ∾ **RUS** 181 Hp 19
Atmore ○ **USA** 86 De 30
Atnbrua ○ **N** 158 Gm 15
Atocha ○ **BOL** 136 Ea 56
Atogafina ○ **G** 332 Gl 45
Atoka ○ **USA** 70 Cp 28
Atome ○ **ANG** 340 Gp 51
Atomic City ○ **USA** 51 Cf 24
Atongo-Bakari ○ **RCA** 321 Hc 43
Atonyia ○ **MEX** 92 Cm 35
Atori ○ **SOL** 290 Nc 50
Atotonilco ○ **MEX** 92 Cn 35
Atotonilco el Alto ○ **MEX** 92 Cl 35
Atoyac ○ **MEX** 92 Cm 37
Atoyac ∾ **MEX** 92 Cn 36
Atoyac ~ **MEX** 92 Cp 36
Ato Zaza ○ **ANG** 332 Ha 49
Atpadi ○ **IND** 238 Kb 37
Atqasuk ○ **USA** 46 Al 9
Atrak ∾ **IR** 222 Jf 27
Atrak ∾ **IR** 222 Jg 27
Åtran ∾ **S** 170 Gn 17
Atrato ∾ **CO** 106 Dk 42
Atsumihantô ◠ **J** 251 Me 28
Atsuta ○ **J** 250 Mg 24
Atsy ○ **RI** 286 Mf 48
Atta ○ **CAM** 320 Gm 42
Aṭ-Ṭafila ○ **JOR** 214 Hk 30
Aṭ-Ṭā'if ○ **KSA** 218 Hn 35
at-Tall ○ **SYR** 208 Hl 29
Attalla ○ **USA** 71 De 28
aṭ-Tamad ○ **ET** 214 Hk 31
aṭ-Tamad ○ **KSA** 214 Hm 33
At Tamimi ○ **LAR** 300 Hd 29
at-Ta'mîn ○ **IRQ** 209 Ja 28
Attâni ○ **IND** 239 Kc 40
Attapu ○ **LAO** 263 Ld 38
aṭ-Tarafiya ○ **KSA** 215 Ja 32
Attavíros △ **GR** 195 Hf 27
Attawapiskat ○ **CDN** 57 Eb 4
Attawapiskat River ∾ **CDN** 7 Eb 4
Attawapiskat River ∾ **CDN** 43 Gb 8
Attawapiskat River ∾ **CDN** 57 De 19
Attawapiskat River ∾ **CDN** 57 Dg 19
at-Tawîl △ **KSA** 214 Hm 31
Attayampatti ○ **IND** 239 Kd 40
at-Tayyara ○ **SUD** 312 Hh 39
Atteridgeville ○ **ZA** 349 Hf 58
Attica ○ **USA** 70 Cn 27
Attica ○ **USA** 71 De 25
Attingal ○ **IND** 239 Kc 41
aṭ-Ṭiwāl ○ **YE** 218 Hp 37
Attock ○ **PK** 223 Jp 29
Attock-Campbellpore ○ **PK** 230 Ka 29
Attu Island ⌂ **USA** 205 Zb 8
At Tullab ○ **LAR** 300 Hd 33
Attur ○ **IND** 239 Kd 40
aṭ-Ṭūr ○ **ET** 301 Hj 31
at-Turba ○ **YE** 218 Hp 39
at-Turba ○ **YE** 218 Ja 39
aṭ Ṭuwaysha ○ **SUD** 312 Hf 39
Atuel ○ **RA** 137 Dp 63
Atuel ∾ **RA** 137 Ea 63
Atuka ○ **RI** 286 Me 48
Atula ○ **USA** 374 Me 57
Atuna ○ **GH** 317 Ge 42
Atura ○ **EAU** 324 Hj 44
Atures ○ **YV** 107 Ea 43
Atutia ∾ **RA** 137 Dn 61
Atvidaberg ○ **S** 170 Gp 16
Atwater ○ **USA** 64 Cb 27
Atwood ○ **USA** 70 Cm 26
Atwood ○ **USA** 71 Dd 26
Atyrau ○ **KZ** 19 Mb 5
Atyrau ○ **KZ** 155 Rb 9
Au.Sable ∾ **USA** 57 De 24
Aua Island ⌂ **PNG** 286 Mh 46
Auasberge △△ **NAM** 348 Ha 57
Auasbila ○ **HN** 97 Df 38
Aubagne la Ciotat ○ **F** 185 Gj 24
Aube ∾ **F** 163 Gj 22
Aúbe ○ **MOC** 344 Hm 54
Aubigny ○ **F** 163 Gh 22
Auburn ○ **USA** 50 Ca 22
Auburn ○ **USA** 60 Dk 24
Auburn ○ **USA** 60 Dn 23
Auburn ○ **USA** 64 Cb 26
Auburn ○ **USA** 70 Cp 25
Auburn ○ **USA** 71 Dc 24
Auburn ○ **USA** 71 Df 29
Auburn ○ **USA** 86 Mf 56
Auburn ○ **AUS** 375 Mm 58
Auburn Range △△ **AUS** 375 Mm 58
Aubusson ○ **F** 184 Gg 23
Aucara ○ **PE** 128 Dl 53
Aucayacu ○ **PE** 116 Dk 50
Auch ○ **F** 184 Gg 24
Auchi ○ **WAN** 320 Gl 42
Auckland ○ **NZ** 383 Nk 64
Auckland Bay ≈ **MYA** 262 Kp 39
Auckland Island ⌂ **NZ** 35 Ta 15
Auden ○ **CDN** 57 Dc 20
Audierne ○ **F** 163 Gd 22
Aue ∾ **D** 174 Gn 20
Auga Azúl ∾ **HN** 96 De 38
Augathella ○ **AUS** 375 Mk 58

Augrabies ○ **ZA** 348 Hb 60
Augrabies Falls ⚲ **ZA** 348 Hc 60
Augsburg ○ **D** 174 Gm 21
Augusta ○ **USA** 51 Cf 22
Augusta ○ **USA** 60 Dp 23
Augusta ○ **USA** 70 Dc 28
Augusta ○ **USA** 71 Dh 29
Augusta ■ **USA** 185 Gp 27
Augusta ○ **AUS** 368 Lh 63
Augustine Island ⌂ **USA** 46 An 15
Augustinópolis ○ **BR** 121 Ek 48
Augusto Montenegro ○ **BR** 120 Ee 47
Augustów ○ **PL** 171 Hd 19
Augustus Downs ○ **AUS** 365 Mf 55
Aukam ○ **NAM** 348 Ha 59
Auki ○ **SOL** 290 Nc 50
Aulīrāipāra ○ **IND** 235 Kk 34
Aulita ∾ **BR** 132 Eh 52
Auliya Dam ∾ **SUD** 312 Hj 38
Ault ○ **USA** 65 Ck 25
Aumo ○ **PNG** 287 Ml 48
Auna ○ **WAN** 320 Gj 40
Aundah ○ **IND** 238 Kc 36
Auob ∾ **ZA** 348 Hc 59
a-'Uqda ○ **SUD** 312 Hj 38
Aurangabâd ○ **IND** 235 Kf 33
Aurangābâd ○ **IND** 238 Kb 36
Auras △ **C** 101 Dk 35
Aure River ∾ **PNG** 287 Mj 49
Aurich(O.) ○ **D** 170 Gk 19
Auriflama ○ **BR** 140 Ej 56
Aurillac ○ **F** 184 Gg 23
Auriya ○ **IND** 234 Kd 32
Aurlandsvangen ○ **N** 158 Gj 15
Aurora ○ **USA** 65 Ck 26
Aurora ○ **USA** 70 Cn 25
Aurora ○ **USA** 70 Db 27
Aurora ○ **USA** 71 Dd 25
Aurora ○ **GUY** 112 Ee 42
Aurora ○ **USA** 56 Da 23
Aurora ○ **BR** 124 Fa 49
Aurora ○ **RP** 267 Ll 37
Aurora ○ **RP** 275 Lm 42
Aurora do Tocantins ○ **BR** 133 El 52
Aurukun ○ **AUS** 365 Mg 52
Aurukun Aboriginal Reserve ••• **AUS** 365 Mg 52
Aus ○ **NAM** 348 Ha 59
Ausa ○ **IND** 238 Kc 36
Austfonna ∾ **N** 158 He 6
Austin ○ **CDN** 56 Cn 21
Austin ○ **USA** 56 Db 24
Austin ○ **USA** 64 Cd 26
Austin ■ **USA** 81 Cp 30
Austin's Post ○ **ZA** 349 He 60
Austral Downs ○ **AUS** 374 Me 56
Australia △ **AUS** 349 Ke 60
Australian Capital Territory ◉ **AUS** 379 Ml 64
Australian Fossil Mammal Site ★ **AUS** 365 Mf 55
Australind ○ **AUS** 368 Lh 62
Austral Islands ⌂ **F** 35 Ba 12
Austria ▪ **A** 174 Gp 22
Autās-Mirim ∾ **BR** 120 Ed 48
Autazes ○ **BR** 120 Ee 47
Autlán ○ **MEX** 92 Ck 36
Autun ○ **F** 163 Gj 22
Auvergne ◉ **F** 185 Gh 23
Auvergne ○ **AUS** 364 Ma 53
Auxerre ○ **F** 163 Gh 22
Auxiliadora ○ **BR** 120 Ee 49
Auyantepuí △ **YV** 112 Ec 43
Ava ○ **USA** 70 Db 27
Ava ○ **MYA** 254 Km 35
Avakubi ○ **RDC** 324 Hf 45
Avallon ○ **F** 163 Gh 22
Avalon ○ **USA** 64 Cc 29
Avalon Peninsula ⌂ **CDN** 61 Eh 22
Avanavero ○ **SME** 113 Ef 43
Avare ○ **BR** 141 Ek 57
Avarskoe Kojsu ∾ **RUS** 202 Jb 24
Ave-Dakpa ○ **GH** 317 Gg 42
Aveg ○ **IR** 209 Jc 28
Aveiro ○ **BR** 120 Eg 47
Aveiro ◉ **P** 184 Gb 25
Avekova ○ **RUS** 205 Yc 6
Aveline Lopes ○ **BR** 124 En 51
Aveline Lopes ○ **BR** 133 Em 51
Avellaneda ○ **RA** 146 Ee 63
Avellino ○ **I** 194 Gp 25
Avenal ○ **USA** 64 Cb 28
Avenue of the Giants ★ **USA** 64 Ca 25
Avery ○ **USA** 51 Cf 23
Aves de Barlovento ⌂ **YV** 107 Ea 40
Avesnes ○ **F** 163 Gh 20
Aves Ridge ♥ **104** Ec 39
Avesta ○ **S** 158 Gp 15
Aveyron ∾ **F** 185 Gh 23
Avezzano ○ **I** 185 Gn 24
Avia Teray ○ **RA** 136 Ed 59
Avignon ○ **F** 185 Gj 24
Ávila ○ **E** 184 Gd 25
Avilés ○ **E** 184 Gc 24
Avissawella ○ **CL** 239 Ke 42
Avoca ○ **AUS** 378 Mh 64
Avoca ○ **AUS** 378 Mk 64
Avon ○ **USA** 51 Cf 22
Avon ○ **USA** 74 Dl 28
Avon ∾ **AUS** 368 Lj 61
Avon Downs ○ **AUS** 374 Me 56
Avon Downs ○ **AUS** 374 Mk 56
Avon Park ○ **USA** 87 Dh 32
Avranches ○ **F** 163 Gf 21
Avsandvgø ∾ **N** 158 Gn 13
Avu Avu ○ **SOL** 290 Nc 50
Avvil ○ **FIN** 159 Hf 11
Awābì ○ **OM** 226 Jg 34
Awaê ○ **CAM** 320 Gm 44
Awagakama River ∾ **CDN** 57 Dg 20
Awakaba ○ **RCA** 321 Hb 41
Awakino ○ **NZ** 383 Nk 65
Awalere River ∾ **NZ** 383 Nj 66
'Awâlî ○ **BRN** 215 Jd 33
Awang ○ **RI** 279 Lj 50
Awanui ○ **NZ** 383 Nj 63
Awar ○ **PNG** 287 Mj 48
Awara Soela ∾ **SME** 113 Eg 44

Awarē ○ **ETH** 328 Ja 41
Awasa ○ **ETH** 325 Hm 41
Āwasa Hāyk' ∾ **ETH** 325 Hm 41
Awash ○ **ETH** 325 Hn 41
Awash Nat. Park ⚲ **ETH** 325 Hm 41
Āwash Wenz ∾ **ETH** 313 Hn 40
Awat ○ **VRC** 230 Ke 25
Āwata Shet' ∾ **ETH** 325 Hm 43
Awbārī ○ **LAR** 297 Gn 32
Awbari Sand Sea ⌂ **LAR** 297 Gm 31
Aw Dheegle ○ **SP** 329 Ja 45
Awdiinle ○ **SP** 328 Np 44
Awe ○ **WAN** 320 Gl 41
Aweil ○ **SUD** 324 Hf 41
Awgu ○ **WAN** 320 Gk 42
Awio ○ **PNG** 287 Mm 49
Āwira Wenz ∾ **ETH** 313 Hm 39
Awisang ○ **RI** 279 Lk 46
Awjilah ○ **LAR** 300 Hc 31
Awka ○ **WAN** 320 Gk 42
Awungi ○ **PNG** 287 Mm 48
Axel Heiberg Island ⌂ **CDN** 43 Fc 2
Axim ○ **GH** 317 Ge 43
Axinim ○ **BR** 120 Ee 48
Axios ∾ **GR** 194 Hd 25
Ax-les-Thermes ○ **F** 184 Gg 24
Ayabene ○ **GQ** 332 Gm 45
Ayacucho ○ **PE** 128 Dl 52
Ayacucho ○ **RA** 146 Ee 64
Ayairi ○ **PE** 128 Dn 53
Ayamé ○ **CI** 317 Ge 43
Ayamiken ○ **GQ** 332 Gm 44
Ayamonte ○ **E** 184 Gc 27
Ayancık ○ **TR** 195 Hk 25
Ayanfure ○ **GH** 317 Ge 43
Ayangba ○ **WAN** 320 Gk 42
Ayapata ○ **PE** 128 Dn 52
Ayapel ○ **CO** 106 Dl 41
Ayas ○ **TR** 195 Hk 26
Ayaviri ○ **PE** 128 Dn 52
Ayazkol ○ **UZB** 223 Jj 24
Aybak ○ **AFG** 223 Jn 27
Ayden ○ **USA** 74 Dk 28
Aydin ○ **TR** 195 Hg 27
Ayerbe ○ **E** 184 Gf 24
Ayer Hitam ○ **MAL** 271 Lb 45
Ayers Rock Uluru △ **AUS** 369 Mb 58
Ayilūr ○ **IND** 239 Kd 40
Ayina ∾ **G** 332 Gn 44
Ayinwafe ○ **GH** 317 Gf 42
Aykel ○ **ETH** 313 Hl 39
Aylesbury ○ **GB** 163 Gf 20
Aylet ○ **ER** 313 Hm 38
Ayllón ○ **E** 184 Ge 25
Aylmer Lake ∾ **CDN** 42 Ec 6
Aymat ○ **ER** 313 Hm 37
Ayn al Ghāzalah ○ **LAR** 300 Hd 29
Ayod ○ **SUD** 324 Hh 41
Ayoni ○ **SUD** 324 Hf 41
Ayopaya ∾ **BOL** 129 Ea 54
Ayos ○ **CAM** 320 Gm 44
'Ayoun el 'Atroûs ○ **RIM** 304 Gb 37
Ayourou ○ **RN** 305 Gg 38
Ayr ○ **GB** 162 Gd 18
Ayr ○ **AUS** 365 Mk 55
Ayranci ○ **TR** 195 Hj 27
Aysha ○ **ETH** 328 Hp 40
Ayungon ○ **RP** 267 Lm 41
Ayutla ○ **MEX** 92 Ck 35
Ayutla ○ **MEX** 93 Cp 37
Ayutla de los Libres ○ **MEX** 92 Cn 37
Ayvacık ○ **TR** 195 Hf 26
Ayvacık ○ **TR** 195 Hl 25
Ayvalık ○ **TR** 195 Hf 26
Āzād Šar ○ **IR** 222 Jf 27
Azaila ○ **E** 184 Gf 25
Azangaro ○ **PE** 128 Dn 53
Azaouagh ∾ **RN** 308 Gj 37
Azazga ○ **DZ** 296 Gh 28
Āzarbāyğan-e Ġharbi ◉ **IR** 209 Jb 26
Āzarbāyğan-e Khāvari ◉ **IR** 209 Jb 26
Azare ○ **WAN** 320 Gm 40
Āzaršahr ○ **IR** 209 Ja 27
Āzaršahr ○ **IR** 209 Ja 27
Azarychy ○ **BY** 171 Hg 19
'Aʾâz ○ **SYR** 195 Hl 27
Azaz △ **DZ** 296 Gh 32
Azazga ○ **DZ** 296 Gh 28
Azeffâl ∾ **RIM** 304 Fn 36
Azemmour ○ **MA** 292 Gb 29
Azerbaijan ▪ **AZ** 202 Jb 25
Azero ∾ **BOL** 129 Ec 55
Azezo ○ **ETH** 313 Hl 39
Azgale ○ **IR** 209 Ja 28
Azilal ○ **MA** 293 Gc 30
Azingo ○ **G** 332 Gl 46
Azirir ∾ **DZ** 296 Gn 32
Aziz ○ **TCH** 309 Ha 37
Azl ○ **BR** 116 Dm 49
Aznâ ○ **IR** 209 Jc 29
Azogues ○ **EC** 116 Dj 47
Azores ⌂ **P** 18 Hb 6
Azov ○ **RUS** 181 Hl 22
Azov Upland △△ **UA** 181 Hl 22
Azrou ○ **MA** 293 Gd 29
Aztec ○ **USA** 65 Ch 27
Aztec Ruins N.M. ★ **USA** 65 Ch 27
Azua ○ **DOM** 101 Dn 36
Azuaga ○ **E** 184 Gd 26
Azúcar ∾ **RCH** 136 Dn 59
Azuer ∾ **E** 184 Ge 26
Azuero Peninsula ⌂ **PA** 97 Dh 42
Azul ○ **MEX** 92 Cn 37
Azul ~ **MEX** 93 Db 37
Azul ○ **RA** 146 Ee 64
Azuma-san △ **J** 251 Mg 27
Azurduy ○ **BOL** 129 Ec 55
Azzaba ○ **DZ** 296 Gk 27
az-Zafra ○ **UAE** 226 Jf 34
Az-Zahrâ ○ **KSA** 215 Jc 32
aẓ-Ẓaidîya ○ **YE** 218 Hp 38
az-Zaqâzîo ○ **ET** 301 Hh 30
az-Zilfi ○ **KSA** 215 Ja 32
az-Zuhra ○ **YE** 218 Hp 38
az-Zūma ○ **SUD** 312 Hh 36
az-Zuqur ⌂ **ER** 218 Hp 38

B. Bartholomew ∾ **USA** 86 Dc 29
B. E. Jordan-Lake ∾ **USA** 74 Dj 28
B.E. Klô'p ∾ **VN** 263 Le 39
B. Grande de Buba ≈ **GNB** 316 Fn 40
B. Rapti ∾ **IND** 234 Kf 32
B. Soltane ○ **TN** 296 Gl 29
B. Touila ○ **TN** 296 Gl 29
Ba ⌂ **FJI** 387 Nl 54
Baa ○ **RI** 282 Lm 51
Baalbeck ★ **RL** 208 Hl 28
Baardheere ○ **SP** 329 Hp 44
Baba ○ **EC** 116 Dj 46
Baba ∾ **RCA** 321 Ha 43
Baba Br. ◠ **TR** 194 He 26
Babaçulândia ○ **BR** 121 Ek 49
Babadag ○ **RO** 175 Hg 23
Babadag △ **AZ** 202 Jc 25
Babadayhan ○ **TM** 222 Jj 27
Babaeski ○ **TR** 194 Hf 25
Bâbâ Gurgur ○ **IRQ** 209 Ja 28
Babahoyo ○ **EC** 116 Dj 46
Babai ~ **NEP** 234 Ke 31
Babalegi ○ **ZA** 349 Hg 58
Babana ○ **RI** 279 Lk 47
Baban Rafi ○ **WAN** 320 Gk 41
Babanûsa ○ **SUD** 312 Hf 40
Babao ○ **VRC** 255 Lc 34
Babase Island ⌂ **PNG** 287 Mn 47
Babat ○ **RI** 278 Lf 48
Babat ○ **RI** 279 Lg 49
Babati ○ **EAT** 337 Hk 48
Babau ○ **RI** 282 Lm 51
Bâbâ Yâdegâr ○ **IR** 209 Jb 28
Babb ○ **USA** 50 Cf 21
Bab-Besen △ **MA** 293 Gd 28
Bâb-e Anâr ○ **IR** 215 Je 31
Babelthuap ⌂ **PAL** 26 Rb 9
Băbeni ○ **RO** 175 He 23
Babenza ○ **RDC** 324 He 45
Baberu ○ **IND** 234 Kd 33
Babetville ○ **RM** 345 Jb 55
Bâbil ◉ **IRQ** 209 Ja 29
Babilé ○ **ETH** 328 Hp 41
Babîna ○ **IND** 234 Kd 33
Babinda ○ **AUS** 365 Mj 54
Babine Lake ∾ **CDN** 42 Db 8
Babo ○ **RI** 283 Mc 47
Bâbol ○ **IR** 222 Je 27
Bâbolsar ○ **IR** 222 Je 27
Babonde ○ **RDC** 324 Hf 44
Baborigame ○ **MEX** 80 Cj 32
Baboua ○ **RCA** 321 Gp 43
Bâbra ○ **IND** 227 Jp 35
Babruysk ○ **BY** 171 Hg 19
Babtai ○ **LT** 171 Hd 18
Bab-Taza △ **MA** 293 Gd 28
Babura ○ **WAN** 320 Gl 40
Bâbusar Pass △ **PK** 230 Ka 28
Babuyan Channel ≈ **RP** 267 Ll 36
Babuyan Island ⌂ **RP** 267 Lm 36
Babylon ★ **IRQ** 209 Ja 29
Bacaadweyn ○ **SP** 328 Jb 42
Bacabal ○ **BR** 112 Ed 45
Bacabal ○ **BR** 121 El 47
Bacabal ○ **BR** 124 En 47
Bacabeira ○ **BR** 121 Em 47
Bacaja ∾ **BR** 121 Ej 48
Bacajar ○ **BR** 121 Ej 47
Bacalar ○ **MEX** 93 Db 36
Bacanora ○ **MEX** 80 Ch 31
Bacău ○ **RO** 175 Hf 22
Bac Ban ○ **VN** 255 Lc 34
Bac Binh ○ **VN** 263 Le 40
Bac Can ○ **VN** 255 Lc 34
Bacchus Marsh ○ **AUS** 379 Mj 64
Bacerac ○ **MEX** 80 Ch 30
Bắc Giang ○ **VN** 255 Ld 34
Bắc Hà ○ **VN** 255 Lc 34
Bachaquero ○ **YV** 107 Dn 41
Bachčysaraj ○ **UA** 175 Hj 23
Bachhrāwān ○ **IND** 234 Ke 32
Báchiniva ○ **MEX** 80 Cj 31
Bach Long Vi ⌂ **VN** 255 Ld 35
Bachmač ○ **UA** 175 Hj 20
Bachu ○ **VRC** 230 Kd 26
Bachuo Akakbe ○ **CAM** 320 Gl 43
Bačka Palanka ○ **SCG** 174 Hb 23
Bačka Topola ○ **SCG** 174 Hb 23
Bäckefors ○ **S** 170 Gn 16
Bäckhammar ○ **S** 170 Gn 16
Backstairs Passage ≈ **AUS** 378 Me 63
Backus ○ **USA** 56 Da 22
Bắc Me ○ **VN** 255 Lc 34
Bắc Ngu'o'n ○ **VN** 255 Lc 34
Bắc Ninh ○ **VN** 255 Ld 35
Bacobampo ○ **MEX** 80 Cg 32
Bacolod ○ **RP** 267 Lm 40
Bactili ○ **SP** 325 Hn 45
Bắc Tô ○ **VN** 263 Ld 38
Bacubirho ○ **MEX** 80 Cj 33
Bacungan ○ **RP** 267 Lk 41
Bacuri ○ **BR** 121 Em 46
Bac Xang ○ **VN** 255 Lc 36
Bad ∾ **USA** 56 Cm 24
Bâd ○ **IR** 222 Je 29
Badā ○ **KSA** 214 Hl 32
Bada △△ **ETH** 325 Hm 42
Bada Barabil ○ **IND** 235 Kg 34
Badagara ○ **IND** 238 Kb 40
Badagri ○ **WAN** 320 Gh 42
Badahšân ◉ **AFG** 223 Jp 27
Badain Jaran Shamo Alashan Shamo ⌂ **VRC** 242 La 27
Badajós ○ **BR** 120 Ec 47
Badajoz ◉ **E** 184 Gc 26
Badaling ★ **VRC** 243 Lh 25
Badalona ○ **E** 184 Gh 25
Badanga ○ **IND** 234 Kh 40
Badau ○ **RI** 278 Ld 47
Bad Camberg ○ **D** 174 Gl 20
Badda Rogghie △ **ETH** 325 Hl 41
Baddeck ○ **CDN** 61 Ed 22
Baddo ∾ **PK** 227 Jl 31

◻Country ▣Capital city ⊙Administrative unit ○Place ♁Island ⛰Mountain range △Mountain ⌓Cape ≈Ocean, Sea ~Lake, River ♆Undersea topography △Glacier ♀National park •••Reservation ★Point of major interest ⌓Landscape

Badeggi ○ WAN 320 Gk 41
Badéguicheri ○ RN 308 Gj 38
Baden ○ CH 174 Gl 22
Baden ○ A 174 Gp 22
Badena ~ SP 337 Hn 46
Baden-Baden ○ D 174 Gl 21
Baden-Württemberg ⊙ D 174 Gl 21
Bādepalli ○ IND 238 Kd 37
Badér ○ RN 308 Gk 38
Badgastein ○ A 174 Gn 22
Badger ○ CDN 61 Ef 21
Badgingarra ○ AUS 368 Lh 61
Badgingarra ♀ AUS 368 Lh 61
Bādgis ⊙ AFG 223 Jk 28
Bad Hersfeld ○ D 174 Gl 20
Badiara ~ SN 304 Fp 38
Badīn ○ PK 227 Jn 33
Badinko ○ RMM 316 Gb 39
Badinn-Ko ~ RMM 316 Gb 39
Badir ○ WAN 320 Gn 40
Bad Ischl ○ A 174 Gn 22
Bad Kissingen ○ D 174 Gm 20
Bad Kreuznach ○ D 163 Gk 21
Badlands ⌓ USA 51 Cl 22
Badlands N.P. ♀ USA 51 Cl 24
Bad Nauheim ○ D 174 Gl 20
Badnāwar ○ IND 234 Kb 34
Badnera ○ IND 234 Kc 35
Bad Neuenahr-Ahrweiler ○ D 163 Gk 20
Bad Neustadt ○ D 174 Gm 20
Bado ○ RI 286 Mf 49
Badoc ○ RP 267 Ll 37
Badogo ○ RMM 316 Gb 40
Badong ○ VRC 243 Lf 30
Ba Đông ○ VN 263 Ld 41
Bad Orb ○ D 174 Gl 20
Badou ○ RT 317 Gg 42
Badoumbé ○ RMM 316 Ga 39
Badplaas ○ ZA 352 Hh 58
Badra ○ IRQ 209 Ja 29
Bad Radkersburg ○ A 174 Gp 22
Bādrah ○ PK 227 Jm 32
Badrānlū ○ IR 222 Jg 27
Bad Reichenhall ○ D 174 Gn 22
Badrinath ○ IND 230 Kd 30
Bad River ~ USA 56 Cm 24
Bad River Ind. Res. ••• USA 56 Dc 22
Badr wa-Hunain ○ KSA 214 Hm 34
Bad Segeberg ○ D 170 Gm 19
Badsīr ○ IR 226 Jg 31
Bad Tölz ○ D 174 Gm 22
Badu ○ VRC 258 Lh 32
Badu Island ♁ AUS 365 Mg 51
Badulla ○ CL 239 Ke 42
Badvel ○ IND 238 Kd 38
Badwater Basin ~ USA 64 Cd 27
Badzére ○ CAM 321 Gp 43
Baédiam ○ RIM 304 Fp 38
Baeza ○ EC 116 Dj 46
Baeza ○ E 184 Ge 27
Bafang ○ CAM 320 Gm 43
Bafatá ○ GNB 316 Fn 39
Baffin Basin ♆ 43 Hb 4
Baffin Bay ≈ 43 Ha 4
Baffin Bay ~ USA 81 Cp 32
Baffin Island ♁ CDN 43 Ha 5
Bafia ○ CAM 320 Gm 43
Bafilo ○ RT 317 Gg 41
Bafing ~ RMM 316 Ga 39
Bafing ~ RG 316 Ga 40
Bafing-Makana ○ RMM 316 Ga 39
Bafoulabé ○ RMM 316 Ga 39
Bafoussam ○ CAM 320 Gm 43
Bāfq ○ IR 226 Jf 30
Bafra ○ TR 195 Hk 25
Bāft ○ IR 226 Jg 31
Bafu Bay ~ LB 316 Gb 43
Bafut ○ CAM 320 Gl 42
Bafwabalinga ○ RDC 324 Hf 45
Bafwabogbo ○ RDC 324 Hf 45
Bafwaboli ○ RDC 324 Hf 45
Bafwasende ○ RDC 324 Hf 45
Baga ○ WAN 321 Gn 39
Bagabag ○ RP 267 Ll 37
Baga-Burul ○ RUS 202 Ja 23
Bagaces ○ CR 97 Df 40
Bagaembo ○ RDC 321 Hb 43
Bagaevskij ○ RUS 181 Hn 22
Bagai ○ PNG 287 Ml 48
Bagaia ○ SUD 312 Hh 40
Bāgalūr ○ IND 238 Kc 39
Bagamanoc ○ RP 267 Ln 39
Bagana ○ WAN 320 Gk 42
Bagandou ○ RCA 321 Ha 44
Baganga ○ RP 275 Lp 42
Bagani ○ NAM 340 Hc 55
Bagansiapiapi ○ RI 270 La 44
Bagaré ○ BF 317 Ge 39
Bagaroua ○ RN 308 Gj 38
Baga Sola ○ TCH 321 Gp 39
Bagassi ○ BF 317 Ge 40
Bagata ○ BF 317 Gf 40
Bagata ○ RDC 333 Ha 47
Bagazan ○ PE 116 Dm 48
Bagbag Island ♁ PNG 287 Mk 48
Bagbe ~ WAL 316 Ga 41
Bagdad ○ USA 64 Cf 28
Bağdād ⊙ IRQ 209 Ja 29
Bagdarin ○ RUS 204 Vb 8
Bage ○ BR 146 Eg 61
Bāgein ○ IR 226 Jg 30
Bāgepalli ○ IND 238 Kc 39
Bagerhat ○ BD 235 Kj 34
Bagestān ○ IR 222 Jh 28
Bageya ○ WAN 320 Gj 39
Bāggirān ○ IR 222 Jh 27
Baggs ○ USA 65 Cj 25
Bāgh ○ IND 234 Kb 34
Baghdad ▣ IRQ 209 Ja 29
Baghelkhand Plateau ⛰ IND 234 Ke 34
Baghlān ○ AFG 223 Jn 27
Baghmara ○ IND 235 Kk 33
Baghpat ○ IND 234 Kc 31
Bāgil ○ YE 218 Hp 38
Baglān ⊙ AFG 223 Jn 28
Bagley ○ USA 56 Da 22
Baglkot ○ IND 238 Kb 37
BaGma ○ IRQ 209 Hp 27
Bagmati ~ NEP 235 Kg 32
Bagnérers-de-Lucrion ○ E 184 Gg 24
Bagnères-d.-B. ○ F 184 Gg 24
Bag Nur ~ VRC 243 Le 26
Bago ○ RP 267 Lm 40
Bagodar ○ IND 235 Kg 33
Bagodo ○ CAM 321 Gn 42
Bagodra ○ IND 227 Jp 34
Bagoé ~ RMM 305 Gc 39
Bagoé ~ RMM 305 Gc 40
Bagomoyo ○ EAT 337 Hm 49
Bagoosaar ○ SP 328 Ja 43
Bagrati ★ GE 202 Hp 24
Bagrationovsk ○ RUS 170 Hc 18
Bagre ○ BR 121 Ej 46
Bagua ○ PE 116 Dj 48
Bagua Grande ○ PE 116 Dj 48
Báguanos ○ C 101 Dl 35
Bagudo ○ WAN 320 Gj 40
Baguinéda ○ RMM 305 Gc 39
Baguio ○ RP 267 Ll 37
Baguio ○ RP 275 Ln 42
Bagyrlaj ~ KZ 181 Jd 21
Bahādorābād ○ IR 226 Jg 31
Bahadurganj ○ NEP 234 Kf 32
Bahādurganj ○ IND 235 Kh 32
Bahamas ♁ BS 87 Dk 32
Bahamas ◻ BS 87 Dl 33
Bahamas National Trust Park ♀ BS 101 Dm 35
Bahār ○ IR 209 Jc 28
Baharagora ○ IND 235 Kh 34
Bahārak ○ AFG 223 Jp 27
Baharampur ○ IND 235 Kj 34
Baharden ○ TM 222 Jg 26
Bahardok ○ TM 222 Jh 26
Bahau ○ MAL 270 Lb 44
Bahaur ○ RI 279 Lg 47
Bahāwalnagar ○ PK 230 Ka 30
Bahāwalpur ○ PK 227 Jp 31
Bahçe ○ TR 195 Hl 27
Baheri ○ IND 234 Kd 31
Bahi ○ EAT 337 Hk 48
Bahia ⊙ BR 125 En 51
Bahía Adventure ~ RCH 152 Dl 68
Bahía Aguirre ~ RA 152 Eb 73
Bahía Anegada ~ RA 147 Ec 66
Bahía Ascunción ~ MEX 75 Ce 32
Bahía Banks ~ EC 128 Dc 46
Bahía Blanca ○ RA 147 Ec 65
Bahía Blanca ~ RA 147 Ed 65
Bahía Buena Vista ~ C 100 Dj 34
Bahía Bustamante ○ RA 152 Ea 68
Bahía Camarones ~ RA 152 Eb 68
Bahía Chamela ~ MEX 92 Ck 36
Bahía Chanco ~ RCH 137 Dm 63
Bahía Chipehua ~ MEX 93 Da 38
Bahía Chiquinata ~ RCH 136 Dn 56
Bahía Coatzacoalcos ~ MEX 93 Da 36
Bahía Conchali ~ RCH 137 Dm 61
Bahía Conquimbo ~ RCH 137 Dn 60
Bahía Creek ○ RA 147 Eb 66
Bahía Cruz ~ RA 152 Eb 68
Bahía da I. Grande ~ BR 141 Em 57
Bahía Damas ~ PA 97 Dh 42
Bahía Darwin ~ RCH 152 Dl 68
Bahía de Adair ~ MEX 75 Cf 30
Bahía de Agiabampo ~ MEX 80 Ch 32
Bahía de Banderas ⌓ MEX 92 Cj 35
Bahía de Banes ~ C 101 Dl 35
Bahía de Bluefields ~ NIC 97 Dg 40
Bahía de Buenventura ~ CO 106 Dk 44
Bahía de Caballos ~ PE 128 Dl 53
Bahía de Caráquez ○ EC 116 Dh 46
Bahía de Chetumal ~ BH 93 Dd 36
Bahía de Cochinos ~ C 100 Dh 34
Bahía de Corrientes ~ C 100 Df 35
Bahía de Guantánamo ~ C 101 Dl 36
Bahía de Jigüey ~ C 100 Dj 34
Bahía de la Ascensión ~ MEX 93 De 36
Bahía de la Glona ~ C 101 Dk 35
Bahía de La Isabela ~ DOM 101 Dn 35
Bahía del Amatique ~ GCA 93 Dd 38
Bahía de La Paz ~ MEX 80 Cg 33
Bahía del Espíritu Santo ~ MEX 93 De 36
Bahía de Lomas ~ RCH 152 Dp 72
Bahía de los Angeles ○ MEX 75 Cf 31
Bahía de Malagueta ~ C 101 Dk 35
Bahía de Manta ~ EC 116 Dh 46
Bahía de Mejillones del Sur ~ RCH 136 Dn 57
Bahía de Neiba ~ DOM 101 Dn 36
Bahía de Nipes ~ C 101 Dl 35
Bahía de Ocoa ~ DOM 101 Dn 36
Bahía de Paita ~ PE 116 Dh 48
Bahía de Panamá ~ PA 97 Dj 41
Bahía de Paracas ~ PE 128 Dk 52
Bahía de Parita ~ PA 97 Dh 41
Bahía de Petacalco ~ MEX 92 Cl 37
Bahía de Salinas ~ CR 96 De 40
Bahía de Salinas ~ PE 128 Dj 51
Bahía de Samaná ~ DOM 101 Dp 36
Bahía de Santa Clara ~ C 100 Dh 34
Bahía de Santa Elena ~ CR 96 De 40
Bahía de Santa Elena ~ EC 116 Dh 47
Bahía de Santiago de Cuba ~ C 101 Dk 36
Bahía de Santos ~ BR 141 El 58
Bahía de Sebastián Vizcaíno ~ MEX 75 Ce 31
Bahía de Sechura ~ PE 116 Dh 48
Bahía Desvelos ~ RA 152 Ea 70
Bahía de Tela ~ HN 96 De 38
Bahía de Yuma ~ DOM 101 Dp 36
Bahía Elisabeth ~ EC 128 Dc 46
Bahía Escocesa ~ DOM 101 Dp 36
Bahía Falsa ~ RA 147 Ec 65
Bahía Guadiana ~ C 100 Df 34
Bahía Guanaquero ~ RCH 137 Dn 61
Bahía Honda ○ C 100 Dg 34
Bahía Inglesa ~ RCH 136 Dn 59
Bahía Inútil ~ RCH 152 Dp 72
Bahía Kino ~ MEX 75 Cf 31
Bahía Kino ○ MEX 80 Cg 31
Bahía Lángare ~ RA 152 Ea 69
Bahía las Cañas ~ RCH 137 Dm 63
Bahía Laura ○ RA 152 Ea 70
Bahía Magdalena ~ MEX 75 Cf 33
Bahía Mansa ○ RCH 147 Dl 66
Bahía Moreno ~ RCH 136 Dn 57
Bahía Nassau ~ RCH 152 Ea 73
Bahía Punta Gorda ~ NIC 97 Dg 40
Bahía Quintero ~ RCH 137 Dm 62
Bahía Rosario ~ MEX 75 Ce 31
Bahía Salvación ~ RCH 152 Dl 71
Bahía San Felipe ~ RCH 152 Dn 72
Bahía San Jorge ~ MEX 75 Cf 30
Bahía San Nicolás ~ PE 128 Dl 53
Bahía San Sebastián ~ RA 152 Dp 72
Bahía Santa Ana ~ MEX 75 Cf 32
Bahía Santa Ines ~ MEX 80 Cg 32
Bahía Santa Maria ~ MEX 75 Cd 30
Bahía San Vicente ~ RCH 137 Dm 64
Bahía Sargento ~ MEX 75 Cf 31
Bahía Sloggett ~ RA 152 Ea 73
Bahía Solano Ciudad Mutís ○ CO 106 Dk 42
Bahía Solano ~ RA 152 Ea 68
Bahía Stokes ~ RCH 152 Dm 73
Bahía Tortugás ○ MEX 75 Ce 32
Bahía Unión ~ RA 147 Ec 65
Bahía Vera ~ RA 152 Eb 68
Bahía Verde ~ RA 147 Ec 65
Bahinga ○ RDC 336 Hf 48
Bahir Dar ○ ETH 313 Hl 40
Bahla ○ OM 226 Jg 34
Bāhla ○ IND 227 Jp 32
Bahl Ab ~ AFG 223 Jm 28
Bahn ○ LB 316 Gb 42
Bahra ○ KSA 218 Hm 35
Bahr Abali ~ TCH 321 Hb 40
Bahraich ○ IND 234 Ke 32
Bahrain ◻ BRN 215 Jd 33
Bahr al-,Arab ~ SUD 312 He 40
Bahr al-Ghazāl ~ SUD 324 Hg 41
Bahr al-Jabel White Nile ~ SUD 324 Hh 41
Bahr Aouk ~ TCH 321 Hb 41
Bahr as-Salam ~ ETH 313 Hl 39
Bahr Azoum ~ TCH 321 Hc 40
Bahr Azrak ~ TCH 321 Hc 40
Bahr az-Zaraf ~ SUD 324 Hh 41
Bahr Baikoré ~ TCH 321 Hc 40
Bahr Bola ~ TCH 321 Hb 40
Bahr Doseo ~ TCH 321 Hb 41
Bahr el Arab ~ SUD 324 Hf 41
Bahr el Ghazal Soro ~ TCH 309 Ha 38
Bahr Erguig ~ TCH 321 Ha 40
Bahriya Oasis ⌓ ET 301 Hg 31
Bahr Kameur ~ RCA 321 Hc 41
Bahr Keita ou Douka ~ TCH 321 Hb 41
Bahr Korbol ~ TCH 321 Ha 40
Bahr Korom ~ TCH 321 Hb 40
Bahr Nzili ~ RCA 313 Hd 40
Bahr Oulu ~ RCA 313 Hd 40
Bahr Salamat ~ TCH 321 Hb 40
Bahr Yūsuf ~ ET 301 Hh 31
Bahšī Kalei ○ AFG 227 Jn 30
Bahū Kalāt ○ IR 226 Jj 33
Baía ~ BR 120 Eh 49
Baía Cabelelo da Velha ~ BR 121 Em 46
Baía de Caxiuanã ~ BR 121 Ej 46
Baía de Guaratuba ~ BR 141 Ek 58
Baia de Inhambane ~ MOC 352 Hk 57
Baía de Marajó ~ BR 121 Ek 46
Baia de Santa Rosa ~ BR 121 Ek 45
Baía de São Marcos ~ BR 121 Em 47
Baia de Setúbal ~ P 184 Gb 26
Baia de Sofala ~ MOC 352 Hk 56
Baía de Todos os Santos ~ BR 125 Fa 52
Baía de Turiaçu ~ BR 121 Em 46
Baía do Bengo ~ ANG 340 Gn 50
Baía do Caeté ~ BR 121 El 46
Baía do Cumã ~ BR 121 Em 47
Baía do Emoraí ~ BR 121 El 46
Baía do Gurupi ~ BR 121 El 46
Baía do Iririaçu ♁ BR 121 Em 46
Baía do Japerica ~ BR 121 El 46
Baía do Lúrio ~ MOC 344 Hn 52
Baía do Maputo ~ MOC 352 Hj 59
Baía do Maracanã ~ BR 121 El 46
Baía dos Lençois ~ BR 121 Em 46
Baía dos Tigres ○ ANG 340 Gm 54
Baía do Tromai ♁ BR 121 Em 46
Baía do Vieira Grande ~ BR 121 Ej 46
Baia Farta ○ ANG 340 Gn 52
Baía Formosa ○ BR 124 Fc 49
Baia Mare ○ RO 175 Hd 22
Baianópolis ○ BR 133 Em 52
Baião ○ BR 121 Ek 47
Baia River ~ PNG 286 Mh 49
Baïbokoum ○ TCH 321 Gp 42
Baidā' Naţil ○ KSA 214 Hn 32
Baidi Cheng ★ VRC 243 Le 30
Baïdou ~ RCA 321 Hc 43
Baie Anantsono ~ RM 353 Hp 57
Baie Boatswain ~ CDN 57 Dj 20
Baie Bradore ~ CDN 61 Ef 20
Baie Chasselup ~ F 386 Ne 56
Baie-Comeau ○ CDN 60 Dp 21
Baie de Boulari ~ F 386 Nf 57
Baie de Burton ~ RDC 336 Hg 48
Baie de Canala ~ F 386 Ne 56
Baie de Châteaubriand ~ F 386 Nf 56
Baie de Corisco ~ G 332 Gl 45
Baie de Fanemotra ~ RM 353 Hp 57
Baie de Gaspé ~ CDN 61 Eb 21
Baie de Gouaro ~ F 386 Ne 56
Baie de l'Allier ~ F 386 Ng 56
Baie de la Seine ~ F 163 Gf 21
Baie de Mahajamba ~ RM 345 Jb 53
Baie de Narinda ~ RM 345 Jb 53
Baie de Rupert ~ CDN 60 Dj 20
Baie de Sandal ~ F 386 Nf 56
Baie des Chaleurs ~ CDN 61 Eb 21
Baie-des-Sables ○ CDN 60 Ea 21
Baie des Sept-Îles ~ CDN 61 Ea 20
Baie de St.-Vinzent ~ F 386 Ne 57
Baie de Téremba ~ F 386 Ne 56
Baie d'Ognat ~ F 386 Nf 56
Baie du Néhoué ~ F 386 Nd 56
Baie Johan Beetz ○ CDN 61 Ec 20
Baie Marguerite ≈ 38 Fa 16
Baie Moar ~ CDN 57 Dj 19
Baie Quinné ~ F 386 Nf 56
Baie-St.Paul ○ CDN 60 Dn 22
Baie-Trinité ○ CDN 60 Ea 21
Baie Verte ○ CDN 61 Ef 21
Ba'īğī ○ IRQ 209 Hp 28
Baihān al-Qaṣāb ○ YE 218 Ja 38
Baihar ○ IND 234 Ke 34
Baihe ○ VRC 243 Lf 29
Baiju Si ★ VRC 235 Kj 31
Baikunthpur ○ IND 234 Kf 34
Baila ○ VRC 235 Kh 31
Baïla ○ SN 316 Fm 39
Baile Atha Cliath Dublin ▣ IRL 163 Gc 19
Băile Herculane ○ RO 194 Hd 23
Bailén ○ E 184 Ge 26
Băileşti ○ RO 194 Hd 24
Bail Hongal ○ IND 238 Kb 38
Bailique ○ BR 121 Ej 47
Ba Illi ○ TCH 321 Ha 40
Ba Illi ~ TCH 321 Ha 40
Bailong Jiang ~ VRC 242 Lc 29
Bailundo ○ ANG 340 Gp 52
Baima ○ VRC 242 La 29
Baimaxue ★ VRC 254 Kp 31
Baimuru ○ PNG 287 Mj 49
Bain ~ RI 286 Mg 49
Baina ○ PNG 286 Mh 49
Bainbridge ○ USA 86 Df 30
Baines Drift ○ RB 349 Hg 57
Baing ○ RI 282 Ll 51
Baining Mts. ⛰ PNG 287 Mn 48
Baiona ○ E 184 Gb 24
Baiquan ○ VRC 205 Wb 9
Bā'ir ○ JOR 214 Hl 30
Bairab Co ~ VRC 231 Kf 28
Baird ○ USA 70 Cn 29
Baird Inlet ~ USA 46 Aj 15
Baird Peninsula ♁ CDN 43 Gc 5
Bairds Table Mountain △ AUS 365 Mh 55
Bairiki ▣ KIR 27 Tb 9
Bairki ○ KIR 27 Tb 9
Bairnsdale ○ AUS 379 Mk 64
Bairo ○ RDC 324 He 45
Baiš ○ KSA 218 Hp 37
Bais ○ RP 267 Lm 41
Baisha ○ VRC 255 Le 36
Baishenzu △ VRC 258 Lk 32
Baishui ○ VRC 243 Le 28
Baissa ○ WAN 320 Gm 42
Baitadi ○ NEP 234 Ke 31
Bait al-Faqīh ○ YE 218 Hp 38
Baitou Shan ⛰ VRC 247 Lp 25
Baixa do Tubarã ~ BR 125 Fa 51
Baixa Grande ○ BR 125 Ep 51
Baixão ○ BR 125 Ep 52
Baixio ○ BR 125 Fb 52
Baixo Guandu ○ BR 141 Ep 55
Baixo Longa ○ ANG 340 Hb 53
Baiyan Si ★ VRC 243 Lf 27
Baiyau ○ PNG 287 Mk 48
Baiyer River ○ PNG 287 Mj 48
Baiyer River N.P. ★ PNG 287 Mj 48
Baiyi ○ VRC 243 Ld 29
Baiyin ○ VRC 242 Lb 27
Baja ○ H 174 Hb 22
Baja California ⌓ MEX 75 Ce 31
Bajada del Agrio ○ RA 147 Dp 65
Baja de Fernão Veloso ~ MOC 344 Hn 53
Baja de Memba ~ MOC 344 Hn 53
Bajanhongor ○ MNG 204 Uc 10
Bajanhongor ○ MNG 204 Uc 9
Bajan Ovoo ○ MNG 204 Ub 10
Bajawa ○ RI 282 Ll 50
Bajie ○ VRC 255 Lc 33
Bajina Bašta ○ SCG 174 Hb 23
Bajío de Ahuichila ○ MEX 81 Cl 33
Bajkal'sk ○ RUS 204 Uc 8
Bajo ○ YV 107 Dp 41
Bajo Caracoles ○ RA 152 Dn 69
Bajo del Gualicho ⌓ RA 147 Eb 67
Bajo de los Menucos ⌓ RA 147 Ea 65
Bajoga ○ WAN 320 Gm 40
Bajo Hondo ○ RA 137 Ea 61
Bajool ○ AUS 375 Mm 57
Bajo Pichanaqui ○ PE 128 Dl 51
Bajos de Haina ○ DOM 101 Dn 36
Bajram-Ali ○ TM 223 Jk 27
Bajram Curri ○ AL 194 Hb 24
Bajsun ○ UZB 223 Jm 26
Bajyrkum ○ KZ 223 Jn 24
Baká ○ NIC 97 Df 39
Bakaba ○ TCH 321 Ha 42
Bakala ○ RCA 321 Hc 42
Bakali ~ RDC 333 Ha 48
Bakaoré ○ TCH 309 Hc 38
Bakau ○ WAG 316 Fm 39
Bakauhuni ○ RI 278 Lc 48
Bakebe ○ CAM 320 Gl 43
Bakel ○ SN 304 Fp 38
Bakelalan ○ MAL 274 Lh 43
Bakelalan ○ MAL 274 Lh 44
Baker ♁ USA 27 Aa 9
Baker ○ USA 51 Ck 22
Baker ○ USA 64 Cd 28
Baker ○ USA 64 Ce 26
Baker ○ USA 74 Dj 26
Baker City ○ USA 50 Cc 23
Bakere ○ RDC 333 Hd 45
Baker Island ♁ USA 42 Da 7
Baker Lake ○ CDN 42 Fb 6
Baker Lake ~ CDN 42 Fb 6
Bakers Creek ○ AUS 375 Ml 56
Bakersfield ○ USA 64 Cc 28
Bakerville ○ ZA 349 Hf 58
Ba Khe ○ VN 255 Lc 35
Bakhtiyārpur ○ IND 235 Kg 33
Bakin Birji ○ RN 308 Gl 38
Bakır Ç. ~ TR 195 Hf 26
Bakkafjörður ○ IS 158 Fn 12
Bakkejord ○ N 158 Hb 11
Bako ○ CI 304 Gc 41
Bako ○ ETH 325 Hl 41
Bako N.P. ♀ MAL 271 Lf 45
Bakori ○ WAN 320 Gk 40
Bakouma ○ RCA 321 Hd 43
Bakoumba ○ G 332 Gn 46
Bakoy ~ RG 316 Gb 40
Bakoye ~ RMM 316 Gb 39
Bakṣaj ~ KZ 202 Jd 22
Baksan ○ RUS 202 Hp 24
Baksan ~ RUS 202 Hp 24
Baku ▣ AZ 202 Jc 25
Baku ○ RDC 324 Hh 44
Bakungan ○ RI 270 Kn 44
Bakuriani ○ GE 202 Hp 25
Bakwa-Kenge ○ RDC 333 Hd 48
Bala ○ CDN 60 Dj 23
Balâ ○ TR 195 Hj 26
Bala ○ SN 304 Fp 38
Balabac ○ RP 266 Lj 41
Balabac ○ RP 274 Lj 42
Balabac Island ♁ RP 274 Lj 42
Balabac Strait ~ MAL 274 Lj 42
Balabac Strait ~ RP 274 Lj 42
Balabagan ○ RP 275 Lm 42
Balabaiba ○ ANG 340 Gn 52
Ba ,labakk ○ RL 208 Hl 29
Balabala ○ RDC 321 Hc 44
Balad al-Mala ○ IRQ 209 Ja 28
Balade ○ IR 222 Jd 27
Bala de Varela ~ GNB 316 Fm 39
Baladjie Lake ~ AUS 368 Lk 61
Balad Rūz ○ IRQ 209 Ja 29
Balad Sonğār ○ IRQ 202 Hn 27
Balagansk ○ RUS 22 Qa 4
Bālāghāt ○ IND 234 Ke 35
Bālāghāt Range ⛰ IND 238 Kb 36
Balaguer ○ E 184 Gg 25
Balahna ○ RUS 181 Hp 17
Balaiberkuak ○ RI 278 Le 46
Balaikarangan ○ RI 271 Le 45
Balaipungut ○ RI 270 La 45
Balaka ○ MW 344 Hk 53
Balakanabat ○ TM 222 Jf 26
Balakéte ○ RCA 321 Hb 42
Balaki ○ RG 316 Ga 39
Balaklija ○ UA 181 Hl 21
Bālākot ○ PK 230 Ka 28
Balakovo ○ RUS 181 Jb 19
Balala ○ ETH 325 Hk 43
Balalai Island ♁ SOL 290 Mp 49
Balama ○ MOC 344 Hm 52
Balam Tākli ○ IND 238 Kb 36
Balancán ○ MEX 93 Dc 37
Balanced Rock ★ USA 50 Ce 24
Balañga ○ RP 267 Ll 38
Balanga ○ RDC 336 Hg 50
Balangala ○ RDC 333 Hb 45
Balangir ○ IND 234 Kf 35
Balangkayan ○ RP 267 Ln 40
Balangoda ○ CL 239 Ke 42
Balao ○ EC 116 Dj 47
Balaoan ○ RP 267 Ll 37
Balapitiya ○ CL 239 Kd 42
Balaraja ○ RI 278 Ld 49
Balarampur ○ IND 235 Kg 34
Balasan ○ RP 267 Lm 40
Balašīhaělektrostal' ○ RUS 171 Hm 18
Bāl Asmar ○ KSA 218 Hp 36
Balašov ○ RUS 181 Hp 20
Balassagyarmat ○ H 174 Hb 21
Balāt ○ ET 301 Hg 33
Balaton ~ H 174 Ha 22
Balatonfüred ○ H 174 Ha 22
Balauring ○ RI 282 Lm 50
Balavé ○ BF 317 Gd 39
Balayan ○ RP 267 Ll 39
Balayan Bay ~ RP 267 Ll 39
Balazote ○ E 184 Ge 26
Balbalan ○ RP 267 Ll 37
Balbina ○ BR 120 Ee 46
Balboa ○ PA 97 Dj 41
Balbriggan ○ IRL 163 Gc 19
Balcad ○ SP 329 Ja 44
Balcanoona ○ AUS 378 Mf 61
Balcarce ○ RA 146 Ee 64
Balcarres ○ CDN 51 Cl 20
Bălceşti ○ RO 194 Hd 23
Balčik ○ BG 195 Hg 24
Balclutha ○ NZ 382 Ng 69
Balde de la Mora ○ RA 137 Eb 61
Bald Head ⌓ AUS 368 Lk 63
Bald Knob ○ USA 70 Dc 28
Bald Mountain △ USA 64 Ce 27
Baldwin ○ USA 56 Db 23
Baldwin ○ USA 57 De 24
Baldwin ○ USA 87 Dg 30
Baldy Mountain △ USA 51 Ch 21
Baldy Mountain △ CDN 56 Cm 20
Bale ~ RMM 316 Gb 40
Bale ○ EAU 324 Hj 45
Balearic Islands ♁ E 184 Gh 26
Baleh ~ MAL 274 Lg 45
Balej ○ RUS 204 Vc 8
Balékoutou ○ TCH 321 Hb 41
Balelesberge ⛰ ZA 352 Hh 59
Bale Mt. National Park ♀ ETH 325 Hm 42
Baleno ○ RP 267 Lm 39
Baler ○ RP 267 Ll 38
Baler Bay ~ RP 267 Ll 38
Baleshwar ○ IND 235 Kh 35
Balestrand ○ N 158 Gk 15
Baléya ○ RMM 316 Gb 39
Baleyara ○ RN 320 Gh 39
Balfes Creek ○ AUS 375 Mj 56
Balfour ○ CDN 50 Cd 21
Balfour ○ ZA 349 Hg 59
Balfour ○ ZA 358 Hf 62
Balfour Downs ○ AUS 360 Ll 57
Balgo ○ AUS 361 Ma 56
Balgonie ○ CDN 51 Ck 20
Balğurašī ○ KSA 218 Hn 36
Balh ○ AFG 223 Jm 27
Balh ⊙ AFG 223 Jm 27
Balh ~ AFG 223 Jm 27
Balh Ab ○ AFG 223 Jm 28
Bālho ○ DJI 313 Hp 39
Bāli ○ IND 227 Ka 33
Bali ♁ RI 279 Lh 49
Bali ○ CAM 320 Gl 43
Baliaga ○ RUS 204 Va 8
Balibi ○ RCA 321 Hc 42
Balicuatro Islands ♁ RP 267 Ln 39
Baliem ~ RI 286 Mf 48
Baliem Valley ⌓ RI 286 Mf 47
Balige ○ RI 270 Kp 44
Baliguda ○ IND 235 Kf 35
Balikesir ○ TR 195 Hf 26
Balikpapan ○ RI 274 Lj 46
Balimbing ○ RI 278 Lc 48
Balimela Reservoir ~ IND 234 Kf 36
Balimo ○ PNG 286 Mh 50
Baling ○ MAL 270 La 43
Balingen ○ D 174 Gl 21
Balingian ○ MAL 274 Lg 44
Balingtan Channel ~ RP 267 Ll 36
Balinn ~ RMM 316 Ga 39
Bali Sea ≈ RI 279 Lh 49
Balitondo ○ RCA 321 Hd 43
Baliza ○ BR 133 Eh 54
Balkan Mountains ⛰ BG 194 Hd 24
Balladonia Motel ○ AUS 369 Lm 62
Ballapūr ○ IND 238 Kc 39
Ballarat ○ AUS 379 Mh 64
Ballaroo ○ AUS 375 Ml 59
Ballater ○ GB 162 Ge 17
Ballé ○ RMM 304 Gb 38
Balleza ○ MEX 80 Cj 32
Ballia ○ IND 235 Kg 33
Ballidu ○ AUS 368 Lj 61
Ballina ○ IRL 162 Gb 18
Ballina ○ AUS 375 Mn 60
Ballinasloe ○ IRL 163 Gb 19
Ballinger ○ USA 81 Cn 30
Ball Lake ~ CDN 56 Db 20
Balloul ○ DZ 293 Gg 28
Ballyhaunis ○ IRL 162 Gb 19
Ballymena ○ GB 162 Gc 18
Ballyshannon ○ IRL 162 Gb 18
Balmaceda ○ RA 152 Dn 68
Balmoral ○ AUS 378 Mg 64
Balmorhea ○ USA 81 Ck 30
Balnearia ○ RA 137 Ec 61
Balneário Camboriú ○ BR 141 Ek 59
Balneario las Grutas ○ RA 147 Eb 66
Balneario Massini ○ RA 147 Ec 66
Balo ○ RI 282 Lm 46
Balo ~ RG 316 Ga 40
Baloa ○ RI 282 Lm 46
Balod ○ IND 234 Ke 35
Balombo ○ ANG 340 Gp 52
Balombo ~ ANG 340 Gp 52
Balong ○ VRC 242 Kn 27
Balong ○ RI 279 Lf 49
Balonne ~ AUS 375 Ml 60
Balos ○ SUD 313 Hk 39
Balotra ○ IND 227 Ka 33
Balqash ○ KZ 22 Nb 5
Balrāmpur ○ IND 234 Kf 32
Balranald ○ AUS 378 Mh 63
Balsa Nova ○ BR 140 Ek 58
Balsapuerto ○ PE 116 Dk 48
Balsas ~ MEX 92 Cm 36
Balsas ○ MEX 92 Cn 36
Balsas ~ MEX 92 Cn 37
Balsas ○ EC 116 Dj 47
Balsas ○ PE 116 Dk 49
Balsas ○ BR 121 El 49
Balsas ~ BR 121 Em 49
Balsas ~ BR 133 El 51
Balsinhas ~ BR 121 Em 50
Balta ○ UA 175 Hg 22
Balta Brăilei ⌓ RO 175 Hg 23
Baltal ○ IND 230 Kb 28
Baltasar Brum ○ ROU 146 Ef 61
Baltasound ○ GB 162 Gf 15
Baltazar ○ YV 107 Ea 44
Bălţi ○ MD 175 Hg 22
Baltic Sea ≈ 170 Ha 18
Baltijsk ○ RUS 170 Hb 18
Baltīm ○ ET 301 Hh 30
Baltimore ○ USA 74 Dk 26
Baltimore ○ IRL 163 Gb 20
Baltimore ○ ZA 349 Hg 57
Baltit ○ PK 230 Kb 27
Baltrum ♁ D 170 Gk 19
Baluan Island ♁ PNG 287 Mk 47
Baluchi ⊙ PK 226 Jk 31
Baluchistan ⌓ IR 226 Jj 32
Baluchistan ⊙ PK 227 Jm 31
Balud ○ RP 267 Lm 39
Balui ⌓ MAL 274 Lh 44
Balūr ○ IND 238 Kb 39
Balurghat ○ IND 235 Kj 33
Balut Island ♁ RP 275 Ln 43
Balvard ○ IR 226 Jg 31
Balvi ○ LV 171 Hf 17
Balwāda ○ IND 234 Kc 34
Balwina Aboriginal Reserve ••• AUS 361 Ma 56
Balygyčan ○ RUS 23 Sb 3
Balygyčan ~ RUS 205 Ya 6
Balzar ○ EC 116 Dj 46
Bam ○ IR 226 Jh 31
Bam ○ TCH 321 Ha 41
Bama ○ VRC 255 Ld 33
Bama ○ WAN 321 Gn 40
Bamaga ○ AUS 365 Mh 51
Bamaji Lake ~ CDN 56 Dc 20
Bamake ○ LB 304 Gc 43
Bamako ▣ RMM 316 Gb 39
Bamba ○ RMM 305 Gf 37
Bamba ~ RCA 321 Hb 43
Bamba ○ EAK 337 Hm 47
Bambadinca ○ GNB 316 Fn 39
Bambalang ○ CAM 320 Gm 43
Bambama ○ RCB 332 Gn 47
Bambamarca ○ PE 116 Dj 49
Bambana ~ NIC 97 Df 39
Bambang ○ RP 267 Ll 37
Bambang ○ RI 278 Lb 48
Bambangando ○ ANG 341 Hd 54
Bambara ○ TCH 321 Hb 41
Bambara-Maoundé ○ RMM 305 Ge 38
Bambari ○ RCA 321 Hc 43
Bambaroo ○ AUS 365 Mj 55
Bambaya ○ RG 316 Fp 40
Bamberg ○ USA 71 Dh 29
Bamberg ○ D 174 Gm 21
Bambesa ○ RDC 324 He 44
Bambesi ○ ETH 325 Hk 41
Bambesi ○ ZW 341 Hg 55
Bambey ○ SN 304 Fm 38
Bambili ○ RDC 324 Hf 44
Bambio ○ RCA 321 Ha 44
Bambisa ○ RDC 324 Hf 43
Bambli ○ LB 316 Gb 43
Bamboesberge ⛰ ZA 349 He 61

Badeggi - Bamboesberge 399

□Country ▣Capital city ⊙Administrative unit ○Place ⌓Island ⛰Mountain range △Mountain ⌒Cape ≈Ocean, Sea ~Lake, River ♆Undersea topography ▲Glacier ♀National park •••Reservation ★Point of major interest ⏢Landscape

Basso △ TCH 309 Hd 37
Basso ○ DY 320 Gh 40
Bass Strait ♆ AUS 379 Mj 65
Bāšt ○ IR 215 Jd 30
Bastak ○ IR 226 Jf 32
Baštanka ○ UA 175 Hj 22
Basti ○ IND 234 Kf 32
Bastia ○ F 185 Gl 24
Basti Maluk ○ PK 227 Jp 31
Bastogne ○ B 163 Gj 20
Bastrop ○ USA 81 Cp 30
Bastrop ○ USA 86 Dc 29
Basua ○ WAN 320 Gl 42
Basunda ○ SUD 313 Hk 39
Başyurt T. △ TR 195 Hh 26
Bat ○ OM 226 Jg 34
Bata ○ GQ 332 Gl 45
Bataan Peninsula ~ RP 267 Ll 38
Batabanó ○ C 100 Dg 34
Batabi ○ WAN 320 Gj 41
Bataf ○ RI 286 Mf 47
Batagaj ○ RUS 205 Wc 5
Batag Island ⌓ RP 267 Ln 39
Bataguaçu ○ BR 140 Eh 56
Batajsk ○ RUS 181 Hm 22
Batakan ○ RI 279 Lh 48
Batak Palace ★ RI 270 Kp 44
Batak Villages ★ RI 270 Kp 44
Batala ○ IND 230 Kb 30
Batalha ○ BR 124 En 48
Batalha ○ BR 124 Fb 50
Batama ○ RDC 324 Hf 45
Batamaj ○ RUS 22 Ra 3
Batamaj ○ RUS 205 Wb 6
Batang ○ RI 278 Le 49
Batangafo ○ RCA 321 Hb 42
Batangas ○ RP 267 Ll 39
Batan Island ⌓ RP 267 Ln 39
Batan Islands ⌓ RP 259 Ll 35
Batas Island ⌓ RP 267 Lk 40
Batatais ○ BR 141 El 56
Batavia ○ USA 60 Dj 24
Batavia Downs ○ AUS 365 Mh 52
Batcham ○ CAM 320 Gl 43
Batchawana ○ CDN 57 Df 22
Batchawana Bay ○ CDN 57 Df 22
Batchelor ○ AUS 364 Mb 52
Batchenga ○ CAM 320 Gm 43
Bătdâmbâng ○ K 263 Lb 39
Bateckij ○ RUS 171 Hh 16
Batéké Plateau ⛰ RCB 332 Gp 47
Batemans Bay ○ AUS 379 Mm 63
Batemba ○ RDC 333 Hd 48
Baté Nafadji ○ RG 316 Gb 40
Bates ○ AUS 369 Mc 61
Batesburg ○ USA 71 Dh 29
Batesville ○ USA 70 Dc 28
Bath ○ USA 60 Dp 24
Bath ○ GB 163 Ge 20
Batha ~ TCH 321 Hb 39
Batha de Laïri ~ TCH 321 Ha 40
Batheaston ○ AUS 375 Ml 57
Bathhurst Aboriginal Reserve ••• AUS 364 Mb 51
Bathinda ○ IND 230 Kb 30
Bathsheba ○ BDS 104 Ee 39
Bá Thu'ó'c ○ VN 255 Lc 35
Bathurst ○ CDN 61 Eb 22
Bathurst ○ ZA 358 Hf 62
Bathurst ○ AUS 379 Ml 62
Bathurst Inlet ○ CDN 6 Db 3
Bathurst Inlet ≈ CDN 42 Eb 5
Bathurst Inlet ○ CDN 47 Cg 11
Bathurst Inlet ≈ CDN 47 Cg 11
Bathurst Island ⌓ CDN 42 Fa 3
Bathurst Island ⌓ AUS 364 Ma 51
Batī ○ ETH 313 Hn 40
Batia ○ DY 317 Gg 40
Batibati ○ RI 279 Lh 47
Batibo ○ CAM 320 Gl 43
Batié ○ BF 317 Ge 41
Batiki ⌓ FJI 387 Nm 54
Bāṭina ⏢ OM 226 Jg 33
Bāṭina ⏢ OM 226 Jg 34
Batiscan ○ CDN 60 Dm 22
Bat Island ⌓ PNG 287 Mk 47
Batkanu ○ WAL 316 Fp 41
Batken ○ KS 223 Jp 25
Batkes ○ RI 283 Mb 49
Bat Khela ○ PK 230 Ka 28
Batlai ○ RUS 202 Jb 24
Bātlāq-e Gāvḫūni ~ IR 222 Je 29
Batlow ○ AUS 379 Ml 63
Batman ○ TR 202 Hn 27
Batna ○ DZ 296 Gk 28
Baṭn al-Ġūl ○ JOR 214 Hk 31
Ba To' ○ VN 263 Le 38
Bato ○ RP 267 Lm 39
Bato Bato ○ RP 275 Lk 43
Batoche N.H.S. ★ CDN 51 Cj 19
Batoka ○ Z 341 Hf 54
Baton Rouge ○ USA 86 Dc 30
Batopilas ○ MEX 80 Cj 32
Batora Ite. Island ⌓ SOL 290 Na 49
Batoua ○ CAM 320 Gn 43
Batouala ○ G 332 Gn 45
Batouri ○ CAM 321 Gp 43
Batovil ~ BR 132 Eh 52
Ba Tri ○ VN 263 Ld 41
Batsari ○ WAN 320 Gk 39
Båtsfjord ○ N 159 Hg 10
Batticaloa ○ CL 239 Ke 42
Batti Malv Island ⌓ IND 262 Kl 41
Battle ~ CDN 51 Cg 19
Battle Camp ○ AUS 365 Mj 53
Battle Creek ~ CDN 51 Ch 21
Battle Creek ○ USA 57 Df 24
Battlefields ○ ZW 341 Hg 55
Battleford ○ CDN 51 Ch 19
Battle Lake ○ USA 56 Da 22
Battle Mountain ○ USA 64 Cd 25
Batuampar ○ RI 278 Lb 46
Batuamparam ○ RI 279 Lh 47
Batu Anpar ○ RI 271 Lc 45
Batuasa ○ RI 283 Ma 47
Batubatu ○ RI 279 Lk 48
Batugade ○ TP 282 Ln 50
Batu Gajah ○ MAL 270 La 43
Batui ○ RI 282 Lm 46
Batuijak ○ RI 270 Kn 43
Batu Islands ⌓ RI 270 Kp 45
Batukangkung ○ RI 270 La 46
Batulicin ○ RI 279 Lh 47
Batumata Point ⌒ PNG 287 Ml 51
Bat'umi ○ GE 202 Hn 25
Batu Pahat ○ MAL 271 Lb 45
Batupanjang ○ RI 270 La 45
Baturaja ○ RI 278 Lb 48
Batu Rakit ○ MAL 271 Lb 43
Baturetno ○ RI 278 Lf 49
Baturi ○ MEX 80 Ch 33
Baturube ○ RI 282 Ll 46
Batusangkar ○ RI 270 La 46
Batu Satu ○ MAL 274 Lg 43
Batyrevo ○ RUS 181 Jb 18
Baú ~ BR 120 Eg 49
Bau ○ MAL 271 Lf 45
Bauana ~ BR 117 Eb 47
Baubau ○ RI 282 Lm 48
Bauchi ○ WAN 320 Gl 40
Baudette ○ USA 56 Da 21
Baudisson Island ⌓ PNG 287 Mm 47
Baudó ~ CO 106 Dk 43
Bauer Basin ♆ 14 Db 11
Bauhinia Downs ○ AUS 364 Md 54
Bauhinia Downs ○ AUS 375 Ml 58
Baukau ○ TP 282 Lp 50
Baungan ○ RI 270 Kp 44
Baures ○ BOL 129 Ec 52
Bauru ○ BR 141 Ek 57
Bauru ○ RDC 333 Hc 45
Bauska ○ LV 171 He 17
Bauta ○ RDC 333 Hc 45
Bautzen ○ D 174 Gp 20
Bavarian Forest ⛰ D 174 Gn 21
Bavon ○ USA 74 Dk 27
Bawa ○ RP 267 Lm 36
Bawal ○ IND 234 Kc 32
Baw Baw ♀ AUS 379 Mk 64
Bawdie ○ GH 317 Ge 43
Bawe ○ RI 283 Mb 46
Bawe ○ RI 283 Md 47
Bawku ○ GH 317 Gf 40
Bawlake ○ MYA 254 Kn 36
Bawo Ofuloa ○ RI 270 Kp 46
Baxkorgan ○ VRC 231 Kk 26
Baxley ○ USA 87 Dg 30
Baxoi ○ VRC 242 Kn 30
Bay ○ RMM 317 Ge 39
Baya-Bwanga ○ RDC 333 Hc 48
Bayadi ○ G 332 Gm 47
Bayaguana ○ DOM 101 Dp 36
Bayala ○ RCB 332 Gn 47
Bayamo ○ C 101 Dk 35
Bayamón ○ USA 104 Ea 36
Bayan ○ VRC 242 Lc 25
Bayan ○ RI 279 Lj 50
Bayanga ○ RCA 321 Ha 44
Bayanga-Didi ○ RCA 321 Gp 43
Bayan Gol ○ VRC 243 Ld 25
Bayan Har Shan ⛰ VRC 242 Km 28
Bayan Har Shan △ VRC 242 Kn 28
Bayan Har Shankou △ VRC 242 Kn 28
Bayan Olji ○ VRC 242 Lc 25
Bayan Shan △ VRC 242 Kn 27
Bayard ○ USA 65 Ch 29
Bayard ○ USA 65 Cl 25
Bayawan ○ RP 267 Lm 41
Bayāżīye ○ IR 222 Jf 29
Baybay ○ RP 267 Ln 40
Bayburt ○ TR 202 Hn 25
Bay City ○ USA 57 Dg 24
Bay City ○ USA 81 Cp 31
Baydaratskaya Bay ≈ RUS 154 Sa 5
Baydhabo ○ SP 329 Hp 44
Baye de l'Oyapock ≈ F 113 Ej 43
Bayern ⊙ D 174 Gm 21
Bayeux ○ BR 124 Fc 49
Bayeux ○ F 163 Gf 21
Bayfield ○ USA 56 Dc 22
Bayındır ○ TR 195 Hf 26
Bayizhan ○ VRC 254 Km 31
Baykan ○ TR 202 Hn 26
Baykonur ○ KZ 155 Sb 9
Bay L'Argent ○ CDN 61 Eg 22
Bay Mills Res. ••• USA 57 Df 22
Bay Minette ○ USA 86 De 30
Baynes Mountains ⛰ NAM 340 Gp 55
Baynūna' h ⏢ UAE 215 Je 34
Bay of Bengal ≈ 238 Kf 37
Bay of Biscay ≈ 184 Gd 23
Bay of Fundy ~ CDN 61 Ea 23
Bay of Harbours ~ GB 147 Ee 72
Bay of Islands ~ CDN 61 Ee 21
Bay of Islands ~ NZ 383 Nk 63
Bay of Plenty ~ NZ 383 Nl 64
Bay of Whales ≈ 38 Ab 17
Bayombong ○ RP 267 Ll 37
Bayonet Point ○ USA 86 Dg 31
Bayonne ○ F 184 Gf 24
Bayota ○ CI 317 Gd 42
Bayou Cane ○ USA 86 Dc 31
Bayou Macon ~ USA 86 Dc 30
Bayovar ○ PE 116 Dh 48
Baypazan ○ TR 195 Hh 25
Bay Port ○ USA 57 Dg 24
Bayramiç ○ TR 195 Hf 26
Bayreuth ○ D 174 Gm 21
Bayrūt Beirut ▣ RL 208 Hk 29
Bay Shore ○ USA 74 Dm 25
Bay Springs ○ USA 86 Dd 30
Bay St. Louis ○ USA 86 Dd 30
Baytown ○ USA 81 Da 31
Bayu ○ RI 270 Kn 43
Bayugan ○ RP 267 Ln 41
Bayum Gol He ~ VRC 242 Kn 27
Bayunglincir ○ RI 278 Lb 47
Bay View ○ NZ 383 Nl 65
Bayzo ○ RN 308 Gj 39
Baza ○ E 184 Ge 27
Bāzār-e Tāle ○ AFG 223 Jn 28
Bazarnye Mataki ○ RUS 181 Jd 18
Bazaruto Archipelago ⌓ MOC 352 Hk 56
Bazavluk ~ UA 175 Hk 22
Bazhong ○ VRC 243 Ld 30
Bazhou ○ VRC 246 Lj 26
Bazmān ○ IR 226 Jk 32
Bāzof ~ IR 222 Jd 29
Bazou ○ CAM 320 Gm 43
Bazré ○ CI 317 Gd 42
Bazuru ○ RDC 324 Hf 44
Beach ○ USA 51 Cl 22
Beachport ○ AUS 378 Mg 64
Beacon ○ AUS 368 Lj 61
Beacon Bay ○ ZA 358 Hf 62
Beacons ♀ GB 163 Ge 20
Beaconsfield ○ AUS 378 Mk 66
Beadmore Reservoir ~ AUS 375 Ml 59
Beadon Point ⌒ AUS 360 Lh 56
Beagle Bay ○ AUS 360 Lm 54
Beagle Bay ~ AUS 360 Lm 54
Beagle Bay Aboriginal Reserve ••• AUS 360 Lm 54
Beagle Gulf ~ AUS 364 Ma 52
Beagle Island ⌓ AUS 368 Lh 60
Bealanana ○ RM 345 Jc 53
Beals Creek ~ USA 70 Cm 29
Beampingaratra ⛰ RM 353 Jb 58
Bear ~ USA 51 Cg 24
Beardmore ○ CDN 57 De 21
Beardstown ○ USA 71 Dc 25
Beardy ~ AUS 375 Mm 60
Bear Lake ~ USA 65 Cg 25
Bear Peninsula ⌓ 38 Db 17
Beas ~ IND 230 Kb 30
Beas d.S. ○ E 184 Ge 26
Beata Island ⌓ DOM 101 Dn 36
Beata Ridge ♆ 101 Dn 37
Beatrice ○ USA 70 Cp 25
Beatrice ○ ZW 341 Hh 55
Beatton River ○ CDN 47 Ca 17
Beatty ○ USA 64 Cd 27
Beattyville ○ CDN 60 Dk 21
Beau Bassin ○ MS 353 Jg 56
Beauchéne Island ⌓ GB 147 Ee 72
Beau Desert ○ AUS 374 Mg 56
Beaudesert ○ AUS 375 Mn 59
Beaufort ○ USA 71 Dh 29
Beaufort ○ MAL 274 Lh 43
Beaufort ○ AUS 378 Mh 64
Beaufort Sea ≈ 42 Cb 4
Beaufort-West ○ ZA 358 Hd 62
Beaumont ○ USA 81 Da 30
Beaumont ○ USA 86 Dd 30
Beaune ○ F 163 Gj 22
Beauséjour ○ CDN 56 Cp 20
Beauty ○ ZA 349 Hf 57
Beauvais ○ F 163 Gg 21
Beauval ○ CDN 42 Ec 7
Beaver ○ USA 46 Bc 11
Beaver ~ USA 46 Bc 13
Beaver ♀ USA 64 Cf 26
Beaver ○ USA 70 Cm 27
Beaver Creek ○ CDN 47 Be 13
Beaver Creek ~ USA 51 Cj 21
Beavercreek ○ USA 71 Dg 26
Beaver Dam ○ USA 57 Dd 24
Beaver Falls ○ USA 71 Dh 25
Beaverhead ~ USA 51 Cf 23
Beaverhead Mountains ⛰ USA 51 Cf 23
Beaver Island ⌓ USA 57 Df 23
Beaver Island ⌓ GB 147 Ed 71
Beavermouth ○ CDN 50 Cc 20
Beaver River ~ USA 51 Cj 21
Beaverton ○ CDN 60 Dj 23
Beāwar ○ IND 234 Kb 32
Beazley ○ RA 137 Ea 62
Bebarama ○ CO 106 Dk 42
Bébédjia ○ TCH 321 Ha 41
Bebedouro ○ BR 141 Ek 56
Bebeka ○ ETH 325 Hk 42
Béboto ○ TCH 321 Ha 41
Béboura ○ RCA 321 Ha 42
Beca ⌓ ER 313 Hn 38
Becal ○ MEX 93 Dd 35
Becanchén ○ MEX 93 Dd 36
Becerrea ○ E 184 Gc 24
Bèchar ○ DZ 293 Ge 30
Becharof Lake ~ USA 46 Al 17
Bechem ○ GH 317 Ge 42
Bechewin Bay ~ USA 46 Ag 17
Becilla d.V. ○ E 184 Gd 24
Beckley ○ USA 71 Dh 27
Bedarra Island ⌓ AUS 365 Mk 55
Bédaya ○ TCH 321 Ha 41
Bedelē ○ ETH 325 Hl 41
Bedēsa ○ ETH 325 Hn 41
Bedford ○ CDN 60 Dm 23
Bedford ○ USA 70 Da 25
Bedford ○ USA 71 De 26
Bedford ○ USA 74 Dj 26
Bedford ○ GB 163 Gf 19
Bedford ○ ZA 358 Hf 62
Bedford Downs ○ AUS 361 Lp 54
Bedi Dat ○ PK 227 Jl 32
Bediondo ○ TCH 321 Ha 41
Bednodem'janovsk ○ RUS 181 Hp 19
Bédo ○ TCH 309 Hb 36
Bédouaram ○ RN 309 Gn 38
Bedourie ○ AUS 374 Mf 58
Beebe ○ USA 70 Dc 28
Beecchal ~ AUS 375 Mj 59
Beechworth ○ AUS 379 Mk 64
Beechy ○ CDN 51 Cj 20
Beeler ○ USA 70 Cm 26
Beenleigh ○ AUS 375 Mn 59
Beersheba ○ IL 214 Hk 30
Beerwah ○ AUS 375 Mn 59
Beestekraal ○ ZA 349 Hf 58
Beetaloo ○ AUS 364 Mc 54
Beeville ○ USA 81 Cp 31
Befale ○ RDC 333 Hc 45
Befandefa ○ RM 353 Hp 57
Befandriana ○ RM 353 Hp 57
Befandriana Ava. ○ RM 345 Jc 53
Befasy ○ RM 353 Ja 56
Beffa ~ DY 320 Gh 41
Befori ○ RDC 333 Hd 45
Befotaka ○ RM 345 Jb 53
Befotaka ○ RM 353 Jb 57
Bega ○ AUS 379 Ml 64
Bega ⌓ FJI 387 Nl 55
Begesin ○ PNG 287 Mj 48
Beggs ○ USA 70 Cp 28
Begna ~ N 158 Gl 15
Begogo ○ RM 353 Jb 57
Bégon ○ RCA 321 Gp 42
Begoro ○ GH 317 Gf 42
Begunicy ○ RUS 171 Hg 16
Begusari ○ IND 235 Kh 33
Beh ~ RI 279 Lj 50
Behābād ○ IR 226 Jj 30
Behara ○ RM 353 Jb 58
Behbahān ○ IR 215 Jd 30
Beheloka ○ RM 353 Hp 57
Béhili ○ RCA 321 Hb 42
Behšahr ○ IR 222 Je 27
Bei'an ○ VRC 205 Wb 9
Béibouo ○ CI 305 Gc 42
Beicheng ○ VRC 204 Wa 9
Beichuan ○ VRC 242 Lc 30
Beidaihe Haibin ★ VRC 246 Lk 26
Beidou ○ VRC 258 Lg 35
Beigi ○ ETH 325 Hk 41
Beihai ○ VRC 255 Le 35
Bei Hulsan Hu ~ VRC 242 Km 27
Bei Jiang ~ VRC 258 Lg 33
Beijing ▣ VRC 243 Lh 26
Beijing Gang ~ VRC 258 Lg 35
Beijing Shi ⊙ VRC 246 Lj 25
Beiliu ○ VRC 255 Lf 34
Béinamar ○ TCH 321 Gp 41
Beipan Jiang ~ VRC 255 Lc 33
Beira ○ MOC 344 Hk 55
Beira Alta ⏢ P 184 Gc 25
Beira Alta ○ ANG 340 Gp 50
Beirut Bayrūt ▣ RL 208 Hk 29
Beiseker ○ CDN 50 Cf 20
Beitan ○ VRC 255 Le 35
Beitbridge ○ ZW 352 Hh 57
Beiuş ○ RO 174 Hd 22
Beizhangdian ○ VRC 243 Lg 27
Beizhen ○ VRC 246 Ll 25
Beja ○ P 184 Gc 27
Beja ○ TN 296 Gl 27
Bejaja ○ DZ 296 Gj 27
Béjar ○ E 184 Gd 25
Bejarn ○ N 158 Gn 12
Beji ~ PK 227 Jn 31
Beji ○ WAN 320 Gk 41
Bejneu ○ KZ 155 Rc 9
Bejsug ~ RUS 202 Hm 23
Bejsugskij liman ~ RUS 181 Hm 22
Bejucal ○ C 100 Dg 34
Bek ~ CAM 321 Gp 44
Beka ○ CAM 321 Gn 41
Béka ○ CAM 321 Gn 42
Béka ○ CAM 321 Gp 42
Bekabad ○ UZB 223 Jn 25
Békamba ○ TCH 321 Ha 41
Bekasi ○ RI 278 Ld 49
Bekdash ○ TM 222 Je 25
Bek-Džar ○ KS 230 Ka 25
Beke ○ RDC 336 Hf 50
Bekenu ○ MAL 274 Lg 43
Békés ○ H 174 Hc 22
Békéscsaba ○ H 174 Hc 22
Bekily ○ RM 353 Ja 58
Bekipay ○ RM 345 Jb 54
Bekitro ○ RM 353 Ja 58
Bekkai ○ J 250 Mj 24
Bekmurat △ TM 222 Jf 25
Bekodoka ○ RM 345 Ja 54
Bek'ojī ○ ETH 325 Hm 42
Bekopaka ○ RM 345 Ja 55
Bekwai ○ GH 317 Gf 42
Bela ~ BR 132 Ee 52
Bela ○ PK 227 Jm 32
Bela ○ IND 234 Kd 32
Bela ○ IND 234 Kf 33
Bélabirim ○ RN 309 Gn 38
Bélabo ○ CAM 321 Gn 43
Bela da Trinidade ○ BR 132 Ee 53
Bela Estrela ○ BR 121 El 48
Belaga ○ MAL 274 Lg 44
Belagonsk ○ RUS 22 Ra 4
Bel Air ○ USA 74 Dk 26
Belaja ○ ETH 313 Hk 40
Belaja ~ RUS 202 Hn 23
Belaja ~ RUS 205 Ja 6
Belaja Berëzka ○ RUS 171 Hj 19
Belaja Glina ○ RUS 181 Hn 22
Belaja Kalitva ○ RUS 181 Hn 21
Belamoty ○ RM 353 Ja 57
Belang ○ RI 275 Ln 45
Belangan ○ RI 279 Lg 47
Bela Palanka ○ SCG 194 Hd 24
Belarus □ BY 171 Hf 19
Belas ○ ANG 340 Gn 50
Belavežskaja pušča ♀ BY 171 He 19
Bela Vista ○ BR 113 Ej 44
Bela Vista ○ BR 140 Ef 57
Bela Vista ○ ANG 332 Gn 49
Bela Vista ○ MOC 352 Hj 59
Belawan ○ RI 270 Kp 44
Belayan ~ RI 274 Lj 45
Bélbéji ○ RN 308 Gk 38
Belčerāg ○ AFG 223 Jl 28
Bełchatów ○ PL 174 Hb 20
Belcher Channel ~ CDN 7 Ea 2
Belcher Channel ≈ CDN 42 Fb 3
Belcher Islands ⌓ CDN 7 Eb 4
Belcher Islands ⌓ CDN 43 Gb 7
Belchite ○ E 184 Gf 25
Belda ○ IND 235 Kh 34
Belden ○ USA 64 Cb 25
Belebej ○ RUS 154 Rb 8
Belebelka ○ RUS 171 Hh 17
Beledweyne ○ SP 328 Ja 43
Beléko-Soba ○ RMM 305 Gc 39
Belel ○ WAN 321 Gn 41
Bélel ○ CAM 321 Gp 42
Belele ○ AUS 368 Lj 59
Belém ○ BR 117 Dp 47
Belém ○ BR 121 Ek 46
Belém ○ BR 124 Fc 49
Belem de São Francisco ○ BR 124 Fa 50
Belen ○ USA 65 Cj 28
Belen ~ PA 97 Dh 41
Belén ○ CO 107 Dm 42
Belén ○ RA 136 Ea 59
Belén ~ RA 136 Ea 59
Beléne ○ RCH 128 Dp 55
Belesc Cogani ○ SP 325 Hn 45
Beles Wenz ~ ETH 313 Hk 40
Beles Wenz ~ ETH 313 Hl 40
Belev ○ RUS 171 Hk 19
Bèlèya ○ RG 316 Ga 40
Beleya Terara ⛰ ETH 313 Hl 40
Belfair ○ USA 50 Ca 22
Belfast ○ USA 60 Dp 23
Belfast ○ GB 162 Gd 18
Belfast ○ ZA 349 Hg 58
Belfield ○ USA 51 Cl 22
Bēlfodiyo ○ ETH 313 Hk 40
Belfort ○ F 163 Gk 22
Belgaum ○ IND 238 Kb 38
Belgica Mountains ⛰ 38 La 17
Belgium □ B 163 Gh 20
Belgo ○ SUD 312 Hj 40
Belgorod ○ RUS 181 Hl 20
Belgrade ○ USA 51 Cg 23
Belgrade ○ USA 56 Da 23
Belgrade ▣ SCG 174 Hb 23
Belgrano ○ RA 136 Eb 58
Belhatti ○ IND 238 Kb 38
Belhaven ○ USA 74 Dk 28
Belhirane ○ DZ 296 Gk 30
Béli ~ BF 305 Gf 38
Beli ○ GNB 316 Fp 40
Beli ○ WAN 320 Gm 42
Bélice ~ I 185 Gn 27
Belidži ○ RUS 202 Jc 25
Belimbing ○ RI 278 Lb 47
Bélinga ○ G 332 Gn 45
Belinskij ○ RUS 181 Hp 19
Belinyu ○ RI 278 Lc 46
Belize □ BH 93 Dd 37
Belize ~ BH 93 Dd 37
Belize ○ ANG 332 Gn 48
Belize Barrier-Reef Reservation ★ BH 93 Dd 37
Belize City ○ BH 93 Dd 37
Beljanica △ SCG 194 Hd 23
Belkar ○ IND 238 Ka 37
Bell ~ CDN 60 Dk 21
Bell ○ ZA 358 Hf 62
Bella ○ CAM 320 Gm 44
Bella Bella ○ CDN 50 Bm 19
Bellac ○ F 163 Gg 22
Bella Coola ○ CDN 50 Bn 19
Bella Flor ○ BOL 129 Ea 51
Bellaire ○ USA 71 Dh 26
Bellary ○ IND 238 Kc 38
Bellata ○ AUS 375 Ml 60
Bellavista ○ PE 116 Dj 48
Bellavista ○ PE 116 Dk 49
Bella Vista ○ PY 140 Eg 59
Bella Vista ○ RA 146 Ee 60
Bella Vista ○ RA 152 Dn 71
Bella Vista do Gurupi ○ BR 121 El 46
Bellburns ○ CDN 61 Ef 20
Belle Anse ○ RH 101 Dm 36
Bellefontaine ○ USA 71 Dg 25
Bellefonte ○ USA 74 Dk 25
Belle Fourche ○ USA 51 Cl 23
Belle Fourche ~ USA 51 Cl 23
Belle Fourche Reservoir ~ USA 51 Cl 23
Belle Fourche River ~ USA 51 Cl 23
Belle Glade ○ USA 87 Dh 32
Belle-Île ⌓ F 163 Ge 22
Belle Isle ⌓ CDN 43 Ja 8
Belle Isle ⌓ CDN 61 Eg 20
Belle Mare ○ MS 353 Jg 56
Bellême ○ F 163 Gg 21
Bellemullet ○ IRL 162 Ga 18
Bellenden Ker ○ AUS 365 Mj 54
Bellenden Ker ♀ AUS 365 Mj 54
Belleterre ○ CDN 60 Dj 22
Belleville ○ CDN 60 Dk 23
Belleville ○ USA 70 Cp 26
Bellevue ○ USA 50 Ca 22
Bellevue ○ USA 70 Da 25
Bellevue ○ USA 71 Dc 24
Bellevue ○ AUS 365 Mh 54
Bellfield ○ AUS 365 Mh 55
Bellingen ○ AUS 379 Mn 61
Bellingham ○ USA 50 Ca 21
Bellinghausen Sea ≈ 38 Eb 16
Bellinzona ○ CH 174 Gl 22
Bell Island ⌓ CDN 61 Eg 20
Bellmead ○ USA 81 Cp 30
Bello ○ CO 106 Dl 42
Bellocq ○ RA 137 Ed 63
Bellona Island ⌓ SOL 290 Nb 51
Bellows Falls ○ USA 60 Dm 24
Bellpat ○ PK 227 Jn 31
Bell Peninsula ⌓ CDN 43 Gb 6
Bellsund ⌓ N 158 Gn 7
Belluno ○ I 174 Gm 22
Bell Ville ○ RA 137 Ec 62
Bellville ○ ZA 358 Hb 62
Belly ~ CDN 51 Cf 21
Belmejo ~ RA 140 Ee 59
Belmira ○ CO 106 Dl 42
Belmond ○ USA 56 Da 24
Belmont ○ ZA 349 Hc 60
Belmont ○ AUS 379 Mm 62
Belmonte ○ BR 125 Fa 53
Belmopan ▣ BH 93 Dd 37
Belmore Creek ~ AUS 365 Mg 55
Belo ○ RM 353 Hp 56
Belobaka ○ RM 345 Ja 55
Belo Campo ○ BR 125 Ep 53
Belogorsk ○ RUS 205 Wb 8
Beloha ○ RM 353 Ja 58
Belo Horizonte ○ BR 141 En 56
Beloit ○ USA 57 Dd 24
Beloit ○ USA 70 Cn 26
Belo Jardim ○ BR 124 Fb 50
Belojarskij ○ RUS 154 Sb 6
Béloko ○ RCA 321 Gp 43
Belo Monte ○ BR 124 Fb 50
Belo Monte do Pontal ○ BR 121 Ej 47
Belomorsk ○ RUS 159 Hk 13
Belomorsko-Baltijskij ~ RUS 159 Hk 13
Belomorsko-Kulojskoje plato ⛰ RUS 159 Hn 13
Belonge ○ RDC 333 Hc 47
Belo Oriente ○ BR 141 En 55
Beloreĉensk ○ RUS 202 Hm 23
Belörem ○ TR 195 Hj 27
Belo Tsiribihina ○ RM 345 Ja 55
Belovo ○ RUS 204 Tc 8
Belowski-Island ⌓ RUS 22 Rb 2
Belozersk ○ RUS 154 Qb 7
Belozersk ○ RUS 159 Hl 15
Belozersko-Kirillovskie grjady ⏢ RUS 159 Hl 15
Belpre ○ USA 70 Cn 27
Bel'skaja vozv. ⛰ RUS 171 Hj 18
Belt ○ USA 51 Cg 22
Belt Bay ~ AUS 374 Me 60
Belterra ○ BR 120 Eg 47
Belton ○ USA 71 Dg 28
Belton ○ USA 81 Cp 30
Belton Lake ~ USA 81 Cp 30
Beluran ○ MAL 274 Lj 43
Beluru ○ MAL 274 Lh 44
Belušja Guba ○ RUS 19 Ma 2
Belvedere ○ I 185 Gp 26
Belvidere ○ USA 71 Dd 24
Belwali ○ LB 316 Gb 42
Belyando ~ AUS 375 Mk 57
Belyi ○ RUS 171 Hj 18
Belyj Jar ○ RUS 204 Tc 7
Belžec ○ PL 175 Hd 20
Belzoni ○ USA 86 Dc 29
Běma ○ RMM 304 Gb 38
Bemaraha ⏢ RM 345 Ja 55
Bemarivo ~ RM 345 Jc 53
Bemarivo ~ RM 345 Jc 54
Bembe ○ ANG 332 Gp 49
Bembeche ⏢ TCH 309 Hb 36
Bembèrèkè ○ DY 320 Gh 40
Bembezi ~ ZW 341 Hg 55
Bembo ○ ANG 340 Ha 51
Bemboka ○ AUS 379 Ml 64
Bemejo ~ RA 137 Dp 60
Bemetāra ○ IND 234 Ke 35
Bemidji ○ USA 56 Da 22
Bemu ○ RI 283 Ma 47
Bemu ○ RI 283 Mb 47
Ben ○ BF 317 Gd 39
Bena ○ USA 56 Da 22
Bena-Dibele ○ RDC 333 Hd 48
Benagerie ○ AUS 378 Mg 61
Benahmed ○ MA 293 Gc 29
Benain ~ RI 282 Ln 50
Bena-Kamba ○ RDC 333 He 47
Benalla ○ AUS 379 Mj 64
Benangin ○ RI 279 Lh 46
Ben Ash Monument ★ USA 51 Cl 23
Benato ○ RM 353 Ja 57
Bena-Tshadi ○ RDC 333 Hd 48
Benavarri ○ E 184 Gg 24
Benavente ○ E 184 Gd 24
Benavides ○ USA 81 Cn 32
Ben Badis ○ DZ 293 Gf 28
Benbonyathe Hill △ AUS 378 Mf 61
Ben Boyd ♀ AUS 379 Mm 64
Bencubbin ○ AUS 368 Lj 61
Bend ○ USA 50 Cb 23
Benda Range ⛰ AUS 378 Mf 62
Bendar Beheštī ○ IR 226 Jj 33
Bende ○ RDC 333 Hd 47
Bendela ○ RDC 333 Ha 47
Bendeleben Mountains ⛰ USA 46 Ag 13
Bendemeer ○ AUS 379 Mm 61
Bendere ○ RDC 333 Hb 44
Bendieuta Creek ~ AUS 378 Mf 61
Bendigo ○ AUS 379 Mj 64
Bend of the Boyne ★ IRL 163 Gc 19
Bendugu ○ WAL 316 Ga 41
Bene ○ MOC 344 Hj 53
Benedictine Monastery ★ AUS 368 Lh 61
Beneditinos ○ BR 124 En 48
Benedito Leite ○ BR 121 Em 49
Bénéna ○ RMM 317 Gd 39
Benenitra ○ RM 353 Ja 57
Benešov ○ CZ 174 Gp 21
Benevento ○ I 194 Gp 25
Benevides ○ BR 121 Ek 46
Benfica ○ BR 141 En 56
Benga ○ MW 344 Hk 52
Bengābād ○ IND 235 Kh 33
Bengala ○ CO 107 Dm 43
Bengāla ○ IND 262 Kl 41
Bengamisa ○ RDC 324 He 45
Bengbis ○ CAM 320 Gn 44
Bengbu ○ VRC 246 Lj 29
Benge ○ USA 50 Cc 22
Benge ○ RDC 324 He 44
Benghazi ○ LAR 300 Hb 29
Bengkalis ○ RI 270 Lb 45
Bengkulu ○ RI 270 La 47
Bengough ○ CDN 51 Ck 20
Bengtsfors ○ S 170 Gm 16
Benguela ○ ANG 340 Gn 52
Ben Guerdane ○ TN 297 Gm 29
Benguerir ○ MA 293 Gc 29
Beni ~ BOL 129 Ea 52
Beni ~ BOL 129 Eb 51
Beni ○ NEP 235 Kf 31
Beni ○ RDC 324 Hg 45
Beni-Abbès ○ DZ 293 Ge 30
Beni Boufran ○ MA 293 Gd 28
Benicarló ○ E 184 Gg 25
Benicássim ○ E 184 Gg 25
Benicito ~ BOL 129 Eb 51
Benidorm ○ E 184 Gg 26
Beni Hammad ★ DZ 296 Gj 28
Beni Haoua ○ DZ 293 Gg 27
Beni Hassan ○ TN 297 Gm 28
Beni Ikhlef ○ DZ 293 Gf 31
Beni Kheddache ○ TN 296 Gm 29
Beni-Mellal ○ MA 293 Gc 29
Benin □ DY 317 Gg 41
Benin ~ WAN 320 Gj 43
Benin City ○ WAN 320 Gj 42
Beni Ounif ○ DZ 293 Gf 29
Beni Saf ○ DZ 293 Gf 28
Benisheikh ○ WAN 321 Gn 40
Beni Slimane ○ DZ 296 Gh 27
Beni Smir △ MA 293 Gf 29
Beni Tajjite Beni-Val ○ MA 293 Ge 29
Benito ○ CDN 56 Cm 20
Benito Juárez ○ RA 146 Ee 64
Benjamin ○ USA 70 Cn 29
Benjamin Aceval ○ PY 140 Ef 58
Benjamin Constant ○ BR 117 Dn 48
Benjamin Hill ○ MEX 80 Cg 30
Benkayang ○ RI 271 Le 45
Benkelman ○ USA 70 Cm 26
Benkovac ○ HR 174 Gp 23
Ben Lawers △ GB 162 Gd 17
Ben Lomond ♀ AUS 378 Mk 66
Ben Macdui △ GB 162 Ge 17
Ben Mehidi ○ DZ 296 Gk 27
Ben More △ GB 162 Gd 17
Bennettsville ○ USA 74 Dj 28
Ben Nevis △ GB 162 Gd 17
Bennichchâb ○ RIM 304 Fn 36
Bennington ○ USA 60 Dm 24
Benoni ○ ZA 349 Hg 59
Benoud ○ DZ 293 Gg 29
Bénoué ~ CAM 321 Gn 41
Bénoué ~ CAM 321 Gn 42
Bénoy ○ TCH 321 Ha 41
Bê'n Quang ○ VN 263 Ld 37
Ben Rinnes △ GB 162 Ge 17
Bensékou ○ DY 320 Gh 40
Ben-Slimane ○ MA 293 Gc 29
Benson ○ USA 56 Da 23
Benson ○ USA 80 Cg 30
Ben S'Rour ○ DZ 296 Gj 28
Bent ○ IR 226 Jh 32
Benta Seretang ○ MAL 270 La 43
Benteng ○ RI 282 Ll 46
Benteng ○ RI 282 Ll 49
Benteng ○ RI 282 Ll 49
Bentiaba ○ ANG 340 Gn 53
Bentiaba ~ ANG 340 Gn 53
Bentick Island ⌓ MYA 262 Kn 40
Bentinck Island ⌓ AUS 365 Mf 54
Bentiu ○ SUD 324 Hg 41
Bentley ○ CDN 50 Ce 19

Basso - Bentley 401

□Country ▣Capital city ⊙Administrative unit ○Place ⛵Island ⛰Mountain range △Mountain ⌒Cape ≈Ocean, Sea ~Lake, River ▿Undersea topography ⩓Glacier ♀National park •••Reservation ★Point of major interest ⏜Landscape

Bento Gomes ~ BR 132 Ef 54
Bento Gonçalves ○ BR 146 Ej 60
Benton ○ USA 64 Cc 27
Benton ○ USA 70 Db 28
Benton ○ USA 71 Dd 27
Benton ○ USA 71 De 29
Bentong ○ MAL 270 La 44
Benton Harbor ○ USA 71 De 24
Bentonville ○ USA 70 Da 27
Bentota ○ CL 239 Kd 42
Bến Tre ○ VN 263 Ld 40
Bent's Old Fort N.H.S. ★ USA 65 Cl 26
Bentuka ○ MAL 274 Lh 43
Benty ○ RG 316 Fp 41
Benua ○ RI 282 Lm 48
Benualawas ○ RI 279 Lh 47
Benue ~ WAN 320 Gk 41
Benue ~ WAN 320 Gm 41
Benue ~ WAN 320 Gn 41
Benut ○ MAL 271 Lb 45
Benwa ○ Z 341 He 51
Benxi ○ VRC 246 Lm 25
Benye ○ RDC 333 Ha 46
Benza ○ ANG 332 Gn 49
Benzdorp ○ SME 113 Eg 44
Ben Zireg ○ DZ 293 Gf 30
Beo ○ RI 275 Lp 43
Beoga ○ RI 286 Me 47
Beohari ○ IND 234 Ke 33
Beoumi ○ CI 317 Gd 42
Beposo ○ GH 317 Gf 43
Beppu ○ J 247 Mb 29
Bequia ⛵ WV 104 Ed 39
Bequimão ○ BR 121 Em 47
Ber ○ RMM 305 Ge 37
Berabevú ○ RA 137 Ec 62
Berahlē ○ ETH 313 Hn 39
Beraketa ○ RM 353 Ja 58
Beramanja ○ RM 345 Jc 52
Bérandjokou ○ RCB 321 Ha 44
Berāni ○ PK 227 Jn 33
Berasia ○ IND 234 Kc 34
Beraspapan ○ RI 279 Lh 46
Berat ○ AL 194 Hb 25
Berau ~ RI 274 Lj 44
Beravina ○ RM 345 Ja 55
Berawan ○ MAL 274 Lh 43
Berbera ○ SP 328 Ja 40
Berbérati ○ RCA 321 Gp 43
Berbice ~ GUY 113 Ee 43
Berchtesgaden ○ D 174 Gn 22
Berdjans'k ○ UA 181 Hl 22
Berdyčiv ○ UA 175 Hg 21
Béré ○ TCH 321 Ha 41
Berea ○ USA 71 Df 27
Béréba ○ BF 317 Ge 40
Berebere ○ RI 275 Ma 44
Bereeda ○ SP 328 Jd 40
bereg Haritona Lapteva ⌒ RUS 204 Tc 4
bereg Prončiščeva ⌒ RUS 204 Va 3
Berehove ○ UA 174 Hd 21
Bereina ○ PNG 287 Mk 50
Bereko ○ EAT 337 Hk 48
Berekua ○ WD 104 Ed 38
Berekum ○ GH 317 Ge 42
Berembang ○ RI 270 La 44
Berenice ○ ET 301 Hk 34
Berens Island ⛵ CDN 56 Cn 19
Berens River ○ CDN 6 Ea 4
Berens River ○ CDN 56 Cn 19
Berens River ~ CDN 56 Db 20
Beresford ○ USA 56 Cp 24
Beresford ○ CDN 61 Ea 22
Berettyóújfalu ○ H 174 Hc 22
Berezhany ○ UA 175 He 21
Berezivka ○ UA 175 Hh 22
Berezna ○ UA 175 Hh 20
Bereznehuvate ○ UA 175 Hj 22
Bereznik ○ RUS 19 Ma 3
Bereznik ○ RUS 154 Qc 6
Bereznik ○ RUS 159 Hp 14
Berezniki ○ RUS 19 Mb 4
Berezniki ○ RUS 154 Rc 7
Berezova ○ RUS 159 Hj 13
Berga ○ E 184 Gg 24
Bergama ○ TR 195 Hf 26
Bérgamo ○ I 185 Gl 23
Bergara Tolosa ○ E 184 Ge 24
Berge ○ N 170 Gl 16
Bergen ○ N 158 Gj 15
Bergen(R.) ○ D 170 Gn 18
Berg en Dal ○ SME 113 Eg 43
Bergerac ○ F 184 Gg 23
Bergsig ○ NAM 348 Gp 56
Bergville ○ ZA 349 Hg 60
Berhait ○ IND 235 Kh 33
Berilo ○ BR 125 En 54
Beringarra ○ AUS 368 Lj 59
Beringovskij ○ RUS 23 Tb 3
Bering Sea ≈ 23 Aa 4
Bering Strait ≈ 46 Ae 13
Bering Strait ▿ 205 Ab 6
Berisso ○ RA 146 Ef 63
Berizal ○ BR 125 Ep 53
Berja ○ E 184 Ge 27
Berkåk ○ N 158 Gm 14
Berkane ○ MA 293 Ge 28
Berkeley ○ USA 64 Ca 26
Berkeley ~ AUS 361 Lp 53
Berkeley Sound ≈ GB 147 Ef 71
Berkner Island ⛵ 38 Ga 17
Berkovica ○ BG 194 Hd 24
Berlengas ~ BR 124 En 49
Berlevåg ○ N 159 Hg 10
Berlin ○ USA 57 Dd 24
Berlin ○ USA 60 Dn 23
Berlin ○ USA 74 Dl 26
Berlin ▣ D 170 Gn 19
Bermagui ○ AUS 379 Mm 64
Bermejillo ○ MEX 81 Cl 33
Bermejo ~ RA 136 Ec 57
Bermejo ~ RA 136 Ed 58
Bermejo ~ RA 137 Ea 61
Bermuda Island ⛵ UK 11 Fb 6
Bermuda Rise ▿ 11 Fb 6
Bern ▣ CH 163 Gk 22
Bernabe Rivera ○ ROU 146 Ef 61
Bérnal ○ RCA 321 Hb 42
Bernalillo ○ USA 65 Cj 28
Bernam ~ MAL 270 La 44
Bernardo ○ USA 65 Cj 28
Bernardo de Irigoyen ○ RA 140 Eg 59
Bernay ○ F 163 Gg 21
Bernese Alps ⛰ CH 163 Gk 22
Berni ~ BOL 129 Ea 52
Bernice ○ USA 70 Db 29
Bernier Bay ≈ CDN 43 Ga 4
Bernier Island ⛵ AUS 368 Lg 58
Berninapass △ CH 174 Gl 22
Bero ~ ANG 340 Gn 53
Beroroha ○ RM 353 Ja 56
Beroun ○ CZ 174 Gn 21
Berra do Bugres ○ BR 132 Ef 53
Berrahal ○ DZ 296 Gk 27
Berrechid ○ MA 293 Gc 29
Berri ○ AUS 378 Mg 63
Berriane ○ DZ 296 Gh 29
Berridale ○ AUS 379 Ml 64
Berrigan ○ AUS 379 Mj 63
Berriozar ○ E 184 Gf 24
Berro ○ BR 124 Fa 49
Berrugas ○ CO 106 Dl 41
Berry Islands ⛵ BS 87 Dj 33
Berryville ○ USA 70 Db 27
Beršad' ○ UA 175 Hg 21
Berseba ○ NAM 348 Ha 59
Berthierville ○ CDN 60 Dm 22
Berthold ○ USA 51 Cl 21
Bertiehaugh ○ AUS 365 Mh 52
Bertolínia ○ BR 121 Em 49
Bertoua ○ CAM 321 Gn 43
Bertrand ○ CDN 61 Eb 22
Bertwell ○ CDN 51 Cl 19
Berunij ○ UZB 223 Jj 25
Beruri ○ BR 120 Ed 47
Beruwala ○ CL 239 Kd 42
Berwick ○ CDN 61 Eb 23
Berwick-upon-Tweed ○ GB 162 Gf 18
Bery ⌒ F 163 Gg 22
Beryl Junction ○ USA 64 Cf 27
Beryslav ○ UA 175 Hj 22
Besal ○ PK 230 Ka 28
Besalampy ○ RM 345 Ja 54
Besançon ○ F 163 Gk 22
Besangi ○ RDC 333 Hc 46
Besarabaien ⏜ MD 175 Hf 21
Besham ○ PK 230 Ka 28
Beshlo ~ ETH 313 Hm 40
Besikama ○ RI 282 Ln 50
Besīma ○ PK 227 Jl 32
Beskids ⛰ SK 174 Hb 21
Beslan ○ RUS 202 Ja 24
Besne ○ IR 226 Jf 31
Besni ○ TR 195 Hl 27
Besoke ○ RDC 333 Hd 46
Bèssao ○ TCH 321 Ha 42
Bessemer ○ USA 71 De 29
Bestjah ○ RUS 205 Wb 6
Beswick ○ AUS 364 Mc 53
Beswick Aboriginal Land ••• AUS 364 Mc 53
Betafo ○ RM 345 Jb 55
Betalevana ○ RM 345 Jc 54
Betanantanana ○ RM 345 Ja 55
Betang ○ VRC 254 Kp 31
Betânia ○ BR 124 Fa 50
Betania ○ BR 129 Ed 53
Betanty Faux Cap ○ RM 353 Ja 58
Betanzos ○ BOL 129 Eb 55
Betanzos ○ E 184 Gb 24
Betarara ○ VU 386 Ng 53
Bétaré-Oya ○ CAM 321 Gp 43
Bete Hor ○ ETH 313 Hm 40
Betein ○ WAN 320 Gl 43
Bétérou ○ DY 317 Gh 41
Bethal ○ ZA 349 Hg 59
Bethanie ○ NAM 348 Ha 59
Bethany ○ USA 70 Da 25
Bethany ○ USA 70 Da 26
Bethel ○ USA 23 Ab 3
Bethel ○ USA 46 Aj 15
Bethel ○ USA 60 Dn 23
Bethel ○ USA 70 Da 28
Bethel ○ USA 74 Dk 28
Bethel Park ○ USA 71 Dh 25
Bethesda ○ USA 74 Dk 26
Bethlehem ○ USA 74 Dl 25
Bethlehem ○ IL 214 Hk 30
Bethlehem ○ ZA 349 Hg 60
Bethulie ○ ZA 349 He 61
Betim ○ BR 133 Em 55
Betioky ○ RM 353 Ja 57
Betong ○ THA 270 La 43
Betong ○ MAL 271 Lf 45
Betongwe ○ RDC 324 Hg 44
Betoota ○ AUS 374 Mg 58
Betou ○ BF 317 Gg 39
Bétou ○ RCB 333 Hb 44
Betroka ○ RM 353 Jb 57
Betsaa ○ RB 341 Hd 55
Bet She'an ○ JOR 208 Hk 29
Betsiaka ○ RM 345 Jc 52
Betsiamites ~ CDN 60 Dn 21
Betsiamites Indian Reservation ••• CDN 60 Dp 21
Betsiboka ~ RM 345 Jb 54
Betsy Bay ○ BS 87 Dm 34
Bettendorf ○ USA 71 Dc 25
Bettiah ○ IND 235 Kg 32
Bettié ○ CI 317 Ge 42
Bettioua ○ DZ 293 Gf 28
Bettles ○ USA 46 An 11
Bettlesdam ○ ZA 349 Hg 59
Betty-Plage ○ RM 345 Jc 54
Betūl ○ IND 234 Kc 35
Betulia ○ CO 107 Dm 42
Betung ○ RI 278 Lc 47
Betwa ~ IND 234 Kd 33
Bêu ○ ANG 332 Gp 49
Beulah ○ USA 51 Cl 22
Beulah ○ AUS 378 Mh 63
Beurkia ○ TCH 309 Ha 38
Beverley ○ CDN 51 Cj 20
Beverley ○ GB 163 Gf 19
Beverley ○ AUS 368 Lj 61
Beverley Springs ○ AUS 361 Ln 54
Beverly ○ CDN 51 Cj 20
Beverly Hills ○ USA 87 Dg 31
Bevoalavo ○ RM 353 Ja 58
Bevoay ○ RM 353 Hp 56
Bewani ○ PNG 286 Mg 47
Bewani ~ RI 286 Mg 47
Bewan Mountains ⛰ PNG 286 Mg 47
Bey Dağ △ TR 195 Hk 26
Bey Dağları △ TR 195 Hh 27
Beyhanlı ○ TR 195 Hl 27
Beylāgan ○ AZ 202 Jb 26
Beylul ○ ER 313 Hp 39
Beyra ○ SP 328 Jb 42
Beyşehir ○ TR 195 Hh 27
Beyşehir Gölü ~ TR 195 Hh 27
Beytüşşebap ○ TR 202 Hp 27
Bezaha ○ RM 353 Ja 57
Bežanicy ○ RUS 171 Hg 17
Bežeck ○ RUS 171 Hl 17
Bežeckij Verh. ⛰ RUS 171 Hl 17
Bezenčuk ○ RUS 181 Jc 19
Bezerra ou Montes Claros ~ BR 133 El 52
Béziers ○ F 185 Gh 24
Bezmein ○ TM 222 Jh 26
Bhābhar ○ IND 227 Jp 33
Bhadgaon ○ IND 234 Kb 35
Bhador ~ IND 227 Jp 35
Bhādrachalam ○ IND 238 Ke 37
Bhadrakh ○ IND 235 Kh 35
Bhadrapur ○ NEP 235 Kh 32
Bhadra Reservoir ~ IND 238 Kb 39
Bhadrāvati ○ IND 238 Kb 39
Bhadwan ○ IND 238 Ka 37
Bhāgalpur ○ IND 235 Kh 33
Bhagirafi ~ IND 230 Kd 30
Bhāgvati ○ IND 238 Kb 38
Bhagwanpur ○ NEP 234 Kf 32
Bhaimsrorgarh ○ IND 234 Kb 33
Bhairab Bazar ○ BD 235 Kk 33
Bhairahawa ○ NEP 235 Kf 32
Bhairi Hol ⛰ PK 227 Jk 33
Bhaisa ○ IND 238 Kc 36
Bhakkar ○ PK 227 Jp 30
Bhaktapur ○ NEP 235 Kg 32
Bhālki ○ IND 238 Kc 36
Bhaluka ○ BD 235 Kk 33
Bhalukpong ○ IND 235 Kl 32
Bhalwāl ○ PK 230 Ka 29
Bhamo ○ MYA 254 Kn 33
Bhanas ○ IND 238 Kb 36
Bhandāra ○ IND 234 Kd 35
Bhanjanagar ○ IND 235 Kg 36
Bhānpura ○ IND 234 Kb 33
Bharatpur ○ IND 234 Kc 32
Bharatpur National Park ♀ IND 234 Kc 32
Bharda ○ NEP 235 Kh 32
Bharūch ○ IND 238 Ka 35
Bhatiapara ○ BD 235 Kj 34
Bhatkal ○ IND 238 Kb 39
Bhātpāra ○ IND 235 Kj 34
Bhaun ○ PK 230 Ka 29
Bhavāni ○ IND 239 Kc 40
Bhavnagar ○ IND 238 Ka 35
Bhawāna ○ PK 230 Ka 30
Bhawānipatna ○ IND 234 Kf 36
Bhera ○ PK 230 Ka 29
Bheri ~ NEP 234 Ke 31
Bheri ~ NEP 235 Kf 31
Bhiavan ○ IND 238 Kb 36
Bhilainagar ○ IND 234 Ke 35
Bhīlwāra ○ IND 234 Kb 33
Bhima ~ IND 238 Kc 37
Bhimāshankar ○ IND 238 Ka 36
Bhīmavaram ○ IND 238 Ke 37
Bhīmunipatnam ○ IND 238 Kf 37
Bhind ○ IND 234 Kd 32
Bhiwandi ○ IND 238 Ka 36
Bhiwani ○ IND 234 Kb 31
Bhognipur ○ IND 234 Kd 32
Bhokar ○ IND 238 Kc 36
Bhol Aha ○ BD 235 Kj 33
Bhongaon ○ IND 234 Kd 32
Bhongīr ○ IND 238 Kd 37
Bhopal ○ IND 234 Kc 34
Bhopālpatnam ○ IND 238 Ke 36
Bhuban ○ IND 235 Kg 35
Bhubaneshwar ○ IND 235 Kg 35
Bhuj ○ IND 227 Jn 34
Bhusāwal ○ IND 234 Kb 35
Bhutan □ BHT 235 Kj 32
Bhutiachang ○ IND 235 Kl 32
Biá ~ BR 117 Ea 48
Biafra ≈ WAN 320 Gl 43
Biak ○ RI 283 Md 46
Biak ⛵ RI 283 Md 46
Biała Podlaska ○ PL 171 Hd 19
Białogard ○ PL 170 Ha 18
Białowieski P.N. ♀ PL 171 Hd 19
Biały Bór ○ PL 170 Ha 19
Białystok ○ PL 171 Hd 19
Bian ~ RI 286 Mg 49
Bianga ○ RCA 321 Hc 43
Biankouma ○ CI 305 Gc 42
Biaora ○ IND 234 Kc 34
Biārjmand ○ IR 222 Jf 27
Biarritz ○ F 184 Gf 24
Biasi ~ RDC 336 Hf 46
Biassini ○ ROU 146 Ef 61
Biata ~ BOL 129 Ea 51
Biau ○ RI 275 Lm 45
Biaza ○ RUS 204 Ta 7
Bibā ○ ET 301 Hh 31
Bibai ○ J 250 Mg 24
Bibala ○ ANG 340 Gm 53
Bibas ○ G 332 Gm 45
Bibbiena ○ I 185 Gm 24
Bibémi ○ CAM 321 Gn 41
Biberach an der Riß ○ D 174 Gl 21
Bibiani ○ GH 317 Ge 42
Bibirevo ○ RUS 171 Hj 17
Biblian ○ EC 116 Dj 47
Biboohra ○ AUS 365 Mj 54
Bibundi ○ CAM 320 Gl 43
Biças ○ BR 141 En 56
Bičevaja ○ RUS 250 Md 22
Bīchena ○ ETH 313 Hl 40
Bicheno ○ AUS 378 Ml 66
Bichhua ○ IND 234 Kd 35
Bichi ○ WAN 320 Gj 39
Bickerton Island ⛵ AUS 364 Me 52
Bida ○ WAN 320 Gj 41
Bidal ○ IND 238 Kc 37
Bidbid ○ OM 226 Jh 34
Biddle ○ USA 51 Ck 23
Bideford ○ GB 163 Gd 20
Bidjovagge ○ N 159 Hd 11
Bidoht ○ IR 222 Jh 28
Bidor ○ MAL 270 La 43
Bieber ○ USA 64 Cb 25
Biéha ○ BF 317 Gf 40
Biel ○ CH 163 Gk 22
Bielefeld ○ D 170 Gl 19
Biella ○ I 185 Gk 23
Biélou ○ CI 305 Gc 41
Bielsa ○ E 184 Gf 24
Bielsko-Biała ○ PL 174 Hb 21
Bielsk Podlaski ○ PL 171 Hd 19
Bienge ○ RDC 333 Hb 48
Biên Hòa ○ VN 263 Ld 40
Biermanskool ○ NAM 340 Gp 55
Biescas ○ E 184 Gf 24
Biesiesvlei ○ ZA 349 He 59
Bieszczadzki ♀ PL 174 Hd 21
Bifoulé ○ CAM 320 Gn 43
Bifoun ○ G 332 Gm 46
Bifuka ○ J 250 Mh 23
Biga ○ TR 195 Hf 25
Bigadiç ○ TR 195 Hg 26
Bigand ○ RA 137 Ed 62
Biga Yarımadası ⏜ TR 194 Hf 26
Big Baldy △ USA 50 Ce 23
Big Bay ○ VU 386 Nf 53
Big Beaver ○ CDN 51 Ck 20
Big Bell ○ AUS 368 Lj 59
Big Belt Mountains ⛰ USA 51 Cg 22
Big Bend ○ SD 352 Hh 59
Big Bend Nat. Park ♀ USA 81 Cl 31
Big Black ~ USA 86 Dd 29
Big Creek ○ USA 50 Ce 23
Big Cypress Indian Reservation ••• USA 87 Dh 32
Big Cypress Swamp ~ USA 87 Dh 32
Big Delta ○ USA 46 Bc 13
Big Desert ⏜ AUS 378 Mg 63
Big Falls ○ USA 56 Da 21
Bigfork ○ USA 50 Ce 21
Biggar ○ CDN 51 Cj 19
Bigge Island ⛵ AUS 361 Ln 53
Biggenden ○ AUS 375 Mn 58
Big Hole ~ USA 51 Cf 23
Big Hole National Battlefield ★ USA 50 Cf 23
Bighorn ~ USA 51 Cj 23
Bighorn Bassin ⏜ USA 51 Ch 23
Bighorn Canyon ♀ USA 51 Ch 23
Bighorn Lake ~ USA 51 Ch 23
Bighorn Mountains ⛰ USA 51 Cj 23
Bight of Bangkok ~ THA 262 La 39
Bight of Benin ≈ WAN 320 Gj 43
Bight of Bonny ≈ WAN 320 Gk 43
Big Island ⛵ CDN 43 Ha 6
Big Island ⛵ CDN 56 Da 21
Big John Creek ~ AUS 378 Mf 61
Big Lake ○ USA 81 Cm 30
Big Lost ~ USA 50 Cf 24
Big Mossy Point ⌒ CDN 56 Cn 19
Big Muddy Creek ~ USA 51 Ck 21
Bignona ○ SN 316 Fm 39
Bigona ○ GNB 316 Fm 39
Bigori ○ SUD 313 Hk 40
Big Pine ○ USA 64 Cc 27
Big Pine Key ○ USA 87 Dh 33
Big Piney ○ USA 70 Db 27
Big Pond ○ CDN 61 Ed 23
Big Rapids ○ USA 57 Df 24
Big River Indian Reservation ••• CDN 51 Cj 19
Big Sable Point ⌒ USA 57 De 23
Big Sandy ○ USA 51 Cg 21
Big Sandy ~ USA 64 Cf 28
Big Sandy Creek ~ USA 65 Cl 26
Big Sandy River ~ USA 65 Ch 25
Big Sky ○ USA 51 Cg 23
Big Smoky Valley ⏜ USA 64 Cd 26
Big Snowy Mountains ⛰ USA 51 Ch 22
Big South Fork Natl. Riv. ♀ USA 71 Df 27
Big Spring ○ USA 70 Cm 29
Bigstore Lake ~ CDN 56 Da 19
Big Sur ○ USA 64 Ca 27
Big Timber ○ USA 51 Ch 23
Big Trout Lake ~ CDN 7 Eb 4
Big Trout Lake ~ CDN 43 Ga 8
Big Trout Lake ○ CDN 56 Dc 19
Biguaçu ○ BR 141 Ek 59
Big Warrambool ~ AUS 375 Ml 60
Big Water ○ USA 65 Cf 27
Big Wells ○ USA 81 Cn 31
Big Wood ~ USA 50 Ce 24
Big Wood Cay ⛵ BS 87 Dk 33
Bihać ○ BIH 174 Gp 23
Bihač ○ BIH 174 Gp 23
Bihar ⊙ IND 235 Kg 33
Biharamulo ○ EAT 336 Hh 47
Biharamulo Game Reservat ••• EAT 336 Hh 47
Bihār Sharīf ○ IND 235 Kg 33
Bihor Massif ⏜ RO 175 Hd 22
Bihoro ○ J 250 Mj 24
Bihta ○ IND 235 Kg 33
Bijāpur ○ IND 238 Kb 37
Bijāpur ○ IND 238 Ke 36
Bijāsuvar ○ AZ 202 Jc 26
Bijbehara ○ IND 230 Kb 29
Bijelo Polje ○ MON 194 Hb 24
Bijie ○ VRC 255 Lc 32
Bijnor ○ IND 234 Kc 31
Bijou Creek ~ USA 65 Ck 26
Bijsk ○ RUS 204 Tc 8
Bikāner ○ IND 227 Ka 31
Bikar ⛵ MH 27 Tb 8
Bikin ○ RUS 205 Wc 9
Bikin ~ RUS 205 Xa 9
Bikin ○ RUS 250 Md 22
Bikin ~ RUS 250 Md 22
Bikini ⛵ MH 27 Ta 8
Bikita ○ ZW 352 Hh 56
Bikok ○ CAM 320 Gm 44
Bikoro ○ RDC 333 Hb 46
Bikou ○ VRC 242 Lc 29
Bikramganj ○ IND 235 Kf 33
Bikubiti △ LAR 300 Hb 34
Bila ~ RI 270 Kp 44
Bilabong Roadhouse ○ AUS 368 Lh 59
Bilaća ○ BIH 194 Hb 24
Bila Cerkva ○ UA 175 Hg 21
Bilād Banī ○ OM 226 Jh 34
Bilala ○ RCB 332 Gn 48
Bilanga ○ BF 317 Gg 39
Bilap Bay ~ IND 262 Kl 40
Bilāspur ○ IND 230 Kc 30
Bilāspur ○ IND 234 Kf 34
Bilassana ○ RG 316 Gb 41
Bilatē Shet' ~ ETH 325 Hm 42
Bilati ~ RDC 336 Hg 46
Bilāwal ○ PK 230 Ka 29
Bilbais ○ ET 301 Hh 30
Bilbao ○ E 184 Ge 24
Bilberatha Hill △ AUS 368 Lj 60
Bilbo Bilbao ○ E 184 Ge 24
Bilecik ○ TR 195 Hh 25
Bīlehsawār ○ IR 209 Jb 26
Bilesha Plain ⏜ EAK 325 Hn 45
Biłgoraj ○ PL 174 Hd 20
Bilgrām ○ IND 234 Kd 32
Bilharghat ○ IND 234 Kf 32
Bilhorod-Dnistrovs'kyj ○ UA 175 Hg 22
Bili ○ RDC 321 Hb 43
Bili ~ RDC 324 Hd 43
Bilibino ○ RUS 205 Za 5
Bilin ○ MYA 262 Kn 37
Biliran Island ⛵ RP 267 Ln 40
Bill ○ USA 51 Ck 24
Billabong Creek ~ AUS 379 Mj 63
Billefjorden ~ N 158 Ha 6
Billiluna ○ AUS 361 Lp 55
Billings ○ USA 51 Ch 23
Billund ○ DK 170 Gl 18
Bill Williams ~ USA 64 Ce 28
Bilma ○ RN 309 Gn 36
Biloela ○ AUS 375 Mm 58
Bilohirs'k ○ UA 175 Hk 23
Biloo ○ SP 329 Hp 45
Bilopilja ○ UA 175 Hk 20
Bilovods'k ○ UA 181 Hm 21
Biloxi ○ USA 86 Dd 30
Bilpa Marea Claypan ~ AUS 374 Mf 58
Bilqās ○ ET 301 Hh 30
Bilthara ○ IND 235 Kf 33
Biltine ○ TCH 309 Hc 38
Biluo Xueshan △ VRC 254 Kp 32
Bilverdī ○ IR 209 Jb 26
Bima ○ RI 279 Lk 50
Bima ~ RDC 324 Hf 44
Bimba ○ CAM 321 Gn 43
Bimbe ○ ANG 340 Gp 51
Bimberi Peak △ AUS 379 Ml 63
Bimbijy ○ AUS 368 Lk 60
Bimbila ○ GH 317 Gg 41
Bimbo ○ RCA 321 Hb 43
Bimey ○ USA 51 Cj 23
Bimini-Gaoure ○ RN 308 Gh 39
Bimini Islands ⛵ USA 87 Dj 33
Bina ○ IND 234 Kd 33
Binaluan ○ RP 267 Lk 40
Binanga ○ RI 270 Kp 45
Binbee ○ AUS 375 Mk 56
Bindapuna ○ PNG 287 Mm 48
Bindé ○ BF 317 Gf 40
Binder ○ TCH 321 Gp 41
Bindi Bindi ○ AUS 368 Lj 61
Bindu ○ RDC 333 Hb 49
Bindura ○ ZW 341 Hh 54
Bin-el-Ouidane ○ MA 293 Gc 29
Binga ○ ZW 341 Hf 54
Bingara ○ AUS 375 Mm 60
Bing Bong ○ AUS 364 Me 53
Binger ○ USA 70 Cn 28
Bingham ○ USA 60 Dp 23
Bingham ○ USA 65 Cj 29
Binghamton ○ USA 60 Dl 24
Bin Ghashīr ○ LAR 297 Gn 29
Binglingsi Shiku ★ VRC 242 Lb 28
Bingöl ○ TR 202 Hn 26
Bingöl Dağları △ TR 202 Hn 26
Bingsjö ○ S 158 Gp 15
Binhai ○ VRC 246 Lk 28
Bình Chánh ○ VN 263 Ld 40
Bình Định ○ VN 263 Le 39
Bình Gia ○ VN 255 Ld 35
Bình Giá ○ VN 263 Ld 40
Bình Long ○ VN 263 Ld 40
Bin-Houyé ○ CI 316 Gb 42
Bình So'n ○ VN 263 Le 38
Bini Erde ○ TCH 309 Hb 35
Binjai ○ RI 270 Kp 44
Binjai ○ RI 271 Le 44
Bin Jawwad ○ LAR 300 Hb 30
Binkolo ○ WAL 316 Ga 41
Bīn Lâm ○ VN 263 Le 38
Binnaway ○ AUS 379 Ml 61
Binscarth ○ CDN 56 Cm 20
Bintagoungou ○ RMM 305 Ge 37
Bint Gubail ○ RL 208 Hk 29
Binthalya ○ AUS 368 Lh 58
Bintuhan ○ RI 278 Lb 48
Bintulu ○ MAL 274 Lg 44
Binuang ○ RI 279 Lh 47
Bin Xian ○ VRC 243 Ld 28
Binyang ○ VRC 255 Le 34
Binz ○ D 170 Gn 18
Binzhou ○ VRC 246 Lk 27
Bio Addo ○ SP 329 Ja 44
Biobío ~ RCH 137 Dm 64
Bioko ⛵ GQ 320 Gk 44
Biosphere 2 ★ USA 65 Cg 29
Biougra ○ MA 292 Gb 30
Bipi Island ⛵ PNG 287 Mk 47
Bipindi ○ CAM 320 Gm 44
Bipok ○ CAM 320 Gm 43
Bīr ○ IND 238 Kb 36
Bi'r Abraq ○ ET 301 Hk 34
Bi'r Abū al-Husain ○ ET 301 Hg 34
Bi'r Abū Garādiq ○ ET 301 Hg 30
Bi'r Abū Hašim ○ ET 301 Hk 34
Bi'r Abū Minqār ○ ET 300 Hf 32
Bi'r Abū Zaïma ○ SUD 312 Hg 38
Birāk ○ LAR 297 Gp 32
Bi'r al ,Alaqah ○ LAR 297 Gp 31
Bi'r al 'Atrun ○ SUD 312 Hf 36
Bi'r al Fakama ○ SUD 313 Hj 37
Bi'r al Fātiyah ○ LAR 297 Gn 31
Bi'r al Ghanam ○ LAR 297 Gn 29
Bi'r al-Gidāmi ○ ET 301 Hj 32
Bi'r al Guzayyil ○ LAR 297 Gm 31
Bi'r al-Hasa ○ ET 301 Hk 34
Bir Ali Ben Khelifa ○ TN 297 Gm 28
Bi'r al Kammūniyah ○ LAR 297 Gp 31
Bi'r Allāq ○ LAR 297 Gm 30
Bi'r al Mastūtah ○ LAR 297 Gn 33
Bi'r al Qāt ○ LAR 297 Gp 31
Bi'r al Qatif ○ LAR 300 He 30
Bi'r al ,Utaylah ○ LAR 297 Ha 30
Bir' Amrâne ○ RIM 304 Gb 34
Bi'r an-Nugaym ○ SUD 313 Hk 36
Bir-Anzarane ○ MA 304 Fn 34
Birao ○ RCA 313 Hd 40
Biratnagar ○ NEP 235 Kh 32
Biratori ○ J 250 Mh 24
Bi'r A'yād ○ LAR 297 Gp 29
Bi'r Baili ○ ET 300 He 30
Bîr Bel Guerdâne ○ RIM 292 Ga 33
Bi'r Bin ,Isa ○ LAR 297 Gp 30
Birchenough Bridge ○ ZW 344 Hj 55
Birch Hills ○ CDN 51 Ck 19
Birchip ○ AUS 378 Mh 63
Birch Island ⛵ CDN 56 Cn 19
Birch Lake ~ CDN 51 Cg 19
Birch Lake ~ CDN 56 Db 20
Birch Mountains ⛰ CDN 42 Eb 7
Birch River ○ CDN 56 Cm 19
Bird ⛵ SY 329 Jf 47
Bird City ○ USA 70 Cm 26
Bi'r Dhu'fān ○ LAR 297 Gp 30
Bir Djedid ○ DZ 296 Gk 29
Birdsville ○ AUS 374 Mf 58
Birdum ○ AUS 364 Mc 53
Birdum Creek ~ AUS 364 Mc 53
Bi'r Durb ○ KSA 214 Hn 33
Birecik ○ TR 195 Hm 27
Bir el Amdar ○ DZ 296 Gk 29
Bir el Ater ○ DZ 296 Gk 28
Bir el Gâreb ○ RIM 304 Fm 35
Bireuen ○ RI 270 Kn 43
Bi'r Fāṭima ○ IRQ 209 Hp 28
Bi'r Fuād ○ ET 301 Hf 30
Bir' Furāwiya ○ SUD 312 Hd 38
Birğand ○ IR 222 Jh 29
Bir-Gandouz ○ MA 304 Fm 35
Birganj ○ NEP 235 Kg 32
Bi'r Gifğāfa ○ ET 301 Hj 30
Birigüi ○ BR 140 Ej 56
Bi'r Guraibī'āt ○ IRQ 215 Ja 31
Bi'r Ḥālida ○ ET 301 Hf 30
Bi'r Hasana ○ ET 301 Hj 30
Bi'r Hasmat 'Umar ○ SUD 301 Hk 35
Bi'r Haṭab ○ SUD 312 Hj 35
Biri ○ SUD 324 Hf 42
Biri ~ SUD 324 Hf 42
Bi'r Ibn Hirmās ○ KSA 214 Hl 31
Birini ○ RCA 321 Hd 42
Biritinga ○ BR 125 Fa 51
Bi'r Jubnī ○ LAR 300 He 30
Birjusa ~ RUS 204 Ub 7
Birkat al-'Amyā' ○ KSA 214 Hp 31
Birkat Qarūn ~ ET 301 Hh 31
Birkat Saira ○ SUD 312 Hd 39
Birkelange ○ SN 304 Fn 38
Birkenhead ○ GB 163 Ge 19
Birkenhead ○ AUS 375 Mk 58
Bi'r Khalaf Allāh ○ LAR 297 Gn 32
Bi'r Kiau ○ SUD 313 Hk 35
Birmaj ○ AZ 202 Jb 26
Birmingham ○ USA 71 De 29
Birmingham ○ GB 163 Gf 19
Bi'r Misāha ○ ET 301 Hf 34
Bîr Mogreïn ○ RIM 292 Ga 33
Bi'r Mūdākim ○ LAR 297 Gn 29
Birnagar ○ IND 235 Kj 34
Bi'r Nāhid ○ ET 301 Hg 30
Bi'r Nauarai ○ SUD 313 Hk 35
Bi'r Nāẓsirah ○ LAR 297 Gm 30
Birney ○ USA 51 Cj 23
Birni ○ DY 317 Gg 41
Birnie ⛵ KIR 35 Aa 10
Birni Gwari ○ WAN 320 Gk 40
Birnim ○ RN 308 Gl 38
Birnin-Keebi ○ WAN 320 Gh 39
Birnin-Konni ○ RN 308 Gj 39
Birnin Kudu ○ WAN 320 Gl 40
Birnin-Yauri ○ WAN 320 Gj 40
Birniwa ○ WAN 320 Gl 39
Birnon ○ IND 235 Kf 33
Biro ○ DY 320 Gh 41
Birobidžan ○ RUS 205 Wc 9
Birofel'd ○ RUS 205 Wc 9
Bir Ounâne ○ RMM 305 Ge 35
Bi'r Qar'āt ad Dibah ○ LAR 296 Gl 31
Bi'r Qaryās ○ LAR 297 Ha 31
Birr ○ IRL 163 Gc 19
Birricannia ○ AUS 375 Mj 56
Birrimba Out Station ○ AUS 364 Mc 53
Birrindudu ○ AUS 364 Ma 55
Bi'r Šalatain ○ ET 301 Hk 34
Bir Senia ○ DZ 293 Gf 29
Birsilpur ○ IND 227 Ka 31
Birtam-Tam ○ MA 293 Gd 29
Bi'r Tarfawi ○ ET 301 Hg 34
Bi'r Taziet ○ LAR 297 Gn 33
Bi'r Tin Abunda ○ LAR 297 Gn 32
Birtle ○ CDN 56 Cm 20
Biruaca ○ YV 107 Ea 42
Birufu ○ RI 286 Mf 48
Bi'r Umm Hibāl ○ ET 301 Hj 34
Birūr ○ IND 238 Kb 39
Biržai ○ LT 171 He 17
Bir Zaltan ○ LAR 300 Hb 31
Bir Zar ○ TN 296 Gl 30
Biša ○ KSA 218 Hp 35
Bisagana ○ WAN 321 Gn 39
Bisalpur ○ IND 234 Kd 31
Bisbee ○ USA 80 Cg 30
Biscarrosse ○ F 184 Gf 23
Biscayne ♀ USA 87 Dh 33
Biscayne Bay ~ USA 87 Dh 33
Bischofshofen ○ A 174 Gn 22
Biscoe Islands ⛵ 38 Fb 16
Biscucuy ○ YV 107 Dn 41
Bisellia ○ SUD 324 Hf 42
Bisen ○ KZ 181 Jb 21
Bisha ○ ER 313 Hl 38
Bishaltar ○ NEP 235 Kg 32
Bishan ○ VRC 255 Ld 31
Bishkek ▣ KS 22 Nb 5
Bishnupur ○ IND 235 Kh 34
Bisho ○ ZA 358 Hf 62
Bishop ○ USA 64 Cc 27
Bishop Aukland ○ GB 162 Ge 18
Bishops Falls ○ CDN 61 Eg 21
Bishop's Stortford ○ GB 163 Gf 20
Bishopville ○ USA 71 Dh 28
Biskotasi Lake ~ CDN 57 Dh 22
Biskra ○ DZ 296 Gj 28
Biskupiec ○ PL 170 Hc 19
Bislig ○ RP 267 Lp 41
Bismarck ○ USA 56 Cm 22
Bismarck Archipelago ⛵ PNG 287 Ml 47
Bismarck Range ⛰ PNG 287 Mj 48
Bismarck Sea ≈ 287 Ml 47
Biso ○ EAU 324 Hh 45
Bison ○ USA 51 Cl 23
Bisono ○ DOM 101 Dn 36
Bispfors ○ S 158 Ha 14
Bisrivier ○ ZA 349 He 61
Bissago Archipelago ⛵ GNB 316 Fm 40
Bissamcuttavk ○ IND 234 Kf 36
Bissau ▣ GNB 316 Fm 40
Bissikrima ○ RG 316 Ga 40

402 Bento Gomes - Bissikrima

□Country ▣Capital city ◉Administrative unit ○Place ◬Island ⛰Mountain range △Mountain ⌓Cape ≈Ocean, Sea ~Lake, River ΨUndersea topography ▲Glacier ♀National park •••Reservation ★Point of major interest ⌒Landscape

Bissorã ○ **GNB** 316 Fn 39
Bistcho Lake ~ **CDN** 47 Cc 15
Bistrița ○ **RO** 175 He 22
Bisún ○ **GQ** 332 Gm 45
Biswān ○ **IND** 234 Ke 32
Bita ~ **CO** 107 Dp 42
Bita ~ **RCA** 324 He 42
Bitagron ○ **SME** 113 Ef 43
Bitam ○ **G** 332 Gm 44
Bitangor ○ **MAL** 271 Lf 44
Bitata ○ **ETH** 325 Hm 43
Bitburg ○ **D** 163 Gk 21
Bitencourt ○ **BR** 117 Dp 46
Bitigiu ○ **ETH** 325 Hn 41
Bitik ○ **KZ** 181 Jd 20
Bitilifondi ○ **RCA** 324 Hf 43
Bitjug ~ **RUS** 181 Hn 20
Bitkine ○ **TCH** 321 Hb 40
Bitlis ○ **TR** 202 Hp 26
Bitola ○ **MK** 194 Hc 25
Bitou ○ **BF** 317 Gf 40
Bitoutouk ○ **CAM** 320 Gm 44
Bitterfontein ○ **ZA** 348 Hb 61
Bitteroot Range ⛰ **USA** 51 Cf 23
Bitterroot ~ **USA** 50 Ce 22
Bitti ○ **I** 185 Gl 25
Bitung ○ **RI** 275 Ln 45
Bituruna ○ **BR** 140 Ej 59
Biu ○ **WAN** 320 Gn 40
Biwako ~ **J** 251 Me 28
Biwat ○ **PNG** 287 Mh 48
Bixby ○ **USA** 70 Da 28
Biyagundi ○ **ER** 313 Hl 38
Biyang ○ **VRC** 243 Lg 29
Biyth ~ **AUS** 364 Md 52
Bizana ○ **ZA** 349 Hg 61
Bizen ○ **J** 251 Md 28
Bizerte ○ **TN** 296 Gl 27
Bizigui ~ **BF** 317 Gf 39
Bj. Bounaama ○ **DZ** 293 Gg 28
Bjala ○ **BG** 194 He 24
Bjarezinski zapavednik ♀ **BY** 171 Hg 18
Bjargtangar ⌓ **IS** 158 Fh 13
Bjelašnica △ **BIH** 194 Hb 24
Bjelovar ○ **HR** 174 Ha 23
Bjerkvik ○ **N** 158 Ha 11
Bjørkåsen ○ **N** 158 Ha 11
Björna ○ **S** 158 Hb 14
Bjørnafjorden ~ **N** 158 Gj 15
Bjorne Peninsula ◬ **CDN** 43 Ga 3
Björnöya ◬ **N** 19 Kb 2
Bjørnstad ○ **N** 159 Hg 11
Bjurholm ○ **S** 158 Hb 14
Bla ○ **RMM** 317 Gd 39
Black ~ **USA** 56 Dc 23
Black ~ **USA** 65 Cg 29
Blackall ○ **AUS** 375 Mj 58
Black Bay ~ **CDN** 57 Dd 21
Black Bay ~ **USA** 74 Dl 27
Black Braes ○ **AUS** 365 Mj 55
Blackbull ○ **AUS** 365 Mg 54
Blackburn ○ **GB** 163 Ge 19
Black Canyon of the Gunnison ♀ **USA** 65 Cj 26
Black Creek ○ **USA** 57 Dd 23
Black Diamond ○ **CDN** 50 Ce 20
Blackdown ○ **AUS** 365 Mh 54
Blackfeet Indian Reservation ••• **USA** 51 Cf 21
Blackfoot ~ **USA** 51 Cf 22
Blackfoot ○ **USA** 51 Cf 24
Blackfoot Indian Reservation ••• **CDN** 51 Cf 20
Blackfoot Reservoir ~ **USA** 51 Cg 24
Black Forest ⛰ **D** 174 Gl 21
Black Hawk ○ **USA** 86 Dc 30
Black Hills ⛰ **USA** 51 Ck 23
Blackie ○ **CDN** 50 Cf 20
Black Island ◬ **CDN** 56 Cp 20
Black Lake ~ **CDN** 42 Ec 7
Black Lake ~ **USA** 46 Aj 17
Black Lake ○ **CDN** 60 Dn 22
Black Mesa △ **USA** 65 Cl 27
Black Mountain △ **USA** 71 Dg 27
Black Mountain △ **AUS** 374 Mf 56
Black Mountains ⛰ **USA** 64 Ce 28
Black Nossob ~ **NAM** 348 Hb 57
Black Point ○ **BS** 87 Dk 33
Black Point ⌓ **AUS** 368 Lh 63
Blackpool ○ **GB** 163 Ge 19
Black Reef ◬ **AUS** 375 Ml 55
Black River ○ **JA** 100 Dj 37
Black River Bay ~ **JA** 100 Dj 37
Black River Fs. ○ **USA** 56 Dc 23
Black River Gorges National Park ★ **MS** 353 Jg 56
Black Rock ○ **USA** 71 Dc 27
Black Rock Desert ⌒ **USA** 64 Cc 25
Blacksburg ○ **USA** 71 Dh 27
Black Sea ≈ 19 Lb 5
Black Sea ≈ 195 Hh 24
Black Sea Lowland ⌒ **UA** 175 Hg 23
Blacks Fork ~ **USA** 65 Cg 25
Blackstone ○ **USA** 74 Dj 27
Black Volta ~ **BF** 317 Ge 39
Black Volta ~ **GH** 317 Ge 41
Blackwater ○ **AUS** 375 Ml 57
Blackwater Creek ~ **AUS** 375 Mj 58
Blackwater Creek ~ **AUS** 379 Mm 62
Blackwater Lake ~ **CDN** 47 Bn 13
Blackwell ○ **USA** 70 Cm 29
Blackwood ~ **AUS** 368 Lh 63
Bladensburg ♀ **AUS** 374 Mh 57
Bladgrond ○ **ZA** 348 Hb 60
Blagodarnyj ○ **RUS** 202 Hp 23
Blagoevgrad ○ **BG** 194 Hd 24
Blagoevo ○ **RUS** 154 Ra 6
Blagoveščenka ○ **RUS** 204 Tb 8
Blagoveščensk ○ **RUS** 205 Wb 8
Blagoveshchenskiy Proliv ≈ **RUS** 205 Xc 3
Blaine ○ **USA** 56 Db 23
Blaine ○ **USA** 70 Cp 26
Blaine Lake ○ **CDN** 51 Cj 19
Blair ○ **USA** 56 Dc 23
Blair ○ **USA** 70 Cp 25
Blair Athol ○ **AUS** 375 Mk 57
Blairbeth ○ **ZA** 349 Hf 58
Blairmore ○ **CDN** 50 Ce 21
Blairsden ○ **USA** 64 Cb 26
Blairsville ○ **USA** 71 Df 28
Blairsville ○ **USA** 74 Dj 25
Blaka ~ **RN** 309 Gn 35
Blaka Laodemi ○ **RN** 309 Gn 35
Blakely ○ **USA** 86 Df 30
Blake Plateau Ψ 87 Dj 30
Blake Point ⌓ **USA** 57 Dd 21
Blama ○ **WAL** 316 Ga 42
Blanca ♀ **PE** 128 Dn 54
Blanca ~ **BOL** 136 Eb 56
Blanca Peek △ **USA** 65 Ck 27
Blanchard ○ **USA** 56 Cp 22
Blanchard Springs Caverns ♀ **USA** 70 Db 27
Blanche Channel ~ **SOL** 290 Na 50
Blanche-Marievallen ~ **SME** 113 Ef 43
Blanchetown ○ **AUS** 378 Mf 63
Blanchisseuse ○ **TT** 104 Ed 40
Blanco ○ **MEX** 80 Ck 32
Blanco ○ **USA** 81 Cn 30
Blanco ~ **PE** 116 Dm 48
Blanco ~ **BOL** 129 Ec 52
Blanco ~ **BOL** 129 Ec 53
Blanco ~ **RA** 137 Dn 61
Blanco ~ **RA** 137 Dp 60
Blanco ~ **RCH** 152 Dm 68
Blanco ~ **RA** 152 Dn 69
Blandá ~ **IS** 158 Fl 13
Bland Creek ~ **AUS** 379 Mk 62
Blanding ○ **USA** 65 Ch 27
Blanes ○ **E** 184 Gh 25
Blanfla ○ **CI** 317 Gd 42
Blangkejeren ○ **RI** 270 Kn 44
Blanquillo ○ **ROU** 146 Eg 62
Blantyre ○ **MW** 344 Hk 53
Blåsjøen ~ **N** 170 Gk 16
Blåsjön ○ **S** 158 Gp 13
Blåvands Huk ⌓ **DK** 170 Gk 18
Blaye ○ **F** 184 Gf 23
Blayney ○ **AUS** 379 Ml 62
Bleaker Island ◬ **GB** 147 Ee 72
Blebo ○ **LB** 316 Gb 43
Bled Tisseras ~ **DZ** 296 Gk 32
Blega ○ **RI** 279 Lg 49
Bleikvassli ○ **N** 158 Gn 13
Blendio ○ **RMM** 305 Gc 40
Blenheim ○ **CDN** 57 Dh 24
Blenheim ○ **AUS** 375 Ml 59
Blenheim ○ **NZ** 383 Nk 66
Blenheim Palace ★ **GB** 163 Ge 20
Blida ○ **DZ** 296 Gh 27
Bligh Water ~ **FJI** 387 Nl 54
Blikaodi ○ **CI** 317 Ge 41
Blind River ○ **CDN** 57 Dg 22
Blitar ○ **RI** 279 Lg 50
Blitchton ○ **USA** 71 Dh 29
Blitta ○ **RT** 317 Gg 41
Blixby ○ **USA** 71 Dc 27
Block Island ◬ **USA** 74 Dn 25
Block Island Sound ~ **USA** 74 Dn 25
Bloemfontein ○ **ZA** 349 He 60
Bloemhof ○ **ZA** 349 He 59
Bloemhof Dam ~ **ZA** 349 He 59
Blois ○ **F** 163 Gg 22
Blolékin ○ **CI** 304 Gc 42
Blöndósbær ○ **IS** 158 Fk 13
Blood Indian Reservation ••• **CDN** 50 Cf 21
Bloods Range ⛰ **AUS** 369 Ma 58
Bloodvein River ~ **CDN** 56 Cp 20
Bloomfield ○ **USA** 65 Cj 27
Bloomfield ○ **USA** 70 Db 25
Bloomfield ○ **USA** 71 De 26
Bloomfield River ○ **AUS** 365 Mj 53
Blooming Prairie ○ **USA** 56 Db 24
Bloomington ○ **USA** 56 Db 23
Bloomington ○ **USA** 71 Dd 25
Bloomington ○ **USA** 71 De 26
Bloomsburg ○ **USA** 74 Dk 25
Bloomsbury ○ **AUS** 375 Ml 56
Blora ○ **RI** 279 Lf 49
Blosseville Kyst ⌒ **DK** 43 La 5
Bloukranspas △ **ZA** 348 Hb 61
Blountstown ○ **USA** 86 Df 30
Blowering ~ **AUS** 379 Ml 63
Blue Earth ○ **USA** 56 Da 24
Bluefield ○ **USA** 71 Dh 27
Bluefields ○ **NIC** 97 Dg 39
Blue Hill ○ **USA** 70 Cn 25
Blue Hills ○ **GB** 101 Dm 35
Blue Hills of Couteau △ **CDN** 61 Ee 22
Blue Hole ★ **BH** 93 De 37
Blue Inlet ~ **CDN** 50 Bp 20
Blue Knob △ **AUS** 379 Mn 61
Blue Lagoon ♀ **Z** 341 Hf 53
Blue Lick Springs ○ **USA** 71 Dg 26
Blue Mesa Reservoir ~ **USA** 65 Cj 26
Blue Mount △ **AUS** 379 Mm 61
Blue Mountain ⛰ **USA** 50 Cc 23
Blue Mountain Lake ○ **USA** 60 Dl 24
Blue Mountain Pass △ **USA** 64 Cd 24
Blue Mountains ⛰ **USA** 74 Dk 25
Blue Mountains ⛰ **JA** 101 Dk 36
Blue Mountains ⛰ **AUS** 379 Ml 62
Blue Mountains ♀ **AUS** 379 Mm 62
Blue Mud Bay ~ **AUS** 364 Md 52
Blue Mud Hill ⛰ **USA** 51 Ck 23
Blue Nile ~ **SUD** 313 Hj 39
Blue Nile ~ **ETH** 313 Hl 40
Blue Nile Falls ~ **ETH** 313 Hl 40
Bluenose Lake ~ **CDN** 47 Ca 11
Blue Ridge ○ **USA** 71 Df 28
Blue Ridge ⛰ **USA** 71 Dg 28
Blue River ○ **CDN** 50 Cc 19
Blue Robin Hill ○ **AUS** 369 Ln 60
Bluesprings Caverns ★ **USA** 71 De 26
Bluewater ○ **USA** 65 Ch 28
Bluewater ○ **AUS** 365 Mk 55
Bluff ○ **USA** 65 Ch 27
Bluff ○ **AUS** 375 Ml 57
Bluff ○ **NZ** 382 Ng 69
Bluff Creek ~ **USA** 70 Cn 27
Bluff Face Range ⛰ **AUS** 361 Lp 54
Bluff Point ⌓ **AUS** 368 Lg 59
Blukwa ○ **RDC** 324 Hh 45
Blumenau ○ **BR** 141 Ek 59
Blunt ○ **USA** 56 Cn 23
Blup Blup Island ◬ **PNG** 287 Mj 47
Bly ○ **USA** 50 Cb 24
Blynn ○ **USA** 50 Ca 21
Blyth ○ **GB** 162 Gf 18
Blyth ~ **AUS** 364 Md 52
Blythe ○ **USA** 64 Ce 29
Blytheville ○ **USA** 71 Dc 28
Blyth Lagoon ~ **AUS** 369 Ln 58
Bø ○ **N** 170 Gl 16
Bo ○ **WAL** 316 Ga 42
Boa ~ **CI** 305 Gc 41
Boa ○ **RDC** 341 Hg 51
Boac ○ **RP** 267 Ll 39
Boaco ○ **NIC** 96 Df 39
Boad Town ○ **GB** 104 Eb 36
Boa Esperança ○ **BR** 112 Ed 44
Boa Esperança ○ **BR** 117 Eb 49
Boa Esperança ○ **BR** 141 Em 56
Boa Esperança do Sul ○ **BR** 141 Ek 57
Boalemo ○ **RI** 282 Lm 46
Boali ○ **RCA** 321 Hb 43
Boana ○ **PNG** 287 Mk 49
Boanamary ○ **RM** 345 Ja 53
Boanda ○ **CAM** 320 Gm 43
Boane ○ **MOC** 352 Hj 59
Boangi ○ **RDC** 333 Hc 46
Boang Island ◬ **PNG** 287 Mn 47
Boario Terme ○ **I** 185 Gl 23
Boat Basin ○ **CDN** 50 Bn 21
Boatlaname ○ **RB** 349 He 57
Boa Viagem ○ **BR** 124 Fa 48
Boa Vista ◬ **CV** 30 Hb 8
Boa Vista ○ **BR** 112 Ed 44
Boa Vista ○ **BR** 117 Eb 46
Boa Vista ○ **BR** 117 Eb 48
Boa Vista ○ **BR** 146 Eh 62
Boa Vista da Tupim ○ **BR** 125 Ep 52
Boa Vista do Ramos ○ **BR** 120 Ef 47
Boayan Island ◬ **RP** 267 Lk 40
Bobadah ○ **AUS** 379 Mk 62
Bobai ○ **VRC** 255 Le 34
Bobbili ○ **IND** 234 Kf 36
Bóbbio ○ **I** 185 Gl 23
Bobene ○ **RDC** 324 He 45
Bobila ○ **RDC** 333 Hc 44
Bobkov ○ **RUS** 181 Hm 20
Bobo ~ **RCA** 321 Hb 42
Bobodioulasso ○ **BF** 317 Gd 40
Bobonaza ~ **EC** 116 Dk 46
Bobonong ○ **RB** 349 Hg 56
Bobotoġ ⛰ **UZB** 223 Jm 27
Bobouaru ○ **TP** 282 Ln 50
Bobr ○ **BY** 171 Hg 18
Bobrowniki ○ **PL** 171 Hd 19
Bobrynec' ○ **UA** 175 Hh 21
Bobuk ○ **SUD** 313 Hk 40
Bobures ○ **YV** 107 Dn 41
Boca Arenal ○ **CR** 97 Df 40
Boca Candelaria ◬ **CO** 106 Dk 44
Boca Chica ○ **DOM** 101 Dp 36
Boca de Anaro ○ **YV** 107 Dn 42
Boca de Arguaca ○ **YV** 107 Ea 42
Boca del Pao ○ **YV** 112 Eb 41
Boca del Rio ○ **MEX** 80 Ch 33
Boca del Rio ○ **PE** 128 Dn 55
Boca del Rio Indio ○ **PA** 97 Dh 41
Boca del Yaqui ~ **MEX** 80 Cg 32
Boca de Pozo Macanao ○ **YV** 112 Eb 40
Boca de Uchire ○ **YV** 112 Eb 40
Boca do Acre ○ **BR** 117 Ea 50
Boca do Capanã ○ **BR** 120 Ed 48
Boca do Carapanatuba ○ **BR** 117 Ec 49
Boca do Iaco ○ **BR** 117 Dp 50
Boca do Jari ○ **BR** 121 Eh 46
Bocaina de Minas ○ **BR** 141 Em 57
Bocaino do Sul ○ **BR** 140 Ek 59
Bocaiúva ○ **BR** 125 En 54
Bocanda ○ **CI** 317 Gd 42
Bocaranga ○ **RCA** 321 Gp 42
Boca Raton ○ **USA** 87 Dh 32
Boca Santa María ~ **MEX** 81 Cp 33
Bocas de Cahuinarí ○ **CO** 117 Dn 46
Bocas del Toro ○ **PA** 97 Dg 41
Bocay ~ **NIC** 97 Df 39
Bochart ○ **CDN** 60 Dm 21
Bochinche ○ **YV** 112 Ed 42
Bocholt ○ **D** 163 Gk 20
Bocoio ○ **ANG** 340 Gn 52
Bocón ○ **YV** 112 Ec 42
Bocono ○ **YV** 107 Dn 41
Boçoroca ○ **BR** 146 Eg 60
Boda ○ **RCA** 321 Ha 43
Böda ○ **S** 170 Ha 17
Bodajbo ○ **RUS** 204 Vb 7
Bodala ○ **RDC** 321 Hd 44
Bodalla ○ **AUS** 379 Mm 64
Bodallin ○ **AUS** 368 Lk 61
Boddington ○ **AUS** 368 Lj 62
Bodélé ⌒ **TCH** 309 Ha 37
Boden ○ **S** 159 Hc 13
Bode-Sadu ○ **WAN** 320 Gj 41
Bodhan ○ **IND** 238 Kc 36
Bodhei ○ **EAK** 337 Hn 46
Bodi ○ **GH** 317 Ge 42
Bodi ○ **DY** 317 Gg 41
Bodingué ~ **RCA** 321 Ha 44
Bodjoki ○ **RDC** 321 Hd 44
Bodjokola ○ **RDC** 321 Hc 44
Bodmin ○ **CDN** 51 Cj 19
Bodmin ○ **GB** 163 Gd 20
Bodø ○ **N** 158 Gn 12
Bodocó ○ **BR** 124 Fa 49
Bodokro ○ **CI** 317 Gd 42
Bodoquena ○ **BR** 140 Ef 56
Bodougou ○ **RG** 316 Gb 41
Bodoupa ○ **RCA** 321 Ha 43
Bodrum ○ **TR** 195 Hf 27
Bodum ○ **S** 158 Ha 14
Boduna ○ **RDC** 321 Hb 43
Boé ○ **GNB** 316 Fn 40
Boende ○ **RDC** 333 Hc 46
Boenze ○ **RDC** 332 Gp 48
Boerne ○ **USA** 81 Cn 31
Boesmansrivier ~ **ZA** 358 Hf 62
Boffa ○ **RG** 316 Fn 40
Bofossou ○ **RG** 316 Gb 41
Boga ○ **RDC** 324 Hg 45
Bogale ○ **MYA** 262 Km 37
Bogalusa ○ **USA** 86 Dd 30
Bogamangon ○ **RCA** 321 Ha 43
Bogan ~ **AUS** 379 Mk 61
Bogandé ○ **BF** 317 Gf 39
Bogan Gate ○ **AUS** 379 Mk 62
Bogangolo ○ **RCA** 321 Hb 43
Bogantungan ○ **AUS** 375 Mk 57
Bogata ○ **USA** 70 Da 29
Bogate Saby ○ **RUS** 181 Jd 18
Bogatoe ○ **RUS** 181 Jd 19
Boğazkale ○ **TR** 195 Hk 25
Boğazlıyan ○ **TR** 195 Hk 26
Bogbonga ○ **RDC** 333 Hb 45
Bogdanovka ○ **RUS** 181 Jd 19
Bogdanovo ○ **RUS** 171 Hj 18
Bogda Shan ⛰ **VRC** 204 Tc 10
Boggabilla ○ **AUS** 375 Ml 60
Boggabri ○ **AUS** 379 Mm 61
Bogia ○ **PNG** 287 Mj 48
Bogilima ○ **RDC** 333 Hb 44
Bognes ○ **N** 158 Gp 11
Boğnūrd ○ **IR** 222 Jg 27
Bogo ○ **RP** 267 Ln 40
Bogo ○ **CAM** 321 Gp 40
Bogoin ○ **RCA** 321 Hb 43
Bogolodza, Khrebet ⛰ **RUS** 250 Md 22
Bogong ♀ **AUS** 379 Mk 64
Bogor ○ **RI** 278 Ld 49
Bogoro ○ **RDC** 324 Hh 45
Bogorodick ○ **RUS** 181 Hm 19
Bogorodsk ○ **RUS** 181 Hp 17
Bogose-Mubea ○ **RDC** 333 Hb 44
Bogoso ○ **GH** 317 Ge 43
Bogotá ▣ **CO** 106 Dl 43
Bogra ○ **BD** 235 Kj 33
Bogučar ○ **RUS** 181 Hn 21
Bogué ○ **RIM** 304 Fn 37
Boğűédia ○ **CI** 305 Gc 42
Boguila ○ **RCA** 321 Ha 42
Bogunda ○ **AUS** 375 Mj 56
Bo Hai ~ **VRC** 246 Lk 26
Bohai Haixia Ψ **VRC** 246 Ll 26
Bohai Wan ~ **VRC** 246 Lj 26
Bohemia ⌒ **CZ** 174 Gp 21
Bohemia Downs ○ **AUS** 361 Lp 55
Bohemia Massif ⛰ **CZ** 174 Gp 21
Bohemian Forest ⛰ **D** 174 Gn 21
Bohena Creek ~ **AUS** 379 Ml 61
Bohicon ○ **DY** 317 Gh 42
Bohlakong ○ **ZA** 349 Hg 60
Bohoduchiv ○ **UA** 175 Hk 20
Bohol ◬ **RP** 267 Ln 41
Bohol Sea ~ **RP** 267 Ln 41
Bohol Strait ~ **RP** 267 Lm 41
Bohong ○ **RCA** 321 Gp 42
Bohongou ○ **BF** 317 Gg 39
Boi ○ **WAN** 320 Gl 41
Bóia ~ **BR** 117 Dp 48
Boiaçu ○ **BR** 120 Ed 46
Boigu Island ◬ **AUS** 286 Mh 50
Boiken ○ **PNG** 286 Mh 47
Boila ○ **MOC** 344 Hm 54
Boina ⌒ **RM** 345 Jb 54
Boipārigūda ○ **IND** 234 Kf 36
Boipeba ○ **BR** 125 Fa 52
Bois ~ **BR** 133 Ek 53
Bois ~ **BR** 133 Ek 54
Bois Blanc Is. ◬ **USA** 57 Df 23
Boise ○ **USA** 50 Cd 24
Boise City ○ **USA** 65 Cl 27
Bois Forte ••• **USA** 56 Db 22
Boissevain ○ **CDN** 56 Cm 21
Boituva ○ **BR** 141 El 57
Bojarka ○ **UA** 175 Hg 20
Bojmurot ○ **UZB** 223 Jm 25
Bojonegoro ○ **RI** 279 Lf 49
Boju ○ **WAN** 320 Gk 42
Boju-Ega ○ **WAN** 320 Gl 42
Bojuru ○ **BR** 146 Ej 61
Bokada ○ **RDC** 321 Hb 43
Bokākhāt ○ **IND** 235 Kl 32
Bokata ○ **RDC** 321 Hd 44
Bokatola ○ **RDC** 333 Hb 46
Boké ○ **RG** 316 Fn 40
Bokele ○ **RDC** 333 Hc 46
Bokhara ~ **AUS** 375 Ml 60
Bokhol Plain ⌒ **EAK** 325 Hm 44
Boki ○ **CAM** 321 Gn 41
Bokin ○ **BF** 317 Gf 39
Bokito ○ **CAM** 320 Gm 43
Bokkeveldberge ⛰ **ZA** 348 Hb 61
Boknafjorden ~ **N** 170 Gj 16
Boko ○ **RCB** 332 Gp 48
Bokode ○ **RDC** 333 Hb 44
Bokoko ○ **RDC** 324 Hf 43
Bokolako ○ **SN** 316 Fp 39
Bokolango ○ **RDC** 333 Hc 45
Bokol Mayo ○ **ETH** 325 Hn 43
Bokondo ○ **RDC** 333 Hb 45
Bokoro ○ **TCH** 321 Ha 39
Boko-Songho ○ **RCB** 332 Gn 48
Bokota ○ **RDC** 333 Hd 46
Boksitogorsk ○ **RUS** 171 Hj 16
Boku ○ **PNG** 290 Mp 49
Boku ○ **RDC** 332 Ha 47
Bokuma ○ **RDC** 333 Hb 46
Bokungu ○ **RDC** 333 Hd 46
Bok Zelenzuk ~ **RUS** 202 Hn 24
Bol' ○ **TCH** 321 Gp 39
Bol. Černigovka ○ **RUS** 181 Jd 19
Bol. Glušica ○ **RUS** 181 Jd 19
Bol. Murata ○ **RUS** 204 Ua 7
Bol. Negatkino ○ **RUS** 181 Jb 18
Bol.Orlovka ○ **RUS** 181 Hn 22
Bol. Zaborov'e ○ **RUS** 171 Hj 16
Bolafa ○ **RDC** 333 Hd 45
Bolaiti ○ **RDC** 333 He 47
Bolama ○ **GNB** 316 Fn 40
Bolama ○ **RDC** 333 Hd 45
Bolaños ~ **MEX** 92 Cl 35
Bolan Pass △ **PK** 227 Jm 30
Bolbec ○ **F** 163 Gg 21
Bold Point ⌓ **RP** 267 Lk 41
Boldyr ○ **UZB** 223 Jm 27
Bole ○ **GH** 317 Ge 41
Bole ○ **ETH** 325 Hl 42
Boleko ○ **RDC** 333 Hb 46
Bolena ○ **RDC** 333 Hb 45
Bolesławiec ○ **PL** 174 Gp 20
Bolgart ○ **AUS** 368 Lj 61
Bolgatanga ○ **GH** 317 Gf 40
Bolhov ○ **RUS** 171 Hk 19
Bolhrad ○ **UA** 175 Hg 23
Boli ○ **VRC** 250 Mb 23
Boli ○ **SUD** 324 Hg 42
Boli ○ **RDC** 336 Hf 46
Bolia ○ **IND** 234 Kb 33
Bolia ○ **RDC** 333 Hb 46
Boliden ○ **S** 159 Hb 13
Bolifar ○ **RI** 283 Mb 47
Bolintin-Vale ○ **RO** 175 He 23
Bolivar ○ **USA** 70 Db 27
Bolivar ○ **USA** 71 Dd 28
Bolívar ○ **CO** 106 Dk 43
Bolivar ○ **CO** 106 Dk 45
Bolivar ○ **PE** 116 Dk 49
Bolivar ○ **BOL** 129 Ea 52
Bolivar ○ **BOL** 129 Ea 54
Bolivar Peninsula ⌒ **USA** 81 Da 31
Bolivia ○ **C** 100 Dj 34
Bolivia □ **BOL** 129 Ea 53
Boljevac ○ **SCG** 194 Hd 24
Boljoon ○ **RP** 267 Lm 41
Bolkar Dağları ⛰ **TR** 195 Hj 27
Bolléne ○ **F** 185 Gj 23
Bollnäs ○ **S** 158 Ha 15
Bollon ○ **AUS** 375 Mk 60
Bolmen ~ **S** 170 Gn 17
Bolnisi ○ **GE** 202 Ja 25
Bolo ○ **RDC** 333 Ha 47
Bolobo ○ **RDC** 332 Ha 47
Bologna ○ **I** 185 Gm 23
Bolognesi ○ **PE** 128 Dl 51
Bologoe ○ **RUS** 171 Hk 17
Bologovo ○ **RUS** 171 Hh 17
Bololedi ~ **EAT** 337 Hk 47
Bolomba ○ **RDC** 333 Hb 45
Bolombo ~ **RDC** 333 Hc 45
Bolonchén de Rejón ○ **MEX** 93 Dc 35
Bolongongo ○ **ANG** 332 Gp 50
Bolonguera ○ **ANG** 340 Gn 52
Bolontio ○ **RI** 275 Lm 45
Bol'šaja Martynovka ○ **RUS** 181 Hn 22
Bol'Šaja Ussurka ~ **RUS** 250 Md 23
Bolšaja Varzuga ~ **RUS** 159 Hl 12
Bol'šakovo ○ **RUS** 170 Hc 18
Bolshezemel'skaya Tundra ⌒ **RUS** 154 Rb 5
Bolshezemel'skaya Tundra ⌒ **RUS** 204 Rb 5
Bolsi ○ **RN** 317 Gg 39
Bolsico ○ **RCH** 136 Dn 57
Bolsoj Anjuj ~ **RUS** 23 Ta 3
Bolsoj Anjuj ~ **RUS** 205 Yc 5
Bol'šoj Balhan ⛰ **TM** 222 Jf 26
Bolsoj Čeremšan ~ **RUS** 181 Jd 18
Bolsoj Enisej ~ **RUS** 204 Ub 8
Bolsoj Irgiz ~ **RUS** 181 Jc 20
Bol'soj Kamen' ○ **RUS** 250 Mc 24
Bolsoj Karaman ~ **RUS** 181 Jb 20
Bolsoj Kuonamka ~ **RUS** 204 Va 5
Bolsoj Uzen' ~ **RUS** 181 Jc 20
Bolsón de Mapimi ⌒ **MEX** 81 Ck 32
Boltodden ⌓ **N** 158 Hb 7
Bolton ○ **USA** 74 Dj 28
Bolton ○ **GB** 163 Ge 19
Bolu ○ **TR** 195 Hh 25
Bolubolu ○ **PNG** 287 Mm 50
Bolzano ○ **I** 174 Gm 22
Boma ○ **RDC** 332 Gn 48
Bomaderry ○ **AUS** 379 Mm 63
Bomadi ○ **WAN** 320 Gj 43
Bomate ○ **RDC** 333 Hb 46
Bombala ○ **AUS** 379 Ml 64
Bombas de Salinas ○ **MEX** 75 Ce 32
Bombay ○ **IND** 238 Ka 36
Bomberai ~ **RI** 283 Mc 47
Bomberai Peninsula ◬ **RI** 283 Mc 47
Bombo ○ **EAU** 324 Hj 45
Bombo ○ **RDC** 332 Gp 48
Bombo ~ **RDC** 332 Gp 48
Bombo-Makuka ○ **RDC** 332 Ha 48
Bomboyo ○ **TCH** 321 Gp 39
Bombura ○ **RDC** 333 Hb 44
Bom Conselho ○ **BR** 124 Fb 50
Bom Despacho ○ **BR** 133 Em 55
Bomdila ○ **IND** 235 Kl 32
Bomet ○ **EAK** 337 Hk 46
Bomi ○ **VRC** 254 Km 31
Bomi ○ **AUS** 375 Ml 60
Bomili ○ **RDC** 324 Hf 45
Bom Jardim ○ **BR** 121 Ej 46
Bom Jardim ○ **BR** 121 El 47
Bom Jardim ○ **BR** 141 En 57
Bom Jardim de Minas ○ **BR** 141 Em 56
Bom Jesus ○ **BR** 121 Em 50
Bom Jesus ~ **BR** 133 Em 51
Bom Jesus ○ **BR** 146 Ej 60
Bom Jesus d. C. ★ **BR** 141 Em 56
Bom Jesus da Lapa ○ **BR** 125 En 52
Bom Jesus de Goiás ○ **BR** 133 Ej 55
Bom Jesus do Galho ○ **BR** 141 En 55
Bom Jesus do Itabapoano ○ **BR** 141 Ep 56
Bømlo ◬ **N** 170 Gj 16
Bomokandi ~ **RDC** 324 Hf 44
Bomokandi ~ **RDC** 324 Hg 44
Bomolu ○ **RDC** 333 Hb 44
Bomongo ○ **RDC** 333 Hb 45
Bom Princípio ○ **BR** 121 El 50
Bom Sucesso ○ **BR** 141 Em 56
Bomu ~ **RDC** 324 Hd 43
Bomu ~ **RDC** 324 Hf 43
Bonāb ○ **IR** 209 Ja 27
Bonaberi ○ **CAM** 320 Gl 43
Bona Bona Island ◬ **AUS** 287 Ml 51
Bona Bona Island ◬ **PNG** 287 Ml 51
Bon Air ○ **USA** 74 Dk 27
Bonaire ◬ **NL** 107 Dp 39
Bonampak ★ **MEX** 93 Dc 37
Bonang ○ **AUS** 379 Ml 64
Bonanza ○ **USA** 65 Ch 26
Bonanza ○ **NIC** 97 Df 38
Bonao ○ **DOM** 101 Dn 36
Bonaparte Archipelago ◬ **AUS** 361 Ln 53
Bonar Bridge ○ **GB** 162 Gd 17
Bonaventure ○ **CDN** 61 Eb 21
Bonavista ○ **CDN** 61 Eh 21
Bonavista Bay ~ **CDN** 61 Eh 21
Bonavista Peninsula ⌒ **CDN** 61 Eh 21
Boncuk D. △ **TR** 195 Hg 27
Bonda ○ **G** 332 Gn 46
Bondari ○ **RUS** 181 Hp 19
Bondo ○ **RDC** 324 Hd 44
Bondo ○ **RDC** 333 Hb 45
Bondo ○ **ANG** 340 Hb 54
Bondoc Peninsula ⌒ **RP** 267 Lm 39
Bondoc Point ⌓ **RP** 267 Lm 39
Bondoukou ○ **CI** 317 Ge 41
Bondoukui ○ **BF** 317 Gd 40
Bondowoso ○ **RI** 279 Lg 49
Bonds Cay ◬ **BS** 87 Dk 33
Bondurant ○ **USA** 51 Cg 24
Bone ~ **RI** 275 Lm 45
Bone ○ **RI** 282 Ll 48
Boné ○ **RMM** 305 Ge 38
Bonebone ○ **RI** 282 Ll 47
Bone-Dumoga National Park ♀ **RI** 275 Lm 45
Bonelipu ○ **RI** 282 Lm 48
Bonelohe ○ **RI** 282 Ll 48
Bonépoupa ○ **CAM** 320 Gm 43
Bonete ~ **RA** 136 Dp 60
Bonfim ○ **BR** 112 Ed 44
Bonfim ○ **BR** 117 Ea 48
Bonfim ○ **BR** 120 Eg 48
Bonfim do Arari ○ **BR** 121 El 47
Bonfinópolis de Minas ○ **BR** 133 Em 54
Bonga ○ **PNG** 287 Mk 49
Bonga ○ **ETH** 325 Hl 42
Bongabon ○ **RP** 267 Ll 38
Bongandanga ○ **RDC** 333 Hc 45
Bongaon ○ **IND** 235 Kj 34
Bongār ○ **IR** 226 Jj 30
Bong Co ~ **VRC** 231 Kk 30
Bongimba ○ **RDC** 333 Hc 47
Bongka ~ **RI** 282 Ll 46
Bongkok ○ **MAL** 270 Lb 43
Bongolava ⌒ **RM** 345 Ja 55
Bongo Massif ⛰ **RCA** 321 Hc 41
Bongor ○ **TCH** 321 Gp 40
Bongouanou ○ **CI** 317 Gd 42
Bonguélé ○ **RCA** 321 Ha 43
Bonham ○ **USA** 70 Cp 29
Boni ○ **RMM** 305 Ge 38
Boni ○ **BF** 317 Ge 40
Boniérédougou ○ **CI** 317 Gd 41
Bonifacio ○ **F** 185 Gl 25
Bonifay ○ **USA** 86 Df 30
Boninal ○ **BR** 125 Ep 52
Bonito ○ **BR** 121 El 46
Bonito ○ **BR** 124 Fc 50
Bonito ○ **BR** 125 Ep 51
Bonito ~ **BR** 133 Ej 54
Bonito ○ **BR** 140 Ef 56
Bon Jesus ○ **ANG** 340 Gn 50
Bonjol ○ **RI** 270 La 45
Bonkoukou ○ **RN** 308 Gh 39
Bonkovac ○ **HR** 174 Gp 23
Bonn ○ **D** 163 Gk 20
Bonne Bay ~ **CDN** 61 Ee 21
Bonnechere ★ **CDN** 60 Dk 23
Bonnechere Caves ★ **CDN** 60 Dk 23
Bonners Ferry ○ **USA** 50 Cd 21
Bonneville ○ **USA** 71 Dg 27
Bonneville Salt Flats ~ **USA** 64 Cf 25
Bonneville Speedway ★ **USA** 64 Cf 25
Bonney Downs ○ **AUS** 360 Lk 57
Bonnie Rock ○ **AUS** 368 Lk 61
Bonny ○ **WAN** 320 Gk 43
Bonoua ○ **CI** 317 Ge 43
Bonshaw ○ **AUS** 375 Mm 60
Bonsoaga ~ **BF** 317 Gg 39
Bontang ○ **RI** 274 Lj 45
Bontebok ★ **ZA** 358 Hc 62
Bonthe ○ **WAL** 316 Fp 42
Bontoc ○ **RP** 267 Ll 37
Bontosunggu ○ **RI** 279 Lk 48
Bonyere ○ **GH** 317 Ge 43
Boobare ○ **AUS** 375 Mj 59
Boodarockin ○ **AUS** 368 Lk 61
Boodie Island Shoals ◬ **AUS** 360 Lh 56
Bookaloo ○ **AUS** 378 Me 61
Book Cliffs ⛰ **USA** 65 Ch 26
Booker T. Washington National Monument ★ **USA** 71 Dh 27
Booko ○ **CI** 304 Gc 41
Boola ○ **RG** 316 Gb 41
Boolardy ○ **AUS** 368 Lj 59
Boolba ○ **AUS** 375 Ml 59
Booligal ○ **AUS** 379 Mj 62
Boomarra ○ **AUS** 365 Mg 55
Boomi ~ **AUS** 375 Ml 60
Boonah ○ **AUS** 375 Mn 60
Boondooma Reservoir ~ **AUS** 375 Mm 59
Boone ○ **USA** 65 Ck 26
Boone ○ **USA** 70 Db 24
Boone ○ **USA** 71 Dh 27
Booneville ○ **USA** 70 Db 28
Booneville ○ **USA** 71 Dd 28
Boonville ○ **USA** 64 Ca 26
Boonville ○ **USA** 70 Db 26
Boonville ○ **USA** 71 De 26
Boopi ~ **BOL** 129 Ea 52
Boorabbin ♀ **AUS** 368 Lk 61
Boorabbin ○ **AUS** 368 Ll 61
Boorama ○ **SP** 328 Hp 41
Boorowa ○ **AUS** 379 Ml 63
Boort ○ **AUS** 379 Mh 64
Boosaaso ○ **SP** 328 Jc 40
Boothbay Harbor ○ **USA** 60 Dp 24
Boothia Peninsula ⌒ **CDN** 7 Ea 2
Boothia Peninsula ◬ **CDN** 42 Fb 4
Booth's ~ **BH** 93 Dd 37
Boothulla ○ **AUS** 375 Mj 59
Booti Booti ♀ **AUS** 379 Mn 62
Booué ○ **G** 332 Gm 46
Bopa ○ **DY** 317 Gg 42
Bopako ○ **RDC** 333 Hc 45
Bopo ○ **WAN** 320 Gk 42
Boqên ○ **VRC** 242 Km 30
Boqueirâ ○ **BR** 133 Em 51
Boqueirão ○ **BR** 116 Dm 49
Boqueirão ○ **BR** 124 Fb 49
Boqueirão do Cesário ○ **BR** 124 Fa 48
Boquerão ○ **BR** 140 Ef 56
Boquerón ○ **C** 101 Dl 36
Boquerón ○ **YV** 107 Dp 41
Boquillas ○ **USA** 81 Cl 31
Boquillas del Carmen ○ **MEX** 81 Cl 31
Boquira ○ **BR** 125 En 52
Bor ○ **RUS** 159 Ja 17
Bor ○ **TR** 195 Hk 27
Bor ○ **RUS** 204 Ua 6
Bor ○ **SUD** 324 Hh 42
Bora ○ **PNG** 286 Mh 49
Bora ⛰ **ETH** 313 Hm 39
Bora Bora ◬ **F** 35 Ba 11
Borabu ○ **THA** 263 Lb 38

Bissorã - Borabu 403

Borah Peak △ USA 50 Cf 23
Borås ○ S 170 Gn 17
Borăzğân ○ IR 215 Jd 31
Borba ○ BR 120 Ee 48
Borbón ○ YV 112 Eb 42
Borbon ○ RP 267 Ln 40
Borçka ○ TR 202 Hn 25
Bordeaux ○ F 184 Gf 23
Bordëbë ○ KS 230 Ka 26
Borden ○ AUS 368 Lk 63
Borden Island ⌒ CDN 42 Ea 3
Borden Peninsula ⌒ CDN 43 Gb 4
Border ○ USA 65 Cg 24
Border Ranges ⛰ AUS 375 Mn 60
Bordertown ○ AUS 378 Mg 64
Borðeyri ○ IS 158 Fk 13
Bord Hûn-e Nou ○ IR 215 Jd 31
Bordighera ○ I 185 Gg 23
Bordj Bou Arreridj ○ DZ 296 Gj 27
Bordj Jenein ○ TN 296 Gl 30
Bordj Messouda ○ DZ 296 Gl 30
Bordj Mokhtar ○ DZ 305 Gg 35
Bordj Omar Driss ○ DZ 296 Gk 31
Bordoloni ○ IND 254 Km 32
Borë ○ ETH 325 Hm 42
Boreda ○ ETH 325 Hl 42
Borensberg ○ S 170 Gp 16
Borgampåd ○ IND 238 Ke 37
Borgarfjörður ○ IS 158 Fp 13
Borgarnes ○ IS 158 Fk 13
Børgefjell △ N 158 Gn 13
Børgefjellet △ N 158 Gn 13
Borger ○ USA 70 Cm 28
Borgholm ○ S 170 Ha 17
Borgi ○ IND 238 Ke 36
Borgu ⌒ DY 320 Gh 41
Borgund ○ N 158 Gk 15
Bori ○ IND 234 Kd 35
Bori ○ DY 317 Gh 41
Bori ○ WAN 320 Gk 43
Boria Tibhu ○ IND 234 Ke 35
Borigumma ○ IND 234 Kf 36
Borisoglebsk ○ RUS 181 Hp 20
Borisovo Sudskoe ○ RUS 171 Hk 16
Boriziny ○ RM 345 Jb 53
Borja ○ PE 116 Dk 48
Borj Bourguiba ○ TN 296 Gl 29
Boû Çtaila ○ RIM 304 Gb 38
Bouctouche ○ CDN 61 Eb 22
Boudamassa ○ TCH 321 Ha 40
Boudiéri ○ BF 317 Gg 39
Boû Djébéha ○ RMM 305 Ge 36
Boudnib ○ MA 293 Ge 30
Boudoua ○ RCA 321 Ha 43
Bouénguidi ⌒ G 332 Gn 46
Bouenza ○ RCB 332 Gn 47
Bougaa ○ DZ 296 Gj 27
Boû Gâdoûm ○ RIM 305 Gc 38
Bougainville Island ⌒ PNG 290 Mp 49
Bougainville Reef ⌒ AUS 365 Mk 53
Bougainville Strait ≈ 290 Mp 49
Bougainville Strait ≈ VU 386 Nf 53
Boughessa ○ RMM 305 Gg 35
Bougounl ○ RMM 305 Gc 40
Bougouriba ～ BF 317 Gd 40
Bougtob ○ DZ 293 Gf 28
Bouira ○ DZ 296 Gj 27
Bou-Ismaïl ○ DZ 296 Gh 27
Bou-Izakarn ○ MA 292 Gb 31
Boujad ○ MA 293 Gc 29
Boujdour ○ MA 292 Fn 32
Bou Kadir ○ DZ 293 Gg 28
Boukân ○ IR 209 Jb 27
Boukô ○ RCA 321 Ha 44
Boukoukola ○ CAM 321 Gn 40
Boukoumbé ○ DY 317 Gg 40
Boukra ○ MA 292 Fp 32
Boulal ○ SN 304 Fn 38
Boulal ○ RMM 305 Gb 38
Boulalbib ○ CAM 321 Gn 41
Boulder ○ USA 51 Cf 22
Boulder ○ USA 51 Cj 24
Boulder ○ USA 65 Ck 25
Boulder ○ USA 368 Ll 61
Boulder City ○ USA 64 Ce 28
Boulé ○ SN 304 Fn 38
Bouli ○ RIM 304 Ga 38
Bouli ⌒ DY 320 Gh 40
Boulia ○ AUS 374 Mf 57
Boulogne-sur-Mer ○ F 163 Gg 20
Boulouba ○ RCA 321 Hc 42
Boulouli ○ RMM 316 Gb 39
Bouloupari ○ F 386 Ne 56
Boulsa ○ BF 317 Gf 39
Boultoum ○ RN 308 Gn 38
Boumalne-du-Dadès ○ MA 293 Gd 30
Boumango ○ G 332 Gn 47
Boumba ～ CAM 321 Gp 44
Boumbé I ○ RCA 321 Gp 43
Boumbé II ～ CAM 321 Gp 43
Boumboum ○ RMM 305 Gf 38
Boumda ○ AUS 378 Ml 64
Bou Mertala ○ RIM 304 Gb 35
Boum Kabir ○ TCH 321 Hb 40
Bou Mréga ○ RIM 304 Ga 37
Bouna ○ CI 317 Gd 41
Boû Nâga ○ RIM 304 Fp 36
Boundary Mountains △△ USA 60 Dn 23
Boundary Peak △ USA 64 Cc 27
Boundiali ○ CI 305 Gc 41
Boundji ○ RCB 332 Gn 46
Boundou ○ SN 316 Fp 39
Boungou ～ RCA 321 Hc 42
Boungou ○ RCA 321 Hc 42
Bounkiling ○ SN 316 Fn 39
Boun Nua ○ LAO 254 La 35
Bountiful ○ USA 65 Cg 25
Bountiful Islands ⌒ AUS 365 Mf 54
Bounty Island ⌒ NZ 35 Tb 14
Bounty Trough ♀ NZ 383 Nl 69
Bouquet ○ F 184 Gf 23
Bourail ○ F 386 Ne 56
Boura ○ BF 317 Ge 40
Bourbonnais ○ F 163 Gh 22
Bourbonne-les-Bains ○ F 163 Gj 21
Bourem ○ RMM 305 Gf 37
Bôurg-en-Bresse ○ F 163 Gj 22
Bourgeneuf ○ F 184 Gg 23

Bote ○ IND 238 Kb 36
Boteka ○ RDC 333 Hb 46
Botemola ○ RDC 333 Hb 47
Boteti ～ RB 349 Hd 56
Botev △ BG 194 He 24
Bothaville ○ ZA 349 Hf 59
Bothwell ○ AUS 378 Mk 67
Botlih ○ RUS 202 Jb 24
Bot Makak ○ CAM 320 Gm 43
Boto-Pasi ○ SME 113 Eg 43
Botoşani ○ RO 175 Hf 22
Botou ○ VRC 246 Lj 26
Botou ○ BF 317 Gg 39
Botro ○ CI 317 Gd 42
Botshabelo ○ ZA 349 Hf 60
Botswana □ RB 349 Hd 56
Bottenhavet ～ S 159 Hb 15
Bottenviken ～ S 159 Hc 13
Botterkloof △ ZA 348 Hb 61
Bottineau ○ USA 56 Cm 21
Bottle Creek ○ GB 101 Dm 35
Botucatu ○ BR 141 Ek 57
Botulu ○ RUS 22 Qb 3
Botumirim ○ BR 125 En 54
Botuporã ○ BR 125 En 52
Botwood ○ CDN 61 Eg 21
Bou ～ CI 317 Gd 41
Bouaflé ○ CI 305 Gc 42
Bou Akba ○ DZ 292 Gc 31
Bouake ○ CI 317 Gd 42
Boualem ○ DZ 293 Gg 29
Bou Ali ○ DZ 293 Gf 32
Bouam ○ CAM 321 Gn 43
Bouânane ○ MA 293 Ge 29
Bouandougou ○ CI 317 Gd 41
Bouanri ○ BF 317 Gg 40
Bouansa ○ RCB 332 Gn 48
Bouar ○ RCA 321 Gp 43
Bouârfa ○ MA 293 Ge 29
Boubélé ○ CI 305 Gc 43
Boubon ○ RN 317 Gg 39
Boubouri ○ CI 317 Gd 43
Bouca ○ RCA 321 Hb 42
Boucaut Bay ～ AUS 364 Md 51
Bouches de Bonifacio ～ F 185 Gf 24
Bouchouaymiy ○ MA 304 Fm 34
Bouderia ～ RM 345 Jb 53
Borja ○ PE 116 Dk 48
Borås...

□ Country ▣ Capital city ⊙ Administrative unit ○ Place ⩓ Island ⋀⋀ Mountain range △ Mountain ⌓ Cape ≈ Ocean, Sea ~ Lake, River ∀ Undersea topography ▲ Glacier ♀ National park ••• Reservation ★ Point of major interest ⌒ Landscape

Buckingham Bay ~ AUS 364 Md 52
Buckingham Downs ○ AUS 374 Mf 57
Buckland ○ USA 46 Aj 13
Buckland River ~ USA 46 Aj 13
Buckley Bay ≈ 38 Sb 17
Bucklin ○ USA 70 Cn 27
Bucksport ○ USA 60 Dp 23
Buco Zau ○ ANG 332 Gn 48
Bucyrus ○ USA 71 Dg 25
Budaka ○ EAU 325 Hj 45
Budalia ○ AUS 374 Mf 57
Budalin ○ MYA 254 Km 34
Budapest ▣ H 174 Hb 22
Búðardalur ○ IS 158 Fk 13
Budaun ○ IND 234 Kd 32
Bud Bud ○ SP 328 Jb 43
Buddabuddah ○ AUS 379 Mk 61
Budd Coast ≈ 38 Qb 16
Buddha ★ J 251 Mf 28
Buddha Park ★ THA 263 Lc 38
Buddhist Mon. ★ IND 234 Kc 34
Budelun Island ⩓ PNG 287 Mn 50
Buděnnovsk ○ RUS 202 Ja 23
Budgewoi ○ AUS 379 Mm 62
Buding ○ RI 278 Ld 47
Buðir ○ IS 158 Fj 13
Budjala ○ RDC 333 Hb 44
Budogošč' ○ RUS 171 Hj 16
Budongquan ○ VRC 231 Kl 28
Budungbudung ~ RI 279 Lk 47
Budva ○ MON 194 Hb 24
Buéa ○ CAM 320 Gl 43
Buedu ○ WAL 316 Ga 41
Buefjorden ~ N 158 Gj 15
Buela ○ ANG 332 Gp 48
Buena Esperanza ○ RA 137 Eb 63
Buenaventura ○ MEX 80 Cj 31
Buenaventura ○ MEX 93 Dd 35
Buenaventura ○ C 101 Dk 35
Buenaventura ○ CO 106 Dk 44
Buena Vista ○ USA 65 Cj 26
Buena Vista ○ USA 74 Dj 27
Buena Vista ○ USA 86 Df 29
Buena Vista ○ YV 107 Dp 42
Buena Vista ○ BOL 129 Ea 51
Buena Vista ○ BOL 129 Ec 54
Buena Vista ○ RA 136 Ea 59
Buena Vista ○ PY 140 Ef 59
Buenavista ○ RP 267 Ll 39
Buenavista ○ RP 275 Lm 42
Buena Vista Island ⩓ SOL 290 Nb 50
Buenavista Tomatlán ○ MEX 92 Cl 36
Buenga ~ ANG 333 Ha 49
Bueno Brandão ○ BR 141 El 57
Buenópolis ○ BR 133 Em 54
Bueno Rahue ~ RCH 147 Dm 66
Buenos Aires ○ CR 97 Dg 41
Buenos Aires ○ CO 106 Dl 43
Buenos Aires ○ CO 117 Dn 47
Buenos Aires ▣ RA 146 Ee 64
Buen Pasto ○ RA 152 Dp 68
Bueramma ○ BR 125 Fa 53
Buesaco ○ CO 106 Dk 45
Bueyeros ○ USA 65 Cl 28
Búfala ○ MEX 80 Ck 32
Bufareh ○ RI 286 Mf 47
Buffalo ○ CDN 51 Cg 20
Buffalo ○ USA 51 Cj 23
Buffalo ○ USA 51 Cl 23
Buffalo ○ USA 56 Cp 22
Buffalo ○ USA 56 Da 23
Buffalo ○ USA 60 Dj 24
Buffalo ○ USA 70 Cn 27
Buffalo ○ USA 70 Db 27
Buffalo ~ USA 70 Db 28
Buffalo ○ USA 81 Da 30
Buffalo Bill Ranch S.H.P. ★ USA 70 Cm 25
Buffalo Bill Reservoir ~ USA 51 Ch 23
Buffalo City East London ○ ZA 358 Hf 62
Buffalo Lake ~ CDN 47 Cc 15
Buffalo Lake ~ CDN 51 Cf 19
Buffalo Natl. Riv. ♀ USA 70 Db 27
Buffalo Range ○ ZW 352 Hh 56
Buffels Drift ○ ZA 349 Hf 57
Buffelsrivier ~ ZA 348 Ha 60
Buffelsrivier ~ ZA 352 Hh 60
Buffé Noir ○ CAM 321 Gn 41
Buford ○ USA 65 Ck 25
Buford ○ USA 86 Df 29
Buftea ○ RO 175 Hf 23
Bug ~ PL 170 Hd 19
Buga ○ CO 106 Dk 44
Buga ○ WAN 320 Gk 41
Bugadi ○ EAU 325 Hj 45
Bugdajly ○ TM 222 Jf 26
Bugene ○ EAT 336 Hh 46
Buggayq ○ KSA 215 Jc 33
Bugi ○ RI 286 Mf 47
Bugingkalo ○ RI 282 Ll 48
Bugiri ○ EAU 325 Hj 45
Bugojno ○ BIH 174 Ha 23
Bugrino ○ RUS 19 Ma 3
Bugrino ○ RUS 154 Ra 5
Bugsuk Island ⩓ RP 266 Lj 41
Bugt Shan △ VRC 242 Kn 27
Buguey ○ RP 267 Ll 36
Bugui Point ⌓ RP 267 Lm 39
Buhairat al-Burullus ~ ET 301 Hh 30
Buhairat al-Manzila ~ ET 301 Hh 30
Buhairat at-Timsāḥ l-Murra ~ ET 301 Hj 30
Buḥairat Nūba ~ SUD 301 Hh 35
Buhairat Šārī ~ IRQ 209 Ja 28
Bu He ~ VRC 242 Kp 27
Buhera ○ ZW 341 Hh 55
Buhl ○ USA 64 Ce 24
Buhlandshahr ○ IND 234 Kc 31
Buhoro ○ EAT 336 Hh 48
Buick ○ CDN 47 Ca 17
Bū'in ○ IR 209 Jc 28
Buin ○ PNG 290 Mp 49
Bui National Park ♀ GH 317 Ge 41
Buinsk ○ RUS 181 Jb 18
Buíque ○ BR 124 Fb 50
Buir Nur ~ MNG 204 Vc 9
Buitepos ○ NAM 348 Hb 57
Buitsivango ~ RB 348 Hc 57
Buiucu ○ BR 120 Ef 48
Buj ○ RUS 171 Hn 16
Bujanovac ○ SCG 194 Hc 24
Bujaraloz ○ E 184 Gf 25
Bujaru ○ BR 121 Ek 46
Buji ○ PNG 286 Mh 50
Bujnaksk ○ RUS 202 Jb 24
Bujumbura ▣ BU 336 Hg 47
Buka ○ UZB 223 Jn 25
Bukaan ○ RI 275 Ll 45
Bukadaban Feng △ VRC 231 Kk 27
Buka Island ⩓ PNG 290 Mp 48
Bukakata ○ EAU 336 Hj 46
Bukalo ○ NAM 341 He 54
Bukama ○ RDC 336 He 50
Bu Kammāsh ○ LAR 297 Gm 29
Bukantov toglari ⋀⋀ UZB 223 Jk 24
Bukavu ○ RDC 336 Hg 47
Bukedea ○ EAU 325 Hk 45
Bukene ○ EAT 336 Hj 48
Bukhara ○ UZB 19 Na 6
Bukhara ○ UZB 223 Jk 26
Bukima ○ EAT 337 Hj 46
Bukit Batu △ MAL 274 Lg 44
Bukitkemuning ○ RI 278 Lc 48
Bukittinggi ○ RI 270 Kp 46
Bükk ⋀⋀ H 174 Hc 22
Bukoba ○ EAT 336 Hh 46
Bukombe ○ EAT 336 Hj 47
Bukrane ○ RI 283 Mb 49
Būl △ IR 215 Je 30
Bula ○ PNG 286 Mg 50
Bula ○ GNB 316 Fn 39
Bula ○ RDC 324 Hg 45
Bula Atumba ○ ANG 332 Gp 50
Bula Derq Plain ⌒ EAK 325 Hm 44
Bulahdelah ○ AUS 379 Mn 62
Bulaka ~ RI 286 Mf 49
Bulalacao Island ⩓ RP 267 Ll 40
Bulalakao ○ RP 267 Ll 39
Bulancak ○ TR 195 Hm 25
Bulanghee ○ VRC 243 Le 26
Bulangu ○ WAN 320 Gl 39
Bulanik ○ TR 202 Hp 26
Būlāq ○ ET 301 Hh 33
Bulawayo ○ ZW 349 Hf 56
Bulaya ○ Z 336 Hg 50
Bulbodney ~ AUS 379 Mk 62
Bulbuta ○ ETH 325 Hm 42
Buldan ○ TR 195 Hg 26
Buldāna ○ IND 234 Kc 35
Buldibuyo ○ PE 116 Dk 50
Buleleng ○ RI 282 Ll 47
Buleleng ○ RI 282 Lm 47
Bulga Downs ○ AUS 368 Lk 60
Bulgan ○ MNG 204 Uc 9
Bulgaria □ BG 194 Hd 24
Bulguksa Temple ★ ROK 247 Ma 28
Buli ○ RI 275 Ma 45
Bū Līfiyat ○ UAE 215 Je 33
Bulimba ○ AUS 365 Mh 54
Bulinga ○ GH 317 Ge 41
Bulisa ○ EAU 324 Hh 44
Buliya ⩓ FJI 387 Nm 55
Bullabulling ○ AUS 368 Ll 61
Bullara ○ AUS 360 Lh 57
Bullaxaar ○ SP 328 Ja 40
Bullecourt ○ AUS 374 Mf 56
Bullfinch ○ AUS 368 Lk 61
Bullhead City ○ USA 64 Ce 28
Bulli ○ AUS 379 Mm 63
Bullita Out Station ○ AUS 364 Mb 54
Bull Mountains ⋀⋀ USA 51 Ch 22
Bullock's Harbour ○ BS 87 Dj 33
Bulloo ~ AUS 374 Mh 60
Bulloo Downs ○ AUS 368 Lk 58
Bullo River ○ AUS 364 Ma 53
Bulls ○ NZ 383 Nk 66
Bulls Bay ~ USA 87 Dj 29
Bull Shoals Lake ~ USA 70 Db 27
Büllsport ○ NAM 348 Ha 58
Bulman ○ AUS 364 Md 52
Bulnes ○ RCH 137 Dm 64
Bulongo ○ RDC 333 Hc 48
Buloo ~ AUS 375 Mj 58
Bulqize ○ AL 194 Hc 25
Bultfontein ○ ZA 349 He 60
Bulu ○ PNG 287 Mn 47
Buluan ○ RP 275 Ln 42
Buluan ~ RP 275 Ln 42
Buluan Lake ~ RP 275 Ln 42
Bulukumba ○ RI 279 Lk 48
Bulukutu ○ RDC 333 Hc 46
Bulula ○ RDC 336 Hf 48
Bulumuri ○ PNG 287 Mm 48
Bulun ~ RUS 205 Yb 5
Bulungu ○ RDC 333 Hb 48
Bulungu ○ RDC 333 Hc 49
Bulunkol ○ VRC 230 Kb 26
Bulusan ○ RP 267 Ln 39
Bulusan Vulcano △ RP 267 Lm 39
Bulwana ○ NAM 348 Hb 58
Buma ~ RDC 333 Ha 47
Bumba ○ RDC 321 Hd 44
Būmbah ○ LAR 300 Hd 29
Bumbire Island ⩓ EAT 336 Hh 46
Bumbuna ○ WAL 316 Ga 41
Bumiayu ○ RI 278 Le 49
Bumi Hills ○ ZW 341 Hg 54
Bumiphol Dam ~ THA 262 Kp 37
Buna ○ EAK 325 Hm 44
Buna ○ RDC 333 Hb 47
Bunabun ○ PNG 287 Mj 48
Bunam ○ PNG 287 Mj 48
Bunbury ○ AUS 368 Lh 62
Buncagaan ○ MNG 204 Ub 9
Buncrana ○ IRL 162 Gc 18
Bunda ○ EAT 337 Hj 47
Bundaberg ○ AUS 375 Mn 58
Bunda Bunda ○ AUS 374 Mh 56
Bundarra ○ AUS 379 Mm 61
Bundeena ○ AUS 374 Mh 59
Bundey ~ AUS 374 Md 57
Bündi ○ IND 234 Kb 33
Bundi ○ PNG 287 Mj 48
Bundibugyo ○ EAU 324 Hh 45
Bundjalung ♀ AUS 375 Mn 60
Bunduqiya ○ SUD 324 Hh 43
Bunga ~ RDC 324 He 45
Bungadi ○ RDC 324 Hf 43
Bungamas ○ RI 278 Lb 47
Bungbulang ○ RI 278 Ld 49
Bungil Creek ~ AUS 375 Ml 59
Bung Kan ○ THA 255 Lb 36
Bungku ○ RI 282 Ll 47
Bungle Bungle Purnululu ♀ AUS 364 Ma 54
Bungo ○ ANG 332 Gp 49
Bungoma ○ EAK 325 Hk 45
Bungo-suido ~ J 247 Mb 29
Bungtlang ○ IND 254 Kl 34
Bungu ○ RDC 333 Hb 46
Bungunya ○ AUS 375 Ml 60
Buni ~ RI 278 Ld 49
Buni ○ WAN 320 Gn 40
Bunia ○ RDC 324 Hh 45
Bunie ○ RDC 324 Hf 44
Bunji ○ PK 230 Kb 28
Bunker ○ USA 70 Dc 27
Bunker Group ⩓ AUS 375 Mn 57
Bunkeya ○ RDC 341 Hf 51
Bunkie ○ USA 86 Db 30
Bunneringee ○ AUS 378 Mg 62
Bunsuru ~ WAN 320 Gk 39
Bunta ○ RI 282 Lm 46
Buntharig ○ THA 263 Lc 38
Buntok ○ RI 279 Lh 46
Bunyakiri ○ RDC 336 Hg 47
Bunya Mountains ♀ AUS 375 Mm 59
Bünyan ○ TR 195 Hk 26
Bunza ○ WAN 320 Gj 39
Buôn Me Thuôt ○ VN 263 Le 39
Bu Plateau ⋀⋀ WAN 320 Gm 40
Buqda Caqable ○ SP 328 Ja 43
Bura ○ EAK 337 Hm 46
Buraan ○ SP 328 Jc 40
Buraen ○ RI 282 Lm 51
Buraika △ YE 219 Jc 38
Burakin ○ AUS 368 Lj 61
Buram ○ SUD 312 He 40
Burang ○ VRC 230 Ke 30
Buranhem ~ BR 125 Fa 54
Burāq ○ SYR 208 Hl 29
Burauen ○ RP 267 Ln 40
Buraydah ○ KSA 214 Hp 32
Burbank ○ USA 64 Cc 28
Burcher ○ AUS 379 Mk 62
Burchun ○ VRC 22 Pa 5
Burco ○ SP 328 Ja 41
Burdalyk ○ TM 223 Jl 26
Burdäspur ○ IND 230 Kb 29
Burdekin Fall Dam ~ AUS 375 Mk 56
Burden ○ USA 70 Cp 27
Burdeos ○ RP 267 Ll 38
Burdulba ○ AUS 364 Mc 52
Burdur ○ TR 195 Hh 27
Burdur G. ~ TR 195 Hh 27
Burē ○ ETH 313 Hl 40
Bureïmi ○ RN 320 Gh 39
Bureinskiy Khrebet ⋀⋀ RUS 205 Wc 9
Burejnskoe vodohranilišče ~ RUS 205 Wc 8
Burell ○ AL 194 Hc 25
Burengapara ○ IND 235 Kk 33
Bureo ~ RCH 137 Dm 64
Búrfell ○ IS 158 Fl 13
Burğ ○ OM 219 Je 36
Burg'al-'Arab ○ ET 301 Hg 30
Burgas ○ BG 195 Hf 24
Burgaw ○ USA 74 Dk 28
Burgdorf ○ USA 50 Ce 23
Burgenland ⊙ A 174 Ha 22
Burgeo ○ CDN 61 Ef 22
Burgeo Bank ∀ 61 Ee 22
Burgersdorp ○ ZA 349 He 61
Burgersfort ○ ZA 349 Hg 58
Burgers Pass △ ZA 358 Hb 62
Burgess Junction ○ USA 51 Cj 23
Burgos ○ E 184 Ge 24
Burgos ○ RP 267 Lk 37
Burgsvik ○ S 170 Hb 17
Burhaiye ○ TR 195 Hf 26
Burhan Budai Shan ⋀⋀ VRC 242 Km 28
Burhānpur ○ IND 234 Kc 35
Buri ○ BR 141 Ek 57
Burias Island ⩓ RP 267 Lm 39
Burias Passage ~ RP 267 Lm 39
Burin ○ CDN 61 Eg 22
Burin Peninsula ⌒ CDN 61 Eg 22
Buri Ram ○ THA 263 Lb 38
Buritama ○ BR 140 Ej 56
Buriti ~ BR 140 Eg 56
Buriti Alegre ○ BR 133 Ek 55
Buriti Bravo ○ BR 124 En 48
Buriticupu ○ BR 121 El 48
Buriticupu ~ BR 121 El 48
Buriti dos Lopes ○ BR 124 Ep 47
Buritirama ○ BR 125 En 51
Buritis ○ BR 133 El 53
Buritj ~ BR 132 Ee 52
Burjassot ○ E 184 Gf 26
Burji ○ WAN 320 Gl 40
Burkburnett ○ USA 70 Cn 28
Burke ○ USA 56 Cn 24
Burke ~ AUS 374 Mg 56
Burke and Wills Roadhouse ○ AUS 365 Mg 55
Burke Channel ~ CDN 50 Bn 20
Burke's Pass △ ZA 348 Ha 60
Burkesville ○ USA 71 Df 27
Burketown ○ AUS 365 Mf 54
Burkeville ○ USA 74 Dj 27
Burkina Faso □ BF 317 Gf 39
Burleigh ○ AUS 374 Mh 56
Burleson ○ USA 70 Cp 29
Burley ○ USA 64 Cf 24
Burlingame ○ USA 70 Da 26
Burlington ○ USA 50 Ca 21
Burlington ○ CDN 60 Dj 24
Burlington ○ USA 60 Dm 23
Burlington ○ CDN 61 Eg 21
Burlington ○ USA 65 Cl 26
Burlington ○ USA 70 Da 26
Burlington ○ USA 71 Dc 25
Burlington ○ USA 74 Dj 27
Burma Myanmar □ MYA 254 Km 34
Burndoo ○ AUS 379 Mh 62
Burnet ○ USA 81 Cn 30
Burnett ~ AUS 375 Mm 58
Burnett Range ⋀⋀ AUS 375 Mm 58
Burnham ○ AUS 374 Mg 57
Burnpur ○ IND 235 Kh 34
Burns ○ USA 50 Cc 24
Burns ○ USA 65 Cj 26
Burnside River ~ CDN 47 Cg 11
Burns Junction ○ USA 64 Cd 24
Burns Lake ○ CDN 42 Db 8
Burntbush ~ CDN 57 Dh 21
Burntbush River ~ CDN 57 Dh 21
Burnt Ranch ○ USA 64 Ca 25
Burny ○ AUS 378 Mj 66
Burqin ○ VRC 204 Tc 9
Burra ○ AUS 378 Mf 62
Burramurra ○ AUS 374 Me 56
Burras ~ PY 136 Ea 57
Burras ~ RA 136 Ea 57
Burrendong Reservoir ~ AUS 379 Ml 62
Burren Junction ○ AUS 379 Ml 61
Burrgum Hill △ AUS 375 Mn 58
Burrinjuck ~ AUS 379 Ml 63
Burris ○ USA 51 Cj 24
Burrton ○ USA 70 Cp 26
Burrum Heads ○ AUS 375 Mn 58
Burruyacu ○ RA 136 Eb 59
Burrville ○ USA 65 Cg 26
Bursa ○ TR 195 Hg 25
Bur Safajah ○ ET 301 Hj 32
Bur Tinle ○ SP 328 Jb 42
Burton ○ USA 57 Dg 24
Burton ○ USA 71 Dh 29
Burträsk ○ S 159 Hc 13
Buru Island ⩓ RI 286 Mh 50
Burūm ○ YE 219 Jc 38
Burumburum ○ WAN 320 Gl 40
Burundi □ BU 336 Hg 47
Buruntuma ○ GNB 316 Fn 39
Bururi ○ BU 336 Hg 47
Bururu ○ RDC 333 Hb 45
Buruti ~ BR 124 En 47
Burwell ○ USA 70 Cn 25
Burwick ○ GB 162 Ge 16
Bury ○ GB 163 Gg 19
Buṣaira ○ SYR 209 Hn 28
Busanga ○ RDC 333 Hc 46
Busanga ○ RDC 341 He 51
Busanga Swamp ⌒ Z 341 He 53
Busango ○ RDC 336 He 50
Būšehr ○ IR 215 Jd 31
Busembatia ○ EAU 325 Hj 45
Būshehr ○ IR 215 Jd 31
Bushenyi ○ EAU 336 Hh 46
Bushy Park ○ AUS 361 Mc 57
Busia ○ EAU 325 Hj 45
Businga ○ RDC 321 Hc 44
Busira ~ RDC 333 Hb 46
Busisi ○ EAT 336 Hj 47
Bus'k ○ UA 175 He 21
Buško jezero ~ BIH 194 Ha 24
Busonga ○ EAK 325 Hk 45
Buṣra aš-Šām ○ SYR 208 Hl 29
Busseri ~ SUD 324 Hf 42
Buston ○ TJ 223 Jn 25
Busuanga ○ RP 267 Lk 39
Busuanga Island ⩓ RP 267 Ll 39
Busu-Bongo ○ RDC 333 Hc 45
Busu-Djanoa ○ RDC 333 Hc 45
Busu-Kwanga ○ RDC 333 Hc 45
Busu-Mandji ○ RDC 321 Hc 44
Busungwe ○ EAU 336 Hh 46
Busunju ○ EAU 324 Hj 45
Busunu ○ GH 317 Gf 41
Busu-Yele ○ RDC 333 Hb 45
But ○ PNG 286 Mh 47
Buta ○ RDC 324 He 44
Butajīra ○ ETH 325 Hm 41
Butak ○ PK 226 Jk 31
Butan ○ RP 267 Ln 41
Buta Ranquil ○ RA 137 Dn 64
Butare ○ RWA 336 Hg 47
Butaritari ⩓ KIR 27 Tb 9
Butat Raya ~ SUD 312 He 40
Butat Raye ~ SUD 312 He 40
Bute ○ AUS 378 Me 62
Bute Giarti ○ ETH 325 Hl 43
Butembo ○ RDC 324 Hg 45
Butha Buthe ○ LS 349 Hg 60
Buthidaung ○ MYA 235 Kl 35
Butiaba ○ EAU 324 Hh 45
Butler ○ USA 71 Df 25
Butler ○ USA 74 Dj 25
Butler ○ USA 86 Dd 29
Butler ○ USA 86 Df 29
Butler ○ AUS 378 Me 63
Butler Creek ~ CDN 57 Dh 20
Butrinti ★ AL 194 Hc 26
Butru ○ AUS 374 Mf 56
Butte ○ USA 51 Cf 22
Butte ○ USA 56 Cn 24
Butterworth ○ MAL 270 La 43
Butterworth ○ ZA 358 Hg 62
Butt of Lewis ⌓ GB 162 Gc 16
Butu ○ RI 279 Lk 47
Butuan ○ RP 267 Ln 41
Butuan Bay ~ RP 267 Ln 41
Butung ⩓ RI 282 Lm 48
Butuo ○ VRC 255 Lb 32
Butuo ○ LB 316 Gb 42
Buturlinovka ○ RUS 181 Hn 20
Butwal ○ NEP 235 Kf 32
Buulo Burte ○ SP 328 Ja 44
Buulo Xaawo ○ SP 325 Hn 44
Buurdhuubo ○ SP 325 Hn 44
Buur Gaabo ○ SP 337 Hn 46
Buur Hakkaba ○ SP 329 Ja 44
Buur Heybe △ SP 329 Ja 44
Buvuma Island ⩓ EAU 325 Hj 45
Buwenge ○ EAU 325 Hj 45
Buxar ○ IND 235 Kf 33
Buxton ○ GUY 113 Ef 42
Büyer A mad-o-kühgīlūye ⊙ IR 215 Jd 30
Buyo ○ CI 305 Gc 42
Büyükmenderes Nehri ~ TR 195 Hg 26
Buyuni ○ EAT 337 Hm 49
Buyun Shan △ VRC 246 Lm 25
Buzan ~ RUS 202 Jc 22
Buzău ○ RO 175 Hf 23
Buzău ~ RO 175 Hf 23
Buzi ○ MOC 344 Hk 55
Buzi ~ MOC 344 Hk 55
Buzi Gonbad ○ AFG 230 Ka 27
Búzios ○ BR 124 Fc 49
Buzuluk ~ RUS 181 Hp 20
Bwagaoia ○ PNG 287 Mn 51
Bwana-Mutombo ○ RDC 333 Hb 49
Bwanga ○ EAT 336 Hh 47
Bwari ○ WAN 320 Gk 41
Bwatnapné ○ VU 386 Nf 53
Bwele-Milonda ○ RDC 333 Hb 49
Bweni ○ EAT 337 Hm 49
Bwiam ○ WAG 316 Fm 39
Byahomľ ○ BY 171 Hf 18
Byam Martin Channel ~ CDN 7 Ea 2
Byam Martin Channel ≈ CDN 42 Ec 3
Byam Martin Island ⩓ CDN 42 Ec 4
Byarezina ~ BY 171 Hg 19
Byaroza ○ BY 171 He 19
Byblos ★ RL 208 Hk 28
Bychav ○ BY 171 Hg 19
Bydgoszcz ○ PL 170 Ha 19
Byerazino ○ BY 171 Hg 19
Byeshankovichy ○ BY 171 Hg 18
Byfield ○ AUS 375 Mm 57
Byfield ♀ AUS 375 Mm 57
Byford ○ AUS 368 Lj 62
Bygdeå ○ S 159 Hc 14
Bygland ○ N 170 Gk 16
Bykle ○ N 170 Gk 16
Bylas ○ USA 65 Cg 29
Bylong ○ AUS 379 Mm 62
Bylot Island ⩓ CDN 43 Gc 4
Bynoe ~ AUS 365 Mg 54
Býrðabungar △ IS 158 Fm 13
Byro ○ AUS 368 Lj 59
Byrock ○ AUS 379 Mk 61
Byron Bay ~ AUS 375 Mn 60
Byron Sound ~ GB 147 Ed 71
Byske ○ S 159 Hc 13
Byskeälven ~ S 159 Hc 13
Bytantaj ~ RUS 205 Wc 5
Bytom ○ PL 174 Hb 20
Bytów ○ PL 170 Ha 18
Byumba ○ RWA 336 Hg 46
Byxelkrok ○ S 170 Ha 17
Bzyb' ~ GE 202 Hn 24

C

C. Sandburg Home N.H.S. ★ USA 71 Dg 28
Caacupé ○ PY 140 Ef 58
Caaguazú ○ PY 140 Eg 58
Caala ○ ANG 340 Gp 52
Caapiranga ○ BR 120 Ed 47
Caapucú ○ PY 140 Ef 59
Caarapó ○ BR 140 Eg 57
Caatiba ○ BR 125 Ep 53
Caatinga ○ BR 133 Em 54
Caazapá ○ PY 140 Ef 59
Cabacal ~ BR 132 Ee 53
Cabaceiras ○ BR 124 Fb 49
Cabadbaran ○ RP 267 Ln 41
Cabaiguán ○ C 100 Dj 34
Cabalete Island ⩓ RP 267 Ll 38
Caballo ○ USA 65 Cj 29
Caballococha ○ PE 117 Dn 47
Caballo Reservoir ~ USA 65 Cj 29
Cabañas ○ C 100 Dg 34
Cabanatuan ○ RP 267 Ll 38
Cabano ○ CDN 60 Dp 22
Cabarete ○ DOM 101 Dn 36
Cabatuan ○ RP 267 Ll 37
Cabaza del Mar ○ RCH 152 Dn 72
Cabazas ○ BOL 129 Ec 55
Cabeça do Apa ○ BR 140 Eg 57
Cabecea do Salsa ~ BR 117 Ec 48
Cabeceiras ○ BR 133 El 53
Cabedelo ○ BR 124 Fc 49
Cabildo ○ RCH 137 Dn 62
Cabimas ○ YV 107 Dn 40
Cabinda ○ ANG 332 Gm 48
Cabinda ⊙ ANG 332 Gm 48
Cabinet Mountains ⋀⋀ USA 50 Cd 21
Cabingaan Island ⩓ RP 275 Ll 43
Cabitutu ~ BR 120 Ef 49
Cabo Aristizábal ⌓ RA 152 Ea 68
Cabo Augusta ⌓ CO 106 Dl 40
Cabo Beata ⌓ DOM 101 Dn 36
Cabo Blanco ⌓ RA 152 Eb 69
Cabo Caçiporé ⌓ BR 113 Ej 44
Cabo Camarón ⌓ HN 100 Df 37
Cabo Carrientes ⌓ CO 106 Dk 43
Cabo Catoche ⌓ MEX 93 De 35
Cabo Codera ⌓ YV 107 Ea 40
Cabo Colonett ⌓ MEX 75 Cd 30
Cabo Corrientes ⌓ MEX 92 Cj 35
Cabo Corrientes ⌓ C 100 Df 35
Cabo Cruz ⌓ C 100 Dj 36
Cabo Daňoso ⌓ RA 152 Ea 70
Cabo de Gracias a Dios ⌓ NIC 97 Dg 38
Cabo de la Vela ⌓ CO 107 Dm 39
Cabo de la Vela ⌓ CO 107 Dm 39
Cabo Delgado ⌓ MOC 344 Hn 51
Cabo del Gata ⌓ E 184 Ge 27
Cabo del Salina ⌓ E 185 Gh 26
Cabo de Palos ⌓ E 184 Gf 27
Cabo de San Antonio ⌓ C 100 Df 35
Cabo de San Francisco ⌓ EC 116 Dh 45
Cabo de San Juan de Guia ⌓ CO 106 Dl 40
Cabo de Santa Marta ⌓ BR 141 Ek 60
Cabo de Santo Agostinho ○ BR 124 Fc 50
Cabo de São Tomé ⌓ BR 141 Ep 56
Cabo de São Vicente ⌓ P 184 Gb 27
Cabo Deseado ⌓ RCH 152 Dl 72
Cabo de Sines ⌓ P 184 Gb 27
Cabo de Sta. Maria ⌓ P 184 Gc 27
Cabo do Norte ⌓ BR 121 Ek 45
Cabo dos Bahías ⌓ RA 152 Eb 68
Cabo dos Búzios ⌓ BR 141 Ep 57
Cabo Dyer ⌓ RCH 152 Dl 70
Cabo Engaño ⌓ DOM 101 Dp 36
Cabo Espichel ⌓ P 184 Gb 26
Cabo Falso ⌓ HN 97 Dg 38
Cabo Guardián ⌓ RA 152 Ea 70
Cabo Gurupi ⌓ BR 121 El 46
Cabo Haro ⌓ MEX 81 Cg 32
Cabo Humos ⌓ RCH 137 Dm 63
Cabo Isabela ⌓ DOM 101 Dn 36
Cabo Jorge ⌓ RCH 152 Dl 71
Cabo Ledo ○ ANG 340 Gn 50
Cabo Maguari ⌓ BR 121 Ek 46
Cabo Manglares ⌓ CO 106 Dj 45
Cabonga ~ CDN 60 Dk 22
Cabo Norte ⌓ EC 128 Dd 46
Caboolture ○ AUS 375 Mn 59
Cabo Orange ⌓ BR 113 Ej 43
Cabo Papuica ⌓ RCH 136 Dn 56
Cabo Peñas ⌓ RA 152 Ea 72
Cabo Primero ⌓ RCH 152 Dk 70
Cabo Quilán ⌓ RCH 147 Dl 67
Cabora Bassa Reservoir ~ MOC 341 Hh 53
Cabo Raper ⌓ RCH 152 Dk 69
Caborca ○ MEX 75 Cf 30
Cabo Rojo ⌓ USA 104 Ea 37
Cabo Samaná ⌓ DOM 101 Dp 36
Cabo San Antonio ⌓ RA 146 Ef 64
Cabo San Juan ⌓ GQ 332 Gl 45
Cabo San Lázaro ⌓ MEX 75 Cf 33
Cabo San Lorenzo ⌓ EC 116 Dh 46
Cabo San Lucas ○ MEX 80 Ch 34
Cabo San Quintín ⌓ MEX 75 Cd 30
Cabo San Rafael ⌓ DOM 101 Dp 36
Cabo Santa Elena ⌓ CR 96 De 40
Cabo Santiago ⌓ RCH 152 Dl 71
Cabosse ○ RCB 332 Gn 44
Cabot ○ USA 70 Db 28
Cabo Tablas ⌓ RCH 137 Dn 61
Cabo Tres Montes ⌓ RCH 152 Dl 69
Cabo Tres Puntas ⌓ RA 152 Eb 69
Cabot Strait ~ CDN 61 Ed 22
Cabourg ○ F 163 Gf 21
Cabo Vigia ⌓ RA 152 Ea 70
Cabra Island ⩓ RP 267 Lk 39
Cabral ○ DOM 101 Dn 36
Cabramurra ○ AUS 379 Ml 63
Cabrera ○ DOM 101 Dp 36
Cabrera ○ CO 106 Dl 44
Cabrera ⩓ E 185 Gh 26
Cabrero ○ RCH 137 Dm 64
Cabreúva ○ BR 141 El 57
Cabrobó ○ BR 124 Fa 50
Cabruta ○ YV 107 Ea 42
Cabuauan Island ⩓ RP 267 Ll 40
Cabuca ○ GNB 316 Fn 39
Cabudare ○ YV 107 Dp 41
Cabugao ○ RP 267 Ll 37
Cabu Lort ⌓ RCH 152 Dl 68
Cabure ○ YV 107 Dp 40
Cabuyaro ○ CO 107 Dm 43
Çaçador ○ BR 140 Ej 59
Čačak ○ SCG 194 Hc 24
Cacao ○ F 113 Eh 43
Caçapava do Sul ○ BR 146 Eh 61
Cacaribaiteri ○ YV 112 Eb 44
Cacequi ○ BR 146 Eg 60
Cáceres ○ BR 132 Ef 54
Cáceres ○ E 184 Gc 26
Cachachi ○ PE 116 Dj 49
Cachapoal ~ RCH 137 Dn 63
Cacharel Chapacura ~ BOL 129 Ec 53
Cachari ○ RA 146 Ee 64
Cache ○ USA 70 Cn 28
Cache Creek ○ CDN 50 Cb 20
Cache Peak △ USA 64 Cf 24
Cacheu ○ GNB 316 Fm 39
Cachi ○ RA 136 Ea 58
Cachimbo ○ BR 120 Eg 50
Cachimbo ○ ANG 340 Hc 50
Cachina ~ RCH 136 Dn 58
Cachingues ○ ANG 340 Ha 52
Cachipo ○ YV 112 Eb 41
Cachira ○ CO 107 Dm 42
Cachoeira ○ BR 125 Fa 52
Cachoeira Alta ○ BR 133 Ej 55
Cachoeira Ana ~ BR 120 Ef 45
Cachoeira Anta ~ BR 133 Ek 52
Cachoeira Araras ~ BR 120 Eg 49
Cachoeira Auasinaua ~ BR 112 Ec 45
Cachoeira Bacuri ~ BR 120 Eh 46
Cachoeira Balbina ~ BR 120 Ee 46
Cachoeira Bula ~ BR 117 Dp 45
Cachoeira Cachoeirinha ~ BR 120 Ed 50
Cachoeira Cajuti ~ BR 120 Eg 46
Cachoeira Campo Grande ~ BR 129 Eb 51
Cachoeira Carreira Comprida ~ BR 133 Ek 51
Cachoeira Costá ~ BR 120 Ed 49
Cachoeira Criminosa ~ BR 120 Ed 46
Cachoeira Criminosa ~ BR 129 Eb 51
Cachoeira Cuma ~ BR 117 Dp 45
Cachoeira Cumaru ~ BR 120 Eg 46
Cachoeira da Andorinha ~ BR 120 Ed 50
Cachoeira da Bolinha ~ BR 120 Ed 46
Cachoeira da Farinha ~ BR 120 Ed 49
Cachoeira da Formosa ~ BR 132 Eh 52
Cachoeira da Gloria ~ BR 120 Ed 50
Cachoeira da Laje ~ BR 129 Eb 51
Cachoeira da Porteira ~ BR 120 Ee 50
Cachoeira das Abelhas ~ BR 129 Ed 51
Cachoeira das Docas ~ BR 133 Eh 53
Cachoeira das Garças ~ BR 132 Eg 53
Cachoeira da Trovoada ~ BR 120 Ef 48
Cachoeira da Viração ~ BR 120 Eg 46
Cachoeira de Coroa ~ BR 121 El 49
Cachoeira de Goiás ○ BR 133 Ej 54
Cachoeira de Saudade ~ BR 132 Eh 53
Cachoeira do Arari ○ BR 121 Ek 46
Cachoeira do Caju ~ BR 120 Ed 46
Cachoeira do Coata ~ BR 120 Ed 50
Cachoeira do Ipui ~ BR 120 Ed 50
Cachoeira do Iracaja ~ BR 129 Eb 51
Cachoeira Dois de Novembro ~ BR 117 Ec 50
Cachoeira Dois Irmãos ~ BR 120 Ee 50
Cachoeira do Onça ~ BR 120 Eg 46
Cachoeira do Oriente ~ BR 117 Eb 50

Buckingham Bay - Cachoeira do Oriente 405

Cachoeira do Patauá 〜 BR 120 Ed 50
Cachoeira do Periquito 〜 BR 120 Ed 49
Cachoeira do Rabalo 〜 BR 132 Eg 55
Cachoeira do Santos 〜 BR 133 Ek 51
Cachoeira dos Índios 〜 BR 112 Ec 45
Cachoeira dos Perdidos 〜 BR 132 Ee 51
Cachoeira do Sul O BR 146 Eh 61
Cachoeira do Tabuleirinho 〜 BR 120 Ef 46
Cachoeira do Tapiú 〜 BR 120 Ef 46
Cachoeira do Tatu 〜 BR 113 Eh 45
Cachoeira do Torino 〜 BR 120 Ef 46
Cachoeira do Urburu 〜 BR 133 Ek 52
Cachoeira du Urçu 〜 BR 112 Ec 45
Cachoeira Grande do Branquinho 〜 BR 120 Ed 47
Cachoeira Grande do Iriri 〜 BR 121 Eh 47
Cachoeira Gregório 〜 BR 112 Ec 45
Cachoeira Guaribas 〜 BR 121 Eh 48
Cachoeira Iauaretê 〜 BR 117 Dp 46
Cachoeira Iauaretê 〜 BR 117 Ea 46
Cachoeira Inferno 〜 BR 120 Eg 47
Cachoeira Ipadu 〜 BR 117 Ea 45
Cachoeira Jutai 〜 BR 120 Ed 49
Cachoeira Lajedao 〜 BR 132 Ee 51
Cachoeira Maçarico 〜 BR 117 Ea 45
Cachoeira Mananá 〜 BR 113 Eh 44
Cachoeira Matamatá 〜 BR 120 Ed 49
Cachoeira Matapi 〜 BR 112 Ec 45
Cachoeira Mongubal Grande 〜 BR 120 Ef 48
Cachoeira Morena 〜 BR 120 Ee 47
Cachoeira Morrinhos 〜 BR 117 Eb 50
Cachoeira Mortandade 〜 BR 121 El 49
Cachoeira Nazaré 〜 BR 129 Ed 51
Cachoeira Nove de Abril 〜 BR 129 Ed 51
Cachoeira Palmeiras 〜 BR 120 Ed 49
Cachoeira Pedemeira 〜 BR 117 Eb 50
Cachoeira Pedra Alta 〜 BR 121 Eh 47
Cachoeira Pequena 〜 BR 121 Ej 47
Cachoeira Periquito 〜 BR 120 Eg 49
Cachoeira Pica-Pau 〜 BR 120 Ee 46
Cachoeira Piranteira 〜 BR 112 Ec 45
Cachoeira Portugal 〜 BR 117 Eb 50
Cachoeira Primeiró do Março 〜 BR 129 Ed 51
Cachoeira Primero Salto 〜 BR 120 Ee 49
Cachoeira Ramos 〜 BR 129 Ed 51
Cachoeira San Roque 〜 BR 129 Ec 51
Cachoeira São Antonio 〜 BR 117 Eb 50
Cachoeiras de Macacú O BR 141 En 57
Cachoeira Seis de Julho 〜 BR 117 Ec 50
Cachoeira Sts. Isabel 〜 BR 121 Ek 49
Cachoeira Tacupare 〜 BR 120 Eg 48
Cachoeira Tambaqui 〜 BOL 117 Eb 50
Cachoeira Taunay 〜 BR 129 Ed 51
Cachoeira Tres Barracas 〜 BR 120 Ed 50
Cachoeira Uacaca 〜 CO 117 Dp 45
Cachoeira Uacura 〜 BR 129 Ed 51
Cachoeira Uapuí 〜 BR 117 Dp 45
Cachoeira Veado 〜 BR 133 Ek 53
Cachoeira Vira-e-Volta 〜 BR 121 Ej 47
Cachoeira Xateturu 〜 BR 121 Eh 49
Cachoeirinha O BR 133 El 55
Cachoeirinha O BR 146 Ej 60
Cachoeria da Curoda 〜 BR 120 Ed 50
Cachueca O ANG 340 Ha 53
Cachuela Esperanza O BOL 129 Eb 51
Cacine O GNB 316 Fn 40
Cacipore 〜 BR 113 Ej 44
Cacique Double O BR 140 Ej 59
Cacoal O BR 129 Ed 51
Cacocum O C 101 Dk 35
Cacolo O ANG 340 Hb 51
Caconda O ANG 340 Gp 52
Cacongo O ANG 332 Gm 48
Cácos O BR 133 Em 52
Caçu O BR 133 Ej 55
Cacuaco O ANG 340 Gn 50
Cacuchi 〜 ANG 340 Ha 52
Cacuilo 〜 ANG 340 Hb 50
Cacula O ANG 340 Gp 53
Caculama O ANG 340 Ha 50
Caculé O BR 125 En 53
Caculuvar 〜 ANG 340 Gp 54
Cacumbi O ANG 340 Hb 51
Cacuso O ANG 340 Gp 50
Cada O RB 341 Hd 55
Cadaado O SP 328 Jb 42
Cadadley O SP 328 Ja 41
Cadale O SP 329 Jb 44
Cadariri 〜 BR 120 Ef 49
Caddo Lake 〜 USA 70 Da 29
Cadena Sal ⛰ PE 128 Dl 51
Cadereyta O MEX 81 Cm 33
Cadiliac O CDN 51 Cj 21
Cadillac O CDN 51 Cj 21
Cadillac O USA 57 Df 23
Cadillac O CDN 60 Dj 21
Cadiz O USA 71 De 27
Cadiz O USA 71 Dh 25
Cádiz O E 184 Gc 27
Cadiz O RP 267 Lm 40
Cadiz Lake 〜 USA 64 Ce 28
Cadlao Island ⌂ RP 267 Lk 40
Cadomin O CDN 50 Cd 19
Cadoux O AUS 368 Lj 61
Caen O F 163 Gf 21
Caernarfon O GB 163 Gd 19
Cáetas O BR 124 Fb 50
Caeté 〜 BR 117 Dp 50
Caeté O BR 141 En 55
Caetité O BR 125 En 53
Caevo O RUS 171 Hl 16
Cafarnaum O BR 125 Ep 51
Cafayate O RA 136 Ea 59
Cafuma 〜 ANG 340 Hb 54
Cagan Aman O RUS 181 Jb 22
Cagayan 〜 RP 267 Ll 37
Cagayan de Oro O RP 267 Ln 41
Cagayan Islands ⌂ RP 266 Lj 41
Cagayan Sulu Island ⌂ RP 274 Lk 42
Cageri O GE 202 Hp 24
Cágliari O I 185 Gl 26
Cagnono Verano O I 194 Gp 25
Cagraray Island ⌂ RP 267 Lm 39
Cagua O YV 107 Ea 40
Caguán 〜 CO 106 Dl 44
Caguán 〜 CO 116 Dl 45
Caguas O USA 104 Ea 36
Çagyl O TM 222 Jf 25
Čah Āb O AFG 223 Jn 27
Cahabón 〜 GCA 93 Dc 38
Çahama O ANG 340 Gp 54
Čahār Borğak O AFG 226 Jk 30
Čahār Mahāll Baḫtiyāri ◉ IR 215 Jd 30
Čāh Ğām O IR 222 Jf 28
Cahir O IRL 163 Gb 19
Cahokia Mounds S.H.S. ★ USA 71 Dc 26
Cahora Bassa O MOC 344 Hj 53
Çahors O F 184 Gg 23
Čah Sagak O IR 223 Jj 29
Cahuacho O PE 128 Dm 53
Cahuapanas O PE 116 Dk 48
Cahuinarí 〜 CO 116 Dm 46
Cahuinarí 〜 CO 117 Dn 46
Cahuison O MEX 80 Ch 31
Cahul O MD 175 Hg 23
Caia O MOC 344 Hk 54
Caiambé O BR 117 Eb 47
Caianda O ANG 341 Hd 51
Caiapo 〜 BR 121 Ek 50
Caiapó 〜 BR 133 Ej 54
Caiapônia O BR 133 Eh 54
Caiari O BR 121 Ek 47
Caibarién O C 100 Dj 34
Caibiran O RP 267 Ln 40
Caicara O YV 112 Ec 41
Caicedonia O CO 106 Dl 43
Caico O BR 124 Fb 49
Caicos Islands ⌂ GB 101 Dm 35
Caicos Passage ≈ 101 Dm 35
Caicumbo O ANG 340 Hc 51
Cái Đầu O VN 263 Lc 40
Caigua O YV 112 Eb 41
Caiguna O AUS 369 Ln 62
Cái Lây O VN 263 Ld 40
Caillou Bay 〜 USA 86 Dc 31
Caima O BR 120 Eh 47
Caimanero O MEX 92 Cj 34
Caimbambo 〜 ANG 340 Gn 52
Caim-Bambo O ANG 340 Gn 52
Caimito O CO 106 Dl 41
Caine 〜 BOL 129 Ea 54
Caine 〜 BOL 129 Eb 55
Cainta O RP 267 Ll 38
Caiongo O ANG 332 Gp 49
Caipe O RA 136 Ea 58
Caipupa O ANG 340 Hb 51
Caird Coast ⌓ 38 Hb 17
Cairns O AUS 365 Mj 54
Cairns Lake 〜 CDN 56 Da 20
Cairo O USA 60 Dl 24
Cairo O USA 86 Df 30
Cairo ▣ ET 301 Hh 31
Cairu O BR 125 Fa 52
Caitou O ANG 340 Gn 53
Caiundo O ANG 340 Ha 53
Caixa 〜 BR 125 En 52
Caiyuan O VRC 255 Lb 32
Cajabamba O EC 116 Dj 46
Cajabamba O PE 116 Dj 49
Cajacay O PE 128 Dk 51
Cajamarca O PE 116 Dj 49
Cajara del Orinoco O YV 107 Ea 42
Cajatambo O PE 128 Dk 51
Cajati O BR 141 Ek 58
Cajazeiras O BR 121 Ej 48
Cajazeiras O BR 124 Fa 49
Cajidiocan O RP 267 Lm 39
Cajones 〜 MEX 93 Cp 37
Cajon Troncoso 〜 RCH 137 Dn 64
Cajuapara 〜 BR 121 El 48
Cajuata O BOL 129 Ea 54
Cajurichic O MEX 80 Ch 31
Cajuru O BR 141 El 56
Caka O VRC 242 Kp 27
Cake Chake O EAT 337 Hm 48
Cala O ZA 349 Hf 61
Calabar O WAN 320 Gl 43
Calabazar de Sagua O C 100 Dj 34
Calabei O RI 279 Lj 50
Calabozo O YV 107 Ea 41
Calabria ◉ I 185 Gp 26
Calacoto O BOL 129 Dp 54
Calafat O RO 194 Hd 24
Calafate O RA 152 Dm 71
Calagua Islands ⌂ RP 267 Lm 38
Calahorra O E 184 Ge 24
Calai O ANG 340 Hb 54
Calais O USA 60 Ea 23
Çalais O F 163 Gg 20
Čalak O UZB 223 Jm 26
Calama O BR 117 Ec 50
Calama O RCH 136 Dp 57
Calamajue O MEX 75 Ce 31
Calamar O CO 106 Dl 40
Calamar O CO 107 Dm 45
Calamarca O BOL 129 Dp 54
Calamba O RP 267 Ll 38
Calamba O ANG 340 Gn 51
Calamian Group ⌂ RP 267 Lk 39
Calamocha O E 184 Gf 25
Calamus Reservoir 〜 USA 70 Cn 25
Calanaque O BR 117 Eb 46
Calandula O ANG 340 Gp 50
Calang O RI 270 Km 43
Calango O PE 128 Dk 52
Calanscio Sand Sea ⌓ LAR 300 Hb 32
Calapan O RP 267 Ll 39
Călărași O RO 175 Hf 23
Călărași O MD 175 Hg 22
Cala Ratjada O E 185 Gh 26
Calarcá O CO 106 Dl 43
Calatambo O RCH 128 Dp 55
Calatayud O E 184 Ge 25
Calatrava O RP 267 Lm 40
Calauit Island ⌂ RP 267 Lk 39
Calayan Island ⌂ RP 267 Ll 36
Calbas 〜 RUS 181 Hm 22
Calbayog O RP 267 Ln 39
Calbuco O RCH 147 Dm 66
Calca O PE 128 Dn 52
Calcasieu 〜 USA 86 Db 30
Calcasieu Lake 〜 USA 86 Db 30
Calceta O EC 116 Dh 46
Calchaquí 〜 RA 136 Ea 58
Calchaquí O RA 137 Ed 60
Calchaquí 〜 RA 137 Ed 60
Calçoene O BR 113 Ej 44
Calçoene 〜 BR 113 Ej 44
Calcutta O IND 235 Kj 34
Caldas O CO 106 Dl 42
Caldas Novas O BR 133 Ek 54
Caldera O CR 97 Df 41
Caldera O RCH 136 Dn 59
Caldıran O TR 202 Hp 26
Caldwell O USA 50 Cd 24
Caldwell O USA 70 Cp 27
Caldwell O USA 71 Dh 26
Caldwell O USA 81 Cp 30
Caledon O ZA 358 Hb 63
Caledon Bay 〜 AUS 364 Me 52
Caledonia O USA 56 Dc 24
Caledonia O CDN 60 Dj 24
Caledonia O CDN 61 Eb 23
Caledonia Hills ⛰ CDN 61 Eb 23
Caledonrivier 〜 ZA 349 Hf 60
Calen O AUS 375 Ml 56
Calequisse O GNB 316 Fm 39
Caleta Agua Duke 〜 RCH 136 Dn 58
Caleta Bandurrias 〜 RCH 136 Dn 58
Caleta Josefina O RCH 152 Dp 72
Caleta la Ligua 〜 RCH 137 Dn 62
Caleta Loa 〜 RCH 128 Dn 55
Caleta Lobos O RCH 136 Dn 56
Caleta los Hornes 〜 RCH 137 Dn 60
Caleta Olivia O RA 152 Ea 69
Caleta Punta Arenas 〜 RCH 136 Dn 56
Caleta Ranquil 〜 RCH 147 Dl 64
Caleta Tontado 〜 RCH 136 Dn 60
Caleta Vitor O RCH 128 Dn 55
Caleufú O RA 137 Eb 63
Caleufú 〜 RA 147 Dn 66
Calexico O USA 64 Ce 29
Calgary O CDN 50 Ce 20
Calhan O USA 65 Ck 26
Calhoun O USA 70 Db 29
Calhoun O USA 71 Df 28
Calhoun City O USA 86 Dd 29
Calhoun Falls O USA 71 Dg 28
Cali O CO 106 Dk 44
Calía 〜 RA 152 Dn 70
Calicoan Island ⌂ RP 267 Ln 40
Calico Ghost Town ★ USA 64 Cd 28
Calicut O IND 239 Kb 40
Calie Corar △ SP 328 Ja 44
Caliente O USA 64 Ce 27
California ◉ USA 64 Cb 25
California O CO 107 Dm 42
California O BR 117 Dn 50
Calik 〜 RI 278 Lc 47
Calilegua O RA 136 Eb 57
Calima O CO 106 Dk 43
Calingasta O RA 137 Dp 61
Calingiri O AUS 368 Lj 61
Calintaan O RP 267 Ll 39
Calion O USA 70 Db 29
Calipatria O USA 64 Ce 29
Calistoga O USA 64 Ca 26
Calitzdorp O ZA 358 Hc 62
Calka O GE 202 Ja 25
Calkiní O MEX 93 Dc 35
Callabonna O AUS 374 Mg 60
Callabonna Creek 〜 AUS 374 Mg 60
Callagiddy O AUS 368 Lh 58
Callahan O USA 64 Ca 25
Callahan O USA 87 Dg 30
Callana 〜 PE 116 Dl 49
Callander O CDN 60 Dj 22
Callawa O AUS 360 Ll 56
Callaway O USA 86 Df 30
Calle Calle 〜 RCH 147 Dm 65
Calles O MEX 92 Cn 34
Calliope O AUS 375 Mm 58
Calliope Range ⛰ AUS 375 Mm 58
Cal Madow ⛰ SP 328 Jc 40
Calmar O CDN 50 Cf 19
Calmar O USA 56 Dc 24
Cal Miskaat ⛰ SP 328 Jc 40
Calnalí O MEX 92 Cn 35
Çalo O TR 195 Hg 26
Calobre O PA 97 Dh 41
Calonda O ANG 340 Hc 50
Calonga 〜 ANG 340 Gp 53
Caloundra O AUS 375 Mn 59
Calpulalpan O MEX 92 Cn 35
Caltagirone O I 185 Gp 27
Caltanissetta O I 185 Gp 27
Calton Hills O AUS 374 Mf 56
Ca Lu O VN 263 Ld 37
Caluango O ANG 340 Hb 50
Calucinga O ANG 340 Ha 51
Calulo O ANG 340 Gp 51
Calunda O ANG 341 Hd 52
Caluquembe O ANG 340 Gp 52
Čalūs O IR 222 Jd 27
Caluula O SP 328 Jd 40
Calvados Chain ⌂ PNG 287 Mn 51
Calvert 〜 AUS 365 Me 54
Calvert Hills O AUS 365 Me 54
Calvert Island ⌂ CDN 50 Bm 20
Calvi O F 185 Gl 24
Calvillo O MEX 92 Cl 35
Calvin O USA 70 Cp 28
Calvinia O ZA 348 Hb 61
Calzada d.C. O E 184 Ge 26
Camabatela O ANG 332 Gp 50
Camaça 〜 BR 117 Ea 49
Camacã O BR 125 Fa 53
Camacari O BR 125 Fa 52
Camacho O MEX 81 Cl 33
Camacupa O ANG 340 Ha 51
Camaguan O YV 107 Ea 41
Camagüey O C 100 Dk 35
Camaipi O BR 121 Ej 45
Camaiú 〜 BR 120 Ee 49
Camamu O BR 125 Fa 52
Çamana O PE 128 Dm 54
Čamanābād O IR 222 Jh 28
Çamanaú 〜 BR 120 Ed 46
Čaman Bīd O IR 222 Jg 27
Çamaniú 〜 BR 120 Ee 48
Čaman Soltān O IR 209 Jc 29
Camapuã O BR 132 Eg 55
Camaquã O BR 146 Eh 61
Camar O RCH 136 Ea 57
Camará O BR 120 Eg 47
Camará O BR 121 Ek 46
Camaragibe O BR 124 Fc 49
Camaraipi 〜 BR 121 Ej 47
Camararé 〜 BR 132 Ee 52
Camargo O MEX 81 Cn 32
Camaron O BOL 136 Eb 56
Camarones 〜 RCH 128 Dp 55
Camarones O RA 152 Ea 68
Camaruã O BR 117 Eb 48
Camas O USA 50 Ca 23
Camatambo O ANG 332 Gp 49
Cà Mau O VN 263 Lc 41
Camaxilo O ANG 340 Hb 50
Cambaju O GNB 316 Fn 39
Camballin O AUS 361 Ln 55
Cambândua O ANG 340 Ha 52
Cambao O CO 106 Dl 43
Cambará do ,Sul O BR 146 Ej 60
Cambisea O PE 128 Dm 51
Cambo 〜 ANG 340 Ha 50
Cambodia □ K 263 Lc 39
Camboon O AUS 375 Mm 58
Cambrai O F 163 Gh 20
Cambria O USA 64 Cb 28
Cambrian Mountains ⛰ GB 163 Ge 19
Cambridge O USA 50 Cd 23
Cambridge O USA 56 Db 23
Cambridge O CDN 57 Dh 24
Cambridge O USA 70 Cm 25
Cambridge O USA 71 Dg 25
Cambridge O USA 71 Dh 25
Cambridge O USA 74 Dk 26
Cambridge O USA 74 Dn 24
Cambridge O JA 100 Dk 36
Cambridge O GB 163 Gf 19
Cambridge O NZ 383 Nk 64
Cambridge Bay O CDN 42 Fa 5
Cambridge Bay O CDN 47 Cj 11
Cambridge Gulf 〜 AUS 364 Ma 53
Cambrils O E 184 Gg 25
Cambuí O BR 141 El 57
Cambulo O ANG 333 Hc 49
Cambundi-Catembo O ANG 340 Ha 51
Camburinga O AUS 364 Me 52
Cambutal O PA 97 Dh 42
Camden O USA 60 Dk 24
Camden O USA 60 Dp 23
Camden O USA 70 Db 29
Camden O USA 71 De 29
Camden O USA 71 Dh 28
Camden O USA 74 Dl 26
Camden O AUS 379 Mm 63
Camdenton O USA 70 Db 27
Cameia O ANG 341 Hc 51
Camela O MEX 92 Ck 36
Camel Creek O AUS 365 Mj 55
Çameli O TR 195 Hg 27
Cam-e Qezel 〜 IR 209 Jb 28
Cameron O USA 65 Cg 28
Cameron O USA 70 Da 26
Cameron O USA 81 Cp 30
Cameron O USA 86 Db 31
Cameron Corner ★ AUS 374 Mg 60
Cameron Highlands ⛰ MAL 270 La 43
Cameroon □ CAM 320 Gm 43
Cametá O BR 121 Ek 47
Camfield O AUS 364 Mb 54
Cami 〜 RA 152 Dp 73
Camiguin Island ⌂ RP 267 Lm 36
Camiguin Island ⌂ RP 267 Ln 41
Camiling O RP 267 Ll 38
Camilla O USA 86 Df 30
Camiña O RCH 128 Dp 55
Camirco O BOL 129 Eb 53
Camiri O BOL 136 Ec 56
Camissombo O ANG 333 Hc 50
Camkani O AFG 223 Jn 29
Camlıdere O TR 195 Hj 25
Çamlıyala O TR 195 Hk 27
Camming O RI 282 Ll 48
Camoapa O NIC 97 Df 39
Camo-Camo O MOC 352 Hk 57
Camocim O BR 124 Ep 47
Camogton O RP 267 Ll 39
Camongua O ANG 340 Ha 51
Camooweal O AUS 365 Mf 55
Camooweal Caves ♀ AUS 374 Mf 56
Camopi O F 113 Eh 44
Camopi 〜 F 113 Eh 44
Camorta Island ⌂ IND 262 Kl 41
Camotes Islands ⌂ RP 267 Ln 40
Camotes Sea 〜 RP 267 Ln 40
Campamento O HN 96 De 38
Campamento Río Grande O YV 112 Ed 41
Campana O RA 146 Ee 63
Campanas O RA 136 Ea 60
Campania ◉ I 194 Gp 25
Campanilla O PE 116 Dk 49
Campaolegre O CO 106 Dl 44
Campaspe O AUS 375 Mk 56
Campbell O USA 64 Ca 27
Campbell O ZA 349 Hd 60
Campbellford O CDN 60 Dk 23
Campbell Plateau ψ 35 Ta 14
Campbell River O CDN 50 Bp 20
Campbell's Bay O CDN 60 Dk 23
Campbellsville O USA 71 Df 27
Campbellton O CDN 61 Ea 22
Campbell Town O AUS 378 Mk 66
Campbelltown O AUS 379 Mm 63
Campbeltown O GB 162 Gd 18
Camp Crook O USA 51 Cl 23
Campeche O MEX 93 Dc 36
Campeche Bank ψ 93 Dc 34
Campechuela O C 101 Dk 35
Campellford O CDN 60 Dj 23
Campell Island ⌂ NZ 35 Ta 15
Campembe 〜 ANG 340 Hc 54
Câmpeni O RO 175 He 22
Camperdown O AUS 378 Mh 65
Camperville O CDN 56 Cm 20
Câm Phá O VN 255 Ld 35
Câmpha O VN 255 Ld 35
Campillos O E 184 Gd 27
Câmpina O RO 175 He 23
Campinaçu O BR 133 Ek 52
Campina da Lagoa O BR 140 Eh 58
Campina do Simão O BR 140 Ej 58
Campina Grande O BR 124 Fb 49
Campinas O BR 141 El 57
Campina Verde O BR 133 Ek 55
Camp Nelson O USA 64 Cc 27
Campo O USA 65 Cl 27
Campo O CAM 320 Gl 44
Campo O MOC 344 Hl 54
Campo Alegre O YV 112 Ec 41
Campo Alegre O BR 124 Fb 50
Campo Alegre de Goiás O BR 133 El 54
Campo Alegre de Lourdes O BR 124 En 50
Campobasso O I 194 Gp 25
Campo Belo O BR 141 Em 56
Campo Bernal O YV 107 Dm 41
Campo Erê O BR 140 Eh 59
Campo Esperanza O PY 140 Ee 57
Campo Formoso O BR 125 Ep 51
Campo Gallo O RA 136 Ec 59
Campo Garay O RA 137 Ed 60
Campo Grande O BR 140 Eg 56
Campo Grande O RA 140 Eg 59
Campo Largo O BR 140 Ek 58
Campo Major O BR 124 En 48
Campo Mourão O BR 140 Eh 58
Campo Novo do Parecis O BR 132 Ef 52
Campos Belos O BR 133 El 52
Campos do Jordão O BR 141 Em 57
Campos dos Parecis ⌓ BR 132 Ee 52
Campo Seco O BR 146 Eg 61
Campo Serio O PE 116 Dl 46
Campos Gerais O BR 141 Em 56
Campos Lindos O BR 121 El 50
Campos Novos O BR 140 Ej 59
Campos Sales O BR 124 Ep 49
Campo Verde O BR 132 Eg 53
Camp Point O USA 71 Dc 25
Câmpulung O RO 175 He 23
Câmpulung Moldovenesc O RO 175 He 22
Camp Verde O USA 65 Cg 28
Camp Wood O USA 81 Cm 31
Cam Ranh O VN 263 Le 40
Camrose O CDN 51 Cf 19
Camú 〜 DOM 101 Dn 36
Camucio O ANG 340 Gn 53
Çamuya 〜 CO 106 Dm 45
Čamzinka O RUS 181 Ja 18
Çan O TR 195 Hf 26
Can. du Ariège 〜 F 184 Gg 24
Can. du Sahel 〜 RMM 305 Gc 39
Canaã O BR 121 Em 49
Canaã 〜 BR 129 Ec 51
Cana Brava 〜 BR 133 Ek 52
Canada □ CDN 56 Db 19
Canada Basin ψ 6 Bb 2
Canada Bay 〜 CDN 61 Ef 20
Cañada Condal 〜 RA 136 Ec 57
Cañada de Gómez O RA 137 Ed 62
Cañada de Luque O RA 137 Ec 61
Cañada el Rosillo 〜 RA 136 Ed 57
Cañada Rica 〜 PY 136 Ec 57
Cañada Rosquín O RA 137 Ed 62
Cañada Seca O RA 137 Ec 63
Canadian O USA 70 Cm 28
Canadian 〜 USA 70 Cp 28
Canadian River 〜 USA 65 Ck 28
Canadian River 〜 USA 70 Cm 28
Cañadó el Pluma 〜 RA 152 Dn 69
Cañadón de las Vacas O RA 152 Dp 71
Cañadón Sacho 〜 RA 152 Dn 68
Cañadón Seco 〜 RA 152 Dn 69
Canagua 〜 YV 107 Dn 41
Canaima O YV 112 Ec 42
Canaima ♀ YV 112 Ec 43
Çanakkale O TR 194 Hf 25
Canal O AUS 375 Ml 58
Canala O F 386 Nf 56
Canal al Desierto 〜 RA 136 Ec 59
Canal Ancho 〜 RCH 152 Dl 71
Canal Baker 〜 RCH 152 Dl 69
Canal Ballenaro 〜 RCH 152 Dn 73
Canal Beagle 〜 RA 152 Dp 73
Canal Castro 〜 RCH 152 Dl 71
Canal Cockburn 〜 RCH 152 Dn 73
Canal Concepción 〜 RCH 152 Dl 71
Canal Darwin 〜 RCH 152 Dl 68
Canal de Ballenas 〜 MEX 75 Cf 31
Canal de Chacao 〜 RCH 147 Dl 66
Canal de Dios 〜 RA 136 Ec 58
Canal de Goncalo 〜 BR 146 Eh 62
Canal de Jambeli 〜 EC 116 Dh 47
Canal de Kellet 〜 MEX 75 Ce 32
Canal de los Tempanos 〜 RA 152 Dm 71
Canal de Morro 〜 EC 116 Dh 47
Canal de Pinta 〜 EC 128 Dc 45
Canal de Pinzon 〜 EC 128 Dc 46
Canal de Puinahua 〜 PE 116 Dl 48
Canal de Salsipuedes 〜 MEX 75 Cf 31
Canal de San Salvador 〜 EC 128 Dc 46
Canal de Tūnis 〜 TN 297 Gm 27
Canal do Gêba 〜 GNB 316 Fm 40
Canal do Gurijuba 〜 BR 121 Ej 45
Canal do Sul 〜 BR 121 Ek 46
Canal du Norte 〜 BR 121 Ej 45
Canal Esteban 〜 RCH 152 Dl 71
Canal Flats O CDN 50 Ce 20
Canal Isabela 〜 EC 128 Dc 46
Canal Jacal 〜 RCH 152 Dm 68
Canal Messier 〜 RCH 152 Dl 70
Canal Moraleda 〜 RCH 152 Dm 68
Canal No. 1 〜 RA 146 Ef 64
Canal No. 11 〜 RA 146 Ee 64
Canal No. 12 〜 RA 146 Ee 64
Canal No. 16 〜 RA 146 Ee 63
Canal No. 2 〜 RA 146 Ef 64
Canal No. 5 〜 RA 146 Ef 64
Canal No. 9 〜 RA 146 Ee 64
Canal Perigoso 〜 BR 121 Ek 46
Canal Pitt 〜 RCH 152 Dl 71
Canal Puyuguapi 〜 RCH 152 Dm 68
Canals O RA 137 Ec 62
Canal San Antinio y Torcuga 〜 RA 137 Ed 62
Canal Smyth 〜 RCH 152 Dl 71
Canal Sormiento 〜 RCH 152 Dl 71
Canal Utarupa 〜 RCH 152 Dl 68
Canal Virgen del Carmen 〜 RA 136 Ec 58
Canal Whiteside 〜 RCH 152 Dn 72
Canamã 〜 BR 132 Ee 51
Cananari 〜 CO 117 Dn 45
Canandaigua O USA 60 Dk 24
Cananea O MEX 80 Cg 30
Cananéia O BR 141 El 58
Cañar O EC 116 Dj 47
Canarana O BR 125 Ep 51
Canarana O BR 133 Eh 52
Canary O AUS 374 Mg 57
Canary Basin ψ 292 Fp 29
Canary Islands ⌂ E 292 Fm 31
Cañas O MEX 92 Cl 36
Cañas O CR 97 Df 40
Cañas 〜 PY 136 Eb 57
Cañasgordas O CO 106 Dl 42
Canastra 〜 BR 133 Ek 51
Canatiba O BR 125 En 52
Canatlán O MEX 80 Ck 33
Cañaveral O PE 116 Dh 47
Cañaveras O E 184 Ge 25
Canavieiras O BR 125 Fa 53
Cañazas O PA 97 Dh 41
Cañazas O PA 97 Dj 41
Canberra ▣ AUS 379 Ml 63
Canby O USA 56 Cp 23
Canby O USA 64 Cb 25
Cancela O BR 124 En 47
Canchungo O GNB 316 Fm 39
Canconga O ANG 340 Hb 52
Cancosa O RCH 129 Dp 55
Cancuc O MEX 93 Db 37
Cancún O MEX 93 De 35
Candarave O PE 128 Dn 54
Candarlı Kōr 〜 TR 195 Hf 26
Candeado O MOC 344 Hj 55
Candeias 〜 BR 117 Ec 50
Candeias O BR 125 Fa 52
Candela O MEX 81 Cm 32
Candelaria O MEX 93 Dc 36
Candelaria 〜 MEX 93 Dc 36
Candelária O BR 146 Eh 60
Candeleda O E 184 Gd 25
Candi ★ RI 270 La 45
Candi Besakih ★ RI 279 Lh 50
Cândido O BR 121 Em 46
Cândido de Abreu O BR 140 Ej 58
Cândido Rondon O BR 140 Eg 58
Cândido Sales O BR 125 Ep 53
Candlour O AUS 365 Mh 55
Cando O CDN 51 Ch 19
Cando O USA 56 Cn 21
Candover O ZA 352 Hj 59
Candulo O MOC 344 Hl 51
Cân Du'ó'c O VN 263 Ld 40
Cane O AUS 360 Lh 57
Cane 〜 AUS 360 Lh 57
Canegrass O AUS 378 Mg 62
Canela Baja O RCH 137 Dn 61
Canelones O ROU 146 Ef 63
Canelos O EC 116 Dk 46
Cañete 〜 PE 128 Dk 52
Cañete O RCH 137 Dm 64
Cañete O E 184 Gf 25
Cangala O ANG 340 Ha 52
Cangalo O ANG 340 Ha 51
Cangamba O ANG 340 Hb 52
Cangandala O ANG 340 Ha 50
Cangas d. N. O E 184 Gc 24
Canghaim 〜 EC 116 Dk 47
Cangoa O ANG 340 Hb 52
Cangombe O ANG 340 Hb 53
Cangrāfa O RIM 304 Fp 37
Cangshan O VRC 246 Lj 28
Canguaretama O BR 124 Fc 49
Canguçu O BR 146 Eh 61
Cangumbe O ANG 340 Hb 51
Cangussu O BR 121 Ek 50
Cangxi O VRC 243 Ld 30
Cangyanshan ★ VRC 243 Lh 27
Cangyuan O VRC 254 Kp 34
Cangzhou O VRC 246 Lj 26
Canhotinho O BR 124 Fb 50
Caniapiscau River 〜 CDN 7 Fb 4
Canicatti O I 185 Gn 27
Canigao Channel 〜 RP 267 Ln 40
Canim Lake O CDN 50 Cb 20
Canindé 〜 BR 124 En 49
Canindé O BR 124 Ep 48
Canindé O BR 124 Fa 48
Canindé São Francisco O BR 124 Fa 50
Canipo Island ⌂ RP 267 Ll 40
Cañita O PA 97 Dj 41
Cañitas O MEX 92 Cl 34
Canjime O ANG 340 Hb 54
Canjufa O GNB 316 Fn 39
Çankın O TR 195 Hj 25
Cankuzo O BU 336 Hh 47
Canmore O CDN 50 Ce 20
Cannanore O IND 238 Kb 40
Cannaore Islands ⌂ IND 239 Ka 40
Canning Hill △ AUS 368 Lj 60
Canning River 〜 USA 46 Bc 9
Cannington Manor Hist.Park ★ CDN 51 Cl 21
Cannon Ball O USA 56 Cm 22
Cannonball River 〜 USA 56 Cm 22

406 Cachoeira do Pataua - Cannonball River

Cannondale Mount △ AUS 375 Ml 58
Cannon Fs. O USA 56 Db 23
Cannonville O USA 65 Cf 27
Cann River O USA 379 Ml 64
Canoa O HN 93 Dd 38
Caño Araguaimujo ～ YV 112 Ed 41
Canoas O MEX 92 Cn 34
Canoas O BR 146 Ej 60
Caño Basame ～ YV 112 Ed 41
Canobie O AUS 365 Mg 55
Caño Colorado O YV 112 Ec 41
Caño el Pinal ～ CO 107 Dn 43
Caño Guaritico ～ YV 107 Dn 42
Canoinhas O BR 140 Ej 59
Caño la Fortele ～ CO 107 Dn 43
Caño Lioni ～ CO 107 Dp 43
Caño los Lobos ～ CO 106 Dl 45
Caño Macare ～ YV 112 Ed 41
Caño Minisiare ～ CO 107 Dp 44
Caño Mono ～ CO 107 Dp 43
Canonaco ～ EC 116 Dk 46
Cañoncito ••• USA 65 Cj 28
Cañon City O USA 65 Ck 26
Caño Toparillo ～ CO 107 Dp 43
Caño Tuparrito ～ CO 107 Dp 43
Canouan △ WV 104 Jd 38
Canowindra O AUS 379 Ml 62
Canso O CDN 61 Ed 23
Canta O PE 128 Dk 51
Cantabria ◉ E 184 Gd 24
Cantalejo O E 184 Ge 25
Cantario ～ BR 129 Ec 51
Cantaura O YV 112 Eb 41
Canterbury ◉ GB 163 Gg 20
Canterbury Bight ～ NZ 383 Nj 68
Cân Tho' O RP 267 Ln 41
Cantilan O RP 267 Ln 41
Canto del Agua O RCH 136 Dn 60
Canto do Buriti O BR 124 En 50
Canton △ KIR 35 Aa 10
Canton O USA 56 Cp 24
Canton O USA 60 Dl 23
Canton O USA 70 Da 29
Canton O USA 70 Dc 25
Canton O USA 71 Df 28
Canton O USA 71 Dk 25
Canton O USA 74 Dk 25
Canton O USA 86 Dc 29
Cantwell O USA 46 Ba 13
Canudos O BR 124 Fa 50
Cañuelas O RA 146 Ee 63
Canumã △ BR 120 Ee 48
Canunda ♀ AUS 378 Mf 64
Canutama O BR 117 Eb 49
Canxixe O MOC 344 Hk 54
Canyon O USA 65 Cl 28
Canyon City O USA 50 Cc 23
Canyon Creek O USA 51 Cf 22
Canyon de Chelly N.M. ♀ USA 65 Ch 28
Canyon Ferry O USA 51 Cg 22
Canyon Ferry Lake ～ USA 51 Cg 22
Canyonlands ♀ USA 65 Cg 26
Canzar O AUS 333 Hc 49
Cao Băng O VN 255 Lc 34
Caohekou O VRC 246 Lm 25
Caojian O VRC 254 Kp 33
Cao Lãnh O VN 263 Lc 40
Caombo O ANG 332 Ha 50
Caonao ～ C 100 Dj 35
Caopiao O VRC 246 Lk 30
Cáorle O I 185 Gn 23
Cao Xian O VRC 243 Lh 28
Cap. Rivadenaira O RCH 136 Dk 46
Cap. Sarmiento O RA 146 Ee 63
Capachica O PE 128 Dp 53
Čapaev O KZ 155 Rb 8
Čapaevski O RUS 181 Jc 19
Capahuari ～ EC 116 Dk 46
Capaia O ANG 340 Hc 50
Capaias O RP 267 Lk 40
Capalonga O RP 267 Lm 38
Capanaparo ～ YV 107 Dp 42
Capanema O BR 121 El 46
Capão Alto O BR 140 Ej 59
Capão Bonito O BR 141 Ek 58
Capão Branco O BR 146 Eh 60
Capão da Canoa O BR 146 Ek 60
Cap Apostolos Andreas △ CY 195 Hk 28
Čaparhär △ AFG 223 Jp 28
Capas O RP 267 Ll 38
Capauari ～ BR 117 Dp 46
Capauari ～ BR 117 Ea 46
Cap-aux-Meules O CDN 61 Ed 22
Capay O RP 267 Lm 39
Cap Bayes ⌐ F 386 Ne 56
Cap Beddouza △ MA 292 Gb 29
Cap Bocage △ F 386 Ne 56
Cap Bonavista △ CDN 61 Eh 21
Cap Bougaroun △ DZ 296 Gk 27
Cap Boyer ⌐ F 386 Ng 56
Capbreton O F 184 Gf 24
Cap-Chat O CDN 61 Ea 21
Cap Corse ⌐ F 185 Gl 24
Cap Dame Marie △ RH 101 Dl 36
Cap de Creus △ E 184 Gh 25
Cap de Flotte ⌐ F 386 Nf 56
Cap de Formentor △ E 184 Gg 26
Cap de la Hague △ F 163 Gf 21
Cap-de-la-Madeleine O CDN 60 Dm 22
Cap de la Nao △ E 184 Gg 26
Cap de Salou △ E 184 Gg 25
Cap-des-Rosiers O CDN 61 Eb 21
Cap des Trois Fourches △ MA 293 Ge 28
Cape ～ AUS 375 Mj 56
Cape Adare △ 38 Tb 17
Cape Agulhas △ ZA 358 Hb 63
Cape Alexander △ SOL 290 Na 49
Cape Angontsy △ RM 345 Jd 53
Cape Ankaboa △ RM 353 Hp 56
Cape Ann △ USA 60 Dn 24
Cape Anorontany △ RM 345 Jc 52
Cape Arid △ AUS 368 Lm 63
Cape Arid ♀ AUS 368 Lm 62
Cape Arnhem △ AUS 365 Me 52
Cape Babaomby △ RM 345 Jc 51
Cape Baring △ CDN 42 Ea 4

Cape Baring △ CDN 47 Cc 11
Cape Barren Island △ AUS 378 Ml 66
Cape Basin ∨ 30 Ka 13
Cape Baskerville △ AUS 360 Ll 54
Cape Bathurst △ CDN 47 Bn 9
Cape Bauer △ AUS 369 Mc 62
Cape Bauld △ CDN 61 Eg 20
Cape Beatrice △ AUS 365 Me 53
Cape Bedford △ AUS 365 Mj 53
Cape Bernier △ AUS 361 Lp 53
Cape Blanche △ AUS 369 Mc 62
Cape Blanco △ USA 50 Bp 24
Cape Bon △ TN 297 Gm 27
Cape Borda △ AUS 378 Me 63
Cape Bossut △ AUS 360 Ll 55
Cape Bougainville △ AUS 361 Ln 52
Cape Bouguer △ AUS 378 Me 64
Cape Bowen △ AUS 365 Me 53
Cape Breton △ CDN 61 Ee 23
Cape Breton Highlands National Park ♀ CDN 61 Ed 22
Cape Breton Island △ CDN 61 Ed 22
Cape Brett △ NZ 383 Nk 63
Cape Brewster △ DK 43 Lb 4
Cape Bululiyan △ RP 266 Lj 41
Cape Butterbee △ 38 Mb 16
Cape Byron △ AUS 375 Mn 60
Cape Calavite △ RP 267 Lk 39
Cape Campbell △ NZ 383 Nk 66
Cape Canaveral △ USA 87 Dh 31
Cape Canaveral △ USA 87 Dh 31
Cape Canaveral Air Station ★ USA 87 Dh 31
Cape Capricorn △ AUS 375 Mm 57
Cape Cargantua △ CDN 57 Df 22
Cape Carnot △ AUS 378 Md 63
Cape Chacon △ USA 42 Da 8
Cape Charles △ USA 74 Dl 27
Cape Chiniak △ USA 46 An 17
Cape Churchill △ CDN 7 Ea 4
Cape Churchill △ CDN 42 Fc 7
Cape Cleare △ USA 46 Bc 15
Cape Clinton △ AUS 375 Mm 57
Cape Coast △ GH 317 Gf 43
Cape Cod Bay ～ USA 74 Dp 25
Cape Cod National Seashore ♀ USA 74 Dp 24
Cape Cod Peninsula ⌐ USA 74 Dp 25
Cape Colbeck △ 38 Ba 17
Cape Combermere △ CDN 43 Gc 3
Cape Comorin △ IND 239 Kc 41
Cape Conran △ AUS 379 Ml 64
Cape Constantine △ USA 46 Aj 15
Cape Cook △ CDN 50 Cb 21
Cape Coral O USA 87 Dg 32
Cape Crawford O AUS 364 Md 54
Cape Croker △ AUS 364 Mc 51
Cape Cross △ NAM 348 Gn 56
Cape Dalhousie △ CDN 47 Bl 9
Cape Dart △ 38 Cb 17
Cape Denbigh △ USA 46 Aj 13
Cape Direction △ AUS 365 Mh 52
Cape Disappointment △ USA 50 Bp 22
Cape Dolphin △ GB 147 Ee 71
Cape Dorchester △ CDN 43 Gc 6
Cape Dorset △ CDN 43 Gc 6
Cape Dromedary △ AUS 379 Mm 64
Cape Du Couedic △ AUS 378 Me 64
Cape Duncan △ CDN 57 Dh 19
Cape Dupuy △ AUS 360 Lh 56
Cape Dussejour △ AUS 364 Ma 53
Cape Dyer △ CDN 7 Fb 3
Cape Dyer △ CDN 43 Hc 5
Cape Egmont △ NZ 383 Nj 65
Cape Elvira △ CDN 42 Eb 4
Cape Encanto △ RP 267 Ll 38
Cape Esteries △ G 332 Gl 45
Cape Farewell △ NZ 383 Nj 66
Cape Fear △ USA 74 Dj 29
Cape Fear ～ USA 74 Dj 29
Cape Finnis △ AUS 378 Md 62
Cape Flattery △ USA 50 Bp 21
Cape Flattery △ AUS 365 Mj 53
Cape Ford △ AUS 364 Ma 52
Cape Forestier △ AUS 378 Ml 67
Cape Formoso △ WAN 329 Gj 43
Cape Foulwind △ NZ 382 Nh 66
Cape Fourcroy △ AUS 364 Ma 52
Cape Fria △ NAM 340 Gm 55
Cape Gambier △ AUS 364 Mb 51
Cape Gantheaume △ AUS 378 Me 64
Cape Gaspé △ CDN 61 Eb 21
Cape George △ CDN 61 Ec 23
Cape Girardeau O USA 71 Dd 27
Cape Girgir △ PNG 287 Mj 47
Cape Graham Moore △ CDN 43 Gc 4
Cape Grenville △ AUS 365 Mh 51
Cape Grey △ AUS 364 Me 52
Cape Gustav Holm △ DK 43 Kc 5
Cape Gwardafuy △ SP 328 Jd 40
Cape Halkett △ USA 46 An 9
Cape Hanpan △ PNG 290 Na 48
Cape Harrison △ CDN 43 Ja 8
Cape Hart △ AUS 378 Me 64
Cape Hatteras △ USA 74 Dl 28
Cape Hatteras National Seashore ♀ USA 74 Dl 28
Cape Hawke △ AUS 379 Mn 62
Cape Helvetius △ AUS 364 Ma 51
Cape Helvetius △ AUS 364 Ma 51
Cape Henrietta Maria △ CDN 43 Gb 7
Cape Hope Islands △ CDN 57 Dj 19
Cape Horn △ RCH 152 Ea 74
Cape Hotham △ AUS 364 Mb 52
Cape Howe △ AUS 379 Mm 64
Cape Hurd △ CDN 57 Dg 23
Cape Hurde △ CDN 57 Dg 23
Cape Ikolik △ USA 46 An 17
Cape Inscription △ AUS 368 Lg 58
Cape Isachsen △ CDN 42 Ec 3
Cape Island △ AUS 361 Kp 53
Cape Jaffa △ AUS 378 Mf 64
Cape Jerius △ AUS 378 Mf 63
Cape Karikari △ NZ 383 Nj 63
Cape Keer-weer △ AUS 365 Mg 52
Cape Keith △ AUS 364 Mb 51
Cape Kellett △ CDN 6 Cb 2
Cape Kellett △ CDN 42 Db 4

Cape Keraudren △ AUS 360 Lk 55
Cape Kidnappers △ NZ 383 Nl 65
Cape Knob △ AUS 368 Lk 63
Cape Knowles △ 38 Ga 17
Cape Krusenstern △ USA 46 Ag 11
Cape Krusenstern National Monument ♀ USA 46 Ag 11
Cape Kumukahi △ USA 75 An 36
Capel O AUS 368 Lh 62
Cape Labrador △ CDN 43 Hc 6
Cape Lambert △ AUS 360 Lj 56
Cape Lambton △ CDN 42 Dc 4
Cape Lambton △ CDN 42 Dc 4
Cape Lannes △ AUS 378 Mf 64
Cape Latouche Treville △ AUS 360 Ll 55
Cape Leeuwin △ AUS 368 Lh 63
Cape Le Grand △ AUS 368 Lm 62
Cape Leveque △ AUS 360 Lm 54
Capelinha O BR 125 En 54
Cape Liptrap △ AUS 379 Mj 65
Cape Lisburne △ USA 23 Ab 3
Cape Lisburne △ USA 46 Ae 11
Capella O BR 125 Fb 51
Capella △ AUS 375 Ml 57
Cape Londonderry △ AUS 361 Lp 52
Capelongo △ ANG 340 Gp 53
Cape Lookout △ USA 50 Bp 23
Cape Lookout △ USA 74 Dk 28
Cape Lookout National Seashore ♀ USA 74 Dk 28
Cape Lopez △ G 332 Gl 46
Cape Lyon △ CDN 47 Ca 11
Cape Maclear △ MW 344 Hk 52
Cape Manifold △ AUS 375 Mm 57
Cape Maria van Diemen △ NZ 383 Nj 63
Cape Masoala △ RM 345 Jd 54
Cape Matáavéa △ VU 386 Nf 53
Cape May △ USA 74 Dl 26
Capembe ～ ANG 340 Hb 54
Cape Melville △ AUS 365 Mj 53
Cape Melville △ AUS 365 Mj 53
Cape Melville △ AUS 365 Mj 53
Cape Mendenhall △ USA 46 Ag 15
Cape Mendocino △ USA 64 Bp 25
Cape Mercy △ CDN 43 Hc 6
Cape Meredith △ GB 147 Ed 72
Cape Mesurado △ LB 316 Ga 43
Cape Mohican △ USA 46 Ae 15
Cape Mordvinof △ USA 46 Ag 17
Cape Moreton △ AUS 375 Mn 59
Cape Murchison △ CDN 43 Hc 6
Cape Muzon △ USA 42 Da 8
Cape Nahoi ～ VU 386 Nf 53
Cape Naturaliste △ AUS 368 Lh 62
Cape Naturaliste △ AUS 378 Ml 66
Capenda-Camulemba △ ANG 340 Hb 50
Cape Nelson △ PNG 287 Ml 50
Cape Nelson △ AUS 378 Mg 65
Cape Newenham △ USA 46 Ag 15
Cape North △ CDN 61 Ed 22
Cape Norvegia △ 38 Ja 17
Cape Nuyts △ AUS 369 Mb 62
Cape of Good Hope △ ZA 358 Hb 63
Cape Ommaney △ USA 42 Cc 7
Cape Otway △ AUS 378 Mh 65
Cape Padrone △ ZA 358 Hf 62
Cape Palliser △ NZ 383 Nk 66
Cape Palmas △ LB 304 Gc 43
Cape Palmerston △ AUS 375 Ml 56
Cape Parry △ CDN 42 Dc 4
Cape Parry △ CDN 47 Bn 9
Cape Pasley △ AUS 369 Lm 62
Cape Peiho △ PNG 287 Ml 48
Cape Peninsula ★ ZA 358 Ha 63
Cape Peron North △ AUS 368 Lg 58
Cape Pierson △ PNG 287 Mm 50
Cape Poinsett △ 38 Qb 16
Cape Portland △ AUS 378 Mk 66
Cape Preston △ AUS 360 Lj 56
Cape Prince Alfred △ CDN 6 Cb 2
Cape Prince Alfred △ CDN 42 Db 4
Cape Prince of Wales △ USA 23 Ab 3
Cape Prince of Wales △ USA 46 Ae 13
Cape Prince of Wales △ USA 205 Ac 5
Cape Queiros ～ VU 386 Nf 53
Cape Race △ CDN 61 Eh 22
Cape Radstock △ AUS 378 Md 62
Cape Range ⌐⌐ AUS 360 Lg 57
Cape Raper △ CDN 43 Hb 5
Cape Reinga △ NZ 383 Nj 63
Cape Resurrection △ USA 46 Ba 15
Cape Riche △ AUS 368 Lk 63
Cape Rodney △ NZ 383 Nk 64
Cape Romano △ USA 87 Dg 33
Cape Romanzof △ USA 46 Ag 15
Cape Ronsard △ AUS 368 Lg 58
Cape Ross △ RP 267 Lk 40
Cape Roxo △ GNB 316 Fm 39
Cape Runaway △ NZ 383 Nl 64
Cape Ruthieres △ AUS 361 Lp 52
Cape Sable △ AUS 365 Mk 53
Cape Sable Island △ CDN 61 Eb 24
Cape Saint Cricq △ AUS 368 Lg 58
Cape Saint Elias △ USA 46 Bc 15
Cape Saint George △ USA 86 Df 31
Cape San Agustin △ RP 275 Lp 42
Cape San Andreas △ AUS 365 Mk 55
Cape San Ildefonso △ RP 267 Lm 38
Cape San Martin △ USA 64 Cb 28
Cape Santa Maria △ BR 87 Dl 34
Cape Sarichef △ USA 46 Ag 17
Cap Escarpé ⌐ F 386 Nf 56
Cape Scott △ CDN 50 Bm 20
Cape Scott △ AUS 364 Ma 52
Cape Sherard △ AUS 378 Ml 62
Cape Shield △ AUS 364 Me 52
Cape Sidmouth △ AUS 365 Mh 52
Çape Skiring △ SN 316 Fm 39
Čápešlü △ IR 222 Jh 27
Cape Spencer △ USA 47 Bg 15
Cape Spencer △ AUS 378 Me 63
Cape Spit △ USA 46 Aj 15
Cape St. Francis △ ZA 358 He 63
Cape St. George △ CDN 61 Ee 21

Cape St. George ♀ PNG 287 Mn 48
Cape St. James △ CDN 42 Da 8
Cape St. Mary's △ CDN 61 Eg 22
Cape St. Paul △ GH 317 Gg 43
Capesterre-Belle-Eau ⌐ F 104 Ed 37
Cape Stewart △ AUS 364 Md 51
Cape Surville △ SOL 290 Nd 51
Cape Talbot △ AUS 361 Lp 52
Cape Tatnam △ CDN 43 Fc 7
Cape Thouin △ AUS 360 Lj 56
Cape Three Points △ GH 317 Ge 43
Cape Town ◪ ZA 358 Ha 62
Cape Tribulation ♀ AUS 365 Mj 54
Cape Turnagain △ NZ 383 Nl 66
Cape Upstart △ AUS 365 Mk 55
Cape Upstart ♀ AUS 365 Mk 55
Cape Vancouver △ USA 46 Ag 15
Cape van Diemen △ AUS 364 Mb 51
Cape van Diemen △ AUS 365 Mf 54
Cape Verde □ CV 316 Fh 38
Cape Verde Archipelago △ CV 316 Fh 38
Cape Verde Basin ∨ 30 Ha 8
Cape Vilanandro △ RM 345 Hp 54
Cape Vincent O USA 60 Dk 23
Cape Vohimena △ RM 353 Ja 58
Cape Voltaire △ AUS 361 Ln 53
Cape Ward Hunt △ PNG 287 Ml 50
Cape Washington △ FJI 387 Nl 55
Cape Wessel △ AUS 364 Me 51
Cape Weymouth △ AUS 365 Mh 52
Cape Wickham △ AUS 379 Mh 65
Cape Wilberforce △ AUS 364 Me 51
Cape Wolstenholme △ CDN 43 Gc 6
Cape York △ AUS 365 Mh 51
Cape York Peninsula ⌐ AUS 365 Mh 51
Cape Young △ NZ 383 Ab 67
Cape Zele'e △ SOL 290 Nc 50
Cap Finnis △ AUS 378 Md 62
Cap Freels △ CDN 61 Eh 21
Cap Garbon △ DZ 293 Gf 28
Cap Gkreko △ CY 195 Hk 28
Cap-Haïtien O RH 101 Dm 36
Capiá ～ BR 124 Fb 50
Capiatá O PY 140 Ef 58
Capibaríbe ～ BR 124 Fb 50
Capilla del Monte O RA 137 Eb 61
Capim △ BR 121 Ek 47
Capim △ BR 121 El 47
Capim Grosso O BR 125 Fa 51
Capinópolis O BR 133 Ek 55
Capinzal O BR 140 Ej 59
Cap Iones O BR 124 Fb 48
Capira O BOL 136 Ec 56
Capirenda O BOL 129 Ea 54
Capitan Baldo O PY 140 Ef 57
Capitán Porto Alegro O BR 146 Eg 60
Capitão Cardoso ～ BR 129 Ed 51
Capitão de Campos O BR 124 Ep 48
Capitão Enéas O BR 125 En 54
Capitão Leônidas Marques O BR 140 Eh 58
Capitão Poço O BR 121 El 46
Capitol O USA 51 Ck 23
Capitol Reef ♀ USA 65 Cg 26
Capivari O BR 132 Ef 55
Capivari ～ BR 141 El 57
Capixaba O BR 125 En 51
Cap Juby ⌐ MA 292 Fp 32
Cap Kormakitis △ CY 195 Hj 28
Caplanovo O RUS 250 Mh 22
Cap Low △ CDN 43 Ga 6
Çaplygin O RUS 181 Hm 19
Čaplynka O UA 175 Hj 22
Cap Mécatina △ CDN 61 Ee 20
Cap Mountain △ CDN 47 Ca 13
Cap Nachtigal ⌐ CAM 320 Gl 44
Cap Ndoua ⌐ F 386 Nf 57
Capo Blanco △ CR 97 Df 41
Capo Carbonare △ I 185 Gl 26
Capoche ～ MOC 344 Hj 53
Capo Falso △ DOM 101 Dn 36
Capolo ～ ANG 340 Gn 51
Capoma ～ RUS 159 Hm 12
Caponda O MOC 344 Hh 53
Capo Rizzuto O I 194 Ha 26
Capo San Diego △ RA 152 Eb 73
Capo San Juan △ RA 152 Ec 73
Capo San Vito △ I 185 Gn 26
Capo Spartivento △ I 185 Gl 26
Capo Vaticano △ I 185 Gp 26
Capps O USA 86 Df 30
Cap Rhir △ MA 292 Ga 30
Capricorn Channel ～ AUS 375 Mm 57
Capricorn Group △ AUS 375 Mn 57
Capricorn Section ♀ AUS 375 Mn 57
Caprivistrip ⌐ NAM 340 Hc 55
Cap Robert △ CDN 61 Ec 21
Cap Rossel △ F 386 Nf 56
Cap Roussin △ F 386 Nf 56
Cap Seize O CDN 61 Ea 21
Cap Serrat △ TN 296 Gf 27
Cap Sim △ MA 292 Ga 30
Cap Spartel △ MA 293 Gc 28
Cap St. John △ CDN 61 Eg 21
Captain Cook O USA 75 Am 36
Captains Flat O AUS 379 Ml 63
Cap Takouch △ DZ 296 Gk 27
Capua O I 185 Gn 25
Capua ～ ANG 340 Hb 53
Capucapu ～ BR 120 Ee 46
Capulin Mountain N.M. ★ USA 65 Cl 27
Capul Island △ RP 267 Lm 39
Capunda O ANG 340 Ha 51
Capunda Cavilongo O ANG 340 Gp 53
Cap Vert △ SN 304 Fm 38
Cap Wabao ⌐ F 386 Nf 56
Cap Whittle △ CDN 61 Ee 20
Cap Wom Nat. Park ★ PNG 286 Mh 47
Caquena O RCH 128 Dp 55

Caquetá ～ CO 106 Dk 45
Caqueta ～ CO 116 Dl 45
Caqueta ～ CO 117 Dn 46
Caqueta ～ CO 117 Dn 46
Caqueza O CO 106 Dm 43
Cara ～ RUS 204 Vc 7
Carabao Island △ RP 267 Ll 39
Carabaya ～ PE 128 Dp 53
Carabinani ～ BR 120 Ec 47
Carabobo ◉ YV 107 Ea 40
Caracal O RO 175 He 23
Caracaraí O BR 121 Ed 45
Caracas ◪ YV 107 Ea 40
Caracel ～ BR 121 El 50
Caracol O BR 124 En 50
Caracol O BR 140 Ef 57
Caracoli O CO 106 Dm 40
Caracollo O BOL 129 Ea 54
Caraculo O ANG 340 Gn 53
Caraga △ RP 275 Lp 42
Carai O BR 125 Ep 54
Caraíva ～ BR 125 Fa 54
Carairo △ BR 120 Ed 47
Caraíva △ BR 125 Fa 54
Carajari ～ BR 120 Eh 48
Carajas O BR 121 El 49
Carajos △ MS 31 Mb 11
Caramat ⌐ CDN 57 De 21
Caramoan O RP 267 Lm 39
Caramoan Peninsula ⌐ RP 267 Lm 39
Caramujo O BR 132 Ef 53
Caranavi O BOL 129 Ea 52
Carandaí O BR 141 En 56
Carandotta O AUS 374 Mf 57
Carangola O BR 141 En 56
Carapajó O BR 121 Ek 47
Cara-Paraná ～ CO 116 Dm 46
Carapebus O BR 141 Ep 57
Carapina O BR 141 Ep 56
Carapo O YV 112 Ec 43
Caraquet O CDN 61 Eb 22
Caratinga O BR 141 En 55
Carauari O BR 117 Ea 48
Caraúbas O BR 124 Fb 48
Caravaca d.I.C. O E 184 Ge 26
Caravela O GNB 316 Fm 40
Caravelas O BR 125 Fa 54
Caraveli O PE 128 Dm 53
Caraz ～ PE 116 Dj 50
Carazinho O BR 146 Eh 60
Carballo O E 184 Gb 24
Carberry O CDN 56 Cn 21
Carbine O AUS 368 Ll 61
Carbó O MEX 80 Cg 31
Carbonale O USA 65 Cj 26
Carbondale O USA 71 Dd 27
Carbondale O USA 74 Dl 25
Carbonear O CDN 61 Eh 22
Carboneras △ E 184 Gf 27
Carbónia O I 185 Gl 26
Carbonita O BR 125 En 54
Carcar O RP 267 Lm 40
Carcarañá O RA 137 Ec 62
Carcarañá ～ RA 137 Ed 62
Carcassonne O F 184 Gh 24
Carcross O CDN 47 Bj 15
Cardabia ～ AUS 360 Lg 57
Čardak O TR 195 Hg 27
Cardamom Mountains ⌐⌐ K 263 Lb 39
Cardeña O E 184 Gd 26
Cárdenas O MEX 92 Cn 35
Cárdenas O MEX 93 Db 36
Cárdenas O C 100 Dh 34
Cardenyabba Creek ～ AUS 374 Mh 60
Cardiff ◪ GB 163 Ge 20
Cardigan O GB 163 Gd 19
Cardigan Bay ～ GB 163 Gd 19
Cardona O ROU 146 Ef 62
Cardoso O BR 140 Ek 56
Cardston O CDN 51 Cf 21
Cardwell O AUS 365 Mk 55
Cardwell Range ⌐⌐ AUS 365 Mj 55
Carefree O USA 71 De 26
Carei O RO 174 Hd 22
Careiro da Várzea O BR 120 Ee 47
Carentan O F 163 Gf 21
Carevo O BG 195 Hf 24
Carey O USA 50 Cf 24
Carey Downs O AUS 368 Lh 58
Careysburg O LB 316 Ga 42
Cargados △ MS 31 Mb 11
Cargèse O F 185 Gl 24
Carhaix-Plouguer ～ F 163 Ge 21
Carhuanca O PE 128 Dm 52
Carhué O RA 137 Ec 64
Cariacica O BR 141 Ep 56
Cariamanga O EC 116 Dj 48
Cariango O ANG 340 Gp 51
Cariati O I 194 Ha 26
Caribbean Sea ～ 97 Dh 38
Caribe ～ MEX 93 Dc 36
Caribia O CO 106 Dk 41
Caribo Lake ～ CDN 50 Cb 19
Cariboo Mountains ⌐⌐ CDN 42 Dc 8
Caribou O USA 60 Dp 22
Caribou River ～ USA 46 Aj 17
Caricaca ～ BR 121 El 49
Carié O BR 124 Fb 50
Carievale O CDN 56 Cm 21
Carigara O RP 267 Ln 40
Carinda O AUS 379 Mk 61
Cariné O BR 124 Ep 47
Cariñena O E 184 Gf 25
Carinhanha O BR 125 En 53
Carinhanha ～ BR 133 Em 53
Caripande O ANG 341 Hd 52
Cariparé O BR 133 Em 51
Caripito O YV 112 Ec 40
Cariquima O RCH 128 Dp 55
Carira O BR 125 Fb 51
Caris ～ YV 112 Eb 41
Caritianas O BR 117 Ec 50
Carius O BR 124 Fa 49
Carleton O CDN 61 Ea 21
Carleton O CDN 61 Eb 22
Carleton O CDN 61 Eb 24
Carleton Place O CDN 60 Dk 23
Carletonville O ZA 349 Hf 59
Carlhuaz O PE 116 Dk 50
Carlin O USA 64 Cd 25

Carlindi O AUS 360 Lk 56
Carlinville O USA 71 Dc 26
Carlisle O USA 71 Dh 28
Carlisle O USA 74 Dk 25
Carlisle O GB 162 Ge 18
Carlo O AUS 374 Mf 57
Carlópolis O BR 140 Ek 57
Carlos Casares O RA 137 Ed 63
Carlos Chagas O BR 125 Ep 54
Carlos Tejedor O RA 137 Ec 63
Carlow ◉ IRL 163 Gc 19
Carloway O GB 162 Gc 16
Carlsbad O USA 64 Cd 29
Carlsbad O USA 65 Ch 29
Carlsbad O USA 81 Cm 30
Carlsbad Caverns National Park ♀ USA 65 Ck 29
Carlsberg Ridge ∨ 31 Mb 9
Carlton O AUS 379 Mk 61
Carlyle O USA 71 Dc 22
Carlyle O CDN 51 Cl 21
Carlyle Lake ～ USA 71 Dd 26
Carmacks O CDN 6 Ca 3
Carmacks O CDN 47 Bg 13
Carmagnola O I 185 Gk 23
Carman O CDN 56 Cn 21
Carmangay O CDN 51 Cf 20
Carmathen O GB 163 Gd 20
Carmaux O F 184 Gh 23
Carmelita O GCA 93 Dc 37
Carmelo O ROU 146 Ee 62
Carmen O USA 80 Cg 30
Carmen O RCH 137 Dn 60
Carmen O RP 267 Ln 41
Carmen Alto O RCH 136 Dp 57
Carmen del Areco O RA 146 Ee 63
Carmen de Patagones O RA 147 Ec 66
Carmí O CDN 50 Cc 21
Carmi O USA 71 Dd 26
Carmichael O AUS 375 Mj 56
Carmichael ～ AUS 375 Mj 57
Carmichael Crag △ AUS 369 Mb 58
Carmila O AUS 375 Ml 56
Carmo de Mata O BR 141 Em 56
Carmo de Paranaíba O BR 133 El 55
Carmolândia O BR 121 Ek 49
Carmona O CR 97 Df 40
Carmona ⌐ E 184 Gd 27
Carnamah O AUS 368 Lh 60
Carnarvon O ZA 358 Hc 61
Carnarvon O AUS 368 Lg 58
Carnarvon O AUS 375 Mk 58
Carnarvon ♀ AUS 375 Mk 58
Carnarvon Range ⌐⌐ AUS 368 Ll 58
Carnarvon Range ⌐⌐ AUS 375 Ml 58
Carnegie O AUS 368 Lm 58
Carnegie Ridge ∨ 96 De 46
Carn Eigei △ GB 162 Gd 17
Carnes O AUS 378 Md 61
Carnic Alps ⌐⌐ A 174 Gn 22
Car Nicobar Island △ IND 262 Kl 41
Carnot O RCA 321 Gp 43
Carnot Bay ～ AUS 360 Ll 54
Carol City O USA 87 Dh 32
Carolina △ KIR 35 Ba 10
Carolina O USA 104 Eb 36
Carolina O CO 106 Dl 42
Carolina O BR 121 El 49
Carolina O RA 349 Kg 59
Carolina Beach O USA 74 Dk 28
Caroline O CDN 50 Ce 19
Caroline Islands △ FSM 27 Rb 9
Caroline Peak △ NZ 382 Nf 68
Caroll O USA 70 Da 24
Carollton O USA 70 Cp 29
Caromecó O RA 146 Ed 65
Caroni ～ YV 112 Ec 43
Carora O YV 107 Dn 40
Caroval O BR 132 Ef 54
Çarovi O BR 146 Eg 60
Carozero O RUS 159 Hm 15
Carpathian Mountains ⌐⌐ SK 174 Hc 21
Carpathian Mountains ⌐⌐ RO 175 He 22
Carpenter Rocks O AUS 378 Mg 64
Carpentras O F 185 Gj 23
Carpina O BR 124 Fc 49
Carpincho ～ PY 140 Ee 57
Carpinteria O USA 64 Cc 28
Carpio O USA 56 Cm 21
Carpolac O AUS 378 Mg 64
Carrabelle O USA 86 Df 31
Carrabin O AUS 368 Lk 61
Čär Räh O AFG 223 Jk 29
Carraipia O CO 107 Dm 40
Carranya O AUS 361 Lp 55
Carrara O I 185 Gm 23
Carrara Range ⌐⌐ AUS 365 Me 55
Carrasquero O YV 107 Dm 40
Carr Boyd Range ⌐⌐ AUS 364 Ma 54
Carriacou △ WG 104 Ed 39
Carriçal O CV 316 Fh 37
Carrieton O AUS 378 Mf 62
Carril O RA 146 Ee 63
Carrington O USA 56 Cn 22
Carrington Island △ USA 64 Cf 25
Carringue O RCH 147 Dm 65
Carrión ～ E 184 Gd 24
Carrizal O CO 107 Dm 40
Carrizal ～ RCH 136 Dn 60
Carrizal O RA 137 Ea 60
Carrizal Bajo O RCH 136 Dn 60
Carrizo ～ RCH 136 Dp 58
Carrizo Creek ～ USA 65 Cl 27
Carrizo Springs O USA 81 Cm 31
Carrizozo O USA 65 Ck 29
Carrollthon O USA 70 Db 26
Carrollton O USA 86 Df 29
Carron River ～ CDN 51 Cl 19
Carrozas O CO 107 Dm 44
Čarrūd O IR 226 Jg 30
Çarşamba O TR 195 Hl 25
Çarsanga O TM 223 Jl 27
Carseland O CDN 50 Cf 20
Carson O USA 56 Cm 22
Carson ～ USA 361 Lp 53
Carson City O USA 64 Cc 26
Carson Sink ～ USA 64 Cc 26
Carstairs O CDN 50 Ce 20
Cartagena O CO 106 Dk 40
Cartagena O E 184 Gf 27

□Country ▣Capital city ◉Administrative unit ○Place ◭Island ⛰Mountain range △Mountain ⌓Cape ≈Ocean, Sea ~Lake, River ▽Undersea topography ⧍Glacier ♀National park •••Reservation ★Point of major interest ⏥Landscape

Çeşme O TR 195 Hf 26
Çeşme Bījār O IR 209 Jb 28
Češme Kabūd O IR 209 Jb 29
Cess Bay ~ LB 316 Gb 43
Cessnock O AUS 379 Mm 62
Cess River ~ LB 316 Gb 43
Cesvaine O LV 171 Hf 17
Cetraro O I 185 Gp 26
Céu Azul O BR 140 Eh 58
Ceuta O YV 107 Dn 41
Ceuta Sebta O E 293 Gd 28
Ceva O I 185 Gl 23
Cévennes ⛰ F 185 Gh 24
Ceyhan O TR 195 Hk 27
Ceyik Dağları △ TR 195 Hh 27
Ceylanpınar O TR 202 Hm 27
Ceylon O CDN 51 Ck 20
Cgengannūr O IND 239 Kc 41
Chaah O MAL 271 Lb 44
Cha-am O THA 262 Kp 39
Chaanba ⏥ DZ 296 Gh 31
Cha'anpu O VRC 255 Lf 31
Chabarovsk O RUS 26 Rb 5
Chabet el Akra ★ DZ 296 Gj 27
Chablé O MEX 93 Dc 37
Chacabuco O RA 137 Ed 63
Chacane O MOC 352 Hk 58
Chacao O RCH 147 Dm 66
Chacarilla ~ RCH 136 Dp 56
Chacay ~ RA 137 Dp 63
Chacay Alto O RCH 137 Dn 60
Chachapoyas O PE 116 Dk 49
Chacharramendi O RA 137 Eb 64
Chache O GH 317 Ge 41
Chachersk O BY 171 Hh 19
Chachevichy Klichaw O BY 171 Hg 19
Chachoeira Tunuí ~ BR 117 Dp 45
Chachoeiro de Itapemirim O BR 141 Ep 56
Chachoengsao O THA 262 La 39
Chack O PK 227 Ka 31
Chaco ~ RCH 136 Dp 58
Chaco ⏥ PY 136 Ed 57
Chaco Austral ⏥ RA 136 Ec 58
Chaco Boreal ⏥ PY 136 Ed 56
Chaco Central ⏥ RA 136 Ec 57
Chaco Culture N.H.P. ♀ USA 65 Ch 27
Chācro O PK 227 Jp 33
Chad □ TCH 309 Gp 38
Chadaouanka O RN 308 Gk 38
Chadin O PE 116 Dj 49
Chadiza O Z 344 Hj 53
Chādor Hills ⛰ IND 238 Ka 35
Chadron O USA 51 Cl 24
Chafo O WAN 320 Gj 40
Chāgai O PK 227 Jl 31
Chāgai Hills ⛰ PK 226 Jk 31
Chāgalamarri O IND 238 Kd 38
Chagcharān O AFG 223 Jl 28
Chagne O ETH 313 Hl 40
Chagos Archipelago ◭ UK 31 Nb 10
Chaguaramal O YV 112 Ec 41
Chaguaramas O TT 104 Ed 40
Chaguaramas O YV 107 Ea 41
Chaguaramas O YV 112 Ec 41
Chahbounia O DZ 296 Gh 28
Chāh Sandan O PK 226 Jk 31
Chai O MOC 344 Hn 51
Chaibāsa O IND 235 Kg 34
Chaibis O NAM 348 Ha 57
Chaillu Mountains ⛰ G 332 Gm 46
Chai Nat O THA 262 Kp 38
Chaîne des Bibans ⛰ DZ 296 Gj 27
Chaitén O RCH 147 Dm 67
Chaiya O THA 262 Kp 41
Chaiyaphum O THA 262 La 38
Chajarí O RA 146 Ee 61
Chajrjuzevo O RUS 23 Sb 4
Chākāi O IND 235 Kh 33
Chākar ~ PK 227 Jn 31
Chakari O ZW 341 Hg 55
Chakdara O PK 223 Jp 28
Chakial O IND 234 Kf 33
Châk Kâmpóng Saôm ~ K 263 Lb 40
Chakkrarat O THA 263 Lb 38
Chak Swari O PK 230 Ka 29
Chakwāl O PK 230 Ka 29
Chakwenga O Z 341 Hg 53
Chala O PE 128 Dl 53
Chala O EAT 336 Hh 49
Chalaco O PE 116 Dj 48
Chalais O F 184 Gf 23
Chalalou O PNG 287 Mk 47
Chalanta O RA 137 Eb 62
Chalatenango O ES 93 Dd 38
Chalaua O MOC 344 Hm 54
Chalbi Desert ⏥ EAK 325 Hl 44
Chalchuapa O ES 93 Dd 38
Chalengkou O VRC 231 Kl 26
Chaleur Bay ~ CDN 61 Eb 22
Chalhuanca O PE 128 Dm 53
Chaling O VRC 258 Lg 32
Chalinze O EAT 337 Hm 49
Chālisgaon O IND 234 Kb 35
Chalkidiki ⏥ GR 194 Hd 25
Chalky Inlet ~ NZ 382 Ne 69
Chalkyitsik O USA 46 Bc 11
Challa O BOL 129 Ea 54
Challakere O IND 238 Kc 38
Challans O F 163 Ge 22
Challapata O BOL 129 Ea 55
Challenger Plateau ▽ NZ 382 Nh 65
Challis O USA 50 Ce 23
Chalmette O USA 86 Dd 31
Châlons-en-Champagne O F 163 Gh 21
Chalon-sur-Saône O F 163 Gj 22
Chaltubo O GE 202 Hp 24
Chá Lugela O MOC 344 Hl 54
Cham O D 174 Gn 21
Chama O USA 65 Cj 27
Chama O Z 344 Hj 51
Chamais Bay ~ NAM 348 Gp 59
Chaman O PK 227 Jm 30
Chamaya ~ PE 116 Dj 49
Chamba O IND 230 Kc 29
Chamba O EAT 344 Hl 51
Chambal ~ IND 234 Kd 32
Chambas O C 100 Dj 34
Chamberlain O CDN 51 Cj 20
Chamberlain O USA 56 Cn 24
Chamberlain ~ AUS 361 Lp 54
Chamberlain Lake ~ USA 60 Dp 22
Chambers O USA 65 Ch 28
Chambers Bay ~ AUS 364 Mb 52
Chambersburg O USA 74 Dk 26
Chambery O F 185 Gj 23
Chambeshi ~ Z 336 Hh 50
Chambira ~ PE 116 Dl 48
Chambishi O Z 341 Hf 52
Chambo O EC 116 Dj 46
Chambord O CDN 60 Dm 21
Chambord ★ F 163 Gg 22
Chambrey O RP 267 Lm 40
Chambri Lakes ~ PNG 286 Mh 48
Chame O PA 97 Dj 41
Chamelecón ~ HN 93 Dd 38
Chametengo O MOC 344 Hk 54
Chamical O RA 137 Ea 61
Cham Ka O THA 254 Kp 36
Ch'amo Hāyk ~ ETH 325 Hl 43
Chamouchouane ~ CDN 60 Dm 21
Champa O RUS 22 Ra 3
Champagne ⏥ F 163 Gj 21
Champagne-Ardenne ◉ F 163 Gh 21
Champaign O USA 71 Dd 25
Champassak O LAO 263 Lc 38
Champerico O GCA 93 Db 38
Champotón O MEX 93 Dc 36
Chāmrājnagar △ IND 238 Kc 39
Chāmrājnagar O IND 238 Kc 40
Chamutete O ANG 340 Ha 53
Chan ◭ VN 263 Le 38
Chañaral O RCH 136 Dn 59
Chança ~ P 184 Gc 27
Chancani O RA 137 Eb 61
Chancay ~ PE 116 Dj 49
Chancay O PE 128 Dk 51
Chan Chan ★ PE 116 Dj 50
Chanchayllo O PE 128 Dk 51
Chancheng O VRC 255 Le 36
Ch'anch'o O ETH 325 Hm 41
Chanco O RCH 137 Dm 63
Chanda O IND 234 Kf 32
Chandalar River ~ USA 46 Ba 11
Chandarpur O IND 234 Kf 35
Chandausi O IND 234 Kd 31
Chāndbāli O IND 235 Kh 35
Chandeleur Islands ◭ USA 86 Dd 31
Chandeleur Sound ~ USA 86 Dd 31
Chanderi O IND 234 Kc 33
Chandigarh O IND 230 Kc 30
Chandipur O IND 235 Kh 35
Chandla O IND 234 Ke 33
Chandler O CDN 61 Eb 21
Chandler O USA 70 Da 29
Chandless ~ BR 117 Dp 50
Chandless ~ BR 132 Ef 51
Chandpur O BD 235 Kk 34
Chandrabhāga ~ IND 230 Kc 29
Chandrapur O IND 235 Kf 34
Chandrapur O IND 238 Kd 36
Chandrasekbarapuram O IND 238 Kd 38
Chanduy O EC 116 Dh 47
Chandvad O IND 234 Kb 35
Chandwa O IND 235 Kg 34
Chandwak O IND 234 Kf 33
Chandyga O RUS 22 Rb 3
Changa O Z 341 Hg 54
Changallo O PE 128 Dl 52
Changamwe O EAK 337 Hm 47
Changanācheri O IND 239 Kc 41
Changane ~ MOC 352 Hj 57
Changara O MOC 344 Hj 54
Changbai O VRC 247 Ma 25
Changbai Shan ⛰ VRC 247 Lp 25
Changcheng O VRC 246 Lj 26
Changdao O VRC 246 Ll 27
Changde O VRC 255 Lf 31
Changdeokgung Palace ★ ROK 247 Lp 27
Changfeng O VRC 246 Lj 29
Changhang O ROK 247 Lp 27
Changhua O RC 259 Ll 33
Changji O VRC 204 Tc 10
Changjiang O VRC 255 Le 36
Changjiang Kou ~ VRC 246 Lm 30
Changjie Si ★ VRC 243 Le 28
Changjin O DVRK 247 Lp 25
Changjin Ho ~ DVRK 247 Lp 25
Changkot Jering O MAL 270 La 43
Changle O VRC 243 Ld 30
Changle O VRC 258 Lk 33
Changli O VRC 246 Lk 26
Changling O VRC 243 Lg 30
Changlun O MAL 270 La 42
Changning O VRC 254 Kp 33
Changning O VRC 255 Lc 31
Changning O VRC 258 Lg 32
Chango O IND 230 Kd 30
Changphu O IND 254 Kn 32
Changpin O RC 259 Ll 34
Changping O VRC 243 Lh 25
Changsan Got ⌓ DVRK 246 Ln 26
Changsha O VRC 258 Lg 31
Changshan O VRC 258 Lk 31
Changshan Qundao ◭ VRC 246 Lm 26
Changshou O VRC 255 Ld 31
Changshu O VRC 246 Ll 30
Changshun O VRC 255 Ld 33
Changsong O DVRK 246 Ln 25
Changsŏng O ROK 247 Lp 28
Changtai O VRC 258 Lj 33
Changting O VRC 258 Lj 33
Changuillo O PE 128 Dl 53
Ch'angwon O ROK 247 Ma 28
Changwu O VRC 255 Lf 34
Changxing O VRC 246 Lk 30
Changxing Dao ◭ VRC 246 Ll 26
Changyang O VRC 255 Lc 32
Changyon O DVRK 246 Ln 26
Changyuan O VRC 243 Lh 28
Changzhi O VRC 243 Lg 27
Changzhou O VRC 246 Lk 30
Channapatna O IND 238 Kc 39
Channarāyapatna O IND 238 Kc 39
Channel Country ⏥ AUS 374 Mg 57
Channel Islands ♀ USA 64 Cb 28
Channel Islands ◭ USA 64 Cb 29
Channel Islands ◭ GB 163 Ge 21
Channel of Gonâve ~ RH 101 Dm 36
Channel of la Mona ~ DOM 101 Dp 37
Channel of Saint Marc ~ RH 101 Dm 36
Channel-Port-aux Basques O CDN 61 Ee 22
Channing O USA 65 Cl 28
Chantada O E 184 Gc 24
Chanthaburi O THA 262 La 39
Chantilly O F 163 Gh 21
Chantrey Inlet ≈ CDN 42 Fb 5
Chanty-Mansijsk O RUS 154 Sb 6
Chanute O USA 70 Da 27
Chaoeira Maracanaí ~ BR 120 Eh 46
Chaohu O VRC 246 Lj 30
Chao Hu ~ VRC 246 Lj 30
Chaource O F 163 Gj 21
Chaoyang O VRC 246 Ll 25
Chaoyang O VRC 258 Lj 34
Chaozhou O VRC 258 Lj 34
Chapada O BR 146 Eh 60
Chapada Araripe ⛰ BR 124 Ep 49
Chapada da Borborema ⏥ BR 124 Fb 49
Chapada das Mangabeiras ⛰ BR 121 El 50
Chapada Diamantina ⛰ BR 125 En 52
Chapada do Apodi ⛰ BR 124 Fa 48
Chapada dos Guimarães O BR 132 Eg 53
Chapada dos Parecis ⛰ BR 129 Ed 52
Chapadão do Sul O BR 133 Eh 55
Chapadinha O BR 124 En 47
Chapais O CDN 60 Dl 21
Chapala O MEX 92 Cl 35
Chapare ~ BOL 129 Eb 54
Chaparral O USA 65 Cj 29
Chaparral O CO 106 Dl 44
Chapecó O BR 140 Eh 59
Chapel Arm O CDN 61 Eh 22
Chapel Hill O USA 74 Dj 28
Chapell O USA 65 Cl 25
Chapelton O JA 101 Dk 36
Chapleau O CDN 57 Dg 22
Chaplin O CDN 51 Cj 20
Chapra O IND 234 Kc 34
Chapra O IND 235 Kg 33
Chapuru O SOL 290 Nb 50
Chapuy O RA 137 Ed 62
Chaquanas O TT 104 Ed 40
Chār O RIM 304 Fp 35
Charache O YV 107 Dn 41
Charadai O RA 140 Ee 59
Charagua O BOL 129 Ec 55
Charalá O CO 107 Dm 42
Charan O IND 238 Kb 37
Charcas O MEX 92 Cm 34
Charco de Peña O MEX 80 Ck 31
Charcos de Risa O MEX 81 Cl 32
Charente ~ F 163 Gg 22
Chari ~ TCH 321 Gp 39
Chārikar O AFG 223 Jn 28
Chariton O USA 70 Db 25
Chariton ~ USA 70 Db 25
Charity O GUY 113 Ee 42
Charkhi Dādri O IND 234 Kb 31
Charki ~ RUS 181 Ja 19
Charleroi O B 163 Gj 20
Charlesbourg O CDN 60 Dn 22
Charles City O USA 56 Db 24
Charles Fuhr O RA 152 Dn 71
Charles Mound △ USA 56 Dc 24
Charleston O USA 71 Dd 26
Charleston O USA 71 Dh 26
Charleston O USA 71 Dh 29
Charleston O USA 71 Dk 29
Charleston O NZ 382 Nh 66
Charleston Peak △ USA 64 Ce 27
Charlestown O USA 71 Df 26
Charlestown O KN 104 Ec 37
Charlestown O IRL 162 Gb 19
Charleville O AUS 375 Mk 59
Charleville-Mézières O F 163 Gh 21
Charlotte O USA 57 Df 24
Charlotte O USA 71 Dh 28
Charlotte O USA 71 Cn 31
Charlotte Amalie O USA 104 Eb 36
Charlotte Harbor ~ USA 87 Dg 32
Charlotte Lake ~ CDN 50 Bp 19
Charlottenberg O S 170 Gn 16
Charlottesville O USA 74 Dj 26
Charlottetown O CDN 61 Ec 22
Charlotteville O TT 104 Ed 40
Charlton O AUS 378 Mh 64
Charlton Island ◭ CDN 43 Gc 8
Charlton Island ◭ CDN 57 Dj 19
Charnley ~ AUS 361 Ln 54
Charolles O F 163 Gj 22
Charouïne O DZ 293 Gf 31
Charovsk O RUS 171 Hn 16
Charron Lake ~ CDN 56 Da 19
Chārsadda O PK 223 Jp 28
Charters Towers O AUS 375 Mk 56
Chartres O F 163 Gg 21
Chās O IND 235 Kh 34
Chaschuil O RA 136 Dp 59
Chaschuil ~ RA 136 Dp 59
Chascomús O RA 146 Ee 63
Chascomús O RA 146 Ef 63
Chashniki O BY 171 Hg 18
Chasicó O RA 147 Dp 66
Chasicó O RA 147 Ec 65
Chasquitambo O PE 128 Dk 51
Chatanga O RUS 22 Qa 2
Chatangskiy Zaliv ~ RUS 22 Qa 2
Chatanika O USA 46 Bc 13
Châteaubriant O F 163 Gf 22
Château-Chinon O F 163 Gh 22
Châteaudun O F 163 Gg 21
Château-Gontier O F 163 Gf 22
Châteaulin O F 163 Gd 21
Châteauneuf-sur-Loire O F 163 Gh 22
Château-Renault O F 163 Gg 22
Châteauroux O F 163 Gg 22
Château-Salins O F 163 Gk 21
Château-Thierry O F 163 Gh 21
Châtellerault O F 163 Gg 22
Chatfield O USA 56 Db 24
Chatham O CDN 57 Dg 24
Chatham O CDN 61 Eb 22
Chatham O USA 70 Db 29
Chatham O GB 163 Gg 20
Chatham Island ◭ AUS 368 Lj 63
Chatham Island ◭ NZ 383 Ab 67
Chatham Islands ◉ NZ 383 Ab 67
Chatham Rise ▽ NZ 383 Nl 67
Châtillon-sur-Indre O F 163 Gg 22
Châtillon-sur-Seine O F 163 Gj 22
Chatman Strait ~ USA 47 Bj 17
Chatra O IND 235 Kg 33
Chatrapur O IND 235 Kg 36
Chatsworth O CDN 57 Dh 23
Chatsworth O USA 71 Df 28
Chatsworth O AUS 374 Mg 56
Chattahoochee ~ USA 86 Df 29
Chattahoochee O USA 86 Df 30
Chattanooga O USA 71 Df 28
Chaudepalle O IND 238 Kd 39
Chaudes-Aigues O F 185 Gh 23
Chaudière ~ CDN 60 Dn 22
Châu Đốc O VN 263 Lc 40
Chauk O MYA 254 Km 35
Chaumont O F 163 Gj 21
Chaunskaya Guba ≈ RUS 205 Za 5
Chaura Island ◭ IND 262 Kl 41
Chauri O IND 238 Ka 38
Chautata O IND 230 Kb 31
Chautaugau Lake ~ USA 60 Dj 24
Chavakachcheri O CL 239 Ke 41
Chavakkad O IND 239 Kb 40
Chavarría O RA 146 Ee 60
Cha-Vat O THA 270 La 42
Chavel O BR 124 Ep 47
Chaves O BR 121 Ek 46
Chaves O P 184 Gc 25
Chaveslândia O BR 133 Ej 55
Chavin de Huántar ★ PE 116 Dk 50
Chavinillo O PE 116 Dk 50
Chavón ~ DOM 101 Dp 36
Chavuma O Z 341 Hd 52
Chavuma Falls ~ ANG 341 Hd 52
Chavuna O EAT 336 Hj 48
Chavusy O BY 171 Hh 19
Chayanta ~ BOL 129 Ea 55
Chaznī O AFG 223 Jn 29
Chazón O RA 137 Ec 62
Cheakamus Indian Reservation ••• CDN 50 Ca 21
Cheb O CZ 174 Gn 20
Chebba O TN 297 Gm 28
Cheboksary O RUS 181 Jb 17
Cheboygan O USA 57 Df 23
Checacupe O PE 128 Dn 53
Ché Ché O GNB 316 Fn 40
Checheng O RC 259 Ll 34
Cheche Pass △ LS 349 Hg 60
Chech'ŏn O ROK 247 Ma 27
Checotak O USA 70 Da 28
Chedabucto Bay ~ CDN 61 Ed 23
Cheduba Island ◭ MYA 254 Kl 36
Cheduba Strait ~ MYA 254 Kl 36
Cheektowaga O USA 60 Dj 24
Cheepash River ~ CDN 57 Dh 20
Cheepie O AUS 375 Mj 59
Cheesman Peak △ AUS 369 Mb 59
Chefchaouen O MA 293 Gd 28
Chefornak O USA 46 Ag 15
Chéfu ~ MOC 352 Hj 57
Chegga O RIM 293 Gd 33
Chegga O DZ 296 Gj 28
Chegutu O ZW 341 Hh 55
Chehalis O USA 50 Ca 22
Chehalis ~ USA 50 Ca 22
Chehong Jiang ~ VRC 255 Lb 32
Cheïrik O RIM 304 Fp 35
Chelan O USA 50 Cc 22
Chelan O CDN 51 Cl 19
Cheleka O ZA 348 Hc 58
Ch'elenk'o O ETH 325 Hn 41
Chelforó O RA 147 Ea 65
Chelghoum el Aïd O DZ 296 Gj 27
Chelinda O MW 344 Hj 51
Cheline O MOC 352 Hk 57
Chellal O DZ 296 Gj 28
Chełm O PL 175 Hd 20
Chełmno O PL 170 Hb 19
Chelmsford O GB 163 Gg 20
Chelmsford Dam ~ ZA 349 Hg 59
Cheltenham O GB 163 Ge 20
Chelvai O IND 238 Ke 36
Chelyabinsk O RUS 154 Sa 7
Chemaïa O MA 292 Gb 29
Chemax O MEX 93 De 35
Chemba O MOC 344 Hk 54
Chembe O Z 341 Hg 51
Chemillé O F 163 Gf 22
Chemnitz O D 174 Gn 20
Chemuumi ~ ZW 341 Hf 55
Chenāb ~ PK 230 Ka 30
Chenāb ~ IND 230 Kb 29
Chenachane O DZ 293 Gd 32
Chenacharte ~ DZ 293 Gd 33
Ch'ench'a O ETH 325 Hl 42
Chencoyi O MEX 93 Dc 36
Cheney O USA 50 Cd 22
Cheney Reservation ~ USA 70 Cn 27
Chengalpattu O IND 238 Kd 39
Chengam O IND 238 Kd 39
Chengbu O VRC 255 Le 32
Chengcheng O VRC 243 Le 28
Chengde O VRC 246 Lj 25
Chengdu O VRC 242 Lc 30
Chenggu O VRC 243 Ld 29
Cheng Hai ~ VRC 254 La 32
Chenghai O VRC 258 Lj 34
Chengjiagang O VRC 246 Lk 28
Chengmai O VRC 255 Le 36
Chengqian O VRC 246 Lj 28
Chengshan Jiano ⌓ VRC 246 Lm 27
Chengwu O VRC 243 Lh 28
Chengxi O VRC 243 Ld 30
Cheng Xian O VRC 243 Lc 29
Chenini O TN 296 Gm 29
Chennai Madras O IND 238 Ke 39
Chenoa O USA 71 Dd 25
Chenxi O VRC 255 Lf 31
Chenzhou O VRC 258 Lg 33
Cheo Reo O VN 263 Le 39
Chepen O PE 116 Dj 49
Chépénéhé O F 386 Nf 56
Chepes O RA 137 Ea 61
Chepo O PA 97 Dj 41
Chepstow O GB 163 Ge 20
Cher ~ F 163 Gg 22
Cheran O MEX 92 Cl 36
Cherangany Hills ⛰ EAK 325 Hk 45
Cheraw O USA 71 Dh 28
Cherbourg O F 163 Gf 21
Cherchell O DZ 296 Gh 27
Cherepovets O RUS 171 Hm 16
Chéri O RN 308 Gm 39
Cheria O DZ 296 Gk 28
Cherkessk O RUS 202 Hn 23
Chermult O USA 50 Cb 24
Cherokee O USA 56 Da 24
Cherokee O USA 70 Cn 27
Cherokee O USA 71 Dg 28
Cherokee Indian Reservation ••• USA 71 Dg 28
Cherokee Lake ~ USA 71 Dg 27
Cherokee Sound O BS 87 Dk 32
Cherrabun O AUS 361 Ln 55
Cherry Creek ~ USA 51 Cl 23
Cherry Creek O USA 56 Cm 23
Cherry Creek O USA 64 Ce 26
Cherry Spring O USA 81 Cn 30
Cherryville O CDN 50 Cc 20
Cherryville O USA 70 Dc 27
Cherskogo, Khrebet ⛰ RUS 22 Rb 3
Cherskogo, Khrebet ⛰ RUS 205 Xa 5
Chervyen' O BY 171 Hg 19
Chesapeake O USA 74 Dk 27
Chesapeake Bay ~ USA 74 Dk 26
Chesea ~ PE 116 Dm 50
Cheshskaya guba ≈ RUS 154 Ra 5
Chest ~ USA 74 Dj 26
Chester O USA 51 Cg 21
Chester O USA 56 Db 24
Chester O CDN 61 Eb 23
Chester O USA 71 Dd 27
Chester O USA 71 Dh 28
Chester O USA 74 Dk 27
Chester O GB 163 Ge 19
Chesterfield O USA 71 Dc 26
Chesterfield O GB 163 Gf 19
Chesterfield Inlet ≈ CDN 42 Fc 6
Chesterfield Inlet O CDN 43 Fc 6
Chesterfield Islands ◭ F 35 Sb 11
Chesterton Range ⛰ AUS 375 Mk 58
Chestertown O USA 60 Dl 24
Chestertown O USA 74 Dk 26
Chesuncook ~ USA 60 Dp 22
Chetaibi O DZ 296 Gk 27
Chetek O USA 56 Dc 23
Chéticamp O CDN 61 Ed 22
Chetlat Island ◭ IND 238 Ka 40
Chetumal O BH 93 Dd 36
Chetwynd O CDN 47 Ca 17
Chevak O USA 46 Ag 15
Chevejecure ~ BOL 129 Eb 53
Chevoit Hills ⛰ GB 162 Ge 18
Chevoit O NZ 383 Nj 67
Chewelah O USA 50 Cd 21
Cheyenne ~ USA 51 Cl 24
Cheyenne O USA 65 Ck 25
Cheyenne O USA 70 Cn 28
Cheyenne Bottoms ~ USA 70 Cn 26
Cheyenne River ~ USA 51 Ck 24
Cheyenne River Ind. Res. ••• USA 56 Cm 23
CheyenneWells O USA 65 Cl 26
Cheyūr O IND 238 Ke 39
Chhāpar O IND 234 Kb 32
Chhatarpur O IND 234 Kd 33
Chhattīsgarh ◉ IND 234 Ke 34
Chhattīsgarh ⏥ IND 234 Ke 35
Chhaygaon O IND 235 Kk 33
Chhindwāra O IND 234 Kd 35
Chhota Udepur O IND 234 Kb 34
Chhukha O BHT 235 Kj 32
Chhura O IND 234 Kf 35
Chía O CO 106 Dl 43
Ch'iaksan ★ ROK 247 Ma 27
Chiamboni O SP 337 Hn 46
Chiange O ANG 340 Gn 53
Chiang Kan O LAO 262 La 37
Chiang Kan O THA 262 La 37
Chiang Kham O THA 254 La 36
Chiang Khong O THA 254 La 35
Chiang Mai O THA 254 Kp 36
Chiang Rai O THA 254 Kp 36
Chian Muan O THA 254 Kp 36
Chiapa ~ MEX 93 Db 37
Chiapa de Corzo O MEX 93 Db 37
Chiasien O RC 259 Ll 34
Chiat'ura O GE 202 Hp 24
Chiautla O MEX 92 Cn 36
Chiavenna O I 174 Gl 22
Chiawa O Z 341 Hg 53
Chiayi O RC 259 Ll 34
Chiba O J 251 Mg 28
Chibabava O MOC 352 Hj 56
Chibbyit O MYA 254 Km 34
Chibemba O ANG 340 Gp 53
Chibembe O Z 344 Hj 52
Chibia O ANG 340 Gn 53
Chibombo O Z 341 He 53
Chibougamau O CDN 60 Dl 21
Chibougamau ~ CDN 60 Dl 21
Chibuto O MOC 352 Hj 58
Chibwika O Z 341 He 52
Chicago O USA 71 De 25
Chicago Hts. O USA 71 De 25
Chicala O ANG 340 Ha 52
Chicala O ANG 340 Hb 51
Chicamba O MOC 344 Hj 55
Chicambi O ANG 340 Gn 52
Chicapa ~ ANG 333 Hc 49
Chicayan O MEX 92 Cn 35
Chicha O TCH 309 Hb 37
Chichagof Island ◭ USA 6 Ca 4
Chichagof Island ◭ USA 47 Bg 17
Chichaoua O MA 292 Gb 30
Chicheng O VRC 243 Lh 25
Chichén Itza ★ MEX 93 Dd 35
Chichibu O J 251 Mf 27
Chichigalpa O NIC 96 De 39
Chickamauge Lake ~ USA 71 Df 28
Chickasha O USA 70 Cp 28
Chicken O USA 46 Be 13
Chiclayo O PE 116 Dj 49
Chico O USA 64 Cb 26
Chico ~ RA 136 Eb 59
Chico ~ RA 147 Dn 67
Chico ~ RA 152 Dn 70
Chico ~ RA 152 Dp 68
Chico ~ RA 152 Dp 70
Chico ~ RA 152 Dp 71
Chico ~ RA 152 Ea 68
Chico O MOC 352 Hj 56
Chicoa O MOC 344 Hj 53
Chicoasén O MEX 93 Db 37
Chicoca O ANG 340 Hc 53
Chicoma Mountain △ USA 65 Cj 27
Chicomba O ANG 340 Gp 53
Chicomo O MOC 352 Hj 58
Chicondua ~ ANG 340 Gn 53
Chicontepec de Tejeda O MEX 92 Cn 35
Chicopee O USA 60 Dm 24
Chicoral O CO 106 Dl 43
Chicoutimi O CDN 60 Dn 21
Chicualacuala O MOC 352 Hh 57
Chicuma O ANG 340 Gp 52
Chicundo O ANG 340 Ha 52
Ch'ida O ETH 325 Hl 42
Chidambaram O IND 239 Kd 40
Chidenguele O MOC 352 Hk 58
Chido O ROK 247 Lp 28
Chidu O SUD 325 Hj 41
Chief Joseph Pass △ USA 50 Cf 23
Chiefland O USA 86 Dg 31
Chief Menominee Mon. ★ USA 71 De 25
Chief's Island ◭ RB 341 Hd 55
Chiemsee ~ D 174 Gn 22
Chiengi O Z 336 Hg 50
Chieng Khu'o'ng O VN 255 Lb 35
Chieo Lan Reservoir ~ THA 262 Kp 41
Chieti O I 194 Gp 24
Chifango O ANG 340 Ha 53
Chifukunya Hills △ Z 341 Hg 53
Chifumage ~ ANG 341 Hc 51
Chifunda O Z 344 Hj 51
Chifunde O MOC 344 Hj 53
Chigamane O MOC 352 Hj 56
Chiginagak Bay ~ USA 46 Al 17
Chigmit Mountains ⛰ USA 46 An 15
Chignecto Bay ~ CDN 61 Eb 23
Chignik O USA 10 Ba 4
Chignik Bay ~ USA 46 Al 17
Chignik Lake O USA 46 Al 17
Chigombe ~ MOC 352 Hj 57
Chigorodo O CO 106 Dk 42
Chiguana O BOL 136 Dp 56
Chigubo O MOC 352 Hj 57
Chihuahua O MEX 80 Cj 31
Chikalda △ IND 234 Kc 35
Chikanda O WAN 320 Gh 41
Chikhli O IND 234 Kd 34
Chikhli O IND 238 Ka 35
Chikjajur O IND 238 Kb 38
Chikmagalūr O IND 238 Kb 39
Chikodi O IND 238 Kb 37
Chikombedzi O ZW 352 Hh 56
Chikuminuk Lake ~ USA 46 Al 15
Chikwa O Z 344 Hj 51
Chikwawa O MW 344 Hk 54
Chikwina O MW 344 Hk 51
Chila O MEX 92 Cp 35
Chila O ANG 340 Gp 52
Chilakalūrupet O IND 238 Ke 37
Chilan O RC 259 Ll 33
Chi Lăng O VN 255 Ld 35
Chilanga O Z 341 Hg 53
Chilanko Forks O CDN 50 Bp 19
Chilapa O MEX 92 Cn 37
Chilapa de Díaz O MEX 92 Cp 36
Chilas O PK 230 Kb 28
Chilaw O CL 239 Kd 42
Chilca O PE 128 Dk 52
Chilcaya O RCH 128 Dp 55
Chilchinbito O USA 65 Cg 27
Chilcoot O USA 64 Cb 26
Chilcotin ~ CDN 50 Bp 19
Childers O AUS 375 Mn 58
Childersburg O USA 71 De 29
Childress O USA 70 Cm 28
Chile □ RCH 137 Dm 62
Chile Chico O RCH 152 Dn 69
Chilecito O RA 137 Ea 60
Chileka O MW 344 Hk 53
Chilembwe O Z 341 Hh 52
Chile Rise ▽ 15 Ea 13
Chilete O PE 116 Dj 49
Chilicothe O USA 71 Dg 26
Chililabombwe O Z 341 Hf 52
Chilko Lake ~ CDN 50 Bp 20
Chilla O EC 116 Dj 47
Chillagoe O AUS 365 Mj 54
Chillajara O BOL 136 Dp 56
Chillán O RCH 137 Dm 64
Chillan ~ RCH 137 Dn 64
Chillar O RA 146 Ee 64
Chillar Well O AUS 361 Mb 56
Chillicothe O USA 70 Db 26
Chillicothe O USA 71 Dd 25
Chillinji O PK 230 Kb 27
Chillūpār O IND 235 Kf 32
Chilmari O BD 235 Kj 33
Chilobwe O MW 344 Hj 52
Chilombo O ANG 341 Hd 52
Chiloquin O USA 50 Cb 24
Chilpancingo O MEX 92 Cm 37
Chilpi O IND 234 Ke 34
Chilton O USA 57 Dd 23
Chiltrepec O MEX 93 Db 36
Chiluage O ANG 341 Hc 50
Chiluango ~ ANG 332 Gn 48
Chilubula O Z 341 Hh 51
Chilumba O MW 344 Hk 51
Chimala O EAT 337 Hj 50
Chimaliro O MW 344 Hk 51
Chimaltenango O GCA 93 Dc 38
Chiman O PA 97 Dj 41
Chimanimani O ZW 344 Hj 55
Chimanimani ♀ ZW 344 Hj 55
Chimayo O USA 65 Ck 28
Chimban O PE 116 Dj 49
Chimbarongo O RCH 137 Dn 63
Chimbinde O ANG 340 Hb 52
Chimbo ~ EC 116 Dj 47
Chimbote O PE 116 Dj 50
Chiméal O K 263 Lb 40
Chimichguá O CO 106 Dl 41
Chimki O RUS 171 Hl 18
Chimney Rock N.H.S. ★ USA 65 Cl 25
Chimoio O MOC 344 Hj 55
Chimolo O ZW 352 Hh 56
Chimumo ~ ANG 340 Ha 54
Chimur O IND 234 Kd 35
China O MEX 81 Cn 33
China ▣ VRC 243 Lg 27
Chinacota O CO 107 Dm 42
Chinampas O MEX 92 Cl 35
Chinandega O NIC 96 De 39

Çeşme - Chinandega 409

□Country ⊡Capital city ⊙Administrative unit ○Place ⌂Island ⛰Mountain range △Mountain ⌓Cape ≈Ocean, Sea ~Lake, River ♆Undersea topography △Glacier ♀National park •••Reservation ★Point of major interest ⏥Landscape

Chinati Peak △ USA 81 Ck 31
Chincha Alta ○ PE 128 Dk 52
Chinchilla ○ AUS 375 Mm 59
Chinchina ○ CO 106 Dl 43
Chinchin Straits ≈ 270 Kp 42
Chincolco ○ RCH 137 Dn 62
Chincoteague Bay ~ USA 74 Dl 26
Chinde ○ MOC 344 Hk 55
Chin Do ⌂ ROK 247 Ln 28
Chindo ○ ROK 247 Lp 28
Chindrikir' ○ PK 230 Kb 27
Chindwinn ~ MYA 254 Km 33
Chindwinn ~ MYA 254 Km 34
Chinegue ○ MOC 344 Hk 52
Chingara ♀ CO 107 Dm 43
Chingo ○ ANG 340 Gn 53
Chingola ○ Z 341 Hf 52
Chingombe ○ Z 341 Hg 53
Chinguar ○ ANG 340 Ha 52
Chingueia ○ ANG 340 Ha 52
Chinguețți ○ RIM 304 Fp 35
Chinguil ○ TCH 321 Hb 40
Chinhama ○ ANG 340 Ha 52
Chinhanda ○ MOC 344 Hj 53
Chinhanguanine ○ MOC 352 Hj 58
Chinhoyi ○ ZW 341 Hh 54
Chiniot ○ PK 230 Ka 30
Chinjan ○ PK 227 Jm 30
Chinju ○ ROK 247 Lp 28
Chinkapook ○ AUS 378 Mh 63
Chinko ~ RCA 324 He 42
Chinle ○ USA 65 Ch 27
Chinmen ○ RC 258 Lk 33
Chinmen Tao ⌂ RC 258 Lk 33
Chinnur ○ IND 238 Kd 36
Chinon ○ F 163 Gg 22
Chinook ○ USA 51 Ch 21
Chino Valley ○ USA 64 Cf 28
Chinpurtar ○ NEP 235 Kh 32
Chinsali ○ Z 341 Hh 51
Chintalnār ○ IND 238 Ke 36
Chintāmani ○ IND 238 Kd 39
Chintheche ○ MW 344 Hj 51
Chinturu ○ IND 238 Ke 37
Chinyama Litapi ○ Z 341 Hd 52
Chioco ○ MOC 344 Hj 54
Chióggia ○ I 185 Gn 23
Chioutneticoe Lake ~ CDN 60 Ea 23
Chipanga ○ MOC 344 Hk 54
Chipasanse ○ Z 336 Hh 50
Chipata ○ Z 344 Hj 52
Chipepo ○ Z 341 Hf 54
Chipili ○ Z 341 Hg 51
Chipindo ○ ANG 340 Gp 52
Chipinge ○ ZW 352 Hj 56
Chipipa ○ ANG 340 Gp 52
Chipiriri ~ BOL 129 Eb 54
Chip Lake ~ CDN 50 Ce 19
Chipley ○ USA 86 Df 30
Chiplūn ○ IND 238 Ka 37
Chipman ○ CDN 51 Cf 19
Chipman ○ CDN 61 Eb 22
Chipman Lake ~ CDN 57 Df 21
Chipogolo ○ EAT 337 Hk 49
Chipoia ○ ANG 340 Hb 52
Chipoka ○ MW 344 Hk 53
Chippewa Fs. ○ USA 56 Dc 23
Chipungo ○ Z 341 Hh 52
Chiputo ○ MOC 344 Hj 53
Chiquian ○ PE 128 Dk 51
Chiquihuitlán ○ MEX 92 Cp 37
Chiquilá ○ MEX 93 De 35
Chiquimula ○ GCA 93 Dd 38
Chiquimulilla ○ GCA 93 Dc 38
Chiquinquirá ○ CO 106 Dl 43
Chira ~ PE 116 Dh 48
Ch'ira ○ ETH 325 Hl 42
Chirāla ○ IND 238 Ke 38
Chiramba ○ MOC 344 Hk 54
Chiredzi ○ ZW 352 Hh 56
Chirfa ○ RN 308 Gn 35
Chirgaon ○ IND 234 Kd 33
Chiriacu ○ PE 116 Dj 48
Chiribiquete ♀ CO 116 Dm 45
Chiricahua National Monument ★ USA 80 Ch 30
Chiricahua Peak △ USA 80 Ch 30
Chirikof Island ⌂ USA 46 An 17
Chirimena ○ YV 107 Ea 40
Chiriqui Grande ○ PA 97 Dg 41
Chiris ~ PE 128 Dl 52
Chirisan ♀ ROK 247 Lp 28
Chirma River ~ PNG 287 Mk 50
Chiromo ○ MW 344 Hk 54
Chirovanga ○ SOL 290 Na 49
Chirripó ~ CR 97 Dg 40
Chirripó del Atlantico ~ CR 97 Dg 41
Chirumanzu ○ ZW 341 Hh 55
Chirundu ○ Z 341 Hg 54
Chisamba ○ Z 341 Hg 53
Chisasibi ○ CDN 43 Gb 8
Chisec ○ GCA 93 Dc 38
Chisekesi ○ Z 341 Hf 54
Chisenga ○ MW 337 Hj 50
Chishi Island ⌂ Z 341 Hg 51
Chisholm ○ USA 56 Db 22
Chishui ○ VRC 255 Lc 31
Chishui He ~ VRC 255 Lc 31
Chishuihejie ○ VRC 255 Lc 32
Chisimba Falls ~ Z 341 Hh 51
Chişinău ⊡ MD 175 Hg 22
Chişineu-Criş ○ RO 174 Hc 22
Chisisa ○ Z 341 He 52
Chisoso ○ Z 341 Hh 51
Chissano ○ MOC 352 Hj 58
Chissinguane ○ MOC 352 Hk 56
Chistian Mandy ○ PK 227 Ka 31
Chistochina ○ USA 46 Bc 13
Chisumbanje ○ ZW 352 Hh 56
Chita ○ BOL 129 Ea 55
Chita ○ EAT 337 Hk 50
Chitado ○ ANG 340 Gn 54
Chitagá ○ CO 107 Dm 42
Chitāpur ○ IND 238 Kc 37
Chitek ○ CDN 51 Ch 19
Chitek Lake ~ CDN 56 Cn 19
Chitembo ○ ANG 340 Ha 52
Chí Thanh ○ VN 263 Le 39
Chitimacha Indian Reservation ••• USA 86 Dc 31
Chitina ○ USA 46 Bc 15
Chitipa ○ MW 337 Hj 50
Chitobe ○ MOC 352 Hj 56
Chitongo ○ Z 341 Hf 54
Chitose ○ J 250 Mg 24
Chitowe ○ EAT 344 Hm 51
Chitradurga ○ IND 238 Kc 38
Chitrakūt ○ IND 234 Ke 33
Chitrāl ○ PK 223 Jp 28
Chitré ○ PA 97 Dh 42
Chittagong ○ BD 235 Kk 34
Chittar ~ IND 239 Kc 41
Chittaranjan ○ IND 235 Kh 34
Chittaurgarh ○ IND 234 Kb 33
Chittivalasa ○ IND 238 Kf 37
Chittoor ○ IND 238 Kd 39
Chitungwiza ○ ZW 341 Hh 55
Chityāl ○ IND 238 Kd 37
Chiulezi ~ MOC 344 Hl 51
Chiumbe ~ ANG 340 Hb 51
Chiumbo ○ ANG 340 Gp 52
Chiume ○ ANG 340 Hc 53
Chiúre ○ MOC 344 Hm 52
Chiúre Novo ○ MOC 344 Hm 52
Chiusa Sclafani ○ I 185 Gn 27
Chiúta ○ MOC 344 Hj 53
Chivacoa ○ YV 107 Dp 40
Chivasingo ○ PNG 287 Mk 49
Chivato ○ RCH 136 Dn 59
Chivay ○ PE 128 Dn 53
Chivé ○ BOL 129 Dp 52
Chivhu ○ ZW 341 Hh 55
Chivilcoy ○ RA 137 Ed 63
Chivirico ○ C 101 Dk 36
Chiviriga ~ ZW 352 Hh 56
Chivolo ○ CO 106 Dl 40
Chivuna ○ Z 341 Hf 54
Chiweta ○ MW 344 Hk 51
Chixoy o Negro ~ GCA 93 Dc 38
Chizarira ♀ ZW 341 Hf 54
Chizarira Hills ⛰ ZW 341 Hf 54
Chizela ○ Z 341 He 52
Chizu ○ J 251 Md 28
Chlef El Asnam ○ DZ 293 Gg 27
Chmel'nyc'kyj ○ UA 175 Hf 21
Chmel'nyk ○ UA 175 Hg 21
Chŏâm Khsant ○ K 263 Lc 38
Choapa ~ RCH 137 Dn 61
Choapan ○ MEX 93 Da 37
Chobe ~ NAM 341 He 54
Chobe ♀ RB 341 He 55
Chocolate Hills ★ RP 267 Lm 41
Chocolate Mountains ⛰ USA 64 Ce 29
Chocontá ○ CO 106 Dm 43
Chocope ○ PE 116 Dj 49
Chocotawhatchee ~ USA 86 Df 30
Choctawhatchee Bay ~ USA 86 De 30
Choctaw Indian Reservation ••• USA 86 Dd 29
Chodavaram ○ IND 238 Kf 37
Cho Do ⌂ DVRK 246 Ln 26
Choele Choel ○ RA 147 Eb 65
Chofombo ○ MOC 341 Hh 53
Chogā Zanbil ★ IR 215 Jc 30
Choiceland ○ CDN 51 Ck 19
Choirokoitia ★ CY 195 Hj 28
Choiseul ⌂ SOL 290 Na 49
Choiseul Sound ~ GB 147 Ee 71
Choix ○ MEX 80 Cf 32
Chojnice ○ PL 170 Ha 19
Chojniki ○ BY 175 Hh 20
Chōkai-san △ J 251 Mf 26
Chok Chai ○ THA 262 La 38
Choke Canyon Lake ~ USA 81 Cn 31
Ch'ok'ē Terara △ ETH 313 Hl 40
Chókwè ○ MOC 352 Hj 58
Cholame ○ USA 64 Cb 28
Chola Shan ⛰ VRC 242 Kp 29
Chola Shan △ VRC 242 Kp 30
Chola Shankou △ VRC 242 Kp 30
Cholchol ~ RCH 147 Dm 65
Cholet ○ F 163 Gf 22
Cholm ○ RUS 171 Hh 17
Cholm-Žirkovskij ○ RUS 171 Hj 18
Cholula ○ MEX 92 Cn 36
Choluteca ○ HN 96 De 39
Choluteca ~ HN 96 De 39
Ch'ŏlwŏn ○ ROK 247 Lp 26
Choma ○ Z 341 Hf 54
Chom Bung ○ THA 262 Kp 39
Chom Phra ○ THA 263 Lb 38
Chom Tong ○ THA 254 Kp 36
Chomūn ○ IND 234 Kb 32
Chona ~ EAT 337 Hj 48
Ch'ŏnan ○ ROK 247 Lp 27
Chonarwa ○ NEP 235 Kh 32
Chon Buri ○ THA 262 La 39
Chonchi ○ RCH 147 Dl 67
Chonchon ○ DVRK 247 Lp 25
Chon Daen ○ THA 262 La 37
Chone ○ EC 116 Dh 46
Chongchon ~ DVRK 247 Ln 26
Chongjin ○ DVRK 247 Ma 25
Ch'ŏngju ○ ROK 247 Lp 27
Chongming ○ VRC 246 Ll 30
Chongmyo Shrine ★ ROK 247 Lp 27
Chongoene ○ MOC 352 Hj 58
Chongorói ○ ANG 340 Gn 52
Chongoyape ○ PE 116 Dj 49
Chong Phan ~ THA 262 Kp 41
Chongpyong ○ DVRK 247 Lp 26
Chongqing ○ VRC 242 Lb 30
Chongqing ○ VRC 255 Ld 31
Chongren ○ VRC 258 Lj 32
Chong Samui ~ THA 262 Kp 41
Ch'ŏngsan Do ⌂ ROK 247 Lp 28
Chong Tao ~ THA 262 Kp 41
Chongwe ○ Z 341 Hg 53
Chongwe ~ Z 341 Hg 53
Chongyang ○ VRC 258 Lh 31
Chongyi ○ VRC 258 Lh 33
Chongzuo ○ VRC 255 Ld 34
Chŏnju ○ ROK 247 Lp 28
Chontalpa ○ MEX 93 Db 37
Cho'n Thành ○ VN 263 Ld 40
Chonuu ○ RUS 23 Sa 3
Cho Oyu △ VRC 235 Kh 31
Chopda ○ IND 234 Kb 35
Chopinzinho ○ BR 140 Eh 58
Chorales del Rosaria ♀ CO 106 Dk 40
Chorkerup ○ AUS 368 Lj 63
Choró ○ BR 124 Fa 48
Choro ~ BR 124 Fa 48
Chorol ○ UA 175 Hj 21
Chorolque ~ BOL 129 Eb 54
Chorolque △ BOL 136 Ea 56
Choromoro ○ RA 136 Eb 59
Chorregon ○ AUS 375 Mh 57
Chorrillos ○ PE 128 Dk 52
Chorro la Libertad ~ CO 117 Dp 46
Chorzów ○ PL 174 Hb 20
Chōshi ○ J 251 Mg 28
Chosica ○ PE 128 Dk 51
Chos Malal ○ RA 137 Dn 64
Chota ○ PE 116 Dj 49
Choteau ○ USA 51 Cf 22
Chotyn ○ UA 175 Hf 21
Chotynec ○ RUS 171 Hk 19
Choûm ○ RIM 304 Fp 35
Chouteau ○ USA 70 Da 27
Chovd ○ MNG 22 Pb 5
Chowan ~ USA 74 Dk 27
Chowchilla ○ USA 64 Cb 27
Choz ~ Z 336 Hj 50
Chozi ○ Z 336 Hj 50
Chrene ★ LAR 300 Hc 29
Chrisman ○ USA 71 Dd 26
Chrisman ○ USA 71 De 26
Christchurch ○ NZ 383 Nj 67
Christiana ○ ZA 349 He 59
Christiansburg ○ USA 71 Dh 27
Christianshåb ○ DK 7 Ga 3
Christiansted ○ USA 104 Eb 37
Christie Bay ~ CDN 42 Eb 6
Christina Lake ○ CDN 50 Cc 21
Christino Castro ○ BR 121 Em 50
Christmas Creek ○ AUS 361 Lp 55
Christmas Creek ~ AUS 361 Lp 55
Christmas Island ⌂ AUS 278 Lc 51
Christmas Valley ○ USA 50 Cb 24
Chromer ○ GB 163 Gg 19
Chromo ○ USA 65 Cj 27
Chrystel Cave ★ USA 56 Db 23
Chuathbaluk ○ USA 46 Al 15
Chuave ○ PNG 287 Mj 49
Chub Cay ○ BS 87 Dj 33
Chubu-Sangaku ♀ J 251 Me 27
Chubut ○ RA 147 Dn 67
Chubut ~ RA 147 Dp 67
Chubut ~ RA 147 Ea 67
Chuchiliga ○ GH 317 Gf 40
Chucuma ○ RA 137 Ea 61
Chucunaque ~ PA 97 Dj 41
Chu Dang Sin △ VN 263 Le 39
Chugach Mountains ⛰ USA 46 Bc 15
Chugchug ~ RCH 136 Dp 57
Chugoku-sanchi ⛰ J 251 Mc 28
Chugui ○ PE 128 Dm 52
Chugwater ○ USA 65 Ck 25
Chuhar Jamāli ○ PK 227 Jm 33
Chuhar Kāna ○ PK 230 Ka 30
Chui ○ BR 146 Eh 62
Chui Chui ○ RCH 136 Dp 57
Ch'uja Do ⌂ ROK 247 Lp 29
Chuka ○ EAK 337 Hl 46
Chukai ○ MAL 271 Lb 43
Chukchi Peninsula ⌂ RUS 23 Aa 3
Chukchi Peninsula ⌂ RUS 46 Ac 11
Chukchi Sea ≈ 23 Aa 3
Chukotskiy Peninsula ⌂ RUS 205 Aa 5
Chukotskoye Nagor'ye ⛰ RUS 23 Tb 3
Chula ○ USA 64 Cd 29
Chulitna ○ USA 46 Ba 13
Chulucanas ○ PE 116 Dh 48
Chulymskaya Ravnina ⏥ RUS 204 Tc 7
Chuma ○ BOL 128 Dp 53
Chuma Shankou △ VRC 242 Kn 30
Chumberland ○ USA 74 Dj 27
Chumbicha ○ RA 137 Ea 60
Chumbo ○ BR 133 El 55
Chumikgiarsa ○ IND 230 Kc 29
Chumphae ○ THA 262 La 37
Chumphon ○ THA 262 Kp 40
Chumpi ○ PE 128 Dm 53
Chumsaeng ○ THA 262 La 38
Chun ○ THA 254 La 36
Chuna ○ PK 230 Ka 30
Chun'an ○ VRC 258 Lk 31
Chunchi ○ EC 116 Dj 47
Ch'unch'ŏn ○ ROK 247 Lp 27
Chunchura ○ IND 235 Kh 34
Chundela ○ ANG 340 Hc 53
Chunga ○ Z 341 Hf 53
Chunga ○ Z 344 Hj 51
Chungara ○ RCH 128 Dp 55
Ch'ungju ○ ROK 247 Lp 27
Ch'ungmu ○ ROK 247 Lp 28
Chungyang Shanmo ⛰ RC 259 Ll 34
Chūniān ○ PK 230 Ka 30
Chunshui ○ VRC 243 Lg 29
Chunwan ○ VRC 255 Lf 34
Chunya ○ EAT 337 Hj 50
Chuŏr Phnum Dângrek ⛰ K 263 Lb 38
Chupadero de Caballo ○ MEX 81 Cm 31
Chu' Pha ○ VN 263 Ld 39
Chu' Prông ○ VN 263 Ld 39
Chuquibamba ○ PE 128 Dm 53
Chuquibambilla ○ PE 128 Dm 53
Chuquicamata ○ RCH 136 Dp 57
Chuquicara ○ PE 116 Dj 50
Chuquis ○ PE 116 Dk 50
Chur ○ CH 174 Gl 22
Churachāndpur ○ IND 254 Kl 33
Churcampa ○ PE 128 Dl 52
Churchbridge ○ CDN 56 Cm 20
Churchill ~ CDN 42 Fb 7
Churchill ○ CDN 42 Fc 7
Churchill ~ CDN 43 Hc 8
Churchill Falls ○ CDN 61 Ec 19
Churchill River ~ CDN 6 Ea 4
Churchill River ~ CDN 61 Ed 19
Churchs Ferry ○ USA 56 Cn 21
Churia Range ⛰ NEP 234 Ke 31
Churia Range ⛰ NEP 235 Kg 32
Churin ○ PE 128 Dk 51
Churit Tso ~ VRC 231 Kg 30
Churu ○ IND 234 Kb 31
Churuguara ○ YV 107 Dp 40
Chu' Sê ○ VN 263 Le 39
Chuska Mountains ⛰ USA 65 Ch 27
Chusmisa ○ RCH 128 Dp 55
Chust ○ UA 175 Hd 21
Chute Akamba ~ RDC 324 Hf 45
Chute Bangu ~ RDC 324 He 44
Chute de la Vina ~ CAM 321 Gn 42
Chute du Tello ~ CAM 321 Gn 42
Chute Kamimbi Fuka ~ RDC 336 He 50
Chute Kiubo ~ RDC 336 Hf 50
Chute Malamba Gungu ~ RDC 341 Hd 50
Chute Mpoumé ~ CAM 320 Gm 44
Chute Mupele ~ RDC 324 He 45
Chute Penge ~ RDC 324 Hg 45
Chute Pogge II ~ RDC 333 Hc 49
Chutes de Billy ~ RMM 316 Gb 39
Chutes de Gozobangui ~ RDC 321 Hd 43
Chutes de Katende ~ RDC 333 Hd 49
Chutes d'Ekom ~ CAM 320 Gm 43
Chutes de la Lobé ~ CAM 320 Gl 44
Chutes de Lancrenon ~ CAM 321 Gp 42
Chutes de l'Au ~ RDC 324 Hh 45
Chutes de Nachtigal ~ CAM 320 Gm 43
Chutes de Ngolo ~ RCA 321 Hd 43
Chutes de Touboutou ~ RCA 321 Gp 43
Chutes du Félou ~ RMM 304 Ga 38
Chutes du Gouina ~ RMM 304 Ga 38
Chutes du Kinkon ~ RG 316 Fp 40
Chutes Gauthiot ~ TCH 321 Gp 41
Chutes Pangu ~ RDC 324 Hf 44
Chutes Tshunga ~ RDC 324 He 45
Chutes Usu ~ RDC 324 He 44
Chute Toky ~ RDC 324 Hg 45
Chute Walfe ~ RDC 333 Hd 48
Chuwangsan ★ ROK 247 Ma 27
Chuxiong ○ VRC 254 La 33
Chuy ○ ROU 146 Eh 62
Chyulu Hills ⛰ EAK 337 Hl 47
Ciamis ○ RI 278 Le 49
Ciancang Shan △ VRC 254 Kp 33
Cianjur ○ RI 278 Ld 49
Cianorte ○ BR 140 Eh 57
Cibadak ○ RI 278 Ld 49
Cibinong ○ RI 278 Ld 49
Cibitoke ○ BU 336 Hg 47
Cibuta △ MEX 80 Cg 30
Cicalengka ○ RI 278 Ld 49
Cícero Dantas ○ BR 125 Fa 51
Cichibu-Tama ♀ J 251 Mf 28
Cicia ⌂ FJI 390 Aa 54
Cicurug ○ RI 278 Ld 49
Cidade Gaúcha ○ BR 140 Eh 57
Cide ○ TR 195 Hj 25
Cidmas ○ RI 278 Lc 49
Ciechanów ○ PL 170 Hc 19
Ciechocinek ○ PL 170 Hb 19
Ciego de Ávila ○ C 100 Dj 35
Ciénaga ○ CO 106 Dl 40
Ciénaga Grande ~ CO 106 Dl 41
Ciénaga Grande de Sta. Marta ~ CO 106 Dl 40
Ciénagas del Catatumbo ♀ YV 107 Dn 41
Ciénaga Zapatosa ~ CO 106 Dm 41
Cieneguilla ○ PY 136 Eb 57
Cienfuegos ○ C 100 Dh 34
Cieszanów ○ PL 175 Hd 20
Cieza ○ E 184 Gf 26
Çifteler ○ TR 195 Hh 26
Cifuentes ○ C 100 Dh 34
Cifuentes ○ E 184 Ge 25
Cifuncho ○ RCH 136 Dn 58
Cihanbeyli ○ TR 195 Hj 26
Cihanbeyli Yaylâsı ⛰ TR 195 Hj 26
Cihuatlán ○ MEX 92 Ck 36
Cijulang ○ RI 278 Le 49
Cikajang ○ RI 278 Ld 49
Cikalong ○ RI 278 Ld 49
Cikalongwetan ○ RI 278 Ld 49
Cikampek ○ RI 278 Ld 49
Čikoj ~ RUS 204 Va 8
Cikotok ○ RI 278 Ld 49
Cilacap ○ RI 278 Le 49
Cilamaya ○ RI 278 Ld 49
Cilangkahan ○ RI 278 Ld 49
Cilaos ○ F 353 Jf 56
Cilat ○ IRQ 209 Jb 29
Čil'či ○ RUS 204 Wa 7
Çıldır ○ TR 202 Hp 25
Çıldır Çayı ~ TR 202 Hp 25
Ciledug ○ RI 278 Le 49
Cili ○ VRC 255 Lf 31
Cilibia ○ RO 175 Hf 23
Čil'mamedkum ⏥ TM 222 Jf 25
Cima ○ USA 64 Ce 28
Cimahi ○ RI 278 Ld 49
Cimarron ○ USA 65 Cj 26
Cimarron ○ USA 65 Ck 27
Cimarron ○ USA 70 Cm 27
Cimarron ~ USA 70 Cn 27
Cimarron River ~ USA 65 Cl 27
Cimişlia ○ MD 175 Hg 22
Cimitarra ○ CO 106 Dm 42
Cimljansk ○ RUS 181 Hn 22
Cimpu ○ RI 282 Ll 47
Çınar ○ TR 202 Hn 27
Cinaruco ~ YV 107 Ea 42
Cinaruco Capanaparo ♀ YV 107 Ea 42
Cincel ~ PY 136 Ea 57
Cincinnati ○ USA 71 Df 26
Çine ○ TR 195 Hg 27
Čingildi ○ UZB 223 Jl 25
Cino ○ UZB 223 Jn 25
Cinque Island ⌂ IND 262 Kl 40
Cintalapa ○ MEX 93 Db 37
Cintra ○ RA 137 Ec 62
Ciotat ○ F 185 Gk 24
Cipa ~ RUS 204 Vb 7
Cipó ~ BR 141 En 55
Cipolândia ○ BR 140 Eg 56
Cipolletti ○ RA 147 Ea 65
Čirčik ○ UZB 223 Jn 25
Čirčik ~ UZB 223 Jn 25
Circle ○ USA 46 Bc 13
Circle ○ USA 51 Ck 22
Circleville ○ USA 71 Dg 26
Circular Reef ⌂ PNG 287 Mk 47
Cirebon ○ RI 278 Le 49
Ciriquiri ~ BR 117 Eb 50
Čirka Kem ~ RUS 159 Hj 14
Cir Kud ○ SP 328 Hp 44
Čirokči ○ UZB 223 Jm 26
Ciró Marina ○ I 194 Ha 26
Cirpan ○ BG 194 He 24
Cisarua ○ RI 278 Ld 49
Cisco ○ USA 65 Ch 26
Cisco ○ USA 70 Cn 29
Cislău ○ RO 175 Hf 23
Cisneros ○ CO 106 Dl 42
Cisnes ~ RCH 152 Dn 68
Cisnes Medio ○ RCH 152 Dm 68
Cisolok ○ RI 278 Ld 49
Cisséla ○ RG 316 Ga 40
Cistern Point ⌓ BS 87 Dk 34
Cistierna ○ E 184 Gd 24
Čistopol' ○ RUS 181 Jd 18
Čita ○ RUS 204 Vb 8
Citaré ~ BR 113 Eg 45
Citra ○ USA 87 Dg 31
Citronelle ○ USA 86 Dd 30
Citrusdal ○ ZA 358 Hb 62
Citrus Heights ○ USA 64 Cb 26
Cittanova ○ I 194 Ha 26
Ciudad ○ MEX 92 Ck 34
Ciudad Acuña ○ MEX 81 Cm 31
Ciudad Altamirano ○ MEX 92 Cm 36
Ciudad Anáhuac ○ MEX 81 Cm 32
Ciudad Bolívar ○ YV 112 Ec 41
Ciudad Camargo ○ MEX 80 Ck 32
Ciudad Colón ○ CR 97 Df 41
Ciudad Constitución ○ MEX 80 Cg 33
Ciudad Cuauhtémoc ○ MEX 93 Db 38
Ciudad Darío ○ NIC 96 De 39
Ciudad del Carmen ○ MEX 93 Db 36
Ciudad del Este ○ PY 140 Eg 58
Ciudad del Maíz ○ MEX 92 Cn 34
Ciudad de Nutrias ○ YV 107 Dp 41
Ciudad Guayana ○ YV 112 Ec 41
Ciudad Guzmán ○ MEX 92 Cl 36
Ciudad Hidalgo ○ MEX 92 Cm 36
Ciudad Juárez ○ MEX 80 Cj 30
Ciudad Lerdo ○ MEX 81 Cl 33
Ciudad M. Alemán ○ MEX 81 Cn 32
Ciudad Madero ○ MEX 81 Cp 34
Ciudad Mante ○ MEX 92 Cn 34
Ciudad Mendoza ○ MEX 92 Cp 35
Ciudad Mutís ○ CO 106 Dk 42
Ciudad Neily ○ CR 97 Dg 41
Ciudad Obregon ○ MEX 80 Ch 32
Ciudad Ojeda ○ YV 107 Dn 40
Ciudad Pemex ○ MEX 93 Db 37
Ciudad Piar ○ YV 112 Ec 42
Ciudad Quesada ○ CR 97 Df 40
Ciudad Real ○ E 184 Ge 26
Ciudad-Rodrigo ○ E 184 Gc 25
Ciudad Sahagún ○ MEX 92 Cn 36
Ciudad Valles ○ MEX 92 Cn 35
Ciudad Victoria ○ MEX 92 Cn 34
Ciutadella ○ E 184 Gh 25
Civil'sk ○ RUS 181 Jb 18
Cívita Castellana ○ I 185 Gn 24
Civitanova Marche ○ I 185 Gn 24
Civitavécchia ○ I 185 Gm 24
Çivril ○ TR 195 Hg 26
Cixi ○ VRC 246 Ll 30
Čiža ○ RUS 159 Ja 12
Cizre ○ TR 202 Hn 27
Čjurupyns'k ○ UA 175 Hj 22
Čkalove ○ UA 175 Hk 22
Čkalovskoe ○ RUS 250 Mc 23
Claerwater Lake ~ USA 71 Dc 27
Clain ~ F 163 Gg 22
Clairemont ○ USA 70 Cm 29
Clair Engle Lake ~ USA 64 Ca 25
Clairon ○ USA 56 Db 24
Clairview ○ AUS 375 Ml 57
Clam Lake ○ USA 56 Dc 22
Clanton ○ USA 71 De 29
Clanville ○ ZA 349 Hf 61
Clanwilliam ○ ZA 358 Hb 62
Claquato Church ★ USA 50 Ca 22
Clara City ○ USA 56 Da 23
Clara Island ⌂ MYA 262 Kn 40
Claravale ○ AUS 364 Mb 53
Claraville ○ AUS 365 Mg 55
Claraville ○ AUS 374 Md 57
Clare ○ USA 57 Df 24
Clare ○ AUS 365 Mk 55
Clare ○ AUS 375 Mj 57
Clare ○ AUS 378 Mf 62
Claremont ○ USA 60 Dm 24
Claremore ○ USA 70 Da 27
Clarence ~ AUS 375 Mn 60
Clarence ○ NZ 383 Nj 67
Clarence Island ⌂ 38 Ga 16
Clarence River ~ NZ 383 Nj 67
Clarence Strait ~ AUS 364 Mb 52
Clarence Town ○ BS 87 Dl 34
Clarendon ○ USA 70 Cm 28
Clarenton ○ USA 51 Ck 24
Clarenville ○ CDN 61 Fg 21
Claresholm ○ CDN 50 Cf 21
Clarie City ○ USA 56 Cp 23
Clarinda ○ USA 70 Da 25
Clarines ○ YV 112 Eb 41
Clario ~ BR 120 Eg 49
Clarion ○ USA 74 Dj 25
Clarion ~ USA 74 Dj 25
Clarje Coast ⏥ 38 Rb 16
Clark ○ USA 56 Cp 23
Clark Canyon Reservoir ~ USA 51 Cf 23
Clarke ~ AUS 365 Mj 55
Clarke City ○ CDN 61 Ea 20
Clarke Island ⌂ AUS 378 Ml 66
Clarke Range ⛰ AUS 375 Mk 56
Clarke River ○ AUS 365 Mj 55
Clarkes Beach ○ CDN 61 Eh 22
Clarkfield ○ USA 56 Cp 23
Clark Fork ○ USA 50 Cd 21
Clark Fork ~ USA 50 Ce 22
Clarkleigh ○ CDN 56 Cn 20
Clark Mountain △ USA 64 Ce 28
Clarks ○ USA 70 Cn 25
Clarksburg ○ USA 71 Dh 26
Clarksdale ○ USA 71 Dc 28
Clark's Harbour ○ CDN 61 Ea 24
Clarks Hill Lake ~ USA 71 Dg 29
Clarkson ○ ZA 358 He 63
Clark's Point ○ USA 46 Al 15
Clarkston ○ USA 50 Cd 22
Clarksville ○ USA 70 Da 29
Clarksville ○ USA 70 Db 28
Clarksville ○ USA 71 De 27
Clarnecy ○ F 163 Gh 22
Claro ~ BR 133 Ej 54
Clarskville ○ USA 74 Dj 27
Claude ○ USA 70 Cm 28
Cláudia ○ BR 132 Eg 51
Claveria ○ RP 267 Ll 36
Claveria ○ RP 267 Lm 39
Claxton ○ USA 71 Dh 29
Claybank ○ CDN 51 Ck 20
Clay Belt ⏥ CDN 43 Gb 8
Clay Belt ⏥ CDN 57 Dh 20
Clay Center ○ USA 70 Cp 25
Clay City ○ USA 71 Dg 27
Claydon ○ CDN 51 Ch 21
Clayoquot Sound ~ CDN 50 Bn 21
Claypan ~ AUS 375 Mj 60
Claypool ○ USA 65 Cg 29
Clay River ~ PNG 287 Mj 48
Clayton ○ USA 50 Ce 23
Clayton ○ USA 65 Cl 27
Clayton ○ USA 70 Da 28
Clayton ○ USA 71 Dg 28
Clayton ○ USA 86 Dc 30
Clayton ○ USA 86 Df 30
Clearfield ○ USA 56 Cm 24
Clearfield ○ USA 64 Cf 25
Clearfield ○ USA 74 Dj 25
Clear Fork ~ USA 70 Cn 29
Clear Lake ○ USA 56 Cp 23
Clear Lake ○ USA 56 Db 23
Clear Lake ○ USA 64 Ca 26
Clear Lake ~ USA 64 Ca 26
Clear Lake Reservoir ~ USA 64 Cb 25
Clearwater ○ CDN 50 Cb 20
Clearwater ~ USA 50 Cd 22
Clearwater ○ USA 86 Dg 31
Clearwater Lake ~ CDN 50 Cb 19
Clearwater Mountains ⛰ USA 50 Ce 22
Cleburne ○ USA 70 Cp 29
Cle Elum ○ USA 50 Cb 22
Clemson ○ USA 71 Dg 28
Clendenin ○ USA 71 Dh 26
Clermont ○ USA 87 Dg 31
Clermont ○ F 163 Gh 21
Clermont ○ AUS 375 Mk 57
Clermont-Ferrand ○ F 185 Gh 23
Clermont-l'Hérault ○ F 185 Gh 24
Cleugh Passage ~ IND 262 Kl 39
Cleve ○ AUS 378 Me 62
Cleveland ○ USA 71 Df 28
Cleveland ○ USA 71 Dg 25
Cleveland ○ USA 81 Da 30
Cleveland ○ USA 86 Dc 29
Cleveland Heights ○ USA 71 Dh 25
Clewiston ○ USA 87 Dh 32
Clifden ○ IRL 163 Ga 19
Clifden ○ NZ 382 Nf 69
Cliff ○ USA 65 Ch 29
Cliffs of Moher ★ IRL 163 Ga 19
Clifton ○ USA 65 Ch 26
Clifton ○ USA 65 Ch 29
Clifton ○ USA 70 Cp 26
Clifton Forge ○ USA 74 Dj 27
Clifton Hills ○ AUS 374 Mf 59
Climax ○ CDN 51 Ch 21
Climax ○ USA 56 Cp 22
Clinch Mountains ⛰ USA 71 Dg 27
Cline River ○ CDN 50 Cd 19
Clines Corners ○ USA 65 Ck 28
Clingmans Dome △ USA 71 Dg 28
Clint ○ USA 80 Cj 30
Clinton ○ USA 50 Ca 22
Clinton ○ CDN 50 Cb 20
Clinton ○ CDN 57 Dh 24
Clinton ○ USA 70 Cn 28
Clinton ○ USA 70 Da 26
Clinton ○ USA 70 Db 28
Clinton ○ USA 71 Dc 25
Clinton ○ USA 71 Dd 25
Clinton ○ USA 71 Dd 27
Clinton ○ USA 71 De 26
Clinton ○ USA 71 Df 24
Clinton ○ USA 71 Dh 28
Clinton ○ USA 74 Dj 28
Clinton ○ USA 86 Dc 29
Clinton ○ NZ 382 Ng 69
Clintonville ○ USA 57 Dd 23
Clio ○ USA 86 Df 30
Clipperton Island ⌂ MEX 10 Db 8
Clocolan ○ ZA 349 Hf 60
Clodomira ○ RA 136 Eb 59
Clonagh ○ AUS 374 Mg 56
Clonbrook ○ GUY 113 Ef 42
Cloncurry ○ AUS 374 Mg 56
Cloncurry Plateau ⏥ AUS 374 Mf 56
Clonmacnoice ★ IRL 163 Gc 19
Clonmel ○ IRL 163 Gc 19
Cloppenburg ○ D 170 Gk 19
Cloquet ○ USA 56 Db 22
Cloquet ~ USA 56 Dc 22
Cloud Peak △ USA 51 Cj 23
Clouds Creek ○ AUS 379 Mn 61
Cloudy ○ USA 70 Da 28
Cloudy Bay ~ NZ 383 Nk 66
Cloverdale ○ USA 64 Ca 26
Clovis ○ USA 65 Cl 28
Cloyne ○ CDN 60 Dk 23
Cluj-Napoca ○ RO 175 Hd 22
Cluny ○ AUS 374 Mf 58
Clute ○ USA 81 Da 31
Clyde ○ USA 56 Cn 21
Clyde ~ GB 162 Ge 18
Clyde ~ AUS 364 Md 52
Clyde Park ○ USA 51 Cg 23
Clyde River ○ CDN 43 Hb 4
Clyde River ○ CDN 61 Eb 24
Cna ~ RUS 181 Hn 19
Cnia del Sacramento ○ ROU 146 Ef 63
Cnori ○ GE 202 Ja 25
Co. Doña Inés ○ RCH 136 Dp 59
Coachella ○ USA 64 Cd 29
Coachella Canal ~ USA 64 Ce 29
Coahuayana ○ MEX 92 Cl 36
Coahuayutla ○ MEX 92 Cm 36
Coal Brook ○ CDN 61 Ee 22
Coalcomán ○ MEX 92 Cl 36
Coalcomán ~ MEX 92 Cl 36
Coaldale ○ CDN 51 Cf 21
Coaldale ○ USA 64 Cc 27
Coalinga ○ USA 64 Cb 27
Coalville ○ USA 65 Cg 25
Coamo ○ USA 104 Ea 36
Coaraci ○ BR 125 Fa 53
Coari ~ BR 117 Eb 48
Coari ○ BR 117 Ec 48
Coari ~ BR 117 Ec 48

410 Chinati Peak - Coari

Coasa ○ **PE** 128 Dn 53
Coast Mountains ⌃⌃ **CDN** 47 Bl 17
Coast Mountains ⌃⌃ **CDN** 50 Bp 20
Coast Mountains ⌃⌃ **USA/CDN** 42 Da 8
Coast Range ⌃⌃ **USA** 50 Ca 23
Coast Range ⌃⌃ **AUS** 375 Mm 57
Coata ○ **PE** 128 Dp 53
Coatbridge ○ **GB** 162 Ge 18
Coatepec ○ **MEX** 92 Cp 36
Coatepeque ○ **GCA** 93 Dc 38
Coatesville ○ **USA** 74 Dl 25
Coaticook ○ **CDN** 60 Dn 23
Coats Island ⌂ **CDN** 43 Gb 6
Coats Land ⌒ 38 Hb 17
Coatzacallo ～ **MEX** 93 Da 37
Coatzacoalcos ○ **MEX** 93 Da 36
Cobán ○ **GCA** 93 Dc 38
Cobar ○ **AUS** 379 Mj 61
Cobargo ○ **AUS** 379 Ml 63
Cobbam ○ **AUS** 378 Mh 61
Cobh ○ **IRL** 163 Gb 20
Cobhain River ～ **CDN** 56 Da 19
Cobija ○ **BOL** 129 Dp 51
Cobleskill ○ **USA** 60 Dl 24
Coboconk ○ **CDN** 60 Dj 23
Cobourg ○ **CDN** 60 Dj 24
Cobourg Peninsula ⌒ **AUS** 364 Mc 51
Cobquecura ○ **RCH** 137 Dn 64
Cobra ○ **AUS** 368 Lj 58
Cobram ○ **AUS** 379 Mj 63
Cobre ○ **MOC** 344 Hk 52
Coburg ○ **D** 174 Gm 20
Coburg Island ⌂ **CDN** 43 Gc 3
Coburn ○ **AUS** 368 Lh 59
Coburn Mountain △ **USA** 60 Dn 23
Coca Puerto Francisco de Orellano ○ **EC** 116 Dk 46
Coca ～ **EC** 116 Dk 46
Cocal ○ **BR** 124 Ep 47
Cocalinho ○ **BR** 121 Em 47
Cocalinho ○ **BR** 133 Ej 53
Cocalzinho des Goiás ○ **BR** 133 Ek 53
Cochabamba ○ **PE** 116 Dj 49
Cochabamba ○ **BOL** 129 Ea 54
Cochamó ○ **RCH** 147 Dm 66
Cochem ○ **D** 163 Gk 20
Cochetopa Hills ⌃⌃ **USA** 65 Cj 27
Cochenour ○ **CDN** 56 Dp 20
Cochin ○ **IND** 239 Kb 41
Cochise ○ **USA** 65 Ch 29
Cochran ○ **USA** 71 Dg 29
Cochrane ○ **CDN** 57 Dh 21
Cochrane ○ **CDN** 57 Dg 23
Cochrane ○ **RCH** 152 Dm 69
Cockburn ⌃ **USA** 57 Dg 23
Cockburn Harbor ○ **GB** 101 Dm 35
Cockburn Island ⌂ **CDN** 57 Dg 23
Cockburn Town ○ **BS** 87 Dl 33
Cockburn Town ○ **GB** 101 Dm 35
Cocklebiddy ○ **AUS** 369 Lp 62
Coco ○ **NIC** 96 De 39
Coco ○ **CR** 96 Df 40
Côco ～ **BR** 121 Ek 50
Cocoa ○ **USA** 87 Dh 31
Cocobeach ○ **G** 332 Gl 45
Cocobeach ○ **GQ** 332 Gl 45
Coco Channel ∿ **IND** 262 Kl 39
Cocoparra ⚘ **AUS** 379 Mk 63
Cocorna ○ **CO** 106 Dl 42
Cocos ○ **BR** 133 Em 53
Cocos Islands ⌂ **AUS** 26 Pb 11
Cocos Ridge ∇ 97 Df 42
Cocula ○ **MEX** 92 Ck 35
Codajás ○ **BR** 120 Ed 47
Codemin ○ **BR** 133 Em 53
Codfish Island ⌂ **NZ** 382 Nf 69
Codó ○ **BR** 124 En 48
Codo de Pozuzo ○ **PE** 116 Dl 50
Codozinho ○ **BR** 121 Em 48
Codpa ○ **RCH** 128 Dp 55
Codrii ⌒ **MD** 175 Hf 21
Codrington ○ **AG** 104 Ed 37
Cody ○ **USA** 51 Ch 23
Cody ○ **USA** 56 Cn 24
Coelemu ○ **RCH** 137 Dn 64
Coelho Neto ○ **BR** 124 En 48
Coen ○ **AUS** 365 Mh 52
Coeroeni ○ **SME** 113 Ef 44
Coëtivy ○ **SY** 31 Mb 10
Coeur d'Alene ○ **USA** 50 Cd 22
Coeur d'Alene ～ **USA** 50 Cd 22
Coeur d'Alene Indian Reservation ••• **USA** 50 Cd 22
Coeur d'Alene Lake ～ **USA** 50 Cd 22
Coffee Bay ○ **ZA** 358 Hg 62
Coffeeville ○ **USA** 86 Df 30
Coffeyville ○ **USA** 70 Da 27
Coffin Bay ○ **AUS** 378 Md 63
Coffin Bay ⚘ **AUS** 378 Md 63
Coffs Harbour ○ **AUS** 379 Mn 61
Cofimvaba ○ **ZA** 358 Hf 62
Cogădăk ○ **IR** 215 Jd 31
Coghlan ○ **ZA** 349 Hg 61
Cognac ○ **F** 184 Gf 23
Cogo ○ **GQ** 332 Gl 45
Cogotí ～ **RCH** 137 Dn 61
Cograjskoe vodohranilišče ～ **RUS** 202 Ja 23
Coguno ○ **MOC** 352 Hk 58
Cohagen ○ **USA** 51 Cj 22
Cohoes ○ **USA** 60 Dm 24
Coig Coyle ～ **RA** 152 Dp 71
Coihaique Alto ○ **RCH** 152 Dn 68
Coihauque ○ **RCH** 152 Dn 68
Coihué ○ **RCH** 137 Dn 64
Coihueco ○ **RCH** 137 Dn 64
Coilumbus ○ **USA** 81 Cp 33
Coimbatore ○ **IND** 239 Kc 40
Coimbra ○ **P** 184 Gb 25
Coín ○ **E** 184 Gd 27
Cöjbalsan ○ **MNG** 204 Vb 9
Cojedes ～ **YV** 107 Dp 41
Cojimíes ○ **EC** 116 Dh 45
Cojoida ○ **YV** 112 Ed 41
Cojr ○ **MNG** 204 Va 9
Cojúa ○ **YV** 107 Dn 40
Cojutepeque ○ **ES** 93 Dd 39
Coke ～ **USA** 65 Cg 24
Col. Vivida ○ **BR** 140 Eh 58
Colac ○ **AUS** 378 Mh 65

Colares ○ **BR** 121 Ek 46
Colatina ○ **BR** 141 Ep 55
Colby ○ **USA** 70 Cm 26
Colbún ○ **RCH** 137 Dn 63
Colca ～ **PE** 128 Dn 53
Colca ～ **PE** 128 Dn 53
Colcabamba ○ **PE** 128 Dm 52
Colchester ○ **GB** 163 Gg 20
Cold Bay ○ **USA** 46 Aj 17
Col de Bana △ **CAM** 320 Gm 43
Col de Gobo △ **RN** 309 Gp 35
Col de Maure △ **F** 185 Gk 23
Col de Sara △ **RN** 308 Gn 35
Col de Tafori △ **RG** 316 Fp 40
Col de Yei Lulu △ **RN** 309 Gp 35
Coldfoot ○ **USA** 46 Ba 11
Cold Lake ○ **CDN** 42 Eb 8
Cold Lake ～ **CDN** 42 Eb 8
Cold Springs ○ **USA** 64 Cc 26
Coldstream ○ **GB** 162 Ge 18
Coldwalter ○ **USA** 70 Cn 27
Coldwater ○ **USA** 71 Df 25
Coleambally ○ **AUS** 379 Mj 63
Coleambally Creek ～ **AUS** 379 Mj 63
Colebrook ○ **USA** 60 Dn 23
Coleen ～ **USA** 46 Be 11
Colekeplaas ○ **ZA** 358 He 62
Coleman ○ **USA** 81 Cn 30
Coleman ～ **AUS** 365 Mg 53
Colenso ○ **ZA** 349 Hg 60
Coleraine ○ **GB** 162 Gc 18
Coleraine ○ **AUS** 378 Mg 64
Coleroon ～ **IND** 239 Kd 40
Colesberg ○ **ZA** 349 He 61
Col es Chandeliers △ **RN** 308 Gn 35
Colfax ○ **USA** 50 Cd 22
Colfax ○ **USA** 64 Cb 26
Colga Downs ○ **AUS** 368 Lk 59
Colider ○ **BR** 132 Eg 51
Coligny ○ **ZA** 349 Hf 59
Colima ○ **MEX** 92 Ck 36
Colin Archer Peninsula ⌒ **CDN** 43 Fc 3
Colinas ○ **BR** 121 Em 49
Colinas de Tocantins ○ **BR** 121 Ek 50
Colinet ○ **CDN** 61 Eh 22
Coll ⌂ **GB** 162 Gc 17
Collacagua ○ **RCH** 136 Dp 56
Collado-Villalba ○ **E** 184 Gd 25
Collarenebri ○ **AUS** 375 Ml 60
Collaroy ○ **AUS** 375 Ml 57
Collbran ○ **USA** 65 Cj 26
Collector ○ **AUS** 379 Ml 63
College ○ **USA** 46 Ba 13
College Station ○ **USA** 81 Cp 30
Collerina ○ **AUS** 375 Mk 60
Collie ○ **AUS** 368 Lj 62
Collier Bay ～ **AUS** 361 Ln 54
Collier Bay Aboriginal Reserve ••• **AUS** 361 Lm 54
Collier Range ⚘ **AUS** 368 Lk 58
Collier Range ⌃⌃ **AUS** 368 Lk 58
Collierville ○ **USA** 71 Df 28
Collines Baoule ⌃⌃ **CI** 317 Gd 42
Collines de Bongouanou ⌃⌃ **CI** 317 Gd 42
Collines de Grabo ⌃⌃ **CI** 305 Gc 43
Collingsville ○ **USA** 71 Df 28
Collingwood ○ **USA** 70 Db 23
Collingwood ○ **NZ** 383 Nj 66
Collingwood Bay ～ **PNG** 287 Ml 50
Collins ○ **CDN** 57 Dd 20
Collins ○ **USA** 70 Db 25
Collins ○ **USA** 70 Db 27
Collins ～ **USA** 86 Dd 30
Collinson Peninsula ⌒ **CDN** 42 Fa 4
Collinsville ○ **USA** 71 Df 28
Collinsville ○ **AUS** 375 Mk 56
Collipulli ○ **RCH** 137 Dm 64
Collo ○ **DZ** 296 Gk 27
Collón Curá ～ **RA** 147 Dm 66
Colmar ○ **F** 163 Gk 21
Colméia ○ **BR** 121 Ek 50
Colmena ○ **RA** 146 Ed 60
Colmenar Viejo ○ **E** 184 Ge 25
Colnett ○ **F** 386 Ne 56
Colniza ○ **BR** 120 Ee 50
Cologne ○ **D** 163 Gk 20
Colombia ○ **MEX** 81 Cn 32
Colombia ○ **C** 101 Dk 35
Colombia ⚐ **CO** 107 Dm 44
Colombier ○ **CDN** 60 Dp 21
Colombo ○ **BR** 140 Ek 58
Colombo ⚐ **CL** 239 Kd 41
Colome ○ **USA** 56 Cn 24
Colón ○ **C** 100 Dh 34
Colón ○ **RA** 137 Ed 62
Colón ○ **RA** 146 Ee 62
Colonelganj ○ **IND** 234 Ke 32
Colonel Hill ○ **BS** 87 Dl 34
Colonett ○ **MEX** 75 Cd 30
Colonia 10 de Julio ○ **RA** 137 Ec 61
Colonia Carlos Pellegrini ○ **RA** 146 Ef 60
Colonia Dora ○ **RA** 136 Ec 60
Colonial ○ **USA** 74 Dk 27
Colônia Leopoldina ○ **BR** 124 Fc 50
Colonia Prosperidad ○ **RA** 146 Ec 61
Colonia St. Teresia ○ **RA** 146 Ee 61
Colonias Unidas ○ **RA** 140 Ee 59
Colonsay ⌂ **GB** 162 Gc 17
Colony ○ **USA** 65 Ck 23
Colorado ○ **USA** 65 Cj 26
Colorado ～ **USA** 81 Co 31
Colorado ○ **CR** 97 Df 40
Colorado ○ **C** 100 Dj 35
Colorado ～ **BOL** 129 Ec 52
Colorado ～ **PY** 136 Eb 57
Colorado ～ **RA** 136 Eb 57
Colorado ～ **RCH** 137 Ea 61
Colorado ～ **BR** 140 Eh 58
Colorado ～ **RA** 147 Ec 65
Colorado City ○ **USA** 65 Cj 26
Colorado City ○ **USA** 65 Ck 27
Colorado City ○ **USA** 70 Cm 29
Colorado Desert ⌒ **USA** 64 Ce 29

Colorado d'Oeste ○ **BR** 129 Ed 52
Colorado Nat. Monument ★ **USA** 65 Cj 26
Colorado Plateau ⌃⌃ **USA** 65 Cg 27
Colorado River ～ **USA** 65 Cg 27
Colorado River Aqueduct ～ **USA** 64 Ce 28
Colorado River Indian Reservation ••• **USA** 64 Ce 28
Colorado Springs ○ **USA** 65 Ck 26
Colotlán ○ **MEX** 92 Cl 34
Colotlipa ○ **MEX** 92 Cn 37
Colquechaca ○ **BOL** 129 Ea 55
Col Quijoux △ **RCA** 321 Hd 41
Colquiri ○ **BOL** 129 Ea 54
Colquitt ○ **USA** 86 Df 30
Colston Park ○ **USA** 375 Ml 56
Columbia ～ **CDN** 50 Cc 20
Columbia ～ **USA** 50 Cc 21
Columbia ○ **USA** 70 Db 26
Columbia ○ **USA** 70 Db 29
Columbia ○ **USA** 71 De 28
Columbia ○ **USA** 71 Df 27
Columbia ○ **USA** 71 Dh 29
Columbia ○ **USA** 74 Dk 26
Columbia ○ **USA** 86 Dd 30
Columbia City ○ **USA** 71 Df 25
Columbia Mountains ⌃⌃ **CDN** 50 Cc 20
Columbia Plateau ⌃⌃ **USA** 64 Cd 24
Columbia Reach ～ **CDN** 50 Cc 19
Columbus ○ **USA** 51 Cl 23
Columbus ○ **USA** 70 Cp 25
Columbus ○ **USA** 70 Da 27
Columbus ○ **USA** 71 Df 26
Columbus ○ **USA** 71 Dg 26
Columbus ○ **USA** 80 Dj 30
Columbus ○ **USA** 86 Dj 29
Columbus ○ **USA** 86 Dd 29
Columbus Bank ∇ 87 Dl 34
Columbus Junction ○ **USA** 70 Dc 25
Columbus Monument ★ **BS** 87 Dl 33
Coluna ○ **BR** 125 En 55
Colville Chanel ～ **NZ** 383 Nk 64
Colville Indian Reservation ••• **USA** 50 Cc 21
Colville River ～ **USA** 46 Ba 3
Colville River ～ **USA** 46 Aj 11
Colville River ～ **USA** 46 An 11
Coma ○ **MEX** 81 Cn 33
Coma ○ **ETH** 325 Hl 41
Comácchio ○ **I** 185 Gn 23
Comácha ○ **MOC** 344 Hj 54
Comal ～ **RI** 278 Le 49
Comalcalco ○ **MEX** 93 Db 36
Comallo ○ **RA** 147 Dn 66
Comanche ○ **USA** 81 Cn 30
Comandante Fontana ○ **RA** 140 Ee 58
Comandante Giribone ○ **RA** 146 Ef 63
Comandante Luis Piedra Buena ○ **RA** 152 Dp 70
Comănești ○ **RO** 175 Hf 22
Comarapa ○ **BOL** 129 Eb 54
Comas ○ **PE** 128 Dl 51
Comau ～ **RCH** 147 Dm 67
Comayagua ○ **HN** 96 De 38
Comayagüela ○ **HN** 96 De 38
Combapata ○ **PE** 128 Dn 53
Combarbala ○ **RCH** 137 Dn 61
Combermere Bay ～ **MYA** 254 Kl 36
Combomune ○ **MOC** 352 Hj 57
Combóvár ○ **H** 174 Ha 22
Comé ～ **DY** 317 Gg 42
Come by Chance ○ **AUS** 379 Ml 60
Comedero ○ **MEX** 80 Cj 33
Comendador ○ **DOM** 101 Dn 36
Comer ○ **USA** 71 Dg 28
Comercinho ○ **BR** 125 En 54
Comet ○ **USA** 374 Md 60
Comet ○ **AUS** 375 Ml 57
Comet ～ **AUS** 375 Ml 58
Cometela ○ **MOC** 352 Hk 56
Comfort ○ **USA** 81 Cn 31
Comilla ○ **BD** 235 Kk 34
Comino ～ **USA** 71 Dc 27
Comitán ○ **MEX** 93 Db 37
Commee ○ **CDN** 57 Dd 21
Commerce ○ **USA** 70 Cp 29
Commercy ○ **F** 163 Gj 21
Commissioner Island ⌂ **CDN** 56 Cp 19
Committee Bay ～ **CDN** 7 Eb 3
Committee Bay ～ **CDN** 43 Ga 5
Commodore Reef ⌂ **RP** 266 Lh 41
Commonwealth Range ⌃⌃ 38 Aa 18
Commoron ～ **AUS** 375 Mm 60
Como ○ **I** 185 Gl 23
Como ～ **RCB** 332 Gp 45
Como Bluff Dinosaur Graveyard ★ **USA** 65 Ck 25
Comodo ○ **ETH** 325 Hn 43
Comodoro ○ **BR** 132 Ee 52
Comodoro Rivadavia ○ **RA** 152 Ea 68
Comoé ～ **CI** 317 Ge 42
Comoé ～ **CI** 317 Ge 43
Comolangma Feng △ **VRC** 235 Kh 32
Comoros ☐ **COM** 345 Hp 51
Comoros Archipelago ⌂ **COM** 345 Hp 51
Comox ○ **CDN** 50 Bp 21
Compeer ○ **CDN** 51 Cg 20
Compiégne ○ **F** 163 Gh 21
Compos dos Goitacazes ○ **BR** 141 En 56
Compostela ○ **MEX** 92 Ck 35
Compostela ○ **Rp** 275 Lp 42
Comrat ○ **MD** 175 Hg 22
Comstock ○ **USA** 81 Cm 31
Comunidad ○ **YV** 107 Ea 44
Comunidad ○ **PE** 128 Dp 52
Cona ～ **RUS** 204 Va 6
Co Nag ～ **VRC** 231 Kk 29
Conakry ⚐ **RG** 316 Fn 41
Conambo ○ **EC** 116 Dk 46
Conambo ～ **EC** 116 Dk 47
Conara ○ **AUS** 378 Mk 66

Conay ○ **RCH** 137 Dn 60
Conay ～ **RCH** 137 Dn 60
Conc. do Coité ○ **BR** 125 Fa 51
Conca ○ **USA** 81 Cn 31
Concán ○ **MEX** 92 Cn 34
Concarneau ○ **F** 163 Gd 22
Conceição ○ **BR** 124 Fa 49
Conceição da Barra ○ **BR** 141 En 57
Conceição de Mácabu ○ **BR** 141 Ek 50
Conceição do Araguaia ○ **BR** 121 Ep 49
Conceição do Canindé ○ **BR** 124 Ep 49
Conceição do Mato Dentro ○ **BR** 141 En 55
Conceição do Mau ○ **BR** 112 Ed 44
Conceição do Tocantins ○ **BR** 133 El 52
Concepción ○ **YV** 107 Dn 40
Concepción ○ **PE** 128 Dl 51
Concepción ○ **RA** 136 Eb 59
Concepción ○ **CDN** 137 Dm 64
Concepción ○ **PY** 140 Ef 57
Concepción de Buenos Aires ○ **MEX** 92 Cl 35
Concepción del Oro ○ **MEX** 81 Cm 33
Concepción del Uruguay ○ **RA** 146 Ee 62
Concepción ○ **RP** 267 Ll 38
Conception Bay ～ **CDN** 61 Eh 22
Conception Bay ～ **NAM** 348 Gp 57
Conception Island ⌂ **BS** 87 Dl 34
Conch ～ **IND** 234 Kd 32
Conchagua ○ **ES** 93 Dd 39
Conchal ○ **BR** 141 Ek 57
Conchas ○ **BR** 141 Ek 57
Conchas Dam ～ **USA** 65 Ck 28
Conchas Lake ～ **USA** 65 Ck 28
Conchi ○ **RCH** 136 Dp 57
Concho River ～ **USA** 81 Cn 30
Concón ○ **RCH** 137 Dn 62
Concord ○ **USA** 60 Dn 24
Concord ○ **USA** 64 Cb 27
Concord ○ **USA** 71 Dh 28
Concordia ○ **USA** 70 Db 26
Concordia ○ **USA** 70 Da 26
Concordia ○ **MEX** 92 Cj 34
Concordia ○ **BR** 140 Ei 48
Concordia ○ **RA** 146 Ee 61
Concórdia do Pará ○ **BR** 121 Ek 47
Concrete ○ **USA** 50 Ca 21
Concuil Grove ○ **USA** 70 Cp 26
Con Cuông ○ **VN** 255 Lc 36
Conda ○ **ANG** 340 Gp 51
Condamine ○ **AUS** 375 Mm 59
Condamine ～ **AUS** 375 Mm 59
Côn Dào ～ **VN** 263 Ld 41
Côn Dào ⌂ **VN** 263 Ld 41
Conde ○ **USA** 56 Cn 23
Conde ○ **BR** 125 Fb 51
Condé ○ **ANG** 340 Gp 51
Condédezi ～ **MOC** 344 Hj 53
Condega ○ **NIC** 96 De 39
Conde Matarazzo ○ **BR** 146 Eh 62
Condeúba ○ **BR** 125 Ep 53
Condingup ○ **AUS** 368 Lm 62
Condobolin ○ **AUS** 379 Mk 62
Condom ○ **F** 184 Gg 24
Condon ○ **USA** 50 Cb 23
Condon ○ **RP** 267 Ll 37
Conecuh ～ **USA** 86 De 30
Conelans Wildman ○ **AUS** 364 Mb 53
Cone Peak △ **AUS** 365 Mh 52
Conesa ○ **RA** 137 Ed 62
Conflict Group ⌂ **PNG** 287 Mm 51
Confolens ○ **F** 163 Gg 22
Confusion Bay ～ **CDN** 61 Eg 20
Confusion Range ⌃⌃ **USA** 64 Cf 26
Confuso ～ **PY** 140 Ee 58
Congaz ○ **MD** 175 Hg 22
Conghua ○ **VRC** 258 Lg 34
Congjiang ○ **VRC** 258 Le 33
Congo ～ **RDC** 332 Ha 47
Congo ～ **RDC** 333 Hb 45
Congo ～ **RDC** 333 Hb 46
Congo Basin ⌒ **RDC** 333 Ha 47
Congonhas ○ **BR** 141 Em 56
Congonhas do Norte ○ **BR** 141 En 55
Congress ○ **USA** 64 Cf 28
Conhello ○ **RA** 137 Ec 63
Conhuas ○ **MEX** 93 Dc 36
Conical Peak △ **USA** 51 Cg 22
Conitaca ○ **MEX** 80 Cj 33
Conjo ～ **ANG** 340 Ha 51
Conjuboy ○ **AUS** 365 Mj 53
Conklin ○ **CDN** 42 Ed 8
Conlara ○ **RA** 137 Eb 62
Connaught ○ **IRL** 162 Gb 19
Conneaut ○ **USA** 71 Dh 25
Connecticut ○ **USA** 60 Dm 24
Connecticut ⊙ **USA** 74 Dm 25
Connell ○ **USA** 50 Cc 22
Connellsville ○ **USA** 74 Dj 26
Connemara ⌒ **IRL** 163 Ga 19
Connemara ⚘ **AUS** 374 Mg 58
Conner ○ **RP** 267 Ll 36
Conners Range ⌃⌃ **AUS** 375 Ml 56
Connersville ○ **USA** 71 Df 26
Connor ○ **USA** 50 Ce 23
Connors ～ **AUS** 375 Ml 57
Conoble Lake ～ **AUS** 379 Mj 62
Conogol ○ **MNG** 204 Vb 9
Conover ○ **USA** 57 Dd 22
Conquista ○ **BOL** 129 Ea 51
Conrad ○ **USA** 51 Cf 21
Conrad ○ **BR** 124 Ea 50
Consata ～ **BOL** 129 Dp 53
Conselheiro Lafaiete ○ **BR** 141 Em 56
Conselheiro Pena ○ **BR** 141 En 56
Consolación del Sur ○ **C** 100 Dg 34
Consort ○ **CDN** 51 Cg 19
Constance Bay ○ **IND** 262 Kl 40
Constância ○ **RO** 175 Hg 23
Constantina ○ **E** 184 Gd 27
Constantine ○ **DZ** 296 Gk 27
Constanza ○ **DOM** 101 Dm 36
Constitución ○ **RCH** 137 Dn 63
Consuegra ○ **SME** 113 Ef 43
Consuelo Peak △ **AUS** 375 Ml 58
Consul ○ **CDN** 51 Ch 21
Consul ○ **BR** 132 Eg 52

Contact ○ **USA** 64 Ce 25
Contagem ○ **BR** 133 Em 55
Contamana ○ **PE** 116 Dl 49
Contas ～ **BR** 125 Ep 52
Contas ～ **BR** 125 Fa 53
Contendas do Sincorá ○ **BR** 125 Ep 52
Contramaestre ○ **C** 101 Dk 35
Contrato ○ **PE** 116 Dj 49
Contumazá ○ **PE** 116 Dj 49
Contwoyto Lake ～ **CDN** 6 Db 3
Contwoyto Lake ～ **CDN** 47 Cg 13
Convención ○ **CO** 107 Dm 41
Conway ○ **USA** 60 Dn 24
Conway ○ **USA** 70 Db 28
Conway ○ **USA** 87 Dj 29
Conway ○ **ZA** 369 Mb 61
Conway ○ **AUS** 375 Ml 56
Conwy ○ **GB** 163 Ge 19
Coober Pedy ○ **AUS** 374 Md 60
Cooinda Motel ○ **AUS** 364 Mc 52
Cook ○ **USA** 56 Db 22
Cook ○ **AUS** 369 Mb 61
Cook Bay ～ 38 Sb 17
Cook Bay ～ **VU** 386 Ng 55
Cook City ○ **USA** 51 Ch 23
Cookeville ○ **USA** 71 Df 27
Cook Inlet ～ **USA** 10 Ba 4
Cook Inlet ～ **USA** 46 An 15
Cook Islands ⌂ **NZ** 35 Ab 11
Cookshire ○ **CDN** 60 Dn 23
Cookstown ○ **GB** 162 Gc 18
Cooktown ○ **AUS** 365 Mj 53
Cook Strait ～ **NZ** 383 Nk 66
Coolabah ○ **AUS** 379 Mk 61
Cooladdi ○ **AUS** 375 Mk 59
Coolah ○ **AUS** 379 Ml 61
Coolamon ○ **AUS** 379 Mk 63
Coolangatta ○ **AUS** 375 Mn 60
Coolgardie ○ **AUS** 368 Ll 61
Coolidge ○ **USA** 65 Cg 29
Coolmunda Reservoir ～ **AUS** 375 Mm 60
Cooloola ⚘ **AUS** 375 Mn 59
Cooma ○ **AUS** 379 Ml 63
Coonabarabran ○ **AUS** 379 Ml 61
Coonalpyn ○ **AUS** 378 Mf 63
Coonamble ○ **AUS** 379 Ml 61
Coonawarra ○ **AUS** 378 Mg 64
Coondapoor ○ **IND** 238 Kb 39
Coongan ～ **AUS** 360 La 56
Coon Rapids ○ **USA** 56 Db 23
Cooper Lake ～ **USA** 81 Cn 30
Cooper Creek ～ **AUS** 374 Mg 59
Coopermine ○ **CDN** 6 Da 3
Cooperstown ○ **USA** 56 Cn 22
Cooper's Town ○ **BS** 87 Dk 32
Coopracandra ⚘ **AUS** 379 Ml 64
Coorabie ○ **AUS** 369 Mc 61
Coorabulka ○ **AUS** 374 Mg 57
Coorada ○ **AUS** 375 Ml 58
Coorong ⚘ **AUS** 378 Mf 64
Coorow ○ **AUS** 368 Lj 60
Cooroy ○ **AUS** 375 Mn 59
Coos Bay ○ **USA** 50 Bp 24
Coose ～ **USA** 71 De 29
Cootamundra ○ **AUS** 379 Ml 63
Copacabana ○ **CO** 106 Dl 42
Copacabana ○ **BOL** 128 Dp 54
Copacabana ○ **BOL** 129 Ed 53
Copahue △ **RA** 137 Dn 64
Copal Urco ○ **PE** 116 Dm 47
Copán ○ **HN** 93 Dd 38
Copán ★ **HN** 93 Dd 38
Cope ○ **USA** 65 Cl 26
Copeland ○ **USA** 70 Cm 27
Copenhagen ⚑ **DK** 170 Gm 18
Copeton Reservoir ～ **AUS** 375 Mm 60
Copiapó ○ **RCH** 136 Dn 59
Copiapó ～ **RCH** 136 Dn 59
Copley ○ **AUS** 378 Mf 61
Coporito ○ **YV** 112 Ed 41
Copperas Cove ○ **USA** 81 Cn 30
Copper Center ○ **USA** 46 Bc 15
Copper Harbor ○ **USA** 57 De 22
Coppermine ○ **CDN** 47 Ce 11
Coppermine Point ⌒ **CDN** 57 Df 22
Coppermine River ～ **CDN** 47 Cc 11
Coppermine River ～ **CDN** 47 Ce 11
Copper River ～ **USA** 46 Bc 13
Copper River ～ **USA** 46 Bc 15
Copperton ○ **ZA** 349 Hd 60
Coqên ○ **VRC** 231 Kg 30
Coqueiro ○ **RP** 181 El 49
Coqueiro ○ **BR** 132 Ef 54
Coquimatlán ○ **MEX** 92 Ck 36
Coquimbo ○ **RCH** 137 Dn 60
Coquitlam ○ **CDN** 50 Ca 21
Corabia ○ **RO** 194 Hc 24
Coração de Jesus ○ **BR** 133 Em 54
Coracora ○ **PE** 128 Dn 53
Corail ○ **RH** 101 Dm 36
Coral ○ **CDN** 57 Dh 20
Coralaque ～ **PE** 128 Dn 54
Coral Bay ～ **AUS** 360 Lg 57
Coral Harbour ○ **CDN** 43 Gb 6
Coral Heights ○ **BS** 87 Dh 33
Coral Sea ∿ 34 Sa 11
Coral Sea Islands Territory ⊙ **AUS** 34 Sa 11
Coral Springs ○ **USA** 87 Dh 32
Corantijn ～ **SME** 113 Ef 43
Coranzuli ○ **PY** 136 Ea 57
Corbett ⚘ **IND** 234 Kd 31
Corbico ○ **BOL** 129 Ea 54
Corbin ○ **USA** 71 Df 27
Corcoran ○ **USA** 64 Cc 27
Corcovado △ **RA** 147 Dn 67
Corda ～ **BR** 121 Em 49
Cord de Vilcanota ⌃⌃ **PE** 128 Dm 52
Cordeiro ○ **BR** 141 En 57
Cordele ○ **USA** 86 Df 29
Cordell ○ **USA** 70 Cn 28

Cordillera de Chilla ⌃⌃ **PE** 128 Dm 53
Cordillera de Huanzo ⌃⌃ **PE** 128 Dm 53
Cordilheira ○ **BR** 146 Eh 61
Cordillera Aznaques ⌃⌃ **BOL** 129 Ea 54
Cordillera Blanca ⌃⌃ **PE** 116 Dk 50
Cordillera Çantabrica ⌃⌃ **E** 184 Gc 24
Cordillera Central ⌃⌃ **PA** 97 Dg 41
Cordillera Central ⌃⌃ **DOM** 101 Dn 36
Cordillera Central ⌃⌃ **USA** 104 Ea 36
Cordillera Central ⌃⌃ **BOL** 129 Ea 55
Cordillera Central ⌃⌃ **E** 184 Gd 25
Cordillera Central ⌃⌃ **RP** 267 Ll 37
Cordillera Chilena ⌃⌃ **RCH** 152 Dm 72
Cordillera Chonaleña ⌃⌃ **NIC** 97 Df 40
Cordillera Darwin ⌃⌃ **RCH** 152 Dn 73
Cordillera de Apolobamba ⌃⌃ **PE/BOL** 128 Dp 53
Cordillera de Carabaya ⌃⌃ **PE** 128 Dn 52
Cordillera de Colangüil ⌃⌃ **RA** 137 Dp 61
Cordillera de Colonche ⌃⌃ **EC** 116 Dh 46
Cordillera de Darwin ⌃⌃ **RCH** 136 Dp 59
Cordillera de Domeyko ⌃⌃ **RCH** 136 Dp 58
Cordillera de Guanacaste ⌃⌃ **CR** 97 Df 40
Cordillera de la Brea ⌃⌃ **RA** 136 Dp 60
Cordillera de la Costa ⌃⌃ **RCH** 137 Dm 64
Cordillera de la Costa ⌃⌃ **RCH** 137 Dn 63
Cordillera del Condor ⌃⌃ **PE** 116 Dj 48
Cordillera de Lipez ⌃⌃ **BOL** 136 Ea 57
Cordillera de los Picachos ⚘ **CO** 106 Dl 44
Cordillera del Tigre ⌃⌃ **RA** 137 Dp 62
Cordillera de Mérida ⌃⌃ **YV** 107 Dn 42
Cordillera de Mochara ⌃⌃ **BOL** 136 Eb 56
Cordillera de Nahuelbuta ⌃⌃ **RCH** 147 Dn 65
Cordillera de Ollita ⌃⌃ **RCH** 137 Dn 61
Cordillera de Pernehué ⌃⌃ **RCH** 137 Dn 64
Cordillera de San Blas ⌃⌃ **PA** 97 Dj 41
Cordillera de San Pablo de Balzar ⌃⌃ **EC** 116 Dh 46
Cordillera de Santa Rosa ⌃⌃ **RA** 137 Dp 60
Cordillera de Suararu ⌃⌃ **BOL** 136 Eb 56
Cordillera de Talamanca ⌃⌃ **CR** 97 Dg 41
Cordillera Entre Ríos ⌃⌃ **HN** 97 Df 38
Cordillera Isabelia ⌃⌃ **NIC** 97 Df 39
Cordillera Negra ⌃⌃ **PE** 116 Dk 50
Cordillera Nombre de Dios ⌃⌃ **HN** 96 De 38
Cordillera Oriental ⌃⌃ **DOM** 101 Dp 36
Cordillera Oriental ⌃⌃ **BOL** 129 Ea 54
Cordillera Patagonica ⌃⌃ **RA** 147 Dn 66
Cordillera Patagonica ⌃⌃ **RCH** 152 Dm 71
Cordillera Real ⌃⌃ **EC** 116 Dj 47
Cordillera Real ⌃⌃ **BOL** 128 Dp 53
Cordillera Septentrional ⌃⌃ **DOM** 101 Dn 36
Cordillera Vilcabamba ⌃⌃ **PE** 128 Dn 52
Cordillera del Viento ⌃⌃ **RA** 137 Dn 64
Cordisburgo ○ **BR** 133 Em 55
Córdoba ○ **RA** 137 Eb 61
Córdoba ○ **RA** 147 Dp 66
Córdoba ○ **E** 184 Gd 27
Cordón de la Llarretas ⌃⌃ **RA** 137 Dp 63
Cordón del Plata ⌃⌃ **RA** 137 Dp 62
Cordón Seler ⌃⌃ **RCH** 152 Dm 69
Cordova ○ **USA** 46 Bc 3
Cordova ○ **USA** 46 Bc 15
Coreau ○ **BR** 124 Ep 47
Coreaú ～ **BR** 124 Ep 47
Coremas ○ **BR** 124 Fa 49
Corfield ○ **AUS** 374 Mh 56
Corfu ⌂ **GR** 194 Hb 26
Corguinho ○ **BR** 132 Eg 55
Coria ○ **E** 184 Gc 26
Coriabo ○ **GUY** 112 Ee 42
Coria del Rio ○ **E** 184 Gc 27
Coribe ○ **BR** 133 Em 52
Corinda ○ **RA** 140 Ee 59
Corinna ○ **AUS** 378 Mj 66
Corinth ○ **USA** 60 Dp 23
Corinth ○ **USA** 71 Dd 28
Corinto ○ **HN** 93 Dd 38
Corinto ○ **NIC** 96 De 39
Corinto ○ **BR** 133 Em 55
Corio Bay ～ **AUS** 375 Mm 57
Corixa Grande ～ **BR** 132 Ee 54
Corixão ～ **BR** 132 Ef 55
Cork Corcaigh ○ **IRL** 163 Gb 20
Cork ○ **AUS** 374 Mh 57
Corleone ○ **I** 185 Gn 27
Corlu ○ **TR** 195 Hf 25
Cornelia ○ **ZA** 349 Hg 59
Cornélio Procópio ○ **BR** 140 Ej 57
Cornell ○ **USA** 56 Dc 22
Corner Brook ○ **CDN** 61 Ee 21
Corner Inlet ～ **AUS** 379 Mk 65
Corniche des Dahra ～ **DZ** 293 Gg 27

□Country ⊡Capital city ◉Administrative unit OPlace ♁Island ⛰Mountain range △Mountain ⌓Cape 〰Ocean, Sea ~Lake, River ♆Undersea topography ▲Glacier ♀National park •••Reservation ★Point of major interest ⏢Landscape

Corning O USA 60 Dk 24
Corning O USA 64 Ca 26
Corning O USA 70 Da 25
Cornish O USA 60 Dn 24
Cornish Creek ~ AUS 375 Mj 57
Čornobyl' O UA 175 Hg 20
Cornoé ~ CI 317 Gd 41
Čornomors'ke O UA 175 Hj 23
Cornwall O CDN 60 Dl 23
Cornwall ⏢ GB 163 Gd 20
Cornwallis Island ♁ CDN 42 Fb 3
Cornwall Island ♁ CDN 42 Fb 3
Čornyj Čeremoš ~ UA 175 He 21
Coro O YV 107 Dp 40
Coroatá O BR 121 Em 48
Corocoro O BOL 129 Dp 54
Coroico ~ BOL 129 Ea 52
Corolla O USA 74 Dl 27
Coromandel O BR 133 El 55
Coromandel O NZ 383 Nk 64
Coromandel ♁ NZ 383 Nk 64
Coromandel Coast ⏢ IND 239 Ke 40
Coron O RP 267 Ll 39
Corona O USA 65 Ck 28
Coronado National Monument ★ USA 80 Cg 30
Coronation O CDN 51 Cg 19
Coronation Gulf ~ CDN 6 Da 3
Coronation Gulf 〰 CDN 47 Ce 11
Coronation Islands ♁ AUS 361 Ln 53
Coron Bay ~ RP 267 Ll 40
Coronda O RA 137 Ed 61
Coronel O RCH 137 Dm 64
Coronel Bogado O PY 140 Ef 59
Coronel Dorrego O RA 147 Ed 65
Coronel Fabriciano O BR 141 En 55
Coronel Martinez O PY 140 Ef 58
Coronel Moldes O RA 137 Eb 62
Coronel Murta O BR 125 En 54
Coronel Oviedo O PY 140 Ef 58
Coronel Pringels O RA 137 Ed 64
Coronel Rodolfo Bunge O RA 137 Ed 64
Coronel Sapucaia O BR 140 Eg 57
Coronel Suárez O RA 137 Ec 64
Coronel Vidal O RA 146 Ef 64
Coron Island ♁ RP 267 Ll 40
Corowa O AUS 379 Mk 63
Corozal O BH 93 Dd 36
Corozal O CO 106 Dl 41
Corpus Christi O USA 81 Cp 32
Corpus Christi Bay ~ USA 81 Cp 32
Corque O BOL 129 Ea 55
Corr. Caro ~ BR 132 Ef 54
Corr. das Cruzes ~ BR 132 Ef 53
Corr. do Tucum ~ BR 132 Ef 53
Corr. Fossa ~ BR 120 Ee 49
Corr. Onça ~ BR 120 Ee 49
Corr. Santa Maria ~ BR 120 Ee 49
Corral O RCH 147 Dm 65
Corral de Bustos O RA 137 Ec 62
Corralejo O E 292 Fp 31
Corrales O MEX 80 Ck 33
Corrane O MOC 344 Hm 53
Corredeira Grande ~ BR 132 Eg 52
Corredeira Salga Rede ~ BR 112 Ec 45
Corredeira Unari ~ BR 117 Dp 45
Corregidor Island ♁ RP 267 Ll 38
Córrego do Ouro O BR 133 Ej 54
Corrego Niutaca ~ BR 140 Ef 56
Corrego Sancho ~ BR 133 Ek 51
Correia Pinto O BR 140 Ej 59
Corrente ~ BR 121 Em 49
Corrente ~ BR 125 En 52
Corrente ~ BR 133 Ej 55
Corrente O BR 133 Em 51
Correntes ~ BR 124 En 48
Correntes O BR 124 Fb 50
Correntes ~ BR 132 Eg 54
Correntina O BR 133 Em 52
Correntoso O RA 147 Dn 66
Corrie Downs O AUS 374 Mg 57
Corrientes ~ PE 116 Dl 47
Corrientes O RA 140 Ee 59
Corrientes ~ RA 146 Ee 60
Corrigan O USA 81 Da 30
Corrigin O AUS 368 Lj 62
Corriverton O GUY 113 Ef 43
Corry O USA 74 Dj 25
Corryong O AUS 379 Mk 64
Corse ◉ F 185 Gl 24
Corsica ♁ F 185 Gl 25
Corsicana O USA 70 Cp 29
Cortázar O MEX 92 Cm 35
Corte O F 185 Gl 24
Cortegana O E 184 Gc 27
Cortes O RP 267 Lp 41
Cortez O USA 65 Ch 27
Cortina d'Ampezzo O I 174 Gn 22
Čortkiv O UA 175 He 21
Cortland O USA 60 Dk 24
Cortland O USA 70 Cp 25
Cortona O I 185 Gm 24
Coruche O P 184 Gb 26
Çoruh Nehri ~ TR 202 Hn 25
Çorum O TR 195 Hk 25
Corumba O BR 132 Ef 55
Corumbá ~ BR 133 El 54
Corumbá de Goiás O BR 133 Ek 53
Corumbaíba O BR 133 Ek 55
Corumbiara Antigo ~ BR 129 Ed 52
Corunna North △ AUS 378 Me 62
Corupá O BR 141 Ek 59
Coruripe O BR 125 Fb 51
Corutuba ~ BR 125 En 53
Corvallis O USA 50 Ca 23
Corwen O GB 163 Ge 19
Corydon O USA 70 Db 25
Corydon O USA 71 De 26
Cosalá O MEX 80 Cj 33
Cosamaloapan O MEX 93 Da 36
Cosapa O BOL 128 Dp 55
Cosapilla O RCH 128 Dp 54
Coscaya O RCH 128 Dp 55
Cosenza O I 185 Gp 26
Coshocton O USA 71 Dh 25
Cosmonaut Sea 〰 38 Kb 16
Cosmo Newbery O AUS 368 Lm 59
Cosmópolis O BR 141 El 57
Cosmos O USA 56 Da 23
Cosne O F 163 Gh 22
Cosoleacaque Jáltipan O MEX 93 Da 36
Cossack O AUS 360 Lj 56
Costa Blanca ⏢ E 184 Gf 27
Costa Brava ⏢ E 185 Gh 25
Costa Daurada ⏢ E 184 Gg 25
Costa de Araujo O RA 137 Dp 62
Costa de la Luz ⏢ E 184 Gc 27
Costa del Azahar ⏢ E 184 Gg 26
Costa del Sol ⏢ E 184 Gd 27
Costa de Ponent ⏢ E 184 Gh 25
Costa Marques O BR 129 Eb 52
Costa Rica □ CR 97 Df 41
Costa Rica O BR 133 Eh 55
Costa Verde ⏢ P 184 Gb 25
Costa Verde ⏢ E 184 Gc 24
Costești O RO 175 He 23
Costești O MD 175 Hf 22
Costilla O USA 65 Ck 27
Cotabambas O PE 128 Dm 52
Cotabato O RP 275 Lm 42
Cotacajes ~ BOL 129 Ea 54
Cotagaita O BOL 136 Eb 56
Cotahuasi O PE 128 Dm 53
Cotahuasi ~ PE 128 Dm 53
Cotaxe ~ BR 141 Ep 55
Coteau des Prairies ⛰ USA 56 Cp 23
Coteau du Missouri ⛰ USA 56 Cm 21
Côte d'Argent ⏢ F 184 Gf 24
Côte d'Azur ⏢ F 185 Gk 24
Côte d'Ivoire □ CI 317 Gc 41
Cotegipe O BR 133 Em 52
Côte Nord ⏢ CDN 61 Ea 20
Cotentin ⏢ F 163 Gf 21
Côtes de Fer O RH 101 Dm 36
Coti ~ BR 117 Eb 50
Cotia ~ BR 117 Eb 50
Cotija O MEX 92 Cl 36
Cotingo ~ BR 112 Ed 43
Coto Nc. de Gredos ♀ E 184 Gd 25
Cotonou O DY 317 Gh 42
Cotopaxi O USA 65 Ck 26
Cotorro O C 100 Dg 34
Cotriguaçu O BR 120 Ee 50
Cottage Grove O USA 50 Ca 24
Cottage Grove O USA 56 Db 23
Cottbus O D 174 Gn 20
Cottica O SME 113 Eg 44
Cotton O USA 56 Db 22
Cottonbush ~ AUS 374 Mf 57
Cottonwood O USA 50 Cd 23
Cottonwood O USA 64 Cf 28
Cotuhe ~ PE 117 Dn 47
Cotuí O DOM 101 Dn 36
Cotulla O USA 81 Cn 31
Couchman Range ⛰ AUS 361 Lp 53
Couffo ~ DY 317 Gg 42
Coulee City O USA 50 Cc 22
Coulman Island ♁ 38 Tb 17
Coulomb Point ⌓ AUS 360 Ll 54
Coulonge ~ CDN 60 Dk 22
Coulta O AUS 378 Md 63
Coulterville O USA 71 Dd 26
Council O USA 50 Cd 23
Council Bluffs O USA 70 Da 25
Council Grove Lake ~ USA 70 Cp 26
Counselors O USA 65 Cj 27
Coupville O USA 50 Ca 21
Courantyne ~ GUY 113 Ef 43
Courantyne ~ GUY 113 Ef 44
Courcibo ~ F 113 Eh 43
Courland Lagoon ~ RUS 170 Hc 18
Courmayeur O I 185 Gk 23
Courtenay O CDN 50 Bp 21
Courtenay O USA 56 Cn 22
Courtney O USA 70 Cp 29
Courtright O CDN 57 Dg 24
Courval O CDN 51 Cj 20
Coushatta O USA 70 Db 29
Coutada do Ambriz ♀ ANG 332 Gn 49
Coutances O F 163 Ge 21
Couto de Magahães ~ BR 133 Eh 52
Couto de Magelhas de Minas O BR 133 En 55
Couto Magalhães O BR 121 Ek 50
Coutras O F 184 Gf 23
Coutts O CDN 51 Cg 21
Cova Figueira O CV 316 Fh 38
Covè O DY 317 Gh 42
Cove Fort O USA 64 Cf 26
Covelo O USA 64 Ca 26
Coventry O GB 163 Gf 19
Covilhã O P 184 Gc 25
Covington O USA 57 Dd 22
Covington O USA 71 Dd 28
Covington O USA 71 Df 26
Covington O USA 71 Dg 29
Covington O USA 71 Dh 27
Covington O USA 86 Dc 30
Cowal Creek O AUS 365 Mh 51
Cowan O CDN 56 Cm 20
Cowansville O CDN 60 Dm 23
Cowcowing Lakes ~ AUS 368 Lj 61
Cowell O AUS 378 Me 62
Cowichan Lake ~ CDN 50 Bp 21
Cowra O AUS 379 Ml 62
Coxcatlán O MEX 92 Cp 35
Coxilha de Santana ⛰ BR 146 Ef 60
Coxim O BR 132 Eg 55
Cox's Bazar O BD 235 Kk 35
Cox's Cove O CDN 61 Ee 21
Coxs Creek ~ AUS 379 Ml 61
Coyah O RG 316 Fp 41
Coyaima O CO 106 Dl 44
Coyame O MEX 80 Ck 31
Coyle ~ RA 152 Dp 71
Coyota ~ GCA 93 Dc 38
Coyotitán O MEX 92 Cj 34
Coyuca de Benitez O MEX 92 Cm 37
Cozad O USA 70 Cn 25
Cozumel O MEX 93 De 35
Craceville O USA 56 Cp 23
Cracow O AUS 375 Mm 58
Craddock Channel ~ NZ 383 Nk 64
Cradle Mount Lake St. Clair ♀ AUS 378 Mj 67
Cradock O ZA 358 He 62
Cradock O AUS 378 Mf 62
Craig O USA 65 Cj 25
Craigie O AUS 365 Mj 55
Craigieburn O AUS 379 Mj 64
Craignure O GB 162 Gc 17
Craik O CDN 51 Ck 20
Craiova O RO 194 Hd 23
Cramond O ZA 348 Hc 59
Cranbourne O AUS 379 Mj 65
Cranbrook O CDN 50 Cd 21
Cranbrook O AUS 368 Lj 63
Crane O USA 50 Cc 24
Crane O USA 81 Cl 30
Crane Lake ~ CDN 51 Ch 20
Cranston O USA 74 Dn 25
Craolândia O BR 121 El 50
Crasna ~ RO 174 Hd 22
Crater Aniakchak ★ USA 46 Al 17
Cratère du Nouveau-Québec △ CDN 43 Ha 6
Crater Lake ~ USA 50 Ca 24
Crater Lake ♀ USA 50 Ca 24
Crater Lake ~ WAN 320 Gm 40
Crater Mountain △ USA 46 Al 13
Crater of Diamonds S.P. ★ USA 70 Db 29
Crater Point ⌓ PNG 287 Mn 48
Craters of the Moon National Monument ★ USA 50 Cf 24
Cratéus O BR 124 Ep 48
Crati ~ I 194 Ha 26
Crato O BR 124 Fa 49
Cravari ou Curucuinazá ~ BR 132 Ef 52
Craven O CDN 51 Ck 20
Cravo Norte O CO 107 Dn 42
Crawford O USA 51 Cl 24
Crawford O USA 71 Dg 29
Crawfordsville O USA 71 De 26
Crawley O GB 163 Gf 20
Creede O USA 65 Cj 27
Creel O MEX 80 Cj 32
Cree Lake ~ CDN 42 Ec 7
Gregory Creek ~ AUS 374 Me 60
Creil O F 163 Gh 21
Crema O I 185 Gl 23
Cremona O I 185 Gm 23
Crepori ~ BR 120 Ef 48
Crepori ~ BR 120 Ef 49
Cres O HR 174 Gp 23
Cres ♁ HR 174 Gp 23
Cresbard O USA 56 Cn 23
Crescent O USA 50 Cb 24
Crescent City O USA 87 Dh 31
Crescent Group ♁ VRC 263 Lf 37
Crescent Head O AUS 379 Mn 61
Crescent Lake ~ USA 65 Cl 25
Crespo O RA 137 Ed 62
Crest O F 185 Gj 23
Crested Butte O USA 65 Cj 26
Creston O CDN 50 Cd 21
Creston O USA 65 Cj 25
Creston O USA 70 Da 25
Crestview O USA 86 De 30
Creswell Downs O AUS 364 Md 54
Creswick O AUS 379 Mh 64
Crete O USA 70 Cp 25
Crete O USA 71 De 25
Crete ♁ GR 194 He 28
Creuse ~ F 163 Gg 22
Crewe O GB 163 Ge 19
Crib O AUS 379 Mj 65
Criciúma O BR 140 Ek 60
Crieff O GB 162 Gd 17
Crimea ⏢ UA 175 Hj 23
Crisfield City O USA 74 Dk 27
Crisostomo ~ BR 133 Ej 51
Cristalândia O BR 133 Ek 51
Cristalina O BR 133 El 54
Cristalino ~ BR 120 Eg 50
Cristalino ~ BR 133 Ej 52
Cristalino ~ BR 133 Ej 53
Cristo O BR 117 Eb 49
Cristópolis O BR 133 Em 52
Criswold O CDN 56 Cm 21
Crixás O BR 133 Ek 51
Crixás O BR 133 Ek 53
Crixás Açu ~ BR 133 Ej 53
Crixás-Açu ~ BR 133 Ej 52
Crixás Mirim ~ BR 133 Ej 52
Crnagora ⛰ MK 194 Hc 24
Crni vrh △ BIH 174 Ha 23
Croajingolor ♀ AUS 379 Ml 64
Croatia □ HR 174 Gp 23
Crocker Range ♀ MAL 274 Lj 43
Crockett O USA 81 Da 30
Crocodile Island ♁ AUS 364 Md 51
Crofton O USA 56 Cp 24
Croker Island ♁ AUS 364 Mc 51
Cromer O CDN 56 Cm 21
Cromína O BR 133 Ek 54
Cromwell O USA 56 Db 22
Cromwell O NZ 382 Ng 68
Crook O USA 65 Cl 25
Crooked ~ USA 50 Cb 23
Crooked Creek O USA 46 Al 15
Crooked Island ♁ BS 87 Dl 34
Crooked River O CDN 51 Cl 19
Crookston O USA 56 Cp 22
Crookwell O AUS 379 Ml 63
Croppa Creek ~ AUS 375 Mm 60
Crosby O USA 51 Cl 21
Crosby O CDN 60 Dk 23
Crosbyton O USA 70 Cm 29
Cross ~ WAN 320 Gl 43
Cross City O USA 86 Dg 31
Crossett O USA 70 Db 29
Crossfield O CDN 50 Ce 20
Cross Lake ~ CDN 42 Fb 7
Cross Plains O USA 70 Cn 29
Cross Sound 〰 USA 47 Bg 15
Crossville O USA 71 Df 28
Crosswind Lake ~ USA 46 Bc 13
Crotone O I 194 Ha 26
Crow Agency O USA 51 Cj 23
Crow Creek ~ USA 65 Ck 25
Crow Creek Ind. Res. ••• USA 56 Cn 23
Crowdy Bay ♀ AUS 379 Mn 61
Crowell O USA 70 Cn 29
Crow Indian Reservation ••• USA 51 Ch 23
Crow Lake O CDN 56 Db 21
Crowl Creek ~ AUS 379 Mj 62
Crowley O USA 86 Db 30
Crown Island ♁ PNG 287 Mk 48
Crownpoint O USA 65 Ch 28
Crown Point O USA 71 De 25
Crows Nest O AUS 375 Mn 59
Croydon O AUS 365 Mh 55
Crozet Basin ♆ 31 Na 13
Crozon O F 163 Gd 21
Cruces O C 100 Dh 34
Crucita O EC 116 Dh 46
Cruilas O MEX 81 Cn 33
Crump Lake ~ USA 50 Cc 24
Crusero O PE 128 Dn 53
Cruta ~ HN 97 Dg 38
Cruz O BR 124 Ep 47
Cruz Alta O BR 146 Eg 60
Cruz de Almas O BR 125 Fa 52
Cruz del Eje O RA 137 Eb 61
Cruzeiro O BR 141 Em 57
Cruzeiro O MOC 352 Hk 56
Cruzeiro d'Oeste O BR 140 Eh 57
Cruzeiro do Sul O BR 116 Dm 49
Cruzinha da Garça O CV 316 Fh 37
Cruz Machado O BR 140 Ej 59
Crysta Falls O USA 57 Dd 22
Crystal Brook O AUS 378 Mf 62
Crystal City O CDN 56 Cn 21
Crystal City O USA 81 Cn 31
Crystal Creek ♀ AUS 365 Mj 55
Crystal Lake O USA 71 Dd 24
Crystal River O USA 86 Dg 31
Crystal River St. Arch. S. ★ USA 86 Dg 31
Crystal Springs O CDN 51 Ck 19
Crystal Springs O USA 86 Dc 29
Crystel Lake Cave ★ USA 71 Dc 24
Ctanacuname ♀ YV 107 Ea 44
Cúa O YV 107 Ea 40
Cuaca O YV 107 Dp 40
Cuácua ~ MOC 344 Hl 54
Cù ,a Cung Hâu ~ VN 263 Ld 41
Cuainia ~ YV 107 Ea 44
Cuaio ~ ANG 340 Hb 53
Cuajinicuilapa O MEX 92 Cn 37
Cuale O ANG 340 Gp 50
Cuamba O MOC 344 Hl 53
Cuanavale ~ ANG 340 Hb 53
Cuando ~ ANG 340 Hc 53
Cuangar O ANG 340 Hb 54
Cuango O ANG 332 Ha 49
Cuango ~ ANG 333 Ha 49
Cuanza ~ ANG 340 Gn 50
Cuanza O ANG 340 Ha 51
Cuao ~ YV 107 Ea 43
Cuarteron Reef ♁ MAL 266 Lg 41
Cuarto ~ RA 137 Eb 62
Cù'a Soi Rap ~ VN 263 Ld 40
Cù'a Sông Bây Háp ~ VN 263 Lc 41
Cuatir ~ ANG 340 Hb 54
Cuatro Caminos O C 100 Dk 35
Cuatro Ciénegas O MEX 81 Cl 32
Cuatro Esquinas O YV 107 Dn 41
Cuauhtémoc O MEX 80 Cj 31
Cuautitlán O MEX 92 Cn 36
Cuautla O MEX 92 Cn 36
Cuba O USA 65 Cj 27
Cuba □ C 100 Dh 35
Cu Bai O VN 263 Ld 37
Cubal ~ ANG 340 Gn 53
Cubal O ANG 340 Gp 52
Cubango ~ ANG 340 Ha 52
Cubaté ~ BR 117 Ea 45
Cubati ~ ANG 340 Ha 53
Cube O EC 116 Dj 45
Cubero O USA 65 Cj 28
Cubia ~ ANG 340 Hc 53
Cubitas O C 100 Dk 35
Çubuk O TR 195 Hj 25
Cubulco O GCA 93 Dc 38
Cuby O USA 70 Dc 26
Cuchi ~ ANG 340 Ha 52
Cuchi O ANG 340 Ha 53
Cuchilla de Haedo ⛰ ROU 146 Ef 62
Cuchilla del Daymán ⛰ ROU 146 Ef 61
Cuchilla Grande ⛰ ROU 146 Eg 62
Cuchilla Grande Inferior ⛰ ROU 146 Ef 62
Cuchillo-Co O RA 147 Eb 65
Cuchivero O YV 112 Eb 42
Cuchivero ~ YV 112 Eb 42
Cucho Ingenio O BOL 129 Eb 55
Cuckadoo O AUS 374 Mg 56
Čučkovo O RUS 171 Hn 18
Cu'c Liêu O VN 263 Ld 40
Cucuí O BR 117 Ea 45
Cucumbi ~ ANG 340 Hb 51
Cucurital O YV 112 Eb 43
Cúcuta O CO 107 Dm 42
Cuddalore O IND 238 Kd 40
Cuddapah O IND 238 Kd 38
Čudniv O UA 175 Hg 20
Čudovo O RUS 171 Hh 16
Cudskoe ozero ~ RUS 171 Hf 16
Cue O AUS 368 Lj 59
Cuebe ~ ANG 340 Ha 53
Cueio ~ ANG 340 Ha 54
Cueiras ~ BR 120 Ed 47
Cuelei ~ ANG 340 Ha 53
Cuéllar O E 184 Gd 25
Cuemba O ANG 340 Hb 52
Cuenca O EC 116 Dj 47
Cuenca O E 184 Ge 25
Cuencamé O MEX 81 Cl 33
Cuengo ~ ANG 340 Hb 50
Cueramaro O MEX 92 Cm 35
Cuernavaca O MEX 92 Cm 36
Cuero O USA 81 Cp 31
Cuero O C 101 Dl 36
Cuervo O USA 65 Ck 28
Cueto O C 101 Dl 35
Cuetzalán O MEX 92 Cp 35
Cueva de la Quebrada del Toro ♀ YV 107 Dp 40
Cueva de los Guácharos ♀ CO 106 Dk 45
Cuevas de Altamira ★ E 184 Gd 24
Cuevas o Cañas ~ RA 136 Eb 58
Cuevo O BOL 136 Ec 56
Cuevo ~ BOL 136 Ec 56
Čugo ~ ANG 332 Ha 49
Čuhloma O RUS 171 Hp 16
Čuhujiv O UA 181 Hl 21
Cuiabá O BR 117 Dp 47
Cuiabá O BR 132 Ef 53
Cuiabá ~ BR 132 Eg 53
Cuiba ~ BR 132 Ef 54
Cuije ~ ANG 340 Ha 50
Cuilapa O GCA 93 Dc 38
Cuilo O ANG 332 Gp 49
Cuílo O ANG 340 Hb 50
Cuilo-Futa O ANG 332 Gp 49
Cuilo Pombo O ANG 332 Gp 49
Cuima O ANG 340 Gp 52
Cuimba O ANG 332 Gp 49
Cuio O ANG 340 Gn 52
Cuiriri ~ ANG 340 Hb 53
Cuito ~ ANG 340 Hb 52
Cuito Cuanavale O ANG 340 Hb 53
Cuitzeo O MEX 92 Cm 35
Cuiú-Cuiú O BR 120 Ef 48
Cuiuni ~ BR 117 Ec 46
Cujar ~ PE 128 Dm 51
Cukas O RI 278 Lc 46
Culamagia O ANG 340 Ha 50
Culan Sancal △ ETH 313 Hk 40
Culasi O RP 267 Ll 40
Culbertson O USA 51 Ck 21
Culbertson O USA 70 Cm 25
Culebra ♁ USA 104 Eb 36
Culebras O PE 116 Dj 50
Culfa O ARM 202 Ja 26
Culgoa ~ AUS 375 Mk 60
Culgoa O AUS 378 Mh 63
Culiacán O MEX 80 Cj 33
Culio ~ ANG 332 Gp 49
Culion O RP 267 Lk 40
Culion Island ♁ RP 267 Lk 40
Culiseu ~ BR 132 Eh 52
Cullera O E 184 Gf 26
Cullinan O ZA 349 Hg 58
Cullmann O USA 71 De 28
Cullulleraine O AUS 378 Mg 63
Čul'man O RUS 204 Wa 7
Culpeper O USA 74 Dj 26
Culpina O BOL 136 Eb 56
Culuene ~ BR 132 Eh 53
Culuene ~ BR 133 Eh 52
Culverden O NZ 383 Nj 67
Čulym O RUS 204 Tb 7
Čulym ~ RUS 204 Tb 7
Cumanā O YV 112 Eb 40
Cumanacoa O YV 112 Eb 40
Cumanayagua O C 100 Dh 34
Cumanda O EC 116 Dj 47
Cumar O SP 328 Ja 44
Cumaral O CO 107 Dm 43
Cumaribo O CO 107 Dp 43
Cumbe O EC 116 Dj 47
Cumberland ~ USA 71 Df 27
Cumberland O USA 71 Dg 27
Cumberland O USA 74 Dj 26
Cumberland Downs O AUS 375 Mk 57
Cumberland Gap N.H.P. ★ USA 71 Dg 27
Cumberland Island ♁ USA 87 Dh 30
Cumberland Island National Seashore ♀ USA 87 Dh 30
Cumberland Islands ♁ AUS 375 Ml 56
Cumberland Peninsula ♁ CDN 43 Hc 5
Cumberland Plateau ⛰ USA 71 Df 28
Cumberland Sound ~ CDN 7 Fb 3
Cumberland Sound 〰 CDN 43 Hb 5
Cumbi O ANG 332 Gn 49
Cumborah O AUS 375 Mk 60
Cumbre del Laudo △ RCH 136 Dp 59
Cumbres de Majalca O MEX 80 Cj 31
Cumbrian Mountains ⛰ GB 162 Ge 18
Cumbum O IND 238 Kd 38
Čumikan O RUS 205 Xa 8
Cuminá ~ BR 113 Eg 45
Cuminá ~ BR 120 Ef 45
Cuminã O BR 120 Ef 46
Cuminapanema ~ BR 120 Eg 46
Cummings O USA 64 Ca 26
Cummins O AUS 378 Md 63
Cummins Range ⛰ AUS 361 Lp 55
Cumnock O GB 162 Gd 18
Cumpas O MEX 80 Ch 30
Çumra O TR 195 Hj 27
Cumueté ~ BR 121 Ej 50
Cumuripa O MEX 80 Ch 31
Čuna ~ RUS 204 Ub 7
Cunani O BR 113 Ej 45
Cuñare O CO 116 Dm 45
Cunauaru ~ BR 117 Ec 47
Cund ~ ANG 340 Ha 52
Cunda dia Baze O ANG 340 Ha 50
Cunday O CO 106 Dl 43
Cundeelee O AUS 369 Lm 61
Cundeelee Aboriginal Reserve ••• AUS 369 Lm 61
Cunderdin O AUS 368 Lj 61
Cunduacán O MEX 93 Db 36
Cunene O ANG 340 Gp 53
Cunene ~ ANG 340 Ha 53
Cúneo O I 185 Gk 23
Cunha O BR 141 Em 57
Cunhãs ~ BR 121 Ek 49
Cunhinga ~ ANG 340 Ha 51
Cunhinga O ANG 340 Ha 52
Cuniuá ~ BR 117 Ea 49
Čunja ~ RUS 204 Ub 6
Cunjamba O ANG 340 Hb 53
Cunnamulla O AUS 375 Mj 60
Cunningham Islands ♁ AUS 364 Me 51
Čun'skij O RUS 204 Ub 7
Cuntima O GNB 316 Fn 39
Cunyu O AUS 368 Ll 59
Cuokkarassa △ N 159 Hd 11
Čupa O RUS 159 Hj 12
Cūpānān O IR 222 Jf 29
Cupari ~ BR 120 Eg 47
Cupari ~ BR 120 Eg 48
Cupica O CO 106 Dk 42
Curaçá O BR 124 Fa 50
Curaça ~ BR 124 Fa 50
Curaçao ♁ NL 107 Dp 39
Curacautín O RCH 147 Dn 65
Curacaví O RCH 137 Dn 62
Curachi O GUY 112 Ed 42
Curácuaro de Morelos O MEX 92 Cm 36
Curahuara de Carangas O BOL 129 Dp 54
Curanilahué O RCH 137 Dm 64
Curanja ~ PE 128 Dn 51
Curapča O RUS 205 Wc 6
Curaual ~ BR 120 Ee 48
Curbur O AUS 368 Lh 59
Curdimurka O AUS 374 Me 60
Čūre O AFG 223 Jl 29
Curepipe O MS 353 Jg 56
Curepto O RCH 137 Dm 63
Curib O RUS 202 Jb 24
Curibaya O PE 128 Dn 54
Curiche Liverpool ~ BOL 129 Ec 53
Curichi Tunas ~ BOL 129 Ed 54
Curicó O RCH 137 Dn 63
Čurilovo O RUS 171 Hh 18
Curimatá ~ BR 121 Em 50
Curimatá O BR 133 Em 51
Curimatá de Baixo ~ BR 117 Eb 48
Curionópolis O BR 121 Ek 48
Curitiba O BR 140 Ek 58
Curitibanos O BR 140 Ej 59
Curiúva O BR 140 Ej 58
Curly Cut Cays ♁ BS 87 Dk 34
Curnamona O AUS 378 Mf 61
Curoca ~ ANG 340 Gn 54
Currais Novos O BR 124 Fb 49
Curral Falso O BR 146 Ej 61
Curralinho O BR 121 Ek 46
Curral Novo O BR 124 Ep 50
Curral Velho O BR 133 Em 52
Curral Velho O CV 316 Fj 37
Currant O USA 64 Ce 26
Currant Mountain △ USA 64 Ce 26
Currarehue O RCH 147 Dn 65
Currat Alto O BR 146 Eh 62
Currawilla O AUS 374 Mg 58
Currawinya O AUS 375 Mj 60
Currawinya ♀ AUS 375 Mj 60
Current Island ♁ BS 87 Dk 33
Currie O USA 64 Ce 25
Currie O AUS 379 Mh 65
Currituck Sound ~ USA 74 Dl 27
Curtea de Argeș O RO 175 He 23
Curtin O AUS 368 Lm 61
Curtin Springs O AUS 369 Mb 58
Curtis O E 184 Gb 24
Curtis Channel ~ AUS 375 Mm 57
Curtis Island ♁ AUS 375 Mm 57
Curu ~ BR 124 Fa 47
Curuá O BR 120 Eg 46
Curuá ~ BR 120 Eg 49
Curuá ~ BR 120 Eg 50
Curuaés ~ BR 120 Eg 50
Curuá ou Cururu ~ BR 133 Eh 53
Curuça ~ BR 116 Dm 49
Curuça O BR 121 El 46
Curucay ~ EC 116 Dl 46
Curucuriari ~ BR 117 Dp 46
Curuduri ~ BR 117 Ec 45
Curué do Sul ~ BR 120 Eh 47
Curuguaty O PY 140 Eg 58
Curumani O CO 107 Dm 41
Curumu O BR 121 Ej 46
Curup O RI 278 Lb 47
Curupá O BR 121 El 50
Curuquetê ~ BR 117 Eb 50
Cururú-Açu ~ BR 120 Ef 50
Cururu ou Cururu-ri ~ BR 120 Ef 49
Cururupu O BR 121 Em 46
Curuzú Cuatiá O RA 146 Ef 60
Curvá ~ BR 120 Eg 47
Curva Grande O BR 121 Em 47
Curvelo O BR 133 Em 55
Cushabatay ~ PE 116 Dl 49
Cushamen O RA 147 Dn 67
Cushing O USA 70 Cp 28
Cusimi O YV 112 Eb 43
Cusis ~ BR 132 Ee 54
Čusovoj O RUS 154 Rc 7
Cusseta O USA 86 Df 29
Cussivi ~ ANG 340 Hc 53
Cusso ~ ANG 340 Gp 53
Čust O UZB 223 Jp 25
Custer O USA 51 Cj 22
Custer O USA 51 Cl 24
Custódia O BR 124 Fb 50
Cutato ~ ANG 340 Ha 51
Cutato O ANG 340 Ha 53
Cut Bank O USA 51 Cf 21
Cutenda O ANG 340 Gp 53
Cutervo O PE 116 Dj 49
Cuthbert O USA 86 Df 30
Cutias O BR 121 Ej 45
Čutove O UA 175 Hk 21
Cuttaburra Creek ~ AUS 375 Mj 60
Cuttack O IND 235 Kg 35
Cutzamala de Prinzón O MEX 92 Cm 36
Cuvango O ANG 340 Ha 53
Cuvelai O ANG 340 Gp 53
Cuvelai ~ ANG 340 Ha 54
Cuvette de la Bénoué ⏢ CAM 321 Gn 41
Cuvier Island ♁ NZ 383 Nk 64
Cuvo ~ ANG 340 Gp 52
Cuxhaven O D 170 Gl 19
Cuya O RCH 128 Dn 55
Cuyahoya Valley N.R.A. ♀ USA 71 Dh 25
Cuyama O USA 64 Cc 28
Cuyo O RP 267 Ll 40
Cuyo East Passage ~ RP 267 Ll 40
Cuyo Islands ♁ RP 267 Ll 40
Cuyo Subterranean National Park ★ RP 267 Ll 40
Cuyo West Passage ~ RP 267 Ll 40
Cuyuni ~ GUY 112 Ed 42
Cuyuni ~ GUY 112 Ee 42
Cuzco O PE 128 Dm 52
Čvrsnica △ BIH 194 Ha 24
Cyangugu O RWA 336 Hg 47
Cyclades ♁ GR 194 He 27
cyganak Mankyclaks ~ KZ 202 Jd 23
Cygnet O AUS 378 Mk 67
Cyhyryn O UA 175 Hj 21
Cynthia O AUS 375 Mm 58
Cynthiana O USA 71 Df 26
Cypress O USA 86 Db 30
Cypress Gardens ★ USA 87 Dh 32
Cypress Hills ⛰ CDN 51 Cg 21
Cyprus □ CY 195 Hk 28
Cyrenaica ⏢ LAR 300 Hc 30
Cyrene O ZW 349 Hg 56
Cyron O AUS 375 Ml 60
Cytherea O AUS 375 Mk 59

412 Corning - Cytherea

□Country ▣Capital city ⊙Administrative unit ○Place ◬Island ⛰Mountain range △Mountain ⌓Cape ≈Ocean, Sea ∼Lake, River ▽Undersea topography ▲Glacier ♀National park •••Reservation ★Point of major interest ⏥Landscape

Czaplinek ○ PL 170 Ha 19
Czarnkow ○ PL 170 Ha 19
Czech Republic □ CZ 174 Gn 20
Czersk ○ PL 170 Ha 19
Częstochowa ○ PL 174 Hb 20
Čžinskij tasķyncu ∼ KZ 181 Jc 20

D

D. Federal ⊙ BR 133 Ek 53
D. L. Garzas ○ MEX 81 Cm 33
Daanbantayan ○ RP 267 Lm 40
Daaquam ○ CDN 60 Dn 22
Dabaga ○ EAT 337 Hk 50
Dabajuro ○ YV 107 Dn 40
Dabakala ○ CI 317 Gd 41
Dabalebo ○ SME 113 Ef 43
Dabaray ○ AFG 227 Jm 30
Dabas ○ H 174 Hb 22
Daba Shan ⛰ VRC 243 Le 29
Dabat ○ ETH 313 Hl 39
Dabatou ○ RG 316 Ga 40
Dabeiba ○ CO 106 Dk 42
Daben ○ VRC 255 Le 36
Dābhāde ○ IND 238 Ka 36
Dabhoi ○ IND 227 Ka 34
Dābhol ○ IND 238 Ka 37
Dabie Shan ⛰ VRC 243 Lh 30
Dabiss ○ RG 316 Fn 40
Dablo ○ BF 317 Gf 39
Dabnou ○ RN 308 Gj 38
Dabo ○ SN 316 Fn 39
Dabola ○ RG 316 Ga 40
Dabolatounka ○ RG 316 Ga 40
Dabou ○ CI 317 Gd 43
Daboya ○ GH 317 Gf 41
Dabra ○ IND 234 Kd 33
Dabsen Hu ∼ VRC 242 Km 27
Dabus Wenz ∼ ETH 313 Hk 40
Dabwa ○ TCH 309 Gn 38
Dắc Glei ○ VN 263 Ld 38
Dachangshan Dao ◬ VRC 246 Lm 26
Dachau ○ D 174 Gm 21
Dacheng ○ VRC 258 Lh 31
Dachenzhuang ○ VRC 246 Lj 26
Dachsteingruppe △ A 174 Gn 22
Dachung Yogma ○ IND 230 Kd 29
Đắc Mil ○ VN 263 Ld 39
Đắc Song ○ VN 263 Ld 39
Dadanawa ○ GUY 112 Ee 44
Dade City ○ USA 87 Dg 31
Dādhar ○ PK 227 Jm 31
Dadong ○ VRC 255 Le 34
Dadra and Nagar Haveli ⊙ IND 238 Ka 35
Dādu ○ PK 227 Jm 32
Daduan ○ VRC 258 Lh 31
Dadu He ∼ VRC 254 Lb 31
Dadukou ○ VRC 246 Lj 30
Daduru Oya ∼ CL 239 Kd 42
Daet ○ RP 267 Lm 38
Dafang ○ VRC 255 Lc 32
Dafanpu ○ VRC 243 Lf 26
Dafeng ○ VRC 246 Ll 29
Dafengding Natural Ecosystem Reserves ♀ VRC 255 Lb 31
Dafoe ○ CDN 51 Ck 20
Dafra ○ TCH 321 Hb 40
Dafter ○ USA 57 Df 22
Daga ○ BHT 235 Kj 32
Daga ∼ ETH 325 Hk 41
Dagaari ○ SP 328 Jb 42
Dagami ○ RP 267 Ln 40
Dagana ○ SN 304 Fn 37
Daga Pos ○ SUD 325 Hk 41
Dagash ○ SUD 312 Hj 36
Dagda ○ LV 171 Hf 17
Dage ○ RDC 321 Hc 44
Dag-e Namadi ∼ AFG 223 Jj 29
Dagestanskie Ogni ○ RUS 202 Jc 24
Dagestanskij zapovednik ♀ RUS 202 Jb 23
Daggaboersnek △ ZA 358 He 62
Daggyai Co ∼ VRC 235 Kg 31
Daglung ○ VRC 235 Kk 31
Dagmar ○ OM 226 Jh 34
Dagohoy ○ RP 267 Ln 41
Dagomys ○ RUS 195 Hm 24
Dagua ○ CO 106 Dk 44
Daguan ○ VRC 255 Lb 32
Daguan ○ VRC 255 Lc 31
Daguit ○ RP 267 Lm 38
Dagupan ○ RP 267 Ll 37
Daguragu-Kurintji Aboriginal Land ••• AUS 364 Mb 54
Dagushan ○ VRC 246 Lm 26
Dagworth ○ AUS 365 Mh 54
Dagworth ○ AUS 374 Mh 56
Dagzê Co ∼ VRC 231 Kh 30
Dagzhuka ○ VRC 235 Kj 31
Dahab ○ ET 214 Hk 31
Dahaban ○ SUD 218 Hm 35
Dahbed ○ UZB 223 Jm 26
Daheba ○ VRC 242 Kp 28
Da Hinggan Ling ⛰ VRC 205 Wb 9
Dahiri ○ CI 317 Gd 43
Dahlak Archipelago ◬ ER 313 Hn 38
Dahle ○ AFG 227 Jl 30
Dāhod ○ IND 234 Kb 34
Dahongliutan ○ VRC 230 Kd 27
Dahra ⏥ LAR 297 Ha 31
Dahr Qualâta ⏥ RIM 305 Gc 37
Dahr Tîchît ⏥ RIM 304 Gb 36
Dahšūr ○ ET 301 Hh 31
Dahūk ○ IRQ 209 Hp 27
Dahūk ○ IRQ 209 Hp 27
Daïet Akhicha ∼ DZ 293 Gg 31
Dai Hai ∼ VRC 243 Lg 25
Dai Island ◬ SOL 290 Nc 49
Daimiel ○ E 184 Ge 26
Daingerfield ○ USA 70 Da 29
Daintree ○ AUS 365 Mj 54
Daintree ♀ AUS 365 Mj 54
Daiquiri ○ C 101 Dl 36
Daireaux ○ RA 137 Ed 64
Dair Mawās ○ ET 301 Hh 32
Dairy Creek ○ AUS 368 Lh 58
Dai-sen △ J 251 Mc 28
Daisengen-dake △ J 250 Mf 25
Daisen-Oki ♀ J 251 Mc 28
Daisetsuzan ♀ J 250 Mh 24
Dai Shan ◬ VRC 246 Lm 30
Daisy ○ USA 70 Da 28
Dai Xian ○ VRC 243 Lg 26
Daiyun Shan ⛰ VRC 258 Lk 33
Dajabón ○ DOM 101 Dn 36
Dajarra ○ AUS 374 Mf 56
Dajing ○ VRC 242 Lb 27
Đaj Loi ○ VN 255 Lc 36
Daka ∼ GH 317 Gf 41
Dakar ▣ SN 304 Fl 38
Dakata Shet' ∼ ETH 328 Hp 42
Dakeshi ○ VRC 235 Kj 31
Dakhla Oasis ⏥ ET 301 Hg 33
Daki Takwas ○ WAN 320 Gj 40
Dak Nông ○ VN 263 Ld 39
Dākoānk ○ IND 270 Kl 42
Dākoānk ○ IND 270 Kl 42
Dakoro ○ RN 308 Gk 38
Dakota City ○ USA 56 Cp 24
Dakovica ○ SCG 194 Hc 24
Dakovo ○ HR 174 Hb 23
Daksum ○ IND 230 Kb 29
Dala ○ SOL 290 Nc 50
Dala ○ ANG 340 Hc 50
Dala ○ ANG 340 Hc 51
Dalaba ○ SN 316 Fp 39
Dalaba ○ RG 316 Fp 40
Dalad Qi ○ VRC 243 Lf 25
Dalahaj ○ RUS 204 Uc 8
Dalälven ∼ S 158 Gp 15
Dalaman Çayı ∼ TR 195 Hg 27
Dalāmi ○ SUD 312 Hh 40
Dalandzadgad ○ MNG 26 Qa 5
Dalangyun ○ MYA 254 Km 36
Dalap-Uliga-Darrit ▣ MH 27 Ta 9
Dalarna ⏥ S 158 Gn 15
Dà Lat ○ VN 263 Le 40
Dālbandīn ○ PK 227 Jl 31
Dalbeg ○ AUS 375 Mk 56
Dalby ○ AUS 375 Mm 59
Dalcahue ○ RCH 147 Dl 67
Dale ○ USA 50 Cc 23
Dale ○ N 158 Gj 15
Dale City ○ USA 74 Dk 26
Dale Hollow Lake ∼ USA 71 Df 27
Dalei Shan ⛰ VRC 242 Kn 26
Dales ○ USA 64 Ca 25
Daletme ○ MYA 235 Kl 35
Dalğā' ○ ET 301 Hh 32
Dalgaranga Hill △ AUS 368 Lj 59
Dalgety Brook ∼ AUS 368 Lj 58
Dalgonally ○ AUS 374 Mg 56
Dalhaki ○ AFG 223 Jm 27
Dalhart ○ USA 65 Cl 27
Dalhousie ○ CDN 61 Ea 21
Dalhousie ○ IND 230 Kb 29
Dali ○ VRC 243 Le 28
Dali ○ VRC 254 La 33
Dali ○ RMM 304 Gc 38
Dalian ○ VRC 246 Ll 26
Daliang Shan ⛰ VRC 255 Lb 31
Dālimb ○ IND 238 Kc 37
Dalkola ○ IND 235 Kh 33
Dallas ○ USA 50 Ca 23
Dallas ○ CDN 56 Cp 20
Dallas ○ USA 70 Cp 29
Dallas City ○ USA 71 Dc 25
Dalli ○ WAN 320 Gm 41
Dall Island ◬ USA 42 Da 8
Dallol Bosso ∼ RN 320 Gh 39
Dalmac ⏥ HR 174 Gp 23
Dalmatia ⏥ HR 174 Gp 23
Dal'nee ○ RUS 250 Mh 22
Dal'negorsk ○ RUS 250 Md 23
Dal'nerčensk ○ RUS 250 Mc 23
Dal'nije Zelency ○ RUS 159 Hl 11
Daloa ○ CI 305 Gc 42
Dalong ○ VRC 255 Le 32
Dalrymple Lake ∼ AUS 375 Mk 56
Dalsmynni ○ IS 158 Fj 13
Dāltenganj ○ IND 235 Kg 34
Dalton ○ USA 65 Cl 25
Dalton ○ ZA 352 Hh 60
Dalu ○ VRC 242 Lc 27
Daludalu ○ RI 270 La 45
Dalupin Island ◬ RP 267 Ln 39
Dalupiri Island ◬ RP 267 Ll 36
Dalu Shan ⛰ VRC 255 Ld 31
Dalvík ○ IS 158 Fl 13
Dalwallinu ○ AUS 368 Lj 61
Daly ∼ AUS 364 Mb 53
Daly River ○ AUS 364 Mb 52
Daly River Aboriginal Land ••• AUS 364 Ma 53
Daly Waters ○ AUS 364 Mc 54
Damad ○ KSA 218 Hp 37
Damagaram-Takaya ○ RN 308 Gl 38
Damaguete ○ RP 267 Lm 41
Dāmān ○ AFG 227 Jl 30
Damān ○ IND 238 Ka 35
Damān and Diu ⊙ IND 227 Jp 35
Da-Man-Hūr ○ ET 301 Hh 30
Damār ○ YE 218 Ja 38
Damara ○ RCA 321 Hb 43
Damardatar ○ RI 279 Lh 47
Damar Laut ○ MAL 270 La 43
Damasak ○ WAN 320 Gn 39
Damas Cays ◬ BS 100 Dh 34
Damascus ▣ SYR 208 Hl 29
Damaturu ○ WAN 320 Gm 40
Damauli ○ NEP 235 Kg 32
Damāvand ○ IR 222 Je 28
Damazine ○ SUD 313 Hk 40
Damba ○ ANG 332 Gp 49
Dambai ○ GH 317 Gg 41
Dambam ○ WAN 320 Gm 40
Damboa ○ WAN 320 Gn 40
Dambulla ○ CL 239 Ke 42
Dame Marie ○ RH 101 Dl 36
Dam Gamad ○ SUD 312 Hf 39
Dāmgān ○ IR 222 Jf 27
Damgarten ○ D 170 Gm 18
Damietta ○ ET 301 Hh 30
Dāmnagar ○ IND 227 Jp 35
Damodar ∼ IND 235 Kh 34
Damoh ○ IND 234 Kd 34
Damongo ○ GH 317 Gf 41
Damortis ○ RP 267 Ll 37
Dampar ○ WAN 320 Gm 41
Damphu ○ BHT 235 Kk 32
Dampier ○ AUS 360 Lj 56
Dampier Archipelago ◬ AUS 360 Lj 56
Dampier Downs ○ AUS 360 Lm 55
Dampier Land ⏥ AUS 360 Lm 54
Dampier Strait ∼ PNG 287 Ml 48
Dam Qu ∼ VRC 231 Kl 29
Damrūr ○ KSA 218 Hm 35
Damt ○ YE 218 Ja 38
Damtang ○ VRC 230 Kf 29
Damtar ○ TCH 321 Ha 40
Damwal ○ ZA 349 Hg 58
Damxung ○ VRC 231 Kk 30
Danané ○ CI 316 Gb 42
Dà Nẵng ○ VN 263 Le 37
Danao ○ RP 267 Lm 40
Danar ○ RI 283 Mc 48
Danau Aiwasa ∼ RI 283 Md 47
Danau Amaru ∼ RI 283 Mc 46
Danau Batur ∼ RI 279 Lh 50
Danau Belajau ∼ RI 279 Lg 47
Danau Diatas ∼ RI 270 La 46
Danau Dibaru ∼ RI 270 La 46
Danau ,Gigi ∼ RI 283 Mc 46
Danau Gita ∼ RI 283 Mc 46
Danau Jati luhur ∼ RI 278 Ld 49
Danau Jembawan ∼ RI 278 Lc 47
Danau Kai ∼ RI 286 Mg 49
Danau Kamakawalar ∼ RI 283 Md 47
Danau Kerinci ∼ RI 270 La 47
Danau Lauttawar ∼ RI 270 Kn 43
Danau Lindu ∼ RI 282 Ll 46
Danau Lindu ∼ RI 368 Ll46
Danau Mahakam ∼ RI 274 Lj 46
Danau Makiri ∼ RI 283 Mc 46
Danau Maninjau ∼ RI 270 La 46
Danau Matano ∼ RI 282 Ll 47
Danau Melintang ∼ RI 274 Lj 46
Danau Mooat ∼ RI 275 Ln 45
Danau Paniai ∼ RI 286 Me 47
Danau Poso ∼ RI 282 Ll 46
Danau Rana ∼ RI 282 Lp 47
Danau Ranau ∼ RI 278 Lb 48
Danau Riamkanan ∼ RI 279 Lh 47
Danau Rombebai ∼ RI 286 Me 46
Danau Rombebai ∼ RI 286 Mf 46
Danau Semayang ∼ RI 274 Lj 46
Danau Sentan ∼ RI 286 Mg 47
Danau Sentarum ∼ RI 274 Lg 45
Danau Singkarak ∼ RI 270 La 46
Danau Sumpa ∼ RI 274 Lg 45
Danau Tanemot ∼ RI 283 Mc 46
Danau Tempe ∼ RI 279 Lk 48
Danau Tigi ∼ RI 286 Me 48
Danau Toba ∼ RI 270 Kp 44
Danau Tondano ∼ RI 275 Ln 45
Danau Towuti ∼ RI 282 Ll 47
Danau Yamur ∼ RI 283 Md 47
Danba ○ VRC 242 La 30
Danbatta ○ WAN 320 Gl 39
Danbury ○ USA 56 Db 22
Danbury ○ USA 74 Dm 25
Danby Lake ∼ USA 64 Ce 28
Dan Chang ○ THA 262 Kp 38
Dancheng ○ VRC 243 Lh 29
Dandara ★ ET 301 Hj 32
Dandaragan ○ AUS 368 Lh 61
Dandau ○ ANG 340 Ha 51
Dandeli ○ IND 238 Kb 38
Dandenong ○ AUS 379 Mj 64
Dando ○ ANG 340 Ha 51
Dandong ○ VRC 246 Lm 25
Daneib ∼ NAM 348 Hc 56
Danesfahan ○ IR 209 Jc 28
Danfeng ○ VRC 243 Lf 29
Dang ○ CAM 321 Gn 43
Danga ○ RMM 305 Ge 37
Danga ○ RDC 324 Hf 44
Dangara ○ TJ 223 Jn 26
Dangchang ○ VRC 242 Lc 28
Dange ○ ANG 332 Gp 49
Dange ∼ ANG 332 Gp 50
Dangerous Cape ⌓ USA 46 An 17
Danggali ♀ AUS 378 Mg 62
Dangila ○ ETH 313 Hl 40
Dangjin Shankou △ VRC 242 Km 26
Dangla Shan ⛰ VRC 231 Kk 29
Dangriga ○ BH 93 Dd 37
Dangshan ○ VRC 246 Lj 28
Dangtu ○ VRC 246 Lk 30
Dan-Gulbi ○ WAN 320 Gk 40
Dangur ○ ETH 313 Hk 40
Dangur ⛰ ETH 313 Hk 40
Dangyang ○ VRC 243 Lf 30
Dan He ∼ VRC 243 Lg 28
Daniel ○ USA 51 Cg 24
Danielskuil ○ ZA 349 Hd 60
Danilov ○ RUS 171 Hn 16
Danilovka ○ RUS 181 Hp 20
Daning ○ VRC 243 Lf 27
Daninghe ★ VRC 243 Le 30
Dan-Issa ○ RN 320 Gk 39
Dānızkānan ○ AZ 202 Jc 25
Danja ○ WAN 320 Gk 40
Danjiangkou ○ VRC 243 Lf 29
Danjiankou Shuiku ∼ VRC 243 Lf 29
Dank ○ OM 226 Jg 34
Dankov ○ RUS 181 Hm 19
Danli ○ HN 96 Dc 39
Dannenberg(E.) ○ D 170 Gm 19
Dannevirke ○ NZ 383 Nl 66
Dannhauser ○ ZA 352 Hh 59
Dano ○ BF 317 Ge 40
Danot ○ ETH 328 Ja 42
Dan Sadau ○ WAN 320 Gk 40
Danskøya ◬ N 158 Gm 6
Dansville ○ USA 60 Dj 24
Danta ○ IND 227 Ka 33
Dantalpalli ○ IND 238 Kd 37
Dantch ○ RT 317 Gg 41
Danube ∼ D 174 Gn 21
Danube ∼ SCG 174 Hb 23
Danube ∼ RO 175 Hf 23
Danube Delta ⏥ RO 175 Hg 23
Danubyu ○ MYA 262 Km 37
Danville ○ USA 70 Db 28
Danville ○ USA 71 De 25
Danville ○ USA 71 Df 27
Danville ○ USA 74 Dj 27
Dan Xian ○ VRC 255 Le 36
Danyang ○ VRC 246 Lk 30
Danyi-Apéyémé ○ RT 317 Gg 42
Danzhai ○ VRC 255 Ld 32
Danzhou ○ VRC 255 Le 33
Dao ○ RP 267 Ll 40
Đảo Phú Quôc ◬ VN 263 Lb 40
Daotanghe ○ VRC 242 La 27
Dao Timi ○ RN 309 Gn 35
Daoud ○ DZ 293 Gf 28
Daoukro ○ CI 317 Ge 42
Dao Xian ○ VRC 255 Lf 33
Daozhen ○ VRC 255 Ld 31
Dapa ○ RP 267 Ln 41
Dapaong ○ BF 317 Gg 40
Dapchi ○ WAN 320 Gm 39
Dapélogo ○ BF 317 Gf 39
Đa Phúc ○ VN 255 Lc 35
Dapitan ○ RP 267 Lm 41
Dāpoli ○ IND 238 Ka 37
Dapolinê ○ IND 254 Km 32
Da Qaidam ○ VRC 242 Km 27
Daqiao ○ VRC 255 Lb 32
Daqin Dao ◬ VRC 246 Ll 26
Daqing ○ VRC 205 Wb 9
Daqu Shan ◬ VRC 246 Lm 30
Dar'a ○ SYR 208 Hl 29
Dar'a ○ SYR 208 Hl 29
Dara ○ SN 304 Fn 38
Dara ∼ SP 329 Hp 45
Dārāb ○ IR 226 Jf 31
Darāban ○ PK 227 Jp 30
Daradou ○ RCA 324 He 43
Darāfisa ○ SUD 312 Hj 39
Daraina ○ RM 345 Jc 52
Dārān ○ IR 222 Jd 29
Darasun ○ RUS 204 Vb 8
Darauli ○ IND 235 Kg 32
Daravica △ SCG 194 Hc 24
Darāw ○ ET 301 Hj 33
Darazo ○ WAN 320 Gm 40
Darband ○ IR 226 Jg 30
Darband -e Hān ○ IRQ 209 Ja 28
Darbhanga ○ IND 235 Kg 33
Darby ○ USA 50 Ce 22
Dar Chioukh ○ DZ 296 Gh 28
Darda ○ AUS 368 Ll 59
Dardanelle ○ USA 70 Db 28
Dardanelle Lake ∼ USA 70 Db 28
Dardanelles ∼ TR 194 Hf 25
Dar el Barka ○ RIM 304 Fn 37
Darende ○ TR 195 Hl 26
Dar es Salaam ○ EAT 337 Hm 49
Dareton ○ AUS 378 Mh 63
Darfield ○ NZ 383 Nj 67
Darfur ⏥ SUD 312 Hd 39
Dargan-Ata ○ TM 223 Jk 25
Dargaville ○ NZ 383 Nj 63
Dargeçit ○ TR 202 Hn 27
Dargo ○ AUS 379 Mk 64
Dargol ○ RN 317 Gg 39
Darhala ○ CI 317 Gd 41
Darhan ○ MNG 204 Va 9
Darién ⏥ PA 97 Dj 41
Darien Calima ○ CO 106 Dk 43
Dārīn ○ KSA 215 Jd 32
Dario Meira ○ BR 125 Fa 53
Darj ○ LAR 297 Gm 30
Darjiling ○ IND 235 Kj 32
Dārjing ○ IND 235 Kg 35
Darkan ○ AUS 368 Lj 62
Darke Peak ○ AUS 378 Me 62
Darlag ○ VRC 242 Kp 29
Darling ○ ZA 358 Hb 62
Darling ∼ AUS 378 Mh 62
Darling Downs ⏥ AUS 375 Mm 59
Darling Range ⛰ AUS 368 Lj 61
Darlington ○ USA 56 Dc 24
Darlington ○ USA 74 Dj 28
Darlington ○ GB 162 Gf 18
Darlington Point ○ AUS 379 Mj 63
Darłowo ○ PL 170 Gp 18
Darlton ○ AUS 379 Mk 61
Darmazār ○ IR 226 Jg 31
Darmstadt ○ D 174 Gl 21
Dār Muğahhar ○ YE 218 Ja 39
Darnah ○ LAR 300 Hd 29
Darnick ○ AUS 379 Mh 62
Darnley Island ◬ AUS 286 Mh 50
Daroca ○ E 184 Gf 25
Darouma ∼ RMM 304 Gb 38
Darou-Mousti ○ SN 304 Fm 38
Darr ∼ AUS 375 Mh 57
Darregaz ○ IR 222 Jh 27
Darregueira ○ RA 137 Ec 64
Darre Sahr ○ IR 209 Jb 29
Darre-ye Bum ○ AFG 223 Jk 28
Darre-ye Šūf ○ AFG 223 Jm 28
Darrington ○ USA 50 Cb 21
Darsah ◬ YE 219 Je 39
Dartmoor ♀ GB 163 Gd 20
Dartmoor ○ AUS 378 Mg 64
Dartmouth ○ CDN 61 Ec 23
Dartmouth ∼ AUS 379 Mk 64
Daru ○ RI 275 Lp 45
Daru ○ PNG 286 Mh 50
Daru ○ WAL 316 Ga 42
Darubia ○ PNG 287 Mm 50
Daruvar ○ HR 174 Ha 23
Darvaz ○ AFG 223 Jp 26
Darvazskij hrebet ⛰ TJ 223 Jp 26
Darvinskij zapovednik ♀ RUS 171 Hl 16
Darvoza ○ UZB 223 Jm 25
Darwāzagei ○ AFG 227 Jm 30
Darwendale ○ ZW 341 Hh 54
Dārwha ○ IND 234 Kc 35
Darwin △ EC 128 Dc 46
Darwin ○ GB 147 Ee 71
Darwin ○ AUS 364 Mb 52
Darwin River ○ AUS 364 Mb 52
Daryāce-e Sistan ∼ IR 226 Jj 30
Daryāče-ye Bāhtegān ∼ IR 215 Je 31
Daryāče-ye Tašk ∼ IR 215 Je 31
Darya Khān ○ PK 227 Jp 30
Daryāpur ○ IND 234 Kc 35
Daryā-ye Namak ∼ IR 222 Jd 28
Dārzīn ○ IR 226 Jg 31
Dās ◬ UAE 215 Je 33
Dasāda ○ IND 227 Jp 34
Dashan ○ VRC 255 Lc 32
Dashapalla ○ IND 235 Kg 35
Dashennongjia △ VRC 243 Lf 30
Dashiqiao ○ VRC 246 Lm 25
Dasht ∼ PK 226 Jk 33
Dasht-i-Tahlāb ⏥ PK 226 Jj 31
Dashuikeng ○ VRC 243 Ld 27
Daska ○ IND 230 Kb 29
Dasoguz ○ TM 222 Jh 25
Dasol Bay ∼ RP 267 Lk 38
Dass ○ WAN 320 Gl 40
Dassa ○ DY 317 Gh 42
Dassabolo ∼ RMM 316 Ga 39
Dassari ○ DY 317 Gg 40
Dassel ○ USA 56 Da 23
Dasseneiland ◬ ZA 358 Ha 62
Dašt-e Abbas ○ IR 209 Jb 29
Dašt-e Kavīr ⏥ IR 222 Je 28
Dašt-e Lūt ⏥ IR 222 Jg 29
Dašt-e Mārgō ⏥ AFG 226 Jk 30
Dašt-e Palang ∼ IR 215 Jd 31
Dāsū ○ PK 230 Ka 28
Datah Dawai ○ RI 274 Lh 45
Datang ○ VRC 255 Le 33
Datca ○ TR 195 Hf 27
Date ○ J 250 Mg 24
Dateland ○ USA 64 Cf 29
Dates Coast ⏥ 38 Sb 17
Datian ○ VRC 258 Lj 33
Datian Ding △ VRC 255 Lf 34
Datil ○ USA 65 Cj 28
Dating ○ VRC 255 Ld 33
Datkan ○ MYA 254 Km 36
Datong ○ VRC 242 La 27
Datong ○ VRC 243 Lg 25
Datong He ∼ VRC 242 La 27
Datong Shan ⛰ VRC 242 Kp 27
Datu Piang ○ RP 275 Ln 42
Daub ○ RI 286 Mg 50
Dāūd Khel ○ PK 223 Jp 29
Daudnagar ○ IND 235 Kg 33
Daugava ∼ LV 171 Hf 17
Daugavpils ○ LV 171 Hf 18
Dauka ○ OM 219 Je 36
Daule ○ EC 116 Dh 46
Daule ∼ EC 116 Dh 46
Daule ○ RI 282 Ll 48
Daumannsodden ⌓ N 158 Gm 6
Daund ○ IND 238 Kb 36
Daung Kyun ◬ MYA 262 Kn 39
Dauphin ○ CDN 56 Cn 20
Dauphina ⏥ F 185 Gj 23
Dauphin Lake ∼ CDN 56 Cn 20
Dauphin River ○ CDN 56 Cn 19
Daura ○ WAN 320 Gl 39
Daus ○ KSA 218 Hn 35
Dausa ○ IND 234 Kc 32
Dăvăçi ○ AZ 202 Jc 25
Dāvangere ○ IND 238 Kb 38
Davao ○ RP 275 Ln 42
Davao Gulf ∼ RP 275 Ln 42
Dāvari ○ IR 226 Jg 32
Dāvarzan ○ IR 222 Jg 27
Davenport ○ USA 50 Cc 22
Davenport ○ USA 71 Dc 25
Davenport Creek ∼ AUS 374 Me 60
Davenport Downs ○ AUS 374 Mg 58
Davenport Range ⛰ AUS 374 Md 56
David ○ PA 97 Dg 41
David City ○ USA 70 Cp 25
Davidson ○ CDN 51 Ck 20
Davidson ○ USA 70 Cn 28
Davinópolis ○ BR 133 El 55
Davis ○ USA 64 Cb 26
Davis ○ USA 74 Dk 28
Davis ∼ AUS 360 Ll 57
Davis Bay ≈ 38 Rb 16
Davis Mountains ⛰ USA 81 Ck 30
Davison ○ USA 57 Dg 24
Davis Sea ≈ 38 Pa 16
Davis Strait ∼ CDN 7 Ga 3
Davo ∼ CI 317 Gd 43
Davos ○ CH 174 Gl 22
Dawa ○ VRC 246 Lm 25
Dawadawa ○ GH 317 Gf 41
Dawa Wenz ∼ ETH 325 Hm 43
Dawhenya ○ GH 317 Gf 43
Dawir ○ SUD 324 Hj 41
Dawn ○ USA 65 Cl 28
Dawson ○ CDN 6 Ca 3
Dawson ○ CDN 47 Bg 13
Dawson ○ USA 56 Cn 22
Dawson ○ USA 86 Df 30
Dawson ∼ AUS 375 Ml 58
Dawson Bay ∼ CDN 56 Cm 19
Dawson Creek ○ CDN 6 Cb 4
Dawson Creek ○ CDN 47 Ca 17
Dawson Range ⛰ AUS 375 Ml 57
Dawu ○ VRC 242 La 30
Dawu ○ VRC 243 Lh 30
Dax ○ F 184 Gf 24
Daxi ○ VRC 259 Ll 31
Da Xian ○ VRC 243 Ld 30
Daxiengmao Reserves ♀ VRC 242 Lb 30
Daxin ○ VRC 255 Ld 34
Daxue Shan ⛰ VRC 254 La 31
Daya Barat Islands ◬ RI 282 Lp 49
Dayao ○ VRC 254 La 33
Daya Wan ∼ VRC 258 Lh 34
Dayboro ○ AUS 375 Mn 59
Dāyet en Nahārāt ○ RMM 305 Ge 37
Dayi ∼ GH 317 Gg 42
Dayl ○ WAN 320 Gk 40
Daylesford ○ AUS 379 Mj 64
Daymān ∼ ROU 146 Ef 61
Dayong ○ VRC 255 Lf 31
Dayr az-Zawr ○ SYR 209 Hm 28
Dayrut ○ ET 301 Hh 32
Daysland ○ CDN 51 Cf 19
Dayton ○ USA 50 Cd 22
Dayton ○ USA 64 Cc 26
Dayton ○ USA 71 Df 26
Dayton ○ USA 71 Df 28
Daytona Beach ○ USA 87 Dh 31
Dayu ○ VRC 258 Lh 33
Dayu ○ RI 279 Lh 46
Dayul Gômpa ○ VRC 254 Kp 31
Da Yunhe ∼ VRC 246 Lj 28
Dayville ○ USA 50 Cc 23
Dazhang Xi ∼ VRC 258 Lk 33
Dazhou Dao ◬ VRC 255 Lf 36
Dazhu ○ VRC 243 Ld 30
Dazkırı ○ TR 195 Hg 27
Dazu ○ VRC 255 Lc 31
Dchira ○ MA 292 Fp 32
De Aar ○ ZA 349 He 61
Dead Lake ∼ USA 56 Da 22
Deadman's Cay ○ BS 87 Dl 34
Deadman's Creek Indian Reservation ••• CDN 50 Cb 20
Dead Sea ∼ IL 214 Hk 30
Dead Sea ∼ IL 214 Hk 30
Deakin ○ AUS 369 Ma 61
Dealesville ○ ZA 349 He 60
Déali ○ SN 304 Fn 38
Deal Island ◬ AUS 379 Mk 65
De'an ○ VRC 258 Lh 31
Dean Channel ∼ CDN 50 Bn 19
Deán Funes ○ RA 137 Eb 61
Dearborn ○ USA 71 Dg 24
Dear Lake ○ CDN 56 Da 19
Deary ○ USA 50 Cd 22
Dease ∼ CDN 47 Bl 15
Dease Arm ∼ CDN 47 Ca 11
Dease Inlet ∼ USA 46 An 9
Dease Lake ○ CDN 42 Db 7
Dease Strait ∼ CDN 6 Db 3
Dease Strait ∼ CDN 42 Eb 5
Dease Strait ≈ CDN 47 Cg 11
Death Valley ♀ USA 64 Cd 27
Death Valley ⏥ USA 64 Cd 27
Death Valley Junction ○ USA 64 Cd 27
Deauville ○ F 163 Gf 21
Debal'ceve ○ UA 181 Hm 21
Debalo ○ SUD 324 Hh 41
de Banhine ♀ MOC 352 Hj 57
Debao ○ VRC 255 Ld 34
Debar ○ MK 194 Hc 25
Debark ○ ETH 313 Hl 39
Debaysima ○ ER 313 Hp 39
Debden ○ CDN 51 Cj 19
Debdou ○ MA 293 Ge 29
Debepare ○ PNG 286 Mg 49
De Beque ○ USA 65 Ch 26
Débéré ∼ BF 317 Ge 39
Debesa ○ AUS 361 Ln 54
Deblin ○ PL 174 Hc 20
Debre Birhan ○ ETH 325 Hm 41
Debrecen ○ H 174 Hc 22
Debre Markos ○ ETH 313 Hl 40
Debre May ○ ETH 313 Hl 40
Debre Sina ○ ETH 325 Hm 41
Debre Tabor ○ ETH 313 Hm 40
Debre Work' ○ ETH 313 Hl 40
Debre Zebīt ○ ETH 313 Hm 40
Debre Zeyit ○ ETH 313 Hk 40
Debre Zeyit ○ ETH 325 Hm 41
Decatur ○ USA 70 Cp 24
Decatur ○ USA 70 Cp 29
Decatur ○ USA 71 Dd 26
Decatur ○ USA 71 De 28
Decatur ○ USA 71 Df 25
Decatur ○ USA 86 Df 29
Deccan ⏥ IND 238 Kb 36
Deception Bay ∼ PNG 287 Mj 49
Deception Pan ∼ RB 349 Hd 56
Deception Point ⌓ AUS 364 Ma 51
Deception Valley ⏥ RB 349 Hd 56
Dechang ○ VRC 254 La 32
Dechu ○ IND 227 Ka 32
Děčín ○ CZ 174 Gp 20
Decize ○ F 163 Gh 22
Decker ○ USA 51 Cj 23
Decorah ○ USA 56 Dc 24
Deda ○ RO 175 He 22
Dedaye ○ MYA 262 Km 37
Deder ○ ETH 325 Hn 41
Dediāpāda ○ IND 238 Ka 35
De Doorns ○ ZA 358 Hb 62
Dédougou ○ BF 317 Ge 39
Dedza ○ MW 344 Hk 53
Dedza Mount △ MW 344 Hk 53
Dee ∼ GB 162 Ge 17
Deep ∼ USA 74 Dj 28
Deep River ○ CDN 60 Dk 22
Deep Springs ○ USA 64 Cd 27
Deepwater ○ USA 70 Db 26
Deepwater ○ AUS 375 Mm 60
Deep Well ○ AUS 374 Md 58
Deerfield Beach ○ USA 87 Dh 32
Deering ○ USA 46 Aj 11
Deer Island ◬ CDN 56 Cp 20
Deer Lake ○ CDN 61 Ef 21
Deer Lake ∼ CDN 61 Ef 21
Deer Lodge ○ USA 51 Cf 22
Deer Park ○ USA 50 Cd 22
Deer Pond ∼ CDN 61 Eg 21
Deer River ○ USA 56 Db 22
Deerton ○ USA 57 De 22
Deerwood ○ USA 56 Db 22
Defferrari ○ RA 146 Ee 65
Defiance ○ USA 71 Df 25
Défilé de Tosaye ⏥ RMM 305 Gf 37
De Forest ○ USA 57 Dd 24
De Funiak Springs ○ USA 86 De 30
Degache ○ TN 296 Gl 28
Degbassa ○ ETH 313 Hl 40
Dêgê ○ VRC 242 Kp 30
Degeh Bur ○ ETH 328 Hp 41
Degeh Medo ○ ETH 328 Hp 42
Dégelis ○ CDN 60 Dp 22
Degema ○ WAN 320 Gk 43
Dêgên ○ VRC 254 Kp 31
Deggendorf ○ D 174 Gn 21
De Goejegebergte ⛰ SME 113 Eg 44
Degollado ○ MEX 92 Cl 35
Degoma ○ ETH 313 Hl 39
Dégrand Saint-Léon ○ F 113 Eh 44
De Gray Lake ∼ USA 70 Db 28
De Grey ∼ AUS 360 Lk 56
Dehalak Desēt ◬ ER 313 Hn 38
Dehāqān ○ IR 215 Jd 30
Dehbārez ○ IR 226 Jg 32
Dehbid ○ IR 215 Je 30
Deh Dašt ○ IR 215 Jd 30
Deheg ○ IR 226 Jf 31
Dehej ○ IND 238 Ka 35
Dehgaon ○ IND 234 Kd 34
Deh Havāk ○ AFG 223 Jn 28
Deh Heir ○ IR 226 Jf 31
Dehiba ○ TN 297 Gm 29
Dehito ∼ PK 227 Jm 33
Dehkanabad ○ UZB 223 Jm 26
Dehlorān ○ IR 209 Jb 29
Deh Molla ○ IR 215 Jc 30
Dehra Dun ○ IND 230 Kc 30
Deh Rāvūd ○ AFG 223 Jl 29
Dehri ○ IND 235 Kg 33
Dehšir ○ IR 215 Je 30
Deh Šū ○ AFG 226 Jk 30
Dehua ○ VRC 258 Lk 33
Deim Bukhit ○ SUD 324 Hf 42
Deira ○ UAE 226 Jf 33
Dej ○ RO 175 He 22
Dejen ○ ETH 313 Hm 40
Dejian ○ VRC 255 Le 31
d'Ejna ○ RUS 159 Hj 11
Dejnau ○ TM 223 Jk 26
De Kalb ○ USA 70 Da 29
De Kalb ○ USA 71 Df 25
Dek'emhāre ○ ER 313 Hm 38
Dekese ○ RDC 333 Hc 47
Dekhlet Nouâdhibou ∼ RIM 304 Fm 35
Dekina ○ WAN 320 Gk 42
Dekoa ○ RCA 321 Hb 42
Delacroix ○ USA 86 Dd 31
de l'Akagera ♀ RWA 336 Hh 46
De Land ○ USA 87 Dh 31

Czaplinek - De Land 413

◻ Country ▣ Capital city ⊙ Administrative unit ○ Place ⛬ Island ⛰ Mountain range △ Mountain ⌓ Cape ≈ Ocean, Sea ∼ Lake, River ♆ Undersea topography ▵ Glacier ♀ National park ••• Reservation ★ Point of major interest ⌒ Landscape

Delano ○ USA 64 Cc 28
Delārām ○ AFG 223 Jk 29
Delareyville ○ ZA 349 He 59
Delavan ○ USA 71 Dd 24
Delaware ○ USA 71 Dg 25
Delaware ∼ USA 74 Dl 25
Delaware ⊙ USA 74 Dl 26
Delaware Bay ∼ USA 74 Dl 26
Delbi ○ SN 304 Fn 38
Del Bonita ○ CDN 51 Cf 21
Delburne ○ CDN 51 Cf 19
Delčev ○ MK 194 Hd 25
Deleau ○ CDN 56 Cm 21
Delegate River ○ AUS 379 Ml 64
Délembé ○ RCA 321 Hd 41
Délép ○ TCH 321 Hb 39
Delfi ★ GR 194 Hd 26
Delfino ○ BR 125 Ep 51
Delfinópolis ○ BR 141 El 56
Delft ○ NL 163 Gh 20
Delft Island ⛬ CL 239 Kd 41
Delfus ○ PE 116 Dk 48
Delfzijl ○ NL 170 Gk 19
Delgo ○ SUD 312 Hh 35
Delhi ○ USA 60 Dl 24
Delhi ○ USA 86 Dc 29
Delhi ○ IND 234 Kc 31
Déli ○ TCH 321 Gp 41
Delicias ○ MEX 80 Ck 31
Delījān ○ IR 222 Jd 28
Delingha ○ VRC 242 Kn 27
Delisle ○ CDN 51 Cj 20
Delisle ○ CDN 60 Dn 21
Delissaville ○ AUS 364 Mb 52
Deliverence Island ⛬ AUS 286 Mg 50
Dell ○ USA 51 Cf 23
Dell Rapids ○ USA 56 Cp 24
Dellys ○ DZ 296 Gh 27
Delmas ○ ZA 349 Hg 59
Delmenhorst ○ D 170 Gl 19
Delnice ○ HR 174 Gp 23
Del Norte ○ USA 65 Cj 27
De Long Mountains ⛰ USA 46 Aj 11
Deloraine ○ CDN 56 Cm 21
Deloraine ○ AUS 378 Mk 66
Delphi ○ USA 71 De 25
Delray Beach ○ USA 87 Dh 32
Del Rio ○ MEX 80 Cg 30
Del Rio ○ USA 81 Cm 31
Delsbo ○ S 158 Ha 15
Delta ○ CDN 50 Ca 21
Delta ○ USA 64 Cf 26
Delta ○ USA 65 Ch 26
Delta Beach ○ CDN 56 Cn 20
Delta del Tigre ○ ROU 146 Ef 63
Delta Downs ○ AUS 365 Mg 54
Delta Junction ○ USA 46 Bc 13
Delta N.W.R. ♀ USA 86 Dd 31
Delton ○ USA 71 Df 28
Delungra ○ AUS 375 Mm 60
Demagiri ○ IND 235 Kl 34
Demak ○ RI 278 Lf 49
Demba ○ RCA 324 He 43
Demba ○ RDC 333 Hd 48
Demba Koli ○ SN 316 Fp 39
Dembecha ○ ETH 313 Hl 40
Dembī ○ ETH 325 Hl 41
Dembī Dolo ○ ETH 325 Hk 41
Dembo ○ CAM 321 Gn 41
Dembo ○ TCH 321 Ha 41
Demidov ○ RUS 171 Hh 18
Deming ○ USA 65 Cj 29
Demini ∼ BR 112 Ec 45
Demini ∼ BR 120 Ec 46
Demirci ○ TR 195 Hg 26
Dem'jánka ∼ RUS 204 Sc 7
Demjansk ○ RUS 171 Hj 17
Demmin ○ D 170 Gn 19
Demnate ○ MA 293 Gc 30
Democracia ○ BR 120 Ed 48
Democratic Republic of the Congo ◻ RDC 333 Hd 47
De Moines ○ USA 65 Ck 27
Demonia ○ GR 194 Hd 27
Demopolis ○ USA 86 Dd 29
Demotte ○ USA 71 De 25
Demta ○ RI 286 Mg 47
Denakil ⌒ ER 313 Hn 38
Denakil Depression ⌒ ETH 313 Hn 39
Denakil Desert ⌒ ETH 313 Hn 39
Denali National Park & Reserve ♀ USA 46 Ba 13
Denan ○ ETH 328 Hp 42
Denbeigh Downs ○ AUS 374 Mg 57
Denbigh ○ CDN 60 Dk 23
Den Chai ○ THA 254 La 36
Dendang ○ RI 278 Ld 47
Dendāra ○ RIM 305 Gc 37
Déndoudi ○ SN 304 Fp 38
Deneba ○ ETH 325 Hm 41
Deng Deng ○ CAM 321 Gn 43
Denge ○ WAN 320 Gj 39
Dengfeng ○ VRC 243 Lg 28
Dengguen ○ VRC 255 Lc 31
Dengi ○ WAN 320 Gl 41
Děngqên ○ VRC 242 Km 30
Denguiro ○ RCA 321 Hd 43
Dengzhou ○ VRC 243 Lg 29
Denham ○ AUS 368 Lg 58
Denham Island ⛬ AUS 365 Mf 54
Denham Range ⛰ AUS 375 Mk 57
Denham Sound ∼ AUS 368 Lg 58
Denham Springs ○ USA 86 Dc 30
Den Helder ○ NL 163 Gh 19
Denia ○ E 184 Gg 26
Denial Bay ∼ AUS 369 Mc 62
Deniliquin ○ AUS 379 Mj 63
Denio Junction ○ USA 64 Cc 25
Denise ⛬ SY 329 Jf 47
Denison ○ USA 70 Cp 29
Deniz ○ TR 195 Hg 27
Denkanikota ○ IND 238 Kc 39
Denman ○ AUS 379 Mm 62
Denmark ◻ DK 170 Gk 18
Denmark ○ AUS 368 Lj 63
Denmark Strait ∼ DK 18 Hb 3
Denmark Strait ≈ 43 La 5
Denmark Strait ∼ IS 158 Fl 12
Denpasar ○ RI 279 Lh 50
Dension ○ USA 70 Da 25
Denton ○ USA 70 Cp 29
Denton ○ USA 74 Dk 26
D'Entrecasteaux ♀ AUS 368 Lh 63
Denu ○ GH 317 Gg 42
Denver ○ USA 65 Ck 26
Denver City ○ USA 65 Cl 29
Deodápolis ○ BR 140 Eg 57
Deogarh ○ IND 235 Kg 35
Deogarh Peak △ IND 234 Kf 34
Deoghar ○ IND 235 Kh 33
Deolāli ○ IND 238 Ka 36
Deoli ○ IND 234 Kd 35
Deolia ○ IND 234 Kb 33
Deo Ông Cô △ VN 263 Le 40
Deori ○ IND 234 Ke 35
Deo Tu Na △ K 263 Ld 39
Déou ○ BF 305 Gf 38
Depālpur ○ IND 234 Kb 34
De Panne ○ B 163 Gh 20
Depapre ○ RI 286 Mg 47
Dépression du Mourdi ⌒ TCH 309 Hc 36
de Puracé ♀ CO 106 Dk 44
Deputatskij ○ RUS 205 Xb 5
Dêqên ○ VRC 231 Kj 30
Deqing ○ VRC 255 Lf 34
De Queen ○ USA 70 Da 29
Dera ○ ETH 325 Hm 41
Dera ∼ SP 325 Hn 45
Dera Bugti ○ PK 227 Jn 31
Dera Ghāzi Khān ○ PK 227 Jp 30
Dera Ismāīl Khān ○ PK 227 Jp 30
Dera Murād Jamali ○ PK 227 Jm 31
Dera Nanak ○ IND 230 Kb 30
Dera Nawāb Sahib ○ PK 227 Jp 31
Derāwar Fort ○ PK 227 Jp 31
Derbent ○ RUS 202 Jc 24
Derbissaka ○ RCA 324 He 43
Derby ○ GB 163 Gf 19
Derby ○ ZA 349 Hf 58
Derby ○ AUS 361 Lm 54
Derby ○ AUS 378 Mk 66
Derdepoort ○ ZA 349 Hf 58
Déréssa ○ TCH 321 Hc 39
Derewo ∼ RI 286 Me 47
Dergačy ○ UA 175 Hk 20
Dergačy ○ RUS 181 Jc 20
De Ridder ○ USA 86 Db 30
Derkūl ∼ KZ 181 Jd 20
Derm ○ NAM 348 Hb 57
Dermott ○ USA 86 Dc 29
Dernia ○ RDC 333 Hb 44
Deror ○ ETH 328 Ja 41
Derramadero ○ C 100 Dj 35
Derre ○ MOC 344 Hl 54
Derri ○ SP 328 Jb 43
Derrry ○ USA 65 Cj 29
Derry ○ USA 60 Dn 24
Derry Downs ○ AUS 374 Md 57
Derudeb ○ SUD 313 Hl 37
De Rust ○ ZA 358 Hd 62
Derventa ○ BIH 174 Ha 23
Derveze ○ TM 222 Jh 25
Derwent ○ CDN 51 Cg 19
Derwent ○ AUS 361 Mc 57
Derwent ∼ AUS 378 Mk 67
Deržavinsk ○ KZ 155 Sb 8
Deržavnyj zapovednik ♀ UA 175 Hg 23
Des ○ PNG 286 Mg 50
Desaguadero ∼ BOL 129 Ea 54
Desaguadero ∼ RA 137 Ea 62
Desagües de los Colorados Salina ∼ RA 137 Ea 60
Des Allemands ○ USA 86 Dc 31
de Santa Marta ♀ CO 107 Dm 40
Des Arc ○ USA 70 Dc 28
Des Arc ○ USA 71 Dc 27
Desbarats ○ CDN 57 Dg 22
Deschutes ∼ USA 50 Cb 23
Desē ○ ETH 313 Hm 40
Deseado ∼ RA 152 Dp 69
Deseado ∼ RA 152 Ea 69
Desecho ○ YV 107 Ea 44
Desert ♀ IND 227 Jp 32
Desert Center ○ USA 64 Ce 29
Desert Hot Springs ○ USA 64 Cd 29
Desert Peak △ USA 64 Cf 25
Desideño Tello ○ RA 137 Ea 61
Desierto de Altar ⌒ MEX 64 Ce 29
Desierto de Mayran ⌒ MEX 81 Cl 33
Desierto de Sechura ⌒ PE 116 Dh 48
Desierto de Vizcaíno ⌒ MEX 75 Cf 32
Desmaraisville ○ CDN 60 Dk 21
De Smet ○ USA 56 Cp 23
Des Moines ○ USA 70 Db 25
Des Moines ∼ USA 70 Db 25
Desna ∼ UA 171 Hj 19
Desnătui ∼ RO 194 Hd 23
Desolation Canyon ⌒ USA 65 Cg 26
Desolation Point ⌓ RP 267 Ln 40
De Soto ○ USA 56 Dc 24
De Soto ○ USA 71 Dc 26
Despatch ○ ZA 358 He 62
Despeñaderos ○ RA 137 Eb 61
Des Plains ○ USA 71 De 24
Despotovac ○ SCG 174 Hc 23
Dessau ○ D 174 Gm 20
Dest. S.Simão ○ BR 129 Ed 53
D'Estrees Bay ∼ AUS 378 Me 63
Desventurados Islands ⛬ RCH 15 Eb 12
Dete ○ ZW 341 Hf 55
Detkovo ○ RUS 171 Hg 16
Detmold ○ D 174 Gl 20
De Tour Village ○ USA 57 Df 22
Detpa ○ AUS 378 Mg 64
Detroit ○ USA 70 Da 29
Detroit ○ USA 71 Df 24
Détroit de Jacques-Cartier ≈ CDN 43 Hc 8
Détroit de Jaques-Cartier ∼ CDN 61 Ec 21
Détroit de Selwyn ∼ VU 386 Nf 54
Détroit d' Honguedo ∼ CDN 61 Eb 21
Detroit Lakes ○ USA 56 Da 22
Dettifoss ★ IS 158 Fm 13
Det Udom ○ THA 263 Lc 38
Detuo ○ VRC 254 Lb 31
Detva ○ SK 174 Hb 21
Deua ♀ AUS 379 Ml 63
Deutschheim S.H.S. ★ USA 70 Dc 26
Deva ○ RO 194 Hd 23
Devadurg ○ IND 238 Kc 37
Devakottai ○ IND 239 Kd 41
Devanhalli ○ IND 238 Kc 39
Devaprayāg ○ IND 230 Kd 30
Devar Hipparg ○ IND 238 Kc 37
Devarshola ○ IND 239 Kc 40
Deveci Dağı △ TR 195 Hk 25
Develi ○ TR 195 Hk 26
Deveril ○ AUS 375 Ml 57
Devgaon ○ IND 234 Kb 36
Devgarh ○ IND 227 Ka 33
Devica ∼ RUS 181 Hn 20
Devils Hole National Monument ★ USA 64 Cd 27
Devils Lake ○ USA 56 Cn 21
Devils Lake Sioux Ind. Res. ••• USA 56 Cn 22
Devil's Point ○ BS 87 Dl 33
Devils Postpile National Monument ★ USA 64 Cc 27
Devils River ∼ USA 81 Cm 31
Devils Tower Natl. Monument ★ USA 51 Ck 23
Devin ○ BG 194 He 25
Devine ○ USA 81 Cn 31
Devipattinam ○ IND 239 Kd 41
Devli ○ IND 234 Kb 33
Devon ○ CDN 50 Ce 19
Devon ⌒ GB 163 Gd 20
Devon ○ ZA 349 Hg 59
Devon Island ⛬ CDN 43 Ga 3
Devonport ○ AUS 378 Mk 66
Devonshire ○ AUS 375 Mj 57
Devrek ○ TR 195 Hh 25
Devure ∼ ZW 341 Hh 55
Dewās ○ IND 234 Kc 34
Dewelē ○ ETH 328 Hp 40
Dewetsdorp ○ ZA 349 Hf 60
Dewey ○ USA 104 Eb 36
Dewey Lake ∼ USA 71 Dg 27
De Witt ○ USA 70 Dc 28
De Witt ○ USA 71 Dc 25
Dexing ○ VRC 258 Lj 31
Dexter ○ USA 70 Cp 27
Dexter ○ USA 71 Dd 27
Dexterville ○ USA 56 Dc 23
Deyang ○ VRC 242 Lc 30
Deyhūk ○ IR 222 Jg 29
Deyyer ○ IR 215 Jd 32
Dez ∼ IR 215 Jc 30
Dezfūl ○ IR 209 Jc 29
Dežgān ○ IR 226 Jf 32
Dezhou ○ VRC 246 Lj 27
Dhaka ▣ BD 235 Kk 34
Dhakia ○ IND 234 Ke 31
Dhalkewar ○ NEP 235 Kh 32
Dham-al-Khayl ○ MA 292 Fp 33
Dhamsala ○ IND 230 Kc 29
Dhamtari ○ IND 234 Ke 35
Dhanāna ○ IND 227 Jp 32
Dhanasar ○ PK 227 Jn 30
Dhanaura ○ IND 234 Kc 31
Dhanbād ○ IND 235 Kh 34
Dhandelhura ○ NEP 234 Ke 31
Dhandhuka ○ IND 227 Ka 34
Dhangarhi ○ NEP 234 Ke 31
Dhankuta ○ NEP 235 Kh 32
Dhanpuri ○ IND 234 Ke 34
Dhanushkodi ○ IND 239 Kd 41
Dhār ○ IND 234 Kb 34
Dharampur ○ IND 238 Ka 35
Dharan Bazar ○ NEP 235 Kh 32
Dharangaon ○ IND 234 Kb 35
Dhārapuram ○ IND 239 Kc 40
Dhāri ○ IND 227 Jp 35
Dharmapuri ○ IND 238 Kc 39
Dharmastala ○ IND 238 Kb 39
Dharmavaram ○ IND 238 Kc 38
Dharmjaygarh ○ IND 234 Kf 34
Dharni ○ IND 234 Kc 35
Dharug ♀ AUS 379 Mm 62
Dharwad ○ IND 238 Kb 38
Dhaulagiri Himal ⛰ NEP 235 Kf 31
Dhauliganga ∼ IND 230 Kd 30
Dhaulpur ○ IND 234 Kc 32
Dhaya ○ DZ 293 Gf 28
Dhebar Lake ∼ IND 234 Kb 33
Dhenkānāl ○ IND 235 Kg 35
Dhërmi ○ AL 194 Hb 25
Dhiinsoor ○ SP 329 Hp 44
Dhofar (Zufār) ⌒ OM 219 Je 36
Dhone ○ IND 238 Kc 38
Dhooble ○ SP 325 Hn 45
Dhorāji ○ IND 227 Jp 35
Dhorpatan ○ NEP 234 Kf 31
Dhrāngadhra ○ IND 227 Jp 34
Dhuburi ○ IND 235 Kj 33
Dhule ○ IND 234 Kb 35
Dhulian ○ IND 235 Kh 33
Dhunche ○ NEP 235 Kg 31
Dhurbo ○ SP 328 Jd 40
Dhuudo ○ SP 328 Jd 41
Dhuusa Mareeb ○ SP 328 Jb 43
Diaba ○ RMM 305 Gd 37
Diabiga ○ BF 317 Gg 40
Diablo Range ⛰ USA 64 Cb 27
Diabo ○ BF 317 Gf 40
Diabugu ○ WAG 316 Fn 39
Diaca ○ MOC 344 Hm 51
Diadema ○ BR 141 El 57
Diadioumbéra ○ RMM 304 Ga 38
Diafarabé ○ RMM 305 Gd 38
Diagbe ○ RDC 324 Hf 43
Diailasasgou ○ RMM 317 Ge 39
Diaka ∼ RMM 305 Gd 38
Diakon ○ RMM 304 Ga 38
Dialafara ○ RMM 316 Ga 39
Dialakoto ○ SN 316 Fp 39
Dialloubé ○ RMM 305 Gd 38
Diamante ○ RA 137 Dp 63
Diamante ∼ RA 137 Ea 63
Diamante ○ RA 137 Ed 62
Diamantina ○ BR 141 En 55
Diamantina ∼ AUS 374 Mg 57
Diamantina Lakes ○ AUS 374 Mg 57
Diamantino ○ BR 132 Ef 53
Diamantino ○ BR 133 Eh 54
Diamantino ∼ BR 133 Eh 54
Diamarakro ○ CI 317 Ge 42
Diambala ○ RCB 332 Gn 48
Diamond Harbour ○ IND 235 Kj 34
Diamond Jennes Peninsula ⛬ CDN 47 Ca 9
Diamond Peak △ USA 50 Ca 24
Diamonds ○ USA 50 Cc 24
Diamou ○ RMM 304 Ga 38
Diampangila ○ RDC 333 Hd 47
Diana ○ SN 316 Fp 39
Dianbai ○ VRC 255 Lf 35
Dian Chi ∼ VRC 254 Lb 33
Diandioume ○ RMM 304 Gb 38
Dianfa ○ CI 305 Gc 41
Diangouté Kamara ○ RMM 304 Gb 38
Dianké-Makam ○ SN 316 Fp 39
Dianópolis ○ BR 133 El 51
Dianra ○ CI 305 Gc 41
Diapaga ○ BF 317 Gg 39
Diaramana ○ RMM 317 Gd 39
Dias ○ MOC 344 Hk 52
Dias Point ⌓ NAM 348 Gp 59
Dīat at Tulūl ⌒ SYR 208 Hl 29
Diavlos Zakinthou ∼ GR 194 Hc 27
Diawala ○ CI 317 Gd 40
Dibā ○ UAE 226 Jg 33
Dibage ○ IRQ 209 Hp 28
Ḍibān ○ JOR 214 Hk 30
Dibaya ○ RDC 333 Hd 49
Dibaya-Lubwe ○ RDC 333 Hb 48
Dibella ○ RN 309 Gn 37
Dibeng ○ ZA 349 Hd 59
Dibete ○ RB 349 Hf 57
Dī Bīn ○ YE 218 Ja 38
Dibini ○ IND 235 Kf 32
Dibiri Island ⛬ PNG 286 Mh 50
Dibis ○ ET 301 Hg 34
Diboli ○ RMM 304 Fp 38
Diboll ○ USA 81 Da 30
Dibrugarh ○ IND 254 Km 32
Dibs ○ SUD 312 He 39
Dickens ○ USA 70 Cm 29
Dickinson ○ USA 51 Cl 22
Dickson ○ RUS 22 Pa 2
Dickson ○ USA 71 De 27
Dickson ○ RUS 204 Tb 4
Dickson land ⛬ N 158 Gp 6
Dickson Mounds ★ USA 71 Dd 25
Dicle Nehri ∼ TR 195 Hn 26
Dida Galgalu Desert ⌒ EAK 325 Hl 44
Didako ○ CI 317 Gd 43
Didēsa Wenz ∼ ETH 325 Hk 41
Didiévi ○ CI 317 Gd 42
Didig Sala ○ ETH 313 Hn 39
Didimótiho ○ GR 194 Hf 25
Didir ○ BF 317 Ge 39
Didjéni ○ RMM 316 Gb 39
Didsbury ○ CDN 50 Ce 20
Dīdwāna ○ IND 234 Kb 32
Didy ○ RM 345 Jc 55
Die ○ F 185 Gj 23
Die Bos ○ ZA 348 Hb 61
Diébougou ○ BF 317 Ge 40
Diê Châu ○ VN 255 Lc 36
Diécké ○ RG 316 Gb 42
Diego de Almagro ○ RCH 136 Dp 59
Diego de Alvar ○ RA 137 Ec 63
Diego Garcia ⛬ UK 31 Nb 10
Diego Lamas ○ ROU 146 Ef 61
Diéma ○ RMM 304 Gb 38
Diemals ○ AUS 368 Lk 60
Diemansputs ○ ZA 348 Hc 60
Diem Tiêu ○ VN 263 Le 39
Điên Biên ○ VN 255 Lb 35
Dienga ○ G 332 Gn 46
Diên Phu'ó'c ○ VN 263 Le 39
Diepholz ○ D 170 Gl 19
Dieppe ○ CDN 61 Eb 22
Dieppe ○ F 163 Gg 21
Dierks ○ USA 70 Da 28
Die Venster △ ZA 358 Hb 62
Dif ○ EAK 325 Hn 45
Diffa ○ RN 320 Gn 39
Difounda ○ G 332 Gm 47
Difuma ○ RDC 333 He 47
Dīg ○ IND 234 Kc 32
Digalu ○ ETH 325 Hm 43
Digba ○ RDC 324 He 43
Digboi ○ IND 254 Km 32
Digby ○ CDN 61 Ea 23
Digha ∼ IRQ 215 Jb 30
Dighton ○ USA 70 Cm 26
Digion ○ F 163 Gh 22
Diğla ∼ IRQ 209 Jb 29
Diglūr ○ IND 238 Kc 36
Digne-l.-B. ○ F 185 Gk 23
Digor ○ TR 202 Hp 25
Digos ○ RP 275 Ln 42
Digras ○ IND 234 Kc 35
Digri ○ PK 227 Jn 33
Digua ○ RCH 137 Dn 64
Diguillin ∼ RCH 137 Dn 64
Digul ∼ RI 286 Mf 49
Digul ∼ RI 286 Mg 48
Digul ∼ RI 286 Mg 49
Digya National Park ♀ GH 317 Gf 42
Dihang or Siang ∼ IND 254 Km 31
Dijon ○ F 163 Gj 22
Dijon ∼ RG 316 Gb 41
Dik ○ TCH 321 Ha 41
Dikanäs ○ S 158 Gp 13
Dikhil ○ DJI 328 Hp 40
Dikili ○ TR 195 Hf 26
Dikirnis ○ ET 301 Hh 30
Dikodougou ○ CI 317 Gd 41
Dikti Oros △ GR 194 He 28
Dikulwe ∼ RDC 341 Hf 51
Dikwa ○ WAN 321 Gn 39
Dila ○ ETH 325 Hm 42
Dilezi Geçidi △ TR 209 Ja 27
Dili ▣ TP 282 Ln 50
Dili ○ RMM 304 Gc 38
Dili ○ RDC 324 Hf 44
Dilia ○ USA 65 Ck 28
Dilia ∼ RN 309 Gn 38
Diliján ○ ARM 202 Ja 25
Dilikot ○ NEP 234 Ke 31
Di Linh ○ VN 263 Ld 40
Diližanskij zapov. ★ ARM 202 Ja 25
Dilj ⛰ HR 174 Ha 23
Dilj △ HR 174 Ha 23
Dilke ○ CDN 51 Ck 20
Dilley ○ USA 81 Cn 31
Dilling ○ SUD 312 Hg 39
Dillingham ○ USA 10 Ab 4
Dillingham ○ USA 46 Al 15
Dillon ○ USA 51 Cf 23
Dillon ○ USA 74 Dj 28
Dilo Djidji ∼ G 332 Gn 46
Dilolo ○ RDC 341 Hd 51
Dilos ★ GR 194 He 27
Dima ○ ETH 313 Hm 40
Dimako ○ CAM 321 Gn 43
Dimāpur ○ IND 254 Kl 33
Dimbaza ○ ZA 358 Hf 62
Dimbelenge ○ RDC 333 Hd 48
Dimbokro ○ CI 317 Gd 42
Dimboola ○ AUS 378 Mh 64
Dimbulah ○ AUS 365 Mj 54
Dimitrievka ○ RUS 181 Hn 19
Dimitrovgrad ○ RUS 181 Jc 18
Dimitrovgrad ○ SCG 194 Hd 24
Dimitrovgrad ○ BG 194 He 24
Dimlang △ WAN 320 Gm 41
Dimlik ∼ TCH 321 Ha 41
Dimmitt ○ USA 65 Cl 28
Dimona ○ IL 214 Hk 30
Dimora ○ AUS 374 Mh 56
Dimovo ○ BG 194 Hd 24
Dimpam ○ CAM 321 Gn 44
Dina ○ PK 230 Ka 29
Dinagat ○ RP 267 Ln 41
Dinagat Island ⛬ RP 267 Ln 40
Dinagat Sound ∼ RP 267 Ln 40
Dinajpur ○ BD 235 Kj 33
Dinalongan ○ RP 267 Ll 37
Dinan ○ F 163 Ge 21
Dinangourou ○ RMM 305 Ge 38
Dinant ○ B 163 Gj 20
Dinapigui ○ RP 267 Lm 37
Dinar ○ TR 195 Hh 27
Dinard ○ F 163 Ge 21
Dinaric Alps ⛰ BIH 174 Ha 23
Dīnchīya Shef ∼ ETH 325 Hl 42
Dindar ♀ SUD 313 Hk 39
Dinde ○ ANG 340 Gn 53
Dinder ∼ SUD 313 Hj 39
Dinder Wenz ∼ ETH 313 Hk 40
Dindi ○ ZW 344 Hj 54
Dindigul ○ IND 239 Kd 40
Dindima ○ WAN 320 Gm 40
Dindiza ○ MOC 352 Hj 57
Dindori ○ IND 234 Ke 34
Dinga ○ PK 230 Ka 29
Dinga ○ RDC 332 Ha 48
Dingalan Bay ∼ RP 267 Ll 38
Ding'an ○ VRC 255 Lc 33
Dingbian ○ VRC 243 Ld 27
Dinge ○ ANG 332 Gn 48
Dingle ○ IRL 163 Ga 19
Dingle Bay ∼ IRL 163 Ga 20
Dingnan ○ VRC 258 Lh 33
Dingo ○ AUS 375 Ml 57
Dingtao ○ VRC 243 Lh 28
Dinguiraye ○ RG 316 Ga 40
Dingwall ○ CDN 61 Ed 22
Dingwall ○ GB 162 Gd 17
Dingxi ○ VRC 242 Lc 28
Dingxiang ○ VRC 243 Lg 26
Dingxiao ○ VRC 255 Lc 33
Dingyuan ○ VRC 246 Lj 29
Dingzhou ○ VRC 243 Lh 26
Dingzi Gang ∼ VRC 246 Ll 27
Dingzikou ○ VRC 231 Kl 26
Dinhata ○ IND 235 Kj 32
Đinh Lập ○ VN 255 Ld 35
Dinira ♀ YV 107 Dn 41
Dinokwe ○ RB 349 Hf 57
Dinorwic ○ CDN 56 Db 21
Dinosaur ○ USA 65 Ch 25
Dinosaur National Monument ♀ USA 65 Ch 25
Dinosaur Provincial Park ♀ CDN 51 Cg 20
Dinsho ○ ETH 325 Hm 42
Dinsmore ○ CDN 51 Cj 20
Dintiteladas ○ RI 278 Lc 48
Dinuba ○ USA 64 Cc 27
Dioila ○ RMM 305 Gc 39
Diomandou ○ RG 316 Gb 41
Diongoï ○ RMM 304 Gb 38
Dionisio ○ BR 141 En 55
Dionósio Cerqueira ○ BR 140 Eh 59
Diorama ○ BR 133 Ej 54
Dioro ○ RMM 317 Gd 39
Dios Irmãos ○ BR 133 Ek 53
Dioulatié-Dougou ○ CI 305 Gc 41
Diouloulou ○ SN 316 Fm 39
Dioumara ○ RMM 304 Gb 38
Dioundiou ○ RN 320 Gh 39
Dioura ○ RMM 305 Gc 38
Diourbel ○ SN 304 Fm 38
Dīpālpur ○ PK 230 Ka 30
Diphu ○ IND 254 Kl 33
Diplo ○ PK 227 Jn 33
Dipolog ○ RP 267 Lm 41
Diporaz D. △ TR 195 Hh 27
Dī Qār ⊙ IRQ 215 Jb 30
Diqdāqa ○ UAE 226 Jf 33
Dir ○ PK 223 Jp 28
Dirangzong ○ IND 235 Kl 32
Dir Di ○ SUD 324 Hg 42
Dirē ○ RMM 305 Ge 37
Dirē Dawa ○ ETH 325 Hn 41
Dirgila ○ RDC 324 He 44
Diriamba ○ NIC 96 De 40
Dirico ○ ANG 340 Hc 54
Dirk Hartog Island ⛬ AUS 368 Lg 58
Dirkou ○ RN 309 Gn 36
Dirrah ○ SUD 312 Hf 39
Dirranbandi ○ AUS 375 Ml 60
Dirty Devil River ∼ USA 65 Cg 26
Disa ○ IND 227 Ka 33
Dis Al ○ NAM 348 Hb 56
Discovery Bay ∼ AUS 378 Mg 65
Disko ⛬ DK 43 Jb 5
Disko Bugt ∼ DK 7 Ga 3
Disko Bugt ≈ DK 43 Jb 5
Dismal Swamp ∼ USA 74 Dk 27
Dišnā ○ ET 301 Hj 32
Disney ○ AUS 375 Mk 56
Disneyland ★ USA 64 Cd 29
Disteghil Sar △ PK 230 Kb 27
Disūq ○ ET 301 Hh 30
Ditang ○ VRC 255 Le 31
Ditin ○ RG 316 Fp 40
Dittmer ○ USA 71 Dc 26
Diu ○ IND 227 Jp 35
Diunoe ○ RUS 202 Hp 23
Dīvāndarre ○ IR 209 Jb 28
Divénié ○ RCB 332 Gm 47
Divide ○ USA 51 Cf 23
Divilican ○ RP 267 Lm 37
Divilvican Bay ∼ RP 267 Lm 37
Divinhe ○ MOC 352 Hk 56
Divinópolis ○ BR 141 Em 56
Divisa ○ PA 97 Dh 41
Divisaderos ○ MEX 80 Ch 31
Divisópolis ○ BR 125 Ep 53
Divo ○ CI 317 Gd 43
Divriği ○ TR 195 Hl 26
Divuma ○ RDC 341 Hd 51
Divundu ○ NAM 340 Hc 55
Dixcove ○ GH 317 Ge 43
Dixon ○ USA 56 Cn 24
Dixon ○ USA 70 Db 26
Dixon ○ USA 71 Dd 25
Dixon Entrance ∼ CDN 6 Ca 4
Dixon Entrance ♆ CDN 42 Da 8
Diyadin ○ TR 202 Hp 26
Diyālā ⊙ IRQ 209 Ja 29
Diyarbakir ○ TR 202 Hn 27
Dizangué ○ CAM 320 Gl 44
Dize ○ IR 209 Ja 27
Dj. Ben Amar ○ DZ 293 Gg 28
Dja ∼ CAM 321 Gn 44
Djado ○ RN 308 Gn 35
Djado Plateau ⛰ RN 297 Gn 35
Djalasiga ○ RDC 324 Hh 44
Djale ∼ RDC 333 Hd 47
Djaluwon Creek ∼ AUS 361 Lp 56
Djamàa ○ DZ 296 Gk 29
Djamandjary ○ RM 345 Jb 52
Djamba ○ RDC 341 Hd 50
Djambala ○ RCB 332 Gp 47
Djanet ○ DZ 296 Gl 29
Djarua ∼ RI 283 Mc 47
Djatkovo ○ RUS 171 Hk 19
Djebel Adrar Soula △ DZ 296 Gk 33
Djebel Aïssa △ DZ 293 Gf 29
Djebel Amour ⛰ DZ 293 Gg 29
Djebel Antar △ DZ 293 Gf 29
Djebel Atafaitafa △ DZ 296 Gk 33
Djebel Babor △ DZ 296 Gj 27
Djebel Ben Tadjine ⛰ DZ 293 Gd 31
Djebel Bou Kahil ⛰ DZ 296 Gh 28
Djebel Fernane △ DZ 296 Gj 28
Djebel Goûfi △ DZ 296 Gk 27
Djebel in Azzene ⛰ DZ 293 Gg 32
Djebel Ksel △ DZ 293 Gg 29
Djebel Ounane △ DZ 296 Gk 33
Djebel Oust △ MA 293 Gf 29
Djebel Serkout △ DZ 308 Gk 34
Djebel Settaf △ DZ 296 Gh 32
Djebel Tebaga ⛰ TN 296 Gl 29
Djebel Telerhteba △ DZ 308 Gk 33
Djebel Tenouchfi △ DZ 293 Gf 28
Djebel Timétrine ⛰ RMM 305 Gf 36
Djebel Touaris △ DZ 293 Ge 31
Djebel Toucha △ DZ 293 Gf 30
Djébok ○ RMM 305 Gg 37
Djebono △ GH 317 Gg 41
Djébrène ○ TCH 321 Hb 40
Djédaa ○ TCH 321 Hb 39
Djéma ○ RCA 324 He 42
Djemila ○ DZ 296 Gj 27
Djeniene Bou Rzeg ○ DZ 293 Gf 29
Djenné ○ RMM 317 Gd 39
Djerba ○ TN 297 Gm 29
Djérem ∼ CAM 321 Gn 42
Djerem ∼ CAM 321 Gn 43
Djermaya ○ TCH 321 Gp 39
Djérnber ○ TCH 321 Ha 40
Djibasso ○ BF 317 Gd 39
Djibo ○ BF 305 Gf 38
Djiborosso ○ CI 305 Gc 41
Djibouti ◻ DJI 313 Hp 40
Djibouti ▣ DJI 328 Hp 40
Djidja ○ DY 317 Gg 42
Djidji ∼ G 332 Gn 46
Djigoué ○ BF 317 Ge 41
Djigouéra ○ BF 317 Gd 40
Djiguéni ○ RIM 304 Gb 38
Djilbe ○ CAM 321 Gp 40
Djiroutou ○ CI 305 Gc 43
Djohong ○ CAM 321 Gp 42
Djoku-Punda ○ RDC 333 Hc 48
Djoli ○ TCH 321 Hb 41
Djolu ○ RDC 333 Hd 45
Djombo ○ RDC 333 Hc 45
Djonâba ○ RIM 304 Fp 37
Djorf Torba ○ DZ 293 Ge 30
Djoua ∼ G 332 Gn 45
Djoubissi ○ RCA 321 Hc 42
Djoué ∼ RCB 332 Gp 47
Djougou ○ DY 317 Gg 41
Djoum ○ CAM 321 Gn 44
Djoumboli ○ CAM 320 Gn 42
Djouna ○ TCH 321 Hc 40
Djugu ○ RDC 324 Hh 45
Djúpivogur ○ IS 158 Fn 13
D'kar ○ RB 349 Hc 56
Dla ∼ RMM 316 Gb 39
Dmitrievka ○ KZ 154 Sb 8
Dmitriev-Lgovskij ○ RUS 171 Hk 19
Dmitrov ○ RUS 171 Hl 17
Dnepr ∼ RUS 171 Hj 18
Dnieper ∼ BY 171 Hh 19
Dnieper ∼ UA 175 Hk 21
Dnieper Upland ⛰ UA 175 Hg 21
Dniester ∼ MD 175 Hg 22
Dnipro-Dzerżyns'k ○ UA 175 Hk 21
Dniprodzerżynske vodoschovijšče ∼ UA 175 Hk 21
Dnipropetrvs'k ○ UA 175 Hk 21
Dniprovs'kyj lyman ∼ UA 175 Hh 22
Dnister ∼ UA 175 He 21
Dnistrovs'kyj lyman ∼ UA 175 Hh 22
Dno ○ RUS 171 Hh 17
Doa ○ MOC 344 Hk 54
Doaktown ○ CDN 61 Ea 22
Doany ○ RM 345 Jc 53
Doba ○ VRC 231 Kj 30
Doba ○ TCH 321 Ha 41
Dobbspet ○ IND 238 Kc 39
Dobbyn ○ AUS 365 Mf 55
Dobe ○ RB 340 Hc 55
Dobele ○ LV 171 Hd 17
Doberai Peninsula ⛬ RI 283 Mc 46
Dobhi ○ IND 235 Kg 33
Dobiegniew ○ PL 170 Gp 19
Dobie River ∼ CDN 56 Dc 20
Dobinga ○ CAM 321 Gn 41
Dobō ○ RI 283 Md 48
Doboj ○ BIH 174 Hb 23
Dobre Miasto ○ PL 170 Hc 18
Dobrič ○ BG 195 Hf 24
Dobrinka ○ RUS 181 Hm 19
Dobrjanka ○ RUS 154 Rc 7
Dobron' ○ UA 174 Hd 21
Dobroteşti ○ RO 175 He 23
Dobrush ○ BY 171 Hh 19
Doc Can Island ⛬ RP 275 Lk 43
Doce ∼ BR 133 Ej 55
Doce ∼ BR 141 En 56

414 Delano - Doce

Doce ∼ BR 141 Ep 55
Docker Creek Kultukatjara ○ AUS 369 Ma 58
Doctor Arroyo ○ MEX 92 Cm 34
Doctor Gonzáles ○ MEX 81 Cn 33
Doctor Mora ○ MEX 92 Cm 35
Doda ○ RI 282 Ll 46
Doda ○ EAT 337 Hm 48
Dodaga ○ RI 275 Ma 45
Dod Ballapur ○ IND 238 Kc 39
Dodecanese ◬ GR 194 Hf 27
Dodge ○ USA 50 Cc 22
Dodge City ○ USA 70 Cm 27
Dodji ○ SN 304 Fn 38
Dodola ○ ETH 325 Hm 42
Dodoma ▣ EAT 337 Hk 49
Dodori ∼ EAK 337 Hn 46
Dodowa ○ GH 317 Gf 43
Dodsen ○ USA 51 Ch 21
Dodson ○ USA 51 Ch 21
Doembang Nangbuat ○ THA 262 Kp 38
Dofa ○ RI 282 Ln 46
Dōğā'ī ○ IR 222 Jh 27
Dogai Coring ∼ VRC 231 Kj 28
Doğanşehir ○ TR 195 Hm 26
Doğansu ○ TR 202 Hp 26
Dogbo ○ CI 305 Gc 43
Dogbo-Tota ○ DY 317 Gg 42
Dog Creek ○ CDN 50 Ca 20
Dōgen Co ∼ VRC 231 Kk 30
Dog Island ◬ USA 86 Df 31
Dog Lake ∼ CDN 56 Cn 20
Dog Lake ∼ CDN 57 Dd 21
Dogō ◬ J 251 Mc 27
Dogo ○ RMM 305 Gc 40
Dogoba ○ SUD 324 Hh 42
Dō Gonbadān ○ IR 215 Jd 30
Dogondoutchi ○ RN 308 Gj 39
Dogoumbo ○ TCH 321 Ha 40
Dōgo-yama △ J 251 Mc 28
Doğubayazıt ○ TR 202 Ja 26
Doğu Karadeniz Dağları ⛰ TR 195 Hm 25
Doğu Menteşe △ TR 195 Hg 27
Dogwood ∼ AUS 375 Ml 59
Doha ▣ Q 215 Jd 33
Doi △ THA 254 Kp 36
Doi Inthanon ♀ THA 254 Kn 36
Doi Inthanon △ THA 254 Kp 36
Dois ○ BR 140 Eh 58
Dois Corregos ○ BR 141 Ek 57
Dois Irmãos do Tocantins ○ BR 121 Ek 50
Dois Riachos ∼ BR 124 Fb 50
Doi Suthep Poi ♀ THA 254 Kp 36
Doka ○ RI 283 Md 49
Doka ○ SUD 313 Hk 39
Dokdo Takeshima ◬ ROK 247 Mb 27
Dokis Indian Reservation ••• CDN 60 Dj 22
Doko ○ RG 316 Gb 40
Doko ○ WAN 320 Gl 39
Dokučaevs'k ○ UA 181 Hl 22
Dokui ○ BF 317 Gd 39
Dolak ◬ RI 286 Mf 49
Doland ○ USA 56 Cn 23
Dolavon ○ RA 147 Eb 67
Dolbeau ○ CDN 60 Dm 21
Dolbel ○ RN 305 Gg 38
Doleib Hill ○ SUD 324 Hh 41
Dolgellau ○ GB 163 Gd 19
Dolia ○ IND 227 Jp 34
Dolinsk ○ RUS 250 Mh 22
Dolit ○ RI 283 Lp 46
Dolleman Island ◬ 38 Fb 16
Dolmen ★ ROK 247 Lp 28
Dolný Kubín ○ SK 174 Hb 21
Dolo ○ RI 279 Lk 46
Dolokmerawan ○ RI 270 Kp 44
Dolok Pinapan △ RI 270 Kp 44
Doloksanggul ○ RI 270 Kp 44
Dolomites ⛰ I 174 Gm 22
Dolores ○ USA 65 Ch 27
Dolores ○ GCA 93 Dd 37
Dolores ○ CO 106 Dl 44
Dolores ○ YV 107 Dp 41
Dolores ○ ROU 146 Ee 62
Dolores ○ RA 146 Ef 64
Dolores ∼ RP 267 Ln 40
Dolores Hidalgo ○ MEX 92 Cm 35
Dolores River ∼ USA 65 Ch 26
Dolphin and Union Strait ∼ CDN 6 Da 3
Dolphin and Union Strait ≈ CDN 47 Cc 11
Dolphin Island ◬ USA 86 Dd 30
Dol Tachi △ THA 262 Kp 37
Đô Lu'o'ng ○ VN 255 Lc 36
Dolyna ○ UA 175 Hd 21
Dolyns'ka ○ UA 175 Hj 21
Dolzanskaja ○ RUS 181 Hl 22
Dolzanskaja ○ UA 181 Hl 22
Doma ○ ZW 341 Hh 54
Dom Aquino ○ BR 132 Eg 53
Domar ○ VRC 230 Ke 29
Domasse ○ MOC 352 Hj 57
Domažlice ○ CZ 174 Gn 21
Dombaj ○ RUS 202 Hn 24
Dombås ○ N 158 Gl 14
Dombe ○ MOC 344 Hj 55
Dombe Grande ○ ANG 340 Gn 52
Dombóvár ○ H 174 Ha 22
Dom Cavati ○ BR 141 En 55
Dom Eliseu ○ BR 121 El 48
Domeyko ○ RCH 137 Dn 60
Domfront ○ F 163 Gf 21
Dominase ○ GH 317 Gf 42
Domingodé ○ CO 106 Dk 42
Domingos Mourão ○ BR 124 Ep 48
Dominica □ WD 104 Ed 38
Dominica ◬ WD 104 Ed 38
Dominical ○ CR 97 Df 41
Dominican Republic □ DOM 101 Dn 35
Dominica Passage ≈ 104 Ed 38
Domiongo ○ RDC 333 Hc 48
Domkirke ★ DK 170 Gm 18
Domkonda ○ IND 238 Kd 36
Domo ○ ETH 328 Jb 42
Domodedovo ○ RUS 171 Hl 18
Domodóssola ○ I 174 Gl 22
Domoni ○ COM 345 Ja 52
Dom Pedrito ○ BR 146 Eg 61
Dom Pedro ○ BR 121 Em 48
Dompem ○ GH 317 Ge 43
Dompu ○ RI 279 Lk 50
Dom Silvério ○ BR 141 En 56
Don ○ MEX 80 Ch 32
Don ∼ RUS 181 Hn 22
Donadeu ○ RA 136 Ec 59
Donald ○ AUS 378 Mh 64
Donaldsonville ○ USA 86 Dc 30
Donauwörth ○ D 174 Gm 21
Donaw ○ UZB 223 Jm 26
Don Benito ○ E 184 Gd 26
Doncaster ○ GB 163 Gf 19
Doncaster ○ AUS 374 Mh 56
Doncaster Indian Reserve ★ CDN 60 Dl 22
Dondaicha ○ IND 234 Kb 35
Dondo ○ RI 282 Ll 50
Dondo ○ RI 282 Lm 46
Dondo ○ RDC 321 Hc 43
Dondo ○ ANG 340 Gp 50
Dondo ○ MOC 344 Hk 55
Donec ∼ RUS 181 Hl 20
Doneck ○ RUS 181 Hm 21
Donegal ○ IRL 162 Gb 18
Donets ∼ UA 181 Hl 21
Donets'k ○ UA 181 Hl 22
Donets Ridge ⛰ UA 181 Hl 21
Dong ○ IND 254 Kn 31
Donga ○ WAN 320 Gm 42
Dong'an ○ VRC 255 Lf 32
Dongara ○ AUS 368 Lh 60
Dongargarh ○ IND 234 Ke 35
Dongchuan ○ VRC 255 Lb 32
Dongco ○ VRC 231 Kg 29
Dong Co ∼ VRC 231 Kg 29
Dong Đăng ○ VN 255 Ld 34
Dongeleksor ○ KZ 155 Sa 9
Dōngelek su k. ∼ KZ 181 Jd 21
Dongfang ○ VRC 255 Le 36
Dongfang ○ VRC 255 Lf 31
Dongfanghong ○ VRC 250 Mc 22
Donggala ○ RI 279 Lk 46
Donggi ○ RI 282 Lm 46
Donggi Cona ∼ VRC 242 Kp 28
Donggou ○ VRC 246 Lm 26
Dongguan ○ VRC 258 Lg 34
Đông Hà ○ VN 263 Ld 37
Donghai ○ VRC 246 Lk 28
Donghai Dao ◬ VRC 255 Lf 35
Dong Hoi ○ VN 263 Ld 37
Dong Hu'ng ○ VN 255 Ld 35
Dongkala ○ RI 282 Ll 48
Dongkeng ○ VRC 258 Lk 32
Dongking ○ VRC 255 Le 36
Dongkou ○ VRC 255 Lf 32
Donglan ○ VRC 255 Ld 33
Donglük ○ VRC 231 Kj 26
Dongmen ○ VRC 255 Ld 34
Dongming ○ VRC 243 Lh 28
Dongning ○ VRC 250 Mb 23
Dongo ○ RDC 333 Hb 44
Dongo ○ ANG 340 Gp 53
Dongola ○ SUD 312 Hh 36
Dongotona Mountains ⛰ SUD 325 Hj 43
Dongou ○ RCB 333 Ha 44
Dongpa ○ VRC 230 Ke 30
Dong Phaya Yen ⛰ THA 262 La 37
Đông Phú ○ VN 263 Ld 40
Dongqiao ○ VRC 231 Kk 30
Dongshan Wan ∼ VRC 258 Lj 34
Dongsha Qundao ◬ VRC 258 Lj 35
Dongsheng ○ VRC 243 Le 26
Dongtai ○ VRC 246 Ll 29
Dongtai Taijnat Hu ∼ VRC 231 Kl 27
Dongting Hu ∼ VRC 258 Lg 31
Dongue ○ ANG 340 Gp 53
Donguila ○ G 332 Gl 45
Dongwe ∼ Z 341 He 52
Dongxiang ○ VRC 258 Lj 31
Dongxing ○ VRC 255 Le 35
Dongxing ○ VRC 255 Le 36
Dongyang ○ VRC 259 Ll 31
Dongying ○ VRC 246 Lk 27
Dongzhai ○ VRC 243 Lg 26
Dongzhi ○ VRC 246 Lj 30
Doniphan ○ USA 71 Dc 27
Don Jiang ∼ VRC 258 Lh 34
Donji Vakuf ○ BIH 174 Ha 23
Donkar ○ BHT 235 Kk 32
Donkerpoort ○ ZA 349 He 61
Donko ○ WAN 320 Gj 40
Don Martin ○ MEX 81 Cm 32
Don Matías ○ CO 106 Dl 42
Dønna ◬ N 158 Gm 12
Donnacona ○ CDN 60 Dn 22
Donnegal Bay ∼ IRL 162 Gb 18
Donnelly ○ CDN 47 Cc 17
Donnybrook ○ ZA 349 Hg 60
Donnybrook ○ AUS 368 Lh 62
Dono Manga ○ TCH 321 Ha 41
Donostia-San Sebastian ○ E 184 Ge 24
Don Quê ○ VN 263 Ld 37
Donqula Dongola ○ SUD 312 Hh 36
Donskoj ○ RUS 181 Hm 19
Doolgunna ○ AUS 368 Lk 58
Doolow ○ ETH 328 Hp 43
Doomadgee ○ AUS 365 Mf 54
Doomadgee Aboriginal Reserve ••• AUS 365 Mf 54
Doongmabulla ○ AUS 375 Mk 57
Dooper ○ USA 70 Da 29
Door Peninsula ◬ USA 57 De 23
Dora ○ USA 65 Cl 29
Dorado ∼ RA 136 Ec 58
Doraga ○ RP 267 Lm 39
Dōrāhāk ○ IR 215 Jd 32
Dorah Pass ⛰ IND 223 Jp 27
Doralē ○ DJI 328 Hp 40
Doranala ○ IND 238 Kd 38
Dorchester ○ GB 163 Ge 20
Dordabis ○ NAM 348 Ha 57
Dordogne ∼ F 184 Gg 23
Dordrecht ○ NL 163 Gh 20
Dordrecht ○ ZA 349 Hf 61
Doreenville ○ NAM 348 Hb 57
Dores do Indaiá ○ BR 133 Em 55
Dorey ○ RMM 305 Gf 38
Dorgali ○ I 185 Gl 25
Dori ○ BF 305 Gf 38
Doring Bay ○ ZA 348 Ha 61
Doringrivier ∼ ZA 358 Hb 62
Dorisvale ○ AUS 364 Mb 53
Dormentes ○ BR 124 Ep 50
Dornoch ○ GB 162 Ge 17
Doro ○ RMM 305 Gf 37
Dorogobuž ○ RUS 171 Hj 18
Doroḥ ○ IR 222 Jj 29
Dorohoi ○ RO 175 Hf 21
Dorohovo ○ RUS 171 Hk 18
Dorolemo ○ RI 275 Ma 45
Döröö nuur ∼ MNG 204 Ua 9
Doropo ○ CI 317 Ge 41
Dorotea ○ S 158 Gp 13
Dorowa ○ ZW 341 Hh 55
Dorra ○ DJI 313 Hp 39
Dorrance ○ USA 70 Cn 26
Dorre Island ◬ AUS 368 Lg 58
Dorrigo ○ AUS 379 Mn 61
Dorrigo ♀ AUS 379 Mn 61
Dorsale Camerounaise ⛰ CAM 320 Gm 42
Dortmund ○ D 163 Gk 20
Dörtyol ○ TR 195 Hk 27
Dorūd ○ IR 209 Jc 29
Doruma ○ RDC 324 Hf 43
Dos Caminos ○ YV 112 Eb 41
Dos de Mayo ○ PE 116 Dl 49
Dos Hermanas ○ E 184 Gd 27
Dōšī ○ AFG 223 Jn 28
Dosi ○ RI 283 Md 48
Dos Lagunas ○ GCA 93 Dd 37
Dô So'n ○ VN 255 Ld 35
Dospat ○ BG 194 He 25
Dosso ○ RN 320 Gh 39
Dothan ○ USA 86 Df 30
Dot Lake ○ USA 46 Bc 13
Dotswood ○ AUS 365 Mk 55
Douai ○ F 163 Gh 20
Douako ○ RG 316 Ga 41
Douala ○ CAM 320 Gl 44
Doualayel ○ CAM 320 Gn 42
Douarnenez ○ F 163 Gd 21
Doubabougou ○ RMM 304 Gb 38
Double Island Point ⌓ AUS 375 Mn 58
Double Mountain △ AUS 375 Mm 57
Double Mountain Fork Brazos River ∼ USA 70 Cm 29
Doubodo ∼ BF 317 Gg 40
Doubs ∼ F 163 Gk 22
Doubtful Bay ∼ AUS 361 Ln 54
Doubtful Island Bay ∼ AUS 368 Lk 63
Doubtful Sound ∼ NZ 382 Nf 68
Doubtless Bay ∼ NZ 383 Nj 63
Doué ∼ SN 304 Fn 37
Douélé ○ CI 305 Gc 42
Douentza ○ RMM 305 Ge 38
Dougga ★ TN 296 Gl 27
Doughboy Bay ∼ NZ 382 Nf 69
Douglas ○ USA 51 Ck 24
Douglas ○ USA 80 Ch 30
Douglas ○ USA 86 Dg 30
Douglas ○ GB 147 Ee 71
Douglas ○ GB 162 Gd 18
Douglas ○ ZA 349 Hd 60
Douglas ○ AUS 364 Mb 52
Douglas ∼ AUS 375 Mj 58
Douglas Creek ∼ AUS 374 Me 60
Douglas Lake ∼ USA 71 Dg 28
Douglas Lake Indian Reservation ••• CDN 50 Cb 20
Douglas Pass ⛰ USA 65 Ch 26
Douglas Point ⌓ CDN 57 Dg 23
Douglas Range ⛰ 38 Fa 16
Douglass ○ USA 70 Cp 27
Dougmuge ○ VRC 255 Lb 34
Dougoulé ○ RN 308 Gm 38
Douhongpo △ VRC 255 Lc 33
Doulatābād ○ AFG 223 Jl 27
Doulatābād ○ IR 226 Jg 31
Doulat Yār ○ AFG 223 Jl 28
Doullens ○ F 163 Gh 20
Doumandzou ○ G 332 Gm 45
Doumba ○ RN 309 Gn 36
Doum Doum ○ TCH 321 Gp 39
Doumé ○ CAM 320 Gn 43
Doumé ○ CAM 321 Gn 43
Doumé ∼ CAM 321 Gp 43
Doumen ○ VRC 258 Lg 34
Douna ○ BF 305 Gf 38
Douna ○ BF 317 Gd 40
Douné ○ RG 316 Ga 40
Dounkassa ○ DY 320 Gh 40
Dounkou ○ BF 317 Ge 39
Douqing ○ VRC 255 Lc 32
Douradina ○ BR 140 Eg 57
Douradina ○ BR 140 Eh 57
Douradoquara ○ BR 133 El 55
Dourados ○ BR 140 Eg 57
Dourbali ○ TCH 321 Gp 40
Dourbeye ○ CAM 321 Gn 40
Dourdoura ○ TCH 321 Hc 40
Douro ○ RMM 305 Ge 38
Douro ∼ RMM 305 Ge 38
Douroum ○ CAM 321 Gn 40
Doussala ○ G 332 Gm 47
Doutoufouk ○ RN 308 Gl 39
Douz ○ TN 296 Gl 29
Dove ○ PNG 287 Ml 50
Dove Creek ○ USA 65 Ch 27
Dovedale ○ RB 349 Hf 57
Dover ○ USA 60 Dn 24
Dover ○ USA 71 De 27
Dover ○ USA 74 Dl 26
Dover ○ GB 163 Gg 20
Dover ○ AUS 378 Mk 67
Dover-Foxcroft ○ USA 60 Dp 23
Doverlândia ○ BR 133 Eh 54
Dovrefjell △ N 158 Gn 6
Dowa ○ MW 344 Hj 52
Dowagiac ○ USA 71 De 24
Dowerin ○ AUS 368 Lj 61
Downey ○ USA 51 Cf 24
Downieville ○ USA 64 Cb 26
Downs ○ USA 70 Cn 26
Dowsk ○ BY 171 Hh 19
Doyle ○ USA 64 Cb 25
Doylestown ○ USA 74 Dl 25
Doyleville ○ USA 65 Cj 26
Doze de Outubro ∼ BR 132 Ee 52
Dozgah ∼ IR 215 Je 31
Dozois ∼ CDN 60 Dk 22
Dr. Pedro P. Peña ○ PY 136 Ec 57
Dra Afratir ⏜ MA 292 Fp 33
Drabonso ○ GH 317 Gf 42
Dracena ○ BR 140 Ej 56
Dragalina ○ RO 175 Hf 23
Drăgăşani ○ RO 175 He 23
Draghoender ○ ZA 349 Hd 60
Draguignan ○ F 185 Gk 24
Drahichyn ○ BY 171 He 19
Drake ○ USA 56 Cm 22
Drakensberg ⛰ LS 349 Hg 61
Drakes Bay ∼ USA 64 Ca 27
Dráma ○ GR 194 He 25
Dramba ○ RDC 324 Hh 44
Drammen ○ N 170 Gl 16
Drangajökull ▲ IS 158 Fj 12
Drar Souttouf ⏜ MA 304 Fn 35
Drau ∼ A 174 Gp 22
Drava ∼ HR 174 Ha 22
Dravograd ○ SLO 174 Gp 22
Drayton ○ USA 56 Cp 21
Drayton Valley ○ CDN 50 Ce 19
Drean ○ DZ 296 Gk 27
Dreikikir ○ PNG 286 Mh 47
Dresden ○ D 174 Gn 20
Dreux ○ F 163 Gg 21
Drevsjø ○ N 158 Gm 15
Drezdenko ○ PL 170 Gp 19
Driggs ○ USA 51 Cg 24
Drimiopsis ○ NAM 348 Hb 57
Drina ∼ BIH 194 Hb 24
Drinkwater ○ CDN 51 Ck 20
Drjanovo ○ BG 194 He 24
Drobeta-Turnu ○ RO 194 Hd 23
Droërivier ○ ZA 358 Hd 62
Drogheda ○ IRL 163 Gc 19
Drohobych ○ UA 175 Hd 21
Droitwich ○ GB 163 Ge 19
Drôme ∼ F 185 Gj 23
Drome ○ PNG 286 Mg 47
Dronne ∼ F 184 Gg 23
Dronning Maud Fjelkjede ⏜ 38 Ca 18
Dronning Maud Land ⏜ 38 Ka 17
Drosh ○ PK 223 Jp 28
Drottningholm Birka ★ S 170 Ha 16
Drovers Cave ♀ AUS 368 Lh 61
Druja ○ LV 171 Hf 18
Drumduff ○ AUS 365 Mh 54
Drume ○ AL 194 Hb 24
Drumheller ○ CDN 51 Cf 20
Drummond ○ USA 51 Cf 22
Drummond ○ USA 56 Dc 22
Drummond ○ USA 57 Dg 22
Drummond Range ⛰ AUS 375 Mk 58
Drummondville ○ CDN 60 Dm 23
Druskininkai ○ LT 171 He 18
Družina ○ RUS 205 Xb 5
Družkivka ○ UA 181 Hl 21
Drvar ○ BIH 174 Ha 23
Dry ∼ AUS 364 Mc 54
Dry Bay ≈ USA 47 Bg 15
Dryberry Lake ∼ CDN 56 Db 21
Dryden ○ CDN 56 Db 21
Dryden ○ USA 81 Cl 30
Drygalski Island ◬ 38 Pb 16
Dry Hartsrivier ∼ ZA 349 He 59
Drysdale Island ◬ AUS 364 Md 51
Drysdale River ○ AUS 361 Lp 53
Drysdale River ∼ AUS 361 Lp 53
Drysdale River ♀ AUS 361 Lp 53
Dry Tortugas ◬ USA 86 Dg 33
Dschang ○ CAM 320 Gm 43
Dua ∼ RDC 321 Hc 44
Duale ∼ RDC 333 Hd 45
Dualla ○ CI 305 Gc 41
Du'an ○ VRC 255 Ld 34
Duangua ∼ MOC 341 Hh 53
Duansban ○ VRC 255 Lc 33
Duaringa ○ AUS 375 Ml 57
Dubā ○ KSA 214 Hk 32
Duba ○ WAN 320 Gj 41
Dubai ○ UAE 226 Jh 33
Dubăsan ○ MD 175 Hg 22
Dubawnt Lake ∼ CDN 6 Db 3
Dubawnt Lake ∼ CDN 42 Fa 6
Dubawnt River ∼ CDN 42 Fa 6
Dubbis ○ USA 51 Cf 23
Dubbo ○ AUS 379 Ml 62
Dubec ○ RUS 171 Hm 16
Dubeibat ○ SUD 312 Hg 39
Dubele ○ RDC 324 Hg 44
Dubie ○ RDC 336 Hg 50
Dublin ○ USA 71 Dg 29
Dublin Baile Atha Cliath ▣ IRL 163 Gc 19
Dubna ○ RUS 171 Hl 17
Dubno ○ UA 175 He 20
Dubo ○ ETH 325 Hl 42
Dubois ○ USA 51 Cf 23
Dubois ○ USA 51 Cj 24
Du Bois ○ USA 74 Dj 25
Dubovka ○ RUS 181 Ja 21
Dubreka ○ RG 316 Fp 41
Dubrovka ○ RUS 171 Hg 17
Dubrovnik ○ HR 194 Ha 24
Dubrovycja ○ UA 175 He 20
Dubulu ○ RDC 321 Hc 43
Dubuque ○ USA 56 Dc 24
Dubwe ○ LB 304 Gc 43
Duchess ○ AUS 374 Mf 56
Ducie ◬ UK 14 Cb 12
Duck ∼ USA 71 De 28
Duck Creek ∼ AUS 360 Lj 57
Duck Lake ○ CDN 51 Cj 19
Duck Mountain ⛰ CDN 56 Cm 20
Duck Valley Indian Reservation ••• USA 64 Cd 24
Duckwater ○ USA 64 Cd 26
Duc Lâp ○ VN 263 Ld 37
Duc Mŷo ○ VN 263 Le 39
Du'c Phô ○ VN 263 Le 38
Du'c Tho ○ VN 255 Lc 36
Duc' Trong ○ VN 263 Le 40
Duda ∼ CO 106 Dl 44
Dudduumo ○ SP 329 Hp 45
Dudhani ○ IND 238 Kc 37
Dūdhi ○ IND 234 Kf 33
Dudhwa National Park ♀ IND 234 Ke 31
Dudignac ○ RA 137 Ed 63
Dudinka ○ RUS 204 Tc 5
Dudley ○ GB 163 Ge 19
Dudorovskij ○ RUS 171 Hk 19
Dūdu ○ IND 234 Kb 32
Dudub ○ ETH 328 Jb 42
Dudypta ∼ RUS 204 Ua 4
Due ○ RDC 333 Hb 48
Duékoué ○ CI 305 Gc 42
Duere ∼ BR 133 Ek 51
Duero ∼ E 184 Ge 25
Duğaimīya ○ KSA 215 Jc 33
Dugbia ○ RDC 324 He 44
Dugdug ○ SUD 324 Hg 41
Dugi ◬ HR 174 Gp 23
Dū Gibla ○ YE 218 Hp 39
Dugum ○ ETH 313 Hm 39
Dugway ○ USA 64 Cf 25
Dugwaya ○ SUD 313 Hk 37
Duham ○ USA 74 Dj 28
Duhau ○ RA 137 Ec 64
Du He ∼ VRC 243 Lf 29
Duḥna ○ KSA 214 Hp 33
Duhovnickoe ○ RUS 181 Jc 19
Duhovščina ○ RUS 171 Hj 18
Duhubi ○ NEP 235 Kh 32
Duida-Marahuaca ♀ YV 112 Eb 44
Duineveld ○ NAM 348 Ha 57
Duisburg ○ D 163 Gk 20
Duitama ○ CO 107 Dm 43
Dujiangyan ○ VRC 242 Lb 30
Dukambiya ○ ER 313 Hl 38
Dūkān ○ IRQ 209 Ja 28
Dūkān Buhairat ∼ IRQ 209 Ja 27
Duke ○ USA 70 Cn 28
Duke of York Island ◬ PNG 287 Mn 48
Dūk Fadiat ○ SUD 324 Hh 42
Dūk Falwil ○ SUD 324 Hh 42
Dukhān ○ Q 215 Jd 33
Duki ○ RUS 205 Xa 8
Dukku ○ WAN 320 Gl 40
Dukku ○ WAN 320 Gm 40
Dukwe ○ RB 349 Hf 56
Dulaiḥān ○ KSA 214 Hn 32
Dulai' Rasīd ○ KSA 214 Hp 33
Dulan ○ VRC 242 Kp 27
Dulce ○ USA 65 Cj 27
Dulce ∼ RA 136 Eb 59
Dulce ∼ RA 136 Ec 60
Dulce ∼ RA 137 Ec 61
Dulce Nombre de Culmi ○ HN 97 Df 38
Dulgalah ∼ RUS 205 Wc 5
Dulhunty ∼ AUS 365 Mh 51
Dulhunty River ∼ AUS 365 Mh 51
Dulia ○ RDC 324 He 44
Dulia ○ RDC 324 Hg 45
Dulkaninna ○ AUS 374 Mf 60
Dullewāla ○ PK 227 Jp 30
Dulovo ○ BG 195 Hf 24
Dululu ○ AUS 375 Mm 57
Duluth ○ USA 56 Db 22
Dūmā ○ SYR 208 Hl 29
Duma ○ RDC 324 Hf 43
Duma ∼ RDC 324 Hf 43
Duma ∼ EAT 337 Hj 47
Dumai ○ RI 270 La 45
Dumalag ○ RP 267 Lm 40
Dumaran Island ◬ RP 267 Lk 40
Dumaresq ∼ AUS 375 Mm 60
Dumas ○ USA 70 Cm 28
Dumas ○ USA 86 Dc 29
Dūmat al-Ğandal ○ KSA 214 Hm 31
Dumba Cambango ○ ANG 340 Ha 51
Dumbéa ○ F 386 Nf 57
Dumbleyung ○ AUS 368 Lj 62
Dumbleyung Lake ∼ AUS 368 Lj 62
Dumbo ○ CAM 320 Gm 42
Dum Duma ○ IND 254 Km 32
Dumfries ○ GB 162 Ge 18
Dumka ○ IND 235 Kh 33
Dumoine ∼ CDN 60 Dk 22
Dumpu ○ PNG 287 Mj 48
Dumri ○ IND 235 Kg 34
Dun ∼ USA 74 Dj 27
Duna ∼ H 174 Hb 22
Duna ○ ANG 340 Hc 52
Dunaföldvár ○ H 174 Hb 22
Dunaj ∼ RO 175 Hg 23
Dunajivci ○ UA 175 Hf 21
Dunajska Streda ○ SK 174 Ha 22
Dunajskie plavni ♀ UA 175 Hg 23
Dunalley ○ AUS 378 Mk 67
Dunaújváros ○ H 174 Hb 22
Dunbar ○ GB 162 Ge 18
Dunbar ○ AUS 365 Mh 54
Dunbeath ○ GB 162 Ge 16
Duncan ○ CDN 50 Ca 21
Duncan ∼ CDN 50 Cd 20
Duncan ○ USA 65 Ch 29
Duncan ○ USA 70 Cp 28
Duncan Passage ∼ IND 262 Kl 40
Duncansby Head ⌓ GB 162 Ge 16
Duncan Town ○ BS 87 Dl 34
Duncanville ○ USA 70 Cp 29
Dunchurch ○ CDN 57 Dh 23
Dundaga ○ LV 170 Hd 17
Dundalk ○ USA 74 Dk 26
Dundalk ○ IRL 162 Gc 18
Dundas Uummannaq ○ DK 43 Hb 3
Dundas Peninsula ◬ CDN 42 Eb 4
Dundas Strait ∼ AUS 364 Mb 51
Dundee ○ USA 70 Cn 29
Dundee ○ GB 162 Ge 17
Dundee ○ ZA 352 Hh 60
Dundret △ S 159 Hc 12
Dune de Pilat ★ F 184 Gf 23
Dunedin ○ NZ 382 Nh 68
Dunedoo ○ AUS 379 Ml 61
Dunes de Dokhara ⏜ DZ 296 Gj 29
Dunfermline ○ GB 162 Ge 17
Dünga Būnga ○ PK 227 Ka 31
Dungannon ○ GB 162 Gc 18
Dūngarpur ○ IND 227 Ka 34
Dungarven ○ IRL 163 Gc 19
Dungas ○ RN 320 Gm 39
Dungkek ○ RI 279 Lg 49
Dungloe ○ IRL 162 Gb 18
Dungog ○ AUS 379 Mm 62
Dungu ○ RDC 324 Hg 44
Dungu ∼ RDC 324 Hg 44
Dungunāb ○ SUD 313 Hl 35
Dunham ∼ AUS 364 Ma 54
Dunham River ∼ AUS 361 Lp 54
Dunkeld ○ AUS 378 Mh 64
Dunken ○ USA 65 Ck 29
Dunkerque ○ F 163 Gg 20
Dunkirk ○ USA 60 Dj 24
Dunk Island ◬ AUS 365 Mk 54
Dunkwa ○ GH 317 Gf 43
Dunlap ○ USA 70 Da 25
Dunlap ○ USA 71 Df 28
Dunmarra ○ AUS 364 Mc 54
Dunmore ○ USA 74 Dl 25
Dunmore Town ○ BS 87 Dk 33
Dunnellon ○ USA 87 Dg 31
Dunning ○ USA 70 Cm 25
Dunnville ○ CDN 60 Dj 24
Dunolly ○ AUS 379 Mh 64
Dunqul ○ ET 301 Hh 34
Dunraven ○ USA 60 Dl 24
Dunrobin ○ AUS 375 Mk 57
Dunsborough ○ AUS 368 Lh 62
Dunseith ○ USA 56 Cm 21
Duntroon ○ NZ 382 Nh 68
Dunyāpur ○ PK 227 Jp 31
Du'o'ng Dông ○ VN 263 Lb 40
Duparquet ○ CDN 60 Dj 21
Du Plessis ○ NAM 348 Hb 56
Dupnica ○ BG 194 Hd 24
Dupree ○ USA 56 Cm 23
Dupuyer ○ USA 51 Cf 21
Duqm ○ OM 219 Jg 36
Duquette ○ USA 56 Db 22
Du Quoin ○ USA 71 Dd 26
Durack ∼ AUS 361 Lp 53
Durack Range ⛰ AUS 361 Lp 54
Dūrāğ ○ AFG 223 Jp 27
Durağan ○ TR 195 Hk 25
Duran ○ USA 65 Ck 28
Durán ○ EC 116 Dj 47
Durance ∼ F 185 Gk 23
Durand ○ USA 56 Dc 23
Durango ○ USA 65 Cj 27
Durango ○ MEX 80 Ck 33
Durango ○ HN 96 Df 38
Durango ○ E 184 Ge 24
Durant ○ USA 70 Cp 29
Durant ○ USA 86 Dd 29
Durazno ○ ROU 146 Ef 62
Durban ○ ZA 352 Hh 60
Durbanville ○ ZA 358 Hb 62
Durchesne ○ USA 65 Cg 25
Durchesne River ∼ USA 65 Cg 25
Durdur ∼ SP 328 Hp 40
Dureji ○ PK 227 Jm 33
Düren ○ D 163 Gk 20
Durg ○ IND 234 Ke 35
Durgapūr ○ IND 235 Kh 34
Durgarajupatnam ○ IND 238 Ke 38
Durham ○ CDN 57 Dh 23
Durham ○ USA 70 Cp 26
Durham ○ GB 162 Ge 18
Durham Downs ○ AUS 374 Mg 59
Duri ○ RI 270 La 45
Durkee ○ USA 50 Cd 23
Ḑurma ○ KSA 215 Jb 33
Durmitor ♀ BIH 194 Hb 24
Durmitor △ MON 194 Hb 24
Durness ○ GB 162 Gd 16
Duro △ ETH 325 Hl 43
Durong South ○ AUS 375 Mm 59
Durra ○ ETH 325 Hl 42
Durrandella ○ AUS 375 Mk 58
Durrës ○ AL 194 Hb 25
Dursunbay ○ TR 195 Hg 26
Duru ○ RDC 324 Hg 43
Duru ∼ RDC 324 Hg 44
Durubu ○ RDC 321 Hh 43
Durukhsi ○ SP 328 Ja 41
D'Urville Island ◬ NZ 383 Nk 66
Duryu San △ DVRK 247 Ma 25
Dūš ○ ET 301 Hh 33
Dū Šaiḥ ○ IRQ 209 Ja 29
Dušak ○ TM 222 Jj 27
Dusey River ∼ CDN 57 De 20
Dushan ○ VRC 255 Ld 33
Dushanbe ▣ TJ 223 Jn 26
Dushore ○ USA 74 Dk 25
Dushutou ○ VRC 246 Lk 28
Dusin ○ PNG 287 Mj 48
Dusky Sound ∼ NZ 382 Ne 68
Düsseldorf ○ D 163 Gk 20
Düstlik ○ UZB 223 Jm 25
Dūst Moḥammad Hān ○ IR 226 Jj 30
Dusun ○ MAL 124 Lk 43
Dusunmudo ○ RI 278 Lb 46
Dusunpasirmajang ○ RI 270 La 46
Dusuntuo ○ RI 270 La 47
Duta ○ Z 341 Hh 51
Dutch John ○ USA 65 Ch 25
Dutch Village ★ USA 57 De 24
Dutsan Wai ○ WAN 320 Gl 40
Dutse ○ WAN 320 Gl 40
Dutsin-Ma ○ WAN 320 Gk 39
Dutton ○ USA 51 Cf 22
Duvan ○ RUS 154 Rc 7
Duvefjorden ∼ N 158 Hd 5
Dūvertepe ○ TR 195 Hg 26
Duvno ○ BIH 194 Ha 24
Duwwa ○ OM 226 Jh 35
Duye ∼ RDC 324 Hg 45
Duyfken Point ⌓ AUS 365 Mg 52
Duyun ○ VRC 255 Ld 32
Düzce ○ TR 195 Hh 25
Dūzdūzān ○ IR 209 Jb 27
Düziçi ○ TR 195 Hl 27
Duziguo Gang △ VRC 255 Lb 31
Dvina Bay ∼ RUS 159 Hm 13
Dvor ○ HR 174 Ha 23
Dwangstan Shuiku ∼ VRC 255 Le 34
Dwarsberg ○ ZA 349 Hf 58
Dwellingup ○ AUS 368 Lj 62
Dwight ○ CDN 60 Dj 23
Dwight ○ USA 71 Dd 25
Dwokwa ○ GH 317 Gf 43
Dworshak Reservoir ∼ USA 50 Cd 22
Dwyka ∼ ZA 358 Hc 62
Dyaul Island ◬ PNG 287 Mm 47
Dyersburg ○ USA 71 Dd 27
Dyersville ○ USA 56 Dc 24
Dyika ○ ZW 341 Hh 55
Dyke Ackland Bay ∼ PNG 287 Ml 50
Dymer ○ UA 175 Hh 20
Dysart ○ AUS 375 Ml 57
Dytiki Elāda ⊙ GR 194 Hc 26
Dytikí Macedonia ⊙ GR 194 Hc 25
Džalilabad ○ AZ 202 Jc 26
Džambul ○ KZ 19 Na 5
Džanga ○ TM 222 Je 25
Džankoj ○ UA 181 Hk 23
Dzaoudzi ○ F 345 Ja 52
Džargalah ○ RUS 205 Wc 5
Džartyrabot ○ TJ 230 Ka 27
Džebel ○ TM 222 Je 26
Džejhun ○ TM 223 Jk 26
Džejnau ○ UZB 223 Jl 26
Dželandy ○ TJ 230 Ka 27
Dzeng ○ CAM 320 Gm 44
Džermuk ○ ARM 202 Ja 26
Dzeržinsk ○ RUS 154 Qc 7
Dzeržinsk ○ RUS 181 Hp 17
Dzhugdzhur, Khrebet ⛰ RUS 22 Rb 4

Doce - Dzhugdzhur, Khrebet 415

□Country ▣Capital city ⊙Administrative unit OPlace ♁Island ⛰Mountain range △Mountain ⌓Cape ≈Ocean, Sea ~Lake, River ▽Undersea topography ▲Glacier ♀National park •••Reservation ★Point of major interest ▭Landscape

Dzhugdzhur, Khrebet ⛰ RUS 205 Wc 7
Działdowo O PL 170 Hc 19
Dzibalchén O MEX 93 Dd 36
Dzilam de Bravo O MEX 93 Dd 35
Dzioua O DZ 296 Gj 29
Džirgatal' O TJ 223 Jp 26
Dzisna O BY 171 Hf 18
Dzitás O MEX 93 Dd 35
Dziuche O MEX 93 Dd 36
Dzjatlava O BY 171 He 19
Džubga O RUS 202 Hm 23
Džurak-Sal ~ RUS 181 Hp 22
Džuryn O UA 175 Hf 21
Džvari O GE 202 Hp 24
Dzyarzhynsk O BY 171 Hf 19

E

E. V. Spence Reservoir ~ USA 70 Cm 29
Eabament Lake ~ CDN 57 De 20
Eads O USA 65 Cl 26
Eagar O USA 65 Ch 28
Eagle O USA 46 Be 13
Eagle O USA 65 Cj 26
Eagle Bend O USA 56 Da 22
Eagle Butte O USA 56 Cm 23
Eagle Creek ~ CDN 51 Cj 20
Eagle Lake ~ CDN 56 Db 21
Eagle Lake ~ USA 64 Cb 25
Eagle Mountain △ USA 56 Dc 22
Eagle Nest O USA 65 Ck 27
Eagle Pass O USA 81 Cm 31
Eagle Passage ~ GB 147 Ee 72
Eagle Peak △ USA 80 Ck 30
Eagle Point O USA 50 Ca 24
Eagle Point ⌓ AUS 287 Ml 51
Eagle Point ⌓ PNG 287 Ml 51
Eagle River O USA 57 Dd 22
Ea H'leo O VN 263 Le 39
Eandja O RDC 333 Hc 46
Earaheedy O AUS 368 Ll 58
Ear Falls O CDN 56 Db 20
Earls Cove O CDN 50 Ca 21
Early O USA 70 Da 24
Earn ~ GB 162 Gd 17
Easley O USA 71 Dg 28
East Alligator ~ AUS 364 Mc 52
East Angus O CDN 60 Dn 23
East Aurora O USA 60 Dj 24
East Bluff ⌓ CDN 43 Hb 6
Eastbourne O GB 163 Gg 20
East Brady O USA 74 Dj 25
East Caicos ♁ GB 101 Dn 35
East Cape ⌓ USA 87 Dh 33
East Caroline Basin ▽ 27 Sa 9
East Cay ♁ PNG 287 Mj 50
East China Sea ≈ 259 Lm 31
Eastend O CDN 51 Ch 21
East End Point ⌓ BS 87 Dk 33
Easter Group ♁ AUS 368 Lg 60
Easter Island ♁ RCH 14 Db 12
Eastern Cordillera ⛰ CO 106 Dl 44
Eastern Cordillera ⛰ PE 116 Dk 48
Eastern Ghats ▭ IND 239 Kc 40
Eastern Group ♁ AUS 369 Ln 62
Eastern Sayan ⛰ RUS 22 Pb 4
Eastern Sayan ⛰ RUS 204 Ua 8
Easterville O CDN 56 Cn 19
East Falkland ♁ GB 147 Ee 71
East Fork ~ USA 46 Bc 11
East Fork Andreafsky ~ USA 46 Aj 13
East Fork Bruneau ~ USA 64 Ce 24
East Frisian Islands ♁ D 170 Gk 19
East Grand Forks O USA 56 Cp 22
Eastham O USA 74 Dp 25
East Haydon O AUS 365 Mg 55
East Holothuria Reef ♁ AUS 361 Lp 52
East Hyden Wheat Bin O AUS 368 Lk 62
East Islands ♁ PNG 287 Mm 47
East Korea Bay ~ DVRK 247 Lp 26
East Lansing O USA 57 Df 24
East Liverpool O USA 71 Dh 25
East London Buffalo City O ZA 358 Hf 62
Eastmain O CDN 7 Fa 4
Eastmain O CDN 57 Dj 19
Eastman O USA 71 Dg 29
East Mariana Basin ▽ 27 Sb 8
Eastmere O AUS 375 Mj 57
Eastnor O ZW 341 Hg 55
Easton O USA 74 Dk 26
Easton O USA 74 Dl 25
East Pacific Rise ▽ 14 Cb 15
East Point ⌓ CDN 57 Dh 20
East Point ⌓ CDN 61 Ed 22
East Point O USA 86 Df 29
Eastpoort O ZA 358 He 62
East Siberian Sea ≈ 205 Yb 3
East St. Louis O USA 71 Dc 26
East Timor □ TP 282 Lp 50
Ea Sup O VN 263 Ld 39
Eateringinn Creek ~ AUS 369 Mc 59
Eation O USA 71 Df 26
Eaton O USA 65 Ck 25
Eaton O USA 71 Df 26
Eaton O AUS 375 Ml 56
Eatonia O CDN 51 Ch 20
Eatonton O USA 71 Dg 29
Eau Claire O USA 56 Dc 23
Eau Claire ~ USA 57 Dd 23
Ebala O PNG 287 Mj 49
Eban O WAN 320 Gj 41
Ebangalakata O RDC 333 Hc 46
Ebano O MEX 92 Cn 34
Ebe ~ WAN 320 Gl 43
Ebejiyin O GQ 332 Gm 44
Ebelle O WAN 320 Gk 42
Ebeltoft O DK 170 Gm 17
Ebem O WAN 320 Gk 43
Ebenezer O CDN 51 Cl 20
Ebensburg O USA 74 Dj 25
Eberswalde O D 170 Gn 19
Ebetsu O J 250 Mg 24
Ebian O VRC 255 Lb 31
Ebinur Hu ~ VRC 204 Tb 9
Ebo O ANG 340 Gp 51
Ebola ~ RDC 321 Hc 44
Ebolowa O CAM 320 Gm 44
Eboman O G 332 Gm 44
Ebomicu O GQ 332 Gm 45
Ebon ♁ MH 27 Ta 9
Ebony O NAM 348 Gp 57
Eboso O G 332 Gm 44
Eboundja O CAM 320 Gl 44
Ebrāhīmābād O IR 226 Jg 31
Ebro O USA 86 Df 30
Ebro ~ E 184 Gf 25
Ecatepec O MEX 92 Cn 36
Ecatepec O MEX 93 Cp 37
Echaporã O BR 140 Ej 57
Echbara O TCH 321 Hc 39
Echigo-sammyaku ⛰ J 251 Mf 27
Echo O USA 65 Cg 25
Echuca O AUS 379 Mj 64
Écija O E 184 Gd 27
Ecijskij massiv △ RUS 205 Wb 5
Ecker ~ RA 152 Dn 69
Eckermann O USA 57 Df 22
Eclipse Island ♁ AUS 368 Lj 63
Eclipse Sound ≈ CDN 43 Gc 4
Ecoole O CDN 50 Bp 21
Ecoporanga O BR 125 Ep 55
Ecuador □ EC 116 Dj 46
Ecuc O GQ 332 Gl 45
Ed O ER 313 Hn 39
Edalābād O IND 234 Kc 35
Ed Damer O SUD 313 Hj 37
Ed Debba O SUD 312 Hh 36
Eddontenajon O CDN 47 Bl 17
Eddystone O CDN 56 Cn 20
Ede O WAN 320 Gj 42
Edéa O CAM 320 Gm 44
Edefors O S 159 Hc 12
Edéia O BR 133 Ek 54
Eden O USA 74 Dj 27
Eden O USA 81 Cn 30
Eden ~ GB 162 Ge 18
Eden O AUS 379 Ml 64
Edenburg O ZA 349 He 60
Edendale O ZA 349 Hg 60
Edendale O NZ 382 Ng 69
Edenderry O IRL 163 Gc 19
Edenhope O AUS 378 Mg 64
Edenton O USA 74 Dk 27
Edenville O ZA 349 Hf 59
Edenwold O CDN 51 Ck 20
Edessa O GR 194 Hd 25
Edgar Ranges ⛰ AUS 360 Lm 55
Edgartown O USA 74 Dn 25
Edgecumbo O NZ 383 Nl 64
Edgeley O USA 56 Cn 22
Edgell Island ♁ CDN 43 Hc 6
Edgemont O USA 51 Cl 24
Edgeøya ♁ N 19 La 3
Edgeøya ♁ N 158 Hc 7
Edgeøyjøkulen ~ N 158 Hd 7
Edgewood O USA 70 Cp 29
Ediliile O AUS 378 Md 63
Edina O USA 70 Db 25
Edina O LB 316 Ga 43
Edinboro O USA 74 Dj 25
Edinburgh O GB 162 Ge 18
Edineţ O MD 175 Hf 21
Edingburg O USA 81 Cn 32
Edingeni O MW 344 Hj 52
Edirne O TR 194 Hf 25
Edith Downs O AUS 374 Mh 56
Edith Falls O AUS 364 Mc 53
Edith-Ronne-Land ▭ 38 Fa 18
Edithvale O AUS 364 Mb 53
Edjeleh O DZ 296 Gl 32
Edmond O USA 70 Cm 26
Edmond O USA 70 Cp 28
Edmonds O USA 50 Ca 22
Edmont O USA 70 Cm 26
Edmonton O CDN 50 Ce 19
Edmundston O CDN 60 Dp 22
Edna O USA 81 Cp 31
Edolo O I 174 Gm 22
Edremit O TR 195 Hf 26
Edremit Kör ~ TR 195 Hf 26
Edson O CDN 50 Cd 19
Edum O GQ 332 Gm 45
Edward ~ AUS 379 Mh 63
Edward Island ♁ AUS 364 Md 53
Edward River O AUS 365 Mg 53
Edward River Kowanyama Aboriginal Reserve ••• AUS 365 Mg 53
Edwards Plateau ⛰ USA 81 Cm 30
Edward VII Peninsula ♁ 38 Bb 17
Edwin O CDN 56 Cn 21
Eek O USA 46 Aj 15
Eel ~ USA 71 Df 25
Eel River ~ USA 64 Bp 25
Eendekuil O ZA 358 Hb 62
Eesti □ EST 171 He 16
Efaté ♁ VU 386 Ng 54
Effie O USA 56 Db 22
Effigy Mounds Natl. Mon. ★ USA 56 Dc 24
Effingham O USA 71 Dd 26
Efon Alaye O WAN 320 Gj 42
Eforie Nord O RO 175 Hg 23
Efremov O RUS 181 Hl 19
Egadi Islands ♁ I 185 Gm 27
Egale Lake O USA 81 Cp 31
Egalite O CDN 60 Dk 23
Egayit O MYA 254 Km 36
Egbe O WAN 320 Gj 41
Egbunda O RDC 324 Hf 44
Eger O H 174 Hc 22
Egersund O N 170 Gk 16
Eggenfelden O D 174 Gn 21
Egg Lagoon O AUS 379 Mj 65
Eg gol ~ MNG 204 Uc 8
Egholo O SOL 290 Na 50
Egilsstaðir O IS 158 Fn 13
Égina O GR 194 Hd 27
Égina ♁ GR 194 Hd 27
Eginbah O AUS 360 Lk 56
Égio O GR 194 Hd 26
Eğirdir O TR 195 Hh 27
Eğirdir Gölü ~ TR 195 Hh 26
Egito O ANG 340 Gp 51
Egito Praia O ANG 340 Gn 51
Eglington Island ♁ CDN 42 Dc 3
Egmont ♀ NZ 383 Nj 65
Egmont Bay ~ CDN 61 Eb 22
Egor'evsk O RUS 171 Hm 18
Egorlyk ~ RUS 202 Hn 23
Egortyk ~ RUS 181 Hn 22
Egoumi O G 332 Gm 46
Egra O IND 235 Kh 35
Eğrigöz D. △ TR 195 Hg 26
Eguia O RP 267 Lk 38
Egvekinot O RUS 205 Zc 5
Egypt □ ET 300 Hf 32
Eha-Amufu O WAN 320 Gk 42
Ehegnadzor O ARM 202 Ja 26
Eh-Eh ~ RA 140 Ee 58
Eia Point ⌓ PNG 287 Mk 49
Eide O N 158 Gk 14
Eidsemub O NAM 348 Ha 58
Eidsvold O AUS 375 Mm 58
Eidsvoll O N 158 Gm 15
Eidukal ~ SUD 313 Hk 36
Eifel ⛰ D 163 Gk 20
Eiffel Flats O ZW 341 Hh 55
Eight Degree Channel ≈ 239 Ka 42
Eight Mile Bay ~ BS 87 Dk 32
Eights Coast ▭ 38 Ea 17
Eighty Mile Beach ▭ AUS 360 Ll 55
Eikefjord O N 158 Gj 15
Eilai O SUD 312 Hh 37
Eildon O AUS 379 Mj 64
Eilerts-de-Haan Mountains ⛰ SME 113 Ef 44
Eileson O USA 46 Bc 13
Einasleigh ~ AUS 365 Mh 54
Einasleigh O AUS 365 Mh 55
Eindayaza O MYA 262 Kn 38
Eindhoven O NL 163 Gj 20
Eindpaal O NAM 348 Hb 58
Ein Mansûr O SUD 312 Hf 38
Einme O MYA 262 Km 37
Eirunepé O BR 117 Dn 49
Eirup O NAM 348 Hb 58
Eiseb ~ NAM 348 Hb 56
Eisenach O D 174 Gm 20
Eisenerz O A 174 Gp 22
Eisenhüttenstadt O D 170 Gp 19
Eisenstadt O A 174 Ha 22
Eišiškės O LT 171 He 18
Eivānakī O IR 222 Je 28
Eivissa Ibiza O E 184 Gg 26
Eivissa Ibiza ♁ E 184 Gg 26
Eja ~ RUS 181 Hn 22
Ejea d. l. C. O E 184 Gf 24
Ejeda O RM 353 Ja 58
Ejido O YV 107 Dn 41
Ejin Horo Qi O VRC 243 Le 26
Ejisu O GH 317 Gf 42
Ej-Jemâa O MA 292 Gb 30
Ejmiatsin O ARM 202 Hp 25
Ejrin O WAN 320 Gh 42
Ejsk O RUS 181 Hm 22
Ejsk O UA 181 Hm 22
Ejule O WAN 320 Gk 42
Ejura O GH 317 Gf 42
Ejutla O MEX 92 Cp 37
Ekalaka O USA 51 Ck 23
Ekamour O RIM 304 Ga 37
Ekang O WAN 320 Gl 43
Ekangar Sarai O IND 235 Kg 33
Ekaterinovka O RUS 181 Ja 19
Ekenäs Tammisaari O FIN 171 Hd 16
Ekerem O TM 222 Je 27
Eket O WAN 320 Gk 43
Ekibastuz O KZ 22 Nb 4
Ekismane O RN 308 Gk 38
Eklingi O IND 227 Ka 33
Ekok O CAM 320 Gl 43
Ekoli O RDC 333 He 46
Ekombe O RDC 333 Hc 45
Ekonamou O RCB 332 Ha 45
Ekondo Titi O CAM 320 Gl 43
Ekouata O G 332 Gl 46
Eksjö O S 170 Gp 17
Eku O WAN 320 Gk 43
Ekuku O RDC 333 Hc 46
Ekukula O RDC 333 Hc 45
Ekuma ~ NAM 340 Gp 55
Ekumakoko O RDC 333 Hd 47
Ekwan Point ⌓ CDN 57 Dg 19
El'dikan O RUS 22 Rb 3
El Abiodh Sidi Cheikh O DZ 293 Gg 29
Ēl Ābrēd O ETH 328 Ja 43
Elabuga O RUS 181 Jd 18
El Adeb Larache O DZ 296 Gl 32
Ēl Āguer ▭ RIM 304 Ga 37
El-Aïoun O MA 293 Ge 28
El Alia O DZ 296 Gj 29
El Alto O PE 116 Dh 48
El Amparo de Apure O YV 107 Dn 42
Elan' O RUS 181 Hp 20
Eland's Bay O ZA 358 Ha 62
Elandsrivier ~ ZA 349 Hg 58
Elanga O RDC 333 Hb 46
Elangay O RN 308 Gh 38
El Angel O EC 116 Dk 45
Elan'-Kolenovskij O RUS 181 Hn 20
El Aouinet O DZ 296 Gk 28
El Aquilar O PY 136 Eb 57
El Arco O MEX 75 Cf 31
El Aricha O DZ 293 Gf 28
El Arish O AUS 365 Mk 54
El Arrouch O DZ 296 Gk 27
El Assaba ⛰ RIM 304 Fp 37
Elassóna O GR 194 Hc 26
El Astillero O E 184 Ge 24
Elat O IL 214 Hk 31
Élavagnon O RT 317 Gg 42
El Avila ♀ YV 107 Ea 40
Elâziğ O TR 195 Hm 26
El Bagre O CO 106 Dl 42
El Bajo O YV 112 Eb 41
El Banco O CO 106 Dm 41
El Barco de Ávila O E 184 Gd 25
El Barreal ~ MEX 80 Cj 30
El Barreal O RA 137 Ea 60
El Barril O MEX 75 Cf 31
El Barril O MEX 92 Cl 34
Elbasan O AL 194 Hc 25
El Baúl O YV 107 Dp 41
El Bayadh O DZ 293 Gg 29
Elbe O USA 50 Ca 22
Elbe ~ D 170 Gm 19
El Beid ~ WAN 321 Gp 39
El Ben O EAK 325 Hn 44
Elberton O USA 71 Dg 28
El Beru Hagai O SP 325 Hn 44
Elbeuf O F 163 Gg 21
El Beyyed O RIM 304 Ga 35
El Bioba O ETH 328 Hp 43
Elbistan O TR 195 Hl 26
Elblag O PL 170 Hb 18
El Blanquero O YV 112 Ec 41
El Bordj O DZ 293 Gg 28
El Bordo O CO 106 Dk 44
El-Borouj O MA 293 Gc 29
El Botalón O YV 107 Dn 40
Elbow O CDN 51 Cj 20
Elbow Lake O USA 56 Cp 23
El Bravo O RA 136 Ec 59
Elbrus O RUS 202 Hp 24
El Burgo de Osma O E 184 Ge 25
El Burro O YV 107 Ea 42
Elburz Mountains ⛰ IR 209 Jc 27
El Caburé O RA 136 Ec 58
El Caín O RA 147 Dp 66
El Cajon O USA 64 Cd 29
El Callao O YV 112 Ed 42
El Campín O CO 107 Dn 43
El Campo O USA 81 Cp 31
El Cantón O YV 107 Dn 42
El Carito O YV 112 Eb 41
El Carmen O GCA 93 Db 38
El Carmen O CO 106 Dj 44
El Carmen O EC 116 Dj 46
El Carmen O BOL 129 Ec 52
El Carmen O RA 136 Eb 58
El Caro O YV 112 Eb 41
El Carril O RA 136 Eb 58
El Carrizal O MEX 80 Cj 30
El Casabe O YV 112 Ec 42
El Casco O MEX 80 Ck 33
El Centro O USA 64 Ce 29
El Cerrito O CO 106 Dk 44
El Cerro O BOL 129 Ed 54
El Chacho O RA 137 Ea 61
El Chaparro O YV 112 Eb 41
El Charancho O RA 137 Eb 64
El Charco O RA 136 Eb 59
Elche d.l.S. O E 184 Ge 26
El Chinero O MEX 75 Ce 30
Elcho Island ♁ AUS 364 Md 51
El Chorro O RA 137 Eb 60
Elchouka O RUS 181 Jd 19
El Cobre O RCH 136 Dn 58
El Cocuy ♀ CO 107 Dm 42
El Colorado O MEX 80 Ch 33
El Colorado O RA 136 Ec 59
El Copé O PA 97 Dh 41
El Corazón Pelileo O EC 116 Dj 46
El Coyote O MEX 75 Cf 32
El Coyte O RCH 152 Dn 68
El Crispín O RA 137 Ec 61
El Cristo O YV 112 Ec 42
El Cruce O GCA 93 Dd 37
El Cruce O PE 116 Dj 49
El Crucero O MEX 75 Ce 31
El Cuy O RA 147 Dp 65
El Cuyo O MEX 93 De 35
Elcy O RUS 171 Hj 17
Elda O E 184 Gf 26
Eldama Ravine O EAK 325 Hk 45
El Darien O CO 106 Dl 42
Elderslie O AUS 374 Mh 57
El Desemboque O MEX 75 Cf 30
El Difícil O CO 106 Dl 41
El Divisorio O RA 147 Ed 65
Eldjarnsstaðir O IS 158 Fl 13
El Djelfa O DZ 296 Gh 28
El Djouf ▭ RIM 304 Gb 36
Eldon O CDN 61 Ec 22
El Doncello O CO 106 Dl 45
Eldorado O USA 70 Cn 28
El Dorado O USA 70 Cp 27
El Dorado O USA 70 Db 29
Eldorado O USA 71 Dd 27
Eldorado O MEX 80 Cj 33
Eldorado O USA 81 Cm 30
El Doradó O YV 112 Ed 42
Eldorado O BR 140 Eg 57
Eldorado O RA 140 Eg 59
Eldorado O BR 141 Ek 58
Eldorado dos Carajás O BR 121 Ek 48
El Dorado Springs O USA 70 Da 27
Eldoret O EAK 325 Hk 45
El Dunuba O EAK 325 Hm 44
El'dzik O TM 223 Jk 26
Elec O RUS 181 Hm 19
Electric Mills O USA 86 Dd 29
Electric Peak △ USA 51 Cg 23
Elefe O WAN 320 Gk 43
Eleja O LV 171 Hd 17
Elektra O USA 70 Cn 29
Elektrėnai O LT 171 He 18
Eleku ~ RDC 333 Hb 46
El Empalme O EC 116 Dj 46
El Empalme ~ EC 116 Dj 46
El Emperado O YV 107 Dn 41
El Encanto O CO 116 Dm 46
El Engenio O PE 128 Dl 53
Elephanta Caves ★ IND 238 Ka 36
Elephant Butte Reservoir ~ USA 65 Cj 29
Elephantine Island ★ ET 301 Hj 33
Elephant Island ♁ 38 Ga 15
Elesbão Veloso O BR 124 En 49
El Escorial ★ E 184 Gd 25
Eleşkirt O TR 202 Hp 26
El Espino O BOL 129 Ec 55
El Estor O GCA 93 Dd 38
El Estrecho O CO 106 Dk 45
Elesvaram O IND 238 Kf 37
El Eucalipto O ROU 146 Ef 61
El Eulma O DZ 296 Gj 27
Eleuthera Island ♁ BS 87 Dk 33
El Fahs O TN 296 Gl 27
El Faouar O TN 296 Gj 29
El Farcya O MA 292 Ga 32
El Faro O MEX 64 Ce 29
El Fasher O SUD 312 He 39
El Fortín O RA 137 Ec 62
Elfrida O USA 80 Ch 30
Elfros O CDN 51 Cl 20
El Fud O ETH 328 Hp 42
El Fuerte O MEX 80 Ch 32
El Fuerte de Samaipata ★ BOL 129 Ec 55
El Gaa Taatzebar ▭ DZ 293 Gh 33
Elgal O EAK 325 Hm 45
El Gallâouîya O RIM 304 Ga 35
El Galpón O RA 136 Eb 58
El Gambole O SP 329 Ja 44
El Garrobo O NIC 96 Df 39
El Geneina O SUD 312 Hd 39
El Gezira ▭ SUD 313 Hj 38
El Gheddiya O RIM 304 Ga 37
El Giara O SP 337 Hn 46
Elgin O USA 50 Cd 23
Elgin O CDN 56 Cm 21
Elgin O USA 56 Cm 22
Elgin O USA 64 Ce 27
Elgin O USA 71 Dd 24
Elgin O USA 71 Df 27
Elgin O USA 81 Cp 30
Elgin O GB 162 Ge 17
El Gleïta O RMM 304 Ga 38
El Gof O ETH 325 Hm 44
El Golfete ~ GCA 93 Dd 38
El Golfo de Santa Clara O MEX 75 Ce 30
El Grullo O MEX 92 Ck 36
El Guácharo ♀ YV 112 Ec 40
El Guaje O MEX 81 Cl 31
El Guamache O YV 112 Ec 40
El Guapo O YV 112 Eb 40
El Guayabo O YV 107 Dm 41
El Guérara O DZ 293 Gf 31
El Guetar O TN 296 Gl 28
El Guettara O RMM 305 Ge 34
El-Hadeb O MA 293 Gc 30
El Hadjar O DZ 296 Gk 27
El Haggounia O MA 292 Fp 32
El Hajeb O MA 293 Gd 29
El-Hamel O DZ 296 Gh 28
El Hamma O TN 296 Gl 29
El Hammâmi ▭ RIM 304 Fp 34
El Haouaria O TN 297 Gm 27
El Haouita O DZ 296 Gh 29
El Hatillo O YV 112 Eb 40
El Higirio O RCH 137 Dn 60
El Homr O DZ 293 Gg 31
Elhovo O BG 194 Hf 24
El Huecu O RA 137 Dn 64
El Huejote O MEX 80 Cj 33
Elias Garcia O ANG 340 Hb 50
Elida O USA 65 Cl 29
Elīda'ar O ETH 313 Hn 39
El Ideal O MEX 93 De 35
El Idrissa O DZ 296 Gh 28
Elie O CDN 56 Cp 21
Eliki Gounda O RN 308 Gl 38
Elila O RDC 333 He 47
Elila ~ RDC 336 Hf 47
Elim O USA 46 Aj 13
Elim O ZA 358 Hb 63
Elim Indian Reservation ••• USA 46 Aj 13
Elingampangu O RDC 333 He 46
Elipa O RDC 333 He 46
Elisa O RA 137 Ed 61
Elisabeth Islands ♁ CDN 7 Ea 1
Eliseu Martins O BR 124 En 50
Elista O RUS 181 Ja 22
Eliye Springs O EAK 325 Hk 44
Elizabeth O USA 74 Dl 25
Elizabeth City O USA 74 Dk 27
Elizabeth Downs O AUS 364 Mb 52
Elizabethton O USA 71 Dg 27
Elizabethtown O USA 71 Df 27
Elizabethtown O USA 74 Dj 28
Elizondo O E 184 Gf 24
Elizovo O RUS 205 Yb 8
El-Jadida O MA 292 Gb 29
El Jaralito O MEX 81 Ck 32
El Jem O TN 297 Gm 28
El Jordán O CO 107 Dn 43
Elk ~ USA 71 Dh 26
Ełk O PL 170 Hd 19
El Kala O DZ 296 Gl 27
El Kantara O DZ 296 Gj 28
El-Katouat O MA 293 Gc 29
Elk City O USA 50 Ce 23
Elk City O USA 70 Cn 28
Elk Creek O USA 64 Ca 26
Elkedra O AUS 374 Md 56
El-Kef O TN 296 Gl 27
El-Kelaa-des-Srarhna O MA 293 Gc 29
Ēl Kerē O ETH 328 Hp 43
Elkford O CDN 50 Ce 21
El-Khaoula O MA 292 Ga 31
Elkhart O USA 70 Cm 27
Elkhart O USA 71 Df 25
Elkhart O USA 81 Da 30
El Khatt ▭ RIM 304 Ga 34
Elkhead Mountains ⛰ USA 65 Cj 25
El Khnâchîch ▭ RMM 305 Gd 35
Elkholm O USA 57 Dd 24
Elkhorn O CDN 56 Cm 21
Elkhorn ~ USA 56 Cn 24
Elkhorn River ~ USA 56 Cn 24
El Khroub O DZ 296 Gk 27
Elkin O USA 71 Dh 27
Elkins O USA 65 Ck 29
Elkins O USA 71 Dh 26
Elk Island ♀ CDN 51 Cf 19
Elk Island ♁ CDN 56 Cp 20
Elk Lake O CDN 57 Dh 22
Elk Mountains ⛰ USA 65 Cj 26
Elko O CDN 50 Ce 21
Elko O USA 64 Ce 25
Ēl K'oran O ETH 328 Ja 43
Elk Point O USA 56 Cp 24
Elk River O USA 50 Cd 22
Elk River O USA 56 Db 23
El-Ksar-el-Kbir O MA 293 Gc 28
El Kseur O DZ 296 Gj 27
El Ksiba O MA 293 Gd 29
El-Ksour O TN 296 Gl 28
Elkwater O CDN 51 Cg 21
Elléba Fonfou O RN 308 Gj 37
Ellef Ringnes Island ♁ CDN 42 Ec 3
Ēl Lēh O ETH 325 Hm 44
El Lein O EAK 337 Hn 46
Ellenbrae O AUS 361 Lp 53
Ellendale O USA 56 Cn 22
Ellensburg O USA 50 Cb 22
Ellesmere Island ♁ CDN 43 Gb 3
El Limón O MEX 92 Cn 34
Elliot O ZA 349 Hf 61
Elliot Heads O AUS 375 Mn 58
Elliot Lake O CDN 57 Dg 22
Elliot Price Conservation Park ♀ AUS 374 Me 60
Elliott O AUS 364 Mc 54
Elliott Key ♁ USA 87 Dh 33
Ellis O USA 50 Ce 23
Ellisras O ZA 349 Hf 57
Elliston O AUS 378 Md 62
Ellora O IND 234 Kb 35
Ellora Caves ★ IND 234 Kb 35
Ellsworth O USA 51 Cl 24
Ellsworth O USA 56 Db 23
Ellsworth O USA 60 Dp 23
Ellsworth O USA 70 Cn 26
Ellsworth Land ▭ 38 Eb 17
Ellsworth Mountains ⛰ 38 Eb 17
Elma O USA 50 Ca 22
El Maad O DZ 296 Gj 27
El Macao O DOM 101 Dp 36
Elma D. △ TR 195 Hj 26
Elmadağ O TR 195 Hj 25
El Mahbas O MA 292 Gb 32
El Maitén O RA 147 Dn 67
Elma Laboid O DZ 296 Gk 28
El Malah O DZ 293 Gf 28
Elmalı O TR 195 Hg 27
El Mallaile O ETH 328 Hp 43
El Mâmoûn O RMM 305 Gf 36
El Mannsour O DZ 293 Gf 32
El Manteco O YV 112 Ec 42
El Manzano O RCH 137 Dn 63
El Maria O PA 97 Dh 42
El Marsa O DZ 293 Gg 27
El Maya O DZ 296 Gh 29
Elm Creek O CDN 56 Cp 21
Elm Creek O USA 70 Cn 25
El Médano O MEX 80 Cg 33
El Medo O ETH 325 Hn 43
El Meghaier O DZ 296 Gj 29
El Mejo O YV 107 Ea 41
Elmeki O RN 308 Gk 37
El Membrillo O RCH 137 Dn 62
El Meniaa O DZ 296 Gh 30
El-Menzel O MA 293 Gd 29
El Mhaïjrât O RIM 304 Fm 36
El Miamo O YV 112 Ed 42
El Miguelito O MEX 81 Cp 33
El Milagro O MEX 81 Cl 31
El Milia O DZ 296 Gk 27
Elmina O GH 317 Gf 43
Elmira O USA 60 Dk 24
Elmo O USA 70 Cp 26
Elmore O AUS 379 Mj 64
El Moro N.M. ★ USA 65 Ch 28
El Morrión O MEX 80 Ck 31
El Mreïti O RIM 304 Gc 34
Elmshorn O D 170 Gl 19
Elm Springs O USA 51 Cl 23
Elmwood O USA 70 Cm 27
El Mzereb O RMM 293 Gc 33
El Nayar O MEX 92 Ck 34
El Negrito O HN 96 De 38
El Nido O RP 267 Lk 40
El Nihuil O RA 137 Dp 63
El'nja O RUS 171 Hj 18
Elnora O CDN 51 Cf 19
El Nula O YV 107 Dn 42
Eloaua Island ♁ PNG 287 Ml 46
El Obeid O SUD 312 Hg 39
Elogbatindi O CAM 320 Gm 44
El Ogla O DZ 296 Gk 29
El Ogla Gasses O DZ 296 Gk 28
Elogo O RCB 332 Gp 45
El Ojito O MEX 80 Cj 32
El Olvio O CO 107 Dn 44
Elongo O RDC 333 Hc 46
Elorza O YV 107 Dp 42
El Oso O YV 112 Eb 43
Elota O MEX 92 Cj 34
El Ouadey ~ TCH 321 Hb 39
El Ouatia O MA 292 Ga 31
El Oued O DZ 296 Gk 29
Eloy O USA 65 Cg 29
Eloy Alfaro O EC 116 Dh 46
El Palito O YV 107 Dp 40
El Palmar O YV 112 Ec 41
El Palmito O MEX 80 Ck 33
El Pao de la Fortuna O YV 112 Ec 42
El Paraíso O HN 96 De 39
El Paso O USA 71 Dd 25
El Paso O USA 80 Cj 30
El Peru O YV 112 Ed 42
Elphinstone O AUS 375 Ml 56
El Pilar O YV 112 Ec 40
El Piñal O CO 106 Dl 41
El Pingo O RA 146 Ee 61
Elpitiya O CL 239 Ke 42
El Pont de Suert O E 184 Gg 24
El Portal O USA 64 Cb 27
El Portezuelo O RA 136 Eb 60
El Porvenir O MEX 80 Cj 30
El Porvenir O PA 97 Dj 41
El Porvenir O YV 107 Dp 42
El Progreso O GCA 93 Dc 38
El Progreso O GCA 93 Dd 38
El Progreso O HN 96 De 38
El Puente O BOL 129 Ec 54
El Puente O BOL 136 Eb 56
El Puerto d. Sta. Maria O E 184 Gc 27
El-Qualidia O MA 292 Gb 29
El Questro O AUS 361 Lp 54
Elquí ~ RCH 137 Dn 61
El Rebalse O MEX 80 Ck 31
El Regalo O YV 107 Dp 41
El Remolino O MEX 81 Cm 31
El Reno O USA 70 Cn 28
El Retamo O RA 137 Eb 62
El Retiro O YV 107 Ea 41
El Reventon O MEX 92 Cm 34
El Reves O MEX 81 Cl 32
El Rey O RA 136 Eb 58
El Rosario O MEX 92 Ck 34
El Rosario O YV 112 Ec 41
Elrose O CDN 51 Ch 20
Elroy O USA 56 Dc 24
El Rucio O MEX 92 Cl 34
Elsa O USA 81 Cp 32
El Sahuaro O MEX 75 Cf 30
El Salado O RCH 136 Dn 59
El Sallado O RA 152 Dp 70
El Salto O MEX 92 Ck 34
El Salto O RCH 137 Dn 63
El Salvador O MEX 81 Cm 33
El Salvador □ ES 93 Dd 39
El Santo O C 100 Dj 34
El Sauce O NIC 96 De 39
El Sauz O MEX 80 Cj 31
El Sauzal O MEX 75 Cd 30
Elsberry O USA 71 Dc 26
El Seco O MEX 92 Cp 35
El Seibo O DOM 101 Dp 36
Elsen Nur ~ VRC 231 Kl 28
Elsey O AUS 364 Mc 53
Elsey ♀ AUS 364 Mc 53
Elsie Hills O AUS 375 Mk 58
El Silencio O YV 112 Ec 41
El Soberbio O BR 140 Eg 59
El Socorro O YV 112 Eb 41
El Sombrero O YV 107 Ea 41
El Sombrero O RA 152 Dp 68
El Sosnedao O RA 137 Dp 63
Elstow O CDN 51 Cj 20
El Sueco O MEX 80 Cj 31
El Tajin ★ MEX 81 Cp 34

416 Dzhugdzhur, Khrebet - El Tajin

El Tala ○ RA 136 Eb 59
El Tamá ♀ YV 107 Dm 42
El Tambo ○ CO 106 Dk 44
El Tarf ○ DZ 296 Gl 27
El Tecolote ○ MEX 81 Cm 33
El Tecuan ○ MEX 92 Ck 35
El Tecuan ○ MEX 92 Ck 36
El Tejar ○ RA 137 Ed 63
El Temasdal ○ MEX 81 Cn 33
El Testerazo ○ MEX 64 Cd 29
Eltham ○ NZ 383 Nk 65
EL Tichlilt ○ RIM 304 Fp 37
El Tigre ○ PA 97 Dh 42
El Tigre ○ CO 106 Dl 42
El Tigre ○ YV 112 Eb 41
El Tigrito ○ YV 112 Eb 41
El Tocuyo ○ YV 107 Dn 41
Èl'ton ○ RUS 181 Jb 21
El Tornito ○ BR 132 Ee 54
El Tortugo ○ MEX 80 Ch 33
El Trigo ○ RA 146 Ee 63
El Triunfo ○ EC 116 Dj 47
El Tuparro ♀ CO 107 Dp 43
El Turbio ○ RA 152 Dm 71
Elu ○ RI 283 Ma 50
Elubo ○ GH 317 Ge 43
Elūru ○ IND 238 Ke 37
El Valle ○ PA 97 Dh 41
El Valle ○ PE 116 Dk 49
El Vapor ○ MEX 93 Db 36
Elvas ○ P 184 Gc 26
El Vergel ○ MEX 80 Cj 32
Elverum ○ N 158 Gm 15
El Viejo ○ NIC 96 De 39
El Vigía ○ YV 107 Dn 41
Elvira ○ RA 146 Ee 63
Elvire ~ AUS 364 Ma 55
Elvita ~ CO 107 Dn 43
El Vivero ○ YV 107 Dp 42
El Volcán ○ RCH 137 Dn 62
El Wak ○ EAK 325 Hn 44
El Wálamo ○ MEX 92 Cj 34
El Warsesa ○ EAK 325 Hm 44
Elwood ○ USA 70 Cm 25
Elwood ○ USA 71 Df 25
Elx ○ E 184 Gf 26
Ely ○ USA 56 Dc 22
Ely ○ USA 64 Ce 26
Ely ○ GB 163 Gg 19
El Yagual ○ YV 107 Dp 42
Elyria ○ USA 71 Dg 25
El Zacate ○ MEX 81 Cl 31
El Zape ○ MEX 80 Cj 33
El Zulia ○ CO 107 Dm 42
El Zurdo ○ RA 152 Dn 71
Émaé ♁ VU 386 Ng 54
Emali ○ EAK 337 Hl 47
Emām Hasan ○ IR 215 Jc 31
Emām Tāqi ○ IR 222 Jh 27
Emån ~ S 170 Gp 17
Emananus Island ♁ PNG 287 Ml 46
Emao ♁ VU 386 Ng 54
Embalsa Cerrón Grande ~ ES 93 Dd 38
Embalse Amaluza ~ EC 116 Dj 47
Embalse Cabra Corral ~ RA 136 Eb 58
Embalse Casa de Piedra ~ RA 147 Ea 65
Embalse Cerros Colorados ~ RA 147 Dp 65
Embalse Cogotí ~ RCH 137 Dn 61
Embalse de Alárcon ~ E 184 Ge 26
Embalse de Al Atazar ~ E 184 Ge 25
Embalse de Alcántara ~ E 184 Gc 26
Embalse de Almendra ~ E 184 Gc 25
Embalse de Buendía ~ E 184 Ge 25
Embalse de El Grado ~ E 184 Gg 24
Embalse de Guri ~ YV 112 Ec 42
Embalse de la Serena ~ E 184 Gd 26
Embalse del Ebro ~ E 184 Gd 24
Embalse del Guárico ~ YV 107 Ea 41
Embalse del Nihuil ~ RA 137 Dp 63
Embalse del Río Tercero ~ RA 137 Eb 62
Embalse de Maquinenza ~ E 184 Gg 25
Embalse de Riaño ~ E 184 Gd 24
Embalse el Cadillal ~ RA 136 Eb 59
Embalse El Cajón ~ HN 96 De 38
Embalse Ezequiel Ramos Mexia ~ RA 147 Dp 65
Embalse Florentino Ameghino ~ RA 147 Ea 67
Embalse los Molinos ~ RA 137 Eb 61
Embalse Paso de las Piedras ~ RA 147 Ec 65
Embalse Playa de Piedra ~ YV 112 Eb 41
Embalse Poechos ~ PE 116 Dh 48
Embalse Rapel ~ RCH 137 Dn 63
Embalse Río Hondo ~ RA 136 Eb 59
Embalse Salto Grande ~ ROU 146 Ef 61
Embalse Yacyretá-Apipé ~ BR 140 Ef 59
Embarcación ○ PY 136 Eb 57
Embarcación ○ RA 136 Eb 57
Embarrass ~ USA 71 Dd 26
Embeipua ○ RI 282 Lm 48
Embetsu ○ J 250 Mg 23
Embi ○ KZ 155 Rc 9
Embi ~ KZ 155 Rc 9
Embilipitiya ○ CL 239 Ke 42
Embira ~ BR 117 Dn 49
Embira ~ BR 117 Dn 50
Embondo ○ RDC 333 Hb 45
Embu ○ EAK 337 Hl 46
Embundo ○ ANG 340 Ha 54
Emden ○ D 170 Gk 19
Emeck ○ RUS 159 Hn 14
Emeishan ○ VRC 255 Lb 31
Emerald ○ AUS 375 Ml 57
Emeriau Point ⌒ AUS 360 Lm 54
Emerson ○ CDN 56 Cp 21
Emet ○ TR 195 Hg 26
Emeti ○ PNG 286 Mh 49
Emi Fezzane ▲ RN 309 Gp 35
Emi Koussi ▲ TCH 309 Hb 36
Emiliano Zapato ○ MEX 93 Dc 37
Emília Romagna ⊙ I 185 Gl 23
Emi Lulu ▲ RN 308 Gm 34
Eminābād ○ IND 230 Kb 29
Emirau Island ♁ PNG 287 Mm 46
Emirdağ ○ TR 195 Hh 26
Emirgazi ○ TR 195 Hj 27
Emmaboda ○ S 170 Gp 17
Emmen ○ NL 170 Gk 19
Emmet ○ AUS 375 Mj 58
Emmetsburg ○ USA 56 Da 24
Emmiganuru ○ IND 238 Kc 38
Emo ○ CDN 56 Db 21
Emory ○ USA 70 Da 29
Emory Peak ▲ USA 81 Cl 31
Empalme ○ MEX 80 Cg 31
Empangeni ○ ZA 352 Hh 60
Empedrado ○ RCH 137 Dm 63
Emperor Range ⛰ PNG 290 Mp 48
Emperor Seamounts Ψ 23 Ta 4
Empire ○ USA 57 De 23
Empire ○ USA 65 Cj 26
Emplawas ○ RI 283 Ma 50
Emporia ○ USA 70 Cp 26
Emporia ○ USA 74 Dk 27
Emporium ○ USA 74 Dj 25
Empress Augusta Bay ≈ PNG 290 Mp 49
Empress Mine ○ ZW 341 Hg 55
Ems ~ D 170 Gk 19
Emsdale ○ CDN 60 Dj 23
Emu Park ○ AUS 375 Mm 57
Emva ○ RUS 154 Rb 6
Ena ○ J 251 Me 28
Enangiperi ○ EAK 337 Hk 46
Enarotali ○ RI 286 Me 47
Encarnación ○ PY 140 Ef 59
Encarnacion de Díaz ○ MEX 92 Cl 35
Encinal ○ USA 81 Cn 31
Encinitas ○ USA 64 Cd 29
Encino ○ USA 65 Ck 28
Encino ○ USA 81 Cn 32
Encón ○ RA 137 Ea 62
Encontrados ○ YV 107 Dm 41
Encounter Bay ≈ AUS 378 Mf 63
Encruzilhada ○ BR 125 Ep 53
Encruzilhada do Sul ○ BR 146 Eh 61
Enda ○ VRC 242 Kn 30
Endau ○ EAK 337 Hm 46
Ende ○ RI 282 Ll 50
Endeavor ○ CDN 51 Cl 19
Endeavour Strait ≈ AUS 365 Mh 51
Endebes ○ EAK 325 Hk 45
Endengue ○ CAM 320 Gn 44
Enderbury ♁ KIR 35 Aa 10
Enderby Island ♁ AUS 360 Lj 56
Enderby Land ⌓ 38 Mb 17
Endiang ○ CDN 51 Cf 20
Endicott ○ USA 60 Dk 24
Endikott Mountains ⛰ USA 46 An 11
Endimari ~ BR 117 Ea 50
Endom ○ CAM 320 Gn 44
Endyalgout Island ♁ AUS 364 Mc 51
Ene ~ PE 128 Dl 51
Eneabba ○ AUS 368 Lh 60
Energía ○ RA 146 Ee 65
Eneri Mondrague ~ TCH 309 Ha 35
Enez ○ TR 194 Hf 25
Enfida ○ TN 297 Gm 27
Enfield ○ CDN 61 Ec 23
Enfield ○ USA 74 Dk 27
Enfield ○ USA 74 Dm 25
Enfok ○ IND 270 Kl 42
Eng. Navarro ○ BR 125 En 54
Engadine ○ USA 57 Df 22
Engaru ○ J 250 Mh 23
Engaruka ○ EAT 337 Hl 47
Engaruki Basin ⌓ EAT 337 Hl 47
Engcobo ○ ZA 349 Hf 61
Engele ○ USA 65 Cj 29
Engel's ○ RUS 181 Jb 20
Engelsbergbruk ★ S 170 Gp 16
Engeringa Creek ~ AUS 374 Md 60
Enghershafu ▲ ER 313 Hm 37
Engineer Group ♁ PNG 287 Mm 51
Engkilili ○ MAL 271 Lf 45
England ○ USA 70 Dc 28
England ⊙ GB 163 Ge 19
Englehart ○ CDN 60 Dj 22
English Bay ≈ USA 46 An 15
English Channel ≈ 163 Ge 20
English Coast ⌓ 38 Fa 17
English Harbour East ○ CDN 61 Eg 22
English River ○ CDN 56 Dc 21
Engoordina ○ AUS 374 Md 58
Engozero ○ RUS 159 Hk 13
Enguié ○ G 332 Gn 46
Engure ○ LV 171 Hd 17
Enguri ~ GE 202 Hn 24
En Hazeva ○ IL 214 Hk 30
Enid ○ USA 70 Cp 27
Enisejsk ○ RUS 204 Ua 7
Eniwa ○ J 250 Mg 24
Eniwetok ♁ MH 27 Ta 8
Enjil ○ MA 293 Gd 29
Enjukovo ○ RUS 171 Hm 16
Enkhuizen ○ NL 163 Gj 19
Enköping ○ S 170 Ha 16
Enmelen ○ RUS 205 Aa 5
Enna ○ I 185 Gp 27
Ennadai Lake ~ CDN 42 Fa 6
Ennada Lake ~ CDN 6 Db 3
En Nahud ○ SUD 312 Hg 39
Ennedi ⛰ TCH 309 Hc 37
Ennedi ⛰ TCH 309 Hd 37
Ennen Tegaham ~ TCH 309 Ha 36
Enneri Bardagué ~ TCH 309 Ha 34
Enneri Ká ~ TCH 309 Ha 36
Enneri Mi ~ TCH 309 Gp 35
Enneri Yébiqué ~ TCH 309 Ha 34
Ennery ○ RH 101 Dm 36
Enngonia ○ AUS 375 Mj 60
Ennis ○ USA 51 Cf 23
Ennis ○ USA 70 Cp 29
Ennis ○ IRL 163 Gb 19
Enniscorthy ○ IRL 163 Gc 19
Enniskillen ○ GB 162 Gb 18
Ennistimon ○ IRL 163 Gb 19
Enns ~ A 174 Gp 22
Enochs ○ USA 65 Cl 29
Enontekiö ○ FIN 159 Hd 11
Enos ▲ GR 194 Hc 26
Enotaevka ○ RUS 181 Jb 22
Enozero ~ RUS 159 Hm 12
Enping ○ VRC 258 Lg 34
Enrekang ○ RI 279 Lk 47
Enrile ○ RP 267 Ll 37
Enschede ○ NL 170 Gk 19
Enseada de Tijucas ≈ BR 141 Ek 59
Ensenada ○ MEX 75 Cd 30
Ensenada ○ RCH 147 Dm 66
Ensenada Chaitén ≈ RCH 147 Dm 67
Ensenada de la Broa ≈ C 100 Dg 34
Ensenada del Pabellón ≈ MEX 80 Cj 33
Ensenada de Mompiche ≈ EC 116 Dh 45
Ensenada de Tumaco ≈ CO 106 Dj 45
Ensenada de Utría ♀ CO 106 Dk 42
Enshi ○ VRC 243 Le 30
Enshū-nada ≈ J 251 Me 28
Ensign ○ USA 70 Cm 27
Entebbe ○ EAU 324 Hj 45
Enterprise ○ CDN 47 Cc 15
Enterprise ○ USA 50 Cd 23
Enterprise ○ USA 86 De 30
En Timadé ○ RIM 304 Ga 36
Entrecasteaux Islands ♁ PNG 287 Mm 50
Entre Lagos ○ RCH 147 Dm 66
Entre Rios ○ BR 120 Ee 48
Entre Rios ○ BR 120 Eg 48
Entre Rios ○ BR 125 Fa 51
Entre Ríos ○ BOL 136 Eb 56
Entrocamento ○ BR 121 El 48
Entronque de San Fernando ○ MEX 80 Ck 32
Entrop ○ RI 286 Mg 47
Entwistle ○ CDN 50 Ce 19
Enugu ○ WAN 320 Gk 42
Enumclaw ○ USA 50 Cb 22
Enurmino ○ RUS 23 Aa 3
Enurmino ○ RUS 46 Ae 11
Envigado ○ CO 106 Dl 42
Enviken ○ S 158 Gp 15
Envira ○ BR 117 Dn 49
Enxudé ○ GNB 316 Fn 40
Enyamba ○ RDC 333 He 47
Enyellé ~ RCB 333 Hb 44
Epako ○ NAM 348 Ha 56
Epanomí ○ GR 194 Hd 25
Epatlán ○ MEX 92 Cn 36
Epe ○ WAN 320 Gj 42
Epembe ○ NAM 340 Gn 54
Epéna ○ RCB 333 Ha 45
Eparnara ○ AUS 374 Md 56
Épernay ○ F 163 Gh 21
Ephemeral Lakes ~ AUS 374 Me 59
Ephraim ○ USA 65 Cg 26
Ephrata ○ USA 50 Cc 22
Ephrata ○ USA 74 Dk 25
Epi ○ RDC 324 Hf 44
Epi ♁ VU 386 Ng 54
Epidavros ★ GR 194 Hd 27
Épinal ○ F 163 Gk 21
Epini ○ RDC 324 Hg 45
Epira ○ GUY 113 Ef 43
Epizana ○ BOL 129 Eb 54
Epoma ○ RCB 332 Gp 45
Epping Forest ○ AUS 375 Mk 57
Epukiro ○ NAM 348 Hb 56
Epukiro ~ NAM 348 Hb 56
Epukiro ~ NAM 348 Hc 56
Epulu ~ RDC 324 Hg 44
Epupa Falls ~ NAM 340 Gn 54
Epuyén ○ RA 147 Dn 67
Eqlīd ○ IR 215 Je 30
Equatorial Guinea □ GQ 332 Gl 45
Erahtur ○ RUS 181 Hn 18
Eralé ○ BR 120 Eh 45
Eram ○ PNG 287 Mh 48
Eran Bay ≈ RP 266 Lj 41
Era River ~ PNG 287 Mj 49
Erave ○ PNG 287 Mh 49
Erave River ~ PNG 287 Mj 49
Eravur ○ CL 239 Ke 42
Erawan ♀ THA 262 Kp 38
Erbaa ○ TR 195 Hl 25
Erçek Gölü ~ TR 202 Hp 26
Erciş ○ TR 202 Hp 26
Erciyes D. ▲ TR 195 Hk 26
Erdek ○ TR 195 Hf 25
Erdemli ○ TR 195 Hk 27
Erdènète ○ MNG 204 Uc 9
Erdi ⌓ TCH 309 Hd 36
Eré ○ TCH 321 Gp 41
Erebato ~ YV 112 Eb 43
Erechim ○ BR 140 Eh 59
Eregik ○ USA 46 Al 15
Ereğli ○ TR 195 Hh 25
Ereğli ○ TR 195 Hk 27
Ereké ~ RCA 321 Ha 42
Erekta ○ PNG 286 Mg 49
Erenhot ○ VRC 26 Ub 5
Erer Wenz ~ ETH 328 Hp 41
Erétria ○ GR 194 Hd 26
Erfoud ○ MA 293 Gd 30
Erfurt ○ D 174 Gm 20
Ergani ○ TR 195 Hm 26
Erg Bourarhet ⌓ DZ 296 Gl 32
Erg Chech ⌓ RIM 305 Gc 34
Erg d'Admer ⌓ DZ 308 Gl 33
Erg Douaouir ⌓ RMM 305 Ge 35
Erg du Djourab ⌓ TCH 309 Ha 37
Erg du Ténéré ⌓ RN 308 Gm 37
Erg el Atchane ⌓ DZ 293 Gf 31
Erg er Raoui ⌓ DZ 293 Ge 31
Erg Iguidi ⌓ RIM 293 Gc 33
Erg I-n-Sâkâne ⌓ RMM 305 Gf 35
Erg Issaouane ⌓ DZ 296 Gk 32
Ergli ○ LV 171 He 17
Erg n' Ataram ⌓ DZ 305 Gg 34
Erg Tifernine ⌓ DZ 296 Gk 32
Ergun Zuoqi ○ VRC 204 Wa 8
Er Hai ~ VRC 254 La 33
Eriba ○ SUD 313 Hl 37
Erick ○ USA 70 Cn 28
Erickson ○ CDN 56 Cm 20
Erie ○ USA 57 Dh 24
Erīgāt ⌓ RMM 305 Gd 36
Erik Eriksenstretet ≈ N 158 He 6
Erik Ridge Ψ 43 Ka 7
Eriksdale ○ CDN 56 Cn 20
Eriksmåla ○ S 170 Gp 17
Erimo ○ J 250 Mh 24
Erimomisaki ⌒ J 250 Mh 25
Erin ○ USA 71 De 27
Erinundra ♀ AUS 379 Ml 64
Eritrea □ ER 313 Hl 37
Erkowit ○ SUD 313 Hl 36
Erlangen ○ D 174 Gm 21
Erlang Shan ▲ VRC 254 Lb 31
Erldunda ○ AUS 369 Mc 58
Erlistoun ○ AUS 368 Lm 60
Erlistoun Creek ~ AUS 368 Ll 59
Ermelo ○ ZA 352 Hh 59
Ermenek ○ TR 195 Hj 27
Ermil Post ○ SUD 312 Hf 39
Ermoúpoli ○ GR 194 He 27
Ernabella ○ AUS 369 Mc 59
Ernakulam ○ IND 239 Kb 41
Ernée ○ F 163 Gf 21
Erode ○ IND 239 Kc 40
Eromanga ○ AUS 374 Mh 59
Erongoberg ⛰ NAM 348 Gp 56
Erong Springs ○ AUS 368 Lj 58
Eroro ○ PNG 287 Ml 50
Errabiddy ○ AUS 368 Lj 58
Er Rachidia ○ MA 293 Gd 30
Errego ○ MOC 344 Hl 54
Er-Remla ○ TN 297 Gm 28
Errittau ○ PNG 287 Mj 49
Errol ○ USA 60 Dn 23
Erromango ♁ VU 386 Ng 55
Ersekë ○ AL 194 Hc 25
Erskine ○ USA 56 Cp 22
Eršov ○ RUS 181 Jc 20
Erta Ale ▲ ETH 313 Hn 39
Ertai ○ VRC 204 Tc 9
Ertil' ○ RUS 181 Hn 20
Ertis ~ KZ 204 Tb 8
Erua ♁ ER 313 Hn 38
Erundu ○ NAM 348 Ha 56
Eruwa ○ WAN 320 Gh 42
Ervália ○ BR 141 En 56
Ervent ○ TM 222 Jh 26
Erzin ○ RUS 204 Ub 8
Erzincan ○ TR 195 Hm 26
Erzurum ○ TR 202 Hn 26
Esa'ala ○ PNG 287 Mm 50
Eşan ~ TR 195 Hg 27
Esan ○ J 250 Mg 25
Esashi ○ J 250 Mf 25
Esashi ○ J 250 Mh 23
Esbjerg ○ DK 170 Gk 18
Esbo ○ FIN 159 He 15
Escada ○ BR 124 Fc 50
Escalante ○ USA 64 Cf 27
Escalante ~ USA 64 Cf 27
Escalante ○ RP 267 Lm 40
Escalante Desert ⌓ USA 64 Cf 27
Escalerilla ○ RCH 136 Dp 56
Escalón ○ MEX 81 Ck 32
Escambia ~ USA 86 De 30
Escanaba ~ USA 57 De 22
Escanaba ○ USA 57 De 23
Escara ○ BOL 129 Dp 55
Escárcega ○ MEX 93 Dc 36
Escarpade Point ⌒ RP 267 Lm 36
Eschwege ○ D 174 Gl 20
Escobar ○ RA 146 Ee 63
Escondido ○ USA 64 Cd 29
Escondido ~ MEX 93 Dd 36
Escondido ~ NIC 97 Df 39
Escott ○ AUS 365 Mf 54
Escravos ○ WAN 320 Gj 43
Escuinapa ○ MEX 92 Cj 34
Escuintla ○ GCA 93 Dc 38
Escuminac ○ CDN 61 Eb 22
Ese ○ RDC 324 Hf 43
Eséka ○ CAM 320 Gm 44
Eseli ○ PNG 287 Ml 48
Esenaj ○ KZ 181 Jd 21
Esence Dağl. ▲ TR 195 Hm 26
Esenyurt ○ TR 195 Hg 25
Esfahān ○ IR 222 Jd 29
Esfahān ⊙ IR 222 Jd 29
Esfarāyen ○ IR 222 Jg 27
Esfolado ~ BR 124 En 49
Eshan ○ VRC 254 Lb 33
Eshimba ○ RDC 333 He 48
Eshowe ○ ZA 352 Hh 60
Esigodini ○ ZW 349 Hg 56
Esil ○ KZ 154 Sb 8
Esim ~ KZ 155 Sb 8
Esira ○ RM 353 Jb 58
Esk ○ AUS 375 Mn 59
Eškameš ○ AFG 223 Jn 27
Eškāšem ○ AFG 223 Jp 27
Eskdale ○ AUS 379 Mk 64
Eskifjörður ○ IS 158 Fn 13
Eskil ○ TR 195 Hj 26
Eskilstuna ○ S 170 Gp 16
Eskimo Lakes ~ CDN 47 Bj 11
Eski-Nookat ○ KS 230 Ka 25
Eskişehir ○ TR 195 Hh 26
Esla ~ E 184 Gd 25
Eslāmābād-e Garb ○ IR 209 Jb 28
Eslām Qal'e ○ IR 222 Jh 28
Eslām Qal'e ○ AFG 223 Jj 28
Eslāmšahr ○ IR 222 Jd 28
Eslöv ○ S 170 Gn 18
Eşme ○ TR 195 Hg 26
Esmeralda ○ C 100 Dj 35
Esmeralda ~ BOL 129 Ea 52
Esmeralda ○ BR 146 Ej 60
Esmeralda ○ AUS 365 Mh 55
Esmeraldas ○ EC 116 Dj 45
Esmeraldas ~ EC 116 Dj 45
Esmeraldas ○ BR 133 Em 55
Esnagami Lake ~ CDN 57 De 20
Esnagi Lake ~ CDN 57 Df 21
Espake ○ IR 226 Jj 32
Espalion ○ F 184 Gh 23
Espanola ○ CDN 57 Dh 22
Espanola ○ USA 65 Cj 28
Espanveita ○ PA 97 Dh 42
Esperança ○ BR 124 Fb 49
Esperance ○ AUS 368 Ll 62
Esperance Bay ≈ AUS 368 Ll 62
Esperantina ○ BR 124 En 47
Esperantinópolis ○ BR 121 Em 48
Esperanza ○ MEX 80 Ch 32
Esperanza ○ PE 117 Dn 50
Esperanza ○ BR 117 Dp 48
Esperanza ○ RA 137 Ed 61
Esperanza ○ RA 152 Dn 71
Espiel ○ E 184 Gd 26
Espigão do Oeste ○ BR 129 Ed 51
Espigão Mestre ⛰ BR 133 El 51
Espinal ○ CO 106 Dl 43
Espinal ○ BR 132 Ee 54
Espinero ○ YV 112 Ec 42
Espinheira ○ ANG 340 Gn 54
Espinho ○ P 184 Gb 25
Espinillo ○ RA 140 Ee 58
Espino ○ CO 107 Dm 42
Espino ○ YV 107 Ea 41
Espinosa ○ BR 125 En 53
Espírito Santo ⊙ BR 141 Ep 55
Espírito Santo do Pinhal ○ BR 141 El 57
Espírito Santo do Turvo ○ BR 140 Ek 57
Espíritu Santo ○ MEX 92 Cm 34
Espíritu Santo ♁ VU 386 Nf 53
Espita ○ MEX 93 Dd 35
Esplanada ○ BR 125 Fb 51
Espoo Esbo ○ FIN 159 He 15
Espungabera ○ MOC 352 Hj 56
Esqābād ○ IR 222 Jg 28
Esquel ○ RA 147 Dn 67
Esquina ○ RCH 128 Dp 55
Esquina ○ RA 146 Ee 61
Esquiú ○ RA 137 Eb 60
Essang ○ RI 275 Lp 43
Essaouira ○ MA 292 Ga 30
Essé ○ CAM 320 Gm 43
Essej ○ RUS 204 Uc 5
Es Semara ○ MA 292 Fp 32
Essen ○ D 163 Gk 20
Essentuki ○ RUS 202 Hp 23
Essequibo ~ GUY 112 Ee 45
Essequibo ~ GUY 113 Ee 42
Essex ○ USA 64 Cd 28
Essex ○ USA 74 Dk 26
Essiama ○ GH 317 Ge 43
Esslingen am Neckar ○ D 174 Gl 21
Esso ○ RUS 205 Yb 7
Est. Las Tablas ○ MEX 92 Cn 34
Estacada ○ USA 50 Ca 23
Estação Catur ○ MOC 344 Hk 52
Eşţahbānāt ○ IR 215 Je 31
Estância ○ BR 125 Fb 51
Estancia Atamisqui ○ RA 136 Ec 60
Estancia Camerón ○ RCH 152 Dp 72
Estancia Carmen ○ RA 152 Dp 73
Estancia La Julia ○ RA 152 Dp 70
Estancia Las Cumbres ○ RCH 152 Dm 71
Estancia María Luisa ○ RA 152 Ea 73
Estancia Marina ○ RA 152 Dp 73
Estancia Policarpo ○ RA 152 Eb 73
Estancia Rocallosa ○ RCH 152 Dm 72
Estandarte ○ BR 121 Em 46
Estanica ○ USA 65 Cj 28
Estanque del Leon ○ MEX 81 Cl 32
Estanques ○ YV 107 Dn 41
Estarca ~ BOL 136 Ea 56
Estcourt ○ ZA 349 Hg 60
Eštehārd ○ IR 222 Jd 28
Esteio ○ BR 146 Ej 60
Estella ○ E 184 Ge 24
Estelli ○ NIC 96 De 39
Estelline ○ USA 70 Cm 28
Estépar ○ E 184 Gd 24
Estepona ○ E 184 Gd 27
Esterhazy ○ CDN 51 Cl 20
Esternay ○ F 163 Gh 21
Estero Bay ≈ USA 64 Cb 28
Estero de Boca ○ EC 116 Dh 47
Estero Real ~ NIC 96 De 39
Esteros del Batel ⌓ RA 146 Ee 60
Esteros del Iberá ⌓ RA 146 Ef 60
Esteros Miriñay ~ RA 146 Ef 60
Estes Park ○ USA 65 Ck 25
Estevan ○ CDN 51 Cl 21
Estherville ○ USA 56 Da 24
Estima ○ MOC 344 Hj 53
Estique ○ PE 128 Dn 54
Estlin ○ CDN 51 Ck 20
Eston ○ CDN 51 Ch 20
Estorilo ○ P 184 Gb 26
Estrecho Asia ≈ RCH 152 Dl 71
Estrecho Blanco ≈ RCH 137 Dn 60
Estrecho de la Maire ≈ RA 152 Eb 73
Estrecho Nelson ≈ RCH 152 Dl 71
Estreito ○ BR 121 El 49
Estrela ○ BR 146 Eh 60
Estrela do Sul ○ BR 133 El 55
Estremoz ○ P 184 Gc 26
Estrirão do Equador ○ BR 117 Dn 48
Estuaire de Gabon ≈ G 332 Gl 45
Estuaire du Cameroun ≈ CAM 320 Gl 44
Esztergom ○ H 174 Hb 22
Etadunna ○ AUS 374 Mf 60
Etaga ○ MOC 344 Hm 54
Etah ○ DK 43 Ha 3
Etah ○ IND 234 Kd 32
Étampes ○ F 163 Gh 21
Etanga ○ NAM 340 Gn 54
Etawah ○ IND 234 Kd 32
Étéké ○ G 332 Gm 46
Etere ○ PNG 286 Mh 50
Ethel ~ AUS 368 Lk 58
Ethelbert ○ CDN 56 Cm 20
Ethel Creek ○ AUS 360 Ll 57
Etheldale ○ AUS 365 Mh 55
Ethiopia □ ETH 325 Hm 41
Etiga ○ RDC 324 Hg 44
Etoliko ○ GR 194 Hc 26
Etolin Strait ≈ USA 46 Ag 15
Etorohaberge ⛰ NAM 340 Gn 54
Etosha ♀ NAM 340 Gp 55
Etosha Pan ~ NAM 340 Ha 55
Etou ○ CAM 321 Gn 44
Etoumbi ○ RCB 332 Gp 45
Etowah ○ USA 71 Df 28
Etowah Mounds S.H.S. ★ USA 71 Df 28
Étretat ○ F 163 Gf 21
Etropole ○ BG 194 He 24
Etsha ○ RB 341 Hd 55
Etsouali ○ RCB 332 Gp 47
Ettaiyāpuram ○ IND 239 Kc 41
Et-Tleta-de-Oued-Laou ○ MA 293 Gd 28
Et-Tnine ○ MA 292 Gb 30
Etumba ○ RDC 333 Hc 47
Etumba ○ RDC 333 He 46
Eturnagaram ○ IND 238 Kd 36
Etzatlan ○ MEX 92 Ck 35
Etzikom Coulée ~ CDN 51 Cg 21
Eua ♁ TO 390 Ac 56
Euaiki ♁ TO 390 Ac 56
Eubalong ○ AUS 379 Mk 62
Euboea ♁ GR 194 Hd 26
Euca ○ BR 113 Ej 44
Eucla ○ AUS 369 Ma 61
Eucla Basin ⌓ AUS 369 Ln 62
Euclid ○ USA 71 Dh 25
Euclides da Cunha ○ BR 125 Fa 51
Euclides da Cunha Paulista ○ BR 140 Eh 57
Eudora ○ USA 86 Dc 29
Eudunda ○ AUS 378 Mf 63
Eufalula ○ USA 86 Df 30
Eufaula ○ USA 70 Da 28
Eufaula Lake ~ USA 70 Da 28
Eufrasio Loza ○ RA 137 Ec 60
Eugene ○ USA 50 Ca 24
Eugênia ~ BR 132 Ee 51
Eugowra ○ AUS 379 Ml 62
Eulo ○ AUS 375 Mj 60
Eumara Springs ○ AUS 365 Mj 55
Eunápolis ○ BR 125 Fa 54
Eungella ○ AUS 375 Ml 56
Eungella ♀ AUS 375 Ml 56
Eunice ○ USA 65 Cl 29
Eunice ○ USA 86 Db 30
Euphrat ~ IRQ 215 Ja 30
Euphrates Euphrat ~ IRQ 209 Hn 28
Eupora ○ USA 86 Dd 29
Eura ○ FIN 159 Hc 15
Eureka ○ CDN 43 Ga 2
Eureka ○ USA 46 Ba 13
Eureka ○ USA 50 Cc 24
Eureka ○ USA 56 Cn 23
Eureka ○ USA 64 Bp 25
Eureka ○ USA 64 Cd 26
Eureka ○ USA 65 Cf 26
Eureka ○ USA 70 Cp 27
Eureka Sound ≈ CDN 7 Eb 2
Eureka Springs ○ USA 70 Db 27
Eurimbla ♀ AUS 375 Mm 58
Eurinilla Creek ~ AUS 378 Mg 61
Europa ○ AUS 379 Mj 64
Eurotunnel ★ GB 163 Gg 20
Euskadi ⊙ E 184 Ge 24
Eutaw ○ USA 86 Dd 29
Euthini ○ MW 344 Hj 51
Eva ○ USA 70 Cm 27
Evadale ○ USA 81 Da 30
Eva Downs ○ AUS 364 Md 55
Evale ○ ANG 340 Gp 54
Evan ○ F 163 Gk 22
Evandale ○ CDN 61 Ea 23
Evangelina ○ ZA 349 Hg 57
Evans ○ USA 65 Ck 25
Evans Strait ≈ CDN 43 Gb 6
Evanston ○ USA 71 De 24
Evanstone ○ USA 65 Cg 25
Evansville ○ CDN 57 Dg 23
Evansville ○ USA 71 De 26
Evant ○ USA 81 Cn 30
Evaton ○ ZA 349 Hf 59
Eva Valley ○ AUS 364 Mc 53
Evensk ○ RUS 205 Yb 6
Everard Junction ○ AUS 369 Ln 58
Everard Ranges ⛰ AUS 369 Mc 59
Everett ○ USA 50 Ca 21
Everett ○ USA 87 Dh 30
Everglades ♀ USA 87 Dh 33
Everglades City ○ USA 87 Dh 33
Evergreen ○ USA 50 Ce 21
Evergreen ○ USA 86 De 30
Evertsberg ○ S 158 Gn 15
Evesham ○ AUS 375 Mh 57
Evianyong ○ GQ 332 Gm 45
Evijärvi ○ FIN 159 Hd 14
Evje ○ N 170 Gk 16
Evla ○ EST 171 Hf 16
Evodoula ○ CAM 320 Gm 43
Evöğli ○ IR 209 Ja 26
Évora ○ P 184 Gb 26
Evreux ○ F 163 Gg 21
Evron ○ F 163 Gf 21
Ewan ○ USA 50 Cd 22
Ewango ○ WAN 320 Gl 42
Ewaso Ngiro ~ EAK 325 Hl 45
Ewasse ○ PNG 287 Mm 48
Ewing ○ USA 56 Cn 24
Ewing ○ USA 70 Dc 26
Exaltación ○ BOL 129 Ea 51
Exaltación ○ BOL 129 Eb 52
Excelsior ○ ZA 349 Hf 60
Excursion Inlet ○ USA 47 Bj 15
Exelsior Springs ○ USA 70 Da 26
Exeter ○ CDN 57 Dh 24
Exeter ○ USA 60 Dn 24
Exeter ○ USA 64 Cc 27
Exeter ○ GB 163 Gd 20
Exloits ~ CDN 61 Ef 21
Exmoor ♀ GB 163 Ge 20
Exmore ○ USA 74 Dl 27
Exmouth ○ AUS 360 Lh 56
Exmouth Gulf ≈ AUS 360 Lh 57
Exmouth Plateau Ψ AUS 360 Lg 55
Expedition Range ⛰ AUS 375 Ml 58
Extrema ○ BR 141 El 57
Extremadura ⊙ E 184 Gc 26
Exu ○ BR 124 Fa 49
Exuma Cays ♁ BS 87 Dk 33
Exuma Cays Land and Sea Park ♀ BS 87 Dk 33
Exuma Sound ≈ BS 87 Dk 33
Eyangu ○ RDC 333 Hd 47
Eyebrow ○ CDN 51 Cj 20
Eyehill Creek ~ CDN 51 Ch 19
Eye Tsaka ~ VRC 231 Kf 30
Eyl ○ SP 328 Jc 42
Eymoutiers ○ F 184 Gg 23
Eyota ○ USA 56 Db 23
Eyre Creek ~ AUS 374 Mf 58
Eyre Mountains ⛰ NZ 382 Ng 68
Eyre Peninsula ♁ AUS 378 Md 62
Eysturoy ♁ DK 162 Gc 14
Ezequiel Montes ○ MEX 92 Cn 35
Ezere ○ LV 170 Hd 17
Ezernieki ○ LV 171 Hf 17
Ezgueret ~ RMM 308 Gh 37
Ezhou ○ VRC 243 Lh 30

El Tala - Ezhou 417

□Country ▣Capital city ⊙Administrative unit ○Place ♁Island ⛰Mountain range △Mountain ⌓Cape ≈Ocean, Sea ~Lake, River ▿Undersea topography ▲Glacier ♣National park •••Reservation ★Point of major interest ⏢Landscape

Ezibeleni ○ **ZA** 349 Hf 61
Ezine ○ **TR** 195 Hf 26
Ezo ○ **SUD** 324 Hf 43
Ezzangbo ○ **WAN** 320 Gl 42
Ez-Zhiliga ○ **MA** 293 Gc 29

F

Faaborg ○ **DK** 170 Gl 18
Fabens ○ **USA** 80 Cj 30
Faber Lake ~ **CDN** 47 Cc 13
Fabriano ○ **I** 185 Gn 24
Facatativá ○ **CO** 106 Dl 43
Fachi ○ **RN** 308 Gm 36
Fāchūd ○ **IND** 238 Kb 36
Facundo ○ **RA** 152 Dn 68
Fada ○ **TCH** 309 Hc 37
Fada-Ngourma ○ **BF** 317 Gg 39
Faddoi ○ **SUD** 324 Hj 41
Fadiffolu Atoll ♁ **MV** 239 Ka 43
Fadugu ○ **WAL** 316 Ga 41
Fa'er ○ **VRC** 255 Lc 32
Fafa ○ **RMM** 305 Gg 38
Fafa Fam ~ **RCA** 321 Hb 42
Fafadun ○ **SP** 325 Hn 44
Fafakouro ○ **SN** 316 Fn 39
Fafen Shet' ~ **ETH** 328 Hp 41
Faga ~ **BF** 317 Gg 39
Fagamalo ○ **WS** 390 Ad 52
Făgăraş ○ **RO** 175 He 23
Fagernes ○ **N** 158 Gl 15
Fagersta ○ **S** 158 Gp 15
Făget ○ **RO** 194 Hd 23
Faghmah ⊙ **YE** 219 Jc 37
Fagih Soleimān ○ **IR** 209 Jb 28
Fagita ○ **RI** 283 Mb 46
Fagrinkotti ○ **SUD** 312 Hh 36
Fagudu ○ **RI** 282 Ln 46
Fagwir ○ **SUD** 324 Hh 41
Fahreğ ○ **IR** 226 Jh 31
Fā'id ○ **ET** 301 Hj 30
Fairān ○ **ET** 301 Hj 31
Fairbaim Reservat ~ **AUS** 375 Mk 57
Fairbanks ○ **USA** 6 Bb 3
Fairbanks ○ **USA** 46 Bc 13
Fairbanks ○ **USA** 56 Dc 22
Fair Bluff ○ **USA** 74 Dj 28
Fairbury ○ **USA** 70 Cp 25
Fair Cape ⌓ **AUS** 365 Mh 52
Fairchild ○ **USA** 56 Dc 23
Fairfax ○ **USA** 56 Cn 24
Fairfax ○ **USA** 70 Da 25
Fairfield ○ **USA** 50 Ce 24
Fairfield ○ **USA** 51 Cg 22
Fairfield ○ **USA** 60 Dp 23
Fairfield ○ **USA** 64 Ca 26
Fairfield ○ **USA** 65 Cf 25
Fairfield ○ **USA** 70 Dc 25
Fairfield ○ **USA** 71 De 29
Fairfield ○ **USA** 81 Cp 30
Fairhill ○ **AUS** 375 Ml 57
Fairhope ○ **USA** 86 Dd 30
Fair' Isle ♁ **GB** 162 Gf 16
Fairlie ○ **NZ** 382 Nh 68
Fairlight ○ **CDN** 56 Cm 21
Fairmont ○ **USA** 56 Da 24
Fairmont ○ **USA** 70 Cp 25
Fairmont ○ **USA** 71 Dh 26
Fairmont Hot Springs ○ **CDN** 50 Ce 20
Fairo ○ **WAL** 316 Ga 42
Fairoaks ○ **USA** 71 Dc 28
Fairport ○ **USA** 57 De 23
Fairvale ○ **CDN** 61 Eb 23
Fairview ○ **CDN** 47 Cc 17
Fairview ○ **USA** 51 Ck 22
Fairview ○ **USA** 57 Dg 23
Fairview ○ **USA** 70 Cn 27
Fairview ○ **USA** 70 Cp 26
Fairview ○ **USA** 70 Da 26
Fairview ○ **AUS** 365 Mj 53
Faisalābād ○ **PK** 230 Ka 30
Faith ○ **USA** 51 Cl 23
Faiyiba ○ **SUD** 312 Hh 38
Faizābād ○ **IND** 234 Kf 32
Fajardo ○ **USA** 104 Eb 36
Faje ○ **WAN** 320 Gj 41
Fakaofo ♁ **NZ** 35 Aa 10
Fakarava ♁ **F** 35 Bb 11
Fakenham ○ **GB** 163 Gg 19
Fakfak ♁ **RI** 283 Mb 47
Fakfak ○ **RI** 283 Mc 47
Fako △ **CAM** 320 Gl 43
Fakse Bugt ~ **DK** 170 Gn 18
Fak Tha ○ **THA** 254 La 36
Fala ~ **RMM** 305 Gd 38
Falaba ○ **WAL** 316 Ga 41
Falagountou ○ **BF** 305 Gg 38
Falaise ○ **F** 163 Gf 21
Falaise d'Angamma ⛰ **TCH** 309 Ha 37
Falaise de Bandiagara ⛰ **RMM** 305 Ge 38
Falaise de l'Aguer-Tay ⛰ **TCH** 309 Ha 35
Falaise de Tambaoura ⛰ **RMM** 316 Ga 39
Falaise de Tiguidit ⏢ **RN** 308 Gk 37
Falaises du Gobnangou ⛰ **BF** 317 Gg 40
Falam ○ **MYA** 254 Kl 34
Falcón ~ **RCH** 152 Dm 70
Falcon Reservoir ~ **USA** 81 Cn 32
Faléa ○ **RMM** 316 Ga 39
Falealupo ○ **WS** 390 Ad 52
Falefapuna ○ **WS** 390 Ae 52
Faléme ~ **SN** 316 Ga 39
Falfurrias ○ **USA** 81 Cn 32
Fali Mountains △ **WAN** 320 Gm 42
Falkat ~ **ER** 313 Hm 37
Falkenberg ○ **S** 170 Gm 17
Falkland Islands ♁ **GB** 147 Ee 71
Falkland Plateau ▿ 15 Ga 15
Falkland Sound ~ **GB** 147 Ed 72
Falköping ○ **S** 170 Gn 16
Fall City ○ **USA** 50 Ca 22
Fall Line Hills ⛰ **USA** 71 Dd 28
Fallon ○ **USA** 51 Ck 22
Fallon ○ **USA** 64 Cc 26
Fallónica ○ **I** 185 Gm 24
Fall River ○ **USA** 74 Dn 25
Fall River Mills ○ **USA** 64 Cb 25
Falls City ○ **USA** 70 Da 25
Falls Reservation ~ **USA** 74 Dj 27
Falmey ○ **RN** 320 Gh 39
Falmouth ○ **USA** 74 Dn 25
Falmouth ○ **JA** 100 Dk 36
Falmouth ○ **AG** 104 Ed 37
Falmouth ○ **GB** 163 Gd 20
Falo ○ **RMM** 305 Gc 39
Falou ○ **RMM** 304 Gb 38
False Bay ~ **ZA** 358 Hb 63
Falsino ~ **BR** 113 Ej 45
Falso Cabo de Hornos ⌓ **RCH** 152 Dp 73
Falster ♁ **DK** 170 Gn 18
Falun ○ **CDN** 50 Cf 19
Falun ○ **S** 158 Gp 15
Fam ~ **RCA** 321 Hb 42
Famaillá ○ **RA** 136 Eb 59
Famalé ○ **RN** 305 Gg 38
Fāmarin ○ **IR** 209 Jc 28
Fambusi ○ **GH** 317 Gf 40
Fame Range ⛰ **AUS** 369 Lm 58
Family Lake ~ **CDN** 56 Da 20
Fana ○ **RMM** 305 Gc 39
Fanado ~ **BR** 125 En 54
Fanambana ~ **RM** 345 Jc 52
Fanambana ○ **RM** 345 Jd 52
Fanchang ○ **VRC** 246 Lk 30
Fandriana ○ **RM** 353 Jb 56
Fang ○ **THA** 254 Kp 36
Fangak ○ **SUD** 324 Hh 41
Fangalawa ○ **PNG** 287 Mm 47
Fangamadou ○ **RG** 316 Ga 41
Fangcheng ○ **VRC** 243 Lg 29
Fangcheng ○ **VRC** 255 Ld 35
Fangliao ○ **RC** 259 Ll 34
Fang Xian ○ **VRC** 243 Lf 29
Fanja Kana ○ **RM** 353 Jb 56
Fanning River ○ **AUS** 365 Mk 55
Fanø ♁ **DK** 170 Gl 18
Fano ○ **I** 185 Gn 24
Fanshi ○ **VRC** 243 Lg 26
Fanūg ○ **IR** 226 Jh 32
Fan Xian ○ **VRC** 243 Lh 28
Fanxue ○ **VRC** 243 Ld 27
Fāqūs ○ **ET** 301 Hh 30
Fara ○ **BF** 317 Ge 40
Faraba ○ **RMM** 316 Ga 39
Faradje ○ **RDC** 324 Hg 44
Farafangana ○ **RM** 353 Jb 57
Faragouaran ○ **RMM** 304 Gc 40
Farāh ⊙ **AFG** 223 Jj 29
Farāh ~ **AFG** 223 Jj 29
Farāh ○ **AFG** 223 Jk 29
Farahābād ○ **IND** 238 Kd 37
Farahalana ○ **RM** 345 Jd 53
Farāhrūd ○ **AFG** 223 Jk 29
Farako ○ **RMM** 305 Gc 40
Farallon de Medinilla ♁ **USA** 27 Sa 8
Farallones de Calí ♣ **CO** 106 Dk 44
Faramana ○ **BF** 317 Gd 39
Faranah ○ **RG** 316 Ga 40
Faraony ~ **RM** 353 Jb 56
Far'aoun ○ **RIM** 304 Fp 36
Farasan Islands ♁ **KSA** 218 Hn 37
Faratshiho ○ **RM** 345 Jb 55
Faraulep ♁ **FSM** 27 Sa 9
Farfenni ○ **WAG** 316 Fn 39
Fargha ~ **SUD** 313 Hk 39
Fargo ○ **USA** 56 Cp 22
Fargo ○ **USA** 86 Dg 30
Farhār ○ **AFG** 223 Jn 27
Fari ○ **RMM** 316 Ga 39
Farias Brito ○ **BR** 124 Fa 49
Faribault ○ **USA** 56 Db 23
Farīdābād ○ **IND** 234 Kc 31
Farīdkot ○ **IND** 230 Kb 30
Faridpur ○ **BD** 235 Kj 34
Farié ○ **RN** 317 Gg 39
Farim ○ **GNB** 316 Fn 39
Farīmān ○ **IR** 222 Jh 28
Farínha ~ **BR** 121 El 49
Färjestaden ○ **S** 170 Ha 17
Farka ○ **RN** 305 Gh 38
Fārkawn ○ **IND** 254 Kl 34
Farkwa ○ **EAT** 337 Hk 48
Farley ○ **USA** 65 Cl 27
Farlo ~ **SN** 304 Fp 38
Farmer ○ **USA** 50 Cc 22
Farmer City ○ **USA** 71 Dd 25
Farmersville ○ **USA** 70 Cp 29
Farmerville ○ **USA** 70 Db 29
Farmington ○ **USA** 60 Dn 23
Farmington ○ **USA** 65 Ch 27
Farmington ○ **USA** 71 Dc 25
Farmington ○ **USA** 71 Dc 27
Farmoreah ○ **RG** 316 Fp 41
Farmville ○ **USA** 74 Dj 27
Farnham ○ **CDN** 60 Dm 23
Farnham ○ **GB** 163 Gf 20
Faro ○ **BR** 120 Ef 47
Faro ○ **P** 184 Gb 27
Faro ~ **CAM** 321 Gn 41
Faro ~ **CAM** 321 Gn 42
Faro de Barima ○ **YV** 112 Ed 41
Faroe Islands ♁ **DK** 162 Gc 14
Fårösund ○ **S** 170 Hb 17
Farquharson Tableland ⏢ **AUS** 368 Lm 59
Farrāšband ○ **IR** 215 Je 31
Farras Creek ~ **AUS** 374 Mg 58
Farroupilha ○ **BR** 146 Ej 60
Farrukhābād ○ **IND** 234 Kd 32
Farrukhnagar ○ **IND** 238 Kd 37
Fārs ⊙ **IR** 215 Jd 30
Fársala ○ **GR** 194 Hd 26
Fārsān ○ **IR** 222 Jd 29
Farson ○ **USA** 51 Cj 24
Fārūğ ○ **IR** 222 Jh 27
Faruraq ○ **IR** 209 Ja 26
Farwell ○ **USA** 65 Cl 28
Fāryāb ⊙ **AFG** 223 Jl 28
Fasā ○ **IR** 215 Je 31
Fasad ○ **OM** 219 Je 36
Fasama ○ **LB** 316 Gb 42
Fašaryk ○ **UZB** 223 Jp 25
Fâs Boye ○ **SN** 304 Fm 38
Fashe ○ **WAN** 320 Gj 41
Fasil Ghebbi ★ **ETH** 313 Hl 39
Fask ○ **MA** 292 Gb 31
Faskruðsjörður ○ **IS** 158 Fp 13
Fassala Néré ○ **RIM** 305 Gd 38
Fassanu ○ **LAR** 297 Gn 30
Fastiv ○ **UA** 175 Hg 20
Fataki ○ **RDC** 324 Hh 44
Fatao ○ **RMM** 304 Gb 38
Fatehābād ○ **IND** 230 Kb 31
Fatehpur ○ **PK** 227 Jp 30
Fatehpur ○ **IND** 234 Ke 33
Fatehpur Sikri ○ **IND** 234 Kc 32
Fatepur ○ **BD** 235 Kk 33
Fatež ○ **RUS** 171 Hk 19
Fatham Five National Marine Park ♣ **CDN** 57 Dh 23
Fatick ○ **SN** 304 Fm 38
Fátima ○ **P** 184 Gb 26
Fatima de Sul ○ **BR** 140 Eg 57
Fatimé ○ **RMM** 317 Gd 39
Fatitet ○ **SUD** 325 Hj 42
Fatsa ○ **TR** 195 Hl 25
Fattasha ○ **SUD** 312 Hh 38
Fatu Hiva ♁ **F** 14 Ca 11
Fatuma ○ **RDC** 336 Hg 49
Fatundu ○ **RDC** 333 Ha 48
Faucett ○ **USA** 70 Da 26
Faulkton ○ **USA** 56 Cn 23
Fauquier ○ **CDN** 50 Cc 21
Faure Island ♁ **AUS** 368 Lg 58
Fauresmith ○ **ZA** 349 He 60
Fauro Island ♁ **SOL** 290 Na 49
Fauske ○ **N** 158 Gp 12
Faux Cap ○ **RM** 353 Ja 58
Faxaflói ~ **IS** 158 Fj 13
Faxälven ~ **S** 158 Ha 14
Faxinal ○ **BR** 140 Ej 58
Faxinal do Soturno ○ **BR** 146 Eh 60
Faya Largeau ○ **TCH** 309 Hb 37
Fayala ○ **RDC** 333 Ha 47
Fayaoué ○ **F** 386 Nf 56
Fayette ○ **USA** 86 Dc 30
Fayetteville ○ **USA** 70 Da 27
Fayetteville ○ **USA** 71 Df 26
Fayetteville ○ **USA** 74 Dj 28
Fayettville ○ **USA** 71 De 28
Faylakah ⌓ **KWT** 215 Jc 31
Fazao ○ **RT** 317 Gg 41
Fazao Mountains ⛰ **RT** 317 Gg 41
Fazeï ○ **RN** 308 Gm 36
Fazenda Foz do Cristalino ○ **BR** 133 Ej 52
Fazenda Santa Lúcia ○ **BR** 132 Eg 54
Fazenda Vista Alegre ○ **BR** 120 Ed 49
Fazilpur ○ **PK** 227 Jp 31
Fco. Beltrão ○ **BR** 140 Eh 59
Fdérik ○ **RIM** 304 Fp 34
Fécamp ○ **F** 163 Gg 21
Federal ○ **RA** 146 Ee 61
Fedovo ○ **RUS** 159 Hm 14
Féfiné ○ **RG** 316 Fn 40
Fehmarn ♁ **D** 170 Gm 18
Feidh Botma ○ **DZ** 296 Gh 28
Feidong ○ **VRC** 246 Lj 30
Feijo ○ **BR** 117 Dn 50
Feilding ○ **NZ** 383 Nk 66
Feira de Santana ○ **BR** 125 Fa 52
Feixi ○ **VRC** 246 Lj 30
Fei Xian ○ **VRC** 246 Lj 28
Feke ○ **TR** 195 Hk 27
Felanitx ○ **E** 185 Gh 26
Felaou ○ **DZ** 308 Gj 36
Feldberg △ **D** 163 Gk 22
Feldkirch ○ **A** 174 Gl 22
Felege Neway ○ **ETH** 325 Hl 42
Félicité ♁ **SY** 329 Jf 48
Felidu Atoll ♁ **MV** 239 Ka 44
Felipe Carrillo Puerto ○ **MEX** 93 De 36
Felixlândia ○ **BR** 133 Em 55
Felixstowe ○ **GB** 163 Gg 20
Feltre ○ **I** 185 Gm 23
Fêmeas ~ **BR** 133 Em 52
Fence Lake ○ **USA** 65 Ch 28
Feng'an ○ **VRC** 258 Lh 34
Fengceng ○ **VRC** 258 Lh 31
Fengcheng ○ **VRC** 246 Ln 25
Fengdu ○ **VRC** 255 Ld 31
Fenggang ○ **VRC** 255 Ld 32
Fenghua ○ **VRC** 259 Ll 31
Fenghuan ○ **VRC** 243 Lh 30
Fenghuang ○ **VRC** 255 Le 32
Fenghuang ○ **VRC** 258 Lj 34
Fenghuangshan ★ **VRC** 246 Ln 25
Fengije ○ **VRC** 243 Le 30
Fengjiu ○ **VRC** 243 Lh 28
Fengliang ○ **VRC** 258 Lj 34
Fengling Guan △ **VRC** 258 Lk 31
Fengpin ○ **RC** 259 Ll 34
Fengpo ○ **VRC** 254 La 34
Fengrun ○ **VRC** 246 Lj 26
Fengshan ○ **VRC** 255 Ld 33
Fengshan ○ **RC** 259 Ll 34
Fengshuba Shuiku ~ **VRC** 258 Lh 33
Fengshun ○ **VRC** 258 Lj 34
Fengton zhai Giant Panda Reserves ♣ **VRC** 242 Lb 30
Feng Xian ○ **VRC** 243 Ld 29
Feng Xian ○ **VRC** 246 Lj 28
Fengxian ○ **VRC** 246 Ll 30
Fengxiang ○ **VRC** 243 Ld 28
Fengxin ○ **VRC** 258 Lh 31
Fengyang ○ **VRC** 246 Lj 29
Fengyuan ○ **RC** 259 Ll 33
Fengzhen ○ **VRC** 243 Lg 25
Fen He ~ **VRC** 243 Lf 27
Feni ○ **BD** 235 Kk 34
Feni Islands ♁ **PNG** 287 Mn 48
Fênix ○ **BR** 140 Eh 57
Fennimore ○ **USA** 56 Dc 24
Fenoarivo Atn. ○ **RM** 345 Jc 54
Fenoarivo Be ○ **RM** 345 Jb 55
Fenshui Guan △ **VRC** 258 Lk 32
Fenstan Shuiku ~ **VRC** 255 Le 31
Fenton ○ **USA** 57 Df 24
Fenyang ○ **VRC** 243 Lf 27
Feodosija ○ **UA** 175 Hk 23
Fera Island ♁ **SOL** 290 Nb 50
Ferapontovo ○ **RUS** 171 Hm 16
Ferdjioua ○ **DZ** 296 Gj 27
Ferdous ○ **IR** 222 Jg 28
Féredou ○ **RG** 316 Gb 41
Fereidūnkenār ○ **IR** 222 Jd 27
Fērfēr ○ **ETH** 328 Ja 43
Fergana ○ **UZB** 22 Nb 5
Fergana ○ **UZB** 223 Jp 25
Fergus Falls ○ **USA** 56 Cp 22
Fergusson Island ♁ **PNG** 287 Mm 50
Fergusson River ○ **AUS** 364 Mc 53
Feriana ○ **TN** 296 Gl 28
Ferkessédougou ○ **CI** 317 Gd 41
Ferland ○ **CDN** 51 Cj 21
Ferland ○ **CDN** 57 Dd 20
Ferlo ~ **SN** 304 Fn 38
Fermo ○ **I** 185 Gn 24
Fermoy ○ **IRL** 163 Gb 19
Fermund ~ **N** 158 Gm 14
Fermundsmarka ♣ **N** 158 Gm 14
Fernandina Beach ○ **USA** 87 Dh 30
Fernando ~ **MEX** 81 Cn 33
Fernando de Noronha ♁ **BR** 15 Ha 10
Fernandópolis ○ **BR** 140 Ej 56
Fernão Veloso ○ **MOC** 344 Hn 53
Ferndale ○ **CDN** 57 Dh 23
Fernie ○ **CDN** 50 Ce 21
Ferokh ○ **IND** 239 Kb 40
Ferrara ○ **I** 185 Gm 23
Ferreira d. Alentejo ○ **P** 184 Gb 26
Ferreira Gomes ○ **BR** 121 Ej 45
Ferreñafe ○ **PE** 116 Dj 49
Ferris ○ **USA** 70 Cp 29
Ferro ~ **BR** 132 Eg 52
Ferrol ○ **E** 184 Gb 24
Ferryland ○ **CDN** 61 Eh 22
Feshi ○ **RDC** 333 Hb 49
Fessenden ○ **USA** 56 Cm 22
Festus ○ **USA** 71 Dc 26
Fété Bowé ○ **SN** 304 Fp 38
Feteşti ○ **RO** 175 Hf 23
Fethiye ○ **TR** 195 Hg 27
Fetisovo ○ **KZ** 155 Rb 10
Fetlar ♁ **GB** 162 Gf 15
Feurs ○ **F** 185 Gj 23
Fevral'sk ○ **RUS** 205 Wc 8
Feyzābād ○ **AFG** 223 Jp 27
Fèz ○ **MA** 293 Gd 28
Fiadanana ○ **RM** 345 Jb 55
Fiambalá ○ **RA** 136 Ea 59
Fiambala ~ **RA** 136 Ea 59
Fian ○ **GH** 317 Ge 40
Fianarantsoa ○ **RM** 353 Jb 56
Fianga ○ **TCH** 321 Gp 41
Fiatt ○ **USA** 71 Dc 25
Fichē ○ **ETH** 325 Hm 41
Fichsburg ○ **ZA** 349 Hf 60
Fichtelberg △ **D** 174 Gn 20
Fichtelgebirge ⛰ **D** 174 Gm 20
Field ~ **AUS** 374 Me 57
Fields ○ **USA** 50 Cc 24
Fier ○ **AL** 194 Hb 25
Fifa ○ **RG** 316 Gb 40
Fife Lake ~ **CDN** 51 Ck 21
Fifinda ○ **CAM** 320 Gl 44
Figeac ○ **F** 184 Gh 23
Figtree ○ **ZW** 349 Hg 56
Figueira da Foz ○ **P** 184 Gb 25
Figueira Torta ○ **BR** 146 Eh 62
Figueres ○ **E** 185 Gh 24
Figueroa ~ **RA** 136 Eb 59
Figueró dos Vinhos ○ **P** 184 Gb 25
Figuig ○ **MA** 293 Gf 29
Figuil ○ **CAM** 321 Gn 41
Fiherenana ~ **RM** 353 Hp 57
Fiji □ **FJI** 387 Nm 55
Fik' ○ **ETH** 328 Hp 41
Fika ○ **WAN** 320 Gm 40
Filabusi ○ **ZW** 349 Hg 56
Filadélfia ○ **BR** 121 El 49
Filadélfia ○ **BR** 125 Ep 51
Filadelfia ○ **BOL** 129 Dp 51
Filadelfia ○ **PY** 136 Ed 57
Filamane ○ **RMM** 304 Gc 40
Filchner Ice Shelf ▲ 38 Ga 17
Filedelfia ○ **CR** 96 Df 40
Filiaşi ○ **RO** 194 Hd 23
Filiatrá ○ **GR** 194 Hc 27
Filim ○ **OM** 226 Jh 35
Filingué ○ **RN** 308 Gh 38
Filipstad ○ **S** 170 Gn 16
Fillmore ○ **CDN** 51 Cl 21
Fillmore ○ **USA** 64 Cc 28
Filóti ○ **GR** 194 He 27
Filtu ○ **ETH** 325 Hn 43
Filtu △ **ETH** 325 Hn 43
Filuo ○ **SOL** 290 Nb 49
Fimi ~ **RDC** 333 Ha 47
Finaly River ~ **CDN** 47 Bn 17
Finca de Chañaral ○ **RCH** 136 Dp 59
Finch'a'ā Dam ~ **ETH** 325 Hl 41
Finch'aya ○ **ETH** 325 Hm 43
Finch Hatton ○ **AUS** 375 Ml 56
Findlay ○ **USA** 71 Dg 25
Fingal ○ **AUS** 378 Mk 66
Finger Lake ~ **CDN** 56 Da 19
Finger Lakes ~ **USA** 60 Dk 24
Fingoe ○ **MOC** 341 Hh 53
Finike ○ **TR** 195 Hg 27
Finisterre Range ⛰ **PNG** 287 Mk 48
Finke ○ **AUS** 374 Md 58
Finke ~ **AUS** 374 Md 58
Finke Bay ~ **AUS** 364 Mb 52
Finke Gorge ♣ **AUS** 369 Mc 58
Finkolo ○ **RMM** 305 Gc 40
Finland ○ **USA** 56 Dc 22
Finland □ **FIN** 159 He 15
Finlay Forks ○ **CDN** 47 Ca 17
Finley ○ **USA** 56 Cp 22
Finley ○ **AUS** 379 Mj 63
Finmark ○ **CDN** 57 Dd 21
Finnmark ⏢ **N** 159 Hd 11
Finnsnes ○ **N** 158 Ha 11
Finnstuga ○ **S** 158 Gp 15
Finote Selam ○ **ETH** 313 Hl 40
Finschhafen ○ **PNG** 287 Mk 49
Finspång ○ **S** 170 Gp 16
Finsteraarhorn △ **CH** 174 Gl 22
Finyolé ○ **CAM** 321 Gn 41
Fionnphort ○ **GB** 162 Gc 17
Fiordo Elefantes ~ **RCH** 152 Dm 69
Fiordo Penuin ~ **RCH** 152 Dl 70
Fırat Nehri ~ **TR** 195 Hm 26
Fire Island National Seashore ♣ **USA** 74 Dm 25
Firgoun ○ **RN** 305 Gg 38
Firjuza ○ **TM** 222 Jg 27
Firmat ○ **RA** 137 Ed 62
Firmeza ○ **PE** 128 Dp 51
Firminy ○ **F** 185 Gh 23
Firou ○ **DY** 317 Gg 40
Fīrozābad ○ **IND** 234 Kd 32
Firozpur ○ **IND** 230 Kb 30
Firsovo ○ **RUS** 250 Mh 22
Firth of Forth ~ **GB** 162 Ge 17
Firth of Lorne ~ **GB** 162 Gc 17
Firth of Tay ~ **GB** 162 Ge 17
Firth of Thames ~ **NZ** 383 Nk 64
Fīrūzābād ○ **IR** 215 Je 31
Fīrūzkūh ○ **IR** 222 Je 28
Firvale ○ **CDN** 50 Bn 19
Fish ~ **NAM** 348 Ha 58
Fisher ○ **AUS** 369 Mb 61
Fisher Strait ≈ **CDN** 43 Gb 6
Fishguard ○ **GB** 163 Gd 20
Fishing Lake ~ **CDN** 56 Da 19
Fish River Canyon ♣ **NAM** 348 Ha 59
Fisīhā Genet ○ **ETH** 325 Hm 43
Fisterra ○ **E** 184 Gb 24
Fitampito ○ **RM** 353 Jb 56
Fitchburg ○ **USA** 60 Dm 24
Fitzcarrald ○ **PE** 128 Dm 51
Fitzgerald ○ **USA** 86 Dg 30
Fitzgerald River ♣ **AUS** 368 Lk 62
Fitzmaurice ~ **AUS** 364 Mb 53
Fitzroy ○ **GB** 147 Ee 71
Fitz Roy ○ **RA** 152 Ea 69
Fitzroy ~ **AUS** 361 Lm 54
Fitzroy ○ **AUS** 364 Mb 53
Fitzroy ~ **AUS** 375 Ml 57
Fitzroy Crossing ○ **AUS** 361 Ln 55
Fitzroy Island ♁ **AUS** 365 Mk 54
Fitzwilliam ♁ **CDN** 57 Dh 23
Fitzwilliam Island ♁ **CDN** 57 Dh 23
Fitzwilliam Strait ~ **CDN** 6 Da 2
Fiuggi ○ **I** 185 Gn 25
Five Points ○ **USA** 64 Cb 27
Five Stars ○ **GUY** 112 Ed 42
Fizi ○ **RDC** 336 Hg 48
Fjällnes ○ **S** 158 Gn 14
Fjellstue ○ **N** 159 Hd 11
Fjerritslev ○ **DK** 170 Gl 17
Fjordland ♣ **NZ** 382 Nf 68
Fkih-Ben-Salah ○ **MA** 293 Gc 29
Flacq ○ **MS** 353 Jg 56
Flagler ○ **USA** 65 Cl 26
Flagstaff ○ **USA** 64 Cf 28
Flagstaff ○ **ZA** 349 Hg 61
Flagstaff Lake ~ **USA** 60 Dn 23
Flambeau ~ **USA** 56 Dc 23
Flambeau Ind. Res. ••• **USA** 56 Dc 22
Fläming ⛰ **D** 170 Gn 19
Flaming Gorge N.R.A. ♣ **USA** 65 Ch 25
Flaming Gorge Res. ~ **USA** 65 Ch 25
Flamingo ○ **USA** 87 Dh 33
Flamingo Point ⌓ **BS** 87 Dl 33
Flannan Isles ♁ **GB** 162 Gb 16
Flatey ♁ **IS** 158 Fj 13
Flathead ~ **USA** 50 Ce 21
Flathead Indian Reservation ••• **USA** 50 Ce 22
Flathead Lake ~ **USA** 50 Cf 22
Flat Island ♁ **RP** 266 Lh 40
Flat Point ⌓ **NZ** 383 Nk 66
Flats ○ **USA** 70 Cm 25
Flat Top ○ **USA** 71 Dh 27
Flé ~ **RG** 316 Gb 40
Flecha Point ⌓ **RP** 275 Lm 42
Flekkefjord ○ **N** 170 Gk 16
Flensburg ○ **D** 170 Gl 18
Flers ○ **F** 163 Gf 21
Fleurance ○ **F** 184 Gg 24
Fleur de Lys ○ **CDN** 61 Ef 20
Fleurieu Pen. ♁ **AUS** 378 Mf 63
Flexal ○ **BR** 120 Eg 46
Flinders ~ **AUS** 365 Mg 54
Flinders Bay ~ **AUS** 368 Lh 63
Flinders Chase ♣ **AUS** 378 Me 63
Flinders Group ♁ **AUS** 365 Mj 53
Flinders Island ♁ **AUS** 378 Md 62
Flinders Island ♁ **AUS** 379 Ml 65
Flinders Peak △ **AUS** 375 Mn 59
Flinders Ranges ♣ **AUS** 378 Mf 61
Flin Flon ○ **CDN** 6 Db 4
Flint ○ **USA** 57 Df 24
Flint ~ **USA** 86 Df 29
Flint Hills ⛰ **USA** 70 Cp 26
Flippin ○ **USA** 70 Db 27
Flisa ○ **N** 158 Gm 15
Flomaton ○ **USA** 86 De 30
Floodwood ○ **USA** 56 Db 22
Flora ○ **USA** 71 Dd 26
Florac ○ **F** 185 Gh 23
Florala ○ **USA** 86 De 30
Flora Valley ○ **AUS** 364 Ma 55
Flor da Serra ○ **BR** 140 Eh 59
Flor de Agosto ○ **PE** 116 Dm 47
Flor del Desierto ○ **RCH** 136 Dp 57
Flor de Punga ○ **PE** 116 Dl 48
Florence ○ **USA** 50 Bp 24
Florence ○ **USA** 56 Cp 23
Florence ○ **USA** 57 Dd 23
Florence ○ **USA** 65 Ck 26
Florence ○ **USA** 70 Cp 26
Florence ○ **USA** 71 De 28
Florence ○ **USA** 71 Dh 28
Florence ○ **I** 185 Gm 24
Florence Junction ○ **USA** 65 Cg 29
Florencia ○ **CO** 106 Dl 45
Florencia ○ **RA** 146 Ee 60
Florencio Sanches ○ **ROU** 146 Ef 62
Flores ○ **GCA** 93 Dc 37
Flores ○ **BR** 124 Fb 49
Flores ♁ **RI** 282 Ll 50
Flores de Goiás ○ **BR** 133 El 53
Flores do Piauí ○ **BR** 124 En 49
Flores Gracía ○ **MEX** 92 Cl 34
Flores Island ♁ **CDN** 50 Bn 21
Flores Sea ≈ **RI** 282 Ll 49
Floresta ○ **BR** 124 Fa 50
Floresta ○ **BR** 140 Eh 57
Floresta do Araguaia ○ **BR** 121 Ek 49
Floresta Nacional Aveiro ♣ **BR** 120 Eg 47
Floreşti ○ **MD** 175 Hg 22
Floresville ○ **USA** 81 Cn 31
Florián ○ **CO** 106 Dl 43
Floriano ○ **BR** 124 En 49
Floriano Peixoto ○ **BR** 117 Ea 50
Florianòpolis ○ **BR** 141 Ek 59
Florida ⊙ **USA** 87 Dh 31
Florida ○ **C** 100 Dj 35
Florida ○ **CO** 106 Dk 44
Florida ○ **ROU** 146 Ef 63
Florida Bay ~ **USA** 87 Dh 33
Floridablanca ○ **CO** 107 Dm 42
Florida City ○ **USA** 87 Dh 33
Florida Keys ♁ **USA** 87 Dh 33
Florien ○ **USA** 86 Db 30
Florina ○ **GR** 194 Hc 25
Florínia ○ **BR** 140 Ej 57
Florissant ○ **USA** 71 Dc 26
Florissant Fossil Beds N.M. ★ **USA** 65 Ck 26
Florø ○ **N** 158 Gj 15
Flower's Cove ○ **CDN** 61 Ef 20
Floyd ~ **USA** 56 Cp 24
Floydada ○ **USA** 70 Cm 29
Fluk ○ **RI** 283 Lp 46
Flumendosa ~ **I** 185 Gl 26
Flying Fish Cove ○ **AUS** 278 Lc 51
Flying Fox Creek ~ **AUS** 364 Mc 53
Fly River ~ **PNG** 286 Mg 49
Fly River ~ **PNG** 286 Mh 50
Fô ○ **BF** 317 Gd 40
Foa ♁ **TO** 390 Ac 55
Foam Lake ○ **CDN** 51 Cl 20
Fô-Bouré ○ **DY** 317 Gh 40
Foča ○ **BIH** 194 Hb 24
Foça ○ **TR** 195 Hf 26
Focşani ○ **RO** 175 Hf 23
Fodé ○ **RCA** 321 Hd 43
Fodékaria ○ **RG** 316 Gb 40
Fogang ○ **VRC** 258 Lg 34
Fog Bay ~ **AUS** 364 Mb 52
Foggaret el ,Arah ○ **DZ** 296 Gh 32
Foggaret ez Zouba ○ **DZ** 296 Gh 32
Fóggia ○ **I** 194 Gp 25
Fogi ○ **RI** 282 Ln 47
Fogo ○ **CDN** 61 Eg 21
Fogo ♁ **CV** 316 Fh 38
Fogo Island ♁ **CDN** 61 Eh 21
Föhr ♁ **D** 170 Gl 18
Foix ○ **F** 184 Gg 24
Fokino ○ **RUS** 171 Hk 19
Fokku ○ **WAN** 320 Gj 40
Folda ~ **N** 158 Gp 12
Folégandros ○ **GR** 194 He 27
Foley ○ **USA** 86 De 30
Foley ○ **RB** 349 Hf 56
Foleyet ○ **CDN** 57 Dg 21
Foley Island ♁ **CDN** 43 Gc 5
Folgefonn ⏢ **N** 170 Gk 16
Folgelevo ○ **KZ** 223 Jn 24
Foligno ○ **I** 185 Gn 24
Folkston ○ **USA** 87 Dh 30
Folkstone ○ **GB** 163 Gg 20
Folldal ○ **N** 158 Gm 14
Follet ○ **USA** 70 Cm 27
Föllinge ○ **S** 158 Gp 14
Folsom ○ **USA** 65 Cl 27
Fomboni ○ **COM** 345 Hp 52
Fome ~ **BR** 124 En 47
Fomena ○ **GH** 317 Gf 42
Fomento ○ **C** 100 Dj 34
Fona ○ **VU** 386 Ng 54
Fond du Lac ••• **USA** 56 Db 22
Fond-du-Lac ○ **CDN** 42 Ec 7
Fon du Lac ○ **USA** 57 Dd 24
Fonéko ○ **RN** 305 Gg 38
Fongolembi ○ **SN** 316 Fp 39
Fonni ○ **I** 185 Gl 25
Fonoifua ♁ **TO** 390 Ac 56
Fonseca ○ **CO** 107 Dm 40
Fontainebleau ○ **F** 163 Gh 21
Fontanīna ○ **ETH** 313 Hm 40
Fontas ○ **CDN** 47 Ca 15
Fonte Boa ○ **BR** 117 Ea 47
Fontenay ★ **F** 163 Gj 22
Fontenay-le-Comte ○ **F** 163 Gf 22
Fontenelle ○ **USA** 65 Cg 25
Fontenelle Reservoir ~ **USA** 65 Cg 24
Font-Romeu ○ **F** 184 Gg 24
Fontur ⌓ **IS** 158 Fn 12
Fo'ondo ○ **SOL** 290 Nc 50
Foping ○ **VRC** 243 Ld 29
Forage Christine ○ **BF** 305 Gf 38
Forari ○ **VU** 386 Ng 54
Forbes ○ **AUS** 379 Ml 62
Forcados ○ **WAN** 320 Gj 43
Ford ~ **USA** 57 De 23
Ford Costantine ○ **AUS** 374 Mg 56
Førde ○ **N** 158 Gj 15
Fordyce ○ **USA** 70 Db 29
Forécariah ○ **RG** 316 Fp 41
Forelhogna △ **N** 158 Gm 14
Foreman ○ **USA** 70 Da 29
Foremost ○ **CDN** 51 Cg 21
Forestburg ○ **CDN** 51 Cf 19
Forest City ○ **USA** 71 Dc 28
Forest Grove ○ **USA** 50 Ca 23
Forest Home ○ **AUS** 365 Mh 55
Forest Lake ○ **USA** 56 Db 23
Forest Strait ~ **MYA** 262 Kp 40
Forestville ○ **CDN** 60 Dp 21
Forfar ○ **GB** 162 Ge 17
Forf Portal ○ **EAU** 324 Hh 45
Forgan ○ **USA** 70 Cm 27
Fork ○ **USA** 50 Bp 22
Fork ~ **USA** 71 De 26
Fork Red ~ **USA** 70 Cn 28
Forlandet nasjonalpark ♣ **N** 158 Gm 6
Forlandsundet ~ **N** 158 Gm 6
Forli ○ **I** 185 Gm 23
Forman ○ **USA** 56 Cp 22
Formation Cave ★ **USA** 51 Cg 24
Formby Bay ~ **AUS** 378 Me 63
Formentera ♁ **E** 184 Gg 26
Formia ○ **I** 185 Gn 25
Formiga ○ **BR** 132 Ef 54
Formiga ○ **BR** 141 Em 56
Formosa ~ **BR** 133 Ek 51
Formosa ○ **BR** 133 Ek 52
Formosa ○ **BR** 133 El 53
Formosa ○ **RA** 140 Ee 59
Formosa do Araguaia ○ **BR** 133 Ek 51
Formosa do Rio Preto ○ **BR** 133 Em 51
Formoso ~ **BR** 133 Ek 52
Formoso ~ **BR** 133 Em 53
Fornells ○ **E** 185 Gj 25
Fornos ○ **MOC** 352 Hk 57
Foro Burunga ○ **SUD** 312 Hd 39
Forqualier ○ **F** 185 Gj 24
Forres ○ **RA** 136 Eb 59
Forrest ○ **USA** 71 Dd 25
Forrest ○ **USA** 86 Dd 29
Forrest ○ **AUS** 369 Ma 61
Forrest ○ **AUS** 379 Mh 65
Forrest Lakes ~ **AUS** 369 Ma 60
Forrest River Aboriginal Reserve ••• **AUS** 361 Lp 53
Forsayth ○ **AUS** 365 Mh 55
Forshaga ○ **S** 170 Gn 16
Forsnes ○ **N** 158 Gl 14
Forssa ○ **FIN** 159 Hd 15

418 Ezibeleni - Forssa

☐ Country ◙ Capital city ◉ Administrative unit ○ Place ⛬ Island ⛰ Mountain range △ Mountain ⌓ Cape ≈ Ocean, Sea ~ Lake, River ♆ Undersea topography ▲ Glacier ♀ National park ••• Reservation ★ Point of major interest ▭ Landscape

Forsyth ○ USA 51 Cj 22
Forsyth Island ⛬ AUS 365 Mf 54
Forsyth Range ⛰ AUS 374 Mh 57
Fort Abbâs ○ PK 227 Ka 31
Fort Abercrombie ★ USA 56 Cp 22
Fort Albany ○ CDN 43 Gb 8
Fort Albany ○ CDN 57 Dh 19
Fort Albercombie State Historic Park ★ USA 46 An 17
Fortaleza ○ BR 117 Eb 50
Fortaleza ○ BR 120 Ee 47
Fortaleza ○ BR 124 Fa 47
Fortaleza ○ BOL 128 Dp 51
Fortaleza ○ BOL 129 Ea 52
Fortaleza dos Nogueiras ○ BR 121 El 49
Fort Amanda ★ USA 71 Df 25
Fort Amherst N.H.S. ★ CDN 61 Ec 22
Fort Apache ○ USA 65 Ch 29
Fort Apache Indian Reservation ••• USA 65 Cg 28
Fort Atkinson ○ USA 57 Dd 24
Fort Augustus ○ GB 162 Gd 17
Fort Battleford ★ CDN 51 Ch 19
Fort Beaufort ○ ZA 358 Hf 62
Fort Beausejour N.H.P. ★ CDN 61 Eb 23
Fort Belknap Indian Reservation ••• USA 51 Ch 21
Fort Benton ○ USA 51 Cg 22
Fort Benton ★ USA 51 Cg 22
Fort Berthold ••• USA 51 Cl 22
Fort Bowie N.H.S. ★ USA 65 Ch 29
Fort Bragg ○ USA 64 Bp 26
Fort Bridger ○ USA 65 Cg 25
Fort Bridger S.H.S. ★ USA 65 Cg 25
Fort Caroline National Monument ★ USA 87 Dh 30
Fort-Chimo Kuujjuaq ○ CDN 43 Hb 7
Fort Chipewyan ○ CDN 42 Eb 7
Fort Collins ○ USA 65 Ck 25
Fort Davis ○ USA 81 Cl 30
Fort Davis N.H.S. ★ USA 81 Cl 30
Fort Defiance ○ USA 65 Ch 28
Fort-de-France ○ F 104 Ed 38
Fort Deposit ○ USA 86 De 30
Fort Dilts Hist.Site ★ USA 51 Cl 22
Fort Dodge ○ USA 56 Da 24
Fort Donelson N.B. ★ USA 71 Dd 27
Forte Carumbo ○ ANG 333 Hb 49
Fort Edwards N.H.S. ★ CDN 61 Eb 23
Fort Erie ○ CDN 60 Dj 24
Fortescue ~ AUS 360 Lj 56
Fortescue Roadhouse ○ AUS 360 Lj 56
Fort F.Steel S.H.S ★ USA 65 Cj 25
Fort Fisher ★ USA 74 Dj 28
Fort Frances ○ CDN 56 Db 21
Fort Franklin ○ CDN 47 Bn 13
Fort Frederica National Monument ★ USA 87 Dh 30
Fort Gadsden S.H.S. ★ USA 86 Df 30
Fort Gaines ★ USA 86 Dd 30
Fort Gaines ○ USA 86 Df 30
Fort Garland ○ USA 65 Ck 27
Fort George ○ CDN 7 Fa 4
Fort George N.H.P. ★ CDN 60 Dj 24
Fort Gibson Lake ~ USA 70 Da 27
Fort Good Hope ○ CDN 6 Cb 3
Fort Hall Indian Reservation ••• USA 51 Cf 24
Fort Hancock ○ USA 80 Ck 30
Forthassa Gharbia ○ DZ 293 Gf 29
Fort Hope ○ CDN 57 Dd 20
Fort Hope ••• CDN 57 De 20
Fort Howard ○ GB 147 Ee 71
Fortin ○ MEX 92 Cp 35
Fortín Avalos Sanchez ○ PY 136 Ed 57
Fortín Carlos A.Lopez ○ PY 140 Ee 56
Fortín Comandante Nowak ○ PY 140 Ee 58
Fortín Defensores del Chaco ○ PY 140 Ee 56
Fortín General Diaz ○ PY 136 Ed 57
Fortín Lagerenza ○ PY 136 Ed 56
Fortín Olmos ○ RA 137 Ed 60
Fortín Pilcomayo ○ RA 136 Ed 57
Fortín Ravelo ○ BOL 129 Ed 55
Fortín Teniente Moises Galeno ○ PY 140 Ee 58
Fortín Tte. Rojas Silva ○ PY 136 Ed 57
Fortí Pozo Hondo ○ PY 136 Ec 57
Fort Jackson ★ USA 71 Dh 28
Fort Jefferson ★ USA 71 Df 26
Fort Jefferson Natl. Mem. ★ USA 86 Dg 33
Fort Kaskaskia S.H.S. ★ USA 71 Dd 26
Fort Kearney S.H.P ★ USA 70 Cn 25
Fort Kearney S.H.P. ★ USA 56 Cn 24
Fort Kent ○ USA 60 Dp 22
Fort Knox ★ USA 71 Df 27
Fort Lamed N.H.S. ★ USA 70 Cn 26
Fort Laramie N.H.S ★ USA 51 Ck 24
Fort Lauderdale ○ USA 87 Dh 32
Fort Liard ○ CDN 6 Cb 3
Fort Liard ○ CDN 47 Ca 15
Fort Liberté ○ RH 101 Dn 36
Fort Mackinac ★ USA 57 Df 23
Fort Macleod ○ CDN 51 Cf 21
Fort Madison ○ USA 70 Dc 25
Fort Massachusetts ★ USA 86 Dd 30
Fort Matanzas National Monument ★ USA 87 Dh 31
Fort Maurepas ••• CDN 56 Cp 20
Fort McAllister S.H.S. ★ USA 87 Dh 30
Fort McDermitt Indian Reservation ••• USA 64 Cd 24
Fort McDowell Indian Reservation ••• USA 65 Cg 29
Fort McKavett ○ USA 81 Cm 30
Fort Mc Murray ○ CDN 6 Da 4
Fort McMurray ○ CDN 42 Eb 7
Fort Mc Pherson ○ CDN 6 Ca 3
Fort McPherson ○ CDN 47 Bj 11
Fort Meade ○ USA 87 Dg 32
Fort Mohave Indian Reservation ••• USA 64 Ce 28
Fort Morgan ○ USA 65 Cl 25
Fort Morgan ★ USA 86 Dd 30
Fort Myers ○ USA 87 Dg 32
Fort Nelson ○ CDN 6 Cb 4
Fort Nelson ○ CDN 47 Ca 15
Fort Nelson River ~ CDN 47 Bn 15
Fort Norman ○ CDN 6 Cb 3
Fort Norman ○ CDN 47 Bn 13
Fort Oglethorpe ○ USA 71 Df 28
Fort Payne ○ USA 71 Df 28
Fort Peck ••• USA 51 Cj 21
Fort Peck ○ USA 51 Cj 22
Fort Peck Lake ~ USA 51 Cj 22
Fort Phil Kearny ★ USA 51 Cj 23
Fort Pierce ○ USA 87 Dh 32
Fort Pierre ○ USA 56 Cm 23
Fort Portal ○ EAU 324 Hh 45
Fort Providence ○ CDN 47 Cc 15
Fort Providence ○ CDN 6 Da 3
Fort Pulaski National Monument ★ USA 87 Dh 30
Fort Qu'Appelle ○ CDN 51 Ck 20
Fort Raleigh N.H.S. ★ USA 74 Dl 28
Fort Randall H.S. ★ USA 56 Cn 24
Fort Reliance ○ CDN 6 Db 3
Fort Resolution ○ CDN 6 Da 3
Fort Resolution ○ CDN 42 Eb 6
Fort Resolution ○ CDN 47 Ce 15
Fortress of Louisbourg N.H.S. ★ CDN 61 Ed 23
Fort Rice S.H.S. ★ USA 56 Cm 22
Fort Ripley ○ USA 56 Da 22
Fort Rixon ○ ZW 341 Hg 55
Fortrose ○ NZ 382 Ng 69
Fort Rupert ○ CDN 7 Fa 4
Fort Rupert Waskaganish ○ CDN 43 Gc 8
Fort Scott ○ USA 70 Da 27
Fort Scott N.H.S. ★ USA 70 Da 27
Fort-Ševčenko ○ KZ 202 Jc 23
Fort Severn ○ CDN 7 Eb 4
Fort Severn ○ CDN 43 Ga 7
Fort Simpson ○ CDN 6 Cb 3
Fort Simpson ○ CDN 47 Ca 15
Fort Smith ○ CDN 6 Da 3
Fort Smith ○ CDN 42 Eb 7
Fort Smith ○ USA 51 Cj 23
Fort Smith ○ USA 70 Da 28
Fort St. James ○ CDN 6 Cb 4
Fort St. John ○ CDN 47 Ca 17
Fort Stanwix National Monument ★ USA 60 Dl 24
Fort Steele ○ CDN 50 Ce 21
Fort Stockton ○ USA 81 Cl 30
Fort Summer ○ USA 65 Ck 28
Fort Summer State Memorial ★ USA 65 Ck 28
Fort Sumter National Monument ★ USA 87 Dj 29
Fort Supply ○ USA 70 Cn 27
Fort Thomas ○ USA 65 Ch 29
Fort Thompson ○ USA 56 Cn 23
Fort Trotten ○ USA 56 Cn 22
Fortul ○ CO 107 Dn 42
Fortuna ○ USA 51 Cl 21
Fortuna ○ USA 64 Bp 25
Fortuna ○ CR 97 Df 40
Fortuna ○ BR 121 Em 48
Fortuna ~ BR 129 Ed 51
Fortune ○ CDN 61 Ef 22
Fortune Bay ~ CDN 61 Eg 22
Fortune Hr. ○ CDN 61 Eg 21
Fort Union N.M. ★ USA 65 Ck 28
Fort Union Trading Post N.H.S. ★ USA 51 Ck 21
Fort Valley ○ USA 86 Df 29
Fort Vermilion ○ CDN 47 Ce 15
Fort Walsh N.H.S. ★ CDN 51 Ch 21
Fort Walton Beach ○ USA 86 De 30
Fort Washakie ○ USA 51 Cj 24
Fort Washita H.S. ★ USA 70 Cp 28
Fort Wayne ○ USA 71 Df 25
Fort Wellington ○ GUY 113 Ef 42
Fort William ○ GB 162 Gd 17
Fort Wingate ○ USA 65 Ch 28
Fort Worth ○ USA 70 Cp 29
Fort Yukon ○ USA 6 Bb 3
Fort Yukon ○ USA 46 Bc 11
Forūdgān ○ IR 222 Jd 29
Forūmad ○ IR 222 Jg 27
Forvik ○ N 158 Gn 13
Fosa de Cariaco ~ YV 112 Eb 40
Foshan ○ VRC 258 Lg 34
Fosnavåg ○ N 158 Gj 14
Foso ○ GH 317 Gf 43
Fossil ○ USA 50 Cb 23
Fossil Butte Nat.Monument ★ USA 65 Cg 25
Fossil Downs ○ AUS 361 Ln 55
Fossong Fontem ○ CAM 320 Gl 43
Foster ○ AUS 379 Mk 65
Fostoria ○ USA 71 Dg 25
Fotadrevo ○ RM 353 Ja 58
Fotokol ○ CAM 321 Gp 39
Fouénan ○ CI 304 Gc 41
Fougamou ○ G 332 Gm 46
Fougères ○ F 163 Gf 21
Fouia ○ SOL 290 Nc 50
Foula ⛬ GB 162 Ge 15
Foulabala ○ RMM 305 Gc 40
Foulamôri ○ RG 316 Fp 39
Foul Bay ~ ET 301 Hk 34
Foulenzem ○ G 332 Gl 46
Fouler ○ USA 65 Ck 26
Foumbadou ○ RG 316 Gb 41
Foumban ○ CAM 320 Gm 43
Foumbot ○ CAM 320 Gm 43
Foumbouni ○ COM 345 Hp 51
Foum-Zguid ○ MA 293 Gc 30
Foundiougne ○ SN 304 Fm 38
Founougo ○ DY 317 Gh 40
Fountain ○ USA 65 Ck 26
Fountain ○ USA 86 Df 30
Fountain's Abbey ★ GB 162 Ge 18
Four Corners ○ USA 51 Ck 23
Four Corners ○ USA 64 Cd 28
Fouriesburg ○ ZA 349 Hg 60
Fourou ○ RMM 305 Gc 40
Fourtown ○ USA 56 Da 21
Fouta Djallon ⛰ RG 316 Fp 40
Foveaux Strait ~ NZ 382 Nf 69
Fowlers Bay ○ AUS 369 Mc 61
Fowlers Bay ~ AUS 369 Mc 62
Fowlers Gap ○ AUS 378 Mg 61
Fowlerton ○ USA 81 Cn 31
Fox ~ USA 71 Dd 25
Foxe Basin ~ CDN 7 Fa 3
Foxe Basin ♆ CDN 43 Gc 5
Foxe Channel ~ CDN 7 Fa 3
Foxe Channel ≈ CDN 43 Gb 5
Foxe Peninsula ▭ CDN 7 Fa 3
Foxe Peninsula ⛬ CDN 43 Gc 6
Fox Glacier ○ NZ 382 Ng 67
Fox Harbour ○ CDN 43 Ja 8
Fox Island ⛬ USA 57 De 23
Foxton ○ NZ 383 Nk 66
Fox Valley ○ CDN 51 Ch 20
Foynøya ⛬ N 158 Hf 5
Foz de Copeá ○ BR 117 Ec 47
Foz de Iguaçu ○ BR 140 Eg 58
Foz de Jaú ○ BR 120 Ed 46
Foz do Cunene ○ ANG 340 Gm 54
Foz do Mamoriá ○ BR 117 Ea 47
Fraga ○ E 184 Gg 25
Fraile Muerto ○ ROU 146 Eg 62
Frambo ○ CI 317 Ge 43
Framingham ○ USA 74 Dn 24
Franca ○ BR 141 El 56
Francavilla ○ I 194 Ha 25
France ☐ F 163 Gg 21
France-Comté ◉ F 163 Gj 22
Frances Lake ~ CDN 47 Bl 13
Franceville ○ G 332 Gn 46
Francis ○ CDN 51 Cl 20
Francisco Aires ○ BR 124 En 49
Francisco de Orellana ○ PE 116 Dm 47
Francisco de Vitoria ○ RA 137 Ec 63
Francisco Dumont ○ BR 133 Em 54
Francisco I. Madero ○ MEX 81 Ck 33
Francisco Rueda ○ MEX 93 Db 37
Francisco Sá ○ BR 125 En 54
Francisco Santos ○ BR 124 Ep 49
Francisco Villa ○ MEX 81 Cn 33
Francisco Zarco ○ MEX 64 Cd 29
Francistown ○ RB 349 Hf 56
Franco da Roche ○ BR 141 El 57
François ○ CDN 61 Ef 22
Francs Peak △ USA 51 Ch 24
Frankenberg(Eder) ○ D 174 Gl 20
Frankfield ○ AUS 375 Mk 57
Frankfort ○ USA 57 De 23
Frankfort ○ USA 71 De 25
Frankfort ○ USA 71 Df 26
Frankfort ○ ZA 349 Hg 59
Frankfurt (Oder) ○ D 170 Gn 19
Frankfurt am Main ○ D 174 Gl 20
Frank Hann ♀ AUS 368 Ll 62
Frankish Alp ⛰ D 174 Gm 21
Frankland ○ AUS 368 Lj 63
Franklin ○ USA 60 Dn 24
Franklin ○ USA 70 Cn 25
Franklin ○ USA 70 Da 27
Franklin ○ USA 71 De 26
Franklin ○ USA 71 De 27
Franklin ○ USA 71 Dg 28
Franklin ○ USA 71 Dh 25
Franklin ○ USA 74 Dk 27
Franklin ○ USA 74 Dl 25
Franklin ○ USA 81 Cp 30
Franklin ○ USA 86 Dc 31
Franklin ○ ZA 349 Hg 61
Franklin ○ AUS 374 Mg 57
Franklin Bay ≈ CDN 47 Bn 11
Franklin D. Roosevelt Lake ~ USA 50 Cc 21
Frankling ○ USA 74 Dj 26
Franklin Harbour ~ AUS 378 Me 62
Franklin Island ⛬ 38 Tb 17
Franklin Lake ~ USA 64 Ce 25
Franklin Lower Gordon Wild Rivers ♀ AUS 378 Mj 67
Franklin Mountains ⛰ CDN 47 Bn 13
Franklin Strait ~ CDN 7 Ea 2
Franklin Strait ≈ CDN 42 Fb 4
Franklinton ○ USA 74 Dj 27
Franklinton ○ USA 86 Dc 30
Franklinville ○ USA 60 Dj 24
Frankton ○ NZ 382 Ng 68
Frannie ○ USA 51 Ch 23
Fransfontein ○ NAM 348 Gp 56
Fransfonteinberge ⛰ NAM 348 Gp 56
Frånsta ○ S 158 Ha 14
Franz ○ CDN 57 Df 21
Franz Josef ○ NZ 382 Ng 67
Franz Josef Land ⛬ RUS 19 Mb 1
Frascati ○ I 185 Gn 25
Fraser ~ CDN 50 Ca 19
Fraser ~ CDN 50 Cb 21
Fraser ~ CDN 50 Cc 19
Fraser ♀ AUS 379 Mj 64
Fraser Basin ▭ CDN 42 Dc 8
Fraserburg ○ ZA 358 Hc 61
Fraserburgh ○ GB 162 Gf 17
Fraserdale ○ CDN 57 Dh 21
Fraser Island ♀ AUS 375 Mn 58
Fraser Island ⛬ AUS 375 Mn 58
Fraser Plateau ▭ CDN 50 Bp 20
Fraser Range ○ AUS 368 Lm 61
Fraserwood ○ CDN 56 Cp 20
Fraustro ○ MEX 81 Cm 33
Fray Bentos ○ ROU 146 Ee 62
Fray Jorge ○ RCH 137 Dm 61
Fredericia ○ DK 170 Gl 18
Frederick ○ USA 56 Cn 23
Frederick ○ USA 74 Dk 26
Fredericksburg ○ USA 74 Dk 26
Fredericksburg ○ USA 81 Cn 30
Fredericktown ○ USA 71 Dc 27
Frederico Westphalen ○ BR 140 Eh 59
Fredericton ○ CDN 61 Ea 23
Frederikshavn ○ DK 170 Gm 17
Frederiksted ○ USA 104 Eb 37
Fredonia ○ USA 60 Dj 24
Fredonia ○ USA 64 Cf 27
Fredonia ○ USA 70 Cp 27
Fredonia ○ CO 106 Dl 43
Fredrika ○ S 158 Ha 13
Fredrikstad ○ N 170 Gm 16
Freeburg ○ USA 70 Db 26
Freedom ○ USA 51 Cg 24
Freehold ○ USA 74 Dl 25
Freeling Heights △ AUS 378 Mf 61
Freeman ○ USA 56 Cp 24
Freemansundet ~ N 158 Hc 6
Freeport ○ USA 71 Dd 24
Freeport ○ USA 74 Dj 25
Freeport ○ USA 81 Da 31
Freeport ○ BS 87 Dj 32
Freer ○ USA 81 Cn 32
Freetown ◙ WAL 316 Fp 41
Frégate ⛬ SY 329 Jf 48
Fregenal d. I. S. ○ E 184 Gc 26
Fregon Aparawatatja ○ AUS 369 Mc 59
Freiberg ○ D 174 Gn 20
Freiburg im Breisgau ○ D 163 Gk 21
Frei Inocêncio ○ BR 141 Ep 55
Frei Orlando ○ BR 133 Em 55
Freire ○ RCH 147 Dm 65
Freirina ○ RCH 136 Dn 60
Freising ○ D 174 Gm 21
Freistadt ○ A 174 Gp 21
Fréjus ○ F 185 Gk 24
Fremantle ○ AUS 368 Lh 62
Fremont ○ USA 64 Cb 27
Fremont ~ USA 65 Cg 26
Fremont ○ USA 70 Cp 25
Fremont ○ USA 71 Dg 25
Fremont Lake ~ USA 51 Ch 24
Fremont Mountains ⛰ USA 50 Cb 24
French Broad ~ USA 71 Dg 27
Frenchglen ○ USA 50 Cc 24
French Guiana ◉ F 113 Eh 43
Frenchman Creek ~ USA 65 Cl 25
Frenchman R. ~ CDN 51 Ch 21
French Pass ○ NZ 383 Nj 66
French Polynesia ◉ F 35 Bb 11
Frenchville ○ USA 60 Dp 22
Frenda ○ DZ 293 Gg 28
Fresco ~ BR 121 Ej 49
Fresco ~ BR 121 Ej 50
Fresco ○ CI 317 Gd 43
Fresia ○ RCH 147 Dm 66
Fresnillo ○ MEX 92 Cl 34
Fresno ○ USA 64 Cc 27
Fresno Reservoir ~ USA 51 Cg 21
Freudenstadt ○ D 174 Gl 21
Frewena ○ AUS 364 Md 55
Freycinet ♀ AUS 378 Ml 67
Freycinet Estuary ~ AUS 368 Lg 59
Freycinet Peninsula ⛬ AUS 378 Ml 67
Frí ○ GR 194 Hf 28
Fria ○ RG 316 Fp 40
Frías ○ RA 136 Eb 60
Fribourg ○ CH 163 Gk 22
Friedrichshafen ○ D 174 Gl 22
Friend ○ USA 70 Cp 25
Friesach ○ A 174 Gn 22
Friona ○ USA 65 Cl 28
Friuli-Venézia-Giúlia ◉ I 174 Gn 22
Frobisher Bay ~ CDN 7 Fb 3
Frobisher Bay ≈ CDN 43 Hb 6
Frohavet ~ N 158 Gl 14
Froid ○ USA 51 Ck 21
Frolovo ○ RUS 181 Hp 21
Frome ~ AUS 374 Me 60
Frome Downs ○ AUS 378 Mf 61
Fromontono del Gargano ⛬ I 194 Ha 25
Frontera ○ MEX 93 Db 36
Frontera ○ E 292 Fl 32
Fronteras ○ MEX 80 Ch 30
Frontier Province ◉ PK 223 Jp 29
Front Range ⛰ USA 65 Ck 25
Front Royal ○ USA 74 Dj 26
Frosinone ○ I 185 Gn 25
Frøya ⛬ N 158 Gl 14
Frozen Strait ≈ CDN 43 Gb 5
Fruta del Leite ○ BR 125 En 54
Frutal ○ BR 141 Ek 56
Frutillar ○ RCH 147 Dm 66
Frýdek-Místek ○ CZ 174 Hb 21
Fua'amotu ○ TO 390 Ac 56
Fucheng ○ VRC 243 Lh 27
Fuding ○ VRC 259 Ll 32
Fuencaliente de la Palma ○ E 292 Fm 31
Fuengirole ○ E 184 Gd 27
Fuente de Cantos ○ E 184 Gc 26
Fuente de Fresno ○ E 184 Gd 26
Fuente Obejuna ○ E 184 Gd 26
Fuerte ~ MEX 80 Ch 32
Fuerte Bulnes ○ RCH 152 Dn 72
Fuerte San Lorenzo ★ PA 97 Dh 41
Fuerteventura ⛬ E 292 Fn 31
Fufeng ○ VRC 243 Ld 28
Fuga Island ⛬ RP 267 Ll 36
Fuglehuken ⌓ N 158 Gm 6
Fugong ○ VRC 254 Kp 32
Fugou ○ VRC 243 Lh 29
Fugu ○ VRC 243 Lf 26
Fuhal ○ VRC 204 Tc 9
Fujairah ○ UAE 226 Jg 33
Fuji ○ J 251 Mf 28
Fujian ◉ VRC 258 Lj 32
Fu Jiang ~ VRC 242 Lc 30
Fujieda ○ J 251 Mf 28
Fuji-Hakone-Izu N.P. ★ J 251 Mf 28
Fujin ○ VRC 250 Mc 22
Fuji-san Fujiyama ★ J 251 Mf 28
Fujisawa ○ J 251 Mf 28
Fujiyama ★ J 251 Mf 28
Fujiyoshida ○ J 251 Mf 28
Fūka ○ ET 301 Hf 30
Fukagawa ○ J 250 Mg 24
Fukuchiyama ○ J 251 Md 28
Fukue ○ J 247 Ma 29
Fukuei Chiao ⌓ RC 259 Ll 33
Fukue-shima ⛬ J 247 Ma 29
Fukui ○ J 251 Md 27
Fukuoka ○ J 247 Ma 29
Fukushima ○ J 250 Mg 25
Fukushima ○ J 251 Mg 27
Fukuyama ○ J 251 Mc 28
Fulacunda ○ GNB 316 Fn 40
Fulanga ⛬ FJI 390 Aa 55
Fulda ○ USA 56 Da 24
Fulda ○ D 174 Gl 20
Fulda ~ D 174 Gl 20
Fuli ○ RC 259 Ll 34
Fuling ○ VRC 255 Ld 31
Fullarton ○ TT 104 Ed 40
Fullerton ○ USA 70 Cn 25
Fullerton ○ USA 71 Dg 26
Fulton ○ USA 60 Dk 24
Fulton ○ USA 71 Dc 25
Fulton ○ USA 71 Dd 27
Fulula ~ RDC 332 Ha 48
Fulunäs ○ S 158 Gn 15
Fumbelo ○ ANG 340 Hb 51
Fumel ○ F 184 Gg 23
Funabashi ○ J 251 Mf 28
Funadomari ○ J 250 Mg 23
Funafuti ⛬ TUV 35 Tb 10
Funan ○ VRC 243 Lh 29
Funäsdalen ○ S 158 Gn 14
Funcal ○ P 292 Fm 29
Fundación ○ CO 106 Dl 40
Fundão ○ BR 141 Ep 55
Fundão ○ P 184 Gc 25
Fundición ○ MEX 80 Ch 32
Fundo ~ BR 124 En 50
Fundo de Figueiras ○ CV 316 Fj 37
Fundong ○ CAM 320 Gm 42
Fundy National Park ♀ CDN 61 Eb 23
Fungurume ○ RDC 341 Hf 51
Funhalouro ○ MOC 352 Hj 57
Funing ○ VRC 246 Lk 29
Funing ○ VRC 255 Lc 34
Funin Shan ⛰ VRC 243 Lf 29
Funsi ○ GH 317 Gf 40
Funtua ○ WAN 320 Gk 40
Funza ○ CO 106 Dl 43
Fuping ○ VRC 243 Lh 26
Fuqing ○ VRC 258 Lk 33
Fuquan ○ VRC 255 Ld 32
Furancungo ○ MOC 344 Hj 53
Furano ○ J 250 Mh 24
Fūrg ○ IR 226 Jf 31
Furmanov ○ RUS 171 Hn 17
Furmanovo ○ KZ 181 Jc 21
Furnace Creek ○ USA 64 Cd 27
Furneaux Group ⛬ AUS 379 Ml 65
Furo Carandazinho ~ BR 132 Ef 54
Furo de Geraldo ~ BR 117 Ec 48
Furo do Jurupari ~ BR 120 Eh 47
Furo do Tajapuru ~ BR 121 Ej 46
Furqlūs ○ SYR 208 Hl 28
Furroli △ ETH 325 Hm 44
Fürstenfeld ○ A 174 Ha 22
Fürstenwalde(S.) ○ D 170 Gn 19
Fürth ○ D 174 Gm 21
Furudal ○ S 158 Gp 15
Furukawa ○ J 251 Mg 26
Fury and Heela Strait ~ CDN 7 Eb 3
Fusagasugá ○ CO 106 Dl 43
Fushë-Krujë ○ AL 194 Hb 25
Fushui ○ VRC 243 Le 28
Fuskam Mata ○ WAN 320 Gl 40
Füssen ○ D 174 Gm 22
Fusui ○ VRC 255 Ld 34
Futaleufú ○ RCH 147 Dn 67
Futaleufú ~ RA 147 Dn 67
Futehjang ○ PK 230 Ka 29
Futrono ○ RCH 147 Dm 66
Futuna ⛬ VU 386 Nh 55
Futuna ⛬ F 390 Aa 53
Fu Xian ○ VRC 243 Le 28
Fuxian Hu ~ VRC 255 Lb 33
Fuxing ○ VRC 258 Lj 31
Fuyang ○ VRC 243 Lh 29
Fuyn ○ VRC 204 Wb 9
Fuyu ○ VRC 205 Wb 9
Fuyuan ○ VRC 205 Wc 9
Fuyuan ○ VRC 255 Lc 33
Fuyu ○ VRC 204 Tc 9
Füzesabony ○ H 174 Hc 22
Fuzhou ○ VRC 258 Lk 32
Fuzhouzhen ○ VRC 246 Ll 26
Füzuli ○ AZ 202 Jb 26
Fyn ⛬ DK 170 Gl 18
Fyresvatn ~ N 170 Gk 16

G

g. Ačkasar △ GE 202 Hp 25
g. Bazardjuzu △ AZ 202 Jb 25
g. Dombaj Ul'gen △ GE 202 Hn 24
g. G'amys △ AZ 202 Jb 25
g. Kapydzjk △ ARM 202 Ja 26
g. Kërmjukej △ AZ 202 Jc 26
g. Lajla △ GE 202 Hp 24
Ga ○ GH 317 Ge 41
Gaalkacyo ○ SP 328 Jb 42
Gaamodebli ○ LB 316 Gb 42
Gaba ○ ETH 328 Hp 42
Gabagaba ○ PNG 287 Mk 50
Ğabal Abadad △ SUD 313 Hk 36
Ğabal Abū Ḍi'āb △ ET 301 Hk 33
Ğabal ad-Dair △ SUD 312 Hh 39
Ğabal Aderuba △ ER 313 Hl 38
Ğabal al-'Aǧma ⛰ ET 301 Hj 31
Ğabal al-'Urf △ ET 301 Hj 32
Ğabal al-Aǧā' ⛰ KSA 214 Hn 32
Ğabal al-Barqa △ ET 301 Hj 33
Ğabal al-Ǧalāla ⛰ ET 301 Hh 31
Ğabal al-Ǧhir △ YE 219 Je 39
Ğabal al-Lauz △ KSA 214 Hk 31
Ğabal al Qahb ⛬ KSA 215 Ja 33
Ğabal al Qamar ⛰ YE 219 Je 38
Ğabal al-Qarā ⛰ OM 219 Je 36
Ğabal al Waǧid ⛰ KSA 218 Ja 36
Ğabal an-Nabi △ YE 218 Hp 38
Ğabal ar-Ruwāq ⛰ SYR 208 Hl 29
Ğabal Asoteriba △ SUD 301 Hl 35
Ğabal Asoteriba △ SUD 313 Hk 37
Ğabal as-Sibā' △ ET 301 Hk 33
Ğabal Atāqa △ ET 301 Hj 31
Ğabal at-Tubaiq ⛰ KSA 214 Hl 31
Ğabal Auliyā ○ SUD 312 Hj 38
Ğabal az-Zalmā' △ KSA 214 Hm 32
Ğabal az-Zanna ○ UAE 215 Je 33
Ğabal Barkal ★ SUD 312 Hh 36
Ğabal Bozi ○ SUD 313 Hj 39
Gabaldon ○ RP 267 Ll 38
Ğabal Duqaila ⛬ YE 218 Hp 37
Ğabal Elba △ ET 301 Hl 34
Ğabal Erba △ SUD 313 Hl 35
Ğabal Ğarf △ ET 301 Hk 34
Ğabal Ğarib △ ET 301 Hj 31
Ğabal Gumbin △ SUD 324 Hh 43
Ğabal Ğurābī △ ET 301 Hg 31
Ğabal Gurad △ SUD 313 Hk 36
Ğabal Gurgei △ SUD 312 He 39
Ğabal Hamāṭa △ ET 301 Hk 34
Ğabal Hamoyet △ SUD 313 Hl 37
Ğabal Hamrīn ⛰ IRQ 209 Hp 28
Ğabal Haybān △ SUD 312 Hh 40
Ğabal Hilāl △ ET 301 Hj 30
Gabal Homot Tohadar △ SUD 313 Hl 36
Ğabal Kaiai △ SUD 313 Hl 36
Ğabal Kasangor △ SUD 325 Hk 43
Ğabal Kuror △ SUD 312 Hh 35
Ğabal Maǧāra △ ET 301 Hj 30
Ğabal Marra △ SUD 312 Hd 39
Ğabal Mazmum ○ SUD 313 Hj 39
Ğabal Mismār △ SUD 313 Hk 36
Ğabal Mubārak △ JOR 214 Hk 30
Ğabal Muqsim △ ET 301 Hj 34
Gabal Mūsa Mount Sinai △ ET 301 Hj 31
Ğabal Muwaiha ⛰ UAE 226 Jf 33
Ğabal Nuqrus △ ET 301 Hk 33
Ğabal Ofreik △ SUD 313 Hk 37
Ğabal os Sarāǧ △ AFG 223 Jn 28
Ğabal-Qatrānī ⛰ ET 301 Hh 31
Ğabal Qattār △ ET 301 Hj 32
Ğabal Radwa △ KSA 214 Hm 33
Ğabal Rāfit △ SUD 312 Hj 35
Ğabal Rašīd ⛰ SYR 208 Hl 28
Ğabal Ra's Madhar △ KSA 214 Hl 33
Ğabal Ṣabbāǧa △ ET 301 Hj 31
Ğabal Ṣabidana △ SUD 313 Hl 36
Ğabal Šā'ib △ ET 301 Hj 32
Ğabal Šammar ⛰ KSA 214 Hm 32
Ğabal Simḥān ⛰ OM 219 Jf 37
Ğabal Sinǧār ⛰ IRQ 202 Hn 27
Ğabal Tallasa △ SUD 312 Hh 40
Ğabal Teljo △ SUD 312 He 38
Ğabal Ūda △ SUD 313 Hl 35
Gabal Umm Ba'ānib △ ET 301 Hj 32
Ğabal Yu'alliq ⛰ ET 301 Hj 30
Gabal Zubair ⛬ YE 218 Hp 38
Gabane ○ RB 349 He 59
Gabarouse ○ CDN 61 Ed 23
Gabba Island ⛬ AUS 286 Mh 50
Gabbs ○ USA 64 Cd 26
Gabela ○ ANG 340 Gp 51
Gabensis ○ PNG 287 Mk 49
Gabès ○ TN 297 Gm 29
Gabi ○ RN 320 Gk 39
Gabia ○ RDC 333 Ha 48
Gabir ○ SUD 324 He 41
Gabiro ○ RWA 336 Hh 46
Gabo Frio ○ BR 141 Ep 57
Gaborone ◙ RB 349 He 58
Gabras ○ SUD 312 Hf 40
Gābrik ○ IR 226 Jh 33
Gābrik ~ IR 226 Jh 33
Gabrovo ○ BG 194 He 24
Gabú ○ GNB 316 Fn 39
Gabu ○ RDC 324 Hf 44
Gabun ☐ G 332 Gm 46
Gacanka Xaafuun ~ SP 328 Jd 40
Gacheta ○ CO 107 Dm 43
Gacko ○ BIH 194 Hb 24
Gačsar ○ IR 222 Jd 28
Gadabeji ○ RN 308 Gk 38
Gadag ○ IND 238 Kb 38
Gadaisu ○ PNG 287 Ml 51
Gada-Woundou ○ RG 316 Ga 40
Gäddede ○ S 158 Gn 13
Gadein ○ SUD 324 Hg 41
Gaden ★ VRC 235 Kk 31
Gadis ~ RI 270 Kp 45
Gadra ○ PK 227 Jp 33
Gadsden ○ USA 71 Df 28
Gadwāl ○ IND 238 Kc 37
Gadzi ○ RCA 321 Ha 43
Găeşti ○ RO 175 He 23
Gaeta ○ I 185 Gn 25
Gaffney ○ USA 71 Dh 28
Gafsa ○ TN 296 Gl 28
Gagal ○ TCH 321 Gp 41
Gagan ○ PNG 290 Mp 48
Gagarawa ○ WAN 320 Gl 39
Gagargarh ○ IND 234 Kf 32
Gagarin ○ UZB 223 Jm 25
Gagarus ○ NAM 340 Gp 55
Gaǧatū ○ AFG 223 Jn 29
Gage ○ USA 70 Cn 27
Gagere ~ WAN 320 Gk 39
Gaggabutan ○ RP 267 Ll 37
Gāğī ○ AFG 223 Jn 29
Gagin ~ IR 226 Jh 33
Gagliano d. Capo ○ I 194 Hb 26
Gagnoa ○ CI 317 Gd 42
Gagnon ○ CDN 60 Dp 20
Ǧaǧōrī ○ AFG 223 Jm 29
Gagra ○ GE 202 Hn 24
Gagrūd ~ IR 222 Jd 28
Ga Hai ~ VRC 242 Kn 27
Gahkom ○ IR 226 Jf 31
Ǧahnīn ○ OM 219 Je 37
Gahrom ○ IR 215 Je 31
Gaibanda ○ BD 235 Kj 33
Gaidak ○ AFG 223 Jm 29
Gaidhøpggen △ N 158 Gk 15
Gail ○ USA 70 Cm 29
Gail ~ A 174 Gn 22
Gaillac ○ F 184 Gg 24
Gaiman ○ RA 147 Eb 67
Gainatseb ○ NAM 348 Gp 56
Gainesville ○ USA 70 Cp 29
Gainesville ○ USA 70 Db 27
Gainesville ○ USA 71 Df 28
Gainesville ○ USA 87 Dg 31
Gairdner ~ AUS 368 Lk 62
Gairesi ~ ZW 344 Hj 54
Gaivota ○ BR 121 Ej 45
Gai Xlan ○ VRC 246 Lm 25
Gajendragarh ○ IND 238 Kb 38
Gajiram ○ WAN 321 Gn 39
Gajny ○ RUS 19 Mb 3
Gajos ○ EAK 325 Hl 44
Gajutino ○ RUS 171 Hm 16
Gajwel ○ IND 238 Kd 37
Gakem ○ WAN 320 Gl 42
Gakou ○ RMM 304 Gb 38
Gakugsa ○ RUS 171 Hl 15
Gala ○ VRC 235 Kj 31
Gala Co ~ VRC 235 Kj 31
Ǧalāǧil ○ KSA 215 Ja 33
Ǧalal al-Batra △ JOR 214 Hk 31
Ǧalal Bāqir △ JOR 214 Hk 31
Galán ○ CO 107 Dm 42
Galana ~ EAK 337 Hm 47
Galanga ○ ANG 340 Gp 52
Galangue ○ ANG 340 Ha 52
Galaosje ○ UZB 223 Jl 26
Galapagos Islands ⛬ EC 128 Dd 45
Galarza ○ RA 146 Ef 60
Galashiels ○ GB 162 Ge 18

Forsyth - Galashiels 419

◻Country ▣Capital city ⊙Administrative unit ○Place ⌂Island ⛰Mountain range △Mountain ⌓Cape ≈Ocean, Sea ~Lake, River ΨUndersea topography ▲Glacier ♀National park •••Reservation ★Point of major interest ⏜Landscape

Galata ○ CY 195 Hj 28
Galaţi ○ RO 175 Hg 23
Galax ○ USA 71 Dh 27
Galbraith ○ AUS 365 Mg 54
Gáldar ○ E 292 Fn 31
Galdiyān ○ IR 209 Ja 27
Galé ○ RMM 316 Gb 39
Gale ○ RDC 321 Hc 44
Galeana ○ MEX 80 Cj 30
Galeana ○ MEX 81 Cm 33
Galegu ○ SUD 313 Hk 39
Galegu ~ SUD 313 Hk 39
Galela ○ RI 275 Lp 45
Galema ○ LB 316 Gb 42
Galena ○ USA 6 Ba 3
Galena ○ USA 46 Al 13
Galena ○ USA 56 Dc 24
Galena Bay ○ CDN 50 Cd 20
Gāleq ○ IR 226 Jk 32
Galera ○ EC 116 Dh 45
Galera ~ BR 132 Ee 53
Galera Point ⌓ TT 104 Ed 40
Galerazamba ○ CO 106 Dl 40
Galesburg ○ USA 71 Dc 25
Galesville ○ USA 56 Dc 23
Galēti Shet' ~ ETH 325 Hn 41
Galeton ○ CDN 57 Dh 20
Galgamuwa ○ CL 239 Kd 42
Galheirã ~ BR 133 Em 52
Galheiros ○ BR 133 El 52
Gali ○ GE 202 Hn 24
Galia ○ BR 140 Ek 57
Galiba ○ IRQ 215 Jb 30
Galibi ○ SME 113 Eg 43
Galič ○ RUS 171 Hn 16
Galicia ⊙ E 184 Gb 24
Galičskaja vozvyšsennosť ⛰ RUS 171 Hn 17
Galiléia ○ BR 141 Ep 55
Galim ○ CAM 320 Gm 43
Galim ○ CAM 320 Gn 42
Galio ○ PNG 287 Mm 48
Galion ○ USA 71 Dg 25
Galital Point ⌓ PNG 286 Mg 50
Galivedu ○ IND 238 Kd 39
Galiwinku ○ AUS 364 Md 51
Gallābāt ○ SUD 313 Hk 39
Gallaorol ○ UZB 223 Jm 26
Gallatin ○ USA 70 Db 26
Gallatin ○ USA 71 De 27
Galle ○ CL 239 Kd 42
Gállego ~ E 184 Gf 24
Gallegos ○ USA 65 Cl 28
Gallegos ~ RA 152 Dn 71
Gallegos ~ RA 152 Dp 71
Galleguillos ○ RCH 136 Dn 59
Gallipoli ○ I 194 Ha 25
Gallipoli ○ AUS 365 Me 55
Gallipolis ○ USA 71 Dg 26
Gällivare ○ S 159 Hb 12
Gallo Mountains ⛰ USA 65 Ch 28
Galloway ⛰ GB 162 Gd 18
Gallup ○ USA 65 Ch 28
Galmi ○ RN 308 Gj 38
Galo Boukoy ○ RCA 321 Gp 43
Galool ○ SP 328 Hp 44
Gal Oya National Park ♀ CL 239 Ke 42
Gālrēz ○ AFG 223 Jn 28
Gal Shiikh ○ SP 328 Jb 40
Galt ○ USA 64 Cb 26
Gal Tardo ○ SP 328 Ja 44
Galtat-Zemmour ○ MA 292 Fp 33
Galūgāh ○ IR 222 Je 27
Galūla ○ IRQ 209 Ja 28
Galung ○ RI 279 Lk 47
Galva ○ USA 71 Dc 25
Galvão ○ BR 140 Eh 59
Galveston ○ USA 81 Da 31
Galveston Island ⌂ USA 81 Da 31
Galvez ~ PE 116 Dm 48
Gálvez ○ RA 137 Ed 62
Galway ○ IRL 163 Gb 19
Galway Bay ~ IRL 163 Gb 19
Galway Downs ○ AUS 374 Mh 58
Gam ○ TJ 223 Jp 26
Gam ○ NAM 348 Hc 56
Gama ○ BR 133 Ek 54
Gama River ~ PNG 286 Mh 49
Gāmasiāb ~ IR 209 Jb 28
Gamawa ○ WAN 320 Gm 39
Gamba ○ G 332 Gm 47
Gamba ○ RDC 333 He 48
Gamba ○ ANG 340 Ha 51
Gambaga ○ GH 317 Gf 40
Gambang ○ MAL 271 Lb 44
Gambara ○ MEX 92 Cl 36
Gambēla ○ ETH 325 Hk 41
Gambela National Park ♀ ETH 325 Hk 42
Gambell ○ USA 46 Ac 13
Gambia ◻ WAG 316 Fm 39
Gambia ~ WAG 316 Fm 39
Gambie ~ RG 316 Fp 39
Gambie ~ SN 316 Fp 39
Gambier Island ⌂ AUS 378 Me 63
Gambier Islands ⌂ F 14 Ca 12
Gambo ○ CDN 61 Eg 21
Gambo ~ RG 316 Ga 40
Gambo ○ RCA 321 Hd 43
Gamboa ○ PA 97 Dj 41
Gamboma ○ RCB 332 Gp 46
Gamboula ○ RCA 321 Gp 43
Gamdou ○ RN 320 Gl 39
Gamelair ~ BR 133 Ej 51
Gameleira ~ BR 133 El 53
Gameleira da Lapa ○ BR 125 En 52
Gamğamāl ○ IRQ 209 Ja 28
Gāmid az-Zinād ○ KSA 218 Hn 36
Gamis ○ NAM 348 Ha 58
Gamkab ~ NAM 348 Ha 60
Gamkahe ○ RI 275 Lp 45
Gamkarivier ~ ZA 358 Hc 62
Gammelstad ○ S 159 Hd 13
Gammon Ranges ♀ AUS 378 Mf 61
Gamoep ○ ZA 348 Hb 60
Gamperé △ CAM 321 Gn 42
Gamr ○ ET 301 Hh 30
Gamra ○ RIM 304 Fp 37
Gamsa ○ ET 301 Hj 32
Gamsār ○ AFG 227 Jk 30
Gamsberg △ NAM 348 Ha 57
Gamud △ ETH 325 Hm 43
Gamūm ○ KSA 218 Hm 35
Gamvik ○ N 159 Hg 10
Ganab ○ NAM 348 Gp 57
Ganado ○ USA 65 Ch 28
Ganamub ○ NAM 340 Gn 55
Gananita ○ SUD 312 Hj 36
Gananoque ○ CDN 60 Dk 23
Ganāt as-Suwais ~ ET 301 Hj 30
Gāncā ○ AZ 202 Ja 25
Ganda ○ ANG 340 Gp 52
Gandajika ○ RDC 333 Hd 49
Gandak ~ IND 235 Kg 32
Gandaq ○ IR 222 Jf 28
Gandara ○ RP 267 Ln 40
Gandarbat ○ IND 230 Kb 28
Gandāva ○ PK 227 Jm 31
Gande ○ WAN 320 Gj 39
Gander ○ CDN 61 Eg 21
Gander ~ CDN 61 Eg 21
Gander Bay ○ CDN 61 Eg 21
Gander Lake ~ CDN 61 Eg 21
Gandesa ○ E 184 Gg 25
Gāndhi Dham ○ IND 227 Jn 34
Gāndhinagar ○ IND 227 Ka 34
Gāndhi Sāgar ~ IND 234 Kb 33
Gāndhi Sāgar Colony ○ IND 234 Kb 33
Gandia ○ E 184 Gf 26
Gandiaye ○ SN 304 Fm 38
Gandō-ko ~ J 250 Mg 26
Gandomak ○ AFG 223 Jn 28
Gandoman ○ IR 215 Jd 30
Gandu ○ BR 125 Fa 52
Gâneb ○ RIM 304 Ga 36
Ganesh △ NEP 235 Kg 31
Ganga ~ IND 234 Kd 31
Ganga Ganges ~ IND 234 Ke 32
Ganga Ganges ~ IND 235 Kf 33
Gangačin ○ IR 209 Ja 27
Gangākher ○ IND 238 Kc 36
Gangala na Bodio ○ RDC 324 Hg 44
Gangán ○ RA 147 Dp 67
Ganganagar ○ IND 227 Ka 31
Gangāpur ○ IND 234 Kb 33
Gangara ○ RN 308 Gl 38
Gangaw ○ MYA 254 Kl 34
Gangca ○ VRC 242 La 27
Gangchang ○ VRC 243 Le 30
Gangdisê Shan ⛰ VRC 230 Kf 30
Ganges ○ F 185 Gh 24
Ganges ~ IND 234 Ke 32
Ganges ~ IND 235 Kg 33
Ganges ~ BD 235 Kk 34
Gangir ~ IR 209 Ja 29
Gang Jiang ~ VRC 258 Lh 32
Gangkha ○ BHT 235 Kj 32
Gango ~ ANG 340 Gp 51
Gangotri ○ IND 230 Kd 30
Gangtok ○ IND 235 Kj 32
Gangu ○ RDC 324 Hd 43
Gangula ○ ANG 340 Gn 51
Gangure ○ MOC 344 Hm 51
Ganhe ○ VRC 204 Wa 8
Gani ○ RI 283 Ma 46
Ganī Hēl ○ AFG 223 Jn 29
Ganjuškino ○ KZ 202 Jc 22
Gankar Punsum △ BHT 235 Kk 32
Gan'kovo ○ RUS 171 Hj 16
Ganluo ○ VRC 255 Lb 31
Gannat ○ F 163 Gh 22
Ganquan ○ VRC 243 Le 27
Gansbaai ○ ZA 358 Hb 63
Gansé ○ CI 317 Ge 41
Gansen ○ VRC 231 Kl 27
Gansu ⊙ VRC 242 Kn 25
Gansu ⊙ VRC 242 Lc 28
Ganta ○ LB 316 Gb 42
Gantang ○ VRC 242 Lc 27
Gantheaume Bay ~ AUS 368 Lg 59
Gantheaume Point ⌓ AUS 360 Ll 54
Gantira ○ RI 282 Ll 47
Ganye ○ WAN 320 Gm 41
Ganyesa ○ ZA 349 Hd 59
Ganyh ~ AZ 202 Jb 25
Ganyu ○ VRC 246 Lk 28
Ganze ~ RDC 333 He 48
Ganzhou ○ VRC 258 Lh 33
Gao ○ RMM 305 Gf 37
Gao ○ BF 317 Ge 40
Gao ○ RDC 324 Hg 44
Gao'an ○ VRC 258 Lh 31
Gaochun ○ VRC 246 Lk 30
Gaofengtao ○ VRC 246 Lj 28
Gaogou ○ VRC 246 Lk 29
Gaohezhen ○ VRC 246 Lj 30
Gaojiabu ○ VRC 243 Lf 26
Gaolan ○ VRC 242 Lb 27
Gaolan ★ VRC 243 Lf 30
Gaomi ○ VRC 246 Lk 27
Gaoping ○ VRC 243 Lg 28
Gaotai ○ VRC 242 Kp 26
Gaotang ○ VRC 246 Lj 27
Gaoua ○ BF 317 Ge 40
Gaoual ○ RG 316 Fp 40
Gao Xian ○ VRC 255 Lc 31
Gaoyi ○ VRC 243 Lh 27
Gaoyou ○ VRC 246 Lk 29
Gaoyou Hu ~ VRC 246 Lk 29
Gaozhou ○ VRC 255 Lf 35
Gap ○ F 185 Gk 23
Gapi ○ RDC 324 Hf 43
Gapuwiyak ○ AUS 364 Md 52
Garabil ⛰ TM 223 Jk 27
Garabinzam ○ RCB 332 Gn 45
Garacad ○ SP 328 Jc 42
Garachico ○ E 292 Fm 31
Garachine ○ PA 97 Dk 41
Garada ○ SUD 312 Hh 36
Garadag ○ SP 328 Jb 41
Gara-Ekar △ DZ 308 Gj 36
Garagoa ○ CO 107 Dm 43
Garah ○ AUS 375 Ml 60
Garaina ○ PNG 287 Mk 49
Gara Khannfoussa △ DZ 296 Gk 32
Garalo ○ RMM 305 Gc 40
Garamba ~ RDC 324 Hg 44
Garampani ○ IND 235 Kl 32
Gara Nasa △ ETH 325 Hk 41
Garandal ○ JOR 214 Hk 30
Garango ○ BF 317 Gf 40
Garanhuns ○ BR 124 Fb 50
Ga-Rankuwa ○ ZA 349 Hf 58
Garapuava ○ BR 133 El 54
Garāra ○ KSA 215 Jb 32
Garasa ○ PNG 287 Ml 50
Garaš ○ JOR 208 Hk 29
Garawe ○ LB 316 Gb 43
Garayalde ○ RA 152 Ea 68
Garba ○ RCA 321 Hc 41
Garbahaarrey ○ SP 325 Hn 44
Garba Tula ○ EAK 325 Hm 45
Garberville ○ USA 64 Bp 25
Garças ou Jacaréguea ~ BR 133 Eh 53
Garchitorena ○ RP 267 Lm 39
Garda ○ I 185 Gm 23
Gardabah ⏜ LAR 300 Hd 31
Gardabani ○ GE 202 Ja 25
Gardandēvāl ○ AFG 223 Jm 28
Gardelegen ○ D 170 Gm 19
Garden City ○ USA 70 Cm 26
Garden City ○ USA 87 Dj 29
Garden Peninsula ⌂ USA 57 De 23
Gardēz ○ AFG 223 Jn 29
Gardiner ○ USA 51 Cg 23
Gardiner ○ CDN 57 Dh 21
Gardiner ○ USA 60 Dp 23
Gardner ○ USA 56 Cp 22
Gardner ○ USA 65 Ck 27
Gardner Plateau ⛰ AUS 361 Ln 53
Gardnerville ○ USA 64 Cc 26
Gárdony ○ H 174 Hb 22
Garessio ○ I 185 Gk 23
Garet el Djenoun ⛰ DZ 296 Gj 33
Gare Tigre ○ F 113 Eh 43
Gar et Tarf ~ DZ 296 Gk 28
Garfield ○ AUS 375 Mj 57
Garford ○ AUS 369 Mc 60
Gargando ○ RMM 305 Gd 37
Gargoni ~ ETH 313 Hn 40
Gargouna ○ RMM 305 Gg 38
Gargždai ○ LT 170 Hc 18
Garhchiroli ○ IND 234 Ke 35
Garhshankar ○ IND 230 Kb 30
Gariāband ○ IND 234 Ke 35
Gariau ○ RI 283 Md 47
Garib ○ NAM 348 Ha 57
Garibaldi ○ BR 146 Ej 60
Gariep Dam ~ ZA 349 He 61
Garies ○ ZA 348 Hb 61
Gariganus ○ NAM 348 Hb 59
Garimari ○ PNG 287 Ml 48
Garinais ○ NAM 348 Hb 59
Garissa ○ EAK 337 Hm 46
Garkida ○ WAN 320 Gn 40
Garladinne ○ IND 238 Kc 38
Garland ○ CDN 56 Cm 20
Garland ○ USA 70 Cp 29
Garmabe ○ SUD 324 Hh 43
Garme ○ IR 222 Jg 27
Garmisch-Partenkirchen ○ D 174 Gm 22
Garmsār ⏜ AFG 226 Jk 30
Garner ○ USA 56 Db 24
Garnett ○ USA 70 Da 26
Garnett ○ USA 71 Dh 29
Garnish ○ CDN 61 Eg 22
Garonne ~ F 184 Gg 24
Garoowe ○ SP 328 Jc 41
Garoua ○ CAM 321 Gn 41
Garoua Boulai ○ CAM 321 Gp 43
Garove Island ⌂ PNG 287 Ml 48
Garrāhi ~ IR 215 Jc 30
Garré ○ RA 137 Ec 64
Garrett ○ USA 51 Ck 24
Garrison ○ USA 51 Cf 22
Garrison ○ USA 56 Db 22
Garro ○ MEX 93 Da 36
Garruchas ○ RA 146 Ef 60
Garry Lake ~ CDN 6 Db 3
Garry Lake ~ CDN 42 Fa 5
Garsala ○ SP 329 Ja 44
Garsen ○ EAK 337 Hm 47
Garsila ○ SUD 312 Hd 39
Garston ○ NZ 382 Ng 68
Gartempe ~ F 163 Gg 22
Garu ○ PNG 287 Ml 48
Garuahi ○ PNG 287 Mm 51
Garūb ○ YE 219 Je 36
Garuma ○ RCH 136 Dp 57
Garusovo ○ RUS 171 Hk 17
Garut ○ RI 278 Ld 49
Garuva ○ BR 141 Ek 59
Garwa ○ IND 235 Kf 33
Garwolin ○ PL 174 Hc 20
Gar Xincun ○ VRC 230 Ke 29
Gary ○ USA 71 De 25
Garyarsa ○ VRC 230 Ke 30
Garza ○ RA 136 Ec 60
Garza Garcia ○ MEX 81 Cm 33
Garzê ○ VRC 242 Kp 30
Garzón ○ CO 106 Dl 44
Gaschiga ○ CAM 321 Gn 41
Gascogny ⏜ F 184 Gf 24
Gasconade ~ USA 70 Dc 26
Gascoyne ~ AUS 368 Lj 58
Gascoyne Junction ○ AUS 368 Lh 58
Gasera ○ ETH 325 Hn 42
Gash ~ ER 313 Hl 38
Gashaka ○ WAN 320 Gm 42
Gasherbrum I △ PK 230 Kc 28
Gasherbrum II △ PK 230 Kc 28
Gas Hu ~ VRC 231 Kk 26
Gashua ○ WAN 320 Gm 39
Gashunchaka ○ VRC 242 Km 27
Ğasim ○ RI 283 Mb 46
Ğāsk ○ IR 226 Jg 33
Gasmata ○ PNG 287 Mm 49
Gaspé ○ CDN 61 Eb 21
Ğaşşān ○ IRQ 209 Ja 29
Gassan ○ BF 317 Ge 39
Gassi Touil ⏜ DZ 296 Gk 31
Gassol ○ WAN 320 Gm 41
Ğašt ○ IR 226 Jj 32
Gastona ~ RA 136 Eb 59
Gastonia ○ USA 71 Dh 28
Gastro ○ RA 147 Dp 67
Gata ○ CV 316 Fj 37
Gatafe ○ E 184 Ge 25
Gatanga ○ RDC 324 Hd 44
Gatanga ○ SUD 324 Hf 42
Gatčina ○ RUS 171 Hg 16
Gate City ○ USA 71 Dg 27
Gates ○ USA 60 Dj 24
Gateshead Island ⌂ CDN 42 Fa 4
Gates of the Arctic National Park&Preserve ♀ USA 46 An 11
Gatesville ○ USA 81 Cp 30
Gateway ○ USA 70 Db 27
Gati-Loumo ○ RMM 305 Gd 38
Gatineau ○ CDN 60 Dk 23
Gatineau ~ CDN 60 Dl 22
Ğatkal ~ KS 223 Jp 25
Gatlinburg ○ USA 71 Dg 28
Ğaţţi ○ KSA 214 Hl 30
Gatton ○ AUS 375 Mn 59
Gaturiano ○ BR 124 Ep 49
Gaua ⌂ VU 386 Nf 53
Gaudan ○ TM 222 Jh 27
Gaujas ♀ LV 171 He 17
Gaula ~ N 158 Gm 14
Gauley Bridge ○ USA 71 Dh 26
Gauley Mountain △ USA 71 Dh 26
Gaurdak ○ TM 223 Jm 27
Gauribidanūr Chik ○ IND 238 Kc 39
Gausta △ N 170 Gl 16
Gavand ○ AFG 223 Jl 28
Gāvbandī ○ IR 215 Je 32
Gāvbast △ IR 215 Je 32
Gávdos ⌂ GR 194 Hd 28
Gave d. Pau ~ F 184 Gf 24
Gāve Rūd ~ IR 209 Jb 28
Gavião ~ BR 125 Ep 53
Gavião ○ BR 125 Fa 51
Gavião ○ P 184 Gc 26
Gavien ○ PNG 287 Mj 47
Gaviota ○ USA 64 Cb 28
Gävle ○ S 158 Ha 15
Gavrilov-Jam ○ RUS 171 Hm 17
Gávrio ○ GR 194 He 27
Gavunipalli ○ IND 238 Kd 39
Gawachab ○ NAM 348 Ha 59
Gawa Island ⌂ PNG 287 Mm 50
Gawa Obo ○ VRC 242 Kn 28
Gāwilgar Hills ⛰ IND 234 Kc 35
Gawler ○ AUS 378 Mf 63
Gawler Ranges ⛰ AUS 378 Md 62
Gawu ○ WAN 320 Gk 41
Gay ○ USA 86 Df 29
Gaya ○ IND 235 Kg 33
Gaya ○ RN 320 Gh 40
Gaya ○ WAN 320 Gl 40
Gayam ○ TCH 321 Ha 41
Gayaza ○ EAU 336 Hh 46
Gayéri ○ BF 317 Gg 39
Gaylord ○ USA 57 Df 23
Gaza ○ IL 208 Hj 30
Ğazāb ○ AFG 223 Jm 29
Ğazā'ir Farasān ⌂ KSA 218 Hn 37
Ğazā'ir Ḫuriyā Muriyā al-Ḫallāniyāt ⌂ OM 219 Jf 37
Gazakh ○ AZ 202 Ja 25
Gazalkent ○ UZB 223 Jn 25
Gazanak ○ IR 222 Jd 28
Gazaoua ○ RN 320 Gk 39
Gazelle Channel ~ PNG 287 Mm 47
Gazelle Peninsula ⌂ PNG 287 Mm 48
Gazerān ○ IR 222 Jd 28
Gazi ○ EAK 337 Hm 48
Gazi Antep ○ TR 195 Hl 27
Gazipaşa ○ TR 195 Hh 27
Ğazipur ○ BD 235 Kk 34
Ğazīrat Abū 'Ali ⌂ KSA 215 Jc 32
Ğazīrat al-Bāṭina ⌂ KSA 215 Jc 32
Ğazīrat an-Nu'mān ⌂ KSA 214 Hk 32
Ğazīrat aṣ-Ṣabāyā ⌂ KSA 218 Hn 36
Ğazīrat Birrīm ⌂ KSA 214 Hl 33
Ğazīrat Dissān ⌂ KSA 218 Hn 37
Ğazīrat Dungunāb ⌂ SUD 313 Hl 35
Ğazīrat Ğawwār ⌂ KSA 214 Hl 33
Ğazīrat Hawār ⌂ BRN 215 Jd 33
Ğazīrat Mukawwa' ⌂ SUD 313 Hl 35
Ğazīrat Sadwān ⌂ ET 301 Hk 32
Ğazīrat Safāğa ⌂ ET 301 Hk 32
Ğazīrat Şağd ⌂ KSA 218 Hn 37
Ğazīrat Şaibāra ⌂ KSA 214 Hl 33
Ğazīrat Sanāfīr ⌂ ET 301 Hk 32
Ğazīrat Tīrān ⌂ ET 301 Hk 32
Ğazīre-ye Abū Mūsā ⌂ IR 226 Jf 33
Ğazīre-ye Forūr ⌂ IR 215 Je 32
Ğazīre-ye Ğabrīn ⌂ IR 215 Jd 32
Ğazīre-ye Ḫārk ⌂ IR 215 Jc 31
Ğazīre-ye Hendorābī ⌂ IR 215 Je 32
Ğazīre-ye Kīš ⌂ IR 215 Je 32
Ğazīre-ye Sirrī ⌂ IR 226 Jf 33
Gazli ○ UZB 223 Jk 25
Ğaznī ⊙ AFG 223 Jm 29
Gazojak ○ TM 223 Jj 25
Gbaboua ○ CAM 321 Gp 42
Gbadolite ○ RDC 321 Hc 43
Gbaïzera ○ RCA 321 Hb 42
Gbalatuai ○ LB 316 Gb 42
Gbanga ○ WAN 320 Gk 41
Gbangbatok ○ WAL 316 Fp 42
Gbanhala ~ RG 316 Gb 41
Gbapleu ○ CI 316 Gb 42
Gbarnga ○ LB 316 Gb 42
Gbatala ○ LB 316 Gb 42
Gbélédan ○ CI 316 Gb 41
Gbengué ○ BF 317 Ge 40
Gberia Timbako ○ WAL 316 Ga 41
Gbérouboué ○ DY 320 Gh 40
Gboko ○ WAN 320 Gl 42
Gbotata ○ LB 316 Gb 42
Gbwado ○ RDC 321 Hc 44
Gdańsk ○ PL 170 Hb 18
Gdor. Igr. Valentín Virasoro ○ RA 140 Ef 59
Gdor. Mayer ○ RA 152 Dn 71
Gdor. Moyano ○ RA 152 Dp 69
Gdor. Solá ○ RA 146 Ee 62
Gdov ○ RUS 171 Hf 16
Gdyel ○ DZ 293 Gf 28
Gdynia ○ PL 170 Hb 18
Geary ○ USA 70 Cn 28
Geba Wenz ~ ETH 325 Hk 41
Gebeit ○ SUD 313 Hl 36
Gebituolatuo ○ VRC 231 Kl 26
Gebre Guracha ○ ETH 325 Hl 41
Gebze ○ TR 195 Hg 25
Gech'a ○ ETH 325 Hk 42
Gedabiet ○ ETH 313 Hl 39
Gedi ○ EAK 337 Hm 47
Gedi Ruins ★ EAK 337 Hn 47
Gediz ○ TR 195 Hg 26
Gediz Nehri ~ TR 195 Hf 26
Gedlegubē ○ ETH 328 Ja 42
Gēdo ○ ETH 325 Hl 41
Gedongratu ○ RI 278 Lc 48
Gedser ○ DK 170 Gm 18
Geelong ○ AUS 379 Mj 65
Geelvink Channel ~ AUS 368 Lg 60
Geesaley ○ SP 328 Jd 40
Geeveston ○ AUS 378 Mk 67
Gēğa Shet' ~ ETH 313 Hn 40
Gegbwema ○ WAL 316 Ga 42
Ge'gyai ○ VRC 230 Ke 29
Geidam ○ WAN 320 Gm 39
Geikie Island ⌂ CDN 57 Dd 20
Geiki Gorge ♀ AUS 361 Ln 55
Geilo ○ N 158 Gl 15
Geirangerfjorden ★ N 158 Gk 14
Geiro ○ EAT 337 Hl 49
Geiser del Tatio ○ RCH 136 Dp 57
Geita ○ EAT 336 Hj 47
Gejiu ○ VRC 255 Lb 34
Gel ~ SUD 324 Hg 42
Gela ○ I 185 Gp 27
Geladaindong △ VRC 231 Kk 29
Geladı ○ ETH 328 Jb 42
Gelai △ EAT 337 Hl 47
Gele ○ RDC 321 Hb 43
Gelendžik ○ RUS 195 Hl 23
Gelemso ○ ETH 325 Hn 41
Gelibolu ○ TR 194 Hf 25
Gelila ○ ETH 325 Hl 41
Gellāb ○ SUD 324 He 41
Gellinsoor ○ SP 328 Jb 42
Gelsenkirchen ○ D 163 Gk 20
Gelumbang ○ RI 278 Lc 47
Gemas ○ MAL 270 Lb 44
Gembogl ○ PNG 287 Mj 48
Gembu ○ WAN 320 Gm 42
Geme ○ RI 275 Lp 43
Gemena ○ RDC 333 Hb 44
Gemerek ○ TR 195 Hl 26
Gemeri Hāyk' ~ ETH 313 Hn 40
Gemi △ ETH 325 Hk 41
Gemlik ○ TR 195 Hg 25
Gemlik Gör ~ TR 195 Hg 25
Gemmeiza ○ SUD 313 Hk 37
Gemmeiza ○ SUD 324 Hg 42
Gemmeiza ○ SUD 324 Hh 43
Gemona d. Fr. ○ I 174 Gn 22
Gemsbok ♀ RB 348 Hc 58
Genalē Wenz ~ ETH 325 Hm 42
Gendarān Bāshī △ IR 209 Jb 26
Gendarme C. Barreto ○ RA 152 Dn 71
General Acha ○ RA 137 Eb 64
General Alvear ○ RA 137 Ea 63
General Alvear Velloso ○ RA 146 Ee 64
General Arenales ○ RA 137 Ed 63
General Ballivián ○ PY 136 Ec 57
General Belgrano ○ RA 146 Ee 63
General Bravo ○ MEX 81 Cn 33
General Cabrera ○ RA 137 Eb 62
General Cepeda ○ MEX 81 Cm 33
General Comacho ○ BOL 128 Dp 54
General Conesa ○ RA 146 Ef 64
General Conesa ○ RA 147 Eb 66
General Elizardo Aquino ○ PY 140 Ef 58
General Enrique Martinez ○ ROU 146 Eh 62
General Eugenio a Garay ○ PY 136 Ec 56
General Güemes ○ RA 136 Eb 58
General José de San Martin ○ RA 140 Ee 59
General Juan Madariaga ○ RA 146 Ef 64
General la Madrid ○ RA 137 Ed 64
General Lavalle ○ RA 137 Ec 62
General Luna ○ RP 267 Lp 41
General M. Belgrano ○ RA 140 Ee 58
General Mansilla ○ RA 146 Ef 63
General Pico ○ RA 137 Eb 63
General Pinedo ○ RA 136 Ed 59
General R. M. Quevedo Palomas ○ MEX 80 Cj 30
General Roca ○ RA 147 Ea 65
General San Martín ○ RA 137 Eb 62
General San Martin ○ RA 147 Ec 65
General Santos ○ RP 275 Ln 42
General Simón Bolívar ○ MEX 81 Cl 33
General Terán ○ MEX 81 Cn 33
General Toševo ○ BG 195 Hg 24
General Treviño ○ MEX 81 Cn 32
General Trías ○ MEX 80 Cj 31
General Viamonte ○ RA 137 Ed 63
General Villegas ○ RA 137 Ec 63
Geneseo ○ USA 60 Dj 24
Geneseo ○ USA 71 Dc 25
Genet ○ ETH 325 Hm 41
Geneva ○ USA 60 Dk 24
Geneva ○ USA 65 Cg 24
Geneva ○ USA 70 Cp 25
Geneva ○ USA 71 Dh 25
Geneva ○ CH 163 Gk 22
Gengma ○ VRC 254 Kp 34
Genil ~ E 184 Gd 27
Genipapo ○ BR 121 Em 49
Genk ○ B 163 Gj 20
Genkai-nada ~ J 247 Ma 29
Genoa ○ I 185 Gl 23
Genoa ○ AUS 379 Ml 64
Genteng ○ RI 278 Ld 49
Genteng ○ RI 279 Lg 50
Genting ○ RI 270 Kn 44
Genyem ○ RI 286 Mg 47
Geogr.Cen.of the 48 Con.States ★ USA 70 Cn 26
Geogr.Center of North America ★ USA 56 Cm 21
Geograph.Center of the U.S.Marker ★ USA 51 Cl 23
Geographe Bay ~ AUS 368 Lh 62
Geographer Channel ~ AUS 368 Lg 58
Geographical Center of the 48 Contiguous States ★ USA 70 Cn 26
Geok-Tepe ○ TM 222 Jg 26
George ○ ZA 358 Hd 62
George ~ AUS 360 Lj 56
George Gill Range ⛰ AUS 369 Mb 58
George Island ⌂ GB 147 Ee 72
George Sound ~ NZ 382 Nf 68
Georgetown ○ USA 71 Df 26
Georgetown ○ USA 74 Dl 26
Georgetown ○ USA 81 Cp 30
Georgetown ○ USA 87 Dj 29
George Town ○ BS 87 Dl 34
Georgetown ○ GB 100 Dh 36
Georgetown ○ WV 104 Ed 39
Georgetown ▣ GUY 113 Ee 42
George Town ○ MAL 270 Kp 43
Georgetown ○ WAG 316 Fn 39
Georgetown ○ AUS 365 Mh 55
Georgetown ○ AUS 378 Mk 66
George V Coast ⏜ 38 Sa 16
George Washington Birthplace National Monument ★ USA 74 Dk 26
George Washington Carver N.M. ★ USA 70 Da 27
George West ○ USA 81 Cn 31
Georgia ⊙ USA 86 Df 29
Georgia ◻ GE 202 Hn 24
Georgiana ○ USA 86 De 30
Georgian Bay ~ CDN 57 Dh 23
Georgievka ○ KZ 204 Tb 9
Georgievsk ○ RUS 202 Hp 23
Georgina ~ AUS 374 Mf 56
Georgina Downs ○ AUS 374 Me 56
Gera ○ D 174 Gm 20
Geradmer ○ F 163 Gk 21
Geráki ○ GR 194 Hd 27
Geraldine ○ USA 51 Cg 22
Geraldine ○ NZ 382 Nh 68
Geraldton ○ AUS 368 Lh 60
Geralton ○ CDN 57 De 21
Geranium ○ AUS 378 Mg 63
Gerāš ○ IR 215 Je 32
Gerber Reservoir ~ USA 50 Cb 24
Gerdau ○ ZA 349 Hf 59
Gerede ○ TR 195 Hh 25
Gerede Çayı ~ TR 195 Hj 25
Gerihun ○ WAL 316 Ga 42
Gerik ○ MAL 270 La 43
Gerlach ○ USA 64 Cc 25
German Bight ~ D 170 Gk 18
German Creek ○ AUS 375 Ml 57
Germania ○ RA 137 Ec 63
Germansen Landing ○ CDN 47 Bn 17
Germantown ○ USA 57 Dd 24
Germantown ○ USA 71 Dd 28
Germany ◻ D 174 Gk 20
Germencik ○ TR 195 Hf 27
Germī ○ IR 209 Jb 26
Germiston ○ ZA 349 Hf 59
Gero ○ J 251 Me 28
Geroliménas ○ GR 194 Hd 27
Gerona ○ RP 267 Ll 38
Gers ~ F 184 Gg 24
Gerūf ○ JOR 214 Hk 30
Gerze ○ TR 195 Hk 25
Gêrzê ○ VRC 231 Kg 29
Geta ○ FIN 170 Hb 15
Geti ○ RDC 324 Hh 45
Gettysburg ○ USA 56 Cn 23
Gettysburg ○ USA 74 Dk 26
Gettysburg N.M.P. ★ USA 74 Dk 26
Getúlio Vargas ○ BR 140 Eh 59
Gevgelija ○ MK 194 Hd 25
Gevrai ○ IND 238 Kb 36
Gewanē ○ ETH 313 Hn 40
Geylegphug ○ BHT 235 Kk 32
Geyve ○ TR 195 Hh 25
Gezhou Ba Gezhou Dam ★ VRC 243 Lf 30
Gezhou Dam ★ VRC 243 Lf 30
Ghaba ○ OM 219 Jg 35
Ghadāmis ○ LAR 296 Gl 30
Ghaddūwah ○ LAR 297 Gp 32
Ghaghara ~ IND 234 Kf 32
Ghaghe Island ⌂ SOL 290 Nb 49
Ghagra ○ IND 235 Kg 34
Ghaibi Dero ○ PK 227 Jm 32
Ghairatganj ○ IND 234 Kd 34
Ghallamane ⏜ RIM 304 Ga 34
Ghana ◻ GH 317 Gf 41
Ghanzi ○ RB 348 Hc 56
Gharb Binna ○ SUD 312 Hg 36
Ghardaïa ○ DZ 296 Gh 29
Ghardimaou ○ TN 296 Gl 27
Gharig ○ SUD 312 Hf 40
Gharyān ○ LAR 297 Gn 29
Ghāt ○ LAR 296 Gm 33
Ghātāl ○ IND 235 Kh 34
Ghātampur ○ IND 234 Ke 32
Ghātsila ○ IND 235 Kh 34
Ghauspur ○ PK 227 Jn 31
Ghazaouet ○ DZ 293 Gf 28
Ghaziābād ○ IND 234 Kc 31
Ghāzīpur ○ IND 234 Kf 33
Ghazluna ○ PK 227 Jm 30
Ghent ○ B 163 Gh 20
Gheorgheni ○ RO 175 He 22
Gherdi ○ IND 238 Kb 37
Ghimpaţi ○ RO 175 He 23
Ghizar ○ PK 230 Ka 27
Ghizar ~ PK 230 Ka 27
Ghizo ○ SOL 290 Na 50
Ghizo Island ⌂ SOL 290 Na 50
Gho Dâ ○ VN 255 Lc 34
Ghomrassen ○ TN 296 Gl 29
Ghoraffa ○ DZ 296 Gk 29
Ghorahi ○ NEP 234 Kf 31
Ghosla ○ IND 234 Kb 34
Ghost Towns ★ USA 50 Ce 23
Ghot ○ IND 238 Ke 36
Ghotanu ○ IND 227 Jp 32
Ghotki ○ PK 227 Jn 32
Ghoveo ○ SOL 290 Nb 50
Ghriss ○ DZ 293 Gg 28
Ghuar ○ IND 227 Jn 34
Ghubaysh ○ SUD 312 Hf 39
Ghubbat al Qamar ~ YE 219 Je 37
Ghumthang ○ NEP 235 Kg 32
Ghutkel ○ IND 234 Ke 35
Giaginskaja ○ RUS 202 Hn 23
GiāiTru'o'ng So'n ⛰ VN 255 Lc 36
Gialalassi ○ SP 328 Ja 44
Giamonaki ○ PNG 287 Ml 50
Giàng ○ VN 263 Ld 38
Giang Trung ⛰ VN 263 Le 39
Giannitsá ○ GR 194 Hd 25
Giant Buddha ★ VRC 255 Lb 31
Giant Forest ○ USA 64 Cc 27
Giant's Causeway ★ GB 162 Gc 18
Gianyar ○ RI 279 Lh 50
Gia Rai ○ VN 263 Lc 41
Giarre ○ I 185 Gp 27
Gia Vúc' ○ VN 263 Le 38
Gibara ○ C 101 Dk 35
Gibb ~ AUS 361 Lp 53
Gibbon ○ USA 50 Cc 23
Gibb River ○ AUS 361 Lp 54
Gibeon ○ NAM 348 Ha 58
Gibē Shet' ~ ETH 325 Hl 42
Gibē Wenz ~ ETH 325 Hl 41
Gibraltar ○ GB 184 Gd 27

420 Galata - Gibraltar

□Country ⊡Capital city ⊙Administrative unit OPlace ♁Island ⩕Mountain range △Mountain ⌒Cape ≈Ocean, Sea ~Lake, River ∀Undersea topography ▲Glacier ♀National park •••Reservation ★Point of major interest ⌓Landscape

Gibraltar Range ♀ AUS 375 Mn 60
Gibson City O USA 71 Dd 25
Gibson Desert ⌓ AUS 361 Ln 57
Gibsons O CDN 50 Ca 21
Gida O WAN 320 Gm 42
Gidam O IND 238 Ke 36
Gidami O ETH 325 Hk 41
Gīdar O PK 227 Jl 31
Giddalur O IND 238 Kd 38
Ǧiddat al-Harāsīs ⌓ OM 219 Jf 36
Giddings O USA 81 Cp 30
Gideån ~ S 158 Hb 14
Gidgee O AUS 368 Lk 59
Gīdolē O ETH 325 Hl 43
Gielnaga del Coro O RA 137 Eb 61
Gien O F 163 Gh 22
Gießen O D 174 Gl 20
Gifford Creek O AUS 368 Lj 58
Gifu O J 251 Me 28
Gigüela ~ E 184 Ge 26
Ǧiḥāna O YE 218 Ja 38
Gihofi O BU 336 Hh 47
Gijón O E 184 Gd 24
Gikongoro O RWA 336 Hg 47
Gila ~ USA 64 Cf 29
Gila Bend O USA 64 Cf 29
Gila Cliff Dwellings N.M. ★ USA 65 Ch 29
Gīlān ⊙ IR 209 Jc 27
Gīlān O AFG 223 Jm 29
Gīlān-e Garb O IR 209 Ja 28
Gila River ~ USA 65 Ch 29
Gila River Indian Reservation ••• USA 65 Cf 29
Gilbert ~ AUS 365 Mg 54
Gilbert Islands ♁ KIR 27 Tb 9
Gilberton O AUS 365 Mh 55
Gilbert River O AUS 365 Mh 55
Gilberts Dome △ AUS 375 Mk 57
Gilbués O BR 121 Em 50
Gildford O USA 51 Cg 21
Gile O MOC 344 Hm 54
Gilead O ZA 349 Hg 57
Giles Meteorological Station O AUS 369 Ma 58
Gilette O USA 51 Ck 23
Gilgandra O AUS 379 Ml 61
Gilgil O EAK 337 Hl 46
Gil Gil Creek ~ AUS 375 Ml 60
Gilgit O PK 230 Kb 28
Gilgit Mountains ⩕ PK 230 Ka 27
Gilgunnia O AUS 379 Mk 62
Gilimanuk O RI 279 Lh 50
Gillam O CDN 42 Fc 7
Gillam O AUS 360 Lk 56
Gillespie O USA 71 Dd 26
Gilliat O AUS 374 Mg 56
Gillroyd O AUS 368 Lh 58
Gills Rock O USA 57 De 23
Gilman O USA 56 Dc 23
Gilman O USA 71 De 25
Gilmer O USA 70 Da 29
Gilort ~ RO 194 Hd 23
Gilo Wenz ~ ETH 325 Hj 42
Gilpo O LB 316 Gb 42
Gilroy O USA 64 Cb 27
Gima O EC 116 Dj 47
Gimbi O ETH 325 Hk 41
Gimi O WAN 320 Gl 41
Gimli O CDN 56 Cp 20
Gimo O S 158 Ha 15
Gimpu O RI 279 Lk 46
Ǧināh O ET 301 Hh 33
Ginchi O ETH 325 Hm 41
Gīnda O ER 313 Hm 38
Ginevrabotnen ~ N 158 Hb 6
Gingin O AUS 368 Lh 61
Gin Gin O AUS 375 Mm 58
Gingindlovu O ZA 352 Hh 60
Gingoog O RP 267 Ln 41
Gingoog Bay ~ RP 267 Ln 41
Gīnīr O ETH 325 Hn 42
Gioás O BR 133 Ej 53
Gióia Táuro O I 185 Gp 26
Giralia O AUS 360 Lh 57
Girard O USA 70 Da 27
Girardot O CO 106 Dl 43
Gira River ~ PNG 287 Mk 50
Gīrau O IRQ 209 Hp 28
Giraul ~ ANG 340 Gn 53
Girbān O SUD 312 Hh 40
Giresun O TR 195 Hm 25
Giresun Dağları ⩕ TR 195 Hm 25
Giri ~ RDC 333 Hb 44
Giri ~ RDC 333 Hb 45
Giridih O IND 235 Kh 33
Girilambone O AUS 379 Mk 61
Giro O WAN 320 Gj 40
Giron O EC 116 Dj 47
Girona O E 185 Gh 24
Gironde ~ F 184 Gf 23
girs'ka miscevisc "Mošens'kadubrava" „★ UA 175 Hh 21
Gīrū O AFG 223 Jn 29
Giru O AUS 365 Mk 55
Girvan O GB 162 Gd 18
Girvas O RUS 159 Hj 14
Girza O ET 301 Hh 31
Gisborne O AUS 379 Mj 64
Gisborne O NZ 383 Nm 65
Gisenyi O RWA 336 Hg 46
Gislaved O S 170 Gn 17
Gisors O F 163 Gg 21
Gissar O TJ 223 Jn 26
Gissar Range ⩕ TJ 223 Jn 26
Gisuru O BU 336 Hh 47
Gitagum O RP 267 Ln 41
Gitarama O RWA 336 Hg 47
Gitata O WAN 320 Gk 41
Gitega O BU 336 Hg 47
Githio O GR 194 Hd 27
Giulianova O I 194 Gp 24
Giurgiu O RO 194 He 24
Giv O IR 222 Jh 29
Givet O B 163 Gj 20
Ǧiwa O WAN 320 Gk 40
Gīyān O IR 215 Je 30
Giyani O ZA 352 Hh 57
Giyaṯī O UAE 215 Je 34
Giyon O ETH 325 Hm 41
Giza O ET 301 Hh 30
Gižduvon O UZB 223 Jl 25
Gizhiginskaya Guba ≈ RUS 205 Yb 6
Gižiga O RUS 23 Ta 3
Gižiga ~ RUS 205 Yc 6
Giżycko O PL 170 Hc 18
Ǧizzīn O RL 208 Hk 29
Gjerde O N 170 Gj 16
Gjirokastër O AL 194 Hc 25
Gjoa Haven O CDN 42 Fb 5
Gjøvik O N 158 Gm 15
Glace Bay O CDN 61 Ee 22
Glaciar Grey ▲ RCH 152 Dm 71
Glaciar San Rafael ▲ RCH 152 Dm 69
Glacier ♀ CDN 50 Cc 20
Glacier Bay ≈ USA 47 Bg 15
Glacier N. P. ♀ USA 50 Cf 21
Glacier Peak △ USA 50 Cb 21
Gladewater O USA 70 Da 29
Gladstone O CDN 56 Cn 20
Gladstone O AUS 375 Mm 57
Gladstone O AUS 378 Mf 62
Gladstone O AUS 378 Ml 66
Gláma △ IS 158 Fj 13
Glåma ~ N 158 Gm 14
Glåma ~ N 158 Gm 15
Glamis O USA 64 Ce 29
Glan O RP 275 Ln 43
Glarner Alpen ⩕ CH 174 Gl 22
Glasgow O USA 51 Cj 21
Glasgow O USA 70 Db 26
Glasgow O USA 71 Df 27
Glasgow O GB 162 Gd 18
Glaslyn O CDN 51 Ch 19
Glassboro O USA 74 Dl 26
Glastonbury O GB 163 Ge 20
Glavinica O BG 194 Hf 24
Glazaniha O RUS 159 Hm 14
Glazier O USA 70 Cm 28
Glazoué O DY 317 Gh 41
Glazov O RUS 154 Rb 7
Gleibat Boukénni O RIM 304 Gb 38
Gleisdorf O A 174 Gp 22
Glélé O CI 305 Gc 43
Glen O USA 60 Dn 23
Glen O ZA 349 Hf 60
Glen O AUS 368 Lj 59
Glenayle O AUS 368 Lm 58
Glenboro O CDN 56 Cn 21
Glenboyle O CDN 47 Bg 13
Glenburgh O AUS 368 Lj 58
Glen Canyon Reservoir ~ USA 65 Cg 27
Glencoe O ZA 349 Hg 60
Glencolumbkille O IRL 162 Gb 18
Glendale O USA 64 Cc 28
Glendale O USA 64 Cf 27
Glendale O USA 64 Cf 29
Glendale O ZW 341 Hh 54
Glendambo O AUS 378 Md 61
Glenden O AUS 375 Ml 56
Glendive O USA 51 Ck 22
Glendo O USA 51 Ck 24
Glendo Reservoir ~ USA 51 Ck 24
Glenelg ~ AUS 378 Mg 64
Glenfield O USA 56 Cn 22
Glengyle O AUS 374 Mf 58
Glen Helen O AUS 361 Mc 57
Glenholme O CDN 61 Eb 23
Glenlivet O ZW 352 Hh 56
Glenlyon Peak △ CDN 47 Bj 13
Glenmire O AUS 375 Mj 58
Glen Mor ⌓ GB 162 Gd 18
Glenmorgan O AUS 375 Ml 59
Glenn Canyon ⌓ USA 65 Cg 27
Glenn Innes O AUS 375 Mm 60
Glenns O USA 74 Dk 27
Glenns Ferry O USA 50 Ce 24
Glennville O USA 64 Cc 28
Glennville O USA 87 Dg 30
Glennwood O USA 65 Ch 29
Glenora O AUS 365 Mh 55
Glenorchy O NZ 382 Ng 68
Glenore O AUS 365 Mg 54
Glenormiston O AUS 374 Mf 57
Glenrio O USA 65 Cl 28
Glenrock O USA 65 Cj 24
Glen Rose O USA 70 Cp 29
Glenrothe O GB 162 Ge 17
Glens Falls O USA 60 Dl 24
Glenties O IRL 162 Gb 18
Glenville O USA 71 Dh 26
Glenwood O USA 56 Da 23
Glenwood O USA 70 Da 25
Glenwood O USA 70 Db 28
Glenwood Springs O USA 65 Cj 26
Glidden O CDN 51 Ch 20
Glidden O USA 56 Dc 22
Glina O HR 174 Gp 23
Glittertinden △ N 158 Gl 15
Gliwice O PL 174 Hb 20
Globe O USA 65 Cg 29
Głogów O PL 174 Ha 20
Glomfjord O N 158 Gn 12
Glommersträsk O S 158 Hb 13
Glorieta O USA 65 Ck 28
Gloster O USA 86 Dc 30
Gloucester O USA 60 Dn 24
Gloucester O USA 74 Dk 27
Gloucester O GB 163 Ge 20
Gloucester O PNG 287 Ml 48
Gloucester O AUS 379 Mn 62
Gloucester Island ♁ AUS 375 Ml 55
Glover Reef ♁ BH 93 De 37
Glovertown O CDN 61 Eg 21
Głubczyce O PL 174 Ha 20
Glubokij O RUS 181 Hn 21
Glymur ~ IS 158 Fk 13
Gmünd O A 174 Gp 21
Gmunden O A 174 Gn 22
Gnaraloo O AUS 360 Lg 57
Gnarp O S 158 Ha 14
Gnibi O SN 304 Fn 38
Gniewkowo O PL 170 Ha 19
Gniezno O PL 170 Ha 19
Gnit O SN 304 Fn 37
Gnjilane O SCG 194 Hc 24
Gnonsamoridou O RG 316 Gb 41
Gnowangerup O AUS 368 Lk 62
Goa ⊙ IND 238 Ka 38
Goageb O NAM 348 Ha 59
Goālpāra O IND 235 Kk 32
Goa Mampu Caves ★ RI 282 Ll 48
Goan O RMM 317 Gd 39
Goari O PNG 287 Mj 49
Goaso O GH 317 Ge 42
Goba O ETH 325 Hn 42
Goba O MOC 352 Hj 59
Gobabedb O NAM 348 Gp 57
Gobabis O NAM 348 Hb 57
Gobālpur O IND 235 Kh 33
Gobari ~ RDC 333 Hb 48
Gobe O G 332 Gl 45
Gobēle Wenz ~ ETH 325 Hn 41
Gobernador Crespo O RA 137 Ed 61
Gobernador Garmendia O RA 136 Eb 59
Gobernador Gregores O RA 152 Dn 70
Gobi Altai Mountains ⩕ MNG 204 Ub 10
Gobindpur O IND 235 Kg 34
Gobo O J 251 Md 29
Gobur O SUD 324 Hh 43
Gobustan O AZ 202 Jc 25
Goce Delčev O BG 194 Hd 25
Gochas O NAM 348 Hb 58
Gōchi O J 247 Mb 28
Go Công Ðông O VN 263 Ld 40
Goðafoss ★ IS 158 Fl 13
Godār-e Alīak △ IR 222 Jg 27
Godār-e Kalmard △ IR 222 Jg 29
Godatair O SUD 324 Hf 41
Godāvari ~ IND 238 Ke 36
Godāvari ~ IND 238 Ke 37
Godāwarī O NEP 234 Ke 31
Godbout O CDN 60 Ea 21
Goddá O IND 235 Kh 33
Godē O ETH 328 Hp 43
Godegode O EAT 337 Hl 49
Goderich O CDN 57 Dg 24
Gōd-e Zere ~ AFG 226 Jj 31
Godfreys Tank O AUS 361 Lp 56
Godhåb Nuuk O DK 43 Jb 6
Godhaven Qeqertarsuaq O DK 43 Ja 5
Godhra O IND 227 Ka 34
Godhyogol O SP 328 Hp 41
Godina O E 184 Gf 25
Godinlabe O SP 328 Jb 43
Godofredo Viana O BR 121 El 46
Godoy Cruz O RA 137 Dp 62
Gods Lake ~ CDN 42 Fc 8
Godthåb O DK 7 Ga 3
Goe O PNG 286 Mg 50
Gog O ETH 325 Hk 42
Gogama O CDN 57 Dh 22
Gogango O AUS 375 Mm 57
Gō-gawa ~ J 251 Mc 28
Gogo O WAN 320 Gl 42
Gogo O AUS 361 Ln 55
Gogoi O MOC 352 Hj 56
Gogounou O DY 320 Gh 40
Gogrial O SUD 324 Hg 41
Gogui O RMM 304 Gb 38
Goha Ts'iyon O ETH 325 Hm 41
Goiana O BR 124 Fc 49
Goiandira O BR 133 Ek 55
Goianésia O BR 121 Ek 47
Goianésia O BR 133 Ek 53
Goiánia O BR 133 Ek 54
Goianinha O BR 124 Fc 49
Goianorte O BR 121 Ek 50
Goiás ⊙ BR 133 Ej 54
Goiatins O BR 121 El 49
Goiatuba O BR 133 Ek 55
Gojeb Wenz ~ ETH 325 Hl 42
Gojo O ETH 325 Hl 41
Gojo-Erê O BR 140 Eh 58
Gojra O PK 230 Ka 30
Gojyō O J 251 Md 28
Gökçe Adasi ♁ TR 194 He 25
Gökova Körfez ~ TR 195 Hf 27
Göksu Çayı ~ TR 195 Hl 26
Göksun O TR 195 Hl 27
Göksu Nehri ~ TR 195 Hj 27
Göktepe O TR 195 Hj 27
Gokwe O ZW 341 Hg 55
Gol O N 158 Gl 15
Golaghāt O IND 235 Kl 32
Golan ⩕ SYR 208 Hk 29
Golana Gof ~ EAK 325 Hm 45
Golbāf O IR 226 Jg 31
Gölbaşı O TR 195 Hj 26
Gölbaşı O TR 195 Hl 27
Golconda O USA 64 Cd 25
Golconda O USA 71 Dd 27
Gölcük O TR 195 Hg 25
Gołdap O PL 170 Hd 18
Gold Bar O CDN 47 Ca 17
Gold Beach O USA 50 Bp 24
Gold Bridge O CDN 50 Ca 20
Gold Coast O AUS 375 Mn 60
Goldcreek O USA 51 Cf 22
Golden O CDN 50 Cd 20
Golden Bay ~ NZ 383 Nj 66
Goldendale O USA 50 Cb 23
Golden Gate O USA 87 Dh 32
Golden Gate Bridge ★ USA 64 Ca 27
Golden Gate Highlands ★ ZA 349 Hg 60
Golden Grove O JA 101 Dk 37
Golden Meadow O USA 86 Dc 31
Golden Spike National History Site ★ USA 64 Cf 25
Golden Valley O ZW 341 Hg 55
Goldfield O USA 64 Cd 27
Gold River O CDN 50 Bn 21
Goldsboro O USA 74 Dk 28
Goldsworthy O AUS 360 Lk 56
Goldthwaite O USA 81 Cn 30
Gōle O IRQ 209 Ja 28
Gōle O TR 202 Hp 25
Golelcha O ETH 325 Hn 41
Goleniów O PL 170 Gp 19
Golestān O AFG 223 Jk 29
Golfa O IR 209 Ja 26
Golf de Sant Jordi ~ E 184 Gg 25
Golf de St. Malo ~ F 163 Ge 21
Golfe de Cintra ∀ 304 Fm 34
Golfe du Lion ~ F 185 Gh 24
Golfete de Coro ~ YV 107 Dn 40
Golf Islands National Seashore ♀ USA 86 Dd 30
Golfito O CR 97 Dg 41
Golfo Almirante Montt ~ RCH 152 Dm 71
Golfo Arcani O I 185 Gl 25
Golfo de Almería ~ E 184 Ge 27
Golfo de Ana María ~ C 100 Dj 35
Golfo de Ancud ~ RCH 147 Dm 67
Golfo de Arauco ~ RCH 137 Dm 64
Golfo de Batabanó ~ C 100 Dg 34
Golfo de Cariaco ~ YV 112 Eb 40
Golfo de Cazones ~ C 100 Dh 35
Golfo de Corcovado ~ RCH 147 Dm 67
Golfo de Cupica ~ CO 106 Dk 42
Golfo de Guacanayabo ~ C 101 Dk 35
Golfo de Guafo ~ RCH 147 Dl 67
Golfo del Darién ~ CO 106 Dk 41
Golfo dell'Asinara ~ I 185 Gl 25
Golfo de Montijo ~ PA 97 Dh 42
Golfo de Morrosquillo ~ CO 106 Dl 41
Golfo de Peñes ~ RCH 152 Dl 69
Golfo de Taraca ~ PE 128 Dp 54
Golfo de Tribugá ~ CO 106 Dk 43
Golfo de Urabá ~ CO 106 Dk 41
Golfo di Gaeta ~ I 185 Gn 25
Golfo di Manfredónia ~ I 194 Ha 25
Golfo di Napoli ~ I 185 Gn 25
Golfo di Policastro ~ I 185 Gp 26
Golfo di S. Eufémia ~ I 185 Gp 26
Golfo di Squillace ~ I 194 Ha 26
Golfo di Trieste ~ I 185 Gn 23
Golfo Nuevo ~ RA 147 Eb 67
Golfo San Esteban ~ RCH 152 Dl 69
Golfo San José ~ RA 147 Eb 67
Golfo San Matías ~ RA 147 Eb 66
Golfo Tres Montes ~ RCH 152 Dl 69
Golfo Trinidad ~ RCH 152 Dl 70
Golf von Mexiko ≈ 86 Dc 32
Gölgeli Dağl. △ TR 195 Hg 27
Golgo di Salerno ~ I 194 Gp 25
Gölhisar O TR 195 Hg 27
Goli O EAU 324 Hh 44
Goliad O USA 81 Cp 31
Goligong Shan △ VRC 254 Kp 33
Golija △ SCG 194 Hc 24
Goliševa O RUS 171 Hg 17
Goljam Perelik △ BG 194 He 25
Gölköy O TR 195 Hl 25
Gölmarmara O TR 195 Hf 26
Golmud O VRC 242 Km 27
Golog Shan △ VRC 242 La 29
Golo Island ♁ RP 267 Ll 39
Golokuati O GH 317 Gg 42
Golomoti O MW 344 Hk 53
Golongosso O RCA 321 Hb 41
Golovnino O RUS 250 Mj 24
Golpāyegān O IR 222 Jd 29
Gol Tappe O IR 209 Ja 27
Gol Tappe O IR 209 Jc 28
Golū ~ IR 222 Je 28
Golungo Alto O ANG 340 Gp 50
Golva O USA 51 Cl 22
Golweyn O SP 329 Ja 45
Goma O RDC 336 Hg 46
Gomang Co ~ VRC 231 Kj 30
Gomati ~ IND 234 Kd 31
Gomati ~ IND 234 Kf 32
Gombad-e Qabūs O IR 222 Jf 27
Gombaki O IR 226 Jh 33
Gombari O RDC 324 Hg 44
Gombe O WAN 320 Gm 40
Gombe ~ EAT 336 Hh 48
Gombe-Matadi O RDC 332 Gp 48
Gombe Stream ♀ EAT 336 Hg 48
Gombi Fulani O WAN 320 Gn 40
Gomboussougou O BF 317 Gf 40
Gómez Farías O MEX 80 Cj 31
Gomez Palacio O MEX 81 Cl 33
Goméz Rendón O EC 116 Dh 47
Gomo Co ~ VRC 231 Kg 28
Gomogomo O RI 283 Md 49
Gomon O CI 317 Gd 43
Gomorovići O RUS 171 Hk 15
Gomoti ~ RB 341 Hd 56
Gonābād O IR 222 Jh 28
Gonaïves O RH 101 Dm 36
Gonam ~ RUS 205 Wb 7
Gonarezhou ♀ ZW 352 Hh 56
Gonatá O CI 305 Gc 42
Gonbad-e Kabūd O IR 222 Jh 27
Gonçalves Dias O BR 121 Em 48
Gonda O IND 234 Kf 32
Gondal O IND 227 Jp 35
Gondē O ETH 325 Hm 42
Gonder O ETH 313 Hl 39
Gondey O TCH 321 Hb 41
Gondia O IND 234 Ke 35
Gondola O MOC 344 Hj 55
Gondolahun O LB 316 Ga 42
Gondola Pt. O CDN 61 Ea 23
Gondom ▲ ETH 325 Hl 41
Gönen O TR 195 Hf 25
Gonga O CAM 321 Gn 43
Gong'an O VRC 243 Lg 30
Gongbo'gyamda O VRC 235 Kl 31
Gongcheng O VRC 255 Lf 33
Gonggar O VRC 235 Kk 31
Gongga Shan △ VRC 254 La 31
Gonghe O VRC 242 La 27
Gongo O TCH 321 Hb 41
Gongolgon O AUS 379 Mk 61
Gongoué O G 332 Gl 46
Gongshan O VRC 254 Kp 32
Gong Xian O VRC 243 Lg 28
Gong Xian O VRC 255 Lc 31
Gonohe O J 250 Mg 25
Gonoruwa O CL 239 Ke 42
Gōnoura O J 247 Ma 29
Gonzales O USA 81 Cp 31
Gonzales O USA 86 Dc 30
Gonzáles ~ PY 140 Ee 57
Gonzáles Chaves O RA 137 Ed 64
Gonzáles Moreno O RA 137 Ec 63
Gonzales Suares O PE 116 Dl 47
González O MEX 92 Cn 34
Gonzanamá O EC 116 Dj 48
Goobang Creek ~ AUS 379 Mk 62
Goobies O CDN 61 Eg 22
Gooch Range ⩕ AUS 360 Lh 57
Goodenough Bay ~ PNG 287 Ml 50
Goodenough Island ♁ PNG 287 Ml 50
Goodeve O CDN 51 Cl 20
Good Hope Mount △ CDN 50 Bp 20
Goodhouse O ZA 348 Hb 60
Gooding O USA 50 Ce 24
Goodland O USA 70 Cm 26
Goodlettsville O USA 71 De 27
Goodnews Bay O USA 46 Aj 15
Goodooga O AUS 375 Mk 60
Goodparla O AUS 364 Mb 52
Goods Lake ~ CDN 6 Ea 4
Goold Island ♁ AUS 365 Mk 55
Goole O GB 163 Gf 19
Goolgowi O AUS 379 Mj 62
Goolwa O AUS 378 Mf 63
Goomader ~ AUS 364 Mc 52
Goomader River ~ AUS 364 Mc 52
Goomalling O AUS 368 Lj 61
Goomeri O AUS 375 Mn 59
Goondiwindi O AUS 375 Ml 60
Goongarrie ♀ AUS 368 Ll 61
Goonyella Mine O AUS 375 Ml 56
Goornong O AUS 379 Mj 64
Goose Bay O CDN 7 Fb 4
Goose Bay O CDN 43 Hc 8
Goose Bay O CDN 61 Ed 19
Goose Creek ~ USA 64 Ce 25
Goose Green O GB 147 Ee 71
Goose Lake ~ CDN 51 Cj 20
Goose Lake ~ USA 64 Cb 25
Goose River ~ CDN 61 Ed 19
Gooty O IND 238 Kc 38
Gopichettipalaiyam O IND 239 Kc 40
Goppe Bazar O MYA 235 Kl 35
Gōr ⊙ AFG 223 Jl 28
gora Addala-Suhgel'meer △ RUS 202 Jb 24
gora Balkon-Myl'k ~ RUS 159 Hl 11
gora Čingikan △ RUS 204 Vb 8
gora Čuguš △ RUS 195 Hm 24
Goradiz O AZ 202 Jb 26
Goradudi Plain ⌓ EAK 325 Hm 44
gora Djuftydag △ RUS 202 Jb 25
gora Dyh-Tau △ RUS 202 Hp 24
gora Ébručorr ~ RUS 159 Hh 12
gora Èl'brus △ RUS 202 Hp 24
gora Èlgoras ~ RUS 159 Hh 11
gora Golaja △ RUS 205 Yb 5
Goragorskij O RUS 202 Ja 24
gora Jagel'urta ~ RUS 159 Hl 12
gora Jamantau △ RUS 154 Rc 8
gora Jumper Uajv ~ RUS 159 Hk 12
gora Kalgalakša ~ RUS 159 Hk 13
Góra Kalwaria O PL 170 Hc 19
gora Kamennik ~ RUS 159 Hk 12
gora Kazbek △ RUS 202 Ja 24
Gorakhpur O IND 235 Kf 32
gora Konžakovskij Kamen' △ RUS 154 Rc 7
gora Ledjanaja △ RUS 205 Zb 6
gora Lednikovaja △ RUS 204 Va 3
gora Mus-Haja △ RUS 205 Xb 6
Goranlega ~ SP 337 Hn 46
gora Očenyrd △ RUS 154 Sa 5
gora Rohmojva ~ RUS 159 Hg 12
gora Skalistyj Golec △ RUS 204 Vc 7
gora Snežnaja △ KS 230 Ka 25
gora Strizament △ RUS 202 Hp 23
gora Valunnaja △ RUS 205 Za 5
Goražde O BIH 194 Hb 24
Gōrband O AFG 223 Jn 28
Gorbea O RCH 147 Dm 65
Gorda Cay ♁ BS 87 Dk 32
Gördes O TR 195 Hg 26
Gordil O RCA 321 Hc 41
Gordon O USA 51 Cl 24
Gordon Downs O AUS 364 Ma 55
Gordon's O BS 87 Dl 34
Gordon's Bay O ZA 358 Hb 63
Gordonsville O USA 74 Dj 26
Gordonvale O AUS 365 Mj 54
Goré O TCH 321 Ha 42
Gorē O ETH 325 Hk 41
Gore O NZ 382 Ng 69
Gore Bay O CDN 57 Dg 23
Göreme ★ TR 195 Hk 26
Gorgadji O BF 305 Gf 38
Gorgān O IR 222 Jf 27
Gorges ★ DZ 296 Gh 27
Gorges du Tarn ★ F 185 Gh 23
Gorgol ~ RIM 304 Fp 37
Gorgol Blanc ~ RIM 304 Fp 37
Gorgol Noire ~ RIM 304 Fp 37
Gorgora O ETH 313 Hl 39
Gorgoram O WAN 320 Gm 39
Gorhiar O PK 227 Jp 33
Gori O GE 202 Ja 25
Goricy O RUS 171 Hl 17
Goris O ARM 202 Jb 26
Gorizia O SLO 185 Gn 23
Gorjačij O RUS 202 Hm 23
Gorjačij Ključ O RUS 202 Hm 23
Gor'kovskoe vodohranilišče ~ RUS 171 Hn 16
Görlitz O D 174 Gp 20
Gōrmā O AFG 223 Jk 28
Gorman O USA 64 Cc 28
Gorna O BG 194 He 24
Gornjackij O RUS 181 Hn 21
Gorno-Altajsk O RUS 204 Tc 8
Gornovodnoe O RUS 250 Md 24
Gornozavodsk O RUS 250 Mg 22
Gornyj O RUS 181 Jc 20
Goro O ETH 325 Hn 42
Gorodec O UA 175 Hf 20
Gorodišče O RUS 181 Ja 19
Gorodovikovsk O RUS 181 Hn 22
Gorogoro O RI 283 Lp 46
Gorohovec O RUS 181 Hp 17
Goroka O PNG 287 Mj 49
Goroke O AUS 378 Mg 64
Gorom-Gorom O BF 305 Gf 38
Gorongosa △ MOC 344 Hj 55
Gorongosa O MOC 344 Hk 55
Gorongosa ~ MOC 352 Hk 56
Gorontalo O RI 275 Lm 45
Goronyo O WAN 308 Gj 39
Goroubi O RN 317 Gg 39
Gorouol ~ BF 305 Gf 38
Gorrie O AUS 364 Mc 53
Goršečnoe O RUS 181 Hl 20
Gōryān O AFG 223 Jj 28
gory Byrranga ⩕ RUS 22 Pa 2
Gory Byrranga ⩕ RUS 204 Tb 4
Gory Prževal'skogo ⩕ RUS 250 Mc 24
Gorzów Wlkp. O PL 170 Gp 19
Goschen Strait ~ PNG 287 Mm 51
Gosford O AUS 379 Mm 62
Goshen O USA 71 Df 25
Goshute Indian Reservation ••• USA 64 Ce 26
Goslar O D 174 Gm 20
Gospić O HR 174 Gp 23
Gossas O SN 304 Fm 38
Gosses O AUS 378 Md 61
Gossi O RMM 305 Gf 38
Gostivar O MK 194 Hc 25
Gostynin O PL 170 Hb 19
Gota O ETH 325 Hn 41
Gotaälv ~ S 170 Gn 17
Göteborg O S 170 Gm 17
Gotel Mountains ⩕ WAN 320 Gm 42
Gotha O D 174 Gm 20
Gothenburg O USA 70 Cm 25
Gothéye O RN 317 Gg 39
Goth Kunda Baklish O PK 227 Jm 33
Gotland ♁ S 170 Hb 17
Gōtland ⌓ S 170 Gn 17
Goto de Doñana ♀ E 184 Gc 27
Gotō rettō ♁ J 247 Ma 29
Gotsa Sandōn ♁ S 170 Hb 16
Göttingen O D 174 Gl 20
Gouandé O DY 317 Gg 40
Gouatchi O RCA 321 Hc 43
Gouaya ~ BF 317 Gf 39
Goubangzi O VRC 246 Ll 25
Gouburn ~ AUS 379 Mm 62
Gouchi O RN 308 Gl 39
Goudar ~ IR 226 Jf 32
Goudge O RA 137 Dp 63
Goudiri O SN 304 Fp 38
Goudoumaria O RN 308 Gm 39
Gouéké O RG 316 Gb 41
Gouiret Moussa O DZ 296 Gh 30
Goukār O IR 209 Jc 28
Goulahonfla O CI 305 Gc 42
Goulais River O CDN 57 Df 22
Goulburn ~ AUS 379 Mj 64
Goulburn ♀ AUS 379 Ml 62
Goulburn O AUS 379 Ml 63
Gould O USA 70 Cn 28
Goulfey O CAM 321 Gp 39
Goulia O CI 305 Gc 40
Goulmima O MA 293 Gd 30
Goumal Kalei O AFG 223 Jn 29
Goumbatou O TCH 321 Hc 40
Goumbi O RN 308 Gh 39
Goumbi O G 332 Gm 46
Goumbou O RMM 305 Gc 38
Gouméré O CI 317 Ge 42
Gouna O CAM 321 Gn 41
Gounda O RCA 321 Hc 41
Gounda ~ RCA 321 Hc 41
Goundam O RMM 305 Ge 37
Goundi O TCH 321 Ha 41
Gounou-Gaya O TCH 321 Gp 41
Goupār O IR 226 Jh 30
Goúra △ GR 194 Hd 27
Gouraid Ǧaramī O AFG 223 Jp 27
Gourak O AFG 223 Jl 29
Gouray O RIM 304 Fp 38
Gouraya O DZ 293 Gg 27
Gourcy O BF 317 Ge 39
Gourdon O F 184 Gg 23
Gouré O RN 308 Gm 38
Gourits ~ ZA 358 Hc 63
Gouritsmond O ZA 358 Hc 63
Gourjhamar O IND 234 Kd 34
Gourma ⌓ BF 317 Gg 40
Gourma-Rharous O RMM 305 Gf 37
Gournay-en-Bray O F 163 Gg 21
Gouro O TCH 309 Hb 36
Gourrama O MA 293 Gd 29
Gouvea O BR 141 En 55
Gouverneur O USA 60 Dl 23
Gouzam O IR 226 Jf 30
Gouzé O RCA 321 Ha 42
Gouzgān ⊙ AFG 223 Jl 27
Gouzon O F 163 Gh 22
Gov. Valadares O BR 141 Ep 55
Gove O USA 70 Cm 26
Gove Peninsula ♁ AUS 364 Me 52
Governador Eugênio Barros O BR 121 Em 48
Governor Generoso O RP 275 Lp 42
Governor's Camp O EAK 337 Hk 46
Governor's Harbour O BS 87 Dk 33
Govinh Ballabh ~ IND 234 Kf 33
Gowan Range ⩕ AUS 375 Mj 58
Gowganda O CDN 57 Dh 22
Goya O RA 146 Ee 60
Göyçay O AZ 202 Jb 25
Goyder O AUS 364 Md 52
Goyder Creek ~ AUS 374 Md 58
Goyders Lagoon ~ AUS 374 Mf 59
Goyllarisquizga O PE 128 Dk 51
Göynük O TR 195 Hh 25
Goyoum O CAM 321 Gn 43
Goẓare O AFG 223 Jk 28
Goz-Beida O TCH 321 Hc 39
Gozha Co ~ VRC 230 Ke 28
Gozo ♁ M 185 Gp 27
Graaf-Reinet O ZA 358 He 62
Graafwater O ZA 358 Hb 62
Grabo O CI 304 Gc 43
Grabouw O ZA 358 Hb 63
Gračanica O BIH 174 Hb 23
Gracefield O CDN 60 Dk 22
Gracias O HN 93 Dd 38
Graciosa ♁ P 18 Ha 6
Gradaús O BR 121 Ej 49
Grado O E 184 Gc 24
Gradsko O MK 194 Hc 25
Grady O USA 65 Cl 28
Grady O USA 70 Dc 28
Grafton O USA 56 Cp 21
Grafton O USA 71 Dh 26
Grafton O AUS 375 Mn 60
Graham O CDN 56 Dc 21
Graham O USA 70 Cn 29
Graham Creek ~ USA 50 Cc 22
Graham Island ♁ CDN 42 Da 8
Graham Island ♁ CDN 43 Fc 3
Grahamstown O ZA 358 Hf 62
Grahovo O RUS 181 Jd 17
Graie O LB 316 Gb 42
Grain Coast ⌓ LB 316 Ga 43
Grainfield O USA 70 Cm 26
Grajagan O RI 279 Lh 50
Grajaú ~ BR 121 El 48
Grajaú O BR 121 Em 47
Grajaú ~ BR 121 Em 48
Grajewo O PL 170 Hd 19
Grajvoron O RUS 175 Hk 20
Gramado O BR 146 Ej 60
Graman O AUS 375 Mm 60
Gramilla O RA 136 Eb 59
Grammos △ GR 194 Hc 25
Gramphoo O IND 230 Kc 29
Grampianfjella △ N 158 Gm 6

Gibraltar Range - Grampianfjella 421

□Country ▣Capital city ◉Administrative unit ○Place 🏝Island ⛰Mountain range △Mountain ⌒Cape ≈Ocean, Sea ~Lake, River ♆Undersea topography ▲Glacier ⚲National park •••Reservation ★Point of major interest ⌓Landscape

Grampian Mountains ⛰ **GB** 162 Gd 17
Grampians ⚲ **AUS** 378 Mh 64
Gramsdale ○ **GB** 162 Gc 17
Gramsh ○ **AL** 194 Hb 25
Granaatboskolk ○ **ZA** 348 Hb 60
Granada ○ **USA** 65 Cl 27
Granada ○ **NIC** 96 Df 40
Granada ○ **CO** 106 Dm 44
Granada ○ **E** 184 Ge 27
Gran Altiplanicie Central ⌓ **RA** 152 Dn 70
Gran Baja de San Julián ⌓ **RA** 152 Dp 70
Gran Bajo del Gualicho ⌓ **RA** 147 Eb 66
Granburry ○ **USA** 70 Cn 29
Granby ○ **CDN** 60 Dm 23
Granby ○ **USA** 65 Ck 25
Gran Canaria 🏝 **E** 292 Fn 32
Gran Chaco ⌓ **RA** 136 Ec 58
Grand ~ **USA** 57 Df 24
Grand ~ **USA** 71 Df 25
Grand Baie ○ **MS** 353 Jg 56
Grand Ballon △ **F** 163 Gk 22
Grand Bank ○ **CDN** 61 Eg 22
Grand-Bassam ○ **CI** 317 Ge 43
Grand Bay-Westfield ○ **CDN** 61 Ea 23
Grand Bend ○ **CDN** 57 Dh 24
Grand-Bérébi ○ **CI** 305 Gc 43
Grand Bourg ○ **F** 104 Ed 38
Grand Bruit ○ **CDN** 61 Ee 22
Grand Caicos 🏝 **GB** 101 Dn 35
Grand Canal ~ **IRL** 163 Gb 19
Grand Canyon ⚲ **USA** 64 Cf 27
Grand Canyon ⌓ **USA** 64 Cf 27
Grand Canyon ○ **USA** 65 Cf 27
Grand Canyon Caverns ★ **USA** 64 Cf 28
Grand Cayman 🏝 **GB** 100 Dh 36
Grand Cess ○ **LB** 316 Gb 43
Grand Coulee ○ **USA** 50 Cc 22
Grand Coulee Dam ★ **USA** 50 Cc 22
Grande ~ **GCA** 93 Dc 38
Grande ~ **YV** 112 Ed 41
Grande ~ **BR** 125 En 51
Grande ~ **PE** 128 Dl 53
Grande ~ **BR** 133 Ej 55
Grande ~ **BR** 133 Em 51
Grande ~ **BR** 133 Em 52
Grande ~ **RA** 136 Ea 59
Grande ~ **RA** 136 Eb 57
Grande ~ **RCH** 137 Dn 61
Grande ~ **RA** 137 Dn 63
Grande ~ **RA** 137 Dp 64
Grande ~ **BR** 141 Ek 56
Grande ~ **BR** 141 El 56
Grande ~ **RA** 152 Dp 72
Grande Anse ○ **WL** 104 Ed 38
Grande Bay ~ **RA** 152 Dp 71
Grande de Lipez ~ **BOL** 136 Ea 56
Grande de Tarja ~ **BOL** 136 Eb 57
Grande de V. Hermoso ~ **RA** 136 Dp 60
Grande-Entreé ○ **CDN** 61 Ed 22
Grande Kabylie ⌓ **DZ** 296 Gh 27
Grande Miquelon 🏝 **F** 61 Ef 22
Grande ó Guapay ~ **BOL** 129 Ec 55
Grande o Guasamayo ~ **RA** 136 Ea 59
Grande ou Funda ~ **BR** 132 Ef 55
Grande Pilcomayo ~ **BOL** 129 Eb 55
Grande Prairie ○ **CDN** 6 Cb 4
Grande Prairie ○ **CDN** 47 Cc 17
Grand Erg de Bilma ⌓ **RN** 308 Gn 37
Grande-Rivière ○ **CDN** 61 Eb 21
Grande Rivière de la Baleine ~ **CDN** 43 Gc 7
Grande Ronde ~ **USA** 50 Cd 23
Grande Sido ~ **TCH** 321 Hb 41
Grande-Terre 🏝 **F** 104 Ed 37
Grande-Vallée ○ **CDN** 61 Eb 21
Grand Falls ○ **CDN** 60 Ea 22
Grandfalls ○ **USA** 81 Cl 30
Grand Falls ~ **EAK** 337 Hl 46
Grand Falls-Windsor ○ **CDN** 61 Eg 21
Grandfather Mountain △ **USA** 71 Dh 27
Grand Forks ○ **CDN** 50 Cc 21
Grand Forks ○ **USA** 56 Cp 22
Grand Gorge ○ **USA** 60 Dl 24
Grand Haven ○ **USA** 57 De 24
Grand Island 🏝 **USA** 57 De 22
Grand Island ○ **USA** 70 Cn 25
Grand Isle ○ **USA** 86 Dd 31
Grand Junction ○ **USA** 65 Ch 26
Grand-Lahou ○ **CI** 317 Gd 43
Grand Lake ○ **CDN** 61 Eb 22
Grand Lake ○ **USA** 86 Db 31
Grand Manan Island 🏝 **CDN** 61 Ea 23
Grand Marais ○ **USA** 56 Dc 22
Grand Marais ○ **USA** 57 Df 22
Grand Mère ○ **CDN** 60 Dm 22
Grand Mesa ⛰ **USA** 65 Ch 26
Grândola ○ **P** 184 Gb 26
Grand-Popo ○ **DY** 317 Gg 42
Grand Portage ○ **USA** 57 Dd 22
Grand Portage Ind.Res. ••• **USA** 56 Dc 22
Grand Portage N.M. ★ **USA** 57 Dd 22
Grand-Pré N.H.S. ★ **CDN** 61 Eb 23
Grand Rapids ○ **CDN** 42 Fb 8
Grand Rapids ○ **CDN** 56 Cn 19
Grand Rapids ○ **USA** 56 Db 22
Grand Rapids ○ **USA** 57 Df 24
Grand Récif de Cook 🏝 **F** 386 Nd 55
Grand Récif de Koumac 🏝 **F** 386 Nd 56
Grand Récif Mathieu 🏝 **F** 386 Ne 56
Grand Récif Mengalia 🏝 **F** 386 Ne 56
Grand Récif Sud 🏝 **F** 386 Nf 57
Grand Remous ○ **CDN** 60 Dk 22
Grand River ~ **USA** 56 Cm 23
Grand-Rivière ○ **F** 104 Ed 38
Grand-Santi ○ **F** 113 Eg 43
Grand Staircase-Escalante National Monument ★ **USA** 64 Cf 27
Grand Teton N.P. ⚲ **USA** 51 Cg 24
Grand Teton Peak △ **USA** 51 Cg 24
Grand Traverse Bay ~ **USA** 57 Df 23
Grand Turk 🏝 **GB** 101 Dn 35
Grand Victoria ○ **CDN** 60 Dk 22
Grandview ○ **USA** 50 Cb 22
Grandview ○ **CDN** 56 Cm 20
Grange Hill ○ **JA** 100 Dj 36
Grangemouth ○ **GB** 162 Gd 18
Granger ○ **USA** 65 Cg 25
Grangeville ○ **USA** 50 Cd 23
Granite Bay ○ **CDN** 50 Bp 20
Granite Falls ○ **USA** 56 Da 23
Granite Pass △ **USA** 51 Ch 23
Granite Peak △ **USA** 51 Cg 23
Granite Peak △ **USA** 64 Cd 25
Granite Peak △ **USA** 64 Cf 26
Granite Peak △ **AUS** 368 Lj 63
Granja ○ **BR** 124 Ep 47
Gran Laguna Salada ~ **RA** 152 Ea 68
Gränna ○ **S** 170 Gp 16
Granollers ○ **E** 184 Gh 25
Gran Pajatén ★ **PE** 116 Dk 49
Gran Pampa Pelada ⌓ **BOL** 136 Ea 56
Gran Pampa Salada ⌓ **BOL** 136 Ea 56
Gran Parasidso △ **I** 185 Gk 23
Gran Quivira ○ **USA** 65 Cj 28
Gran Rio ~ **SME** 113 Eg 44
Gran Sasso d'Italia ⛰ **I** 185 Gn 24
Grant ○ **USA** 65 Ck 26
Grant ○ **USA** 70 Cm 25
Gran Tarajal ○ **E** 292 Fn 31
Grant City ○ **USA** 70 Da 25
Grantham ○ **GB** 163 Gf 19
Grant-Kohrs Ranch N.H.S. ★ **USA** 51 Cf 22
Grant Range ⛰ **USA** 64 Ce 27
Grants ○ **USA** 65 Cj 28
Grantsburg ○ **USA** 56 Db 23
Grants Pass ○ **USA** 50 Ca 24
Grantsville ○ **USA** 64 Cf 25
Granville ○ **USA** 60 Dm 24
Granville ○ **F** 163 Ge 21
Grão Mogol ○ **BR** 125 En 54
Graskop ○ **ZA** 352 Hh 58
Gräsö 🏝 **S** 170 Hb 15
Graspan ○ **ZA** 349 He 60
Grasse ○ **F** 185 Gk 24
Grasslands ⚲ **CDN** 51 Cj 21
Grasslands ⌓ **CDN** 51 Cj 21
Grass Range ○ **USA** 51 Ch 22
Grass Valley ○ **USA** 64 Cb 26
Grassy ○ **AUS** 378 Mj 66
Grassy Lake ○ **CDN** 51 Cg 21
Grates Point ⌒ **CDN** 61 Eh 21
Graton ○ **USA** 56 Cn 23
Gravatá ○ **BR** 124 Fc 50
Gravataí ○ **BR** 146 Ej 60
Gravelbourg ○ **CDN** 51 Cj 21
Gravelotte ○ **ZA** 352 Hh 58
Gravenhurst ○ **CDN** 60 Dj 23
Grave Peak △ **USA** 50 Ce 22
Gravesend ○ **AUS** 375 Mm 60
Gravsted ★ **DK** 170 Gl 18
Gray ○ **USA** 70 Dg 29
Gray ○ **F** 163 Gj 22
Grayling ○ **USA** 46 Aj 13
Grayling ○ **USA** 57 Df 23
Grayrocks Reservoir ~ **USA** 51 Ck 24
Grays Harbor ~ **USA** 50 Bp 22
Grays Lake ~ **USA** 51 Cg 24
Grayson ○ **USA** 71 Dg 26
Graz ○ **A** 174 Gp 22
Great Artesian Basin ⌓ **AUS** 374 Mg 58
Great Australian Bight ♆ **AUS** 369 Lp 63
Great Bahama Bank ♆ 87 Dj 33
Great Bahama Island 🏝 **BS** 87 Dj 32
Great Barrier Island 🏝 **NZ** 383 Nk 64
Great Barrier Reef ♆ **AUS** 365 Mh 51
Great Basalt Wall ⚲ **AUS** 375 Mj 56
Great Basin ⌓ **USA** 64 Cd 25
Great Basin ⚲ **USA** 64 Ce 26
Great Bear Lake ~ **CDN** 6 Cb 3
Great Bear Lake ~ **CDN** 47 Ca 11
Great Bear River ~ **CDN** 47 Bn 13
Great Bend ○ **USA** 70 Cn 26
Great Britain 🏝 **GB** 162 Gf 17
Great Coco Island 🏝 **MYA** 262 Kl 38
Great Divide Basin ⌓ **USA** 51 Ch 24
Great Dividing Range ⛰ **AUS** 365 Mh 52
Great Duck 🏝 **CDN** 57 Dg 23
Great Duck Island 🏝 **CDN** 57 Dg 23
Great Eastern Erg ⌓ **DZ** 296 Gj 31
Greater Antilles 🏝 100 Dh 35
Greater St. Lucia Wetland Park ⚲ **ZA** 352 Hj 60
Great Exhibition Bay ~ **NZ** 383 Nj 63
Great Exuma Island 🏝 **BS** 87 Dk 34
Great Falls ○ **USA** 51 Cg 22
Great Falls ~ **GUY** 113 Ee 44
Great Guana Cay 🏝 **BS** 87 Dk 33
Great Harbour Cay 🏝 **BS** 87 Dj 33
Great Inagua Island 🏝 **BS** 101 Dm 35
Great Island 🏝 **NZ** 383 Nj 63
Great Kambung Swamp ~ **AUS** 379 Mh 63
Great Kei ~ **ZA** 358 Hf 62
Great Keppel Island 🏝 **AUS** 375 Mm 57
Great Lake ~ **AUS** 378 Mk 66
Great Limpopo Transfrontier Park ⚲ 352 Hh 57
Great Mercury Island 🏝 **NZ** 383 Nk 64
Great Nicobar Island 🏝 **IND** 270 Kl 42
Great Ouse ~ **GB** 163 Gg 19
Great Palm Island 🏝 **AUS** 365 Mk 55
Great Papuan Plateau ⛰ **PNG** 286 Mh 49
Great Plains ⌓ **CDN** 51 Cj 19
Great Plains ⌓ **USA** 65 Cl 25
Great Rattling Brook ~ **CDN** 61 Ef 21
Great Ruaha ~ **EAT** 337 Hk 49
Great Ruaha ~ **EAT** 337 Hl 49
Great Sacandaga ~ **USA** 60 Dl 24
Great Sale Cay 🏝 **BS** 87 Dj 32
Great Salt Lake ~ **USA** 64 Cf 25
Great Salt Lake Desert ⛰ **USA** 64 Cf 25
Great Salt Plains Lake ~ **USA** 70 Cn 27
Great Sand Dunes N.M. ⚲ **USA** 65 Ck 27
Great Sand Hills ⛰ **CDN** 51 Ch 20
Great Sand Sea ⌓ **LAR** 300 Hd 31
Great Sandy Desert ⌓ **USA** 50 Cb 24
Great Sandy Desert ⌓ **AUS** 360 Lm 56
Great Sea Reef ≈ **FJI** 387 Nm 54
Great Slave Lake ~ **CDN** 6 Da 3
Great Slave Lake ~ **CDN** 42 Eb 6
Great Slave Lake ~ **CDN** 47 Ce 15
Great Smoky Mountains ⚲ **USA** 71 Df 28
Great Smoky Mountains ⛰ **USA** 71 Dg 28
Great Ungarian Plain ⌓ **H** 174 Hc 22
Great Victoria Desert ⌓ **AUS** 369 Lp 59
Great Visrivier ~ **ZA** 358 Hf 62
Great Wash Cliffs ⛰ **USA** 64 Ce 28
Great Western Erg ⌓ **DZ** 293 Gf 30
Great Western Torres Islands 🏝 **MYA** 262 Kn 40
Great Yarmouth ○ **GB** 163 Gg 19
Great Zimbabwe National Monument ★ **ZW** 352 Hh 56
Gréboun △ **RN** 308 Gl 35
Greece □ **GR** 194 Hc 26
Greefield ○ **USA** 71 Df 26
Greegully Creek ~ **AUS** 361 Lm 55
Greeley ○ **USA** 65 Ck 25
Greeley ○ **USA** 70 Cn 25
Greely Fjord ~ **CDN** 7 Eb 1
Greemville ○ **USA** 86 De 30
Green ○ **USA** 50 Ca 24
Greenbank ○ **CDN** 60 Dj 23
Green Bay ○ **USA** 57 De 23
Green Bay ~ **USA** 57 De 23
Green Bay ~ **CDN** 61 Eg 21
Greenbush ○ **USA** 56 Cp 21
Green Cape ⌒ **AUS** 379 Mm 64
Greencastle ○ **USA** 71 De 26
Greencastle ○ **USA** 74 Dj 26
Green Cay 🏝 **BS** 87 Dk 34
Greene ○ **USA** 60 Dl 24
Greenfield ○ **USA** 57 De 24
Greenfield ○ **USA** 60 Dm 24
Greenfield ○ **USA** 70 Da 25
Greenfield ○ **USA** 70 Db 27
Greenfield ○ **USA** 71 Dc 26
Greenfield ○ **USA** 71 Df 26
Green Head ○ **AUS** 368 Lh 61
Green Island 🏝 **AUS** 365 Mk 54
Green Island Bay ~ **RP** 267 Lk 40
Green Islands 🏝 **PNG** 287 Mn 48
Greenland ◉ **DK** 7 Ga 2
Greenland ◉ **DK** 43 Jb 4
Greenland ○ **USA** 57 Dd 22
Greenland Basin ♆ 18 Jb 2
Greenland Sea ♆ 18 Hb 3
Greenly Island 🏝 **AUS** 378 Md 63
Green Mountains ⛰ **USA** 60 Dm 24
Greenock ○ **GB** 162 Gd 18
Greenough ○ **AUS** 368 Lh 60
Greenouth ~ **AUS** 368 Lh 60
Green River ~ **USA** 51 Cg 24
Green River ○ **USA** 65 Cg 26
Green River ○ **USA** 65 Ch 25
Green River ○ **PNG** 286 Mg 47
Green River Bassin ⌓ **USA** 65 Cg 24
Greensboro ○ **USA** 71 De 29
Greensboro ○ **USA** 71 Dg 29
Greensboro ○ **USA** 74 Dj 27
Greensburg ○ **USA** 70 Cn 27
Greensburg ○ **USA** 71 Df 26
Greensburg ○ **USA** 74 Dj 25
Green Swamp ~ **USA** 74 Dj 28
Greenup ○ **USA** 71 Dd 26
Greenvale ○ **AUS** 365 Mj 55
Green Valley ○ **USA** 80 Cg 30
Greenville ○ **USA** 60 Dp 23
Greenville ○ **USA** 64 Cb 25
Greenville ○ **USA** 70 Cp 29
Greenville ○ **USA** 70 Dc 28
Greenville ○ **USA** 71 Dd 26
Greenville ○ **USA** 71 Df 25
Greenville ○ **USA** 71 Dg 27
Greenville ○ **USA** 71 Dh 25
Greenville ○ **USA** 74 Dk 28
Greenville ○ **USA** 86 Dc 29
Greenville ○ **USA** 86 Dg 30
Greenville ○ **LB** 316 Gb 43
Greenwich ○ **USA** 71 Dg 25
Greenwich ○ **GB** 163 Gf 20
Greenwood ○ **USA** 71 De 26
Greenwood ○ **USA** 71 Dg 28
Greenwood ○ **USA** 86 Dc 29
Greer ○ **USA** 71 Dg 28
Greers Ferry Lake ~ **USA** 70 Db 28
Gregoria Pérez de Denis ○ **RA** 136 Ed 60
Gregório ~ **BR** 117 Dn 49
Gregorio ~ **BR** 117 Dn 50
Gregorio Aznarez ○ **ROU** 146 Eg 63
Gregorio Méndez ○ **MEX** 93 Dc 37
Gregory ○ **USA** 56 Cn 24
Gregory ⚲ **AUS** 364 Mb 54
Gregory ~ **AUS** 365 Mf 55
Gregory Downs ○ **AUS** 365 Mf 55
Gregory Lake ~ **AUS** 361 Lp 56
Gregory Range ⛰ **AUS** 360 Ll 56
Gregory Range ⛰ **AUS** 365 Mh 55
Gregory Springs ○ **AUS** 365 Mj 55
Greifswald ○ **D** 170 Gn 18
Gremiha ○ **RUS** 159 Hm 11
Gremjač'e ○ **RUS** 181 Hn 20
Grená ○ **DK** 170 Gm 17
Grenada ○ **USA** 86 Dd 29
Grenada □ **WG** 104 Ed 39
Grenada Basin ♆ 104 Ec 39
Grenen 🏝 **DK** 170 Gm 17
Grenfell ○ **CDN** 51 Cl 20
Grenfell ○ **AUS** 379 Ml 62
Grenivík ○ **IS** 158 Fl 13
Grenoble ○ **F** 185 Gj 23
Grenora ○ **USA** 51 Ck 21
Grenville ○ **USA** 65 Cl 27
Grenville ○ **WG** 104 Ed 39
Gresham ○ **USA** 50 Ca 23
Gresik ○ **RI** 279 Lg 49
Gressåmoen ⚲ **N** 158 Gn 13
Grevená ○ **GR** 194 Hc 25
Grey ~ **CDN** 61 Ef 22
Greybull ○ **USA** 51 Cj 23
Greybull River ~ **USA** 51 Ch 23
Greylingstad ○ **ZA** 349 Hg 59
Greymouth ○ **NZ** 382 Nh 67
Grey Ranges ⛰ **AUS** 374 Mh 60
Grey River ○ **CDN** 61 Ef 22
Greyton ○ **ZA** 358 Hb 63
Greytown ○ **ZA** 352 Hh 60
Gribanovskij ○ **RUS** 181 Hn 20
Gribingui ~ **RCA** 321 Hb 42
Gribouo ○ **CI** 305 Gc 42
Gridino ○ **RUS** 159 Hk 13
Gridley ○ **USA** 64 Cb 26
Griekwastad Griquatown ○ **ZA** 349 Hd 60
Griffin ○ **CDN** 51 Cl 21
Griffin ○ **USA** 86 Df 29
Griffith ○ **AUS** 379 Mk 63
Griffiths Point ⌒ **CDN** 42 Db 3
Grijalva ~ **MEX** 93 Db 36
Grimari ○ **RCA** 321 Hc 43
Grimsby ○ **CDN** 60 Dj 24
Grimsby ○ **GB** 163 Gf 19
Grimselpass △ **CH** 174 Gl 22
Grimsey 🏝 **IS** 158 Fm 12
Grimstad ○ **N** 170 Gl 16
Grimsvötn ▲ **IS** 158 Fm 13
Grindavík ○ **IS** 158 Fj 14
Grinkiskis ○ **LT** 171 Hd 18
Grinnell Peninsula 🏝 **CDN** 7 Ea 2
Grinnell ○ **USA** 70 Db 25
Grinnel Peninsula 🏝 **CDN** 42 Fb 3
Grinsted ○ **DK** 170 Gl 18
Grintavec △ **SLO** 174 Gp 22
Grise Fiord ○ **CDN** 43 Ga 3
Grisslehamn ○ **S** 170 Hb 15
Grivița ○ **RO** 175 Hf 23
Grizim ~ **DZ** 293 Ge 33
Grizzly Bear Mountain △ **CDN** 47 Ca 13
Grjazi ○ **RUS** 181 Hm 19
Grjaznovo ○ **RUS** 171 Hl 18
Grjazovec ○ **RUS** 171 Hn 16
Grl. Enrique Mosconi ○ **PY** 136 Ec 57
Grois Island 🏝 **CDN** 61 Eg 20
Groauras ~ **BR** 124 Ep 47
Grobina ○ **LV** 170 Hc 17
Groblersdal ○ **ZA** 349 Hg 58
Groblershoop ○ **ZA** 349 Hd 60
Groenrivier ~ **ZA** 348 Ha 61
Groenriviersmond ○ **ZA** 348 Ha 61
Groesbeek ○ **ZA** 349 Hg 57
Grójec ○ **PL** 174 Hc 20
Gromballa ○ **TN** 297 Gm 27
Grong ○ **N** 158 Gn 13
Groningen ○ **SME** 113 Eg 43
Groningen ○ **NL** 170 Gk 19
Gronlid ○ **CDN** 51 Ck 19
Grønlingrotten ⚲ **N** 158 Gn 12
Grootberg ⛰ **NAM** 340 Gn 55
Grootberg ○ **NAM** 340 Gp 55
Groot Bergrivier ~ **ZA** 358 Hb 62
Grootdraai Dam ~ **ZA** 349 Hg 59
Grootdrink ○ **ZA** 349 Hc 60
Grootduin ⌓ **NAM** 348 Hb 57
Groote Eylandt 🏝 **AUS** 365 Me 53
Grootfontein ○ **NAM** 340 Hb 55
Grootfontein ○ **NAM** 348 Ha 58
Groot Henar ○ **SME** 113 Ef 43
Groot Karasberge ⛰ **NAM** 348 Hb 59
Grootkraal ○ **ZA** 358 Hc 62
Groot Letaba ~ **ZA** 352 Hh 57
Groot Marico ○ **ZA** 349 Hf 58
Grootrivier ~ **ZA** 358 Hc 62
Grootrivier ~ **ZA** 358 Hd 62
Groot Swartberge ⛰ **ZA** 358 Hd 62
Groot vloer ~ **ZA** 348 Hc 60
Groot Waterberg ⛰ **NAM** 348 Ha 56
Groot Winterhoekberge ⛰ **ZA** 358 He 62
Gropakehn ○ **LB** 316 Gb 43
Gros Morne △ **CDN** 61 Ee 21
Gros-Morne ○ **RH** 101 Dm 36
Gros Morne National Park ⚲ **CDN** 61 Ee 21
Gross Aub ○ **NAM** 348 Hb 59
Großer Arber △ **D** 174 Gn 21
Großer Priel △ **A** 174 Gp 22
Grosseto ○ **I** 185 Gm 24
Großglockner ▲ **A** 174 Gn 22
Gross Ums ○ **NAM** 348 Hb 57
Groswater Bay ~ **CDN** 7 Ga 4
Grotte de Lascaux ★ **F** 184 Gg 23
Grotte du Pech-Marie ★ **F** 184 Gg 23
Grotto of the Redempton ★ **USA** 56 Da 24
Grouard ○ **CDN** 47 Cc 17
Groumania ○ **CI** 317 Ge 42
Groundhog River ~ **CDN** 57 Dg 21
Group Aceton 🏝 **F** 14 Bb 12
Grouse Creek ○ **USA** 64 Cf 25
Grove City ○ **USA** 71 Dg 26
Grove Hill ○ **USA** 86 Dd 30
Grover ○ **USA** 51 Cg 24
Grover Beach ○ **USA** 64 Cb 28
Groznyy ○ **RUS** 202 Ja 24
Grudzdžiai ○ **LT** 171 Hd 17
Grudziądz ○ **PL** 170 Hb 19
Grumantbyen ○ **N** 158 Gp 6
Grumeti ~ **EAT** 337 Hk 47
Grums ○ **S** 170 Gn 16
Grünau ○ **NAM** 348 Hb 59
Grundarfjöður ○ **IS** 158 Fh 13
Grundy ○ **USA** 71 Dg 27
Grupe ○ **GH** 317 Ge 41
Grupo Sagua Baracoa ⛰ **C** 101 Dl 35
Grutness ○ **GB** 162 Gf 16
Gruver ○ **USA** 70 Cm 27
Gryfice ○ **PL** 170 Gp 19
Grygla ○ **USA** 56 Da 21
Gryllefjord ○ **N** 158 Ha 11
Grytøya 🏝 **N** 158 Ha 11
Grytviken ○ **UK** 15 Ha 15
Gstaad ○ **CH** 163 Gk 22
Guabito ○ **PA** 97 Dg 41
Guacamayas ○ **CO** 106 Dl 44
Guacara ○ **YV** 107 Dp 40
Guacautey ○ **YV** 112 Ed 43
Guachaca ○ **CO** 106 Dm 40
Guachara ○ **YV** 107 Dp 42
Guachipas ○ **RA** 136 Eb 58
Guachochic ○ **MEX** 80 Cj 32
Guachucal ○ **CO** 116 Dk 45
Guaco ○ **CO** 107 Dn 44
Guacu Boi ○ **BR** 146 Ef 60
Guadalajara ○ **MEX** 92 Cl 35
Guadalajara ○ **E** 184 Ge 25
Guadalcanal ○ **E** 184 Gd 26
Guadalcanal 🏝 **SOL** 290 Nc 51
Guadalcázar ○ **MEX** 92 Cm 34
Guadalimar ~ **E** 184 Ge 26
Guadálmez ~ **E** 184 Gd 26
Guadalope ~ **E** 184 Gf 25
Guadalquivir ~ **E** 184 Gd 27
Guadalupe ○ **USA** 64 Cb 28
Guadalupe ○ **MEX** 81 Cm 33
Guadalupe ~ **USA** 81 Cn 30
Guadalupe ○ **MEX** 92 Cl 34
Guadalupe ○ **PE** 116 Dj 49
Guadalupe ○ **BR** 124 En 49
Guadalupe ○ **E** 184 Gd 26
Guadalupe Bravos ○ **MEX** 80 Cj 30
Guadalupe Mountains ⛰ **USA** 65 Ck 29
Guadalupe Mountains National Park ⚲ **USA** 80 Ck 30
Guadalupe Peak △ **USA** 80 Ck 30
Guadalupe Victoria ○ **MEX** 64 Ce 29
Guadalupe Victoria ○ **MEX** 81 Ck 33
Guadalupe Victoria ○ **MEX** 81 Cp 33
Guadalupe y Calvo ○ **MEX** 80 Cj 32
Guadeloupe 🏝 **F** 104 Ed 37
Guadeloupe Passage ≈ 104 Ed 37
Guadelupe de Bahues ○ **MEX** 80 Ck 32
Guadiana ~ **P** 184 Gc 27
Guadiana ~ **E** 184 Gd 26
Guadiana Menor ~ **E** 184 Ge 27
Guadix ○ **E** 184 Ge 27
Guaduas ○ **CO** 106 Dl 43
Guaíba ○ **BR** 146 Ej 61
Guaicu ○ **BR** 133 Em 54
Guáimaro ○ **C** 101 Dk 35
Guaina ○ **YV** 112 Ec 43
Guainía ~ **CO** 107 Dp 44
Guaíra ○ **BR** 140 Eg 58
Guaíra ○ **BR** 141 Ek 56
Guairacá ○ **BR** 140 Eh 57
Guajara ○ **BR** 116 Dm 49
Guajará ~ **BR** 120 Eh 47
Guajará-Mirim ○ **BR** 129 Eb 51
Guajeru ○ **BR** 125 Ep 53
Guajira Peninsula 🏝 **CO** 107 Dn 39
Gualaceo ○ **EC** 116 Dj 47
Gualán ○ **GCA** 93 Dd 38
Gualaquiza ○ **EC** 116 Dj 47
Gualcuna ○ **RCH** 137 Dn 60
Gualeguay ~ **RA** 146 Ee 61
Gualeguay ○ **RA** 146 Ee 62
Gualeguay ~ **RA** 146 Ee 62
Gualeguaychu ○ **RA** 146 Ee 62
Gualeguaychu ~ **RA** 146 Ee 62
Gualjaina ○ **RA** 147 Dn 67
Guallatiri ○ **RCH** 128 Dp 55
Guam 🏝 **USA** 27 Sa 8
Guamá ~ **BR** 121 Ek 46
Guamá ○ **BR** 121 El 47
Guamal ○ **CO** 106 Dl 41
Guamal ○ **CO** 106 Dm 44
Guaminí ○ **RA** 137 Ec 64
Guamo ○ **CO** 106 Dl 43
Guamote ○ **EC** 116 Dj 46
Guamuchil ○ **MEX** 80 Ch 33
Guamués ~ **CO** 116 Dk 45
Gua Musang ○ **MAL** 270 La 43
Gu'an ○ **VRC** 246 Lj 26
Guanabacoa ○ **C** 100 Dg 34
Guanabo ○ **C** 100 Dg 34
Guanaceví ○ **MEX** 80 Cj 33
Guanaco Muerto ○ **RA** 137 Eb 61
Guanaco Sombriana ○ **RA** 137 Ec 60
Guanajay ○ **C** 100 Dg 34
Guanajuato ○ **MEX** 92 Cm 35
Guanajuñ ○ **YV** 112 Ec 43
Guanambi ○ **BR** 125 En 53
Guanare ○ **YV** 107 Dp 41
Guanare ~ **YV** 107 Dp 41
Guanarito ○ **YV** 107 Dp 41
Guanay ○ **BOL** 129 Dp 53
Guanchil ~ **RA** 136 Ea 59
Guandacol ○ **RA** 137 Dp 60
Guandi ~ **BR** 141 Ep 55
Guandiping ○ **VRC** 255 Lf 31
Guang'an ○ **VRC** 243 Ld 30
Guangchang ○ **VRC** 258 Lh 32
Guangde ○ **VRC** 246 Lk 30
Guangdong ◉ **VRC** 258 Lg 33
Guanghai ○ **VRC** 258 Lg 35
Guanghan ○ **VRC** 242 Lb 30
Guangji ○ **VRC** 242 Lb 30
Guanglu Dao 🏝 **VRC** 246 Lm 26
Guangmao Shan △ **VRC** 254 La 32
Guangning ○ **VRC** 258 Lg 34
Guangrao ○ **VRC** 246 Lk 27
Guangsheng Si ★ **VRC** 243 Lf 27
Guangshui ○ **VRC** 243 Lg 30
Guangshun ○ **VRC** 255 Ld 32
Guangxi Zhuangzu Zizhiqu ◉ **VRC** 255 Ld 33
Guangyang ○ **VRC** 258 Lj 31
Guangyuan ○ **VRC** 243 Lc 29
Guangze ○ **VRC** 258 Lj 32
Guangzhou ○ **VRC** 258 Lg 34
Guanhães ○ **BR** 141 En 55
Guaniamo ~ **YV** 112 Ec 42
Guánica ○ **USA** 104 Ea 37
Guanipa ~ **YV** 112 Ec 41
Guanling ○ **VRC** 255 Lc 33
Guanocó ○ **YV** 112 Ec 40
Guanqiao ○ **VRC** 243 Lc 27
Guanta ○ **YV** 112 Eb 40
Guanta ○ **RCH** 137 Dn 60
Guantánamo ○ **C** 101 Dl 35
Guantánamo Bay ○ **USA** 101 Dl 36
Guantao ○ **VRC** 243 Lh 27
Guanyun ○ **VRC** 246 Lk 28
Guapi ○ **CO** 106 Dk 44
Guapiara ○ **BR** 141 Ek 58
Guápiles ○ **CR** 97 Dg 40
Guapó ○ **BR** 133 Ek 54
Guaporé ~ **BOL** 129 Ed 52
Guaporé ~ **BR** 132 Ee 53
Guaporé ○ **BR** 146 Eh 60
Guaqui ○ **BOL** 128 Dp 54
Guará ~ **BR** 133 Em 52
Guarabira ○ **BR** 124 Fc 49
Guaraci ○ **BR** 141 Ek 56
Guaraciaba de Cardro ○ **BR** 140 Eh 59
Guaraciaba do Norte ○ **BR** 124 Ep 48
Guaraí ○ **BR** 121 Ek 50
Guarajambala ~ **HN** 93 Dd 39
Guaramacal ⚲ **YV** 107 Dn 41
Guaramuri ○ **GUY** 112 Ee 42
Guaranda ○ **EC** 116 Dj 46
Guaraniaçu ○ **BR** 140 Eh 58
Guaranoco ○ **YV** 112 Ec 41
Guarantã do Norte ○ **BR** 120 Eg 50
Guarapari ○ **BR** 141 Ep 56
Guarapuava ○ **BR** 140 Eh 58
Guaraquecaba ○ **BR** 141 Ek 58
Guararapes ○ **BR** 140 Ej 56
Guaratinga ○ **BR** 125 Fa 54
Guaratinguetá ○ **BR** 141 Em 57
Guaratuba ○ **BR** 141 Ek 58
Guarayos ○ **BOL** 128 Dp 52
Guarda ○ **P** 184 Gc 25
Guarda Mor ○ **BR** 133 El 54
Guardia Mitre ○ **RA** 147 Ec 66
Guardo ○ **E** 184 Gd 24
Guarenas ○ **YV** 107 Ea 40
Guari ○ **PNG** 287 Mk 50
Guariba ~ **BR** 120 Ed 49
Guariba ~ **BR** 120 Ed 50
Guariba ○ **BR** 141 Ek 56
Guaribas ○ **BR** 124 En 50
Guárico ~ **YV** 107 Ea 41
Guarinuma ○ **CO** 107 Dp 44
Guaruja ○ **BR** 141 El 58
Guarulhos ○ **BR** 141 El 57
Guasave ○ **MEX** 80 Ch 33
Guasca ○ **CO** 106 Dm 43
Guasdualito ○ **YV** 107 Dn 42
Guasimas ○ **MEX** 80 Cg 32
Guasipati ○ **YV** 112 Ec 42
Guasopa ○ **PNG** 287 Mn 50
Guatacondo ○ **RCH** 136 Dp 56
Guatacondo ~ **RCH** 136 Dp 56
Guatemala □ **GCA** 93 Dc 38
Guatemala Basin ♆ 11 Db 9
Guatemala Basin ♆ 96 Da 39
Guatemala City ▣ **GCA** 93 Dc 38
Guatire ○ **YV** 107 Ea 40
Guatopo ⚲ **YV** 107 Ea 40
Guaviare ~ **CO** 107 Dp 44
Guavi River ~ **PNG** 286 Mh 49
Guaxupé ○ **BR** 141 El 56
Guayabal ○ **C** 101 Dk 35
Guayabal ○ **YV** 107 Ea 41
Guayabero ~ **CO** 107 Dm 44
Guayaguas ○ **RA** 137 Ea 61
Guayaguayare ○ **TT** 104 Ed 40
Guayalejo ~ **MEX** 92 Cn 34
Guayama ○ **USA** 104 Ea 37
Guayape ~ **HN** 96 De 38
Guayapo ~ **YV** 107 Ea 43
Guayaquil ○ **EC** 116 Dh 47
Guayaramerin ○ **BOL** 129 Eb 51
Guayas ~ **CO** 106 Dl 45
Guaycurú ~ **RA** 140 Ee 59
Guayllabamba ~ **EC** 116 Dj 45
Guaymallén ○ **RA** 137 Dp 62
Guaytacama ○ **EC** 116 Dj 46
Guayubin ○ **DOM** 101 Dn 36
Guba ○ **ETH** 313 Hk 40
Guba Buor Khaya ≈ **RUS** 205 Wc 4
Gubaha ○ **RUS** 154 Rc 7
Guban ⌓ **SP** 328 Hp 40
Gubat ○ **RP** 267 Ln 39
Ģubatsaa Hills ⛰ **RB** 341 Hd 55
Ǧubba ○ **KSA** 214 Hn 32
Gubbi ○ **IND** 238 Kc 39
Gubbio ○ **I** 185 Gn 24
Guben ○ **D** 174 Gp 20
Gubi ○ **WAN** 320 Gl 40
Gubio ○ **WAN** 320 Gn 39
Gubkin ○ **RUS** 181 Hl 20
Gucha ~ **EAK** 337 Hk 46
Gucheng ○ **VRC** 243 Lf 28
Gucheng ○ **VRC** 243 Lf 29
Ģūčki ○ **IR** 222 Jh 27
Ǧūda ○ **KSA** 215 Jc 33
Gūdalūr ○ **IND** 239 Kc 40
Gudalur ○ **IND** 239 Kc 41
Ģudaut'a ○ **GE** 202 Hn 24
Ģudayyidat ○ **KSA** 214 Hn 30
Ǧudayyidat Ḥāmir ○ **IRQ** 214 Hn 30
Gudbrandsdalen ⌓ **N** 158 Gl 15
Gudekota ○ **IND** 238 Kc 38
Gudenå ~ **DK** 170 Gl 17
Gudermes ○ **RUS** 202 Jb 24
Gudgaon ○ **IND** 234 Kc 35
Gudivāda ○ **IND** 238 Ke 37
Gudiyattam ○ **IND** 238 Kd 39
Gudong ○ **VRC** 254 Kp 33
Gudryolum ○ **TM** 222 Jf 27
Gūdūr ○ **IND** 238 Kd 38
Gudvangen ○ **N** 158 Gk 15
Gueasson ○ **RG** 316 Gb 42
Guechémé ○ **RN** 320 Gh 39
Gueckedou ○ **RG** 316 Ga 41
Guéjar ~ **CO** 107 Dm 44
Guelb er Richat △ **RIM** 304 Ga 35
Guéléhé ○ **TCH** 321 Hb 41
Guélengdeng ○ **TCH** 321 Gp 40
Guéléninkoro ○ **RMM** 316 Gb 40
Guelltat Sidi Saad ○ **DZ** 293 Gg 28
Guelma ○ **DZ** 296 Gk 27
Guelmine ○ **MA** 292 Ga 31
Guelph ○ **CDN** 57 Dh 24
Guendo ○ **RMM** 305 Gc 39
Guéné ○ **DY** 320 Gh 40
Guenguel ~ **RA** 152 Dn 68
Guenté Paté ○ **SN** 304 Fn 38
Guépaouo ○ **CI** 317 Gd 42
Güeppi ○ **PE** 116 Dl 46
Güer Aike ○ **RA** 152 Dp 71
Guérande ○ **F** 163 Ge 22
Guerara ○ **DZ** 296 Gj 29
Guercif ○ **MA** 293 Ge 28
Guéréda ○ **TCH** 309 Hd 38
Guéret ○ **F** 163 Gg 22
Guernsey ○ **USA** 51 Ck 24

422 Grampian Mountains - Guernsey

□Country ▣Capital city ⊙Administrative unit OPlace ⌂Island ⛰Mountain range △Mountain ⌓Cape ≈Ocean, Sea ~Lake, River ▿Undersea topography ▲Glacier ♀National park •••Reservation ★Point of major interest ⌒Landscape

Guernsey ⌂ GB 163 Ge 21
Guernsey Reservoir ~ USA 51 Ck 24
Guérou O RIM 304 Fp 37
Guerrero O MEX 81 Cm 31
Guerrero O MEX 81 Cn 32
Guerrero Negro O MEX 75 Ce 32
Gueskérou O RN 321 Gn 39
Guéssabo O CI 305 Gc 42
Guéssésso O CI 304 Gc 42
Guessou-Sud O DY 320 Gh 40
Guestecitas O CO 107 Dm 40
Guetéma O RMM 304 Gb 38
Guéyo O CI 305 Gc 43
Guézaoua O RN 308 Gl 38
Gūge O IR 222 Jd 29
Gugē △ ETH 325 Hl 42
Gugu ⛰ ETH 325 Hm 41
Gugu △ ETH 325 Hn 41
Guguan ⌂ USA 27 Sa 8
Guhāgar O IND 238 Ka 37
Guiana Basin ▿ 11 Ga 8
Guiana Highlands ⛰ YV 112 Eb 43
Guiaviare ~ CO 107 Dm 44
Guibéroua O CI 305 Gc 42
Guibes O NAM 348 Ha 59
Guichi O VRC 246 Lj 30
Guichón O ROU 146 Ef 62
Guidan O RN 320 Gk 39
Guidari O TCH 321 Ha 41
Guider O CAM 321 Gn 41
Guidiguir O RN 308 Gl 39
Guidiguis O CAM 321 Gp 40
Guidimouni O RN 308 Gl 39
Guiding O VRC 255 Ld 32
Guidong O VRC 258 Lg 33
Guidouma O G 332 Gm 46
Guiers Lake ~ SN 304 Fn 37
Guigang O VRC 255 Le 34
Guiglo O CI 304 Gc 42
Guihua O VRC 242 Lc 30
Guihulngan O RP 267 Lm 40
Guijá O MOC 352 Hj 58
Guijuelo O E 184 Gd 25
Guilderton O AUS 368 Lh 61
Guildford O GB 163 Gf 20
Guilin O VRC 255 Lf 33
Guillestre O F 185 Gk 23
Guilmaro O DY 317 Gg 40
Guimarães O BR 121 Em 47
Guimarães O P 184 Gb 25
Guimarânia O BR 133 El 55
Guimaras Island ⌂ RP 267 Lm 40
Guimaras Strait ≈ RP 267 Lm 40
Guimba O RP 267 Ll 38
Guin O USA 71 De 28
Guinas O NAM 340 Ha 55
Guinchos Cay ⌂ BS 87 Dk 34
Guindulman O RP 267 Ln 41
Guiné O BR 125 Ep 52
Guinea □ RG 316 Fp 40
Guinea-Bissau □ GNB 316 Fm 39
Gûines O C 100 Dg 34
Guingamp O F 163 Ge 21
Guinguinéo O SN 304 Fm 38
Guiping O VRC 255 Le 34
Guir O RMM 305 Ge 36
Güira de Melena O C 100 Dg 34
Guiratinga O BR 132 Eh 54
Güiria O YV 112 Ec 40
Guirvas O SN 304 Fn 38
Guisa O C 101 Dk 35
Guishi Shuiku ~ VRC 255 Lf 33
Guissat O RN 308 Gk 37
Guissèr Mechra-Benâbbou O MA 293 Gc 29
Guissoumalé O RMM 316 Gb 39
Guitri O CI 317 Gd 43
Guiuan O RP 267 Ln 40
Guivi ⌂ FIN 159 Hf 11
Guixi O VRC 258 Lj 31
Guiyang O VRC 255 Ld 32
Guiyang O VRC 258 Lg 33
Guizhou ⊙ VRC 255 Lc 32
Gujarant ⊙ IND 227 Jp 34
Gujarat ⊙ IND 227 Jp 34
Gujar Khān O PK 230 Ka 29
Gujiao O VRC 243 Lg 27
Gujrānwāla O IND 230 Kb 29
Gujrat O PK 230 Ka 29
Gujri O IND 234 Kb 34
Gukovo O RUS 181 Hn 21
Gulargambone O AUS 379 Ml 61
Gulbarga O IND 238 Kc 37
Gulbene O LV 171 Hf 17
Gulbub O ER 313 Hm 37
Gul'ča O KS 230 Ka 25
Gulča ~ KS 230 Ka 26
Guledagudda O IND 238 Kb 37
Gulf Country ⌒ AUS 365 Mg 55
Gulf Dulce ~ CR 97 Dg 41
Gulf of Aden ≈ SP 328 Ja 40
Gulf of Alaska ≈ 6 Bb 4
Gulf of Amatique ~ HN 93 Dd 38
Gulf of Anadyr ≈ RUS 205 Zc 6
Gulf of Antalya ~ TR 195 Hh 27
Gulf of Aqabah ≈ 214 Hk 31
Gulf of Bone ≈ RI 282 Ll 47
Gulf of Boothia ~ CDN 7 Ea 2
Gulf of Boothia ≈ CDN 43 Fb 5
Gulf of Bothnia ≈ FIN 158 Hb 14
Gulf of Cádiz ≈ E 184 Gc 27
Gulf of California ≈ 75 Ce 30
Gulf of Campeche ≈ 93 Da 36
Gulf of Carpentaria ▿ AUS 365 Mf 52
Gulf of Chiriquí ~ PA 97 Dg 41
Gulf of Corinth ~ GR 194 Hd 26
Gulf of Coronado ~ CR 97 Dg 41
Gulf of Darién ~ PA 104 Dk 41
Gulf of Drin ~ AL 194 Hb 25
Gulf of Finland ≈ FIN 171 He 16
Gulf of Fonseca ~ HN 96 De 39
Gulf of Gabès ~ TN 297 Gm 28
Gulf of Gdańsk ~ PL 170 Hb 18
Gulf of Genoa ~ I 185 Gl 23
Gulf of Gonâve ~ RH 101 Dm 36
Gulf of Guayaquil ~ EC 116 Dh 47
Gulf of Guinea ≈ 317 Gg 43
Gulf of Hallāniyāt ~ OM 219 Jf 37
Gulf of Hammamet ~ TN 297 Gm 27
Gulf of Honduras ~ HN 96 De 37
Gulf of Kachchh ~ IND 227 Jn 34
Gulf of Khambhāt ~ IND 238 Ka 35
Gulf of Maine ≈ 60 Dp 24
Gulf of Mannar ~ IND 239 Kd 41
Gulf of Martaban ~ MYA 262 Kn 38
Gulf of Masira ~ OM 219 Jh 35
Gulf of Mexico ≈ 86 Db 33
Gulf of Nicoya ~ CR 97 Df 41
Gulf of Ob ~ RUS 22 Nb 3
Gulf of Ob ≈ RUS 154 Sc 5
Gulf of Oman ≈ OM 226 Jh 33
Gulf of Panamá ~ PA 97 Dj 42
Gulf of Papagayo ~ CR 97 Df 40
Gulf of Papua ≈ 287 Mj 50
Gulf of Paria ~ YV 112 Ec 40
Gulf of Riga ≈ LV 171 Hd 17
Gulf of Saint Lawrence ≈ 61 Ec 21
Gulf of San Jorge ~ RA 152 Ea 69
Gulf of San Miguel ~ PA 97 Dj 41
Gulf of Santa Catalina ~ USA 64 Cc 29
Gulf of Sidra ≈ 297 Ha 29
Gulf of Suez ~ ET 301 Hj 31
Gulf of Tadjoura ~ DJI 328 Hp 40
Gulf of Taganrog ~ RUS 181 Hl 22
Gulf of Tarant ~ I 194 Ha 25
Gulf of Thailand ≈ 262 La 40
Gulf of Tolo ≈ RI 282 Lm 47
Gulf of Tomini ≈ RI 282 Ll 46
Gulf of Tonkin ≈ VN 255 Ld 35
Gulf of Tunis ~ TN 297 Gm 27
Gulf of València ~ E 184 Gg 26
Gulf of Venezuela ~ YV 107 Dn 40
Gulf of Venice ~ I 185 Gn 23
Gulfo of Tehuantepec ~ MEX 93 Da 38
Gulfport O USA 86 Dd 30
Gulf Shores O USA 86 De 30
Gulf St. Vincent ~ AUS 378 Mf 63
Gulgong O AUS 379 Ml 62
Guliston O UZB 223 Jn 25
Gul Kach O PK 227 Jn 30
Gulkana O USA 46 Bc 13
Gulkana River ~ USA 46 Bc 13
Gul'kevič O RUS 202 Hn 23
Güllab D. ~ TR 195 Hm 27
Gullfoss ★ IS 158 Fl 13
Gulliver O USA 57 De 23
Gull Lake ~ CDN 51 Cf 19
Gull Lake O CDN 51 Ch 20
Gull Lake ~ USA 56 Da 22
Güllük Körfez ~ TR 195 Hf 27
Gully O USA 56 Da 22
Gulmar Kale ★ TR 202 Hp 27
Gulmit O PK 230 Kb 27
Gülnar O TR 195 Hj 27
Gülpınar O TR 195 Hf 26
Gülşehir O TR 195 Hk 26
Gulu O EAU 324 Hj 44
Gulumba Gana O WAN 321 Gp 40
Guluwuru Island ⌂ AUS 364 Me 51
Gulwe O EAT 337 Hl 49
Gumaira O UAE 226 Jf 33
Gumal ~ PK 227 Jn 30
Gumani Hurasagar ~ BD 235 Kj 33
Gumare O RB 341 Hd 56
Gumawana Island ⌂ PNG 287 Mm 50
Gumba O RDC 321 Hc 44
Gumbiro O EAT 344 Hk 51
Gumbo Gumbo Creek ~ AUS 375 Mh 59
Gumel O WAN 320 Gl 39
Gumi O RI 275 Lp 45
Gumine O PNG 287 Mj 49
Gumla O IND 235 Kg 34
Gumlu O AUS 365 Mk 55
Gummersbach O D 163 Gk 20
Gummi O WAN 320 Gj 39
Gümüşhane O TR 195 Hm 25
Guna O IND 234 Kc 33
Gunam Ronda O IND 238 Kd 39
Guna Terara △ ETH 313 Hm 40
Gun Barrel City O USA 70 Cp 29
Gundagai O AUS 379 Ml 63
Gundāla O IND 238 Ke 37
Gundji O RDC 333 Hc 44
Gundlupet O IND 238 Kc 40
Gündoğmuş O TR 195 Hh 27
Gunga O ANG 340 Hb 53
Gungi O RDC 333 Hb 49
Gungo O ANG 340 Gp 51
Gungu O RDC 333 Hb 48
Gunisao Lake ~ CDN 56 Cn 19
Gunisao River ~ CDN 56 Cn 19
Güniya O RL 208 Hk 29
Gunn O CDN 50 Ce 19
Gunna O SUD 324 Hf 42
Gunnab O NAM 348 Ha 59
Gunnarn O S 158 Ha 13
Gunnawarra O AUS 365 Mj 54
Gunnbjørn Fjeld △ DK 43 Kc 5
Gunnedah O AUS 379 Mm 61
Gunning O AUS 379 Ml 63
Gunnison O USA 65 Cg 26
Gunnison O USA 65 Cj 26
Gunnison River ~ USA 65 Ch 26
Gunn Point ⌓ AUS 364 Mb 52
Gunpowder O AUS 365 Mf 55
Günsang O VRC 230 Kf 30
Gunt ~ TJ 223 Jp 27
Gunta O WAN 320 Gl 40
Guntakal O IND 238 Kc 38
Guntersville O USA 71 De 28
Gunterville Lake ~ USA 71 De 28
Guntur O IND 238 Ke 37
Gununa O AUS 365 Mf 54
Gunung Abohgalong △ RI 270 Kn 43
Gunung Agung △ RI 279 Lh 50
Gunung Angemuk △ RI 286 Mf 47
Gunung Antares △ RI 286 Mg 48
Gunung Api △ RI 279 Lk 50
Gunung Argopuro △ RI 279 Lg 49
Gunung Arjuna △ RI 279 Lg 49
Gunung Aurbunak △ RI 279 Lh 47
Gunung Awu △ RI 275 Ln 44
Gunung Bakayan △ RI 274 Lj 44
Gunung Balease △ RI 282 Ll 47
Gunung Basakan △ RI 274 Lj 44
Gunung Batukau △ RI 279 Lh 50
Gunung Benom △ MAL 270 La 44
Gunung Besar △ MAL 271 Lb 44
Gunung Bintang △ MAL 270 La 43
Gunung Boliohutu △ RI 275 Lm 45
Gunung Bulawa △ RI 275 Lm 45
Gunung Chamah △ MAL 270 La 43
Gunung Cirema △ RI 278 Le 49
Gunung Dako △ RI 275 Ll 45
Gunung Dempo △ RI 278 Lb 47
Gunung Dom △ RI 286 Me 47
Gunung Gading N.P. ♀ RI 271 Le 45
Gunung Gagau △ MAL 270 Lb 43
Gunung Gandadiwata △ RI 279 Lk 47
Gunung Guguang △ RI 274 Lj 44
Gununghalu O RI 278 Ld 49
Gunung Harun △ MAL 274 Lh 43
Gunung Irau △ RI 283 Mc 46
Gunung Kambuno △ RI 279 Lk 47
Gunung Kaplamada △ RI 282 Lp 47
Gunung Karoni △ RI 282 Ll 47
Gunung Katoposo △ RI 282 Ll 46
Gunung Kemal △ RI 274 Lj 45
Gunung Kerinci △ RI 270 La 46
Gunung Kinabalu △ MAL 274 Lj 42
Gunung Korbu △ MAL 270 La 43
Gunung Kujat △ RI 274 Lj 44
Gunung Kwoka △ RI 283 Mc 46
Gunung Lawit △ RI 274 Lg 45
Gunung Ledang △ MAL 270 Lb 44
Gunung Lembu △ RI 270 Kn 43
Gunung Lesung △ RI 274 Lh 45
Gunung Leuser △ RI 270 Kn 44
Gunung Liangpran △ RI 274 Lh 45
Gunung Lompobatang △ RI 279 Lk 48
Gunung Lompopana △ RI 279 Lk 46
Gunung Lumut △ RI 274 Lj 46
Gunung Malea △ RI 270 Kp 45
Gunung Malino △ RI 275 Ll 45
Gunung Marapi △ RI 270 La 46
Gunung Masura △ RI 270 La 47
Gunung Mebo △ RI 283 Mc 46
Gunung Mekongga △ RI 282 Ll 47
Gunung Menyapa △ RI 274 Lh 45
Gunung Merapi O RI 278 Lf 49
Gunung Mulu ♀ MAL 274 Lh 43
Gunung Mulu △ MAL 274 Lh 44
Gunung Murud △ MAL 274 Lh 44
Gunung Niut △ RI 271 Le 45
Gunung Noring △ MAL 270 La 43
Gunung Porekautimbu △ RI 282 Ll 46
Gunung Rantemario △ RI 279 Lk 47
Gunung Raung △ RI 279 Lg 50
Gunung Raya △ RI 279 Lg 46
Gunung Rinjani △ RI 279 Lj 50
Gunung Saran △ RI 271 Lf 46
Gunung Sebayan △ RI 271 Lf 46
Gunung Sidole △ RI 279 Lk 46
Gunung Sihabuhabu △ RI 270 Kp 44
Gunungsitoli O RI 270 Kn 45
Gunung Slamet △ RI 278 Le 49
Gunung Solat △ RI 275 Lp 45
Gunung Sonjol △ RI 275 Ll 45
Gunung Tahan △ MAL 270 Lb 43
Gunung Takan △ RI 279 Lj 50
Gunung Talaman △ RI 270 Kp 45
Gunung Tambora △ RI 279 Lj 50
Gunung Tapis △ MAL 271 Lb 43
Gunung Tenamatura △ RI 282 Ll 46
Gunung Tentolomatinan △ RI 275 Ll 45
Gunung Tibau △ RI 274 Lh 45
Gunung Trus Madi △ MAL 274 Lj 43
Gunungtua O RI 270 Kp 45
Gunung Tumpu △ RI 282 Lm 46
Gunung Tumputiga △ RI 282 Lm 46
Gunung Ubia △ RI 286 Me 48
Gunung Umsini △ RI 283 Mc 46
Gunung Wanggameti △ RI 282 Ll 51
Gunupur O IND 235 Kf 36
Guocheng O VRC 242 Lc 27
Guodao O VRC 243 Lf 27
Guodao O VRC 243 Lg 27
Guo He ~ VRC 246 Lj 29
Guoquanyan △ VRC 242 Lb 30
Guoyang O VRC 243 Lh 29
Gurage △ ETH 325 Hm 41
Gurān O IR 226 Jf 32
Gurayquirajo ~ RA 146 Ee 61
Gurba ~ RDC 324 Hf 43
Gurbantünggüt Shamo ⌒ VRC 204 Tc 10
Gurd Abu Muharrik ⌒ ET 301 Hg 31
Gurdon O USA 70 Db 29
Guree Creek ~ AUS 360 Lj 57
Gurenici O RUS 171 Hj 15
Gurgaon O IND 234 Kc 31
Gurguéia ~ BR 121 Em 50
Gurguéia ~ BR 124 En 49
Gurib ~ NAM 348 Ha 59
Gurig ♀ AUS 364 Mb 51
Gurig National Park ♀ AUS 364 Mb 51
Gūrīn O IRQ 209 Hp 27
Gürina O YV 112 Ec 40
Gurinhatã O BR 133 Ek 55
Gurjaani O GE 202 Ja 25
Gurla Mandhate △ VRC 230 Ke 30
Gurlan O UZB 222 Jj 25
Gurm O AFG 223 Jp 27
Gurner O AUS 361 Mb 57
Guro O MOC 344 Hj 54
Gürpinar O TR 202 Hp 26
Gurri O SUD 321 Hd 39
Gursahaygani O IND 234 Kd 32
Guru O VRC 235 Kj 31
Gurué O MOC 344 Hl 53
Gurun O MAL 270 La 43
Gürün O TR 195 Hl 26
Gurupa O BR 121 Ej 46
Gurupi ~ BR 121 El 47
Gurupi ~ BR 121 El 48
Gurupi O BR 133 Ek 51
Guru Sikhar Mount Abu △ IND 227 Ka 33
Guruve O ZW 341 Hh 54
Guruzāla O IND 238 Kd 37
Gusau O WAN 320 Gk 39
Gusev O RUS 170 Hd 18
Gushan ★ VRC 258 Lk 32
Gusher O USA 65 Ch 25
Gushgy O TM 223 Jk 28
Gushi O VRC 242 Kn 30
Gushi O VRC 243 Lh 29
Gushiegu O GH 317 Gf 41
Gushikawar O J 259 Lp 32
Gus'-Hrustal'nyj O RUS 181 Hn 18
Gusi O RI 283 Mc 47
Gūš Lāġar O IR 223 Jj 28
Gúspini O I 185 Gl 26
Gustav Adolf land ⌂ N 158 Hc 6
Gustavfjellet △ N 158 Ha 6
Gustavia O F 104 Ec 37
Gustavo Sotelo O MEX 75 Cf 30
Gustavsberg O S 170 Hb 16
Gustavus O USA 47 Bg 15
Gustav V land ⌂ N 158 Hb 5
Gusuku sites ★ J 259 Lp 32
Gütersloh O D 163 Gk 20
Guthalungra O AUS 365 Mk 55
Guthrie O USA 65 Ch 29
Guthrie O USA 70 Cm 29
Guthrie O USA 70 Cp 28
Guthrie O USA 71 De 27
Gutian O VRC 258 Lk 32
Gutiérrez Zamora O MEX 81 Cp 34
Gutsuo O VRC 235 Kh 31
Guttaiyūr O IND 238 Kc 40
Guttenberg O USA 56 Dc 24
Gutu O ZW 341 Hh 55
Guwahati O IND 235 Kk 32
Ġuwaifāt O UAE 215 Jd 33
Guwaiza O UAE 226 Jf 33
Guwayr O SUD 313 Hj 37
Guyana □ GUY 112 Ed 43
Guyanas O MEX 80 Cg 32
Guyandotte ~ USA 71 Dg 26
Guyenne ⌒ F 184 Gf 23
Guy Fawkes River ♀ AUS 379 Mn 61
Guyī O ETH 325 Hk 41
Guymon O USA 70 Cm 27
Guynemer O CDN 56 Cn 20
Guyra O AUS 379 Mm 61
Guyu O ZW 349 Hg 56
Guyuan O VRC 243 Ld 27
Güzelsu O TR 202 Hp 26
Guzhen O VRC 246 Lj 29
Guzhen O VRC 259 Ll 32
Guzmán O MEX 80 Cj 30
Guzor O UZB 223 Jm 26
Gvādar O IR 226 Jj 33
Gvadar Bay ~ PK 226 Jj 33
Gvardejsk O RUS 170 Hc 18
Gvasjugi O RUS 250 Me 22
Gwa O MYA 262 Km 37
Gwaai O ZW 341 Hf 55
Gwaai River ~ ZW 341 Hf 55
Gwabegar O AUS 379 Ml 61
Gwada O WAN 320 Gk 41
Gwadabawa O WAN 308 Gj 39
Gwādar O PK 226 Jk 33
Gwagwalada O WAN 320 Gk 41
Gwalangu O RDC 333 Hb 44
Gwalior O IND 234 Kc 32
Gwalishtap O PK 226 Jk 31
Gwamba O WAN 320 Gh 40
Gwanda O ZW 349 Hg 56
Gwane O RDC 324 He 43
Gwaram O WAN 320 Gl 40
Gwarif O RI 286 Mf 47
Gwarzo O WAN 320 Gk 40
Gwasero O WAN 320 Gh 41
Gwayi ~ ZW 341 Hf 55
Gwembe O Z 341 Hf 54
Gwendje O RDC 333 Hb 44
Gweru O ZW 341 Hg 55
Gweru ~ ZW 341 Hg 55
Gweta O RB 349 He 56
Gwi O WAN 320 Gk 41
Gwinn O USA 57 De 22
Gwinner O USA 56 Cn 22
Gwoza O WAN 321 Gn 40
Gwydir ~ AUS 375 Ml 60
Gyaca O VRC 235 Kl 31
Gyangze O VRC 235 Kj 31
Gyaring Co ~ VRC 231 Kj 30
Gyaring Hu ~ VRC 242 Kn 28
Gyda O RUS 204 Ta 4
Gydanskaja guba ~ RUS 22 Nb 2
Gydanskaya Guba ~ RUS 204 Ta 4
Gydanskiy Peninsula ⌂ RUS 22 Nb 2
Gydanskiy Poluostrov ⌂ RUS 204 Sc 4
Gyitang O VRC 242 Kn 30
Gympie O AUS 375 Mn 59
Gyobinchan O MYA 254 Km 35
Gyobingauk O MYA 254 Km 36
Gyöngyös O H 174 Hb 22
Győr O H 174 Ha 22
Gypsum Palace O AUS 379 Mj 62
Gypsumville O CDN 56 Cn 20
Gyumri O ARM 202 Hp 25

H

h. Roman-Koš △ UA 175 Hk 23
H. S. Trumann Reservation ~ USA 70 Db 26
Há O VN 255 Ld 35
Häädemeste O EST 171 Hd 16
Haakon VII land ⌂ N 158 Gn 6
Haalenberg O NAM 348 Gp 59
Ha'ano ⌂ TO 390 Ac 55
Ha'apai Group ⌂ TO 390 Ac 55
Haapajärvi O FIN 159 He 14
Haapsalu O EST 171 Hd 16
Haarlem O NL 163 Gh 19
Haarlem O ZA 358 Hd 62
Haastberget △ N 158 Hc 6
Haast Bluff O AUS 361 Mb 57
Haast Pass △ NZ 382 Ng 68
Haasts Bluff Aboriginal Land ••• AUS 361 Ma 57
Haast Village O NZ 382 Ng 67
Haaway O SP 329 Hp 45
Hab ~ PK 227 Jm 33
Habarane O CL 239 Ke 42
Habar Cirir O SP 328 Ja 43
Ḥabarūt O OM 219 Je 36
Habaswein O EAK 325 Hm 45
Ḥābībābād O IR 222 Jd 29
Habob ~ SUD 313 Hk 36
Habraykhoun O LAO 263 Lc 38
Habšān O UAE 215 Je 34
Hachijyo-shima ⌂ J 251 Mf 29
Hachinohe O J 250 Mg 25
Hachiōji O J 251 Mf 28
Hachita O USA 80 Cf 30
Hackberry O USA 64 Cf 28
Hackney O GUY 113 Ee 42
Haco O ANG 340 Gp 51
Hacufera O MOC 352 Hj 56
Ḥāḍa O KSA 214 Hn 34
Hadagalli O IND 238 Kb 38
Hadaliya O SUD 313 Hl 37
Hadashville O CDN 56 Da 21
Ḥadbaram O OM 219 Jf 37
Ḥaddā' O KSA 218 Hm 35
Ḥaddād Banī Malik O KSA 218 Hn 35
Haddumati Atoll ⌂ MV 239 Ka 44
Hadejia O WAN 320 Gl 39
Hadejia ~ WAN 320 Gl 39
Ḥadera O IL 208 Hk 29
Haderslev O DK 170 Gl 18
Hadgaon O IND 238 Kc 36
Hadibū O YE 219 Je 39
Hadihui O VRC 243 Lf 27
Hadilik O VRC 231 Kh 27
Hadım O TR 195 Hj 27
Hadjač O UA 175 Hk 20
Hadjer Bandala O TCH 321 Hc 40
Hadjer el Hamis O TCH 321 Gp 39
Hadley Bay ~ CDN 6 Db 2
Hadley Bay ≈ CDN 42 Ec 4
Ḥaḍnān O IRQ 209 Hp 27
Hà Đong O VN 255 Lc 35
Ḥadrānīya O IRQ 209 Hp 28
Hadrian's Wall ★ GB 162 Ge 18
Hadseløya ⌂ N 158 Gn 11
Hadsund O DK 170 Gm 17
Hadyžensk O RUS 202 Hm 23
Hae O THA 254 La 36
Haeinsa Temple ★ ROK 247 Lp 28
Haeju O DVRK 247 Ln 27
Hae-nam O ROK 247 Lp 28
Haenertsburg O ZA 349 Hg 57
Ḥafar al-Bāṭin O KSA 215 Ja 31
Hafford O CDN 51 Cj 19
Haffouz O TN 296 Gl 28
Hafik O TR 195 Hl 26
Hafirat al-'Aida O KSA 214 Hm 32
Ḥāfirat Nisāḥ O KSA 215 Jb 33
Ḥāfizābād O PK 230 Ka 30
Hafnarfjörður O IS 158 Fk 14
Haftgel O IR 215 Jc 30
Hagadera O EAK 325 Hn 45
Ḥağar aš-Šarqī ⛰ OM 226 Jh 34
Hagar Banga O SUD 313 Hd 40
Hagari ~ IND 238 Kc 38
Ḥağda O YE 218 Hp 39
Hagebro O DK 170 Gl 17
Hagemeister Island ⌂ USA 46 Aj 15
Hagen O D 163 Gk 20
Hāgere Hiywet O ETH 325 Hl 41
Hāgere Selam O ETH 325 Hm 42
Hagerman O USA 50 Ce 24
Hagermann O USA 65 Ck 29
Hagerstown O USA 74 Dj 26
Hagfors O S 158 Gn 15
Ḥağğa O YE 218 Hp 38
Ḥāgg'Abd Allāh O SUD 313 Hj 38
Ḥaǧǧiābād O IR 226 Jf 31
Hagi O J 247 Mb 28
Ha Giang O VN 255 Lc 34
Haguaçu da Bahia O BR 125 Em 51
Haguenau O F 163 Gk 21
Hahaya O COM 345 Hp 51
Haho O BF 317 Ge 40
Haho ~ RT 317 Gg 42
Hai'an O VRC 246 Ll 29
Hai'an O VRC 255 Lf 35
Haib O NAM 348 Hb 60
Haib ~ NAM 348 Hb 60
Ḥaibar O KSA 214 Hm 33
Ḥaibar al-Ganūb O KSA 218 Hp 36
Haicheng O VRC 246 Lm 25
Haidargarh O IND 234 Ke 32
Hải Du'o'ng O VN 255 Ld 35
Haieng O VRC 258 Lh 34
Haifa O IL 208 Hk 29
Haifeng O VRC 258 Lh 34
Haig O AUS 369 Lp 61
Haigler O USA 70 Cm 25
Haikang O VRC 255 Le 35
Haikou O VRC 255 Lf 35
Ḥā'il O KSA 214 Hn 32
Hailar O VRC 204 Vc 9
Hailey O USA 50 Ce 24
Hailing Dao ⌂ VRC 255 Lf 35
Hailuoto Karlö ⌂ FIN 159 Hd 13
Haima' O OM 219 Jg 36
Haimen O VRC 246 Ll 30
Hainan ⊙ VRC 255 Le 36
Hainan Dao ⌂ VRC 255 Le 36
Haines O USA 47 Bj 15
Haines O USA 50 Cc 23
Haines Junction O CDN 47 Bg 15
Hainin O YE 218 Jc 38
Haining O VRC 246 Ll 30
Hai Ninh O VN 255 Ld 35
Hải Phong O VN 255 Ld 35
Haïré Lao O SN 304 Fn 37
Haitan Dao ⌂ VRC 259 Lk 33
Haiti □ RH 101 Dm 37
Haitou O VRC 255 Le 36
Haiyan O VRC 242 La 27
Haiyan O VRC 246 Ll 30
Haiyang O VRC 246 Ll 27
Haiyuan O VRC 242 Lc 27
Haizhou Wan ~ VRC 246 Lk 28
Hajdarkan O KS 223 Jp 26
Hajeb El Ayoun O TN 296 Gl 28
Hajiki-saki ⌓ J 251 Mf 26
Hajnówka O PL 171 Hd 19
Hajo Do ⌂ ROK 247 Ln 28
Hajsyn O UA 175 Hg 21
Hajvoron O UA 175 Hg 21
Hajyr O RUS 205 Wc 4
Haka O MYA 254 Kl 34
Hakalau O USA 75 An 36
Hakkâri O TR 202 Hp 27
Hakkâri Dağları ⛰ TR 202 Hp 27
Hakkulabad O UZB 223 Jp 25
Hakodate O J 250 Mg 25
Hakosberge ⛰ NAM 348 Gp 57
Hakskeenpan ~ ZA 348 Hc 59
Hakui O J 251 Me 27
Hakusan ♀ J 251 Me 27
Haku-san △ J 251 Me 27
Hāla O PK 227 Jn 33
Halabǧa O IRQ 209 Ja 28
Halā'ib O ET 301 Hl 34
Halali O NAM 340 Ha 55
Ḥālat 'Ammār O KSA 214 Hk 31
Halberstadt O D 174 Gm 20
Halbrite O CDN 51 Cl 21
Halden O N 170 Gm 16
Haldia O IND 235 Kh 34
Haldwāni O IND 234 Kd 31
Hale ~ AUS 374 Md 57
Haleakala Crater △ USA 75 Am 35
Haleakala Natl. Park ♀ USA 75 An 35
Haleiwa O USA 75 Al 35
Ha Lejone O LS 349 Hg 60
Haleyville O USA 71 De 28
Hal Flood Range ⛰ 38 Ca 17
Halfmoon Bay O CDN 50 Ca 21
Halfmoon Bay (Oban) O NZ 382 Ng 69
Half Moon Lake ~ AUS 369 Mc 61
Halfway O USA 50 Cd 23
Halfway Point ⌓ CDN 57 Dh 20
Halgen O SP 328 Ja 43
Ḥalḥal O IR 209 Jc 27
Halhgol O MNG 204 Vc 9
Ḥalībān O KSA 215 Ja 34
Haliburton Highland ⛰ CDN 60 Dj 23
Ḥalīd O IRQ 209 Ja 29
Halifax O CDN 61 Ec 23
Halifax O AUS 365 Mk 55
Halifax Bay ~ AUS 365 Mk 55
Ḥalīǧ Abu Ḥašhā'ifa ~ ET 301 Hf 30
Ḥalīg al-'Arab ~ et 301 Hg 30
Ḥalīg al-Kuwait ~ KWT 215 Jb 31
Ḥalīǧ as-Sallūm ~ ET 300 He 30
Ḥalīǧ aṭ-Ṭīna ~ ET 301 Hj 30
Halīl Rūd ~ IR 226 Jh 32
Halilulik O RI 282 Ln 50
Haliyāl O IND 238 Kb 38
Hálki ⌂ GR 195 Hf 27
Halkída O GR 194 Hd 26
Halkirk O CDN 51 Cf 19
Halland ⌒ S 170 Gn 17
Hallandale Beach O USA 87 Dh 33
Hallasan ★ ROK 247 Lp 29
Hallasan △ ROK 247 Lp 29
Hall Beach O CDN 43 Gb 5
Halle O D 174 Gm 20
Halleck O USA 64 Ce 25
Hallein O A 174 Gn 22
Hallen O S 158 Gn 14
Hallett O AUS 378 Mf 62
Hallettsville O USA 81 Cp 31
Halliday O USA 51 Cl 22
Hallingdal ⌒ N 158 Gl 15
Hallingskarvet △ N 158 Gk 15
Hall in Tirol O A 174 Gm 22
Hall Islands ⌂ FSM 27 Sb 9
Hall Lake ~ CDN 43 Gb 5
Hällnäs O S 158 Hb 13
Hallock O USA 56 Cp 21
Hall Peninsula ⌂ CDN 43 Hb 6
Hall Point ⌓ AUS 364 Mc 51
Hällristningar ★ S 170 Gm 16
Halls Creek O AUS 361 Lp 55
Halls Gap O AUS 378 Mh 64
Halls Lake O CDN 60 Dj 23
Hallstavik O S 170 Hb 15
Halmahera Sea ≈ RI 275 Ma 45
Halmstad O S 170 Gn 17
Halndi O LB 316 Ga 42
Hālol O IND 227 Ka 34
Ha Long Bay ★ VN 255 Ld 35
Hälsingland ⌒ S 158 Gp 15
Halstad O USA 56 Cp 22
Halt Assini O GH 317 Ge 43
Haltdalen O N 158 Gm 14
Haltiatunturi △ S 159 Hc 11
Haltom City O USA 70 Cp 29
Halvad O IND 227 Jp 34
Halvmåneøya ⌂ N 158 Hd 7
Halvø ⌓ DK 7 Fb 2
Halvø ⌓ DK 43 Hb 3
Ḥalwān al Ḥunfa △ KSA 214 Hm 31
Ham ~ NAM 348 Hb 60
Hamab O NAM 348 Hb 60
Hamada O J 247 Mb 28
Hamada de la Daoura ⌒ DZ 293 Gd 31
Hamada de Tindouf ⌒ DZ 292 Gb 32
Hamada du Drâa ⌒ DZ 293 Gc 31
Hamada du Guir ⌒ MA 293 Ge 30
Hamada ed Douakel ⌒ DZ 293 Gc 32
Hamâda el Harich ⌒ RMM 305 Gd 34
Hamadān O IR 209 Jc 28
Hamadān ⊙ IR 209 Jc 28
Hamada Tounassine ⌒ DZ 293 Gc 31
Hamaguir O DZ 293 Ge 30
Hamāh O SYR 208 Hl 28
Hamale O GH 317 Ge 40
Hamamah O LAR 300 Hc 29
Hamamasu O J 250 Mg 24
Hamamatsu O J 251 Me 28
Hamamed en Nasla ⌒ LAR 297 Gm 30
Hamar O N 158 Gm 15
Hamasaka O J 251 Md 28
Hamatombetsu O J 250 Mh 23
Hambantota O CL 239 Ke 42
Hamburg O USA 60 Dj 24
Hamburg O USA 70 Da 25
Hamburg O USA 70 Db 29
Hamburg O D 170 Gm 19
Hamburg O ZA 358 Hf 62
Hämeenlinna O FIN 159 Hd 15
Hamelin O AUS 368 Lh 59
Hamelin Pool ~ AUS 368 Lg 59
Hameln O D 170 Gl 19
Hamen Wan ~ VRC 258 Lj 34
Hamer Koke O ETH 325 Hl 43
Hamerro-Hadad O ETH 328 Hp 42
Hamersley Range ⛰ AUS 360 Ll 56
Hamersley Range O AUS 360 Lj 57
Hamersley Range ♀ AUS 360 Lk 57
Hamhung O DVRK 247 Lp 26
Hami O VRC 204 Ua 10
Hamīd O SUD 312 Hh 35
Ḥamīdiya O SYR 208 Hk 28
Ḥamīdīye O IR 215 Jc 30
Hamilton O UK 161 Fb 6
Hamilton O USA 46 Aj 13
Hamilton O USA 50 Ce 22
Hamilton O CDN 57 Dh 24
Hamilton O USA 70 Da 26
Hamilton O USA 71 Dd 28
Hamilton O USA 71 Df 26
Hamilton O USA 81 Cn 30

Guernsey - Hamilton 423

□Country ▣Capital city ⊙Administrative unit OPlace ⛰Island ⛰Mountain range △Mountain ⌓Cape ≈Ocean, Sea ~Lake, River ♆Undersea topography ⛰Glacier ♀National park •••Reservation ★Point of major interest ⌓Landscape

Hamilton O AUS 378 Mh 64
Hamilton O AUS 378 Mk 67
Hamilton O NZ 383 Nk 64
Hamilton Dome O USA 51 Cj 24
Hamilton Downs O AUS 361 Mc 57
Hamilton Hotel O AUS 374 Mg 57
Hamilton Island ⛰ AUS 375 Ml 56
Hamim O UAE 226 Jf 34
Hamina O FIN 159 Hf 15
Hamiota O CDN 56 Cm 20
Hami Pendi ⌓ VRC 204 Ua 10
Ḥamir O YE 218 Hp 38
Hamirpur O IND 234 Ke 33
Ḥamīs al-Bahr O KSA 218 Hn 36
Hamlet O USA 74 Dj 28
Hamlin O USA 70 Cm 29
Hamlin O USA 70 Da 25
Hamlin O USA 71 Dg 26
Hâm Luông ~ VN 263 Ld 40
Hamm O D 163 Gk 20
Hammamet O TN 297 Gm 27
Hammam-Lif O TN 297 Gm 27
Hammer O CDN 57 Dh 22
Hammerdal O S 158 Gp 14
Hammerfest O N 159 Hd 10
Hammer Springs O NZ 383 Nj 67
Hammilton Sound ~ CDN 61 Eg 21
Hammon O USA 70 Cn 28
Hammond O USA 71 De 25
Hammond O USA 86 Dc 30
Hammonton O USA 74 Dl 26
Hamoine O MOC 352 Hk 57
Hamoud O RMM 304 Ga 38
Hampden O CDN 61 Ef 21
Hampi O IND 238 Kc 38
Hampton O USA 60 Dn 24
Hampton O CDN 61 Eb 23
Hampton O USA 70 Db 24
Hampton O USA 70 Db 29
Hampton O USA 71 Dh 29
Hampton O USA 74 Dk 27
Hampton Bays O USA 74 Dm 25
Hampton Butte △ USA 50 Cb 24
Hamra O SUD 312 Hg 40
Hamrat al-Wuzz O SUD 312 Hh 38
Hamrat as Shaykh O SUD 312 Hf 38
Hams Fork ~ USA 65 Cg 25
Ham Thuân Nam O VN 263 Ld 40
Hāmūn-e Jāz Mūriān ~ IR 226 Jh 32
Hāmūn-e Pūzak ~ AFG 226 Jj 30
Hāmūn-e Sāberi ~ AFG 226 Jj 30
Hāmūn-i-Māshkel ~ PK 226 Jk 31
Ham Yên O VN 255 Lc 34
Hamyski O RUS 202 Hm 23
Han O GH 317 Ge 40
Hana O USA 75 An 35
Hānābād O AFG 223 Jn 27
Hanadet Bet Touadjine ⌓ DZ 293 Gf 30
Hanahai Hills ⛰ RB 349 Hc 57
Hanak O TR 202 Hp 25
Ḥān al-Baġdādī O IRQ 209 Hp 29
Hanalei O USA 75 Al 34
Ḥān al-Maḥāwīl O IRQ 209 Ja 29
Hà Nam O VN 255 Lc 35
Hanamaki O J 250 Mg 26
Hanapepe O USA 75 Al 35
Hānaqīn O IRQ 209 Ja 28
Han ar-Rahba O IRQ 214 Hp 30
Ḥanāṣir O SYR 208 Hl 28
Hanaus O NAM 348 Ha 58
Hâncesti O MD 175 Hg 22
Hanceville O CDN 50 Ca 20
Hancheng O VRC 243 Le 28
Hanchuan O VRC 243 Lg 30
Hancock O USA 74 Dl 25
Handa O J 251 Me 28
Handöl O S 158 Gn 14
Handan O VRC 243 Lh 27
Handeni O EAT 337 Hl 48
Handsworth O AUS 375 Mk 58
Handwara O IND 230 Kb 28
Handyga O RUS 205 Xa 6
Hanestad O N 158 Gm 15
Ḥān-e Taḥtī O IR 209 Ja 26
Hanford O USA 64 Cc 27
Hāngal O IND 238 Kb 38
Han Gang ~ ROK 247 Lp 27
Hanger Wenz ~ ETH 325 Hl 41
Hanggin Qi O VRC 243 Le 26
Hanging Rock ⛰ AUS 360 Ll 57
Hanglong O VRC 255 Ld 33
Hangö O FIN 171 Hd 16
Hangu O PK 223 Jp 29
Hangzhou O VRC 246 Ll 30
Hangzhou Wan ~ VRC 246 Ll 30
Hanhovuz O TM 223 Jj 27
Hanhovuz sur hovdany ~ TM 223 Jj 27
Hani O TR 202 Hn 26
Hania O GR 194 Hd 28
Ḥaniḍ O KSA 215 Jc 32
Haniš al-Kabīr ⛰ ER 313 Hp 39
Hanja ~ ANG 340 Gn 52
Han Jiang ~ VRC 258 Lj 33
Hanka O UZB 223 Jj 25
Han Kalāle O IR 222 Jf 27
Hankey O ZA 358 He 62
Hankinson O USA 56 Cp 22
Hanko Hangö O FIN 171 Hd 16
Hanksville O USA 65 Cg 26
Hanley O CDN 51 Cj 20
Hanmer O CDN 57 Dh 22
Han Mugida O IRQ 209 Hp 29
Hann ~ AUS 361 Lp 54
Hann ~ AUS 365 Mh 53
Hanna O CDN 51 Cg 20
Hannaford O USA 56 Cn 22
Hannah Bay ~ CDN 57 Dh 20
Hannibal O USA 70 Dc 26
Hannik O SUD 312 Hj 36
Hannock O USA 74 Dk 25
Hannoversch Münden O D 174 Gl 20
Hanöbukten ~ S 170 Gp 18
Hanoi ▣ VN 255 Lc 35
Hanover O CDN 57 Dh 23
Hanover O USA 74 Dk 26
Hanover O D 170 Gl 19
Hanover Road O ZA 349 He 61
Hansa Bay ~ PNG 287 Mj 48
Hānsdiha O IND 235 Kh 33
Hanse O IND 230 Kc 29
Hanshou O VRC 258 Lg 31
Han Shui ~ VRC 243 Le 29
Han Shui ~ VRC 243 Lf 29
Han Shui ~ VRC 243 Lg 30
Hānsi O IND 234 Kb 31
Hansnes O N 159 Hb 10
Hanson ~ AUS 361 Mc 56
Hanson Bay ~ NZ 383 Ab 67
Hānsot O IND 238 Ka 35
Hanstholm O DK 170 Gk 17
Hantai O VRC 258 Lg 31
Hantajskoe vodohranilišče ~ RUS 204 Tc 5
Hantamsberg ⛰ ZA 348 Hb 61
Hantsavichy O BY 171 He 19
Hanumana O IND 234 Kf 33
Hanumāngarh O IND 227 Ka 31
Hanyin O VRC 243 Le 29
Hanyuan O VRC 255 Lb 31
Ḥān Yūnis O IL 301 Hj 30
Hanzhong O VRC 243 Ld 29
Ḥān Zūr O IRQ 209 Ja 28
Hao ⛰ F 35 Bb 11
Haora O IND 235 Kh 34
Haotan O VRC 243 Le 27
Haoud el Hamra O DZ 296 Gk 30
Haouich O TCH 321 Hc 39
Haouza O MA 292 Ga 32
Hapakant O MYA 254 Kn 33
Haparanda O S 159 Hd 13
Hapolio O IND 235 Kl 32
Happy O USA 65 Cl 28
Happy Camp O USA 64 Ca 25
Happy Jack O USA 65 Cg 28
Happy Valley O AUS 374 Mh 57
Hāpur O IND 234 Kc 31
Haquira O PE 128 Dm 53
Har ~ MNG 204 Ua 9
Harabali O RUS 181 Jb 22
Haraḍ O KSA 215 Jc 33
Haraḍ O YE 218 Hp 37
Haradok O BY 171 Hg 18
Haraǧa O KSA 218 Hp 37
Haragu O PNG 286 Mh 49
Haramachi O J 251 Mg 27
Harānaq O IR 222 Jf 29
Harantim O BR 125 Ep 53
Harappa O PK 230 Ka 30
Harare ▣ ZW 341 Hh 54
Harāt O IR 226 Jf 30
Harat ⛰ ER 313 Hm 37
Harāvaǧān O IR 226 Jf 30
Haraz Djombo O TCH 309 Hb 39
Haraz-Mangueigne O TCH 321 Hc 41
Harbel O LB 316 Ga 42
Harbin O VRC 204 Wa 9
Harbor Beach O USA 57 Dg 24
Harbour Breton O CDN 61 Ef 22
Harbour Deep O CDN 61 Ef 20
Harbour Grace O CDN 61 Eh 22
Harbour View O JA 101 Dk 37
Harcourt O CDN 61 Eb 22
Harcourt O AUS 379 Mj 64
Harda O IND 234 Kc 34
Hardali O IND 238 Kb 39
Hardangerfjorden ~ N 158 Gk 15
Hardangerjøkulen ~ N 158 Gk 15
Hardangervidda ♀ N 158 Gk 15
Hardangervidda ⛰ N 158 Gk 15
Hardeeville O USA 71 Dh 29
Hardey ~ AUS 360 Lj 57
Hardibo Hāyk' ~ ETH 313 Hm 40
Hardin O USA 51 Cj 23
Hardin O USA 71 Dc 26
Harding O ZA 349 Hg 61
Harding ~ AUS 360 Lj 56
Hardingsburg O USA 71 De 27
Hardisty O CDN 51 Cg 19
Hardoi O IND 234 Ke 32
Hardwicke Bay ~ AUS 378 Me 63
Hardy O USA 70 Dc 27
Hardy O USA 71 Dc 27
Hare Bay ~ CDN 61 Eg 20
Hare Bay O CDN 61 Eg 21
Hārer O ETH 328 Hp 41
Hāresābād O IR 222 Jg 27
Hareto O ETH 325 Hl 41
Harewa O ETH 328 Hp 41
Hargele O ETH 328 Hp 43
Hargeysa O SP 328 Hp 41
Har Hu ~ VRC 242 Kn 26
Hari ~ RI 270 La 46
Hari ~ RI 278 Lb 46
Haría O E 292 Fp 31
Ḥarīb O YE 218 Ja 38
Haribomo O RMM 305 Ge 37
Haridwar O IND 234 Kd 31
Harihar O IND 238 Kb 38
Harihari O NZ 382 Nh 67
Harilek ~ RI 278 Lb 47
Harina-nada ♆ J 251 Md 28
Haripa O IND 239 Kc 41
Haripur O PK 230 Ka 29
Hari Rūd ~ IR 223 Jj 27
Harirūd ~ AFG 223 Jj 28
Harisal O IND 234 Kc 35
Harischandra Range ⛰ IND 238 Ka 36
Harjavalta O FIN 159 Hc 15
Härjedalen ⌓ S 158 Gn 14
Harkány O H 174 Ha 23
Harkidum O IND 230 Kd 30
Harlan O USA 70 Da 25
Harlan O USA 71 Dg 27
Harlan County Lake ~ USA 70 Cn 25
Harlem O USA 51 Ch 21
Harlin O AUS 375 Mn 59
Harlingen O USA 81 Cp 32
Harlingen O NL 163 Gj 19
Harlovka O RUS 159 Hl 11
Harlovka ~ RUS 159 Hl 11
Harlowton O USA 51 Ch 22
Harmancık O TR 195 Hg 26
Härmänkyla O FIN 159 Hg 13
Harmanli O BG 194 He 25
Harmil ⛰ ER 313 Hn 37
Harnāi O PK 227 Jm 30
Harney Basin ⌓ USA 50 Cc 24
Harney Lake ~ USA 50 Cc 24
Harney Peak △ USA 51 Cl 24
Härnösand O S 158 Hb 14
Haro O E 184 Ge 24
Haro ~ SP 325 Hn 45
Harobo O J 250 Mg 23
Harold Byrd Range ⛰ 38 Cb 18
Harovskaja grjada ⛰ RUS 171 Hn 16
Harpanahalli O IND 238 Kb 38
Harper O USA 50 Cd 24
Harper O USA 70 Cn 27
Harper O LB 304 Gc 43
Harpers Ferry N.H.P. ★ USA 74 Dj 26
Harrai O IND 234 Kd 34
Harran O TR 195 Hm 27
Harrand O PK 227 Jn 31
Ḥarrat al-'Uwairiḍ ⌓ KSA 214 Hl 32
Ḥarrat al-Buqūm ⌓ KSA 218 Hn 35
Ḥarrat Ḥaḍan ⌓ KSA 218 Hn 35
Ḥarrat Haibar ⌓ KSA 214 Hm 33
Ḥarrat Rahaṭ ⌓ KSA 214 Hm 34
Harricana ~ CDN 60 Dj 20
Harriman O USA 71 Df 28
Harrington O USA 50 Cc 22
Harrington O AUS 379 Mn 61
Harrington Harbour O CDN 61 Ee 20
Harris O CDN 51 Cj 20
Harrisburg O USA 71 Dc 28
Harrisburg O USA 71 Dd 27
Harrisburg O USA 74 Dk 25
Harrishill O CDN 56 Da 21
Harris Lake ~ AUS 369 Lm 61
Harrismith O ZA 349 Hg 60
Harrison O USA 51 Cl 24
Harrison O USA 57 Df 24
Harrison O USA 70 Db 27
Harrison O USA 71 Df 26
Harrison Bay ≈ USA 46 An 9
Harrisonburg O USA 74 Dj 26
Harrison Lake ~ CDN 50 Cb 21
Harrisville O USA 57 Dg 23
Harrisville O USA 71 Dh 26
Harrodsburg O USA 71 Df 27
Harrogate O CDN 50 Cd 20
Harrogate O GB 162 Gf 18
Harrow O AUS 378 Mg 64
Ḥar Rūd ~ IR 209 Jc 27
Harry's Harbour O CDN 61 Ef 21
Harry Strunk Lake ~ USA 70 Cm 25
Harsāni O IND 227 Jp 33
Harsīn O IR 209 Jb 28
Harşit Çayı ~ TR 195 Hm 25
Hârşova O RO 175 Hg 23
Harstad O N 158 Gp 11
Harsūsud O IND 234 Kc 34
Hart O USA 65 Cl 28
Hartbeesfontein O ZA 349 Hf 59
Hartebeestrivier ~ ZA 348 Hc 60
Hårteigen △ N 158 Gk 15
Hartford O USA 57 Dd 24
Hartford O USA 71 De 27
Hartford O USA 74 Dm 25
Hartford O USA 86 De 30
Hartford City O USA 71 Df 25
Hartkjølen △ N 158 Gn 13
Hart Lake ~ USA 50 Cc 24
Hartlepool O GB 162 Gf 18
Hart Mount △ CDN 56 Cm 19
Hart Mountain National Antelope Refuge ♀ USA 50 Cc 24
Hartol O FIN 159 Hf 15
Hartseer O NAM 348 Ha 56
Hartsel O USA 65 Ck 26
Hartselle O USA 71 De 28
Harts Range O AUS 374 Md 57
Harts Range ⛰ AUS 374 Md 57
Hartsrivier ~ ZA 349 He 59
Hartsville O USA 71 Dh 28
Hartswater O ZA 349 He 59
Hartwell O USA 71 Dg 28
Hartwell Lake ~ USA 71 Dg 28
Haruchas O NAM 348 Ha 58
Haruku O RI 283 Ma 47
Hārūnābād O PK 227 Ka 31
Harur O IND 238 Kd 39
Har Us nuur ~ MNG 204 Ua 9
Harūt Rūd ~ AFG 223 Jj 29
Harvard O USA 71 Dd 24
Harvest Home O AUS 375 Mk 56
Harvey O USA 56 Cn 22
Harvey O AUS 368 Lh 62
Harwich O GB 163 Gg 20
Haryana ⊙ IND 234 Kb 31
Haryn' ~ BY 175 Hf 20
Harz Mountains ⛰ D 174 Gm 20
Hāš O IR 226 Jj 31
Hasama O J 251 Mg 26
Hasan O RUS 250 Mb 24
Hasanābād O IR 222 Jd 28
Hasan D. △ TR 195 Hk 26
Hasankeyf O TR 202 Hn 27
Hasan Kuli O TM 222 Je 27
Hasanparti O IND 238 Kd 36
Hasanpur O IND 234 Kd 31
Hasavjurt O RUS 202 Jb 24
Hasaweb ~ NAM 348 Ha 58
Hashab O SUD 312 He 39
Hāsilpur O PK 227 Ka 31
Haskanit O SUD 312 Hf 40
Haskell O USA 70 Cn 29
Haskovo O BG 194 He 25
Hasnābād O IND 235 Kj 34
Hassa O TR 195 Hl 27
Hassan O IND 238 Kc 39
Hassayampa ~ USA 64 Cf 29
Hâssei Mbârek O RIM 304 Ga 37
Hassel ♀ AUS 368 Lk 63
Hassela O S 158 Ha 14
Hasselt O B 163 Gj 20
Hassi Bahbah O DZ 296 Gh 28
Hassi Barouda O DZ 293 Gg 31
Hassi Bedjedjene O DZ 296 Gl 32
Hassi Bedoud O MA 293 Ge 29
Hassi Bel Guebbour O DZ 296 Gk 31
Hassi Berrekhem O DZ 296 Gj 29
Hassi bou Bernous O DZ 293 Ge 32
Hassi-Delaa O DZ 296 Gh 29
Hassi-el-Ahmar O MA 293 Ge 29
Hassi el Alimar O DZ 293 Gg 28
Hassi el Belrem O DZ 296 Gh 32
Hassi el Khannfous O DZ 296 Gh 31
Hassi el Khebi O DZ 293 Gd 31
Hassi el Krenig O DZ 296 Gh 32
Hassi el Mounir O DZ 293 Gc 31
Hassi Fahl O DZ 296 Gh 30
Hassi Fouïni O RIM 305 Gc 37
Hassi Habadra O DZ 296 Gj 32
Hassi Himana O DZ 293 Ge 31
Hassi Ifertas O LAR 297 Gm 31
Hassi Imoulaye O DZ 296 Gl 31
Hassi in Akeouet O DZ 296 Gl 32
Hassi Inifel O DZ 296 Gh 31
Hassi Kord Meriem O DZ 293 Ge 31
Hassi Mahzez O DZ 293 Gd 31
Hassi Maraket O DZ 296 Gh 30
Hassi Messaoud O DZ 296 Gj 30
Hassi Moussa O DZ 293 Gg 31
Hassi Ntsel O DZ 296 Gk 32
Hassi-Onuz O MA 292 Ga 31
Hassi Ras el Erg O DZ 296 Gh 31
Hassi R'Mel O DZ 296 Gh 29
Hassi Safiet Iniguel O DZ 296 Gh 30
Hassi Settala O DZ 296 Gh 29
Hassi Tabankort O DZ 296 Gk 31
Hassi Tabelbalet O DZ 296 Gk 32
Hassi Tartrat O DZ 293 Gc 32
Hässleholm O S 170 Gn 17
Hassman O USA 56 Db 21
Hastings O USA 56 Db 23
Hastings O USA 57 Df 24
Hastings O USA 70 Cn 25
Hastings O GB 163 Gg 20
Hastings ~ AUS 379 Mn 61
Hastings O NZ 383 Nl 65
Haštpar O IR 209 Jc 27
Hastrūd O IR 209 Jc 27
Hašuri O GE 202 Hp 25
Hasvik O N 159 Hc 10
Haswell O USA 65 Cl 26
Hasy Hague O LAR 297 Gm 32
Hasy in Āgiuel O LAR 297 Gm 32
Hat'ae Do ⛰ ROK 247 Ln 28
Hatanga O RUS 204 Uc 4
Hatanga ~ RUS 204 Uc 4
Hatay Antakya O TR 195 Hl 27
Hatch O USA 64 Cf 27
Hatch O USA 65 Cj 29
Hatches Creek O AUS 374 Md 56
Hatchie ~ USA 71 Dd 28
Hateg O RO 194 Hd 23
Hateruma-shima ⛰ J 259 Lm 33
Hatfield O AUS 379 Mh 62
Hatgal O MNG 204 Uc 8
Hat Gamaria O IND 235 Kg 34
Hat Head ♀ AUS 379 Mn 61
Hathras O IND 234 Kd 32
Hà Tiên O VN 263 Lc 40
Hatikali O IND 254 Kl 33
Hatiman O J 251 Me 28
HàTĩnh O VN 255 Lc 36
Hatkamba O IND 238 Ka 37
Hat Nai Yang O THA 262 Kn 41
Hato Corozal O CO 107 Dn 42
Hato Mayor O DOM 101 Dp 36
Hatpaas O RI 282 Lp 49
Hatra ★ IRQ 209 Hp 28
Hatta O IND 234 Kd 33
Hattah O AUS 378 Mh 63
Hattah-Kulkyne ♀ AUS 378 Mh 63
Hatteras O USA 74 Dl 28
Hatteras Island ⛰ USA 74 Dl 28
Hatteras Plain ♆ 11 Fa 7
Hattfjelldal O N 158 Gn 13
Hattiesburg O USA 86 Dd 30
Hattieville O BH 93 Dd 37
Hatton-Dikoya O CL 239 Ke 42
Hattushash ★ TR 195 Hk 26
Ḥatūnābād O IR 226 Jf 30
Ḥatūnīya O SYR 202 Hn 27
Hatutea ⛰ F 14 Bb 10
Hatvan O H 174 Hb 22
Hat Yai O THA 270 La 42
Hatyngnah O RUS 205 Ya 5
Hatyrka O RUS 205 Zc 6
Hatzfeldhafen O PNG 287 Mj 48
Hau ~ RI 279 Lk 47
Haugesund O N 170 Gj 16
Hâu Giang ~ VN 263 Lc 40
Hauhui O SOL 290 Nc 50
Haukeligrend O N 170 Gk 16
Haukivesi ⌓ FIN 159 Hg 14
Haukivuori O FIN 159 Hf 14
Haumonía O RA 136 Ed 59
Haur-Abdallāh ~ IRQ 215 Jc 31
Hauraha O SOL 290 Nc 51
Hauraki Gulf ~ NZ 383 Nk 64
Haur al-Habbānīya ~ IRQ 209 Hp 29
Haur al-Ḥammar ~ IRQ 215 Jb 30
Haur al-Hawīza ~ IRQ 215 Jb 30
Haur as-Ṣa'dīya ~ IRQ 209 Jb 29
Haur as Šubaika ~ IRQ 209 Ja 29
Haur as Suwaiqīa ~ IRQ 209 Ja 29
Haur Dalmg ~ IRQ 209 Ja 29
Haur Dayāt ~ SUD 313 Hl 35
Hauser Lake ~ USA 51 Cg 22
Hautajärvi O FIN 159 Hg 12
Ḥautat Banī Tamīn O KSA 215 Jb 34
Hautavaara O RUS 171 Hh 15
Haute-Normandie ⊙ F 163 Gg 21
Hauterive O CDN 60 Dp 21
Hauts Plateaux de l'Ouest ⛰ CAM 320 Gl 42
Havana O USA 71 Dc 25
Havana La Habana ▣ C 100 Dg 34
Havasi O UZB 223 Jn 25
Havasu Lake ~ USA 64 Ce 28
Havasupai Indian Reservation ••• USA 64 Cf 28
Have Etoe O GH 317 Gg 42
Havel ~ D 170 Gn 19
Haveli O PK 230 Ka 30
Havelian O PK 230 Ka 28
Havelock O CDN 60 Dl 23
Havelock O USA 74 Dk 28
Havelock O NZ 383 Nj 66
Havelock Island ⛰ IND 262 Kl 40
Haven O USA 70 Cp 27
Haverfordwest O GB 163 Gd 20
Haverhill O USA 60 Dn 24
Hāveri O IND 238 Kb 38
Havilah O AUS 375 Mk 56
Havlíčkův Brod O CZ 174 Gp 21
Havøysund O N 159 Hd 10
Havre O USA 51 Ch 21
Havre-Aubert O CDN 61 Ed 22
Havre-St.-Pierre O CDN 61 Ec 20
Havza O TR 195 Hk 25
Haw ~ USA 74 Dj 28
Hawaii ⊙ USA 75 Am 35
Hawaii ⛰ USA 75 An 36
Hawaiian Ridge ⛰ USA 75 Al 35
Hawaii Volcanoes National Park ♀ USA 75 An 36
Hawalli O KWT 215 Jb 31
Hawera O NZ 383 Nk 65
Hawi O USA 75 An 35
Hawick O GB 162 Ge 18
Ḥawīǧat Arbān O IRQ 209 Hp 28
Hawke Bay ~ NZ 383 Nl 65
Hawker O AUS 378 Mf 61
Hawke's Bay O CDN 61 Ef 20
Hawkesbury O CDN 60 Dl 23
Hawkesbury Point ⌓ AUS 364 Md 51
Hawkesville O USA 71 De 27
Hawkins O USA 56 Dc 23
Hawkinsville O USA 71 Dg 29
Hawk Junction O CDN 57 Df 21
Hawk Springs O USA 65 Ck 25
Hawley O USA 56 Cp 22
Hawston O ZA 358 Hb 63
Hawthorn O USA 87 Dg 31
Hawthorne O USA 64 Cc 26
Hawzēn O ETH 313 Hm 38
Haxtun O USA 65 Cl 25
Hay ~ AUS 374 Me 57
Hay O AUS 379 Mj 63
Haya O RI 283 Ma 47
Haya O SUD 313 Hl 36
Haya'er O VRC 231 Kl 27
Haybān O SUD 312 Hh 40
Hayden Peak △ USA 50 Cd 24
Hayes Halvø ⌓ DK 7 Fb 2
Hayes ⌓ DK 43 Ha 3
Hayes O USA 56 Cm 23
Hayes Creek O AUS 364 Mb 52
Hayes River ~ CDN 42 Fc 7
Hayfork O USA 64 Ca 25
Hayiang Dao ⛰ VRC 246 Lm 26
Hāyk' O ETH 313 Hm 40
Hāyk' Hāyk' ~ ETH 313 Hm 40
Haykota O ER 313 Hl 38
Haymana O TR 195 Hj 26
Hayrabolu O TR 195 Hf 25
Hay River O CDN 6 Da 3
Hay River ~ CDN 47 Ca 15
Hay River O CDN 47 Cc 15
Hays O USA 70 Cn 26
Hays O YE 218 Hp 39
Hay Springs O USA 51 Cl 24
Haystack Peak △ USA 64 Cf 26
Haysville O USA 70 Cp 27
Hayward O USA 56 Dc 22
Hayward O USA 64 Cb 27
Haywood Channel ~ MYA 254 Kl 36
Hayy al-Maḥaṭṭa O KSA 215 Jb 33
Ḥaz'alīya an-Našwa O IRQ 215 Jb 30
Ḥazarābād O IR 222 Je 27
Hazard O USA 70 Cn 27
Hazard O USA 71 Dg 27
Hazāribāg O IND 235 Kg 34
Hazaribagh Range ⛰ IND 234 Kf 34
Hāzāribag National Park ♀ IND 235 Kg 33
Hazārmani O AFG 223 Jm 28
Hazelgreen O USA 56 Dc 24
Hazelton O CDN 6 Cb 4
Hazen O USA 56 Cm 22
Hazen Bay ~ USA 46 Ag 15
Hazen Strait ~ CDN 42 Eb 3
Hazīpur O IND 235 Kg 33
Hazlehurst O USA 86 Dc 30
Hazlehurst O USA 86 Dg 30
Hazlet O CDN 51 Ch 20
Hazleton O USA 74 Dl 25
Hazoras O UZB 223 Jj 25
Hazoua O TN 296 Gk 29
Ḥażrat-e Solṭān O AFG 223 Jm 27
Headingly O AUS 374 Mf 56
Headlands O ZW 341 Hh 55
Head of Bight ~ AUS 369 Mb 61
Headquarters O USA 50 Ce 22
Head Smashed in Buffalo Jump ★ CDN 50 Cf 21
Healdsburg O USA 64 Ca 26
Healesville O AUS 379 Mj 64
Healy O USA 46 Ba 13
Healy O USA 70 Cm 26
Heany Junction O ZW 349 Hg 56
Hearne O USA 81 Cp 30
Hearst O CDN 57 Dg 21
Heart River ~ USA 56 Cm 22
Hearts Content O CDN 61 Eh 22
Heath ~ BOL 128 Dp 52
Heathcote O AUS 379 Mj 64
Heavener O USA 70 Da 28
Hebbale O IND 238 Kb 39
Hebbronville O USA 81 Cn 32
Hebei ⊙ VRC 243 Lh 26
Hebel O AUS 375 Mk 60
Heber O USA 65 Cg 28
Hebera O RI 283 Ma 46
Heber City O USA 65 Cg 25
Heber Springs O USA 70 Dc 28
Hebgert Lake ~ USA 51 Cg 23
Hebi O VRC 243 Lg 28
Hebron O CDN 43 Hc 7
Hebron O USA 70 Cp 25
Hebron O IL 214 Hk 30
Heby O S 170 Ha 16
Hecate Strait ~ CDN 42 Da 8
Hecelchakán O MEX 93 Dc 35
Hechevarría O C 101 Dl 35
Hechi O VRC 255 Le 33
Hechuan O VRC 243 Ld 30
Hecla O CDN 56 Cp 20
Hecla and Griper Bay ≈ CDN 42 Eb 3
Hecla Island ⛰ CDN 56 Cp 20
Hector O USA 56 Da 23
Hector Tejada O PE 128 Dn 53
Heddal ★ N 170 Gl 16
Hede O S 158 Gn 14
Heerenveen O NL 163 Gj 19
Heer land ⛰ N 158 Ha 7
Heerlen O NL 163 Gk 20
Hefei O VRC 246 Lj 30
Hefeng O VRC 255 Le 31
Heffley Creek O CDN 50 Cb 20
Hegang O VRC 205 Wc 9
Hegang O VRC 250 Ma 22
Heggadadevankote O IND 238 Kc 39
Hegigio River ~ PNG 286 Mh 49
Hehel O VRC 230 Kf 27
Heho O MYA 254 Kn 35
Hehua O VRC 243 Lf 30
Heide O D 170 Gl 18
Heidelberg O USA 86 Dd 30
Heidelberg O D 174 Gl 21
Heidelberg O ZA 349 Hg 59
Heidelberg O ZA 358 Hc 63
Heidenheim a.d.Brenz O D 174 Gm 21
Heights O USA 74 Dk 27
Heihe O VRC 205 Wb 9
Hei He ~ VRC 242 Kp 26
Heijiang O VRC 255 Le 35
Heilbron O ZA 349 Hf 59
Heilbronn O D 174 Gl 21
Heilongjiang ⊙ VRC 204 Wa 9
Heilong Jiang ~ VRC 205 Wb 9
Heimaey ⛰ IS 158 Fk 14
Heimahe O VRC 242 Kp 27
Heimdal O N 158 Gl 14
Heina Islands ⛰ PNG 287 Mj 46
Heināvesi O FIN 159 Hg 14
Heinola O FIN 159 Hf 15
Heinze Chaung ~ MYA 262 Kn 38
Heirābād O AFG 223 Jm 27
Heirane O DZ 293 Gf 32
Heishan Shuiku ~ VRC 243 Lh 30
Heitorai O BR 133 Ek 53
Hejaz ⛰ KSA 214 Hm 33
Hejian O VRC 246 Lj 26
Hejiang O VRC 255 Lc 31
Hejin O VRC 243 Lf 28
Hekimhan O TR 195 Hl 26
Hekla △ IS 158 Fl 13
Hekou O VRC 242 Lb 27
Hekou O VRC 243 Lh 30
Hekou O VRC 255 Lb 34
Helagsfjällen △ S 158 Gn 14
Helan O VRC 243 Ld 26
Helan Shan ⛰ VRC 242 Lc 26
Helanshan ★ VRC 243 Ld 26
Helena O USA 51 Cf 22
Helena O USA 71 Dc 28
Helena O NAM 348 Hc 56
Helena Island ⛰ USA 71 Dh 29
Helen Reef ⛰ PAL 26 Rb 9
Helen Springs O AUS 364 Mc 55
Helensville O NZ 383 Nk 64
Helgoland ⛰ D 170 Gk 18
Helgoländer Bucht ~ D 170 Gk 18
Helle ~ IR 215 Jd 31
Helleland O N 170 Gk 16
Hellin O E 184 Gf 26
Hellingdalelvi ~ N 158 Gl 15
Hells Canyon ⌓ USA 50 Cd 23
Hell's Gate ♀ EAK 337 Hl 46
Helmand ~ AFG 223 Jl 29
Helmand ⊙ AFG 226 Jk 30
Helmeringhausen O NAM 348 Ha 58
Helmond O NL 163 Gj 20
Helmsdale O GB 162 Ge 16
Helper O USA 65 Cg 26
Helsingborg O S 170 Gn 17
Helsinger O DK 170 Gm 17
Helsingfors Helsinki ▣ FIN 159 He 15
Helsinki Helsingfors ▣ FIN 159 He 15
Helspoort O ZA 358 Hd 62
Helvecia O RA 137 Ed 61
Hembe O RDC 333 Hd 45
Hemet O USA 64 Cd 29
Hemingford O USA 51 Cl 24
Hemnesberget O N 158 Gn 12
Hempstead O USA 74 Dm 25
Hempstead O USA 81 Cp 30
Hemse O S 170 Hb 17
Hemsedal O N 158 Gl 15
Hemsö ⛰ S 158 Hb 14
Hemudu Wenhua Yizhi ★ VRC 259 Ll 31
Henan ⊙ VRC 243 Lf 29
Hen and Chicken Group ⛰ NZ 383 Nk 63
Henares ~ E 184 Ge 25
Henasi-saki ⌓ J 250 Mf 25
Henbury O AUS 369 Mc 58
Henbury Meteorite Craters ♀ AUS 369 Mc 58
Hendek O TR 195 Hh 25
Henderson ⛰ UK 14 Cb 12
Henderson O USA 60 Dk 24
Henderson O USA 64 Ce 27
Henderson O USA 70 Da 29
Henderson O USA 71 Dd 28
Henderson O USA 71 De 27
Henderson O USA 74 Dj 27
Henderson O RA 137 Ed 64
Hendersonville O USA 71 De 27
Hendersonville O USA 71 Dg 28
Hendīǧān O IR 215 Jc 30
Hendorābī O IR 215 Je 32
Hendrina O ZA 349 Hg 59
Ḥenǧān O AFG 223 Jn 28
Henǧān ⛰ IR 226 Jf 32
Henganofi O PNG 287 Mj 49
Hengchun O RC 259 Ll 34
Hengduan Shan ⛰ VRC 254 Kp 31
Hengduan Shan ⛰ VRC 254 Kp 32
Hengshan △ VRC 243 Lg 26
Hengshan O VRC 258 Lg 32
Hengshan △ VRC 258 Lg 32
Hengshui O VRC 243 Lh 27
Heng Xian O VRC 243 Lg 28
Heng Xian O VRC 255 Le 34
Hengyang O VRC 258 Lg 32
Heničes'k O UA 175 Hk 22
Hennaya O DZ 293 Gf 28
Hennebont O F 163 Ge 22
Hennenman O ZA 349 Hf 59
Hennessey O USA 70 Cp 27
Henrietta O USA 70 Cn 29
Henry O USA 56 Cp 23
Henry O USA 71 Dd 25
Henry ~ AUS 360 Lh 57
Henryetta O USA 70 Cp 28
Henry Kater Peninsula ⌓ CDN 43 Hb 5
Henry Lawrence Island ⛰ IND 262 Kl 39
Henrys Fk. ~ USA 51 Cg 24
Henties Bay O NAM 348 Gp 57
Henvey Inlet Indian Reservation ••• CDN 57 Dh 23
Henzada O MYA 262 Km 37
Heping O VRC 258 Lh 33
Heppner O USA 50 Cc 23
Hepu O VRC 255 Le 35
Hèraðsvötn ~ IS 158 Fl 13
Herāme O IR 215 Je 31
Herāt ⊙ AFG 223 Jj 29
Herāt O AFG 223 Jk 28
Herbagat O SUD 313 Hl 36

424 Hamilton - Herbagat

Herbert ～ **AUS** 365 Mj 55
Herberton ○ **AUS** 365 Mj 54
Herbertpur ○ **IND** 230 Kc 30
Herbert River Falls ～ **AUS** 365 Mj 53
Herbertsdale ○ **ZA** 358 Hc 63
Herbert Vale ○ **AUS** 365 Mf 55
Herbert Wash ～ **AUS** 369 Ln 58
Herceg-Novi ○ **MON** 194 Hb 24
Hercílio Luz ★ **BR** 140 Ek 60
Herciliópolis ○ **BR** 140 Ej 59
Hercules Bay ～ **PNG** 287 Mk 49
Herðubreið △ **IS** 158 Fm 13
Heredia ○ **CR** 97 Df 40
Hereford ○ **USA** 51 Cl 23
Hereford ○ **USA** 65 Cc 26
Hereford ○ **USA** 65 Cl 28
Hereford ○ **GB** 163 Ge 19
Herekino ○ **NZ** 383 Nj 63
Hereroland ○ **NAM** 348 Hb 56
Herford ○ **D** 170 Gl 19
Herington ○ **USA** 70 Cp 26
Heriot Bay ○ **CDN** 50 Bp 20
Hèrlèn gol ～ **MNG** 204 Vc 9
Herlen He ～ **VRC** 204 Vc 9
Hermanas ○ **MEX** 81 Cm 32
Herma Ness ⌒ **GB** 162 Gf 15
Hermann ○ **USA** 70 Dc 26
Hermannsburg ○ **AUS** 361 Mc 57
Hermannsburg Aboriginal Land ••• **AUS** 361 Mc 57
Hermanusdorings ○ **ZA** 349 Hf 58
Hermidale ○ **AUS** 379 Mk 61
Hermiston ○ **USA** 50 Cc 23
Hermitage ○ **CDN** 61 Eg 22
Hermitage ○ **USA** 70 Db 29
Hermitage Bay ～ **CDN** 61 Ef 22
Hermit Islands ⌃ **PNG** 287 Mj 46
Hermon ○ **ZA** 358 Hb 62
Hermosillo ○ **MEX** 80 Cg 31
Herná Majia Miraval ○ **RA** 136 Ec 61
Hernandarias ○ **RA** 146 Ee 61
Hernando ○ **RA** 137 Ec 62
Hernando ○ **USA** 71 De 29
Heroica Zitácuaro ○ **MEX** 92 Cm 35
Herold ○ **ZA** 358 Hd 63
Herold's Bay ～ **ZA** 358 Hd 63
Heron Island ⌃ **AUS** 375 Mm 57
Heron Lake ○ **USA** 56 Da 24
Herradura ○ **MEX** 92 Cm 34
Herradura ○ **RA** 140 Ee 59
Herrera d. P. ○ **E** 184 Gd 24
Herrera del Duque ○ **E** 184 Gd 26
Herrin ○ **USA** 71 Dd 27
Hertzogville ○ **ZA** 349 He 60
Herval ○ **BR** 140 Eg 57
Herval ○ **BR** 140 Eg 57
Hervey ⌃ **NZ** 35 Ba 11
Hervey Bay ○ **AUS** 375 Mn 58
Hervey Bay ～ **AUS** 375 Mn 58
Herveys Range △ **AUS** 379 Ml 62
Herzliyya ○ **IL** 208 Hh 29
Hesadi ○ **IND** 235 Kg 34
Heşärak ○ **AFG** 223 Jn 28
Heshan ○ **VRC** 258 Lg 34
Heshun ○ **VRC** 243 Lg 27
Hesperia ○ **USA** 57 De 24
Hesperia ○ **USA** 64 Cd 28
Hessen ⊙ **D** 174 Gl 20
Heta ～ **RUS** 204 Ua 4
Hetaude ○ **NEP** 235 Kg 32
Hetch Hetchy Aqueduct ～ **USA** 64 Cb 27
Hetovo ○ **RUS** 159 Hp 14
Hettinger ○ **USA** 51 Cl 23
Hevealândia ○ **BR** 120 Ed 48
Hevi Dzodze ○ **GH** 317 Gg 42
Hevsgöl nuur ～ **MNG** 204 Ub 8
Hewitt ○ **USA** 81 Cp 30
Hexham ○ **GB** 162 Ge 18
He Xian ○ **VRC** 246 Lk 30
He Xian ○ **VRC** 255 Lf 33
Heyang ○ **VRC** 243 Le 28
Heyfield ○ **AUS** 379 Mk 64
Heyuan ○ **VRC** 258 Lh 34
Heywood ○ **AUS** 378 Mg 65
Heze ○ **VRC** 243 Lh 28
Hezîî ○ **IR** 222 Jh 28
Hezuozhen ○ **VRC** 242 Lb 28
Hg. Diên ○ **VN** 263 Ld 37
Hhohho ⊙ **SD** 352 Hh 58
Hi.-Bou-Allala ○ **DZ** 293 Ge 30
Hi. Brahim △ **MA** 292 Gb 31
Hi. Daoula ○ **DZ** 296 Gj 29
Hi.-el-Kerma ○ **MA** 292 Gb 31
Hi. Fougani ○ **DZ** 293 Gd 30
Hi. Hadour ○ **DZ** 293 Gf 30
Hialeah ○ **USA** 87 Dh 33
Hiawatha ○ **USA** 70 Da 26
Hibberdene ○ **ZA** 349 Hf 61
Hibbing ○ **USA** 56 Db 22
Hibernia Reef ⌃ **AUS** 282 Lm 51
Hibiny ～ **RUS** 159 Hj 12
Hichinbrook Island ⌃ **AUS** 365 Mk 55
Hickman ○ **USA** 71 Dd 27
Hickmann ○ **PY** 136 Ec 57
Hickory ○ **USA** 71 De 28
Hidaka ○ **J** 250 Mh 24
Hidaka-sammyaku △ **J** 250 Mh 24
Hidalgo ○ **MEX** 80 Ck 32
Hidalgo ○ **MEX** 81 Cm 32
Hidalgo del Parral ○ **MEX** 80 Ck 32
Hida-sammyaku △ **J** 251 Me 27
Hiddensee △ **D** 170 Gn 18
Hidden Valley ○ **AUS** 364 Ma 53
Hidden Valley ○ **AUS** 364 Mc 54
Hidden Valley ○ **AUS** 365 Mj 55
Hidden Valley ○ **AUS** 375 Mk 56
Hidrolândia ○ **BR** 124 Ep 48
Hiên ○ **VN** 263 Ld 38
Hienghéne ○ **F** 386 Ne 56
Hierkinn ○ **N** 158 Gk 14
Hierro ⌃ **E** 292 Fl 32
Higashi-Hiroshima ○ **J** 251 Mc 28
Higashi-Osaka ○ **J** 251 Md 28
Higashi-suidō ～ **J** 247 Ma 29
Higgins ○ **USA** 70 Cm 27
Higginsville ○ **USA** 70 Da 26
Higginsville ○ **AUS** 368 Ll 61
High Atlas △ **MA** 292 Gb 30

Highborn Cay ⌃ **BS** 87 Dk 33
Highbury ○ **AUS** 365 Mh 54
Highbury ○ **AUS** 375 Mj 57
High Dam ★ **ET** 301 Hj 34
Highflats ○ **ZA** 349 Hf 61
High Island ⌃ **USA** 81 Da 31
High Lakes ○ **USA** 51 Cf 19
Highland Park ○ **USA** 71 De 24
Highland Plains ○ **AUS** 365 Mf 55
High Level ○ **CDN** 47 Cc 15
High Plateaus △ **DZ** 293 Gf 29
High Point ○ **USA** 71 Df 28
High Prairie ○ **CDN** 50 Da 4
High River ○ **CDN** 50 Cf 20
High Rock ○ **BS** 87 Dj 32
High Rock Lake ～ **USA** 71 Dh 28
High Rolling Mountains △ **RP** 267 Ll 39
High Springs ○ **USA** 86 Dg 31
High Tatra △ **SK** 174 Hb 21
Higuera de Zaragoza ○ **MEX** 80 Ch 33
Higuerote ○ **YV** 107 Ea 40
Hiiumaa ⌃ **EST** 170 Hc 16
Hiko ○ **USA** 64 Ce 27
Hikone ○ **J** 251 Md 28
Hikurangi ○ **NZ** 383 Nk 63
Hikurangi △ **NZ** 383 Nl 64
Hikurangi Trench ～ **NZ** 383 Nl 66
Hila ○ **RI** 283 Lp 47
Hilbre ⌃ **CDN** 56 Cn 20
Hildale ○ **USA** 64 Cf 27
Hildalgo ○ **MEX** 81 Cn 33
Hildesheim ○ **D** 170 Gl 19
Hilger ○ **USA** 51 Ch 22
Hili ○ **UAE** 226 Jf 33
Hilisimaetano ○ **RI** 270 Kn 45
Hill City ○ **USA** 50 Ce 24
Hill City ○ **USA** 51 Cl 24
Hill City ○ **USA** 56 Db 22
Hill City ○ **USA** 70 Cn 26
Hill Creek Extension ••• **USA** 65 Ch 26
Hilléket ○ **TCH** 321 Hc 39
Hill End ○ **AUS** 379 Ml 62
Hillerød ○ **DK** 170 Gm 18
Hilli ○ **BD** 235 Kj 33
Hills ○ **USA** 57 Dj 24
Hillsboro ○ **USA** 56 Cp 22
Hillsboro ○ **USA** 65 Cj 29
Hillsboro ○ **USA** 71 Dd 26
Hillsboro ○ **USA** 71 Dg 26
Hillsboro ○ **USA** 81 Cp 30
Hillsborough ○ **USA** 74 Dj 27
Hillsborough ○ **WG** 104 Ed 39
Hillsborough Bay ～ **CDN** 61 Ec 22
Hillside ○ **USA** 64 Cf 28
Hillside ○ **AUS** 360 Lk 56
Hillsport ○ **CDN** 57 Df 21
Hillston ○ **AUS** 379 Mj 62
Hillsville ○ **USA** 71 Dh 27
Hilo ○ **USA** 75 An 36
Hilok ○ **RUS** 204 Vb 8
Hiltaba ○ **AUS** 378 Md 62
Hilton ○ **USA** 60 Dj 24
Hilton ○ **AUS** 374 Mf 56
Hilton Head Island ⌃ **USA** 71 Dh 29
Hilvan ○ **TR** 195 Hm 27
Hilversum ○ **NL** 163 Gj 19
Himachal △ **USA** 50 Ci 23
Himachal Pradesh ⊙ **IND** 230 Kc 30
Himalaya △ **VRC** 230 Kd 29
Himalaya △ **NEP/VRC** 235 Kf 31
Himal Chuli △ **NEP** 235 Kg 31
Himanka ○ **FIN** 159 Hd 13
Himatnagar ○ **IND** 227 Ka 34
Himbirti ○ **ER** 313 Hm 38
Himeji ○ **J** 251 Md 28
Himi ○ **J** 251 Me 27
Himora ○ **ETH** 313 Hl 38
Hin ○ **THA** 262 La 37
Hinatuan ○ **RP** 267 Lp 41
Hinatuan Passage ～ **RP** 267 Ln 41
Hinche ○ **RH** 101 Dn 36
Hinchinbrook Island ⌃ **USA** 46 Bc 15
Hinchinbrook Island ♀ **AUS** 365 Mk 55
Hinda ○ **RCB** 332 Gn 48
Hindaun ○ **IND** 234 Kc 32
Hinds Lake ～ **CDN** 61 Ef 21
Hindubaágh ○ **PK** 227 Jn 30
Hindu Kush △ **AFG** 223 Jn 28
Hindupur ○ **IND** 238 Kc 39
Hinesville ○ **USA** 87 Dh 30
Hinganghåt ○ **IND** 234 Kd 35
Hingol ～ **PK** 227 Jl 33
Hingoli ○ **IND** 238 Kc 36
Hingon ○ **USA** 71 Dh 27
Hingoraja ○ **PK** 227 Jn 32
Hiniđán ○ **PK** 227 Jm 33
Hınıs ○ **TR** 202 Hn 26
Hinkley ○ **USA** 56 Db 23
Hinlopenrenna ♥ **N** 158 Gp 5
Hinlopenstretet ～ **N** 158 Ha 5
Hinnøya △ **N** 158 Gp 11
Hinoba-an ○ **RP** 267 Lm 41
Hinogyaung ○ **MYA** 262 Km 37
Hinojo ○ **RA** 137 Ed 64
Hinomi-sa ⌒ **J** 251 Mc 28
Hinsdale ○ **USA** 51 Cj 21
Hinton ○ **USA** 50 Cd 19
Híos ⌃ **GR** 194 Hb 26
Híos ○ **GR** 195 Hf 26
Hipólito ○ **MEX** 81 Cm 33
Hir ○ **IR** 222 Jd 27
Hirado ○ **J** 247 Ma 29
Hirado ○ **J** 250 La 29
Hirafok ○ **DZ** 308 Gj 34
Hirakůd Reservoir ～ **IND** 235 Kf 35
Hiraman ～ **EAK** 337 Hm 46
Hiranai ○ **J** 250 Mg 25
Hirara ○ **J** 259 Ln 33
Hirata ○ **J** 251 Mf 28
Hiratsuka ○ **J** 247 Mf 28
Hiré ○ **CI** 317 Gd 42
Hirfanlı Brj. ～ **TR** 195 Hj 26
Hiripitiya ○ **CL** 239 Ke 42
Hiriyur ○ **IND** 238 Kc 39
Hirna ○ **ETH** 325 Hn 41
Hiro'o ○ **J** 250 Mh 24
Hirosaki ○ **J** 250 Mf 25
Hiroshima ○ **J** 247 Mb 28
Hirs'kyj Tikyč ～ **UA** 175 Hh 21
Hirtshals ○ **DK** 170 Gl 17
Hisår ○ **IND** 234 Kb 31

Hisawa ○ **J** 251 Md 29
Hisiu ○ **PNG** 287 Mk 50
Hislaviči ○ **RUS** 171 Hj 18
Hişn aş Şahâbî ○ **LAR** 300 Hc 30
Hisor togʻlari △ **UZB** 223 Jm 26
Hispaniola ⌃ **101** Dm 37
Hispaniola Trough ～ **101** Dn 35
Hît ○ **IRQ** 209 Hp 29
Hita ○ **J** 247 Mg 29
Hitachi ○ **J** 251 Mg 27
Hitoyoshi ○ **J** 247 Mg 29
Hitra ⌃ **N** 158 Gj 14
Hiva Oa ⌃ **F** 14 Ca 10
Hiwassee Lake ～ **USA** 71 Df 28
Hixon ○ **CDN** 50 Ca 19
Hjalmaren ～ **S** 170 Gp 16
Hjargas nuur ～ **MNG** 204 Ua 9
Hjellset ○ **N** 158 Gk 14
Hjemmeluft ★ **N** 159 Hd 11
Hjo ○ **S** 170 Gp 16
Hjørring ○ **DK** 170 Gl 17
Hkakabo Ràzi △ **MYA** 254 Kn 31
Hkyenhpa ○ **MYA** 254 Kn 32
Hlabisa △ **ZA** 352 Hh 60
Hlegu ○ **MYA** 262 Kn 37
Hlobyne ○ **UA** 175 Hj 21
Hluchiv ○ **UA** 175 Hk 20
Hluhluwe ○ **ZA** 352 Hj 59
Hlusk ○ **BY** 171 Hg 19
Hlu̇thi ○ **SD** 352 Hh 59
Hlybokaye ○ **BY** 171 Hf 18
Hnalân ○ **VN** 255 Hb 13
Hniliĵ Tikič ～ **UA** 175 Hh 21
Ho ○ **GH** 317 Gg 42
Hòa Bình ○ **VN** 255 Lc 35
Hòa Bình ○ **VN** 263 Ld 37
Hoài Nho'n ○ **VN** 263 Le 38
Hoanik ～ **NAM** 340 Gn 55
Hoare Bay ～ **CDN** 43 Hc 5
Hoarusib ～ **NAM** 340 Gn 55
Hoaseb ⌒ **NAM** 348 Hb 57
Hoback Jct. ○ **USA** 51 Cg 24
Hobart ○ **DVRK** 247 Lp 25
Hobart ○ **USA** 70 Cn 27
Hobart ○ **AUS** 378 Mk 67
Hobbs ○ **USA** 65 Cl 29
Hobhouse ○ **ZA** 349 Hf 60
Hobo ○ **CO** 106 Dl 44
Hobro ○ **DK** 170 Gl 17
Hobyo ○ **SP** 328 Jc 43
Hochgolling △ **A** 174 Gn 22
Ho Chi Minh Saigon ○ **VN** 263 Ld 40
Hochveld ⌒ **NAM** 348 Ha 56
Hoctún ○ **MEX** 93 Dd 35
Hoda̱ Àfarîn ○ **IR** 209 Jb 27
Hodal ○ **IND** 234 Kc 32
Hodgenville ○ **USA** 71 Df 27
Hodges Gardens ★ **USA** 86 Db 30
Hodgson ○ **CDN** 51 Cj 20
Hodgson ○ **CDN** 56 Cp 20
Hodgson Downs ○ **AUS** 364 Md 53
Hodgson River ○ **AUS** 364 Md 53
Hodh ⌒ **RIM** 304 Gb 37
Hodick Mountains △ **38** Da 18
Hódmezővásárhely ○ **H** 174 Hc 22
Hodmo ～ **SP** 328 Jd 40
Hodo Dan ⌒ **DVRK** 247 Lp 26
Hodonín ○ **CZ** 174 Ha 21
Hodq Shamo △ **VRC** 243 Ld 25
Hodžambas ○ **TM** 223 Jl 26
Hodzana ～ **USA** 46 Ba 11
Hodža-Obigarm ○ **TJ** 223 Jn 26
Hoeyang ○ **DVRK** 247 Lp 26
Hof ○ **D** 174 Gm 20
Hoffman's Cay ⌃ **BS** 87 Dk 33
Höflðakaupstaður Skagaströnd ○ **IS** 158 Fk 13
Hofmeyr ○ **ZA** 349 He 61
Höfn ○ **IS** 158 Fn 13
Hofsjökull ⧊ **IS** 158 Fl 13
Hofsós ○ **IS** 158 Fl 13
Höfu ○ **J** 247 Mb 29
Höganäs ○ **S** 170 Gn 17
Hogan Island △ **AUS** 379 Mk 65
Hogatza River ～ **USA** 46 An 11
Hogback Mountain △ **USA** 65 Ck 25
Högby ○ **S** 170 Ha 17
Hoggar △ **DZ** 308 Gj 34
Hog Harbour ○ **VU** 386 Nf 53
Hoghu ○ **VRC** 258 Lg 31
Hog Island ○ **GUY** 113 Ee 42
Högsby ○ **S** 170 Gp 17
Hohental ○ **NAM** 340 Ha 55
Hohenwald ○ **USA** 71 De 28
Hohe Tauern △ **A** 174 Gn 22
Hohoe ○ **GH** 317 Gg 42
Hoholitna River ～ **USA** 46 Al 15
Hoh Sai Hu ～ **VRC** 231 Kl 28
Hòhuku ○ **J** 247 Mb 28
Hoh Xil Hu ～ **VRC** 231 Kk 28
Hoh Xil Shan △ **VRC** 231 Kh 28
Höi An ○ **VN** 263 Le 38
Hoima ○ **EAU** 324 Hh 45
Hoisington ○ **USA** 70 Cn 26
Hoja Wajeer ○ **SP** 337 Hn 46
Hoka ○ **RI** 283 Ma 49
Hokitika ○ **NZ** 382 Nh 67
Hokkaidō ⌃ **J** 250 Mj 24
Hokksund ○ **N** 170 Gl 16
Hokmâbâd ○ **IR** 222 Jg 27
Hokua ○ **VU** 386 Nf 53
Hola ○ **EAK** 337 Hm 46
Holalagondi ○ **IND** 238 Kc 38
Hola Prystan' ○ **UA** 175 Hj 22
Holbæk ○ **DK** 170 Gm 18
Holbrook ○ **USA** 64 Cf 24
Holbrook ○ **USA** 65 Ck 29
Holbrook ○ **AUS** 379 Mk 63
Holden ○ **CDN** 51 Cf 19
Holden ○ **USA** 65 Cf 26
Holden ○ **USA** 70 Da 26
Holdenville ○ **USA** 70 Cp 28
Holdrege ○ **USA** 70 Cn 25
Holguín ○ **C** 101 Dk 35
Holhol ○ **DJI** 328 Hp 40
Hollabrunn ○ **A** 174 Gp 21
Holland ○ **CDN** 56 Cn 21
Holland ○ **USA** 57 De 24
Høllen ○ **N** 170 Gk 16
Hollick-Kenyon Plateau △ **38** Db 17
Hollis ○ **USA** 70 Cn 28
Hollister ○ **USA** 64 Cb 27
Holloko ★ **H** 174 Hb 21
Holly ○ **USA** 65 Cl 26

Holly Ridge ○ **USA** 74 Dk 28
Holly Springs ○ **USA** 71 Dd 28
Hollywood ★ **USA** 57 Dn 23
Hollywood ○ **USA** 87 Dh 32
Holma ○ **WAN** 321 Gn 41
Holman Island ○ **CDN** 47 Cc 9
Hólmavík ○ **IS** 158 Fk 13
Holme ○ **N** 158 Gj 15
Holme Park ○ **ZA** 349 Hg 58
Holmes Reefs ⌃ **AUS** 365 Mk 54
Holmfors ○ **S** 158 Hb 13
Holmia ○ **GUY** 112 Ee 43
Holmogarskaja ○ **RUS** 159 Hn 14
Holmön ⌃ **S** 159 Hc 14
Holmsk ○ **RUS** 250 Mg 22
Holmskij ○ **RUS** 202 Hm 23
Holmsund ○ **S** 159 Hc 14
Holmudden ○ **S** 170 Hb 17
Holoog ○ **NAM** 348 Ha 59
Holopaw ○ **USA** 87 Dh 31
Holroyd ～ **AUS** 365 Mh 53
Holstebro ○ **DK** 170 Gl 17
Holstein ○ **USA** 56 Da 25
Holsteinsborg ○ **DK** 43 Jb 5
Holter Lake ～ **USA** 51 Cg 22
Holton ○ **USA** 70 Da 26
Holt Rock ○ **AUS** 368 Lk 62
Holuwon ○ **RI** 286 Mf 48
Holy Cross ○ **USA** 46 Aj 13
Holyhead ○ **GB** 163 Gd 19
Holyoke ○ **USA** 65 Cl 25
Hope Vale ○ **AUS** 365 Mj 53
Holyrood ○ **CDN** 61 Eh 22
Holyrood ○ **USA** 70 Cn 26
Hom ～ **NAM** 348 Hb 60
Homa Bay ～ **EAK** 337 Hk 46
Homâm ○ **IR** 209 Jc 27
Hombetsu ○ **J** 250 Mh 24
Hombori ○ **RMM** 305 Ge 38
Hombori ○ **RMM** 305 Gf 38
Homeb ⌒ **NAM** 348 Gf 57
Home Bay ～ **CDN** 7 Fb 3
Home Bay ～ **CDN** 43 Hb 5
Homedale ○ **USA** 50 Cd 24
Home Hill ○ **AUS** 365 Mk 55
Homein ○ **IR** 209 Jc 29
Homer ○ **USA** 10 Ba 4
Homer ○ **USA** 46 An 15
Homer ○ **USA** 70 Db 29
Homerville ○ **USA** 86 Dg 30
Homer Youngs Peak △ **USA** 57 Cf 23
Homestead ○ **USA** 87 Dh 33
Homestead N.M. of America ★ **USA** 70 Cp 27
Hominy ○ **USA** 70 Cp 27
Homnäbâd ○ **IND** 238 Kc 37
Homodji ○ **RN** 309 Go 37
Homonhon Island ⌃ **RP** 267 Ln 40
Homs ○ **SYR** 208 Hl 28
Homyel' ○ **BY** 171 Hh 19
Honâvar ○ **IND** 238 Kb 38
Honaz D. △ **TR** 195 Hg 27
Honda ○ **CO** 106 Dl 43
Honda Bay ～ **RP** 267 Lk 41
Hòn Đât ○ **VN** 263 Lc 40
Hondeklipbaai ○ **ZA** 348 Ha 61
Hondo ○ **USA** 65 Ck 29
Hondo ○ **USA** 81 Cn 31
Hondo ～ **MEX** 93 Dd 36
Hondo ○ **J** 247 Ma 29
Hondō ～ **VRC** 100 Dg 34
Honduras ⌒ **HN** 96 De 38
Hønefoss ○ **N** 158 Gl 15
Honesdale ○ **USA** 74 Di 25
Honey Lake ～ **USA** 64 Cb 25
Honfleur ○ **F** 163 Gf 21
Hong'an ○ **VRC** 243 Lh 30
Hongch'ŏn ○ **ROK** 247 Lp 27
Hongde ○ **VRC** 243 Ld 27
Hongdong ○ **VRC** 243 Lf 27
Hồng Gai ～ **VN** 255 Ld 35
Hongfeng Hu ～ **VRC** 255 Ld 32
Hong He ～ **VRC** 243 Lh 29
Hong Hu ～ **VRC** 258 Lg 31
Hongjiang ○ **VRC** 255 Le 32
Hong Kong ⊙ **VRC** 258 Lh 34
Hong Kong Island ⌃ **VRC** 258 Lh 34
Hongliuyuan ○ **VRC** 242 La 26
Hongmen ○ **VRC** 246 Lk 30
Hongmenhe ○ **VRC** 243 Le 27
Hồng Ngự ○ **VN** 263 Lc 40
Hongor ○ **MNG** 204 Va 9
Hongshan ○ **VRC** 243 Lg 30
Hongshui He ～ **VRC** 255 Ld 33
Hongū ○ **J** 251 Md 29
Hongwei ○ **VRC** 258 Lj 31
Hongwon ○ **DVRK** 247 Lp 26
Hongya ○ **VRC** 255 Lb 31
Hongyuan ○ **VRC** 242 Lb 29
Hongze Hu ～ **VRC** 246 Lk 29
Hongzhi Liang △ **VRC** 243 Le 28
Honiara ⌖ **SOL** 290 Nb 50
Honiton ○ **GB** 163 Ge 20
Honjō ○ **J** 250 Mf 26
Honnah ○ **USA** 6 Ca 4
Honnali ○ **IND** 238 Kb 38
Honningsvåg ○ **N** 159 He 10
Honokaa ○ **USA** 75 An 35
Honolulu ○ **USA** 75 Al 35
Honoria ○ **PE** 116 Dl 50
Hòn Rái ⌃ **VN** 263 Lc 41
Honshū ⌃ **J** 251 Md 27
Hòn Tân ○ **VN** 255 Lc 35
Hòn Thô Chu ⌃ **VN** 263 Lb 41
Hòn Tre △ **VN** 263 Le 39
Honu̇u ～ **RUS** 205 Xb 5
Hood ～ **USA** 64 Eb 5
Hood Bay ～ **PNG** 287 Mk 51
Hood Point ⌒ **AUS** 368 Lk 63
Hood River ○ **USA** 50 Cb 23
Hoogeveen ○ **NL** 170 Gk 19
Hooker ○ **USA** 70 Cm 27
Hooker Creek ○ **AUS** 364 Mb 55
Hooker Creek Aboriginal Land ••• **AUS** 364 Mb 55
Hook Island ⌃ **AUS** 375 Ml 56
Hook Reef ⌃ **AUS** 375 Ml 55
Hoonah ○ **USA** 47 Bj 15
Hoopa Valley Indian Reservation ••• **USA** 64 Ca 25

Hooper ○ **USA** 65 Ck 27
Hooper ○ **USA** 70 Cp 25
Hooper Bay ～ **USA** 23 Ab 3
Hooper Bay ～ **USA** 46 Ag 15
Hooper Bay ～ **USA** 46 Ag 15
Hoopeston ○ **USA** 71 De 25
Hoopstad ○ **ZA** 349 He 59
Hoover ○ **USA** 51 Cl 23
Hoover ○ **USA** 71 Dh 24
Hoover Dam ★ **USA** 64 Ce 27
Hopa ○ **TR** 202 Hn 25
Ho-pang ○ **MYA** 254 Kp 34
Hope ○ **USA** 71 Db 29
Hope ○ **CDN** 50 Cb 21
Hope ○ **USA** 64 Ce 29
Hope ○ **USA** 65 Ck 29
Hope ○ **USA** 70 Db 29
Hope ○ **NAM** 348 Ha 59
Hope ～ **AUS** 368 Lk 59
Hope Campbell Lake ～ **AUS** 369 Ln 60
Hopefield ○ **ZA** 358 Hb 62
Hope Island △ **CDN** 57 Dh 23
Hopelchén ○ **MEX** 93 Dd 36
Hopen ⌃ **N** 19 La 3
Hopen ⌃ **N** 158 Gk 14
Hopen ⌃ **N** 158 He 7
Hopenbanken ♥ **N** 158 Hf 7
Hoper ～ **RUS** 181 Hp 19
Hopetoun ○ **AUS** 368 Ll 62
Hopetoun ○ **AUS** 378 Mg 63
Hopetown ○ **ZA** 349 Hd 60
Hopewell ○ **USA** 74 Dk 27
Hopewell Cape ○ **CDN** 61 Eb 23
Hopewell Culture N.H.P. ★ **USA** 71 Dg 26
Hopi ••• **USA** 65 Cg 27
Hopín ○ **MYA** 254 Kn 33
Hopkinsville ○ **USA** 71 De 27
Hopland ○ **USA** 64 Ca 26
Hoquiam ○ **USA** 50 Bp 22
Hor ～ **RUS** 205 Xa 9
Hor ～ **RUS** 250 Me 22
Hora Hoverla △ **UA** 175 He 21
Horana ○ **CL** 239 Ke 42
Horasan ○ **TR** 202 Hp 25
Hórby ○ **S** 170 Gn 18
Horcones ～ **RA** 136 Eb 58
Horeilândia ○ **BR** 124 Fa 49
Hör-e Mûsá ～ **IR** 215 Jc 30
Horezu ○ **RO** 175 He 23
Horinger ○ **VRC** 243 Lf 25
Horinsk ○ **RUS** 204 Va 8
Horizontina ○ **BR** 140 Eg 59
Horki ○ **BY** 171 Hh 18
Horlivka ○ **UA** 181 Hl 21
Horlog Hu ～ **VRC** 242 Kn 27
Hormoz △ **IR** 226 Jg 32
Hormoz ⊙ **IR** 226 Jf 32
Hormozgân ⊙ **IR** 226 Jf 32
Hormūd ○ **IR** 226 Jg 32
Horn △ **A** 174 Gp 21
Hornaday River ～ **CDN** 47 Ca 11
Hornavan ～ **S** 158 Ha 12
Hornbjarg ⌃ **IS** 158 Fj 12
Horncontos ○ **PA** 97 Dg 41
Horndal ○ **S** 158 Ha 15
Hornell ○ **USA** 60 Dh 24
Hornell ○ **USA** 60 Dk 24
Hornepayne ○ **CDN** 57 Df 21
Hornindalsvaten ～ **N** 158 Gk 15
Horn Island ⌃ **USA** 86 Dd 30
Horn Island ⌃ **AUS** 365 Mh 51
Horno Islands △ **PNG** 287 Mk 47
Horns ～ **MEX** 80 Ch 32
Horn Plateau △ **CDN** 6 Cb 3
Horn Plateau △ **CDN** 47 Ca 13
Hornsby ○ **AUS** 379 Mm 62
Hornsund ～ **N** 158 Gp 7
Hornsundtind △ **N** 158 Ha 7
Horodnja ○ **UA** 175 Hh 20
Horodok ○ **UA** 175 Hd 21
Horodok ○ **UA** 175 He 21
Horol' ○ **RUS** 250 Me 23
Horoquetas ○ **CF** 97 Dg 40
Horra ○ **VRC** 231 Kk 30
Horrocks ○ **AUS** 368 Lh 60
Horsburg Atoll ⌃ **MV** 239 Ka 43
Horse Creek ○ **USA** 65 Ck 25
Horse Creek ○ **USA** 65 Ck 25
Horsefly ○ **CDN** 50 Cb 19
Horsefly Lake ～ **CDN** 50 Cb 19
Horseheads ○ **USA** 60 Dk 24
Horse Island ⌃ **CDN** 56 Cn 19
Horse Island ⌃ **CDN** 61 Eg 20
Horsens ○ **DK** 170 Gl 18
Horseshoe Bend ○ **USA** 50 Cd 24
Horseshoe Bend Nat. Mil. Pk. ★ **USA** 86 Df 29
Horsham ○ **AUS** 378 Mh 64
Horten ○ **N** 170 Gm 16
Hortobágy ⌒ **H** 174 Hc 22
Hortobágyi ⍋ **H** 174 Hc 22
Horton Lake ～ **CDN** 47 Ca 11
Horton River ～ **CDN** 47 Bn 11
Horton River ～ **CDN** 6 Cb 2
Horwood Lake ～ **CDN** 57 Dg 22
Horyn ～ **UA** 175 He 21
Horyuji ★ **J** 251 Md 28
Hosa'ina ○ **ETH** 325 Hl 42
Hôsämand ○ **AFG** 223 Jn 29
Hosanagara ○ **IND** 238 Kb 39
Hosdurg ○ **IND** 238 Kb 39
Hosdurga ○ **IND** 238 Kc 39
Hoseinâbâd ○ **IR** 209 Jb 28
Hoseinâbâd ○ **IR** 226 Jj 30
Hoseiniye-ye Nârdin ○ **IR** 209 Jb 29
Hošeutovo ○ **RUS** 181 Jb 22
Hoshâb ○ **PK** 227 Jk 32
Hoshangâbâd ○ **IND** 234 Kc 34
Hoshiârpur ○ **IND** 230 Kb 30
Hôsib ～ **SUD** 313 Hk 36
Hôsi ○ **AFG** 223 Jn 29
Hosiârpur ○ **IND** 230 Kb 30
Hoskins ○ **PNG** 287 Mm 48
Hoskote ○ **IND** 238 Kc 39
Hospah ○ **USA** 65 Cj 28
Hospås-Rûd ○ **AFG** 226 Jk 30
Hospet ○ **IND** 238 Kc 38
Hospicia ○ **PE** 128 Dn 55

Hospicio ★ **MEX** 92 Cl 35
Hosrovio ○ **IRQ** 209 Ja 28
Hosséré Gode △ **CAM** 321 Gn 41
Hosséré Vokre △ **CAM** 321 Gn 41
Hosston ○ **USA** 70 Db 29
Host ○ **AFG** 223 Jn 29
Hosur ○ **IND** 238 Kc 39
Hoşu ○ **IND** 238 Kc 39
Hôş Yeiláq ○ **IR** 222 Jf 27
Hot ○ **THA** 254 Kp 36
Hotahudo ○ **TP** 282 Ln 50
Hotan ○ **VRC** 230 Kd 27
Hotan He ～ **VRC** 230 Ke 26
Hotazel ○ **ZA** 349 Hd 59
Hô Thác Ba ～ **VN** 255 Lc 35
Hoti ○ **RI** 283 Mb 47
Hoṯbe ○ **IR** 209 Jc 26
Hoṯbe Sarâ ○ **IR** 209 Jc 26
Hotchkiss ○ **USA** 65 Cj 26
Hot Springs ★ **USA** 50 Bp 22
Hot Springs ○ **USA** 50 Ce 23
Hot Springs ○ **USA** 51 Cl 24
Hot Springs ○ **USA** 70 Db 28
Hot Springs ○ **USA** 70 Db 28
Hot Springs ○ **USA** 51 Dg 28
Hot Springs Natl. P. ★ **USA** 70 Db 28
Hottah Lake ～ **CDN** 47 Cc 13
Hottentotskloof ○ **ZA** 358 Hb 62
Hot Water Beach ♀ **NZ** 383 Nk 64
Houailou ○ **F** 386 Ne 56
Houeïriye ○ **RIM** 305 Gc 37
Houghton ○ **USA** 56 Dc 21
Houghton ○ **USA** 57 Dd 22
Houghton Lake ～ **USA** 57 Df 23
Houghton Lake ～ **USA** 57 Df 23
Houhai ○ **VRC** 255 Lf 35
Houhu ○ **VRC** 243 Lf 35
Houlton ○ **USA** 60 Ea 22
Houma ○ **USA** 86 Dc 31
Houma ○ **VRC** 243 Lf 28
Houma ○ **TO** 390 Ac 56
Houmt Souk Jerba ○ **TN** 297 Gm 29
Houndé ○ **BF** 317 Ge 40
Houston ○ **USA** 46 Ba 15
Houston ○ **USA** 70 Db 27
Houston ○ **USA** 81 Cp 31
Houston ○ **USA** 86 Dd 29
Houston Point △ **CDN** 57 Dh 19
Hout Bay ○ **ZA** 358 Hb 63
Houtkraal ○ **ZA** 349 He 61
Houtman Abrolhos ⌃ **AUS** 368 Lg 60
Houzi-e Soltân ～ **IR** 222 Jd 28
Hova ○ **S** 170 Gn 16
Hovd ～ **MNG** 204 Ua 9
Hovden ○ **N** 170 Gk 16
Hovenweep N.M. ★ **USA** 65 Ch 27
Hovoro ○ **SOL** 290 Na 50
Howakil △ **ER** 313 Hn 38
Howakil Bay ～ **ER** 313 Hn 38
Howard ○ **USA** 56 Cp 24
Howard ○ **USA** 57 Dd 23
Howard City ○ **USA** 57 Df 24
Howard Island △ **AUS** 364 Md 52
Howard Springs ○ **AUS** 364 Mb 52
Howards Springs △ **AUS** 364 Mb 52
Howardville ○ **USA** 71 Dd 27
Howell ○ **USA** 57 Df 24
Howes ○ **USA** 51 Cl 23
Howe Sound ～ **CDN** 50 Ca 21
Howick ○ **ZA** 352 Hh 60
Howick Group ⌃ **AUS** 365 Mj 53
Howison ○ **USA** 86 Dd 30
Howland ⌃ **USA** 27 Aa 9
Howlong ○ **AUS** 379 Mk 63
Hoxie ○ **USA** 70 Cm 26
Hoy ⌃ **GB** 162 Ge 16
Hőy ○ **IR** 209 Ja 26
Hoyerswerda ○ **D** 174 Gp 20
Høylandet ○ **N** 158 Gm 13
Hpangpai ○ **MYA** 254 Kp 34
Hpawngtut ○ **MYA** 254 Kn 33
Hradec Králové ○ **CZ** 174 Gp 20
Hradyz'k ○ **UA** 175 Hj 21
Hrami ～ **GE** 202 Ja 25
Hrazdan ○ **ARM** 202 Ja 25
Hrebet Karagaz △ **TM** 222 Jf 26
Hrebinka ○ **UA** 175 Hj 20
Hrebyn ～ **UA** 159 Ll 33
Hsuen Shan △ **VRC** 259 Ll 33
Hsukushima Shrine ★ **J** 247 Mb 28
Htingu ○ **MYA** 254 Kn 33
Hua'an ○ **VRC** 258 Lj 33
Huab ～ **NAM** 340 Gp 55
Huabu ○ **VRC** 258 Lk 31
Huacalera △ **RA** 136 Eb 57
Huacaña ○ **PE** 128 Dm 53
Huacaya ○ **BOL** 136 Ec 56
Huacaya ○ **BOL** 136 Ec 56
Huacaybamba ○ **PE** 116 Dk 50
Huachabamba ○ **BOL** 129 Dj 55
Huachacalla ○ **BOL** 128 Dp 55
Huachi ○ **VRC** 243 Le 27
Huachipato ○ **RCH** 137 Dm 64
Huacho ○ **PE** 128 Dk 51
Huacrachuco ○ **PE** 116 Dk 50
Huacullani ○ **PE** 128 Dp 54
Huaguén ○ **RCH** 137 Dn 62
Huahaizi ○ **VRC** 242 Km 26
Huahanting Shiku ～ **VRC** 246 Lj 30
Hua Hin ○ **THA** 262 Kp 39
Huahuas ～ **NIC** 97 Df 38
Huaia-Miçu ～ **BR** 132 Eh 51
Huai'an ○ **VRC** 243 Lh 25
Huaibei ○ **VRC** 246 Lj 29
Huaibin ○ **VRC** 243 Lh 29
Huai He ～ **VRC** 243 Lg 26
Huaihua ○ **VRC** 255 Lf 32
Huaiji ○ **VRC** 255 Lf 34
Huailai ○ **VRC** 243 Lh 25
Huai Na ～ **THA** 262 La 37
Huainan ○ **VRC** 246 Lj 29
Huairen ○ **VRC** 243 Lg 26
Huaiyang ○ **VRC** 243 Lh 29
Huaiyin ○ **VRC** 246 Lk 29
Huai Yot ○ **THA** 270 Kp 42

Huaiyuan ○ **VRC** 246 Lj 29
Huajuapan ○ **MEX** 80 Ck 33
Huajuapan ○ **MEX** 92 Cp 36
Huaki ○ **RI** 282 Lp 49
Hualapai Indian Reservation ••• **USA** 64 Cf 28
Hualien ○ **RC** 259 Ll 34
Huallaga ~ **PE** 116 Dk 48
Huallaga ~ **PE** 116 Dk 50
Huallaga ~ **PE** 128 Dk 51
Huallanca ○ **PE** 116 Dj 50
Hualong ○ **VRC** 242 Lb 27
Huamachuco ○ **PE** 116 Dj 49
Huamali ○ **PE** 128 Dl 51
Huamani ○ **PE** 128 Dl 52
Huamantla ○ **MEX** 92 Cp 35
Huambo ○ **PE** 128 Dm 53
Huambo ○ **ANG** 340 Gp 52
Huamboya ○ **EC** 116 Dj 46
Huampami ○ **PE** 116 Dj 48
Huamuxtitlán ○ **MEX** 92 Cn 37
Huanan ○ **VRC** 250 Mb 22
Huancabamba ○ **PE** 116 Dj 48
Huancabamba ~ **PE** 116 Dj 48
Huancane ○ **PE** 128 Dp 53
Huancano ○ **PE** 128 Dl 52
Huanca Sancos ○ **PE** 128 Dl 52
Huancavelica ○ **PE** 128 Dl 52
Huancayo ○ **PE** 128 Dl 52
Huanchon ○ **PE** 128 Dk 51
Huangchuan ○ **VRC** 243 Lh 29
Huanggang ○ **VRC** 243 Lh 30
Huanggang Shan △ **VRC** 258 Lj 32
Huang He ~ **VRC** 242 La 27
Huang He ~ **VRC** 243 Ld 25
Huang He ~ **VRC** 243 Lh 28
Huang He ~ **VRC** 246 Lj 27
Huanghe Kou ~ **VRC** 246 Lk 27
Huanghua ○ **VRC** 246 Lj 26
Huanginaoyuan ○ **VRC** 255 Lf 32
Huanglianyu △ **VRC** 258 Lj 33
Huangling ○ **VRC** 243 Le 28
Huanglong ○ **VRC** 243 Le 28
Huanglong Si ★ **VRC** 242 Lb 29
Huangmei ○ **VRC** 243 Lh 30
Huangpi ○ **VRC** 243 Lh 30
Huangping ○ **VRC** 255 Ld 32
Huangsha ○ **VRC** 258 Lk 32
Huangshan ★ **VRC** 246 Lj 30
Huangshan ○ **VRC** 258 Lk 31
Huangshi ○ **VRC** 243 Lh 30
Huang Shui ~ **VRC** 242 La 27
Huang Shui ~ **VRC** 242 Lb 27
Huangtu Gaoyuan ⌒ **VRC** 243 Ld 27
Huangyan ○ **VRC** 259 Ll 31
Huangyuan ○ **VRC** 242 La 27
Huangzhong ○ **VRC** 242 La 27
Huangzhu ○ **VRC** 255 Lf 36
Huaning ○ **VRC** 255 Lb 33
Huanquelén ○ **RA** 137 Ec 64
Huanqueros ○ **RA** 137 Ed 61
Huanren ○ **VRC** 247 Ln 25
Huanta ○ **PE** 128 Dl 52
Huanuco ○ **PE** 116 Dk 50
Huanuni ○ **BOL** 129 Ea 55
Huanusco ○ **MEX** 92 Cl 35
Huan Xian ○ **VRC** 243 Ld 27
Huanza ○ **PE** 128 Dk 51
Huaping ○ **VRC** 254 La 32
Huaping Yü ♁ **RC** 259 Ll 33
Huaqiao ○ **VRC** 243 Ld 30
Huaquillas ○ **EC** 116 Dh 47
Huara ○ **RCH** 136 Dp 56
Huaral ○ **PE** 128 Dk 51
Huaráz ○ **PE** 116 Dk 50
Huari ○ **PE** 116 Dk 50
Huarina ○ **BOL** 129 Dp 54
Huarmey ○ **PE** 128 Dj 51
Huarochiri ○ **PE** 128 Dk 52
Huarocondo ○ **PE** 128 Dm 52
Huarong ○ **VRC** 258 Lg 31
Huasabas ○ **MEX** 80 Ch 31
Huasaga ○ **EC** 116 Dk 47
Huasagà ~ **PE** 116 Dk 47
Hua Sai ○ **THA** 262 La 41
Huascarán △ **PE** 116 Dk 50
Huasco ○ **RCH** 136 Dn 60
Huasco ~ **RCH** 136 Dn 60
Huashan ○ **VRC** 255 Ld 33
Huashaoying ○ **VRC** 243 Lh 25
Huashixian ○ **VRC** 242 Kp 28
Huatabampo ○ **MEX** 80 Cg 32
Huatugou ○ **VRC** 231 Kk 26
Huatulco ○ **MEX** 93 Da 38
Huatusco ○ **MEX** 92 Cp 35
Huauchinango ○ **MEX** 92 Cn 35
Huaura ~ **PE** 128 Dk 51
Huautla ○ **MEX** 92 Cn 35
Huautla de Jiménez ○ **MEX** 92 Cp 36
Huaxi ★ **VRC** 255 Ld 32
Hua Xian ○ **VRC** 243 Lh 28
Hua Xian ○ **VRC** 258 Lg 34
Huayabamba ~ **PE** 116 Dk 49
Huayacocotla ○ **MEX** 92 Cn 35
Huayin ○ **VRC** 243 Le 28
Huaying ○ **VRC** 243 Ld 30
Huayllay ○ **PE** 128 Dk 51
Huaynamota ~ **MEX** 92 Ck 34
Huayuan ○ **VRC** 255 Le 31
Huazhou ○ **VRC** 255 Lf 35
Hubbard ○ **USA** 70 Db 24
Hubbard Creek Reservation ~ **USA** 70 Cn 29
Hubbard Lake ~ **USA** 57 Dg 23
Hubbell Trading Post N.H.S. ★ **USA** 65 Cg 28
Hub Chauk ○ **PK** 227 Jm 33
Hubei ⊙ **VRC** 243 Lf 30
Hubli ○ **IND** 238 Kb 38
Hucal ○ **RA** 137 Eb 64
Huchine ♁ **F** 35 Ba 11
Huckitta ○ **AUS** 374 Md 57
Hudat ○ **ETH** 325 Hm 43
Huddersfield ○ **GB** 163 Gf 19
Hudiksvall ○ **S** 158 Ha 15
Hudi Quan ★ **VRC** 254 Kp 32
Hudson ○ **USA** 60 Dm 24
Hudson ○ **USA** 71 Df 25
Hudson ~ **USA** 74 Dm 25
Hudson Bay ≈ **CDN** 43 Fc 6
Hudson Bay ○ **CDN** 51 Cl 19
Hudson Falls ○ **USA** 60 Dm 24
Hudson Mountains ⛰ 38 Ea 17
Hudson's Hope ○ **CDN** 47 Ca 17
Hudson Strait ~ **CDN** 7 Fa 3
Hudson Strait ≈ **CDN** 43 Ha 6
Hudwirt Lake ~ **CDN** 56 Da 19
Hūdžajli ○ **UZB** 155 Rc 10
Huê ○ **VN** 263 Ld 37
Hueco ○ **USA** 80 Ck 30
Huedin ○ **RO** 175 Hd 22
Huehuetenango ○ **GCA** 93 Dc 38
Huejucar ○ **MEX** 92 Cl 34
Huejuquilla El Alto ○ **MEX** 92 Ck 34
Huejutla de Reyes ○ **MEX** 92 Cn 35
Huelma ○ **E** 184 Ge 27
Huelva ○ **E** 184 Gc 27
Huencuecho Sur ○ **RCH** 137 Dn 63
Huéneja ○ **E** 184 Ge 27
Huenque ~ **PE** 128 Dp 54
Huepil ○ **RCH** 137 Dn 64
Hueque ~ **YV** 107 Dp 40
Huércal-Overa ○ **E** 184 Gf 27
Huerfano River ~ **USA** 65 Ck 27
Huertecillas ○ **MEX** 81 Cm 33
Huesca ○ **E** 184 Gf 24
Huéscar ○ **E** 184 Ge 27
Huetamo de Nuñez ○ **MEX** 92 Cm 36
Huftarøy ♁ **N** 158 Gj 15
Hugh ~ **AUS** 374 Md 58
Hugh Butler Lake ~ **USA** 70 Cm 25
Hughenden ○ **CDN** 51 Cg 19
Hughenden ○ **AUS** 375 Mj 56
Hughes ○ **USA** 46 An 11
Hughes ○ **RA** 137 Ed 62
Hugli ~ **IND** 235 Kj 35
Hugo ○ **USA** 70 Da 29
Hugo Lake ~ **USA** 70 Da 29
Hugoton ○ **USA** 70 Cm 27
Huguangyan ★ **VRC** 255 Le 35
Huguochang ○ **VRC** 255 Lc 31
Hui'an ○ **VRC** 258 Lk 33
Hui'anpu ○ **VRC** 243 Ld 27
Huib Hoch Plateau ⛰ **NAM** 348 Ha 59
Huichang ○ **VRC** 258 Lh 33
Huichon ○ **DVRK** 247 Ln 25
Huichuan ○ **VRC** 242 Lb 28
Huidong ○ **VRC** 254 Lb 32
Huidong ○ **VRC** 258 Lh 34
Huilai ○ **VRC** 258 Lj 34
Huili ○ **VRC** 254 Lb 32
Huillapima ○ **RA** 136 Ea 60
Huilong ○ **VRC** 255 Lf 32
Huimbayoc ○ **PE** 116 Dk 49
Huimin ○ **VRC** 246 Lj 27
Huinca Renancó ○ **RA** 137 Eb 63
Huining ○ **VRC** 242 Lc 28
Huishui ○ **VRC** 255 Ld 32
Huiten Nur ~ **VRC** 231 Kl 28
Huitong ○ **VRC** 255 Le 32
Huitoyacu ~ **PE** 116 Dk 47
Huittinen ○ **FIN** 159 Hd 15
Huixtepec ○ **MEX** 92 Cp 36
Huixtla ○ **MEX** 93 Db 38
Huiyang ○ **VRC** 258 Lh 34
Huize ○ **VRC** 255 Lb 32
Huizhou ○ **VRC** 258 Lh 34
Huji ○ **VRC** 243 Lg 30
Hujra Shāh Meqeem ○ **PK** 230 Ka 30
Hukeri ○ **IND** 238 Kb 37
Hukkajärvi ○ **FIN** 159 Hg 13
Hukou ○ **VRC** 258 Lj 31
Hukuntsi ○ **RB** 349 Hc 58
Hula ○ **PNG** 287 Mk 51
Hula ○ **NZ** 383 Nk 64
Hulahula ~ **USA** 46 Bc 11
Hulaiba ○ **KWT** 215 Jb 30
Ḥulaiș ○ **KSA** 214 Hm 34
Hulane ○ **RI** 283 Lp 47
Hulekal ○ **IND** 238 Kb 38
Hulett ○ **USA** 51 Ck 23
Hulhuta ○ **RUS** 181 Jb 22
Hulin ○ **VRC** 250 Mc 23
Huliyar ○ **IND** 238 Kc 39
Hull ♁ **KIR** 35 Aa 10
Hull ○ **CDN** 60 Dk 23
Hull ○ **USA** 71 Dc 26
Hullehgush ○ **PK** 230 Kb 27
Hūlm ○ **AFG** 223 Jm 27
Hulun Nur ~ **VRC** 204 Vc 9
Ḥulwān ○ **ET** 301 Hh 31
Humacao ○ **USA** 104 Eb 36
Humahuaca ○ **PY** 136 Eb 57
Humahuaca ○ **RA** 136 Eb 57
Humaitá ○ **BR** 117 Ec 49
Humaitá ○ **BOL** 129 Ea 51
Humansdorp ○ **ZA** 358 He 63
Ḥumari ○ **SUD** 313 Hk 37
Humay ○ **PE** 128 Dl 52
Humaya Lobos ~ **MEX** 80 Cj 33
Humbe ○ **ANG** 340 Gp 54
Humberto de Campos ○ **BR** 124 En 47
Humberto Primo ○ **RA** 137 Ed 61
Humbert River ○ **AUS** 364 Mb 54
Humboldt ○ **CDN** 51 Ck 19
Humboldt ○ **USA** 56 Cp 24
Humboldt ○ **USA** 56 Da 24
Humboldt ~ **USA** 64 Cc 25
Humboldt ○ **USA** 71 Dd 28
Humboldt ○ **PE** 116 Dl 50
Humboldt Bay ~ **USA** 64 Bp 25
Humboldt Gletscher ▲ **DK** 43 Hc 3
Humboldt Salt Marsh ~ **USA** 64 Cd 26
Hume ○ **USA** 64 Cc 27
Humenné ○ **SK** 174 Hc 21
Humeston ○ **USA** 70 Db 25
Humirim ○ **BR** 133 Eh 55
Humocaro ○ **YV** 107 Dn 41
Humpata ○ **ANG** 340 Gn 53
Humphrey ○ **USA** 51 Cf 23
Humphrey ○ **USA** 70 Cp 25
Humphreys Peak △ **USA** 65 Cg 28
Humptulips ○ **USA** 50 Ca 22
Humpty Doo ○ **AUS** 364 Mb 52
Hūn ○ **LAR** 297 Gp 31
Húnaflói ~ **IS** 158 Fk 13
Hunan ○ **VRC** 205 Wc 9
Hunan ⊙ **VRC** 255 Lf 32
Hunchun ○ **VRC** 250 Mb 24
Hundested ○ **DK** 170 Gm 18
Hundred Islands ★ **RP** 267 Lk 37
Hunedoara ○ **RO** 194 Hd 23
Hunga Ha'apai ♁ **TO** 390 Ac 56
Hungary ◻ **H** 174 Hb 22
Hunga Tonga ♁ **TO** 390 Ac 56
Hungerford ○ **AUS** 375 Mj 60
Hungnam ○ **DVRK** 247 Lp 26
Hungry Horse Reservoir ~ **USA** 50 Ce 21
Hungund ○ **IND** 238 Kc 37
Hu'ng Yên ○ **VN** 255 Ld 35
Ḥūnīk ○ **IR** 226 Jj 30
Huni Valley ○ **GH** 317 Ge 43
Hunkuyi ○ **WAN** 320 Gk 40
Huns ○ **NAM** 348 Ha 59
Hūnsār ○ **IR** 222 Jd 29
Hunsberge ⛰ **NAM** 348 Ha 59
Hunsrück ⛰ **D** 163 Gk 21
Hunsur ○ **IND** 238 Kc 39
Hunter ○ **USA** 70 Cn 26
Hunter ~ **AUS** 379 Mm 62
Hunter Island ♁ **CDN** 50 Bm 20
Hunter Island ♁ **AUS** 378 Mj 66
Hunters ○ **USA** 50 Cc 21
Huntingdon ○ **CDN** 60 Dl 23
Huntingdon ○ **USA** 71 Dd 28
Huntingdon ○ **USA** 74 Dj 25
Huntington ○ **USA** 65 Cg 26
Huntington ○ **USA** 71 Df 25
Huntington ○ **USA** 71 Dg 26
Huntington Beach ○ **USA** 64 Cc 29
Huntly ○ **GB** 162 Ge 17
Huntly ○ **NZ** 383 Nk 64
Huntsville ○ **CDN** 60 Dj 23
Huntsville ○ **USA** 70 Db 27
Huntsville ○ **USA** 71 De 28
Huntsville ○ **USA** 81 Da 30
Hunucma ○ **MEX** 93 Dc 35
Hunyuan ○ **VRC** 243 Lg 26
Hunza ~ **PK** 230 Kb 27
Huoi Mo ○ **LAO** 254 Lb 36
Huolingol ○ **VRC** 204 Vc 9
Huonfels ○ **AUS** 365 Mh 55
Huong He ○ **LAO** 255 Lc 35
Hu'o'ng Khé ○ **VN** 255 Lc 36
Hu'o'ng So'n ○ **VN** 255 Lc 36
Huon Gulf ~ **PNG** 287 Mk 49
Huon Peninsula ♁ **PNG** 287 Mk 49
Huonville ○ **AUS** 378 Mk 67
Huoqiu ○ **VRC** 246 Lj 29
Huoshan ○ **VRC** 246 Lj 30
Huozhou ○ **VRC** 243 Lf 27
Ḥūr ○ **IR** 222 Jf 29
Huraba ○ **RI** 270 Kp 45
Ḥuraimilā ○ **KSA** 215 Jb 33
Ḥuraiș ○ **KSA** 215 Jb 33
Hurdiyo ○ **SP** 328 Jd 40
Hurdsfield ○ **USA** 56 Cm 22
Huri Hills ⛰ **EAK** 325 Hl 44
Hurkett ○ **CDN** 57 Dd 21
Hurki ○ **BY** 171 Hh 18
Hurlimbo ○ **GH** 317 Ge 43
Hurman Çayı ~ **TR** 195 Hl 26
Huron ○ **USA** 56 Cn 23
Hurricane ○ **USA** 64 Cf 27
Hurso ○ **ETH** 325 Hn 41
Hurtado ○ **RCH** 137 Dn 61
Hurtado ~ **RCH** 137 Dn 61
Husainābād ○ **IND** 235 Kf 33
Ḥusain al-Gāfūs ○ **IRQ** 209 Ja 29
Húsavík ○ **IS** 158 Fm 13
Ḥūsf ○ **IR** 222 Jh 29
Husheib ○ **SUD** 313 Hk 38
Huși ○ **RO** 175 Hf 22
Huskisson ○ **AUS** 379 Mm 63
Huskvarna ○ **S** 170 Gp 17
Huslia ○ **USA** 46 Al 13
Husum ○ **S** 158 Hb 14
Husum ○ **D** 170 Gl 18
Hūṯ ○ **YE** 218 Hp 37
Hutan Melintang ○ **MAL** 270 La 44
Hutchinson ○ **USA** 56 Da 23
Hutchinson ○ **USA** 70 Cn 26
Hutchinson ○ **ZA** 349 Hd 61
Hutjena ○ **PNG** 290 Mp 48
Hutou ○ **VRC** 250 Mc 22
Huttonsville ○ **USA** 71 Dh 26
Huu ○ **RI** 279 Lk 50
Huwan ○ **VRC** 243 Lh 30
Huxi Xincun ○ **VRC** 242 La 25
Huy ○ **B** 163 Gj 20
Huzestān ⊙ **IR** 215 Jc 30
Huzhou ○ **VRC** 246 Ll 30
Huzūrābād ○ **IND** 238 Kd 36
Ḥvāğe ○ **IR** 209 Jb 26
Hvalynsk ○ **RUS** 181 Jb 19
Hvammstangi ○ **IS** 158 Fk 13
Hvar ○ **HR** 194 Ha 24
Hvar ♁ **HR** 194 Ha 24
Hvojnaja ○ **RUS** 171 Hk 16
Hvolsvöllur ○ **IS** 158 Fk 14
Ḥvormūğ ○ **IR** 215 Jd 31
Hvorostjanka ○ **RUS** 181 Jc 19
Hvostovo ○ **RUS** 250 Mh 22
Hwange ○ **ZW** 341 Hf 55
Hwange ♀ **ZW** 341 Hf 55
Hwaseong ★ **ROK** 247 Lp 27
Hwedza ○ **ZW** 341 Hh 55
Hyannis ○ **USA** 65 Cl 25
Hyannis ○ **USA** 74 Dn 25
Hycklinge ○ **S** 170 Gp 17
Hyden ○ **AUS** 368 Lk 62
Hyder ○ **USA** 64 Cf 29
Hyderābād ○ **PK** 227 Jm 33
Hyderabad ○ **IND** 238 Kd 37
Hydrographer Passage ~ **AUS** 375 Mm 56
Hyères ○ **F** 185 Gk 24
Hyesan ○ **DVRK** 247 Ma 25
Hyland Bay ~ **AUS** 364 Ma 52
Hyltebruk ○ **S** 170 Gn 17
Hyndmar Peak △ **USA** 50 Ce 24
Hyong-sen △ **J** 251 Md 28
Hyrynsalmi ○ **FIN** 159 Hg 13
Hysham ○ **USA** 51 Cj 22
Hythe ○ **CDN** 47 Cc 17
Hyuga ○ **J** 247 Mb 29
Hyūga-nada ~ **J** 247 Mb 29
Hyvanger ○ **N** 158 Gj 15
Hyypio ○ **FIN** 159 Hf 12

I

Iá ~ **BR** 117 Ea 46
Iaciara ○ **BR** 133 El 53
Iaco ~ **BR** 117 Dp 50
Iaçu ○ **BR** 125 Ep 52
Iakora ○ **RM** 353 Jb 57
Ia Krâng Po'C ~ **VN** 263 Ld 38
Ialibu ○ **PNG** 286 Mh 49
Ialomița ~ **RO** 175 Hf 23
Ianabinda ○ **RM** 353 Ja 57
Ianca ○ **RO** 175 Hf 23
Iapim ○ **BR** 116 Dm 49
Iaranjal do Jari ○ **BR** 121 Eh 46
Iași ○ **RO** 175 Hf 22
Iaškul' ○ **RUS** 181 Ja 22
Iauarete ○ **BR** 117 Dp 45
Iba ○ **RP** 267 Lk 38
Ibadan ○ **WAN** 320 Gh 42
Ibague ○ **CO** 106 Dl 43
Ibaiti ○ **BR** 140 Ej 57
Ibanabuiú ○ **BR** 124 Fa 48
Ibanda ○ **EAU** 336 Hh 46
Ibañez ~ **RCH** 152 Dm 69
Ibanga ○ **RDC** 336 Hf 47
Ibar ~ **SCG** 194 Hc 24
Ibarej ~ **BOL** 129 Eb 53
Ibarra ○ **EC** 116 Dj 45
Ibb ○ **YE** 218 Ja 39
Ibba ~ **SUD** 324 Hg 42
Ibba ○ **SUD** 324 Hg 43
Ibembo ○ **RDC** 324 Hd 44
Ibenga ~ **RCB** 321 Ha 44
Iberia ○ **USA** 70 Db 26
Iberia ○ **PE** 128 Dp 51
Iberian Basin ▼ 18 Ja 5
Ibestad ○ **N** 158 Ha 11
Ibeto ○ **WAN** 320 Gj 40
Ibi ○ **E** 184 Gf 26
Ibi ○ **WAN** 320 Gl 41
Ibiá ○ **BR** 133 El 55
Ibiaí ○ **BR** 133 Em 54
Ibibebo ○ **BOL** 136 Ec 56
Ibicaraí ○ **BR** 125 Fa 53
Ibicuitinga ○ **BR** 124 Fa 48
Ibimirim ○ **BR** 124 Fb 50
Ibina ~ **RDC** 324 Hg 45
Ibipeba ○ **BR** 125 En 51
Ibipitanga ○ **BR** 125 En 52
Ibiporâ ○ **BR** 140 Ej 57
Ibiquera ○ **BR** 125 Ep 52
Ibiraba ○ **BR** 125 En 51
Ibiraci ○ **BR** 141 El 56
Ibirama ○ **BR** 140 Ek 59
Ibirité ○ **BR** 141 Em 56
Ibiruba ○ **BR** 146 Eh 60
Ibitiara ○ **BR** 125 En 52
Ibitinga ○ **BR** 141 Ek 56
Ibitira ○ **BR** 125 En 53
Ibitirama ○ **BR** 141 Ep 56
Ibity △ **RM** 353 Jb 56
Ibiza Eivissa ○ **E** 184 Gg 26
Ibiza Eivissa ♁ **E** 184 Gg 26
Ibó ○ **BR** 124 Fa 50
Ibo ○ **MOC** 344 Hn 52
Ibohamane ○ **RN** 308 Gj 38
Iboko ○ **RDC** 333 Hb 46
Ibonma ○ **RI** 283 Mc 47
Ibotirama ○ **BR** 125 En 52
Ibra ○ **OM** 226 Jh 34
İbradi ○ **TR** 195 Hh 27
,Ibrī ○ **OM** 226 Jg 34
Ibšawāy ○ **ET** 301 Hh 31
Ibuacu ○ **BR** 124 Ep 48
Ibusuki ○ **J** 247 Mb 30
Içá ~ **BR** 117 Dp 47
Ica ○ **PE** 128 Dl 53
Ica ~ **PE** 128 Dl 53
Icaboe Island ♁ **NAM** 348 Gp 59
Içana ~ **BR** 117 Dp 45
Içana ○ **BR** 117 Ea 45
Içana ~ **BR** 117 Ea 45
Icaño ○ **RA** 137 Eb 60
Icapuí ○ **BR** 124 Fb 48
Içara ○ **BR** 140 Ek 60
Icaraíma ○ **BR** 140 Eh 57
Icaral ○ **BR** 124 Fa 47
Icatu ○ **BR** 121 Em 47
Içel Mersin ○ **TR** 195 Hk 27
Iceland ◻ **IS** 158 Fk 13
Iceland Plateau ▼ 18 Ja 3
Icém ○ **BR** 141 Ek 56
Ichalkaranji ○ **IND** 238 Kb 37
Iche ○ **MA** 293 Gf 29
Icheu ○ **WAN** 320 Gk 42
Ichhāwar ○ **IND** 234 Kc 34
Ichigemskiy Khrebet ⛰ **RUS** 205 Yb 6
Ichilo ~ **BOL** 129 Eb 54
Ichi-Nomiya ○ **J** 251 Me 28
Ichinoseki ○ **J** 250 Mg 26
Ichmul ○ **MEX** 93 Dd 35
Ichoa ~ **BOL** 129 Eb 53
Ichuña ○ **PE** 128 Dn 54
Icó ○ **BR** 124 Fa 49
Icoca ○ **ANG** 332 Ha 49
Iconha ○ **BR** 141 Ep 56
Icy Cape ⌓ **USA** 46 Aj 9
Icy Cape ⌓ **USA** 46 Be 15
Icy Strait ~ **USA** 47 Bj 15
Ida ○ **IND** 227 Ka 34
Idabato ○ **CAM** 320 Gl 43
Idabel ○ **USA** 70 Da 29
Idabo ○ **ETH** 325 Hn 42
Idaga Hamus ○ **ETH** 313 Hm 38
Ida Grove ○ **USA** 56 Da 24
Idah ○ **WAN** 320 Gk 42
Idaho ⊙ **USA** 50 Cd 23
Idaho City ○ **USA** 50 Ce 24
Idaho Falls ○ **USA** 51 Cg 24
Idaiatuba ○ **BR** 141 El 57
Idalia ○ **USA** 65 Cl 26
Idalia ♀ **AUS** 375 Mj 58
Ida Mountains △ **GR** 194 He 28
Ida-Oumarkt ○ **MA** 292 Gb 31
Idāppādi ○ **IND** 239 Kc 40
Idar-Oberstein ○ **D** 163 Gk 21
Ida Valley ○ **AUS** 368 Ll 60
'Idd al-Ghanam ○ **SUD** 312 He 40
Ideles ○ **DZ** 308 Gj 34
Idenao ○ **CAM** 320 Gl 43
Idenburg ~ **RI** 286 Mf 47
Idfū ○ **ET** 301 Hj 33
Idi ○ **RI** 270 Kn 43
Idi-Iroko ○ **WAN** 320 Gh 42
Idiofa ○ **RDC** 333 Hb 48
Idiriya ○ **MA** 292 Ga 32
Iditarod ○ **USA** 46 Al 13
Idlib ○ **SYR** 208 Hl 28
Idodi ○ **EAT** 337 Hk 49
Idohuo ○ **RDC** 324 Hg 45
Idongo ○ **RCA** 321 Hc 42
Idra ○ **GR** 194 Hd 27
Idra ♁ **GR** 194 Hd 27
Idrija ○ **SLO** 174 Gp 22
Idumbe ○ **RDC** 333 Hc 48
Idutywa ○ **ZA** 358 Hg 62
Iecava ○ **LV** 171 He 17
Iepê ○ **BR** 140 Ej 57
Ieper ○ **B** 163 Gh 20
Ierápetra ○ **GR** 194 He 28
Ie-shima ♁ **J** 259 Lp 32
Ifakara ○ **EAT** 337 Hl 50
Ifaki ○ **WAN** 320 Gj 42
Ifalik ♁ **FSM** 27 Sa 9
Ifanadiana ○ **RM** 353 Jb 56
Ifanirea ○ **RM** 353 Jb 57
Ifaty ○ **RM** 353 Hp 57
Ife ○ **WAN** 320 Gj 42
Ifenat ○ **TCH** 321 Hb 39
Iferouâne ○ **RN** 308 Gl 36
Ifetesene △ **DZ** 296 Gj 33
Iffley ○ **AUS** 365 Mg 55
Ifjord ○ **N** 159 Hf 10
Ifon ○ **WAN** 320 Gj 42
Ifould Lake ~ **AUS** 369 Mc 61
Ifrane ○ **MA** 293 Gd 29
Ifunda ○ **EAT** 337 Hk 49
Igabi ○ **WAN** 320 Gk 40
Igaluit ○ **CDN** 7 Fb 3
Igalula ○ **EAT** 337 Hj 48
Iganga ○ **EAU** 325 Hj 45
Iganna ○ **WAN** 320 Gh 42
Igapó ○ **BR** 124 Fb 50
Igaporã ○ **BR** 125 En 52
Igara Acimã ~ **BR** 117 Ea 49
Igara Irá ~ **BR** 117 Dp 46
Igara Mangutiri ~ **BR** 117 Ea 50
Igara Mururé ~ **BR** 121 Ej 50
Igara Nhoquim ~ **BR** 121 Ej 50
Igara Novo Mundo ~ **BR** 129 Ec 51
Igara Pantanal ~ **BR** 120 Ef 49
Igara Paraná ~ **CO** 116 Dm 46
Igarapava ○ **BR** 133 El 55
Igarapé-Açu ○ **BR** 121 El 46
Igarapé Agua Blanca ~ **BR** 120 Ee 50
Igarapé Capitão ~ **BR** 117 Eb 49
Igarapé Citiari ~ **BR** 117 Eb 49
Igarapé do Anamã ~ **BR** 120 Ed 47
Igarapé do Anil ~ **BR** 120 Ef 50
Igarapé do Limão ~ **BR** 120 Eg 49
Igarapé do Pombal ~ **BR** 120 Eh 49
Igarapé Grande ○ **BR** 121 Em 48
Igarapé Iauiari ~ **BR** 117 Dp 45
Igarapé Ipixuma ~ **BR** 117 Ea 48
Igarapé Ipixuna ~ **BR** 121 Eh 48
Igarapé Irá ~ **BR** 117 Dp 46
Igarapé Muiuçu ou Puiuçu ~ **BR** 120 Ee 49
Igarapé Natupi ~ **BR** 120 Ed 49
Igarapé Pacutinga ~ **BR** 120 Ee 50
Igarapé Prata ~ **BR** 120 Ef 48
Igarapé San José ~ **BR** 121 Eh 48
Igarapé São Francisco ~ **BR** 117 Dp 50
Igarapé Serra Encantada ~ **BR** 121 Eh 49
Igarapé Terra Preta ~ **BR** 120 Ee 48
Igarapé Triunfo ~ **BR** 121 Eh 49
Igarassu ○ **BR** 124 Fc 49
Igara Tabocal ~ **BR** 117 Ec 49
Igara Turi ~ **BR** 117 Dp 46
Igarite ○ **BR** 125 En 51
Igarka ○ **RUS** 204 Tc 5
Igarpé-Min ○ **BR** 121 Ek 47
Igawa ○ **EAT** 337 Hk 50
Igaz Dağları ⛰ **TR** 195 Hj 25
Igbeti ○ **WAN** 320 Gj 41
Igbogo ○ **WAN** 320 Gj 42
Igboho ○ **WAN** 320 Gh 41
Igbo-Ora ○ **WAN** 320 Gh 42
Iğdır ○ **TR** 202 Hp 26
Igherm ○ **MA** 292 Gb 30
Ighil Tzane ○ **DZ** 293 Gg 28
Iglédias ○ **I** 185 Gl 26
Igli ○ **DZ** 293 Ge 30
Ignace ○ **CDN** 56 Dc 21
Ignacio ○ **USA** 65 Cj 27
Ignacio Allende ○ **MEX** 81 Cl 33
Ignatovo ○ **RUS** 159 Hl 15
Ignatovo ○ **RUS** 159 Hl 15
İğneada ○ **TR** 195 Hg 25
Igolo ○ **DY** 317 Gh 42
Igoma ○ **EAT** 337 Hj 49
Igombe ~ **EAT** 337 Hj 48
Igornachoix Bay ~ **CDN** 61 Ee 20
Igoumenítsa ○ **GR** 194 Hc 26
Igra ○ **RUS** 154 Rb 7
Igrim ○ **RUS** 154 Sa 6
Igrim ○ **RUS** 204 Sa 6
Igrita ○ **WAN** 320 Gk 43
Iguaçu ~ **BR** 140 Eh 58
Iguaçu ~ **BR** 140 Eh 59
Iguaçu Falls ♀ **RA** 140 Eg 58
Iguaí ○ **BR** 125 Ep 53
Iguala de la Independencia ○ **MEX** 92 Cn 36
Iguape ○ **BR** 141 El 58
Iguapeí ~ **BR** 132 Ee 53
Iguará ~ **BR** 124 En 47
Iguatemi ○ **BR** 140 Eg 57
Iguatemi ~ **BR** 140 Eg 57
Iguatu ○ **BR** 124 Fa 49
Iguéla ○ **G** 332 Gl 46
Iguetti ○ **RIM** 292 Gb 33
Iguguno ○ **EAT** 337 Hk 48
Iguídi Ouan Kasa ⌒ **LAR** 308 Gm 33
Iguitu ○ **BR** 125 En 51
Igumnovskaja ○ **RUS** 171 Hp 15
Igunga ○ **EAT** 337 Hj 48
Iharana ○ **RM** 345 Jd 52
Ihavadiffulu Atoll ♁ **MV** 239 Ka 42
Ihelum ~ **PK** 230 Ka 28
Ihelum ~ **PK** 230 Ka 29
Iherir ○ **DZ** 296 Gl 33
Iheya ○ **J** 259 Ma 32
Iheya-shima ♁ **J** 259 Lp 32
Ihiala ○ **WAN** 320 Gk 43
Ihitsa ○ **LAR** 297 Gn 33
Ihosy ○ **RM** 353 Jb 57
İhtiyarşahap Dağları ⛰ **TR** 202 Hp 26
Ihu ○ **PNG** 287 Mj 49
Ihuari ○ **PE** 128 Dk 51
Ihugh ○ **WAN** 320 Gl 42
Iida ○ **J** 251 Me 28
Iidaan ○ **SP** 328 Jc 42
Iide-san △ **J** 251 Mf 27
Iijoki ~ **FIN** 159 Hf 13
Iisalmi ○ **FIN** 159 Hf 14
Iiyama ○ **J** 251 Mf 27
Iizuka ○ **J** 247 Mb 29
Ija ~ **RUS** 204 Uc 8
Ījajī ○ **ETH** 325 Hl 41
Ijebu-Igbo ○ **WAN** 320 Gj 42
Ijebu-Ode ○ **WAN** 320 Gj 42
Ijevan ○ **ARM** 202 Ja 25
Ijkharrah ○ **LAR** 300 Hc 31
Ijoukak ○ **MA** 292 Gb 30
IJsselmmeer ~ **NL** 163 Gj 19
Ijuí ○ **BR** 146 Eh 60
Ikaalinen ○ **FIN** 159 Hd 15
Ikalamavony ○ **RM** 353 Jb 56
Ikanbujimal ○ **VRC** 231 Kj 26
Ikanda ○ **RDC** 333 Hc 47
Ikang ○ **WAN** 320 Gl 43
Ikare ○ **WAN** 320 Gj 42
Ikaría ♁ **GR** 194 He 27
Ikauna ○ **IND** 234 Kf 32
Ikebe ○ **WAN** 320 Gk 42
Ikeda ○ **J** 250 Mh 24
Ikeja ○ **WAN** 320 Gh 42
Ikela ○ **RDC** 333 Hd 46
Ikelemba ~ **RDC** 333 Hb 45
Ikelenge ○ **Z** 341 He 51
Ikem ○ **WAN** 320 Gk 42
Ikènguè ○ **G** 332 Gl 46
Ikere ○ **WAN** 320 Gj 42
Iki ♁ **J** 247 Ma 29
Ikire ○ **WAN** 320 Gj 42
Ikirun ○ **WAN** 320 Gj 42
Ikizu ○ **EAT** 337 Hk 46
Ikobé ○ **G** 332 Gm 46
Ikola ○ **EAT** 336 Hh 49
Ikole ○ **WAN** 320 Gj 42
Ikom ○ **WAN** 320 Gl 42
Ikomu ○ **WAN** 320 Gh 41
Ikongo ○ **RM** 353 Jb 56
Ikonongo ○ **RDC** 333 Hb 45
Ikoo ○ **EAK** 337 Hm 46
Ikopa ~ **RM** 345 Jb 54
Ikorodu ○ **WAN** 320 Gh 42
Ikot Ekpene ○ **WAN** 320 Gk 43
Ikoto ○ **SUD** 325 Hj 43
Ikoy ~ **G** 332 Gm 46
Ikozi ○ **RDC** 336 Hf 47
Ikpikpuk River ~ **USA** 46 An 9
Ikrjanoe ○ **RUS** 181 Jb 22
Ikutha ○ **EAK** 337 Hm 47
Ila ○ **WAN** 320 Gj 42
Ilaga ○ **RI** 286 Me 48
Ilagan ○ **RP** 267 Ll 37
Ilaiyānkudi ○ **IND** 239 Kd 41
Ilaka ○ **RM** 345 Jc 55
Īlām ○ **IR** 209 Jb 29
Īlām ⊙ **IR** 209 Jb 29
Ilan ○ **RC** 259 Ll 33
Ilaro ○ **WAN** 320 Gh 42
Ilaura ○ **PNG** 287 Mk 49
Ilave ○ **PE** 128 Dp 54
Ilave ~ **PE** 128 Dp 54
Iława ○ **PL** 170 Hb 19
Ilawe ○ **WAN** 320 Gj 42
Ilbenge ○ **RUS** 204 Wa 6
Ilbilbie ○ **AUS** 375 Ml 56
Ile-Ala-Toosu ⛰ **KS** 230 Ka 26
Île Art ♁ **F** 386 Nd 55
Île aux Coudres ♁ **CDN** 60 Dn 22
Île-à-Vache ♁ **RH** 101 Dm 36
Île Baaba ♁ **F** 386 Ne 56
Île Balabio ♁ **F** 386 Ne 56
Île Beautemps-Beaupré ♁ **F** 386 Ne 56
Ilebo ○ **RDC** 333 Hc 48
Île Brion ♁ **CDN** 61 Ed 22
Ile Corisco ♁ **G** 332 Gl 45
Île d'Ambre ♁ **MS** 353 Jg 56
Île de France ⊙ **F** 163 Gh 21
Île de Gorée ★ **SN** 304 Fm 38
Île de Groix ♁ **F** 163 Ge 22
Île de la Gonâve ♁ **RH** 101 Dm 36
Île de la Tortue ♁ **RH** 101 Dm 36
Île de Noirmoutier ♁ **F** 163 Ge 22
Île de Ré ♁ **F** 163 Gf 22
Île des Genévriers ♁ **CDN** 61 Ee 20
Île des Pins ♁ **F** 386 Nf 57
Île de St. Pierre ♁ **F** 61 Ef 22
Île d'Oléron ♁ **F** 184 Gf 23
Île d'Orleans ♁ **CDN** 60 Dn 22
Île d'Ouessant ♁ **F** 163 Gd 21
Île Ducos ♁ **F** 386 Ne 57
Île Dudune ♁ **F** 386 Nf 56
Île du Gros Mécatina ♁ **CDN** 61 Ee 20
Île du Petit Mécatina ♁ **CDN** 61 Ee 20
Île d'Yeu ♁ **F** 163 Ge 22
Ile Esomba ♁ **RDC** 333 Hc 44
Île Europa ♁ **F** 353 Hn 57
Île Grande Cayemite ♁ **RH** 101 Dm 36
Île Grimault ♁ **F** 386 Ne 56
Ile Idjiwi ♁ **RDC** 336 Hg 47
Île Igué ♁ **F** 386 Nd 55
Île Juân de Nova ♁ **RM** 345 Hp 54
Île Kiji ♁ **RIM** 304 Fm 36
Île Koutoumo ♁ **F** 386 Nf 57
Ileksa ~ **RUS** 159 Hl 14
Île Lamaque ♁ **CDN** 61 Eb 22
Île Léliogat ♁ **F** 386 Nf 56
Île Madame ♁ **CDN** 61 Ed 23
Île Neba ♁ **F** 386 Nd 56
Île Nié ♁ **F** 386 Nf 56
Île Ouen ♁ **F** 386 Nf 57
Île Pott ♁ **F** 386 Nd 55
Iles ○ **CO** 116 Dk 45
Ilesa ○ **WAN** 320 Gh 41
Ilesa ○ **WAN** 320 Gj 42
Îles Belep ♁ **F** 386 Nd 55
Îles de la Madeleine ♁ **CDN** 61 Ec 22
Iles de Los ♁ **RG** 316 Fp 41
Îles de Mingan ♁ **CDN** 61 Eb 20
Îles d'Gyères ♁ **F** 185 Gk 24
Îles du Roi-Georges ♁ **F** 35 Bb 11
Îles du Salut ♁ **F** 113 Eh 43
Îles Monger ♁ **CDN** 61 Ee 20
Îles Ste. Marie ♁ **CDN** 61 Ee 20
Iles Tristao ♁ **GNB** 316 Fn 40
Ile Sumba ♁ **RDC** 333 Hb 45
Île Tidra ♁ **RIM** 304 Fm 36
Île Tiga ♁ **F** 386 Nf 56
Île Toupéti ♁ **F** 386 Nf 56
Île Vandé ♁ **F** 386 Nd 56
Ilford ○ **CDN** 6 Ea 4
Ilford ○ **AUS** 379 Ml 62
Ilfracombe ○ **AUS** 375 Mj 57
Ilgaz ○ **TR** 195 Hj 25
Ilgın ○ **TR** 195 Hh 26
Ilha Aaratuba ♁ **BR** 120 Ed 47
Ilha Anajás ♁ **BR** 121 Ej 46

426 Huaiyuan - Ilha Anajás

Ilha Apeú ♁ **BR** 121 El 46
Ilha Aramaca ♁ **BR** 117 Dp 48
Ilha Arapiri ♁ **BR** 120 Eg 46
Ilha Autaz ♁ **BR** 120 Ee 47
Ilha Cacumba ♁ **BR** 125 Fa 54
Ilha Cajutuba ♁ **BR** 121 El 46
Ilha Cannpatal ♁ **BR** 124 En 47
Ilha Caviana de Dentro ♁ **BR** 121 Ej 45
Ilha Caviana de Fora ♁ **BR** 121 Ej 45
Ilha Cipotuba ♁ **BR** 120 Ec 47
Ilha Comprida ♁ **BR** 141 El 58
Ilha Cruz ♁ **BR** 125 Fa 53
Ilha Cuxiuara ♁ **BR** 120 Ed 47
Ilha da Botija ♁ **BR** 117 Ec 48
Ilha da Iobaca ♁ **MOC** 352 Hj 59
Ilha da Laguna ♁ **BR** 121 Ej 46
Ilha da Mutuoca ♁ **BR** 121 Em 46
Ilha das Araras ♁ **BR** 120 Ed 48
Ilha das Flores ○ **BR** 125 Fb 51
Ilha das Galinhas ♁ **GNB** 316 Fn 40
Ilha da Trinidade ♁ **BR** 120 Ee 47
Ilha de Boipeba ♁ **BR** 125 Fa 52
Ilha de Bubaque ♁ **GNB** 316 Fn 40
Ilha de Carache ♁ **GNB** 316 Fm 40
Ilha de Caravela ♁ **GNB** 316 Fm 40
Ilha de Casuarina ♁ **MOC** 344 Hm 54
Ilha de Curari ♁ **BR** 120 Ed 47
Ilha de Itamaracá ♁ **BR** 124 Fc 49
Ilha de Itaparica ♁ **BR** 125 Fa 52
Ilha de Jeta ♁ **GNB** 316 Fm 40
Ilha de Maracá ♁ **BR** 113 Ej 44
Ilha de Marajó ⏥ **BR** 121 Ej 46
Ilha de Moçambique ♁ **MOC** 344 Hn 53
Ilha de Orango ♁ **GNB** 316 Fm 40
Ilha de Orangozinho ♁ **GNB** 316 Fn 40
Ilha de Pecixe ♁ **GNB** 316 Fm 40
Ilha de San Francisco ♁ **BR** 141 Ek 59
Ilha de Santa Catarina ♁ **BR** 141 Ek 59
Ilha de Santa Rita ♁ **BR** 120 Ef 47
Ilha de São Sebastiãn ♁ **BR** 141 Em 57
Ilha de Serraia ♁ **BR** 121 Ej 46
Ilha de Tinharé ♁ **BR** 125 Fa 52
Ilha de Uno ♁ **GNB** 316 Fm 40
Ilha do Bacuri ♁ **BR** 121 Ek 47
Ilha do Baílique ♁ **BR** 121 Ek 45
Ilha do Bananal ♁ **BR** 133 Ej 51
Ilha do Cabo Frio ♁ **BR** 141 Ep 57
Ilha do Caiuárias ♁ **BR** 124 En 47
Ilha do Coro ♁ **BR** 120 Ec 47
Ilha do Curuá ♁ **BR** 121 Ej 45
Ilha do Huqui ♁ **BR** 120 Eg 47
Ilha do Ibo ♁ **MOC** 344 Hn 52
Ilha do Marapiti ♁ **BR** 120 Ed 48
Ilha do Pará ♁ **BR** 121 Ej 46
Ilha dos Macacos ♁ **BR** 121 Ej 46
Ilha dos Marínheiros ♁ **BR** 146 Eh 61
Ilha do Timbotuba ♁ **BR** 117 Ea 47
Ilha Formosa ♁ **GNB** 316 Fm 40
Ilha Grande ♁ **BR** 141 Em 57
Ilha Grande de Gurupa ♁ **BR** 121 Ej 46
Ilha Grande de S. Isabel ♁ **BR** 124 Ep 47
Ilha Ipixuna ♁ **BR** 117 Ec 47
Ilha Itarana ♁ **BR** 121 El 46
Ilha Jacaré ♁ **BR** 120 Ee 48
Ilha Janauçu ♁ **BR** 121 Ej 45
Ilha Macalòè ♁ **MOC** 344 Hn 51
Ilha Mangunca ♁ **BR** 121 Em 46
Ilha Marengo ou Pavilhão ♁ **BR** 120 Ef 50
Ilha Martin Vaz ♁ **BR** 30 Hb 12
Ilha Matemo ♁ **MOC** 344 Hn 52
Ilha Menfunvo ♁ **MOC** 344 Hn 52
Ilha Mexiana ♁ **BR** 121 Ek 46
Ilha Muturí ♁ **BR** 121 Ej 46
Ilha Panamin ♁ **BR** 117 Eb 47
Ilha Paru ♁ **BR** 120 Eg 46
Ilha Pupunhas ♁ **BR** 117 Ec 49
Ilha Quifuqui ♁ **MOC** 344 Hn 51
Ilha Quipaco ♁ **MOC** 344 Hn 52
Ilha Qurimba ♁ **MOC** 344 Hn 52
Ilha Rongui ♁ **MOC** 344 Hn 51
Ilha Roxa ♁ **GNB** 316 Fn 40
Ilha S. Jorge ♁ **BR** 121 Em 46
Ilha Santana ♁ **BR** 124 En 47
Ilhas de São João ♁ **BR** 121 Em 46
Ilhas Desertas ♁ **P** 292 Fm 29
Ilhas do Aquiqui ♁ **BR** 121 Eh 46
Ilhas do Bazaruto ♁ **MOC** 352 Hk 56
Ilha Solteira ○ **BR** 140 Ej 56
Ilhas Selvagens ♁ **P** 292 Fn 30
Ilha Tecomaji ♁ **MOC** 344 Hn 51
Ilha Tijoca ♁ **BR** 121 Ek 46
Ilha Trocana ♁ **BR** 120 Ee 48
Ilha Tupinambarana ♁ **BR** 120 Ee 47
Ilha Urubu ♁ **BR** 120 Ef 47
Ilha Urucuri ♁ **BR** 121 Eh 46
Ilha Urutaí ♁ **BR** 121 Ej 46
Ilha Vanizi ♁ **MOC** 344 Hn 51
Ilhéu do Meio ♁ **GNB** 316 Fn 40
Ilhéus ○ **BR** 125 Fa 53
Ilhéus Secos ou do Rombo ♁ **CV** 316 Fh 38
Iliamna Lake ~ **USA** 46 Al 15
Il' ič ○ **KZ** 223 Jn 25
Ilıca ○ **TR** 202 Hn 26
Ilicínia ○ **BR** 141 Em 56
Iligan ○ **RP** 267 Ln 41
Iligan Bay ~ **RP** 267 Ln 41
Iligan Point ⌓ **RP** 267 Lm 36
Ilimo ○ **PNG** 287 Mk 50
Ilin Island ♁ **RP** 267 Ll 39
Il'ino ○ **RUS** 171 Hh 18
Ilirneskiy Kryazh ⏥ **RUS** 205 Za 5
Ilistaja ~ **RUS** 250 Mc 23
Ilısu Baraj ~ **TR** 202 Hn 27
Ilısu Brj. ~ **TR** 202 Hn 27
Iliwa ~ **GUY** 112 Ee 44
Iljara ○ **EAK** 337 Hn 46
Iljio ○ **WAN** 320 Gh 42
Ilkoma ○ **EAT** 337 Hk 47
Illapel ○ **RCH** 137 Dn 61
Illapel ~ **RCH** 137 Dn 61
Illara Creek ~ **AUS** 369 Mc 58
Illawong ○ **AUS** 368 Lh 60
Île Anvers ♁ 38 Fb 16
Île Charcot ♁ 38 Fa 16
Île Joinville ♁ 38 Ga 16
Illéla ○ **RN** 308 Gj 38
Illela ○ **WAN** 308 Gj 39
Iller ~ **D** 174 Gm 22
Illes Balears ⊙ **E** 184 Gg 26
Illescas ○ **MEX** 92 Cl 34
Illgen City ○ **USA** 56 Dc 22
Illica ○ **TR** 195 Hf 26
Illičivs'k ○ **UA** 175 Hh 22
Illinois ~ **USA** 50 Ca 24
Illinois ⊙ **USA** 71 Dc 26
Illinois ~ **USA** 71 Dc 26
Illizi ○ **DZ** 296 Gl 32
Illora ○ **E** 184 Gd 27
Illueca ○ **E** 184 Gf 25
Ilnik ○ **USA** 46 Al 17
Ilo ○ **PE** 128 Dn 54
Ilobasco ○ **ES** 93 Dd 39
Ilobi ~ **RCB** 321 Ha 44
Ilobu ○ **WAN** 320 Gj 42
Iloca ○ **RCH** 137 Dm 63
Iloc Island ♁ **RP** 267 Lk 40
Ilog ~ **RP** 267 Lm 41
Iloilo ○ **RP** 267 Lm 40
Ilomantsi ○ **FIN** 159 Hh 14
Ilonga ○ **EAT** 337 Hl 50
Ilorin ○ **WAN** 320 Gj 41
Ilovlja ○ **RUS** 181 Hp 21
Ilovlja ~ **RUS** 181 Ja 20
Ilula ○ **EAT** 337 Hj 47
Ilulissat Jakobshavn ○ **DK** 43 Jb 5
Ilur ○ **RI** 283 Mb 48
Ilushi ○ **WAN** 320 Gk 42
Ilwaco ○ **USA** 50 Bp 22
Ilwendo ○ **Z** 341 Hd 54
Imabari ○ **J** 251 Mc 28
Imajõ ○ **J** 251 Me 28
Imakane ○ **J** 250 Mf 24
Imala ○ **MOC** 344 Hm 53
İmamoğlu ○ **TR** 195 Hk 27
Imandi ○ **RI** 275 Lm 45
Imandra ~ **RUS** 159 Hj 12
Imanombo ○ **RM** 353 Ja 58
Imari ○ **J** 247 Ma 29
Imassogo ○ **BF** 317 Ge 39
Imata ○ **PE** 128 Dn 53
Imatra ○ **FIN** 159 Hg 15
Imbassaí ○ **BR** 125 Fb 52
Imbituba ○ **BR** 141 Ek 60
Imbituva ○ **BR** 140 Ej 58
Imborditure Creek ~ **AUS** 374 Me 56
Imbwae ○ **Z** 341 He 54
Iménas ○ **RMM** 305 Gg 37
Imerina Imady ○ **RM** 353 Jb 56
Imese ○ **RDC** 321 Hb 44
Imī ○ **ETH** 328 Hp 42
Imi-n-Tanoute ○ **MA** 292 Gb 30
İmişly ○ **AZ** 202 Jb 26
Imja Do ♁ **ROK** 247 Ln 28
Imjin ~ **DVRK** 247 Lp 26
Imlay ○ **USA** 64 Cc 25
Imlay City ○ **USA** 57 Dg 24
Imlily ○ **MA** 304 Fn 34
Immokalee ○ **USA** 87 Dh 32
Immouzzer-des-Ida-Outanane ○ **MA** 292 Gb 30
Imnaha ○ **USA** 50 Cd 23
Imnaha ~ **USA** 50 Cd 23
Imo ~ **WAN** 320 Gk 43
Ímola ○ **I** 185 Gm 23
Imonda ○ **PNG** 286 Mg 47
Imotski ○ **HR** 194 Ha 24
Imouzèr-du-Kandar ○ **MA** 293 Gd 29
Imperatriz ○ **BR** 121 El 48
Imperia ○ **I** 185 Gl 24
Imperial ○ **USA** 70 Cm 25
Imperial ~ **RCH** 147 Dm 65
Imperial Beach ○ **USA** 64 Cd 29
Imperieuse Reef ♁ **AUS** 360 Lk 54
Impfondo ○ **RCB** 333 Ha 45
Imphāl ○ **IND** 254 Kl 33
Impulo ○ **ANG** 340 Gn 52
Impulo ~ **ANG** 340 Gn 52
İmranlı ○ **TR** 195 Hl 26
İmroz ○ **TR** 194 He 25
Imtān ○ **SYR** 208 Hl 29
Imuris ○ **MEX** 80 Cg 30
Imuruan Bay ~ **RP** 267 Lk 40
Imusho ○ **Z** 341 Hd 54
Ina ⌓ **PL** 170 Gp 19
I-n-Abangharit ○ **RN** 308 Gj 37
Inachab ○ **NAM** 348 Ha 59
Inácio Martins ○ **BR** 140 Ej 58
I-n-Adiattafene ○ **RMM** 305 Ge 38
In Afellahlah ○ **DZ** 308 Gl 34
Inaja ○ **BR** 120 Ee 48
Inaja ~ **BR** 121 Ej 50
Inaja ○ **BR** 124 Fb 50
I-n-Aleī ○ **RMM** 305 Ge 37
Inambari ~ **PE** 128 Dn 52
Inambari ○ **PE** 128 Dp 52
In Amenas ○ **DZ** 296 Gl 31
In Amguel ○ **DZ** 308 Gj 34
Inangahua ○ **NZ** 382 Nh 66
Inanwatan ○ **RI** 283 Mc 47
Iñapari ○ **PE** 128 Dp 51
Inari Ânâr ○ **FIN** 159 Hf 11
Inarijärvi Ânarjaävri ~ **FIN** 159 Hf 11
In Atteï ○ **DZ** 308 Gk 35
Inauini ~ **BR** 117 Ea 50
Inawashiro-ko ~ **J** 251 Mg 27
In Azaoua ○ **RN** 308 Gk 35
In Belbel ○ **DZ** 293 Gg 32
Inca ~ **RA** 136 Dp 60
Inca ○ **E** 185 Gh 26
Inca de Oro ○ **RCH** 136 Dp 59
Incahuasi ○ **PE** 116 Dj 49
Incahuasi ○ **RA** 136 Ea 58
Inchbonnie ○ **NZ** 382 Nh 67
Inch'ŏn ○ **ROK** 247 Lp 27
Inchope ○ **MOC** 344 Hj 55
Incinillas ○ **E** 184 Ge 24
Incomati ~ **MOC** 352 Hj 58
Incuyo ○ **PE** 128 Dm 53
Indaial ○ **BR** 140 Ek 59
Indalsälven ~ **S** 158 Gp 14
Inda Medhanī ○ **ETH** 313 Hm 39
Indaparapeo ○ **MEX** 92 Cm 36
Indapur ○ **IND** 238 Kb 36
Indara Pint ○ **IND** 270 Kl 42
Indara Point ○ **IND** 270 Kl 42
Indargarh ○ **IND** 234 Kb 33
Inda Silasē ○ **ETH** 313 Hm 38
Indaw ○ **MYA** 254 Kn 35
I-n-Délimane ○ **RMM** 305 Gg 38
Indenpendence ○ **USA** 71 Dh 27
Independece Rock S.H.S. ★ **USA** 51 Cj 24
Independence ○ **USA** 56 Db 22
Independence ○ **USA** 56 Dc 24
Independence ○ **USA** 64 Cc 27
Independence ○ **USA** 70 Cp 27
Independence ○ **USA** 70 Da 26
Independence Hall ★ **USA** 74 Dl 26
Independence Mine ★ **USA** 46 Ba 15
Independence Mountains ⛰ **USA** 64 Cd 25
Independência ○ **BR** 124 Ep 48
Independencia ○ **BOL** 129 Ea 54
Independenia ○ **RO** 175 Hg 23
Inderbor ○ **KZ** 181 Jd 21
Indi ○ **IND** 238 Kb 37
India □ **IND** 238 Kb 38
Indiana ⊙ **USA** 71 De 26
Indiana ○ **USA** 74 Dj 25
Indianapolis ○ **USA** 71 De 26
Indian Cabins ○ **CDN** 47 Cc 15
Indian Head ○ **CDN** 51 Cl 20
Indian Head ○ **USA** 74 Dk 26
Indian Ocean ≈ 31 Na 11
Indianola ○ **USA** 70 Db 25
Indianola ○ **USA** 86 Dc 29
Indianópolis ○ **BR** 133 El 55
Indian Peak △ **USA** 64 Cf 26
Indian Res. ••• **USA** 57 Dd 23
Indian Reservation Fort Albany ••• **CDN** 57 Dg 19
Indian Reservation Long Lake ••• **CDN** 57 De 21
Indian River Bay ~ **USA** 74 Dl 26
Indian Springs ○ **USA** 64 Ce 27
Indian Trail Caverns ★ **USA** 71 Dg 25
Indian Wells ○ **USA** 65 Cg 28
Indiara ○ **BR** 133 Ej 54
Indiaroba ○ **BR** 125 Fb 51
Indibir ○ **ETH** 325 Hl 41
Indígena de Vaupes ••• **CO** 117 Dn 45
Indigirka ~ **RUS** 23 Sa 3
Indigirka ~ **RUS** 205 Xc 5
Indio ○ **USA** 64 Cd 29
Indio ~ **NIC** 97 Df 40
Indio Rico ○ **RA** 147 Ed 65
Indira Gandhi Nahar ~ **IND** 227 Ka 32
Indispensable Reefs ⏥ **SOL** 290 Nb 52
Indispensable Strait ~ **SOL** 290 Nc 50
Indombo ○ **G** 332 Gn 45
Indonesia □ **RI** 278 Le 48
Indooroopilly ○ **AUS** 369 Mc 60
Indore ○ **IND** 234 Kb 34
Indragiri ~ **RI** 278 Lb 46
Indramayu ○ **RI** 278 Le 49
Indrapura ○ **RI** 270 Kp 44
Indravati ~ **IND** 234 Kf 36
Indravati ~ **IND** 238 Ke 36
Indus ~ **PK** 227 Jn 31
Indus ~ **PK** 227 Jn 33
Indus ~ **PK** 227 Jp 30
Indus ~ **PK** 227 Jp 31
Indus ~ **PK** 230 Ka 28
Indus ~ **PK** 230 Ka 29
Indus ~ **IND** 230 Kd 29
Indus ~ **VRC** 230 Ke 29
Indwe ○ **ZA** 349 Hf 61
İnebola ○ **TR** 195 Hj 25
İnebolu ○ **TR** 195 Hj 24
I-n-Echaï ○ **RMM** 305 Gf 35
In Ecker ○ **DZ** 308 Gj 33
İnegöl ○ **TR** 195 Hg 26
Ineguha ○ **ETH** 328 Hp 41
Inékar ○ **RMM** 308 Gh 38
Ineu ○ **RO** 174 Hd 22
Inewari ○ **ETH** 325 Hm 41
Inez ○ **USA** 71 Dg 27
Inezgane ○ **MA** 292 Gb 30
In Ezzane ○ **DZ** 308 Gm 34
Infanta ○ **RP** 267 Ll 38
I-n-Farba ○ **RIM** 304 Ga 38
Infiernillo ○ **MEX** 92 Cl 36
Inga ○ **BR** 124 Fc 49
Ingal ○ **RN** 308 Gk 37
Ingallen Creek ~ **AUS** 361 Mc 56
Ingāna ○ **IRQ** 209 Ja 28
Inganda ○ **RDC** 333 Hc 46
Ingauk ○ **MYA** 262 Kn 37
Ingawa ○ **WAN** 320 Gl 39
Ingende ○ **RDC** 333 Hb 46
Ingeniero Chanourdie ○ **RA** 146 Ee 60
Ingeniero G.N. Juárez ○ **RA** 136 Ec 57
Ingeniero Jacobacci ○ **RA** 147 Dp 66
Ingeniero Moneta ○ **RA** 146 Ee 62
Ingenio Mora ○ **BOL** 129 Ec 55
Ingham ○ **AUS** 365 Mj 55
In Ghar ○ **DZ** 293 Gg 32
Ingleche ○ **MOC** 352 Hj 57
Inglefield Bredning ≈ **DK** 43 Ha 3
Inglefield Land ⏥ **DK** 43 Ha 3
Ingleses do Rio Vermelho ○ **BR** 141 Ek 59
Ingleside ○ **USA** 81 Cp 32
Inglewood ○ **AUS** 375 Mm 60
Inglewood ○ **NZ** 383 Nk 65
Ingoda ~ **RUS** 204 Vb 8
Ingólfshöfði ⌓ **IS** 158 Fm 14
Ingolo ○ **RCB** 332 Gn 47
Ingolstadt ○ **D** 174 Gm 21
Ingomar ○ **USA** 51 Cj 22
Ingonish ○ **CDN** 61 Ed 22
Ingore ○ **GNB** 316 Fn 39
Ingrāj Bazār ○ **IND** 235 Kj 33
Ingrid Christensen Coast ⏥ 38 Nb 17
Ingwe ○ **Z** 341 Hf 52
Ingwempisi ~ **ZA** 352 Hh 59
Inhaca ○ **MOC** 352 Hj 59
Inhafenga ○ **MOC** 352 Hj 56
Inhambane ○ **MOC** 352 Hk 57
Inhambupe ○ **BR** 125 Fa 51
Inhambupe ~ **BR** 125 Fa 51
Inhaminga ○ **MOC** 344 Hk 55
Inhamissiba ~ **MOC** 352 Hj 57
Inhamitanga ○ **MOC** 344 Hk 55
Inharrime ○ **MOC** 352 Hk 58
Inharrime ~ **MOC** 352 Hk 58
Inhassoro ○ **MOC** 352 Hk 56
Inhaúmas ○ **BR** 133 Em 52
In Herene ○ **LAR** 296 Gm 32
Inhul ~ **UA** 175 Hj 22
Inhulec ~ **UA** 175 Hj 22
Inhúma ○ **BR** 124 Ep 49
Inhumas ○ **BR** 133 Ek 54
Iniriada ~ **CO** 107 Dn 44
Inírida ~ **CO** 107 Dp 44
Inja ○ **RUS** 23 Sa 4
Inja ○ **RUS** 204 Tc 8
Inje ○ **ROK** 247 Ma 26
Injibara ○ **ETH** 313 Hl 40
I-n-Jitane ○ **RN** 308 Gk 37
Injune ○ **AUS** 375 Ml 58
Inkerman ○ **AUS** 365 Mg 54
Inkisi ~ **RDC** 332 Gp 48
Inkouéle ○ **RCB** 332 Gp 46
Inkster ○ **USA** 56 Cp 21
Inland Kaikoura Range ⛰ **NZ** 383 Nj 67
Inn ~ **A** 174 Gm 22
Innahas Chebbi ~ **DZ** 296 Gh 32
Innamincka ○ **AUS** 374 Mg 59
Inner Hebrides ♁ **GB** 162 Gc 17
Innes National Park ♀ **AUS** 378 Me 63
Inneston ○ **AUS** 378 Me 63
Innesvale ○ **AUS** 364 Mb 53
Innisfail ○ **CDN** 50 Ce 19
Innisfail ○ **AUS** 365 Mk 54
Innoko River ~ **USA** 46 Al 13
Innsbruck ○ **A** 174 Gm 22
Innwood ○ **USA** 56 Cp 24
Inobonto ○ **RI** 275 Lm 45
Inoca ○ **BOL** 128 Dp 54
Inocência ○ **BR** 133 Eh 55
Inongo ○ **RDC** 333 Hb 46
Inoni ○ **RCB** 332 Gp 47
I-n-Ouagar ○ **RN** 308 Gk 37
Inowrocław ○ **PL** 170 Ha 19
I-n-Quezzam ○ **DZ** 308 Gj 36
Inquisivi ○ **BOL** 129 Ea 54
Inriville ○ **RA** 137 Ec 62
In Salah ○ **DZ** 296 Gh 32
Insar ○ **RUS** 181 Ja 19
Insein ○ **MYA** 262 Km 37
Însurăţei ○ **RO** 175 Hf 23
Inta ○ **RUS** 154 Sa 5
I-n-Tadéra ○ **RN** 308 Gk 35
I-n-Tebezas ○ **RMM** 305 Gg 37
I-n-Tedeïni ○ **RN** 308 Gl 37
I-n-Telli ○ **RMM** 308 Gh 37
I-n-Témegui ○ **RMM** 305 Gg 37
Intendente Alvear ○ **RA** 137 Ec 63
Interior ○ **USA** 56 Cm 24
Interlaken ○ **CH** 163 Gk 22
International Falls ○ **USA** 56 Db 21
Interview Island ♁ **IND** 262 Kl 39
Intich'o ○ **ETH** 313 Hm 38
I-n-Tillit ○ **RMM** 305 Gf 38
Intuto ○ **PE** 116 Dl 47
Inúbia ○ **BR** 125 En 52
Inubō-saki ⌓ **J** 251 Mg 28
Inukjuak Port Harrison ○ **CDN** 43 Gc 7
Inuo ○ **PNG** 286 Mh 49
Inuvik ○ **CDN** 6 Ca 3
Inuvik ○ **CDN** 47 Bj 11
Inuya ~ **PE** 128 Dm 51
Inveraray ○ **GB** 162 Gd 17
Invercargill ○ **NZ** 382 Ng 69
Inverell ○ **AUS** 375 Mm 60
Inverleigh ○ **AUS** 365 Mg 55
Inverleigh ○ **AUS** 379 Mh 65
Inverloch ○ **AUS** 379 Mj 65
Inverness ○ **CDN** 61 Ed 22
Inverness ○ **USA** 87 Dg 31
Inverness ○ **GB** 162 Gd 17
Inverurie ○ **GB** 162 Ge 17
Inverway ○ **AUS** 364 Ma 54
Investigator Channel ~ **MYA** 262 Kn 39
Investigator Strait ~ **AUS** 378 Me 63
Inwood ○ **CDN** 56 Cp 20
Inwood ○ **USA** 56 Cp 24
Inyarinyi Kenmore Park ○ **AUS** 369 Mc 59
Inyathi ○ **ZW** 341 Hg 55
Inyo Mountains ⛰ **USA** 64 Cc 27
Inyonga ○ **EAT** 336 Hj 49
Inzá ○ **CO** 106 Dk 44
Inza ○ **RUS** 181 Jb 19
In-Zakèt ○ **RMM** 305 Gf 37
Inžavino ○ **RUS** 181 Hp 19
Inzia ~ **RDC** 333 Ha 48
In Ziza ○ **DZ** 305 Gh 34
Ioánnina ○ **GR** 194 Hc 26
Iokanga ~ **RUS** 159 Hl 12
Io Kazan Retto ♁ **J** 27 Sa 7
Iola ○ **USA** 70 Da 27
Iomba ○ **PNG** 287 Mj 49
Iona ○ **ANG** 340 Gn 54
Ionava ○ **LT** 171 He 18
Ione ○ **USA** 64 Cb 26
Iongo ○ **ANG** 340 Ha 50
Ionia ○ **USA** 57 Df 24
Ionian Islands ♁ **GR** 194 Hb 26
Ionian Sea ≈ 194 Ha 27
Iónioi Níso ⊙ **GR** 194 Hb 26
Ioniveem ~ **RUS** 46 Ac 13
Iori ~ **GE** 202 Ja 25
Iori ○ **PNG** 287 Mj 49
Ios ○ **GR** 194 He 27
Ios ♁ **GR** 194 He 27
Iō-shima ♁ **J** 247 Mb 30
Iouigharacène △ **MA** 293 Gc 29
Iouîk ○ **RIM** 304 Fm 36
Iowa ⊙ **USA** 56 Da 24
Iowa ~ **USA** 56 Db 24
Iowa City ○ **USA** 70 Dc 25
Iowa Falls ○ **USA** 70 Db 24
Iowa Park ○ **USA** 70 Cn 29
Iowa Sac and Fox Indian Reservation ••• **USA** 70 Da 26
Ipala ○ **GCA** 93 Dd 38
Ipameri ○ **BR** 133 Ek 54
Ipanema ~ **BR** 124 Fb 50
Ipanema ○ **BR** 141 Ep 55
Ipao ○ **VU** 386 Nh 55
Iparia ○ **PE** 116 Dl 50
Ipatinga ○ **BR** 141 En 55
Ipatovo ○ **RUS** 202 Hp 23
Ipauçu ○ **BR** 140 Ek 57
Ipaumirim ○ **BR** 124 Fa 49
Ipeke ○ **RDC** 333 Hb 47
Ipek Geç △ **TR** 202 Hp 26
Iperu ○ **WAN** 320 Gh 42
Ipiaçu ○ **BR** 133 Ek 55
Ipiales ○ **CO** 116 Dk 45
Ipiaú ○ **BR** 125 Fa 53
Ipil ○ **RP** 275 Lm 42
Ipira ○ **BR** 125 Fa 52
Ipiranga ~ **BR** 120 Eg 50
Ipiros ⊙ **GR** 194 Hc 26
Ipita ○ **BOL** 129 Ec 55
Ipitinga ~ **BR** 120 Eh 45
Ipixuma ~ **BR** 116 Dm 49
Ipixuna ○ **BR** 117 Dn 49
Ipixuna ~ **BR** 117 Ec 49
Ipixuna do Pará ○ **BR** 121 El 47
Ipixuna ou Paraná Pixuna ~ **BR** 117 Ec 49
Ipoh ○ **MAL** 270 La 43
Ipojuca ○ **BR** 124 Fc 50
Iporã ○ **BR** 133 Ej 54
Iporanga ○ **BR** 141 Ek 58
Ipota ○ **VU** 386 Ng 55
Ippy ○ **RCA** 321 Hc 42
Ipswich ○ **USA** 56 Cn 23
Ipswich ○ **GB** 163 Gg 19
Ipswich ○ **AUS** 375 Mn 59
Ipu ○ **BR** 124 Ep 48
Ipumirim ○ **BR** 140 Eh 59
Ipurupuro ~ **BOL** 129 Eb 53
Iqaluit ○ **CDN** 43 Hb 6
Iqe ○ **VRC** 242 Km 26
Iquipi ○ **PE** 128 Dm 53
Iquique ○ **RCH** 136 Dn 56
Iquitos ○ **PE** 116 Dm 47
Iraan ○ **USA** 81 Cm 30
Ira Banda ○ **RCA** 321 Hd 43
Iracema ○ **BR** 124 Fa 48
Iracoubo ○ **F** 113 Eh 43
Irado ♁ **J** 247 Ma 29
Iraël' ○ **RUS** 154 Rc 6
Iraí de Minas ○ **BR** 133 El 55
Irajuba ○ **BR** 125 Ep 52
Iraka ○ **WAN** 320 Gl 40
Iráklio ○ **GR** 194 He 28
Iramaia ○ **BR** 125 Ep 52
Iran □ **IR** 222 Je 28
Iranduba ○ **BR** 120 Ed 47
Īrānšahr ○ **IR** 226 Jj 32
Irapuato ○ **MEX** 92 Cm 35
Iraq □ **IRQ** 209 Hp 29
Iraquara ○ **BR** 125 Ep 52
Irará ○ **BR** 125 Fa 52
Irarraren ⏥ **DZ** 296 Gj 32
Irati ○ **BR** 140 Ej 58
Irauçuba ○ **BR** 124 Fa 47
Irbes Saurums Kura kurk ≈ 170 Hc 17
Irbid ○ **JOR** 208 Hk 29
Irebue ○ **RDC** 333 Ha 46
Irecê ○ **BR** 125 En 51
Ireland ♁ **IRL** 162 Gb 18
Ireland □ **IRL** 163 Ga 19
Irene ○ **RA** 147 Ed 65
Iretama ○ **BR** 140 Eh 58
Ireupuow ○ **VU** 386 Ng 55
Irgakly ○ **RUS** 202 Ja 23
Irhil M'Goun △ **MA** 293 Gc 30
Iri ○ **ROK** 247 Lp 28
Iriaki ○ **RI** 283 Md 47
Iriba ○ **TCH** 309 Hd 38
Iriki ~ **MA** 293 Gc 31
Iriklinskoe vodohranilišče ~ **RUS** 155 Rc 8
Iringa ○ **EAT** 337 Hk 49
Iriomote-shima ♁ **J** 259 Lm 33
Iriona ○ **HN** 97 Df 38
Iriri ~ **BR** 120 Eg 49
Iriri ~ **BR** 120 Eg 50
Iriri ~ **BR** 120 Eh 48
Iriri Nôvo ~ **BR** 120 Eh 50
Irish Sea ≈ 162 Gd 19
Irkeštam ○ **KS** 230 Ka 26
Irkutsk ○ **RUS** 204 Uc 8
Irma ○ **CDN** 51 Cg 19
Irmo ○ **USA** 71 Dh 28
Irnogou ~ **CI** 317 Ge 41
Irobo ○ **CI** 317 Gd 43
Ironasiteri ○ **YV** 112 Eb 45
Irondequoit ○ **USA** 60 Dj 24
Irondro ○ **RM** 353 Jb 56
Iron Knob ○ **AUS** 378 Me 62
Iron Mountain ○ **USA** 57 De 23
Iron Range ♀ **AUS** 365 Mh 52
Iron Range N.P. ♀ **AUS** 365 Mh 52
Iron River ○ **USA** 57 Dd 22
Ironton ○ **USA** 71 Dc 27
Ironton ○ **USA** 71 Dg 26
Ironwood ○ **USA** 56 Dc 22
Iroquois Falls ○ **CDN** 57 Dh 21
Irō-saki ⌓ **J** 251 Mf 28
Irrawaddy ~ **MYA** 254 Km 35
Irrawaddy ~ **MYA** 254 Km 36
Irrawaddy ~ **MYA** 254 Kn 34
Irrtuia ○ **BR** 121 El 46
'Irsāl ○ **RL** 208 Hl 28
Iršava ○ **UA** 175 Hd 21
Irtysh ~ **KZ** 22 Nb 4
Irtysh ~ **RUS** 22 Nb 4
Irtysh ~ **RUS** 154 Sb 7
Irtysh ~ **RUS** 204 Sc 8
Irtyšsk ○ **KZ** 204 Ta 8
Irumu ○ **RDC** 324 Hg 45
Irún ○ **E** 184 Gf 24
Iruña ○ **E** 184 Gf 24
Irupana ○ **BOL** 129 Ea 54
Irurzun ○ **E** 184 Gf 24
Irvine ○ **USA** 64 Cd 29
Irvine ○ **USA** 71 Dg 27
Irving ○ **USA** 70 Cp 29
Irving ○ **USA** 70 Db 25
Irwin ~ **AUS** 368 Lh 60
Isa ○ **WAN** 320 Gk 39
Isaac ~ **AUS** 375 Ml 57
Isaac Lake ~ **CDN** 50 Cb 19
Isaaq Jilible ~ **SP** 325 Hn 45
Isabel ○ **USA** 56 Cm 23
Isabela ○ **USA** 104 Ea 36
Isabela ○ **RP** 275 Ll 42
Isabela de Sagua ○ **C** 100 Dj 34
Isabella ○ **USA** 56 Dc 22
Isabella Ind. Res. ••• **USA** 57 Df 24
Isabella Lake ~ **USA** 64 Cc 28
Isabel Pass △ **USA** 46 Bc 13
Isabel Rubio ○ **C** 100 Df 34
Isabel Segunda ○ **USA** 104 Eb 36
Isaccea ○ **RO** 175 Hg 23
Isachsen ○ **CDN** 42 Ec 3
Isafara ○ **TJ** 223 Jp 25
Isafjörddur ○ **DK** 18 Hb 3
Ísafjörður ○ **IS** 158 Fj 12
Isahaya ○ **J** 247 Mb 29
Isaka ○ **RDC** 333 Ha 47
Isa Khel ○ **PK** 223 Jp 29
Isakly ○ **RUS** 181 Jd 18
Isambe ○ **RDC** 336 Hf 46
Isanagar ○ **IND** 234 Ke 32
Isandja ○ **RDC** 333 Hc 47
Isanga ○ **RDC** 333 Hd 46
Isangano ♀ **Z** 341 Hh 51
Isangi ○ **RDC** 324 He 45
Isango ○ **RDC** 336 Hg 46
Isanlu-Makatu ○ **WAN** 320 Gj 41
Īšan Şalīb ○ **IRQ** 215 Ja 30
Isar ~ **D** 174 Gm 21
İscehisar ○ **TR** 195 Hh 26
Ischia ○ **I** 185 Gn 25
Isdell ~ **AUS** 361 Ln 54
Ise ○ **J** 251 Me 28
Išeevka ○ **RUS** 181 Jc 18
Iseke ○ **EAT** 337 Hk 49
Isende ○ **RDC** 333 Hc 46
Iseo ○ **I** 185 Gl 23
Isère ~ **F** 185 Gk 23
Isérnia ○ **I** 194 Gp 25
Ise-shima ★ **J** 251 Me 28
Ise-wan ♆ **J** 251 Me 28
Iseyin ○ **WAN** 320 Gh 42
Isfjordbanken ♆ **N** 158 Gm 7
Isfjorden ~ **N** 158 Gn 6
Isha ○ **PK** 223 Jp 29
Ishasha ○ **EAU** 336 Hg 46
Ishiara ○ **EAK** 337 Hl 46
Ishigaki ○ **J** 259 Ln 33
Ishigaki-shima ♁ **J** 259 Ln 33
Ishikari ○ **J** 250 Mg 24
Ishikari ~ **J** 250 Mg 24
Ishikari-wan ~ **J** 250 Mg 24
Ishikawa ○ **J** 259 Lp 32
Ishinomaki ○ **J** 251 Mg 26
Ishinowaki-wan ~ **J** 250 Mg 26
Ishinowaki-wan ~ **J** 251 Mg 26
Ishioka ○ **J** 251 Mg 27
Ishizuchi-sen △ **J** 251 Mc 29
Ishpeming ○ **USA** 57 De 22
Ishurdi ○ **BD** 235 Kj 33
Isikari-sammyaku ⛰ **J** 250 Mh 24
Išim ○ **RUS** 19 Na 4
Išim ○ **RUS** 154 Sb 7
Isimbira ○ **EAT** 336 Hj 49
Isiolo ○ **EAK** 325 Hl 45
Isipingo ○ **ZA** 349 Hh 61
Isiro ○ **RDC** 324 Hf 44
Isisford ○ **AUS** 375 Mj 58
Iskar ~ **BG** 194 Hd 24
Iškašim ○ **TJ** 223 Jp 27
Iškeeve ○ **RUS** 181 Jd 18
İskenderun ○ **TR** 195 Hk 27
İskenderun Körfezi ~ **TR** 195 Hk 27
İskilip ○ **TR** 195 Hk 25
Iskitim ○ **RUS** 204 Tb 8
Iskushuban ○ **SP** 328 Jd 40
Isla ○ **MEX** 93 Da 37
Isla Aji ♁ **CO** 106 Dk 44
Isla Aldea ♁ **RCH** 152 Dl 70
Isla Alejandro Selkirk ♁ **RCH** 147 Dh 62
Isla Alexander Selkirk ♁ **RCH** 15 Eb 13
Isla Altamura ♁ **MEX** 80 Ch 33
Isla Amantani ♁ **PE** 128 Dp 53
Isla Angamos ♁ **RCH** 152 Dl 70
Isla Angel de la Guarda ♁ **MEX** 75 Cf 31
Isla Apipé Grande ♁ **RA** 140 Ef 59
Isla Aracuba ♁ **BR** 117 Ea 46
Isla Arena ♁ **MEX** 75 Cf 32
Isla Baltra ♁ **EC** 128 Dc 46
Isla Benjamin ♁ **RCH** 152 Dl 68
Isla Bermejo ♁ **RA** 147 Ec 65
Isla Blanca ♁ **MEX** 93 De 35
Isla Blanquilla ♁ **YV** 112 Eb 40
Isla Brincanco ♁ **PA** 97 Dh 42
Isla Byron ♁ **RCH** 152 Dl 69
Isla Campana ♁ **RCH** 152 Dl 70
Isla Capitán Aracena ♁ **RCH** 152 Dn 73
Isla Carlos ♁ **RCH** 152 Dm 73
Isla Carmen ♁ **MEX** 80 Cg 33
Isla Cayambre ♁ **CO** 106 Dk 44
Isla Cedros ♁ **MEX** 75 Ce 31
Isla Cerralvo ♁ **MEX** 80 Ch 33
Isla Chaffers ♁ **RCH** 152 Dl 68
Isla Chañaral ♁ **RCH** 137 Dm 60
Isla Chatham ♁ **RCH** 152 Dl 71
Isla Chiquitina ♁ **PE** 128 Dj 51
Isla Choros ♁ **RCH** 137 Dn 60
Isla Clarence ♁ **RCH** 152 Dn 72
Isla Coche ♁ **YV** 112 Ec 40
Isla Colón ♁ **PA** 97 Dg 41
Isla Contoy ♁ **MEX** 93 De 35
Isla Cubagua ♁ **YV** 112 Eb 40
Isla Cumchao ♁ **RCH** 147 Dm 67
Isla Cutano ♁ **RCH** 152 Dl 68
Isla Dawson ♁ **RCH** 152 Dn 72
Isla de Aguada ○ **MEX** 93 Dc 36
Isla de Caño ♁ **CR** 97 Df 41
Isla de Cébago ♁ **PA** 97 Dh 42
Isla de Chiloé ♁ **RCH** 147 Dl 67
Isla de Chincha ♁ **PE** 128 Dk 52
Isla de Coiba ♁ **PA** 97 Dg 42
Isla de Cozumel ♁ **MEX** 93 De 35
Isla de Guanaja ♁ **HN** 100 Df 37
Isla de la Juventud ♁ **C** 100 Dg 35
Isla del Alborán ♁ **E** 293 Ge 28
Isla de la Plata ♁ **EC** 116 Dh 46
Isla del Carmen ♁ **MEX** 93 Db 36
Isla del Coco ♁ **CR** 15 Eb 9
Isla del Maiz Grande ♁ **NIC** 97 Dg 39
Isla de los Césares ♁ **RA** 147 Ec 66
Isla de los Estados ♁ **RA** 152 Eb 73
Isla de los Riachos ♁ **RA** 147 Ec 66
Isla del Pillo ♁ **RA** 137 Ed 62
Isla del Santa ♁ **PE** 116 Dj 50
Isla del Venado ♁ **NIC** 97 Dg 40
Isla de Macabi ♁ **PE** 116 Dh 49
Isla de Maiz Pequeña ♁ **NIC** 97 Dg 39
Isla de Margarita ♁ **YV** 112 Eb 40
Isla de Ometepe ♁ **NIC** 97 Df 40
Isla de Providencia ♁ **CO** 97 Dh 39
Isla de Rey ♁ **PA** 97 Dj 41
Isla de Roatán ♁ **HN** 96 De 37
Isla de Salamanca ♀ **CO** 106 Dl 40
Isla de San Andrés ♁ **CO** 97 Dh 39

Isla de San Ignacio ◬ MEX 80 Ch 33
Isla des Idolo ◬ MEX 81 Cp 34
Isla Desolación ◬ RCH 152 Dl 72
Isla Desterrada ◬ MEX 93 Dc 34
Isla de Utila ◬ HN 96 De 37
Isla Diego de Almagro ◬ RCH 152 Dl 71
Isla do Mel ◬ BR 141 Ek 58
Isla Duque de York ◬ RCH 152 Dl 71
Isla El Tigre ◬ HN 96 De 39
Isla El Vieja ◬ HN 96 De 39
Isla Esmeralda ◬ RCH 152 Dl 70
Isla Española ◬ EC 128 Dd 46
Isla Espíritu Santo ◬ MEX 80 Cg 33
Isla Fernandina ◬ EC 128 Dc 46
Isla Ferrol ◬ PE 116 Dj 50
Isla Flamenco ◬ RA 147 Ec 66
Isla Gama ◬ RA 147 Ec 66
Isla Garrido ◬ RCH 152 Dl 68
Isla Gordon ◬ RCH 152 Dp 73
Isla Gorgona ♀ CO 106 Dj 44
Isla Gorgona ◬ CO 106 Dj 44
Isla Grande de Tierra del Fuego ◬ RCH 152 Dp 72
Isla Guadalupe ◬ MEX 75 Cc 31
Isla Guafo ◬ RCH 147 Dl 67
Isla Guamblin ◬ RCH 152 Dl 68
Isla Guardian Brita ◬ RCH 152 Dm 73
Isla Hanover ◬ RCH 152 Dl 71
Islahiye O TR 195 Hl 27
Isla Holbox ◬ MEX 93 De 35
Isla Hoste ◬ RCH 152 Dp 73
Isla Humos ◬ RCH 152 Dl 68
Isla Ipun ◬ RCH 152 Dl 68
Isla Isabela ◬ MEX 92 Cj 35
Isla Isabela ◬ EC 128 Dc 46
Isla Isauilias ◬ RCH 152 Dl 68
Isla J. Stuvan ◬ RCH 152 Dl 69
Isla Jabalí ◬ RA 147 Ec 66
Isla James ◬ RCH 152 Dl 68
Isla Javier ◬ RCH 152 Dl 69
Isla Jicarón ◬ PA 97 Dg 42
Isla Jorge Montt ◬ RCH 152 Dl 71
Isla Juana Ramirez ◬ MEX 81 Cp 34
Isla La Tortuga ◬ YV 112 Eb 40
Isla la Viuda ◬ PE 116 Dj 50
Isla Lennox ◬ RCH 152 Ea 73
Isla Level ◬ RCH 152 Dl 68
Isla l'Hermite ◬ RCH 152 Ea 73
Isla Lobos ◬ MEX 80 Cg 32
Isla Lobos de Afuera ◬ PE 116 Dh 49
Isla Lobos de Tierra ◬ PE 116 Dh 49
Isla Londonderry ◬ RCH 152 Dn 73
Isla Loreto ◬ CO 117 Dn 47
Islamābād ▣ PK 230 Ka 29
Isla Madre de Dios ◬ RCH 152 Dl 71
Isla Magdalena ◬ MEX 75 Cf 33
Isla Magdalena ◬ RCH 152 Dm 68
Isla Malpelo ◬ CO 15 Eb 9
Isla Manuel Rodríguez ◬ RCH 152 Dl 72
Isla Marchena ◬ EC 128 Dc 45
Isla Margarita ◬ CO 106 Dl 41
Isla María Cleofas ◬ MEX 92 Cj 35
Isla María Madre ◬ MEX 92 Cj 35
Isla María Magdalena ◬ MEX 92 Cj 35
Isla Maxorca ◬ PE 128 Dj 51
Isla Meanguera ◬ HN 96 De 39
Isla Melchor ◬ RCH 152 Dl 68
Isla Merino Jarpa ◬ RCH 152 Dl 69
Islāmgarh O PK 227 Jp 32
Isla Mocha ◬ RCH 147 Dm 65
Isla Mona ◬ USA 104 Ea 36
Isla Monserat ◬ MEX 80 Cg 33
Isla Montuosa ◬ PA 97 Dg 42
Islamorada O USA 87 Dh 33
Isla Mornington ◬ RCH 152 Dk 70
Islampur O IND 235 Kg 33
Islāmpur O IND 235 Kj 32
Isla Mujeres ◬ MEX 93 De 35
Isla Nalcayes ◬ RCH 152 Dm 69
Isla Navarino ◬ RCH 152 Ea 73
Island Bay ~ RP 266 Lk 41
Island Lagoon ~ AUS 378 Me 61
Island Lake ~ CDN 42 Fc 8
Island Park Reservoir ~ USA 51 Cg 23
Island Pond O USA 60 Dn 23
Island Pond ~ CDN 61 Ef 21
Isla Noir ◬ RCH 152 Dm 73
Isla Nueva ◬ RCH 152 Ea 73
Isla Nuñez ◬ RCH 152 Dl 72
Isla Ochidro ◬ RCH 152 Dl 70
Isla Orchila ◬ YV 107 Ea 40
Isla Owen ◬ RCH 152 Dl 71
Isla Parida ◬ PA 97 Dg 41
Isla Patricio Lynch ◬ RCH 152 Dl 70
Isla Pérez ◬ MEX 93 Dc 34
Isla Picton ◬ RCH 152 Ea 73
Isla Pinta ◬ EC 128 Dc 45
Isla Pinzon ~ EC 128 Dc 46
Isla Prat ◬ RCH 152 Dl 70
Isla Puná ◬ EC 116 Dh 47
Isla Redonda ◬ YV 112 Ed 41
Isla Refugio ◬ RCH 147 Dm 67
Isla Riesco ◬ RCH 152 Dm 72
Isla Rivero ◬ RCH 152 Dl 68
Isla Robinson Crusoe ◬ RCH 15 Fa 13
Isla Róbinson Crusoe Más a Tierra ◬ RCH 147 Dj 62
Isla Romero ◬ RCH 152 Dl 68
Isla San Ambrosio ◬ RCH 15 Fa 12
Isla San Cristóbal ◬ EC 128 Dd 46
Isla San Esteban ◬ MEX 75 Cf 31
Isla San Felix ◬ RCH 15 Eb 12
Isla San Gallán ◬ PE 128 Dk 52
Isla San Jerónimo ◬ RA 146 Ee 60
Isla San José ◬ MEX 80 Cg 33
Isla San José ◬ PA 97 Dj 41
Isla San Juanito ◬ MEX 92 Cj 35
Isla San Lorenzo ◬ MEX 75 Cf 31
Isla San Lorenzo ◬ PE 128 Dk 52
Isla San Pedro ◬ RCH 147 Dm 67
Isla San Pedro Nolasco ◬ MEX 80 Cg 31
Isla San Salvador ◬ EC 128 Dc 46
Isla Santa Catalina ◬ MEX 80 Cg 33
Isla Santa Clara ◬ RCH 147 Dj 62
Isla Santa Cruz ◬ MEX 80 Cg 33
Isla Santa Cruz ◬ EC 128 Dc 46
Isla Santa Fé ◬ EC 128 Dc 46
Isla Santa Inís ◬ RCH 152 Dm 72
Isla Santa Margarita ◬ MEX 75 Cf 33
Isla Santa Maria ◬ EC 128 Dc 46
Isla Santa María ◬ RCH 147 Dl 64
Isla Santa Rosa ◬ EC 116 Dj 45
Islas Chargneau ◬ RCH 152 Dl 72
Islas Chauques ◬ RCH 147 Dm 67
Islas de la Bahía ◬ HN 96 De 37
Islas del Maiz ◬ NIC 97 Dg 39
Islas de Lobos ◬ MEX 81 Cp 34
Islas de San Bernardo ◬ CO 106 Dk 41
Islas de Sotavento ⌒ YV 107 Ea 40
Isla Serrano ◬ RCH 152 Dl 70
Islas Gilbert ◬ RCH 152 Dn 73
Islas Guaitecas ◬ RCH 147 Dl 67
Islas Siari ◬ MEX 80 Cg 32
Islas Simpson ◬ RCH 152 Dm 68
Islas Los Frailes ◬ YV 112 Ec 40
Islas Los Testigos ◬ YV 112 Ec 40
Islas Magil ◬ RCH 152 Dm 73
Islas Marías ◬ MEX 92 Cj 35
Isla Soledad ◬ CO 106 Dj 44
Islas Pajaros ◬ RCH 137 Dn 60
Islas Rennell ◬ RCH 152 Dl 71
Islas Revillagigedo ◬ MEX 10 Da 8
Islas Santanilla ◬ HN 100 Dg 37
Islas Secas ◬ PA 97 Dh 42
Islas Socorro ◬ MEX 10 Da 8
Islas Stewart ◬ RCH 152 Dm 73
Islas Stosch ◬ RCH 152 Dl 70
Islas Tachichilte ◬ MEX 80 Ch 33
Isla Talavera ◬ RA 140 Ef 59
Isla Talcan ◬ RCH 147 Dm 67
Isla Tiburón ◬ MEX 75 Cf 31
Isla Tigre ◬ PE 117 Dn 47
Isla Toba ◬ RA 152 Eb 68
Isla Tobejuba ◬ YV 112 Ed 41
Isla Tomás ◬ RCH 152 Dp 73
Isla Traiguen ◬ RCH 152 Dm 68
Isla Tranqui ◬ RCH 147 Dm 67
Isla Trinidad ◬ RA 147 Ed 65
Isla Umbú O PY 140 Ee 59
Isla Uvas ◬ PA 97 Dh 42
Isla van der Meulen ◬ RCH 152 Dl 70
Isla Victoria ◬ RCH 152 Dl 68
Isla Wagner ◬ RCH 152 Dl 69
Isla Watermann ◬ RCH 152 Dn 73
Isla Wellington ◬ RCH 152 Dl 70
Isla Wolfaston ◬ RCH 152 Ea 73
Islay O PE 128 Dm 54
Islay ◬ GB 162 Gc 18
Isla Yacireta ◬ PY 140 Ef 59
Isle au Haut ◬ USA 60 Dp 24
Isle of Lewis ◬ GB 162 Gc 16
Isle of Man ◬ GB 162 Gd 18
Isle of Skilly ◬ GB 163 Gc 21
Isle of Skye ◬ GB 162 Gc 17
Isle of Wight ◬ GB 163 Gf 20
Isle Royale ♀ USA 57 Dd 22
Isle Royale ◬ USA 57 Dd 22
Isles Dernieres ◬ USA 86 Dc 31
Isleta ••• USA 65 Cj 28
Isleta O CO 107 Ea 44
Isle Woodah ◬ AUS 364 Me 52
Ismael Cortinas O ROU 146 Ef 62
Ismā'īlīya O ET 301 Hj 30
Ismayıllı O AZ 202 Jc 25
Isnā O ET 301 Hj 33
Isoanala O RM 353 Ja 57
Isoka O Z 344 Hj 51
Isola Alicudi ◬ I 185 Gn 26
Isola Asinara ◬ I 185 Gk 25
Isola d'Elba ◬ I 185 Gm 24
Isola di C.,R. O I 194 Ha 26
Isola di Caoráia ◬ I 185 Gl 24
Isola di Capri ◬ I 185 Gn 25
Isola di Giglio ◬ I 185 Gm 24
Isola di Lampedusa ◬ I 185 Gn 28
Isola di Linosa ◬ I 185 Gn 28
Isola di Montecristo ◬ I 185 Gm 24
Isola di Pantelleria ◬ I 185 Gn 27
Isola di Pianosa ◬ I 185 Gm 24
Isola di San Pietro ◬ I 185 Gk 26
Isola di Sant'Antioco ◬ I 185 Gk 26
Isola d'Ischia ◬ I 185 Gn 25
Isola di Ustica ◬ I 185 Gn 26
Isola Favignana ◬ I 185 Gm 27
Isola Filicudi ◬ I 185 Gp 26
Isola Levanzo ◬ I 185 Gn 26
Isola Lipari ◬ I 185 Gp 26
Isola Maréttimo ◬ I 185 Gm 27
Isola Stromboli ◬ I 185 Gp 26
Isola Vulcano ◬ I 185 Gp 26
Isole di Ponza ◬ I 185 Gn 25
Isole Trémiti ◬ I 194 Gp 24
Isongole O EAT 337 Hj 50
Isopa O EAT 336 Hh 50
Isorana O RM 353 Jb 56
Iso Vietonen ~ FIN 159 He 12
Isparta O TR 195 Hh 27
İsperih O BG 194 Hf 24
Ispica O I 185 Gp 27
Ispir O TR 202 Hn 25
Israel □ IL 208 Hj 30
Israelite Bay O AUS 369 Lm 62
Israelite Bay ~ AUS 369 Lm 62
Isra-tu ◬ ER 313 Hm 37
Issa O RUS 181 Ja 19
Issaba O DY 317 Gh 42
Issangele O CAM 320 Gl 43
Issano O GUY 112 Ee 43
Isseke O EAT 337 Hk 49
Issia O CI 305 Gc 42
Issimu O RI 275 Lm 45
Issinga O G 332 Gl 46
Issoire O F 185 Gh 23
Issoro O SUD 324 Hj 44
Issoudun O F 163 Gh 22
Issuna O EAT 337 Hk 48
Istanbul O TR 195 Hg 25
Istfjord Radio O N 158 Gm 6
Istfjordrenna ▾ N 158 Gm 7
Istgāh-e Nāīn O IR 222 Je 29
Isthmus ⌒ CDN 42 Fc 5
Isthmus of Tehuantepec ⌒ MEX 93 Da 37
Istiéa O GR 194 Hd 26
Istisu O AZ 202 Ja 26
Istmina O CO 106 Dk 43
Istmo Malagua ◬ CO 106 Dk 43
Istria ⌒ HR 185 Gn 23
Isulan O RP 275 Ln 42
Isumrud ~ PNG 287 Mj 48
Iswepe O ZA 352 Hh 59
Itabaiana O BR 124 Fc 49
Itabaiana O BR 125 Fb 51
Itabaianinha O BR 125 Fb 51
Itabaliza O BR 133 El 51
Itabela O BR 125 Fa 54
Itaberá O BR 141 Ek 57
Itaberaba O BR 125 Ep 52
Itaberaí O BR 133 Ek 54
Itabira O BR 141 En 55
Itabirito O BR 141 En 56
Itaboca O BR 117 Ec 48
Itaboraí O BR 141 En 57
Itabuna O BR 125 Fa 53
Itacaiúna ~ BR 121 Ek 48
Itacaiunas ~ BR 121 Ej 49
Itacaja O BR 121 El 50
Itacambira O BR 125 En 54
Itacarambi O BR 133 Em 53
Itacaré O BR 125 Fa 53
Itacaruare O RA 140 Eg 59
Itacoatiara O BR 120 Ee 47
Itaetê O BR 125 Ep 52
Itagi O BR 125 Ep 53
Itaguaí O BR 141 En 57
Itaguaje O BR 140 Eh 57
Itaguara O BR 141 Em 56
Itaguari ~ BR 133 Em 53
Itagüí O CO 106 Dl 42
Itah Lake ~ AUS 379 Mj 63
Ita Ibaté O RA 140 Ef 59
Itaim ~ BR 124 Ep 49
Itainópolis O BR 124 Ep 49
Itainzinho ~ BR 124 Ep 49
Itaiopolis O BR 140 Ej 59
Itaipú Reservoir ~ BR 140 Eg 58
Itaisen-Suomenlahti ♀ FIN 159 Hf 15
Itaituba O BR 117 Ec 48
Itaituba O BR 120 Ef 48
Itajá O BR 133 Ej 55
Itajaí O BR 141 Ek 59
Itajubá O BR 141 Em 57
Itajubaquara O BR 125 En 51
Itaju do Colônia O BR 125 Fa 53
Itajuípe O BR 125 Fa 53
Itakhoia O BD 235 Kk 33
Italy O USA 70 Cp 29
Italy □ I 185 Gm 23
Itamaraju O BR 125 Fa 54
Itamarandiba O BR 125 En 54
Itamarati O BR 117 Dp 49
Itambacuri O BR 125 Ep 55
Itambe O BR 124 Fc 49
Itambé O BR 125 Ep 53
Itamirim O BR 125 En 53
Itampolo O RM 353 Hp 58
Itanagar O IND 235 Kl 32
Itanagé O BR 125 En 52
Itanagra O BR 125 Fa 52
Itang O ETH 325 Hk 41
Itanhaém O BR 141 El 58
Itanhauā ~ BR 117 Eb 48
Itanhém ~ BR 125 Ep 54
Itanhém ~ BR 125 Fa 54
Itanhomi O BR 141 Ep 55
Itaobim O BR 125 Ep 54
Itaocata O BR 141 En 56
Itapaci O BR 133 Ek 53
Itapacurá ~ BR 120 Eg 48
Itapagé O BR 124 Fa 47
Itapagipe O BR 133 Ek 55
Itapaiúna O BR 132 Ef 51
Itaparaná ~ BR 117 Ec 49
Itaparica O BR 125 Fa 52
Itapebi O BR 125 Fa 53
Itapecerica O BR 141 Em 56
Itapecerica da Serra O BR 141 El 57
Itapecuru Mirim O BR 121 Em 47
Itapera O BR 124 En 47
Itapermirim O BR 141 Ep 56
Itaperuna O BR 141 En 56
Itapetinga O BR 125 Ep 53
Itapetininga O BR 141 Ek 57
Itapeva O BR 141 Ek 58
Itapevi O BR 141 El 57
Itapicuru ~ BR 121 Em 47
Itapicuru ~ BR 121 Em 49
Itapicuru ~ BR 125 Fa 51
Itapicuru-Acu ~ BR 125 Ep 51
Itapicuru-Mirim ~ BR 125 Ep 51
Itapipoca O BR 124 Fa 47
Itapiranga O BR 120 Ee 47
Itapiranga O BR 140 Eh 59
Itapirapuã O BR 133 Ej 53
Itapirapuã △ BR 141 Ek 58
Itapiúna O BR 124 Fa 48
Itápolis O BR 141 Ek 56
Itaporã O BR 140 Eg 57
Itaporanga O BR 124 Fa 49
Itaporanga O BR 140 Ek 57
Itapuã O BR 146 Ej 61
Itapuranga O BR 133 Ej 53
Itaquai ~ BR 117 Dn 48
Itaquai ~ BR 117 Dn 49
Itaqui O BR 146 Ef 60
Itaquyry O PY 140 Eg 58
Itarana O BR 141 Ep 55
Itararé O BR 140 Ek 58
Itarema O BR 124 Fa 47
Itaruã do Oeste O BR 117 Ec 50
Itāsi O IND 234 Kc 34
Itata ~ RCH 137 Dm 64
Itati O RA 140 Ee 59
Itatiba O BR 141 El 57
Itatinga O BR 141 Ek 57
Itatira O BR 124 Fa 48
Itatupã O BR 121 Ej 46
Itaú O BR 124 Fb 48
Itaúba O BR 132 Eg 51
Itauçu O BR 133 Ek 54
Itaueira O BR 124 En 49
Itaueira ~ BR 124 En 49
Itaum O BR 140 Eg 57
Itaúmas O BR 141 Fa 55
Itaúna O BR 121 Em 47
Itaúna O BR 141 Em 56
Itbayat Island ◬ RP 259 Ll 35
Ite O PE 128 Dn 54
Itéa O GR 194 Hd 26
Iten O EAK 325 Hk 45
Itenecito ~ BOL 129 Eb 52
Itenes o Guaporé ~ BOL 129 Ec 52
Itete O EAT 337 Hl 50
Itezhi-Tezhi O Z 341 Hf 53
Ithaca O USA 60 Dk 24
Itháki O GR 194 Hc 26
Itháki ◬ GR 194 Hc 26
Itigi O EAT 337 Hk 48
Itiki O IND 238 Kb 38
Itimbiri ~ RDC 321 Hd 44
Itinga ~ BR 121 El 48
Itipo O RDC 333 Hb 46
Itiquira O BR 132 Eg 54
Itiquira ~ BR 132 Eg 54
Itiquira ou Piquiri ~ BR 132 Ef 54
Itirapuão O BR 141 El 56
Itiúba O BR 125 Fa 51
Itkillik River ~ USA 46 Ba 9
Itō O J 251 Mf 28
Itobe O WAN 320 Gk 42
Itobo O EAT 337 Hj 48
Itoculo O MOC 344 Hn 53
Itoigawa O J 251 Me 27
Itoko O RDC 333 Hc 46
Itomampy ~ RM 353 Jb 57
Itonamas ~ BOL 129 Eb 52
Itquiy O MA 292 Fp 32
Ittoqqortoormiit O DK 43 Lb 4
Itu O BR 141 El 57
Itu O WAN 320 Gl 43
Ituaçu O BR 125 Ep 52
Ituango O CO 106 Dl 42
Ituberá O BR 125 Fa 52
Itui ~ BR 117 Dn 48
Itui ~ BR 117 Dn 49
Ituiutaba O BR 133 Ek 55
Itula O RDC 336 Hf 47
Itulissat O DK 7 Ga 3
Itumba O EAT 337 Hj 49
Itumba O EAT 337 Hj 50
Itumbiara O BR 133 Ek 55
Itungi O EAT 337 Hj 50
Ituni O GUY 113 Ee 43
Ituporanga O BR 140 Ek 59
Iturama O BR 133 Ej 55
Iturbide O MEX 81 Cn 33
Ituri ~ RDC 324 Hg 44
Itutinga O BR 141 Em 56
Ituverava O BR 141 El 56
Ituxi ~ BR 117 Eb 49
Ituxi ~ BR 117 Eb 50
Ituzaingo O RA 140 Ef 59
Itwangi O EAT 337 Hj 47
Itzehoe O D 170 Gl 19
Iuka O USA 71 Dd 28
Iul'tim O RUS 205 Aa 5
Iuluti O MOC 344 Hm 53
Ivabah O RI 270 Kn 44
Ivaí ~ BR 140 Eh 57
Ivaí O BR 140 Ej 58
Ivaiporã O BR 140 Ej 58
Ivakoany ⛰ RM 353 Jb 57
Ivalo Avvil O FIN 159 Hf 11
Ivalojoki ~ FIN 159 Hf 11
Ivangorod O RUS 171 Hg 16
Ivanhoe O AUS 379 Mj 62
Ivanjica O SCG 194 Hb 24
Ivanovo O RUS 171 Hg 17
Ivanovo O RUS 171 Hn 17
Ivanteevka O RUS 181 Jc 19
Ivanuškova O RUS 22 Qb 4
Ivato O RM 353 Jb 56
Ivatsevichy O BY 171 He 19
Ivdel' O RUS 154 Sa 6
Ivindo ~ G 332 Gn 45
Ivinheima ~ BR 140 Eh 56
Ivinhema O BR 140 Eh 57
Ivisan O RP 267 Lm 40
Ivittuut O DK 43 Jc 6
Ivohibe O RM 353 Jb 57
Ivon ~ BOL 129 Ea 51
Ivondro ~ RM 345 Jc 55
Ivori River ~ PNG 287 Mj 49
Ivorogbo O WAN 320 Gk 43
Ivory Coast ⌒ CI 317 Gd 43
Ivrindi O TR 195 Hf 26
Ivujivik O CDN 43 Gc 6
Ivuna O EAT 336 Hj 50
Ivvavik National Park ♀ CDN 47 Be 11
Iwa Island ◬ PNG 287 Mm 50
Iwaizumi O J 250 Mg 26
Iwaki O J 251 Mg 27
Iwakuni O J 251 Mc 28
Iwala O RDC 333 Hd 47
Iwamizawa O J 250 Mg 24
Iwanai O J 250 Mg 24
Iwano-Frankivs'k O UA 175 He 21
Iwantja O AUS 369 Mc 59
Iwanuma O J 250 Mg 26
Iwanuma O J 251 Mg 26
Iwatebu O PNG 286 Mh 49
Iwate-san △ J 250 Mg 26
Iwe O RDC 333 He 47
Iwo O WAN 320 Gj 42
Iwopin O WAN 320 Gj 42
Iwungu O RDC 333 Hb 48
Iwupataka O AUS 361 Mc 57
Ixcaquixtla O MEX 92 Cp 35
Ixhuatán O MEX 93 Da 37
Ixiamas O BOL 129 Dp 52
Ixmiquilpan O MEX 92 Cn 35
Ixopo O ZA 349 Hh 61
Ixtapa O MEX 92 Cm 37
Ixtapa O MEX 92 Cp 36
Ixtapan de la Sal O MEX 92 Cm 36
Ixtepec O MEX 93 Da 37
Ixtlahuaca O MEX 92 Cp 35
Ixtlahuacán del Río O MEX 92 Cl 35
Ixtlán de Juárez O MEX 93 Cp 37
Ixtlán del Río O MEX 92 Ck 35
'Iyāl Bakhīt O SUD 312 Hg 39
Iyayi O EAT 337 Hk 50
Iyo O J 251 Mc 29
Iyo-nada ~ J 247 Mb 29
Izabal Lake ~ GCA 93 Dd 38
Izadḫvast O IR 215 Je 30
Izamal O MEX 93 Dd 35
Izberbaš O RUS 202 Jb 24
Izborsk O RUS 171 Hf 17
Ize O IR 215 Jc 30
Izena-shima ◬ J 259 Lp 32
Izevsk O RUS 19 Mb 4
Izhevsk O RUS 154 Rb 7
Izjum O UA 181 Hl 21
Izkī O OM 226 Jg 34
Ižma O RUS 154 Rb 5
Ižma ~ RUS 154 Rb 6
Izmajil O RO 175 Hg 23
İzmir O TR 195 Hf 26
İzmit O TR 195 Hg 25
İznik O TR 195 Hg 25
İznik Gölü ~ TR 195 Hg 25
Izobil'nyj O RUS 202 Hn 23
Izra' O SYR 208 Hl 29
Izra' O SYR 208 Hl 29
Iztapa O GCA 93 Dc 39
Izúcar de Matamoros O MEX 92 Cn 36
Izu-hanto ◬ J 251 Mf 28
Izuhara O J 247 Ma 28
Izumi O J 251 Mg 26
Izumo O J 251 Mc 28
Izu-shotō ◬ J 251 Mf 28
Izu Trench ▾ 251 Mh 28

J

J. Bou Ladiab △ TN 296 Gl 29
J. H. Ken Reservoir ~ USA 74 Dj 27
J. Redmond Reservoir ~ USA 70 Cp 26
Jaab Lake ~ CDN 57 Dg 20
Jaala O FIN 159 Hf 15
Jabal Adar Gwagwa △ ET 301 Hk 34
Jabal Akakus ⛰ LAR 308 Gm 33
Jabal al-'Adiriyāt ⛰ JOR 214 Hl 30
Jabal al-Akhdar ⛰ OM 226 Jg 34
Jabal al-Ḥašā' △ YE 218 Ja 39
Jabal al Gardah ⛰ LAR 300 Hd 33
Jabal al Hasāwinah ⛰ LAR 297 Gn 31
Jabal al Hawa'ish ⛰ LAR 300 Hd 33
Jabal Ali O UAE 226 Jf 33
Jabal al Maruf ⛰ LAR 300 Hb 33
Jabal Arknu △ LAR 300 He 34
Jabal as Sawdā' ⛰ LAR 297 Gp 31
Jabal at-Tīh ⛰ ET 301 Hj 31
Jabal Bin Ghanimah ⛰ LAR 309 Gp 33
Jabal Ḍurān △ YE 218 Ja 38
Jabal Isbil △ YE 218 Ja 38
Jabal Katrinah △ ET 301 Hj 31
Jabal Manar △ YE 218 Ja 38
Jabal Nafūsah ⛰ LAR 297 Gm 30
Jabal Nuqayy ⛰ LAR 300 Hb 34
Jabal Nuqum △ YE 218 Ja 38
Jabalpur O IND 234 Kd 34
Jabal Sabir △ YE 218 Ja 39
Jabal Tadrart ⛰ DZ 296 Gl 33
Jabal Tammū △ RN 309 Gp 34
Jabal Tarhuni △ LAR 300 Hd 34
Jabal Thamer △ YE 218 Ja 39
Jabal Tuwayq ⛰ KSA 215 Ja 33
Jabal Tuwayq ⛰ KSA 218 Ja 35
Jabal Uweinat △ LAR 300 He 35
Jabal Waddān △ LAR 297 Ha 31
Jabal Zalṭan ⛰ LAR 300 Hb 31
Jabarona O SUD 312 Hf 37
Jabillo O CR 97 Dg 41
Jabiru O AUS 364 Mc 52
Jabitaca O BR 124 Fb 49
Jablah O SYR 208 Hl 28
Jablanica O BG 194 He 24
Jablon ~ RUS 205 Za 5
Jablonica O SK 174 Ha 21
Jabo O WAN 320 Gj 39
Jaboatão dos Guararapes O BR 124 Fc 50
Jaborandi O BR 133 Em 52
Jabotá ~ BR 132 Eg 52
Jabuticabal O BR 141 Ek 56
Jabuticatubas O BR 141 En 55
Jaca O E 184 Gf 24
Jacal O SP 328 Jb 43
Jacala O MEX 92 Cn 35
Jacana O BR 124 Fb 49
Jacaraú O BR 124 Fc 49
Jacaré ~ BR 117 Ec 49
Jacaré O BR 125 Ep 51
Jacareacanga O BR 120 Ef 49
Jacaré Grande O BR 125 En 53
Jacarei ~ BR 124 Ep 47
Jacareí O BR 141 El 57
Jaceel ~ SP 328 Jd 40
Jáchal ~ RA 137 Dp 61
Jáchymov O CZ 174 Gn 20
Jaciara O BR 132 Eg 53
Jacinto O BR 125 Ep 54
Jaci Paraná O BR 117 Eb 50
Jaciparaná ~ BR 117 Eb 50
Jacitara O BR 117 Eb 47
Jackhead O CDN 56 Cp 20
Jackman O USA 60 Dn 23
Jacksboro O USA 70 Cn 29
Jackson O USA 51 Cg 24
Jackson O USA 56 Da 24
Jackson O USA 57 Df 24
Jackson O USA 64 Cb 26
Jackson O USA 71 Dd 27
Jackson O USA 71 Dg 26
Jackson O USA 86 Dd 30
Jackson O USA 86 Df 29
Jackson Arm O CDN 61 Ef 21
Jacksonboro O USA 71 Dh 29
Jackson Lake ~ USA 51 Cg 24
Jacksonville O USA 70 Db 28
Jacksonville O USA 71 Dc 26
Jacksonville O USA 74 Dk 28
Jacksonville O USA 84 Da 30
Jacksonville O USA 86 Df 29
Jacksonville O USA 86 Dg 30
Jacksonville O USA 87 Dh 30
Jacksonville Beach O USA 87 Dh 30
Jacmel O RH 101 Dm 36
Jacó O CR 97 Df 41
Jacobābād O PK 227 Jn 31
Jacobina O BR 125 Ep 51
Jacobina O BR 132 Ef 54
Jacob Lake O USA 65 Cf 27
Jacona O MEX 92 Cl 36
Jacqueville O CI 317 Gd 43
Jacquinot Bay ~ PNG 287 Mm 48
Jacuba ~ BR 133 Eh 55
Jacuipe ~ BR 125 Fa 51
Jacuí ~ BR 146 Eh 61
Jacundá ~ BR 117 Ec 50
Jacunda ~ BR 121 Ej 47
Jacundá O BR 121 Ek 48
Jacup O AUS 368 Lk 62
Jacupiranga O BR 141 Ek 58
Jacurici ~ BR 125 Fa 51
Jada O WAN 321 Gn 41
Jadebusen ≈ D 170 Gl 19
Jadib O YE 219 Je 36
Jādū O LAR 297 Gn 30
Jaén O PE 116 Dj 48
Jaén O E 184 Ge 27
Jāfarābād O IND 227 Jp 35
Jafarābād O IND 234 Kb 35
Jafarābād △ IND 234 Kb 35
Jaffna O CL 239 Kd 41
Jaffna Lagoon ~ CL 239 Ke 41
Jagalūr O IND 238 Kc 38
Jagbahur O WAL 316 Fp 41
Jagdalpur O IND 234 Kf 36
Jagdaqi O VRC 204 Wa 8
Jagdīspur O IND 234 Ke 32
Jaggang O VRC 230 Kd 29
Jaggayyapeta O IND 238 Ke 37
Jagodnoje O RUS 23 Sa 3
Jagtial O IND 238 Kd 36
Jagua O C 100 Dh 34
Jaguapitã O BR 140 Ej 57
Jaguaquara O BR 125 Fa 52
Jaguarão O BR 146 Eh 62
Jaguarão ~ BR 146 Eh 62
Jaguarari O BR 125 Ep 51
Jaguaré O BR 141 Ep 55
Jaguaretama O BR 124 Fa 48
Jaguari O BR 146 Eg 60
Jaguariaíva O BR 140 Ek 58
Jaguariba ~ BR 124 Fa 49
Jaguaribe ~ BR 124 Ep 49
Jaguaribe O BR 124 Fa 48
Jaguaruana O BR 124 Fb 48
Jaguaruna O BR 141 Ek 60
Jagüe ~ RA 136 Dp 60
Jagüey Grande O C 100 Dh 34
Jahānābād O IND 235 Kg 33
Jahangiraba O IND 234 Kd 31
Jahārah O KSA 214 Hm 32
Jahotyn O UA 175 Hh 20
Jahun O WAN 320 Gl 39
Jaiba O BR 125 En 53
Jaicós O BR 124 Ep 49
Jailolo O RI 275 Lp 45
Jainagar O IND 234 Kf 34
Jainpur O IND 234 Ke 34
Jaintiapur O BD 235 Kk 33
Jaipur O IND 234 Kb 32
Jaipur O IND 254 Km 32
Jairi O CAM 320 Gm 42
Jaisalmer O IND 227 Jp 32
Jaisinghnagar O IND 234 Ke 34
Jājapur O IND 235 Kh 35
Jājapur Road O IND 235 Kh 35
Jajpan O UZB 223 Jp 25
Jākar O BHT 235 Kk 32
Jakarta ▣ RI 278 Ld 48
Jakenan O RI 278 Lf 49
Jäkkvik O S 158 Ha 12
Jakobshavn Ilulissat O DK 43 Jb 5
Jakob's Ladder Great Falls ~ GUY 113 Ee 44
Jakobstad Pietarsaari O FIN 159 Hc 14
Jakpa O WAN 320 Gj 43
Jakutsk O RUS 204 Wc 6
Jakymivka O UA 175 Hk 22
Jal O USA 65 Cl 29
Jalālābād O AFG 223 Jp 28
Jalālpur Pīrwāla O PK 227 Jp 31
Jalán ~ HN 96 De 38
Jalandhar O IND 230 Kb 30
Jalang O RI 282 Ll 48
Jalapa O MEX 93 Db 37
Jalapa O GCA 93 Dd 38
Jalapa de Díaz O MEX 93 Cp 36
Jalasjärvi O FIN 159 Hd 14
Jalaté ~ MEX 93 Dc 37
Jalaud ~ RP 267 Lm 40
Jalaun O IND 234 Kd 32
Jales O BR 140 Ej 56
Jaleswar O IND 235 Kh 35
Jālgaon O IND 234 Kc 35
Jalgaon O IND 238 Kb 36
Jalingo O WAN 320 Gm 41
Jālna O IND 238 Kb 36
Jálon ~ E 184 Ge 25
Jalor O IND 227 Ka 33
Jalostotitlan O MEX 92 Cl 35
Jalpa O MEX 92 Cl 35
Jalpāiguri O IND 235 Kj 32
Jalpan O MEX 92 Cn 35
Jalu O LAR 300 Hc 31
Jaluit ◬ MH 27 Ta 9
Jama O EC 116 Dh 46
Jamaame O SP 329 Hp 45
Jāmai O IND 234 Kd 34
Jamaica □ JA 101 Dk 37
Jamaica Channel ≈ 101 Dl 37
Jamal O C 101 Dl 35
Jamalpur O BD 235 Kk 33
Jamalwal O PK 227 Jn 30
Jamanxim ~ BR 120 Ef 48
Jamanxim ~ BR 120 Eg 49
Jamanxim ~ BR 120 Eg 50
Jamari ~ BR 117 Ec 50
Jamari O WAN 320 Gm 40
Jamarovka O RUS 204 Va 8
Jamb O IND 234 Kd 35
Jamba O ANG 340 Ha 53
Jamba ~ ANG 340 Hb 50
Jambi Telanaipura O RI 278 Lb 46
Jamboeye ~ RI 270 Kn 43
Jambol O BG 194 Hf 24
Jambusar O IND 227 Ka 34
James ~ USA 56 Cn 23
Jamesābād O PK 227 Jn 33
James Bay ~ CDN 7 Eb 4
James Bay ≈ CDN 43 Gb 8
James Bay ~ CDN 57 Dh 19
James Corner O EAT 337 Hk 50
Jameson Land ⌒ DK 43 Lb 4
James Range ⛰ AUS 369 Mc 58
James River ~ USA 56 Cp 24
Jamestown O USA 56 Cn 22
Jamestown O USA 60 Dj 24
Jamestown O USA 71 Df 27
Jamestown O USA 87 Dj 29
Jamestown O ZA 349 Hf 61
Jamestown O AUS 378 Mf 62
Jamestown Reservoir ~ USA 56 Cn 22
Jamieson O AUS 379 Mk 64
Jamiltepec O MEX 92 Cp 36

428 Isla de San Ignacio - Jamiltepec

Jam Jodhpur ○ **IND** 227 Jn 35
Jamkhandi ○ **IND** 238 Kb 37
Jāmkhed ○ **IND** 238 Kb 36
Jamm ○ **RUS** 171 Hg 16
Jammaladugu ○ **IND** 238 Kd 38
Jammu ○ **IND** 230 Kb 29
Jammu and Kashmir ◉ **PK** 230 Kb 28
Jāmnagar ○ **IND** 227 Jn 34
Jampangkulon ○ **RI** 278 Ld 49
Jampiľ ○ **UA** 175 He 21
Jampiľ ○ **UA** 175 Hg 21
Jampue ○ **RI** 279 Lk 47
Jāmpur ○ **PK** 227 Jp 31
Jämsä ○ **FIN** 159 He 15
Jamshedpur ○ **IND** 235 Kg 34
Jamtari ○ **WAN** 320 Gm 42
Jämtland ◉ **S** 158 Gn 14
Jamu ○ **ETH** 325 Hk 42
Jāmui ○ **IND** 235 Kj 33
Jāmŭi ○ **IND** 235 Kh 33
Jamuna 〜 **BD** 235 Kj 33
Jamundi ○ **CO** 106 Dk 44
Jana 〜 **RUS** 22 Rb 3
Jana ○ **RUS** 205 Wc 5
Janaia do Sul ○ **BR** 140 Ej 57
Janakpur ○ **NEP** 235 Kg 32
Janāna △ **UAE** 215 Je 33
Janakpur ○ **NEP** 235 Kg 32
Jandaíra ○ **BR** 125 En 53
Jandeira ○ **BR** 125 En 53
Jandira ○ **BR** 132 Ee 53
Janaúba ○ **BR** 125 En 53
Jandatuba 〜 **BR** 117 Dn 48
Jandiatuba 〜 **BR** 117 Dp 48
Jandowae ○ **AUS** 375 Mm 59
Jandrakinot ○ **RUS** 46 Ac 13
Janeiro 〜 **BR** 133 Em 51
Janesville ○ **USA** 57 Dd 24
Jangada ○ **BR** 132 Ef 53
Jangamo ○ **MOC** 352 Hk 58
Jangaon ○ **IND** 238 Kd 37
Jangiabad ○ **UZB** 223 Jn 25
Jangier ○ **UZB** 223 Jn 25
Jangijul ○ **UZB** 223 Jn 25
Jangikišlok ○ **UZB** 223 Jm 25
Jangikurgan ○ **UZB** 223 Jp 25
Jangipur ○ **IND** 235 Kj 33
Jangirabad ○ **UZB** 223 Jm 25
Jang Tawang ○ **IND** 235 Kk 32
Janiopolis ○ **BR** 140 Eh 58
Janišcevo ○ **RUS** 159 Hl 15
Jan Kempdorp ○ **ZA** 349 He 59
Jan Mayen ⌅ **N** 18 Jb 2
Janos ○ **MEX** 80 Ch 30
Jansenville ○ **ZA** 358 He 62
Jantan ○ **RI** 283 Md 47
Jantelco ○ **MEX** 92 Cn 36
Jantho ○ **RI** 270 Km 43
Jantingue ○ **MOC** 352 Hj 58
Januária ○ **BR** 133 Em 53
Jao 〜 **RB** 341 Hd 55
Jaora ○ **IND** 234 Kb 34
Japan □ **J** 250 Mh 25
Japan Trench ▿ **J** 251 Mh 27
Japaratinga ○ **BR** 124 Fc 50
Japeri ○ **BR** 141 En 57
Japerica ○ **RI** 121 El 46
Japura ○ **BR** 117 Ea 46
Japurá 〜 **BR** 117 Ea 46
Japurá 〜 **BR** 117 Eb 47
Jaque ○ **PA** 97 Dj 42
Jaquitinhonha 〜 **BR** 125 En 54
Jarāblus ○ **SYR** 195 Hl 27
Jaraguá ○ **BR** 133 Ek 53
Jaraguá do Sul ○ **BR** 141 Ek 59
Jaraguari ○ **BR** 140 Eg 56
Jarahueca ○ **C** 100 Dj 34
Jaraniyo ○ **ETH** 313 Hm 40
Jarânwäla ○ **PK** 230 Ka 30
Jarauçu 〜 **BR** 121 Eh 47
Jarcevo ○ **RUS** 171 Hj 18
Jardim ○ **BR** 124 Fa 49
Jardim ○ **BR** 140 Ef 56
Jardim do Serido ○ **BR** 124 Fb 49
Jardin América ○ **RA** 140 Ef 59
Jardine 〜 **AUS** 365 Mh 51
Jardine River 〜 **AUS** 365 Mh 51
Jardine River ⚑ **AUS** 365 Mh 51
Jardines de la Reina ⌂ **C** 100 Dj 35
Jari 〜 **BR** 117 Ec 48
Jari 〜 **BR** 120 Eh 45
Jari 〜 **BR** 121 Eh 46
Jari ○ **BR** 146 Eg 60
Jarita ○ **MEX** 81 Cn 32
Järna ○ **S** 170 Ha 16
Jarnema ○ **RUS** 159 Hm 14
Jarosław ○ **PL** 174 Hd 20
Järpen ○ **S** 158 Gn 14
Jarqurghon ○ **UZB** 223 Jm 27
Jarrahdale ○ **AUS** 368 Lj 62
Jarso ○ **ETH** 325 Hk 41
Jartai ○ **VRC** 243 Lc 26
Jartai Yanchi 〜 **VRC** 242 Lc 26
Jaru ○ **BR** 129 Ec 51
Jaru 〜 **BR** 129 Ec 51
Jaruma ○ **BOL** 129 Dp 55
Järvenpää ○ **FIN** 159 He 15
Jarvis ⌅ **USA** 35 Ab 10
Jary ○ **RUS** 154 Sb 5
Jasaan ○ **RP** 267 Ln 41
Jashpurnagar ○ **IND** 235 Kg 34
Jasiira ⌅ **SP** 329 Ja 45
Jasikan ○ **GH** 317 Gg 42
Jašiūnai ○ **LT** 171 He 18
Jaslo ○ **PL** 174 Hc 21
Jasnogrosk ○ **RUS** 171 Hl 18
Jasnomorskij ○ **RUS** 250 Mg 22
Jason Islands ⌅ **GB** 147 Ed 71
Jasper △ **CDN** 50 Cb 19
Jasper ○ **CDN** 50 Cc 19
Jasper ○ **USA** 60 Db 24
Jasper ○ **USA** 70 Db 27
Jasper ○ **USA** 71 De 26
Jasper ○ **USA** 71 Df 28
Jasper ○ **USA** 81 Da 30
Jasper ○ **USA** 86 Dg 30
Jasrāna ○ **IND** 234 Kd 32
Jastrebac △ **SCG** 194 Hc 24
Jastrowie ○ **PL** 170 Ha 19
Jasubibeteri ○ **YV** 112 Eb 44

Jászberény ○ **H** 174 Hb 22
Jataí ○ **BR** 133 Ej 54
Jatapu 〜 **BR** 120 Ed 45
Jataratuba ○ **BR** 125 Fb 51
Jateí ○ **BR** 140 Eg 57
Jath ○ **IND** 238 Kb 37
Jati ○ **PK** 227 Jn 33
Jatibarang ○ **RI** 278 Le 49
Jatibonico ○ **C** 100 Dj 35
Jatiwangi ○ **RI** 278 Lf 49
Jatoba ○ **BR** 132 Eg 52
Jatuarana ○ **BR** 120 Ee 47
Jaú ⌅ **BR** 120 Ec 46
Jaú 〜 **BR** 120 Ed 46
Jaú ○ **BR** 141 Ek 57
Jauapen 〜 **BR** 120 Ed 46
Jauaperi 〜 **BR** 120 Ed 45
Jaua-Sarisariñama ⚑ **YV** 112 Eb 43
Jauco ○ **C** 101 Dl 35
Jauharābād ○ **PK** 230 Ka 29
Jauja ○ **PE** 128 Dl 51
Jaumave ○ **MEX** 92 Cn 34
Jaunpiebalga ○ **LV** 171 He 17
Jaunpur ○ **IND** 234 Kf 33
Jaupaci ○ **BR** 133 Ej 54
Jauquara 〜 **BR** 132 Ef 53
Jaurdi ○ **AUS** 368 Ll 61
Jauru ○ **BR** 132 Ee 53
Jauru ○ **BR** 132 Eg 55
Jauru 〜 **BR** 132 Eg 55
Java ⌅ **RI** 278 Le 49
Javan ○ **TJ** 223 Jn 26
Javari 〜 **BR** 120 Eh 46
Javier de Viana ○ **ROU** 146 Ef 61
Jävre ○ **S** 159 Hc 13
Jawi ○ **RI** 278 Le 46
Jawor ○ **PL** 174 Ha 20
Jaworzno ○ **PL** 174 Hb 20
Jay ○ **USA** 70 Da 27
Jayamkondacholapuram ○ **IND** 239 Kd 40
Jayanca ○ **PE** 116 Dj 49
Jayapura ○ **RI** 286 Mg 47
Jayton ○ **USA** 70 Cm 29
Jażelbicy ○ **RUS** 171 Hj 16
Jazykovo ○ **RUS** 181 Jb 18
Jbel Aqachi △ **MA** 293 Gd 29
Jbel Azourki △ **MA** 293 Gc 30
Jbel Bani △ **MA** 292 Gc 31
Jbel Bou Iblane △ **MA** 293 Gd 29
Jbel Bou Naceur △ **MA** 293 Gd 29
Jbel Grouz △ **DZ** 293 Gf 29
Jbel Tazzeka △ **MA** 293 Gd 28
Jbel Toubkal △ **MA** 292 Gc 30
Jean ○ **USA** 64 Ce 28
Jean Rabel ○ **RH** 101 Dm 36
Jebala △ **MA** 293 Gd 28
Jebba ○ **WAN** 320 Gj 41
Jebel Ouarkziz △ **MA** 292 Ga 31
Jeberos ○ **PE** 116 Dk 48
Jebiniana ○ **TN** 297 Gm 28
Jebri ○ **PK** 227 Jl 32
Jedburgh ○ **GB** 162 Ge 18
Jeddore Cape ⌒ **CDN** 61 Ec 23
Jedrzejów ○ **PL** 174 Hc 20
Jeedamya ○ **AUS** 368 Ll 60
Jefawa ○ **SUD** 313 Hd 40
Jefferson ○ **USA** 70 Da 26
Jefferson ○ **USA** 70 Db 28
Jefferson ○ **USA** 70 Db 28
Jefferson City ○ **USA** 70 Db 26
Jefferson City ○ **USA** 71 Dg 27
Jeffersonville ○ **USA** 60 Dm 23
Jeffersonville ○ **USA** 71 Df 26
Jeffrey City ○ **USA** 65 Cj 24
Jeffrey's Bay ○ **ZA** 358 Hd 62
Jef-Jef el Kébir △ **TCH** 309 Hc 35
Jega ○ **WAN** 320 Gj 39
Jege ○ **WAN** 320 Gj 41
Jejevo ○ **SOL** 290 Nb 50
Jeju ○ **ROK** 247 Lp 29
Jeju Do ⌅ **ROK** 247 Ln 29
Jejuí- Guazu 〜 **PY** 140 Ef 58
Jeju Strait 〜 **ROK** 247 Lp 29
Jēkabpils ○ **LV** 171 He 17
Jekimoviči ○ **RUS** 171 Hj 18
Jelei ○ **RI** 278 Lf 47
Jelenec' ○ **UA** 175 Hn 22
Jelenia Góra ○ **PL** 174 Gp 20
Jelgava ○ **LV** 171 Hd 17
Jeli ○ **MAL** 270 La 43
Jellico ○ **USA** 71 Df 27
Jelling ○ **DK** 170 Gl 18
Jelmusibak ○ **RI** 279 Lh 46
Jelsa ○ **HR** 194 Ha 24
Jema ○ **GH** 317 Gg 42
Jemâa-Ida-Oussemlal ○ **MA** 292 Gb 31
Jema Shet' 〜 **ETH** 325 Hm 41
Jember ○ **RI** 279 Lg 50
Jemberem ○ **GNB** 316 Fn 40
Jemca ○ **RUS** 159 Hn 14
Jemez Pueblo ○ **USA** 65 Cj 28
Jemilčyne ○ **UA** 175 Hf 20
Jemma ○ **WAN** 320 Gl 40
Jempang 〜 **RI** 274 Lj 46
Jemuluang ○ **MAL** 271 Lb 44
Jen ○ **WAN** 320 Gm 41
Jena ○ **D** 174 Gm 20
Jenakijeve ○ **UA** 181 Hl 21
Jenda ○ **MW** 344 Hj 52
Jendouba ○ **TN** 296 Gl 28
Jeneponto ○ **RI** 279 Lk 48
Jenerhodar ○ **UA** 175 Hk 22
Jenin ○ **JOR** 208 Ha 29
Jenipapo ○ **BR** 120 Ee 45
Jenisejsk ○ **RUS** 22 Pb 4
Jenisejskij zaliv 〜 **RUS** 22 Nb 2
Jenkins ○ **USA** 71 Dg 27
Jenks ○ **USA** 70 Da 28
Jenner ○ **CDN** 51 Cg 20
Jenner ○ **USA** 64 Ca 26
Jennings ○ **USA** 86 Db 30
Jenny ○ **SME** 113 Ef 43
Jenolan Caves ★ **AUS** 379 Ml 62
Jens Munk Island ⌅ **CDN** 43 Gb 5
Jepara ○ **RI** 278 Lf 49
Jeparit ○ **AUS** 378 Ma 64
Jequié ○ **BR** 125 Ep 52
Jequitinhanha 〜 **BR** 125 Ep 54
Jequitaí ○ **BR** 133 Em 54
Jequitaí 〜 **BR** 133 Em 54
Jequitiba ○ **BR** 141 En 55

Jequitinhonha ○ **BR** 125 Ep 54
Jerada ○ **MA** 293 Ge 28
Jerangle ○ **AUS** 379 Ml 63
Jerantut ○ **MAL** 270 Lb 44
Jerba Island ⌅ **TN** 297 Gm 29
Jerdera ○ **RI** 283 Mc 49
Jerecuaro ○ **MEX** 92 Cm 35
Jérémie ○ **RH** 101 Dl 36
Jeremoabo ○ **BR** 124 Fa 51
Jerer Shet' 〜 **ETH** 328 Hp 41
Jerez 〜 **MEX** 92 Cl 34
Jerez de García Salinas ○ **MEX** 92 Cl 34
Jerez de I. C. ○ **E** 184 Gc 26
Jerez de la Frontera ○ **E** 184 Gc 27
Jerggul ○ **N** 159 He 11
Jericho ○ **AUS** 375 Mk 57
Jericoacoara ○ **BR** 124 Ep 47
Jerilderie ○ **AUS** 379 Mj 63
Jerko La △ **VRC** 230 Ke 30
Jerome ○ **USA** 50 Ce 24
Jerome ○ **USA** 87 Dh 32
Jeropol ○ **RUS** 23 Ta 3
Jerramungup ○ **AUS** 368 Lk 63
Jersey ⌅ **GB** 163 Ge 21
Jersey City ○ **USA** 74 Dl 25
Jerseyville ○ **USA** 71 Dc 26
Jerši ○ **RUS** 171 Hk 18
Jertih ○ **MAL** 270 Lb 43
Jerumenha ○ **BR** 124 En 49
Jerusalem ◙ **IL** 214 Hk 30
Jervis Bay ○ **AUS** 379 Mm 63
Jervis Bay 〜 **AUS** 379 Mm 63
Jervis Inlet 〜 **CDN** 50 Ca 21
Jervois ○ **AUS** 374 Ne 57
Jesenice ○ **SLO** 174 Gp 22
Jeseník ○ **CZ** 174 Ha 20
Jesi ○ **I** 185 Gn 24
Jesinskaja ○ **RUS** 171 Hn 15
Jesmond ○ **CDN** 50 Ca 20
Jessamine Creek 〜 **AUS** 374 Mh 57
Jessej ○ **RUS** 22 Qa 3
Jessheim ○ **N** 158 Gm 15
Jessore ○ **BD** 235 Kj 34
Jesup ○ **USA** 87 Dg 30
Jesús Carranza ○ **MEX** 93 Da 37
Jesús María ○ **RA** 137 Eb 61
Jesús Menendez ○ **C** 101 Dk 35
Jet ○ **USA** 70 Cn 27
Jetmore ○ **USA** 70 Cm 26
Jetpur ○ **IND** 227 Jp 35
Jevargi ○ **IND** 238 Kc 37
Jevnaker ○ **N** 158 Gm 15
Jevpatorija ○ **UA** 175 Hj 23
Jewel Cave Natl. Monument ★ **USA** 51 Ck 24
Jeypore ○ **IND** 234 Kf 36
Jezerce △ **AL** 194 Hb 24
Jezioro Mamry 〜 **PL** 170 Hc 18
Jezioro Śniardwy 〜 **PL** 170 Hc 19
Jhābuz ○ **IND** 234 Kb 34
Jhajharr ○ **IND** 234 Kc 31
Jhajjar ○ **IND** 234 Kc 31
Jhal ○ **PK** 227 Jm 31
Jhālawār ○ **IND** 234 Kc 33
Jhamat ○ **PK** 223 Jp 29
Jhang ○ **PK** 227 Kp 30
Jhânsi ○ **IND** 234 Kd 33
Jharkhand ◉ **IND** 235 Kg 34
Jharol ○ **IND** 227 Ka 33
Jhatpat ○ **PK** 227 Jn 31
Jhelum ○ **PK** 230 Ka 29
Jhenida ○ **BD** 235 Kj 34
Jhudo ○ **PK** 227 Jn 33
Jhunjhunūn ○ **IND** 234 Kb 31
Jí´pyrskij ○ **RUS** 23 Ta 4
Jiading ○ **VRC** 246 Ll 30
Jiahe ○ **VRC** 258 Lg 33
Jiajiang ○ **VRC** 255 Lc 31
Jialing Jiang 〜 **VRC** 243 Ld 29
Jiamusi ○ **VRC** 250 Mb 22
Ji'an ○ **VRC** 258 Lh 32
Jianchang ○ **VRC** 246 Lk 25
Jianchuan ○ **VRC** 254 Kp 32
Jiande ○ **VRC** 258 Lk 31
Jiangaosh △ **MYA** 254 Kp 33
Jiangbei ○ **VRC** 255 Ld 31
Jiangcheng Hanibu 〜 **VRC** 254 La 34
Jiange ○ **VRC** 242 Lc 30
Jianghong ○ **VRC** 255 Le 35
Jianghua ○ **VRC** 255 Lf 33
Jiangjin ○ **VRC** 255 Lc 31
Jiangkou ○ **VRC** 255 Le 32
Jiangkouzhen ○ **VRC** 243 Le 30
Jiangle ○ **VRC** 258 Lj 32
Jiangling ○ **VRC** 243 Lg 30
Jiangluo ○ **VRC** 243 Lc 29
Jiangmen ○ **VRC** 258 Lg 34
Jiangshan ○ **VRC** 258 Lk 31
Jiangsu ◉ **VRC** 246 Lk 29
Jiangxi ◉ **VRC** 258 Lk 32
Jiangyin ○ **VRC** 246 Ll 30
Jiangyong ○ **VRC** 255 Lf 33
Jiangyou ○ **VRC** 242 Lc 30
Jianhe ○ **VRC** 255 Le 32
Jianli ○ **VRC** 258 Lj 31
Jianmen Gong ★ **VRC** 242 Lc 29
Jianning ○ **VRC** 258 Lj 32
Jian'ou ○ **VRC** 258 Lk 32
Jianshi ○ **VRC** 243 Le 30
Jianshui ○ **VRC** 255 Lb 34
Jianyang ○ **VRC** 242 Lc 30
Jianyang ○ **VRC** 258 Lj 32
Jiaojiang ○ **VRC** 259 Ll 31
Jiaokou ○ **VRC** 243 Lf 27
Jiaoling ○ **VRC** 258 Lh 33
Jiaonan ○ **VRC** 246 Lk 28
Jiaotelo ○ **VRC** 235 Kh 31
Jiaozhou ○ **VRC** 246 Lk 28
Jiaozou ○ **VRC** 243 Lg 28
Jiashan ○ **VRC** 246 Lj 29
Jiashi ○ **VRC** 230 Kc 26
Jia Tsuo La △ **VRC** 235 Kh 31
Jia Xian ○ **VRC** 243 Lf 26
Jia Xian ○ **VRC** 243 Lg 29
Jiaxing ○ **VRC** 246 Ll 30
Jiayu ○ **VRC** 258 Lj 31
Jiayu Gong ★ **VRC** 242 Kn 26
Jiayuguan ○ **VRC** 242 Kn 26
Jiazhou Wan 〜 **VRC** 246 Ll 28
Jiberu ○ **WAN** 320 Gn 41
Jibiya ○ **WAN** 320 Gk 39
Jicarilla ••• **USA** 65 Cj 28
Jichang ○ **VRC** 255 Lc 32
Jičín ○ **CZ** 174 Gp 20
Jiddah ○ **KSA** 218 Hm 35

Jidhi ○ **SP** 328 Hp 40
Jieshi ○ **VRC** 258 Lh 34
Jieshi Wan 〜 **VRC** 258 Lh 34
Jieshi Wang ○ **VRC** 258 Lh 34
Jieshou ○ **VRC** 243 Lh 29
Jiexi ○ **VRC** 258 Lh 34
Jiexiu ○ **VRC** 243 Lf 27
Jieyang ○ **VRC** 258 Lh 34
Jieznas ○ **LT** 171 He 18
Jiga ○ **ETH** 313 Hl 40
Jiggalong ○ **AUS** 360 Ll 57
Jiggalong Aboriginal Land ••• **AUS** 360 Ll 57
Jigonshan ★ **VRC** 243 Lh 30
Jigong Shan △ **VRC** 254 Kp 32
Jiguaní ○ **C** 101 Dk 35
Jihlava ○ **CZ** 174 Gp 21
Jihlava 〜 **CZ** 174 Ha 21
Jihur ○ **ETH** 325 Hm 41
Jiiqley ○ **SP** 328 Ja 43
Jije ○ **VRC** 255 Lc 31
Jijiga ○ **ETH** 328 Hp 41
Jijona ○ **E** 184 Gf 26
Jilamo ○ **HN** 94 De 38
Jilf Kabir Plateau △ **ET** 300 He 34
Jilib ○ **SP** 329 Hp 45
Jīma ○ **ETH** 325 Hl 42
Jimani ○ **DOM** 101 Dn 36
Jimata ○ **ETH** 325 Hl 41
Jimbe ○ **Z** 341 He 51
Jimei ○ **VRC** 258 Lk 33
Jiménez ○ **MEX** 80 Ck 32
Jiménez ○ **MEX** 81 Cm 31
Jiménez ○ **RP** 267 Lm 41
Jiménez de Teul ○ **MEX** 92 Cl 34
Jimeta ○ **WAN** 320 Gl 41
Jimi River 〜 **PNG** 287 Mj 48
Jimna Range △ **AUS** 375 Mn 59
Jimo ○ **VRC** 246 Ll 27
Jimpir ○ **PK** 227 Jm 33
Jimulco ○ **MEX** 81 Cl 33
Jinan ○ **VRC** 246 Lj 27
Jinchang ○ **VRC** 242 Lb 26
Jincheng ○ **VRC** 243 Lg 28
Jincheng ○ **VRC** 255 Ll 33
Jinchuan ○ **VRC** 242 La 30
Jind ○ **IND** 234 Kc 31
Jindabyne ○ **AUS** 379 Ml 64
Jindare ○ **AUS** 364 Mb 53
Jindřichův Hradec ○ **CZ** 174 Gp 21
Jinfo Shan △ **VRC** 255 Lc 31
Jingbian ○ **VRC** 243 Le 27
Jingchen ○ **VRC** 258 Lj 33
Jingchuan ○ **VRC** 243 Ld 28
Jingde ○ **VRC** 246 Lk 30
Jingdezhen ○ **VRC** 258 Lj 31
Jingdong ○ **VRC** 254 La 34
Jinggangshan ★ **VRC** 258 Lh 32
Jinggu ○ **VRC** 254 La 34
Jinghe ○ **VRC** 204 Tb 10
Jinghong ○ **VRC** 254 La 34
Jingjiang ○ **VRC** 246 Ll 29
Jingle ○ **VRC** 243 Lf 26
Jingmen ○ **VRC** 243 Lg 30
Jingning ○ **VRC** 243 Lc 28
Jingshan ○ **VRC** 243 Lg 30
Jingta ○ **VRC** 243 Lb 27
Jingtieshan ○ **VRC** 242 Kn 26
Jingtie Shan △ **VRC** 242 Kn 26
Jingxi ○ **VRC** 255 Ld 34
Jing Xian ○ **VRC** 246 Lk 30
Jingxiang ○ **VRC** 246 Lj 28
Jingxing ○ **VRC** 243 Lh 27
Jingyan ○ **VRC** 255 Lc 31
Jingyu ○ **VRC** 247 Lp 25
Jingyu Hu 〜 **VRC** 231 Kj 27
Jingyuan ○ **VRC** 242 Lc 27
Jingzhou ○ **VRC** 255 Le 32
Jinhua ○ **VRC** 258 Lk 31
Jining ○ **VRC** 246 Lj 28
Jinja ○ **EAU** 325 Hj 45
Jinka ○ **ETH** 325 Hl 43
Jinka ○ **AUS** 374 Md 57
Jinkou ○ **VRC** 243 La 30
Jinning ○ **VRC** 254 La 33
Jinniu ○ **VRC** 243 Lh 30
Jinotega ○ **NIC** 96 Df 39
Jinotepe ○ **NIC** 96 De 40
Jinping ○ **VRC** 255 Ld 34
Jinping ○ **VRC** 255 Le 32
Jinqian He 〜 **VRC** 243 Le 29
Jinsha ○ **VRC** 255 Ld 32
Jinsha Jiang 〜 **VRC** 242 Kn 29
Jinsha Jiang 〜 **VRC** 255 Lb 32
Jinshanlin ★ **VRC** 246 Lj 26
Jinshatan ○ **VRC** 243 Lg 26
Jinshi ○ **VRC** 255 Lf 31
Jinshiqiao ○ **VRC** 255 Lf 32
Jin Si ★ **VRC** 243 Lg 27
Jins Shan ○ **VRC** 243 Lf 30
Jinta ○ **VRC** 242 Kp 26
Jintan ○ **VRC** 246 Lk 30
Jintang ○ **VRC** 242 Lc 30
Jintotolo Channel 〜 **RP** 267 Lm 40
Jintur ○ **IND** 238 Kc 36
Jinxi ○ **VRC** 243 Li 25
Jinxi ○ **VRC** 258 Lj 32
Jinxian ○ **VRC** 258 Lk 31
Jinyun ○ **VRC** 258 Lk 31
Jinzhai ○ **VRC** 246 Lj 30
Jinzhong Shan △ **VRC** 255 Lc 33
Jinzhou ○ **VRC** 246 Ll 26
Jinzhou ○ **VRC** 246 Ll 26
Ji-Paraná ○ **BR** 129 Ed 51
Jipijapa ○ **EC** 116 Dh 46
Jiquí ○ **C** 100 Dj 35
Jiquilpan ○ **MEX** 92 Cl 36
Jiquiriçá ○ **BR** 125 Fa 52
Jiqzhi ○ **VRC** 242 La 29
Jiri ○ **NEP** 235 Kh 32
Jirja ○ **ET** 301 Hh 32
Jirriban ○ **SP** 328 Jc 42
Jishan ○ **VRC** 243 Lf 28
Jishou ○ **VRC** 255 Le 32
Jisr ○ **SYR** 208 Hl 28
Jitarning ○ **AUS** 368 Lk 62
Jitra ○ **MAL** 270 La 42
Jitaúna ○ **BR** 125 Fa 52
Jiu 〜 **RO** 194 Hd 24
Jiu 〜 **RO** 194 Hd 24
Jiucai Ling △ **VRC** 255 Lf 33
Jiuchang ○ **VRC** 255 Lc 32
Jiuchang ○ **VRC** 255 Ld 32
Jiuhuashan ★ **VRC** 246 Lj 30

Jiujiang ○ **VRC** 258 Lj 31
Jiulihu ★ **VRC** 258 Lk 33
Jiuling Shan △ **VRC** 258 Lh 31
Jiulongpo ○ **VRC** 255 Ld 31
Jiulong Shan △ **VRC** 258 Lk 31
Jiuquan ○ **VRC** 242 Kp 26
Jiurongcheng ○ **VRC** 246 Lm 27
Jiusuo ○ **VRC** 255 Le 36
Jiuxu ○ **VRC** 255 Ld 33
Jiuzhaigou ★ **VRC** 242 La 29
Jivundu ○ **Z** 341 He 52
Jiwani ○ **PK** 226 Jj 33
Jixi ○ **VRC** 205 Wc 9
Jixi ○ **VRC** 246 Lk 30
Jixi ○ **VRC** 250 Mb 23
Ji Xian ○ **VRC** 243 Lf 27
Ji Xian ○ **VRC** 246 Lj 25
Jixian ○ **VRC** 250 Mb 22
Jiyang ○ **VRC** 246 Lj 27
Jiyuan ○ **VRC** 243 Lg 28
Jizan ○ **KSA** 218 Hp 37
Jizzakh ○ **UZB** 223 Jm 25
Jlam ○ **NEP** 235 Kh 32
Joaíma ○ **BR** 125 Ep 54
Joal-Fadiout ○ **SN** 304 Fm 38
Joana ○ **YV** 112 Ed 41
Joana Coeli ○ **BR** 121 Ek 48
Joana Câmara ○ **BR** 124 Fb 48
João Arregui ○ **BR** 146 Ef 60
João Câmara ○ **BR** 124 Fb 48
João Fagundes ○ **BR** 146 Ef 61
João Lisboa ○ **BR** 121 El 48
João Monlevade ○ **BR** 141 En 55
João Neiva ○ **BR** 141 Ep 55
João Pessoa ○ **BR** 124 Fc 49
João Pinheiro ○ **BR** 133 El 54
João Pires ○ **BR** 125 Ep 52
Joaquim ○ **BR** 121 Em 49
Joaquim Gomes ○ **BR** 124 Fc 50
Joaquín V. González ○ **RA** 137 Ec 59
Jobabo ○ **C** 101 Dk 35
Jobele ○ **WAN** 320 Gk 42
Jocoli ○ **RA** 137 Dp 62
Jocotepec ○ **MEX** 92 Cl 35
Jódar ○ **E** 184 Ge 27
Jodensavanne ○ **SME** 113 Eg 43
Jodhpur ○ **IND** 227 Ka 32
Jodiya ○ **IND** 227 Jp 34
Joe Batts Arm ○ **CDN** 61 Eg 21
Jõetsu ○ **J** 251 Me 27
Jof ○ **TN** 297 Gm 30
Jofane ○ **MOC** 352 Hk 56
Jogana ○ **WAN** 320 Gl 40
Jogbani ○ **IND** 235 Kh 32
Jõgeva ○ **EST** 171 Hf 16
Joggins ○ **CDN** 61 Eb 23
Jogindarnagar ○ **IND** 230 Kc 30
Jogipet ○ **IND** 238 Kc 37
Jogoghopa ○ **IND** 235 Kj 33
Johán ○ **PK** 227 Jm 31
Johanna River 〜 **PNG** 287 Mf 48
Johannesburg ○ **ZA** 349 Hf 59
Johi ○ **GUY** 113 Ee 45
John Day 〜 **USA** 50 Cb 23
John Day Fossil Beds ★ **USA** 50 Cc 23
John Days Fossil Beds National Monument ★ **USA** 50 Cb 23
John Martin Reservoir 〜 **USA** 65 Cl 27
Johnson ○ **USA** 70 Cm 27
Johnson City ○ **USA** 71 Dg 27
Johnson City ○ **USA** 81 Cn 30
Johnsons Crossing ○ **CDN** 47 Bj 15
Johnston ○ **USA** 71 Dg 29
Johnstone Hill △ **AUS** 361 Ma 57
Johnstone South ○ **AUS** 365 Mk 54
Johnstown ○ **USA** 60 Dl 24
Johnstown ○ **USA** 74 Dj 25
Johor ◉ **MAL** 271 Lb 45
Johor Bharu ○ **MAL** 271 Lb 45
Joigny ○ **F** 163 Gh 21
Joinville ○ **BR** 141 Ek 59
Joinville ○ **F** 163 Gj 21
Jojutla ○ **MEX** 92 Cn 36
Jokau ○ **ETH** 325 Hj 41
Jokau ○ **ETH** 325 Hk 41
Jokkmokk ○ **S** 159 Hb 12
Jõkulsá á Brú 〜 **IS** 158 Fn 13
Jõkulsá á Fjöllum 〜 **IS** 158 Fm 12
Joliet ○ **USA** 51 Ck 23
Joliet ○ **USA** 71 Dd 25
Joliette ○ **CDN** 60 Dm 22
Joli Island △ **RP** 275 Ll 43
Jolo Island △ **RP** 275 Ll 43
Jolo ○ **RP** 275 Ll 42
Jolon ○ **USA** 64 Cb 28
Jomalig Island △ **RP** 267 Lm 38
Jombang ○ **RI** 279 Lf 49
Jombo 〜 **ANG** 340 Hb 51
Jomda ○ **VRC** 242 Kp 30
Jommon ○ **RI** 283 Md 47
Jomo Lhari △ **BHT** 235 Kj 32
Jomsom ○ **NEP** 235 Kf 31
Jonê ○ **VRC** 242 Lb 29
Jonesboro ○ **USA** 70 Db 28
Jonesboro ○ **USA** 71 Dc 28
Jonesport ○ **USA** 60 Ea 23
Jones Sound 〜 **CDN** 7 Eb 2
Jones Sound 〜 **CDN** 43 Ga 3
Jonesville ○ **USA** 86 Dc 30
Jonglei Canal 〜 **SUD** 324 Hh 42
Jongshan ○ **VRC** 255 Le 31
Jonišakis ○ **LT** 171 Hd 17
Jõnkõping ○ **S** 170 Gn 17
Jonquière ○ **CDN** 60 Dn 21
Jonuta ○ **MEX** 93 Db 36
Jonzac ○ **F** 184 Gf 23
Joplin ○ **USA** 70 Da 27
Jorabat ○ **IND** 235 Kk 33
Jordan ○ **USA** 51 Cj 22
Jordan ○ **USA** 56 Db 23
Jordan 〜 **IL** 208 Hk 29
Jordan ○ **JOR** 208 Hk 29
Jordan ○ **RP** 267 Lm 40
Jordânia ○ **BR** 125 Ep 53
Jordan Bay 〜 **CDN** 61 Eb 24
Jordan Valley ○ **USA** 50 Cd 24
Jorf ○ **MA** 293 Ge 29
Jorgucat ○ **AL** 194 Hc 26
Jorhât ○ **IND** 235 Kl 32
Joriapani ○ **NEP** 234 Ke 31
Jõrn ○ **S** 159 Hc 13
Joroinen ○ **FIN** 159 Hf 14

Jorong ○ **RI** 279 Lh 48
Jorskoe ploskogor'e △ **GE** 202 Ja 25
Joru ○ **WAL** 316 Ga 42
Jos ○ **WAN** 320 Gl 41
Jose Abad Santos ○ **RP** 275 Ln 43
José Battle 4 Ordoñez ○ **ROU** 146 Eg 62
José Bonifacio ○ **BR** 140 Ek 56
José Cardel ○ **MEX** 93 Cp 36
José de la Costa ○ **YV** 107 Dp 40
José de San Martín ○ **RA** 152 Dn 68
José E. Rodo ○ **ROU** 146 Ef 62
Joselândia ○ **BR** 132 Ef 54
José Pedro Varela ○ **ROU** 146 Eg 62
Joseph ○ **USA** 50 Cd 23
Joseph Bonaparte Gulf 〜 **AUS** 364 Ma 53
Josephstaal ○ **PNG** 287 Mj 48
José Rodrigues ○ **BR** 121 Ej 48
Joshimath ○ **IND** 230 Kd 30
Joshin-Etsu-Plateau ⚑ **J** 251 Mf 27
Joshipur ○ **IND** 235 Kg 35
Joshua Tree ⚑ **USA** 64 Cd 29
Jos Plateau △ **WAN** 320 Gl 41
Jostedalsbreen △ **N** 158 Gk 15
Jostedalsbreen Nasjonalpark ⚑ **N** 158 Gk 15
Jotaiana ○ **YV** 112 Ed 41
Jotunheimen ⚑ **N** 158 Gl 15
Joubertberge △ **NAM** 340 Gn 55
Joubertina ○ **ZA** 358 Hd 62
Joulter Cays △ **BS** 87 Dj 33
Jourdanton ○ **USA** 81 Cn 31
Joutsa ○ **FIN** 159 Hf 15
Joutsijärvi ○ **FIN** 159 Hg 12
Jovellanos ○ **C** 100 Dh 34
Joviânia ○ **BR** 133 Ek 54
Jowhar ○ **SP** 329 Ja 44
Joyabaj ○ **GCA** 93 Dc 38
Joya de Ceren ★ **ES** 93 Dd 39
Jreïda ○ **RIM** 304 Fm 36
Jreïf ○ **RIM** 304 Fp 37
Juaben ○ **GH** 317 Gf 42
Juajialing ○ **VRC** 242 Lc 28
Juami 〜 **BR** 117 Ea 46
Juanacatlán ○ **MEX** 92 Cl 35
Juan Aldama ○ **MEX** 81 Cl 33
Juan Bautista Alberdi ○ **RA** 136 Eb 59
Juan E. Barra ○ **RA** 137 Ed 64
Juan Fernández Islands △ **RCH** 15 Eb 13
Juangcheng ○ **VRC** 243 Lh 28
Juan Guerra ○ **PE** 116 Dk 49
Juan I. Lacaze ○ **ROU** 146 Ef 63
Juani Island △ **EAT** 337 Hm 50
Juan Jorba ○ **RA** 137 Eb 62
Juán José Perez ○ **BOL** 128 Dp 53
Juanjui ○ **PE** 116 Dk 49
Juankoski ○ **FIN** 159 Hg 14
Juan R. Cháve ○ **PY** 140 Ef 58
Juan Sola ○ **RA** 136 Ec 57
Juan W. Gez ○ **RA** 137 Ea 62
Juapon ○ **GH** 317 Gg 42
Juara ○ **BR** 132 Ef 51
Juárez ○ **MEX** 80 Ca 30
Juárez ○ **MEX** 81 Cm 32
Juárez ○ **MEX** 93 Db 37
Juari 〜 **BR** 121 Ej 49
Juazeiro ○ **BR** 124 Ep 50
Juazeiro do Norte ○ **BR** 124 Fa 49
Juazohn ○ **LB** 316 Gb 43
Juba 〜 **BR** 132 Ef 53
Jūbā ○ **SUD** 324 Hh 43
Jubail ○ **RL** 208 Hk 28
Juberina ○ **YV** 112 Ed 41
Jubilee Lake ○ **CDN** 61 Eg 21
Jubilee Lake 〜 **AUS** 369 Lp 60
Jucá 〜 **BR** 124 Ep 49
Júcar 〜 **E** 184 Gf 26
Jucás ○ **BR** 124 Fa 49
Juchipila ○ **MEX** 92 Cl 35
Juchitán ○ **MEX** 92 Cn 37
Juchitán ○ **MEX** 93 Da 37
Juciapé ○ **BR** 125 Ep 52
Jucuri ○ **BR** 124 Fb 48
Jucuruçu ○ **BR** 125 Ep 54
Jucuruçu 〜 **BR** 125 Fa 54
Jucurutu ○ **BR** 124 Fb 49
Judenburg ○ **A** 174 Gp 22
Judith 〜 **USA** 51 Ch 22
Judoma 〜 **RUS** 205 Xa 7
Juglong ○ **AUS** 379 Ml 63
Juhaviči ○ **RUS** 171 Hg 17
Ju He 〜 **VRC** 243 Lf 30
Juhnev ○ **RUS** 171 Hp 15
Juhnov ○ **RUS** 171 Hk 18
Juigalpa ○ **NIC** 97 Df 39
Juína ○ **BR** 132 Ee 51
Juinamirim 〜 **BR** 132 Ee 51
Juiná ou Zui-Uina 〜 **BR** 132 Ee 52
Juist △ **D** 170 Gk 19
Juiz de Fora ○ **BR** 141 En 56
Jujun ○ **RI** 270 La 47
Jukkasjärvi ○ **S** 159 Hc 12
Jukleggi ○ **N** 158 Gl 15
Julaca ○ **BOL** 136 Ea 56
Julau ○ **MAL** 271 Lf 45
Jule ○ **N** 158 Gn 13
Julesberg ○ **USA** 65 Cl 25
Juli ○ **PE** 128 Dp 53
Juliaca ○ **PE** 128 Dn 53
Julia Creek ○ **AUS** 374 Mg 56
Julian ○ **USA** 64 Cd 29
Julian Alps △ **SLO** 174 Gn 22
Julianehåb Qaqortoq ○ **DK** 43 Jc 6
Juliasdale ○ **ZW** 344 Hj 55
Júlio de Castilhos ○ **BR** 146 Eg 60
Julpa 〜 **BOL** 129 Eb 55
Julong Shan △ **VRC** 243 Lf 30
Juma 〜 **BR** 120 Ee 47
Juma 〜 **BR** 120 Ee 47
Juma 〜 **RUS** 159 Hj 13
Jumbilla ○ **PE** 116 Dk 48
Jumilla ○ **E** 184 Gf 26
Jumi Pozo ○ **RA** 137 Eb 60
Jumla ○ **NEP** 234 Kf 31
Jump 〜 **USA** 56 Dc 23
Juna ○ **BR** 132 Ee 51
Juna Downs ○ **AUS** 360 Lk 57
Jūnâgadh ○ **IND** 227 Jp 36
Junâgarh ○ **IND** 234 Kf 36
Junan ○ **VRC** 246 Lk 28
Juncal ○ **RCH** 136 Dp 58

Junction ○ USA 81 Cn 30
Junction Bay ~ AUS 364 Mc 51
Junction City ○ USA 50 Ca 23
Junction City ○ USA 56 Cp 24
Junction City ○ USA 70 Cp 26
Junction City ○ USA 70 Db 29
Jundah ○ AUS 374 Mh 58
Jundiaí ○ BR 141 El 57
Juneau ○ USA 6 Ca 4
Juneau ○ USA 47 Bj 15
Junee ○ AUS 375 Ml 57
Junee ○ AUS 379 Mk 63
June Lake ○ USA 64 Cc 27
Jungar Qi ○ VRC 243 Lf 26
Jungfrau △ CH 163 Gk 22
Junggar Pendi ⌒ VRC 204 Tc 9
Jungue ○ ANG 340 Gp 51
Juniata ~ USA 74 Dk 25
Junín ○ CO 116 Dj 45
Junín ○ PE 128 Dl 51
Junin ○ RCH 128 Dn 55
Junín ○ RA 137 Ed 63
Junín de los Andes ○ RA 147 Dn 65
Junleri ○ WAN 320 Gm 41
Junlian ○ VRC 255 Lc 31
Junnar ○ IND 238 Ka 36
Juno ○ USA 81 Cm 30
Junosuando ○ S 159 Hd 12
Junqoley ○ SUD 324 Hh 42
Junsele ○ S 158 Ha 14
Juntas ○ CR 97 Df 40
Juntas ○ RCH 136 Dp 60
Juntura ○ USA 50 Cc 24
Juntusranta ○ FIN 159 Hg 13
Juorkuna ○ FIN 159 Hf 13
Jupati ~ BR 121 Ej 45
Jupiter ~ CDN 61 Ec 21
Juquiá ○ BR 141 El 58
Jur ~ SUD 324 Hg 41
Jura ⟁ GB 162 Gc 17
Juradó ○ CO 106 Dk 42
Juramento ○ BR 125 En 54
Jura Mountains ⛰ F/CH 163 Gk 22
Jurbarkas ○ LT 170 Hd 18
Jurege ~ MOC 344 Hm 51
Juremal ○ BR 124 Ep 50
Jur'ev-Pol'skij ○ RUS 171 Hm 17
Jurga ○ RUS 204 Tb 7
Jurien ○ AUS 368 Lh 61
Jurien Bay ~ AUS 368 Lh 61
Juriepe ~ YV 107 Dp 42
Jurilovka ○ RO 175 Hg 23
Jurjung-Haja ○ RUS 204 Vb 4
Jūrmala ○ LV 171 Hd 17
Jurong ○ VRC 246 Lk 30
Juruá ~ BR 116 Dm 49
Juruá ~ BR 117 Dp 49
Jurua ○ BR 117 Ea 47
Juruá ~ BR 117 Ea 48
Jurua ~ BR 117 Eb 47
Juruana ~ BR 132 Ee 51
Juruazinho ~ BR 117 Ec 50
Juruena ~ BR 120 Ee 49
Juruena ~ BR 120 Ee 50
Juruena ○ BR 132 Ee 51
Juruena o' Ananina ~ BR 132 Ee 52
Jurupari ~ BR 117 Dn 49
Juruti ○ BR 120 Ef 47
Juscimeira ○ BR 132 Eg 54
Juškozero ○ RUS 159 Hj 13
Jussara ○ BR 125 Ep 51
Jussara ○ BR 133 Ej 53
Justa ~ RCH 136 Dn 59
Justiniano Posse ○ RA 137 Ec 62
Justo Daract ○ RA 137 Eb 62
Justozero ○ RUS 159 Hj 14
Jutaí ○ BR 117 Ea 47
Jutaí ~ BR 117 Ea 47
Jüterbog ○ D 174 Gn 20
Juti ○ BR 140 Eg 57
Jutiapa ○ GCA 93 Dd 38
Jutiapa ○ HN 96 De 38
Juticalpa ○ HN 96 De 38
Juuka ○ FIN 159 Hg 14
Juva ○ FIN 159 Hf 15
Juwana ○ RI 278 Lf 49
Ju Xian ○ VRC 246 Lk 28
Juxtlahuaca ○ MEX 92 Cn 37
Juye ○ VRC 243 Lh 28
Juzkuduk ○ UZB 223 Jk 24
Juž Morava ~ SCG 194 Hc 24
Južne ○ UA 175 Hh 22
Južno-Aličurskij hrebet ⛰ TJ 230 Ka 27
Juzno-Golodnostepskij kanal ~ UZB 223 Jn 25
Južno-Kuril'sk ○ RUS 250 Mj 23
Južno Sachalinsk ○ RUS 26 Sa 5
Južnyj ○ RUS 202 Ja 23
Juzzak ○ PK 226 Jj 31
Jwaneng ○ RB 349 He 58
Jwathit ○ MYA 254 Km 34
Jylland ⌒ DK 170 Gl 18
Jyväskylä ○ FIN 159 He 14

K

K. I. Alakol' ~ KZ 204 Tb 9
K 2 △ PK 230 Kc 28
Kaabong ○ EAU 325 Hk 44
Kaahka ○ TM 222 Jh 27
Kaala-Gomen ○ F 386 Nd 56
Kaamanen ○ FIN 159 Hf 11
Kaapmuiden ○ ZA 352 Hh 58
Kaaresuvanto ○ FIN 159 Hd 11
Kaarina ○ FIN 159 Hd 15
Kaart ⌒ RMM 316 Gb 39
Kaavi ○ FIN 159 Hg 14
Kabacan ○ RP 275 Ln 42
Kabaklyoba ○ TM 223 Jk 26
Kabala ○ WAL 316 Ga 41
Kabale ○ EAU 336 Hg 46
Kabalo ○ RDC 336 Hf 49
Kabambare ○ RDC 336 Hf 48
Kaban Brj. ~ TR 195 Hm 26
Kabanga ○ RDC 333 Hb 49
Kabango ○ RDC 336 Hf 49
Kabangu ○ RDC 341 Hd 51
Kabania Lake ~ CDN 57 Dd 19
Kabanjahe ○ RI 270 Kp 44
Kabankalan ○ RP 267 Lm 40
Kabara ○ RMM 305 Ge 37
Kabara ⟁ FJI 390 Aa 55
Kabare ○ RI 283 Mb 46
Kabare ○ RDC 336 Hg 47
Kabare ○ RDC 336 Hg 49
Kabarnet ○ EAK 325 Hk 45
Kabasalan ○ RP 275 Lm 42
Kabau ○ RI 282 Ln 47
Kabba ○ WAN 320 Gk 42
Kabe ○ WAN 320 Gj 40
Kaberamaido ○ EAU 325 Hj 45
Kabeya ○ RDC 333 Hd 49
Kabeya ○ RDC 336 Hg 48
Kabī ○ ETH 313 Hm 40
Kabia ~ TCH 321 Gp 41
Kabika River ~ CDN 60 Dj 21
Kabinakagami Lake ~ CDN 57 Df 21
Kabin Buri ○ THA 262 La 38
Kabinda ○ RDC 333 He 49
Kabir ○ RI 282 Ln 50
Kabīrwāla ○ PK 227 Jp 30
Kabkābīya ○ SUD 312 He 39
Kabna ○ SUD 312 Hj 36
Kabo ○ RCA 321 Hb 42
Kabolaa ○ RI 283 Mb 46
Kabombo ~ Z 341 He 52
Kabompo ○ Z 341 Hd 52
Kabondo-Dianda ○ RDC 336 He 50
Kabongo ○ RDC 333 He 49
Kabou ○ RT 317 Gg 41
Kabou ○ RCA 321 Hc 43
Kabrai ○ IND 234 Kd 33
Kabrousse ○ SN 316 Fm 39
Kabšān ○ KSA 214 Hp 33
Kabūd Rāhang ○ IR 209 Jc 28
Kābul ⛰ AFG 223 Jn 28
Kabul ▣ AFG 223 Jn 28
Kābul ~ AFG 223 Jn 28
Kabulamwanda ○ Z 341 Hf 53
Kabumbu ○ RDC 336 Hf 48
Kabunda ○ RDC 341 Hg 52
Kabundi ○ RDC 341 Hf 51
Kabunga ○ RDC 336 Hf 46
Kaburuang ○ RI 275 Lp 44
Kabūshīya ○ SUD 313 Hj 37
Kabūtarhan ○ IR 226 Jg 30
Kabuzal Island ⟁ MYA 262 Kn 39
Kabwe ○ Z 341 Hg 53
Kabwum ○ PNG 287 Mk 49
Kačanik ○ SCG 194 Hc 24
Kacepi ○ RI 283 Ma 46
Kach ○ PK 227 Jm 30
Kachako ○ WAN 320 Gl 40
Kacheh Kūh ⛰ PK 226 Jj 31
Kachekabwe ○ RB 341 He 55
Kachernak Bay ≈ USA 46 An 15
Kachia ○ WAN 320 Gk 41
Kachīsī ○ ETH 313 Hl 41
Kacholola ○ Z 341 Hh 53
Kachovka ○ UA 175 Hj 22
Kachulu ○ MW 344 Hk 53
Kachung ○ EAU 324 Hj 45
Kaçkar D. △ TR 202 Hn 25
Kačug ○ RUS 204 Va 8
Kada ○ AFG 226 Jk 30
Kadambūr ○ IND 239 Kc 41
Kadan Kyun ⟁ MYA 262 Kp 39
Kaddam ○ IND 238 Kd 36
Kaddam Dam ~ IND 238 Kd 36
Kade ○ GH 317 Gf 42
Kadéï ~ RCA 321 Gp 43
Kadiana ○ RMM 305 Gc 40
Kadiaso ○ CI 305 Gc 41
Kadijivka ○ UA 181 Hm 21
Kadina ○ AUS 378 Me 62
Kadınhanı ○ TR 195 Hh 26
Kadiolo ○ RMM 317 Gd 40
Kadiri ○ IND 238 Kd 38
Kadirli ○ TR 195 Hl 27
Kadkan ○ IR 222 Jh 28
Kadoka ○ USA 56 Cm 24
Kadoma ○ ZW 341 Hg 55
Kadovar Island ⟁ PNG 287 Mj 47
Kadugli ○ SUD 312 Hg 40
Kaduj ○ RUS 171 Hm 16
Kaduna ~ WAN 320 Gj 41
Kaduna ○ WAN 320 Gk 40
Kaduna ~ WAN 320 Gk 41
Kadung Ga ○ MYA 254 Kn 32
Kadūr ○ IND 238 Kc 39
Kadykčan ○ RUS 23 Sa 3
Kaechon ○ DVRK 247 Ln 26
Kaédi ○ RIM 304 Fp 37
Kaélé ○ CAM 321 Gp 40
Kaena Point ⌓ USA 75 Al 35
Kaeng Khlo ○ THA 263 Lb 37
Kaesŏng ○ DVRK 247 Lp 26
Kaevanga ○ SOL 290 Nb 50
Kafakumba ○ RDC 341 Hd 50
Kafan ○ ARM 202 Jb 26
Kafanchan ○ WAN 320 Gl 41
Kaffrine ○ SN 304 Fn 38
Kafia Kingi ○ SUD 324 He 41
Kafin-Chana ○ WAN 308 Gj 39
Kafin Hausa ○ WAN 320 Gl 39
Kafirnigan ~ UZB 223 Jn 27
Kåfjord ○ N 159 He 10
Kafolo ○ CI 317 Gd 41
Kafountine ○ SN 316 Fm 39
Kafr ○ ET 301 Hg 30
Kafr as-Saiḫ ○ ET 301 Hh 30
Kafu ~ EAU 324 Hh 45
Kafubu ~ RDC 341 Hg 51
Kafue ♀ Z 341 He 53
Kafue ~ Z 341 Hf 52
Kafue ~ Z 341 Hf 53
Kafue ○ Z 341 Hg 53
Kafue Flats ⌒ Z 341 Hf 53
Kafukule ○ MW 344 Hj 51
Kafulwe ○ Z 336 Hg 50
Kafuya ~ RDC 336 Hf 48
Kaga ○ J 251 Me 27
Kaga Bandoro ○ RCA 321 Hb 42
Kagadi ○ EAU 324 Hh 45
Kagagi Lake ~ CDN 56 Db 21
Kagaľnik ~ RUS 181 Hn 22
Kagan ○ UZB 223 Jl 26
Kagān ○ PK 230 Ka 28
Kagara ~ EAT 336 Hh 46
Kagaré ○ BF 317 Gf 39
Kagarko ○ WAN 320 Gk 41
Kagau ○ PNG 287 Mh 49
Kagera ~ EAT 336 Hh 46
Kaggi ○ IND 238 Kb 39
Kagianagami Lake ~ CDN 57 De 20
Kagitumba ○ RWA 336 Hh 46
Kağızman ○ TR 202 Hp 25
Kagmar ○ SUD 312 Hh 38
Kagologolo ○ RI 270 Kp 46
Kagombo ○ RDC 341 Hf 51
Kagoshima ○ J 247 Ma 30
Kagoshima-wan ≈ J 247 Mb 30
Kāgū ~ IR 226 Jj 33
Kahama ○ EAT 336 Hj 47
Kahān ○ PK 227 Jn 31
Kahao ○ NAM 340 Gp 55
Kahayan ~ RI 279 Lg 46
Kahemba ○ RDC 333 Hb 49
Kahīr ○ IR 226 Jh 33
Kahīrī ○ IR 226 Jj 32
Kāhna Nau ○ PK 230 Kb 30
Kahnplay ○ LB 316 Gb 42
Kahnūg ○ IR 226 Jg 32
Kahnwia ○ LB 316 Gb 43
Kahone ○ SN 304 Fn 38
Kahoolawe ⟁ USA 75 Am 35
Kahramanmaraş ○ TR 195 Hl 27
Kahrīzak ○ IR 222 Jd 28
Kahror Pakka ○ PK 227 Jp 31
Kâhta ○ TR 195 Hm 27
Kahuku Point ⌓ USA 75 Al 35
Kahului ○ USA 75 Am 35
Kahunge ○ EAU 324 Hh 45
Kahurangi ♀ NZ 383 Nj 66
Kahurangi Point ⌓ NZ 382 Nh 66
Kaiam ○ PNG 287 Mh 49
Kaiama ○ WAN 320 Gh 41
Kaiapit ○ PNG 287 Mk 49
Kaiapoi ○ NZ 383 Nj 67
Kaibab Indian Reservation ••• USA 64 Cf 27
Kai Beab ○ RI 286 Mf 49
Kaibola ○ PNG 287 Mm 50
Kaibul-Lamioa ★ IND 254 Kl 33
Kaiemothia ○ SUD 325 Hk 43
Kaieteur ♀ GUY 112 Ee 43
Kaieteur Falls ~ GUY 112 Ee 43
Kaifeng ○ VRC 243 Lg 28
Kaihua ○ VRC 258 Lk 31
Kaikohe ○ NZ 383 Nj 63
Kaikoura ○ NZ 383 Nj 67
Kaikoura Peninsula ⟁ NZ 383 Nj 67
Kailahun ○ WAL 316 Ga 41
Kailash △ VRC 230 Ke 30
Kaileuna Island ⟁ PNG 287 Mm 50
Kaili ○ VRC 255 Ld 32
Kailua ○ USA 75 Am 35
Kailua-Kona ○ USA 75 Am 36
Kaima ○ RI 286 Mf 48
Kaimana ○ RI 283 Mc 47
Kaim River ~ PNG 286 Mg 49
Kaimur Range ⛰ IND 234 Ke 33
Kainab ~ NAM 348 Hb 59
Kainan ○ J 251 Md 29
Kainantu ○ PNG 287 Mj 49
Kaindu ○ Z 341 Hf 53
Kaingiwa ○ WAN 320 Gh 39
Kainji Dam ~ WAN 320 Gj 41
Kainji Reservoir ~ WAN 320 Gj 40
Kaipara Harbour ~ NZ 383 Nk 64
Kaiping ○ VRC 258 Lg 34
Kairāna ○ IND 234 Kc 31
Kairiu Island ⟁ PNG 286 Mh 47
Kairouan ○ TN 297 Gm 28
Kais ~ RI 283 Mc 46
Kaiserslautern ○ D 163 Gk 21
Kaiserstuhl △ D 163 Gk 21
Kaisho ○ EAT 336 Hh 46
Kaišiadorys ○ LT 171 He 18
Kaisosi ○ EAU 324 Hh 45
Kaisut Desert ⌒ EAK 325 Hl 45
Kait ○ PNG 287 Mn 48
Kaita ○ EAU 325 Hk 43
Kaitaia ○ NZ 383 Nj 63
Kaitangata ○ NZ 382 Ng 69
Kaiteriteri ○ NZ 383 Nj 66
Kaithal ○ IND 234 Kc 31
Kaititja-Walpiri Aboriginal Land ••• AUS 364 Mc 55
kai Tkráki ⊙ GR 194 He 25
Kaitumälven ~ S 159 Hb 12
Kaiwai ○ IND 234 Kc 33
Kaiwatu ○ RI 282 Lp 50
Kaiwi Channel ~ USA 75 Am 35
Kai Xian ○ VRC 243 Le 30
Kaiyang ○ VRC 255 Ld 32
Kaiyuan ○ VRC 255 Lb 34
Kaiyuh Mountains ⛰ USA 46 Al 13
Kajaani ○ FIN 159 Hf 13
Kajabbi ○ AUS 374 Mg 56
Kajang ○ RI 282 Ll 48
Kajang-Sungai Chua ○ MAL 270 La 44
Kajo Kaji ○ SUD 324 Hh 44
Kajrafkkum ○ TJ 223 Jn 25
Kajrakkumskoe vodohranilisce ~ TJ 223 Jn 25
Kajuru ○ WAN 320 Gk 40
Kākā ○ SUD 312 Hj 40
Kakabeka Falls ○ CDN 56 Dc 21
Kakadu ♀ AUS 364 Mc 52
Kakaha ○ USA 75 Al 35
Kakakee ○ USA 71 Dd 25
Kakamas ○ ZA 348 Hc 60
Kakamega ○ EAK 325 Hk 45
Kakamoéka ○ RCB 332 Gm 48
Kākān ○ AFG 223 Jp 27
Kakanda ○ RDC 341 Hf 51
Kakasa ○ PNG 287 Ml 50
Kakata ○ LB 316 Ga 42
Kakching ○ MYA 254 Km 33
Kake ○ USA 47 Bj 17
Kake ○ J 251 Mc 28
Kakegawa ○ J 251 Mf 28
Kakera ○ RDC 336 Hg 49
Kakhovka Reservoir ~ UA 175 Hj 22
Kākī ○ IR 215 Jd 31
Kakielo ○ RDC 341 Hg 52
Kakimba ○ RDC 336 Hg 48
Kakināda ○ IND 238 Kf 37
Kakisa Lake ~ CDN 47 Cc 15
Kakkar ○ PK 227 Jm 32
Kakken-sen △ J 251 Md 28
Kakobola ○ RDC 333 Hb 48
Kakogawa ○ J 251 Md 28
Kakonko ○ EAT 336 Hh 47
Kakowip ○ IND 235 Kj 35
Kakpin ○ CI 317 Ge 41
Kaktovik ○ USA 46 Be 9
Kakuma ○ EAK 325 Hk 44
Kakumbi ○ Z 341 Hh 52
Kakumiro ○ EAU 324 Hh 45
Kakunodate ○ J 250 Mg 26
Kakus ○ NAM 348 Hb 57
Kakwala ○ RDC 341 Hd 51
Kala ○ WAN 321 Gp 39
Kala ○ EAT 336 Hh 50
Kalaat Khasba ○ TN 296 Gl 28
Kālābāgh ○ PK 223 Jp 29
Kalabahi ○ RI 282 Ln 50
Kalabakan ○ MAL 274 Lj 43
Kalabi ○ EAU 325 Hj 44
Kalabo ○ Z 341 Hd 53
Kalābsha ★ ET 301 Hj 34
Kalabua ○ RDC 333 Hd 49
Kalač ○ RUS 181 Hn 20
Kalač-na-Donu ○ RUS 181 Hp 21
Kaladar ○ CDN 60 Dk 23
Kalafgān ○ AFG 223 Jn 27
Kalafilia ○ RG 316 Gb 41
Kalahari Desert ⌒ RB 348 Hc 57
Kalahari Gemsbok ♀ ZA 348 Hc 58
Kalaigaon ○ IND 235 Kl 32
Kalaihum ○ TJ 223 Jp 26
Kalaj ○ WAG 316 Fn 39
Kalajoki ○ FIN 159 Hd 13
Kalaldi ○ CAM 321 Gn 42
Kalale ○ DY 320 Gh 40
Kala-I-Mor ○ TM 223 Jk 28
Kalām ○ PK 230 Ka 28
Kalamata ○ GR 194 Hd 27
Kalamazoo ~ USA 57 De 24
Kalamazoo ○ USA 57 Df 24
Kalamba ○ RDC 333 Ha 46
Kalambáka ○ GR 194 Hc 26
Kalambo ~ EAT 336 Hh 50
Kalamits'ka zatoka ~ UA 175 Hj 23
Kalana ○ RMM 316 Gb 40
Kalang ~ IND 235 Kl 32
Kalangali ○ EAT 337 Hj 49
Kala Oya ~ CL 239 Ke 41
Kälarne ○ S 158 Gp 14
Kalasin ○ THA 263 Lb 37
Kalāt ○ IR 226 Jh 33
Kalāt ○ PK 227 Jm 31
Kalāte-ye Siyāh ○ IR 226 Jj 31
Kalatungan Mountains △ RP 275 Ln 42
Kalaupapa ○ USA 75 Am 35
Kalaus ~ RUS 202 Hp 23
Kalaw ○ MYA 254 Kn 35
Kalbā ○ UAE 226 Jg 33
Kalbarri ○ AUS 368 Lg 59
Kalbarri ♀ AUS 368 Lh 59
Kaldakvistl ~ IS 158 Fl 13
Kale ○ TR 195 Hg 27
Kalé ○ RMM 316 Ga 39
Ka Lea ⌓ USA 75 An 36
Kalecık ○ TR 195 Hj 25
Kalehe ○ RDC 336 Hg 47
Kalema ○ RDC 333 He 48
Kalemie ○ RDC 336 Hg 48
Kalemyo ○ MYA 254 Kl 34
Kāl-e Namaksar ~ IR 222 Jj 29
Kalengwa ○ Z 341 He 52
Kalēnoe ○ KZ 181 Jd 21
Kāl-e Šūr ~ IR 222 Jg 28
Kāl-e Šūr ~ IR 222 Jh 27
Kāl-e Sūr e Sabzevār ~ IR 222 Jg 27
Kāl-e Sūr Gağarm ~ IR 222 Jg 27
Kalevala ○ RUS 159 Hh 13
Kalewa ○ MYA 254 Km 34
Kaleybar ○ IR 209 Jb 26
Kalf ~ NAM 348 Ha 58
Kálfafell ○ IS 158 Fl 14
Kálfafellsstaður ○ IS 158 Fn 13
Kalghatgi ○ IND 238 Kb 38
Kalgin Island ⟁ USA 46 An 15
Kalgo ○ WAN 320 Gj 39
Kalgoorlie ○ AUS 368 Ll 61
Kal'i ○ RUS 159 Hp 14
Kali ~ NEP 234 Ke 31
Kali ○ RMM 316 Ga 39
Kali ○ AUS 368 Lj 59
Kaliakair ○ BD 235 Kj 33
Kalian ○ RP 275 Ln 42
Kalianda ○ RI 278 Lc 48
Kalibo ○ RP 267 Lm 40
Kali Gandaki ~ NEP 235 Kf 31
Kaliganj ○ BD 235 Kj 34
Kalima ○ RDC 336 Hf 47
Kalimantan Borneo ⟁ RI 274 Lf 46
Kálimnos ○ GR 194 Hf 27
Kálimnos ⟁ GR 194 Hf 27
Kalina ○ EAT 336 Hh 48
Kalinga ○ IND 235 Kg 35
Kalinga ○ AUS 365 Mh 53
Kalininabad ○ TJ 223 Jn 27
Kaliningrad ○ RUS 170 Hb 18
Kalininsk ○ RUS 181 Ja 20
Kalinjra ○ IND 234 Kb 34
Kalinkavichy ○ BY 171 Hg 19
Kalinko ○ RG 316 Ga 40
Kālinmpang ○ IND 235 Kj 32
Kalip ○ PNG 287 Mm 48
Kaliro ○ EAU 325 Hj 45
Kalis ○ SP 328 Jc 41
Kalisat ○ RI 279 Lg 50
Kalisizo ○ EAU 336 Hh 46
Kalispell ○ USA 50 Ce 21
Kalisz ○ PL 174 Hb 20
Kaliuda ○ RI 282 Ll 51
Kalivia ○ GR 194 Hd 27
Kalivta ~ RUS 181 Hn 21
Kaliwungu ○ RI 278 Lf 49
Kalix ○ S 159 Hd 13
Kalixälven ~ S 159 Hc 12
Kaljazin ○ RUS 171 Hl 17
Kalkan ○ TR 195 Hg 27
Kalkaringji ○ AUS 364 Mb 54
Kalkaska ○ USA 57 Df 23
Kalkbank ○ ZA 349 Hg 57
Kalkfeld ○ NAM 348 Gp 56
Kalkfontein Dam ~ ZA 349 He 60
Kalkrand ○ NAM 348 Ha 58
Kalkuni ○ GUY 113 Ef 43
Kalkwerf ○ ZA 349 Hc 60
Kallakkurichchi ○ IND 238 Kd 40
Kallam ○ IND 238 Kc 36
Kallambella ○ IND 238 Kc 39
Kallār ○ IRQ 209 Ja 28
Kallar ○ IND 238 Kb 39
Kallar Kahār ○ PK 230 Ka 29
Kalli ○ EST 171 He 16
Kallidaikurichchi ○ IND 239 Kc 41
Kallislahti ○ FIN 159 Hg 15
Kallsjön ~ S 158 Gn 14
Kalmali ○ IND 238 Kc 37
Kalmar ○ S 170 Gp 17
Kalmarsund ~ S 170 Ha 17
Kalmeta ○ AUS 365 Mg 55
Kal'mius ~ UA 181 Hl 22
Kalmunai ○ CL 239 Ke 42
Kalmykovo ○ KZ 181 Jd 21
Kālna ○ IND 235 Kj 34
Kalni ~ BD 235 Kk 33
Kalocsa ○ H 174 Hb 22
Kalo Kalo ○ PNG 287 Mm 50
Kaloke ○ LB 304 Gc 43
Kalokitting ○ SUD 312 He 39
Kaloko ○ RDC 333 He 49
Kālol ○ IND 227 Ka 34
Kalole ○ RDC 336 Hf 47
Kaloleni ○ EAK 337 Hm 47
Kalomo ○ Z 341 Hf 54
Kalomo ~ Z 341 Hf 54
Kalosi ○ RI 279 Lk 47
Kalossia ○ EAK 325 Hk 45
Kalounka ○ RG 316 Fn 40
Kalpáki ○ GR 194 Hc 26
Kalpeni Island ⟁ IND 239 Ka 40
Kalpitiya ○ CL 239 Kd 41
Kalskag ○ USA 46 Aj 15
Kaltag ○ USA 46 Al 13
Kaltungo ○ WAN 320 Gm 41
Kaluga ○ RUS 171 Hl 18
Kālu Khuhar ○ PK 227 Jm 33
Kaluluma ○ MW 344 Hj 52
Kalulushi ○ Z 341 Hf 52
Kalumburu ○ AUS 361 Lp 53
Kalumburu Aboriginal Land ••• AUS 361 Lp 53
Kalumengongo ~ RDC 336 Hf 50
Kalundborg ○ DK 170 Gm 18
Kalundu ○ RDC 336 Hg 47
Kalundwe ○ RDC 333 He 49
Kalungu ~ Z 336 Hj 50
Kalungwishi ~ Z 336 Hg 50
Kalūr Kot ○ PK 223 Jp 29
Kaluš ○ UA 175 He 21
Kalvakurti ○ IND 238 Kd 37
Kalvarija ○ LT 171 Hd 18
Kalwi ○ MYA 262 Kn 37
Kalyān ○ IND 238 Ka 36
Kalyandrug ○ IND 238 Kc 38
Kalynivka ○ UA 175 Hg 21
Kam ~ NAM 348 Ha 57
Kama ~ RUS 154 Rc 7
Kama ~ RUS 181 Jd 18
Kama ○ PNG 287 Mm 47
Kamaday ○ TCH 321 Hc 40
Kamaishi ○ J 250 Mg 26
Kamakhya Dispur ○ IND 235 Kk 32
Kamakwie ○ WAL 316 Fp 41
Kamal ○ RI 279 Lg 49
Kamālia ○ PK 230 Ka 30
Kamalpur ○ IND 235 Kk 33
Kaman ○ TR 195 Hj 26
Kamangu ○ Z 344 Hj 51
Kamani ~ SME 113 Ef 44
Kamanjab ○ NAM 340 Gp 55
Kamanyola ○ RDC 336 Hg 47
Kamāraj ○ IR 215 Jd 31
Kamarān ○ YE 218 Hp 38
Kamarān ⟁ YE 218 Hp 38
Kamarang ○ GUY 112 Ed 43
Kamarata ○ YV 112 Ec 43
Kāmāreddi ○ IND 238 Kd 36
Kama Reservoir ~ RUS 154 Rc 7
Kamaria Falls ~ GUY 113 Ee 42
Kamaron ○ WAL 316 Ga 41
Kamaru ○ RI 282 Lm 48
Kamaši ○ UZB 223 Jm 26
Kamativi ○ ZW 341 Hf 55
Kamba ○ WAN 320 Gh 40
Kamba ○ ETH 325 Hl 42
Kambalda ○ AUS 368 Ll 61
Kambang ○ RI 270 La 46
Kamberatoro ○ PNG 286 Mg 47
Kambia ○ WAL 316 Fp 41
Kambolé ○ RT 317 Gg 41
Kambot ○ PNG 287 Mj 48
Kambove ○ RDC 341 Hf 51
Kambuku ○ PNG 287 Mn 48
Kambūt ○ LAR 300 He 30
Kamchatka ⟁ RUS 23 Sb 4
Kamchatka ⟁ RUS 205 Ya 7
Kamchatka Basin ψ RUS 205 Yc 7
Kamchatskiy Zaliv ≈ RUS 205 Yc 7
Kamdesh ○ AFG 223 Jp 28
Kameasi ○ RI 282 Ll 46
Kameel ○ ZA 349 He 59
Kamelik ~ RUS 181 Jc 20
Kamen' ○ BY 171 Hg 18
Kamende ○ RDC 333 He 49
Kameng ○ AFG 223 Jl 28
Kamenka ○ RUS 159 Hp 13
Kamenka ○ RUS 171 Hh 18
Kamenka ○ RUS 181 Hp 19
Kamenka ○ KZ 181 Jd 20
Kamennogorsk ○ RUS 171 Hg 15
Kameno ○ BG 195 Hf 24
Kamen'-Rybolov ○ RUS 250 Mc 23
Kamenskoe ○ RUS 205 Za 6
Kamensk-Šahtinskij ○ RUS 181 Hn 21
Kamensk-Ural'skiy ○ RUS 154 Sa 7
Kame Ruins ★ ZW 349 Hg 56
Kameshia ○ RDC 336 Hf 50
Kameškovo ○ RUS 171 Hn 17
Kâmet △ VRC 230 Kd 30
Kamiah ○ USA 50 Cd 22
Kamień Pomorski ○ PL 170 Gp 18
Kamiesberge Range ⛰ ZA 348 Hb 61
Kamieskroon ○ ZA 348 Ha 61
Kamiis ○ J 250 Mg 25
Kamiji ○ RDC 333 Hd 49
Kamikawa ○ J 250 Mh 24
Kami-Khoshi ⟁ J 247 Ma 30
Kamileroi ○ AUS 365 Mg 55
Kamiloops Plateau ⛰ CDN 50 Cb 21
Kamina ○ RT 317 Gg 41
Kamina ○ RDC 336 He 48
Kamina ○ RDC 336 He 50
Kamina Base ○ RDC 336 He 50
Kamin'-Kašyrs'kyj ○ UA 175 He 20
Kaminokuni ○ J 250 Mf 25
Kamino-shima ⟁ J 247 Ma 28
Kamioka ○ J 251 Me 27
Kamishak Bay ≈ USA 46 An 15
Kami-Shiroro ○ J 250 Mh 24
Kamitsushima ○ J 247 Ma 28
Kamituga ○ RDC 336 Hf 47
Kami-Yaku ○ J 247 Mb 30
Kam'janec'-Podil's'kyj ○ UA 175 Hf 21
Kam'jani Mohyly ★ UA 175 Hk 22
Kam'jani Mohyly ★ UA 181 Hl 22
Kam'janka ○ UA 175 Hh 21
Kam'janka ○ UA 175 Hh 22
Kamjong ○ IND 254 Km 33
Kamloops ○ CDN 50 Cb 20
Kamloops Indian Reservation ••• CDN 50 Cb 20
Kammanassieberge ⛰ ZA 358 Hd 62
Kāmoke ○ PK 230 Kb 30
Kamola ○ RDC 336 Hf 49
Kamoro ~ RM 345 Jb 54
Kamoto ○ Z 341 Hh 52
Kamp 52 ○ SME 113 Ef 43
Kampala ○ SUD 324 He 41
Kampala ▣ EAU 324 Hj 45
Kampar ○ MAL 270 La 43
Kampar ~ RI 271 Lb 45
Kamparkan ~ RI 270 La 45
Kamparkiri ~ RI 270 La 45
Kampene ○ RDC 336 Hf 47
Kamphaeng Phet ○ THA 262 Kp 37
Kamphambale ○ MW 344 Hj 52
Kampi Katoto ○ EAT 337 Hj 49
Kampli ○ IND 238 Kc 38
Kamponde ○ RDC 333 Hd 49
Kâmpóng Cham ○ K 263 Lc 39
Kâmpóng Chhnăng ○ K 263 Lc 39
Kâmpóng Saôm ○ K 263 Lb 40
Kâmpóng Spoē ○ K 263 Lc 40
Kâmpóng Thum ○ K 263 Lc 39
Kâmpóng Trach ○ K 263 Lc 40
Kâmpôt ○ K 263 Lb 40
Kampsey ○ AUS 379 Mn 61
Kampti ○ BF 317 Ge 40
Kampumbu ○ Z 344 Hj 51
Kampun ~ RI 286 Mf 48
Kampung Ayer Puteh ○ MAL 271 Lb 43
Kampung Balok ○ MAL 271 Lb 44
Kampung Benta ○ MAL 271 Lb 44
Kampung Berang ○ MAL 271 Lb 43
Kampung Buloh ○ MAL 270 Lb 43
Kampung Gajah ○ MAL 270 La 43
Kampung Jambu ○ MAL 270 Lb 43
Kampung Jerangau ○ MAL 271 Lb 43
Kampung Kerau ○ MAL 270 Lb 44
Kampung Kubu Baru ○ MAL 270 La 44
Kampung Leban Chondong ○ MAL 271 Lb 44
Kampung Nibong ○ MAL 270 La 43
Kampung Penarik ○ MAL 270 Lb 43
Kampung Perlis ○ MAL 270 La 42
Kampung Raja ○ MAL 270 Lb 43
Kampung S. Ayer Deras ○ MAL 270 Lb 43
Kampung Sedili Kechil ○ MAL 271 Lc 45
Kampung Sepat ○ MAL 271 Lb 43
Kampung Sook ○ MAL 274 Lj 43
Kampung Tahan ○ MAL 270 Lb 43
Kampung Tekek ○ MAL 271 Lc 44
Kampung Telok Ramunia ○ MAL 271 Lc 45
Kamqua ○ ZA 348 Hc 58
Kamsack ○ CDN 51 Cl 20
Kamsar ○ RG 316 Fn 40
Kamskoe Ust'e ○ RUS 181 Jc 18
Kamsuuma ○ SP 329 Hp 45
Kamtchatka ⟁ RUS 205 Yb 8
Kamtchatka Basin ψ 23 Ta 4
Kāmthi ○ IND 234 Kd 35
Kamtsha ~ RDC 333 Hb 48
Kamudi ○ IND 239 Kd 41
Kamuli ○ EAU 324 Hj 45
Kamungu ○ RDC 333 He 49
Kamutambai ~ RDC 333 Hd 49
Kāmyārān ○ IR 209 Jb 28
Kamyshin ○ RUS 181 Ja 20
Kamys-kůjmasy ~ KZ 181 Jc 21
Kamyzjak ○ RUS 202 Jc 22
Kan ○ UZB 223 Jm 26
kan. Širokij ~ RUS 202 Hp 23
Kana ~ ZW 341 Hf 55
Kanab ○ USA 64 Cf 27
Kanab Creek ~ USA 64 Cf 27
Kanacea ⟁ FJI 390 Aa 54
Kanadej ○ RUS 181 Jb 19
Kanaka ○ RI 283 Mc 47
Kanakapura ○ IND 238 Kc 39
Kanal Dnjaprovskaja-Buhski ~ BY 171 He 19
kanal im. Lenina ~ RUS 202 Ja 24
Kanal Levaja Vetv' ~ RUS 202 Hn 23
kanal Levaja Vetv' ~ RUS 202 Hp 23
Kanan ○ RI 279 Lk 47
Kananga ○ RDC 333 Hd 48
Kananga Boyd ♀ AUS 379 Ml 62
Kananggar ○ RI 282 Ll 51
Kananto ○ GH 317 Ge 41
Kanaš ○ RUS 181 Jb 18
Kanawha ~ USA 71 Dg 26
Kanazawa ○ J 251 Md 27
Kanbalu ○ MYA 254 Km 34
Kanbe ○ MYA 262 Km 37
Kanbi ○ BF 317 Gf 39
Kanchana Buri ○ THA 262 Kp 39
Kanchanadit ○ THA 262 Kp 41
Kanchanpur ○ NEP 235 Kh 32
Kanchenjunga △ NEP 235 Kh 32
Kanchibya ~ Z 341 Hh 51
Kānchipuram ○ IND 238 Kd 39
Kandahār ○ AFG 227 Jl 30
Kandahār ○ IND 238 Kc 36
Kandalakša ○ RUS 159 Hj 12
Kandalakšskaja guba ~ RUS 159 Hj 12
Kandang ○ RI 270 Kn 44
Kandangan ○ RI 279 Lh 47
Kandanghaur ○ RI 278 Ld 49
Kandare ○ WAN 320 Gk 41
Kandavu ⟁ FJI 387 Nl 55
Kandavu Passage ~ FJI 387 Nm 55
Kande ○ RT 317 Gg 41
Kandéko ~ RCB 332 Ha 45
Kandep ○ PNG 286 Mh 48
Kāndi ○ IND 235 Kj 34
Kandi ○ DY 320 Gh 40
Kandiadiou ○ SN 316 Fm 39
Kandiafara ○ RG 316 Fn 40
Kandiāro ○ PK 227 Jn 32
Kandika ○ RG 316 Fp 39
Kandil Bouzou ○ RN 308 Gm 38
Kandıra ○ TR 195 Hh 25

430 Junction - Kandıra

□ Country ▣ Capital city ⊙ Administrative unit O Place ♁ Island ⛰ Mountain range △ Mountain ⌓ Cape ≈ Ocean, Sea ~ Lake, River ♆ Undersea topography ⟁ Glacier ♀ National park ••• Reservation ★ Point of major interest ⏜ Landscape

Kandja O RCA 321 Hc 43
Kandkhot O PK 227 Jn 31
Kāndla O IND 227 Jp 34
Kando ~ RDC 341 Hf 51
Kandos O AUS 379 Ml 62
Kandreho O RM 345 Ja 54
Kandrian O PNG 287 Ml 49
Kandukūr O IND 238 Kd 38
Kandy O CL 239 Ke 42
Kane O USA 74 Dj 25
Kane Basin ≈ DK 7 Fb 2
Kane Basin ♆ DK 43 Hb 3
Kanel O SN 304 Fp 38
Kaneohe O USA 75 Am 35
Kanevskaja O RUS 181 Hm 22
Kanferandé O RG 316 Fn 40
Kang O AFG 226 Jj 30
Kang O RB 349 Hd 57
Kangaba O RMM 316 Gb 40
Kangahun O WAL 316 Fp 41
Kangal O TR 195 Hl 26
Kangān O IR 215 Je 32
Kangān Čam ~ IR 209 Jb 29
Kangar O MAL 270 La 42
Kangaré O RMM 316 Gb 40
Kangaroo Island ♁ AUS 378 Me 63
Kangaroo Valley O AUS 379 Mm 63
Kangasniemi O FIN 159 He 14
Kangāvar O IR 209 Jc 28
Kangding O VRC 242 La 30
Kangdong O DVRK 247 Lp 26
Kangen ~ SUD 325 Hj 42
Kangerlussuaq Søndre Strømfjord O DK 7 Ga 3
Kanggye O DVRK 247 Lp 25
Kanghwa O ROK 247 Lp 27
Kanghwa Do ♁ ROK 247 Ln 27
Kangi O SUD 324 Hf 41
Kangiqsujuaq O CDN 7 Fa 3
Kangirsuk O CDN 7 Fb 3
Kangkir O VRC 230 Kd 27
Kang Kra Chan ★ THA 262 Kp 39
Kangmar O VRC 235 Kj 31
Kangnŭng O ROK 247 Ma 27
Kango O G 332 Gm 45
Kangondi O EAK 337 Hl 46
Kangrinboqê Feng Kailash △ VRC 230 Ke 30
Kangto △ IND 235 Kl 32
Kangz'gyai △ VRC 242 Kn 26
Kanha National Park ♀ IND 234 Ke 34
Kani O J 251 Me 28
Kani O MYA 254 Km 34
Kani O CI 305 Gc 41
Kaniama O RDC 333 Hd 49
Kaniasso O CI 305 Gc 41
Kanibadam O TJ 223 Jp 25
Kanibes ~ NAM 348 Ha 58
Kaniet Islands ♁ PNG 287 Mj 46
Kanigiri O IND 238 Kd 38
Kanin, poluostrov ♁ RUS 159 Ja 12
Kanin Kamen' ⛰ RUS 159 Hj 11
Kanin Nos O RUS 19 Ma 3
Kanin Nos O RUS 154 Qc 5
Kanin Nos O RUS 159 Hp 11
Kanin Peninsula ♁ RUS 154 Qc 5
Kanioumé O RMM 305 Ge 38
Kanita O J 250 Mg 25
Kaniva O AUS 378 Mg 64
Kanivs'ke vodoschovyšče ~ UA 175 Hh 21
Kanji-dong O DVRK 247 Ma 25
Kanjirapalli O IND 239 Kc 41
Kanjiroba △ NEP 234 Kf 31
Kanjiža O SCG 174 Hb 22
Kanjiža O SCG 174 Hc 22
Kankalabé O RG 316 Ga 40
Kankan O RG 316 Gb 40
Kankara O WAN 320 Gk 40
Kankelaba ~ RMM 305 Gc 40
Kānker O IND 234 Ke 35
Kankesanturai O CL 239 Kd 41
Kankha ~ IND 235 Kf 33
Kankiya O WAN 320 Gk 39
Kankossa O RIM 304 Ga 38
Kankyidaung O MYA 262 Km 37
Kanmaw Kyun ♁ MYA 262 Kp 40
Kanna O MYA 254 Kn 36
Kannad O IND 234 Kb 35
Kannapolis O USA 71 Dh 28
Kanniyākumari O IND 239 Kc 41
Kannus O FIN 159 Hd 14
Kano O J 247 Mb 28
Kano O WAN 320 Gl 39
Kanona O Z 341 Hh 52
Kanoni O RDC 341 Hf 51
Kanono O NAM 341 Hd 54
Kanopolis Lake ~ USA 70 Cp 26
Kanoroba O CI 305 Gc 41
Kanosh O USA 64 Cf 26
Kanouri ⏜ RN 308 Gn 38
Kano Vlei O NAM 340 Hb 55
Kanowit O MAL 274 Lg 44
Kanoya O J 247 Mb 30
Kanozero ~ RUS 159 Hk 12
Kanpur O IND 234 Kd 32
Kansanshi O Z 341 Hf 52
Kansas ⊙ USA 70 Cm 26
Kansas O USA 70 Da 27
Kansas City O USA 70 Da 26
Kansenia O RDC 341 He 51
Kansk O RUS 204 Ub 7
Kantalai O CL 239 Ke 41
Kantang O THA 270 Kp 42
Kantchari O BF 317 Gg 39
Kantche O RN 320 Gl 39
Kantemirovka O RUS 181 Hm 21
Kantharalak O THA 263 Lc 38
Kanthi O IND 235 Kh 35
Kanthidaw O MYA 262 Km 37
Kantunil O MEX 93 Dd 35
Kanuku Mountains ⛰ GUY 112 Ee 44
Kanur O IND 238 Kc 38
Kanus O NAM 348 Hb 59
Kanuworalak Buri O THA 262 Kp 38
Kanye O RB 349 He 58
Kanyemba O ZW 341 Hh 53
Kanyilombi O Z 341 He 52
Kanys-Kija O KS 223 Jp 25
Kanyu O RB 349 He 56
Kao O RI 275 Lp 45
Kao O RN 308 Gj 38
Kao ♁ TO 390 Ac 55
Kao Chaison O THA 270 La 42
Kao Chason O THA 270 La 42
Kaôh Kông ♁ K 263 Lb 40
Kaôh Rŭng ♁ K 263 Lb 40
Kaôh Rŭng Sâmlŏem ♁ K 263 Lb 40
Kaohsiung O RC 258 Lk 34
Kaohsiung O RC 259 Ll 34
Kaôh Tang ♁ K 263 Lb 40
Kaôh Thmei ♁ K 263 Lb 40
Kaoka O SOL 290 Nc 50
Kaokoland ⏜ NAM 340 Gn 54
Kaoko Otavi O NAM 340 Gn 55
Kaolack O SN 304 Fm 38
Kaolo O SOL 290 Nb 50
Kaoma O Z 341 He 53
Kaouadja O RCA 321 Hd 42
Kaouadja ~ RCA 324 Hd 41
Kaouara O CI 317 Gd 40
Kapa O MYA 262 Kp 39
Kapa ♁ TO 390 Ad 55
Kapaa O USA 75 Al 34
Kapadvanj O IND 227 Ka 34
Kapai O PNG 287 Mj 49
Kapaimari O PNG 286 Mh 48
Kapaku O RI 279 Lk 50
Kapalabuaya O RI 283 Lp 46
Kap Alexander ⌓ DK 7 Fa 2
Kap Alexandra ⌓ DK 43 Ha 3
Kapalua O USA 75 Am 35
Kap Ambai ♁ RI 286 Me 46
Kapandae O GH 317 Gf 41
Kapande ~ RDC 341 Hf 51
Kapandun O GH 317 Gf 40
Kapanga O RDC 341 Hd 50
Kapangan O RP 267 Ll 37
Kapapa O RDC 336 Hg 50
Kapatu O Z 336 Hh 50
Kapatu ~ EAT 337 Hk 48
Kapau River ~ PNG 287 Mk 49
Kapchorwa O EAU 325 Hk 45
Kapedo O EAK 325 Hk 45
Kapema O RDC 341 Hg 51
Kapenguria O EAK 325 Hk 45
Kap Farvel ⌓ DK 18 Gb 4
Kap Farvel Uummannarsuaq ⌓ DK 43 Ka 7
Kapia O RDC 333 Hb 48
Kapichira Falls ~ MW 344 Hk 53
Kaping Hsi ~ RC 259 Ll 34
Kapip O PK 227 Jn 30
Kapiri Mposhi O Z 341 Hg 52
Kapīsa ⊙ AFG 223 Jn 28
Kapiskau River ~ CDN 57 Df 20
Kapiskong Lake ~ CDN 57 Dh 21
Kapit O MAL 274 Lg 45
Kapitau O RI 286 Mf 47
Kapiti Island ♁ NZ 383 Nk 66
Kapiura River ~ PNG 287 Mm 48
Kaplan O USA 86 Db 31
Kap Morris Jesup ⌓ DK 18 Ha 1
Kapoe O THA 262 Kp 41
Kapoeta O SUD 325 Hj 43
Ka Poh ★ THA 262 Kp 40
Kapona O RDC 336 Hg 49
Kaporo O MW 337 Hj 50
Kaposvár O H 174 Ha 22
Kappadokien ⏜ TR 195 Hk 27
Kappar O PK 226 Jk 33
Kappelshamm O S 170 Ha 17
Kappelskär O S 170 Hb 16
Kapp Laura ⌓ N 158 Hf 5
Kapp Platen ⌓ N 158 Hd 5
Kapp's Farm O NAM 348 Ha 57
Kapsabet O EAK 325 Hk 45
Kapsowar O EAK 325 Hk 45
Kaptai O BD 235 Kl 34
Kaptai Reservoir ~ BD 235 Kl 34
Kapuas ~ RI 271 Lf 45
Kapuas ~ RI 279 Lh 47
Kapulo O RDC 336 Hg 50
Kapuskasing O CDN 57 Dg 21
Kapuskasing River ~ CDN 57 Dg 21
Kapustin Jar Pologoe O RUS 181 Ja 21
Kaputa O Z 336 Hg 50
Kaputirr O EAK 325 Hk 44
Kapuvár O H 174 Ha 22
Kap York ⌓ DK 7 Fb 2
Kap York ⌓ DK 43 Hb 3
Kar. Masel'ga O RUS 159 Hj 14
Kara O RT 317 Gg 41
Kara ~ RT 317 Gg 41
Karabekaul O TM 223 Jk 26
Kara-Bogaz-Gol ~ TM 222 Je 25
Karabogazgöl O TM 222 Je 25
Karabük O TR 195 Hj 25
Karabula O RUS 204 Ub 7
Karaburun O TR 195 Hf 26
Karabutak O KZ 155 Sa 9
Karacabey O TR 195 Hg 25
Karaca Dağ. △ TR 195 Hm 27
Karačaevsk O RUS 202 Hn 24
Karacaköy O TR 195 Hg 25
Karaçal T. △ TR 195 Hj 27
Karacasu O TR 195 Hg 27
Karačev O RUS 171 Hk 19
Karāchi O PK 227 Jm 33
Karaçoban O TR 202 Hp 26
Karād O IND 238 Ka 37
Kara Dağ. △ TR 195 Hj 27
Karaga O GH 317 Gf 41
Karaginskiy Zaliv ≈ RUS 205 Yc 7
Karagüney Dağı ⛰ TR 195 Hj 25
Karagwe O EAT 336 Hh 46
Karahalı O TR 195 Hg 26
Karaiai O PNG 287 Ml 48
Karaj O IR 222 Jd 28
Karajagi O IND 238 Kb 37
Karak O MAL 270 Lb 44
Kara-Kabak O KS 230 Ka 26
Kara-Kala O TM 222 Jg 26
Karakax He ~ VRC 230 Ke 27
Karakaya Brj. ~ TR 195 Hm 26
Karakeçi O TR 195 Hm 27
Karakoram ⏜ PK 230 Kb 27
Kara K'orē O ETH 313 Hm 40
Karakoro ~ RMM 304 Ga 38
Karakul O UZB 223 Jk 26
Kara-Kul' O KS 230 Ka 25
Kara-Kul'dža O KS 230 Ka 25
Karakum ⏜ TM 222 Jg 25
Karakum Canal ~ TM 222 Jg 26
Karakum Canal ~ TM 223 Jk 27
Karakum Desert ⏜ UZB 223 Jl 26
Karal O TCH 321 Gp 39
Karalundi O AUS 368 Lk 59
Karama ~ RI 279 Lk 47
Karamadai O IND 239 Kc 40
Karaman O TR 195 Hj 27
Karamay O VRC 204 Tc 9
Karamba O NAM 348 Hb 56
Karambu O RI 279 Lh 47
Karamea O NZ 382 Nh 66
Karamea Bight ~ NZ 382 Nh 66
Karamet Nijaz O TM 223 Jl 27
Karamyk O KS 223 Jp 26
Karang O SN 316 Fm 39
Karangampel O RI 278 Le 49
Karangana O RMM 317 Gd 39
Karangnunggal O RI 278 Ld 49
Karangoua ~ RCB 332 Gn 45
Karangua O Z 341 Hf 52
Kāranja O IND 234 Kc 35
Karanji O IND 234 Kd 35
Karanpur O IND 227 Ka 31
Karap O PNG 287 Mj 48
Karapınar O TR 195 Hj 27
Karara O AUS 375 Mm 60
Kara-Sal ~ RUS 181 Hp 22
Karasburg O NAM 348 Hb 60
Kara Sea ≈ 19 Na 2
Karasjok O N 159 He 11
Kara Strait ~ RUS 19 Mb 3
Karasu O TR 195 Hh 25
Karasu ~ TR 202 Hn 26
Karasu-Aras Dağl. ⛰ TR 202 Hn 26
Karasuk O RUS 204 Ta 8
Karasuk Hills ⛰ EAK 325 Hk 44
Kara-Suu O KS 230 Ka 25
Karât O IR 222 Jj 28
Karataş O TR 195 Hk 27
Karatas O KZ 223 Jn 25
Karatina O EAK 337 Hl 46
Karatsu O J 247 Ma 29
Karatu O EAT 337 Hk 47
Karaul O RUS 204 Tb 4
Karaulbazar O UZB 223 Jl 26
Karauli O IND 234 Kc 32
Karauwi O PNG 287 Mj 49
Karavan O KS 223 Jp 25
Karavānsarāy-ye Šams O IR 226 Jf 30
Karavas O GR 194 Hd 27
Karawa O RDC 321 Hc 44
Karawanella O CL 239 Ke 42
Karawang O RI 278 Ld 49
Karawari River ~ PNG 286 Mh 48
Karayazı O TR 202 Hp 26
Karaye O WAN 320 Gk 40
Karbala O IRQ 209 Hp 29
Karbālā ⊙ IRQ 214 Hn 30
Kårböle O S 158 Gp 14
Karchat O PK 227 Jm 33
Kardámila O GR 194 He 26
Kardha O IND 234 Kd 35
Karditsa O GR 194 Hc 26
Kardiva Channel ~ MV 239 Ka 43
Kärdla O EST 170 Hd 16
Kărdžali O BG 194 He 25
Kareeberge ⛰ ZA 349 Hd 61
Kareebospoort △ ZA 349 Hd 61
Karegari O PNG 286 Mh 48
Karelien ⏜ RUS 159 Hg 15
Karema O PNG 287 Mk 50
Karema O EAT 336 Hh 49
Karepol'e O RUS 159 Hp 13
Karera O IND 234 Kc 33
Karesuando O S 159 Hc 11
Kārevāndar O IR 226 Jj 32
Kargal O IND 238 Kb 38
Kargasok O RUS 204 Tb 7
Kargat O RUS 204 Ta 7
Kargı O TR 195 Hk 25
Kargil O IND 230 Kc 28
Kargopol' O RUS 154 Qb 6
Kargopol' O RUS 159 Hm 15
Karguéri O RN 308 Gm 39
Kargūški O IR 226 Jg 32
Karhe ~ IR 215 Jc 30
Kari O WAN 320 Gm 40
Karia O PNG 287 Mm 47
Karianga O RM 353 Jb 57
Kariba O ZW 341 Hg 54
Kariba Reservoir ~ Z 341 Hf 54
Kariega ~ ZA 358 Hd 62
Kariés O GR 194 He 25
Karigasniemi O FIN 159 Hf 11
Karijini ♀ AUS 360 Lk 57
Kārīkāl O IND 239 Kd 40
Karima O SUD 312 Hh 37
Karimama O DY 320 Gh 39
Karimata Strait ≈ 278 Ld 46
Karimganj O IND 254 Kl 33
Karīmnagar O IND 238 Kd 36
Karimui O PNG 287 Mj 49
Karin O SP 328 Ja 40
Karin O SP 328 Jc 40
Karina O WAL 316 Ga 41
Karis O FIN 159 Hd 15
Karisimbi △ RWA 336 Hg 46
Káristos O GR 194 He 26
Kariya O J 251 Me 28
Kāriyāpatti O IND 239 Kd 41
Karizanga ★ IND 235 Kl 32
Karjat O IND 238 Kb 36
Karjo ~ EAK 325 Hk 45
Kārkal O IND 238 Kb 39
Kar Kar Island ♁ PNG 287 Mk 48
Karkh O PK 227 Jm 32
Karkinit Gulf ~ UA 175 Hj 23
Karkkila O FIN 159 Hd 15
Karkonosze ⛰ PL 174 Gp 20
Karksi-Nuia O EST 171 He 16
Karleby O FIN 159 Hd 14
Karlgarin O AUS 368 Lk 62
Karling O SUD 312 Hh 39
Karlıova O TR 202 Hn 26
Karlivka O UA 175 Hk 21
Karlmarsund ~ S 170 Ha 17
Karlobag O HR 174 Gp 23
Karlovac O HR 174 Gp 23
Karlovo O BG 194 He 24
Karlovy Vary O CZ 174 Gn 20
Karlsborg O S 170 Gp 16
Karlshamn O S 170 Gp 17
Karlskoga O S 170 Gp 16
Karlskrona O S 170 Gp 17
Karlsruhe O D 174 Gl 21
Karlstad O USA 56 Cp 21
Karlstad O S 170 Gn 16
Karluk O USA 46 An 17
Karma O SUD 312 Hh 36
Karma O RN 317 Gg 39
Karma ~ TCH 321 Ha 40
Karmāla O IND 238 Kb 36
Karmé O TCH 321 Gp 39
Karmina O UZB 223 Jl 25
Karmøy ♁ N 170 Gj 16
Karnah O UZB 223 Jl 26
Karnāl O IND 234 Kc 31
Karnali ~ NEP 234 Ke 31
Karnaou △ TCH 309 Ha 35
Karnaphuli Reservoir ~ BD 254 Kl 34
Karnare O BG 194 He 24
Karnataka ⊙ IND 238 Kb 38
Karnivá O CZ 174 Hb 21
Karnobat O BG 194 Hf 24
Karnprayāg O IND 230 Kd 30
Karoi O ZW 341 Hg 54
Karo La △ VRC 235 Kk 31
Karonga O MW 337 Hj 50
Karong Tso ~ VRC 231 Kg 30
Karonie O AUS 368 Lm 61
Karoo ⏜ ZA 358 Hc 62
Karoo ♀ ZA 358 Hd 62
Karoonda O AUS 378 Mf 63
Karor O PK 227 Jp 30
Karora O SUD 313 Hm 37
Karos O ZA 348 Hc 60
Karosa O RI 279 Lk 46
Kárpathio Pélagos ~ GR 195 Hf 28
Kárpathos O GR 195 Hf 28
Kárpathos ♁ GR 195 Hf 28
Karpeníssi O GR 194 Hc 26
Karpina O HR 174 Gp 22
Karratha O AUS 360 Lj 56
Karratha Roadhouse O AUS 360 Lj 56
Karrats Fjord ≈ DK 43 Ja 4
Karredouw O ZA 358 He 62
Karridale O AUS 368 Lh 63
Kars O TR 202 Hp 25
Kärsämäki O FIN 159 He 13
Kārsava O LV 171 Hf 17
Karshi O WAN 320 Gk 41
Karši O UZB 19 Na 6
Kartabu O GUY 113 Ee 42
Kartaly O RUS 154 Rc 8
Karthala △ COM 345 Hp 51
Kartingan ~ RI 279 Lg 47
Kārtnen ⊙ A 174 Gn 22
Kartuzy O PL 170 Ha 18
Karu O PNG 287 Mn 47
Karubaga O RI 286 Mf 47
Karubeamsberge ⛰ NAM 348 Ha 57
Karubwe O Z 341 Hg 53
Karuh O AFG 223 Jk 28
Karumba O AUS 365 Mg 54
Kārumbhar Island ♁ IND 227 Jn 34
Karumei O J 250 Mg 25
Karumwa O EAT 336 Hj 47
Kārūn ~ IR 209 Jc 29
Karungu O EAK 337 Hk 46
Karunjie O AUS 361 Lp 54
Karūr O IND 239 Kd 40
Karuzi O BU 336 Hh 47
Karvia O FIN 159 Hd 14
Karviná O CZ 174 Hb 21
Kārwār O IND 238 Ka 38
Kas O TR 195 Hg 27
Kas O SUD 312 Hd 39
Kasa ~ ARM 202 Ja 25
Kasa O VRC 242 La 30
Kasa O RP 267 Ll 36
Kasa O RDC 333 Hb 46
Kasaba O Z 341 Hg 51
Kasabi O RDC 336 Hg 50
Kasabonika O CDN 57 Dd 19
Kāsaf Rūd ~ IR 222 Jj 27
Kasai O J 251 Md 28
Kasaji O RDC 341 Hd 51
Kāsa Khurd O IND 238 Ka 36
Kasama O Z 341 Hh 51
Kasan O UZB 223 Jl 26
Kasane O RB 341 He 54
Kasanga O EAT 336 Hh 50
Kasangor O SUD 325 Hj 43
Kasangulu O RDC 332 Gp 48
Kasanka ♀ Z 341 Hh 52
Kasansa O RDC 333 Hd 49
Kasansaj O UZB 223 Jp 25
Kāsaragod O IND 238 Kb 39
Kasari O J 259 Ma 31
Kasaro ~ SUD 312 Hg 39
Kašary O RUS 181 Hn 21
Kasasi O WAL 316 Ga 41
Kasayi ~ RDC 333 Hb 47
Kasba Lake ~ CDN 6 Db 3
Kasba Lake ~ CDN 42 Fa 6
Kasba-Tadla O MA 293 Gc 29
Kasdir O DZ 293 Gf 29
Kaseda O J 247 Mb 30
Kasei ~ RDC 333 Hc 49
Kasempa O Z 341 He 52
Kasem Wenz ~ ETH 325 Hm 41
Kasenga O RDC 333 Hb 47
Kasenga O RDC 341 Hg 51
Kasengu O RDC 324 Hh 44
Kasenye O RDC 324 Hh 45
Kasese O EAU 324 Hg 45
Kasese O RDC 336 Hf 46
Kaset Sombun O THA 262 La 37
Kāsganj O IND 234 Kd 32
Kashabowie O CDN 56 Dc 21
Kāshān O IR 222 Jd 29
Kashechewan O CDN 57 Dh 19
Kashi O VRC 230 Kc 26
Kashileshi ~ RDC 341 Hd 51
Kashima O J 251 Mg 28
Kashima-nada ~ J 251 Mg 27
Kashinatpu O BD 235 Kj 34
Kashīpur O IND 234 Kd 31
Kashitu O Z 341 Hg 52
Kashiwa O J 251 Mf 28
Kashiwazaki O J 251 Me 27
Kāshmor O PK 227 Jn 31
Kasia O IND 235 Kf 32
Kasidishi ~ RDC 341 Hd 50
Kasigi O PNG 286 Mh 49
Kasigluk O USA 46 Aj 15
Kasimbar O RI 282 Ll 46
Kasimov O RUS 181 Hn 18
Kašin O RUS 171 Hl 17
Kasindi O RDC 324 Hg 45
Kaškadarja ~ UZB 223 Jl 26
Kaškarancy O RUS 159 Hk 12
Kaskas O SN 304 Fn 37
Kaskaskia ~ USA 71 Dd 26
Kaskinen O FIN 159 Hc 14
Kaslo O CDN 50 Cd 21
Kāšmar O IR 222 Jh 28
Kasoba O RDC 333 Hc 49
Kasompe O Z 341 He 52
Kasongo O RDC 336 Hf 48
Kasongo-Lunda O RDC 333 Ha 49
Kaspi O GE 202 Ja 24
Kaspian Depression ⏜ KZ 155 Rb 9
Kaspijsk O RUS 202 Jb 24
Kassala O SUD 313 Hl 38
Kassama O RMM 316 Ga 39
Kassándra ♁ GR 194 Hd 26
Kassándria O GR 194 Hd 25
Kaššary O RUS 181 Hn 21
Kassel O D 174 Gl 20
Kasserine O TN 296 Gl 28
Kássos ♁ GR 194 Hf 28
Kassoum O BF 317 Ge 39
Kastamonu O TR 195 Hj 25
Kastéli O GR 194 Hd 28
Kastomoe O RUS 181 Hm 20
Kastoriá O GR 194 Hc 25
Kastsyukovichy O BY 171 Hh 19
Kasuga O J 247 Mb 29
Kasuga O J 251 Md 28
Kasuku ~ RDC 333 He 47
Kasula O Z 341 Hf 53
Kasulu O EAT 336 Hh 48
Kasumbulesa O RDC 341 Hf 52
Kasumi O J 251 Md 28
Kasumigaura ~ J 251 Mf 28
Kasumkent O RUS 202 Jb 25
Kasumpti O IND 230 Kc 30
Kasungu O MW 344 Hj 52
Kasungu ♀ MW 344 Hj 52
Kasūr O PK 230 Kb 30
Kat O IR 215 Jc 30
Kataba O Z 341 He 54
Katabaie O RDC 333 Hd 49
Katagum O WAN 320 Gm 39
Katakakishi O RDC 341 Hd 50
Katako-Kombe O RDC 333 He 47
Katakwi O EAU 325 Hj 45
Katamatite O AUS 379 Mj 64
Katana O RI 275 Lp 45
Katana O RDC 336 Hg 47
Katanda O RDC 333 Hd 49
Katanga O RDC 333 Hc 49
Katangi O IND 234 Kd 34
Katangi O IND 234 Kd 35
Katangli O RUS 23 Sa 4
Katanning O AUS 368 Lj 62
Katanti O RDC 336 Hf 47
Kataouâne O RIM 305 Gc 37
Katápola O GR 194 He 27
Kata Tjutal △ AUS 369 Mb 58
Katavi ♀ EAT 336 Hh 49
Katavía O GR 195 Hf 28
Katcha O WAN 320 Gk 41
Katchall Island ♁ IND 270 Kl 42
Katchamba O RT 317 Gg 41
Kateel River ~ USA 46 Al 13
Katèn ~ RUS 250 Me 22
Katende O RDC 333 Hd 49
Katenge O RDC 333 Hd 49
Katengo O RDC 336 Hg 48
Katere O NAM 340 Hc 55
Kateríni O GR 194 Hd 25
Katesh O EAT 337 Hk 48
Katete O Z 344 Hj 53
Katghora O IND 234 Kf 34
Katha O MYA 254 Kn 33
Kathang O IND 254 Km 32
Katherine ~ AUS 364 Mc 52
Katherine O AUS 364 Mc 53
Kathiawar Peninsula ⏜ IND 227 Jn 34
Kathleen Lake ~ CDN 57 Dg 21
Kathmandu ▣ NEP 235 Kg 32
Kathu O ZA 349 Hd 59
Kathua O IND 230 Kb 29
Kati O RMM 316 Gb 39
Katiati O PNG 287 Mj 48
Katiéna O RMM 317 Gd 39
Katihar O IND 235 Kh 33
Katima Mulilo O NAM 341 Hd 54
Katimik Lake ~ CDN 56 Cn 19
Katin O WAN 320 Gk 41
Katingan ~ RI 279 Lg 46
Katini O RDC 333 Hb 49
Katiola O CI 317 Gd 41
Katiti Aboriginal Land ••• AUS 369 Mb 58
Katiu ♁ F 35 Bb 11
Katla O SUD 312 Hg 40
Katlanova O MK 194 Hc 25
Katmai National Park & Preserve ♀ USA 46 An 15
Kato O GUY 112 Ee 43
Katoa O TCH 321 Gp 40
Kātoda O IND 234 Kb 33
Katoka O RDC 341 Hd 51
Katombe O RDC 333 Hc 48
Katompi O RDC 336 Hf 49
Katondwe O Z 341 Hh 53
Katonga ~ EAU 324 Hh 45
Katonga O RDC 341 Hd 51
Katoomba O AUS 379 Ml 62
Katoto O EAT 336 Hh 48
Katowice O PL 174 Hb 20
Katoya O IND 235 Kj 34
Katrancik Dağı △ TR 195 Hh 27
Katrineholm O S 170 Ha 16
Katse O EAK 337 Hm 46
Katse Dam ~ LS 349 Hg 60
Katséna ~ CAM 320 Gm 42
Katsepy O RM 345 Ja 53
Katshungu O RDC 336 Hf 47
Katsina O WAN 320 Gk 39
Katsina-Ala O WAN 320 Gl 42
Katsuta O J 251 Mg 27
Katsuura O J 251 Md 29
Katsuura O J 251 Mg 28
Kattakišlok O UZB 223 Jm 26
Kattakūrgon O UZB 223 Jm 26
Kattankudi O CL 239 Ke 42
Kattarakara O IND 239 Kc 41
Kattawami Lake ~ CDN 57 Dh 21
Kattegat ~ DK 170 Gm 17
Katui O NZ 383 Nj 63
Katumba O RDC 333 He 49
Katumbi O MW 344 Hj 51
Katun ~ RUS 204 Tc 8
Katundu O Z 341 He 54
Katupa O RI 279 Lk 50
Kātūria O IND 235 Kh 33
Katwe O EAU 336 Hg 46
Katwe O RDC 341 Hf 51
Katy O USA 81 Da 31
Kauai ♁ USA 75 Al 34
Kauai Channel ~ USA 75 Al 35
Kaufman O USA 70 Cp 29
Kaugel River ~ PNG 287 Mj 49
Kauhajoki O FIN 159 Hc 14
Kaukauna O USA 57 Dd 23
Kaukauveld ⏜ NAM 340 Hc 55
Kaukonen O FIN 159 He 12
Kauksi O EST 171 Hf 16
Kaulakahi Channel ~ USA 75 Ak 34
Kaumalapau Harbor O USA 75 Am 35
Kauman O RI 279 Lg 49
Kaunakakai O USA 75 Am 35
Kaunas O LT 171 Hd 18
Kaup O PNG 287 Mj 47
Kaupena O PNG 287 Mj 49
Kaupo O USA 75 Am 35
Kaurai O PNG 287 Mn 50
Kaura-Namoda O WAN 320 Gk 39
Kauro ~ EAK 325 Hl 45
Kaustinen O FIN 159 Hd 14
Kautokeino O N 159 Hd 11
Kauwa O WAN 321 Gn 39
Kau-Ye Kyun ♁ MYA 262 Kp 40
Kavadarci O MK 194 Hd 25
Kavak O TR 195 Hk 25
Kavála O GR 194 He 25
Kavalerovo O RUS 250 Md 23
Kāvali O IND 238 Ke 38
Kavango Land ⏜ NAM 340 Hb 55
Kavār O IR 215 Je 31
Kavaratti O IND 239 Ka 40
Kavaratti Island ♁ IND 239 Ka 40
Kavarna O BG 195 Hg 24
Kavevka O RUS 159 Hm 12
Kavi O IND 227 Ka 34
Kavieng O PNG 287 Mm 47
Kavimba O RB 341 He 55
Kavinga O Z 344 Hj 52
Kavir-e ~ IR 226 Jf 31
Kavir- e Abarqū ~ IR 215 Je 30
Kavir- e Darre Anğir ~ IR 222 Jf 29
Kavir-e Haǧǧ Ali Qoli ~ IR 222 Jf 28
Kavir-e Namak ~ IR 222 Jg 28
Kavir- e Siyāh-Kūh ~ IR 222 Je 29
Kavkazskij zapovednik ♀ RUS 202 Hn 24
Kávos O GR 194 Hb 26
Kawa O RI 283 Ma 47
Kawagoe O J 251 Mf 28
Kawaihae O USA 75 Am 35
Kawaikini △ USA 75 Al 34
Kawajena O SUD 324 Hg 42
Kawakawa O NZ 383 Nk 63
Kawala O MYA 254 Km 32
Kawali O RI 278 Le 49
Kawambu O PNG 287 Mm 47
Kawambwa O Z 336 Hg 50
Kawana O Z 341 He 52
Kawangkoan O RI 275 Ln 45
Kawanoe O J 251 Mc 28
Kawant O IND 227 Ka 34
Kāwardha O IND 234 Ke 34
Kawarga ~ RI 286 Mf 49
Kawartha Lakes ~ CDN 60 Dj 23
Kawasa O RDC 341 Hg 51
Kawasaki O J 251 Mf 28
Kawatipoli O MYA 254 Kn 36
Kawatiri O NZ 383 Nj 66
Kawauchi O J 250 Mg 25
Kawau Island ♁ NZ 383 Nk 64
Kawaya O RDC 336 Hg 50
Kawaya O ZW 341 Hg 54
Kawayan O RP 267 Ln 40
Kaweka △ NZ 383 Nl 65
Kawene O CDN 56 Dc 21
Kawe Rapids ~ Z 341 Hh 53
Kawerau O NZ 383 Nl 65
Kawhia O NZ 383 Nk 65
Kawich Peak △ USA 64 Cd 26
Kawinaw Lake ~ CDN 56 Cn 19
Kawkpalut O MYA 262 Kn 37
Kawkwreik O MYA 262 Kp 37
Kaw Lake ~ USA 70 Cp 27
Kawlin O MYA 254 Km 34
Kawltang O MYA 254 Km 33
Kawm Umbu O ET 301 Hj 33
Kaxgar He ~ VRC 230 Kc 26
Kaya O BF 317 Gf 39
Kayaapu O RI 278 Lb 48
Kayak Island ♁ USA 46 Bc 15
Kayambi O Z 337 Hj 50
Kayan ~ RI 274 Lj 44
Kayanga ~ SN 316 Fn 39
Kāyankulam O IND 239 Kc 41
Kayanza O BU 336 Hg 47
Kayar O SN 304 Fm 38
Kayasa O RI 275 Lp 45
Kayasan ★ ROK 247 Ma 28
Kayattār O IND 239 Kc 41
Kaycee O USA 51 Cj 24
Kayembe-Mukulu O RDC 341 Hd 50
Kayenta O USA 65 Cg 27
Kayenzi O EAT 337 Hj 47
Kayere O RDC 336 Hg 50
Kayes O RMM 304 Ga 38
Kayima O WAL 316 Ga 41
Kayli O SUD 313 Hk 40
Kaynabayongo O RDC 336 Hg 46
Kayokwe O BU 336 Hg 47
Kayonza O RWA 336 Hh 46
Kayrunnera O AUS 378 Mh 61
Kayser Gebergte ⛰ SME 113 Ef 44
Kayseri O TR 195 Hk 26
Kayuagung O RI 278 Lc 47
Kayuku O RI 282 Ll 46
Kayunga O EAU 324 Hj 45
Kayuputeh O RI 271 Le 45
Kayuyu O RDC 336 Hf 47
Kayville O CDN 51 Ck 20
Kazabazua O CDN 60 DK 23
Kazača Lopen' O UA 175 Hk 20
Kazačje O RUS 22 Rb 2
Kazakhstan □ KZ 155 Rb 9
Kazamabika O G 332 Gm 46
Kazan' O RUS 181 Jc 18
Kazandzik O TM 222 Jf 26
Kazanlăk O BG 194 He 24
Kazan River ~ CDN 42 Fa 6
Kazaure O WAN 320 Gl 39
Kazbegi O GE 202 Ja 24
Kaz Dağı △ TR 195 Hf 26
Kazembe O Z 344 Hj 52
Kāzerūn O IR 215 Jd 31

□Country ▣Capital city ⊙Administrative unit OPlace ⌂Island ⛰Mountain range △Mountain ⌓Cape ≈Ocean, Sea ~Lake, River ΨUndersea topography ▲Glacier ♀National park •••Reservation ★Point of major interest ⌒Landscape

Kāzi Ahmad O PK 227 Jm 32
Kazi-Magomed O AZ 202 Jc 25
Kāzimkarabekir O TR 195 Hj 27
Kazincbarcika O H 174 Hc 21
Kaziza O RDC 341 Hd 51
Kaztalovka O KZ 181 Jc 21
Kazuma Pan ♀ ZW 341 He 55
Kazumba O RDC 333 Hc 49
Kazungula O Z 341 He 54
Kazuno O J 250 Mg 25
Kbombole O SN 304 Fm 38
Ké O G 332 Gm 45
Kéa ⌂ GR 194 He 27
Keaau O USA 75 An 36
Keahole Point ⌓ USA 75 Am 36
Kearney O USA 70 Cn 25
Keating Point ⌓ IND 262 Kl 41
Keban O TR 195 Hm 26
Keban Brj. ~ TR 195 Hm 26
Kebara O RCB 332 Gp 47
Kebasen O RI 278 Le 49
Kebbe O WAN 320 Gj 39
Kébémer O SN 304 Fm 38
Kébila O RMM 305 Gc 40
Kebili O TN 296 Gl 29
Kebnekaise △ S 158 Hb 12
K'ebri Dehar O ETH 328 Ja 42
Kebumen O RI 278 Le 49
Kech ~ PK 226 Jk 32
K'ech'a Terara △ ETH 325 Hm 42
Kéché O RCA 321 Hc 41
Kechika River ~ CDN 47 Bn 15
Kecskemét O H 174 Hb 22
Kedainiai O LT 171 He 18
Kédédéssé O TCH 321 Ha 40
Kedgwick O CDN 60 Ea 22
Kedi O IND 230 Kc 30
Kediri O RI 279 Lf 49
Kédougou O SN 316 Fp 39
Kedrovaja △ VRC 250 Mb 23
Kędzierzyn-Koźle O PL 174 Ha 20
Keekorok O EAK 337 Hk 46
Keel O IRL 162 Ga 18
Keele Peak △ CDN 47 Bl 13
Keele River ~ CDN 47 Bn 13
Keeling Island ⌂ AUS 26 Pb 11
Keelung O RC 259 Ll 33
Keene O USA 60 Dm 24
Keep River ♀ AUS 364 Ma 53
Keetmannshoop O NAM 348 Ha 59
Keezhik Lake ~ CDN 57 Dd 20
Kefaloniá ⌂ GR 194 Hc 26
Kefamenanu O RI 282 Ln 50
Keffi O WAN 320 Gk 41
Kefin Hausa O WAN 320 Gl 39
Keflavík O IS 158 Fj 13
Kegaska O CDN 61 Ed 20
Kehena O USA 75 An 36
Kehia O RDC 336 Hg 49
Kehl O D 163 Gk 21
Kéibo O BF 317 Gf 39
Keila O EST 171 He 16
Keimoes O ZA 348 Hc 60
Kei Mouth O ZA 358 Hg 62
Keipene O LV 171 He 17
Keiskammarivier ~ ZA 358 Hf 62
Keïta O RN 308 Gj 38
Keitele O FIN 159 He 14
Keitele ⌓ FIN 159 He 14
Keith O AUS 378 Mg 64
Keith Arm ~ CDN 47 Ca 13
Keithville O USA 70 Db 29
Keiyasi O FJI 387 Nl 54
Keizer O USA 50 Ca 23
Kejaman O MAL 274 Lg 44
Kejimkujik National Park ♀ CDN 61 Eb 23
Kejvy ⛰ RUS 159 Hl 12
Kėkajgyr O KS 230 Kb 25
Kėk-Art O KS 230 Kb 25
Keke O PNG 287 Mk 50
Kéké ~ RCA 321 Hc 43
Kékes △ H 174 Hb 22
Kekirawa O CL 239 Ke 41
Kekri O IND 234 Kb 33
Kekrima ~ RG 316 Fp 40
Kelabo O PNG 286 Mh 48
K'elafo O ETH 328 Ja 43
Kelai ~ RI 274 Lj 45
Kélakam O RN 308 Gm 39
Kelambakkam O IND 238 Ke 39
Kelan O VRC 243 Lf 26
Kelang O MAL 270 La 44
Kelapa O RI 278 Lc 46
Këlcyrë O AL 194 Hc 25
Kel'da ~ RUS 159 Hp 13
Keleft O AFG 223 Jl 27
Kelem O ETH 325 Hk 43
Keles O UZB 223 Jn 25
Keles ~ KZ 223 Jn 25
Keléya O RMM 305 Gc 40
Kelian O MAL 271 Lf 44
Kelibia O TN 297 Gm 27
Kelifskij Uzboj ⌒ TM 223 Jk 27
Kelkit O TR 195 Hm 25
Kelkıt Çayı ~ TR 195 Hm 25
Kella ⌂ SOL 290 Nb 48
Kellé O RN 308 Gm 38
Kéllé O RCB 332 Gp 46
Kellerberrin O AUS 368 Lj 61
Keller Lake ~ CDN 47 Ca 13
Kellett Strait ≈ CDN 42 Ea 3
Kellogg O USA 50 Cd 22
Kelmė O LT 171 Hd 18
Kelmet O ER 313 Hm 37
Kelo O TCH 321 Gp 41
Kelongwa O Z 341 Hf 52
Kelowna O CDN 50 Cc 21
Kelso O USA 50 Ca 22
Kelu O VRC 255 Le 35
Kelua O RI 279 Lh 47
Kelume O RI 278 Lc 46
Kelvin O USA 65 Cg 29
Kelvington O CDN 51 Cl 19
Kelvin Island ⌂ CDN 57 Dd 21
Kelwa O PK 227 Jl 33
Kem O RUS 159 Hk 13
Kem' ~ RUS 159 Hk 13
Kemah O TR 195 Hm 26
Kemâliye O TR 195 Hm 26
Kemasik O MAL 271 Lb 43
Kemba O RCA 321 Hd 43
Kembangjanggut O RI 274 Lj 45
Kembani O RI 282 Lm 46
Kembé O RCA 321 Hc 43
Kembe O RDC 341 Hf 51
Kembéra O RG 316 Fp 40
Kembolcha O ETH 313 Hm 40
Kemdéré O TCH 321 Hb 41
Kemer O TR 195 Hg 27
Kemer O TR 195 Hh 27
Kemerovo O RUS 204 Tc 7
Kemi O FIN 159 He 13
Kemijärvi O FIN 159 Hf 12
Kemijervi ~ FIN 159 Hf 12
Kemijoki ~ FIN 159 Hf 12
Kemkara O RUS 205 Xa 7
Kemlja O RUS 181 Ja 18
Kemmare River ~ IRL 163 Ga 20
Kemmerer O USA 65 Cg 25
Kempele O FIN 159 He 13
Kempendjaji O RUS 204 Vc 6
Kemp Peninsula ⌂ 38 Ga 17
Kemps Bay O BS 87 Dk 33
Kempten (Allgäu) O D 174 Gm 22
Kempton O AUS 378 Mk 67
Kemptville O CDN 60 Dl 23
Kemubu O MAL 270 La 43
Ken ~ IND 234 Ke 33
Kenadsa O DZ 293 Ge 30
Kenai O USA 6 Ba 3
Kenai O USA 46 Ba 15
Kenai Fjords National Parks ♀ USA 46 Ba 15
Kenai Peninsula ⌂ USA 46 Ba 15
Kenalia O PNG 286 Mh 50
Kenamuke Swamp ~ SUD 325 Hj 42
Kenansville O USA 87 Dh 32
Kenār Daryā O IR 222 Jd 27
Kenari O RI 279 Lk 50
Kenaston O CDN 51 Cj 20
Kendal O GB 162 Ge 18
Kendal O RI 278 Lf 49
Kendall O USA 70 Cm 27
Kendall O USA 87 Dh 33
Kendall ~ AUS 365 Mg 53
Kendallville O USA 71 Df 25
Kendari O RI 282 Lm 47
Kendawangan O RI 278 Le 47
Kèndégué O TCH 321 Hb 40
Kendrāpāra O IND 235 Kh 35
Kendrew O ZA 358 He 62
Kendu Bay O EAK 337 Hk 46
Kendujhargarh O IND 235 Kg 35
Kendungwuni O RI 278 Le 49
Kenema O WAL 316 Ga 42
Kenenkou O RMM 305 Gc 39
Kenewa O PNG 286 Mh 50
Kenge O RDC 333 Ha 48
Keng Tung O MYA 254 Kp 35
Kenhardt O ZA 348 Hc 60
Kéniéba O RMM 316 Ga 39
Kéniébandi O RMM 316 Ga 39
Keningau O MAL 274 Lj 43
Kénitra O MA 293 Gc 28
Kenli O VRC 246 Lk 27
Kenmare O USA 51 Cl 21
Kenmare O IRL 163 Gb 20
Kenmore Park O AUS 369 Mc 59
Kennebec ~ USA 60 Dn 23
Kennebunk O USA 60 Dn 24
Kennedy O CDN 51 Cl 21
Kennedy O USA 81 Cp 31
Kennedy O ZW 341 Hf 55
Kennedy ~ AUS 365 Mj 53
Kennedy O AUS 365 Mj 55
Kennedy Channel ≈ 7 Fb 1
Kennedy Peak △ MYA 254 Kl 34
Kennedy Range ⛰ AUS 368 Lh 58
Kennedy's Vale O ZA 349 Hg 58
Kenner O USA 86 Dc 30
Kennesaw Mtd. N.B.P. ★ USA 86 Df 29
Kenneth Range ⛰ AUS 360 Lj 57
Kennett O USA 71 Dc 27
Kennewick O USA 50 Cc 22
Keno O CDN 47 Bj 13
Keno City O CDN 6 Ca 3
Kenogami River ~ CDN 57 Df 20
Kenora O CDN 56 Da 21
Kenosha O USA 57 De 24
Kenscoff O RH 101 Dm 36
Kensington O CDN 61 Ec 22
Kensington Downs O AUS 375 Mj 57
Kent O USA 50 Ca 22
Kent O USA 50 Cb 23
Kent O USA 71 Dh 25
Kent O USA 81 Ck 30
Kent O WAL 316 Fp 41
Kentani O ZA 358 Hg 62
Kent Group ⌂ AUS 379 Mk 65
Ken Thao O LAO 262 La 37
Kenting ★ RC 259 Ll 34
Kent Junction O CDN 61 Eb 22
Kentland O USA 71 De 25
Kenton O USA 71 Dg 25
Kenton-on-Sea O ZA 358 Hf 62
Kent Peninsula ⌂ CDN 47 Cg 11
Kentriki Macedonia ⊙ GR 194 Hd 25
Kentucky ⊙ USA 71 De 27
Kentucky ~ USA 71 Df 27
Kentucky Lake ~ USA 71 Dd 27
Kentville O CDN 61 Eb 23
Kentwood O USA 86 Dc 30
Kenya □ EAK 325 Hk 45
Kenyasi Mohn O GH 317 Ge 42
Kenyon O USA 56 Db 23
Kenzou O CAM 321 Gp 43
Keokuk O USA 70 Dc 25
Kepa O RUS 159 Hj 13
Kepahiang O RI 278 Lb 47
Kepanjen O RI 279 Lg 50
Kepelekese ~ RDC 333 Hc 49
Kepi O RI 286 Mf 49
Kepi Gjuhëzës ⌓ AL 194 Hb 25
Kepina ~ RUS 159 Hn 13
Kepino O RUS 159 Hn 13
Kępno O PL 174 Ha 20
Kepp ~ AUS 364 Ma 53
Keppel Bay ~ AUS 375 Mm 57
Keppel Island ⌂ GB 147 Ed 71
Keppel Sands O AUS 375 Mm 57
Kepsut O TR 195 Hg 26
Kepudori O RI 283 Md 46
Kepulauan Aru ⌂ RI 283 Md 48
Kepulauan Ayu ⌂ RI 283 Mb 45
Kepulauan Babar ⌂ RI 283 Ma 49
Kepulauan Badas ⌂ RI 271 Ld 45
Kepulauan Banda ⌂ RI 283 Ma 48
Kepulauan Bonerate ⌂ RI 282 Ll 49
Kepulauan Boo ⌂ RI 283 Ma 46
Kepulauan Bowokan ⌂ RI 282 Lm 47
Kepulauan Fam ⌂ RI 283 Ma 46
Kepulauan Goraici ⌂ RI 275 Lp 45
Kepulauan Gorong ⌂ RI 283 Mb 48
Kepulauan Jin ⌂ RI 283 Md 49
Kepulauan Kai ⌂ RI 283 Mc 48
Kepulauan Kangean ⌂ RI 279 Lh 49
Kepulauan Karimata ⌂ RI 278 Le 46
Kepulauan Karimunjawa ⌂ RI 278 Lf 48
Kepulauan Kumamba ⌂ RI 286 Mf 46
Kepulauan Laut Kecil ⌂ RI 279 Lh 48
Kepulauan Leti ⌂ RI 283 Ma 50
Kepulauan Lingga ⌂ RI 271 Lc 45
Kepulauan Loloda Utara ⌂ RI 275 Lp 44
Kepulauan Lucipara ⌂ RI 283 Lp 48
Kepulauan Macan ⌂ RI 282 Ll 49
Kepulauan Malukalukuang ⌂ RI 279 Lj 48
Kepulauan Mamboor ⌂ RI 283 Md 47
Kepulauan Masalima ⌂ RI 279 Lj 48
Kepulauan Moor ⌂ RI 283 Md 47
Kepulauan Nanusa ⌂ RI 275 Lp 43
Kepulauan Nusela ⌂ RI 283 Mb 46
Kepulauan Paidaido ⌂ RI 286 Me 46
Kepulauan Pasitelu ⌂ RI 282 Ll 49
Kepulauan Pisang ⌂ RI 283 Mb 47
Kepulauan Riau ⌂ RI 271 Lc 45
Kepulauan Sabalana ⌂ RI 279 Lk 49
Kepulauan Salabangka ⌂ RI 282 Lm 47
Kepulauan Sangihe ⌂ RI 275 Ln 44
Kepulauan Santengar ⌂ RI 279 Lj 49
Kepulauan Sariga ⌂ RI 283 Mc 47
Kepulauan Sermata ⌂ RI 283 Ma 50
Kepulauan Sula ⌂ RI 282 Ln 46
Kepulauan Talaud ⌂ RI 275 Lp 44
Kepulauan Tayandu ⌂ RI 283 Mb 48
Kepulauan Tempelan ⌂ RI 271 Ld 45
Kepulauan Tiworo ⌂ RI 282 Lm 48
Kepulauan Tukangbesi ⌂ RI 282 Ln 48
Kepulauan Valse Pisang ⌂ RI 283 Mb 47
Kepulauan Watubela ⌂ RI 283 Mb 48
Kepulauan Widi ⌂ RI 283 Ma 46
Kerala ⊙ IND 239 Kb 40
Kerama-rettō ⌂ J 259 Lp 32
Keram River ~ PNG 287 Mj 48
Kerang O RI 279 Lj 47
Kerang O AUS 379 Mh 63
Keranirhat O BD 235 Kl 34
Keravat O PNG 287 Mm 48
Kerawa O WAN 321 Gn 40
Kerby O USA 50 Ca 24
Kerčens'ka pr. ~ RUS 195 Hl 23
Kerch O UA 195 Hl 23
Kerchouel O RMM 305 Gg 37
Kéré O RCA 324 He 43
Kéré ~ RCA 324 Hf 43
Kerein Hills O AUS 379 Mk 62
Kerema O PNG 287 Mj 49
Keremeos O CDN 50 Cc 21
Keremeos Range Indian Reservation ••• CDN 50 Cb 21
Kérémou O DY 317 Gh 40
Keren O ER 313 Hm 38
Kerend O IR 209 Jb 28
Kerens O USA 70 Cp 29
Kereru Range ⛰ PNG 287 Mj 49
Keret' O RUS 159 Hj 12
Kerewan O WAG 316 Fm 39
Kerguelen ⌂ F 31 Na 14
Keria Landing O GUY 113 Ee 42
Kericho O EAK 337 Hk 46
Keri Kera O SUD 312 Hj 39
Kerio ~ EAK 325 Hl 44
Keriya He ~ VRC 230 Ke 27
Kerkenah ⌂ TN 297 Gm 28
Kerki O TM 223 Jl 27
Kerkiči O TM 223 Jl 27
Kerkikeri O NZ 383 Nk 63
Kérkira O GR 194 Hb 26
Kerkouane ★ TN 297 Gm 27
Kermadec Islands ⌂ NZ 35 Aa 13
Kermān ⊙ IR 226 Jf 31
Kermān O IR 226 Jg 30
Kermānšāhan O IR 226 Jf 30
Kermānšāh O IR 209 Jb 28
Kermānshāh ⊙ IR 209 Jb 28
Kermāšah O IR 215 Jd 30
Kermit O USA 81 Cl 30
Kernijoki ~ FIN 159 Hf 12
Kérou O DY 317 Gh 40
Kerouané O RG 316 Gb 41
Kerrobert O CDN 51 Ch 20
Kerrville O USA 81 Cn 30
K'ersa O ETH 325 Hn 41
Kershaw O USA 71 Dh 28
Kersinyané O RIM 304 Ga 38
Kertamulia O RI 278 Le 46
Kertosono O RI 279 Lg 49
Kerugoya O EAK 337 Hl 46
Keryneia O CY 195 Hj 28
Kerzaz O DZ 293 Gf 31
Kesagami Lake ~ CDN 57 Dh 20
Kesagami River ~ CDN 57 Dh 20
Kesälahti O FIN 159 Hg 15
Keşan O TR 194 Hf 25
Keşem O AFG 223 Jp 27
Kesennuma O J 250 Mg 26
Keshod O IND 227 Jp 35
Keskin O TR 195 Hj 26
Kes'ma O RUS 171 Hl 16
Kestell O ZA 349 Hg 60
Kesten'ga O RUS 159 Hh 13
Keswick O CDN 60 Dj 23
Keswick O GB 162 Ge 18
Keszthely O H 174 Ha 22
Ket ~ RUS 204 Tc 7
Keta O GH 317 Gg 43
Keta Lagoon ~ GH 317 Gg 43
Ketama O MA 293 Gd 28
Ketanggungan O RI 278 Le 49
Ketapang O RI 278 Le 46
Ketapang O RI 279 Lg 49
Ketaun O RI 270 La 47
Ketčenary O RUS 181 Ja 22
Ketchikan O USA 42 Da 7
Ketchum O USA 50 Ce 24
Kete-Krachi O GH 317 Gf 42
Ketesso O CI 317 Ge 43
Keti Bandar O PK 227 Jm 33
Kétou O DY 320 Gh 42
Kętrzyn O PL 170 Hc 18
Ketsko-Tymskaya Ravnina ⌒ RUS 204 Tb 6
Ketta O RCB 332 Gp 45
Kétté O CAM 321 Gp 43
Kettering O USA 71 Df 26
Kettle ~ CDN 50 Cc 21
Kettle ~ USA 50 Cc 21
Kettle Falls O USA 50 Cc 21
Keudemane O RI 270 Kn 43
Keuka Lake ~ USA 60 Dk 24
Keur Madiabel O SN 316 Fm 39
Keur Massène O RIM 304 Fm 37
Keur Momar Sar O SN 304 Fn 38
Keuruu O FIN 159 He 14
Kévé O RT 317 Gg 42
Kewa O PNG 286 Mh 49
Kewanee O USA 71 Dd 25
Kewapante O RI 282 Lm 50
Kewaunee O USA 57 De 23
Keweenaw Bay ~ USA 57 Dd 22
Keweenaw Bay Ind. Res. ••• USA 57 Dd 22
Keweenaw Peninsula ⌂ USA 57 De 22
K'ey Āfer O ETH 325 Hl 43
Keyala O SUD 325 Hj 43
Keya Paha River ~ USA 56 Cm 24
Key Biscayne ⌓ USA 87 Dh 33
Keyes O CDN 56 Cn 20
Keyhole Reservoir ~ USA 51 Ck 23
Key Largo O USA 87 Dh 33
Keyling Inlet ~ AUS 364 Ma 53
Keyser O USA 74 Dj 26
Keystone ~ USA 70 Cp 27
Keysville O USA 74 Dj 27
Keytesville O USA 70 Db 26
Key West O USA 87 Dh 33
Kežma O RUS 204 Uc 7
Kežmarok O SK 174 Hc 21
Kgalagadi Transfrontier Park ♀ ZA 348 Hc 58
Kgama-Kgama-Pan ~ RB 341 He 55
Kgokgole ~ ZA 349 Hd 59
Khabarovsk O RUS 205 Xa 9
Khabou O RIM 304 Fp 38
Khabrat al Dawish O KWT 215 Jb 31
Khagaria O IND 235 Kh 33
Khairāgarh O IND 234 Ke 35
Khairapa O IND 227 Ka 32
Khairpur O PK 227 Jn 32
Khairpur O PK 227 Ka 31
Khajuraho O IND 234 Kd 33
Khajuri Kachari O PK 223 Jn 29
Khakhea O RB 349 Hd 58
Khakurdi O IND 234 Kb 35
Khalfallah O DZ 293 Gg 28
Khalij al Būmbah ~ LAR 300 Hd 29
Khalopyenichy O BY 171 Hg 18
Khambhāliya O IND 227 Jn 34
Khambhat O IND 227 Ka 34
Khāmgaon O IND 234 Kc 35
Khamis O KSA 218 Hp 36
Kham Khuan Kaeo O THA 263 Lc 38
Khammam O IND 238 Ke 37
Khampat O MYA 254 Km 34
Kham Ta Kla O THA 263 Lb 37
Khamti O MYA 254 Km 33
Khan ~ NAM 348 Gp 57
Khan ~ NAM 348 Ha 56
Khānāpur O IND 238 Kb 38
Khandala O IND 238 Kc 36
Khandwa O IND 234 Kc 35
Khānewāl O PK 227 Jp 30
Khāngāh Dogran O PK 230 Ka 30
Khangai Mountains ⛰ MNG 204 Ub 9
Khāngarh O PK 227 Jp 31
Khangar Sidi Nadji O DZ 296 Gk 28
Khanna O IND 230 Kc 30
Khanom O THA 262 Kp 41
Khānpur O PK 227 Jn 32
Khānpur O PK 227 Jp 31
Khao Chmao ★ THA 262 La 39
Khao Kha Khaeng △ THA 262 Kp 37
Khao Kheaw ♀ THA 262 La 38
Khao Laen Reservoir ~ THA 262 Kp 38
Khao Sok ♀ THA 262 Kp 41
Khapalu O PK 230 Kc 28
Khaptada National Park ♀ NEP 234 Ke 31
Kharagpur O IND 235 Kh 34
Khārān O PK 227 Jl 31
Kharar O IND 230 Kc 30
Khārdung La △ IND 230 Kc 28
Kharga al-Ḫāriğa O ET 301 Hh 33
Khargon O IND 234 Kb 35
Khāriān O PK 230 Ka 29
Khariār O IND 234 Kf 35
Kharikhola O NEP 235 Kh 32
Khārk O IR 215 Jd 31
Kharkiv O UA 181 Hl 20
Kharsia O IND 234 Kf 34
Khartoum ▣ SUD 312 Hj 38
Khartoum North O SUD 312 Hj 38
Khashm al-Qirba O SUD 313 Hk 38
Khashm alQirba Dam ~ SUD 313 Hk 38
Khāsi-Jaintia Hills ⛰ IND 235 Kk 33
Khatal O IND 234 Kf 33
Khatanskiy Zaliv ≈ RUS 204 Va 4
Khātegaon O IND 234 Kc 34
Khatoli O IND 234 Kb 33
Khatt et Toueïrja ~ RIM 304 Fn 36
Khaudum O NAM 340 Hc 55
Khaudum ~ NAM 340 Hc 55
Khaur O PK 230 Ka 29
Khāvda O IND 227 Jn 34
Khazzān ar-Ruṣayriṣ ~ SUD 313 Hk 40
Khed O IND 238 Ka 37
Kheda O IND 227 Ka 34
Khemis-des-Zemamra O MA 292 Gb 29
Khemis Miliana O DZ 296 Gh 27
Khemisset O MA 293 Gc 29
Khemmarat O THA 263 Lc 37
Khenchela O DZ 296 Gk 28
Khenifra O MA 293 Gd 29
Kherālu O IND 227 Ka 34
Kherba O DZ 293 Gg 27
Kheri O IND 234 Kc 35
Kherrata O DZ 296 Gj 27
Kherson O UA 175 Hj 22
Kherwara O IND 227 Ka 34
Khe Sanh O VN 263 Ld 37
Khett Atoui ~ RIM 304 Fn 35
Khe Ve O VN 263 Lc 37
Khewra O PK 230 Ka 29
Khipro O PK 227 Jn 33
Khiu O PK 227 Jp 30
Khiva O UZB 222 Jj 25
Khlong Ngae O THA 270 La 42
Khlong Thom O THA 270 Kp 42
Khobi O GE 202 Hn 24
Khodoriv O UA 175 He 21
Khok Chang O THA 263 Lb 37
Khok Kloi O THA 262 Kn 41
Khok Pho O THA 270 La 42
Khok Samrong O THA 262 La 38
Khomas Highland ⛰ NAM 348 Ha 57
Khome Island ⌂ EAU 336 Hj 46
Khomeynišahr O IR 222 Jd 29
Khon O THA 262 Kp 37
Khondmal Hills ⛰ IND 234 Kf 36
Khong Chiam O THA 263 Lc 38
Khong Khi Sua O THA 262 La 38
Khon Kaen O THA 263 Lb 37
Khor Abū Sunt ~ SUD 312 Hh 35
Khor Adar ~ SUD 324 Hj 41
Khor' Angar O DJI 313 Hp 39
Khorāsān ⊙ IR 222 Jg 28
Khorasgān O IR 222 Jd 29
Khor Baraka ~ SUD 313 Hl 37
Khordha O IND 235 Kg 35
Khor Duleyb ~ SUD 313 Hj 40
Khor Fakkan O UAE 226 Jg 33
Khor Gandze O VRC 242 Kp 30
Khorixas O NAM 348 Gp 56
Khor Nyanding ~ SUD 324 Hj 41
Khorramābād O IR 209 Jc 29
Khorramshahr O IR 215 Jc 30
Khor Tumat ~ SUD 313 Hk 40
Khorug O TJ 223 Jp 27
Khor Veveno ~ SUD 324 Hj 42
Khossanto O SN 316 Fp 39
Khost O PK 227 Jm 30
Khotol Mountain △ USA 46 Al 13
Khouribga O MA 293 Gc 29
Khreum O MYA 254 Kl 35
Khuang Nai O THA 263 Lc 38
Khubus O ZA 348 Ha 60
Khuchinarai O THA 263 Lc 37
Khudabad O PK 230 Kb 27
Khudiān O PK 230 Kb 30
Khudžand O TJ 223 Jn 25
Khukhan O THA 263 Lc 38
Khulna O BD 235 Kj 34
Khumaga O RB 349 He 56
Khunaniwāla O PK 227 Jp 30
Khunti O IND 235 Kg 34
Khun Yuam O THA 254 Kn 36
Khuraburi O THA 262 Kp 41
Khurai O IND 234 Kd 33
Khurayt O SUD 312 Hf 39
Khurja O IND 234 Kc 31
Khushāb O PK 230 Ka 29
Khuwei O SUD 312 Hg 39
Khuzdār O PK 227 Jm 32
Khwazakhela O PK 223 Jp 28
Khyber Pass ★ AFG 223 Jp 28
Khyriv O UA 175 Hd 21
Kia O SOL 290 Nb 49
Kia ⌂ FJI 387 Nm 54
Kiakalamu O RDC 336 Hf 50
Kiama O AUS 379 Mm 63
Kiamba O RP 275 Ln 43
Kiambere Reservoir ~ EAK 337 Hl 46
Kiambi O RDC 336 Hg 49
Kiambu O EAK 337 Hl 46
Kiamichi ~ USA 70 Da 28
Kiamichi Mountain ⛰ USA 70 Da 28
Kiampanjang O RI 274 Lj 44
Kiana O USA 46 Aj 11
Kiana O AUS 364 Me 54
Kiandarat O RI 283 Mb 47
Kiandra O AUS 379 Ml 63
Kiangdom O IND 230 Kd 29
Kiangwe ~ RDC 336 Hf 48
Kiantjärvi ~ FIN 159 Hg 13
Kia Ora O AUS 378 Mf 62
Kiáto O GR 194 Hd 26
Kiau Point ⌓ PNG 287 Mk 48
Kibaha O EAT 337 Hm 49
Kibakwe O EAT 337 Hl 49
Kibala O ANG 332 Gn 49
Kibali ~ RDC 324 Hg 44
Kibandi O RDC 332 Gn 48
Kibangou O RCB 332 Gm 47
Kibau O EAT 337 Hk 50
Kibawe O RP 275 Ln 42
Kibaya O EAT 337 Hl 48
Kibbanahalli O IND 238 Kc 39
Kibene O PNG 286 Mh 49
Kiberege O EAT 337 Hl 49
Kibi O GH 317 Gf 42
Kibish O SUD 325 Hk 43
Kibiti O EAT 337 Hm 49
Kibiya O WAN 320 Gl 40
Kibo △ EAT 337 Hl 47
Kiboga O EAU 324 Hh 45
Kiboko ~ EAK 337 Hl 47
Kibombo O RDC 333 He 47
Kibondo O EAT 336 Hh 47
Kibraj O UZB 223 Jn 25
Kibre Mengist O ETH 325 Hm 43
Kıbrıscık O TR 195 Hh 25
Kibungo O RWA 336 Hh 47
Kibunzi O RDC 332 Gn 48
Kibuye O RWA 336 Hg 47
Kibwesa O EAT 336 Hg 49
Kibwezi O EAK 337 Hl 47
Kičevo O MK 194 Hc 25
Kichčik O RUS 23 Sb 4
Kichha O IND 234 Kd 31
Kichimiloo ~ AUS 375 Mj 60
Kichwamba O EAU 336 Hh 46
Kickapoo Indian Reservation ••• USA 70 Da 26
Kickene Özen ~ KZ 181 Jc 21
Kičmengskij Gorodok O RUS 154 Ra 7
Kidal O RMM 305 Gg 36
Kidapawan O RP 275 Ln 42
Kidatu O EAT 337 Hl 49
Kidd's Beach O ZA 358 Hf 62
Kidepo ~ SUD 325 Hj 43
Kidepo National Park ♀ SUD 325 Hj 44
Kidete O EAT 337 Hl 49
Kidira O SN 304 Fp 38
Kidston O AUS 365 Mj 55
Kiel O D 170 Gm 18
Kielce O PL 174 Hc 20
Kieler Bucht ~ D 170 Gm 18
Kiembara O BF 317 Ge 39
Kienge O RDC 341 Hf 51
Kiên Lu'o'ng O VN 263 Lc 40
Kieta O PNG 290 Mp 49
Kiev ▣ UA 175 Hg 20
Kievka ~ RUS 250 Mc 24
Kiev Reservoir ~ UA 175 Hh 20
Kifaya O RG 316 Fp 39
Kiffa O RIM 304 Ga 37
Kifingi O RDC 336 Hf 50
Kifissiá O GR 194 Hd 26
Kifrī O IRQ 209 Ja 28
Kifuankese O RDC 333 Hd 48
Kifusa O RDC 333 He 49
Kigač ~ KZ 202 Jc 22
Kigali ▣ RWA 336 Hh 46
Kiğı O TR 202 Hn 26
Kigille O SUD 325 Hk 41
Kignan O RMM 317 Gd 40
Kigoma O EAT 336 Hg 48
Kigosi ~ EAT 336 Hh 47
Kigumo O EAK 337 Hl 46
Kihei O USA 75 Am 35
Kihelkona O EST 170 Hc 16
Kihikihi O NZ 383 Nk 65
Kihnu ⌂ EST 171 Hd 16
Kihurio O EAT 337 Hl 48
Kii-hantō ⌂ J 251 Md 29
Kiiminki O FIN 159 Hf 13
Kii-Nagashima O J 251 Me 28
Kii-sanchi ⛰ J 251 Md 29
Kii-suidō ~ J 251 Md 29
Kijabé O EAK 337 Hl 46
Kijang O RI 271 Lc 45
Kijiado O EAK 337 Hl 46
Kijungu O EAT 337 Hl 48
Kika O DY 320 Gh 41
Kikagati O EAU 336 Hh 46
Kikai-shima ⌂ J 259 Mb 31
Kikale O EAT 337 Hm 49
Kikamba O RDC 336 Hf 47
Kikambala O EAK 337 Hm 47
Kikinda O SCG 174 Hc 23
Kikole O RDC 336 Hg 50
Kikombo O EAT 337 Hk 49
Kikonai O J 250 Mg 25
Kikondja O RDC 336 Hf 50
Kikori O PNG 287 Mj 49
Kikori River ~ PNG 287 Mh 49
Kikwit O RDC 333 Hb 48
Kilaguni O EAK 337 Hm 47
Kilakkarai O IND 239 Kd 41
Kilala O EAK 337 Hl 47
Kilauea Crater ★ USA 75 An 36
Kilauea Lighthouse ★ USA 75 Al 34
Kilboghamn O N 158 Gn 12
Kilbuck Mountains ⛰ USA 46 Al 15
Kilchipur O IND 234 Kc 33
Kilcoy O AUS 375 Mn 59
Kildare O IRL 163 Gc 19
Kildonan O ZW 341 Hh 54
Kildurk O AUS 364 Ma 54
Kilembe O RDC 333 Hb 48
Kilembe O RDC 336 Hf 49
Kilembi O RDC 336 Hf 48
Kilembwe O RDC 341 Hf 51
Kileo O RDC 333 He 48
Kilgore O USA 70 Da 29
Kilgoris O EAK 337 Hk 46
Kilia O PNG 287 Mm 50
Kiliba O RDC 336 Hg 47
Kilibo O DY 317 Gh 41
Kili Bulak O VRC 231 Kl 29
Kilifas O PNG 286 Mg 47
Kilifi O EAK 337 Hm 47
Kilija O UA 175 Hg 23
Kilikkollūr O IND 239 Kc 41
Kilim O TCH 321 Hb 40
Kilimanjaro ♀ EAT 337 Hl 47
Kilimatinde O EAT 337 Hk 48
Kilinailau Islands ⌂ PNG 290 Mp 48
Kilindoni O EAT 337 Hm 49
Kilingi-Nõmme O EST 171 He 16
Kilíni O GR 194 Hc 27
Kilis O TR 195 Hl 27
Kiliuda Bay ≈ USA 46 An 17
Kilju O DVRK 247 Ma 25
Kilkee O IRL 163 Gb 19
Kilkenny O IRL 163 Gc 19
Kilkís O GR 194 Hd 25
Killaloe Station O CDN 60 Dj 23
Killaly O CDN 51 Cl 20
Killam O CDN 51 Cg 19
Killarney O AUS 375 Mj 57
Killarney O CDN 56 Cn 21
Killarney O CDN 57 Dh 23
Killarney O IRL 163 Gb 19
Killarney O AUS 364 Mb 54
Killarney Prov. Park ♀ CDN 57 Dh 22
Killdeer O CDN 51 Cj 21
Killdeer O USA 51 Cl 22
Killeen O USA 81 Cp 30
Killin O GB 162 Gd 17
Kilmarnock O GB 162 Gd 18
Kilmore O AUS 379 Mj 64
Kilogbe O WAN 320 Gh 40
Kilokaka O SOL 290 Nb 50
Kilombero ~ EAT 337 Hl 50
Kilosa O EAT 337 Hl 49
Kilpisjärvi O FIN 159 Hc 11
Kilrush O IRL 163 Gb 19
Kiluan O RI 278 Lc 48
Kilubi ~ RDC 336 He 50
Kilubi O RDC 336 Hf 48
Kilunguye ~ RDC 336 Hf 48
Kilwa O RDC 336 Hg 50
Kilwa Kivinje O EAT 337 Hm 50
Kilwa Masoko O EAT 337 Hm 50

432 Kāzi Ahmad - Kilwa Masoko

Kilwat ○ RI 283 Mc 48
Kim ○ USA 65 Cl 27
Kim ~ CAM 320 Gm 43
Kim ○ TCH 321 Gp 41
Kimaan ○ RI 286 Mf 50
Kimamba ○ EAT 337 Hl 49
Kimana ○ EAK 337 Hl 47
Kimano II ○ RDC 336 Hg 48
Kimba ○ RCB 332 Gp 47
Kimba ○ AUS 365 Mh 53
Kimba ○ AUS 378 Me 62
Kimball ○ USA 56 Cn 24
Kimball ○ USA 56 Da 23
Kimball ○ USA 65 Cl 25
Kimbao ○ RDC 333 Ha 48
Kimbe ○ PNG 287 Ml 48
Kimbe Bay ~ PNG 287 Mm 48
Kimberley ○ CDN 50 Cd 21
Kimberley ○ ZA 349 He 60
Kimberley Aboriginal Land ••• AUS 361 Lp 53
Kimberley Downs ○ AUS 361 Ln 54
Kimberley Plateau ⛰ AUS 361 Ln 54
Kimbirila Sud ○ CI 316 Gb 41
Kimchaek ○ DVRK 247 Ma 25
Kimenga ~ RCB 332 Gn 47
Kími ○ GR 194 He 26
Kimilili ○ EAK 325 Hk 45
Kimisi ○ EAT 336 Hh 47
Kimjongsuk-up ○ DVRK 247 Lp 25
Kimobetsu ○ J 250 Mg 24
Kimongo ○ RCB 332 Gn 48
Kimovsk ○ RUS 181 Hm 19
Kimparana ○ RMM 317 Gd 39
Kimpese ○ RDC 332 Gp 48
Kimry ○ RUS 171 Hl 17
Kim So'n ○ VN 255 Ld 35
Kīmūn al-Maṭā'ina ○ ET 301 Hh 33
Kimuta Island 🏝 PNG 287 Mn 51
Kimvula ○ RDC 332 Gp 48
Kin ○ J 259 Lp 32
Kina ○ RDC 336 Hf 50
Kinabalu ⚲ MAL 274 Lj 42
Kinabatangan ~ MAL 274 Lj 43
Kinangaly △ RM 345 Ja 55
Kinango ○ EAK 337 Hm 48
Kinara ○ RI 283 Mc 47
Kinbasket Lake ~ CDN 50 Cc 19
Kincaid ○ CDN 51 Cj 21
Kincardine ○ CDN 57 Dg 23
Kinchega ⚲ AUS 378 Mh 62
Kinchil ○ MEX 93 Dc 35
Kinda ○ RDC 336 He 50
Kindamba ○ RCB 332 Gp 47
Kindeje ○ ANG 332 Gn 49
Kinder ○ USA 86 Db 30
Kindersley ○ CDN 51 Ch 20
Kindi ○ BF 317 Ge 39
Kindi ○ RDC 333 Ha 48
Kindia ○ RG 316 Fp 40
Kindu ○ RDC 333 He 47
Kinel' ○ RUS 181 Jd 19
Kinel' Čerkasy ○ RUS 181 Jd 19
Kinel'skie jary ⛰ RUS 181 Jd 19
Kineshma ○ RUS 171 Hp 17
Kinesi ○ EAT 337 Hj 46
King ~ AUS 379 Mk 64
Kinga ○ RDC 341 Hd 51
Kinganga ○ RDC 332 Gn 48
Kingani ○ RCB 332 Gn 47
Kingaroy ○ AUS 375 Mm 59
King Ash Bay ○ AUS 364 Me 53
King Christian Island 🏝 CDN 42 Fa 3
King City ○ USA 64 Cb 27
King Cove ○ USA 46 Aj 17
King Edward ~ AUS 361 Lp 53
King Edward VIII Bay ≈ 38 Na 16
Kingfisher ○ USA 70 Cp 28
Kingfisher Island 🏝 AUS 361 Ln 54
King George Bay ~ GB 147 Ed 71
King Georg Sound ~ AUS 368 Lk 63
Kingisepp ○ RUS 171 Hg 16
King Island 🏝 CDN 50 Bn 19
King Island 🏝 USA 205 Ac 6
King Island 🏝 AUS 379 Mj 65
Kingissseppa ○ EST 170 Hd 16
King Junction ○ AUS 365 Mh 53
King Lear △ USA 64 Cc 25
King Leopold Ranges ⛰ AUS 361 Ln 54
Kingman ○ USA 64 Ce 28
Kingman ○ USA 70 Cn 27
Kingombe ○ RDC 333 He 47
Kingombe ○ RDC 336 Hf 47
Kingoonya ○ AUS 378 Md 61
Kingoué ○ RCB 332 Gn 47
Kingri ○ PK 227 Jn 30
King Salmon ○ USA 46 Al 15
Kingsburg ○ ZA 349 Hh 61
Kings Canyon ⚲ USA 64 Cc 27
Kings Canyon ⚲ AUS 369 Mb 58
Kingscote ○ ZA 349 Hg 61
Kingscote ○ AUS 378 Me 63
Kings Cove ○ CDN 61 Eh 21
Kingsford ○ USA 57 Dd 23
Kingslake ⚲ AUS 379 Mj 64
Kingsland ○ USA 87 Dh 30
Kings Landing Hist. Settlement ★ CDN 60 Ea 23
Kingsley ○ ZA 352 Hh 60
Kings-Mountain ○ USA 71 Dh 28
King Sound ~ AUS 361 Lm 54
Kings Peak △ USA 65 Cg 25
Kingsport ○ USA 71 Dg 27
Kings's Lynn ○ GB 163 Gg 19
Kingston ○ CDN 60 Dk 23
Kingston ○ USA 74 Dm 25
Kingston ▣ JA 101 Dk 36
Kingston ○ AUS 378 Mk 67
Kingston S.E. ○ AUS 378 Mf 64
Kingston-upon Hull ○ GB 163 Gf 19
Kingstown ▣ WV 104 Ed 39
Kingstree ○ USA 87 Dj 29
Kingsville ○ USA 81 Cp 32
Kingswood ○ USA 74 Dj 26
Kingswood ○ ZA 349 He 59
Kingungi ○ RDC 333 Ha 48
Kingwaya ○ RDC 333 Ha 48
King William Island 🏝 CDN 42 Fb 5
King Williams Town ○ LB 316 Gb 43
King William's Town ○ ZA 358 Hf 62
Kingwood ○ USA 74 Dj 26
Kingwood ○ USA 81 Da 31
Kiniama ○ RDC 341 Hg 51
Kınık ○ TR 195 Hf 26
Kinim ○ PNG 287 Mj 48
Kinirapoort ○ ZA 349 Hg 61
Kinjhar Lake ~ PK 227 Jm 33
Kinkala ○ RCB 332 Gp 48
Kinkasan-Shima ⌓ J 251 Mg 26
Kinkosi ○ RDC 332 Gp 48
Kinmundy ○ USA 71 Dd 26
Kinna ○ S 170 Gn 17
Kinna ○ EAK 325 Hm 45
Kinnaird Head △ GB 162 Ge 17
Kinnear ○ USA 51 Cj 24
Kinniya ○ CL 239 Ke 41
Kino-gawa ~ J 251 Md 28
Kinomoto ○ J 251 Me 28
Kinoosao ○ CDN 42 Fa 7
Kinrara ○ AUS 365 Mj 55
Kinsarvik ○ N 158 Gk 15
Kinshasa ▣ RDC 332 Gp 48
Kinsley ○ USA 70 Cn 27
Kinston ○ USA 74 Dk 28
Kintampo ○ GH 317 Gf 41
Kintap ○ RI 279 Lh 47
Kintinnian ○ RG 316 Gb 40
Kintyre 🏝 GB 162 Gc 18
Kinwat ○ IND 238 Kc 36
Kinyeti △ SUD 324 Hj 44
Kinyinya ○ BU 336 Hh 47
Kioa 🏝 FJI 387 Nm 54
Kiokluk Mountains ⛰ USA 46 Al 15
Kiosk ○ CDN 60 Dj 22
Kiowa ○ USA 65 Ck 26
Kiowa ○ USA 70 Cn 27
Kiowa ○ USA 70 Cp 28
Kipaila ○ RDC 336 Hg 49
Kipaka ○ RDC 336 Hf 48
Kiparissía ○ GR 194 Hc 27
Kipemba ○ RDC 332 Gp 48
Kipembawe ○ EAT 337 Hj 49
Kipengere Range ⛰ EAT 337 Hj 50
Kipili ○ EAT 336 Hh 49
Kipini ○ EAK 337 Hn 47
Kipkelion ○ EAK 337 Hk 46
Kipling ○ CDN 51 Cl 20
Kipnuk ○ USA 46 Ag 15
Kipti ○ UA 175 Hh 20
Kipushi ○ RDC 341 Hf 51
Kipushia ○ RDC 341 Hg 52
Kirakira ○ SOL 290 Nc 51
Kirandul ○ IND 238 Ke 36
Kirané ○ RIM 304 Ga 38
Kiranomena ○ RM 345 Jb 55
Kiranūr ○ IND 238 Kd 40
Kirā Panagia 🏝 GR 194 He 26
Kirbyville ○ USA 86 Db 30
Kireevsk ○ RUS 181 Hl 19
Kirenga ~ RUS 204 Va 7
Kirensk ○ RUS 204 Va 7
Kiri ○ RDC 333 Hb 46
Kiriab ○ RI 286 Me 46
Kiriaini ○ EAK 337 Hl 46
Kiribati ◻ KIR 27 Aa10
Kırıkhan ○ TR 195 Hl 27
Kırıkkale ○ TR 195 Hj 26
Kirillov ○ RUS 171 Hm 16
Kirillovo ○ RUS 250 Mh 22
Kirinda ○ CL 239 Ke 42
Kirishima-yaku ★ J 247 Mb 30
Kiriši ○ RUS 171 Hj 16
Kirit ○ SP 328 Jb 41
Kiritappu ○ J 250 Mj 24
Kiritimati 🏝 KIR 14 Ba 9
Kiriwina Island 🏝 PNG 287 Mm 50
Kirkalocka ○ AUS 368 Lj 60
Kirkcaldy ○ GB 162 Ge 17
Kirkenes ○ N 159 Hg 11
Kirkimbie ○ AUS 364 Ma 54
Kirkland ○ USA 50 Ca 22
Kirkland Lake ○ CDN 60 Dj 21
Kırklareli ○ TR 195 Hf 25
Kirksville ○ USA 70 Db 25
Kirkūk ○ IRQ 209 Ja 28
Kirkvollen ○ N 158 Gm 14
Kirkwall ○ GB 162 Ge 16
Kirkwood ○ USA 71 Dc 26
Kirkwood ○ ZA 358 He 62
Kırobası ○ TR 195 Hj 27
Kirov ○ RUS 171 Hk 18
Kirovo-Čepeck ○ RUS 154 Rb 7
Kirovohrad ○ UA 175 Hh 21
Kirovsk ○ RUS 159 Hj 12
Kirovsk ○ RUS 171 Hh 16
Kirovs'ke ○ UA 175 Hk 23
Kirovskij ○ RUS 23 Sb 4
Kirovskij ○ RUS 202 Jc 23
Kirovskij ○ TJ 223 Jn 27
Kirovskij ○ RUS 250 Mc 23
Kirpili ~ RUS 202 Hm 23
Kirsanov ○ RUS 181 Hp 19
Kırşehir ○ TR 195 Hk 26
Kirtachi ○ RN 320 Gh 39
Kirtāka ○ AFG 227 Jf 30
Kirthar ⚲ PK 227 Jm 33
Kirthar Range ⛰ PK 227 Jm 32
Kiru ○ WAN 320 Gl 40
Kiruk ○ RI 286 Mf 50
Kiruna ○ S 159 Hb 12
Kirundo ○ BU 336 Hh 47
Kirundu ○ RDC 333 He 46
Kirwin Reservation ~ USA 70 Cn 26
Kiryandongo ○ EAU 324 Hh 45
Kiryū ○ J 251 Mf 27
Kiržač ○ RUS 171 Hm 17
Kiš ○ IR 215 Je 32
Kisa ○ S 170 Gp 17
Kisa ○ RDC 336 Hg 46
Kisaki ○ EAT 337 Hl 49
Kisanga ○ RDC 324 Hf 44
Kisanga ○ EAT 337 Hl 49
Kisangani ○ RDC 324 He 45
Kisangire ○ EAT 337 Hm 49
Kisantete ○ RDC 333 Ha 48
Kisantu ○ RDC 332 Gp 48
Kisaran ○ RI 270 Kp 44
Kisarawe ○ EAT 337 Hm 49
Kisarazu ○ J 251 Mf 28
Kisasi ○ EAT 337 Hm 48
Kiselëvsk ○ RUS 204 Tc 8
Kisenge ○ RDC 341 Hd 51
Kisengwa ○ RDC 336 Hf 48
Kisha ○ RB 349 Hd 58
Kishanganj ○ IND 235 Kh 32
Kishangar ○ IND 227 Jp 32
Kishangarh ○ IND 234 Kb 32
Kishangarh ○ IND 234 Kd 33
Kishinde ○ RDC 333 He 49
Kishiwada ○ J 251 Md 28
Kishtwar ○ IND 230 Kb 29
Kiši ○ WAN 320 Gh 41
Kisigo ~ EAT 337 Hk 49
Kisii ○ EAT 336 Hh 49
Kisii ○ EAK 337 Hk 46
Kisiju ○ EAT 337 Hm 49
Kisima ○ EAK 325 Hl 45
Kisiwani ○ EAT 337 Hl 48
Kiska Island 🏝 USA 23 Tb 4
Kiskőrös ○ H 174 Hb 22
Kiskunfélegyháza ○ H 174 Hb 22
Kiskunhalas ○ H 174 Hb 22
Kislino ○ RUS 171 Hg 16
Kislovodsk ○ RUS 202 Hp 24
Kismaayo ○ SP 329 Hp 46
Kisogwa ○ EAT 336 Hh 47
Kisomoro ○ EAU 324 Hh 45
Kisoro ○ EAU 336 Hg 46
Kiso-sammyaku ⛰ J 251 Me 28
Kisose ○ RDC 333 He 49
Kissen ~ RG 316 Fp 40
Kissidougou ○ RG 316 Ga 41
Kissimmee ○ USA 87 Dh 31
Kistanje ○ HR 174 Gp 23
Kisuki ○ J 251 Mc 28
Kisumu ○ EAK 337 Hk 46
Kisvárda ○ H 174 Hd 21
Kita ○ RMM 316 Gb 39
Kitāf ○ YE 218 Ja 37
Kitahiyama ○ J 250 Mf 24
Kitaibaraki ○ J 251 Mg 27
Kitakami ○ J 250 Mg 26
Kitakami ~ J 250 Mg 26
Kitakami-kōti ⛰ J 250 Mg 26
Kitakata ○ J 251 Mf 27
Kitakyūshū ○ J 247 Mb 29
Kitale ○ EAK 325 Hk 45
Kitambwe ○ RDC 333 He 47
Kitami ○ J 250 Mh 24
Kitami-sammyaku ⛰ J 250 Mh 23
Kitanda ○ RDC 336 Hf 49
Kitangari ○ EAT 344 Hm 51
Kitani ○ EAK 337 Hl 47
Kitava Island 🏝 PNG 287 Mm 50
Kitaya ○ EAT 344 Hm 51
Kit Carson ○ USA 65 Cl 26
Kitchener ○ CDN 57 Dh 24
Kitchener ○ AUS 369 Ln 61
Kitchigama ~ CDN 60 Dj 20
Kiteba ○ RDC 333 He 49
Kitee ○ FIN 159 Hh 14
Kitendwe ○ RDC 336 Hg 49
Kitenga ○ RDC 333 Ha 48
Kitenge ○ RDC 336 Hf 46
Kitengo ○ RDC 333 He 49
Kitgum ○ EAU 324 Hj 44
Kithira ○ GR 194 Hd 27
Kíthnos 🏝 GR 194 He 27
Kitika ○ RCA 321 Hd 43
Kitimat ○ CDN 42 Db 8
Kitinen ~ FIN 159 Hf 12
Kitiwak ~ EAT 337 Hk 50
Kitlilā ○ FIN 159 He 12
Kitmore Range ⛰ AUS 361 Ma 57
Kitob ○ UZB 223 Jm 26
Kitou ○ J 251 Md 29
Kitsamby ~ RM 345 Jb 55
Kitsuki ○ J 247 Mb 29
Kittanning ○ USA 74 Dj 25
Kitt Peak National Observatory ★ USA 65 Cf 29
Kitty Hawk ○ USA 74 Dl 27
Kitui ○ EAK 337 Hm 46
Kitunda ○ EAT 337 Hj 49
Kitungu ○ RDC 336 He 50
Kitutu ○ RDC 336 Hf 47
Kitwe ○ Z 341 Hg 52
Kitzbühel ○ A 174 Gn 22
Kiu ○ EAK 337 Hl 46
Kiu Lem Reservoir ~ THA 254 Kp 36
Kiunga ○ PNG 286 Mg 49
Kiunga ○ EAK 337 Hn 46
Kiuruvesi ○ FIN 159 Hf 14
Kivalina ○ USA 46 Ag 11
Kivalina River ~ USA 46 Ag 11
Kiviõli ○ EST 171 Hf 16
Kivori-Kui ○ PNG 287 Mk 50
Kiwaba N'zogi ○ ANG 340 Ha 50
Kiwai Island 🏝 PNG 286 Mh 50
Kiwayuu Bay ~ EAK 337 Hn 47
Kiwele ○ RDC 341 Hg 51
Kiwijärvi ~ FIN 159 He 14
Kiyāmaki Dāğ △ IR 209 Ja 26
Kiyāsar ○ IR 222 Je 27
Kiyāt ○ KSA 218 Hn 36
Kiyawa ○ WAN 320 Gl 40
Kizhake Chalakudi ○ IND 239 Kc 40
Kızılcahamam ○ TR 195 Hj 25
Kızılırmak ~ TR 195 Hj 25
Kizil'jurt ○ RUS 202 Jb 24
Kizil Kaja ○ TM 222 Jf 25
Kiziltašskij liman ~ RUS 195 Hl 23
Kızıltepe ○ TR 202 Hn 27
Kizimkazi ○ EAT 337 Hm 49
Kizi Pogost ★ RUS 159 Hk 14
Kizljar ○ RUS 202 Jb 24
Kizljarskij zaliv ~ RUS 202 Jb 23
Kizyl Atrek ○ TM 222 Jf 27
Kizyl Baudak ○ TM 222 Jh 24
Kjalvaz ○ AZ 202 Jc 26
Kjascicy ○ BY 171 Hg 18
Kjøllefjord ○ N 159 Hf 10
Kjøpsvik ○ N 158 Ha 11
Kjusjur ○ RUS 204 Wb 4
Kjustendil ○ BG 194 Hd 24
Klaarstroom ○ ZA 358 Hd 62
Kladanj ○ BIH 174 Hb 23
Kladar ○ RI 286 Me 50
Kladno ○ CZ 174 Gn 20
Klaeng ○ THA 262 La 39
Klagenfurt ○ A 174 Gp 22
Klain Swartberge ⛰ ZA 358 Hc 62
Klaipėda ○ LT 170 Hc 18
Klakah ○ RI 279 Lg 49
Klamath ○ USA 64 Bp 25
Klamath ~ USA 64 Ca 25
Klamath Falls ○ USA 50 Cb 24
Klamath Mountains ⛰ USA 64 Ca 25
Klampo ○ RI 274 Lj 45
k-l Aralsor ~ KZ 181 Jb 21
Klarälven ~ S 158 Gn 15
Klaten ○ RI 278 Lf 49
Klatovy ○ CZ 174 Gn 21
Klawer ○ ZA 348 Hb 61
Klay ○ LB 316 Ga 42
Klein Aub ○ NAM 348 Ha 57
Kleinbegin ○ ZA 349 Hc 60
Kleine Sundainseln 🏝 RI 279 Lj 49
Klein-Karas ○ NAM 348 Hb 59
Klein Letaba ~ ZA 352 Hh 57
Klein Nauas ○ NAM 348 Ha 57
Kleinpoort ○ ZA 358 He 62
Kleinsee ○ ZA 348 Ha 60
Klekovača △ BIH 174 Ha 23
Kléla ○ RMM 317 Gd 40
Klerksdorp ○ ZA 349 Hf 59
Klésso ○ BF 317 Gd 40
Kletnja ○ RUS 171 Hj 19
Kleve ○ D 163 Gk 20
Klickitat ~ USA 50 Cb 22
Klimavichy ○ BY 171 Hh 19
Klimovsk ○ RUS 171 Hl 18
Klimpfjäll ○ S 158 Gp 13
Klin ○ RUS 171 Hl 17
Klina ○ SCG 194 Hc 24
Klincy ○ RUS 171 Hh 19
Klinghardsberg ⛰ NAM 348 Gp 59
Klinochchi ○ CL 239 Ke 41
Klínovec △ CZ 174 Gn 20
Klinsko-Dmitrovskaja grjada ⛰ RUS 171 Hk 17
Klintehamn ○ S 170 Ha 17
Klipfontein ○ ZA 358 He 62
Klippberget △ S 158 Hb 13
Klipplaat ○ ZA 358 He 62
Kliprand ○ ZA 348 Hb 61
Kliprivier ~ ZA 349 Hg 59
Klis ○ HR 194 Ha 24
Klis ○ RI 283 Lp 50
Kljavino ○ RUS 181 Jd 18
Kljaz'ma ~ RUS 171 Hn 17
Ključ ○ BIH 174 Ha 23
Ključi ○ RUS 202 Hm 23
Ključi ○ RUS 205 Yc 7
Kłodzko ○ PL 174 Ha 20
Klondike Region ⏜ USA 46 Be 13
Klosterneuburg ○ A 174 Gp 21
K-l Tudakul ~ UZB 223 Jl 26
Kluane ○ CDN 47 Bg 15
Kluane Lake ~ CDN 47 Bg 15
Kluane Natural Park ⚲ CDN 47 Bg 15
Kluang ○ MAL 271 Lb 44
Kluczbork ○ PL 174 Hb 20
Kludang ○ BRU 274 Lh 43
Klungkung ○ RI 279 Lh 50
Klymovo ○ RUS 171 Hj 19
k-l Žaltyr ~ KZ 202 Jd 22
Knarvik ○ N 158 Gj 15
Knewstubb Lake ~ CDN 42 Dc 8
Kneža ○ BG 194 He 24
Knight Inlet ~ CDN 50 Bn 20
Knight Island 🏝 USA 46 Bc 15
Knin ○ HR 174 Ha 23
Knippa ○ USA 81 Cn 31
Knjaginino ○ RUS 181 Ja 18
Knjaževac ○ SCG 194 Hd 24
Knobby Head ⌓ AUS 368 Lh 60
Knokke-Heist ○ B 163 Gh 20
Knox ○ USA 71 De 25
Knox Coast ⏜ 38 Qa 16
Knoxville ○ USA 70 Db 25
Knoxville ○ USA 71 Df 27
Knoxville ○ USA 86 Df 29
Knud Rasmussen Land ⏜ DK 7 Fb 2
Knud Rasmussen Land ⏜ DK 43 Hc 3
Knutshø △ N 158 Gl 14
Knysna ○ ZA 358 Hd 63
Knysna National Lake Area ⚲ ZA 358 Hd 63
Ko ⛰ RUS 250 Me 22
Koaba ○ DY 317 Gg 40
Koalla ○ BF 317 Gf 39
Koamb ○ CAM 321 Gn 44
Koaru ○ PNG 287 Mj 50
Koba ○ RI 278 Ld 47
Kobe ○ J 251 Md 28
Kobe ○ RI 275 Lp 45
Kobeľaky ○ UA 175 Hk 21
Kobenni ○ RIM 304 Gb 38
Kobi ○ RI 283 Ma 47
Kobi ○ CAM 321 Gp 43
Koblagué ○ TCH 321 Ha 41
Koblenz ○ D 163 Gk 20
Kobli ○ DY 317 Gg 40
K'obo ○ ETH 313 Hm 39
Kobona ○ RUS 171 Hh 15
Kobou ○ BF 305 Gf 38
Kobovashi ○ J 247 Mb 30
Kobryn ○ BY 171 He 19
Kobuk ○ USA 46 Al 11
Kobuk River ~ USA 46 An 11
Kobuk Valley National Park ⚲ USA 46 Aj 11
K'obulet'i ○ GE 202 Hn 25
Koca ~ TR 195 Hg 25
Kocaeli İzmit ○ TR 195 Hg 25
Kocaeli Yarımmadası ⌓ TR 195 Hg 25
Kočani ○ MK 194 Hd 25
Koçarlı ○ TR 194 Hf 27
Kočečum ~ RUS 204 Uc 5
Kočetovka ○ RUS 181 Hm 19
Kočevje ○ SLO 174 Gp 23
Kŏch'ang ○ ROK 247 Lp 28
Ko Chang ⚲ THA 262 La 39
Ko Chang 🏝 THA 262 La 40
Koch Bihar ○ IND 235 Kj 32
Kochi ○ J 251 Mc 29
Koch Island 🏝 CDN 43 Gc 5
Kocjubyns'ke ○ UA 175 Hg 20
Kočkoma ○ RUS 159 Hj 13
Kočubej ○ RUS 202 Jb 23
Kodār ○ IND 238 Kd 37
Kodari ○ NEP 235 Kg 32
Kodarma ○ IND 235 Kg 33
Kodi ○ RI 279 Lk 50
Kodiak ○ USA 10 Ba 4
Kodiak ○ USA 46 An 17
Kodiak Island 🏝 USA 46 An 17
Kodibeleng ○ RB 349 He 57
Kodina ~ RUS 159 Hm 14
Kodinar ○ IND 227 Jp 35
Kodino ○ RUS 159 Hm 14
Kodjari ○ BF 317 Gg 40
Kodok ○ SUD 324 Hj 41
Koébonou ○ CI 317 Ge 41
Koēs ○ NAM 348 Hb 58
Kofa Mountains ⛰ USA 64 Ce 29
Kofarnikhon ○ TJ 223 Jn 26
Koffiefontein ○ ZA 349 He 60
Koforidua ○ GH 317 Gf 42
Kōfu ○ J 251 Mf 28
Koga ○ J 251 Mf 27
Kogalym ○ RUS 154 Sc 6
Kogalym ○ RUS 204 Sc 6
Kogan ○ AUS 375 Mm 59
Køge ○ DK 170 Gn 18
Køge Bugt ~ DK 170 Gn 18
Kogon ~ RG 316 Fn 40
Kogon ~ RG 316 Fp 40
Koğür ○ IR 222 Jd 27
Kohan ○ PK 227 Jm 31
Kohāt ○ PK 223 Jp 29
Kohila ○ EST 171 He 16
Kohil'nik ~ UA 175 Hg 22
Kohima ○ IND 254 Km 33
Kōh-i-Mārān △ PK 227 Jm 31
Ko Hinh ○ LAO 255 Lb 35
Koh-i-Patandar ⛰ PK 227 Jl 32
Kohler Range ⛰ 38 Da 17
Kohtla-Järve ○ EST 171 Hf 16
Kohŭng ○ ROK 247 Lp 28
Koichab ~ NAM 348 Gp 59
Koichab Pan ~ NAM 348 Gp 59
Koidu ○ WAL 316 Ga 41
Koihoa ○ IND 262 Kl 41
Koïla Kabé ~ SN 316 Ga 39
Koil Island 🏝 PNG 287 Mj 47
Koilkuntla ○ IND 238 Kd 38
Koimekeah ○ IND 270 Kl 42
Koindu ○ WAL 316 Ga 41
Koito ○ EAK 337 Hm 47
Kojda ○ RUS 159 Hp 12
Kojda ~ RUS 159 Hp 12
Kŏje Do 🏝 ROK 247 Ma 28
Kŏjin ○ ROK 247 Ma 26
Kojmatdag ⛰ TM 222 Jf 25
Kojonup ○ AUS 368 Lj 62
K'ok'a ○ ETH 325 Hm 41
K'ok'a Gidib ~ ETH 325 Hm 41
K'ok'a Hāyk' ~ ETH 325 Hm 41
Kokand ○ UZB 19 Na 5
Kokand ○ UZB 223 Jp 25
Kokas ○ RI 283 Mc 47
Kokatha ○ AUS 378 Md 61
Kokča ○ UZB 223 Jl 25
Kokemäki ○ FIN 159 Hc 15
Kokenau ○ RI 286 Me 48
Kokerboom ○ NAM 348 Hb 60
Kokerit ○ GUY 112 Ee 42
Kokgrukluk River ~ USA 46 Al 15
Ko Khra Thong 🏝 THA 262 Kn 41
Kokkola Karleby ○ FIN 159 Hd 14
Koko ○ WAN 320 Gj 40
Koko ○ WAN 320 Gj 42
Kokoda ○ PNG 287 Mk 50
Kokofata ○ RMM 316 Gb 39
Kokolik River ~ USA 46 Aj 11
Kokologo ○ BF 317 Gf 39
Kokomo ○ USA 71 De 25
Kokonselk ⌓ FIN 159 Hf 15
Kokopo ○ PNG 287 Mn 48
Kokoro ○ PNG 287 Mk 49
Kokoro ~ RG 316 Gb 39
Kokosa ○ ETH 325 Hm 42
Kokoulo ~ RG 316 Fp 40
Kokpekty ○ KZ 204 Tb 9
Kokrajhar ○ IND 235 Kk 32
Kokrines ○ USA 46 An 13
Kokrines Hills ⛰ USA 46 An 13
Koksan ○ DVRK 247 Lp 26
Kokshetau ○ KZ 19 Na 4
Kokstad ○ ZA 349 Hg 61
Kokumbo ○ CI 317 Gd 42
Kŏkŭm Do 🏝 ROK 247 Lp 28
Ko Kut 🏝 THA 263 Lb 40
Kokwo ○ SUD 325 Hk 43
Kol ○ PNG 287 Mj 48
Kola ○ RUS 159 Hj 11
Kola ○ LB 316 Gb 42
Kolāchi ~ PK 227 Jm 32
Kolahun ○ LB 316 Ga 41
Kolaka ○ RI 282 Ll 48
Kolan ~ AUS 375 Mm 58
Ko Lanta 🏝 THA 270 Kp 42
Kola Peninsula 🏝 RUS 159 Hk 12
Kolār ○ IND 238 Kc 39
Kolar Gold Fields ○ IND 238 Kd 39
Kolari ○ FIN 159 Hd 12
Kolåsen ○ S 158 Gn 14
Kolasib ○ IND 254 Kl 33
Kolašin ○ MON 194 Hb 24
Kolattupuzha ○ IND 239 Kc 41
Kolāyat ○ IND 227 Ka 32
Kolbio ○ EAK 337 Hn 46
Kol'čugino ○ RUS 171 Hm 17
Kolda ○ SN 316 Fn 39
Koldaga ○ TCH 321 Ha 41
Kolding ○ DK 170 Gl 18
Kole ○ RDC 324 He 44
Kole ○ RDC 333 Hb 47
Kole ○ RDC 333 Hd 47
Kolebira ○ IND 235 Kg 34
Kolenté ~ RG 316 Fp 41
Kolentén ○ RG 316 Fp 40
Koležma ○ RUS 159 Hk 13
Kolhāpur ○ IND 238 Ka 37
Kolhāpur ○ IND 238 Kd 37
Kolhozabad ○ TJ 223 Jn 27
Koliba ○ CI 305 Gc 41
Koliba ~ RG 316 Fp 39
Kolín ○ CZ 174 Gp 20
Kolinbiné ~ RMM 304 Ga 38
K'olito ○ ETH 325 Hm 42
Kolka ○ LV 170 Hd 17
köl Küsmüryn ~ KZ 154 Sb 8
Kolky ○ UA 175 He 20
Kollegal ○ IND 238 Kc 39
Kollo ○ RN 320 Gh 39
Kolmanskop ○ NAM 348 Gp 59
Kolno ○ PL 170 Hc 19
Kolo ○ PL 170 Hb 19
Kolo ○ EAT 337 Hk 48
Koloa ○ USA 75 Al 35
Kolobane ○ SN 304 Fn 38
Kolobeke ○ RDC 333 Hb 46
Kołobrzeg ○ PL 170 Gp 18
Kolokani ○ RMM 316 Gb 39
Koloko ○ BF 317 Gd 40
Kolomak ○ UA 175 Hk 21
Kolombangara Island 🏝 SOL 290 Na 49
Kolomna ○ RUS 171 Hm 18
Kolomonyi ○ RDC 333 Hd 48
Kolomyja ○ UA 175 He 21
Kolondiéba ○ RMM 305 Gc 40
Kolonedale ○ RI 282 Ll 47
Kolongotomo ○ RMM 305 Gc 39
Kolonia ▣ FSM 27 Sb 9
Kolono ○ RI 282 Lm 48
Kolossa ~ RMM 305 Gc 39
Kolozero ~ RUS 159 Hj 11
Kolpaševo ○ RUS 204 Tb 7
Kolpino ○ RUS 171 Hh 16
Kolpny ○ RUS 181 Hl 19
Kolpós Ágion Oros ~ GR 194 Hd 25
Kolpós Kassándras ~ GR 194 Hd 25
Kolpur ○ PK 227 Jm 31
Kol'skij zaliv ~ RUS 159 Hj 11
Kolu ○ ETH 325 Hk 43
Kolubara ~ SCG 174 Hb 23
Kolumadulu Atoll 🏝 MV 239 Ka 44
Kolvereid ○ N 158 Gm 13
Kolvica ○ RUS 159 Hj 12
Kolwezi ○ RDC 341 He 51
Kolyma ~ RUS 23 Sb 3
Kolyma ~ RUS 205 Ya 5
Kolyma ~ RUS 205 Yc 5
Kolyma Plain ⏜ RUS 205 Ya 5
Kolymna Plain ⏜ RUS 23 Sb 3
Kolymskaya Guba ≈ RUS 205 Ya 4
Kolymskoye Nagor'ye ⛰ RUS 23 Sb 3
Kolymskoye Nagor'ye ⛰ RUS 205 Ya 6
Kolyšlej ○ RUS 181 Ja 19
Kolyuchinskaya Guba ~ RUS 46 Ac 11
Kom △ BG 194 Hd 24
Kom ~ CAM 320 Gm 44
Kom ○ EAK 325 Hm 45
Komadougou Gana ~ WAN 320 Gm 39
Komadougou-Yobe ~ WAN 321 Gn 39
Komaio ○ PNG 286 Mh 49
Komanda ○ RDC 324 Hg 45
Komandorskie Ostrova 🏝 RUS 23 Ta 4
Komandorskije ostrova 🏝 RUS 205 Za 7
Komárno ○ SK 174 Ha 22
Komárom ○ H 174 Ha 22
Komatipoort ○ ZA 352 Hh 58
Komatirivier ~ ZA 352 Hh 58
Komatsu ○ J 251 Md 27
Kombat ○ NAM 340 Ha 55
Kombissiri ○ BF 317 Gf 39
Komboltindi ○ CAM 320 Gl 43
Kombongou Kondio ○ BF 317 Gg 40
Kome Island 🏝 EAT 336 Hj 47
Komering ~ RI 278 Lc 47
Komfane ○ RI 283 Md 48
Komga ○ ZA 358 Hf 62
Komi ⌓ RUS 154 Ra 6
Komin-Yanga ○ BF 317 Gg 40
Komo ○ PNG 286 Mh 49
Komo ~ G 332 Gm 45
Komo 🏝 FJI 390 Aa 55
Komodo ○ RI 279 Lk 50
Komodo 🏝 RI 279 Lk 50
Komodo National Park ⚲ RI 279 Lk 50
Komodou ○ RG 316 Gb 41
Komono ○ RCB 332 Gn 47
Komoro ○ J 251 Mf 27
Komosi ○ RDC 321 Hb 43
Komotiní ○ GR 194 He 25
Kompa ○ DY 320 Gh 39
Kompiam ○ PNG 287 Mh 48
Komsberge ⛰ ZA 358 Hc 62
Komsomol'sk-na-Amure ○ RUS 22 Rb 4
Komsomolabad ○ TJ 223 Jn 26
Komsomol'sk ○ RUS 171 Hm 17
Komsomol'skij ○ RUS 181 Ja 18
Komsomol'skij ○ RUS 202 Ja 23
Komsomol'sk-na-Amure ○ RUS 205 Xa 8
Komukanti ○ NAM 340 Ha 55
Kŏmun Do 🏝 ROK 247 Lp 28
Kon ○ CAM 320 Gm 43
Kona ~ AFG 223 Jp 28
Kona ○ RN 320 Gl 39
Kona ○ WAN 320 Gm 41
Konakovo ○ RUS 171 Hl 17
Konar ◉ AFG 223 Jp 28
Konārak ○ IR 226 Jj 33
Konārak ○ IND 235 Kh 36
Konār Tahte ○ IR 215 Jd 31
Konda ~ RUS 154 Sb 7
Konda ~ RUS 204 Sb 7
Kondagaon ○ IND 238 Ke 36
Kondinin ○ AUS 368 Lk 62
Kondio ○ BF 317 Gg 40
Kondoa Irangi ○ EAT 337 Hk 48
Kondololo ○ RDC 324 He 45
Kondopoga ○ RUS 159 Hk 14
Kondrovo ○ RUS 171 Hk 18
Kondue ○ RDC 333 Hd 48
Konduga ○ WAN 321 Gn 40
Koné ○ F 386 Ne 56
Koneng ○ RI 270 Kn 43
Kōne-Urgenč ○ TM 222 Jh 24
Kōneurgenč ○ TM 155 Rc 10
Konevo ○ RUS 159 Hm 14
Kong ○ CI 317 Gd 41
Kong ○ CAM 320 Gn 43
Kongakut ~ USA 46 Be 11
Kongasso ○ CI 305 Gc 42
Kongbo ○ RCA 321 Hc 43
Kong Christian IX Land ⏜ DK 18 Hb 2
Kong Christian IX Land ⏜ DK 43 Kb 5
Kong Christian X Land ⏜ DK 18 Ha 3
Kong Christian X Land ⏜ DK 43 Kc 4
Kongelai ○ EAK 325 Hk 45
Kong Frederik VIII Land ⏜ DK 18 Hb 2
Kong Frederik VI Kyst ⏜ DK 18 Gb 3
Kong Frederik VI Kyst ⏜ DK 43 Ka 6
Kong Fu ★ VRC 246 Lj 28
Kong Karls Land 🏝 N 19 La 2
Kong Karls land 🏝 N 158 Hf 6
Kongola ○ NAM 341 Hd 54
Kongolo ○ RDC 333 He 48
Kongolo ○ RDC 336 Hf 48

Kilwat - Kongolo 433

□Country ▣Capital city ⊙Administrative unit ○Place ♁Island ⛰Mountain range △Mountain ⌒Cape ≈Ocean, Sea ~Lake, River ΨUndersea topography ⛰Glacier ⚲National park •••Reservation ★Point of major interest ⌓Landscape

Kongor ○ SUD 324 Hh 42
Kongoussi ○ BF 317 Gf 39
Kongsberg ○ N 170 Gl 16
Kongsfjorden ~ N 158 Gm 6
Kongsøya ♁ N 158 Hg 6
Kongsvinger ○ N 158 Gm 15
Kongur Shan △ VRC 230 Kb 26
Kongwa ○ EAT 337 Hl 49
Koni ○ RDC 341 Hf 51
Konikans ○ ZA 348 Hb 61
Konimeh ○ UZB 223 Jl 25
Konin ○ PL 170 Hb 19
Konina ○ RMM 305 Gc 39
Konjic ○ BIH 194 Ha 24
Konka ~ UA 175 Hk 22
Könkämäälven ~ S 159 Hc 11
Könkämäeno ~ FIN 159 Hc 11
Konkče ~ AFG 223 Jp 27
Konkiep ~ NAM 348 Ha 59
Konko ○ RDC 341 Hf 51
Konkoma ○ ETH 325 Hm 43
Konkoso ○ WAN 320 Gj 40
Konkouré ○ RG 316 Fp 40
Kona ○ RMM 305 Ge 38
Konnonkoski ○ FIN 159 He 14
Konnūr ○ IND 238 Kb 37
Konobougou ○ RMM 305 Gc 39
Konogogo ○ PNG 287 Mm 47
Konongo ○ GH 317 Gf 42
Konos ○ PNG 287 Mm 47
Konoša ○ RUS 19 Ma 3
Konoša ○ RUS 154 Qb 6
Konoša ○ RUS 171 Hn 15
Kōnosu ○ J 251 Mf 27
Konotop ○ UA 175 Hj 20
Kon Plong ○ VN 263 Le 38
Konqi He ~ VRC 231 Kj 25
Konsankoro ○ RG 316 Gb 41
Konséguéla ○ RMM 317 Gd 39
Końskie ○ PL 174 Hc 20
Konso ○ ETH 325 Hl 43
Konsotami ○ RG 316 Fp 40
Konstantinovsk ○ RUS 181 Hn 22
Konta ○ IND 238 Ke 37
Kontagora ○ WAN 320 Gj 40
Kontcha ○ CAM 320 Gn 42
Kontiolahti ○ FIN 159 Hg 14
Kontiomäki ○ FIN 159 Hg 13
Kontous ⌓ RN 308 Gl 38
Kon Tum ○ VN 263 Ld 38
Konya ○ TR 195 Hj 27
Konza ○ EAK 337 Hl 46
Konzi ~ RDC 333 Ha 48
Konzloduj ○ BG 194 Hd 24
Kooi Reservoir ~ NEP 235 Kh 32
Kookooligit Mountains ⛰ USA 46 Ae 13
Kookynie ○ AUS 368 Ll 60
Koolatah ○ AUS 365 Mh 53
Kooline ○ AUS 360 Lj 57
Koolpinyah ○ AUS 364 Mb 52
Koolyanobbing ○ AUS 368 Lk 61
Koomboolomba ○ AUS 365 Mj 54
Koondoo ○ AUS 375 Mj 58
Koongie Park ○ AUS 361 Lp 55
Koopmansfontein ○ ZA 349 He 60
Koor ○ RI 283 Mc 46
Koorawatha ○ AUS 379 Ml 63
Koorda ○ AUS 368 Lj 61
Kooskia ○ USA 50 Ce 22
Kootenay ~ CDN 50 Ce 20
Kootenay ⚲ CDN 50 Ce 20
Kootenay ~ USA 50 Ce 21
Kootenay Bay ○ CDN 50 Cd 21
Kootenay Indian Reservation ••• CDN 50 Ce 21
Kootenay Lake ~ CDN 50 Cd 21
Koo Wee Rup ○ AUS 379 Mj 65
Koozata Lagoon ~ USA 46 Ae 13
Kopa ○ Z 341 Hh 51
Kopanzu ○ LB 316 Gb 42
Kopaskaja ○ RUS 181 Hm 22
Kópasker ○ IS 158 Fm 12
Kópavogur ○ IS 158 Fk 13
Ko Payang ♁ THA 262 Kn 41
Koper ○ SLO 185 Gn 23
Kopet Dağ ⛰ IR 222 Jg 26
Kop Geç △ TR 202 Hn 25
Ko Phangan ♁ THA 262 La 41
Ko Phi ♁ THA 270 Kp 42
Ko Phuket ♁ THA 270 Kn 42
Kopiago ○ PNG 286 Mh 48
Köping ○ S 170 Gp 16
Kopingué ○ CI 317 Ge 41
Koporokendié-Na ○ RMM 305 Ge 38
Koppa ○ IND 238 Kb 39
Koppal ○ IND 238 Kc 38
Koppang ○ N 158 Gm 15
Kopparberg ○ S 170 Gp 16
Koppies ○ ZA 349 Hf 59
Koppieskraalpan ~ ZA 348 Hc 59
Koprivnica ○ HR 174 Ha 22
Koprū Irm. ~ TR 195 Hh 27
Kor ~ IR 215 Je 30
Ko Ra ♁ THA 262 Kp 41
Kora ⚲ EAK 337 Hm 46
Korača ○ RUS 181 Hl 20
Ko Racha Noi ♁ THA 270 Kn 42
Ko Racha Yai ♁ THA 270 Kn 42
K'orahē ○ ETH 328 Ja 42
Ķorakata cuķurligi ⌓ UZB 223 Jl 25
Korangal ○ IND 238 Kc 37
Korannaberg ⛰ ZA 349 Hd 59
Korān-o-Mogān ○ AFG 223 Jp 28
Koraon ○ IND 234 Kf 33
Koraput ○ IND 234 Kf 36
Korasa ○ SOL 290 Na 49
Koratagere ○ IND 238 Kc 39
Ko Rawi ♁ THA 270 Kp 42
Korbach ○ D 174 Gl 20
Korbeniči ○ RUS 171 Hk 15
Korbol ○ TCH 321 Ha 41
Korçë ○ AL 194 Hc 25
Korčula ○ HR 194 Ha 24
Korčula ♁ HR 194 Ha 24
Korda ○ IND 227 Jp 34
Kordestān ⊙ IR 209 Jb 28
Kordié ○ BF 317 Ge 39
Kord-Kuy ○ IR 222 Jf 27
Kordofan ⌓ SUD 312 Hg 39
Kore ○ RI 279 Lk 50
Korea Bay ≈ 246 Lm 26
Korea Strait ≈ 247 Ma 29
Korec' ○ UA 175 Hf 20
Korem ○ ETH 313 Hm 39
Korémaïrwa ○ RN 320 Gh 39
Korenevo ○ RUS 175 Hk 20
Korenovsk ○ RUS 202 Hm 23
Korf ○ RUS 205 Za 6
Korgen ○ N 158 Gn 12
Korgom ○ RN 320 Gl 39
Korhogo ○ CI 317 Gd 41
Koribundu ○ WAL 316 Ga 42
Korientze ○ RMM 305 Ge 38
Kórinthos ○ GR 194 Hd 27
Korioume ○ RMM 305 Ge 37
Koripobi ○ PNG 290 Mp 49
Korissía ○ GR 194 He 27
Korithi ○ GR 194 Hc 27
Korkodon ○ RUS 23 Sb 3
Korkodon ~ RUS 205 Yb 6
Korkut ○ TR 202 Hn 26
Korkuteli ○ TR 195 Hh 27
Korla ○ VRC 204 Tc 10
Kornaka ○ RN 308 Gk 38
Kornárno ○ SK 174 Ha 22
Kornati ⚲ HR 194 Gp 24
Kornati ♁ HR 194 Gp 24
Koro ○ CI 305 Gc 41
Koro ○ RMM 305 Ge 38
Koro ♁ FJI 387 Nm 54
Koroba ○ PNG 286 Mh 48
Korodiga ○ EAT 337 Hl 48
Köroğlu Dağları ⛰ TR 195 Hh 25
Korogwe ○ EAT 337 Hm 48
Korohane ○ RN 308 Gk 38
Korolevu ○ FJI 387 Nl 55
Koronadal ○ RP 275 Ln 42
Korondziba ○ ZW 341 Hf 55
Koronga ○ RMM 304 Gc 38
Koróni ○ GR 194 Hc 27
Koronti ○ RI 282 Lm 48
Koror ▣ PAL 26 Rb 9
Kőrös ~ H 174 Hc 22
Korosamer River ~ PNG 286 Mh 48
Koro Sea ≈ FJI 387 Nm 54
Korosten' ○ UA 175 Hg 20
Korostyšiv ○ UA 175 Hg 20
Korotčaevo ○ RUS 204 Ta 5
Koro Toro ○ TCH 309 Hb 37
Korovou ○ SOL 290 Mp 49
Korovou ○ FJI 387 Nm 54
Korpilahti ○ FIN 159 He 14
Korsakow ○ RUS 250 Mh 22
Korsimoro ○ BF 317 Gf 39
Korskrogen ○ S 158 Gp 15
Korsnas ○ FIN 159 Hc 14
Korsør ○ DK 170 Gm 18
Kortala ○ SUD 312 Hh 39
Kortrijk ○ B 163 Gh 20
Korumburra ○ AUS 379 Mj 65
Korup ○ CAM 320 Gl 43
korvonsaroj Raboti Malik ★ UZB 223 Jl 26
Korwai ○ IND 234 Kd 33
Koryakskoye Nagor'ye ⛰ RUS 23 Ta 3
Korycin ○ PL 171 Hd 19
Kós ♁ GR 194 Hf 27
Kós ○ GR 195 Hf 27
Kosa ○ ETH 325 Hl 42
Kosa Arabats'ka Strilka ⌓ UA 175 Hk 22
Kosaja Gora ○ RUS 171 Hl 18
Ko Samet ⚲ THA 262 La 39
Ko Samui ○ THA 262 Kp 41
Ko Samui ♁ THA 262 La 41
Kościan ○ PL 170 Ha 19
Kościerzyna ○ PL 170 Ha 18
Kosciusko ○ USA 86 Dd 29
Kosciusko ⚲ AUS 379 Ml 64
Kose ○ EST 171 He 16
Köse ○ TR 195 Hm 25
Köse Dağları ⛰ TR 195 Hl 25
Kosha ○ SUD 312 Hh 35
Kosi ~ NEP 235 Kh 32
Ko Si Boya ♁ THA 270 Kp 42
Košice ○ SK 174 Hc 21
Kōšim ~ KZ 181 Jd 21
Ko Similan ♁ THA 262 Kn 41
Koskaecodde Lake ~ CDN 61 Eg 22
Košk-e Kohne ○ AFG 223 Jk 28
Koški ○ RUS 181 Jd 18
Košoba ○ TM 222 Je 25
Kosong ○ DVRK 247 Ma 26
Kosovo ⌓ SCG 194 Hc 24
Kosovska Mitrovica ○ SCG 194 Hc 24
Kosso ○ CI 317 Gd 43
Kossou ○ CI 317 Gd 42
Kósta ○ GR 194 Hd 27
Kostanaj ○ KZ 154 Sa 8
Koster ○ ZA 349 Hf 58
Kostjantynivka ○ UA 181 Hl 21
Kostomukša ○ RUS 159 Hh 13
Kostopil' ○ UA 175 Hf 20
Kostroma ~ RUS 171 Hn 16
Kostroma ○ RUS 171 Hn 17
Kostrzyn ○ PL 170 Gp 19
Kosubuke ○ RDC 333 Hd 48
Ko Surin Nua ♁ THA 262 Kn 41
Ko Surin Tai ♁ THA 262 Kn 41
Koszalin ○ PL 170 Ha 18
Kőszeg ○ H 174 Ha 22
Kota ○ IND 234 Kb 33
Kota ○ IND 234 Kf 34
Kotaagung ○ RI 278 Lc 48
Kota Baharu ○ MAL 270 Lb 42
Kotabangun ○ RI 274 Lj 46
Kotabaru ○ RI 270 La 46
Kotabaru ○ RI 279 Lj 47
Kotabatu ○ RI 271 Lf 46
Kota Belud ○ MAL 274 Lj 42
Kotabumi ○ RI 278 Lc 48
Kota Cascades ~ DY 317 Gg 40
Kot Addu ○ PK 227 Jp 30
Kota Kinabalu ○ MAL 274 Lh 42
Kota Kinabula ○ MAL 274 Lh 43
Kotamangalam ○ IND 239 Kc 40
Kota Maruda ○ MAL 274 Lj 42
Kota Marudu ○ MAL 274 Lj 42
Kotamobagu ○ RI 275 Lm 45
Kota Nopan ○ RI 270 Kp 45
Ko Tao ♁ THA 262 Kp 40
Kotapinang ○ RI 270 La 45
Ko Tarutao ♁ THA 270 Kp 42
Kota Tampan ○ MAL 270 La 43
Kota Tinggi ○ MAL 271 Lb 45
Kotcho Lake ~ CDN 47 Ca 15
Kot Chutta ○ PK 227 Jp 31
Kot Diji ○ PK 227 Jn 32
Kotel-e Čita Kandaw △ AFG 223 Jn 29
Kotel-e Nīl △ AFG 223 Jm 28
Kotel-e Ounay △ AFG 223 Jn 28
Kotel-e Robāt-e Mīrzā △ AFG 223 Jj 28
Kotel-e Šibar △ AFG 223 Jm 28
Kotel-e Šorḫ △ AFG 223 Jj 28
Kotel-e Šotorḫūn △ AFG 223 Jl 28
Kotel-e Spālang △ AFG 223 Jn 28
Kotel'nič ○ RUS 154 Ra 7
Kotel'nikovo ○ RUS 181 Hp 22
Kotel'va ○ UA 175 Hk 20
Kotemaori ○ NZ 383 Nl 65
Kotido ○ EAU 325 Hk 44
Kotīra ○ PK 227 Jm 32
Kotka ○ FIN 159 Hf 15
Kot Kapūra ○ IND 230 Kb 30
Kotlas ○ RUS 154 Ra 6
Kotlik ○ USA 46 Aj 13
Kot Mūmin ○ PK 230 Ka 29
Kotna ○ PNG 287 Mj 48
Koto ○ CAM 320 Gl 43
Kotobi ○ CI 317 Gd 42
Kotongoro ○ TCH 321 Hb 41
Koton-Karifi ○ WAN 320 Gk 41
Kotor ○ MON 194 Hb 24
Kotouba ○ CI 317 Ge 41
Kotoula ○ CI 305 Gc 40
Kotovo ○ RUS 181 Ja 20
Kotovsk ○ UA 175 Hg 22
Kotovsk ○ RUS 181 Hn 19
Kot Pūtli ○ IND 234 Kc 32
Kotri ○ PK 227 Jn 33
Kotri ~ IND 238 Ke 36
Kot Shākir ○ PK 227 Jp 30
Kottagūdem ○ IND 238 Ke 37
Kottakota ○ IND 238 Kd 39
Kottayam ○ IND 239 Kc 41
Kotte ○ CL 239 Kd 42
Kotto ~ RCA 321 Hc 43
Kotto ~ RCA 321 Hd 41
Kotto ~ RCA 321 Hd 42
Kottūru ○ IND 238 Kc 38
Kotu ♁ TO 390 Ac 55
Kotu Group ♁ TO 390 Ac 56
Kotuj ~ RUS 204 Uc 4
Kotuj ~ RUS 204 Uc 5
Koturdepe ○ TM 222 Je 26
Kotwa ○ ZW 344 Hj 54
Kotzebue ○ USA 23 Ab 3
Kotzebue ○ USA 46 Ag 11
Kotzebue Sound ≈ USA 23 Ab 3
Kotzebue Sound ≈ USA 46 Ai 11
Kouaga ~ RMM 304 Ga 38
Kouakourou ○ RMM 305 Gd 38
Kouandé ○ DY 317 Gg 40
Kouango ○ RCA 321 Hc 43
Kouankan ○ RG 316 Gb 41
Kouaoua ○ F 386 Ne 56
Kouassi-Datékro ○ CI 317 Ge 42
Kouba Olanga ○ TCH 309 Hb 38
Koubia ○ RG 316 Ga 40
Kouchibouguac National Park ⚲ CDN 61 Eb 22
Koudougou ○ BF 317 Ge 39
Kouéré ○ BF 317 Gd 40
Koufey ○ RN 309 Gn 38
Kouga ~ ZA 358 Hd 62
Kougaberge ⛰ ZA 358 Hd 62
Kougnohou ○ RT 317 Gg 42
Kougouleu ○ G 332 Gl 45
Koui ○ RCA 321 Gp 42
Kouibli ○ CI 305 Gc 42
Kouilou ~ RCB 332 Gn 48
Kouinine ○ DZ 296 Gk 29
Kouka ○ BF 317 Gd 40
Kouka ○ RT 317 Gg 41
Kouki ○ RCA 321 Ha 42
Koukou ○ TCH 313 Hd 40
Koukourou ~ RCA 321 Hb 42
Koukourou ~ RCA 321 Hc 42
Koula ○ RMM 304 Gc 39
Koulamoutou ○ G 332 Gn 46
Koulbo ○ TCH 321 Hc 39
Koulbous ○ SUD 309 Hd 38
Koulé ○ RG 316 Gb 42
Koulé Ekou △ DY 317 Gh 41
Koulikoro ○ RMM 305 Gc 39
Koulou ○ RN 320 Gh 39
Koulouguidi ○ RMM 316 Ga 39
Koulountou ~ SN 316 Fp 39
Koulouoko ~ BF 317 Gf 39
Koum ○ CAM 321 Gp 41
Kouma ○ RCA 321 Hb 42
Kouma ~ RCA 321 Hb 43
Koumac ○ F 386 Ne 56
Koumameyong ○ G 332 Gm 45
Koumantou ○ RMM 305 Gc 40
Koumba ~ RG 316 Fp 40
Koumbala ○ RCA 321 Hc 41
Koumbala ~ RCA 321 Hc 41
Koumbia ○ RG 316 Fp 40
Koumbia ○ BF 317 Ge 40
Koumbri ○ BF 317 Gf 39
Koumogo ○ TCH 321 Hb 41
Koumongou ○ BF 317 Gg 40
Koumongou ~ BF 317 Gg 40
Koumou ~ RCA 321 Hd 41
Koumpentoum ○ SN 304 Fn 38
Koumra ○ TCH 321 Ha 41
Kounahiri ○ CI 317 Gd 42
Koundara ○ RG 316 Fp 39
Koundé ○ RCA 321 Gp 42
Koundian ○ RMM 316 Ga 39
Koundian ○ RG 316 Gb 40
Koundjourou ○ TCH 321 Hb 39
Koundou ○ RG 316 Ga 41
Koundougou ○ BF 317 Gd 40
Koun-Fao ○ CI 317 Ge 42
Koungheul ○ SN 316 Fn 39
Koungouri ○ TCH 321 Hb 40
Kouniana ○ RMM 317 Gd 39
Kounkané ○ SN 316 Fn 39
Kountze ○ USA 81 Da 30
Kouoro ○ RMM 317 Gd 39
Koup ○ ZA 358 Hc 62
Kouraqué ○ RMM 316 Ga 39
Kourémélé ○ RMM 316 Gb 40
Kourgou ○ TCH 321 Ha 41
Kourgui ○ CAM 321 Gp 40
Kouri ○ RMM 317 Gd 39
Kouri Kouri ○ TCH 321 Gp 39
Kourkéto ○ RMM 304 Ga 38
Kourou ○ F 113 Eh 43
Kourouba ○ RMM 316 Gb 39
Kouroudjél ○ RIM 304 Ga 37
Kourougui ~ BF 317 Ge 39
Kouroukoto ○ RMM 316 Ga 39
Kourouma ○ BF 317 Gd 40
Kourouninnkoto ○ RMM 316 Ga 39
Kouroussa ○ RG 316 Gb 40
Koussa Arma ○ RN 309 Gn 37
Koussanar ~ SN 304 Fp 38
Koussanar ○ SN 316 Fn 39
Koussane ○ SN 304 Fp 38
Koussané ○ RMM 304 Ga 38
Kousseri ○ CAM 321 Gp 39
Koussountou ○ RT 317 Gg 41
Koutaba ○ CAM 320 Gm 43
Koutia Gaïdi ○ SN 304 Fn 38
Koutiala ○ RMM 317 Gd 39
Kouto ○ CI 305 Gc 41
Kouvola ○ FIN 159 Hf 15
Kouyou ~ RCB 332 Gp 46
Kouyou ~ RCB 333 Ha 46
Kovalam ○ IND 239 Kc 41
Kovarzino ○ RUS 159 Hm 15
Kovdor ○ RUS 159 Hh 12
Kovdozero ~ RUS 159 Hh 12
Kovel' ○ UA 175 He 20
Kovillur ○ IND 239 Kc 41
Kovilpatti ○ IND 239 Kc 41
Kovkula ○ RUS 159 Hm 14
Kovrov ○ RUS 171 Hn 17
Kovūr ○ IND 238 Ke 38
Kovylkino ○ RUS 181 Hp 18
Kowanyama ○ AUS 365 Mg 53
Kowares ○ NAM 340 Gp 55
Kowloon ○ VRC 258 Lh 34
Koyakskoye Nagor'ye ⛰ RUS 205 Za 6
Koyama ○ RG 316 Gb 42
Ko Yao Yai ♁ THA 270 Kp 42
Köyceğiz ○ TR 195 Hg 27
Koyna Reservoir ~ IND 238 Ka 37
Koyuk ○ USA 46 Aj 13
Koyuk River ~ USA 46 Aj 13
Koyukuk ○ USA 46 Al 13
Koyukuk River ~ USA 46 Al 13
Koža ~ RUS 159 Hl 14
Koza ○ CAM 321 Gn 40
Kozan ○ TR 195 Hk 27
Kozáni ○ GR 194 Hc 25
Kozara ⚲ BIH 174 Ha 23
Kozel'sk ○ RUS 171 Hk 19
Kozienice ○ PL 174 Hc 20
Kozjatyn ○ UA 175 Hg 21
Kozlovka ○ RUS 181 Jb 18
Kozluk ○ TR 202 Hn 26
Koz'modem'jansk ○ RUS 159 Ja 17
Kožuf ⛰ MK 194 Hd 25
Kōzu-shima ♁ J 251 Mf 28
Kpako ~ DY 320 Gh 40
Kpalimé ○ RT 317 Gg 42
Kpandu ○ GH 317 Gg 42
Kpassa ~ GH 317 Gg 42
Kpedze ○ GH 317 Gg 42
Kpéssi ○ RT 317 Gg 41
Kpété Béna ○ RT 317 Gg 42
Kpetoe ○ RT 317 Gg 42
Kpong ○ GH 317 Gf 42
Kr. Barrikady ○ RUS 181 Jb 22
Kraairi ~ ZA 349 Hf 61
Kraankuil ○ ZA 349 Hd 60
Krabbé ○ RA 137 Ed 64
Krabi ○ THA 262 Kp 41
Krâchéh ○ K 263 Ld 39
Kracnooskil's'k vodoschovijšče ~ UA 181 Hl 21
Kragerø ○ N 170 Gl 16
Kragujevac ○ SCG 194 Hc 24
Krajenskie ○ PL 170 Ha 19
Krajnovka ○ RUS 202 Jb 24
Krakatau Islands ♁ RI 278 Lc 49
Krakatau Volcan △ RI 278 Lc 49
Krakau ○ PL 174 Hc 20
Kraków ○ PL 174 Hc 20
Kralendijk ○ NL 107 Dp 39
Kraljevo ○ SCG 194 Hc 24
Kramators'k ○ UA 181 Hl 21
Kramfors ○ S 158 Ha 14
Kramskoye Reservoir ~ RUS 19 Mb 4
Kraníđi ○ GR 194 Hd 27
Kranj ○ SLO 174 Gp 22
Krankaanpää ○ FIN 159 Hd 15
Kranskop ○ ZA 352 Hh 60
Kranuan ○ THA 263 Lb 37
Kranzberg ○ NAM 348 Gp 56
Krapina ○ HR 174 Gp 22
Kraskino ○ RUS 250 Mb 24
Krāslava ○ LV 171 Hf 18
Krasn. Jar ○ RUS 181 Ja 20
Krasnaja Jaruga ○ RUS 175 Hk 20
Krasnaja Poljana ○ RUS 195 Hm 24
Krasnapollye ○ BY 171 Hh 19
Krasnen ○ RUS 205 Zb 6
Kraśnik ○ PL 174 Hc 20
Krasnoarmejsk ○ RUS 171 Hm 17
Krasnoarmejskoe ○ RUS 181 Jc 19
Krasnoarmijs'k ○ UA 181 Hl 21
Krasnodar ○ RUS 202 Hm 23
Krasnodarskoe vodohranilišče ~ RUS 202 Hm 23
Krasnodon ○ UA 181 Hm 21
Krasnoe ○ RUS 171 Hh 18
Krasnoe Znamja ○ TM 223 Jk 27
Krasno Gorbatka ○ RUS 181 Hn 18
Krasnogorodsk ○ RUS 171 Hg 17
Krasnogorskij ○ RUS 181 Jc 17
Krasnogvardejski ○ UZB 223 Jm 26
Krasnohorivka ○ UA 181 Hl 21
Krasnohrad ○ UA 175 Hk 21
Krasnohvardijs'ke ○ UA 175 Hk 23
Krasno Jar ○ RUS 202 Jc 23
Krasnokamensk ○ RUS 204 Vc 8
Krasnokamsk ○ RUS 154 Rb 7
Krasno Luč ○ UA 181 Hm 21
Krasnopavlivka ○ UA 181 Hl 21
Krasnoperekops'k ○ UA 175 Hj 23
Krasnopilja ○ UA 175 Hk 20
Krasnoščel'e ○ RUS 159 Hl 12
Krasnoslobodsk ○ RUS 181 Hp 18
Krasnoslobodsk ○ RUS 181 Ja 21
Krasnovodsk ○ TM 222 Je 25
Krasnovodskij zaliv ≈ TM 222 Je 26
Krasnovodsk platosy ⛰ TM 222 Je 25
Krasnoyarsk ○ RUS 22 Pb 4
Krasnoyarsk ○ RUS 204 Ua 7
Krasnoyarsk Reservoir ~ RUS 204 Tc 8
Krasnoznamjans'kyj kanal ~ UA 175 Hj 22
Krasnyj Cholm ○ RUS 171 Hl 16
Krasnyj Jar ○ RUS 181 Jc 19
Krasnyj Kut ○ RUS 181 Jb 20
Krasnystaw ○ PL 175 Hd 20
Krasoarmejsk ○ RUS 181 Ja 20
Krasuha ○ RUS 171 Hk 16
Kratke Range ⛰ PNG 287 Mj 49
Krau ○ RI 286 Mg 47
Krečetovo ○ RUS 159 Hm 15
Krefeld ○ D 163 Gk 20
Kremenchuk ○ UA 175 Hj 21
Kremenchuk Reservoir ~ UA 175 Hj 21
Kremenec' ○ UA 175 He 20
Kreminci ○ UA 175 He 21
Kreminna ○ UA 181 Hl 21
Kreml' ★ RUS 202 Jc 22
Kremmling ○ USA 65 Cj 26
Krems an der Donau ○ A 174 Gp 21
Krestcy ○ RUS 171 Hj 16
Krestjanskij ○ UZB 223 Jn 25
Krestovaja Guba ○ RUS 19 Mb 2
Krestovoe ○ RUS 205 Yc 5
Kresty ○ RUS 171 Hl 18
Kretinga ○ LT 170 Hc 18
Kribi ○ CAM 320 Gl 44
Kriel ○ ZA 349 Hg 59
Krim-Krim ○ TCH 321 Gp 41
Krims'ky hory ⛰ UA 175 Hj 23
Krishna ~ IND 238 Kb 37
Krishna ○ IND 238 Kc 37
Krishnadevipera ○ IND 238 Kf 37
Krishnagiri ○ IND 238 Kd 39
Krishnanagar ○ IND 235 Kj 34
Krishnārājanagara ○ IND 238 Kb 39
Krishnaraja Sagar ~ IND 238 Kc 39
Krishnarajpet ○ IND 238 Kc 39
Kristiansand ○ N 170 Gl 16
Kristianstad ○ S 170 Gp 18
Kristiansund ○ N 158 Gk 14
Kristinehamn ○ S 170 Gn 16
Kristinestad ○ FIN 159 Hc 14
Kríti ⊙ GR 194 Hd 28
Kriva Palanka ○ MK 194 Hd 24
Krivodol ○ BG 194 Hd 24
Krivyj Rih ○ UA 175 Hj 21
krjaz Vetrenyj pojas ⛰ RUS 159 Hk 14
Krk ♁ HR 174 Gp 23
Krka ~ HR 194 Ha 24
Krkonoše ⛰ CZ 174 Gp 20
Krkonossky ⚲ CZ 174 Gp 20
Krnov ○ CZ 174 Ha 20
Krokek ○ S 170 Ha 16
Krokodilrivier ~ ZA 349 Hf 58
Krokom ○ S 158 Gp 14
Króksfjarðarnes ○ IS 158 Fj 13
Krolevec' ○ UA 175 Hj 20
Kroměříž ○ CZ 174 Ha 21
Kromy ○ RUS 171 Hk 19
Krong Buk ○ VN 263 Le 39
Krŏng Kaôh Kŏng ○ K 263 Lb 40
Krŏng Pa ○ VN 263 Le 39
Kronockij Zaliv ≈ RUS 205 Yc 8
Kronoki ○ RUS 23 Ta 4
Kronprins Christian Land ⌓ DK 18 Hb 1
Kronštadt ○ RUS 171 Hg 16
Kroonstad ○ ZA 349 Hf 59
Kropotkin ○ RUS 202 Hm 23
Krośniewice ○ PL 170 Hb 19
Krosno ○ PL 174 Hc 21
Krosno Odrzańskie ○ PL 170 Gp 19
Krotoszyn ○ PL 174 Ha 20
Krotz Springs ○ USA 86 Dc 30
Krško ○ SLO 174 Gp 22
Krüger ⚲ ZA 352 Hh 57
Krugersdorp ○ ZA 349 Hf 59
Krui ○ RI 278 Lb 48
Kruidfontein ○ ZA 358 Hc 62
Krumë ○ AL 194 Hc 24
Krumovgrad ○ BG 194 He 25
Kruševac ○ SCG 194 Hc 24
Krutec ~ RUS 181 Ja 19
Kruzof Island ♁ USA 47 Bg 17
Kryazh Chekanovskogo ⛰ RUS 204 Wa 4
Kryazh Polousnyy ⛰ RUS 205 Xb 5
Kryazh Pronchishcheva ⛰ RUS 204 Vb 4
Kryichaw ○ BY 171 Hh 19
Krylovo ○ RUS 170 Hc 18
Krym ⊙ UA 175 Hj 23
Krymsk ○ RUS 195 Hl 23
Krynica ○ PL 174 Hc 21
Kryve Ozero ○ UA 175 Hh 22
Ksar Chellala ○ DZ 296 Gh 28
Ksar el Boukhari ○ DZ 296 Gh 28
Ksar el Hirane ○ DZ 296 Gh 29
Ksar Ghilane ○ TN 296 Gl 29
Kšenskij ○ RUS 181 Hl 20
Ksour Essaf ○ TN 297 Gm 28
Kstovo ○ RUS 159 Ja 17
Kuah ○ MAL 270 Kp 42
Kuala ~ RI 270 Kp 44
Kuala Belait ○ BRU 274 Lh 43
Kuala Dungan ○ MAL 271 Lb 43
Kualakapus ○ RI 279 Lh 47
Kualakeriau ○ RI 274 Lg 45
Kuala Krai ○ MAL 270 La 43
Kuala Kurau ○ MAL 270 La 43
Kuala Lipis ○ MAL 270 Lb 43
Kuala Lumpur ▣ MAL 270 La 44
Kuala Penyu ○ MAL 274 Lh 43
Kuala Perak ~ MAL 270 La 43
Kuala Pilah ○ MAL 270 Lb 44
Kuala Selangor ○ MAL 270 La 44
Kualasimpang ○ RI 270 Kp 43
Kuala Tatau ○ MAL 274 Lg 44
Kuala Terengganu ○ MAL 271 Lb 43
Kuala Tomani ○ MAL 274 Lh 43
Kualatungka ○ RI 278 Lb 46
Kualepembuang ○ RI 279 Lg 47
Kuamut ~ MAL 274 Lj 43
Kuancheng ○ VRC 246 Lk 25
Kuandang ○ RI 275 Lm 45
Kuandian ○ VRC 246 Ln 25
Kuangfu ○ RC 259 Ll 34
Kuantan ○ MAL 271 Lb 44
Kua Ruins ★ EAT 337 Hm 49
Kuban' ~ RUS 202 Hn 23
Kubārā ○ OM 226 Jg 34
Kubbum ○ SUD 313 Hd 40
Kubeai ○ PNG 286 Mh 49
Kubena ~ RUS 171 Hn 15
Kubira ○ PNG 286 Mh 50
Kubkain ○ PNG 286 Mh 48
Kubokawa ○ J 251 Mc 29
Kūbonān ○ IR 226 Jf 30
Kubuna ○ PNG 287 Mk 50
Kubutambahan ○ RI 279 Lh 50
Kubutsa ○ SD 352 Hh 59
Kūčeşfahān ○ IR 209 Jc 27
Kučevo ○ SCG 174 Hc 23
Kuchaiburi ○ IND 235 Kg 34
Kucharo-ko ~ J 250 Mj 24
Kuching ○ MAL 271 Lf 45
Kuchino-Erabu-shima ♁ J 247 Ma 30
Kuchino-shima ♁ J 259 Ma 31
Kudāl ○ IND 238 Ka 37
Kudan ○ WAN 320 Gk 40
Kudang ○ WAG 316 Fn 39
Kudani ○ GH 317 Gg 40
Kudat ○ MAL 274 Lj 42
Kudatini ○ IND 238 Kc 38
Kudene ○ RI 283 Md 49
Kūderu ○ IND 238 Kc 38
Kudever' ○ RUS 171 Hg 17
Kudiakam Pan ~ RB 349 He 56
Kudi-Boma ○ RDC 332 Gn 48
Kudirkos Naumiestis ○ LT 171 Hd 18
Kudjip ○ PNG 287 Mj 48
Kudligi ○ IND 238 Kc 38
Kudu ○ WAN 320 Gj 41
Kudumane ○ RB 341 He 55
Kudus ○ RI 278 Lf 49
Kuet ~ RI 270 Kn 44
Kufstein ○ A 174 Gm 22
Kuganavolok ○ RUS 159 Hl 14
Kūhak ○ IR 226 Jj 30
Kūhak ○ IR 226 Jk 32
Kuḥaylī ○ SUD 312 Hj 36
Kūh-e Ālādāğ ⛰ IR 222 Jg 27
Kūh-e Alīgūg △ IR 215 Jd 30
Kūh-e Alvand △ IR 209 Jc 28
Kūh-e Bāḫarz ⛰ IR 222 Jh 28
Kūh-e Baḫūn △ IR 226 Jg 32
Kūh-e Bampošt ⛰ IR 226 Jk 32
Kūh-e Barādar-e Šāh △ IR 209 Jb 27
Kūh-e Bārān ⛰ IR 222 Jh 29
Kūh-e Barğovein ⛰ IR 222 Jg 27
Kūh-e Barm Fīruz △ IR 215 Jd 30
Kūh-e Bāyir Govein ⛰ IR 222 Jg 27
Kūh-e Bazmān △ IR 226 Jh 31
Kūh-e Bīnālūd ⛰ IR 222 Jh 27
Kūh-e Bonkahar △ IR 215 Je 30
Kūh-e Dālāhānī △ IR 209 Jb 28
Kūh-e Damāvand ★ IR 222 Je 28
Kūh-e Darband ⛰ IR 226 Jg 30
Kūh-e Ešger ⛰ IR 222 Jg 28
Kūh-e Estand △ IR 226 Jh 30
Kūh-e Ğamšīdzāī ⛰ IR 226 Jj 31
Kūh-e Gebal Bārez ⛰ IR 226 Jg 31
Kūh-e Hazār △ IR 226 Jg 31
Kūh-e Hūrān △ IR 226 Jg 32
Kūh-e Hvāğe Mohammad ⛰ AFG 223 Jn 28
Kūh-e Kābir ⛰ IR 209 Jb 29
Kūh-e Kalār △ IR 215 Jd 30
Kūh-e Karkas △ IR 222 Jd 29
Kūh-e Kārūn △ IR 215 Jd 30
Kūh-e Kum ⛰ IR 215 Je 31
Kūh-e Lālezār △ IR 226 Jg 31
Kūh-e Madvār △ IR 226 Jf 30
Kūh-e Mālmand ⛰ AFG 223 Jk 29
Kūh-e Māršenān △ IR 222 Je 29
Kūh-e Masāhīm △ IR 226 Jf 30
Kūh-e Mazār ⛰ AFG 223 Jl 29
Kūh-e Mehe ⛰ IR 226 Jh 31
Kūh-e Mīrzā 'Arab △ IR 222 Jj 29
Kūh-e Mūrgūm △ IR 222 Jg 29
Kūh-e Nāybānd △ IR 222 Jg 29
Kūh-e Noḫonč △ IR 226 Jj 32
Kūh-e Palangān ⛰ IR 226 Jj 30
Kūh-e Parou △ IR 209 Jb 28
Kūh-e Puhal-e Ḫamīr ⛰ IR 226 Jf 32
Kūh-e Safīd Ḫers ⛰ AFG 223 Jp 27
Kūh-e Šāh △ IR 226 Jh 30
Kūh-e šahand △ IR 209 Jb 27
Kūh-e Šāh-e Gūlak △ IR 209 Jc 28
Kūh-e Šāh Ğahān ⛰ IR 222 Jh 27
Kūh-e Šāhū ⛰ IR 209 Jb 28
Kuh-e Sayyad ○ AFG 223 Jl 27
Kūh-e Segoch △ IR 226 Jg 30
Kūh-e Sendān Dāğ ⛰ IR 209 Jc 27
Kūh-e Sorḫ ⛰ IR 222 Jg 28
Kūh-e Taftān △ IR 226 Jj 31
Kūh-e Taḫt-e Soleiman △ IR 222 Jd 27
Kūh-e Tašāk △ IR 215 Jd 31
Kūh-e-Vāhān ⛰ AFG 230 Ka 27
Kūh-e Varzarīn △ IR 209 Jb 29
Kūh-e Zarde △ IR 222 Jc 29
Kūhhā-ye Bašākerd ⛰ IR 226 Jh 32
Kūhhā-ye Kūhpāye ⛰ IR 226 Jg 30
Kūhhā-ye Sabalān ⛰ IR 209 Jb 26
Kūhhā-ye Tāleš ⛰ IR 209 Jb 27
Kūhīn ○ IR 209 Jc 27
Kuhmo ○ FIN 159 Hg 13
Kūh Mobārak ○ IR 226 Jg 33
Kuhmoinen ○ FIN 159 He 15
Kuhmuh ○ RUS 202 Jb 24
Kūhpāye ○ IR 222 Je 29
Kūhrang ~ IR 222 Jd 29
Kūh-Rud Mountains ⛰ IR 222 Jd 28
Kui ○ PNG 287 Mk 49
Kui Buri ○ THA 262 Kp 39
Kuibyšev ○ RUS 181 Jc 18
Kuiseb ~ NAM 348 Gp 57
Kuiseb ~ NAM 348 Ha 57
Kuitan ○ VRC 258 Lh 34
Kuito ○ ANG 340 Ha 52
Kuiu Island ♁ USA 47 Bj 17
Kuivastu ○ EST 171 Hd 16
Kuixingyan ★ VRC 258 Lj 33
Kuixiang ○ VRC 255 Lb 32
Kujama ○ WAN 320 Gk 40
Kujbyšev ○ RUS 204 Ta 7
Kujdusun ○ RUS 205 Xb 6
Kuji ○ J 250 Mg 25
Kuji ~ J 251 Mg 27
Kujolri ○ ROK 247 Ma 27
Kujši ķumlar ★ UZB 223 Jk 24

434 Kongor - Kujši ķumlar

Kujūkuri-nada ～ **J** 251 Mg 28	Kungälv ○ **S** 170 Gm 17	Kushikino ○ **J** 247 Ma 30	Kyaikto ○ **MYA** 262 Kn 37
Kujwa ○ **ROK** 247 Lp 29	Kŭngerlussung ～ **DK** 7 Ga 3	Kushimoto ○ **J** 251 Md 29	Kyaka ○ **EAT** 336 Hh 46
Kukaklek Lake ～ **USA** 46 An 15	Kunggyu Co ～ **VRC** 230 Kf 30	Kushiro ○ **J** 250 Mj 24	Kyancutta ○ **AUS** 378 Md 62

Lábrea ○ **BR** 117 Eb 49
Labrieville ○ **CDN** 60 Dn 20
...

Lagamar O BR 133 El 55
Lagan ~ S 170 Gn 17
Lagan' O RUS 202 Jb 23
Lagarto O BR 125 Fb 51
La Gateada O NIC 97 Df 39
Lagaw O RP 267 Ll 37
Lagbar O SN 304 Fn 38
Lagdo O CAM 321 Gn 41
Lagen ~ N 158 Gm 15
Lages O USA 64 Ce 25
Lages O BR 140 Ej 59
Lageuen O RI 270 Km 43
Lagh Bogal ~ EAK 325 Hn 45
Lagh Bor ~ EAK 325 Hm 44
Lagh Bor ~ EAK 325 Hn 45
Lagh Isiolo ~ EAK 325 Hl 45
Lagh Kutulo ~ EAK 325 Hn 44
Laghonat O DZ 296 Gh 29
La Gi O VN 263 Ld 40
Lagkor Co ~ VRC 231 Kg 29
Laglan O AUS 375 Mk 57
La Gloria O MEX 81 Cn 32
La Gloria O USA 81 Cn 32
La Gloria O CO 106 Dl 41
Lağmān ⊙ AFG 223 Jp 28
Lågneset ⌓ N 158 Gn 7
Lagoa Antiga da Rabeca ~ BR 132 Ee 53
Lagoa Arari ~ BR 121 Ek 46
Lagoa Baia Grande ~ BOL 129 Ed 53
Lagoa Acará ~ BR 117 Ec 49
Lagoa Casamento ~ BR 146 Ej 61
Lagoa Chiguive ~ MOC 352 Hk 57
Lagoa Chuali ~ MOC 352 Hj 58
Lagoa da Prata O BR 133 Em 55
Lagoa de Canoa O BR 124 Fb 50
Lagoa Dongane ~ MOC 352 Hk 58
Lagoa do Peixe ~ BR 146 Ej 61
Lagoa dos Quadros ~ BR 146 Ek 60
Lagoa Dourada O BR 141 Em 56
Lagoa Grande O BR 124 Ep 50
Lago Agrio O EC 116 Dk 45
Lago Aiapuá ~ BR 117 Ec 48
Lagoa Itapera ~ BR 146 Ek 60
Lago Amanã ~ BR 117 Eb 47
Lagoa Manueira ~ BR 146 Eh 62
Lagoa Amaramba ~ MOC 344 Hk 53
Lagoa Marrangua ~ MOC 352 Hj 58
Lagoa Mirim ~ BR 141 Ek 60
Lago Anamã ~ BR 120 Ed 47
Lago Ananta ~ PE 128 Dn 53
Lago Aníbal Pinto ~ RCH 152 Dm 72
Lagoa Novo ~ BR 121 Ej 45
Lago Apinacocha ~ PE 128 Dm 53
Lagoa Piti ~ MOC 352 Hj 59
Lagoa Poelela ~ MOC 352 Hk 58
Lagoa Preta O BR 125 Ep 53
Lago Argentino ~ RA 152 Dm 71
Lago Aricota ~ PE 128 Dn 54
Lagoa Sombrio ~ BR 146 Ek 60
Lagoa Tartaruga ~ BR 121 Ek 46
Lagoa Uembje ~ MOC 352 Hj 58
Lagoa Verde O BR 121 Em 47
Lagoa Vermelho O BR 146 Ej 60
Lago Ayarde ~ RA 136 Ed 58
Lago Badajós ~ BR 120 Ec 47
Lago Banamana ~ MOC 352 Hj 57
Lago Blanco ~ RA 152 Dn 68
Lago Blanco ~ RCH 152 Dn 72
Lago Budi ~ RCH 147 Dm 65
Lago Buenos Aires ~ RA 152 Dn 69
Lago Caburgua ~ RCH 147 Dn 65
Lago Calafquen ~ RCH 147 Dm 65
Lago Campos ~ PY 136 Ed 56
Lago Cardiel ~ RA 152 Dn 70
Lago Carri Lafquen Grande ~ RA 147 Dp 66
Lago Chapo ~ RCH 147 Dm 66
Lago Chioa ~ PE 116 Dl 50
Lago Cochrane ~ RCH 152 Dm 69
Lago Colhué Huapi ~ RA 152 Dp 68
Lago Conceptión ~ BOL 129 Ec 53
Lago Conceptión ~ BOL 129 Ed 54
Lago Cóndor ~ RA 152 Dn 71
Lago Corico ~ RCH 147 Dm 65
Lago das Onças ~ BR 132 Ef 54
Lago de Arapa ~ PE 128 Dn 53
Lago de Atitlán ~ GCA 93 Dc 38
Lago de Brasilia ~ BR 133 El 53
Lago de Coari ~ BR 117 Ec 48
Lago de Coipose ~ BOL 129 Dp 55
Lago de Erepecuru ~ BR 120 Ef 46
Lago de Guzmán ~ MEX 80 Cj 30
Lago de Junín ~ PE 128 Dl 51
Lagodekhi O GE 202 Ja 25
Lago de la Laja ~ RCH 137 Dn 64
Lago del Sello ~ RA 152 Dn 69
Lago del Tigre ~ GCA 93 Dc 37
Lago del Toro ~ RCH 152 Dm 71
Lago de Poopó ~ BOL 129 Ea 55
Lago de San Lui ~ BOL 129 Eb 52
Lago de Valencia ~ YV 107 Ea 40
Lago de Yojoa ~ HN 93 Dd 38
Lago di Bolsena ~ I 185 Gm 24
Lago di Bracciano ~ I 185 Gn 24
Lago di Como ~ I 174 Gl 22
Lago di Garda ~ I 185 Gm 23
Lago Dilolo O ANG 341 Hc 51
Lago d'Iseo ~ I 185 Gm 23
Lago di Trasimeno ~ I 185 Gn 24
Lago do Bacuri ~ BR 124 En 47
Lago do Coco O BR 121 Ek 50
Lago do Rei ~ BR 120 Ee 47
Lago Elena ~ RCH 152 Dl 69
Lago Enriquillo ~ DOM 101 Dn 36
Lago Fagnano Cami ~ RA 152 Dp 73
Lago Faia ~ BR 141 Ep 57
Lago Fontana ~ RA 152 Dn 68
Lago Futalaufquen ~ RA 147 Dn 67
Lago Gaiba ~ BR 132 Ef 54
Lago Gatún ~ PA 97 Dh 41
Lago General Carrera ~ RCH 152 Dm 69
Lago General Vintter ~ RA 147 Dn 67
Lago Ghio ~ RA 152 Dn 69
Lago Grande ~ RA 152 Dp 69
Lago Grande de Manacapuru ~ BR 120 Ed 47
Lago Grande do Curuai ~ BR 120 Eg 47
Lago Huachi ~ BOL 129 Ec 53
Lago Huatunas ~ BOL 129 Ea 52
Lago Huechulafquén ~ RA 147 Dn 65
Lago Huinaimarca ~ BOL 129 Dp 54
Lago Inuria ~ PE 116 Dl 50
Lago Janauacá ~ BR 120 Ed 47
Lago Jari ~ BR 117 Ec 48
Lago Jucumarini ~ PE 128 Dn 54
Lago la Banca Grande ~ RA 147 Ec 65
Lago Lagunillas ~ PE 128 Dn 53
Lago Lanalhué ~ RCH 137 Dm 64
Lago Languí Layo ~ PE 128 Dn 53
Lago La Plata ~ RCH 152 Dn 68
Lago Llanquihue ~ RCH 147 Dm 66
Lago Loriscota ~ PE 128 Dp 54
Lago Macucocha ~ PE 128 Dm 53
Lago Mamiá ~ BR 117 Ec 48
Lago Mamori ~ BR 120 Ed 47
Lago Manaquiri ~ BR 120 Ed 47
Lago Mandioré ~ BOL 132 Ef 55
Lago Manhali ~ MOC 352 Hk 57
Lago Menéndez ~ RA 147 Dn 67
La Gomera ♁ E 292 Fm 31
Lago Miratuba ~ BR 120 Ee 47
Lago Musters ~ RA 152 Dp 68
Lago Nahuel Huapi ~ RA 147 Dn 66
Lagon d'Ouvéa ~ F 386 Nf 56
Lago Nhamanene ~ MOC 352 Hk 57
Lago Niassa ~ MOC 344 Hk 52
Lagonoy Gulf ~ RP 267 Lm 39
Lago Ofhidro ~ RCH 152 Dp 72
Lago O'Higgins ~ RCH 152 Dm 70
Lagoon Point ⌓ USA 46 Aj 17
Lago Orcococha ~ PE 128 Dl 52
Lago Pacucha ~ PE 128 Dm 52
Lago Pañe ~ PE 128 Dn 53
Lago Panguipulli ~ RCH 147 Dm 65
Lago Parinacochas ~ PE 128 Dm 53
Lago Pellegrini ~ RA 147 Ea 65
Lago Piorini ~ BR 117 Ec 47
Lago Pirehueico ~ RCH 147 Dm 65
Lago Posadas O RA 152 Dm 69
Lago Presidente Ríos ~ RCH 152 Dl 69
Lago Puelo ~ RA 147 Dn 67
Lago Pueyrredón ~ RA 152 Dn 69
Lago Puyehue ~ RCH 147 Dm 66
Lago Ranco O RCH 147 Dm 66
Lago Ranco ~ RCH 147 Dm 66
Lago Riñihue ~ RCH 147 Dm 65
Lago Rogagua ~ BOL 129 Ea 52
Lago Rogoaguado ~ BOL 129 Ea 52
Lago Rogoaguado ~ BOL 129 Eb 52
Lago Rupanco ~ RCH 147 Dm 66
Lagos O P 184 Gb 27
Lagos O WAN 320 Gh 42
Lagosa O EAT 336 Hg 48
Lago San Martin ~ RA 152 Dm 70
Lagos de Moreno O MEX 92 Cm 35
Lago Seco ~ RA 152 Dn 70
Lago Shibinacocha ~ PE 128 Dn 52
Lagos Lagoon ~ WAN 320 Gh 42
Lago Strobel ~ RA 152 Dn 70
Lago Suches ~ PE 128 Dn 54
Lago Taciuã ~ BR 120 Ed 48
Lago Tefé ~ BR 117 Eb 47
Lago Todds los Santos ~ RCH 147 Dm 66
Lago Trinidad ~ PY 136 Ed 56
Lago Uberaba ~ BR 132 Ef 54
La Gouera O MA 304 Fm 35
Lago Uru Uru ~ BOL 129 Ea 55
Lago Velcho ~ RCH 147 Dm 67
Lago Viedma O RA 152 Dm 70
Lago Viedma ~ RA 152 Dm 70
Lago Vilama ~ PY 136 Ea 57
Lago Villarrica ~ RCH 147 Dm 65
Lago Vintter O RA 152 Dn 68
Lågøya ♁ N 158 Ha 5
Lago Yulton ~ RCH 152 Dm 68
Lago Yusala ~ BOL 129 Ea 52
La Grande O USA 50 Cc 23
La Grange O USA 71 Df 26
La Grange O USA 81 Cp 31
La Grange O USA 86 Df 29
Lagrange Mission O AUS 360 Ll 55
La Gran Sabana ⏢ YV 112 Ed 43
La Grita O YV 107 Dm 41
La Gruta O RA 140 Eg 59
La Guardia O RCH 136 Dp 59
La Guardia O RA 137 Eb 60
Lagudri O RI 270 Kn 45
L'Agulhas O ZA 358 Hc 63
Laguna O USA 65 Cj 28
Laguna ••• USA 65 Cj 28
Laguna ~ RCH 137 Dn 61
Laguna O BR 141 Ek 60
Laguna Abra ~ RA 147 Ef 66
Laguna Alajuela ~ PA 97 Dj 41
Laguna Bayano ~ PA 97 Dj 41
Laguna Bismuna ~ NIC 97 Dg 38
Laguna Blanco ~ RCH 152 Dp 73
Laguna Calchaquí las Aves ~ RA 137 Ed 60
Laguna Chasicó ~ RA 147 Ec 65
Laguna Chichancanab ~ MEX 93 Dd 36
Laguna Chila ~ MEX 92 Cn 34
Laguna Colorada ~ BOL 136 Ea 57
Laguna Curicó ~ RA 147 Eb 66
Laguna de Agua Brava ~ MEX 92 Ck 34
Laguna de Bay ~ RP 267 Ll 38
Laguna de Brus ~ HN 97 Df 38
Laguna de Caratasca ~ HN 97 Df 38
Laguna de Castillos ~ ROU 146 Eh 63
Laguna de Catemaco ~ MEX 93 Da 36
Laguna de Chapala ~ MEX 92 Cl 35
Laguna de Chautengo O MEX 92 Cn 37
Laguna de Chiriquí ~ PA 97 Dg 41
Laguna de Cuitzeo ~ MEX 92 Cm 35
Laguna de la Cocha ~ CO 116 Dk 45
Laguna del Caimanero ~ MEX 92 Cj 34
Laguna del Carmen ~ MEX 93 Da 36
Laguna del Cisne ~ RA 136 Ec 60
Laguna del Este ~ MEX 93 Dc 36
Laguna del Maule ~ RCH 137 Dn 64
Laguna del Monte ~ RA 137 Ec 64
Laguna de Los Mexicanos ~ MEX 80 Cj 31
Laguna del Palmar ~ RA 137 Ed 60
Laguna del Rey O MEX 81 Cl 32
Laguna de Luna ~ RA 146 Ef 60
Laguna de Perlas ~ NIC 97 Dg 39
Laguna de Pila ~ RA 146 Ef 64
Laguna de Pozuelo ~ PY 136 Ea 57
Laguna de Rocha ~ ROU 146 Eg 63
Laguna de San Andrés ~ MEX 81 Cp 34
Laguna de Santa María ~ MEX 80 Cj 30
Laguna de Tacarigua ♀ YV 112 Eb 40
Laguna de Tamiahua ~ MEX 81 Cp 34
Laguna de Términos ~ MEX 93 Dc 36
Laguna de Tres Palos ~ MEX 92 Cn 37
Laguna de Wounta ~ NIC 97 Dg 39
Laguna dos Barros ~ BR 146 Ej 60
Laguna El Cuervo ~ MEX 80 Ck 31
Laguna El Guaje ~ MEX 81 Cl 31
Laguna Epecuén ~ RA 137 Ec 64
Laguna Galarza ~ RA 146 Ef 60
Laguna Góez ~ RA 137 Ed 63
Laguna Grande ~ RCH 137 Dn 60
Laguna Grande O RA 152 Dn 70
Laguna Guatimape ~ MEX 80 Ck 33
Laguna Iberá ~ RA 146 Ef 60
Laguna Inferior ~ MEX 93 Da 37
Laguna la Amarga ~ RA 147 Ea 65
Laguna la Argentina ~ RA 146 Ef 64
Laguna la Brava ~ RA 137 Ec 62
Laguna la Dulce ~ RA 137 Ea 64
Laguna Larga ~ RA 137 Ec 61
Laguna las Tunas Grandes ~ RA 137 Ec 63
Laguna Limpia O RA 140 Ee 59
Laguna los Mistoles ~ RA 137 Ec 61
Laguna Madre ~ USA 81 Cp 32
Laguna Madre ~ MEX 81 Cp 33
Laguna Mar Chiquita ~ RA 137 Ec 61
Laguna Mar Chiquita ~ RA 137 Ed 63
Laguna Mar Chiquita ~ RA 146 Ef 64
Laguna Melincue ~ RA 137 Ed 62
Laguna Merin ~ ROU 146 Eh 62
Laguna Mitla ~ MEX 92 Cm 37
Laguna Morán ~ RA 146 Ee 62
Laguna Negro ~ ROU 146 Eh 63
laguna Nèskynpil'gyn ~ RUS 46 Ac 11
laguna Nutaugé ~ RUS 46 Aa 11
Laguna Ojo de Liebre ~ MEX 75 Ce 32
Laguna Pahára ~ NIC 97 Dg 38
Laguna Paiva O RA 137 Ed 61
Laguna Playa Noriega ~ MEX 80 Cg 31
Laguna Pueblo Viejo ~ MEX 92 Cn 34
Laguna Ramon Grande ~ PE 116 Dh 48
Lagunas O PE 116 Dl 48
Lagunas O RCH 136 Dp 56
Laguna Salado ~ RA 146 Ef 64
Laguna San Ignacio O MEX 75 Cf 32
Laguna San Marcos ~ MEX 92 Cn 37
Lagunas Saladas ~ RA 136 Ec 60
Laguna Superior ~ MEX 93 Da 37
Laguna Tembladoras ~ MEX 93 Db 38
laguna Tènkérgynpil'gyn ~ RUS 46 Aa 11
Laguna Ttati ~ RA 146 Ef 60
Laguna Urre Lyuquén ~ RA 147 Eb 65
Laguna Vera ~ PY 140 Ef 59
Laguna Verde O YV 107 Ea 42
Laguna Verde ~ RA 147 Dp 67
Laguna Yema O RA 136 Ed 58
Laguna y Salina Llancañelo ~ RA 137 Dp 63
Lagune Aby ~ CI 317 Ge 43
Lagune Bay ~ CI 317 Ge 43
Lagune Ebrié ~ CI 317 Gd 43
Lagune Ndogo ~ G 332 Gm 47
Lagune Nkomi ~ G 332 Gl 46
Lagune Tadio ~ CI 317 Gd 43
Lagunillas O YV 107 Dn 40
Lagunillas O BOL 129 Ec 55
La Gygnes Lake ~ USA 70 Da 26
Lah O IND 230 Kc 28
Laha O RI 282 Lp 47
La Habana Havana ▣ C 100 Dg 34
Lahad Datu O MAL 124 Lk 43
La Hai O VN 263 Le 39
Lahaina O USA 75 Am 35
Lahār O IND 234 Kd 32
Lahat O RI 278 Lb 47
Lahe O MYA 254 Km 32
Lahemaa ♀ EST 171 He 16
La Hermosa O CO 107 Dn 43
Lahewa O RI 270 Kn 45
Lahiğ O YE 218 Ja 39
Lāhīğān O IR 209 Jc 27
La Higuera O RCH 137 Dn 60
Lahiti O FIN 159 He 15
Lahn ~ D 174 Gl 20
Laholmsbukten ~ S 170 Gn 17
La Honda O CO 106 Dk 42
Lahore O PK 230 Kb 30
La Horqueta O MEX 93 Da 37
La Horqueta O YV 112 Ec 41
La Horqueta O YV 112 Ed 42
Lahotan Reservoir ~ USA 64 Cc 26
Lahri O PK 227 Jn 31
La Huacana O MEX 92 Cm 36
La Huerra O MEX 92 Ck 36
La Huerta O RCH 137 Dn 63
Laï O TCH 321 Ha 41
Laiagam O PNG 286 Mh 48
Laiama O PNG 287 Ml 49
Lai'an O VRC 246 Lk 29
Lai Châu O VN 255 Lb 34
Laifeng O VRC 255 Le 31
Laihia O FIN 159 Hd 14
Lai-hka O MYA 254 Kn 35
Lailā O KSA 218 Jb 34
Lailaba O WAN 320 Gj 39
Laila Outka △ MA 293 Gd 28
Laimu O RI 283 Ma 47
Laingsburg O ZA 358 Hc 62
Laingsnek △ ZA 349 Hg 59
Lainioälven ~ S 159 Hd 12
Lairg O GB 162 Gd 16
Lai River ~ PNG 287 Mj 48
Lais O RI 270 La 47
Laisälven ~ S 158 Ha 13
Laisamis O EAK 325 Hl 45
Laiševo O RUS 181 Jc 18
Laiwu O VRC 246 Lj 27
Laiwui O RI 283 Lp 46
Laixi O VRC 246 Ll 27
Laiyang O VRC 246 Ll 27
Laiyuan O VRC 243 Lh 26
Laizhou O VRC 246 Ll 27
Laja O BOL 129 Dp 54
Laja ~ RCH 137 Dm 64
La Jagua O C 100 Dj 35
La Jagua de Ibirico O CO 107 Dm 41
Laja Larga O YV 107 Ea 42
Lajamanu Hooker Creek O AUS 364 Mb 55
La Jaram ⏢ MA 292 Ga 32
Lajas O PE 116 Dj 49
Lajas ~ RA 136 Ea 59
Laje O BR 125 Fa 52
Lajeado O BR 146 Eh 60
Lajeado Grande O BR 146 Ej 60
Lajedão O BR 125 Ep 54
Lajedo O BR 124 Fb 50
La Jerónima O RA 152 Dm 71
Lajes O BR 124 Fb 48
Lajinha O BR 141 Ep 56
Lajitas O USA 81 Cl 31
Lajkovac O SCG 174 Hb 23
La Joya de los Sachas O EC 116 Dk 46
La Junta O USA 65 Cl 27
Laka Chew Bahir Lake Stephanie ~ ETH 325 Hl 43
Lakamané O RMM 304 Gb 38
Lake Abbé ~ ETH 313 Hn 40
Lake Abert ~ USA 50 Cb 24
Lake Abitibi ~ CDN 57 Dh 21
Lake Acraman ~ AUS 378 Md 62
Lake Albacutya ~ AUS 378 Mg 63
Lake Albert ~ EAU 324 Hh 45
Lake Albert ~ AUS 378 Mf 63
Lake Alexandrina ~ AUS 378 Mf 63
Lake Alma O CDN 51 Ck 20
Lake Almanor ~ USA 64 Cb 25
Lake Amadeus ~ AUS 369 Mb 58
Lake Amboseli ~ EAK 337 Hl 47
Lake Anec ~ AUS 361 Ma 57
Lake Anna ~ USA 74 Dk 26
Lake Annean ~ AUS 368 Lk 59
Lake Aougoundou ~ RMM 305 Ge 38
Lake Argyle O AUS 364 Ma 54
Lake Argyle ~ AUS 364 Ma 54
Lake Ar Razzāzah ~ IRQ 209 Hp 29
Lake Arrowhead ~ USA 70 Cn 29
Lake Arthur O USA 86 Db 30
Lake Ashtabula ~ USA 56 Cp 22
Lake Assad ~ SYR 209 Hm 28
Lake Athabasca ~ CDN 6 Db 4
Lake Ath Tharthar ~ IRQ 209 Hp 29
Lake Auld ~ AUS 361 Lm 57
Lake Austin ~ AUS 368 Lk 59
Lake Avon ~ AUS 379 Mm 63
Lake Avu ~ PNG 286 Mg 49
Lake Baker ~ AUS 369 Lp 59
Lake Ballard ~ AUS 368 Ll 60
Lake Balqash ~ KZ 22 Nb 5
Lake Bangala ~ ZW 352 Hh 56
Lake Bangweulu ~ Z 341 Hg 51
Lake Baringo ~ EAK 325 Hl 45
Lake Barkley ~ USA 71 Dd 27
Lake Barlee ~ AUS 368 Lk 60
Lake Baykal ~ RUS 22 Qa 4
Lake Baykal ~ RUS 204 Va 8
Lake Beachêne ~ CDN 60 Dj 22
Lake Bedford ~ AUS 369 Lm 59
Lake Benmore ~ NZ 382 Nh 68
Lake Bennett ~ AUS 361 Mb 57
Lake Benton O USA 56 Cp 23
Lake Betty ~ AUS 361 Lp 55
Lake Biddy O AUS 368 Lk 62
Lake Bindegolly ~ AUS 375 Mj 60
Lake Bisina ~ EAU 325 Hj 45
Lake Bistineau ~ USA 70 Db 29
Lake Blanche ~ AUS 360 Lm 57
Lake Blanche ~ AUS 374 Mf 60
Lake Boga O AUS 379 Mh 63
Lake Bogoria ~ EAK 325 Hl 45
Lake Bolac O AUS 378 Mh 64
Lake Bonney ~ AUS 378 Mf 64
Lake Borgne ~ USA 86 Dd 30
Lake Bosumtwi ~ GH 317 Gf 42
Lake Breaden ~ AUS 369 Ln 58
Lake Brewster ~ AUS 379 Mk 62
Lake Brown ~ AUS 368 Lk 61
Lake Brownwood ~ USA 81 Cn 30
Lake Brunner ~ NZ 382 Nh 67
Lake Buchanan ~ AUS 368 Lm 58
Lake Buchanan ~ AUS 375 Mj 56
Lake Buck ~ AUS 364 Mb 55
Lake Buloke ~ AUS 378 Mh 64
Lake Bunyanyi ~ EAU 336 Hg 46
Lake Burera ~ RWA 336 Hg 46
Lake Burigi ~ EAT 336 Hh 46
Lake Burkanoko ~ AUS 375 Mj 60
Lake Burnside ~ AUS 368 Lm 58
Lake Burrumbeet ~ AUS 378 Mh 64
Lake Buyo ~ CI 305 Gc 42
Lake C. W. McConaughy ~ USA 65 Cl 25
Lake Cadibarrawirracanna ~ AUS 374 Md 60
Lake Callabonna ~ AUS 374 Mf 60
Lake Callara ~ AUS 374 Me 60
Lake Carey ~ AUS 368 Lm 60
Lake Cargelligo O AUS 379 Mk 62
Lake Carmody ~ AUS 368 Lk 62
Lake Carnegie ~ AUS 368 Lm 59
Lake Caroline ~ AUS 374 Me 58
Lake Chad ~ RN 321 Gn 39
Lake Champlain ~ USA 60 Dm 23
Lake Charles O USA 86 Db 30
Lake Charlevoix ~ USA 57 Df 23
Lake Chelan ~ USA 50 Cb 21
Lake Chilika ~ IND 235 Kg 36
Lake Chilwa ~ MW 344 Hk 53
Lake Chinta ~ MOC 344 Hk 53
Lake Chippewa ~ USA 56 Dc 23
Lake Christopher ~ AUS 369 Lp 58
Lake City O USA 56 Cp 23
Lake City O USA 65 Cj 26
Lake City O USA 86 Dg 30
Lake City O USA 87 Dj 29
Lake Claire ~ CDN 42 Eb 7
Lake Clark ~ USA 46 An 15
Lake Clark National Park & Preserve ♀ USA 46 An 15
Lake Cobb ~ AUS 369 Lp 58
Lake Coleridge ~ NZ 382 Nh 67
Lake Conroe ~ USA 81 Da 30
Lake Constance ~ 174 Gl 22
Lake Conway ~ AUS 374 Md 60
Lake Corangamite ~ AUS 378 Mh 65
Lake Corpus Christi ~ USA 81 Cn 31
Lake Country O CDN 50 Cc 20
Lake Cowal ~ AUS 379 Mk 62
Lake Cowan ~ AUS 368 Lm 61
Lake Crowley ~ USA 64 Cc 27
Lake Crystel O USA 56 Da 23
Lake Cumberland ~ USA 71 Df 27
Lake Cunningham ~ ZW 349 Hg 56
Lake Cyohoha Sud ~ BU 336 Hg 47
Lake Dakataua ~ PNG 287 Mm 48
Lake Darlot ~ AUS 368 Ll 59
Lake Dartmouth ~ AUS 375 Mj 59
Lake Debo ~ RMM 305 Gd 38
Lake Deborah ~ AUS 368 Lk 61
Lake Deborah East ~ AUS 368 Lk 61
Lake Deborah West ~ AUS 368 Lk 61
Lake De Burgh ~ AUS 364 Md 55
Lake Dennis ~ AUS 361 Ma 56
Lake Dey-Dey ~ AUS 369 Mb 60
Lake Diefenbaker ~ CDN 51 Cj 20
Lake Disappointment ~ AUS 360 Lm 57
Lake District ♀ GB 162 Gd 18
Lake Do ~ RMM 305 Ge 38
Lake Dora ~ AUS 360 Lm 57
Lake Dundas ~ AUS 368 Ll 62
Lake Dutton ~ AUS 378 Me 61
Lake Echo O CDN 61 Ec 23
Lake Edward ~ EAU 336 Hg 46
Lake Eildon ~ AUS 379 Mk 64
Lake Eliza ~ AUS 378 Mf 64
Lake Ellesmere ~ NZ 383 Nj 67
Lake Elwell ~ USA 51 Cg 21
Lake Erie ~ CDN/USA 57 Dh 24
Lake Erie ~ CDN/USA 71 Dh 24
Lake Etamunbanie ~ AUS 374 Mf 59
Lake Eucumbene ~ AUS 379 Ml 64
Lake Everard ~ AUS 378 Md 61
Lake Eyasi ~ EAT 337 Hk 47
Lake Eyre ♀ AUS 374 Me 60
Lake Eyre Basin ⏢ AUS 374 Me 59
Lake Eyre North ~ AUS 374 Me 60
Lake Eyre South ~ AUS 374 Me 60
Lake Faguibine ~ RMM 305 Gd 37
Lake Farnham ~ AUS 369 Lp 58
Lake Fati ~ RMM 305 Ge 37
Lakefield ♀ AUS 365 Mh 53
Lakefield O AUS 365 Mj 53
Lake Fleur de May ~ CDN 61 Eb 19
Lake Florence ~ AUS 374 Mf 60
Lake Fork Reservation ~ USA 70 Da 29
Lake Francis Case ~ USA 56 Cn 24
Lake Frome ~ AUS 378 Mf 61
Lake Gairdner ~ AUS 378 Md 61
Lake Gairdner ♀ AUS 378 Md 61
Lake Galilee ~ AUS 375 Mj 57
Lake Garnpung ~ AUS 378 Mh 62
Lake Garou ~ RMM 305 Ge 37
Lake Geneva ~ CH 163 Gk 22
Lake George O USA 60 Dm 24
Lake George ~ USA 87 Dh 31
Lake George ~ EAU 324 Hh 45
Lake George ~ AUS 361 Lm 57
Lake George ~ AUS 378 Mf 64
Lake George ~ AUS 379 Ml 63
Lake Gidgi ~ AUS 369 Lp 60
Lake Giles ~ AUS 368 Lk 60
Lake Gillen ~ AUS 369 Ln 59
Lake Gilles ~ AUS 378 Me 62
Lake Gilmore ~ AUS 368 Ll 62
Lake Gogebic ~ USA 57 Dd 22
Lake Goorly ~ AUS 368 Lj 61
Lake Gordon ~ AUS 378 Mk 67
Lake Grace O AUS 368 Lk 62
Lake Grace North ~ AUS 368 Lk 62
Lake Grace South ~ AUS 368 Lk 62
Lake Granby ~ USA 65 Ck 25
Lake Grandin ~ CDN 47 Cc 13
Lake Granger ~ USA 81 Cp 30
Lake Greenwood ~ USA 71 Dh 28
Lake Greeson ~ USA 70 Db 28
Lake Gregory ~ AUS 368 Lk 58
Lake Gregory ~ AUS 374 Mf 60
Lake Gruszka ~ AUS 369 Ln 58
Lake Hamilton ~ AUS 378 Md 63
Lakehamu River ~ PNG 287 Mk 49
Lake Hancock ~ AUS 369 Ln 58
Lake Hanson ~ AUS 378 Me 61
Lake Harbour O CDN 43 Hb 6
Lake Haribomo ~ RMM 305 Ge 37
Lake Haridon Bight ~ AUS 368 Lg 59
Lake Harris ~ AUS 378 Md 61
Lake Hart ~ AUS 378 Me 61
Lake Harvey ~ AUS 368 Lj 61
Lake Hauroko ~ NZ 382 Nf 68
Lake Havasu City O USA 64 Ce 28
Lake Hawea O NZ 382 Ng 68
Lake Hawea ~ NZ 382 Ng 68
Lake Hillman ~ AUS 368 Lj 61
Lake Hindmarsh ~ AUS 378 Mg 64
Lake Hoar ~ AUS 369 Lm 58
Lake Hope ~ AUS 368 Ll 62
Lake Hope or Panda ~ AUS 374 Mf 60
Lake Hopkins ~ AUS 369 Ma 58
Lake Houston ~ USA 81 Da 30
Lake Howitt ~ AUS 374 Mf 59
Lake Hume ~ AUS 379 Mk 64
Lake Huron ~ CDN 57 Dg 23
Lake Huron ~ CDN/USA 57 Dg 23
Lake Ihema ~ RWA 336 Hh 46
Lake Ikimba ~ EAT 336 Hh 46
Lake Illawarra ~ AUS 379 Mm 63
Lake Ilma ~ AUS 369 Lp 60
Lake Isabella O USA 64 Cc 28
Lake Itaska O USA 56 Da 22
Lake Itezhi-Tezhi ~ Z 341 He 53
Lake J.B.Thomas ~ USA 70 Cm 29
Lake Jackson O USA 81 Da 31
Lake Jeffries ~ AUS 368 Lm 59
Lake Jipe ~ EAK 337 Hl 47
Lake Jones ~ AUS 361 Lp 55
Lake Jones ~ AUS 369 Ln 58
Lake Joseph ~ CDN 60 Dj 23
Lake Julius ~ AUS 374 Mf 56
Lake Kabara ~ RMM 305 Gd 38
Lake Kamplombo ~ Z 341 Hg 51
Lake Katubu ~ PNG 286 Mh 49
Lake Keene ~ AUS 369 Lm 58
Lake Keepit ~ AUS 379 Mm 61
Lake Kemp ~ USA 70 Cn 29
Lake Kenering ~ MAL 270 La 43
Lake Kijanebalola ~ EAU 336 Hh 46
Lake King O AUS 368 Lk 62
Lake King ~ AUS 368 Lk 62
Lake Kissimmee ~ USA 87 Dh 32
Lake Kitangiri ~ EAT 337 Hk 48
Lake Kittakittaooloo ~ AUS 374 Mf 59
Lake Kivu ~ RDC 336 Hg 46
Lake Knowee ~ USA 71 Dg 28
Lake Koocanusa ~ CDN 50 Ce 21
Lake Koodnanie ~ AUS 374 Mf 59
Lake Koolkootinnie ~ AUS 374 Me 59
Lake Koraou ~ RMM 305 Ge 38
Lake Kosi ~ ZA 352 Hj 59
Lake Kossou ~ CI 317 Gd 42
Lake Kwania ~ EAU 324 Hj 45
Lake Kwinina ~ PNG 286 Mg 49
Lake Kyoga ~ EAU 324 Hj 45
Lake Laberge ~ CDN 47 Bj 15
Lake Labyrinth ~ AUS 378 Md 61
Lake Ladoga ~ RUS 171 Hh 15
Lake Lagdo ~ CAM 321 Gn 41
Lake Lanagan ~ AUS 361 Lp 55
Lake Lanao ~ RP 275 Ln 42
Lakeland O USA 86 Dg 30
Lakeland O USA 87 Dg 31
Lakeland Downs O AUS 365 Mj 53
Lake Lavon ~ USA 70 Cp 29
Lake Leaghur ~ AUS 378 Mh 62
Lake Leckhart ~ AUS 368 Lk 62
Lake Lefroy ~ AUS 368 Ll 61
Lake Lewisville ~ USA 70 Cp 29
Lake Liambezi ~ NAM 341 He 54
Lake Limestone ~ USA 81 Cp 30
Lake Lindon B. Johnson ~ USA 81 Cn 30
Lake Livingston ~ USA 81 Da 30
Lake Logipi ~ EAK 325 Hl 44
Lake Louise ~ USA 46 Bc 13
Lake Louise O CDN 50 Cd 20
Lake Lucerne ~ CH 174 Gl 22
Lake Lusiwasi ~ Z 341 Hh 52
Lake Mabesi ~ WAL 316 Ga 42
Lake MacDonald ~ AUS 361 Ma 57
Lake Macfarlane ~ AUS 378 Me 62
Lake Machattie ~ AUS 374 Mf 58
Lake Mackay ~ AUS 361 Ma 57
Lake Mackay Aboriginal Land ••• AUS 361 Ma 56
Lake MacLeod ~ AUS 368 Lg 58
Lake Macquarie ~ AUS 379 Mm 62
Lake Magadi ~ EAK 337 Hl 47
Lake Magenta ~ AUS 368 Lk 62
Lake Maggiore ~ I 174 Gl 22
Lake Mahinerangi ~ NZ 382 Ng 68
Lake Mai-Ndombe ~ RDC 333 Hb 47
Lake Mainit ~ RP 267 Ln 41
Lake Maitland ~ AUS 368 Ll 59
Lake Malata ~ AUS 378 Md 63
Lake Malawi ~ MW 344 Hk 51
Lake Malawi ♀ MW 344 Hk 52
Lake Malombe ~ MW 344 Hk 53
Lake Managua ~ NIC 96 De 39
Lake Manantali ~ RMM 316 Ga 39
Lake Manapouri ~ NZ 382 Nf 68
Lake Manitoba ~ CDN 56 Cn 20
Lake Manjirenji ~ ZW 352 Hh 56
Lake Manyane ~ ZW 341 Hh 54
Lake Manyara ~ EAT 337 Hk 47
Lake Maracaibo ~ YV 107 Dn 40

436 Lagamar - Lake Maracaibo

Lake Marion ~ USA 71 Dh 29
Lake Marmion ~ AUS 368 Ll 60
Lake Martin ~ USA 86 Df 29
Lake Mason ~ AUS 368 Lk 59
Lake Maurepas ~ USA 86 Dc 30
Lake Maurice ~ AUS 369 Mb 60
Lakemba △ FJI 390 Aa 55
Lake Mbakaou ~ CAM 321 Gn 42
Lakemba Passage ~ FJI 390 Aa 55
Lake Mburo ♀ EAU 336 Hh 46
Lake McGregor ~ CDN 51 Cf 20
Lake McLernon ~ AUS 361 Lp 55
Lake McMillan ~ USA 65 Ck 29
Lake Mead ~ USA 64 Ce 28
Lake Melville ~ CDN 7 Ga 4
Lake Meramangye ~ AUS 369 Mc 60
Lake Meranda ~ AUS 368 Ll 59
Lake Meridith ~ USA 70 Cm 28
Lake Michigan ~ USA 57 De 24
Lake Mills ♀ USA 56 Da 24
Lake Minchumina ◎ USA 46 An 13
Lake Minchumina ~ USA 46 An 13
Lake Mindona ~ AUS 378 Mb 62
Lake Minigwal ~ AUS 369 Lm 60
Lake Mipia ~ AUS 378 Mf 58
Lake Mistassini ~ CDN 43 Ha 8
Lake Mohave ~ USA 64 Ce 28
Lake Mokoan ~ AUS 379 Mk 64
Lake Mondurran ~ AUS 375 Mm 58
Lake Monowai ~ NZ 382 Nf 68
Lake Moondarra ~ AUS 374 Mf 56
Lake Moore ~ AUS 368 Lj 60
Lake Moultrie ~ USA 71 Dh 29
Lake Muhazi ~ RWA 336 Hh 46
Lake Mulapula ~ AUS 374 Mf 60
Lake Mungo ~ AUS 378 Mb 62
Lake Murray ~ USA 71 Dh 28
Lake Murray ~ PNG 286 Mg 49
Lake Murray ~ PNG 286 Mg 49
Lake Mutirikwe ~ ZW 352 Hh 56
Lake Mweru ~ RDC 336 Hg 50
Lake Mweru Wantipa ~ Z 336 Hg 50
Lake Nabberu ~ AUS 368 Ll 58
Lake Naivasha ~ EAK 337 Hk 46
Lake Nakuru ~ EAK 337 Hk 46
Lake Nash ◎ AUS 374 Me 56
Lake Nasser ~ ET 301 Hj 34
Lake Nasser ~ ET 301 Hj 34
Lake Natron ~ EAT 337 Hl 47
Lake Neale ~ AUS 369 Mb 58
Lake Nerka ~ USA 46 Al 15
Lake Newell ~ AUS 369 Lp 58
Lake Ngami ~ RB 349 Hd 56
Lake Niangay ~ RMM 305 Ge 38
Lake Nicaragua ~ NIC 97 Df 40
Lake Nipigon ~ CDN 57 Dd 21
Lake Nipissing ~ CDN 60 Dj 22
Lake Noondie ~ AUS 368 Lk 60
Lake Norman ~ USA 71 Dh 28
Lake Ntomba ~ RDC 333 Ha 46
Lake Numalla ~ AUS 375 Mj 60
Lake Oahe ~ USA 56 Cm 23
Lake Oconee ~ USA 71 Dg 29
Lake of Bays ~ CDN 60 Dj 23
Lake of the Ozarks ~ USA 70 Db 26
Lake Ogascana ~ CDN 60 Dj 22
Lake Ohau ~ NZ 382 Ng 68
Lake Ohrid ~ AL 194 Hc 25
Lake Okeechobee ~ USA 87 Dh 32
Lake Onega ~ RUS 171 Hk 15
Lake Ontario ~ CDN/USA 60 Dj 24
Lake Opeta ~ EAU 325 Hk 45
Lake Oro ~ RMM 305 Gd 37
Lake O'the Pines ~ USA 70 Da 29
Lake Owyhee ~ USA 50 Cd 24
Lake Palestine ~ USA 70 Da 29
Lake Panache ~ CDN 57 Dh 22
Lake Panache ~ CDN 57 Dh 22
Lake Paringa ◎ NZ 382 Ng 67
Lake Park ◎ USA 86 Dg 30
Lake Patman ~ USA 70 Da 29
Lake Pedder ~ AUS 383 Mf 67
Lake Peipus ~ EST 171 Hf 16
Lake Philippi ~ AUS 374 Mf 58
Lake Piso ~ LB 316 Ga 42
Lake Placid ◎ USA 60 Dj 23
Lake Placid ◎ USA 87 Dh 32
Lake Pleasant ◎ USA 60 Dj 24
Lake Poinsett ~ USA 56 Cp 23
Lake Pontchartrain ~ USA 86 Dc 30
Lakeport ◎ USA 64 Ca 26
Lake Poteriteri ~ NZ 382 Nf 69
Lake Powell ~ USA 64 Cf 27
Lake Poygan ~ USA 57 Dd 23
Lake Prespa ~ MK 194 Hc 25
Lake Providence ◎ USA 86 Dc 30
Lake Pukaki ~ NZ 382 Nh 67
Lake Puntawolana ~ AUS 374 Mf 60
Lake Raeside ~ AUS 368 Lm 60
Lake Rara National Park ♀ NEP 235 Kf 31
Lake Ray Robert ~ USA 70 Cp 29
Lake Rebecca ~ AUS 368 Lm 61
Lake Red Rock ~ USA 70 Db 25
Lake Roe ~ AUS 368 Lm 61
Lake Rosa ~ BS 101 Dm 35
Lake Rosseau ~ CDN 60 Dj 23
Lake Rossignol ~ CDN 61 Eb 23
Lake Rotoroa ~ NZ 383 Nj 66
Lake Rotorua ~ NZ 383 Nl 64
Lake Rukwa ~ EAT 336 Hh 49
Lake Rweru ~ BU 336 Hh 47
Lake Sagara ~ EAT 336 Hh 48
Lake Sakakawea ~ USA 51 Cl 22
Lake Scugog ~ CDN 60 Dj 23
Lake Scutari ~ AL 194 Hb 24
Lake Seabrook ~ AUS 368 Lk 61
Lake Sélingue ~ RMM 316 Gb 40
Lake Seminole ~ USA 86 De 30
Lakes Entrance ◎ AUS 379 Ml 64
Lake Sevan ~ ARM 202 Ja 26
Lake Sharpe ~ AUS 368 Ll 62
Lake Shelbyville ~ USA 57 De 26
Lakeshore ◎ USA 64 Cc 27
Lake Short ~ AUS 374 Mf 59
Lake Sibaya ~ ZA 352 Hj 59
Lakeside ◎ USA 50 Bp 24
Lakeside ◎ USA 74 Dk 27
Lake Sidney Lanier ~ USA 71 Dg 28

Lake Simcoe ~ CDN 60 Dj 23
Lake Sinclair ~ USA 71 Dg 29
Lake Sprenger ~ AUS 369 Ln 58
Lake St.Claire ~ USA 57 Dg 24
Lake St.Joseph ~ CDN 56 Dc 20
Lake St. Lucia ~ ZA 352 Hj 60
Lake St. Martin ~ CDN 56 Cn 20
Lake Stamford ~ USA 70 Cn 29
Lake Stephanie ~ ETH 325 Hl 43
Lake Summer ~ NZ 383 Nj 67
Lake Sumner ~ NZ 383 Nj 67
Lake Superior ~ USA 57 Dd 22
Lake Sylvester ~ AUS 364 Me 55
Lake Szega ~ PNG 286 Mg 49
Lake Taal ~ RP 267 Ll 38
Lake Tahoe ~ USA 64 Cb 26
Lake Talquin ~ USA 86 Df 30
Lake Tana ~ ETH 313 Hl 39
Lake Tanda ~ RMM 305 Gd 38
Lake Tanganyika ~ RDC 336 Hg 48
Lake Tarrabool ~ AUS 364 Md 55
Lake Taupo ~ NZ 383 Nk 65
Lake Tawakoni ~ USA 70 Da 29
Lake Tay ~ AUS 368 Ll 62
Lake Te Anau ~ NZ 382 Nf 68
Lake Tekapo ~ NZ 382 Nh 67
Lake Tekapo ~ NZ 382 Nh 67
Lake Télé ~ RMM 305 Ge 37
Lake Temagami ~ CDN 57 Dh 22
Lake Temengor ~ MAL 270 La 43
Lake Te Nggano ~ SOL 290 Nc 51
Lake Tes ~ VU 386 Nf 53
Lake Texana ~ USA 81 Cp 31
Lake Texoma ~ USA 70 Cp 29
Lake Throssel ~ AUS 369 Ln 59
Lake Titicaca ~ PE 128 Dp 53
Lake Togo ~ RT 317 Gg 42
Lake Torquinie ~ AUS 374 Mf 58
Lake Torrens ~ AUS 378 Mb 61
Lake Torrens ♀ AUS 378 Me 61
Laketown ◎ USA 65 Cg 25
Lake Travis ~ USA 81 Cn 30
Lake Tschida ~ USA 51 Cl 22
Lake Turkana ~ EAK 325 Hk 44
Lake Tyrrell ~ AUS 378 Mh 63
Lake Uloowaranie ~ AUS 374 Mf 59
Lake Urana ~ AUS 378 Mk 63
Lake Urmia ~ IR 209 Ja 27
Lake Valley ~ USA 64 Ce 26
Lake Van ~ TR 202 Hp 26
Lake Victoria ~ EAT 336 Hj 46
Lake Victoria ~ AUS 378 Mg 62
Lakeview ◎ USA 50 Cb 24
Lake Village ~ USA 51 Cg 23
Lake Village ◎ USA 86 Dc 27
Lake Violet ~ AUS 368 Ll 59
Lake Waikare ~ NZ 383 Nk 64
Lake Wairarapa ~ NZ 383 Nk 66
Lake Wakatipu ~ NZ 382 Ng 68
Lake Walcott ~ USA 64 Cf 24
Lake Wales ◎ USA 87 Dh 32
Lake Wallambin ~ AUS 368 Lj 61
Lake Wamala ~ EAU 324 Hh 45
Lake Wanaka ~ NZ 382 Ng 68
Lake Wappapello ~ USA 71 Dc 27
Lake Warrakalanna ~ AUS 374 Mf 60
Lake Warrandirinna ~ AUS 374 Me 59
Lake Wateree ~ USA 71 Dh 28
Lake Waukarlycarly ~ AUS 360 Lm 56
Lake Way ~ AUS 368 Ll 59
Lake Wellington ~ AUS 379 Mk 65
Lake Wells ~ AUS 368 Lm 59
Lake White ~ AUS 361 Ma 56
Lake Wills ~ AUS 361 Ma 56
Lake Windamere ~ AUS 379 Ml 62
Lake Winifred ~ AUS 360 Lm 57
Lake Winnebago ~ USA 57 Dd 24
Lake Winnipeg ~ CDN 6 Ea 4
Lake Winnipeg ~ CDN 42 Fb 8
Lake Winnipeg ~ CDN 56 Cn 19
Lake Winnipegosis ~ CDN 6 Db 4
Lake Winnipegosis ~ CDN 56 Cm 19
Lake Winnipesaukee ~ USA 60 Dn 24
Lake Wisdom ~ PNG 287 Mk 48
Lake Wivenhoe ~ AUS 375 Mn 59
Lakewood ◎ USA 65 Ck 26
Lakewood ◎ USA 65 Ck 29
Lakewood ◎ USA 74 Dl 25
Lake Woods ~ AUS 364 Mc 54
Lake Worth ◎ USA 87 Dh 32
Lake Wyangala ~ AUS 379 Ml 62
Lake Wyara ~ AUS 375 Mj 60
Lake Xau ~ RB 349 He 56
Lake Yamma Yamma ~ AUS 374 Mg 59
Lake Yindarlgooda ~ AUS 368 Lm 61
Lake Younghusband ~ AUS 378 Me 61
Lake Zaysan ~ KZ 22 Pa 5
Lake Zaysan ~ KZ 204 Tb 9
Lakhcheb ◎ RIM 304 Ga 36
Lakhdaria ◎ DZ 296 Gh 27
Lakhimpur ◎ IND 234 Ke 32
Lakhipur ◎ IND 254 Kl 33
Lakhnâdon ◎ IND 234 Kd 34
Lakhpat ◎ IND 232 Jm 34
Lākhra ◎ PK 227 Jm 33
Lakhya ~ BD 235 Kg 33
Lakin ◎ USA 70 Cm 27
Lakinsk ◎ RUS 171 Hm 17
Lakki ◎ PK 223 Jp 29
Lakonikós Kolpós ~ GR 194 Hd 27
Lakota ◎ USA 56 Cn 21
Lakota ◎ USA 56 Da 24
Lakota ◎ CI 317 Gd 43
Laksefjorden ~ N 159 Hf 10
Lakselv ◎ N 159 He 11
Laksfossen ~ N 158 Gn 13
Lakshadweep ◎ IND 239 Ka 40
Lakshadweep Islands △ IND 239 Ka 40
Lakshadweep Sea ~ 239 Kb 41
Lakshimpur ◎ BD 235 Kk 34
Lakshmipur ◎ IND 262 Kl 39
Laktaši ◎ BIH 174 Ha 23
Lakuan ◎ RI 275 Ll 45
Lala ◎ RP 275 Lm 42
La Labor ◎ HN 93 Dd 38

Lalafuta ~ Z 341 He 53
Lalago ◎ EAT 337 Hj 47
La Laguna ◎ RA 137 Ec 62
La Laguna ◎ E 292 Fm 31
La Laja ◎ RA 137 Cp 34
La Laja ◎ YV 112 Ed 43
La Laja ◎ RCH 137 Dm 64
La Laja ◎ RCH 137 Dn 60
Lâlâ Muisâ ~ PK 230 Ka 29
Lalang ◎ RI 278 Lc 47
Lalapansi ◎ ZW 341 Hg 55
Lalara ◎ G 332 Gm 45
Lalaua ◎ MOC 344 Hm 53
Lalaua ◎ MOC 344 Hm 53
Lalbert ◎ AUS 378 Mh 63
Lalbiti ◎ NEP 235 Kg 32
L'Alcúdia ◎ E 184 Gf 26
Laleham ◎ AUS 375 Ml 57
Lâlezâr ~ IR 226 Jg 31
Lâlganj ◎ IND 234 Ke 32
Lālganj ◎ IND 234 Kf 33
Lālī ◎ IR 209 Jc 29
Lalibela ◎ ETH 313 Hm 39
La Libertad ◎ ES 93 Dd 39
La Libertad ◎ HN 96 De 38
La Libertad ◎ EC 116 Dh 47
La Ligua ◎ RCH 137 Dn 61
La Ligua ◎ RCH 137 Dn 62
Laliki ◎ RI 282 Lp 49
La Lima ◎ HN 96 De 38
Lalín ◎ E 184 Gb 24
Lalindu ~ RI 282 Ll 47
La Línea ◎ E 184 Gd 27
Lalitpur ◎ IND 234 Kd 33
Lalla Rookh ◎ AUS 360 Lk 56
Lal-lo ◎ RP 267 Ll 36
La Loche ◎ CDN 42 Ec 7
Lâlsot ◎ IND 234 Kc 32
Laluagon ◎ RI 282 Ll 46
La Macarena ◎ CO 107 Dm 44
La Madera ◎ YV 112 Ec 41
La Madrid ◎ RA 137 Eb 60
La Madrugada ◎ RA 152 Ea 69
la Maiella △ I 194 Gp 24
Lamainong ◎ RI 270 Kn 44
La Majada ◎ RA 137 Eb 60
Lamalaga ◎ MA 304 Fm 34
Lamalera ◎ RI 282 Lm 50
Lamaline ◎ CDN 61 Ef 22
La Mancha ◎ E 184 Ge 26
La Manuela ◎ RA 137 Ec 64
Lamap ◎ VU 386 Nf 54
Lamar ◎ USA 65 Cl 26
Lamar ◎ USA 70 Da 27
La Margarita del Norte ◎ MEX 81 Cl 32
La Marque ◎ USA 81 Da 31
La Marsa ◎ TN 297 Gm 27
Lamas ◎ PE 116 Dk 49
La Masica ◎ HN 96 De 38
La Maya ◎ C 101 Dl 35
Lamballe ◎ F 163 Ge 21
Lambaréné ◎ G 332 Gm 46
Lambari ◎ BR 133 Em 55
Lambarí ◎ BR 141 Em 56
Lambaro Angan ◎ RI 270 Km 43
Lambayeque ◎ PE 116 Dh 49
Lambert's Bay ◎ ZA 358 Ha 62
Lambi ◎ SOL 290 Nb 50
Lambualano ◎ RI 282 Lm 48
Lambumbu Bay ~ VU 386 Nf 54
Lamdesar ◎ RI 283 Mb 49
Lamé ◎ TCH 321 Gp 41
Lame Deer ◎ USA 51 Cj 23
Lamego ◎ P 184 Gc 25
Lameguapi ◎ RCH 147 Dl 66
Lamend ◎ USA 70 Cm 26
Lameroo ◎ AUS 378 Mg 63
La Mesa ◎ USA 64 Cd 29
La Mesa ◎ USA 65 Cj 29
Lamesa ◎ USA 70 Cn 29
La Mesa ◎ CO 106 Dl 43
La Mesa ◎ YV 107 Dn 40
La Mesilla ◎ GCA 93 Dc 38
Lami ◎ FJI 387 Nm 55
Lamía ◎ GR 194 Hd 26
Lamindo ◎ SUD 324 Hh 43
Lamington ♀ AUS 375 Mn 60
La Misión ◎ MEX 64 Cd 29
Lamison ◎ USA 71 De 29
Lamitan ◎ RP 275 Lm 42
Lammeulo ◎ RI 270 Km 43
Lamon Bay ~ RP 267 Lm 38
Lamongan ◎ RI 279 Lg 49
La Montaña ~ PE 116 Dl 49
La Mora ◎ MEX 81 Cl 32
La Mora ◎ RA 137 Ea 63
La Morita ◎ MEX 80 Ck 31
La Mosquitia ~ HN 97 Df 38
Lampa ~ PE 128 Dm 53
Lampa ◎ PE 128 Dn 53
Lampanaih ◎ RI 270 Km 43
Lam Pao Reservoir ~ THA 263 Lb 37
Lampasas ◎ USA 81 Cn 30
Lampedusa ◎ I 185 Gn 28
Lamphun ◎ THA 254 Kp 36
Lamphun ◎ THA 254 Kp 36
Lam Plaimat ◎ THA 263 Lb 38
Lampman ◎ CDN 51 Cl 21
Lamu ◎ EAK 337 Hn 47
Lamud ◎ PE 116 Dj 49
Lamu Island △ EAK 337 Hn 47
la Mula △ I 185 Gp 26
Lamutskoe ◎ RUS 205 Za 5
Lan' ~ BY 171 Hf 19
Lanai △ USA 75 Am 35
Lanai City ◎ USA 75 Am 35
Lanaka ◎ CY 195 Hj 28
La Navecilla ◎ MEX 80 Ck 32
Lanbi Kyun △ MYA 262 Kn 40
Lancang ◎ VRC 254 Kp 34
Lancang Jiang ~ VRC 254 La 34

Lancaster ◎ USA 56 Dc 24
Lancaster ◎ USA 60 Dn 23
Lancaster ◎ USA 64 Cc 28
Lancaster ◎ USA 70 Db 25
Lancaster ◎ USA 71 Dg 26
Lancaster ◎ USA 71 Dh 28
Lancaster ◎ USA 71 Dg 26
Lancaster ◎ GB 162 Ge 19
Lancaster Sound ~ CDN 7 Eb 2
Lancaster Sound ~ CDN 43 Fc 4
Lance Creek ◎ USA 51 Cj 24
Lancelin ◎ AUS 368 Lh 61
Lancester ◎ USA 71 Dg 26
Lanciano ◎ I 194 Gp 24
Lanco ◎ RCH 147 Dm 65
Lancones ◎ PE 116 Dh 48
Landak ~ RI 271 Le 45
Landau ◎ D 174 Gn 21
Land Between The Lakes ♀ USA 71 Dd 27
Landeck ◎ A 174 Gm 22
Landegode △ N 158 Gn 12
Lander ◎ USA 51 Cj 24
Lander ◎ AUS 361 Mc 57
Landete ◎ E 184 Gf 26
Landfell Island △ IND 262 Kl 39
Landi ◎ RG 316 Ga 41
Landía Playa ◎ E 292 Fn 31
Landi Kotal ◎ PK 223 Jp 28
Landis ◎ CDN 51 Ch 19
Landless Corner ◎ Z 341 Hg 53
Landor ◎ AUS 368 Lj 58
Landri Sales ◎ BR 124 En 49
Landsberg am Lech ◎ D 174 Gm 21
Landsdowne ◎ IND 234 Kd 31
Land's End ~ GB 163 Gc 20
Landshut ◎ D 174 Gn 21
Landskrona ◎ S 170 Gn 18
La Negra ◎ RCH 136 Dn 57
La Negra ◎ RA 146 Ea 61
Lanett ◎ USA 86 Df 29
La Nevadita ◎ CO 107 Dm 40
Lanfiéra ◎ BF 317 Ge 39
Lang ◎ USA 56 Cn 21
Langa ◎ CO 107 Dm 40
La'nga Co ~ VRC 230 Ke 30
Langa-Langa ◎ RDC 332 Ha 47
Langano Häyk' ~ ETH 325 Hm 42
Langarüd ◎ IR 222 Jd 27
Langatabiki ◎ F 113 Eg 43
Langberg △ ZA 349 Hd 60
Langbinsi ◎ GH 317 Gd 40
Langdon ◎ USA 56 Cn 21
Langeac ◎ F 185 Gh 23
Langebaan ◎ ZA 358 Ha 62
Langeland △ DK 170 Gm 18
Langenburg ◎ CDN 56 Cm 20
Langeoog △ D 170 Gk 18
Langesund ◎ N 170 Gl 16
Langfang ◎ VRC 246 Lj 26
Langford ◎ CDN 50 Ca 21
Langfry ◎ USA 81 Cm 31
Langgam ◎ RI 270 La 45
Langgapayung ◎ RI 270 La 45
Langgur ◎ RI 283 Mc 48
Langham ◎ CDN 51 Cj 19
Langjökull △ IS 158 Fk 13
Langka ◎ RI 270 Kn 43
Langkobale ◎ RI 282 Ll 47
Langkon ◎ MAL 274 Lj 42
Langlade △ CDN 61 Ee 21
Langlade ou Petit Miquelon △ F 61 Ef 22
Langlo ~ AUS 375 Mj 58
Langlo Crossing ◎ AUS 375 Mj 59
Langmusi ◎ VRC 242 Lb 28
Lango ◎ RCB 332 Gp 45
Langon ◎ F 184 Gf 23
Langøya △ N 158 Gp 11
Langqên Zangbo ~ VRC 230 Ke 30
Langres ◎ F 163 Gj 22
Langruth ◎ CDN 56 Cn 20
Langsa ◎ RI 270 Kp 43
Lang So'n ◎ VN 255 Ld 35
Lang Suan ◎ THA 262 Kp 41
Langtang ◎ NEP 235 Kg 31
Langtang ◎ WAN 320 Gl 41
Langtang Nat. Park ♀ NEP 235 Kg 31
Langtao ◎ MYA 254 Kn 32
Långträsk ◎ S 158 Hb 13
Langu ◎ THA 270 Kp 42
Languedoc ~ F 185 Gh 24
Languedoc-Roussillon ⊙ F 185 Gh 23
Languiñeo ◎ RA 147 Dn 67
Langxi ◎ VRC 246 Lk 30
Langzhong ◎ VRC 243 Lc 30
Laniel ◎ CDN 60 Dj 22
Lanigan ◎ CDN 51 Ck 20
Lanjut ◎ RI 278 Lc 46
Lankadonkhang ◎ VRC 230 Ke 30
Lankao ◎ VRC 243 Lh 28
Lankapatti ◎ IND 254 Kl 33
Lânkâran ◎ AZ 202 Jc 26
Lanlacuni Bajo ◎ PE 128 Dn 52
Lannemezan ◎ F 184 Gg 24
Lannion ◎ F 163 Ge 21
La Noria ◎ MEX 92 Cj 34
La Rana ◎ C 100 Dj 34
Lanquin ◎ GCA 93 Dd 38
Lansdale ◎ USA 74 Dl 25
Lansdowne ◎ AUS 361 Lp 54
Lansdowne House ◎ CDN 57 De 19
L'Anse ◎ USA 57 Dd 22
L'Anse aux Meadows N.H.S. ★ CDN 61 Eg 20
Lansford ◎ USA 56 Cm 21
Lansing ◎ USA 56 Dc 24
Lansing ◎ USA 57 De 24
Lansjärv ◎ S 159 Hc 12
Lantau ◎ WAN 320 Gm 39
Lantian ◎ VRC 243 Le 28
Lantz Corners ◎ USA 74 Dj 25
Lanu ◎ RI 275 Ll 45
Lanusei ◎ I 185 Gl 26
Lanuza Bay ~ RP 267 Lp 41
Lanxi ◎ VRC 205 Wb 9
Lanxi ◎ VRC 258 Lk 31
Lan Xian ◎ VRC 243 Lf 26
Lan Yü △ RC 259 Ll 34
Lanya ◎ PE 128 Dp 53
Lanzarote △ E 292 Fp 31
Lanzhou ◎ VRC 242 Lb 27
Laoag ◎ RP 267 Ll 36
Laoang ◎ RP 267 Ln 39

Lào Cai ◎ VN 255 Lb 34
La Ochoa ◎ MEX 81 Cl 33
La Ofelia ◎ RA 147 Dn 65
Laohekou ◎ VRC 243 Lf 29
Laokas ◎ THA 321 Gp 41
Laon ◎ F 163 Gh 21
Laona ◎ RI 282 Ll 48
La Oroya ◎ PE 128 Dl 51
Laos ■ LAO 255 Lb 36
Laoshan ★ VRC 246 Ll 27
Laouda ◎ CI 317 Gd 42
Laoudi-Ba ◎ CI 317 Ge 41
La'oueïssi ◎ RIM 304 Fp 37
Lapa ◎ BR 140 Ek 58
Lapachito ◎ RA 140 Ee 59
Lapac Island △ RP 275 Ll 43
Lapai ◎ WAN 320 Gk 41
Lapalisse ◎ F 163 Gh 22
La Palma ◎ MEX 92 Ck 34
La Palma ◎ PA 97 Dj 41
La Palma ◎ C 100 Dg 34
La Palma ◎ CO 106 Dl 43
La Palma ◎ E 292 Fm 31
La Palma del Condado ◎ E Gc 27
La Palmarita ◎ CO 100 Dj 35
La Palmita ◎ CO 106 Dl 44
La Paloma ◎ ROU 146 Eg 63
La Pampita ◎ RCH 137 Dn 60
La Paragua ◎ YV 122 Ec 42
Laparan Island △ RP 275 Ll 43
Lapataia ◎ RA 152 Dp 73
Lapau ◎ RI 282 Ll 50
Lapau ◎ PNG 287 Mm 48
La Paz ◎ MEX 80 Cg 33
La Paz ◎ HN 96 De 38
La Paz ◎ CO 107 Dm 40
La Paz ◎ BOL 128 Dp 54
La Paz ◎ RA 137 Ea 62
La Paz ◎ RA 146 Ee 61
La Paz ◎ ROU 146 Ef 63
La Paz ◎ RP 267 Ln 40
La Paz Centro ◎ NIC 96 De 39
Lapdah Leptis Magna ★ LAR 297 Gp 29
La Pedrera ◎ CO 117 Dp 46
Lapeenranta ◎ FIN 159 Hf 15
Lapeer ◎ USA 57 Dg 24
La Perla ◎ MEX 80 Ck 31
La Pérouse Strait ~ RUS/J 205 Xb 9
La Pérouse Strait ~ RUS/J 250 Mg 23
La Pesca ◎ MEX 81 Cp 34
La Piedad ◎ MEX 92 Cl 35
La Pila ◎ MEX 92 Cm 35
Lapine ◎ USA 86 Df 30
Lapining Island △ RP 267 Ln 40
Lapinlahti ◎ FIN 159 Hf 14
La Pintada ◎ PA 97 Dh 41
La Place ◎ USA 86 Dc 30
La Placita ◎ MEX 92 Cf 36
Lapland ~ S/FIN 158 Hb 13
La Plant ◎ USA 56 Cm 23
La Plata ◎ USA 70 Db 25
La Plata ◎ CO 106 Dk 44
La Plata ◎ RA 146 Ee 62
la Pobla de Segur ◎ E 184 Gg 24
La Poile ◎ CDN 61 Ee 21
La Porte ◎ USA 64 Cb 26
La Porte ◎ USA 71 De 25
La Porte ◎ USA 81 Da 31
La Poyata ◎ CO 107 Dm 43
Laporte ◎ USA 74 Dk 25
La Pryor ◎ USA 81 Cm 31
Lapseki ◎ TR 194 Hf 25
Laptev Sea ~ RUS 22 Qb 2
Laptev Sea ~ 22 Qb 2
Lapua ◎ FIN 159 Hd 14
La Puerta ◎ RA 137 Ec 61
Lapu Lapu ◎ RP 267 Lm 40
La Punilla ◎ RCH 137 Dn 64
La Punta ◎ CO 107 Dm 41
La Punta ◎ RA 137 Eb 60
La Purisima ◎ MEX 75 Cf 32
Laqiyat Arba'in ◎ SUD 312 Hf 35
Laqiyat 'Umran ◎ SUD 312 Hg 36
Laqui ◎ PE 128 Dl 53
La Quiaca ◎ PY 136 Eb 57
L'Aquila ◎ I 185 Gn 24
Lâr ◎ IR 226 Jf 32
Lara ~ G 332 Gm 45
Lara ◎ AUS 379 Mj 65
Larabanga ◎ GH 317 Gd 41
Larache ◎ MA 293 Gc 28
Laragh ◎ IRL 163 Gc 19
Lârak △ IR 226 Jg 32
La Ramada ◎ RA 136 Eb 59
Laramanay ◎ TCH 321 Gp 41
Laramate ◎ PE 128 Dl 53
Laramie ◎ USA 65 Ck 25
Laramie Mountains △ USA 65 Cj 24
Laramie Peak △ USA 51 Ck 24
Laramie River ~ USA 65 Ck 25
La Rana ◎ C 100 Dj 34
Laranjal ◎ BR 117 Eb 46
Laranjeiras do Sul ◎ BR 140 Eh 58
Larantuka ◎ RI 282 Lm 50
Larat ◎ RI 283 Mb 49
Larba ◎ DZ 296 Gh 27
Lârbro ◎ S 170 Hb 17
Larde ◎ MOC 344 Hm 54
Larder Lake ◎ CDN 60 Dj 21
Lare ◎ EAK 325 Hl 45
Laredo ◎ USA 81 Cn 32
Laredo ◎ E 184 Ge 24
Laredo Sound ~ CDN 50 Bm 19
La Reforma ◎ MEX 81 Cm 32
La Reforma ◎ C 100 Dj 34
La Reforma ◎ YV 112 Ed 42
La Reforma ◎ RA 146 Ee 63
La Reine ◎ CDN 60 Dj 21
La Réole ◎ F 184 Gf 23
Lâr-e Polûr ◎ IR 222 Jd 28
Lares ◎ PE 128 Dp 53
Largeau ◎ TCH 309 Hb 37
Largo ◎ USA 86 Dg 32
Largo ◎ BR 125 Ep 51
Lariang ◎ RI 279 Lk 46
Lariang ~ RI 279 Lk 46

La Ribera ◎ MEX 80 Ch 34
Larimore ◎ USA 56 Cp 22
La Rioja ◎ RA 137 Ea 60
La Rioja ⊙ E 184 Ge 24
Larissa ◎ GR 194 Hd 26
Lar'jak ◎ RUS 204 Ta 6
Lârkâna ◎ PK 227 Jn 32
Lark Harbour ◎ CDN 61 Ee 21
Larkspur ◎ USA 65 Ck 26
Laro ◎ BF 317 Ge 40
Laro ◎ CAM 320 Gn 41
La Robla ◎ E 184 Gd 24
La Roche ◎ B 163 Gj 20
La Roche ◎ F 386 Ng 56
la Rochelle ◎ F 163 Gf 22
La Roche-sur-Yon ◎ F 163 Gf 22
La Roda ◎ E 184 Ge 26
La Romaine ◎ CDN 61 Ed 20
La Romana ◎ DOM 101 Dp 36
La Ronge ◎ CDN 42 Ec 7
Laropi ◎ EAU 324 Hh 44
La Rosa ◎ YV 107 Dp 41
Larose ◎ USA 86 Dc 31
La Rosita ◎ MEX 81 Cm 31
La Rosita ◎ NIC 97 Df 39
La Rosita ◎ CO 107 Dn 43
Larrainzar ◎ MEX 93 Db 37
Larrimah ◎ AUS 364 Mc 53
Larroque ◎ RA 146 Ee 62
Larry Point △ AUS 360 Lk 55
Larrys River ◎ CDN 61 Ed 23
Lars Christensen Land △ 38 Na 17
Larsen Ice Shelf △ 38 Fb 16
Larvik ◎ N 170 Gl 16
La Sagra △ E 184 Ge 27
Lasahata ◎ RI 283 Ma 47
Lasahau ◎ RI 282 Lm 48
La Sal ◎ USA 65 Ch 26
Lasalimu ◎ RI 282 Lm 48
Lasanga Island △ PNG 287 Mk 49
Las Animas ◎ CO 65 Cl 27
Las Animas ◎ CO 106 Dk 43
Lasarat ◎ ETH 328 Hp 40
Las Armas ◎ RA 146 Ef 64
La Sarre ◎ CDN 60 Dj 21
las Arrias ◎ RA 137 Ec 61
la Sau d'Urgell ◎ E 184 Gg 24
Las Bocas ◎ MEX 80 Ch 32
Las Bonitas ◎ YV 112 Eb 42
Las Breas ◎ RCH 137 Dn 60
Las Cabreras ◎ C 101 Dk 35
Lascano ◎ EC 116 Dh 46
Lascano ◎ ROU 146 Eg 63
Las Catitas ◎ RA 137 Dp 62
Lasceilles ◎ AUS 378 Mh 63
L'Ascension ◎ CDN 60 Dl 22
Las Chapas ◎ RA 147 Ea 67
Las Choapas ◎ MEX 93 Da 37
La Scie ◎ CDN 61 Eg 21
Las Coloradas ◎ MEX 81 Cm 32
Las Conchas ◎ MEX 80 Cg 31
Las Conchas ◎ MEX 80 Ck 31
Las Condes ◎ RCH 137 Dn 62
Las Cruces ◎ USA 65 Cj 29
Las Cruces ◎ MEX 93 Db 37
Las Cuevas ◎ RA 137 Dn 62
Lasem ◎ RI 279 Lf 49
La Serena ◎ RCH 137 Dn 60
Las Flores ◎ RA 137 Dp 61
Las Flores ◎ RA 146 Ee 64
Las Gamas ◎ RA 137 Ed 60
Las Garcitas ◎ RA 140 Ee 59
Las Garzas ◎ RA 146 Ee 61
Las Gatos ◎ USA 64 Ca 27
Las Hediondas ◎ RCH 137 Dn 60
Las Heras ◎ RA 152 Dp 69
Las Hermanas ◎ YV 112 Ed 41
Las Hermosas ♀ CO 106 Dl 44
Lashio ◎ MYA 254 Kn 34
Las Horquetas ◎ RA 152 Dn 70
Las Hortensias ◎ RCH 147 Dm 65
Lasibu ◎ PNG 287 Mm 48
La Sierpe ◎ C 100 Dj 35
La Sila △ I 194 Ha 26
L'Asile ◎ RH 101 Dm 36
Łask ◎ PL 174 Hb 20
Laškargâh ◎ AFG 227 Jl 30
Las Lajas ◎ RA 147 Dn 65
Las Lajitas ◎ RA 136 Eb 58
Las Leñas ◎ RA 137 Dn 63
Las Lomas ◎ PE 116 Dh 48
Las Lomitas ◎ RA 136 Ed 58
Las Maravillas ◎ MEX 93 Db 37
Las Margaritas ◎ MEX 93 Db 37
Las Martinas ◎ C 100 Df 35
Las Mercedes ◎ CO 107 Dm 41
Las Mercedes ◎ YV 107 Ea 41
Las Mercedes ◎ YV 107 Ea 43
Las Nayas ◎ RP 267 Ln 39
Las Nutrias ◎ RA 146 Ee 65
Las Orquídeas ♀ CO 106 Dk 42
La Sortija ◎ RA 146 Ed 65
Las Palmas ◎ PE 116 Dl 50
Las Palmas de Gran Canaria ◎ E 292 Fm 31
Las Palomas ◎ USA 65 Cj 29
Las Pedroñeras ◎ E 184 Ge 26
Las Peñas ◎ MEX 92 Cl 36
Las Petas ◎ BR 132 Ee 54
La Spézia ◎ I 185 Gl 23
Las Piedras ◎ PE 128 Dn 51
Las Piedras ◎ PE 128 Dp 52
Las Piedras ◎ ROU 146 Ef 63
Las Pipinas ◎ RA 146 Ef 63
Las Plumas ◎ RA 147 Ea 67
Las Pocitas ◎ MEX 80 Cg 33
Las Rosas ◎ MEX 93 Db 37
Las Rosas ◎ RA 137 Ed 62
Lassance ◎ BR 133 Em 54
Lassen Peak △ USA 64 Cb 25
Lassen Volcanic ♀ USA 64 Cb 25
Lassio ~ G 332 Gn 46
Las Tablas ◎ PA 97 Dh 42
Last Chance ◎ USA 65 Cl 26
Last Mountain Lake ~ CDN 51 Ck 20
Las Toscas ◎ RA 137 Ed 63
Las Toscas ◎ RA 146 Ee 60
Las Toscas ◎ ROU 146 Eg 62
Lastoursville Bonda ◎ G 332 Gn 46

Lastovo ⚲ **HR** 194 Ha 24
Las Tres Matas ○ **YV** 112 Eb 41
Las Trincheras ○ **YV** 112 Eb 42
Las Trojes ○ **HN** 97 Df 38
Las Tunas ○ **C** 101 Dk 35
Lasu ○ **PNG** 287 Mn 48
Las Varas ○ **MEX** 80 Ch 31
Las Varas ○ **MEX** 92 Ck 35
Las Varillas ○ **RA** 137 Ec 61
Las Vegas ○ **USA** 64 Ce 27
Las Vegas ○ **USA** 65 Ck 28
Las Ventanas ○ **YV** 107 Ea 42
Las Ventas c.P.A. ○ **E** 184 Gd 26
Las Viboras ○ **RA** 136 Eb 58
Las Yaras ○ **PE** 128 Dn 54
Latacunga ○ **EC** 116 Dj 46
Latah Creek 〜 **USA** 50 Cd 22
Latakia, Al Lādhiqīyah ○ **SYR** 208 Hk 28
La Tapoa 〜 **BF** 317 Gg 39
La Tapoa ○ **RN** 320 Gh 39
Lataro ⚲ **VU** 386 Nf 53
Latas ○ **RCH** 136 Dp 57
Latchford ○ **CDN** 57 Dh 22
Late ⚲ **TO** 390 Ac 55
La Templadera del Derrumbe ○ **MEX** 80 Cj 33
Lateriquique 〜 **PY** 132 Ee 55
Latham ○ **AUS** 368 Lj 60
Lathan ○ **IND** 254 Kn 32
Lathi ⚲ **VU** 386 Nf 53
Lathu ⚲ **VU** 386 Nf 53
Latiéouol 〜 **SN** 304 Fn 38
Latina ○ **I** 185 Gn 25
La Tinaja ○ **MEX** 92 Cp 36
La Tinaja ○ **MEX** 93 Cp 36
La Tinaja de Bartolo ○ **MEX** 80 Ck 33
La Tirana ○ **RCH** 136 Dp 56
Latodo ○ **RI** 282 Ll 49
La Toison ○ **RH** 101 Dm 36
La Tola ○ **EC** 116 Dj 45
La Toma ○ **RA** 137 Eb 62
Latoma ○ **RI** 282 Ll 47
La Tontouta ○ **F** 386 Nf 57
Latorre ○ **RCH** 137 Dn 60
Latou ○ **RI** 282 Ll 47
Latouche ⚲ **USA** 46 Bc 15
Látrar ○ **IS** 158 Fj 12
La Trinitaria ○ **MEX** 93 Db 37
Latrobe ○ **USA** 74 Dj 25
Latrobe ○ **AUS** 378 Mk 66
La Troncal ○ **EC** 116 Dj 47
Lat-Suhanra ⚑ **PK** 227 Ka 31
Latu ○ **RI** 283 Ma 47
La Tunia ○ **CO** 106 Dm 45
La Tuque ○ **CDN** 60 Dm 22
Lãtũr ○ **IND** 238 Kc 36
Latvia □ **LV** 171 He 17
Lau ○ **WAN** 320 Gm 41
Laucala ⚲ **FJI** 390 Aa 54
Laudar ○ **YE** 218 Ja 39
Lauderdale ○ **USA** 86 Dd 29
Lauenburg/E. ○ **D** 170 Gm 19
Laughlin ○ **USA** 64 Ce 28
Lauhkaung ○ **MYA** 254 Kp 33
Lauiya Nandangarh ○ **IND** 235 Kg 32
Launceston ○ **GB** 163 Gd 20
Launceston ○ **AUS** 378 Mk 66
Launglen ○ **MYA** 262 Kn 39
La Unión ○ **MEX** 92 Cl 36
La Unión ○ **MEX** 93 Dd 37
La Unión ○ **HN** 96 De 38
La Unión ○ **ES** 96 De 39
La Unión ○ **EC** 116 Dh 46
La Unión ○ **CO** 116 Dk 48
La Unión ○ **PE** 116 Dk 50
La Unión ○ **RCH** 147 Dm 66
La Unión ○ **RA** 152 Dm 71
La Unión ○ **E** 184 Gf 27
Launlonbok Islands ⚲ **MYA** 262 Kn 39
Laupahoehoe ○ **USA** 75 An 35
Lauqa ○ **KSA** 214 Hp 31
Laura ○ **AUS** 365 Mj 53
La Urbana ○ **YV** 107 Ea 42
Laurel ○ **USA** 51 Ch 23
Laurel ○ **USA** 74 Dk 26
Laurel ○ **USA** 86 Dd 30
Laureles ○ **ROU** 146 Ef 61
Laurenço ○ **BR** 113 Ej 44
Laurens ○ **USA** 71 Dg 28
Laurentian Mountains △△ **CDN** 60 Dm 22
Laurentians ○ **CDN** 60 Dk 22
Laurí ○ **MYA** 254 Km 33
Lau Ridge ♥ 35 Aa 12
Laurinburg ○ **USA** 74 Dj 28
Laurium ○ **USA** 57 Dd 22
Lauro de Freitas ○ **BR** 125 Fa 52
Lauro Sodré ○ **BR** 120 Ec 47
Lausanne ○ **CH** 163 Ga 22
Lautaro Vilcún ○ **RCH** 147 Dm 65
Lautem ○ **TP** 282 Lp 50
Lautoka ⚲ **FJI** 387 Nl 54
Laut Selat ○ **RI** 279 Lj 47
Laut Sulawesi 〜 **RI** 279 Lj 44
La Uvita ○ **CO** 107 Dm 42
Lava Beds National Monument ★ **USA** 64 Cb 25
Laval ○ **CDN** 60 Dm 23
Laval ○ **F** 163 Gf 22
Lavalle ○ **RA** 136 Eb 60
La Vallita ○ **C** 100 Dj 35
Lãvãn ⚲ **IR** 215 Je 32
Lavanggu ○ **SOL** 290 Nc 51
Lavanono ○ **RM** 353 Ja 58
Lavaur ○ **F** 184 Gg 24
La Vega ○ **DOM** 101 Dm 36
La Vega ○ **CO** 106 Dk 44
La Veguita ○ **YV** 107 Dp 41
La Venta ○ **MEX** 93 Dd 37
La Ventana ○ **MEX** 92 Cm 34
La Ventosa ○ **MEX** 93 Da 37
La Vergareña ○ **YV** 112 Ec 42
La Verkin ○ **USA** 64 Cf 27
La Vernia ○ **USA** 81 Cn 31
Laverton ○ **AUS** 368 Lm 60
La Veta ○ **USA** 65 Ck 27
Lavia ○ **FIN** 159 Hd 15
La Victoria ○ **YV** 107 Dp 42
La Victoria ○ **YV** 107 Dp 42
Lavik ○ **N** 158 Gj 15
La Vila Joiosa ○ **E** 184 Gf 26
Lavillette ○ **CDN** 61 Eb 22

La Vilos ○ **RCH** 137 Dn 61
Lavina ○ **USA** 51 Ch 22
La Viña ○ **RA** 136 Eb 58
La Viña ○ **RA** 136 Eb 59
La Violeta ○ **RA** 137 Ed 62
La Virgen ○ **NIC** 97 Df 40
La Virginia ○ **CO** 106 Dk 43
La Viuda ○ **YV** 112 Ec 41
Lavradol ○ **BR** 132 Ef 52
Lavras ○ **BR** 141 Em 56
Lavrio ○ **GR** 194 He 27
Lavumisa ○ **SD** 352 Hh 59
Lavushi Manda ⚑ **Z** 341 Hh 52
Lawang ○ **RI** 279 Lg 49
Lawan Gopeng ○ **MAL** 270 La 43
Lawarai-Pass △ **PK** 223 Jp 28
Lawas ○ **MAL** 274 Lh 43
Lawksawk ○ **MYA** 254 Kn 35
Lawn Bay 〜 **CDN** 61 Eg 23
Lawngmasu ○ **IND** 254 Kl 34
Lawngngaw ○ **MYA** 254 Kn 32
Lawn Hill ○ **AUS** 365 Mf 55
Lawn Hill ⚑ **AUS** 365 Mf 55
Lawowa ○ **RI** 282 Lm 48
Lawra ○ **GH** 317 Gg 41
Lawrence ○ **CDN** 60 Dl 23
Lawrence ○ **USA** 60 Dn 23
Lawrence ○ **USA** 70 Da 26
Lawrence ○ **NZ** 382 Ng 68
Lawrenceburg ○ **USA** 71 De 28
Lawrenceville ○ **USA** 71 Dd 26
Lawrenceville ○ **USA** 71 Dg 29
Lawrenceville ○ **USA** 74 Dk 27
Lawtha ○ **MYA** 254 Km 34
Lawton ○ **USA** 56 Cn 21
Lawton ○ **USA** 70 Cn 28
Laxong Co 〜 **VRC** 231 Kg 28
Lay ○ **TP** 437 Gf 39
Laya ○ **BRG** 316 Fp 41
Laya Dula ○ **RG** 316 Ga 41
Layaworng Ga ○ **MYA** 254 Kn 33
La Ye ○ **CO** 106 Dl 41
La Ye ○ **YV** 107 Dp 42
La Yilleguera ○ **YV** 107 Ea 42
Layo ○ **PE** 128 Dn 53
Layton ○ **USA** 65 Cf 25
La Zarca ○ **MEX** 80 Ck 33
Lazarev ○ **RUS** 205 Xb 8
Lazarevskoe ○ **RUS** 195 Hm 24
Lázaro Cárdenas ○ **MEX** 75 Ce 30
Lázaro Cárdenas ○ **MEX** 92 Cl 37
Lázaro Cárdenas ○ **MEX** 93 Dd 36
Lazdijai ○ **LT** 171 Hd 18
Lãze ○ **IR** 215 Je 32
Lazio ◉ **I** 185 Gn 24
Lazo ○ **RUS** 206 Mc 24
Léach ○ **K** 263 Lb 39
Lead ○ **USA** 51 Ch 23
Leader ○ **CDN** 51 Ch 20
Leadore ○ **USA** 50 Cf 23
Leadville ○ **USA** 65 Cj 26
League City ○ **USA** 81 Da 31
Leakey ○ **USA** 81 Cn 31
Lea Lea ○ **PNG** 287 Mk 50
Leamington ○ **CDN** 71 Dg 24
Leander ○ **USA** 81 Cn 30
Leander Point ◠ **AUS** 368 Lh 60
Leandra ○ **ZA** 349 Hg 59
Leandro ○ **BR** 121 Em 48
Learmonth ○ **AUS** 360 Lh 57
Leary ○ **USA** 86 Df 30
Leavenworth ○ **USA** 50 Cb 22
Leavenworth ○ **USA** 70 Da 26
Łeba ○ **PL** 170 Ha 18
Lebak ○ **RP** 275 Lm 42
Lébamba ○ **G** 332 Gm 47
Lébango ○ **RCB** 332 Gp 45
Lébango 〜 **RCB** 332 Gp 45
Lebanon ○ **USA** 50 Ca 23
Lebanon ○ **USA** 60 Dm 24
Lebanon ○ **USA** 70 Cn 26
Lebanon ○ **USA** 70 Db 27
Lebanon ○ **USA** 71 De 28
Lebanon ○ **USA** 71 Df 27
Lebanon ○ **USA** 74 Dk 25
Lebanon ○ **RL** 208 Hk 28
Lebanon Mountains △△ **RL** 208 Hk 29
Lebap ○ **TM** 223 Jj 25
Lebedjan' ○ **RUS** 181 Hm 19
Lebedyn ○ **UA** 175 Hk 20
Lebel-sur-Quévillon ○ **CDN** 60 Dk 21
Lebida ○ **RDC** 332 Ha 47
Lébiri ○ **G** 332 Gn 46
le Blanc ○ **F** 163 Gg 22
Lebo ○ **USA** 70 Da 26
Lebo ○ **RDC** 333 Ha 47
Leboma ○ **RDC** 333 Ha 47
Lébombi ○ **G** 332 Gn 47
Lebombo Mountains △△ **ZA** 352 Hj 59
Leboni ○ **RI** 282 Ll 47
Lebon Régis ○ **BR** 140 Ej 59
Le Borgne ○ **RH** 101 Dm 36
Łebork ○ **PL** 170 Ha 18
Lebowakgomo ○ **ZA** 349 Hg 58
Lebrita d. Barr. ○ **E** 184 Gc 27
Lebu ○ **RCH** 137 Dm 64
Lecce ○ **I** 194 Hb 25
Lecco ○ **I** 185 Gl 23
Le Center ○ **USA** 56 Db 23
Lechang ○ **VRC** 258 Lg 32
le Chateau ○ **F** 163 Gh 20
Lechenicho ○ **E** 184 Ge 24
Lechang ○ **VRC** 258 Lg 32
Lechuguilla Cave ★ **USA** 65 Ck 29
Łęczna ○ **PL** 175 Hd 20
Łęczyca ○ **PL** 170 Hb 19
Ledes ○ **E** 184 Gf 24
Ledmozero ⚲ **RUS** 159 Hh 13
Ledo ○ **IND** 254 Km 32
Ledong ○ **VRC** 255 Le 36
Ledu ○ **VRC** 242 Lb 27
Leduc ○ **CDN** 51 Cf 19
Leeanne ○ **IRL** 163 Gb 19
Leech Lake 〜 **USA** 56 Db 22
Leech Lake ••• **USA** 56 Da 22
Leeds ○ **GB** 163 Gf 19
Leeds ○ **USA** 71 De 29
Leeds ○ **GUY** 113 Ef 42
Leego ○ **GB** 163 Gf 19
Leek ○ **GB** 163 Gf 19
Leemann ○ **AUS** 368 Lh 60
Leeper ○ **USA** 71 Dc 27

Leer(O.) ○ **D** 170 Gk 19
Leesburg ○ **USA** 74 Dk 26
Leesburg ○ **USA** 87 Dg 31
Leesville ○ **USA** 86 Db 30
Leeton ○ **AUS** 379 Mk 63
Leeudoridgstad ○ **ZA** 349 Hf 59
Leeu-Gamka ○ **ZA** 358 Hc 62
Leeupoort ○ **ZA** 349 Hf 58
Leeuwarden ○ **NL** 163 Gj 19
Leeuwin-Naturaliste ⚑ **AUS** 368 Lh 62
Leeuwrivier ○ **ZA** 358 Hd 62
Leeward Islands ⚲ **USA** 104 Ec 37
Leeward Islands ⚲ **CV** 316 Fh 38
le Faouët ○ **F** 163 Ge 21
Lefeque ○ **RA** 147 Dn 67
le Ferlo ⌒ **SN** 304 Fn 38
Léfini 〜 **RCB** 332 Gp 46
Lefkáda ○ **GR** 194 Hc 26
Lefkáda ⚲ **GR** 194 Hc 26
Le François ○ **F** 104 Ed 38
Leganes ○ **E** 184 Gd 25
Legaspi ○ **RP** 267 Lm 39
Legendre Island ⚲ **AUS** 360 Lj 56
Legion Mine 〜 **ZW** 349 Hg 56
Legionowo ○ **PL** 170 Hc 19
Legkraal ○ **ZA** 349 Hg 57
Legnano ○ **I** 185 Gl 23
Legnica ○ **PL** 174 Ha 20
Leguan Island ⚲ **GUY** 113 Ee 42
Legune ○ **AUS** 364 Ma 53
Le Havre ○ **F** 163 Gf 21
Lehena ○ **GR** 194 Hc 27
Lehigh Acres ○ **USA** 87 Dh 32
Lehighton ○ **USA** 74 Dl 25
Lehman ○ **USA** 65 Cl 29
Lehman Caves ★ **USA** 64 Ce 26
Lehututu ○ **RB** 349 Hc 57
Leiah ○ **PK** 227 Jp 30
Leibnitz ○ **A** 174 Gp 22
Leicester ○ **GB** 163 Gf 19
Leichhardt ⚲ **AUS** 365 Mf 54
Leichhardt Range △△ **AUS** 375 Mk 56
Leiden ○ **NL** 163 Gh 19
Leigh Creek ○ **AUS** 378 Me 61
Leigh Creek South ○ **AUS** 378 Mf 61
Leigong Shan △ **VRC** 255 Le 32
Leimebamba ○ **PE** 116 Dk 49
Leimus ○ **HN** 97 Df 38
Leine 〜 **D** 170 Gm 19
Leinster ◉ **IRL** 163 Gc 19
Leinster ○ **AUS** 368 Ll 60
Leipzig ○ **D** 174 Gn 20
Leiria ○ **P** 184 Gb 26
Leirvik ○ **N** 170 Gj 16
Leishan ○ **VRC** 255 Le 32
Leitre ○ **PNG** 286 Mg 47
Leiyang ○ **VRC** 258 Lg 32
Leizhou Bandao ⌒ **VRC** 255 Lf 35
Leizhou Wan 〜 **VRC** 255 Lf 35
Lek 〜 **NL** 163 Gj 20
Leka ⚲ **N** 158 Gm 13
Lékana ○ **RCB** 332 Gp 47
Lekatero ○ **RDC** 333 Hd 46
Lékila ○ **G** 332 Gn 46
Lekki Legoon 〜 **WAN** 320 Gj 42
Leknes ○ **N** 158 Gn 11
Lékoni ○ **G** 332 Gp 46
Lékoni 〜 **G** 332 Gp 46
Leksand ○ **S** 158 Gp 15
Leksozero 〜 **RUS** 159 Hh 14
Lela ○ **RI** 282 Lm 50
Lélali ○ **RCB** 332 Gn 47
Le Lamentin ○ **F** 104 Ed 38
le Lavandou ○ **F** 185 Gk 24
Lelehudi ○ **PNG** 287 Mm 51
Lelepa ⚲ **VU** 386 Nf 54
Lely Geberge △△ **SME** 113 Eg 43
Lelystad ○ **NL** 163 Gj 19
Lemankoa ○ **PNG** 290 Mp 48
Le Mans ○ **F** 163 Gg 21
Lema Shilindi ○ **ETH** 325 Hn 43
Lematang 〜 **RI** 278 Lb 47
Lembal. Amb. Anjafy △ **RM** 345 Jc 54
Lembalemban'i Marovoalavo △△ **RM** 345 Jc 54
Lembar ○ **RI** 279 Lh 50
Lembé ○ **CAM** 320 Gn 43
Lembeni ○ **EAT** 337 Hl 47
Lembo ○ **RI** 282 Lm 47
Lemery ○ **RP** 267 Ll 39
Lemesos ○ **CY** 195 Hj 28
Lemfu ○ **RDC** 332 Gp 48
Lemhi ○ **USA** 50 Cf 23
Lemhi Range △△ **USA** 50 Cf 23
Lemieux Islands ⚲ **CDN** 43 Hb 6
Lemluia ○ **MA** 292 Fp 32
Lemmon ○ **USA** 51 Cl 23
Lemolemo ○ **RI** 283 Ma 46
Le-Mont-Dore ○ **F** 185 Gh 23
Lempa 〜 **ES** 96 Dd 39
Lêmpäälä ○ **FIN** 159 Hd 15
Lemper ○ **RI** 274 Lj 46
Lemsford ○ **CDN** 51 Ch 20
Lemsid ○ **MA** 292 Fn 32
Lemu ○ **WAN** 320 Gk 41
Le Mure ○ **F** 185 Gj 23
Lemvig ○ **DK** 170 Gk 17
Lemyethna ○ **MYA** 262 Km 37
Lena ○ **USA** 86 Db 30
Lena 〜 **RUS** 204 Va 8
Lena 〜 **RUS** 204 Vb 7
Lena 〜 **RUS** 204 Wa 5
Lena 〜 **RUS** 204 Wb 4
Lena 〜 **RUS** 205 Wb 6
Lena Delta ⌒ **RUS** 204 Wb 4
Lenakel ○ **VU** 386 Ng 55
Lençóis ○ **BR** 125 Ep 52
Lençóis Paulista ○ **BR** 141 Ek 57
Lenda 〜 **RDC** 324 Hg 45
Lende ○ **IR** 215 Jd 33
Lendepas ○ **NAM** 348 Hb 58
Lendery 〜 **RUS** 159 Hh 14
Lengguru 〜 **RI** 283 Md 47

Lenghu ○ **VRC** 231 Kl 26
Lenglong Ling △△ **VRC** 242 La 27
Lenglong Ling 〜 **VRC** 242 La 27
Lengoué 〜 **RCB** 332 Gp 45
Lengshui Jiang ○ **VRC** 255 Lf 32
Leng Sú Sin ○ **VN** 254 Lb 34
Lengulu ○ **RDC** 324 Hf 44
Lengwe ⚑ **MW** 344 Hk 54
Lenhovda ○ **S** 170 Gp 17
Lenine ○ **UA** 175 Hk 23
Leningradskij ○ **RUS** 205 Zc 5
Leninogorsk ○ **RUS** 181 Jd 18
Leninsk ○ **KZ** 155 Sa 9
Leninsk ○ **RUS** 181 Ja 21
Leninsk ○ **UZB** 230 Ka 25
Leninskij ○ **TJ** 223 Jn 26
Leninskoe ○ **RA** 147 Dn 68
Leninskoe ○ **RUS** 205 Wc 9
Leninskoe ○ **KS** 230 Ka 25
Lenkau ○ **PNG** 287 Mk 47
Lenkivci ○ **UA** 175 Hf 21
Lenmalu ○ **RI** 283 Mb 46
Leno-Angarskij Plato ⌒ **RUS** 204 Uc 7
Lenoir ○ **USA** 71 Dh 28
Lenoir City ○ **USA** 71 Df 28
Lenore Lake 〜 **CDN** 51 Ck 19
Lenox ○ **USA** 70 Da 25
Lens ○ **F** 163 Gh 20
Lensk ○ **RUS** 204 Vb 6
Lenswood ○ **AUS** 56 Cm 19
Lenti ○ **H** 174 Ha 22
Lentiira ○ **FIN** 159 Hg 13
Lentini ○ **I** 185 Gp 27
Lenya 〜 **MYA** 262 Kp 40
Léo ○ **BF** 317 Ge 40
Leoben ○ **A** 174 Gp 22
Léogâne ○ **RH** 101 Dm 36
Léok ○ **RI** 275 Ll 45
Leola ○ **USA** 56 Cn 23
Leominster ○ **USA** 60 Dm 24
Leominster ○ **GB** 163 Ge 19
León ○ **MEX** 92 Cm 35
León ○ **NIC** 96 De 39
León ◉ **E** 184 Gd 24
Léona ○ **SN** 304 Fm 38
Leonard ○ **USA** 81 Da 29
Leonardville ○ **NAM** 348 Hb 57
Leoncio Prado ○ **PE** 116 Dl 47
Leonhard ○ **USA** 56 Cp 22
Leónidio ○ **GR** 194 Hd 27
Leonora ○ **AUS** 368 Ll 60
León Viejo ★ **NIC** 96 De 39
Leopold and Astrid Coast ⌒ 38 Pa 16
Leopold Downs ○ **AUS** 361 Ln 54
Leopoldina ○ **BR** 141 En 56
Leopoldo de Bulhões ○ **BR** 133 Ek 54
Leoti ○ **USA** 70 Cm 26
Léoua ○ **RCA** 321 Hc 43
Leova ○ **MD** 175 Hg 22
le Palais ○ **F** 163 Ge 22
Lepangun ○ **RI** 279 Lk 48
Lepaterique ○ **HN** 96 De 38
Lepau ○ **RI** 282 Ll 50
Lepeľ ○ **BY** 171 Hg 18
Lephephe ○ **RB** 349 He 57
Leping ○ **VRC** 258 Lj 31
Le Port ○ **F** 353 Jf 56
Lépoura ○ **GR** 194 He 26
Leppävirta ○ **FIN** 159 Hf 14
Lepsius Point ◠ **PNG** 287 Mk 48
Leptis Magna ★ **LAR** 297 Gp 29
Leptokariá ○ **GR** 194 Hd 25
le Puy-en-Velay ○ **F** 185 Gh 23
Leqceiba ○ **RIM** 304 Fp 37
Lequena ○ **RCH** 136 Dp 56
Léraba 〜 **CI** 317 Gd 41
Léraba Occidentale 〜 **BF** 317 Gd 40
Lercara Friddi ○ **I** 185 Gn 27
Lerdo de Tejada ○ **MEX** 93 Da 36
Lere ○ **WAN** 320 Gl 40
Léré ○ **TCH** 321 Gp 41
Leré ○ **MEX** 92 Cn 36
Lerma 〜 **E** 184 Gd 24
Lerneb ○ **RMM** 305 Gd 37
Leros ⚲ **GR** 194 Hf 27
Leross ○ **CDN** 51 Cl 20
Lerum ○ **S** 170 Gn 17
Lerwick ○ **GB** 162 Gf 15
Ler Zerai ○ **SUD** 312 Hf 40
les Abymes ○ **F** 104 Ed 37
les Andelys ○ **F** 163 Gg 21
Lesau ○ **PNG** 287 Mk 46
les Baux ○ **F** 185 Gj 24
Les Cayes ○ **RH** 101 Dm 36
Les Ecrins △ **F** 185 Gk 23
Les Escoumins ○ **CDN** 60 Dp 21
Leshan ○ **VRC** 255 Lc 31
Lesjaskog ○ **N** 158 Gk 14
Leskina ○ **RUS** 204 Ta 4
Lesko ○ **PL** 174 Hd 21
Leskovac ○ **SCG** 194 Hc 24
Leskovik ○ **AL** 194 Hc 25
Leslie ○ **USA** 70 Db 28
Lesnoj Voronež 〜 **RUS** 181 Hn 19
Lesosibirsk ○ **RUS** 204 Ua 7
Lesotho □ **LS** 349 Hf 60
Lesozavodsk ○ **RUS** 206 Mc 23
Lesportes de Fer ★ **DZ** 296 Gj 27
les Sables-d'Olonnes ○ **F** 163 Gf 22
Les Saintes ⚲ **F** 104 Ec 38
Lessé 〜 **RCA** 321 Hb 43
Lesser Antilles ⚲ 104 Eb 38
Lesser Caucasus △△ **GE** 202 Hp 25
Lesser Slave Lake 〜 **CDN** 42 Ea 7
Lesser Sunda Islands ⚲ **RI** 279 Lj 49
Lestijärvi 〜 **FIN** 159 He 14
Les Trois Ilets ○ **F** 104 Ed 38
Les Trois Rivières ○ **RCA** 324 He 42
Lesvos ⚲ **GR** 194 He 26
Leszno ○ **PL** 174 Ha 20
Letaba 〜 **ZA** 352 Hh 57
Le Tampon ○ **F** 353 Jf 56
Letelinger ○ **CDN** 56 Cp 21
Letfata ○ **RIM** 304 Fp 37
Lethbridge ○ **CDN** 51 Cf 21

Lethem ○ **GUY** 112 Ee 44
Lethlakane ○ **RB** 349 He 56
Letiahau 〜 **RB** 349 Hd 56
Letiahau Pan 〜 **RB** 349 Hd 56
Leticia ○ **CO** 117 Dn 48
Leting ○ **VRC** 246 Lk 26
Letkhokpin ○ **MYA** 254 Kn 34
Letlhakeng ○ **RB** 349 He 58
Letnij bereg ⌒ **RUS** 159 Hl 13
Letoda ○ **RI** 283 Ma 50
Letohatchee ○ **USA** 71 De 29
Le Touquet-Paris-Plage ○ **F** 163 Gg 20
Letpadan ○ **MYA** 262 Km 37
Letpan ○ **MYA** 254 Kl 36
Letsitele ○ **ZA** 352 Hh 57
Letsok-Aw Kyun ⚲ **MYA** 262 Kn 40
Letta ○ **CAM** 321 Gn 43
Letterkenny ○ **IRL** 162 Gb 18
Letwurung ○ **RI** 283 Ma 49
Léua ○ **ANG** 340 Hf 51
Leuanrua ○ **SOL** 290 Nb 48
Leupp ○ **USA** 65 Cg 28
Leura ○ **AUS** 375 Ml 57
Leuven ○ **B** 163 Gj 20
Levajok ○ **N** 159 He 11
Levan ○ **USA** 65 Cg 26
Levanger ○ **N** 158 Gm 14
Levasi 〜 **RUS** 202 Jb 24
Levelland ○ **USA** 65 Cl 29
Levelock ○ **USA** 46 Al 15
Lever 〜 **BR** 133 Ej 51
le Verdon 〜 **F** 184 Gf 23
Leverkusen ○ **D** 163 Gk 20
Levice ○ **SK** 174 Hb 21
Levídi ○ **GR** 194 Hd 27
le Vigan ○ **F** 185 Gh 24
Levin ○ **NZ** 383 Nk 66
Levinópolis ○ **BR** 133 Em 53
Levis ○ **CDN** 60 Dn 22
Levroux ○ **F** 163 Gg 22
Levski ○ **BG** 194 He 24
Levuka ○ **FJI** 387 Nm 54
Lewe ○ **MYA** 254 Km 36
Lewellen ○ **USA** 65 Cl 25
Lewis ⚲ **GB** 162 Gd 15
Lewis and Clark Lake 〜 **USA** 56 Cp 24
Lewisburg ○ **USA** 71 De 28
Lewisburg ○ **USA** 74 Dj 26
Lewis Pass △ **NZ** 382 Nh 67
Lewisporte ○ **CDN** 61 Eg 21
Lewis Range △△ **AUS** 361 Ma 56
Lewis Smith Lake 〜 **USA** 71 De 28
Lewiston ○ **USA** 50 Cd 22
Lewiston ○ **USA** 60 Dn 23
Lewiston ○ **USA** 65 Cj 25
Lewistown ○ **USA** 51 Ch 22
Lewistown ○ **USA** 71 Dc 25
Lewistown ○ **USA** 74 Dk 25
Lewisville ○ **USA** 70 Db 29
Lexington ○ **USA** 50 Cc 23
Lexington ○ **USA** 70 Cn 25
Lexington ○ **USA** 71 De 28
Lexington ○ **USA** 71 Df 26
Lexington ○ **USA** 71 Df 28
Lexington ○ **USA** 71 Dj 27
Lexington Park ○ **USA** 74 Dk 26
Leyburn ○ **AUS** 375 Mm 60
Leye ○ **VRC** 255 Ld 33
Leyte ⚲ **RP** 267 Ln 40
Leyte Gulf 〜 **RP** 267 Ln 40
Lezama ○ **YV** 107 Ea 41
Lezhë ○ **AL** 194 Hb 25
Lezhi ○ **VRC** 242 Lc 30
Ľgov ○ **RUS** 175 Hk 20
Lha Metundo ⚲ **MOC** 344 Hn 51
Lhari ○ **VRC** 231 Kl 30
Lhasa ○ **VRC** 235 Kk 31
Lhazê ○ **VRC** 235 Kh 31
Lhokkruet ○ **RI** 270 Kn 43
Lhokseumawe ○ **RI** 270 Kn 43
Lhoksukon ○ **RI** 270 Kn 43
Lhorong ○ **VRC** 242 Km 30
I'Hospitalet ○ **E** 184 Gj 25
Lhotse △ **NEP** 235 Kh 32
Lhozhag ○ **VRC** 235 Kh 31
Lhünzê ○ **VRC** 246 Ln 30
Lianddovery ○ **GB** 163 Ge 19
Lianelli ○ **GB** 163 Gd 20
Liang ○ **RI** 282 Lm 46
Lianga ○ **RP** 267 Lp 41
Lianga Bay 〜 **RP** 267 Lp 41
Liangcheng ○ **VRC** 242 Lg 26
Liangcheng ○ **VRC** 246 Lk 28
Lianghe ○ **VRC** 255 Le 31
Lianghe ○ **VRC** 255 Lf 32
Lianghekou ○ **VRC** 242 Ld 30
Liangping ○ **VRC** 243 Le 30
Liangshan ○ **VRC** 243 Lh 28
Lianhua ○ **VRC** 258 Lg 32
Lianhua Shan △△ **VRC** 258 Lh 34
Lianjiang ○ **VRC** 255 Lf 35
Lianjiang ○ **VRC** 258 Lj 33
Lianping ○ **VRC** 258 Lh 33
Lianshan ○ **VRC** 258 Lg 32
Liantang ○ **VRC** 255 Lf 33
Lian Xian ○ **VRC** 255 Lf 33
Lianyuan ○ **VRC** 255 Lf 32
Lianyungang ○ **VRC** 246 Lk 28
Liaocheng ○ **VRC** 243 Lh 27
Liaodong Bandao ⌒ **VRC** 246 Lm 26
Liaodong Wan 〜 **VRC** 246 Ll 25
Liaozhong ○ **VRC** 246 Lm 25
Līāquatpur ○ **PK** 227 Jp 31
Liard 〜 **CDN** 42 Ea 6
Liard Plateau ⌒ **CDN** 42 Bl 15
Liard River ○ **CDN** 47 Bn 15
Liard River ⚑ **CDN** 47 Ca 16
Liazhou Wan 〜 **VRC** 246 Lk 27
Líbano ○ **CO** 106 Dl 43
Líbano ○ **RA** 137 Ed 64
Libby ○ **USA** 50 Ce 21
Libenge ○ **RDC** 333 Hb 44
Liberal ○ **USA** 70 Cm 27
Liberdade 〜 **BR** 133 Eh 51
Liberec ○ **CZ** 174 Gp 20
Liberia ○ **CR** 97 Df 40
Liberia □ **LB** 316 Ga 42
Libertad ○ **YV** 107 Dp 41

Libertad ○ **RA** 146 Ef 61
Libertad ○ **ROU** 146 Ef 63
Libertas ○ **ZA** 349 Hf 60
Liberty ○ **USA** 71 Df 27
Liberty ○ **USA** 74 Dl 25
Liberty ○ **USA** 81 Da 30
Libmanan ○ **RP** 267 Lm 39
Libode ○ **ZA** 349 Hg 61
Liboi ○ **EAK** 325 Hn 45
Liboko ○ **RDC** 321 Hc 44
Liboumba 〜 **G** 332 Gn 45
Libourne ○ **F** 184 Gf 23
Librazhid ○ **AL** 194 Hc 25
Libreville ⬛ **G** 332 Gl 45
Libro Point ◠ **RP** 267 Lk 40
Libuganon 〜 **RP** 275 Ln 42
Libya □ **LAR** 297 Gn 31
Libyan Desert ⌒ **LAR** 300 Hd 32
Licata ○ **I** 185 Gn 27
Licenciado Matienzo ○ **RA** 146 Ee 64
Lichang ○ **VRC** 243 Lg 30
Licheng ○ **VRC** 243 Lg 27
Lichfield ○ **GB** 163 Gf 19
Lichinga ○ **MOC** 344 Hk 52
Lichtenburg ○ **ZA** 349 Hf 59
Lichuan ○ **VRC** 243 Le 30
Liciro ○ **MOC** 344 Hl 54
Lícis 〜 **LV** 170 Hd 17
Licking 〜 **USA** 70 Dc 27
Licking 〜 **USA** 71 Df 26
Licosa ◠ **I** 185 Gp 26
Licuare 〜 **MOC** 344 Hl 54
Licungo 〜 **MOC** 344 Hl 53
Lida ○ **USA** 64 Cd 27
Lida ○ **BY** 171 Hf 18
Liden ○ **S** 158 Ha 14
Lidfontein ○ **NAM** 348 Hb 58
Lidia 〜 **PE** 128 Dn 51
Lidji 〜 **RDC** 332 Ha 47
Lidjombo ○ **RCA** 321 Ha 44
Lidköping ○ **S** 170 Gn 16
Lido ○ **RN** 320 Gb 39
Lido di Ostia ○ **I** 185 Gm 25
Lizdbark ○ **PL** 170 Hb 18
Liebenthal ○ **CDN** 51 Ch 20
Liechtenstein □ **FL** 174 Gl 22
Liège ○ **B** 163 Gj 20
Lieksa 〜 **FIN** 159 Hh 14
Liemian ○ **VRC** 243 Lh 30
Lienz ○ **A** 174 Gn 22
Liepāja ○ **LV** 170 Hc 17
Lietnik ○ **USA** 46 Ae 13
Liezen ○ **A** 174 Gn 22
Lifjell △ **N** 158 Gn 16
Lifou ⚲ **F** 386 Nf 56
Lifuka ⚲ **TO** 390 Ac 55
Lifune 〜 **ANG** 332 Gp 50
Ligao ○ **RP** 267 Lm 39
Ligatne ○ **LV** 171 He 17
Ligbo ○ **RDC** 324 Hg 44
Ligfoot Lake 〜 **AUS** 368 Lm 60
Light ○ **PP** 267 Ln 40
Lighthouse Reef ⚲ **BH** 96 De 37
Lightning Ridge ○ **AUS** 375 Mk 60
Ligonha 〜 **MOC** 344 Hl 53
Ligonier ○ **USA** 71 Df 26
Ligowola ○ **EAT** 344 Hl 51
Ligua 〜 **RCH** 137 Dn 62
Ligui ○ **MEX** 80 Cg 33
Ligunga ○ **EAT** 344 Hl 51
Ligurta ○ **USA** 64 Ce 29
Liguria ◉ **I** 185 Gl 23
Ligurian Sea 〜 **I** 185 Gk 24
Lihir Group ⚲ **PNG** 287 Mn 47
Lihoslavl' ○ **RUS** 175 Hk 17
Lihovskoj ○ **RUS** 181 Hn 21
Lihue ○ **USA** 75 Al 35
Lihula ○ **EST** 171 Hd 16
Lijiang ○ **VRC** 254 La 32
Lijiang ★ **VRC** 255 Lf 37
Lijiang ○ **VRC** 255 Lf 33
Lik ○ **LAO** 255 Lb 36
Likala ○ **RDC** 333 Hb 45
Likame 〜 **RDC** 321 Hc 44
Likati ○ **RDC** 324 Hd 44
Likati ○ **RDC** 324 Hd 44
Likely ○ **CDN** 50 Cb 19
Likely ○ **USA** 64 Cc 25
Likete ○ **RDC** 333 Hc 46
Likisia ○ **TP** 282 Ln 50
Likoma ⚲ **MW** 344 Hk 51
Likouala 〜 **RCB** 332 Gp 45
Likouala aux Herbes 〜 **RCB** 333 Ha 45
Likoula 〜 **RCB** 332 Ha 46
Liku ○ **RI** 271 Le 45
Likum ○ **PNG** 287 Mk 47
Likuyu ○ **EAT** 344 Hl 51
Lilarea ○ **AUS** 375 Mj 57
L'Ile-d'Entrée ⚲ **CDN** 61 Ed 22
L'Ile-Rousse ○ **F** 185 Gl 24
Lilia ○ **VRC** 258 Lg 32
Lilla ○ **PK** 230 Ka 29
Lille ○ **F** 163 Gh 20
Lille Bælt 〜 **DK** 170 Gl 18
Lillehammer ○ **N** 158 Gm 15
Lillesand ○ **N** 170 Gl 16
Lillestrøm ○ **N** 170 Gm 16
Lillooet ○ **CDN** 50 Ca 20
Lillooet ⚲ **CDN** 50 Cb 20
Lilo ○ **RDC** 333 He 46
Lilongwe ⬛ **MW** 344 Hj 52
Lilo Viejo ○ **RA** 136 Ec 59
Liloy ○ **RP** 267 Ln 41
Lim 〜 **RCA** 321 Gp 42
Lima ○ **USA** 71 Df 26
Lima 〜 **P** 184 Gb 25
Lima ○ **PY** 141 Ef 57
Lima 〜 **P** 184 Gb 25
Lima ○ **OM** 226 Jg 33
Lima ⬛ **PE** 128 Dk 52
Limache ○ **RCH** 137 Dn 62
Limache ○ **RA** 137 Ec 60
Limã 〜 **BR** 121 Ed 45
Limão do Curuá ○ **BR** 121 Ej 45
Limapuare ○ **BR** 141 Em 56
Limapuluh ○ **RI** 270 Kp 44
Limar 〜 **RCH** 137 Dn 61
Limassa ○ **RCA** 321 Hc 43
Limavady ○ **GB** 162 Gc 18
Limay 〜 **RA** 147 Dp 65
Limba Limba 〜 **EAT** 336 Hj 49
Limbang ○ **MAL** 274 Lh 43
Limbani ○ **PE** 128 Dp 53
Limbaša ○ **RDC** 321 Hd 43
Limbaži ○ **LV** 171 He 17

□Country ▣Capital city ⊙Administrative unit OPlace ♁Island ⛰Mountain range △Mountain ⌓Cape ≈Ocean, Sea ~Lake, River ᴪUndersea topography ▲Glacier ♀National park •••Reservation ★Point of major interest ⏜Landscape

Limbdi O IND 227 Jp 34
Limbé O RH 101 Dm 36
Limbé Victoria O CAM 320 Gl 44
Limbe O MW 344 Hk 53
Limbla O AUS 374 Md 57
Limboto O RI 275 Lm 45
Limbovka O RUS 159 Hn 12
Limbunya O AUS 364 Ma 54
Limburg a.d. Lahn O D 163 Gk 20
Lime Acres O ZA 349 Hd 60
Limedsforsen O S 158 Gn 15
Limeira O BR 141 El 57
Limerick O CDN 51 Cj 21
Limerick Luimheach O IRL 163 Gb 19
Limingen ~ N 158 Gn 13
Limmen Bight ~ AUS 364 Md 53
Limmen Bight Aboriginal Land ••• AUS 364 Md 53
Limmfjorden ~ DK 170 Gl 17
Limnos ♁ GR 194 He 25
Limoeiro O BR 124 Fc 49
Limoeiro de Ajuru O BR 121 Ek 46
Limoeiro do Norte O BR 124 Fa 48
Limoges O F 184 Gg 23
Limon O USA 65 Cl 26
Limón O CR 97 Dg 41
Limón O EC 116 Dj 47
Limonar O C 101 Dl 35
Limousin ⊙ F 184 Gg 23
Limoux O F 184 Gh 24
Limpio O PY 140 Ef 58
Limpopo ~ MOC 352 Hj 57
Limuru O EAK 337 Hl 46
Līna O KSA 215 Hp 31
Linaälven ~ S 159 Hc 12
Linahamari O RUS 159 Hh 11
Lin'an O VRC 246 Lk 30
Linapacan Island ♁ RP 267 Lk 40
Linapacan Strait ~ RP 267 Lk 40
Linares O MEX 81 Cn 33
Linares O RCH 137 Dn 63
Linares O E 184 Ge 26
Linariá O GR 194 He 26
Lincang O VRC 254 Kp 34
Linchang O VRC 243 Le 29
Linchuan O VRC 258 Lh 32
Lincoln O USA 60 Dm 23
Lincoln O USA 60 Dp 23
Lincoln O USA 64 Cb 26
Lincoln O USA 70 Cn 26
Lincoln O USA 70 Cp 25
Lincoln O USA 71 Dd 25
Lincoln O GB 163 Gf 19
Lincoln Boyhood Natl. Mem. ★ USA 71 De 26
Lincoln Caverns ★ USA 74 Dj 25
Lincoln City O USA 50 Bp 23
Lincoln National Park ♀ AUS 378 Me 63
Lincoln Park O USA 71 Dg 24
Lincolton O USA 71 Dh 28
Lincon O RA 137 Ed 63
Lindagadan O MYA 254 Km 35
Lindau O D 174 Gl 22
Linde ~ RUS 204 Wa 5
Lindela O MOC 352 Hk 58
Lindeman Group ♁ AUS 375 Ml 56
Linden O USA 70 Da 29
Linden O GUY 113 Ee 42
Lindesness ⌓ N 170 Gk 17
Lindi ~ RDC 324 He 45
Lindi ~ RDC 336 Hf 46
Lindi O EAT 337 Hm 50
Lindi Bay ~ EAT 337 Hm 50
Lindis Pass △ NZ 382 Ng 68
Lindley O ZA 349 Hf 59
Lindos O GR 195 Hg 27
Lindsay O USA 51 Ck 22
Lindsay O CDN 60 Dj 23
Lindsay O USA 64 Cc 27
Lindsborg O USA 70 Cp 26
Linduri O VU 386 Nf 53
Line Islands ♁ 27 Ab 9
Linejnoe O RUS 181 Jb 22
Linek O RP 275 Lm 42
Lineville O USA 70 Db 25
Linfé O CAM 320 Gm 43
Linfen O VRC 243 Lf 27
Linganamakki Reservoir ~ IND 238 Kb 38
Lingayen Gulf ~ RP 267 Ll 37
Lingbao O VRC 243 Lf 28
Lingbi O VRC 246 Lj 29
Lingen(E.) O D 170 Gk 19
Lingig O RP 267 Lp 41
Lingle O USA 51 Ck 24
Lingole O RCB 332 Gp 48
Lingomo O RDC 333 Hc 45
Lingqi ★ VRC 258 Lk 31
Lingqiu O VRC 243 Lg 26
Lingshan O VRC 255 Le 34
Lingshan Dao ♁ VRC 246 Ll 28
Lingshi O VRC 243 Lf 27
Lingshui O VRC 255 Le 36
Lingsugār O IND 238 Kc 37
Lingtai O VRC 243 Ld 28
Linguère O SN 304 Fn 38
Lingui O VRC 255 Le 33
Lingwu O VRC 243 Ld 26
Ling Xian O VRC 258 Lg 32
Lingyuan O VRC 246 Lk 25
Linhai O VRC 259 Ll 31
Linhares O BR 141 Fa 55
Linhe O VRC 243 Ld 25
Linhemo O ANG 340 Ha 52
Linkiring O SN 316 Fp 39
Link Lakes ~ AUS 368 Lm 59
Linköping O S 170 Gp 16
Linkou O VRC 205 Wc 9
Linkou O VRC 250 Ma 23
Linli O VRC 255 Lf 31
Linn O USA 70 Dc 26
Linpeng O VRC 255 Ld 34
Linqing O VRC 243 Lh 27
Linqu O VRC 246 Lk 27
Linquan O VRC 243 Lh 29
Lins O BR 140 Ek 56
Linsan O RG 316 Fp 40
Linshu O VRC 246 Lk 28
Linshui O VRC 243 Ld 30
Linstead O JA 101 Dk 36
Linta ~ RM 353 Ja 58
Lintang O MAL 124 Lk 43
Lintao O VRC 242 Lb 28
L-in-Techerène O RMM 305 Gf 35
Linton O USA 56 Cm 22
Linton O USA 71 De 26
Lintong O VRC 243 Le 28
Lin Xian O VRC 243 Lf 26
Lin Xian O VRC 243 Lg 27
Linxiang O VRC 258 Lg 31
Linxiashi O VRC 242 Lb 28
Linyandi O NAM 341 Hd 55
Linyanti ~ RB 341 Hd 55
Linyati Swamp ~ NAM 341 Hd 55
Linyi O VRC 246 Lj 27
Linyi O VRC 246 Lk 28
Linz O A 174 Gn 21
Linze O VRC 242 Kp 26
Linzhen O VRC 243 Le 27
Línzor O RCH 136 Dp 57
Lioma O MOC 344 Hl 53
Lions Den O ZW 341 Hg 54
Lioto O RCA 321 Hc 43
Liouesso O RCB 332 Gp 45
Lipa O RP 267 Ll 39
Lipale O MOC 344 Hl 54
Lipari O I 185 Gp 26
Lipari Islands ♁ I 185 Gp 26
Lipcani O MD 175 Hf 21
Lipeck O RUS 181 Hm 19
Lipeo ~ PY 136 Eb 57
Liperi O FIN 159 Hg 14
Lipin Bor O RUS 159 Hm 15
Liping O VRC 255 Le 32
Lipki O RUS 181 Hl 19
Lipljan O SCG 194 Hc 24
Lipno O PL 170 Hb 19
Lipova O RO 174 Hc 22
Lippe ~ D 174 Gl 20
Lippstadt O D 174 Gl 20
Lipton O CDN 51 Cl 20
Liptougou O BF 317 Gg 39
Lipu O VRC 255 Lf 33
Liqu O VRC 242 Lb 28
Lira O EAU 324 Hj 44
Liranga O RCB 333 Ha 46
Lircay O PE 128 Dl 52
Lirung O RI 275 Lp 44
Lisala O RDC 333 Hc 44
Lisbon O USA 56 Cn 22
Lisbon O USA 71 Dh 25
Lisbon ▣ P 184 Gb 26
Lisburne Peninsula ♁ USA 46 Ag 11
Lishan O VRC 243 Ld 30
Lishan ★ VRC 243 Lf 28
Lishi O VRC 243 Lf 27
Lishi O VRC 255 Lc 31
Lishui O VRC 259 Lk 31
Lisieux O F 163 Gg 21
Lisitu O EAT 337 Hk 50
Liski O RUS 181 Hm 20
Lismore O AUS 375 Mn 60
Lismore O AUS 378 Mh 64
Lisnaskea O GB 162 Gc 18
Lissadell O AUS 364 Ma 54
Lištica O BIH 194 Ha 24
Listowel O CDN 57 Dh 24
Listowel O IRL 163 Gb 19
Listrvjanka O RUS 204 Va 8
Lita O EC 116 Dj 45
Litang O VRC 254 La 31
Litang O VRC 255 Le 34
Litani ~ SME 113 Eg 44
Lītāni ~ RL 208 Hk 29
Litchfield O USA 56 Da 23
Litchfield ♀ AUS 364 Mb 52
Litchville O USA 56 Cn 22
Lithgow O AUS 379 Mm 62
Lithuania □ LT 170 Hd 18
Litipāra O IND 235 Kh 33
Litoměřice O CZ 174 Gn 20
Litomyšl O CZ 174 Gp 21
Little ~ USA 70 Da 28
Little Abitibi Lake ~ CDN 57 Dh 21
Little Abitibi River ~ CDN 57 Dh 20
Little Andaman ♁ IND 262 Kl 40
Little Bahama Bank ᴪ 87 Dj 32
Little Barrier Island ♁ NZ 383 Nk 64
Little Bay O CDN 61 Ee 22
Little Belt Mountains ⛰ USA 51 Cg 22
Little Bighorn Battlefield ★ USA 51 Cj 23
Little Bighorn Battlefield N.M. ★ USA 51 Cj 23
Little Blue River ~ USA 70 Cn 25
Little Cayman ♁ GB 100 Dh 36
Little Coco Island ♁ MYA 262 Kl 39
Little Colorado River ~ USA 65 Cg 28
Little Current O CDN 57 Dh 23
Little Current River ~ CDN 57 De 20
Little Desert ♀ AUS 378 Mg 64
Little Desert ⏜ AUS 378 Mg 64
Little Diomede Island ♁ USA 46 Ae 11
Little Exuma Island ♁ BS 87 Dl 34
Little Falls O USA 56 Da 23
Little Falls O USA 60 Dl 24
Littlefield O USA 64 Cf 27
Littlefield O USA 65 Cl 29
Little Fork O USA 56 Db 21
Little Fork River ~ USA 56 Db 21
Little Fort O CDN 50 Cb 20
Little Gold ~ AUS 361 Lp 55
Little Grand Rapids O CDN 56 Da 19
Little Harbour O BS 87 Dk 33
Little Humboldt ~ USA 64 Cd 25
Little Inagua Island ♁ BS 101 Dm 35
Little Karoo ⏜ ZA 358 Hc 62
Little Lake O USA 64 Cc 28
Little Marais O USA 56 Dc 22
Little Missouri River ~ USA 51 Ck 23
Little Missouri River ~ USA 51 Cl 22
Little Nicobar Island ♁ IND 270 Kl 42
Little Powder River ~ USA 51 Ck 23
Little Ragged Island ♁ BS 87 Dl 34
Little Rock O USA 70 Db 28
Little Ruaha ~ EAT 337 Hk 50
Little Sable Point ⌓ USA 57 De 24
Little Sandy Desert ⏜ AUS 368 Ll 58
Little San Salvador Island ♁ BS 87 Dk 33
Little Scarcies of Kaba Mabole ~ WAL 316 Fp 41
Little Sioux ~ USA 56 Da 24
Little Snake River ~ USA 65 Ch 25
Littleton O USA 60 Dn 23
Littleton O USA 65 Ck 26
Littletown O USA 65 Ck 26
Little Wabash ~ USA 71 Dd 26
Little White River ~ CDN 57 Dg 22
Litunde O MOC 344 Hk 52
Liuba O VRC 243 Ld 29
Liuchiu Yü ♁ RC 259 Ll 34
Liuheng Dao ♁ VRC 259 Lm 31
Liujiachang O VRC 243 Lf 30
Liujiang O VRC 255 Le 33
Liujiaxia Shiku ★ VRC 242 Lb 28
Liujing O VRC 255 Lf 34
Liuli O EAT 344 Hk 51
Liulin O VRC 243 Lf 27
Liuliu O SOL 290 Na 49
Liupan Shan ⛰ VRC 243 Lc 27
Liupanshui O VRC 255 Lc 32
Liúpo O MOC 344 Hm 53
Liushilipu O VRC 243 Lh 29
Liuwa Plain ♀ Z 341 Hd 53
Liuxu O VRC 255 Le 34
Liuyang O VRC 258 Lg 31
Liuzhai O VRC 255 Ld 33
Liuzhano Shan ⛰ VRC 255 Lc 34
Liuzhi O VRC 255 Lc 32
Liuzhou O VRC 255 Le 33
Liuzhuang O VRC 246 Ll 29
Livádi O GR 194 He 27
Livadiá O GR 194 Hd 26
Livadija O UA 175 Hk 23
Līvāni O LV 171 Hf 17
Lively Island ♁ GB 147 Ee 72
Livengood O USA 46 Ba 13
Live Oak O USA 86 Dg 30
Livermore Falls O USA 60 Dn 23
Liverpool O CDN 61 Eb 24
Liverpool O GB 163 Ge 19
Liverpool O AUS 379 Mm 62
Liverpool Bay ~ CDN 47 Bl 11
Liverpool Range ⛰ AUS 379 Ml 61
Livingston O USA 51 Cg 23
Livingston O USA 71 Df 27
Livingston O USA 81 Da 30
Livingston O USA 86 Dd 29
Livingstone O Z 341 He 54
Livingstone Island ♁ 38 Fb 16
Livingstone Mountains ⛰ EAT 337 Hk 50
Livingstonia O MW 344 Hk 51
Livno O BIH 194 Ha 24
Livny O RUS 181 Hl 19
Livonia O USA 57 Dg 24
Livorno O I 185 Gl 24
Livramento de Nossa Senhora O BR 125 En 52
Liwa O RI 278 Lc 48
Liwa O TCH 309 Gp 39
Liwale O EAT 337 Hl 50
Liwonde O MW 344 Hk 53
Liwonde ♀ MW 344 Hk 53
Li Xian O VRC 242 Lb 30
Li Xian O VRC 242 Lc 28
Lixin O VRC 246 Lj 29
Lixoúri O GR 194 Hc 26
Liyang O VRC 246 Lk 30
Li Yubu O SUD 324 Hf 43
Lizarda O BR 121 El 50
Lizard Island ♀ AUS 365 Mj 53
Lizard Island ♁ AUS 365 Mj 53
Lizums O LV 171 Hf 17
Lizzie Webber Reef ♁ MAL 266 Lg 41
Ljahovskie ostrova ♁ RUS 205 Xa 4
Ljaki O AZ 202 Jb 25
Ljamca O RUS 159 Hl 13
Ljangar O AFG 230 Ka 27
Ljuban' O RUS 171 Hh 16
Ljubanskae vdsh. ~ BY 171 Hg 19
Ljubar O UA 175 Hf 21
Ljubašivka O UA 175 Hh 22
Ljubercy O RUS 171 Hm 18
Ljubešiv O UA 175 He 20
Ljubljana ▣ SLO 174 Gp 22
Ljubomľ O UA 175 He 20
Ljubytino O RUS 171 Hj 16
Ljudinovo O RUS 171 Hk 19
Ljugarn O S 170 Hb 17
Ljungan ~ S 158 Ha 14
Ljungby O S 170 Gn 17
Ljungdalen O S 158 Gn 14
Ljusan ~ S 158 Gp 15
Ljusdal O S 158 Ha 15
Llallagua O BOL 129 Ea 55
Llandrindod Wells O GB 163 Ge 19
Llanes O E 184 Gd 24
Llanquihué O RCH 147 Dm 66
Llangurig O GB 163 Ge 19
Llano O USA 81 Cn 30
Llano ~ USA 81 Cn 30
Llanobajo O CO 106 Dk 44
Llano del Quimal ⏜ RCH 136 Dp 57
Llano el Guaje ⏜ MEX 81 Cl 32
Llano Estacado ⏜ USA 65 Cl 29
Llanos ⏜ CO 107 Dn 44
Llanos de Chiquitos ⏜ BOL 129 Ec 55
Llanos de Guarayos ⏜ BOL 129 Eb 53
Llanos de la Rioja ⏜ RA 137 Ea 60
Llanos de los Caballos Mesteños ⏜ MEX 81 Ck 31
Llanos de Mojos ⏜ BOL 129 Eb 53
Llanura Costera de Golfo ⏜ MEX 81 Cn 33
Llao Llao O RA 147 Dn 66
Llata O PE 116 Dk 50
Llaylla O PE 128 Dl 51
Lleida O E 184 Gg 25
Llera O MEX 92 Cn 34
Llerena O E 184 Gc 26
Iley ⏜ EAK 325 Hl 45
Lleyn Peninsula ♁ GB 163 Gd 19
L'Liaoyang O VRC 246 Lm 25
Llica O BOL 129 Dp 55
Llico O RCH 137 Dm 64
Llíria O E 184 Gf 26
Lljucmajor O E 184 Gh 26
Lloyd O USA 51 Ch 21
Lloyd Bay ~ AUS 365 Mh 52
Lloydminster O CDN 51 Ch 19
Lluta O PE 128 Dm 54
Lluta ~ RCH 128 Dp 55
Loa O USA 65 Cg 26
Loa ~ RCH 136 Dp 56
Loa ~ RCH 136 Dp 57
Loanda O BR 140 Eh 57
Loanda ~ ANG 340 Ha 50
Loandji ~ RDC 333 Hb 48
Loange ~ RDC 333 Hb 49
Loange ~ RDC 333 Hc 48
Loango O RDC 332 Gn 48
Loanja ~ Z 341 He 54
Loão Chagas O ANG 341 Hd 51
Loay O RP 267 Lm 41
Lobato O BR 141 Em 57
Lobatse O RB 349 He 58
Lobaye ~ RCA 321 Ha 43
Lobeke ~ CAM 321 Gp 44
Lobería O RA 146 Ee 65
Lobi O RDC 321 Hd 43
Lobios O E 184 Gb 25
Lobira O SUD 325 Hj 43
Lobito O ANG 340 Gn 52
Lobitos O PE 116 Dh 48
Lobo O RI 283 Mc 47
Lobo ~ CAM 321 Gn 44
Loboko O RCB 332 Ha 46
Lobo Lodge O EAT 337 Hk 46
Lobos O RA 146 Ee 63
Lobskoe O RUS 159 Hk 14
Lobu O RI 282 Lm 46
Lobuja O RUS 205 Ya 5
Locarno O CH 174 Gl 22
Locate O USA 51 Ck 22
Lochboisdale O GB 162 Gc 17
Loches O F 163 Gg 22
Loch Fyne ~ GB 162 Gd 18
Lochgilphead O GB 162 Gd 17
Lochiel O ZA 352 Hh 59
Lochinvar ♀ Z 341 Hf 53
Lochinver O GB 162 Gd 16
Loch Linnhe ~ GB 162 Gd 17
Loch Lomond ~ GB 162 Gd 17
Lochmaddy O GB 162 Gc 17
Loch Ness ~ GB 162 Gd 17
Lochów O PL 170 Hc 19
Lochsa ~ USA 50 Ce 22
Loch Sport O AUS 379 Mk 65
Lock O AUS 378 Md 62
Lockhart O USA 81 Cp 31
Lockhart O AUS 379 Mk 63
Lockhart River O AUS 365 Mh 52
Lockhart River Aboriginal Reserve ••• AUS 365 Mh 52
Lock Haven O USA 74 Dk 25
Lockney O USA 70 Cm 28
Lockport O USA 60 Dj 24
Lôc Ninh O VN 263 Ld 40
Locri O I 194 Ha 26
Locumba O PE 128 Dn 54
Locumba ~ PE 128 Dn 54
Locust ~ USA 70 Db 25
Lod O IL 214 Hk 30
Lodejnoe Pole O RUS 171 Hj 15
Lodève O F 185 Gh 24
Lodge Creek ~ USA 51 Ch 21
Lodge Grass O USA 51 Cj 23
Lodgepole O CDN 50 Ce 19
Lodgepole Creek ~ USA 65 Ck 25
Lodhrān O PK 227 Jp 31
Lodi O USA 64 Cb 26
Lodi O I 185 Gl 23
Lodi O RDC 333 Hc 48
Lodié ~ G 332 Gn 46
Løding O N 158 Gn 12
Lødingen O N 158 Gp 11
Lodja O RDC 333 Hd 47
Lodmalasin △ EAT 337 Hk 47
Lodrani O IND 227 Jp 34
Lodwar O EAK 325 Hk 44
Łódź O PL 174 Hb 20
Loei O THA 262 La 37
Loeka ~ RDC 321 Hd 44
Loémé ~ RCB 332 Gm 48
Loeng Nok Tha O THA 263 Lc 37
Loeriesfontein O ZA 348 Hb 61
Lofa River ~ LB 316 Ga 42
Lofé O SN 304 Fm 38
Lofoten ♁ N 158 Gn 12
Lofty Range ⛰ AUS 368 Lk 58
Log O RUS 181 Hp 21
Loga O RN 308 Gh 39
Loga O SUD 324 Hh 43
Logan O USA 65 Cg 25
Logan O USA 65 Cl 28
Logan O USA 71 Dh 27
Logan Pass △ USA 50 Cf 21
Logansport O USA 71 De 25
Lōgar ⊙ AFG 223 Jn 28
Lōgar ~ AFG 223 Jn 28
Lögdeälven ~ S 158 Hb 14
Loge ~ ANG 332 Gp 49
Logona ~ TCH 321 Gp 40
Logone Birni O CAM 321 Gp 40
Logone Gana O TCH 321 Gp 40
Logone Occidental ~ TCH 321 Gp 41
Logone Oriental ~ TCH 321 Ha 41
Logone Tandjilé ~ TCH 321 Gp 41
Logroño O E 184 Ge 24
Lohagara O BD 235 Kj 34
Lohāghāt O IND 234 Kd 31
Lohardaga O IND 235 Kg 34
Lohéac O F 163 Ge 22
Lohiniva O FIN 159 He 12
Lohja O FIN 159 Hd 15
Lohjanan O RI 274 Lj 46
Lohr O D 174 Gl 21
Loiborsoit O EAT 337 Hl 47
Loi-kaw O MYA 254 Kn 36
Loile ~ RDC 333 Hc 46
Loilo ~ RDC 333 Hd 45
Loimaa O FIN 159 Hd 15
Loima Hills ⛰ EAK 325 Hk 44
Loire ⊙ F 163 Gf 22
Loire ~ F 163 Gf 22
Loi Song △ MYA 254 Kn 34
Loita Hills ⛰ EAK 337 Hk 46
Loja O EC 116 Dj 48
Loja O E 184 Gd 27
Lojmola O RUS 171 Hh 15
Lokabatan O AZ 202 Jc 25
Lokalama O RDC 333 Hb 47
Lokalema O RDC 321 Hd 44
Lokandu O RDC 333 He 47
Lokan tekojärvi ~ FIN 159 Hf 12
Lokata O RI 283 Mb 46
Lokichar O EAK 325 Hk 44
Lokichar ~ EAK 325 Hk 44
Lokichogio O EAK 325 Hk 43
Lokila O RDC 333 He 47
Lokitaung O EAK 325 Hk 43
Loknja O RUS 171 Hh 17
Loko O WAN 320 Gk 41
Lokoja O WAN 320 Gk 42
Lokola O RDC 333 Hc 46
Lokolo ~ RDC 333 Hb 46
Lokomby O RM 353 Jb 57
Lokomo O CAM 321 Gp 44
Lokomo ~ CAM 321 Gp 44
Lokona O RDC 333 Hd 46
Lokono O PNG 287 Mm 47
Lokori O EAK 325 Hl 45
Lokoro ~ RDC 333 Hb 46
Lokossa O DY 317 Gg 42
Lokot O RUS 171 Hk 19
Lokoti O CAM 321 Gp 42
Lokoundjé ~ CAM 320 Gm 44
Loksa O EST 171 He 16
Loksiati O SME 113 Eg 43
Loks Land ♁ CDN 43 Hc 6
Lokutu O RDC 333 Hd 45
Lokwakangola O EAK 325 Hk 44
Loky ~ RM 345 Jc 52
Lol ~ SUD 324 Hf 41
Lola O RG 316 Gb 42
Lola O ANG 340 Gn 53
Lole ~ RDC 333 Hb 47
Lolengi O RDC 333 Hc 45
Lolgorien O EAK 337 Hk 46
Lolland ♁ DK 170 Gm 18
Lolo O USA 50 Ce 22
Lolobata O RI 275 Ma 45
Lolobau Island ♁ PNG 287 Mm 48
Lolodorf O CAM 320 Gm 44
Lolo Hot Springs O USA 50 Ce 22
Lolol O RCH 137 Dn 63
Lolo Pass △ USA 50 Ce 22
Lolui Island ♁ EAU 337 Hj 46
Lolvavana Passage ~ VU 386 Ng 53
Lolwane O ZA 349 Hd 59
Lolworth O AUS 375 Mj 56
Lolworth Range ⛰ AUS 375 Mj 56
Lom O N 158 Gl 15
Lom O BG 194 Hd 24
Lom ~ CAM 321 Gp 42
Loma O ETH 325 Hl 42
Loma Alta O USA 81 Cm 31
Loma Bonita O MEX 93 Da 36
Lomako ~ RDC 333 Hc 45
Lomaloma O FJI 390 Aa 54
Lomami ~ RDC 324 He 45
Lomami O RDC 333 Hd 46
Lomami ~ RDC 333 He 46
Loma Mountains △ WAL 316 Ga 41
Loman O USA 56 Db 21
Lomas O PE 128 Dl 53
Lomas ~ PE 128 Dl 53
Loma San Martín △ RA 147 Dp 65
Lomas Coloradas ⏜ RA 147 Ea 67
Lomas de Arena O MEX 80 Ck 30
Lomas de Vallejos O RA 140 Ee 59
Lomas de Zamora O RA 146 Ee 63
Lomaum O ANG 340 Gp 52
Lomba ~ ANG 340 Hb 53
Lombadina O AUS 360 Lm 54
Lombang O RI 279 Lk 47
Lombardia ⊙ I 185 Gl 23
Lombe O RI 282 Lm 48
Lombe ~ ANG 340 Ha 50
Lomblen ♁ RI 282 Lm 50
Lombo O RDC 321 Hb 43
Lombok ♁ RI 279 Lh 50
Lombok Basin ᴪ RI 279 Lh 51
Lomé ▣ RT 317 Gg 42
Lomela ~ RDC 333 Hc 46
Lomela O RDC 333 Hd 47
Lometa O USA 81 Cn 30
Lomfjorden ~ N 158 Ha 6
Lomié O CAM 321 Gn 44
Loming O SUD 324 Hj 43
Lomond O CDN 51 Cf 20
Lomphat O K 263 Ld 39
Lompoc O USA 64 Cb 28
Lompoul O SN 304 Fm 38
Lom Sak O THA 262 La 37
Łomża O PL 170 Hc 19
Lonand O IND 238 Kb 36
Lonar O IND 238 Kc 36
Lonāvale O IND 238 Ka 36
Lončakovo O RUS 250 Md 22
Loncoche O RCH 147 Dm 65
Loncopangue O RCH 137 Dn 64
Loncopue O RA 147 Dn 65
Londa O IND 238 Kb 38
Londela-Kayes O RCB 332 Gn 48
Londengo O ANG 340 Gn 52
Londiani O EAK 337 Hk 46
Londolovit O PNG 287 Mn 47
London O CDN 57 Dh 24
London O USA 71 Df 27
London O USA 71 Dg 26
London ▣ GB 163 Gf 20
Londonderry O GB 162 Gc 18
Londrina O BR 140 Ej 57
Lonely Mine O ZW 341 Hg 55
Lone Pine O USA 64 Cc 27
Lonesome ♀ AUS 375 Ml 58
Long O THA 254 Kp 36
Longá ~ BR 124 Ep 47
Longa ~ ANG 340 Gp 51
Longa O ANG 340 Hb 53
Long'an O VRC 243 Le 27
Longana O VU 386 Nf 53
Longaškino O RUS 205 Ya 4
Long Bay ~ USA 87 Dj 29
Long Bay ~ JA 101 Dk 36
Long Beach O USA 64 Cc 29
Long Beach O USA 87 Dj 29
Longbow O CDN 56 Da 21
Long Branch O USA 74 Dm 25
Long Cay ♁ BS 87 Dl 34
Long Cay ♁ BH 96 De 37
Longchang O VRC 255 Lc 31
Longchuan O VRC 258 Lh 33
Long Creek O USA 50 Cc 23
Long Đất O VN 263 Ld 40
Longe ~ ANG 332 Gp 49
Longford O IRL 163 Gc 19
Longford O AUS 378 Mk 66
Longhui O VRC 255 Lf 32
Longido O EAT 337 Hl 47
Longikis O RI 279 Lj 46
Longing O VRC 254 Kp 33
Longiram O RI 279 Lh 46
Long Island ♁ CDN 61 Ea 23
Long Island ♁ USA 74 Dm 25
Long Island ♁ BS 87 Dl 34
Long Island ♁ PNG 287 Mk 48
Long Island ♁ AUS 375 Ml 57
Long Island Sound ~ USA 74 Dm 25
Longkou O VRC 246 Lk 27
Longlac O CDN 57 De 21
Long Lake ~ USA 56 Cm 22
Long Lake ~ CDN 57 De 21
Long Lama O MAL 274 Lh 44
Long Lellang O MAL 274 Lh 44
Longlin O VRC 255 Lc 33
Longling O VRC 254 Kp 33
Longmen O VRC 255 Lf 35
Longmen O VRC 258 Lg 34
Longmen Shiku ★ VRC 243 Lf 28
Longmont O USA 65 Ck 25
Long Mỹ O VN 263 Lc 41
Longnan O VRC 258 Lh 33
Longo O G 332 Gn 46
Longonjo O ANG 340 Gp 52
Longonot △ EAK 337 Hl 46
Longotea O PE 116 Dk 49
Long Pine O USA 56 Cn 24
Long Point ⌓ CDN 56 Cn 19
Long Point O CDN 57 Dh 24
Long Point ⌓ CDN 57 Dh 24
Long Point ⌓ CDN 61 Ee 21
Long Point ⌓ RP 266 Lk 41
Long Point ⌓ NZ 382 Ng 69
Long Point Bay ~ CDN 57 Dh 24
Long Prairie O USA 56 Da 23
Longquan O VRC 258 Lk 32
Long Range Mountains ⛰ CDN 61 Ee 22
Longreach O AUS 375 Mj 57
Longs Reefs ♁ PNG 287 Mm 51
Longs Creek O CDN 61 Ea 23
Long Seridan O MAL 274 Lh 43
Longshan O VRC 258 Lg 34
Longsheng O VRC 255 Lf 33
Longshou-Shan ⛰ VRC 242 La 26
Longs Peak △ USA 65 Ck 25
Long Thành O VN 263 Ld 40
Longton O AUS 375 Mj 56
Longueuil O CDN 60 Dm 23
Long Valley Junction O USA 64 Cf 27
Longview O USA 50 Ca 22
Longview O CDN 50 Ce 20
Longview O USA 70 Da 29
Longwy O F 163 Gj 21
Longxi O VRC 242 Lc 28
Long Xian O VRC 243 Ld 28
Long Xuyên O VN 263 Lc 40
Longyan O VRC 258 Lj 33
Longyao O VRC 243 Lh 27
Longyearbyen O N 158 Gp 6
Longyou O VRC 258 Lk 31
Longzhou O VRC 255 Ld 34
Loni Kand O IND 238 Kb 36
Lonkonia ~ RDC 333 Hd 47
Lonoke O USA 70 Dc 28
Lonquimay O RCH 147 Dn 65
Lonsdale O USA 56 Db 23
Lons-de-Saunier O F 163 Gj 22
Lontou O RMM 304 Ga 38
Lontra ~ BR 121 Ek 49
Lontra ~ BR 140 Eh 56
Lontue ~ RCH 137 Dn 63
Lonua ~ RDC 333 Hd 45
Looc O RP 267 Lm 39
Lookout Pass △ USA 50 Ce 22
Lookout Point ⌓ AUS 365 Mj 53
Looma O AUS 361 Ln 55
Loon O CDN 57 Dd 21
Loon O RP 267 Lm 41
Loongana O AUS 369 Lp 61
Loop River ~ USA 70 Cn 25
Lootsberg Pass △ ZA 349 He 61
Lop O VRC 230 Ke 27
Lopary O RM 353 Jb 57
Lopatino O RUS 181 Ja 19
Lopburi O THA 262 La 38
Lopez O CO 106 Dk 44
Lopez O RP 267 Lm 39
Lop Nur ~ VRC 231 Kk 25
Lopon ~ RDC 333 Hc 45
Lopori ~ RDC 333 Hc 45
Lopphavet ~ N 159 Hc 10
Lora ~ YV 107 Dm 41
Lora Creek ~ AUS 374 Md 60
Lorain O USA 71 Dg 25
Lorana O RI 282 Ll 47
Lorca O E 184 Gf 27
Lordegān O IR 215 Jd 30
Lord Howe Island ♁ AUS 35 Sb 13
Lord Howe Rise ᴪ 35 Ta 12
Lord Loughborough Island ♁ MYA 262 Kn 40
Lordsburg O USA 65 Ch 29
Lore O TP 282 Lp 50
Lore Lindu National Park ♀ RI 282 Ll 46
Lorella O AUS 364 Md 53
Lorena O BR 141 Em 57
Lorengau O PNG 287 Mk 46
Lorentz ~ RI 286 Mf 48
Lorentz National Park ♀ RI 286 Me 48
Lore Rūd ~ AFG 223 Jm 29
Lorestān ⊙ IR 209 Jb 29
Loreto O MEX 80 Cg 32
Loreto O MEX 92 Cm 34
Loreto O EC 116 Dk 46
Loreto O CO 117 Dn 47
Loreto O BR 121 Em 49
Loreto O BOL 129 Eb 53
Loreto O I 185 Gn 24
Loreto O RP 267 Ln 40
Lorian Swamp ~ EAK 325 Hm 45
Lorica O CO 106 Dk 41
Lorient O F 163 Ge 22
Lorimers O GB 101 Dn 35
Loring O USA 51 Cj 21
Lorne O AUS 375 Mk 58
Lorne O AUS 379 Mh 65
Lorneville O CDN 61 Ea 23
Loronyo O SUD 324 Hj 43
Loropéni O BF 317 Ge 40
Lörrach O D 163 Gk 22
Lorraine ⊙ F 163 Gj 21
Lorraine O AUS 365 Mf 55
Loruk O EAK 325 Hl 45
Lorukumu O EAK 325 Hk 44
Lorzot O TN 297 Gm 30
Los O S 158 Gp 15
Los Alamos O USA 65 Cj 28
Los Aldamas O MEX 81 Cn 32
Los Amates O GCA 93 Dd 38

Limbdi - Los Amates 439

Los Amores ○ RA 146 Ee 60
Los Andes ○ RCH 137 Dn 62
Los Angeles ○ USA 64 Cc 29
LosÁngeles ○ RCH 137 Dm 64
Los Angeles Aqueduct ∼ USA 64 Cc 28
Losari ○ RI 278 Le 49
Los Asientos ○ PA 97 Dh 42
Los Aztecas ○ MEX 92 Cn 34
Los Banos ○ USA 64 Cb 27
Los Barrancos ○ YV 112 Ec 41
Los Barriles ○ MEX 80 Ch 34
Los Barros ○ RCH 137 Dn 64
Los Blancos ○ RA 136 Ec 57
Los Canelos ○ RCH 152 Dn 72
Los Caribes ○ YV 112 Ed 43
Los Castillos ○ YV 112 Ec 41
Los Chiles ○ CR 97 Df 40
Los Chorchos ○ MEX 92 Ck 35
Los Cinuelos ○ DOM 101 Dn 36
Los Corrales ○ MEX 75 Cf 31
Los Cristianos ○ E 292 Fm 32
Los Gaviotas ○ YV 112 Ec 41
Los Güires ○ YV 112 Ed 41
Los Herreras ○ MEX 81 Cn 33
Los Indios ○ C 101 Dl 35
Lošinj ⌂ HR 185 Gn 23
Los Jobillos ○ DOM 101 Dn 36
Los Jories ○ RA 136 Ec 60
Los Kahós ♀ CO 106 Dk 42
Los Lagos ○ RCH 147 Dm 65
Los Llanos de Aridane ○ E 292 Fl 31
Los Loros ○ RCH 136 Dn 59
Los Lunas ○ USA 65 Cj 28
Los Menucos ○ RA 147 Dp 66
Los Mochis ○ MEX 80 Ch 33
Los Molinos ○ USA 64 Ca 25
Los Monos ○ RA 152 Dp 69
Los Moscas ○ RA 146 Ee 62
Los Muenmos ○ RCH 147 Dm 66
Los Navalmorales ○ E 184 Gd 26
Los Negrones ○ YV 107 Dm 40
Los Nevados ♀ CO 106 Dl 43
Los Norteños ○ MEX 75 Cf 30
Loso ∼ RDC 333 Hb 46
Losomba ○ RDC 333 He 47
Losoni ○ RI 282 Lm 47
Los Pozos ○ PA 97 Dh 42
Los Puentes ○ MEX 80 Cj 33
Los Reyes Salgado ○ MEX 92 Cl 36
Los Rodriguez ○ MEX 81 Cm 32
Los Roques ○ YV 107 Ea 40
Los Roques Archipelago ⌂ YV 107 Ea 40
Los Santos ○ PA 97 Dh 42
Los Sauces ○ RCH 137 Dm 64
Lossogonoi Plateau ⩘ EAT 337 Hl 47
Los Tábanos ○ RA 146 Ee 60
Los Taques ○ YV 107 Dn 40
Los Teques ○ YV 107 Ea 40
Lost Hills ○ USA 64 Cc 28
Lost River ○ CDN 60 Dl 23
Lost River Range ⩘ USA 50 Ce 23
Lost River Range △ USA 50 Ce 23
Los Troncos ○ BOL 129 Ec 54
Lost Trail Pass △ USA 50 Ce 23
Losuia ○ PNG 287 Mm 50
Losuk ○ PNG 287 Mm 47
Los Vientos ○ RCH 136 Dp 58
Los Yébenes ○ E 184 Gd 26
Lot ∼ F 184 Gg 23
Lotfābād ○ IR 222 Jh 27
Lothair ○ USA 51 Cg 21
Lotia ○ IND 234 Kd 34
Loto ○ RDC 333 Hd 47
Loto ∼ RDC 333 Hd 47
Lotofaga ○ WS 390 Ae 53
Lotoi ∼ RDC 333 Hb 46
Lotta ∼ RUS 159 Hg 11
Lotukel △ SUD 325 Hj 43
Louangphrabang ○ LAO 254 Lb 36
Loubetsi ○ RCB 332 Gn 47
Loubomo ○ RCB 332 Gn 48
Loubougoula ○ RMM 317 Gd 40
Loudenville ○ USA 71 Dg 25
Loudi ○ VRC 255 Lf 32
Loudima ○ RCB 332 Gn 48
Loudima ∼ RCB 332 Gn 48
Loudon ○ F 163 Gg 22
Louéssé ∼ RCB 332 Gn 47
Louétsi ∼ G 332 Gm 47
Louga ○ SN 304 Fm 38
Lough Dergh ∼ IRL 163 Gb 19
Lougheed Island ⌂ CDN 42 Ec 3
Lough Foyle ∼ IRL 162 Gc 18
Lough Gorrib ∼ IRL 163 Gb 19
Lough Neagh ∼ GB 162 Gc 18
Loughrea ○ IRL 163 Gb 19
Lough Ree ∼ IRL 163 Gc 19
Lougou ○ DY 320 Gh 40
Louhi ○ RUS 159 Hj 12
Louingui ○ RCB 332 Gp 48
Louisa ○ USA 71 Dg 26
Louisa Downs ○ AUS 361 Lp 55
Louisbourg ○ CDN 61 Ee 23
Louisburg ○ USA 74 Dj 27
Louise ○ USA 81 Cp 31
Louiseville ○ CDN 60 Dm 22
Louisiade Archipelago ⌂ PNG 287 Mn 51
Louisiana ○ USA 70 Dc 26
Louisiana ◉ USA 86 Db 30
Lou Island ⌂ PNG 287 Mk 47
Louis Trichardt ○ ZA 349 Hg 57
Louisville ○ USA 70 Cp 25
Louisville ○ USA 71 Df 26
Louisville ○ USA 71 Dg 29
Louisville ○ USA 86 Dd 29
Loukoléla ○ RCB 333 Ha 46
Loukouo ○ RCB 332 Gp 47
Loulan Gucheng ★ VRC 231 Kj 25
Louléma ○ RCB 332 Gm 48
Loulouni ○ RMM 317 Gd 40
Lou Lou Park ○ AUS 375 Mk 57
Loum ○ CAM 320 Gl 43
Loumbol ∼ SN 304 Fp 38
Loumou ○ RCB 332 Gp 48
Loup City ○ USA 70 Cn 25
Lourdes ○ CDN 61 Ee 21
Lourdes ○ F 184 Gf 24
Lour-Escale ○ SN 304 Fn 38
Lousserie ○ RIM 304 Ga 37
Louta ○ BF 317 Ge 39
Louth ○ GB 163 Gf 19
Louth ○ AUS 379 Mj 61
Loutra ○ GR 194 He 27
Loutrá Epidsoú ○ GR 194 Hd 26
Louvakou ○ RCB 332 Gn 48
Louviers ○ F 163 Gg 21
Louvincourt ○ CDN 60 Dk 21
Louwsburg ○ ZA 352 Hh 59
Louxiao Shan ⩘ VRC 258 Lg 32
Lövånger ○ S 159 Hc 13
Loveč ○ BG 194 He 24
Lovelady ○ USA 81 Da 30
Loveland ○ USA 65 Ck 25
Lovell ○ USA 51 Ch 23
Lovelock ○ USA 64 Cc 25
Lóvere ○ I 185 Gm 23
Loverna ○ CDN 51 Ch 20
Loving ○ USA 65 Ck 29
Loving ○ USA 70 Cn 29
Lovington ○ USA 65 Cl 29
Lovisa ○ FIN 159 Hf 15
Lövnäsvallen ○ S 158 Gn 15
Lovoi ∼ RDC 336 He 50
Lovozero ○ RUS 159 Hk 11
Lovozero ∼ RUS 159 Hk 12
Lóvua ○ ANG 333 Hc 49
Lovua ∼ RDC 333 Hc 49
Low ○ CDN 60 Dk 23
Lowa ∼ RDC 336 Hf 46
Low Bay ∼ GB 147 Ee 72
Lowell ○ USA 50 Ce 22
Lowell ○ USA 60 Dn 24
Lowelli ○ SUD 325 Hj 43
Löwen ∼ NAM 348 Hb 59
Lower Arrow Lake ∼ CDN 50 Cc 21
Lower Brule Ind. Res. ••• USA 56 Cm 23
Lower Ft.Garry N.H.P. ★ CDN 56 Cp 20
Lower Glenelg ♀ AUS 378 Mg 65
Lower Gwelo ○ ZW 341 Hg 55
Lower Hutt ○ NZ 383 Nk 66
Lower Lake ○ USA 64 Ca 26
Lower Lake ∼ USA 64 Cc 25
Lower Loteni ○ ZA 349 Hg 60
Lower Lough Erne ∼ GB 162 Gc 18
Lower Peninsula ⌓ USA 57 Df 23
Lower Red Lake ∼ USA 56 Da 22
Lower Sabie ○ ZA 352 Hh 58
Lower Sioux Ind. Res. ••• USA 56 Da 23
Lower Valley of Awash ★ ETH 313 Hn 40
Lower Valley of the Omo ★ ETH 325 Hl 43
Lower Zambezi ♀ Z 341 Hg 53
Lowestoft ○ GB 163 Gg 19
Łowicz ○ PL 170 Hb 19
Lowman ○ USA 50 Ce 23
Lowrie Channel ∼ AUS 364 Me 53
Low Rocky Point ⌓ AUS 378 Mj 67
Lowry Pueblo Ruins ★ USA 65 Ch 27
Low Tatra ⩘ SK 174 Hb 21
Lowville ○ USA 60 Dl 24
Loxton ○ ZA 349 Hd 61
Loxton ○ AUS 378 Mg 63
Loya ∼ RDC 336 Hf 46
Loyada ○ DJI 328 Hp 40
Loyalty Islands ⌂ F 386 Nf 56
Loyangalani ○ EAK 325 Hl 44
Loyds ∼ CDN 61 Ef 21
Loyengo ○ SD 352 Hh 59
Loyoro ○ EAU 325 Hk 44
Loza ∼ RM 345 Jb 53
Loznica ○ SCG 174 Hb 23
Loznicy ○ RUS 171 Hh 17
Lozova ○ UA 175 Hk 21
Lšinj ⌂ HR 185 Gn 23
Lua ∼ RDC 333 Hb 44
Luabo ○ RDC 336 Hf 50
Luabo ○ MOC 344 Hk 55
Luabu ∼ RDC 333 Hb 47
Luacano ○ ANG 341 Hc 51
Luachimo ○ ANG 333 Hc 49
Luachimo ∼ ANG 340 Hc 50
Luaco ○ ANG 333 Hc 49
Lua-Dekere ∼ RDC 321 Hb 43
Luahula ∼ RDC 341 Hd 50
Luala ∼ MOC 344 Hk 54
Lualaba Congo ∼ RDC 333 He 46
Luali ○ RDC 332 Gn 48
Luama ∼ RDC 336 Hf 48
Luambala ∼ MOC 344 Hk 52
Luambe ♀ Z 344 Hj 52
Luambimba ∼ Z 341 Hd 52
Luambo ○ RDC 341 Hf 51
Luampa ○ Z 341 He 53
Luampa ∼ Z 341 He 53
Luampa Kuta ○ Z 341 He 53
Lu'an ○ VRC 246 Lj 30
Luanchuan ○ VRC 243 Lf 29
Luanda ◙ ANG 340 Gn 50
Luando ∼ ANG 340 Ha 51
Luando ○ ANG 340 Hb 51
Luanginga ∼ Z 341 Hd 53
Luang Namtha ○ LAO 254 La 35
Luango ∼ ANG 332 Gn 48
Luangue ○ ANG 340 Hb 50
Luangue ∼ ANG 340 Hb 50
Luanguinga ∼ ANG 340 Hc 52
Luangundo ∼ ANG 340 Hc 54
Luangwa ∼ Z 336 Hh 50
Luangwa ○ Z 341 Hh 53
Luangwa ∼ MOC 341 Hh 53
Luanjing ○ VRC 242 Lc 27
Luanping ○ VRC 246 Lj 25
Luanshya ○ Z 341 Hf 52
Luan Xian ○ VRC 246 Lk 26
Luanza ○ RDC 336 Hg 50
Luapula ∼ RDC 341 Hg 51
Luapula ○ Z 341 Hg 52
Luaraca ○ E 184 Gc 24
Luashi ○ RDC 341 Hd 51
Luashi ∼ RDC 341 Hd 51
Luassingua ∼ ANG 340 Hb 53
Luatamba ○ ANG 340 Hc 52
Luatize ∼ MOC 341 Hh 53
Luatize ∼ MOC 344 Hl 52
Luau ○ ANG 341 Hd 51
Lua-Vindu ∼ RDC 333 Hb 44
Luba ○ GQ 320 Gl 44
Lubalo ○ ANG 340 Hb 50
Lubalo ∼ ANG 340 Hb 50
Lubamba ○ RDC 336 Hf 48
Lubana ez. ∼ LV 171 Hf 17
Lubang ○ RP 267 Ll 39
Lubang Island ⌂ RP 267 Lk 39
Lubango ○ ANG 340 Gn 53
Lubansenshi ∼ Z 341 Hh 51
Lubanza ○ RDC 333 Hc 48
Lubao ○ RP 267 Ll 38
Lubao ○ RDC 333 He 48
Lubartów ○ PL 174 Hd 20
Lübben ○ D 174 Gp 20
Lubbock ○ USA 70 Cm 29
Lubec ○ USA 60 Ea 23
Lübeck ○ D 170 Gm 19
Lubefu ○ RDC 333 He 48
Lubefu ∼ RDC 333 He 48
Lubembe ∼ RDC 333 Hc 49
Lubero ○ RDC 336 Hg 46
Lubero ∼ RDC 336 Hg 46
Lubi ∼ RDC 333 Hd 49
Lubilaji ∼ RDC 341 Hd 50
Lubilandji ∼ RDC 333 Hd 49
Lubile ○ RDC 336 Hf 47
Lubile ∼ RDC 336 Hg 49
Lubin ○ PL 174 Ha 20
Lubishi ∼ RDC 333 He 49
Lubishi ○ Z 341 Hh 51
Lublin ○ PL 174 Hd 20
Lubliniec ○ PL 174 Hb 20
Lubny ○ UA 175 Hj 20
Lubok Antu ○ MAL 271 Lf 45
Lubompo ○ Z 341 Hf 53
Lubongola ○ RDC 336 Hf 47
Lubu ∼ Z 341 Hh 51
Lubudi ∼ RDC 333 Hc 48
Lubudi ○ RDC 336 He 50
Lubue ∼ RDC 333 Hb 48
Lubukalung ○ RI 270 Kp 46
Lubukbargalung ○ RI 270 La 46
Lubuklinggau ○ RI 278 Lb 47
Lubukpakam ○ RI 270 Kp 44
Lubuk Sikaping ○ RI 270 La 45
Lubule ∼ RDC 336 Hg 50
Lubumbashi ○ RDC 341 Hf 51
Lubundji ∼ RDC 333 Hc 48
Lubungu ○ Z 341 Hf 53
Lubutu ○ RDC 336 Hf 46
Lubutu ∼ RDC 336 Hf 46
Lubwe ○ Z 341 Hg 51
Lucala ○ ANG 340 Gp 50
Lucala ∼ ANG 340 Gp 50
Lucan ○ CDN 57 Dh 24
Lucanas ○ PE 128 Dl 53
Lucano ○ E 184 Gc 24
Lucapa ○ ANG 340 Hc 50
Lucas ○ USA 70 Db 25
Lucas do Rio Verde ○ BR 132 Eg 52
Lucca ○ I 185 Gm 24
Lucea ○ JA 100 Dj 36
Lucedale ○ USA 86 Dd 30
Lučegorsk ○ RUS 250 Md 22
Lucena ○ E 184 Gd 27
Lucena ○ RP 267 Ll 39
Lučenec ○ SK 174 Hb 21
Lucerne ○ CH 163 Gk 22
Lucerne Valley ○ USA 64 Cd 28
Lucero ○ MEX 80 Cj 30
Lucheng ○ VRC 243 Lg 27
Lucheng ○ VRC 255 Ld 33
Luchenza ○ MW 344 Hk 53
Luchering ∼ MOC 344 Hk 52
Luchimva ∼ MOC 344 Hk 53
Luchuan ○ VRC 255 Le 34
Lüchun ○ VRC 254 Lb 34
Lucie ○ PE 128 Dn 53
Lucie ○ GUY 113 Ef 44
Lucie ∼ SME 113 Ef 44
Lucindale ○ AUS 378 Mg 64
Lucio V. Mansilla ○ RA 137 Eb 60
Lucira ○ ANG 340 Gn 52
Luck ○ USA 56 Db 23
Luc'k ○ UA 175 He 20
Luckau ○ D 174 Gn 20
Luckeesarai ○ IND 235 Kh 33
Luckhoff ○ ZA 349 He 60
Lucknow ○ IND 234 Ke 32
Lucknow ○ AUS 374 Mg 57
Lucky ○ USA 70 Db 29
Lucky Bay ○ AUS 378 Me 62
Lucky Lake ○ CDN 51 Cj 20
Lucma ○ PE 116 Dj 49
Lucma ○ PE 128 Dm 52
Luçon ○ F 163 Gf 22
Lücongpo ○ VRC 243 Lf 30
Lucossa ○ ANG 332 Gp 49
Lucre ○ PE 128 Dn 52
Lucunga ○ ANG 332 Gp 49
Lucunga ∼ ANG 332 Gp 49
Lucusse ○ ANG 340 Hc 52
Lucy Creek ○ AUS 374 Me 57
Lüderitz ○ NAM 348 Gp 59
Lüderitz Bay ∼ NAM 348 Gp 59
Ludhiana ○ IND 230 Kb 30
Ludian ○ VRC 255 Lb 32
Ludimbi ∼ RDC 333 He 48
Luding ○ VRC 254 La 31
Ludington ○ USA 57 De 24
Ludlow ○ USA 51 Cf 23
Ludlow ○ USA 60 Dm 24
Ludlow ○ USA 64 Cd 28
Ludlow ○ USA 65 Ck 27
Ludlow ○ GB 163 Ge 19
Ludogorie ⩘ BG 194 Hf 24
Ludowici ○ USA 87 Dh 30
Luduş ○ RO 175 He 22
Ludvika ○ S 158 Gp 15
Ludwigsburg ○ D 174 Gl 21
Ludwigshafen a.Rh. ○ D 163 Gk 21
Ludwigslust ○ D 170 Gm 19
Ludza ○ LV 171 Hf 17
Luebo ○ RDC 333 Hc 48
Luebo ∼ RDC 333 Hc 48
Lueki ○ RDC 333 He 47
Lueki ∼ RDC 333 He 48
Luele ∼ ANG 340 Hc 50
Luemba ○ RDC 336 Hg 47
Luembe ∼ RDC 333 He 49
Luembe ∼ ANG 340 Hc 51
Luena ○ RDC 336 He 50
Luena ○ ANG 340 Hb 51
Luena ∼ ANG 340 Hc 51
Luena ∼ Z 341 Hd 53
Luena ○ Z 341 Hh 51
Luena Flats ⌓ Z 341 Hd 53
Luengué ○ ANG 340 Hc 54
Luengué ∼ ANG 340 Hc 54
Luenha ∼ MOC 344 Hj 54
Lueo ∼ RDC 341 Hd 51
Lueta ○ RDC 333 Hd 49
Lueta ∼ RDC 333 Hd 50
Lueti ∼ ANG 340 Hc 53
Lüeyang ○ VRC 243 Ld 29
Lufeng ○ VRC 254 La 33
Lufeng ○ VRC 258 Lh 34
Lufico ○ ANG 332 Gn 49
Lufije ∼ ANG 340 Hc 51
Lufimi ∼ RDC 333 Ha 48
Lufira ∼ RDC 336 Hf 50
Luf Island ⌂ PNG 287 Mj 46
Lufkin ○ USA 81 Da 30
Lufu ∼ RDC 332 Gn 48
Lufu ○ RDC 332 Gp 48
Lufuba ∼ Z 336 Hh 50
Lufubu ○ Z 336 Hg 50
Lufuige ∼ ANG 341 Hd 52
Lufukwe ∼ RDC 336 Hf 50
Lufupa ∼ RDC 341 He 51
Lufupa ∼ Z 341 He 53
Lufwa ∼ RDC 336 Hf 50
Lufwango ∼ RDC 336 Hf 48
Luga ○ RUS 171 Hg 16
Lugait ○ RP 267 Ln 41
Luganga ○ EAT 337 Hk 49
Lugano ○ CH 174 Gl 22
Luganville ○ VU 386 Nf 53
Lugard's Falls ∼ EAK 337 Hm 47
Lugazi ○ EAU 324 Hj 45
Lugela ○ MOC 344 Hl 54
Lugenda ∼ MOC 344 Hl 52
Lughaye ○ SP 328 Hp 40
Lugo ○ E 184 Gc 24
Lugogo ∼ EAU 324 Hj 45
Lugoj ○ RO 174 Hc 23
Lugu ○ VRC 231 Kg 29
Lugu △ IND 235 Kg 34
Lugu ○ VRC 254 Lb 31
Lugulu ∼ RDC 336 Hf 47
Luguruka ○ EAT 337 Hl 50
Lugus Island ⌂ RP 275 Ll 43
Luhanka ○ FIN 159 He 15
Luhan Shan ⩘ VRC 254 Lb 32
Luhans'k ○ UA 181 Hm 21
Luhatahata ○ RDC 333 Hd 49
Luhe ○ VRC 246 Lk 29
Luhe ○ VRC 258 Lh 34
Luhebu ○ NAM 340 Hb 55
Luhira ∼ EAT 337 Hl 50
Luhit ∼ IND 254 Kn 32
Luhoho ∼ RDC 336 Hg 46
Luhovicy ○ RUS 171 Hm 18
Luhulu ∼ RDC 336 Hg 46
Luhuo ○ VRC 242 La 30
Lui ∼ ANG 340 Ha 50
Lui ∼ Z 341 Hd 54
Luia ○ ANG 333 Hc 50
Luia ∼ ANG 341 Hc 50
Luia ∼ MOC 344 Hj 53
Luiana ○ ANG 341 Hd 54
Luiana ∼ ANG 341 Hd 54
Luido ○ MOC 352 Hk 56
Luie ∼ RDC 333 Ha 48
Luika ∼ RDC 336 Hf 48
Luiko ∼ RDC 336 Hg 48
Luilaka ∼ RDC 333 Hc 47
Luilu ∼ RDC 333 Hd 46
Luilu ∼ RDC 333 Hd 49
Luimbale ○ ANG 340 Gp 52
Luimheach ○ IRL 163 Gb 19
Luinga ○ ANG 340 Gp 50
Luinshui ○ VRC 246 Lk 29
Luio ∼ ANG 340 Hc 52
Luís Correia ○ BR 124 Ep 47
Luishia ○ RDC 341 Hf 51
Luis Moya ○ MEX 92 Cl 34
Luís Viana ○ BR 124 Ep 50
Luitpold Coast ⌓ 38 Ha 17
Luiza ○ RDC 333 Hd 49
Luiza ∼ RDC 341 Hd 50
Luizavo ∼ ANG 341 Hd 51
Luizi ○ RDC 336 Hf 49
Luizi ∼ RDC 336 Hf 49
Lujan ○ RA 136 Eb 59
Luján ○ RA 137 Eb 62
Luján ○ RA 146 Ee 63
Luján ∼ RA 146 Ee 63
Luján de Cuyo ○ RA 137 Dp 62
Lujiang ○ VRC 246 Lj 30
Luka ∼ RDC 336 Hg 47
Lukafu ○ RDC 341 Hf 51
Lukala ○ RDC 332 Gp 48
Lukalaba ○ RDC 333 Hd 49
Lukanga Swamp ⌓ Z 341 Hf 53
Lukashi ∼ RDC 333 He 48
Lukasu ○ RDC 336 He 50
Lukedi ∼ RDC 333 Hd 47
Lukene ∼ RDC 333 Hc 47
Lukenga ○ RDC 336 Hg 48
Lukenie ∼ RDC 333 Hb 47
Lukeville ○ USA 75 Cf 30
Lukimwa ∼ EAT 344 Hk 51
Lukojanov ○ RUS 181 Ja 18
Lukolela ○ RDC 333 Ha 46
Lukolela ○ RDC 333 He 48
Lukolini ○ EAT 336 Hj 49
Lukonzolwa ○ RDC 336 Hg 50
Lukoshi ∼ RDC 341 Hd 51
Lukosi ∼ EAT 337 Hl 50
Lukovit ○ BG 194 He 24
Lukovnikovo ○ RUS 171 Hk 17
Łuków ○ PL 174 Hd 20
Luksagu ○ RI 282 Lm 46
Lukubi ○ RDC 341 Hg 52
Lukufo ∼ RDC 336 Hg 49
Lukuga ∼ RDC 336 Hf 48
Lukuga ∼ RDC 336 Hg 48
Lukula ○ RDC 332 Gn 48
Lukula ∼ RDC 332 Gn 48
Lukula ○ RDC 336 Hf 49
Lukulu ∼ RDC 336 Hg 49
Lukulu ○ Z 341 Hd 53
Lukulu ∼ Z 341 Hh 51
Lukumburu ○ EAT 337 Hk 50
Lukuni ○ RDC 333 Ha 48
Lukusashi ∼ Z 341 Hh 53
Lukushi ∼ RDC 336 Hf 49
Lukusuzi ∼ Z 344 Hj 52
Lukusuzi ♀ Z 344 Hj 52
Lukuswa ∼ RDC 336 Hf 49
Lukuzye ∼ Z 344 Hj 52
Lukwasa ○ IND 234 Kc 33
Lula ○ USA 71 Dc 28
Lula ∼ RDC 333 Hc 47
Luleå ○ S 159 Hd 13
Luleälven ∼ S 159 Hc 12
Lüleburgaz ○ TR 195 Hf 25
Luliang ○ VRC 255 Lb 33
Lüliang Shan ⩘ VRC 243 Lf 27
Luliāni ○ PK 230 Kb 30
Lulimba ○ RDC 336 Hg 48
Lulindi ∼ RDC 336 Hf 48
Luling ○ USA 81 Cp 31
Lulo ∼ ANG 340 Hb 50
Lulonga ○ RDC 332 Gn 49
Lulonga ∼ RDC 333 Hb 45
Lulu ∼ RDC 324 He 45
Lulua ∼ RDC 333 Hc 48
Lulua ∼ RDC 341 Hd 50
Luma ○ WAN 320 Gj 40
Luma Cassai ○ ANG 340 Hb 51
Lumaco ○ RCH 147 Dm 65
Lumajang ○ RI 279 Lg 50
Lumajangdong Co ∼ VRC 230 Ke 28
Lumana ○ RDC 336 Hf 47
Lumangwe Falls ∼ Z 336 Hg 50
Lumata ○ RDC 341 Hf 52
Lumbala ∼ ANG 341 Hc 52
Lumbala-Caquengue ○ ANG 341 Hc 52
Lumbala N'guimbo ○ ANG 341 Hc 53
Lumbe ∼ Z 341 He 53
Lumber ∼ USA 74 Dj 28
Lumbermen's Mon. ★ USA 57 Df 23
Lumberton ○ USA 74 Dj 28
Lumberton ○ USA 86 Dd 30
Lumbila ○ EAT 337 Hk 50
Lumbini ○ NEP 235 Kf 32
Lumbo ○ MOC 344 Hn 53
Lumbovskij zaliv ∼ RUS 159 Hn 12
Lumbrera ○ RA 136 Eb 58
Lumby ○ CDN 50 Cc 20
Lumding ○ IND 254 Kl 33
Lumege ∼ ANG 340 Hc 51
Lumene ∼ RDC 333 Ha 48
Lumeta ○ ANG 340 Hb 54
Lumholtz ♀ AUS 365 Mj 55
Lumi ○ PNG 286 Mg 47
Lumpkin ○ USA 86 Df 29
Lumpur ∼ RI 278 Lc 47
Lumsden ○ CDN 51 Ck 20
Lumsden ○ CDN 61 Eh 21
Lumsden ○ NZ 382 Ng 68
Lumuna ∼ ANG 340 Hc 54
Lumut ○ BRU 274 Lh 43
Lumwana ○ Z 341 He 51
Lun ○ MNG 204 Uc 9
Luna ○ USA 65 Ch 29
Luna ∼ BR 120 Ed 48
Lunahuana ○ PE 128 Dk 52
Lunan ○ VRC 255 Lb 33
Lunavada ○ IND 227 Ka 34
Lund ○ CDN 50 Bp 21
Lund ○ USA 64 Cf 26
Lund ○ S 170 Gn 18
Lundazi ○ Z 344 Hj 52
Lundazi ∼ Z 344 Hj 52
Lundu ○ MAL 271 Le 45
Lundu ○ Z 344 Hj 51
Lüneburg ○ D 170 Gm 19
Lüneburger Heide ⌓ D 170 Gl 19
Lunenburg ○ CDN 61 Eb 23
Lunenburg ○ USA 74 Dj 27
Lunéville ○ F 163 Gk 21
Lunga ∼ Z 341 Hf 52
Lunga Lunga ○ EAK 337 Hm 48
Lunge ○ ANG 340 Ha 52
Lunggar ○ VRC 231 Kg 30
Lungi ○ WAL 316 Fp 41
Lunglei ○ IND 235 Kl 34
Lungo ○ MOC 344 Hn 53
Lungué-Bungo ∼ ANG 340 Hb 52
Lunguengu ○ RDC 336 Hf 47
Lunguto ○ RI 275 Ll 45
Lungwebungu ∼ ANG 340 Hc 52
Luni ∼ IND 227 Jp 33
Lunin ○ BY 171 Hf 19
Luninyets ○ BY 171 Hf 19
Lūnkaransa ○ IND 227 Ka 31
Lunsar ○ WAL 316 Fp 41
Lunsemfwa ∼ Z 341 Hg 53
Lunsemfwa ○ Z 341 Hg 53
Lunsemfwa Falls ∼ Z 341 Hg 53
Luntai ○ VRC 204 Tb 10
Lunyere ∼ EAT 344 Hk 51
Lunyuk ○ RI 279 Lj 50
Lunzi ∼ Z 344 Hj 51
Luo ○ RI 282 Ll 46
Luo ∼ MOC 344 Hl 54
Luobei ○ VRC 250 Mb 22
Luobuzhuang ○ VRC 231 Kh 26
Luochuan ○ VRC 243 Le 28
Luodian ○ VRC 255 Ld 33
Luoding ○ VRC 255 Lf 34
Luo He ∼ VRC 243 Lf 28
Luohe ○ VRC 243 Lh 29
Luoma Hu ∼ VRC 246 Lk 28
Luonan ○ VRC 243 Le 28
Luongo ∼ Z 341 Hg 51
Luoning ○ VRC 243 Lf 28
Luoping ○ VRC 255 Lc 33
Luoshan ○ VRC 243 Lh 29
Luotian ○ VRC 243 Lh 30
Luoxu ○ VRC 255 Le 34
Luoyang ○ VRC 243 Lg 28
Luoyuan ○ VRC 258 Lk 32
Luozi ○ RDC 332 Gn 48
Lupa ∼ EAT 337 Hj 50
Lupa Market ○ EAT 337 Hj 50
Lupande ∼ Z 341 Hh 52
Lupane ○ ZW 341 Hf 55
Lupar ∼ MAL 271 Lf 45
Luperon ○ DOM 101 Dn 36
Lupilichi ○ MOC 344 Hk 51
Lupingo ○ EAT 344 Hk 51
Lupire ○ ANG 340 Hb 53
Lupiro ○ EAT 337 Hl 50
Lupon ○ RP 275 Ln 42
Lupuka ○ Z 341 Hd 54
Lupula ○ ANG 340 Ha 53
Luputa ○ RDC 333 Hd 49
Lupweji ∼ RDC 336 He 50
Luquembo ○ ANG 340 Ha 51
Luray ○ USA 70 Cn 26
Lureco ∼ MOC 344 Hl 52
Luremo ○ ANG 333 Ha 50
Luri ○ RI 279 Lj 47
Luribay ○ BOL 129 Ea 54
Lurin ∼ PE 128 Dk 51
Lúrio ∼ MOC 344 Hm 52
Lúrio ○ MOC 344 Hn 52
Luruaco ○ CO 106 Dl 40
Lusahang ○ EAT 336 Hh 47
Lusaka ○ RDC 333 He 49
Lusaka ◙ Z 341 Hg 53
Lusako ○ RDC 336 Hf 48
Lusamba ○ RDC 333 He 48
Lusambo ○ RDC 333 Hd 48
Lusancay Island ⌂ PNG 287 Ml 50
Lusanga ○ RDC 333 Hb 48
Lusangi ○ RDC 336 Hf 48
Lusenga Plain ♀ Z 336 Hg 50
Lushan ○ VRC 243 Lg 29
Lushan △ VRC 246 Lj 27
Lushan ★ VRC 258 Lj 31
Lushi ○ VRC 243 Lf 28
Lushipuka ∼ RDC 341 Hg 51
Lushnjë ○ AL 194 Hb 25
Lushoto ○ EAT 337 Hm 48
Lushui ○ VRC 254 Kp 33
Lushui ★ VRC 258 Lj 31
Lüshun ○ VRC 246 Ll 26
Lusibi ○ Z 341 He 54
Lusikisiki ○ ZA 349 Hg 61
Lusinga ○ RDC 336 Hf 50
Lusitania ○ CO 106 Dl 44
Lusiwasi ○ Z 341 Hh 52
Lusk ○ USA 51 Ck 24
Lussanhando ∼ MOC 344 Hl 52
Lussenga ○ ANG 332 Gn 49
Lusutfu ∼ SD 352 Hh 59
Luswaka ○ RDC 336 Hf 50
Lü Tao ⌂ RC 259 Ll 34
Lutembo ○ ANG 340 Hc 52
Luth ○ SUD 324 Hh 42
Luther Lake ∼ CDN 57 Dh 23
Lutherstadt Wittenberg ○ D 174 Gn 20
Luti ○ SOL 290 Na 49
Lutiba ○ RDC 336 Hg 46
Lutlut ○ MYA 262 Kp 39
Lutombe ○ ZW 352 Hh 57
Luton ○ GB 163 Gf 20
Lutong ○ MAL 274 Lg 43
Lutope ∼ ZW 341 Hg 55
Lutsen ○ USA 56 Dc 22
Lutshima ○ RDC 333 Hb 48
Lutshima ∼ RDC 333 Hb 49
Lutshuadi ∼ RDC 333 Hc 48
Lutuai ○ ANG 340 Hb 52
Lutumba ○ ZW 352 Hh 57
Lutunguru ○ RDC 336 Hg 46
Lützow-Holm Bay ≈ 38 Lb 16
Lutzputs ○ ZA 348 Hc 60
Lutzville ○ ZA 348 Hb 61
Luuq ○ SP 328 Hp 44
Luveira ∼ RDC 341 He 51
Luverne ○ USA 56 Cp 24
Luverne ○ USA 86 De 30
Luvia ∼ RDC 336 Hf 49
Luvidjo ∼ RDC 336 Hf 49
Luvilombo ∼ RDC 336 Hf 50
Luvo ○ ANG 332 Gn 48
Luvua ∼ RDC 336 Hg 49
Luvua ∼ ANG 341 Hd 51
Luvuei ○ ANG 340 Hc 52
Luvunzo ∼ RDC 336 Hg 49
Luwawa ○ MW 344 Hj 52
Luwe ∼ RDC 336 Hg 50
Luwego ∼ EAT 344 Hl 51
Luwembe ○ Z 341 Hh 53
Luwingu ○ Z 341 Hg 51
Luwishi ∼ Z 341 Hf 52
Luwombwa ∼ Z 341 Hg 52
Luwuk ○ RI 282 Lm 46
Luwumbu ∼ Z 344 Hj 51
Luxembourg □ L 163 Gj 21
Luxembourg ◙ L 163 Gk 21
Luxeuil ○ F 163 Gk 22
Luxi ○ VRC 254 Kp 33
Luxi ○ VRC 255 Lb 33
Luxi ○ VRC 255 Lf 31
Luxikegongba ○ VRC 231 Kh 30
Luxor ○ ET 301 Hj 33
Luyamba ○ RDC 336 Hf 47
Luyi ○ VRC 243 Lh 29
Luz ○ BR 133 Em 55
Luzhai ○ VRC 255 Le 33
Luzhou ○ VRC 255 Lc 31
Luzi ○ RDC 333 Hb 48
Luzi ○ ANG 340 Hc 52
Luziâna ○ BR 133 Ek 54
Luzilândia ○ BR 124 En 47
Luzon ⌂ RP 267 Ll 38
Luzon Sea ≈ 266 Lj 39
Luzon Strait ≈ RP 259 Ll 35
Luzy ○ F 163 Gh 22
L'viv ○ UA 175 Hd 21
Lwakhaka ○ EAK 325 Hk 45
Lwela ○ Z 341 Hg 51
Lwela ∼ Z 341 Hg 51
Lyantonde ○ EAU 336 Hh 46
Lycksele ○ S 158 Hb 13
Lydenburg ○ ZA 352 Hh 58
Lydon ∼ AUS 360 Lh 57
Lyefchytsy ○ BY 175 Hf 20
Ly Hoa ○ VN 263 Ld 37
Lykso ○ ZA 349 Hd 59
Lyman ○ USA 70 Da 25
lyman Moločnyj ∼ UA 175 Hk 22
Lyme Bay ∼ GB 163 Ge 20
Lyme Regis ○ GB 163 Ge 20
Lynchburg ○ USA 74 Dj 27
Lynches ∼ USA 71 Dh 28
Lynd ∼ AUS 365 Mh 54
Lynden ○ USA 50 Ca 21
Lyndhurst ○ AUS 365 Mj 55
Lyndhurst ○ AUS 378 Mf 61
Lyndon ○ AUS 360 Lh 57
Lyndon ∼ AUS 360 Lh 57
Lyndonville ○ USA 60 Dn 23
Lyness ○ GB 162 Ge 16
Lyngdal ○ N 170 Gk 16
Lyngen ∼ N 159 Hc 11
Lyngseidet ○ N 159 Hb 11
Lynher Reef ⌓ AUS 360 Ll 53
Lynn ○ USA 71 Df 26
Lynn ○ USA 81 Cn 32
Lynndyl ○ USA 64 Cf 26
Lynn Haven ○ USA 86 Df 30
Lynn Lake ○ CDN 42 Fa 7
Lynton ○ GB 163 Ge 20
Lynton ○ AUS 368 Lh 60
Lynx Lake ∼ CDN 42 Ec 6
Lyon ○ F 185 Gj 23
Lyons ○ USA 70 Cn 26
Lyons ○ USA 71 Dg 29
Lyons ∼ AUS 368 Lj 58
Lyons River ○ AUS 368 Lh 58
Lyra Reef ⌂ PNG 287 Mn 46
Lysefjord ∼ N 170 Gk 16
Lysekil ○ S 170 Gm 16
Lysite ○ USA 51 Cj 24
Lyskovo ○ RUS 181 Ja 18
Lysyčans'k ○ UA 181 Hl 21
Lysye Gory ○ RUS 181 Ja 20

440 Los Amores - Lysye Gory

□Country ▣Capital city ⊙Administrative unit OPlace ♁Island ⛰Mountain range △Mountain ⌓Cape ≈Ocean, Sea ~Lake, River ♆Undersea topography ▲Glacier ♀National park •••Reservation ★Point of major interest ⏢Landscape

Lyttelton O NZ 383 Nj 67
Lytton O CDN 50 Cb 20
Lyuban' O BY 171 Hg 19

M

M. Etna △ I 185 Gp 27
M. i. Tomorrit △ AL 194 Hc 25
M. Linas △ I 185 Gl 26
Ma ~ MYA 254 Kp 34
Ma'alot-Tarshiha O IL 208 Hk 29
Maamba O Z 341 Hf 54
Ma'ān O JOR 214 Hk 30
Ma'an O CAM 320 Gm 44
Maana'oba ♁ SOL 290 Nc 50
Maaninkavaara O FIN 159 Hf 12
Maanselkä ⏢ FIN 159 Hg 12
Ma'anshan O VRC 246 Lk 30
Maardu O EST 171 He 16
Maarianhamina O FIN 159 Hc 15
Ma'arrat an-Nūmān O SYR 208 Hl 28
Maas ~ NL 163 Gj 20
Maasim O RP 275 Ln 43
Maasin O RP 267 Ln 40
Maasstroom O ZA 349 Hg 57
Maastricht O NL 163 Gj 20
Maasupa O SOL 290 Nc 50
Maatsuyker Islands ♁ AUS 378 Mj 67
Maba O RI 275 Ma 45
Ma'bad O IR 222 Jf 28
Mabaia O ANG 332 Gn 49
Mabalane O MOC 352 Hj 57
Mabana O RDC 324 Hg 45
Mabanda O BU 336 Hg 48
Ma'bar O YE 218 Ja 38
Mabaruma O GUY 112 Ee 41
Mabé ~ CAM 320 Gm 42
Mabein O MYA 254 Kn 34
Mabel Creek O AUS 374 Md 60
Mabel Downs O AUS 361 Lp 54
Mabélé O CAM 321 Gn 42
Mabelle O USA 70 Cn 29
Mabenga O RDC 333 Hb 47
Mabenge O RDC 324 He 43
Mabeta O CAM 320 Gl 44
Mabo O SN 316 Fn 39
Mabopane O ZA 349 Hf 58
Mabote O MOC 352 Hj 57
Mabou O CDN 61 Ed 22
Mabrouk O RMM 305 Gf 36
Mabrous O RN 297 Gn 35
Mabrūk O LAR 297 Ha 30
Mabuiag Island ♁ AUS 286 Mh 50
Mabuki O EAT 337 Hj 47
Mabula O ZA 349 Hf 58
Mabur ~ RI 286 Mf 49
Mabura O GUY 113 Ee 43
Mabutsane O RB 349 Hd 58
Mača O RUS 22 Qb 4
Maçacara O BR 125 Fa 51
Macachin O RA 137 Eb 64
Macado d. C. O P 184 Gc 25
Macaé O BR 141 Ep 57
Macaene O MOC 352 Hj 58
Macaíba O BR 124 Fc 48
Macajalar Bay ≈ RP 267 Ln 41
Macajuba O BR 125 Ep 52
Macalister O AUS 365 Mg 55
MacAlpine Lake ~ CDN 42 Fa 5
Maçambará O BR 146 Eg 60
Macamic O CDN 60 Dj 21
Macanao O YV 112 Eb 40
Macandze O MOC 352 Hj 57
Maçangana ~ BR 129 Ec 51
Macanillal O YV 107 Dp 42
Macapá O BR 121 Ej 45
Macapillo O RA 136 Ec 58
Macará O EC 116 Dj 48
Macaracas O PA 97 Dh 42
Macarani O BR 125 Ep 53
Macarao ♀ YV 107 Ea 40
Macari O PE 128 Dn 53
Macaroni O AUS 365 Mg 54
Macarretane O MOC 352 Hj 58
Macarthur O AUS 378 Mh 65
Macas O EC 116 Dj 47
Macatanja O MOC 344 Hi 54
Macaú O BR 124 Fb 48
Macau O VRC 258 Lg 34
Macau ⊙ VRC 258 Lg 34
Macauá ~ BR 128 Dp 51
Macauari O BR 120 Ee 46
Macaúbas O BR 125 En 52
Macaya O BOL 128 Dp 55
Macaza ~ CDN 60 Dl 22
Mac Cluer Gulf ~ RI 283 Mc 47
Macdiarmid O CDN 57 Dd 21
Macdonald Downs O AUS 374 Md 57
MacDonnell ⛰ AUS 361 Mb 57
Macdonnell Peninsula ♁ AUS 378 Mf 63
Macduff O GB 162 Ge 17
Macedonia □ MK 194 Hc 25
Macedonia ⏢ GR 194 Hc 25
Maceió O BR 124 Fc 50
Macenta O RG 316 Gb 41
Macerata O I 185 Gn 24
Mac Gregor Range ⛰ AUS 374 Mh 59
Mach O PK 227 Jm 31
Machacalis O BR 125 Ep 54
Machacamarca O BOL 129 Ea 55
Machachi O EC 116 Dj 46
Machadinho O BR 117 Ec 50
Machadinho ~ BR 120 Ed 50
Machado ~ BR 129 Ed 51
Machado O BR 141 Em 56
Machadodorp O ZA 352 Hh 58
Machado ou Ji-Paraná ~ BR 117 Ec 50
Machado ou Ji-Paraná ~ BR 129 Ed 51
Machagai O RA 140 Ee 59
Machaila O MOC 352 Hj 57
Machakos O EAK 337 Hl 46
Machala O EC 116 Dj 47
Machaneng O RB 349 Hf 57
Machang O VRC 255 Ld 32
Machanga O MOC 352 Hk 56
Machaquilá ~ GCA 93 Dd 37
Machawaian Lake ~ CDN 57 De 20
Macheke O ZW 341 Hh 55
Macheng O VRC 243 Lh 30
Mācherla O IND 238 Kd 37
Machesse O MOC 344 Hk 55
Māchgaon O IND 235 Kh 35
Machias O USA 60 Ea 23
Machile ~ Z 341 He 54
Machilīpatnam O IND 238 Ke 37
Machina O WAN 320 Gl 39
Machiques O YV 107 Dm 40
Machok O WAN 320 Gl 41
Machu Picchu ★ PE 128 Dm 52
Machupo ~ BOL 129 Eb 52
Macia O MOC 352 Hj 58
Maciel O PY 140 Ef 59
Măcin O RO 175 Hg 23
Macintyre ~ AUS 375 Ml 60
Mack O USA 65 Ch 26
Maçka O TR 195 Hm 25
Mackay O USA 50 Cf 24
Mackay O AUS 375 Ml 56
MacKay Lake ~ CDN 42 Eb 6
Mackenzie ~ AUS 375 Ml 57
Mackenzie Bay ≈ CDN 6 Ca 3
MacKenzie Bay ≈ CDN 47 Bg 11
Mackenzie King Island ♁ CDN 6 Da 2
Mackenzie King Island ♁ CDN 42 Eb 3
Mackenzie Mountains ⛰ CDN 6 Ca 3
Mackenzie Mountains ⛰ CDN 47 Bj 13
MacKenzie Reservoir ~ USA 70 Cm 28
Mackenzie River ~ CDN 6 Cb 3
Mackenzie River ~ CDN 47 Bj 11
Mackenzie River Delta ⏢ CDN 47 Bj 11
Mackinaw City O USA 57 Df 23
Mackinnon Road O EAK 337 Hm 47
Macklin O CDN 51 Ch 19
Macks Inn O USA 51 Cg 23
Macksville O AUS 379 Mn 61
Maclean O AUS 375 Mn 60
Maclean Strait ≈ CDN 42 Ec 3
Maclear O ZA 349 Hg 61
Macleay ~ AUS 379 Mn 61
Macmillan ~ CDN 47 Bj 13
Maco O RP 275 Ln 42
Maçobere O MOC 352 Hj 56
Macocola O ANG 332 Ha 49
Macomb O USA 71 Dc 25
Macomér O I 185 Gl 25
Macomia O MOC 344 Hm 52
Macon O USA 70 Db 26
Macon O USA 71 Dg 26
Macon O USA 86 Dd 29
Macon O USA 86 Df 29
Mâcon O F 163 Gj 22
Macondo O ANG 341 Hd 52
Macondo ~ ANG 341 Hd 52
Macoppe O RI 282 Ll 48
Macossa O MOC 344 Hj 54
Macovane O MOC 352 Hk 56
Mac Phrik O THA 262 Kp 37
Macquarie ~ AUS 379 Mk 61
Macquarie Harbour ≈ AUS 378 Mj 67
Macquarie Island ♁ AUS 34 Sb 15
Macquarie Ridge ♆ 34 Sb 15
Mac Robertson Land ⏢ 38 Mb 17
Macroon O IRL 163 Gb 20
Macrorie O CDN 51 Cj 20
Mactan Island ♁ RP 267 Lm 40
Macuira ♀ CO 107 Dn 39
Macuma O EC 116 Dk 47
Macumba ~ AUS 374 Me 59
Macururé O BR 124 Fa 50
Macururé ~ BR 124 Fa 50
Macusani O PE 128 Dn 53
Macuspana O MEX 93 Db 37
Macuze O MOC 344 Hl 54
Macva Shrine ★ THA 262 Kp 37
Madadeni O ZA 352 Hh 59
Madagascar □ RM 345 Ja 54
Madagascar Basin ♆ 31 Mb 12
Madagli O WAN 321 Gn 40
Madagoi ~ SP 329 Hp 45
Ma Đa Gui O VN 263 Ld 40
Madak O PK 227 Jl 32
Madakasīra O IND 238 Kc 39
Madalena O BR 124 Fa 48
Madama O RN 297 Gn 35
Madamba O RP 275 Lm 42
Madana O TCH 321 Ha 41
Madanapalle O IND 238 Kd 39
Madang O PNG 287 Mj 48
Madanganj O BD 235 Kk 34
Madaoua O RN 308 Gj 38
Madarounfa O RN 320 Gk 39
Madau Island ♁ PNG 287 Mn 50
Madavaram O IND 238 Ke 37
Madawa O PNG 287 Mn 51
Madaya O MYA 254 Kn 34
Madbar O SUD 324 Hh 42
Maddūr O IND 238 Kc 39
Madeir O SUD 324 Hg 42
Madeira ~ BR 117 Ec 49
Madeira ~ BR 120 Ee 48
Madeira ~ BOL 129 Eb 51
Madeira ♁ P 292 Fm 29
Madeirinha ~ BR 129 Ed 51
Madeline Island ♁ USA 56 Dc 22
Madera O USA 64 Cb 27
Madera O MEX 80 Ch 31
Madero O SP 337 Hn 46
Madgaon O IND 238 Ka 38
Madhpur O BD 235 Kk 33
Madhuban O IND 235 Kg 32
Madhubani O IND 235 Kh 32
Madhugiri O IND 238 Kc 39
Madhupur O IND 235 Kh 33
Madhya Phadesh ⊙ IND 234 Kc 34
Madibira O EAT 337 Hk 50
Madibogo O ZA 349 He 59
Madidi ~ BOL 129 Dp 52
Madidi ~ BOL 129 Ea 52
Madigan Gulf ~ AUS 374 Me 60
Madikeri O IND 238 Kb 39
Madill O USA 70 Cp 29
Madimba O RDC 332 Gp 48
Madimba O ANG 332 Gp 49
Ma'din O SYR 209 Hm 28
Madina O RMM 304 Gc 40
Madina O RMM 316 Gb 39
Madinani O CI 305 Gc 41
Madina-Salambandé O RG 316 Ga 40
Madīnat al Abyar O LAR 300 Hc 29
Madīnat as-Sādāt O ET 301 Hh 30
Madīnat aš-Širq O YE 218 Hp 38
Madīnat Nāṣir O ET 301 Hj 33
Madina-Woula O RG 316 Fp 41
Madingo-Kayes O RCB 332 Gm 48
Madingou O RCB 332 Gn 48
Madingrin O CAM 321 Gp 41
Madi Opei O EAU 325 Hj 44
Madirovalo O RM 345 Jb 54
Madison ~ USA 51 Cg 23
Madison O USA 56 Cp 23
Madison O USA 57 Dd 24
Madison O USA 70 Cp 25
Madison O USA 70 Cp 26
Madison O USA 71 Df 26
Madison O USA 71 Dh 26
Madisonville O USA 71 De 27
Madisonville O USA 81 Cp 30
Madiun O RI 279 Lf 49
Madja O RCA 313 Hd 40
Mado Gashi O EAK 325 Hm 45
Madoi O VRC 242 Kp 28
Madol O SUD 324 Hf 41
Madona O LV 171 He 17
Madonie ⛰ I 185 Gn 27
Madra Dağı ⛰ TR 195 Hf 26
Madraka O KSA 214 Hm 34
Madras O USA 50 Cb 23
Madras O IND 238 Ke 39
Madre de Dios O PE 128 Dn 52
Madre de Dios ~ PE 128 Dp 52
Madrid O USA 86 Df 30
Madrid ⊙ E 184 Ge 25
Madrid ▣ E 184 Ge 25
Madrid O RP 267 Ln 41
Madridejos O E 184 Ge 26
Madruga O C 100 Dh 34
Madu O SUD 312 Hf 38
Maduda O RDC 332 Gn 48
Madula O RDC 324 He 45
Madura O AUS 369 Lp 61
Madurai O IND 239 Kd 41
Madurankuli O CL 239 Kd 42
Madurāntakam O IND 238 Kd 39
Maduru Oya Reservoir ~ CL 239 Ke 42
Madyan O PK 230 Ka 28
Madziwa Mine O ZW 341 Hh 54
Maebashi O J 251 Mf 27
Mae Chaem O THA 254 Kp 36
Mae Charim O THA 254 La 36
Mãe do Rio O BR 121 El 47
Mae Hong Son O THA 254 Kp 36
Mae Khajan O THA 254 Kp 36
Maelang O RI 275 Lm 45
Maelhada O P 184 Gb 25
Mae Nam Khwae Noi ~ THA 262 Kp 38
Mae Nam Ping ~ THA 262 Kp 37
Maengsan O DVRK 247 Lp 26
Mae Pok O THA 262 Kp 37
Mae Sai O MYA 254 Kp 35
Mae Sariang O THA 254 Kp 36
Mae Sot O THA 262 Kp 37
Maestro de Campo Island ♁ RP 267 Ll 39
Mae Su O THA 254 Kn 36
Mae Suai O THA 254 Kp 36
Mae Suya O THA 254 Kp 36
Mae Taeng O THA 254 Kp 36
Mae Tub Reservoir ~ THA 262 Kp 37
Maevarano ~ RM 345 Jc 53
Maevatanana O RM 345 Jb 54
Maevo O RUS 171 Hg 17
Maewo ♁ VU 386 Ng 53
Mafa O RI 275 Lp 45
Mafeking O CDN 56 Cm 19
Maféré O CI 317 Ge 43
Mafeteng O LS 349 Hf 60
Maffin O RI 286 Mf 46
Mafia Channel ~ EAT 337 Hm 49
Mafia Island ♁ EAT 337 Hm 49
Mafikeng O ZA 349 He 58
Mafil O RCH 147 Dm 65
Mafra O BR 140 Ej 59
Mafrak O KSA 214 Hm 34
Mafraq O YE 218 Hp 39
Maga O CAM 321 Gp 40
Magadan O RUS 23 Sa 4
Magadan O RUS 205 Ya 7
Magadi O EAK 337 Hl 46
Maǧāġa O ET 301 Hh 31
Magalakwin ~ ZA 349 Hg 57
Magalhães Barata O BR 121 El 46
Magamba O RCA 321 Hd 43
Magandene O MOC 352 Hj 57
Magangué O CO 106 Dl 41
Magano ~ RP 275 Ln 42
Magao O TCH 321 Gp 40
Magara Ku ★ VRC 242 Km 26
Magara O BU 336 Hg 47
Magaret Creek ~ AUS 374 Me 60
Magaria O RN 320 Gl 39
Magarida O PNG 287 Ml 51
Magat ~ RP 267 Ll 37
Magaw O MYA 254 Kn 36
Magazine Mountain △ USA 70 Db 28
Magba O CAM 320 Gm 43
Magbakele O RDC 321 Hd 44
Magbuntoso O WAL 316 Fp 41
Magburaka O WAL 316 Ga 41
Magdalena O USA 65 Cj 28
Magdalena O MEX 80 Cg 30
Magdalena O MEX 92 Cl 35
Magdalena ~ CO 106 Dl 40
Magdalena ~ CO 106 Dl 42
Magdalena ~ CO 106 Dl 44
Magdalena O BOL 129 Eb 52
Magdalena O RA 146 Ef 63
Magdeburg O D 170 Gm 19
Magé O BR 141 En 57
Magelang O RI 278 Le 49
Magerøya ♁ N 159 He 10
Magetan O RI 278 Lf 49
Maggieville O AUS 365 Mg 54
Maghama O RIM 304 Fp 38
Maghnia O DZ 293 Gf 28
Magic Hot Springs ★ USA 64 Ce 24
Magic Reservoir ~ USA 50 Ce 24
Magindrano O RM 345 Jc 53
Magistral'nyj O RUS 204 Va 7
Máglie O I 194 Hb 25
Magnetic Island ♀ AUS 365 Mk 55
Magnetic Island ♁ AUS 365 Mk 55
Magnitogorsk O RUS 154 Rc 8
Magnolia O USA 70 Db 29
Mago ♁ FJI 390 Aa 54
Màgoé O MOC 341 Hh 53
Magog O CDN 60 Dm 23
Magou ~ DY 317 Gg 40
Magoura O DZ 293 Gf 28
Magoye O Z 341 Hf 54
Magpie ~ CDN 61 Eb 20
Magra O DZ 296 Gj 28
Magrath O CDN 51 Cf 21
Magrur O SUD 312 Hh 38
Magṭā Lahjar O RIM 304 Fp 37
Magu ~ BR 124 En 47
Maguan O VRC 255 Lc 34
Magude O MOC 352 Hj 58
Magueyal O MEX 81 Cl 32
Magugon O MYA 262 Km 37
Magumeri O WAN 321 Gn 39
Magunge O ZW 341 Hg 54
Maguohe O VRC 255 Lb 33
Magura O BD 235 Kj 34
Magwe O MYA 254 Km 35
Magwe O SUD 324 Hj 43
Magyichaung O MYA 235 Kl 35
Maǧz O YE 218 Hp 37
Mahābād O IR 209 Ja 27
Mahābaleshwar O IND 238 Ka 37
Mahabe O RM 345 Ja 54
Mahabo O RM 353 Ja 56
Māhad O IND 238 Ka 36
Mahadday Weeyne O SP 329 Ja 44
Mahādeo Range ⛰ IND 238 Ka 37
Mahagi O RDC 324 Hh 44
Mahagi Port O RDC 324 Hh 44
Mahaicony O GUY 113 Ef 42
Maḥā'il O KSA 218 Hn 36
Mahaing O MYA 254 Km 35
Mahajamba ~ RM 345 Jb 53
Mahajanga Majunga O RM 345 Ja 53
Mahajilo ~ RM 345 Ja 55
Mahakam ~ RI 274 Lh 45
Mahal O IND 238 Kd 39
Mahalapye O RB 349 Hf 57
Mahale Mountains ⛰ EAT 336 Hg 49
Mahalevona O RM 345 Jc 53
Maḥallāt O IR 222 Jd 29
Mahalona O RI 282 Ll 47
Mahambo O RM 345 Jc 54
Mahamūd-e'Rāqī O AFG 223 Jn 28
Māhān O IR 226 Jg 30
Mahanadi ~ IND 234 Kf 35
Mahānadi Delta ⏢ IND 235 Kh 35
Mahananda ~ BD 235 Kj 33
Mahango ~ NAM 340 Hc 55
Mahanoro O RM 345 Jc 55
Maha Oya O CL 239 Ke 42
Mahārājganj O IND 235 Kf 32
Maharashtra ⊙ IND 238 Ka 36
Mahāsamund O IND 234 Ke 35
Maha Sarakham O THA 263 Lb 37
Mahasolo O RM 345 Jb 55
Mahatalaky O RM 353 Jb 58
Maḥaṭṭat 10 O SUD 313 Hj 36
Maḥaṭṭat 2 O SUD 312 Hh 35
Maḥaṭṭat 5 O SUD 312 Hj 35
Maḥaṭṭat 6 O SUD 312 Hj 35
Maḥaṭṭat 8 O SUD 312 Hj 35
Maḥaṭṭat Dab'a O JOR 214 Hl 30
Maḥaṭṭat Ṭalāṭa O ET 301 Hj 30
Mahavavy ~ RM 345 Jb 53
Mahavavy ~ RM 345 Jc 52
Mahavelona O RM 345 Jc 54
Mahawelatota O CL 239 Ke 42
Mahaxai O LAO 263 Lc 37
Mahazoma O RM 345 Jb 54
Maḥbūb O SUD 312 Hg 39
Mahbūbābād O IND 238 Kd 37
Mahbūbnagar O IND 238 Kc 37
Mahḍa O OM 226 Jf 33
Mahd ad-Dahab O KSA 214 Hn 34
Mahdia O GUY 112 Ee 43
Mahdia O TN 297 Gm 28
Mahdīšahr O IR 222 Je 28
Mahe O IND 238 Kb 40
Mahé ♁ SY 329 Jf 48
Mahébourg O MS 353 Jg 56
Mahendragarh O IND 234 Kb 31
Mahenge O EAT 337 Hl 50
Mahesāna O IND 227 Ka 34
Maheshpur O IND 235 Kh 33
Maḥfar al-Buṣayya O IRQ 215 Ja 30
Maḥfar al-Ḥammām O SYR 209 Hm 28
Mahi ~ IND 234 Kb 34
Mahia Peninsula ♁ NZ 383 Nm 65
Māhīdašt O IR 209 Jb 28
Mahila O RDC 336 Hg 48
Mahilyow O BY 171 Hg 19
Mahin O WAN 320 Gj 42
Mahina O RMM 316 Ga 39
Mahitsy O RM 345 Jb 55
Mahmiya O SUD 313 Hj 37
Mahmūd Jiq O IR 209 Jb 27
Maḥmūr O IRQ 209 Hp 28
Mahne O IR 222 Jh 28
Mahnomen O USA 56 Da 22
Mahoba O IND 234 Kd 33
Mahón Maó O E 185 Gj 26
Mahone Bay ≈ CDN 61 Eb 23
Mahony Lake ~ CDN 47 Bn 13
Mahood Lake ~ CDN 50 Cb 20
Mahoua O TCH 321 Hb 40
Mahrauni O IND 234 Kd 33
Mahres O TN 297 Gm 28
Mahulu O RDC 336 Hf 46
Mahuneni O RI 275 Ln 44
Mahur Island ♁ PNG 287 Mn 47
Mahuta O WAN 320 Gj 40
Mahuva O IND 227 Jp 35
Mahwah O IND 234 Kc 32
Maiama O PNG 287 Mk 49
Maiana ♁ KIR 27 Tb 9
Maica ~ CDN 60 Dk 20
Maicao O CO 107 Dm 40
Maici ~ BR 117 Ec 49
Maici ~ BR 120 Ed 49
Maicimirim ~ BR 117 Ec 49
Maicuru ~ BR 113 Eg 45
Maicuru ~ BR 120 Eg 46
Maidī O YE 218 Hp 37
Maidi O RI 275 Lp 45
Maidstone O CDN 51 Ch 19
Maidstone O GB 163 Gg 20
Maiduguri O WAN 321 Gn 40
Maif'a O YE 218 Jb 38
Maigatari O WAN 320 Gl 39
Mai Gudo △ ETH 325 Hl 42
Maihar O IND 234 Ke 33
Maihara O J 251 Md 28
Maiinchi O WAN 320 Gj 39
Maijdi O BD 235 Kk 34
Maijishan Shiku ★ VRC 243 Lc 28
Maika ~ RDC 324 Hg 44
Maikala Range ⛰ IND 234 Ke 34
Maiko ~ RDC 336 Hf 46
Maikonkele O WAN 320 Gk 41
Maikoro O TCH 321 Ha 41
Mai Kussa River ~ PNG 286 Mh 50
Mailani O IND 234 Ke 31
Mailepalli O IND 238 Kd 37
Mailin ~ RA 136 Ec 60
Maillstream Chichester ♀ AUS 360 Lj 56
Mailsi O PK 227 Ka 31
Maimana O AFG 223 Jl 28
Maimará O RA 136 Eb 57
Maimón O DOM 101 Dn 36
Maimoon Palace ★ RI 270 Kp 44
Main ~ CDN 61 Ef 21
Main ~ D 174 Gl 22
Main à Dieu O CDN 61 Ee 22
Mainau ★ D 174 Gl 22
Main Brook O CDN 61 Ef 20
Main Channel ~ CDN 57 Dg 23
Main-Donau-Kanal ~ D 174 Gm 21
Maine ⊙ USA 60 Dn 23
Maine ⏢ F 163 Gf 22
Maïné-Soroa O RN 296 Gn 39
Maing Kwan O MYA 254 Kn 32
Mainit O RP 267 Lm 41
Mainit O RP 267 Ln 41
Mainland O CDN 61 Ee 21
Mainland ♁ GB 162 Gf 15
Mainling O VRC 254 Km 31
Mainoru O AUS 364 Md 53
Mainpuri O IND 234 Kd 32
Maintirano O RM 345 Hp 55
Mainz O D 174 Gl 21
Maio ♁ CV 316 Fj 38
Maiparu O YV 112 Ed 42
Maipo ~ RCH 137 Dn 62
Mai Pu O RA 137 Dp 62
Maipú O RA 146 Ef 64
Maiqū' O KSA 214 Hn 32
Maiquetía O YV 107 Ea 40
Mairana O BOL 129 Ec 55
Mairi O BR 125 Ep 51
Mairinque O BR 141 El 57
Maisān ⊙ IRQ 215 Jb 30
Maisí O C 101 Dl 35
Maiskhal Island ♁ BD 235 Kk 35
Maitembge O RB 349 Hf 56
Maitencillo O RCH 137 Dm 61
Maitland ~ AUS 360 Lj 56
Maitland O AUS 378 Me 63
Maitland O AUS 379 Mm 62
Maiurno O SUD 313 Hj 39
Maiwa O RI 279 Lk 47
Maizho Kunggar O VRC 235 Kk 31
Maizuru O J 251 Md 28
Maja ~ RUS 205 Wc 7
Maja ~ RUS 205 Xa 7
Majagua O C 100 Dj 35
Majahual O MEX 93 De 36
Majalengka O RI 278 Le 49
Majda O RUS 159 Hn 12
Majdanpek O SCG 194 Hd 23
Majeicodoteri Platanal O YV 112 Eb 44
Majenang O RI 278 Le 49
Majene O RI 279 Lk 47
Majes ~ PE 128 Dm 54
Majgaon O IND 234 Kf 34
Majholi O IND 234 Ke 33
Majī O ETH 325 Hk 42
Majiahewan O VRC 243 Lc 27
Majiang O VRC 255 Ld 32
Majid O RI 275 Lm 46
Majie O VRC 255 Lc 34
Maji Moto O EAT 337 Hk 46
Majkapčigaj O KZ 204 Tc 9
Majli-Saj O KS 230 Ka 25
Majmeča ~ RUS 204 Ub 4
Majn ~ RUS 205 Zb 6
Majo ~ MEX 80 Ch 32
Majoli O SME 113 Eg 44
Major O CDN 51 Ch 20
Major Isidoro O BR 124 Fb 50
Majskij O RUS 202 Ja 24
Majunga O RM 345 Ja 53
Majuro ♁ MH 27 Tb 9
Maka O SN 316 Fn 39
Maka O LB 316 Ga 42
Makabana O RCB 332 Gn 47
Makado O ZW 349 Hg 56
Maka Gouye O SN 316 Fn 39
Makaha O USA 75 Al 35
Makah Indian Reservation ••• USA 50 Bp 21
Makak O CAM 320 Gm 44
Makaka O RCB 332 Gn 47
Makalamabedi O RB 349 Hd 56
Makale O RI 279 Lk 47
Makalondi O RN 317 Gg 39
Makalu △ NEP 235 Kh 32
Makamba O BU 336 Hg 48
Makambako O EAT 337 Hk 50
Makanjila O MW 344 Hk 52
Makanya O EAT 337 Hl 48
Makarfi O WAN 320 Gk 40
Makari O CAM 321 Gp 39
Makariki O RI 283 Ma 47
Makarora O NZ 382 Ng 68
Makarov Dvor O RUS 171 Hn 15
Makarska O HR 194 Ha 24
Makasa O Z 336 Hh 50
Makassar Ujung Pandang O RI 279 Lk 48
Makassar Strait ♆ RI 274 Lj 46
Makassar Strait ≈ RI 279 Lj 47
Makat O KZ 155 Rb 9
Makaya O RDC 333 Hb 47
Makekeda O RDC 324 Hf 44
Makemo ♁ F 35 Bb 11
Makeni O WAL 316 Fp 41
Makere O EAT 336 Hh 48
Makgadikgadi-Nxai Pan ♀ RB 341 He 55
Makgadikgadi Pans ⏢ RB 349 He 56
Makhachkala O RUS 202 Jb 24
Makhaleng ~ LS 349 Hf 60
Makhdumnagar O IND 234 Kf 32
Makhtal O IND 238 Kc 37
Makhu O IND 230 Kb 30
Maki O RI 283 Md 47
Makijivka O UA 181 Hl 21
Makilimbo O RDC 324 Hf 44
Makina O SOL 290 Nc 50
Makī National Park ♀ ETH 325 Hl 43
Makīnat Šihan O OM 219 Je 36
Makindu O EAK 337 Hl 47
Makkovik O CDN 43 Hc 7
Makó O H 174 Hc 22
Mako O SN 316 Fp 39
Makogai ♁ FJI 387 Nm 54
Makokibatan Lake ~ CDN 57 De 20
Makokou O G 332 Gn 45
Makonde Plateau ⛰ EAT 344 Hm 51
Makongo O GH 317 Gf 41
Makongolosi O EAT 337 Hj 50
Makopong O RB 349 Hd 58
Makor O CAM 321 Gn 42
Makoro O RDC 324 Hg 44
Makoua O TCH 321 Hc 41
Makoua O RCB 332 Gp 46
Makoubi O RCB 332 Gn 47
Makoulou Tréchot O RCB 332 Gp 47
Makov O RUS 202 Jc 22
Makovo O RUS 202 Jc 22
Makrān Coast Range ⛰ PK 226 Jk 33
Maks al-Qiblī O ET 301 Hh 33
Maksudangarh O IND 234 Kc 33
Maktau O EAK 337 Hl 47
Makthar O TN 296 Gl 28
Mākū O IR 209 Ja 26
Makuende O RDC 336 Hf 49
Makunduchi O EAT 337 Hm 49
Makung O RC 258 Lk 34
Makungu O EAT 337 Hk 50
Makungviro O EAT 337 Hl 50
Makunudu Atoll ♁ MV 239 Ka 42
Makurau ♁ VU 386 Ng 54
Makurazaki O J 247 Ma 30
Makurdi O WAN 320 Gl 42
Makutano O EAK 325 Hk 44
Makutano O EAK 337 Hl 46
Makuti O ZW 341 Hg 54
Makuyuni O EAT 337 Hl 47
Makwassie O ZA 349 Hf 59
Makwate O RB 349 Hf 57
Māl O RIM 304 Fp 37
Mal. Anjuj ~ RUS 205 Yc 5
Mala O PE 116 Dk 52
Mala ~ PE 116 Dk 52
Mala O RI 283 Mb 46
Malaba O EAK 325 Hk 45
Malabang O RP 275 Ln 42
Malabar Coast ⏢ IND 238 Ka 38
Malabo O GQ 320 Gl 44
Malabo ▣ GQ 320 Gl 44
Malabungan O RP 266 Lj 41
Malabwe O Z 341 He 54
Malacacheta O BR 125 En 54
Malacca O IND 262 Kl 41
Malad △ ER 313 Hm 37
Malad City O USA 65 Cf 24
Maladzyechna O BY 171 Hf 18
Málaga O CO 107 Dm 42
Málaga O E 184 Gd 27
Malagarasi ~ EAT 336 Hh 47
Malagarasi O EAT 336 Hh 48
Malaimbandy O RM 353 Ja 56
Malaita ♁ SOL 290 Nc 50
Malaita O ZA 349 Hg 58
Malaja Bykovka O RUS 181 Jb 20
Malaja Uzen' O RUS 181 Jb 20
Malaja Uzen' ~ RUS 181 Jb 20
Malaja Višera O RUS 171 Hj 16
Malakāl O SUD 324 Hh 41
Malakanagiri O IND 238 Ke 36
Mālākānd Pass △ PK 223 Jp 28
Malake O IR 215 Je 32
Malakheti O NEP 234 Ke 31
Malakula ♁ VU 386 Nf 54
Malakwa O CDN 50 Cc 20
Malakwāl O PK 230 Ka 29
Malala O PNG 287 Mj 48
Malala O PNG 287 Mk 48
Malalaua O PNG 287 Mk 50
Malam O PNG 286 Mh 50
Malamala O RI 282 Ll 47
Malambo O EAT 337 Hk 47
Malammaduri O WAN 320 Gl 39
Malampaka O EAT 337 Hj 47
Malanda O AUS 365 Mj 54
Malandji O RDC 333 Hd 48
Malang O RI 279 Lg 49
Malanga O MOC 344 Hl 52
Malangani O EAT 337 Hk 50
Malangbong O RI 278 Le 49
Malanje O ANG 340 Ha 50
Malantouen O CAM 320 Gm 43
Malanut Bay ≈ RP 266 Lj 41
Malanville O DY 320 Gh 40
Malapatan O RP 275 Ln 43
Malappuram O IND 239 Kc 40
Malār O PK 227 Jl 32
Malarba O CAM 320 Gn 42
Mälaren ~ S 170 Ha 16
Malargüe O RA 137 Dp 63
Malargüe ~ RA 137 Dp 63
Malasait O PNG 287 Mm 48
Malaso ~ RI 279 Lk 47
Malaspina Glacier ▲ USA 47 Be 15
Malatya O TR 195 Hm 26
Malaut O IND 230 Kb 30
Malavalli O IND 238 Kc 39
Malāvī O IR 209 Jb 29
Malawi □ MW 344 Hj 52
Malay O RP 267 Ll 40
Malaybalay O RP 267 Ln 41
Malāyer O IR 209 Jc 28
Malay Peninsula ♁ MAL 271 Lb 43
Malaysia □ MAL 271 Le 44
Malazán O RA 137 Ea 61
Malazgirt O TR 202 Hp 26
Malbazza O RN 308 Gj 39
Malbhanguwa O NEP 234 Ke 31
Malbon O AUS 374 Mg 56
Malbon Vale O AUS 374 Mf 56
Malbooma O AUS 378 Mc 61
Malbork O PL 170 Hb 19
Malbrán O RA 137 Ec 60

Lyttelton - Malbrán 441

Marcapata ○ PE 128 Dn 52
Marcelândia ○ BR 132 Eg 51
Marcelino ○ BR 117 Ea 45
Marcelino Ramos ○ BR 140 Eh 59
March ○ SK 174 Ha 21
Marcha ○ RUS 22 Ra 3
Marche ○ BR 117 Ea 45
Marche ◅ F 184 Gg 23
Marche ◅ I 185 Gn 24
Marchinbar Island ⏹ AUS 364 Me 51
Marciac ○ F 184 Gf 24
Marcionílio Sousa ○ BR 125 Ep 52
Marco ○ BR 124 Fc 46
Marco ○ USA 87 Dh 33
Marco ◉ I 185 Gn 24
Marco Rondon ○ BR 129 Ed 52
Marcoux ○ USA 56 Cp 22
Marcos Paz ○ RA 146 Ee 63
Marcus ○ USA 56 Da 24
Mârdâkan ○ AZ 202 Jd 25
Mardān ○ PK 230 Ka 28
Mar de Ajó ○ RA 146 Ef 64
Mar de Espanha ○ BR 141 En 56
Mar del Plata ○ RA 146 Ef 64
Mardiān ○ AFG 223 Jm 27
Mardie ○ AUS 360 Lj 56
Mardie Island ⏹ AUS 360 Lh 56
Mardin ○ TR 202 Hn 27
Mardin Daglari ⚊ TR 202 Hn 27
Mare ∼ RI 282 Ll 48
Mare ∼ F 386 Ng 56
Maré ◅ F 386 Ng 56
Marea del Portillo ○ C 101 Dk 36
Mare de Tizi ∼ RCA 313 Hd 40
Mareeba ○ AUS 365 Mj 54
Mareeq ○ SP 328 Jb 44
Marekesa ○ RDC 324 Hf 45
Maréna ○ RMM 304 Ga 38
Marendet ○ RN 308 Gk 37
Marengâb ○ IR 222 Jd 28
Marenge ○ RDC 336 Hg 48
Marengo ○ CDN 51 Cn 20
Marennes ○ F 184 Gf 23
Marerano ○ RM 353 Ja 56
Mareth ○ TN 297 Gm 29
Mar'evka ○ RUS 181 Jc 19
Marfa ○ USA 81 Ck 30
Margaree Forks ○ CDN 61 Ed 22
Margaret ∼ AUS 361 Lg 55
Margaret Lake ∼ CDN 47 Cc 15
Margaret River ○ AUS 368 Lh 62
Margarida ○ BR 140 Ef 55
Margarima ○ PNG 286 Mh 49
Margaritovo ○ RUS 181 Hm 22
Marghita ○ RO 174 Hd 22
Margilan ○ UZB 223 Jp 25
Margosatibug ○ RP 275 Lm 42
Margua ∼ CO 107 Dm 42
Marguerite ○ CDN 50 Ca 19
Marha ∼ RUS 204 Vc 5
Marhamat ○ UZB 230 Ka 25
Marhanec' ○ UA 175 Hk 22
Marhoum ○ DZ 293 Gd 29
Mari ○ PNG 286 Mg 50
Maria ◅ F 35 Ba 12
Maria ○ PE 116 Dk 49
Maria ○ MOC 344 Hl 54
Maria da Fé ○ BR 141 Em 57
María Elena ○ RCH 136 Dp 57
Maria Esther ○ RA 152 Dp 70
Maria Ignacia ○ RA 146 Ee 64
Maria Island ⏹ AUS 364 Md 53
Maria Island ⏹ AUS 378 Ml 67
Maria Island ⏹ AUS 378 Ml 67
Mariakani ○ EAK 337 Hm 47
María Linda ∼ GCA 93 Dc 39
Marialva ○ P 184 Ge 25
Marian ○ AUS 375 Ml 56
Mariani ○ IND 254 Km 32
Marianna ○ USA 71 Dc 28
Marianna ○ USA 86 Df 30
Marianno I. Loza ○ RA 146 Ee 60
Marianópolis ○ BR 121 Em 48
Mariánské Lázné ○ CZ 174 Gn 21
Mariapolis ○ CDN 56 Cn 21
Mariaqua ○ BR 120 Ef 47
Mariarano ○ RM 345 Jb 53
Marias ∼ USA 51 Cg 21
Marias Pass △ USA 51 Cf 21
María Teresa ○ RA 137 Ed 63
Maria Teresa ○ ANG 340 Gn 50
Mariazell ○ A 174 Gp 22
Ma'rib ○ YE 218 Ja 38
Maribo ○ DK 170 Gm 18
Maribor ○ SLO 174 Gp 22
Maricá ○ BR 141 En 57
Mariça ∼ BG 194 He 24
Maricao ○ USA 104 Ea 36
Maricopa ○ USA 64 Cc 28
Marico ∼ RB 349 Hf 58
Maridi ○ SUD 324 Hg 43
Maridi ∼ SUD 324 Hg 43
Marié ∼ BR 117 Dp 46
Marié ∼ BR 117 Ea 46
Marie-Byrd-Land ◅ 38 Cb 17
Marie-Galante ⏹ F 104 Ed 38
Mariehamn Maarianhamina ◉ FIN 159 Hc 15
Mariel ○ C 100 Dg 34
Marienberg ○ PNG 287 Mj 48
Mariental ○ NAM 348 Hb 58
Mariepaué ∼ BR 120 Ed 48
Mariestad ○ S 170 Gn 16
Marietta ○ USA 70 Cp 29
Marietta ○ USA 71 Dd 26
Marietta ○ USA 86 Df 29
Mariga ∼ WAN 320 Gj 40
Marigot ○ F 104 Ec 36
Marigot ○ RH 101 Dm 36
Marigot ○ WD 104 Ed 38
Marihatag ○ RP 267 Lp 41
María Eugenia ○ RA 137 Ed 61
Mariinsk ○ RUS 204 Tc 7
Marijampolé ○ LT 171 Hd 18
Marikal ○ IND 238 Kc 37
Marília ○ BR 140 Ek 57
Marimari ∼ BR 120 Ee 48
Marimba ○ ANG 340 Ha 50
Marimbona ∼ RM 345 Jc 54

Marimbondo ○ BR 124 Fb 50
Marimia ○ BR 140 Ej 57
Ma'rina Horka ○ BY 171 Hf 19
Marina Plains ○ AUS 365 Mb 53
Marinduque Island ⏹ RP 267 Ll 39
Marine ◉ ET 313 Hf 38
Marine ∼ ER 313 Hn 38
Marine ♀ EAK 337 Hn 47
Marineland of Florida ★ USA 87 Dh 31
Marinette ○ USA 57 De 23
Maringá ○ BR 140 Ej 57
Maringa ∼ RDC 332 Hc 45
Marion ○ USA 70 Cp 26
Marion ○ USA 70 Dc 24
Marion ○ USA 71 Dd 27
Marion ○ USA 71 De 25
Marion ○ USA 71 De 29
Marion ○ USA 71 Dg 25
Marion ○ USA 71 Dg 28
Marion ○ USA 71 Dj 26
Marion Downs ○ AUS 374 Mf 57
Marion Lake ∼ USA 70 Cp 26
Marion Reef ⏹ AUS 375 Mn 55
Maripa ○ YV 113 Ee 42
Maripasoula ○ F 113 Eg 44
Maripipi Island ⏹ RP 267 Ln 40
Mariposa ○ USA 64 Cc 27
Mariquita ○ BR 133 Em 52
Mariquita ○ CO 106 Dl 43
Marisa ∼ RI 275 Ll 45
Mariscal Cáceres ○ PE 128 Dl 52
Marischalltown ○ USA 56 Db 24
Mariscal de Juárez ○ MEX 92 Cn 37
Marita Downs ○ AUS 375 Mh 57
Marite ○ ZA 352 Hl 58
Marittimo ⏹ I 185 Gp 26
Marituba ○ BR 120 Ec 47
Mariupol' ∼ UA 181 Hl 22
Mariusa ♀ YV 113 Ed 41
Mârîvân ○ IR 209 Jb 28
Mariveles ○ RP 267 Ll 38
Mariveles Reef ⏹ 266 Lg 41
Mârjamaa ○ EST 171 He 16
Markala ○ RMM 305 Gc 39
Markam ∼ VRC 254 Kp 31
Markandeh ★ AFG 223 Jm 28
Mârkâpur ○ IND 238 Kd 38
Markara ○ ARM 202 Hp 25
Markazi ◈ IR 222 Jd 28
Marked Tree ○ USA 71 Dc 28
Marken ○ ZA 349 Hg 57
Markham ○ CDN 60 Dj 24
Markham Bay ∼ PNG 287 Mk 49
Markham River ∼ PNG 287 Mk 49
Markit ○ VRC 230 Kc 26
Markivka ∼ UA 181 Hm 21
Markounda ○ RCA 321 Ha 42
Markovac ○ SCG 174 Hc 23
Markovo ○ RUS 23 Tb 3
Markovo ○ RUS 171 Hn 16
Markovo ○ RUS 205 Zb 6
Markoye ○ BF 305 Ge 38
Marks ○ RUS 181 Ja 20
Marktoberdorf ○ D 174 Gm 22
Marktredwitz ○ D 174 Gm 21
Mark Twain Lake ∼ USA 70 Dc 26
Marla ○ AUS 369 Mc 59
Marlandy Hill △ AUS 368 Lj 60
Marlborough ○ USA 74 Dn 24
Marlborough ∼ GB 163 Gf 20
Marlborough ○ AUS 375 Ml 57
Marlborough Sounds ∼ NZ 383 Nj 66
Marlborouth ○ GUY 113 Ee 42
Marlin ○ USA 81 Cp 30
Marlinton ○ USA 71 Dh 26
Marlo ○ AUS 379 Ml 64
Marlow ○ USA 70 Cn 28
Marmagao ○ IND 238 Ka 38
Marmande ○ F 184 Gg 23
Marmara Adasi ⏹ TR 195 Hf 25
Marmaraereğlisi ○ TR 195 Hf 25
Marmaris ○ TR 195 Hg 27
Marmarth ○ USA 51 Cl 22
Marmelo ∼ BR 117 Ea 50
Marmelos ○ BR 120 Ed 49
Marmelos ∼ BR 120 Ed 50
Mar Menor ∼ E 184 Gf 27
Marmion Lake ∼ CDN 56 Dc 21
Marmolada △ I 174 Gm 22
Marmot Bay ∼ USA 46 An 15
Marmot Island ⏹ USA 46 Ba 15
Mar Muerto ∼ MEX 93 Da 37
Marmul ○ OM 219 Jf 36
Marne-la-Vallée ○ F 163 Gh 21
Marneuli ○ GE 202 Ja 25
Marnoo ○ AUS 378 Mh 64
Maro ○ TCH 321 Hb 41
Maroa ○ YV 107 Ea 44
Maroala Ambanjabe ○ RM 345 Jb 53
Maroantsetra ○ RM 345 Jc 53
Maroelaboom ○ NAM 340 Hb 55
Maroharatra ○ RM 353 Jb 56
Marojezy ♀ RM 345 Jc 53
Marokau ⏹ F 35 Bb 11
Marolambo ○ RM 353 Jb 56
Maromandia ○ RM 345 Jc 53
Maromokotro △ RM 345 Jc 52
Marondera ○ ZW 341 Hh 55
Marongora ○ ZW 341 Hg 54
Maroni ∼ F 113 Eg 44
Maron Island ⏹ PNG 287 Mj 46
Maroochydore ○ AUS 375 Mn 59
Maros ∼ RO 174 Hc 22
Maros ○ RI 279 Lk 48
Maroseranana ○ RM 345 Jc 55
Marotandrano ○ RM 345 Jc 54
Marou ○ SOL 290 Nc 51
Maroua ○ CAM 321 Gp 40
Marouíni ∼ F 113 Eh 44
Marova ○ BR 120 Ec 46
Marovato ○ RM 345 Jb 53
Marovato ○ RM 345 Jc 52
Marovoay ○ RM 345 Ja 54
Marovoay ○ RM 345 Jb 54
Marowini ∼ SME 113 Eg 43
Marqua ∼ AUS 374 Me 57
Marquard ○ ZA 349 Hf 60
Marquesas Keys ⏹ USA 87 Dg 33
Marquetto ○ USA 57 De 23
Marquez ○ USA 81 Cp 30
Marquises Islands ◅ F 14 Ca 10
Marqūq ○ SUD 324 Hh 41
Marracuene ○ MOC 352 Hj 58
Marrakech ○ MA 292 Gc 30
Marrât ○ KSA 215 Ja 33
Marrawah ○ AUS 378 Mj 66

Marree ○ AUS 374 Mf 60
Marromeu ○ MOC 344 Hk 55
Marroonah ○ AUS 360 Lh 57
Marrupa ○ MOC 344 Hl 52
Marryville ○ USA 86 Db 30
Marsá al Burayqah ○ LAR 300 Hb 30
Marsabit ♀ EAK 325 Hl 44
Marsabit ○ EAK 325 Hm 44
Marsā I-'Alam ○ ET 301 Hk 33
Marsala ○ I 185 Gn 27
Marsā Matrūh ○ ET 301 Hf 30
Marsā Mubārak ○ ET 301 Hk 33
Marsassoum ○ SN 316 Fm 39
Marsden ○ AUS 379 Mk 62
Marseille ○ F 185 Gj 24
Marshall ○ USA 46 Aj 15
Marshall ○ USA 56 Da 23
Marshall ○ USA 57 Df 24
Marshall ○ USA 70 Da 29
Marshall ○ USA 70 Db 26
Marshall ○ USA 70 Db 28
Marshall ○ USA 71 Dd 26
Marshall ○ LB 316 Ga 42
Marshall ∼ AUS 374 Me 57
Marshall Bennet Islands ⏹ PNG 287 Mn 50
Marshall Islands ◻ MH 27 Ta 8
Marshalltown ○ USA 56 Db 24
Marshfield ○ USA 56 Dc 23
Marshfield ○ USA 57 De 23
Marshfield ○ USA 70 Db 27
Marsh Harbour ○ BS 87 Dk 32
Mars Hill ○ USA 60 Ea 22
Marsh Island ⏹ USA 86 Db 31
Marsimang ∼ RI 283 Mb 47
Marsimang Tanjung ◠ RI 283 Mb 47
Marsoui ○ CDN 61 Ea 21
Mârsta ○ S 170 Ha 16
Martaban ○ MYA 262 Kn 37
Martap ○ CAM 321 Gp 42
Martapura ○ RI 278 Lb 48
Martapura ○ RI 279 Lk 47
Marte ○ WAN 321 Gp 39
Marten River ∼ CDN 57 Dh 22
Martensøya ⏹ N 158 Hc 5
Martha ○ GR 194 He 28
Marthaguy ∼ AUS 379 Mk 61
Martha's Vineyard ⏹ USA 74 Dn 25
Martigny ○ CH 163 Gk 22
Martigues ○ F 185 Gj 24
Martil ○ MA 293 Gd 28
Martin ○ USA 56 Cm 24
Martin ○ USA 71 Dd 27
Martin ○ SK 174 Hb 21
Martinborough ∼ NZ 383 Nk 66
Martindopolis ○ BR 140 Ej 57
Martínez de la Torre ○ MEX 81 Cp 34
Martínez de Tineo ○ RA 136 Ec 57
Martinho Campos ○ BR 133 Em 55
Martinique ◻ F 104 Ed 38
Martinique Passage ▽ 104 Ed 38
Martinsburg ○ USA 74 Dj 26
Martinsville ○ CDN 51 Cj 19
Martinsville ○ USA 71 De 26
Martinsville ○ USA 74 Dj 27
Marton ○ NZ 383 Nk 66
Martos ○ E 184 Ge 27
Marttila ○ FIN 159 Hd 15
Martûba ○ LAR 300 Hd 29
Martuni ○ ARM 202 Ja 25
Martynovo ○ KZ 181 Jd 20
Maru ○ WAN 320 Gk 39
Maruanum ∼ BR 121 Ej 45
Marudi ○ MAL 274 Lk 45
Marulaneng Hoedspruit ○ ZA 352 Hh 58
Marungu ⚊ RDC 336 Hg 49
Marupa ∼ BR 120 Ed 48
Marupa ○ PNG 287 Mn 48
Marutéa ⏹ F 14 Ca 12
Marutea ⏹ F 35 Bb 11
Mâruteru ○ IND 238 Ke 37
Maru'ura ○ SOL 290 Nc 50
Marvão ○ P 184 Gc 26
Marvast ○ IR 215 Je 30
Marv Dasht ○ IR 215 Je 31
Marve ○ AFG 223 Jk 28
Marwayne ○ CDN 51 Cg 19
Mary ∼ TM 223 Jj 27
Mary ∼ AUS 361 Lp 55
Mary ∼ AUS 364 Mb 52
Maryal Bai ○ SUD 324 Hf 41
Mary Anne-Group ⏹ AUS 360 Lh 56
Mary Anne Passage ≈ AUS 360 Lh 56
Mary Ann Point ◠ AUS 368 Lk 63
Maryborough ○ AUS 375 Mn 58
Maryborough ○ AUS 379 Mh 64
Marydale ○ ZA 349 Hd 60
Maryfield ○ USA 50 Cb 23
Mary River ∼ AUS 364 Mb 52
Marysvale ○ USA 65 Cf 26
Marysville ○ USA 64 Cb 26
Marysville ○ USA 70 Cp 26
Marysville ○ USA 71 Dg 25
Maryvale ○ AUS 365 Mj 55
Maryvale ○ AUS 374 Md 58
Maryville ○ USA 70 Da 25
Maryville ○ USA 71 Dg 28
Marzagão ○ BR 133 Ek 54
Marzanābād ○ IR 222 Jd 27
Marzargão ○ BR 132 Eg 53
Marzuq ○ LAR 297 Gn 33
Maşabb Rašid ∼ ET 301 Hh 30
Masachapa ○ NIC 96 De 40
Masada N.P. ★ IL 214 Ha 30
Masagaweyn ○ SP 328 Jb 44
Masagua ○ GCA 93 Dc 38
Masaguara ○ HN 96 De 38
Masahunga ○ EAT 337 Hk 47
Masai Mara ♀ EAK 337 Hk 46
Masai Steppe ◅ EAT 337 Hl 48
Masaka ○ EAU 336 Hk 46
Ma'sal ○ MEX 80 Cj 31
Masally ○ AZ 202 Jc 26
Masama ○ RB 349 Hf 57
Masamba ○ RI 282 Ll 47
Masan ○ ROK 247 Ma 28
Masanga ○ RDC 333 Hd 46
Masapun ○ RI 282 Lp 49
Masasi ○ EAT 344 Hm 51

Masatepe ○ NIC 96 De 40
Masaya ○ NIC 96 De 39
Masbate ○ RP 267 Lm 39
Masbate ○ RP 267 Lm 39
Masbate ⏹ RP 267 Lm 39
Mascara ○ DZ 293 Gf 28
Mascarene Basin ▽ 31 Mb 11
Mascarene Plateau ▽ 31 Mb 10
Mascota ○ MEX 92 Ck 35
Mascota ∼ MEX 92 Ck 35
Masel'gskaja ○ RUS 159 Hk 14
Maseru ◉ LS 349 Hf 60
Masfut ○ UAE 219 Jh 33
Masged-e Abolfazl ★ IR 226 Jh 32
Masged-e Soleimân ★ IR 215 Jc 30
Mashala ○ RDC 333 Hd 48
Mashansha ○ PE 128 Dm 51
Mashari ○ NAM 348 Nc 54
Mashava ○ ZW 352 Hh 56
Mashhad ○ IR 222 Jh 27
Mashi ○ VRC 255 Lf 31
Mashike ○ J 250 Mg 24
Mâshkel ∼ PK 226 Jk 31
Mâshkel ∼ PK 226 Jk 31
Mashkode ○ CDN 57 Dg 22
Mashowingrivier ∼ ZA 349 Hd 59
Mashra' ar-Raqq ○ SUD 324 zHg 41
Masi ∼ N 159 Hd 11
Masia ○ EAT 337 Hj 49
Masia-Mbio ○ RDC 333 Ha 48
Masi-Manimba ○ RDC 333 Ha 48
Masindi ○ EAU 324 Hh 45
Masindi Port ○ EAU 324 Hj 45
Masinga Reservoir ∼ EAK 337 Hl 46
Masingbi ○ WAL 316 Ga 41
Masinloc ○ RP 267 Lk 38
Masira ○ OM 226 Jh 35
Masira Channel ∼ OM 226 Jh 35
Masis ○ ARM 202 Ja 25
Masisi ○ RDC 336 Hg 46
Maskane ○ SYR 209 Hm 27
Maskelyne Islands ⏹ VU 386 Nf 54
Maso ○ PNG 287 Mm 49
Masohi ○ RI 283 Ma 47
Masoko ○ EAT 337 Hj 50
Masoller ○ ROU 146 Ef 61
Masomeloka ∼ RM 353 Jc 56
Mason ○ USA 57 Df 24
Mason ○ USA 81 Cn 30
Mason Bay ∼ NZ 382 Nf 69
Mason City ○ USA 70 Db 24
Maspalomas ○ E 292 Fn 32
Massa ○ I 185 Gm 23
Massabi ○ ANG 341 Hd 51
Massachusets ◈ USA 60 Dm 24
Massachusetts Bay ∼ USA 60 Dn 24
Massaguet ○ TCH 321 Gp 39
Massakori ○ TCH 321 Gp 39
Massalassef ○ TCH 321 Ha 40
Massama ○ WAN 320 Gk 39
Massa Mar ○ I 185 Gm 24
Massangano ○ ANG 340 Gn 50
Massangena ○ MOC 352 Hj 56
Massango ○ ANG 332 Ha 50
Massangulo ○ MOC 344 Hk 52
Massapê ○ BR 124 Ep 47
Massaranduba ○ BR 141 Ek 59
Massarole ○ SP 328 Ja 44
Massassa-Lewémé ○ RCB 332 Gn 47
Massau ○ PNG 333 Ha 49
Mâsselvfossen ∼ N 158 Hb 11
Massenya ○ TCH 321 Ha 40
Masset ○ CDN 42 Da 8
Massey ○ CDN 57 Dg 22
Massey Sound ≈ CDN 42 Fc 3
Massif Central ⚊ F 185 Gj 23
Massif d'Abo ⚊ TCH 309 Gp 34
Massif d'Atafi ⚊ RN 309 Gp 34
Massif de Dahra ⚊ DZ 293 Gg 27
Massif de la Hotte ⚊ RH 101 Dl 36
Massif de la Selle △ RH 101 Dm 36
Massif de L'Aures ⚊ DZ 296 Gj 28
Massif de l'Ouarsenis ⚊ DZ 293 Gg 28
Massif de Taghouaji ⚊ RN 308 Gl 37
Massif de Tchingou △ F 386 Ne 56
Massif de Termit ⚊ RN 308 Gm 37
Massif de Tsaratanana ⚊ RM 345 Jc 52
Massif du Kapka ⚊ TCH 309 Hc 38
Massif du Manengouba △ CAM 320 Gl 43
Massif du Mbam △ CAM 320 Gm 42
Massif du Tamgué ⚊ RG 316 Fp 39
Massif Tabulaire ⚊ F 113 Eh 44
Massigui ○ RMM 305 Gc 40
Massili ∼ BF 317 Gf 39
Massillon ○ USA 71 Dh 25
Massina ○ RMM 317 Gd 39
Massinga ○ MOC 344 Hk 53
Massingir ○ MOC 352 Hh 57
Massosse ○ ANG 340 Ha 53
Maštaga ○ AZ 202 Jd 25
Masterton ○ NZ 383 Nk 66
Mastûj ∼ PK 223 Jp 28
Mastûra ○ KSA 214 Hm 34
Masty ○ BY 171 He 19
Masuda ○ J 247 Mb 28
Masuguru ○ EAT 344 Hm 51
Mâsur ○ IR 209 Jc 29
Masvingo ∼ ZW 352 Hh 56
Masyâf ○ SYR 208 Hl 28
Mata Bia △ TP 282 Lp 50
Matabungkay ○ RP 267 Ll 39
Mataca ○ MOC 344 Hl 52
Matacawa Levu ⏹ FIJI 387 Nl 54
Matachewan ○ CDN 57 Dh 22
Matachic ○ MEX 80 Cj 31
Matacú ○ BOL 129 Ed 54
Mata d. São João ○ BR 125 Fa 52
Matadi ○ RDC 332 Gn 48
Matador ○ USA 70 Cm 29
Matagalpa ○ NIC 97 Df 39
Matagami ○ CDN 60 Dh 21
Matagorda Bay ∼ USA 81 Da 31

Matagorda Peninsula ⏹ USA 81 Cp 31
Mataiva ⏹ F 35 Ba 11
Matakali ○ RI 279 Lk 47
Matakana Island ⏹ NZ 383 Nl 64
Matakaoa Point ◠ NZ 383 Nm 64
Matakawau ○ NZ 383 Nm 64
Matala ○ GR 194 He 28
Matala ○ IND 238 Kc 37
Matala ○ ANG 340 Gp 53
Matalan Point ◠ RP 275 Lm 42
Matale ○ CL 239 Ke 42
Matale ○ RDC 336 Hg 47
Matali ○ GUY 113 Ee 43
Matam ○ SN 304 Fp 38
Mata Mata ○ ZA 348 Hc 58
Matamey ○ RN 320 Gl 39
Matamoros ○ MEX 92 Cm 35
Matamoros ○ MEX 81 Cn 33
Ma'tan ○ LAR 300 Hd 34
Ma'tan as Sarah ○ LAR 309 Hc 35
Matanda ∼ Z 341 Hg 51
Matandu ∼ EAT 337 Hm 50
Matane ○ CDN 60 Ea 21
Matanga ○ RI 282 Lm 46
Matankari ○ RN 308 Gk 39
Matano ∼ RI 282 Ll 47
Matansa ○ C 100 Dh 34
Matanzas ○ C 100 Dh 34
Matanzas ∼ YV 112 Ec 41
Matão ○ BR 141 Ek 56
Matajojo ○ ROU 146 Ef 61
Matapedia ○ CDN 60 Ea 22
Matapedia ∼ CDN 61 Ea 21
Matapi ○ BR 121 Ej 45
Matapuri ○ NZ 383 Nk 63
Mataquito ∼ RCH 137 Dm 63
Matará ○ PE 116 Dj 49
Mataram ○ RA 136 Ec 60
Matara ○ CL 239 Ke 43
Matara ○ ER 313 Hm 38
Mataraca ∼ BR 124 Fc 49
Mataram ○ RI 279 Lh 50
Mataranka ○ AUS 364 Mc 53
Mataró ○ E 184 Gh 25
Mataso ⏹ VU 386 Ng 54
Matata ○ RDC 336 Hf 47
Matatiele ∼ ZA 349 Hg 61
Matatindoe Point ◠ RP 266 Lj 41
Mataurá ∼ BR 120 Ed 48
Matausu ∼ RI 282 Ll 48
Matawai ∼ NZ 383 Nl 65
Matawin ∼ CDN 60 Dm 22
Matchai ○ ANG 340 Hc 51
Mateev Kurgan ○ RUS 181 Hm 22
Mategua ○ BOL 129 Ec 52
Matehuala ○ MEX 92 Cm 34
Mateiros ○ BR 133 El 51
Matekwe ○ EAT 344 Hm 51
Matelot ○ TT 104 Ed 40
Matema ○ EAT 337 Hk 50
Matema ○ MOC 344 Hj 53
Matenge ○ MOC 344 Hj 53
Matete ○ RDC 324 Hg 45
Matetsi ○ ZW 341 Hf 55
Matetsi ∼ ZW 341 Hf 55
Mateur ○ TN 296 Gl 27
Mátézalka ○ H 175 Hd 22
Matha ○ F 184 Gf 23
Matheson ○ CDN 57 Dh 21
Mathis ○ USA 81 Cp 31
Mathiston ○ USA 86 Dd 29
Mathoura ○ AUS 379 Mj 63
Mathura ○ IND 234 Kc 32
Mati ○ RP 275 Lp 41
Matia ∼ EAK 337 Hm 46
Matiakoali ○ BF 317 Gg 39
Matiali ○ IND 235 Kj 32
Matias Cordoso ○ BR 125 En 53
Matias Olimpio ○ BR 124 En 47
Matías Romero ○ MEX 93 Da 37
Matibane ○ MOC 344 Hn 53
Maticora ∼ YV 107 Dn 40
Matiguás ○ NIC 97 Df 39
Matilde ○ RA 137 Ed 61
Matilla ○ RCH 136 Dp 56
Matima ○ RB 349 He 56
Matinenda Lake ∼ CDN 57 Dg 22
Matinha ○ BR 141 Ek 58
Mâtli ○ PK 227 Jn 33
Matnog ○ RP 267 Lm 39
Mato ○ BR 124 Em 48
Mato Grosso ◉ BR 132 Ee 52
Mato Grosso ○ BR 132 Ef 53
Mato Grosso do Sul ◉ BR 132 Ef 55
Mato Grosso Plateau ◅ BR 132 Eg 53
Matola ○ MOC 352 Hj 58
Matondo ○ ZW 349 Hg 56
Matong Mountains ⚊ SUD 324 Hj 43
Matope ○ MW 344 Hk 53
Matopo ○ ZW 349 Hg 56
Matos ∼ BOL 129 Eb 53
Mato Verde ○ BR 125 En 53
Mátra ⚊ H 174 Hb 22
Matrah ○ OM 226 Jh 34
Matrouha ○ TN 296 Gm 29
Matru ○ WAL 316 Fp 42
Matsari ○ CAM 320 Gn 40
Matsiatra ∼ RM 353 Ja 56
Matsiloje ○ RB 349 Hf 56
Matsue ○ J 251 Mc 28
Matsuka Achouka ○ G 332 Gl 46
Matsu Liehtao ⏹ RC 259 Ll 32
Matsumoto ○ J 251 Me 27
Matsu Temple ★ RC 259 Ll 34
Matsuyama ○ J 251 Mc 29
Matsuzaka ○ J 251 Me 28
Mattagami ∼ CDN 57 Dg 20
Mattagami River ∼ CDN 57 Dg 20
Mattamuskeet Lake ∼ USA 74 Dk 28
Mattawa ○ USA 50 Cc 22
Mattawa ○ CDN 60 Dj 22
Mattawamkeag ○ USA 60 Dp 23
Mattawitchewan River ∼ CDN 57 Dg 21

Matterhorn △ USA 64 Ce 25
Matterhorn △ CH 163 Gk 22
Matthews ○ USA 71 Dh 28
Matthews Range △ EAK 325 Hl 45
Matthews Ridge ○ GUY 112 Ed 42
Matthew Town ○ BS 101 Dl 35
Mattice ○ CDN 57 Dg 21
Mattili ○ IND 234 Kf 36
Mattô ○ J 251 Me 27
Mattoon ○ USA 71 Dd 26
Matucana ○ PE 116 Dk 51
Matugama ○ CL 239 Ke 42
Matukar ○ PNG 287 Mj 48
Matuku ⏹ FIJI 387 Nm 55
Matundu ○ RDC 324 Hd 43
Matupi ○ MYA 235 Kl 35
Matupi ○ MYA 235 Kl 35
Matuquinha ○ RDC 324 Hd 43
Ma'tuq ○ SUD 312 Hj 38
Maturín ○ YV 112 Ec 41
Matusadona ♀ ZW 341 Hg 54
Matveevka ○ RUS 181 Jc 18
Maty-Centre ○ RCB 332 Gp 47
Mau ∼ IND 234 Ke 33
Mau ○ IND 235 Kf 32
Maúa ○ BR 141 El 57
Maua ○ EAK 325 Hl 45
Maúa ○ MOC 344 Hl 52
Mauban ○ RP 267 Ll 38
Mauberge ○ F 163 Gh 20
Ma-u-bin ○ MYA 262 Kn 37
Maubisse ○ TP 282 Ln 50
Maud ○ USA 70 Da 29
Maude ○ AUS 379 Mj 63
Maué ○ ANG 340 Hb 54
Maués ○ BR 120 Ef 47
Maués ∼ BR 120 Ef 47
Maués-Mirim ∼ BR 120 Ef 47
Maugani ○ IND 234 Ke 33
Maugris ○ RIM 304 Fn 36
Maui ⏹ USA 75 Am 35
Mauk ○ RI 278 Ld 49
Maulamyaing ○ MYA 262 Kn 37
Maule ∼ RCH 137 Dm 63
Maullín ○ RCH 147 Dm 66
Maumee ○ USA 71 Df 25
Maumere ○ RI 282 Ln 50
Maun ○ RB 341 Hd 55
Mauna Kea △ USA 75 Am 36
Maunaloa ○ USA 75 Am 35
Mauna Loa △ USA 75 Am 36
Maungmagan Islands ⏹ MYA 262 Kn 38
Maungu ○ EAK 337 Hm 47
Maugaq ○ KSA 214 Hn 32
Mau Ranīpur ○ IND 234 Kd 33
Mauri ∼ BOL 128 Dp 54
Mauriac ○ F 185 Gh 23
Maurine ○ USA 51 Cl 22
Mauritania ◻ RIM 292 Ga 33
Mauritius ◻ MS 353 Jg 55
Mauritius ⏹ MS 353 Jg 55
Maury Mountains ⚊ USA 50 Cb 24
Mauston ○ USA 56 Dc 24
Maute ⌂ NZ 35 Ba 12
Mauterndorf ○ A 174 Gn 22
Mavelikara ○ IND 239 Kc 41
Mavengue ○ ANG 340 Hb 54
Mavila ○ PE 128 Dp 51
Mavinga ○ ANG 340 Hc 53
Mavita ○ MOC 352 Hj 55
Mavúe ○ MOC 352 Hj 56
Mavuji ∼ EAT 337 Hm 50
Mavunga ∼ ANG 341 Hc 52
Mavuradonha ⚊ ZW 341 Hh 54
Mawa ○ RDC 324 Hf 44
Mawai ○ MAL 271 Lb 45
Mawan ○ PNG 287 Mj 48
Mawanella ○ CL 239 Ke 42
Mawang ○ VRC 255 Le 31
Mawangdui Hanmu ★ VRC 258 Lg 31
Mawasangka ○ RI 282 Lm 48
Mâwat ○ IRQ 209 Ja 28
Mawdin ○ MYA 262 Km 38
Mawefan ○ RI 283 Md 47
Mawhun ○ MYA 254 Km 33
Mawlaik ○ MYA 254 Kn 34
Max ○ USA 56 Cm 22
Maxaas ○ SP 328 Ja 43
Maxcanú ○ MEX 93 Dc 35
Máximo Gómez ○ C 100 Dh 34
Maxixe ○ MOC 352 Hk 57
Maxwelton ○ AUS 374 Mh 56
May- ∼ AUS 361 Ln 54
Mayabander ○ IND 262 Kl 39
Mayaca ∼ YV 112 Eb 45
Mayaguana Island ⏹ BS 87 Dm 34
Mayaguana Passage ≈ 87 Dm 34
Mayagüez ○ USA 104 Ea 36
Mayahi ∼ RN 308 Gk 39
Mayala ○ RDC 333 Ha 49
Mayama ○ RCB 332 Gp 47
Mayamba ○ RDC 333 Ha 48
Maya Mountains ⚊ BH 93 Dd 37
Mayanabo ○ C 101 Dk 35
Mayang ○ VRC 255 Le 32
Mayanja ∼ EAU 324 Hh 45
Mayankwa ∼ Z 341 Hd 53
Mayari ○ C 101 Dl 35
Maybell ○ USA 65 Ch 25
Maych'ew ○ ETH 313 Hn 40
Maycoba ○ MEX 80 Ch 31
May Dara Shet' ∼ ETH 313 Hl 40
Maydena ○ AUS 378 Mk 67
Maydh ○ SP 328 Jb 40
May Downs ○ AUS 375 Ml 57
Mayenne ○ F 163 Gf 21
Mayenne ∼ F 163 Gf 21
Mayer Samou ∼ SN 316 Fp 39
Mayersville ○ USA 70 Da 26
Mayfair ○ CDN 51 Cj 19
Mayfield ○ USA 71 Dd 27
Mayhill ○ USA 65 Ck 29
May-Jirgui ∼ RN 308 Gl 39
Maykop ○ RUS 202 Hn 23
Maymont ○ CDN 51 Cj 19
Maymyo ○ MYA 254 Kn 34
Maynas ◅ PE 116 Dk 47
Mayne ∼ AUS 374 Mg 57
Mayneside ○ AUS 374 Mh 57
Mâyni ○ IND 238 Kb 37
Mayo ∼ MEX 80 Ch 32
Mayo ○ USA 86 Dg 30
Mayo ∼ PE 116 Dk 49
Mayo ∼ RA 152 Dn 68
Mayo ○ RA 152 Dn 68
Mayo Bay ∼ RP 275 Lp 42

Mayo Betwa O **WAN** 320 Gn 41
Mayo Butale O **WAN** 320 Gm 42
Mayo Darlé O **CAM** 320 Gm 42
Mayo Déo O **CAM** 321 Gn 42
Mayo Djoi O **CAM** 321 Gp 41
Mayo Godi O **CAM** 321 Gp 41
Mayo Kebbi O **TCH** 321 Gn 41
Mayo Kébi O **CAM** 321 Gn 41
Mayoko O **RCB** 332 Gn 47
Mayo Lidi O **CAM** 321 Gp 41
Mayo Louti O **CAM** 321 Gp 41
Mayombé O **G** 332 Gm 47
Mayon Vulcano △ **RP** 267 Lm 39
Mayor Buratovich O **RA** 147 Ec 65
Mayor Rey O **CAM** 321 Gp 41
Mayor Island ⏷ **NZ** 383 Nl 64
Mayor Otano O **PY** 140 Eg 59
Mayor Pablo Lagerenza O **PY** 129 Ed 55
Mayo Selbe O **WAN** 320 Gm 41
Mayo Tiel O **CAM** 321 Gm 41
Mayotte ⏷ **F** 345 Ja 52
May Pen O **JA** 101 Dk 37
Mayrara Point O **RP** 267 Ll 36
May River O **PNG** 286 Mg 48
Maysville O **USA** 71 Dg 26
Maytiguid Island ⏷ **RP** 267 Lk 40
Mayu ∼ **RI** 286 Mf 49
Mayumba O **G** 332 Gm 47
Mayumba ◁ **RDC** 336 Hg 49
Mayum La △ **VRC** 230 Kf 30
Mâyûm ◉ **IND** 235 Kd 40
Mayville O **USA** 56 Cp 22
Maywood O **USA** 70 Cm 25
Maza O **RA** 137 Ec 64
Mazabuka O **Z** 341 Hf 53
Mazagão O **BR** 121 Ej 46
Mazagão Velho O **BR** 121 Ej 46
Mazama O **USA** 50 Cb 21
Mazamari O **PE** 128 Dl 51
Mazan O **PE** 116 Dm 47
Mazandarān ◉ **IR** 222 Jd 27
Mazao O **RDC** 341 Hd 50
Mazar O **VRC** 230 Kc 27
Mazara d. Vallo O **I** 185 Gn 27
Mazâr-e Adschaeb ★ **AFG** 223 Jm 27
Mazarredo O **RA** 152 Ea 69
Mazarron O **E** 184 Gf 27
Mazar Tag △ **VRC** 230 Kd 26
Mazaruni ∼ **GUY** 112 Ea 43
Mazarwala O **VRC** 230 Kc 27
Mazatán O **MEX** 80 Cf 32
Mazatán O **MEX** 93 Db 38
Mazatenango O **GCA** 93 Dc 38
Mazatlán O **MEX** 92 Cf 34
Mazatzal Mountains ◿◿ **USA** 65 Cg 28
Mazcalapa ∼ **MEX** 93 Db 38
Mazeikiai O **LT** 170 Hd 17
Mazela O **CI** 304 Gc 40
Mazimechopes ∼ **MOC** 352 Hj 58
Mazingo O **G** 332 Gn 45
Mazocahui O **MEX** 80 Cg 31
Mazoco O **MOC** 344 Hk 51
Mazo-Cruz O **PE** 128 Dp 54
Mazoe ∼ **MOC** 344 Hj 54
Mazomora O **EAT** 337 Hm 49
Mazoula O **DZ** 296 Gk 31
Mazowe O **ZW** 341 Hh 54
Mazowe O **ZW** 341 Hh 54
Mazra'eh Akhund O **IR** 215 Je 30
Mazrûb O **SUD** 312 Hg 39
Mazunga O **ZW** 349 Hg 56
Mazur Miao ★ **VRC** 258 Lk 33
Mazyr O **BY** 171 Hg 19
Mazzamitla O **MEX** 92 Cl 34
Mba O **CAM** 320 Gn 42
Mbabala Island ⏷ **Z** 341 Hg 51
Mbabane ◙ **SD** 352 Hh 59
Mbacha O **WAN** 320 Gl 42
Mbadi O **G** 332 Gm 47
Mbagne O **SN** 304 Fn 37
Mbahiakro O **CI** 317 Gd 42
Mbaïki O **RCA** 333 Hb 44
Mbakana O **RDC** 332 Ha 48
Mbakaou O **CAM** 320 Gn 42
Mbaké O **SN** 304 Fm 38
Mbako O **RCA** 321 Gp 43
Mbala O **Z** 336 Hh 50
Mbalabala O **ZW** 349 Hg 56
Mbalageti ∼ **EAT** 337 Hk 47
Mbalam O **CAM** 321 Gn 44
Mbalambala O **EAK** 337 Hm 46
Mbale O **EAU** 325 Hk 45
Mbali O **RCA** 321 Ha 42
Mbali ∼ **RCA** 321 Hd 42
Mbali-Iboma O **RDC** 333 Ha 47
Mbalmayo O **CAM** 320 Gm 44
Mbalo O **SOL** 290 Nc 50
Mbam ∼ **CAM** 320 Gm 43
Mbama O **CAM** 320 Gn 43
Mbama O **RCB** 332 Gp 46
Mbamba Bay O **EAT** 344 Hk 51
Mbambanakira O **SOL** 290 Nb 50
Mbandaka O **RDC** 333 Ha 45
Mbandjok O **CAM** 320 Gm 43
Mbandza O **RCB** 332 Gp 45
Mbane O **SN** 304 Fn 37
Mbang O **CAM** 321 Gp 44
Mbanga O **SOL** 290 Na 50
Mbanga O **CAM** 320 Gl 43
Mbangala ∼ **EAT** 344 Hm 51
Mbanika Island ⏷ **SOL** 290 Nb 50
M'banza Congo O **ANG** 332 Gp 49
Mbanza-Ngungu O **RDC** 332 Gp 48
Mbar O **SN** 304 Fm 38
Mbarakoma O **SOL** 290 Na 50
Mbarangandu ∼ **EAT** 344 Hl 51
Mbarara O **EAU** 336 Hk 46
Mbaraugandu ∼ **EAT** 344 Hl 51
Mbari ∼ **RCA** 321 Hd 43
Mbata O **RCA** 333 Hb 44
Mbati O **Z** 341 Hh 51
Mbatuna O **SOL** 290 Nb 50
Mbava ∼ **SOL** 290 Na 49
Mbazwana O **ZA** 352 Hk 58
Mbé O **CAM** 321 Gn 42
Mbé O **G** 332 Gm 45
Mbé O **RCB** 332 Gn 46
Mbéloba O **RCA** 321 Hc 43
Mbemkuru ∼ **EAT** 337 Hm 50

Mbengue O **CI** 317 Gd 41
Mbengwi O **CAM** 320 Gl 42
M'Beni O **COM** 345 Hp 51
Mbéré ∼ **CAM** 321 Gp 42
Mberengwa O **ZW** 349 Hg 56
Mbéwé O **CAM** 321 Gn 43
Mbeya O **EAT** 337 Hj 50
Mbeya O **Z** 344 Hj 51
Mbi ∼ **RCA** 321 Ha 43
Mbiama O **WAN** 320 Gk 43
Mbigou O **G** 332 Gm 46
Mbinda O **RCB** 332 Gn 47
Mbini O **GQ** 332 Gl 45
Mbita O **CAM** 321 Gp 42
Mbitao O **CAM** 321 Gm 43
Mbiyi O **ZW** 352 Hh 56
Mbizi O **ZW** 352 Hh 56
Mbo O **RCA** 321 Ha 41
Mbobo O **MW** 344 Hk 52
Mboké O **CAM** 320 Gn 43
Mboko O **RDC** 336 Hg 47
Mbokonumbeta Island ⏷ **SOL** 290 Nb 50
Mbokou ∼ **RCA** 324 Hf 43
Mbomo O **RCB** 332 Gp 45
Mbomou ∼ **RCA** 324 Hd 43
Mbomou ∼ **RCA** 324 Hf 43
Mbon O **RCB** 332 Gp 47
Mboné O **RG** 316 Ga 40
Mbonge O **CAM** 320 Gl 43
Mbopo O **SOL** 290 Na 50
Mborokua ⏷ **SOL** 290 Nb 50
Mboroma O **Z** 341 Hg 53
Mborong O **RI** 282 Ll 50
Mbot O **CAM** 320 Gn 42
Mbouda O **CAM** 320 Gm 43
Mboula O **CAM** 321 Gn 42
Mbouma O **CAM** 321 Gn 44
Mboune O **SN** 304 Fp 38
Mbour O **SN** 304 Fm 38
Mbout O **RIM** 304 Fp 37
Mboutou ∼ **RCA** 324 He 42
Mbozi O **EAT** 337 Hj 50
Mbrés O **RCA** 321 Hb 42
Mbu ∼ **CAM** 321 Gn 43
Mbudi O **RDC** 332 Ha 48
Mbugwe O **EAT** 337 Hk 47
Mbuji-Mayi O **RDC** 333 Hd 49
Mbuji-Mayi ◉ **RDC** 333 Hd 49
Mbuke Islands ⏷ **PNG** 287 Mk 47
Mbulo Island ⏷ **SOL** 290 Nb 50
Mbulu O **EAT** 337 Hk 47
Mbuma O **SOL** 290 Nc 50
Mburucuyá O **RA** 146 Ee 60
Mbuyuni O **EAT** 337 Hl 48
Mbuzi O **Z** 344 Hj 52
Mbwamaji O **EAT** 337 Hm 49
Mc. Arthur ∼ **CAM** 320 Gn 43
McAdam N.P. ★ **PNG** 287 Mk 49
Mc Alester O **USA** 70 Dd 28
Mcallen O **USA** 81 Cn 32
McArthur O **USA** 71 Dg 26
McBride O **CDN** 50 Cb 19
McCall O **USA** 50 Cd 23
McCamey O **USA** 81 Cl 30
McCammon O **USA** 51 Cf 24
McCandless O **USA** 71 Dh 25
McCarthy O **USA** 46 Be 15
McClintock Channel ∼ **CDN** 42 Fa 4
McClintock Range ◿◿ **AUS** 361 Lp 55
Mc Clintock Channel ∼ **CDN** 6 Db 2
McCluer Island ⏷ **AUS** 364 Mc 51
Mc Clure Strait ∼ **CDN** 6 Cb 2
Mc Clusky O **USA** 56 Cm 22
McComb O **USA** 86 Dc 30
McConnelsburg O **USA** 74 Dj 26
McCook O **USA** 70 Cm 25
McCormick O **USA** 71 Dg 29
McCreary O **CDN** 56 Cn 20
McDermitt O **USA** 64 Cd 25
McDonough O **USA** 86 Dd 29
McDouall Peak O **AUS** 374 Md 60
McDougall Mills O **CDN** 56 Dc 20
McDougall's Bay O **ZA** 348 Ha 60
Mc Dougall Sound ∼ **CDN** 7 Ea 2
McDowell Lake ∼ **CDN** 56 Db 19
McCensk O **RUS** 181 Hl 19
McFarland O **USA** 64 Cc 28
McGehee O **USA** 86 Dc 29
McGill O **USA** 64 Ce 26
Mc Grath O **USA** 6 Ba 3
McGrath O **USA** 46 Al 13
McGregor O **USA** 51 Cl 21
McGregor O **USA** 56 Db 22
Mc Gregor O **USA** 81 Cp 30
McHenry O **AUS** 365 Mh 51
McHenry River ∼ **AUS** 365 Mh 51
Mcherrah O **DZ** 293 Gd 32
Mchinga O **EAT** 337 Hm 50
Mchinji O **MW** 344 Hj 52
M'Chouneche O **DZ** 296 Gk 28
McIlwraith Range ◿◿ **AUS** 365 Mh 52
Mc Innes Lake ∼ **CDN** 56 Db 19
McIntosh O **USA** 56 Cm 23
Mcintyre Bay ∼ **CDN** 57 Dd 21
McKay Lake ∼ **CDN** 57 De 21
McKay Range ◿◿ **AUS** 360 Lm 57
Mc Kean ⏷ **KIR** 35 Aa 10
McKenzie O **USA** 71 Dd 27
McKenzie Bridge O **USA** 50 Ca 23
McKinlay O **AUS** 374 Mg 56
McKinleyville O **USA** 64 Bg 25
Mc Kinney O **USA** 70 Cp 29
McKinney Mountain △ **USA** 81 Cl 31
McKittrick O **USA** 64 Cc 28
McLaren Creek O **AUS** 361 Mc 56
McLaren Vale O **AUS** 378 Me 63
McLaughlin O **USA** 56 Cm 23
McLean O **USA** 70 Cm 28
Mc Leansboro O **USA** 71 Dd 26
McLeese Lake O **CDN** 50 Cb 19
McLeod Bay ∼ **CDN** 42 Eb 6
M'Clure Strait ∼ **CDN** 6 Cb 2
McMasterville O **CDN** 60 Dm 23
McMinnville O **USA** 50 Ca 23
McMinnville O **USA** 71 De 28
McPhee Res. ∼ **USA** 65 Ch 27
McPherson O **USA** 70 Cn 26
McPherson △ **AUS** 375 Mn 60

McPhersons Pillar △ **AUS** 369 Ln 58
McRae O **USA** 71 Dg 29
McTavish Arm ∼ **CDN** 47 Cc 13
McVicar Arm ∼ **CDN** 47 Ca 13
Mdandu O **EAT** 337 Hk 50
Mdantsane O **ZA** 358 Hf 62
M'Doukal O **DZ** 296 Gj 28
M' Drac ∼ **VN** 263 Le 39
Meacham O **CDN** 51 Ck 19
Mead O **CDN** 57 Dg 21
Meade O **USA** 70 Cm 27
Meade Peak △ **USA** 65 Cg 24
Meade River O **USA** 46 Al 9
Meadji O **CI** 305 Gc 43
Meadow O **USA** 65 Cl 29
Meadowbank O **AUS** 365 Mj 55
Meadow Creek O **CDN** 50 Cd 20
Meadow Lake O **CDN** 42 Ec 8
Meadow Valley Wash ∼ **USA** 64 Ce 27
Meadville O **USA** 71 Dh 25
Meadville O **USA** 86 Dc 30
Mealy Mountains ◿◿ **CDN** 43 Ja 8
Meana O **TM** 222 Jj 27
Meander River O **CDN** 47 Cc 15
Mearim ∼ **BR** 121 El 49
Mearim ∼ **BR** 121 Em 47
Mearim ∼ **BR** 121 Em 47
Meath Peak O **CDN** 51 Ck 19
Meaux O **F** 163 Gh 21
Mebridege ∼ **ANG** 332 Gn 49
Mecanhelas O **MOC** 344 Hk 53
Mecaya ∼ **CO** 116 Dl 45
Mecca O **USA** 64 Cd 29
Mecca O **KSA** 218 Hm 35
Mecequesse ∼ **MOC** 344 Hl 53
Mechang O **MAL** 270 La 43
Mechâra O **ETH** 325 Hn 41
Mechelen O **B** 163 Gj 20
Mecheria O **DZ** 293 Gf 29
Mechigmenskiy Zaliv ∼ **RUS** 46 Ac 13
Mechra Bel-Ksiri O **MA** 293 Gd 28
Mechroha O **DZ** 296 Gk 27
Mecitözü O **TR** 195 Hk 25
Meckenburger Bucht ∼ **D** 170 Gm 18
Mecklenburg-Vorpommern ◉ **D** 170 Gm 19
Meconta O **MOC** 344 Hm 53
Mecubúri O **MOC** 344 Hm 53
Mecubûri ∼ **MOC** 344 Hm 53
Mecúfi O **MOC** 344 Hn 52
Mecula O **MOC** 344 Hl 52
Medak O **IND** 234 Kc 35
Medan O **RI** 270 Kp 44
Medart O **USA** 86 Df 30
Medawachchiya O **CL** 239 Ke 41
Medd Allah O **RIM** 305 Gd 38
Médéa O **DZ** 296 Gh 27
Medeiros O **BR** 133 El 55
Medellín O **CO** 106 Dk 42
Medelpad ∼ **S** 158 Gp 14
Méderdra O **RIM** 304 Fn 37
Medford O **USA** 50 Ca 24
Medford O **USA** 56 Dc 23
Medgidia O **RO** 175 Hg 23
Medi O **SUD** 324 Hh 43
Media Luna O **RA** 137 Ea 63
Medianeira O **BR** 140 Eg 58
Mediaş O **RO** 175 He 22
Medicilândia O **BR** 121 Eh 47
Medicine Bow O **USA** 65 Cj 25
Medicine Bow Mountains ◿◿ **USA** 65 Cj 25
Medicine Bow Peak △ **USA** 65 Cj 25
Medicine Hat O **CDN** 51 Cg 20
Medicine Lake ∼ **USA** 51 Ck 21
Medicine Lodge O **USA** 70 Cn 27
Medicine Lodge ∼ **USA** 70 Cn 27
Medina O **USA** 71 Dg 25
Medina ∼ **USA** 81 Cn 31
Medina O **BR** 125 Ep 54
Medina O **KSA** 214 Hm 33
Medina del Campo O **E** 184 Gd 25
Medina del Ríoseco O **E** 184 Gd 25
Médina Gounas O **SN** 316 Fp 39
Médina-Sidonia O **E** 184 Gd 27
Médina-Yorofoula O **SN** 316 Fn 39
Medinîpur O **IND** 235 Kh 34
Mediouna O **MA** 293 Gc 29
Mediterranean Sea ∼ **∼** 184 Gg 27
Médoc ⌒ **F** 184 Gf 23
Médok O **VRC** 254 Km 31
Médok ★ **VRC** 254 Km 31
Medora O **USA** 51 Cl 22
Medrissa O **DZ** 293 Gg 28
Medvedica ∼ **RUS** 181 Hp 20
Medvež'egorsk O **RUS** 159 Hk 14
Medvež'i o-va ⏷ **RUS** 205 Yc 4
Medvežka O **RUS** 205 Yc 5
Medyn' O **RUS** 171 Hk 18
Medyn O **RUS** 171 Hk 18
Meekatharra O **AUS** 368 Lk 59
Meeker O **USA** 65 Ch 26
Meeladeen O **SP** 328 Jc 40
Meeline O **AUS** 368 Lj 60
Meelpaeg Lake ∼ **CDN** 61 Ef 21
Meerut O **IND** 234 Kc 31
Meerzorg O **SME** 113 Eg 43
Meeteetse O **USA** 51 Ch 23
Mega O **RI** 283 Mb 46
Mêga O **ETH** 325 Hm 43
Mêga Escarpment ⌒ **ETH** 325 Hl 43
Megalo O **ETH** 325 Hn 41
Megalópoli O **GR** 194 Hc 27
Megama O **MOC** 344 Hm 52
Megamo O **RI** 283 Mb 46
Megaruma ∼ **MOC** 344 Hm 53
Megeitia O **SUD** 312 Hh 38
Megéve O **F** 185 Gk 23
Megezez △ **ETH** 325 Hm 41
Meghalaya ◉ **IND** 235 Kk 33
Meghna ∼ **BD** 235 Kk 34
Mégiscane ∼ **CDN** 60 Dk 21
Mégiste ⏷ **TR** 195 Hj 27
Megri O **ARM** 202 Jb 26
Meguidene O **DZ** 293 Gg 31
Mehakit O **RI** 279 Lj 47
Mehāl Mêda O **ETH** 313 Hm 40
Mehamn O **N** 159 Hf 10
Méhana O **RN** 305 Gg 38

Mehar O **PK** 227 Jm 32
Mehdia O **DZ** 293 Gg 28
Mehekar O **IND** 234 Kc 35
Meherpur O **BD** 235 Kj 34
Mehmani O **IR** 226 Jg 32
Mehrâbpur O **PK** 227 Jm 31
Mehrân O **IR** 209 Jb 29
Mehrân ∼ **IR** 215 Je 32
Mehrân O **IR** 226 Jf 32
Mehrgarh ★ **PK** 227 Jm 31
Mehtarlâm O **AFG** 223 Jp 28
Meia Meia O **EAT** 337 Hk 48
Meia Ponte ∼ **BR** 133 Ek 54
Meia Ponte ∼ **BR** 133 Ek 55
Meibod O **IR** 222 Je 29
Meidânšahr O **AFG** 223 Jn 28
Meidougou O **CAM** 321 Gp 42
Meiganga O **CAM** 321 Gp 42
Meighen Island ⏷ **CDN** 42 Fa 2
Meigu O **VRC** 255 Lb 31
Meiktila O **MYA** 254 Kn 35
Meili Xue Shan △ **VRC** 254 Kp 31
Meimand O **IR** 215 Jd 30
Meime O **IR** 222 Je 29
Meiningen O **D** 174 Gl 20
Meinmagwe ∼ **MYA** 254 Kl 36
Meio ∼ **BR** 121 Ej 48
Meio ∼ **BR** 124 Fb 49
Meio ∼ **BR** 125 Fa 54
Meio ∼ **BR** 133 Em 52
Meiringen O **CH** 174 Gj 22
Meishan O **VRC** 242 Lb 30
Meißen O **D** 174 Gn 20
Meitan O **VRC** 255 Ld 32
Mei Xian O **VRC** 243 Ld 28
Meizhou O **VRC** 258 Lj 33
Meizhou Dao ⏷ **VRC** 258 Lk 33
Mejia O **PE** 128 Dn 54
Mejillones O **RCH** 136 Dn 57
Mejnypil'gyno O **RUS** 23 Tb 3
Mejnypil'gyno O **RUS** 205 Zc 6
Meka O **AUS** 368 Lj 59
Mékambo O **G** 332 Gp 45
Mekane Selam O **ETH** 313 Hm 40
Mek'elê O **ETH** 313 Hm 39
Mékhé O **SN** 304 Fm 38
Meki O **ETH** 325 Hm 41
Mékié ∼ **CAM** 320 Gn 43
Me-kin O **MYA** 254 Kp 35
Mekmene Ben Amar O **DZ** 293 Gf 29
Mekomo O **CAM** 320 Gm 44
Mekong ∼ **VRC** 242 Km 29
Mekong ∼ **VRC** 254 Kp 32
Mekong ∼ **VRC** 254 Kp 32
Mekong ∼ **VRC** 254 Kp 32
Mekong ∼ **LAO** 254 La 36
Mekong ∼ **LAO** 254 La 36
Mekong ∼ **LAO** 254 La 36
Mekong ∼ **CAM** 255 Lc 36
Mekong ∼ **THA** 263 Lc 38
Mekong ∼ **K** 263 Lc 39
Mekoryuk O **USA** 23 Ab 3
Mekoryuk O **USA** 46 Ag 15
Mékrou ∼ **DY** 317 Gg 40
Melado ∼ **RCH** 137 Dn 63
Melak O **RI** 279 Lh 46
Melaka O **MAL** 270 Lb 44
Melaka ◉ **MAL** 271 Lb 44
Melanesia Basin ♥ **∼** 27 Ta 9
Melaque O **MEX** 92 Ck 34
Melati O **RI** 278 Lf 49
Melati ∼ **MOC** 352 Hj 57
Melbourne O **USA** 70 Dc 27
Melbourne O **USA** 87 Dh 31
Melbourne O **AUS** 379 Mj 64
Melbourne Island ⏷ **CDN** 47 Cj 11
Melchett Lake ∼ **CDN** 57 De 20
Melchor de Mencos O **GCA** 93 Dd 37
Meldrum Bay ∼ **CDN** 57 Dg 23
Melé O **RCA** 321 Hc 41
Mele Bay ∼ **VU** 386 Nf 54
Meleck O **RUS** 204 Ua 7
Melela O **MOC** 344 Hl 53
Melenki O **RUS** 181 Hn 18
Melet Irm ∼ **TR** 195 Hl 25
Melfi O **TCH** 321 Ha 40
Mélfi O **I** 185 Gp 25
Melfort O **CDN** 51 Ck 19
Melgaco O **BR** 121 Ej 46
Melhus O **N** 158 Gm 14
Melili ◉ **EAK** 337 Hk 46
Melilla O **E** 293 Ge 28
Melinca O **RCH** 147 Dm 67
Melincué O **RA** 137 Ec 62
Melipeuco O **RCH** 147 Dn 65
Melipilla O **RCH** 137 Dn 62
Melita O **CDN** 56 Cm 21
Melita ∼ **RCH** 137 Dn 63
Melito di Porto Salvo O **I** 194 Gp 27
Melitopol' O **UA** 175 Hk 22
Melka Deka O **ETH** 328 Hp 42
Melka Guba O **ETH** 325 Hn 43
Melka Meri O **ETH** 325 Hn 43
Melkbosstrand O **ZA** 358 Ha 62
Melkrivier O **ZA** 349 Hg 57
Mella O **C** 101 Dk 35
Mellam O **SUD** 312 He 39
Mellen O **USA** 56 Dc 22
Mellerud O **S** 170 Gn 16
Mellette O **USA** 56 Cn 23
Mellit O **SUD** 312 He 38
Mellizos O **RCH** 136 Dp 57
Mellvville Hills ◿◿ **CDN** 47 Bn 11
Melmoth O **ZA** 352 Hh 60
Mélník O **CZ** 174 Gp 20
Melo O **PY** 140 Ee 56
Melo O **ROU** 146 Eg 62
Melo O **G** 332 Gm 44
Meloco O **MOC** 344 Hm 52
Melolo O **RI** 282 Ll 50
Melozitna River ∼ **USA** 46 An 13
Melrose O **CDN** 61 Ed 23
Melrose O **USA** 65 Cl 28
Melrose O **USA** 368 Ll 59
Melrose O **AUS** 378 Mf 62
Melstone O **USA** 51 Ch 22
Melton ∼ **FIN** 159 He 12
Melton O **AUS** 379 Mj 64
Melũli ∼ **MOC** 344 Hm 53
Melun O **F** 163 Gh 21
Melur O **IND** 239 Kd 40
Melvern Lake ∼ **USA** 70 Da 26

Melville O **CDN** 51 Cl 20
Melville O **USA** 86 Dc 30
Melville Bay ∼ **AUS** 364 Me 52
Melville Bugt ∼ **DK** 43 Hc 3
Melville Island ⏷ **CDN** 6 Da 2
Melville Island ⏷ **CDN** 42 Eb 3
Melville Island ⏷ **AUS** 364 Mb 51
Melville Island Aboriginal Reserve •••
AUS 364 Mb 51
Melville Peninsula ⌒ **CDN** 43 Gb 5
Melville Sound ∼ **CDN** 47 Cg 11
Memala O **RI** 279 Lg 46
Mé Maoya △ **F** 386 Ne 56
Memâri O **IND** 235 Kh 34
Memba O **MOC** 344 Hn 53
Membeca O **BR** 132 Ef 52
Memboro O **RI** 279 Lk 50
Memel O **ZA** 349 Hg 59
Memmingen O **D** 174 Gm 22
Memo O **YV** 107 Ea 41
Mempawah O **RI** 271 Le 45
Memphis O **USA** 70 Cm 28
Memphis O **USA** 70 Db 25
Memphis O **USA** 71 Db 28
Memphis ★ **ET** 301 Hh 31
Mena O **USA** 70 Da 28
Ména O **RMM** 305 Gc 39
Menaa O **DZ** 296 Gj 28
Menabe ∼ **RM** 353 Ja 56
Menaka O **RMM** 308 Gh 38
Mename ∼ **RI** 282 Lc 46
Menanga O **RI** 282 Lo 46
Menangina O **AUS** 368 Ll 60
Menarandra ∼ **RM** 353 Ja 58
Menarbu O **RI** 283 Md 47
Menard O **USA** 81 Cn 30
Menawashei O **SUD** 312 He 39
Menchia O **TN** 296 Gl 29
Mendala △ **RI** 278 Lc 47
Mendebo ◿◿ **ETH** 325 Hm 42
Mendelejevsk O **RUS** 181 Je 18
Mendenhall O **USA** 86 Dc 30
Mendes ∼ **BR** 121 Em 46
Mendes O **DZ** 293 Gg 28
Méndez O **MEX** 81 Cn 33
Méndez O **EC** 116 Dj 47
Mendi O **PNG** 287 Mh 49
Mendi O **ETH** 325 Hk 41
Mendiya-Plage O **MA** 293 Gc 28
Mendocino O **USA** 64 Bp 26
Mendooran O **AUS** 379 Ml 61
Mendopolo O **SUD** 324 Hh 43
Mendota O **USA** 64 Cb 27
Mendota O **USA** 71 Dd 25
Mendoza O **PE** 116 Dk 49
Mendoza O **RA** 137 Dp 62
Mene de Mauroa O **YV** 107 Dn 40
Mene Grande O **YV** 107 Dn 41
Menemen O **TR** 194 Hf 26
Menengai △ **EAK** 337 Hk 46
Menesjärvi O **FIN** 159 He 11
Meng ∼ **CAM** 321 Gn 42
Menga O **ANG** 340 Gp 51
Mengcheng O **VRC** 246 Lj 29
Menggala O **RI** 278 Lc 49
Menggari O **RI** 283 Md 46
Menghai O **VRC** 254 La 35
Mengla ∼ **VRC** 254 La 35
Menglian O **VRC** 254 Kp 34
Menglong O **VRC** 254 La 35
Mengong O **CAM** 320 Gm 44
Meng Shan ◿◿ **VRC** 246 Lj 27
Mengshan O **VRC** 255 Lf 33
Ménguémé O **CAM** 320 Gm 44
Mengwi O **RI** 279 Lh 50
Mengxing O **VRC** 254 La 35
Mengyan O **VRC** 255 Le 32
Mengyin O **VRC** 246 Lj 28
Mengzi O **VRC** 255 Lb 34
Menindee O **AUS** 378 Mh 62
Menindee Lake ∼ **AUS** 378 Mh 62
Meningie O **AUS** 378 Mf 63
Menjalin O **RI** 271 Le 45
Menkerja O **RUS** 204 Wa 5
Menneval O **CDN** 60 Ea 22
Menominee O **USA** 57 De 23
Menominee O **USA** 57 De 23
Menominee Ind. Res. ••• **USA** 57 Dd 23
Menominee Falls O **USA** 57 Dd 24
Menomonie O **USA** 56 Dc 23
Menongue O **ANG** 340 Ha 53
Mentangula O **MOC** 344 Hk 52
Mentawai Islands ⏷ **RI** 270 Kp 46
Mentawai Strait ∼ **RI** 270 Kp 45
Menton O **F** 185 Gk 24
Mentor O **USA** 71 Dh 25
Menyamya Bulolo O **PNG** 287 Mk 49
Menyuan O **VRC** 242 La 27
Menzel Bourguiba O **TN** 296 Gl 27
Menzel Chaker O **TN** 297 Gm 28
Menzelinsk O **RUS** 181 Je 18
Menzel Temime O **TN** 297 Gm 27
Menzies O **AUS** 368 Ll 60
Meob Bay ∼ **NAM** 348 Gp 58
Meoqui O **MEX** 80 Ck 31
Meota O **CDN** 51 Ch 19
Mepala O **ANG** 332 Gn 49
Mepica O **MOC** 344 Hl 53
Meponda O **MOC** 344 Hk 52
Meppen O **D** 170 Gj 19
Mepuse ∼ **MOC** 344 Hk 54
Mera O **EC** 116 Dj 46
Mera O **PNG** 287 Mk 48
Merak O **RI** 278 Lc 48
Merama Hill O **EAU** 336 Hh 46
Mérang O **G** 332 Gl 46
Merangin ∼ **RI** 278 Lb 47
Merano O **I** 174 Gm 22
Merapah O **AUS** 365 Mh 52
Meratswe ∼ **RB** 349 He 57
Merauke O **RI** 286 Mg 50
Merauke ∼ **RI** 286 Mg 50
Mercan Dağları ◿◿ **TR** 195 Hm 26
Mercara O **IND** 239 Kc 39
Mercedes O **USA** 81 Cp 32
Mercedes O **RA** 146 Ee 60
Mercedes O **RA** 146 Ee 63
Mercedes O **ROU** 146 Ef 62
Mercer O **USA** 56 Dc 22
Merchants Bay ∼ **CDN** 43 Hc 5
Mercoya O **RMM** 304 Gb 38

Mercury Islands ⏷ **NZ** 383 Nl 64
Mereb Wenz ∼ **ER** 313 Hm 38
Merecure O **YV** 107 Dp 42
Meredith O **USA** 65 Cj 26
Meredith O **USA** 379 Mj 64
Meredoua O **DZ** 293 Gg 33
Merefa O **UA** 175 Hk 21
Mereksen O **DZ** 296 Gl 31
Mere Lava ⏷ **VU** 386 Ng 53
Merga O **SUD** 312 Hf 36
Mergui O **MYA** 262 Kp 39
Mergui Archipelago ⏷ **MYA** 262 Kn 39
Méri O **TR** 194 Hf 25
Meri O **CAM** 321 Gp 40
Meriç N. Ergene ∼ **TR** 194 Hf 25
Mérida O **MEX** 93 Dd 35
Mérida ◉ **YV** 107 Dn 41
Mérida O **E** 184 Gc 26
Meriden O **USA** 74 Dm 25
Meridian O **USA** 81 Cp 30
Meridian O **USA** 86 Dd 30
Meridja O **DZ** 293 Ge 30
Merikarvia O **FIN** 159 Hc 15
Merimbula O **AUS** 379 Ml 64
Meringur O **AUS** 378 Mg 63
Merino Downs O **AUS** 375 Mj 57
Merivale O **AUS** 375 Ml 58
Merka O **SP** 329 Ja 45
Merkânam O **IND** 238 Kd 39
Merkiné O **LT** 171 He 18
Merluna O **AUS** 365 Mh 52
Mernoo Bank ♥ **∼** 383 Nk 67
Meroe Royal City ★ **SUD** 313 Hj 37
Merolia O **AUS** 368 Lm 60
Meropoh O **MAL** 270 Lb 43
Merouana O **DZ** 296 Gj 28
Merowe O **SUD** 312 Hh 36
Merredin O **AUS** 368 Lj 61
Merriam O **USA** 71 Df 25
Merrill O **USA** 50 Cb 24
Merrill O **USA** 57 Dd 23
Merriman O **USA** 56 Cm 24
Merriman O **ZA** 349 Hd 61
Merritt O **CDN** 50 Cb 20
Merritt Island O **USA** 87 Dh 31
Merritt Reservoir ∼ **USA** 56 Cm 24
Merriwa O **AUS** 379 Mm 62
Mersa Fatma O **ER** 313 Hm 38
Mersa Tek'lay O **ER** 313 Hm 37
Mersey ∼ **AUS** 378 Mk 66
Mersin O **TR** 195 Hk 27
Mersing O **MAL** 271 Lb 44
Merta O **IND** 234 Kb 32
MerthyrTydfil O **GB** 163 Ge 20
Merti O **EAK** 325 Hm 45
Mértola O **P** 184 Gc 27
Merton O **AUS** 379 Mj 63
Mertoutek O **DZ** 308 Gj 33
Mertule Maryam O **ETH** 313 Hm 40
Mertzon O **USA** 81 Cm 30
Meru O **EAK** 325 Hl 45
Meru △ **EAK** 325 Hm 46
Merume Mountains ◿◿ **GUY** 112 Ed 42
Merunga O **ANG** 340 Gp 54
Meruóco O **BR** 124 Ep 47
Merweville O **ZA** 358 Hc 62
Merzifon O **TR** 195 Hk 25
Mesa O **USA** 50 Cc 22
Mesa O **USA** 65 Cg 29
Mesa O **MOC** 344 Hm 52
Mesa de Yambí ∼ **CO** 117 Dn 45
Mesai ∼ **CO** 116 Dm 45
Mesa Verde ⌒ **USA** 65 Ch 27
Mesalo ∼ **MOC** 344 Hm 52
Mescalero O **USA** 65 Ck 29
Mescalero Apache ••• **USA** 65 Ck 29
Meščerskaja nizmennosť ◿◿ **RUS** 171 Hm 18
Meschede O **D** 174 Gl 20
Meschetti O **SP** 325 Hn 45
Mescit Dağları △ **TR** 202 Hn 25
Meseta Baya △ **RA** 147 Dp 65
Meseta de Jaua △ **YV** 112 Eb 43
Meseta de las Vizcachas ⌒ **RA** 152 Dm 71
Meseta del Canquel ⌒ **RA** 152 Dp 68
Meseta del Guengul ⌒ **RA** 152 Dn 68
Meseta de Montemayor ⌒ **RA** 152 Dp 67
Meseta de Zohlaguna ◿◿ **MEX** 93 Dd 36
Meseta el Muerte ⌒ **RA** 152 Dm 70
Meseta el Pedrero ⌒ **RA** 152 Dp 69
Mesĝinšahr O **IR** 209 Jb 26
Mesick O **USA** 57 Dl 23
Meškân O **IR** 222 Jh 27
Mesklip O **ZA** 348 Ha 60
Meslo O **ETH** 325 Hm 42
Mesna ∼ **RUS** 159 Ja 11
Mesopotamia ∼ **RA** 146 Ee 61
Mesopotamia ∼ **SYR** 209 Hn 28
Mesquaie Ind. Settlement ••• **USA** 70 Db 25
Mesquite O **USA** 64 Ce 27
Mesquite O **USA** 70 Cp 29
Messaad O **DZ** 296 Gh 29
Messabi Range ◿◿ **USA** 56 Da 22
Messaména O **CAM** 321 Gn 44
Messeied O **MA** 292 Ga 32
Messelesek O **RI** 282 Lm 46
Messina O **I** 185 Gp 26
Messina O **ZA** 349 Hg 57
Messinge ∼ **MOC** 344 Hk 52
Messiniakós Kólpós ∼ **GR** 194 Hc 27
Messondo O **CAM** 320 Gm 44
Mestghanem O **DZ** 293 Gf 28
Mestia O **GE** 202 Hp 24
Meşudiye O **TR** 195 Hl 25
Mesuji ∼ **RI** 278 Lc 48
Meta ∼ **CO** 107 Dm 43
Meta ∼ **RA** 146 Ee 63
Meta ∼ **YV** 107 Ea 42
Metagama O **CDN** 57 Dg 22
Meta Incognita Peninsula ⌒ **CDN** 43 Ha 6
Metairie O **USA** 86 Dc 31

Meta Lake ～ **CDN** 57 De 20	Middelpos ○ **ZA** 358 Hc 61	Mileura ○ **AUS** 368 Lj 59	Mineral Wells ○ **USA** 70 Cn 29	Mirimire ○ **YV** 107 Dp 40
Metaline Falls ○ **USA** 50 Cd 21	Middelwit ○ **ZA** 349 Hf 58	Milé Wenz ～ **ETH** 313 Hn 40	Minersville ○ **USA** 64 Cf 26	Mirim Lagoon ～ **BR** 146 Eh 62
Metán ○ **RA** 136 Eb 58	Middle Akali Lake ～ **USA** 64 Cc 25	Milford ○ **USA** 60 Dm 24	Minfeng ○ **VRC** 230 Kf 27	Mírina ○ **GR** 194 He 26
Metanca ○ **MOC** 344 Hl 53	Middle America Trench ▽ 93 Da 39	Milford ○ **USA** 64 Cf 26	Minga ○ **RDC** 341 Hf 51	Miriñay ～ **RA** 146 Ef 60
Metapán ○ **ES** 93 Dc 38	Middle Andaman ⌂ **IND** 262 Kl 39	Milford ○ **USA** 74 Di 25	Minga ○ **Z** 341 Hh 53	Miringoni ○ **COM** 345 Np 52
Metaponto ○ **I** 194 Ha 25	Middlecamp ○ **AUS** 378 Mg 62	Milford ○ **USA** 74 Dl 26	Mingàçevir ○ **AZ** 202 Jb 25	Mirinzal ○ **BR** 121 Em 47
Metchum ～ **CAM** 320 Gl 42	Middlebury ○ **NL** 163 Gh 20	Milford Lake ～ **USA** 70 Cp 26	Mingàçevir Reservoir ～ **AZ** 202 Jb 25	Miriscal Estigarribia ○ **PY** 136 Ed 57
Metema ○ **ETH** 313 Hl 39	Middlebury ○ **USA** 60 Dm 23	Milford Sound ○ **NZ** 382 Nf 68		Miritiparaná ～ **CO** 117 Dn 46
Metengobalame ～ **MOC** 344 Hj 53	Middlecamp ○ **AUS** 378 Mg 62	Milford Sound ～ **NZ** 382 Nf 68	Mingala ○ **RCA** 321 Hc 43	Mirjan ○ **IND** 238 Kb 38
Meteor Creek ～ **AUS** 375 Ml 58	Middle Fork ～ **USA** 46 Ba 11	Milgarra ○ **AUS** 365 Mg 55	Minganja ○ **ANG** 340 Hb 52	Mirnyj ○ **RUS** 204 Vb 6
Metepec ○ **MEX** 92 Cn 35	Middle Fork Salmon ～ **USA** Ce 23	Milgun ○ **AUS** 368 Lk 58	Mingao ○ **CO** 107 Ea 44	Mirong ○ **VRC** 254 La 34
Meteran ○ **PNG** 287 Ml 47	Middle Gate ○ **USA** 64 Cd 26	Milhana ○ **MOC** 344 Hm 53	Mingary ○ **AUS** 378 Mg 62	Mírpur Batoro ○ **PK** 227 Jn 33
Metetí ○ **PA** 97 Dk 41	Middle Island ⌂ **AUS** 368 Lm 63	Milhãt ○ **IRQ** 209 Hp 28	Mingbulok ○ **UZB** 223 Jk 24	Mirpur Khâs ○ **PK** 227 Jn 33
Methana ○ **GR** 194 Hd 27	Middle Loup River ～ **USA** 56 Cm 24	Miliana ○ **DZ** 296 Gh 27	Mingela ○ **AUS** 365 Mk 55	Mirpur Matheio ○ **PK** 227 Jn 33
Methóni ○ **GR** 194 Hc 27		Miliakapiti ○ **AUS** 364 Mb 51	Mingenew ○ **AUS** 368 Lh 60	Mirpur Sakro ○ **PK** 227 Jn 33
Metil ○ **MOC** 344 Hm 54	Middlemarch ○ **NZ** 382 Nh 68	Milim ○ **PNG** 287 Mn 48	Minggang ○ **VRC** 243 Lh 29	Mirra Mitta Bore ○ **AUS** 374 Mf 59
Metionga Lake ～ **CDN** 56 Dc 21	Middlemount ○ **AUS** 375 Ml 57	Milingimbi ○ **AUS** 364 Md 52	Minghoshan ○ **VRC** 231 Km 25	Mirrasol d'Oeste ○ **BR** 132 Ee 53
Metkovič ○ **HR** 194 Ha 24	Middle Park ○ **AUS** 365 Mh 55	Milk River ～ **USA** 51 Cj 21	Mingin ○ **MYA** 254 Km 34	Mírrngadja Village ○ **AUS** 364 Md 52
Mètlaoui ○ **TN** 296 Gl 28	Middleport ○ **USA** 71 Dg 26	Millaa Millaa ○ **AUS** 365 Mj 54	Ming Ming ○ **PNG** 287 Mk 48	
Metlili Chaamba ～ **DZ** 296 Gh 29	Middle Racoon ～ **USA** 70 Da 25	Millaroo ○ **AUS** 365 Mk 56	Mingoyo ○ **EAT** 344 Hm 51	Mirrote ○ **MOC** 344 Hm 54
Metoro ○ **RI** 278 Lc 48	Middle Reef ⌂ **SOL** 290 Nc 52	Millas ○ **F** 185 Gh 24	Mingue ○ **CAM** 320 Gn 43	Mirsaale ○ **SP** 328 Jc 43
Metro ○ **RI** 278 Lc 48	Middle Ridge ⌒ **CDN** 61 Eg 21	Millau ○ **F** 185 Gh 23	Minguri ○ **MOC** 344 Hn 53	Mirsale ○ **SP** 328 Jb 43
Metropolis ○ **USA** 71 Dd 27	Middlesboro ○ **USA** 71 Df 27	Millbridge ○ **USA** 60 Ea 23	Mingxi ○ **VRC** 258 Lj 32	Mirtna ○ **AUS** 375 Mk 55
Metsera ○ **RDC** 333 He 47	Middlesborough ○ **GB** 162 Gf 18	Millcreek ○ **USA** 57 Dh 24	Minhe Huizu Tuzu Zizhixian ○ **VRC** 242 Lb 27	Mirtoan Sea ～ **GR** 194 Hd 27
Métsovo ○ **GR** 194 Hc 26	Middleton ○ **AUS** 374 Mg 57	Milledgeville ○ **USA** 71 Dg 29		Miruka ○ **EAK** 337 Hk 46
Mettuppâlaiyam ○ **IND** 239 Kc 40	Middleton ○ **AUS** 378 Mk 67	Mille Lacs Lake ～ **USA** 56 Db 22		Miruro ○ **MOC** 341 Hh 53
Mettūr ○ **IND** 238 Kd 40	Middletown ○ **USA** 57 Dd 24	Millen ○ **USA** 71 Dh 29	Minh Hải ○ **VN** 263 Lc 41	Mirzapur ○ **IND** 234 Kf 33
Metu ○ **ETH** 325 Hk 41	Middletown ○ **USA** 71 Df 26	Miller ○ **USA** 56 Cn 23	Minhla ○ **MYA** 254 Km 36	Misaki ○ **J** 251 Mc 29
Metuge ○ **MOC** 344 Hm 52	Middletown ○ **USA** 74 Dl 25	Miller ○ **USA** 70 Cn 25	Minhla ○ **MYA** 262 Km 37	Misaki ○ **J** 251 Md 28
Metz ○ **F** 163 Gk 21	Midelt ○ **MA** 293 Gd 29	Miller ○ **ZA** 358 Hd 62	Minho ～ **E** 184 Gb 24	Misaki ○ **EAT** 337 Hj 48
Meulaboh ○ **RI** 270 Km 43	Mid-Indian-Basin ▽ 31 Nb 10	Millerovo ○ **RUS** 181 Hm 21	Minicoy Island ⌂ **IND** 239 Ka 41	m-i Sakyndyk ◠ **KZ** 202 Jd 23
Meuse ～ **F** 163 Gj 21	Mid-Indian Ridge ▽ 31 Na 12	Millersburg ○ **USA** 71 Dh 25	Minidoka ○ **USA** 50 Cf 24	Misantla ○ **MEX** 92 Cp 36
Mexcaltitán ○ **MEX** 92 Ck 35	Midi-Pyrénées ◎ **F** 184 Gg 24	Millersburg ○ **USA** 74 Dk 25	Minigua ○ **CI** 316 Gb 41	Misau ○ **WAN** 320 Gm 40
Mexia ○ **USA** 81 Cn 30	Midland ○ **USA** 57 Df 24	Millers Creek ～ **AUS** 374 Md 60	Minilya ～ **AUS** 360 Lh 57	Misawa ○ **J** 250 Mg 25
Mexican Hat ○ **USA** 65 Cg 27	Midland ○ **CDN** 60 Dj 23	Millers Creek Reservation ～ **USA** 70 Cn 29	Minilya Roadhouse ○ **AUS** 360 Lg 57	Miscou Centre ○ **CDN** 61 Eb 22
Mexican Water ○ **USA** 65 Ch 27	Midland ○ **AUS** 368 Lh 61			Miscou Island ⌂ **CDN** 61 Eb 22
Mexico ○ **USA** 70 Db 26	Midland ○ **USA** 70 Db 26	Millicent ○ **AUS** 378 Mg 64	Mining Area Yampi Sound ★ **AUS** 361 Lm 54	Misele ○ **RDC** 333 Ha 48
Mexico Basin ▽ 93 Da 34	Midongy ⌒ **RM** 353 Jb 57	Millington ○ **USA** 71 Dd 28	Miniota ○ **CDN** 56 Cm 20	Mishagua ～ **PE** 128 Dm 51
Mexico Bay ～ **USA** 60 DK 24	Midongy Atsimo ○ **RM** 353 Jb 57	Millinocket ○ **USA** 60 Dp 23	Minissa ○ **BF** 317 Ge 39	Mishaleyi ○ **VRC** 230 Ke 26
Mexico City ◉ **MEX** 92 Cn 36	Midouze ～ **F** 184 Gf 24	Mill Island ⌂ **CDN** 43 Gc 6	Miniss Lake ～ **CDN** 56 Dc 20	Mishamo ○ **EAT** 336 Hh 48
Meyâmei ○ **IR** 222 Jf 27	Mid-Pacific Mountains ▽ 27 Sb 7	Millmerran ○ **AUS** 375 Mm 59	Ministro Ramos Mexía ～ **RA** 147 Ea 66	Mishan ○ **VRC** 250 Mb 23
Meyanodas ○ **RI** 283 Mb 49	Midsandur ○ **IS** 158 Fk 13	Millpoo ○ **PE** 128 Dl 52		Mi-shima ⌂ **J** 247 Mb 28
Meydancik ○ **TR** 202 Hp 25	Midsayap ○ **RP** 275 Ln 42	Millrose ○ **AUS** 368 Ll 59	Minj ○ **PNG** 287 Mj 48	Misima Island ⌂ **PNG** 287 Mn 51
Meyersdale ○ **USA** 74 Dj 26	Midu ○ **VRC** 254 La 33	Mills Lake ～ **CDN** 47 Cc 15	Minjilang ○ **AUS** 364 Mc 51	Miski ○ **SUD** 312 He 38
Mezaligon ○ **MYA** 262 Km 37	Midway ～ **USA** 86 Df 29	Millston ○ **USA** 56 Dc 23	Minlaton ○ **AUS** 378 Me 63	Miskolc ○ **H** 174 Hc 21
Mezdra ○ **BG** 194 Hd 24	Midway Range ～ **CDN** 50 Cc 21	Millstream ○ **AUS** 360 Lj 56	Minle ○ **VRC** 242 La 26	Mismâr ○ **SUD** 313 Hk 36
Mezhdurečensk ○ **RUS** 204 Tc 8	Midwest ○ **USA** 51 Cj 24	Millungera ○ **AUS** 365 Mg 55	Minmaya ○ **J** 250 Mg 25	Misrak Gashemo ○ **ETH** 328 Ja 41
Mezen' ～ **RUS** 154 Qc 5	Midwest City ○ **USA** 70 Cp 28	Millville ○ **USA** 74 Dl 26	Minna ○ **WAN** 320 Gk 41	Misrikh ○ **IND** 234 Ke 32
Mezen' ○ **RUS** 159 Ja 13	Midyat ○ **TR** 202 Hn 27	Millwood ○ **USA** 71 Dg 25	Minneapolis ○ **USA** 56 Da 23	Missanabie ○ **CDN** 57 Df 21
Mezen' ～ **RUS** 154 Qc 5	Midyobo ○ **GQ** 332 Gm 45	Millwood Lake ～ **USA** 70 Db 29	Minneapolis ○ **USA** 70 Cp 26	Misseni ○ **RMM** 305 Gc 40
Mezenskaja guba ～ **RUS** 159 Hp 12	Miechów ○ **PL** 174 Hc 20	Milly Milly ○ **AUS** 368 Lj 59	Minnedosa ○ **CDN** 56 Cn 20	Missinaibi Lake ～ **CDN** 57 Dg 21
	Międzyrzec Podlaski ○ **PL** 175 Hd 20	Milne Bay ～ **PNG** 287 Mm 51	Minneola ○ **USA** 70 Cm 27	Missinaibi River ～ **CDN** 57 Dg 20
Mézessé ○ **CAM** 320 Gn 44	Międzyrzecz ○ **PL** 170 Gp 19	Milnesand ○ **USA** 65 Cl 29	Minnesota ◎ **USA** 56 Da 22	Mission ○ **CDN** 50 Ca 21
Mezón ○ **PY** 136 Eb 57	Mielec ○ **PL** 174 Hc 20	Milo ○ **USA** 60 Dp 23	Minnesota ～ **USA** 56 Da 23	Mission ○ **USA** 56 Cm 24
Mezquital ○ **MEX** 81 Cp 33	Miélékouka ○ **RCB** 332 Gf 45	Milo ○ **ETH** 313 Hn 40	Minnewaukan ○ **USA** 56 Cn 21	Mission ○ **USA** 81 Cn 32
Mezquital ○ **MEX** 92 Ck 34	Miembwe ○ **EAT** 337 Hl 50	Milo ～ **RG** 316 Gb 40	Minnie Creek ～ **AUS** 368 Lh 58	Mission Beach ○ **AUS** 365 Mk 54
Mezquital ～ **MEX** 92 Ck 34	Miena ○ **AUS** 378 Mk 67	Milo ○ **EAT** 337 Hk 50	Minnies ○ **AUS** 365 Mh 54	Missira ○ **SN** 316 Fp 39
Mfou ○ **CAM** 320 Gn 44	Miengwe ○ **Z** 341 Hg 52	Milogradovo ○ **RUS** 250 Md 24	Minnipa ○ **AUS** 378 Md 62	Missisagi River ～ **CDN** 57 Dg 22
Mfouati ○ **RCB** 332 Gn 48	Mier ○ **MEX** 81 Cn 32	Milos ○ **GR** 194 He 27	Minnitaki Lake ～ **CDN** 56 Db 21	Missicabi ～ **CDN** 60 Dj 20
Mfum ○ **WAN** 320 Gl 43	Mieres ○ **E** 184 Gc 24	Mílos ⌂ **GR** 194 He 27	Minkrnri ○ **RMM** 305 Ge 37	Mississauga ○ **CDN** 60 Dj 24
Mgangerabeli Plains ⌒ **EAK** 337 Hm 46	Mier y Noriega ○ **MEX** 92 Cm 34	Milparinka ○ **AUS** 374 Mg 60	Minong ○ **USA** 56 Dc 22	Mississippi ◎ **USA** 86 Dc 29
Mgende ○ **EAT** 336 Hm 49	Mierzeja Helska ⌂ **PL** 170 Hb 18	Milsanka ravnina ～ **AZ** 202 Jb 25	Minorca ⌂ **E** 185 Gj 26	Mississippi River ～ **USA** 56 Db 22
Mgeta ～ **EAT** 337 Hm 49	Migdol ○ **ZA** 349 He 59	Milton ○ **USA** 60 Dn 23	Minot ○ **USA** 56 Cm 21	Mississippi River Delta ⌂ **USA** 86 Dd 31
Mgne. de Nganha △ **CAM** 321 Gn 42	Migiole ○ **EAT** 337 Hk 49	Milton ○ **USA** 74 Dk 25	Minqing ○ **VRC** 258 Lk 32	
	Migori ～ **EAK** 337 Hk 46	Milton ○ **USA** 86 De 30	Minquan ○ **VRC** 243 Lh 28	Mississippi Sound ～ **USA** 86 Dd 30
Mgori ○ **EAT** 337 Hk 48	Migre ○ **SUD** 313 Hk 38	Milton ～ **NZ** 382 Ng 69	Min Shan △ **VRC** 242 Lb 29	Missoula ○ **USA** 50 Cf 22
Mgunga ○ **EAT** 337 Hl 49	Miguasha Park ★ **CDN** 61 Ea 21	Milton-Freewater ○ **USA** 50 Cc 23	Minsk ◉ **BY** 171 Hf 19	Missour ○ **MA** 293 Ge 29
Mhamid ○ **MA** 293 Gd 31	Miguel Alemán ○ **MEX** 80 Cj 31	Milton Keynes ○ **GB** 163 Gf 19	Mińsk Maz. ○ **PL** 170 Hc 19	Missouri City ○ **USA** 81 Da 31
Mhangura ○ **ZW** 341 Hg 54	Miguel Alves ○ **BR** 124 En 48	Miltou ○ **TCH** 321 Ha 40	Minta ○ **CAM** 320 Gn 43	Missouri ◎ **USA** 70 Db 26
Mhasvád ○ **IND** 238 Kb 37	Miguel Auza ○ **MEX** 81 Cl 33	Miluo ○ **VRC** 258 Lg 31	Mintable ○ **AUS** 369 Mc 59	Missouri River ～ **USA** 56 Cn 24
Mhlatuze ～ **ZA** 352 Hh 60	Miguel Calmon ○ **BR** 125 Ep 51	Milwaukee ○ **USA** 57 De 24	Minter City ○ **USA** 86 Dc 29	Missouri Valley ○ **USA** 70 Da 25
Mhluzi ○ **ZA** 349 Hg 58	Miguel Leão ○ **BR** 124 En 48	Mimili ○ **AUS** 369 Mc 59	Minto ○ **CDN** 56 Cn 21	Mistake Creek ～ **AUS** 364 Ma 54
Mhow ○ **IND** 234 Kb 34	Miguelópolis ○ **BR** 141 Ek 56	Mimi ～ **CAM** 320 Gn 43	Minto ○ **CDN** 61 Ea 22	Mistassibi ～ **CDN** 60 Dm 21
Miabi ○ **RDC** 333 Hd 49	Miguel Pereira ○ **BR** 141 En 57	Miminoso ○ **TJ** 223 Jp 26	Minto II ○ **CAM** 321 Gn 44	Mistassini ○ **CDN** 60 Dl 20
Miagao ○ **RP** 267 Lm 40	Migues ○ **ROU** 146 Eg 63	Mimongo ○ **G** 332 Gm 46	Minton ○ **CDN** 51 Ck 20	Mistawak ～ **CDN** 60 Dj 21
Miahuatlán ○ **MEX** 92 Cp 37	Mihajlov ○ **RUS** 171 Hm 18	Mimoun ○ **DZ** 293 Gf 28	Minturn ○ **USA** 65 Cj 26	Mistawasis Indian Reservation ••• **CDN** 51 Cj 19
Miajadas ○ **E** 184 Gd 26	Mihajlovka ○ **RUS** 181 Hp 20	Mimoutou ○ **RCB** 332 Ha 44	Minůdast ○ **IR** 222 Jf 27	
Miamère ○ **RCA** 321 Hb 41	Mihajlovka ○ **RUS** 250 Mc 24	Mina ○ **USA** 64 Cc 26	Minusinsk ○ **RUS** 204 Tc 8	Mistelbach ○ **A** 174 Ha 21
Miami ○ **USA** 70 Cm 28	Mihajlovo ○ **BG** 194 Hd 24	Mina ～ **RI** 282 Ln 50	Minvoul ○ **G** 332 Gn 44	Misterei ○ **SUD** 321 Hd 39
Miami ○ **USA** 70 Da 27	Mihalıçcık ○ **TR** 195 Hh 26	Minâ' 'Abdallâh ○ **KWT** 215 Jc 31	Min Xian ○ **VRC** 242 Lc 28	Mistras ★ **GR** 194 Hd 27
Miami ○ **USA** 87 Dh 33	Mihnevo ○ **RUS** 171 Hm 18	Mínáb ○ **IR** 226 Jg 32	Mio ○ **USA** 57 Df 23	Misumba ○ **RDC** 333 Hc 48
Miami Beach ○ **USA** 87 Dh 33	Mihumo Chini ○ **EAT** 337 Hm 50	Mina Clavero ○ **RA** 137 Eb 61	Miố ～ **J** 247 Mb 29	Misumi ○ **J** 247 Mb 29
Miami Canal ～ **USA** 87 Dh 33	Mijek ○ **MA** 304 Fp 34	Minaçu ○ **BR** 133 Ek 52	Miquelon ○ **CDN** 60 Dk 21	Mita Hills Dam ～ **Z** 341 Hg 53
Miân Channûn ○ **PK** 230 Ka 30	Mikese ○ **EAT** 337 Hl 49	Minaki ○ **CDN** 56 Da 20	Miquelon ○ **F** 61 Ef 22	Mitande ○ **MOC** 344 Hl 53
Miandrivazo ○ **RM** 345 Ja 55	Miki ○ **RDC** 336 Hg 47	Mina la Casualidad ○ **RA** 136 Dp 58	Miquihuana ○ **MEX** 81 Cn 34	Mitare ～ **YV** 107 Dn 40
Miangas ⌂ **RI** 275 Lp 43	Mikikani ○ **EAT** 344 Hm 51		Mira ～ **EC** 116 Dj 45	Mitatib ○ **SUD** 313 Hk 38
Miani ○ **PK** 230 Ka 29	Mikínes ★ **GR** 194 Hd 27	Mina la Juanita ○ **RCH** 137 Dn 63	Mira ～ **EC** 116 Dj 45	Mitchell ○ **USA** 56 Cm 23
Miani Hor ～ **PK** 227 Jm 33	Mikkeli ○ **FIN** 159 Hf 15	Minami-Alp ★ **J** 251 Mf 28	Mira ○ **P** 184 Gb 25	Mitchell ○ **USA** 51 Cl 24
Mianmian Shan △ **VRC** 254 La 32	Mikonos ○ **GR** 194 He 27	Minami- Daitō- Jima ⌂ **J** 26 Rb 7	Mira ○ **I** 185 Gn 23	Mitchell ～ **AUS** 375 Mh 58
Mianning ○ **VRC** 254 Lb 31	Míkonos ⌂ **GR** 194 He 27	Minamikayabe ～ **J** 250 Mg 25	Mirabela ○ **BR** 133 Em 54	Mitchell and Alice Rivers ⚲ **AUS** 365 Mh 53
Miânwâli ○ **PK** 223 Jp 29	Mikshevichy ○ **BY** 171 Hf 19	Minam-Tane ○ **AT** 247 Ma 30	Miracema ○ **BR** 141 En 56	
Mianyang ○ **VRC** 242 Lc 30	Mikulov ○ **CZ** 174 Ha 21	Minam Tori ⌂ **J** 27 Sb 7	Miracema do Tocantins ○ **BR** 121 Ek 50	Mitchell Lake ～ **USA** 71 De 29
Mianzhu ○ **VRC** 242 Lb 30	Mikumi ○ **EAT** 337 Hl 49	Minas ○ **C** 101 Dk 35		Mitchell Range △ **AUS** 364 Md 52
Miao ○ **RDC** 333 Hd 49	Mikumi ⚲ **EAT** 337 Hl 49	Minas ○ **ROU** 146 Eg 63	Mirador ○ **BR** 116 Dm 48	Mitchell River ～ **AUS** 361 Ln 53
Miaodao Qundao ⌂ **VRC** 246 Ll 27	Mikumi Lodge ○ **EAT** 337 Hl 49	Minas ○ **RI** 270 La 45	Mirador ○ **BR** 121 Em 49	Mitchell River ～ **AUS** 361 Mh 53
Miao Li ○ **RC** 259 Ll 33	Mikun´ ○ **RUS** 19 Ma 3	Minâ' Sa'ud ○ **KWT** 215 Jc 31	Miraflores ○ **CO** 117 Dn 45	Mitchell River ～ **AUS** 379 Mk 64
Miao Ling △ **VRC** 255 Ld 32	Mila ○ **DZ** 296 Gk 27	Minas Basin ～ **CDN** 61 Eb 23	Miraflores ○ **BR** 117 Eb 47	Mitchelltown ○ **IRL** 163 Ga 19
Miaozu ○ **VRC** 255 Ld 33	Milaca ○ **USA** 56 Db 23	Minas de Barroteran ○ **MEX** 81 Cm 32	Miragoâne ○ **RH** 101 Dm 36	Mithankot ○ **PK** 227 Jp 31
Miass ○ **RUS** 154 Sa 8	Miladummadulu Atoll ⌂ **MV** 239 Ka 42		Miraj ○ **IND** 238 Kb 37	Mitha Tiwâná ○ **PK** 223 Jp 29
Miastko ○ **PL** 170 Ha 19	Milagres ○ **BR** 124 Fa 49	Minas de Corrales ○ **ROU** 146 Eg 63	Miramar ○ **RA** 146 Ef 65	Mithi ○ **PK** 227 Jn 33
Mibalaie ○ **RDC** 333 Hc 48	Milagres ○ **BR** 133 Ep 51	Minas de Matahambre ○ **C** 100 Df 34	Miramar ○ **USA** 64 Ce 29	Míthimna ○ **GR** 194 He 26
Mibenge ○ **Z** 341 Hg 51	Milagro ○ **EC** 116 Dj 47	Minas do Mimoso ○ **BR** 125 Ep 51	Miramichi ～ **CDN** 61 Ea 22	Mitiamo ○ **AUS** 379 Mj 64
Mibu Island ⌂ **PNG** 286 Mm 47	Milagros ○ **RP** 267 Lm 39	Minas Gerais ◎ **BR** 125 En 54	Miramichi ○ **CDN** 61 Eb 22	Mitiaro ⌂ **NZ** 35 Ba 11
Mica ○ **ZA** 352 Hh 58	Milan ○ **USA** 57 Dg 24	Minas Novas ○ **BR** 125 En 54	Miramichi Bay ～ **CDN** 61 Eb 22	Mitilíni ○ **GR** 194 Hf 26
Mica Creek ～ **CDN** 50 Cc 19	Milan ○ **USA** 70 Db 25	Minatitlán ○ **MEX** 92 Ck 36	Miran ○ **PK** 227 Jp 32	Mitji ～ **SN** 316 Fp 39
Micáucha ○ **MOC** 344 Hk 55	Milan ○ **USA** 71 Dd 28	Minatitlán ○ **MEX** 93 Da 37	Miranda ○ **YV** 107 Dp 40	Mitla ★ **MEX** 93 Cp 37
Miccosukee Indian Reservation ••• **USA** 87 Dh 32	Milan ○ **I** 185 Gl 23	Minbu ○ **MYA** 254 Km 35	Miranda ○ **BR** 140 Ef 56	Mito ○ **J** 251 Mg 27
	Milando ○ **ANG** 340 Ha 50	Minchika ○ **WAN** 321 Gn 40	Miranda ～ **BR** 140 Ef 56	Mitoko ○ **RDC** 331 Hc 44
Michalovce ○ **SK** 174 Hc 21	Milang ○ **AUS** 378 Mf 63	Minchinâbâd ○ **PK** 230 Ka 30	Miranda de Ebro ○ **E** 184 Ge 24	Mitomani ○ **EAT** 344 Hm 51
Michelago ○ **AUS** 379 Ml 63	Milange ○ **RDC** 336 Hf 47	Mindanao ⌂ **RP** 267 Lp 41	Miranda do Norte ○ **BR** 121 Em 47	Mitra Peak △ **NZ** 382 Nf 68
Miches ○ **DOM** 101 Dp 36	Milange ○ **MOC** 344 Hk 54	Mindanao ～ **RP** 275 Lp 42	Miranda Downs ○ **AUS** 365 Mg 54	Mitrofania Island ⌂ **USA** 46 Al 17
Michigan ◎ **USA** 57 De 23	Milango ～ **RI** 275 Ll 45	Mindelo ○ **CV** 316 Fh 37	Mirandela ○ **BR** 125 Fa 51	Mitsamiouli ○ **COM** 345 Hp 51
Michigan City ○ **USA** 71 De 25	Milanoa ○ **RM** 345 Jc 52	Minden ○ **CDN** 60 Dj 23	Mirandela ○ **P** 184 Gc 25	Mitsinjo ○ **RM** 345 Ja 54
Michikamau Lake ～ **CDN** 7 Fb 4	Milas ○ **TR** 195 Hf 27	Minden ○ **USA** 70 Cn 25	Mirandiba ○ **BR** 124 Fa 50	Mits'iwa ○ **ER** 313 Hm 38
Michilla ○ **RCH** 136 Dn 57	Milazzo ○ **I** 185 Gp 26	Minden ○ **USA** 70 Db 29	Miranda ○ **BR** 140 Ej 56	Mits'iwa Channel ～ **ER** 313 Hm 38
Michipicoten Bay ～ **CDN** 57 Df 21	Milbank ○ **USA** 56 Cp 23	Minden ○ **D** 170 Gl 19	Mirani ○ **AUS** 375 Ml 56	Mitta Mitta ～ **AUS** 379 Mk 64
Michipicoten Island ⌂ **CDN** 57 Df 22	Milbanke Sound ～ **CDN** 50 Bm 19	Minderoo ○ **AUS** 360 Lh 56	Mirante ○ **BR** 125 Ep 53	Mittweida ○ **D** 170 Go 20
Michurinsk ○ **RUS** 181 Hm 19	Milden ○ **CDN** 51 Cj 20	Mindif ○ **CAM** 321 Gp 40	Mirante do Paranapanema ○ **BR** 141 Ek 56	m-i Tubḩaragan ◠ **KZ** 202 Jc 23
Mico ～ **NIC** 97 Dj 39	Mildura ○ **AUS** 378 Mh 63	Mindik ○ **PNG** 287 Mk 48		Mitumba Mountains △ **RDC** 336 Hg 47
Micomeseng ○ **GQ** 332 Gm 45	Mile ○ **VRC** 255 Lb 33	Mindiptana ○ **RI** 286 Mg 48	Mira Por Vos ⌂ **BS** 87 Dl 34	
Miconge ○ **ANG** 332 Ge 48	Milé ○ **ETH** 313 Hn 40	Mindona ～ **AUS** 378 Mh 62	Mir Bačče Kût ○ **AFG** 223 Jn 28	Mitwaba ○ **RDC** 336 Hf 50
Micronesia ⌂ **FSM** 27 Sa 8	Milepa ○ **EAT** 336 Hh 50	Mindoro Strait ～ **RP** 267 Ll 39	Miravalles △ **E** 184 Gc 24	Mityana ○ **EAU** 324 Hj 45
Micronesia ◎ **FSM** 27 Sa 9	Miles ○ **USA** 81 Cm 30	Mindoro ⌂ **RP** 267 Lk 39	Miravelles △ **E** 184 Gc 24	Mitzic ○ **G** 332 Gn 45
Midale ○ **CDN** 51 Cl 21	Miles ○ **AUS** 375 Mm 59	Mindouli ○ **RCB** 332 Gn 48	Mirbât ○ **OM** 219 Jf 37	Mius ～ **RUS** 181 Hm 22
Midar ○ **MA** 293 Ge 28	Miles City ○ **USA** 51 Cj 22	Mindourou ○ **CAM** 321 Gn 44	Mirebalais ○ **RH** 101 Dm 36	Mixco ○ **GCA** 93 Dc 38
Midas ○ **USA** 64 Cd 25	Mi'léso ○ **ETH** 325 Hn 41	Minduri ○ **BR** 141 Em 56	Mirělhěft ○ **MA** 292 Ga 31	Mixteco ～ **MEX** 92 Cn 37
Mid-Atlantic Ridge ▽ 30 Ja 11	Milestone ○ **CDN** 51 Ck 20	Mine ○ **J** 247 Ma 28	Miria ○ **RN** 308 Gl 39	Mixtlán ○ **MEX** 92 Ck 35
Middelburg ○ **ZA** 349 He 61	Milesville ○ **USA** 56 Cm 23	Mine Centre ○ **CDN** 56 Db 21	Miriâlgûda ○ **IND** 238 Kd 37	Miya ○ **WAN** 320 Gl 40
Middelburg ○ **ZA** 349 Hg 58	Mineola ○ **USA** 70 Da 29	Mineiros ○ **BR** 133 Eh 54	Miriam Vale ○ **AUS** 375 Mm 58	Miyake-shima ⌂ **J** 251 Mf 28
		Mineral ○ **USA** 64 Cb 25		Miyako ○ **J** 250 Mg 26
		Mineral'nye Vody ○ **RUS** 202 Hp 23		Miyakonojō ○ **J** 247 Mb 30

				Miyako-rettō ⌂ **J** 259 Ln 33
				Miyako-shima ⌂ **J** 259 Ln 33
				Miyândoâb ○ **IR** 209 Jb 27
				Miyâne ○ **IR** 209 Jb 27
				Miyazaki ○ **J** 247 Mb 30
				Miyazu ○ **J** 251 Md 28
				Miyi ○ **VRC** 254 La 32
				Miyoshi ○ **J** 251 Mc 28
				Miyun ○ **VRC** 246 Lj 25
				Mizan Teferî ○ **ETH** 325 Hk 42
				Mizdah ○ **LAR** 297 Ha 30
				Mizen Head ◠ **IRL** 163 Ga 20
				Mizhi ○ **VRC** 243 Lf 27
				Mizil ○ **RO** 175 Hf 23
				Mizo Hills △ **IND** 254 Kl 34
				Mizoram ◎ **IND** 254 Kl 34
				Mizpah ○ **USA** 51 Ck 22
				Mizpé-Ramon ○ **IL** 214 Hk 30
				Mizque ○ **BOL** 129 Eb 54
				Mizque ～ **BOL** 129 Eb 54
				Mizur ○ **RUS** 202 Hp 24
				Mizusawa ○ **J** 250 Mg 26
				Mjakit ○ **RUS** 23 Sb 3
				Mjölby ○ **S** 170 Gp 16
				Mjörn ～ **S** 170 Gn 17
				Mørsa ～ **RUS** 181 Hm 22
				Mkanga ○ **EAT** 337 Hk 49
				Mkasi ～ **Z** 336 Hj 50
				Mkata ～ **EAT** 337 Hl 49
				Mkata ～ **EAT** 337 Hm 48
				Mkoani ○ **EAT** 337 Hm 48
				Mkokotoni ○ **EAT** 337 Hn 47
				Mkondoa ～ **EAT** 337 Hl 49
				Mkowe ○ **EAK** 337 Hn 47
				Mkunumbi ○ **EAK** 337 Hn 47
				Mkuranga ○ **EAT** 337 Hm 49
				Mkushi ～ **Z** 341 Hg 52
				Mkushi River ○ **Z** 341 Hg 52
				Mkuze ～ **ZA** 352 Hh 59
				Mkuze ～ **ZA** 352 Hh 59
				Mkwaja ○ **EAT** 337 Hm 48
				Mladá Boleslav ○ **CZ** 174 Gp 20
				Mladenovac ○ **SCG** 174 Hc 23
				Mlandizi ○ **EAT** 337 Hm 49
				M'lang ○ **RP** 275 Ln 42
				Mlawa ○ **PL** 170 Hc 19
				Mlenganapass ～ **ZA** 349 Hg 61
				Mlibizi ～ **ZW** 341 Hf 55
				Mligasi ～ **EAT** 337 Hm 48
				Mljet ⚲ **HR** 194 Ha 24
				Mljet ⌂ **HR** 194 Ha 24
				Mmabatho ○ **ZA** 349 He 58
				Mmadinare ○ **RB** 349 Hf 56
				Mmamabula ○ **RB** 349 Hf 57
				Mmashoro ○ **RB** 349 Hf 56
				Mmathethe ○ **RB** 349 He 58
				Mmatshumo ○ **RB** 349 He 56
				Mnamuk ○ **RI** 282 Lg 47
				Mnanzi ○ **EAT** 337 Hm 48
				Mo ～ **GH** 317 Gg 41
				Mo ～ **CAM** 320 Gl 43
				Moa ○ **C** 101 Dl 35
				Moa ～ **BR** 116 Dm 49
				Moa ～ **WAL** 316 Ga 42
				Moab ○ **USA** 65 Ch 26
				Moabi ○ **G** 332 Gm 47
				Moaghan ○ **IRL** 162 Gc 18
				Moa Island ⌂ **AUS** 365 Mh 51
				Moala ⌂ **FJI** 387 Nm 55
				Moala Group ⌂ **FJI** 387 Nm 55
				Mo'allemán ○ **IR** 222 Jf 28
				Moamba ○ **MOC** 352 Hj 58
				Moaña ○ **E** 184 Gb 24
				Moanda ○ **G** 332 Gm 46
				Moanda ～ **RDC** 333 Hb 44
				Moapa ○ **USA** 64 Ce 27
				Moares ○ **BR** 146 Eh 61
				Moatize ○ **MOC** 344 Hj 54
				Moba ○ **RDC** 336 Hg 49
				Mobârake ○ **IR** 222 Jd 29
				Mobaye ○ **RCA** 321 Hc 43
				Mobayi-Mbongo ○ **RDC** 321 Hc 43
				Mobdoua ～ **RIM** 305 Gc 38
				Mobena ○ **RDC** 333 Hb 45
				Moberly ○ **USA** 70 Db 26
				Mobile ○ **USA** 65 Cf 29
				Mobile ○ **USA** 86 Dd 30
				Mobile Bay ～ **USA** 86 De 30
				Mobridge ○ **USA** 56 Cm 23
				Mobuisi ○ **RDC** 333 Hb 45
				Moca ○ **DOM** 101 Dn 36
				Moçambique ○ **MOC** 344 Hn 53
				Moč Châu ○ **VN** 255 Lc 35
				Moce ⌂ **FJI** 390 Aa 55
				Mochima ▽ **YV** 112 Eb 40
				Mochudi ○ **RB** 349 Hf 58
				Mochumi ○ **PE** 116 Dh 49
				Moçimboa da Praia ○ **MOC** 344 Hn 51
				Mocímboa do Rovuma ○ **MOC** 344 Hm 51
				Môco △ **ANG** 340 Gp 52
				Mocoa ○ **CO** 116 Dk 45
				Mococa ○ **BR** 141 El 56
				Mocoduene ○ **MOC** 352 Hk 57
				Moções ～ **BR** 121 Ek 46
				Mocojuba ○ **BR** 121 Ek 47
				Mocomoco ○ **BOL** 129 Dp 53
				Mocorito ○ **MEX** 80 Cj 33
				Mocotó ○ **BR** 121 El 47
				Moctezuma ○ **MEX** 80 Ch 31
				Moctezuma ○ **MEX** 80 Cj 32
				Moctezuma ～ **MEX** 92 Cn 34
				Moctezuma ○ **MEX** 92 Cn 35
				Mocuba ○ **MOC** 344 Hl 54
				Mocupe ○ **PE** 116 Dj 49
				Modale ○ **RDC** 321 Hd 44
				Modderrivier ○ **ZA** 349 He 60
				Modena ○ **I** 185 Gm 23
				Modesto ○ **USA** 64 Cb 27
				Modigjo ○ **CI** 305 Gc 42
				Mododiče ○ **BIH** 174 Hb 23
				Moe ○ **AUS** 379 Mk 65
				Moebase ○ **MOC** 344 Hm 54
				Moeko ～ **RDC** 333 Hb 44
				Moengo ○ **SME** 113 Eg 43
				Moenkopi Wash ～ **USA** 65 Cg 27
				Moeraki ○ **NZ** 382 Nh 68
				Moerkesung ○ **VRC** 231 Kg 30
				Moers ○ **D** 163 Gk 20
				Moessoba ○ **RMM** 305 Gc 39
				Moffat ○ **GB** 162 Ge 18

□Country ▣Capital city ◉Administrative unit ○Place ♁Island ⩕Mountain range △Mountain ⌓Cape ≈Ocean, Sea ~Lake, River ♆Undersea topography ▲Glacier ♀National park •••Reservation ★Point of major interest ⌒Landscape

Moffit ○ USA 56 Cm 22
Mofu ○ Z 341 Hh 51
Moga ○ RDC 336 Hf 47
Mogadishu ▣ SP 329 Ja 45
Mogadouro ○ P 184 Gc 25
Mogalo ○ RDC 333 Hb 44
Mogami ~ J 251 Mf 26
Moganshan ★ VRC 246 Lk 30
Mogaung ○ MYA 254 Kn 33
Moğen ○ IR 222 Jf 27
Moghrar ○ DZ 293 Gf 29
Mogincual ○ MOC 344 Hn 53
Mogna ○ RA 137 Dp 61
Mogoča ○ RUS 204 Vc 8
Mogok ○ MYA 254 Kn 34
Mogollon ○ USA 65 Ch 29
Mogroum ○ TCH 321 Gp 40
Mogwadi Dendron ○ ZA 349 Hg 57
Mogwase ○ ZA 349 Hf 58
Mohács ○ H 174 Hb 22
Mohale's Hoek ○ LS 349 Hf 61
Mohall ○ USA 56 Cm 21
Mohammadābād ○ IR 222 Jd 29
Moḥammadābād ○ IR 226 Jf 30
Moḥammadābād ○ IR 226 Jg 31
Mohammad Āgā ○ AFG 223 Jn 28
Mohammadia ○ DZ 293 Gg 28
Mohammedia ○ MA 293 Gc 29
Mohana ○ IND 235 Kg 36
Mohanganj ○ BD 235 Kk 33
Mohania ○ IND 235 Kf 33
Mohawk ○ USA 57 Dd 22
Mohe Xilinji ○ VRC 204 Wa 8
Mohelnice ○ CZ 174 Ha 21
Mohenjo Daro ★ PK 227 Jn 32
Moho ○ PE 128 Dp 53
Mohol ○ IND 238 Kb 37
Mohon Peak △ USA 64 Cf 28
Mohoro ○ EAT 337 Hm 50
Mohovaja, gora △ RUS 159 Ja 11
Mohyliv-Podil's'kyj ○ UA 175 Hf 21
Moila Point ⌓ PNG 290 Mp 49
Moili ♁ COM 345 Hp 52
Moimba ○ ANG 340 Gn 54
Moin ○ CR 97 Dg 41
Moincêr ○ VRC 230 Ke 30
Moindou ○ F 386 Ne 56
Moinga ○ EAT 344 Hk 51
Mo i Rana ○ N 158 Gn 12
Moirang ○ IND 254 Kl 33
Moiseevskaja ○ RUS 171 Hn 15
Moisie ○ CDN 61 Ea 20
Moisie ~ CDN 61 Ea 20
Moissac ○ F 184 Gg 23
Moïssala ○ TCH 321 Ha 41
Moitaco ○ YV 112 Eb 42
Moîto ○ TCH 321 Ha 39
Mojave ○ USA 64 Cc 28
Mojave ~ USA 64 Cd 28
Mojave Desert ⌒ USA 64 Cd 28
Mojave National Preserve ♀ USA 64 Ce 28
Moji d. Cruzes ○ BR 141 El 57
Moji-Guaçu ○ BR 141 El 57
Moji-Mirim ○ BR 141 El 57
Mojiquiçaba ○ BR 125 Fa 54
Mojo ○ ETH 325 Hm 41
Mojokerto ○ RI 279 Lg 49
Moju ~ BR 121 Ek 46
Moju ~ BR 121 Ek 47
Mōka ○ J 251 Mg 27
Mokāma ○ IND 235 Kg 33
Mokambo ○ RDC 341 Hg 52
Mokamole ○ ZA 349 Hg 57
Mokaria ○ RDC 321 Hd 44
Mokelumne ~ USA 64 Cb 26
Mokengo ○ RDC 333 Hb 48
Mokgomane ○ RB 349 He 58
Mokhotlong ○ LS 349 Hf 60
Mokimbo ○ RDC 336 Hg 49
Moknine ○ TN 297 Gm 28
Mokokchung ○ IND 254 Km 32
Mokolo ○ CAM 321 Gn 40
Mokolo ○ RDC 333 Hb 45
Mokolo ~ ZA 349 Hf 58
Mokombe ~ RDC 333 Hd 46
Mokoreta ○ NZ 382 Ng 69
Mokp'o ○ ROK 247 Ln 28
Mokrous ○ RUS 181 Jb 20
Mokša ~ RUS 181 Hn 18
Mokūkī ○ AFG 223 Jj 28
Mokwa ○ WAN 320 Gj 41
Mola ~ GH 317 Gf 41
Molakalmuru ○ IND 238 Kc 38
Molalatau ○ RB 349 Hg 57
Molalla ○ USA 50 Ca 23
Molat ♁ HR 174 Gp 23
Molde ○ N 158 Gk 14
Moldova □ MD 175 Hf 22
Moldova Nouă ○ RO 174 Hc 23
Moldoveanu △ RO 175 He 23
Mole ~ AUS 375 Mm 60
Molegbe ○ RDC 321 Hc 43
Mole Island ♁ PNG 287 Mk 47
Mole Lake Ind. Res. ••• USA 57 Dd 23
Mole National Park ♀ GH 317 Gf 41
Molepolole ○ RB 349 He 58
Molėtai ○ LT 171 He 18
Molfetta ○ I 194 Ha 25
Molibagu ○ RI 275 Lm 45
Molina ○ RCH 137 Dn 63
Molina ○ E 184 Gf 25
Molina de Segura ○ E 184 Gf 26
Moline ○ USA 70 Cp 27
Moline ○ USA 71 Dc 25
Moliro ○ RDC 336 Hh 50
Molise ◉ I 194 Gp 25
Mollendo ○ PE 128 Dm 54
Mollepata ○ PE 128 Dm 52
Molo ~ EAK 325 Hk 45
Molo ○ EAK 337 Hk 46
Moločna ~ UA 175 Hk 22
Molócuè ○ MOC 344 Hl 53
Molócuè ~ MOC 344 Hl 53
Molodo ○ RMM 305 Gc 38
Mologa ~ RUS 171 Hl 16
Molokai ♁ USA 75 Am 35
Molong ○ AUS 379 Ml 62
Molopo ~ RB 349 Hd 58
Moloporivier ○ ZA 349 Hd 58
Moloundou ○ CAM 332 Gp 44
Molteno ○ ZA 349 Hf 61
Moltenopass △ ZA 358 Hd 62
Moluccas ♁ RI 275 Lp 46
Molucca Sea ≈ RI 282 Lm 46
Molumbo ○ MOC 344 Hl 53
Molwe ○ RDC 341 He 51
Molyneux Bay ~ NZ 382 Ng 69
Moma ~ RUS 205 Xb 5
Moma ○ MOC 344 Hm 54
Momaligi ○ WAL 316 Fp 42
Momats ~ RI 286 Mf 48
Momba ○ Z 341 Hf 53
Mombaca ○ BR 124 Fa 48
Mombasa ○ EAK 337 Hm 48
Mombetsu ○ J 250 Mh 23
Mombo ○ EAT 337 Hm 48
Mombo ~ ANG 340 Hc 51
Mombongo ○ RDC 333 Hd 45
Momboyo ~ RDC 333 Hb 46
Mombum ○ RI 286 Mf 50
Mome-á-l'Eau ○ F 104 Ed 37
Momo ○ G 332 Gm 45
Momote ○ PNG 287 Mk 47
Mompog Passage ~ RP 267 Ll 39
Mompono ○ RDC 333 Hc 45
Mompós Santa Cruz de Mompox ○ CO 106 Dl 41
Momskiy Khrebet ⩕ RUS 205 Xb 5
Møn ♁ DK 170 Gn 18
Mon ○ IND 254 Km 32
Mon ~ MYA 254 Km 35
Mon. of St. Caterine ★ ET 214 Hk 31
Monaco □ MC 185 Gk 24
Monaco ▣ MC 185 Gk 24
Monahans ○ USA 81 Cl 30
Monana ○ G 332 Gn 46
Monapo ○ MOC 344 Hn 53
Monapo ~ MOC 344 Hn 53
Mona Quimbundo ○ ANG 340 Hb 50
Monarch ○ USA 51 Cg 22
Monarch Islands ♁ GB 162 Gb 17
Monarch Mountain △ CDN 50 Bn 20
Monashee Mountains ⩕ CDN 50 Cc 20
Monaši ○ UA 175 Hg 22
Monasterace Marina ○ I 194 Ha 26
Monastir ○ I 185 Gl 26
Monastir ○ TN 297 Gm 28
Monastyrščina ○ RUS 171 Hh 18
Monatélé ○ CAM 320 Gm 43
Monboré ○ CAM 321 Gp 41
Monção ○ BR 121 Em 47
Mončegorsk ○ RUS 159 Hj 12
Mönchengladbach ○ D 163 Gk 20
Monchy ○ CDN 51 Cj 21
Monchy ○ CDN 51 Cl 20
Moncks Corner ○ USA 71 Dh 29
Monclova ○ MEX 81 Cm 32
Monclova ○ MEX 93 Dc 36
Moncton ○ CDN 61 Eb 22
Mondaí ○ BR 140 Eh 59
Mondamin ○ USA 70 Da 25
Monde ~ P 184 Gb 25
Mondego ~ P 184 Gb 25
Mondjamboli ○ RDC 321 Hc 44
Mondjuku ○ RDC 333 Hc 46
Mondo ○ TCH 309 Gp 39
Mondombe ○ RDC 333 Hd 46
Mondómo ○ CO 106 Dk 44
Mondono ○ RI 282 Lm 46
Mondorobé ○ G 332 Gl 46
Mondovi ○ USA 56 Dc 23
Mondovì ○ I 185 Gk 23
Mondrian Island ♁ AUS 368 Lm 63
Monduli ○ EAT 337 Hl 47
Moné ~ CAM 320 Gl 43
Monemvassía ○ GR 194 Hd 27
Moneragala ○ CL 239 Ke 42
Monet ○ CDN 60 Dl 21
Monett ○ USA 70 Db 27
Monfalcone ○ I 185 Gn 23
Monforte ○ E 184 Gc 24
Monforte ○ P 184 Gc 26
Monga ○ RDC 321 Hd 43
Mongala ~ RDC 333 Hb 44
Mongalla ○ SUD 324 Hh 43
Mongar ○ BHT 235 Kk 32
Mongbwalu ○ RDC 324 Hg 45
Mongemputu ○ RDC 333 Hc 47
Mongeri ○ WAL 316 Ga 41
Mongers Lake ~ AUS 368 Lj 60
Mongge ○ RI 283 Mc 46
Monggui ○ RI 283 Md 46
Mŏng Hpayak ○ MYA 254 Kp 35
Mŏng Hsan ○ MYA 254 Kn 35
Mŏng Ka ○ MYA 254 Kp 35
Mŏng Kung ○ MYA 254 Kn 35
Mongla ○ BD 235 Kj 34
Mŏng Mit ○ MYA 254 Kn 34
Mŏng Nai ○ MYA 254 Kn 35
Mongo ○ TCH 321 Hb 39
Mongolia □ MNG 204 Ub 9
Mongomo ○ GQ 332 Gm 45
Mongonu ○ WAN 321 Gn 39
Mongororo ○ TCH 313 Hd 40
Mongotang ○ VRC 254 Kp 31
Mongoumba ○ RCA 333 Hb 44
Mŏng Pan ○ MYA 254 Kp 35
Mŏng Ton ○ MYA 254 Kp 35
Mongu ○ Z 341 Hd 53
Mongua ○ ANG 340 Gp 54
Mŏnguel ○ RIM 304 Fp 37
Mŏng Yai ○ MYA 254 Kp 34
Mŏng Yang ○ MYA 254 Kp 35
Mŏng Yawng ○ MYA 254 La 35
Mŏng Yu ○ MYA 254 Kp 34
Moni ○ RI 282 Ll 50
Monianga ○ RDC 333 Hb 44
Moniteau ○ USA 57 Dd 23
Monida ○ USA 51 Cf 23
Monida Pass ○ USA 51 Cf 23
Monida Pass △ USA 51 Cf 23
Monieka ○ RDC 333 Hc 46
Monimpébougou ○ RMM 305 Gd 38
Moni River ~ PNG 287 Ml 50
Monitcello ○ USA 71 Df 27
Monitor Range ⩕ USA 64 Cd 26
Moñitos ○ CO 106 Dk 41
Monje ○ RA 137 Ed 62
Monjolos ○ BR 133 Em 55
Monkayo ○ RP 275 Ln 42
Monkey Bay ○ MW 344 Hk 53
Monkey Hill △ AUS 379 Ml 62
Monkey Mia ○ AUS 368 Lg 58
Mońki ○ PL 171 Hd 19
Monkira ○ AUS 374 Mg 58
Monkoto ○ RDC 333 Hc 46
Monmouth ○ USA 50 Ca 23
Monmouth ○ USA 71 Dc 25
Mono ~ RT 317 Gg 41
Monobamba ○ PE 128 Dl 51
Monodoñedo ○ E 184 Gc 24
Monogororo ○ TCH 313 Hd 40
Mono Island ♁ SOL 290 Mp 49
Mono Lake ~ USA 64 Cc 26
Monólithos ○ GR 195 Hg 27
Monolon ○ AUS 378 Mh 61
Monopamba ○ CO 116 Dk 45
Monou ○ TCH 309 Hd 37
Monowai ○ NZ 382 Nf 68
Monroe ○ USA 50 Cb 22
Monroe ○ USA 57 Dd 24
Monroe ○ USA 70 Db 25
Monroe ○ USA 70 Db 29
Monroe ○ USA 71 Dg 25
Monroe ○ USA 71 Dg 29
Monroe ○ USA 71 Dh 28
Monroe City ○ USA 70 Dc 26
Monroe Lake ~ USA 71 De 26
Monroeville ○ USA 74 Dj 25
Monroeville ○ USA 86 De 30
Monrovia ▣ LB 316 Ga 42
Mons ○ B 163 Gj 20
Monsefú ○ PE 116 Dh 49
Monsenhor Gil ○ BR 124 En 48
Monsidão ○ BR 133 Em 51
Møns Klint ★ DK 170 Gn 18
Monsombougou ○ RMM 304 Ga 38
Montagne-au-Perche ○ F 163 Gg 21
Montagnes Françaises △ F 113 Eg 43
Montagnes Noires ⩕ RH 101 Dm 36
Montagu ○ ZA 358 Hc 62
Montague ○ CDN 61 Ec 22
Montague Island ♁ USA 46 Bc 15
Montague Island ♁ AUS 379 Mm 64
Montague Sound ~ AUS 361 Ln 53
Montaigu ○ F 163 Gf 22
Montajtas ○ KZ 223 Jn 24
Montalbán ○ E 184 Gf 25
Montalto △ I 194 Gp 26
Montalvânia ○ BR 133 Em 53
Montana ◉ USA 51 Cg 22
Montana ○ BG 194 Hd 24
Montaña de Yoro △ HN 96 De 38
Montañas de Colón ⩕ HN 97 Df 38
Montañas de Comayagua ⩕ HN 96 De 38
Montañas del Norte de Chiapas ⩕ MEX 93 Db 37
Montañas del Patuca ⩕ HN 97 Df 38
Montandón ○ RCH 136 Dp 59
Montanha ○ BR 125 Ep 55
Montargis ○ F 163 Gh 21
Montauban ○ F 184 Gg 23
Montauk ○ USA 74 Dn 25
Montauk Point ⌓ USA 74 Dn 25
Mont Baldy △ USA 65 Ch 29
Montbard ○ F 163 Gh 22
Montbéliard ○ F 163 Gk 22
Mont Bellevue de'Inini △ F 113 Eh 44
Mont Blanc △ F 185 Gk 23
Mont-Boré ○ F 386 Nf 57
Montbrison ○ F 185 Gh 23
Montceau-les-Mines ○ F 163 Gj 22
Mont-de- Marsan ○ F 184 Gf 24
Montdidier ○ F 163 Gh 21
Mont du Metal △ DZ 308 Gl 35
Mont du Niaguouelé △ RG 316 Gb 40
Monteagle ○ USA 71 Df 28
Monteagle ○ AUS 375 Mk 57
Monteagudo ○ BOL 129 Eb 55
Monte Albán ★ MEX 92 Cp 36
Monte Alegre ○ BR 120 Eg 46
Montealegre ○ P 184 Gc 25
Monte Alegre de Goiás ○ BR 133 El 52
Monte Alegre de Minas ○ BR 133 Ek 55
Monte Alegre de Sergipe ○ BR 125 Fb 51
Monte Alegre do Piauí ○ BR 121 Em 50
Monte Aprazível ○ BR 140 Ej 56
Monte Azul ○ BR 125 En 53
Montebello ○ CDN 60 Dl 23
Montebello Islands ♁ AUS 360 Lh 56
Monte Belo ○ ANG 340 Gp 52
Monte Buckland △ RA 152 Eb 73
Monte Burney △ RCH 152 Dm 72
Monte Campana △ RA 152 Eb 73
Monte-Carlo ○ F 185 Gk 24
Monte Carmelo ○ BR 133 El 55
Monte Caseros ○ RA 146 Ee 61
Monte Castelo ○ BR 140 Ej 59
Monte Cátria △ I 185 Gn 24
Montecello ○ USA 71 De 25
Monte Cervati △ I 194 Gp 25
Monte Cervialto △ I 194 Gp 25
Monte Chiperone △ MOC 344 Hk 54
Monte Cinto △ F 185 Gl 24
Monte Comán ○ RA 137 Ea 63
Monte Creek ○ CDN 50 Cc 20
Monte Cristi ○ DOM 101 Dn 36
Montecristi ○ EC 116 Dh 46
Monte Cristo ○ BOL 129 Ed 53
Monte Darwin △ RCH 152 Dp 73
Monte del Gennargentu △ I 185 Gl 26
Monte Dinero ○ RA 152 Dp 72
Monte Dourado ○ BR 121 Eh 46
Monte do Urucum △ BR 132 Ef 55
Monte Eremita △ I 194 Gp 25
Monte Escobedo ○ MEX 92 Cl 34
Monte Falterona △ I 185 Gm 24
Montego Bay ○ JA 100 Dj 36
Montego Bay ~ JA 100 Dj 36
Monte Grande ○ NIC 96 Df 39
Monte Grande ⌒ BOL 129 Ec 54
Monte Grande △ BR 132 Ee 55
Monte Hall Dyke △ RCH 152 Dl 72
Monte Hermoso ○ RA 147 Ed 65
Monte Incudine △ F 185 Gl 25
Monte Inés △ RA 152 Dp 70
Monteiro ○ BR 124 Fb 49
Monte Jervis △ RCH 152 Dl 70
Monte Jesi △ MOC 344 Hk 52
Monte Ladrillero △ RCH 152 Dm 72
Montelibano ○ CO 106 Dl 42
Montelimar ○ NIC 96 De 40
Montélimar ○ F 185 Gj 23
Monte Lindo ~ PY 140 Ee 57
Monte Lindo ~ PY 140 Ed 57
Monte Lindo Grande ~ RA 140 Ee 58
Montello ○ USA 57 Dd 24
Montello ○ USA 64 Ce 25
Monte Mabu △ MOC 344 Hl 54
Monte Macá △ RCH 152 Dm 68
Monte Melimoyu △ RCH 147 Dm 67
Monte Mepalue △ MOC 344 Hm 53
Monte Miletto △ I 194 Gp 25
Monte Mitra △ GQ 332 Gl 45
Montemorelos ○ MEX 81 Cn 33
Montemor-o-Novo ○ P 184 Gb 26
Monte Namuli △ MOC 344 Hl 53
Montenegro ○ BR 146 Ej 60
Montenegro □ MON 194 Hb 24
Montenge-Boma ○ RDC 333 Hb 44
Monte Patria ○ RCH 137 Dn 61
Montepellier ○ F 185 Gh 24
Monte Perdido △ E 184 Gf 24
Montepío ○ MEX 93 Da 36
Monte Plata ○ DOM 101 Dp 36
Montepuez ~ MOC 344 Hm 52
Montepulciano ○ I 185 Gm 24
Monte Quemado ○ RA 136 Ec 58
Montequez ○ MOC 344 Hm 52
Monte Rasu △ I 185 Gl 25
Monterey ○ USA 64 Ca 27
Monterey ○ USA 74 Dj 26
Monterey Bay ~ USA 64 Ca 27
Monteria ○ CO 106 Dk 41
Montero ○ BOL 129 Ec 54
Monteros ○ RA 136 Eb 59
Monte Rosa △ I 185 Gk 23
Monte Rotondo △ F 185 Gl 24
Monterrey ○ MEX 81 Cm 33
Monterrico ○ GCA 93 Dc 39
Montes Altos ○ BR 121 El 48
Monte Santo ○ BR 125 Fa 51
Monte Santo de Minsa ○ BR 141 El 56
Monte Sarmiente △ RCH 152 Dn 73
Monte Scholl △ RA 152 Dp 70
Montes Claros ○ BR 125 En 54
Montes de Oca ○ RA 147 Ec 65
Montes de Onzole ⩕ EC 116 Dj 45
Montes de Toledo ⩕ E 184 Gd 26
Monte Servino △ I 185 Gk 23
Monte Sirino △ I 194 Gp 25
Montesquieu Islands ♁ AUS 361 Ln 53
Monte Terminillo △ I 185 Gn 24
Monte Tetris △ RA 152 Dm 70
Monte Triste △ RA 147 Eb 67
Monteverde ★ CR 97 Df 40
Monte Victoria △ RCH 152 Dn 72
Montevideo ○ USA 56 Da 23
Montevideo ▣ ROU 146 Ef 63
Monteville ○ CDN 57 Dh 22
Monte Viso △ I 185 Gk 23
Monte Vista ○ USA 65 Cj 27
Monte Voltarino △ I 194 Gp 25
Monte Warton △ RCH 152 Dm 72
Montezuma ○ USA 86 Df 29
Montezuma ○ BR 125 En 53
Mont Gangan ⩕ RG 316 Fp 40
Montgomery ○ USA 71 De 29
Montgomery City ○ USA 70 Dc 26
Mont Guédi △ TCH 321 Hb 39
Mont Guyot △ USA 71 Dg 28
Monti ○ I 185 Gl 25
Mont Iboundji △ G 332 Gm 46
Monticello ○ USA 65 Ch 27
Monticello ○ USA 65 Cj 29
Monticello ○ USA 70 Dc 24
Monticello ○ USA 71 Dg 29
Monticello ○ USA 74 Dl 25
Monticello ○ USA 86 Dc 29
Montichiari ○ I 185 Gm 23
Montijo ○ E 184 Gc 26
Montilla ○ E 184 Gd 27
Montima ~ RDC 321 Hc 44
Montipa ○ ANG 340 Gn 53
Montividiu ○ BR 133 Ej 54
Mont Joli ○ CDN 60 Dp 21
Mont Kadiondola △ RG 316 Ga 40
Mont Koronga △ RT 317 Gg 41
Mont Laurier ○ CDN 60 Dl 22
Mont Lozere △ F 185 Gh 23
Montluçon ○ F 163 Gg 22
Mont Mabanda △ G 332 Gm 47
Montmagny ○ CDN 60 Dn 22
Montmartre ○ CDN 51 Cl 20
Mont Mézenc △ F 185 Gj 23
Mont Mimongo △ G 332 Gm 46
Mont Morris ○ AUS 375 Mj 58
Mont Moubolo ○ RN 308 Gm 36
Mont Mpélé △ G 332 Gm 47
Mont Niénokoué △ CI 305 Gc 43
Monto ○ AUS 375 Mm 58
Montoro ○ E 184 Gd 26
Mont Pelée △ F 104 Ed 38
Montpelier ○ USA 60 Dm 23
Montpelier ○ USA 65 Cg 24
Montreal ○ CDN 60 Dl 23
Montreal Lake Indian Reservation ••• CDN 51 Cj 19
Montreal River ~ CDN 57 Dg 22
Montreuil ○ F 163 Gg 20
Montreux ○ CH 163 Gk 22
Montrose ○ USA 65 Ch 26
Montrose ○ USA 74 Dk 25
Montrose ○ USA 86 Dc 29
Montrose ○ GB 162 Ge 17
Mont Ross △ F 31 Na 14
Montrouis ○ RH 101 Dm 36
Mont Sainte Odile ★ F 163 Gk 21
Monts Bleus ⩕ RDC 324 Hh 45
Monts Chic-Chocs ⩕ CDN 60 Ea 21
Monts de Cristal ⩕ G 332 Gm 45
Monts de Daïa ⩕ DZ 293 Gf 28
Monts de Oulad Naïl ⩕ DZ 296 Gh 28
Monts des Ksour ⩕ DZ 293 Gf 29
Monts des Nementcha ⩕ DZ 296 Gk 28
Monts de Tlemcen ⩕ DZ 293 Gf 28
Monts du Hombori ⩕ RMM 305 Ge 38
Monts du Mouydir ⩕ DZ 296 Gj 33
Monts du Zab ⩕ DZ 296 Gj 28
Montserrat ♁ GB 104 Ec 37
Monts Gautier ⩕ DZ 308 Gl 34
Montsinéry ○ F 113 Eh 43
Monts Madingues ⩕ RMM 316 Gb 39
Monts Mugtia ⩕ RDC 336 Hg 49
Monts Notre-Dame ⩕ CDN 60 Dn 23
Monts Otish △ CDN 60 Dn 19
Mont-St.-Pierre ○ CDN 61 Eb 21
Monts Totomaï ⩕ RN 297 Gn 35
Mont Toussoro △ RCA 321 Hd 41
Monturaqui ○ RCH 136 Dp 58
Mont Ventoux △ F 185 Gj 23
Mont Vernon ○ AUS 368 Lk 58
Monument Draw River ~ USA 65 Cl 29
Monument Rocks ★ USA 70 Cm 26
Monument Valley ⌒ USA 65 Cg 27
Monywa ○ MYA 254 Km 34
Monza ○ I 185 Gl 23
Monza ○ VRC 231 Kl 29
Monze ○ Z 341 Hf 54
Monzón ○ PE 116 Dk 50
Monzón ○ E 184 Gg 25
Mooifontein ○ NAM 348 Ha 58
Mooi River ○ ZA 349 Hg 60
Mooirivier ~ ZA 352 Hh 60
Moojeeba ○ AUS 365 Mh 53
Mookane ○ RB 349 Hf 57
Mooketsi ○ ZA 352 Hh 57
Mookgopong Naboomspruit ○ ZA 349 Hg 58
Mooki ~ AUS 379 Mm 61
Moola ~ MOC 344 Hk 51
Mooloo Downs ○ AUS 368 Lj 58
Mooloogool ○ AUS 368 Lk 59
Mooloolooo Out Station ○ AUS 364 Mb 54
Moomba ○ AUS 374 Mg 59
Moomin Creek ~ AUS 375 Ml 60
Moonan Flat ○ AUS 379 Mm 61
Moonaree ○ AUS 378 Md 61
Moonbi Range ⩕ AUS 379 Mm 61
Moonda Lake ~ AUS 374 Mg 58
Moonie ~ AUS 375 Ml 60
Moonie ○ AUS 375 Mm 59
Moonlight Head ⌓ AUS 378 Mh 65
Moonta ○ AUS 378 Me 63
Moonya ○ AUS 375 Mj 57
Moora ○ AUS 368 Lh 61
Moorarie ○ AUS 368 Lj 58
Moorcroft ○ USA 51 Ck 23
Moore ○ USA 51 Ch 22
Moore ○ USA 70 Cp 28
Moore ~ AUS 368 Lh 61
Moore Haven ○ USA 87 Dh 32
Moore Home St. Mem. ★ USA 71 Dd 26
Moore Park ○ AUS 375 Mn 58
Moore River ♀ AUS 368 Lh 61
Moores Creek N.B. ★ USA 74 Dj 28
Moore's Island ♁ BS 87 Dk 32
Mooresville ○ USA 71 Dh 28
Mooreville ○ USA 71 De 26
Moorhead ○ USA 51 Ck 23
Moorhead ○ USA 56 Cp 22
Moornanyah Lake ~ AUS 379 Mh 62
Moose ○ USA 51 Cg 24
Moose Island ♁ CDN 56 Cp 20
Moose Jaw ○ CDN 51 Ck 20
Mooselookmeguntic Lake ~ USA 60 Dn 23
Moose Mountain △ CDN 51 Cl 21
Moose Pass ○ USA 46 Ba 15
Moose River ~ CDN 57 Dg 20
Mooshead Lake ~ USA 60 Dn 23
Moosomin ○ CDN 56 Cm 20
Moosonee ○ CDN 57 Dh 20
Mootwingee ♀ AUS 378 Mh 61
Mootwinge Historical Site (Aboriginal Rock Art) ★ AUS 378 Mg 61
Mopán ~ GCA 93 Dd 37
Mopane ○ ZA 349 Hg 57
Mopeia ○ MOC 344 Hk 55
Mopipi ○ RB 349 He 56
Mopti ○ RMM 305 Gd 38
Moqor ○ AFG 223 Jm 29
Moquegua ○ PE 128 Dn 54
Moquegua ~ PE 128 Dn 54
Moquehuá ○ RA 146 Ee 63
Mór ○ H 174 Hb 22
Mora ○ USA 56 Db 23
Mora ○ USA 65 Ck 28
Mora ○ S 158 Gp 15
Mora ○ P 184 Gb 26
Mora ○ E 184 Ge 26
Mora ○ CAM 321 Gp 40
Moradabad ○ IND 234 Kd 31
Morada Nova ○ BR 124 Fa 48
Morada Nova de Minas ○ BR 133 Em 55
Morado ~ RCH 136 Dn 59
Morafenobe ○ RM 345 Ja 54
Morag ○ PL 170 Hb 19
Moraine State Park ♀ USA 74 Dj 25
Morais de Almeida ○ BR 120 Eg 49
Moraleja ○ P 184 Gc 25
Morales ○ GCA 93 Dd 38
Moramanga ○ RM 345 Jc 55
Moran ○ USA 70 Da 27
Moran ~ AUS 361 Ln 53
Moranbah ○ AUS 375 Ml 57
Moran Junction ○ USA 51 Cg 24
Morant Bay ○ JA 101 Dk 37
Morant Point ⌓ JA 101 Dk 37
Morarano ○ RM 345 Jb 54
Mora River ~ USA 65 Ck 28
Moratalla ○ E 184 Ge 26
Moratuwa ○ CL 239 Kd 42
Moravia ⌒ CZ 174 Gp 21
Morávia ⩕ MOC 341 Hh 53
Morawa ~ CZ 174 Ha 21
Morawa ○ AUS 368 Lj 60
Morawhanna ○ GUY 112 Ee 41
Moray Downs ○ AUS 375 Mk 56
Moray Firth ~ GB 162 Ge 17
Morazán ○ HN 96 De 38
Morbeng Soekmekaar ○ ZA 349 Hg 57
Morbi ○ IND 227 Jp 34
Mörbylånga ○ S 170 Ha 17
Morden ○ CDN 56 Cn 21
Mordovo ○ RUS 181 Hn 19
Mordovskij zopovednik ♀ RUS 181 Hp 18
Mor'e ○ RUS 171 Hh 15
Moreau ~ USA 56 Cm 23
Morecambe ○ GB 162 Ge 18
Moree ○ AUS 375 Ml 60
Morehead ○ PNG 286 Mg 50
Morehead City ○ USA 74 Dk 28
Morehead River ~ PNG 286 Mg 50
Moreheand ○ USA 71 Dg 26
Morelia ○ MEX 92 Cm 36
Morelia ○ CO 106 Dl 45
Morell ○ CDN 61 Ec 22
Morella ○ E 184 Gf 25
Morella ○ AUS 375 Mh 57
Morelos ○ MEX 81 Cl 31
Morelos ○ MEX 81 Cm 31
Morelos ○ MEX 92 Cl 34
Morena ○ IND 234 Kd 32
Morenero ○ YV 112 Ec 41
Moreno ○ BR 124 Fc 50
Moreno ○ RA 146 Ee 63
Moresby Island ♁ CDN 42 Da 8
Moretele ~ ZA 349 Hf 58
Moreton ○ AUS 365 Mh 52
Moreton Bay ~ AUS 375 Mn 59
Moreton Island ♁ AUS 375 Mn 59
Morez ○ F 163 Gj 22
Morfou ○ CY 195 Hj 28
Morgāb ○ AFG 223 Jk 28
Morġab ~ AFG 223 Jl 28
Morgābrūb ~ AFG 223 Jk 28
Morgan ○ AUS 378 Mf 63
Morgan City ○ USA 86 Dc 31
Morganfield ○ USA 71 De 27
Morgan Hill ○ USA 64 Cb 27
Morganton ○ USA 71 Dh 28
Morgantown ○ USA 71 De 27
Morgantown ○ USA 74 Dj 26
Morgan Vale ○ AUS 378 Mg 62
Morgenzon ○ ZA 349 Hg 59
Morghab ~ TM 223 Jk 27
Mori ○ J 250 Mg 24
Moriarty ○ USA 65 Cj 28
Moribaya ○ RG 316 Gb 41
Morichal Largo ~ YV 112 Ec 41
Morichal Viejo ○ CO 107 Dn 44
Morigio Island ♁ PNG 287 Mj 49
Morijo ○ EAK 337 Hk 46
Moriki ○ WAN 320 Gk 39
Morioka ○ J 250 Mg 26
Morire ○ MOC 344 Hk 54
Mori River ~ PNG 287 Ml 50
Morjen ~ PK 226 Jk 31
Morkoka ~ RUS 204 Vb 6
Morlaix ○ F 163 Ge 21
Morley ○ CDN 50 Ce 20
Morne Diablotin △ WD 104 Ed 38
Morne Trois Pitons N.P. ★ WD 104 Ed 38
Morney ○ AUS 374 Mg 58
Mornington Island ♁ AUS 365 Mf 54
Moro ○ USA 50 Cb 23
Moro ○ PE 116 Dj 50
Moro ○ PK 227 Jm 32
Moroak ○ AUS 364 Mc 53
Morobe ○ PNG 287 Mk 49
Morobo ○ SUD 324 Hh 44
Morocco □ MA 293 Gc 29
Morococha ○ PE 116 Dk 51
Morodougou ○ RG 316 Gb 40
Morogoro ○ EAT 337 Hl 49
Moro Gulf ~ RP 275 Lm 42
Moroleón ○ MEX 92 Cm 35
Morombe ○ RM 353 Hp 56
Morón ○ C 100 Dj 34
Morón ○ YV 107 Dp 40
Morón ○ RA 146 Ee 63
Mörön ○ MNG 204 Uc 9
Morona ~ PE 116 Dk 48
Morón d.l.F. ○ E 184 Gd 27
Morondava ○ RM 353 Hp 56
Morondo ○ CI 305 Gc 41
Moroni ▣ COM 345 Hp 51
Moronou ○ CI 317 Gd 42
Moroto ○ EAU 325 Hk 44
Morouba ○ RCA 321 Hb 42
Morowali ○ RI 282 Ll 46
Morozovsk ○ RUS 181 Hn 21
Morpará ○ BR 125 En 51
Morreesburg ○ ZA 358 Hb 62
Morrestes ○ BR 141 Ek 58
Morrilton ○ USA 70 Db 28
Morrin ○ CDN 51 Cf 20
Morrinhos ○ BR 124 Ep 47
Morrinhos ○ BR 133 Ek 54
Morrinsville ○ NZ 383 Nk 64
Morris ○ CDN 56 Cp 21
Morrison Bay ~ MYA 262 Kp 39
Morristown ○ USA 56 Cm 23
Morristown ○ USA 56 Da 23
Morristown ○ USA 71 Dg 27
Morrisville ○ USA 60 Dm 23
Morro ○ EC 116 Dh 47
Morro Bay ○ USA 64 Cb 28
Morro Campo do Padre △ BR 140 Ek 59
Morro Chico ○ RCH 152 Dn 72
Morrocoy ♀ YV 107 Dp 40
Morro de Curoca △ ANG 340 Gn 54
Morro do Chapéu ○ BR 125 Ep 51
Morro do Copão Doce △ BR 140 Ej 59
Morro do Moleque △ BR 140 Ek 60
Morro do Pilar ○ BR 141 En 55
Morropón ○ PE 116 Dj 48
Morro River ~ WAL 316 Ga 42
Morros ○ BR 124 En 47
Morrua ○ MOC 344 Hl 54
Morrumbala ○ MOC 344 Hk 54
Morrumbene ○ MOC 352 Hk 57
Mors ⌒ DK 170 Gl 17
Moršansk ○ RUS 181 Hn 19
Morsi ○ IND 234 Kd 35
Morstone ○ AUS 365 Mf 55
Mørsvikbotn ○ N 158 Gp 12
Mortagne ○ F 184 Gf 23
Mortes ~ BR 133 Ej 52
Mortes ~ BR 133 Ej 53
Mortesoro ○ SUD 313 Hk 40
Mortlake ○ AUS 378 Mh 65
Mortlock Islands ♁ PNG 290 Na 48
Morton ○ USA 50 Ca 22
Morton ♀ AUS 379 Mm 63
Mortugaba ○ BR 125 En 53
Moruga ○ TT 104 Ed 40
Moruita ○ EAU 325 Hk 45
Morundah ○ AUS 379 Mk 63
Morungu ○ EAT 336 Hh 48
Moruongete △ EAU 325 Hk 44
Moruppatti ○ IND 239 Kd 40
Moruya ○ AUS 379 Mm 63
Morvan ⌒ F 163 Gh 22

446 Moffit - Morvan

Morven O AUS 375 Mk 59
Morwell O AUS 379 Mk 65
Mosa O PNG 287 Mm 48
Mosambique □ MOC 344 Hl 53
Mosby O USA 51 Cj 22
Mosca O USA 65 Cj 27
Moščnyi ostrov ◭ RUS 171 Hf 16
Mosconi O RA 137 Ed 63
Moscow O USA 50 Cd 22
Moscow O USA 71 Dd 28
Moscow ▣ RUS 171 Hl 18
Mosel ~ D 163 Gk 21
Moselebe ~ RB 349 He 58
Moser River O CDN 61 Ec 23
Moses Lake O USA 50 Cc 22
Mosetse O RB 349 Hf 56
Mošgān O IR 226 Jf 31
Mosgiel O NZ 382 Nh 68
Moshaneng O RB 349 He 58
Moshesh's Ford O ZA 349 Hf 61
Moshi O EAT 337 Hl 47
Moshi Rest Camp O Z 341 He 53
Mosi-Oa-Tunya ♀ Z 341 He 54
Mosite O RDC 333 Hd 45
Mosjøen O N 158 Gn 13
Moskenesøya ◭ N 158 Gn 12
Moskosel O S 158 Hb 13
Moskovskij O TJ 223 Jn 27
Moskow O USA 70 Cm 27
Moskva ~ RUS 171 Hl 18
Mosna O RO 175 He 22
Mošok O RUS 181 Hn 18
Mosomane O RB 349 He 57
Mosonmagyaróvár O H 174 Ha 22
Mosopa O RB 349 He 58
Mosqueiro O BR 121 Ek 46
Mosqueiro O BR 125 Fb 51
Mosquera O CO 106 Dj 44
Mosquero O USA 65 Cl 28
Mosquito ~ PY 140 Ee 57
Mosquito Coast ⏢ NIC 97 Dg 39
Mosquito Gulf ~ PA 97 Dh 41
Mosquito Lagoon ~ USA 87 Dh 31
Moss O N 170 Gm 16
Mossaka O RCB 333 Ha 46
Mossbank O CDN 51 Ck 20
Moss Bluff O USA 86 Db 30
Mossburn O NZ 382 Nf 68
Mosselbaai O ZA 358 Hd 63
Mossendjo O RCB 332 Gn 47
Mossgiel O AUS 379 Mj 62
Mossman O AUS 365 Mj 54
Mossoró O BR 124 Fb 48
Mossoró ~ BR 124 Fb 48
Mossuril O MOC 344 Hn 53
Moss Vale O AUS 379 Mm 63
Most O CZ 174 Gn 20
Mostar O BIH 194 Ha 24
Mostardas O BR 146 Ej 61
Mosteiro de Batalha ★ P 184 Gb 26
Móstoles O E 184 Gd 25
Mosul O IRQ 209 Hp 27
Møsvatnet ~ N 170 Gk 16
Mot'a O ETH 313 Hl 40
Motaba ~ RCB 321 Ha 44
Motagua ~ GCA 93 Dd 38
Motala O S 170 Gp 16
Motigu O GH 317 Ge 41
Motihari O IND 235 Kg 32
Motilla d.P. O E 184 Gf 26
Motiti Island ◭ NZ 383 Nl 64
Motley O USA 56 Da 22
Motloutse ~ RB 349 Hf 56
Motloutse ~ RB 349 Hg 57
Motobu O J 259 Lp 32
Motopi O RB 349 He 56
Motorina Island ◭ PNG 287 Mn 51
Motor Speedway ★ USA 71 De 26
Motozintla de Mendoza O MEX 93 Db 38
Motril O E 184 Ge 27
Motru O RO 194 Hd 23
Mott O USA 51 Cl 22
Motto do Padre △ BR 133 Ek 54
Motueka O NZ 383 Nj 66
Motuhora Island ◭ NZ 383 Nl 64
Motul O MEX 93 Dd 36
Motupe O PE 116 Dj 49
Motupiko O NZ 383 Nj 66
Moturiki ◭ FJI 387 Nm 54
Motu River ~ NZ 383 Nl 65
Motygino O RUS 204 Ua 7
Motykleika O RUS 23 Sa 4
Mou O F 386 Nf 56
Moucha Island ◭ DJI 328 Hp 40
Mouchalagane ~ CDN 60 Dp 19
Mouchard O F 163 Gj 22
Mouchoir Bank ▽ 101 Dn 35
Mouchoir Passage ≈ 101 Dn 35
Moudjéria O RIM 304 Fp 37
Moudros O GR 194 He 26
Mouenda O G 332 Gm 47
Mougamou O G 332 Gn 46
Mouila O G 332 Gm 46
Moujia O RN 308 Gj 38
Mouka O RCA 321 Hc 42
Moukoumbi O G 332 Gn 46
Moul O RN 297 Gn 38
Moula ~ TCH 321 Ha 41
Moulamein O AUS 379 Mj 63
Moulares O TN 296 Gl 28
Moulay Bouâzza O MA 293 Gc 29
Moulay-Bousselhamo O MA 293 Gc 28
Moulay Idriss O MA 293 Gd 29
Mould Bay O CDN 42 Ea 3
Moulèngui-Binza O G 332 Gm 47
Moulhoule O DJI 313 Hp 39
Moulins O F 163 Gh 22
Mouloud O DJI 328 Hp 40
Moulton Neel O USA 71 De 28
Moultrie O USA 86 Df 30
Moulvi Bazar O BD 235 Kk 33
Moulvouday O CAM 321 Gp 40
Mouly O F 386 Nf 56
Mounanko O CAM 320 Gl 44
Mound City O USA 56 Cn 23
Moundou O TCH 321 Gp 41
Moundsville O USA 71 Dh 26
Moungoudou O RCB 332 Gn 47
Moungoundi O RCB 332 Gm 47
Moŭng Roessei O K 263 Lb 39
Mounguel O CAM 321 Gn 42
Mouniandjé ~ G 332 Gn 45
Mount Abbot △ AUS 375 Mk 56
Mount Abu △ IND 227 Ka 33
Mount Adam △ GB 147 Ed 71
Mount Adams △ USA 50 Cb 22
Mount Agnamala △ RP 267 Ll 36
Mount Agou △ RT 317 Gg 42
Mount Aha △ RB 340 Hc 55
Mountain O USA 57 Dd 23
Mountain City O USA 64 Ce 25
Mountain City O USA 71 Dh 27
Mountain Grove O USA 70 Db 27
Mountain Home O USA 50 Cd 24
Mountain Home O USA 70 Db 27
Mountains Bamboutos ⛰ CAM 320 Gl 43
Mountains Boutourou ⌓ CI 317 Ge 41
Mountain Springs O USA 64 Ce 28
Mountains Toura △ CI 305 Gc 42
Mountain Valley O AUS 364 Mc 53
Mountain View O USA 70 Db 28
Mountain Village O USA 46 Aj 13
Mountain Zebra ★ ZA 358 He 62
Mount Aiome △ PNG 287 Mj 48
Mount Airy O USA 71 Dh 27
Mount Albert Edward △ PNG 287 Mk 50
Mount Alice West △ AUS 368 Ll 59
Mount Allen △ NZ 382 Nf 69
Mount Alma △ AUS 375 Mm 57
Mount Amung △ PNG 287 Mk 49
Mount Anglem △ NZ 382 Nf 69
Mount Anne △ AUS 378 Mk 67
Mount Apo △ RP 275 Ln 42
Mount Aragats △ ARM 202 Ja 25
Mount Ararat △ TR 202 Ja 26
Mount Arden △ AUS 378 Me 62
Mount Arnhurst △ AUS 360 Lp 55
Mount Aspiring ♀ NZ 382 Ng 68
Mount Aspiring △ NZ 382 Ng 68
Mount Atouat △ LAO 263 Ld 38
Mount Augustus O AUS 368 Lj 58
Mount Augustus ♀ AUS 368 Lj 58
Mount Augustus △ AUS 368 Lj 58
Mount Ayanganna △ GUY 112 Ed 43
Mount Ayliff O ZA 349 Hg 61
Mount Ayr O USA 70 Da 25
Mount Baco △ RP 267 Ll 39
Mount Bagong △ AUS 379 Mk 64
Mount Bajimba △ AUS 375 Mn 60
Mount Baker △ USA 50 Cb 21
Mount Balbi △ PNG 290 Mp 49
Mount Ball △ AUS 361 Lp 55
Mount Banda Banda △ AUS 379 Mn 61
Mount Bangeta △ PNG 287 Mk 49
Mount Barker O AUS 368 Lj 63
Mount Barker △ AUS 378 Mf 63
Mount Barloweerie △ AUS 368 Lj 59
Mount Barnett O AUS 361 Ln 54
Mount Barrington △ AUS 379 Mm 62
Mount Beadell △ AUS 369 Ln 58
Mount Beauty O AUS 379 Mk 64
Mount Behn △ AUS 364 Ma 54
Mount Bennett △ AUS 360 Lj 57
Mount Binga △ MOC 344 Hj 55
Mount Blackburn △ USA 46 Ck 15
Mount Bodangora △ AUS 379 Ml 62
Mount Bona △ USA 46 Be 15
Mount Bonaparte △ USA 50 Cc 21
Mount Booroondara △ AUS 379 Mj 61
Mount Bosavi △ PNG 286 Mh 49
Mount Brassey △ AUS 374 Md 57
Mount Brazeau △ CDN 50 Cd 19
Mount Bresnahan △ AUS 360 Lj 57
Mount Brockman O AUS 360 Lj 57
Mount Brockman △ AUS 360 Lj 57
Mount Bruce △ AUS 360 Lk 57
Mount Bryan △ AUS 378 Mf 62
Mount Buffalo ♀ AUS 379 Mk 64
Mount Buller △ AUS 379 Mk 64
Mount Bundey △ AUS 364 Mb 52
Mount Burges △ AUS 368 Ll 61
Mount Burgess △ CDN 47 Bg 11
Mount Busa △ RP 275 Ln 42
Mount Cairns △ AUS 374 Md 56
Mount Callahan △ USA 64 Cd 26
Mount Cameroun △ CAM 320 Gl 43
Mount Canlaon △ RP 267 Lm 40
Mount Cann △ AUS 379 Ml 64
Mount Canobolis △ AUS 379 Ml 62
Mount Capitoah △ RP 267 Ln 39
Mount Carleton △ CDN 61 Ea 22
Mount Carmel O USA 71 Dd 26
Mount Carmel Junction O USA 64 Cf 27
Mount Carrol O USA 71 Dd 24
Mount Carter △ AUS 365 Mh 52
Mount Catherine △ AUS 375 Ml 58
Mount Cecil △ AUS 369 Mc 58
Mount Cecil Rhodes △ AUS 368 Ll 58
Mount Celia O AUS 368 Lm 60
Mount Cetaceo △ RP 267 Ll 37
Mount Charles △ AUS 368 Lj 59
Mount Charles △ AUS 369 Lp 58
Mount Chiginagak △ USA 46 Al 17
Mount Clere O AUS 368 Lj 58
Mount Cleveland △ USA 50 Ce 21
Mount Cockburn △ AUS 361 Mb 57
Mount Cockburn North △ AUS 364 Ma 53
Mount Columbia △ CDN 50 Cd 19
Mount Connelly △ AUS 361 Lp 53
Mount Connor △ AUS 361 Ln 53
Mount Cook O NZ 382 Ng 67
Mount Cook △ NZ 382 Ng 67
Mount Cook ♀ NZ 382 Nh 67
Mount Cooke △ AUS 368 Lj 62
Mount Coole ♀ AUS 365 Mj 53
Mount Coolon O AUS 375 Mk 56
Mount Coricudgy △ AUS 379 Mm 62
Mount Cradle △ AUS 378 Mj 66
Mount Currie Indian Reservation ••• CDN 50 Ca 20
Mount Curwood △ USA 57 Dd 22
Mount Dalrymple △ AUS 375 Ml 56
Mount Dangoua △ RCA 324 Hf 42
Mount Darwin O ZW 341 Hh 54
Mount Davidson △ AUS 361 Mb 56
Mount de Babel △ CDN 60 Dp 20
Mount Deering △ AUS 369 Ma 58
Mount Denison △ USA 46 An 15
Mount Denison △ AUS 361 Mc 57
Mount Desert Island ◭ USA 60 Dp 23
Mount Dick △ AUS 375 Mj 56
Mount Doonerek △ USA 6 Bb 3
Mount Dora O USA 87 Dh 31
Mount Doreen O AUS 361 Mb 57
Mount Douglas O AUS 375 Mk 56
Mount Downton △ CDN 50 Bp 19
Mount Duau △ PNG 287 Mj 49
Mount Dutton △ USA 65 Cf 27
Mount East △ AUS 368 Lm 60
Mount Eba O AUS 378 Md 61
Mount Ebenezer O AUS 369 Mc 58
Mount Eccles ♀ AUS 378 Mg 65
Mount Edgar O AUS 360 Ll 56
Mount Edgar △ AUS 360 Ll 56
Mount Edith Clavell △ CDN 50 Cc 19
Mount Eduni △ CDN 47 Bl 13
Mount Egerton △ AUS 368 Lj 58
Mount Egmont △ NZ 383 Nj 65
Mount Elbert △ USA 65 Cj 26
Mount Elgon △ EAU 325 Hk 45
Mount Elizabeth △ AUS 361 Lp 54
Mount Ellen △ USA 65 Cg 26
Mount Ellery △ AUS 379 Ml 64
Mount Elliot △ AUS 365 Mk 55
Mount Elliott △ AUS 361 Lp 56
Mount Elvire △ AUS 360 Lj 60
Mount Embi △ PNG 286 Mh 48
Mount Erebus △ 38 Tb 17
Mount Eruki △ PNG 287 Mj 49
Mount Essendon △ AUS 368 Ll 58
Mount Evans △ USA 51 Cf 22
Mount Evelyn △ AUS 364 Mc 52
Mount Everest △ NEP 235 Kh 32
Mount Everett △ USA 60 Dm 24
Mount Exmouth △ AUS 379 Ml 61
Mount Fairweather △ USA 47 Bg 15
Mount Famham △ CDN 50 Cd 20
Mount Farquharson △ AUS 364 Ma 54
Mount Feathertop △ AUS 379 Mk 64
Mount Field ♀ AUS 378 Mk 67
Mount Finnigan △ AUS 365 Mj 53
Mount Fletcher O ZA 349 Hg 61
Mount Florance O AUS 360 Lj 56
Mount Floyd △ USA 64 Cf 28
Mount Forest O CDN 57 Dh 24
Mount Forrest △ AUS 368 Lk 60
Mount Frankland ♀ AUS 368 Lj 63
Mount Fraser O AUS 368 Lk 58
Mount Fraser △ AUS 368 Lk 58
Mount Frederick △ AUS 360 Lj 57
Mount Frere O ZA 349 Hg 61
Mount Gambier O AUS 378 Mg 64
Mount Gardiner △ AUS 361 Mc 57
Mount Gardiner △ AUS 375 Ml 57
Mount Garnet O AUS 365 Mj 54
Mount Gascoyne △ AUS 368 Lj 58
Mount Gilruth △ AUS 364 Mc 52
Mount Giluwe △ PNG 287 Mh 48
Mount Goldsworthy △ AUS 360 Lk 56
Mount Gould △ AUS 368 Lj 58
Mount Graham △ USA 65 Ch 29
Mount Gratwick △ AUS 360 Lk 56
Mount Grenfell △ AUS 379 Mj 61
Mount Hack △ AUS 378 Mf 61
Mount Hagen O PNG 287 Mj 48
Mount Halcon △ RP 267 Ll 39
Mount Hale △ AUS 368 Lj 58
Mount Halifax △ AUS 365 Mk 55
Mount Hann △ AUS 361 Ln 53
Mount Harris △ AUS 369 Ma 58
Mount Hawkes △ 38 Gb 18
Mount Hayes △ USA 46 Bc 13
Mount Hebron O USA 64 Cb 25
Mount Herbert △ AUS 361 Ln 54
Mount Hinkley △ AUS 369 Ma 59
Mount Hogart △ AUS 374 Me 56
Mount Hollister △ AUS 360 Lg 57
Mount Hood △ USA 50 Cb 23
Mount Hope O AUS 378 Md 63
Mount Hope O AUS 379 Mj 62
Mount Hopeless O AUS 374 Mf 60
Mount House O AUS 361 Ln 54
Mount Howship △ AUS 364 Mc 52
Mount Hoy △ AUS 361 Mc 57
Mount Hoyo △ RDC 324 Hg 45
Mount Humboldt △ F 386 Nf 56
Mount Hutt O NZ 382 Nh 67
Mount Ida O USA 70 Db 28
Mount Ida O AUS 368 Ll 60
Mount Illbillee △ AUS 369 Mc 59
Mount Inglis △ AUS 375 Ml 58
Mount Isa O AUS 374 Mf 56
Mount Isarog △ RP 267 Lm 39
Mount J. Cartier △ CDN 61 Ea 21
Mount Jackson △ AUS 368 Lk 61
Mount Jackson △ AUS 368 Lk 61
Mount Jefferson △ USA 64 Cd 26
Mount Joffre △ CDN 50 Ce 20
Mount Johnson △ AUS 369 Ln 58
Mount Joy △ CDN 47 Bj 13
Mount Juliana △ SME 113 Ef 44
Mount Junction △ AUS 364 Ma 55
Mount Kagora △ WAN 320 Gl 41
Mount Kaichui △ SOL 290 Nc 50
Mount Kalourat △ SOL 290 Nc 50
Mount Kamale △ CAM 321 Gn 40
Mount Kanangio △ PNG 287 Mj 48
Mount Kaputar ♀ AUS 379 Ml 61
Mount Karé △ RCA 321 Ha 42
Mount Karimui △ PNG 287 Mj 49
Mount Karoma △ PNG 286 Mh 48
Mount Katmai △ USA 46 An 15
Mount Kavendou △ RG 316 Fp 40
Mount Kaye △ AUS 379 Ml 64
Mount Keith O AUS 368 Ll 59
Mount Kendall △ NZ 383 Nj 66
Mount Kenevi △ PNG 287 Mk 50
Mount Kenya ♀ EAK 337 Hl 46
Mount Kenya △ EAK 337 Hl 46
Mount Kiangarow △ AUS 375 Mm 59
Mount Kilimanjaro ⛰ EAT 337 Hl 47
Mount Kintore △ AUS 369 Mb 59
Mount Klotz △ CDN 47 Bg 13
Mount Kopé △ CI 305 Gc 43
Mount Kosciusko △ AUS 379 Ml 64
Mount Koupé △ CAM 320 Gl 43
Mount Kubonitu △ SOL 290 Nb 50
Mount Kulal △ EAK 325 Hl 44
Mount Kusiwigasi △ PNG 286 Mg 48
Mount Lacy △ AUS 361 Ln 54
Mount Lambell △ AUS 364 Mc 52
Mount Lamington △ PNG 287 Ml 50
Mount Laptz △ AUS 361 Lp 54
Mount Larcom O AUS 375 Mm 57
Mount Lefo △ CAM 320 Gm 43
Mount Le Grand △ AUS 368 Lm 62
Mount Leichhardt △ AUS 361 Mc 56
Mount Leisler △ AUS 361 Ma 57
Mount Leonard Darwin △ RI 286 Me 48
Mount Lesueur △ AUS 368 Lh 61
Mount Liebig △ AUS 361 Mb 57
Mount Lindsay △ AUS 369 Ma 59
Mount Lister △ 38 Ta 17
Mount Livermore △ USA 81 Ck 30
Mount Lofty Ranges ⛰ AUS 378 Mf 63
Mount Logan △ CDN 47 Be 15
Mount Lookout △ AUS 365 Mj 55
Mount Loughlen △ AUS 374 Md 57
Mount Lucy △ AUS 361 Mc 57
Mount Luke △ AUS 368 Lj 59
Mount Lulworth △ AUS 368 Lj 59
Mount Lynn △ USA 64 Ca 25
Mount Macdonald △ VU 386 Ng 54
Mount Madden Wheat Bin O AUS 368 Lk 62
Mount Madley △ AUS 369 Lm 58
Mount Magnet O AUS 368 Lj 60
Mount Maiden △ AUS 368 Lm 59
Mount Maitabi △ SOL 290 Na 49
Mount Makarakomburu △ SOL 290 Nb 50
Mount Malindang △ RP 267 Lm 41
Mount Mantalingajan △ RP 266 Lj 41
Mount Marcus Baker △ USA 46 Bc 15
Mount Marcy △ USA 60 Dl 23
Mount Margaret △ AUS 360 Lj 56
Mount Margaret △ AUS 374 Md 60
Mount Markham △ 38 Sb 18
Mount Marum △ VU 386 Ng 54
Mount Marvine △ USA 65 Cg 26
Mount Mary O AUS 378 Mf 63
Mount McGuire △ USA 50 Ce 23
Mount McKinley △ USA 6 Ba 3
Mount McKinley △ USA 46 An 13
Mount McLoughlin △ USA 50 Ca 24
Mount Meharry △ AUS 360 Lk 57
Mount Mengam △ PNG 287 Mj 48
Mount Menzies △ 38 Na 17
Mount Merrimerriwa △ AUS 379 Mj 62
Mount Meru △ EAT 337 Hl 47
Mount Michael △ PNG 287 Mj 49
Mount Michelson △ USA 46 Be 11
Mount Miller △ USA 46 Be 15
Mount Mitchel △ USA 71 Dg 28
Mount Molloy O AUS 365 Mj 54
Mount Morbanipari △ PNG 286 Mh 48
Mount Morgan △ USA 64 Cc 27
Mount Morgan O AUS 375 Mm 57
Mount Moroto △ EAU 325 Hk 44
Mount Mpamphala △ MW 344 Hj 51
Mount Mulgrave O AUS 365 Mh 54
Mount Mulligan O AUS 365 Mj 54
Mount Murchison △ AUS 368 Lj 59
Mount Murchisson △ WAN 320 Gl 41
Mount Nansen △ CDN 47 Bg 13
Mount Napier △ AUS 364 Ma 54
Mount Narryer △ AUS 368 Lj 59
Mount Nellie △ AUS 361 Ln 54
Mount Nelson △ PNG 287 Mk 50
Mount Nesselrode △ CDN 47 Bj 15
Mount Ngaoui △ CAM 321 Gp 42
Mount Ngauruhoe △ NZ 383 Nk 65
Mount Nicholson △ AUS 375 Ml 58
Mount Norfolk △ AUS 378 Mj 66
Mount Norman △ AUS 365 Mh 55
Mount Norris Bay ~ AUS 364 Mc 51
Mountnorris Bay ~ AUS 364 Mc 51
Mount Nyangani △ ZW 344 Hj 55
Mount Nymagee △ AUS 379 Mk 61
Mount Octy △ AUS 374 Md 56
Mount Okora △ WAN 320 Gk 42
Mount Oku △ CAM 320 Gm 42
Mount Olga Kata Tjutal △ AUS 369 Mb 58
Mount Olive O USA 74 Dj 28
Mount Olympus △ USA 50 Ca 22
Mount Ord △ AUS 361 Ln 54
Mount Ossa △ AUS 378 Mj 66
Mount Oweenee △ AUS 365 Mj 55
Mount Padbury O AUS 368 Lk 58
Mount Palgrave △ AUS 360 Lh 57
Mount Panie △ F 386 Ne 56
Mount Parker △ AUS 364 Ma 54
Mount Parsons △ AUS 364 Md 52
Mount Pascoe △ AUS 368 Ll 59
Mount Patterson △ CDN 47 Bj 13
Mount Patterson △ AUS 368 Lk 58
Mount Pattullo △ CDN 47 Bl 17
Mount Peale △ USA 65 Ch 26
Mount Peko △ CI 305 Gc 42
Mount Penot △ VU 386 Nf 54
Mount Percy △ AUS 361 Ln 54
Mount Perry O AUS 375 Mm 58
Mount Pfizner △ AUS 361 Mc 57
Mount Pierre Trudeau △ CDN 6 Bb 3
Mount Pinatubo △ RP 267 Ll 38
Mount Pleasant O USA 57 Df 24
Mount Pleasant O USA 65 Cg 26
Mount Pleasant O USA 70 Da 29
Mount Pleasant O USA 70 Dc 25
Mount Pleasant O USA 87 Dj 29
Mount Pulog ★ RP 267 Ll 37
Mount Pulog △ RP 267 Ll 37
Mount Ragang △ RP 275 Ln 42
Mount Rainier ♀ USA 50 Cb 22
Mount Rainier △ USA 50 Cb 22
Mount Ratz △ CDN 47 Bj 17
Mount Rawlinson △ AUS 369 Lp 58
Mount Redcliffe △ AUS 368 Ll 60
Mount Remarkable △ AUS 361 Lp 54
Mount Remarkable ♀ AUS 378 Me 62
Mount Revelstoke ♀ CDN 50 Cc 20
Mount Richmond ♀ AUS 378 Mg 65
Mount Richmond △ NZ 383 Nj 66
Mount Ritter △ USA 64 Cc 27
Mount Robe △ AUS 378 Mg 61
Mount Robinson △ AUS 360 Lk 57
Mount Robson △ CDN 50 Cc 19
Mount Rogers △ USA 71 Dh 27
Mount Rogers N.R.A. ♀ USA 71 Dh 27
Mount Rollestone △ NZ 382 Nh 67
Mount Roosevelt △ CDN 47 Bn 15
Mount Roraima △ GUY 112 Ed 43
Mount Ruapehu △ NZ 383 Nk 65
Mount Rupert O ZA 349 He 60
Mount Rushmore Nat. Mon. ★ USA 51 Cl 24
Mount Russell △ USA 46 An 13
Mount Ryan △ AUS 365 Mh 53
Mount Ryan △ AUS 379 Ml 62
Mount Saint Helens △ USA 50 Ca 22
Mount Samson △ AUS 360 Lj 57
Mount-Sandiman O AUS 368 Lh 58
Mount Sanford O AUS 364 Mb 54
Mount Sapocoy △ RP 267 Ll 37
Mount Savalou △ DY 317 Gg 41
Mount Scott △ AUS 375 Ml 56
Mount Selfton △ NZ 382 Nh 67
Mount Selinda O ZW 352 Hj 56
Mount Shasta O USA 64 Ca 25
Mount Shasta △ USA 64 Ca 25
Mount Shenton △ AUS 369 Lm 59
Mount Sicapoo △ RP 267 Ll 36
Mount Sidley △ 38 Cb 17
Mount Silisili △ WS 390 Ad 52
Mount Simpson △ PNG 287 Ml 50
Mount Sinai △ ET 301 Hj 31
Mount Singleton △ AUS 361 Mb 56
Mount Singleton △ AUS 368 Lj 60
Mount Sisa △ PNG 286 Mh 49
Mount Skinner O AUS 374 Md 57
Mount Soder △ AUS 361 Mc 57
Mount Somers O NZ 382 Nh 67
Mount Squires △ AUS 369 Lp 59
Mount St. Elias △ USA 47 Be 15
Mount St. Gregory △ CDN 61 Ee 21
Mount St. Helens Natural Volcanic Monument ♀ USA 50 Ca 22
Mount Stanley △ EAU 324 Hg 45
Mount Steele △ CDN 47 Be 15
Mount Sterling O USA 71 Dc 26
Mount Sterling O USA 71 Dg 26
Mount Stewart △ AUS 375 Mj 56
Mount Strong △ PNG 287 Mk 50
Mount Strzelecki ♀ AUS 378 Mk 66
Mount Stuart O AUS 360 Lj 57
Mount Suckling △ PNG 287 Ml 50
Mount Sulen △ PNG 286 Mh 47
Mount Sullivan △ AUS 364 Mb 54
Mount Sunflower △ USA 65 Cl 26
Mount Surprise O AUS 365 Mj 55
Mount Swan O AUS 374 Md 57
Mount Swan △ AUS 374 Md 57
Mount Tabayog △ RP 267 Ll 37
Mount Tabletop △ AUS 375 Mk 57
Mount Tabwemasana △ VU 386 Nf 53
Mount Tafel △ SME 113 Ef 44
Mount Talbot △ AUS 369 Lp 59
Mount Tamboritha △ AUS 379 Mk 64
Mount Tanami △ AUS 361 Ma 56
Mount Taraka △ PNG 290 Mp 49
Mount Tasman △ NZ 382 Nh 67
Mount Tavani △ VU 386 Ng 54
Mount Theo △ AUS 361 Mb 56
Mount Thuilliero △ IND 270 Kl 42
Mount Thuillieró △ IND 270 Kl 42
Mount Tipron △ USA 64 Ce 28
Mount Tip Tree △ AUS 365 Mj 54
Mount Tobin △ USA 64 Cd 25
Mount Tonkoui △ CI 304 Gc 42
Mount Tops △ AUS 361 Mc 56
Mount Torbert △ USA 46 An 15
Mount Trumbull O USA 64 Cf 27
Mount Tukosmera △ VU 386 Ng 55
Mount Tutoko △ NZ 382 Nf 68
Mount Ulawun △ PNG 287 Mm 48
Mount Unbunmaroo △ AUS 374 Mg 57
Mount Union O USA 64 Cf 28
Mount Union O USA 74 Dj 25
Mount Usborne △ GB 147 Ee 71
Mount Vancouver △ CDN 47 Be 15
Mount Vangunu △ SOL 290 Nb 50
Mount Veniaminof △ USA 46 Aj 17
Mount Vernon O USA 50 Ca 21
Mount Vernon O USA 50 Cc 23
Mount Vernon O USA 71 Dd 26
Mount Vernon O USA 71 Dg 25
Mount Vernon O USA 71 Dg 29
Mount Vesuvius △ I 194 Gp 25
Mount Victor △ AUS 378 Mf 61
Mount Victoria ♀ MYA 254 Kl 35
Mount Victoria △ MYA 254 Kl 35
Mount Victoria △ PNG 287 Mk 50
Mount Victory △ PNG 287 Ml 50
Mount Vitumbi △ MW 344 Hj 51
Mount Waddington △ CDN 50 Bp 20
Mount Walker O AUS 368 Lk 62
Mount Walker △ AUS 375 Mj 56
Mount Wall △ AUS 360 Lj 57
Mount Walton △ AUS 368 Lk 61
Mount Wamtakin △ PNG 286 Mg 48
Mount Warning △ AUS 375 Mn 60
Mount Washington △ USA 60 Dn 23
Mount Webb △ AUS 361 Ma 57
Mount Wedge O AUS 361 Mb 57
Mount Wedge O AUS 378 Md 62
Mount Wedge Central △ AUS 361 Mb 57
Mount Wells △ AUS 361 Lp 54
Mount White △ AUS 365 Mh 52
Mount Whitney △ USA 64 Cc 27
Mount Wilhelm △ PNG 287 Mj 48
Mount William △ AUS 378 Mh 64
Mount William ♀ AUS 378 Ml 66
Mount William Lambert △ AUS 369 Ln 58
Mount Willingdon △ CDN 50 Cd 20
Mount Windsor O AUS 374 Mg 57
Mount Woodroffe △ AUS 369 Mb 59
Mount Yawaioutou △ GH 317 Gg 42
Mount Yule △ PNG 287 Mk 50
Mount Zeil △ AUS 361 Mc 57
Mount Ziama △ RG 316 Gb 41
Mouping O VRC 246 Ll 27
Moura O BR 120 Ed 46
Moura O P 184 Gc 26
Moura O AUS 375 Mm 58
Mouray O TCH 321 Hc 40
Mourdi ⏢ TCH 309 Hd 37
Mourdiah O RMM 305 Gc 38
Mouri Mountains △ WAN 320 Gm 41
Mousgougou O TCH 321 Hb 40
Moussadey O RN 308 Gh 39
Moussafoyo O TCH 321 Hb 41
Moussaya O RG 316 Fp 41
Moussaya O RG 316 Gb 40
Moussoro O TCH 321 Ha 39
Moutainair O USA 65 Cj 28
Mouths of the Amazon ~ BR 121 Ek 45
Mouths of the Ganges ≈ 235 Kj 35
Mouths of the Indus ~ PK 227 Jm 33
Mouths of the Irrawaddy ~ MYA 262 Km 38
Mouths of the Mekong ~ VN 263 Ld 41
Moûtiers O F 185 Gk 23
Moutong O RI 275 Ll 45
Moutourous O CAM 321 Gp 40
Mouyondzi O RCB 332 Gn 47
Moville O USA 56 Cp 24
Mowasi O GUY 113 Ee 43
Moweaqua O USA 71 Dd 26
Mowewe O RI 282 Ll 47
Moxey Town O BS 87 Dk 33
Moxoto ~ BR 124 Fb 50
Moyahua O MEX 92 Cl 35
Moyalē O ETH 325 Hm 44
Moyamba O WAL 316 Fp 41
Moyen Atlas ⛰ MA 293 Gc 29
Moyeni O LS 349 Hf 61
Moyie O CDN 50 Ce 21
Moyie Springs O USA 50 Cd 21
Moyo O EAU 324 Hh 44
Moyobamba O PE 116 Dk 49
Moyowosi ~ EAT 336 Hh 47
Møysalen △ N 158 Gp 11
Moyu O VRC 230 Kd 27
Možaisk O RUS 171 Hk 18
Mozambicano ⌓ MOC 352 Hk 56
Mozambique Channel ≈ MOC 344 Hn 55
Mozarak O TCH 321 Ha 39
Mozdok O RUS 202 Ja 24
Mozdūrān O IR 223 Jj 27
Mpala O RDC 336 Hg 49
Mpala O RDC 341 He 51
Mpam ~ CAM 320 Gm 43
Mpama ~ RCB 332 Gp 46
Mpana O GH 317 Gf 41
Mpanda O EAT 336 Hh 49
Mpanga O EAT 337 Hl 49
Mpase O RDC 333 Hc 46
Mpassa ~ G 332 Gn 46
Mpata O RDC 333 Hb 48
Mpataba O GH 317 Ge 43
Mpatora O EAT 337 Hm 50
Mpepaya O EAT 344 Hk 51
Mphaki O LS 349 Hf 61
Mpiéla O RMM 304 Gc 39
Mpigi O EAU 324 Hj 45
Mpika O Z 341 Hh 51
Mpitimbo O EAT 344 Hk 51
Mpo O RDC 333 Hb 47
Mpoko ~ RCA 321 Ha 43
Mpoko O RDC 333 Hb 47
Mponde ~ EAT 337 Hk 48
Mponela O MW 344 Hj 52
Mpongwe O Z 341 Hg 52
Mporaloko O G 332 Gl 46
Mporokoso O Z 336 Hg 50
Mpoukou ~ RCB 332 Gn 47
Mpouop ~ CAM 321 Gn 44
Mpouya O RCB 332 Gp 47
Mpraeso O GH 317 Gf 42
Mpui O EAT 336 Hh 50
Mpulo O Z 341 Hg 52
Mpulungu O Z 336 Hh 50
Mpumalanga ◉ ZA 352 Hh 60
Mpume O RDC 333 Hb 48
Mpungu O NAM 340 Hb 54
Mpwapwa O EAT 337 Hl 49
Mrara O DZ 296 Gj 29
Mrčajevci O SCG 194 Hc 24
Mrkonjić Grad O BIH 174 Ha 23
M'saken O TN 297 Gm 28
Msak Mallat ⛰ LAR 297 Gm 33
Msak Mustafit ⌓ LAR 297 Gm 33
Msandile ~ Z 344 Hj 52
Msangasi ~ EAT 337 Hm 48
Msanzara ~ Z 341 Hh 53
Msata O EAT 337 Hm 49
Msembe O EAT 337 Hk 49
M'Sila O DZ 296 Gj 28
Msima ~ EAT 336 Hh 49
Msoro O Z 341 Hh 52
Msta ~ RUS 171 Hj 16
Msta ~ RUS 171 Hk 17
Mstsislaw O BY 171 Hh 18
Msuka O EAT 337 Hm 48
Msuna O ZW 341 Hf 55
Mtakuja O EAT 336 Hh 49
Mtama O EAT 344 Hm 51
Mtambo ~ EAT 336 Hh 49
Mtandikeni O EAT 337 Hm 48
Mtangano Island ◭ EAU 337 Hj 46
Mtera Dam ~ EAT 337 Hk 49
Mtito Andei O EAK 337 Hl 47
Mtonya O EAT 344 Hk 51
Mto Wa Mbu O EAT 337 Hk 47
Mtskheta O GE 202 Ja 25
Mtubatuba O ZA 352 Hj 60
Mtwara O EAT 344 Hn 51
Muadiala O RDC 333 Hc 49
Muaguide O MOC 344 Hm 52
Mualádzi O MOC 344 Hj 53
Mualama O MOC 344 Hm 54
Mualatalang O RI 278 Lb 47
Muaná O BR 121 Ek 46
Muanda O RDC 332 Gn 48
Muangai O ANG 340 Hb 52
Muang Gnômmarat O LAO 255 Lc 37
Muang Hiam O LAO 255 Lb 35
Muang Hôngsa O LAO 254 La 36
Muang Houn O LAO 254 La 35
Muang Huang O LAO 255 Lb 36
Muang Khammouan O LAO 263 Lc 37
Muang Không O LAO 263 Lc 38
Muang Khôngxédôn O LAO 263 Lc 38
Muang Khoua O LAO 254 Lb 35
Muang May O LAO 263 Ld 38
Muang Namo O LAO 254 La 35
Muang Nan O LAO 254 La 36

Morven - Muang Nan 447

Muang Ou Tai ○ **LAO** 254 La 34
Muang Pakbèng ○ **LAO** 254 La 36
Muang Pak-Cay ○ **LAO** 254 La 36
Muang Pakxan ○ **LAO** 255 Lb 36
Muang Pakxong ○ **LAO** 263 Ld 38
Muang Phalan ○ **LAO** 263 Lc 37
Muang Phin ○ **LAO** 263 Ld 37
Muang Phiang ○ **LAO** 254 La 36
Muang Phôn-Hông ○ **LAO** 254 Lb 36
Muang Samsip ○ **THA** 263 Lc 38
Muang Sing ○ **LAO** 254 La 35
Muang Souy ○ **LAO** 255 Lb 36
Muang Xaignabouri ○ **LAO** 254 La 36
Muang Xay ○ **LAO** 254 La 35
Muang Xépôn ○ **LAO** 263 Ld 37
Muanza ○ **MOC** 344 Hk 55
Muanzanza ○ **RDC** 333 Hc 49
Muar ○ **MAL** 270 Lb 44
Muara ○ **RI** 270 La 46
Muara ○ **MAL** 274 Lh 43
Muaraaman ○ **RI** 278 Lb 47
Muarabeliti ○ **RI** 278 Lb 47
Muarabinuangeun ○ **RI** 278 Lc 49
Muarabulian ○ **RI** 278 Lb 46
Muarabungo ○ **RI** 278 Lb 46
Muaradua ○ **RI** 278 Lc 48
Muaraenim ○ **RI** 278 Lb 47
Muarainu ○ **RI** 279 Lh 46
Muarajawa ○ **RI** 274 Lj 46
Muara Koman ○ **RI** 279 Lh 46
Muaralakitan ○ **RI** 278 Lb 47
Muaranayan ○ **RI** 279 Lh 46
Muarapayang ○ **RI** 279 Lh 46
Muararupit ○ **RI** 278 Lb 47
Muarasiberut ○ **RI** 270 Kp 46
Muarasimatalu ○ **RI** 270 Kp 46
Muarasoma ○ **RI** 270 Kp 45
Muaratebo ○ **RI** 278 Lb 46
Muaratembesi ○ **RI** 278 Lb 46
Muarateweh ○ **RI** 279 Lh 46
Muarawahau ○ **RI** 274 Lj 45
Muaro Takus Ruins ★ **RI** 270 La 45
Muatua ○ **MOC** 344 Hm 53
Muávula ○ **MOC** 344 Hl 54
Muazi ～ **MOC** 344 Hj 55
Mubambe ○ **RDC** 341 He 51
Mubayira ○ **ZW** 341 Hh 55
Mubende ○ **EAU** 324 Hh 45
Mubi ○ **WAN** 321 Gn 40
Mubo ○ **VRC** 243 Ld 27
Mubrani ○ **RI** 283 Mc 46
Mucaba ○ **ANG** 332 Gp 49
Mucajaí ○ **BR** 112 Ed 44
Mucajaí ～ **BR** 112 Ed 44
Mucanha ～ **MOC** 341 Hh 53
Muccan ○ **AUS** 360 Lk 56
Mucelo ～ **MOC** 344 Hk 55
Muchea ○ **AUS** 368 Lh 61
Muchena ○ **MOC** 344 Hj 53
Muchinga Escarpment ⏥ **Z** 341 Hg 53
Muchinga Mountains ⛰ **Z** 341 Hh 52
Muchinka ○ **Z** 341 Hh 52
Muchuan ○ **VRC** 255 Lb 31
Muckadilla ○ **AUS** 375 Ml 59
Muckaty ○ **AUS** 364 Mc 55
Muco ～ **CO** 107 Dn 43
Mucojo ○ **MOC** 344 Hn 52
Muconda ○ **ANG** 340 Hc 51
Mucope ○ **ANG** 340 Gp 54
Mucubela ○ **MOC** 344 Hl 54
Mucuchachi ○ **YV** 107 Dn 41
Mucucuaú ～ **BR** 120 Ed 45
Mucugé ○ **BR** 125 Ep 52
Mucuim ～ **BR** 117 Eb 49
Mucuim ～ **BR** 117 Eb 50
Mucumbura ○ **MOC** 341 Hh 54
Mucumbura ～ **ZW** 341 Hh 54
Mucupia ○ **MOC** 344 Hk 55
Múcure ○ **YV** 112 Eb 41
Mucuri ～ **BR** 125 Ep 54
Mucuri ○ **BR** 141 Fa 55
Mucuri ～ **BR** 141 Fa 55
Mucusso ○ **ANG** 340 Hc 54
Mucussueje ○ **ANG** 341 Hc 51
Mūd ○ **IR** 222 Jh 29
Mudaibi ○ **OM** 226 Jh 34
Mudaisis ○ **OM** 226 Jf 34
Mudanya ○ **TR** 195 Hg 25
Mudarraq ○ **KSA** 214 Hp 32
Mudawwa ○ **JOR** 214 Hk 31
Mudayy ○ **OM** 219 Je 36
Mud Bay ○ **CDN** 50 Bp 21
Mūdbidri ○ **IND** 238 Kb 39
Muddebihāl ○ **IND** 238 Kc 37
Muddus ♀ **S** 159 Hc 12
Muddy Gap ○ **USA** 65 Cj 24
Mudgal ○ **IND** 238 Kc 38
Mudgee ○ **AUS** 379 Ml 62
Mudgeeraba ○ **AUS** 375 Mn 60
Mudhol ○ **IND** 238 Kb 37
Mudigere ○ **IND** 238 Kb 39
Mudigubba ○ **IND** 238 Kc 38
Mudjumbuli ○ **RDC** 321 Hc 44
Mud Lake ～ **USA** 56 Cp 21
Mudon ○ **MYA** 262 Kn 37
Mudukulattūr ○ **IND** 239 Kd 41
Mudumu ♀ **NAM** 341 Hd 54
Muecate ○ **MOC** 344 Hm 53
Mueda ○ **MOC** 344 Hm 51
Muelle de los Bueyes ○ **NIC** 97 Df 39
Mueller Range ⛰ **AUS** 361 Lp 55
Muemba ○ **MOC** 344 Hk 52
Muenda ～ **MOC** 344 Hl 53
Muende ○ **MOC** 344 Hj 53
Muerto ～ **PY** 136 Ec 57
Muezerskij ○ **RUS** 159 Hh 14
Mufulira ○ **Z** 341 Hg 52
Mufu Shan △ **VRC** 258 Lg 31
Muğaira ○ **KSA** 214 Hm 32
Mugang ○ **VRC** 255 Lc 34
Mugango ○ **EAT** 337 Hj 46
Muğanskaja ravnina ⏥ **AZ** 202 Jc 26
Mugār ○ **IR** 222 Je 29
Muger ○ **ETH** 325 Hm 41
Muger Wenz ～ **ETH** 325 Hm 41
Muggon ○ **AUS** 368 Lh 59
Mughal Sarai ○ **IND** 234 Kf 33
Mughsail ○ **OM** 219 Je 36
Mugina ○ **BU** 336 Hg 48
Muğla ○ **TR** 195 Hg 27
Muguia ○ **MOC** 344 Hm 52
Muhagiria ○ **SUD** 312 He 40
Muhaiwīr ○ **IRQ** 209 Hn 29
Muhala ○ **RDC** 336 Hg 48
Muḥammadīya ○ **IRQ** 209 Hp 29
Muhammed Qol ○ **SUD** 313 Hl 35
Muḥāt ○ **KSA** 218 Hp 37
Muheza ○ **EAT** 337 Hm 48
Mühlhausen ○ **D** 174 Gm 20
Mühlig-Hofman Mountains ⛰ 38 Jb 17
Muhoro ○ **EAK** 337 Hj 46
Muhos ○ **FIN** 159 He 13
Muhu ♁ **EST** 171 Hd 16
Muhula ○ **MOC** 344 Hm 53
Muhutwe ○ **EAT** 336 Hh 46
Muhuvesi ～ **EAT** 344 Hl 51
Mũi Ba Làng An ⌓ **VN** 263 Le 38
Mũi Cà Mau ⌓ **VN** 263 Lc 41
Muico ○ **MOC** 344 Hm 52
Mũi Dôc ⌓ **VN** 263 Ld 37
Muidumbe ○ **MOC** 344 Hm 51
Muié ○ **ANG** 340 Hc 53
Mũi Kê Gà ⌓ **VN** 263 Le 40
Mũi La Gan ⌓ **VN** 263 Le 40
Mũi Lai ⌓ **VN** 263 Ld 37
Mũi Nam Trâm ⌓ **VN** 263 Le 38
Muine ○ **ANG** 340 Hc 54
Muira ～ **MOC** 344 Hj 54
Mui Rô'ng Quèn ⌓ **VN** 255 Lc 36
Muiron Islands ♁ **AUS** 360 Lg 56
Muisne ○ **EC** 116 Dj 45
Muite ○ **MOC** 344 Hm 53
Muitos Capões ○ **BR** 146 Ej 60
Muizenberg ○ **ZA** 358 Hb 63
Mūjnak ○ **UZB** 155 Rc 10
Muju ○ **ROK** 247 Lp 27
Mujuí dos Campos ○ **BR** 120 Eg 47
Mukačeve ○ **UA** 174 Hd 21
Mukah ○ **MAL** 271 Lf 44
Mukala ○ **RDC** 333 Ha 48
Mukana ○ **RDC** 336 Hf 50
Mukanga ○ **RDC** 333 Hc 49
Mukawa ○ **PNG** 287 Ml 50
Mukdahan ○ **THA** 263 Lc 37
Mukebo ○ **RDC** 336 Hg 49
Mukeriān ○ **IND** 230 Kb 30
Muke T'uri ○ **ETH** 325 Hm 41
Mukinbudin ○ **AUS** 368 Lk 61
Mukomuko ○ **RI** 270 La 47
Mu Ko Phi Phi ♀ **THA** 270 Kp 42
Mukosa ○ **ZW** 344 Hj 54
Mukry ○ **TM** 223 Jl 27
Muksu ～ **TJ** 223 Jp 26
Muktsar ○ **IND** 230 Kb 30
Mukuku ○ **Z** 341 Hg 52
Mukulakulu ○ **RDC** 336 He 50
Mukunsa ○ **Z** 336 Hg 50
Mukupa Koama ○ **Z** 336 Hh 50
Mukutawa River ～ **CDN** 56 Cn 19
Mukwe ○ **NAM** 340 Hc 55
Mūl ○ **IND** 234 Kd 35
Mula ～ **PK** 227 Jm 31
Mulaku Atoll ♁ **MV** 239 Ka 44
Mulaley ○ **AUS** 379 Ml 61
Mulanay ○ **RP** 267 Lm 39
Mulanje Mountains △ **MW** 344 Hk 53
Mulanje Mountains ○ **MW** 344 Hk 54
Mulatos ○ **CO** 106 Dk 41
Mulawa ○ **PK** 230 Ka 29
Mulbāgal ○ **IND** 238 Kd 39
Mulchen ○ **RCH** 137 Dm 64
Mulchole ○ **IND** 238 Kc 40
Mule Alcantarilla ○ **E** 184 Gf 27
Muleba ○ **EAT** 336 Hh 46
Mulegá ○ **MEX** 75 Cf 32
Mulembe ○ **RDC** 336 Hg 47
Mulenda ○ **RDC** 333 He 48
Mulengu ○ **Z** 336 Hh 50
Muleshoe ○ **USA** 65 Cl 28
Muleta ～ **RP** 275 Ln 42
Mulevala ○ **MOC** 344 Hl 54
Mulga Creek ～ **AUS** 379 Mk 61
Mulgildie ○ **AUS** 375 Mm 58
Mulgul ○ **AUS** 368 Lk 58
Mulhacén △ **E** 184 Ge 27
Mulhouse ○ **F** 163 Gk 22
Muli ～ **RI** 286 Mf 49
Mulia ○ **RI** 286 Me 47
Mulifanua ○ **WS** 390 Ad 52
Mulilansolo ○ **Z** 341 Hh 51
Muling ○ **VRC** 250 Mb 23
Mūlki ○ **IND** 238 Kb 39
Mull ♁ **GB** 162 Gc 17
Mullaittivu ○ **CL** 239 Ke 41
Mullen ○ **USA** 56 Cm 24
Mullens ○ **USA** 71 Dh 27
Muller Range ⛰ **PNG** 286 Mh 48
Mullewa ○ **AUS** 368 Lh 60
Mulligan ～ **AUS** 374 Mf 57
Mullingar ○ **IRL** 163 Gc 19
Mullins ○ **USA** 74 Dj 28
Mullsjö ○ **S** 170 Gn 17
Mulobezi ○ **Z** 341 He 54
Mulondo ○ **ANG** 340 Gp 53
Mulonga Plain ⏥ **Z** 341 Hd 54
Mulongoie ～ **RDC** 336 Hf 48
Mulshi Lake ～ **IND** 238 Ka 36
Multai ○ **IND** 234 Kd 35
Multān ○ **PK** 227 Jp 30
Multia ○ **FIN** 159 He 14
Muluk ○ **PNG** 287 Mk 48
Mulungu ～ **RDC** 341 Hd 50
Mulungushi ○ **Z** 341 Hg 53
Mulungushi Dam ～ **Z** 341 Hg 53
Mulurulu Lake ～ **AUS** 378 Mh 62
Mulyungarie ○ **AUS** 378 Mg 61
Muma ○ **RDC** 321 Hd 44
Mumbai Bombay ○ **IND** 238 Ka 36
Mumbeji ○ **Z** 341 Hd 52
Mumbleberry Lake ～ **AUS** 374 Mf 58
Mumbondo ○ **ANG** 340 Gp 51
Mumbué ○ **ANG** 340 Ha 52
Mumbwa ○ **Z** 341 Hf 53
Mume ○ **RDC** 336 Hf 50
Mumena ○ **RDC** 341 Hf 51
Mumeng ○ **PNG** 287 Mk 49
Mumi ○ **RI** 283 Md 46
Mumias ○ **EAK** 325 Hk 45
Mummballup ○ **AUS** 368 Lj 62
Mumoma ○ **RDC** 333 Hd 49
Mumulusan ○ **RI** 282 Lm 46
Mun ○ **RI** 283 Mc 48
Muna ○ **MEX** 93 Dd 35
Muna ～ **RUS** 204 Vc 5
Munaya ～ **CAM** 320 Gl 43
Muncakabau ○ **RI** 278 Lc 48
Munchique ♀ **CO** 106 Dk 44
Muncho Lake ○ **CDN** 47 Bn 15
Muncie ○ **USA** 71 Df 25
Munda ○ **PK** 227 Jp 30
Munda ○ **SOL** 290 Na 50
Mundabullangana ○ **AUS** 360 Lj 56
Mundare ○ **CDN** 51 Cf 19
Mundaring ○ **AUS** 368 Lj 61
Munday ○ **USA** 70 Cn 29
Mundgod ○ **IND** 238 Kb 38
Mundico Coelho ○ **BR** 120 Ef 49
Mundiwindi ○ **AUS** 360 Ll 57
Mundo Novo ○ **BR** 125 Ep 51
Mundo Novo ○ **BR** 140 Eg 57
Mundoonen Range ⛰ **AUS** 379 Ml 63
Mundra ○ **IND** 227 Jn 34
Mundrabilla ○ **AUS** 369 Lp 61
Mundrabilla Motel ○ **AUS** 369 Ma 61
Mundri ○ **SUD** 324 Hh 43
Mundubbera ○ **AUS** 375 Mm 58
Mūndwa ○ **IND** 227 Ka 32
Munenga ○ **ANG** 340 Gp 50
Munera ○ **E** 184 Ge 26
Munfordville ○ **USA** 71 Df 27
Mungaboom ○ **AUS** 364 Md 54
Mungallala ○ **AUS** 375 Mk 59
Mungallala Creek ～ **AUS** 375 Mk 60
Mungana ○ **AUS** 365 Mj 54
Mungaoli ○ **IND** 234 Kc 33
Mungári ○ **MOC** 344 Hj 54
Mungbere ○ **RDC** 324 Hg 44
Mungelia ○ **IND** 234 Ke 34
Munger ○ **IND** 235 Kh 33
Mungeranie ○ **AUS** 374 Mf 60
Mungindi ○ **AUS** 375 Ml 60
Munglinup ○ **AUS** 368 Ll 62
Mungo ○ **ANG** 340 Ha 51
Mungo ♀ **AUS** 378 Mh 62
Mungra ○ **IND** 234 Kf 33
Munhango ○ **ANG** 340 Hb 52
Munich ○ **D** 174 Gm 21
Muniengashi ～ **RDC** 341 Hg 52
Munim ～ **BR** 124 En 47
Muniungu ○ **RDC** 333 Ha 48
Muniz Freire ○ **BR** 141 Ep 56
Munkedal ○ **S** 170 Gm 16
Munkfors ○ **S** 170 Gn 16
Munkumpu ○ **Z** 341 Hf 52
Munmarlary ○ **AUS** 364 Mc 52
Munnikspoort △ **ZA** 358 Hc 62
Munning Point ⌓ **NZ** 383 Ab 67
Munnt ○ **IND** 239 Kc 40
Munsan ○ **ROK** 247 Lp 27
Munse ○ **RI** 282 Lm 48
Munster ⦿ **IRL** 163 Gb 19
Münster ○ **D** 163 Gk 20
Munte ○ **RI** 274 Lk 45
Munte ○ **RI** 275 Lk 45
Munteme ○ **EAU** 324 Hh 45
Munţii Zarandului △ **RO** 174 Hc 22
Muntok ○ **RI** 278 Lc 47
Muntu ○ **EAU** 324 Hj 45
Muntu ○ **RDC** 333 Hb 47
Munukata ○ **J** 247 Mb 29
Munyamedzi ～ **Z** 341 Hh 52
Munyati ～ **ZW** 341 Hg 54
Munzur Vadisi Milli Parkı ♀ **TR** 195 Hm 26
Muoco ○ **MOC** 344 Hl 52
Muodoslompolo ○ **S** 159 Hd 11
Muohyang San △ **DVRK** 247 Lp 25
Mu'o'ng Cha ○ **VN** 255 Lb 35
Mu'o'ng Lam ○ **VN** 255 Lc 36
Mu'o'ng Lói ○ **VN** 255 Lb 35
Mu'o'ng Mu'o'n ○ **VN** 255 Lb 35
Mu'o'ng Tè ○ **VN** 255 Lb 34
Muonio ○ **FIN** 159 Hd 12
Muonioälven ～ **S** 159 Hd 12
Muonionjok ～ **FIN** 159 Hd 12
Mupa ○ **ANG** 340 Gp 54
Mupamadzi ～ **Z** 341 Hh 52
Muqakoori ○ **SP** 328 Ja 43
Muqšin ○ **OM** 219 Jf 36
Muquém ○ **BR** 133 Ek 53
Muqui ～ **BR** 129 Ec 51
Muqui ○ **BR** 141 Ep 56
Mura ○ **BR** 120 Ee 47
Murabek ○ **UZB** 223 Jl 26
Muradiye ○ **TR** 202 Hp 26
Murafa ～ **UA** 175 Hg 21
Murakami ○ **J** 251 Mf 26
Muralgarra ○ **AUS** 368 Lj 60
Muramgaon ○ **IND** 234 Ke 35
Muramvya ○ **BU** 336 Hg 47
Muranga ○ **EAK** 337 Hl 46
Murangering ○ **EAK** 325 Hk 44
Muraré ～ **BR** 113 Eh 45
Murat Dağı △ **TR** 195 Hg 26
Murat Nehri ～ **TR** 202 Hn 26
Muravera ○ **I** 185 Gl 26
Murça ○ **P** 184 Gc 25
Mürče Ḥūrt ○ **IR** 222 Jd 29
Murchison Range ⛰ **AUS** 364 Md 55
Murchison ～ **AUS** 368 Lh 59
Murchison ○ **AUS** 379 Mj 64
Murchison ○ **NZ** 383 Nj 66
Murchison Falls ～ **EAU** 324 Hh 44
Murchison Falls ♀ **EAU** 324 Hh 44
Murchison Island ♁ **CDN** 57 Dd 20
Murchison Roadhouse ○ **AUS** 368 Lh 59
Murcia ○ **E** 184 Gf 27
Murcia ⦿ **E** 184 Gf 27
Mur-de-Rostrenen ○ **F** 163 Ge 21
Murdo ○ **USA** 56 Cm 24
Murdochville ○ **CDN** 61 Eb 21
Mureji ○ **WAN** 320 Gj 41
Mureş ～ **RO** 174 Hc 22
Muret ○ **F** 184 Gg 24
Murewa ○ **ZW** 341 Hh 54
Murfreesboro ○ **USA** 70 Db 28
Murfreesboro ○ **USA** 71 De 28
Murfreesboro ○ **USA** 74 Dk 27
Murgab ○ **TJ** 230 Ka 26
Murgab ～ **TJ** 230 Ka 26
Murgenella ○ **AUS** 364 Mc 51
Murgha Kibzai ○ **PK** 227 Jn 30
Murgon ○ **AUS** 375 Mm 59
Murgoo ○ **AUS** 368 Lj 59
Murgud ○ **IND** 238 Kb 37
Muri ○ **IND** 235 Kg 34
Muriaé ○ **BR** 141 En 56
Muri Cêtar ○ **VRC** 242 La 27
Muricilândia ○ **BR** 121 Ek 49
Muricizal ～ **BR** 121 Ek 49
Muriege ○ **ANG** 340 Hc 50
Muritiba ○ **BR** 125 Fa 52
Müritz ～ **D** 170 Gn 19
Murizidié Pass △ **LAR** 309 Gp 34
Murmansk ○ **RUS** 159 Hh 11
Murmanskij bereg ⏥ **RUS** 159 Hj 11
Murmaši ○ **RUS** 159 Hj 11
Muro ○ **I** 194 Gp 25
Muro ○ **PNG** 287 Mj 49
Murom ○ **RUS** 181 Hn 18
Muroran ○ **J** 250 Mg 24
Muros ○ **E** 184 Gb 24
Muroto ○ **J** 251 Md 29
Muroto-saki ⌓ **J** 251 Md 29
Murphy ○ **USA** 71 Dg 28
Murphysboro ○ **USA** 71 Dd 27
Murra Murra ○ **AUS** 375 Mk 60
Murray ○ **USA** 71 Dd 27
Murray ～ **AUS** 368 Lj 62
Murray ～ **AUS** 378 Mf 63
Murray Downs ○ **AUS** 374 Md 56
Murray Harbour ○ **CDN** 61 Ec 22
Murray Island ♁ **AUS** 286 Mh 50
Murray Range ⛰ **PNG** 286 Mh 49
Murraysburg ○ **ZA** 349 Hd 61
Murray Sunset ♀ **AUS** 378 Mg 63
Murray Town ○ **AUS** 378 Mf 62
Murrayville ○ **AUS** 378 Mg 63
Murree ○ **PK** 230 Ka 29
Murrí ～ **CO** 106 Dk 42
Murrieta ○ **USA** 64 Cd 29
Murroa ○ **MOC** 344 Hl 54
Murro Agudo ○ **BR** 141 Ek 56
Murrumbidgee ～ **AUS** 379 Mj 63
Murrumburrah ○ **AUS** 379 Ml 63
Murrupula ○ **MOC** 344 Hm 53
Murrurundi ○ **AUS** 379 Mm 61
Murshidābād ○ **IND** 235 Kj 33
Murtajāpur ○ **IND** 234 Kc 35
Murtle Lake ～ **CDN** 50 Cc 19
Murtlock Islands ♁ **FSM** 27 Sb 9
Murtoa ○ **AUS** 378 Mh 64
Murtovaara ○ **FIN** 159 Hg 13
Muru ～ **BR** 117 Dn 50
Muruat ○ **IND** 238 Ka 36
Muruken ○ **PNG** 287 Mj 48
Murupara ○ **NZ** 383 Nl 65
Murupu ○ **BR** 112 Ed 44
Mururani ○ **NAM** 340 Hb 55
Mururoa ♁ **F** 14 Ca 12
Murwāra ○ **IND** 234 Ke 34
Murwillumbah ○ **AUS** 375 Mn 60
Mürzzuschlag ○ **A** 174 Gp 22
Muş ○ **TR** 202 Hn 26
Musa Ālī Terara △ **ER** 313 Hp 39
Musadi ○ **RDC** 333 Hd 47
Musaia ○ **WAL** 316 Ga 41
Musaimīr ○ **YE** 218 Ja 39
Mūsa Khel ○ **PK** 223 Jp 29
Mūsa Khel Bāzār ○ **PK** 227 Jn 30
Musallim ～ **OM** 219 Jg 35
Mūsā Qal'e ～ **AFG** 223 Jl 29
Musa River ～ **PNG** 287 Ml 50
Musashi ○ **J** 247 Mb 29
Musawa ○ **WAN** 320 Gk 39
Muscat ◙ **OM** 226 Jh 34
Muscatine ○ **USA** 71 Dc 25
Muscle Shoals ○ **USA** 71 De 28
Musenge ○ **RDC** 336 Hg 46
Musenge ○ **RDC** 341 Hd 50
Musengezi ～ **ZW** 341 Hh 54
Musgrave ○ **AUS** 365 Mh 53
Musgrave Harbour ○ **CDN** 61 Eh 21
Musgrave Range ⛰ **AUS** 369 Mb 59
Mushayfāt ○ **SUD** 312 Hh 40
Mushenge ○ **RDC** 333 Hc 48
Mushie ○ **RDC** 333 Ha 47
Mushima ○ **Z** 341 He 53
Mushipashi ○ **Z** 341 Hh 51
Mushota ○ **Z** 336 Hg 50
Mushu Island ♁ **PNG** 286 Mh 47
Mushumbi Pools ○ **ZW** 341 Hh 54
Musi ～ **RI** 278 Lc 47
Musin ○ **WAN** 320 Gh 42
Mūsīyan ○ **IR** 209 Jb 29
Muskegon ○ **USA** 57 De 24
Muskgon ～ **USA** 57 De 24
Muskingum ～ **USA** 71 Dg 26
Muskogee ○ **USA** 70 Da 28
Musoma ○ **EAT** 337 Hj 46
Musondweji ～ **Z** 341 He 52
Musongoie ○ **RDC** 336 He 50
Musontov ○ **UZB** 223 Jl 25
Musoshi ○ **RDC** 341 Hf 51
Musquodoboit ○ **CDN** 61 Ec 23
Mussau Island ♁ **PNG** 287 Ml 46
Musselshell ～ **USA** 51 Cj 22
Mussende ○ **ANG** 340 Ha 51
Musserra ○ **ANG** 332 Gn 49
Mussolo ○ **ANG** 340 Ha 50
Mussuma ～ **ANG** 340 Hc 53
Mussuma ○ **ANG** 341 Hc 53
Mustafābād ○ **PK** 230 Ka 30
Mustafa Kemal Paşa ○ **TR** 195 Hg 25
Mustahil ○ **ETH** 328 Ja 43
Mustang ○ **NEP** 235 Kf 31
Mustang ～ **NEP** 235 Kf 31
Mustang Island ♁ **USA** 81 Cp 32
Mustique ♁ **WV** 104 Ed 39
Mustjala ○ **EST** 170 Hc 16
Mustvee ○ **EST** 171 Hf 16
Musu Dan ⌓ **DVRK** 247 Ma 25
Muswellbrook ○ **AUS** 379 Mm 62
Mut ○ **TR** 195 Hj 27
Mūt ○ **ET** 301 Hg 33
Mutakala ○ **EAU** 336 Hh 46
Mutale ～ **ZA** 352 Hh 57
Mutanda ○ **Z** 341 Hf 52
Mutando ○ **MOC** 344 Hj 54
Mutare ○ **ZW** 344 Hj 55
Mutarnee ○ **AUS** 365 Mk 55
Muteta ○ **RDC** 336 Hg 50
Mutha ○ **EAK** 337 Hm 46
Mutianyu ★ **VRC** 246 Lj 25
Mutici ○ **BR** 124 Fb 50
Mutiene ○ **RDC** 332 Ha 48
Mutimutema ○ **ZW** 341 Hg 54
Muting ○ **RI** 286 Mg 49
Mutinglupa ○ **RP** 267 Ll 38
Mutir ○ **EAU** 324 Hh 44
Mutki ○ **TR** 202 Hn 26
Mutoko ○ **ZW** 344 Hj 54
Mutombo-Mukulu ○ **RDC** 336 He 50
Mutomo ○ **EAK** 337 Hl 46
Mutorashanga ○ **ZW** 341 Hh 54
Mutoto ○ **RDC** 333 Hd 48
Mutsamudu ○ **COM** 345 Ja 52
Mutshatsha ○ **RDC** 341 He 51
Mutsu ○ **J** 250 Mg 25
Muttaburra ○ **AUS** 375 Mj 57
Mutton Bay ○ **CDN** 61 Ee 20
Mutúali ○ **MOC** 344 Hl 53
Mutum ～ **BR** 117 Dp 48
Mutum ～ **BR** 117 Dp 49
Mutum ○ **BR** 141 Ep 55
Mutumbi ○ **RDC** 336 Hg 49
Mutum Biyu ○ **WAN** 320 Gm 41
Mutumbo ○ **ANG** 340 Ha 52
Mutum Daya ○ **WAN** 320 Gm 41
Mutum ou Madeira ～ **BR** 132 Eg 54
Mutum Paraná ○ **BR** 117 Eb 50
Mutungu-Tan ○ **RDC** 333 Ha 49
Mutur ○ **CL** 239 Ke 41
Mutu-wan ～ **J** 250 Mg 25
Mutwanga ○ **RDC** 324 Hg 45
Muurola ○ **FIN** 159 He 12
Mu us Shamo ⏥ **VRC** 243 Ld 26
Muvattupula ○ **IND** 239 Kc 41
Muwassam ○ **YE** 218 Hp 37
Muwo Island ♁ **PNG** 287 Mm 50
Muxima ○ **ANG** 332 Gn 50
Muyinga ○ **BU** 336 Hh 47
Muy Muy ○ **NIC** 96 Df 39
Muyombe ○ **Z** 344 Hj 51
Muyuka ○ **CAM** 320 Gl 43
Muyumba ○ **RDC** 336 Hf 49
Muzaffarābād ○ **PK** 230 Ka 28
Muzaffargarh ○ **PK** 227 Jp 30
Muzaffarnagar ○ **IND** 234 Kc 31
Muzaffarpur ○ **IND** 235 Kg 32
Muzambinho ○ **BR** 141 El 56
Muze ○ **MOC** 341 Hh 53
muzej-usad'ba "Tarhany" ★ **RUS** 181 Hp 19
Muzerabani ○ **ZW** 341 Hh 54
Muzhen ○ **VRC** 246 Lj 29
Muzizi ～ **EAU** 324 Hh 45
Muzo ○ **CO** 106 Dl 43
Múzquiz ○ **MEX** 81 Cm 32
Muztag △ **VRC** 231 Kh 27
Muztagata △ **VRC** 230 Kb 26
Muzur ○ **TR** 195 Hk 26
Mvangan ○ **CAM** 320 Gm 44
Mvolo ○ **SUD** 324 Hg 42
Mvometo ○ **EAT** 337 Hl 49
Mvoung ～ **G** 332 Gn 45
Mvouti ○ **RCB** 332 Gn 48
Mvuha ○ **EAT** 337 Hl 49
Mvuma ○ **ZW** 341 Hh 55
Mvurwi ○ **ZW** 341 Hh 54
Mvuvye ～ **Z** 341 Hh 53
Mwadi-Kalumbu ○ **RDC** 333 Hb 49
Mwadingusha ○ **RDC** 341 Hf 51
Mwafwe ～ **Z** 341 He 52
Mwaga ○ **EAT** 337 Hl 50
Mwaleshi ～ **Z** 341 Hh 51
Mwambo ○ **EAT** 344 Hn 51
Mwambwa ～ **Z** 344 Hj 51
Mwami ○ **ZW** 341 Hg 54
Mwana-Ndeke ○ **RDC** 336 Hf 48
Mwango ○ **RDC** 333 Hd 49
Mwanisenga ○ **EAT** 336 Hj 48
Mwanza ○ **RDC** 336 Hf 49
Mwanza ○ **EAT** 336 Hj 47
Mwanza ○ **MW** 344 Hk 53
Mwanza Gulf ～ **EAT** 336 Hj 47
Mwanzangoma ～ **RDC** 333 Hd 48
Mwarazi ～ **ZW** 344 Hj 55
Mwaru ～ **EAT** 337 Hk 48
Mwatate ○ **EAK** 337 Hm 47
Mwatate ～ **EAK** 337 Hm 47
Mweka ○ **RDC** 333 Hc 48
Mwembeshi ～ **Z** 341 Hf 53
Mwenda ○ **Z** 341 Hg 51
Mwenda ○ **Z** 341 Hg 52
Mwene-Bijl ○ **RDC** 341 Hd 50
Mwene-Ditu ○ **RDC** 333 Hd 49
Mwenezi ○ **ZW** 352 Hh 56
Mwenezi ～ **ZW** 352 Hh 56
Mwenga ○ **RDC** 336 Hg 47
Mweru Wantipa ♀ **Z** 336 Hg 50
Mweshi ○ **Z** 341 Hg 51
Mwilambwe ○ **RDC** 336 He 50
Mwimbi ○ **EAT** 336 Hh 50
Mwingi ○ **EAK** 337 Hm 46
Mwinilunga ○ **Z** 341 He 51
Mwitikiri ○ **EAT** 337 Hk 49
Mwogo ～ **RWA** 336 Hg 47
Mwombezhi ～ **Z** 341 He 52
Myaing ○ **MYA** 254 Km 35
Myall Lakes ♀ **AUS** 379 Mn 62
Myanaung ○ **MYA** 254 Km 36
Myanmar Burma ◻ **MYA** 254 Km 34
Myaungmya ○ **MYA** 262 Km 37
Mychajlivka ○ **UA** 175 Hk 22
Myingyan ○ **MYA** 254 Km 35
Myinmoletkat Taung △ **MYA** 262 Kp 39
Myitkyina ○ **MYA** 254 Kn 33
Myittha ○ **MYA** 254 Km 35
Mykolaiv ○ **UA** 175 Hh 22
Mykolajiv ○ **UA** 175 Hf 21
Mymensingh ○ **BD** 235 Kk 33
Mynämäki ○ **FIN** 159 Hc 15
Mynfontein ○ **ZA** 349 Hd 61
Myohaung ○ **MYA** 235 Kl 35
Myola ○ **PNG** 287 Mk 50
Myola ○ **AUS** 365 Mj 55
Mýrdalsjökull ⧋ **IS** 158 Fl 14
Myre ○ **N** 158 Gp 11
Myrgorod ○ **UA** 175 Hj 21
Myri ○ **IS** 158 Fm 13
Myronivka ○ **UA** 175 Hh 21
Myrtle Beach ○ **USA** 87 Dj 29
Myrtleford ○ **AUS** 379 Mk 64
Myrtle Point ○ **USA** 50 Ca 24
mys Aleksandra ⌓ **RUS** 205 Xa 8
mys Aniva ⌓ **RUS** 205 Xb 9
mys Aniva ⌓ **RUS** 250 Mh 22
mys Billingsa ⌓ **RUS** 205 Zc 5
mys Buor-Haja ⌓ **RUS** 205 Wc 4
mys Čeljuskin ⌓ **RUS** 22 Qa 2
mys Čeljuskin ⌓ **RUS** 204 Uc 3
mys Čukotskij ⌓ **RUS** 23 Aa 5
mys Čukotskij ⌓ **RUS** 46 Ac 13
mys Čukotskij ⌓ **RUS** 205 Ab 6
mys Cypnavolok ⌓ **RUS** 159 Hj 11
mys Dežneva ⌓ **RUS** 23 Ab 3
mys Dežneva ⌓ **RUS** 46 Ae 11
mys Elizavety ⌓ **RUS** 205 Xb 8
mys Enkèn ⌓ **RUS** 205 Xb 7
mys Geka ⌓ **RUS** 205 Zc 6
mys Južnyj ⌓ **RUS** 205 Yb 7
mys Kanin Nos ⌓ **RUS** 154 Qc 5
Myškin ○ **RUS** 171 Hl 17
mys Krigujgun ⌓ **RUS** 46 Ae 13
mys Kril'on ⌓ **RUS** 250 Mg 23
mys Lajdennyi ⌓ **RUS** 159 Ja 11
Myślenice ○ **PL** 174 Hc 21
mys Lopatka ⌓ **RUS** 23 Sb 4
mys Lopatka ⌓ **RUS** 205 Yb 8
mys Navarin ⌓ **RUS** 205 Zc 6
mys Nygčigėn ⌓ **RUS** 46 Ae 13
Mys Oljutorskij ⌓ **RUS** 23 Tb 4
mys Oljutorskij ⌓ **RUS** 205 Zb 6
Mỹ So'n ★ **VN** 263 Le 38
Mysore ○ **IND** 238 Kc 39
mys Orlovskij ⌓ **RUS** 159 Hn 12
mys Ozenoj ⌓ **RUS** 205 Yc 7
mys Paksa ⌓ **RUS** 204 Vb 4
Mys Šelagskij ⌓ **RUS** 23 Ta 2
mys Šelagskij ⌓ **RUS** 205 Zb 4
mys Serdce-Kamen' ⌓ **RUS** 46 Ae 11
mys Svjatoj Nos ⌓ **RUS** 159 Hm 11
mys Svjatoj Nos ⌓ **RUS** 205 Xa 4
mys Terpenija ⌓ **RUS** 205 Xb 9
Mystery Caves ★ **USA** 56 Db 24
mys Voronov ⌓ **RUS** 159 Hn 12
mys Želanija ⌓ **RUS** 19 Na 2
Myszyniec ○ **PL** 170 Hc 19
Mỹ Tho ○ **VN** 263 Lc 40
Mytišči ○ **RUS** 171 Hl 17
Myton ○ **USA** 65 Cg 25
Mývatn ★ **IS** 158 Fm 13
Mzenga ○ **EAT** 337 Hm 49
Mziha ○ **EAT** 337 Hl 48
Mzimba ○ **MW** 344 Hj 51
Mzuzu ○ **MW** 344 Hk 51

N

Naala ○ **TCH** 321 Gp 39
Naalehu ○ **USA** 75 An 36
Nāal Hiyyon ～ **IL** 214 Hk 31
Nāal Paran ～ **IL** 214 Hk 30
Na'am ○ **SUD** 324 Hg 41
Na'ām ～ **SUD** 324 Hg 43
Naama ○ **DZ** 293 Gf 29
Na'ama ○ **ET** 301 Hk 32
Naantali ○ **FIN** 159 Hc 15
Nababeep ○ **ZA** 348 Ha 60
Nabadeed ○ **SP** 328 Hp 41
Nabalāt ○ **SUD** 312 Hh 38
Naban Shuiku ～ **VRC** 255 Le 34
Nabar ○ **TCH** 309 Hc 36
Nabarlek ○ **AUS** 364 Mc 52
Nabas ○ **RP** 267 Lm 40
Nabatīya ○ **RL** 208 Hk 29
Nabavatu ○ **FJI** 387 Nm 54
Nabeerera ○ **EAT** 337 Hl 48
Naberežnye Čelny ○ **RUS** 181 Je 18
Nabesna ○ **USA** 46 Be 13
Nabeul ○ **TN** 297 Gm 27
Nabġa ○ **UAE** 226 Jf 33
Nabgunhe ★ **VRC** 254 Kp 34
Nabiac ○ **AUS** 379 Mn 62
Nabies ○ **ZA** 348 Hc 60
Nabilque ～ **BR** 140 Ef 56
Nabingora ○ **EAU** 324 Hh 45
Nabire ○ **RI** 283 Md 47
Nabisar ○ **PK** 227 Jn 33
Nablus ○ **JOR** 208 Hk 29
Nabogwe ○ **EAT** 336 Hh 47
Nabou ○ **BF** 317 Ge 40
Nabouwalu ○ **FJI** 387 Nm 54
Nabq ○ **ET** 214 Hk 31
Nabusanke ○ **EAU** 324 Hh 45
Nacala ○ **MOC** 344 Hn 53
Načalovo ○ **RUS** 202 Jc 22
Nacaome ○ **HN** 96 De 39
Nacaroa ○ **MOC** 344 Hm 53
Nacebe ○ **BOL** 129 Ea 51
Naches ○ **USA** 50 Cb 22
Nachingwea ○ **EAT** 344 Hm 51
Nāchna ○ **IND** 227 Jp 32
Náchod ○ **CZ** 174 Ha 20
Nachuge ○ **IND** 262 Kl 40
Nackara ○ **AUS** 378 Mf 62
Nacogdoches ○ **USA** 81 Da 30
Nacori Chico ○ **MEX** 80 Ch 31
Nacozari de García ○ **MEX** 80 Ch 30
Nacula ♁ **FJI** 387 Nl 54
Nacuñán ○ **RA** 137 Ea 63
Nadawli ○ **GH** 317 Ge 40
Nāder Šāh Kūt ○ **AFG** 223 Jp 28
Nadi ○ **FJI** 387 Nl 54
Nadiād ○ **IND** 227 Ka 34
Nadoba ○ **BF** 317 Gg 40
Nadojata ～ **RUS** 204 Sb 4
Nador ○ **MA** 293 Ge 28
Nadsori ○ **FJI** 387 Nm 55
Naduri ○ **FJI** 387 Nm 54
Nadvima ○ **UA** 175 He 21
Nadvojce ○ **RUS** 159 Hj 14
Nadym ○ **RUS** 154 Sc 5
Nadzab ○ **PNG** 287 Mk 49
Nā'ebābād ○ **AFG** 223 Jm 27
Naejahgsan ★ **ROK** 247 Lp 28
Nafadji ○ **SN** 316 Ga 39
Nafi ○ **KSA** 215 Hp 33
Nafplio ○ **GR** 194 Hd 27
Nafūd ad-Daḥī ⏥ **KSA** 218 Ja 35
Nafūd al-'Uraik ⏥ **KSA** 214 Hp 33
Nafūd as-Sirr ⏥ **KSA** 215 Ja 33
Nāg ○ **PK** 227 Jl 32
Nag 'Hammādi ○ **ET** 301 Hh 33
Naga ♁ **J** 247 Ma 29
Naga ○ **RP** 267 Lm 39
Naga ○ **RP** 267 Lm 40
Nagafābād ○ **IR** 222 Jd 29
Nagagami Lake ～ **CDN** 57 Df 21
Nagaj ○ **IND** 238 Kb 37
Nagāland ⦿ **IND** 254 Km 32
Nagamangala ○ **IND** 238 Kc 39
Nagambie ○ **AUS** 379 Mj 64
Nagandana ○ **CI** 305 Gc 40
Nagano ○ **J** 251 Mf 27
Nagaoka ○ **J** 251 Mf 27
Nagaon ○ **IND** 235 Kl 32
Nagappattinam ○ **IND** 239 Kd 40
Nagar ○ **IND** 234 Kc 32

448 Muang Ou Tai - Nagar

◻Country ▣Capital city ⊙Administrative unit ○Place ♁Island ⋀⋀Mountain range △Mountain ⌒Cape ≈Ocean, Sea ~Lake, River ♆Undersea topography ⩓Glacier ♀National park •••Reservation ★Point of major interest ⌓Landscape

Nagara ○ RMM 304 Ga 38
Nagarhole National Park ♀ IND 238 Kb 40
Nagarjuna Sāgar ~ IND 238 Kd 37
Nagar Karnūl ○ IND 238 Kd 37
Nagarote ○ NIC 96 De 39
Nagar Pārkar ○ PK 227 Jp 33
Nagarzê ○ VRC 235 Kk 31
Nagasaki ○ J 247 Ma 29
Nagato ○ J 247 Mb 28
Nāgaur ○ IND 227 Ka 32
Nāgbhīr ○ IND 234 Kd 35
Nāgda ○ IND 234 Kb 34
Nage ○ RI 282 Ll 50
Nageezi ○ USA 65 Ch 27
Nāgercoil ○ IND 239 Kc 41
Nagichot ○ SUD 325 Hj 43
Nagina ○ IND 234 Kd 31
Nago ○ J 259 Ma 32
Nago ○ PNG 286 Mg 49
Nāgod ○ IND 234 Ke 33
Nagorno-Karabakh ⊙ AZ 202 Jb 25
Nagornyg ○ RUS 205 Zc 6
Nagoya ○ J 251 Me 28
Nagp'e ○ RUS 171 Hm 17
Nāgpur ○ IND 234 Kd 35
Nagqu ○ VRC 235 Kl 30
Nagua ○ DOM 101 Dp 36
Nagum ○ PNG 286 Mh 47
Nagyatád ○ H 174 Ha 22
Nagykanizsa ○ H 174 Ha 22
Nagystad ○ H 174 Ha 22
Naha ○ J 259 Lp 32
Na Haeo ○ THA 262 La 37
Nahafalia ○ USA 86 Dd 29
Nāhan ○ IND 230 Kc 30
Nahang ~ IR 226 Jk 32
Na Hang ○ VN 255 Lc 34
Nahanni National Park ♀ CDN 47 Bn 15
Nahariyya ○ IL 208 Hk 29
Naheleg ♁ ER 313 Hn 37
Nahia Lō ○ VN 255 Lc 35
Nahl ~ IR 226 Jh 30
Nahodka ○ RUS 250 Mc 24
Nahr al-Qāsh ~ SUD 313 Hl 38
Nahr az-Zāb ~ IRQ 209 Hp 27
Nahr az-Zābas ~ IRQ 209 Hp 28
Nahr Bārū ~ SUD 325 Hj 41
Nahuatzen ○ MEX 92 Cm 36
Nahuel Mapá ○ RA 137 Ea 63
Nahunta ○ USA 87 Dg 30
Nahuo ○ VRC 255 Lf 35
Naica ○ MEX 80 Ck 32
Naicam ○ CDN 51 Ck 19
Nā'id Abar ○ KSA 218 Hp 37
Nā'if al-Āğil ○ IRQ 215 Ja 30
Naihbawi ○ IND 254 Kl 34
Naij Tal ○ VRC 242 Km 28
Naikliu ○ RI 282 Lm 50
Nailaga ○ FJI 387 Nl 54
Naima ○ SUD 312 Hj 38
Nain ○ CDN 7 Fb 4
Nain ○ CDN 43 Hc 7
Nāīn ○ IR 222 Je 29
Naini Tāl ○ IND 234 Kd 31
Nainpur ○ IND 234 Kd 34
Nairai ♁ FJI 387 Nm 54
Nairn ○ GB 162 Gd 17
Nairobi ♀ EAK 337 Hl 46
Nairobi ▣ EAK 337 Hl 46
Naitaba ♁ FJI 390 Aa 54
Naivasha ○ EAK 337 Hl 46
Najas ~ C 100 Dk 35
Nájera ○ E 184 Ge 24
Najībābād ○ IND 234 Kd 31
Najopue ○ MOC 344 Hl 53
Najrān ○ KSA 218 Ja 37
Naju ○ ROK 247 Lp 28
Naka ~ J 251 Mg 27
Nakadori-shima ♁ J 247 Ma 29
Nakagawa ○ J 250 Mg 23
Nakamura ○ J 251 Mc 29
Nakanai Mountains ⋀⋀ PNG 287 Mm 48
Nakanno ○ RUS 204 Va 6
Nakano-shima ♁ J 251 Mc 27
Nakano-shima ♁ J 259 Ma 31
Nakashibetsu ○ J 250 Mj 24
Nakasongola ○ EAU 324 Hj 45
Naka-Tane ○ J 247 Mb 30
Nakatsu ○ J 247 Mb 29
Nakatsugawa ○ J 251 Me 28
Nak'fa ○ ER 313 Hm 37
Nakhchyvan ⊙ ARM 202 Ja 26
Nakhon Nayok ○ THA 262 La 38
Nakhon Pathom ○ THA 262 Kp 39
Nakhonphanom ○ THA 263 Lc 37
Nakhon Ratchasima ○ THA 262 La 38
Nakhon Sawan ○ THA 262 Kp 38
Nakhon si Thammarat ○ THA 262 Kp 41
Nakhon Thai ○ THA 262 La 37
Nakhtarāna ○ IND 227 Jn 34
Naki-Est ○ BF 317 Gg 40
Nakina ○ CDN 43 Ga 8
Nakina ○ CDN 57 De 20
Nakitoma ○ EAU 324 Hj 45
Nakkala ○ CL 239 Ke 42
Nakło ○ PL 170 Ha 19
Naknek ○ USA 10 Ba 4
Naknek ○ USA 46 Al 15
Nako ○ BF 317 Ge 40
Nakonde ○ Z 336 Hj 50
Nakong-Atinia ○ GH 317 Gf 40
Nakop ○ ZA 348 Hc 60
Nakotombetsu ○ J 250 Mh 23
Nakskov ○ DK 170 Gm 18
Nakuru ○ EAK 337 Hl 46
Nakusp ○ CDN 50 Cc 20
Nāl ~ PK 227 Jl 32
Nālatvād ○ IND 238 Kc 37
Nalázi ○ MOC 352 Hj 58
Nalbarra ○ AUS 368 Lj 60
Nal'čik ○ RUS 202 Hp 24
Nalgonda ○ IND 238 Kd 37
Nali ○ VRC 255 Le 35
Näljänkä ○ FIN 159 Hf 13
Nallıhan ○ TR 195 Hh 25
Nalong ○ MYA 254 Kn 33
Nalpāktos ○ GR 194 Hc 26
Nālūt ○ LAR 297 Gm 30
Nama ○ RI 283 Mb 48
Nama ~ NAM 340 Hc 55
Namaacha ○ MOC 352 Hh 58
Namacunde ○ ANG 340 Gp 54
Namacurra ○ MOC 344 Hl 54
Namadgi ♀ AUS 379 Ml 63
Namai ○ NEP 234 Kf 32
Namakia ○ RM 345 Ja 53
Nāmakkal ○ IND 239 Kd 40
Namaklwe ○ MYA 254 Kp 36
Namaksār ~ AFG 223 Jj 29
Namakzār-e Šahdād ~ IR 226 Jg 30
Namaland ⌓ NAM 348 Ha 59
Namanga ○ EAK 337 Hl 47
Namangahn ○ UZB 22 Nb 5
Namangan ○ UZB 223 Jp 25
Namapa ○ MOC 344 Hm 52
Nama Pan ○ NAM 340 Hc 55
Namaponda ○ MOC 344 Hm 53
Namaqualand ⌓ ZA 348 Ha 60
Namas ○ RI 286 Mg 48
Namasagali ○ EAU 324 Hj 45
Namasale ○ EAU 324 Hj 45
Namatanai ○ PNG 287 Mn 47
Namba ○ ANG 340 Gp 51
Nambare ○ EAK 325 Hk 45
Nambazo ○ MW 344 Hk 53
Nambe ••• USA 65 Ck 28
Namber ○ RI 283 Md 46
Nambi ○ AUS 368 Ll 60
Nambour ○ AUS 375 Mn 59
Nambu ○ VRC 242 Lc 30
Nambuangongo ○ ANG 332 Gn 50
Nambucca Heads ○ AUS 379 Mn 61
Nambung ♀ AUS 368 Lh 61
Namche Bazar ○ NEP 235 Kh 32
Nam Chon Reservoir ~ THA 262 Kp 38
Namco ○ VRC 231 Kk 30
Nam Co ~ VRC 231 Kk 30
Namcy ○ RUS 205 Wb 6
Nam Đinh ○ VN 255 Ld 35
Nametil ○ MOC 344 Hm 53
Namhae Do ♁ ROK 247 Ma 28
Namhan ~ ROK 247 Lp 27
Nami ○ MAL 270 La 43
Namialo ○ MOC 344 Hm 53
Namib Desert ⌓ ANG 340 Gm 54
Namib Desert ⌓ ANG 340 Gm 54
Namib Desert ⌓ NAM 348 Gp 57
Namibe ○ ANG 340 Gn 53
Namibia ◻ NAM 348 Gp 57
Namib-Naukluft Park ♀ NAM 348 Gp 58
Namie ○ J 251 Mg 27
Namies ○ ZA 348 Hb 60
Namīn ○ IR 202 Jc 26
Namina ○ MOC 344 Hm 53
Namioka ○ J 250 Mg 25
Namiquipa ○ MEX 80 Cj 31
Namiranga ○ MOC 344 Hn 51
Namiroe ~ MOC 344 Hm 53
Namitete ○ MW 344 Hj 53
Namjagbarwa Feng △ VRC 254 Km 31
Namlan ○ MYA 254 Kn 34
Namlea ○ RI 283 Hj 47
Namling ○ VRC 235 Kj 31
Nam Ngum Reservoir ~ LAO 254 Lb 36
Namo ○ RI 279 Lk 46
Namoi ~ AUS 379 Ml 61
Namon ○ RT 317 Gg 41
Namonuito Atoll ♁ FSM 27 Sa 9
Namorona ○ RM 353 Jc 56
Namorrói ○ MOC 344 Hl 53
Nam Ou ~ LAO 254 Lb 35
Nampa ○ USA 50 Cd 24
Nampagan ○ MYA 254 Km 33
Nampala ○ RMM 305 Gd 38
Nam Pat ○ THA 262 La 37
Nam Pawn ~ MYA 254 Kn 35
Nampevo ○ MOC 344 Hl 54
Nampo ○ DVRK 247 Ln 26
Nam Poon ○ THA 254 La 36
Nampuecha ○ MOC 344 Hn 52
Nampula ○ MOC 344 Hm 53
Namrole ○ RI 282 Lp 47
Namru ○ VRC 230 Ke 30
Namsos ○ N 158 Gm 13
Namsskogan ○ N 158 Gn 13
Nam Taung ~ MYA 254 Kp 35
Namtha ○ MYA 254 Km 33
Nam Theun ○ LAO 263 Lc 37
Nam Tok Chat Trakan ♀ THA 262 La 37
Namtu ○ MYA 254 Kn 34
Namudi ○ PNG 287 Ml 50
Namuka-i-Lau ♁ FJI 390 Aa 55
Namukumbo ○ Z 341 Hf 53
Namuno ○ MOC 344 Hm 52
Namur ○ CDN 60 Dl 23
Namur ○ B 163 Gj 20
Namutoni ○ NAM 340 Ha 55
Namwala ○ Z 341 Hf 53
Namwera ○ MW 344 Hk 53
Namwŏn ○ ROK 247 Lp 28
Namysłów ○ PL 174 Ha 20
Nan ○ THA 254 La 36
Nana ○ CAM 321 Gp 42
Nana ~ RCA 321 Gp 42
Nana Bakassa ○ RCA 321 Ha 42
Nana Bakassa ~ RCA 321 Ha 42
Nana Barya ~ RCA 321 Ha 42
Nana Barya ~ TCH 321 Ha 42
Nana Candundo ○ ANG 341 Hd 51
Nanae ○ J 250 Mg 25
Nanaimo ○ CDN 50 Bp 21
Nanambinia ○ AUS 369 Lm 62
Nanango ○ AUS 375 Mm 59
Nanao ○ J 251 Me 27
Nan'ao Dao ♁ VRC 258 Lj 34
Nanay ~ PE 116 Dm 47
Nanchang ○ VRC 258 Lh 31
Nancheng ○ VRC 258 Lj 32
Nanchong ○ VRC 243 Ld 30
Nanchuan ○ VRC 255 Ld 31
Nancowry Island ♁ IND 270 Kl 42
Nancy ○ F 163 Gk 21
Nanda Devi ★ IND 230 Kd 30
Nanda Devi △ IND 230 Kd 30
Nandai ○ F 386 Ne 56
Nandaime ○ NIC 96 Df 40
Nandalur ○ IND 238 Kd 38
Nandaly ○ AUS 378 Mh 63
Nandan ○ VRC 255 Ld 33
Nanded ○ IND 238 Kc 36
Nandewar Range ⋀⋀ AUS 379 Mm 61
Nāndghāt ○ IND 234 Ke 35
Nandi ○ ZW 352 Hh 56
Nandigāma ○ IND 238 Ke 37
Nandi Hills ○ IND 238 Kc 39
Nandikotkūr ○ IND 238 Kd 38
Nanding Hé ~ VRC 254 Kp 34
Nandipadu ○ IND 238 Kd 38
Nandom ○ GH 317 Ge 40
Nandouta ○ RT 317 Gg 41
Nandowrie ○ AUS 375 Mk 58
Nāndūra ○ IND 234 Kc 35
Nandurbār ○ IND 234 Kb 35
Nandyal ○ IND 238 Kd 38
Nanfeng ○ VRC 258 Lj 32
Nangade ○ MOC 344 Hm 51
Nanga Eboko ○ CAM 320 Gm 43
Nangalala ○ AUS 364 Md 52
Nangalao Island ♁ RP 267 Ll 40
Nanganga ○ EAT 344 Hm 51
Nanga Pinoh ○ RI 271 Lf 46
Nangarhār ⊙ AFG 223 Jn 28
Nangaroro ○ RI 282 Ll 50
Nanga Tayap ○ RI 271 Lf 46
Nangbéto Reservoir ~ RT 317 Gg 42
Nangiloc ○ AUS 378 Mh 63
Nangin ○ MYA 262 Kp 40
Nangnim Mountains ⋀⋀ DVRK 247 Lp 25
Nango ○ J 247 Mb 29
Nangolet ○ SUD 325 Hj 43
Nangomba ○ EAT 344 Hm 51
Nangong ○ VRC 243 Lh 27
Nangqên ○ VRC 242 Kn 29
Nang Rong ○ THA 263 Lb 38
Nānguneri ○ IND 239 Kc 41
Nangurukuru ○ EAT 337 Hm 50
Nang Xian ○ VRC 235 Kl 31
Nanhua ○ VRC 254 La 33
Nanhui ○ VRC 246 Ll 30
Nanjangūd ○ IND 238 Kc 39
Nanje ○ VRC 243 Lh 27
Nanjian ○ VRC 254 La 33
Nanjiang ○ VRC 243 Ld 29
Nanjing ○ VRC 246 Lk 29
Nanjirinji ○ EAT 337 Hm 50
Nanjuyod ○ RP 267 Lm 41
Nankang ○ VRC 258 Lh 33
Nankoku ○ J 251 Mc 29
Nankova ○ ANG 340 Hb 54
Nanling ○ VRC 246 Lk 30
Nan Ling ⌓ VRC 255 Lf 33
Nanlixa ○ MOC 344 Hl 52
Nanning ○ VRC 255 Ld 34
Nannup ○ AUS 368 Lh 62
Nano ~ DY 320 Gh 41
Nanoro ○ BF 317 Ge 39
Nanpan Jiang ~ VRC 255 Lb 33
Nanpara ○ IND 234 Ke 32
Nanping ○ VRC 255 Lf 31
Nanping ○ VRC 258 Lk 32
Nansebo ○ ETH 325 Hm 42
Nansen Sound ~ CDN 7 Ea 1
Nanshan Island ♁ RP 266 Lh 40
Nanshui Shuiku ~ VRC 258 Lg 33
Nansio ○ EAT 337 Hj 47
Nanterre ○ F 163 Gh 21
Nantes ○ F 163 Gf 22
Nanton ○ CDN 50 Ce 20
Nanton ○ GH 317 Gf 41
Nantong ○ VRC 246 Ll 29
Nantong Kuangqu ○ VRC 255 Ld 31
Nantou ○ RC 259 Ll 34
Nantua ○ F 163 Gj 23
Nantucket ○ USA 74 Dn 25
Nantucket Island ♁ USA 74 Dp 25
Nantucket Shoals ~ USA 74 Dn 25
Nantucket Sound ~ USA 74 Dn 25
Nantulo ○ MOC 344 Hm 52
Nantwich ○ GB 163 Ge 19
Nanuku Passage ~ FJI 390 Aa 54
Nanumanga ♁ TUV 35 Tb 10
Nanumea ♁ TUV 35 Tb 10
Nanuque ○ BR 125 Ep 54
Nanutarra Roadhouse ○ AUS 360 Lh 57
Nan Xiang ○ VRC 258 Lg 31
Nanxiao ○ VRC 255 Le 34
Nanxijiang ★ VRC 259 Ll 31
Nanxiong ○ VRC 258 Lh 33
Nanyamba ○ EAT 344 Hm 51
Nanyang ○ VRC 243 Lg 29
Nanyang Hu ~ VRC 246 Lj 28
Nanyi Hu ~ VRC 246 Lk 30
Nan-Yō ○ J 251 Mf 26
Nanyuki ○ EAK 325 Hl 45
Nanzes ○ NAM 348 Hb 59
Nanzhai ○ VRC 255 Le 32
Nanzhang ○ VRC 243 Lf 30
Nanzhao ○ VRC 243 Lg 29
Nanzhila ○ Z 341 He 54
Nanzhila ~ Z 341 Hf 54
Naogaon ○ BD 235 Kj 33
Naolinco ○ MEX 92 Cp 36
Não-me Toque ○ BR 146 Eh 60
Naos ○ NAM 348 Ha 57
Náoussa ○ GR 194 Hd 25
Naozhoudao ♁ VRC 255 Lf 35
Napa ○ USA 64 Ca 26
Napadogan ○ CDN 60 Ea 22
Napaha ○ MOC 344 Hm 52
Napanee ○ CDN 60 Dh 23
Napanwainami ○ RI 283 Md 47
Napan-yaur ○ RI 283 Md 47
Napaskiak ○ USA 46 Aj 15
Napeitom ○ EAK 325 Hl 45
Napen △ N 170 Gk 16
Napido ○ RI 283 Md 46
Napier ○ ZA 358 Hb 63
Napier ○ NZ 383 Nl 65
Napier Broom Bay ~ AUS 361 Lp 52
Napier Downs ○ AUS 361 Ln 54
Napier Mountains ⋀⋀ 38 Mb 16
Napier Peninsula ♁ AUS 364 Md 52
Napier Range ⋀⋀ AUS 361 Ln 54
Naples ○ USA 86 Dg 32
Naples ○ I 185 Gn 25
Napo ~ EC 116 Dk 46
Napo ~ PE 116 Dm 47
Napo ○ VRC 255 Lc 34
Napoleon ○ USA 56 Cm 22
Napoleon ○ USA 71 Df 25
Nappamerrie ○ AUS 374 Mg 59
Nappanee ○ USA 71 De 25
Napperby ○ AUS 361 Mc 57
Napuka ♁ F 35 Bb 11
Naqāda ○ ET 301 Hj 33
Naqade ○ IR 209 Ja 27
Naqil al-Farda △ YE 218 Ja 38
Nara ○ J 251 Md 28
Nara ○ RMM 305 Gc 38
Nāra Canal ~ PK 227 Jn 32
Narach ○ BY 171 Hf 18
Naracoorte ○ AUS 378 Mg 64
Naracoorte Caves (Australien Fossil Mammal Site) ★ AUS 378 Mg 64
Naradhan ○ AUS 379 Mk 62
Naraini ○ IND 234 Ke 33
Nārāinpur ○ IND 238 Ke 36
Nārājānkher ○ IND 238 Kc 36
Nara Moru ○ EAK 337 Hl 46
Naran ○ PK 230 Ka 28
Narang ○ AFG 223 Jp 28
Naranjal ○ EC 116 Dj 47
Naranjito ○ EC 116 Dj 47
Naranjo ○ MEX 80 Ch 33
Naranjos ○ MEX 81 Cp 34
Narao ○ J 247 Ma 29
Narasannapeta ○ IND 235 Kg 36
Narasapuram ○ IND 238 Ke 37
Narasaraopet ○ IND 238 Kd 37
Narasimharajapura ○ IND 238 Kb 39
Narathiwat ○ THA 270 La 42
Nara Visa ○ USA 65 Cl 28
Naravuka ○ FJI 387 Nm 54
Narayangadh ○ NEP 235 Kg 32
Narayani ~ NEP 234 Kf 32
Narbonne ○ F 185 Gh 24
Narcondam Island ♁ IND 262 Km 39
Naré ○ RA 137 Ed 61
Narega Island ♁ PNG 287 Ml 48
Naregal ○ IND 238 Kb 38
Narembeen ○ AUS 368 Lk 62
Naréna ○ RMM 316 Gb 39
Nares Plain ♆ 11 Fb 7
Nargund ○ IND 238 Kb 38
Nāri ~ PK 227 Jm 31
Narian Mar ○ RUS 19 Mb 3
Narib ○ NAM 348 Ha 58
Nariep ○ ZA 348 Ha 61
Narimanov ○ RUS 181 Jb 22
Narin Nur ○ VRC 243 Le 26
Narita ○ J 251 Mg 28
Nar'jan-Mar ○ RUS 154 Rb 5
Narkatiāganj ○ IND 235 Kg 32
Narmada ~ IND 234 Kd 34
Narmada ~ IND 238 Ka 35
Narnak-e ~ IR 226 Jf 31
Nārnaul ○ IND 234 Kb 31
Narob ~ NAM 348 Ha 58
Naro-Fominsk ○ RUS 171 Hl 18
Naro Island ♁ RP 267 Lm 40
Narok ○ EAK 337 Hk 46
Narooma ○ AUS 379 Mm 64
Narowāl ○ IND 230 Kb 29
Nærøyfjorden ~ N 158 Gk 15
Nārpes ○ FIN 159 Hc 14
Narrabri ○ AUS 379 Ml 61
Narran ~ AUS 375 Mk 60
Narrandera ○ AUS 379 Mk 63
Narran Lake ~ AUS 375 Mk 60
Narrien Range ⋀⋀ AUS 375 Mk 57
Narrogin ○ AUS 368 Lj 62
Narromine ○ AUS 379 Ml 62
Narsimhapur ○ IND 234 Kd 34
Narsinghgarh ○ IND 234 Kc 34
Narsipatnam ○ IND 238 Kf 37
Narssarssuaq ○ DK 43 Jc 6
Naru ♁ J 247 Ma 29
Narubis ○ NAM 348 Hb 59
Naruto ○ J 251 Md 28
Narva ○ EST 171 Hf 16
Narva Bay ~ EST 171 Hf 16
Narvik ○ N 158 Ha 11
Narvskoe vodohranilišče ~ RUS 171 Hg 16
Narwietooma ○ AUS 361 Mc 57
Naryilco ○ AUS 374 Mg 60
Naryn-Huduk ○ RUS 202 Jb 23
Naryškino ○ RUS 171 Hk 19
Năsăud ○ RO 175 He 22
Naschiti ○ USA 65 Ch 27
Nāshik ○ IND 238 Ka 36
Nashino ~ EC 116 Dk 46
Nashua ○ USA 51 Cj 21
Nashua ○ USA 56 Db 24
Nashua ○ USA 60 Dn 24
Nashville ○ USA 70 Da 29
Nashville ○ USA 71 De 27
Nashwauk ○ USA 56 Db 22
Nasia ○ GH 317 Gf 40
Nasia ~ GH 317 Gf 40
Našice ○ HR 174 Ha 23
Nasijärvi ~ FIN 159 Hd 15
Nasipit ○ RP 267 Ln 41
Nāşir ○ SUD 325 Hj 41
Nasīrābād ○ PK 226 Jk 33
Nasīrābād ○ PK 227 Jn 31
Nasīrbād ○ IR 222 Jj 28
Nasmah ○ LAR 297 Gn 30
Nasondoye ○ RDC 341 He 51
Nasorolevu △ FJI 387 Nm 54
Nāsriganj ○ IND 235 Kg 33
Naşriyān ○ IR 209 Jb 29
Nāsrullāhganj ○ IND 234 Kc 34
Nass ○ IRL 163 Gc 19
Nassarawa ○ WAN 320 Gk 41
Nassau ♁ NZ 35 Ab 11
Nassau ▣ BS 87 Dk 33
Nassau ~ AUS 365 Mg 53
Nassian ○ CI 317 Gd 41
Nass River ~ CDN 47 Bj 18
Nastapoka Islands ♁ CDN 43 Gc 7
Næstved ○ DK 170 Gm 18
Nasugbu ○ RP 267 Ll 38
Nasuraghena ○ SOL 290 Nd 51
Nasva ○ RUS 171 Hh 17
Nata ○ PA 97 Dh 41
Nata ○ RB 349 Hf 56
Nata ~ RB 349 Hf 56
Nataboti ○ RI 282 Lp 47
Natal ○ BR 121 Ek 48
Natal ○ BR 124 Fc 48
Natal ○ RI 270 Kp 45
Natal Basin ♆ 31 Lb 13
Natal Drakensberg ♀ ZA 349 Hg 60
Natanz ○ IR 222 Jd 29
Natar ○ RI 278 Lc 48
Natashquan ~ CDN 61 Ed 20
Natchamba ○ RT 317 Gg 41
Natchez ○ USA 86 Dc 30
Natchitoches ○ USA 86 Db 30
Nate ○ IND 238 Ka 37
Natewa Bay ~ FJI 387 Nm 54
Natha Gali ○ PK 230 Ka 28
Nathalia ○ AUS 379 Mj 64
Nathan River ○ AUS 364 Md 53
Na Thawi ○ THA 270 La 42
Nāthdwāra ○ IND 227 Ka 33
Nathenje ○ MW 344 Hj 53
Nathorst land ♁ N 158 Gp 7
Nathrop ○ USA 65 Cj 26
Natih ○ OM 226 Jg 34
Natimuk ○ AUS 378 Mg 64
Natingui ○ BR 140 Ej 58
Natitingou ○ DY 317 Gg 40
Natividade ○ BR 133 El 51
Natmauk ○ MYA 254 Km 35
Natoma ○ USA 70 Cn 26
Natore ○ BD 235 Kj 33
Natovi ○ FJI 387 Nm 54
Nātra ○ S 158 Hb 14
Nattam ○ IND 239 Kd 40
Nattavaara ○ S 159 Hc 12
Natuna Islands ♁ RI 271 Ld 43
Natuna Sea ≈ 271 Ld 44
Natural Bridges N.M. ★ USA 65 Cg 27
Naturaliste Channel ~ AUS 368 Lg 58
Naturaliste Plateau ♆ AUS 368 Lf 62
Naturita ○ USA 65 Ch 26
Naturkanaoka Pan ~ NAM 340 Gp 55
Nau ○ TJ 223 Jn 25
Nauabu ○ PNG 287 Ml 51
Naubise ○ NEP 235 Kg 32
Nauchas ○ NAM 348 Ha 57
Naudesberg Pass △ ZA 358 He 62
Naudesnek △ ZA 349 Hf 61
Nauela ○ MOC 344 Hl 53
Naugarh ○ IND 234 Kf 32
Naujan ○ RP 267 Ll 39
Naujan Lake ~ RP 267 Ll 39
Naukan ○ RUS 46 Ae 13
Naukluft ⋀⋀ NAM 348 Ha 58
Naukot ○ PK 227 Jn 33
Naulila ○ ANG 340 Gp 54
Naumburg ○ D 174 Gm 20
Nauna Island ♁ PNG 287 Ml 47
Naungmo ○ MYA 254 Km 33
Nauru ◻ NAU 35 Ta 10
Naushahro Firoz ○ PK 227 Jn 32
Nauta ○ PE 116 Dm 48
Nautanwa ○ NEP 235 Kf 32
Nautla ○ MEX 93 Cp 35
Nauzerus ○ NAM 348 Ha 57
Nava ○ MEX 81 Cm 31
Nava ~ RDC 324 Hf 44
Navahrudak ○ BY 171 He 19
Navahrudskae uzvyšša ⋀⋀ BY 171 He 19
Navajo ••• USA 65 Cg 27
Navajo City ○ USA 65 Cj 27
Navajo N.M. ★ USA 65 Cg 27
Navajo Reservoir ~ USA 65 Cj 27
Naval ○ RP 267 Ln 40
Navalmoral d.l.M. ○ E 184 Gd 26
Navan ○ IRL 163 Gc 19
Navapara ○ BD 235 Kj 34
Navapolatsk ○ BY 171 Hf 18
Navapur ○ IND 238 Ka 35
Navarra ⊙ E 184 Ge 24
Navarro ○ RA 146 Ee 63
Navašino ○ RUS 181 Hp 18
Navasota ○ USA 81 Cp 30
Navasota ~ USA 81 Cp 30
Navau ♁ FJI 390 Aa 54
Nāve ○ AFG 223 Jm 29
Naverre ○ USA 86 Da 30
Navia ○ E 184 Gc 24
Naviraí ○ BR 140 Eg 57
Naviti ♁ FJI 387 Nl 54
Naviu Island ♁ PNG 286 Mh 50
Navlakhi ○ IND 227 Jp 34
Navlja ○ RUS 171 Hk 19
Năvodari ○ RO 175 Hg 23
Navojoa ○ MEX 80 Ch 32
Na Vong ○ LAO 255 Lb 35
Nāvor ○ AFG 223 Jm 29
Nāvor ~ AFG 223 Jm 29
Navrongo ○ GH 317 Gf 40
Navsāri ○ IND 238 Ka 35
Navua ○ FJI 387 Nm 55
Nāwa ○ IND 234 Kb 32
Nawābshāh ○ PK 227 Jn 32
Nawāda ○ IND 235 Kg 33
Na Wai ○ THA 254 Kp 36
Nawa Kot ○ PK 227 Jp 31
Nāwalkal ○ IND 238 Kc 37
Nawalpur ○ NEP 235 Kg 32
Nawāpāra ○ IND 234 Kf 35
Nawar ○ RT 317 Gg 41
Nawinda Kuta ○ Z 341 He 54
Nawngawn ○ MYA 254 Kp 35
Nawnghkio ○ MYA 254 Kn 34
Nawngleng ○ MYA 254 Kp 34
Nawoiy ○ UZB 223 Jl 25
Naxçıvan ○ ARM 202 Ja 26
Náxos ○ GR 194 He 27
Náxos ♁ GR 194 He 27
Naya Chor ○ PK 227 Jn 33
Nayak ○ AFG 223 Jm 28
Nayar ○ MEX 92 Ck 34
Nāyband ○ IR 222 Jg 29
Nayoro ○ J 250 Mh 23
Nayouri ○ BF 317 Gg 39
Nayuchi ○ MW 344 Hk 53
Nazaré ○ BR 113 Ej 44
Nazaré ○ BR 121 El 49
Nazaré ○ BR 125 Fa 52
Nazaré ○ P 184 Gb 26
Nazaré da Mata ○ BR 124 Fc 49
Nazaré do Piauí ○ BR 124 En 49
Nazareth ○ CO 106 Dl 43
Nazareth ○ IL 208 Hk 29
Nazas ○ MEX 81 Ck 33
Nazas ~ MEX 81 Ck 33
Nazca ○ PE 128 Dl 53
Nazcalines ★ PE 128 Dl 53
Nazca Ridge ♆ 128 Dj 55
Naze ○ J 259 Ma 31
Nazilli ○ TR 195 Hg 27
Nazirhati ○ BD 235 Kk 34
Nazko ○ CDN 50 Ca 19
Nazombe ○ MOC 344 Hm 51
Nazran ○ RUS 202 Ja 24
Nazrēt ○ ETH 325 Hm 41
Nbâk ○ RIM 304 Fn 37
Nbeiket el Ahouâch ○ RIM 305 Gc 37
Ncanaha ○ ZA 358 He 62
Ncaute ○ NAM 340 Hb 55
Nchalo ○ MW 344 Hk 54
Nchelenge ○ Z 336 Hg 50
Ncojane ○ RB 348 Hc 57
Ncue ○ GQ 332 Gm 44
Ndaki ○ RMM 305 Gf 38
Ndala ○ EAT 337 Hj 48
Ndalambo ○ EAT 336 Hj 50
N'dalatando ○ ANG 340 Gp 50
Ndali ○ DY 320 Gh 41
Ndanda ○ RCA 321 Hd 43
Ndanda ○ EAT 344 Hm 51
Ndande ○ SN 304 Fm 38
Ndangane ○ SN 304 Fm 38
Ndarapo Swamp ~ EAK 337 Hm 47
Ndarassa ○ RCA 321 Hd 42
Ndareda ○ EAT 337 Hk 48
Ndébougou ○ RMM 305 Gd 38
Ndedu ○ RDC 324 Hg 44
Ndeji ○ WAN 320 Gj 41
Ndekesha ○ RDC 333 Hc 49
Ndéko ~ RCB 333 Ha 46
Ndélé ○ RCA 321 Hc 41
Ndélélé ○ CAM 321 Gp 43
Ndembera ~ EAT 337 Hk 50
Ndendé ○ G 332 Gm 47
Ndeundekat sur-Mer ○ SN 304 Fm 38
Ndia ○ SN 304 Fp 38
Ndiago ○ SN 304 Fm 37
Ndian ~ CAM 320 Gl 43
Ndikiniméki ○ CAM 320 Gm 43
Ndim ○ RCA 321 Gp 42
Ndindi ○ SN 304 Fm 38
Ndindi ○ G 332 Gm 47
Ndioum ○ SN 304 Fn 37
Ndioum Guènt ○ SN 304 Fn 38
Ndiya ○ WAN 320 Gk 43
N'djamena ▣ TCH 321 Gp 39
Ndji ~ RCA 321 Hd 42
Ndjim ~ CAM 320 Gm 43
Ndjolé ○ G 332 Gm 46
Ndjoundou ○ RCB 333 Ha 46
Ndjwé ~ CAM 321 Gp 44
Ndofane ○ SN 316 Fm 39
Ndok ○ CAM 321 Gp 42
Ndokama ○ CAM 320 Gm 43
Ndokayo ○ CAM 321 Gp 43
Ndoki ~ RCB 332 Ha 45
Ndola ○ Z 341 Hg 52
Ndom ○ CAM 320 Gm 43
Ndongolo ○ G 332 Gm 45
Ndop ○ CAM 320 Gm 43
Ndora Mountains △ WAN 320 Gm 42
Ndorola ○ BF 317 Gd 40
Ndoto Mountains ⋀⋀ EAK 325 Hl 45
Ndoukou ○ RCA 321 Hc 43
Ndoumbou ○ RCA 321 Ha 42
Ndoussi ○ CI 317 Gd 43
Ndu ○ CAM 320 Gm 42
Ndu ○ RDC 321 Hd 43
Ndumbwe ○ EAT 344 Hm 51
Ndumo ○ ZA 352 Hj 59
Ndurumo ~ EAT 337 Hk 48
Nduye ○ RDC 324 Hg 45
Ndzouani ♁ COM 345 Ja 52
Neabul Creek ~ AUS 375 Mk 59
Neah Bay ○ USA 50 Bp 21
Neale Junction ○ AUS 369 Ln 60
Neales ~ AUS 374 Me 60
Neales Creek ~ AUS 374 Md 59
Néa Moudaniá ○ GR 194 Hd 25
Nea Pafos ★ CY 195 Hj 28
Neápoli ○ GR 194 Hc 25
Neápoli ○ GR 194 Hd 27
Neapoli ○ GR 194 He 28
Nearchuss Passage ~ MYA 262 Kn 39
Near Islands ♁ USA 205 Zb 8
Nebbou ○ BF 317 Gf 40
Nebe ○ RI 282 Lm 50
Nebelat el Hagana ○ SUD 312 Hg 39
Nebine Creek ~ AUS 375 Mk 60
Nebo ○ AUS 375 Ml 56
Nebraska ⊙ USA 65 Cl 25
Nebraska City ○ USA 70 Cp 25
Nebrodi ⋀⋀ I 185 Gp 27
Nečajane ○ UA 175 Hh 22
Necedah ○ USA 56 Dc 23
Nechako Plateau ⌓ CDN 42 Db 8
Neche ○ USA 56 Cp 21
Neches ~ USA 81 Da 30
Nechi ○ CO 106 Dl 41
Nechi ~ CO 106 Dl 42
Nechisar N.P. ♀ ETH 325 Hl 43
Neckar ~ D 174 Gl 21
Necochea ○ RA 146 Ee 65
Necoclí ○ CO 106 Dk 41
Necungas ○ MOC 344 Hk 54
Nédéley ○ TCH 309 Hb 38
Nederland ○ USA 65 Ck 26
Nederland ○ USA 81 Da 31
Nederlandse Antillen ⊙ NL 107 Dp 39
Nedrata ○ ETH 313 Hm 40
Nedryhajliv ○ UA 175 Hk 20
Nedumangad ○ IND 239 Kc 41
Nedunkeni ○ CL 239 Ke 41
Nedveži ostrova ♁ RUS 23 Ta 2
Needles ○ CDN 50 Cc 21
Needles ○ USA 64 Ce 28
Needs Creek ○ AUS 368 Lk 58
Neenah ○ USA 57 Dd 23
Neepawa ○ CDN 56 Cn 20
Neerim ○ AUS 379 Mj 64
Nefasīt ○ ER 313 Hm 38
Nefas Mewch'a ○ ETH 313 Hm 40
Neffatia ○ TN 297 Gm 29
Nefhi Shet' ~ ER 313 Hm 38
Nefta ○ TN 296 Gk 29
Neftçala ○ AZ 202 Jc 26
Neftejugansk ○ RUS 154 Sb 6
Neftekumsk ○ RUS 202 Ja 23
Nefza ○ TN 296 Gl 27
Negage ○ ANG 332 Gp 49
Négala ○ RMM 316 Gb 39
Néganssi ○ DY 320 Gh 40
Negār ○ IR 226 Jg 31
Negara ○ RI 279 Lh 47
Negara ~ RI 279 Lh 47
Negele ○ ETH 325 Hm 42
Negēlē ○ ETH 325 Hm 43
Negev ⌓ IL 214 Hk 30
Negezi ○ EAT 337 Hj 47
Negiralama ○ RI 270 La 44

Nagara - Negiralama 449

Negola O ANG 340 Gp 53
Negomane O MOC 344 Hm 51
Negombo O CL 239 Kd 42
Negotin O SCG 194 Hd 23
Negotino O MK 194 Hd 25
Negril O JA 100 Dj 36
Negrine O DZ 296 Gk 28
Negro ~ NIC 96 De 39
Negro ~ YV 107 Dm 41
Negro ~ BR 117 Ea 45
Negro ~ RA 117 Ea 46
Negro ~ BOL 117 Eb 50
Negro ~ BR 117 Ec 46
Negro ~ BR 120 Ed 47
Negro ~ BOL 129 Ea 52
Negro ~ BR 132 Ef 55
Negro ~ PY 140 Ee 57
Negro ~ RA 140 Ee 58
Negro ~ PY 140 Ef 58
Negro ~ ROU 146 Ef 62
Negro ~ ROU 146 Eg 62
Negro ~ RA 147 Ea 65
Negros O RP 267 Lm 41
Negru O RO 195 Hg 24
Neguac O CDN 61 Eb 22
Nehaevskij O RUS 181 Hn 20
Nehalem O USA 50 Bp 23
Nehalem ~ USA 50 Ca 23
Nehāvand O IR 209 Jc 28
Nehbandān O IR 209 Jh 30
Nehone O ANG 340 Ha 53
Neiafu O TO 390 Ad 56
Neiba O DOM 101 Dn 36
Neiden O N 159 Hg 11
Neijiang O VRC 255 Lc 31
Neilburg O CDN 51 Ch 19
Neilersdrif O ZA 348 Hc 60
Neilsville O USA 56 Dc 23
Nei Monggol Zizhiqu ◉ VRC 26 Qa 5
Neina O NAM 340 Ha 55
Neineis O NAM 348 Gp 56
Neiríz O IR 226 Jf 31
Neisip O NAM 348 Ha 59
Neiße O D 174 Gp 20
Neiva O CO 106 Dl 44
Neixiang O VRC 243 Lf 29
Neizār O IR 222 Jd 28
Nejime O J 247 Mb 30
Nejo O ETH 325 Hk 41
Nek'emte O ETH 325 Hl 41
Nekljudovo O RUS 181 Ja 17
Nekob O MA 293 Gd 30
Nekoma O USA 56 Cn 21
Neksø O DK 170 Gp 18
Nelamangala O IND 238 Kc 39
Nelia O AUS 374 Mh 56
Nelidovo O RUS 171 Hj 17
Neligh O USA 56 Cp 24
Nellimo O FIN 159 Hf 11
Nellore O IND 238 Ke 38
Nel'ma O RUS 250 Mf 22
Nelson O CDN 50 Cd 21
Nelson O USA 56 Dc 23
Nelson O USA 70 Cn 25
Nelson O USA 74 Dk 25
Nelson O RA 137 Ed 61
Nelson O NZ 383 Nj 66
Nelson Bay O AUS 379 Mn 62
Nelsonia O USA 74 Dl 27
Nelson Islands ⚓ USA 46 Ag 15
Nelson Lakes ♀ NZ 383 Nj 67
Nelson River ~ CDN 6 Ea 4
Nelson River ~ CDN 42 Fc 7
Nelspruit O ZA 352 Hh 58
Néma O RIM 305 Gc 37
Nemaiah Valley ••• CDN 50 Ca 20
Neman ~ RUS 171 Hd 18
Nemanyere O AUS 379 Lk 61
Nembrala O RI 282 Lm 51
Néméyong O CAM 321 Gn 43
Nemiscau O CDN 60 Dk 20
Némiscau ~ CDN 60 Dk 20
Nemours O F 163 Gh 21
Nemrut Dağı ▲ TR 195 Hm 26
Nemunas ~ LT 170 Hc 18
Nemunas ~ LT 170 Hd 18
Nemuro O J 250 Mj 24
Nemuro-hanto ⚓ J 250 Mj 24
Nemuro-Kaikyō ~ J 250 Mj 24
Nemyriv O UA 175 Hg 21
Nenagh O IRL 163 Gb 19
Nenane O USA 46 Ba 13
Nenggiri ~ MAL 270 La 43
Nengo ~ ANG 341 Hc 53
Nengonengo ⚓ F 35 Bb 11
Nen Jiang ~ VRC 204 Wa 9
Nenjiang O VRC 204 Wb 9
Nenoksa O RUS 159 Hm 13
Neo O J 251 Me 28
Neodesha O USA 70 Cp 27
Neolithic Monuments ★ GB 162 Ge 16
Néo Petrítsi O GR 194 Hd 25
Neópolis O BR 125 Fb 51
Neosho ~ USA 70 Da 26
Neosho O USA 70 Da 27
Nepa O RUS 204 Va 7
Nepal □ NEP 235 Kg 32
Nepalganj O NEP 234 Ke 31
Nepara O NAM 340 Hb 54
Nepean O CDN 60 Dl 23
Nepeña O PE 116 Dj 50
Nephi O USA 65 Cf 26
Nephin Beg Range ▲ IRL 162 Gb 18
Nepisiguit ~ CDN 61 Ea 22
Nepisiguit Bay ~ CDN 61 Eb 22
Nepoko ~ RDC 324 Hf 44
Nepoko ~ RDC 324 Hf 44
Nepomuceno O BR 141 En 56
Népoui O F 386 Ne 56
Neptune O USA 74 Dm 25
Neptune Island ⚓ AUS 378 Md 63
Nérac O F 184 Gg 23
Neragon Island ⚓ USA 46 Ag 15
Nerča ~ RUS 204 Vc 8
Nerehta O RUS 171 Hn 17
Nereta O LV 171 He 17
Neretva ~ BIH 194 Ha 24
Neriquinha O ANG 340 Hc 53
Nerja O E 184 Ge 27
Nerjungri O RUS 204 Wa 7
Nerľ ~ RUS 171 Hl 17
Nerľ ~ RUS 171 Hm 17
Nerla O IND 238 Kb 37

Nerópolis O BR 133 Ek 54
Nerren Nerren O AUS 368 Lh 59
Nerrima O AUS 361 Ln 55
Nes O N 158 Gm 15
Nes' O RUS 159 Ja 12
Nes' ~ RUS 159 Ja 12
Nēšābūr O IR 222 Jh 27
Nesebăr O BG 195 Hf 24
Nesøya ⚓ N 158 Gn 12
Ness City O USA 70 Cn 26
Nessona O MOC 344 Hk 55
Nestaocano ~ CDN 60 Dm 20
Nesterov O UA 175 Hd 20
Nesterovo O RUS 171 Hm 16
Néstos ~ GR 194 He 25
Netaar O RI 286 Mg 47
Netanya O IL 208 Ha 29
Netarhāt O IND 235 Kg 34
Nétéboulou O SN 316 Fp 39
Netherlands □ NL 163 Gh 19
Netia O MOC 344 Hm 53
Neto ~ I 194 Ha 26
Netrakona O BD 235 Kk 33
Nettilling Lake ~ CDN 43 Ha 5
Nettitiling Lake ~ CDN 7 Fa 3
Nett Lake ~ USA 56 Db 21
Neubrandenburg O D 170 Gn 19
Neuchâtel O CH 163 Gk 22
Neuenkirchen O D 163 Gk 21
Neufchâteau O B 163 Gj 21
Neufchâteau O F 163 Gj 21
Neufchâtel-en-Bray O F 163 Gg 21
Neumarkt in der Oberpfalz O D 174 Gm 21
Neumünster O D 170 Gm 18
Neuquén O RA 137 Dp 64
Neuquén O RA 147 Dp 65
Neuras ~ NAM 348 Ha 58
Neuruppin O D 170 Gn 19
Neuschwabenland ⌒ 38 Jb 17
Neuschwanstein ★ D 174 Gm 22
Neuse ~ USA 74 Dk 28
Neuser ~ USA 74 Dk 28
Neusiedler See ~ A 174 Ha 22
Neustadt an der Aisch O D 174 Gm 21
Neustrelitz O D 170 Gn 19
Neuwied O D 163 Gk 20
Neva ~ RUS 171 Hh 16
Nevada ◉ USA 64 Cc 26
Nevada O USA 70 Da 27
Nevada del Huila ▲ CO 106 Dk 44
Nevada de Oumbal ▲ CO 116 Dj 45
Nevado Allincapac ▲ PE 128 Dn 52
Nevado Ampato ▲ PE 128 Dn 53
Nevado Ancohuma ▲ BOL 129 Dp 53
Nevado Ausangate ▲ PE 128 Dn 52
Nevado Coropuna ▲ PE 128 Dm 53
Nevado de Acay ▲ RA 136 Ea 58
Nevado de Cachí ▲ RA 136 Ea 58
Nevado de Chañi ▲ RA 136 Ea 58
Nevado de Colima ▲ MEX 92 Ck 36
Nevado de Huila ▼ CO 106 Dl 44
Nevado del Illimani ▲ BOL 129 Ea 54
Nevado de Longaví ▲ RCH 137 Dn 64
Nevado del Ruíz ▲ CO 106 Dl 43
Nevado de Putre ▲ RCH 128 Dp 55
Nevado de Sajama ▲ BOL 128 Dp 54
Nevado de Tolima ▲ CO 106 Dl 43
Nevado Huayana ▲ BOL 128 Dp 54
Nevado Huayna Potosí ▲ BOL 129 Dp 54
Nevado Ojos de Salado ▲ RA 136 Dp 59
Nevado Queva ▲ RA 136 Ea 58
Nevado Salcantay ▲ PE 128 Dn 52
Neveľ O RUS 171 Hg 17
Nevel'sk O RUS 205 Xb 9
Nevel'sk O RUS 250 Mg 22
Nevers O F 163 Gh 22
Nevertire O AUS 379 Mk 61
Neves ~ BR 121 Em 49
Nevesinje O BIH 194 Ha 24
Neville O CDN 51 Cj 21
Nevis ⚓ KN 104 Ec 37
Nevşehir O TR 195 Hk 26
Nevvinnomyssk O RUS 202 Hn 23
New ~ USA 71 Dh 27
New ~ GUY 113 Ef 44
Newala O EAT 344 Hm 51
New Albany O USA 71 Dd 28
New Albany O USA 71 De 26
New Alton Downs O AUS 374 Mf 59
New Amsterdam O GUY 113 Ef 42
Newark O USA 60 Dk 24
Newark O USA 71 Dg 25
New Athens O USA 71 Dc 26
Newaygo O USA 57 Df 24
New Bedford O USA 74 Dn 25
Newberg O USA 50 Ca 23
New Bern O USA 74 Dk 28
Newberry O USA 57 Df 22
Newberry O USA 71 Dh 28
Newbery Aboriginal Reserve ••• AUS 368 Lm 60
New Bight O BS 87 Dl 33
Newborn O USA 71 Dd 27
New Bosten O USA 71 Dc 25
New Boston O USA 70 Da 29
New Braunfels O USA 81 Cn 31
New Bridgen O CDN 51 Cg 20
New Britain ⚓ PNG 287 Mm 48
New Britain Trench ▼ 287 Ml 49
New Brunswick ◉ CDN 61 Ea 22
New Buffalo O USA 71 De 25
Newburgh O USA 74 Dl 25
New Bussa O WAN 320 Gj 41
New Caledonia ◉ F 386 Nd 56
New Caledonia ⚓ F 386 Nd 56
Newcastle O USA 51 Ck 24
Newcastle O USA 70 Cn 24
New Castle O USA 71 Dh 25
New Castle O USA 71 Dh 25
Newcastle O CDN 61 Ea 22
Newcastle O ZA 349 Hg 59
Newcastle ◉ AUS 379 Mm 62
Newcastle Creek ~ AUS 364 Mc 54
Newcastle-upon-Tyne O GB 162 Gf 18

Newcastle Waters O AUS 364 Mc 54
Newcastle West O IRL 163 Gb 19
New City O USA 74 Dm 25
Newcomb O USA 65 Ch 27
Newdale O CDN 56 Cm 20
New Delamere O AUS 364 Mb 53
New Delhi ⊡ IND 234 Kc 31
New Denver O CDN 50 Cd 21
New Dixie O AUS 365 Mh 53
Newell O USA 51 Cl 23
New England ◉ USA 51 Cl 22
New England O USA 56 Cm 23
New England ♀ AUS 379 Mn 61
New England Range ▲ AUS 379 Mm 61
New Featherstone O ZW 341 Hh 55
Newfoundland ◉ CDN 7 Fb 4
Newfoundland ◉ CDN 43 Hc 8
Newfoundland ◉ CDN 60 Dn 20
Newfoundland Basin ▼ 18 Gb 5
Newfoundland Evaporation Basin ~ USA 64 Cf 25
New Galloway O GB 162 Gd 18
New Georgia ⚓ SOL 290 Na 50
New Georgia Group ⚓ SOL 290 Na 50
New Georgia Sound ~ SOL 290 Na 49
New Germany O CDN 61 Eb 23
New Glasgow O CDN 61 Ec 23
New Guinea ⚓ RI 286 Me 47
New Guinea Trench ▼ 286 Me 46
Newhalen O USA 46 Al 15
New Halfa O SUD 313 Hk 38
New Hampshire ◉ USA 60 Dn 24
New Hampton O USA 56 Db 24
New Hanover ⚓ PNG 287 Ml 47
New Hanover O ZA 352 Hh 60
New Harmony O USA 71 Dd 26
New Haven O USA 74 Dm 25
New Hazelton O CDN 42 Bh 7
New Hebrides ⚓ VAN 386 Ne 53
New Hebrides Trench ▼ 35 Ta 11
New Iberia O USA 86 Dc 30
New Ireland ⚓ PNG 287 Mm 47
New Island ⚓ GB 147 Ed 71
New Jersey ◉ USA 74 Dl 26
Newkirk O USA 65 Ck 28
New Leipzig O USA 51 Cl 22
New Liskeard ◉ CDN 57 Dh 22
New Liskeard O CDN 60 Dj 22
New London O USA 57 Dd 23
New London O USA 74 Dm 25
New Madrid O USA 71 Dc 27
Newman O AUS 360 Lk 57
Newmark O USA 74 Dk 26
Newmarket O CDN 60 Dj 23
Newmarket O IRL 163 Gb 19
Newmarket O GB 163 Gg 19
New Martinsville O USA 71 Dh 26
New Meadows O USA 50 Cd 23
New Mexico ◉ USA 65 Ch 29
New Mirpur O PK 230 Ka 29
Newnan O USA 86 Df 29
New Norfolk O AUS 378 Mk 67
New Orleans O USA 86 Dd 30
New Philadelphia O USA 71 Dg 25
New Plymouth O NZ 383 Nj 65
Newport O USA 50 Bp 23
Newport O USA 50 Cd 21
Newport O USA 60 Dm 23
Newport O USA 70 Dc 28
Newport O USA 71 Dg 28
Newport O USA 71 Dj 28
Newport O GB 163 Ge 20
Newport O GB 163 Gf 20
Newport News O USA 74 Dk 27
New Port Richey O USA 86 Dg 31
New Providence Island ⚓ BS 87 Dk 33
New Quay O GB 163 Gd 20
Newquay O GB 163 Gd 20
New Raymer O USA 65 Ck 25
New Richmond O USA 56 Db 23
New Richmond O CDN 61 Eb 21
New Roads O USA 86 Dc 30
New Rochelle O USA 74 Dm 25
New Rockford O USA 56 Cn 22
New Ross O IRL 163 Gc 19
Newry O USA 62 Gc 18
Newry O AUS 364 Ma 54
Newry Island ⚓ AUS 375 Ml 56
New Salem O USA 56 Cm 22
New Siberia ⚓ RUS 23 Sa 2
New Siberian ⚓ RUS 205 Xc 3
New Siberian Islands ⚓ RUS 22 Rb 2
New Smyrna Beach O USA 87 Dh 31
New South Wales ◉ AUS 378 Mh 62
New Stuyahok O USA 46 Al 15
Newtok O USA 46 Ag 15
Newton O USA 70 Cp 26
Newton O USA 70 Db 25
Newton O USA 71 Dd 26
Newton O USA 71 Dh 28
Newton O USA 86 Dd 29
Newton O GB 163 Ge 19
Newton Mills O CDN 61 Ec 23
Newtonmore O GB 162 Gd 17
Newtontoppen ▲ N 158 Ha 6
New Town O USA 51 Cl 22
New Ulm O USA 56 Da 23
Newwark O GB 163 Gf 19
New Waterford O CDN 61 Ed 22
New Westminster O CDN 50 Ca 21
New York ◉ USA 60 Dl 24
New York O USA 74 Dm 25
New Zealand □ NZ 383 Nj 65
Nexapa ~ MEX 92 Cn 36
Nexpa ~ MEX 92 Cl 36
Neyyāttinkara O IND 239 Kc 41
Nezahualcóyotl O MEX 92 Cm 36
Neznanovo O RUS 181 Hn 18
Nezperce O USA 50 Cd 22
Nez Perce Indian Reservation ••• USA 50 Cd 22
Ngabang O RI 271 Le 45
Ngabe O RCB 332 Gp 47
Ngabu O MW 344 Hk 54

Ngabwe O Z 341 Hf 52
Ngadda River ~ WAN 321 Gn 39
Ngadiluwih O RI 279 Lf 49
Ngakobo O RCA 321 Hc 43
Ngala O WAN 321 Gn 39
Ngalda O WAN 320 Gm 40
Ngalipaeng O RI 275 Ln 44
Ngalo O RDC 321 Hc 43
Ngam O TCH 321 Ha 40
Ngama O CAM 320 Gm 43
Ngambé O CAM 320 Gm 43
Ngambé Tikar O CAM 320 Gm 43
Ngambwe Falls ~ Z 341 Hd 54
Ngamdu O WAN 320 Gn 40
Ngamo O ZW 341 Hf 55
Nganda O SN 316 Fn 39
Ngangala O SUD 324 Hh 43
Ngangla Ringco ~ VRC 230 Kf 30
Nganglong Kangri ▲▲ VRC 230 Ke 29
Nganglong Kangri △ VRC 230 Ke 29
Ngangzé ~ VRC 231 Kh 30
Nganji O RDC 336 Hf 47
Nganjuk O RI 279 Lf 49
Nganzi O ANG 332 Gn 48
Ngao O THA 254 La 36
Ngaou Ndal O CAM 321 Gn 42
Ngaoundéré O CAM 321 Gn 42
Ngapali O MYA 254 Km 36
Ngara O EAT 336 Hh 47
Ngara O MW 344 Hk 51
Ngarama O RWA 336 Hh 46
Ngarangou O TCH 321 Gp 39
Ngaras O RI 278 Lb 48
Ngarimbi O EAT 337 Hm 49
Ngaruawahia O NZ 383 Nk 64
Ngaso Plain ~ EAK 325 Hl 44
Ngasumet O EAT 337 Hl 48
Ngathaingyaung O MYA 262 Km 37
Ngato O CAM 321 Gp 44
Ngau ⚓ FJI 387 Nm 55
Ngawi O RI 279 Lf 49
Ngawihi O NZ 383 Nk 66
Ngayu ~ RDC 324 Hf 45
Ngazidja ⚓ COM 345 Hp 51
Ngazun O MYA 254 Km 35
Ngbala O RCB 332 Gp 45
Ngbi Lôc O VN 255 Lc 36
Ngerengere O EAT 337 Hm 49
Ngezi ~ ZW 341 Hg 55
Nggatokae Island ⚓ SOL 290 Nb 50
Nggela ⚓ SOL 290 Nc 50
Nggela Pile ⚓ SOL 290 Nc 50
Nggelelevu ⚓ FJI 390 Aa 54
Ngidinga O RDC 332 Gp 48
Ngilmina O RI 282 Ln 51
Ngina O RDC 324 Hf 44
Ngina O RDC 333 Ha 47
Nginyang O EAK 325 Hl 45
Ngo O RCB 332 Gp 47
Ngoako Ramalepe Duiwelskloof O ZA 352 Hh 57
Ngoassé O CAM 320 Gm 44
Ngong O CAM 321 Gn 41
Ngong O EAK 337 Hl 46
Ngonga O CAM 320 Gm 43
Ngonye Falls ~ Z 341 Hd 54
Ngora O EAU 325 Hj 45
Ngorengore O EAK 325 Hl 45
Ngoring Hu ~ VRC 242 Kn 28
Ngoro O CAM 320 Gm 43
Ngorongoro Crater ★ EAT 337 Hk 47
Ngororero O RWA 336 Hg 46
Ngoso O RDC 333 Hb 48
Ngoto O RCA 321 Ha 45
Ngotwane ~ RB 349 Hf 58
Ngouanga ~ RCA 324 He 42
Ngoubou-Ngoubou O RCB 332 Gn 46
Ngoulemakong O CAM 320 Gm 44
Ngoulonkila O RCB 332 Gp 47
Ngouma O RMM 305 Ge 38
Ngouni ~ G 332 Gm 46
Ngounié ~ G 332 Gm 46
Ngounié ~ G 332 Gm 47
Ngoura O CAM 321 Gp 42
Ngoura O TCH 321 Ha 39
Ngouri O TCH 321 Gp 39
Ngourti O RN 297 Gn 38
Ngoussa O DZ 296 Gj 29
Ngouyè Pété O SN 304 Fn 37
Ngouyo O RCA 324 He 43
Ngozi O BU 336 Hg 47
Ngquba O RDC 341 Hf 51
Ngudu O EAT 336 Hj 47
Nguélémendouka O CAM 321 Gn 43
Nguema O RDC 333 Hd 49
Ngui O RCA 321 Hd 42
Nguia Bouar O RCA 321 Gp 43
Nguigmi O RN 297 Gn 38
Nguila O CAM 320 Gm 43
Nguini O RN 308 Gl 38
Nguiu O AUS 364 Mb 51
Ngukurr O AUS 364 Md 53
Ngumbo ⚓ VU 386 Ng 54
Ngundu O ZW 352 Hh 56
Ngunut O EAT 337 Hm 46
Ngunut O RI 279 Lg 50
Ngurore O WAN 320 Gn 42
Nguru O WAN 320 Gn 41
Nguti O CAM 320 Gl 43
Nguyakro O CI 317 Gd 42
Ngwanalekau Hills ▲▲ RB 349 Hd 56

Ngwedaung O MYA 254 Kn 36
Ngwesi O ZW 349 Hf 56
Ngweze ~ Z 341 He 54
Ngwo O CAM 320 Gl 42
Nhabe ~ RB 349 Hd 56
Nhachengue O MOC 352 Hk 57
Nhacra O GNB 316 Fn 40
Nhamalabue O MOC 344 Hk 54
Nhamatanda O MOC 344 Hj 55
Nhamunda O BR 120 Ef 46
Nhamunda ~ BR 120 Ef 46
Nhandeara O BR 140 Ej 56
Nhandu ~ BR 120 Eg 50
Nhandugue ~ MOC 344 Hj 55
Nharêa O ANG 340 Ha 51
Nha Trang O VN 263 Le 39
Nhecolândia O BR 132 Ef 55
Nhia ~ ANG 340 Gp 51
Nhill O AUS 378 Mg 64
Nhlangano O SD 352 Hh 59
Nho Quan O VN 255 Lc 35
Nhulunbuy O AUS 365 Me 52
Nhu' Xuân O VN 255 Lc 36
Niababri O CI 305 Gc 43
Niable O CI 317 Ge 42
Niackhar O SN 304 Fm 38
Niada O RCA 321 Hc 43
Niafounké O RMM 305 Gd 38
Niagara O USA 56 Cn 22
Niagara Falls O CDN 60 Dj 24
Niagara Falls ★ USA 71 Dj 24
Niague O CI 305 Gc 43
Niah ~ MAL 271 La 44
Niah N.Pulau ★ MAL 274 La 44
Niakaramandougou O CI 317 Gd 41
Niambézaria O CI 317 Gd 43
Niamey ⊡ RN 308 Gh 39
Niamina O RMM 305 Gc 39
Niampak O RI 275 Lp 43
Niamtougou O RT 317 Gg 41
Niandakoro O RG 316 Gb 40
Niandan ~ RG 316 Gb 41
Nianfasa O CI 305 Gc 41
Niangandu O EAT 337 Hl 49
Niangara O RDC 324 Hf 44
Niangoloko O BF 317 Gd 40
Nia-Nia O RDC 324 Hf 45
Nianing O SN 304 Fm 38
Niantanina O RG 316 Gb 40
Niaotoga ⚓ VRC 243 Lh 30
Niaoshu Shan △ VRC 242 Lb 28
Niapidou O CI 305 Gc 43
Niapu O RDC 324 Hf 44
Niari ~ RCB 332 Gn 47
Niaro O SUD 312 Hh 40
Niau ⚓ F 35 Bb 11
Nibong Tebal O MAL 270 La 43
Nicaragua □ NIC 97 Df 39
Nicastro O I 185 Gp 26
Nice O F 185 Gk 24
Niceville O USA 86 De 30
Nichinan O J 247 Mb 30
Nicholas Channel ~ 100 Dh 34
Nicholasville O USA 71 Df 27
Nicholson O AUS 364 Ma 55
Nicholson O AUS 365 Me 52
Nicholson Range ▲▲ AUS 368 Lj 59
Nichols Town O BS 87 Dj 33
Nička O TM 223 Jk 27
Nickarieriver ~ SME 113 Ef 43
Nickol Bay ~ AUS 360 Lj 56
Nicman O CDN 60 Ea 22
Nicobar ⚓ IND 262 Km 41
Nicola Mameet Indian Reservation ••• CDN 50 Cb 20
Nicolás Bruzzone O RA 137 Eb 63
Nicolás Levalle O RA 147 Ec 65
Nicondocho ~ MOC 344 Hm 52
Nicosia □ CY 195 Hj 28
Nicosia O I 185 Gp 27
Nicoya O CR 97 Df 40
Nicoya Peninsula ⚓ CR 97 Df 41
Nictau O CDN 61 Ea 22
Nicuadala O MOC 344 Hl 54
Nicupa O MOC 344 Hm 53
Nida O LT 170 Hc 18
Nidadavole O IND 238 Ke 37
Nidelva ~ N 170 Gl 16
Nidri O GR 194 Hc 26
Nidubrolu O IND 238 Ke 37
Nidzica O PL 170 Hc 19
Nieauwoudtville O ZA 348 Hb 61
Niebüll O D 170 Gl 18
Niedere Tauern ▲ A 174 Gn 22
Niederösterreich ◉ A 174 Gp 21
Niedersachsen ◉ D 170 Gk 19
Niedersächsisches Wattenmeer ♀ D 170 Gk 19
Niefang O GQ 332 Gm 45
Niellé O CI 317 Gd 40
Niellim O TCH 321 Ha 41
Niem O RCA 321 Gp 42
Niemba O RDC 336 Hg 48
Niemba O RDC 336 Hg 49
Niemelane O RIM 304 Fp 36
Nienburg O D 170 Gl 19
Nièri Ko ~ SN 316 Fp 39
Nietverdiend O ZA 349 Hf 59
Nieu-Bethesda O ZA 349 He 61
Nieuw Amsterdam O SME 113 Ef 43
Nieuw Nickerie O SME 113 Ef 42
Nieuwpoort O NL 107 Dp 39
Nieva ~ PE 116 Dk 48
Nieves O MEX 81 Cl 33
Niğde O TR 195 Hk 27
Nigel O ZA 349 Hg 59
Niger □ RN 308 Gl 37
Niger ~ WAN 320 Gk 43
Niger ~ WAN 320 Gk 43
Niger Delta ~ WAN 320 Gj 43
Nigeria □ WAN 320 Gk 40
Nighāsan O IND 234 Ke 31
Night Hawk Lake ~ CDN 57 Dh 21
Nightmute O USA 46 Ag 15
Nihama O J 251 Mc 29
Nihing ~ PK 227 Jl 31
Nihkoni O J 251 Mg 27
Niigata O J 251 Mf 27
Niihau ⚓ USA 75 Ak 35
Nijima ⚓ J 251 Mf 28
Niimi O J 251 Mc 28
Niitsu O J 251 Mf 27

Nijgarh O NEP 235 Kg 32
Nijmegen O NL 163 Gj 20
Nikel' O RUS 159 Hh 11
Nikiniki O RI 282 Ln 50
Nikiski O USA 46 Ba 15
Nikkaluokta O S 158 Hb 12
Nikki O DY 320 Gh 41
Nikkō ⚓ J 251 Mf 27
Nikko ★ J 251 Mf 27
Nikoemvon O CAM 320 Gm 44
Nikol'skoje O RUS 23 Ta 4
Nikolaevo O RUS 171 Hg 16
Nikolaevsk O RUS 181 Ja 20
Nikolaevsk-na-Amure O RUS 205 Xa 8
Nikolai O USA 46 An 13
Nikolajevsk-na-Amure O RUS 23 Sa 4
Nikolo-L'vovskoe O RUS 250 Mb 24
Nikol'skoe O RUS 181 Ja 19
Nikonga ~ EAT 336 Hh 47
Nikopol O UA 175 Hk 22
Nikopol O BG 194 He 24
Niko'sk O RUS 181 Ja 19
Niksar O TR 195 Hl 25
Nikšić O MON 194 Hb 24
Nikumaroro ⚓ KIR 35 Aa 10
Nikunau ⚓ KIR 35 Tb 10
Nilakkottai O IND 239 Kc 40
Niland O USA 64 Ce 29
Nilanga O IND 238 Kc 36
Nile ~ ET 301 Hh 31
Niles O USA 71 De 25
Nilópolis O BR 141 En 57
Nilsiä O FIN 159 Hf 14
Nilt O PK 230 Kb 27
Nīmach O IND 234 Kb 33
Nīmbāhera O IND 234 Kb 33
Nimba Mountains ▲ RG 316 Gb 42
Nimbin O AUS 375 Mn 60
Nîmes O F 185 Gh 24
Nimjat O RIM 304 Fn 37
Nim Ka Thāna O IND 234 Kb 32
Nimmitabel O AUS 379 Ml 64
Nimröz ◉ AFG 226 Jk 30
Nimrud O IRQ 209 Hp 27
Nimule O SUD 324 Hj 44
Nimule National Park ♀ SUD 324 Hj 44
Nina O NAM 348 Hb 57
Ninawî ◉ IRQ 209 Hn 28
Ninda O ANG 340 Hc 53
Nindigully O AUS 375 Ml 60
Nine Degree Channel ~ IND 239 Ka 41
Ninette O CDN 56 Cn 21
Ninette O NAM 348 Hb 57
Ninety Mile Beach ⚓ AUS 379 Mk 65
Ninety Mile Beach ⚓ NZ 383 Nj 63
Ninety Six N.H.S. ★ USA 71 Dg 28
Ningaloo ⚓ AUS 360 Lg 57
Ningaloo Cape Range ♀ AUS 360 Lg 57
Ningan O VRC 255 Lb 32
Ningbo O VRC 259 Ll 31
Ningde O VRC 258 Lk 32
Ningdu O VRC 258 Lh 32
Ningera O PNG 286 Mg 47
Ningerum O PNG 286 Mg 48
Ningguo O VRC 246 Lk 30
Ninghai O VRC 259 Ll 31
Ninghe O VRC 246 Lj 26
Ninghua ~ VRC 258 Lj 32
Ningi O WAN 320 Gl 40
Ningjin O VRC 246 Lj 27
Ningjing Shan ▲▲ VRC 242 Kn 30
Ningming O VRC 255 Ld 34
Ningqiang O VRC 243 Ld 29
Ningshan O VRC 243 Le 29
Ningwu O VRC 243 Lg 26
Ningxia Huizu Zizhiqu ◉ VRC 242 Lc 27
Ning Xian O VRC 243 Ld 28
Ningxiang O VRC 258 Lg 31
Ningyuan O VRC 255 Lf 33
Ninh Binh O VN 255 Ld 35
Ninh Hòa O VN 263 Le 39
Ninh So'n O VN 263 Le 40
Ninia O RI 286 Mf 48
Ninigo Islands ⚓ PNG 287 Mh 46
Ninilchik O USA 46 Ba 15
Niniwe ★ IRQ 209 Hp 27
Ninochmida O GE 202 Hp 25
Ninohe O J 250 Mg 25
Nintao O TUV 35 Tb 10
Nioaque O BR 140 Eg 56
Niobrara ~ USA 56 Cn 24
Niobrara River ~ USA 51 Cl 24
Niodio O SN 316 Fm 39
Niofouin O SN 305 Gc 41
Nioka O RDC 324 Hh 44
Nioka O RDC 333 Hd 48
Niokolo-Koba O SN 316 Fp 39
Niono O RMM 305 Gd 38
Niorenge ~ MOC 344 Hl 52
Nioro O RMM 304 Gb 38
Nioro du Rip O SN 316 Fn 39
Niort O F 163 Gf 22
Nioût O RIM 305 Gc 37
Nipa O PNG 286 Mh 48
Nipāni O IND 238 Kb 37
Nipawin O CDN 51 Cl 19
Nipele ~ NAM 340 Ha 55
Niphad O IND 234 Kb 35
Nipigon O CDN 57 Dd 21
Nipigon Bay ~ CDN 57 Dd 21
Nipiodi O MOC 344 Hl 54
Nipissing ~ CDN 60 Dj 22
Nipoué River ~ LB 316 Gb 42
Nipton O USA 64 Ce 28
Niquelândia O BR 133 Ek 53
Niquero O C 101 Dk 35
Nir O IR 209 Jb 27
Nira O IND 238 Kb 36
Nirmal O IND 238 Kd 36
Niš O SCG 194 Hd 24
Nis O AFG 223 Jf 29
Niša O KSA 215 Ja 31
Nišab O YE 218 Jb 38
Nisaka ⚓ J 247 Ma 29
Nišan O UZB 223 Jl 26
Nishi O VRC 255 Lf 31
Nishi-no-Omote O J 247 Mb 30
Nishino-shima ⚓ J 251 Mc 27

□ Country ▣ Capital city ⊙ Administrative unit ○ Place ⛰ Island ⩕ Mountain range △ Mountain ⌓ Cape ≋ Ocean, Sea ~ Lake, River ▾ Undersea topography ▲ Glacier ♀ National park ••• Reservation ★ Point of major interest ⏥ Landscape

Nishi-Okoppe ○ **J** 250 Mh 23
Nishi-Suidō ~ **ROK** 247 Ma 28
Niskakoski ○ **RUS** 159 Hg 11
Nisko ○ **PL** 174 Hd 20
Nissan Island ⛰ **PNG** 290 Mp 48
Nisséko ○ **BF** 317 Ge 40
Nisser ~ **N** 170 Gl 16
Nissiros ⛰ **GR** 195 Hf 27
Nissum Fjord ~ **DK** 170 Gk 17
Ništūn ○ **YE** 219 Je 38
Nita Downs ○ **AUS** 360 Ll 55
Nitchequon ○ **CDN** 60 Dn 19
Niterói ○ **BR** 141 En 57
Nitmiluk Katherine Gorge ♀ **AUS** 364 Mc 53
Nitra ○ **SK** 174 Hb 21
Nitro ○ **USA** 71 Dh 26
Niuafo'ou ⛰ **F** 390 Ac 53
Niuatoputapu ⛰ **TO** 35 Aa 11
Niu' Aunofo Point ⌓ **TO** 390 Ac 56
Niuchang ○ **VRC** 255 Lc 33
Niue ⛰ **NZ** 35 Ab 11
Niue ⛰ **NZ** 390 Af 55
Niulakita ⛰ **TUV** 35 Tb 11
Niutoushan ○ **VRC** 246 Lk 30
Niutou Shan ⛰ **VRC** 259 Ll 31
Nivala ○ **FIN** 159 He 14
Nive ~ **AUS** 375 Mk 58
Niwai ○ **IND** 234 Kb 32
Nixa ○ **USA** 70 Db 27
Nixon ○ **USA** 64 Cc 26
Nixon ○ **USA** 81 Cp 31
Niyrakpak Lagoon ~ **USA** 46 Ae 13
Niž. Tunguska ~ **RUS** 22 Pb 3
Niz. Zolotica ○ **RUS** 159 Hm 13
Nizāmābād ○ **IND** 238 Kd 36
Nizgan ~ **AFG** 223 Jl 29
Nizhnevartovsk ○ **RUS** 204 Ta 6
Nizhniy Novgorod ○ **RUS** 181 Ja 17
Nizi ○ **RDC** 324 Hh 45
Niziām Sāgar ~ **IND** 238 Kd 36
Nizip ○ **TR** 195 Hl 27
Nižneimatskoje ○ **RUS** 22 Pa 3
Nižnekamsk ○ **RUS** 181 Jd 18
Nižnekamsk Reservoir ~ **RUS** 154 Rb 7
Nižne-Kolymsk ○ **RUS** 205 Yc 5
Nižneudinsk ○ **RUS** 204 Ub 8
Nižnij Lomov ○ **RUS** 181 Hp 19
Nižnij Odes ○ **RUS** 154 Rb 6
Nižnij Tagil ○ **RUS** 154 Sa 7
Nižnjaja Tunguska ~ **RUS** 204 Ua 5
Nižnjaja Tunguska ~ **RUS** 204 Uc 6
Nizwa ○ **OM** 226 Jg 34
Nižyn ○ **UA** 175 Hj 20
Nizzana ○ **ET** 214 Hk 30
Njagan ○ **RUS** 19 Na 3
Njagan' ○ **RUS** 154 Sa 6
Njaiama-Sewafe ○ **WAL** 316 Ga 41
Njandoma ○ **RUS** 171 Hn 15
Njau ○ **WAG** 316 Fn 39
Njenje ~ **EAT** 337 Hl 50
Njinjo ○ **EAT** 337 Hm 50
Njoko ~ **Z** 341 He 54
Njombe ~ **EAT** 337 Hk 49
Njombe ○ **EAT** 337 Hk 50
Njoro ○ **EAK** 337 Hk 46
Njuja ~ **RUS** 204 Vb 6
Njurba ○ **RUS** 204 Vc 6
Njurunda ○ **S** 158 Ha 14
Nkalagu ○ **WAN** 320 Gk 42
Nkam ~ **CAM** 320 Gm 43
Nkam ~ **G** 332 Gm 45
Nkambe ○ **CAM** 320 Gm 42
Nkaw ○ **RDC** 333 Hb 47
Nkayi ○ **RCB** 332 Gn 48
Nkayi ○ **ZW** 341 Hg 55
Nkeni ~ **RCB** 332 Gp 47
Nkhata Bay ○ **MW** 344 Hk 51
Nkhotakota ○ **MW** 344 Hj 52
Nkola ○ **RCB** 332 Gm 47
Nkolabona ○ **G** 332 Gm 45
Nkole ○ **Z** 341 Hh 51
Nkomfap ○ **WAN** 320 Gl 42
Nkomi ~ **G** 332 Gl 46
Nkondwe ○ **EAT** 336 Hh 48
Nkongjok ○ **CAM** 320 Gm 43
Nkongsamba ○ **CAM** 320 Gm 43
Nkon Ngok ○ **CAM** 320 Gm 43
Nkoranza ○ **GH** 317 Gf 42
Nkoteng ○ **CAM** 321 Gn 43
Nkoué ○ **RCB** 332 Gp 48
Nkoul ○ **CAM** 321 Gn 44
Nkubu ○ **EAK** 337 Hl 46
Nkundi ○ **EAT** 336 Hh 49
Nkurenkuru ○ **NAM** 340 Hb 54
Nkwanta ○ **GH** 317 Gg 41
Nmai Hka ~ **MYA** 254 Kp 33
n-Nā'ī ○ **KSA** 214 Hp 32
Nnewi ○ **WAN** 320 Gk 43
No. 24 Well ○ **AUS** 360 Lm 57
No.35 Well ○ **AUS** 361 Ln 57
Noanama ○ **CO** 106 Dk 43
Noatak ○ **USA** 23 Ab 3
Noatak ○ **USA** 46 Aj 11
Noatak River ~ **USA** 46 Aj 11
Nobeoka ○ **J** 247 Mb 29
Nobéré ○ **BF** 317 Gf 40
Noble's Trail Monument ★ **USA** 56 Cn 23
Noboribetsu ○ **J** 250 Mg 24
Nobres ○ **BR** 132 Ef 53
Nochixtlán ○ **MEX** 92 Cp 36
Nockatunga ○ **AUS** 374 Mh 59
Noda ○ **J** 250 Mg 25
Nodaway ~ **USA** 70 Da 25
Noenieput ○ **ZA** 348 Hc 59
Noetinger ○ **RA** 137 Ec 62
Noga ~ **AUS** 375 Ml 57
Nogales ○ **MEX** 80 Cg 30
Nogales ○ **USA** 80 Cg 30
Nogales ○ **MEX** 80 Ch 30
Nogales ○ **RCH** 137 Dn 62
Nōgata ○ **J** 247 Mb 29
Nogent-le-Rotrou ○ **F** 163 Gg 21
Nogent-sur-Seine ○ **F** 163 Gh 21
Noginsk ○ **RUS** 171 Hm 18
Nogliki ○ **RUS** 205 Xb 8
Nogoa ~ **AUS** 375 Mk 58
Nogoyá ○ **RA** 146 Ee 62
Noguira ~ **RA** 140 Ee 59
Nohar ○ **IND** 230 Kb 31
Noheji ○ **J** 250 Mg 25
Noire ~ **CDN** 60 Dk 22
Noirmoutier ○ **F** 163 Ge 22
Nojabr'sk ○ **RUS** 204 Ta 6
Nojack ○ **CDN** 50 Ce 19
Nojima-saki ⌓ **J** 251 Mf 28
Nokaneng ○ **RB** 341 Hd 55
Nokha ○ **IND** 227 Ka 32
Nokia ○ **FIN** 159 Hd 15
Nok Kundi ○ **PK** 226 Jk 31
Nokomis ○ **CDN** 51 Ck 20
Nokou ○ **TCH** 309 Gp 38
Nokuku ○ **VU** 386 Nf 53
Nola ○ **I** 194 Gp 25
Nola ○ **RCA** 321 Gp 44
Noling ~ **RI** 282 Ll 47
Nolin River Lake ~ **USA** 71 De 27
Noll ○ **ZA** 358 Hd 62
Nom ○ **VRC** 204 Ua 10
Nomad ○ **PNG** 286 Mh 49
Nomad River ~ **PNG** 286 Mh 49
Nomane ○ **PNG** 287 Mj 49
Nombre de Dios ○ **MEX** 92 Ck 34
Nome ○ **USA** 23 Ab 3
Nome ○ **USA** 46 Ag 13
Nomhon ○ **VRC** 242 Kn 27
Nomtsas ○ **NAM** 348 Ha 58
Nomuka ⛰ **TO** 390 Ac 56
Nomuka Group ⛰ **TO** 390 Ac 56
Nonacho Lake ~ **CDN** 42 Ec 6
Nonant-le-Pin ○ **F** 163 Gg 21
Non Champa ○ **THA** 263 Lb 37
Nondo ○ **Z** 336 Hh 50
Nong Bua ○ **THA** 262 La 38
Nong Bua Daeng ○ **THA** 262 La 37
Nong Bua Khok ○ **THA** 262 La 38
Nong Bua Lamphu ○ **THA** 263 Lb 37
Nong Khae ○ **THA** 262 La 38
Nong Khai ○ **THA** 263 Lb 37
Nongoma ○ **ZA** 352 Hh 59
Nong Phai ○ **THA** 262 La 37
Nong Phok ○ **THA** 263 Lc 37
Nong Phu ○ **THA** 263 Lc 37
Nongra Lake ~ **AUS** 364 Ma 55
Nong Rua ○ **THA** 263 Lb 37
Nonoava ○ **MEX** 80 Cj 32
Nonogasta ○ **RA** 137 Ea 60
Non Thai ○ **THA** 262 La 38
Nonton ○ **GB** 162 Gf 18
Nooleeye ○ **SP** 328 Jb 43
Noolyeana Lake ~ **AUS** 374 Me 59
Noonaman ○ **AUS** 364 Mb 52
Noondoonia ○ **AUS** 369 Lm 62
Noonkabah ○ **AUS** 361 Ln 55
Noonyereena Hill △ **AUS** 368 Lk 58
Noordoewer ○ **NAM** 348 Ha 60
Noorvik ○ **USA** 46 Aj 11
Noosa Heads ○ **AUS** 375 Mn 59
Nootka Island ⛰ **CDN** 50 Bn 21
Nootka Sound ~ **CDN** 50 Bn 21
Noqui ○ **ANG** 332 Gn 48
Nøra ○ **N** 158 Gm 14
Nora ○ **S** 158 Ha 15
Norah ⛰ **ER** 313 Hm 37
Norala ○ **RP** 275 Ln 42
Norassoba ○ **RG** 316 Gb 40
Norba ○ **VRC** 242 Kp 30
Norberto de la Riesta ○ **RA** 146 Ee 63
Norcatur ○ **USA** 70 Cm 26
Nordaustlandet ⛰ **N** 19 La 3
Nordaustlandet ⛰ **N** 158 Hb 6
Nordberg ○ **N** 158 Gk 15
Nordby ○ **DK** 170 Gm 18
Norden ○ **D** 170 Gk 19
Nordenskiöld land ⛰ **N** 158 Gn 7
Norderney ⛰ **D** 170 Gk 19
Norderstedt ○ **D** 170 Gm 19
Nordeste ○ **ANG** 333 Hc 49
Nordfjordeid ○ **N** 158 Gj 15
Nordfjorden ~ **N** 158 Gj 15
Nordfjorden ~ **N** 158 Gp 6
Nordfold ○ **N** 158 Gp 12
Nordhausen ○ **D** 174 Gm 20
Nordhorn ○ **D** 170 Gk 19
Nordkap ⌓ **N** 159 He 10
Nordkapp ⌓ **N** 158 Hb 5
Nordkynhalvøya ⛰ **N** 159 Hf 10
Nördlingen ○ **D** 174 Gm 21
Nordmaling ○ **S** 158 Hb 14
Nordman ○ **USA** 50 Cd 21
Nord-Ostsee-Kanal ~ **D** 170 Gl 19
Norðoyar ⛰ **DK** 162 Gc 14
Nord-Pas-de-Calais ⊙ **F** 163 Gg 20
Nordre ○ **N** 159 Hf 10
Nordre Strømfjord ≋ **DK** 43 Jb 5
Nordrhein-Westfalen ⊙ **D** 163 Gk 20
Norðurflóður ≋ **IS** 158 Fk 12
Nordvestspitsbergen nasjonalpark ♀ **N** 158 Gm 6
Nordvik ○ **RUS** 22 Qb 2
Nordvik ○ **RUS** 204 Va 4
Norfolk ⛰ **AUS** 35 Ta 12
Norfolk ○ **USA** 56 Cp 24
Norfolk ○ **USA** 74 Dk 27
Norfolk Ridge ▾ 18 Ja 3
Norgara ○ **ETH** 313 Hl 39
Norgate ○ **CDN** 56 Cn 20
Norheimsund ○ **N** 158 Gj 15
Norias ○ **MEX** 81 Cl 33
Norias ○ **USA** 81 Cp 32
Norilsk ○ **RUS** 22 Pa 3
Noril'sk ○ **RUS** 204 Tc 5
Normal ○ **USA** 71 Dd 25
Norman ○ **USA** 70 Cp 28
Norman ~ **AUS** 365 Mg 54
Normanby ~ **AUS** 365 Mj 53
Normanby Island ⛰ **PNG** 287 Mm 50
Normandia ○ **BR** 112 Ee 44
Normandin ○ **CDN** 60 Dm 21
Normandy ○ **USA** 81 Cm 31
Normandy ⏥ **F** 163 Gf 21
Norman's Cay ⛰ **BS** 87 Dk 33
Normansland Point ⌓ **CDN** 57 Dh 19
Normanton ○ **AUS** 365 Mg 54
Normanville ○ **AUS** 378 Mf 63
Norman Wells ○ **CDN** 47 Bn 13
Normétal ○ **CDN** 60 Dj 21
Norquay ○ **CDN** 51 Cl 20
Norquinco ○ **RA** 147 Dn 66
Norra Borgafjällen △ **S** 158 Gp 13
Norråker ○ **S** 158 Gp 13
Norranside ○ **AUS** 374 Mf 57
Norra Storfjället △ **S** 158 Gp 12
Norrbotten ⏥ **S** 159 Hc 13
Norris ○ **USA** 51 Cg 23
Norristown ○ **USA** 74 Dl 25
Norrköping ○ **S** 170 Ha 16
Norrtälje ○ **S** 170 Hb 16
Norseman ○ **AUS** 368 Ll 62
Norskebanken ▾ **N** 158 Gn 5
Norsup ○ **VU** 386 Nf 54
Nortelândia ○ **BR** 132 Ef 53
North ○ **USA** 71 Dh 29
North Adams ○ **USA** 60 Dm 24
Northam ○ **ZA** 349 Hf 58
Northam ○ **AUS** 368 Lj 61
North American Basin ▾ 11 Fb 6
Northampton ○ **USA** 60 Dm 24
Northampton ○ **GB** 163 Gf 19
Northampton ○ **AUS** 368 Lh 60
North Andaman ⛰ **IND** 262 Kl 39
North Arm ~ **CDN** 42 Eb 6
North Arm ~ **CDN** 47 Ce 13
North Arm ○ **GB** 147 Ee 72
North Augusta ○ **USA** 71 Dg 29
North Balabac Strait ~ **RP** 266 Lj 41
North Banda Basin ≋ **RI** 282 Lm 47
North Bannister ○ **AUS** 368 Lj 62
North Battleford ○ **CDN** 51 Ch 19
North Bay ○ **CDN** 60 Dj 22
North Bay ~ **IND** 262 Kl 41
North Bend ○ **USA** 50 Bp 24
North Bend ○ **USA** 70 Cp 25
North Bimini ⛰ **USA** 87 Dj 33
North Branch ○ **USA** 56 Db 23
North Caicos ⛰ **GB** 101 Dn 35
North Canadian ~ **USA** 70 Cn 28
North Cape ⌓ **NZ** 383 Nj 63
North Caribou Lake ~ **CDN** 43 Fc 8
North Carolina ⊙ **USA** 71 Dg 28
North Cascades ♀ **USA** 50 Cb 21
North Channel ~ **CDN** 57 Dg 22
North Channel ~ **GB** 162 Gd 18
North Charleston ○ **USA** 71 Dh 29
North Creek ○ **AUS** 374 Me 60
North Dakota ⊙ **USA** 51 Cl 22
North East ○ **USA** 57 Dh 24
Northeast Cape ⌓ **USA** 46 Ae 13
Northeast Pacific Basin ▾ 10 Ba 5
Northeast Point ⌓ **CDN** 61 Eg 20
Northeast Point ⌓ **BS** 101 Dm 35
Northeast Providence Channel ~ **BS** 87 Dk 33
Northern Cay ⛰ **BH** 93 De 37
Northern Cheyenne Indian Reservation ••• **USA** 51 Cj 23
Northern Circars ⩕ **IND** 238 Ke 37
Northern Dvina ~ **RUS** 19 Ma 3
Northern Dvina ~ **RUS** 154 Qc 6
Northern Ireland ⊙ **GB** 162 Gc 18
Northern Lau Group ⛰ **FJI** 390 Aa 54
Northern Light Lake ~ **CDN** 56 Dc 21
Northern Mariana Islands ⛰ **USA** 27 Sb 8
Northern Sporades ⛰ **GR** 194 Hd 26
Northern Territory ⊙ **AUS** 364 Mb 55
Northfield ○ **USA** 56 Db 23
North Flinders Ranges ⩕ **AUS** 378 Mf 61
North Fork ○ **USA** 50 Ce 23
North Fork Clearwater ~ **USA** 50 Ce 22
North Fork Holston ~ **USA** 71 Dg 27
North Fork John Day ~ **USA** 50 Cc 23
North Fork Kuskokwim ~ **USA** 46 An 13
North Fork Payette ~ **USA** 50 Cd 23
North Fork Red River ~ **USA** 70 Cm 28
NorthFork Solomon ~ **USA** 70 Cm 26
North Fork Solomon River ~ **USA** 70 Cm 26
North French River ~ **CDN** 57 Dh 20
North Frisian Islands ⛰ **D** 170 Gk 18
Northgate ○ **CDN** 51 Cl 21
North Gate ○ **RB** 341 Hd 55
North Goulburn Island ⛰ **AUS** 364 Mc 51
North Head ○ **CDN** 61 Ea 23
North Head ○ **AUS** 365 Mh 55
North Head ⌓ **AUS** 368 Lh 61
Northhome ○ **USA** 56 Da 22
North Horr ○ **EAK** 325 Hl 44
North Island ⛰ **USA** 87 Dj 29
North Island ⛰ **EAK** 325 Hk 43
North Island ⛰ **AUS** 365 Me 53
North Island ⛰ **AUS** 368 Lg 60
North Island ⛰ **NZ** 383 Nj 64
North Korea □ **DVRK** 247 Ma 26
North Lakhimpur ○ **IND** 254 Km 32
Northland Plateau ▾ 383 Nl 63
North Las Vegas ○ **USA** 64 Ce 27
North Lincoln Land ⛰ **CDN** 43 Gb 3
North Little Rock ○ **USA** 70 Db 28
North Loup ~ **USA** 56 Cm 24
North Loup River ~ **USA** 56 Cm 24
North Luangwa ♀ **Z** 344 Hj 51
North Lyons ○ **AUS** 368 Lj 58
North Male Atoll ⛰ **MV** 239 Ka 43
North Malosmadulu Atoll ⛰ **MV** 239 Ka 43
North Milk ~ **CDN** 51 Cf 21
North Nilandu Atoll ⛰ **MV** 239 Ka 44
North Peninsula ⛰ **CDN** 57 Dd 20
North Peron Island ⛰ **AUS** 364 Ma 52
North Platte ~ **USA** 65 Cl 25
North Platte ○ **USA** 70 Cm 25
North Platte River ~ **USA** 51 Cj 24
North Point ⌓ **USA** 57 Dg 23
North Point ⌓ **CDN** 61 Ec 22
North Point ⌓ **WAN** 320 Gj 43
North Point ⌓ **AUS** 378 Mj 66
North Pole ⌓ 38 Pb 18
North Pole ○ **USA** 46 Bc 13
Northport ○ **USA** 50 Cd 21
North Port ○ **USA** 57 Df 23
North Powder ○ **USA** 50 Cd 23
North Reef ⛰ **SOL** 290 Nc 52
North River ~ **PNG** 286 Mg 47
North Rom ○ **USA** 64 Cf 27
North Rona ⛰ **GB** 162 Gd 16
North Santiam ~ **USA** 50 Ca 23
North Saskatchewan ~ **CDN** 51 Ch 19
North Sea ≋ 162 Gh 17
North Sentinel Island ⛰ **IND** 262 Kl 40
North Siberian Lowland ⏥ **RUS** 22 Pb 3
North Siberian Lowland ⏥ **RUS** 204 Tc 4
North Solitary Island ⛰ **AUS** 375 Mn 60
North Star ○ **CDN** 47 Cc 17
North Star ○ **AUS** 375 Mm 60
North Stradbroke Island ⛰ **AUS** 375 Mn 59
North Sydney ○ **CDN** 61 Ed 22
North Taranaki Bight ~ **NZ** 383 Nj 65
North Thompson ~ **CDN** 50 Cb 20
North Twin Island ⛰ **CDN** 57 Dh 19
North Twin Lake ~ **CDN** 61 Ef 21
North Uist ⛰ **GB** 162 Gc 17
Northumberland ♀ **GB** 162 Ge 18
Northumberland Island ⛰ **AUS** 375 Ml 56
Northumberland Strait ~ **CDN** 61 Eb 22
North Umpqua ~ **USA** 50 Ca 24
North Vancouver ○ **CDN** 50 Ca 21
North West Basin ⏥ **AUS** 360 Lh 57
North West Cape ⌓ **AUS** 360 Lg 56
North West Frontier Province ⊙ **PK** 223 Jp 28
Northwest Gander ~ **CDN** 61 Eg 21
Northwest Highlands ⩕ **GB** 162 Gd 17
North West Island ⛰ **AUS** 375 Mm 57
Northwest Pacific Basin ▾ 27 Sb 5
North West Point ⌓ **GB** 100 Dh 36
Northwest Point ⌓ **BS** 101 Dl 35
Northwest Providence Channel ~ **USA** 87 Dj 32
North West River ○ **CDN** 61 Ed 19
Northwest Territories ⊙ **CDN** 6 Cb 3
Northwest Territory ⊙ **CDN** 47 Bl 11
North Wichita River ~ **USA** 70 Cm 29
North Wilkesboro ○ **USA** 71 Dh 27
Northwood ○ **USA** 56 Cn 22
Northwood ○ **USA** 56 Db 24
North York Moors ♀ **GB** 162 Gf 18
Norton ○ **USA** 70 Cn 26
Norton ○ **USA** 71 Dg 27
Norton ○ **ZW** 341 Hh 54
Norton Bay ~ **USA** 46 Aj 13
Norton Peak △ **USA** 50 Ce 24
Norton Shores ○ **USA** 57 De 24
Norton Sound ~ **USA** 23 Ab 3
Norton Sound ~ **USA** 46 Aj 13
Nortonville ○ **USA** 56 Cn 22
Nortonville ○ **USA** 71 De 27
Norwalk ○ **USA** 64 Cc 29
Norwalk ○ **USA** 70 Da 25
Norwalk ○ **USA** 71 Dg 25
Norwalk ○ **USA** 74 Dm 25
Norway ○ **USA** 60 Dn 23
Norway □ **N** 158 Gk 16
Norway House ○ **CDN** 42 Fb 8
Norwegian Basin ▾ 18 Jb 3
Norwegian Bay ~ **CDN** 7 Ea 2
Norwegian Bay ~ **CDN** 43 Fc 3
Norwich ○ **USA** 60 Dl 24
Norwich ○ **USA** 74 Dm 25
Norwich ○ **GB** 163 Gg 19
Norwood ○ **USA** 56 Db 23
Norwood ○ **USA** 71 Df 26
Nosara ○ **CR** 96 Df 41
Noshiro ○ **J** 250 Mf 25
Nosop ~ **RB** 348 Hc 58
Noṣratābād ○ **IR** 226 Jh 31
Nossa Senhora da Glória ○ **BR** 125 Fb 51
Nossa Senhora das Dores ○ **BR** 125 Fb 51
Nossa Senhora do Livramento ○ **BR** 132 Ef 53
Nossa Senhora do Socorro ○ **BR** 125 Fb 51
Nossob ○ **NAM** 348 Ha 57
Nossob ~ **NAM** 348 Hb 57
Nossob ~ **RB** 348 Hc 58
Nossob Camp ○ **ZA** 348 Hc 58
Nossumbougou ○ **RMM** 316 Gc 39
Nosy Ankao ⛰ **RM** 345 Jc 52
Nosy Be ⛰ **RM** 345 Jb 52
Nosy Boraha Sainte-Marie ⛰ **RM** 345 Jd 54
Nosy Mitsio ⛰ **RM** 345 Jc 52
Nosy Radama ⛰ **RM** 345 Jb 52
Nosy Varika ○ **RM** 353 Jc 56
Nothaburi ○ **THA** 262 La 39
Notintsila ○ **ZA** 349 Hg 61
Noto ○ **I** 185 Gp 27
Notocote ○ **MOC** 344 Hm 54
Notodden ○ **N** 170 Gl 16
Noto-hantō ⛰ **J** 251 Me 27
Noto-shima ⛰ **J** 251 Me 27
Notre Dame Bay ~ **CDN** 61 Ej 21
Notre-Dame-du-Nord ○ **CDN** 60 Dj 22
Notse ○ **RT** 317 Gg 42
Nottawasaga Bay ~ **CDN** 57 Dh 23
Nottaway ~ **CDN** 60 Dj 20
Nottingham ○ **GB** 163 Gf 19
Nottingham Downs ○ **AUS** 374 Mh 56
Nottingham Island ⛰ **CDN** 43 Gc 6
Nottoway ~ **USA** 74 Dk 27
Nouâdhibou ○ **RIM** 304 Fm 35
Nouakchott ▣ **RIM** 304 Fm 36
Nouâmghâr ○ **RIM** 304 Fm 36
Noubandegān ○ **IR** 215 Je 31
Noubarān ○ **IR** 209 Jc 28
Nouhao ~ **BF** 317 Gf 40
Nouméa ○ **F** 386 Nf 57
Noumoukiédougou ○ **BF** 317 Gd 41
Noun ~ **CAM** 320 Gm 43
Nouna ○ **BF** 317 Gd 39
Nouna ~ **G** 332 Gn 45
Noupoort ○ **ZA** 349 He 61
Noušahr ○ **IR** 222 Jd 27
Nousūd ○ **IR** 209 Ja 28
Nov. Igirma ○ **RUS** 204 Uc 7
Nova Almada ○ **MOC** 344 Hk 55
Nova Almeida ○ **BR** 141 Ep 56
Nova Alvorada do Sul ○ **BR** 140 Eg 56
Nova Andradina ○ **BR** 140 Eh 57
Nova Aurora ○ **BR** 140 Eh 58
Nova Brasilândia ○ **BR** 132 Eg 53
Nova Caipemba ○ **ANG** 332 Gp 49
Nova Canaã do Norte ○ **BR** 132 Eg 51
Nova Chaves ○ **MOC** 344 Hm 53
Nova Coimbra ○ **MOC** 344 Hk 52
Nova Crixás ○ **BR** 133 Ej 53
Nova Cruz ○ **BR** 124 Fc 49
Nova Esperança ○ **BR** 140 Eh 57
Nova Esperança ○ **ANG** 332 Gp 49
Nova Friburgo ○ **BR** 141 En 57
Nova Golegã ○ **MOC** 352 Hk 56
Nova Granada ○ **BR** 140 Ek 56
Nova Iguaçu ○ **BR** 141 En 57
Nova Itaipe ○ **BR** 125 Ep 52
Novaja Ladoga ○ **RUS** 171 Hh 15
Nova Jorque ○ **BR** 121 Em 49
Nova Kachovka ○ **UA** 175 Hj 22
Novalukoml' ○ **BY** 171 Hg 18
Nova Macajuba ○ **BR** 121 El 46
Nova Mambone ○ **MOC** 352 Hk 56
Nova Módica ○ **BR** 141 Ep 55
Nova Monte Verde ○ **BR** 132 Ef 51
Nova Nabúri ○ **MOC** 344 Hm 54
Nova Odesa ○ **UA** 175 Hh 22
Nova Olímpia ○ **BR** 140 Eh 57
Nova Olinda ○ **BR** 121 Ek 49
Nova Olinda do Norte ○ **BR** 120 Ee 47
Nova Prata ○ **BR** 146 Ej 60
Nova Resende ○ **BR** 141 El 56
Nova Roma ○ **BR** 133 El 52
Novarra ○ **I** 185 Gl 23
Nova Russas ○ **BR** 124 Ep 48
Nova Santarém ○ **MOC** 344 Hk 52
Nova Scotia ⊙ **CDN** 61 Eb 24
Nova Serrana ○ **BR** 133 Em 55
Nova Soure ○ **BR** 125 Fa 51
Novato ○ **USA** 64 Ca 26
Nova Venécia ○ **BR** 141 Ep 55
Nova Viçosa ○ **BR** 125 Fa 54
Nova Viseu ○ **MOC** 344 Hl 52
Nova Vodelaha ○ **UA** 175 Hk 21
Nova Xavantina ○ **BR** 133 Eh 53
Novaya Zemlya ⏥ **RUS** 19 Mb 2
Novaya Zemlya ⛰ **RUS** 154 Rb 4
Nova Zagora ○ **BG** 194 Hf 24
Nové Zámky ○ **SK** 174 Hb 22
Novgorod ○ **RUS** 171 Hh 16
Novgorodka ○ **RUS** 171 Hg 17
Novhorodka ○ **UA** 175 Hj 21
Novhorod-Siverskyj ○ **UA** 175 Hj 20
Novikovo ○ **RUS** 250 Mh 22
Novillero ○ **MEX** 92 Ck 34
Novi Pazar ○ **SCG** 194 Hc 24
Novi Pazar ○ **BG** 195 Hf 24
Novi Sad ○ **SCG** 174 Hb 23
Novi Sanžary ○ **UA** 175 Hh 21
Novlensko ○ **RUS** 171 Hm 16
Novo ~ **BR** 120 Ef 49
Novo ~ **BR** 120 Eg 49
Novo ~ **BR** 121 Eh 48
Novo Acordo ○ **BR** 121 El 50
Novo Acre ○ **BR** 125 Ep 52
Novo Airão ○ **BR** 120 Ed 47
Novoaleksandrovsk ○ **RUS** 202 Hn 23
Novoanninskij ○ **RUS** 181 Hp 20
Novo Aripuanã ○ **BR** 120 Ed 48
Novoazovs'k ○ **UA** 181 Hm 22
Novobogat ○ **KZ** 202 Jd 22
Novo Brasilândia ○ **BR** 129 Ec 51
Novočeboksarsk ○ **RUS** 181 Jb 17
Novočerkassk ○ **RUS** 181 Hn 22
Novo Cruzeiro ○ **BR** 125 Ep 54
Novočuguevka ○ **RUS** 250 Mc 23
Novodvinsk ○ **RUS** 154 Qc 6
Novodvinsk ○ **RUS** 159 Hn 13
Novoe Mašozero ○ **RUS** 159 Hj 13
Novo Hamburgo ○ **BR** 146 Ej 60
Novohoperskij ○ **RUS** 181 Hn 20
Novo Horizonte ○ **BR** 140 Ek 56
Novohrad-Volyns'kyj ○ **UA** 175 Hf 20
Novokačalinsk ○ **RUS** 250 Mb 23
Novokašpirskij ○ **RUS** 181 Jb 19
Novokažaly ○ **KZ** 155 Sa 9
Novokujbyševsk ○ **RUS** 181 Jc 19
Novokuznetsk ○ **RUS** 204 Tc 8
Novo Lima ○ **BR** 141 En 55
Novo Mesto ○ **SLO** 174 Gp 23
Novomičurinsk ○ **RUS** 171 Hm 18
Novomihajlovskij ○ **RUS** 202 Hm 23
Novomoskovs'k ○ **UA** 175 Hk 21
Novo-Moskovsk ○ **RUS** 171 Hm 18
Novonikolaevskij ○ **RUS** 181 Hp 20
Novo Oriente ○ **BR** 117 Ec 50
Novo Oriente ○ **BR** 124 Ep 48
Novopavlovsk ○ **RUS** 202 Hp 24
Novo Pensamento ○ **BR** 120 Ec 46
Novopetrovskoe ○ **RUS** 171 Hl 17
Novopokrovka ○ **RUS** 250 Md 23
Novopokrovskaja ○ **RUS** 202 Hn 23
Novo Progresso ○ **BR** 120 Eg 49
Novopskov ○ **UA** 181 Hm 21
Novo Repartimento ○ **BR** 121 Ej 48
Novorossiysk ○ **RUS** 195 Hl 23
Novorybnaja ○ **RUS** 204 Va 4
Novoržev ○ **RUS** 171 Hg 17
Novo São Joaquim ○ **BR** 133 Eh 53
Novoseľe Capeľka ○ **RUS** 171 Hg 16
Novoselickoe ○ **RUS** 202 Hp 23
Novoselivs'ke ○ **UA** 175 Hj 23
Novoselycja ○ **UA** 175 He 21
Novosemejkino ○ **RUS** 181 Jd 19
Novošešminsk ○ **RUS** 181 Jd 18
Novoshakhtinsk ○ **RUS** 181 Hm 22
Novosibirsk ○ **RUS** 22 Nb 4
Novosibirsk ○ **RUS** 204 Tb 7
Novosibirskoe vodohranilišče ~ **RUS** 204 Tb 8
Novosokoľniki ○ **RUS** 171 Hg 17
Novotrojic'ke ○ **UA** 175 Hj 22
Novoukrajinka ○ **UA** 175 Hh 21
Novouľjanovsk ○ **RUS** 181 Jc 18
Novouzensk ○ **RUS** 181 Jc 20
Novovolyns'k ○ **UA** 175 He 20
Novozavidovskij ○ **RUS** 171 Hl 17
Novozybkov ○ **RUS** 171 Hj 19
Nový Bor ○ **CZ** 174 Gp 20
Novyi Port ○ **RUS** 154 Sc 5
Novyj Buh ○ **UA** 175 Hj 22
Nový Jičín ○ **CZ** 174 Hb 21
Novyj Oskol ○ **RUS** 181 Hl 20
Novyj Uojan ○ **RUS** 204 Vb 7
Novyj Urengoj ○ **RUS** 154 Sc 5
Novyj Uzen' ○ **KZ** 155 Rb 10
Nowa Nowa ○ **AUS** 379 Ml 64
Nowa Sól ○ **PL** 174 Gp 20
Nowata ○ **USA** 70 Da 27
Nowe ○ **PL** 170 Hb 19
Nowendoc ○ **AUS** 379 Mm 61
Nowgong ○ **IND** 234 Kd 33
Nowogard ○ **PL** 170 Gp 19
Nowood Creek ~ **USA** 51 Cj 24
Nowra ○ **AUS** 379 Mm 63
Nowshera ○ **PK** 223 Jp 29
Nowy Sącz ○ **PL** 174 Hc 21
Noxubee N.W.R. ♀ **USA** 86 Dd 29
Noya ~ **G** 332 Gl 45
Noyant ○ **F** 163 Gf 22
Noyes Island ⛰ **USA** 42 Da 7
Noyon ○ **F** 163 Gh 21
Nozay ○ **F** 163 Gf 22
Nqoga ~ **RB** 341 Hd 55
Nritu Ga ○ **MYA** 254 Kn 32
Nsa ○ **RCB** 332 Gp 47
Nsadzu ○ **Z** 344 Hj 53
Nsakaluba ○ **Z** 341 Hg 51
Nsalamu ○ **Z** 341 Hh 52
Nsalu Caves ★ **Z** 341 Hh 52
Nsama ○ **Z** 336 Hg 50
Nsanje ○ **MW** 344 Hk 54
Nsawam ○ **GH** 317 Gf 43
Nsawkaw ○ **GH** 317 Ge 42
Nsele ~ **RDC** 332 Gp 48
Nsemi ○ **CAM** 321 Gn 43
Nsiza ○ **ZW** 341 Hg 55
Nsoc ○ **GQ** 332 Gm 45
Nsoko ○ **SD** 352 Hh 59
Nsombo ○ **Z** 341 Hg 51
Nsontin ○ **RDC** 333 Ha 47
Nsukka ○ **WAN** 320 Gk 42
Nsung ○ **GQ** 332 Gm 45
Ntambu ○ **Z** 341 He 52
Ntandembele ○ **RDC** 333 Ha 47
Ntatrat ○ **RIM** 304 Fn 37
Ntcheu ○ **MW** 344 Hk 53
Ntchisi ○ **MW** 344 Hj 52
Ntem ~ **CAM** 320 Gm 44
Ntem ~ **G** 332 Gm 44
Nterguent ○ **RIM** 304 Fp 36
Nthalire ○ **MW** 344 Hj 51
Nthunga ○ **MW** 344 Hj 52
Ntimaru ○ **EAK** 337 Hk 46
Ntiona ○ **TCH** 309 Gp 38
Ntokou ○ **RCB** 332 Gp 45
Ntoum ○ **G** 332 Gl 45
Ntui ○ **CAM** 320 Gm 43
Ntungamo ○ **EAU** 336 Hg 46
Ntusi ○ **EAU** 324 Hh 45
Ntwetwe Pan ~ **RB** 349 He 56
Ntywenka ○ **ZA** 349 Hg 61
Nuakata Island ⛰ **PNG** 287 Mm 51
Nuaneteze ~ **MOC** 352 Hh 57
Nuangan ○ **RI** 275 Ln 45
Nuangola ○ **USA** 74 Dk 25
Nūba ⏥ **SUD** 312 Hh 36
Nuba Mountains ⩕ **SUD** 312 Hh 39
Nubian Desert ⏥ **SUD** 312 Hh 35
Nuble ~ **RCH** 137 Dn 64
Nuboai ○ **RI** 286 Me 47
Nucuray ~ **PE** 116 Dk 48
Nudo Chicllaraza △ **PE** 128 Dl 52
Nudo de Paramillo △ **CO** 106 Dk 42
Nueces Plains ⏥ **USA** 81 Cn 31
Nueces River ~ **USA** 81 Cn 31
Nueltin Lake ~ **CDN** 6 Ea 4
Nueltin Lake ~ **CDN** 42 Fb 6
Nuestra Sr. del Rosario de Caá Cati ○ **RA** 140 Ef 59
Nueva Alejandria ○ **PE** 116 Dm 48
Nueva Arcadia ○ **HN** 93 Dd 38
Nueva Ciudad Guerrero ○ **MEX** 81 Cn 32
Nueva Coahuila ○ **MEX** 93 Dc 37
Nueva Constitución ○ **RA** 137 Ea 63
Nueva Era ○ **RP** 267 Ll 37
Nueva Esperanza ○ **RA** 136 Eb 59
Nueva Florida ○ **YV** 107 Dp 41
Nueva Galia ○ **RA** 137 Eb 63
Nueva Gerona ○ **C** 100 Dg 35
Nueva Guinea ○ **NIC** 97 Df 40
Nueva Imperial ○ **RCH** 147 Dm 65
Nueva Italia ○ **RA** 137 Ed 62
Nueva Lubecka ○ **RA** 152 Dn 68
Nueva Ocotepeque ○ **HN** 93 Dd 38
Nueva Palmira ○ **ROU** 146 Ee 62
Nueva Pompeya ○ **RA** 136 Ed 58
Nueva Rosita ○ **MEX** 81 Cm 32
Nueva San Salvador ○ **ES** 93 Dd 39
Nuevitas ○ **C** 101 Dk 35
Nuevo Andoas ○ **PE** 116 Dk 47
Nuevo Casas Grandes ○ **MEX** 80 Cj 30
Nuevo Italia ○ **PY** 140 Ef 58
Nuevo Laredo ○ **MEX** 81 Cn 32
Nuevo Riaño ○ **E** 184 Gd 24
Nuevo Rocafuerte ○ **EC** 116 Dl 46
Nuevo Turino ○ **RA** 137 Ed 61
Nuguaçu ○ **BR** 125 Ep 51
Nuguria Islands ⛰ **PNG** 290 Mp 47
Nuḫaib ○ **IRQ** 209 Hn 29
Nuhaida ○ **OM** 226 Jg 34
Nuhaka ○ **NZ** 383 Nl 65
Nui ⛰ **TUV** 35 Tb 10
Nuiqsut ○ **USA** 46 Ba 9
Núi Thán ○ **VN** 263 Le 38
Nu Jiang ~ **VRC** 242 Km 30
Nu Jiang ~ **VRC** 254 Kp 33
Nukaat ○ **RI** 283 Mb 49
Nūkābād ○ **IR** 226 Jj 31
Nuka Island ⛰ **USA** 46 Ba 15
Nukey Bluff △ **AUS** 378 Md 62
Nukhayla Merga ○ **SUD** 312 Hf 36
Nukiki ○ **SOL** 290 Na 49
Nuku ○ **PNG** 286 Mh 47
Nuku'alofa ▣ **TO** 390 Ac 56
Nukufetau ⛰ **TUV** 35 Tb 10
Nuku Hiva ⛰ **F** 35 Bb 10
Nukuhu ○ **PNG** 287 Ml 48
Nukumanu Islands ⛰ **PNG** 290 Nb 48
Nukunono ⛰ **NZ** 35 Aa 10
Nukus ○ **UZB** 19 Mb 5
Nukus ○ **UZB** 222 Jh 24
Nulato ○ **USA** 46 Al 13
Nullagine ○ **AUS** 360 Ll 56

Nishi-Okoppe - Nullagine 451

□Country ▣Capital city ⊙Administrative unit ○Place ▵Island ⛰Mountain range △Mountain ⌓Cape ≋Ocean, Sea ~Lake, River ΨUndersea topography ⩟Glacier ♀National park •••Reservation ★Point of major interest ⌒Landscape

Nullagine ~ **AUS** 360 Ll 56
Nullarbor ♀ **AUS** 369 Ma 61
Nullarbor Plain ⛰ **AUS** 369 Ln 61
Nullarbor Roadhouse ○ **AUS** 369 Mb 61
Num ○ **NEP** 235 Kh 32
Numaligarh ○ **IND** 235 Kl 32
Numan ○ **WAN** 320 Gm 41
Numancia ★ **E** 184 Ge 25
Numatinna ~ **SUD** 324 Hf 42
Numazu ○ **J** 251 Mf 28
Numbi ○ **RDC** 336 Hg 46
Numbulwar ○ **AUS** 364 Md 53
Numedal ⌒ **N** 158 Gl 15
Numery ○ **AUS** 374 Md 57
Numil Downs ○ **AUS** 365 Mg 55
Nunavik ▵ **DK** 7 Ga 2
Nunavik ▵ **DK** 43 Ja 4
Nunavut ⊙ **DK** 6 Db 3
Nunavut ⊙ **CDN** 47 Cc 11
Nunavut Territory ⊙ **CDN** 42 Fa 5
Nundle ○ **AUS** 379 Mm 61
Nundo de Sunipani △ **PE** 128 Dn 53
Nundroo ○ **AUS** 369 Mc 61
Nungarin ○ **AUS** 368 Lk 61
Nungo ○ **MOC** 344 Hl 52
Nungwaia ○ **PNG** 286 Mh 47
Nungwe Bay ○ **EAT** 337 Hj 47
Nunivak Island ▵ **USA** 10 Ab 4
Nunivak Island ▵ **USA** 46 Ag 15
Nunkapasi ○ **IND** 235 Kg 35
Nunligran ○ **RUS** 205 Aa 6
Nuno ○ **USA** 65 Ck 25
Ñuñoa ○ **PE** 128 Dn 53
Nun River ~ **WAN** 320 Gk 43
Nuoro ○ **I** 185 Gl 25
Nupfure ~ **ZW** 341 Hg 54
Nuporanga ○ **BR** 141 El 56
Nuqāb ○ **YE** 218 Ja 38
Nuquí ○ **CO** 106 Dk 43
Nūr ○ **IR** 222 Jd 27
Nūrābād ○ **IR** 209 Jb 28
Nūrābād ○ **IR** 209 Jb 29
Nūrābād ○ **IR** 215 Jd 30
Nurata ○ **UZB** 223 Jl 25
Nurato tog tizmasi ⛰ **UZB** 223 Jl 25
Nur Dağları ⛰ **TR** 195 Hk 27
Nurei ○ **SUD** 312 Hd 39
Nurek ○ **TJ** 223 Jn 26
Nuremberg ○ **D** 174 Gm 21
Nūr Gāma ○ **PK** 227 Jm 31
Nurhak ○ **TR** 195 Hl 27
Nurhak D. △ **TR** 195 Hl 26
Nuri ○ **MEX** 80 Ch 31
Nuri ★ **SUD** 312 Hh 36
Nuriootpa ○ **AUS** 378 Mf 63
Nurlat ○ **RUS** 181 Jd 18
Nurmes ○ **FIN** 159 Hg 14
Nurmijärvi ○ **FIN** 159 Hg 14
Nurobod ○ **UZB** 223 Jm 26
Nūrpur ○ **PK** 227 Jp 30
Nurse Cay ▵ **BS** 87 Dl 34
Nusa Dua ○ **RI** 279 Lh 50
Nusa Penida ▵ **RI** 279 Lh 50
Nusawulan ○ **RI** 283 Mc 48
Nusaybin ○ **TR** 202 Hn 27
Nushagak Bay ~ **USA** 46 Al 15
Nushagak Peninsula ▵ **USA** 46 Aj 15
Nushagak River ~ **USA** 46 Al 15
Nu Shan ⛰ **VRC** 254 Kp 32
Nushki ○ **PK** 227 Jm 31
Nutepel'men ○ **RUS** 46 Ac 11
Nutrioso ○ **USA** 65 Ch 29
Nutt ○ **USA** 65 Cj 29
Nuttal ○ **PK** 227 Jn 31
Nutwood Downs ○ **AUS** 364 Md 53
Nuu ○ **EAK** 337 Hl 46
Nuuk Godhåb ⊙ **DK** 43 Jb 6
Nuupas ○ **FIN** 159 Hf 12
Nuussuaq ○ **DK** 43 Hc 3
Nuussuaq Halvø ⌓ **DK** 7 Ga 2
Nuussuaq Halvø ▵ **DK** 43 Jb 4
Nuwaibi' al-Muzayyina ○ **ET** 214 Hk 31
Nuwara Eliya ○ **CL** 239 Ke 42
Nuwefontein ○ **NAM** 348 Hb 59
Nuweh ○ **RI** 286 Mf 49
Nuwerus ○ **ZA** 348 Hb 61
Nuweveldberge ⛰ **ZA** 358 Hc 62
Nuy ○ **ZA** 358 Hb 62
Nuyts Archipelago ▵ **AUS** 369 Mc 62
Nūyudupeta ○ **IND** 238 Kd 39
Nūzvīd ○ **IND** 238 Ke 37
Nwa ○ **CAM** 320 Gm 42
Nwanetsi ○ **ZA** 352 Hh 58
Nwangalala ○ **RDC** 341 Hf 51
Nxai Pan ~ **RB** 341 He 55
Nxamasere ~ **RB** 340 Hc 55
Nxamasere ○ **RB** 341 Hc 55
Nya ~ **TCH** 321 Gp 41
Nyaake ○ **LB** 304 Gc 43
Nyabessano ○ **CAM** 320 Gm 44
Nyabing ○ **AUS** 368 Lk 62
Nyabisindu ○ **RWA** 336 Hg 47
Nyadire ~ **ZW** 344 Hj 54
Nyagassola ○ **RG** 316 Gb 39
Nya-Ghezi ○ **RDC** 336 Hg 47
Nyahanga ○ **EAT** 337 Hj 47
Nyahua ~ **EAT** 337 Hj 48
Nyahururu ○ **EAK** 325 Hl 45
Nyah West ○ **AUS** 378 Mh 63
Nyaingêntanglha Feng △ **VRC** 231 Kk 30
Nyainqêntanglha Shan ⛰ **VRC** 231 Kk 30
Nyainrong ○ **VRC** 231 Kl 29
Nyakanazi ○ **EAT** 336 Hh 47
Nyakanura ○ **EAT** 336 Hh 47
Nyak Co ~ **VRC** 230 Kd 29
Nyala ○ **SUD** 312 He 39
Nyalam ○ **VRC** 235 Kh 31
Ny Ålesund ○ **N** 158 Gm 6
Nyali ○ **G** 332 Gm 47
Nyalikungu ○ **EAT** 337 Hj 47
Nyamaluma ○ **Z** 341 Hh 52
Nyamandhlovu ○ **ZW** 341 Hf 55
Nyamapanda ○ **ZW** 344 Hj 54
Nyamassila ○ **RT** 317 Gg 41
Nyambarongo ~ **RWA** 336 Hg 46
Nyamirembe ○ **EAT** 336 Hh 47
Nyamkalika ○ **EAT** 336 Hh 48
Nyamlell ○ **SUD** 324 Hf 41
Nyamoko ○ **CAM** 320 Gm 43
Nyamtumbo ○ **EAT** 344 Hk 51
Nyanga ~ **G** 332 Gm 47
Nyanga ○ **RCB** 332 Gn 47
Nyanga ○ **ZW** 344 Hj 55
Nyanga ♀ **ZW** 344 Hj 55
Nyangadzi ~ **ZW** 344 Hj 54
Nyangamara ○ **EAT** 344 Hm 51
Nyangana ○ **NAM** 340 Hc 55
Nyanza-Lac ○ **BU** 336 Hg 48
Nyasa ○ **RDC** 336 Hf 48
Nyassar ○ **CAM** 321 Gp 42
Nyaungkhashe ○ **MYA** 262 Kn 37
Nyaunglebin ○ **MYA** 262 Kn 37
Nyaung U ○ **MYA** 254 Km 35
Nyavizh ○ **BY** 171 Hf 19
Nyazura ○ **ZW** 341 Hh 55
Nyazwidzi ~ **ZW** 341 Hh 55
Nybergsund ○ **N** 158 Gm 15
Nyborg ○ **DK** 170 Gm 18
Nybro ○ **S** 170 Gp 17
Nycla ○ **RUS** 154 Sc 5
Nyda ○ **RUS** 22 Nb 3
Nye ~ **G** 332 Gm 44
Nyeri ○ **EAK** 337 Hl 46
Ny-Friesland ⌒ **N** 158 Ha 6
Nyibiam ○ **WAN** 320 Gl 41
Nyiel ○ **SUD** 324 Hh 42
Nyikine ○ **SN** 316 Fm 39
Nyima ○ **VRC** 231 Kh 30
Nyimba ○ **Z** 341 Hh 53
Nyingchi ○ **VRC** 254 Km 31
Nyiragongo △ **RDC** 336 Hg 46
Nyírbátor ○ **H** 174 Hc 22
Nyíregyháza ○ **H** 174 Hc 22
Nyiri Desert ⌒ **EAK** 337 Hl 47
Nyiru Range ⛰ **EAK** 325 Hl 44
Nykia ♀ **MW** 344 Hj 51
Nykøbing ○ **DK** 170 Gl 17
Nykøbing Falster ○ **DK** 170 Gm 18
Nyköping ○ **S** 170 Ha 16
Nylrivier ~ **ZA** 349 Hg 58
Nylstroom ○ **ZA** 349 Hg 58
Nymagee ○ **AUS** 379 Mk 62
Nynäshamm ○ **S** 170 Hb 16
Nyngan ○ **AUS** 379 Mk 61
Nyoman ~ **BY** 171 He 19
Nyoma rap ○ **IND** 230 Kd 29
Nyon ○ **CH** 163 Gk 22
Nyong ~ **CAM** 320 Gl 44
Nyong ~ **CAM** 321 Gn 43
Nyons ○ **F** 185 Gj 23
Nyos ~ **CAM** 320 Gm 42
Nyrud ○ **RUS** 159 Hg 11
Nysa ○ **PL** 174 Ha 20
Nysa Łużycka ~ **PL** 174 Gp 20
Nyudō-saki ⌓ **J** 250 Mf 25
Nyumbaya Mungo Reservoir ~ **EAT** 337 Hl 47
Nyunzu ○ **RDC** 336 Hf 48
Nyž. Sirohozy ○ **UA** 175 Hk 22
Nzako ○ **RCA** 321 Hd 43
Nzako ~ **RCA** 321 Hd 43
Nzambi ○ **RCB** 332 Gm 47
Nzambi ○ **RDC** 333 Ha 46
Nzara ○ **SUD** 324 Hg 43
Nzassi ○ **RCB** 332 Gm 48
Nzébéla ○ **RG** 316 Gb 41
Nzega ○ **EAT** 337 Hj 48
Nzérékoré ○ **RG** 316 Gb 42
N'Zeto ○ **ANG** 332 Gn 49
Nzi ~ **CI** 317 Gd 41
Nzi ~ **CI** 317 Gd 42
Nzima ○ **EAT** 336 Hj 47
Nzo ~ **CI** 304 Gc 42
Nzoia ~ **EAK** 325 Hk 45
Nzoo ○ **RG** 316 Gb 42
Nzoro ○ **RCA** 321 Gp 42
Nzoro ~ **RDC** 324 Hh 44

O

O.T. Downs ○ **AUS** 364 Md 54
o. Žiloj ▵ **AZ** 209 Jd 25
O'Chiese Indian Reservation ••• **CDN** 50 Ce 19
Oahu ▵ **USA** 75 Am 35
Oakbank ○ **AUS** 378 Mg 62
Oak Bay ○ **CDN** 50 Ca 21
Oak-Bluff ○ **CDN** 56 Cp 21
Oakburn ○ **CDN** 56 Cm 20
Oak Creek ○ **USA** 65 Cj 25
Oakdale ○ **USA** 64 Cb 27
Oakdale ○ **USA** 86 Db 30
Oakes ○ **USA** 56 Cn 22
Oakey ○ **AUS** 375 Mm 59
Oakey Creek ~ **AUS** 375 Mm 59
Oak Grove ○ **USA** 71 Dh 29
Oak Grove ○ **USA** 86 Dc 29
Oak Harbor ○ **USA** 50 Ca 21
Oak Hill ○ **USA** 71 Dh 27
Oak Hill ○ **USA** 87 Dh 31
Oak Hills ○ **AUS** 365 Mj 55
Oakhurst ○ **USA** 64 Cc 27
Oak Lake ~ **CDN** 56 Cm 21
Oakland ○ **USA** 64 Ca 27
Oakland ○ **USA** 70 Cp 25
Oakland ○ **USA** 70 Da 25
Oakland ○ **USA** 71 Dc 28
Oakland ○ **USA** 74 Dj 26
Oaklands ○ **AUS** 379 Mk 63
Oak Lawn ○ **USA** 71 Dd 25
Oaklay ○ **USA** 70 Cm 26
Oakley ○ **USA** 64 Cf 24
Oakover ~ **AUS** 360 Ll 56
Oak Point ○ **CDN** 56 Cp 20
Oakridge ○ **USA** 50 Ca 24
Oak Ridge ○ **USA** 71 Df 27
Oakshade ○ **USA** 71 Df 25
Oakview ○ **CDN** 56 Cn 20
Oakwood ○ **USA** 70 Cn 28
Oamaru ○ **NZ** 382 Nh 68
Oanāq Thule ○ **DK** 7 Fb 2
Oara Cāy ~ **IR** 209 Jc 28
Oarānqū ~ **IR** 209 Jb 27
Oasis ○ **USA** 64 Ce 25
Oatlands ○ **AUS** 378 Mk 67
Oaw Island ▵ **AUS** 369 Ln 62
Oaxaca de Juárez ○ **MEX** 92 Cp 37
Ob ~ **RUS** 19 Na 3
Ob ~ **RUS** 22 Nb 3
Ob ~ **RUS** 22 Pa 4
Ob ~ **RUS** 154 Sb 5
Ob ~ **RUS** 204 Sb 5
Ob ~ **RUS** 204 Sb 6
Ob ~ **RUS** 204 Sc 6
Ob ~ **RUS** 204 Ta 7
Ob ~ **RUS** 204 Tb 7
Oba ○ **CDN** 57 Df 21
Obaba ○ **RCB** 332 Ha 46
Obaha ○ **PNG** 287 Ml 50
Obais ~ **RI** 286 Mf 49
Obala ○ **CAM** 320 Gm 43
Obalapuram ○ **IND** 238 Kc 38
Obama ○ **J** 251 Md 28
Obamska ~ **CDN** 60 Dj 20
Oban ○ **GB** 162 Gd 17
Oban ○ **WAN** 320 Gl 43
Oban ○ **AUS** 374 Mf 56
Obanazawa ○ **J** 251 Mg 26
Öbe ○ **AFG** 223 Jk 28
Obed ○ **CDN** 50 Cd 19
Obehie ○ **WAN** 320 Gk 43
Obeliai ○ **LT** 171 He 18
Obera ○ **RA** 140 Eg 59
Oberlin ○ **USA** 70 Cm 26
Oberon ○ **AUS** 379 Ml 62
Oberösterreich ⊙ **A** 174 Gn 21
Oberstdorf ○ **D** 174 Gm 22
Obi ○ **WAN** 320 Gl 41
Óbidos ○ **BR** 120 Eg 46
Óbidos ○ **BR** 120 Eg 46
Óbidos ○ **P** 184 Gb 26
Obigarm ○ **TJ** 223 Jn 26
Obihiro ○ **J** 250 Mh 24
Obihingou ~ **TJ** 223 Jp 26
Obilebit ~ **PY** 140 Ee 56
Obira ○ **J** 250 Mg 23
Obíspo Trejo ○ **RA** 137 Ec 61
Obitočna kosa ▵ **UA** 181 Hl 22
Oblačnaja △ **RUS** 250 Md 24
Obluč'e ○ **RUS** 205 Wc 9
Obninsk ○ **RUS** 171 Hk 18
Obo ○ **VRC** 242 La 27
Obo ○ **RCA** 324 Hf 43
Oboa △ **EAU** 325 Hk 45
Obobogorab ○ **ZA** 348 Hc 59
Obock ○ **DJI** 328 Hp 40
Obogu ○ **GH** 317 Gf 42
Obojan ○ **RUS** 175 Hk 20
Obokote ○ **RDC** 336 Hf 46
Oboli ○ **RCB** 332 Gp 46
Obolo ○ **WAN** 320 Gk 42
Obonga Lake ~ **CDN** 57 Dd 21
Obout ○ **CAM** 320 Gm 44
Obouya ○ **RCB** 332 Gp 46
Obozerskij ○ **RUS** 159 Hn 14
Obrenovac ○ **SCG** 174 Hb 23
Obrovac ○ **HR** 174 Gp 23
Obruk Yaylâsı ⛰ **TR** 195 Hj 26
Obščij syrt ⛰ **RUS** 181 Jc 20
Observatorio de Astronómico Nacional ★ **MEX** 75 Ce 30
Obshchiy Syrt ⛰ **RUS** 155 Rb 8
Obubra ○ **WAN** 320 Gl 42
Obuchiv ○ **UA** 175 Hh 20
Obudu ○ **WAN** 320 Gl 42
Obudu Cattle Ranch ○ **WAN** 320 Gl 42
Obytočna zatoka ~ **UA** 175 Hk 22
Obzor ○ **BG** 195 Hf 24
Očakiv ○ **UA** 175 Hh 22
Ocala ○ **USA** 87 Dg 31
Ocampo ○ **MEX** 81 Cl 32
Ocampo ○ **MEX** 92 Cm 35
Ocaña ○ **CO** 107 Dm 41
Ocana ○ **E** 184 Ge 26
Ocara ○ **BR** 124 Fa 48
Ocate ○ **USA** 65 Ck 27
Occidental ⛰ **PE** 116 Dk 52
Ocean City ○ **USA** 74 Dl 26
Ocean Falls ○ **CDN** 50 Bn 19
Oceano ○ **USA** 64 Cb 28
Ocean Shores ○ **USA** 50 Bp 22
Oceanside ○ **USA** 64 Cd 29
Ocean Springs ○ **USA** 86 Dd 30
Ocha ○ **RUS** 23 Sa 4
Och'amch'ire ○ **GE** 202 Hn 24
Ochiai ○ **J** 251 Mc 28
Ochobo ○ **WAN** 320 Gk 42
Ocho Rios ○ **JA** 101 Dk 36
Ochotsk ○ **RUS** 23 Sa 4
Ochtyrka ○ **UA** 175 Hk 20
Ocilla ○ **USA** 86 Dg 30
Ockelbo ○ **S** 158 Ha 15
Ocmulgee ~ **USA** 71 Dg 29
Ocmulgee National Monument ★ **USA** 71 Dg 29
Ocoña ○ **PE** 128 Dm 54
Ocoña ~ **PE** 128 Dm 54
Oconee ~ **USA** 71 Dg 29
Ocongate ○ **PE** 128 Dn 52
Oconto ○ **USA** 57 De 23
Oconto ○ **USA** 70 Cm 25
Ocoroni ○ **MEX** 80 Ch 33
Ocoruro ○ **PE** 128 Dn 53
Ocós ○ **GCA** 93 Db 38
Ocosingo ○ **MEX** 93 Db 37
Ocotal ○ **NIC** 96 De 39
Ocotillo ○ **USA** 64 Cd 29
Ocotillo Wells ○ **USA** 64 Cd 29
Ocotlán ○ **MEX** 92 Cp 37
Ocozocoautla ○ **MEX** 93 Db 37
Ocracoke ○ **USA** 74 Dl 28
Ocreza ~ **P** 184 Gc 26
Ocros ○ **PE** 128 Dm 52
Octolán ○ **MEX** 92 Cl 35
Ocú ○ **PA** 97 Dh 42
Ocua ○ **MOC** 344 Hm 52
Ocumare del Tuy ○ **YV** 107 Ea 40
Ocuri ○ **BOL** 129 Eb 55
Oda ○ **GH** 317 Gf 43
Ódáðahraun ⛰ **IS** 158 Fm 13
Odaejin ○ **DVRK** 247 Ma 25
Odaesan ★ **ROK** 247 Ma 27
Ōdate ○ **J** 250 Mg 25
Odawara ○ **J** 251 Mf 28
Odemira ○ **P** 184 Gb 27
Odendaalsrus ○ **ZA** 349 Hf 59
Odense ○ **DK** 170 Gl 18
Oder ~ **D** 170 Gp 19
Oderbruch ⌒ **D** 170 Gn 19
Odessa ○ **USA** 50 Cc 22
Odessa ○ **USA** 81 Cl 30
Odessa ○ **UA** 175 Hh 22
Odienné ○ **CI** 304 Gc 41
Odila ~ **NAM** 340 Ha 54
Odiongan ○ **RP** 267 Ll 39
Odjala ○ **G** 332 Gn 46
Odoev ○ **RUS** 181 Hl 19
Odŏngk ○ **K** 263 Lc 40
O'Donnell ~ **AUS** 361 Lp 55
Odorheiu Secuiesc ○ **RO** 175 He 22
Odra ~ **PL** 170 Gp 19
Odrus ~ **SUD** 313 Hl 36
Odzema ○ **RCB** 332 Ha 46
Odzi ○ **ZW** 344 Hj 55
Odzi ~ **ZW** 344 Hj 55
Odziba ○ **RCB** 332 Gp 47
Oedmis ○ **TR** 195 Hg 26
Oeiras ○ **BR** 124 En 49
Oeiras do Para ○ **BR** 121 Ek 46
Oelemari ~ **SME** 113 Eg 44
Oelrichs ○ **USA** 51 Cl 24
Oelwein ○ **USA** 56 Dc 24
Oeno ▵ **UK** 14 Ca 12
Oenpelli ○ **AUS** 364 Mc 52
Oezel Uzan ~ **IR** 209 Jc 27
Of ○ **TR** 202 Hn 25
Ofa ○ **WAN** 320 Gj 41
O'Fallon Creek ~ **USA** 51 Ck 22
Ofaqin ○ **IL** 214 Hk 30
Ófærafoss ★ **IS** 158 Fl 14
Ofcolaco ○ **ZA** 352 Hh 58
Offenbach ○ **D** 174 Gl 20
Offenburg ○ **D** 163 Gk 21
Officer Creek ~ **AUS** 369 Mc 59
Offoué ~ **G** 332 Gm 46
Offumpo ○ **CI** 317 Gd 43
Oficina Alemania ○ **RCH** 136 Dp 58
Ofoase ○ **GH** 317 Gf 42
Ofotfjorden ~ **N** 158 Ha 11
Ofunato ○ **J** 250 Mg 26
Oga ○ **J** 250 Mf 26
Ogaden ⌒ **ETH** 328 Hp 42
Oga-hanto ▵ **J** 250 Mf 26
Ōgaki ○ **J** 251 Me 28
Ogallala ○ **USA** 65 Cl 25
Ogan ~ **RI** 278 Lc 48
Ogani ○ **WAN** 320 Gk 43
Ogasawara ▵ **J** 27 Sa 7
Ogawara-ko ~ **J** 250 Mg 25
Ogba ○ **WAN** 320 Gj 42
Ogbomoso ○ **WAN** 320 Gh 41
Ogden ○ **USA** 65 Cg 25
Ogdensburg ○ **USA** 60 Dl 23
Ogea Levu ▵ **FJI** 390 Aa 55
Ogea Oriki ▵ **FJI** 390 Aa 55
Ogeechee ~ **USA** 71 Dg 29
Ogema ○ **CDN** 51 Ck 20
Ogema ○ **USA** 56 Cp 22
Ogembo ○ **EAK** 337 Hk 46
Ogeoué ~ **G** 332 Gm 46
Ogi ○ **J** 251 Mf 27
Ogies ○ **ZA** 349 Hg 59
Ogilvie River ○ **CDN** 47 Bg 13
Oglanly ○ **TM** 222 Jf 26
Oglat Beraber ○ **DZ** 293 Ge 30
Oglat el Faci ○ **DZ** 293 Gd 32
Oglat el Faci ○ **DZ** 293 Gf 32
Oglat el Khnâchîch ○ **RMM** 305 Ge 35
Oglat Marhboura ○ **DZ** 293 Gf 29
Oglive Mountains ⛰ **CDN** 47 Be 11
Ogmore ○ **AUS** 375 Ml 57
Ognon ~ **F** 163 Gk 22
Ogoja ○ **WAN** 320 Gl 42
Ogoki ○ **CDN** 57 Df 20
Ogoki Lake ~ **CDN** 57 De 20
Ogoki Reservation ••• **CDN** 57 Dd 20
Ogoki River ~ **CDN** 57 Dd 20
Ogooué ~ **G** 332 Gl 46
Ogooué ~ **G** 332 Gn 46
Ogooué ~ **RCB** 332 Gn 47
Ogou ~ **RT** 317 Gg 41
Ogoulou ~ **G** 332 Gm 46
Ogre ○ **LV** 171 He 17
Ogulin ○ **HR** 174 Gp 23
Ogun ○ **WAN** 320 Gj 41
Ogurugu ○ **WAN** 320 Gk 42
Oğuzeli ○ **TR** 195 Hl 27
Ogwashi Uku ○ **WAN** 320 Gk 42
Oha ○ **RUS** 205 Xb 8
Ohai ○ **NZ** 382 Nf 68
Ohakune ○ **NZ** 383 Nk 65
Ohalia ○ **WAN** 320 Gk 43
Ohanet ○ **DZ** 296 Gl 31
Ohi △ **GR** 194 He 26
Ohio ⊙ **USA** 71 Dg 25
Ohio ~ **USA** 71 Dh 26
Ohonua ○ **TO** 390 Ac 56
Ohota ~ **RUS** 205 Xb 7
Ohotsk ○ **RUS** 205 Xb 7
Ohotskoe ○ **RUS** 250 Mh 22
Ohře ~ **CZ** 174 Gn 20
Ohrid ○ **MK** 194 Hc 25
Ohrigstad ○ **ZA** 352 Hh 58
Ohura ○ **NZ** 383 Nk 65
Ohwaka ○ **EAT** 337 Hm 49
Oiapoque ○ **F** 113 Eh 44
Oiapoque ~ **BR** 113 Eh 44
Oiba ○ **CO** 107 Dm 42
Oicha ○ **RDC** 324 Hg 45
Oigawa ~ **J** 251 Mf 28
Oijärvi ○ **FIN** 159 Hf 13
Oil City ○ **USA** 70 Db 29
Oil City ○ **USA** 74 Dj 25
Oildale ○ **USA** 64 Cc 28
Oilton ○ **USA** 81 Cn 32
Oimjakon ○ **RUS** 23 Sa 3
Oise ~ **F** 163 Gh 21
Oisina ○ **RI** 282 Lm 51
Oíta ○ **RA** 137 Ea 61
Oita ○ **J** 247 Mb 29
Ojai ○ **USA** 64 Cc 28
Oje de Ague ○ **MEX** 80 Cj 31
Ojinaga ○ **MEX** 81 Ck 31
Ojiya ○ **J** 251 Mf 27
Ojocaliente ○ **MEX** 92 Cl 34
Ojo de Carrizo ○ **MEX** 80 Ck 31
Ojo de Laguna ○ **MEX** 80 Cj 31
Ojokkuduk ○ **UZB** 223 Jl 25
Ojos Negros ○ **MEX** 75 Cd 30
Oj-Tal ○ **KS** 230 Ka 25
Oju ○ **WAN** 320 Gl 42
Ojuelos de Jalisco ○ **MEX** 92 Cm 35
Ojyl ○ **KZ** 155 Rb 9
Ok △ **IS** 158 Fk 13
Oka ~ **RUS** 171 Hl 18
Oka ~ **RUS** 204 Uc 8
Oka ○ **WAN** 320 Gj 42
Okaba ○ **RI** 286 Mf 50
Oka-Don Plain ⛰ **RUS** 181 Hn 19
Okahandja ○ **NAM** 348 Ha 56
Okakarara ○ **NAM** 348 Ha 56
Okali ○ **RCB** 332 Gp 46
Okali ○ **RCB** 332 Gp 47
Okanagan Falls ○ **CDN** 50 Cc 21
Okanagan Indian Reservation ••• **CDN** 50 Cc 20
Okanagan Lake ~ **CDN** 50 Cc 21
Okanagan Range ⛰ **CDN** 50 Cb 21
Okanagan Valley ⌒ **CDN** 50 Cc 21
Okandjambo ○ **NAM** 340 Gn 55
Okangoho ○ **NAM** 348 Ha 56
Okangwati ○ **NAM** 340 Gn 54
Okankolo ○ **NAM** 340 Ha 55
Okano ~ **G** 332 Gm 45
Okanogan ○ **USA** 50 Cb 21
Okanogan ~ **USA** 50 Cc 21
Okanono ○ **NAM** 348 Gp 56
Okapa ○ **PNG** 287 Mj 49
Okāra ○ **PK** 230 Ka 30
Okarche ○ **USA** 70 Cp 28
Okata ○ **WAN** 320 Gh 41
Okato ○ **NZ** 383 Nj 65
Okatumba ○ **NAM** 340 Gn 55
Okaukuejo ○ **NAM** 340 Gp 55
Okavango ~ **NAM** 340 Hb 54
Okavango ~ **RB** 341 Hd 55
Okavango Delta ⌒ **RB** 341 Hd 55
Okave ○ **NAM** 348 Ha 56
Okaya ○ **J** 251 Mf 27
Okayama ○ **J** 251 Mc 28
Okay Creek ○ **AUS** 375 Ml 57
Okazaki ○ **J** 251 Me 28
Okazize ○ **NAM** 348 Ha 56
Okdarjo ~ **UZB** 223 Jl 25
Okeechobee ○ **USA** 87 Dh 32
Okefenokee N.W.R. ♀ **USA** 87 Dg 30
Okefenokee Swamp ~ **USA** 87 Dg 30
Okehamten ○ **GB** 163 Gd 20
Oke-Iho ○ **WAN** 320 Gh 41
Okélataka ○ **RCB** 332 Gp 46
Okemah ○ **USA** 70 Cp 28
Okene ○ **WAN** 320 Gk 42
Okha ○ **IND** 227 Jn 34
Okha Māthi ○ **IND** 227 Jn 35
Oki ○ **RI** 282 Lp 47
Okiep ○ **ZA** 348 Ha 60
Okigwe ○ **WAN** 320 Gk 43
Oki Kaikyo ~ **J** 251 Mc 28
Okinawa ○ **J** 259 Lp 32
Okinawa Islands ▵ **J** 259 Ma 32
Okinawa-shima ▵ **J** 259 Ma 32
Okino-Daitō-shima ▵ **J** 26 Rb 7
Okinoerabu-shima ▵ **J** 259 Ma 32
Okino-shima ▵ **J** 251 Mc 29
Oki-shoto ▵ **J** 251 Mc 27
Okitipupa ○ **WAN** 320 Gj 42
Okkan ○ **MYA** 262 Km 37
Okkūrgan ○ **UZB** 223 Jn 25
Oklahoma ⊙ **USA** 70 Cn 28
Oklahoma City ○ **USA** 70 Cn 28
Oklan ○ **RUS** 205 Za 6
Oklanskoye Plato ⛰ **RUS** 205 Yc 6
Okmulgee ○ **USA** 70 Cp 28
Oko ○ **WAN** 320 Gj 42
Ok Ohm River ~ **PNG** 286 Mh 48
Okok ~ **EAU** 325 Hj 44
Okola ○ **CAM** 320 Gm 43
Okollo ○ **EAU** 324 Hh 44
Okolona ○ **USA** 71 Df 26
Okombahe ○ **NAM** 348 Gp 56
Okondja ○ **G** 332 Gn 46
Okondjatu ○ **NAM** 348 Hb 56
Okongo ○ **NAM** 340 Ha 54
Okoppe ○ **J** 250 Mh 23
Okotoks ○ **CDN** 50 Cf 20
Okoyo ○ **RCB** 332 Gp 46
Okpala-Ngwa ○ **WAN** 320 Gk 43
Okpara ~ **DY** 320 Gh 41
Okpo ○ **MYA** 254 Km 36
Okrika ○ **WAN** 320 Gk 43
Okrouyo ○ **CI** 305 Gc 43
Oksapmin ○ **PNG** 286 Mh 48
Øksfjord ○ **N** 159 Hd 10
Okskij Gos. Zapovednik ♀ **RUS** 181 Hn 18
Oksovskij ○ **RUS** 159 Hm 14
Okstindan △ **N** 158 Gn 13
Okstindane △ **N** 158 Gp 6
Ok Tedi River ~ **PNG** 286 Mg 49
Oktemberjan ○ **ARM** 202 Hp 25
Oktjabr'shij ○ **RUS** 159 Hk 12
Oktjabr'sk ○ **KZ** 155 Rc 9
Oktjabr'sk ○ **RUS** 181 Jc 19
Oktjabrskij ○ **RUS** 154 Rb 8
Oktjabr'skij ○ **RUS** 171 Hl 15
Oktjabr'skij ○ **RUS** 171 Hp 15
Oktjabr'skij ○ **RUS** 181 Jc 18
Oktjabr'skij ○ **RUS** 205 Ya 8
Oktos ○ **UZB** 223 Jl 26
Oktumkum ⌒ **TM** 222 Je 25
Oktwin ○ **MYA** 254 Kn 36
Oku ○ **J** 259 Ma 32
Oku ~ **RDC** 336 Hf 46
Okua ○ **WAN** 320 Gk 42
Okuchi ○ **J** 247 Mb 29
Okulovka ○ **RUS** 171 Hj 16
Okundi ○ **WAN** 320 Gl 42
Okushiri ○ **J** 250 Mf 24
Okushiri-tō ▵ **J** 250 Mf 24
Okuta ○ **WAN** 320 Gh 41
Okwa ~ **RB** 348 Hc 57
Okwa ~ **RB** 349 Hd 57
Ola ○ **RUS** 23 Sb 4
Ola ○ **USA** 50 Cd 23
Ola ○ **USA** 70 Db 28
Olá ○ **PA** 97 Dh 41
Olacapato ○ **RA** 136 Ea 58
Ólafsfjörður ○ **IS** 158 Fl 12
Ólafsvík ○ **IS** 158 Fh 13
Olaf V land ⌒ **N** 158 Hb 6
Olancha ○ **USA** 64 Cc 27
Olanchito ○ **HN** 96 De 38
Öland ▵ **S** 170 Ha 17
Olary ○ **AUS** 378 Mg 62
Olathe ○ **USA** 70 Da 26
Olavarría ○ **RA** 137 Ed 64
Ólbia ○ **I** 185 Gl 25
Olcott ○ **USA** 60 Dj 24
Old Barns ○ **CDN** 61 Ec 23
Old Cork ○ **AUS** 374 Mg 57
Old Crow ○ **CDN** 47 Be 11
Old Delamere ○ **AUS** 364 Mb 53
Old Dongola ★ **SUD** 312 Hh 36
Oldeani ○ **EAT** 337 Hk 47
Oldeani △ **EAT** 337 Hk 47
Oldenburg ○ **D** 170 Gk 19
Oldenburg (H.) ○ **D** 170 Gm 18
Olderdalen ○ **N** 159 Hc 11
Olderfjord ○ **N** 159 He 10
Oldest Christian Mission Site ★ **CDN** 60 Dn 21
Old Faithful Geysir ★ **USA** 51 Cg 23
Oldfield ~ **AUS** 368 Ll 62
Old Forge ○ **USA** 60 Dl 24
Old Fort Parker St. Hist. Site ★ **USA** 70 Cp 30
Oldham ○ **GB** 163 Ge 19
Old Harbor ○ **USA** 46 An 17
Old Herbert Vale ○ **AUS** 365 Mf 55
Old Horse Springs ○ **USA** 65 Ch 29
Oldman ~ **CDN** 50 Ce 21
Old Mkushi ○ **Z** 341 Hg 53
Oldoiniyo Orok △ **EAK** 337 Hl 47
Ol-Doinyo Sabuk ♀ **EAK** 337 Hl 46
Old Parakylia ○ **AUS** 378 Me 61
Old Perlican ○ **CDN** 61 Eh 21
Old Reef ▵ **AUS** 375 Ml 55
Olds ○ **CDN** 50 Ce 20
Old Station ○ **USA** 64 Cb 25
Old Wives Lake ~ **CDN** 51 Cj 20
Old Women Mountains ⛰ **USA** 64 Ce 28
Olean ○ **USA** 60 Dj 24
Olecko ○ **PL** 170 Hd 18
Oleiros ○ **P** 184 Gc 26
Olëkma ○ **RUS** 204 Wa 7
Olëkma ~ **RUS** 204 Wa 7
Olëkminsk ○ **RUS** 204 Wa 6
Oleksandrivka ○ **UA** 175 Hj 21
Olenëk ~ **RUS** 204 Va 5
Olenëk ○ **RUS** 204 Vb 5
Olenëk ~ **RUS** 204 Vc 5
Olenëk ~ **RUS** 204 Wa 4
Olenekskiy Zaliv ≋ **RUS** 204 Vc 4
Olenica ○ **RUS** 159 Hk 12
Olenino ○ **RUS** 171 Hj 17
Olenjok ~ **RUS** 22 Ra 2
Olenogorsk ○ **RUS** 159 Hj 11
Ol Eoinyo Lengai △ **EAT** 337 Hk 47
Oleśnica ○ **PL** 174 Ha 20
Olevs'k ○ **UA** 175 Hf 20
Ol'ga ○ **RUS** 250 Md 24
Olgastretet ~ **N** 158 Hd 6
Olgij ○ **MNG** 22 Pa 5
Ol'ginsk ○ **RUS** 205 Wc 8
Ölgiy ○ **MNG** 204 Ua 9
Olho d'Água das Flores ○ **BR** 124 Fb 50
Ol'hovka ○ **RUS** 181 Ja 21
Oli ~ **DY** 320 Gh 40
Oli ○ **WAN** 320 Gj 41
Olib ▵ **HR** 174 Gp 23
Olifants ~ **NAM** 348 Ha 57
Olifants ~ **NAM** 348 Hb 57
Olifants ○ **ZA** 352 Hh 58
Olifantshoek ○ **ZA** 349 Hd 59
Olifantsrivier ~ **ZA** 358 Hb 62
Ólimbia ○ **GR** 194 Hc 27
Ólimbos ○ **GR** 195 Hf 28
Olimpia Colina ○ **BR** 141 Ek 56
Olinalá ○ **MEX** 92 Cn 37
Olinda ○ **BR** 124 Fc 50
Olindina ○ **BR** 125 Fa 51
Olinga ○ **MOC** 344 Hl 54
Olio ○ **AUS** 374 Mh 56
Oliva ○ **RA** 137 Ec 62
Oliva ○ **E** 184 Gf 26
Oliva d. I. F. ○ **P** 184 Gc 26
Oliveira ○ **BR** 141 Em 56
Oliveira dos Brejinhos ○ **BR** 125 En 52
Olivenza ○ **E** 184 Gc 26
Olivet ○ **USA** 56 Cp 24
Olivia ○ **USA** 56 Da 23
Ol Keju Ado ~ **EAK** 337 Hl 47
Olla ○ **USA** 86 Db 30
Ollagüe ○ **RCH** 136 Dp 56
Olmedo ○ **E** 184 Gd 25
Olmos ○ **PE** 116 Dj 48
Olney ○ **USA** 70 Cn 29
Olney ○ **USA** 71 Dd 26
Oloči ○ **RUS** 204 Vc 8
Olodio ○ **CI** 305 Gc 43
Olofström ○ **S** 170 Gp 17
Oloibiri ○ **WAN** 320 Gk 43
Oloiserri ○ **EAK** 337 Hl 47
Oloitokitok ○ **EAK** 337 Hl 47
Oloj ~ **RUS** 205 Yc 5
Ololdou ○ **SN** 304 Fp 38
Olomane ~ **CDN** 61 Ed 20
Olomburi ○ **SOL** 290 Nc 50
Olomouc ○ **CZ** 174 Ha 21
Olonec ○ **RUS** 171 Hj 15
Olongapo ○ **RP** 267 Lk 38
Olorgesailie National Monument ★ **EAK** 337 Hl 46
Oloron-Ste.-Marie ○ **F** 184 Gf 24
Oloyskiy Khrebet ⛰ **RUS** 205 Yc 5
Ol'sa ○ **RUS** 171 Hh 18
Olsztyn ○ **PL** 170 Hc 19
Olsztynek ○ **PL** 170 Hc 19
Olt ~ **RO** 175 He 23
Olten ○ **CH** 163 Gk 22
Olteniţa ○ **RO** 175 Hf 23
Oltu ○ **TR** 202 Hn 25
Oltu Çayı ~ **TR** 202 Hn 25
Ol Tukai ○ **EAK** 337 Hl 47
Oluanpi ○ **RC** 259 Ll 35
Olukbaşı ○ **TR** 195 Hk 27
Olur ○ **TR** 202 Hp 25
Olutanga ○ **RP** 275 Lm 42
Olutanga Island ▵ **RP** 275 Lm 42
Olvera ○ **E** 184 Gd 27
Olympia ○ **USA** 50 Ca 22
Olympic Dam ○ **AUS** 378 Me 61
Olympic Mountains ⛰ **USA** 50 Ca 22
Olympic National Park ♀ **USA** 50 Bp 21
Olympos △ **GR** 194 Hd 25
Olympos △ **CY** 195 Hj 28
Olyutorskiy Poluostrov ▵ **RUS** 205 Za 6
Olyutorskiy Zaliv ≋ **RUS** 205 Za 6
Om' ~ **RUS** 204 Ta 7
Ōma ○ **J** 250 Mg 25
Omachi ○ **J** 251 Me 27
Omae-saki ⌓ **J** 251 Me 28
Ōmagari ○ **J** 250 Mg 26
Omagh ○ **GB** 162 Gc 18
Omaha ○ **USA** 70 Cp 25
Omaha ○ **USA** 70 Db 27
Omaha Indian Reservation ••• **USA** 70 Cp 25
Omak ○ **USA** 50 Cc 21
Omakau ○ **NZ** 382 Ng 68
Omakwia ○ **GUY** 113 Ee 43
Oman □ **OM** 226 Jg 33
Omanga ○ **RDC** 333 He 47

452 Nullagine - Omanga

□Country ▣Capital city ⊙Administrative unit ○Place ⌂Island ⛰Mountain range △Mountain ⌒Cape ≈Ocean, Sea ∼Lake, River ▽Undersea topography ▲Glacier ♀National park •••Reservation ★Point of major interest ⌓Landscape

Omapere ○ **NZ** 383 Nj 63
Omarama ○ **NZ** 382 Nh 68
Omaruru ∼ **NAM** 348 Gp 56
Omaruru ○ **NAM** 348 Ha 56
Omás ○ **PE** 116 Dk 52
Ōma-saki ⌒ **J** 250 Mg 25
Omatako ∼ **NAM** 340 Hb 55
Omatako ○ **NAM** 348 Ha 56
Omatako △ **NAM** 348 Ha 56
Omate ○ **PE** 128 Dn 54
Omati ○ **PNG** 287 Mh 49
Omati River ∼ **PNG** 286 Mh 49
Omba ∼ **RI** 283 Md 48
Ombala ○ **ANG** 340 Gp 54
Ombella ∼ **RCA** 321 Hb 43
Ombotozu △ **NAM** 348 Ha 56
Omboué ○ **G** 332 Gl 46
Ombrone ∼ **I** 185 Gm 24
Ombu ○ **RA** 137 Ed 61
Ombuku ∼ **NAM** 340 Gn 54
Omčak ○ **RUS** 23 Sa 3
Omchi ○ **TCH** 309 Ha 35
Omdurman ○ **SUD** 312 Hh 38
Omega ○ **NAM** 341 Hd 55
Omeo ○ **AUS** 379 Mk 64
Ometepec ○ **MEX** 92 Cn 37
Omi ∼ **BOL** 129 Eb 52
Ōmi-Hachiman ○ **J** 251 Me 28
Omineca Mountains ⛰ **CDN** 42 Db 7
Omitara ○ **NAM** 348 Hb 57
Ōmiya ○ **J** 251 Mf 28
Ommanney Bay ≈ **CDN** 42 Fa 4
Omoa ○ **HN** 93 Dd 38
Omoku ○ **WAN** 320 Gk 43
Omoloj ∼ **RUS** 205 Wc 4
Omolon ○ **RUS** 23 Sb 3
Omolon ∼ **RUS** 23 Sb 3
Omolon ∼ **RUS** 205 Yb 5
Omolon ○ **RUS** 205 Yc 6
Omolon ∼ **RUS** 205 Yc 6
Omo National Park ♀ **ETH** 325 Hk 42
Omono ∼ **J** 250 Mg 26
Omo Wenz ∼ **ETH** 325 Hl 42
Ompah ○ **CDN** 60 Dk 23
Ompupa ○ **ANG** 340 Gn 54
Omsk ○ **RUS** 22 Nb 4
Omsk ○ **RUS** 204 Sc 7
Omsukčan ○ **RUS** 205 Yb 6
Omsukchanskiy Khrebet ⛰ **RUS** 205 Ya 6
Ōmu ○ **J** 250 Mh 23
Omu-Aran ○ **WAN** 320 Gj 41
Omuo ○ **WAN** 320 Gj 42
Omuramba Ovambo ∼ **NAM** 340 Ha 55
Ōmura-wan ∼ **J** 247 Ma 29
Omurtag ○ **BG** 194 Hf 24
Ōmuta ○ **J** 247 Mb 29
Omutinskij ○ **RUS** 154 Sb 7
Oña ○ **EC** 116 Dj 47
Oña ○ **E** 184 Ge 24
Ona-Dikombe ○ **RDC** 333 He 47
Onaman Lake ∼ **CDN** 57 De 21
Onamia ○ **USA** 56 Da 23
Onang ○ **RI** 279 Lk 47
Onanhasang ○ **RI** 270 Kp 45
Onaping ○ **CDN** 57 Dh 22
Onaping Lake ∼ **CDN** 57 Dh 22
Onava ○ **USA** 56 Cp 24
Onaway ○ **USA** 57 Df 23
Onças ○ **BR** 120 Eg 46
Oncativo ○ **RA** 137 Ec 61
Oncocua ○ **ANG** 340 Gn 54
Onda ○ **E** 184 Gf 26
Ondangwa ○ **NAM** 340 Ha 54
Ondas ∼ **BR** 133 Em 52
Ondaw ○ **MYA** 254 Km 34
Onderombapa ○ **NAM** 348 Hb 57
Ondjiva ○ **ANG** 340 Gp 54
Ondo ○ **WAN** 320 Gj 42
Ondobe ○ **NAM** 340 Ha 54
Ondores ○ **PE** 116 Dk 51
Öndörhaan ○ **MNG** 204 Vb 9
Ondozero ○ **RUS** 159 Hj 14
Ondozero ∼ **RUS** 159 Hj 14
Oneata ⌂ **FJI** 390 Aa 55
Onega ∼ **RUS** 159 Hl 14
Onega ○ **RUS** 159 Hm 14
Onega Bay ∼ **RUS** 159 Hk 13
Önege ○ **KZ** 181 Jb 21
Oneida ○ **USA** 60 Dl 24
Oneida ○ **USA** 71 Df 27
Oneida Lake ∼ **USA** 60 Dk 24
O'Neill ○ **USA** 56 Cn 24
Onema ○ **RDC** 333 He 48
Onema-Okolo ○ **RDC** 333 Hd 47
Onema Ututu ○ **RDC** 333 Hd 47
Oneonta ○ **USA** 60 Dl 24
Oneonta ○ **USA** 71 De 28
Oneşti ○ **RO** 175 Hf 22
Onezhskiy Poluostrov ⌂ **RUS** 154 Qb 6
Onezskij p-ov. ⌓ **RUS** 159 Hl 13
Onga ○ **G** 332 Gp 46
Ongeri ○ **RDC** 333 He 48
Ongersrivier ∼ **ZA** 349 Hd 61
Ongjin ○ **DVRK** 247 Ln 27
Ongka ○ **RI** 275 Ll 45
Ongkharak ○ **THA** 262 La 38
Ongoka ○ **RDC** 333 He 46
Ongole ○ **IND** 238 Ke 38
Ongon ○ **PE** 116 Dk 50
Ongongoro ○ **NAM** 348 Hb 56
Onhne ○ **MYA** 262 Kn 37
Oni ○ **GE** 202 Hp 24
Onibe ∼ **RM** 345 Jc 54
Onida ○ **USA** 56 Cm 23
Onie ú Olin ∼ **RA** 152 Dn 69
Onilahy ∼ **RM** 353 Ja 57
Onin Peninsula Fakfak ⌂ **RI** 283 Mb 47
Onitsha ○ **WAN** 320 Gk 42
Onive ∼ **RM** 345 Jb 55
Onkivesi ⌒ **FIN** 159 Hf 14
Ōno ○ **J** 251 Me 28
Ono ⌂ **FJI** 387 Nm 55
Onoilau ⌂ **FJI** 390 Aa 56
Onoko ○ **TCH** 321 Gp 40
Onomichi ○ **J** 251 Mc 28
Onon ∼ **RUS** 204 Vb 8
Onoto ○ **YV** 112 Eb 41
Onseepkans ○ **ZA** 348 Hb 60
Onslow ○ **AUS** 360 Lh 56
Onslow Bay ∼ **USA** 74 Dk 28
Ontake-san △ **J** 251 Me 28
Ontar ○ **VU** 386 Nf 53
Ontario ⊙ **CDN** 43 Fc 8
Ontario ○ **USA** 50 Cd 23
Ontario ⊙ **CDN** 56 Dc 21
Ontario ○ **USA** 64 Cd 29
Ontario Peninsula ⌓ **CDN** 57 Dh 24
Ontmoeting ○ **ZA** 348 Hc 59
Ontonagon ○ **USA** 57 Dd 22
Onverwacht ○ **SME** 113 Eg 43
Onwul River ∼ **WAN** 320 Gl 42
Onyx Cave ★ **USA** 70 Db 27
Oobagooma ○ **AUS** 360 Ln 54
Oodnadatta ○ **AUS** 374 Md 59
Oodweyne ○ **SP** 328 Ja 41
Ooldea Range ⛰ **AUS** 369 Mb 61
Oolloo ○ **AUS** 364 Mb 52
Oologah Lake ∼ **USA** 70 Da 27
Ooratippra ○ **AUS** 374 Me 56
Oorindi ○ **AUS** 374 Mg 56
Oostermoed ○ **ZA** 349 Hf 58
Opaka ○ **BG** 194 Hf 24
Opala ○ **RUS** 23 Sb 4
Opala ○ **RDC** 333 He 46
Opang ○ **RI** 283 Lp 46
Opari ○ **SUD** 324 Hj 44
Opasatika ○ **CDN** 57 Dg 21
Opasatika Lake ∼ **CDN** 57 Dg 21
Opatija ○ **HR** 174 Gp 23
Opatów ○ **PL** 174 Hc 20
Opava ○ **CZ** 174 Ha 21
Opelika ○ **USA** 86 Df 29
Opelousas ○ **USA** 86 Db 30
Open Bay ○ **PNG** 287 Mm 48
Open Bay ∼ **PNG** 287 Mm 48
Opeongo Lake ∼ **CDN** 60 Dj 23
Opheim ○ **USA** 51 Cj 21
Ophir ○ **USA** 46 Al 13
Ophthalmia Range ⛰ **AUS** 360 Lk 57
Opienge ○ **RDC** 324 Hf 45
Opikeigen Lake ∼ **CDN** 57 Dd 20
Opillja ⛰ **UA** 175 He 21
Opišn'a ○ **UA** 175 Hk 21
Opobo ○ **WAN** 320 Gk 43
Opočka ○ **RUS** 171 Hg 17
Opole ○ **PL** 174 Ha 20
Oponono Lake ∼ **NAM** 340 Gp 55
Opon Valley ○ **GH** 317 Gf 43
Opopeo ○ **MEX** 92 Cm 36
Opotiki ○ **NZ** 383 Nl 65
Opp ○ **USA** 86 De 30
Oppdal ○ **N** 158 Gl 14
Opportunity ○ **USA** 50 Cd 22
Optatija ○ **HR** 185 Gn 23
Optima Lake ∼ **USA** 70 Cm 27
Opunake ○ **NZ** 383 Nj 65
Opuwo ○ **NAM** 340 Gn 55
Ora ∼ **VU** 386 Nf 53
Oraba ○ **EAU** 324 Hh 44
Oracle ○ **USA** 65 Cg 29
Oradea ○ **RO** 174 Hd 22
Öræfajökull △ **IS** 158 Fm 13
Orah ○ **WAN** 320 Gj 42
Orai ○ **IND** 234 Kd 33
Oral ○ **KZ** 19 Mb 4
Oral ○ **KZ** 155 Rb 8
Oral ∼ **KZ** 155 Rb 9
Oral ∼ **KZ** 181 Jd 21
Oran ○ **DZ** 293 Gf 28
Oranapai ○ **GUY** 112 Ee 42
Orange ○ **USA** 74 Dj 26
Orange ○ **USA** 86 Db 30
Orange ○ **F** 185 Gj 23
Orange ∼ **ZA** 348 Ha 60
Orange ∼ **NAM** 348 Hb 60
Orange ∼ **ZA** 349 Hd 60
Orange ∼ **LS** 349 Hg 60
Orange ○ **AUS** 379 Ml 62
Orangeburg ○ **USA** 71 Dh 29
Orange Creek ○ **AUS** 369 Mc 58
Orange Park ○ **USA** 87 Dh 30
Orangerie Bay ∼ **PNG** 287 Ml 51
Orangeville ○ **CDN** 57 Dh 24
Orange Walk ○ **BH** 93 Dd 36
Orangi ∼ **EAT** 337 Hk 47
Orania ○ **ZA** 349 He 60
Oranienburg ○ **D** 170 Gn 19
Oranjefontein ○ **ZA** 349 Hf 57
Oranje Mountains ⛰ **SME** 113 Eg 44
Oranjemund ○ **NAM** 348 Ha 60
Oranjestad ○ **NL** 104 Ec 37
Oranjestad ○ **NL** 107 Dn 39
Oranjeville ○ **ZA** 349 Hg 59
Oransbari ○ **RI** 283 Md 46
Oranžeri ○ **RUS** 202 Jb 23
Orapa ○ **RB** 349 He 56
Oras ○ **RP** 267 Ln 39
Orattanādu ○ **IND** 239 Kd 40
Oravo Sur ∼ **CO** 107 Dn 43
Orbetello ○ **I** 185 Gm 24
Órbigo ∼ **E** 184 Gd 24
Orbost ○ **AUS** 379 Ml 64
Orcadas ○ **GB** 38 Gb 16
Orcopampa ○ **PE** 128 Dm 53
Orcutt ○ **USA** 64 Cb 28
Ord ○ **USA** 70 Cn 25
Ord ∼ **AUS** 364 Ma 54
Ordes ○ **E** 184 Gb 24
Ordoqui ○ **RA** 137 Ed 63
Ordos Mu us Shamo ⌓ **VRC** 243 Ld 26
Ord River ○ **AUS** 364 Ma 54
Ordu ○ **TR** 195 Hl 25
Ordway ○ **USA** 65 Cl 26
Ore ○ **WAN** 320 Gj 42
Örebro ○ **S** 170 Gp 16
Oredež ○ **RUS** 171 Hh 16
Oregon ⊙ **USA** 50 Ca 24
Oregon ○ **USA** 70 Da 26
Oregon ○ **USA** 71 Dg 25
Oregon Caves ★ **USA** 50 Ca 24
Orehovo-Zuevo ○ **RUS** 171 Hm 18
Orel ○ **RUS** 181 Hl 19
Orel' ∼ **UA** 181 Hl 21
Orellana ○ **PE** 116 Dj 48
Orellana ○ **PE** 116 Dl 49
Orem ○ **USA** 65 Cg 25
Ore Mountains ⛰ **D** 174 Gn 20
Ören ○ **TR** 195 Hg 27
Orenburg ○ **RUS** 19 Mb 4
Orenburg ○ **RUS** 155 Rb 8
Oreresan ○ **PNG** 287 Ml 50
Øresund ≈ 170 Gn 18
Orewa ○ **NZ** 383 Nk 64
Organabo ○ **F** 113 Eh 43
Organ Pipe Cactus National Mon. ♀ **USA** 64 Cf 29
Orgūn ○ **AFG** 223 Jn 29
Orhaneli ○ **TR** 195 Hg 26
Orhangazi ○ **TR** 195 Hg 25
Orhei ○ **MD** 175 Hg 22
Orhon gol ∼ **MNG** 204 Uc 9
Orialen ○ **RG** 316 Gb 40
Orica ○ **HN** 96 De 38
Orichiv ○ **UA** 175 Hk 22
Orick ○ **USA** 64 Bp 25
Orida ○ **RN** 296 Gn 35
Ørie ○ **N** 170 Gm 16
Orient ○ **USA** 50 Cc 21
Oriente ○ **RA** 146 Ed 65
Orihuela ○ **E** 184 Gf 26
Orillia ○ **CDN** 60 Dj 23
Orin ○ **USA** 51 Ck 24
Orinduik ○ **BR** 112 Ed 43
Orinoca ○ **BOL** 129 Ea 55
Orinoco ∼ **CO** 107 Ea 43
Orinoco ∼ **YV** 107 Ea 44
Orinoco ∼ **YV** 112 Eb 42
Orinoco ∼ **YV** 112 Eb 44
Orinoco ∼ **YV** 112 Ec 41
Orinoco Delta ⌓ **YV** 112 Ec 41
Oriomo ○ **PNG** 286 Mh 50
Oriomo Plateau ⛰ **PNG** 286 Mg 50
Orisaare ○ **EST** 171 Hd 16
Orissa ⊙ **IND** 235 Kg 35
Orissa Coast Canal ∼ **IND** 235 Kh 35
Oristano ○ **I** 185 Gl 26
Orito ○ **CO** 116 Dk 45
Orituco ∼ **YV** 107 Ea 41
Orivesi ○ **FIN** 159 He 15
Oriximiná ○ **BR** 120 Eg 46
Orizaba ○ **MEX** 92 Cp 35
Orizona ○ **BR** 133 Ek 54
Orjanovo ○ **BG** 194 He 24
Orkadiéré ○ **SN** 304 Fp 38
Orkanger ○ **N** 158 Gl 14
Örkelljunga ○ **S** 170 Gn 17
Orkla ∼ **N** 158 Gl 14
Orkney ○ **ZA** 349 Hf 59
Orkney Islands ⌂ **GB** 162 Ge 16
Orla ○ **USA** 81 Cl 30
Orlameš ○ **AFG** 223 Jm 27
Orland ○ **USA** 64 Ca 26
Orlândia ○ **BR** 141 El 56
Orlando ○ **USA** 87 Dh 31
Orleanais ⌓ **F** 163 Gg 22
Orleãns ○ **BR** 140 Ek 60
Orléans ○ **F** 163 Gg 22
Orleans Farm ○ **AUS** 368 Lm 62
Orlik ○ **RUS** 204 Ub 8
Örlögstaden ★ **S** 170 Gp 16
Orlov Gaj ○ **RUS** 181 Jb 20
Orlovskij ○ **RUS** 181 Hp 22
Orlovskij zaliv ∼ **RUS** 159 Hn 12
Orlu ○ **WAN** 320 Gk 43
Orman Reef ⌂ **AUS** 286 Mh 50
Ormāra ○ **PK** 227 Jl 33
Ormiston Gorge ♀ **AUS** 361 Mc 57
Ormoc ○ **RP** 267 Ln 40
Ormond Beach ○ **USA** 87 Dh 31
Ormtjern ♀ **N** 158 Gl 15
Orne ∼ **F** 163 Gf 21
Ørnes ○ **N** 158 Gn 12
Örnsköldsvik ○ **S** 158 Ha 14
Oro ∼ **RA** 140 Ee 59
Orocó ○ **BR** 124 Fa 50
Orocue ○ **CO** 107 Dn 43
Orodara ○ **BF** 317 Gd 40
Orodel ○ **RO** 194 Hd 23
Orofino ○ **USA** 50 Cd 22
Orogrande ○ **USA** 65 Cj 29
Orom ○ **EAU** 325 Hj 44
Oromocto ○ **CDN** 61 Ea 23
Oron ○ **WAN** 320 Gl 43
Orondo ○ **USA** 50 Cb 22
Oroners ○ **AUS** 365 Mh 53
Orono ○ **USA** 60 Dp 23
Oronoque ○ **GUY** 113 Ef 44
Oronoque ∼ **GUY** 113 Ef 45
Orope ○ **YV** 107 Dm 41
Oropesa ○ **E** 184 Gd 26
Oroquieta ○ **RP** 267 Lm 41
Orós ○ **BR** 124 Fa 49
Orosháza ○ **H** 174 Hc 22
Orosmayo ∼ **PY** 136 Ea 57
Orotina ○ **CR** 97 Df 41
Orotukan ○ **RUS** 23 Sb 3
Orotukan ○ **RUS** 205 Ya 6
Oro Valley ○ **USA** 65 Cg 29
Oroville ○ **USA** 50 Cc 21
Oroville ○ **USA** 64 Cb 26
Oroville Reservoir ∼ **USA** 64 Cb 26
Oroviţa ○ **RO** 174 Hc 23
Orr ○ **USA** 56 Db 21
Orreaga ○ **E** 184 Gf 24
Orroroo ○ **AUS** 378 Mf 62
Orsa ○ **S** 158 Gp 15
Orsha ○ **BY** 171 Hh 18
Orsk ○ **RUS** 19 Mb 4
Orsk ○ **RUS** 155 Rc 8
Orşova ○ **SCG** 194 Hd 23
Ørsta ○ **N** 158 Gj 14
Ortaca ○ **TR** 195 Hg 27
Ortaköy ○ **TR** 195 Hk 26
Orte ○ **I** 185 Gn 24
Ortega ○ **CO** 106 Dl 44
Orteguaza ∼ **CO** 116 Dl 45
Orthez ○ **F** 184 Gf 24
Ortho ∼ **BOL** 129 Ea 51
Ortigueira ○ **BR** 140 Ej 58
Ortigueira ○ **E** 184 Gb 24
Ortiz ○ **MEX** 80 Cg 31
Ortiz ○ **YV** 107 Ea 41
Ortler △ **I** 174 Gm 22
Ortona ○ **I** 194 Gp 24
Ortonville ○ **USA** 56 Cp 23
Oru ○ **CO** 107 Dm 41
Orūmīyeh ○ **IR** 209 Ja 27
Orupembe ○ **NAM** 340 Gn 55
Oruro ○ **BOL** 129 Ea 54
Orust ⌂ **S** 170 Gm 16
Orūzgān ○ **AFG** 223 Jm 29
Orūzgān ⊙ **AFG** 223 Jm 29
Orvieto ○ **I** 185 Gn 24
Orwell ○ **USA** 71 Dh 25
Orzūīye ○ **IR** 226 Jg 31
Oržycja ∼ **UA** 175 Hj 21
Orzysz ○ **PL** 170 Hc 19
Oš ○ **UZB** 22 Nb 5
Oš ○ **KS** 230 Ka 25
Osa ○ **RUS** 154 Rc 7
Osage ○ **USA** 56 Db 24
Osage ∼ **USA** 70 Da 26
Osage Indian Reservation ••• **USA** 70 Cp 27
Ōsaka ○ **J** 251 Md 28
Osamba ○ **NAM** 348 Hb 57
Osa Peninsula ⌂ **CR** 97 Df 41
Osasco ○ **BR** 141 El 57
Osborne ○ **USA** 70 Cn 26
Osby ○ **S** 170 Gn 17
Osca ∼ **BOL** 129 Eb 54
Oscar II land ⌂ **N** 158 Gn 6
Oscar Soto Máynes ○ **MEX** 80 Cj 31
Osceola ○ **USA** 70 Cp 25
Osceola ○ **USA** 70 Db 25
Osceola ○ **USA** 71 Dd 28
Óschiri ○ **I** 185 Gl 25
Oscoda ○ **USA** 57 Dg 23
Oscuro ○ **USA** 65 Cj 29
Oshakati ○ **NAM** 340 Gp 54
Oshamambe ○ **J** 250 Mf 24
Oshawa ○ **CDN** 60 Dj 24
Oshikango ○ **NAM** 340 Gp 54
Oshikuku ○ **NAM** 340 Gp 54
Ōshima ○ **J** 251 Mf 28
Ōshima ⌂ **J** 251 Mf 28
Ō-shima ⌂ **J** 250 Mf 25
Oshima-hantō ⛰ **J** 250 Mg 24
Oshivelo ○ **NAM** 340 Ha 55
Oshkosh ○ **USA** 57 Dd 24
Oshkosh ○ **USA** 65 Cl 25
Oshogbo ○ **WAN** 320 Gj 42
Oshwe ○ **RDC** 333 Hb 47
Osiān ○ **IND** 227 Ka 32
Osijek ○ **HR** 174 Hb 23
Osima ○ **PNG** 286 Mg 47
Osinniki ○ **RUS** 204 Tc 8
Oskaloosa ○ **USA** 70 Db 25
Oskarshamn ○ **S** 170 Ha 17
Oskélanéo ○ **CDN** 60 Dl 21
Öskemen ○ **KZ** 204 Tb 9
Os'kino ○ **RUS** 181 Hm 20
Oskū ○ **IR** 209 Jb 27
Oslo ▣ **N** 158 Gm 15
Oslofjorden ∼ **N** 170 Gm 16
Osmānābād ○ **IND** 238 Kc 36
Osmancık ○ **TR** 195 Hk 25
Osmaneli ○ **TR** 195 Hh 25
Osmaniye ○ **TR** 195 Hl 27
Os'mino ○ **RUS** 171 Hg 15
Osmond Beach ○ **USA** 87 Dh 31
Osnabrück ○ **D** 170 Gl 19
Osnaburgh House ○ **CDN** 56 Dc 20
Oso ∼ **RDC** 336 Hf 46
Osório ○ **BR** 146 Ej 60
Osório da Fonseca ○ **BR** 120 Ee 47
Osorno ○ **RCH** 147 Dm 66
Osorno ○ **E** 184 Gd 24
Ososo ○ **WAN** 320 Gk 42
Osoyoos ○ **CDN** 50 Cc 21
Osoyoos Indian Reservation ••• **CDN** 50 Cc 21
Osøyra ○ **N** 158 Gj 15
Osprey Reef ⌂ **AUS** 365 Mk 52
Ossabaw Island ⌂ **USA** 87 Dh 30
Ossélé ○ **RCB** 332 Gp 46
Osso ○ **RDC** 336 Hf 46
Ossora ○ **RUS** 23 Ta 4
Ošta ○ **RUS** 171 Hk 15
Ostaškov ○ **RUS** 171 Hj 17
Östavall ○ **S** 158 Gp 14
Oste ∼ **D** 170 Gl 19
Ostend ○ **B** 163 Gh 20
Oster ∼ **RUS** 171 Hj 19
Österbotten ⌓ **FIN** 159 Hd 14
Österbybruk ○ **S** 158 Ha 15
Osterdalen ⌓ **N** 158 Gm 15
Östergötland ⌓ **S** 170 Gp 16
Östersjön ∼ **S** 170 Ha 16
Östersund ○ **S** 158 Gp 14
Östhammar ○ **S** 170 Hb 15
Ostiglia ○ **I** 185 Gm 23
Oštorīnān ○ **IR** 209 Jc 28
Ostraja △ **RUS** 250 Mc 23
Ostrava ○ **CZ** 174 Ha 21
Ostróda ○ **PL** 170 Hb 19
Ostrogožsk ○ **RUS** 181 Hm 20
Ostrohz ○ **UA** 175 Hf 20
Ostrołęka ○ **PL** 170 Hc 19
Ostrov ○ **RUS** 159 Hl 15
Ostrov ○ **RUS** 171 Hg 17
Ostrova Arkticheskogo Instituta ⌂ **RUS** 22 Pa 2
ostrova Arkticheskogo Instituta ⌂ **RUS** 204 Ta 3
ostrova Černye Brat'ja ⌂ **RUS** 205 Xc 9
ostrova de-Longa ⌂ **RUS** 205 Xc 3
ostrova Izvestij CIK ⌂ **RUS** 204 Tb 3
ostrov Ajon ⌂ **RUS** 23 Ta 3
ostrov Ajon ⌂ **RUS** 205 Za 5
ostrova Komsomol'skoj Pravdy ⌂ **RUS** 204 Va 3
ostrov Anzerskij ⌂ **RUS** 159 Hl 13
ostrova Petra ⌂ **RUS** 204 Vb 3
ostrov Arakamčečen ⌂ **RUS** 46 Ac 13
ostrova Sergeja Kirova ⌂ **RUS** 204 Tc 3
ostrov Atlasova ⌂ **RUS** 205 Ya 8
ostrova Žochova ⌂ **RUS** 23 Sb 2
ostrov Bel'kovskij ⌂ **RUS** 205 Wc 3
ostrov Belyj ⌂ **RUS** 204 Sb 4
ostrov Belyy ⌂ **RUS** 22 Nb 2
ostrov Bennett ⌂ **RUS** 22 Sa 2
ostrov Bennetta ⌂ **RUS** 205 Xc 3
ostrov Beringa ⌂ **RUS** 205 Za 7
ostrov Bol. Begičév ⌂ **RUS** 22 Qb 2
ostrov Bol. Begičev ⌂ **RUS** 204 Vb 4
ostrov Bol. Ljachovskij ⌂ **RUS** 22 Sa 2
ostrov Bol. Ljahovskij ⌂ **RUS** 205 Xb 4
ostrov Bol. Šantar ⌂ **RUS** 205 Xa 8
ostrov Bol.šoj. Setnoj ⌂ **RUS** 202 Jc 23
ostrov Bol.Zjudostinskij ⌂ **RUS** 202 Jc 23
ostrov Bol'ševik ⌂ **RUS** 204 Uc 3
ostrov Bol'shevik ⌂ **RUS** 22 Qa 2
ostrov Čečen ⌂ **RUS** 202 Jb 23
ostrov Faddeevskij ⌂ **RUS** 205 Xb 3
ostrov Genrietty ⌂ **RUS** 205 Yb 3
ostrov Gogland ⌂ **RUS** 171 Hf 15
ostrov Graham Bell ⌂ **RUS** 19 Na 1
ostrov Hall ⌂ **RUS** 19 Mb 1
ostrov Iturup ⌂ **RUS** 205 Xc 10
ostrov Iturup Etorofu ⌂ **RUS** 250 Mk 23
ostrov Jackson ⌂ **RUS** 19 Mb 1
ostrov Karaginskiy ⌂ **RUS** 23 Ta 4
ostrov Karaginskiy ⌂ **RUS** 205 Yc 7
ostrov Karl Alexander ⌂ **RUS** 19 Mb 1
ostrov Ketoj ⌂ **RUS** 205 Ya 9
ostrov Kil'din ⌂ **RUS** 159 Hk 11
ostrov Kolgujev ○ **RUS** 19 Ma 3
ostrov Kolguyev ⌂ **RUS** 154 Ra 5
ostrov Komsomolec ⌂ **RUS** 22 Pb 1
ostrov Kotel'nyi ⌂ **RUS** 205 Xa 3
ostrov Kunašir ⌂ **RUS** 205 Xc 10
ostrov Kunašir Kunashiri ⌂ **RUS** 250 Mk 23
ostrov Mal. Ljahovskij ⌂ **RUS** 205 Xb 4
ostrov Maly Ljachovskij ⌂ **RUS** 22 Rb 2
ostrov Maly Taymyr ⌂ **RUS** 22 Qa 2
ostrov Malyy Taymyr ⌂ **RUS** 204 Va 3
ostrov Mc Clintock ⌂ **RUS** 19 Mb 1
ostrov Mednyi ⌂ **RUS** 205 Za 8
ostrov Moneron ⌂ **RUS** 205 Xa 9
ostrov Moneron ⌂ **RUS** 250 Mg 22
ostrov Moristyj ∼ **RUS** 202 Jb 23
ostrov Morskoj Birjučok ∼ **RUS** 202 Jb 23
ostrov Moržovec ⌂ **RUS** 159 Hn 12
ostrov Ogurčinskij ⌒ **TM** 222 Je 26
ostrov Oktjabr'skoj Reveljucii ⌂ **RUS** 204 Ub 3
ostrov Oktjabrskoj Revoljucii ⌂ **RUS** 22 Pb 2
ostrov Olenij ⌂ **RUS** 22 Nb 2
ostrov Olenij ⌂ **RUS** 159 Hk 13
ostrov Olenij ⌂ **RUS** 204 Ta 4
ostrov Onekotan ⌂ **RUS** 23 Sb 5
ostrov Onekotan ⌂ **RUS** 205 Ya 9
ostrov Paddejevskij ⌂ **RUS** 22 Sa 2
ostrov Paramušil ⌂ **RUS** 23 Sb 4
ostrov Paramušir ⌂ **RUS** 205 Ya 8
ostrov Pežostrov ⌂ **RUS** 159 Hj 12
ostrov Rudolf ⌂ **RUS** 19 Mb 1
ostrov Russkij ⌂ **RUS** 22 Pb 2
ostrov Russkij ⌂ **RUS** 204 Ua 3
ostrov Salisbury ⌂ **RUS** 19 Mb 1
ostrov Šiaškotan ⌂ **RUS** 23 Sb 5
ostrov Šiaškotan ⌂ **RUS** 205 Ya 9
ostrov Sibirjakova ⌂ **RUS** 204 Ta 4
ostrov Sibirjakovo ⌂ **RUS** 22 Nb 2
ostrov Sigovec ⌂ **RUS** 159 Hk 14
ostrov Sikotan Shikotan ⌂ **RUS** 250 Mk 24
ostrov Simušir ⌂ **RUS** 23 Sb 5
ostrov Simušir ⌂ **RUS** 205 Ya 9
Ostrovskoe ○ **RUS** 171 Hn 17
ostrov Šmidta ⌂ **RUS** 22 Pa 1
ostrov Šokal'skogo ⌂ **RUS** 204 Sc 4
ostrov Sosnovec ⌂ **RUS** 159 Hn 12
ostrov Stolbovoj ⌂ **RUS** 205 Wc 4
ostrov Šumšu ⌂ **RUS** 205 Yb 8
ostrov Svedtrup ⌂ **RUS** 22 Pa 2
ostrov Sverdrup ⌂ **RUS** 204 Ta 4
ostrov Tjulenij ∼ **RUS** 202 Jb 23
ostrov Urup ⌂ **RUS** 205 Xc 9
ostrov Ušakova ⌂ **RUS** 22 Pa 1
ostrov Valaan ⌂ **RUS** 171 Hh 15
ostrov Vaygach ⌂ **RUS** 154 Rc 4
ostrov Velikij ⌂ **RUS** 159 Hj 12
ostrov Vil'kickogo ⌂ **RUS** 22 Nb 2
ostrov Vil'kickogo ⌂ **RUS** 204 Sc 4
ostrov Vize ⌂ **RUS** 22 Nb 2
ostrov Yttygran ⌂ **RUS** 46 Ac 13
ostrov Žannetty ⌂ **RUS** 205 Yb 3
ostrov Zelenyj Habomai ⌂ **RUS** 250 Mk 24
ostrov Zjudev ⌂ **RUS** 202 Jc 23
ostrov Žohova ⌂ **RUS** 205 Ya 3
Ostrowiec Świętokrzyski ○ **PL** 174 Hc 20
Ostrów Maz. ○ **PL** 170 Hc 19
Ostrów Wlkp. ○ **PL** 174 Ha 20
Osttirol ⌓ **A** 174 Gn 22
O'Sullivan Lake ∼ **CDN** 57 De 20
Ōsumi-hantō ⌂ **J** 247 Mb 30
Ōsumi-kaikyō ∼ **J** 247 Mb 30
Ōsumi-shotō ⌂ **J** 247 Mb 30
Osuna ○ **E** 184 Gd 27
Osurovo ○ **RUS** 171 Hm 17
Oswego ○ **USA** 60 Dk 24
Oswego ○ **USA** 70 Da 27
Oświęcim ○ **PL** 174 Hb 21
Ōta ○ **J** 251 Mc 28
Otacilio Costa ○ **BR** 140 Ej 59
Otago Peninsula ⌂ **NZ** 382 Nh 68
Otaki ○ **NZ** 383 Nk 66
Otakw ∼ **RI** 286 Me 48
Otakwa ○ **RI** 286 Me 48
Otampes ○ **F** 163 Gh 21
Otaru ○ **J** 250 Mg 24
Otavalo ○ **EC** 116 Dj 45
Otavi ○ **NAM** 340 Ha 55
Otawa ○ **USA** 71 Dd 25
Otchinjau ○ **ANG** 340 Gn 54
Oterkpolu ○ **GH** 317 Gf 42
Oteros ∼ **MEX** 80 Ch 32
O'The Cherokees ∼ **USA** 70 Da 27
Othello ○ **USA** 50 Cc 22
Oti ○ **RI** 279 Lk 46
Oti ∼ **BF** 317 Gg 40
Otjahevita ○ **NAM** 348 Ha 56
Otjikondo ○ **NAM** 340 Gp 55
Otjimbingwe ○ **NAM** 348 Gp 57
Otjinene ○ **NAM** 348 Hb 56
Otjinhungwa ○ **NAM** 340 Gn 54
Otjisemba ○ **NAM** 348 Ha 56
Otjitambi ○ **NAM** 340 Gp 55
Otjitanda ○ **NAM** 340 Gn 54
Otjituuo ○ **NAM** 340 Hb 55
Otjiu ○ **NAM** 340 Gn 55
Otjiwarongo ○ **NAM** 348 Ha 56
Otjomatemba ○ **NAM** 340 Gn 55
Otjondeka ○ **NAM** 340 Gp 55
Otjosundu ○ **NAM** 348 Ha 56
Otjozondjou ∼ **NAM** 348 Hb 56
Otoca ○ **PE** 128 Dl 53
Otog Qi ○ **VRC** 243 Ld 26
Otog Qian Qi ○ **VRC** 243 Ld 26
Otoineppu ○ **J** 250 Mg 23
Otok ⌂ **HR** 174 Gp 23
Otola ○ **DY** 317 Gg 41
Otomi ○ **J** 259 Lm 33
Otong Java Islands ⌂ **SOL** 290 Nb 48
Otorohanga ○ **NZ** 383 Nk 65
Otoskwin River ∼ **CDN** 57 Dd 20
Otosquen ○ **CDN** 56 Cm 19
Otoyo ○ **J** 251 Mc 29
Otra ∼ **N** 170 Gk 16
Otradnaja ○ **RUS** 202 Hn 23
Otradnyj ○ **RUS** 181 Jd 19
Otranto ○ **I** 194 Hb 25
Otse ○ **RB** 349 He 59
Otselic ○ **USA** 60 Dk 24
Ōtsu ○ **J** 251 Md 28
Ōtsuki ○ **J** 251 Mf 28
Otta ○ **N** 158 Gl 15
Otta ∼ **N** 158 Gl 15
Ottapidāram ○ **IND** 239 Kd 41
Ottawa ∼ **CDN** 60 Dj 22
Ottawa ▣ **CDN** 60 Dl 23
Ottawa ○ **USA** 70 Da 26
Ottawa ○ **USA** 71 Df 25
Ottawa Islands ⌂ **CDN** 7 Eb 4
Ottawa Islands ⌂ **CDN** 43 Gb 7
Ottawa River ∼ **CDN** 60 Dj 22
Ottenby ○ **S** 170 Ha 17
Otter ○ **USA** 51 Cj 23
Otter ○ **CDN** 61 Ec 21
Otter Creek ○ **USA** 86 Dg 31
Ottosdal ○ **ZA** 349 He 59
Ottumwa ○ **USA** 70 Db 25
Otu ○ **CAM** 320 Gl 43
Otukamamoan Lake ∼ **CDN** 56 Db 21
Otukpa ○ **WAN** 320 Gk 42
Otumpa ○ **RA** 136 Ec 59
Otuquis ∼ **BR** 132 Ee 55
Oturkpo ○ **WAN** 320 Gl 42
Otu Tolu Group ⌂ **TO** 390 Ac 56
Otuzco ○ **PE** 116 Dj 49
Otway ♀ **AUS** 379 Mh 65
Otway Range ⛰ **AUS** 378 Mh 65
Oua ∼ **G** 332 Gn 45
Ouachita ∼ **USA** 70 Da 28
Ouachita Mountains ⛰ **USA** 70 Da 28
Ouaco ○ **F** 386 Ne 56
Ouadâne ○ **RIM** 304 Ga 35
Ouadda ○ **RCA** 321 Hd 41
Ouadi Achim ∼ **TCH** 309 Hb 38
Ouadi Enné ∼ **TCH** 309 Hb 38
Ouadi Fama ∼ **TCH** 309 Hc 38
Ouadi Haddad ∼ **TCH** 309 Hb 38
Ouadi Haouach ∼ **TCH** 309 Hc 37
Ouadi Ouagat ∼ **TCH** 309 Hc 38
Ouadi Rimé ∼ **TCH** 309 Hb 39
Ouad Nâga ○ **RIM** 304 Fn 36
Ouadou ∼ **RIM** 304 Ga 38
Ouagadougou ▣ **BF** 317 Gf 39
Ouahabou ○ **BF** 317 Ge 40
Ouahigouya ○ **BF** 317 Ge 39
Ouaka ∼ **RCA** 321 Hc 42
Ouaka ∼ **RCA** 321 Hc 43
Ouaklé ○ **DY** 317 Gg 41
Oualâta ○ **RIM** 305 Gc 37
Oualia ○ **RMM** 316 Ga 39
Ouallam ○ **RN** 305 Gh 38
Ouallen ○ **DZ** 293 Gg 33
Ouana Wagny ∼ **G** 332 Gn 46
Ouanary ○ **F** 113 Ej 43
Ouanda Djallé ○ **RCA** 321 Hd 41
Ouandago ○ **RCA** 321 Hb 42
Ouandja ○ **RCA** 321 Hd 41
Ouandja ∼ **RCA** 321 Hd 41
Ouando ○ **RCA** 324 He 42
Ouango ○ **RCA** 321 Hd 43
Ouangolodougou ○ **CI** 317 Gd 41
Ouaninou ○ **CI** 316 Gb 41
Ouanzerbé ○ **RN** 305 Gg 38
Ouara ∼ **RCA** 324 Hf 42
Ouareau ∼ **CDN** 60 Dl 22
Ouargaye ○ **BF** 317 Gg 40
Ouaritoufoulout ○ **RMM** 308 Gh 37
Ouarkla ○ **CAM** 321 Gp 41
Ouarkoye ○ **BF** 317 Ge 39
Ouartu S. Elena ○ **I** 185 Gl 26
Ouarzazate ○ **MA** 293 Gc 30
Ouassa Bamvélé ○ **CAM** 320 Gn 43
Ouatagouna ○ **RMM** 305 Gg 38
Ouatcha ○ **RN** 320 Gl 39
Ouatéré Galafondo ○ **RCA** 321 Hb 43
Oubangui ∼ **RCA** 321 Hb 43
Oudtshoom ○ **ZA** 358 Hc 62
Ouê'a ○ **DJI** 328 Hp 40
Oued Aguemour ∼ **DZ** 296 Gj 32
Oued Amadror ∼ **DZ** 296 Gk 33
Oued Assaq ∼ **MA** 292 Fn 33
Oued Barika ∼ **DZ** 296 Gj 28
Oued Besbes ∼ **DZ** 296 Gj 28
Oued Bou Ali ∼ **DZ** 296 Gh 30
Oued Chebaba ∼ **DZ** 296 Gh 31
Oued Chlef ∼ **DZ** 293 Gg 27
Oued Daoura ∼ **DZ** 293 Gd 30
Oued Djedi ∼ **DZ** 296 Gh 28
Oued Drâa ∼ **MA** 292 Gb 31
Oued Drâa ∼ **MA** 293 Gc 30
Oued el Abiod ○ **RIM** 304 Fp 37
Oued el Arab ∼ **DZ** 296 Gk 28
Oued el Attar ∼ **DZ** 296 Gj 29
Oued el Fahl ∼ **DZ** 296 Gh 30
Oued El Gharbi ∼ **DZ** 293 Gg 29
Oued el Hadjadj ∼ **DZ** 296 Gj 31
Oued el Hallaïl ∼ **DZ** 296 Gk 28
Oued el Ham ∼ **DZ** 296 Gh 28
Oued el-Hamra ∼ **RIM** 292 Gb 32
Oued El Kebir ∼ **TN** 296 Gl 28
Oued el Khatt ∼ **MA** 292 Fp 33
Oued el Korima ∼ **DZ** 293 Gf 29
Oued el Ma ∼ **RIM** 292 Gb 33
Oued en Nsa ∼ **DZ** 296 Gh 29
Oued es Seggeur ∼ **DZ** 293 Gg 29
Oued Fessi ∼ **TN** 297 Gm 29
Oued Garfa ∼ **RIM** 304 Fp 38
Oued Grou ∼ **MA** 293 Gc 29
Oued Guélaour ∼ **RIM** 304 Fp 37
Oued Guir ∼ **DZ** 293 Ge 30
Oued Ilafergh ∼ **DZ** 305 Gg 35
Oued in Sokki ∼ **DZ** 296 Gh 31
Oued Irharhar ∼ **DZ** 296 Gj 32
Oued Isly ∼ **MA** 293 Gf 28
Oued Ittel ∼ **DZ** 296 Gj 28
Oued Jenein ∼ **TN** 296 Gl 30
Oued Khârroûb ∼ **RIM** 304 Gb 34
Oued Laouni ∼ **DZ** 308 Gj 35
Oued l-Asyūṭī ∼ **ET** 301 Hh 32
Oued Massine ∼ **DZ** 296 Gh 32
Oued Mehaïguene ∼ **DZ** 296 Gh 29
Oued Meirir ∼ **DZ** 293 Gf 28
Oued Mejerda ∼ **TN** 296 Gl 27
Oued Mellal ∼ **MA** 293 Gc 29

Omapere - Oued Mellal 453

Oued Mellegue ∾ **DZ** 296 Gl 27	Ouro Amat ○ **SN** 304 Fp 38	Ozark Plateau △ **USA** 70 Da 27	Pacitan ○ **RI** 278 Lf 50	Pajule ○ **EAU** 324 Hj 44
Oued Melloulou ∾ **MA** 293 Ge 29	Ouro Branco ○ **BR** 125 Ep 51	Ożarów ○ **PL** 174 Hc 20	Packsaddle ○ **AUS** 378 Mg 61	Pakan ○ **MAL** 271 Lf 45
Oued Meskiana ∾ **DZ** 296 Gk 28	Ourofane ○ **RN** 308 Gl 38	Özd ○ **H** 174 Hc 21	Packwood ○ **USA** 50 Cb 22	Pakashkan Lake ∾ **CDN** 56 Dc 21
Oued Messaoud ∾ **DZ** 293 Gf 31	Ouro Fino ○ **BR** 141 El 57	Ozerki ○ **RUS** 181 Jb 17	Paclenika ♀ **HR** 174 Gp 23	Pakawau ○ **NZ** 383 Nj 66
Oued Metlili ∾ **DZ** 296 Gh 31	Ouro Preto ∾ **BR** 129 Eb 51	ozero Bab'e ∾ **RUS** 159 Hm 12	Păc Ma ∾ **VN** 254 Lb 34	Pak Charang ○ **THA** 263 Lb 38
Oued Mial ∾ **DZ** 296 Gh 31	Ouro Prêto ○ **BR** 141 En 56	ozero Baskunčak ∾ **RUS** 181 Jb 21	Paco do Lumiar ∾ **BR** 121 Em 47	Pakenham ○ **AUS** 379 Mj 65
Oued Mina ∾ **DZ** 293 Gg 28	Ouro Preto d'Oeste ○ **BR** 129 Ec 51	ozero Beloe ∾ **RUS** 159 Hl 15	Pacorá ○ **BR** 97 Dj 41	Paki ○ **WAN** 320 Gl 40
Oued Mya ∾ **DZ** 296 Gj 30	Ouro Sogui ∾ **SN** 304 Fp 38	ozero Bol'šaya Saga ∾ **RUS** 181 Ja 22	Pacoti ○ **BR** 124 Fa 48	Pakima ○ **RDC** 333 He 47
Oued Namous ∾ **DZ** 296 Gh 28	Oursi ○ **BF** 305 Gf 38	ozero Botkul' ∾ **RUS** 181 Jb 21	Pacoval ○ **BR** 120 Eg 47	Pakistan □ **PK** 227 Jm 31
Oued Ouerrha ∾ **MA** 293 Gd 28	Ouse ∾ **GB** 163 Gf 19	ozero Bustah ∾ **RUS** 205 Xb 4	Pac Seng ○ **LAO** 255 Lb 35	Pak Kad ○ **THA** 255 Lb 36
Oued Oumer-Rbia ∾ **MA** 292 Gb 29	Oussoumbidiagna ○ **RMM** 304 Ga 38	ozero Čany ∾ **RUS** 204 Ta 8	Pacuí ○ **BR** 133 Em 54	Paklenica ♀ **HR** 174 Gp 23
Oued Ouret ○ **DZ** 296 Gl 33	Oussouye ○ **SN** 316 Fm 39	ozero Chaskakshor ∾ **TM** 223 Jl 27	Pad ∾ **MAL** 274 Lh 43	Pakokku ○ **MYA** 254 Km 35
Oued Retem ∾ **DZ** 296 Gj 29	Outamba-Kilimi N.P. ♀ **WAL** 316 Fp 41	ozero Činozero ∾ **RUS** 159 Hh 14	Padag ∾ **PK** 227 Jl 31	Pakovskij ○ **KZ** 155 Sa 8
Oued Rhiou ○ **DZ** 293 Gg 28	Outardes ∾ **CDN** 60 Dp 21	ozero Čudzjavr ∾ **RUS** 159 Hk 11	Padalere ○ **RI** 282 Lm 47	Pakowki Lake ∾ **CDN** 51 Cg 21
Oued Rhir ○ **DZ** 296 Gk 29	Outat-Oulad-el-Haj ∾ **MA** 293 Ge 29	ozero El'ton ∾ **RUS** 181 Jb 21	Padam ○ **IND** 230 Kc 29	Pakpattan ○ **PK** 230 Ka 30
Oued Rhumel ∾ **DZ** 296 Gk 27	Outeid Arkass ∾ **RMM** 305 Gd 37	ozero Hanka ∾ **RUS** 205 Wc 9	Padampur ○ **IND** 234 Kf 35	Pak Phanang ○ **THA** 262 La 41
Oued Saoura ∾ **DZ** 293 Gf 31	Outeiro Maior △ **P** 184 Gb 24	ozero Hanka ∾ **RUS** 250 Mc 23	Padang ○ **RI** 270 Kp 46	Pakri ○ **NEP** 234 Kf 32
Oued Sebou ∾ **MA** 293 Gc 28	Outeniequaberge △ **ZA** 358 Hc 62	ozero Il'men ∾ **RUS** 171 Hh 16	Padangpanjang ○ **RI** 270 Kp 45	Pak Tho ○ **THA** 262 Kp 39
Oued Sefioum ∾ **DZ** 293 Gf 28	Outer Hebrides △ **GB** 162 Gb 17	ozero Jalpuh ∾ **UA** 175 Hg 23	Padang Sidempuan ○ **RI** 270 Kp 45	Pak Thong Chai ○ **THA** 262 La 38
Oued Sidi Hasseur ∾ **DZ** 293 Gg 28	Outer Island △ **USA** 56 Dc 22	ozero Jangozero ∾ **RUS** 159 Hm 14	Padany ○ **RUS** 159 Hj 14	Paktikä ◎ **AFG** 223 Jn 29
Oued Siliana ∾ **TN** 296 Gl 27	Outes ○ **E** 184 Gb 24	ozero Jaroto ∾ **RUS** 154 Sc 5	Padauiri ∾ **BR** 112 Eb 45	Paktyä ◎ **AFG** 223 Jn 29
Oued Soummam ∾ **DZ** 296 Gj 27	Outjo ○ **NAM** 348 Gg 56	ozero Jaroto ∾ **RUS** 204 Sc 5	Padcaya ○ **BOL** 129 Eb 56	Pakuanratu ○ **RI** 278 Lc 47
Oued Sud ∾ **MA** 292 Gb 30	Outlook ○ **CDN** 51 Cj 20	ozero Jašil'kul ∾ **TJ** 230 Ka 27	Paddington ○ **AUS** 379 Mj 62	Pakuli ○ **RI** 279 Lk 46
Oued Tadant ∾ **DZ** 308 Gk 34	Outokumpu ○ **FIN** 159 Hg 14	ozero Karakul ∾ **TJ** 230 Ka 26	Paden City ○ **USA** 71 Dh 26	Pakwach ○ **EAU** 324 Hh 44
Oued Tadjataret ∾ **DZ** 308 Gl 34	Outoul ○ **DZ** 308 Gj 34	ozero Kargalyshor ∾ **TM** 223 Jl 27	Padeniya ○ **CL** 239 Ke 42	Pakwash Lake ∾ **CDN** 56 Db 20
Oued Tafassasset ∾ **DZ** 308 Gl 34	Ouvéa △ **F** 386 Nf 56	ozero Keret' ∾ **RUS** 159 Hj 13	Paderborn ○ **D** 174 Gl 20	Pakxé ○ **LAO** 263 Lc 38
Oued Tagrina ∾ **DZ** 308 Gk 35	Ouyen ○ **AUS** 378 Mh 63	ozero Kolvickoe ∾ **RUS** 159 Hj 12	Pâderu ○ **IND** 234 Kf 36	Pala ○ **TCH** 321 Gp 41
Oued Takalo ∾ **DZ** 308 Gk 34	Ou Yiang ∾ **VRC** 259 Ll 31	ozero Koolen ∾ **RUS** 46 Ac 13	Padibe ○ **EAU** 324 Hj 44	Palacios ○ **USA** 81 Cp 31
Oued Takisset ∾ **DZ** 297 Gm 33	Ouzibi ∾ **G** 332 Gm 47	ozero Krasnoe ∾ **RUS** 205 Zb 6	Padilla ○ **MEX** 81 Cn 34	Palacios ○ **BOL** 129 Eb 54
Oued Tamanrasset ∾ **DZ** 305 Gg 34	Ova △ **G** 332 Gm 46	ozero Kronockoe ∾ **RUS** 205 Yb 8	Padilla ○ **BOL** 129 Eb 55	Palacios ○ **RA** 137 Ed 61
Oued Tarfa ∾ **ET** 301 Hh 31	Ovalau △ **FJI** 387 Nm 54	ozero Kytaj ∾ **UA** 175 Hg 23	Padjelanta ♀ **S** 158 Ha 12	Palacode ○ **IND** 238 Kc 39
Oued Tari ∾ **DZ** 296 Gh 33	Ovalle ○ **RCH** 137 Dn 61	ozero Labaz ∾ **RUS** 204 Ub 4	Padmanābhapuram ○ **IND** 239 Kc 41	Palafrugell ○ **E** 185 Gm 25
Oued Tekhammat ∾ **DZ** 296 Gd 32	Ovamboland △ **NAM** 340 Gp 55	ozero Lača ∾ **RUS** 159 Hm 15		Palagruža △ **HR** 194 Ha 24
Oued Tekouiat ∾ **DZ** 308 Gk 34	Ovan ○ **G** 332 Gn 45	ozero Melkoe ∾ **RUS** 204 Ua 5	Padova ○ **I** 185 Gm 23	Palahana ○ **IND** 234 Ke 33
Oued Tenuchchad ∾ **MA** 292 Gb 32	Ovar ○ **P** 184 Gb 25	ozero Mogotoevo ∾ **RUS** 205 Xc 4	Padrauna ○ **IND** 235 Kf 32	Palakau ○ **PNG** 287 Ml 46
Oued Tichkatine ∾ **DZ** 308 Gj 35	Owau Island △ **SOL** 290 Na 49	ozero Nero ∾ **RUS** 171 Hm 17	Padre Angel Buodo ○ **RA** 137 Eb 64	Palala ○ **LB** 316 Gb 42
Oued Tigzerte ∾ **MA** 292 Gb 31	Ovejería ○ **RA** 137 Ea 63	ozero Njuk ∾ **RUS** 159 Hh 13	Padre Bernardo ○ **BR** 133 Ek 53	Palala ○ **ZA** 349 Hg 58
Oued Tilia ∾ **DZ** 293 Gg 32	Oveng ○ **CAM** 320 Gn 44	ozero Pjasino ∾ **RUS** 22 Pa 5	Padre Island △ **USA** 81 Cp 32	Palälak ○ **AFG** 226 Jk 30
Oued Timeldjame ∾ **DZ** 296 Gh 31	Overflowing River ∾ **CDN** 56 Cm 19	ozero Pjasino ∾ **RUS** 204 Tc 5	Padre Island National Seashore ♀ **USA** 81 Cp 32	Palamakoloi ○ **RB** 349 Hd 57
Oued Timissit ∾ **DZ** 296 Gl 31	Øvergård ○ **N** 159 Hb 11	ozero Sarezckoe ∾ **TJ** 230 Ka 26		Palamau National Park ♀ **IND** 235 Kg 34
Oued Tin Amzi ∾ **DZ** 308 Gj 35	Överkalix ○ **S** 159 Hd 12	ozero Sasyk ∾ **UA** 175 Hj 23	Padre Paraíso ○ **BR** 125 Ep 54	
Oued Tin Hadjène ∾ **DZ** 308 Gk 33	Overland Park ○ **USA** 70 Da 26	ozero Seliger ∾ **RUS** 171 Hj 17	Padron ○ **E** 184 Gb 24	Palamós ○ **E** 185 Gn 25
Oued Tin Tarabine ∾ **DZ** 308 Gk 35	Overton ○ **USA** 64 Ce 27	ozero Srednee Kujto ∾ **RUS** 159 Hh 13	Paducah ○ **USA** 70 Dm 28	Palana ○ **RUS** 23 Ta 4
Oued Tirahart ∾ **DZ** 308 Gk 34	Övertorneå ○ **S** 159 Hd 12		Paducah ○ **USA** 71 Dd 27	Palana ○ **RUS** 205 Yb 7
Oued Tirhemar ∾ **DZ** 296 Gk 32	Overum ○ **S** 170 Gg 16	ozero Sundozero ∾ **RUS** 159 Hj 14	Paegnyöngdo △ **ROK** 246 Ln 27	Palanan ○ **RP** 267 Lm 37
Oued Tirine ∾ **DZ** 308 Gl 34	Oviedo ○ **DOM** 101 Dn 36	ozero Suojarv ∾ **RUS** 159 Hk 14	Paekdu San △ **DVRK** 247 Ma 25	Palanan Bay ≈ **RP** 267 Lm 37
Oued Tisnale ∾ **DZ** 296 Gj 31	Oviedo Uvléu ○ **E** 184 Gc 24	ozero Taymyr ∾ **RUS** 204 Uc 4	Paeroa ○ **NZ** 383 Nk 64	Palancia ∾ **E** 184 Gc 25
Oued Tlelat ○ **DZ** 293 Gf 28	Ovödij ○ **MNG** 204 Ub 9	ozero Tunajča ∾ **RUS** 250 Mh 22	Paestum ★ **I** 194 Gp 25	Palangan ○ **RP** 267 Lm 37
Oued Torset ∾ **DZ** 296 Gl 33	Ovongo ○ **ZA** 349 Hh 61	ozero Undozero ∾ **RUS** 159 Hm 14	Paete ○ **RP** 267 Ll 38	Palangkaraya ○ **RI** 279 Lg 47
Oued Touil ∾ **DZ** 296 Gh 28	Øvre ♀ **N** 159 He 11	ozero Velikoe ∾ **RUS** 171 Hl 17	Paez ○ **CO** 106 Dl 44	Palani ○ **IND** 239 Kc 40
Oued Tournde ∾ **DZ** 308 Gm 34	Øvre ○ **S** 159 Hc 11	ozero Vodlozero ∾ **RUS** 159 Hl 14	Pafos ○ **CY** 195 Hj 28	Palanro ○ **RI** 279 Lk 48
Oued Zazii ∾ **DZ** 308 Gj 35	Øvre Dividal ♀ **N** 159 Hb 11	ozero Vože ∾ **RUS** 159 Hm 15	Pafúri ∾ **MOC** 352 Hh 57	Palanpur ○ **IND** 227 Ka 33
Oued Zâzir ∾ **DZ** 308 Gj 35	Øvre Pasvik ♀ **RUS** 159 Hg 11	ozero Zorkal ∾ **TJ** 230 Ka 27	Pafuri ∾ **ZA** 352 Hh 57	Palapye ○ **RB** 349 Hf 57
Oued Zegrir ∾ **DZ** 296 Gk 29	Ovruč ○ **UA** 175 Hg 20		Pafuri Gate ○ **ZA** 352 Hh 57	Palasamudram ○ **IND** 238 Kc 39
Oued-Zem ○ **MA** 293 Gc 29	Owaka ○ **NZ** 382 Ng 69	Ozerskij ○ **RUS** 250 Mh 22	Paga ○ **HR** 174 Gp 23	Palasan Island △ **RP** 267 Lm 38
Oued Zenati ○ **DZ** 296 Gk 27	Owalama Range △ **PNG** 287 Mk 50	Ozery ○ **RUS** 171 Hm 18	Pagadenbaru ○ **RI** 278 Ld 49	Palasbari ○ **BD** 235 Kj 33
Oued Zeroud ∾ **TN** 296 Gl 28		Ozhiski Lake ∾ **CDN** 57 Dd 20	Pagadian ○ **RP** 275 Lm 42	Palatka ○ **RUS** 23 Sb 3
Oued Ziz ∾ **MA** 293 Gd 30	Owando ○ **RCB** 332 Gp 46	Ožidaevo ∾ **RUS** 250 Mh 22	Pagadian Bay ≈ **RP** 275 Lm 42	Palatka ○ **USA** 87 Dh 31
Oued Zmertène ∾ **TN** 296 Gl 29	Owase ○ **J** 251 Md 28	Ozieri ○ **I** 185 Gl 25	Pagan △ **MYA** 254 Km 35	Palau □ **PAL** 26 Rb 9
Oued Zousfana ∾ **DZ** 293 Gf 30	Owasso ○ **USA** 70 Cp 27	Ozinki ○ **RUS** 181 Jc 20	Pagan △ **USA** 27 Sa 8	Palau ○ **MEX** Cm 32
Ouéléssébougou ○ **RMM** 305 Gc 40	Owatonna ○ **USA** 56 Db 23	Ožogina ∾ **RUS** 205 Xc 5	Paganzo ○ **RA** 137 Ea 61	Palau ○ **I** 185 Gl 25
Ouéllé ○ **CI** 317 Gd 42	Owego ○ **USA** 60 Dk 24	Ozona ○ **USA** 81 Cm 30	Pagaralam ○ **RI** 278 Lb 48	Palaui Island △ **RP** 267 Lm 36
Ouémé Affon ∾ **DY** 317 Gg 41	Owen ○ **USA** 56 Dc 23	Ozuluama ○ **MEX** 81 Cp 34	Pagassitikós Kólpos ≈ **GR** 194 Hd 26	Palaui Island △ **PAL** 26 Rb 9
Ouémé ○ **DY** 320 Gh 41	Owena ○ **WAN** 320 Gj 42	Ozurgeti ○ **GE** 202 Hp 25		Palauk ○ **MYA** 262 Kp 39
Ouen el Melah ∾ **DZ** 296 Gj 31	Owendo ○ **G** 332 Gl 45		Pagatan ○ **RI** 279 Lh 47	Palaw ∾ **MYA** 262 Kp 38
Ouenkoro ○ **RMM** 317 Ge 39	Owen Falls Dam ∾ **EAU** 324 Hj 45	**P**	Pagawyun ∾ **MYA** 262 Kp 38	Palawan △ **RP** 267 Lk 41
Ouénou ○ **DY** 320 Gh 41	Owenga ○ **NZ** 383 Ab 68		Page ○ **USA** 56 Cp 22	Palawan Passage ≈ **RP** 266 Lj 41
Ouenza ○ **DZ** 296 Gl 28	Owens ∾ **USA** 64 Cc 27	Pa ○ **BF** 317 Ge 40	Page ○ **USA** 64 Cf 27	Paläyankottai ○ **IND** 239 Kc 41
Oué-Oué ○ **DY** 317 Gh 41	Owens ○ **USA** 74 Dk 26	Pa. Arara ∾ **BR** 120 Ed 47	Page ○ **USA** 70 Da 28	Palazzolo Acreide ○ **I** 185 Gp 27
Ouessa ○ **BF** 317 Ge 40	Owensboro ○ **USA** 71 De 27	Pa. Autaz Mirim ∾ **BR** 120 Ee 47	Pageland ○ **USA** 71 Dh 28	Palbe ○ **GH** 317 Gf 41
Ouèssè ○ **DY** 317 Gh 41	Owens Lake ∾ **USA** 64 Cd 27	Pa. do Mamori ∾ **BR** 120 Ee 47	Pagelaran ○ **RI** 278 Ld 49	Palca ∾ **RA** 137 Dp 60
Ouezzane ○ **MA** 293 Gd 28	Owen Sound ○ **CDN** 57 Dh 23	Pa. do Panelão ∾ **BR** 117 Ec 48	Pagerdewa ○ **RI** 278 Lc 47	Palcamayo ○ **PE** 128 Dl 51
Oufrane ○ **DZ** 293 Gg 31	Owen Springs ○ **AUS** 361 Mc 59	Pa. do Ramos ∾ **BR** 120 Ef 47	Pagergunung ○ **RI** 278 Lc 47	Palcazú ∾ **PE** 128 Dl 51
Ougarou ○ **BF** 317 Gg 39	Owen Stanley Range △ **PNG** 287 Mk 50	Pa. Mirim do Abufari ∾ **BR** 117 Ec 48	Pagimana ○ **RI** 282 Lm 46	Paleiochora ○ **GR** 194 Hd 28
Oughterard ○ **IRL** 163 Gb 19		Pa. Urariá ∾ **BR** 120 Ee 47	Pagman ○ **AFG** 223 Jn 28	Paleleh ○ **RI** 275 Ll 45
Ouham ∾ **TCH** 321 Ha 41	Owensville ○ **USA** 71 Df 26	Paama △ **VU** 386 Ng 54	Pagoh ○ **MAL** 270 Lb 44	Palembang ○ **RI** 278 Lc 47
Ouham ∾ **RCA** 321 Ha 42	Owenton ○ **USA** 71 Df 26	Paarl ○ **ZA** 358 Hb 62	Pago Pago ○ **USA** 35 Aa 11	Palena ∾ **RCH** 147 Dm 67
Ouidah ○ **DY** 317 Gh 42	Owerri ○ **WAN** 320 Gk 43	Pabal ○ **IND** 238 Kb 36	Pagosa Springs ○ **USA** 65 Cj 27	Palena ○ **RCH** 147 Dn 67
Ouidi ○ **RN** 297 Gn 38	Owikeno Lake ∾ **CDN** 50 Bn 20	Pabal-ri ○ **DVRK** 247 Ma 25	Pagri ○ **VRC** 235 Kj 32	Palenchuo ○ **YV** 112 Ea 41
Ouinardène ○ **RMM** 305 Gd 37	Owo ∾ **WAN** 320 Gj 42	Pabedaná ○ **IR** 226 Jg 30	Paguyaman ○ **RI** 275 Lm 45	Palencia ○ **E** 184 Gd 25
Oujâf ○ **RIM** 304 Gc 37	Owode ○ **WAN** 320 Gj 42	Pabellones ∾ **MEX** 92 Cl 34	Pagwa River ○ **CDN** 57 Df 20	Palen Lake ∾ **USA** 64 Ce 29
Oujda ○ **MA** 293 Ge 28	Owosso ○ **USA** 57 Df 24	Pabna ○ **BD** 235 Kj 33	Pagwi ○ **PNG** 286 Mh 48	Palenque ○ **MEX** 93 Db 37
Oujeft ○ **RIM** 304 Fp 35	Owutu ○ **WAN** 320 Gk 43	Pabradé ○ **LT** 171 He 18	Pahala ○ **USA** 75 Am 36	Palenque ★ **MEX** 93 Db 37
Oukaimeden ○ **MA** 292 Gc 30	Owyhee ○ **USA** 64 Ce 25	Pab Range △ **PK** 227 Jm 32	Pahang ∾ **MAL** 271 Lb 44	Palenque ○ **PA** 97 Dj 41
Oukal ○ **AFG** 223 Jj 29	Owyhee ∾ **USA** 64 Cd 25	Pacaás Novos △ **BR** 129 Eb 51	Paharpur ★ **BD** 235 Kj 33	Paleohora ∾ **YV** 107 Dm 40
Oukraal ○ **ZA** 358 Hb 63	Owyhee Mountains △ **USA** 50 Cd 24	Pacacocha ∾ **PE** 128 Dm 52	Pahaska Tepee ○ **USA** 51 Ch 23	Paleokastrisa ♀ **GR** 194 Hb 26
Oukré ○ **RIM** 304 Ga 37		Pacaembu ○ **BR** 140 Ej 56	Pahn Wrool ○ **LB** 316 Gb 43	Palermo ○ **CO** 106 Dl 44
Oulacca ○ **AUS** 375 Ml 59	Owyhee Ridge △ **USA** 50 Cd 24	Pacahuaras ∾ **BOL** 129 Ea 51	Pahoa ○ **USA** 75 An 36	Palermo ○ **I** 185 Gn 26
Oulad-Teïma ○ **MA** 292 Gb 30	Oxapampa ○ **PE** 128 Dl 51	Pacajá ○ **BR** 121 Ej 47	Pahokee ○ **USA** 87 Dh 32	Paleski radyjacyjna-ěkalagicny zapavednik ♀ **BY** 175 Hg 20
Oulainen ○ **FIN** 159 He 13	Oxbow ○ **CDN** 51 Cl 21	Pacajá ∾ **BR** 121 Ej 47	Pahotun River ∾ **PNG** 286 Mh 50	
Oulanka ♀ **FIN** 159 Hg 12	Oxelösund ○ **S** 170 Ha 16	Pacajás ○ **BR** 121 Ej 47	Pahrump ○ **USA** 64 Ce 27	Palestina ○ **CO** 106 Dk 43
Ould Yenjé ○ **RMM** 304 Ga 38	Oxenhope ○ **AUS** 375 Mj 56	Pacajus ○ **BR** 124 Fa 48	Pahtakor ○ **UZB** 223 Jm 25	Palestina ○ **EC** 116 Dh 46
Oued Allenda ○ **DZ** 296 Gk 29	Oxford ○ **CDN** 61 Ec 23	Pacapausa ○ **PE** 128 Dm 53	Pai ○ **THA** 254 Kp 36	Palestina ○ **RCH** 136 Dp 57
Oued Djellal ○ **DZ** 296 Gj 28	Oxford ○ **USA** 71 Dd 28	Pacaraima Mountains △ **YV** 112 Ec 44	Paia ○ **USA** 75 Am 35	Palestine ○ **USA** 81 Da 30
Ouli ○ **CAM** 321 Gp 43	Oxford ○ **USA** 71 Df 26		Paicuru ∾ **BR** 121 Eh 46	Paletwa ○ **MYA** 235 Kl 35
Oulmes ○ **MA** 293 Gc 29	Oxford ○ **USA** 74 Dj 27	Pacaraima Mountains △ **GUY** 112 Ed 43	Paide ○ **EST** 171 He 16	Palezgir ○ **IND** 239 Kc 40
Oulnina Hill △ **AUS** 378 Mf 62	Oxford ○ **USA** 70 Dc 26		Paiewa ○ **PNG** 287 Mk 49	Palgharr ○ **IND** 238 Ka 36
Oulo Uleåborg ○ **FIN** 159 He 13	Oxford ○ **GB** 163 Gf 20	Pacaraos ○ **PE** 116 Dk 51	Paihia ○ **NZ** 383 Nk 63	Palgrat ○ **IND** 239 Kc 40
Oulujärvi ∾ **FIN** 159 Hf 13	Oxford ○ **AUS** 378 Mk 67	Pacasmayo ○ **PE** 116 Dj 49	Paijan ○ **PE** 116 Dj 49	Palha ∾ **BR** 129 Ed 51
Oulujoki ∾ **FIN** 159 He 13	Oxford ○ **NZ** 383 Nj 67	Pacatuba ○ **BR** 124 Fa 48	Päijänne ∾ **FIN** 159 He 15	Palhano ∾ **BR** 124 Fa 48
Oumache ○ **DZ** 296 Gj 28	Oxkutzcab ○ **MEX** 93 Dd 35	Pãc Bó ○ **VN** 255 Lc 34	Paiko ○ **WAN** 320 Gk 41	Palheta ○ **BR** 117 Eb 47
Ouma ∾ **G** 332 Gm 46	Oxley Downs ○ **AUS** 379 Mj 63	Pace ○ **USA** 86 De 30	Paiku Co ∾ **VRC** 235 Kg 31	Pâli ○ **IND** 227 Ka 33
Oum-Chalouba ○ **TCH** 309 Hc 38	Oxnard ○ **USA** 64 Cc 28	Pacet ○ **RI** 278 Ld 49	Pail ○ **PK** 230 Ka 29	Pali ○ **IND** 234 Ke 34
Oumcheggag ○ **MA** 292 Fp 32	Oya ∾ **MAL** 271 Lf 44	Pachacámac ★ **PE** 116 Dk 52	Paila ○ **MEX** 81 Cl 33	Palian ○ **THA** 270 Kp 42
Oum Djerane ○ **DZ** 293 Gg 28	Oyabi ○ **RCB** 332 Gp 46	Pachačí ○ **RUS** 23 Ta 3	Paila ∾ **BOL** 129 Ec 54	Palimbang ○ **RP** 275 Lm 42
Oumé ○ **CI** 317 Gd 42	Oyama △ **J** 251 Mf 27	Pachačí ○ **RUS** 205 Za 6	Pailastunturi ♀ **FIN** 159 Hd 11	Palisade ○ **USA** 70 Cm 25
Oum el Achar ○ **DZ** 292 Gb 31	Oyamakonskoye Nagor'ye △ **RUS** 205 Xb 6	Pachaconas ○ **PE** 128 Dm 53	Pailín ○ **K** 263 Lb 39	Palisades Reservoir ∾ **USA** 51 Cg 24
Oum el Bouaghi ○ **DZ** 296 Gk 27		Pachala ○ **SUD** 325 Hk 42	Paillaco ○ **RCH** 147 Dm 66	
Oum-Hadjer ○ **TCH** 321 Hb 39	Oyan ○ **G** 332 Gm 45	Pachan ○ **RI** 279 Lg 49	Pailon ○ **BOL** 129 Ec 54	Pallina ○ **IND** 238 Kp 54
Oumm el Khezz ○ **RIM** 304 Ga 37	Oyapock ∾ **F** 113 Eh 44	Pachía ○ **PE** 128 Dn 54	Paimpol ○ **F** 163 Gf 21	Pallisa ○ **EAU** 325 Hj 45
Ounara ○ **MA** 292 Gb 30	Oyem ○ **G** 332 Gm 45	Pachino ○ **I** 185 Gp 27	Paina ○ **PNG** 287 Mj 49	Palliser Bay ≈ **NZ** 383 Nk 66
Ounasjoki ∾ **FIN** 159 He 12	Oyen ○ **CDN** 51 Cg 20	Pachitea ∾ **PE** 128 Dl 50	Painan ○ **RI** 270 La 46	Palm ∾ **NAM** 340 Gn 55
Oundou ∾ **RG** 316 Ga 40	Oyeren ∾ **N** 170 Gm 16	Pacho ○ **CO** 106 Dl 43	Paine ○ **RCH** 137 Dn 62	Palma △ **BR** 133 El 52
Ounianga Kébir ○ **TCH** 309 Hc 36	Oyé Yeska ○ **TCH** 309 Hb 36	Pachuca ○ **MEX** 92 Cn 35	Painedaw ○ **MYA** 262 Kn 38	Palma ○ **MOC** 344 Hn 51
Ounianga Sérir ○ **TCH** 309 Hc 36	Oyo ○ **WAN** 320 Gj 42	Paciá ∾ **BR** 117 Eb 49	Paineiras ○ **BR** 133 Em 55	Palma del Río ○ **E** 184 Gd 27
Ountivou ○ **RT** 317 Gg 42	Oyo ○ **RCB** 332 Ha 46	Pacific ○ **USA** 71 Dc 26	Painesville ○ **USA** 71 Dg 25	Palmanate ○ **IND** 235 Kg 35
Ouogo ○ **RCA** 321 Ha 42	Oyotún ○ **PE** 116 Dj 49	Pacifica ○ **USA** 64 Ca 27	Paint Rock ○ **USA** 81 Cn 30	Pallasca ○ **PE** 116 Dk 50
Ouray ○ **USA** 65 Cj 27	Oyou Bezzé Denga ∾ **RN** 297 Gn 37	Pacific Grove ○ **USA** 64 Ca 27	Paintsville ○ **USA** 71 Dg 27	Pallas-ja Ounastunturin ♀ **FIN** 159 He 11
Ouré-Kaba ○ **RG** 316 Ga 40		Pacific Ocean ≈ 10 Ab 6	Paipa ○ **CO** 107 Dm 43	
Ourém ○ **BR** 121 El 46	Øyrlandsodden ⌒ **N** 158 Gp 7	Pacific Ranges △ **CDN** 50 Bn 20	Paipote ∾ **RCH** 136 Dn 59	Pallina ○ **BD** 235 Kj 33
Ourense ○ **E** 184 Gc 24	Oyster Island △ **MYA** 254 Kl 36	Pacific Rim ♀ **CDN** 50 Bn 21	Paipote ○ **RCH** 136 Dn 59	Palliser Bay ○ **BD** 235 Kj 33
Ouri ○ **TCH** 309 Hb 35	Oysterville ○ **USA** 50 Bp 22		Paisha ○ **RC** 258 Lk 34	Palm ○ **USA** 82 Dd 30
Ouricuri ○ **BR** 124 Ep 49	Ožalp ○ **TR** 202 Hp 26	Pacijan Island △ **RP** 267 Ln 40	Paisley ○ **USA** 50 Cb 24	Palma ○ **E** 184 Gh 26
Ourikéla ○ **RMM** 317 Gd 39	Ozamis ○ **RP** 267 Lm 41		Paisley ○ **GB** 162 Gd 18	Palma ∾ **F** 333 Ha 47
Ourilândia do Norte ○ **BR** 121 Ej 49	Ozamiz ○ **RP** 267 Lm 41		Paita ○ **PE** 116 Dh 48	Palma del Río ○ **E** 184 Gd 27
Ourinhos ○ **BR** 140 Ek 57	Ozark ∾ **USA** 70 Db 28		Païta ○ **F** 386 Nf 56	Palmaner ○ **IND** 238 Kc 39
Ourini ○ **TCH** 309 Hd 37	Ozark ○ **USA** 70 Db 28		Paiton ○ **RI** 279 Lg 49	Palmar ∾ **YV** 107 Dm 40
Ourlal ○ **DZ** 296 Gj 28	Ozark ○ **USA** 86 Df 30		Pajapita ○ **GCA** 93 Db 38	Palmar ○ **EC** 116 Dh 47
Ouro ∾ **BR** 133 Ek 52	Ozark Natl. Scenic Riverways ♀ **USA** 70 Dc 27		Pajarito ○ **CO** 107 Dm 43	Palmares ∾ **BR** 124 Fc 50
			Pájaro ∾ **CO** 107 Dm 40	Palmar Grande ○ **RA** 140 Ee 59
			Pajeú ∾ **BR** 124 Fa 50	Palmarito ○ **YV** 107 Dn 42
			Pajeú ∾ **BR** 124 Fa 50	Palmar Norte ○ **CR** 97 Dg 41
			Pajtug ○ **UZB** 230 Ka 25	

Palmas ○ **BR** 133 Ek 51
Palmas ○ **BR** 140 Ej 59
Palmas de Monte Alto ○ **BR** 125 En 53
Palma Sola ○ **RA** 136 Eb 58
Palma Soriano ○ **C** 101 Dl 35
Palm Bay ○ **USA** 87 Dh 31
Palm Coast ○ **USA** 87 Dh 31
Palm Cove ○ **AUS** 365 Mj 54
Palmdale ○ **USA** 64 Cc 28
Palmeira ○ **BR** 140 Ej 58
Palmeira ○ **BR** 133 El 51
Palmeira ○ **BR** 140 Eh 59
Palmeira d'Oeste ○ **BR** 140 Ej 56
Palmeira dos Indios ○ **BR** 124 Fb 50
Palmeirândia ○ **BR** 121 Em 47
Palmeiras ○ **BR** 124 En 49
Palmeiras ∾ **BR** 121 Ek 49
Palmeiras ∾ **BR** 133 Ej 53
Palmeiras ∾ **BR** 133 El 51
Palmeiras de Goiás ○ **BR** 133 Ek 54
Palmeiras do Jovari ○ **BR** 116 Dm 48
Palmeirópolis ○ **BR** 133 Ek 52
Palmer △ **USA** 46 Ba 15
Palmer ○ **AUS** 365 Mj 54
Palmer ∾ **AUS** 369 Mc 58
Palmer Lake ○ **USA** 65 Ck 26
Palmerston △ **NZ** 35 Ab 11
Palmerston ○ **NZ** 382 Nh 68
Palmerston North ○ **NZ** 383 Nk 66
Palmerville ○ **AUS** 365 Mh 53
Palmeta ∾ **RA** 140 Ee 59
Palmetto ∾ **USA** 86 Dg 32
Palm Grove ♀ **AUS** 375 Ml 58
Palm Harbor ○ **USA** 86 Dg 31
Palmillas ○ **MEX** 81 Cn 34
Palmira ○ **CO** 106 Dk 44
Palmira ○ **YV** 107 Dm 41
Palmira ○ **EC** 116 Dj 47
Palmira ○ **RA** 137 Dp 62
Palm Islands △ **AUS** 365 Mk 55
Palmiste ○ **RH** 101 Dm 36
Palmital ○ **BR** 140 Eh 58
Palmital ○ **BR** 140 Ej 57
Palm Passage ≈ **AUS** 365 Mk 55
Palm Springs ○ **USA** 64 Cd 29
Palm Tree Creek ∾ **AUS** 375 Ml 58
Palm Valley ○ **USA** 87 Dh 30
Palmyra △ **USA** 27 Ab 9
Palmyra ○ **USA** 71 De 26
Palmyra ○ **SYR** 209 Hm 28
Palmyras Point ⌒ **IND** 235 Kh 35
Palo ○ **RP** 267 Ln 40
Palo Alto ○ **USA** 64 Ca 27
Palo Blanco ○ **RA** 136 Dp 59
Palo Duro Canyon ∾ **USA** 70 Cm 28
Paloemeu ○ **SME** 113 Eg 44
Paloemeu ∾ **SME** 113 Eg 44
Palo Flores ○ **YV** 107 Dn 41
Paloh ○ **MAL** 271 Lb 44
Paloich ○ **SUD** 312 Hj 40
Palomares ○ **MEX** 93 Da 37
Palomas ○ **MEX** 80 Cj 30
Palomas ○ **ROU** 146 Ef 61
Palomino ○ **CO** 107 Dm 40
Palomitas ○ **RA** 136 Eb 58
Palompon ○ **RP** 267 Ln 40
Palopo ○ **RI** 282 Ll 47
Palora ○ **EC** 116 Dk 46
Palos ○ **C** 100 Dh 34
Palos Blancos ○ **BOL** 136 Ec 56
Palotina ○ **BR** 140 Eh 58
Palouse ○ **USA** 50 Cd 22
Palouse ∾ **USA** 50 Cd 22
Palo Verde ○ **USA** 64 Ce 29
Palpa ○ **PE** 128 Dl 53
Palpalá ○ **RA** 136 Eb 58
Palparara ○ **AUS** 374 Mg 58
Palpite ○ **C** 100 Dh 34
Paltamo ○ **FIN** 159 Hf 13
Palu ○ **RI** 279 Lk 46
Palu △ **RI** 282 Ll 50
Palu ○ **TR** 202 Hn 26
Paluan Bay ≈ **RP** 267 Ll 39
Palwal ○ **IND** 234 Kc 31
Pama ∾ **BF** 317 Gg 40
Pama ∾ **RCA** 321 Ha 43
Pamaguá ○ **BR** 133 Em 51
Pamaibá ∾ **BR** 124 En 49
Pamanukan ○ **RI** 278 Ld 49
Pamanzi-Bé ⌀ **F** 345 Ja 52
Pamarama ○ **BR** 124 En 48
Pâmban Island △ **IND** 239 Kd 41
Pambarra ∾ **MOC** 352 Hk 56
Pambeguwa ○ **WAN** 320 Gl 40
Pamdai ○ **RI** 286 Me 46
Pamekasan ○ **RI** 279 Lg 49
Pameue ○ **RI** 270 Kn 43
Pameungpeuk ○ **RI** 278 Ld 49
Pâmidi ○ **IND** 238 Kc 38
Pamiers ○ **F** 184 Gg 24
Pamir ∾ **TJ** 223 Jp 26
Pamir △ **AFG** 230 Ka 27
Pamlico ∾ **USA** 74 Dk 28
Pamlico Sound ≈ **USA** 74 Dk 28
Pamoni ∾ **YV** 112 Eb 44
Pampa ○ **USA** 70 Cm 28
Pampã ∾ **BR** 125 Ep 54
Pampa Alta ∾ **RA** 137 Eb 64
Pampa Aullagas ○ **BOL** 129 Ea 55
Pampa Blanca ∾ **RA** 136 Eb 58
Pampachiri ○ **PE** 128 Dm 53
Pampa del Agua Amarga ∾ **RA** 147 Dp 65
Pampa de la Matanzilla ∾ **RA** 137 Dp 64
Pampa de la Varita ∾ **RA** 137 Ea 63
Pampa la Yoya ∾ **PE** 128 Dn 54
Pampa del Castillo ∾ **RA** 152 Dp 68
Pampa del Castillo ∾ **RA** 152 Dp 68
Pampa del Diamante ∾ **RA** 137 Dp 63
Pampa del Indio ○ **RA** 140 Ee 59
Pampa del Infierno ○ **RA** 136 Ed 59
Pampa de los Guanacos ○ **RA** 136 Ed 59
Pampa del Tamarugal ∾ **RCH** 136 Dp 56

Parque Nacional Llanganates ⚲ **EC** 116 Dj 46
Parque Nacional Llica ⚲ **BOL** 129 Dp 55
Parque Nacional Llullaillaco ⚲ **RCH** 136 Dp 58
Parque Nacional Los Alerces ⚲ **RA** 147 Dn 67
Parque Nacional Los Glaciares ⚲ **RA** 152 Dm 70
Parque Nacional Los Huemules ⚲ **RCH** 152 Dm 68
Parque Nacional Los Mármoles ⚲ **MEX** 92 Cn 35
Parque Nacional Machalilla ⚲ **EC** 116 Dh 46
Parque Nacional Manú ⚲ **PE** 128 Dn 51
Parque Nacional Manuel Antonio ⚲ **CR** 97 Df 41
Parque Nacional Marinho de Abrolhos ⚲ **BR** 125 Fa 54
Parque Nacional Marítimo-Terrestre de Cabrera ⚲ **E** 185 Gh 26
Parque Nacional Nahuelbuta ⚲ **RCH** 137 Dm 64
Parque Nacional Nahuel Huapi ⚲ **RA** 147 Dn 66
Parque Nacional Nevado de Colima ⚲ **MEX** 92 Cl 36
Parque Nacional Nevado de Tolúca ⚲ **MEX** 92 Cn 36
Parque Nacional Nevado de Tres Cruces ⚲ **RCH** 136 Dp 59
Parque Nacional Noel Kempff Mercado ⚲ **BOL** 129 Ed 53
Parque Nacional Padocarpus ⚲ **EC** 116 Dj 48
Parque Nacional Palo Verde ⚲ **CR** 97 Df 40
Parque Nacional Pan de Azúcar ⚲ **RCH** 136 Dn 59
Parque Nacional Perito Moreno ⚲ **RA** 152 Dn 70
Parque Nacional Pico de Orizaba ⚲ **MEX** 92 Cp 35
Parque Nacional Pico de Tancitaro ⚲ **MEX** 92 Cl 36
Parque Nacional Portobello ⚲ **PA** 97 Dj 41
Parque Nacional Punta Sal ⚲ **HN** 96 De 38
Parque Nacional Queulat ⚲ **RCH** 152 Dm 68
Parque Nacional Quitralco ⚲ **RCH** 152 Dm 68
Parque Nacional Rayón ⚲ **MEX** 92 Cm 36
Parque Nacional Río Abiseo ⚲ **PE** 116 Dk 49
Parque Nacional Río Azul ⚲ **GCA** 93 Dd 37
Parque Nacional Río Pilcomayo ⚲ **RA** 140 Ee 58
Parque Nacional Sangay ⚲ **EC** 116 Dj 46
Parque Nacional Santa de Ayes Laguna Colorada ⚲ **BOL** 136 Ea 57
Parque Nacional Santa-Rosa ⚲ **CR** 97 Df 40
Parque Nacional Saslaya ⚲ **NIC** 97 Df 39
Parque Nacional Serra da Capivara ⚲ **BR** 124 En 50
Parque Nacional Serranías San Luis ⚲ **PY** 140 Ef 57
Parque Nacional Sierra de San Pedro Mártir ⚲ **MEX** 75 Ce 30
Parque Nacional Tikal ⚲ **GCA** 93 Dd 37
Parque Nacional Tolhuaca ⚲ **RCH** 147 Dn 65
Parque Nacional Torres del Paine ⚲ **RCH** 152 Dm 71
Parque Nacional Tortuguero ⚲ **CR** 97 Dg 40
Parque Nacional Tunari ⚲ **BOL** 129 Ea 54
Parque Nacional Villarica ⚲ **RA** 147 Dn 65
Parque Nacional Viñales ⚲ **C** 100 Dg 34
Parque Nacional Vol. Baru ⚲ **PA** 97 Dg 41
Parque Nacional Yanachaga-Chemillén ⚲ **PE** 128 Dl 51
Parque Nacional Yasuni ⚲ **EC** 116 Dk 46
Parque Nacional Ybyuí ⚲ **PY** 140 Ef 59
Parque Nacional Zoquiapán y Anexas ⚲ **MEX** 92 Cn 36
Parque Natural de Cuyabeno ⚲ **EC** 116 Dj 46
Parral ○ **RCH** 137 Dm 64
Parramatta ○ **AUS** 379 Mm 62
Parramore Island ◬ **USA** 74 Dl 27
Parras de la Fuente ○ **MEX** 81 Cl 33
Parrita ○ **CR** 97 Df 41
Parrsboro ○ **CDN** 61 Eb 23
Parrs Halt ○ **ZA** 349 Hf 57
Parry Bay 〰 **CDN** 43 Gb 5
Parry Island ◬ **CDN** 57 Dh 23
Parry Islands ◬ **CDN** 42 Ea 3
Parryøya ◬ **N** 158 Hc 5
Parry Peninsula ◬ **CDN** 47 Bn 11
Parry Sound ○ **CDN** 57 Dh 23
Pārsābād ○ **IR** 209 Jb 26
Parsoburan ○ **RI** 270 Kp 44
Parsons ○ **USA** 70 Da 27
Parson's Pond ○ **CDN** 61 Ef 20
Parsons Range ⛰ **AUS** 364 Md 52
Partābpur ○ **IND** 234 Kf 34
Partāwal ○ **IND** 235 Kf 32
Pårtefjällen △ **S** 158 Ha 12
Parthenay ○ **F** 163 Gf 22
Pārtibanur ○ **IND** 239 Kd 41
Partizansk ○ **RUS** 250 Mc 24
Párto Acre ○ **BR** 117 Ea 50
Partridge River ∼ **CDN** 57 Dh 20
Partūr ○ **IND** 238 Kc 36
Paru ∼ **YV** 112 Eb 43
Paru ∼ **BR** 113 Eg 45
Paru ∼ **BR** 120 Eh 46
Paru de Este ∼ **BR** 113 Eg 45
Paruna ○ **AUS** 378 Mg 63
Parur ○ **IND** 239 Kc 40
Paruro ○ **PE** 128 Dn 52
Parvān ⊙ **AFG** 223 Jn 28
Pārvatipuram ○ **IND** 234 Kf 36
Parvatsar ○ **IND** 234 Kb 32
Paryang ○ **VRC** 230 Kf 30
Parys ○ **ZA** 349 Hf 59
Paša ○ **RUS** 171 Hj 15
Pasadena ○ **CDN** 61 Ef 21
Pasadena ○ **USA** 64 Cc 28
Pasadena ○ **USA** 81 Da 31
Pasaje ○ **EC** 116 Dj 47
Pasaje o Juramento ∼ **RA** 136 Eb 58
Pasān ○ **IND** 234 Kf 34
Pasanauri ○ **GE** 202 Ja 24
Pasapuat ○ **RI** 270 La 47
Pasarbantal ○ **RI** 270 La 47
Pasarbembah ○ **RI** 270 La 47
Pasārgād ○ **IR** 215 Je 30
Pasarsibuhuan ○ **RI** 270 Kp 45
Pasartalo ○ **RI** 278 Lb 48
Pasarwajo ○ **RI** 282 Lm 48
Pasawug ○ **MYA** 254 Kn 36
Pascagoula ○ **USA** 86 Dd 30
Pascagoula ∼ **USA** 86 Dd 30
Pascani ○ **RO** 175 Hf 22
Pasco ○ **USA** 50 Cc 22
Pasco Island ◬ **AUS** 360 Lh 56
Pasewalk ○ **D** 170 Gn 19
Pasiere ○ **LV** 171 Hf 17
Pasig ○ **RP** 267 Ll 38
Pasinler ○ **TR** 202 Hn 25
Pasión ∼ **GCA** 93 Dc 37
Pasir Pengaraian ○ **RI** 270 La 45
Pasir Puteh ○ **MAL** 270 Lb 43
Paska Dinh ○ **LAO** 255 Lc 36
Paskenta ○ **USA** 64 Ca 26
Paškovskij ○ **RUS** 202 Hm 23
Pašman ◬ **HR** 194 Gp 24
Pasmore ∼ **AUS** 378 Mf 61
Pasni ○ **PK** 226 Jk 33
Paso ○ **RI** 283 Ma 47
Paso Bermejo △ **RCH** 137 Dn 62
Paso de Hachado △ **RA** 147 Dn 65
Paso de Huaytiquina △ **RCH** 136 Ea 57
Paso de Icalma △ **RA** 147 Dn 65
Paso de Indios ○ **RA** 147 Dp 67
Paso del Agua Negra △ **RA** 137 Dp 61
Paso de la Laguna ○ **RA** 146 Ee 61
Paso de Lesca ○ **C** 100 Dj 35
Paso del Indio ∼ **RCH** 152 Dl 70
Paso de los Libres ○ **RA** 146 Ef 60
Paso de los Toros ○ **ROU** 146 Ef 62
Paso del Planchon △ **RCH** 137 Dn 63
Paso del Rey ○ **RA** 137 Eb 62
Paso del Sapo ○ **RA** 147 Dp 67
Paso de Ménende △ **RCH** 147 Dm 67
Paso de Ovejas ○ **MEX** 92 Cp 36
Paso de Patria ○ **PY** 140 Ee 59
Paso de San Francisco △ **RCH** 136 Dp 59
Paso Mamuil Mulal △ **RA** 147 Dn 65
Paso Maule o Pehuenche △ **RA** 137 Dn 64
Paso Real de San Diego ○ **C** 100 Dg 34
Paso Robles ○ **USA** 64 Cb 28
Pasquia Hills ◬ **CDN** 51 Cl 19
Pasrur ○ **IND** 230 Kb 29
Passagem Franca ○ **BR** 124 En 49
Passage Pan ∼ **RB** 349 Hd 56
Passamaquoddy Bay ∼ **CDN** 61 Ea 23
Passau ○ **D** 174 Gn 21
Passe d'Amogjâr △ **RIM** 304 Fp 35
Passe de Djoûk △ **RIM** 304 Fp 37
Passe de Korizo △ **TCH** 309 Gp 34
Passe de la Sarcelle ∼ **F** 386 Nf 57
Passe de Salvador △ **RN** 296 Gn 34
Passe de Soufa △ **RIM** 304 Ga 38
Passi ○ **RP** 267 Lm 40
Passi ○ **SN** 316 Fm 39
Passira ○ **BR** 124 Fc 50
Pass Lake ○ **CDN** 57 Dd 21
Passo da Guarda ○ **BR** 146 Eg 61
Passo del Brennero Brennerpass △ **I** 174 Gm 22
Passo dello Stelvio △ **I** 174 Gm 22
Passo di Resia Reschenpass △ **A** 174 Gm 22
Passo Fundo ○ **BR** 146 Eh 60
Passos ○ **BR** 141 El 56
Pastavy ○ **BY** 171 Hf 18
Pasteur ○ **RA** 137 Ec 63
Pasto ○ **CO** 116 Dk 45
Pastol Bay ∼ **USA** 46 Aj 13
Pastos Bons ○ **BR** 121 Em 49
Pastura ○ **USA** 65 Ck 28
Pasuruan ○ **RI** 279 Lg 49
Pasvalys ○ **LT** 171 Hd 17
Pasvikelva ∼ **RUS** 159 Hg 11
Pata ○ **CO** 117 Dn 46
Pata ○ **SN** 316 Fn 39
Pata ○ **RCA** 321 Hc 41
Patacamaya ○ **BOL** 128 Dp 54
Patadkal ○ **IND** 238 Kb 38
Patagonia ▭ **RA** 152 Dn 71
Pata Island ◬ **RP** 275 Ll 43
Pataiya ○ **IND** 239 Kc 40
Patakata ○ **IND** 235 Kk 33
Patambalu ○ **RDC** 333 Hb 47
Patamuté ○ **BR** 124 Fa 50
Patan ○ **IND** 227 Jp 34
Patan ○ **NEP** 235 Kg 32
Pātan ○ **IND** 238 Ka 37
Patani ○ **RI** 275 Ma 45
Patas ○ **IND** 238 Kb 36
Patawanga Lake ∼ **CDN** 57 Dd 20
Patchogue ○ **USA** 74 Dm 25
Patea ○ **NZ** 383 Nk 65
Pategi ○ **WAN** 320 Gj 41
Pate Island ◬ **EAK** 337 Hn 47
Patelão ∼ **BR** 132 Ef 51
Paternó ○ **I** 185 Gp 27
Paternoster ○ **ZA** 358 Ha 62
Pateros ○ **USA** 50 Cb 21
Paterson ○ **USA** 50 Cc 23
Paterson ○ **USA** 74 Dl 25
Paterson ○ **ZA** 358 He 62
Paterson Inlet ∼ **NZ** 382 Ng 69
Paterson Range ⛰ **AUS** 360 Lm 56
Pathalaia ○ **NEP** 235 Kg 32
Pathalgaon ○ **IND** 235 Kf 34
Pathānkot ○ **IND** 230 Kb 29
Patharkot ○ **NEP** 235 Kg 32
Pathfinder Reservoir ∼ **USA** 51 Cj 24
Pathin ○ **THA** 262 Kp 40
Pāthrud ○ **IND** 238 Kb 36
Pathum Thanni ○ **THA** 262 La 38
Pathvant Range ⛰ **USA** 64 Cf 26
Pati ○ **GE** 202 Hn 24
Pati ○ **RI** 278 Lf 49
Patía ∼ **CO** 106 Dj 45
Patiala ○ **IND** 230 Kc 30
Patio Chiquito ○ **CO** 107 Dn 43
Patkai Range ⛰ **IND** 254 Km 32
Pátmos ○ **GR** 194 Hf 27
Pátmos ◬ **GR** 194 Hf 27
Patna ○ **IND** 235 Kg 33
Patnitola ○ **BD** 235 Kj 33
Patnonongan Island ◬ **RP** 267 Lm 38
Patnos ○ **TR** 202 Hp 26
Pato ○ **CO** 106 Dl 42
Pato Branco ○ **BR** 140 Eh 59
Patoka ∼ **USA** 71 De 26
Patomskoye Nagor'ye ⛰ **RUS** 204 Vb 7
Patonga ○ **EAU** 325 Hj 44
Patonga ○ **AUS** 364 Mc 52
Patos ○ **BR** 124 Fb 49
Patos ∼ **RA** 137 Dp 62
Patos de Minas ○ **BR** 133 El 55
Patos du São José ∼ **BR** 132 Ef 52
Patos Lagoon ∼ **BR** 146 Ej 61
Patquia ○ **RA** 137 Ea 61
Pátra ○ **GR** 194 Hc 26
Patraikos Kólpos 〰 **GR** 194 Hc 26
Patrakeevka ○ **RUS** 159 Hn 13
Patreksfjörður ○ **IS** 158 Fj 13
Patricia ○ **CDN** 51 Cg 20
Patricia ○ **USA** 56 Cm 24
Patricia ○ **USA** 65 Cl 29
Patridge ∼ **CDN** 57 Dh 20
Patrimonjo ○ **BR** 133 Ek 55
Patrocínio ○ **BR** 133 El 55
Pattamada ○ **IND** 239 Kc 41
Pattani ○ **THA** 270 La 42
Pattaya ○ **THA** 262 La 39
Patten ○ **USA** 60 Dp 23
Patterson ○ **USA** 50 Cf 23
Patterson ○ **USA** 64 Cb 27
Patterson ○ **USA** 87 Dg 30
Patterson ∼ **AUS** 364 Mb 52
Patti ○ **I** 185 Gp 26
Pattoki ○ **PK** 230 Ka 30
Patton ○ **USA** 71 Dd 27
Pattonsburg ○ **USA** 70 Da 25
Pattukkottai ○ **IND** 239 Kd 40
Patu ○ **BR** 124 Fb 49
Patuakhali ○ **BD** 235 Kk 34
Patuca ∼ **HN** 97 Df 38
Paturau Mangarakau ○ **NZ** 382 Nh 66
Pátzcuaro ○ **MEX** 92 Cm 36
Patzimaro ○ **MEX** 92 Cl 35
Pau ○ **F** 184 Gf 24
Pauanui ○ **NZ** 383 Nk 64
Paucarcolla ○ **PE** 128 Dn 53
Paucartambo ∼ **PE** 128 Dl 51
Paucartambo ○ **PE** 128 Dn 52
Pau d'Arco ∼ **BR** 121 Ej 49
Pau d'Arco ○ **BR** 121 Ek 49
Pau de Ferros ○ **BR** 124 Fa 49
Pauh ○ **RI** 278 Lb 47
Pauillac ○ **F** 184 Gf 23
Pauini ∼ **BR** 117 Dp 49
Pauini ○ **BR** 117 Ea 49
Pauini ∼ **BR** 117 Ec 46
Pauk ○ **MYA** 254 Km 35
Paukkaung ○ **MYA** 254 Km 36
Paulatuk ○ **CDN** 47 Bn 11
Paulau Sipura ◬ **RI** 270 Kp 47
Paulaya ∼ **HN** 97 Df 38
Paulina ○ **USA** 50 Cc 23
Paulina Peak △ **USA** 50 Cb 24
Paulino Neves ○ **BR** 124 En 47
Paulista ○ **BR** 124 Fc 50
Paulistana ○ **BR** 124 Ep 50
Paulo Alfonso ○ **BR** 124 Fa 50
Paulo do Faria ○ **BR** 140 Ek 56
Paulo Ramos ○ **BR** 121 Em 48
Paulpietersburg ○ **ZA** 352 Hh 59
Paul Roux ○ **ZA** 349 Hf 60
Pauls Valley ○ **USA** 70 Cp 28
Paungdawthi ○ **MYA** 262 Kn 37
Paungde ○ **MYA** 254 Km 36
Pauni ○ **IND** 234 Kd 35
Paup ○ **PNG** 286 Mh 47
Pauri ○ **IND** 234 Kc 33
Pausa ○ **PE** 128 Dm 53
Pauto ∼ **CO** 107 Dn 43
Pauwasi ∼ **RI** 286 Mg 47
Pāvagada ○ **IND** 238 Kc 38
Pavão ○ **BR** 125 Ep 54
Pāve ○ **IR** 209 Jb 28
Pavia ○ **I** 185 Gl 23
Pavilion ○ **CDN** 50 Ca 20
Pāvilosta ○ **LV** 170 Hc 17
Pavlodar ○ **KZ** 204 Ta 8
Pavlof Volcano △ **USA** 46 Aj 17
Pavlohrad ○ **UA** 181 Hj 21
Pavlovac ○ **HR** 174 Ha 23
Pavlovka ○ **RUS** 181 Jb 19
Pavlovo ○ **RUS** 181 Hp 18
Pavlovsk ○ **RUS** 171 Hh 16
Pavlovsk ○ **RUS** 181 Hn 20
Pavlovskaja ○ **RUS** 181 Hm 22
Pavlyš ○ **UA** 175 Hj 21
Pavullo nel Frignano ○ **I** 185 Gm 23
Pavuvu Island ◬ **SOL** 290 Nb 50
Pawan ∼ **RI** 271 Lf 46
Pawāyān ○ **IND** 234 Ke 32
Pawhuska ○ **USA** 70 Cp 27
Pawnee ○ **USA** 70 Cp 27
Pawnee City ○ **USA** 70 Cp 25
Pawnee Indian Village S.H.S ★ **USA** 70 Cn 26
Paw Paw ○ **USA** 71 De 24
Pawtucket ○ **USA** 74 Dn 25
Pawut ○ **MYA** 262 Kp 39
Paxi ◬ **GR** 194 Hb 26
Paxiúbe ∼ **BR** 120 Ed 50
Paxson ○ **USA** 46 Bc 13
Payagyi ○ **MYA** 262 Kn 37
Payakumbuh ○ **RI** 270 La 46
Payar ○ **SN** 304 Fn 38
Payarheisalam ○ **RI** 275 Lp 45
Payeti ○ **RI** 282 Ll 50
Payette ○ **USA** 50 Cd 23
Payette ∼ **USA** 50 Cd 23
Paynes Find ○ **AUS** 368 Lj 60
Paynesville ○ **USA** 56 Da 23
Paynesville ○ **AUS** 379 Mk 64
Payogasta ○ **RA** 136 Ea 58
Paysandú ○ **ROU** 146 Ee 62
Pays de la Centre ⊙ **F** 163 Gg 21
Pays de la Loire ⊙ **F** 163 Gg 21
Payson ○ **USA** 65 Cg 28
Payyānnur ○ **IND** 238 Kb 39
Paz ∼ **BOL** 129 Ea 54
Pazar ○ **TR** 202 Hn 25
Pazarcık ○ **TR** 195 Hl 27
Pazardžik ○ **BG** 194 Hd 24
Paz de Ariporo ○ **CO** 107 Dn 43
Paz del Rio ○ **CO** 107 Dm 43
Pazha ○ **PK** 227 Jn 31
Pazos Kanki ○ **RA** 137 Ec 63
Pcič ∼ **BY** 171 Hg 19
Pe ○ **MYA** 262 Kp 39
Pea ∼ **USA** 86 Dd 30
Peace Memorial ★ **J** 251 Mc 28
Peace River ∼ **CDN** 6 Da 6
Peace River ∼ **CDN** 47 Ca 17
Peace River ○ **CDN** 47 Cc 17
Peace River ∼ **CDN** 47 Cc 17
Peace River ∼ **USA** 87 Dh 32
Peach Springs ○ **USA** 64 Cf 28
Peachtree City ○ **USA** 86 Df 29
Peak Baboquivari △ **USA** 80 Cg 30
Peak Carstensz △ **RI** 286 Me 48
Peak Charles ⚲ **AUS** 368 Ll 62
Peak Charles △ **AUS** 368 Ll 62
Peak District ⚲ **GB** 163 Gf 19
Peake ○ **AUS** 378 Mf 63
Peake Creek ∼ **AUS** 374 Md 60
Peake Hill △ **AUS** 360 Lk 56
Peak Hill ○ **AUS** 368 Lk 58
Peak Hill ○ **AUS** 379 Mk 62
Peal Sound 〰 **CDN** 7 Ea 2
Pearce ○ **USA** 80 Ch 30
Pearce Point ⌓ **AUS** 364 Ma 53
Pearisburg ○ **USA** 71 Dh 27
Pearl ∼ **USA** 86 Dc 30
Pearland ○ **USA** 81 Da 31
Pearl City ○ **USA** 75 Am 35
Pearl Harbor ★ **USA** 75 Al 35
Pearsall ○ **USA** 81 Cn 31
Pearson ○ **USA** 86 Dg 30
Pearson Island ◬ **AUS** 378 Md 62
Pearston ○ **ZA** 358 He 62
Peary Channel 〰 **CDN** 42 Fa 3
Peary Land ▭ **DK** 18 Ha 1
Pease ∼ **USA** 70 Cn 28
Peba ∼ **BR** 121 Ek 49
Pebane ○ **MOC** 344 Hm 54
Pebas ○ **PE** 117 Dn 47
Pebble Island ◬ **GB** 147 Ee 71
Peč ○ **SCG** 194 Hc 24
Pecangakan ○ **RI** 278 Lf 49
Peçanha ○ **BR** 141 En 55
Pecan Island ○ **USA** 86 Db 31
Pečenga ○ **RUS** 159 Hh 11
Pečeniz'ke vodoschovyšče ∼ **UA** 181 Hl 21
Pechora ∼ **RUS** 19 Mb 3
Pechora ∼ **RUS** 154 Rb 5
Pechora ○ **RUS** 154 Rc 5
Pechora ∼ **RUS** 154 Rc 6
Pechorskoye More 〰 **RUS** 154 Rb 5
Pečory ○ **RUS** 171 Hf 17
Pecos ○ **USA** 81 Cl 30
Pecos Plains ▭ **USA** 65 Ck 29
Pecos River ∼ **USA** 65 Ck 28
Pécs ○ **H** 174 Hb 22
Pedasi ○ **PA** 97 Dj 42
Pedda Arikatla ○ **IND** 238 Kd 38
Peddapalli ○ **IND** 238 Kd 36
Peddie ○ **ZA** 358 Hf 62
Pedernales ○ **DOM** 101 Dm 36
Pedernales ○ **YV** 112 Ec 41
Pedernales ○ **RCH** 136 Dp 59
Pederneiras ○ **BR** 141 Ek 57
Pé de Serra ○ **BR** 125 Fa 51
Pedirka ○ **AUS** 374 Md 59
Pedra ○ **BR** 124 Fb 50
Pedra Azul ○ **BR** 125 Ep 54
Pedra Badejo ○ **CV** 316 Fj 38
Pedra Branca ○ **BR** 124 Fa 48
Pedra de Amolar ∼ **BR** 121 El 50
Pedra do Feitiço ○ **ANG** 332 Gn 48
Pedra Grande ○ **BR** 125 Ep 54
Pedra Lume ○ **CV** 316 Fj 37
Pedra Preta ○ **BR** 132 Eg 54
Pedras Grandes ○ **BR** 141 Ek 60
Pedras Tonhosas ◬ **STP** 332 Gk 45
Pedregal ∼ **MEX** 93 Db 37
Pedregal ○ **YV** 107 Dn 40
Pedregal ∼ **YV** 107 Dn 40
Pedregal ○ **BR** 146 Eg 61
Pedregulho ○ **BR** 141 El 56
Pedreira ∼ **BR** 121 Ej 45
Pedreiras ○ **BR** 121 Em 48
Pedreiras ○ **BR** 146 Eh 61
Pedriceña ○ **MEX** 80 Ck 33
Pedro Alexandre ○ **BR** 124 Fa 50
Pedro Alonso ○ **BR** 121 Ek 50
Pedro Antunes ○ **BR** 146 Eh 61
Pedro Avelino ○ **BR** 124 Fb 48
Pedro Bank ⋎ 100 Dj 37
Pedro Barros ○ **BR** 141 El 58
Pedro Betancourt ○ **C** 100 Dh 34
Pedro Canário ○ **BR** 141 Fa 55
Pedro Carbo ○ **EC** 116 Dh 46
Pedro Cays ◬ **JA** 100 Dj 37
Pedro de Valdivia ○ **RCH** 136 Dp 57
Pedro Gomes ○ **BR** 132 Eg 55
Pedro II ○ **BR** 124 Ep 48
Pedro Juan Caballero ○ **PY** 140 Ef 57
Pedro Luro ○ **RA** 147 Ec 65
Pedro Montoya ○ **MEX** 92 Cm 35
Pedro Osório ○ **BR** 146 Eh 61
Peebinga ○ **AUS** 378 Mg 63
Peebles ○ **GB** 162 Ge 18
Peedamulla ○ **AUS** 360 Lh 56
Pee Dee ∼ **USA** 74 Dj 28
Pee Dee River ∼ **USA** 87 Dj 29
Peekskill ○ **USA** 74 Dm 25
Peel ○ **GB** 162 Gd 18
Peel River ∼ **CDN** 6 Ca 3
Peel River ∼ **CDN** 47 Bj 11
Peel Sound 〰 **CDN** 42 Fb 4
Peeramudlayeppa Lake ∼ **AUS** 374 Me 59
Peera Peera Poolanna Lake ∼ **AUS** 374 Me 59
Peerless ○ **USA** 51 Ck 21
Peers ○ **CDN** 50 Ce 19
Peetz ○ **USA** 65 Cl 25
Pegasus Bay ∼ **NZ** 383 Nj 67
Pegatan ○ **RI** 279 Lg 47
Pego ○ **E** 184 Gf 26
Pegu ○ **MYA** 262 Kn 37
Peguis Indian Reservation ••• **CDN** 56 Cn 20
Pegunungan Abuki ⛰ **RI** 282 Ll 47
Pegunungan Balingara △ **RI** 282 Ll 46
Pegunungan Balingara △ **RI** 282 Ll 46
Pegunungan Border ⛰ **RI** 286 Mg 47
Pegunungan Fakfak ⛰ **RI** 283 Mc 47
Pegunungan Foja ⛰ **RI** 286 Mf 47
Pegunungan Gauttier ⛰ **RI** 286 Mf 47
Pegunungan Hose ⛰ **MAL** 274 Lg 44
Pegunungan Jayawijaya ⛰ **RI** 286 Mf 48
Pegunungan Kumafa ⛰ **RI** 283 Mc 47
Pegunungan Mekongga ⛰ **RI** 282 Ll 47
Pegunungan Müller ⛰ **RI** 274 Lg 45
Pegunungan Muratus ⛰ **RI** 279 Lh 47
Pegunungan Paleleh ⛰ **RI** 275 Ll 45
Pegunungan Pusat Gajo ⛰ **RI** 270 Kn 43
Pegunungan Schwaner ⛰ **RI** 271 Lf 46
Pegunungan Sergeulangit ⛰ **RI** 270 Kn 44
Pegunungan Sudirman ⛰ **RI** 286 Me 47
Pegunungan Tamrau ⛰ **RI** 283 Mc 46
Pegunungan Tineba ⛰ **RI** 282 Ll 46
Pegunungan Tineba ⛰ **RI** 282 Ll 46
Pegunungan Tiyo ⛰ **RI** 283 Md 48
Pegunungan Van Rees ⛰ **RI** 286 Me 47
Pegunungan Wondiwoi ⛰ **RI** 283 Md 47
Péhonko ○ **DY** 317 Gh 40
Pehowa ○ **IND** 230 Kc 31
Pehowa Road ○ **IND** 234 Kc 31
Pehuajó ○ **RA** 137 Ed 63
Pehuén-Co ○ **RA** 147 Ed 65
Peigan Indian Reservation ••• **CDN** 50 Cf 21
Peili ○ **SUD** 324 Hf 42
Peinan Hsi ∼ **RC** 259 Ll 34
Peixa ∼ **BR** 133 Ej 53
Peixes ou de São Francisco ∼ **BR** 132 Ef 51
Peixe ∼ **BR** 133 Eh 54
Peixe ○ **BR** 133 Ek 51
Peixe ∼ **BR** 133 Ek 53
Peixe Couro ou Aquinabo ∼ **BR** 132 Eg 54
Pei Xian ○ **VRC** 246 Lj 28
Peixoto de Azevedo ○ **BR** 132 Eg 51
Peixoto de Azevedo ∼ **BR** 132 Eg 51
Peka ○ **SOL** 290 Nb 51
Pekabata ○ **RI** 279 Lk 47
Pekalongan ○ **RI** 278 Le 49
Pekan ○ **MAL** 271 Lb 44
Pekanbaru ○ **RI** 270 La 45
Pekin ○ **USA** 56 Cn 22
Pekin ○ **USA** 71 Dd 25
Pekinga ○ **DY** 320 Gh 39
Pekkala ○ **FIN** 159 Hf 12
Peklino ○ **RUS** 171 Hj 19
Pekul'ney, Khrebet ⛰ **RUS** 205 Zb 5
Péla ○ **RG** 316 Gb 42
Pelabuhanratu ○ **RI** 278 Ld 49
Pelawanbesan ○ **RI** 274 Lj 45
Pelébina ○ **DY** 317 Gg 41
Pelechuco ○ **BOL** 128 Dp 53
Pelee ◬ **CDN** 71 Dg 25
Pelei ○ **RI** 282 Lm 46
Peleihari ○ **RI** 279 Lh 47
Pelejo ○ **PE** 116 Dl 49
Pelekech Range ⛰ **EAK** 325 Hk 44
Pelelu Tepu ○ **SME** 113 Eg 44
Pelenge ○ **RDC** 333 Hd 47
Pelézi ○ **CI** 305 Gc 42
Pelham ○ **AUS** 365 Mh 55
Pelhřimov ○ **CZ** 174 Gp 21
Pelican Lake ∼ **CDN** 56 Cm 19
Pelicano ∼ **RCH** 137 Dn 60
Pelican Rapids ○ **USA** 56 Cp 22
Pelikan Lake ∼ **USA** 56 Db 22
Pelkosenniemi ○ **FIN** 159 Hf 12
Pella ○ **USA** 70 Db 25
Pell City ○ **USA** 71 De 29
Pellegrini ○ **RA** 137 Ec 64
Pello ○ **FIN** 159 He 12
PellstonCharlevoix ○ **USA** 57 Df 23
Pellworm ◬ **D** 170 Gl 18
Pelly Bay 〰 **CDN** 43 Fc 5
Pelly Bay ○ **CDN** 43 Ga 5
Pelly Crossing ○ **CDN** 47 Bg 13
Pelly River ∼ **CDN** 47 Bj 13
Pelmadulla ○ **CL** 239 Ke 42
Peloponnese ⊙ **GR** 194 Hc 27
Pelopónnissos ⊙ **GR** 194 Hc 27
Pelotas ○ **BR** 146 Eh 61
Pelsart Island ◬ **AUS** 368 Lh 60
Pelsor ○ **USA** 70 Db 28
Pem ○ **PNG** 287 Ml 50
Pemadumcook Lake ∼ **USA** 60 Dp 23
Pemalang ○ **RI** 278 Le 49
Pemangkat ○ **RI** 271 Le 45
Pematang Purba ○ **RI** 270 Kp 45
Pematangsiantar ○ **RI** 270 Kp 44
Pemba ○ **Z** 341 Hf 54
Pemba ○ **MOC** 344 Hn 52
Pemba Channel ∼ **EAT** 337 Hm 48
Pemba Island ◬ **EAT** 337 Hm 48
Pembe ○ **MOC** 352 Hk 57
Pemberton ○ **CDN** 50 Ca 20
Pemberton ○ **AUS** 368 Lj 63
Pembina ∼ **CDN** 50 Cd 19
Pembina ○ **USA** 56 Cp 21
Pembina River ∼ **CDN** 56 Cn 21
Pembine ○ **USA** 57 Dd 23
Pembre ○ **RI** 286 Me 49
Pembrobeshire Coast ⚲ **GB** 163 Gd 20
Pembroke ○ **CDN** 60 Dk 23
Pembroke ○ **GB** 163 Gd 20
Pemgze ○ **VRC** 258 Lj 31
Pemir ○ **IND** 235 Kl 32
Pemuco ○ **RCH** 137 Dm 64
Pen ○ **IND** 238 Ka 36
Pen. de Paracas ◬ **PE** 116 Dk 52
Peña Blanca ○ **RCH** 136 Dn 59
Peñaflor ○ **RCH** 137 Dn 62
Penalva ○ **BR** 121 Em 47
Penampang ○ **MAL** 274 Lj 43
Penápolis ○ **BR** 140 Ej 56
Peñaranda de Bracamonte ○ **E** 184 Gd 25
Peñarroya △ **E** 184 Gf 25
Peñarroya-Pueblonuevo ○ **E** 184 Gd 26
Peñas Blancas ○ **NIC** 97 Df 40
Penascola Mountains ⛰ 38 Ha 18
Pench National Park ⚲ **IND** 234 Kd 35
Pendé ∼ **RCA** 321 Gp 42
Pendé ∼ **TCH** 321 Ha 42
Pendembu ○ **WAL** 316 Fp 41
Pendembu ○ **WAL** 316 Ga 41
Pender ○ **USA** 56 Cp 24
Pender Bay ∼ **AUS** 360 Lm 54
Pendjan ∼ **DY** 317 Gg 40
Pendjua ○ **RDC** 333 Hb 46
Pendleton ○ **USA** 50 Cc 23
Pendleton ○ **USA** 71 Df 26
Pendopo ○ **RI** 278 Lb 47
Pend Oreille ∼ **USA** 50 Cd 21
Pend Oreille Lake ∼ **USA** 50 Cd 22
Penebel ○ **RI** 279 Lh 50
Penedo ○ **BR** 125 Fb 51
Pene-Katamba ○ **RDC** 333 He 46
Pene-Mende ○ **RDC** 336 Hg 48
Penetanguishene ○ **CDN** 57 Dh 23
Peng'an ○ **VRC** 243 Ld 30
Pengang ∼ **IND** 238 Kd 36
Pengastulan ○ **RI** 279 Lh 50
Pengchia Yü ◬ **RC** 259 Ll 33
Penge ○ **RDC** 324 Hf 44
Pengkou ○ **VRC** 258 Lj 33
Penglai ○ **VRC** 246 Ll 27
Penglai ○ **VRC** 255 Lf 36
Pengshan ○ **VRC** 242 Lb 30
Pengshui ○ **VRC** 255 Le 31
Penguin ○ **AUS** 378 Mk 66
Penguin Islands ◬ **CDN** 61 Ef 22
Pengxi ○ **VRC** 243 Lc 30
Penhalonga ○ **ZW** 344 Hj 55
Pen Hills ○ **USA** 74 Dj 25
Penhoek Pass △ **ZA** 349 Hf 61
Péni ○ **BF** 317 Gd 40
Peniche ○ **P** 184 Gb 26
Penies ◬ **FJI** 387 Nm 54
Peninga ○ **RUS** 159 Hj 14
Peninsula ◬ **NZ** 383 Nk 64
Península Antonio Varas ◬ **RCH** 152 Dm 71
Península Brecknock ◬ **RCH** 152 Dn 73
Península Brunswick ◬ **RCH** 152 Dn 72
Península Córdoba ◬ **RCH** 152 Dm 72
Península de Araya ◬ **YV** 112 Eb 40
Península de Guanahacabibes ◬ **C** 100 Df 34
Península de Muños Gamero ◬ **RCH** 152 Dm 72
Península de Paria ⚲ **YV** 112 Ec 40
Península de Paria ◬ **YV** 112 Ec 40
Península de Taitao ◬ **RCH** 152 Dl 69
Península de Tumbes ◬ **RCH** 137 Dm 64
Península de Vizcaíno ◬ **MEX** 75 Ce 32
Península de Zapata ▭ **C** 100 Dh 34
Península dos Tigres ◬ **ANG** 340 Gm 54
Península Dumas ◬ **RCH** 152 Dp 73
Península El Palmar ◬ **MEX** 93 Dc 36
Península Hardy ◬ **RCH** 152 Dp 73
Península Huequi ◬ **RCH** 147 Dm 67
Península Mitre ◬ **RA** 152 Ea 73
Península Paraguaná ▭ **YV** 107 Dn 39
Península Roca ◬ **RCH** 152 Dm 71
Península Rous ◬ **RCH** 152 Dp 73
Península S. Martin ◬ **RCH** 152 Dl 70
Península San Juan del Gozo ◬ **ES** 93 Dd 39
Península Sisquelan ◬ **RCH** 152 Dl 69
Península Skyring ◬ **RCH** 152 Dl 68
Península Staines ◬ **RCH** 152 Dm 71
Península Swett ◬ **RCH** 152 Dl 70
Península Tres Montes ◬ **RCH** 152 Dl 69
Península Valiente ◬ **PA** 97 Dh 41
Península Verde ◬ **RA** 147 Ed 65
Península Wharton ◬ **RCH** 152 Dl 70
Península Wilcock ◬ **RCH** 152 Dl 71
Péninsule de Gaspé ▭ **CDN** 61 Ea 21
Péninsule d'Ungava ◬ **CDN** 43 Gc 6
Peninular Lake ∼ **CDN** 57 Dd 20
Penjabungan Tonga ○ **RI** 270 Kp 45
Pénjamo ○ **MEX** 92 Cl 35
Pennādam ○ **IND** 239 Kd 40
Pennant ○ **CDN** 51 Ch 20

□Country ▣Capital city ◉Administrative unit ○Place ♁Island ⛰Mountain range △Mountain ⌓Cape ≈Ocean, Sea ~Lake, River ΨUndersea topography ▲Glacier ♀National park •••Reservation ★Point of major interest ⌒Landscape

Penner ~ IND 238 Kc 38
Penneshaw ○ AUS 378 Me 63
Pennsylvania ◉ USA 74 Dj 25
Penn Yan ○ USA 60 Dk 24
Penny Strait ~ CDN 7 Ea 2
Penny Strait ≈ CDN 42 Fb 3
Peno ○ RUS 171 Hj 17
Penoka ○ LB 304 Gc 43
Penola ○ AUS 378 Mg 64
Peñón Blanco ○ MEX 81 Ck 33
Penong ○ AUS 369 Mc 61
Penonomé ○ PA 97 Dh 41
Penrhyn Tongareva ♁ NZ 35 Ba 10
Penrhyn Basin Ψ 14 Ba 10
Penrith ○ GB 162 Ge 18
Penrith ○ AUS 379 Mm 62
Pensa ○ BF 317 Gf 39
Pensacola ○ USA 86 De 30
Pensacola Bay ~ USA 86 De 30
Penshurst ○ AUS 378 Mh 64
Pensilvania ○ CO 106 Dl 43
Pentecost ♁ VU 386 Ng 53
Pentecost Downs Karunjie ○ AUS 361 Lp 54
Pentecostes ○ BR 124 Fa 47
Pentecost Range ⛰ AUS 361 Lp 53
Penticton ○ CDN 50 Cc 21
Penticton Indian Reservation ••• CDN 50 Cb 21
Pentland ○ AUS 375 Mj 56
Pentland Firth ~ GB 162 Ge 16
Pentwater ○ USA 57 De 24
Penukonda ○ IND 238 Kc 38
Penwegon ○ MYA 254 Kn 36
Penza ○ RUS 181 Ja 19
Penzance ○ GB 163 Gd 20
Penzele ○ RDC 333 Hb 46
Penzhinskaya Guba ≈ RUS 205 Yc 6
Penžina ~ RUS 23 Ta 3
Penžina ~ RUS 205 Za 6
Peoria ○ USA 65 Cf 29
Peoria ○ USA 71 Dd 25
Pepa ○ RDC 336 Hg 49
Pepani ~ ZA 349 Hd 59
Pependicular Cliffs ⌒ AUS 369 Ln 62
Pepita ou Port Alegre ~ BR 121 Eh 50
Peque ○ CO 106 Dl 42
Pequeri ~ BR 132 Eg 54
Pequot Lakes ○ USA 56 Da 22
per. Bicanekskij △ ARM 202 Ja 26
Perabumulih ○ RI 278 Lc 47
Peraconi ~ BR 120 Ee 47
Peraguaizinho ~ BR 132 Ef 53
Peraiyur ○ IND 239 Kc 41
Perambalūr ○ IND 239 Kd 40
Perāmeri ⌓ FIN 159 Hd 13
Perbaungan ○ RI 270 Kp 44
Perbulan ○ RI 270 Kn 44
Percé ○ CDN 61 Eb 21
Percival Lakes ~ AUS 361 Ln 56
Perdekop ○ ZA 349 Hg 59
Perdita ~ BR 121 El 50
Perdizes ○ BR 133 El 55
Perdões ○ BR 141 Em 56
Perdue ○ CDN 51 Cj 19
Perédaka ○ RG 316 Fp 40
Pereira ○ CO 106 Dl 43
Pereira Barreto ○ BR 140 Ej 56
Pereiro ○ BR 124 Fa 49
Perejaslav-Chmel'nyc'kyj ○ UA 175 Hh 20
Perejaslavka ○ RUS 250 Md 22
Pereljub ○ RUS 181 Jd 20
Peremetnoe ○ KZ 181 Jd 20
Peremyšl' ○ RUS 171 Hk 18
Perené ~ PE 128 Dl 51
Perenjori ○ AUS 368 Lj 60
Perenka ○ FIN 159 Hg 13
Pèrèrè ○ DY 320 Gh 41
Pereščepyne ○ UA 175 Hk 21
Pereslavl'-Zalesskij ○ RUS 171 Hm 17
pereval Akbajtal △ TJ 230 Ka 26
pereval Anzob △ TJ 223 Jn 26
pereval Čyiyrčyk △ KS 230 Ka 25
pereval Harami △ RUS 202 Jb 24
pereval Kajtezek △ TJ 230 Ka 27
pereval Krestovyi △ GE 202 Ja 24
pereval Kyzyl-Art △ TJ 230 Ka 26
pereval Najzataš △ TJ 230 Ka 27
pereval Taldyk △ KS 230 Ka 26
Perevoz ○ RUS 181 Ja 18
Perez ○ RA 137 Ed 62
Pergamino ○ RA 137 Ed 62
Pergamon ★ TR 195 Hf 26
Perham ○ USA 56 Da 22
Perho ○ FIN 159 He 14
Periá ~ BR 124 En 47
Peribán de Ramos ○ MEX 92 Cl 36
Péribonca ~ CDN 60 Dn 20
Péribonka ○ CDN 60 Dn 21
Perico ○ USA 65 Cl 27
Perico ○ C 100 Dh 34
Pericos ○ MEX 80 Cj 33
Périgueux ○ F 184 Gg 23
Perija ♀ YV 107 Dm 41
Peri Lake ~ AUS 379 Mh 61
Perim ♁ YE 218 Hp 39
Peringat ○ MAL 270 Lb 42
Periquen ○ YV 112 Ed 43
Peri Suyu ~ TR 202 Hn 26
Perito Moreno ○ RA 152 Dn 69
Peritoro ○ BR 121 Em 48
Perm ○ RUS 19 Mb 4
Perm ○ RUS 154 Rc 7
Perma ○ DY 317 Gg 40
per Maruhskij △ RUS 202 Hn 24
Përmet ○ AL 194 Hc 25
Pernambuco ◉ BR 124 Ep 50
Pernambut ○ IND 238 Kd 39
Pernatty Lagoon ~ AUS 378 Me 61
Pernik ○ BG 194 Hd 24
Perniö ○ FIN 159 Hd 15
Perola ○ BR 140 Eh 57
Peronne ○ F 163 Gh 21
Perote ○ MEX 92 Cp 35
Peroto ○ BOL 129 Eb 53
Perpignan ○ F 185 Gh 24
Perquilauquén ~ RCH 137 Dn 64
Perrault Falls ○ CDN 56 Db 20
Perrinvale ○ AUS 368 Ll 60
Perriyar ~ IND 239 Kc 40
Perros-Guirec ○ F 163 Ge 21
Perry ○ CDN 57 Df 22
Perry ○ USA 70 Cp 27
Perry ○ USA 70 Da 25
Perry ○ USA 70 Dc 26
Perry ○ USA 71 Dg 29
Perry Hall ○ USA 74 Dk 26
Perry Lake ~ USA 70 Da 26
Perryton ○ USA 70 Cm 27
Perryville ○ USA 46 Al 17
Perryville ○ USA 71 Dc 27
Persepolis ★ IR 215 Je 31
Perseverancia ○ BOL 129 Ec 53
Persian Gulf ≈ IR 215 Jc 31
Pertek ○ TR 195 Hm 26
Perth ○ CDN 60 Dk 23
Perth ○ GB 162 Ge 17
Perth ○ AUS 368 Lh 61
Perth ○ AUS 378 Mk 66
Perth-Amboy ○ USA 74 Dl 25
Perth-Andover ○ CDN 60 Ea 22
Perth Basin Ψ AUS 368 Lg 61
Pertominsk ○ RUS 159 Hm 13
Pertuis Breton ~ F 163 Gf 22
Pertuis d'Antiocha ~ F 163 Gf 22
Peru ○ USA 71 Dd 25
Peru ▣ PE 128 Dl 53
Perú ○ BOL 129 Ea 52
Peru Basin Ψ 15 Ea 11
Peru-Chile-Trench Ψ 15 Eb 10
Peru-Chile-Trench Ψ 136 Dn 59
Perúgia ○ I 185 Gn 24
Perugorría ○ RA 146 Ee 60
Peruíbe ○ BR 141 El 58
Perumpāvūr ○ IND 239 Kc 40
Perundurai ○ IND 239 Kc 40
Pervari ○ TR 202 Hp 27
Pervomais'kyj ○ UA 175 Hk 21
Pervomajs'k ○ UA 175 Hh 21
Pervomajsk ○ RUS 181 Hp 18
Pervomajskoe ○ RUS 171 Hg 15
Pervomajskij ○ RUS 181 Hm 19
Pervosovetsk ○ KZ 181 Jd 20
Pervoural'sk ○ RUS 154 Rc 7
Pesace River ○ CDN 6 Da 4
Pésaro ○ I 185 Gn 24
Pescado ~ PY 136 Eb 57
Pesčanoe ○ RUS 159 Hk 14
Pescara ○ I 194 Gp 24
Peshāwar ○ PK 223 Jp 29
Peshkop ○ AL 194 Hc 25
Peshú Islands ♁ RC 258 Lk 34
peski Gurydangdan ⌒ TM 222 Jh 27
peski Sějunagsak ⌒ TM 222 Jf 26
Pesqueira ○ BR 124 Fb 50
Peštera ○ BG 194 He 24
Pestovo ○ RUS 171 Hk 16
Pestravka ○ RUS 181 Jc 19
Petah Tiqwa ○ IL 208 Hk 29
Petäjävesi ○ FIN 159 He 14
Petaling Jaya ○ MAL 270 La 44
Petaluma ○ USA 64 Ca 26
Petaquillas ○ MEX 92 Cn 37
Petarbar ○ IND 235 Kg 34
Petare ○ YV 107 Ea 40
Petatlán ○ MEX 92 Cm 37
Petauke ○ Z 341 Hh 53
Petawawa ○ CDN 60 Dk 23
Petcacab ○ MEX 93 Dd 36
Pété ○ CAM 321 Gp 40
Petén Itza Lake ~ GCA 93 Dd 37
Petenwell ~ USA 56 Dc 23
Peterbell ○ CDN 57 Dg 21
Peterborough ○ CDN 60 Dj 23
Peterborough ○ GB 163 Gf 19
Peterborough ○ AUS 378 Mf 62
Peterborough ○ AUS 378 Mh 65
Peterhead ○ GB 162 Gf 17
Peter Island ♁ 38 Ea 16
Petermann Aboriginal Land ••• AUS 369 Ma 58
Petermann Ranges ⛰ AUS 369 Ma 58
Peter Pond Lake ~ CDN 6 Db 4
Peter Pond Lake ~ CDN 42 Ec 7
Petersburg ○ USA 6 Ca 4
Petersburg ○ USA 42 Da 7
Petersburg ○ USA 74 Dj 26
Peter's Mine ○ GUY 112 Ee 42
Pétionville ○ RH 101 Dm 36
Petit-Bourg ○ F 104 Ed 37
Petite Forte ○ CDN 61 Eg 22
Petite Kabylie ⌒ DZ 296 Gj 27
Petit Goâve ○ RH 101 Dm 36
Petit Lac Manicouagan ~ CDN 60 Ea 20
Petit Point ⌓ AUS 368 Lg 58
Petit-Rocher ○ CDN 61 Ea 22
Petit-Saguenay ○ CDN 60 Dn 21
Petlād ○ IND 227 Ka 34
Peto ○ MEX 93 Dd 35
Petoh ○ MAL 271 Lb 44
Petorca ~ RCH 137 Dn 62
Petoskey ○ USA 57 Df 23
Petra ★ JOR 214 Hk 30
Petras Negras ○ BOL 129 Ec 52
Petre Bay ~ NZ 383 Ab 67
Petrič ○ BG 194 Hd 25
Petrified Wood Park ★ USA 51 Cl 23
Petrified Forest ♀ USA 65 Ch 28
Petro ○ PK 227 Jp 32
Petrodvorec ○ RUS 171 Hg 16
Petrohué ○ RCH 147 Dm 66
Petrolândia ○ BR 124 Fa 50
Petrolia ○ USA 64 Bp 25
Petrolina ○ BR 124 Ep 50
Petrolina de Goiás ○ BR 133 Ek 54
Petropavlovsk ○ KZ 19 Na 4
Petropavlovsk-Kamchatskiy ○ RUS 205 Yb 8
Petroquímica ○ RA 152 Ea 68
Petroșani ○ RO 194 Hd 23
Petrovac ○ SCG 174 Hc 23
Petrovo ○ RUS 171 Hk 16
Petrovsk ○ RUS 181 Ja 19
Petrov Val ○ RUS 181 Ja 20
Petrozavodsk ○ RUS 171 Hk 15
Petrusburg ○ ZA 349 He 60
Petrus Steyn ○ ZA 349 Hg 59
Petrusville ○ ZA 349 He 61
Petuški ○ RUS 171 Hm 18
Peulla ○ RCH 147 Dm 66
Peumo ○ RCH 137 Dn 63
Peureulak ○ RI 270 Kn 43
Peusangan ~ RI 270 Kn 43
Pevek ○ RUS 23 Tb 3
Pevek ○ RUS 205 Zb 5
Pézenas ○ F 185 Gh 24
Pezu ○ PK 223 Jp 29
Pforzheim ○ D 174 Gl 21
Phāgi ○ IND 234 Kb 32
Phaileng ○ IND 254 Kl 34
Phaisali ○ THA 262 La 38
Phalodi ○ IND 227 Ka 32
Phalombe ○ MW 344 Hk 53
Phāltan ○ IND 238 Kb 37
Phan ○ THA 254 Kp 36
Phangnga ○ THA 262 Kp 41
Phanom ○ THA 262 Kp 41
Phanom Dong Rak ⛰ THA 263 Lb 38
Phanom Sarakham ○ THA 262 La 39
Phan Rang ○ VN 263 Le 40
Phan Thiêt ○ VN 263 Le 40
Phapon ○ MYA 262 Km 37
Pharenda ○ IND 235 Kf 32
Pharr ○ USA 81 Cn 32
Phatthalung ○ THA 270 Kp 42
Phayakhapun Phiasi ○ THA 263 Lb 38
Phayao ○ THA 254 Kp 36
Phayuha Khiri ○ THA 262 La 38
Phedra ○ SME 113 Eg 43
Phenix City ○ USA 86 Df 29
Phet Buri ~ THA 262 Kp 39
Phetchabun ○ THA 262 La 37
Phetchaburi ○ THA 262 Kp 39
Phibun Mangsahan ○ THA 263 Lc 38
Phichit ○ THA 262 La 37
Philadelphia ○ USA 74 Dk 26
Philadelphia ○ USA 86 Dd 29
Philae ★ ET 301 Hj 34
Philip ○ USA 56 Cm 23
Philippeville ○ B 163 Gj 20
Philippines ▣ RP 267 Lm 38
Philippine Sea ≈ RP 267 Lm 38
Philippine Sea ≈ RP 267 Ln 37
Philippine Trench Ψ RP 267 Lp 39
Philippolis ○ ZA 349 He 61
Philipsburg ○ USA 51 Cf 22
Philipsburg ○ USA 70 Cn 26
Philipsburg ○ USA 70 Db 27
Philipsburg ○ NL 104 Ec 36
Philip Smith Mountains ⛰ USA 46 Ba 11
Philipstown ○ ZA 349 He 61
Phillip Creek ○ AUS 364 Mc 55
Phillip Creek Station ○ AUS 364 Mc 55
Phillip Island ♁ AUS 379 Mj 65
Phillips ○ USA 56 Dc 23
Phillips Mountains ⛰ 38 Ca 17
Phillips Range ⛰ AUS 361 Ln 54
Philpots Island ♁ CDN 43 Gc 4
Phippsøya ♁ N 158 Hb 5
Phitsanulok ○ THA 262 Kp 37
Phitshane ○ RB 349 He 58
Phnom Penh ▣ K 263 Lc 40
Phoenix ○ USA 65 Cf 29
Phoenix Islands ♁ KIR 35 Aa 10
Phon ○ THA 263 Lb 38
Phon ○ THA 263 Lc 37
Phoncharoen ○ THA 263 Lb 37
Phonda ○ IND 238 Ka 37
Phôngsali ○ LAO 254 Lb 35
Phong Thô ○ VN 255 Lb 34
Phong Thong ○ THA 263 Lb 37
Phon Sa Yan ○ LAO 255 Lb 36
Phop Phra ○ THA 262 Kp 37
Phou Khoun ○ LAO 254 Lb 36
Phrae ○ THA 254 La 36
Phranakhon Si Ayutthaya ○ THA 262 La 38
Phran Kratai ○ THA 262 Kp 37
Phra Pathom Chedi ★ THA 262 Kp 39
Phú Bai ○ VN 263 Ld 37
Phù Cát ○ VN 263 Le 38
Phuket ○ THA 270 Kp 42
Phu Khieo ○ THA 262 La 37
Phu Lan Chang ○ THA 263 Lc 37
Phulbari ○ BD 235 Kj 33
Phum ♁ GB 162 Gc 17
Phumĭ Bâ Kêv ○ K 263 Ld 39
Phumĭ Bham ○ K 263 Lc 39
Phumĭ Boeng Préav ○ K 263 Lb 40
Phumĭ Bung Lung ○ K 263 Ld 39
Phumĭ Chhlong ○ K 263 Lc 39
Phumĭ Chŏâm Sla ○ K 263 Lb 40
Phumĭ Chŏng Kai ○ K 263 Lb 39
Phumĭ Dei Lo ○ K 263 Lc 40
Phumĭ Kâmpóng Strâlaun ○ K 263 Lc 38
Phumĭ Kâmpóng Trâbêk ○ K 263 Lc 39
Phumĭ Kdŏl Kraôm ○ K 263 Lb 39
Phumĭ Khley ○ K 263 Lc 39
Phumĭ Khna ○ K 263 Lc 40
Phumĭ Khna Krau Phnŭma ○ K 263 Lc 39
Phumĭ Krêk ○ K 263 Lc 40
Phumĭ Leu ○ K 263 Ld 39
Phumĭ Mlu Prey ○ K 263 Lc 39
Phumĭ Peng Méas ○ K 263 Lc 39
Phumĭ Phsa Rôméas ○ K 263 Lc 40
Phumĭ Ponley ○ K 263 Lc 39
Phumĭ Prêk Khsay ○ K 263 Lc 40
Phumĭ Pring ○ K 263 Lc 39
Phumĭ Sala Vichey ○ K 263 Lc 39
Phumĭ Sâmraông ○ K 263 Lb 38
Phumĭ Suŏng ○ K 263 Lc 40
Phumĭ Taek Sŏk ○ K 263 Lb 39
Phumĭ Thalabârivăt ○ K 263 Lc 39
Phumĭ Thkov ○ K 263 Lb 39
Phumĭ Thmâ Pôk ○ K 263 Lb 39
Phumĭ Véal Rénh ○ K 263 Lb 40
Phu' Nong ○ VN 263 Ld 39
Phunphin ○ THA 262 Kp 41
Phuntsholing ○ BHT 235 Kj 32
Phu'ó'c So'n ○ VN 263 Ld 38
Phú Qúy ♁ VN 263 Le 40
Phurkia ○ IND 230 Kd 30
Phu Tho ○ VN 255 Lc 35
Phutnaditjhaba ○ ZA 349 Hg 60
Phuttaisong ○ THA 263 Lb 38
Phu Yen △ THA 262 La 37
Piaca dos Mineiros ○ BR 133 Eh 55
Piacenza ○ I 185 Gl 23
Piamonte ○ CO 106 Dl 42
Piana-Mwanga ○ RDC 336 Hf 49
Piancó ~ BR 124 Fa 49
Pian Creek ~ AUS 375 Ml 60
Piangil ○ AUS 378 Mh 63
Pianguan ○ VRC 243 Lf 26
Piankan ○ RDC 333 Ha 47
Piaski ○ PL 175 Hd 20
Piatraneamț ○ RO 175 He 22
Piauí ~ BR 124 Em 49
Piauí ◉ BR 124 En 50
Piauí ~ BR 124 En 50
Piave ~ I 174 Gm 22
Piaxtla ~ MEX 80 Cj 33
Piaxtla ○ MEX 92 Cj 34
Pibor ~ SUD 325 Hj 42
Pibor Post ○ SUD 325 Hj 42
Pica ○ RCH 136 Dp 56
Picacho del Diablo △ MEX 75 Ce 30
Pičaevo ○ RUS 181 Hp 19
Picanco ○ BR 124 Fb 49
Picardie ◉ F 163 Gg 21
Picayune ○ USA 86 Dd 30
Pic d'Aneto △ E 184 Gg 24
Pic de Guéra △ TCH 321 Hb 40
Pic de Tibé △ RG 316 Gb 41
Pic du Midi d'Ossau △ F 184 Gf 24
Piceno ○ I 185 Gn 24
Pich ○ MEX 93 Dc 36
Pichaman ○ RCH 137 Dm 63
Pichana ~ RA 137 Eb 61
Pichanal ○ PY 136 Eb 57
Pichanal ○ RA 136 Eb 57
Pichar ○ IND 234 Kc 33
Picher ○ USA 70 Da 27
Pichilemu ○ RCH 137 Dm 63
Pichilingú ○ MEX 80 Cg 33
Pichi Mahuida ○ RA 147 Eb 65
Pichis ~ PE 128 Dl 51
Pichucalco ○ MEX 93 Db 37
Pickerel Lake ~ CDN 56 Dc 21
Pickertaramoor ○ AUS 364 Mb 51
Pickle Lake ○ CDN 7 Eb 4
Pickstown ○ USA 56 Cn 24
Pickwick Lake ~ USA 71 Dd 28
Pico ♁ P 18 Hb 6
Pico Aitana △ E 184 Gf 26
Pico Ascotan ó del Jardin △ BOL 136 Dp 56
Pico Basilé △ GQ 320 Gl 44
Pico Bolívar △ YV 107 Dn 41
Pico Bonito △ HN 96 De 38
Pico Columna △ PA 97 Dj 41
Pico Cristóbal Colón △ CO 106 Dm 40
Pico da Bandeira △ BR 141 En 56
Pico da Neblina △ BR 112 Eb 45
Pico de Orizaba △ MEX 92 Cp 35
Pico de Salamanca ○ RA 152 Ea 68
Pico de Teide △ E 292 Fm 31
Pico do Carlo △ CV 316 Fh 38
Pico Kazer △ RCH 152 Ea 73
Pico Lowry △ MEX 75 Ce 32
Pico Pedra Azul △ BR 141 Ep 56
Pico Rondon △ BR 120 Ec 45
Picos ○ BR 124 Ep 49
Pico São Mateus △ BR 141 Ep 56
Picos de Europa △ E 184 Gd 24
Picota ○ PE 116 Dk 49
Pico Tabatinga △ BR 120 Ec 45
Pico Tamacuari △ BR 112 Eb 45
Pico Truncado ○ RA 152 Ea 69
Pico Turquino △ C 101 Dk 36
Pic River ~ CDN 57 De 21
Pic Tiska △ DZ 308 Gl 34
Picton ○ CDN 60 Dk 24
Picton ○ AUS 379 Mm 63
Picton ○ NZ 383 Nk 66
Pictou ○ CDN 61 Ec 23
Pictou Island ♁ CDN 61 Ec 23
Pic Toussidé △ TCH 309 Ha 35
Pictured Rocks Natl.Lakeshore ♀ USA 57 De 22
Picuí ○ BR 124 Fb 49
Picunda ○ GE 202 Hn 24
Picún Leufú ○ RA 147 Dp 65
Pidando ♁ DVRK 246 Ln 26
Pidarak ○ PK 226 Jk 33
Piedade ○ BR 141 El 57
Pie de Pepé ○ CO 106 Dk 43
Piedmont ○ USA 86 Df 29
Piedrabuena ○ E 184 Gd 26
Piedra del Águila ○ RA 147 Dn 66
Piedra Echada ○ RA 147 Ec 65
Piedras Altas ○ BR 146 Eh 61
Piedras Blancas ○ CR 97 Dg 41
Piedras Negras ○ MEX 81 Cm 31
Piedras Negras ○ RCH 147 Dm 66
Piedra Sola ○ ROU 146 Ef 62
Piedritas ○ MEX 81 Cl 31
Piedritas ○ RA 137 Ec 63
Pie Islands ♁ CDN 57 Dd 21
Piekenaarskloof △ ZA 358 Hb 62
Pieksämäki ○ FIN 159 Hf 14
Piéla ○ BF 317 Gf 39
Pielavesi ○ FIN 159 Hf 14
Pielinen ~ FIN 159 Hg 14
Pieljekaise ♀ S 158 Gp 12
Pieman ~ AUS 378 Mj 66
Piemonte ◉ I 185 Gk 23
Pienaarsrivier ○ ZA 349 Hf 58
Piendamó ○ CO 106 Dk 44
Pieniężno ○ PL 170 Hb 18
Pieres ○ RA 146 Ee 65
Pierre ○ USA 56 Cm 23
Pierre Lake ~ CDN 57 Dh 21
Pierreville ○ TT 104 Ed 40
Pierson ○ CDN 56 Cm 21
Pierson ○ USA 87 Dh 31
Piešťany ○ SK 174 Ha 21
Pietarsaan ○ FIN 159 Hc 14
Pietermaritzburg ○ ZA 352 Hh 60
Pietersburg Polokwane ○ ZA 349 Hg 57
Pietlo ○ LB 316 Gb 43
Pie Town ○ USA 65 Ch 28
Piet Plessis ○ ZA 349 He 59
Piet Retief ○ ZA 352 Hh 59
Pietroșani ○ RO 194 He 24
Pieve di Cadore ○ I 174 Gn 22
Pifaina ○ BR 141 El 56
Pifo ○ EC 116 Dj 46
Pigeon ○ USA 74 Dj 25
Pigeon Hole ○ AUS 364 Mb 54
Pigeon Lake ~ CDN 50 Cf 19
Pigeon River ○ CDN 57 Dd 21
Piggott ○ USA 71 Dc 27
Piggs Peak ○ SD 352 Hh 58
Pigu ○ GH 317 Gf 41
Pigüé ○ RA 137 Ec 64
Pigŭm Do ♁ ROK 247 Ln 28
Pihtipudas ○ FIN 159 He 14
Pijijiapan ○ MEX 93 Db 38
Pikalevo ○ RUS 171 Hk 16
Pikangikum ○ CDN 56 Da 20
Pikangikum Lake ~ CDN 56 Db 20
Piketberg ○ ZA 358 Hb 62
Piketon ○ USA 71 Dg 26
Pikeville ○ USA 71 Df 28
Pikeville ○ USA 71 Dg 27
Pikien Rio ~ SME 113 Eg 44
pik Karasak △ VRC 230 Ka 26
pik Kommunizma △ TJ 223 Jp 26
pik Lenina △ KS 230 Ka 26
Pikounda ○ RCB 332 Ha 45
pik Piramidal'nyj △ TJ 223 Jp 26
pik Revoljucii △ TJ 230 Ka 26
Pila ○ RA 146 Ee 64
Piła ○ PL 170 Ha 19
Pilaga ~ RA 140 Ee 58
Pila Kyun ♁ MYA 262 Kn 40
Pilane ○ RB 349 He 58
Pilanesberg ♀ ZA 349 Hf 58
Pilanesberg △ ZA 349 Hf 58
Pilani ○ IND 234 Kb 31
Pilão Arcado ○ BR 124 En 50
Pilar ○ RA 137 Ec 61
Pilar ○ PY 140 Ee 59
Pilar ○ RA 146 Ee 63
Pilar ○ IND 238 Ka 38
Pilar ○ RP 267 Lp 41
Pilas Group ♁ RP 275 Ll 42
Pilas Island ♁ RP 275 Ll 42
Pilaya ~ BOL 136 Eb 56
Pilbara ⌒ AUS 360 Lj 57
Pilbarra Point ⌓ VU 386 Ng 55
Pilcaniqeu ○ RA 147 Dn 66
Pilcomayo ~ BOL 129 Eb 55
Pilcomayo ~ PY 136 Ed 57
Pilcomayo ~ PY 140 Ee 58
Pilcomayo ~ RA 140 Ee 58
Pilcopata ○ PE 128 Dn 52
Pileälven ~ S 158 Ha 12
Pileru ○ IND 238 Kd 39
Pilga ○ AUS 360 Lk 56
Pilibhit ○ IND 234 Kd 31
Pilliga ○ AUS 379 Ml 61
Pilluna ○ PE 116 Dk 49
Pilocomayo ~ BOL 136 Ec 56
Pilón ○ C 101 Dk 36
Pílos ○ GR 194 Hc 27
Pilot Point ○ USA 10 Ab 4
Pilot Point ○ USA 46 Al 17
Pilot Rock ○ USA 50 Cc 23
Pilot Station ○ USA 46 Aj 15
Pimba ○ AUS 378 Me 61
Pimbee ○ AUS 368 Lh 58
Pimenta Bueno ○ BR 129 Ed 51
Pimenteiras ○ BR 124 Ep 49
Pimenteiras d'Oeste ○ BR 129 Ed 52
Pimentel ○ PE 116 Dh 49
Pimpalgaon Basvant ○ IND 238 Ka 35
Piná ~ BR 121 El 46
Pina ○ GH 317 Gf 40
Pinaleno Mountains ⛰ USA 65 Cg 29
Piñalito ○ CO 106 Dm 44
Pinamalayan ○ RP 267 Ll 39
Pinamar ○ RA 146 Ef 64
Pinamula ○ RI 275 Ll 45
Pinanga ○ RDC 333 Hb 47
Pınarbaşı ○ TR 195 Hl 26
Pinar del Río ○ C 100 Dg 34
Pınarhisar ○ TR 195 Hf 25
Pincher Creek ○ CDN 50 Ce 21
Pinchollo ○ PE 128 Dn 53
Pińczów ○ PL 174 Hc 20
Pinda ○ MOC 344 Hk 54
Pindaí ○ BR 125 En 53
Pindal ○ EC 116 Dh 48
Pindalba ~ BR 133 Eh 53
Pindar ○ AUS 368 Lh 60
Pindarama do Tocantins ○ BR 133 El 51
Pindaré ~ BR 121 El 48
Pind Dādar Khān ○ PK 230 Ka 29
Pindi Bhattiān ○ PK 230 Ka 30
Pindi Gheb ○ PK 230 Ka 29
Pindiu ○ PNG 287 Mk 49
Pindolo ○ RI 282 Ll 47
Pindos Mountains ⛰ GR 194 Hc 26
Pindusi ○ RUS 159 Hk 14
Pine ○ USA 50 Ce 24
Pine Apple ○ USA 86 De 30
Pine Bluff ○ USA 70 Db 28
Pine Bluffs ○ USA 65 Ck 25
Pine Creek ○ AUS 364 Mb 52
Pine Creek Indian Reservation ••• CDN 56 Cm 19
Pinedale ○ USA 51 Ch 24
Pine Dock ○ CDN 56 Cp 20
Pinefield ○ BS 87 Dm 34
Pine Flat Lake ~ USA 64 Cc 27
Pinega ~ RUS 154 Ra 6
Pinega ○ RUS 159 Hp 13
Pinega ~ RUS 159 Hp 13
Pine Grove ○ AUS 368 Lh 59
Pine Hill ○ AUS 361 Mc 57
Pinehurst ○ USA 64 Cc 27
Pinehurst ○ USA 74 Dj 28
Pineimuta River ~ CDN 57 Dd 19
Pineiro Machado ○ BR 146 Eh 61
Pine Island Bay ≈ 38 Db 17
Pineland ○ USA 86 Db 30
Pinellas Park ○ USA 86 Dg 32
Pine Point ○ CDN 6 Da 3
Pine Point ○ CDN 47 Ce 15
Pine Portage ○ CDN 57 Dd 21
Piñera ○ ROU 146 Ef 62
Pine RichIndian Reservation ••• USA 51 Cl 24
Pine Ridge ○ USA 51 Cl 24
Pine Ridge ○ USA 64 Cc 27
Pine Springs ○ USA 80 Ck 30
Pinetop-Lakeside ○ USA 65 Ch 28
Pinetown ○ ZA 352 Hh 60
Pineville ○ USA 71 Dg 27
Pineville ○ USA 86 Db 30
Piney ○ CDN 56 Cp 21
Piney Buttes ⌒ USA 51 Cj 22
Pingal ○ PK 230 Ka 27
Ping'an ○ VRC 242 La 27
Pingaring ○ AUS 368 Lk 62
Pingba ○ VRC 255 Ld 32
Pingchang ○ VRC 243 Ld 30
Pingdingshan ○ VRC 243 Lg 29
Pingdu ○ VRC 246 Lk 27
Pingelly ○ AUS 368 Lj 62
Pingguo ○ VRC 255 Ld 34
Pinghe ○ VRC 258 Lj 33
Pinghu ○ VRC 246 Ll 30
Pingjiang ○ VRC 255 Le 32
Pingjiang ○ VRC 258 Lg 31
Pingle ○ VRC 255 Lf 33
Pingli ○ VRC 243 Le 29
Pingliang ○ VRC 243 Ld 28
Pingling ○ VRC 258 Lh 34
Pinglu ○ VRC 243 Lg 26
Pingluo ○ VRC 243 Ld 26
Pingnan ○ VRC 255 Lf 34
Pingnan ○ VRC 258 Lk 32
Pingquan ○ VRC 246 Lk 25
Pingree ○ USA 56 Cn 22
Pingrup ○ AUS 368 Lk 62
Pingshan ○ VRC 243 Lg 26
Pingshi ○ VRC 258 Lg 33
Pingtang ○ VRC 255 Ld 33
Pingtung ○ RC 259 Ll 34
Pinguanjie ○ VRC 255 Lb 34
Pingvallavatn ~ IS 158 Fk 13
Pingvellir ○ IS 158 Fk 13
Pingwang ○ VRC 246 Ll 30
Pingwu ○ VRC 242 Lc 29
Pingxiang ○ VRC 255 Ld 34
Pingxiang ○ VRC 258 Lg 32
Pingyang ○ VRC 259 Ll 32
Pingyao ○ VRC 243 Lg 27
Pingyi ○ VRC 246 Lj 28
Pingyin ○ VRC 246 Lj 27
Pingyu ○ VRC 243 Lh 29
Pingyuan ○ VRC 258 Lh 33
Pinha ○ BR 146 Ej 61
Pinhalzinho ○ BR 140 Eh 59
Pinhão ○ BR 140 Ej 58
Pinheiro ○ BR 121 Em 47
Pinheiros ○ BR 141 Ep 55
Pinhél ○ BR 120 Eg 47
Pinhuã ~ BR 117 Eb 49
Pinillos ○ CO 106 Dl 41
Pinipel Island ♁ PNG 290 Mp 48
Pinjarra ○ AUS 368 Lj 62
Pinkha ○ MYA 254 Km 33
Pinkhwun ○ MYA 254 Kn 35
Pink Mountain ○ CDN 47 Ca 17
Pinlebu ○ MYA 254 Km 34
Pinnacles ○ AUS 368 Ll 60
Pinnacles National Monument ★ USA 64 Cb 27
Pinnaroo ○ AUS 378 Mg 63
Pinogana ○ PA 97 Dk 41
Pinogu ○ RI 275 Lm 45
Pinoh ~ RI 271 Lf 46
Pinon ○ USA 65 Ck 29
Pinos ○ MEX 92 Cm 34
Pinotepa Nacional ○ MEX 92 Cn 37
Pinrang ○ RI 279 Lk 47
Pinsk ○ BY 171 He 19
Pintadas ○ BR 125 Fa 51
Pintado ○ BR 124 En 50
Pintado ~ BR 133 Ej 52
Pintados ○ RCH 136 Dp 56
Pinto ○ RA 137 Ec 60
Pintoyacu ~ EC 116 Dk 46
Pinturas ~ RA 152 Dn 69
Pintuyan ○ RP 267 Ln 41
Piñuelas ○ CO 106 Dl 40
Pioacho de la Laguna ○ MEX 80 Cg 34
Pioche ○ USA 64 Ce 27
Piodi ○ RDC 333 He 49
Pio IX ○ BR 124 Ep 49
Pioka ○ RDC 332 Gp 48
Piombino ○ I 185 Gm 24
Pioneer Huron City ★ USA 57 Dg 23
Pioneer Mountains ⛰ USA 51 Cf 23
Pioneer Woman Monument ★ USA 70 Cp 27
Pioneiros d'Oeste ○ BR 133 Eh 53
Piorini ○ BR 117 Ec 47
Piorini ~ BR 117 Ec 47
Piotrków Tribunalski ○ PL 174 Hb 20
Pio XII. ○ BR 121 Em 47
Pipah Range ⛰ AUS 374 Mf 56
Pipalyatjara ○ AUS 369 Ma 59
Piparia ○ IND 234 Kd 34
Pipe Spring National Monument ★ USA 64 Cf 27
Pipestone ○ CDN 56 Cm 21
Pipestone ○ USA 56 Cp 24
Pipestone Creek ~ CDN 51 Cl 20
Pipestone Nat. Mon. ★ USA 56 Cp 23
Pipi ~ RCA 321 Hd 41
Pipili ○ IND 235 Kg 35
Pipiriki ○ NZ 383 Nk 65
Piplān ○ PK 223 Jp 29
Piplod ○ IND 227 Ka 34
Pippingarra ○ AUS 360 Lk 56
Pippingarra Aboriginal Reserve ••• AUS 360 Lk 56
Pipri ○ IND 234 Kf 33
Piprod ○ IND 234 Ke 34
Piqua ○ USA 71 Df 25
Piqua Historic Area ★ USA 71 Df 25
Piquet Carneiro ○ BR 124 Fa 48
Piquete ○ BR 141 Em 57
Piquiri ~ BR 140 Eh 58
Pira ○ DY 317 Gg 41
Pirabeiraba ○ BR 141 Ek 59
Piraca ~ BR 133 Ek 54
Piracaia ○ BR 141 El 57
Piracanjuba ○ BR 133 Ek 54
Piracanjuba ~ BR 133 Ek 54
Piracicaba ○ BR 141 Ek 57
Piracuruca ○ BR 124 Ep 47
Pirada ○ GNB 316 Fn 39
Piraeus ○ GR 194 Hd 27
Piraí do Sul ○ BR 140 Ej 58
Pirajiba ○ BR 125 En 52
Piraju ○ BR 140 Ek 57
Pirajuí ○ BR 140 Ek 57
Pirambu ○ BR 125 Fb 51
Piram Island ♁ IND 238 Ka 35
Piranga ○ BR 141 En 56
Piranha ~ BR 117 Eh 49
Piranhas ~ BR 120 Ef 49
Piranhas ~ BR 121 Ek 50
Piranhas ○ BR 124 Fb 49
Piranhas ○ BR 124 Fb 50
Piranhas ○ BR 133 Eh 54
Piranhas ~ BR 133 Ej 54

Penner - Piranhas 457

Piranji ~ BR 124 Fa 48
Pīrānšahr O IR 209 Ja 27
Pira Paraná ~ CO 117 Dn 46
Pirapemas O BR 121 Em 47
Pirapora O BR 133 Em 54
Pirapozinho O BR 140 Ej 57
Piraquara O BR 141 Ek 58
Piraraja O ROU 146 Eg 62
Pirassununga O BR 141 El 57
Piratinga ~ BR 133 El 53
Piratini O BR 146 Eh 61
Piratucu ~ BR 120 Ef 47
Piray ~ BOL 129 Ec 54
Pirenópolis O BR 133 Ek 53
Pires do Rio O BR 133 Ek 54
Pirgí O GR 194 Hf 26
Pírgos O GR 194 Hc 27
Pírgos O GR 194 He 28
Piriá O BR 121 Ej 46
Piriápolis O ROU 146 Eg 63
Pirica ~ RA 136 Ea 59
Pirimapun O RI 286 Mf 49
Piripá O BR 125 Ep 53
Piripiri O BR 124 En 48
Piritiba O BR 125 Ep 51
Piriyapatna O IND 238 Kb 39
Pir Mangho O PK 227 Jm 33
Pirmasens O D 163 Gk 21
Pirna O D 174 Gn 20
Piro O MOC 344 Hk 55
Pironé O RA 140 Ee 58
Pirot O SCG 194 Hd 24
Pirpainti O IND 235 Kh 33
Pir Panchal Range ⛰ IND 230 Kb 28
Pirttikoski O FIN 159 Hf 12
Piru O RI 283 Ma 47
Pisa O I 185 Gm 24
Pisac O PE 128 Dn 52
Pisagua O RCH 128 Dn 55
Pisanda O CO 106 Dk 45
Pisba ♀ CO 107 Dm 43
Pišča O UA 175 Hd 20
Pisco O PE 116 Dk 52
Pisco Elquí O RCH 137 Dn 61
Piscovo O RUS 171 Hn 17
Písek O CZ 174 Gp 21
Pishan O VRC 230 Kd 27
Pishīn O PK 227 Jm 30
Pishin Lora ~ PK 227 Jl 31
Pishin Lora ~ PK 227 Jm 30
Pīshūkān O PK 226 Jk 33
Pīšīn O IR 226 Jj 32
Piso Firme O BOL 129 Ed 52
Pisqui ~ PE 112 Dl 49
Pissila O BF 317 Gf 39
Piste O MEX 93 Dd 35
Pisticci O I 194 Ha 25
Pistóia O I 185 Gm 24
Pistolet Bay ≈ CDN 61 Eg 20
Pisuerga ~ E 184 Gd 24
Pisz O PL 170 Hc 19
Pit ~ USA 64 Cb 25
Pita O RG 316 Fp 40
Pital O MEX 93 Dc 36
Pitalito O CO 106 Dk 45
Pitanga O BR 140 Ej 58
Pitangueiras O BR 141 Ek 56
Pitangui O BR 133 Em 55
Pitarpunga Lake ~ AUS 378 Mh 63
Pitas O MAL 274 Lj 42
Pitcairn ♁ UK 14 Ca 12
Pitcairn Islands ♁ UK 14 Cb 12
Pitche O GNB 316 Fn 39
Pitea O S 159 Hc 13
Piteälven ~ S 159 Hc 13
Pitești O RO 175 He 23
Pithāpuram O IND 238 Kf 37
Pithara O AUS 368 Lj 61
Pithiviers O F 163 Gh 21
Piti ~ EAT 337 Hj 49
Pitigliano O I 185 Gm 24
Pitinga ~ BR 120 Ee 46
Pitjantjatjara Aboriginal Land ••• AUS 369 Mb 59
Pitkjaranta O RUS 171 Hh 15
Pitlochry O GB 162 Ge 17
Pitoa O CAM 321 Gn 41
Piton des Neiges △ F 353 Jf 56
Pit River O RI 286 Mf 48
Pitrufquen O RCH 147 Dm 65
Pitt ♁ NZ 35 Aa 14
Pitt Island ♁ CDN 42 Db 8
Pitt Island ♁ NZ 383 Ab 68
Pittsburg O USA 70 Da 27
Pittsburg O USA 71 Df 27
Pittsburgh O USA 71 Dh 25
Pittsburgh O USA 74 Dj 25
Pittsfield O USA 60 Dm 24
Pittsfield O USA 60 Dp 23
Pittsfield O USA 71 Dc 26
Pitts Town O BS 87 Dl 34
Pitt Strait ≈ NZ 383 Ab 68
Pittsworth O AUS 375 Mm 59
Pitu ~ EAT 337 Hk 50
Pituil O RA 136 Ea 60
Pituil ~ RA 136 Ea 60
Pium O BR 133 Ek 51
Pium ~ BR 133 Ek 51
Piúma O BR 141 Ep 56
Piumhí O BR 141 El 56
Piura O PE 116 Dh 48
Piura ~ PE 116 Dh 48
Piva ~ MON 194 Hb 24
Pivabiska Lake ~ CDN 57 Dg 21
Pivdennyj Buh ~ UA 175 Hg 21
Pivijay O CO 106 Dl 40
Pivnično-Krymsky kanal ~ UA 175 Hj 22
Pi Xian O VRC 242 Lb 30
Pi Xian O VRC 246 Lj 28
Pixoyal O MEX 93 Dc 36
Pixtun O MEX 93 Dc 36
Pizacoma O PE 128 Dp 54
Piz Bernina △ I 174 Gl 22
Pizhi O WAN 320 Gj 41
Pizzo O I 194 Ha 26
Pjandž O TJ 223 Jn 27
Pjandz ~ UZB 223 Jn 27
Pjandž ~ AFG 223 Jp 26
Pjandž ~ TJ 230 Ka 27
Pjaozero ~ RUS 159 Hh 13
Pjat'-Jah O RUS 154 Sc 6
Pjatychatky O UA 175 Hj 21
Pjóðgarður Skaftafell ♀ IS 158 Fm 13
Plaçabuçu O BR 125 Fb 51
Placentia O CDN 61 Eg 22
Placentia Bay ≈ CDN 61 Eg 22
Placer O RP 267 Lm 40
Placer O RP 267 Ln 41
Placerville O USA 64 Cb 26
Placerville O USA 65 Ch 27
Placetas O C 100 Dj 34
Plácido de Castro O BR 129 Ea 51
Placongo O RCB 332 Gn 47
Plain City O USA 71 Dg 25
Plains O USA 50 Ce 22
Plains O USA 65 Cl 29
Plains O USA 70 Cm 27
Plains of San Augustin ⛰ USA 65 Ch 29
Plainted Desert ⌓ USA 64 Cf 27
Plainview O USA 56 Cp 24
Plainview O USA 56 Db 23
Plainview O USA 70 Cm 28
Plainville O USA 70 Cn 26
Plainwell O USA 57 Df 24
Plaiyam O IND 239 Kc 40
Plaju O RI 278 Lc 47
Plampang O RI 279 Lj 50
Plana Cays ♁ BS 87 Dm 34
Planadas O CO 106 Dl 44
Planaltina O BR 133 El 53
Planalto O BR 140 Eh 58
Planalto O BR 140 Eh 59
Planalto de Angonia ⛰ MOC 344 Hj 53
Planalto de Lichinga ⛰ MOC 344 Hk 52
Planalto Maracanaquará ⌓ BR 120 Eh 45
Planalto Moçambicano ⌓ MOC 344 Hl 53
Planas ~ CO 107 Dn 43
Planco O ROU 146 Eg 62
Plandi ~ BF 317 Gd 40
Planeta Rica O CO 106 Dl 41
Planet Downs O AUS 365 Mf 55
Plankinton O USA 56 Cn 24
Plano O USA 70 Cp 29
Plano Alto O BR 146 Ef 60
Planta Esmeralda O RCH 136 Dn 58
Plant City O USA 87 Dg 32
Planura O BR 141 Ek 56
Plaquemine O USA 86 Dc 30
Plaridel O RP 267 Lm 41
Plasencia O E 184 Gc 24
Plaster Rock O CDN 60 Ea 22
Plastun O RUS 250 Me 23
Plata de Azufre O RA 137 Dn 63
Platanal O YV 112 Eb 44
Platbakkies O ZA 348 Hb 61
Plateau des Bolovens ⛰ LAO 263 Ld 38
Plateau du Fadnoun ⛰ DZ 296 Gk 32
Plateau du Rekkam ⛰ MA 293 Ge 29
Plateau of Tibet ⌓ VRC 231 Kg 29
Plateau Sud-Camerounais ⌓ CAM 321 Gn 43
Plateros O MEX 92 Cl 34
Platina O USA 64 Ca 25
Platinum O USA 10 Ab 4
Platinum O USA 46 Aj 15
Plato O CO 106 Dl 41
Plato de Sopa O RCH 136 Dp 58
plato Kaplankyr ⛰ UZB 222 Jg 25
Plato Kystyk ⛰ RUS 204 Wa 4
Platón Sánchez O MEX 92 Cn 35
Platte O USA 56 Cn 24
Platte River ~ USA 70 Cn 25
Platteville O USA 56 Dc 24
Plattsburgh O USA 60 Dl 23
Plattsmouth O USA 70 Cp 25
Platveld O NAM 348 Ha 56
Plauen O D 174 Gn 20
Plavinas O LV 171 He 17
Plavsk O RUS 181 Hl 19
Playa Blanca O E 292 Fp 31
Playa Dayaniguas O C 100 Dg 34
Playa del Carmen O MEX 93 De 35
Playa las Cañas O C 100 Dg 34
Playa Lauro Villar O MEX 81 Cp 33
Playa Rosario O C 100 Dg 34
Playas O EC 116 Dh 47
Playa Vicente O MEX 93 Da 37
Plây Ku O VN 263 Ld 38
Plaza Huincul O RA 147 Dp 65
Pleasanton O USA 70 Da 26
Pleasanton O USA 81 Cn 31
Pleasent View O USA 65 Ch 27
Pledger Lake ~ CDN 57 Df 20
Plenty O CDN 51 Ch 20
Plenty ~ AUS 374 Md 57
Plentywood O USA 51 Ck 21
Plered O RI 278 Ld 49
Pleseck O RUS 159 Hn 14
Plessisville O CDN 60 Dn 22
Pleszew O PL 174 Ha 20
Plettenberg Bay O ZA 358 Hd 63
Pleven O BG 194 He 24
Plevna Downs O AUS 374 Mh 59
Plitvica O HR 174 Gp 23
Plitvička Jezera ♀ HR 174 Gp 23
Pljevlja O MON 194 Hb 24
Ploče O HR 194 Ha 24
Płock O PL 170 Hb 19
Ploëmel O F 163 Ge 22
Ploiești O RO 175 Hf 23
Plomb du Cantal △ F 184 Gh 23
Płońsk O PL 170 Hc 19
Ploskos' O RUS 171 Hh 17
Ploty O PL 170 Gp 19
Plovdiv O BG 194 He 24
Plummer O USA 50 Cd 22
Plumridge Lakes ~ AUS 369 Ln 60
Plumtree O ZW 349 Hf 56
Plungė O LT 170 Hc 18
Plyeshchanitsy O BY 171 Hf 18
Plymouth O USA 50 Cc 23
Plymouth O USA 57 Dd 24
Plymouth O USA 71 De 25
Plymouth O USA 74 Dk 28
Plymouth O USA 74 Dn 26
Plymouth O GB 104 Ec 37
Plymouth O TT 104 Ed 40
Plymouth O GB 163 Gd 20
Plzeň O CZ 174 Gn 21
Pniewy O PL 170 Gp 19
Po ~ I 185 Gm 23
Poan High Knob △ USA 71 Dg 27
Poatina O AUS 378 Mk 66
Pobè O DY 320 Gh 42
Población O RCH 137 Dn 63
Poblet ★ E 184 Gg 25
Poča O RUS 159 Hm 14
Pocahontas O CDN 50 Cc 19
Pocahontas O USA 56 Da 24
Pocahontas O USA 71 Dc 27
Pocatello O USA 51 Cf 24
Poccha ~ PE 116 Dk 50
Počep O RUS 171 Hj 19
Pocetas O YV 107 Dn 42
Pochutla O MEX 93 Cp 38
Pocinhos O BR 124 Fb 49
Počinok O RUS 171 Hj 18
Počitelj ★ BIH 194 Ha 24
Pocklington Trough ▿ 290 Mp 52
Pocoata O BOL 129 Ea 55
Poço de Fora O BR 124 Fa 50
Poções O BR 125 Ep 53
Pocomoke O USA 74 Dk 26
Pocone O BR 132 Ef 54
Poço Redondo O BR 124 Fb 50
Poços de Caldas O BR 141 El 56
Poço Verde O BR 125 Fa 51
Pocrane O BR 141 Ep 55
Podbereze'e O RUS 171 Hh 16
Podbereze'e O RUS 171 Hh 17
Podborov'e O RUS 171 Hg 17
Poděbrady O CZ 174 Gp 20
Podgorenski O RUS 181 Hm 20
Podgorica ▣ MON 194 Hb 24
Podile O IND 238 Kd 38
Podkamennaja ~ RUS 22 Pb 3
Podkamennaja-Tunguska ~ RUS 204 Ub 6
Podkova O BG 194 He 25
Podlomka ~ RUS 159 Hl 14
Podoľsk O RUS 171 Hl 18
Podor O SN 304 Fn 37
Podporož'e O RUS 171 Hk 15
Podril'ska vysočyna ⛰ UA 175 He 21
Podyem-Mihajlovka O RUS 181 Jd 19
Pofadder O ZA 348 Hb 60
Pogo O CI 317 Gd 40
Pogoanele O RO 175 Hf 23
Pogoreluša O RUS 171 Hh 17
Pogost O RUS 159 Hn 14
Pogradec O AL 194 Hc 25
Pograničnyj O RUS 250 Mb 23
Poguba ~ BR 132 Eg 54
Poh O RI 282 Lm 46
P'ohang O ROK 247 Ma 27
Pohénégamook O CDN 60 Dp 22
Pohjanmaa Österbotten ⌓ FIN 159 Hd 14
Pohjols O FIN 159 He 13
Pohvistnevo O RUS 181 Jd 19
Poie O RDC 333 Hd 47
Poi Island ♁ SOL 290 Nc 51
Poindimié O F 386 Ne 56
Point Alexander ⌒ AUS 364 Me 52
Point à Luc ⌒ CDN 60 Ea 21
Point Arena O USA 64 Bp 26
Point Arena ⌒ USA 64 Bp 26
Point Arguello ⌒ USA 64 Cb 28
Point au Fer ⌒ USA 86 Dc 31
Point Austin ⌒ AUS 365 Mg 54
Point Banks ⌒ USA 46 An 15
Point Barrow ⌒ USA 46 Al 9
Point Berliet △ RN 308 Gl 35
Point Brown ⌒ AUS 369 Mc 62
Point Buchon ⌒ USA 64 Cb 28
Point Calimere ⌒ IND 239 Kd 40
Point Culver ⌒ AUS 369 Ln 62
Point d'Entrecasteaux ⌒ AUS 368 Lh 63
Point Detour ⌒ USA 57 De 23
Point Dover ⌒ AUS 369 Ln 62
Pointe Aouara ⌒ F 113 Eh 43
Pointe-à-Pitre O F 104 Ed 37
Pointe au Baril Station O CDN 57 Dh 23
Pointe-au-Père O CDN 60 Dp 21
Pointe Aux Barques ⌒ USA 57 Dg 23
Pointe Aux Pins ⌒ CDN 57 Dh 24
Pointe Béhague ⌒ F 113 Ej 43
Pointe de la Fougère Rouge ⌒ CDN 57 Dh 20
Pointe de l'Ouest ⌒ CDN 61 Eb 21
Pointe de Penmarc'h △ F 163 Gd 22
Pointe de Souellaba ⌒ CAM 320 Gl 44
Pointe du Cheval Blanc ⌒ RH 101 Dm 36
Pointe du Raz △ F 163 Gd 21
Pointe du Sud ⌒ CDN 61 Ec 21
Pointe Goyeau ⌒ CDN 57 Dj 20
Pointe Heath ⌒ CDN 61 Ed 21
Pointe Indienne ⌒ RCB 332 Gm 48
Pointe Lefèvre ⌒ F 386 Nf 56
Pointe Longue ⌒ CDN 57 Dj 19
Pointe Noire O F 104 Ec 37
Pointe-Noire O RCB 332 Gm 48
Pointe Pelee ⌒ CDN 71 Dg 25
Pointe Police O SY 329 Jf 48
Pointe Pongara ⌒ G 332 Gl 45
Pointe Quest ⌒ RH 101 Dm 36
Pointe Sallatouk ⌒ RG 316 Fp 41
Point Harbor O USA 74 Dl 27
Point Hibbs ⌒ AUS 378 Mj 67
Point Hicks ⌒ AUS 379 Ml 64
Point Hope O USA 23 Ab 3
Point Hope ⌒ USA 46 Ae 11
Point Jahleel ⌒ AUS 364 Mb 51
Point Lake ~ CDN 6 Da 3
Point Lake ~ CDN 42 Eb 5
Point Lay O USA 46 Ag 11
Point Malcom ⌒ AUS 369 Lm 62
Point Marsden ⌒ AUS 378 Me 63
Point Mornington ⌒ AUS 379 Mj 65
Point of Rocks O USA 65 Ch 25
Point Parent O CDN 61 Ed 20
Point Pedro O CL 239 Ke 41
Point Pleasant O USA 71 Dg 26
Point Pleasant O USA 74 Dl 25
Point Pleasant O USA 74 Dl 26
Point Quobba ⌒ AUS 368 Lg 58
Point Renfrew O CDN 50 Bp 21
Point Reyes ⌒ USA 64 Ca 27
Point Reyes National Seashore ♀ USA 64 Ca 26
Point Saint George ⌒ USA 64 Bp 25
Point Salvation Aboriginal Reserve ••• AUS 369 Ln 60
Point Sir Isaac ⌒ AUS 378 Md 63
Point Somes ⌒ NZ 383 Ab 67
Point Stuart O AUS 364 Mb 52
Point Sur ⌒ USA 64 Ca 27
Poire River ~ PNG 286 Mg 47
Poissonnier Point ⌒ AUS 360 Lk 55
Poitiers O F 163 Gg 22
Poitou ⌓ F 163 Gf 22
Poitou-Charentes ⊙ F 163 Gf 22
Pojezierze Mazurskie ⌓ PL 170 Hb 19
Pojlu O AZ 202 Jb 25
Pojuca O BR 125 Fa 52
Pokaran O IND 227 Jp 32
Pokataroo O AUS 375 Ml 60
Pokhara O NEP 235 Kf 31
Pokigron O SME 113 Eg 43
Po-kil Do ♁ ROK 247 Lp 28
Pokka O FIN 159 He 11
Poko O RDC 324 Hf 44
Pokok Sena O MAL 270 La 42
Pokomoke Sound ≈ USA 74 Dk 27
Pokrovs'ke O UA 181 Hl 22
Pokuma O Z 341 Hf 54
Pola O RUS 171 Hh 17
Pola O RP 267 Ll 39
Polacca Wash ~ USA 65 Cg 27
Polače O HR 194 Ha 24
Polackaja nižina ⌓ BY 171 Hf 18
Pola de Lena O E 184 Gd 24
Pola de Siero O E 184 Gd 24
Poladpur O IND 238 Ka 37
Polān O IR 226 Jj 33
Polanco O RP 267 Lm 41
Poland □ PL 170 Ha 19
Polar Plateau ⛰ 38 Fb 18
Polatlı O TR 195 Hj 26
Polatsk O BY 171 Hg 18
Polavaram O IND 238 Ke 37
Polcura ~ RCH 137 Dn 64
Pol-e Alam O AFG 223 Jn 28
Poleang ~ RI 282 Ll 48
Polebridge O USA 50 Ce 21
Pol-e Fasā O IR 215 Je 31
Pol-e Homrī O AFG 223 Jn 28
Pol-e Safīd O IR 222 Je 27
Polessk O RUS 170 Hc 18
Polewali O RI 279 Lk 47
Polgahawela O CL 239 Ke 42
Poli O CY 195 Hj 28
Poli O RC 259 Ll 34
Poli O CAM 321 Gn 41
Policemans Point O AUS 378 Mf 64
Policoro O I 194 Ha 25
Polígiros O GR 194 Hd 25
Polihnitos O GR 194 He 26
Polikastro O GR 194 Hd 25
Polis'ke O UA 175 Hg 20
Poljarnoe O RUS 23 Sa 2
Poljarnoe O RUS 205 Xc 4
Poljarnyj O RUS 159 Hj 11
Poljarnyje Zori O RUS 159 Hj 12
Poljarnyl O RUS 205 Zc 5
Pollāchi O IND 239 Kc 40
Pollença O E 185 Gh 26
Pollilo O RP 267 Ll 38
Pollilo Island ♁ RP 267 Ll 38
Pollilo Strait ≈ RP 267 Ll 38
Pollock O USA 86 Db 30
Pollock Pines O USA 64 Cb 26
Pol'noj Voron ~ RUS 181 Hn 19
Polo O USA 71 Dd 25
Polochic ~ GCA 93 Dc 38
Polohy O UA 181 Hl 22
Polokwane O ZA 349 Hg 57
Polomolok O RP 275 Ln 42
Polonnaruwa O CL 239 Ke 42
Poloone O UA 175 Hf 20
Polson O USA 50 Ce 22
Poltava O UA 175 Hk 21
Põltsamaa O EST 171 Hf 16
Poluj ~ RUS 154 Sb 5
Poluj ~ RUS 204 Sb 5
Poluostrov Chelyuskin ♁ RUS 204 Uc 3
Poluostrov Lisyanskogo ♁ RUS 205 Xc 7
Poluostrov Pyagina ♁ RUS 205 Ya 7
poluostrov Rybačij ♁ RUS 159 Hj 11
Poluostrov Taygonos ⌒ RUS 23 Ta 3
Poluostrov Taygonos ♁ RUS 205 Yc 6
Poluostrov Yamal ⌓ RUS 19 Na 2
Poluostrov Yamal ♁ RUS 204 Sb 4
Poluostrov Yavay ♁ RUS 204 Sc 4
Polūr O IND 238 Kd 39
Polvadera O USA 65 Cj 28
Polyuc O MEX 93 Dd 36
Poma O RDC 333 He 46
Pomabamba O PE 116 Dk 50
Pomacanchi O PE 128 Dn 52
Pomahuaca O PE 116 Dj 48
Pomaro O MEX 92 Cl 36
Pombal O BR 124 Fb 49
Pombal O P 184 Gb 26
Pombangi O RI 282 Ll 47
Pombas ~ BR 120 El 49
Pombuige ~ ANG 340 Gp 51
Pomene O MOC 352 Hk 57
Pomerania ⌓ PL 170 Ha 19
Pomeranian Bay ≈ D 170 Gn 18
Pomeroy O USA 50 Cd 22
Pomeroy O ZA 352 Hh 60
Pomična O UA 175 Hh 21
Pomio O PNG 287 Mm 48
Pomona O USA 64 Cd 29
Pomona O USA 70 Da 26
Pomona O NAM 348 Gp 59
Pomona Lake ~ USA 70 Da 26
Pomorskije bereg ⌓ RUS 159 Hk 13
Pompano Beach O USA 87 Dh 32
Pompei ★ I 194 Gp 25
Pompéia O BR 140 Ej 57
Pompeu O BR 133 Em 55
Pompey Reefs ♁ AUS 375 Mm 56
Pompeys Pillar ★ USA 51 Ch 22
Pompeys Pillar O USA 51 Cj 23
Pom Phra Chunlachomkiao O THA 262 La 39
Pompué ~ MOC 344 Hj 54
Ponape ♁ FSM 27 Sb 9
Ponass Lake ~ CDN 51 Cl 19
Ponca O USA 56 Cp 24
Ponca City O USA 70 Cp 27
Ponce O USA 104 Ea 37
Poncha Springs O USA 65 Cj 26
Ponchatoula O USA 86 Dc 30
Poncitlán O MEX 92 Cl 35
Pond Creek O USA 70 Cp 27
Pondicherry ⊙ IND 238 Kb 40
Pondicherry ⊙ IND 238 Kd 40
Pondicherry ⊙ IND 238 Kf 37
Pond Inlet O CDN 43 Gc 4
Pondosa O USA 64 Cb 25
Ponds Creek ~ AUS 375 Mj 58
Poneloya O NIC 96 De 39
Ponérihouen O F 386 Ne 56
Ponferrada O E 184 Gc 24
Pônfi ~ MOC 344 Hj 53
Pongaí O BR 140 Ek 56
Pongaroa O NZ 383 Nl 66
Pong Chi O THA 262 La 37
Ponge O RDC 333 He 48
Pong Nam Ron O THA 263 Lb 39
Pongo ~ SUD 324 Hf 41
Pongo de Cumbinama ~ PE 116 Dj 48
Pongo de Paquipachango ~ PE 128 Dl 51
Pongola O ZA 352 Hh 59
Pongola ~ ZA 352 Hh 59
Pongolapoortdam ~ ZA 352 Hj 59
Poni ~ BF 317 Ge 40
Ponio ~ RCH 137 Dn 61
Ponio O BF 317 Gg 40
Ponna O MYA 254 Km 35
Ponnaiyar ~ IND 238 Kd 39
Ponnāni O IND 239 Kb 40
Ponneri O IND 238 Ke 39
Ponoj O RUS 159 Hn 12
Ponoj ~ RUS 159 Hn 12
Ponoka O CDN 50 Cf 19
Ponorogo O RI 279 Lf 49
Ponrang O RI 282 Ll 47
Ponson Island ♁ RP 267 Ln 40
Ponta Albina ⌒ ANG 340 Gm 53
Ponta Cambu ⌒ BR 113 Ej 44
Ponta Coconho ⌒ BR 124 Fc 48
Ponta Comboriú ⌒ BR 141 El 58
Ponta Corumbaú ⌒ BR 125 Fa 54
Ponta da Pescada ⌒ BR 113 Ej 44
Ponta da Sinagoga ⌒ CV 316 Fh 37
Ponta das Palmeirinhas ⌒ ANG 340 Gn 50
Ponta das Salinas ⌒ ANG 340 Gn 53
Ponta de Baleia ⌒ BR 125 Fa 54
Ponta de Juatinga ⌒ BR 141 Em 57
Ponta Delgada O P 18 Hb 6
Ponta de Mata O YV 112 Ec 41
Ponta de Mucuripe ⌒ BR 124 Fa 47
Ponta de Pedras O BR 121 Ek 46
Ponta de Santo Antônio ⌒ BR 124 Fc 49
Ponta do Boi ⌒ BR 141 Em 57
Ponta do Conselho ⌒ BR 125 Fa 52
Ponta do Costa ⌒ BR 113 Ej 43
Ponta do Guará ⌒ BR 121 Ek 45
Ponta do Mutá ⌒ BR 125 Fa 52
Ponta do Ouro O MOC 352 Hj 59
Ponta dos Castelhanos ⌒ BR 141 Em 57
Ponta dos Castelhanos ⌒ BR 141 Ep 56
Ponta dos Indio O BR 113 Ej 43
Ponta dos Mangues Secos ⌒ BR 124 En 47
Ponta dos Meros ⌒ BR 141 Em 57
Ponta do Sol O CV 316 Fh 37
Ponta do Una ⌒ BR 141 El 58
Ponta Grande ⌒ BR 125 Fa 54
Ponta Grossa O BR 140 Ej 58
Ponta Grossa da Marambaia ⌒ BR 141 Em 57
Ponta Guaiuru ⌒ BR 121 Em 46
Ponta Jericoacoara ⌒ BR 124 Ep 47
Pontal O BR 141 El 56
Pontalina O BR 133 Ek 54
Ponta Macalonga ⌒ MOC 344 Hm 54
Ponta Macovane ⌒ MOC 352 Hk 56
Ponta Metacaua ⌒ MOC 344 Hn 52
Ponta Mondub ⌒ BR 141 El 58
Pont-à-Mousson O F 163 Gj 21
Ponta Negra ⌒ BR 124 Fc 48
Ponta Norte ⌒ CV 316 Fj 37
Pontão O BR 121 Ek 49
Ponta Pelindã ⌒ GNB 316 Fm 40
Ponta Porã O BR 140 Eg 57
Pontarlier O F 163 Gj 22
Ponta São Sebastião ⌒ MOC 352 Hk 57
Pontas de Pedras O BR 124 Fc 49
Ponta Tarafo ⌒ CV 316 Fj 38
Ponta Timbue ⌒ MOC 344 Hk 55
Pont du Gard ★ F 185 Gh 24
Ponte Alta ~ BR 133 El 51
Ponte Alta do Tocantins O BR 133 El 51
Ponteareas O E 184 Gb 24
Ponte Branca O BR 133 Eh 54
Ponte d. S. O P 184 Gc 26
Ponte Firme O BR 133 El 55
Ponte Nova O BR 141 En 56
Pontes e Lacerda O BR 132 Ee 53
Ponte Serrada O BR 140 Ej 59
Pontevedra O E 184 Gb 24
Pontiac O USA 57 Dg 24
Pontiac O USA 71 Dd 25
Pontianak O RI 278 Le 46
Pontian Kecil O MAL 271 Lb 45
Pontic Mountains ⛰ TR 195 Hk 25
Pontivy O F 163 Ge 21
Ponto do Murici ⌒ BR 121 Em 47
Pontoise O F 163 Gg 21
Ponton Creek ~ AUS 368 Lm 60
Pontorson O F 163 Gf 21
Pontotoc O USA 71 Dd 28
Pontrémoli O I 185 Gm 23
Pont-St.-Esprit O F 185 Gj 23
Ponuga O PA 97 Dh 42
Pony Express Stat. S.H.S. ★ USA 70 Cp 26
Ponza O I 185 Gn 25
Poochera O AUS 378 Md 62
Poole O GB 163 Ge 20
Pool Malebo ~ RDC 332 Gp 48
Poolowanna Lake ~ AUS 374 Me 59
Poonamallee O IND 238 Kd 39
Pooncarie O AUS 378 Mh 62
Pooneryn O CL 239 Kd 41
Poopó O BOL 129 Ea 55
Pooppeloe Lake ~ AUS 379 Mh 61
Poor Knights Islands ♁ NZ 383 Nk 63
Poorman O USA 46 An 13
Poor Man Indian Reservation ••• CDN 51 Ck 20
Popa Falls ~ NAM 340 Hc 55
Popayan O CO 106 Dk 44
Popil'nja O UA 175 Hg 21
Popiltah Lake ~ AUS 378 Mg 62
Popio Lake ~ AUS 378 Mh 62
Poplar Bluff O USA 71 Dc 27
Poplarfield O CDN 56 Cp 20
Poplar Hill O CDN 56 Da 19
Poplar Point ⌒ CDN 56 Cn 19
Poplar Point O CDN 56 Cp 20
Poplar River ~ USA 51 Ck 21
Poplar River ~ CDN 56 Cn 19
Poplarville O USA 86 Dd 30
Popokabaka O RDC 332 Ha 48
Pópoli O I 185 Gn 24
Popomguine O SN 304 Fm 38
Popondetta O PNG 287 Ml 50
Popovka O RUS 181 Hn 21
Popovo O BG 194 Hf 24
Popov Porog O RUS 159 Hj 14
Poprad O SK 174 Hc 21
Poptún O GCA 93 Dd 37
Porāli ~ PK 227 Jm 32
Poranga O BR 124 Ep 48
Porangahau O NZ 383 Nl 66
Porangatu O BR 133 Ek 52
Porbandar O IND 227 Jn 35
Porčaman O AFG 223 Jk 29
Porciúngula O BR 141 En 56
Porco O BOL 129 Eb 55
Porcos ~ BR 133 Em 52
Porcupine Gorge ♀ AUS 375 Mj 56
Porcupine River ~ USA 6 Bb 3
Porcupine River ~ USA 46 Be 11
Pordenone O I 174 Gn 22
Pore O CO 107 Dm 43
Porecatu O BR 140 Ej 57
Poreče O RUS 171 Hk 18
Poreckoe O RUS 181 Jb 18
Porga O DY 317 Gg 40
Porgera O PNG 286 Mh 48
Porhov O RUS 171 Hg 17
Pori O FIN 159 Hc 15
Porirua O NZ 383 Nk 66
Pórisvatn ~ IS 158 Fl 13
Porjus O S 159 Hb 12
Porlakshöfn O IS 158 Fk 14
Porlamar O YV 112 Ec 40
Pormatkku O FIN 159 Hc 15
Pormissão O BR 140 Ek 56
Pormpuraaw Edward River O AUS 365 Mg 53
Pornic O F 163 Ge 22
Porog O RUS 159 Hm 14
Poro Island ♁ RP 267 Ln 40
Poro Island ♁ SOL 290 Na 49
Poroma O PNG 286 Mh 49
Poronajsk O RUS 23 Sa 5
Poronajsk O RUS 205 Xb 9
Porong O RI 279 Lg 49
Póros O GR 194 Hc 26
Porosozero O RUS 159 Hh 14
Porpise Bay ≈ 38 Ra 16
Porquis Junction O CDN 57 Dh 21
Porsangen ~ N 159 He 10
Porsangerhalvøya ♁ N 159 He 10
Porsea O RI 270 Kp 44
Porsgrunn O N 170 Gl 16
Pórshöfn O IS 158 Fn 12
Porsuk Çayı ~ TR 195 Hh 26
Porta ~ BR 121 Ej 49
Port Adelaide O AUS 378 Me 63
Portadown O GB 162 Gc 18
Portage O USA 46 Ba 15
Portage O USA 57 Dd 24
Portage O CDN 61 Eb 22
Portage O USA 71 Df 24
Portage O NZ 383 Nk 66
Portage-la-Prairie O CDN 56 Cn 20
Portageville O USA 60 Dj 24
Portal O USA 51 Cl 21
Port Alberni O CDN 50 Bp 21
Port Albert O AUS 379 Mk 65
Port Albert O NZ 383 Nk 64
Portales O USA 65 Cl 28
Port Alexander O USA 47 Bj 17
Port Alfred O ZA 358 Hf 62
Port Allegany O USA 74 Dj 25
Port Alma O AUS 375 Mm 57
Port Alsworth O USA 46 Al 15
Port Angeles O USA 50 Ca 21
Port Antonio O JA 101 Dk 36
Port-à-Piment O RH 101 Dl 36
Port Arthur O USA 81 Da 31
Port Arthur O AUS 378 Mk 67
Port Askaig O GB 162 Gc 18
Port au Choix O CDN 61 Ef 20
Port au Choix N.H.P. ★ CDN 61 Ef 20
Port Augusta O AUS 378 Me 62
Port au Port Bay ≈ CDN 61 Ee 21
Port au Port Peninsula ♁ CDN 61 Ee 21
Port-au-Prince ▣ RH 101 Dm 36
Port Austin O USA 57 Dg 23
Port-Barcarès O F 185 Gh 24
Port Bell O EAU 324 Hj 45
Port Bickerton O CDN 61 Ed 23
Port Blair O IND 262 Kl 40
Port Blandford O CDN 61 Eg 21
Port Bolivar O USA 81 Da 31
Port Broughton O AUS 378 Me 62
Port Burwell O CDN 43 Hc 6
Port Burwell O CDN 57 Dh 24
Port Campbell O AUS 378 Mh 65
Port Campbell ♀ AUS 378 Mh 65
Port -Cartier O CDN 61 Ea 21
Port Chalmers O NZ 382 Nh 68
Port Charlotte O USA 87 Dg 32
Port Clinton O USA 71 Dg 25
Port Clyde O USA 60 Dp 24
Port Colborne O CDN 60 Dj 24
Port-Daniel O CDN 61 Eb 21
Port Davey ~ AUS 378 Mj 67
Port-de-Paix O RH 101 Dm 36
Port Dickson O MAL 270 La 44

Port Douglas O **AUS** 365 Mj 54
Port Edward O **ZA** 349 Hh 61
Porteira O **BR** 120 Ef 46
Porteirinha O **BR** 125 En 53
Portél O **BR** 121 Ej 46
Portelândia O **BR** 124 Ee 53
Port Elgin O **CDN** 57 Dh 23
Port Elgin O **CDN** 61 Eb 22
Port Elizabeth O **ZA** 358 He 62
Port Ellen O **GB** 162 Gc 18
Porteno O **RA** 140 Ee 58
Porterville O **USA** 64 Cc 27
Porterville O **RCH** 137 Dm 64
Porterville O **ZA** 358 Hc 62
Portezuelo O **RCH** 137 Dm 64
Port Essington O **AUS** 364 Mb 51
Port Essington O **AUS** 364 Mb 51
Port Fairy O **AUS** 378 Mh 65
Port Fitzroy O **NZ** 383 Nk 64
Port Fourchon O **USA** 86 Dc 31
Port Gentil O **G** 332 Gj 46
Port Germein O **AUS** 378 Me 62
Port Gibson O **USA** 86 De 30
Port Grosvenor O **ZA** 349 Hg 61
Port-Harcourt O **WAN** 326 Gg 43
Port Hardy O **CDN** 50 Bm 20
Port Harrison Inukjuak O **CDN** 43 Gc 7
Port Hastings O **CDN** 61 Ed 23
Port Hedland O **AUS** 360 Lk 56
Port Heiden O **USA** 46 Al 17
Port Hope O **CDN** 60 Dj 24
Port Howe O **BS** 87 Dl 33
Port Huron O **CDN** 57 Dg 24
Port Huron O **USA** 57 Dg 24
Portimão O **P** 184 Gb 27
Port Isabel O **USA** 81 Cp 32
Port Jackson O **AUS** 379 Mm 62
Port Jackson O **NZ** 383 Nk 64
Port Jervis O **USA** 74 Dl 25
Port Kaituma O **GUY** 113 Ef 42
Port Kenny O **AUS** 378 Md 62
Portland O **USA** 50 Ca 23
Portland O **USA** 60 Dn 24
Portland O **USA** 71 Df 25
Portland O **USA** 81 Cp 32
Portland O **AUS** 378 Mg 65
Portland Bay ∼ **AUS** 378 Mg 65
Portland Bight ∼ **JA** 101 Dk 37
Portland Island △ **NZ** 383 Nl 65
Portland Point ⌣ **JA** 101 Dk 37
Portland Roads O **AUS** 365 Mh 52
Port Langdo ∼ **AUS** 365 Mh 52
Port Laoise O **IRL** 163 Gc 19
Port Lavaca O **USA** 81 Cp 31
Port Leamington O **CDN** 61 Ef 21
Port Lincoln O **AUS** 378 Md 63
Port Lions O **USA** 46 An 17
Portlock Reefs △ **PNG** 287 Mj 50
Port Loko O **WAL** 316 Fg 41
Port Loring O **CDN** 60 Dj 23
Port Louis □ **MS** 353 Gg 56
Port-Louis O **F** 104 Ed 37
Port MacDonnell O **AUS** 378 Mg 65
Port Macquarie O **AUS** 379 Mn 61
Port Mansfield O **USA** 81 Cp 32
Port Maria O **JA** 101 Dk 36
Port Maurant O **GUY** 113 Ef 42
Port Mayaca O **USA** 87 Dn 32
Port Mc Arthur ∼ **AUS** 365 Me 54
Port McNeill O **CDN** 50 Bn 20
Port Mellon O **CDN** 50 Ca 21
Port Menier O **CDN** 61 Ed 22
Port Moller O **USA** 10 Ab 4
Port Moller O **USA** 46 Aj 17
Portmore O **JA** 101 Dk 37
Port Moresby ⬛ **PNG** 287 Mk 50
Port Musgrave ∼ **AUS** 365 Mg 51
Portnaguran O **GB** 162 Gc 16
Port Neill O **AUS** 378 Me 63
Port Nelson ≈ **CDN** 43 Fc 7
Port Nelson O **BS** 87 Dl 34
Portneuf O **CDN** 60 Dn 21
Port Nolloth O **ZA** 348 Ha 60
Pôrto O **BR** 124 En 47
Pôrto O **P** 184 Gb 25
Porto O **F** 185 Gl 24
Porto Alegre O **BR** 125 Ep 52
Porto Alegre O **BR** 146 Ej 61
Portoalegre O **P** 184 Gc 26
Porto Alegre do Norte O **BR** 133 Eh 51
Porto Amazonas O **BR** 140 Ej 58
Porto Amboim O **ANG** 340 Gn 51
Porto Arari O **BR** 121 Ej 45
Portobelo O **PA** 97 Dj 41
Porto Braga O **BR** 117 Eb 47
Porto Braga O **BR** 140 Ef 56
Porto Busch O **BR** 140 Ee 56
Porto Caiúa O **BR** 140 Eh 57
Porto Camará O **BR** 121 Ek 46
Porto Camargo O **BR** 140 Eh 57
Port O'Conner O **USA** 81 Cp 31
Porto Cristo O **E** 185 Gk 26
Porto de Mocambo ∼ **MOC** 344 Hn 53
Porto de Pedras O **BR** 124 Fc 50
Porto do Caititu O **BR** 121 Em 48
Porto do Mangue O **BR** 124 Fb 48
Porto do Moz O **BR** 121 Eh 46
Portos dos Gaúchos O **BR** 132 Ef 51
Porto dos Mosteiros O **CV** 316 Fc 48
Porto Esperidão O **BR** 132 Ee 53
Porto Estrela O **BR** 132 Ef 53
Portoferráio O **I** 185 Gi 24
Port of Ness O **GB** 162 Gc 16
Porto Franco O **BR** 121 El 49
Port of Spain ⬛ **TT** 104 Ed 40
Porto Grande O **BR** 121 Ej 45
Portogruaro O **I** 185 Gn 23
Porto Henrique O **MOC** 352 Hj 59
Porto Jofre O **BR** 132 Ee 53
Port-Olry O **VU** 386 Nf 53
Porto Moniz O **P** 292 Fm 29
Porto Mosquito O **CV** 316 Fj 38
Porto Nacional O **BR** 133 Ek 51
Porto-Novo ⬛ **DY** 320 Gh 42
Port Orange O **USA** 87 Dn 31
Port Orchard O **USA** 50 Ca 22
Porto Rico O **BR** 140 Ef 56
Porto Rolha O **BR** 129 Eb 51
Porto Sant ♠ **P** 292 Fm 29
Porto São José O **BR** 140 Eh 57
Porto Seguro O **BR** 125 Fa 54
Porto Tórres O **I** 185 Gk 25
Porto União O **BR** 140 Ej 59
Porto Válter O **BR** 116 Dm 50

Porto-Vecchio O **F** 185 Gl 25
Porto Velho O **BR** 117 Ec 50
Portoviejo O **EC** 116 Dh 46
Port Xavier O **BR** 140 Eg 59
Port Oxford O **USA** 64 Bm 25
Portpatrick O **GB** 162 Gd 18
Port Phillip Bay ∼ **AUS** 379 Mj 64
Port Pirie O **AUS** 378 Me 62
Port Radium O **CDN** 6 Da 3
Port Radium O **CDN** 47 Cc 11
Port Rowan O **CDN** 57 Dh 24
Port Royal N.H.P. ★ **USA** 60 Ea 23
Port Royal Sound ∼ **USA** 71 Dh 29
Portrush O **GB** 162 Gc 18
Port Said O **ET** 301 Hj 30
Port Salemo O **USA** 87 Dn 32
Port Salut O **RH** 101 Di 36
Port Sanilac O **USA** 57 Dg 24
Port Shepstone O **ZA** 349 Hh 61
Portsmouth O **USA** 60 Dn 24
Portsmouth O **USA** 71 Dg 26
Portsmouth O **USA** 74 Dk 27
Portsmouth O **WD** 104 Ed 38
Portsmouth O **GB** 163 Gf 20
Port St. Joe O **USA** 86 Df 31
Port St. John O **USA** 87 Dh 31
Port St. Johns O **ZA** 349 Hg 61
Port St. Lucie O **USA** 87 Dh 32
Port Stanley O **CDN** 57 Dh 24
Port Stephens O **GB** 147 Ed 72
Port Stephens ∼ **AUS** 379 Mn 62
Port Sudan O **SUD** 313 Hi 36
Port Sulphur O **USA** 86 Dd 31
Port Talbot O **GB** 163 Ge 20
Port Tewfik O **ET** 301 Hj 31
Porttipahdan tekojärvi ∼ **FIN** 159 Hf 11
Port Townsend O **USA** 50 Ca 21
Portugal ❑ **P** 184 Ga 25
Portuguesa □ **YV** 107 Dp 41
Portuguesa □ **YV** 107 Ea 41
Portumna O **IRL** 163 Gb 19
Port-Vato O **VU** 386 Nf 54
Port Victoria O **EAK** 325 Hj 45
Port Victoria O **AUS** 378 Me 63
Port-Vila ⬛ **VU** 386 Ng 54
Port Vincent O **AUS** 378 Me 63
Port Waikato O **NZ** 383 Nk 64
Port Wakefield O **AUS** 378 Mf 63
Port Warrender O **AUS** 361 Ln 53
Port Washington O **USA** 57 De 24
Port Welshpool O **AUS** 379 Mk 65
Port Wing O **USA** 56 Dc 22
Porumamilla O **IND** 238 Kd 38
Porvenir O **RCH** 152 Dn 72
Porvoo Borga O **FIN** 159 He 15
Porzo Hondo O **RA** 136 Eb 59
Posadas O **RA** 140 Ef 59
Pošehon'e O **RUS** 171 Hm 16
Posio O **FIN** 159 Hg 12
Poso O **RI** 282 Ll 46
Poso del Tigre O **BOL** 129 Ed 54
Posol O **TR** 202 Hp 25
Posõng O **ROK** 247 Lg 28
Posorja O **EC** 116 Dh 47
Posse O **BR** 133 El 53
Possel O **RCA** 321 Hb 43
Possession Island △ **NAM** 348 Gp 59
Possoš O **RUS** 181 Hm 20
Possum Kingdom Lake ∼ **USA** 70 Cn 29
Post O **USA** 70 Cm 29
Posta Cambio a Zalazar O **RA** 136 Ed 58
Posta Km. 45 O **RA** 136 Ed 58
Posta Lencina O **RA** 136 Ed 58
Post Arinda O **GUY** 112 Ea 43
Post Falls O **USA** 50 Cd 22
Postmasburg O **ZA** 348 Hd 60
Postojna O **SLO** 174 Gp 23
Posto Uaçá O **BR** 113 Ej 44
Postrervalle O **BOL** 129 Ec 55
Postville O **USA** 56 Dc 24
Pota O **RI** 282 Ll 50
Pótam O **MEX** 80 Cg 32
Potamos O **GR** 194 Hd 28
Potawatomi Indian Reservation •••
USA 70 Cp 26
Potchefstroom O **ZA** 349 Hf 59
Poté O **BR** 125 Ep 54
Poteau O **USA** 70 Da 28
Poteet O **USA** 81 Cn 31
Potenji O **BR** 124 Ep 49
Poteny ∼ **BR** 124 Fb 48
Potenza O **I** 194 Gp 25
Potfontein O **ZA** 349 Hd 61
Potgietersrus O **ZA** 349 Hg 58
Potholes Reservoir ∼ **USA** 50 Cc 22
Poti ∼ **BR** 124 En 48
Poti O **BR** 124 Ep 48
P'oti O **GE** 202 Hn 24
Potimalal O **RA** 137 Dp 64
Potin O **IND** 235 Kl 32
Potiraguá O **BR** 125 Fa 53
Potiskum O **WAN** 320 Gm 40
Pot Jostler Creek ∼ **AUS** 374 Mg 57
Pot Mountain △ **USA** 50 Ce 22
Potol Point ⌣ **RP** 267 Ll 40
Potomac ∼ **USA** 74 Dk 26
Potoru O **WAL** 316 Ga 42
Potosi O **USA** 71 Dc 27
Potosí O **NIC** 96 De 39
Potosí O **BOL** 129 Eb 55
Pototan O **RP** 267 Lm 40
Potrerillos O **RA** 137 Dp 62
Potrerillos Abajo O **PA** 97 Dg 41
Potrero ∼ **MEX** 81 Ck 31
Potrero de Gallegos O **MEX** 92 Cl 34
Potrero Seco O **MEX** Dn 59
Presa Alvaro Obregón ∼ **MEX** 80 Ch 32
Potsdam ⬤ **D** 170 Gn 19
Potsdam O **USA** 60 Dl 23
Pottro O **PE** 116 Dk 48
Pottstown O **USA** 74 Dk 25
Pottsville O **USA** 74 Dk 25
Pottuvil O **CL** 235 Ke 42
Põţurge O **TR** 195 Hm 26
Potvinsuom ♀ **FIN** 159 Hg 14
Pouch Cove O **CDN** 61 Eh 22
Pouébo O **F** 386 Ne 56
Pouéré O **RCB** 332 Gp 46
Pougol O **RCA** 321 Gp 42

Poultney O **USA** 60 Dm 24
Poum O **F** 386 Nd 56
Pouma O **CAM** 320 Gm 44
Poumalé O **RCA** 321 Hb 43
Pouni O **BF** 317 Ge 40
Pourerere O **NZ** 383 Nl 66
Pouso Alegre O **BR** 141 El 57
Poûthišät O **K** 263 Lb 39
Pouto O **NZ** 383 Nj 64
Pouytenga O **BF** 317 Gf 39
Povalval O **PNG** 287 Mm 47
Poveneckij zaliv ∼ **RUS** 159 Hk 14
Poverty Bay ∼ **NZ** 383 Nm 65
Povlâr O **IR** 215 Je 30
Povungnituk O **CDN** 7 Fa 4
Powderhorn O **USA** 65 Cj 26
Powder River ∼ **USA** 51 Ck 23
Powder River Pass △ **USA** 51 Cj 23
Powderville O **USA** 51 Ck 23
Powell O **USA** 51 Cn 23
Powell Creek O **AUS** 364 Mc 55
Powell Creek ∼ **AUS** 375 Mh 58
Powell Point ⌣ **BS** 87 Dk 33
Powell Point ⌣ **USA** 65 Cf 27
Powell River O **CDN** 50 Bp 21
Powers O **USA** 57 De 23
Powerview O **CDN** 56 Cp 20
Powhatan O **USA** 86 Db 30
Poxoréo O **BR** 132 Eg 53
Poyang Hu ∼ **VRC** 258 Lj 31
Pozanti O **TR** 195 Hk 27
Požarevac O **SCG** 174 Hc 23
Poza Rica O **MEX** 92 Cp 34
Pozas de Santa Ana O **MEX** 92 Cm 34
Požega O **HR** 174 Ha 23
Požega O **SCG** 194 Hb 24
Poznań O **PL** 170 Ha 19
Pozo O **RA** 136 Ea 59
Pozo Almonte O **RCH** 136 Dp 56
Pozo Colorado O **PY** 140 Ee 57
Pozo del Molle O **RA** 137 Ec 62
Pozo del Tigre O **RA** 136 Ed 58
Pozo del Zorro O **RA** 136 Ec 57
Pozo de Maza O **RA** 136 Ed 57
Pozo Dulce O **RA** 137 Ec 60
Pozo Herrera O **RA** 136 Ec 60
Pozuzo ∼ **PE** 116 Dl 50
Pozuzo O **PE** 128 Dl 51
Pozzuoli O **I** 185 Gn 25
Pra ∼ **GH** 317 Gf 43
Prachin Buri O **THA** 262 La 39
Prachuap Khirikhan O **THA** 262 Kp 40
Pracupi ∼ **BR** 121 Ej 47
Pradéd △ **CZ** 174 Ha 20
Pradelles O **F** 185 Gh 23
Pradesh ⬤ **IND** 234 Kd 33
Prado O **BR** 121 Eh 48
Prado O **BR** 125 Fa 54
Pradópolis O **BR** 141 Ek 56
Prague O **USA** 70 Cp 28
Prague ⬛ **CZ** 174 Gp 21
Praia ⬛ **CV** 316 Fj 38
Praia do Bilene O **MOC** 352 Hj 58
Praia do Xai-Xai O **MOC** 352 Hj 58
Praia Grande O **BR** 141 El 57
Praínha O **BR** 120 Eh 46
Praínha O **BR** 121 Ej 47
Prainha Nova O **BR** 120 Ed 49
Prairie O **AUS** 375 Mj 56
Prairie City O **USA** 50 Cc 23
Prairie Dog Creek ∼ **USA** 70 Cm 26
Prairie Dog Town Fk. Red River ∼ **USA** 70 Cm 28
Prairie Downs O **AUS** 360 Lk 57
Prairie du Chien O **USA** 56 Dc 24
Prairie Grove O **USA** 70 Da 28
Prairie River O **CDN** 51 Cl 19
Praja Grande O **BR** 146 Ej 60
Prakhon Chai O **THA** 263 Lb 38
Prambanan ★ **RI** 278 Lf 49
Prampram O **BR** 317 Gg 43
Pran Buri O **THA** 262 Kp 39
Pran Buri Reservoir ∼ **THA** 262 Kp 39
Prándarjökull △ **IS** 158 Fn 13
Pranhita ∼ **IND** 238 Kd 36
Prántij O **IND** 227 Ka 34
Prapat O **RI** 270 Kp 44
Prasat O **THA** 263 Lb 38
Praslin △ **SY** 329 Jf 48
Prata O **BR** 133 Ek 55
Prata O **BR** 133 Ek 55
Prata ∼ **BR** 133 El 54
Prato O **I** 185 Gm 24
Prats-de-Mollo O **F** 184 Gh 24
Pratt O **USA** 70 Cn 27
Prattville O **USA** 71 De 29
Pratudão ∼ **BR** 133 Em 52
Praya O **RI** 279 Lj 50
Praydinsk O **RUS** 170 Hc 18
Prazaroki O **BY** 171 Hf 18
Prečipice △ **AUS** 375 Mm 58
Prečistoe O **RUS** 171 Hh 18
Predbaykal'skaya Padina ∼ **RUS** 204 Va 8
Predporožnyj O **RUS** 205 Xb 5
Preeceville O **CDN** 51 Cl 20
Preh Khmér O **K** 263 Lc 39
Preili O **LV** 171 Hf 17
Premier Downs O **AUS** 369 Ln 61
Prentice O **USA** 56 Dc 23
Prentiss O **USA** 86 Dd 30
Preparis Island △ **MYA** 262 Kl 38
Pres. de la Plaza O **RA** 140 Ef 59
Presa A. L. Mateos ∼ **MEX** 80 Cj 33
Presa Alacranes ∼ **C** 100 Dh 34
Presa Alvaro Obregón ∼ **MEX** 80 Ch 32
Presa Benito Juárez ∼ **MEX** 93 Da 37
Presa Bogonias ∼ **MEX** 92 Cm 35
Presa de la Angostura ∼ **MEX** 80 Ch 30
Presa de la Angostura ∼ **MEX** 93 Db 37
Presa de la Boquilla ∼ **MEX** 80 Ck 32
Presa del Hanabanilla ∼ **C** 100 Dh 34

Presa del Infiernillo ∼ **MEX** 92 Cm 36
Presa F. Zarco ∼ **MEX** 81 Cl 33
Presa Francisco Madeiro ∼ **MEX** 80 Ck 31
Presa J.O. de Dominguez ∼ **MEX** 80 Ch 32
Presa la Amistad ∼ **MEX** 81 Cm 31
Presa Luis L. León ∼ **MEX** 80 Ck 31
Presa M. Hidalgo ∼ **MEX** 80 Ch 32
Presa Macúzari ∼ **MEX** 80 Ch 32
Presa Marte Goméz ∼ **MEX** 81 Cn 32
Presa Miguel Alemán ∼ **MEX** 93 Cp 36
Presa Nezahualcoyotl ∼ **MEX** 93 Db 37
Presa Plutarco Elias Calles ∼ **MEX** 80 Cg 31
Presa Venustiano Carranza ∼ **MEX** 81 Cm 32
Presa Vicente Guerrero ∼ **MEX** 81 Cn 34
Presa Zaza ∼ **C** 100 Dj 35
Prescot O **USA** 70 Db 29
Prescott O **USA** 50 Cf 22
Prescott O **USA** 64 Cf 28
Prescott O **USA** 70 Db 28
Prescott Island △ **CDN** 42 Fb 4
Prescott Valley O **USA** 64 Cf 28
Preservation Inlet ∼ **NZ** 382 Ne 69
Presho O **USA** 51 Cl 24
Presidencia Roque Sáenz Peña O **RA** 136 Ed 59
Presidente Bernardes O **BR** 140 Eh 57
Presidente Dutra O **BR** 121 Em 48
Presidente Epitácio O **BR** 140 Eh 56
Presidente Figueiredo O **BR** 120 Ee 47
Presidente Jânio Quadros O **BR** 125 Ep 53
Presidente Juscelino O **BR** 121 Em 47
Presidente Juscelino O **BR** 133 Em 55
Presidente Kennedy O **BR** 121 Ek 50
Presidente Médici O **BR** 129 Ed 51
Presidente Olegário O **BR** 133 El 55
Presidente Prudente O **BR** 140 Ej 56
Presidente Vargas O **BR** 124 En 47
Presidente Venceslau O **BR** 140 Eh 56
Presidio O **USA** 81 Ck 31
Presidio O **MEX** 92 Ck 34
Prešov O **SK** 174 Hc 21
Presque Isle O **USA** 60 Dp 22
Press Lake O **CDN** 56 Dc 21
Preston O **USA** 56 Db 24
Preston O **USA** 64 Ce 26
Preston O **USA** 65 Cg 24
Preston O **USA** 70 Db 27
Preston O **GB** 163 Ge 19
Prestonburg O **USA** 71 Dg 27
Preto ∼ **BR** 112 Eb 45
Preto O **BR** 117 Eb 46
Preto ∼ **BR** 117 Ec 50
Preto ∼ **BR** 120 Ec 46
Preto ∼ **BR** 124 En 47
Prêto ∼ **BR** 125 Fa 52
Prêto ∼ **BR** 133 El 53
Prêto ∼ **BR** 133 El 54
Prêto ∼ **BR** 133 En 51
Prêto ∼ **BR** 140 Ek 56
Preto da Eva ∼ **BR** 120 Ee 47
Preto do Candeias ∼ **BR** 117 Ec 50
Preto do Crespo ∼ **BR** 117 Ec 50
Preto do Igapó-Açu ∼ **BR** 120 Ed 48
Pretoria ⬛ Tshwane ⬛ **ZA** 349 Hf 58
Pretrópolis O **BR** 141 En 57
Preveza O **GR** 194 Hc 26
Prey Vêng O **K** 263 Lc 40
Priangarskoe Plato ∼ **RUS** 204 Ub 7
Priargunsk O **RUS** 204 Vc 8
Příbram O **CZ** 174 Gn 21
Pribrežnyj Khrebet ∼ **RUS** 205 Wc 7
Price O **USA** 71 Dg 27
Price O **USA** 65 Cf 26
Price Island △ **CDN** 50 Bm 19
Price River ∼ **USA** 65 Cg 26
Prichard O **USA** 50 Cd 22
Prichard O **USA** 86 Dd 30
Priddis O **CDN** 50 Ce 20
Priego d.C. O **E** 184 Gf 27
Priekule O **LV** 171 Hd 17
Prienai O **LT** 171 Hd 18
Prieska O **ZA** 349 Hd 60
Priest Lake ∼ **USA** 50 Cd 21
Priest River O **USA** 50 Cd 21
Prievidza O **SK** 174 Hb 21
Prijedor O **BIH** 174 Ha 23
Prijepolje O **SCG** 194 Hb 24
Prikro O **CI** 317 Ge 42
Prilenskoye Plato ∼ **RUS** 204 Vb 6
Prilep O **MK** 194 Hc 25
Priluki O **RUS** 181 Hl 22
Primošten O **HR** 194 Gp 24
Primavera O **BR** 121 El 46
Primavera do Leste O **BR** 132 Eg 53
Primeira Cruz O **BR** 124 En 47
Primeiro de Maio O **BR** 140 Ej 57
Primero ∼ **RA** 137 Ec 61
Primorsk O **RUS** 159 Hg 15
Primorsk O **RUS** 181 Hl 22
Primorsko-Ahtarsk O **RUS** 181 Hl 22
Primrose ∼ **RUS** 202 Jb 23
Prince Albert O **CDN** 51 Ck 19
Prince Albert O **ZA** 358 Hc 62
Prince Albert Mountains ⌂ **38** Sb 17
Prince Albert Peninsula O **CDN** 42 Ea 4
Prince Albert Sound ∼ **CDN** 6 Da 2
Prince Albert Sound ≈ **CDN** 47 Cc 9
Prince Alexander Mountains ⌂ **PNG** 286 Mh 47

Prince Charles Island △ **CDN** 7 Fa 3
Prince Charles Island △ **CDN** 43 Gc 5
Prince Charles Mountains ⌂ **38** Na 17
Prince Edward Island ⊚ **CDN** 61 Ec 22
Prince Edward Island ⊚ **CDN** 61 Ec 22
Prince Edward Island National Park ⚲ **CDN** 61 Ec 22
Prince Edward Peninsula O **CDN** 60 Dk 24
Prince Frederick O **USA** 74 Dk 26
Prince George O **CDN** 42 Dc 8
Prince Gustav Adolf Sea ∼ **CDN** 6 Db 2
Prince Gustav Adolf Sea ∼ **38** 42 Ec 3
Prince Harald Coast ⌒ **38** Lb 16
Prince of Wales Island △ **USA** 6 Ca 4
Prince of Wales Island △ **CDN** 6 Ea 2
Prince of Wales Island △ **USA** 42 Da 7
Prince of Wales Island △ **CDN** 42 Fa 4
Prince of Wales Island △ **AUS** 365 Mg 51
Prince of Wales Strait ∼ **CDN** 6 Da 2
Prince of Wales Strait ∼ **CDN** 42 Da 3
Prince Olav Coast ⌒ **38** Ma 16
Prince Patrick Island △ **CDN** 6 Da 2
Prince Patrick Island △ **CDN** 42 Da 2
Prince Regent ∼ **AUS** 361 Ln 53
Prince Regent Inlet ∼ **CDN** 7 Ea 2
Prince Regent Inlet ∼ **CDN** 43 Fc 4
Prince Rupert O **CDN** 42 Dg 8
Princesa Isabel O **BR** 124 Fa 49
Princess Astrid Coast ⌒ **38** Kb 17
Princess Charlotte Bay ∼ **AUS** 365 Mh 53
Princess Harbour O **CDN** 56 Cp 20
Princess Island △ **CDN** 42 Db 8
Princess Island △ **CDN** 50 Bm 19
Princess Martha Coast ⌒ **38** Ja 17
Princess Ragnhild Coast ⌒ **38** La 17
Princess Ranges ⌂ **AUS** 368 Ll 59
Princeton O **CDN** 50 Db 21
Princeton O **USA** 70 Db 25
Princeton O **USA** 70 Dd 29
Princeton O **USA** 71 Dd 25
Princeton O **USA** 71 Dh 27
Princeton O **USA** 74 Df 25
Princetown O **USA** 56 Db 23
Princetown O **AUS** 378 Mh 65
Prince William Sound ∼ **USA** 46 Bc 15
Principe △ **STP** 332 Gk 45
Príncipe da Beira O **BOL** 129 Eb 52
Princton O **USA** 71 De 27
Prineville O **USA** 50 Cb 23
Pringamosa O **CO** 106 Dl 43
Pringgabaya O **RI** 279 Lj 50
Pringle Bay O **ZA** 358 Hb 63
Pringsewu O **RI** 278 Lc 48
Prins Christian Sund ∼ **DK** 18 Gb 3
Prins Karlsforland △ **N** 158 Gm 6
Prins Oscars land △ **N** 158 Hd 5
Prinzapolka ∼ **NIC** 97 Df 39
Priozërsk O **RUS** 171 Hh 15
Pripet ∼ **BY** 175 Hj 20
Pripjat' ∼ **UA** 175 Hh 20
Prišib O **AZ** 202 Jd 26
Priština O **SCG** 194 Hc 24
Pritchett O **USA** 65 Cl 27
Pritzwalk O **D** 170 Gm 19
Privas O **F** 185 Gj 23
Providnnyj Buh ∼ **UA** 175 Hg 21
Privolž'e O **RUS** 181 Jc 19
Privolžsk O **RUS** 171 Hm 17
Prizren O **SCG** 194 Hc 24
Prjaža O **RUS** 171 Hj 15
Probolinggo O **RI** 279 Lg 49
Procupine Hills ⌂ **CDN** 51 Cl 19
Proddatür O **IND** 238 Kd 38
Produjevo O **SCG** 194 Hc 24
Profesor-van-Blommestein Lake ∼ **SME** 113 Eg 43
Profeta ∼ **RCH** 136 Dp 58
Progreso O **MEX** 81 Cm 32
Progreso O **MEX** 93 Dd 35
Progreso O **PE** 128 Dn 53
Prohladnyj O **RUS** 202 Hp 24
Prokop'evsk O **RUS** 204 Tb 8
Prokopjevsk O **RUS** 22 Pa 4
Prokuplje O **SCG** 194 Hc 24
prol. Dmitrija Lapteva ∼ **RUS** 22 Rb 2
prol. Sann ikova ∼ **RUS** 22 Rb 2
Proletarsk O **RUS** 181 Hn 22
Proletarskoe vodohranilišče ∼ **RUS** 181 Hn 22
Proliv Dmitriya Lapteva ∼ **RUS** 205 Xa 2
proliv Longa ∼ **RUS** 23 Tb 2
proliv Longa ∼ **RUS** 205 Zc 4
Proliv Sannikova ∼ **RUS** 205 Xa 4
proliv Senjavina ∼ **RUS** 204 Ub 3
Proliv Vil'kickogo ∼ **RUS** 22 Pa 1
Prome O **MYA** 254 Km 36
Promežutočnyj O **RUS** 205 Zb 5
Promissão O **BR** 132 Ej 56
Promontono del Gargano △ **I** 194 Ha 25
Promyslovka O **RUS** 202 Jb 23
Pronin O **RUS** 181 Hn 21
Pronja ∼ **BY** 171 Hh 18
Pronja ∼ **RUS** 181 Hn 18
Prophet River ∼ **CDN** 47 Ca 15
Propiá O **BR** 125 Fb 51
Propriano O **F** 185 Gl 25
Prosperine O **AUS** 375 Ml 56
Prospect O **AUS** 365 Mg 55
Prosperidad O **RP** 267 Ln 41
Prosperidad O **CO** 107 Dm 40
Prosser O **USA** 50 Cc 22
Prostějov O **CZ** 174 Ha 21
Protection O **USA** 70 Cn 27
Protoka ∼ **RUS** 202 Hm 23
Provence ⌒ **F** 185 Gj 24

Provence-Alpes-Côte d'Azur ⊚ **F** 185 Gk 23
Provenir O **BOL** 129 Dp 51
Providence O **USA** 71 Dd 27
Providence O **USA** 74 Dn 25
Providence Bay O **CDN** 57 Dg 23
Providenciales △ **GB** 101 Dm 35
Providenija O **RUS** 205 Ab 6
Provincetown O **USA** 74 Dn 24
Provins O **F** 163 Gh 21
Provo O **USA** 65 Cg 25
Provost O **CDN** 51 Cg 19
Prozor O **BIH** 194 Ha 24
Prūm O **D** 163 Gk 20
Prundu O **RO** 175 Hf 23
Prungle O **AUS** 378 Mh 63
Pruszków O **PL** 170 Hc 19
Prut ∼ **RO** 175 Hf 22
Pruzhany O **BY** 171 Hd 19
Prydz Bay ∼ **38** Nb 16
Pryluky O **UA** 175 Hj 20
Prymors'k O **UA** 181 Hl 22
Pryor O **USA** 51 Ch 23
Pryor Creek O **USA** 70 Da 27
Prypjacki dzjaržavny zapavednik ⚲ **BY** 175 Hg 20
Pryp'jat' ∼ **UA** 175 He 20
Przasnysz O **PL** 170 Hc 19
Przedbórz O **PL** 174 Hb 20
Przemyśl O **PL** 174 Hd 21
Prževalsk O **KS** 22 Nb 5
Psahná O **GR** 194 Hd 26
Psará O **GR** 194 Hd 27
Psári O **GR** 194 Hd 27
Psebaj O **RUS** 202 Hn 23
Psël ∼ **RUS** 181 Hl 20
Pskem ∼ **UZB** 223 Jp 25
Pskent O **UZB** 223 Jn 25
Pskov O **RUS** 171 Hg 17
Pskovskoe ozero ∼ **RUS** 171 Hg 16
Pt. McLeay O **AUS** 378 Mf 63
Pt. Pelee Natl. Park ⚲ **CDN** 71 Dh 24
Pte. Riv. de L'Artibonite ∼ **RH** 101 Dm 36
Pteri △ **GR** 194 Hc 26
Ptolemaida O **GR** 194 Hc 25
Ptuj O **SLO** 174 Gp 22
Pual O **I** 185 Gl 26
Puán O **RA** 137 Ec 64
Pu'an O **VRC** 255 Lc 33
Puas O **PNG** 287 Mm 47
Pubei O **VRC** 255 Le 34
Pubnico O **CDN** 61 Ea 24
Pucallpa O **PE** 116 Dl 50
Pucara O **PE** 128 Dn 53
Pucara ∼ **PE** 128 Dn 53
Pucauro O **PE** 117 Dn 47
Puceskrogs O **LV** 170 Hd 17
Pucheng O **VRC** 243 Le 28
Pucheng O **VRC** 258 Lk 32
Puchini O **BOL** 129 Ea 54
Puchón O **ROK** 247 Lp 27
Puciosa O **RO** 175 He 23
Pucio Point ⌣ **RP** 267 Ll 40
Pucón O **RCH** 147 Dn 65
Pucté O **MEX** 93 Dd 35
Púcuro O **PA** 104 Dk 42
Pudasjärvi ∼ **FIN** 159 Hf 13
Pu de Sancy △ **F** 184 Gh 23
Pudozž O **RUS** 171 Hi 15
Pudož △ **RUS** 171 Hl 15
Pudu Chattram O **IND** 239 Kc 40
Pudu He ∼ **VRC** 255 Lb 33
Pudukkottai O **IND** 239 Kd 40
Pudur O **IND** 239 Kc 40
Puebla O **MEX** 92 Cn 36
Puebla de Alcocar O **E** 184 Gd 26
Puebla de Sanabria O **E** 184 Gc 24
Pueblo O **USA** 65 Ck 26
Pueblo Bello O **CO** 107 Dm 40
Pueblo Bonito Ruins ★ **USA** 65 Cj 27
Pueblo del Carmen O **ROU** 146 Ef 62
Pueblo Hundido O **RCH** 137 Dn 63
Pueblo Ledesma O **RA** 136 Eb 57
Pueblo Nueva Tiquisate O **GCA** 93 Dc 38
Pueblo Nuevo O **YV** 107 Ea 40
Pueblo Nuevo O **CO** 107 Dp 44
Pueblo Pintado O **USA** 65 Cj 28
Pueblo Viejo O **HN** 96 De 38
Puebloviejo O **EC** 116 Di 46
Puelche O **RCH** 147 Dm 66
Puelches O **RA** 147 Ea 65
Puelén O **RA** 137 Ea 64
Puelo ∼ **RCH** 147 Dn 66
Puente Alto O **RCH** 137 Dn 63
Puente de Ixtla O **MEX** 92 Cn 36
Puente del Inca O **RA** 137 Dp 62
Puente-Genil O **E** 184 Gd 27
Puente Nacional O **CO** 106 Dm 43
Pu'er O **VRC** 254 La 34
Puerco River ∼ **USA** 65 Ch 28
Puerta de Lerma O **RA** 136 Eb 58
Puertecitos O **MEX** 75 Ce 30
Puerto O **E** 184 Gf 27
Puerto Acosta O **BOL** 128 Dp 53
Puerto Aisén O **RCH** 152 Dm 68
Puerto Alegre O **RA** 137 Ea 60
Puerto Angel O **MEX** 93 Cp 38
Puerto Arica O **PE** 116 Dl 46
Puerto Arista O **MEX** 93 Da 38
Puerto Armuelles O **PA** 97 Dg 42
Puerto Arturo O **RCH** 152 Dp 73
Puerto Asís O **CO** 116 Dk 45
Puerto Ayacucho O **YV** 107 Ea 43
Puerto Ayora O **EC** 128 Dc 46
Puerto Bahia Negra O **PY** 140 Ee 56
Puerto Banegas O **BOL** 129 Ec 54
Puerto Baquerizo Moreno O **EC** 128 Dd 46
Puerto Barrios O **GCA** 93 Dd 38
Puerto Bermudez O **PE** 128 Dl 51
Puerto Berrío O **CO** 106 Dl 42
Puerto Bolívar O **EC** 116 Dh 47
Puerto Bolívar O **CO** 107 Dm 39
Puerto Boyacá O **CO** 106 Dl 43
Puerto Busch O **BOL** 140 Ee 56

Puerto Cabello ○ YV 107 Dp 40
Puerto Cabezas ○ NIC 97 Dg 39
Puerto Canoa ○ BOL 129 Ea 52
Puerto Carabuco ○ BOL 128 Dp 53
Puerto Cararé ○ CO 106 Dl 42
Puerto Cárdenas ○ RCH 147 Dm 67
Puerto Carreño ○ CO 107 Ea 42
Puerto Castilla ○ HN 100 Df 37
Puerto Catatumbo ○ YV 107 Dm 41
Puerto Chacabuco ○ RCH 152 Dm 68
Puerto Chicama ○ PE 116 Dj 49
Puerto Cisnes ○ RCH 152 Dm 68
Puerto Coig ○ RA 152 Dp 71
Puerto Colón ○ PY 140 Ef 57
Puerto Constanza ○ RA 146 Ee 62
Puerto Cortés ○ MEX 75 Cf 33
Puerto Cortés ○ HN 96 De 38
Puerto Costés ○ CR 97 Dg 41
Puerto Cumarebo ○ YV 107 Dp 40
Puerto de Cayo ○ EC 116 Dh 46
Puerto de la Cruz ○ E 292 Fm 31
Puerto del Rosario ○ E 292 Gb 31
Puerto de Maranchon △ E 184 Ge 25
Puerto de San Just △ E 184 Gf 25
Puerto Deseado ○ RA 152 Eb 69
Puerto Eden ○ RCH 152 Dl 70
Puerto Escondido ○ MEX 92 Cp 38
Puerto Esperanza ○ C 100 Dg 34
Puerto Esperanza ○ BOL 129 Ea 52
Puerto Esperanza ○ RA 140 Eg 59
Puerto Espinoza ○ CO 116 Dl 46
Puerto Estrella ○ CO 107 Dn 39
Puerto Ferreira ○ BR 141 El 56
Puerto Francisco de Orellano ○ EC 116 Dk 46
Puerto Fuy ○ RCH 147 Dn 65
Puerto Gaitán ○ CO 107 Dm 43
Puerto Galilea ○ PE 116 Dk 47
Puerto Grande ○ EC 116 Dh 47
Puerto Grether ○ BOL 129 Eb 54
Puerto Gutierrez ○ CO 106 Dl 43
Puerto Heath ○ BOL 129 Dp 52
Puerto Humbria ○ CO 116 Dk 45
Puerto Inca ○ PE 116 Dl 50
Puerto Ing. Ibañez ○ RCH 152 Dm 69
Puerto Inírida ○ CO 107 Ea 44
Puerto Itambey ○ PY 140 Eg 58
Puerto Izozog ○ BOL 129 Ec 55
Puerto Japones ○ BOL 129 Dp 54
Puerto Juárez ○ MEX 93 De 35
Puerto la Cruz ○ YV 112 Eb 40
Puerto la Victoria ○ PY 140 Ee 57
Puerto le Esperanza ○ PY 140 Ee 57
Puerto Leguia ○ PE 128 Dn 52
Puerto Leguizamo ○ CO 116 Dl 46
Puerto Lempira ○ HN 97 Dg 38
Puerto Libertad ○ MEX 75 Cf 31
Puerto Limón ○ CO 116 Dk 45
Puertollano ○ E 184 Gd 26
Puerto Llifén ○ RCH 147 Dm 66
Puerto Lobos ○ RA 147 Eb 66
Puerto Lopez ○ YV 107 Dn 40
Puerto López ○ EC 116 Dh 46
Puerto Madero ○ MEX 93 Db 38
Puerto Madero ○ MEX 93 De 36
Puerto Madryn ○ RA 147 Eb 67
Puerto Magdalena ○ MEX 75 Cf 33
Puerto Maldonado ○ PE 128 Dp 52
Puerto Marques ○ MEX 92 Cn 37
Puerto Miriti ○ CO 117 Dp 46
Puerto Montt ○ RCH 147 Dm 66
Puerto Morazán ○ NIC 96 De 39
Puerto Morona ○ EC 116 Dk 47
Puerto Murtinho ○ BR 140 Ef 56
Puerto Mutis ○ PA 97 Dh 42
Puerto Napo ○ EC 116 Dk 46
Puerto Nare ○ CO 106 Dl 42
Puerto Nariño ○ CO 107 Dp 43
Puerto Natales ○ RCH 152 Dm 71
Puerto Navarino ○ RCH 152 Dp 73
Puerto Ninfas ○ RA 147 Eb 67
Puerto Nuevo ○ CO 107 Dp 43
Puerto Obaldia ○ PA 97 Dk 41
Puerto Octay ○ RCH 147 Dm 66
Puerto Olaya ○ CO 106 Dl 42
Puerto Orobayaya ○ BOL 129 Ec 52
Puerto Ospina ○ CO 116 Dl 45
Puerto Padre ○ C 101 Dk 35
Puerto Páez ○ YV 107 Ea 42
Puerto Palomas ○ MEX 93 Da 37
Puerto Patiño ○ BOL 129 Eb 54
Puerto Peñasco ○ MEX 75 Cf 30
Puerto Piña ○ PA 97 Dj 42
Puerto Pinasco ○ PY 140 Ef 57
Puerto Pirámides ○ RA 147 Eb 67
Puerto Pizana ○ PE 116 Dk 49
Puerto Pizarro ○ CO 116 Dm 46
Puerto Plata ○ DOM 101 Dn 36
Puerto Porfía ○ CO 107 Dm 43
Puerto Portillo ○ PE 116 Dm 50
Puerto Prado ○ PE 128 Dl 51
Puerto Princesa ○ RP 267 Lk 41
Puerto Princesa Subterranean River ★ RP 267 Lk 41
Puerto Puyugapi ○ RCH 152 Dm 68
Puerto Quijarro ○ BOL 132 Ef 54
Puerto Quimba ○ PA 97 Dj 41
Puerto Raúl Marín Balmaceda ○ RCH 147 Dm 67
Puerto Rico ♁ USA 104 Ea 36
Puerto Rico ○ PE 128 Dl 52
Puerto Rico ○ BOL 129 Ea 51
Puerto Rico ○ RA 140 Eg 59
Puerto Rico Trench ⩡ 11 Fb 8
Puerto Rico Trench ⩡ 104 Ea 36
Puerto Rondón ○ CO 107 Dn 42
Puerto Saavedra ○ RCH 147 Dm 65
Puerto San Andesito ○ MEX 75 Cf 33
Puerto Sandino ○ NIC 96 De 39
Puerto San Julián ○ RA 152 Ea 70
Puerto San Martín ○ PE 116 Dk 52
Puerto Santa Cruz ○ RA 152 Dp 71
Puerto Saucedo ○ BOL 129 Ec 52
Puerto Siles ○ BOL 129 Eb 52
Puerto Suarez ○ BOL 132 Ef 55
Puerto Turumbán ○ GUY 112 Ed 42
Puerto Vallarta ○ MEX 92 Cj 35
Puerto Varas ○ RCH 147 Dm 66
Puerto Velasco Ibarra ○ EC 128 Dc 46
Puerto Victoria ○ PE 116 Dl 50
Puerto Viejo ○ CR 97 Dg 40
Puerto Villamil ○ EC 128 Dc 46
Puerto Villarroel ○ BOL 129 Eb 54
Puerto Vinte e Dois ○ BR 117 Ec 47
Puerto Visser ○ RA 152 Ea 68
Puerto Weber ○ RCH 152 Dm 71
Puerto Williams ○ RCH 152 Ea 73
Puerto Yungay ○ RCH 152 Dm 70
Puesto Arturo ○ PE 116 Dm 46
Puesto Avanzado ○ PE 116 Dk 47
Pugačev ○ RUS 181 Jc 19
Puge ○ VRC 254 Lb 32
Puger ○ RI 279 Lg 50
Puget Sound ~ USA 50 Ca 22
Puglia ⊙ I 194 Ha 25
Puica ○ PE 128 Dm 53
Puig ○ SUD 324 Hg 41
Puig Major △ E 184 Gh 26
Pujehun ○ WAL 316 Ga 42
Pujiang ○ VRC 242 Lb 30
Pujiang ○ VRC 259 Lk 31
Pujonryong Mountains ⩕ DVRK 247 Lp 26
Pujonryong Sanmaek ⩕ DVRK 247 Lp 25
Pukalani ○ USA 75 Am 35
Puk'ansan ★ ROK 247 Lp 27
Pukapuka ♁ F 14 Ca 11
Pukapuka ♁ NZ 35 Ab 11
Pukarua ♁ F 14 Ca 11
Pukaskava ♣ CDN 57 De 21
Pukatja Ernabella ○ AUS 369 Mc 59
Pukchong ○ DVRK 247 Ma 25
Pukë ○ AL 194 Hb 24
Pukekohe ○ NZ 383 Nk 64
Pukenui ○ NZ 383 Nj 63
Pukota ○ Z 341 Hg 52
Puksubaek △ DVRK 247 Lp 25
Pula ○ HR 185 Gn 23
Pulai ○ RI 274 Lk 45
Pulaksama ○ RI 270 Kn 44
Pulandian Wan ≈ VRC 246 Ll 26
Pulanduta Point ⌓ RP 267 Lm 40
Pulangi ~ RP 275 Ln 42
Pulangpisau ○ RI 279 Lg 47
Pularumpi ○ AUS 364 Mb 51
Pulaski ○ USA 60 Dk 24
Pulaski ○ USA 71 De 28
Pulaski ○ USA 71 Dh 27
Pulau ○ RI 270 La 47
Pulau Adi ♁ RI 283 Mc 48
Pulau Aduar ♁ RI 283 Md 48
Pulau Ahus ♁ RI 274 Lj 44
Pulau Aiduma ♁ RI 283 Mc 48
Pulau Airabu ♁ RI 271 Ld 44
Pulau Ambelau ♁ RI 283 Lp 47
Pulau Ambon ♁ RI 283 Lp 47
Pulau Ambon ♁ RI 283 Ma 47
Pulau Amutu Beser ♁ RI 283 Mc 47
Pulau Angramios ♁ RI 283 Md 47
Pulau Atauro ♁ RI 282 Ln 50
Pulau Aur ♁ MAL 271 Lc 44
Pulau Awai ♁ RI 286 Me 46
Pulau Babar ♁ RI 283 Ma 50
Pulau Babi ♁ RI 270 Kn 44
Pulau Bacan ♁ RI 283 Lp 46
Pulau Bago ♁ RI 270 Kn 44
Pulau Bahubulu ♁ RI 282 Lm 47
Pulau Bakung ♁ RI 271 Lc 45
Pulau Balambangan ♁ MAL 274 Lj 42
Pulau Banawaya ♁ RI 279 Lk 49
Pulau Banda ♁ RI 283 Mb 48
Pulau Banding ○ MAL 270 La 43
Pulau Banggai ♁ RI 282 Lm 46
Pulau Banggi ♁ MAL 274 Lj 42
Pulau Bangka ♁ RI 275 Ln 45
Pulau Bangka ♁ RI 278 Ld 47
Pulau Bangkaru ♁ RI 270 Kn 44
Pulau Bangkudulis ♁ RI 274 Lj 44
Pulau Bangkulu ♁ RI 282 Lm 46
Pulau Basu ♁ RI 278 Lb 46
Pulau Batam ♁ RI 271 Lb 45
Pulau Batanta ♁ RI 283 Mb 46
Pulau Batuata ♁ RI 282 Lm 49
Pulau Batudaka ♁ RI 282 Ll 46
Pulau Baun ♁ RI 283 Md 49
Pulau Bawal ♁ RI 278 Le 47
Pulau Bawean ♁ RI 279 Lg 48
Pulau Baya ♁ MAL 274 Lh 42
Pulau Belangbelang ♁ RI 282 Ll 49
Pulau Belangbelang ♁ RI 283 Lp 46
Pulau Belitung ♁ RI 278 Ld 47
Pulau Bengkalis ♁ RI 270 Lb 45
Pulau Benua ♁ RI 271 Ld 45
Pulau Bepondi ♁ RI 283 Md 46
Pulau Besar ♁ MAL 271 Lc 44
Pulau Besar ♁ RI 282 Lm 50
Pulau Biaro ♁ RI 275 Ln 44
Pulau Binongko ♁ RI 282 Lm 49
Pulau Bintan ♁ RI 271 Lc 45
Pulau Bisa ♁ RI 283 Lp 46
Pulau Boano ♁ RI 283 Lp 47
Pulau Bonerate ♁ RI 282 Ll 49
Pulau Breueh ♁ RI 270 Km 43
Pulau Bromsi ♁ RI 286 Me 46
Pulau Bruit ♁ MAL 271 Lf 44
Pulau Bum Bum ♁ MAL 274 Lk 43
Pulau Bunyu ♁ RI 274 Lj 44
Pulau Buru ♁ RI 282 Lp 47
Pulau Buton Butung ♁ RI 282 Lm 48
Pulau Combol ♁ RI 271 Lb 45
Pulau Dagasuli ♁ RI 275 Lp 44
Pulau Dai ♁ RI 283 Ma 49
Pulau Damar ♁ RI 283 Ma 46
Pulau Damar ♁ RI 283 Ma 49
Pulau Daweloor ♁ RI 283 Mb 49
Pulau Dawera ♁ RI 283 Mb 49
Pulau Dayang Bunting ♁ MAL 270 Kp 42
Pulau Deli ♁ RI 278 Lc 49
Pulau Doangdoangan Besar ♁ RI 279 Lj 48
Pulau Doi ♁ RI 275 Lp 44
Pulau Enggano ♁ RI 278 Lb 48
Pulau Gag ♁ RI 283 Ma 46
Pulau Gam ♁ RI 283 Ma 46
Pulau Gami ♁ RI 283 Mb 46
Pulau Gaya ♁ MAL 274 Lk 43
Pulau Gebe ♁ RI 283 Ma 46
Pulau Gelam ♁ RI 278 Le 47
Pulau Genteng ♁ RI 279 Lg 49
Pulau Gomugomu ♁ RI 283 Lp 46
Pulau Gomumu ♁ RI 283 Lp 46
Pulau Gorong ♁ RI 283 Mb 47
Pulau Gunungapi ♁ RI 282 Lp 49
Pulau Halmahera ♁ RI 275 Ma 45
Pulau Haruku ♁ RI 283 Ma 47
Pulau Hasil ♁ RI 283 Ma 46
Pulau Jambongan ♁ MAL 274 Lj 42
Pulau Jeudin ♁ RI 283 Md 49
Pulau Kabaena ♁ RI 282 Ll 48
Pulau Kaburuang ♁ RI 275 Lp 44
Pulau Kahatola ♁ RI 275 Lp 45
Pulau Kai ♁ RI 283 Mc 48
Pulau Kai Besar ♁ RI 283 Mc 48
Pulau Kai Dulah ♁ RI 283 Mc 48
Pulau Kaimeer ♁ RI 283 Mc 48
Pulau Kaipuri ♁ RI 286 Me 46
Pulau Kai Tanimbar ♁ RI 283 Mc 49
Pulau Kakaban ♁ RI 274 Lk 44
Pulau Kakabia ♁ RI 282 Lm 49
Pulau Kalao ♁ RI 282 Ll 49
Pulau Kalaotoa ♁ RI 282 Ll 49
Pulau Kaledupa ♁ RI 282 Lm 48
Pulau Kanawi ♁ MAL 274 Lj 43
Pulau Kangean ♁ RI 279 Lh 49
Pulau Karakelong ♁ RI 275 Lp 43
Pulau Karamian ♁ RI 279 Lh 48
Pulau Karas ♁ RI 283 Mc 47
Pulau Karimata ♁ RI 278 Le 46
Pulau Karimun ♁ RI 271 Lb 45
Pulau Kasiruta ♁ RI 283 Lp 46
Pulau Kasiui ♁ RI 283 Mb 48
Pulau Kataman ○ RI 271 Lb 45
Pulau Kawe ♁ RI 283 Mb 46
Pulau Kayoa ♁ RI 275 Lp 45
Pulau Kayupangang ♁ RI 282 Ll 49
Pulau Kayyad ♁ RI 282 Ll 49
Pulau Kelang ♁ RI 283 Lp 47
Pulau Kisar ♁ RI 283 Lp 50
Pulau Koba ♁ RI 283 Md 49
Pulau Kobroor ♁ RI 283 Md 49
Pulau Kofiau ♁ RI 283 Ma 46
Pulau Kola ♁ RI 283 Md 48
Pulau Komba ♁ RI 282 Lm 49
Pulau Komoran ♁ RI 286 Mf 50
Pulau Komponaone ♁ RI 282 Lm 48
Pulau Kundur ♁ RI 271 Lb 45
Pulau Kur ♁ RI 283 Mb 48
Pulau Laag ♁ RI 286 Me 48
Pulau Labengke ♁ RI 282 Lm 47
Pulau Labobo ♁ RI 282 Lm 47
Pulau Labuan ♁ MAL 274 Lh 43
Pulau Lagong ♁ RI 271 Le 44
Pulau Lakor ♁ RI 283 Ma 50
Pulau Langkawi ♁ MAL 270 Kp 42
Pulau Lantigiang ♁ RI 282 Ll 49
Pulau Larat ♁ RI 283 Mc 49
Pulau Latalata ♁ RI 283 Lp 46
Pulau Laut ♁ RI 271 Ld 43
Pulau Laut ♁ RI 279 Lj 47
Pulau Lawin ♁ RI 283 Ma 46
Pulau Leer ♁ RI 283 Md 49
Pulau Legundi ♁ RI 278 Lc 48
Pulau Lembeh ♁ RI 275 Ln 45
Pulau Lepar ♁ RI 278 Ld 47
Pulau Leti ♁ RI 283 Lp 50
Pulau Letong ♁ RI 271 Lc 44
Pulau Liat ♁ RI 278 Ld 47
Pulau Lifamatola ♁ RI 282 Lp 46
Pulau Limbo ♁ RI 282 Ln 46
Pulau Lingga ♁ RI 278 Lc 46
Pulau Lintea Tiwolu ♁ RI 282 Lm 48
Pulau Liran ♁ RI 282 Ln 50
Pulau Liukanglu ♁ RI 282 Ll 48
Pulau Madu ♁ RI 282 Ll 49
Pulau Madura ♁ RI 279 Lg 49
Pulau Maikoor ♁ RI 283 Md 49
Pulau Makian ♁ RI 275 Lp 45
Pulau Mallawli ♁ MAL 274 Lj 42
Pulau Manawoka ♁ RI 283 Mb 48
Pulau Mandioli ♁ RI 283 Lp 46
Pulau Mandul ♁ RI 274 Lj 44
Pulau Mangoe ♁ RI 282 Ln 46
Pulau Manin ♁ RI 274 Lj 44
Pulau Manipa ♁ RI 283 Lp 47
Pulau Mansinam ♁ RI 283 Md 46
Pulau Mansuar ♁ RI 283 Mb 46
Pulau Mantehage ♁ RI 275 Ln 45
Pulau Manui ♁ RI 282 Lm 47
Pulau Manupampi ♁ RI 283 Md 46
Pulau Maopora ♁ RI 283 Lp 49
Pulau Mapur ♁ RI 271 Lc 45
Pulau Maputi ♁ RI 275 Lk 45
Pulau Maransabadi ♁ RI 283 Md 47
Pulau Maratua ♁ RI 274 Lk 44
Pulau Maru ♁ RI 283 Mb 49
Pulau Masalembu Besar ♁ RI 279 Lh 48
Pulau Masela ♁ RI 283 Ma 50
Pulau Masi-Masi ♁ RI 286 Mf 46
Pulau Masoni ♁ RI 282 Lm 46
Pulau Matak ♁ RI 271 Lc 44
Pulau Maya ♁ RI 278 Le 46
Pulau Mayu ♁ RI 275 Lp 45
Pulau Melilis ♁ RI 282 Lm 46
Pulau Mendanau ♁ RI 278 Ld 47
Pulau Mendol ♁ RI 271 Lb 45
Pulau Merampi ♁ RI 275 Lp 43
Pulau Mesanak ♁ RI 271 Lc 45
Pulau Miang Besar ♁ RI 274 Lj 45
Pulau Midai ♁ RI 271 Ld 44
Pulau Mios-Num ♁ RI 283 Md 46
Pulau Misool ♁ RI 283 Ma 46
Pulau Miti ♁ RI 275 Ma 45
Pulau Moa ♁ RI 283 Ma 50
Pulau Moeilijk ♁ RI 283 Ma 46
Pulau Molu ♁ RI 283 Mb 49
Pulau Monadotura ♁ RI 275 Ln 45
Pulau Morotai ♁ RI 275 Lp 44
Pulau Moti ♁ RI 275 Lp 45
Pulau Moyo ♁ RI 279 Lj 50
Pulau Muari ♁ RI 283 Lp 46
Pulau Muna ♁ RI 282 Lm 48
Pulau Musala ♁ RI 270 Kp 45
Pulau Namatote ♁ RI 283 Mc 47
Pulau Nambolaki ♁ RI 279 Lk 49
Pulau Namwaan ♁ RI 283 Mb 49
Pulau Natuna Besar ♁ RI 271 Le 43
Pulau Neu ♁ RI 283 Md 49
Pulau Nias ♁ RI 270 Kn 45
Pulau Nila ♁ RI 283 Ma 49
Pulau Nirumoar ♁ RI 286 Mf 46
Pulau Numfoor ♁ RI 283 Md 46
Pulau Nunukan Timur ♁ RI 274 Lj 44
Pulau Nusa Barung ♁ RI 279 Lg 50
Pulau Nusa Laut ♁ RI 283 Ma 47
Pulau Obi ♁ RI 283 Lp 46
Pulau Obilatu ♁ RI 283 Lp 46
Pulau Ogar ♁ RI 283 Mc 47
Pulau Padamaran ♁ RI 282 Ll 48
Pulau Padang ♁ RI 270 Lb 45
Pulau Padea-Besar ♁ RI 282 Lm 47
Pulau Pagai ○ RI 270 Kp 47
Pulau Pagai Selatan ♁ RI 270 Kp 47
Pulau Paliat ♁ RI 279 Lh 49
Pulau Panaitan ♁ RI 278 Lc 49
Pulau Pandam ♁ RI 282 Ll 48
Pulau Pangkor ♁ MAL 270 La 43
Pulau Panjang ♁ RI 271 Le 44
Pulau Panjang ♁ RI 274 Lk 44
Pulau Panjang ♁ RI 278 Ld 48
Pulau Panjang ♁ RI 283 Mb 48
Pulau Parang ♁ RI 283 Mb 47
Pulau Pasi ♁ RI 282 Ll 49
Pulau Pejantan ♁ RI 271 Ld 45
Pulau Pekin ♁ RI 274 Lj 44
Pulau Pelapis ♁ RI 278 Le 46
Pulau Peleng ♁ RI 282 Lm 46
Pulau Pemanggil ♁ MAL 271 Lc 44
Pulau Penambula ♁ RI 283 Md 49
Pulau Penang ♁ MAL 270 Kp 43
Pulau Penebangan ♁ RI 278 Le 46
Pulau Perhentian Besar ♁ MAL 270 Lb 43
Pulau Pinabasan ♁ RI 274 Lj 44
Pulau Pini ♁ RI 270 Kp 45
Pulau Pisang ♁ RI 283 Ma 46
Pulau Poat ♁ RI 282 Lm 46
Pulau Pulasi ♁ RI 282 Ll 49
Pulau Puteran ♁ RI 279 Lg 49
Pulau Raas ♁ RI 279 Lh 49
Pulau Raja ♁ RI 279 Lg 49
Pulau Rakit ♁ RI 278 Le 48
Pulau Rangsang ♁ RI 271 Lb 45
Pulau Rantau Tebingtinggi ♁ RI 270 Lb 45
Pulau Ratewo ♁ RI 283 Md 47
Pulau Rau ♁ RI 275 Lp 44
Pulau Rawa ♁ MAL 271 Lb 44
Pulau Redang ♁ MAL 271 Lb 43
Pulau Romang ♁ RI 283 Lp 49
Pulau Rooin ♁ RI 283 Md 47
Pulau Rumberpon ♁ RI 283 Md 46
Pulau Run ♁ RI 283 Ma 48
Pulau Runduma ♁ RI 282 Ln 48
Pulau Rupat ♁ RI 270 La 45
Pulau Sabalana ♁ RI 279 Lk 49
Pulau Sabaru ♁ RI 279 Lk 49
Pulau Sabuda ♁ RI 283 Mb 47
Pulau Sabuntun ♁ RI 279 Lh 49
Pulau Sago ♁ RI 282 Lm 47
Pulau Sailusbesar ♁ RI 279 Lj 49
Pulau Sakala ♁ RI 279 Lj 49
Pulau Sakar ♁ MAL 274 Lk 43
Pulau Salawati ♁ RI 283 Mb 46
Pulau Salibabu ♁ RI 275 Lp 44
Pulau Salue Besar ♁ RI 282 Lm 46
Pulau Salue Kecil ♁ RI 282 Lm 47
Pulau Samosir ♁ RI 270 Kp 44
Pulau Sanana ♁ RI 282 Lp 47
Pulau Sanding ♁ RI 270 La 47
Pulau Sangiang ♁ RI 278 Lc 48
Pulau Sangihe ♁ RI 275 Ln 44
Pulau Saparua ♁ RI 283 Ma 47
Pulau Sapudi ♁ RI 279 Lh 49
Pulau Sapuka-Besar ♁ RI 279 Lk 49
Pulau Satengar ♁ RI 279 Lj 49
Pulau Sayafi ♁ RI 275 Ma 45
Pulau Sayang ♁ RI 275 Ma 45
Pulau Sebangka ♁ RI 271 Lc 45
Pulau Sebatic ♁ RI 274 Lj 43
Pulau Sebatik ♁ RI 274 Lj 43
Pulau Sebesi ♁ RI 278 Lc 49
Pulau Sebuku ♁ RI 279 Lj 47
Pulau Sedanau ♁ RI 271 Ld 44
Pulau Seho ♁ RI 282 Ln 46
Pulau Selaru ♁ RI 283 Mb 50
Pulau Selayar ♁ RI 282 Ll 48
Pulau Selayar ♁ RI 278 Lc 46
Pulau Selayar ♁ RI 282 Ll 48
Pulau Seliu ♁ RI 278 Ld 47
Pulau Selu ♁ RI 283 Mb 49
Pulau Seluan ♁ RI 271 Ld 43
Pulau Semiai ♁ RI 283 Mc 47
Pulau Sempu ♁ RI 279 Lg 50
Pulau Sera ♁ RI 283 Mb 49
Pulau Seram Ceram ♁ RI 283 Ma 47
Pulau Seram Laut ♁ RI 283 Mb 47
Pulau Serasan ♁ RI 271 Le 44
Pulau Seraya ♁ RI 271 Le 44
Pulau Sermata ♁ RI 283 Ma 50
Pulau Serpanjang ♁ RI 279 Lh 49
Pulau Serua ♁ RI 283 Mb 49
Pulau Serutu ♁ RI 278 Le 46
Pulau Siantan ♁ RI 271 Lc 44
Pulau Siau ♁ RI 275 Ln 44
Pulau Siberut ♁ RI 270 Kp 46
Pulau Sibu ♁ MAL 271 Lc 44
Pulau Simatang ♁ RI 275 Ll 45
Pulau Simeuleu ♁ RI 270 Km 44
Pulau Simuk ♁ RI 270 Kn 46
Pulau Singkep ♁ RI 278 Lb 46
Pulau Siumpu ♁ RI 282 Lm 48
Pulau Subi Besar ♁ RI 271 Le 44
Pulau Subi Kecil ♁ RI 271 Le 44
Pulau Sugi ♁ RI 271 Lb 45
Pulau Supiori ♁ RI 283 Md 46
Pulau Taam ♁ RI 283 Mc 48
Pulau Tabuan ♁ RI 278 Lc 48
Pulau Tahulandang ♁ RI 275 Ln 44
Pulau Taitaitanopo ♁ RI 270 La 47
Pulau Talatakoh ♁ RI 282 Lm 46
Pulau Taliabu ♁ RI 282 Ln 47
Pulau Talisei ♁ RI 275 Ln 45
Pulau Tambalongang ♁ RI 282 Ll 49
Pulau Tambelan Besar ♁ RI 271 Ld 45
Pulau Tambisan ♁ MAL 274 Lk 43
Pulau Tanahbala ♁ RI 270 Kp 46
Pulau Tanahjampea ♁ RI 282 Ll 49
Pulau Tanahmasa ♁ RI 270 Kp 46
Pulau Tanakeke ♁ RI 279 Lk 48
Pulau Taneti ♁ RI 283 Lp 46
Pulau Tanjung Buaya ♁ RI 274 Lk 45
Pulau Tanjungsaleh ♁ RI 278 Le 46
Pulau Tapat ♁ RI 283 Lp 46
Pulau Tarakan ♁ RI 274 Lj 44
Pulau Tayandu ♁ RI 283 Mc 48
Pulau Temjang ♁ RI 271 Lc 45
Pulau Tenggol ♁ MAL 271 Lb 43
Pulau Ternate ♁ RI 275 Lp 45
Pulau Teun ♁ RI 283 Ma 49
Pulau Tidore ♁ RI 275 Lp 45
Pulau Tifore ♁ RI 275 Lp 45
Pulau Tiga ♁ MAL 274 Lh 43
Pulau Timbang ♁ MAL 274 Lk 43
Pulau Timbun Mata ♁ MAL 274 Lk 43
Pulau Timpaus ♁ RI 282 Lm 46
Pulau Tinggi ♁ MAL 271 Lc 44
Pulau Tioman ♁ MAL 271 Lc 44
Pulau Tioor ♁ RI 283 Mb 48
Pulau Toade ♁ RI 275 Ln 44
Pulau Tobalai ♁ RI 283 Ma 46
Pulau Togian ♁ RI 282 Ll 46
Pulau Tolonuu ♁ RI 275 Ma 45
Pulau Tomea ♁ RI 282 Lm 48
Pulau Torobi ♁ RI 283 Ma 46
Pulau Trangan ♁ RI 283 Mc 49
Pulau Tuangku ♁ RI 270 Kn 44
Pulau Tunda ♁ RI 278 Ld 48
Pulau Ujir ♁ RI 283 Md 48
Pulau Unauna ♁ RI 282 Ll 46
Pulau Uwi ♁ RI 271 Ld 45
Pulau Vroolijk ♁ RI 283 Ma 46
Pulau Waar ♁ RI 283 Md 47
Pulau Waigeo ♁ RI 283 Mb 46
Pulau Waiji ♁ RI 283 Mb 46
Pulau Waleabahi ♁ RI 282 Lm 46
Pulau Waleacodi ♁ RI 282 Ll 46
Pulau Waleakodi ♁ RI 282 Ll 46
Pulau Walir ♁ RI 283 Mc 48
Pulau Wamar ♁ RI 283 Mc 48
Pulau Wangiwangi ♁ RI 282 Lm 48
Pulau Warakaraket ♁ RI 283 Mb 47
Pulau Warilau ♁ RI 283 Md 48
Pulau Wasir ♁ RI 283 Md 48
Pulau Wayam ♁ RI 275 Mb 45
Pulau Weeim ♁ RI 283 Mb 46
Pulau Weh ♁ RI 270 Km 43
Pulau Wetan ♁ RI 283 Ma 49
Pulau Wetar ♁ RI 282 Ln 49
Pulau Wokam ♁ RI 283 Md 48
Pulau Workai ♁ RI 283 Md 49
Pulau Wotap ♁ RI 283 Mb 49
Pulau Wowoni ♁ RI 282 Lm 47
Pulau Wowoni ♁ RI 282 Lm 48
Pulau Wuliaru ♁ RI 283 Mb 49
Pulau Yamdena ♁ RI 283 Mb 49
Pulau Yapen ♁ RI 286 Me 46
Pulau Yu ♁ RI 283 Ma 46
Puławy ○ PL 174 Hc 20
Pulicat ○ IND 238 Ke 39
Pulicat Lake ~ IND 238 Ke 39
Pulie River ~ PNG 287 Ml 48
Pulingom ○ IND 238 Kb 39
Pulivendla ○ IND 238 Kd 38
Puliyangudi ○ IND 239 Kc 41
Pulkkila ○ FIN 159 He 13
Pullmann ○ USA 50 Cd 22
Pullo ○ PE 128 Dm 53
Pulmoddai ○ CL 239 Ke 41
Pulo Buda ♁ MYA 262 Kp 40
Pulozero ○ RUS 159 Hj 11
Pulpul ○ PNG 287 Mm 48
Pułtusk ○ PL 170 Hc 19
Pulu ○ VRC 230 Ke 27
Pülümür ○ TR 195 Hm 26
Pulwama ○ IND 230 Kb 29
Puma ○ EAT 337 Hk 48
Puma Yumco ~ VRC 235 Kk 31
Pumbi ○ RDC 321 Hd 44
Puna ○ EC 116 Dj 47
Puna de Alacama ⌒ RA 136 Dp 59
Punakaiki ○ NZ 382 Nh 67
Punakha ○ BHT 235 Kj 32
Punalūr ○ IND 239 Kc 41
Punāsa ○ IND 234 Kc 34
Punata ○ BOL 129 Eb 54
Puncac Jaya Peak Carstensz △ RI 286 Me 48
Puncak Mandala △ RI 286 Mg 48
Puncak Trikora △ RI 286 Mf 48
Puncak Yamin △ RI 286 Mf 48
Punch ○ IND 230 Kb 29
Punda Maria ○ ZA 352 Hh 57
Pundanhar ○ MOC 344 Hn 51
Pune ○ IND 238 Ka 36
Pungalina ○ AUS 365 Me 54
Punganuru ○ IND 238 Kd 39
Pungo Andongo ○ ANG 340 Gp 50
Püngoe ~ MOC 344 Hj 55
Punia ○ RDC 336 Hf 46
Puning ○ VRC 258 Lj 34
Punjab ⊙ PK 227 Jp 30
Punjab ⊙ IND 230 Kb 30
Punkaharju ○ FIN 159 Hg 15
Punkalaidun ○ FIN 159 Hd 15
Punkin Center ○ USA 65 Cl 26
Puno ○ PE 128 Dn 53
Punta Abreojos ○ MEX 75 Cf 32
Punta Aguja ⌓ PE 116 Dh 48
Punta Alcalde ⌓ RCH 136 Dn 60
Punta Alegre ○ C 100 Dj 34
Punta Alegro ⌓ BR 146 Eh 62
Punta Alice ⌓ I 194 Ha 26
Punta Allen ○ MEX 93 De 36
Punta Alta ⌓ EC 116 Dh 46
Punta Alta ○ RA 147 Ec 65
Punta Ancón ⌓ EC 116 Dh 47
Punta Anegada ⌓ PA 97 Dh 42
Punta Angamos ⌓ RCH 136 Dn 57
Punta Animas ⌓ RCH 136 Dn 59
Punta Arenas ⌓ RCH 136 Dn 56
Punta Arenas ○ RCH 152 Dn 72
Punta Baja ⌓ MEX 75 Cf 31
Punta Ballena ⌓ EC 116 Dh 46
Punta Ballenita ⌓ RCH 136 Dn 58
Punta Baru ⌓ CO 106 Dl 40
Punta Burica ⌓ PA 97 Dg 42
Punta Bustamante ⌓ RA 152 Dp 71
Punta Cabeza Mechuda ⌓ MEX 80 Cg 33
Punta Cachos ⌓ RCH 136 Dn 59
Punta Calera ⌓ RCH 147 Dl 65
Punta Cana ○ DOM 101 Dp 36
Punta Canoas ⌓ CO 106 Dl 40
Punta Cantagalo ⌓ BR 141 Ek 59
Punta Capana ⌓ YV 107 Dn 40
Punta Cardón ○ YV 107 Dn 40
Punta Caribaná ⌓ CO 106 Dk 41
Punta Carnera ⌓ EC 116 Dh 47
Punta Carrizal ⌓ RCH 137 Dn 60
Punta Castro ⌓ RA 147 Eb 67
Punta Catalina ⌓ RCH 152 Dp 72
Punta Catedral ⌓ CR 97 Df 41
Punta Celarain ⌓ MEX 93 De 35
Punta Charambirá ⌓ CO 106 Dk 43
Punta Chivato ⌓ MEX 80 Cg 32
Punta Clara ⌓ RA 147 Eb 67
Punta Cobija ⌓ RCH 136 Dn 57
Punta Coco ⌓ CO 106 Dj 44
Punta Coles ⌓ PE 128 Dn 54
Punta Colorada ⌓ MEX 75 Cf 31
Punta Consepción ⌓ MEX 80 Cg 32
Punta Cosigüina ⌓ NIC 93 Dd 39
Punta Cristóbal ⌓ EC 128 Dc 46
Punta Cruces ⌓ CO 106 Dk 42
Punta Curuçá ⌓ BR 121 Ek 46
Punta da Estaca de Bares △ E 184 Gc 24
Punta das Desertas ⌓ BR 146 Ej 61
Punta das Reyes ⌓ RCH 136 Dn 58
Punta de Arenas ⌓ RA 152 Dp 72
Punta de Atalaia ⌓ BR 121 El 46
Punta de Balosto ⌓ RA 136 Ea 59
Punta de Bombón ⌓ PE 128 Dn 54
Punta de Chérrepe ⌓ PE 116 Dh 49
Punta de Concon ⌓ RCH 137 Dm 62
Punta de Díaz ⌓ RCH 136 Dn 60
Punta de Guañape ⌓ PE 116 Dj 50
Punta de Imbituba ⌓ BR 141 Ek 60
Punta del Agua ○ RA 137 Ea 63
Punta del Diablo ⌓ ROU 146 Eh 63
Punta del Este ⌓ ROU 146 Eg 63
Punta Delgada ⌓ RCH 152 Dn 72
Punta Delgado ○ RA 147 Ec 67
Punta de Lilles ⌓ RCH 137 Dm 62
Punta de los Llanos ○ RA 137 Ea 61
Punta del Viento ○ RCH 137 Dn 60
Punta de Maisí ⌓ C 101 Dl 35
Punta de Piedras ○ YV 112 Eb 40
Punta de Quatipuru ⌓ BR 121 El 46
Punta de Santarém ⌓ BR 121 Ej 45
Punta Desengaño ⌓ RA 152 Ea 70
Punta de Tapes ⌓ BR 146 Ej 61
Punta de Traela ⌓ RCH 137 Dm 62
Punta do Latinos ⌓ BR 146 Eh 62
Punta do Picão ⌓ BR 141 En 57
Punta do Porto Belo ⌓ BR 141 Ek 59
Punta do Rapa ⌓ BR 141 Ek 59
Punta Dungeness ⌓ RA 152 Dp 72
Punta Espada ⌓ CO 107 Dn 39
Punta Estrada ⌓ RA 152 Dp 71
Punta Europa ⌓ GQ 320 Gl 44
Punta Foca ⌓ RA 152 Eb 69
Punta Frieta ○ MEX 75 Ce 31
Punta Frontera ⌓ MEX 93 Db 36
Punta Galera ⌓ EC 116 Dh 45
Punta Gallinas ⌓ CO 107 Dn 39
Punta Gorda ○ BH 93 Dd 37
Punta Gorda ⌓ NIC 97 Dg 38
Punta Gorda ⌓ RCH 128 Dn 55
Punta Grande ⌓ RCH 136 Dn 58
Punta Gruesa ⌓ RCH 136 Dn 56
Punta Guaricana ⌓ BR 141 Ek 58
Punta Guascama ⌓ CO 106 Dj 44
Punta Guiones ⌓ CR 96 Df 41
Punta Hereda ⌓ PE 116 Dh 48
Punta Herrero ○ MEX 93 De 36
Punta Holohit ⌓ MEX 93 Dd 35
Punta Hornillos ⌓ PE 128 Dm 54
Punta José Díaz ⌓ BR 141 Ek 59
Punta la Leona ⌓ EC 116 Dh 46
Punta Lavapié ⌓ RCH 147 Dl 64
Punta la Vieja ⌓ RCH 137 Dm 63
Punta Lengua de Vaca ⌓ RCH 137 Dm 61
Punta Lobos ⌓ RCH 128 Dn 55
Punta Lobos ⌓ RCH 136 Dn 56
Punta Lobos ⌓ RCH 136 Dn 60
Punta Lobos ⌓ RCH 137 Dm 63
Punta Lobos ⌓ RA 147 Ed 65
Punta Lucretia ⌓ C 101 Dl 35
Punta Magdalena ⌓ CO 106 Dk 44
Punta Malabrigo ⌓ PE 116 Dh 49
Punta Maldonado ⌓ MEX 92 Cn 37
Punta Malpelo ⌓ PE 116 Dh 47
Punta Manglares ⌓ CO 106 Dk 43
Punta Manzanillo ⌓ YV 107 Dp 40
Punta Maraguay ⌓ YV 107 Dn 40
Punta Mariato ⌓ PA 97 Dh 42
Punta Marumbi ⌓ BR 141 Ek 58
Punta Marzo ⌓ CO 97 Dj 42
Punta Medanosa ⌓ RA 152 Eb 70
Punta Mita ⌓ MEX 92 Ck 35
Punta Mogotes ⌓ RA 146 Ef 65
Punta Molas ⌓ MEX 93 De 35
Punta Molles ⌓ RCH 137 Dn 62
Punta Mono ⌓ NIC 97 Dg 40
Punta Montes ⌓ RA 152 Dp 71
Punta Morro ⌓ MEX 93 Dc 36
Punta Morro ⌓ RCH 136 Dn 59
Punta Negra ⌓ BH 93 Dd 37
Punta Negra ⌓ PE 116 Dh 48
Punta Negra ⌓ RA 146 Ee 65
Punta Nimún ⌓ MEX 93 Dc 35
Punta Norte ⌓ RA 147 Ec 67
Punta Norte del Cabo San Antonio ⌓ RA 146 Ef 64
Punta Novales ⌓ RA 152 Ea 68
Punta Nueva ○ YV 112 Ec 42
Punta Oscura ⌓ GQ 320 Gl 44
Punta Palenque ⌓ DOM 101 Dn 36
Punta Paracas ⌓ PE 116 Dk 52
Punta Pariñas ⌓ PE 116 Dh 48
Punta Patache ⌓ RCH 136 Dn 56
Punta Pedernales ⌓ EC 116 Dh 45
Punta Pedras ⌓ RA 146 Ef 63
Punta Perlas ⌓ NIC 97 Dg 39
Punta Piaroa ○ YV 112 Eb 44
Punta Piaxtla ⌓ MEX 92 Cj 34
Punta Pichalo ⌓ RCH 128 Dn 55
Punta Piedras ⌓ RA 146 Ef 63
Punta Pizarro ⌓ CO 106 Dk 43
Punta Pozos ⌓ RA 152 Eb 69
Punta Protos ⌓ RCH 137 Dn 60
Punta Púlpito ⌓ MEX 80 Cg 32
Punta Quiroga ⌓ RA 147 Eb 67
Punta Rebordelo ⌓ BR 121 Ek 45
Punta Refugio ⌓ MEX 75 Cf 31
Punta Remedios ⌓ ES 93 Dc 39
Puntarenas ○ CR 97 Df 40
Punta Reyes ⌓ CO 106 Dj 44

460 Puerto Cabello - Punta Reyes

□ Country ▣ Capital city ⊙ Administrative unit ○ Place ⛰ Island ⋀⋀ Mountain range △ Mountain ⌓ Cape ≈ Ocean, Sea ~ Lake, River ♆ Undersea topography ▲ Glacier ♀ National park ••• Reservation ★ Point of major interest ⌓⌓ Landscape

Punta Roca Partida ⌓ MEX 93 Da 36
Punta Roja ⌓ RA 152 Eb 68
Punta Saliente ⌓ RCH 137 Dn 61
Punta Salinas ⌓ PE 128 Dj 51
Punta San Bernardo ⌓ CO 106 Dk 41
Punta San Carlos ⌓ MEX 75 Cf 32
Punta San Juan ⌓ PE 128 Dl 53
Punta San Juan de Lima ⌓ MEX 92 Ck 36
Punta San Marcial ⌓ MEX 80 Cg 33
Punta San Pedro ⌓ RCH 136 Dn 58
Punta San Roque ⌓ MEX 75 Ce 32
Punta Santa Lagarda ⌓ MEX 80 Cg 32
Punta Santa Maria ⌓ ROU 146 Eg 63
Punta Santiago ⌓ GQ 320 Gl 44
Punta São Simão ⌓ BR 146 Ej 61
Punta Sierra ⌓ RA 147 Eb 66
Punta Solano ⌓ CO 106 Dk 42
Punta Sur ⌓ RA 146 Ef 64
Punta Tepopa ⌓ MEX 75 Cf 31
Punta Tetas ⌓ RCH 136 Dn 57
Punta Tinoja ⌓ PE 128 Dm 54
Punta Tombo ⌓ RA 152 Eb 68
Punta Topocalma ⌓ RCH 137 Dm 63
Punta Toro ⌓ RCH 137 Dm 62
Punta Tumbes ⌓ RCH 137 Dm 64
Punta Verde ⌓ EC 116 Dj 45
Punta Zamora ⌓ PE 116 Dj 50
Punta Zamuro ⌓ YV 107 Dp 40
Punta Zapotilán ⌓ MEX 93 Da 36
Punto de Manga △ E 184 Gd 25
Punto Fijo ○ YV 107 Dn 40
Punto M.O.P. ○ YV 112 Ec 44
Punto Seco ○ CO 106 Dl 44
Punto Silvanía ○ CO 117 Dn 45
Punto Tejada ○ CO 106 Dk 44
Punxsutawney ○ USA 74 Dj 25
Puolanka ○ FIN 159 Hf 13
Pùonta dos Camboios ⌓ BR 141 Fa 55
Pupi ○ VRC 258 Lg 31
Puponga ○ NZ 383 Nj 66
Pupri ○ IND 235 Kg 32
Pupuan ○ RI 279 Lh 50
Puquina ○ PE 128 Dn 54
Puquío ○ PE 128 Dl 53
Pur ~ RUS 204 Ta 5
Puranpur ○ IND 234 Ke 31
Purari River ~ PNG 287 Mj 49
Purbolinggo ○ RI 278 Le 49
Purcell ○ USA 70 Cp 28
Purcell Mountains ⋀⋀ CDN 50 Cd 20
Pure ~ CO 117 Dp 47
Purepero ○ MEX 92 Cm 36
Pureté ou Purata ~ BR 117 Dp 47
Purgatoire River ~ USA 65 Cl 27
Puri ○ IND 235 Kg 36
Puri ○ ANG 332 Gp 49
Puricaure ○ YV 107 Dn 40
Purificación ○ MEX 92 Ck 36
Purificación ~ MEX 92 Ck 36
Purificacion ○ CO 106 Dl 44
Pūrna ~ IND 234 Kc 35
Pūrna ○ IND 238 Kc 36
Pūrnia ○ IND 235 Kh 33
Purnong ○ AUS 378 Mf 63
Purnululu ♀ AUS 364 Ma 54
Purple Downs ○ AUS 378 Me 61
Purranque ○ RCH 147 Dm 66
Purros ○ NAM 340 Gn 55
Puruándiro ○ MEX 92 Cm 35
Puruarán ○ MEX 92 Cm 36
Puruey ○ YV 112 Eb 42
Puruí ~ BR 117 Dp 46
Puruí ~ BR 117 Dp 47
Purukcahu ○ RI 279 Lh 46
Puruliya ○ IND 235 Kh 34
Purureche ○ YV 107 Dn 40
Purus ~ BR 117 Dp 50
Purus ~ BR 117 Ea 49
Purus ~ BR 117 Eb 48
Purus ~ BR 117 Eb 49
Purus ~ BR 120 Ed 48
Purutu Island ⛰ PNG 286 Mh 50
Purvachal ⌓⌓ IND 254 Kl 34
Purwakarta ○ RI 278 Ld 49
Purwodadi ○ RI 278 Le 49
Purwokerto ○ RI 278 Le 49
Purworejo ○ RI 278 Le 49
Purzell Mountain △ USA 46 Al 11
Pusa ○ MAL 271 Lf 45
Pūsako ○ IR 226 Jh 32
Pusan ○ ROK 247 Ma 28
Pusesāvli ○ IND 238 Kb 37
Pushkar ○ IND 234 Kb 32
Puškin ○ RUS 171 Hg 16
Puškino ○ RUS 171 Hl 17
Puškino ○ RUS 181 Jb 20
Pušlahta ○ RUS 159 Hl 13
Pušno ○ RUS 159 Hk 13
Püspökladány ○ H 174 Hc 22
Pustaza ~ EC 116 Dk 47
Pustoška ○ RUS 171 Hg 17
Pustunich ○ MEX 93 Dc 36
Pusuga ○ GH 317 Gg 41
Putai ○ RC 259 Lk 34
Putai ○ RC 259 Ll 34
Putamayo ~ EC 116 Dl 45
Putao ○ MYA 254 Kn 32
Putian ○ VRC 258 Lk 33
Putina ○ PE 128 Dn 53
Putina ~ PE/BOL 128 Dp 53
Putnam ○ USA 70 Cn 28
Putnam ○ USA 74 Dm 25
Putončany ○ RUS 204 Ua 6
Putrajaya ▣ MAL 270 La 44
Putre ○ RCH 128 Dp 55
Putsonderwater ○ ZA 349 Hc 60
Puttalam ○ CL 239 Kd 41
Puttalam Lagoon ~ CL 239 Kd 41
Puttgarden ○ D 170 Gm 18
Puttur ○ IND 238 Kb 39
Puttur ○ IND 238 Kd 39
Putty ○ AUS 379 Mm 62
Putumayo ~ CO 116 Dm 46
Putumayo ~ CO 117 Dn 47
Putungan ○ RP 267 Ll 38
Putuoshan ★ VRC 246 Lm 30
Putussibau ○ RI 274 Lg 45
Putyvl ○ UA 175 Hk 20
Puuhonua o Honaunau Natl. Hist. P. ★ USA 75 Am 36
Puukohola Heiau Natl. Hist. P. ★ USA 75 Am 36
Puulavesi ~ FIN 159 Hf 15
Puumala ○ FIN 159 Hg 15
Puuwai ○ USA 75 Ak 35
Puyang ○ VRC 243 Lh 28
Puy de Dôme △ F 185 Gh 23
Puyo ○ EC 116 Dk 46
Puzino ○ RUS 205 Wc 9
Puzino ○ RUS 250 Mb 22
Pweto ○ RDC 336 Hg 50
Pwllhelio ○ GB 163 Gd 19
Pyachanung ○ MYA 235 Kl 35
Pyanangazu ○ MYA 254 Kn 35
Pyasina ~ RUS 22 Pa 2
Pyasina ~ RUS 204 Tc 4
Pyasinskiy Zaliv ≈ RUS 204 Tb 4
Pyattigorsk ○ RUS 202 Hp 23
Pyawbwe ○ MYA 254 Km 35
Pyechin ○ MYA 254 Kl 35
Pyetrykaw ○ BY 171 Hg 19
Pyhäjärvi ○ FIN 159 He 14
Pyhäjoki ○ FIN 159 He 13
Pyhäjoki ~ FIN 159 He 13
Pyhäntä ○ FIN 159 Hf 13
Pyhätunturi △ FIN 159 Hf 12
Pyingaing ○ MYA 254 Km 34
Pyinmana ▣ MYA 254 Km 36
Pymatuning ~ USA 71 Dh 25
Pymatuning Reservoir ~ USA 71 Dh 25
Pyonggang ○ DVRK 247 Lp 26
Pyongsan ○ DVRK 247 Ln 26
Pyongsong ○ DVRK 247 Ln 26
P'yŏngt'aek ○ ROK 247 Lp 27
Pyongyang ▣ DVRK 247 Ln 26
Pyote ○ USA 81 Cl 30
Pyramid ○ RI 286 Mf 47
Pyramiden ○ N 158 Ha 6
Pyramid Hill ○ AUS 379 Mj 64
Pyramid Lake ~ USA 64 Cc 26
Pyramid Lake ~ AUS 368 Ll 62
Pyramid Lake Indian Reservation ••• USA 64 Cc 25
Pyramids of Abū Sīr ★ ET 301 Hh 31
Pyramids of Dahšūr ★ ET 301 Hh 31
Pyramids of Giza ★ ET 301 Hh 31
Pyramids of Saggara ★ ET 301 Hh 31
Pyrenees ⋀⋀ F 184 Gf 24
Pyrjatyn ○ UA 175 Hj 20
Pyrzyce ○ PL 170 Gp 19
Pytalovo ○ RUS 171 Hf 17
Pyt'-Jah ○ RUS 204 Sc 6
Pyttegga △ N 158 Gk 14
Pyu ○ MYA 254 Kn 36

Q

Q. Shemona ○ RL 208 Hk 29
Qaanaaq Thule ○ DK 43 Hb 3
Qab ○ VRC 243 Ld 26
Qacha's Nek ○ LS 349 Hg 61
Qadam ○ SUD 312 Hg 40
Qadamgāh ○ IR 222 Jh 27
Qadir Purrān ○ PK 227 Jp 30
Qadub ○ YE 219 Je 39
Qafa ○ OM 219 Je 37
Qagan Nur ○ VRC 243 Le 26
Qagan Tahoi ○ VRC 242 Km 28
Qagcaka ○ VRC 230 Ke 29
Qahāvand ○ IR 209 Jc 28
Qaidam He ~ VRC 242 Kn 27
Qāimšahr ○ IR 222 Je 27
Qaişār ○ AFG 223 Jl 28
Qala'an-Nahl ○ SUD 313 Hk 39
Qalansīya ○ YE 219 Je 39
Qalāt ○ AFG 223 Jm 29
Qal'at al-Mu'azzam ○ KSA 214 Hl 32
Qal'at Hamīdī ○ IRQ 209 Hp 29
Qal'at Sālih ○ IRQ 215 Jb 30
Qal at Sukkar ○ IRQ 215 Jb 30
Qal' e Dize ○ IRQ 209 Ja 27
Qal'e Kāh ○ AFG 223 Jj 29
Qa'le-ye ○ AFG 230 Ka 27
Qalhāt ○ OM 226 Jh 34
Qaltī al Khudeirā ○ SUD 312 Hf 37
Qaltī al Adusa ○ SUD 312 Hf 37
Qaltī Immaseri ○ SUD 312 He 38
Qalyūb ○ ET 301 Hh 30
Qamarlēb ○ VRC 242 Km 28
Qambar ○ PK 227 Jm 32
Qamdo ○ VRC 242 Kn 30
Qamea ⛰ FJI 390 Aa 54
Qamīnis ○ LAR 300 Hb 30
Qamşar ○ IR 222 Jd 29
Qanā ○ KSA 214 Hn 32
Qandahār ⊙ AFG 227 Jl 30
Qandala ○ SP 328 Jc 40
Qaqortoq Jilianehåb ○ DK 43 Jc 6
Qaşr Ahmad ○ LAR 297 Gp 29
Qāra ○ KSA 214 Hn 31
Qāra ○ ET 300 Hf 31
Qara-Āgāç ~ IR 215 Je 31
Qarabāğ ○ AFG 223 Jj 28
Qarabāğ ○ AFG 223 Jn 28
Qara Çay ~ IR 209 Jc 28
Qara Çay ~ IR 222 Jd 28
Qara Dāğ ⋀⋀ IRQ 209 Ja 28
Qara Dāğ ⋀⋀ IR 209 Jb 26
Qaraghandy ○ KZ 22 Nb 5
Qarah Dāğ ⋀⋀ IRQ 209 Hp 27
Qaran ○ VRC 231 Kg 26
Qara Qash ~ IND 230 Kd 28
Qarārat al Hayyirah ~ LAR 297 Gp 32
Qarārat al Kalb ~ LAR 297 Gp 32
Qara Sū ~ IR 209 Jb 26
Qārat al Hārah ⋀⋀ LAR 297 Gp 32
Qārat as Sab'ah ⋀⋀ LAR 297 Ha 32
Qārat Khālaf Allāh △ LAR 297 Ha 32
Qardho ○ SP 328 Jc 41
Qare Āgāğ ○ IR 209 Jb 27
Qare Şū ~ IR 222 Jd 27
Qare Ziyā'od-Dīn ○ IR 209 Ja 26
Qarhan ○ VRC 242 Km 27
Qarokŭl ○ TJ 230 Ka 26
Qarqan He ~ VRC 231 Kh 26
Qarshi ○ UZB 223 Jl 26
Qaryat Abū Nujaym ○ LAR 297 Gp 30
Qaryat al Fa'idiyah ○ LAR 300 Hc 29
Qaryat al-'Ulyā ○ KSA 215 Jb 32
Qaryat Shumaykh ○ LAR 297 Gn 30
Qaşabe △ IR 209 Jb 26
Qasar bu Hadi ○ LAR 297 Ha 30
Qasir al Kharrūbah ○ LAR 300 Hc 29
Qasr al-Farāfira ○ ET 300 Hf 32
Qasr al Jady ○ LAR 300 He 30
Qaşr al Qarn ○ LAR 300 He 30
Qaşr 'Amiq ○ IRQ 209 Hn 29
Qaşr ash Shaqqah ○ LAR 300 He 30
Qasr-e Qand ○ IR 226 Jj 32
Qasr-e Šīrīn ○ IR 209 Ja 28
Qasr Khulayf ○ LAR 297 Gn 32
Qaşr Larocu ○ LAR 297 Gn 32
Q Ata ○ IL 208 Hk 29
Qa'taba ○ YE 218 Ja 39
Qaţana ○ SYR 208 Hl 29
Qaţana ○ SYR 208 Hl 29
Qatar □ Q 215 Jd 33
Qatarkŭhi Pasi Alaj ⋀⋀ TJ 223 Jp 26
Qatārkŭhi Qarama ⋀⋀ TJ 223 Jn 25
Qatarkŭhi Sariqŭl ⋀⋀ TJ 230 Ka 26
Qaţrūye ○ IR 226 Jf 31
Qattara Depression ⌓⌓ ET 300 Hf 31
Qawām al-Ḥamza ○ IRQ 215 Ja 30
Qawz Ragab ○ SUD 313 Hk 37
Qāyen ○ IR 222 Jh 29
Qaysan ○ SUD 313 Hk 40
Qazvīn ○ IR 209 Jc 27
Qeqertarsuaq Godhaven ○ DK 43 Ja 5
Qerri ○ SUD 312 Hj 37
Qeshm ⛰ IR 226 Jg 32
Qešm ○ IR 226 Jg 32
Qezel Alān ★ IR 222 Jf 27
Qianheshangyuan ○ VRC 243 Le 27
Qianjiang ○ VRC 243 Lg 30
Qianjiang ○ VRC 255 Le 31
Qianjin ○ VRC 250 Mc 22
Qian-Ling ★ VRC 243 Ld 28
Qianshan ★ VRC 246 Lm 25
Qian Shan ⋀⋀ VRC 246 Lm 25
Qianshin ○ VRC 246 Lj 30
Qianwei ○ VRC 255 Lb 31
Qianxi ○ VRC 255 Ld 32
Qian Xian ○ VRC 243 Le 28
Qianyang ○ VRC 243 Ld 28
Qianyang ○ VRC 255 Lf 32
Qiaochuan ○ VRC 243 Ld 27
Qiaojdang ○ VRC 255 Ld 34
Qiaojia ○ VRC 255 Lb 32
Qiaowan ○ VRC 242 Kn 25
Qichun ○ VRC 243 Lh 30
Qidam Pendi ⌓⌓ VRC 231 Kl 26
Qidong ○ VRC 246 Ll 30
Qidong ○ VRC 258 Lg 32
Qiemo Qaran ○ VRC 231 Kg 26
Qift ○ ET 301 Hj 33
Qijiang ○ VRC 255 Ld 31
Qikou ○ VRC 259 Ll 31
Qila Didār Singh ○ PK 230 Ka 29
Qila Lādgasht ○ PK 226 Jk 32
Qila Saifullāh ○ PK 227 Jm 30
Qilian ○ VRC 242 La 26
Qilian Shan ⋀⋀ VRC 242 Kn 26
Qilian Shan △ VRC 242 Kp 26
Qilu Hu ~ VRC 255 Lb 33
Qilwa ○ KSA 218 Hn 36
Qimbala ○ ANG 332 Gp 48
Qimen ○ VRC 258 Lj 31
Qina ○ ET 301 Hj 32
Qin'an ○ VRC 242 Lc 28
Qing. Bingmayong Huaqingchi ★ VRC 243 Le 28
Qingdao Tsingtao ○ VRC 246 Ll 27
Qing Donling ★ VRC 246 Lj 25
Qinghai ⊙ VRC 231 Kl 27
Qinghai Hu ~ VRC 242 Kp 27
Qinghai Nanshan ⋀⋀ VRC 242 Kp 27
Qinghe ○ VRC 243 Lh 27
Qingjian ○ VRC 243 Lf 27
Qingkou ○ VRC 255 Ld 32
Qinglong ○ VRC 246 Lk 25
Qingping ○ VRC 255 Le 35
Qingpu ○ VRC 246 Ll 30
Qingshui ○ VRC 242 Kp 26
Qingshuihe ○ VRC 243 Lf 26
Qingtang ○ VRC 258 Lg 33
Qingtian ○ VRC 259 Ll 31
Qingtongxia ○ VRC 243 Lc 26
Qingxu ○ VRC 243 Lg 27
Qingyang ○ VRC 243 Ld 27
Qingyang ○ VRC 246 Lj 30
Qingyang ○ VRC 258 Lg 34
Qingyuan ○ VRC 258 Lg 34
Qingyuanshan ★ VRC 258 Lk 33
Qingzhen ○ VRC 255 Ld 32
Qingzhou ○ VRC 246 Lk 27
Qin He ~ VRC 243 Lg 28
Qinhuangdao ○ VRC 246 Lk 26
Qinling Shan ⋀⋀ VRC 242 Lc 28
Qinshizui ○ VRC 242 La 27
Qintang ○ VRC 255 Le 34
Qinwanglao Shan △ VRC 255 Ld 33
Qin Xian ○ VRC 243 Lg 27
Qinyang ○ VRC 243 Lg 28
Qinzhou ○ VRC 255 Le 34
Qinzhou Wan ~ VRC 255 Le 35
Qionghai ○ VRC 255 Lf 36
Qionglai ○ VRC 242 Lb 30
Qionglai Shan ⋀⋀ VRC 242 Lb 30
Qiongzhong ○ VRC 255 Le 36
Qiongzhou Haixia ~ VRC 255 Lf 35
Qiqihar ○ VRC 204 Wa 9
Qīr ○ IR 215 Je 31
Qisha ○ VRC 255 Le 35
Qishu ○ VRC 243 Le 30
Qišn ○ YE 219 Jd 38
Qitaihe ○ VRC 205 Wc 9
Qitaihe ○ VRC 250 Mb 23
Qitian Ling △ VRC 258 Lg 33
Qiubei ○ VRC 255 Lb 33
Qiujin ○ VRC 258 Lh 31
Qixia ○ VRC 246 Ll 27
Qiyang ○ VRC 255 Lf 32
Qoğūr ○ IR 209 Jb 27
Qom ○ IR 222 Jd 28
Qomse ○ IR 222 Jd 29
Qonggyai ○ VRC 235 Kk 31
Qooriga Neegro ~ SP 328 Jc 42
Qora Mouth ○ ZA 358 Hg 62
Qorve ○ IR 209 Jb 28
Qoryooley ○ SP 329 Ja 45
Qostanay ○ KZ 19 Na 4
Qoţābād ○ IR 215 Je 31
Qoţūr ○ IR 209 Ja 26
Quabbin ~ USA 60 Dm 24
Quachita ~ USA 70 Db 28
Quadi Qadisha ★ RL 208 Hl 28
Quaidabad ○ PK 223 Jp 29
Quairading ○ AUS 368 Lj 61
Quakertown ○ USA 74 Dl 25
Quambone ○ AUS 379 Mk 61
Quamby ○ AUS 374 Mg 56
Quanah ○ USA 70 Cn 28
Quân Đảo Nam Du ⛰ VN 263 Lc 41
Quảng Ngãi ○ VN 263 Le 38
Quango Fitini ○ CI 317 Ge 41
Quan Hóa ○ VN 255 Lc 35
Quankwa ○ RB 340 Hc 55
Quanzhou ○ VRC 255 Lf 33
Quanzhou ○ VRC 258 Lk 33
Quanzijing ○ VRC 242 Lc 26
Qu'Appelle ○ CDN 51 Cl 20
Qu'Appelle ~ CDN 51 Cl 20
Qu'Appelle River ~ CDN 51 Cj 20
Quaraí ○ BR 146 Ef 61
Quargla ○ DZ 296 Gj 30
Quarkoye ○ BF 317 Ge 39
Quarryville ○ CDN 61 Eb 22
Quartz Lake ~ CDN 57 Df 20
Quartzsite ○ USA 64 Ce 29
Quasair ,Amra ★ JOR 214 Hl 30
Quasiginguanit Christianshåb ○ DK 7 Ga 3
Quatorze de Abril ~ BR 129 Ed 51
Quatro Bocas ○ BR 121 Ek 47
Quayvara ○ IRQ 209 Hp 28
Quba ○ AZ 202 Jc 25
Qūčān ○ IR 222 Jh 27
Qudaih ○ KSA 215 Jc 32
Qué ~ ANG 340 Gp 53
Queanbeyan ○ AUS 379 Ml 63
Québec ⊙ CDN 43 Ha 8
Québec ○ CDN 60 Dn 20
Quebec ○ CDN 60 Dn 22
Quebo ○ GNB 316 Fn 40
Quebracho ○ ROU 146 Ef 61
Quebradade Aroma ~ RCH 128 Dp 55
Quebradade Tana ó Camiña ~ RCH 128 Dp 55
Quebrada Sotomayo ~ BOL 136 Ea 56
Quebra de Arriba ○ YV 107 Dn 40
Quedas ○ MOC 344 Hj 55
Quedas de Agua da Binga ~ ANG 340 Gn 51
Quedas de Monte Negro ~ ANG 340 Gn 54
Quedas do Iguaçu ○ BR 140 Eh 58
Quedas do Ruacana ~ ANG 340 Gp 54
Quedlinburg ○ D 174 Gm 20
Qued M'Zab ~ DZ 296 Gj 29
Queen Alexandra Range ⋀⋀ 38 Ta 18
Queen Charlotte ○ CDN 42 Da 8
Queen Charlotte Bay ~ GB 147 Ed 71
Queen Charlotte Islands ⛰ CDN 42 Da 8
Queen Charlotte Sound ≈ CDN 42 Da 8
Queen Charlotte Sound ~ CDN 50 Bm 20
Queen Charlotte Strait ~ CDN 50 Bn 20
Queen Elizabeth ♀ EAU 336 Hg 46
Queen Elizabeth Islands ⛰ CDN 42 Ea 3
Queen Mary Coast ⌓⌓ 38 Pb 16
Queen Maud Gulf ~ CDN 6 Db 3
Queen Maud Gulf ≈ CDN 42 Fa 5
Queen Parry Islands ⛰ CDN 6 Da 2
Queensburg ○ ZA 352 Hh 60
Queenscliff ○ AUS 379 Mj 65
Queenstown ○ ZA 349 Hf 61
Queenstown ○ AUS 378 Mj 67
Queenstown ○ NZ 382 Ng 68
Queets ○ USA 50 Bp 22
Quéguoa ○ F 386 Ne 56
Queguay Grande ~ ROU 146 Ef 62
Quehue ○ PE 128 Dn 53
Quehué ○ RA 137 Eb 64
Queidār ○ IR 209 Jc 27
Queilén ○ RCH 147 Dm 67
Queimadas ○ BR 124 Fc 49
Queimadas ○ BR 125 Fa 51
Queirós ○ BR 140 Ej 56
Quéla ○ ANG 340 Ha 50
Quélé ○ CI 305 Gc 40
Quelimane ○ MOC 344 Hl 54
Quelite ○ MEX 92 Cj 34
Quellón ○ RCH 147 Dm 67
Quellouno ○ PE 128 Dm 52
Quelo ○ ANG 332 Gn 49
Quemado ○ USA 65 Ch 28
Quembo ~ ANG 340 Hb 53
Quemchi ○ RCH 147 Dm 67
Quemú-Quemú ○ RA 137 Ec 64
Quenns Channel ~ AUS 364 Ma 53
Queñoal ~ PY 136 Ea 57
Quenquén Salado ~ RA 146 Ed 65
Quepe ~ RCH 147 Dm 65
Quepos ○ CR 97 Df 41
Quequén ○ RA 146 Ee 65
Quequén Grande ~ RA 146 Ee 65
Querari ~ CO 107 Dn 45
Querari ○ CO 117 Dn 45
Quereco ○ PE 128 Dl 52
Querência do Norte ○ BR 140 Eh 57
Querétaro ○ MEX 92 Cm 35
Querobamba ○ PE 128 Dm 52
Querocotillo ○ PE 116 Dj 49
Quesnel ○ CDN 50 Ca 19
Quesnel Lake ~ CDN 50 Cb 19
Quê So'n ○ VN 263 Ld 38
Quesso ○ RCB 332 Ha 45
Questa ○ USA 65 Ck 27
Quetico Lake ~ CDN 56 Db 21
Quetta ○ PK 227 Jm 30
Queupán Paileman ○ RA 147 Eb 66
Queve ~ ANG 340 Gp 51
Quevedo ○ EC 116 Dj 46
Quevedo ~ EC 116 Dj 46
Quezaltenango ○ GCA 93 Dc 38
Quezon ○ RP 266 Lk 41
Quezon City ○ RP 267 Ll 38
Qufu ○ VRC 246 Lj 28
Quiabaya ○ BOL 129 Dp 53
Quiandéua ○ BR 121 El 47
Quibala ○ ANG 340 Gp 51
Quibaxe ○ ANG 332 Gp 50
Quibdó ○ CO 106 Dk 43
Quiberon ○ F 163 Ge 22
Quíbor ○ YV 107 Dp 41
Quicabo ○ ANG 340 Gn 50
Quiclgou ○ VRC 242 Km 28
Quiculungo ○ ANG 332 Gp 50
Quidico ○ RCH 147 Dm 65
Quiiroga ○ RA 137 Ed 63
Quijingue ○ BR 125 Fa 51
Quijotoa ○ USA 65 Cf 29
Quila ○ MEX 80 Cj 33
Quilandi ○ IND 239 Kb 40
Quilca ○ PE 128 Dm 54
Qu Ileg ○ DK 43 Ka 6
Quilenda ○ ANG 340 Gp 51
Quilengues ○ ANG 340 Gn 53
Quillacollo ○ BOL 129 Ea 54
Quillagua ○ RCH 136 Dp 56
Quillan ○ F 184 Gh 24
Quillen ~ RCH 147 Dm 65
Quill Lake ○ CDN 51 Ck 19
Quill Lakes ~ CDN 51 Ck 20
Quilmes ○ RA 146 Ee 63
Quilombo ○ BR 140 Eh 59
Quilon ○ IND 239 Kc 41
Quilpie ○ AUS 375 Mj 59
Quilpue ○ RCH 137 Dn 62
Quilua ○ MOC 344 Hm 54
Quimantag ⋀⋀ VRC 231 Kk 27
Quimbaya ○ CO 106 Dk 43
Quimbele ○ ANG 332 Ha 49
Quimili ○ RA 136 Ec 59
Quimome ~ BOL 129 Ed 54
Quimper ○ F 163 Gd 22
Quinabucasan Point ⌓ RP 267 Lm 38
Quinapondan ○ RP 267 Ln 40
Quinault ○ USA 50 Ca 22
Quinault Indian Reservation ••• USA 50 Bp 22
Quince Mil ○ PE 128 Dn 52
Quincy ○ USA 64 Cb 26
Quincy ○ USA 70 Dc 26
Quincy ○ USA 71 Dn 24
Quincy ○ USA 86 Df 30
Quines ○ RA 137 Eb 62
Quinga ○ MOC 344 Hn 53
Quingshuihe ○ VRC 242 Kn 29
Quingshui He ~ VRC 242 Lc 27
Quingshui Jiang ~ VRC 255 Le 32
Quinhagak ○ USA 46 Aj 15
Quinhámel ○ GNB 316 Fm 40
Quiniluban Islands ⛰ RP 267 Ll 40
Quinindé ○ EC 116 Dj 45
Quinjalca ○ PE 116 Dk 49
Quinn ~ USA 64 Cc 25
Quintero ○ RCH 137 Dn 62
Quintin Banderas ○ C 100 Dh 34
Quinto ~ RA 137 Eb 63
Quinzau ○ ANG 332 Gn 49
Quionga ○ MOC 344 Hn 51
Quipapa ○ BR 124 Fb 50
Quipeio ○ ANG 340 Gp 52
Quipungo ○ ANG 340 Gp 53
Quira ○ VRC 230 Ke 27
Quiriego ○ MEX 80 Ch 32
Quirigua ★ GCA 93 Dd 38
Quirihué ○ RCH 137 Dm 64
Quirima ○ ANG 340 Hb 51
Quirindi ○ AUS 379 Mm 61
Quirinópolis ○ BR 133 Ej 55
Quiriquiri ○ YV 112 Ec 41
Quiroga ○ MEX 92 Cm 36
Quiroga ○ BOL 129 Eb 55
Quiroz ○ YV 107 Dn 40
Quiruvilca ○ PE 116 Dj 50
Quissanga ○ MOC 344 Hn 52
Quissico ○ MOC 352 Hk 58
Quissongo ○ ANG 340 Gp 51
Quitandinha ○ BR 140 Ek 58
Quitapa ○ ANG 340 Hb 51
Quiterajo ○ MOC 344 Hn 51
Quitéria ~ BR 133 Ej 55
Quiterianópolis ○ BR 124 Ep 48
Quiteve ○ ANG 340 Gp 54
Quitilipi ○ RA 136 Ed 59
Quitman ○ USA 70 Da 29
Quitman ○ USA 86 Dg 30
Quito ▣ EC 116 Dj 46
Quitovac ○ MEX 75 Cf 30
Quivolgo ○ RCH 137 Dm 63
Quixadá ○ BR 124 Fa 48
Quixaxe ○ MOC 344 Hn 53
Quixeramobim ○ BR 124 Fa 48
Quizenga ○ ANG 340 Gp 50
Qujiang ○ VRC 258 Lg 33
Qujing ○ VRC 255 Lb 33
Qumar He ~ VRC 231 Kl 28
Qumar Heyan ○ VRC 231 Kl 28
Qungtag ○ VRC 231 Kh 30
Quobba ○ AUS 368 Lg 58
Quoin Head ⌓ AUS 368 Lg 58
Quoin Island ⛰ AUS 364 Ma 53
Quorn ○ AUS 378 Mf 62
Quray ○ USA 65 Ch 25
Qurayd ○ SUD 312 Hh 40
Qurayyāt ○ OM 226 Jh 34
Qurdūd ○ SUD 312 Hg 40
Qureida ○ SUD 312 He 40
Qŭrgonteppa ○ TJ 223 Jn 27
Qurnat as-Saudā' △ RL 208 Hk 28
Qūs ○ ET 301 Hj 33
Qusaiba ○ IRQ 209 Hn 28
Qusar ○ AZ 202 Jc 25
Qusayr ○ ET 301 Hk 32
Qusum ○ VRC 235 Kl 31
Qutūf ○ UAE 215 Je 34
Quwu Shan ⋀⋀ VRC 242 Lc 27
Qu Xian ○ VRC 243 Ld 30
Qūxū ○ VRC 235 Kk 31
Quyang ○ VRC 243 Lh 26
Quyanghai Shuiku ~ VRC 258 Lg 33
Quỳnh Lu'u ○ VN 255 Lc 36
Quy Nhon ○ VN 263 Le 39
Quzhou ○ VRC 258 Lk 31
Qyzylorda ○ KZ 19 Na 5
Qyzylorda ○ KZ 155 Sb 10
qz-Zalaf ○ SYR 208 Hl 29

R

R. Bellona ⛰ F 35 Sb 12
R. des Outaouai ~ CDN 60 Dj 22
R.io Ntem ○ GQ 320 Gl 44
R. Mégiscane ~ CDN 60 Dk 21
R. S. Kerr Lake ~ USA 70 Da 28
R. Waswanipi ~ CDN 60 Dk 21
Raab ~ A 174 Gp 22
Raahe Brahestad ○ FIN 159 Hd 13
Raanes Peninsula ⛰ CDN 43 Ga 3
Raas Binna ⌓ SP 328 Jd 40
Raas Caluula ⌓ SP 328 Jd 40
Raas Gabbac ⌓ SP 328 Jd 41
Raas Khansir ⌓ SP 328 Ja 40
Raas Macbar ⌓ SP 328 Jd 41
Raas Xaafuun ⌓ SP 328 Jd 40
Raatama ○ FIN 159 He 11
Rab ○ HR 174 Gp 23
Rab ⛰ HR 174 Gp 23
Rába ~ H 174 Ha 22
Raba ○ VRC 242 Kp 30
Raba ○ RI 279 Lk 50
Rabaa ○ DZ 296 Gl 30
Rabaable ○ SP 328 Jc 41
Rabac ○ HR 185 Gn 23
Rabah ○ WAN 320 Gj 39
Rabak ○ SUD 312 Hj 39
Rabal ○ RI 283 Md 49
Raballas ○ RA 152 Dn 69
Rabaraba ○ PNG 287 Ml 50
Rabat ▣ MA 293 Gc 29
Rabaul ○ PNG 287 Mm 48
Rabbit Ears Pass △ USA 65 Cj 25
Rabbit Flat Roadhouse ○ AUS 361 Mb 56
Rabi ⛰ FJI 390 Aa 54
Rabia ○ RI 283 Mb 46
Rābiğ ○ KSA 214 Hm 34
Rabkavi Banhatti ○ IND 238 Kb 37
Rabka-Zdrój ○ PL 174 Hc 21
Râbniţa ○ MD 175 Hg 22
Rabočeostrovsk ○ RUS 159 Hk 13
Rabun Bald △ USA 71 Dg 28
Rabwah ○ PK 230 Ka 30
Rabyanah ○ LAR 300 Hd 33
Raccoon Cay ⛰ BS 87 Dl 34
Raceland ○ USA 86 Dc 31
Rachal ○ USA 81 Cn 32
Rachel ○ USA 64 Ce 27
Rach Gia ○ VN 263 Lc 41
Rachid ○ RIM 304 Ga 36
Rachiv ○ UA 175 He 21
Racibórz ○ PL 174 Ha 20
Racine ○ USA 57 De 24
Radā' ○ YE 218 Ja 38
Radaul Coro ~ CO 117 Dn 46
Radaul Solarte ~ CO 117 Dn 46
Radaul Tonímucu ~ CO 117 Dn 46
Rădăuţio ○ RO 175 He 22
Radechiv ○ UA 175 He 20
Radford ○ USA 71 Dh 27
Rādham ○ PK 227 Jm 32
Rādhanpur ○ IND 227 Jp 34
Radisčevo ○ RUS 181 Jb 19
Radisson ○ CDN 51 Cj 19
Radium Hot Springs ○ CDN 50 Cd 20
Radium Springs ○ USA 65 Cj 29
Radom ○ PL 174 Hc 20
Radom ○ SUD 324 He 41
Radomsko ○ PL 174 Hb 20
Radomyšl' ○ UA 175 Hg 20
Radovis ○ MK 194 Hd 25
Radstadt ○ A 174 Gn 22
Radun ○ RUS 159 Hh 11
Radužnyj ○ RUS 204 Ta 6
Radviliškis ○ LT 171 Hd 18
Radville ○ CDN 51 Ck 20
Radzi ○ VRC 242 Kn 30
Radzyň Podlaski ○ PL 174 Hd 20
Rae ○ CDN 6 Da 3
Rāe Bareli ○ IND 234 Ke 32
Rae-Edzo ○ CDN 47 Cc 13
Rae Isthmus ⌓⌓ CDN 43 Ga 5
Rae River ~ CDN 47 Cc 11
Raes Junction ○ NZ 382 Ng 68
Rae Strait ~ CDN 7 Ea 3
Raetihi ○ NZ 383 Nk 65
Rafaela ○ RA 137 Ed 61
Rafael Freyre ○ C 101 Dk 35
Rafah ○ ET 301 Hj 30
Rafaï ○ RCA 324 Hd 43
Raffingora ○ ZW 341 Hh 54
Rafhā' ○ KSA 214 Hp 31
Rafsai ○ MA 293 Gd 28
Rafsanğān ○ IR 226 Jf 30
Raft ~ USA 64 Cf 24
Raga ○ SUD 324 He 41
Ragama ○ CL 239 Kd 42
Ragged Island ⛰ BS 87 Dl 34
Raghwan ○ KSA 218 Hm 35
Raglan ○ NZ 383 Nk 64
Ragland ○ USA 65 Cl 28
Ragley ○ USA 86 Db 30
Rago ○ USA 70 Cn 27
Rago ♀ N 158 Gp 12
Ragusa ○ I 186 Gp 27
Raha ○ RI 282 Lm 48
Rahachow ○ BY 171 Hh 19
Rahad ~ ETH 313 Hl 39
Rahad al-Bardī ○ SUD 313 Hd 40
Rahama ○ WAN 320 Gl 40
Rāhatgarh ○ IND 234 Kd 34
Raheita ○ ER 313 Hp 39
Rahib ○ SUD 312 Hf 37
Rahim ki Bāzār ○ PK 227 Jn 33
Rahīmyār Khān ○ PK 227 Jp 31
Rahmanovka ○ RUS 181 Jc 20
Rāholt ○ N 158 Gm 15
Rahouia ○ DZ 293 Gg 28
Raiatea ⛰ F 35 Ba 11
Rāichūr ○ IND 238 Kc 37
Raida ○ YE 218 Hp 38
Raiganj ○ IND 235 Kj 33
Raigarh ○ IND 235 Kf 35
Raijua ⛰ RI 282 Ll 51
Raikal ○ IND 238 Kd 36
Railroad Valley ⌓⌓ USA 64 Ce 26
Rainbow ○ AUS 378 Mh 63
Rainbow Beach ○ AUS 375 Mn 58

Punta Roca Partida - Rainbow Beach 461

□Country ⊡Capital city ◉Administrative unit ○Place ⬦Island ᐃᐃMountain range ᐃMountain ◭Cape ≈Ocean, Sea ∼Lake, River ∇Undersea topography ⊠Glacier ⚑National park •••Reservation ★Point of major interest ▱Landscape

Rainbow Bridge N.M. ★ USA 65 Cg 27	Râmšir ○ IR 215 Jc 30	Rare ∼ EAK 337 Hm 47
Rainbow Lake ○ CDN 47 Cc 15	Ramsjö ○ S 158 Gp 14	Rarotonga ⬦ NZ 35 Ba 12
Rainy Lake ∼ CDN 56 Db 21	Râmtek ○ IND 234 Kd 35	Ra's Abū Dāra ◭ ET 301 Hl 34
Rainy River ∼ CDN 56 Da 21	Ramu ○ BD 235 Kl 35	Ra's Abū Madd ◭ KSA 214 Hl 33
Rainy River ∼ USA 56 Da 21	Ramu ○ EAK 325 Hn 44	Ra's Abū Raşâş ◭ OM 219 Jh 35
Raipur ○ IND 234 Ke 33	Ramu Natl. Park ★ PNG 287 Mj 48	Ra's Abū Şağara ◭ SUD 313 Hl 35
Raipur ○ IND 234 Ke 35	Ramu River ∼ PNG 287 Mj 48	Rasa Island ⬦ RP 267 Lk 41
Raipur Khas ○ IND 234 Kd 32	Ramwik ○ S 158 Ha 14	Ra's al-Barr ◭ ET 301 Hh 30
Ra'is ○ KSA 214 Hm 34	Ramygala ○ LT 171 Hd 18	Ra's al-Bayâḍ ◭ YE 218 Hp 38
Raisio ○ FIN 159 Hc 15	Ran ○ WAN 321 Gp 39	Ra's al Hilâl ◭ LAR 300 Hd 29
Raisūt ○ OM 219 Je 36	Rânahu ○ PK 227 Jn 33	Ra's al-Kabš ◭ OM 226 Jh 35
Rai Valley ○ NZ 383 Nj 66	Rana Pratap Sâgar ∼ IND 234 Kb 33	Ra's al-Kalb ◭ YE 219 Jb 37
Raivavaé ⬦ F 35 Bb 12	Ranau ○ MAL 274 Lj 43	Ra's al-Khaimah ○ UAE 226 Jf 33
Râiwind ○ PK 230 Ka 30	Rancagua ○ RCH 137 Dn 63	Ra's an-Naqb ○ JOR 214 Hk 31
Rajada ○ BR 124 Ep 50	Rancharia ○ BR 140 Ej 57	Ra's 'Asîs ◭ SUD 313 Hm 36
Râjahmundry ○ IND 238 Ke 37	Rancheria ∼ CO 107 Dm 40	Ra's aš-Şaṭṭ ◭ IR 215 Jd 31
Râjâkhera ○ IND 234 Kd 32	Ranchester ○ USA 51 Cj 23	Ra's aṭ-Ṭarfa ◭ KSA 218 Hp 37
Râjampet ○ IND 238 Kd 38	Ranchi ○ IND 235 Kh 34	Ra's Banâs ◭ ET 301 Hk 34
Rajang ∼ MAL 271 Lf 44	Rânchi Plateau ᐃ IND 235 Kg 34	Ra's Barîḍ ◭ KSA 214 Hl 33
Rajang ∼ MAL 272 Lg 44	Rancho Cordova ○ USA 64 Cb 26	Ra's Bir ◭ DJI 328 Hp 40
Râjanpur ○ PK 227 Jn 31	Rancho Velho ○ BR 146 Ej 61	Ras Dashen Terara ᐃ ETH 313 Hn 39
Râjâpalaiyam ○ IND 239 Kc 41	Ranchuelo ○ C 100 Dh 34	Ra's Degayê ◭ ER 313 Hp 39
Râjapur ○ IND 238 Ka 37	Randa ○ DJI 328 Hp 40	Ra's-e Barkan ◭ IR 215 Jc 31
Rajasthan ◉ IND 227 Jp 32	Randado ○ USA 81 Cn 32	Ra's-e Fâste ◭ IR 226 Jj 33
Rajasthan ⊙ IND 227 Jp 32	Randale ∼ DJI 313 Hp 39	Ra's-e Halîle ◭ IR 215 Jd 31
Rajgarh ○ IND 234 Kb 31	Randazzo ○ I 185 Gp 27	Raseiniai ○ LT 171 Hd 18
Râjgarh ○ IND 234 Kc 32	Randberge ᐃᐃ ZA 352 Hh 59	Ras el Ma ◭ DZ 293 Gf 28
Rajin ○ DVRK 248 Mb 24	Randers ○ DK 170 Gm 17	Râs el Mâ ○ RMM 305 Gd 37
Râjkot ○ IND 227 Jp 34	Randfontein ○ ZA 349 Hf 59	Ra's-e Šenâs ◭ IR 226 Jj 33
Râjmahal ○ IND 235 Kh 33	Randijaure ∼ S 158 Hb 12	Ra's Fartak ◭ YE 219 Je 38
Rajmahal Hills ᐃᐃ IND 235 Kh 33	Randolph ○ USA 56 Cp 24	Ra's Ğârib ○ ET 301 Hj 31
Râj-Nândgaon ○ IND 234 Ke 35	Randolph ○ USA 70 Da 26	Rasha ∼ VRC 242 Kp 30
Râjpiipla ○ IND 238 Ka 35	Randowaya ○ RI 286 Me 46	Rashâd ○ SUD 312 Hh 40
Raj Samand ○ IND 227 Ka 33	Randsfjorden ∼ N 158 Gm 15	Ra's Hâtibah ◭ KSA 214 Hm 34
Rajshahi ○ BD 235 Kj 33	Randudongkal ○ RI 278 Le 49	Rasht ○ IR 209 Jc 27
Raka ∼ CHN 235 Kg 31	Râne ○ S 159 Hd 13	Ra's Hûn ◭ IND 239 Kd 40
Rakaia ∼ NZ 382 Nh 67	Rânelva ∼ S 159 Hc 12	Rašîdîya ○ SYR 209 Hn 27
Rakaia ○ NZ 383 Nj 67	Ranérou ○ SN 304 Fp 38	Râsipuram ○ IND 239 Kd 40
Rakaposhi ᐃ PK 230 Kb 27	Raneue ○ RT 270 Km 43	Rasirik ○ PNG 287 Mn 47
Rakav ∼ BY 171 Hf 19	Ranfurly ○ CDN 51 Cg 19	Rasi Salai ○ THA 263 Kl 38
Rakhni ○ PK 227 Jn 31	Rang ○ K 263 Ld 39	Râs Jaddi ◭ PK 226 Jk 33
Rakhshân ∼ PK 227 Jl 32	Rangamati ○ BD 235 Kl 34	Râs Jiwani ◭ PK 226 Jj 33
Rakiraki ○ FJI 387 Nm 54	Rangaranga ○ RI 282 Lm 46	Râsk ○ IR 226 Jj 33
Rakitnoe ○ RUS 250 Md 23	Rangely ○ USA 65 Ch 25	Raška ○ SCG 194 Hc 24
Rako ∼ SP 328 Jc 41	Rangers Valley ○ AUS 375 Mj 57	Ra's Karaba ◭ KSA 214 Hl 33
Rakom ○ THA 263 Kl 34	Ranges ᐃᐃ AUS 374 Md 57	Ra's Kasr ◭ SUD 313 Hm 36
Rakops ○ RB 349 He 56	Ranges Valley ○ AUS 374 Mg 56	Ras Kigomasha ◭ EAT 337 Hm 48
Rakovnik ○ CZ 174 Gn 20	Rangia ○ IND 235 Kk 32	Ras Lanuf ○ LAR 300 Hb 30
Rakovskaja ○ RUS 159 Hn 14	Rangiora ○ NZ 383 Nj 67	Ra's Madrakah ◭ OM 219 Jg 36
Rakvere ○ EST 171 Hf 16	Rangiroa ⬦ F 35 Bb 11	Ra's Mâlân ◭ PK 227 Jl 33
Rakwa ○ RI 283 Md 47	Rangitaiki River ∼ NZ 383 Nl 65	Ra's Mâmî ◭ YE 219 Jf 39
Ralco ○ RCH 137 Dn 64	Rangitikei River ∼ NZ 383 Nl 65	Ra's Muâri ◭ PK 227 Jm 33
Râlegaon ○ IND 234 Kd 35	Rangkasbitung ○ RI 278 Ld 49	Ras Muhammad ⚑ ET 301 Hk 32
Raleigh ○ USA 74 Dj 28	Rangnim ∼ DVRK 247 Lp 25	Ras Muhammad Natl. Park ⚑ ET 301 Hk 32
Raleigh ○ USA 86 Dj 29	Rangnom ○ SUD 324 Hh 41	Ra's Musadam ◭ OM 226 Jg 32
Raleigh Bay ≈ USA 74 Dl 28	Rangoon ○ MYA 262 Kn 37	Ra's Mušairib ◭ UAE 215 Jd 33
Raleighvallen ∼ SME 113 Ef 43	Rangpur ○ BD 235 Kj 32	Rasmussen Basin ∇ CDN 42 Fb 5
Ralls ○ USA 70 Cm 29	Rangpur Can ∼ PK 227 Jp 30	Ras Ngomeni ◭ EAK 337 Hn 47
Ralodero ○ PK 227 Jl 31	Ranguna Cay ⬦ BH 93 Dd 37	Râs Nouâdhibou ◭ RIM 304 Fm 35
Râls Köh ᐃᐃ PK 227 Jl 31	Ranguna Cay ⬦ BH 96 De 37	Râs Nuh ◭ PK 226 Jk 33
Rama ○ NY 97 Df 39	Rânibennur ○ IND 238 Kb 38	Raso ⬦ CV 316 Fh 37
Râmabhadrapuram ○ IND 234 Kf 36	Râniganj ○ IND 235 Kh 32	Rason Lake ∼ AUS 369 Ln 60
Rama Caída ○ RA 137 Dp 63	Râniganj ○ IND 235 Kh 34	Raso Real de Macaira ○ YV 107 Ea 41
Râmachandraparam ○ IND 238 Kf 37	Rânikhetî ○ IND 234 Kd 31	Ra's Ormâra ◭ PK 227 Jl 33
Ramagiri ○ IND 238 Kc 38	Ranikot ★ PK 227 Jn 33	Ra's Rahmat ◭ ER 313 Hp 39
Ramah ○ USA 65 Ch 28	Rânipettai ○ IND 238 Kd 39	Ra's Rakan ◭ Q 215 Jd 32
Ramah Navajo ••• USA 65 Ch 28	Rânipur ○ PK 227 Jn 32	Râša ○ YE 218 Jb 38
Râmak ○ AFG 223 Jn 29	Râniya ○ IRQ 209 Ja 27	Ra's Sâğir ◭ OM 219 Jg 35
Râmallâh ○ IL 214 Hk 30	Ranken Store ○ AUS 365 Me 55	Rass Ajdir ◭ TN 297 Gm 29
Ramallo ○ RA 137 Ed 62	Rankin ○ USA 81 Cm 30	Rassakazovo ○ RUS 181 Hn 19
Râmanâthapuram ○ IND 239 Kd 41	Rankins Springs ○ AUS 379 Mk 62	Ra's Šarbitât ◭ OM 219 Jg 36
Râmânuj Ganj ○ IND 235 Kf 34	Rankoshi ○ J 250 Mg 24	Ra's Šarwain ◭ YE 219 Jd 38
Ramardon ○ RI 283 Md 46	Rannes ○ AUS 375 Ml 58	Ras Shaka ◭ EAK 337 Hn 47
Ramasamudram ○ IND 238 Kc 39	Rann of Kachchh ∼ IND 227 Jn 33	Ra's Šu'b ◭ YE 219 Je 39
Ramatlabama ○ ZA 349 He 58	Rano ○ WAN 320 Gl 40	Ra's Tafarît ◭ RIM 304 Fm 35
Ramayampet ○ IND 238 Ke 36	Ranobe ∼ RM 345 Ja 54	Ra's Tannûra ◭ KSA 215 Jd 32
Râmâypatnan ○ IND 238 Ke 38	Ranohira ○ RM 345 Jc 53	Rastatt ○ D 174 Gl 21
Rambouillet ○ F 163 Gg 21	Ranoke ○ CDN 57 Dh 20	Ra's Terma ◭ ER 313 Hp 39
Rambre ○ MYA 254 Kl 36	Ranomafana ○ RM 345 Jc 55	Raštwâr ○ IR 222 Jh 28
Rambutyo Island ⬦ PNG 287 Mk 47	Ranong ○ THA 262 Kp 41	Rastigaissa ᐃ N 159 He 10
Ramea Island ⬦ CDN 61 Ef 22	Ranongga ⬦ SOL 290 Na 50	Râs Timirist ◭ RIM 304 Fm 36
Rame Head ᐃ AUS 379 Ml 64	Ranot ○ THA 270 La 42	Râstoci ○ RO 175 Hd 22
Ramena ○ RM 345 Jc 52	Ranotsara ○ RM 353 Jb 57	Rasūlnagar ○ PK 230 Ka 29
Rameški ○ RUS 171 Hl 17	Ranquil del Norte ○ RA 137 Dp 64	Ra's Warfallah ◭ LAR 297 Gp 31
Râmeswaram ○ IND 239 Kd 41	Ransiki ○ RI 283 Md 46	Ratangarh ○ IND 234 Kb 31
Ramezän Kalak ○ IR 226 Jj 33	Ransom ○ USA 70 Cm 26	Râtansbyn ○ S 158 Gn 14
Râmgarh ○ IND 227 Jp 32	Rantabe ○ RM 345 Jc 53	Ratcatchers Lake ∼ AUS 378 Mh 62
Râmgarh ○ IND 234 Kf 34	Rantabe ∼ RM 345 Jc 53	Ratcha Buri ○ THA 262 Kp 39
Râmgarh ○ IND 235 Kg 34	Rantau ○ RI 279 Lh 47	Ratcliff ○ USA 70 Da 28
Râmgarh ○ BD 235 Kk 34	Rantaubalai ○ RI 279 Lh 47	Ratcliff City ○ USA 70 Cp 28
Râmhormoz ○ IR 215 Jc 30	Rantaupanjang ○ RI 278 Ld 46	Râth ○ IND 234 Kd 33
Ramis Shef ∼ ETH 325 Hn 41	Rantauprapat ○ RI 270 Kp 44	Rathdrum ○ USA 50 Cd 22
Ramkan ○ IR 226 Jg 32	Rantengli ○ RI 279 Lk 47	Rathedaung ○ MYA 235 Kl 35
Ramkhamhung ⚑ THA 262 Kp 37	Rantoul ○ USA 71 Dd 25	Rathenow ○ D 170 Gn 19
Raml ○ IRQ 209 Ja 28	Rantsila ○ FIN 159 He 13	Râtische Alpen ᐃ CH 174 Gl 22
Ramla ○ IL 214 Hk 30	Rantyirrity Point ○ AUS 364 Md 53	Ratlâm ○ IND 234 Kb 34
Ramlat al-Ğâfa ≈ KSA 219 Jf 35	Ranua ○ FIN 159 Hf 13	Ratnachuli ᐃ NEP 235 Kg 31
Ramlat al-Wahiba ≈ OM 226 Jh 34	Ranya ar-Rawdah ○ KSA 218 Hp 35	Ratnâgiri ○ IND 238 Ka 37
Ramlat as Sab atayn ≈ YE 218 Ja 38	Rao ○ SN 304 Fm 38	Ratnapura ○ CL 239 Ke 42
Ramlat Zallâf ≈ LAR 297 Gn 32	Raohe ○ VRC 205 Wc 9	Ratne ○ UA 175 He 20
Ramlu ᐃ ER 313 Hn 39	Raohe ○ VRC 250 Mc 22	Rato ∼ BR 120 Ef 48
Ramnaga ○ IND 234 Ke 32	Raon-l'Etap ○ F 163 Gk 21	Raton ○ USA 65 Ck 27
Ramnagar ○ IND 234 Kd 31	Raoping ○ VRC 258 Lj 34	Raton Pass ᐃ USA 65 Ck 27
Râmnagar ○ IND 234 Kd 33	Raoul ⬦ NZ 35 Aa 12	Rattaphum ○ THA 270 Kp 42
Râmnicu Sârat ○ RO 175 He 23	Rapa ⬦ F 35 Bb 12	Rattlesnake Creek ∼ USA 70 Cn 27
Râmnicu Vâlcea ○ RO 175 He 23	Rapa Nui Easter Island ⬦ RCH 14 Db 12	Rattray ○ GB 162 Ge 17
Ramon ○ USA 65 Ca 28	Râpar ○ IND 227 Jp 34	Råttvik ○ S 158 Gp 15
Ramona ○ USA 64 Cd 29	Rapel ∼ RCH 137 Dn 62	Ratzeburg ○ D 170 Gm 19
Ramos ∼ MEX 80 Ck 34	Rapelje ○ USA 51 Ch 23	Rau ○ RI 270 La 45
Ramos ○ BR 121 Eh 46	Rapid City ○ USA 51 Cl 23	Raub ○ MAL 270 La 44
Ramos Island ⬦ RP 266 Lj 41	Rapide Blanc ○ CDN 60 Dm 22	Rauch ○ RA 146 Ee 64
Ramos Otero ○ RA 146 Ee 63	Rapides de l'Éléphant ∼ RDC 321 Hb 43	Raudal Aguas Verdes ∼ CO 116 Dm 45
Ramotswa ○ RB 349 He 56	Rapides Gembele ∼ RDC 321 Hd 44	Raudal Chiribiquete ∼ CO 116 Dm 45
Rampart ○ USA 46 Ba 13	Rapides Coemani ∼ CO 116 Dm 46	Raudal Coro ∼ CO 117 Dn 46
Râmpur ○ IND 227 Ka 34	Rápidos M'Pupa ∼ ANG 340 Hb 54	Raudal Cumaral ∼ CO 107 Dn 44
Râmpur ○ IND 230 Kc 30	Râpina ○ EST 171 Hf 16	Raudal Curucu ∼ CO 117 Dn 45
Rampur ○ IND 234 Kd 31	Rapla ○ EST 171 He 16	Raudal de la Sal ∼ CO 116 Dm 46
Rampur ○ IND 234 Ke 34	Rapness ○ GB 162 Ge 16	Raudal del Embudo ∼ CO 116 Dm 45
Râmpur ○ IND 235 Kg 35	Rappahannock ∼ USA 74 Dk 26	Raudal de Rayao ∼ CO 107 Dp 44
Rampur Hât ○ IND 235 Kj 33	Rappang ○ RI 279 Lk 47	Raudal el Turbón ∼ CO 117 Dn 45
Rams ○ UAE 226 Jf 33	Rapti ∼ NEP 234 Ke 32	Raudal Guacamaya ∼ CO 107 Dp 44
Râmsar ○ IR 222 Jd 27	Rapulo ∼ BOL 129 Ea 52	Raudal Hacha ∼ CO 116 Dm 45
Ramsay Lake ∼ CDN 57 Dg 22	Rapur ○ IND 238 Kd 38	Raudal Huitoto ∼ CO 116 Dm 45
Râmše ○ IR 215 Je 30	Rapu-Rapu Island ⬦ RP 267 Ln 39	Raudal Las Chulas ∼ CO 107 Dp 44
Ramsele ○ S 158 Gp 14	Raqdalin ○ LAR 297 Gm 29	Raudal Macuna ∼ CO 117 Dn 46
Râmsen ○ IND 227 Ka 33	Raquette ∼ USA 60 Dl 23	Raudal Mandi ∼ CO 117 Dn 45
Ramsey ○ USA 70 Dd 26	Raragala Island ⬦ AUS 364 Md 51	Raudal Palito ∼ CO 117 Dn 45
Ramsey ○ GB 162 Gg 18	Raragala Island ⬦ AUS 364 Me 51	
Ramsgate ○ GB 163 Gg 20		
Ramsgate ○ ZA 349 Hh 61		
Ramsing ○ IND 254 Km 31		

Raudal Qinché ∼ CO 117 Dn 46	Redding ○ USA 64 Ca 25	Renovo ○ USA 74 Dk 25
Raudal Samuro ∼ CO 107 Dp 44	Redditt ○ CDN 56 Da 21	Renqiu ○ VRC 246 Lj 26
Raudal Tonimucu ∼ CO 117 Dn 46	Red Earth ○ CDN 51 Cl 19	Renshou ○ VRC 242 Lc 30
Raudal Tucunare ∼ CO 117 Dp 45	Redención ∼ CO 107 Dp 44	Rentína ○ GR 194 Hd 25
Raudal Yupurari ∼ CO 117 Dn 45	Redenção ○ BR 121 Ej 49	Renton ○ USA 50 Ca 22
Raudat Habbâs ∼ KSA 215 Hp 31	Redenção ○ BR 124 Fa 48	Rentoul River ∼ PNG 286 Mh 49
Raufarhöfn ○ IS 158 Fn 12	Redenção do Gurguéia ○ BR 121 Em 50	Renwick ○ NZ 383 Nj 66
Raukumara Range ᐃᐃ NZ 383 Nl 65	Redentora ○ BR 140 Eh 59	Reo ○ RI 282 Ll 50
Raul Pialo ○ BR 146 Eg 61	Redeyef ○ TN 296 Gk 28	Réo ○ BF 317 Ge 39
Raul Soares ○ BR 141 En 56	Redford ○ USA 56 Cn 23	Reodhar ○ IND 227 Ka 33
Rauma ○ FIN 159 Hc 15	Redford ○ USA 81 Ck 31	Repalle ○ IND 238 Ke 38
Rauma ∼ N 158 Gk 14	Red Hill ᐃ AUS 360 Lj 56	Repatriação ● BR 120 Ed 46
Raunsepna ○ PNG 287 Mm 48	Red Hills ᐃ USA 70 Cn 27	Repartição ● P 128 Dn 54
Raurkela ○ IND 235 Kg 34	Red Indian Lake ∼ CDN 61 Ef 21	Repartimento ● BR 120 Ed 47
Rausu ○ J 250 Mj 23	Redington ○ USA 65 Cg 29	Repentigny ○ CDN 60 Dm 23
Râut ∼ MD 175 Hf 22	Redinha ○ BR 124 Fc 48	Represa Barìri ∼ BR 141 Ek 57
Rautalampi ○ FIN 159 Hf 14	Redkino ○ RUS 171 Hk 17	Represa Capivara ∼ BR 140 Ej 57
Rautavaara ○ FIN 159 Hf 14	Red Lake ○ CDN 6 Ea 4	Represa de Água Vermelha ∼ BR 133 Ej 55
Ravalli ○ USA 50 Ce 22	Red Lake ∼ CDN 56 Da 20	Represa de Balbina ∼ BR 120 Ee 46
Râvand ○ IR 222 Jd 28	Red Lake ∼ USA 56 Da 21	Represa de Barra Bonita ∼ BR 141 Ek 57
Ravânsar ○ IR 209 Jb 28	Red Lake ○ USA 56 Da 22	Represa de Foz de Areala ∼ BR 140 Ej 58
Râvar ○ IR 226 Jg 30	Red Lake ∼ CDN 56 Db 20	Represa de Furnas ∼ BR 141 Em 56
Rava Rus'ka ○ UA 175 Hd 20	Red Lake River ∼ USA 56 Da 21	Represa de India Muerta ∼ ROU 146 Eg 62
Ravat ○ KS 223 Jp 26	Redlands ○ USA 64 Cd 28	Represa de Jurumirim ∼ BR 141 Ek 57
Ravendale ○ USA 64 Cb 25	Red Lodge ○ USA 51 Ch 23	Represa del Palmar ∼ ROU 146 Ef 62
Ravenna ○ USA 70 Cn 25	Redmond ○ USA 50 Cb 23	Represa del Río Negro ∼ ROU 146 Eg 62
Ravenna ○ I 185 Gn 23	Redmond ○ USA 65 Cf 27	Represa de Passo Fundo ∼ BR 140 Eh 59
Ravensborne Creek ∼ AUS 375 Mj 58	Red Mountain ○ USA 64 Cd 28	Represa de Passo Real ∼ BR 146 Eh 60
Ravenshoe ○ AUS 365 Mj 54	Red Mountain Pass ᐃ USA 65 Cj 27	Represa de Salto Santiago ∼ BR 140 Eh 58
Ravensthorpe ○ AUS 368 La 62	Red Oak ○ USA 70 Da 25	Represa de Samuel ∼ BR 117 Ec 50
Ravenswood ○ AUS 375 Mk 56	Redon ○ F 163 Ge 22	Represa de Tucuruí ∼ BR 121 Ek 48
Ravi ∼ PK 230 Ka 30	Redondela ○ E 184 Gb 24	Represa de Xanvantes ∼ BR 140 Ek 57
Râvi ∼ PK 230 Kb 30	Redoubt Volcano ᐃ USA 46 An 15	Represa di Acaray ∼ BR 140 Eg 58
Ravnina ○ TM 222 Jk 27	Red Pheasant ••• CDN 51 Ch 19	Represa do Boa Esperança ∼ BR 124 En 49
Ravo ∼ SOL 290 Nc 51	Red River ∼ USA 70 Cn 28	Represa do Rio Manso ∼ BR 132 Eg 53
Râwa ○ IRQ 209 Hp 28	Red River ∼ VN 255 Lc 34	Represa Emboracacao ∼ BR 133 El 55
Rawa Aopa Watumohae ⚑ RI 282 Ll 48	Red River of the North ∼ USA 56 Cp 21	Represa Ibitinga ∼ BR 141 Ek 56
Rawa Aopa Watumohae National Park ⚑ RI 282 Ll 48	Red Rock ○ USA 51 Cf 23	Represa Itutinga ∼ BR 141 Em 56
Rawalak ∼ PK 230 Ka 29	Red Rock ○ USA 70 Cp 27	Represa Jupiá ∼ BR 140 Ej 56
Râwalpindi ○ PK 230 Ka 29	Red Rock Pass ᐃ USA 51 Cg 23	Represa Nova Ponte ∼ BR 133 El 55
Rawa Maz. ∼ PL 174 Hb 20	Redscar Bay ≈ PNG 287 Mk 50	Represa Paraibuna ∼ BR 141 Em 57
Râwânduz ○ IRQ 209 Ja 27	Red Sea ≈ 31 Lb 8	Represa Peixoto ∼ BR 141 El 56
Rawang ○ MAL 270 La 44	Red Sea ≈ 313 Hm 35	Represa Pincón de Boygorri ∼ ROU 146 Ef 62
Rawarra ∼ RI 283 Mc 46	Red Springs ○ USA 70 Db 27	Represa Promissão ∼ BR 140 Ek 56
Rawas ∼ RI 283 Mc 46	Redstone ○ CDN 50 Ca 19	Represa Salto Osório ∼ BR 140 Eh 58
Rawas ○ RI 278 Lb 47	Redstone River ∼ CDN 47 Bn 13	Represa Tres Irmãos ∼ BR 140 Ej 56
Rawicz ○ PL 174 Ha 20	Redvers ○ CDN 56 Cm 21	Represa Três Marias ∼ BR 133 Em 55
Rawlinna ○ AUS 369 Ln 61	Redwater Creek ∼ USA 51 Ck 22	Republic ○ USA 50 Cc 21
Rawlins ○ USA 65 Cj 25	Red Wing ○ USA 56 Db 23	Republican River ∼ USA 70 Cn 25
Rawlinson Range ᐃᐃ AUS 369 Lp 58	Redwood ○ USA 86 Dc 29	Republic of South Africa □ ZA 349 Hd 59
Rawson ○ RA 147 Eb 67	Redwood Falls ○ USA 56 Da 23	Republic of the Congo □ RCB 332 Gp 46
Rawu ∼ VRC 254 Kn 31	Redwood N.P. ⚑ USA 64 Bp 25	Repulse Bay ○ CDN 43 Ga 5
Ray ○ USA 51 Cl 21	Reed City ○ USA 57 Df 24	Repulse Bay ≈ CDN 43 Ga 5
Râyadrug ○ IND 238 Kc 38	Reeder ○ USA 51 Cl 22	Repulse Bay ≈ AUS 375 Ml 56
Rayagada ○ IND 234 Kf 36	Reedpoint ○ USA 51 Ch 23	Repununi ∼ GUY 112 Ee 44
Rayakottai ○ IND 238 Kc 39	Reedsburg ○ USA 56 Dc 24	Requena ○ YV 112 Eb 42
Râyât ○ IRQ 209 Ja 27	Reedsport ○ USA 50 Bp 24	Requena ○ PE 116 Dm 48
Râyin ○ IR 226 Jg 31	Reedville ○ USA 74 Dk 27	Requena ∼ E 184 Gf 25
Raymond ○ USA 50 Ca 22	Reedy Springs ○ AUS 365 Mj 55	Rera ○ BR 112 Ed 43
Raymond ○ CDN 51 Cf 21	Reefton ○ NZ 382 Nh 67	Reriutaba ○ BR 124 Ep 48
Raymond ○ USA 71 Dd 26	Réeggio di Calabria ○ I 194 Gp 26	Rés. Baskatong ∼ CDN 60 Dl 22
Raymond ○ USA 86 Dc 29	Reese ∼ USA 64 Cd 26	Rés. Nac. de Cijara ⚑ E 184 Gd 26
Raymond Terrace ○ AUS 379 Mm 62	Refahiye ○ TR 195 Hm 26	Reşadiye ○ TR 195 Hl 25
Raymondville ○ USA 81 Cp 32	Reform ○ USA 86 Dd 29	Reschenpass ᐃ A 174 Gm 22
Raymore ○ USA 51 Ck 20	Refugio ○ USA 81 Cp 32	Resen ○ MK 194 Hc 25
Ray Mountains ᐃᐃ USA 46 Ba 13	Regalia ○ MA 293 Gd 28	Resende ○ BR 141 Em 57
Reynolds Pass ᐃ USA 51 Cg 22	Regen ○ D 174 Gn 21	Reserva ○ BR 140 Ej 58
Rayo Cortado ○ RA 137 Ec 61	Regen ∼ D 174 Gn 21	Reserva de Sian Ka'an ⚑ MEX 93 De 36
Rayón ○ MEX 80 Cg 31	Regência ○ BR 141 Fa 55	Reserva Indigena ••• PA 97 Dh 41
Rayón ○ MEX 80 Cg 35	Regensburg ○ D 174 Gn 21	Reserva Indigena Predio Putumayo ••• CO 116 Dl 46
Rayón ○ MEX 93 Dp 37	Regente Feijo ○ BR 140 Ej 57	Reserva Nacional dos Craós ⚑ BR 121 El 50
Rayong ○ THA 262 La 39	Reggane ○ DZ 293 Gf 32	Reserva Nacional Junín ⚑ PE 128 Dl 51
Razan ○ IR 209 Jc 28	Reggou ○ MA 293 Ge 29	Reserva Nacional Paracas ⚑ PE 116 Dk 53
Razdol'naja ∼ RUS 250 Mb 23	Reghin ○ RO 175 He 22	Reserva Natural de Cabo Blanco ★ CR 97 Df 41
Razdol'noe ○ RUS 250 Mc 24	Regina ○ CDN 51 Ck 20	Reserve ○ USA 51 Ck 21
Râzeqân ○ IR 209 Jc 28	Regina Beach ○ CDN 51 Ck 20	Reserve ○ CDN 51 Cl 19
Razgrad ○ BG 194 Hd 24	Régina ○ F 113 Eh 43	Réserve ⚑ AUS 374 Mg 59
Razlog ○ BG 194 Hd 25	Registro ○ BR 141 El 58	Réserve de Fina ••• RMM 316 Gb 39
Razmak ○ PK 223 Jn 29	Regocijo ○ MEX 92 Ck 34	Réserve du Dja ⚑ CAM 321 Gn 44
Reading ○ USA 74 Dl 26	Regola ○ RI 283 Ma 50	Réserve Faunique de Pipineau Labelle ⚑ CDN 60 Dl 22
Reading ○ GB 163 Gf 20	Regone ○ MOC 344 Hm 54	Réserve Naturelle Intégrale Dite Sanctuaire des Addax ⚑ RN 308 Gl 36
Readstown ○ USA 56 Dc 24	Regway ○ CDN 51 Ck 20	Réserves Naturelle National de l'Air et du Ténéré ⚑ RN 308 Gl 36
Realico ○ RA 137 Eb 63	Rehli ○ IND 234 Kd 34	Réservoir Cabonga ∼ CDN 60 Dk 22
Reao ⬦ F 14 Ca 11	Rehoboth ○ NAM 348 Ha 57	Réservoir Decelles ∼ CDN 60 Dj 22
Reardan ○ USA 50 Cc 22	Reḥovot ○ IL 214 Hk 30	Réservoir de La Grande Deux ∼ CDN 43 Gc 8
Reatplains ○ CAN/USA 51 Cj 20	Reid ○ AUS 369 Ma 61	Réservoir Dozois ∼ CDN 60 Dk 22
Rebiana Sand Sea ≈ LAR 300 Hb 33	Reidsville ○ USA 74 Dj 27	Réservoir Gouin ∼ CDN 60 Dl 21
Reboly ○ RUS 159 Hh 14	Reigate ○ GB 163 Gf 20	Réservoir Manicrois ∼ CDN 60 Dp 21
Rebun ○ J 250 Mg 23	Reims ○ F 163 Gj 21	Réservoir Outardes Quatre ∼ CDN 60 Dp 20
Rebun-tö ⬦ J 250 Mg 23	Reindeer Island ⬦ CDN 56 Cn 19	Réservoir Pipmuacan ∼ CDN 60 Dm 22
Rebun-tö ∼ J 205 Xa 9	Reindeer Lake ∼ CDN 6 Db 4	Réservoir Taureau ∼ CDN 60 Dm 22
Recalde ○ RA 137 Ed 64	Reindeer Lake ∼ CDN 42 Fa 7	Resistencia ○ RA 140 Ee 59
Rechéachic ○ MEX 80 Cf 32	Reinosa ○ E 184 Gd 24	
Recife ○ BR 124 Fc 50	Reinsdyrflya ⬦ N 158 Gn 6	
Récif de la Gazelle ⬦ F 386 Ne 56	Reisaelva ∼ N 159 Hc 11	
Récif Petrie ⬦ F 386 Ne 55	Reitz ○ ZA 349 Hg 59	
Récifs de l'Astrolabe ⬦ F 386 Ne 55	Reivilo ○ ZA 349 He 59	
Reconquista ○ RA 146 Ee 60	Rejaf ○ SUD 324 Hh 43	
Recreio ○ BR 141 En 56	Reliance ○ CDN 42 Ec 6	
Recreo ○ RA 137 Eb 60	Remada ○ TN 297 Gm 29	
Recuay ○ PE 116 Dk 50	Remanso ○ BR 124 En 50	
Rèčyca ○ BY 171 Hg 19	Rembang ○ RI 279 Lf 49	
Recz ○ PL 170 Gp 19	Remedios ○ MEX 80 Cg 33	
Red ∼ AUS 365 Mh 54	Remedios ○ PA 97 Dg 41	
Red Bank ○ CDN 61 Eb 22	Remedios ∼ C 100 Dj 34	
Red Bank ○ AUS 378 Mh 64	Remer ○ USA 56 Db 22	
Red Bay ○ USA 71 Dd 28	Remeš ○ IR 226 Jh 32	
Redbank ○ AUS 378 Mh 63	Rémidos ○ BR 30 Ha 10	
Redberry Lake ∼ CDN 51 Cj 19	Remígio ○ BR 124 Fb 49	
Redbird ○ USA 51 Ck 24	Rémire ○ F 113 Eh 43	
Red Bluf ○ USA 64 Ca 25	Remna ○ N 158 Gm 15	
Red Bluff Lake ∼ USA 81 Cl 30	Renaico Malleco ∼ RCH 147 Dm 65	
Red Bud ○ USA 71 Dc 26	Renca ○ RA 137 Eb 62	
Red Butte ᐃ USA 65 Cf 28	Rend Lake ∼ USA 71 Dd 26	
Redcliff ○ ZW 341 Hg 55	Rendo ○ ETH 328 Hp 42	
Red Cliff ᐃ USA 340 Md 57	Rendova ⬦ SOL 290 Na 50	
Red Cliffs ○ AUS 378 Mh 63	Rendsburg ○ D 170 Gl 18	
Red Cloud ○ USA 70 Cn 25	Renfrew ○ CDN 60 Dk 23	
Red Deer ○ CDN 50 Ce 20	Rengat ○ RI 278 Lb 47	
Red Deer ∼ CDN 51 Cf 20	Rengel ○ RI 279 Lf 49	
Red Deer ∼ CDN 51 Ch 20	Rengo ○ RCH 137 Dn 63	
Red Deer ∼ CDN 51 Ci 19	Renhe ○ VRC 243 Ld 30	
Red Deer Lake ∼ CDN 56 Cn 19	Renhua ○ VRC 258 Lg 33	
Red Deer Valley Badlands ▱ CDN 51 Cf 20	Renhuai ○ VRC 255 Ld 32	
Reddersburg ○ ZA 349 Hf 60	Renigunta ○ IND 238 Kd 39	
Red Devil ○ USA 46 Al 15	Reñihue ○ RCH 147 Dm 67	
	Rennell Island ⬦ SOL 290 Nc 51	
	Rennes ○ F 163 Ge 21	
	Rennie ○ CDN 56 Da 21	
	Reno ○ RI 279 Lf 49	
	Reno ∼ I 185 Gn 23	
	Reno ○ USA 64 Cc 26	
	Renosterrivier ∼ ZA 349 Hf 59	
	Renosterrivier ∼ ZA 358 Hc 61	

Roma ○ **S** 170 Hb 17
Roma ○ **LS** 349 Hf 60
Roma ○ **AUS** 375 Ml 59
Romaine 〜 **CDN** 61 Ec 20
Roman ○ **RO** 175 Hf 22
Roman ⊡ **RO** 194 He 24
Romania ⊡ **RO** 194 Hd 23
Romanovka ○ **RUS** 204 Vb 8
Romans ○ **F** 185 Gj 23
Romblon ⚲ **RP** 267 Lm 39
Romblon Island ⚲ **RP** 267 Lm 39
Romblon Strait 〜 **RP** 267 Lm 39
Rome ○ **USA** 68 Dl 24
Rome ○ **USA** 71 Df 28
Rome ◉ **I** 185 Gm 25
Romeo ○ **USA** 57 Dg 24
Romeroville ○ **USA** 65 Ck 28
Romita ○ **MEX** 92 Cm 35
Rommani ○ **MA** 293 Gc 29
Romney ○ **USA** 71 Dg 25
Romney ○ **USA** 74 Dj 26
Romny ○ **UA** 175 Hj 20
Rømø ⚲ **DK** 170 Gl 18
Romodan ○ **UA** 175 Hj 20
Romorantin-Lanthenay ○ **F** 163 Gg 22
Rompin 〜 **MAL** 271 Lb 44
Romsdalen ☆ **N** 158 Gk 14
Ronan ○ **USA** 50 Ce 22
Roncador Reef ♦ **SOL** 290 Nb 49
Ronda ○ **E** 184 Gd 27
Ronde ⚲ **WG** 104 Ed 39
Rønde ○ **DK** 170 Gm 17
Rondeslottet △ **N** 158 Gl 15
Rondon △ **BR** 140 Eh 57
Rondon do Pará ○ **BR** 131 Ek 48
Rondonia Mato Grosso ◉ **BR** 129 Eb 51
Rondonópolis ○ **BR** 132 Eg 54
Rond-Point de Gaulle △ **TCH** 309 Ha 36
Rondu ○ **PK** 230 Kb 28
Rong'an ○ **VRC** 255 Le 33
Rongchang ○ **VRC** 255 Lc 31
Rongcheng ○ **VRC** 246 Lm 27
Rongjiang ○ **VRC** 255 Le 33
Rongkong ○ **RI** 282 Ll 47
Rong Kwang ○ **THA** 254 La 36
Rongshui ○ **VRC** 255 Le 33
Rong Xian ○ **VRC** 255 Lc 33
Rong Xian ○ **VRC** 255 Lf 34
Rønne ○ **DK** 170 Gp 18
Ronne Bay 〜 **38** Fa 17
Ronneby ○ **S** 170 Gp 17
Ronne Ice Shelf ⊿ **38** Fb 17
Rono ○ **RI** 283 Md 49
Ron Phibun ○ **THA** 262 Kp 41
Ronuro 〜 **BR** 132 Eg 52
Roodepoort ○ **ZA** 349 Hf 59
Rooiberg ○ **ZA** 349 Hg 60
Rooibokkraal ○ **ZA** 349 Hf 58
Rooikloof △ **ZA** 358 Hc 62
Rooikop ○ **NAM** 348 Gp 57
Rooipan ○ **ZA** 349 He 60
Rooiputs ○ **ZA** 348 Hc 59
Rooirand 🗻 **NAM** 348 Ha 58
Róo Mulatos ○ **BOL** 129 Ea 55
Roosevelt ○ **USA** 65 Cg 25
Roosevelt ○ **USA** 65 Cg 29
Roosevelt ○ **USA** 70 Cn 28
Roosevelt 〜 **BR** 120 Ed 49
Roosevelt 〜 **BR** 120 Ed 50
Roosevelt Island ⚲ **38** Ba 17
Roosville ○ **CDN** 50 Ce 21
Root 〜 **USA** 56 Dc 24
Roper 〜 **AUS** 364 Md 53
Roper Bar ○ **AUS** 364 Md 53
Roper Valley ○ **AUS** 364 Md 53
Roquefort ○ **F** 184 Gf 23
Roquetas de Mar ○ **E** 184 Ge 27
Roraima ◉ **BR** 120 Ed 45
Rori ○ **RI** 286 Me 46
Røros ○ **N** 158 Gm 14
Rørøy ○ **N** 158 Gm 13
Rørvik ○ **N** 158 Gm 13
Ros' 〜 **UA** 175 Hh 21
Rosadive Yanmad ⚲ **TR** 195 Hf 27
Rosal' ○ **RUS** 171 Hm 18
Rosalia ○ **USA** 50 Cd 22
Rosamorada ○ **MEX** 92 Ck 34
Rosana ○ **BR** 140 Eh 57
Rosano ○ **DOM** 101 Dn 36
Rosario ○ **MEX** 75 Cd 30
Rosario ○ **MEX** 80 Ch 32
Rosário ○ **BR** 121 Em 47
Rosario ○ **RCH** 130 Dn 59
Rosario ○ **PY** 136 Ea 57
Rosario 〜 **RA** 136 Eb 52
Rosarío ○ **RA** 137 Ed 62
Rosario ○ **PY** 140 Ef 58
Rosario ○ **RP** 267 Ll 37
Rosario ○ **RP** 267 Ll 39
Rosario de la Frontera ○ **RA** 136 Eb 58
Rosario del Ingre ○ **BOL** 136 Eb 55
Rosario del Tala 〜 **RA** 146 Ee 62
Rosário do Sul ○ **BR** 146 Eg 61
Rosario Oeste ○ **BR** 132 Ef 53
Rosarito ○ **MEX** 64 Cd 29
Rosarito ○ **MEX** 75 Ce 31
Rosarito ○ **MEX** 80 Cg 32
Rosas ○ **CO** 106 Dk 44
Rosa Zárate Quinindé 〜 **EC** 116 Dj 45
Roscoe ○ **USA** 70 Cm 29
Roscoe River ○ **CDN** 47 Ca 11
Roscoff ○ **F** 163 Gd 21
Roscommon ○ **USA** 57 Df 23
Roscommon ○ **IRL** 163 Gb 19
Roscrea ○ **IRL** 163 Gc 19
Rose ☆ **USA** 35 Ab 11
Rose ○ **USA** 56 Cn 24
Rose 〜 **AUS** 364 Md 53
Roseau 〜 **USA** 56 Db 21
Roseau ◉ **WD** 104 Ed 38
Roseau River 〜 **USA** 56 Db 21
Rosebery ○ **AUS** 378 Mf 65
Rose Blanche ○ **CDN** 61 Ee 22
Rosebud 〜 **USA** 56 Cm 24
Rose Bud ○ **USA** 70 Db 28
Rosebud ○ **USA** 81 Cp 30

Rosebud Creek 〜 **USA** 51 Cj 23
Rosebud Indian Reservation ••• **USA** 56 Cm 24
Roseburg ○ **USA** 50 Ca 24
Rosedale ○ **USA** 86 Dc 29
Rosedale ○ **AUS** 375 Mk 57
Rose Island ⚲ **BS** 87 Dk 33
Roselare ○ **B** 163 Gh 20
Rosenberg ○ **USA** 81 Cp 31
Rosenburg ○ **CDN** 56 Cp 20
Rosendal ○ **N** 170 Gj 16
Rosendal ⚲ **BS** 87 Dk 33
Rosenheim ○ **D** 174 Gn 22
Rose Prairie ○ **CDN** 47 Ca 17
Roses ○ **E** 185 Gh 24
Rosetown ○ **CDN** 51 Ch 20
Rosetta ○ **ET** 301 Hh 30
Rosetta ○ **ZA** 349 Hg 60
Rose Valley ○ **CDN** 51 Cl 19
Rosevelt Piek △ **SME** 113 Eg 44
Roseville ○ **USA** 64 Cb 26
Roseville ○ **USA** 64 Cb 26
Rosewood ○ **AUS** 364 Ma 54
Rosh Pinah ○ **NAM** 348 Ha 59
Rosignol ○ **GUY** 113 Ef 42
Roşiori de Vede ○ **RO** 175 He 23
Roskilde ○ **DK** 170 Gm 18
Roslavl' ○ **RUS** 171 Hj 19
Rosmead ○ **ZA** 349 He 61
Rossano ○ **I** 194 Ha 26
Ross Barnett Reservation 〜 **USA** 86 Dd 29
Ross-Bay Junction ○ **CDN** 61 Ea 19
Ross-Béthio ○ **SN** 304 Fm 37
Rossburn ○ **CDN** 56 Cm 20
Rossel Island ⚲ **PNG** 290 Mp 51
Ross Ice Shelf ⊿ **38** Ab 18
Rössing ○ **NAM** 348 Gp 57
Ross Island ⚲ **38** Ga 16
Ross Island ⚲ **38** Tb 17
Rossiter Bay 〜 **AUS** 368 Lm 63
Rossland ○ **CDN** 50 Cc 21
Rosslare ○ **IRL** 163 Gc 19
Rosso ○ **RIM** 304 Fn 37
Rossosh' ○ **RUS** 181 Hm 22
Rossouw ○ **ZA** 349 Hf 61
Rossport ○ **CDN** 57 De 21
Ross River ○ **CDN** 47 Bj 15
Ross River ○ **AUS** 374 Md 57
Rosston ○ **USA** 70 Cm 27
Røssvatnet 〜 **N** 158 Gn 13
Rossville ○ **AUS** 365 Mj 53
Røst ⚲ **N** 158 Gm 12
Rostäk ○ **IR** 215 Je 32
Rostān ○ **IR** 215 Jb 30
Rostāq ○ **AFG** 223 Jn 27
Rosthern ○ **CDN** 51 Cj 19
Rostock ○ **D** 170 Gm 18
Rostov ○ **RUS** 171 Hm 17
Rostov na-Donu 〜 **RUS** 181 Hm 22
Roswell ○ **USA** 65 Ck 29
Roswell ○ **USA** 71 Df 28
Rota ⚲ **USA** 27 Sa 8
Rothak ○ **IND** 234 Kc 31
Rothenburg ob derTauber ○ **D** 174 Gl 21
Rotherham ○ **GB** 163 Gf 19
Rothesay ○ **GB** 162 Gd 18
Rothsay ○ **USA** 56 Cp 22
Roti ○ **RI** 282 Lm 51
Roti Island ⚲ **RI** 282 Lm 51
Roto ○ **AUS** 379 Mj 62
Rotorua ○ **NZ** 383 Nl 65
Rotterdam ○ **NL** 163 Gh 20
Rottnest Island ⚲ **AUS** 368 Lh 62
Rottweil ○ **D** 174 Gl 21
Roubaix ○ **F** 163 Gh 20
Rouen ○ **F** 163 Gg 21
Roufaer 〜 **RI** 286 Me 47
Rough River Lake 〜 **USA** 71 De 27
Rough Rock ○ **USA** 65 Ch 27
Rouhia ○ **TN** 296 Gl 28
Roumsiki ○ **CAM** 321 Gn 40
Round Maker Indian Reservation •••
Round Mountain ○ **CDN** 51 Ch 19
Round Mountain △ **USA** 64 Cd 26
Round Mountain △ **AUS** 379 Mn 61
Round Pond 〜 **CDN** 61 Ef 21
Round Rock ○ **USA** 81 Cp 30
Round Spring ○ **USA** 70 Dc 27
Roundup ○ **USA** 51 Ch 22
Round Valley Indian Reservation •••
USA 64 Ca 26
Roura ○ **F** 113 Eh 43
Route 66 ★ **USA** 64 Cf 28
Rouxville ○ **ZA** 349 Hf 61
Rouyn-Noranda ○ **CDN** 60 Dj 21
Rovaniemi ○ **FIN** 159 He 12
Rovdino ○ **RUS** 171 Hp 15
Rovereto ○ **I** 185 Gm 23
Roversi ○ **RA** 136 Ed 59
Rovigo ○ **I** 185 Gm 23
Rovinj ○ **HR** 185 Gn 23
Rovnoe ○ **RUS** 181 Jb 20
Rovuma 〜 **MOC** 344 Hk 51
Rovuma 〜 **MOC** 344 Hm 51
Rowenta ○ **AUS** 375 Md 60
Rowley Island ⚲ **CDN** 43 Gc 5
Rowley Shelf ♦ **AUS** 360 Lj 55
Roxas ○ **RP** 267 Lk 40
Roxas ○ **RP** 267 Ll 37
Roxas ○ **RP** 267 Ll 39
Roxas ○ **RP** 267 Lm 40
Roxboro ○ **USA** 74 Dj 27
Roxborough Downs ○ **AUS** 374 Mf 57
Roxburgh ○ **NZ** 382 Ng 68
Roy ○ **USA** 65 Cf 25
Roy ○ **USA** 65 Ck 28
Royal ♀ **AUS** 379 Mm 62
Royal Chitawan Nat. Park ♀ **NEP** 235 Kg 32
Royal City ★ **SUD** 313 Hj 37
Royal Gorge ★ **USA** 65 Ck 26
Royal Island ⚲ **BS** 87 Dk 33
Royal Natal ♀ **ZA** 349 Hg 60
Royal Palace ★ **DY** 317 Gg 42
Royal Palaces ★ **DY** 317 Gg 42
Royalton ○ **USA** 56 Da 23
Royal Tunbridge Wells ○ **GB** 163 Gg 20
Royan ○ **F** 184 Gf 23
Roy Hill ○ **AUS** 360 Lk 57
Roy Hill △ **AUS** 360 Lk 57
Røyrvik ○ **N** 158 Gn13

Royston ○ **USA** 71 Dg 28
Rožaje ○ **MON** 194 Hc 24
Różan ○ **PL** 170 Hc 19
Rozdol'ne ○ **UA** 175 Hj 23
Rozdyl'na ○ **UA** 175 Hh 22
Rozivka ○ **UA** 181 Hl 22
Rožňava ○ **SK** 174 Hc 21
Rtišcevo ○ **RUS** 181 Hp 19
Ruacana 〜 **NAM** 340 Gp 54
Ruacana Falls 〜 **NAM** 340 Gp 54
Ruaha ⚲ **EAT** 337 Hk 49
Ruahine Range 🗻 **NZ** 383 Nl 66
Ruakaka ○ **NZ** 383 Nk 63
Ruangwa ○ **EAT** 344 Hm 51
Ruapuke Island ⚲ **NZ** 382 Ng 69
Ruashi ○ **RDC** 341 Hf 51
Ruatahuna ○ **NZ** 383 Nl 65
Ruatotia ○ **NZ** 383 Nm 64
Ruavatu ○ **NZ** 383 Nj 64
Ruawai ○ **NZ** 383 Nj 64
Rubafu ○ **EAT** 336 Hh 46
Rubcovsk ○ **RUS** 204 Tb 8
Rubeho Mountains 🗻 **EAT** 337 Hl 49
Rubens ○ **RA** 152 Dn 71
Rubeshibe ○ **J** 250 Mh 24
Rubi ○ **RDC** 324 He 44
Rubi 〜 **RDC** 324 He 44
Rubiataba ○ **BR** 133 Ek 53
Rubicon 〜 **USA** 64 Cb 26
Rubim ○ **BR** 125 Ep 54
Rubio ○ **YV** 107 Dm 42
Rubondo Island ♀ **EAT** 336 Hh 47
Rubondo Island ⚲ **EAT** 336 Hh 47
Ruby ○ **USA** 46 An 13
Ruby ○ **USA** 50 Cd 21
Ruby Dome △ **USA** 64 Ce 25
Ruby Lake 〜 **USA** 64 Ce 25
Ruby Mountains 🗻 **USA** 64 Ce 26
Ruby Plains ○ **AUS** 361 Lp 55
Rubyvale ○ **AUS** 375 Mk 57
Rucava ○ **LV** 170 Hc 17
Rucheng ○ **VRC** 258 Lg 33
Ruči'i ○ **RUS** 159 Hn 12
Rūd ○ **IR** 222 Jh 28
Rudall 〜 **AUS** 360 Lm 57
Rudall △ **AUS** 378 Me 62
Rudall River ♀ **AUS** 360 Lm 57
Rūdbar ○ **IR** 209 Jc 27
Rudewa ⚲ **EAT** 344 Hk 51
Rūdhāne ye Cangūle 〜 **IRQ** 209 Jb 29
Rudköping ○ **DK** 170 Gm 18
Rudnaja Pristan' ○ **RUS** 250 Md 23
Rudnja ○ **RUS** 171 Hh 19
Rudnyj ○ **KZ** 154 Sa 8
Rudnyy ○ **KZ** 19 Na 4
Rudong ○ **VRC** 246 Ll 29
Rūdsar ○ **IR** 222 Jd 27
Rudyard ○ **USA** 51 Cg 21
Ruen △ **BG** 194 Hd 24
Ruenya 〜 **ZW** 344 Hj 54
Rufa'a ○ **SUD** 313 Hj 38
Ruffec ○ **F** 163 Gg 22
Rufiji 〜 **EAT** 337 Hm 49
Rufino ○ **RA** 137 Ec 63
Rufisque ○ **SN** 304 Fm 37
Rufrufua ○ **RI** 283 Mc 47
Rufunsa ○ **Z** 341 Hg 51
Rugao ○ **VRC** 246 Ll 29
Rugby ○ **USA** 56 Cn 21
Rügen ⚲ **D** 170 Gn 18
Rugheiwa ○ **SUD** 312 Hh 37
Ruhengen ○ **RWA** 336 Hg 46
Ruhnu ⚲ **EST** 171 Hd 17
Ruhudji 〜 **EAT** 337 Hk 50
Ruhuhu 〜 **EAT** 344 Hk 51
Ruhuwa 〜 **VRC** 259 Ll 32
Rui Barbosa ○ **BR** 125 Ep 52
Ruichang ○ **VRC** 258 Lh 31
Ruicheng ○ **VRC** 243 Lf 28
Ruidoso ○ **USA** 80 Ck 30
Ruidoso 〜 **USA** 65 Ck 29
Ruijin ○ **VRC** 258 Lh 33
Ruili ○ **VRC** 254 Kn 33
Ruins ★ **EAT** 337 Hm 50
Ruins of Bamboro ⚲ **K** 263 Lc 39
Ruins of Sampanago ★ **MYA** 254 Kn 33
Ruiru ○ **EAK** 337 Hl 46
Ruitersbos ○ **ZA** 358 Hc 62
Rūjiena ○ **LV** 171 He 17
Ruka ○ **FIN** 159 Hg 12
Rukanga ○ **EAK** 337 Hm 47
Rukarara 〜 **RWA** 336 Hg 47
Ruki 〜 **RDC** 333 Hb 46
Rukua ○ **RI** 282 Ln 48
Rulenge ○ **EAT** 336 Hh 47
Ruleville ○ **USA** 86 Dc 29
Rulex ○ **USA** 70 Cn 29
Ruma ○ **SCG** 174 Hb 23
Ruma 〜 **WAN** 320 Gk 39
Rumāh ○ **KSA** 215 Jb 33
Rumahbaru ○ **RI** 270 Km 43
Rumahkai ○ **RI** 283 Ma 47
Rumah Kulit ○ **MAL** 274 Lh 44
Rumahtinggih ○ **RI** 286 Mg 49
Rumaila ○ **IRQ** 215 Jb 30
Rumbek ○ **SUD** 324 Hg 42
Rum Cay ⚲ **BS** 87 Dl 34
Rumeila ○ **SUD** 313 Hk 39
Rumford ○ **USA** 60 Dn 23
Rumia ○ **PL** 170 Hb 18
Rum Jungle ○ **AUS** 364 Mb 52
Rummāna ○ **ET** 301 Hj 30
Rumoi ○ **J** 250 Mg 24
Rumonge ○ **BU** 336 Hg 47
Rumphi ○ **MW** 344 Hj 51
Rumpi Hills △ **CAM** 320 Gl 43
Rumson ○ **USA** 74 Dm 25
Rumuruti ○ **EAK** 325 Hl 45
Runan ○ **VRC** 243 Lh 29
Runaway Bay ⚲ **JA** 101 Dk 36
Runazi ○ **EAT** 336 Hh 47
Runde 〜 **ZW** 352 Hj 55
Runde 〜 **ZW** 352 Hj 56
Runde ○ **RI** 270 Kn 44
Rungu ○ **RDC** 324 Hf 44
Rungwa 〜 **EAT** 336 Hh 49
Runn 〜 **S** 158 Gp 15
Runnymede ○ **AUS** 374 Mh 56
Runton Range 🗻 **AUS** 360 Lm 57
Ruokolaahti ○ **FIN** 159 Hg 15

Ruoqiang ○ **VRC** 231 Kh 26
Ruo Shui 〜 **VRC** 242 Kp 25
Ruovesi ○ **FIN** 159 Hd 15
Rupanyup ○ **AUS** 378 Mh 64
Rupert ○ **USA** 51 Cf 24
Rupert ○ **USA** 71 Dh 26
Rupia ○ **EAT** 337 Hl 50
Ruponda ○ **EAT** 344 Hm 51
Rupisi ○ **ZW** 352 Hj 56
Ruqqunda ○ **SUD** 312 Hh 38
Rurópolis ○ **BR** 120 Eg 48
Rurutu ⚲ **F** 35 Ba 12
Rusa'a ○ **AFG** 223 Jp 27
Rusape ○ **ZW** 341 Hj 55
Ruşayna Dam 〜 **SUD** 313 Hk 40
Ruse ○ **BG** 194 Hf 24
Rusera ○ **IND** 235 Kh 33
Rus'ka ○ **UA** 175 He 22
Rus Rus ○ **HN** 97 Df 38
Rush Center ○ **USA** 70 Cn 26
Rush Creek 〜 **USA** 65 Cl 26
Rushinga ○ **ZW** 344 Hj 54
Rush Springs ○ **USA** 70 Cp 28
Rushville ○ **USA** 51 Cl 24
Rushville ○ **USA** 71 Dc 25
Rushville ○ **USA** 71 Df 26
Rushworth ○ **AUS** 379 Mj 64
Rusksele ○ **S** 158 Hb 13
Rus Rus ○ **HN** 97 Df 38
Russas ○ **BR** 124 Fb 48
Russell ○ **CDN** 56 Cm 20
Russell ○ **USA** 70 Cn 26
Russell ○ **USA** 71 Dg 26
Russell ○ **NZ** 383 Nk 63
Russell Islands ⚲ **SOL** 290 Nb 50
Russell Lake 〜 **USA** 71 Dg 28
Russellville ○ **USA** 70 Db 28
Russellville ○ **USA** 71 Dg 28
Russel Range 🗻 **AUS** 369 Lm 62
Russel Springs ○ **USA** 70 Cm 26
Russelville ○ **USA** 71 Dg 28
Russia ⊡ **RUS** 154 Qc 7
Russian 〜 **USA** 64 Ca 26
Russian Mission ○ **USA** 46 Aj 15
Rust'avi ○ **GE** 202 Ja 25
Rust de Winter ○ **ZA** 349 Hg 58
Rust de Winter Dam 〜 **ZA** 349 Hg 58
Rustefjelbma ○ **N** 159 Hf 10
Rustenburg ○ **ZA** 349 Hf 58
Rustic ○ **USA** 65 Ck 25
Ruston ○ **USA** 70 Db 29
Ruta ○ **RI** 283 Lp 46
Rutana ○ **BU** 336 Hg 47
Ruteng ○ **RI** 282 Ll 50
Rutenga ○ **ZW** 352 Hh 56
Rutherglen ○ **AUS** 379 Mk 64
Rutland ○ **USA** 60 Dm 24
Rutland Island ⚲ **IND** 262 Kl 40
Rutland Plains ○ **AUS** 365 Mg 53
Rutog ○ **VRC** 230 Kd 29
Rutshuru ○ **RDC** 336 Hg 46
Rutukira 〜 **EAT** 344 Hk 51
Rutul ○ **RUS** 202 Jb 25
Ru'us al-Gibāl △ **OM** 216 Jg 32
Ruvu ○ **EAT** 337 Hm 49
Ruvubu 〜 **EAT** 336 Hh 47
Ruvuma 〜 **EAT** 344 Hm 51
Ruwase 〜 **ZW** 341 Hh 55
Ruweis ○ **UAE** 215 Je 33
Ruwenzori ♀ **EAU** 324 Hg 45
Ruwenzori 🗻 **EAU** 324 Hg 45
Ruwī ○ **OM** 226 Jh 34
Ruya 〜 **ZW** 341 Hh 54
Rü-ye ○ **AFG** 223 Jm 28
Ruyigi ○ **BU** 336 Hh 47
Ruyuan ○ **VRC** 258 Lg 33
Ruza ○ **RUS** 171 Hl 18
Ruzaevka ○ **RUS** 181 Ja 18
Ruzhany ○ **BY** 171 He 19
Ruzhou ○ **VRC** 243 Lg 28
Ružomberok ○ **SK** 174 Hb 21
Rwamagana ○ **RWA** 336 Hh 47
Rwanda ⊡ **RWA** 336 Hg 47
Ryazan' ○ **RUS** 171 Hm 18
Rybinsk ○ **RUS** 171 Hm 16
Rybinsk Reservoir 〜 **RUS** 171 Hm 16
Rybnik ○ **PL** 174 Hb 20
Rybnoe ○ **RUS** 171 Hm 18
Rycroft ○ **CDN** 47 Cc 17
Ryegate ○ **USA** 51 Ch 22
Rye Patch Reservoir 〜 **USA** 64 Cc 25
Ryfsk ○ **RUS** 175 Hk 20
Rylstone ○ **AUS** 379 Ml 62
Rynda 〜 **RUS** 159 Hl 11
Ryn-kum 〜 **KZ** 181 Jb 21
Ryn-kum 〜 **KZ** 181 Jb 21
Ryohaku-sanchi 🗻 **J** 251 Me 28
Ryōtsu ○ **J** 251 Mf 26
Rypin ○ **PL** 170 Hb 19
Rysana Pan 〜 **RB** 349 He 56
Rytinki ○ **FIN** 159 Hf 13
Rytkuči ○ **RUS** 205 Za 5
Ryukyu Islands ⚲ **J** 259 Lp 32
Ryukyu Trench ♦ **26** Ra 7
Rzeszów ○ **PL** 174 Hd 21
Ržev ○ **RUS** 171 Hl 17

S.F.Powder River 〜 **USA** 51 Cj 24
S. Hamadouche 〜 **DZ** 293 Gf 28
Sa'a ○ **SOL** 290 Nc 50
Saa ○ **CAM** 320 Gm 43
Sa'ādatābād ○ **IR** 215 Je 30
Sa'adatābād ○ **IR** 226 Jf 31
Saakow ○ **SP** 329 Hp 45
Saale 〜 **D** 174 Gm 20
Saalfeld ○ **D** 174 Gm 20
Saanen ○ **CDN** 50 Ca 21
Saanich ○ **CDN** 50 Ca 21
Saarbrücken ○ **D** 163 Gk 21
Sääre ○ **EST** 170 Hc 16
Saaremaa ⚲ **EST** 170 Hc 16
Saarijärvi ○ **FIN** 159 He 14
Saariselkä △ **FIN** 159 Hf 11
Saarivaara ○ **FIN** 159 Hg 13
Saarland ◉ **D** 163 Gk 21
Saarlouis ○ **D** 163 Gk 21
Saartuz ○ **TJ** 223 Jl 27
Saatly ○ **AZ** 202 Jc 26
Saba ⚲ **NL** 104 Ec 37
Sababa 〜 **BR** 121 Em 46
Sab 'Ābār ○ **SYR** 208 Hl 29

Sadd al-Āli High Dam ★ **ET** 301 Hj 34
Sadd-e Eskandar ★ **IR** 222 Jf 27
Saddleback Pass △ **ZA** 352 Hh 58
Saddle Mountain △ **USA** 51 Cf 23
Saddle Peak △ **IND** 262 Kl 39
Şa Đéc ○ **VN** 263 Lc 40
Sādegān ○ **IR** 215 Jc 30
Sadh ○ **OM** 219 Jf 37
Sadi ○ **ETH** 325 Hk 41
Sadi ○ **ETH** 325 Hn 43
Sadio ○ **RN** 304 Fn 38
Sadiola ⊙ **RMM** 316 Ga 39
Sādiqābād ⊙ **PK** 227 Jp 31
Sadiyyat ⚲ **UAE** 215 Jf 33
Sado 〜 **P** 184 Gb 26
Sado-Kaik yō 〜 **J** 251 Mf 27
Sado-shima ⚲ **J** 251 Mf 26
Sadova ○ **RO** 194 Hd 24
Sadovoe ○ **RUS** 181 Ja 22
Sadrinsk ○ **RUS** 154 Sa 7
Safad △ **ETH** 313 Hl 39
Safāga ⚲ **KSA** 214 Hm 32
Safané ⊙ **BF** 317 Ge 39
Safar ○ **AFG** 227 Jl 30
Şaffle ○ **S** 170 Gn 16
Safford ○ **USA** 65 Ch 29
Safi ○ **JOR** 214 Hl 30
Safi ○ **MA** 292 Gb 29
Safi ○ **TCH** 309 Ha 38
Safia 〜 **PNG** 287 Ml 50
Şafidār △ **IR** 215 Je 31
Şäfītā ○ **SYR** 208 Hl 28
Safonovo ○ **RUS** 171 Hj 18
Safotu ○ **WS** 390 Ad 52
Şafrā' ○ **AFG** 209 Hn 28
Safrab ○ **UZB** 223 Jm 26
Safranbolu ○ **TR** 195 Hj 25
Saga ○ **VRC** 235 Kg 31
Saga ○ **J** 247 Mb 29
Saga ○ **RI** 283 Mb 47
Sagabari ○ **RMM** 316 Gb 39
Sagai ○ **PK** 227 Jm 30
Sagaing ○ **MYA** 254 Km 35
Sâgallou ○ **DJI** 328 Hp 40
Sagamu ○ **WAN** 320 Gh 42
Sagan ○ **VRC** 230 Kd 27
Sagana ○ **EAK** 337 Hl 46
Sāgand ○ **IR** 222 Jf 29
Sāgar ○ **IND** 234 Kd 34
Sāgar ○ **IND** 238 Kb 38
Sagaredžo ○ **GE** 202 Ja 25
Sagarmatha Mount Everest △ **NEP** 235 Kh 32
Sagarmatha Nat. Park ♀ **NEP** 235 Kh 32
Sagasia ○ **PNG** 286 Mh 50
Sagastyr ○ **RUS** 204 Wb 4
Sagata ○ **SN** 304 Fm 38
Sagaisirk ⚲ **USA** 46 Ba 11
Sagauli Bāzar ○ **IND** 235 Kg 32
Sagay ○ **RP** 267 Lm 40
Sage ○ **USA** 65 Cg 25
Sagua de Tánamo ○ **C** 101 Dl 35
Sagua la Grande ○ **C** 100 Dh 34
Saguenay 〜 **CDN** 60 Dn 21
Saguia el-Hamra 〜 **MA** 292 Fp 32
Saguia el-Hamra 〜 **MA** 292 Ga 32
Sagunt ○ **E** 184 Gf 26
Sagure ○ **ETH** 325 Hm 42
Sagwon ○ **USA** 46 Ba 11
Sagyz ○ **KZ** 155 Rb 9
Şāh ○ **UAE** 215 Je 34
Sah ○ **RMM** 305 Gd 38
Sahaba ○ **SUD** 312 Hh 36
Şāhābād ○ **IND** 234 Kd 33
Sahagún ○ **CO** 106 Dl 41
Sahara 〜 **RN** 308 Gk 36
Saharan Atlas 🗻 **DZ** 293 Gf 29
Saharanpur ○ **IND** 234 Kc 31
Saharsa ○ **IND** 235 Kh 33
Sahaswan ○ **IND** 234 Kd 31
Şābā ○ **SYR** 208 Hl 29
Şāhbā ⊙ **SYR** 208 Hl 29
Sāh Budāg △ **IR** 209 Jb 29
Şahbuz ○ **ARM** 202 Ja 26
Şābdād ○ **IR** 226 Jg 30
Saheib ○ **SUD** 312 He 40
Sahel ⌂ **RN** 308 Gk 38
Şāh Gùj ○ **AFG** 223 Jm 29
Şahibganj ○ **IND** 235 Kh 33
Şahibpur ○ **IND** 227 Ka 34
Şāhiliya ○ **IRQ** 209 Hp 29
Sahiwal ○ **PK** 230 Ka 29
Şāh Küh △ **IR** 222 Jf 27
Şāhlābād ○ **IR** 222 Jh 29
Şahm ○ **OM** 226 Jg 33
Şahne ○ **IR** 209 Jb 28
Şāhovskaja ○ **RUS** 171 Hk 18
Şahrā at-Tīh ⌂ **ET** 301 Hj 30
Şahrak ○ **IR** 215 Je 30
Şahrak ○ **IR** 222 Jd 28
Şahrak ○ **AFG** 223 Jl 28
Sahra Marzuq ⌂ **LAR** 297 Gn 33
Şahrā ,Surt ⌂ **LAR** 297 Ha 30
Şahrazūr ○ **IRQ** 209 Ja 28
Şahr-e Bābak ○ **IR** 226 Jf 30
Şahr-e Kord ○ **IR** 222 Jd 29
Şahr-e Nou ○ **IR** 223 Jj 28
Şahr-e Şafā ○ **AFG** 227 Jm 30
Sahrestan ○ **TJ** 223 Jn 26
Şahrīvar ○ **IR** 222 Jd 28
Şahrīyar ○ **IR** 222 Jd 28
Şāh Rūd 〜 **IR** 222 Jf 27
Şahrūd ○ **IR** 222 Jf 27
Sahu ○ **RI** 275 Lp 45
Sahuaripa ○ **MEX** 80 Ch 31
Sahuayacaneito ○ **MEX** 80 Ch 31
Sahuayo ○ **MEX** 92 Cl 35
Sahul Banks ♦ **AUS** 360 Lm 52
Sahul Shelf ♦ **AUS** 361 Ln 52
Sahy ○ **H** 174 Hb 22
Sai 〜 **IND** 234 Ke 32
Sai ○ **J** 250 Mg 25

Şai ∼ **RI** 271 Lf 45
Saʿīb ad-Dāṭ ∼ **KSA** 214 Hp 33
Saʿīb Hisb ∼ **IRQ** 215 Hp 30
Sai Buri ○ **THA** 270 La 42
Saïda ○ **DZ** 293 Gg 28
Saïdia ○ **MA** 293 Ge 28
Saidor ○ **PNG** 287 Mk 48
Saidpur ○ **IND** 234 Kf 33
Saidpur ○ **BD** 235 Kj 33
Saigo ○ **J** 251 Mc 27
Saigon Ho Chi Minh ○ **VN** 263 Lc 40
Şaih ○ **IRQ** 209 Hp 28
Saiha ○ **IND** 254 Kl 34
Şaiḩ ʿÁbid ○ **IRQ** 209 Jb 29
Şaiḩ Aḩmad ○ **IRQ** 209 Ja 29
Şaiḩ Fāris ○ **IRQ** 209 Jb 29
Şaiḩūt ○ **YE** 219 Jd 38
Saikanosy Ampasindava ⌂ **RM** 345 Jb 52
Saikanosy Masoala ⌂ **RM** 345 Jd 53
Saikhoa Ghāt ○ **IND** 254 Km 32
Saiki ○ **J** 247 Mb 29
Sailāna ○ **IND** 234 Kb 34
Sailolof ○ **RI** 283 Mb 46
Saimaa △ **FIN** 159 Hf 15
Saimaa ∼ **RUS** 171 Hh 15
Sain Alto ○ **MEX** 92 Cl 34
Saindak ○ **PK** 226 Jj 31
Sainsoutou ○ **SN** 316 Ga 39
Saint Affrique ○ **F** 184 Gh 23
Saint Albert ○ **CDN** 50 Cf 19
Saint-André ○ **F** 353 Jf 56
Saint Andrew ○ **GB** 162 Ge 17
Saint Anne ○ **USA** 71 Cg 24
Saint Anthony ○ **USA** 51 Cg 24
Saint-Armand-Montrond ○ **F** 163 Gh 22
Saint Arnaud ○ **NZ** 383 Nj 66
Saint Avold ○ **F** 163 Gk 21
Saint Benedict ○ **CDN** 51 Ck 19
Saint-Benoit ○ **F** 353 Jf 56
Saint-Brieuc ○ **F** 163 Ge 21
Saint Brieux ○ **CDN** 51 Ck 19
Saint-Céré ○ **F** 184 Gg 23
Saint Charles ○ **USA** 65 Cg 24
Saint Claude ○ **F** 163 Gj 22
Saint Croix ⌂ **USA** 104 Eb 37
Saint-Denis ○ **F** 353 Jf 56
Saint-Die ○ **F** 163 Gk 21
Saint-Dizier ○ **F** 163 Gj 21
Sainte-Anne ○ **F** 104 Ed 37
Sainte-Elie ○ **F** 113 Eh 43
Sainte Marie ○ **F** 104 Ed 38
Sainte-Marie ⌂ **RM** 345 Jd 54
Sainte-Maure-d.-T. ○ **F** 163 Gg 22
Sainte Menehould ○ **F** 163 Gj 21
Saint-Emilion ○ **F** 184 Gf 23
Sainte Rose du Lac ○ **CDN** 56 Cn 20
Saintes ○ **F** 184 Gf 23
Saint-Étienne ○ **F** 185 Gh 23
Saint-Flour ○ **F** 185 Gh 23
Saint Francis Islands ⌂ **AUS** 369 Mc 62
Saint-Gaudens ○ **F** 184 Gg 24
Saint George ○ **USA** 64 Cf 27
Saint George ○ **AUS** 375 Ml 60
Saint George Basin ∼ **AUS** 361 Ln 53
Saint George's ◉ **WG** 104 Ec 39
Saint-Georges ○ **F** 113 Ej 43
Saint George's Channel ∼ **GB** 163 Gc 20
Saint-Girons ○ **F** 184 Gg 24
Saint Guénolé ○ **F** 163 Gd 22
Saint Helens ○ **USA** 50 Ca 23
Saint-Helier ○ **GB** 163 Ge 21
Sainthiya ○ **IND** 235 Kh 34
Saint-Jean d'Angély ○ **F** 184 Gf 23
Saint-Jean-de-Monts ○ **F** 163 Ge 22
Saint Jo ○ **USA** 70 Cp 29
Saint John ○ **CDN** 60 Ea 23
Saint John ⌂ **USA** 104 Eb 36
Saint John ∼ **LB** 316 Gb 42
Saint Johns ○ **USA** 65 Ch 28
Saint-Joseph ○ **F** 353 Jf 56
Saint-Joseph ○ **F** 386 Nf 56
Saint Kilda ⌂ **GB** 162 Gb 17
Saint Kitts ⌂ **KN** 104 Ec 37
Saint Laurent du Maroni ○ **F** 113 Eh 43
Saint Lawrence ∼ **CDN** 60 Dp 21
Saint Lawrence ○ **AUS** 375 Ml 57
Saint Lawrence Island ⌂ **USA** 23 Ab 3
Saint Lazare ○ **CDN** 56 Cm 20
Saint-Lô ○ **F** 163 Gf 21
Saint Louis ○ **SN** 304 Fm 37
Saint-Louis ○ **F** 163 Gk 22
Saint Lucia ⊡ **WL** 104 Ed 39
Saint Lucia Channel ∼ **←** 104 Ed 38
Saint-Malo ○ **F** 163 Ge 21
Saint Marc ○ **RH** 101 Dm 36
Saint Maries ○ **USA** 50 Cd 22
Saint Mary ∼ **CDN** 50 Cd 21
Saint Mary ○ **USA** 50 Cl 21
Saint Marys Peak ⌂ **AUS** 378 Mf 61
Saint Matthew Island ⌂ **USA** 23 Aa 3
Saint Matthias Group ⌂ **PNG** 287 Ml 46
Saint-Méen ○ **F** 163 Ge 21
Saint Michael ○ **USA** 23 Ab 3
Saint Michael ○ **USA** 46 Aj 13
Saint Michel de L'Attalaye ○ **RH** 101 Dm 36
Saint-Nazaire ○ **F** 163 Ge 22
Saint Omer ○ **F** 163 Gh 20
Saint Paul ♀ **RP** 267 Lk 40
Saint-Paul ○ **F** 353 Jf 56
Saint Peterburg ○ **RUS** 171 Hg 15
Saint Peter Island ⌂ **AUS** 369 Mc 62
Saint Peter Port ○ **GB** 163 Ge 21
Saint-Philippe ○ **F** 353 Jf 56
Saint Pierre ○ **F** 104 Ed 38
Saint-Pierre ○ **F** 353 Jf 56
Saint-Pierre Bank ♥ 61 Ef 22
Saint-Pol de Léon ○ **F** 163 Gd 21
Saint Pourcain ○ **F** 163 Gh 22
Saint-Quentin ○ **F** 163 Gh 21
Saint Regis ○ **USA** 50 Ce 22
Saint Thomas ⌂ **USA** 104 Eb 36

Saint Vidgeen ○ **AUS** 364 Md 53
Saint Vincent ⌂ **WV** 104 Ed 39
Saint Vincent Island ⌂ **USA** 74 Ec 30
Saint Vincent and the Grenadines ⊡ **WV** 104 Ec 39
Saint Vincent Passage ∼ **WV** 104
Saint Walburg ○ **CDN** 51 Ch 19
Saint-Yrielx-la-Perche ○ **F** 184 Gg 23
Saipal △ **NEP** 234 Ke 31
Saipan ⌂ **USA** 27 Sa 8
Saipina ○ **BOL** 129 Eb 55
Saito ○ **J** 247 Mb 29
Saiton ○ **RP** 267 Lm 41
Saiʿūn ○ **YE** 219 Jc 38
Sai Yok ♀ **THA** 262 Kp 38
Saja ○ **ETH** 325 Hl 42
Sajama △ **BOL** 128 Dp 55
Sajama ∼ **BOL** 129 Dp 55
Sajano ∼ **RUS** 204 Tc 8
Sajat ○ **TM** 223 Jk 26
Sajkyn ○ **KZ** 181 Jb 21
Sajmak ○ **TJ** 230 Kb 27
Sajnšand ∼ **MNG** 26 Qb 5
Saka ○ **MA** 293 Ge 28
Saka ○ **ETH** 325 Hl 41
Sakabinda ○ **RDC** 341 He 51
Sa Kaeo ○ **THA** 262 La 39
Sakai ○ **J** 247 Ma 29
Sakai ○ **J** 251 Md 28
Sakaide ○ **J** 251 Mc 28
Sakaiminato ○ **J** 251 Mc 28
Sakákah ○ **KSA** 214 Hn 31
Sakaleona ∼ **RM** 353 Jc 56
Sakania ○ **RDC** 341 Hg 52
Sakaraha ○ **RM** 353 Ja 57
Sakar Island ⌂ **PNG** 287 Ml 48
Sakarya Adapazari ○ **TR** 195 Hh 25
Sakarya Nehri ∼ **TR** 195 Hh 25
Sakassou ○ **CI** 317 Gd 42
Sake ○ **RDC** 336 Hg 46
Saketa ○ **RI** 283 Lp 46
Sakété ○ **DY** 320 Ga 42
Saketi ○ **RI** 278 Lc 49
Sakhalin ⌂ **RUS** 23 Sa 4
Sakhalin ⌂ **RUS** 205 Xb 8
Sakhalinskiy Zaliv ∼ **RUS** 205 Xb 8
Sakhonnakhon ○ **THA** 263 Lc 37
Saki ○ **WAN** 320 Gh 41
Şäki ○ **AZ** 202 Jb 25
Şäkiai ○ **LT** 171 Hd 18
Sakiet Si Youssef ○ **TN** 296 Gl 27
Sakiramke ○ **RI** 286 Mg 50
Sak Lek ○ **THA** 262 La 37
Saklepie ○ **LB** 316 Gb 42
Sakleshpur ○ **IND** 238 Kb 39
Sakoamadinika ○ **RM** 345 Jb 54
Sakrānd ○ **PK** 227 Jn 32
Sakri ○ **IND** 234 Kb 35
Sakrivier ○ **ZA** 358 Hc 61
Sakrivier ∼ **ZA** 358 Hc 61
Saks ○ **USA** 86 Df 29
Saku ○ **J** 251 Mf 27
Saky ○ **UA** 175 Hj 23
Sal △ **CV** 30 Hb 8
Sal ∼ **RUS** 181 Hp 22
Sal ∼ **CV** 316 Fj 37
Sala ○ **S** 170 Ha 16
Sala ○ **EAT** 336 Hh 49
Salaberry-de-Valleyfield ○ **CDN** 60 Dl 23
Salacgrīva ○ **LV** 171 Hd 17
Saladas ○ **RA** 146 Ea 60
Saladillo ○ **RA** 137 Ec 60
Saladillo ○ **RA** 146 Ea 63
Salado ∼ **RA** 136 Ea 60
Salado ∼ **RA** 137 Dc 59
Salado ∼ **RA** 137 Ea 63
Salado ∼ **RA** 137 Ea 61
Salado ∼ **RA** 137 Ec 60
Salado ∼ **RA** 137 Ed 61
Salado ∼ **RA** 137 Ed 63
Salado ∼ **RA** 140 Ea 58
Salado ∼ **RA** 146 Ea 59
Salado o Chadileuvu ∼ **RA** 137 Éa 64
Salado o Curacó ∼ **RA** 137 Eb 65
Salado Viejo ∼ **RA** 136 Ea 60
Salaga ○ **GH** 317 Gf 41
Salagle ○ **SP** 329 Hp 45
Şalāḩaddin ⊛ **IRQ** 209 Hp 28
Salahleh ○ **SP** 328 Ja 41
Salajwe ○ **RB** 349 Ne 57
Salal ○ **TCH** 309 Ha 38
Salâla ○ **SUD** 313 Hl 35
Salâlah ○ **OM** 219 Jf 37
Salamá ○ **GCA** 93 Dc 38
Salamá ○ **HN** 96 De 38
Salamanca ○ **USA** 60 Dj 24
Salamanca ○ **MEX** 92 Cm 35
Salamanca ○ **RCH** 137 Dn 61
Salamanca ○ **E** 184 Ga 25
Salamaua ○ **PNG** 287 Mk 49
Salamina ○ **CO** 106 Dl 40
Salamina ○ **CO** 106 Dl 43
Salamo ○ **PNG** 287 Mm 50
Şalamzār ○ **IR** 222 Ja 29
Sãlang Tunnel ★ **AFG** 223 Jn 28
Salantai ○ **LT** 170 Hc 17
Salar Aguas Calientes ∼ **RCH** 136 Ea 57
Salar de Aguilar ∼ **RCH** 136 Dp 58
Salar de Antofalla ∼ **RA** 136 Ea 58
Salar de Arizaro ∼ **RA** 136 Ea 58
Salar de Ascotán ∼ **RCH** 136 Dp 57
Salar de Atacama ∼ **RCH** 136 Dp 57
Salar de Bella Vista ∼ **RCH** 136 Dp 56
Salar de Calientes ∼ **RCH** 136 Ea 57
Salar de Caucharí ∼ **RA** 136 Ea 57
Salar de Coposa ∼ **BOL** 129 Dp 55
Salar de Huasco ∼ **RCH** 136 Dp 56
Salar de la Empexa ∼ **BOL** 136 Dp 56
Salar de la Isla ∼ **RCH** 136 Dp 58
Salar de la Laguna ∼ **BOL** 136 Dp 56
Salar de la Mina ∼ **RA** 136 Ea 59

Salar del Hombre Muerto ∼ **RA** 136 Ea 58
Salar de Llamara ∼ **RCH** 136 Dn 56
Salar de Maricunga ∼ **RCH** 136 Dp 59
Salar de Pajonales ∼ **RCH** 136 Dp 58
Salar de Pedernales ∼ **RCH** 136 Dp 59
Salar de Pocitos ∼ **RA** 136 Ea 58
Salar de Río Grande ∼ **RA** 136 Dp 58
Salar de Surire ∼ **RCH** 128 Dp 55
Salar de Uyuni ∼ **BOL** 136 Ea 56
Salar Grande ∼ **RCH** 136 Dp 59
Salar Pocitos ∼ **RA** 136 Ea 58
Salar Punta Negra ∼ **RCH** 136 Dp 58
Salas d. l. ○ **E** 184 Ge 24
Salâšbil ∼ **YE** 219 Jc 37
Salata ○ **RI** 316 Gb 42
Salatiga ○ **RI** 278 Lf 49
Salavat ○ **RUS** 154 Rc 8
Salavãtãbãd ○ **IR** 209 Jb 28
Salay ○ **RP** 267 Ln 41
Salazar ○ **RA** 137 Ec 64
Salazie ○ **F** 353 Jf 56
Salcabamba ○ **PE** 128 Dl 52
Salcedo ○ **DOM** 101 Dn 36
Salcha ○ **USA** 46 Bc 13
Saldaña ∼ **CO** 106 Dl 44
Saldaña ∼ **CO** 106 Dl 44
Saldaña ○ **E** 184 Ga 24
Saldanha ○ **ZA** 358 Ha 62
Saldanha Bay ∼ **ZA** 358 Ha 62
Saldillo ∼ **RA** 137 Ec 62
Saldus ○ **LV** 170 Hd 17
Salé ○ **MA** 293 Ge 28
Sale ○ **AUS** 379 Mk 65
Salechard ○ **RUS** 19 Na 3
Salechard ○ **RUS** 154 Sb 5
Salée ○ **RIM** 304 Fn 38
Sâlehãbãd ○ **IR** 209 Jb 28
Salehard ○ **RUS** 154 Sb 5
Salehard ○ **RUS** 204 Sb 5
Salelologa ○ **WS** 390 Ad 52
Salem ○ **USA** 50 Ca 23
Salem ○ **USA** 54 Cp 24
Salem ○ **USA** 60 Dn 24
Salem ○ **USA** 70 Db 27
Salem ○ **USA** 70 Dc 27
Salem ○ **USA** 71 Dd 26
Salem ○ **USA** 71 Dh 25
Salem ○ **USA** 74 Dl 26
Salem ○ **USA** 86 Dg 31
Salem ○ **IND** 238 Kd 40
Salem ○ **RI** 283 Mc 46
Salémata ○ **SN** 316 Fp 39
Salemi ○ **I** 185 Gn 27
Salerno ○ **I** 185 Gn 26
Sales ○ **BR** 140 Ek 56
Salesópolis ○ **BR** 141 Em 57
Salet ○ **RI** 278 Lc 47
Saleye ○ **CI** 317 Ge 41
Salgir ∼ **UA** 175 Hk 23
Şalgótarján ○ **H** 174 Hb 21
Salgovaara ○ **RUS** 159 Hj 14
Salgueiro ○ **BR** 124 Fa 50
Salgyr ∼ **UA** 175 Hk 23
Salḩad ○ **SYR** 208 Hl 29
Salí ∼ **RA** 136 Eb 59
Sali ○ **VRC** 254 Kp 32
Sali ○ **DZ** 293 Gf 31
Salida ○ **USA** 65 Ck 26
Şalîf ad-Ḏahī ○ **YE** 218 Hp 38
Salihli ○ **TR** 195 Hg 26
Salihorsk ○ **BY** 171 Hf 19
Şaliķénié ○ **SN** 316 Fn 39
Şalîm ○ **OM** 219 Jf 36
Salìma ○ **MW** 344 Hk 52
Salimi ○ **RDC** 341 Hd 50
Salima ○ **MOC** 344 Hl 52
Şalmo ∼ **MYA** 254 Km 35
Salina ○ **USA** 70 Cp 26
Salina Colorada Grande ∼ **RA** 147 Ec 65
Salina Cruz ○ **MEX** 93 Da 37
Salina d. Ronda ∼ **E** 184 Gd 27
Salina de Guayatayoc ∼ **PY** 136 Eb 57
Salina de Guayatayoc ∼ **RA** 136 Eb 57
Salina de la Laguna Verde ∼ **RA** 136 Dp 59
Salina del Gualicho ∼ **RA** 147 Eb 66
Salina Grande ∼ **RA** 137 Ea 64
Salina Point ⌒ **BS** 87 Dl 34
Salinas ○ **USA** 64 Cb 27
Salinas ○ **USA** 64 Cb 27
Salinas ○ **MEX** 92 Cm 34
Salinas ○ **MEX** 93 Dc 37
Salinas ○ **EC** 116 Dh 47
Salinas ∼ **BR** 124 En 49
Salinas ∼ **BR** 125 En 54
Salinas ∼ **BOL** 136 En 56
Salinas-Aguada ⌒ **PE** 128 Dn 54
Salinas Chicas ∼ **RA** 147 Ec 65
Salinas de Ambargasta ∼ **RA** 137 Eb 60
Salinas de Garci ∼ **BOL** 129 Ea 55
Salinas dos Colorados ∼ **RA** 137 Ea 60
Salinas de Atacama ∼ **RCH** 136 Ea 61
Salinas de Mascasín ∼ **RA** 137 Eb 62
Salinas Grandes ∼ **RA** 136 Ea 57
Salinas Grandes ∼ **RA** 137 Eb 60
Salinas Grandes ∼ **RA** 137 Ec 64
Salinas Grandes ∼ **RA** 147 Eb 67
Salinas Grandes ∼ **RA** 147 Eb 63
Salinas Pueblo Mission N.M. ★ **USA** 65 Cj 28
Salinas Victoria ○ **MEX** 81 Cm 32
Salina Trapalcó ∼ **RA** 147 Ea 65
Saline ∼ **USA** 70 Cn 26
Saliópolis ○ **BR** 121 El 46
Salisbury ∼ **CDN** 61 Eb 22
Salisbury ○ **USA** 71 Dg 26
Salisbury ○ **USA** 74 Dl 26
Salisbury ○ **GB** 163 Ge 20

Salisbury Channel ∼ **EAU** 337 Hj 46
Salisbury Island ⌂ **CDN** 43 Gc 6
Salisbury Island ⌂ **AUS** 369 Lm 63
Salish Mountains △ **USA** 50 Ce 21
Salitral ○ **PE** 116 Dj 48
Salitral ○ **RA** 147 Gc 65
Salitral de la Perra ∼ **RA** 137 Ea 64
Salitral de las Barrancas ∼ **RA** 147 Ec 65
Salitre ○ **EC** 116 Dj 46
Salitre ∼ **BR** 124 Ep 50
Salitre ∼ **BR** 125 Ep 51
Şalka ○ **WAN** 320 Gj 40
Şalkar ○ **KZ** 155 Rc 9
Şalla ∼ **FIN** 159 Hg 12
Salliqueló ○ **RA** 137 Ec 64
Sallisaw ○ **USA** 70 Da 28
Sällom ○ **SUD** 313 Hl 35
Salluit ○ **CDN** 51 Dl 38
Sally's Cove ○ **CDN** 61 Ee 21
Salmãs ○ **IR** 209 Ja 26
Salmi ○ **RUS** 171 Hh 15
Salmo ○ **CDN** 50 Cd 21
Salmon ○ **USA** 50 Ce 23
Salmon ∼ **USA** 50 Ce 23
Salmon Arm ○ **CDN** 50 Cc 20
Salmon Falls Creek ∼ **USA** 64 Ce 25
Salmon Falls Reservoir ∼ **USA** 64 Ce 24
Salmon Gums ○ **AUS** 368 Ll 62
Salmon Sea ≈ 287 Ml 49
Salmon River Mountains △ **USA** 50 Ce 23
Salo ○ **FIN** 159 Hd 15
Salo ○ **RCA** 321 Ha 44
Salomon ∼ **USA** 70 Cp 26
Salomon Sea ≈ 287 Ml 49
Salon-de-P. ○ **F** 185 Gj 24
Salonga ∼ **RDC** 333 Hc 46
Salonta ○ **RO** 174 Hc 22
Salor ∼ **E** 184 Gc 26
Saloum ∼ **SN** 304 Fn 38
Salpausselkä ∼ **FIN** 159 He 15
Salragún ○ **E** 184 Ga 24
Salsacata ○ **RA** 137 Eb 61
Sal'sk ∼ **RUS** 181 Hn 22
Sal'skij ○ **RUS** 171 Hk 15
Sal'sko-Manyčskaja grjada △ **RUS** 181 Hn 22
Salso ∼ **I** 185 Gn 27
Salsomaggiore ○ **I** 185 Gl 23
Salt ∼ **USA** 65 Cg 29
Salt ○ **E** 184 Gh 24
Salta ○ **RA** 136 Eb 58
Salt Basin ∼ **USA** 80 Ck 30
Saltcoats ○ **CDN** 51 Cl 20
Saltee Island ⌂ **IRL** 163 Gc 19
Salteeiva ∼ **N** 158 Gf 12
Saltfjell Svartisen ♀ **N** 158 Gp 12
Salt Fork Brazos River ∼ **USA** 70 Cn 29
Salt Fork Of Arkansas ∼ **USA** 70 Cp 28
Salt Fork Red River ∼ **USA** 70 Cm 28
Saltillo ○ **MEX** 81 Cm 33
Salt Lake ∼ **AUS** 378 Mh 61
Salt Lake City ○ **USA** 65 Cg 25
Salto ○ **RA** 137 Ed 63
Salto ○ **ROU** 146 Ef 61
Salto ○ **RA** 137 Ed 63
Salto Angel Angel Falls ★ **YV** 112 Ec 42
Salto da Divisa ○ **BR** 125 Ep 53
Salto da Morena ∼ **BR** 120 Se 49
Salto do Guaíra ○ **BR** 140 Eg 58
Salto do Jacuí ○ **BR** 146 Eh 60
Salto do Jirau ∼ **BR** 117 Eb 50
Salton City ○ **USA** 64 Ce 29
Salton Sea ∼ **USA** 64 Ce 29
Salto Nihuil ∼ **RA** 137 Dp 63
Salto Palmar ∼ **PY** 140 Ee 58
Salto Primeiro ∼ **BR** 132 Eg 53
Salto Primeiro de Abril ∼ **BR** 129 Ed 51
Salto Tequendama ∼ **CO** 117 Dn 46
Salt Pan ∼ **NAM** 348 Hb 59
Salt Range △ **PK** 230 Ka 29
Saltsjöbaden ○ **S** 170 Hb 16
Salt Sts.Marie ○ **CDN** 57 Df 22
Saluda ○ **USA** 71 Dh 29
Saluda ∼ **USA** 71 Dg 28
Salus ○ **RI** 275 Lp 45
Saluzzo ○ **I** 185 Gk 23
Salvador ○ **BR** 125 Fa 52
Salvaleón de Higüey ○ **DOM** 101 Dp 36
Salvaterra ○ **BR** 121 Ek 46
Salvatierra ○ **MEX** 92 Cm 35
Salwã Baḩrī ∼ **ET** 301 Hj 33
Salween (Thanlwin) ∼ **MYA** 254 Kp 35
Salyan ○ **AZ** 202 Jc 26
Salyersville ○ **USA** 71 Dg 27
Salzburg ○ **A** 174 Gn 22
Salzburg ⊛ **A** 174 Gn 22
Salzgitter ○ **D** 170 Gm 19
Salzwedel ○ **D** 170 Gm 19
Sam ○ **G** 332 Gm 45
Sama ∼ **PE** 128 Dn 54
Sama ○ **PE** 128 Dn 55
Samachique ○ **MEX** 80 Cj 33
Samagaigai ○ **NAM** 340 Hb 55
Samã'il ○ **OM** 226 Jh 34
Samakhvalavichy ○ **BY** 171 Hf 19
Samakoulou ○ **RMM** 316 Gb 39
Samal ○ **RP** 275 Ln 42
Samal Island ⌂ **RP** 275 Ln 42
Sãmalkot ○ **IND** 238 Kf 37
Samalusi ○ **LAR** 300 Hc 29
Samãlzâl ∼ **ET** 291 Jn 30
Saman ○ **PNG** 290 Mp 51
Samana Cay ⌂ **BS** 87 Dm 34

Samaná Peninsula ⌂ **DOM** 101 Dp 36
Samandağı ○ **TR** 195 Hk 27
Samanga ○ **EAT** 337 Hm 50
Samangán ⊛ **AFG** 223 Jm 27
Samangán ○ **AFG** 223 Jm 27
Samanturai ○ **CL** 239 Ke 42
Samar ∼ **RP** 267 Ln 40
Samara ∼ **RUS** 155 Rb 8
Samara ○ **UA** 175 Hk 21
Samara ○ **RUS** 181 Jd 19
Samara ○ **RUS** 250 Xa 9
Samariapo ○ **YV** 107 Ea 43
Samarinda ○ **RI** 274 Lj 46
Samarkand ○ **UZB** 19 Na 6
Samarkand ○ **UZB** 223 Jm 26
Samarkölinin ∼ **KZ** 181 Jd 21
Sãmarrã' ∼ **IRQ** 209 Hp 28
Samar Sea ∼ **RP** 267 Ln 39
Samarskoe vodorhranilišče ∼ **RUS** 181 Jc 18
Samaru ○ **WAN** 320 Gk 40
Samastïpur ○ **IND** 235 Kg 33
Samasuma Island ⌂ **PNG** 287 Mj 46
Samate ○ **RI** 283 Mb 46
Samatiguila ○ **CI** 304 Gc 41
Sâmatra ○ **IND** 227 Jn 34
Samaxı ○ **AZ** 202 Jc 25
Samaysa Dheer ○ **SP** 328 Jc 40
Samba ○ **IND** 230 Kb 29
Samba ∼ **RI** 279 Lg 46
Samba ○ **BF** 317 Ge 39
Samba ○ **RDC** 333 Hc 45
Samba ○ **RDC** 336 Hf 48
Samba Caju ○ **ANG** 340 Gp 50
Sambailo ○ **RG** 316 Fp 39
Sambalpur ○ **IND** 235 Kg 35
Sambao ∼ **RM** 345 Ja 54
Sambas ∼ **RI** 271 Le 45
Sambas ∼ **RI** 271 Le 45
Sambava ○ **RM** 345 Jd 53
Sambazõ ∼ **MOC** 344 Hk 55
Sambir ○ **UA** 175 Hd 21
Sambito ∼ **BR** 124 Ep 49
Sambo ○ **ANG** 340 Gp 52
Samboja ○ **RI** 274 Lj 46
Samborombón ∼ **RA** 146 Ef 63
Samborombón Bay ∼ **RA** 146 Ef 63
Samborondón ○ **EC** 116 Dj 46
Sambriàl ○ **IND** 230 Kb 29
Sambriano ∼ **RM** 345 Jc 53
Samburu ○ **EAK** 337 Hm 47
Sambusu ○ **NAM** 340 Hb 54
Samch'ok ○ **ROK** 247 Ma 27
Samch'ŏnp'o ○ **ROK** 247 Ma 28
Samdrup Jonkhar ○ **BHT** 235 Kk 32
Same ○ **EAT** 337 Hl 48
Samevloeiing ○ **ZA** 348 Hc 59
Samfya ○ **Z** 341 Hg 51
Şamḫa ∼ **YE** 219 Je 39
Sámi ○ **GR** 194 Hc 26
Sami ○ **IND** 227 Jp 34
Samia ○ **RN** 308 Gl 38
Samïrã' ○ **KSA** 214 Hn 32
Samiria ∼ **PE** 116 Dl 48
Samiţa ○ **KSA** 218 Hp 37
Samjiyon ○ **DVRK** 247 Ma 25
Samkir ○ **AZ** 202 Ja 25
Şammalladenmäki ∼ **FIN** 159 Hc 15
Sam Muang ∼ **THA** 262 La 37
Sam Nám ∼ **VN** 255 Lb 35
Samnú ○ **LAR** 297 Gp 32
Samo ○ **PNG** 287 Mn 47
Samoa ⌂ **WS** 35 Aa 11
Samoa Islands ⌂ **USA** 35 Ab 11
Samoded ○ **RUS** 159 Hn 14
Samojlovka ○ **RUS** 181 Hp 20
Samokov ○ **BG** 194 Hd 24
Samoqe ○ **RG** 316 Gb 42
Sámos ○ **GR** 194 Hf 27
Samothraki ○ **GR** 194 He 25
Samothráki ⌂ **GR** 194 He 25
Sampa ○ **GH** 317 Ge 42
Sampacho ○ **RA** 137 Eb 62
Sampaga ○ **RI** 279 Lk 47
Sampang ○ **RI** 279 Lg 49
Sampara ∼ **RI** 282 Lm 48
Sampelga ○ **BF** 317 Gg 39
Sampit ○ **RI** 279 Lg 47
Sampit ∼ **RI** 279 Lg 47
Sampolawa ○ **RI** 282 Ln 48
Sampun ○ **PNG** 287 Mn 48
Sampwe ○ **RDC** 336 Hf 50
Samreboe ○ **GH** 317 Ge 43
Samsam ○ **SUD** 313 Hk 39
Samsang ○ **VRC** 230 Kf 30
Samsherpur ○ **IND** 238 Ka 36
Samsø ⌂ **DK** 170 Gm 18
Sâm So'n ○ **VN** 255 Lc 36
Samson Indian Reservation ••• **CDN** 51 Cf 19
Samsun ○ **TR** 195 Hl 25
Samtredia ○ **GE** 202 Hp 24
Samucumbi ○ **ANG** 340 Hb 52
Samuhū ○ **RA** 136 Ep 59
Samulondo ○ **RDC** 341 Hd 50
Samundri ○ **PK** 230 Ka 30
Samur ∼ **RUS** 202 Jc 25
Samur–Abşeron Kanalı ∼ **AZ** 202 Jc 25
Samut Prakan ○ **THA** 262 La 39
Samut Sakhon ○ **THA** 262 Kp 39
Samut Songkhram ○ **THA** 262 Kp 39
Saña ○ **PE** 116 Dj 49
Saña ∼ **PE** 116 Dj 49
Sanã ○ **YE** 219 Jc 37
Sanaa ⊡ **YE** 218 Ja 38
Sanaba ○ **RMM** 304 Gb 38
Sanaba ○ **BF** 317 Gd 39
Sanaga ∼ **CAM** 321 Gl 43
San Agusin ○ **YV** 107 Ea 42
San Agustín de Valle Fértil ○ **RA** 137 Ea 62
San Alberto ○ **CO** 107 Dm 42

San Alejandro ○ **PE** 116 Dl 50
Sanana ○ **RI** 282 Ln 47
Sanandağ ○ **IR** 209 Jb 28
Sanando ○ **RMM** 305 Gc 39
San Andrés ○ **CO** 97 Dh 39
San Andrés ○ **C** 101 Dk 35
San Andrés ○ **CO** 106 Dk 42
San Andrés ∼ **RCH** 136 Dp 59
San Andrés ○ **RP** 267 Lm 39
San Andrés de Giles ○ **RA** 146 Ee 63
San Andrés de Sotavento ○ **CO** 106 Dl 41
San Andres Mountains △ **USA** 65 Cj 29
San Andres Point ⌒ **RP** 267 Ll 39
San Andrés Tuxtla ○ **MEX** 93 Da 36
San Andrés y Sauces ○ **E** 292 Fm 31
San Andros ○ **BS** 87 Dj 33
Sananduva ○ **BR** 140 Ej 59
San Angelo ○ **USA** 81 Cm 30
Sanankoroba ○ **RMM** 316 Gc 39
San Antón ○ **PE** 128 Dn 53
San Antoni del Golfo ○ **YV** 112 Ec 40
San Antonio ○ **USA** 65 Cj 29
San Antonio ○ **USA** 81 Cn 31
San Antonio ○ **BH** 93 Dd 37
San Antonio ○ **CO** 106 Dj 45
San Antonio ○ **YV** 107 Ea 44
San Antonio ○ **RCH** 137 Dm 62
San Antonio ○ **RA** 137 Ea 62
San Antonio Bay ∼ **USA** 81 Cp 31
San Antonio Bay ∼ **RP** 266 Lj 41
San Antonio de Alcalá ○ **MEX** 80 Ck 31
San Antonio de Areco ○ **RA** 146 Ee 63
San Antonio de Getucha ○ **CO** 116 Dl 45
San Antonio de los Cobres ○ **RA** 136 Ea 58
San Antonio del Sur ○ **C** 101 Dl 35
San Antonio de Tamanaco ○ **YV** 107 Ea 41
San Antonio Oeste ○ **RA** 147 Eb 66
San Antonio River ∼ **USA** 81 Cp 31
San Antonio Villalongín ○ **MEX** 92 Cm 36
Sanarate ○ **GCA** 93 Dc 38
Sanaroa Island ⌂ **PNG** 287 Mm 50
San Augustin ○ **MEX** 75 Ce 31
Sanâw ○ **YE** 219 Jd 37
Sanãwad ○ **IND** 234 Kc 34
Sanba ○ **VRC** 254 Kp 31
San Bartolo ○ **PE** 116 Dk 52
San Bartolomé d. T. ○ **E** 292 Fn 32
Sanbei Yangchang ○ **VRC** 243 Ld 26
San Benito ○ **USA** 81 Cp 32
San Benito ○ **GCA** 93 Dc 37
San Benito ○ **NIC** 96 De 39
San Benito Abad ○ **CO** 106 Dl 41
San Benito Mountain △ **USA** 64 Cb 27
San Bento do Sul ○ **BR** 140 Ek 59
San Bernardina Strait ∼ **RP** 267 Ln 39
San Bernardino ○ **USA** 64 Cd 28
San Bernardo ○ **MEX** 80 Ch 32
San Bernardo ○ **RA** 136 Ed 60
San Bernardo ○ **RCH** 137 Dn 62
San Bernardo ○ **RA** 137 Ed 64
San Bernardo del Viento ○ **CO** 106 Dk 41
San Blas ○ **MEX** 80 Ch 32
San Blas ○ **MEX** 80 Ck 34
San Blas ○ **MEX** 81 Cm 32
San Blas ○ **MEX** 92 Ck 35
San Blas Islands ⌂ **PA** 97 Dj 41
San Borja ○ **BOL** 129 Ea 52
Sanborn ○ **USA** 56 Da 23
San Buenaventura ○ **MEX** 81 Cm 32
San Buenaventura ○ **BOL** 129 Ea 52
Sança ○ **MOC** 344 Hk 54
San Carlos ○ **MEX** 75 Cf 33
San Carlos ○ **MEX** 80 Cg 31
San Carlos ○ **MEX** 81 Cm 31
San Carlos ○ **MEX** 81 Cn 33
San Carlos ○ **NIC** 97 Df 40
San Carlos ∼ **CR** 97 Df 40
San Carlos ○ **PA** 97 Dj 41
San Carlos ○ **YV** 107 Dp 41
San Carlos ○ **RCH** 137 Dn 64
San Carlos ○ **RA** 137 Dp 62
San Carlos ○ **RA** 137 Ec 60
San Carlos ○ **ROU** 146 Eg 63
San Carlos ○ **RP** 267 Ll 38
San Carlos ○ **RP** 267 Lm 40
San Carlos Bay ∼ **USA** 87 Dg 32
San Carlos de Bolívar ○ **RA** 137 Ed 64
San Carlos de Guaroa ○ **CO** 107 Dm 44
San Carlos del Meta ○ **YV** 107 Ea 42
San Carlos del Zulia ○ **YV** 107 Dn 41
San Carlos de Río Negro ○ **YV** 112 Dp 45
San Carlos Indian Reservation ••• **USA** 65 Cg 29
San Carlos Park ○ **USA** 87 Dh 32
San Carlos Reservoir ∼ **USA** 65 Cg 29
San Carlos Reservoir ∼ **USA** 65 Cg 29
San Carols ∼ **PY** 140 Ee 57
San Cayetano ○ **RA** 146 Ee 65
Sancha ○ **VRC** 243 Lf 26
Sancha ○ **VRC** 255 Le 33
Sanchakou ○ **VRC** 230 Kd 26
Sánchez Magallanes ○ **MEX** 93 Db 36
Sanchi ○ **IND** 234 Kc 34
Sãnchor ○ **IND** 227 Jp 33
San Christóbal ∼ **RCH** 136 Dn 57
San Clara ○ **CDN** 56 Cm 20
San Clemente ○ **USA** 64 Cc 29
San Clemente ○ **RCH** 137 Dn 63
San Clemente del Tuyú ○ **RA** 146 Ef 64

San Clemente Island ♁ USA 64 Cc 29
Sanclerlândia ○ BR 133 Ej 54
Sanco Point ⌓ RP 267 Lp 41
San Cosme y Damián ○ PY 140 Ef 59
San Cristóbal ○ GCA 93 Dc 38
San Cristóbal ○ PA 97 Dh 41
San Cristóbal ○ C 100 Dg 34
San Cristobal ○ DOM 101 Dn 36
San Cristóbal ○ YV 107 Dm 42
San Cristobal ○ RCH 136 Dp 57
San Cristobal ○ RA 137 Ed 61
San Cristobal ♁ SOL 290 Nc 51
San Cristóbal de las Casas ○ MEX 93 Db 37
San Cristobal Trench ♆ SOL 290 Nc 51
Sancti Spíritu ○ RA 137 Ec 63
Sancti Spíritus ○ C 100 Dj 35
Sand ○ N 170 Gj 16
Sand ~ ZA 349 Hg 57
Sandai ○ RI 271 Lf 46
Sandakan ○ MAL 274 Lk 43
Sandakan ○ RI 278 Le 50
Sandama ○ RMM 316 Gb 39
Sandando ○ ANG 340 Hc 51
Sandane ○ N 158 Gk 15
Sandanski ○ BG 194 Hd 25
Sandaré ○ RMM 304 Ga 38
Sand Arroyo ~ USA 65 Cl 27
Sanday ♁ GB 162 Ge 16
Sandbank Lake ~ CDN 57 Dg 20
Sandberg ○ ZA 358 Hb 62
Sand Draw ○ USA 51 Ch 24
Sandefjord ○ N 170 Gm 16
Sandégue ○ CI 317 Ge 42
Sandema ○ GH 317 Gf 40
Sânderão ○ IND 227 Ka 33
Sanders ○ USA 65 Ch 28
Sanderson ○ USA 81 Cl 30
Sandersville ○ USA 71 Dg 29
Sandfire Roadhouse ○ AUS 360 Ll 55
Sandfløgga △ N 170 Gk 16
Sandford Lake ~ CDN 56 Dc 21
Sand Hills ⩕ USA 51 Cl 24
Sandhornøy ♁ N 158 Gn 12
Sandia ○ PE 128 Dp 53
San Diego ○ USA 64 Cd 29
San Diego ○ MEX 80 Cj 30
San Diego ○ USA 81 Cn 32
Sandıklı ○ TR 195 Hh 26
Sandila ○ IND 234 Ke 32
Sand Lake ~ CDN 56 Da 20
Sandnes ○ N 170 Gj 16
Sandnessjøen ○ N 158 Gm 12
Sando ○ PE 128 Dm 53
Sandoa ○ RDC 341 Hd 50
Sandomierz ○ PL 174 Hc 20
San Domingos do Capim ○ BR 121 El 46
Sandougou ~ SN 316 Fn 39
Sandover ~ AUS 374 Md 56
Sandovo ○ RUS 171 Hl 16
Sandoway ○ MYA 254 Kl 36
Sandoy ♁ DK 162 Gc 15
Sandoyal ○ USA 71 Dd 26
Sand Pass △ USA 64 Cf 26
Sand Point ○ USA 46 Aj 17
Sandpoint ○ USA 50 Cd 21
Sandrakatsy ○ RM 345 Jc 54
Sandrakota ~ RM 345 Jc 53
Sandratsino ~ RM 345 Jc 54
Sand River ~ PNG 286 Mg 47
Sandrivier ~ ZA 349 Hf 60
Sand Springs ○ USA 70 Cp 27
Sandstone ○ USA 56 Db 22
Sandstone ○ AUS 368 Lk 59
Sandur ○ IND 238 Kc 38
Sandusky ○ USA 57 Dg 24
Sandvicken ○ S 158 Ha 15
Sandvig ○ DK 170 Gp 18
Sandvika ○ N 158 Gm 14
Sandvika ○ N 158 Gn 13
Sandwich Harbour ○ NAM 348 Gp 57
Sandwich Harbour Lagoon ~ NAM 348 Gp 57
Sandwig ○ BD 235 Kk 34
Sandy ○ USA 65 Cg 25
Sandy Bight ~ AUS 369 Lm 62
Sandy Cape ⌓ AUS 375 Mn 58
Sandy Creek ~ AUS 375 Mj 57
Sandy Creek ~ AUS 379 Mj 62
Sandy Desert ⌂ PK 226 Jk 31
Sandy Hills ⩕ USA 70 Da 29
Sandykači ○ TM 223 Jk 27
Sandy Lake ○ CDN 56 Da 19
Sandy Lake ~ CDN 56 Db 19
Sandy Lake ~ CDN 61 Ef 21
Sandy Point ○ BS 87 Dk 32
San Estanislao ○ CO 106 Dl 40
San Estanislao ○ PY 140 Ef 58
San Esteban ○ HN 96 Df 38
San Evaristo ○ MEX 80 Cg 33
San Felipe ○ MEX 75 Ce 30
San Felipe ○ MEX 92 Cm 35
San Felipe ○ MEX 93 Dd 35
San Felipe ○ YV 107 Dp 40
San Felipe ○ CO 112 Ea 45
San Felipe ○ RCH 137 Dn 62
San Felipe de Vichayal ○ PE 116 Dh 48
San Félix ○ YV 107 Dn 40
San Felix do Araguaia ○ BR 133 Ej 51
San Félix do Piauí ○ BR 124 En 48
San Fernando ○ USA 64 Cc 28
San Fernando ○ MEX 75 Ce 30
San Fernando ○ MEX 81 Cn 33
San Fernando ○ TT 104 Ed 40
San Fernando ○ RA 136 Ea 59
San Fernando ○ RCH 137 Dn 63
San Fernando ○ E 184 Gc 27
San Fernando ○ RP 267 Ll 37
San Fernando de Apure ○ YV 107 Ea 42
San Fernando de Atabapo ○ YV 107 Ea 43
Sånfj. ★ S 158 Gn 14
Sanford ○ USA 60 Dn 24
Sanford ○ USA 74 Dj 28
Sanford ○ USA 87 Dh 31
Sanford ~ AUS 368 Lj 59
San Francesc d.F. ○ E 184 Gg 26
San Francisco ○ USA 64 Ca 27
San Francisco ○ ES 93 Dd 39
San Francisco ○ YV 107 Dn 40
San Francisco ○ PE 128 Dm 52
San Francisco ○ BOL 129 Eb 54
Sân Francisco ○ BR 133 Em 53
San Francisco ~ RA 137 Dp 61
San Francisco ○ RA 137 Ec 61
San Francisco ○ RP 267 Ln 41
San Francisco Bay ~ USA 64 Ca 27
San Francisco Creek ~ USA 81 Cl 31
San Francisco de Bellocq ○ RA 146 Ed 65
San Francisco de Borja ○ MEX 80 Cj 32
San Francisco de Laishi ○ RA 140 Ee 59
San Francisco de la Paz ○ HN 96 De 38
San Francisco del Chañar ○ RA 137 Eb 60
San Francisco del Oro ○ MEX 80 Cj 32
San Francisco del Rincón ○ MEX 92 Cm 35
San Francisco de Macoris ○ DOM 101 Dn 36
San Francisco de Mostaza ○ RCH 137 Dn 62
San Francisco do Sul ○ BR 141 Ek 59
Sang ○ GH 317 Gf 41
Sanga ○ RMM 305 Ge 38
Sanga ○ BF 317 Gg 40
Sanga ○ EAU 336 Hh 46
Sanga ○ ANG 340 Gp 51
Sanga ○ MOC 344 Hk 52
Sanga ~ MOC 344 Hk 55
San Gabriel ○ EC 116 Dk 45
San Gabriel Mixtepec ○ MEX 92 Cp 36
Sangama ○ EAT 336 Hj 50
Sangameshwar ○ IND 238 Ka 37
Sangamner ○ IND 238 Kb 36
Sangamon ~ USA 71 Dc 25
Sangān ○ IR 222 Jj 28
Sanganer ○ IND 234 Kb 32
Sangar ○ RUS 22 Ra 3
Sangar ○ RUS 205 Wb 6
Sangardo ○ RG 316 Ga 41
Sangarédi ○ RG 316 Fp 40
Sangarh ~ PK 227 Jp 30
Sangata ○ RI 274 Lj 45
Sangāv ○ IRQ 209 Ja 28
Sangbast ○ IR 222 Jh 28
Sangbé ○ CAM 320 Gn 42
Sangbor ○ AFG 223 Jk 28
Sange ○ RDC 336 Hg 49
Sangeang ♁ RI 279 Lk 50
San Genaro ○ RA 137 Ed 62
San Germán ○ USA 104 Ea 36
Sanggan He ~ VRC 243 Lh 25
Sanggau ○ RI 271 Lf 45
Sangha ~ CAM 333 Ha 45
Sānghar ○ PK 227 Jn 32
Sanghona ○ GNB 316 Fn 40
San Gil ○ CO 107 Dm 42
San Gimignano ○ I 185 Gm 24
Sangin ○ AFG 223 Jl 29
San Giovanni in Fiore ○ I 194 Ha 26
Sangiran ★ RI 278 Lf 49
Sangju ○ ROK 247 Lp 27
Sangkha Buri ○ THA 262 Kp 38
Sangkulirang ○ RI 274 Lj 45
Sângkŭm Ândet ○ K 263 Ld 39
Sangli ○ IND 238 Kb 37
Sangmelima ○ CAM 320 Gn 44
Sango ○ ZW 352 Hh 56
Sangôl ○ TR 195 Hg 26
Sangola ○ IND 238 Kb 37
Sangolquí ○ EC 116 Dj 46
Sangonera ~ E 184 Gf 27
Sangouani ○ CI 305 Gc 41
Sangouiné ○ CI 304 Gc 42
Sangowo ○ RI 275 Ma 44
Sangraduoro ~ BR 132 Ef 53
Sangre de Cristo Mountain ⩕ USA 65 Ck 26
San Gregorio ○ MEX 93 Db 38
Sangre Grande ○ TT 104 Ed 40
Sangrūr ○ IND 230 Kb 30
Sangsang ○ VRC 235 Kh 31
Sangue ~ BR 132 Ee 51
Sanguéya ○ RG 316 Fn 40
Sanguiana ○ RG 316 Ga 40
San Guillermo ○ RP 267 Ll 37
Sangutane ~ MOC 352 Hj 57
Sangutane ○ MOC 352 Hj 58
Sangwali ○ NAM 341 Hd 55
Sangwir River ~ LB 316 Gb 43
Sangzhi ○ VRC 255 Le 31
San Hilario ○ RA 140 Ee 59
Sâni ○ RIM 304 Ga 37
Sanibel ○ USA 87 Dg 32
Sanibel Island ♁ USA 87 Dg 32
San Ignacio ○ MEX 75 Cf 31
San Ignacio ○ MEX 80 Cg 32
San Ignacio ○ MEX 81 Cl 32
San Ignacio ○ MEX 92 Cj 34
San Ignacio ○ BH 93 Dd 37
San Ignacio ○ CR 97 Df 41
San Ignacio ○ YV 112 Ed 43
San Ignacio ○ PE 116 Dj 48
San Ignacio ○ PY 140 Ef 59
San Ignacio ○ RA 140 Eg 59
San Ignacio de Moxos ○ BOL 129 Eb 53
San Ignacio de Velasco ○ BOL 129 Ed 54
Sani Pass △ ZA 349 Hg 60
San Isidro ○ YV 112 Ed 42
San Isidro ○ RA 146 Ee 63
San Isidro ○ RP 267 Ln 40
San Isidro de El General ○ CR 97 Df 41
San Jacinto ○ PE 116 Dh 48
San Jaime ○ RA 146 Ee 61
San Javier ○ BOL 129 Eb 53
San Javier ~ RA 146 Ee 60
San Javier ○ RA 146 Ee 61
San Javier ○ E 184 Gf 27
San Javier de Loncomilla ○ RCH 137 Dn 63
Sanje ○ EAU 336 Hh 46
Sanjia ○ VRC 255 Lf 35
Sanjiang ○ VRC 255 Le 33
Sanjiaotang ○ VRC 259 Ll 31
Sanjō ○ J 251 Mf 27
San Joaquin ~ USA 64 Cb 27
San Joaquín ○ YV 112 Eb 41
San Joaquín ~ BOL 129 Ec 52
San Joaquin ○ RA 137 Ec 63
San Joaquin Valley ⌂ USA 64 Cb 27
San Jon ○ USA 65 Cl 28
San Jorge ~ CO 106 Dl 41
San Jorge ○ CO 107 Dp 43
San Jorge ○ RA 137 Ec 61
San Jorge ○ ROU 146 Eg 62
San Jorge Island ♁ SOL 290 Nb 50
San Jose ○ USA 64 Cb 27
San Jose ○ USA 71 Dd 25
San José ○ MEX 80 Cg 32
San José ○ GCA 93 Dc 39
San José ▣ CR 97 Df 41
San José Albán ○ CO 106 Dk 45
San José ○ YV 107 Dm 41
San José ○ PY 140 Ef 58
San José ○ RA 140 Eg 59
San Jose ~ RCH 147 Dm 65
San Jose ○ RP 267 Ll 38
San Jose ○ RP 267 Ll 39
San José d. l. Lajas ○ C 100 Dg 34
San José d. Pinhais ○ BR 141 Ek 58
San José de Buja ○ YV 112 Ec 41
San José de Chimbo ○ EC 116 Dj 46
San JosédeChiquitos ○ BOL 129 Ed 54
San José de Comondú ○ MEX 80 Cg 33
San José de Dimas ○ MEX 80 Cg 31
San José de Feliciano ○ RA 146 Ee 61
San José de Gracia ○ MEX 75 Cf 32
San José de Gracia ○ MEX 80 Ch 32
San José de Guajademi ○ MEX 75 Cf 32
San José de Guanipa El Tigrito ○ YV 112 Eb 41
San José de Guaribe ○ YV 112 Eb 41
San José de Guaviare ○ CO 107 Dm 44
San José de Jachál ○ RA 137 Dp 61
San José de la Dormida ○ RA 137 Ec 61
San José del Alto ○ PE 116 Dj 48
San José de la Madquina ○ RCH 147 Dm 65
San José del Cabo ○ MEX 80 Ch 34
San José del Monte ○ RP 267 Ll 38
San José del Morro ○ RA 137 Eb 62
San José de Maipo ○ RCH 137 Dn 62
San José de Mayo ○ ROU 146 Ef 63
San José de Ocoa ○ DOM 101 Dn 36
San José de Quero ○ PE 128 Dl 52
San José de Raices ○ MEX 81 Cm 33
San José do Ausentes ○ BR 146 Ej 60
San José do Xingu ○ BR 133 Eh 51
San José Iturbide ○ MEX 92 Cm 35
San José Norte ○ RA 136 Ea 59
San Juan ★ USA 50 Ca 21
San Juan ~ NIC 97 Df 40
San Juan ○ DOM 101 Dn 36
San Juan ~ DOM 101 Dn 36
San Juán ○ USA 104 Ea 36
San Juán ~ CO 106 Dk 43
San Juan ~ YV 112 Ec 41
San Juan ○ PE 128 Dl 53
San Juan ○ BOL 129 Ed 55
San Juan ○ RCH 136 Dp 57
San Juan ~ BOL 136 Eb 56
San Juan ~ RCH 137 Dn 60
San Juan ○ RA 137 Dp 61
San Juan ~ RA 137 Dp 61
San Juan ~ RA 137 Ea 62
San Juan ~ PY 140 Ee 57
San Juan ~ ROU 146 Ef 63
San Juan ○ RP 267 Ln 40
San Juan Bautista ○ PY 140 Ef 59
San Juan Bautista ○ RCH 147 Dj 62
San Juan d'Alacant ○ E 184 Gf 26
San Juan de Arama ○ CO 106 Dm 44
San Juán de Flores ○ HN 96 De 38
San Juan de Guadelupe ○ MEX 81 Cl 33
San Juan de la Costa ○ MEX 80 Cg 33
San Juán del Caite ○ HN 93 Dd 38
San Juan del César ○ CO 107 Dm 40
San Juán de Limay ○ NIC 96 De 39
San Juan de los Cayos ○ YV 107 Dp 40
San Juan de los Galdanos ○ YV 112 Ec 40
San Juan de los Lagos ○ MEX 92 Cl 35
San Juan de los Morros ○ YV 107 Ea 41
San Juan de los Planes ○ MEX 80 Ch 34
San Juan del Río ○ MEX 81 Ck 33
San Juan del Río ○ MEX 92 Cm 35
San Juán del Sur ○ NIC 96 Df 40
San Juan de Manpiare ○ YV 107 Ea 43
San Juan de Tocoma ○ YV 112 Ec 42
San Juan de Yanac ○ PE 128 Dl 52
San Juan Evangelista ○ MEX 93 Da 37
San Juan Islands ♁ USA 50 Ca 21
San Juanito ○ MEX 80 Cj 32
San Juan Mountain ⩕ USA 65 Cj 27
San Juan Nepomuceno ○ CO 106 Dl 41
San Juan River ~ USA 65 Cj 27
San Juan y Martínez ○ C 100 Df 34
San Julián ○ BOL 129 Ec 54
San Justo ○ RA 137 Ed 61
Sankamış ○ TR 202 Hp 25
Sankarani ~ RG 316 Gb 40
Sankarankovil ○ IND 239 Kc 41
Şankaya ○ TR 195 Hk 26
Sankha ○ THA 263 Lb 38
Sankt Anton ○ A 174 Gm 22
Sankt Gallen ○ CH 174 Gl 22
Sankt Moritz ○ CH 174 Gl 22
Sankt Peter-Ording ○ D 170 Gl 18
Sankt Pölten ○ A 174 Gp 21
Sankuru ~ RDC 333 Hc 48
Sankuru ~ RDC 333 Hd 48
San Leonardo de Yagüe ○ E 184 Ge 25
Sanlifan ○ VRC 243 Lh 30
Sanli Urfa ○ TR 195 Hm 27
San Loren ○ PY 140 Ef 58
San Lorenzo ○ USA 65 Cj 29
San Lorenzo ~ MEX 80 Cj 33
San Lorenzo ○ HN 96 De 39
San Lorenzo ○ CO 107 Dn 42
San Lorenzo ○ EC 116 Dh 46
San Lorenzo ○ EC 116 Dj 45
San Lorenzo ○ PE 128 Dp 51
San Lorenzo ○ RA 137 Ed 62
San Lorenzo ○ RA 146 Ee 60
San Lourdes ○ BOL 129 Dp 51
Sanlúcar de Barrameda ○ E 184 Gc 27
Sanlúcar la Mayor ○ E 184 Gc 27
San Luis ○ MEX 64 Ce 29
San Luis ○ USA 64 Ce 29
San Luis ○ USA 65 Ck 27
San Luís ○ GCA 93 Dd 37
San Luís ○ C 101 Dk 35
San Luis ○ CO 106 Dl 42
San Luis ○ YV 107 Dp 40
San Luis ○ PE 116 Dk 50
San Luís ○ RCH 136 Dp 59
San Luis ○ RA 137 Ea 62
San Luis ○ ROU 146 Eh 62
San Luis ○ RP 267 Ln 40
San Luis Canal ~ USA 64 Cb 27
San Luis del Cordero ○ MEX 81 Ck 33
San Luis del Palmar ○ RA 140 Ee 59
San luis de Shuaro ○ PE 128 Dl 51
San Luis Obispo ○ USA 64 Cb 28
San Luis Potosí ○ MEX 92 Cm 34
San Luis Reservoir ~ USA 64 Cb 27
San Luis Valley ⌂ USA 65 Cj 27
San Luiz de la Paz ○ MEX 92 Cm 35
Sanluri ○ I 185 Gl 26
San Marcos ♁ MEX 80 Cg 32
San Marcos ○ USA 81 Cn 30
San Marcos ○ MEX 92 Cn 37
San Marcos ○ GCA 93 Db 38
San Marcos ○ CO 106 Dl 41
San Marcos de Colón ○ HN 96 De 39
San Mariano ○ RP 267 Lm 37
San Marino □ RSM 185 Gm 24
San Marino ▣ RSM 185 Gn 24
San Marino ○ AUS 374 Md 60
San Martín ○ CO 106 Dm 44
San Martin ~ BOL 129 Ec 52
San Martin ○ RA 137 Ea 60
San Martín Chalchicuautla ○ MEX 92 Cn 35
San Martín de los Andes ○ RA 147 Dn 66
San Mateo ○ USA 64 Ca 27
San Mateo ○ USA 65 Cj 28
San Mateo ○ YV 112 Eb 41
San Mateo ○ EC 116 Dj 45
San Mateo Ixtatán ○ GCA 93 Dc 38
San Mateo Matengo ○ MEX 92 Cn 36
San Mateo Mountains ⩕ USA 65 Cj 28
San Matías ○ BR 132 Ee 54
Sanmen ○ VRC 259 Ll 31
Sanmen Wan ~ VRC 259 Ll 31
Sanmenxia ○ VRC 243 Lf 28
San Miguel ○ USA 64 Cb 28
San Miguel ○ USA 80 Cg 30
San Miguel ~ MEX 80 Cj 32
San Miguel ○ MEX 81 Cl 31
San Miguel ○ ES 93 Dd 39
San Miguel ○ PA 97 Dj 41
San Miguel ○ YV 112 Eb 41
San Miguel ○ EC 116 Dj 45
San Miguel ~ CO 116 Dk 45
San Miguel ○ PE 128 Dm 52
San Miguel ~ BOL 129 Ec 54
San Miguel ~ BOL 129 Ed 54
San Miguel ○ BR 133 Eh 52
San Miguel ○ RA 146 Ee 63
San Miguel ○ RA 146 Ef 60
San Miguel ○ RP 275 Lm 42
San Miguel Aloapan ○ MEX 92 Cp 37
San Miguel Bay ~ RP 267 Lm 39
San Miguel de Allende ○ MEX 92 Cm 35
San Miguel de Baga ○ C 101 Dk 35
San Miguel de Huachi ○ BOL 129 Ea 52
San Miguel del Monte ○ RA 146 Ee 63
San Miguel de los Bancos ○ EC 116 Dj 45
San Miguel de Pallaques ○ PE 116 Dj 49
San Miguel de Salcedo ○ EC 116 Dj 46
San Miguel de Tucumán ○ RA 136 Eb 59
San Miguel d'Oeste ○ BR 140 Eh 59
San Miguél do Guamá ○ BR 121 El 46
San Miguelito ○ MEX 80 Ch 30
San Miguelito ○ NIC 97 Df 40
San Miguelito ○ BOL 129 Dp 51
San Miguel River ~ USA 65 Ch 26
Sanming ○ VRC 258 Lj 32
San Narcisco ○ RP 267 Lk 38
Sännfjället △ S 158 Gn 14
San Nicolás ○ MEX 80 Ch 31
San Nicolas ○ MEX 81 Cm 33
San Nicolas ○ BOL 129 Eb 53
San Nicolas de los Arroyos ○ RA 137 Ed 62
San Nicolás de Tolentino ○ E 292 Fm 31
San Nicolas Island ♁ USA 64 Cc 29
San Nicolás Tolentino ○ MEX 92 Cm 34
Sânnicolau Mare ○ RO 174 Hc 22
Sannieshof ○ ZA 349 He 59
Sanniquellie ○ LB 316 Gb 42
Sannohe ○ J 250 Mg 25
Sano Eyre ~ RCH 152 Dl 70
Sanok ○ PL 174 Hd 21
San Onofre ○ CO 106 Dl 41
Sanoyea ○ LB 316 Ga 42
San Pablo ○ USA 64 Ca 26
San Pablo ○ C 100 Dj 35
San Pablo ○ CO 106 Dl 42
San Pablo ○ YV 107 Ea 42
San Pablo ~ PE 116 Dj 48
San Pablo ○ PE 116 Dj 49
San Pablo ~ BOL 129 Ec 53
San Pablo ○ RCH 147 Dm 66
San Pablo ○ RP 267 Ll 38
San Pablo de Lipez ○ BOL 136 Ea 56
San Pascual ○ RP 267 Lm 39
San Pedro ○ MEX 75 Cf 31
San Pedro ○ MEX 80 Cg 34
San Pedro ○ MEX 80 Ck 31
San Pedro ~ MEX 92 Ck 34
San Pedro ~ GCA 93 Dc 37
San Pedro ○ BH 93 De 37
San Pedro ~ C 100 Dj 35
San Pedro ○ YV 112 Eb 40
San Pedro ~ BOL 129 Ea 55
San Pedro ○ BOL 129 Ec 54
San Pedro ○ RCH 136 Dp 56
San Pedro ○ RA 136 Eb 58
San Pedro ○ RA 136 Eb 59
San Pedro ○ RCH 137 Dm 64
San Pedro ○ PY 140 Ef 58
San Pedro ○ RA 140 Eg 59
San Pedro ○ RA 146 Ee 62
San Pedro ○ RP 267 Lm 39
San Pédro ○ CI 305 Gc 43
San Pedro de Atacama ○ RCH 136 Dp 57
San Pedro de Buena Vista ○ BOL 129 Eb 55
San Pedro de Curahuara ○ BOL 128 Dp 54
San Pedro de la Cueva ○ MEX 80 Ch 31
San Pedro de la Roca ★ C 101 Dk 36
San Pedro de Las Bocas ○ YV 112 Ec 42
San Pedro de las Colonias ○ MEX 81 Cl 33
San Pedro de Lloc ○ PE 116 Dj 49
San Pedro del Norte ○ NIC 97 Df 39
San Pedro del Paraná ○ PY 140 Ef 59
San Pedro de Macoris ○ DOM 101 Dp 36
San Pedro de Quemes ○ BOL 136 Dp 56
San Pedro de Urabá ○ CO 106 Dk 41
San Pedro el Alto ○ MEX 93 Cp 37
San Pedro Huamelula ○ MEX 93 Da 37
San Pedro Lagunillas ○ MEX 92 Ck 35
San Pedro Norte ○ RA 137 Eb 61
San Pedro River ~ USA 65 Cg 29
San Pedro Sacatepéquez ○ GCA 93 Dc 38
San Pedro Sula ○ HN 93 Dd 38
San Petro ○ PE 128 Dn 51
San Petro de Cachi ○ PE 128 Dl 52
San Petro de Colalao ○ RA 136 Eb 59
San Piero a.S. ○ I 185 Gm 23
Sanpoku ○ J 251 Mf 26
Sanpoli ~ USA 50 Cc 21
Sanqingshan ★ VRC 258 Lj 31
Sanquianga ♀ CO 106 Dj 44
San Quintín ○ MEX 75 Cd 30
Sanra Ana de Yacuma ○ BOL 129 Eb 52
San Rafael ○ USA 64 Ca 27
San Rafael ○ MEX 80 Cg 31
San Rafael ○ MEX 80 Ck 32
San Rafael ○ MEX 81 Cm 33
San Rafael ~ MEX 81 Cn 34
San Rafael ○ CR 97 Df 40
San Rafael ○ CO 112 Ea 45
San Rafael ○ PE 116 Dk 51
San Rafael ○ BOL 128 Dp 52
San Rafael ○ BOL 129 Ed 54
San Rafael ~ BR 132 Ee 55
San Rafael ○ RA 137 Dp 63
San Rafael de Canagua ○ YV 107 Dp 41
San Rafael de Curiapo ○ YV 112 Ed 41
San Rafael del Moján ○ YV 107 Dn 40
San Rafael de Onoto ○ YV 107 Dp 41
San Rafael de Yuma ○ DOM 101 Dp 36
San Rafael Mountains ⩕ USA 64 Cb 28
San Rafael River ~ USA 65 Cg 26
San Ramón ○ CR 97 Df 40
San Ramón ○ PE 128 Dl 51
San Ramon ○ BOL 129 Eb 52
San Ramón ○ BOL 129 Ec 53
San Ramón ~ BOL 129 Ed 53
San Ramón ○ RCH 136 Dn 59
San Ramón ○ RA 137 Ea 61
San Ramón ○ ROU 146 Ef 63
San Ramón de la Nueva Oran ○ PY 136 Eb 57
San Remo ○ I 185 Gk 24
San Remo ○ AUS 379 Mj 65
San Roberto ○ MEX 81 Cm 33
San Roque ○ E 184 Gd 27
San Roque ○ RP 267 Ll 38
San Roque ○ RP 267 Ln 39
San Saba ○ USA 81 Cn 30
San Saba ~ USA 81 Cn 30
Sansalé ○ RG 316 Fn 40
San Salvador ♁ BS 87 Dl 33
San Salvador ▣ ES 93 Dd 39
San Salvador ○ RA 146 Ee 61
San Salvador ○ RA 146 Ef 60
San Salvador ~ ROU 146 Ef 62
San Salvador de Jujuy ○ RA 136 Eb 58
Sansanding ○ RMM 317 Gd 39
Sansanne-Mango ○ BF 317 Gg 40
Sansārpur ○ IND 234 Ke 31
San Sebastián ○ USA 104 Ea 36
San Sebastián ○ RA 152 Dp 72
San Sebastian ○ E 184 Ge 25
San Sebastian de la Gomera ○ E 292 Fm 31
San Sebastião do Vaturna ○ BR 120 Ee 47
San Sebatian de Yali ○ NIC 96 De 39
Sansepolcro ○ I 185 Gn 24
San Severo ○ I 194 Gp 25
Sansha Wan ~ VRC 259 Ll 32
Sanshui ○ VRC 258 Lg 34
Sansibar ♁ EAT 337 Hm 49
San Silvestre ○ YV 107 Dn 41
San Simon ○ USA 65 Ch 29
San Simón ~ BOL 129 Ec 52
Sanso ○ RMM 305 Gc 40
Sanstad ○ N 158 Gl 14
Sansui ○ VRC 255 Le 32
Sansundi ○ RI 283 Md 46
Sansu-ri ○ DVRK 247 Lp 25
Santa ○ PE 116 Dj 50
Santa ~ PE 116 Dj 50
Santa Adélia ○ BR 141 Ek 56
Santa Ana ○ USA 64 Cd 29
Santa Ana ○ MEX 80 Cg 30
Santa Ana ○ MEX 80 Ch 32
Santa Ana ○ ES 93 Dd 38
Santa Ana ○ HN 96 De 39
Santa Ana ○ C 100 Dj 34
Santa Ana ○ CO 106 Dl 41
Santa Ana ○ CO 106 Dl 44
Santa Ana ~ YV 107 Dm 41
Santa Ana ○ YV 112 Eb 41
Santa Ana ○ EC 116 Dh 46
Santa Ana ○ PE 128 Dl 53
Santa Ana ○ BR 132 Ee 55
Santa Ana ○ RA 140 Eg 59
Santa Ana ○ RP 267 Lm 36
Santa Ana Island ♁ SOL 290 Nd 51
Santa Anita ○ MEX 80 Ch 34
Santa Anna ○ USA 81 Cn 30
Santa Bárbara ○ USA 64 Cb 28
Santa Bárbara ○ MEX 80 Ck 32
Santa Barbara ○ HN 93 Dd 38
Santa Bárbara ○ DOM 101 Dp 36
Santa Bárbara ○ CO 106 Dl 43
Santa Bárbara ○ YV 107 Dn 42
Santa Bárbara ○ YV 107 Ea 44
Santa Bárbara ○ YV 112 Eb 41
Santa Bárbara ○ YV 112 Ec 41
Santa Bárbara ○ YV 112 Ec 42
Santa Barbara ~ BOL 129 Ed 54
Santa Bárbara ○ RCH 137 Dn 64
Santa Bárbara ○ BR 141 En 55
Santa Barbara Channel ~ USA 64 Cb 28
Santa Barbara do Sul ○ BR 146 Eh 60
Santa Barbara Island ♁ USA 64 Cc 29
Santa Brígida ○ BR 124 Fa 50
Santa Catalina ○ RA 136 Eb 58
Santa Catalina ○ RP 267 Lm 41
Santa Catalina Island ♁ USA 64 Cc 29
Santa Catarina ○ MEX 75 Ce 31
Santa Catarina ○ MEX 81 Cm 33
Santa Catarina ○ MEX 92 Cn 37
Santa Catarina ⊙ BR 140 Eh 59
Santa Catarina ○ CV 316 Fj 38
Santa Cecilia ○ BR 140 Ej 59
Santa Clara ○ C 100 Dj 34
Santa Clara ○ YV 112 Eb 41
Santa Clara ○ BR 121 Ej 46
Santa Clara ○ BR 132 Ee 54
Santa Clara ~ BR 132 Ee 54
Santa Clara ○ RA 136 Eb 58
Santa Clarita ○ USA 64 Cc 28
Santa Clotilde ○ PE 116 Dm 47
Santa Cruz ○ USA 64 Ca 27
Santa Cruz ○ CR 96 Df 40
Santa Cruz ○ YV 107 Dp 42
Santa Cruz ○ YV 112 Ed 42
Santa Cruz ○ PE 116 Dk 51
Santa Cruz ○ PE 116 Dl 48
Santa Cruz ○ BR 124 Ep 50
Santa Cruz ○ BR 124 Fb 49
Santa Cruz ~ PY 136 Eb 57
Santa Cruz ○ RA 136 Eb 57
Santa Cruz ○ RCH 137 Dn 63
Santa Cruz ○ BR 140 Ef 56
Santa Cruz ○ BR 141 El 56
Santa Cruz ~ RA 152 Dn 71
Santa Cruz ○ RA 152 Dp 71
Santa Cruz ○ RP 267 Lk 38
Santa Cruz ○ RP 267 Ll 39
Santa Cruz ○ RP 275 Ln 42
Santa Cruz Cabrália ○ BR 125 Fa 54
Santa Cruz d.N. ○ C 100 Dh 34
Santa Cruz de Bucaral ○ YV 107 Dp 40
Santa Cruz de la Palma ○ E 292 Fm 31
Santa Cruz de la Sierra ○ BOL 129 Ec 54
Santa Cruz del Quiché ○ GCA 93 Dc 38
Santa Cruz del Sur ○ C 100 Dk 35
Santa Cruz de Mompox ○ CO 106 Dl 41
Santa Cruz de Tenerife ○ E 292 Fm 31
Santa Cruz do Arari ○ BR 121 Ek 46
Santa Cruz do Capibaribe ○ BR 124 Fb 49
Santa Cruz do Sul ○ BR 146 Eh 60
Santa Cruz do Xingu ○ BR 133 Eh 51
Santa Cruz Island ♁ SOL 35 Ta 11
Santa Cruz Island ♁ USA 64 Cc 28
Santa Deustua ○ PE 128 Dl 53
Santa do Salitre ○ BR 133 El 55
Santa Eduwiges ○ MEX 80 Cg 31
Santa Efigênia de Minas ○ BR 141 En 55

466 San Clemente Island - Santa Efigênia de Minas

Santa Elena O MEX 81 Cl 32
Santa Elena O YV 112 Ec 41
Santa Elena O PE 116 Dl 49
Santa Elena O RA 137 Ed 64
Santa Elena O RA 146 Ee 61
Santa Elena de Uairén O YV 112 Ed 43
Santa Eleodora O RA 137 Ec 63
Santa Eugenia O E 184 Gb 24
Santa Eulalia O MEX 81 Cm 31
Santa Fe O USA 65 Ck 28
Santa Fé O PA 97 Dh 41
Santa Fé O CO 107 Dm 42
Santa Fé O PE 116 Dm 48
Santa Fé O RA 137 Ed 61
Santafe O E 184 Ge 27
Santa Fe O RP 267 Ll 39
Santa Fe de Bogotá Bogotá ▣ CO 106 Dl 43
Santa Fé del Pino O MEX 81 Cl 31
Santa Fé de Minas O BR 133 Em 54
Santa Fé do Sul O BR 140 Ej 56
Santa Filomena O BR 121 Em 50
Santa Helena O BR 121 Em 47
Santa Helena O BR 140 Eg 58
Santa Helena de Cusima O CO 107 Dm 43
Santa Helena de Goiás O BR 133 Ej 54
Santai O VRC 242 Lc 30
Santa Ines O USA 64 Cb 28
Santa Inés O YV 107 Dp 40
Santa Inés O YV 112 Eb 41
Santa Inês O BR 121 Em 47
Santa Inês O BR 125 Fa 52
Santa Isabel ~ GCA 93 Dd 38
Santa Isabel O PA 97 Dj 41
Santa Isabel O EC 116 Dj 47
Santa Isabel O PE 116 Dl 48
Santa Isabel O RA 137 Ea 64
Santa Isabel ◭ SOL 290 Nb 49
Santa Isabel d'Oeste O BR 140 Eh 58
Santa Isabel do Para O BR 121 Ek 46
Santa Isabel do Rio Negro O BR 117 Eb 46
Santa Juliana O BR 133 El 55
Santa La Cuata ⚲ YV 107 Dn 41
Santa Lucía O C 100 Df 34
Santa Lucía O RA 137 Dp 61
Santa Lucía O RA 146 Ee 60
Santa Lucía ~ RA 146 Ee 60
Santa Lucía O ROU 146 Ef 63
Santa Lucía O ROU 146 Eg 63
Santa Lucia Range ⛰ USA 64 Cb 27
Santa Luisa O RCH 136 Dn 58
Santa Luz O BR 121 Em 50
Santaluz O BR 125 Fa 51
Santa Luzia O BR 120 Ed 45
Santa Luzia O BR 121 Em 48
Santa Luzia O BR 124 Fb 49
Santa Luzia O BR 125 Fa 53
Santa Luzia O BR 141 En 55
Santa Luzia ◭ CV 316 Fh 37
Santa Luzia do Pará O BR 121 El 46
Santa Luzia do Paruá O BR 121 Em 47
Santa Magdalena O RA 137 Eb 63
Santa Maria O USA 64 Cb 28
Santa Maria ~ MEX 92 Cm 35
Santa María O HN 96 De 38
Santa María O CR 97 Df 41
Santa María ~ PA 97 Dh 41
Santa María O CO 107 Dm 43
Santa María O YV 107 Dn 41
Santa Maria O YV 112 Ec 40
Santa Maria O BR 120 Ee 48
Santa Maria ~ BR 121 Ek 49
Santa María ~ RA 136 Eb 59
Santa Maria O BR 146 Eh 60
Santa Maria O CV 316 Fj 37
Santa Maria O ANG 340 Gn 52
Santa Maria da Boavista O BR 124 Ep 50
Santa Maria das Barreiras O BR 121 Ek 50
Santa María de Ipire O YV 112 Eb 41
Santa Maria de Jebitá O BR 141 Ep 55
Santa María del Oro O MEX 80 Ck 33
Santa María de Los Guaicas O YV 112 Eb 44
Santa María del Río O MEX 92 Cm 35
Santa María del Valle O PE 116 Dk 50
Santa María de Nanay O PE 116 Dm 47
Santa María de Nieva O PE 116 Dk 48
Santa Maria de Vitória O BR 133 Em 52
Santa Maria do Para O BR 121 El 46
Santa Maria do Suaçui O BR 125 En 55
Santa Maria Huatulco O MEX 93 Cp 38
Santa Marta O CO 106 Dl 40
Santa Marta O ANG 340 Gn 52
Santa Monica O USA 64 Cc 29
Santan O RI 274 Lj 46
Santana O CO 107 Dm 42
Santana O BR 121 Ej 46
Santana ~ BR 124 En 50
Santana O BR 133 Em 52
Santana O P 292 Fm 29
Santana da Boa Vista O BR 146 Eh 61
Santana de Ipanema O BR 124 Fb 50
Santana de Pirapama O BR 133 Em 55
Santana do Acaraú O BR 124 Ep 47
Santana do Araguaía O BR 121 Ej 50
Santana do Itarare O BR 140 Ek 57
Santana do Livramento O BR 146 Ef 61
Santana do Manhuaçu O BR 141 En 56
Santana do Matos O BR 124 Fb 48
Santander O CO 106 Dk 44
Santander O E 184 Ge 24
Santander O RP 267 Lm 41
Santander Jiménez O MEX 81 Cn 33
Santa Nevada ⚲ YV 107 Dn 41
Santantadibe ~ RB 341 Hd 55
Sant Antíoco O I 185 Gk 26
Sant Antoni O E 184 Gg 26
Santanyi O E 185 Gh 26
Santao △ VU 386 Ng 55
Santa Oballa O E 184 Gd 26
Santa Paula O USA 64 Cc 28
Santa Pilomena O BR 124 Ep 50
Santa Pola O E 184 Gf 26
Santa Quitéria O BR 124 Ep 48
Santa Quitéria do Maranhão O BR 124 En 47
Santarám O P 184 Gb 26
Santarém O BR 120 Eg 47
Santarém Novo O BR 121 El 46
Santa Rita O MEX 80 Cg 33
Santa Rita O HN 96 De 38
Santa Rita O PA 97 Dh 41
Santa Rita O YV 107 Dn 40
Santa Rita O CO 107 Dp 43
Santa Rita O YV 107 Ea 41
Santa Rita O YV 112 Ec 41
Santa Rita O BR 117 Dp 47
Santa Rita O BR 124 Fc 49
Santa Rita ~ RA 136 Eb 58
Santa Rita de Caldas O BR 141 El 57
Santa Rita de Cássia O BR 133 Em 51
Santa Rita do Araguaia O BR 133 Eh 54
Santa Rita do Sul O BR 146 Ej 61
Santa Rosa O USA 64 Ca 26
Santa Rosa O USA 65 Cg 29
Santa Rosa O USA 65 Ck 28
Santa Rosa O CO 106 Dk 45
Santa Rosa O YV 107 Dp 42
Santa Rosa O CO 107 Dp 44
Santa Rosa O YV 112 Eb 41
Santa Rosa O EC 116 Dj 47
Santa Rosa O PE 128 Dn 53
Santa Rosa O BOL 129 Ea 51
Santa Rosa O BOL 129 Ea 52
Santa Rosa ~ BOL 129 Ea 54
Santa Rosa O RA 137 Eb 64
Santa Rosa O BR 140 Eg 59
Santa Rosa O RA 146 Ee 60
Santa Rosa Beach O USA 86 De 30
Santa Rosa de Amonadona O YV 112 Ea 45
Santa Rosa de Copán O HN 93 Dd 38
Santa Rosa del Conlara O RA 137 Eb 62
Santa Rosa de Lima O ES 93 Dd 39
Santa Rosa de los Pastos Grandes O RA 136 Ea 58
Santa Rosa de Quijos O EC 116 Dk 46
Santa Rosa de Viterbo O BR 141 El 56
Santa Rosa do Tocantins O BR 133 Ek 51
Santa Rosa Island ◭ USA 64 Cb 29
Santa Rosa Lake ~ USA 65 Ck 28
Santa Rosalía O MEX 75 Cf 32
Santa Rosalia O YV 112 Eb 42
Šantarskie ostrova ◭ RUS 205 Xa 7
Santa Si ★ VRC 254 Kp 33
Santa Sylvina O RA 136 Ed 59
Santa Teresa O MEX 81 Cn 33
Santa Teresa O YV 107 Ea 40
Santa Teresa ~ BR 133 Ek 51
Santa Teresa ~ BR 133 Ek 52
Santa Teresa O RA 137 Ed 62
Santa Teresa d. G. O I 185 Gl 25
Santa Teresa de Goiás O BR 133 Ek 52
Santa Teresita O RA 146 Ef 64
Santa Terezinha O BR 133 Ej 51
Santa Terezinha de Goiás O BR 133 Ek 53
Santa Theresa O AUS 374 Md 58
Santa Theresa Aboriginal Land ••• AUS 374 Md 57
Santa Victoria O PY 136 Ec 57
Santa Vitória do Palmar O BR 146 Eh 62
Santchou O CAM 320 Gl 43
Santee ~ USA 87 Dj 29
Santee Indian Reservation ••• USA 56 Cp 24
Santiago O MEX 80 Ch 34
Santiago ~ MEX 81 Cl 33
Santiago O MEX 81 Cm 33
Santiago O PA 97 Dh 41
Santiago O CO 107 Dm 42
Santiago O EC 116 Dj 47
Santiago ~ PE 116 Dk 47
Santiago O PE 128 Dl 53
Santiago O BR 132 Ee 55
Santiago ▣ RCH 137 Dn 62
Santiago O BR 146 Eg 60
Santiago O RP 267 Ll 37
Santiago ◭ CV 316 Fj 38
Santiago Atitlán O GCA 93 Dc 38
Santiago Chazumba O MEX 92 Cp 35
Santiago d. T. O E 292 Fm 31
Santiago de Cao O PE 116 Dj 49
Santiago de Chocorvos O PE 128 Dl 52
Santiago de Chuco O PE 116 Dj 50
Santiago de Compostela O E 184 Gb 24
Santiago de Cuba O C 101 Dl 35
Santiago del Estero O RA 136 Eb 59
Santiago de los Caballeros O DOM 101 Dn 36
Santiago de Machaca O BOL 128 Dp 54
Santiago Ixcuintla O MEX 92 Ck 35
Santiago los Caballeros O MEX 80 Cj 33
Santiago Mountains ⛰ USA 81 Cl 30
Santiago Papasquiaro O MEX 80 Ck 33
Santiago Papasquiaro ~ MEX 80 Ck 33
Santiago Peak △ USA 81 Cl 31
Santiago Tamazola O MEX 92 Cn 37
Santiago Tuxtla O MEX 93 Da 36
Santiago Yosondúa O MEX 92 Cp 36
San Tiburcio O MEX 81 Cm 33
Santigi O RI 275 Ll 45
Santiguila O RMM 305 Gc 39
Säntis △ CH 174 Gl 22
Sant Joan de Labritja O E 184 Gg 26
Santo Andre O BR 141 El 57
Santo André O ANG 340 Gp 52
Santo Ângelo O BR 146 Eg 60
Santo Ant. de Lisboa O BR 124 Ep 49
Santo Ant. do Amparo O BR 141 Em 56
Santo Ant. do Monte O BR 141 Em 56
Santo Antònio do Içá O BR 117 Ea 47
Santo Antão ◭ CV 30 Hb 8
Santo Antão ◭ CV 316 Fh 37
Santo Antonio O BR 120 Ed 47
Santo Antônio O BR 124 Fc 49
Santo Antonio ~ BR 133 Ek 51
Santo António O CV 316 Fj 38
Santo Antônio da Platina O BR 140 Ej 57
Santo Antonio de Leverger O BR 132 Ef 53
Santo Antônio de Pádua O BR 141 En 56
Santo Antônio de Patrulha O BR 146 Ej 60
Santo Antônio dos Lopes O BR 121 Em 48
Santo Antônio do Sudoeste O BR 140 Eh 58
Santo Corrazón O BR 132 Ee 54
Santo Domingo O MEX 92 Cm 34
Santo Domingo ~ MEX 92 Cp 36
Santo Domingo ~ MEX 93 Dc 37
Santo Domingo O NIC 97 Df 39
Santo Domingo O C 100 Dh 34
Santo Domingo ▣ DOM 101 Dn 36
Santo Domingo ~ YV 107 Dn 41
Santo Domingo O RA 136 Ec 58
Santo Domingo de los Colerados O EC 116 Dj 46
Santo Domingo Pueblo O USA 65 Cj 28
Santo Estêvão O BR 125 Fa 52
Santo Inácio do Piauí O BR 124 Ep 49
Santo Lugares O RA 136 Ec 59
San Tomé O YV 112 Eb 41
Santópolis do Aguapeí O BR 140 Ej 56
Santoríni ◭ GR 194 He 27
Santos O BR 141 El 57
Santos O AUS 374 Mg 60
Santos Dumont O BR 141 En 56
Santos Mercado O BOL 117 Ea 50
Santos Plateau ▾ 15 Gb 12
Santo Thomas O RP 275 Ln 42
Santo Tirso O P 184 Gb 25
Santo Tomás O MEX 80 Cj 31
Santo Tomás O NIC 97 Df 39
Santo Tomas O PA 97 Dg 41
Santo Tomás △ EC 128 Dc 46
Santo Tomás O PE 128 Dm 53
Santo Tomás ~ PE 128 Dm 53
Santo Tomas O RP 275 Ln 42
Santo Tomé O RA 137 Ed 61
Santo Tomé O RA 146 Ef 60
Santuario de la Coromonto O YV 107 Dp 41
Sanur O RI 279 Lh 50
San Vicente O MEX 75 Cd 30
San Vicente O ES 93 Dd 39
San Vicente O YV 107 Ea 43
San Vicente O YV 112 Ec 40
San Vicente del Caguan O CO 106 Dl 44
San Vicente de Tagua O RCH 137 Dn 63
San Vicente Tancuayalab O MEX 92 Cn 35
San Victor O GUY 112 Ed 42
San Victor O RA 146 Ee 61
San Vincente O BOL 136 Ea 56
San Vincente de Cañete O PE 116 Dk 52
San Vito O CR 97 Dg 41
San Xavier Indian Reservation ••• USA 80 Cg 30
Sanya O VRC 255 Le 36
Sanya Juu O EAT 337 Hl 47
Sanyangkeng O VRC 258 Lk 31
Sanyat ad Daffah O LAR 300 He 30
Sanyati O ZW 341 Hg 54
Sanyati ~ ZW 341 Hg 54
Sanying O VRC 243 Lc 27
San Ysidro O USA 65 Cj 28
Sanyuan O VRC 243 Le 28
Sanza Pombo O ANG 332 Gp 49
São Amaro O BR 125 Fa 52
São André O BR 133 El 54
Sao Ant. de Jesus O BR 125 Fa 52
São Antônia O BR 112 Ed 44
São Antônio O BR 121 Ej 45
São Antônio ~ BR 141 En 55
São Antônio O STP 332 Gk 45
São Antônio da Abunari O BR 120 Ed 46
São Antônio das Missões O BR 146 Eg 60
São Antônio do Jacinto O BR 125 Ep 54
São Bartolomeu ~ BR 133 El 54
São Benedito ~ BR 120 Ef 50
São Benedito ~ BR 120 Eg 50
São Benedito do Rio Preto O BR 124 En 47
São Bento O BR 121 Em 47
São Bento do Norte O BR 124 Fb 48
Sao Bento do Una O BR 124 Fb 50
São Bernardo O BR 124 En 47
São Borja O BR 146 Eg 60
São Caetano de Odivelas O BR 121 Ek 46
São Caitano O BR 124 Fb 50
São Canuto O BR 146 Eg 60
São Carlos O BR 140 Eh 59
São Carlos O BR 141 Ek 57
Sao Comba Dão O P 184 Gb 25
São Cristóvão O BR 125 Fb 51
São Cristóvão O ANG 340 Gn 52
São Cruz ~ BR 133 El 54
São Desidério O BR 133 Em 52
São Domingos O BR 133 El 52
São Domingos ~ BR 133 El 52
Sao Domingos O GNB 316 Fm 39
São Domingos da Maranhão O BR 121 Em 48
Sao Domingos do Azeitão O BR 121 Em 49
São Felício O BR 113 Eh 45
São Felipe O BR 112 Ea 45
São Felix de Balsas O BR 121 Em 49
São Felix do Xingu O BR 121 Ej 49
São Ferrnando ~ BR 132 Ee 54
São Fidélis O BR 141 Ep 56
São Filipe O CV 316 Fh 38
São Francisco ~ BR 124 Ep 50
São Francisco ~ BR 124 Fb 50
São Francisco ~ BR 125 En 51
São Francisco ~ BR 125 En 53
São Francisco ~ BR 125 Ep 53
São Francisco ~ BR 133 Em 53
São Francisco ~ BR 133 Em 54
São Francisco ~ BR 133 Em 55
São Francisco ~ BR 141 El 56
São Francisco de Assis O BR 146 Eg 60
São Francisco de Paula O BR 146 Ej 60
São Francisco do Maranhão O BR 124 En 49
São Gabriel O BR 146 Eg 61
São Gabriel da Cachoeira O BR 117 Dp 46
São Gabriel da Cachoeira O BR 117 Ea 46
São Gabriel da Palha O BR 141 Ep 55
São Gabriel d'Oeste O BR 132 Eg 55
São Geraldo do Araguia O BR 121 Ek 49
São Gonçalo O BR 141 En 57
São Gonçalo do Abaeté O BR 133 Em 55
São Gonçalo do Amarante O BR 124 Fa 47
São Gonçalo do Rio O BR 141 En 55
São Gonçalo do Supucaí O BR 141 Em 56
São Gotardo O BR 133 El 55
Sao Hill O EAT 337 Hk 50
São Inácio O BR 140 Eh 57
São Jerônimo Butiá O BR 146 Eh 61
São Jerônimo da Serra O BR 140 Ej 57
São João O BR 117 Ea 46
São João O BR 120 Ed 48
São João ~ BR 125 Ep 54
São João ~ BR 133 Ej 52
São João Batista O BR 121 Em 47
São João da Alicança O BR 133 El 53
São João da Baliza O BR 120 Ee 45
São João da Barra ~ BR 120 Ee 50
São João da Barra O BR 141 Ep 56
São João da Paracajuba O BR 121 Ej 46
São João da Ponte O BR 125 En 53
São João de Araguaia O BR 121 Ek 48
São João de Cortes O BR 121 Em 47
São João del Rei O BR 141 Em 56
São João de Meriti O BR 141 En 57
São João do Caçiporé O BR 113 Ej 44
São João do Caiuá O BR 140 Eh 57
São João do Paraíso O BR 125 En 53
São João do Piauí O BR 124 En 50
São João do Sabuji O BR 124 Fb 49
São João dos Patos O BR 124 En 49
São João Evangelista O BR 141 En 55
São Joaquim O BR 117 Dp 46
São Joaquim O BR 117 Ea 46
São Joaquim O BR 146 Ej 60
São Joaquim da Barra O BR 141 El 56
Sao Jorge ◭ P 18 Ha 6
São Jorge do Jvaí O BR 140 Eh 57
São Jorge do Limpopo O MOC 352 Hj 57
São José O BR 121 Ek 47
São José O BR 141 Ek 59
São José d. Campos O BR 141 El 57
São José de Anauá O BR 120 Ed 45
São José de Boa Vista O BR 141 El 56
São José de Mipibu O BR 124 Fc 49
São José de Piranhas O BR 124 Fa 49
São José de Ribamar O BR 121 Em 47
São José do Barreiro O BR 141 Em 57
São José do Belmonte O BR 124 Fa 49
São José do Cerrito O BR 140 Ej 59
São José do Egito O BR 124 Fb 49
São José do Norte O BR 146 Eh 62
São José do Peixe O BR 124 En 49
São José do Prado O BR 125 Fa 54
São José do Rio Claro O BR 132 Ef 52
São José do Rio Preto O BR 140 Ek 56
São José dos Dourados ~ BR 140 Ej 56
São Lourenço ~ BR 132 Ef 54
São Lourenço ~ BR 132 Eg 54
São Lourenço O BR 141 Em 57
São Lourenço do Sul O BR 146 Ej 61
São Lucas O ANG 340 Ha 51
São Luis O BR 121 Em 47
São Luís de Montes Belos O BR 133 Ej 54
São Luís do Curu O BR 124 Fa 47
São Luis do Paraitinga O BR 141 Em 57
São Luis do Quitunde O BR 124 Fc 50
São Luis do Tapajós O BR 120 Ef 48
São Luis Gonzaga O BR 146 Eg 60
São Luis Gonzaga do Maranhão O BR 121 Em 48
São Luzia do Paçuí O BR 121 Ej 45
São Manuel O BR 141 Ek 57
São Manuel ou Teles Pires ~ BR 120 Ef 50
São Marco ~ BR 133 El 54
São Marcos O BR 146 Ej 60
São Mateus O BR 141 Fa 55
São Mateus do Maranhão O BR 121 Em 47
São Mateus do Sul O BR 140 Ej 58
São Miguel ◭ P 18 Hb 6
São Miguel O BR 121 Ej 45
São Miguel ~ BR 132 Ef 52
São Miguel Arcanjo O BR 141 El 57
São Miguel das Missões O BR 146 Eg 60
São Miguel do Araguaia O BR 133 Ej 52
São Miguel do Iquaçu O BR 140 Eg 58
São Miguel dos Campos O BR 124 Fb 50
São Miguel dos Macacos O BR 121 Ej 46
São Miguel do Tapuio O BR 124 Ep 48
Saona Island ◭ DOM 101 Dp 36
Saône ~ F 163 Gk 22
Saoner O IND 234 Kd 35
São Nicolau ◭ CV 30 Hb 8
São Nicolau ~ BR 124 Ep 48
São Nicolau O BR 146 Eg 60
São Nicolau ◭ CV 316 Fj 37
São Onofre ~ BR 125 En 52
São Paulo ◭ BR 30 Hb 9
São Paulo ⊙ BR 140 Ej 56
São Paulo O BR 141 El 57
São Paulo de Olivença O BR 117 Dp 47
São Pedro O BR 117 Dp 46
São Pedro O BR 117 Ea 46
São Pedro O BR 121 Ej 47
São Pedro ~ BR 124 Ep 49
São Pedro ~ BR 129 Ed 51
São Pedro ~ BR 133 El 54
São Pedro O BR 141 Ek 57
São Pedro O CV 316 Fh 37
São Pedro da Aldeia O BR 141 En 57
São Pedro da Garça O BR 133 Em 54
Sao Pedro do Piauí O BR 124 En 48
São Pedro dos Crentes O BR 121 El 49
São Pedro do Sul O BR 146 Eg 60
São Raimundo das Mangabeiras O BR 121 Em 49
São Raimundo Nonanto O BR 124 En 50
São Ramão O BR 133 Em 54
São Romão O BR 117 Ea 48
São Sebastião O BR 141 Em 57
São Sebastião da Boa Vista O BR 121 Ek 46
São Sebastião do Caí O BR 146 Ej 60
São Sebastião do Maranhão O BR 125 En 55
São Sebastião do Paraíso O BR 141 El 56
Sao Sebastião do Passe O BR 125 Fa 52
São Sebastião dos Poções O BR 133 Em 53
São Sebastião do Tocantins O BR 121 Ek 48
São Sepé O BR 146 Eh 61
São Simao O BR 133 Ej 55
São Simão ou Branca ~ BR 129 Ec 52
São Teotónio O P 184 Gb 27
São Tiago ◭ CV 30 Hb 8
São Tomé O BR 124 Fc 49
São Tomé O BR 141 Ep 57
São Tomé ▣ STP 332 Gk 45
São Tomé and Principe □ STP 332 Gk 45
São Valentim O BR 140 Eh 59
São Vicente O BR 121 Ej 46
São Vicente ~ BR 124 Ep 49
São Vicente O BR 132 Eg 53
São Vicente O BR 141 El 57
São Vicente do Sul O BR 146 Eg 60
São Vicente Ferrer O BR 121 Em 47
São Vicento ◭ CV 30 Hb 8
Sapang O MAL 274 Lk 43
Sapão ~ BR 133 Em 51
Saparua O RI 283 Ma 47
Sapé O BR 124 Fc 49
Sape O RI 279 Lk 50
Sapele O WAN 320 Gj 43
Sapelo Island ◭ USA 87 Dh 30
Sapěrnoe O RUS 171 Hg 15
Sápes O GR 194 He 25
Sapiranga O BR 146 Ej 60
Sapiranga do Sul O BR 146 Ej 60
Šapki O RUS 171 Hh 16
Sapo ~ SUD 324 Hf 41
Sapoba O WAN 320 Gj 42
Sapodilla Cays ◭ BH 93 Dd 37
Saponé O BF 317 Gf 39
Sapo-Sapo O RDC 333 Hd 48
Saposoa O PE 116 Dk 49
Sapoti ~ BR 120 Ed 49
Sapouy O BF 317 Gf 40
Sappho O USA 50 Bp 21
Sapporo O J 250 Mg 24
Sapri O I 194 Gp 25
Sapucaí ~ BR 141 Ek 56
Sapucaia O BR 120 Ef 47
Sapucaia O BR 121 Ek 49
Sapucaia O BR 141 En 57
Sapulpa O USA 70 Cp 28
Sapulu O RI 279 Lg 49
Sapulut O MAL 274 Lj 43
Sapwe O RDC 341 Hg 51
Saqadī O SUD 313 Hj 39
Sāqain O YE 218 Hp 37
Šāqīya O IRQ 209 Hp 28
Šaqlāwa O IRQ 209 Ja 27
Saqqat al-Harīta ▭ KSA 218 Jb 37
Saqqez O IR 209 Jb 27
Šaqr O YE 219 Jd 38
Šaqrā O KSA 215 Ja 33
Šaqrā' O YE 218 Ja 39
Saqū O IR 226 Jg 32
Sarā O IR 202 Jc 26
Sara O RP 267 Lm 40
Sara O RI 283 Mc 47
Sara O BF 317 Ge 40
Sarāb O IR 209 Jb 27
Sarabaya O BOL 128 Dp 55
Sarāb Dōre O IR 209 Jb 29
Šaraburi O THA 262 La 38
Šaraf al-Ba'l O KSA 214 Hk 31
Sarafara ~ SUD 312 Hh 40
Saraf Doungous O TCH 321 Hb 39
Saraféré O RMM 305 Ge 38
Šarafğegān O IR 222 Jd 28
Šarafhāne O IR 209 Ja 26
Sarafšan O UZB 223 Jk 25
Saraguro O EC 116 Dj 47
Sarahs O IR 223 Jj 27
Sarahuru O ZW 352 Hh 56
Sarai O RUS 181 Hn 19
Saraipālia O IND 234 Kf 35
Sarajevo ▣ BIH 194 Hb 24
Sara-Kawa O RT 317 Gg 41
Saraland O USA 86 Dd 30
Saramacca ~ SME 113 Eg 43
Saramati △ IND 254 Km 33
Saran O AFG 223 Jn 29
Saranac Lake O USA 60 Dl 23
Saranda O EAT 337 Hk 48
Sarande O AL 194 Hc 26
Sarandi O BR 140 Eh 59
Sarandi del Yi O ROU 146 Eg 62
Sarandi de Navarro O ROU 146 Ef 62
Sarandi Grande O ROU 146 Ef 62
Sarang O IND 254 Km 32
Sarangani Bay ~ RP 275 Ln 43
Sarangani Islands ◭ RP 275 Ln 43
Sārangpur O IND 234 Kc 34
Saransk O RUS 181 Ja 18
Sarāpāli O IND 235 Kg 35
Sarapul O RUS 19 Mb 4
Sarapul O RUS 154 Rb 7
Saraqeb O SYR 208 Hl 28
Sarār O YE 219 Jd 38
Sarare ~ YV 107 Dn 42
Sarare ~ BR 132 Ee 53
Sarasota O USA 87 Dg 32
Sarata ~ UA 175 Hg 22
Saratoga O USA 65 Cj 25
Saratoga Hot Springs ★ USA 65 Cj 25
Saratoga Springs O USA 60 Dl 24
Saratok O MAL 271 Lf 45
Saratov O RUS 181 Jb 20
Sarāvān O IR 226 Jk 32
Saravan O LAO 263 Ld 38
Saray O TR 195 Hf 25
Saraya O SN 316 Ga 39
Šarāyān O IR 222 Jh 29
Sarbakty O KZ 204 Ta 8
Sarbāz O IR 226 Jj 32
Sarbāz ▭ IR 226 Jj 32
Sarbiše O IR 222 Jh 29
Sarco O RCH 137 Dn 60
Sarda ~ NEP 234 Ke 31
Sardanga O RUS 204 Vc 6
Sardara O KZ 223 Jm 25
Sardara Sukojmasi ~ KZ 223 Jn 25
Sardārshahr O IND 234 Kb 31
Sardašt O IR 209 Ja 27
Sardašt O IR 215 Jd 30
Sarde Band ~ AFG 223 Jn 29
Sardegna ⊙ I 185 Gl 25
Sardinas O MEX 80 Ck 32
Sardinata O CO 107 Dm 41
Sardinia ◭ I 185 Gl 25
Sardinien ◭ I 185 Gk 25
Sardis Lake ~ USA 70 Da 28
Sar'ein O IR 209 Jb 26
Saré-Kali O RG 316 Fp 40
Sareks ⚲ S 158 Ha 12
Saré Ndiaye O SN 316 Fn 39
Sar-e Pol O AFG 223 Jl 27
Sar-e Pol ~ AFG 223 Jl 27
Sar-e Pol-e Zahāb O IR 209 Ja 28
Saréyamou O RMM 305 Ge 37
Sargapur O IND 238 Kc 37
Sargasso Sea ≈ 11 Fa 7
Sargento Ayte Victor Sanabria O RA 136 Ed 58
Sargents O AUS 364 Mb 52
Sargodha O PK 230 Ka 30
Sarh O TCH 321 Hb 41
Sarhala O CI 305 Gc 41
Sārī O IR 222 Je 27
Sariā ~ BR 117 Eb 49
Saria ◭ GR 195 Hf 28
Saria O IND 230 Kb 29
Sariba Island ◭ PNG 287 Mm 51
Saric O MEX 80 Cg 30
Šārif O YE 219 Jd 37
Sarigan ◭ USA 27 Sa 8
Sarikei O MAL 271 Lf 44
Sarina O CDN 57 Dg 24
Sarina O AUS 375 Ml 56
Sarinleey O SP 325 Hn 44
Saripari O RI 279 Lh 46
Sarīr ▭ LAR 309 Ha 33
Sarīr al Qattūsah ▭ LAR 297 Gp 32
Sariri O PNG 287 Ml 50
Sarīr Tibesti ▭ LAR 309 Ha 34
Sarīr Umm ,Illah ▭ LAR 297 Gn 32
Sariwon O DVRK 247 Ln 26
Sar'ja O RUS 154 Ra 7
Sark ◭ GB 163 Ge 21
Sarkari Tala O IND 227 Jp 32
Šarki Karaağaç O TR 195 Hh 26
Sarkin O KZ 181 Jd 21
Sarkinkudu O WAN 320 Gl 41
Şarkışla O TR 195 Hl 26

Santa Elena - Şarkışla 467

□Country ▣Capital city ⊙Administrative unit OPlace ♁Island ⛰Mountain range △Mountain ⌓Cape ≈Ocean, Sea ~Lake, River ♆Undersea topography ▲Glacier ♀National park •••Reservation ★Point of major interest ⌒Landscape

Şarköy O TR 195 Hf 25
Šarlat Char ⛰ PK 227 Jm 31
Şarlat-I.-Can. O F 184 Gg 23
Şarlauk O TM 222 Jf 26
Šarma O KSA 214 Hk 31
Sarmanovo O RUS 181 Je 18
Sărmăşel Gară O RO 175 He 22
Sarmette O VU 386 Nf 54
Sarmi O RI 286 Mf 46
Sarmiento O RA 137 Eb 61
Şarmiento O RA 152 Dp 68
Šarmuhīya O IRQ 215 Jb 30
Särna O S 158 Gn 15
Särnstugan O S 158 Gn 15
Sarny O UA 175 Hf 20
Saroako O RI 282 Ll 47
Sarōbī O AFG 223 Jn 28
Sarolangun O RI 278 Lb 47
Saroma O J 250 Mh 24
Saromako ~ J 250 Mh 23
Saronikós Kolpós ≈ GR 194 Hd 27
Sarore O RI 286 Mg 50
Saros Kōrfezi ≈ TR 194 Hf 25
Sarota O PNG 287 Mk 50
Sarpinskie ozero ~ RUS 181 Ja 21
Sarpsborg O N 170 Gm 16
Sarrapio O YV 112 Eb 42
Sarrèguemines O F 163 Gk 21
Sarria O E 184 Gc 24
Sarro O RMM 317 Gd 39
Sarstún ~ GCA 93 Dd 38
Sartane O F 185 Gl 25
Sartang ~ RUS 205 Wc 5
Sartell O USA 56 Da 23
Sarthe ~ F 163 Gf 22
Sarubetsu O J 250 Mh 24
Sarufutsu O J 250 Mh 23
Saruwaged Range ⛰ PNG 287 Mk 49
Sárvár O H 174 Ha 22
Sarvestān O IR 215 Je 31
Šary O KSA 214 Hp 32
Saryagaš O KZ 223 Jn 25
Saryarka ⌒ KZ 22 Nb 5
Sarygamyš kŏli ~ TM 222 Jg 25
Saryjazinskoe vodohranilišče ~ TM 223 Jk 27
Sarykamys O KZ 155 Rb 9
Sarykamyšskaja kotlovina ⌒ UZB 222 Jg 24
Sarykŭdyk O KZ 181 Jd 21
Sarykul' O UZB 223 Jm 26
Sary syganak k-l ~ KZ 181 Jc 21
Sary-Taš O KS 230 Ka 26
Sasabe O USA 80 Cg 30
Sasabeneh O ETH 328 Hp 42
Sasarām O IND 235 Kf 33
Sasebo O J 247 Ma 29
Saskatchewan ⊙ CDN 6 Db 4
Saskatchewan ~ CDN 42 Fa 8
Saskatchewan O CDN 51 Cf 19
Saskatchewan ⊙ CDN 51 Ch 20
Saskatoon O CDN 51 Cj 19
Sasolburg O ZA 349 Hf 59
Sasoma O IND 230 Kc 28
Sasovo O RUS 181 Hn 18
Sassandra ~ CI 305 Gc 41
Sassandra O CI 305 Gc 43
Sassandra O CI 305 Gc 43
Sassari O I 185 Gk 25
Sassélé O RCA 321 Ha 43
Sassie Island ♁ AUS 365 Mh 51
Sassnitz O D 170 Gn 18
Sassoumbouroum O RN 320 Gl 39
Sass Town O LB 316 Gb 43
Sastre O RA 137 Ec 61
Sāsvad O IND 238 Kb 36
Sasykkul' O TJ 230 Ka 27
Sata O J 247 Mb 30
Satadougoux O RMM 316 Ga 39
Satagaj O RUS 204 Wa 6
Satama-Sokoura O CI 317 Gd 42
Sata misaki ⌓ J 247 Mb 30
Satāna O IND 238 Ka 35
Sātāra O IND 238 Ka 37
Satara O ZA 352 Hh 58
Satéma O RCA 321 Hc 43
Satevo O MEX 80 Cj 32
Sathing Phra O THA 270 La 42
Satilla ~ USA 86 Dg 30
Satipo O PE 128 Dl 51
Satiri O BF 317 Gd 40
Satiwāla O PK 230 Ka 30
Satlui ~ IND 230 Kb 30
Satlui ~ IND 230 Kc 30
Satluj ~ IND 230 Kb 30
Satna O IND 234 Ke 33
Sato O J 247 Ma 30
Sátoraljaújhely O H 174 Hc 21
Sātpura Range ⛰ IND 234 Kb 35
Satrokala O RM 353 Ja 57
Satsuma-Hantō ♁ J 247 Ma 30
Satsunan Islands ♁ J 259 Ma 32
Sattahip O THA 262 La 39
Satt al-Arab ~ IRQ 215 Jb 30
Sattenapalle O IND 238 Ke 37
Satthwa O MYA 254 Km 36
Satti O IND 230 Kc 28
Sattūr O IND 239 Kc 41
Satuk O THA 263 Lb 38
Satu Mare O RO 175 Hd 22
Şatun O THA 270 Kp 42
Šatura O RUS 171 Hm 18
Satwas O IND 234 Kc 34
Şatymangalam O IND 239 Kc 40
Šaubak O JOR 214 Hk 30
Sauce O RA 146 Ee 61
Sauce Blanco O RA 147 Eb 66
Sauce Chico ~ RA 147 Ec 65
Saucillo O MEX 80 Ck 32
Sauda O N 170 Gk 16
Saudade O BR 117 Eb 48
Sauðárkrókur O IS 158 Fk 13
Saudavel O BR 125 En 52
Saúde O BR 125 Ep 51
Saudi Arabia □ KSA 214 Hm 32
Saueninã ~ BR 132 Ee 52
Sauêruiná ou Papagaio ~ BR 132 Ee 52
Saujil O RA 136 Ea 60
Sauk Centre O USA 56 Da 23
Sauk City O USA 57 Dd 24
Saukorem O RI 283 Mc 46
Saül O F 113 Eh 44
Saulieu O F 163 Gh 22
Saulkrasti O LV 170 Hd 17
Sault O F 185 Gj 23
Sault Ste.Marie O USA 57 Df 22
Saumarez Reef ♁ AUS 375 Mn 56
Saumlaki O RI 283 Mb 50
Saumur O F 163 Gf 22
Saundatti O IND 238 Kb 38
Saunders Point △ AUS 369 Ln 59
Saunyi ~ EAT 337 Hl 48
Sauquira O OM 219 Jg 36
Sauren O PNG 287 Ml 48
Sauri Hill △ WAN 320 Gk 40
Saurimo O ANG 340 Hc 50
Sauriwaunawa O GUY 112 Ee 44
Sausi O PNG 287 Mj 48
Sausu O RI 282 Ll 46
Sautar O ANG 340 Hb 51
Sautatá O CO 106 Dk 42
Saut Grand Canori ~ F 113 Eh 44
Saut Macague ~ F 113 Eh 44
Sauzal O RCH 137 Dm 63
Savá O HN 96 De 38
Sava ~ SLO 174 Gp 22
Sava ~ HR 174 Ha 23
Savage O USA 51 Ck 22
Savage River O AUS 378 Mj 66
Savai'i ♁ WS 35 Aa 11
Savai'i ♁ WS 390 Ad 52
Savalou O DY 317 Gg 42
Savane O MOC 344 Hk 55
Savanna O USA 71 Dc 24
Savanna ~ USA 71 Dg 28
Savannah O USA 71 Dd 28
Savannah O USA 71 Dh 29
Savannah ~ USA 71 Dh 29
Savannah Downs O AUS 365 Mg 55
Savannakhét O LAO 263 Lc 37
Savanna-la-Mar O JA 100 Dj 36
Savant Lake O CDN 56 Dc 20
Savant Lake ~ CDN 56 Dc 20
Savantvāti O IND 238 Ka 38
Savanūr O IND 238 Kb 38
Savaştepe O TR 195 Hf 26
Savate O ANG 340 Ha 54
Save ~ F 184 Gg 24
Sâve O IR 222 Jd 28
Savè O DY 317 Gh 41
Save ~ ZW 341 Hh 55
Save ~ ZW 352 Hj 56
Save O MOC 352 Hk 56
Savelugu O GH 317 Gf 41
Săveni O RO 175 Hf 22
Saverne O F 163 Gk 21
Savigliano O I 185 Gk 23
Savinskij O RUS 159 Hn 14
Şavitaipale O FIN 159 Hf 15
Šavnik O MON 194 Hb 24
Savoie ⊙ F 185 Gk 23
Savo Island ♁ SOL 290 Nb 50
Savona O CDN 50 Cb 20
Savona O I 185 Gl 23
Savonlinna O FIN 159 Hg 15
Savonranta O FIN 159 Hg 14
Savoonga O USA 46 Ae 13
Savoonga O USA 205 Ab 6
Savory ~ AUS 360 Ll 57
Savot O UZB 222 Jj 25
Sāvsjö O S 170 Gp 17
Savusavu O FJI 387 Nm 54
Savusavu Bay ≈ FJI 387 Nm 54
Savuti ~ RB 341 Hd 55
Savuti O RB 341 He 55
Saw O MYA 254 Km 35
Sawadori O RI 286 Me 46
Sawahlunto O RI 270 La 46
Sawai O RI 283 Ma 47
Sawai Mādhopur O IND 234 Kc 32
Sawaleke O FJI 387 Nm 54
Sawam Khalok O THA 262 Kp 37
Şawang Dan Din O THA 263 Lb 37
Šawāq O KSA 214 Hl 32
Sawara O J 251 Mg 28
Sawāri O IRQ 209 Hp 28
Sawatch Mountains ⛰ USA 65 Cj 26
Sawhaj O ET 301 Hh 32
Sawi O THA 262 Kp 40
Sawilo O LB 316 Ga 42
Sawka O MYA 254 Kn 35
Sawkanah O LAR 297 Gp 31
Sawla O GH 317 Ge 41
Sawmill Bay ~ CDN 47 Cc 13
Sawmills O ZW 341 Hg 55
Sawqirah Bay ≈ OM 219 Jg 36
Sawtooth Range ⛰ USA 50 Ce 23
Sawu O RI 282 Ll 51
Sawu Island ♁ RI 282 Ll 51
Sawu Sea ≈ RI 282 Ll 50
Sawyer O USA 70 Cn 27
Saxby Downs O AUS 374 Mh 56
Saxon O USA 56 Dc 22
Say O RMM 317 Gd 39
Say O RN 320 Gh 39
Sayabec O CDN 60 Ea 21
Sāyalkudi O IND 239 Kd 41
Sayán O PE 116 Dk 51
Sayaxché O GCA 93 Dc 37
Sayda Sidon O RL 208 Hk 29
Sayengga O RI 283 Mc 47
Saylac O SP 328 Hp 40
Sayre O USA 70 Cn 28
Sayre O USA 74 Dk 25
Say Tha Ni O LAO 254 Lb 36
Sayula O MEX 92 Cl 36
Sayula O MEX 93 Da 37
Sayward O CDN 50 Bp 20
Sazaka O J 251 Mf 27
Šāzand O IR 209 Jc 29
Sazin O PK 230 Ka 28
Sazonovo O RUS 171 Hk 16
Sbaa O DZ 293 Gf 31
Sbeitla O TN 296 Gl 28
Scaddan O AUS 368 Ll 62
Scalea O I 185 Gp 26
Scalloway O GB 162 Gf 15
Scammon Bay O USA 46 Ag 15
Scamp Hill △ AUS 369 Lp 58
Scandia O CDN 51 Cf 20
Şcandia O USA 70 Cn 26
Šćara ~ BY 171 He 19
Scarborough O TT 104 Ed 40
Scarborough O GB 162 Gf 18
Scarborough Shoal ♁ RP 266 Lj 38
Scarface Peak △ USA 50 Cd 23
Şcawfell Island ♁ AUS 375 Ml 56
Ščekino O RUS 181 Hl 19
Ščelkovo O RUS 171 Hm 18
Schaffhausen O D 163 Gk 22
Schefferville O CDN 43 Hb 7
Schefferville O CDN 7 Fb 4
Schell Creek Range ⛰ USA 64 Ce 26
Schenectady O USA 60 Dl 24
Schidni Karpaty ⛰ UA 175 Hd 21
Schiermonnikoog ♁ NL 170 Gk 19
Schleswig O D 170 Gl 18
Schleswigholst. Wattenmeer ♀ D 170 Gl 18
Schleswig-Holstein ⊙ D 170 Gl 18
Schlip O NAM 348 Ha 57
Schluderns O I 174 Gm 22
Schmidtsdrif O ZA 349 Hd 60
Schoenchen O USA 70 Cn 26
Schongau O D 174 Gm 22
Schoombee O ZA 349 He 61
Schouten Island ♁ AUS 378 Ml 67
Schouten Islands ♁ PNG 287 Mj 47
Schrader Range ⛰ PNG 287 Mj 48
Schroffenstein △ NAM 348 Hb 59
Schulenburg O USA 81 Cp 31
Schuls O CH 174 Gm 22
Schurz O USA 64 Cc 26
Schuyler O USA 70 Cp 25
Schwäbisch Hall O D 174 Gl 21
Schwarzrand ⛰ NAM 348 Ha 58
Schwedt O D 170 Gn 19
Schweinfurt O D 174 Gm 20
Schweizer Reneke O ZA 349 He 59
Schwerin O D 170 Gm 19
Schwerin Mural Crescent ⛰ AUS 369 Ma 58
Schwyz O CH 174 Gl 22
Şciacca O I 185 Gn 27
Ščigry O RUS 181 Hl 20
Scioto ~ USA 71 Dg 26
Scipio O USA 65 Cg 26
Scobey O USA 51 Ck 21
Scole O GB 163 Gg 19
Scone O AUS 379 Mm 62
Scoresby Land ⌒ DK 18 Hb 2
Scoresby Land ⌒ DK 43 La 4
Scoresby Sund ≈ DK 43 La 4
Ščors O UA 175 Hh 20
Scotia Ridge ♆ 15 Ga 15
Scotia Sea ≈ 15 Gb 15
Scotland O USA 74 Dk 26
Scotland ⊙ GB 162 Gd 17
Scotstown O CDN 60 Dn 23
Scottburgh O ZA 349 Hh 61
Scott City O USA 70 Cm 26
Scott City O USA 71 Dd 27
Scott Point ⌓ AUS 365 Me 52
Scott Reef ⌓ AUS 360 Lm 53
Scottsbluff O USA 65 Cl 25
Scottsboro O USA 71 De 28
Scottsburg O USA 71 Df 26
Scottsdale O USA 65 Cg 29
Scottsdale O AUS 378 Mk 66
Scottsville O USA 71 De 27
Scottville O USA 57 De 24
Scotty's Junction O USA 64 Cd 27
Scout Mountain △ USA 51 Cf 24
Scranton O USA 74 Dk 25
Scuol Schuls O CH 174 Gm 22
Seabra O BR 125 Ep 52
Seaford O USA 74 Dl 26
Seaforth O AUS 375 Ml 56
Sea Islands ♁ USA 87 Dh 30
Seal ~ CDN 42 Fb 7
Sea Lake O AUS 378 Mh 63
Seal Cove O CDN 61 Ef 21
Seale O USA 86 Df 29
Sealion Islands ♁ GB 147 Ee 72
Sealy O USA 81 Cp 31
Sea of Azov ≈ UA 175 Hk 22
Sea of Azov ≈ UA/RUS 181 Hl 22
Sea of Crete ≈ GR 194 Hd 28
Sea of Hebrides ≈ GB 162 Gc 17
Sea of Japan ≈ 250 Mc 26
Sea of Marmara ≈ TR 195 Hg 25
Sea of Okhotsk ≈ 205 Xc 7
Sea Park O ZA 349 Hh 61
Seara O BR 140 Eh 59
Searchlight O USA 64 Ce 28
Searchmont O CDN 57 Df 22
Searcy O USA 70 Dc 28
Seaside O USA 50 Bp 23
Seaside O USA 64 Cb 27
Seaspray O AUS 379 Mk 65
Seattle O USA 50 Ca 22
Seaward Kaikoura Range ⛰ NZ 383 Nj 67
Seba O RI 282 Ll 51
Sébaco O NIC 96 De 39
Sebago Lake ~ USA 60 Dn 24
Sebak O RI 283 Mc 46
Sebastian O USA 87 Dh 32
Sebastopol O USA 64 Ca 26
Sebauh O MAL 274 Lg 44
Sebba O BF 317 Gg 39
Sebderat O ER 313 Hl 38
Sebdou O DZ 293 Gf 28
Sébé ~ G 332 Gn 46
Şébé ~ G 332 Gp 46
Sebekino O RUS 181 Hl 20
Sébékoro O RMM 316 Gb 39
Şebergăn O AFG 223 Jl 27
Seberida O RI 278 Lb 46
Sebeş O RO 194 Hd 23
Sébéte O RMM 305 Gc 38
Şebež O RUS 171 Hg 17
Sebie O RDC 333 Hb 47
Sebina O RB 349 Hf 56
Şebinkarahisar O TR 195 Hm 25
Şebit O EAK 325 Hk 45
Sebkha Ain Belbela ~ DZ 293 Gd 32
Sebkha Azzel Matti ~ DZ 293 Gf 31
Sebkha de Timimoun ~ DZ 293 Gf 31
Sebkha de Tindouf ~ DZ 293 Gc 32
Sebkha El Kebira ~ DZ 293 Gf 28
Sebkha el Mellah ~ DZ 293 Gf 31
Sebkha Mekerrhane ~ DZ 293 Gg 32
Sebkha Ndrhamcha ~ RIM 304 Fn 36
Sebkha Oumm Debua ~ MA 292 Fp 32
Sebkhat Tah ~ MA 292 Fp 31
Sebkhet Afouidich ~ MA 304 Fn 35
Sebkhet Aghzoumal ~ MA 292 Fp 33
Sebkhet Audal ~ MA 292 Fp 32
Sebkhet Chemchâm ~ RIM 304 Fp 35
Sebkhet En Noual ~ TN 296 Gl 28
Sebkhet Gallanmane ~ RIM 304 Gb 34
Sebkhet Iguetti ~ RIM 292 Gb 33
Sebkhet Oumm ed Droûs Guebli ~ RIM 304 Ga 34
Sebkhet Oumm ed Droûs Telli ~ RIM 292 Ga 33
Sebkhet Sidi El Hani ~ TN 297 Gm 28
Sebkhet Tanouzkka ~ MA 304 Fn 34
Sebkhet Tidsit ~ MA 304 Fn 34
Sebol O GCA 93 Dc 38
Seboto Point ⌓ RP 275 Lm 42
Seboyeta O USA 65 Cj 28
Sebree O USA 71 De 27
Sebring O USA 87 Dh 32
Şebta O E 293 Gd 28
Šebunino O RUS 250 Mg 22
Sebuyau O MAL 271 Lf 45
Sechura O PE 116 Dh 48
Seco ~ RA 136 Eb 59
Seco ~ RA 152 Ea 70
Seco de las Peñas ~ RA 137 Dp 63
Second Mesa O USA 65 Cg 28
Secretary Island ♁ NZ 382 Nf 68
Secunderābād O IND 238 Kc 37
Sécure ~ BOL 129 Ea 52
Sécure ~ BOL 129 Eb 53
Seda O LT 170 Hd 17
Sedalia O USA 70 Db 26
Sedan O USA 65 Cl 27
Sedan O USA 70 Cp 27
Sedan O F 163 Gj 21
Sedan O AUS 375 Mh 58
Sedan O AUS 378 Mf 63
Seddon O NZ 383 Nk 66
Sedeh O IR 222 Jh 29
Sedgefield O ZA 358 Hd 62
Sedgwick O USA 70 Cp 27
Sédhiou O SN 316 Fn 39
Sedič ~ IR 226 Jh 33
Sedič ~ IR 226 Jh 33
Sedoa O RI 282 Ll 46
Sedok O RUS 202 Hn 23
Sedom O IL 214 Hk 30
Sedona O USA 65 Cg 28
Sedrata O DZ 296 Gk 27
Şedro Woolley O USA 50 Ca 21
Šeduva O LT 171 Hd 18
Seeheim O NAM 348 Ha 59
Seeis O NAM 348 Ha 57
Seeis ~ NAM 348 Ha 57
Seekaskootch Indian Reservation ••• CDN 51 Cg 19
Seekoegat O ZA 358 Hd 62
Seekoeivier ~ ZA 349 He 61
Seeley Lake O USA 50 Cf 22
Seemore Downs O AUS 369 Ln 61
Seferihisar O TR 194 Hf 26
Sefīdābe O IR 226 Jj 30
Sefid Rūd ~ IR 209 Jc 27
Sefophe O RB 349 Hg 57
Sefrou O MA 293 Gd 29
Segag O ETH 328 Hp 42
Ségala O RMM 304 Ga 38
Segama ~ MAL 274 Lk 43
Segamat O MAL 270 Lb 44
Segara Anakan ~ RI 278 Le 49
Ségbana O DY 320 Gh 40
Segbwema O WAL 316 Ga 42
Segen Wenz ~ ETH 325 Hl 43
Segera O EAT 337 Hm 48
Segeri O RI 279 Lk 48
Seget O RI 283 Mb 46
Segeža O RUS 159 Hj 14
Seghe O SOL 290 Na 50
Segnān O AFG 223 Jp 27
Ségou O RMM 305 Gc 39
Segovia O CO 106 Dl 42
Segovia O E 184 Gd 25
Segozero ~ RUS 159 Hj 14
Segré O F 163 Gf 22
Segué O RMM 317 Ge 39
Seguedine O RN 297 Gn 35
Seguéla O RMM 305 Gc 38
Seguéla O CI 305 Gc 42
Séguénéga O BF 317 Gf 39
Seguin O USA 81 Cp 31
Segunda ~ RA 137 Ec 61
Segura O P 184 Gc 26
Segura d. Canajo ~ E 184 Ge 26
Sehithwa O RB 349 Hd 56
Sehonghong O LS 349 Hg 60
Sehore O IND 234 Kc 34
Sehulea O PNG 287 Mm 51
Sehwān O PK 227 Jm 32
Seia O P 184 Gc 25
Seibert O USA 65 Cl 26
Seigals Creek O AUS 365 Me 54
Şeih-Alī O AFG 223 Jn 28
Seikan Tunnel ★ J 250 Mf 25
Seikoyu O MYA 254 Km 35
Seiland ♁ N 159 Hd 10
Seiling O USA 70 Cn 27
Seille ~ F 163 Gj 22
Seinäjoki O FIN 159 Hd 14
Seine ~ F 163 Gg 21
Seival O BR 146 Eh 61
Sejaka O RI 279 Lj 47
Sejenane O TN 296 Gl 27
Sejm ~ RUS 175 Hk 20
Sejmčan O RUS 23 Sb 3
Sejmčan O RUS 205 Ya 6
Sejny O PL 171 Hd 18
Sejorong O RI 279 Lj 50
Seka O ETH 325 Hl 42
Seka Banza O RDC 332 Gn 48
Sekayam ~ RI 271 Lk 45
Sekayu O RI 278 Lb 47
Seke O RDC 333 He 48
Sekenke O EAT 337 Hk 48
Seki O J 251 Me 28
Sekibisho-shima ♁ J 259 Ln 33
Sekoma O RB 349 Hd 58
Sekondi O GH 317 Gf 43
Sek'ot'a O ETH 313 Hm 39
Şekpiegu O GH 317 Gf 41
Šeksna O RUS 171 Hm 16
Sela Dingay O ETH 325 Hm 41
Sela Nok O MYA 254 Km 32
Selaphum O THA 263 Lb 37
Selapiu Island ♁ PNG 287 Mm 47
Selassi O RI 283 Mc 47
Selat Alas ~ RI 279 Lj 50
Selat Aruri ~ RI 283 Md 46
Selat Bali ~ RI 279 Lh 50
Selat Bangka ~ RI 278 Lc 47
Selat Bengalis ~ RI 270 La 45
Selat Berhala ~ RI 278 Lc 46
Selat Boano ~ RI 283 Lp 47
Selat Bungalaut ~ RI 270 Kp 47
Selat Buol ~ RI 275 Ll 45
Selat Buton ~ RI 282 Lm 48
Selat Combo ~ RI 271 Lc 45
Selat Dampier ~ RI 283 Mb 46
Selat Durian ≈ 271 Lb 46
Selat Gaspar ~ RI 278 Ld 47
Selat Jailolo ~ RI 283 Ma 46
Selat Kabaena ~ RI 282 Ll 48
Selat Karimata ~ RI 278 Le 47
Selat Lombok ~ RI 279 Lh 50
Selat Madura ~ RI 279 Lg 49
Selat Mangole ~ RI 282 Ln 47
Selat Manipa ~ RI 283 Lp 47
Selat Morotai ~ RI 275 Ma 44
Selat Muna ~ RI 282 Lm 48
Selat Nautilus ~ RI 283 Mc 48
Selat Nerong ~ RI 283 Mc 48
Selat Obi ~ RI 283 Lp 46
Selat Ombai ~ RI 282 Ln 50
Selat Padang ~ RI 271 Lb 45
Selat Panaitan ~ RI 278 Lc 49
Selat Panjan ~ RI 271 Lb 45
Selatpanjang O RI 270 Lb 45
Selat Patinti ~ RI 283 Lp 46
Selat Peleng ~ RI 282 Lm 46
Selat Romang ~ RI 282 Lp 49
Selat Roti ~ RI 282 Lm 51
Selat Rupat ~ RI 270 La 45
Selat Sageurin ~ RI 283 Mb 46
Selat Salue Timpaus ~ RI 282 Lm 46
Selat Sanding ~ RI 270 La 47
Selat Sape ~ RI 279 Lk 50
Selat Selayar ~ RI 282 Ll 48
Selat Sele ~ RI 283 Mb 46
Selat Siberut ~ RI 270 Kp 46
Selat Sikakap ~ RI 270 La 47
Selat Singapore ≈ 271 Lb 45
Selat Sumba ♆ RI 279 Lk 50
Selat Sunda ~ RI 278 Ld 48
Selat Tiworo ~ RI 282 Lm 48
Selat Walea ~ RI 282 Lm 46
Selat Wetar ~ RI 282 Ln 50
Selat Woinui ~ RI 283 Md 46
Selat Yapen ~ RI 283 Md 46
Selawik O USA 46 Al 11
Selawik River ~ USA 46 Al 11
Sélba O BF 305 Gf 38
Selbu O N 158 Gm 14
Selby O USA 56 Cn 23
Selçuk O TR 195 Hf 26
Selden O USA 70 Cm 26
Seldovia O USA 46 Ba 15
Selebi-Phikwe O RB 349 Hf 57
Selemdža ~ RUS 205 Wc 8
Selendi O TR 195 Hg 26
Selengei O EAK 337 Hl 47
Sèlèngè mörön ~ MNG 204 Uc 9
Selenginsk O RUS 204 Va 8
Selenginsk ~ RUS 204 Va 8
Sélestat O F 163 Gk 21
Seleti O SN 316 Fm 39
Selfoss O IS 158 Fk 14
Sel'gi O RUS 159 Hj 14
Sélibabi O RIM 304 Fp 38
Seligman O USA 64 Cf 28
Sélim O RCA 324 Hf 43
Seling O IND 254 Kl 34
Sélinnkegni O RMM 304 Ga 38
Selinsgrove O USA 74 Dk 25
Selinunte ★ I 185 Gn 27
Selizarovo O RUS 171 Hj 17
Selkämeri ⌓ FIN 159 Hc 15
Selkirk O CDN 56 Cp 20
Selkirk Mountains ⛰ USA 50 Cd 21
Sellersburg O USA 71 De 26
Sells O USA 75 Cf 30
Selma O USA 64 Cc 27
Selma O USA 71 De 29
Selmer O USA 71 Dd 28
Selong O RI 279 Lj 50
Selouane O MA 293 Ge 28
Sélouma O RG 316 Ga 40
Selous O ZW 341 Hh 55
Selous Game Reserve ••• EAT 337 Hl 50
Selsele-ye Pīr-e Šūrān ⛰ IR 226 Jj 31
Selsele-ye Safid Kūh ⛰ AFG 223 Jj 28
Selsele-ye Siyāh Kūh ⛰ AFG 223 Jk 29
Selu O IND 238 Kc 36
Selva Alegre O EC 116 Dj 45
Selvas ⌒ BR 117 Dm 49
Selvíra O BR 140 Ej 56
Selway ~ USA 50 Ce 22
Selway Falls ~ USA 50 Ce 22
Selwyn O AUS 374 Mg 56
Selwyn Mountains ⛰ CDN 47 Bj 13
Selwyn Range ⛰ AUS 374 Mg 56
Semangka ~ RI 278 Lc 48
Semarang O RI 278 Lf 49
Sematan O MAL 271 Le 45
Semau Island ♁ RI 282 Lm 51
Sembabule O EAU 336 Hh 46
Sembakung ~ RI 274 Lj 44
Sembalia O RI 279 Lj 50
Sembatti O IND 239 Kc 40
Sembe O LB 316 Ga 42
Sembé O RCB 332 Gp 45
Sembehun O WAL 316 Fp 42
Semberong ~ MAL 271 Lb 44
Şemdinli O TR 209 Ja 27
Sémé O CI 305 Gc 40
Semei O SUD 312 Hh 39
Semenivka O UA 171 Hj 19
Semey O KZ 204 Tb 8
Semichi Islands ♁ USA 205 Zb 8
Semidi Islands ♁ USA 46 Al 17
Sémien O CI 305 Gc 42
Semikarakorsk O RUS 181 Hn 22
Semillero O GCA 93 Dc 39
Semiluki O RUS 181 Hm 20
Seminoe Dam O USA 65 Cj 24
Seminoe Reservoir ~ USA 65 Cj 24
Seminole O USA 65 Cl 29
Seminole O USA 70 Cp 28
Semirara Islands ♁ RP 267 Ll 39
Semīrom O IR 215 Jd 30
Semitau O RI 271 Lf 45
Semlac O ZA 349 Hd 58
Semliki ~ RDC 324 Hg 45
Semna O SUD 312 Hh 35
Semnān O IR 222 Je 28
Semnān ⊙ IR 222 Je 28
Semolale O RB 349 Hg 56
Sempol O RI 279 Lh 49
Şemporna O MAL 274 Lk 43
Šemšak O IR 222 Jd 28
Semu ~ EAT 337 Hk 47
Semurut O RI 274 Lj 45
Sĕmža O RUS 159 Ja 12
Senachwine Lake ~ USA 71 Dd 25
Senador José Porfíro O BR 121 Ej 47
Senador Pompeu O BR 124 Fa 48
Sen'afē O ER 313 Hm 38
Senaki O GE 202 Hp 24
Sena Madureira O BR 117 Dp 50
Senamrae O PNG 286 Mg 48
Senanayaka Samudra ~ CL 239 Ke 42
Senanga O Z 341 Hd 54
Senatobia O USA 71 Dd 28
Senayang O RI 278 Lc 46
Sendafa O ETH 325 Hm 41
Sendai O J 247 Ma 30
Sendai O J 251 Mg 26
Sendégué O RMM 305 Gd 38
Sendhwa O IND 234 Kb 35
Seneca O USA 50 Cc 23
Seneca O USA 56 Cn 23
Seneca O USA 70 Cp 26
Seneca O USA 71 Dg 28
Seneca Caverns ★ USA 74 Dj 26
Seneca Falls O USA 60 Dk 24
Seneca Lake ~ USA 60 Dk 24
Seneca Lake ~ USA 71 Dh 26
Senegal ~ RIM 304 Fn 37
Senegal □ SN 304 Fn 38
Senekal O ZA 349 Hf 60
Seney O USA 57 Df 22
Seney Natl. Wildlife Refuge ••• USA 57 De 22
Senga O MW 344 Hk 52
Sengang O WAN 320 Gj 43
Senge O RDC 321 Hd 44
Sengerema O EAT 337 Hj 47
Sênggê Zangbo Indus ~ VRC 230 Ke 29
Senggigi O RI 279 Lh 50
Sengkang O RI 282 Ll 48
Sengoshe O RB 341 Hd 55
Senguerr ~ RA 152 Dn 68
Senguerr ~ RA 152 Dp 68
Sengwa ~ ZW 341 Hg 54
Senhora do Porto O BR 141 En 55
Senhor do Bonfim O BR 125 Ep 51
Senigállia O I 185 Gn 24
Senirkent O TR 195 Hh 26
Senj O HR 174 Gp 23
Senja ♁ N 158 Ha 11
Senkaku-shotō ♁ J 259 Lm 33
Senkanse O BF 317 Gf 40
Sènko O RG 316 Gb 41
Senkobo O Z 341 He 54
Senlis O F 163 Gh 21
Senmonorom O K 263 Ld 39
Sennār O SUD 313 Hj 39
Sennār Dam ~ SUD 313 Hj 39
Senneterre O CDN 60 Dk 21
Sennoj O RUS 181 Jb 19
Seno Aisén ~ RCH 152 Dm 68
Seno Almirantazgo ~ RCH 152 Dp 73
Seno Año Nuevo ~ RCH 152 Dp 73
Seno Otway ~ RCH 152 Dn 72
Seno Reloncaví ~ RCH 147 Dm 66
Seno Skyring ~ RCH 152 Dm 72
Senqu Orange ~ LS 349 Hg 60
Sens O F 163 Gh 21
Senta O SCG 174 Hc 23
Sento Sé O BR 124 Ep 50
Sentrum O ZA 349 Hf 58
Senuda O RI 279 Lg 47
Senye O GQ 332 Gl 45
Seonath ~ IND 234 Ke 35
Seoni O IND 234 Kd 34
Seoni Mālwa O IND 234 Kc 34
Seorinārāyan O IND 234 Kf 35
Seoul ▣ ROK 247 Lp 27
Sepa O RI 283 Ma 47
Sepako O RB 341 Hf 55
Sepang O RI 282 Ll 50
Separ O USA 65 Ch 29
Separation Point ⌓ NZ 383 Nj 66
Sepasu O RI 274 Lj 45
Sepatini ~ BR 117 Eb 49
Şepeteri O WAN 320 Gh 41
Šepetivca O UA 175 Hf 20
Sepiddašt O IR 209 Jc 29
Şepik River ~ PNG 286 Mg 48
Şepit O UA 175 He 22
Sepo O DVRK 247 Lp 26
Sepo O RI 275 Ma 45
Sępólno Krajeńskie O PL 170 Ha 19
Sepon O IND 254 Km 32
Sepotuba ~ BR 132 Ef 53
Sept-des-Gzoula O MA 292 Gb 29
Sept-Îles O CDN 61 Ea 20
Sepupa O RB 341 Hc 55
Seputih ~ RI 278 Lc 48
Sequoia N.P. ♀ USA 64 Cc 27
Şequoyah's Cabin ★ USA 70 Da 28
Serabad ~ UZB 223 Jm 26
Serabad O UZB 223 Jm 27
Serabu O WAL 316 Fp 42
Şerafettin Dağl. ⛰ TR 202 Hn 26
Serafimović O RUS 181 Hp 21
Serahs O TM 223 Jj 27
Seram O IND 238 Kc 37
Serang ~ RI 278 Ld 49
Serang ~ RI 278 Lf 49
Seraran O RI 283 Mc 47
Serasan Strait ≈ 271 Le 45
Serath O CDN 51 Ck 20
Serbia □ SCG 174 Hc 23
Serca O VRC 242 Km 30
Serchip O IND 254 Kl 34
Serdo O ETH 313 Hn 40
Serdobsk O RUS 181 Ja 19
Seredka O RUS 171 Hf 16
Sérédou O RG 316 Gb 41

468 Şarköy - Sérédou

□ Country ▣ Capital city ⊙ Administrative unit O Place ⌂ Island ⛰ Mountain range △ Mountain ⌓ Cape ≈ Ocean, Sea ~ Lake, River Ψ Undersea topography ▲ Glacier ⚲ National park ••• Reservation ★ Point of major interest ⏢ Landscape

Şereflikoçhisar O TR 195 Hj 26
Serekunda O WAG 316 Fm 39
Seremban O MAL 270 La 44
Serengeti ⚲ EAT 337 Hk 47
Serengeti Plain ⏢ EAT 337 Hk 47
Serenje O Z 341 Hg 52
Sereno ~ BR 121 El 49
Séres O GR 194 Hd 25
Seret ~ UA 175 He 21
Sergač O RUS 181 Ja 18
Sergeevka O RUS 250 Mc 24
Sergeevsk O RUS 181 Jd 19
Sergiev-Posad O RUS 171 Hm 17
Sergipe ⊙ BR 125 Fb 51
Seria O BRU 274 Lh 43
Serian O MAL 271 Lf 45
Seribudolok O RI 270 Kp 44
Sérifos ⌂ GR 194 He 27
Serik O TR 195 Hh 27
Serikambelo O RI 283 Lp 47
Serikbuya O VRC 230 Kc 26
Seringapatam Reef ⌂ AUS 360 Lm 52
Sermowai ~ RI 286 Mg 47
Seroglazka O RUS 181 Jb 22
Seronera Lodge O EAT 337 Hk 47
Seronga O RB 341 Hd 55
Serouenout O DZ 308 Gk 33
Serov O RUS 154 Sa 7
Serowe O RB 349 Hf 57
Serpa O P 184 Gc 27
Serpent ~ RMM 304 Gb 38
Serpent's Mouth ≈ 104 Ed 41
Serpuhov O RUS 171 Hl 18
Serra O BR 141 Ep 56
Serra Azul ⛰ BR 132 Eg 53
Serra Bom Jesus do Gurguéia ⛰ BR 121 Em 50
Serra Branca O BR 124 Fb 49
Serra Cafema △ ANG 340 Gn 54
Serra da Bodoquena ⛰ BR 140 Ef 56
Serra da Capivara ⛰ BR 133 Em 53
Serra da Chella ⛰ ANG 340 Gn 54
Serra da Divisões ⛰ BR 133 Ej 54
Serra da Gardunha ⛰ P 184 Gc 25
Serra da Ibiapaba ⛰ BR 124 Ep 47
Serra da Mantigueira ⛰ BR 141 El 57
Serra da Mesa Reservoir ~ BR 133 Ek 53
Serra das Alparcatas ⛰ BR 121 Em 49
Serra das Araras ⛰ BR 132 Ef 53
Serra das Araras O BR 133 Em 53
Serra das Encantadas ⛰ BR 146 Eh 61
Serra das Marrecas ⛰ BR 124 Ep 50
Serra da Tabatinga ⛰ BR 133 Em 51
Serra de Divisor ⛰ BR 116 Dm 49
Serra de Estrela ⛰ P 184 Gb 25
Serra de Maracajú ⛰ BR 140 Eg 56
Serra de Paraná Piacaba ⛰ BR 140 Ek 58
Serra de Santa Bárbara ⛰ BR 129 Ed 53
Serra de São Jerônimo ⛰ BR 132 Eg 54
Serra de Traíra ⛰ BR 117 Dp 46
Serra de Uneiuxi ⛰ BR 117 Ea 46
Serra do Almeirim ⛰ BR 120 Eh 46
Serra do Baturite ⛰ BR 124 Ep 48
Serra do Cachimbo ⛰ BR 120 Ef 49
Serra do Caiapó ⛰ BR 133 Eh 54
Serra do Canguçu ⛰ BR 146 Eh 61
Serra do Capauari ⛰ BR 117 Dp 46
Serra do Chaparaó ⛰ BR 141 En 56
Serra do Chifre ⛰ BR 125 Ep 54
Serra do Estrondo ⛰ BR 121 Ek 50
Serra do Gurupi ⛰ BR 121 Ek 48
Serra dois Irmãos ⛰ BR 124 Ep 50
Serra do Jatapu ⛰ BR 120 Ee 46
Serra do Mar ⛰ BR 141 Ek 59
Serra do Navio O BR 121 Ej 45
Serra do Norte ⛰ BR 132 Ee 51
Serra do Ouricana ⛰ BR 125 Ep 53
Serra do Penitente ⛰ BR 121 El 50
Serra do Ramalho O BR 125 En 52
Serra do Roncador ⛰ BR 133 Ej 52
Serra dos Aimorés ⛰ BR 125 Ep 54
Serra dos Aimorés ⛰ BR 141 Ep 55
Serra dos Apiacás ⛰ BR 120 Ef 50
Serra dos Caiabis ⛰ BR 132 Ef 51
Serra dos Carajás ⛰ BR 121 Ej 49
Serra do Seringa ⛰ BR 121 Ej 49
Serra dos Gradaús ⛰ BR 121 Ej 50
Serra dos Três Irmãos ⛰ BR 117 Eb 50
Serra dos Xavantes ⛰ BR 133 Ek 52
Serra do Tiracambu ⛰ BR 121 El 48
Serra do Tombador ⛰ BR 132 Ee 51
Serra do Traíra ⛰ BR 117 Dp 46
Serra Dourada O BR 125 En 52
Serra Dourada ⛰ BR 133 Ek 52
Serra do Uruçui ⛰ BR 121 Em 50
Serra do Valentim ⛰ BR 124 En 48
Serra Geral de Goiás ⛰ BR 133 El 51
Serra Geral do Paranã ⛰ BR 133 El 53
Serra Grande ⛰ BR 124 Ep 48
Serra Lombarda ⛰ BR 113 Ej 44
Serra Mecula △ MOC 344 Hl 51
Serrana O BR 141 El 56
Serranía de Ayapel ⛰ CO 106 Dl 42
Serranía de Baudo ⛰ CO 106 Dk 42
Serrania de Caiza ⛰ BOL 136 Ec 56
Serranía de Imata ⛰ YV 112 Ed 42
Serranía de la Cerbatana ⛰ YV 107 Ea 42
Serranía de la Macarena ⛰ CO 106 Dl 44
Serranía de la Neblina ⚲ YV 112 Ea 45
Serranía del Darién ⛰ PA 104 Dk 41
Serranía del Sapo ⛰ PA 97 Dj 42
Serranía de Mapichí ⛰ YV 107 Ea 43
Serranía de Naquen ⛰ BR 107 Dp 45
Serranía de San Lucas ⛰ CO 106 Dl 42
Serranías del Burro ⛰ MEX 81 Cl 31
Serranias Huapi ⛰ NIC 97 Df 39
Serrania Turagua ⛰ YV 112 Eb 42
Serranópolis O BR 133 Eh 55
Serra Paranaquara ⛰ BR 120 Eh 46
Serra Preta O BR 125 Fa 52
Serraria O BR 121 El 47
Serra San Bruno O I 194 Ha 26
Serra São Francisco ⛰ BR 125 Ep 51
Serra Talhada O BR 124 Fa 50
Serres O F 185 Gj 23
Serrinha O BR 125 Fa 51
Serro O BR 141 En 55
Serrolândia O BR 125 Ep 51
Sertã O P 184 Gb 26
Sertânia O BR 124 Fb 50
Sertanópolis O BR 140 Ej 57
Sertão de Camapuã ⏢ BR 133 Eh 55
Sertãozinho O BR 141 Ek 56
Sêrtar O VRC 242 La 29
Serti O WAN 320 Gm 42
Sēru O ETH 325 Hn 42
Serui O RI 286 Me 46
Seruini ~ BR 117 Ea 50
Serule O RB 349 Hf 56
Seruyan ~ RI 279 Lg 47
Servia O GR 194 Hc 25
Sêrxü O VRC 242 Kp 29
Sesayap O RI 274 Lj 44
Sesayap ~ RI 274 Lj 44
Sesayap ⚲ RI 274 Lj 44
Seščinskij O RUS 171 Hj 19
Sese O RDC 324 He 44
Seseganaga Lake ~ CDN 56 Dc 20
Sese Islands ⌂ EAU 336 Hj 46
Sesenge O RDC 324 Hg 44
Sesepe O RI 283 Ma 46
Sesfontein O NAM 340 Gn 55
Seshego O ZA 349 Hg 57
Sesheke O Z 341 He 54
Sesimbra O P 184 Gb 26
Sešma ~ RUS 181 Jd 18
Sesriem O NAM 348 Gp 58
Sessa O ANG 340 Hc 52
Seštamad O IR 222 Jg 28
Sestri O I 185 Gl 23
Sestriere O I 185 Gk 23
Sesuntepeque O ES 93 Dd 39
Sète O F 185 Gh 24
Sete de Setembro ~ BR 133 Eh 52
Sete Lagoas O BR 133 Em 55
Setenta ⏢ RA 152 Dp 69
Setermoen O N 158 Ha 11
Setesdal ⏢ N 170 Gk 16
Seti ~ NEP 234 Ke 31
Sétif O DZ 296 Gj 27
Setlagole O ZA 349 He 59
Seto-naikai ★ J 251 Mc 28
Seto-nai-kai ~ J 251 Mc 28
Setouchi O J 259 Ma 31
Setpe O KZ 155 Rb 10
Settat O MA 293 Gc 29
Setté Cama O G 332 Gl 47
Settiya O IND 239 Kd 40
Settlers O ZA 349 Hg 58
Setto O DY 317 Gh 42
Setúbal O P 184 Gb 26
Setubinha O BR 125 En 54
Seulimeum O RI 270 Km 43
Sevan O ARM 202 Ja 25
Sevaré O RMM 305 Gd 38
Sevaruyo O BOL 129 Ea 55
Sevastopol O UA 175 Hj 23
Sevčenko Šyg. ~ KZ 155 Sa 9
Seven Emu O AUS 365 Me 54
Seven Lakes O USA 65 Ch 28
Severin O RO 194 Hd 23
Severn ~ CDN 43 Ga 8
Severn ~ GB 163 Ge 20
Severn O ZA 349 Hd 59
Severn ~ AUS 375 Mm 60
Severnaya Zemlya ⌂ RUS 22 Pb 1
Severn River ~ CDN 6 Ea 4
Severnye uvaly ⛰ RUS 154 Ra 7
Severobajkal'sk O RUS 204 Va 7
Severo Donec' ~ UA 181 Hm 21
Severodonec'k O UA 181 Hm 21
Severodvinsk O RUS 159 Hm 13
Severo Enisejsk O RUS 204 Ua 6
Severo-Kuril'sk O RUS 23 Sb 4
Severo Kuril'sk O RUS 205 Yb 8
Severomorsk O RUS 159 Hj 11
Severo Sos'va ~ RUS 154 Sa 6
Severo-Zadonsk O RUS 171 Hm 18
Severskij Don ~ RUS 181 Hn 22
Severy O USA 70 Cp 27
Sevettijarvi O FIN 159 Hf 11
Sevier ~ USA 64 Cf 26
Sevier O USA 65 Cf 26
Sevier Bridge Reservoir ~ USA 65 Cg 26
Sevier Desert ⏢ USA 64 Cf 26
Sevier Lake ~ USA 64 Cf 26
Sevilla O CO 106 Dl 43
Seville O E 184 Gd 27
Sevlievo O BG 194 He 24
Sevsk O RUS 171 Hk 19
Sewa ~ WAL 316 Fp 42
Sewa ~ WAL 316 Ga 41
Seward O USA 46 Ba 15
Seward O USA 70 Cp 25
Seward Peninsula ⌂ USA 46 Ag 13
Sewdāyah ⏢ LAR 297 Ha 31
Sewell O RCH 137 Dn 63
Sewerimabu O PNG 286 Mh 50
Sey O RA 136 Ea 57
Seychelles □ SY 329 Jf 48
Seydişehir O TR 195 Hh 27
Seyðisfjörður O IS 158 Fp 13
Seyhan Brj. ~ TR 195 Hk 27
Seyhan Nehri ~ TR 195 Hk 27
Seyitgazi O TR 195 Hh 26
Seymour O USA 70 Cn 29
Seymour O USA 71 Df 26
Seymour O ZA 358 Hf 62
Seymour O AUS 379 Mj 64
Seymour Arm O CDN 50 Cc 20
Seyyedābād O IR 222 Jg 27
Seyyedābād O AFG 223 Jn 29
Seyyedān O IR 209 Jb 28
Sez ⊙ VRC 258 Lg 34
Sézanne O F 163 Gh 21
Sezín O MYA 254 Kn 33
Sfakia O GR 194 He 28
Sfântu Gheorghe O RO 175 He 23
Sfântu Gheorghe O RO 175 Hg 23
Sfax O TN 297 Gm 28
Sfinári O GR 194 Hd 28
Sfissifa O DZ 293 Gf 29
Sfizef O DZ 293 Gf 28
Shaanxi ⊙ VRC 243 Ld 29
Shabaqua Corners O CDN 56 Dc 21
Shabasha O SUD 312 Hj 38
Shabaskwia Lake ~ CDN 57 Dd 20
Shabqadar O PK 223 Jp 28
Shabunda O RDC 336 Hf 47
Shache O VRC 230 Kc 26
Shackelton Ice Shelf ▲ 38 Pb 16
Shackleton Range ⛰ 38 Ja 18
Shādan Lund O PK 227 Jp 30
Shadaogou O VRC 255 Le 31
Shadehill Reservoir ~ USA 51 Cl 23
Shādi ~ PK 226 Jk 33
Shafter O USA 64 Cc 28
Shafter O USA 81 Ck 31
Shagein △ EAT 337 Hm 48
Shagwa O WAN 320 Gj 40
Shāhāda O IND 234 Kb 35
Shah Alam O MAL 270 La 44
Shāhāpur O IND 238 Ka 36
Shahara O YE 218 Hp 37
Shahar Sultān O PK 227 Jp 31
Shahāt Chrene ★ LAR 300 Hc 29
Shāhbandar O PK 227 Jm 33
Shāhbāz Kalāt O PK 226 Jk 32
Shahda Bohotleh O SP 328 Jb 41
Shāhdādkot O PK 227 Jm 32
Shāhdāpur O PK 227 Jn 33
Shahdol O IND 234 Ke 34
Shahe O VRC 243 Lh 27
Shahe O VRC 246 Lk 27
Shāhganj O IND 234 Kf 32
Shahistagani O BD 235 Kk 33
Shahjahānpur O IND 234 Kd 32
Shāh Kot O PK 230 Ka 30
Shāhpur O PK 230 Ka 29
Shāhpur O IND 234 Kb 32
Shaighālū O PK 227 Jn 30
Shaikhpura O IND 235 Kg 33
Shakargarn O IND 230 Kb 29
Shakawe O RB 341 Hc 55
Shaker Village ★ USA 71 Df 27
Shakespeare Island ⌂ CDN 57 Dd 21
Shakhty O RUS 181 Hn 22
Shakotan-hantō ⌂ J 250 Mf 24
Shaktoolik O USA 46 Aj 13
Shaktoolik River ~ USA 46 Aj 13
Shalaanbood O SP 329 Ja 45
Shala Hāyk' ~ ETH 325 Hm 42
Shalalth O CDN 50 Ca 20
Shalī al-Fīl O SUD 313 Hk 40
Shallow Lake ~ AUS 374 Mf 58
Shaluli Shan ⛰ VRC 242 Kp 30
Shama ~ EAT 336 Hj 49
Shambe O SUD 324 Hh 42
Shamboyacu O PE 116 Dk 49
Shambu O ETH 325 Hl 41
Shamganj O BD 235 Kk 33
Shamli O IND 234 Kc 31
Shamman O SUD 313 Hk 39
Shamokin O USA 74 Dk 25
Shamputa O Z 341 Hf 53
Shamrock O USA 70 Cm 28
Shamsābād O IND 238 Kd 37
Shamshergani O NEP 234 Ke 31
Shamva O ZW 341 Hh 54
Shandan O VRC 242 La 26
Shandon Downs O AUS 364 Md 54
Shandong ⊙ VRC 246 Lj 27
Shandong Bandao ⌂ VRC 246 Ll 27
Shangani ~ ZW 341 Hf 55
Shangani O ZW 341 Hg 55
Shangani-Tiyabenzi Dam ~ ZW 341 Hg 55
Shangbahe O VRC 243 Lh 30
Shangcai O VRC 243 Lh 29
Shangcheng O VRC 243 Lh 30
Shangchuan Dao ⌂ VRC 258 Lg 35
Shanggao O VRC 258 Lh 31
Shanghai O VRC 246 Ll 30
Shanghai Shi ⊙ VRC 246 Ll 30
Shanghang O VRC 258 Lj 33
Shanghe O VRC 246 Lj 27
Shangnan O VRC 243 Lf 29
Shangombo O Z 341 Hd 54
Shangqiu O VRC 243 Lh 28
Shangrao O VRC 258 Lj 31
Shangtu O VRC 258 Lh 31
Shangwu O WAN 320 Gj 40
Shangying O VRC 255 Ld 34
Shangyou Yichang ~ VRC 230 Ke 25
Shangyu O VRC 246 Ll 30
Shangzhou O VRC 243 Le 29
Shanhaiguan ★ VRC 246 Lk 25
Shanhaiguan O VRC 246 Lk 26
Shani O WAN 320 Gm 40
Shaniko O USA 50 Cb 23
Shankou O VRC 255 Le 35
Shankou O VRC 255 Lf 31
Shannon O IRL 163 Gb 19
Shannon ~ IRL 163 Gb 19
Shannon O AUS 368 Lj 63
Shanti Niketan O IND 235 Kh 34
Shantou O VRC 258 Lj 34
Shanusi O PE 116 Dk 49
Shanwei O VRC 258 Lh 34
Shanxi ⊙ VRC 243 Lf 26
Shan Xian O VRC 246 Lj 28
Shanyang O VRC 243 Le 29
Shanyin O VRC 243 Lg 26
Shaodong O VRC 255 Lf 32
Shaoguan O VRC 258 Lg 33
Shaoshan O VRC 258 Lg 32
Shaowu O VRC 258 Lj 32
Shaoxing O VRC 259 Ll 31
Shaoyang O VRC 255 Lf 32
Shapembe O RDC 333 Hc 48
Shaping O VRC 255 Le 34
Shāpur O IND 238 Kc 37
Shāpur Chākar O PK 227 Jn 32
Sharafa O SUD 312 Hf 39
Sharan Jogīzai O PK 227 Jn 30
Sharbot Lake O CDN 60 Dk 23
Share O WAN 320 Gj 41
Shargalle O WAN 320 Gl 39
Shari O J 250 Mj 24
Shari ~ RDC 324 Hh 44
Sharīf Ya'qūb O SUD 313 Hj 38
Sharjah O UAE 226 Jf 33
Sharkawshchyna O BY 171 Hf 18
Shark Bay ~ AUS 368 Lg 58
Sharkh O OM 226 Jh 35
Sharm el Sheikh O ET 301 Hj 32
Sharon O USA 71 Dh 25
Sharon Springs O USA 70 Cm 26
Sharqpur O PK 230 Ka 30
Sharwangai O PK 223 Jn 29
Shasha O WAN 320 Gj 42
Shasha O ETH 325 Hk 42
Shashani ~ ZW 349 Hg 56
Shashe O RB 349 Hf 56
Shashe ~ RB 349 Hf 56
Shashemenē O ETH 325 Hm 42
Shashi O VRC 243 Lg 30
Shasta ~ USA 64 Ca 25
Shatahkung O MYA 254 Kp 32
Shatawī O SUD 313 Hh 38
Shatskiy Rise Ψ 27 Sb 6
Shaunavon O CDN 51 Ch 21
Shaw ~ AUS 360 Lk 56
Shawano O USA 57 Dd 23
Shaweneetown S.H.S. ★ USA 71 Dd 27
Shawinigan O CDN 60 Dm 22
Shawnee O USA 70 Cp 28
Shawnee O USA 70 Da 26
Shawneetown O USA 71 Dd 27
Shawo O VRC 243 Lh 30
Shayang O VRC 243 Lg 30
Shay Gap O AUS 360 Ll 56
Shayhk Sadin O SUD 312 Hh 38
Shaykh Gok O SUD 312 Hj 40
Shchuchiy Khrebet ⛰ RUS 205 Zb 6
Shchuchyn O BY 171 He 19
Shea O GUY 112 Ee 44
Shebeli ~ ETH 328 Hp 43
Shebeli ~ SP 329 Ja 44
Sheboygan O USA 57 De 24
Shebshi Mountains ⛰ WAN 320 Gm 41
Shediac O CDN 61 Eb 22
Sheenjek River ~ USA 46 Bc 11
Sheep Mountain △ USA 65 Cj 25
Sheep Range ⛰ USA 64 Ce 27
Sheep Springs O USA 65 Ch 27
Sheet Harbour O CDN 61 Ec 23
Sheffield O USA 81 Cm 30
Sheffield O GB 163 Gf 19
Sheffield O NZ 383 Nj 67
Shegyin O MYA 262 Kn 37
Shēh Husēn O ETH 325 Hn 42
Sheho O CDN 51 Cl 20
Shehong O VRC 242 Lc 30
Sheikh Hasan O ETH 313 Hk 39
Sheila O AUS 374 Mf 56
Shekhupūra O PK 230 Kb 30
Shekī O ETH 325 Hl 42
Shelbina O USA 70 Db 26
Shelburne O CDN 57 Dh 23
Shelburne O CDN 61 Eb 24
Shelburne Bay ~ AUS 365 Mh 51
Shelburne Museum ★ USA 60 Dm 23
Shelby O USA 51 Cg 21
Shelby O USA 71 Dh 28
Shelbyville O USA 71 Dd 26
Shelbyville O USA 71 De 28
Shelbyville O USA 71 Df 26
Shelden O USA 56 Cp 24
Sheldon O ZA 358 He 62
Sheldon Point O USA 46 Ag 14
Shelikhov Gulf ≈ RUS 205 Yb 6
Shelikof Strait ~ USA 10 Ba 4
Shell Beach O USA 86 Dd 31
Shellbrook O CDN 51 Cj 19
Shellen O WAN 320 Gn 41
Shellharbour O AUS 379 Mm 63
Shell Lake O CDN 51 Cj 19
Shell Lakes ~ AUS 369 Lp 60
Shellmouth O CDN 56 Cm 20
Shelter Cove O USA 64 Bp 25
Sheltikof Strait ≈ USA 46 An 17
Shelton O USA 50 Ca 22
Shemgang O BHT 235 Kk 32
Shemkhiya O SUD 312 Hj 36
Shenandoah O USA 70 Da 25
Shenandoah ~ USA 74 Dj 26
Shenandoah Nat. P. ★ USA 74 Dj 26
Shendam O WAN 320 Gl 41
Shendi O SUD 313 Hj 37
Shenge O WAL 316 Fp 42
Shengsi ⌂ VRC 246 Lm 30
Sheng Xian O VRC 259 Ll 31
Shenjiamen O VRC 259 Lm 31
Shenmu O VRC 243 Lf 26
Shennongjia ★ VRC 243 Lf 30
Sheno O ETH 325 Hm 41
Shentang Shan △ VRC 255 Lf 34
Shen Xian O VRC 243 Lh 26
Shenzhen O VRC 258 Lh 34
Sheo O IND 227 Jp 32
Sheokhala O IND 235 Kh 34
Sheopur O IND 234 Kc 33
Shepahua O PE 128 Dm 51
Shepherd Island ⌂ VU 386 Ng 54
Shepparton O AUS 379 Mj 64
Sherbro Island ⌂ WAL 316 Fp 42
Sherbrooke O CDN 60 Dn 23
Sherbro River ~ WAL 316 Fp 42
Sherburne Reef ⌂ PNG 287 Ml 47
Sherda O TCH 309 Ha 35
Sheridan O USA 50 Ca 23
Sheridan O USA 51 Cj 23
Sheridan O USA 70 Db 28
Sheridan Lake O USA 65 Cl 26
Sheringa O AUS 378 Md 62
Sherlock ~ AUS 360 Lj 56
Sherlock O AUS 378 Mf 63
Sherman O USA 70 Cp 29
Sherman Basin ~ CDN 42 Fb 5
Sherman Mills O USA 60 Dp 23
Sherman Reservoir ~ USA 70 Cn 25
Sherpur O BD 235 Kj 33
s-Hertogenbosch O NL 163 Gj 20
Sherwood O RB 349 Hf 57
Sherwood Park O CDN 51 Cf 19
Shetland Islands ⌂ GB 162 Gf 15
Shevgaon O IND 238 Kb 36
She Xian O VRC 243 Lg 27
She Xian O VRC 258 Lk 31
Sheyang O VRC 246 Ll 29
Sheyenne Natl. Grassland ⚲ USA 56 Cp 22
Sheyenne River ~ USA 56 Cn 22
Shibām O YE 219 Jc 38
Shibata O J 251 Mf 27
Shibecha O J 250 Mj 24
Shibetsu O J 250 Mh 23
Shibing O VRC 255 Le 32
Shibushi O J 247 Mb 30
Shibuyunje O Z 341 Hf 53
Shicheng O VRC 258 Lj 32
Shichinohe O J 250 Mg 25
Shidao O VRC 246 Lm 27
Shigong Si ★ VRC 243 Le 27
Shihezi O VRC 204 Tc 10
Shiikh O SP 328 Ja 41
Shijiazhuang O VRC 243 Lh 26
Shikārpur O PK 227 Jn 32
Shikārpur O IND 238 Kb 38
Shikengkong △ VRC 258 Lg 33
Shikine-shima ⌂ J 251 Mf 28
Shikohābād O IND 234 Kd 32
Shikoku ⌂ J 251 Mc 29
Shikoku-sanchi ⛰ J 251 Mc 29
Shikotsu-ko ~ J 250 Mg 24
Shilabo O ETH 328 Ja 42
Shilipu O VRC 243 Lg 30
Shillong O IND 235 Kk 33
Shiloango ~ RDC 332 Gn 48
Shimabara O J 247 Mb 29
Shimba Hills ⚲ EAK 337 Hm 48
Shimbiris △ SP 328 Jb 40
Shimen O VRC 255 Lf 31
Shimian O VRC 254 Lb 31
Shimizu O J 250 Mh 24
Shimizu O J 251 Mf 28
Shimla O IND 230 Kc 30
Shimoda O J 251 Mf 28
Shimoga O IND 238 Kb 39
Shimo-Khoshi ⌂ J 247 Ma 30
Shimokita-hanto ⌂ J 250 Mg 25
Shimo-Koshiki O J 247 Ma 30
Shimong O IND 254 Km 31
Shimoni O EAK 337 Hm 48
Shimonoseki O J 247 Mb 28
Shimono-shima ⌂ J 247 Ma 28
Shimuwini O ZA 352 Hh 57
Shinan O VRC 255 Le 34
Shinano ~ J 251 Mf 27
Shindand O AFG 223 Jk 29
Shinga O RDC 333 He 47
Shingana O RDC 341 Hg 52
Shingbwiyang O MYA 254 Kn 32
Shingerdar Stupa ★ PK 230 Ka 28
Shingleton O USA 57 De 22
Shingletown O USA 64 Cb 25
Shingū O J 251 Me 29
Shingwedzi O ZA 352 Hh 57
Shingwedzi ~ ZA 352 Hh 57
Shinjō O J 251 Mg 26
Shinkafe O WAN 320 Gk 39
Shinnston O USA 71 Dh 26
Shinyanga O EAT 337 Hj 47
Shiogama O J 251 Mg 26
Shiojiri O J 251 Me 27
Shiono-misaki ⌓ J 251 Md 29
Ship Bottom O USA 74 Dl 26
Shiping O VRC 254 Lb 34
Shipkila △ IND 230 Kd 30
Shippagan O CDN 61 Eb 22
Shiprock O USA 65 Ch 27
Shipu O VRC 259 Ll 31
Shipwreck Coast ⏢ ZA 358 Hf 63
Shiqian O VRC 255 Le 32
Shiqiao O VRC 246 Lk 30
Shiquan O VRC 243 Le 29
Shiquanhe O VRC 230 Kd 29
Shirahama O J 251 Md 29
Shirakami ★ J 250 Mg 25
Shirakawa O J 251 Mg 27
Shirane-san △ J 251 Mf 27
Shiranuka O J 250 Mh 24
Shiraro O ETH 313 Hm 38
Shiraroi O J 250 Mg 24
Shirati O EAT 337 Hk 46
Shiratori O J 251 Me 28
Shirdi O IND 238 Kb 36
Shiretoko ⚲ J 250 Mj 23
Shiretokohanto ⌓ J 205 Xb 10
Shiretokohanto ⌂ J 250 Mj 23
Shiretokomisaki ⌓ J 250 Mj 23
Shirinthorn Reservoir ~ THA 263 Lc 38
Shiripuno ~ EC 116 Dk 46
Shirley O USA 70 Db 28
Shirley O NAM 348 Hb 58
Shiroishi O J 251 Mg 27
Shirpur O IND 234 Kb 35
Shirya-saki ⌓ J 250 Mg 25
Shishaldin Volcano △ USA 46 Ag 17
Shishi O VRC 258 Lk 33
Shīshīnda O ETH 325 Hk 42
Shishmaref O USA 46 Ag 11
Shishou O VRC 258 Lg 31
Shismaref O USA 23 Ab 3
Shiura O J 250 Mg 25
Shivpuri O IND 234 Kc 33
Shivwitta Plateau ⏢ USA 64 Cf 27
Shiwan Dash ⏢ VRC 255 Ld 35
Shiwa Ngandu O Z 341 Hh 51
Shiwulidun O VRC 243 Ld 27
Shixing O VRC 258 Lh 33
Shiyan O VRC 243 Lf 29
Shizhu O VRC 243 Le 30
Shizhu O VRC 259 Ll 31
Shizilu O VRC 255 Le 35
Shizong O VRC 255 Lc 33
Shizuishan O VRC 243 Lc 26
Shizuishan O VRC 243 Ld 26
Shizunai O J 250 Mg 24
Shizuoka O J 251 Me 28
Shklow O BY 171 Hg 18
Shkodër O AL 194 Hb 24
Shkumbin ~ AL 194 Hc 25
Shoal Bay O IND 262 Kl 40
Shoalhaven ~ AUS 379 Mm 63
Shoal Lake O CDN 56 Cm 20
Shoalwater Bay ~ AUS 375 Mm 57
Shōbara O J 251 Mc 28
Shoga O EAT 337 Hj 50
Sholingnur O IND 238 Kd 39
Shoranūr O IND 239 Kc 40
Shorap O PK 227 Jl 33
Shoreacres O CDN 50 Cc 21
Shorkot O PK 230 Ka 30
Shorobe O RB 341 Hd 55
Shortland Island ⌂ SOL 290 Mp 49
Shoshone O USA 50 Ce 24
Shoshone O USA 64 Cd 28
Shoshone Mountains ⛰ USA 64 Cd 26
Shoshone River ~ USA 51 Ch 23
Shoshong O RB 349 Hf 57
Shoshoni O USA 51 Cj 24
Shott Ech Chergui ~ DZ 293 Gf 28
Shott el Djerid ~ TN 296 Gl 29
Shott El Fedjaj ~ TN 296 Gl 29
Shott el Gharsa ~ TN 296 Gk 28
Shott el Hodna ~ DZ 296 Gj 28
Shott el Malah ~ DZ 296 Gj 29
Shott Melrhir ~ DZ 296 Gk 28
Shott Merouane ~ DZ 296 Gk 29
Shou Xian O VRC 246 Lj 29
Shouyang O VRC 243 Lg 27
Shovelanna Hill △ AUS 360 Lk 57
Showil ~ SUD 312 Hh 38
Show Low O USA 65 Cg 28
Shreveport O USA 70 Da 29
Shrewsbury O GB 163 Ge 19
Shrines of Ise ★ J 251 Me 28
Shuajingsi O VRC 242 Lb 29
Shuangfeng O VRC 258 Lg 32
Shuanggou O VRC 243 Lg 29
Shuanghe O VRC 243 Lf 30
Shuangjiang O VRC 254 Kp 34
Shuanglin Si ★ VRC 243 Lf 27
Shuanglin Si ★ VRC 243 Lg 27
Shuangpai O VRC 255 Lf 33
Shuangpaishan O VRC 258 Lg 32
Shuangpai Shuiku ~ VRC 255 Lf 33
Shuanyashan O VRC 205 Wc 9
Shuanyashan O VRC 250 Mb 22
Shubuta O USA 86 Dd 30
Shucheng O VRC 246 Lj 30
Shudanzhuang O VRC 231 Kg 27
Shufu O VRC 230 Kb 26
Shuganu O IND 254 Kl 33
Shuikou O VRC 255 Le 33
Shujāābād O PK 227 Jp 31
Shule O VRC 230 Kc 26
Shule He ~ VRC 231 Km 25
Shullsburg O USA 56 Dc 24
Shumagin Island ⌂ USA 10 Ba 4
Shumilina O BY 171 Hg 18
Shunchang O VRC 258 Lj 32
Shunde O VRC 258 Lg 34
Shungnak O USA 46 Al 11
Shuozhou O VRC 243 Lg 26
Shurugwi O ZW 341 Hh 55
Shushufindi Central O EC 116 Dk 46
Shuswap ~ CDN 50 Cc 20
Shuswap Lake ~ CDN 50 Cc 20
Shute Harbour O AUS 375 Ml 56
Shuttleworth O AUS 375 Mk 57
Shuyak Island ⌂ USA 46 An 15
Shuyang O VRC 246 Lk 28
Shwebo O MYA 254 Km 34
Shwedaung O MYA 254 Km 36
Shwedaung O MYA 254 Kn 35
Shwemyo O MYA 254 Km 35
Shymkent O KZ 19 Na 5
Shyok O IND 230 Kc 28
Shyok ~ PK 230 Kc 28
Shyok ~ IND 230 Kd 28
Shyshchytsy O BY 171 Hf 19
Si O RMM 317 Gd 39
Si. Amor Bou Hajla O TN 296 Gl 28
Siabuwa O ZW 341 Hf 54
Siāhān Range ⛰ PK 226 Jk 32
Siak ~ RI 270 La 45
Siālkot O IND 230 Kb 29
Sialum O PNG 287 Mk 49
Siaman O PNG 287 Mn 48
Sianhala O CI 305 Gc 40
Siapa O YV 107 Ea 44
Siapa o Matapire ~ YV 112 Ea 45
Siara O PNG 290 Mp 48
Siare ~ CO 107 Dn 44
Siare Guajibos O CO 107 Dn 44
Siargao Island ⌂ RP 267 Lp 41
Siasi O RP 275 Ll 43
Siasiada O PNG 287 Mm 51
Siasibabole O Z 341 Hf 54
Siasi Island ⌂ RP 275 Ll 43
Siaton Point ⌓ RP 267 Lm 41
Siavonga O Z 341 Hg 54
Siay O RP 275 Lm 42
Siba O IRQ 215 Jb 30
Sibabai O RI 270 La 47
Sibaj O RUS 154 Rc 8
Sibalay Aricha O BD 235 Kj 34
Sibanicú O C 101 Dk 35
Sibayo O PE 128 Dn 53
Sibayu O RI 274 Lk 45
Sibayu O RI 275 Lk 45
Sibdu O SUD 312 Hf 40
Şibelanga O RI 270 Kp 44
Šibenik O HR 194 Gp 24
Siberia ⏢ RUS 22 Pb 3
Siberia ⏢ RUS 204 Ub 6
Siberimanua O RI 270 Kp 47
Sibi O PK 227 Jm 31
Sibi O RMM 316 Gb 39
Sibidiri O PNG 286 Mh 50
Sibigo O RI 270 Km 44
Sibiloi National Park ⚲ EAK 325 Hl 43
Šibīn Al-Kūm O ET 301 Hh 30
Sibinda O NAM 341 Hd 54
Sibircevo O RUS 250 Mc 23
Sibiti O RCB 332 Gn 47
Sibiti ~ EAT 337 Hk 47
Sibiu O RO 175 He 23

Şereflikoçhisar - Sibiu 469

Sīb Kūh ⛰ IR 215 Je 32
Sibley O USA 56 Da 24
Sibolga O RI 270 Kp 45
Siboluton O RI 275 Ll 45
Siborang O RI 270 Kp 45
Siborongborong O RI 270 Kp 44
Sibr O OM 219 Jf 37
Sibsagar O IND 254 Km 32
Sibu O MAL 271 Lf 44
Sibuco O RP 275 Ll 42
Sibuguey ≈ RP 275 Lm 42
Sibuguey Bay ≈ RP 275 Lm 42
Si Bun Ruang O THA 263 Lb 37
Siburan O MAL 271 Lf 45
Sibut O RCA 321 Hb 43
Sibutu Group ◬ RP 274 Lk 43
Sibutu Island ◬ RP 274 Lk 43
Sibutu Passage ≈ RP 274 Lk 43
Sibuyan Island ◬ RP 267 Lm 39
Sibuyan Sea ≈ RP 267 Lm 39
Sibwesa O EAT 336 Hh 49
Sicamous O CDN 50 Cc 20
Sica Sica O BOL 129 Ea 54
Sicasica ⛰ BOL 129 Ea 54
Siccus ~ AUS 378 Mf 61
Sicheng Dao ◬ VRC 246 Lm 26
Si Chomphu O THA 263 Lb 37
Sichon O THA 262 Kp 41
Sichote-Alin ⛰ RUS 250 Md 23
Sichote-Alin' ⛰ RUS 26 Rb 5
Sichuan ⊙ VRC 255 Lb 31
Sicília ⊙ I 185 Gn 27
Sicilian Channel ≈ I 185 Gm 26
Sicily ◬ I 185 Gn 27
Sico Tinto o Negro ~ HN 97 Df 38
Sicuani O PE 128 Dn 53
Sicunusa O SD 352 Hh 59
Sidangoli O RI 275 Lp 45
Siddāpur O IND 238 Kb 38
Siddhapur O IND 227 Ka 34
Siddipet O IND 238 Kd 36
Sideia Island ◬ PNG 287 Mm 51
Sidéradougou O BF 317 Gd 40
Sidhauli O IND 234 Ke 32
Sidhi O IND 234 Ke 33
Sidhnūr O IND 238 Kc 38
Sīdī ,Abdarrahmān O ET 301 Hg 30
Sidi Aïssa O DZ 296 Gh 28
Sidi Akhfennir O MA 292 Ga 31
Sidi Ali O DZ 293 Gg 27
Sidi-Allal-el-Babravi O MA 293 Gc 28
Sīdī as Ṣayd O LAR 297 Gn 29
Sīdī Barrānī O ET 300 He 30
Sidi Bel Abbes O DZ 293 Gf 28
Sidi-Bennour O MA 292 Gb 29
Sidi-Bettache O MA 293 Gc 29
Sidi Boubekeur O DZ 293 Gg 28
Sidi Bouzid O TN 296 Gl 28
Sidi-Hajjaj O MA 293 Gc 29
Sidi-Harazem O MA 293 Gd 29
Sidi Ifni O MA 292 Ga 31
Sidi-Kacem O MA 293 Gd 28
Sidikalang O RI 270 Kn 44
Sidi Khaled O DZ 296 Gj 28
Sīdī Khalīfah O LAR 300 Hb 29
Sidikila O RG 316 Gb 40
Sidi Mokhtâr O RMM 305 Ge 36
Sidi-Mokhtar O MA 292 Gb 30
Sidi Moussa ~ DZ 296 Gj 32
Sidi-Moussa O MA 292 Gb 29
Sidi-Slimane O MA 293 Gc 28
Sidi-Smaïl O MA 292 Gb 29
Sidi Yousset O TN 297 Gm 28
Sidlaghatta O IND 238 Kc 39
Sidli O IND 235 Kk 32
Sidney O CDN 50 Ca 21
Sidney O USA 51 Ck 22
Sidney O USA 60 Dl 24
Sidney O USA 65 Cl 25
Sidney O USA 71 Df 25
Sido O RMM 304 Gc 40
Sido O RCA 321 Hb 41
Sidoarjo O RI 279 Lg 49
Sidon O RL 208 Hk 29
Sidondo O RI 279 Lk 46
Sidrolândia O BR 140 Eg 56
Sidwadweni O ZA 349 Hg 61
Siedlce O PL 170 Hd 19
Siegen O D 174 Gl 20
Siékorolé O RMM 316 Gb 40
Siembra O RI 283 Mc 47
Siemiatycze O PL 171 Hd 19
Siěmpang O K 263 Ld 38
Siěm Réap O K 263 Lb 39
Siena O I 185 Gm 24
Sieradz O PL 174 Hb 20
Sierpc O PL 170 Hb 19
Sierra Ambargasta ⛰ RA 137 Ec 60
Sierra Añueque ⛰ RA 147 Dp 66
Sierra Balmaceda ⛰ RCH 152 Dn 72
Sierra Barmeja ⛰ E 184 Gd 27
Sierra Blanca △ USA 65 Ck 29
Sierra Blanca O USA 80 Ck 30
Sierra Blanca de la Totora ⛰ RA 147 Dp 66
Sierra Cavalonga ⛰ PY 136 Ea 57
Sierra Chica O RA 137 Ed 64
Sierra Colorada ⛰ RA 136 Eb 58
Sierra Colorada O RA 147 Ea 66
Sierra Cuadrada ⛰ RA 152 Dp 68
Sierra Cuntamana ⛰ PE 116 Dl 49
Sierra d. Alcaraz ⛰ E 184 Ge 26
Sierra D. Tejeda ♀ E 184 Ge 27
Sierra da Fartura ⛰ BR 140 Eh 59
Sierra de Aguas Calientes ⛰ RA 136 Ea 59
Sierra de Alto Pencoso ⛰ RA 137 Ea 62
Sierra de Amambay ⛰ PY 140 Eg 57
Sierra de Ancasti ⛰ RA 137 Eb 60
Sierra de Auca Mahuida ⛰ RA 137 Dp 64
Sierra de Bahoruco ⛰ DOM 101 Dn 36
Sierra de Calalaste ⛰ RA 136 Ea 59
Sierra de Carapé ⛰ ROU 146 Eg 63
Sierra de Chipchihua ⛰ RA 147 Dp 67
Sierra de Cura Malal ⛰ RA 137 Ec 64
Sierra de Famatina ⛰ RA 136 Ea 60
Sierra de Guadarrama ⛰ E 184 Gd 25
Sierra de Guampí ⛰ YV 112 Eb 43
Sierra de Juarez ⛰ MEX 64 Ce 29
Sierra de Lacandón ⛰ GCA 93 Dc 37
Sierra de la Giganta ⛰ MEX 80 Cg 32
Sierra de Lágrima ⛰ MEX 80 Ck 30
Sierra de la Macarena ♀ CO 106 Dm 44
Sierra de la Neblina ⛰ YV 112 Eb 45
Sierra de la Punilla ⛰ RA 137 Dp 61
Sierra de las Minas ⛰ GCA 93 Dc 38
Sierra de la Ventana O RA 147 Ed 65
Sierra del Carmen ⛰ USA 81 Cl 31
Sierra del Centinela ⛰ RA 136 Eb 58
Sierra del Gata ⛰ E 184 Gc 25
Sierra del Nevado ⛰ RA 137 Dp 63
Sierra de los Cuchumatanes ⛰ GCA 93 Dc 38
Sierra de los Frailes ⛰ MEX 92 Cj 34
Sierra de los Llanos ⛰ RA 137 Ea 61
Sierra de los Tuxtla ⛰ MEX 93 Da 36
Sierra del Tontal ⛰ RA 137 Dp 61
Sierra del Volcán ⛰ RA 146 Ee 64
Sierra Del Xistral △ E 184 Gc 24
Sierra del Zamuro ⛰ YV 112 Ec 43
Sierra de Maigualida ⛰ YV 112 Eb 43
Sierra de Manchao ⛰ RA 136 Ea 60
Sierra de Misiones ⛰ RA 140 Eg 59
Sierra de Neiba ⛰ DOM 101 Dn 36
Sierra de Ocoa ⛰ DOM 101 Dn 36
Sierra de Perijá ⛰ CO 107 Dm 41
Sierra de San Antonio ⛰ MEX 80 Cg 30
Sierra de San Boria ⛰ MEX 75 Cf 31
Sierra de San Luis ⛰ RA 137 Ea 62
Sierra de Sanogasta ⛰ RA 137 Ea 60
Sierra de San Pedro ⛰ E 184 Gc 26
Sierra de San Pedro Mártir ⛰ MEX 75 Ce 30
Sierra de Segura ⛰ E 184 Ge 27
Sierra de Susapampa ⛰ RA 137 Eb 61
Sierra de Tatul ⛰ RCH 137 Dn 60
Sierra de Unturán ⛰ YV 112 Eb 44
Sierra de Unturán ⛰ YV 112 Eb 45
Sierra de Valle Fertil ⛰ RA 137 Dp 60
Sierra de Velasco ⛰ RA 137 Ea 60
Sierra do Boqueirão ⛰ BR 146 Eg 60
Sierra do Espigão ⛰ BR 140 Ej 59
Sierra do Mucajaí ⛰ BR 112 Ed 44
Sierra el Catire ⛰ YV 112 Ec 42
Sierra el Humo △ MEX 75 Cf 30
Sierra El Nido ⛰ MEX 80 Cj 31
Sierra Geral ⛰ BR 140 Ej 58
Sierra Gorda O RCH 136 Dp 57
Sierra Grande O RA 147 Eb 66
Sierra Huancache ⛰ RA 147 Dn 67
Sierra la Blanca ⛰ RA 136 Ea 59
Sierra La Encantada ⛰ MEX 81 Cl 31
Sierra la Esperanza ⛰ HN 96 Df 38
Sierra Leone □ WAL 316 Fp 41
Sierra Leone Basin ▾ 30 Ja 9
Sierra Leone Rise ▾ 30 Hb 9
Sierra Libre ⛰ MEX 80 Cg 31
Sierra los Ajos ⛰ MEX 80 Cg 30
Sierra Madre ⛰ RP 267 Ll 38
Sierra Madre de Chiapas ⛰ MEX 93 Db 37
Sierra Madre del Sur ⛰ MEX 92 Cm 37
Sierra Madre Occidental ⛰ MEX 80 Ch 30
Sierra Madre Oriental ⛰ MEX 81 Cl 31
Sierra Madrona ⛰ E 184 Gd 26
Sierra Maestra ⛰ C 101 Dk 36
Sierra Mojada O MEX 81 Cl 32
Sierra Morena ⛰ E 184 Gc 27
Sierra Nevada ⛰ USA 64 Cb 26
Sierra Nevada ⛰ E 184 Ge 27
Sierra Nevada de Santa Marta ⛰ CO 106 Dm 40
Sierra Parima ⛰ BR 112 Eb 44
Sierra Peyuami ⛰ YV 112 Ec 43
Sierra Pire Mahuida ⛰ RA 147 Dp 67
Sierra San Luis ♀ YV 107 Dp 40
Sierras de Córdoba ⛰ RA 137 Eb 62
Sierra Sta. Victoria ⛰ PY 136 Eb 57
Sierra Tapirapeco ⛰ YV 112 Eb 45
Sierraville O USA 64 Cb 26
Sierra Vista O USA 80 Cg 30
Sierra Vizcaíno ⛰ MEX 75 Ce 32
Sierre de Miahuatlán ⛰ MEX 92 Cp 36
Siete Puntas ~ PY 140 Ee 57
Sif O YE 219 Jc 38
Sifahandra O RI 270 Kn 45
Sīfenī O ETH 313 Hn 39
Sif Fatima O DZ 296 Gl 30
Sifié O CI 305 Gc 42
Sífnos ◬ GR 194 He 27
Sig O DZ 293 Gf 28
Sigatal O MAL 274 Lj 43
Sigatoka O FJI 387 Nl 55
Sigatoka ~ FJI 387 Nl 55
Sigenti O RI 275 Ll 45
Sighetu Marmației O RO 175 Hd 22
Sighișoara O RO 175 He 22
Sigira O YE 219 Jf 39
Sigiriya O CL 239 Ke 41
Sigli O RI 270 Kn 43
Siglufjörður O IS 158 Fl 12
Signal Hill N.H.P. ★ CDN 61 Eh 22
Sigony O RUS 181 Jc 19
Sigor O EAK 325 Hk 45
Sigourney O USA 70 Db 25
Siguanea O C 100 Dg 35
Siguatepeque O HN 96 De 38
Sigüenza O E 184 Ge 25
Siguiri O RG 316 Gb 40
Sigulda O LV 171 He 17
Siguri Falls ~ EAT 337 Hl 50
Sigutlat Lake ~ CDN 50 Bn 19
Şihām O YE 218 Hp 38
Sihany O RUS 181 Jb 19
Sihāwā O IND 234 Ke 35
Sihong O VRC 246 Lk 29
Sihora O IND 234 Kd 34
Sihuas O PE 116 Dk 50
Sihui O VRC 258 Lg 34
Siikajoki O FIN 159 He 13
Siilinjärvi O FIN 159 Hf 14
Siirt O TR 202 Hn 27
Sijeme ⛰ HR 174 Gp 23
Sijiao Shan ◬ VRC 246 Lm 30
Sika O IND 227 Jn 34
Sikandra Rao O IND 234 Kc 32
Sikar O IND 234 Kb 32
Sikasso O RMM 317 Gd 40
Sikensi O CI 317 Gd 43
Sikereti O NAM 340 Hc 55
Sikeston O USA 71 Dd 27
Sikhoraphum O THA 263 Lb 38
Sikia O GR 194 He 26
Síkinos ◬ GR 194 He 27
Sikkim ⊙ IND 235 Kj 32
Sikonge O EAT 336 Hj 48
Sikongo O Z 341 Hd 53
Sikopo Island ◬ SOL 290 Na 49
Sikoro O EAU 325 Hk 45
Sikthjah O RUS 204 Wa 5
Siktjah O RUS 204 Wb 5
Sikuto O RI 275 Ll 45
Sikwane O RB 349 Hf 59
Sil ~ E 184 Gc 24
Sila O UAE 215 Jd 33
Sila O PNG 287 Ml 50
Şilago O RP 267 Ln 40
Šilalė O LT 170 Hd 18
Silango O PNG 287 Mm 48
Şilao O MEX 92 Cm 35
Šilauliai O LT 171 Hd 18
Silavatturai O CL 239 Kd 41
Silay O RP 267 Lm 40
Silchar O IND 254 Kl 33
Silda O IND 235 Kh 34
Şile O TR 195 Hg 25
Šilera ~ IND 238 Ke 37
Silesia O USA 51 Ch 23
Silesian Lowland ⏥ PL 174 Gp 20
Silet O DZ 308 Gj 34
Silheti O IND 234 Ke 35
Silhoutte ◬ SY 329 Jf 48
Siliana O TN 296 Gl 27
Silifke O TR 195 Hk 27
Siliguri O IND 235 Kj 32
Silil O SP 328 Hp 40
Siling Co ~ VRC 231 Kj 30
Silistra O BG 175 Hf 23
Silivri O TR 195 Hg 25
Şiljan ~ S 158 Gp 15
Şilka O RUS 204 Vc 8
Şilka ~ RUS 204 Vc 8
Šilkan O RUS 23 Sa 4
Silkeborg O DK 170 Gl 17
Silk Road ★ VRC 230 Kf 27
Silkwood O AUS 365 Mk 54
Sillamäe O EST 171 Hf 16
Sillānwāli O PK 230 Ka 30
Silli O BF 317 Ge 40
Şillod O IND 234 Kb 35
Šil'naja Balka O KZ 181 Jc 20
Siloams Sprs. O USA 70 Da 27
Silobela O ZW 341 Hg 55
Şilong O VRC 255 Le 34
Šilovo O RUS 181 Hn 18
Silowana Plains ⏥ Z 341 Hd 54
Silsand O N 158 Ha 11
Siltar O LAR 297 Ha 30
Siluas O RI 271 Le 45
Siluko O WAN 320 Gj 42
Şiluko ~ WAN 320 Gj 42
Šilutė O LT 170 Hc 18
Silutshana O ZA 352 Hh 60
Silva O USA 71 Dc 27
Silva ~ BR 133 Ej 52
Silvan O TR 202 Hn 26
Silvan Brj. ~ TR 202 Hn 26
Sīlvāne O IR 209 Ja 27
Silvânia O BR 133 Ek 54
Silvanópolis O BR 133 Ek 51
Silver Bank ▾ 101 Dp 35
Silver City O USA 65 Ch 29
Silver City O USA 74 Dj 28
Silver Dollar O CDN 56 Dc 21
Silver Islet O CDN 57 Dd 21
Silver Lake O USA 50 Cb 24
Silver Park O CDN 51 Ck 19
Silver Peak O USA 64 Cd 27
Silver Springs O USA 64 Cc 26
Silver Star Mine O AUS 365 Mf 55
Silverthorne O USA 65 Cj 26
Silverthrone Mountain △ CDN 50 Bn 20
Silverton O USA 50 Ca 23
Silverton O USA 65 Cj 27
Silverton O USA 70 Cm 28
Silverton O AUS 378 Mg 61
Silves O BR 120 Ee 47
Silves O P 184 Gb 27
Silvia O CO 106 Dk 44
Sima O COM 345 Ja 52
Simakalo O RI 270 La 47
Simalugiri O IND 254 Km 32
Şimanggang O MAL 271 Lf 45
Šimanovsk O RUS 205 Wb 8
Simao O VRC 254 La 34
Simão Dias O BR 125 Fb 51
Simão Pereira O BR 141 En 56
Simara Island ◬ RP 267 Lm 39
Simav O TR 195 Hg 26
Simav ~ TR 195 Hg 26
Simba O RDC 333 Hd 45
Simbabwe □ ZW 341 Hf 55
Simbai O PNG 287 Mj 48
Simberi Island ◬ PNG 287 Mm 47
Simbo ◬ SOL 290 Na 50
Simbo O EAT 336 Hg 48
Simcoe O CDN 57 Dh 24
Simdega O IND 235 Kg 34
Sīmēn ♀ ETH 313 Hm 39
Sīmēn ⛰ ETH 313 Hm 39
Simenti O SN 316 Fp 39
Simferopol' O UA 175 Hj 23
Simga O IND 234 Ke 35
Simhadripuram O IND 238 Kd 38
Simi O GR 195 Hf 27
Simi ◬ GR 195 Hf 27
Simianona ~ RM 345 Jc 54
Similigurha O IND 234 Kf 36
Similipal National Park ♀ IND 235 Kh 35
Simindou O RCA 321 Hd 42
Simiri O RN 305 Gh 38
Simiriundui O GUY 112 Ed 42
Simitli O BG 194 Hd 25
Simi Valley O USA 64 Cc 28
Simiyu ~ EAT 337 Hj 47
Simla O USA 65 Ck 26
Simmie O CDN 51 Ch 21
Simmler O USA 64 Cc 28
Simmons Peak △ USA 50 Ce 22
Simo O FIN 159 He 13
Simões O BR 124 Ep 49
Simões Filho O BR 125 Fa 52
Simojärvi ~ FIN 159 Hf 12
Simojovel O MEX 93 Db 37
Simonbondo O RCB 332 Gn 47
Simon's Town O ZA 358 Ha 63
Simpang O RI 278 Lb 46
Simpang Kanan ~ RI 270 Kp 44
Simpangkawat O RI 270 Kp 44
Simpang Kiri ~ RI 270 Kn 44
Simpang Lembing O MAL 271 Lb 44
Simpang Lima O MAL 270 La 44
Simpang Pertang O MAL 270 Lb 44
Simpangsukarame O RI 278 Lc 48
Simpele O FIN 159 Hg 15
Simplício Mendes O BR 124 Ep 49
Simplonpass △ CH 163 Gk 22
Simpsom ~ RCH 152 Dm 68
Simpson O CDN 51 Ck 20
Simpson Desert ⏥ AUS 374 Me 58
Simpson Desert ♀ AUS 374 Mf 58
Simpson Islands ◬ CDN 57 De 21
Simpson Peninsula ◬ CDN 43 Ga 5
Simpsons ♀ AUS 361 Mc 57
Simpsonville O USA 71 Dg 28
Şimrishamm O S 170 Gp 18
Šimsk O RUS 171 Hh 16
Simunjan O MAL 271 Lf 45
Simunul ◬ RP 275 Lk 43
Simunye O SD 352 Hh 59
Sina O PE 128 Dp 53
Sinabang O RI 270 Kn 44
Sina Daqha O SP 328 Jb 43
Sinadipan O RP 267 Ll 37
Sinai ⏥ ET 301 Hj 31
Sinaia O RO 175 He 23
Sinaloa ~ MEX 80 Cj 33
Sinaloa de Leyva O MEX 80 Ch 33
Sinamaica O YV 107 Dn 40
Sinametella O ZW 341 Hf 55
Sinan O VRC 255 Le 32
Şinanpaşa O TR 195 Hg 26
Šināș O OM 226 Jg 33
Sīnāwan O LAR 297 Gm 30
Sinawongourou O DY 317 Gh 40
Sinazongwe O Z 341 Hf 54
Sinbaungwe O MYA 254 Km 36
Sínbo O MYA 254 Kn 33
Sincan O TR 195 Hl 26
Sincelejo O CO 106 Dl 41
Sincerin O CO 106 Dl 40
Sinchaingbyin O MYA 235 Kl 35
Sinclair O CDN 56 Cm 21
Sind Indus ~ IND 230 Kd 29
Sind ~ IND 234 Kd 32
Sinda O Z 341 Hh 53
Sīndand ~ AFG 223 Jk 29
Sindangan O RP 267 Lm 41
Sindangan Bay ~ RP 267 Lm 41
Sindangbarang O RI 278 Ld 49
Sindara O G 332 Gm 46
Sindarë O UZB 223 Jn 25
Sindari O IND 227 Jp 33
Sindh ⊙ PK 227 Jn 32
Sindia O SN 304 Fm 38
Sindian O SN 316 Fm 39
Sindou O BF 317 Gd 40
Sinee morco cyganaķy ~ KZ 202 Jc 22
Sinegorsk O RUS 250 Mh 22
Sinegorskie O RUS 181 Hn 22
Sinendé O DY 320 Gh 40
Sines O P 184 Gb 27
Sinettä O FIN 159 He 12
Singa O SUD 313 Hj 39
Singako O TCH 321 Hb 41
Singapore ▣ SGP 271 Lb 45
Singapore □ SGP 271 Lc 45
Singaraja O RI 279 Lh 50
Singaung O MYA 254 Km 35
Sing Buri O THA 262 La 38
Singida O EAT 337 Hk 48
Singilej O RUS 181 Jc 19
Singiro △ EAU 336 Hh 46
Singkawang O RI 271 Le 45
Singkil O RI 270 Kn 44
Singleton O AUS 379 Mm 62
Singou ~ BF 317 Gg 40
Singrobo O CI 317 Gd 42
Singuédeze ~ MOC 352 Hh 57
Singye O DVRK 247 Lp 26
Sinharaja Forest Reserve ♀ CL 239 Ke 42
Sin Hô O VN 255 Lb 34
Sinhung O DVRK 247 Lp 25
Sinie Lipjagi O RUS 181 Hm 20
Siniloan O RP 267 Ll 38
Siniscola O I 185 Gl 25
Siniy, Khrebet ⛰ RUS 250 Mc 23
Sinj O HR 194 Ha 24
Sinjai O RI 282 Ll 48
Sinjaja ~ RUS 204 Wa 6
Sinjembela O Z 341 Hd 54
Sinkāt O SUD 313 Hl 36
Sinkiang ⊙ VRC 231 Kg 27
Sinmido ◬ DVRK 246 Ln 26
Sinnamary O F 113 Eh 43
Sinnamary ~ F 113 Eh 43
Sinnar O IND 238 Kb 36
Sinnūris O ET 301 Hh 31
Sinop O BR 132 Eg 52
Sinop O TR 195 Hk 24
Sinsicap O PE 116 Dj 49
Sinta O RG 316 Fp 40
Sintang O RI 271 Lf 45
Sint Estatius ◬ NL 104 Ec 37
Sint Maarten ◬ NL 104 Ec 37
Sint Nicolaas O NL 107 Dp 39
Sinton O USA 81 Cp 31
Sintong O RI 270 La 45
Sintra O P 184 Gb 26
Sintra O CI 305 Gc 42
Sinú ~ CO 106 Dk 41
Sinuiju O DVRK 246 Ln 25
Sinujiif O SP 328 Jc 41
Sinungu O Z 341 Hd 53
Sioma O Z 341 Hd 54
Sioma Ngwezi ♀ Z 341 Hd 54
Sion O CH 163 Gk 22
Siota O SOL 290 Nc 50
Sioux Center O USA 56 Cp 24
Sioux City O USA 56 Cp 24
Sioux Falls O USA 56 Cp 24
Sioux Ind. Mus. ★ USA 56 Cm 24
Sioux Lookout O CDN 56 Dc 20
Sioux Narrows O CDN 56 Da 21
Sioux Rapids O USA 56 Da 24
Sipacate O GCA 93 Dc 39
Sipalay O RP 267 Lm 41
Sipaliwini O SME 113 Ef 44
Sipao O YV 112 Eb 42
Sipilou O CI 316 Gb 42
Sipirok O RI 270 Kp 45
Şipitang O MAL 274 Lh 43
Šipovles ★ RUS 181 Hn 20
Sipsey Fork ~ USA 71 De 28
Sipuca ~ RCH 136 Dp 56
Sipupus O RI 270 Kp 45
Siquia ~ NIC 97 Df 39
Siquijor O RP 267 Lm 41
Siquijor Island ◬ RP 267 Lm 41
Siquirres O CR 97 Dg 40
Siquisique O YV 107 Dp 40
Siquita O YV 107 Ea 43
Şira ~ N 170 Gk 16
Šira O RUS 204 Tc 8
Şīra O IND 238 Kc 39
Šīraāz O IR 215 Je 31
Şirāb O OM 219 Jg 35
Šīr Abu Nu'air ◬ UAE 226 Jf 33
Sīrač O IR 226 Jg 30
Si Racha O THA 262 La 39
Sirajganj O BD 235 Kj 33
Sirakoro O RMM 316 Gb 39
Sirakorola O RMM 304 Gc 39
Siramana O RG 316 Gb 40
Şiran O TR 195 Hm 25
Širana O CI 304 Gc 41
Sirasso O CI 305 Gc 41
Siraway O RP 275 Ll 42
Sirba ~ BF 317 Gg 39
Sirba ~ RN 317 Gg 39
Sīr Banī Yās ◬ UAE 215 Je 33
Sirbin O ET 301 Hh 30
Sīrdān O IR 209 Jc 27
Sīrē O ETH 325 Hl 41
Sirē O ETH 325 Hm 41
Sire O EAT 336 Hh 48
Sir Edward Pellew Group ◬ AUS 365 Me 53
Siref O TCH 321 Hc 39
Siren O USA 56 Db 23
Sirena O CR 97 Dg 41
Siret O RO 175 Hf 22
Şiret ~ RO 175 Hf 23
Šīrgāh O IR 222 Je 27
Sīrğān O IR 226 Jf 31
Sirğān ~ IR 226 Jf 31
Şirha O IND 235 Kg 32
Šīr Ḥān O AFG 223 Jn 27
Sīrīk O IR 226 Jg 32
Sirikit Reservoir ~ THA 254 La 36
Şirinhaém O BR 124 Fc 50
Širin Tagāb ~ AFG 223 Jl 27
Sirinumu L. ~ PNG 287 Mk 50
Sirisa O PNG 286 Mg 50
Siriwo ~ RI 283 Md 47
Sir Joseph Banks Group ◬ AUS 378 Me 63
Sirkazhi O IND 239 Kd 40
Sīr Kūh △ IR 215 Je 30
Sirnak O TR 202 Hp 27
Sirohi O IND 227 Ka 33
Sirombu O RI 270 Kn 45
Sironcha O IND 238 Ke 36
Sirong O VRC 255 Le 33
Sirong O RI 282 Lm 46
Sironj O IND 234 Kc 33
Síros ◬ GR 194 He 27
Sir Robert Campbell Island ◬ MYA 262 Kp 40
Sirsa O IND 230 Kb 31
Sirsāla O IND 238 Kc 36
Sirsi O IND 238 Kb 38
Sirsilla O IND 238 Kd 36
Sirsiri O SUD 324 Hh 43
Sirte O LAR 297 Ha 30
Siruguppa O IND 238 Kc 38
Siruma O RP 267 Lm 38
Şirūr O IND 238 Kb 36
Šīrvān O IR 222 Jg 27
Sirvanskaja ravnina ⏥ AZ 202 Jb 25
Širvintos O LT 171 He 18
Sirwā O YE 218 Ja 38
Sisa O PE 116 Dk 49
Sisak O HR 174 Ha 23
Si Sa Ket O THA 263 Lc 38
Sisal O MEX 93 Dc 35
Si Samrong O THA 262 Kp 37
Si Satchanalai O THA 262 Kp 37
Si satchanalei ♀ THA 262 Kp 37
Si Sawat O THA 262 Kp 38
Sishen O ZA 349 Hd 59
Sishiliang O VRC 243 Le 26
Sishui O VRC 246 Lj 28
Sisian O ARM 202 Ja 26
Sisi Bargaon O IND 254 Km 32
Sisimiut Holsteinsborg O DK 43 Jb 5
Siskiyou Mountains ⛰ USA 64 Ca 25
Si Songkhram O THA 263 Lb 37
Sisŏphŏn O K 263 Lb 39
Sissano O PNG 286 Mh 47
Sisseton O USA 56 Cp 23
Sisseton Indian Reservation ••• USA 56 Cp 23
Sissi O TCH 321 Hb 40
Sissili ~ BF 317 Gf 40
Sīstan-ō-Bālūčestan ⊙ IR 226 Jh 32
Sisteron O F 185 Gk 23
Sisters O USA 50 Cb 23
Sistranda O N 158 Gl 14
Sitakili O RMM 316 Ga 39
Sitalike O EAT 336 Hh 49
Sitampiky O RM 345 Ja 54
Sitang O VRC 242 La 27
Sītāpur O IND 234 Ke 32
Sitasjaure ~ S 158 Ha 12
Sitawan O MAL 270 La 43
Siteki O SD 352 Hh 59
Si That O THA 263 Lb 37
Sithmarhi O IND 235 Kg 32
Sithoniá ◬ GR 194 He 26
Sitiá O BR 124 Fa 48
Sitidgi Lake ~ CDN 47 Bj 11
Sitiecito O C 100 Dh 34
Sitila O MOC 352 Hk 57
Sitio da Abadia O BR 133 El 53
Sitio do Mato O BR 125 En 52
Sitio Novo O BR 121 El 48
Sítio Novo de Tocantins O BR 121 El 48
Sitionuevo O CO 106 Dl 40
Sitka O USA 47 Bj 17
Sitkalidak Island ◬ USA 46 An 17
Sitka Sound ≈ USA 47 Bg 17
Sitole Mt. △ PNG 286 Mh 48
Sitoti O Z 341 Hd 54
Sitting Bull Burial Site ★ USA 56 Cm 22
Sitting Bull Mon. ★ USA 56 Cm 23
Sittona O ER 313 Hl 38
Sittoung ~ MYA 254 Kn 36
Sittwe O MYA 235 Kl 35
Situbondo O RI 279 Lh 49
Sitwe O Z 344 Hj 51
Si-u O MYA 254 Kn 34
Siulakderas O RI 270 La 46
Siuna O NIC 97 Df 39
Siuna O RI 282 Lm 46
Siuri O IND 235 Kh 34
Sivaganga O IND 239 Kd 41
Sivakka O FIN 159 Hg 14
Sivas O TR 195 Hl 26
Sivé O RIM 304 Fp 38
Siver Bank Passage ≈ 101 Dn 35
Siverek O TR 195 Hm 27
Siverskij O RUS 171 Hg 16
Siverskiy Khrebet ⛰ RUS 205 Yb 5
Sivolândia O BR 132 Eg 55
Sivrihisar O TR 195 Hh 26
Siwa O RI 282 Ll 47
Sīwa O ET 300 He 31
Siwan O IND 235 Kg 32
Sixaola O CR 97 Dg 41
Sixaola ~ PA 97 Dg 41
Si Xian O VRC 246 Lj 29
Six Lakes O USA 57 Df 24
Siyabuswa O ZA 349 Hg 58
Siyāh △ IR 215 Jd 31
Siyana O IND 234 Kd 31
Siyān Češme O IR 209 Ja 26
Siyang O VRC 246 Lk 29
Siyang O VRC 255 Ld 34
Siyäzän O AZ 202 Jc 25
Siyeteb O SUD 313 Hk 36
Sjain O RUS 250 Md 22
Sjamža O RUS 171 Hn 16
Sjarednelimanskaja nižina ⛰ BY 171 He 19
Sjas'stroj O RUS 171 Hj 15
Sjenica O SCG 194 Hc 24
Sjöbo O S 170 Gn 18
Sjøholt O N 158 Gk 14
Sjojacha O RUS 204 Sc 4
Sjuøyane ◬ N 158 Hc 5
Skaap ~ NAM 348 Ha 57
Skadovs'k O UA 175 Hj 22
Skafell Pike △ GB 162 Ge 18
Skagaströnd O IS 158 Fk 13
Skagaströnd O IS 158 Fk 13
Skagen O DK 170 Gm 17
Skagern ~ S 170 Gn 16
Skagerrak ~ N 170 Gl 17
Skagway O USA 6 Ca 4
Skagway O USA 47 Bg 15
Skålan O S 158 Gn 14
Skaland O N 158 Ha 11
Skälderviken ~ S 170 Gn 17
Skalholt O IS 158 Fk 13
Skalistyj hrebet ⛰ RUS 202 Hn 23
Skanderborg O DK 170 Gm 17
Skånland O N 158 Ha 11
Skardu O PK 230 Kb 28
Skare O N 170 Gk 16
Skärgårdshavets ♀ FIN 159 Hc 15
Skarstind △ N 158 Gl 14
Skarżysko-Kamienna O PL 174 Hc 20
Skaymat O MA 292 Fn 33
Skeena ~ CDN 42 Db 8
Skeena Mountains ⛰ CDN 42 Db 7
Skeena Mountains ⛰ CDN 47 Bl 17
Skeena River ~ CDN 47 Bl 17
Skegness O GB 163 Gg 19
Skeiðarársandur ⏥ IS 158 Fm 14
Skeldon O GUY 113 Ef 43
Skeleton Coast Park ♀ NAM 340 Gn 55
Skellefteå O S 159 Hc 13
Skellefteälven ~ S 158 Hb 13
Skelleftehamn O S 159 Hc 13
Skellig Michael ★ IRL 163 Ga 20
Skhira O TN 297 Gm 28
Skhirat O MA 293 Gc 29
Skhour-des-Rahamna O MA 293 Gc 29
Ski O N 170 Gm 16
Skíathos O GR 194 Hd 26
Skiathos ◬ GR 194 Hd 26
Skiatook Lake ~ USA 70 Cp 27
Skibotn O N 159 Hc 11
Skien O N 170 Gl 16
Skierniewice O PL 174 Hb 20
Skikda O DZ 296 Gk 27
Skipskop O ZA 358 Hc 63
Skipton O GB 162 Ge 19
Skipton O AUS 378 Mh 64
Skíros O GR 194 He 26
Skíros ◬ GR 194 He 26
Skive O DK 170 Gl 17
Skjalfandafljót ~ IS 158 Fm 13
Skjern O DK 170 Gl 18

470 Sīb Kūh - Skjern

◻ Country ▣ Capital city ⊙ Administrative unit O Place ♁ Island ⛰ Mountain range △ Mountain ⌒ Cape ≈ Ocean, Sea ~ Lake, River ▼ Undersea topography ▲ Glacier ♀ National park ••• Reservation ★ Point of major interest ⌓ Landscape

Skjervøy O N 159 Hc 11
Skjolden O N 158 Gk 15
Škocjanske jama ★ SLO 185 Gn 23
Skogmo O N 158 Gm 13
Skokie O USA 71 Dd 25
Sköllersta O S 170 Gp 16
Skón O K 263 Lc 40
Skópelos O GR 194 Hd 26
Skópelos ♁ GR 194 Hd 26
Skopin O RUS 181 Hm 19
Skopje ▣ MK 194 Hc 25
Skosai O RI 286 Mg 47
Skoura O MA 293 Gc 30
Skövde O S 170 Gn 16
Skovorodino O RUS 204 Wa 8
Skowhegan O USA 60 Dn 23
Skownan O CDN 56 Cn 20
Skriveri O LV 171 He 17
Skrunda O LV 170 Hd 17
Skudeneshavn O N 170 Gj 16
Skukuza O ZA 352 Hh 58
Skull Valley Indian Reservation ••• USA 64 Cf 25
Skutvik O N 158 Gp 12
Skwentna O USA 46 Ba 15
Skwierzyna O PL 170 Gp 19
Skyline Caverns ★ USA 74 Dj 26
Skyvra O UA 175 Hg 21
Slade Point ⌒ AUS 365 Mg 51
Slagnäs O S 158 Ha 13
Slana O USA 46 Bc 13
Slancy O RUS 171 Hg 16
Slasi Island ♁ RP 275 Ll 43
Slate Islands ♁ CDN 57 De 21
Slatina O HR 174 Ha 23
Slatina O RO 175 He 23
Slaton O USA 70 Cm 29
Slave ~ CDN 42 Eb 6
Slave Coast ⌓ 317 Gg 43
Slave Lake O CDN 42 Eb 7
Slave Lake ~ CDN 50 Ca 21
Slave River ~ CDN 47 Ce 15
Slavianka O RUS 205 Xa 9
Slavjanka O RUS 250 Mb 24
Slavjansk-na-Kubani O RUS 202 Hm 23
Slavonsky Brod O HR 174 Hb 23
Slavuta O UA 175 Hf 20
Slawharad O BY 171 Hh 19
Slawi O RI 278 Le 49
Sławno O PL 170 Ha 18
Slayton O USA 56 Da 24
Sleaford Bay ~ AUS 378 Md 63
Sleeper Islands ♁ CDN 43 Gb 7
Sleeping Bear Dunes N.L. ♀ USA 57 De 23
Sleepy Eye O USA 56 Da 23
Sleetmute O USA 46 Al 15
Slidell O USA 86 Dd 30
Slide Mountain △ USA 60 Dl 24
Sligo O IRL 162 Gb 18
Slim O DZ 296 Gh 28
Slim River O MAL 270 La 44
Slissel'burg O RUS 171 Hh 16
Slite O S 170 Hb 17
Slīteres rezervāts ♀ LV 170 Hd 17
Sliven O BG 194 Hf 24
Sljeme △ HR 174 Gp 23
Sloan O USA 56 Cg 24
Slobozia O RO 175 Hf 23
Slocan O CDN 50 Cd 21
Slogien △ N 158 Gk 14
Slonim O BY 171 He 19
Sloping Point ⌒ AUS 360 Lj 56
Slovakia ◻ SK 174 Ha 21
Slovakian Oro Mountains ⛰ SK 174 Hb 21
Slovarodima O RUS 22 Ra 4
Slovenia ◻ SLO 185 Gn 23
Slovjans'k O UA 181 Hl 21
Słowinski Park Narodowy ♀ PL 170 Ha 18
Sluč ~ UA 175 Hf 20
Sluderns O I 174 Gm 22
Slunj O HR 174 Gp 23
Słupsk O PL 170 Ha 18
Slurry O ZA 349 He 58
Slutsk O BY 171 Hf 19
Småland ⌓ S 170 Gn 17
Smålandsstenar O S 170 Gn 17
Small Malaita ♁ SOL 290 Nc 50
Smallwood Reservoir ~ CDN 43 Hc 8
Smalyavichy O BY 171 Hf 18
Smarhon' O BY 171 Hf 18
Smeaton O CDN 51 Ck 19
Smederevo O SCG 174 Hc 23
Smethport O USA 74 Dj 25
Smila O UA 175 Hh 21
Smiley O CDN 51 Ch 20
Smiltene O LV 171 He 17
Smirnenski O BG 194 Hd 24
Smith O CDN 6 Da 4
Smith ~ USA 51 Cg 22
Smith Arm ~ CDN 47 Ca 11
Smith Bay ≈ CDN 43 Gc 3
Smith Center O USA 70 Cn 26
Smithfield O USA 74 Dj 28
Smithfield O ZA 349 Hf 61
Smith Island ♁ IND 262 Kl 39
Smith Mountain Lake ~ USA 74 Dj 27
Smith Point ⌒ AUS 364 Mc 51
Smith River O USA 64 Bp 25
Smiths Bay ~ CDN 7 Fa 2
Smiths Falls O CDN 60 Dl 23
Smiths Ferry O USA 50 Cd 23
Smithton O AUS 378 Mj 66
Smithville O USA 86 Df 30
Smjadovo O BG 194 Hf 24
Smojlovo O RUS 171 Hg 17
Smoky ~ CDN 42 Ea 8
Smoky Bay ~ AUS 369 Mc 62
Smoky Bay O AUS 378 Md 62
Smoky Cape ⌒ AUS 379 Mn 61
Smoky Falls O CDN 57 Dg 20
Smoky Falls ~ CDN 57 Dg 20
Smoky Hill River ~ USA 70 Cm 26
Smoky Hills ⌓ USA 70 Cn 26
Smoky River ~ CDN 47 Cc 17
Smøla ♁ N 158 Gk 14
Smolensk O RUS 171 Hj 18
Smolensk-Moscow Upland ⛰ RUS 171 Hj 18
Smolikas △ GR 194 Hc 25
Smoljan O BG 194 He 25
Smoljaninovo O RUS 250 Mc 24
Smoot O USA 51 Cg 24
Smooth Rock Falls O CDN 57 Dh 21
Smörfjöll △ IS 158 Fn 13
Smyrna O USA 74 Dl 26
Smyšljaevsk O RUS 181 Jd 19
Sna. del Rincón ~ RA 136 Ea 58
Snabai O RI 283 Md 46
Snæfell △ IS 158 Fn 13
Snæfellsjökull ▲ IS 158 Fh 13
Snake Island ♁ AUS 379 Mk 65
Snake River ~ USA 56 Cm 24
Snake River Canyon ★ USA 50 Cc 22
Snake River Plain ⌓ USA 50 Ce 24
Snåsa O N 158 Gn 13
Snåsvatnet ~ N 158 Gn 13
Sneeuberg ⛰ ZA 349 He 61
Sněžka △ CZ 174 Gp 20
Snihurivka O UA 175 Hj 22
Snižne O UA 181 Hm 22
Snøhetta △ N 158 Gl 14
Snoqualmie Pass △ USA 50 Cb 22
Snota △ N 158 Gl 14
Snøtoppen △ N 158 Hb 5
Snowdon △ GB 163 Gd 19
Snowdonia ♀ GB 163 Gd 19
Snowflake O USA 65 Cg 28
Snow Hill O USA 74 Dl 26
Snow Hill Island ♁ 38 Ga 16
Snowtown O AUS 378 Mf 62
Snowy ~ AUS 379 Ml 64
Snowy Mountains ⛰ AUS 379 Ml 64
Snowy River ♀ AUS 379 Ml 64
Snowyside Peak △ USA 50 Ce 24
Snug Corner O BS 87 Dm 34
Snuŏl O K 263 Ld 39
Snyder O USA 70 Cn 28
Snyder O USA 70 Cp 25
Soacha O CO 106 Dl 43
Soalala O RM 345 Ja 54
Soân ~ PK 230 Ka 29
Soanierana-Ivongo O RM 345 Jc 54
Soari River ~ PNG 286 Mh 49
Soa-Siu O RI 275 Lp 45
Soatá O CO 107 Dm 42
Soavina O RM 353 Jb 56
Soavina O RM 353 Jc 56
Soavinandriana O RM 345 Jb 55
Sob ~ UA 175 Hg 21
Soba O WAN 320 Gk 40
Sobaek Mountains ⛰ ROK 247 Lp 28
Sobaeksan ★ ROK 247 Ma 27
Sobangouma O RMM 305 Ge 38
Sobát ~ SUD 324 Hj 41
Sobger ~ RI 286 Mg 48
Sobinka O RUS 181 Hn 18
Sobni △ ETH 313 Hm 38
Sobol O USA 70 Da 28
Sobradinho O BR 133 Ek 53
Sobradinho O BR 146 Eh 60
Sobradinho Reservoir ~ BR 125 En 51
Sobrado ~ BR 133 El 52
Sobral O BR 124 Ep 47
Socavão O BR 140 Ek 58
Socha O CO 107 Dm 42
Socha O PE 116 Dl 46
Sochaczew O PL 170 Hc 19
Sochi O RUS 195 Hm 24
Society Islands ♁ F 35 Ba 11
Socompa O RA 136 Dp 58
Socorro O USA 65 Cj 29
Socorro O CO 107 Dm 42
Socorro O BR 141 El 57
Socorro do Piauí O BR 124 En 49
Socota O PE 116 Dj 49
Socotra ♁ YE 219 Jf 39
Sóc Trăng O VN 263 Lc 41
Soda Lake ~ USA 64 Ce 28
Sodankylä O FIN 159 Hf 12
Soda Springs O USA 51 Cg 24
Soddy-Daisy O USA 71 Df 28
Sodere O ETH 325 Hm 41
Söderfors O S 158 Ha 15
Söderhamn O S 158 Ha 15
Söderköping O S 170 Ha 16
Södertälje O S 170 Ha 16
Sodiri O SUD 312 Hg 38
Sodium O ZA 349 Hd 61
Sodo O ETH 325 Hl 42
Södra O FIN 159 Hc 14
Sodwana Bay ♀ ZA 352 Hj 59
Soe O RI 282 Ln 50
Soeng Sari O THA 263 Lb 38
Sofala O MOC 352 Hk 56
Sofara O RMM 305 Gd 38
Sofia O USA 65 Cl 27
Sofia ▣ BG 194 Hd 24
Sofia ~ RM 345 Jb 53
Sofijivka O UA 175 Hk 21
Sofijsk O RUS 205 Xa 8
Sofporog O RUS 159 Hh 13
Soğā'abād O IR 222 Jd 29
Sogakofe O GH 317 Gg 43
Sogamoso ~ CO 107 Dm 42
Sogamoso O CO 107 Dm 43
Soğanlı ~ TR 195 Hj 25
Sogeram River ~ PNG 287 Mj 48
Sogeri O PNG 287 Mk 50
Sogndal O N 158 Gk 15
Sognefjorden ~ N 158 Gj 15
Sognesjøen ~ N 158 Gj 15
Sogod O RP 267 Ln 40
,Sogoubéni O RG 316 Gb 41
Sŏguip'o O ROK 247 Lp 29
Söğütlü Çayı ~ TR 195 Hl 26
Sog Xian O VRC 235 Kl 30
Soh O UZB 223 Jp 26
Sohagi O IND 234 Ke 33
Soheil O IR 222 Je 29
Sohela O IND 234 Kf 35
Sohm Plain ▼ 11 Ga 6
Sohós O GR 194 Hd 25
Sohŭksan Do ♁ ROK 246 Ln 28
Soin O BF 317 Ge 39
Soissons O F 163 Gh 21
Sōja O J 251 Mc 28
Sojana O RUS 159 Hp 13
Sojat O IND 227 Ka 33
Šojda ~ RUS 159 Hl 15
Šojna O RUS 154 Qc 5
Šojna' O RUS 159 Ja 12
Sojoton Point ⌒ RP 267 Lm 41
Sok ~ RUS 181 Jd 19
Sokch'o O ROK 247 Ma 26
Söke O TR 195 Hf 27
Sokele O RDC 336 He 50
Sokhumi O GE 202 Hn 24
Soko O CI 317 Ge 42
Soko Banja O SCG 194 Hc 24
Sokodé O RT 317 Gg 41
Sokode Etoe O GH 317 Gg 42
Sokol O RUS 171 Hm 16
Sokol O RUS 205 Ya 7
Sokol O RUS 250 Mh 22
Sokółka O PL 171 Hd 19
Sokołów Podlaski O PL 170 Hd 19
Sokone O SN 316 Fm 39
Sokosti △ FIN 159 Hf 11
Sokoto O RMM 305 Gc 38
Sokoto O WAN 320 Gj 39
Sokoto ~ WAN 320 Gj 39
Sokša O RUS 171 Hk 15
Sokskie jary ⛰ RUS 181 Jd 19
Sola O C 100 Dk 35
Sola de Vega O MEX 92 Cp 36
Solan O IND 230 Kc 30
Solana Beach O USA 64 Cd 29
Solander Island ♁ NZ 382 Nf 69
Solânea O BR 124 Fc 49
Solano O YV 112 Ea 45
Solāpur O IND 238 Kb 37
Solberg O S 158 Ha 14
Sol'cy O RUS 171 Hg 16
Soldado Monge O EC 116 Dj 47
Soldatna O USA 46 Ba 15
Soldatskaja Tašla O RUS 181 Jb 19
Sol de Julio O RA 137 Ec 60
Soldier Point ⌒ AUS 364 Mb 51
Soledad O USA 64 Cb 27
Soledad O CO 106 Dl 40
Soledad O YV 112 Ec 41
Soledad de Doblado O MEX 93 Cp 36
Soledad Díez Gutiérrez O MEX 92 Cm 34
Soledade O BR 124 Fb 49
Soledade O BR 146 Eh 60
Soledar O UA 181 Hm 21
Sølen △ N 158 Gm 15
Solënyj O RUS 181 Jb 22
Solenzara O F 185 Gl 25
Solenzo O BF 317 Gd 39
Šolgara O AFG 223 Jm 27
Solhābād O IR 222 Jg 28
Solhan O TR 202 Hn 26
Soligalič O RUS 171 Hp 16
Solikamsk O RUS 154 Rc 7
Solimões ~ BR 117 Dp 47
Solimões ~ BR 120 Ed 47
Solingen O D 163 Gk 20
Solita O CO 116 Dl 45
Solitaire O NAM 348 Gp 57
Soljanka O RUS 181 Jc 20
Sollefteå O S 158 Ha 14
Sóller O E 184 Gh 26
Solnečnogorsk O RUS 171 Hl 17
Solo Surakarta O RI 278 Lf 49
Solo ~ RI 278 Lf 49
Solo ~ RI 279 Lg 49
Solodniki O RUS 181 Ja 21
Šolohovskij O RUS 181 Hn 21
Solok O RI 270 La 46
Sololá O GCA 93 Dc 38
Sololo O EAK 325 Hm 44
Solomon O USA 70 Cp 26
Solomon Islands ♁ SOL 290 Mp 49
Solomon Islands ◻ SOL 290 Na 49
Solončak Gijoklenkui ~ TM 222 Jg 25
Solone O UA 175 Hk 21
Solonópole O BR 124 Fa 48
Solon Sprs. O USA 56 Dc 22
Solor ♁ RI 282 Lm 50
Solothurn O CH 163 Gk 22
Soloveckie O RUS 159 Hk 13
Soloveckie o-va ★ RUS 159 Hk 13
Solsona O E 184 Gg 24
Solsona O RP 267 Ll 36
Soltānābād O IR 222 Jg 27
Soltān Bakvā O AFG 223 Jk 29
Soltānīye O IR 209 Jc 27
Soltau O D 170 Gl 19
Solusi O ZW 349 Hf 56
Sölvesborg O S 170 Gp 17
Solwezi O Z 341 Hf 52
Soma O TR 195 Hf 26
Sōma O J 251 Mg 27
Somabhula O ZW 341 Hg 55
Somadougou O RMM 305 Gd 38
Somalia ◻ SP 329 Hp 44
Somali Basin ▼ 31 Ma 10
Somali Plateau ⌓ ETH 325 Hn 41
Somalomo O CAM 320 Gn 44
Somba O RI 279 Lk 47
Sombo O RDC 324 He 44
Sombo O ANG 340 Hc 50
Sombo ~ ANG 340 Hc 50
Sombor O SCG 174 Hb 23
Sombrerete O MEX 92 Cl 34
Sombrero O RCH 152 Dp 72
Sombrero Channel ≈ 270 Kl 42
Sombrero Channel ~ IND 270 Kl 42
Sombrio O BR 140 Ek 60
Som Det O THA 263 Lb 37
Somero O FIN 159 Hd 15
Somers O USA 50 Ce 21
Somerset O CDN 56 Cn 21
Somerset O USA 71 Df 27
Somerset O USA 74 Dj 26
Somerset O AUS 365 Mh 51
Somerset Aboriginal Reserve ••• AUS 365 Mh 51
Somerset-East O ZA 358 He 62
Somerset Island ♁ CDN 7 Ea 2
Somerset Island ♁ CDN 42 Fc 4
Somerset West O ZA 358 Hb 63
Somerton O USA 64 Ce 29
Somerville O USA 71 Dd 28
Somerville O USA 74 Dl 25
Somerville O USA 81 Cp 30
Somerville Lake ~ USA 81 Cp 30
Somes Bar O USA 64 Ca 25
Somil O ANG 340 Hc 53
Somino O RUS 171 Hk 16
Somme ~ F 163 Gg 20
Sommen ~ S 170 Gp 17
Sommerset O USA 65 Cj 26
Sommerset O USA 71 Df 24
Sømna ♁ N 158 Gm 13
Somokoro O CI 317 Gd 41
Somosomo O FJI 390 Aa 54
Somosomo Strait ~ FJI 387 Nm 54
Somotillo O NIC 96 De 39
Somoto O NIC 96 De 39
Sompeta O IND 235 Kg 36
Som Poi O THA 263 Lb 38
Somra O MYA 254 Km 33
Son ~ IND 235 Kf 33
Son ~ IND 235 Kg 33
Soná O PA 97 Dh 42
Sona O BOL 129 Ea 51
Sonaco O GNB 316 Fn 39
Sonaimur O BD 235 Kk 34
Sonanga O RMM 305 Gc 39
Sonapur O IND 235 Kf 35
Sonar ~ IND 234 Kd 33
Sonbong O DVRK 250 Mb 24
Sønderborg O DK 170 Gl 18
Sondershausen O D 174 Gm 20
So'n Đong O VN 255 Ld 35
Søndre Strømfjord O DK 7 Ga 3
Sondrio O I 174 Gl 22
Sondu O EAK 337 Hk 46
Sonepat O IND 234 Kc 31
Song O MAL 274 Lg 45
Song O WAN 320 Gn 41
Songa O RI 283 Lp 46
Songa O RDC 336 He 50
Sông Ba ~ VN 263 Le 38
Sông Ba ~ VN 263 Le 39
Sông Câu O VN 263 Le 39
Sông Đà ~ VN 254 Lb 34
Sông Đà ~ VN 255 Lc 35
Song D'ông Nai ~ VN 263 Ld 40
Songea O EAT 344 Hk 51
Songgat ~ RI 286 Mg 47
Songhua ~ VRC 250 Mb 22
Songhua Jiang ~ VRC 205 Wb 9
Songir O IND 234 Kb 35
Songjiang O VRC 246 Ll 30
Songkhla O THA 270 La 42
Songkou O VRC 258 Lk 33
Song Ling ⛰ VRC 246 Lk 25
Sông Lũy O VN 263 Ld 40
Songming O VRC 255 Lb 33
Sŏngnam O ROK 247 Lp 27
Songnim O DVRK 247 Ln 26
Songnisan ★ ROK 247 Lp 27
Songo O SUD 324 He 41
Songo O ANG 332 Gp 49
Songo O MOC 344 Hj 53
Songololo O RDC 332 Gn 48
Songo Mnara Island ♁ EAT 337 Hm 50
Songow Lagoon ~ GH 317 Gg 43
Songpan O VRC 242 Lb 29
Song Phinong O THA 262 Kp 38
Song Shan △ VRC 243 Lg 28
Songwe O RDC 336 Hf 47
Songwe O RDC 336 Hf 48
Songwe ~ EAT 337 Hj 50
Song Xian O VRC 243 Lf 28
Songyang O VRC 258 Lk 31
Songyu ★ ROK 247 Ma 27
Songzi O VRC 243 Lf 30
So'n Hiệp O VN 263 Le 39
Sonjo O EAT 337 Hk 47
Sonkajärvi O FIN 159 Hf 14
Sonkwale Mountains △ WAN 320 Gl 42
So'n La O VN 255 Lc 35
Sonmiāni Bay ~ PK 227 Jm 33
Sonneberg O D 174 Gm 20
Sono ~ BR 121 El 50
Sono ~ BR 133 El 51
Sono ~ BR 133 Em 54
Sonoita O MEX 75 Cf 30
Sonoita O USA 80 Cg 30
Sonoma Range ⛰ USA 64 Cd 25
Sonora O USA 64 Cb 27
Sonora O MEX 64 Ce 29
Sonora O USA 81 Cm 30
Sonora O BR 132 Eg 54
Sonora Desert ⌓ USA 64 Ce 29
Sonora Pass △ USA 64 Cc 26
Sonqor O IR 209 Jb 28
Sonsón O CO 106 Dl 43
Sonsonate O ES 93 Dc 39
Sonsorol ♁ PAL 26 Rb 9
Sonstraal O ZA 349 Hd 59
Sonta O RDC 341 Hg 51
So'n Tây O VN 255 Lc 35
Sooke O CDN 50 Bp 21
Sooyac O SP 329 Hp 45
Sopachuy O BOL 129 Eb 55
Sopau O PNG 287 Mn 47
Sop Hao O LAO 255 Lc 35
Sop Huai O THA 254 Kp 36
Sopinho O MOC 344 Hl 54
Sop Moei O THA 262 Kp 37
Sopore O IND 230 Kb 28
Sopot O PL 170 Hb 18
Soppero O S 159 Hc 11
Sop Prap O THA 262 Kp 37
Sopron O H 174 Ha 22
Sora O I 185 Gn 25
Sorab O IND 238 Kb 38
Sorāh O PK 227 Jn 32
Sŏraksan ★ ROK 247 Ma 26
Sŏraksan △ ROK 247 Ma 26
Sora Mboum O CAM 321 Gp 42
Soras ~ PE 128 Dm 53
Sorata O BOL 129 Dp 53
Sōrath ⌓ IND 227 Jn 35
Sorati ~ J 250 Mh 24
Sorau O WAN 321 Gn 41
Sorbas O E 184 Ge 27
Sore O F 184 Gf 23
Sorel O CDN 60 Dm 23
Sorell O AUS 378 Mk 67
Sorere O EAU 325 Hj 45
Sorezaru Point ⌒ SOL 290 Na 49
Sørflatanger O N 158 Gm 13
Sorfta O ETH 325 Hm 42
Sórgono O I 185 Gl 25
Sorgun O TR 195 Hk 26
Sorh-ō-Pārsā O AFG 223 Jn 28
Sori O DY 320 Gh 40
Soria O E 184 Ge 25
Sorido O RI 283 Md 46
Sørkapp land ♁ N 158 Ha 7
Sørkappøya ♁ N 158 Ha 7
Soro O PK 227 Jm 30
Soro O IND 235 Kh 35
Soro ~ TCH 309 Ha 38
Sorobango O CI 317 Ge 41
Soroca O MD 175 Hf 21
Sorocaba O BR 141 El 57
Sorokino O RUS 171 Hg 17
Sorokskaja guba ~ RUS 159 Hk 13
Sorol ♁ FSM 27 Sa 9
Sorombéo O CAM 321 Gp 41
Sorong O RI 283 Mb 46
Sørœr O N 159 Hc 10
Sororó ~ BR 121 Ek 48
Soroti O EAU 325 Hj 45
Sørøya ♁ N 159 Hd 10
Sørøysundet ~ N 159 Hc 10
Sorraia ~ P 184 Gb 26
Sorrento O CDN 50 Cc 20
Sorrento O I 194 Gp 25
Sorriso O BR 132 Eg 52
Sorsele O S 158 Ha 13
Sorsogon O RP 267 Lm 39
Sørspitsbergen nasjonalpark ♀ N 158 Gp 7
Sørstraumen O N 159 Hd 11
Sort O E 184 Gg 24
Sortavala O RUS 171 Hh 15
Sortland O N 158 Gp 11
Sørvågen O N 158 Gn 12
Sørvágur O DK 162 Gc 14
Sŏsan O ROK 247 Lp 27
Sŏsan Haean ♀ ROK 247 Ln 27
Sosnogorsk O RUS 154 Rb 6
Sosnove O UA 175 Hf 20
Sosnovka O RUS 159 Hm 12
Sosnovo O RUS 171 Hh 15
Sosnovyi Bor O RUS 171 Hg 15
Sosnovyj O RUS 159 Hh 13
Sosnowiec O PL 174 Hb 20
Sosnycja O UA 175 Hj 20
Soso Bay ~ FJI 387 Nm 55
Sosquehanna ~ USA 74 Dk 25
Sosso O RCA 321 Gp 44
Šostka O UA 175 Hj 20
Sosúa O DOM 101 Dn 36
Sot ~ RUS 171 Hn 16
Sota ~ DY 320 Gh 40
Sotian O RMM 305 Gc 40
Sotik O EAK 337 Hk 46
Sotkamo O FIN 159 Hg 13
Soto O RA 137 Eb 61
Soto la Marina O MEX 81 Cn 34
Sotomayor O CO 106 Dk 45
Sotondideri O RI 283 Md 46
Sotouboua O RT 317 Gg 41
Sotuta O MEX 93 Dd 35
Souanké O RCB 321 Gp 44
Soubakaniédougou O BF 317 Gd 40
Soubakgétou ♁ DY 317 Gh 41
Soubané O RG 316 Fn 40
Soubéira O BF 317 Gf 39
Soubré O CI 305 Gc 43
Souchang O VRC 258 Lk 31
Soudan O AUS 374 Me 56
Souf ⌓ DZ 296 Gk 29
Soufflets ~ CDN 61 Ef 20
Soufriére O WL 104 Ed 39
Sougai O RI 279 Lh 49
Sougueur O DZ 293 Gg 28
Souhoulé O RG 316 Gb 42
Souillac O MS 353 Jg 56
Souk Ahras O DZ 296 Gk 27
Souk-el-Arba-du-Rharb O MA 293 Gc 28
Souk-el-Kella O MA 293 Gd 28
Souk-Jemmaâ-des-Oulad-Abbo O MA 293 Gc 29
Soukoukoutane O RN 308 Gh 38
Souk-Tleta-des-Akhasass O MA 292 Gb 31
Soulac O F 184 Gf 23
Soulis Pond ~ CDN 61 Eg 21
Souma'e Sara O IR 209 Jc 27
Sounding Creek ~ CDN 51 Cg 20
Sounga O G 332 Gl 47
Soungrougrou ~ SN 316 Fn 39
Soúnio O GR 194 He 27
Souquéta O RG 316 Fp 40
Source de Congo ~ RDC 341 Hf 51
Source of the Nile ~ BU 336 Hg 47
Soure O BR 121 Ek 46
Sour El Ghozlane O DZ 296 Gh 27
Souris O CDN 56 Cm 21
Souris O CDN 61 Ec 22
Souris River ~ USA 56 Cm 21
Sourou ~ RMM 317 Ge 39
Souroukaha O CI 317 Gd 41
Sousa O BR 124 Fa 49
Sousse O TN 297 Gm 28
Soutelo O E 184 Gb 24
South Alligator ~ AUS 364 Mc 52
Southampton O CDN 57 Dh 23
Southampton O GB 163 Gf 20
Southampton Island ♁ CDN 7 Eb 3
Southampton Island ♁ CDN 43 Ga 6
South Andaman ♁ IND 262 Kl 40
South Andros Island ♁ BS 100 Dj 34
South Aulatsivik Island ♁ CDN 43 Hc 7
South Australia ⊙ AUS 374 Md 60
South Australian Basin ▼ 34 Ra 13
South Australian Basin ▼ 369 Mc 65
South Baldy △ USA 65 Cj 29
South Banda Basin ▼ 282 Lp 49
South Baymouth O CDN 57 Dg 23
South Bend O USA 71 De 25
South Bimini ♁ USA 87 Dj 33
South Boston O USA 74 Dj 27
South Branch Potomac ~ USA 74 Dj 26
Southbridge O USA 60 Dm 24
South Bruny Island ♁ AUS 378 Mk 67
South Caicos ♁ GB 101 Dm 35
South Carolina ⊙ USA 71 Dh 28
South Charleston O USA 189 Dh 26
South China Sea ≈ 258 Lg 35
South China Sea ≈ 263 Ld 41
South Cove O USA 64 Ce 27
South Dakota ⊙ USA 51 Cl 23
Southeast Cape ⌒ USA 46 Ae 13
South East Cape ⌒ AUS 378 Mk 67
Southeastern Taurus Mountains ⛰ TR 195 Hm 27
Southeast Indian Ridge ▼ 34 Pb 14
South East Islands ♁ AUS 369 Lm 63
Southeast Pacific Basin ▼ 15 Ea 15
South East Point ⌒ AUS 379 Mk 65
Southend O CDN 42 Fa 7
South End ⌒ AUS 360 Lh 56
Southend-on-Sea O GB 163 Gg 20
Southern Alps ⛰ NZ 382 Ng 68
Southern Cross O AUS 368 Lk 61
Southern Cross Club O GB 100 Dh 36
Southern Indian Lake ~ CDN 6 Ea 4
Southern Indian Lake ~ CDN 42 Fb 7
Southern Kashiji ~ Z 341 Hd 52
Southern Lau Group ♁ FJI 390 Aa 55
Southern Lueti ~ Z 341 Hd 53
Southern National Park ♀ SUD 324 Hg 42
Southern Pines O USA 74 Dj 28
Southern Uplands ⛰ GB 162 Gd 18
Southern Ute ••• USA 65 Ch 27
Southesk Tablelands ⌓ AUS 361 Lp 56
Southey O CDN 51 Ck 20
South Fidji Basin ▼ 35 Tb 12
South Fork O USA 65 Cj 27
South Fork John Day ~ USA 50 Cc 23
South Fork Kuskokwim ~ USA 46 An 13
South Fork Owyhee ~ USA 50 Cd 24
South Fork Republican River ~ USA 65 Cl 26
South Fork Solomon River ~ USA 70 Cm 26
South Fork White River ~ USA 56 Cm 24
South Galway O AUS 374 Mg 58
South Gate O RB 341 Hd 55
South Georgia ♁ UK 15 Ha 15
South Goulburn Island ♁ AUS 364 Mc 51
South Hanik Lake ~ CDN 6 Ea 3
South Hatia Island ♁ BD 235 Kk 34
South Haven O USA 57 De 24
South Henik Lake ~ CDN 42 Fb 6
South Hill O USA 74 Dj 27
South Horr O EAK 325 Hl 44
South Island ♁ NZ 382 Ng 67
South Island N.P. ♀ EAK 325 Hl 44
South Koel ~ IND 235 Kg 34
South Korea ◻ ROK 247 Ma 27
South Lake O CDN 61 Ed 22
South Lake Tahoe O USA 64 Cb 26
South Loup ~ USA 70 Cn 25
South Loup River ~ USA 70 Cn 25
South Luangwa ♀ Z 341 Hh 52
South Male Atoll ♁ MV 239 Ka 44
South Malosmadulu Atoll ♁ MV 239 Ka 43
South Milford O CDN 61 Eb 23
South Nahanni River ~ CDN 47 Bn 13
South Nilandu Atoll ♁ MV 239 Ka 44
Southold O USA 74 Dm 25
South Orkneys ♁ GB 38 Gb 16
South Pacific Ocean ≈ 35 Aa 13
South Pass △ USA 65 Ch 24
South Peron Island ♁ AUS 364 Ma 52
South Platte ~ USA 65 Ck 26
South Platte River ~ USA 65 Cl 25
South Pole ⌓ 38 Fb 18
Southport O USA 74 Dk 29
Southport O GB 163 Ge 19
Southport O AUS 378 Mk 67
South Reef ♁ SOL 290 Nc 52
South Rukuru ~ MW 344 Hj 51
South Saskatchewan ~ CDN 51 Cg 20
South Shetlands Islands ⛰ 38 Ga 16
South Shields O GB 162 Gf 18
South Sioux City O USA 56 Cp 24
South Solitary Island ♁ AUS 379 Mn 61
South Stradbroke Island ♁ AUS 375 Mn 59
South Taranaki Bight ~ NZ 383 Nk 66
South Thompson ~ CDN 50 Cb 20
South Tucson O USA 65 Cg 29
South Turkana-N.P. ♀ EAK 325 Hk 45
South Twin Island ♁ CDN 57 Dh 19
South Twin Lake ~ CDN 61 Eg 21
South Uist ♁ GB 162 Gc 17
South West ♀ AUS 378 Mj 67
South West Cape ⌒ AUS 378 Mj 67
Southwest Cape ⌒ NZ 382 Nf 69
Southwest Gander ~ CDN 61 Eg 21
Southwest Miramichi ~ CDN 61 Ea 22
Southwest Pacific Basin ▼ 35 Aa 14
Southwest Point ⌒ BS 87 Dk 33
South West Rocks O AUS 379 Mn 61
Souto Soares O BR 125 Ep 52
Soutpan O ZA 349 He 60
Soutpansberg ⛰ ZA 349 Hg 57
Soutpansnek △ ZA 358 He 62
Soutrivier ~ ZA 348 Hb 61
Soutrivier ~ ZA 348 Hc 60
Søværoy O N 158 Gn 12
Sovdezero O RUS 159 Hj 14
Soverato O I 194 Ha 26
Sovetsk O RUS 170 Hc 18
Sovetskaja O RUS 202 Hn 23
Sovetskaja O RUS 202 Hp 23
Sovetskaja Gavan O RUS 26 Rb 5
Sovetskaj Gavan O RUS 205 Xa 9
Sovpol'e O RUS 159 Hp 13
Soweto O ZA 349 Hf 59
Soyaló O MEX 93 Db 37
Sōya-misaki ⌒ J 250 Mg 23
Soyo O ANG 332 Gn 49
Sož ~ BY 171 Hh 19
Spa O B 163 Gj 20
Spain ◻ E 184 Gc 25
Spalding O AUS 378 Mf 62
Spallumcheen O CDN 50 Cc 20
Spanish ~ CDN 57 Dh 22
Spanish River Indian Reserve ••• CDN 57 Dg 22
Spanish Town O JA 101 Dk 37

Skjervøy - Spanish Town 471

□ Country ▣ Capital city ⊙ Administrative unit O Place ♁ Island ⩕ Mountain range △ Mountain ⌓ Cape ≈ Ocean, Sea ~ Lake, River ♆ Undersea topography ▵ Glacier ♀ National park ••• Reservation ★ Point of major interest ⌒ Landscape

Sparke Range ⩕ AUS 361 Ln 55
Sparks O USA 64 Cc 26
Sparta O USA 56 Dc 24
Sparta O USA 71 Df 28
Sparta O USA 71 Dg 29
Sparta O USA 71 Dh 27
Spartanburg O USA 71 Dh 28
Spárti O GR 194 Hd 27
Sparwood O CDN 50 Ce 21
Spas-Demensk O RUS 171 Hk 18
Spas-Klepiki O RUS 181 Hn 18
Spasskaja Guba O RUS 159 Hj 14
Spassk-Dal'nij O RUS 250 Mc 23
Spassk-Rjazanskij O RUS 181 Hn 18
Spearfish O USA 51 Cl 23
Spearhole Creek ~ AUS 360 Lk 57
Spearman O USA 70 Cm 27
Speedwell Island ♁ GB 147 Ed 72
Speightstown O BDS 104 Ed 39
Speke Gulf ~ EAT 337 Hj 47
Spence Bay O CDN 42 Fc 5
Spencer O USA 56 Cn 24
Spencer O USA 56 Da 24
Spencer O USA 71 De 26
Spencer O USA 71 Dh 26
Spencer ~ AUS 378 Me 62
Spencer Gulf ♆ AUS 378 Me 63
Spences Bridge O CDN 50 Cb 20
Spessart ⩕ D 174 Gl 21
Spey ~ GB 162 Ge 17
Speyer O D 174 Gl 21
Sphinx ★ ET 301 Hh 31
Spicer Islands ♁ CDN 43 Gc 5
Spiekeroog ♁ D 170 Gk 18
Spinazzola O I 194 Ha 25
Spin Bōldak O AFG 227 Jl 30
Spirit Lake O USA 56 Da 24
Spiritwood O CDN 51 Cj 19
Spiro O USA 70 Da 28
Spitak O ARM 202 Hp 25
Spit Point ⌓ AUS 360 Lk 56
Spitsbergen ⌒ N 158 Gp 6
Spitsbergen Bank ♆ 19 Kb 2
Spitskopvlei O ZA 358 He 62
Spittal an der Drau O A 174 Gn 22
Split O HR 194 Ha 24
Spofford O USA 81 Cm 31
Spokane ~ USA 50 Cc 22
Spokane O USA 50 Cd 22
Spokane House ★ USA 50 Cd 22
Spokane Indian Reservation ••• USA 50 Cc 22
Špola O UA 175 Hh 21
Spoleto O I 185 Gn 24
Spoon ~ USA 71 Dd 25
Spooner O USA 56 Dc 23
Spotted Horse O USA 51 Ck 23
Sprague ~ USA 50 Cb 24
Sprague O USA 50 Cd 22
Spratly Island ♁ 263 Lf 41
Spray O USA 50 Cc 23
Spree ~ D 174 Gp 20
Sprengisandur ⩕ IS 158 Fl 13
Spring O AUS 368 Lk 59
Springbok O ZA 348 Ha 60
Spring Creek O USA 64 Ce 25
Spring Creek O AUS 365 Mj 55
Springdale O USA 50 Cd 21
Springdale O CDN 61 Ef 21
Springdale O USA 70 Da 27
Springer O USA 65 Ck 27
Springfield O USA 50 Ca 23
Springfield O USA 60 Dm 24
Springfield O USA 65 Cl 27
Springfield O USA 70 Db 27
Springfield O USA 71 Dc 26
Springfield O USA 71 Dd 26
Springfield O USA 71 Dg 26
Springfontein O ZA 349 He 61
Spring Garden O GUY 113 Ee 42
Spring Green O USA 56 Dc 24
Springhill O CDN 61 Eb 23
Springhill O USA 70 Db 29
Spring Hill O USA 86 Dg 31
Springlake O USA 65 Cl 28
Spring Lake Dunn O USA 74 Dj 28
Springrale O AUS 374 Mg 57
Springs O ZA 349 Hg 59
Springs Junction O NZ 383 Nj 67
Springsure O AUS 375 Ml 58
Springtown O USA 70 Cp 29
Springvale O AUS 361 Lp 54
Spring Vale O AUS 365 Me 55
Spring Valley O CDN 51 Ck 20
Spring Valley O ZA 358 Hf 62
Springview O USA 56 Cm 24
Springville O USA 60 Dj 24
Springville O USA 65 Cg 25
Springville O USA 71 De 29
Springwater O CDN 51 Ch 20
Spring Way O USA 64 Cf 25
Spruce Grove O CDN 50 Ce 19
Spruce Home O CDN 51 Ck 19
Spruce Knob △ USA 74 Dj 26
Spruce Mountain △ USA 64 Ce 25
Spruce Pine O USA 71 Dg 28
Spur O USA 70 Cm 29
Squamish O CDN 50 Ca 21
Squarnish ~ CDN 50 Ca 20
Squilax O CDN 50 Cc 20
Sragen O RI 278 Lf 49
Srbica O SCG 194 Hc 24
Srbobran O SCG 174 Hb 23
Sredec O BG 195 Hf 24
Sredinnyy Khrebet ⩕ RUS 23 Sb 4
Sredinnyy Khrebet ⩕ RUS 205 Yb 8
Srednekolymsk O RUS 23 Sb 3
Sredne Russkaya Vozvyshennost' ⩕ RUS 154 Qb 8
Sremska Mitrovica O SCG 174 Hb 23
Srê Sbov O K 263 Ld 39
Sretensk O RUS 204 Vc 8
Sribne O UA 175 Hj 20
Sri Dungargarh O IND 234 Kb 31
Sri Jayawardanapura Kotte O CL 239 Kd 42
Srīkakulam O IND 235 Kf 36
Sri Kālahasti O IND 238 Kd 39
Sri Lanka □ CL 239 Ke 41
Srinagar O IND 230 Kb 28
Srinakarin ♀ THA 262 Kp 38
Srinakarin Reservoir ~ THA 262 Kp 38
Srinivāspur O IND 238 Kd 39
Sriparumbudur O IND 238 Kd 39
Srīrampūr O IND 238 Kb 36
Srirangam O IND 239 Kd 40
Srirangapatnam O IND 238 Kc 39
Srīsailam O IND 238 Kd 37
Sri Toi O PK 227 Jn 30
Srivaikuntam O IND 239 Kc 41
Srīvardhan O IND 238 Ka 36
Śrīvilliputtūr O IND 239 Kc 41
Środa Wlkp. O PL 170 Ha 19
Srungavarapukota O IND 234 Kf 36
St. Adolphe O CDN 56 Cp 21
St. Albans O CDN 61 Ef 22
St. Albans O USA 71 Dg 26
St. Albans O GB 163 Gf 20
St. Albert Dome △ PNG 286 Mg 48
St.-Alexandre O CDN 60 Dp 22
St. Ambroise O CDN 56 Cn 20
St.-Ambroise O CDN 60 Dn 21
St. Andrew Bay ~ USA 86 De 30
St. Andrew's O CDN 61 Ee 22
St. Andrew Sound ~ USA 87 Dh 30
St. Ann's Bay ~ CDN 61 Ed 22
St. Ann's Bay O JA 101 Dk 36
St. Anthony O CDN 61 Eg 20
St. Arnaud O AUS 378 Mh 64
St. Augustin O CDN 61 Ee 20
St. Augustin ~ CDN 61 Ee 20
St. Augustine O USA 71 Dc 25
St. Augustine O USA 87 Dh 31
St. Augustin Nord-Ouest ~ CDN 61 Ee 20
St. Bride's O CDN 61 Eg 22
St.-Bruno O CDN 60 Dn 21
St. Carles de la Ràpita O E 184 Gg 25
St. Catharines O CDN 60 Dj 24
St. Catherines Island ♁ USA 87 Dh 30
St. Charles O USA 70 Dc 28
St. Charles O USA 71 Dc 26
St. Charles O USA 71 Dd 25
St. Charles O USA 74 Dk 26
St. Claire ~ CDN 57 Dg 24
St. Cloud O USA 56 Da 23
St. Cloud O USA 87 Dh 31
St. Croix ~ USA 56 Db 23
St. Croix Falls O USA 56 Db 23
St. Croix Island Nat. Mon. ★ CDN 60 Ea 23
St. Croix S.P. ★ USA 56 Db 23
St. Denis O F 163 Gh 21
St. Dominique-du-Rosaire O CDN 60 Dj 21
St. Edmunds O GB 163 Gg 19
St. Elias Mountains ⩕ CDN 47 Be 15
St.-Esprit O CDN 60 Dm 23
St.-Félicien O CDN 60 Dm 21
St. Feliu de Guíxols O E 185 Gh 25
St. Francis O USA 60 Dp 22
St. Francis O USA 70 Cm 26
St. Francis Bay ~ NAM 348 Gp 58
St. Francis Bay ~ ZA 358 He 63
St. Francisville O USA 86 Dc 30
St.-Francuis ~ CDN 60 Dm 22
St.-Gabriel O CDN 60 Dm 22
St. George O CDN 61 Ea 23
St. George O USA 71 Dh 29
St. George Island ♁ USA 86 Df 31
St. George's O CDN 61 Ee 21
St.-Georges O CDN 60 Dn 22
St. George's Bay ~ CDN 61 Ed 23
St. George's Channel ~ PNG 287 Mn 47
St.-Gérard O CDN 60 Dn 23
St. Helena ♁ UK 30 Jb 11
St. Helena Bay ~ ZA 358 Ha 62
St. Helena Sound ~ USA 71 Dh 29
St. Helens O AUS 378 Ml 66
St. Helens Point ⌓ AUS 378 Ml 66
St.-Hyacinthe O CDN 60 Dm 23
St. Ignace O USA 57 Df 23
St. Ignace Islands ♁ CDN 57 Dd 21
St. James O USA 56 Da 23
St. James O USA 71 Dc 27
St. Jean-d.M. O F 185 Gk 23
St.-Jean-de-Dieu O CDN 60 Dp 22
St.-Jean-de-Luz O F 184 Gf 24
St.-Jean-Port-Joli O CDN 60 Dn 22
St.-Jean-sur-Richelieu O CDN 60 Dm 23
St.-Jerôme O CDN 60 Dm 23
St. Joe O USA 70 Db 27
St. John ~ USA 60 Dp 22
St. John ~ CDN 60 Ea 22
St. John O USA 70 Cn 26
St. John Island ♁ CDN 61 Ef 20
St. John River ~ LB 316 Gb 42
St. John's O CDN 61 Eh 22
St. Johns O USA 71 Df 24
St. Johns ~ USA 87 Dh 30
St. John's ▣ AG 104 Ec 37
St. Johnsbury O USA 60 Dm 23
St. John's Island ♁ ET 301 Hl 34
St. Joseph O USA 70 Da 26
St. Joseph O USA 71 De 28
St. Joseph O USA 86 Dc 30
St. Joseph Peninsula ⌒ USA 86 Df 31
St. Joseph Point ⌓ USA 86 Df 31
St. Jovite O CDN 60 Dl 22
St. Kitts and Nevis □ KN 104 Ec 37
St. Lawrence O CDN 61 Eg 22
St. Lawrence Island ♁ USA 46 Ae 13
St. Lawrence Island ♁ USA 205 Ab 6
St. Lazare O CDN 56 Cm 20
St. Léonard O CDN 60 Ea 22
St.-Leu O F 353 Jf 56
St. Louis O USA 71 Dc 26
St.-Louis-de-France O CDN 60 Dm 22
St. Louis River ~ USA 56 Db 22
St. Lucia O ZA 352 Hj 60
St.-Malachie O CDN 60 Dn 22
St. Margaret Bay ~ CDN 61 Ef 20
St. Marks O USA 86 Df 30
St. Martins O CDN 61 Eb 23
St. Marys O USA 46 Aj 15
St. Mary's ~ CDN 61 Ec 23
St. Marys O USA 70 Da 26
St. Marys O USA 71 Dh 26
St. Marys O USA 71 Dh 26
St. Marys O USA 74 Dj 25
St. Mary's O Z 341 Hf 52
St. Marys O AUS 378 Ml 66
St. Mary's Bay ~ CDN 61 Eg 22
St.-Maurice ~ CDN 60 Dm 21
St.-Michel-des-Saints O CDN 60 Dl 22
St.-Niklaas O B 163 Gh 20
St. Pamphile O CDN 60 Dp 22
St.-Pascal O CDN 60 Dp 22
St. Paul ♁ F 31 Nb 13
St. Paul O USA 56 Db 23
St. Paul O CDN 61 Ef 20
St. Paul O USA 70 Cn 25
St. Paul O USA 70 Db 28
St. Paul O USA 71 Dg 27
St.-Paul-du-Nord O CDN 60 Dp 21
St. Paul Île ♁ CDN 61 Ed 22
St. Pauls O USA 74 Dj 28
St. Peter O USA 56 Da 23
St. Peter's O CDN 61 Ed 23
St. Peter's Bay O CDN 61 Ec 22
St. Petersburg O USA 86 Dg 32
St.-Philémon O CDN 60 Dn 22
St. Pierre O CDN 61 Ef 22
St. Pierre and Miquelon ⊙ F 61 Ef 22
St.-Quentin O F 163 Gh 21
St.-Raymond O CDN 60 Dn 22
St. Savin O F 163 Gg 22
St. Sebastian Bay ~ ZA 358 Hc 63
St.-Siméon O CDN 60 Dn 21
St. Simons Island ♁ USA 87 Dh 30
St. Stephen O CDN 60 Ea 23
St. Stephens Hist. Site ★ USA 86 Dd 30
St. Teresa O USA 86 Df 31
St. Thomas O USA 56 Cp 21
St. Thomas O CDN 57 Dh 24
St.-Tite O CDN 60 Dm 22
St. Tropez O F 185 Gk 24
St.-Urbain O CDN 60 Dn 22
St. Vincent Island ♁ USA 86 Df 31
St. Vincent's O CDN 61 Eh 22
St.-Yvon O CDN 61 Eb 21
St.-Zénon O CDN 60 Dl 22
Sta. Eulária d.R. O E 184 Gg 26
Sta. Isabel O MEX 93 Db 37
Sta. Olalla del Cala O E 184 Gc 27
Sta. Rosa de la Roca O BOL 129 Ed 53
Sta. Victoria O PY 136 Eb 57
Staaten ~ AUS 365 Mh 54
Staaten River ♀ AUS 365 Mh 54
Stabbursdalen ♀ N 159 Hd 10
Stade O D 170 Gl 19
Staduhino O RUS 205 Za 5
Stafafell O IS 158 Fn 13
Stafford O GB 163 Ge 19
Stagit ~ USA 50 Cb 21
Stalowa Wola O PL 174 Hc 20
Stamford O USA 70 Cn 29
Stamford O USA 74 Dm 25
Stamford O GB 163 Gf 19
Stamford O AUS 375 Mh 56
Stampriet O NAM 348 Hb 58
Stamsund O N 158 Gn 11
Stanberry O USA 70 Da 25
Stanbridge O AUS 379 Mj 62
Standerton O ZA 349 Hg 59
Standing Rock ••• USA 56 Cm 22
Standish O USA 57 Dg 23
Standish O USA 64 Cb 25
Stanford O USA 51 Cg 22
Stanford O USA 71 Df 27
Stanger O ZA 352 Hh 60
Stangford O GB 162 Gd 18
Stanhope O AUS 379 Mj 64
Staniard Creek O BS 87 Dj 33
Stanislaus ~ USA 64 Cb 26
Stanley O USA 50 Ce 23
Stanley O USA 51 Cl 21
Stanley O GB 147 Ef 71
Stanley O AUS 378 Mj 66
Stanley Reservoir ~ IND 238 Kc 40
Stanovoye Nagor'ye ⩕ RUS 22 Qb 4
Stanovoy Khrebet ⩕ RUS 22 Ra 4
Stanovoy Khrebet ⩕ RUS 204 Wa 7
Stanovoy Nagor'ye ⩕ RUS 204 Vb 7
Stansmore Range ⩕ AUS 361 Lp 56
Stanthorpe O AUS 375 Mm 60
Stanton O USA 70 Cm 29
Stanwell O AUS 375 Mm 57
Stanwood O USA 71 Dc 25
Stanyčno-Luhans'ke O UA 181 Hm 21
Stapleford O ZW 344 Hj 55
Stapleton O USA 70 Cm 25
Star. Poltavka O RUS 181 Jb 20
Staraja Majna O RUS 181 Jc 18
Staraja Toropa O RUS 171 Hh 17
Stara Zagora O BG 194 He 24
Starbuck ♁ KIR 35 Ba 10
Starbuck O USA 56 Da 23
Star City O USA 70 Db 29
Starcke O AUS 365 Mj 53
Stargard Szcz. O PL 170 Gp 19
Starica O RUS 171 Hk 17
Starica O RUS 181 Ja 21
Starja Russa O RUS 171 Hh 16
Stark O USA 70 Da 27
Starke O USA 87 Dg 31
Starkville O USA 86 Dd 29
Starnberg O D 174 Gm 21
Starnberger See ~ D 174 Gm 22
Starobil's'k O UA 181 Hm 21
Starogard Gd. O PL 170 Hb 18
Starokostjantyniv O UA 175 Hf 21
Staro Kulatka O RUS 181 Jb 19
Starominskaja O RUS 181 Hm 22
Starotitarovskaja O RUS 195 Hl 23
Star Trek ~ RUS 202 Jb 24
Start Point △ GB 163 Ge 20
Staryi Oskol O RUS 181 Hl 20
Staryya Darohi O BY 171 Hg 19
State College O USA 74 Dj 25
State Line O USA 86 Dd 30
Statesboro O USA 71 Dg 29
Statesville O USA 71 Dh 28
Staton Island ♁ USA 74 Dl 25
Statton O USA 65 Cl 26
Statue of Liberty ★ USA 74 Dm 25
Staunton O USA 74 Dj 26
Stavanger O N 170 Gj 16
Stavkirke ★ N 158 Gk 15
Stavropol' O RUS 202 Hp 23
Stawell O AUS 378 Mh 64
Stawiski O PL 170 Hd 19
Stayton O USA 50 Ca 23
St -Barthélémy ♁ F 104 Ec 37
Ste.-Agathe-des-Monts O CDN 60 Dl 22
Ste.-Angèle-de Merici O CDN 60 Dp 21
Ste.Anne O CDN 56 Cp 21
Ste.-Anne-de-Beaupré O CDN 60 Dn 22
Ste.-Anne-des-Monts O CDN 61 Ea 21
Ste.-Anne-du-Lac O CDN 60 Dl 22
Ste.-Croix O CDN 60 Dn 22
Ste.-Eulalie O CDN 60 Dm 22
Ste.-Justine O CDN 60 Dn 22
Ste.-Marguerite ~ CDN 61 Ea 20
Ste.-Marie O CDN 60 Dn 22
Ste.Rose du Lac O CDN 56 Cn 20
Steamboat O USA 50 Ca 24
Steamboat Springs O USA 65 Cj 25
Stebbins O USA 46 Aj 13
Steckfontein ★ ZA 349 Hf 59
Steelpoortrivier ~ ZA 349 Hg 58
Steenkampsberge ⩕ ZA 349 Hg 58
Steens Mountain ⩕ USA 50 Cc 24
Steenstrup Gletscher ▵ DK 43 Ja 3
Steep Point ⌓ AUS 368 Lg 59
Steeprock O CDN 56 Cn 20
Stefansson Island ♁ CDN 6 Db 2
Stefansson Island ♁ CDN 42 Ec 4
Steiermark ⊙ A 174 Gp 22
Steilloopbrug O ZA 349 Hg 57
Steilrandberge ⩕ NAM 340 Gn 54
Steinbach O CDN 56 Cp 21
Steinen ~ BR 132 Eg 52
Steinhausen O NAM 348 Hb 56
Steinkjer O N 158 Gm 13
Steinkopf O ZA 348 Ha 60
Stella O ZA 349 He 59
Stella Maris O BS 87 Dl 34
Stellarton O CDN 61 Ec 23
Stelle Island ♁ 38 Ga 17
Stellenbosch O ZA 358 Hb 62
Stelvio ♀ I 174 Gm 22
Stenbibhöjden △ S 158 Ha 13
Stenda O D 170 Gm 19
Stenness O GB 162 Ge 15
Stenon Kásu ~ GR 194 Hf 28
Stenón Kithéron ~ GR 194 Hd 28
Stenungsund O S 170 Gm 16
Stepanavan O ARM 202 Ja 25
Stepan Razin O AZ 202 Jd 25
Stephen O USA 56 Cp 21
Stephens O USA 70 Db 29
Stephenville O CDN 61 Ee 21
Stephenville O USA 70 Cn 29
Stephenville Crossing O CDN 61 Ee 21
Stepnoe O RUS 181 Jb 20
Steréa Atikí ⊙ GR 194 Hd 26
Sterkfontein Dam ~ ZA 349 Hg 60
Sterkspruit O ZA 349 Hf 61
Sterkstroom O ZA 349 Hf 61
Sterling O USA 56 Cn 22
Sterling O USA 65 Cl 25
Sterling O USA 70 Cn 26
Sterling O ZA 358 Hc 61
Sterling City O USA 81 Cm 30
Sterling Heights O USA 57 Dg 24
Sterlitamak O RUS 154 Rc 8
Stérnes O GR 194 He 28
Stes.-Maries-de-la-Mer O F 185 Gj 24
Stetin Bay ~ PNG 287 Mm 48
Stettiner Haff ~ D 170 Gn 19
Stettler O CDN 51 Cf 19
Steubenville O USA 71 Dh 25
Stevenage O GB 163 Gf 20
Stevenson O USA 50 Ca 23
Stevenson Creek ~ AUS 374 Md 59
Stevensons Peak △ AUS 369 Mb 58
Stevens Port O USA 57 Dd 23
Stevens Village O USA 46 Ba 13
Stevensville O USA 50 Ce 22
Stewart O USA 6 Ca 4
Stewart O CDN 42 Db 7
Stewart Crossing O CDN 47 Bg 13
Stewart Island ♁ NZ 382 Ng 69
Stewart Islands ♁ SOL 290 Nd 50
Stewarts Point O USA 64 Ca 26
Stewart Valley O CDN 51 Cj 20
Stewartville O USA 56 Db 24
Steynsburg O ZA 349 He 61
Steynsrus O ZA 349 Hf 59
Steyr O A 174 Gp 21
Steytlerville O ZA 358 Hd 62
Sth. Baymouth O CDN 57 Dg 23
Stigler O USA 70 Da 28
Stikine ~ USA 42 Da 7
Stikine Plateau ⌒ USA 42 Da 7
Stile O DZ 296 Gj 28
Stilfontein O ZA 349 Hf 59
Stilfser Joch Passo dello Stelvio △ I 174 Gm 22
Still Bay O ZA 358 Hc 63
Stillwater ~ USA 51 Cg 23
Stillwater O USA 64 Cc 26
Stillwater O USA 70 Cp 27
Stillwater O NZ 382 Nh 67
Stillwater Hudson O USA 56 Db 23
Stilo O I 194 Ha 26
Stilwell O USA 70 Da 28
Stinnett O USA 70 Cm 28
Stintino O I 185 Gk 25
Štip O MK 194 Hd 25
Stirling O CDN 60 Dk 23
Stirling O GB 162 Gd 17
Stirling O AUS 361 Mc 56
Stirling O AUS 365 Mg 54
Stirling North O AUS 378 Me 62
Stirling Range ⩕ AUS 368 Lj 63
Stjørdal O N 158 Gm 14
Stockbridge O USA 86 Df 29
Stockbridge Indian Reservation ••• USA 57 Dd 23
Stockdale O USA 81 Cp 31
Stockerau O A 174 Gp 21
Stockholm O CDN 51 Cl 20
Stockholm ▣ S 170 Hb 16
Stockport O AUS 374 Mf 57
Stockton O USA 64 Cb 26
Stockton O USA 70 Cn 26
Stockton O USA 70 Db 27
Stockton O USA 71 Dd 24
Stockton O USA 86 Dg 30
Stockton Island ♁ USA 56 Dc 22
Stockton Lake ~ USA 70 Da 27
Stockton Plateau ⩕ USA 81 Cl 30
Stockville O USA 70 Cm 25
Stöde O S 158 Ha 14
Stoffberg O ZA 349 Hg 58
Stogovo △ MK 194 Hc 25
Stohld ~ UA 175 He 20
Stoke-on-Trent O GB 163 Ge 19
Stokes Point ⌓ AUS 378 Mh 66
Stokes Range ⩕ AUS 364 Mb 53
Stokkvågen O N 158 Gn 12
Stokmarknes O N 158 Gn 11
Stolac O BIH 194 Hb 24
Stolin O BY 175 Hf 20
Stöllet O S 158 Gn 15
Stompneuspunt ⌓ ZA 358 Ha 62
Stone O USA 64 Cf 24
Stone Forest ★ VRC 255 Lb 33
Stoneham O USA 65 Cl 25
Stonehaven O GB 162 Ge 17
Stonehenge ★ GB 163 Ge 20
Stonehenge O AUS 374 Mh 58
Stonepynten ⌓ N 158 He 7
Stones River N.B. ★ USA 71 De 28
Stonewall O CDN 56 Cp 20
Stoney Point ⌓ AUS 374 Mg 59
Stœng Trêng O K 263 Lc 39
Stonington O USA 60 Dp 23
Stony Creek O USA 74 Dk 27
Stony Indian Reservation ••• CDN 50 Ce 20
Stony Rapids O CDN 42 Ec 7
Stony River O USA 46 Al 15
Stooping River ~ CDN 57 Dg 20
Stopanja O SCG 194 Hc 24
Stopem Blockem Range ⩕ AUS 365 Mj 55
Stora O S 158 Gp 13
Storå O S 170 Gp 16
Stora Lulevatten ~ S 158 Hb 12
Storås O N 158 Gl 14
Stora Sjöfallets ♀ S 158 Ha 12
Storavan ~ S 158 Hb 13
Storby O FIN 170 Hb 15
Stord ♁ N 170 Gj 16
Store Bælt ~ DK 170 Gm 18
Støren O N 158 Gm 14
Store Sotra ♁ N 170 Gj 15
Storfjordbanken ♆ N 158 Hc 7
Storfjorden ~ N 158 Hb 7
Storfjordrenna ♆ N 158 Hc 7
Storfors O S 170 Gp 16
Storjord O N 158 Gp 12
Storkerson Peninsula ♁ CDN 42 Ec 4
Storklinten △ S 159 Hc 13
Storlien O S 158 Gn 14
Storm Bay ~ AUS 378 Mk 67
Stormberg O ZA 349 Hf 61
Stormberg △ ZA 349 Hf 61
Storm Lake O USA 56 Da 24
Stormrivier O ZA 358 Hd 62
Stormsvlei O ZA 358 Hb 63
Stornoway O CDN 60 Dn 23
Stornoway O GB 162 Gc 16
Storøya ♁ N 158 Hg 5
Storsåtern O S 158 Gn 14
Storsjö O S 158 Gn 14
Storsjøen ~ N 158 Gm 15
Storsjön ~ S 158 Gn 14
Storslett O N 159 Hc 11
Storsteinhalvøya ♁ N 158 Ha 5
Storsteinnes O N 159 Hb 11
Stortoppen △ S 158 Ha 12
Storuman ~ S 158 Gp 13
Storuman O S 158 Ha 13
Storvindeln ~ S 158 Ha 13
Story City O USA 70 Db 24
Stöttingfjället △ S 158 Ha 13
Stoughton O CDN 51 Cl 21
Stoŭng O K 263 Lc 39
Stout Lake ~ CDN 56 Da 19
Stowbtsy O BY 171 Hf 19
Strabane O GB 162 Gc 18
Strahan O AUS 378 Mj 67
Strait of Belle Isle ~ CDN 61 Ef 20
Strait of Bonifacio ~ I 185 Gl 25
Strait of Canso ~ CDN 61 Ed 23
Strait of Dover ~ GB 163 Gg 20
Strait of Georgia ~ CDN 50 Ca 21
Strait of Gibraltar ~ MA 293 Gd 28
Strait of Hormuz ~ OM 226 Jg 32
Strait of Juan de Fuca ~ USA 50 Bp 21
Strait of Magellan ~ RCH 15 Fb 15
Strait of Magellan ~ RCH 152 Dp 72
Strait of Malacca ≈ 270 Kp 43
Strait of Messina ~ I 194 Gp 26
Strait of Otranto ~ I 194 Hb 25
Straits of Florida ≈ 87 Dh 34
Straits of Mackinac ~ USA 57 Df 23
Strakonice O CZ 174 Gn 21
Stralsund O D 170 Gn 18
Strand O ZA 358 Hb 63
Strandfontein O ZA 348 Ha 61
Strangways ~ AUS 364 Mc 53
Stranraer O GB 162 Gd 18
Strasbourg O CDN 51 Ck 20
Strasbourg O USA 65 Ck 26
Strasbourg O F 163 Gk 21
Strasburg O USA 56 Cm 22
Stratford O CDN 57 Dh 24
Stratford O USA 64 Cc 27
Stratford O USA 65 Cl 27
Stratford O NZ 383 Nk 65
Stratford upon Aven O GB 163 Gf 19
Strathburn O AUS 365 Mh 53
Strathfillan O AUS 374 Mh 57
Strathgordon O AUS 365 Mh 53
Strathgordon O AUS 378 Mj 67
Strathhaven O AUS 365 Mh 53
Strathleven O AUS 365 Mh 53
Strathmore O CDN 51 Cf 20
Strathmore O AUS 365 Mh 54
Strathmore O AUS 375 Mk 56
Strathroy O CDN 57 Dh 24
Stratton O USA 60 Dn 23
Stratton O USA 65 Cl 26
Straubing O D 174 Gn 21
Straumsjøen O N 158 Gn 11
Strawberry O USA 65 Cg 28
Strawn O USA 70 Cn 29
Streaky Bay ~ AUS 369 Mc 62
Streaky Bay O AUS 378 Md 62
Streatfield Lake ~ CDN 57 De 19
Streatham O AUS 378 Mh 64
Streator O USA 71 Dd 25
Streich Mound O AUS 369 Lm 61
Strelley O AUS 360 Lk 56
Strel'na O RUS 159 Hm 12
Strel'na ~ RUS 159 Hm 12
Strenči O LV 171 He 17
Stresa O I 185 Gl 23
Streymoy ♁ DK 162 Gc 14
Strickland River ~ PNG 286 Mh 48
Stroeder O RA 147 Ec 66
Strofiliá O GR 194 Hd 26
Strokkurgeysir ★ IS 158 Fk 13
Stromness O GB 162 Gd 16
Strömstad O S 170 Gm 16
Strömsvattudal ⌒ S 158 Gp 13
Strong O USA 70 Db 29
Strong City O USA 70 Cp 26
Stronsay ♁ GB 162 Ge 16
Stroud O AUS 379 Mm 62
Stroudsburg O USA 74 Dl 25
Struan O CDN 51 Cj 19
Struer O DK 170 Gl 17
Struga O MK 194 Hc 25
Struis Bay ~ ZA 358 Hc 63
Struma ~ BG 194 Hd 25
Strumica O MK 194 Hd 25
Strydenburg O ZA 349 Hd 60
Strydpoortberge ⩕ ZA 349 Hg 58
Stryj O UA 175 Hd 21
Stryj ~ UA 175 Hd 21
Stryker O USA 50 Ce 21
Strzelecki Creek ~ AUS 374 Mg 60
Strzelno O PL 170 Hb 19
Stuart O USA 56 Cn 24
Stuart O USA 70 Da 25
Stuart O USA 71 Dh 27
Stuart O USA 87 Dh 32
Stuart Bluff Range ⩕ AUS 361 Mc 57
Stuart Creek ~ AUS 374 Me 60
Stuart Island ♁ USA 46 Aj 13
Stuart Lake ~ CDN 42 Dc 8
Stuart Range ⩕ AUS 374 Md 60
Study Butte O USA 81 Cl 31
Stupino O RUS 171 Hl 18
Sturgeon ~ CDN 57 Dh 22
Sturgeon Bay ~ CDN 56 Cn 19
Sturgeon Bay O USA 57 De 23
Sturgeon Falls O CDN 60 Dj 22
Sturgeon Lake ~ CDN 56 Dc 21
Sturgis O USA 51 Cl 23
Sturgis O USA 71 Df 25
Štúrovo O SK 174 Hb 22
Sturt ♀ AUS 374 Mg 60
Sturt Bay ~ AUS 378 Me 63
Sturt Creek O AUS 364 Ma 55
Sturt Creek ~ AUS 364 Ma 55
Sturt Desert ⌒ AUS 374 Mg 60
Stutterheim O ZA 358 Hf 62
Stuttgart O USA 70 Dc 28
Stuttgart O D 174 Gl 21
Stykk Shólmsbær O IS 158 Fj 13
Styr O N 158 Gk 15
Styr ~ UA 175 He 20
Suachevi O GE 202 Hp 25
Suai O TP 282 Ln 50
Šu'aib Gayyāda ~ IRQ 209 Hn 29
Šu'aib Gayyāda ~ IRQ 209 Hn 29
Suain O PNG 286 Mh 47
Suakin O SUD 313 Hl 36
Suakin Archipelago ♁ SUD 313 Hm 36
Suam ~ EAK 325 Hk 45
Suana O RDC 333 Hc 49
Suao O RC 259 Ll 33
Sua Pan ~ RB 349 He 56
Suan Phung O THA 262 Kp 39
Suapi O BOL 129 Ea 52
Suapure ~ YV 107 Ea 42
Sua Súa O YV 112 Ed 42
Suavanao O SOL 290 Nb 49
Suay Riĕng O K 263 Lc 40
Subang O RI 278 Ld 49
Subankata O IND 235 Kk 32
Suban Point ⌓ RP 267 Lm 39
Şubansiri ~ IND 235 Kl 31
Šūbarkūdyk O KZ 155 Rc 9
Subarnarekha ~ IND 235 Kh 34
Subate O LV 171 Hf 17
Subei O VRC 242 Km 26
Sublett O USA 64 Cf 24
Sublette O USA 70 Cm 27
Şubotica O SCG 174 Hb 22
Šubra Al-Haima O ET 301 Hh 30
Subrahmanya O IND 238 Kb 39
Sucatinga O BR 124 Fa 48
Suceava O RO 175 Hf 22
Suchbataar O MNG 26 Qa 5
Suches O PE 128 Dp 53
Suchiapa ~ MEX 93 Db 37
Suchil O MEX 92 Cl 34
Suchixtepec O MEX 93 Cp 37
Sucio ~ CO 106 Dk 42
Sucre O CO 106 Dl 41
Sucre O EC 116 Dh 46
Sucre O BOL 129 Eb 55
Sucúa O EC 116 Dj 47
Sucundun O BR 120 Ee 49
Sucunduri ~ BR 120 Ee 49
Sucunduri ~ BR 120 Ee 50
Sucupira do Norte O BR 121 Em 49
Sucuriju O BR 121 Ek 45
Sucuriú ~ BR 133 Eh 55
Suda O RUS 171 Hm 16
Sudak O UA 175 Hk 23
Sudan O USA 65 Cl 28
Sudan □ SUD 312 Hf 38
Sudbury O CDN 57 Dh 22
Sudd Dinka ⌒ SUD 324 Hh 41
Suddie O GUY 113 Ee 42
Sudeten ⩕ CZ 174 Gp 20
Sūd Ğān O IR 222 Jd 29
Sudislavl' O RUS 171 Hn 17
Suðuroy ♁ DK 162 Gc15
Sudža O RUS 175 Hk 20
Sue ~ SUD 324 Hg 42
Sue ~ SUD 324 Hg 43
Sueca O E 184 Gf 26
Suemez Island ♁ USA 42 Da 7
Suez O ET 301 Hj 30
Suez Canal ★ ET 301 Hj 30
Sūf ~ AFG 223 Jm 28
Sufetula ★ TN 296 Gl 28
Suffern O USA 74 Dl 25

472 Sparke Range - Suffern

Suffield ○ CDN 51 Cg 20
Suffolk ○ USA 74 Dk 27
Sufijon mašiti ★ UZB 223 Jl 25
Süfiyān ○ IR 209 Jb 26
Şūg al-Ġarrāhī ○ YE 218 Hp 38
Sugar 〜 USA 57 Dd 24
Sugar Land ○ USA 81 Cp 31
Sugarloaf Mount △ AUS 379 Ml 62
Sugbai Passage 〜 RP 275 Ll 43
Sugbongkogon ○ RP 267 Ln 41
Sugbongkogon Salay ○ RP 267 Ln 41
Suge La △ VRC 235 Kk 31
Sugerloaf Mountain △ USA 60 Dn 23
Sugihwaras ○ RI 278 Lb 48
Suğla Gölü 〜 TR 195 Hh 27
Sugluk ○ CDN 43 Gc 6
Sugoj 〜 RUS 205 Yb 6
Suğra ○ SYR 198 Hj 27
Sugu ○ WAN 320 Gm 41
Suguian ○ RI 279 Lk 48
Sugun ○ VRC 230 Kc 26
Sugut 〜 MAL 274 Lj 42
Suguta 〜 EAK 325 Hl 45
Suhait ○ VRC 242 Lc 26
Şuḥār ○ OM 226 Jg 33
Sühbaatar ○ MNG 204 Va 8
Suheli Par ⚓ IND 239 Ka 40
Suhiniči ○ RUS 171 Hk 18
Suhl ○ D 174 Gm 20
Suhodol ○ RUS 181 Jd 19
Suhona 〜 RUS 154 Qc 6
Suhona 〜 RUS 171 Hp 16
Şuhut ○ TR 195 Hh 26
Suiá-Miçu 〜 BR 133 Eh 51
Suiá Missu 〜 BR 133 Eh 52
Suibin ○ VRC 250 Mb 22
Suichang ○ VRC 258 Lk 31
Suichuan ○ VRC 258 Lh 32
Suide ○ VRC 243 Le 27
Suifenhe ○ VRC 250 Mb 23
Suigam ○ IND 227 Jg 33
Suihua ○ VRC 205 Wb 9
Suijiang ○ VRC 255 Lc 31
Suining ○ VRC 242 Lc 30
Suining ○ VRC 246 Lj 29
Suining ○ VRC 255 Lf 32
Suir 〜 IRL 163 Cg 19
Suixi ○ VRC 255 Lf 35
Suiyang ○ VRC 250 Mb 23
Suiyang ○ VRC 255 Ld 32
Suizhong ○ VRC 246 Li 25
Şuizhou ○ VRC 243 Lg 30
Šuja ○ RUS 171 Hj 15
Šuja ○ RUS 171 Hm 14
Sujālpur ○ IND 234 Kc 34
Šujawal ○ PK 227 Jn 33
Šujostrov ⚓ RUS 159 Hk 13
Šukābād ○ IR 209 Jc 29
Sukabumi ○ RI 278 Ld 49
Sukadana ○ RI 271 Lf 46
Sukadana ○ RI 278 Lc 48
Sukagawa ○ J 251 Mg 27
Sukaraja ○ RI 278 Le 49
Sukaraja ○ RI 278 Lf 49
Sukareja ○ RI 278 Le 49
Sukeva ○ FIN 159 Hf 14
Sukhothai ○ THA 262 Kp 37
Suki ○ PNG 287 Me 47
Sukkertoppen Maniitsoq ○ DK 43 Jb 5
Sukkozero ○ RUS 159 Hj 14
Sukkur ○ PK 227 Jn 32
Sukses ○ NAM 348 Ha 56
Suksun ○ RUS 154 Rc 7
Sukumo ○ J 251 Mc 29
Sukur ★ WAN 321 Gn 40
Sukwa ○ RDC 333 Hc 45
Sukwane ○ RB 349 He 56
Sula ⚓ N 158 Gj 15
Sula ○ UA 175 Hj 21
Sūlagiri ○ IND 238 Kd 39
Sulaib aṭ-Tarfa' ○ KSA 214 Hn 31
Sulaiman ⌒⌒ PK 227 Jn 31
Sulakyurt ○ TR 195 Hj 25
Sulak 〜 RUS 202 Ja 24
Sulat 〜 RP 267 Ln 40
Sulawesi Celebes ⚓ RI 282 Lm 47
Sule ⚓ SOL 290 Nc 50
Sulechów ○ PL 170 Gp 19
Suleia ○ WAN 320 Gk 41
Sulejów ○ PL 174 Hb 20
Sule Skerry ⚓ GB 162 Gd 16
Šullič ○ AFG 223 Jm 28
Suliki ○ RI 270 La 46
Sulina ○ RO 175 Hg 23
Sulima ○ WAL 316 Ga 42
Sulitjelma △ N 158 Gf 12
Sulitjelma △ S 158 Ha 12
Suljukta ○ KS 223 Jn 26
Sulkava ○ FIN 159 Hg 15
Sullana ○ PE 116 Dh 48
Sulligent ○ USA 86 Dd 29
Sullivan ○ USA 71 Dc 26
Sullivan ○ USA 74 Dc 27
Sullivan Lake 〜 CDN 51 Cg 20
Sullorsuaq Vaigat 〜 DK 43 Ja 4
Sully ○ F 163 Gh 22
Sulmona ○ I 186 Gn 25
Sulop ○ RP 275 Ln 42
Sulphur ○ USA 64 Cc 25
Sulphur ○ USA 70 Cp 28
Sulphur 〜 USA 70 Da 28
Sulphur ○ USA 86 Db 30
Sulphur Creek 〜 USA 51 Cl 23
Sulphur Springs ○ USA 70 Da 29
Sultan ○ CDN 57 Dg 22
Sultandağ △ TR 195 Hh 26
Sultan Dağları △ TR 195 Hh 26
Sultan Hamud ○ EAK 337 Hl 46
Sultanhanı ○ TR 195 Hj 26
Sultan Kudarat ○ RP 275 Ln 42
Sultānpur ○ IND 234 Kc 34
Sultānpur ○ IND 234 Kc 34
Sultan-Ubajs ⌒⌒ UZB 223 Jj 24
Sultepec ○ MEX 92 Cm 36
Suluán Island ⚓ RP 267 Lp 40
Sulu Archipelago ⚓ RP 275 Ll 43

Suluistyk 〜 TJ 230 Kb 27
Sülüklü ○ TR 195 Hj 26
Sululta ○ ETH 325 Hm 41
Sulumei River 〜 PNG 286 Mh 48
Suluntah ○ LAR 300 Hc 29
Sulūq ○ LAR 300 Hc 30
Sülūru ○ IND 238 Ke 39
Sulusaray ○ TR 195 Hk 26
Sulu Sea 〜 RP 267 Lk 41
Sulzberger Bay 〜 38 Bb 17
Sumaianyar ○ RI 279 Lj 47
Šūmär ○ IR 209 Ja 29
Sumatra ○ USA 86 Df 31
Sumatra ⚓ RI 278 Ld 49
Şumauma ○ BR 120 Ed 49
Sumava ♀ CZ 174 Gn 21
Sumba ⚓ RI 279 Lk 51
Sumba ○ ANG 332 Gn 49
Sumbar 〜 TM 222 Jg 26
Sumbawa ⚓ RI 279 Lj 50
Sumbawa ⚓ RI 279 Lk 50
Sumbawabesar ○ RI 279 Lj 50
Sumbawanga ○ EAT 336 Hh 49
Sumbe ○ ANG 340 Gn 51
Sumbi ○ RDC 332 Gn 48
Sumbu ○ Z 336 Hh 50
Sumbu ○ Z 336 Hh 50
Sumbuya ○ WAL 316 Ga 42
Sumé ○ BR 124 Fb 49
Sumedang ○ RI 278 Ld 49
Šumen ○ BG 194 Hf 24
Şumenep ○ RI 279 Lg 49
Sumerlja ○ RUS 181 Jb 18
Sumidouro Grande 〜 BR 132 Ef 53
Summerdown ○ NAM 348 Hb 56
Summerfield ○ USA 70 Cp 25
Summer Lake 〜 USA 50 Cb 24
Summerland ○ CDN 50 Cb 21
Summerlea ○ NZ 382 Nh 66
Summerside ○ CDN 61 Eb 22
Summerstrand ○ ZA 358 He 63
Summersville ○ USA 70 Dc 27
Summerville ○ USA 71 Dh 26
Summerville ○ USA 71 Df 28
Summerville ○ USA 71 Dh 29
Summit ○ USA 56 Cp 23
Summit ○ USA 86 Dc 30
Summit Lake ○ CDN 47 Bn 15
Summit Mountain △ USA 64 Cd 26
Summit Peak △ USA 65 Cj 27
Sumner ○ USA 70 Db 26
Sumner ○ USA 86 Dc 29
Sumozero 〜 RUS 159 Hk 14
Šürgaz ○ IR 226 Jh 31
Şürgaz ○ IR 226 Jh 31
Surgut ○ NEP 234 Kh 33
Surgut ○ RUS 154 Sc 6
Surhandar'ja 〜 UZB 223 Jm 26
Surhandar'ja 〜 UZB 223 Jm 26
Surhob 〜 TJ 223 Jp 26
Suriago Strait 〜 RP 267 Ln 40
Suriäpet ○ IND 238 Kd 37
Surigao ○ RP 267 Ln 41
Surin ○ THA 263 Lb 38
Suriname □ SME 113 Ef 43
Surinda ○ RUS 204 Ub 6
Surovikino ○ RUS 181 Hp 21
Surray ○ CDN 50 Ca 21
Surrey ○ USA 56 Cm 21
Surrey ○ USA 74 Dk 27
Surskoe ○ RUS 181 Jb 18
Surt Sirte ○ LAR 297 Ha 30
Surskoe ○ RUS 181 Jb 18
Sürüç ○ TR 195 Hm 27
Suruga-wan 〜 J 251 Mf 28
Surulangun ○ RI 278 Lb 47
Surumu 〜 BR 112 Ed 44
Şurwakima Falls 〜 GUY 112 Ed 42
Süş ○ IR 209 Jc 29
Susa ○ CO 106 Dm 43
Susa ○ I 185 Gk 23
Susa ○ J 247 Mb 28
Süsah ○ LAR 300 Hc 29
Susaki ○ J 251 Mc 29
Süsangerd ○ IR 215 Jc 30
Susanville ○ USA 64 Cb 25
Suşehri ○ TR 195 Hm 25
Sušensko vodohraniliŝče 〜 RUS 204 Tc 8
Susitna River 〜 USA 46 Ba 13
Susoh ○ RI 270 Kn 44
Susong ○ VRC 246 Lj 30
Suspiro ○ BR 146 Eg 61
Susquehanna 〜 USA 74 Dk 25
Susques ○ RA 136 Ea 57
Sussex ○ CDN 61 Eb 23
Süstar ○ IR 209 Jc 29
Sustut Peak △ CDN 47 Bn 17
Sustut River 〜 CDN 47 Bn 17
Susua ○ RI 282 Ll 47
Susuka ○ SOL 290 Na 49
Susuman ○ RUS 205 Xa 6
Susuman ○ RUS 205 Xc 6
Susunu ○ RI 283 Mc 47
Susupe ○ USA 27 Sa 8
Susurluk ○ TR 195 Hg 26
Susuz ○ TR 202 Hp 25
Suswe ○ ZW 344 Hj 54
Sunkosh 〜 BHT 235 Kj 32
Sutherland ○ USA 70 Cm 25
Sutherland ○ ZA 358 Hc 62
Sutherlin ○ USA 50 Ca 24
Sutlei 〜 PK 227 Jn 31
Sunnynook ○ CDN 51 Cg 20
Sunnyside ○ USA 50 Cc 22
Sunnyside ○ USA 56 Cd 22
Sunnyvale ○ USA 64 Ca 27
Sun Prairie ○ USA 57 Dd 24
Sunset Beach ○ USA 50 Bp 22
Sunset Country ○ AUS 378 Mg 63
Sunset Crater Volcano National Monument ♀ USA 64 Cf 28
Suntai ○ WAN 320 Gm 42
Suntar ○ RUS 221 Qb 3
Suntar 〜 RUS 204 Vc 6
Suntar-Khayata, Khrebet ⌒⌒ RUS 205 Xa 6
Suntar-Khayata, Khrebet ⌒⌒ RUS 205 Xa 6

Suntsar ○ PK 226 Jk 33
Suntu ○ ETH 325 Hl 41
Sunwu ○ VRC 205 Wb 9
Sunxi ⚓ USA 16 Ln 27
Sunyani ○ GH 317 Ge 42
Sunža 〜 RUS 202 Ja 24
Sun Zhongshan Guju ★ VRC 258 Lg 34
Suô'i Rút ○ VN 255 Lc 35
Suojarvi ○ RUS 159 Hj 14
Suomenlinna ★ FIN 159 He 15
Suomenselkä ⌒⌒ FIN 159 He 14
Suô-nada 〜 J 247 Mb 28
Suonenjoki ○ FIN 159 Hf 14
Supamo 〜 YV 112 Ec 42
Supaul ○ IND 235 Kh 32
Superior ○ USA 56 Dc 22
Superior ○ USA 65 Cg 29
Superior ○ USA 70 Cn 25
Supetar ○ HR 194 Ha 24
Suphan Buri ○ THA 262 Kp 38
Süphan D. △ TR 202 Hp 26
Supia ○ CO 106 Dl 43
Supplejack Downs ○ AUS 364 Mb 55
Suqa-al-Gamal ○ SUD 312 Hf 39
Sūq aš-Šuyūḥ ○ IRQ 215 Jb 30
Suqian ○ VRC 246 Lk 29
Sūq Suwaiq ○ KSA 214 Hm 33
Suqu ○ VRC 258 Lh 34
Sür ○ RL 208 Hk 29
Sür ○ IR 215 Jd 31
Sür ○ IR 215 Je 31
Sür ○ IR 215 Je 32
Sür ○ IR 222 Jd 28
Sür ○ IR 222 Jh 28
Sür ○ IR 222 Jh 28
Şür ○ OM 226 Jh 34
Sura 〜 RUS 181 Ja 18
Sura ○ ETH 325 Hn 42
Sūrāb ○ IR 222 Jc 29
Sūrāb ○ PK 227 Jm 31
Surabaya ○ RI 278 Lc 48
Surabaya ○ RI 279 Lg 49
Surakarta ○ RI 278 Lf 49
Suramana ○ RI 279 Lk 46
Surat ○ IND 234 Ka 35
Süratgarh ○ IND 227 Ka 31
Suratkal ○ IND 238 Kb 39
Şurat Thani ○ THA 262 Kp 41
Sürav 〜 BY 171 Hh 19
Suraž ○ RUS 171 Hj 18
Surazh ○ BY 171 Hh 18
Şurbiton ○ AUS 375 Mk 57
Surcubamba ○ PE 128 Dl 52
Surendranagar ○ IND 227 Jp 34

Suwailih ○ JOR 208 Hk 29
Suwalki ○ PL 171 Hd 18
Suwannee 〜 USA 86 Dg 30
Suwanose-shima ⚓ J 259 Ma 31
Suwarrow ⚓ NZ 35 Ab 11
Suwŏn ○ ROK 247 Lp 27
Suyckutambo ○ PE 128 Dn 53
Suyo ○ PE 116 Dh 48
Sûza ○ IR 226 Jf 32
Suzdal' ○ RUS 171 Hm 17
Suzhou ○ VRC 246 Lj 29
Suzhou ○ VRC 246 Ll 30
Suzu ○ J 251 Me 27
Suzuka ○ J 251 Me 28
Suzu-misaki ⌒ J 251 Me 27
Svaljava ○ UA 175 Hd 21
Svappavaara ○ S 159 Hc 12
Svartfioljlekelen ⚓ N 159 Hc 10
Svartisen △ N 158 Gn 12
Svataya Volya ○ BY 171 He 19
Svatove ○ UA 181 Hm 21
Sveagruva ○ N 158 Ha 7
Svealand ○ S 170 Gn 16
Sveg ○ S 158 Gn 14
Svenčionys ○ LT 171 He 18
Svendborg ○ DK 170 Gm 18
Svendsen Peninsula ⌒ CDN 43 Gb 3
Svenes ○ N 170 Gl 16
Svenskøya ⚓ N 158 He 6
Svenstavik ○ S 158 Gn 14
Sverdlovs'k ○ UA 181 Hn 21
Sverdrup Islands ⚓ CDN 7 Ea 2
Sverdrup Islands ⚓ CDN 42 Fb 3
Svetlaja ○ RUS 250 Mf 22
Svetlogorsk ○ RUS 170 Hb 18
Svetlograd ○ RUS 202 Hp 23
Svetlyj Jar ○ RUS 181 Ja 21
Svetogorsk ○ RUS 171 Hg 15
Svetskij ○ RUS 154 Sa 6
Svidník ○ SK 174 Hc 21
Sviiga 〜 RUS 181 Jc 18
Svilengrad ○ BG 194 Hf 25
Svincovyj Rudnik ○ TM 223 Jm 26
Svislač ○ BY 171 Hd 19
Svištov ○ BG 194 He 24
Svitlovods'k ○ UA 175 Hj 21
Svoboda ○ BY 171 Hd 19
Svobodnyj ○ RUS 205 Wb 8
Svôlvær ○ N 158 Gp 11
Svyatohirs'k ★ VRC 231 Kf 30
Swabian Alp ⌒⌒ D 174 Gl 21
Swaershoek ○ ZA 358 He 62
Swain Reefs ⚓ AUS 375 Mn 56
Swains ⚓ USA 35 Aa 11
Swainsboro ○ USA 71 Dg 29
Swakop 〜 NAM 348 Ha 56
Swakopmund ○ NAM 348 Gp 57
Swakopmund ○ NAM 348 Gp 57
Swan 〜 CDN 51 Ci 19
Swana-Mume ○ RDC 341 Hf 51
Swan Hill ○ AUS 378 Mh 63
Swan Island ⚓ USA 70 Dc 28
Swan Lake 〜 CDN 56 Cm 19
Swan Lake 〜 USA 50 Cf 22
Swan Lake 〜 USA 56 Da 23
Swan Plain ○ CDN 56 Cm 19
Swan Reach ○ AUS 378 Mf 63
Swanquarter ○ USA 74 Dk 28
Swan River ○ CDN 56 Cm 20
Swan River 〜 AUS 376 Lg 62
Swansea ○ GB 162 Gf 19
Swansea ○ USA 71 Dg 28
Swansea ○ USA 163 Gd 20
Swansea ○ AUS 378 Mk 67
Swanson Reservoir 〜 USA 70 Cm 25
Swanton ○ USA 60 Dm 23
Swan Valley ○ USA 51 Cg 24
Swartberg ⌒⌒ ZA 349 Hg 61
Swartbooisdrift ○ NAM 340 Gn 54
Swartkolkvloer 〜 ZA 358 Hc 61
Swartmodder ○ ZA 348 Hc 59
Swartruggens ○ ZA 349 Hf 58
Swartruggens ⌒⌒ ZA 358 Hb 62
Swasiland □ SD 352 Hh 59
Swāt 〜 PK 223 Jp 28
Swāt ○ PK 230 Ka 28
Swate ○ WAN 320 Gh 40
Sweden □ S 158 Gn 14
Swedru ○ GH 317 Gf 43
Sweers Island ⚓ AUS 365 Mf 54
Sweetgrass ○ USA 51 Cf 21
Sweet Grass Indian Reservation ••• CDN 51 Ch 19
Sweet Home ○ USA 50 Ca 23
Sweetwater ○ KIR 14 Ba 9
Sweetwater ○ USA 70 Cn 28
Sweetwater River 〜 USA 51 Ch 24
Sweetwater Station ○ USA 65 Ch 24
Swellendam ○ ZA 358 Hc 63
Świdnica ○ PL 174 Ha 20
Świebodzin ○ PL 170 Gp 19
Świecie ○ PL 170 Hb 19
Swift Current ○ CDN 51 Cj 20
Swift Current Creek 〜 CDN 51 Ch 21
Swifts Creek ○ AUS 379 Mk 64
Swindon ○ GB 163 Ge 20
Swinoujście ○ PL 170 Gp 19
Swiss Historical Village ★ USA 56 Cd 22
Switzerland □ CH 163 Gk 22
Syanno ○ BY 171 Hg 18
Syari-dake △ J 250 Mj 24
Syčevka ○ RUS 171 Hk 18
Sydney ⚓ KIR 35 Aa 10
Sydney ○ CDN 61 Ed 22
Sydney ○ AUS 379 Mm 62
Syktyvkar ○ RUS 19 Mb 3
Syktyvkar ○ RUS 154 Rb 6
Sylacauga ○ USA 71 De 29
Sylhet ○ BD 235 Kk 33
Sylva 〜 RUS 171 Dg 28
Sylvania ○ CDN 51 Df 25
Sylvania ○ CDN 71 Dh 25
Sylvania ○ USA 360 Ll 57
Sylvan Lake ○ CDN 50 Ce 19
Sylvia ○ USA 70 Cn 27
Syndassko ○ RUS 204 Va 4
Synder ○ USA 70 Cm 29
Synder ○ USA 70 Cp 29

Syne'nykove ○ UA 175 Hk 21
Synnfjell △ N 158 Gl 15
Synnot Range ⌒⌒ AUS 361 Ln 54
Syō-gawa 〜 J 251 Me 27
Syracuse ○ USA 60 Dk 24
Syracuse ○ USA 70 Cm 26
Syracuse ○ USA 70 Cp 25
Syracuse ○ I 185 Gp 27
Syr Dariya 〜 KZ 155 Sa 9
Syrdar'ja 〜 UZB 223 Jn 25
Syre ○ USA 56 Cp 22
Syria □ SYR 208 Hl 28
Syriam ○ MYA 262 Kn 37
Syrian Desert ⌒ SYR 209 Hm 29
Syrjajeve ○ UA 175 Hg 22
Syroke ○ UA 175 Hj 22
Sysmä ○ FIN 159 He 15
Sysola 〜 RUS 154 Rb 6
Syzran' ○ RUS 181 Jb 19
Szamotuły ○ PL 170 Ha 19
Szarvas ○ H 174 Hc 22
Szczecin ○ PL 170 Gp 19
Szczecinek ○ PL 170 Ha 19
Szczekociny ○ PL 174 Hb 20
Szczytno ○ PL 170 Hc 19
Szeged ○ H 174 Hc 22
Székes-Fehérvár ○ H 174 Hb 22
Szekszárd ○ H 174 Hb 22
Szentes ○ H 174 Hc 22
Szigetvár △ H 174 Ha 23
Szolnok ○ H 174 Hc 22
Szombathely ○ H 174 Ha 22
Sztabin ○ PL 171 Hd 19

T

T.Roosevelt (North Unit) ♀ USA 51 Cl 22
T.Roosevelt (South Unit) ♀ USA 51 Cl 22
Tâba ⚓ KSA 214 Hp 32
Tâba ○ ET 301 Hk 31
Tabaconas ○ PE 116 Dj 48
Tabala ○ RP 267 Lm 39
Tabāla ○ KSA 218 Hp 35
Tabankort ○ RMM 305 Gg 37
Tabankulu ○ ZA 349 Hg 61
Tabaq ○ SUD 313 Hj 35
Tabaquén ○ CO 107 Dp 44
Tabarğal ○ KSA 214 Hm 30
Tabar Group ⚓ PNG 287 Mn 47
Tabar Island ⚓ PNG 287 Mm 47
Tabarka ○ TN 296 Gi 27
Tabas ○ IR 222 Jg 29
Tabatinga ○ BR 117 Dp 48
Tabelbala ○ DZ 293 Ge 31
Taber ○ CDN 51 Cf 21
Taberdga ○ DZ 296 Gk 28
Tabernas ○ E 184 Ge 27
Tabert ○ GB 162 Gc 17
Tabia Tsaka 〜 VRC 231 Kf 30
Tabibuga ○ PNG 287 Mj 48
Tabina ○ RP 275 Lm 42
Tabiteuea ⚓ KIR 35 Tb 10
Tabla ○ RN 308 Gk 39
Tablas Island ⚓ RP 267 Ll 39
Tablas Strait 〜 RP 267 Ll 39
Tablat ○ DZ 296 Gh 27
Table Cape ⌒ NZ 383 Nm 65
Table Head ⌒ CDN 61 Ea 22
Tableland ○ AUS 361 Lp 54
Table Rock 〜 USA 70 Db 27
Tabletop △ AUS 361 Lm 57
Tabletop △ AUS 368 Lk 60
Tabligbo ○ RT 317 Gg 42
Tabmas ○ USA 86 Dm 23
Tabola ○ RUS 202 Jc 22
Taboco 〜 BR 132 Eg 55
Tabone ○ RI 279 Lk 47
Tabong ○ MYA 254 Kn 32
Tabora ○ EAT 336 Hj 48
Tabor City ○ USA 74 Dj 28
Tabou ○ CI 305 Gc 43
Tabou ○ BF 317 Ge 40
Tabou ○ FJI 390 Aa 55
Tabrīz ○ IR 209 Jb 27
Tabubil ○ PNG 286 Mg 48
Tabudarat ○ RI 279 Lj 47
Tabūk ⚓ KSA 214 Hl 31
Tabuk ○ RP 267 Ll 37
Tabul ○ RP 275 Ll 43
Tabuleiro ○ BR 146 Eg 61
Tabuneran ⚓ KIR 14 Ba 9
Tabür ○ SUD 313 Hd 40
Tacabamba ○ PE 116 Dj 49
Tacajó ○ C 101 Dk 35
Tacalaya ○ PE 128 Dn 54
Tacañitas ○ RA 136 Ec 60
Tacaratu ○ BR 124 Fa 50
Tacheng ○ VRC 204 Tb 9
Tachibana-wan 〜 J 247 Ma 29
Tachilek ○ MYA 254 Kp 35
Tachiumet ○ LAR 297 Hb 32
Tachtojamsk ○ RUS 23 Sb 3
Tacinskij ○ RUS 181 Hn 21
Tacipi ○ RI 282 Ll 48
Tacloban ○ RP 267 Ln 40
Tacoda Sekan ○ MYA 254 Kn 36
Tacoma ○ USA 50 Ca 22
Taco Pozo ○ RA 136 Ec 58
Tacuane ○ MOC 344 Hl 54
Tacuaras ○ PY 146 Ef 57
Tacurong ○ RP 275 Ln 42
Tacuato ○ YV 107 Dn 40
Tacutu 〜 BR 112 Ed 44
Tacutu 〜 BR 112 Ed 44
Tadahadi ○ SOL 290 Nc 51
Taddert ○ MA 293 Gc 30
Tadélaka ○ RN 308 Gl 38
Tademaït Plateau ⌒⌒ DZ 293 Gg 31
Tadenet Lake 〜 CDN 47 Bn 11
Tādepallegūdem ○ IND 238 Ke 37
Tadewa ○ RI 278 Lk 50
Tadine ○ F 386 Nf 56
Tadjentourt △ DZ 296 Gl 32
Tadjmout ○ DZ 296 Gh 33
Tadjouna ○ DZ 293 Gg 29
Tadjoura ○ DJI 328 Hp 40
Tadmur Palmyra ○ SYR 209 Hm 28

Tadoba National Park ★ IND 234 Kd 35
Tadohae Haesang ★ ROK 247 Ln 28
Tadohae Haesang ♀ ROK 247 Lp 28
Tadoussac ○ CDN 60 Dp 21
Tadpatri ○ IND 238 Kc 38
Tadrart Akakus ★ LAR 297 Gm 33
Taduno ○ RI 282 Lm 46
Taebaek Mountains ⌒⌒ DVRK 247 Lp 26
Taech'on ○ ROK 247 Lp 27
Taech'ŏngdo ○ ROK 246 Ln 27
Taedong 〜 DVRK 247 Ln 26
Taegu ○ ROK 247 Ma 28
Taehan Haehyŏp 〜 ROK 247 Ma 28
Taehüksan Do ⚓ ROK 247 Ln 28
Taejŏng ○ ROK 247 Lp 29
Taejŏnpyŏngdo ○ ROK 247 Ln 27
T'aepaek ○ ROK 247 Ma 27
Taera ○ SOL 290 Na 49
Tafalla ○ E 184 Gf 24
Tafédek ○ RN 308 Gk 37
Tafelberg △ ZA 358 Hb 62
Tafermaar ○ RI 283 Mc 49
Tafilalt ⌒ MA 293 Gd 30
Tafinkar ○ RMM 305 Gg 38
Tafiré ○ CI 317 Gd 41
Tafo Mpaem ○ GH 317 Gf 42
Tafraoute ○ MA 292 Gb 31
Tafreš ○ IR 209 Jc 28
Taft ○ USA 64 Cc 28
Taft ○ IR 226 Jf 30
Taga ○ WS 390 Ad 52
Tagab ○ SUD 312 Hh 36
Tagagawik River 〜 USA 46 Al 13
Taĝänet Keyna ⌒⌒ RMM 305 Ge 36
Taganito ○ RP 267 Ln 41
Taganrog ○ RUS 181 Hm 22
Tagânt ⌒⌒ RIM 304 Fp 37
Taĝarak ○ IR 209 Jc 26
Tagarev △ TM 222 Jg 26
Tagari River 〜 PNG 286 Mh 49
Tagaytay ○ RP 267 Ll 38
Tagbara ○ RCA 321 Hc 43
Tagbilaran ○ RP 267 Lm 41
Taghajit ○ RN 308 Gl 36
Tago ○ RP 267 Lp 41
Tagoûrâret ⌒⌒ RIM 305 Ge 37
Tagpait ○ RP 267 Lk 41
Tagua 〜 CO 106 Dl 44
Taguá ○ BR 133 Em 51
Taguaruçu 〜 BR 140 Eg 56
Taguas 〜 RA 137 Dp 60
Taguatinga ○ BR 133 Ek 53
Taguatinga ○ BR 133 El 52
Tagula ○ PNG 287 Mn 51
Tagula Islands ⚓ PNG 287 Mn 51
Tagum ○ RP 275 Ln 42
Tahafo ○ RI 275 Lp 45
Tahalra ⌒ DZ 308 Gj 34
Tahär ⚓ AFG 223 Jn 27
Taharoa ○ NZ 383 Nk 65
Tahar-Souk ○ MA 293 Gd 28
Tahat △ DZ 308 Gj 34
Taheke ○ NZ 383 Nj 63
Taheman ○ VRC 230 Kb 27
Tahifet ○ DZ 308 Gk 34
Tahiti ⚓ F 35 Bb 11
Tahleguah ○ USA 70 Da 28
Tahoka ○ USA 70 Cm 29
Taholah ○ USA 50 Bp 22
Tahomi ○ LB 316 Gb 43
Tahoua ○ RN 308 Gk 38
Tahquamenon Falls S.P. ♀ USA 57 Df 22
Tahrami ○ LAR 309 Gp 33
Tahr-e-Ĝamšid ○ IR 215 Je 31
Tahsis ○ CDN 50 Bn 21
Tahta ○ TM 222 Jh 25
Tahta ○ ET 301 Hh 32
Tahta-Bazar ○ TM 223 Jk 28
Tahtakūpir ○ UZB 155 Sa 10
Tahtalı Dağları △ TR 195 Hk 27
Tah-te Suleimān ⌒⌒ IR 209 Jb 27
Tahuamanú 〜 PE 128 Dn 51
Tahuamanu ○ BOL 129 Dp 51
Tahuata ⚓ F 35 Bb 11
Tahulandang ○ RI 275 Ln 44
Tahuna ○ RI 275 Ln 44
Taï ○ CI 305 Gc 43
Taiama ○ WAL 316 Ga 42
Tai'an ○ VRC 246 Lj 27
Taibai ○ VRC 243 Le 29
Taibai Shan △ VRC 243 Ld 29
Taibet ○ DZ 296 Gh 29
Taibique ○ E 292 Fm 32
Taichung ○ RC 259 Li 33
Taigetos ⌒⌒ GR 194 Hd 27
Taigu ○ VRC 243 Lg 27
Taihang Shan ⌒⌒ VRC 243 Lg 28
Taihape ○ NZ 383 Nk 65
Taihe ○ VRC 243 Lh 29
Taihe ○ VRC 258 Lh 32
Taihu 〜 VRC 246 Lj 30
Tai Hu 〜 VRC 246 Ll 30
Taihu ○ VRC 246 Ll 30
Taijiang ○ VRC 255 Le 32
Taikang ○ VRC 243 Lh 28
Taikky ○ MYA 262 Kn 37
Tailai ○ VRC 204 Wa 9
Tailem Bend ○ AUS 378 Mf 63
Tailing ○ GUY 112 Ed 42
Taim ○ BR 146 En 62
Taimā' ⚓ KSA 214 Hm 32
Taimatī ○ PA 97 Dj 41
Taimushan ★ VRC 259 Ll 32
Tainan ○ RC 259 Lk 34
Tainan ○ RC 259 Li 34
Tainhas ○ BR 146 Ej 60
Taining ○ VRC 258 Lj 32
Tainzhu ○ VRC 255 Le 32
Taió ○ BR 140 Ek 59
Taiobeiras ○ BR 125 En 53
Taiof Island ⚓ PNG 290 Mp 48
Taipei ○ RC 259 Ll 33
Taiping ○ VRC 255 Ld 34
Taiping ○ VRC 258 Lk 33
Taiping ○ MAL 270 La 43
Taipong ○ GUY 112 Ed 43
Tairua ○ NZ 383 Nk 64
Tais ○ RI 278 Lb 48
Taisha ○ EC 116 Dk 47

Taisha ○ J 251 Mc 28
Taishan ★ VRC 246 Lj 27
Taishan ○ VRC 258 Lg 34
Taishi ○ RC 259 Ll 34
Taishun ○ VRC 258 Lk 32
Taita Hills ⛰ EAK 337 Hm 47
Taitung ○ RC 259 Ll 34
Taivalkoski ○ FIN 159 Hf 13
Taiwan ◘ RC 259 Ll 34
Taiwan ♁ RC 259 Ll 34
Taiwan Strait ≈ RC 258 Lk 34
Tai Xian ○ VRC 246 Ll 29
Taixing ○ VRC 246 Ll 29
Taiyuan ○ VRC 243 Lg 27
Taizhou ○ VRC 246 Lk 29
Ta'izz ○ YE 218 Hp 39
Tajen ○ RC 259 Ll 34
Taji ○ IND 235 Kl 32
Tajicaringa ○ AUS 379 Mk 64
Tajikistan ◘ TJ 223 Jn 26
Tajima ○ J 251 Mf 27
Tajimi ○ J 251 Me 28
Tajique ○ USA 65 Cj 28
Tāj Mahāl ★ IND 234 Kd 32
Tajmura ~ RUS 204 Ub 6
Tajo ~ E 184 Ge 25
Tājpur ○ IND 235 Kg 33
Tajšet ○ RUS 204 Ub 7
Tajuña ~ E 184 Ge 25
Tājūr' ○ LAR 297 Gn 29
Tak ○ THA 262 Kp 37
Takāb ○ IR 209 Jb 27
Takaba ○ EAK 325 Hn 44
Takachiho ○ J 247 Mb 29
Takahashi ○ J 251 Mc 28
Takaka ○ NZ 383 Nj 66
Takalar ○ RI 279 Lk 48
Takalou ○ TCH 321 Hb 40
Takama ○ GUY 113 Ee 43
Takamaka ○ SY 329 Jf 48
Takamatsu ○ J 251 Md 28
Takanabe ○ J 247 Mb 29
Takanosu ○ J 250 Mf 25
Takaoka ○ J 251 Me 27
Takapuna ○ NZ 383 Nk 64
Takara-shima ♁ J 259 Ma 31
Takasaki ○ J 251 Mf 27
Takatokwane ○ RB 349 Hd 58
Takatsuki ○ J 251 Md 28
Takaungu ○ EAK 337 Hm 47
Takayama ○ J 251 Me 27
Takefu ○ J 251 Md 28
Takengon ○ RI 270 Kn 43
Takeo ○ K 263 Lc 40
Take Shima ♁ J 247 Mb 27
Takeshima Dokdo ♁ J 247 Mb 27
Take-shima ♁ J 247 Mb 30
Takestān ○ IR 209 Jc 27
Taketa ○ J 247 Mb 29
Tak Fa ○ THA 262 La 38
Takhro ○ THA 263 Lb 38
Takht-i-Bahi ★ PK 230 Ka 28
Takht-i-Sulaiman △ PK 227 Jn 30
Takiéta ○ RN 308 Gl 39
Takijuk Lake ~ CDN 42 Eb 5
Takikawa ○ J 250 Mg 24
Takikro ○ GH 317 Ge 42
Takinoue ○ J 250 Mh 23
Takis ○ PNG 287 Mm 48
Takiyuak Lake ~ CDN 47 Ce 11
Takla Lake ~ CDN 47 Bn 17
Taklamakan Desert ⏜ VRC 230 Ke 26
Takli Dhokeshwar ○ IND 238 Kb 36
Taknis ○ LAR 300 Hc 29
Takobanda ○ RCA 321 Hc 42
Takoradi ○ GH 317 Gf 43
Takorka ○ RN 308 Gk 39
Takoutala ○ SN 304 Fp 38
Takpamba ○ RT 317 Gg 41
Takpoima ○ LB 316 Ga 42
Takrīt ○ IRQ 209 Hp 28
Taksimo ○ RUS 204 Vb 7
Taku ~ CDN 47 Bj 15
Takuapa ○ THA 262 Kp 41
Takum ○ WAN 320 Gl 42
Takundi ○ RDC 332 Ha 48
Tāl ○ IND 234 Kb 34
Tala ○ MEX 92 Cl 35
Tala ~ RA 136 Eb 59
Tala ○ ROU 146 Eg 63
Tāla ○ IND 234 Ke 34
Tala ○ EAK 337 Hl 46
Talachyn ○ BY 171 Hg 18
Talagang ○ PK 230 Ka 29
Talaganta ○ RCH 137 Dn 62
Talaimannar ○ CL 239 Kd 41
Talaivasal ○ IND 239 Kd 40
Talakalla ○ IND 238 Kb 38
Talamba ○ PK 230 Ka 30
Talanga ○ HN 96 De 38
Talangbetutu ○ RI 278 Lc 47
Talangpadang ○ RI 278 Lb 47
Talang Selengku ○ RI 278 Lc 47
Talara ○ PE 116 Dh 48
Talaroo ○ AUS 365 Mh 55
Talasea ○ PNG 287 Mm 48
Talata Mafara ○ WAN 320 Gj 39
Talat at-Timiat ○ KSA 214 Hp 31
Talavera de la Reino ○ E 184 Gd 26
Talawana ○ AUS 360 Ll 57
Talawanta ○ AUS 365 Mg 55
Talawdī ○ SUD 312 Hh 40
Talbot Islands ♁ AUS 286 Mh 50
Talbotton ○ USA 86 Df 29
Talbragar ~ AUS 379 Ml 62
Talca ○ RCH 137 Dn 63
Talcahuano ○ RCH 137 Dm 64
Tālcher ○ IND 235 Kg 35
Talcho ○ RN 308 Gh 38
Taldalt ○ MA 292 Gb 31
Taldisay ○ KZ 155 Rc 8
Taldom ○ RUS 171 Hl 17
Tale ○ GH 317 Gf 41
Taleex ○ SP 328 Jc 41
Talegaon ○ IND 234 Kd 35
Tālem ○ IR 209 Jc 27
Tāleqān ○ AFG 223 Jn 27
Tāleqān Rūd ~ AFG 223 Jn 27
Taley ○ RCA 321 Ha 42
Talguharai ○ SUD 313 Hk 36
Talhār ○ PK 227 Jn 33
Talibon ○ RP 267 Ln 40
Talicherla ○ IND 238 Kd 38
Talihina ○ USA 70 Da 28
Tālīkota ○ IND 238 Kc 37
Talimardžan ○ UZB 223 Jl 26
Talimarjan suv ambari ~ UZB 223 Jl 26
Taling Chan ○ THA 262 La 39
Taliouine ○ MA 293 Gc 30
Taliparamba ○ IND 238 Kb 39
Talipaw ○ RP 275 Ll 43
Tali Post ○ SUD 324 Hh 43
Talisayan ○ RP 267 Ln 41
Talisayan ○ RI 274 Lk 45
Taliwang ○ RI 279 Lj 50
Talkeetna ○ USA 46 Ba 13
Talkeetna Mountains ⛰ USA 46 Ba 13
Talladega ○ USA 71 De 29
Tall'Afar ○ IRQ 209 Hp 27
Tallahassee ○ USA 86 Df 30
Tall al-Laḥm ○ IRQ 215 Jb 30
Tall al-Manūk △ SYR 209 Hm 29
Tallangatta ○ AUS 379 Mk 64
Tall Birāk ○ SYR 209 Hn 27
Tallering Peak △ AUS 368 Lh 60
Tall Huqna ○ IRQ 209 Hp 27
Tallinn ⊡ EST 171 He 16
Tallkalā ○ AFG 223 Jk 29
Tallkalah ○ SYR 208 Hl 28
Tall Kūšik ○ SYR 209 Hn 27
Tallulah ○ USA 86 Dc 29
Tall ,Uwaināt ○ IRQ 209 Hp 27
Talmest ○ MA 292 Gb 30
Talnah ○ RUS 204 Tc 5
Talnoe ○ UA 175 Hh 21
Taloard ○ IR 215 Jd 30
Taloda ○ IND 234 Kb 35
Talon ○ RUS 205 Xc 7
Talovaja ○ RUS 181 Hn 20
Talovka ○ RUS 205 Za 6
Talovka ~ RUS 205 Za 6
Talras ○ RN 308 Gl 38
Talsi ○ LV 170 Hd 17
Talsinnt ○ MA 293 Ge 29
Taltal ○ RCH 136 Dn 58
Taltal ~ RCH 136 Dn 58
Taltson ~ CDN 42 Eb 6
Talu ○ RI 270 Kp 45
Taludaa ○ RI 275 Lm 45
Taluk ○ RI 270 La 46
Talusan ○ RP 275 Lm 42
Talwood ○ AUS 375 Ml 60
Tam ~ F 184 Gg 24
Tama ○ USA 70 Db 25
Tamadanet ○ DZ 296 Gl 31
Tamale ○ GH 317 Gf 41
Tamanco ○ PE 116 Dl 48
Tamandourirt ○ RMM 305 Gf 36
Tamanduá ○ BR 125 En 54
Tamanhint ○ LAR 297 Gp 32
Tamani ○ RMM 305 Gc 39
Tamaniquá ○ BR 117 Eb 47
Taman Negara Natl. Park ⚘ MAL 270 Lb 43
Tamano ○ J 251 Mc 28
Tamanrasset ○ DZ 308 Gj 34
Tamanrasset ○ RN 308 Gj 38
Tamanredjo ○ SME 113 Eg 43
Tamanskij zaliv ~ UA 195 Hl 23
Tamarac ○ USA 87 Dh 32
Tamarack Island ♁ CDN 56 Cp 20
Tamarac N.W.R. ⚘ USA 56 Da 22
Tamarike ○ RI 286 Mg 50
Tamarindo ○ CR 96 Df 40
Ṯamarīt ○ OM 219 Jf 37
Tamarou ○ DY 320 Gh 41
Tamási ○ H 174 Hb 22
Tamaso ○ SUD 312 Hj 39
Tamassoumit ○ RIM 304 Fp 36
Tamatama ○ YV 112 Eb 44
Tamatave ○ RM 345 Jc 55
Tamaya ~ PE 116 Dm 50
Tamazula ○ MEX 92 Cj 33
Tamazula ○ MEX 92 Cl 36
Tamazulapán ○ MEX 92 Cp 36
Tamazunchale ○ MEX 92 Cn 35
Tambach ○ EAK 325 Hk 45
Tambacounda ○ SN 316 Fp 39
Tambakara ○ RMM 304 Ga 38
Tambakboyo ○ RI 279 Lf 49
Tambaqui ○ BR 117 Ec 48
Tambar ○ AUS 379 Ml 61
Tambara ○ MOC 344 Hj 54
Tambaram ○ IND 238 Ke 39
Tambarga ○ BF 317 Gg 40
Tambawel ○ WAN 320 Gj 39
Tambe ○ ANG 340 Gp 52
Tambea ○ RI 282 Ll 48
Tambea ○ SOL 290 Nb 50
Tambej ○ RUS 204 Sc 4
Tambellup ○ AUS 368 Lj 63
Tâmbeubui ○ IND 262 Kl 40
Tambillo ○ PE 128 Dm 54
Tambillo ~ RCH 136 Dp 56
Tambo ○ PA 97 Dh 41
Tambo ~ PE 128 Dm 51
Tambo ~ PE 128 Dn 54
Tambo ○ RDC 336 Hf 50
Tambo ○ AUS 375 Mk 58
Tambobamba ○ PE 128 Dm 52
Tambo Grande ○ PE 116 Dh 48
Tambo Grande ○ PE 116 Dj 48
Tambohorano ○ RM 345 Hp 54
Tambopata ~ PE 128 Dp 52
Tambo Pucacuro ○ PE 116 Dl 47
Tambor ○ ANG 340 Gn 54
Tambores ○ ROU 146 Ef 61
Tamboril ○ BR 124 Ep 48
Tamboryacu ~ PE 116 Dl 46
Tambo Tanbillo ○ BOL 129 Ea 55
Tamboura ○ RCA 324 He 43
Tambov ○ RUS 181 Hn 19
Tambugo ○ RP 267 Ll 37
Tambul ○ PNG 287 Mh 48
Tambulan ○ RI 279 Lk 46
Tambunan ○ MAL 274 Lj 43
Tambura ○ SUD 324 Hf 43
Tambuttegama ○ CL 239 Ke 41
Tâmchekket ○ RIM 304 Ga 37
Tamdibulak ○ UZB 223 Jl 25
Tamdytou toglari △ UZB 155 Sa 10
Tame ○ CO 107 Dn 42
Tamegroute ○ MA 293 Gd 30
Tamelelt ○ MA 293 Gc 30
Tamelhat ○ DZ 296 Gk 29
Tamenglong ○ IND 254 Kl 33
Tameque ○ LB 316 Gb 43
Tamesi ~ MEX 81 Cn 35
Tamesna ⏜ RN 308 Gj 36
Tamezret ○ TN 296 Gl 29
Tamiahua ○ MEX 81 Cp 34
Tamica ○ RUS 159 Hm 13
Tamil Nādu ⊙ IND 239 Kc 40
Tamitatoala ~ BR 132 Eg 52
Tamitatoala ~ BR 132 Eh 52
Tamjang ~ RI 270 Kn 43
Tam Ký ○ VN 263 Le 38
Tamluk ○ IND 235 Kh 34
Tamnūn ○ YE 219 Jd 38
Tamou ○ RN 320 Gh 39
Tampa ○ USA 86 Dg 31
Tampa ○ ANG 340 Gn 53
Tampa ~ ANG 340 Gn 53
Tampa Bay ~ USA 86 Dg 32
Tampéna ○ RN 317 Gg 39
Tampere ○ FIN 159 Hd 15
Tampico ○ MEX 81 Cp 34
Tampin ○ MAL 270 Lb 44
Tampo ○ RI 282 Lm 48
Tampoketsan'i ⛰ RM 345 Jb 54
Tampoketsan'i Beveromay ⛰ RM 345 Jb 54
Tampokets Kamoro ⛰ RM 345 Jb 54
Tamri ○ MA 292 Ga 30
Tamshiyacu ○ PE 116 Dm 48
Tamu ○ MYA 254 Km 33
Ṯamūd ○ YE 219 Jc 37
Tamuin ○ MEX 81 Cn 34
Tamulol ○ RI 283 Mb 46
Tamworth ○ AUS 379 Mm 61
Tana ○ N 159 Hf 10
Tana ~ N 159 Hg 10
Tana ~ EAK 337 Hl 46
Tanabe ○ J 251 Md 29
Tanaberu ○ RI 282 Ll 48
Tanabi ○ BR 140 Ek 56
Tanacross ○ USA 46 Bc 13
Tanaf ○ SN 316 Fn 39
Tanafjorden ~ N 159 Hg 10
TaN-Ahenet ⏜ DZ 305 Gg 34
Tanahgrogot ○ RI 274 Lj 46
Tanahmerah ○ RI 283 Mc 47
Tanah Rata ○ MAL 270 La 43
Tānai ○ PK 223 Jn 29
Tanai ~ MYA 254 Kn 32
Tanakpur ○ IND 234 Kd 31
Tanamalwila ○ CL 239 Ke 42
Tanama River ~ USA 6 Bb 3
Tanambe ○ RM 345 Jc 54
Tanami Desert ⏜ AUS 364 Mb 55
Tân An ○ VN 263 Ld 40
Tanana ○ USA 46 An 13
Tanana River ~ USA 46 Bc 13
Tanandava ○ RM 353 Hp 56
Tanantou ○ RG 316 Gb 41
Tancheng ○ VRC 246 Lj 28
Tanchon ○ DVRK 247 Ma 25
Tancuime ○ MEX 92 Cn 35
Tānda ○ IND 234 Kb 34
Tanda ○ CI 317 Ge 42
Tandag ○ RP 267 Lp 41
Tandalti ○ SUD 312 Hh 39
Tăndărei ○ RO 175 Hf 23
Tanderiouel ~ RMM 305 Gf 38
Tandi ○ IND 230 Kc 29
Tandik ○ MAL 274 Lj 42
Tandil ○ RA 146 Ee 64
Tandjouaré ○ BF 317 Gg 40
Tāndliānwāla ○ PK 230 Ka 30
Tando Ādam ○ PK 227 Jn 33
Tando Allāhyār ○ PK 227 Jn 33
Tando Bāgo ○ PK 227 Jn 33
Tando Ikram ○ PK 227 Jn 33
Tando Jam ○ PK 227 Jn 33
Tando Muhammad Khān ○ PK 227 Jn 33
Tandou Lake ~ AUS 378 Mh 62
Tando Zinze ○ ANG 332 Gn 48
Tandula Tank ~ IND 234 Ke 35
Tandung ○ RI 279 Lk 47
Tāndūr ○ IND 238 Kd 37
Tanega-shima ♁ J 247 Mb 30
Taneichi ○ J 250 Mg 25
Tan Emellel ○ DZ 296 Gl 32
Tanete ○ RI 282 Ll 48
Tanezrouft ⏜ DZ 305 Gg 34
Tang ○ IR 226 Jh 33
Tanga ○ TCH 309 Hb 37
Tanga ○ EAT 337 Hm 48
Tangadee ○ AUS 368 Lk 58
Tangail ○ BD 235 Kk 33
Tanga Islands ♁ PNG 287 Mn 47
Tangale Peak △ WAN 320 Gm 41
Tangalle ○ CL 239 Ke 43
Tangangire ○ EAT 337 Hk 47
Tangara ○ BR 124 Fb 49
Tangará da Serra ○ BR 132 Ef 53
Tangarana ~ PE 116 Dl 47
Tangarare ○ SOL 290 Nb 50
Tangaye ○ BF 317 Ge 39
Tangerang ○ RI 278 Ld 49
Tanggu ○ VRC 246 Lj 26
Tangguantun ○ VRC 246 Lj 26
Tanggula Dangla Shan ⛰ VRC 231 Kk 29
Tanggula Shan △ VRC 231 Kk 29
Tanggula Shankou △ VRC 231 Kl 29
Tanghe ○ VRC 243 Lg 29
Tangi ○ PK 223 Jp 28
Tangier ○ MA 293 Gc 28
Tangjiatai ○ VRC 242 Lc 27
Tangkak ○ MAL 270 Lb 44
Tang La △ VRC 235 Kj 32
Tangmai ○ VRC 242 Km 30
Tangorin ○ AUS 375 Mj 56
Tangoutranat ○ RMM 305 Ge 37
Tangra Yumco ~ VRC 231 Kh 30
Tangse ○ IND 230 Kd 29
Tangse ○ RI 270 Km 43
Tangshan ○ VRC 246 Lk 26
Tangu ○ PNG 287 Mj 48
Tangua ○ CO 116 Dk 45
Tangue River Reservoir ~ USA 51 Cj 23
Tanguieta ○ DY 317 Gg 40
Tanguin-Dassouri ○ BF 317 Gf 39
Tangulbei ○ EAK 325 Hl 45
Tangung ○ RI 274 Lj 44
Tangwang ~ VRC 250 Ma 22
Tangyuan ○ VRC 250 Mb 22
Tangyung Tso ~ VRC 231 Kh 30
Tanhaçu ○ BR 125 Ep 52
Tanh Hòa ○ VN 263 Ld 40
Tân Hiệp ○ VN 263 Lc 40
Tánh Linh ○ VN 263 Ld 40
Tani ○ K 263 Lc 40
Taniantaweng Shan ⛰ VRC 242 Kn 30
Tanimbar Islands ♁ RI 283 Mb 50
Taninga ○ MOC 352 Hj 58
Taninthari ○ MYA 262 Kp 39
Taninthari (Tenasserim) ~ MYA 262 Kp 39
Tanipaddi ○ IND 238 Kd 39
Tanisapata ○ RI 283 Mb 47
Tanjay ○ RP 267 Lm 41
Tanjung ○ RI 271 Lf 45
Tanjung ○ RI 279 Lh 47
Tanjung ○ RI 279 Lj 47
Tanjung ○ RI 279 Lj 50
Tanjung Aikar ⌓ RI 283 Md 46
Tanjung Api ⌓ RI 271 Le 45
Tanjung Api Reserve ★ RI 282 Ll 46
Tanjung Api Reserve ⌓ RI 282 Ll 46
Tanjung Aro Usu ⌓ RI 283 Mb 50
Tanjungaru ○ RI 279 Lj 47
Tanjung Arus ⌓ RI 368 Ll 45
Tanjung Ayami ⌓ RI 283 Md 47
Tanjung Ayu ⌓ RI 274 Lj 46
Tanjung Baginda ⌓ RI 278 Ld 47
Tanjungbalai ○ RI 270 Kp 44
Tanjung Bangkai ⌓ RI 271 Le 45
Tanjung Baram ⌓ MAL 274 Lg 43
Tanjung Basu ⌓ RI 278 Lb 46
Tanjung Bateeputin ⌓ RI 270 Km 43
Tanjungbatu ○ RI 274 Lj 44
Tanjung Batu ⌓ RI 274 Lk 44
Tanjung Batuhitam ⌓ RI 282 Lm 46
Tanjung Bawang ⌓ RI 278 Le 46
Tanjung Berikat ⌓ RI 278 Ld 47
Tanjung Bira ⌓ RI 279 Lh 48
Tanjung Borang ⌓ RI 283 Mc 48
Tanjung Bugel ⌓ RI 278 Lf 49
Tanjung Bulupulu ⌓ RI 282 Ll 47
Tanjung Butung ⌓ RI 282 Lm 48
Tanjung Cangkuang ⌓ RI 278 Lc 49
Tanjung Carat ⌓ RI 278 Lc 47
Tanjung Cina ⌓ RI 278 Lc 48
Tanjung Cool ⌓ RI 286 Mf 50
Tanjung Dadi ⌓ RI 283 Mb 46
Tanjung Dampelas ⌓ RI 274 Lk 45
Tanjung Datu ⌓ MAL 271 Le 44
Tanjung Datuk ⌓ RI 271 Lb 45
Tanjung Dehegila ⌓ RI 275 Ma 45
Tanjung Dehekolano ⌓ RI 282 Lp 46
Tanjung Deilubun ⌓ TP 282 Lp 50
Tanjung De Jongs ⌓ RI 286 Mf 49
Tanjung Dewa ⌓ RI 270 Km 44
Tanjung Dewa ⚘ RI 279 Lj 47
Tanjung D'Urville ⌓ RI 286 Me 46
Tanjung Ela ⌓ RI 282 Ln 51
Tanjung Fet Dome ⌓ RI 283 Ma 46
Tanjung Flesko ⌓ RI 275 Ln 45
Tanjung Goram ⌓ RI 282 Lm 48
Tanjung Gunung ⌓ RI 271 Le 45
Tanjung Haya ⌓ RI 283 Ma 47
Tanjung Ilingelyo ⌓ RI 283 Ma 46
Tanjung Indramayu ⌓ RI 278 Le 49
Tanjung Indrapura ⌓ RI 270 La 47
Tanjung Iskanawatu ⌓ RI 282 Lp 49
Tanjung Jabunk ⌓ RI 278 Lc 46
Tanjung Jambair ⌓ RI 270 Kn 43
Tanjung Jenemejai ⌓ RI 282 Ll 47
Tanjung Kai ⌓ RI 279 Lk 47
Tanjung Kait ⌓ RI 278 Ld 47
Tanjung Kandi ⌓ RI 275 Ll 45
Tanjung Karang ○ MAL 270 La 44
Tanjung Keluang ⌓ RI 278 Lf 47
Tanjung Kerbau ⌓ RI 278 Lb 47
Tanjung Kokoe ⌓ RI 282 Ll 48
Tanjung Kopondai ⌓ RI 282 Lm 50
Tanjung Korongwaah ⌓ RI 286 Mg 47
Tanjung Ladongi ⌓ RI 282 Ll 47
Tanjung Langundu ⌓ RI 279 Lk 50
Tanjung Lasoni ⌓ RI 282 Lm 47
Tanjung Layar ⌓ RI 279 Lj 48
Tanjung Lelai ⌓ RI 275 Ma 45
Tanjung Lesung ⌓ RI 278 Lc 49
Tanjung Lia ⌓ RI 283 Lp 47
Tanjung Libobo ⌓ RI 283 Ma 46
Tanjung Liongsong ⌓ RI 279 Lj 50
Tanjunglolo ○ RI 270 La 46
Tanjung Lumut ⌓ RI 278 Ld 47
Tanjung Malacu ⌓ RI 279 Lg 48
Tanjung Malim ○ MAL 270 La 44
Tanjung Mangkalihat ⌓ RI 274 Lk 45
Tanjung Mangkok ⌓ RI 279 Lj 47
Tanjung Manimbaya ⌓ RI 274 Lk 45
Tanjung Manundi ⌓ RI 283 Md 46
Tanjung Marsimang ⌓ RI 283 Mb 47
Tanjung Mata ⌓ RI 279 Lj 50
Tanjung Medang ⌓ RI 270 La 44
Tanjung Memori ⌓ RI 283 Md 46
Tanjung Momfafa ⌓ RI 283 Mb 46
Tanjung Namaa ⌓ RI 283 Ma 47
Tanjung Nasong ⌓ MAL 274 Lh 43
Tanjung Ngabordamiu ⌓ RI 283 Mc 49
Tanjung Ngoni ⌓ RI 283 Md 49
Tanjung Ngunju ⌓ RI 282 Ll 51
Tanjung Nipanipa ⌓ RI 282 Lm 47
Tanjung Padangtikar ⌓ RI 278 Le 46
Tanjung Palpetu ⌓ RI 282 Ln 47
Tanjung Panang ⌓ RI 275 Ll 45
Tanjungpandan ○ RI 278 Ld 47
Tanjung Pandendelisa ⌓ RI 282 Ll 46
Tanjung Pangga ⌓ RI 279 Lh 50
Tanjung Pangkah ⌓ RI 279 Lg 49
Tanjung Panjang ⌓ RI 275 Ll 45
Tanjung Papisoi ⌓ RI 283 Mc 48
Tanjung Pasir ⌓ MAL 271 Lf 44
Tanjung Pemali ⌓ RI 282 Lm 46
Tanjung Pemali ⌓ RI 282 Lm 48
Tanjung Pemarung ⌓ RI 274 Lj 46
Tanjung Pentanciangan ⌓ RI 279 Lj 47
Tanjung Perapat ⌓ MAL 274 Lh 43
Tanjung Perkat ⌓ RI 278 Lc 46
Tanjung Pertandangan ⌓ RI 270 La 44
Tanjung Perupuk ⌓ RI 274 Lk 45
Tanjung Peureulak ⌓ RI 270 Kn 43
Tanjungpinang ○ RI 271 Lc 45
Tanjung Pulisan ⌓ RI 275 Ln 45
Tanjungpura ○ RI 270 Kp 44
Tanjung Purwo ⌓ RI 279 Lh 50
Tanjung Puting ⌓ RI 279 Lf 47
Tanjung Putus ⌓ RI 278 Le 46
Tanjungraja ○ RI 278 Lc 47
Tanjung Ranbausawa ⌓ RI 286 Me 47
Tanjung Rangas ⌓ RI 279 Lk 47
Tanjung Rangasa ⌓ RI 279 Lk 47
Tanjung Raya ⌓ RI 270 Kn 44
Tanjung Raya ⌓ RI 278 Ld 46
Tanjungredeb ○ RI 274 Lj 44
Tanjung Sabra ⌓ RI 283 Mc 47
Tanjung Salangketo ⌓ RI 282 Ll 48
Tanjung Salipolo ⌓ RI 279 Lk 47
Tanjung Samal ⌓ RI 283 Ma 47
Tanjung Sambar ⌓ RI 278 Le 47
Tanjung Samia ⌓ RI 275 Lm 45
Tanjung Samuk ⌓ RI 278 Lc 46
Tanjung Sangau ⌓ RI 278 Lc 46
Tanjung Santigi ⌓ RI 267 Ll 4
Tanjung Santigi ⌓ RI 275 Ll 45
Tanjung Santigi ⌓ RI 282 Lm 46
Tanjung Saribi ⌓ RI 283 Md 46
Tanjung Sasar ⌓ RI 279 Lk 50
Tanjung Sekopong ⌓ RI 278 Lc 48
Tanjung Sele ⌓ RI 283 Mb 46
Tanjung Selokan ⌓ RI 278 Lc 47
Tanjungselor ○ RI 274 Lj 44
Tanjung Semuntai ⌓ RI 274 Lk 45
Tanjung Senebui ⌓ RI 270 La 44
Tanjung Sepat ○ MAL 270 La 44
Tanjung Sipang ⌓ MAL 271 Lf 45
Tanjung Soos ⌓ RI 283 Mb 46
Tanjung Sopi ⌓ RI 275 Ma 44
Tanjung South ⌓ RI 279 Lh 48
Tanjung Sugul ⌓ MAL 274 Lj 42
Tanjung Sugut ⌓ MAL 274 Lj 42
Tanjung Tagopah ⌓ RI 283 Mc 47
Tanjung Tapaulama ⌓ RI 282 Lm 47
Tanjung Tongerai ⌓ RI 283 Mc 47
Tanjunguban ○ RI 271 Lc 45
Tanjung Vals ⌓ RI 286 Me 50
Tanjung Waka ⌓ RI 282 Lp 47
Tanjung Wararisbari ⌓ RI 286 Me 46
Tanjung Watukebo ⌓ RI 283 Mc 48
Tanjung Watupati ⌓ RI 283 Ma 50
Tanjung Wayamli ⌓ RI 275 Ma 45
Tanjung Weduar ⌓ RI 283 Mc 49
Tanjung Yamtu ⌓ RI 283 Mb 46
Tanjurer ~ RUS 205 Zc 5
Tānk ○ PK 223 Jp 29
Tankwa ~ ZA 358 Hc 62
Tankwa-Karoo ⚘ ZA 358 Hb 62
Tān Ky ○ VN 255 Lc 36
Tanlay ○ F 163 Gj 22
Tan Minh ○ VN 263 Ld 40
Tanna ♁ VU 386 Ng 55
Tannum Sands ○ AUS 375 Mm 57
Tannu-Ola, Khrebet ⛰ RUS 204 Tc 8
Tano ~ GH 317 Ge 42
Tanon Strait ~ RP 267 Lm 41
Tanot ○ IND 227 Jp 32
Tanougou ○ DY 317 Gg 40
Tanout ○ RN 308 Gl 38
Tān Phu ○ VN 263 Ld 40
Tanque Novo ○ BR 125 En 52
Tansarga ○ BF 317 Gg 40
Tansen ○ NEP 235 Kf 32
Tanshui ★ RC 259 Ll 33
Tansilla ○ BF 317 Gd 39
Tanṭā ○ ET 301 Hh 30
Tantamayo ○ PE 116 Dk 50
Tan-Tan ○ MA 292 Ga 31
Tantoyuca ○ MEX 92 Cn 35
Tanūmah ○ KSA 218 Hp 36
Tanumbirini ○ AUS 364 Md 54
Tanumshede ○ S 170 Gm 16
Tanunak ○ USA 46 Ag 15
Tanxi ○ VRC 255 Le 32
Tanyan ○ MYA 254 Kp 34
Ta-nyaung ○ MYA 254 Km 35
Tanzania ◘ EAT 336 Hj 48
Taocun ○ VRC 246 Ll 27
Tao He ~ VRC 242 Lb 28
Taojiang ○ VRC 258 Lg 31
Taonan ○ VRC 204 Wa 9
Taongi ♁ MH 27 Ta 8
Taopa ○ RI 275 Ll 45
Taormina ○ I 185 Gp 27
Taos ○ USA 65 Ck 27
Taos Pueblo ★ USA 65 Ck 27
Taouârdeï ○ RMM 305 Gg 37
Taoudenni ○ RMM 305 Ge 34
Taounate ○ MA 293 Gd 28
Taourirt ○ MA 293 Ge 28
Taouz ○ MA 293 Gd 30
Taoyuan ○ VRC 255 Lf 31
Taoyuan ○ RC 259 Ll 33
Taoyuan Dongling ★ VRC 258 Lj 33
Tapa ○ EST 171 He 16
Tapachula ○ MEX 93 Db 38
Tapaiuna ~ BR 132 Ef 51
Tapajós ~ BR 120 Ee 49
Tapajós ~ BR 120 Ef 48
Tapajós ~ BR 120 Eg 47
Tapajós ~ BR 120 Eg 48
Tapaktuan ○ RI 270 Kn 44
Tapalpa ○ MEX 92 Ck 36
Tapalqué ○ RA 146 Ee 64
Tapan ○ RI 270 La 47
Tapanahony ~ SME 113 Eg 44
Tapanatepec ○ MEX 93 Da 37
Tapaneco ~ MEX 92 Cn 37
Tapanui ○ NZ 382 Ng 68
Tapauá ~ BR 117 Eb 48
Tapauá ○ BR 117 Ec 48
Tapaué ~ BR 117 Ea 48
Tapaung ○ MYA 254 Kn 34
Tapebicuá ○ RA 146 Ef 60
Tapejara ○ BR 146 Eh 60
Tapena ○ PE 128 Dp 54
Tapenaga ~ RA 140 Ee 59
Tapera ○ BR 120 Ec 46
Tapera ~ BR 120 Ed 45
Tapera ○ BR 146 Eh 60
Taperoá ○ BR 124 Fb 49
Tapes ○ BR 146 Ej 61
Tapeta ○ LB 316 Gb 42
Taphan ○ THA 262 La 37
Tapi ~ IND 234 Kb 35
Tapi ~ IND 234 Kc 35
Tapi Aike ○ RA 152 Dn 71
Tapian ○ RI 274 Lj 46
Tapiantana Channel ~ RP 275 Ll 42
Tapiantana Group ♁ RP 275 Lm 42
Tapiche ~ PE 116 Dl 49
Tapinbini ○ RI 271 Lf 46
Tapini ○ PNG 287 Mk 50
Tapira ○ BR 133 El 55
Taplejung ○ NEP 235 Kh 32
Tapó-Caparo ⚘ YV 107 Dn 42
Tapol ○ TCH 321 Gp 41
Tappahannock ○ USA 74 Dk 27
Tapu ○ NZ 383 Nk 64
Tapul ○ RP 275 Ll 43
Tapul Group ♁ RP 275 Ll 43
Tapul Island ♁ RP 275 Ll 43
Ṭāqa ○ OM 219 Jf 37
Taq-e Bostān ○ IR 209 Jb 28
Taqṭaq ○ IRQ 209 Ja 28
Taquara ○ BR 146 Ej 60
Taquaralto ○ BR 133 Ek 51
Taquari ~ BR 132 Ef 55
Taquari ~ BR 132 Eg 55
Taquari ○ BR 146 Eh 60
Taquaritinga ○ BR 141 Ek 56
Taquarituba ○ BR 141 Ek 57
Tar ~ USA 74 Dj 28
Tara ○ RUS 204 Sc 7
Tara ○ Z 341 Hf 54
Tara ○ AUS 375 Mm 59
Tarabuco ○ BOL 129 Eb 55
Taraco ○ PE 128 Dp 53
Tarag ○ IND 238 Kb 37
Tarāghin ○ LAR 297 Gp 33
Taraira ~ BR 117 Dp 46
Taraire ○ BOL 136 Ec 56
Tarajim ○ WAN 320 Gm 39
Tarakan ○ RI 274 Lj 44
Tarakbits ○ PNG 286 Mg 48
Tarakurgan ○ UZB 223 Jp 25
Taralga ○ AUS 379 Ml 63
Taramana ○ RI 282 Ln 50
Tarama-shima ♁ J 259 Ln 33
Tarancón ○ E 184 Ge 25
Tarangire ⚘ EAT 337 Hk 48
Tarangire ~ EAT 337 Hl 48
Taranna ○ AUS 378 Mk 67
Táranto ○ I 194 Ha 25
Tarapaca ○ CO 117 Dp 47
Tarapacá ○ RCH 128 Dp 55
Tarapoto ○ PE 116 Dk 49
Tārāpur ○ IND 238 Ka 36
Tarapuy ○ EC 116 Dk 46
Tarara ○ PNG 290 Mp 49
Tarare ○ F 185 Gj 23
Tararua Range ⛰ NZ 383 Nk 66
Tarasa Dwip Island ♁ IND 262 Kl 41
Tarascon ○ F 185 Gj 24
Tarat ○ DZ 296 Gl 32
Tarata ○ PE 128 Dn 54
Tarauacá ~ BR 117 Dn 49
Tarauaca ○ BR 117 Dn 50
Tarauacá ~ BR 117 Dn 50
Tarawai Island ♁ PNG 286 Mh 47
Tarawara ♁ KIR 27 Tb 9
Tarazona ○ E 184 Ge 25
Tarbaj ○ EAK 325 Hn 44
Tarbela Reservoir ~ PK 230 Ka 28
Tarbes ○ F 184 Gg 24
Tarboro ○ USA 74 Dk 28
Tarbrax ○ AUS 374 Mh 56
Tarcoola ○ AUS 378 Md 61
Tardie ○ AUS 368 Lj 59
Tardun ○ AUS 368 Lh 60
Taree ○ AUS 379 Mn 61
Tarfaya ○ MA 292 Fp 32
Targa ○ RN 308 Gj 37
Tārgovişte ○ RO 175 He 23
Tārgovište ○ BG 194 Hf 24
Tārgu Frumos ○ RO 175 Hf 22
Targuist ○ MA 293 Gd 28
Tārgu Jiu ○ RO 194 Hd 23
Tārgu Mureş ○ RO 175 He 22
Tārgu Secuiesc ○ RO 175 He 22
Tarhūnah ○ LAR 297 Gn 29
Tari ○ PNG 286 Mh 48
Taria ~ BOL 136 Eb 56
Tarib ○ KSA 218 Hp 36
Tariba ○ YV 107 Dm 42
Tarica ○ PE 116 Dk 50
Ṭarīf ○ UAE 215 Je 33
Tarifa ○ E 184 Gd 27
Tarija ○ BOL 136 Eb 56
Tarikere ○ IND 238 Kb 39
Tariku Rouffaer ~ RI 286 Me 47
Tariku Van Daalen ~ RI 286 Me 47
Tarīm ○ YE 219 Jc 37
Tarim Basin ⏜ VRC 204 Tb 10
Tarim Basin ⏜ VRC 230 Ke 26
Tarime ○ EAT 337 Hk 46
Tarim He ~ VRC 231 Kf 25
Tarimoro ○ MEX 92 Cm 35
Taring ○ RI 270 Kn 44
Taripa ○ RI 282 Ll 46
Taritatu Idenburg ~ RI 286 Mf 47
Tarka ~ ZA 358 He 62
Tarkastad ○ ZA 358 Hf 62
Tarkio ○ USA 70 Da 25
Tarko-Sale ○ RUS 204 Ta 6
Tarkwa ○ GH 317 Ge 43
Tarlac ○ RP 267 Ll 38
Tarlton Downs ○ AUS 374 Me 57
Tarma ○ PE 128 Dl 51
Tarmidā ○ KSA 215 Ja 33
Tarn ~ F 184 Gh 24
Tārnaby ○ S 158 Gp 13
Tarnak Rūd ~ AFG 227 Jl 30
Tārnāveni ○ RO 175 Hd 22
Tarnobrzeg ○ PL 174 Hc 20
Tarnogskij Gorodok ○ RUS 171 Hp 15
Tarnów ○ PL 174 Hc 20
Taroa ○ CO 107 Dn 39
Taroko ○ RC 259 Ll 33
Taroko ★ RC 259 Ll 33
Tarok Tso ~ VRC 231 Kf 30
Taron ○ PNG 287 Mn 48
Taroom ○ AUS 375 Ml 58
Taroudant ○ MA 292 Gb 30
Taroum ○ RN 305 Gh 38
Tarquinia ○ I 185 Gm 24
Tarrafal ○ CV 316 Fh 37
Tarrafal ○ CV 316 Fh 38
Tarragona ○ E 184 Gg 25
Tarragona ○ RP 275 Lp 42
Tarrajākka ~ S 158 Ha 12
Tarraleah ○ AUS 378 Mk 67
Tarras ○ NZ 382 Ng 68
Tárrega ○ E 184 Gg 25
Tarso Emissi △ TCH 309 Hb 35

474 Taisha - Tarso Emissi

□Country ▣Capital city ◉Administrative unit ○Place ◬Island ⩕Mountain range △Mountain ⌒Cape ≈Ocean, Sea ~Lake, River ▿Undersea topography △Glacier ♀National park •••Reservation ★Point of major interest ⏥Landscape

Tarso Lango ⩕ TCH 309 Hb 35
Tarso Tieroko △ TCH 309 Ha 35
Tarsus ○ TR 195 Hk 27
Tartagal ○ PY 136 Ec 57
Tartagal ~ PY 136 Ec 57
Tärtär ○ AZ 202 Jb 25
Tärtär ~ AZ 202 Jb 25
Tartarugalzinho ○ BR 121 Ej 45
Tartu ○ EST 171 Hf 16
Ţarţūs ○ SYR 208 Hk 28
Tarucani ○ PE 128 Dn 54
Tarum ~ RI 278 Ld 49
Tarusa ○ RUS 171 Hl 18
Tarusan ○ RI 270 La 46
Tarutung ○ RI 270 Kp 45
Tarutyne ○ UA 175 Hg 22
Tarves ○ AUS 375 Mj 58
Tarvo ~ BOL 129 Ed 53
Ţarwāniya ○ UAE 226 Jf 34
Taschereau ○ CDN 60 Dj 21
Taseko Lakes ~ CDN 50 Ca 20
Taš Guzar ○ AFG 223 Jm 27
Tashigang ○ BHT 235 Kk 32
Tashkent ▣ UZB 223 Jn 25
Tasik Bera ~ MAL 270 Lb 44
Tasik Kenyir ~ MAL 270 Lb 43
Tasikmalaya ○ RI 278 Ld 49
Tašir ○ ARM 202 Ja 25
Taşkent ○ TR 195 Hj 27
Taškepriskoe vodohranilišče ~ TM 223 Jk 27
Tasker ○ RN 308 Gm 38
Taşköprü ○ TR 195 Hk 25
Taskul ○ PNG 287 Mm 47
Taš-Kumyr ○ KS 230 Ka 25
Tasman Bay ≈ NZ 383 Nj 66
Tasman Head ⌒ AUS 378 Mk 67
Tasmanien ◉ AUS 378 Mh 67
Tasman Mountains ⩕ NZ 383 Nj 66
Tasman Peninsula ◬ AUS 378 Ml 67
Tasman Plateau ▿ 34 Sa 14
Tasman Point ⌒ AUS 364 Me 53
Tăşnad ○ RO 174 Hd 22
Taşova ○ TR 195 Hl 25
Tassara ○ RN 308 Gj 37
Tassa-Takorat ○ RN 308 Gj 37
Tasserest ○ RMM 308 Gh 38
Tassili du Hoggar ⩕ DZ 308 Gj 35
Tassili n'Ajjer ⩕ DZ 296 Gk 33
Tassiné ~ DY 320 Gh 40
Tasso Fragoso ○ BR 121 Em 50
Tāsūkī ○ IR 226 Jj 30
Tata ○ H 174 Hb 22
Tata ○ MA 293 Gc 31
Tatabánya ○ H 174 Hb 22
Tatajuba ○ BR 116 Dm 49
Tatakoto ◬ F 35 Bb 11
Tatali ○ GH 317 Gg 41
Tatamá ♀ CO 106 Dk 43
Tata Mailau △ TP 282 Ln 50
Tatamba ○ SOL 290 Nb 50
Tatandica ○ MOC 344 Hj 55
Tataouine ○ TN 297 Gm 29
Tatarbunary ○ UA 175 Hg 23
Tatarsk ○ RUS 204 Ta 7
Tatarskiy Proliv ≈ RUS 23 Sa 4
Tatarskiy Proliv ≈ RUS 205 Xb 8
Tatau ○ MAL 274 Lg 44
Tatau Island ◬ PNG 287 Mm 47
Tatawa ○ RI 283 Md 47
Tate ~ AUS 365 Mh 54
Tateyama ○ J 251 Mf 28
Tate-yama △ J 251 Me 27
Tathlina Lake ~ CDN 47 Cc 15
Tathra ♀ AUS 368 Lh 60
Tathra ○ AUS 379 Mm 64
Tati ~ RB 349 Hf 56
Tatiščevo ○ RUS 181 Ja 20
Tatkan ○ MYA 254 Km 35
Tat Kha ○ THA 262 La 37
Tatla Lake ○ CDN 50 Bp 20
Taţlīţ ○ KSA 218 Hp 36
Tatokou ○ RN 308 Gl 38
Tattakarai ○ IND 238 Kc 40
Tattannagaripalli ○ IND 238 Kc 39
Tatu ○ NZ 383 Nk 65
Tatuí ○ BR 141 Ek 57
Tatuke ○ LB 316 Gb 43
Tatum ○ USA 65 Cl 29
Taturgou ○ VRC 230 Kc 27
Tatvan ○ TR 202 Hp 26
Tau ○ N 170 Gk 16
tau. Mūgodžor ⩕ KZ 155 Rc 9
Tauá ○ BR 124 Ep 49
Ta Uân Xê ○ VN 263 Le 38
Tauari ○ BR 121 El 46
Taubaté ○ BR 141 Em 57
Tauberbischofsheim ○ D 174 Gl 21
tau Bescoky △ KZ 155 Rb 10
Tauca ○ PE 116 Dj 50
Taufikia ○ SUD 324 Hh 41
Tauini ~ BR 120 Ee 45
Taulihawa ○ NEP 234 Kf 32
Tauliya ○ IRQ 209 Hn 29
Taumarunui ○ NZ 383 Nk 65
Taumaturgo ○ BR 116 Dm 50
Taum Sauk Mountain △ USA 71 Dc 27
Taung ○ ZA 349 He 59
Taungdwingyi ○ MYA 254 Km 35
Taunggyi ○ MYA 254 Kn 35
Taungtha ○ MYA 254 Km 35
Taungup ○ MYA 254 Km 36
Taunton ○ USA 74 Dn 25
Taunton ○ GB 163 Ge 20
Taupo ○ NZ 383 Nl 65
Taurage ○ LT 170 Hd 18
Tauranga ○ NZ 383 Nl 64
Tauranga Harbour ≈ NZ 383 Nl 64
Tauri River ~ PNG 287 Mj 49
Tauroa Point ⌒ NZ 383 Nj 63
Taurus Mountains ⩕ TR 195 Hh 27
Tauta ○ PNG 287 Mj 48
Tauyskaya Guba ≈ RUS 205 Xc 7
Tavai ○ PY 140 Eg 59
Tavanei River ~ PNG 287 Ml 51
Tavara ○ SOL 290 Na 50
Tavas ○ TR 195 Hg 27
Tavda ○ RUS 19 Na 4
Tavda ~ RUS 154 Sa 7
Taveta ○ EAT 337 Hk 50
Taveta ○ EAK 337 Hl 47
Taveuni ◬ FJI 390 Aa 54
Tavira ○ P 184 Gc 27
Tavistock ○ GB 163 Gd 20
Tavoliere ⏥ I 194 Gp 25
Tavolo ○ PNG 287 Mm 49
Tavoy ○ MYA 262 Kp 38
Tavşanlı ○ TR 195 Hg 26
Tavua ○ FJI 387 Nl 54
Tavuki ○ FJI 387 Nl 55
Tavu Na Sici ◬ FJI 390 Aa 55
Tawaeli ○ RI 279 Lk 46
Tāwa Reservoir ~ IND 234 Kd 34
Tawargeri ○ IND 238 Kc 38
Tawas City ○ USA 57 Dg 23
Tawau ○ MAL 274 Lj 43
Tawilah ○ SUD 312 He 39
Tawi Tawi Group ◬ RP 275 Ll 43
Tawi Tawi Island ◬ RP 275 Lk 43
Tawma ○ MYA 254 Km 34
Tawu ○ RC 259 Ll 34
Tāwūq ○ IRQ 209 Ja 28
Tawūq Çay ~ IRQ 209 Ja 28
Tāwurghā' ○ LAR 297 Gp 29
Taxco ○ MEX 92 Cn 36
Taxila ○ PK 230 Ka 29
Taxkorgan ○ VRC 230 Kb 27
Tay ~ GB 162 Ge 17
Tayabamba ○ PE 116 Dk 50
Tayabas Bay ≈ RP 267 Ll 39
Tayahua ○ MEX 92 Cl 34
Tayan ○ RI 271 Lf 46
Tāyebād ○ IR 223 Jj 28
Tayeeglow ○ SP 328 Ja 43
Taykan ○ LAR 300 Hb 30
Tayler ○ USA 70 Cn 25
Tayler ○ USA 81 Cp 30
Tayler Park ○ USA 65 Cj 26
Taylor ○ USA 46 Ag 13
Taylor ○ USA 65 Cg 28
Taylor River ~ USA 65 Cj 26
Taylors Island ○ USA 74 Dk 26
Taymyr Peninsula ⏥ RUS 22 Pb 2
Taymyr Peninsula ◬ RUS 204 Ua 4
Tây Ninh ○ VN 263 Ld 40
Tayoltita ○ MEX 80 Ck 33
Tayrona ♀ CO 106 Dl 40
Tay So'n ○ VN 263 Le 39
Tây So'n ○ VN 263 Le 39
Taytay ○ RP 267 Lk 40
Taytay Bay ≈ RP 267 Lk 40
Tayu ○ RI 278 Lf 49
Ta Yü ◬ RC 258 Lk 34
Tayuling ○ RC 259 Ll 33
Tayyāna ○ SYR 209 Hn 28
Taz ~ RUS 22 Pa 3
Taz ~ RUS 204 Ta 6
Taz ~ RUS 204 Tb 5
Taza ○ MA 293 Ge 28
Tazenakht ○ MA 293 Gc 30
Tazerzaït ⏥ RN 308 Gj 36
Tazewell ○ USA 71 Dh 27
Tāzirbū ○ LAR 300 Hc 33
Tazlina Lake ~ USA 46 Bc 15
Tazolé ○ RN 308 Gl 37
Tazovskij ○ RUS 204 Ta 5
Tazovskij Poluostrov ◬ RUS 154 Sc 5
Tazovskij Poluostrov ⏥ RUS 204 Sc 5
Tazrouk ○ DZ 308 Gk 34
Tazungdan ○ MYA 254 Kn 32
Tazzarine ○ MA 293 Gd 30
T'bilisi ▣ GE 202 Ja 25
Tchabal Gangdaba ⩕ CAM 321 Gn 42
Tchabal Mbabo △ CAM 320 Gn 42
Tchadaoua ○ RN 320 Gk 39
Tchamba ○ RT 317 Gg 41
Tchamba ○ CAM 321 Gn 41
Tchaourou ○ DY 317 Gh 41
Tchériba ○ BF 317 Ge 39
Tchetti ○ DY 317 Gg 42
Tchibanga ○ G 332 Gm 47
Tchie ○ TCH 309 Hb 37
Tchin Garaguene ○ RN 308 Gk 38
Tchin-Salatine ○ RN 308 Gj 37
Tchin-Tabaredene ○ RN 308 Gj 38
Tcholliré ○ CAM 321 Gp 41
Tchuba ○ USA 86 Dc 29
Tczew ○ PL 170 Hb 18
Teá ~ BR 117 Eb 46
Teacapan ○ MEX 92 Cj 34
Te Akau ○ NZ 383 Nk 64
Te Anau ○ NZ 382 Nf 68
Teapa ○ MEX 93 Db 37
Te Araroa ○ NZ 383 Nm 64
Te Aroha ○ NZ 383 Nk 64
Te Awamutu ○ NZ 383 Nk 64
Teba ○ RI 286 Me 46
Tebaram ○ RN 308 Gj 38
Tébe ○ G 332 Gn 46
Tebedu ○ MAL 271 Lf 45
Teberda ○ RUS 202 Hn 24
Tebessa ○ DZ 296 Gk 28
Tebesselamane ○ RMM 305 Gg 37
Tebicuary ~ PY 140 Ef 59
Tebingtingg ○ RI 278 Lb 47
Tebingtinggi ○ RI 270 Kp 44
Tebingtinggi ◬ RI 270 Lb 45
Tebo ~ RI 270 La 46
Tébourba ○ TN 296 Gl 27
Téboursouk ○ TN 296 Gl 27
Tecalitlán ○ MEX 92 Cl 36
Tecamachalco ○ MEX 92 Cn 36
Tecámbaro ○ MEX 92 Cm 36
Tecate ○ MEX 64 Cd 29
Tecer Dağl. ⩕ TR 195 Hl 26
Techiman ○ GH 317 Ge 42
Techimpolo ○ ANG 340 Ha 53
Techirimba ○ ANG 340 Gp 51
Techissanha ○ ANG 340 Ha 53
Techongolola ○ ANG 340 Ha 51
Tecka ○ RA 147 Dn 67
Tecka ~ RA 147 Dn 67
Tecoh ○ MEX 93 Dd 35
Tecojate ○ GCA 93 Dc 39
Tecolotlán ○ MEX 92 Ck 35
Tecomán ○ MEX 92 Ck 36
Tecoripa ○ MEX 80 Cg 31
Tecpan de Galeana ○ MEX 92 Cm 37
Tecpatán ○ MEX 93 Db 37
Tecuala ○ MEX 92 Ck 34
Tecuci ○ RO 175 Hf 23
Tecumseh ○ USA 70 Cp 25
Tecunara ~ BR 133 Ej 51
Ted ○ SP 328 Hp 43
Tedjen ○ TM 222 Jj 27
Tedjen ~ TM 222 Jj 27
Téermoli ○ I 194 Gp 25
Tees ○ CDN 51 Cf 19
Tees ~ GB 162 Ge 18
Tefé ~ BR 117 Ea 48
Tefé ○ BR 117 Eb 47
Tefé ~ BR 117 Eb 48
Tefenni ○ TR 195 Hg 27
Teffedest ⩕ DZ 296 Gj 33
Tegal ○ RI 278 Le 49
Tegalombo ○ RI 278 Lf 50
Tegernsee ○ D 174 Gm 22
Tegguidda-n-Tessoum ○ RN 308 Gj 37
Teghra ○ IND 235 Kh 33
Tegina ○ WAN 320 Gk 40
Tégouma ~ RN 308 Gm 38
Tegucigalpa ▣ HN 96 De 38
Teg Wani ~ ZW 341 Hf 55
Tehachapi ○ USA 64 Cc 28
Tehek Lake ~ CDN 42 Fb 6
Téhini ○ CI 317 Ge 41
Tehrān ◉ IR 222 Je 28
Tehri ○ IND 230 Kd 30
Tehuacan ○ MEX 92 Cp 35
Tehuantepec ○ MEX 93 Da 37
Tehuantepec ~ MEX 93 Da 37
Tehuantepec Ridge ▿ 11 Ea 8
Teil ○ SN 304 Fn 38
Teiskot ○ RMM 305 Gg 37
Teiti ○ SUD 312 Hh 36
Teixeira ○ BR 124 Fb 49
Teixeira de Freitas ○ BR 125 Ep 54
Teixeira Soares ○ BR 140 Ej 58
Tejakula ○ RI 279 Lh 50
Teji ○ ETH 325 Hm 41
Tejkovo ○ RUS 171 Hn 17
Tejo ~ BR 116 Dm 50
Tejo ~ P 184 Gb 26
Tejon Pass △ USA 64 Cc 28
Tekadu ○ PNG 287 Mk 49
Te Kaha ○ NZ 383 Nl 64
Te Karaka ○ NZ 383 Nl 65
Tekax ○ MEX 93 Dd 35
Tekezē Wenz ~ ETH 313 Hm 39
Tekirdağ ○ TR 195 Hf 25
Tekit ○ MEX 93 Dd 35
Tekkali ○ IND 235 Kg 36
Tekman ○ TR 202 Hn 26
Teknaf ○ BD 235 Kl 35
Tekoa ○ USA 50 Cd 22
Tékro ○ TCH 309 Hc 36
Teku ○ RI 282 Lm 46
Te Kuiti ○ NZ 383 Nk 65
Tela ○ HN 96 De 38
Tela ○ RDC 341 Hg 52
Tela ○ Z 341 Hg 52
Telagapulang ○ RI 279 Lg 47
Telagh ○ DZ 293 Gf 28
Telanaipura ○ RI 278 Lb 46
Telaqua Lake ~ USA 46 An 15
Telarah ○ AUS 375 Mk 57
Telares ○ RA 137 Ec 60
Télatai ○ RMM 305 Gg 37
T'elavi ○ GE 202 Ja 25
Tel Aviv-Jaffa ○ IL 208 Hk 29
Telč ○ CZ 174 Gp 21
Telchac Puerto ○ MEX 93 Dd 35
Telde ○ E 292 Fn 32
Tele ~ RDC 324 He 44
Telefomin ○ PNG 286 Mg 48
Telegraph Range ⩕ CDN 50 Ca 19
Telekitonga ◬ TO 390 Ac 56
Telêmaco Borba ○ BR 140 Ej 58
Télemsès ○ RN 308 Gj 38
Telemzane ○ DZ 296 Gj 29
Telen ~ RI 274 Lj 45
Teleneşti ○ MD 175 Hg 22
Teleormer ~ RO 175 He 23
Telerghma ○ DZ 296 Gk 27
Teles Pires ou São Manuel ~ BR 132 Eg 52
Telfer ○ AUS 360 Lm 56
Teliata Point ⌒ PNG 287 Mk 48
Téliméle ○ RG 316 Fp 40
Tellxtlahuaca ○ MEX 92 Cp 36
Tell Atlas ⩕ DZ 293 Gf 28
Tell City ○ USA 71 De 26
Teller ○ USA 46 Ag 13
Tellico Lake ~ USA 71 Df 28
Tellis ○ TCH 309 Ha 38
Tell Tamr ○ SYR 209 Hn 27
Telok Intan ○ MAL 270 La 43
Teloloapan ○ MEX 92 Cn 36
Telsang ○ IND 238 Kb 37
Telsen ○ RA 147 Ea 67
Telšiai ○ LT 170 Hd 18
Teltelē ○ ETH 325 Hl 43
Teluk Adang ≈ RI 274 Lj 46
Teluk Airhitam ≈ RI 278 Lf 47
Teluk Apar ≈ RI 279 Lj 47
Teluk Balikpapan ≈ RI 274 Lj 46
Telukbatang ○ RI 278 Le 46
Telukbayur ○ RI 270 La 46
Teluk Bayur ≈ RI 270 La 46
Telukbayur ○ RI 274 Lj 44
Teluk Belimbing ≈ RI 278 Lc 48
Teluk Bengkunat ≈ RI 278 Lb 48
Teluk Berau Mac Cluer Gulf ≈ RI 283 Mc 47
Teluk Bilang ≈ RI 275 Ll 45
Teluk Bima ≈ RI 279 Lk 50
Teluk Bintuni ≈ RI 283 Mc 47
Telukbutun ○ RI 271 Le 43
Teluk Cenderawasih ≈ RI 283 Md 47
Telukdalam ○ RI 270 Kn 45
Teluk Darvel ≈ MAL 274 Lk 43
Teluk Datu ≈ MAL 271 Lf 45
Teluk Dondo ≈ RI 275 Ll 45
Teluk Galela ≈ RI 275 Lp 45
Teluk Gorontalo ≈ RI 275 Lm 45
Teluk Grajagan ≈ RI 279 Lg 50
Teluk Kaibus ≈ RI 283 Mb 46
Teluk Kampa ≈ RI 278 Lc 46
Teluk Kamrau ≈ RI 283 Mc 47
Teluk Kao ≈ RI 275 Lp 45
Teluk Kimanis ≈ MAL 274 Lh 43
Teluk Klabat ≈ RI 278 Lc 46
Teluk Kolowana-Watobo ≈ RI 282 Lm 48
Teluk Kotawaringin ≈ RI 278 Lf 47
Teluk Kumai ≈ RI 279 Lf 47
Teluk Kumbar ○ MAL 270 Kp 43
Teluk Labuk ≈ MAL 274 Lj 42
Teluk Lampung ≈ RI 278 Lc 48
Teluk Mandar ≈ RI 279 Lk 47
Teluk Marudu ≈ MAL 274 Lj 42
Teluknibung ○ RI 270 Kp 44
Teluk Nuri ≈ RI 278 Le 46
Teluk Painan ≈ RI 270 La 46
Teluk Palu ≈ RI 279 Lk 46
Teluk Pedang ≈ RI 282 Lm 50
Teluk Pelabuhan Ratu ≈ RI 278 Ld 49
Teluk Penanjung ≈ RI 278 Le 49
Teluk Penyu ≈ RI 278 Le 49
Teluk Piru ≈ RI 283 Ma 47
Teluk Rembang ≈ RI 278 Lf 49
Teluk Saleh ≈ RI 279 Lj 50
Teluk Sampit ≈ RI 279 Lg 47
Teluk Sandakan ≈ MAL 274 Lj 43
Teluk Sankulirang ≈ RI 274 Lk 45
Teluk Santong ≈ RI 279 Lj 50
Teluk Sebakor ≈ RI 283 Mc 47
Teluk Sebanganu ≈ RI 279 Lg 47
Teluk Sebuku ≈ RI 274 Lj 44
Teluk Sekatak ≈ RI 274 Lj 44
Teluk Semangka ≈ RI 278 Lc 48
Teluk Sibolga ≈ RI 270 Kp 45
Teluk Sindih. ≈ RI 282 Ll 50
Teluk Sukadana ≈ RI 278 Le 46
Teluk Tambu ≈ RI 274 Lk 45
Teluk Triton ≈ RI 283 Mc 47
Teluk Walckenaer ≈ RI 286 Mf 47
Teluk Wandammen ≈ RI 283 Md 47
Teluk Waromge ≈ RI 283 Mb 46
Teluk Waropen ≈ RI 286 Me 46
Teluk Waropen ≈ RI 286 Me 47
Teluk Waworada ≈ RI 279 Lk 50
Teluk Weda ≈ RI 275 Ma 45
Teluk Yos Sudarso ≈ RI 286 Mg 47
Telupid ○ MAL 274 Lj 43
Tely ~ RDC 324 Hf 44
Téma ○ BF 317 Gf 39
Téma ○ GH 317 Gg 43
Temacine ○ DZ 296 Gj 29
Temagami ○ CDN 60 Dj 22
Temanggung ○ RI 278 Lf 49
Temascaltepec ○ MEX 92 Cm 36
Tematangi ◬ F 35 Bb 12
Temax ○ MEX 93 Dd 35
Temba ○ ZA 349 Hg 58
Tembagapura ○ RI 286 Me 48
Tembenči ~ RUS 204 Ub 5
Tembesi ~ RI 278 Lb 47
Tembilahan ○ RI 278 Lb 46
Tembisa ○ ZA 349 Hg 59
Tembito ○ RI 275 Ll 45
Tembladera ○ PE 116 Dj 49
Temblador ○ YV 112 Ec 41
Tembo ○ RDC 333 Ha 49
Tembo Aluma ○ ANG 333 Ha 49
Tembwe ○ Z 344 Hj 51
Temcha ~ ETH 313 Hl 40
Temecula ○ USA 64 Cd 29
Temelon ○ GQ 332 Gm 45
Téméra ○ RMM 305 Gf 37
Temerloh ○ MAL 270 Lb 44
Teminabuan ○ RI 283 Mb 46
Temirtau ○ KZ 22 Nb 4
Témiscamie ~ CDN 60 Dm 20
Témiscaming ○ CDN 60 Dj 22
Temki ○ TCH 321 Hb 40
Temnikov ○ RUS 181 Hp 18
Temo ○ MEX 93 Db 37
Temora ○ AUS 379 Mk 63
Témoris ○ MEX 80 Ch 32
Tempe ○ USA 65 Cg 29
Tempeh ○ RI 279 Lg 50
Tempestad ○ PE 116 Dl 46
Témpio Pausánia ○ I 185 Gl 25
Temple ○ USA 81 Cp 30
Temple Amara ★ SUD 312 Hh 35
Temple Bay ≈ AUS 365 Mh 52
Temple of Abydos ★ ET 301 Hh 32
Temple of Horus ★ ET 301 Hj 33
Temple of Kawa ★ SUD 312 Hh 36
Temples of Musawwarat ★ SUD 313 Hj 37
Temples of Naga ★ SUD 313 Hj 37
Templeton ○ NZ 383 Nj 67
Tempoal de Sánchez ○ MEX 92 Cn 35
Tempué ○ ANG 340 Hb 52
Temrjuk ○ RUS 195 Hl 23
Temryjukskij zaliv ≈ RUS 195 Hl 23
Temuco ○ RCH 147 Dm 65
Temuka ○ NZ 382 Nh 68
Ten. Portela ○ BR 140 Eh 59
Tena ○ EC 116 Dk 46
Tenabó ○ MEX 93 Dc 35
Ténado ○ BF 317 Ge 39
Tenaha ○ USA 81 Da 30
Tenakee Springs ○ USA 47 Bg 17
Tenāli ○ IND 238 Ke 37
Tenancingo ○ MEX 92 Cn 36
Ténarunga ◬ F 14 Ca 12
Tenasserim Island ◬ MYA 262 Kn 39
Tenassorim ~ MYA 262 Kp 39
Tenaun ○ RCH 147 Dm 67
Tenby ○ GB 163 Gd 20
Tendaba ○ WAG 316 Fm 39
Tendaho ○ ETH 313 Hn 40
Ten Degree Cannel ≈ IND 262 Kl 41
Tendō ○ J 251 Mg 26
Tendouk ○ SN 316 Fm 39
Tendrara ○ MA 293 Gf 29
Tendrivs'ka Kosa ⏥ UA 175 Hh 22
Tendūkheda ○ IND 234 Kd 34
Téné ○ RMM 317 Gd 39
Ténenkou ○ RMM 305 Gd 38
Ténéré du Tafassasset ⏥ RN 308 Gm 35
Tenerife ◬ E 292 Fm 31
Ténès ○ DZ 293 Gg 27
Tengahdai ○ RI 282 Lm 50
Tengchong ○ VRC 254 Kp 33
Tenggarong ○ RI 274 Lj 46
Tengger Shamo ⏥ VRC 242 Lb 26
Tengréla ○ CI 305 Gc 40
Te-n-Guembo ○ RIM 304 Gb 37
Teng Xian ○ VRC 255 Lf 34
Tengzhou ○ VRC 246 Lj 28
Teniente General J. C. Sánchez ○ RA 140 Ee 58
Tenindewa ○ AUS 368 Lh 60
Tenkasi ○ IND 239 Kc 41
Tenke ○ RDC 341 Hf 51
Tenkiller Ferry Lake ~ USA 70 Da 28
Tenkodogo ○ BF 317 Gf 40
Tenlāu ○ IND 270 Kl 42
Tenlāu ○ IND 270 Kl 42
Ten Mile Lake ~ CDN 61 Ef 20
Ten Mile Pond ~ CDN 61 Eh 21
Tennant Creek ○ AUS 364 Mc 55
Tennessee ◉ USA 71 Dd 28
Tennessee ~ USA 71 Dd 28
Teno ~ RCH 137 Dn 63
Teno ~ FIN 159 Hf 11
Tenochtitlán ○ MEX 93 Da 37
Tenom ○ MAL 274 Lh 43
Tenosique ○ MEX 93 Dc 37
Tenoûmer △ RIM 304 Ga 34
Tensas River N.W.R. ♀ USA 86 Dc 29
Ten Sleep ○ USA 51 Cj 23
T'enta ○ ETH 313 Hm 40
Tente ○ RI 279 Lk 50
Tentena ○ RI 282 Ll 46
Tenterfield ○ AUS 375 Mn 60
Ten Thousand Islands ◬ USA 87 Dh 33
Teocaltiche ○ MEX 92 Cl 35
Teocuitatlán de Corona ○ MEX 92 Cl 35
Teodoro Sampaio ○ BR 125 Fa 52
Teodoro Sampaio ○ BR 140 Eh 57
Teofilândia ○ BR 125 Fa 51
Teófilo Otoni ○ BR 125 Ep 54
Teofipol' ○ UA 175 Hf 21
Te One ○ NZ 383 Ab 67
Teotihuacán ★ MEX 92 Cn 36
Teotitlán del Camino ○ MEX 92 Cp 35
Teotônio Vilela ○ BR 124 Fb 50
Tepa ○ GH 317 Ge 42
Tepalcatepec ○ MEX 92 Cl 36
Tepatitlán ○ MEX 92 Cl 35
Tepeaca ○ MEX 92 Cp 36
Tepechitlán ○ MEX 92 Cl 35
Tepecoacuilco ○ MEX 92 Cn 36
Tepehuanes ○ MEX 80 Cj 33
Tepeji del Río ○ MEX 92 Cn 36
Tepelenë ○ AL 194 Hb 25
Tepere ○ MOC 344 Hm 52
Tepetzintla ○ MEX 81 Cp 34
Tēpī ○ ETH 325 Hk 42
Tepic ○ MEX 92 Ck 35
Tepich ○ MEX 93 Dd 35
Teplice ○ CZ 174 Gn 20
Teploe ○ RUS 181 Hl 19
Tëplyi Kljuc ○ RUS 205 Xa 6
Te Puke ○ NZ 383 Nl 64
Tepuxtla ○ MEX 92 Cj 34
Tequila ○ MEX 92 Cl 35
Tequisistlán ○ MEX 93 Da 37
Tequisquiapan ○ MEX 92 Cn 35
Téra ○ RN 305 Gg 38
Teradomari ○ J 251 Mf 27
Teraina ◬ KIR 14 Ba 9
Terakeka ○ SUD 324 Hh 43
Téramo ○ I 185 Gn 24
Terán ○ CO 106 Dj 45
Terang ○ AUS 378 Mh 65
Terapo ○ PNG 287 Mk 50
Teratani ~ PK 227 Jn 31
Terawera ○ NZ 383 Nl 65
Tercan ○ TR 202 Hn 26
Terceira ◬ P 18 Hb 6
Terceiro Acampamento ○ BR 113 Eh 45
Tercero ~ RA 137 Ec 62
Terebo ○ PNG 287 Mh 47
Terebovlja ○ UA 175 He 21
Te Reinga ○ NZ 383 Nl 65
Terek ○ RUS 202 Ja 24
Terek Alikazgan ~ RUS 202 Jb 24
Terekli-Mekteb ○ RUS 202 Ja 23
Térékolé ~ RMM 304 Ga 38
Teren'ga ○ RUS 181 Jb 19
Terenos ○ BR 140 Eg 56
Teresina ○ BR 124 En 48
Tereška ~ RUS 181 Jb 20
Teresópolis ○ BR 141 En 57
Terezinha de Goiás ○ BR 133 El 52
Teriberka ○ RUS 159 Hk 11
Teriberka ~ RUS 159 Hk 11
Terin Kot ○ AFG 223 Jl 29
Termachivka ○ UA 175 Hg 20
Termas del Chillán ○ RCH 137 Dn 64
Termas del Flaco ○ RCH 137 Dn 63
Termas de Rio Hondo ○ RA 136 Eb 59
Terme ○ TR 195 Hl 25
Termesse ○ RG 316 Fp 39
Termez ○ UZB 223 Jm 27
Términi Imerese ○ I 185 Gn 26
Termit ○ RN 308 Gm 37
Termit-Kaoboul ○ RN 308 Gm 38
Termo ○ USA 64 Cb 25
Ternata ○ RI 275 Lp 45
Ternej ○ RUS 250 Me 23
Terni ○ I 185 Gn 24
Ternopil' ○ UA 175 He 21
Terou ~ DY 317 Gg 41
Terowie ○ AUS 378 Mf 62
Terpaima ♀ YV 107 Dp 41
Terra Alta ○ BR 121 Ek 46
Terra Boa ○ BR 140 Eh 57
Terrace ○ CDN 42 Db 8
Terrace Bay ○ CDN 57 De 21
Terrace Bay ○ NAM 340 Gn 55
Terracina ○ I 185 Gn 25
Terra de Araia ○ BR 146 Ej 60
Terra Firma ○ ZA 349 Hd 58
Terråk ○ N 158 Gn 13
Terralba ○ I 185 Gl 26
Terra Nova ○ BR 124 Fa 50
Terra Nova do Norte ○ BR 132 Eg 51
Terra Nova National Park ♀ CDN 61 Eg 21
Terra Santa ○ BR 120 Ef 47
Terrassa ○ E 184 Gg 25
Terra Vermelha ○ BR 140 Ef 56
Terrebonne ○ CDN 60 Dl 23
Terre Haute ○ USA 71 De 26
Terrell ○ USA 70 Cp 29
Terreton ♀ USA 51 Cf 24
Terrier Rouge ○ RH 101 Dm 36
Terry ○ USA 51 Ck 22
Terry Hie Hie ○ AUS 375 Mm 60
Terryville ○ USA 74 Dm 25
Terscheling ◬ NL 163 Gj 19
Terşef ○ TCH 321 Ha 39
Terskij bereg ⏥ RUS 159 Hl 12
Teruel ○ CO 106 Dl 44
Teruel ○ E 184 Gf 25
Terujak ○ RI 270 Kn 43
Terujak ○ MAL 274 Lj 43
Tervel ○ BG 195 Hf 24
Tervo ○ FIN 159 Hf 14
Tervola ○ FIN 159 He 12
Tesalia ○ CO 106 Dl 44
Teselima ○ GH 317 Ge 41
Teseny ○ ER 313 Hl 38
Tes-Hein ~ MNG 204 Ub 9
Teshekpuk Lake ~ USA 46 An 9
Teshikaga ○ J 250 Mj 24
Teshio ~ J 250 Mh 23
Teshio-santi ⩕ J 250 Mg 23
Teslin ○ CDN 47 Bj 15
Teslin Lake ~ CDN 47 Bj 15
Tesouras ~ BR 133 Ej 53
Tessalit ○ RMM 305 Gg 35
Tessaoua ○ RN 320 Gk 39
Tesséroukane ○ RN 308 Gk 36
Tessiner Alpen ⩕ CH 174 Gl 22
Tessit ○ RMM 305 Gg 38
Tessounfat ○ RMM 305 Gg 35
Testour ○ TN 296 Gl 27
Têt ~ F 185 Gh 24
Tété Manovo ~ RCA 321 Hc 41
Tete ○ MOC 344 Hj 54
Tetehui ○ PNG 287 Mj 49
Tête Jaune Cache ○ CDN 50 Cc 19
Tetepare ◬ SOL 290 Na 50
Tetere ○ SOL 290 Nc 50
Tetere ○ SOL 290 Nc 51
Teteriv ~ UA 175 Hg 20
Tetijiv ○ UA 175 Hg 21
Tétini ⩕ RG 316 Gb 41
Tetjuši ○ RUS 181 Jc 18
Tetlin ○ USA 46 Be 13
Tetlin Indian Reservation ••• USA 46 Be 13
Teton ~ USA 51 Cg 22
Tetouan ○ MA 293 Gd 28
Tetovo ○ MK 194 Hc 24
Teturi ○ RDC 324 Hg 45
Teuco ~ RA 136 Ec 57
Teul ○ MEX 92 Cl 35
Teulada ○ I 185 Gl 26
Teulon ○ CDN 56 Cp 20
Teunom ○ RI 270 Km 43
Teuquito ~ RA 136 Ec 57
Te Urewera ♀ NZ 383 Nl 65
Teuri-tō ◬ J 250 Mg 23
Teutoburger Wald ⩕ D 170 Gk 19
Teutônia ○ BR 146 Ej 60
Teutonic Mining Centre ○ AUS 368 Ll 60
Tévere ~ I 185 Gn 24
Teverya ○ IL 208 Hk 29
Tevriz ○ RUS 204 Sc 7
Te Waewae Bay ≈ NZ 382 Nf 69
Tewah ○ RI 279 Lg 46
Tewantin ○ AUS 375 Mn 59
Tēwo ○ VRC 242 Lb 28
Texada Island ◬ CDN 50 Bp 21
Texarkana ○ USA 70 Db 29
Texas ◉ USA 81 Cl 30
Texas ○ AUS 375 Mm 60
Texas City ○ USA 81 Da 31
Texcoco ○ MEX 92 Cn 36
Texel ◬ NL 163 Gj 19
Texhoma ○ USA 70 Cm 27
Texmelucán ○ MEX 92 Cn 36
Teyateyaneng ○ LS 349 Hf 60
Teymurlu ○ IR 209 Ja 27
Teziutlán ○ MEX 92 Cp 35
Tezontepec ○ MEX 92 Cn 35
Tezpur ○ IND 235 Kl 32
Tezu ○ IND 254 Kn 32
Tfaritiy ○ MA 292 Ga 32
Thabana Ntlenyana △ LS 349 Hg 60
Thaba 'Nchu ○ ZA 349 Hf 60
Thaba Putsoa ⩕ LS 349 Hf 61
Thaba Tseka ○ LS 349 Hg 60
Thabeikkyin ○ MYA 254 Km 34
Thabazimbi ○ ZA 349 Hf 58
Tha Bo ○ THA 263 Lb 37
Tha Champa ○ THA 263 Lc 37
Thach An ○ VN 255 Ld 34
Tha Chana ○ THA 262 Kp 41
Thach Tru ○ VN 263 Le 38
Thādiq ○ KSA 215 Ja 33
Thagaya ○ MYA 254 Kn 36
Thái Bình ○ VN 255 Ld 35
Thái Hoà ○ VN 255 Lc 36
Thailand □ THA 262 La 39
Thái Nguyên ○ VN 255 Lc 35
Thakadu ○ RB 349 Hf 56
Thakaundrove ◬ FJI 387 Nm 54
Thakurgaon ○ BD 235 Kj 32
Thal ○ PK 223 Jp 29
Thala ○ TN 296 Gl 28
Thalang ○ THA 270 Kp 42
Thal Canal ~ PK 227 Jp 30
Thale Luang ~ THA 270 La 42
Thallon ○ AUS 375 Ml 60
Thalpar ○ PK 230 Kb 28
Thamad Bū Hashīshah ○ LAR 300 Hb 32
Thamaga ○ RB 349 He 58
Tha Mai ○ THA 262 La 39
Thames ○ GB 163 Gg 20
Thames ○ NZ 383 Nk 64
Thames R. ~ CDN 57 Dh 24
Thamesville ○ CDN 57 Dh 24
Tham Than ♀ THA 262 Kp 38
Thanatpin ○ MYA 262 Kn 37
Thanbyuzayat ○ MYA 262 Kn 38
Thane ○ IND 238 Ka 36
Thăng Bình ○ VN 263 Le 38
Thangoo ○ AUS 360 Lm 55
Thanh Hóa ○ VN 255 Lc 36
Thanh So'n ○ VN 255 Lc 35
Thanjavur ○ IND 239 Kd 40
Thankot ○ NEP 235 Kg 32
Than Kyun ◬ MYA 262 Kn 41
Than Uyên ○ VN 255 Lb 35
Thanyit ○ MYA 254 Km 33
Thanze ○ MYA 262 Km 37
Thaoge ~ RB 341 Hd 55
Thào Phi Tung ○ VN 255 Lc 34
Thap Put ○ THA 262 Kp 41
Thap Sakae ○ THA 262 Kp 40
Tharād ○ IND 227 Jp 33
Tharaka ○ EAK 337 Hl 46
Thar Desert ⏥ PK 227 Jn 32
Thargomindah ○ AUS 375 Mh 60
Tha Sae ○ THA 262 Kp 40
Tha Sala ○ THA 262 Kp 41
Tha Song Yang ○ THA 262 Kp 37
Thassos ○ GR 194 He 25
Thassos ◬ GR 194 He 25
Thatcher ○ USA 65 Ck 27

Tarso Lango - Thatcher 475

Thât Khê ○ **VN** 255 Ld 34	Thoury ○ **F** 163 Gh 21	Tiémé ○ **CI** 305 Gc 41	Timms Hill △ **USA** 56 Dc 23	Tiruvattiyur ○ **IND** 238 Ke 39	Todos Santos ○ **BOL** 129 Eb 54
Thatmako ○ **GR** 194 Hd 26	Thousand Springs ∿ **USA** 64 Ce 25	Tiémélékro ○ **CI** 317 Gd 42	Timni ○ **PNG** 287 Mk 49	Tiruvŭru ○ **IND** 238 Ke 37	Toéguin ○ **BF** 317 Gf 39
Thaton ○ **MYA** 262 Kn 37	Thracian Sea ∾ **GR** 194 He 25	Tiên Giang ∿ **VN** 263 Lc 40	Timoforo ○ **RI** 283 Mc 46	Tis ○ **IR** 226 Jj 33	Toekornstigstuwmeer ∿ **SME** 113 Ef 43
That Phanom ○ **THA** 263 Lc 37	Three Forks ○ **USA** 51 Cg 23	Tienie ○ **LB** 316 Ga 42	Timok ∿ **SCG** 194 Hd 24	Tisdale ○ **CDN** 51 Ck 19	Toeni ○ **BF** 317 Ge 39
Thatta ○ **PK** 227 Jm 33	Three Gorges Reservoir ∿ **VRC** 243 Le 30	Tiéningboué ○ **CI** 317 Gd 41	Timon ○ **BR** 124 En 48	Tisgaon ○ **IND** 238 Kb 36	Toéssé ○ **BF** 317 Gf 40
Tha Tum ○ **THA** 263 Lb 38	Three Hills ○ **CDN** 51 Cf 20	Tienko ○ **CI** 305 Gc 40	Timor ⌂ **RI** 282 Ln 50	Tisgui-Remz ○ **MA** 292 Gb 31	Tofield ○ **CDN** 51 Cf 19
Thaungalut ○ **MYA** 254 Km 33	Three Hummock Island ⌂ **AUS** 378 Mj 66	Tiên Yên ○ **VN** 255 Ld 35	Timor Sea ∾ 282 Ln 51	Tishomingo ○ **USA** 70 Cp 28	Tofino ○ **CDN** 50 Bn 21
Tha Uthen ○ **THA** 263 Lc 37	Three Kings Island ⌂ **NZ** 383 Nj 63	Tiera ○ **BF** 317 Gd 40	Timote ○ **RA** 137 Ec 63	Tissamaharama ○ **CL** 239 Ke 42	Tofua ⌂ **TO** 390 Ac 55
Tha Wang Pha ○ **THA** 254 La 36	Three Rivers ○ **USA** 71 Df 25	Tiéré ○ **RMM** 317 Gd 40	Timoudi ○ **DZ** 293 Gf 31	Tista ○ **DZ** 293 Gg 32	Toganaly ○ **AZ** 202 Jb 25
Thayawthadangyi Kyun ⌂ **MYA** 262 Kn 39	Three Rivers ○ **USA** 81 Cn 31	Tieri ○ **AUS** 375 Mf 57	Timpas ○ **USA** 65 Cl 27	Tisza ∿ **H** 174 Hc 21	Togba ○ **RIM** 304 Ga 37
Thayer ○ **USA** 70 Da 27	Three Sister Islands ⌂ **SOL** 290 Nd 51	Tierra Amarilla ○ **USA** 65 Cj 27	Timpton ○ **RUS** 205 Wb 7	Tit ○ **DZ** 293 Gg 32	Togga Ceel Madoobe ∿ **SP** 328 Jc 41
Thayer ○ **USA** 70 Dc 27	Three Sisters ○ **ZA** 349 Hd 61	Tierra Blanca ○ **MEX** 93 Cp 36	Timra ○ **S** 158 Ha 14	Titao ○ **BF** 317 Ge 39	Togga Dhud ∿ **SP** 328 Jc 40
Thaygon ○ **MYA** 262 Kn 37	Three Sisters △ **AUS** 374 Mg 58	Tierra Colorada ○ **MEX** 92 Cn 37	Tina △ **ZA** 349 Hg 61	Tit-Ary ○ **RUS** 204 Wb 4	Togga Dhuudo ∿ **SP** 328 Jd 41
Thayne ○ **USA** 51 Cg 24	Three Springs ○ **AUS** 368 Lh 60	Tierralta ○ **CO** 106 Dk 41	Tinaca Point ⌓ **RP** 275 Ln 43	Tite ○ **GNB** 316 Fn 40	Togga Giael ∿ **SP** 328 Jd 40
The Alley ○ **JA** 101 Dk 37	Three Ways Roadhouse ○ **AUS** 364 Md 55	Tie Siding ○ **USA** 65 Cj 25	Tinaco ○ **YV** 107 Ea 41	Titlagarh ○ **IND** 234 Kf 35	Togga Giawl ∿ **SP** 328 Jd 40
The Alps △ **AUS** 375 Ml 57	Throckmorton ○ **USA** 70 Cn 29	Tieta-de-Sidi-Bouguedra ○ **MA** 292 Gb 29	Ti-n-Aguelhaj Tangoutranat ○ **RMM** 305 Ge 37	Titwaifuru ○ **RI** 286 Mf 47	Togga Jidali ∿ **SP** 328 Jb 40
Thebes ○ **GR** 194 Hd 26	Throssell Range ⌒ **AUS** 360 Ll 56	Tieté ○ **BR** 140 Ej 56	Ti-n-Akof ○ **BF** 305 Gf 38	Ti-Tree ○ **AUS** 361 Mc 57	Togga Nugaal ∿ **SP** 328 Jc 41
Thebes ★ **ET** 301 Hj 33	Thua ∿ **EAK** 337 Hm 46	Tieté ∿ **BR** 141 El 57	Tin Alkoum ○ **DZ** 296 Gl 33	Titu ○ **RO** 175 He 23	Togga Silil ∿ **SP** 328 Hp 40
The Big Dry Creek ∿ **USA** 51 Cj 22	Thuân Châu ○ **VN** 255 Lb 35	Tieté ∿ **BR** 141 Gf 57	Tinambung ○ **RI** 279 Lk 47	Titule ○ **RDC** 324 He 44	Togga Tog Dheet ∿ **SP** 328 Ja 41
The Bight of Acklins ∿ **BS** 87 Dl 34	Thud Point ⌓ **AUS** 365 Mg 52	Tiffin ○ **USA** 71 Dg 25	Tinamburg ○ **RI** 279 Lk 47	Titusville ○ **USA** 74 Dj 25	Togga Weyne ∿ **SP** 328 Jd 40
The Brothers ⌂ **YE** 219 Je 39	Thuir ○ **ZW** 349 Hg 56	Tiflêt ○ **MA** 293 Gc 29	Tinaroo Falls Reservoir ∿ **AUS** 365 Mj 54	Titusville ○ **USA** 87 Dh 31	Togi ○ **J** 251 Me 27
The Caves ○ **AUS** 375 Mm 57	Thul ○ **PK** 227 Jn 31	Tifton ○ **USA** 86 Dg 30	Tiva ∿ **EAK** 337 Hm 46	Tiva ∿ **EAK** 337 Hm 46	Togiak ○ **USA** 46 Aj 15
The Dalles ○ **USA** 50 Cb 23	Thule Qaanaaq ○ **DK** 43 Hb 3	Tifu ○ **RI** 282 Lp 47	Tivoli ○ **USA** 81 Cp 31	Tivoli ○ **USA** 81 Cp 31	Togiak Bay ∿ **USA** 46 Aj 15
Thedford ○ **USA** 70 Cm 25	Thun ○ **CH** 163 Gk 22	Tiga Reservation ••• **WAN** 320 Gl 40	Tivoli ○ **I** 185 Gn 25	Tiva ∿ **EAK** 337 Hm 46	Togian Islands ⌂ **RI** 282 Ll 46
The English Company's Islands ⌂ **AUS** 364 Me 51	Thunderlarra ○ **AUS** 368 Lj 60	Tiger ○ **USA** 50 Cd 21	Tiwa ∿ **EAK** 337 Hm 46	Tiwuronto ○ **RI** 282 Ll 50	Togo ○ **CDN** 56 Cn 20
The Entrance ○ **AUS** 379 Mk 62	Thunder Bay ○ **CDN** 57 Dd 21	Tiger Island ⌂ **GUY** 113 Ee 42	Tixmucuy ○ **MEX** 93 Dc 36	Tixmucuy ○ **MEX** 93 Dc 36	Togo ○ **USA** 56 Db 22
The Everglades ∿ **USA** 87 Dh 33	Thunder Bay ∿ **CDN** 57 Dd 21	Tighenif ○ **DZ** 293 Gg 28	Tixtla ○ **MEX** 92 Cn 37	Togo ○ **PNG** 286 Mh 50	Togo ○ **PNG** 286 Mh 50
The Forty Fours ⌂ **NZ** 383 Ac 67	Thunder Bay ∿ **USA** 57 Dg 23	Tighina ○ **MD** 175 Hg 22	Tizayuca ○ **MEX** 92 Cn 36	Tizayuca ○ **MEX** 92 Cn 36	Togo ○ **RDC** 324 Hg 44
The Grampians ⌒ **AUS** 378 Mh 64	Thung Muang ○ **THA** 254 La 36	Tigîl ○ **RUS** 23 Sb 4	Tizimín ○ **MEX** 93 Dd 35	Tizimín ○ **MEX** 93 Dd 35	Togoba ○ **PNG** 287 Mg 48
The Great Oasis ∿ **ET** 301 Hk 34	Thung Salaeng Luang ⛺ **THA** 262 La 37	Tignère ○ **CAM** 320 Gn 42	Tizi-n-Essako ○ **RMM** 308 Gh 36	Tizi-n-Essako ○ **RMM** 308 Gh 36	Togobala ○ **RG** 316 Gb 41
The Gums ○ **AUS** 375 Mm 59	Thung Song ○ **THA** 262 Kp 41	Tignish ○ **CDN** 61 Ec 22	Tizi-n-Tairhemt △ **MA** 293 Gd 29	Tizi-n-Tairhemt △ **MA** 293 Gd 29	Togo Hills ⌒ **GH** 317 Gg 42
The Hague ○ **NL** 163 Gh 19	Thung Yai ○ **THA** 262 Kp 41	Tigre ∿ **YV** 112 Ec 41	Tizi-n-Tarhatine △ **MA** 293 Gc 30	Tizi-n-Tarhatine △ **MA** 293 Gc 30	Togoromá ○ **CO** 106 Dk 43
The Haven ○ **ZA** 358 Hg 62	Thungyai-Huai Kha Khaeng ⛺ **THA** 262 Kp 38	Tigre ∿ **PE** 116 Dl 47	Tizi Ouzou ○ **DZ** 296 Gj 27	Tizi Ouzou ○ **DZ** 296 Gj 27	Togtoh ○ **VRC** 243 Lf 25
The Horn △ **AUS** 379 Mk 64	Thunkar ○ **BHT** 235 Kk 32	Tigre ∿ **RA** 146 Ee 63	Tiznados ∿ **YV** 107 Ea 41	Tiznados ∿ **YV** 107 Ea 41	Toguéré-Koumbé ○ **RMM** 305 Gd 38
Theinkun ○ **MYA** 262 Kp 40	Thuraiyur ○ **IND** 239 Kd 40	Tigris ∿ **IRQ** 209 Jb 29	Tiznit ○ **MA** 292 Gb 31	Tiznit ○ **MA** 292 Gb 31	Togwotee Pass △ **USA** 51 Cg 24
The Johnston Lakes ∿ **AUS** 368 Ll 62	Thuraria ○ **RIM** 304 Ga 36	Tiguent ○ **RIM** 304 Fn 37	Tižtiž ○ **IR** 209 Jb 28	Tižtiž ○ **IR** 209 Jb 28	Tohat ∿ **DZ** 293 Gf 32
Thekkadi ○ **IND** 239 Kc 41	Thurles ○ **IRL** 163 Gb 19	Tiguézéfene ○ **RN** 308 Gh 38	Tjamdado ○ **RUS** 250 Mj 23	Tjamdado ○ **RUS** 250 Mj 23	Tohiatso ○ **UZB** 222 Jh 24
The Lakes ⛺ **AUS** 379 Mk 64	Thursday Island ○ **AUS** 365 Mg 51	Tiguili ○ **TCH** 321 Hb 40	Tjatino ○ **RUS** 250 Mj 23	Tjatino ○ **RUS** 250 Mj 23	Tohma ∿ **TR** 195 Hf 26
Thelon River ∿ **CDN** 42 Fa 6	Thursday Island ⌂ **AUS** 365 Mg 51	Tigzirt ○ **DZ** 296 Gj 27	Tjeggelvas ∿ **S** 158 Ha 12	Tjeggelvas ∿ **S** 158 Ha 12	Tohmajarvi ○ **FIN** 159 Hh 14
The Lynd Junction ○ **AUS** 365 Mj 55	Thurso ○ **GB** 162 Ge 16	Tihâmah ∿ **YE** 218 Hp 38	Tjørn △ **S** 170 Gm 17	Tjørn △ **S** 170 Gm 17	Tohoro O'Odham Indian Reservation ••• **USA** 65 Cf 29
Theme ○ **MYA** 254 Kn 36	Thurston Island ⌂ 38 Ea 16	Thâmat aš-Šám ∿ **KSA** 218 Hm 36	Tjorn △ **S** 170 Gm 17	Tjorn △ **S** 170 Gm 17	Tohoun ○ **RT** 317 Gg 42
Thenia ○ **DZ** 296 Gh 27	Thurston Lake ∿ **CDN** 47 Bn 17	Tihivinskaja grjada ⌒ **RUS** 171 Hj 16	Tjulander araly ⌂ **KZ** 155 Rb 9	Tjulander araly ⌂ **KZ** 155 Rb 9	Toibalawe ○ **IND** 262 Kl 40
Theniet el Had ○ **DZ** 296 Gh 28	Thybørøn ○ **DK** 170 Gk 17	Tihoi ○ **NZ** 383 Nk 65	Tjulanderaraly △ **KZ** 202 Jd 23	Tjulanderaraly △ **KZ** 202 Jd 23	Toili ○ **RI** 282 Lm 46
Theodore ○ **CDN** 51 Cl 20	Thylo ○ **MW** 344 Hk 54	Thoreck ○ **RUS** 202 Hn 23	Tlacoapa ○ **MEX** 92 Cn 37	Tlacoapa ○ **MEX** 92 Cn 37	Toiru River ∿ **PNG** 287 Mm 48
Theodore ○ **USA** 86 Dd 30	Thylungra ○ **AUS** 374 Mh 59	Thosuco ○ **MEX** 93 Dd 35	Tlacolula ○ **MEX** 93 Cp 37	Tlacolula ○ **MEX** 93 Cp 37	Toivakka ○ **FIN** 159 Hf 14
Theodore ○ **AUS** 375 Mm 58	Thymania ○ **AUS** 374 Mf 57	Tihuatlan ○ **MEX** 81 Cp 34	Tlacotalpan ○ **MEX** 93 Cp 36	Tlacotalpan ○ **MEX** 93 Cp 36	Toivala ∿ **FIN** 159 Hf 14
Theodor Roosevelt Lake ∿ **USA** 65 Cg 29	Thyou ○ **BF** 317 Ge 40	Tihvin ○ **RUS** 171 Hj 16	Tlacotepec ○ **MEX** 92 Cn 37	Tlacotepec ○ **MEX** 92 Cn 37	Tojo ○ **J** 251 Mc 28
The Pas ○ **CDN** 6 Db 4	Thyrrhenian Sea ∾ 185 Gm 26	Tijamuchi ∿ **BOL** 129 Eb 53	Tlahualillo de Zaragoza ○ **MEX** 81 Cl 32	Tlahualillo de Zaragoza ○ **MEX** 81 Cl 32	Tojtepa ○ **UZB** 223 Jn 25
The Pennines ⌒ **GB** 162 Ge 18	Tiadiaye ○ **SN** 304 Fm 38	Tijeras ∿ **USA** 65 Cj 28	Tlahuac ○ **MEX** 92 Cn 36	Tlahuac ○ **MEX** 92 Cn 36	Tok ○ **USA** 46 Be 13
The Pilot △ **AUS** 379 Ml 64	Tiahuanaco ○ **BOL** 129 Dp 54	Tijĩ ○ **LAR** 297 Gm 29	Tlahuilltepa ○ **MEX** 92 Cn 35	Tlahuilltepa ○ **MEX** 92 Cn 35	Tokachi ∿ **J** 250 Mj 24
Thep Sa Thit ○ **THA** 262 La 38	Tiahuanaco ★ **BOL** 129 Dp 54	Tijuana ○ **MEX** 64d Cd 29	Tlalamabele ○ **RB** 349 Hf 56	Tlalamabele ○ **RB** 349 Hf 56	Tokachi-dake △ **J** 250 Mh 24
Theran △ **IR** 222 Jd 28	Tianchang ○ **VRC** 246 Lk 29	Tijucas ∿ **BR** 141 Ek 59	Tlalixcoyan ○ **MEX** 92 Cp 36	Tlalixcoyan ○ **MEX** 92 Cp 36	Tokaj ○ **H** 174 Hc 21
Therhi ○ **PK** 227 Jn 32	Tiandong ○ **VRC** 255 Ld 33	Tijucu ∿ **BR** 133 Ek 55	Tlalnepantla ○ **MEX** 92 Cn 36	Tlalnepantla ○ **MEX** 92 Cn 36	Tôkamachi ○ **J** 251 Mf 27
Thermaikós Kólpos ∿ **GR** 194 He 25	Tian'e ○ **VRC** 255 Ld 33	Tikal △ **GCA** 93 Dd 37	Tlaltenango ○ **MEX** 92 Cl 35	Tlaltenango ○ **MEX** 92 Cl 35	Tokanui ○ **NZ** 382 Ng 69
Thermopolis ○ **USA** 51 Cj 24	Tianeti ○ **GE** 202 Ja 24	Tikamgarh ○ **IND** 234 Kd 33	Tlapa ○ **MEX** 92 Cn 37	Tlapa ○ **MEX** 92 Cn 37	Tokapalle ○ **IND** 238 Kd 38
The Rock ○ **AUS** 379 Mk 63	Tianfanjie ○ **VRC** 258 Lj 31	Tikanlik ○ **VRC** 231 Kh 25	Tlapacoyan ○ **MEX** 92 Cn 35	Tlapacoyan ○ **MEX** 92 Cn 35	Tokar ○ **SUD** 313 Hl 38
Theron Mountains ⌒ 38 Ja 18	Tiangol ∿ **SN** 304 Fn 38	Tikaré ○ **BF** 317 Gf 39	Tlaquepaque ○ **MEX** 92 Cl 35	Tlaquepaque ○ **MEX** 92 Cl 35	Tokara-kaikyŏ ∿ **J** 247 Mb 30
The Sisters ⌂ **NZ** 383 Ab 67	Tiangol Louggguéré ∿ **SN** 304 Fn 38	Tikchik Lakes ∿ **USA** 46 Al 15	Tlaxcala ○ **MEX** 92 Cn 36	Tlaxcala ○ **MEX** 92 Cn 36	Tokara-retto ⌂ **J** 259 Ma 31
The Snares ⌂ **NZ** 382 Nf 69	Tianguá ○ **BR** 124 Ep 47	Tikem ○ **TCH** 321 Gp 41	Tlaxiaco ○ **MEX** 92 Cn 37	Tlaxiaco ○ **MEX** 92 Cn 37	Tokat ○ **TR** 195 Hl 25
Thessalía Elláda ◎ **GR** 194 Hc 26	Tiangué Bori ○ **RG** 316 Fp 40	Tiki Basin ♥ 14 Ca 11	Tlemcen ○ **DZ** 293 Gf 28	Tlemcen ○ **DZ** 293 Gf 28	Tŏkchŏkto ⌂ **ROK** 247 Ln 27
Thessalon ○ **CDN** 57 Df 22	Tianjin ○ **VRC** 246 Lj 26	Tiko ○ **CAM** 320 Gl 43	Tlhakgameng ○ **ZA** 349 He 59	Tlhakgameng ○ **ZA** 349 He 59	Tokchon ○ **DVRK** 247 Ln 27
Thessaloniki ○ **GR** 194 Hd 26	Tianjin Shi ◎ **VRC** 246 Lj 26	Tikota ○ **IND** 238 Kb 37	Tljarata ○ **RUS** 202 Jb 24	Tljarata ○ **RUS** 202 Jb 24	Tokelau Islands ⌂ **NZ** 35 Aa 10
Thessaly ◎ **GR** 194 Hc 26	Tianjun ○ **VRC** 242 Kp 27	Tikša ○ **RUS** 159 Hj 13	Tlokoeng ○ **LS** 349 Hg 60	Tlokoeng ○ **LS** 349 Hg 60	Tokmak ○ **UA** 175 Hk 22
Thetford ○ **GB** 163 Gg 19	Tiankoura ○ **BF** 317 Ge 40	Tikseozero ∿ **RUS** 159 Hh 12	Tlokweng ○ **RB** 349 Hf 59	Tlokweng ○ **RB** 349 Hf 59	Tokomaru Bay ○ **NZ** 383 Nm 65
Thetford Mines ○ **CDN** 60 Dn 22	Tianlin ○ **VRC** 255 Ld 33	Tiksi ○ **RUS** 205 Wb 4	Tmassah ○ **LAR** 297 Gp 32	Tmassah ○ **LAR** 297 Gp 32	Tokoro ○ **NZ** 250 Mj 23
The Triangle ⌒ **MYA** 254 Kn 33	Tianmen ○ **VRC** 243 Lg 30	Tiku ○ **RI** 270 Kp 46	Toak ○ **VU** 386 Ng 54	Toak ○ **VU** 386 Ng 54	Tokoroa ○ **NZ** 383 Nk 65
Theunissen ○ **ZA** 349 Hf 60	Tianmu Shan ⌒ **VRC** 246 Lk 30	Tiladummati Atoll ⌂ **MV** 239 Ka 42	Toamasina Tamatave ○ **RM** 345 Jc 55	Toamasina Tamatave ○ **RM** 345 Jc 55	Tokorozawa ○ **RG** 316 Gb 41
The Valley ○ **GB** 104 Ec 36	Tianmustian ★ **VRC** 246 Lk 30	Tilaiya ○ **IND** 235 Kg 33	Tioga ○ **VRC** 242 Kn 30	Tioga ○ **VRC** 242 Kn 30	Toksook Bay ○ **USA** 46 Aj 15
Thevenard Island ⌂ **AUS** 360 Lh 56	Tiananshan ★ **VRC** 259 Ll 31	Tilakväda ○ **IND** 238 Ka 35	Tioga Pass △ **USA** 64 Cc 27	Tioga Pass △ **USA** 64 Cc 27	Toksovo ○ **RUS** 171 Hh 15
The Wash ∿ **GB** 163 Gg 19	Tiantai ○ **VRC** 259 Ll 31	Tilama ∿ **RCH** 137 Dn 62	Tionesta ○ **USA** 74 Dj 25	Tionesta ○ **USA** 74 Dj 25	Toktogul sus s. ∿ **KS** 230 Ka 25
The Woodlands ○ **USA** 81 Da 30	Tiantangzhai ★ **VRC** 243 Lh 30	Tilantongo ○ **MEX** 92 Cp 36	Tiop ○ **RI** 270 La 47	Tiop ○ **RI** 270 La 47	Tokunoshima ⌂ **J** 259 Ma 32
The Yellow Mountain ⌒ **AUS** 379 Mk 62	Tianyanghaijao ★ **VRC** 255 Le 36	Tilarán ○ **CR** 97 Df 40	Tioribougou ○ **RMM** 316 Gb 39	Tioribougou ○ **RMM** 316 Gb 39	Tokuno-shima ⌂ **J** 259 Ma 32
Thiamis ○ **GR** 194 Hc 26	Tianyang ○ **VRC** 255 Ld 34	Tilburg ○ **NL** 163 Gj 20	Tiou ○ **BF** 317 Ge 39	Tiou ○ **BF** 317 Ge 39	Tokushima ○ **J** 251 Md 28
Thiang Dao ○ **THA** 254 Kp 36	Tianzhu ○ **VRC** 242 Lb 27	Tilbury ○ **CDN** 57 Dg 24	Tiouilît ○ **RIM** 304 Fm 36	Tiouilît ○ **RIM** 304 Fm 36	Tokuyama ○ **J** 247 Mb 28
Thibodaux ○ **USA** 86 Dc 31	Tiaret ○ **DZ** 293 Gg 28	Tilden ○ **USA** 70 Cp 25	Tiouki ○ **RMM** 305 Gd 38	Tiouki ○ **RMM** 305 Gd 38	Tokwe ∿ **ZW** 341 Hh 55
Thief River Falls ○ **USA** 56 Cp 21	Tiaret ○ **TN** 296 Gm 30	Tilden ○ **USA** 81 Cn 31	Tipaza ○ **DZ** 296 Gh 27	Tipaza ○ **DZ** 296 Gh 27	Tokwe ∿ **ZW** 352 Hh 56
Thiers ○ **F** 185 Gh 23	Tías ○ **E** 292 Fp 31	Tilemsen ○ **MA** 292 Ga 31	Tipitapa ○ **NIC** 96 De 39	Tipitapa ○ **NIC** 96 De 39	Tokyo ⊡ **J** 251 Mf 28
Thies ○ **SN** 304 Fm 38	Tiaski ○ **SN** 304 Fn 38	Tilemsi Valley ∿ **RMM** 305 Gg 38	Tipperary ○ **IRL** 163 Gb 19	Tipperary ○ **IRL** 163 Gb 19	Tôkyô-wan ∿ **J** 251 Mf 28
Thika ○ **EAK** 337 Hl 46	Tiassale ○ **CI** 317 Gd 43	Tilghman ○ **USA** 74 Dk 26	Tipperary ○ **AUS** 364 Mb 52	Tipperary ○ **AUS** 364 Mb 52	Tokzar ○ **AFG** 223 Jm 28
Thikombia ⌂ **FJI** 390 Aa 53	Tibaji ○ **BR** 140 Ej 58	Tiličiki ○ **RUS** 23 Ta 3	Tipton ○ **USA** 70 Db 26	Tipton ○ **USA** 70 Db 26	Tol ○ **PNG** 287 Mm 48
Thikri ○ **IND** 234 Kb 34	Tibati ○ **CAM** 320 Gn 42	Tiligba ○ **RDC** 324 He 44	Tipton ○ **USA** 71 Dc 25	Tipton ○ **USA** 71 Dc 25	Tolabit ○ **RI** 275 Lp 45
Thillé Boubakar ○ **SN** 304 Fn 37	Tibau ○ **BR** 124 Fp 48	Tillaberi ○ **RN** 305 Gg 38	Tiptonville ○ **USA** 71 Dd 27	Tiptonville ○ **USA** 71 Dd 27	Tolaga Bay ○ **NZ** 383 Nm 65
Thilogne ○ **SN** 304 Fp 38	Tibau do Sul ○ **BR** 124 Fc 49	Tillamook ○ **USA** 50 Bp 23	Tiptūr ○ **IND** 238 Kc 39	Tiptūr ○ **IND** 238 Kc 39	Tôlanaro ○ **RM** 353 Jb 58
Thimphu ⊡ **BHT** 235 Kj 32	Tibba ○ **PK** 227 Jp 30	Tillamook Bay ∿ **USA** 50 Bp 23	Tipuani ○ **BOL** 129 Dp 53	Tipuani ○ **BOL** 129 Dp 53	Tolapalca ∿ **BOL** 129 Ea 55
Thingsat ○ **IND** 254 Kl 33	Tiberghamine ○ **DZ** 293 Gg 31	Tillanchang Dwip ⌂ **IND** 262 Kl 41	Tipuani ○ **EC** 116 Dl 46	Tipuani ○ **EC** 116 Dl 46	Tolé ○ **PA** 97 Dh 41
Thio ○ **F** 386 Nf 56	Tibet ◎ **VRC** 231 Kj 30	Tillia ○ **RN** 308 Gj 38	Tipuru ○ **GUY** 112 Ee 43	Tipuru ○ **GUY** 112 Ee 43	Tolé ○ **RCA** 321 Gp 42
Thionville ○ **F** 163 Gk 21	Tibiri ○ **RN** 320 Gh 39	Tillsonburg ○ **CDN** 57 Dh 24	Tiputini ○ **EC** 116 Dl 46	Tiputini ○ **EC** 116 Dl 46	Toledo ○ **USA** 50 Ca 23
Thira ○ **GR** 194 He 27	Tibiri ○ **RN** 320 Gh 39	Tilmans Corner ○ **USA** 86 Dd 30	Tiquicheo ○ **MEX** 92 Cm 36	Tiquicheo ○ **MEX** 92 Cm 36	Toledo ○ **USA** 71 Dg 25
Thíra Santorini ⌂ **GR** 194 He 27	Tibni ○ **SYR** 209 Hn 28	Tiloa ○ **RN** 305 Gh 38	Tiquié ∿ **BR** 117 Dp 45	Tiquié ∿ **BR** 117 Dp 45	Toledo ○ **BOL** 129 Ea 55
Thiruvarur ○ **IND** 239 Kd 40	Tibro ○ **S** 170 Gm 16	Tilomonte ○ **RCH** 136 Dp 57	Tirana ⊡ **AL** 194 Hb 25	Tirana ⊡ **AL** 194 Hb 25	Toledo ○ **BR** 140 Eh 58
Thisted ○ **DK** 170 Gl 17	Tibtan Lake ∿ **USA** 86 Dd 30	Tilpa ○ **AUS** 379 Mj 61	Tiraoue ○ **BR** 308 Gh 36	Tiraoue ○ **BR** 308 Gh 36	Toledo ○ **RP** 267 Lm 40
Thistle Island ⌂ **AUS** 378 Me 63	Tibú ○ **CO** 107 Dm 41	Tilrhemt ○ **DZ** 296 Gh 29	Tiraque ○ **BOL** 129 Eb 54	Tiraque ○ **BOL** 129 Eb 54	Toledo Bend Reservoir ∿ **USA** 86 Db 30
Thjórsá ⌂ **IS** 158 Fk 14	Tibung ○ **RI** 279 Lk 47	Tiltil ○ **RCH** 137 Dn 62	'Tirarè Shet' ∿ **ETH** 313 Hm 39	'Tirarè Shet' ∿ **ETH** 313 Hm 39	Tolga ○ **DZ** 296 Gj 28
Thjórsá ∿ **IS** 158 Fl 13	Tica ○ **MOC** 344 Hk 55	Tima ○ **ET** 301 Hn 32	Tirari Desert ∿ **AUS** 374 Mf 60	Tirari Desert ∿ **AUS** 374 Mf 60	Tolhuin ○ **RA** 152 Ea 73
Thlewiaza River ∿ **CDN** 42 Fb 6	Ticaboo ○ **USA** 65 Cg 27	Timahdite ○ **MA** 293 Gd 29	Tirasberge ⌒ **NAM** 348 Ha 58	Tirasberge ⌒ **NAM** 348 Ha 58	Toliara Tuléar ○ **RM** 353 Hp 57
Thoen ○ **THA** 262 Kp 37	Ticao Island ⌂ **RP** 267 Lm 39	Timalchara ○ **BR** 128 Dp 55	Tiraspol ○ **MD** 175 Hg 22	Tiraspol ○ **MD** 175 Hg 22	Tolitoli ○ **RI** 275 Ll 45
Thoeng ○ **THA** 254 La 36	Ticao Passage ∾ **RP** 267 Lm 39	Timane ∿ **PY** 136 Ed 56	Tire ○ **NZ** 383 Nk 64	Tire ○ **NZ** 383 Nk 64	Tofjatti ○ **RUS** 181 Jc 19
Thohoyandou ○ **ZA** 352 Hh 57	Tichît ○ **RIM** 304 Gb 36	Timanskij Krjaž ⌒ **RUS** 19 Ma 3	Tire ○ **TR** 195 Hf 26	Tire ○ **TR** 195 Hf 26	Toljmačovo ○ **RUS** 171 Hg 16
Thomas ○ **AUS** 368 Lj 58	Tichla ○ **MA** 304 Fn 35	Timan Ridge ⌒ **RUS** 19 Na 3	Tiredolu ○ **TR** 195 Hm 25	Tiredolu ○ **TR** 195 Hm 25	Tolo ○ **RDC** 333 Hb 47
Thomaston ○ **USA** 86 Df 29	Ticho ○ **ETH** 325 Hm 42	Timan Ridge ⌒ **RUS** 154 Ra 5	Tiree ⌂ **GB** 162 Gc 17	Tiree ⌂ **GB** 162 Gc 17	Tolokiwa Island ⌂ **PNG** 287 Mk 48
Thomaston Corner ○ **CDN** 60 Ea 23	Ticonderoga ○ **USA** 60 Dm 24	Timargarha ○ **PK** 223 Jp 28	Tirere ○ **PNG** 286 Mh 50	Tirere ○ **PNG** 286 Mh 50	Tolono ○ **USA** 71 Dd 26
Thomasville ○ **USA** 71 Dh 28	Ticul ○ **MEX** 93 Dd 35	Timaru ○ **NZ** 382 Nh 68	Tirhatimine ○ **DZ** 296 Gh 33	Tirhatimine ○ **DZ** 296 Gh 33	Tolsan Do ⌂ **ROK** 247 Lp 28
Thomasville ○ **USA** 86 Dd 30	Tidal River ○ **AUS** 379 Mk 65	Timau ○ **EAK** 325 Hl 45	Tirich Mir △ **IND** 223 Jp 27	Tirich Mir △ **IND** 223 Jp 27	Toltén ○ **RCH** 147 Dm 65
Thomasville ○ **USA** 86 Dg 30	Tidarméné ○ **RMM** 308 Gh 37	Timâveni ○ **RO** 175 He 22	Tiriri ○ **RG** 323 Hj 45	Tiriri ○ **RG** 323 Hj 45	Toltén ∿ **RCH** 147 Dm 65
Thomonde ○ **RH** 101 Dm 36	Tiddim ○ **MYA** 254 Kl 34	Timba ○ **CO** 106 Dk 44	Tiro ○ **RG** 316 Ga 41	Tiro ○ **RG** 316 Ga 41	Tolú ○ **CO** 106 Dl 41
Thompson ○ **CDN** 42 Fb 7	Tiddis ★ **DZ** 296 Gk 27	Timbaki ○ **GR** 194 He 28	Tirol ◎ **A** 174 Gm 22	Tirol ◎ **A** 174 Gm 22	Toluca ○ **MEX** 92 Cn 36
Thompson ∿ **CDN** 42 Fb 7	Tidikelt Plateau ∿ **DZ** 293 Gg 32	Timbalier Bay ∿ **USA** 86 Dc 31	Tiros ○ **BR** 133 Em 55	Tiros ○ **BR** 133 Em 55	Toluviejo ○ **CO** 106 Dl 41
Thompson ○ **USA** 70 Db 25	Tidjikja ○ **RIM** 304 Ga 36	Timbaúba ○ **BR** 124 Fc 49	Tiros ○ **BR** 194 He 27	Tiros ○ **BR** 194 He 27	Tolwe ○ **ZA** 349 Hg 57
Thompson Falls ○ **USA** 50 Ce 22	Tiébissou ○ **CI** 317 Gd 42	Timbedgha ○ **RIM** 304 Gb 37	Tirso ∿ **I** 185 Gl 25	Tirso ∿ **I** 185 Gl 25	Tom ∿ **RUS** 204 Tc 8
Thompson Pass △ **USA** 46 Bc 15	Tiéblé ○ **BF** 317 Gd 42	Timber Creek ○ **AUS** 364 Mb 53	Tirthahalli ○ **IND** 238 Kb 39	Tirthahalli ○ **IND** 238 Kb 39	Toma ∿ **RA** 136 Ea 59
Thomson ∿ **USA** 71 Dg 24	Tiéfora ○ **BF** 317 Gd 40	Timber Mill ○ **AUS** 364 Mc 51	Tiruchchendūr ○ **IND** 239 Kd 41	Tiruchchendūr ○ **IND** 239 Kd 41	Toma ○ **BF** 317 Ge 39
Thomson ○ **AUS** 374 Mh 58	Tiegba ○ **CI** 317 Gd 43	Timbiras ○ **BR** 124 En 48	Tiruchirappalli ○ **IND** 239 Kd 40	Tiruchirappalli ○ **IND** 239 Kd 40	Tomah ○ **USA** 56 Dc 24
Thomson Dam ∿ **AUS** 379 Mk 64	Tieli ○ **VRC** 205 Wb 9	Timbó ○ **BR** 140 Ek 59	Tiruchengodu ○ **IND** 239 Kc 40	Tiruchengodu ○ **IND** 239 Kc 40	Tomahawk ○ **USA** 57 Dd 23
Thong Pha Phum ○ **THA** 262 Kp 38	Tielong ○ **IND** 230 Kd 28	Timbo ○ **RG** 316 Ga 40	Tirukkalukkunram ○ **IND** 238 Ke 39	Tirukkalukkunram ○ **IND** 238 Ke 39	Tomakas ○ **NAM** 340 Gn 55
Thongwa ○ **MYA** 262 Kn 37	Tiéma ○ **CI** 305 Gc 41	Timboon ○ **AUS** 378 Mh 65	Tirukkovilūr ○ **IND** 238 Kd 40	Tirukkovilūr ○ **IND** 238 Kd 40	Tomakomai ○ **J** 250 Mg 24
Thôn Hai ○ **VN** 263 Ld 37	Tiemba ○ **CI** 305 Gc 41	Timboroa ○ **EAK** 325 Hk 45	Tirukkovilūr ○ **IND** 239 Kd 40	Tirukkovilūr ○ **IND** 239 Kd 40	Tomales Bay ∿ **USA** 64 Ca 26
Thonon ○ **F** 163 Gk 22	Tiembedga ∿ **RIM** 304 Ga 36	Timboy ○ **BOL** 136 Eb 56	Tirumakudal ○ **IND** 238 Kc 39	Tirumakudal ○ **IND** 238 Kc 39	Tomamae ○ **J** 250 Mg 24
Thoreau ○ **USA** 65 Ch 28	Tien ○ **CI** 305 Gc 41	Timbuktu ○ **RMM** 305 Ge 37	Tirumala ○ **IND** 238 Kd 38	Tirumala ○ **IND** 238 Kd 38	Tomanivi △ **FJI** 387 Nl 54
Thorndale ○ **ZA** 349 Hg 57	Tién ○ **CI** 305 Gc 41	Timbulun ○ **RI** 270 La 46	Tirumangalam ○ **IND** 239 Kc 41	Tirumangalam ○ **IND** 239 Kc 41	Tomar ○ **BR** 117 Ec 46
Thorne ○ **CDN** 60 Dj 22	Tierra Blanca ○ **USA** 254 Kl 34	Timbuni ∿ **RI** 283 Mc 46	Tirunelveli ○ **IND** 239 Kc 41	Tirunelveli ○ **IND** 239 Kc 41	Tomar ○ **P** 184 Gb 26
Thornhill ○ **GB** 162 Ge 18	Tiddis ★ **DZ** 296 Gk 27	Timbunke ○ **PNG** 286 Mh 48	Tiruntani ○ **PE** 116 Dl 49	Tiruntani ○ **PE** 116 Dl 49	Tomari ○ **RUS** 250 Mg 22
Thornton ○ **USA** 50 Cd 22	Tiébissou ○ **CI** 317 Gd 42	Timehrie ○ **GUY** 113 Ee 42	Tirupati ○ **IND** 238 Kd 39	Tirupati ○ **IND** 238 Kd 39	Tomarza ○ **TR** 195 Hk 26
Thornton ○ **USA** 86 Dc 29	Tidjikja ○ **RIM** 304 Ga 36	Timelluline ○ **DZ** 296 Gl 31	Tiruparankundram ○ **IND** 239 Kc 41	Tiruparankundram ○ **IND** 239 Kc 41	Tomas ∿ **PE** 128 Dl 52
Thorntonia ○ **AUS** 365 Mf 55	Tigmad ○ **DZ** 296 Gk 28	Timgad ★ **DZ** 296 Gk 28	Tiruppadūr ○ **IND** 239 Kd 40	Tiruppadūr ○ **IND** 239 Kd 40	Tomašewska ○ **UA** 174 Hd 20
Thôt Nôt ○ **VN** 263 Lc 40	Timia ○ **RN** 308 Gj 36	Timia ○ **RN** 308 Gj 36	Tiruppattūr ○ **IND** 238 Kd 39	Tiruppattūr ○ **IND** 238 Kd 39	Tomaševka ○ **UA** 174 Hc 19
Thou ○ **BF** 317 Ge 39	Timiaouine ○ **DZ** 308 Gi 35	Timiaouine ○ **DZ** 308 Gi 35	Tiruppur ○ **IND** 239 Kc 40	Tiruppur ○ **IND** 239 Kc 40	Tomaszewska ○ **UA** 174 Hd 20
Thouars ○ **F** 163 Gf 22	Timika ○ **RI** 286 Me 48	Timika ○ **RI** 286 Me 48	Tirürangani ○ **IND** 239 Kb 40	Tirürangani ○ **IND** 239 Kb 40	Tomás ○ **PE** 128 Dl 52
Thouet ∿ **F** 163 Gf 22	Timimoun ○ **DZ** 293 Gf 31	Timimoun ○ **DZ** 293 Gf 31	Tirutturaippūndi ○ **IND** 239 Kd 40	Tirutturaippūndi ○ **IND** 239 Kd 40	Tomarovka ○ **RUS** 175 Hk 20
Thoufi ○ **DZ** 296 Gk 28	Timiş ∿ **RO** 174 Hc 23	Timiş ∿ **RO** 174 Hc 23	Tiruvalaru ○ **IND** 239 Kd 40	Tiruvalaru ○ **IND** 239 Kd 40	Tomarza ○ **TR** 195 Hk 26
	Timişoara ○ **RO** 174 Hc 23	Timişoara ○ **RO** 174 Hc 23	Tiruvalla ⌂ **IND** 239 Kc 41	Tiruvalla ⌂ **IND** 239 Kc 41	Tomas ∿ **PE** 128 Dl 52
	Tiemba ○ **CI** 305 Gc 41	Timmins ○ **CDN** 57 Dh 21	Tiruvannāmalai ○ **IND** 238 Kd 39	Tiruvannāmalai ○ **IND** 238 Kd 39	Tomás Garrido ○ **MEX** 93 Dd 36

□Country ▣Capital city ◉Administrative unit OPlace ♁Island ⛰Mountain range △Mountain ⌓Cape ≈Ocean, Sea ~Lake, River ΨUndersea topography ▲Glacier ♀National park •••Reservation ★Point of major interest ⌒Landscape

Tomaszów Lubelski O PL 175 Hd 20
Tomaszów Maz. O PL 174 Hc 20
Tomat O SUD 312 Hf 40
Tomat O SUD 313 Hk 38
Tomatán O MEX 75 Ce 31
Tomatlán O MEX 92 Ck 36
Tombe O ANG 340 Ha 52
Tombel O CAM 320 Gl 43
Tombigbee ~ USA 71 Dd 28
Tomboco O ANG 332 Gn 49
Tombokro O CI 317 Gd 42
Tombolo O RI 279 Lk 48
Tombouctou Timbuktu O RMM 305 Ge 37
Tombstone O USA 80 Cg 30
Tombua O ANG 340 Gm 53
Tom Burke O ZA 349 Hg 57
Tomé O RCH 137 Dm 64
Tomé-Açu O BR 121 Ek 47
Tomelilla O S 170 Gn 18
Tomelloso O E 184 Ge 26
Tomi ~ RCA 321 Hb 43
Tomiko O CDN 60 Dj 22
Tomina ~ BOL 129 Eb 55
Tominé ~ RG 316 Fp 39
Tomingley O AUS 379 Mk 62
Tomini O RI 275 Ll 45
Tominián O RMM 317 Gd 39
Tomioka O J 251 Mf 27
Tomkinson Ranges ⛰ AUS 369 Ma 59
Tomma ♁ N 158 Gn 12
Tommot O RUS 205 Wb 7
Tomo ~ CO 107 Dn 43
Tomo ~ CO 107 Dp 43
Tomochic O MEX 80 Ch 31
Tomohon O RI 275 Ln 45
Tomori O RCA 321 Gp 44
Tomorlog O VRC 231 Kk 26
Tompira O RI 282 Ll 47
Tompi Seleka O ZA 349 Hg 58
Tompkins O CDN 51 Ch 20
Tompkinsville O USA 71 De 27
Tompo O RI 275 Ll 45
Tom Price O AUS 360 Lj 57
Tomsk O RUS 204 Tb 7
Toms River O USA 74 Dl 26
Tomu O RI 283 Mc 47
Tomu River ~ PNG 286 Mh 49
Tonalá O MEX 92 Cl 35
Tonalá O MEX 93 Db 37
Tonami O J 251 Me 27
Tonantins O BR 117 Ea 47
Tonasket O USA 50 Cc 21
Tonate O F 113 Eh 43
Tonb-e Borzog ♁ IR 226 Jf 32
Tondano O RI 275 Ln 45
Tonde O Z 341 Hg 52
Tønder O DK 170 Gl 18
Tondi O IND 239 Kd 41
Tondibi O RMM 305 Gf 37
Tondigamé Goulbi ~ RN 320 Gh 39
Tondiji O RMM 316 Ga 39
Tondi Kiwindi O RN 305 Gg 38
Tondon O RG 316 Fp 40
Tondong O RI 279 Lk 47
Tondoro O NAM 340 Hb 54
Tonekābon O IR 222 Jd 27
Tong O SUD 324 Hg 42
Tong ~ SUD 324 Hg 43
Tonga O CAM 320 Gm 43
Tonga O SUD 324 Hh 41
Tonga □ TO 390 Ab 56
Tongaat O ZA 352 Hh 60
Tonga Islands ♁ TO 390 Ad 55
Tongaland ⌒ ZA 352 Hj 59
Tong'an O VRC 258 Lj 33
Tongareva ♁ NZ 35 Ba 10
Tongariki ♁ VU 386 Ng 54
Tongariro ♀ NZ 383 Nk 65
Tongatapu ♁ TO 390 Ac 56
Tongatapu Group ♁ TO 390 Ac 56
Tonga Trench Ψ 390 Ac 57
Tongbai O VRC 243 Lg 29
Tongbai Shan ⛰ VRC 243 Lg 29
Tongcheng O VRC 246 Lj 30
Tongcheng O VRC 258 Lg 31
Tongchon O DVRK 247 Lp 26
Tongchuan O VRC 243 Le 28
Tongdao O VRC 255 Le 32
Tongde O VRC 242 La 28
Tongehatan Point ⌓ RP 275 Lk 43
Tonggu O VRC 258 Lh 31
Tong'guan O VRC 243 Lf 28
Tongguzbasti O VRC 230 Kf 26
Tonggu Zhang △ VRC 258 Lj 33
Tonghae O ROK 247 Ma 27
Tonghai O VRC 255 Lb 33
Tonghaiko O VRC 243 Lg 30
Tong Island ♁ PNG 287 Mk 47
Tongjiang O VRC 243 Ld 30
Tongjiang O VRC 250 Mc 22
Tongko O RI 282 Ll 46
Tongku O RI 282 Ll 46
Tongliang O VRC 255 Ld 31
Tongling O VRC 246 Lj 30
Tonglu O VRC 258 Lk 31
Tongmu O VRC 258 Lg 32
Tongnan O VRC 243 Lc 30
Tongo O RCB 332 Ha 46
Tongoa ♁ VU 386 Ng 54
Tongobory O RM 353 Ja 57
Tongomayél O BF 305 Gf 38
Tongren O VRC 242 La 28
Tongren O VRC 255 Le 32
Tongsa O BHT 235 Kk 32
Tongshan O VRC 258 Lh 31
Tongshi O VRC 255 Le 36
Tongtian He Zhiqu ~ VRC 242 Km 28
Tongue ~ USA 51 Cj 23
Tongue O GB 162 Gd 16
Tongue of the Ocean ~ BS 87 Dk 33
Tongue River ~ USA 51 Cj 23
Tonguro ~ BR 133 Eh 52
Tongxiang O VRC 246 Ll 30
Tongxin O VRC 243 Lc 27
Tongyu O VRC 243 Lg 27
Tongzi O VRC 255 Ld 31
Tónichi O MEX 80 Ch 31
Tonila O MEX 92 Cl 36
Tonina O CO 107 Ea 44
Tonk O IND 234 Kb 32
Tonka O RMM 305 Ge 37
Tonkawa O USA 70 Cp 27
Tonkensval ~ SME 113 Ef 43
Tonkoro O AUS 374 Mh 57
Tônle Kông ~ K 263 Ld 39
Tonle San ~ K 263 Ld 38
Tonle Sap ~ K 263 Lb 39
Tônle Srepok ~ K 263 Ld 39
Tōno O J 250 Mg 26
Tonono O PY 136 Ec 57
Tonopah O USA 64 Cd 26
Tonoro O YV 112 Ec 41
Tonosí O PA 97 Dh 42
Tonosyō O J 251 Md 28
Tonotha O RB 349 Hf 56
Tonozero ~ RUS 159 Hh 13
Ton Sai O THA 270 La 42
Tønsberg O N 170 Gl 16
Tonsina O USA 46 Bc 15
Tonstad O N 170 Gk 16
Tontelbos O ZA 358 Hc 61
Tonto ~ MEX 92 Cp 36
Tonto National Monument ★ USA 65 Cg 29
Tonumea ♁ TO 390 Ac 56
Tonya O TR 195 Hm 25
Toobanna O AUS 365 Mk 55
Toodos ⛰ CY 195 Hj 28
Toodyay O AUS 368 Lj 61
Tooele O USA 65 Cf 25
To'Okona O PNG 287 Mk 49
Toolebuc O AUS 374 Mg 57
Toolondo O AUS 378 Mg 64
Tooloombilla O AUS 375 Ml 58
Toompine O AUS 375 Mj 59
Toomula O AUS 365 Mk 55
Tooncatchyin Creek ~ AUS 374 Mf 60
Toonerville O USA 65 Cl 27
Toowoomba O AUS 375 Mm 59
Topeka O USA 70 Cp 26
Topía O MEX 80 Cj 33
Topia ~ RCA 321 Ha 43
Toplița O RO 175 He 22
Topola O SCG 174 Hc 23
Topoli O RDC 324 Hf 44
Topolinoe O RUS 205 Xa 6
Topolobampo O MEX 80 Ch 33
Topolovgrad O BG 194 He 24
Topolovka O RUS 205 Yb 6
Toppenish O USA 50 Cb 22
Tops ♀ AUS 379 Mm 62
Topsfield O USA 60 Ea 23
Top Springs O AUS 364 Mb 54
Topura O PNG 287 Mm 51
Tor O ETH 325 Hj 42
Toramarkog O VRC 242 Kn 29
Torata O PE 128 Dn 54
Torbanlea O AUS 375 Mn 58
Torbat-e Gām O IR 222 Jj 28
Torbāt-e Heidarīye O IR 222 Jh 28
Torbay O AUS 368 Lj 63
Tordesillas O E 184 Gd 25
Tōre O S 159 Hd 13
Torell land ♁ N 158 Ha 7
Torgaj O KZ 155 Sa 9
Torgaj ustirti ⛰ KZ 155 Sa 8
Torgaj zylgasy ⌒ KZ 155 Sa 9
Torgau O D 174 Gn 20
Torgun ~ RUS 181 Jb 20
Toricueije O BR 133 Eh 53
Toriparu O BR 132 Eh 54
Tori-shima ♁ J 259 Ma 32
Torit O SUD 324 Hj 43
Toritama O BR 124 Fb 50
Toriud O IR 222 Jf 28
Torkestan Mountains ⛰ AFG 223 Jk 28
Tormosin O RUS 181 Hp 21
Tornado Mountain ⛰ CDN 50 Ce 21
Torneälven ~ S 159 Hc 12
Torneträsk ~ S 159 Hb 11
Torngat Mountains ⛰ CDN 43 Hc 7
Tornio O FIN 159 He 13
Tornionjoki ~ FIN 159 Hd 12
Tornquist O RA 147 Ec 65
Torntabacken ♁ S 170 Gp 17
Toro O E 184 Gd 25
Toro O EAU 324 Hh 45
Torobuku O RI 282 Lm 48
Torodi O RN 317 Gg 39
Torok O TCH 321 Gp 41
Törökbálint O H 174 Hb 22
Torokina O PNG 290 Mp 49
Torokoroba O RMM 305 Gc 39
Törökszentmiklós O H 174 Hc 22
Torola ~ HN 93 Dd 39
Toronto O CDN 60 Dj 24
Toropec O RUS 171 Hh 17
Toroq O IR 222 Jh 27
Tororo O EAU 325 Hj 45
Torquato Severo O BR 146 Eg 61
Torquay O CDN 51 Cl 21
Torquay O GB 163 Ge 20
Torra Bay O NAM 348 Gn 56
Torrance O USA 64 Cc 29
Torrealba O YV 112 Eb 41
Torre d. Greco O I 194 Gp 25
Torre de Moncorvo O P 184 Gc 25
Torrelaguna O E 184 Ge 25
Torrelavega O E 184 Gd 24
Torremolinos O E 184 Gd 27
Torrens Creek O AUS 375 Mj 56
Torrens Creek ~ AUS 375 Mj 57
Torrent O E 184 Gf 26
Torreon O USA 65 Cj 28
Torreon O MEX 81 Cl 33
Torreón de Cañas O MEX 80 Ck 32
Torre-P. O E 184 Gf 27
Torres O BR 140 Ek 60
Torres del Paine O RCH 152 Dm 71
Torres Strait ≈ 286 Mg 50
Torres Vedras O P 184 Gb 26
Torrevieja O E 184 Gf 26
Torrey O USA 65 Cg 26
Torricelli Mountains ⛰ PNG 286 Mh 47
Torrijos O E 184 Gd 25
Torrington O USA 51 Ck 24
Torrington O USA 74 Dm 25
Tor Rock △ AUS 364 Mc 52
Torron ~ S 158 Gn 14
Torsby O S 158 Gn 15
Tórshavn O DK 162 Gc 14
Torsö ♁ S 170 Gn 16
Tortel O RCH 152 Dm 69
Tortiya O CI 317 Gd 41
Tortola ♁ GB 104 Eb 36
Tortoli O I 185 Gl 26
Tortona O I 185 Gl 23
Tortosa O E 184 Gg 25
Tortuguilla O C 101 Dl 36
Tortum O TR 202 Hn 25
Torue O RI 282 Ll 46
Torugart O KS 230 Kb 25
Torul O TR 195 Hm 25
Toruń O PL 170 Hb 19
Tõrva O EST 171 He 17
Torvarkovskij O RUS 181 Hm 19
Torwood O AUS 365 Mh 54
Tory Hill O CDN 60 Dj 23
Tory Island ♁ IRL 162 Gb 18
Toržkovskaja grjada ⛰ RUS 171 Hk 17
Toržok O RUS 171 Hk 17
Torzym O PL 170 Gp 19
Tosagua O EC 116 Dh 46
Tosa-Shimizu O J 251 Mc 29
Tosa-wan ~ J 251 Mc 29
Tosca O ZA 349 Hd 58
Toscana ◉ I 185 Gm 24
Toshām O IND 234 Kb 31
Toshima ♁ J 251 Mf 28
Toshino-Kumano ★ J 251 Md 29
Toshka Lakes ~ ET 301 Hh 34
Tosi O SUD 312 Hh 40
Toškŭrgon O UZB 223 Jm 26
Tosno O RUS 171 Hh 16
Toson Hu ~ VRC 242 Kn 27
Tostado O RA 137 Ed 60
Tõstamaa O EST 171 Hd 16
Tošviska O RUS 154 Rb 5
Tosya O TR 195 Hk 25
Tot O EAK 325 Hk 45
Totaranui O NZ 383 Nj 66
Toteng O RB 349 Hd 56
Totías O SP 328 Ja 44
Tot'ma O RUS 154 Qc 7
Tot'ma O RUS 171 Hp 16
Totness O SME 113 Ef 43
Toto O WAN 320 Gk 41
Toto O ANG 332 Gp 49
Totoalejos O RA 137 Eb 60
Totok O RI 275 Ln 45
Totolán O MEX 92 Cl 35
Totolapan O MEX 92 Cm 36
Totolapan O MEX 93 Cp 37
Totonicapán O GCA 93 Dc 38
Totora O BOL 129 Dp 54
Totora O BOL 129 Eb 54
Totoral O RCH 136 Dn 59
Totoral ~ RCH 136 Dn 59
Totoral ~ RCH 136 Dn 60
Totoras O RA 137 Ed 62
Totota O LB 316 Ga 42
Totoya ♁ FJI 390 Aa 55
Tottan Hills ⛰ 38 Ja 17
Tottenham O AUS 379 Mk 62
Tottori O J 251 Mc 28
Totumito O YV 107 Dn 42
Touâjîl O RIM 304 Fp 34
Touâret O RN 308 Gk 35
Touba O SN 304 Fn 38
Touba O CI 304 Gc 41
Toubacouta O SN 316 Fm 39
Toubéré Bafal O SN 304 Fp 38
Touboro O CAM 321 Gp 42
Toucy O F 163 Gh 22
Toueyyirât O RMM 305 Ge 37
Tougan O BF 317 Ge 39
Touggourt O DZ 296 Gk 29
Tougnifili O RG 316 Fn 40
Tougouri O BF 317 Gf 39
Tougué O RG 316 Ga 40
Touho O F 386 Ne 56
Toujl O RIM 304 Ga 38
Toukoto O RMM 316 Gb 39
Toul O F 163 Gj 21
Toulépleu O CI 316 Gb 42
Touliu O RC 259 Ll 34
Toulon O F 185 Gj 24
Toulounga O TCH 321 Hb 40
Toulouse O F 184 Gg 24
Toumbélaga O RN 308 Gk 38
Toumodi O CI 317 Gd 42
Toumoundjila O RG 316 Gb 40
Touna O RMM 305 Gc 40
Tounfafi O RN 308 Gj 38
Toungbon O MYA 254 Km 34
Toungoo O MYA 254 Kn 36
Toungour O TCH 309 Hb 37
Toura ~ BF 317 Gf 39
Touragondī O AFG 223 Jj 28
Tourassine O RIM 292 Ga 33
Tourba O TCH 321 Gp 39
Tourîne O RIM 304 Ga 34
Tournai O B 163 Gh 20
Tournavista O PE 116 Dl 50
Tournhout O B 163 Gj 20
Tourni O BF 317 Gd 40
Tournon-s.-R. O F 185 Gj 23
Tournus O F 163 Gj 22
Touros O BR 124 Fc 48
Touroua O CAM 321 Gn 41
Touroug O MA 293 Gd 30
Tourougoumbé O RMM 304 Gb 38
Tours O F 163 Gg 22
Toussiana O BF 317 Gd 40
Toutes Aides O CDN 56 Cn 20
Toutoukro O CI 317 Gd 41
Touwsrivier O ZA 358 Hc 62
Touwsrivier ~ ZA 358 Hc 62
Tovar O YV 107 Dn 41
Tovdalselva ~ N 170 Gk 16
Tovuz O AZ 202 Ja 25
Towada O J 250 Mg 25
Towada Hachimantai ★ J 250 Mg 25
Towada-Hachimantai ♀ J 250 Mg 26
Towadal-ko ~ J 250 Mg 25
Towakaima O GUY 112 Ee 42
Towanda O USA 74 Dk 25
Towari O RI 282 Ll 48
Towaya O RI 279 Lk 46
Towe O LB 316 Gb 42
Tower O USA 56 Cp 22
Towera O AUS 360 Lh 57
Towerhill Creek ~ AUS 375 Mj 56
Tower Peak △ AUS 369 Lm 62
Towla O ZW 349 Hg 56
Towner O USA 56 Cm 21
Towns ~ AUS 364 Md 53
Townsend O USA 51 Cg 22
Townshend Island ♁ AUS 375 Mm 57
Townsville O AUS 365 Mk 55
Towot O SUD 325 Hk 42
Towrana O AUS 368 Lh 58
Towson O USA 74 Dk 26
Toxkan He ~ VRC 230 Kd 25
Toyah O USA 81 Cl 30
Tōya-ko ~ J 250 Mg 24
Toyama O J 251 Me 27
Toyama-wan ~ J 251 Me 27
Toyohashi O J 251 Me 28
Toyokawa O J 251 Me 28
Toyooka O J 251 Md 28
Toyota O J 251 Me 28
Toyotomi O J 250 Mg 23
Tozeur O TN 296 Gl 29
Tqvarch'eli O GE 202 Hn 24
Trà Bông O VN 263 Le 38
Trabzon O TR 195 Hm 25
Tracadie-Sheila O CDN 61 Eb 22
Tracy O USA 56 Da 23
Tracy O USA 64 Cb 27
Traer O USA 70 Db 24
Tragacete O E 184 Gf 25
Traiguén O RCH 147 Dm 65
Trail O CDN 50 Cd 21
Traine ~ AUS 361 Lp 54
Traipu O BR 124 Fb 50
Trairão ~ BR 121 Ej 49
Trairi O BR 124 Fa 47
Trakai O LT 171 He 18
Trakan Phut Phon O THA 263 Lc 38
Trakoščan ★ HR 174 Gp 22
Tralee O IRL 163 Ga 19
Tramandai O BR 146 Ej 61
Trà My O VN 263 Le 38
Tranås O S 170 Gp 17
Trang O THA 270 Kp 42
Trắng Bàng O VN 263 Ld 40
Trangie O AUS 379 Mk 62
Tranoroa O RM 353 Ja 58
Trānsāh O IR 209 Jb 27
Trænstaven ♁ N 158 Gm 12
Transua O CI 317 Ge 42
Transylvanian Alps ⛰ RO 194 Hd 23
Trà Ôn O VN 263 Lc 41
Trápani O I 185 Gn 26
Traralgon O AUS 379 Mk 65
Trârza ⌒ RIM 304 Fn 37
Trásos Montes ⌒ P 184 Gc 25
Trat O THA 263 Lb 39
Travaillant Lake ~ CDN 47 Bl 11
Travellers Lake ~ AUS 378 Mg 62
Travellers Village O AUS 369 Ma 61
Travemünde O D 170 Gm 18
Traverse City O USA 57 Df 23
Travesía del Tunuyán ⌒ RA 137 Ea 62
Travesía Puntara ⌒ RA 137 Ea 63
Travessia da Onça ~ BR 121 Eh 48
Trà Vinh O VN 263 Ld 41
Travis O USA 81 Cp 30
Trawas O RI 278 Lb 47
Trayning O AUS 368 Lj 61
Treasure Island O USA 86 Dg 32
Treasury Islands ♁ SOL 290 Mp 49
Třebíč O CZ 174 Gp 21
Trebinje O BIH 194 Hb 24
Trebisacce O I 194 Ha 26
Trebišov O SK 174 Hc 21
Treesbank O CDN 56 Cn 21
Trego O USA 56 Dc 23
Treinta y Tres O ROU 146 Eg 62
Trelew O RA 147 Eb 67
Trelleborg O S 170 Gn 18
Tremonton O USA 65 Cf 25
Trena O ETH 313 Hn 40
Trenary O USA 57 De 22
Trenche ~ CDN 60 Dm 21
Trenčín O SK 174 Hb 21
Trenggalek O RI 279 Lf 49
Trenque Lauquen O RA 137 Ec 63
Trent O USA 70 Cm 29
Trentino-Alto Ádige ◉ I 174 Gm 22
Trento O I 174 Gm 23
Trento O RP 267 Lp 41
Trenton O CDN 60 Dk 23
Trenton O CDN 61 Ec 23
Trenton O USA 70 Cm 25
Trenton O USA 70 Db 25
Trenton O USA 74 Dl 25
Trepassey O CDN 61 Eh 22
Trepassey Bay ~ CDN 61 Eh 22
Tres Arboles O ROU 146 Ef 62
Tres Arroyos O RA 146 Ed 65
Tres Bicos O BR 140 Ej 58
Tres Bocas O YV 107 Dm 41
Tres Bocas O RA 146 Ee 62
Tres Carros O RA 152 Dp 70
Três Casas O BR 117 Ec 49
Tres Cerros △ RA 147 Dn 67
Três Corações O BR 141 Em 56
Três de Maio O BR 140 Eg 59
Tres Esquinas O CO 116 Dl 45
Tres Isletas O RA 136 Ed 59
Três Lagoas O BR 140 Ej 56
Tres Lagos O RA 152 Dn 70
Três Marias O BR 133 Em 55
Tres Mojones O RA 136 Ed 59
Tres Morros O RA 136 Eb 57
Tres Palmas O CO 106 Dk 41
Três Palmeiras O BR 140 Eh 59
Três Passos O BR 140 Eg 59
Tres Picos O MEX 93 Db 38
Tres Piedras O USA 65 Cj 27
Três Pontas O BR 141 Em 56
Tres Puntas ⌓ GCA 93 Dd 38
Três Ranchos O BR 133 El 55
Três Rios O BR 141 En 57
Tres Unidos O PE 116 Dl 48
Tres Valles O MEX 93 Cp 36
Três Vendas O BR 146 Eg 61
Treuer Range ⛰ AUS 361 Mb 57
Trevelín O RA 147 Dn 67
Treviso O BR 140 Ek 60
Treviso O I 185 Gm 23
Triang O MAL 270 Lb 44
Triangle O CDN 47 Cc 17
Triangle O ZW 352 Hh 56
Tribugá O CO 106 Dk 43
Tribune O USA 70 Cm 26
Trichur O IND 239 Kc 40
Tri City O USA 50 Ca 24
Trida O AUS 379 Mj 62
Trier O D 163 Gk 21
Trieste O I 185 Gn 23
Triglav △ SLO 174 Gn 22
Triglavski Narodni Park ♀ SLO 174 Gn 22
Tríkala O GR 194 Hc 26
Trikkandiyur O IND 239 Kb 40
Trillbar O AUS 368 Lj 58
Trincheras O MEX 80 Cg 30
Trincomalee O CL 239 Ke 41
Trindade ♁ BR 30 Ha 12
Trindade O BR 124 Ep 49
Trindade O BR 133 Ek 54
Tring O PNG 287 Mh 47
Trinidad O USA 65 Ck 27
Trinidad O C 100 Dh 35
Trinidad ♁ TT 104 Ed 40
Trinidad O CO 107 Dn 43
Trinidad O BOL 129 Eb 53
Trinidad O PY 140 Ef 59
Trinidad O ROU 146 Ef 62
Trinidad and Tobago □ TT 104 Ed 40
Trinity ~ USA 64 Ca 25
Trinity O USA 81 Da 30
Trinity Bay ~ CDN 61 Eh 22
Trinity Island ♁ USA 10 Ba 4
Trinity Islands ♁ USA 46 An 17
Trinity Range ⛰ USA 64 Cc 26
Trinkat Island ♁ IND 262 Kl 41
Trinkitāt O SUD 313 Hl 36
Tripitapa ~ NIC 97 Df 39
Trípoli O GR 194 Hd 27
Tripoli O RL 208 Hk 28
Tripoli ▣ LAR 297 Gn 29
Tripolitania ⌒ LAR 297 Gm 30
Tripp O USA 56 Cp 24
Tripura ◉ IND 235 Kk 34
Tristan da Cunha ♁ UK 30 Ja 13
Triste Gulf ~ YV 107 Ea 40
Trisuli ~ NEP 235 Kg 31
Trisuli Bazar O NEP 235 Kg 32
Triunfo O BR 146 Ej 60
Triunvirato O RA 137 Ed 63
Trivalea-Moșteni O RO 175 He 23
Trivandrum O IND 239 Kb 41
Trnava O SK 174 Ha 21
Trobriand Islands ♁ PNG 287 Mm 50
Trocoman ~ RA 137 Dn 64
Trofors O N 158 Gn 13
Trogir O HR 194 Ha 24
Troick O RUS 154 Sa 8
Troicko-Pečorsk O RUS 154 Rc 6
Trois-Pistoles O CDN 60 Dp 21
Trois Rivières O RH 101 Dm 36
Trois-Rivières Three Rivers O CDN 60 Dm 22
Trojan O BG 194 He 24
Trollhättan O S 170 Gn 16
Trombetas ~ BR 113 Ef 45
Trombetas ~ BR 120 Ef 46
Tromelin ♁ F 31 Mb 11
Trompsburg O ZA 349 He 61
Tromsø O N 158 Hb 11
Trona O USA 64 Cd 28
Troncoso O MEX 92 Cl 34
Trondheim O N 158 Gm 14
Trondheimsfjorden ~ N 158 Gl 14
Tropas ~ BR 120 Ef 49
Trostjanec' O UA 175 Hk 20
Trotters O USA 51 Cl 22
Trotus ~ RO 175 Hf 22
Troughton Island ♁ AUS 361 Lp 52
Troup O USA 70 Da 29
Trout O CDN 61 Ee 21
Troutbeck O ZW 344 Hj 55
Trout Creek O USA 50 Ce 22
Trout Creek O CDN 60 Dj 23
Trout Lake ~ CDN 47 Ca 15
Trout Lake O USA 50 Cb 23
Trout Lake ~ CDN 56 Db 20
Trout Lake O USA 57 Df 22
Trout Peak △ USA 51 Ch 23
Troy O USA 50 Cd 21
Troy O USA 60 Dm 24
Troy O USA 70 Da 26
Troy O USA 71 Dc 26
Troy O USA 71 Df 25
Troy O USA 86 Df 30
Troya ~ RA 136 Ea 59
Troya ~ RA 137 Dp 60
Troyes O F 163 Gj 21
Troy Peak △ USA 64 Ce 26
Trpanj O HR 194 Ha 24
Truando ~ CO 106 Dk 42
Truant Island ♁ AUS 364 Me 51
Truant Island ♁ AUS 365 Me 51
Trubčevsk O RUS 171 Hj 19
Truchas Peek △ USA 65 Ck 27
Truckee O USA 64 Cb 26
Truck Islands ♁ FSM 27 Sb 9
Trujillo O USA 65 Ck 28
Trujillo O HN 96 De 38
Trujillo O PE 116 Dj 50
Trujillo O E 184 Gd 26
Trumon O RI 270 Kn 44
Trung Khann O VN 255 Ld 34
Trunkey O AUS 379 Ml 62
Truro O CDN 61 Ec 23
Truro O GB 163 Gd 20
Trusan O MAL 274 Lh 43
Trutch O CDN 47 Ca 17
Truth or Consequences O USA 65 Cj 29
Trutnov O CZ 174 Gp 20
Tryon O USA 70 Cm 25
Tryon Island ♁ AUS 375 Mm 57
Tryphena O NZ 383 Nk 64
Trzebnica O PL 174 Ha 20
Tsadumu O IND 238 Kd 39
Tsagaan Chulunta O VRC 231 Kl 26
Tsamai O WAN 308 Gj 39
Tsama I O RCB 332 Gp 46
Tsandi O NAM 340 Gp 54
Tsangano O MOC 344 Hk 53
Tsaramandroso O RM 345 Jb 54
Tsaratanana O RM 345 Jb 54
Tsaraxaibis O NAM 348 Hb 59
Tsarisberge ⛰ NAM 348 Ha 58
Tsau O RB 349 Hd 56
Tsauchab ~ NAM 348 Gp 58
Tsavo O EAK 337 Hm 47
Tsavo ~ EAK 337 Hm 47
Tsavo East ♀ EAK 337 Hm 47
Tsavo West ♀ EAK 337 Hm 47
Tsawah O LAR 297 Gm 33
Tseikuru O EAK 337 Hm 46
Tsembo O RCB 332 Gn 47
Tseminyu O IND 254 Km 33
Tsentral'no-Tungusskoye Plato ⛰ RUS 204 Ub 7
Tsentral'noyakutskaya Ravnina ⌒ RUS 204 Vc 6
Tses O NAM 348 Hb 58
Tsévié O RT 317 Gg 42
Tshabong O RB 349 Hd 59
Tshako O RDC 341 Hd 50
Tshala O RDC 341 Hd 50
Tshane O RB 349 Hc 58
Tshaneni O SD 352 Hh 59
Tshela O RDC 332 Gn 48
Tshenga-Oshwe O RDC 333 Hd 47
Tshesebe O RB 349 Hf 56
Tshibala O RDC 333 Hc 49
Tshibamba O RDC 341 Hd 50
Tshibeke O RDC 336 Hg 47
Tshibuka O RDC 333 Hc 49
Tshibumbula O RDC 333 Hc 48
Tshibwika O RDC 341 Hc 50
Tshidilamolomo O ZA 349 He 58
Tshie O RDC 333 Hd 50
Tshikapa O RDC 333 Hc 49
Tshikula O RDC 333 Hc 49
Tshilenge O RDC 333 Hd 49
Tshileo O RDC 333 Hd 49
Tshimbalanga O RDC 341 Hd 50
Tshimbane O RDC 333 Hb 47
Tshimboko O RDC 333 He 49
Tshimbulu O RDC 333 Hd 49
Tshimbungu O RDC 341 Hd 50
Tshindji O RDC 341 Hd 50
Tshipise O ZA 352 Hf 57
Tshisenda O RDC 341 Hf 52
Tshisenge O RDC 333 Hc 49
Tshisonge O RDC 333 Hd 50
Tshitadi O RDC 333 Hc 49
Tshitanzu O RDC 333 Hd 50
Tshofa O RDC 333 He 48
Tshokwane O ZA 352 Hh 58
Tsholotsho O ZW 341 Hf 55
Tshopo O RDC 324 He 45
Tshopo ~ RDC 324 Hf 45
Tshuapa ~ RDC 333 Hc 46
Tshuapa ~ RDC 333 He 47
Tshwane Pretoria ▣ ZA 349 Hf 58
Tsiafaiavona △ RM 345 Jb 55
Tsiaki O RCB 332 Gn 47
Tsimafana O RM 345 Ja 55
Tsimazava O RM 353 Ja 56
Tsimlyansk Reservoir ~ RUS 181 Hp 22
Tsineng O ZA 349 Hd 59
Tsingtao O VRC 246 Ll 27
Tsingy de Bamaraha Strict. N.R. ♀ RM 345 Ja 55
Tsinjomorona ~ RM 345 Jc 53
Tsintsabis O NAM 340 Ha 55
Tsiombe O RM 353 Ja 58
Tsiribihina ~ RM 345 Ja 55
Tsiroanomandidy O RM 345 Ja 55
Tsitondroina O RM 353 Ja 56
Tsitsib O NAM 340 Hb 55
Tsitsikamma ♀ ZA 358 He 63
Tsitsutl Peak △ CDN 50 Bp 19
Tsivory O RM 353 Jb 58
Ts'khinvali O GE 202 Hp 24
Tsoe O RB 349 He 56
Tsogstsalu O IND 230 Kd 28
Tsolo O ZA 349 Hg 61
Tsomo ~ ZA 349 Hf 61
Tsomo O ZA 358 Hf 62
Tso Morari ~ IND 230 Kd 29
Tsondab ~ NAM 348 Gp 58
Tsootsha O RB 348 Hc 57
Tsu O J 251 Me 28
Tsubata O J 251 Me 27
Tsuchiura O J 251 Mg 27
Tsugaru-Kaikyō ~ J 250 Mf 25
Tsuli O ZW 341 Hf 55
Tsumbiri O RDC 332 Ha 47
Tsumeb O NAM 340 Ha 55
Tsumis Park O NAM 348 Ha 57
Tsumkwe O NAM 340 Hc 55
Tsuruga O J 251 Md 28
Tsuruoka O J 251 Mf 26
Tsushima ♁ J 247 Ma 28
Tsuyama O J 251 Mc 28
Tswaane O RB 348 Hc 57
t-Taḥtā O RL 208 Hk 29
Tuakau O NZ 383 Nk 64
Tual O RI 283 Mc 48
Tuam O IRL 163 Gb 19
Tuambli O CI 316 Gb 42
Tuam Island ♁ PNG 287 Ml 48
Tuamotu Islands ♁ F 35 Bb 11
Tuần Giáo O VN 255 Lb 35
Tuanxi O VRC 255 Ld 32
Tuapse O RUS 202 Hm 23
Tuaran O MAL 274 Lj 42
Tuare O RI 282 Ll 46
Tua River ~ PNG 287 Mj 49
Tuatapere O NZ 382 Nf 69
Tuba ~ RUS 204 Tc 8
Tuba City O USA 64 Cf 27
Tuban O RI 279 Lg 49
Tubarão O BR 141 Ek 60
Tūbās O JOR 208 Hk 29
Tubau O MAL 274 Lg 44
Tubbataha Reef Marine Park ★ RP 267 Lk 41
Tubbataha Reefs ♁ RP 267 Lk 41
Tubek ⌒ KZ 202 Jd 23
Tubeya O RDC 333 Hd 49
Tubili Point ⌓ RP 267 Ll 39
Tübingen O D 174 Gl 21
Tub-Karagan ⌓ KZ 202 Jd 23
Tubmonburg O LB 316 Ga 42
Tubruq O LAR 300 He 29
Tubuali ♁ F 35 Bb 12
Tuburan O RP 267 Lm 40
Tucacas O YV 107 Dp 40
Tucano O BR 125 Fa 51
Tucavaca ~ BR 132 Ee 55
Tucheng O VRC 255 Lc 32
Tuchola O PL 170 Ha 19
Tuckanarra O AUS 368 Lk 59
Tucker Bay ~ 38 Tb 17
Tucson O USA 65 Cg 29
Tucuco O YV 107 Dm 41
Tucumã O BR 121 Ej 49
Tucumcari O USA 65 Ck 28
Tucuña O CO 117 Dn 45
Tucupido O YV 112 Eb 41
Tucupita O YV 112 Ed 41
Tucurui O BR 121 Ej 47
Tucu-Tucu O RA 152 Dn 70
Tudela O RP 267 Lm 41
Tudu O EST 171 Hf 16
Tudun Wada O WAN 320 Gl 40

Tomaszów Lubelski - Tudun Wada 477

□Country ▣Capital city ⊙Administrative unit OPlace ⌂Island ⛰Mountain range △Mountain ⌒Cape ≈Ocean, Sea ~Lake, River ▽Undersea topography ⊿Glacier ♀National park •••Reservation ★Point of major interest ▭Landscape

Tuena O AUS 379 Ml 63
Tueré ~ BR 121 Ej 48
Tuetue O RI 282 Lm 48
Tufanbeyli O TR 195 Hl 26
Tufi O PNG 287 Ml 50
Tug O VRC 243 Le 26
Tugela ~ ZA 352 Hh 60
Tuguegarao O RP 267 Ll 37
Tugur O RUS 205 Xa 8
Tugyl O MYA 262 Km 37
Tui O E 184 Gb 24
Tuichi ~ BOL 128 Dp 53
Tuilibigeal O AUS 379 Mk 62
Tuineje O E 292 Fp 31
Tuisen O IND 254 Kl 34
Tuitán O MEX 81 Ck 33
Tujmazy O RUS 154 Rb 8
Tuki Point O SOL 290 Na 49
Tukola Tolha O VRC 242 Km 28
Tükrah O LAR 300 Hc 29
Tuktoyaktuk O CDN 6 Ca 3
Tuktoyaktuk O CDN 47 Bj 11
Tukums O LV 171 Hd 17
Tukuyu O EAT 337 Hj 50
Tula O MEX 81 Cn 34
Tula O RUS 171 Hl 18
Tula O EAK 337 Hm 46
Tula ~ EAK 337 Hm 46
Tulancingo O MEX 92 Cn 36
Tulare Lake Bed O USA 64 Cc 27
Tulare Lake Bed ~ USA 64 Cc 28
Tularosa O USA 65 Cj 29
Tulate O GCA 93 Dc 38
Tula Yiri O WAN 320 Gm 41
Tulbagh O ZA 358 Hb 62
Tulcan O EC 116 Dk 45
Tulcea O RO 175 Hg 23
Tulčin O UA 175 Hg 21
Tulé O YV 107 Dm 40
Tuléar O RM 353 Hp 57
Tulehu O RI 283 Ma 47
Tulemalu Lake ~ CDN 42 Fb 6
Tule River Indian Reservation ••• USA 64 Cc 27
Tulga O AUS 374 Mh 57
Tulia O USA 70 Cm 28
Tuli Block ▭ RB 349 Hf 57
Tuljāpur O IND 238 Kc 37
Tullahoma O USA 71 De 28
Tullamore O AUS 379 Mk 62
Tulle O F 184 Gg 23
Tullos O USA 86 Db 30
Tullus O SUD 312 He 40
Tully O AUS 365 Mj 54
Tully Range ⛰ AUS 374 Mh 57
Tuloma ~ RUS 159 Hj 11
Tulsa O USA 70 Cp 27
Tulsipur O NEP 234 Kf 31
Tulsipur O IND 234 Kf 32
Tulu O PNG 287 Mk 46
Tuluá O CO 106 Dk 43
Tulu Āmara Terera △ ETH 325 Hl 41
Tuluksak O USA 46 Aj 15
Tūlūl al-Ašaqif ⛰ JOR 208 Hl 29
Tulum O MEX 93 De 35
Tulumayo ~ PE 128 Dl 51
Tulume O RDC 333 Hd 49
Tulun O RUS 204 Ub 8
Tulungagung O RI 279 Lf 50
Tulu Wefel △ ETH 325 Hk 41
Tuma ~ NIC 97 Df 39
Tuma O RUS 181 Hn 18
Tumacacori National Monument ★ USA 80 Cg 30
Tumaco O CO 106 Dj 45
Tumair O KSA 215 Ja 33
Tuma Island ⌂ PNG 287 Mm 50
Tumannyj O RUS 159 Hk 11
Tumany O RUS 23 Sb 3
Tumba O S 170 Ha 16
Tumba O RDC 333 Hd 47
Tumba O RDC 333 Hd 49
Tumbanglahung O RI 279 Lg 46
Tumbangsamba O RI 279 Lg 46
Tumbarumba O AUS 379 Mk 63
Tumbengu ~ RDC 333 Hd 46
Tumbes O PE 116 Dh 47
Tumbler Ridge O CDN 47 Ca 17
Tumbwe O RDC 341 Hf 51
Tumby Bay O AUS 378 Me 63
Tumd Youyi O VRC 243 Lf 25
Tumeremo O YV 112 Ed 42
Tumgaon O IND 234 Kf 35
Tumkūr O IND 238 Kc 39
Tumlingtan O NEP 235 Kh 32
Tumpat O MAL 270 Lb 42
Tumsar O IND 234 Kd 35
Tumu O GH 317 Ge 40
Tumuc-Humac-Mountains ⛰ BR 113 Eg 44
Tumupasa O BOL 128 Dp 53
Tumureng O GUY 112 Ed 42
Tumut O AUS 379 Ml 63
Tuna O GH 317 Ge 41
Tunaida O ET 301 Hg 33
Tunapuna O TT 104 Ed 40
Tunas de Zaza O C 100 Dj 35
Tunchang O VRC 255 Le 36
Tunchang O VRC 255 Lf 36
Tuncurry O AUS 379 Mn 62
Tun-de O MYA 262 Km 37
Tundulu O Z 336 Hg 50
Tunduma O EAT 336 Hj 50
Tunduru O EAT 344 Hl 51
Tundza ~ BG 194 Hf 24
Tunga O WAN 320 Gl 41
Tungabhadra ~ IND 238 Kb 39
Tungabhadra ~ IND 238 Kc 38
Tungabhadra Reservoir ~ IND 238 Kb 38
Tungaru O SUD 312 Hh 40
Tungawan O RP 275 Lm 42
Tungaztarim O VRC 231 Kf 27
Tungho O RC 259 Ll 34
Tungi O BD 235 Kk 34
Tungkil Island ⌂ RP 275 Ll 43
Tungo O WAN 320 Gm 41
Tungshih O RC 259 Ll 33
Tungsten O CDN 47 Bl 15
Tunguru O EAT 337 Hj 47
Tunguskaja vozvyšennost ⛰ RUS 159 Hh 13
Tunguwatu O RI 283 Md 48
Tuni O IND 238 Kf 37
Tunica O USA 71 Dc 28
Tunis ▣ TN 296 Gm 27
Tunisia □ TN 296 Gl 29
Tunja O CO 107 Dm 43
Tunkal ~ RI 278 Lb 46
Tunnel Creek ♀ AUS 361 Ln 54
Tunnsjøen ~ N 158 Gn 13
Tunqiu O VRC 255 Le 33
Tuntum O BR 121 Em 48
Tuntutuliak O USA 46 Aj 15
Tunuyan O RA 137 Dp 62
Tunuyán ~ RA 137 Dp 62
Tunuyán ~ RA 137 Ea 62
Tunuyán Viejo ~ RA 137 Ea 62
Tuoa CRiver ~ PNG 287 Mj 49
Tuo Jiang ~ VRC 255 Lc 31
Tuoji Dao ⌂ VRC 246 Ll 26
Tuŏl Kruŏs O K 263 Lb 39
Tu'o'ng Du'o'ng O VN 255 Lc 36
Tuotuo He ~ VRC 231 Kk 28
Tuotuo Heyan O VRC 231 Kl 28
Tupã O BR 140 Ej 56
Tupaciguara O BR 133 Ek 55
Tupambaé O ROU 146 Eg 62
Tupana ~ BR 120 Ed 48
Tupanaci O BR 124 Fa 50
Tupanantinga O BR 124 Fb 50
Tupanciretã O BR 146 Eg 60
Tuparro ~ CO 107 Dp 43
Tupelo O USA 71 Dd 28
Tupelo N.B. ★ USA 71 Dd 28
Tupilco O MEX 93 Db 36
Tupim ~ BR 125 Ep 52
Tupiratins O BR 121 Ek 50
Tupitina O MEX 92 Cl 36
Tupiza O BOL 136 Eb 56
Tupiza ~ BOL 136 Eb 56
Tupper Lake O USA 60 Dl 23
Tupran O IND 238 Kd 37
Tupungato O RA 137 Dp 62
Tupure O YV 107 Dn 40
Túquerres O CO 116 Dk 45
Tuqu Gang ~ VRC 255 Le 36
Tura O RUS 22 Qa 3
Tura ~ PA 104 Dk 42
Tura ~ RUS 154 Sa 7
Tura O RUS 204 Uc 6
Tura O VRC 231 Kh 27
Tura O IND 235 Kk 33
Turaba O KSA 214 Hp 31
Turaba O KSA 218 Hn 35
Turaif O KSA 214 Hm 30
Turama River ~ PNG 286 Mh 49
Turangi O NZ 383 Nk 65
Turan Lowland ▭ KZ/UZB/TM 155 Sa 10
Turbaco O CO 106 Dl 40
Turbat O PK 226 Jk 33
Turbio ~ MEX 92 Cl 35
Turbio ~ RCH 136 Dp 59
Turbio ~ RCH 137 Dn 60
Turbio ~ RA 152 Dn 71
Turbo O CO 106 Dk 41
Turco O BOL 129 Dp 55
Turco ~ BOL 129 Dp 55
Turda O RO 175 Hd 22
Tŭrda O SUD 312 Hg 40
Turee Creek ~ AUS 360 Lj 57
Turee Creek O AUS 360 Lk 57
Turéia ⌂ F 14 Ca 12
Turek O PL 170 Hb 19
Turen O RI 279 Lg 50
Turgeon ~ CDN 60 Dj 21
Turgutlu O TR 195 Hf 26
Turhal O TR 195 Hl 25
Turi ~ BR 117 Ea 46
Tūri O EST 171 He 16
Turia ~ E 184 Gf 25
Turiaçu O BR 121 Em 46
Turiaçu ~ BR 121 Em 47
Turiamo O YV 107 Ea 40
Turiani O EAT 337 Hl 49
Túriba ⌂ YV 107 Ea 42
Turin O CDN 51 Cf 21
Turin O I 185 Gk 23
Turka O UA 175 Hd 21
Turkana ⛰ EAK 325 Hk 44
Türkeminskij zaliv ~ TM 222 Je 26
Turkey ~ USA 56 Dc 24
Turkey O USA 70 Cm 28
Turkey □ TR 195 Hh 26
Turkey Creek Warmun O AUS 364 Ma 54
Turkey Mountain △ AUS 375 Mm 59
Türkmenabat O TM 223 Jk 26
Türkmenbashi O TM 222 Je 25
Turkmenistan □ TM 222 Jf 26
Türkoğlu O TR 195 Hl 27
Turks Island Passage ≈ 101 Dn 35
Turks Islands ⌂ GB 101 Dn 35
Turku Åbo O FIN 159 Hc 15
Turkwel ~ EAK 325 Hk 44
Turkwel Gorge Reservation ~ EAK 325 Hk 45
Turlock O USA 64 Cb 27
Turmalina O BR 125 En 54
Turmero O YV 107 Ea 40
Turneffe Island ⌂ BH 96 De 37
Turner O USA 51 Ch 21
Turner ~ AUS 360 Lk 56
Turners Peninsula ⌂ WAL 316 Fp 42
Turnu Măgurele O RO 194 He 24
Turpan O VRC 204 Tc 10
Turpan Pendi ▭ VRC 204 Tc 10
Turpin O USA 70 Ck 27
Turrialba O CR 97 Dg 41
Turro O BR 140 Ek 60
Tursăq O IRQ 209 Ja 29
Tursunzade O TJ 223 Jm 26
Türtkŭl O UZB 223 Jj 25
Turtleford O CDN 51 Ch 19
Turtle Island ⌂ WAL 316 Fp 42
Turtle Islands ⌂ RP 274 Lk 42
Turtle Lake ~ CDN 51 Ch 19
Turtle Lake O USA 56 Db 23
Turtle Mountain ••• USA 56 Cn 21
Turuchipa ~ BOL 129 Eb 55
Turuepano ♀ YV 112 Ec 40
Turugart Shankou △ VRC 230 Kb 25
Turuhansk O RUS 204 Tc 5
Turuna ~ BR 113 Ef 45
Turva ★ TR 194 Hf 26
Turvânia O BR 133 Ej 54
Turvo ~ BR 133 Ej 54
Turvo ~ BR 140 Ek 56
Turwi ~ ZW 352 Hh 56
Tuscaloosa O USA 71 De 29
Tuscan Archipelago ⌂ I 185 Gl 24
Tuscánia O I 185 Gm 24
Tuscarora O USA 64 Cd 25
Tuscola O USA 71 Cn 29
Tuscola O USA 71 Dd 26
Tuscumbia O USA 71 Dd 28
Tusenøyane ⌂ N 158 Hc 7
Tuskegee O USA 71 De 29
Tuskegee Institute N.H.S. ★ USA 86 Df 29
Tutaev O RUS 171 Hm 17
Tutak O TR 202 Hp 26
Tutera O E 184 Gf 24
Tuticorin O IND 239 Kd 41
Tutóia O BR 124 En 47
Tutong O BRU 274 Lh 43
Tutrakan O BG 175 Hf 23
Tuttle O USA 56 Cn 22
Tuttle Creek Lake ~ USA 70 Cp 26
Tutuaca O MEX 80 Cj 31
Tutuala O TP 283 Lp 50
Tutuba ⌂ VU 386 Nf 53
Tutuila Island ⌂ USA 390 Ae 53
Tutula ⌂ USA 35 Aa 11
Tutume O RB 349 Hf 56
Tuul gol ~ MNG 204 Va 9
Tuusniemi O FIN 159 Hf 14
Tuvalu □ TUV 35 Tb 10
Tūwal O KSA 214 Hm 34
Tuxcueca O MEX 92 Cl 35
Tuxford O CDN 51 Ck 20
Tuxpan O MEX 81 Cp 34
Tuxpan O MEX 92 Ck 35
Tuxpan O MEX 92 Cl 36
Tuxpan ~ MEX 92 Cn 35
Tuxtepec O MEX 93 Cp 36
Tuxtla Gutiérrez O MEX 93 Db 37
Tuyên Quang O VN 255 Lc 35
Tuy Hòa O VN 263 Le 39
Tuy Phong O VN 263 Le 40
Tuz Gölü ~ TR 195 Hj 26
Ṭūz Ḫurmātū O IRQ 209 Ja 28
Tuzigoot National Monument ★ USA 65 Cf 28
Tuzla O BIH 174 Hb 23
Tuzla Çayı ~ TR 202 Hn 26
Tuzlaca O TR 202 Hp 26
Tuzohn O LB 316 Gb 42
Tveitsund O N 170 Gk 16
Tver' O RUS 171 Hl 17
Tvøroyri O DK 162 Gc15
TV Tower ★ USA 56 Cp 22
Tweed ~ GB 162 Ge 18
Tweed Heads O AUS 375 Mn 60
Tweefontein O ZA 358 Hb 62
Tweeling O ZA 349 Hg 59
Twee Rivier O NAM 348 Hb 58
Tweespruit O ZA 349 Hf 60
Twentynine Palms O USA 64 Cd 28
Twee Town O LB 316 Gb 43
Tweya O RDC 333 Hb 46
Twilight Cove ~ AUS 369 Ln 62
Twillingate O CDN 61 Eg 21
Twin Bridges O USA 51 Cf 23
Twin Buttes Reservation ~ USA 81 Cm 30
Twin Falls O USA 64 Ce 24
Twingi O Z 341 Hg 51
Twin Hill O USA 46 Aj 15
Twin Peaks △ USA 50 Ce 23
Twin Peaks △ USA 368 Lh 59
Twinppe O MYA 254 Kn 34
Twizel O NZ 382 Nh 68
Two Fold Bay ~ AUS 379 Mm 64
Two Harbors O USA 56 Dc 22
Two Hills O CDN 51 Cg 19
Two Rivers O USA 57 De 23
Two Rocks O AUS 368 Lh 61
Tychy O PL 174 Hb 20
Tyélé O RMM 304 Gc 39
Tygh Valley O USA 50 Cb 23
Tyler O USA 70 Da 29
Tylertown O USA 86 Dc 30
Tylihul's'kyj lyman ~ UA 175 Hh 22
Tymovskoe O RUS 205 Xb 8
Tynda O RUS 204 Wa 7
Tyndall O USA 56 Cp 24
Tyner O USA 71 Df 27
Tynset O N 158 Gm 14
Tyre ★ RL 208 Hk 29
Tyrifi ~ N 158 Gl 15
Tyrma O RUS 205 Wc 8
Tyrnyvanz O RUS 202 Hp 24
Tyrone O USA 65 Ch 29
Tyrone O USA 74 Dj 25
Tyrrhenisches Meer ≈ 185 Gm 26
Tysnesøy ⌂ N 158 Gj 15
Tyumen O RUS 154 Sb 7
Tzaneen O ZA 352 Hh 57
Tzasar O IND 230 Kc 29
Tzinteel O MEX 93 Db 37
Tziscao O MEX 93 Dc 37
Tzonconejo ~ MEX 93 Dc 37
Tzucacab O MEX 93 Dd 35

U

U. Genteng ⌒ RI 278 Ld 49
U. Kakat ⌒ RI 270 Kn 44
U. Pamanukan ⌒ RI 278 Ld 49
U. Pidie ⌒ RI 270 Km 43
U. Tamiang ⌒ RI 270 Kp 43
Uaco Cungo O ANG 340 Gp 51
Ua Huka ⌂ F 14 Ca 10
Uamba O ANG 332 Ha 49
Uanda O AUS 375 Mj 56
Uangando ~ ANG 340 Ha 54
Uape O MOC 344 Hl 54
Ua Pou ⌂ F 35 Bb 10
Uapumba Island ⌂ PNG 286 Mh 50
Uarges △ EAK 325 Hl 45
Uarini ~ BR 117 Ea 48
Uarini O BR 117 Eb 47
Uaroo O AUS 360 Lh 57
Uatuma ~ BR 120 Ee 47
Uaupés ~ BR 117 Ea 45
Uauú O BR 124 Fa 50
Uavala ~ ANG 340 Ha 54
Ub O SCG 174 Hc 23
Ubá O BR 141 En 56
Uba O WAN 321 Gn 40
Ubaí O BR 133 Em 54
Ubai O PNG 287 Mm 48
Ubaila O IRQ 209 Hm 29
Ubaila O IRQ 209 Hn 29
Ubaíra O BR 125 Fa 52
Ubaitaba O BR 125 Fa 53
Ubajara O BR 124 Ep 47
Ubajay O RA 146 Ee 61
Ubaldino Taques O BR 140 Ej 59
Ubangi ~ RDC 333 Ha 45
Ubangui ~ RDC 321 Hb 43
Ubangui ~ RDC 321 Hc 43
Ubaporanga O BR 141 En 55
Ubarc' ~ BY 175 Hg 20
Ubatã O BR 125 Fa 53
Ubate O CO 106 Dl 43
Ubatuba O BR 141 Em 57
Ubauro O PK 227 Jn 31
Ube O J 247 Mb 29
Úbeda O E 184 Ge 27
Uberaba O BR 133 Ek 55
Uberaba ~ BR 133 Ek 55
Uberlândia O BR 112 Ee 45
Uberlândia O BR 133 Ek 55
Ubiaja O WAN 320 Gk 42
Ubierna O E 184 Ge 24
Ubina O BOL 136 Ea 56
Ubirr O AUS 364 Mc 52
Ubol Rat Reservoir ~ THA 263 Lb 37
Ubon Ratchathani O THA 263 Lc 38
Ubovka O RUS 250 Md 23
Ubud O RI 279 Lh 50
Ubundu O RDC 333 He 46
Uč-Adir O TM 223 Jk 26
Ucapinima O CO 117 Dp 45
Ucar O AZ 202 Jb 25
Ucayali ~ PE 116 Dl 49
Ucayali ~ PE 116 Dl 50
Ucayali ~ PE 116 Dm 48
Uch O PK 227 Jp 31
Ucharonidge O AUS 364 Md 54
Uchiurawan ~ J 250 Mg 24
Uchiza O PE 116 Dk 50
Uchquduq O UZB 223 Jk 24
Uchta O RUS 154 Rb 6
Uchta O RUS 159 Hm 15
Uckurgan O UZB 223 Jp 25
Ucluelet O CDN 50 Bp 21
Ucross O USA 51 Cj 23
Učtagankum ▭ TM 222 Jg 25
Ucua O ANG 332 Gp 50
Učur ~ RUS 205 Wc 7
Uda ~ RUS 205 Wc 8
Udačnyj O RUS 204 Vb 5
Udagamandalam O IND 239 Kc 40
Udaia O IND 235 Kh 35
Udaipur O IND 227 Ka 33
Udaipur O IND 235 Kk 34
Udalguri O IND 235 Kk 32
Uda Walawe National Park ♀ CL 239 Ke 42
Uda Walawe Reservoir ~ CL 239 Ke 42
Udayd O SUD 313 Hk 38
Udbina O HR 174 Gp 23
Uddevalla O S 170 Gm 16
Uddjäure ~ S 158 Ha 13
Udegi O WAN 320 Gk 41
Udgir O IND 238 Kc 36
Udhampur O IND 230 Kb 29
Udi O WAN 320 Gk 42
Udila O RDC 333 Hd 47
Udine O I 185 Gn 23
Udispattu O CL 239 Ke 42
Udobnaja O RUS 202 Hn 23
Udomlja O RUS 171 Hk 17
Udon Thani O THA 263 Lb 37
Udskaya Guba ≈ RUS 205 Xa 8
Udubo O WAN 320 Gm 40
Udumalaippettai O IND 239 Kc 40
Udupi O IND 238 Kb 39
Udu Point ⌒ FJI 390 Aa 54
Udy ~ UA 175 Hk 20
Uebonti O RI 282 Ll 46
Ueca △ ETH 325 Hl 41
Ueda O J 251 Mf 27
Uekuli O RI 282 Ll 46
Uele ~ RDC 321 Hd 44
Uelzen O D 170 Gm 19
Uere ~ BR 117 Ea 48
Uere ~ RDC 324 He 44
Uere ~ RDC 324 Hf 43
Ufa ~ RUS 154 Rc 7
Ufa O RUS 154 Rc 8
Ufeyn O SP 328 Jc 40
Uftjuga ~ RUS 154 Ra 6
Ugab ~ NAM 340 Ha 55
Ugab ~ NAM 348 Gn 56
Ugăle O LV 170 Hc 17
Ugalla O EAT 336 Hh 48
Ugalla ~ EAT 336 Hh 48
Uganda □ EAU 336 Hh 46
Ugashik Bay ~ USA 46 Al 17
Ugashik Lake ~ USA 46 Al 17
Ugep O WAN 320 Gl 43
Ughelli O WAN 320 Gj 43
Ugie O ZA 349 Hg 61
Uglič O RUS 171 Hm 17
Ugo O WAN 320 Gk 42
Ugol'nye Kopi O RUS 205 Zc 6
Ugra O RUS 171 Hk 18
Ugra ~ RUS 171 Hk 18
Uherské Hradiště O CZ 174 Ha 21
Uhl O WAN 320 Gk 42
Uhlenhorst O NAM 348 Ha 57
Uholovo O RUS 181 Hn 19
Uhrichsville O USA 71 Dh 25
Uhunbab O UZB 230 Ka 25
Uib O NAM 340 Ha 55
Uig O GB 162 Gc 17
Uige O ANG 332 Gp 49
Uiha ⌂ TO 390 Ac 55
Uijŏngbu O ROK 247 Lp 27
Uiju O DVRK 246 Ln 25
Uintah and Ouray Indian Res. ••• USA 65 Cg 25
Uinta Mountain ⛰ USA 65 Cg 25
Uinta River ~ USA 65 Ch 25
Uiraúná O BR 124 Fa 49
Uis Mine O NAM 348 Gp 56
Uisŏng O ROK 247 Ma 27
Uitenhage O ZA 358 He 62
Uitkyk O ZA 348 Hb 60
Ujae ⌂ MH 27 Ta 9
Ujaly O TJ 223 Jn 26
Ujar O RUS 204 Ua 7
Ujelang ⌂ MH 27 Ta 9
Ujhāni O IND 234 Kd 32
Uji O J 251 Md 28
Uji-guntō ⌂ J 247 Ma 30
Ujiji O EAT 336 Hg 48
Ujjain O IND 234 Kb 34
Ujohbilang O RI 274 Lh 45
Ujungbatu O RI 270 La 45
Ujungberung O RI 278 Ld 49
Ujungkulon National Park ♀ RI 278 Lc 49
Ujung Pandang Makassar O RI 279 Lk 48
Ukara Island ⌂ EAT 337 Hj 46
Ukata O WAN 320 Gj 40
Ukehe O WAN 320 Gk 42
Ukerewe Island ⌂ EAT 336 Hj 47
Ukhrul O IND 254 Km 33
Ukiah O USA 50 Cc 23
Ukiah O USA 64 Ca 26
Uki Island ⌂ SOL 290 Nc 51
Uklāna O IND 230 Kb 31
Ukmergė O LT 171 He 18
Ukraine □ UA 175 Hg 21
Uku ⌂ J 247 Ma 29
Uku O ANG 340 Gp 51
Ukwatutu O RDC 324 Hf 43
Ula O TR 195 Hg 27
Ulaanbaatar ▣ MNG 204 Va 9
Ulaangom O MNG 204 Ua 8
Ulahan-Bom, Khrebet ⛰ RUS 205 Xa 6
Ulaim az-Zama △ KSA 214 Hn 31
Ulamona O PNG 287 Mm 48
Ulan O VRC 242 Kp 27
Ulang ~ AFG 223 Jk 29
Ulanhot O VRC 204 Wa 9
Ulan-Udè O RUS 204 Va 8
Ulan Ul Hu ~ VRC 231 Kk 28
Ulapara O BD 235 Kj 33
Ularbemban O RI 271 Lb 45
Ulawa Island ⌂ SOL 290 Nc 50
Ulaya O EAT 337 Hl 49
Ulcinj O MON 194 Hb 25
Ulco O ZA 349 He 60
Uleåborg O FIN 159 He 13
Ulefoss O N 170 Gl 16
Ulete O EAT 337 Hk 50
Uliastaj O MNG 204 Ub 9
Ulindi ~ RDC 336 Hf 46
Ulindi ~ RDC 336 Hg 47
Ulinskiy Khrebet ⛰ RUS 205 Xa 7
Ulithi ⌂ FSM 26 Rb 8
Ul'janovka O UA 175 Hg 21
Ul'janovo O RUS 170 Hd 18
Ul'janovo O UZB 223 Jn 25
Ul'janovsk O RUS 181 Jc 18
Uljin O ROK 247 Ma 27
Ülken Özen ~ KZ 181 Jc 21
Ulla ~ E 184 Gb 24
Ulladulla O AUS 379 Mm 63
Ullāl O IND 238 Kb 39
Ullapool O GB 162 Gd 17
Ullared O S 170 Gn 17
Ulla Ulla O BOL 128 Dp 53
Ullawarra O AUS 360 Lj 57
Ulloma O BOL 129 Dp 54
Ullsfjorden ~ N 158 Hb 11
Ullŭng △ ROK 247 Mb 27
Ullŭng Do ⌂ ROK 247 Mb 27
Ulm O USA 51 Cg 22
Ulm O USA 51 Ch 22
Ulm O D 174 Gl 21
Ulongwé O MOC 344 Hk 53
Ulricehamm O S 170 Gn 17
Ulsan O ROK 247 Ma 28
Ulsanman ▽ ROK 247 Ma 28
Ulster ⊙ IRL 162 Gb 18
Ultima O AUS 378 Mh 63
Ulu O RUS 205 Wb 6
Ulu O MYA 262 Kp 40
Ulu O SUD 313 Hj 40
Ulúa ~ HN 93 Dd 38
Ulubat Gökü ~ TR 195 Hg 25
Uluçinar O TR 195 Hk 27
Uludağ △ TR 195 Hg 25
Uludere O TR 202 Hp 27
Uluggat O VRC 230 Kb 26
Uluguru Mountains ⛰ EAT 337 Hl 49
Uluinggalau △ FJI 387 Nm 54
Ulundi O ZA 352 Hh 60
Ulungur He ~ VRC 204 Tc 9
Uluputur O PNG 287 Mn 47
Uluru Ayers Rock ♀ AUS 369 Mb 58
Uluru Ayers Rock △ AUS 369 Mb 58
Ulus O TR 195 Hj 25
Ulu Tiram O MAL 271 Lb 45
Ulva O AUS 375 Mj 56
Ulveah ⌂ VU 386 Ng 54
Ulverstone O AUS 378 Mk 66
Ulysses O USA 70 Cm 27
Ulz gol ~ MNG 204 Vb 9
Uma O RDC 324 He 45
Uma ~ RDC 324 Hf 45
Umaish O WAN 320 Gk 41
Umala O BOL 129 Dp 54
Umán O MEX 93 Dd 35
Uman' O UA 175 Hh 21
Umanak Fjord ≈ DK 43 Jb 4
Umarga O IND 238 Kc 37
Umari ~ BR 117 Eb 63
Umaria O IND 234 Ke 34
Umarkhed O IND 238 Kc 36
Umarkot O PK 227 Jn 33
Umarkote O IND 234 Kf 36
Umaroona Lake ~ AUS 374 Me 59
Umatilla Indian Reservation ••• USA 50 Cc 23
Umba O RUS 159 Hk 12
Umba ~ EAT 337 Hm 48
Umbai O MAL 270 Lb 44
Umbakumba O AUS 365 Me 52
Umbelasha ~ SUD 324 Hd 41
Umboi Island ⌂ PNG 287 Mk 48
Umbozero ~ RUS 159 Hk 12
Umbraj O IND 238 Ka 37
Umbria ⊙ I 185 Gn 24
Umbukul O PNG 287 Ml 47
Umburanas O BR 125 Ep 51
Ume ~ ZW 341 Hg 54
Umeå O S 159 Hc 14
Umeälven ~ S 158 Hb 13
Umenede O WAN 320 Gk 42
Umeru Rapids ~ SME 113 Ef 44
Uminat O USA 46 An 11
Umirim O BR 124 Fa 47
Umiujaq O CDN 43 Gc 7
Umium O PNG 287 Ml 48
Umlazi O ZA 352 Hh 60
Umm al Aranib O LAR 297 Gp 32
Umm al-Aštān O UAE 215 Je 34
Umm al-Birak O KSA 214 Hm 34
Umm al-Ğamāğim O KSA 215 Ja 32
Umm al-Qaiwain O UAE 226 Jf 33
Umm an-Nār O UAE 226 Jf 33
Umm Ashar aš-Šarqīyā O KSA 215 Ja 32
Umm as Samīm ~ OM 219 Jf 35
Umm Badr O SUD 312 Hg 38
Umm Barbit O SUD 312 Hj 40
Umm Bel O SUD 312 Hg 39
Umm Buru O SUD 312 Hd 38
Umm Dafag O SUD 313 Hd 40
Umm Dam O SUD 312 Hh 39
Umm Defeis O SUD 312 Hg 39
Umm Dubban O SUD 312 Hg 38
Umm Ḥarāz O SUD 312 Hd 39
Umm Ḥarāz O SUD 312 Hd 39
Umm Ḥawsh O SUD 312 Hf 39
Umm Hītan O SUD 312 Hh 40
Umm Inderaba O SUD 312 Hh 38
Umm Keiredim O SUD 312 Hg 39
Umm Lağğ O KSA 214 Hl 33
Umm Marahik O SUD 312 He 39
Umm Mirdi O SUD 312 Hj 36
Umm Qasr O IRQ 215 Jb 30
Umm Qozein O SUD 312 Hf 38
Umm Qulaita O YE 218 Jb 39
Umm Qurein O SUD 312 Hg 37
Umm Rumetia O SUD 312 Hh 37
Umm Ruwaba O SUD 312 Hh 39
Umm Sa'ad O LAR 300 He 30
Umm Sagung O SUD 324 Hg 41
Umm Sa'id O Q 215 Jd 33
Umm Sayyāla O SUD 312 Hh 38
Umm Shugeira O SUD 312 Hg 39
Umnak Island ⌂ USA 10 Ab 4
Umpqua ~ USA 50 Ca 24
Umpuhua O MOC 344 Hl 53
Umran O KSA 215 Jc 33
Umrer O IND 234 Kd 35
Umtata O ZA 349 Hg 61
Umtata Dam ~ ZA 349 Hg 61
Umtentu O ZA 349 Hh 61
Umuahia O WAN 320 Gk 43
Umuarama O BR 140 Eh 57
Umuda Island ⌂ PNG 286 Mh 50
Umu-Duru O WAN 320 Gk 43
Umutu O WAN 320 Gk 43
Umwukwe Range ⛰ ZW 341 Hh 54
Umzimkulu O ZA 349 Hg 61
Umzimkulu ~ ZA 349 Hg 61
Umzimvubu ~ ZA 349 Hg 61
Umzingwani ~ ZW 349 Hg 56
Umzinto O ZA 349 Hh 61
Una O BR 125 Fa 53
Una O RUS 159 Hm 13
Una ~ BIH 174 Ha 23
Una O IND 227 Jp 35
Una O IND 230 Kc 30
Unadilla O USA 71 Dg 29
Unaðsdalur O IS 158 Fj 12
Unai O BR 133 El 54
'Unaiza Unayzah O KSA 215 Ja 32
Unalakleet O USA 46 Aj 13
Unalakleet River ~ USA 46 Aj 13
Unalaska O USA 10 Ab 4
Unalaska Island ⌂ USA 10 Ab 4
Unango O MOC 344 Hk 52
Unare ~ YV 112 Eb 41
Unari O FIN 159 He 12
Unawari O RI 283 Md 47
Unayzah O KSA 215 Ja 32
Uncompahgre Peak △ USA 65 Cj 26
Uncompahgre Plateau ⛰ USA 65 Ch 26
Undandita O AUS 361 Mb 57
Underberg O ZA 349 Hg 60
Underbool O AUS 378 Mg 63
Unduma ~ BOL 129 Ea 52
Undur O RI 283 Mb 47
Unea Island ⌂ PNG 287 Ml 48
Uneča O RUS 171 Hj 19
Uneí ~ BR 117 Ea 46
Uneiuxi ~ BR 117 Ea 46
Unga Island ⌂ USA 46 Aj 17
Ungarie O AUS 379 Mk 62
Ungava Bay ~ CDN 7 Fb 4
Ungava Bay ≈ CDN 43 Hb 7
Ungerum O PNG 286 Mg 49
Ungheni O MD 175 Hf 22
Ungwana Bay ~ EAK 337 Hn 47
Unhe O ANG 341 Hc 54
Uniab ~ NAM 340 Gn 55
União O BR 124 En 48
União da Vitória O BR 140 Ej 59
União dos Palmares O BR 124 Fb 50
Unimak O USA 10 Ab 4
Unimak Island ⌂ USA 10 Ab 4
Unimak Island ⌂ USA 46 Ag 17
Unini ~ BR 120 Ec 46
Union O USA 71 Dc 26
Union O USA 71 Dh 27
Unión ~ MEX 92 Cm 36
Union ⌂ WV 104 Ed 39
Unión O RA 137 Eb 63
Union Center O USA 51 Cl 23
Union Creek O USA 50 Ca 24
Uniondale O ZA 358 Hd 62
Unión de Tula O MEX 92 Ck 35
Unión Hidalgo O MEX 93 Da 37
Unión Juárez O MEX 93 Db 38
Union's End O ZA 348 Hc 58
Union Springs O USA 86 Df 29
Uniontown O USA 74 Dj 26
Unionville O USA 70 Db 25
United Kingdom □ GB 162 Gg 18
United States of America □ USA 10 Cb 5
Unites Arab Emirates □ UAE 226 Jf 34
Unity O USA 50 Cc 23
Unity O CDN 51 Ch 19
Universal City O USA 81 Cn 31
University of Virginia ★ USA 74 Dj 27
University Park O USA 65 Cj 29
Unmet O VU 386 Nf 54
Unnão O IND 234 Ke 32
Uno ~ BR 124 Fb 50
Uno O GNB 316 Fm 40
Unpongkor O VU 386 Ng 55
Unsan O DVRK 247 Ln 25
Unskaja guba ~ RUS 159 Hm 13
Untion City O USA 71 Dd 27
Ünye O TR 195 Hl 25
Uông Bí O VN 255 Ld 35

478 Tuena - Uông Bí

◘ Country ▣ Capital city ⊙ Administrative unit O Place ♁ Island ⛰ Mountain range △ Mountain ⌓ Cape ≈ Ocean, Sea ~ Lake, River ▿ Undersea topography ▲ Glacier ♀ National park ••• Reservation ★ Point of major interest ▭ Landscape

Uotsuri-shima ♁ J 259 Lm 33
Uozo O J 251 Me 27
Upala O CR 97 Df 40
Upanema O BR 124 Fb 48
Upata O YV 112 Ec 41
Upernavik O DK 43 Ja 4
Upham O USA 56 Cm 21
Upi O RP 275 Ln 42
Upington O ZA 348 Hc 60
Upolu ♁ WS 35 Aa 11
Upolu Point ⌓ USA 75 An 35
Upper Arrow Lake ~ CDN 50 Cc 20
Upper Canada Vill. ★ CDN 60 Dl 23
Upper Humber ~ CDN 61 Ef 21
Upper Hut O NZ 383 Nk 66
Upper Klamath Lake ~ USA 50 Ca 24
Upper Lake O USA 64 Ca 26
Upper Lake ~ USA 64 Cb 25
Upper May ~ PNG 286 Mg 48
Upper Peninsula ▭ USA 57 De 22
Upper Red Lake ~ USA 56 Da 21
Upper Sioux Indian Reservation ••• USA 56 Da 23
Upper Sundusky O USA 71 Dg 25
Upper Twin Lake ~ CDN 57 De 20
Uppland ▭ S 158 Ha 15
Uppsala O S 170 Ha 16
Upsala O CDN 56 Dc 21
Upshi O IND 230 Kc 29
Upstart Bay ~ AUS 365 Mk 55
Upton O USA 51 Ck 23
'Uqlat aṣ-Ṣuqūr O KSA 214 Hp 33
Uqlat Ibn Ğabrain O KSA 214 Hn 32
'Uqlat Ibn Ğabrain O KSA 214 Hn 32
Ur ★ IRQ 215 Ja 30
Uracoa O YV 112 Ec 41
Urad Qianqi O VRC 243 Le 25
Uraguba O RUS 159 Hj 11
Urahoro O J 250 Mh 24
Uraim ~ BR 121 El 47
Urakawa O J 250 Mh 24
Ural ~ KZ 19 Mb 4
Ural ~ RUS 155 Rc 8
Uralla O AUS 379 Mm 61
Ural Mountains ⛰ RUS 19 Mb 4
Ural Mountains ⛰ RUS 154 Rc 8
Ural Mountains ⛰ RUS 204 Sa 5
Ural-Tau, Khrebet ⛰ RUS 154 Rc 8
Urama O YV 107 Dp 40
Uran O IND 238 Ka 36
Urana O AUS 379 Mk 63
Urandangi O AUS 374 Mf 56
Urandi O BR 125 En 53
Uranium City O CDN 42 Ec 7
Uranopolis O GR 194 Hd 25
Uraricuera ~ BR 112 Ed 44
Uravakonda O IND 238 Kc 38
Urawa O J 251 Mf 28
Urbana O USA 71 Dd 25
Urbana O USA 71 Df 25
Urbandale O USA 70 Da 25
Urbano Noris O C 101 Dk 35
Urbano Santos O BR 124 En 47
Urbino O I 185 Gn 24
Urcos O PE 128 Dn 52
Urcubamba ~ PE 116 Dj 48
Urdalsnutten △ N 170 Gk 16
Urdaneta O RP 267 Ll 38
Urdinarrain O RA 146 Ee 62
Ure O WAN 320 Gk 41
Urema ~ RI 283 Md 47
Ures O MEX 80 Cg 31
Urganch O UZB 19 Na 5
Urganch O UZB 222 Jj 25
Ürgüp O TR 195 Hk 26
Urgut O UZB 223 Jm 26
Urho O VRC 204 Tc 9
Urho Kekkosen ♀ FIN 159 Hf 11
Uri O IND 230 Kb 28
Uriah O USA 86 De 30
Uriapuru O BR 132 Ee 53
Uribante ~ YV 107 Dn 42
Uribe O CO 106 Dk 44
Uribe O CO 106 Dl 44
Uribia O CO 107 Dm 40
Urubici O BR 140 Ek 60
Urica O YV 112 Eb 41
Urich O USA 70 Da 26
Uriman O YV 112 Ec 43
Urimará O BR 124 Fa 50
Urjupinsk O RUS 181 Hn 20
Urla O TR 194 Hf 26
Urmetan O TJ 223 Jn 26
Urmi ~ RUS 205 Wc 9
Urnes O N 158 Gk 15
Uroh ~ RI 279 Lk 47
Ụromi O WAN 320 Gk 42
Üroteppa O TJ 223 Jn 26
Urrao O CO 106 Dk 42
Urru Co ~ VRC 231 Kh 30
Ursano O RI 283 Ma 47
Urṭayyān O KSA 214 Hn 31
Uru ~ BR 133 Ek 53
Uru ~ RDC 336 Hf 46
Uruá ~ BR 120 Ed 49
Uruachic O MEX 80 Ch 32
Uruaçu O BR 133 Ek 53
Uruanã O BR 133 Ek 53
Uruapan O MEX 75 Cd 30
Uruapan O MEX 92 Cl 36
Uruará O BR 120 Eh 47
Uruará ~ BR 120 Eh 47
Uruba Grande ~ BR 133 Ek 51
Urubamba ~ PE 128 Dm 51
Urubamba O PE 128 Dm 52
Urubamba ~ PE 128 Dm 52
Urubaxi ~ BR 117 Eb 46
Urucará O BR 120 Ef 47
Urucu ~ BR 117 Eb 48
Urucu ~ BR 120 Ee 49
Uruçuí O BR 121 Em 49
Urucuia O BR 133 Em 54
Urucuia ~ BR 133 Em 54
Uruçuí Preto ~ BR 121 Em 50
Uruçuí Vermelho ~ BR 121 Em 50
Urucuriana ~ BR 120 Eg 45
Urucurituba O BR 120 Ee 47
Uruena ~ RA 136 Eb 59
Uruguai ~ BR 140 Eh 59
Uruguaiana O BR 146 Ef 60
Uruguay ~ RA 146 Ee 61
Uruguay ~ RA 146 Ee 62
Uruguay ◘ ROU 146 Ef 62
Uruguinha O BR 121 Ej 45
Uruma Omba ~ RI 283 Md 48
Urumaco O YV 107 Dn 40
Ürümqi ⊙ VRC 204 Tc 10
Uruoca O BR 124 Ep 47
Urup ~ RUS 202 Hn 23
Urupá ~ BR 129 Ec 51
Urupadi ~ BR 120 Ef 47
Urupês O BR 140 Ek 56
Urupuca ~ BR 125 Ep 55
'Urūq Ḥibāka ▭ KSA 219 Jd 35
'Urūq Subai ▭ KSA 214 Hp 34
'Urūq Subai ▭ KSA 214 Hp 34
'Urūq Subai ▭ KSA 218 Hp 35
Uruquay ~ RA 146 Ef 61
Urus-Martan O RUS 202 Ja 24
Uruwira O EAT 336 Hh 49
Urziceni O RO 175 Hf 23
Us O NAM 348 Ha 57
Usa ~ RUS 154 Rc 5
Usa O J 247 Mb 29
Usagara O EAT 337 Hj 47
'Usaila O KSA 215 Ja 33
'Ušaira O KSA 215 Ja 33
Uşak O TR 195 Hg 26
Usakos O NAM 348 Gp 57
Usambara Mountains ⛰ EAT 337 Hm 48
Usangu Flats ▭ EAT 337 Hj 50
Ušaral O KZ 204 Tb 9
Usa River O EAT 337 Hl 47
Ušče O SCG 194 Hc 24
Usedom ♁ D 170 Gn 18
Useless Loop O AUS 368 Lg 59
Usengi O EAK 337 Hk 46
'Usfān O KSA 218 Hm 35
Ust'-Jansk O RUS 205 Xa 4
Ust'-Kujga O RUS 205 Xa 4
Ust'-Omčug O RUS 205 Xc 6
Ushaa O Z 341 Hd 53
Ushachy O BY 171 Hg 18
Ushagat Island ♁ USA 46 Ba 15
Ushibuka O J 247 Ma 29
Ushuaia O RA 152 Dp 73
Ushurekchen, Khrebet ⛰ RUS 205 Yb 5
Usilampatti O IND 239 Kc 40
Usim O RI 283 Mc 46
Usino O PNG 287 Mj 48
Usinsk O RUS 154 Rc 5
Üsküdar O TR 195 Hg 25
Usman' O RUS 181 Hm 19
Usoke O EAT 336 Hj 48
Usol'e-Sibirskoe O RUS 204 Uc 8
Uson O RP 267 Lm 39
Uspallata O RA 137 Dp 62
Uspanapa ~ MEX 93 Da 37
Usquil O PE 116 Dj 49
Ussel O F 184 Gh 23
Ussuri ~ VRC 205 Wc 9
Ussuri ~ RUS 250 Mc 23
Ussurijsk O RUS 250 Mc 24
Ust'Bol'šereck O RUS 23 Sb 4
Ust'-Čaun O RUS 23 Tb 3
Ust'-Kamenogorsk O KZ 22 Pa 4
Ust'-Kut O RUS 22 Qa 4
Usta O USA 51 Cl 23
Usta Muhammad O PK 227 Jm 31
Ustamurot O UZB 223 Jl 24
Ust'-Barguzin O RUS 204 Va 8
Ust'-Cil'ma O RUS 154 Rb 5
Ust'-Džeguta O RUS 202 Hp 23
Ust'e O RUS 171 Hm 16
Ust'Ilimsk O RUS 22 Pb 4
Ust'Ilimsk O RUS 204 Uc 7
Usti Man'ya O RUS 154 Sa 6
Ústí n.L. O CZ 174 Gp 20
Ustirt Šakraj ~ KZ 155 Rc 9
Ustjužna O RUS 171 Hk 16
Ustka O PL 170 Ha 18
Ust-Kamchatsk O RUS 23 Ta 4
Ust-Kamchatsk O RUS 205 Yc 7
Ust'-Kulom O RUS 154 Rb 6
Ust'-Kut O RUS 204 Va 7
Ust'-Labinsk O RUS 202 Hm 23
Ust'-Luga O RUS 171 Hf 16
Ust'-Maja O RUS 205 Wc 6
Ust'-Nera O RUS 205 Xb 6
Ust'-Olenëk O RUS 204 Wa 4
Ust'-Ordynskij O RUS 204 Va 8
Ust'-Pinega O RUS 159 Hn 13
Ust'-Reka O RUS 159 Hl 15
Ustrzyki Gorne O PL 174 Hd 21
Ust'-Sobolevka O RUS 250 Mf 22
Ust'Tym O RUS 204 Ta 7
Ustupo Yantupo O PA 97 Dj 41
Ust'-Vaga O RUS 159 Hp 14
Ustyurt Plateau ▭ KZ/UZB 19 Mb 5
Ustyurt Plateau ⛰ KZ/UZB 155 Rb 10
Usu O RI 282 Ll 47
Usuki O J 247 Mb 29
Usulután O ES 93 Dd 39
Usumacinta ~ MEX 93 Db 36
Usutu O ZA 349 Hg 57
Ušycja ~ UA 175 Hf 21
Uta O RI 286 Me 48
Uta ~ RI 286 Me 48
Utah ⊙ USA 64 Cf 26
Utah Lake ~ USA 65 Cf 25
Utah Lake ~ AUS 379 Mj 61
Uṭaiṭiya O KSA 215 Ja 33
Utan O RI 279 Lj 50
Utara Baliem Vriendschaps ~ RI 286 Mf 48
Utarabarat O RI 286 Mf 48
'Utayyiq O KSA 215 Jc 32
Ute Creek ~ USA 65 Cl 27
Utegi O EAT 337 Hk 46
Utembo ~ ANG 340 Hc 54
Ute Mountain ••• USA 65 Ch 27
Utena O LT 171 He 18
Utengule O EAT 337 Hk 50
Uteni O RUS 204 Wa 8
Ute Reservoir ~ USA 65 Cl 28
Utete O EAT 337 Hm 50
Uthai Thani O THA 262 Kp 38
Uthal O PK 227 Jm 33
U Thong O THA 262 Kp 38
U Thumphon O LAO 263 Lc 37
Utiariti O BR 132 Ee 52
Utica O USA 60 Dl 24
Utica O USA 71 Dg 25
Utica O CO 106 Dl 43
Utiel O E 184 Gf 26
Utike O RDC 336 Hf 46
Utila O HN 96 De 37
Utinga O BR 125 Ep 52
Utinga ~ BR 125 Ep 52
Utiruyacu ~ PE 116 Dl 48
Utljuks'kyj lyman ~ UA 175 Hk 22
Utnūr O IND 238 Kd 36
Utopia O AUS 374 Md 57
Utopia Aboriginal Land ••• AUS 374 Md 57
Utorgoš O RUS 171 Hg 16
Utraula O IND 234 Kf 32
Utrecht O NL 163 Gj 19
Utrecht O ZA 352 Hh 59
Utrera O E 184 Gd 27
Utrik ♁ MH 27 Tb 8
Utsjoki O FIN 159 Hf 11
Uttangarai O IND 238 Kd 39
Uttaradit O THA 262 Kp 37
Uttaramerūr O IND 238 Kd 39
Uttaranchal ⊙ IND 230 Kd 30
Uttarkashi O IND 230 Kd 30
Uttarkashi ⊙ IND 234 Kd 31
Utuado O USA 104 Ea 36
Utuana O EC 116 Dj 48
Utukok River ~ USA 46 Aj 9
Ututwa O EAT 337 Hk 47
Uummannaq Dundas O DK 43 Hb 3
Uummannarsuaq Kap Farvel ⌓ DK 43 Ka 7
Uusikaupunki O FIN 159 Hc 15
Uusimaa ▭ FIN 159 He 15
Uutapi Ombalantu O NAM 340 Gp 54
Uvá ~ CO 107 Dn 44
Uvá ~ CO 107 Dp 44
Uvalde O USA 81 Cn 31
Uvarovo O RUS 181 Hp 20
Uvat O RUS 154 Sb 7
Uverito O YV 112 Eb 41
Uviéu O E 184 Gc 24
Uvinza O EAT 336 Hh 48
Uvira O RDC 336 Hg 47
Uvs nuur ~ MNG 204 Ua 8
Uvungu O RDC 333 He 47
Uwajima O J 251 Mc 29
Uwa-kai ~ J 251 Mc 29
Uwakeka O RI 283 Lp 49
Uwapa O RI 283 Md 47
Uwebu O RI 286 Mf 49
Uweinat O LAR 300 He 35
Uxin Ju O VRC 243 Le 26
Uxin Qi O VRC 243 Le 26
Uxmal ★ MEX 93 Dd 35
Uyilankulam O CL 239 Kd 41
Uyo O WAN 320 Gk 43
'Uyūn O KSA 215 Jc 33
'Uyun al-Ğiwā' O KSA 214 Hp 32
Uyuni O BOL 136 Ea 56
Už ~ UA 175 Hg 20
Uzan Qoli ~ IR 209 Jb 28
Uzbekistan ◘ UZB 223 Jj 25
Uzboj ~ TM 222 Jg 26
Uzcátegui O YV 107 Dn 42
Uzerche O F 184 Gg 23
Uzgen O KS 230 Ka 25
Užhorod O UA 174 Hd 21
Užice O SCG 194 Hb 24
Uzlovaja O RUS 171 Hl 18
Üzümlü O TR 195 Hm 26
Uzunköprü O TR 194 Hf 25
Užur O RUS 204 Tc 7

V

V. Lelija △ BIH 194 Hb 24
V. Plana O SCG 194 Hc 23
V. Troglav △ BIH 194 Ha 24
Vaala O FIN 159 Hf 13
Vaalajärvi O FIN 159 He 12
Vaalbos ♀ ZA 349 Hd 60
Vaal Dam ~ ZA 349 Hg 59
Vaalplaas O ZA 349 Hg 58
Vaalrivier ~ ZA 349 He 60
Vaalwater O ZA 349 Hg 58
Vaasa Vasa O FIN 159 Hc 14
Vabalninkas O LT 171 He 18
Vác O H 174 Hb 22
Vaca Guzman O BOL 129 Ec 55
Vacaria O BR 146 Ej 60
Vacaville O USA 64 Ca 26
Vacha O MOC 344 Hl 53
Vači O RUS 202 Jb 24
Vāda O IND 238 Ka 36
Vādāsinor O IND 227 Ka 34
Väddö ♁ S 170 Hb 15
Vader O USA 50 Ca 22
Vadodara O IND 227 Ka 34
Vado del Yeso O C 101 Dk 35
Vadsø O N 159 Hg 10
Vaduz ▣ FL 174 Gl 22
Vadvetjåkka ♀ N 158 Hb 11
Vaga ~ RUS 154 Qc 6
Vaga O RUS 171 Hp 15
Vaga O RCB 332 Gp 46
Vågaholmen O N 158 Gn 12
Vagar ♁ DK 162 Gc 14
Vaghena Island ♁ SOL 290 Na 49
Vågsfjorden ~ N 158 Ha 11
Váh ~ SK 174 Ha 21
Vah ~ RUS 204 Ta 6
Vaha O SOL 290 Nb 49
Vāhān O AFG 230 Ka 27
Vāhān ~ AFG 230 Ka 27
Vahš ~ TJ 223 Jn 26
Vahš ~ UZB 223 Jn 27
Vaiaku O TUV 35 Tb 10
Vaiaku ▣ TUV 35 Tb 10
Vaigai ~ IND 239 Kc 40
Vaikam O IND 239 Kc 41
Vail O USA 65 Cj 26
Vailala River ~ PNG 287 Mj 49
Vaippar ~ IND 239 Kc 41
Vaisāli O IND 235 Kg 33
Vajdaguba O RUS 159 Hj 11
Vakaga ~ RCA 321 Hd 41
Vakarel O BG 194 Hd 24
Vaku O RDC 332 Gn 48
Vakuta ♁ PNG 287 Mm 50
Vakuta Island ♁ PNG 287 Mm 50
Val. Meziříčí O CZ 174 Hb 21
Valachchenai O CL 239 Ke 42
Valadeces O MEX 81 Cn 32
Valavanur O IND 238 Kd 40
Valcheta O RA 147 Ea 66
Valdai Hills ⛰ RUS 171 Hh 17
Valdaj O RUS 159 Hk 14
Valdaj O RUS 171 Hj 17
Val-de-Bois O CDN 60 Dl 23
Valdemarsvik O S 170 Ha 16
Valdemoro O E 184 Gd 25
Valdepeñas O E 184 Ge 26
Valdés Peninsula ♁ RA 147 Ec 67
Valdez O USA 6 Bb 3
Valdez O USA 46 Bc 15
Val-d'Isère O F 185 Gk 23
Valdivia O CO 106 Dl 42
Valdivia O RCH 147 Dm 65
Val-d'Or O CDN 60 Dk 21
Valdosta O USA 86 Dg 30
Valdres ▭ N 158 Gl 15
Vale O USA 50 Cd 23
Valemount O CDN 50 Cc 19
Valença O BR 125 Fa 52
Valença O BR 141 En 57
Valença do Piauí O BR 124 Ep 49
Valencay O F 163 Gg 22
Valence O F 185 Gj 23
Valencia O YV 107 Dp 40
València O E 184 Gf 26
Valencia O RP 275 Ln 42
Valencia d. D. J. O E 184 Gd 24
Valencia de Alcántara O E 184 Gc 26
Valenciana ⊙ E 184 Gf 26
Valenciennes O F 163 Gh 20
Valentine O USA 56 Cm 24
Valentine O USA 80 Ck 30
Valera O YV 107 Dn 41
Valera O PE 116 Dk 48
Valerio O MEX 80 Cj 32
Valesdir O VU 386 Nf 54
Valga O EST 171 Hf 17
Valiyannur O IND 239 Kb 40
Valjevo O SCG 194 Hb 23
Valka O LV 171 He 17
Valkeakoski O FIN 159 He 15
Valky O UA 175 Hk 21
Vallabhipur O IND 227 Jp 35
Valladolid O MEX 93 Dd 35
Valladolid O EC 116 Dj 48
Valladolid O E 184 Gd 25
Valldal O N 158 Gk 14
Valle O USA 65 Cf 28
Valle ~ RA 136 Ec 58
Valle Alcaraz O RA 146 Ee 61
Vallecillos O MEX 81 Cm 32
Valle d'Aosta ⊙ I 185 Gk 23
Valle de Bravo O MEX 92 Cm 36
Valle de Chapalcó ▭ RA 137 Eb 64
Valle de Chaschuil ▭ RA 136 Dp 59
Valle de la Pascua O YV 107 Ea 41
Valle de Lerma ▭ RA 136 Eb 58
Valle del Río Bermejo ▭ RA 137 Dp 61
Valle del Río Deseado ▭ RA 152 Dp 69
Valle de Rosario O MEX 80 Cj 32
Valle de Santiago O MEX 92 Cm 35
Valle de Zaragoza O MEX 80 Cj 32
Valledupar O CO 107 Dm 40
Vallée de Azaouagh ▭ RMM 308 Gh 37
Vallée de l'Ahzar ▭ RMM 308 Gh 38
Vallée de Tarka ▭ RN 308 Gk 38
Vallée du Dadès ▭ MA 293 Gc 30
Vallée du Drâa ▭ MA 293 Gc 30
Vallée du Goulbin Kaba ▭ WAN 308 Gk 39
Valle Fértil ▭ RA 137 Ea 61
Vallegrande O BOL 129 Eb 55
Valle Grande O RA 136 Eb 57
Valle Hermoso O MEX 81 Cn 33
Valle Hermoso O MEX 93 Dd 36
Vallehermoso O E 292 Fm 31
Vallejo O USA 64 Ca 26
Valle Longitudinal ▭ RCH 137 Dm 64
Vallenar O RCH 136 Dn 60
Valle Rico O PA 97 Dh 42
Valles Calchaquies ▭ RA 136 Ea 58
Valletta ▣ M 185 Gp 28
Valley O USA 51 Ch 23
Valley City O USA 56 Cn 22
Valley East O CDN 57 Dh 22
Valley Falls O USA 50 Cb 24
Valley Falls O USA 70 Da 26
Valley Mills O USA 81 Cp 30
Valley of the Kings ★ ET 301 Hj 33
Valley Springs O USA 56 Cp 24
Valleyview O CDN 47 Cc 17
Vallgrund O FIN 159 Hc 14
Vallgrund ♁ FIN 159 Hc 14
Vallo della Lucánia O I 194 Gp 25
Valls O E 184 Gg 25
Val Marie O CDN 51 Cj 21
Valmiera O LV 171 He 17
Valmora O USA 65 Ck 28
Valod O IND 238 Ka 35
Valozhyn O BY 171 Hf 18
Val-Paradis O CDN 60 Dj 21
Valparaíso O USA 71 De 25
Valparaíso O MEX 92 Cl 34
Valparaíso O CO 116 Dk 45
Valparaíso O RCH 137 Dm 62
Valparaíso O BR 140 Ej 56
Valpoy O IND 238 Kb 38
Valsād O IND 238 Ka 35
Valset O N 158 Gl 14
Valsjöbyn O S 158 Gn 13
Valsrivier ~ ZA 349 Hf 59
Valtimo O FIN 159 Hg 14
Valujki O RUS 181 Hl 20
Valverde O E 292 Fm 32
Valverde del Camino O E 184 Gc 27
Valverde del Fresno O E 184 Gc 25
Vammala O FIN 159 Hd 15
Van O TR 202 Hp 26
Vanadzor O ARM 202 Ja 25
Vananda O USA 51 Cj 22
Vanapa River ~ PNG 287 Mk 50
Vânători O RO 194 Hd 23
Vanavana ♁ F 35 Bb 12
Vanavara O RUS 204 Uc 6
Van Buren O USA 60 Dp 22
Van Buren O USA 70 Da 28
Van Buren O USA 71 Dc 27
Vân Canh O VN 263 Le 39
Vanceboro O USA 60 Ea 23
Vanceboro O USA 74 Dk 28
Vanceburg O USA 71 Dg 26
Vancourt O USA 81 Cm 30
Vancouver O CDN 50 Ca 21
Vancouver O USA 50 Ca 23
Vancouver Island ♁ CDN 50 Bn 21
Vancouver Island Ranges ⛰ CDN 50 Bp 21
Vanda O FIN 159 He 15
Van Daalen ~ RI 286 Me 47
Vandalia O USA 71 Dd 26
Vandavāsi O IND 238 Kd 39
Vanderbijlpark O ZA 349 Hf 59
Vanderhoof O CDN 42 Db 8
Vanderkloof Dam ~ ZA 349 He 61
Vanderlin Island ♁ AUS 365 Me 53
Van de Wal ~ RI 286 Mf 47
Van Diemen Gulf ~ AUS 364 Mb 51
Vandry O CDN 60 Dm 22
Vandyks drif O ZA 349 Hg 59
Vanegas O MEX 92 Cm 34
Vänern ~ S 170 Gn 16
Vänersborg O S 170 Gn 16
Vaneteze ~ MOC 352 Hj 58
Vangaindrano O RM 353 Jb 57
Vango O RDC 321 Hd 44
Vangunu Island ♁ SOL 290 Nb 50
Vanha Kirkko ★ FIN 159 He 14
Vanh Ninh O VN 263 Le 39
Van Horn O USA 80 Ck 30
Vani O IND 238 Ka 35
Vanillas O RCH 136 Dn 58
Vanimo O PNG 286 Mg 47
Vāniyambādi O IND 238 Kd 39
Vânju Mare O RO 194 Hd 23
Vankarem O RUS 23 Aa 3
Vankarem O RUS 205 Aa 5
Van Keulenfjorden ~ N 158 Gp 7
Văn Lân O VN 263 Le 40
Van Mai O VN 255 Lc 35
Van Mijenfjorden ~ N 158 Gp 7
Vann ♁ N 159 Hb 10
Vännäs O S 158 Hb 14
Vannes O F 163 Ge 22
Văn Quan O VN 255 Ld 35
Van Reenen O ZA 349 Hg 60
Vanrhynsdorp O ZA 348 Hb 61
Vanrook O AUS 365 Mg 54
Vānsada O IND 238 Ka 35
Vansbro O S 158 Gn 15
Vansittart Bay ~ AUS 361 Lp 52
Vansittart Island ♁ CDN 43 Gb 5
Vanstadensrus O ZA 349 Hf 61
Vantaa Vanda O FIN 159 He 15
Vanua Balavu ♁ FJI 390 Aa 54
Vanua Levu ♁ FJI 387 Nm 54
Vanuatu ◘ VU 386 Ng 53
Vanua Vatu ♁ FJI 390 Aa 55
Van Wert O USA 71 Df 25
Van Wyksdorp O ZA 358 Hc 62
Van Wyksvlei O ZA 358 Hc 61
Van Zylsrus O ZA 349 Hd 59
Vao O F 386 Nf 57
Vaparai O IND 239 Kc 40
Va Phu Temple ★ LAO 263 Lc 38
Vara O S 170 Gn 16
Varadero O C 100 Dh 34
Varaklani O LV 171 Hf 17
Varalé O CI 317 Ge 41
Varāmīn O IR 222 Jd 28
Vārānasi O IND 234 Kf 33
Varangerfjorden ~ N 159 Hg 10
Varangerhalvøya ♁ N 159 Hg 10
Varas O AFG 223 Jm 28
Varavani O IND 239 Kd 41
Varaždin O HR 174 Ha 22
Varberg O S 170 Gm 17
Vardar ~ MK 194 Hc 25
Vardåvard O IR 222 Jd 28
Varde O DK 170 Gl 18
Vardenis O ARM 202 Ja 25
Varejonal O MEX 80 Cj 33
Varela O RA 137 Ea 63
Varela O GNB 316 Fm 39
Varese O I 185 Gl 23
Váreza da Palma O BR 133 Em 54
Vårgårda O S 170 Gn 17
Vargem Alta O BR 141 Ep 56
Vargem Bonita O BR 141 El 56
Vargem Grande O BR 124 En 47
Varginha O BR 141 Em 56
Varirata N. P. ★ PNG 287 Mk 50
Varillas O RCH 136 Dp 58
Varkaus O FIN 159 Hf 14
Varmahlíð O IS 158 Fk 13
Värmland ▭ S 170 Gn 16
Varna O BG 194 Hf 24
Värnamo O S 170 Gp 17
Varnek O RUS 154 Rc 5
Varnyany O BY 171 Hf 18
Varoš O BIH 174 Ha 23
Værøy ♁ N 158 Gn 12
Varsag O AFG 223 Jp 27
Varsinais Suomi ▭ FIN 159 Hd 15
Varto O TR 202 Hn 26
Varvarco O RA 137 Dn 64
Várzea Alegre O BR 124 Fa 49
Várzea do Poço O BR 125 Ep 51
Várzea Grande O BR 124 En 49
Várzea Grande O BR 132 Ef 53
Varzeão O BR 140 Ek 58
Varzelândia O BR 125 En 53
Varzino O RUS 159 Hl 11
Varzuga ~ RUS 159 Hl 12
Vasa O FIN 159 Hc 14
Vāsad O IND 227 Ka 34
Vasai O IND 238 Ka 36
Vasconcelos O MEX 93 Da 37
Vasil'evka O RUS 250 Md 22
Vāšīr O AFG 223 Jk 29
Vasjugan ~ RUS 204 Ta 7
Vaslui O RO 175 Hf 22
Vassako ~ RCA 321 Hb 41
Vassar O USA 57 Dg 24
Vassouvas O BR 141 En 57
Västansjö O S 158 Gp 13
Västbacka O S 158 Gp 15
Västerås O S 170 Gp 16
Västerboten ▭ S 159 Hc 14
Västergötland ▭ S 170 Gn 16
Västerhaninge O S 170 Hb 16
Västervik O S 170 Ha 17
Vasto O I 194 Gp 24
Vasvár O H 174 Ha 22
Vasylivka O UA 175 Hk 22
Vasyl'kiv O UA 175 Hh 20
Vasyuganskaya Ravnina ▭ RUS 204 Ta 7
Vatican City O I 185 Gm 25
Vat Luang Temple ★ LAO 263 Lc 38
Vatnajökull ▲ IS 158 Fm 13
Vatolatsaka O RM 353 Hp 57
Vatomandry O RM 345 Jc 55
Vatondrangy △ RM 353 Jb 56
Vatra Dornei O RO 175 He 22
Vattaikundu O IND 239 Kc 40
Vättern ~ S 170 Gp 16
Vatua ♁ FJI 390 Aa 55
Vatu-i-ra Channel ~ FJI 387 Nm 54
Vatukoula O FJI 387 Nl 54
Vatulele ♁ FJI 387 Nl 55
Vatu Vara ♁ FJI 390 Aa 54
Vaughan Springs O AUS 361 Mb 57
Vaughn O USA 51 Cg 22
Vaughn O USA 65 Ck 28
Vaupés ~ CO 116 Dm 45
Vaupés ~ BR 117 Dp 45
Vauxhall O CDN 51 Cf 20
Vava'u ♁ TO 35 Ba 11
Vava'u ♁ TO 390 Ac 55
Vava'u Group ♁ TO 390 Ac 55
Vavoua O CI 305 Gc 42
Vavuniya O CL 239 Ke 41
Vawkavysk O BY 171 He 19
Växjö O S 170 Gp 17
Vaza Barris ~ BR 125 Fa 51
Vaza-Barris ~ BR 124 Fa 50
Vāzaḥā/Wāzaḥwa O AFG 223 Jn 29
Vazante ~ BR 132 Ef 55
Vazante O BR 133 El 54
Vázelay O F 163 Gh 22
Vázquez O C 101 Dk 35
Vda. da Redençao ~ BR 125 En 51
Vda. do Buriti ~ BR 125 En 51
Vda. Pimenterra ~ BR 124 En 50
Vdo. de Côcos ~ BR 133 Em 52
vdp. Padun ~ RUS 159 Hl 12
Vedāranniyam O IND 239 Kd 40
Vedia O RA 137 Ed 63
Vedinho ~ BR 133 Ej 54
Vefsna ~ N 158 Gn 13
Vega O USA 65 Cl 28
Vega ♁ N 158 Gm 13
Vega Baja O USA 104 Ea 36
Vega de Alatorre O MEX 93 Cp 35
Vegreville O CDN 51 Cf 19
Vegueta O PE 116 Dk 51
Vehova O PK 227 Jp 30
Veimandu Channel ~ MV 239 Ka 45
Veintiocho de Mayo O EC 116 Dj 47
Veiros O BR 121 Eh 47
Veiru O PNG 287 Mj 49
Veis O IR 215 Jc 30
Vejer d.l.Fr. O E 184 Gc 27
Vejle O DK 170 Gl 18
Vel. Bereznyj O UA 174 Hd 21
Vel. Byčkiv O UA 175 Hd 21
Vel. Lepetycha O UA 175 Hk 22
Vela Luka O HR 194 Ha 24
Velāpur O IND 238 Kb 37
Velasco Ibarra El Empalme O EC 116 Dj 46
Velasco Ibarra El Empalme ~ EC 116 Dj 46
Vélaz O RA 140 Ee 59
Velcho ~ RCH 147 Dm 67
Velddrif O ZA 358 Hb 62
Velebitskikanal ~ HR 174 Gp 23
Velenje O SLO 174 Gp 22
Veles O MK 194 Hc 25
Vélez O CO 106 Dm 42
Vélez-Malaga O E 184 Gd 27
Vélez R. O E 184 Ge 27
Velha Goa O IND 238 Ka 38
Velhas ~ BR 133 Em 54
Velikaja ~ RUS 205 Zc 6
Velikaja Guba O RUS 159 Hk 14
Velikaja Kema O RUS 250 Me 23
Velikie Luki O RUS 171 Hh 17
Veliko Tărnovo O BG 194 He 24
Velille O PE 128 Dn 53
Vélingara O SN 304 Fn 38
Vélingara O SN 316 Fn 39
Velíž O RUS 171 Hh 18
Vèl Kal' O RUS 23 Aa 3
Vella Lavella Island ♁ SOL 290 Na 49
Vellankulam O CL 239 Kd 41
Velloorsdrif O NAM 348 Hb 60
Vellore O IND 238 Kd 39
Vel'sk O RUS 154 Qc 6
Vel'sk O RUS 171 Hp 15
Velva O USA 56 Cm 21
Velyka Pysarivka O UA 175 Hk 20
Vemasse O TP 282 Lp 50
Vemelho ~ BR 133 Ej 53
Vempalle O IND 238 Kd 38
Venado Tuerto O RA 137 Ec 62
Venamo ~ GUY 112 Ed 42
Venâncio Aires O BR 146 Eh 60
Venda Nova do Imigrante O BR 141 Ep 56
Vendée ▭ F 163 Gf 22
Vendôme O F 163 Gg 22
Veneral O CO 106 Dk 44
Venetie O USA 46 Bc 11
Venev O RUS 171 Hm 18
Venézia-Giúlia ⊙ I 174 Gn 22
Venezuela ◘ YV 107 Dp 41
Venezuela Basin ▿ 104 Ea 38
Vengurla O IND 238 Ka 38
Venice O USA 86 Dd 31
Venice O USA 87 Dg 32
Venice O I 185 Gn 23
Venjan O S 158 Gn 15
Venkatagiri O IND 238 Kd 39
Venlo O NL 163 Gk 20
Ventanas O EC 116 Dj 46
Ventania O BR 140 Ej 58
Ventanilla O PE 116 Dk 51
Ventersburg O ZA 349 Hf 60
Ventersdorp O ZA 349 Hf 59
Venterstad O ZA 349 He 61
Ventspils O LV 170 Hc 17
Ventuari ~ YV 107 Ea 43
Ventuari ~ YV 112 Eb 43
Ventura O USA 64 Cc 28
Venustiano Carranza O MEX 92 Ck 36
Venustiano Carranza O MEX 93 Db 37
Veppur O IND 239 Kd 40
Vera O BR 132 Eg 52

Uotsuri-shima - Vera 479

Vera ○ RA 137 Ed 60
Vera ○ E 184 Gf 27
Veracruz ⊙ MEX 93 Cp 36
Verano ○ I 194 Gp 25
Veranópolis ○ BR 146 Ej 60
Verao ⌂ VU 386 Ng 54
Verāval ○ IND 227 Jp 35
Verchn'aja Chortica ○ UA 175 Hk 22
Verdalsøra ○ N 158 Gm 14
Verde ~ USA 64 Cf 28
Verde ~ MEX 92 Cl 35
Verde ~ PY 132 Ee 55
Verde ~ BR 132 Ef 52
Verde ~ BR 132 Ef 55
Verde ~ BR 132 Eg 52
Verde ~ BR 132 Eh 55
Verde ~ BR 133 Eh 54
Verde ~ BR 133 Ej 54
Verde ~ BR 133 Ej 55
Verde ~ BR 133 El 54
Verde ~ PY 136 Ed 57
Verde ~ PY 140 Ee 57
Verde ~ BR 140 Eh 56
Verde Grande ~ BR 125 En 53
Verde Grande ~ BR 125 En 54
Verde Island ⌂ RP 267 Ll 39
Verde Island Passage ~ RP 267 Ll 39
Verdigre ○ USA 56 Cn 24
Verdigris ~ USA 70 Da 27
Verdon ~ F 185 Gk 24
Verdun ○ F 163 Gj 21
Vereeniging ○ ZA 349 Hf 59
Verena ○ ZA 349 Hg 58
Vereščagino ○ RUS 204 Ta 6
Vergara ○ ROU 146 Eg 62
Vergemont ○ AUS 374 Mh 57
Vergennes ○ USA 60 Dm 23
Verh. Baskunčak ○ RUS 181 Jb 21
Verhalen ○ USA 81 Cl 30
Verhnee Ondomozero ~ RUS 159 Hm 12
Verhneimbatsk ○ RUS 204 Ta 6
Verhnetulomski ○ RUS 159 Hh 11
Verhnetulomskoe vodohranilišče ~ RUS 159 Hg 11
Verhojansk ○ RUS 205 Wc 5
Véria ○ GR 194 Hd 25
Verín ○ E 184 Gc 25
Verkhoyanskiy Khrebet ⛰ RUS 22 Ra 2
Verkhoyanskiy Khrebet ⛰ RUS 205 Wb 5
Verkykerskop ○ ZA 349 Hg 59
Verla ★ FIN 159 Hf 15
Verlegenhuken ⌓ N 158 Gp 5
Vermelho ~ BR 121 Ej 49
Vermelho ~ BR 121 Ek 49
Vermilion ○ CDN 51 Cg 19
Vermilion ○ USA 71 Dg 25
Vermilion Bay ○ CDN 56 Db 21
Vermilion Bay ~ USA 86 Db 31
Vermilion Lake ~ CDN 56 Db 21
Vermilion Range ⛰ USA 56 Db 22
Vermillion ○ USA 56 Cp 24
Vermillion River ~ USA 56 Cp 24
Vermillon ~ CDN 60 Dm 22
Vermont ⊙ USA 60 Dm 24
Vernal ○ USA 65 Ch 25
Verndalen ○ S 158 Gn 14
Verner ○ CDN 57 Dh 22
Verneuil ○ F 163 Gg 21
Verneuk Pan ~ ZA 348 Hc 60
Vernon ○ CDN 50 Cc 20
Vernon ○ USA 64 Cf 25
Vernon ○ USA 70 Cn 28
Vernon ○ F 163 Gg 21
Vernon Center ○ USA 56 Da 24
Vernon Islands ⌂ AUS 364 Mb 52
Vero Beach ○ USA 87 Dh 32
Verona ○ USA 56 Cn 22
Verona ○ USA 57 Dd 24
Verona ○ I 185 Gm 23
Verónica ○ RA 146 Ef 63
Veron Range ⛰ PNG 287 Mn 48
Versailles ○ USA 70 Db 26
Versailles ○ USA 71 Df 26
Versailles ○ F 163 Gg 21
Versalles ○ BOL 129 Ec 52
Vertentes ○ BR 133 Ej 51
Vertientes ○ C 100 Dj 35
Vertijievka ○ UA 175 Hh 20
Vértiz ○ RA 137 Ec 63
Verulam ○ ZA 352 Hh 60
Verviers ○ B 163 Gj 20
Vervins ○ F 163 Gh 21
Ves'egonsk ○ RUS 171 Hl 16
Vesele ○ UA 175 Hk 22
Veselovskoe vodohranilišče ~ RUS 181 Hn 22
Veselynove ○ UA 175 Hh 22
Vešenskaja ○ RUS 181 Hn 21
Veskšino ○ RUS 171 Hh 17
Vesoul ○ F 163 Gj 22
Vestavia Hills ○ USA 71 De 29
Vestbygd ○ N 170 Gk 16
Vesterålen ⌂ N 158 Gp 11
Vesterø Havn ○ DK 170 Gm 17
Vestfjorden ~ N 158 Gn 12
Vestfonna ~ N 158 Hb 6
Vestmannaeyjar ○ IS 158 Fk 14
Vestmannaeyjar ⌂ IS 158 Fk 14
Vestvågøy ⌂ N 158 Gn 11
Vetauua ⌂ FJI 390 Aa 53
Vetlanda ○ S 170 Gp 17
Vetluga ~ RUS 154 Ra 7
Vetrivier ~ ZA 349 Hf 60
Vevay ○ USA 71 Df 26
Vévi ○ GR 194 Hc 25
Veyo ○ USA 64 Cf 27
Vézère ~ F 184 Gg 23
Viacha ○ BOL 129 Dp 54
Viai Island ⌂ PNG 287 Mj 47
Vialadougou ○ CI 305 Gc 41
Viale ○ RA 137 Ed 61
Viamão ○ BR 146 Ej 61
Vian ○ USA 70 Da 28
Viana ○ BR 121 Em 47
Viana ○ BR 141 Ep 56
Viana ○ ANG 340 Gn 50
Viana do Castelo ○ P 184 Gb 25
Viangphoukha ○ LAO 254 La 35
Vianópolis ○ BR 133 Ek 54
Viaréggio ○ I 185 Gl 24
Via River ~ PNG 287 Ml 48
Viborg ○ DK 170 Gl 17
Vibo Valéntina ○ I 185 Gp 26
Vic ○ E 184 Gh 25
Vicam ○ MEX 80 Cg 32
Vicente Guerrero ○ MEX 92 Ck 34
Vicente Guerrero ○ MEX 93 Dd 36
Vicente Guerrero ○ MEX 93 De 35
Vicente Noble ○ DOM 101 Dn 36
Vicenza ○ I 185 Gm 23
Vicertópolis ○ BR 140 Ej 56
Vichada ~ CO 107 Dn 43
Vichada ~ CO 107 Dp 43
Vichadero ○ ROU 146 Eg 61
Vichy ○ F 163 Gh 22
Vici ○ USA 70 Cn 27
Vicksburg ○ USA 86 Dc 29
Viçosa ○ BR 124 Fb 50
Viçosa ○ BR 141 En 56
Viçosa do Ceara ○ BR 124 Ep 47
Victor ○ USA 51 Cg 24
Victor ○ USA 56 Cp 23
Victor ○ USA 65 Ck 26
Victor Harbor ○ AUS 378 Mf 63
Victoria ○ CDN 50 Ca 21
Victoria ○ USA 81 Cp 31
Victoria ○ CO 106 Dl 43
Victoria ○ BOL 129 Ea 51
Victoria ○ RCH 147 Dm 65
Victoria ○ RCH 152 Dp 72
Victoria ○ VRC 258 Lh 34
Victoria ○ RP 267 Ll 39
Victoria ○ CAM 320 Gl 44
Victoria ▣ SY 329 Jf 48
Victoria ~ AUS 364 Mb 54
Victoria ⊙ AUS 378 Mh 64
Victoria Beach ○ CDN 56 Cp 20
Victoria Falls ○ ZW 341 He 54
Victoria Island ⌂ CDN 6 Da 2
Victoria Island ⌂ CDN 42 Eb 4
Victoria Island ⌂ CDN 47 Ce 11
Victoria Lake ~ CDN 61 Ef 21
Victoria Land ▭ 38 Sb 17
Victoria Nile ~ EAU 324 Hh 44
Victoria Peak △ BH 93 Dd 37
Victoria River Downs ○ AUS 364 Mb 54
Victoria River Roadhouse ○ AUS 364 Mb 53
Victorias ○ RP 267 Lm 40
Victoria Strait ~ CDN 6 Db 3
Victoria Strait ≈ CDN 42 Fa 5
Victoria Vale ○ AUS 365 Mh 55
Victoriaville ○ CDN 60 Dn 23
Victoria West ○ ZA 349 Hd 61
Victorica ○ RA 137 Eb 64
Victor Rosales ○ MEX 92 Cl 34
Victorville ○ USA 64 Cd 28
Vicuña ○ RCH 137 Dn 61
Vicuña ○ RCH 152 Dp 73
Vicuña Mackenna ○ RA 137 Eb 62
Vida ○ USA 51 Ck 22
Vidal ○ USA 64 Ce 28
Vidal ○ PE 116 Dm 47
Vidalia ○ USA 71 Dg 29
Vidalia ○ USA 86 Dc 30
Vidamlya ○ BY 171 Hd 19
Vida Nova ○ BR 121 Ej 46
Vidapanakallu ○ IND 238 Kc 38
Vidareidi ○ DK 162 Gc 14
Videira ○ BR 140 Ej 59
Vidin ○ BG 194 Hd 24
Vidisha ○ IND 234 Kc 34
Vidor ○ USA 81 Da 30
Vidzy ○ BY 171 Hf 18
Viedgesville ○ ZA 349 Hf 61
Viedma ○ RA 147 Ec 66
Viejo ~ RA 137 Ec 60
Vielha Mirajan ○ E 184 Gg 24
Vienn ~ F 163 Gg 22
Vienna ○ USA 70 Db 26
Vienna ○ USA 71 Dd 27
Vienna ○ USA 71 Dh 26
Vienna ▣ A 174 Ha 21
Vienne ~ F 163 Gg 22
Vienne ○ F 185 Gj 23
Vientiane ▣ LAO 263 Lb 36
Vieques ⌂ USA 104 Eb 36
Vieremä ○ FIN 159 Hf 14
Vierzon ○ F 163 Gg 22
Viesca ○ MEX 81 Cl 33
Viesite ○ LV 171 He 17
Vieste ○ I 194 Ha 25
Vietas ○ S 158 Hb 12
Vietnam □ VN 255 Lb 35
Viêt Trì ○ VN 255 Lc 35
Viêt Vinh ○ VN 255 Lc 34
Vieux Fort ○ WL 104 Ed 39
Vieytes ○ RA 146 Ef 63
Vigan ○ RP 267 Ll 37
Vigevano ○ I 185 Gl 23
Vigia ○ BR 121 Ek 46
Vigia Chico ○ MEX 93 De 36
Vigia del Fuerta ○ CO 106 Dk 42
Viginia ○ USA 56 Db 22
Vigo ○ E 184 Gb 24
Vihāri ○ PK 230 Ka 30
Vihiti ○ FIN 159 He 15
Vihren △ BG 194 Hd 25
Viitna ○ EST 171 He 16
Vijayanagar ○ IND 227 Ka 34
Vijayawada ○ IND 238 Ke 37
Vik ○ IS 158 Fl 14
Vikajärvi ○ FIN 159 Hf 12
Vikārābād ○ IND 238 Kc 37
Vikenara Point ⌓ SOL 290 Nb 50
Viking ○ CDN 51 Cf 19
Vikna ⌂ N 158 Gm 13
Viksdalen ○ N 158 Gk 15
Viktoria ○ M 185 Gp 27
Vila Arco-Íris ○ BR 121 El 47
Vila Coutinho ○ MOC 344 Hk 53
Vila da Ribeira Brava ○ CV 316 Fh 37
Vila de Sal-Rei ○ CV 316 Fj 37
Vila de Sena ○ MOC 344 Hk 54
Vila do Carmo ○ BR 120 Ed 49
Vila do Conde ○ P 184 Gb 25
Vila do Maio ○ CV 316 Fj 38
Vila do Pôrto Novo ○ CV 316 Fh 37
Vila Franca de Xira ○ P 184 Gb 26
Vila Gomes da Costa ○ MOC 352 Hj 58
Vilakalaka ○ VU 386 Nf 53
Vilalba ○ E 184 Gc 24
Vila Martins ○ BR 117 Dp 49
Vila Nazaré ○ BR 117 Eb 47
Vilāni ○ LV 171 Hf 17
Vilankulo ○ MOC 352 Hk 57
Vilanova ○ E 184 Gb 24
Vila Nova ○ ANG 340 Gp 52
Vila Nova da Fronteira ○ MOC 344 Hk 54
Vila Nova de Gaia ○ P 184 Gb 25
Vila Nova do Sul ○ BR 146 Eh 61
Vilanova i la Geltrú ○ E 184 Gg 25
Vila Nova Sintra ○ CV 316 Fh 38
Vila Real ○ P 184 Gc 25
Vila Real ○ P 184 Gc 27
Vila-real ○ E 184 Gf 26
Vilar Formoso ○ E 184 Gc 25
Vila Rica ○ BR 121 Ej 50
Vilarinho do Monte ○ BR 121 Ej 46
Vila Santissima ○ BR 129 Ed 53
Vila Tambaquí ○ BR 117 Eb 47
Vila Tepequem ○ BR 112 Ed 44
Vila Vehla ○ BR 113 Ej 44
Vilavila ○ PE 128 Dn 53
Vilca ○ PE 128 Dl 52
Vilcabamba ○ EC 116 Dj 48
Vilcashuaman ○ PE 128 Dm 52
Vilches ○ E 184 Ge 26
Vilcún ~ RCH 147 Dm 65
Vilelas ○ RA 136 Ec 59
Vile Velha de Rodao ○ P 184 Gc 26
Vilfranca del P. ○ E 184 Gg 25
Vilha Velha ○ BR 141 Ep 56
Vilhelmina ○ S 158 Gp 13
Vilhena ○ BR 129 Ed 52
Viljandi ○ EST 171 He 16
Viljoenskroen ○ ZA 349 Hf 59
Viljuj ~ RUS 204 Va 5
Viljuj ~ RUS 204 Wa 6
Viljujsk ○ RUS 204 Wa 6
Viljujskoe vodohranilišče ~ RUS 204 Vb 6
Viljujskoje vodohranilišče ~ RUS 22 Qb 3
Vilkija ○ LT 171 Hd 18
Villa Abecia ○ BOL 136 Eb 56
Villa Ahumada ○ MEX 80 Cj 30
Villa Alemana ○ RCH 137 Dn 62
Villa Ana ○ RA 146 Ee 60
Villa Angela ○ RA 136 Ed 59
Villa Atuel ○ RA 137 Dp 63
Villa Azueta ○ MEX 93 Da 36
Villaba ○ RP 267 Ln 40
Villa Berthet ○ RA 136 Ed 59
Villablino ○ E 184 Gc 24
Villa Brana ○ RA 136 Ec 59
Villa Bruzual ○ YV 107 Dp 41
Villa Cañas ○ RA 137 Ed 62
Villacañas ○ E 184 Ge 26
Villa Candelaria ○ RA 137 Ec 60
Villa Carlos Paz ○ RA 137 Eb 61
Villacarrillo ○ E 184 Ge 26
Villach ○ A 174 Gn 22
Villa Constitución ○ RA 137 Ed 62
Villa Corona ○ MEX 92 Ck 35
Villa de Cazones ○ MEX 81 Cp 34
Villa de Cos ○ MEX 92 Cl 34
Villa de Cura ○ YV 107 Ea 41
Villa de Garcia ○ MEX 81 Cm 33
Villa de Leiva ○ CO 107 Dm 43
Villa del Rosario ○ YV 107 Dm 40
Villa del Rosario ○ RA 137 Ec 61
Villa de Reyes ○ MEX 92 Cm 35
Villadiego ○ E 184 Gd 24
Villa Dolores ○ RA 137 Eb 62
Villa Figueroa ○ RA 136 Ec 59
Villa Flores ○ MEX 93 Db 37
Villafranca d. B. ○ E 184 Gc 24
Villa General Belgrano ○ RA 137 Eb 61
Villa General Güemes ○ RA 140 Ee 58
Villa General Roca ○ RA 137 Ea 62
Villa General San Martin ○ RA 137 Dp 61
Villa Gesell ○ RA 146 Ef 64
Villagran ○ MEX 92 Cm 35
Villa Grove ○ USA 65 Ck 26
Villaguay ○ RA 146 Ee 61
Villa Hermosa ○ MEX 92 Cl 35
Villahermosa ○ MEX 93 Db 37
Villa Hidalgo ○ MEX 80 Ch 30
Villa Hidalgo ○ MEX 80 Ck 32
Villa Hidalgo ○ MEX 92 Cl 35
Villa Huidobra ○ RA 137 Eb 63
Villa Insurgentes ○ MEX 75 Cf 33
Villa Juárez ○ MEX 80 Ch 32
Villa Juárez ○ MEX 92 Cm 34
Villa Larca ○ RA 137 Eb 62
Villalbin ○ PY 140 Ee 59
Villaldama ○ MEX 81 Cm 32
Villa Lola ○ YV 112 Ec 42
Villalonga ○ RA 147 Ec 65
Villalpando ○ E 184 Gd 25
Villa Mainero ○ MEX 81 Cn 33
Villa María ○ RA 137 Ec 62
Villa Martin ○ BOL 136 Ea 56
Villamartín ○ E 184 Gd 27
Villa Mascardi ○ RA 147 Dn 66
Villa Matoque ○ RA 136 Ec 58
Villa Mazán ○ RA 136 Ea 60
Villa Media Agua ○ RA 137 Dp 61
Villa Mercedes ○ RA 137 Eb 62
Villa Mills ○ CR 97 Df 41
Villamontes ○ BOL 136 Ec 56
Villa Neriti ○ BR 120 Ee 48
Villanueva ○ MEX 92 Cl 34
Villanueva ○ CO 107 Dm 40
Villa Nueva ○ RA 137 Dp 61
Villanueva d.l.C. ○ E 184 Gc 27
Villanueva d.l.Infantes ○ E 184 Ge 26
Villanueva-de Cordoba ○ E 184 Gd 26
Villa Ocampo ○ MEX 80 Ck 32
Villa Ocampo ○ RA 146 Ee 60
Villa Ojo de Agua ○ RA 137 Ec 60
Villa Olivia ○ PY 140 Ef 59
Villa Ortega ○ RCH 152 Dn 68
Villapinzón ○ CO 107 Dm 43
Villa Reducción ○ RA 137 Ec 62
Villa Regina ○ RA 147 Ea 65
Villarrica ○ PY 140 Ef 59
Villarrica ○ RCH 147 Dm 65
Villarrobledo ○ E 184 Ge 26
Villa Salvadorita ○ NIC 96 De 39
Villa San Martin ○ RA 136 Eb 60
Villa Santa Rita de Catuna ○ RA 137 Ea 61
Villa Talavera ○ BOL 129 Eb 55
Villa Toquepala ○ PE 128 Dn 54
Villatoya ○ E 184 Gf 26
Villa Tunari ○ BOL 129 Eb 54
Villa Union ○ MEX 81 Cm 31
Villa Unión ○ MEX 92 Cj 34
Villa Unión ○ MEX 92 Ck 34
Villa Unión ○ RA 137 Dp 60
Villa Valeria ○ RA 137 Eb 63
Villa Vásquez ○ DOM 101 Dn 36
Villavicencio ○ CO 106 Dl 43
Villaviciosa ○ E 184 Gd 24
Villazón ○ BOL 136 Eb 57
Villefranche-de-Rouergue ○ F 184 Gg 23
Villefranche-s.-S. ○ F 185 Gj 23
Ville-Marie ○ CDN 60 Dj 22
Villena ○ E 184 Gf 26
Villeneuve-s.-Lot ○ F 184 Gg 23
Ville Platte ○ USA 86 Db 30
Villeroy ○ CDN 60 Dn 22
Villiers ○ ZA 349 Hg 59
Villingen-Schwenningen ○ D 174 Gl 21
Villisca ○ USA 70 Da 25
Villupuram ○ IND 238 Kd 39
Vilnes ○ N 158 Gj 15
Vilnius ▣ LT 171 He 18
Vil'njans'k ○ UA 175 Hk 22
Vil'nohir'k ○ UA 175 Hk 21
Vilque ○ PE 128 Dn 53
Vils ~ D 174 Gm 21
Vilyeyka ○ BY 171 Hf 18
Vimioso ○ P 184 Gc 25
Vimmerby ○ S 170 Gp 17
Vina ~ CAM 321 Gn 42
Viña del Mar ○ RCH 137 Dm 62
Vinalhaven Island ⌂ USA 60 Dp 23
Vinarós ○ E 184 Gg 25
Vincennes ○ USA 71 De 26
Vincennes Bay ≈ 38 Qa 16
Vincente Guerrero ○ MEX 75 Cd 30
Vinces ○ EC 116 Dj 46
Vinchina ○ RA 136 Dp 60
Vinchina ~ RA 137 Dp 60
Vindelälven ~ S 158 Ha 13
Vindeln ○ S 159 Hc 13
Vindhya Range ⛰ IND 234 Kb 34
Vineland ○ USA 74 Dl 26
Vingåker ○ S 170 Gp 16
Vinh ○ VN 255 Lc 36
Vinhais ○ P 184 Gc 25
Vinh Cây Du'o'ng ~ VN 263 Lc 40
Vinhedo ○ BR 141 El 57
Vĩnh Hy ○ VN 263 Le 40
Vĩnh Kim ○ VN 263 Le 38
Vinh Lôc ○ VN 255 Lc 35
Vĩnh Long ○ VN 263 Lc 40
Vinh Pham Thiêy ~ VN 263 Ld 40
Vinh Thanh ○ VN 263 Lc 41
Vĩnh Yên ○ VN 255 Lc 35
Vinita ○ USA 70 Da 27
Vinkovci ○ HR 174 Hb 23
Vinnycja ○ UA 175 Hg 21
Vinstra ○ N 158 Gl 15
Vinton ○ USA 70 Db 24
Vinukonda ○ IND 238 Kd 37
Vinza ○ RCB 332 Gp 47
Viola ○ USA 70 Cp 27
Viola ○ USA 71 Dc 25
Violaineville ○ G 332 Gm 45
Vioolsdrif ○ ZA 348 Ha 60
Vipbya Mountains ⛰ MW 344 Hj 52
Vipos ~ RA 136 Eb 59
Vir ○ TJ 223 Jp 27
Virac ○ RP 267 Ln 39
Virachey ○ K 263 Ld 39
Virac Point ⌓ RP 267 Ln 39
Viraganur ○ IND 239 Kd 40
Viramgām ○ IND 227 Jp 34
Viranşehir ○ TR 195 Hm 27
Virarājendrapet ○ IND 238 Kb 39
Virāwah ○ PK 227 Jp 33
Virden ○ CDN 56 Cm 21
Vire ○ F 163 Gf 21
Virei ○ ANG 340 Gn 53
Virgem da Lapa ○ BR 125 En 54
Virgin ~ USA 64 Ce 27
Virgin Gorda ⌂ GB 104 Eb 36
Virginia ○ USA 71 Dc 26
Virginia ⊙ USA 74 Dj 27
Virginia ○ IRL 162 Gc 19
Virginia ○ ZA 349 Hf 60
Virginia ○ AUS 378 Mf 63
Virginia Beach ○ USA 74 Dl 27
Virginia Dale ○ USA 65 Ck 25
Virgin Islands ⌂ GB 104 Eb 36
Virgin Islands ⌂ USA 104 Eb 36
Virgin Passage ~ USA 104 Eb 36
Virgolândia ○ BR 141 En 55
Virida Tábua Salitre ~ BR 125 Ep 51
Virihaure ~ S 158 Ha 12
Virovitica ○ HR 174 Ha 23
Virra ○ FIN 159 Hd 14
Virrória ○ I 185 Gp 27
Virtsu ○ EST 171 Hd 16
Viru ○ PE 116 Dj 50
Virudó ○ CO 106 Dk 43
Virudunagar ○ IND 239 Kc 41
Vis ○ HR 194 Ha 24
Vis ⌂ HR 194 Ha 24
Visaginas ○ LT 171 He 18
Visalia ○ USA 64 Cc 27
Visayan Sea ~ RP 267 Lm 40
Visby ○ S 170 Ha 17
Viscount Melville Sound ~ CDN 6 Da 2
Viscount Melville Sound ≈ CDN 42 Eb 4
Viscu ○ BR 121 El 46
Višegrad ○ BIH 194 Hb 24
Viseu ○ P 184 Gc 25
Vishākhapatnam ○ IND 238 Kf 37
Visicsa ~ BOL 129 Ea 55
Viški ○ LV 171 Hf 17
Visočica △ HR 174 Gp 23
Visoko ○ BIH 194 Ha 24
Visrivier ~ ZA 358 Hc 61
Vista ○ USA 64 Cd 29
Vista ⌂ CV 316 Fj 38
Vista Alegre ○ BR 117 Dp 45
Vista Alegre ○ ANG 332 Gp 50
Vista Flores ○ RA 137 Dp 62
Vistula ~ PL 174 Hc 20
Visuvisu Point ⌓ SOL 290 Na 49
Visvirr ○ RCH 128 Dp 54
Vit ~ BG 194 He 24
Vita ○ CDN 56 Cp 21
Vita ○ IND 238 Kb 37
Vitasaari ○ FIN 159 He 14
Viterbo ○ I 185 Gm 24
Viterlinden △ S 158 Hb 13
Vithalapur ○ IND 227 Ka 34
Vitiaz Strait ~ PNG 287 Mk 48
Vitigudino ○ E 184 Gc 25
Viti Levu ⌂ FJI 387 Nl 54
Vitim ~ RUS 204 Vb 7
Vitim ~ RUS 204 Vb 8
Vitolište ○ MK 194 Hc 25
Vitóna ○ BR 146 Eg 60
Vitor ○ PE 128 Dn 54
Vitória ○ BR 117 Eb 47
Vitória ○ RA 137 Ed 62
Vitória ○ BR 141 Ep 56
Vitória d. Sto. Antão ○ BR 124 Fc 50
Vitória da Conquista ○ BR 125 Ep 53
Vitória do Jari ○ BR 121 Eh 46
Vitória do Mearim ○ BR 121 Em 47
Vitória do Xingu ○ BR 121 Eh 47
Vitoria Gasteiz ○ E 184 Ge 24
Vitorino Freire ○ BR 121 Em 48
Vitosa △ BG 194 Hf 24
Vitré ○ F 163 Gf 21
Vitry-le-Francois ○ F 163 Gj 21
Vitshumbi ○ RDC 336 Hg 46
Vitsyebsk ○ BY 171 Hh 18
Vittangi ○ S 159 Hc 12
Vittel ○ F 163 Gj 21
Vittorio Véneto ○ I 185 Gn 23
Viudas de Oriente ○ MEX 92 Cm 34
Viveiro ○ E 184 Gc 24
Vivi ~ RUS 204 Ub 5
Vivian ○ USA 56 Cm 24
Vivien ○ CDN 56 Cp 21
Vivo ○ ZA 349 Hg 57
Vivonne Bay ~ AUS 378 Me 64
Viwa ⌂ FJI 387 Nl 54
Vizcaíno ○ MEX 75 Cf 32
Vizianagaram ○ IND 234 Kf 36
Vizille ○ F 185 Gj 23
Vizinhos ○ BR 140 Eh 58
Vizzini ○ I 185 Gp 27
Vjalozero ~ RUS 159 Hk 12
Vjartsilja ○ RUS 159 Hh 14
Vjatka ~ RUS 154 Ra 7
Vjatke ~ RUS 154 Rb 7
Vjatskie Poljany ○ RUS 181 Jd 17
Vjazemskij ○ RUS 205 Wc 9
Vjazemskij ○ RUS 250 Md 22
Vjaz'ma ○ RUS 171 Hk 18
Vjazniki ○ RUS 181 Hp 17
Vlaanderen ⊙ B 163 Gj 20
Vladičin Han ○ SCG 194 Hd 24
Vladikavkaz ○ RUS 202 Ja 24
Vladimir ○ RUS 171 Hn 17
Vladivostok ○ RUS 250 Mb 24
Vladyčnoe ○ RUS 171 Hm 16
Vlasenica ○ BIH 174 Hb 23
Vlieland ⌂ NL 163 Gj 19
Vlorë ○ AL 194 Hb 25
Vltava ~ CZ 174 Gp 21
Vobkent ○ UZB 223 Jl 25
Vod. nadrž Lipno ~ CZ 174 Gp 21
Vodla ~ RUS 171 Hl 15
Vogan ○ RT 317 Gg 42
Vogelsberg ⛰ D 174 Gl 20
Vogelweide ○ NAM 348 Hb 57
Voh ○ F 386 Ne 56
Vohilava ○ RM 353 Jb 57
Vohilengo ○ RM 345 Jc 54
Vohimena ○ RM 345 Jc 54
Vohimena ⛰ RM 353 Jb 58
Vohipeno ○ RM 353 Jb 57
Vohitra ~ RM 345 Jc 55
Voi ○ VN 255 Ld 36
Voi ○ EAK 337 Hm 47
Voi ~ EAK 337 Hm 47
Voinica ○ RUS 159 Hh 13
Voinjama ○ LB 316 Gb 41
Voiron ○ F 185 Gj 23
Vojejkov Ice Shelf △ 38 Ra 16
Vojvodina ▭ SCG 174 Hb 23
Vokeo Island ⌂ PNG 287 Mj 47
Volborg ○ USA 51 Cj 23
Volcán Altar △ EC 116 Dj 46
Volcán Antisana △ EC 116 Dj 46
Volcán Antofalla △ RA 136 Ea 58
Volcán Antuco △ RCH 137 Dn 64
Volcán Arenal △ CR 97 Df 40
Volcán Azufral △ CO 116 Dk 45
Volcán Baru △ PA 97 Dg 41
Volcán Calbuco △ RCH 147 Dm 66
Volcán Callagui △ RCH 137 Dn 64
Volcán Cayambe △ EC 116 Dk 45
Volcán Ceboruco △ MEX 92 Ck 35
Volcán Chachani △ PE 128 Dn 54
Volcán Chillán △ RCH 137 Dn 64
Volcán Chimborazo △ EC 116 Dj 46
Volcán Concepción △ NIC 96 Df 40
Volcán Copahue △ RCH 137 Dn 64
Volcán Corcovado △ RCH 147 Dm 67
Volcán Cosigüina △ NIC 93 Dd 39
Volcán Cotopaxi △ EC 116 Dj 46
Volcán de San Salvador △ ES 93 Dd 39
Volcán de San Vicente △ ES 93 Dd 39
Volcán Descabezado △ RCH 137 Dn 63
Volcán Domuyo △ RA 137 Dn 64
Volcán Doña Juana △ CO 106 Dk 45
Volcán G. Pincincha △ EC 116 Dj 46
Volcán Galán △ RA 136 Ea 58
Volcán Guallatiri △ RCH/BOL 128 Dp 55
Volcán Huequi △ RCH 147 Dm 67
Volcán Illiniza △ EC 116 Dj 46
Volcán Isluga △ RCH/BOL 128 Dp 55
Volcán Lascár △ RCH 136 Ea 57
Volcán Las Tres Virgenes △ MEX 75 Cf 32
Volcán Lincancabur △ RCH 136 Dp 57
Volcán Llaima △ RCH 147 Dn 65
Volcán Llullaillaco △ RCH 136 Dp 58
Volcán Maipo △ RCH 137 Dp 63
Volcán Minchinmávida △ RCH 147 Dm 67
Volcán Miravallas △ CR 97 Df 40
Volcán Misti △ PE 128 Dn 54
Volcán Momotombo △ NIC 96 De 39
Volcano ○ USA 75 An 36
Volcán Ollagüe △ BOL 136 Dp 56
Volcán Osorno △ RCH 147 Dm 66
Volcán Peteroa △ RCH 137 Dn 63
Volcán Pichupichu △ PE 128 Dn 54
Volcán Popocatépetl △ MEX 92 Cn 36
Volcán Puracé △ CO 106 Dk 44
Volcán Putana △ RCH 136 Dp 57
Volcán Puyehue △ RCH 147 Dm 66
Volcán San Cristobal △ NIC 96 De 39
Volcán Sangay △ EC 116 Dj 47
Volcán San José △ RCH 137 Dp 62
Volcán San Pedro △ RCH 136 Dp 56
Volcán Santa Maria △ GCA 93 Dc 38
Volcán Santa Maria △ CR 97 Df 40
Volcán Sotará △ CO 106 Dk 44
Volcán Sumaco △ EC 116 Dk 46
Volcán Tacora △ PE 128 Dp 54
Volcán Tajumulco △ GCA 93 Dc 38
Volcán Ticsani △ PE 128 Dn 54
Volcán Tromen △ RA 137 Dn 64
Volcán Tungurahua △ EC 116 Dj 46
Volcán Villarrica △ RCH 147 Dm 65
Volga ~ RUS 154 Qc 7
Volga ○ RUS 171 Hm 17
Volga ~ RUS 181 Jb 20
Volga Upland ▭ RUS 155 Qc 9
Volga Upland ▭ RUS 181 Ja 21
Volgo-Baltijskij kanal ~ RUS 159 Hl 15
Volgodonsk ○ RUS 181 Hp 22
Volgo-Donskoi kanal ~ RUS 181 Hp 21
Volgograd ○ RUS 181 Hp 21
Volgograd Reservoir ~ RUS 181 Ja 21
Volhov ○ RUS 171 Hj 16
Volhov ~ RUS 171 Hj 16
Volksrust ○ ZA 349 Hg 59
Volnovacha ○ UA 181 Hl 22
Voločanka ○ RUS 204 Ua 4
Voloček ○ RUS 159 Hn 14
Voločys'k ○ UA 175 Hf 21
Volodarsk ○ RUS 181 Hp 17
Volodarskij ○ RUS 202 Jc 22
Volodymyr-Volyns'kyj ○ UA 175 He 20
Vologda ○ RUS 19 Ma 4
Vologda ○ RUS 154 Qc 7
Vologda ○ RUS 171 Hn 16
Volokolamsk ○ RUS 171 Hk 17
Volokonovka ○ RUS 181 Hl 20
Volop ○ ZA 349 Hd 60
Vólos ○ GR 194 Hd 26
Volosovo ○ RUS 171 Hg 16
Volot ○ RUS 171 Hh 17
Vol'sk ○ RUS 181 Jb 19
Volstruisleegte ○ ZA 358 Hd 62
Volta ~ GH 317 Gg 43
Volta Blanche ~ BF 317 Gf 39
Volta Blanche ~ BF 317 Gf 40
Volta Lake ~ GH 317 Gf 41
Volta Redonda ○ BR 141 Em 57
Volta Rouge ~ BF 317 Gf 40
Volterra ○ I 185 Gm 24
Voltsberg △ SME 113 Ef 43
Voltti ○ FIN 159 Hd 14
Volubilis ★ MA 293 Gd 28
Volunteer Point ⌓ GB 147 Ef 71
Volyns'ka vysočyna ⛰ UA 175 He 20
Volžsk ○ RUS 181 Jc 18
Volžskiy ○ RUS 181 Ja 21
Volžsko-Kamskij zapov. ♀ RUS 181 Jc 17
Vom ○ WAN 320 Gl 41
Vonavona ⌂ SOL 290 Na 50
Vondrove ○ RM 353 Ja 56
Vondrozo ○ RM 353 Jb 57
Vonga ○ RUS 159 Hp 13
Vónitsa ○ GR 194 Hc 26
Von Lindequist Gate ○ NAM 340 Ha 55
Von Otterøyane ⌂ N 158 Hc 6
Vontimitta ○ IND 238 Kd 38
Voorspoed ○ ZA 349 Hd 59
Vopnafjörður ○ IS 158 Fn 13
Vopnafjörður ~ IS 158 Fn 13
Voranava ○ BY 171 He 18
Vorarlberg ⊙ A 174 Gl 22
Vordingborg ○ DK 170 Gm 18
Vorenža ○ RUS 159 Hk 14
Vorkuta ○ RUS 154 Sa 5
Vorma ~ N 158 Gm 15
Vormsi ⌂ EST 171 Hd 16
Vorona ~ RUS 181 Hp 19
Voronež ~ RUS 181 Hm 19
Voroncovo ○ RUS 204 Tb 4
Voronezh ○ RUS 181 Hm 20
Voron'ja ~ RUS 159 Hk 11
Vorotynec ○ RUS 181 Ja 17
Vorozba ○ UA 175 Hk 20
Vorpommersche Boddenlandschaft ♀ D 170 Gn 18
Vorskl ~ RUS 181 Hl 20
Vorskla ~ UA 175 Hk 21
Vorsma ○ RUS 181 Hp 18
Vorstershoop ○ ZA 349 Hd 58
Võrtsjärv jv. ~ EST 171 He 16
Võru ○ EST 171 Hf 17
Vosburg ○ ZA 349 Hd 61
Vose ○ TJ 223 Jn 27
Vosges ⛰ F 163 Gk 22
Voskresensk ○ RUS 171 Hm 18
Voskresenskoe ○ RUS 171 Hl 17
Voso ~ RI 282 Lp 47
Voss ○ N 158 Gk 15
Vostochnyy Siniy, Khrebet ⛰ RUS 250 Mc 24
Vostock ⌂ KIR 35 Ba 10
Vostočnoe Munozero ○ RUS 159 Hk 12
Vostok ○ RUS 205 Xa 9
Vostok ○ RUS 250 Md 22
Voteche ○ MOC 352 Hk 57
Votkinsk ○ RUS 154 Rb 7
Votuporanga ○ BR 140 Ek 56
Vouzela ○ P 184 Gb 25
Vouziers ○ F 163 Gj 21
Vovčans'k ○ UA 181 Hl 20
Vovodo ~ RCA 324 He 42
voz. Čornae ~ BY 171 He 19
voz. Sporavskoe ~ BY 171 Hf 19
voz. Vyhanaščanskoe ~ BY 171 Hf 19

480 Vera - voz. Vyhanaščanskoe

O Country ▣ Capital city ⊙ Administrative unit O Place ♁ Island ⛰ Mountain range △ Mountain ⌓ Cape ≈ Ocean, Sea ~ Lake, River ▿ Undersea topography ❄ Glacier ♀ National park ••• Reservation ★ Point of major interest ▭ Landscape

Vožega O RUS 171 Hn 15
Voznesens'k O UA 175 Hh 22
Voznesenskoe O RUS 181 Hn 18
Vozroždenie O RUS 181 Jc 19
Vraca O BG 194 Hd 24
Vrbas ~ BIH 174 Ha 23
Vrede O ZA 349 Hg 59
Vredenburg O ZA 358 Ha 62
Vredendal O ZA 348 Hb 61
Vredeshoop O NAM 348 Hb 59
Vreed-en-Hoop O GUY 113 Ee 42
Vriddhāchalam O IND 239 Kd 40
Vriendschaps ~ RI 286 Mf 48
Vršac O SCG 174 Hc 23
Vryburg O ZA 349 He 59
Vryheid O ZA 352 Hh 59
Vsevoložsk O RUS 171 Hh 15
Vuadil O UZB 223 Jp 25
Vube O RDC 324 Hf 44
Vuka ~ HR 174 Hb 23
Vuktyl O RUS 154 Rc 6
Vulavu O SOL 290 Nb 50
Vulcan O CDN 51 Cf 20
Vumba Mountains ⛰ ZW 344 Hj 55
Vundúzi ~ MOC 344 Hj 55
Vũng Tàu O VN 263 Ld 40
Vunisea O FJI 387 Nm 55
Vuntut National Park ♀ CDN 47 Be 11
Vuokatti O FIN 159 Hf 13
Vuollerim O S 158 Hb 12
Vuolvojaure ~ S 158 Hb 12
Vuotso O FIN 159 Hf 11
Vuottas O S 159 Hc 12
Vurnary O RUS 181 Jb 18
Vuti O ZW 341 Hg 54
Vwawa O EAT 337 Hj 50
Vyaparla O IND 238 Kd 37
Vybor O RUS 171 Hg 17
Vyborg O RUS 171 Hg 15
Vyčegda ~ RUS 154 Rb 6
Vydropužsk O RUS 171 Hk 17
Vyerkhnyadzvinsk O BY 171 Hg 18
Vyezžij Log O RUS 204 Ua 7
Vygozero ~ RUS 159 Hk 14
Vyksa O RUS 181 Hp 18
Vylkove O UA 175 Hg 23
Vym ~ RUS 154 Rb 6
Vyrica O RUS 171 Hh 16
Vyšhorod O UA 175 Hh 20
Vyšnij Voloček O RUS 171 Hk 17
Vysokaye O BY 171 Hd 19
Vytegra O RUS 171 Hl 15

W

W. Bill Dannelly Reservoir ~ USA 71 De 29
W. F. George Reservation ~ USA 86 Df 30
W. Rice River ~ USA 56 Cp 22
Wa O GH 317 Ge 40
Waajid O SP 328 Hp 44
Waal ~ NL 163 Gj 20
Waala O F 386 Nd 55
Waanyi-Garawa Aboriginal Reserve ••• AUS 365 Me 55
Waat O SUD 324 Hj 41
Wabag O PNG 286 Mh 48
Wabakimi Lake ~ CDN 56 Dc 20
Wabamun Lake ~ CDN 50 Ce 19
Wabasca ~ CDN 42 Eb 7
Wabash ~ USA 71 De 26
Wabash O USA 71 Df 25
Wabasha O USA 56 Dc 23
Wabassi River ~ CDN 57 De 20
Wabē Gestro ~ ETH 325 Hn 42
Wabē Mena ~ ETH 325 Hn 43
Wabigoon Lake ~ CDN 56 Db 21
Wabimeig Lake ~ CDN 57 Df 20
Wabinosh Lake ~ CDN 57 Dd 20
Waboma Island ♁ PNG 287 Mn 50
Wabuda Island ♁ PNG 286 Mh 50
Waccasassa Bay ≈ USA 86 Dg 31
Wach'īlē O ETH 325 Hm 43
Waci O RI 275 Ma 45
Waco O CDN 61 Eb 20
Waco O USA 81 Cp 30
Waconda Lake ~ USA 70 Cn 26
Wad O PK 227 Jm 32
Wada'ah O SUD 312 He 39
Wad al-Abbas O SUD 313 Hj 39
Wadalei O PNG 287 Mm 50
Wad al-Haddad O SUD 313 Hj 39
Wad an-Nail O SUD 313 Hj 39
Wadayama O J 251 Md 28
Wad Banda O SUD 312 Hg 39
Wad Ban Naqa O SUD 313 Hj 37
Wadbiliga ♀ AUS 379 Ml 64
Waddān O LAR 297 Ha 31
Waddenzee ≈ NL 163 Gj 19
Waddikee O AUS 378 Md 62
Waddy Point ⌓ AUS 375 Mn 58
Wadena O CDN 51 Cl 20
Wadena O USA 56 Da 22
Wadesboro O USA 71 Dh 28
Wadeye O AUS 364 Ma 53
Wad Hassib O SUD 312 Hf 40
Wadhope O CDN 56 Da 20
Wādī Abū Dawn ~ SUD 313 Hj 36
Wādī Abū Khinzīr ~ SUD 312 Hh 38
Wādī Adana ~ YE 218 Ja 38
Wādī al-'Aqīq ~ KSA 214 Hn 33
Wādī al-'Arīš ~ ET 301 Hj 30
Wādī al Awrā ~ LAR 297 Ha 31
Wādī al Ayn ~ OM 226 Jg 34
Wādī al-Bāṭin ~ KSA 215 Ja 31
Wādī al Fārigh ~ LAR 300 Hb 30
Wādī al Fāt ~ LAR 297 Gp 31
Wādī al-Ġarīr ~ KSA 214 Hp 33
Wādī al Ġauf ~ YE 218 Ja 37
Wādī al-Ghalla ~ SUD 312 Hg 40
Wādī al-Ġina ~ KSA 214 Hl 30
Wādī al-Ġiz' ~ YE 219 Jd 37
Wādī al-Ġizl ~ KSA 214 Hl 32
Wādī al-Hamḍ ~ KSA 214 Hl 33
Wādī al-Hanākiya ~ KSA 214 Hn 33
Wādī al-Hawad ~ SUD 313 Hj 37
Wādī al-Ḥurr ~ IRQ 214 Hp 30
Wādī al Kū ~ SUD 312 He 39
Wādī al-Milk ~ SUD 312 Hh 37
Wādī al-Ua'ilī ★ KSA 214 Hm 30
Wādī 'Amd ~ YE 218 Jb 38
Wādī 'Amīq ~ IRQ 209 Hn 29
Wādī 'Amūr ~ SUD 313 Hk 36
Wādī Andam ~ OM 226 Jh 34
Wādī an Nashū' ~ LAR 297 Gn 32
Wādī ,Araba ~ ET 301 Hj 31
Wādī ,Ar'ar ~ KSA 214 Hn 30
Wādī ar-Radd ~ SYR 209 Hn 27
Wādī ar-Rīma ~ KSA 214 Hn 33
Wādī ar-Rišā' ~ KSA 214 Hp 33
Wādī ash Shāṭi ~ LAR 297 Gn 32
Wādī ash Shu'bah ~ LAR 300 Hd 30
Wādī ash Shubayrimah ~ LAR 297 Ha 32
Wādī Asmara ~ KSA 214 Hn 32
Wādī aš-Ša'ba ~ KSA 214 Hn 32
Wādī as-Sirḥān ~ KSA 214 Hl 30
Wādī Aswad ~ OM 226 Jg 34
Wādī Atina ~ OM 219 Je 36
Wādī Azūm ~ SUD 312 Hd 39
Wādī az Zimām ~ LAR 297 Gp 31
Wādī az-Zuhūr ~ OM 219 Jf 37
Wādī Bā'ir ~ JOR 214 Hl 30
Wādī Baiš ~ KSA 218 Hp 37
Wādī Banā ~ YE 218 Ja 39
Wādī Banī Hašbal O KSA 218 Hp 36
Wādī Barjūj ~ LAR 297 Gn 33
Wādī Barkol ~ SUD 312 Hh 37
Wādī Bayy al Kabīr ~ LAR 297 Gp 30
Wādī Bīša ~ KSA 218 Hp 35
Wādī Bīša ~ KSA 218 Hp 36
Wādī Damā ~ KSA 214 Hk 32
Wādī Daur'an ~ YE 218 Jc 38
Wādī d-Dahsa ~ ET 301 Hh 32
Wādī Derbeikan ~ SUD 313 Hk 36
Wādī el Hamim ~ LAR 300 Hd 30
Wādī Faǧr ~ KSA 214 Hl 31
Wādī Faiḥān ~ KSA 214 Hp 31
Wādī Fegoh ~ ET 301 Hk 34
Wādī Ġabǵaba ~ ET 301 Hj 34
Wādī Gadūn ~ OM 219 Je 36
Wādī Ghadūn ~ OM 219 Jg 36
Wādī Habauna ~ KSA 218 Ja 37
Wādī Hadramaut ~ YE 219 Jd 38
Wādī Halfā O SUD 301 Hh 35
Wādī Halfain ~ OM 226 Jg 34
Wādī Hāmir ~ IRQ 214 Hn 30
Wādī Hamir ~ YE 219 Jc 38
Wādī Harāwah ~ LAR 297 Ha 30
Wādī Haurān ~ IRQ 209 Hp 29
Wādī Hudain ~ ET 301 Hk 34
Wādī Hudra ~ YE 219 Jc 37
Wādī Huwār ~ SUD 312 He 37
Wādī Huwayt ~ SUD 313 Hj 35
Wādī Ibib ~ ET 301 Hk 34
Wādī Ibra ~ SUD 312 He 40
Wādī Faysal ~ LAR 297 Gn 30
Wādī Irawan ~ LAR 297 Gm 32
Wādī Kaja ~ TCH 321 Hd 39
Wādī Kbīr ~ LAR 297 Gp 30
Wādī Kirbikān ~ SUD 313 Hj 36
Wādī Kunayr ~ LAR 297 Gp 32
Wādī l-'Allāqī ~ ET 301 Hj 34
Wādī Langeb ~ SUD 313 Hl 36
Wādī Langeb ~ SUD 313 Hl 37
Wādī l-'Arabao ~ JOR 214 Hk 30
Wādī l-'Arīš ~ ET 301 Hj 31
Wādil-Batha ~ OM 226 Jh 34
Wādī l-Ġadaf ~ IRQ 209 Hn 29
Wādī l-Ġadaf ~ JOR 214 Hl 30
Wādī l-Hail ~ SYR 209 Hm 28
Wādī l-Hasā ~ JOR 214 Hl 30
Wādī l-Haurān ~ IRQ 209 Hm 29
Wādī l-Hirr ~ IRQ 214 Hp 30
Wādī l-Miyā ~ SYR 209 Hm 28
Wādī l-Muġib ~ JOR 214 Hk 30
Wādī l-Ubayy ~ IRQ 209 Hp 29
Wādī l-'Ubayyiḍ ~ IRQ 214 Hn 30
Wādī l-Ulyā O OM 226 Jg 34
Wādī Maḥya ~ YE 218 Jc 37
Wādī Majrūr ~ SUD 312 Hf 37
Wādī Maur ~ YE 218 Hp 38
Wādī Maymūn ~ LAR 297 Gm 30
Wādī Mugal ~ SUD 313 Hk 36
Wādī Muheit ~ SUD 312 Hj 37
Wādī Muqaddam ~ SUD 312 Hh 37
Wādī Muqšin ~ OM 219 Jf 36
Wādī Mūsa O JOR 214 Hk 30
Wādī Nabi ~ SUD 313 Hj 35
Wādī Naǧrān ~ KSA 218 Ja 37
Wādī Natāš ~ ET 301 Hj 33
Wādī n-Naṭrūn ~ ET 301 Hg 30
Wādī Oko ~ SUD 313 Hk 35
Wādī Qarqaraut ~ YE 219 Jd 38
Wādī Qarzah ~ LAR 297 Gp 30
Wādī Qinā ~ ET 301 Hj 32
Wādī Qitbit ~ OM 219 Jf 36
Wādī Raima ~ YE 218 Hp 38
Wādī Reseida ~ SUD 313 Hj 35
Wādī Rikat ~ OM 219 Jg 36
Wādī r-Raṭqa ~ IRQ 209 Hn 29
Wādī Sāhūq ~ KSA 214 Hn 33
Wādī Sawfajjin ~ LAR 297 Gp 30
Wādī Seidna O SUD 312 Hj 38
Wādī Shurshūt ~ LAR 297 Gm 30
Wādī Sihan ~ OM 219 Je 36
Wādī ṣ-Ṣawāb ~ SYR 209 Hn 28
Wādī Surdūd ~ YE 218 Hp 38
Wādī Tamat ~ LAR 297 Ha 30
Wādī Tanezzruft ~ LAR 297 Gm 33
Wādī Targhalāt ~ LAR 297 Gp 29
Wādī Tātit ~ KSA 218 Hp 35
Wādī Tayin ~ OM 226 Jh 34
Wādī Tayyāl ~ KSA 214 Hm 31
Wādī T Haurān ~ IRQ 209 Hm 29
Wādī Tinis ~ LAR 297 Gm 33
Wādī t-Tārtār ~ IRQ 209 Hp 28
Wādī t-Tawīl ~ IRQ 209 Hn 29
Wādī t-Tūbal ~ IRQ 209 Hp 29
Wādī Tubǧa ~ KSA 214 Hm 33
Wādī Wouri ~ TCH 309 Gp 35
Wādī Yadat ~ SUD 313 Hk 37
Wādī Zabīd ~ YE 218 Hp 38
Wādī Zamzam ~ LAR 297 Gp 30
Wādī Zazamt ~ LAR 297 Gp 30
Wādī z-Zaidūn ~ ET 301 Hj 33
Wadley O USA 71 Dg 29
Wad Medani O SUD 313 Hj 38
Wadonari O J 259 Ma 32
Wadsworth O USA 64 Cc 26
Waenhuiskrans O ZA 358 Hc 63
Wafangdian O VRC 246 Lm 26
Wagait Aboriginal Reserve ••• AUS 364 Mb 52
Waga River ~ PNG 286 Mh 49
Wagarville O USA 86 Dd 30
Wagau O PNG 287 Mk 49
Wagener O USA 71 Dh 29
Wageningen O SME 113 Ef 43
Wager Bay ≈ CDN 43 Ga 5
Wagga Wagga O AUS 379 Mk 63
Waghete O RI 286 Me 47
Wagin O AUS 368 Lj 62
Wagner O USA 56 Cn 24
Wagner O BR 125 Ep 52
Wagny ~ G 332 Gn 46
Wagoner O USA 70 Da 28
Wagon Mound O USA 65 Ck 27
Wagontire O USA 50 Ce 24
Wągrowiec O PL 170 Ha 19
Wahabu O GH 317 Ge 40
Wahai O RI 283 Ma 47
Wahala O RT 317 Gg 42
Wāhāt al Jalu ▭ LAR 300 Hc 31
Wāhāt al Jufra ▭ LAR 297 Ha 31
Wāhāt al Kufra ▭ LAR 300 Hd 33
Wah Cantonment O PK 230 Ka 29
Wahi O PK 227 Jm 33
Wahiawa O USA 75 Am 35
Wahlbergøya ♁ N 158 Hb 6
Wahlenbergfjorden ~ N 158 Hb 6
Wahoo O USA 70 Cp 25
Wahpeton O USA 56 Cp 22
Wah Pong O MYA 254 Kp 35
Wahroonga O AUS 368 Lh 58
Wai O IND 238 Ka 37
Waialua O USA 75 Al 35
Waian O RC 258 Lk 34
Waianae O USA 75 Al 35
Waiau O NZ 383 Nj 67
Waibakul O RI 279 Lk 50
Waibula O PNG 287 Ml 50
Waidhān O IND 234 Kf 33
Waidhofen an der Thaya O A 174 Gp 21
Waigen Lakes ~ AUS 369 Ma 59
Waihau Bay O NZ 383 Nl 64
Waiheke Island ♁ NZ 383 Nk 64
Waihi O NZ 383 Nk 64
Waikabubak O RI 279 Lk 50
Waikaia O NZ 382 Ng 68
Waikanae O NZ 383 Nk 66
Waikaremoana O NZ 383 Nl 65
Waikari O NZ 383 Nj 67
Waikawa O NZ 382 Ng 69
Waikerie O AUS 378 Mg 63
Wailapa O VU 386 Nf 53
Wailuku O USA 75 Am 35
Wailutu O RI 283 Mb 49
Waimangura O RI 279 Lk 50
Waimate O NZ 382 Nh 68
Waimea O USA 75 An 36
Waimenda O RI 282 Ll 47
Wai Menge ~ PNG 286 Mg 49
Wainganga ~ IND 234 Kd 35
Waingapu O RI 282 Ll 50
Wainwright O USA 23 Ab 2
Wainwright O USA 46 Aj 9
Wainwright O CDN 51 Cg 19
Wainwright Inlet ~ USA 46 Al 9
Waipa O RI 286 Me 47
Waipara O NZ 383 Nj 67
Waipukurau O NZ 383 Nl 66
Wair O RI 283 Mc 48
Waira O PNG 287 Mj 49
Wairaha ~ SOL 290 Nc 50
Wairau River ~ NZ 383 Nj 66
Wairoa O NZ 383 Nl 65
Wairo River ~ PNG 286 Mh 48
Waisa O PNG 287 Mj 49
Waitabula O RI 279 Lk 50
Waitakaruru O NZ 383 Nk 64
Waitaki ~ NZ 382 Nh 68
Waitaki ~ NZ 382 Nh 68
Waitangi O NZ 383 Ab 68
Waitara O NZ 383 Nk 65
Waitiki Landing O NZ 383 Nj 63
Waitomo Caves ♀ NZ 383 Nk 65
Waitsburg O USA 50 Cc 22
Waiuku O NZ 383 Nk 64
Waiwhare O NZ 383 Nl 65
Waje O WAN 320 Gk 41
Wajima O J 251 Me 27
Wajir O EAK 325 Hn 45
Waka O ETH 325 Hl 42
Waka O RDC 333 Hc 45
Wakai O PK 226 Jk 32
Wakasa-wan ≈ J 251 Md 28
Wakatin O RI 282 Lp 47
Wakat Tapai O MAL 271 Lb 43
Wakaw O CDN 51 Ck 19
Wakaya ♁ FJI 387 Nm 54
Wakayama O J 251 Md 28
Wa Keeny O USA 70 Cn 26
Wakefield O USA 57 Dd 22
Wakefield O CDN 60 Dk 23
Wakefield O USA 74 Dk 26
Wakefield ~ AUS 378 Mf 63
Wakema O MYA 262 Km 37
Wakerstrom O ZA 352 Hh 59
Wakkanai O RUS 23 Sa 5
Wakkanai O J 205 Xb 9
Wakkanai O J 250 Mg 23
Wako O PNG 287 Ml 49
Wakomata Lake ~ CDN 57 Dg 22
Wakoo O AUS 379 Mj 63
Wakool ~ AUS 379 Mh 63
Wakunai O PNG 290 Mp 48
Wala ~ EAT 336 Hj 48
Wālājāpet O IND 238 Kd 39
Walambele O GH 317 Ge 40
Walanae ~ RI 279 Lk 48
Wal Athiang O SUD 324 Hg 42
Wałbrzych O PL 174 Ha 20
Walbundrie O AUS 379 Mk 63
Walcha O AUS 379 Mm 61
Walcott O USA 65 Cj 25
Walcott Inlet ~ AUS 361 Ln 54
Wałcz O PL 170 Ha 19
Waldburg O AUS 368 Lj 58
Waldburg Range ⛰ AUS 368 Lj 58
Waldegrave Island ♁ AUS 378 Md 62
Waldegrave Islands ♁ AUS 378 Md 62
Walden O USA 65 Cj 25
Waldenburg O USA 71 Dc 28
Waldersee O CDN 56 Cn 20
Waldo O USA 87 Dg 31
Waldport O USA 50 Bp 23
Waldron O USA 70 Db 28
Wales O USA 23 Ab 3
Wales O USA 46 Ag 13
Wales ⊙ GB 163 Gd 19
Wales O USA 205 Ac 5
Wales Island ♁ CDN 43 Ga 5
Walewale O GH 317 Gf 40
Walgett O AUS 379 Ml 61
Walgra O AUS 374 Mf 56
Walgreen Coast ⌓ 38 Db 17
Walgun O AUS 360 Ll 57
Walhalla O USA 56 Cp 21
Walhalla O USA 71 Dg 28
Walikale O RDC 336 Hg 46
Walis Island ♁ PNG 286 Mh 47
Walker O USA 56 Da 22
Walker ~ USA 64 Cc 26
Walker ~ AUS 364 Md 52
Walker Bay ≈ ZA 358 Hb 63
Walker Lake ~ USA 64 Cc 26
Walker River Indian Reservation ••• USA 64 Cc 26
Walkerville O AUS 379 Mj 65
Wall O USA 51 Cl 23
Wallabi Island ♁ AUS 368 Lg 60
Wallaby Plateau ▿ 34 Qa 12
Wallace O USA 50 Cd 22
Wallace O USA 56 Cp 23
Wallace O USA 70 Cm 25
Wallace O USA 74 Dj 28
Wallaceburg O CDN 57 Dg 24
Wallacetown O NZ 382 Ng 69
Wallal Downs O AUS 360 Ll 55
Wallam Creek ~ AUS 375 Mk 60
Wallareenya O AUS 360 Lk 56
Wallaroo O AUS 378 Me 62
Walla Walla O USA 50 Cc 22
Wallekraal O ZA 348 Ha 61
Wallhallow O AUS 364 Md 54
Walli O PE 128 Dn 53
Wallis ♁ F 390 Ab 52
Wallis and Futuna ⊙ F 390 Ab 52
Walliser Alpen ⛰ CH 163 Gk 22
Wallis Lake ~ AUS 379 Mn 62
Wallonie ⊙ B 163 Gj 20
Wallowa Mountains ⛰ USA 50 Cd 23
Wallumbilla O AUS 375 Ml 59
Walmanpa-Warlpiri Aboriginal Land ••• AUS 364 Mc 55
Walnut O USA 71 Dd 28
Walnut Canyon National Monument ~ USA 64 Cf 28
Walnut Cove O USA 71 Dh 27
Walnut Creek ~ USA 70 Cm 26
Walnut Grove O USA 56 Da 23
Walnut Ridge O USA 71 Dc 27
Walpawa O NZ 383 Nl 65
Walpole O AUS 368 Lj 63
Walpole ♁ F 386 Ng 57
Walpole I. Ind. Res. ••• CDN 71 Dg 24
Walpole-Nornalup ♀ AUS 368 Lj 63
Walsall O GB 163 Gf 19
Walsenburg O USA 65 Ck 27
Walsh O CDN 51 Cg 21
Walsh O USA 65 Cl 27
Walsh ~ AUS 365 Mj 54
Walt Disney World ★ USA 87 Dh 31
Walterboro O USA 71 Dh 29
Waltham Station O CDN 60 Dk 22
Walthill O USA 56 Cp 24
Waltman O USA 51 Cj 24
Walton O USA 71 Df 26
Walung O IND 254 Kn 31
Walungu O RDC 336 Hg 47
Walvis Bay O NAM 348 Gp 57
Walvis Bay ≈ NAM 348 Gp 57
Walvis Ridge ▿ 30 Jb 13
Wamal O RI 286 Mf 50
Wamaza O RDC 336 Hf 48
Wamba O WAN 320 Gl 41
Wamba O RDC 324 Hg 44
Wamba O EAK 325 Hl 45
Wamba ~ RDC 333 Ha 48
Wamba-Luadi O RDC 333 Ha 49
Wamba Mountains ⛰ WAN 320 Gm 42
Wambung O AUS 364 Mb 53
Wamena O RI 286 Mf 48
Wamera Island ♁ PNG 287 Mm 50
Wames O RA 137 Ed 63
Wami ~ EAT 337 Hm 49
Wamis O LAR 297 Gn 30
Wampembe O EAT 336 Hh 49
Wamsutter O USA 65 Cj 25
Wāna O PK 223 Jn 29
Wanaaring O AUS 375 Mh 60
Wanaka O NZ 382 Ng 68
Wanapitei O CDN 57 Dh 22
Wanapitei Lake ~ CDN 57 Dh 22
Wanapitei River ~ CDN 57 Dh 22
Wana River ~ PNG 287 Mk 50
Wanasabari O RI 282 Lm 48
Wanau O RI 283 Mc 46
Wanblee O USA 56 Cm 24
Wanbu O VRC 258 Lh 31
Wandagee O AUS 360 Lh 57
Wandammen Peninsula ⌓ RI 283 Md 47
Wanda Shan ⛰ VRC 250 Mb 23
Wanderlândia O BR 121 Ek 49
Wanderley O BR 125 En 52
Wando O ROK 247 Lp 28
Wando O PNG 286 Mg 50
Wandoan O AUS 375 Mm 59
Wandokai O PNG 287 Mk 49
Wang O PNG 287 Mn 47
Wanga O RDC 324 Hg 44
Wanga Mountains ⛰ WAN 320 Gm 42
Wanganui O NZ 383 Nk 65
Wanganui ~ NZ 383 Nk 65
Wangaratta O AUS 379 Mk 64
Wangary O AUS 378 Md 63
Wangasi-Turu O GH 317 Gf 41
Wangawol O AUS 368 Ll 59
Wangcang O VRC 243 Ld 29
Wangdi Phodrang O BHT 235 Kj 32
Wangerooge ♁ D 170 Gk 18
Wanggao O VRC 255 Lf 33
Wanggar O RI 283 Md 47
Wanggar ~ RI 283 Md 47
Wangi O IND 238 Kb 36
Wangianna O AUS 374 Me 60
Wangjiang O VRC 246 Lj 30
Wangjie O VRC 255 La 34
Wangmo O VRC 255 Ld 33
Wang Nam Yen O THA 262 La 39
Wangon O RI 278 Le 49
Wangpang Yang ~ VRC 246 Ll 30
Wang Sam Mo O THA 263 Lb 37
Wang Saphung O THA 262 La 37
Wang Thong O THA 262 La 37
Wang Wiset O THA 270 Kp 42
Wangziguan O VRC 242 Lc 29
Wan Hsa-la O MYA 254 Kp 35
Wani O IND 238 Kd 36
Wanie-Rukula O RDC 324 He 45
Wanington O USA 86 De 30
Wānkāner O IND 227 Jp 34
Wan Kongmöng O MYA 254 Kp 35
Wanleweeyn O SP 329 Ja 44
Wanlong O VRC 242 Lc 30
Wan Long O MYA 254 Kp 34
Wanna O AUS 360 Lj 57
Wanna Lakes ~ AUS 369 Lp 60
Wannarra O AUS 368 Lj 60
Wannia O VRC 258 Lj 31
Wanning O VRC 255 Lf 36
Wanparti O IND 238 Kd 37
Wanshan Qundao ♁ VRC 258 Lh 35
Wansra O RI 283 Md 46
Wantang O VRC 255 Lb 34
Wantoat O PNG 287 Mk 49
Wan Xian O VRC 243 Le 30
Wanyuan O VRC 243 Ld 29
Wanzai O VRC 258 Lh 31
Waogena O RI 282 Lm 48
Wapanucka O USA 70 Cp 28
Wapato O USA 50 Cb 22
Wapella O CDN 56 Cm 20
Wapello O USA 71 Dc 25
Wapenamanda O PNG 287 Mh 48
Wapet Camp O AUS 360 Lh 56
Wāpi O IND 238 Ka 35
Wapi Pathum O THA 263 Lb 38
Wapoga ~ RI 286 Me 47
Wapotih O RI 282 Lp 47
Wappapello O USA 71 Dc 27
Waprak O RI 283 Md 47
Wapuli O GH 317 Gf 41
Wara O WAN 320 Gj 40
Warakei O NZ 383 Nl 65
Warakuma O AUS 369 Ma 58
Warandab O ETH 328 Ja 42
Waranga Basin ~ AUS 379 Mj 64
Warangal O IND 238 Kd 36
Waratah O AUS 378 Mj 66
Waratah Bay ≈ AUS 379 Mj 65
Wara Wara Mountains ⛰ WAL 316 Fp 41
Warbreccan O AUS 374 Mh 58
Warburg O CDN 50 Ce 19
Warburton O ZA 352 Hh 59
Warburton O AUS 369 Lp 59
Warburton O AUS 379 Mj 64
Warburton Creek ~ AUS 374 Mf 59
Warburton Range ⛰ AUS 369 Lp 59
Warburton Range Aboriginal Land ••• AUS 369 Lp 58
Warburton Range Aboriginal Reserve ••• AUS 369 Lp 59
Ward O NZ 383 Nk 66
Wardak ⊙ AFG 223 Jn 28
Wardang Island ♁ AUS 378 Me 63
Warden O ZA 349 Hg 59
Warden Ridge ⛰ USA 71 Df 28
Wardha O IND 234 Kd 35
Wardha ~ IND 234 Kd 35
War Dhugulle O SP 329 Ja 44
Ward Hunt Strait ~ PNG 287 Ml 50
Wardo O RI 283 Md 46
Ware O CDN 47 Bn 17
Warego Mine O AUS 364 Mc 55
Waren O RI 286 Me 47
Waren ~ RI 286 Me 47
Waren(M.) O D 170 Gn 19
Warenda O AUS 374 Mg 57
War Galoh O SP 328 Jb 42
Warialda O AUS 375 Mm 60
Waria River ~ PNG 287 Mk 49
Wāri Godri O IND 238 Kb 36
Warilau O RI 283 Md 48
Warin Chamrap O THA 263 Lc 38
Warkopi O RI 283 Md 46
Warman O CDN 51 Cj 19
Warmandi O RI 283 Mc 46
Warmbad O NAM 348 Hb 60
Warmbaths O ZA 349 Hf 58
Warmfontein O NAM 348 Hb 59
Warminster O USA 74 Dl 25
Warm Springs O USA 50 Cb 23
Warm Springs O USA 64 Cd 26
Warm Springs O USA 74 Dj 26
Warm Springs Indian Reservation ••• USA 50 Cb 23
Warmun O AUS 364 Ma 54
Warn O RI 274 Lj 46
Warnemünde O D 170 Gm 18
Warner O CDN 51 Cf 21
Warner Lakes ~ USA 50 Cc 24
Warner Peak △ USA 50 Cc 24
Warner Range ⛰ USA 64 Cb 25
Warner Robins O USA 71 Dg 29
Warnes O BOL 129 Ec 54
Warnow ~ D 170 Gm 19
Warooka O AUS 378 Me 63
Waroona O AUS 368 Lh 62
Waropko O RI 286 Mg 48
Warora O IND 234 Kd 35
Warra O AUS 375 Mm 59
Warrabri O AUS 374 Md 56
Warracknabeal O AUS 378 Mh 64
Warragul O AUS 379 Mj 65
Warrakunta Point ⌓ AUS 364 Md 53
Warralong Aboriginal Reserve ••• AUS 360 Lk 56
Warrawagine O AUS 360 Ll 56
Warrego ~ AUS 375 Mj 59
Warrego Range ⛰ AUS 375 Mj 58
Warren O USA 51 Ch 23
Warren O CDN 56 Cp 20
Warren O USA 56 Cp 21
Warren O USA 70 Db 29
Warren O USA 71 Dg 24
Warren O USA 71 Dh 25
Warren O USA 74 Dj 25
Warren O AUS 379 Mk 61
Warrensburg O USA 70 Db 26
Warrenton O USA 71 Dg 29
Warrenton O USA 74 Dj 26
Warrenton O ZA 349 He 60
Warren Vale O AUS 365 Mg 55
Warri O WAN 320 Gj 43
Warri ~ WAN 320 Gj 43
Warriedar O AUS 368 Lj 60
Warriedar Hill △ AUS 368 Lj 60
Warrier O USA 71 De 29
Warriner Creek ~ AUS 374 Me 60
Warrington O GB 163 Ge 19
Warri Warri Creek ~ AUS 374 Mg 60
Warrnambool O AUS 378 Mh 65
Warroad O USA 56 Da 21
Warroora O AUS 360 Lg 57
Warrumbungle ♀ AUS 379 Ml 61
Warrumbungle Range ⛰ AUS 379 Ml 61
Warruwi O AUS 364 Mc 51
Warsa O RI 283 Md 46
Warsaw O USA 70 Db 26
Warsaw O USA 71 Df 25
Warsaw O USA 74 Dj 28
Warsaw O USA 74 Dk 27
Warsaw ▣ PL 170 Hc 19
Warshi O IND 238 Kc 36
Warshiikh O SP 329 Ja 44
Warta ⌓ PL 170 Ha 19
Warta ~ PL 170 Ha 19
Waru O RI 283 Mb 47
Warud O IND 234 Kd 35
Waruta ~ RI 286 Mg 47
Warwick O USA 70 Cp 28
Warwick O USA 74 Dn 25
Warwick O USA 86 Df 30
Warwick O GB 163 Gf 19
Warwick O AUS 375 Mn 60
Warwick Channel ~ AUS 364 Me 53
Warwick Downs O.S. O AUS 374 Mf 56
Waryor ~ RI 283 Mc 46
Wasagaming O CDN 56 Cm 20
Wasagu O WAN 320 Gj 40
Wasai O RI 283 Mb 46
Wasatch Plateau ⛰ USA 65 Cg 26
Wasatch Range ⛰ USA 51 Cg 24
Wasco O USA 50 Cb 23
Wasco O USA 64 Cc 28
Wase O WAN 320 Gl 41
Waseca O USA 56 Db 23
Washago O CDN 60 Dj 23
Was Hāmid O SUD 312 Hj 37
Washāp O PK 226 Jk 32
Washburn O USA 56 Cm 22
Washim O IND 234 Kc 35
Washington ⊙ USA 50 Ca 22
Washington O USA 64 Cf 27
Washington O USA 70 Cp 26
Washington O USA 71 Dc 25
Washington O USA 71 Dc 26
Washington O USA 71 De 26
Washington O USA 71 Dg 26
Washington O USA 71 Dg 29
Washington O USA 71 Dh 25
Washington O USA 74 Dk 28
Washington D. C. ▣ USA 74 Dk 26
Washington Islands ♁ USA 57 De 23
Washi River ~ CDN 57 De 20
Washita ~ USA 70 Cp 28
Washkish O USA 56 Da 21
Washow Bay ~ CDN 56 Cp 20
Washowng O MYA 254 Kn 33
Washpool ♀ AUS 375 Mn 60
Washtucna O USA 50 Cc 22
Wāshūk O PK 227 Jl 32
Wasian O RI 283 Mc 46
Wasile O RI 275 Lp 45
Wasilla O USA 46 Ba 15
Wāsit ⊙ IRQ 209 Ja 29
Wasjabo O SME 113 Ef 43
Waskaganish O CDN 60 Dj 20
Wasletan O RI 283 Mb 49
Waspam O NIC 97 Df 38
Waspuk ~ NIC 97 Df 38
Wassadou O SN 316 Fn 39
Wassamu O J 250 Mh 24
Wasserburg a.Inn O D 174 Gn 21
Wassou O RG 316 Fp 40
Wasta O USA 51 Cl 23
Wasu O PNG 287 Mk 48
Wasum O PNG 287 Ml 49
Waswanipi ~ CDN 60 Dk 21
Waswanipi Indian Reserve ••• CDN 60 Dk 21
Wata O RI 282 Ll 47
Watalgan O AUS 375 Mn 58
Watambayoli O RI 282 Ll 46
Watampone Bone O RI 282 Ll 48
Watansoppeng O RI 279 Lk 48
Watarais O PNG 287 Mk 49
Watarrka ♀ AUS 369 Mb 58
Watee O SOL 290 Nd 51
Waterberge ⛰ ZA 349 Hf 58
Waterbury O USA 74 Dm 25
Wateree ~ USA 71 Dh 29
Waterford O IRL 163 Gc 19
Waterford O ZA 358 He 62
Waterford O AUS 374 Mg 57
Waterhen O CDN 56 Cn 20
Waterhen Lake ~ CDN 56 Cn 19
Waterhouse ~ AUS 364 Mc 53
Waterloo O CDN 57 Dh 24
Waterloo O CDN 60 Dk 23
Waterloo O USA 70 Cp 25
Waterloo O USA 70 Db 24
Waterloo O WAL 316 Fp 41
Waterloo O AUS 364 Ma 54
Waterport O ZA 349 Hg 57
Watersmeet O USA 57 Dd 22
Waterton Glacier International Peace Park ♀ USA 50 Ce 21
Waterton Lakes ♀ CDN 50 Ce 21
Waterton Park O CDN 50 Cf 21
Watertown O USA 56 Cp 23
Watertown O USA 57 Dd 24
Watertown O USA 60 Dl 24
Waterval-Boven O ZA 352 Hh 58
Water Valley O USA 71 Dd 28
Waterville O USA 60 Dp 23
Waterville O USA 70 Cp 26
Waterville O IRL 163 Ga 20
Watford O GB 163 Gf 20
Watford City O USA 51 Cl 22
Watheroo ♀ AUS 368 Lh 61
Watheroo O AUS 368 Lj 61
Watmuri O RI 283 Mb 49
Watoa Island ♁ PNG 287 Mm 50
Watom Island ♁ PNG 287 Mm 48
Watonga O USA 70 Cn 28
Watpi O PNG 287 Mn 48

Vožega - Watpi 481

Watri O **RMM** 304 Gb 38
Watrous O **CDN** 51 Ck 20
Watrupun O **RI** 283 Ma 49
Watsa O **RDC** 324 Hg 44
Watseka O **USA** 71 De 25
Watsi O **RDC** 333 Hc 46
Watsikengo O **RDC** 333 Hc 46
Watson O **CDN** 51 Ck 19
Watson O **USA** 86 Dc 29
Watson O **AUS** 369 Mf 61
Watson O **AUS** 365 Mg 52
Watson Lake O **CDN** 6 Cb 3
Watson Lake ~ **CDN** 47 Bl 15
Watsonville O **USA** 64 Ca 27
Wattegama O **CL** 239 Ke 42
Wattiwarriganna Creek ~ **AUS** 374 Md 60
Watts-Bar Lake ~ **USA** 71 Df 28
Watunea O **RI** 282 Lm 48
Watutau O **RI** 282 Ll 46
Wau O **RI** 283 Mc 46
Wau O **PNG** 287 Mk 49
Wâu O **SUD** 324 Hf 42
Wau O **SUD** 324 Hg 42
Waubra O **AUS** 379 Mf 65
Wauchope O **AUS** 379 Mn 61
Wauchope Roadhouse O **AUS** 361 Mc 56
Waukaringa O **AUS** 378 Mf 62
Waukegan O **USA** 71 De 24
Waukesha O **USA** 57 Dd 23
Waupaca O **USA** 57 Dd 23
Waupun O **USA** 70 Cn 28
Waurika O **USA** 70 Cn 28
Waurika Lake ~ **USA** 70 Cn 28
Wausau O **USA** 57 Dd 23
Wausaukee O **USA** 57 Dd 23
Wauseon O **USA** 71 Df 25
Wautoma O **USA** 57 Dd 23
Wauwatosa O **USA** 57 Dd 24
Wave Hill O **AUS** 368 Mb 54
Waverley O **NZ** 383 Nk 65
Waverly O **USA** 56 Db 24
Waverly O **USA** 60 Dk 24
Waverly O **USA** 70 Db 26
Waverly O **USA** 71 Dd 27
Waverly O **USA** 71 Dd 27
Wave Rock ★ **AUS** 368 Lk 62
Wavre O **B** 163 Gj 20
Wawa O **CDN** 57 Df 22
Wawa ~ **NIC** 97 Df 38
Wawa O **WAN** 320 Gj 41
Wawalalindu O **RI** 282 Ll 47
Wawalalindu O **RI** 282 Lm 47
Wâw al Kabīr O **LAR** 297 Ha 33
Wawanesa O **CDN** 56 Cm 21
Wâw an Nâmûs O **LAR** 297 Ha 33
Wawiwa Island ⌂ **PNG** 287 Mm 50
Wawoi River ~ **PNG** 287 Mh 49
Waworada O **RI** 279 Lk 50
Wawotobi O **RI** 282 Ll 47
Waxahachie O **USA** 70 Cp 29
Waxxari O **VRC** 231 Kh 26
Waya ⌂ **FJI** 387 Nl 54
Wayabula O **RI** 275 Ma 44
Wayan O **USA** 51 Cg 24
Waycross O **USA** 87 Dg 30
Waygay O **RI** 282 Ln 47
Wayhaya O **RI** 282 Ln 46
Wayne O **USA** 56 Cp 24
Waynesboro O **USA** 71 Dd 28
Waynesboro O **USA** 87 Df 29
Waynesboro O **USA** 74 Dj 26
Waynesboro O **USA** 86 Dd 30
Waynesburg O **USA** 71 Dh 26
Waynesville O **USA** 70 Db 27
Waynesville O **USA** 71 Dg 28
Waynoka O **USA** 70 Cn 27
Wayongon O **MYA** 254 Km 33
Wayu O **EAK** 337 Hm 46
Waza O **CAM** 321 Gp 40
Wazah O **AFG** 223 Jn 29
Wazīrābād O **PK** 230 Ka 29
Wâzirr O **TN** 297 Gm 30
Wé O **CAM** 320 Gm 42
Wé O **F** 386 Nf 56
Weagamow Lake O **CDN** 56 Dc 19
Weagamow Lake ~ **CDN** 56 Dc 19
Weam O **PNG** 286 Mg 50
Weasua O **LB** 316 Ga 42
Weatherford O **USA** 70 Cn 28
Weatherford O **USA** 70 Cp 28
Weaverville O **USA** 64 Ca 25
Webequie O **CDN** 57 De 19
Weber O **NZ** 383 Nl 66
Weber Basin ♥ **USA** 283 Mb 48
Webi Jubba ~ **SP** 328 Hp 43
Webster O **USA** 56 Cp 23
Webster City O **USA** 70 Db 24
Webster Reservation ~ **CDN** 57 Dh 20

Cn 26
Webster Springs O **USA** 71 Dh 26
Webuye O **EAK** 325 Hk 45
Wech 'echa O **ETH** 313 Hm 41
Wedau O **PNG** 287 Mm 51
Weddell Island ⌂ **GB** 147 Ed 71
Wedderburn O **AUS** 379 Mh 64
Weddin Mountain ⌂ **AUS** 379 Mj 63
Wedel Jarlsberg land ⌂ **N** 158 Gp 7
Wedell Sea ≈ **38** Gb 17
Wedge Island ⌂ **AUS** 368 Lh 61
Wedowee O **USA** 86 Df 29
Wed Weil O **SUD** 324 Hf 41
Weed O **USA** 64 Ca 25
Weelarrana O **AUS** 360 Ll 57
Weelhamby Lake ~ **AUS** 388 Lj 60
Weenen O **ZA** 352 Hh 60
Weethalle O **AUS** 379 Mk 62
Wee Waa O **AUS** 379 Ml 61
Wegdraai O **NAM** 348 Hb 58
Wegdraai O **ZA** 349 Hc 60
Wegener Ice ⌂ **38** Jb 17
Wegorzewo O **PL** 170 Hc 18
Weiden in der Oberpfalz O **D** 174 Gm 21
Weifang O **VRC** 246 Lk 27
Weihai O **VRC** 246 Lm 27
Wei He ~ **VRC** 243 Lh 28
Weihui O **VRC** 243 Lh 28
Weila O **GH** 317 Ge 41
Weilmoringle O **AUS** 375 Mk 60
Weimar O **D** 174 Gm 20
Weinan O **VRC** 243 Le 28
Weini ~ **GUY** 112 Ee 41
Weining O **VRC** 254 Lc 32
Weipa O **AUS** 365 Mg 52
Weipa South O **AUS** 365 Mg 52
Weipa South O **AUS** 365 Mh 52

Weir ~ **AUS** 375 Ml 60
Weirton O **USA** 71 Dh 25
Weiser O **USA** 50 Cd 23
Weishan O **VRC** 246 Lj 28
Weishan Hu ~ **VRC** 246 Lj 28
Weishi O **VRC** 243 Lh 28
Weixi O **VRC** 254 Kp 32
Wei Xian O **VRC** 243 Lh 27
Weixin O **VRC** 255 Lc 32
Weiyuan O **VRC** 242 Lc 28
Weiyuan O **VRC** 255 Lc 31
Weizhou Dao ⌂ **VRC** 255 Le 35
Weko O **RDC** 324 He 45
Welanpela O **CL** 239 Ke 43
Welatam O **MYA** 254 Kp 32
Welbedacht Dam ~ **ZA** 349 Hf 60
Welch O **USA** 71 Dh 27
Weldiya O **ETH** 313 Hm 40
Weldon O **USA** 74 Dk 27
Weld Range ⌂ **AUS** 368 Lj 59
Welench'iti O **ETH** 325 Hm 41
Weleri O **RI** 278 Lf 49
Weligama O **CL** 239 Ke 43
Welisara O **CL** 239 Kd 42
Wel Jara O **EAK** 337 Hm 46
Welk'itē O **ETH** 325 Hl 41
Welkom O **ZA** 349 Hf 59
Wellawaya O **CL** 239 Ke 42
Wellesley Islands ⌂ **AUS** 365 Mf 54
Wellington O **CDN** 60 Dk 24
Wellington O **USA** 64 Cc 26
Wellington O **USA** 65 Cg 26
Wellington O **USA** 65 Ck 25
Wellington O **USA** 70 Cp 27
Wellington O **ZA** 348 Hb 61
Wellington O **AUS** 379 Ml 62
Wellington ⊞ **NZ** 383 Nk 66
Wellington Channel ~ **CDN** 7 Ea 2
Wellington Channel ~ **CDN** 42 Fc 3
Wellman O **USA** 65 Cl 29
Wells O **USA** 64 Ce 25
Wellsboro O **USA** 74 Dk 25
Wellsford O **NZ** 383 Nk 64
Wellston O **USA** 70 Cp 28
Wellston O **USA** 71 Dg 26
Wellsville O **USA** 64 Ce 25
Wellsville O **USA** 70 Dc 26
Welmel Shet ~ **ETH** 325 Hn 43
Wels O **A** 174 Gn 21
Welshpool O **GB** 163 Ge 19
Welverdiend O **NAM** 348 Hb 58
Welwel O **ETH** 328 Ja 42
Wema O **RDC** 333 He 46
Wembere ~ **EAT** 337 Hj 48
Wenago O **ETH** 325 Hm 42
Wenasage River ~ **CDN** 56 Db 20
Wenatchee O **USA** 50 Cb 22
Wenatchee Mountains ⌂ **USA** 50 Cb 22
Wenceslao Escalante O **RA** 137 Ec 62
Wenceslau Braz O **BR** 140 Ek 57
Wenchang O **VRC** 243 Ld 29
Wenchang O **VRC** 255 Lf 36
Wencheng O **VRC** 259 Ll 32
Wenchi O **GH** 317 Ge 42
Wenchiki O **GH** 317 Gf 40
Wench'i Shet ~ **ETH** 313 Hm 40
Wenchuan O **VRC** 242 Lb 30
Wenden O **USA** 64 Cf 29
Wendeng O **VRC** 246 Ll 27
Wendi O **RI** 282 Ln 46
Wendo O **ETH** 325 Hm 42
Wéndou-Mbôrou O **RG** 316 Fn 40
Wenga O **RDC** 333 Hb 45
Weng'an O **VRC** 255 Ld 32
Wenge O **RDC** 324 He 44
Wenjiazhen O **VRC** 258 Lh 31
Wenlock O **AUS** 365 Mh 52
Wenlock ~ **AUS** 365 Mh 52
Wenquan O **VRC** 231 Ke 29
Wenquan O **VRC** 242 Kp 28
Wenshan O **VRC** 255 Lb 34
Wen Shang O **VRC** 246 Lj 28
Wenshui O **VRC** 243 Lf 27
Wenshui O **VRC** 255 Ld 31
Wentworth O **USA** 56 Cp 23
Wentworth O **CDN** 61 Ec 23
Wentworth O **AUS** 378 Mg 63
Wentzville O **USA** 71 Dc 26
Wenxi O **VRC** 243 Lf 28
Wen Xian O **VRC** 242 Lc 29
Wenzhou O **VRC** 259 Ll 32
Wenzhou Wa ~ **VRC** 259 Ll 32
Wepener O **ZA** 349 Hf 60
Wera ~ **D** 174 Gm 20
Werda O **RB** 349 Hd 58
Werdēr O **ETH** 328 Ja 42
Were Ilu O **ETH** 313 Hm 40
Wernadinga O **AUS** 365 Mf 55
Werner Lake O **CDN** 56 Da 20
Werota O **ETH** 313 Hl 40
Werribee O **AUS** 379 Mj 64
Werrikimbie ♀ **AUS** 379 Mn 61
Werris Creek O **AUS** 379 Mm 61
Wesel O **D** 163 Gk 20
Weser ~ **D** 170 Gl 19
Wesley O **USA** 60 La 23
Wesleyville O **CDN** 61 Eh 21
Wessel Islands ⌂ **AUS** 364 Me 51
Wesselsbron O **ZA** 349 Hf 59
Wessington Springs O **USA** 56 Cn 23
West O **USA** 51 Cg 23
West Australian Basin ♥ **34** Qa 12
West Baine ~ **AUS** 364 Ma 54
West Bay ~ **GB** 100 Dh 36
West Bend O **USA** 57 Dd 24
West Bengal O **IND** 235 Kj 34
Westboro O **USA** 56 Dc 23
West Branch O **USA** 57 Df 23
Westbrook O **USA** 60 Dn 24
Westbury O **AUS** 375 Mj 57
Westby O **USA** 56 Dc 24
West Caicos Island ⌂ **GB** 101 Dm 35
West Cape Howe △ **AUS** 368 Lj 63
West Caroline Basin ♥ **26** Rb 9
West Coast ♀ **ZA** 358 Ha 62
West Columbia O **USA** 81 Da 31
West End O **BS** 87 Dj 32
West End O **GB** 100 Dh 36

Westerberg O **ZA** 349 Hd 60
Westerland O **D** 170 Gl 18
Westerly O **USA** 74 Dn 25
Western O **USA** 70 Cp 25
Western Australia O **AUS** 360 Ll 57
Western Cordillera ⌂ **CO** 106 Dk 45
Western Cordillera ⌂ **PE** 128 Dk 50
Western Cordillera ⌂ **PE** 128 Dn 50
Western Creek ~ **AUS** 375 Mm 59
Western Desert ~ **ET** 300 Hf 31
Western Entrance ~ **PNG** 290 Mp 49
Western Ghats ⌂ **IND** 238 Ka 35
Western Ghats ⌂ **IND** 238 Kb 38
Western Port ~ **AUS** 379 Mj 65
Western Sahara ~ **MA** 292 Fn 33
Western Sayan ⌂ **RUS** 22 Pb 4
Western Sayan ⌂ **RUS** 204 Tc 8
Westerville O **USA** 71 Dg 25
Westerwald ⌂ **D** 163 Gk 20
West European Basin ♥ **18** Hb 5
West Falkland ⌂ **GB** 147 Ed 71
Westfield O **USA** 60 Dm 24
Westfield O **CDN** 60 Ea 23
West Fiji Basin ♥ **35** Tb 11
West Fork ~ **USA** 51 Cj 21
West Fork Des Moines ~ **USA** 56 Da 24
West Frankfort O **USA** 71 Dd 27
West Frisian Islands ⌂ **NL** 163 Gj 19
Westgate O **AUS** 375 Mk 59
West Glacier O **USA** 50 Ce 21
West Group ⌂ **AUS** 368 Ll 63
West Holothuria Reef ⌂ **AUS** 361 Ln 52
Westhope O **USA** 56 Cm 21
West Ice Shelf ⌂ **38** Pa 16
West Island ⌂ **AUS** 364 Me 53
West Jordan O **USA** 65 Cf 25
West Liberty O **USA** 71 Dd 27
West Lunga ~ **Z** 341 He 52
West Lunga ♀ **Z** 341 He 52
Westmar O **AUS** 375 Ml 59
West Mariana Basin ♥ **26** Rb 8
West Memphis O **USA** 71 Dc 28
Westminster O **USA** 74 Dk 26
Westmoreland O **AUS** 365 Mf 54
Westmoreland O **USA** 64 Cx 26
West Mount Barren ⌂ **AUS** 368 Lk 63
West Nicholson O **ZW** 349 Hg 56
Weston O **USA** 51 Ck 23
Weston O **USA** 65 Cg 24
Weston O **USA** 70 Da 26
Weston O **USA** 71 Dh 26
Weston O **USA** 86 Dd 28
Weston O **GB** 163 Ge 20
West Palm Beach O **USA** 87 Dh 32
West Plains O **USA** 70 Dc 27
West Point O **CDN** 61 Eb 22
West Point O **USA** 61 Ed 24
West Point O **USA** 70 Cp 25
West Point O **USA** 74 Dk 27
West Point O **USA** 86 Dd 29
Westpoint O **GB** 147 Ed 71
West Point ~ **WAN** 320 Gl 43
West Point O **AUS** 378 Md 63
West Point △ **AUS** 378 Mj 66
West Point Lake ~ **USA** 86 Df 29
Westport O **USA** 50 Bp 22
Westport O **USA** 56 Ca 22
Westport O **NZ** 382 Nn 66
Westport O **NL** 107 Dp 39
Westray ⌂ **GB** 162 Ge 16
Westree O **CDN** 57 Dh 22
West Road (Blackwater) ~ **CDN** 50 Bp 19
West Siberian Plain ⌂ **RUS** 154 Sa 6
West Siberian Plain ⌂ **RUS** 204 Sc 6
West Thumb O **USA** 51 Cg 23
West Union O **USA** 56 Dc 24
West Union O **USA** 71 Dg 26
West Valley City O **USA** 65 Cf 25
Westville O **CDN** 61 Ec 23
West Virginia O **USA** 71 Dh 26
Westwego O **USA** 86 Dc 31
West Wendover O **USA** 64 Ce 25
Westwood O **USA** 64 Cb 25
Westwood O **AUS** 375 Ml 57
West Wyalong O **AUS** 379 Mk 62
West Yarmouth O **USA** 74 Dn 25
West Yellowstone O **USA** 51 Cg 23
Wetaskiwin O **CDN** 57 Cf 19
Wete O **EAT** 337 Hm 48
Wet Mountains ⌂ **USA** 65 Ck 26
Wetumka O **USA** 70 Cp 28
Weto O **WAN** 320 Gk 42
Wetzlar O **D** 174 Gl 20
Wevok O **USA** 46 Ag 11
Wewak O **PNG** 286 Mh 47
Wexford O **IRL** 163 Gc 19
Weymouth O **CDN** 61 Ea 23
Weymouth O **GB** 163 Ge 20
Weymouth Bay ~ **AUS** 365 Mh 52
Weyto ~ **ETH** 325 Hl 43
Whakatane O **NZ** 383 Nl 64
Whale Bay ~ **USA** 47 Bg 17
Whale Bay ~ **MYA** 262 Kp 40
Whale Cay ⌂ **BS** 87 Dk 33
Whale Cove O **CDN** 42 Fc 6
Whangamata O **NZ** 383 Nk 64
Whanganui ♀ **NZ** 383 Nk 65
Whangarei O **NZ** 383 Nk 63
Wharton O **USA** 81 Da 31
Wharton Basin ♥ **34** Pb 11
Wheatland O **USA** 51 Ck 24
Wheatland O **USA** 64 Cb 26
Wheatland Reservoir No.2 ~ **USA** 65 Ck 25
Wheaton O **USA** 56 Cp 23
Wheeler O **USA** 70 Cm 28
Wheeler Peak △ **USA** 65 Ck 27
Wheelers Point O **USA** 56 Da 21
Wheeling O **USA** 71 Dh 25
Whela Creek ~ **AUS** 368 Lj 59
Wheller Lake ~ **USA** 71 De 28
Whidbey Island ⌂ **USA** 50 Ca 21
Whim Creek O **AUS** 360 Lj 56
Whistler O **CDN** 50 Ca 20
Whitbourne O **CDN** 61 Eg 22

Whitby O **CDN** 60 Dj 24
Whitby O **GB** 162 Gf 18
White Bay ~ **CDN** 61 Ef 20
White Bear ~ **CDN** 61 Ef 21
White Butte △ **USA** 51 Cl 22
White Cape Mountain △ **USA** 60 Dp 23
White City O **USA** 50 Ca 24
White City O **USA** 50 Ck 24
Whiteclay O **USA** 51 Cl 24
Whiteclay Lake ~ **CDN** 57 Dd 20
White Cliffs O **AUS** 378 Mh 61
Whitecourt O **CDN** 56 Da 20
Whitedog O **CDN** 56 Da 20
White Earth ~ **USA** 56 Cm 22
Whitefish O **USA** 50 Ce 21
Whitefish O **CDN** 57 Dh 22
Whitefish Bay ~ **USA** 57 Df 22
Whitefish Lake ~ **USA** 50 Ce 21
Whitefish Lake Ind.Res. ~ **CDN** 57 Dh 22
Whitefish Point O **USA** 57 Df 22
Whitehall O **USA** 51 Cf 23
Whitehall O **USA** 56 Dc 23
Whitehall O **USA** 60 Dm 24
Whitehorse O **CDN** 6 Ca 3
Whitehorse O **USA** 51 Ch 19
Whitehorse O **USA** 56 Cm 23
White Horse Pass △ **USA** 64 Ce 25
White Island ⌂ **CDN** 43 Ga 5
White Island ⌂ **NZ** 383 Nl 64
White Lake ~ **USA** 56 Cn 24
White Lake ~ **CDN** 57 Df 21
White Lake ~ **USA** 86 Db 31
White Lake ~ **USA** 368 Ll 58
Whiteman O **USA** 70 Cm 25
Whiteman Range ⌂ **PNG** 287 Ml 48
Whitemark O **AUS** 378 Ml 66
White Mountain O **USA** 23 Ab 3
White Mountains ⌂ **USA** 60 Dn 23
White Mountains ⌂ **USA** 64 Cc 27
Whitemouth O **CDN** 56 Da 21
White Nile ~ **SUD** 312 Hj 38
White Nile ~ **SUD** 324 Hh 41
White Otter ~ **CDN** 56 Db 20
White Pass △ **USA** 47 Bj 15
White Riv. N.W.R. ~ **USA** 70 Dc 28
White River ~ **CDN** 47 Be 13
White River O **USA** 56 Cn 24
White River O **CDN** 57 Df 21
White River ~ **USA** 70 Cm 29
White River Junction O **USA** 60 Dm 24
White Rock O **CDN** 50 Ca 21
Whitesand ~ **CDN** 51 Cl 20
Whitesands River ~ **USA** 51 Cl 29
White Sands N.M. ♀ **USA** 65 Cj 29
White Sands Space Harbor ★ **USA** 65 Cj 29
White Sea ~ **159** Hl 13
Whites Lake ~ **CDN** 61 Ec 23
White Sulphur Springs O **USA** 51 Cg 22
White Sulphur Springs O **USA** 71 Dh 27
White Swan O **USA** 50 Cb 22
White Umfolozi ~ **ZA** 352 Hh 60
Whiteville O **USA** 74 Dj 28
White Volta ~ **GH** 317 Gf 41
Whitewater O **USA** 57 Dd 24
Whitewater O **USA** 65 Ch 26
Whitewater Baldy △ **USA** 65 Ch 29
Whitewater Bay ~ **USA** 87 Dh 33
Whitewater Lake ~ **CDN** 57 Dd 20
Whitewood O **USA** 51 Cl 23
Whitewood O **AUS** 375 Mh 56
Whitfield O **AUS** 379 Mk 64
Whitianga O **NZ** 383 Nk 64
Whitlash O **USA** 51 Cg 21
Whitley City O **USA** 71 Df 27
Whitman O **USA** 56 Cm 22
Whitmann Mission N.H.S. ★ **USA** 50 Cc 23
Whitmore Mountains △ **38** Ea 18
Whitney O **CDN** 60 Dj 23
Whitney Point O **USA** 60 Dl 24
Whitsunday Island ⌂ **AUS** 375 Ml 56
Whitsunday Passage ~ **AUS** 375 Ml 56
Whittier O **USA** 46 Ba 15
Whittlesea O **ZA** 358 Hf 62
Whittlesea O **AUS** 379 Mj 64
Whitula Creek ~ **AUS** 374 Mh 58
Wholdaia Lake ~ **CDN** 6 Db 3
Wholdaia Lake ~ **CDN** 42 Ec 6
Why O **USA** 64 Cf 29
Whyalla O **AUS** 378 Me 62
Whycocomagh O **CDN** 61 Ed 23
Wiang Chai O **THA** 254 La 36
Wiang Sa O **THA** 254 La 36
Wiang Sa O **THA** 262 Kp 41
Wiangshan O **VRC** 259 Ll 31
Wiarton O **CDN** 57 Dh 23
Wiawer O **EAU** 325 Hj 44
Wiawso O **GH** 317 Ge 42
Wibaux O **USA** 51 Ck 22
Wichita O **USA** 70 Cp 27
Wichita Falls O **USA** 70 Cn 29
Wichita Mountains ⌂ **USA** 70 Cn 28
Wick O **GB** 162 Ge 16
Wickenburg O **USA** 64 Cf 29
Wickepin O **AUS** 368 Lj 62
Wickes O **USA** 70 Da 28
Wickham O **AUS** 360 Lj 56
Wickham ~ **AUS** 364 Mb 54
Wickliffe O **USA** 71 Dd 27
Wicklow O **IRL** 163 Gc 19
Wicklow Mountains ⌂ **IRL** 163 Gc 19
Wide Bay ~ **USA** 46 Al 17
Wide Bay ~ **PNG** 287 Mm 48
Wide Opening ~ **BS** 87 Dj 33
Wideru O **PNG** 287 Mk 49
Widgee Mountain △ **AUS** 375 Mn 59
Widjefjorden ~ **N** 158 Gp 6
Widmark Peninsula △ **PNG** 287 Ml 48
Wieliczka O **PL** 174 Hc 20
Wiembe ~ **USA** 71 Dh 20
Wien ⊞ **A** 174 Gp 22
Wiener Neustadt O **A** 174 Gp 22
Wiesbaden O **D** 163 Gk 20
Wiga Hill △ **WAN** 320 Gm 40
Wiggins O **USA** 65 Ck 25
Wiggins O **USA** 86 Dd 30
Wik'ro O **ETH** 313 Hm 39

Wikwemikong Indian Reserve ~ **CDN** 57 Dh 23
Wilber O **USA** 70 Cp 25
Wilbert O **CDN** 51 Ch 19
Wilbrunga Range ⌂ **AUS** 361 Ma 56
Wilbur O **USA** 50 Cc 22
Wilburton O **USA** 70 Da 28
Wilcannia O **AUS** 378 Mh 61
Wildcat Hill △ **CDN** 51 Cl 19
Wild Coast ~ **ZA** 358 Hg 62
Wild Horse O **CDN** 51 Cg 21
Wild Horse Hill △ **USA** 70 Cm 25
Wildspitze △ **A** 174 Gm 22
Wildwood O **USA** 74 Dl 26
Wilge ~ **ZA** 349 Hg 59
Wilhelmina Mountains ⌂ **SME** 113 Ef 44
Wilhelmøya ⌂ **N** 158 Hc 6
Wilhelmshaven O **D** 170 Gk 19
Wilhelmstal O **NAM** 348 Ha 56
Wilkes-Barre O **USA** 74 Dl 25
Wilkes Land ⌂ **38** Qb 16
Wilkie O **CDN** 51 Ch 19
Wilkinson Lakes ~ **AUS** 369 Mc 60
Wilkins Strait ~ **CDN** 42 Eb 3
Willamette ~ **USA** 50 Ca 24
Willandra ♀ **AUS** 379 Mj 62
Willandra Creek ~ **AUS** 379 Mj 62
Willapa Bay ~ **USA** 50 Bp 22
Willapa Hills ⌂ **USA** 50 Ca 22
Willard O **USA** 65 Cj 28
Willard O **USA** 71 Dg 25
Willard O **MEX** 65 Cj 29
Willare Bridge O **AUS** 361 Lm 54
Willcox O **USA** 65 Ch 29
Willemstad ⊞ **NL** 107 Dp 39
Willen O **CDN** 56 Cm 20
Willeroo O **AUS** 364 Mb 53
Williambury O **AUS** 360 Lh 57
William Creek O **AUS** 374 Me 60
Williamez Peninsula △ **PNG** 287 Ml 48
Williams O **USA** 64 Ca 26
Williams O **USA** 65 Cf 28
Williams O **AUS** 368 Lj 62
Williamsburg O **USA** 70 Db 25
Williamsburg O **USA** 74 Dj 26
Williams Island ⌂ **BS** 87 Dj 33
Williams Lake O **CDN** 50 Ca 19
Williamson O **USA** 71 Dg 27
Williamsport O **USA** 74 Dk 25
Williamston O **USA** 74 Dk 28
Williamstown O **USA** 71 Dg 26
William's Town O **BS** 87 Dl 34
Willigboro O **USA** 74 Dl 25
Willimantic O **USA** 74 Dm 25
Willimac O **USA** 51 Cj 21
Williston O **USA** 51 Cl 22
Williston O **USA** 71 Dh 29
Williston O **USA** 87 Dg 31
Williston O **ZA** 358 Hc 61
Williston Lake ~ **CDN** 47 Bn 17
Willits O **USA** 64 Ca 26
Willmar O **USA** 56 Da 23
Willmington O **USA** 71 Dd 25
Willochra Creek ~ **AUS** 378 Me 61
Willow O **USA** 46 Ba 15
Willowbrook O **CDN** 51 Cl 20
Willow Bunch O **CDN** 51 Ck 20
Willow Creek O **USA** 50 Ca 23
Willow Creek O **CDN** 51 Ch 21
Willow Creek ~ **USA** 64 Ca 25
Willow Lake ~ **CDN** 47 Cc 13
Willowmore O **ZA** 358 Hd 62
Willowra O **AUS** 361 Mc 56
Willow Ranch O **USA** 64 Cc 25
Willows O **USA** 64 Ca 26
Willow Springs O **USA** 70 Dc 27
Willow Tree O **AUS** 379 Mm 61
Willsboro O **USA** 60 Dm 23
Wills Creek ~ **USA** 374 Mf 57
Wilmer O **USA** 86 Dd 30
Wilmington O **USA** 71 Dg 26
Wilmington O **USA** 74 Dl 26
Wilmington O **AUS** 378 Mf 62
Wilmot O **USA** 71 Dh 25
Wilow River O **USA** 56 Db 22
Wilpattu National Park ♀ **CL** 239 Kd 41
Wilpena Creek ~ **AUS** 378 Mf 61
Wilson O **USA** 74 Dk 28
Wilson ~ **AUS** 361 Lp 54
Wilson ~ **AUS** 374 Mh 59
Wilson Creek ~ **USA** 50 Cc 22
Wilson Island ⌂ **IND** 262 Kl 39
Wilson Lake ~ **USA** 70 Cn 27
Wilson's Cr. N.B.P. ★ **USA** 70 Db 27
Wilsons Promontory ♀ **AUS** 379 Mk 65
Wilton O **USA** 56 Cm 22
Wilton ~ **AUS** 364 Md 53
Wiluna O **AUS** 368 Lk 59
Winamac O **USA** 71 De 25
Winburg O **ZA** 349 Hf 60
Winchelsea O **AUS** 379 Mh 65
Winchester O **USA** 50 Cd 22
Winchester O **USA** 51 Cj 24
Winchester O **CDN** 60 Dl 23
Winchester O **USA** 71 De 28
Winchester O **USA** 71 Df 27
Winchester O **USA** 74 Dj 26
Winchester O **GB** 163 Gf 20
Windabout Lake ~ **AUS** 378 Me 61
Wind Cave Natl. Park ♀ **USA** 51 Cl 24
Windhoek ⊞ **NAM** 348 Ha 57
Windidda O **AUS** 368 Lm 59
Windidda Aboriginal Reserve ~ **AUS** 368 Lm 59
Windjana Gorge ♀ **AUS** 361 Ln 54
Wind Mountain △ **USA** 65 Cj 29
Windom O **USA** 56 Da 24
Windora O **AUS** 374 Mg 58
Window on China ★ **RC** 259 Ll 33
Window Rock O **USA** 65 Ch 28
Wind River ~ **USA** 51 Ch 24
Wind River Indian Reservation ~ **USA** 51 Ch 24
Wind River Plc. O **USA** 65 Ch 24
Wind River Range ⌂ **USA** 51 Cg 24

Windsor O **CDN** 61 Eb 23
Windsor O **USA** 64 Ca 26
Windsor O **CDN** 71 Dg 24
Windsor O **USA** 74 Dk 27
Windsor O **GB** 163 Gf 20
Windsor O **AUS** 368 Lk 60
Windsorton Road O **ZA** 349 He 60
Windthorst O **USA** 70 Cn 29
Windward Islands ⌂ **CV** 316 Fh 37
Windward Passage ~ **101** Dl 36
Windy Harbour O **AUS** 368 Lh 63
Wing O **USA** 56 Cm 22
Wingate Mountains ⌂ **AUS** 364 Mb 53
Wingham O **CDN** 57 Dh 24
Wingham O **AUS** 379 Mn 61
Wingon O **MYA** 254 Km 34
Winifred O **USA** 51 Ch 22
Winiperu O **GUY** 113 Ee 42
Winisk O **CDN** 43 Ga 7
Winisk ~ **CDN** 7 Eb 4
Winisk Lake ~ **CDN** 43 Ga 8
Winkelman O **USA** 65 Cg 29
Winkler O **CDN** 56 Cp 21
Winneba O **GH** 317 Gf 43
Winnebago O **USA** 56 Da 24
Winnebago Indian Reservation ~ **USA** 56 Cp 24
Winnecke Creek ~ **AUS** 364 Mb 55
Winnemucca O **USA** 64 Cc 25
Winnemucca Lake ~ **USA** 64 Cc 25
Winner O **USA** 56 Cm 24
Winnfield O **USA** 86 Db 30
Winnibigoshish Lake ~ **USA** 56 Db 22
Winnie O **USA** 81 Da 31
Winning O **AUS** 360 Lh 57
Winnipeg O **CDN** 56 Cp 21
Winnipeg Beach O **CDN** 56 Cp 20
Winnipegosis O **CDN** 56 Cn 20
Winnsboro O **USA** 70 Da 29
Winona O **USA** 56 Dc 23
Winona O **USA** 56 Db 22
Winona O **USA** 65 Cg 28
Winona O **USA** 70 Da 27
Winona O **USA** 86 Dd 29
Winsboro O **USA** 70 Db 29
Winslow O **USA** 65 Cg 28
Winslow O **USA** 74 Dn 24
Winslow O **USA** 74 Dm 25
Winsted O **USA** 60 Dp 24
Winston-Salem O **USA** 71 Dh 27
Winterberg O **D** 174 Gl 20
Winterberge ⌂ **ZA** 358 He 62
Winter Garden O **USA** 87 Dh 31
Winter Harbour O **CDN** 50 Bm 20
Winter Haven O **USA** 87 Dh 31
Winter Island ⌂ **CDN** 43 Gb 5
Winters O **USA** 81 Cn 30
Winterset O **USA** 70 Db 24
Winterthur O **CH** 174 Gl 22
Winthrop O **USA** 50 Cb 21
Winthrop O **USA** 56 Da 23
Winton ~ **AUS** 374 Mh 57
Winton O **NZ** 382 Ng 69
Wintua O **VU** 386 Nf 54
Winyaw Bay ~ **USA** 81 Da 30
Wipembe ~ **MOC** 352 Hj 56
Wipim O **PNG** 286 Mh 50
Wirawila O **CL** 239 Ke 42
Wirliyajarrayi Aboriginal Land ~ **AUS** 361 Mc 56
Wirrabara O **AUS** 378 Mf 62
Wirrulla O **AUS** 378 Md 61
Wiscasset O **USA** 60 Dp 24
Wisconsin O **USA** 56 Dc 23
Wisconsin ~ **USA** 56 Dc 24
Wisconsin Dells O **USA** 57 Dd 24
Wisconsin Rapids O **USA** 56 Dc 23
Wisdom O **USA** 51 Cf 23
Wisemans Ferry O **AUS** 379 Mm 62
Wishart O **CDN** 51 Ck 20
Wishaw O **GB** 162 Ge 18
Wishek O **USA** 56 Cn 22
Wisil O **SP** 328 Jc 43
Wisil Dabaro O **SP** 328 Jc 42
Wisła ~ **PL** 174 Hc 20
Wiślica O **PL** 174 Hc 20
Wismar O **D** 170 Gm 19
Wisner O **USA** 70 Cp 25
Wissembourg O **F** 163 Gk 21
Wisznice O **PL** 175 Hd 20
Witbank O **ZA** 349 Hg 58
Witbooisvlei O **NAM** 348 Hb 58
Witfonteinrand ⌂ **ZA** 349 Hf 58
Witjira ♀ **AUS** 374 Md 59
Wit Kei ~ **ZA** 358 Hf 62
Witkransnek △ **ZA** 349 He 61
Witless Bay O **CDN** 61 Eh 22
Witpütz O **NAM** 348 Ha 59
Witrivier O **ZA** 352 Hh 58
Witsand O **ZA** 358 Hc 63
Wittabrenna Creek ~ **AUS** 374 Mh 60
Witteberge ⌂ **ZA** 349 Hf 60
Witteberge ⌂ **ZA** 358 Hc 62
Witteklip O **ZA** 358 He 62
Wittenberg O **USA** 57 Dd 23
Wittenberge O **D** 170 Gm 19
Wittenoom O **AUS** 360 Lk 57
Wittenoom Gorge ★ **AUS** 360 Lk 57
Wittman O **USA** 64 Cf 29
Wittstock O **D** 170 Gn 19
Witu O **PNG** 287 Ml 48
Witu O **EAK** 337 Hn 47
Witu Islands ⌂ **PNG** 287 Ml 48
Witvlei O **NAM** 348 Hb 57
Witwater O **ZA** 348 Hb 61
Witwatersberge △ **NAM** 348 Gp 57
Witwatersrand ⌂ **ZA** 349 Hf 59
Władysławowo O **PL** 170 Ha 18
Wlingi O **RI** 279 Lg 50
Włocławek O **PL** 170 Hb 19
Włodawa O **PL** 175 Hd 20
Włoszczowa O **PL** 174 Hb 20
Wobulenzi O **EAU** 324 Hj 45
Woburn O **CDN** 60 Dn 23
Wodonga O **AUS** 379 Mk 64
Woe O **GH** 317 Gg 43
Woganmic O **PNG** 287 Ml 48
Wogerlin Hill △ **AUS** 368 Lj 62
Wohlthatmassiv ⌂ **38** Kb 17
Woitape O **PNG** 287 Mk 50

□Country ▣Capital city ⊙Administrative unit ○Place ♁Island ⛰Mountain range △Mountain ⌓Cape ≈Ocean, Sea ~Lake, River ♆Undersea topography ▲Glacier ♀National park •••Reservation ★Point of major interest ⌔Landscape

Wolcott ○ USA 65 Cj 26
Woleai ♁ FSM 27 Sa 9
Woleu ~ G 332 Gm 45
Wolf ~ USA 57 Dd 23
Wolf △ EC 128 Dc 45
Wolf Bay ○ CDN 61 Ed 20
Wolf Creek ○ USA 50 Ca 24
Wolf Creek ○ USA 51 Cg 22
Wolf Creek ~ AUS 361 Lp 55
Wolf Creek Meteorite Crater ♀ AUS 361 Lp 55
Wolf Creek Pass △ USA 65 Cj 27
Wolfe Island ♁ CDN 60 Dk 23
Wolf Point ○ USA 51 Ck 21
Wolfsburg ○ D 170 Gm 19
Wolfville ○ CDN 61 Eb 23
Wolgast ○ D 170 Gn 18
Wolin ♁ PL 170 Gp 19
Wolkefit Pass △ ETH 313 Hl 39
Wollaston Lake ~ CDN 6 Db 4
Wollaston Lake ~ CDN 42 Ec 7
Wollaston Peninsula ♁ CDN 47 Cc 11
Wollemi ♀ AUS 379 Mm 62
Wollogorang ○ AUS 365 Me 54
Wollombi ○ AUS 379 Mm 62
Wollomombi ○ AUS 379 Mm 61
Wollondilly ~ AUS 379 Mm 63
Wollongong ○ AUS 379 Mm 63
Wolmaransstad ○ ZA 349 He 59
Wologisi Range ⛰ LB 316 Gb 41
Wolong ★ VRC 242 Lb 30
Wołów ○ PL 174 Ha 20
Wolseley ○ CDN 51 Cl 20
Wolseley ○ ZA 358 Hb 62
Wolsey ○ USA 56 Cn 23
Wolsztyn ○ PL 170 Gp 19
Wolverhampton ○ GB 163 Ge 19
Wolwefontein ○ ZA 358 He 62
Wombil Downs ○ AUS 375 Mk 60
Womer ○ USA 70 Cn 25
Womer ○ USA 70 Cn 26
Wonderfontein ○ ZA 349 Hg 58
Wondinong ○ AUS 368 Lk 59
Wongan Hills ○ AUS 368 Lj 61
Wonganoo ○ AUS 368 Ll 59
Wongoondy ○ AUS 368 Lh 60
Wŏnju ○ ROK 247 Lp 27
Wonnangatta ~ AUS 379 Mk 64
Wono ○ RI 279 Lk 47
Wonogiri ○ RI 278 Lf 49
Wonoka ○ AUS 378 Me 61
Wonosari ○ RI 278 Le 50
Wonosobo ○ RI 278 Le 49
Wonreli ○ RI 283 Lp 50
Wonsan ○ DVRK 247 Lp 26
Wonyulgunna Hill △ AUS 368 Lk 58
Woodanilling ○ AUS 368 Lj 62
Wood Bay ≈ 38 Tb 17
Woodbridge ○ CDN 56 Cp 21
Woodbridge ○ GB 163 Gg 19
Wood Buffalo National Park ♀ CDN 47 Ce 15
Woodburn ○ USA 50 Ca 23
Woodburn ○ AUS 375 Mn 60
Woodbury ○ USA 86 Df 29
Woodenbong ○ AUS 375 Mn 60
Wooden Shoe Village ○ USA 57 Df 24
Woodfjorden ~ N 158 Gn 6
Woodford ○ AUS 375 Mn 59
Woodgate ○ AUS 375 Mn 58
Woodgreen ○ AUS 374 Md 57
Wood Islands ○ CDN 61 Ec 23
Wood Lake ○ USA 56 Cm 24
Woodlake ○ USA 64 Cc 27
Woodland ○ USA 50 Ca 23
Woodland ○ USA 64 Ca 26
Woodland Park ○ USA 65 Ck 26
Woodlands ○ AUS 368 Lk 58
Woodlark Island ♁ PNG 287 Mn 50
Wood Mountain ○ CDN 51 Cj 21
Woodmurra Creek ~ AUS 374 Md 59
Wood River ~ USA 46 Ba 13
Wood River ~ CDN 51 Cj 21
Woodruff ○ USA 57 Dd 23
Woodruff ○ USA 65 Cg 25
Woods ~ USA 56 Da 21
Woodsfield ○ USA 71 Dh 26
Woods Landing ○ USA 65 Ck 25
Woodson ○ USA 70 Cn 29
Woods Peak △ AUS 365 Mj 54
Woodstock ○ CDN 57 Dh 24
Woodstock ○ CDN 60 Ea 22
Woodstock ○ USA 71 Dd 24
Woodstock ○ USA 74 Dj 26
Woodstock ○ AUS 365 Mk 55
Woodstock ○ AUS 374 Mg 57
Woodstock Dam ~ ZA 349 Hg 60
Woodsville ○ USA 60 Dn 23
Woodville ○ USA 81 Da 30
Woodville ○ USA 86 Dc 30
Woodville ○ NZ 383 Nk 66
Woodward ○ USA 70 Cn 27
Woody Pt. ○ CDN 61 Ee 21
Wooi ○ RI 283 Md 46
Woolfield ○ AUS 375 Mh 56
Woolgoolga ○ AUS 379 Mn 61
Wooli ○ AUS 375 Mn 60
Woolla Downs ○ AUS 361 Mc 57
Woolner ○ AUS 364 Mb 52
Woolnorth Point ⌓ AUS 378 Mj 66
Woolyeenyer Hill △ AUS 368 Ll 62
Woomelang ○ AUS 378 Mh 63
Woomera ○ AUS 378 Me 61
Woomerangee Hill △ AUS 368 Lg 59
Woonsucket ○ USA 74 Dm 25
Woorabinda ○ AUS 375 Ml 58
Wooramel ~ AUS 368 Lh 58
Wooramel Roadhouse ○ AUS 368 Lh 58
Woorkabing Hill △ AUS 368 Lj 62
Woorndoo ○ AUS 378 Mh 64
Wooster ○ USA 71 Dg 25
Woraksan ★ ROK 247 Ma 27
Worcester ○ USA 60 Dn 24
Worcester ○ ZA 358 Hb 62
Worcester Range ⛰ 38 Sb 17
Worchester ○ GB 163 Ge 19
Worden ○ USA 50 Ca 24
Wori ○ RI 275 Ln 45
Workington ○ GB 162 Gd 18
Worland ○ USA 51 Ch 23
World Largest Mineral Hot Sprs. ★ USA 51 Ch 24
Worms ○ D 174 Gl 21
Worthington ○ USA 56 Da 24
Wosimi ○ RI 283 Md 47
Wotho ♁ MH 27 Ta 8
Wotje ♁ MH 27 Tb 9
Wotu ○ RI 282 Ll 47
Woumbou ○ CAM 321 Gp 43
Wounded Knee Massacre ★ USA 51 Cl 24
Wour ○ TCH 309 Gp 35
Woyamdero Plain ⌔ EAK 325 Hm 45
Wozhang Shan △ VRC 254 Lb 33
Wrangel Island ♁ RUS 23 Aa 2
Wrangel Island ♁ RUS 205 Zc 4
Wrangell ○ USA 6 Ca 4
Wrangell ○ USA 47 Bj 17
Wrangell Mountains ⛰ USA 46 Be 15
Wrangell-St. Elias National Park & Preserve ♀ USA 46 Be 13
Wray ○ USA 65 Cl 25
Wrens ○ USA 71 Dg 29
Wrentham ○ CDN 51 Cf 21
Wreyham ○ GB 163 Ge 19
Wriedijk ○ SME 113 Eg 43
Wright ○ USA 51 Ck 24
Wright ○ RP 267 Ln 40
Wrightsville ○ USA 71 Dg 29
Wrigley ○ CDN 47 Bn 13
Wrigley Gulf ≈ 38 Cb 17
Wrocław ○ PL 174 Ha 20
Wrotham Park ○ AUS 365 Mh 54
Wroxton ○ CDN 51 Cl 20
Września ○ PL 170 Ha 19
Wu'an ○ VRC 243 Lh 27
Wubin ○ AUS 368 Lj 61
Wubu ○ VRC 243 Lf 27
Wuchang ○ VRC 243 Lh 30
Wuchuan ○ VRC 255 Ld 31
Wuchuan ○ VRC 255 Lf 35
Wuda ○ VRC 243 Ld 26
Wudangshan ★ VRC 243 Lf 29
Wudang Shan ⛰ VRC 243 Lf 29
Wuday'ah ○ KSA 218 Jb 37
Wudil ○ WAN 320 Gl 40
Wuding ○ VRC 254 Lb 33
Wuding He ~ VRC 243 Le 26
Wudu ○ VRC 242 Lc 29
Wufeng ○ VRC 243 Lf 30
Wugang ○ VRC 255 Lf 32
Wugong ○ VRC 243 Le 28
Wugong Shan △ VRC 258 Lg 32
Wuhai ○ VRC 243 Ld 26
Wuhan ○ VRC 243 Lh 30
Wuhe ○ VRC 246 Lj 29
Wuhu ○ VRC 246 Lk 30
Wuhua ○ VRC 258 Lh 34
Wŭjang ○ VRC 230 Kd 29
Wuji ○ VRC 243 Lh 26
Wu Jiang ~ VRC 255 Ld 32
Wu Jiang ~ VRC 255 Le 31
Wukari ○ WAN 320 Gl 42
Wulai ★ RC 259 Ll 33
Wular Lake ~ IND 230 Kb 28
Wuleidao Wan ~ VRC 246 Ll 27
Wulgo ○ WAN 321 Gn 39
Wuli ○ VRC 231 Kl 28
Wulian Feng ⛰ VRC 255 Lb 32
Wulichuan ○ VRC 243 Lf 29
Wuling Shan ⛰ VRC 255 Le 32
Wulingyuan ★ VRC 255 Lf 31
Wuljan ○ VRC 246 Lk 28
Wulong ○ VRC 255 Ld 31
Wulugu ○ GH 317 Gf 40
Wuluhan ○ RI 279 Lg 50
Wulur ○ RI 283 Ma 49
Wum ○ CAM 320 Gm 42
Wumeng Shan ⛰ VRC 255 Lb 33
Wuming ○ VRC 255 Le 34
Wunagak ○ SUD 324 Hj 41
Wundanyi ○ EAK 337 Hm 47
Wunen ○ RI 286 Mf 47
Wuning ○ VRC 258 Lh 31
Wunna ~ IND 234 Kd 35
Wunnummin Lake ○ CDN 57 Dd 19
Wun Rog ○ SUD 324 Hg 41
Wun Shwai ○ SUD 324 Hg 41
Wuntho ○ MYA 254 Km 34
Wupatki National Monument ★ USA 65 Cg 28
Wuping ○ VRC 258 Lj 33
Wuppertal ○ D 163 Gk 20
Wuppertal ○ ZA 358 Hb 62
Wuqi ○ VRC 243 Ld 27
Wuqia ○ VRC 230 Kb 26
Wurarga ○ AUS 368 Lj 60
Wurno ○ WAN 308 Gj 39
Wuruma Reservoir ~ AUS 375 Mm 58
Würzburg ○ D 174 Gl 21
Wuse ○ WAN 320 Gl 41
Wushan ○ VRC 242 Lc 28
Wushan ○ VRC 243 Le 30
Wushan ○ VRC 246 Lj 29
Wusheng Guan △ VRC 243 Lh 30
Wushishi ○ WAN 320 Gj 41
Wushizen ○ VRC 255 Le 35
Wusuli Jiang ~ VRC 250 Mc 22
Wutai ○ VRC 243 Lg 26
Wutan ○ VRC 255 Lf 31
Wutongqiao ○ VRC 255 Lb 31
Wutung ○ PNG 286 Mg 47
Wuvulu Island ♁ PNG 286 Mh 46
Wuwei ○ VRC 242 Lb 27
Wuwei ○ VRC 246 Lj 30
Wuwu ○ PNG 287 Mk 49
Wuxi ○ VRC 243 Le 30
Wuxi ○ VRC 246 Ll 30
Wuxu ○ VRC 255 Le 34
Wuxuan ○ VRC 255 Le 34
Wuxue ○ VRC 258 Lh 31
Wuyang ○ VRC 243 Lg 29
Wuyi ○ VRC 255 Lb 32
Wuyishan ○ VRC 258 Lj 32
Wuyi Shan ⛰ VRC 258 Lj 33
Wuyuan ○ VRC 258 Lj 31
Wuzhai ○ VRC 243 Lf 26
Wuzhi ○ VRC 243 Lg 28
Wuzhi Shan ⛰ VRC 255 Le 36
Wuzhi Shan △ VRC 255 Le 36
Wuzhong ○ VRC 243 Ld 27
Wuzhou ○ VRC 255 Lf 34
Wyaaba Creek ~ AUS 365 Mh 54
Wyalkatchem ○ AUS 368 Lj 61
Wyandotte Caves ★ USA 71 De 26
Wyandra ○ AUS 375 Mk 59
Wycheproof ○ AUS 378 Mh 64
Wyemandoo Hill △ AUS 368 Lk 60
Wyena ○ AUS 375 Mk 56
Wyloo ○ AUS 360 Lj 57
Wymore ○ USA 70 Cp 25
Wynbring ○ AUS 369 Mc 61
Wyndham ○ AUS 364 Ma 53
Wyndmere ○ USA 56 Cp 22
Wynne ○ USA 71 Dc 28
Wynniatt Bay ≈ CDN 42 Eb 4
Wynyard ○ CDN 51 Ck 20
Wynyard ○ AUS 378 Mj 66
Wyola ○ USA 51 Cj 23
Wyola Lake ~ AUS 369 Mb 60
Wyoming ⊙ USA 51 Ch 24
Wyoming ○ USA 57 Df 24
Wyoming ○ USA 71 Dc 24
Wyoming Range ⛰ USA 51 Cg 24
Wyperfeld ♀ AUS 378 Mg 63
Wyralinu Hill △ AUS 368 Lm 62
Wyseby ○ AUS 375 Ml 58
Wyszków ○ PL 170 Hc 19
Wytheville ○ USA 71 Dh 27
Wyzyna Małopolska ⛰ PL 174 Hc 20
Wždāi Mauba ~ YE 219 Jd 37

X

X. Dôn ○ VN 263 Lc 37
Xaafuun ○ SP 328 Jd 40
Xaçmaz ○ AZ 202 Jc 25
Xagquka ○ VRC 235 Kl 30
Xaidulla ○ VRC 230 Kc 27
Xainza ○ VRC 231 Kj 30
Xai-Xai ○ MOC 352 Hj 58
Xalapa ○ MEX 92 Cp 36
Xalin ○ SP 328 Jc 41
Xalpatláhuac ○ MEX 92 Cn 37
Xa Mát ○ VN 263 Ld 40
Xamavera ○ ANG 340 Hc 54
Xambioia ○ BR 121 Ek 49
Xam Hua ○ LAO 255 Lb 35
Xamindele ○ ANG 332 Gn 49
Xá-Muteba ○ ANG 340 Ha 50
Xanagas ○ RB 348 Hc 57
Xanda ○ SP 328 Jd 40
Xandel ○ ANG 340 Ha 50
Xangongo ○ ANG 340 Gp 54
Xankändi ○ AZ 202 Jb 26
Xanlar ○ AZ 202 Jb 25
Xánthi ○ GR 194 He 25
Xanxerê ○ BR 140 Eh 59
Xapuri ~ BR 128 Dp 51
Xapuri ○ BR 129 Dp 51
Xararheere ○ SP 328 Jb 43
Xarlag ○ VRC 243 Le 27
Xassengue ○ ANG 340 Hb 51
Xátiva ○ E 184 Gf 26
Xaudum ~ RB 340 Hc 55
Xavante Vertentes ~ BR 133 Ej 51
Xavantina ○ BR 140 Eh 56
Xavantinho ~ BR 133 Ej 51
Xcalak ○ MEX 93 De 36
Xêgar ○ VRC 235 Kh 31
Xeitongmoin ○ VRC 235 Kj 31
Xenia ○ USA 71 Dg 26
Xeriuni ~ BR 120 Ed 46
Xeruâ ~ BR 117 Dp 49
Xésavang ○ LAO 263 Lc 37
Xhumo ○ RB 349 He 56
Xiachuan Dao ♁ VRC 258 Lg 35
Xiadong ○ VRC 255 Le 34
Xiahe ○ VRC 242 Lb 28
Xiamen ○ VRC 258 Lj 33
Xiamen Wan ~ VRC 258 Lk 33
Xi'an ○ VRC 243 Le 28
Xianfeng ○ VRC 243 Lf 28
Xianfeng ○ VRC 255 Le 31
Xiangcheng ○ VRC 243 Lg 29
Xiangcheng ○ VRC 254 Kp 31
Xiangfan ○ VRC 243 Lg 30
Xianggyin ○ VRC 258 Lg 31
Xianghondian Shuiku ~ VRC 243 Lh 30
Xiang Jiang ~ VRC 258 Lg 32
Xiangkhoang ○ LAO 255 Lb 36
Xiang Ngeun ○ LAO 254 Lb 36
Xiangning ○ VRC 243 Lf 28
Xiangshui ○ VRC 246 Lk 28
Xiangtan ○ VRC 258 Lg 32
Xiangtangshan Shiku ★ VRC 243 Lg 27
Xiangxiang ○ VRC 258 Lg 32
Xiangzhou ○ VRC 255 Le 34
Xianju ○ VRC 259 Ll 31
Xianning ○ VRC 258 Lh 31
Xianshan Gang ~ VRC 259 Ll 31
Xianxia Ling ⛰ VRC 258 Lk 31
Xianyang ○ VRC 243 Le 28
Xianyou ○ VRC 258 Lk 33
Xiaochikou ○ VRC 258 Lh 31
Xiaogan ○ VRC 243 Lg 30
Xiaohe ○ VRC 243 Le 29
Xiaojiahe ○ VRC 250 Mc 22
Xiaojin ○ VRC 242 Lb 30
Xiaokouzi ★ VRC 243 Lc 26
Xiaomei Guan △ VRC 258 Lh 33
Xiaonanchuan ○ VRC 231 Kl 28
Xiao Shan ⛰ VRC 243 Lf 28
Xiaoshan ○ VRC 246 Ll 30
Xiaowutai Shan △ VRC 243 Lh 26
Xiao Xian ○ VRC 246 Lj 28
Xiapu ○ VRC 259 Ll 32
Xiasi ○ VRC 255 Ld 33
Xia Xian ○ VRC 243 Lf 28
Xiaxiyu ○ VRC 243 Lg 26
Xiayi ○ VRC 246 Lj 28
Xiazhai ○ VRC 255 Lc 33
Xiazhuang ○ VRC 243 Lh 29
Xichang ○ VRC 255 Lb 32
Xichiang ○ VRC 255 Lc 35
Xichong ○ VRC 243 Lc 30
Xichou ○ VRC 255 Lc 34
Xichuan ○ VRC 243 Lf 29
Xicoténcatl ○ MEX 81 Cn 34
Xicotepec ○ MEX 81 Cp 34
Xide ○ VRC 254 Lb 31
Xie ~ BR 117 Ea 45
Xienfeng ○ VRC 258 Lh 33
Xifeng ○ VRC 255 Ld 32
Xifengzhen ○ VRC 243 Ld 28
Xigazê ○ VRC 235 Kj 31
Xihua ○ VRC 243 Lh 29
Xiis ○ SP 328 Jb 40
Xi Jiang ~ VRC 255 Lf 34
Xijin Shuiku ~ VRC 255 Le 34
Xijir Ulan Hu ~ VRC 231 Kk 28
Xijishui ○ VRC 242 Lc 27
Xijji ○ VRC 243 Lc 28
Xilin ○ VRC 255 Lc 33
Xilinji Mohe ○ VRC 204 Wa 8
Xilitla ○ MEX 92 Cn 35
Xime ○ GNB 316 Fn 40
Xinanjiang Shuiku ~ VRC 258 Lk 31
Xincai ○ VRC 243 Lh 29
Xinchang ○ VRC 259 Ll 31
Xincheng ○ VRC 243 Lh 26
Xinchuan Gang ~ VRC 246 Ll 29
Xinfeng ○ VRC 258 Lh 33
Xinfengjiang Shuiku ~ VRC 258 Lh 34
Xingaloot ○ SP 328 Jc 41
Xing'an ○ VRC 255 Lf 33
Xingan ○ VRC 258 Lh 32
Xingcheng ○ VRC 246 Ll 25
Xinge ○ ANG 340 Hb 51
Xingguo ○ VRC 258 Lh 32
Xinghua ○ VRC 246 Lk 29
Xinghua Wan ~ VRC 258 Lk 33
Xingkai Hu ~ VRC 250 Mc 23
Xinglong ○ VRC 246 Lj 25
Xingning ○ VRC 258 Lh 33
Xingod ○ SP 328 Jc 42
Xingren ○ VRC 255 Lc 33
Xingrenbu ○ VRC 242 Lc 27
Xingshan ○ VRC 243 Lf 30
Xingtai ○ VRC 243 Lh 27
Xingtang ○ VRC 243 Lh 26
Xingu ~ BR 121 Eh 47
Xingu ~ BR 121 Eh 48
Xingu ~ BR 121 Eh 49
Xingu ~ BR 121 Eh 50
Xingu ~ BR 132 Eh 51
Xinguara ○ BR 121 Ej 49
Xingwen ○ VRC 255 Lc 31
Xing Xian ○ VRC 243 Lf 26
Xingxiuhai ♀ VRC 242 Kn 28
Xingyi ○ VRC 255 Lc 33
Xinhuang ○ VRC 255 Le 32
Xining ○ VRC 242 La 27
Xiniujiao ○ VRC 255 Le 35
Xinji ○ VRC 243 Lh 27
Xinjin ○ VRC 242 Lb 30
Xinjin ○ VRC 246 Ln 28
Xinlong ○ VRC 242 La 30
Xinning ○ VRC 255 Lf 32
Xinping ○ VRC 255 Ld 32
Xinshao ○ VRC 255 Lb 33
Xintai ○ VRC 246 Lj 28
Xintao ○ VRC 243 Lg 30
Xintian ○ VRC 258 Lg 33
Xinxiang ○ VRC 243 Lg 28
Xinxim ~ BR 120 Eh 50
Xinxing ○ VRC 255 Lg 36
Xinxing ○ VRC 258 Lg 34
Xinxu ○ VRC 255 Ld 34
Xinyang ○ VRC 243 Lh 29
Xinye ○ VRC 243 Lg 29
Xinyi ○ VRC 246 Lk 28
Xinyi ○ VRC 255 Lf 34
Xinying ○ VRC 255 Le 36
Xinyu ○ VRC 258 Lh 32
Xinzhao Shan △ VRC 243 Ld 26
Xinzheng ○ VRC 243 Lg 28
Xinzhou ○ VRC 243 Lg 26
Xinzuotang ○ VRC 258 Lh 34
Xiongyuecheng ○ VRC 246 Lm 25
Xipamanu ~ BOL 129 Dp 51
Xiping ○ VRC 243 Lf 29
Xiping ○ VRC 243 Lg 29
Xique-Xique ○ BR 125 En 51
Xırdalan ○ AZ 202 Jc 25
Xiryang ○ VRC 243 Lg 27
Xishan ★ VRC 243 Lh 30
Xishaqundao Paracel Islands ♁ VRC 263 Lf 37
Xis huangbanna ⌔ VRC 254 La 34
Xishui ○ VRC 243 Lh 30
Xishui ○ VRC 255 Ld 31
Xitole ○ GNB 316 Fn 40
Xiuning ○ VRC 258 Lj 31
Xiushan ○ VRC 255 Le 31
Xiushui ○ VRC 258 Lh 31
Xiuwen ○ VRC 255 Ld 32
Xiuwu ○ VRC 243 Lg 28
Xiuyan ○ VRC 246 Lm 25
Xiuying ○ VRC 255 Lf 35
Xiwu ○ VRC 242 Kn 29
Xixabangma Feng △ VRC 235 Kg 31
Xixé ~ BR 120 Eh 50
Xixia ○ VRC 243 Lf 29
Xi Xian ○ VRC 243 Lf 27
Xixiang ○ VRC 243 Ld 29
Xixón ○ E 184 Gd 24
Xizhong Dao ♁ VRC 246 Ll 26
Xocavänd ○ AZ 202 Jb 26
Xochiapa ○ MEX 93 Da 37
Xochicalco ★ MEX 92 Cn 36
Xochimilco ○ MEX 92 Cn 36
Xonxa Dam ~ ZA 349 Hf 61
Xorkol ○ VRC 231 Kk 26
Xpujil ○ MEX 93 Dd 36
Xuan'en ○ VRC 243 Le 30
Xuanhan ○ VRC 243 Ld 30
Xuanhua ○ VRC 243 Lh 25
Xuân Lôc ○ VN 263 Ld 40
Xuanwei ○ VRC 255 Lc 32
Xuanzhong Si ★ VRC 243 Lf 27
Xuanzhou ○ VRC 246 Lk 30
Xuchang ○ VRC 243 Lg 28
Xudat ○ AZ 202 Jc 25
Xuddur ○ SP 328 Jb 41
Xuddur ○ SP 328 Hp 43
Xuebao Ding △ VRC 242 Lb 29
Xuefeng Shan ⛰ VRC 255 Lf 32
Xueshan △ VRC 242 Lc 27
Xugana Lodge ○ RB 341 Hd 55
Xugui ○ VRC 242 Kn 28
Xumishan Shiku ★ VRC 243 Lc 27
Xun He ~ VRC 243 Le 29
Xunhua ○ VRC 242 Lb 28
Xun Jiang ~ VRC 255 Lf 34
Xunwu ○ VRC 258 Lh 33
Xun Xian ○ VRC 243 Lh 28
Xunxiao ○ VRC 258 Lj 34
Xunyang ○ VRC 243 Le 29
Xunyi ○ VRC 243 Le 28
Xupu ○ VRC 255 Lf 32
Xuru Co ~ VRC 231 Kh 30
Xushui ○ VRC 243 Lh 26
Xuwen ○ VRC 255 Le 35
Xuyi ○ VRC 246 Lk 29
Xuyong ○ VRC 255 Lc 31
Xuzhou ○ VRC 246 Lj 28
Xyatil ○ MEX 93 Dd 36

Y

Y. Kinneret ~ JOR 208 Hk 29
Yaak ○ USA 50 Ce 21
Yaamba ○ AUS 375 Mm 57
Ya'an ○ VRC 255 Lb 31
Yaaq Braaway ○ SP 329 Hp 45
Yabassi ○ CAM 320 Gm 43
Yabayo ○ CI 305 Gc 43
Yabe ○ J 247 Mb 29
Yabebyry ○ PY 140 Ef 59
Yabelo ○ ETH 325 Hl 43
Yabia ○ RDC 321 Hd 44
Yablonovyy Khrebet ⛰ RUS 22 Qa 4
Yablonovyy Khrebet ⛰ RUS 204 Vb 8
Yabucoa ○ USA 104 Eb 37
Yabus ~ ETH 325 Hk 41
Yacambú ♀ YV 107 Dp 41
Yacaré Norte ~ PY 140 Ee 57
Yacata ♁ FJI 390 Aa 54
Yacheng ○ VRC 255 Le 36
Yacimiento Río Turbio ○ RA 152 Dm 71
Yacuiba ○ BOL 136 Ec 56
Yacuma ~ BOL 129 Ea 52
Yacuma ~ BOL 129 Eb 52
Yadé Massif ⛰ RCA 321 Gp 42
Yādgīr ○ IND 238 Kc 37
Yadibikro ○ CI 317 Gd 42
Yadma ○ KSA 218 Ja 36
Yadong ○ VRC 235 Kj 32
Yadua ♁ FJI 387 Nm 54
Yaeyama-rettō ♁ J 259 Lm 33
Yafran ○ LAR 297 Gn 29
Yaghan Basin ♆ 15 Fb 15
Yagishiri-tō ♁ J 250 Mg 23
Yagoua ○ CAM 321 Gp 40
Yagradagzê Shan △ VRC 242 Km 28
Yaguachi Nuevo ○ EC 116 Dj 47
Yaguajay ○ C 100 Dj 34
Yaguaraparo ○ YV 112 Ec 40
Yaguas ~ PE 117 Dn 47
Yaguerón ~ ROU 146 Eh 62
Yaha ○ THA 270 La 42
Yahekou ○ VRC 243 Lg 29
Yahualica ○ MEX 92 Cl 35
Yahuma ○ RDC 333 Hd 45
Yahyalı ○ TR 195 Hk 26
Yaibrai ○ VRC 242 Lb 26
Yaili ○ PE 128 Dl 52
Yaita ○ J 251 Mg 27
Yajalón ○ MEX 93 Db 37
Yajiang ○ VRC 254 La 31
Yaka ○ RCA 321 Hb 43
Yakabindie ○ AUS 368 Ll 59
Yakamul ○ PNG 286 Mh 47
Yakana ○ RDC 333 Hd 45
Yakassé-Attobrou ○ CI 317 Ge 42
Yakeshi ○ VRC 204 Wa 9
Yakfıkebir ○ TR 195 Hm 25
Yakima ~ USA 50 Cb 22
Yakima ○ USA 50 Cb 22
Yakima Indian Reservation ••• USA 50 Cb 22
Yakmach ○ PK 227 Jk 31
Yako ○ BF 317 Ge 39
Yakobi Island ♁ USA 47 Bg 17
Yakoma ○ RDC 321 Hd 43
Yaku ○ J 247 Mb 30
Yaku ★ J 247 Mb 30
Yakumo ○ J 250 Mg 24
Yakushima ★ J 247 Mb 30
Yaku-shima ♁ J 247 Mb 30
Yakutat ○ USA 6 Bb 4
Yakutat ○ USA 47 Be 15
Yakutat Bay ≈ USA 47 Be 15
Yakutia ⛰ RUS 204 Vc 5
Yakutsk ○ RUS 22 Ra 3
Yala ○ THA 270 La 42
Yala ○ GH 317 Gf 40
Yala ○ EAK 337 Hk 45
Yala ~ EAK 337 Hk 46
Yalaki ○ RDC 333 Hd 45
Yala National Park ♀ CL 239 Ke 42
Yalardy ○ AUS 368 Lh 59
Yalata ○ AUS 369 Mb 61
Yalata Aboriginal Land ••• AUS 369 Mb 61
Yalbalgo ○ AUS 368 Lh 58
Yale ○ USA 50 Ca 22
Yale ○ CDN 50 Cb 21
Yale ○ USA 57 Dg 24
Yaleko ○ RDC 324 He 45
Yalgo ○ BF 317 Gf 39
Yalgoo ○ AUS 368 Lj 60
Yalgorup ♀ AUS 368 Lh 62
Yali ○ CO 106 Dl 42
Yali ~ BF 317 Gg 39
Yaligimba ○ RDC 321 Hd 44
Yalimbongo ○ RDC 321 Hd 44
Yalinga ○ RCA 321 Hd 42
Yalingi River ~ PNG 286 Mh 47
Yallalong ○ AUS 368 Lh 59
Yalleroi ○ AUS 375 Mj 58
Yaloké ○ RCA 321 Ha 43
Yalomanga ○ RDC 333 Hd 46
Yalong Jiang ~ VRC 254 La 31
Yalongwa ○ RDC 333 Hd 45
Yalon Jiang ~ VRC 242 Kp 29
Yaloogarrie Creek ~ AUS 361 Mb 56
Yalova ○ TR 195 Hg 25
Yalta ○ UA 175 Hj 23
Yaltubung ○ RI 283 Ma 49
Yalufi ○ RDC 324 He 45
Yalu Jiang ~ VRC 246 Ln 25
Ya ,lujiang Kou ~ DVRK 246 Ln 26
Yālūr ○ AFG 223 Jp 27
Yamada ○ J 250 Mh 26
Yamagata ○ J 251 Mf 26
Yamaguchi ○ J 247 Mb 28
Yamakawa ○ J 251 Mc 29
Yamanashi ○ J 251 Mf 28
Yamarna ○ AUS 369 Lm 60
Yamarna Aboriginal Reserve ••• AUS 369 Lm 59
Yamasá ○ DOM 101 Dn 36
Yamasaki ○ J 251 Md 28
Yamato Basin ♆ 251 Md 27
Yamato Rise ♆ 251 Mc 27
Yamatsuri ○ J 251 Mg 27
Yamba ○ BF 317 Gg 39
Yamba ○ AUS 375 Mn 60
Yambah ○ AUS 361 Mc 57
Yambala ○ RCA 321 Hc 42
Yambarran Range ⛰ AUS 364 Mb 53
Yamba-Tchangsou ○ TCH 321 Gp 41
Yamba-Yamba ○ RDC 336 Hf 48
Yambéring ○ RG 316 Fp 40
Yambio ○ SUD 324 Hg 43
Yambuya ○ RDC 324 He 45
Yame ○ J 247 Mb 29
Yamethin ○ MYA 254 Km 35
Yamīn ○ IRQ 215 Jb 30
Yamisolo ○ RDC 321 Hd 44
Yamon ○ PE 116 Dj 49
Yamoussoukro ▣ CI 317 Gd 42
Yampa ○ USA 65 Cj 25
Yampa River ~ USA 65 Cj 25
Yamskaya Guba ≈ RUS 205 Ya 7
Yamuna ~ IND 230 Kd 30
Yamuna ~ IND 234 Ke 33
Yamunanagar ○ IND 230 Kc 30
Yamzho Yumco ~ VRC 235 Kk 31
Yan ○ MAL 270 La 43
Yana ○ WAL 316 Fp 41
Yanaba Island ♁ PNG 287 Mm 50
Yanac ○ AUS 378 Mg 64
Yanacu Grande ~ PE 116 Dl 48
Yanadani ○ J 251 Mc 29
Yanagava ○ J 247 Mb 29
Yanahuanca ○ PE 116 Dk 51
Yanai ○ J 251 Mc 29
Yanam ○ IND 238 Kf 37
Yan'an ○ VRC 243 Le 27
Yanaoca ○ PE 128 Dn 53
Yanatil ~ PE 128 Dm 52
Yanbu' al-Bahr ○ KSA 214 Hl 33
Yanbu' al-Sinaiyah ○ KSA 214 Hl 34
Yanbu' an-Nahl ○ KSA 214 Hl 33
Yancannia ○ AUS 378 Mh 61
Yancannia Creek ~ AUS 374 Mh 60
Yanchang ○ VRC 243 Lf 27
Yancheng ○ VRC 246 Ll 29
Yanchep ○ AUS 368 Lh 61
Yanchep ♀ AUS 368 Lh 61
Yanchi ○ VRC 243 Ld 27
Yanco Cr. ~ AUS 379 Mj 63
Yanco Glen ○ AUS 378 Mg 61
Yanda Creek ~ AUS 379 Mj 61
Yandal ○ AUS 368 Ll 59
Yandama Creek ~ AUS 374 Mg 60
Yandangshan ★ VRC 259 Ll 31
Yandang Shan ⛰ VRC 259 Ll 32
Yandaxkak ○ VRC 231 Kj 26
Yandev ○ WAN 320 Gl 42
Yandeyarra ○ AUS 360 Lk 56
Yandeyarra Aboriginal Reserve ••• AUS 360 Lk 56
Yandina ○ SOL 290 Nb 50
Yandja ○ RDC 333 Ha 46
Yandon ○ MYA 262 Km 37
Yandongi ○ RDC 321 Hd 44
Yanfeng ○ VRC 255 Lb 31
Yanfolia ○ RMM 316 Gb 40
Yanga ○ CAM 321 Gp 44
Yangalia ○ RCA 321 Hc 42
Yangambi ○ RDC 324 He 45
Yangamo ○ CAM 321 Gn 43
Yangara ~ TCH 309 Hb 35
Yangas ○ PE 116 Dk 51
Yangasso ○ RMM 317 Gd 39
Yangbajain ○ VRC 231 Kk 30
Yangbajain ★ VRC 231 Kk 30
Yangcheng ○ VRC 243 Lg 28
Yangchun ○ VRC 255 Lf 34
Yangcun ○ VRC 258 Lh 34
Yangdok ○ DVRK 247 Lp 26
Yanggandu ○ RI 286 Mg 50
Yang He ~ VRC 243 Lh 25
Yangjiang ○ VRC 255 Lf 35
Yangmingshan ★ RC 259 Ll 33
Yangpu Gang ~ VRC 255 Le 36
Yangquan ○ VRC 243 Lg 27
Yangquangu ○ VRC 243 Lf 27
Yangqu Shan △ VRC 243 Lg 27
Yangshan ○ VRC 258 Lg 33
Yangshuo ○ VRC 255 Lf 33
Yangtze ~ VRC 243 Le 30
Yangtze ~ VRC 246 Lk 29
Yangudi Rassa ♀ ETH 313 Hn 40
Yangxi ○ VRC 255 Lf 35
Yangxin ○ VRC 258 Lh 31
Yang-Yang ○ SN 304 Fn 38
Yangyuan ○ VRC 243 Lh 25
Yangzhou ○ VRC 246 Lk 29
Yanhe ○ VRC 255 Le 31
Yanhu ○ VRC 230 Kf 29
Yanice Irmağı ~ TR 195 Hj 25
Yanjin ○ VRC 255 Lc 31
Yanjing ○ VRC 254 Kp 31
Yank ○ CDN 50 Cd 21
Yankok ○ PNG 286 Mh 47
Yankoman ○ GH 317 Ge 43
Yankton ○ USA 56 Cp 24
Yankton Indian Reservation ••• USA 56 Cn 24
Yanling ○ VRC 243 Lh 28
Yanling ○ VRC 255 Lb 33
Yannarie ~ AUS 360 Lh 57
Yano-Indigirskaya Nizmennost' ⌔ RUS 205 Wc 4
Yanonge ○ RDC 324 He 45
Yanqing ○ VRC 246 Lj 25
Yanqul ○ OM 226 Jg 34
Yanrey ○ AUS 360 Lh 57
Yanshan ○ VRC 246 Lj 26
Yanshan ○ VRC 255 Lc 34
Yanshan ○ VRC 258 Lj 31
Yanskiy Zaliv ≈ RUS 205 Wc 4
Yansoribo ○ RI 283 Mc 46
Yantabulla ○ AUS 375 Mj 60
Yantai ○ VRC 246 Ll 27
Yanting ○ VRC 242 Lc 30
Yantou ○ VRC 259 Ll 31
Yantzaza ○ EC 116 Dj 47
Yanuca ♁ FJI 390 Aa 54
Yanwodao ★ VRC 250 Mc 22
Yanzikou ○ VRC 255 Lc 32
Yaodian ○ VRC 243 Le 27
Yaolin ★ VRC 258 Lk 31
Yaoundé ▣ CAM 320 Gm 44
Yaowang Gang ~ VRC 246 Ll 29

Wolcott - Yaowang Gang 483

Yao Xian ○ VRC 243 Le 28
Yap ⛬ FSM 26 Rb 9
Yapacana ♀ YV 107 Ea 44
Yapacani ~ BOL 129 Eb 54
Yapacáraí ○ PY 140 Ef 58
Yapei ○ GH 317 Gf 41
Yapiroa ○ BOL 129 Ec 55
Yappar ~ AUS 365 Mg 55
Yappirãla ○ IND 238 Kd 38
Yap Trench Ψ 26 Rb 9
Yaputih ○ RI 283 Ma 47
Yaqaga ⛬ FJI 387 Nm 54
Yaqeta ⛬ FJI 387 Nl 54
Yaque del Norte ~ DOM 101 Dn 36
Yaqui ○ MEX 80 Cg 32
Yaqui ~ MEX 80 Cg 32
Yar ~ RI 286 Mf 49
Yara ○ C 101 Dk 35
Yaraka ○ AUS 374 Mh 58
Yardımlı ○ AZ 202 Jc 26
Yaré Lao ○ SN 304 Fn 37
Yaren ○ NAU 35 Ta 10
Yaren ▣ NAU 35 Ta 10
Yargatti ○ IND 238 Kb 37
Yari ~ CO 116 Dm 45
Yari ~ CO 116 Dm 46
Yarim ○ YE 218 Ja 38
Yaritagua ○ YV 107 Dp 41
Yarkant He ~ VRC 230 Kc 27
Yarkant He ~ VRC 230 Kd 26
Yarkhun ~ PK 230 Ka 27
Yarle Lake ~ AUS 369 Mb 61
Yarlung Zangbo Jiang ~ VRC 235 Kh 31
Yarlung Zangbo Jiang Brahmaputra ~ VRC 235 Kl 31
Yarmouth ○ CDN 61 Ea 24
Yarnek ○ RUS 154 Rc 5
Yäro Lund ○ PK 227 Jn 32
Yaroslavl' ⊙ RUS 171 Hm 17
Yaroupi ~ F 113 Eh 44
Yarrabubba ○ AUS 368 Lk 59
Yarraloola ○ AUS 360 Lh 56
Yarram ○ AUS 379 Mk 65
Yarraman ○ AUS 375 Mm 59
Yarra Yarra Lakes ~ AUS 368 Lh 60
Yarrie ○ AUS 360 Ll 56
Yarronvale ○ AUS 375 Mj 59
Yarrowitch ○ AUS 379 Mm 61
Yarrowmere ○ AUS 375 Mj 56
Yarumal ○ CO 106 Dl 42
Yasa ○ RDC 333 Hc 47
Yasawa ⛬ FJI 387 Nl 54
Yasawe Group ⛬ FJI 387 Nl 54
Yasendu ○ RDC 324 He 45
Yashi ○ WAN 320 Gk 39
Yashikera ○ WAN 320 Gh 41
Yasothon ○ THA 263 Lb 38
Yass ○ AUS 379 Ml 63
Yass ~ AUS 379 Ml 63
Yāsūğ ○ IR 215 Jd 30
Yasuni ~ EC 116 Dl 46
Yati ○ RN 297 Gn 35
Yata ○ BOL 129 Ea 52
Yata ~ BOL 129 Eb 51
Yata ~ BOL 129 Eb 52
Yata ~ RCA 321 Hd 41
Yatağan ○ TR 195 Hg 27
Yatako ○ BF 305 Gg 38
Yaté ○ F 386 Nf 57
Yates Center ○ USA 70 Cp 27
Yathkyed Lake ~ CDN 6 Ea 3
Yathkyed Lake ~ CDN 42 Fb 6
Yatolema ○ RDC 324 He 45
Yatsushiro ○ J 247 Mb 29
Yatsushiro-kai ~ J 247 Mb 29
Yatsu-t △ J 251 Mf 28
Yatta ○ EAK 337 Hl 46
Yatta Plateau ⛰ EAK 337 Hl 47
Yatúa ~ YV 117 Ea 45
Yauca ○ PE 128 Dl 53
Yauca ~ PE 128 Dl 53
Yáuco ○ USA 104 Ea 36
Yauri ○ PE 128 Dn 53
Yaurisque ○ PE 128 Dm 52
Yautepec ○ MEX 93 Cp 37
Yauyos ○ PE 128 Dl 52
Yāval ○ IND 234 Kb 35
Yavari ~ PE 117 Dn 48
Yavari Mirim ~ PE 116 Dm 48
Yávaros ○ MEX 80 Ch 32
Yavatmāl ○ IND 234 Kc 35
Yaveri ~ PE 116 Dm 48
Yavero ó Paucartambo ~ PE 128 Dm 52
Yavi ○ PY 136 Eb 57
Yavineto ~ PE 116 Dl 46
Yaviza ○ PA 106 Dk 41
Yavuzeli ○ TR 195 Hl 27
Yawata-hama ○ J 251 Mc 29
Yawatongguzlangar ○ VRC 231 Kf 27
Yawimu ○ RI 286 Mf 49
Yawngo ○ MYA 254 Kp 34
Yawri Bay ~ WAL 316 Fp 41
Yaxcaba ○ MEX 93 Dd 35
Yaxing ○ VRC 255 Le 36
Yayama ○ RDC 333 Hd 46
Yazd ⊙ IR 222 Je 29
Yazd ○ IR 226 Jf 30
Yazdān ○ IR 223 Jj 29
Yāzdavān ~ AFG 226 Jk 30
Yazmān ○ PK 227 Jp 31
Yazoo City ○ USA 86 Dc 29
Yby Yaú ○ PY 140 Ef 57
Ye ○ MYA 262 Kn 38
Yea ○ AUS 379 Mj 64
Yebawmi ○ MYA 254 Km 33
Yebbi-Bou ○ TCH 309 Ha 35
Yebbi Souma ○ TCH 309 Ha 35
Yebok ○ MYA 254 Kl 36
Yebya ○ MYA 254 Km 35
Yecheng ○ VRC 230 Kc 27
Yecla ○ E 184 Gf 26
Yeelanna ○ AUS 378 Md 63
Yeelirrie ○ AUS 368 Ll 59
Yegguebo ○ RN 297 Gn 36
Yegros ○ PY 140 Ef 59
Yégué ○ RT 317 Gg 41
Yegyi ○ MYA 262 Km 37
Yei ○ SUD 324 Hh 43
Yei ~ SUD 324 Hh 43
Yeji ○ VRC 243 Lh 30
Yeji ○ GH 317 Gf 41
Yekaterinburg ○ RUS 154 Sa 7
Yekepa ○ LB 316 Gb 42
Yekokora ~ RDC 333 Hc 45
Yelahanka ○ IND 238 Kc 39
Yele ○ WAL 316 Ga 41
Yélimané ○ RMM 304 Ga 38
Yell ⛬ GB 162 Gf 15
Yellandu ○ IND 238 Ke 37
Yellāpur ○ IND 238 Kb 38
Yellowdine ○ AUS 368 Lk 61
Yellow Grass ○ CDN 51 Ck 20
Yellowknife ○ CDN 42 Eb 6
Yellow River ~ PNG 286 Mg 47
Yellow Sea ≈ 246 Lm 27
Yellowstone ○ USA 51 Cg 23
Yellowstone ~ USA 51 Cj 22
Yellowstone Lake ~ USA 51 Cg 23
Yellowstone National Park ♀ USA 51 Cg 23
Yellowstone River ~ USA 51 Ck 22
Yelm ○ USA 50 Ca 22
Yelma ○ AUS 368 Ll 59
Yelvertoft ○ AUS 374 Mf 56
Yelwa ○ WAN 320 Gj 40
Yelwa ○ WAN 320 Gl 41
Yema ○ RDC 332 Gn 48
Yema Manshan ⛰ VRC 242 Km 26
Yemassee ○ USA 71 Dh 29
Yembo ○ ETH 325 Hk 41
Yemen ☐ YE 218 Ja 38
Yen ○ TCH 309 Hb 36
Yen ○ CAM 320 Gn 44
Yenagoa ○ WAN 320 Gk 43
Yenangyaung ○ MYA 254 Km 35
Yên Bái ○ VN 255 Lc 35
Yenda ○ AUS 379 Mk 63
Yende Milimou ○ RG 316 Ga 41
Yendéré ○ BF 317 Gd 40
Yendi ○ GH 317 Gf 41
Yéneganou ○ RCB 332 Gh 47
Yengchang ○ VRC 231 Kj 30
Yenge ~ RDC 333 Hc 46
Yengema ○ WAL 316 Ga 41
Yengil ○ IND 235 Kl 32
Yengisar ○ VRC 230 Kc 26
Yengo ○ RCB 332 Gp 45
Yengo ♀ AUS 379 Mm 62
Yên Hung ○ VN 255 Lb 35
Yenihisar ○ TR 195 Hf 27
Yenişehir ○ TR 195 Hg 25
Yenisey ~ RUS 22 Pa 3
Yenisey ~ RUS 204 Tc 5
Yenisey ~ RUS 204 Ua 7
Yeniseyskiy Zaliv ≈ RUS 204 Ta 4
Yéno ○ G 332 Gm 46
Yên Vhâu ○ VN 255 Lc 35
Yeola ○ IND 234 Kb 35
Yeo Lake ~ AUS 369 Ln 60
Yeoval ○ AUS 379 Ml 62
Yeovil ○ GB 163 Ge 20
Yeppoon ○ AUS 375 Mm 57
Yerba Buena ○ PE 128 Dn 54
Yercard ○ IND 238 Kd 40
Yerevan ▣ ARM 202 Ja 25
Yergara ○ IND 238 Kc 38
Yergeni Hills ⛰ RUS 181 Hp 21
Yerington ○ USA 64 Cc 26
Yerköy ○ TR 195 Hk 26
Yermak Plateau Ψ 18 Ka 1
Yermala ○ IND 238 Kb 36
Yesan ○ ROK 247 Lp 27
Yeshin ○ MYA 254 Km 34
Yeşilhisar ○ TR 195 Hk 26
Yeşil-ırmak ~ TR 195 Hl 25
Yeşilova ○ TR 195 Hg 27
Yesterday River ~ CDN 57 Dh 20
Yet ○ ETH 328 Hp 43
Yetman ○ AUS 375 Mm 60
Ye-u ○ MYA 254 Km 34
Yevlax ○ AZ 202 Jb 25
Ye Xian ○ VRC 243 Lg 29
Yeyik ○ VRC 231 Kf 27
Yhú ○ PY 140 Eg 58
Yibin ○ VRC 255 Lc 31
Yichang ○ VRC 243 Lf 30
Yicheng ○ VRC 243 Lf 28
Yicheng ○ VRC 243 Lg 30
Yichuan ○ VRC 243 Le 27
Yichuan ○ VRC 243 Lg 28
Yichun ○ VRC 205 Wb 9
Yichun ○ VRC 258 Lh 32
Yifeng ○ VRC 258 Lh 31
Yığılca ○ TR 195 Hh 25
Yihuang ○ VRC 258 Lh 32
Yijun ○ VRC 243 Le 28
Yilan ○ VRC 250 Ma 22
Yıldızeli ○ TR 195 Hl 26
Yiliang ○ VRC 255 Lb 33
Yiliang ○ VRC 255 Lc 32
Yilong ○ VRC 243 Ld 30
Yilou ○ BF 317 Gf 39
Yilui ○ PNG 286 Mh 47
Yima ○ VRC 243 Lf 28
Yimen ○ VRC 254 La 33
Yimni River ~ PNG 286 Mh 47
Yinchuan ○ VRC 243 Ld 26
Yindi ○ AUS 368 Lm 61
Yingawunarri Aboriginal Land ••• AUS 364 Mc 54
Yingcheng ○ VRC 243 Lg 30
Yingde ○ VRC 258 Lg 33
Yinggehai ○ VRC 255 Le 36
Ying He ~ VRC 243 Lh 29
Yingjing ○ VRC 255 Lb 31
Yingkou ○ VRC 246 Ll 25
Yingkou Dashiqiao ○ VRC 246 Lm 25
Yingpan ○ VRC 255 Le 35
Yingshan ○ VRC 243 Ld 30
Yingshang ○ VRC 246 Lj 29
Yingshang ○ VRC 255 Lc 33
Yingtan ○ VRC 258 Lj 31
Yingui ○ CAM 320 Gm 43
Ying Xian ○ VRC 243 Lg 26
Yining ○ VRC 22 Pa 5
Yinjiang ○ VRC 255 Le 31
Yinnietharra ○ AUS 368 Lj 58
Yinxu ★ VRC 243 Lh 27
Yi'ong Co ~ VRC 242 Km 30
Yi'ong Zangbo ~ VRC 242 Km 30
Yipinglang ○ VRC 254 La 33
Yiqikai ○ VRC 242 Kp 28
Yirga Alem ○ ETH 325 Hm 42
Yirga Ch'efē ○ ETH 325 Hm 42
Yirié ○ RG 316 Gb 41
Yirol ○ SUD 324 Hh 42
Yirrkala ○ AUS 365 Me 52
Yishui ○ VRC 246 Lk 28
Yity ○ OM 226 Jh 34
Yiwu ○ VRC 259 Lk 31
Yi Xian ○ VRC 243 Lh 26
Yi Xian ○ VRC 246 Ll 25
Yixing ○ VRC 246 Lk 30
Yiyang ○ VRC 258 Lg 31
Yiyang ○ VRC 258 Lj 31
Yiyuan ○ VRC 246 Lk 27
Yizhang ○ VRC 258 Lg 33
Yizheng ○ VRC 246 Lk 29
Yizhou ○ VRC 255 Le 33
Yizu Daizu ○ VRC 254 La 34
Yläne ○ FIN 159 Hd 15
Yli-Näljänkä ○ FIN 159 Hg 13
Ylitornio ○ FIN 159 Hd 12
Ylivieska ○ FIN 159 Hd 13
Ylöjärvi ○ FIN 159 Hd 15
Yoakum ○ USA 81 Cp 31
Yoboki ○ DJI 328 Hp 40
Yoco ○ YV 112 Ec 40
Yoder ○ USA 65 Ck 26
Yof Pickine ○ SN 304 Fm 38
Yogoum ○ TCH 309 Hb 37
Yog Point ⌒ RP 267 Ln 38
Yogya ○ RI 278 Lf 49
Yogyakarta Yogya ○ RI 278 Lf 49
Yoho ♀ CDN 50 Cd 20
Yoichi ○ J 250 Mg 24
Yokadouma ○ CAM 321 Gp 44
Yokate-shima ⛬ J 259 Ma 31
Yokkaichi ○ J 251 Me 28
Yoko ○ CAM 320 Gn 43
Yokoboué ○ CI 317 Gd 43
Yokohama ○ J 250 Mg 25
Yokohama ○ J 251 Mf 28
Yokosuka ○ J 251 Mf 28
Yokote ○ J 250 Mg 26
Yola ○ WAN 321 Gn 41
Yolombo ○ RDC 333 Hd 46
Yolöten ○ TM 223 Jk 27
Yomadu ○ WAL 316 Ga 41
Yombi ○ G 332 Gm 46
Yomou ○ RG 316 Gb 42
Yomuka ○ RI 286 Mf 49
Yonago ○ J 251 Mc 28
Yonaguni-shima ⛬ J 259 Lm 33
Yoneshiro ~ J 250 Mg 25
Yonezawa ○ J 251 Mf 27
Yong'an ○ VRC 258 Lj 33
Yongchang ○ VRC 242 La 26
Yongcheng ○ VRC 246 Lj 29
Yongchuan ○ VRC 255 Lc 31
Yongdeng ○ VRC 242 Lb 27
Yongding ○ VRC 258 Lj 33
Yŏngdŏk ○ ROK 247 Ma 27
Yongfeng ○ VRC 258 Lh 32
Yongfu ○ VRC 255 Le 33
Yongjing ○ VRC 242 Lb 27
Yŏngju ○ ROK 247 Ma 27
Yongkang ○ VRC 259 Lk 31
Yongle Gong ★ VRC 243 Lf 28
Yongning ○ VRC 243 Lc 26
Yongofondo ○ RCA 321 Hd 43
Yong Peng ○ MAL 271 Lb 44
Yongping ○ VRC 243 Le 27
Yongren ○ VRC 254 La 32
Yongshun ○ VRC 255 Le 31
Yongtai ○ VRC 258 Lk 33
Yongxin ○ VRC 258 Lg 32
Yongxing ○ VRC 258 Lg 32
Yongxiu ○ VRC 258 Lh 31
Yongzhou ○ VRC 255 Lf 32
Yonibana ○ WAL 316 Fp 41
Yonkers ○ USA 74 Dl 25
Yonne ~ F 163 Gh 21
Yonoféré ○ SN 304 Fn 38
Yoonzoy ○ SP 329 Hp 46
Yopal ○ CO 107 Dm 43
Yopales ○ YV 112 Ec 41
Yopie ○ LB 316 Gb 42
Yopurga ○ VRC 230 Kc 26
Yorito ○ HN 96 De 38
York ○ USA 70 Cp 25
York ○ USA 71 Dh 28
York ○ USA 74 Dk 26
York ~ USA 74 Dk 27
York ○ USA 86 Dd 29
York ○ GB 162 Gf 19
York ○ AUS 368 Lj 61
Yorke Peninsula ⛬ AUS 378 Me 63
Yorketown ○ AUS 378 Me 63
Yorkeys Knob ○ AUS 365 Mj 54
York Factory ○ CDN 42 Fc 7
Yorkshire Dales ♀ GB 162 Ge 18
Yorkshire Downs ○ AUS 374 Mh 56
York Sound ~ AUS 361 Ln 53
Yorkton ○ CDN 51 Cl 20
Yoro ○ HN 96 De 38
Yorobougoula ○ RMM 305 Gc 40
Yoron ○ J 259 Ma 32
Yoron-shima ⛬ J 259 Ma 32
Yorosso ○ RMM 317 Gd 39
Yorubaland Plateau ⛰ WAN 320 Gh 41
Yosemite ♀ USA 64 Cc 26
Yoshkar-Ola ○ RUS 154 Ra 7
Yŏsu ○ ROK 247 Lp 28
Yosua ○ PNG 286 Mh 48
Yōtei-Shan △ J 250 Mg 24
Youangarra ○ AUS 368 Lk 60
Youanmi Downs ○ AUS 368 Lk 60
Yoube ○ ETH 328 Ja 42
Youdunzi ○ VRC 231 Kk 26
Youghal ○ IRL 163 Gc 20
You Jiang ~ VRC 255 Ld 34
Youkounkoun ○ RG 316 Fp 39
Young ○ CDN 51 Ck 20
Young ○ ROU 146 Ef 62
Young ○ AUS 379 Ml 63
Youngou ~ RCA 321 Hc 42
Youngs Cove ○ CDN 61 Eb 23
Youngstown ○ USA 71 Dh 25
Youngstwon ○ CDN 51 Cg 20
Youssoufia ○ MA 292 Gb 29
Youvarou ○ RMM 305 Gd 38
You Xian ○ VRC 258 Lg 32
Youyang ○ VRC 255 Le 31
Yowa ~ RDC 321 Hc 44
Yowah Creek ~ AUS 375 Mj 59
Yozgat ○ TR 195 Hk 26
Ypsilanti ○ USA 71 Dg 24
Ysabel Channel ~ PNG 287 Ml 46
Ystad ○ S 170 Gn 18
Ystannah-Hočo ○ RUS 204 Wa 4
Ytterhogdal ○ S 158 Gp 14
Ytterjeppo ○ FIN 159 Hc 14
Yuabao Shan △ VRC 255 Le 33
Yuanjiang ○ VRC 254 La 34
Yuan Jiang ~ VRC 254 Lb 34
Yuan Jiang ~ VRC 255 Lf 31
Yuanjiang ○ VRC 258 Lg 31
Yuanlin ○ RC 259 Ll 34
Yuanling ○ VRC 255 Lf 31
Yuanmou ○ VRC 254 La 33
Yuanping ○ VRC 243 Lg 26
Yuanqu ○ VRC 243 Lf 28
Yuantan ○ VRC 246 Lj 30
Yuanyang ○ VRC 254 Lb 34
Yuat River ~ PNG 287 Mh 48
Yuba ○ USA 70 Cp 29
Yuba City ○ USA 64 Cb 26
Yūbari ○ J 250 Mh 24
Yubdo ○ ETH 325 Hk 41
Yūbetsu ○ J 250 Mh 23
Yubetu-dake △ J 250 Mg 24
Yucatan Basin Ψ 100 De 35
Yucatan Channel ≈ 100 De 35
Yucatan Peninsula ⛬ MEX 93 Dd 35
Yucatón ○ MEX 93 De 35
Yucca ○ USA 64 Ce 28
Yucca House N.M. ★ USA 65 Ch 27
Yuci ○ VRC 243 Lg 27
Yuclong ○ VRC 258 Lg 31
Yucumo ○ BOL 129 Ea 52
Yudu ○ VRC 258 Lh 33
Yuechi ○ VRC 243 Ld 30
Yuelai ○ VRC 243 Le 30
Yuelai ○ VRC 250 Mb 22
Yuendumu ○ AUS 361 Mb 57
Yuendumu Aboriginal Land ••• AUS 361 Mb 57
Yueqing ○ VRC 259 Ll 31
Yuexi ○ VRC 246 Lj 30
Yueyaguan Mingshashan ★ VRC 242 Km 26
Yueyang ○ VRC 258 Lg 31
Yugia ○ VRC 242 Km 26
Yüglük D. △ TR 195 Hj 27
Yugorskiy Poluostrov ⛬ RUS 154 Sa 5
Yugorskiy Poluostrov ⛬ RUS 204 Sa 5
Yuhe ○ VRC 243 Le 27
Yuhe ○ VRC 255 Lc 32
Yuhuan Dao ⛬ VRC 259 Ll 31
Yuin ○ AUS 368 Lj 59
Yuinmery ○ AUS 368 Lk 60
Yu Jiang ~ VRC 255 Le 34
Yuki ○ RDC 333 Hb 47
Yukon Delta ⌓ USA 46 Ag 13
Yukon Plateau ⛰ CDN 47 Bg 13
Yukon River ~ USA 6 Ba 3
Yukon River ~ USA 46 Aj 13
Yukon River ~ USA 46 Bc 11
Yukon River ~ CDN 47 Bg 13
Yukon Territory ⊙ CDN 47 Bg 13
Yüksekova ○ TR 209 Ja 27
Yukuhashi ○ J 247 Mb 29
Yulara ○ AUS 369 Mb 58
Yule ~ AUS 360 Lk 56
Yuleba ○ AUS 375 Ml 59
Yulee ○ USA 87 Dh 30
Yule Island ⛬ PNG 287 Mk 50
Yuli ○ VRC 204 Tc 10
Yuli ○ RC 259 Ll 34
Yuli ○ WAN 320 Gm 41
Yulin ○ VRC 243 Le 26
Yulin ○ VRC 255 Le 34
Yulin Ku ★ VRC 231 Km 25
Yulong Xue Shan △ VRC 254 La 32
Yuma ○ USA 64 Ce 29
Yuma ○ USA 65 Cl 25
Yumbe ○ EAU 324 Hh 44
Yumbel ○ RCH 137 Dm 64
Yumbi ○ RDC 332 Ha 46
Yumbi ○ RDC 336 Hf 46
Yumbo ○ CO 106 Dk 44
Yumen ○ VRC 242 Kn 26
Yumenguan ○ VRC 231 Kl 25
Yumenguan ★ VRC 231 Kl 25
YumenZhen ○ VRC 242 Kn 25
Yuna ~ DOM 101 Dn 36
Yuna ○ AUS 368 Lh 60
Yunak ○ TR 195 Hh 26
Yunan ○ VRC 255 Lf 34
Yuncheng ○ VRC 243 Lf 28
Yuncheng ○ VRC 246 Lj 28
Yundamindera ○ AUS 368 Lm 60
Yunfu ○ VRC 255 Lf 34
Yungang Shiku ★ VRC 243 Lg 25
Yungas ⌓ BOL 129 Ea 53
Yungay ○ PE 116 Dj 50
Yungay ○ RCH 137 Dn 64
Yunguyo ○ PE 128 Dp 54
Yunhe ○ VRC 258 Lk 31
Yunkai Dash ⛰ VRC 255 Le 34
Yunkanjini Aboriginal Land ••• AUS 361 Mb 57
Yunlong ○ VRC 254 Kp 33
Yunmeng ○ VRC 243 Lg 30
Yunnan ⊙ VRC 254 Kp 32
Yunomae ○ J 247 Mb 29
Yunta ○ AUS 378 Mf 62
Yuntaishan ★ VRC 246 Lk 28
Yunwu Shan ⛰ VRC 255 Lf 34
Yun Xian ○ VRC 243 Lf 29
Yunxian ○ VRC 254 Kp 33
Yunxiao ○ VRC 258 Lj 34
Yunyang ○ VRC 243 Le 30
Yunyang ○ VRC 243 Lg 29
Yuping ○ VRC 255 Ld 32
Yuping ○ VRC 255 Le 32
Yuqian ○ VRC 246 Lk 30
Yuquanshan ★ VRC 243 Lf 30
Yura ○ PE 128 Dn 54
Yura ○ BOL 136 Ea 56
Yura ~ BOL 136 Eb 56
Yuratsishki ○ BY 171 Hf 18
Yuraygir ♀ AUS 375 Mn 60
Yurécuaro ○ MEX 92 Cl 35
Yurimaguas ○ PE 116 Dk 48
Yuriria ○ MEX 92 Cm 35
Yuruan ~ YV 112 Ed 42
Yurubi ♀ YV 107 Dp 40
Yuruz ~ PE 116 Dm 50
Yuscarán ○ HN 96 De 39
Yushan ○ VRC 258 Lk 31
Yushan ★ RC 259 Ll 34
Yu Shan △ RC 259 Ll 34
Yushe ○ VRC 243 Lg 27
Yushu ○ VRC 242 Kn 29
Yusufeli ○ TR 202 Hn 25
Yusupalik Tag ⛰ VRC 231 Kj 26
Yutian ○ VRC 230 Ke 27
Yuto ○ RA 136 Eb 57
Yuwang ○ VRC 243 Ld 27
Yuxi ○ VRC 254 Lb 33
Yuxikou ○ VRC 246 Lj 30
Yuyao ○ VRC 246 Ll 30
Yuzawa ○ J 250 Mg 26
Yuzhno-Kamyshovyy Khrebet ⛰ RUS 250 Mh 22
Yuzhno-Sakhalinsk ○ RUS 250 Mh 22
Yuzhou ○ VRC 243 Lg 28
Yvetot ○ F 163 Gg 21
Ywama ○ MYA 254 Kn 35
Ywathit ○ MYA 254 Km 36
Ywathitke ○ MYA 235 Kl 35

Z

Zaachila ○ MEX 92 Cp 36
Záarate ○ RA 146 Ee 63
Zabalocce ○ BY 171 Hh 19
Zabīd ○ YE 218 Hp 38
Zabłudów ○ PL 171 Hd 19
Zābol ⊙ AFG 223 Jm 29
Zābol ○ IR 226 Jj 30
Zābolī ○ IR 226 Jj 32
Zabré ○ BF 317 Gf 40
Zaburun'e ○ KZ 202 Jd 22
Zaburunje cyganaky ~ KZ 202 Jc 22
Zabūt ○ YE 219 Je 38
Žabzugu ○ GH 317 Gg 41
Zacapa ○ GCA 93 Dd 38
Zacapa ○ HN 93 Dd 38
Zacapu ○ MEX 92 Cm 36
Zacatal ○ MEX 93 Dc 36
Zacatecas ○ MEX 92 Cl 34
Zacatecoluca ○ ES 93 Dd 39
Zacatepec ○ MEX 92 Cn 36
Zacatlán ○ MEX 92 Cp 35
Zachidnyj Buh ~ UA 174 Hd 20
Zacoalco de Torres ○ MEX 92 Cl 35
Zacualpan ○ MEX 92 Cm 36
Zacualtipán ○ MEX 92 Cn 35
Zadar ○ HR 174 Gp 23
Zadetkale Kyun ⛬ MYA 262 Kp 40
Zadetky Kyun ⛬ MYA 262 Kn 41
Zadié ~ G 332 Gn 45
Zadoi ○ VRC 242 Km 29
Zadonsk ○ RUS 181 Hm 19
Zaēr Zaīane ⌓ MA 293 Gc 29
Za'farāna ○ ET 301 Hj 31
Zafarqand ○ IR 222 Je 29
Zafarwāl ○ IND 230 Kb 29
Zafra ○ E 184 Gc 26
Zag ○ MA 292 Gb 31
Zagai Island ⛬ AUS 286 Mh 50
Żagań ○ PL 174 Gp 20
Zagaou ⌓ TCH 309 Hc 38
Zagaou ⌓ TCH 312 Hd 38
Zāge ○ IR 209 Jc 29
Zaghouan ○ TN 296 Gm 27
Zagné ○ CI 305 Gc 42
Zagora ○ MA 293 Gd 30
Zagreb ▣ HR 174 Gp 23
Zagros Mountains ⛰ IR 209 Jc 29
Zaharodze ⌓ BY 171 He 19
Zāhedān ○ IR 226 Jj 31
Zahirābād ○ IND 238 Kc 37
Zahir Pir ○ PK 227 Jp 31
Zahla ○ RL 208 Hk 29
Zahmet ○ TM 223 Jk 27
Zahrān ○ KSA 218 Hp 37
Zahrat al Baṭn ⛰ IRQ 214 Hp 30
Zahrez Chergui ~ DZ 296 Gh 28
Zahrez Gharbi ~ DZ 296 Gh 28
Zāhū ○ IRQ 209 Hp 27
Zaila ○ RDC 336 He 50
Zainsk ○ RUS 181 Je 18
Zaïo ○ MA 293 Ge 28
Zajaa ○ MNG 204 Ub 10
Zaječar ○ SCG 194 Hd 24
Zajmišče ○ RUS 181 Ja 21
Zaka ○ ZW 352 Hh 56
Zakamensk ○ RUS 204 Uc 8
Zaki Biam ○ WAN 320 Gl 42
Zákinthos ○ GR 194 Hc 27
Zákinthos ⛬ GR 194 Hc 27
Zakopane ○ PL 174 Hb 21
Zakouma ○ TCH 321 Hb 40
Zakou Shankou △ VRC 242 Kp 27
Zala ○ ANG 332 Gp 49
Zalaegerszeg ○ H 174 Ha 22
Zalamea d.l.S. ○ E 184 Gd 26
Zalanga ○ WAN 320 Gm 40
Zalău ○ RO 175 Hd 22
Zalegošč' ○ RUS 181 Hl 19
Zaleščyky ○ UA 175 He 21
Zalew Szczeciński ~ PL 170 Gp 19
Zalew Wiślany ~ PL 170 Hb 18
zal faddeja ≈ RUS 22 Qa 2
Zalingei ○ SUD 312 Hd 39
Zaliv Akademii ≈ RUS 205 Xa 8
Zaliv Aniva ≈ RUS 205 Xb 9
zaliv Aniva ≈ RUS 250 Mh 22
Zaliv Faddeya ≈ RUS 204 Va 3
Zaliv Korfa ≈ RUS 205 Za 6
Zaliv Krasin ≈ RUS 205 Zc 4
zaliv Mordvinova ~ RUS 250 Mh 22
zaliv Petra Velikogo ~ RUS 250 Mb 24
Zaliv Terpeniya ≈ RUS 205 Xb 9
Zaliv Tollya ≈ RUS 204 Ub 3
Zalki ○ IND 238 Kb 37
Zaltan ○ LAR 300 Hb 31
Žaltyrkōl k-l ~ KZ 181 Jd 21
Zalut ○ MYA 262 Kp 39
Zama ○ RN 308 Gh 38
Zamak ○ YE 218 Jb 37
Zama Lake ~ CDN 47 Cc 15
Zamantı Irmağı ~ TR 195 Hk 26
Zamay ○ CAM 321 Gn 40
Žambaj a-l ⛬ KZ 202 Jc 22
Zambales Mountains ⛰ RP 267 Lk 38
Žambejiti ○ KZ 155 Rb 8
Zambeke ○ RDC 324 He 44
Zambezi ~ ANG 341 Hd 51
Zambezi ○ Z 341 Hd 52
Zambezi ~ Z 341 Hd 52
Zambezi ♀ ZW 341 He 54
Zambezi ~ MOC 344 Hk 54
Zambezi Deka ○ ZW 341 Hf 55
Zambezi Escarpment ⛰ ZW 341 Hg 54
Zambia ☐ Z 340 He 53
Zamboanga ○ RP 275 Lm 42
Zamboanga Peninsula ⌓ RP 275 Lm 42
Zamboanguita ○ RP 267 Lm 41
Zambrano ○ HN 96 De 38
Zambrów ○ PL 170 Hd 19
Zambué ○ MOC 341 Hh 53
Zamek Krzyżacki ★ PL 170 Hb 18
Zamfara ~ WAN 320 Gj 39
Zamīnān ○ IR 226 Jk 32
Zamora ○ MEX 92 Cl 36
Zamora ~ EC 116 Dj 47
Zamora ○ EC 116 Dj 48
Zamora ○ E 184 Gd 25
Zamość ○ PL 175 Hd 20
Zampi ○ RDC 333 Hb 47
Zamza ~ RCA 321 Hc 42
Zan ○ TCH 321 Hb 40
Zanaga ○ RCB 332 Gn 47
Žanakala ○ KZ 181 Jd 21
Žana Kazan ○ KZ 181 Jc 21
Zanda ○ VRC 230 Kd 30
Zandamela ○ MOC 352 Hk 58
Zanderij ○ SME 113 Eg 43
Zanesville ○ USA 71 Dh 26
Zanfla ○ CI 317 Gd 42
Zangāreddigūdem ○ IND 238 Ke 37
Zangasso ○ RMM 317 Gd 39
Zangdo ○ VRC 231 Kh 30
Zanggān Rūd ~ IR 209 Jb 27
Zango ○ WAN 320 Gl 39
Zanjān ○ IR 209 Jc 27
Zanjān ⊙ IR 209 Jc 27
Zanjitas ○ RA 137 Ea 62
Zankoji ★ J 251 Me 29
Zanthus ○ AUS 369 Lm 61
Zantiebougou ○ RMM 305 Gc 40
Zanvar Čāy ~ IR 209 Ja 26
Žanybek ○ KZ 181 Jb 21
Zanzibar ○ EAT 337 Hm 49
Zanzibar Channel ~ EAT 337 Hm 48
Zanzibar Island Sansibar ⛬ EAT 337 Hm 49
Zanzra ○ CI 305 Gc 42
Zaonežskij zaliv ~ RUS 159 Hk 14
Zaoro-Songou ○ RCA 321 Ha 43
Zao-san △ J 251 Mg 26
Zaouatanlaz ○ DZ 296 Gl 33
Zaouia Sidi Moussa ○ DZ 296 Gk 31
Zaoyang ○ VRC 243 Lg 29
Zaozhuang ○ VRC 246 Lj 28
Zapadnaja Dvina ○ RUS 171 Hh 17
Zapadnoe ○ KZ 154 Sb 8
Zapaï ○ RDC 324 He 43
Zapala ○ RA 147 Dn 65
Zapallar ○ RCH 137 Dn 62
Zapata ○ USA 81 Cn 32
Zapiga ○ RCH 128 Dp 55
Zapľusie ○ RUS 171 Hg 16
Zapoljarnyj ○ RUS 159 Hh 11
Zapopan ○ MEX 92 Cl 35
Zaporižžja ○ UA 175 Hk 22
Zapotillo ○ EC 116 Dh 48
Zapotlanejo ○ MEX 92 Cl 35
Zapovednik Černye zemli ⌓ RUS 181 Jb 22
zapovednik Teberdinskij ♀ RUS 202 Hn 24
Zapovednyj ○ RUS 250 Mc 24
Zaqatala ○ AZ 202 Jb 25
Za Qu Mekong ~ VRC 242 Km 29
Zar ○ IR 226 Jg 32
Zar ○ RIM 304 Fn 37
Zara ○ TR 195 Hl 26
Zarafšan tiz ⛬ UZB 223 Jm 26
Zarafšon ~ UZB 223 Jk 26
Zaragoza ○ MEX 80 Cj 30
Zaragoza ○ MEX 81 Cm 31
Zaragoza ○ MEX 92 Cm 35
Zaragoza ○ MEX 92 Cp 35
Zaragoza ○ E 184 Gf 25
Zarajsk ○ RUS 171 Hm 18
Zarand ○ IR 226 Jg 30
Zaranj ○ AFG 226 Jj 30
Zaranou ○ CI 317 Ge 42
Zarasai ○ LT 171 He 18
Zaraza ○ YV 112 Eb 41
Zarcero ○ CR 97 Df 40
Zard ○ PK 227 Jl 31
Zarepe ○ SOL 290 Na 49
Zarghat ○ KSA 214 Hn 32
Zarghūn △ PK 227 Jm 30
Zargūnšahr ○ AFG 223 Jn 29
Zari ○ WAN 320 Gn 39
Zaria ○ WAN 320 Gk 40
Zarične ○ UA 175 He 20
Zaris ○ NAM 348 Ha 58
Zarishoogte Pass △ NAM 348 Ha 58
Zarmal ○ AFG 223 Jn 29
Zarqa ~ JOR 208 Hk 29
Zarqa ○ JOR 214 Hl 30
Zarqā ○ SUD 312 Hg 39
Zarrin ○ IR 222 Jf 29
Zarrīnābād ○ IR 209 Jb 27
Zarrīnābād ○ IR 209 Jc 28
Zarrīne Rūd ~ IR 209 Jb 27
Zarrīnšahr ○ IR 222 Jd 29
Zaruma ○ EC 116 Dj 47
Zarumilla ○ PE 116 Dh 47
Zarza d. G. ○ E 184 Gc 25
Zarzaïtine ○ DZ 296 Gl 31
Zarzal ○ CO 106 Dk 43
Zarzis ○ TN 297 Gm 29
Žaskar ⌓ IND 230 Kc 29
Zaškiv ○ UA 175 Hh 21
Zastron ○ ZA 349 Hf 61
Zaunguzskie Garagum ⌓ TM 222 Jg 25
Zavāre ○ IR 222 Je 29
Zavarthošuu ○ MNG 204 Vb 9
Zavhan gol ~ MNG 204 Ua 9
Zavitinsk ○ RUS 205 Wb 8
Zawīlah ○ LAR 297 Gp 32
Zāwiyat al Mukhayla ○ LAR 300 Hd 29
Zāwiyat Masus ○ LAR 300 Hc 30
Zayat ○ MYA 254 Km 34
Zayethon ○ MYA 254 Km 35
Zaysan ○ KZ 22 Pa 5
Zayū ○ VRC 254 Kn 31
Zaza ~ C 100 Dj 34
Zazafotsy ○ RM 353 Jb 57
Zaziatou ○ RN 320 Gh 39
Zbaraž ○ UA 175 He 21
Zbruč ~ UA 175 Hf 21

484 Yao Xian - Zbruč

Ždanovka ○ RUS 181 Jb 20
Žďár n. Sáz. ○ CZ 174 Gp 21
Zealand ○ DK 170 Gm 18
Zēbāk ○ AFG 223 Jp 27
Zeballos ○ CDN 50 Bn 21
Zeballos △ RA 152 Dn 69
Zebediela ○ ZA 349 Hg 58
Zebulon ○ USA 74 Dj 28
Ze Doca ○ BR 121 El 47
Zeehan ○ AUS 378 Mj 66
Zêêk ○ AFG 223 Jn 29
Zeekoegat ○ ZA 349 Hg 58
Zeerust ○ ZA 349 He 58
Zefat ○ IL 208 Hk 29
Zefre ○ IR 222 Je 29
Zegoua ○ RMM 317 Gd 40
Zéguédéguin ○ BF 317 Gf 39
Zeidābād ○ IR 226 Jf 31
Zeidskoe vodohranilisce ～ TM 223 Jl 27
Zeja ○ RUS 205 Wb 8
Zeja ～ RUS 205 Wb 8
Zejskoe vodohranilišče ～ RUS 205 Wb 8
Zékog ○ VRC 242 La 28
Zelenčukskaja ○ RUS 202 Hn 24
Zelenoborskij ○ RUS 159 Hh 12
Zelenodoľsk ○ RUS 181 Jc 18
Zelenoe ○ KZ 181 Jd 21
Zelenogorsk ○ RUS 171 Hg 15
Zelenogradsk ○ RUS 170 Hc 18
Zelenokumsk ○ RUS 202 Hp 23
Železnja ○ RUS 171 Hl 18
Železnodorožnyi ○ RUS 170 Hc 18
Železnogorsk ○ RUS 171 Hk 19
Železnovodsk ○ RUS 202 Hp 23
Zelfana ○ DZ 296 Gj 29
Zelina ○ HR 174 Gp 22
Zembra △ TN 297 Gm 27
Zemio ○ RCA 324 He 43
Zemlja Bunge ⌒ RUS 205 Xb 3
Zemlja Alexandra ⌒ RUS 19 Ma 1
Zemlya Georga ⌒ RUS 19 Mb 1
Zemlya Wilczek ⌒ RUS 19 Na 1
Zemmora ○ DZ 293 Gg 28
Zemmour ○ MA 292 Fp 33
Zempoaltepetl △ MEX 93 Cp 37
Zendeğan ○ AFG 223 Jj 28
Zengcheng ○ VRC 258 Lg 34
Zengfeng ○ VRC 255 Lc 33
Zenguele ○ ANG 332 Gp 49
Zenia ○ USA 64 Ca 25
Zenica ○ BIH 174 Ha 23
Zentsūji ○ J 251 Mc 28
Zenza do Itombe ○ ANG 340 Gp 50
Zeona ○ USA 51 Cl 23
Zepče ○ BIH 174 Hb 23
Zephyrhills ○ USA 87 Dg 31
Zepita ○ PE 128 Dp 54
Zepu ○ VRC 230 Kc 26
Zeralda ○ DZ 296 Gh 27
Zeravšan ～ TJ 223 Jn 26
Zeravshan Range ⌒ TJ 223 Jm 26
Žerd' ○ RUS 159 Ja 13
Žerdevka ○ RUS 181 Hn 20

Zeribet el Oued ○ DZ 296 Gk 28
Zernograd ○ RUS 181 Hn 22
Zešârt ○ RUS 154 Ra 6
Zestap'oni ○ GE 202 Hp 24
Zêtang ○ VRC 235 Kk 31
Zetikara ○ KZ 154 Sa 8
Zetysaj ○ KZ 223 Jn 25
Zgierz ○ PL 174 Hb 20
Zgorzelec ○ PL 174 Gp 20
Zhag'yab ○ VRC 242 Kn 30
Zhalantun ○ VRC 204 Wa 9
Zhanang ○ VRC 235 Kk 31
Zhangcunpu ○ VRC 243 Lh 29
Zhanghe Shuiku ～ VRC 243 Lf 30
Zhanghuang ○ VRC 255 Le 35
Zhangjiachuan ○ VRC 243 Lc 28
Zhangjiagang ○ VRC 246 Ll 30
Zhangjiakou ○ VRC 243 Lh 25
Zhangping ○ VRC 258 Lj 33
Zhangpu ○ VRC 258 Lj 33
Zhangqiu ○ VRC 243 Lj 27
Zhangye ○ VRC 242 La 26
Zhangzhou ○ VRC 258 Lj 33
Zhangzhu ○ VRC 258 Lh 31
Zhanjiang ○ VRC 255 Le 35
Zhaojue ○ VRC 255 Lb 31
Zhao Ling ★ VRC 243 Le 28
Zhaoping ○ VRC 255 Lf 33
Zhaoqing ○ VRC 255 Lf 34
Zhaotong ○ VRC 255 Lb 32
Zhao Xian ○ VRC 243 Lh 27
Zha po Gang ～ VRC 255 Lf 35
Zhargun Khel ○ PK 223 Jp 29
Zhari Namco ～ VRC 231 Kg 30
Zhaxi Co ～ VRC 231 Kg 29
Zhaxigang ○ VRC 230 Kd 29
Zhaxilhünbo Si ★ VRC 235 Kj 31
Zhazhi ○ VRC 242 La 30
Zhecheng ○ VRC 243 Lh 28
Zheduo Shankou △ VRC 242 La 30
Zhehai ○ VRC 255 Lb 32
Zhejiang ◉ VRC 258 Lk 31
Zhejue ○ VRC 255 Lb 32
Zhelang ○ VRC 258 Lh 34
Zhen'an ○ VRC 243 Le 29
Zhenba ○ VRC 243 Ld 29
Zhenbao Ding △ VRC 255 Lf 32
Zheng'an ○ VRC 255 Ld 31
Zhenghe ○ VRC 258 Lk 32
Zhengxiong ○ VRC 255 Lc 32
Zhengyang ○ VRC 243 Lh 29
Zhengzhou ○ VRC 243 Lg 28
Zhenhai ○ VRC 258 Lj 33
Zhenjiang ○ VRC 246 Lk 29
Zhenkang ○ VRC 254 Kp 34
Zhenping ○ VRC 243 Lg 28
Zhenyuan ○ VRC 243 Ld 28
Zhenyuan ○ VRC 254 La 34
Zhenyuan ○ VRC 255 Le 32
Zhexi Shuiku ～ VRC 255 Lf 31
Zhezqazghan ○ KZ 19 Na 5
Zhichengshi ○ VRC 243 Lf 30
Zhidan ○ VRC 243 Le 27
Zhidol ○ VRC 242 Km 29
Zhigan ○ VRC 230 Kf 30

Zhijiang ○ VRC 243 Lf 30
Zhijiang ○ VRC 255 Le 32
Zhijin ○ VRC 255 Lc 32
Zhiqu ～ VRC 242 Km 28
Zhlobin ○ BY 171 Hg 19
Zhob ○ PK 227 Jn 30
Zhob ～ PK 227 Jn 30
Zhodzina ○ BY 171 Hf 18
Zhombe ○ ZW 341 Hg 55
Zhongba ○ VRC 235 Kg 31
Zhongba ○ VRC 258 Lh 34
Zhongbujie ○ VRC 258 Lj 31
Zhongdan ○ VRC 254 Kp 32
Zhongdian ○ VRC 254 Kp 32
Zhongjiang ○ VRC 242 Lc 30
Zhongning ○ VRC 242 Lc 27
Zhongshan ○ VRC 255 Lf 33
Zhongshan ○ VRC 258 Lg 34
Zhongwei ○ VRC 242 Lc 27
Zhong Xian ○ VRC 243 Ld 30
Zhongxiang ○ VRC 243 Lg 30
Zhongxin Gang ～ VRC 246 Ll 29
Zhongxingqiao ○ VRC 246 Ll 29
Zhongzhai ○ VRC 259 Lm 31
Zhoudangfan ○ VRC 243 Lh 30
Zhoukou ○ VRC 243 Lh 29
Zhoukoudian Yesanpo ★ VRC 243 Lh 26
Zhouning ○ VRC 258 Lk 32
Zhoushan ○ VRC 259 Ll 31
Zhoushan Qundano ～ VRC 246 Ll 30
Zhoushan Qundao ⌒ VRC 246 Lm 30
Zhouzhi ○ VRC 243 Le 28
Zhowagoin ○ VRC 254 Kn 31
Zhuanghe ○ VRC 246 Lm 26
Zhucheng ○ VRC 246 Lk 28
Zhud ○ EC 116 Dj 47
Zhuggu ○ VRC 242 Lc 29
Zhuhai ○ VRC 258 Lg 34
Zhuji ○ VRC 259 Ll 31
Zhujiang Kou ～ VRC 258 Lg 34
Zhumadian ○ VRC 243 Lg 29
Zhuozhou ○ VRC 246 Lj 26
Zhuozi Shan △ VRC 243 Ld 26
Zhushan ○ VRC 243 Lf 29
Zhuxi ○ VRC 243 Le 29
Zhuzhou ○ VRC 258 Lg 32
Ziama Mansouria ○ DZ 296 Gj 27
Žiar ○ SK 174 Hb 21
Ziârat ○ PK 227 Jm 30
Zia Town ○ LB 304 Gc 43
Ziba ○ EAT 337 Hj 48
Ziban ～ DZ 296 Gj 28
Zibo ○ VRC 246 Lk 27
Zichang ○ VRC 243 Le 27
Zielona Góra ○ PL 174 Gp 20
Ziftá ○ ET 301 Hh 30
Žigalovo ○ RUS 204 Va 8
Zigansk ○ RUS 204 Wa 5
Zigerbent ○ TM 223 Jj 25
Zighan ○ LAR 300 Hc 33
Zighout Youcef ○ DZ 296 Gk 27

Zigon ○ MYA 254 Km 34
Zigon ○ MYA 254 Km 36
Zigong ○ VRC 255 Lc 31
Ziguéy ○ TCH 309 Gp 38
Ziguinchor ○ SN 316 Fm 39
Zigzag ○ USA 50 Cb 23
Zihuatanejo ○ MEX 92 Cm 37
Zijin ○ VRC 258 Lh 34
Zilairskoye Plato ⌒ RUS 155 Rc 8
Zile ○ TR 195 Hk 25
Žilina ○ SK 174 Hb 21
Zilinda ○ RUS 204 Vb 5
Zilkale ○ TR 202 Hn 25
Zillah ○ LAR 297 Ha 31
Zilupe ○ LV 171 Hf 17
Zima ○ RUS 204 Uc 8
Zimapán ○ MEX 92 Cn 35
Zimatlán ○ MEX 92 Cp 36
Zimba ○ Z 341 Hf 54
Zimmi ○ WAL 316 Ga 42
Zimnicea ○ RO 194 He 24
Zimnij bereg ⌒ RUS 154 Qc 5
Zimnij bereg ⌒ RUS 159 Hn 13
Zimovniki ○ RUS 181 Hp 22
Zina ○ CAM 321 Gp 40
Zinapécuaro ○ MEX 92 Cm 36
Zinder ○ RN 308 Gl 39
Zinğibār ○ YE 218 Ja 39
Ziniaré ○ BF 317 Gf 39
Zin'kiv ○ UA 175 Hk 20
Zinna ○ WAN 320 Gn 41
Zinzana ○ RMM 317 Gd 39
Zio ～ RT 317 Gg 42
Zion ○ USA 57 De 24
Zion ⚑ USA 64 Cf 27
Ziope ○ GH 317 Gg 42
Zipaquirá ○ CO 106 Dl 43
Zira ～ EAT 337 Hj 50
Ziracuaretiro ○ MEX 92 Cl 36
Zirapup ○ IND 234 Kc 34
Žirnovsk ○ RUS 181 Ja 20
Ziro ○ IND 235 Kl 32
Zitácuano ○ MEX 92 Cm 36
Zitenga ○ BF 317 Gf 39
Zitong ○ VRC 242 Lc 30
Zitouna ○ DZ 296 Gk 27
Zittau ○ D 174 Gp 20
Zitundo ○ MOC 352 Hj 59
Ziway Häyk' ～ ETH 325 Hm 41
Ziwu Liang △ VRC 243 Le 28
Zixi ○ VRC 258 Lj 32
Zixing ○ VRC 258 Lg 33
Ziyā Ābād ○ IR 209 Jc 28
Ziya He ～ VRC 246 Lj 26
Ziyang ○ VRC 242 Lc 30
Ziyang ○ VRC 243 Le 29
Ziyuan ○ VRC 255 Lf 32
Zizdra ○ RUS 171 Hk 19
Zizhong ○ VRC 255 Lc 31
Zizhou ○ VRC 243 Le 27
Zlatica ○ BG 194 He 24
Zlatograd ○ BG 194 He 25
Zlatoust ○ RUS 154 Rc 7

Zlatoustovsk ○ RUS 22 Rb 4
Zlín ○ CZ 174 Ha 21
Zlitan ○ LAR 297 Gp 29
Złoczew ○ PL 174 Hb 20
Z'Malet el Emir ○ DZ 296 Gh 28
Zmievka ○ RUS 181 Hl 19
Znamenka ○ RUS 171 Hk 18
Znamenka ○ RUS 181 Hn 19
Znam'janka ○ UA 175 Hj 21
Žnin ○ PL 170 Ha 19
Znojmo ○ CZ 174 Ha 21
Zoa ○ CAM 320 Gn 43
Zoar Village ★ USA 71 Dh 25
Zobia ○ RDC 324 He 44
Zóbuè ○ MOC 344 Hk 53
Zoébefang ○ CAM 320 Gm 44
Zoétété ○ CAM 320 Gm 44
Zogang ○ VRC 254 Kn 31
Zogbodomè ○ DY 317 Gh 42
Zogoré ○ BF 317 Ge 39
Zohre ～ IR 215 Jd 30
Zoigê ○ VRC 242 Lb 29
Zolfo Springs ○ USA 87 Dh 32
Zolochiv ○ UA 175 He 21
Zolote ○ UA 181 Hm 21
Zolotica ⌒ RUS 159 Hn 13
Zolotonoša ○ UA 175 Hj 21
Zolotuha ○ RUS 181 Jb 22
Zomanda ～ RM 353 Ja 56
Žomba ○ MW 344 Hk 53
Žomboj ○ UZB 223 Jm 26
Zongia ○ RDC 324 He 44
Zongo ○ RDC 321 Hb 43
Zonguldak ○ TR 195 Hh 25
Zongyang ○ VRC 246 Lj 30
Zonkeldi ○ UZB 223 Jk 25
Zonkwa ○ WAN 320 Gl 41
Zoo Baba ○ RN 297 Gn 36
Zoquitlán ○ MEX 93 Cp 37
Zorgo ○ BF 317 Gf 39
Zorita ○ E 184 Gd 26
Zoro ○ WAN 320 Gm 40
Zorritos ○ PE 116 Dh 47
Zorzor ○ LB 316 Gb 42
Zou ～ DY 317 Gg 42
Zouan-Hounien ○ CI 316 Gb 42
Zouar ○ TCH 309 Ha 35
Zouérat ○ RIM 304 Fp 34
Zoûgh ○ RIM 305 Gc 37
Zouireg ○ DZ 293 Gg 29
Zoulabot ○ CAM 321 Gp 44
Zoulouma ○ RCA 321 Hc 43
Zouping ○ VRC 246 Lj 30
Zoushan Dao ⌒ VRC 246 Lm 30
Zoushi ○ VRC 255 Lf 31
Zouzoudinga ○ RN 296 Gn 34
Žovten' ○ UA 175 Hh 22
Žovti Vody ○ UA 175 Hj 21
Zrenjanin ○ SCG 174 Hc 23
Zuata ○ YV 112 Eb 41
Zuata ～ YV 112 Eb 41
Zuba ○ WAN 320 Gk 41
Zubcov ○ RUS 171 Hk 17
Zubova Poljana ○ RUS 181 Hp 18
Zubovo ○ RUS 159 Hl 15

Zubovo ○ RUS 171 Hk 18
Zudáñez ～ BOL 129 Eb 55
Zuénoula ○ CI 305 Gc 42
Zuera ○ E 184 Gf 25
Zuevka ○ RUS 154 Rb 7
Zug ○ CH 174 Gl 22
Zugdidi ○ GE 202 Hn 24
Zugspitze △ D 174 Gm 22
Zújar ～ E 184 Gd 26
Žukovka ○ RUS 171 Hj 19
Žukovskij ○ RUS 171 Hm 18
Zula ○ ER 313 Hm 38
Zula Bahir Selat' ～ ER 313 Hm 38
Zulia ～ CO 107 Dm 41
Zulūma ○ YE 219 Jc 38
Žuma ○ UZB 223 Jm 26
Zumba ○ EC 116 Dj 48
Zumbagua ○ EC 116 Dj 46
Zumbo ○ MOC 341 Hh 53
Zumberge Coast ⌒ 38 Eb 17
Zumbrota ○ USA 56 Db 23
Zumpango ○ MEX 92 Cn 36
Zumpango del Río ○ MEX 92 Cn 37
Zungeru ○ WAN 320 Gk 41
Zunhua ○ VRC 246 Lk 25
Zuni ••• USA 65 Ch 28
Zuni Pueblo ○ USA 65 Ch 28
Zuo Jiang ～ VRC 255 Ld 34
Zuoquan ○ VRC 243 Lg 27
Zuoyun ○ VRC 243 Lg 26
Zur ○ MNG 204 Ub 9
Zurak ○ WAN 320 Gm 41
Zuri ～ BOL 129 Ea 54
Zürich ○ CH 174 Gl 22
Zürichsee ～ CH 174 Gl 22
Zurmi ○ WAN 320 Gk 39
Zuru ○ WAN 320 Gj 40
Žusaly ○ KZ 155 Sa 9
Zutiua ～ BR 121 El 48
Zutiua ～ BR 121 Em 48
Zuunharaa ○ MNG 204 Va 9
Zuurberg ⚑ ZA 358 He 62
Zuwārah ○ LAR 297 Gn 29
Zuytdorp Cliffs ⌒ AUS 368 Lg 59
Zuytdrop ⚑ AUS 368 Lh 59
Zvenigovo ○ RUS 181 Jb 17
Zvenyhorodka ○ UA 175 Hh 21
Zvishavane ○ ZW 352 Hh 56
Zvolen ○ SK 174 Hb 21
Zvornik ○ BIH 174 Hb 23
Zwartkop ○ ZA 358 Hc 61
Zwedru ○ LB 316 Gb 42
Zwelitsha ○ ZA 358 Hf 62
Zwettl ○ A 174 Gp 21
Zwickau ○ D 174 Gn 20
Zwierzyniec ○ PL 175 Hd 20
Zwinglì ○ ZA 349 Hf 58
Zwoleń ○ PL 174 Hc 20
Zwolle ○ USA 86 Db 30
Zwolle ○ NL 170 Gk 19
Zyrjanka ○ RUS 205 Xc 5
Zyrjanovsk ○ KZ 204 Tb 9
Žytomyr ○ UA 175 Hf 20

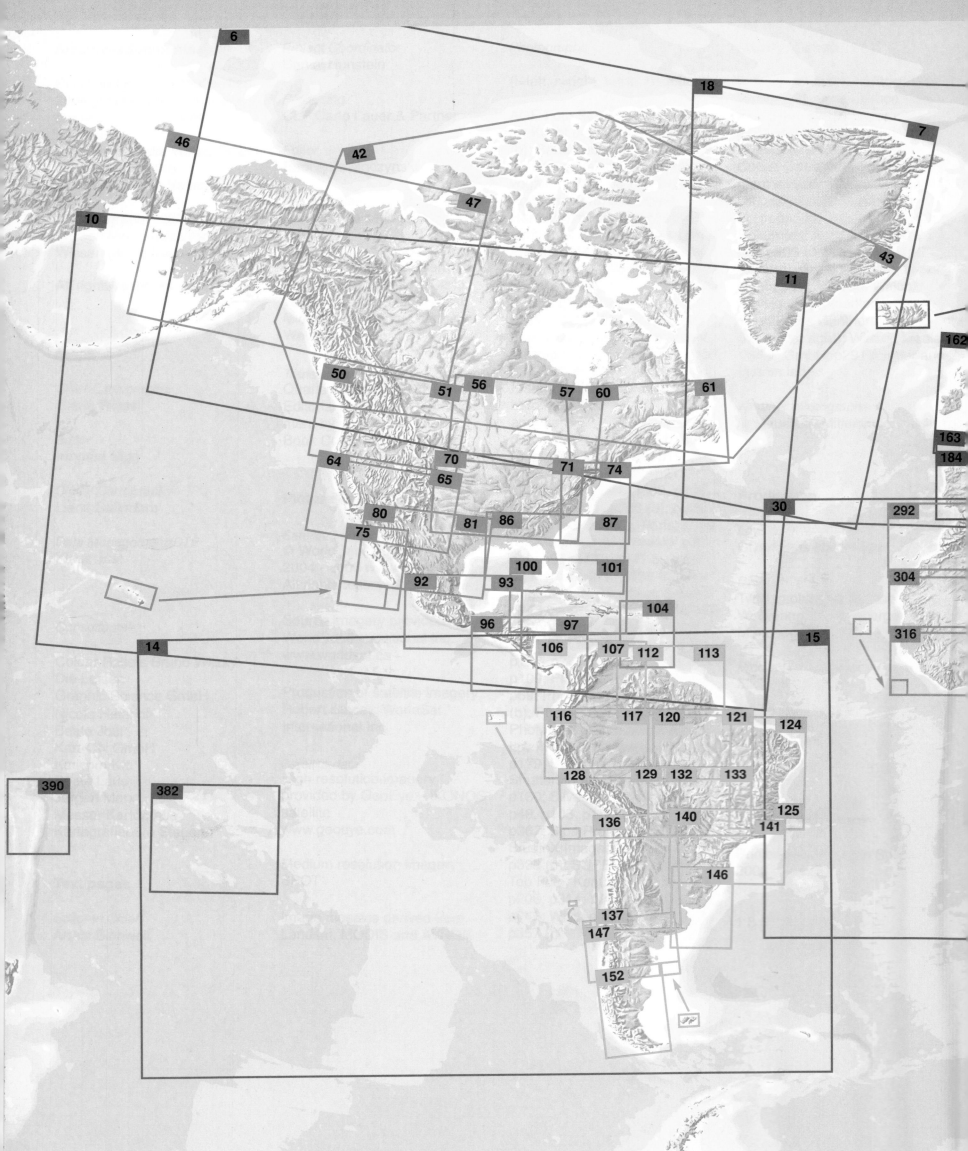

6
18
7
46
42
47
11
43
10
162
163
184
50
51
56
57
60
61
30
292
64
70
65
71
74
87
304
80
81
86
87
75
316
100
101
92
93
104
15
96
97
14
106
107
112
113
116
117
120
121
124
390
382
128
129
132
133
125
136
140
141
146
137
147
152